DICTIONARY OF NEWFOUNDLAND ENGLISH

EDITED BY
G.M. STORY
W.J. KIRWIN
J.D.A. WIDDOWSON

Dictionary of Newfoundland English
Second edition
with supplement

UNIVERSITY OF TORONTO PRESS
TORONTO BUFFALO LONDON

First edition
© University of Toronto Press 1982
Reprinted 1982, 1983 (twice)

Second edition
© University of Toronto Press 1990
Toronto   Buffalo   London
Printed in Canada

ISBN 0-8020-5887-6 (cloth)
ISBN 0-8020-6819-7 (paper)

Distributed in Newfoundland by Breakwater

Canadian Cataloguing in Publication Data

Main entry under title:

Dictionary of Newfoundland English

2nd ed. with supplement.
Includes bibliographical references.
ISBN 0-8020-5887-6 (bound) ISBN 0-8020-6819-7 (pbk.)

1. English language – Dialects – Newfoundland –
Dictionaries. 2. English language – Provincialisms –
Newfoundland – Dictionaries. I. Story, G.M.
(George Morley), 1927–   . II. Kirwin, W.J. (William
James), 1925–   . III. Widdowson, J.D.A. (John David
Allison), 1935–   .

PE3245.N4D5 1990   427'.9718   C90-094709-8

The first edition was published with the help of a grant from the Canadian Federation for
the Humanities, using funds provided by the Social Sciences and Humanities Research
Council of Canada, and a grant from the Publications Fund of University of Toronto Press.

Preface

The Dictionary which is now presented to the public is part of a plan conceived at Memorial University more than two decades ago by members of the Department of English in which the languages (especially the English language), the place- and family-names, and the folklore of Newfoundland were to be subjected to a scrutiny worthy of their importance for Newfoundlanders and their interest to others in the English-speaking world.

None of these had previously been studied with the rigour that critical scholarship demands; nor, when we began our work, were there available those preliminary and ancillary studies or even facilities upon which critical scholarship customarily builds. Work on our part of the project had, therefore, to proceed partly in tandem with that of our colleagues, and we should like to record before acknowledgement of other debts our overriding gratitude for the companionship of E.R. Seary in the initiation of the whole enterprise, and his encouragement of and participation in the progress of its discrete parts; to Herbert Halpert for his continuous and lively interest in our work, and particularly for his creation in the University's Folklore and Language Archive of an exemplary collection from which much of the oral material in the Dictionary is drawn; to Agnes O'Dea, for many years the director of the Centre for Newfoundland Studies in the University Library, who assembled virtually from scratch the materi-

als for the printed record in our work, and who compounded this debt by setting her hand as well to a Bibliography of Newfoundland which has proceeded side by side with the Dictionary; and to our colleagues, some of them our former students, in other disciplines at the University who during the progress of our work have gradually expanded the investigation of Newfoundland history and society, language, geography and natural science, and enabled us to draw upon their findings.

The Dictionary would have been impossible to complete in the time it has taken without this shared scholarship; and its deficiencies, where they are not attributable to our own errors of knowledge and judgement, reside in the very nature of the enterprise itself: the collecting for and editing of the first dictionary of Newfoundland English. Other scholars will, in due course, carry the work further: collect from sources we have omitted, produce critical editions of the printed and manuscript texts we have used, undertake more intensive studies in the field of etymology, and complete the investigation of the phonology and grammar of Newfoundland English. Meanwhile, the present work is offered in the belief that it will fulfil the expectations of general readers in Newfoundland and elsewhere in Canada, meet many of the demands of scholars in various fields engaged in the study of the region and satisfy, in some measure, the long-expressed interest of our fellow-lexicographers in the English-speaking world.

The core of the work is, of course, the alphabetical list of words, phrases and idioms derived from both printed and oral sources and presented with dated quotations in a manner familiar to users of historical dictionaries. Preceding this is a Bibliography of the sources from which our evidence has been drawn and to which the references in the main body of the Dictionary are keyed; and the whole is accompanied by an Introduction in which we set forth a statement of the nature and scope of the work, present a discussion of English language variation in Newfoundland (a discussion for which W.J. Kirwin has particular responsibility), comment on special problems relating to the sources, and explain certain matters of editorial policy and lay-out.

The execution of the work has been a shared task of the three editors, though particular responsibilities were assumed by one or another of us at different stages with general co-ordination by G.M. Story. The collecting of the material in our files was a common effort, with G.M. Story and W.J. Kirwin jointly excerpting the printed sources and also the unpublished documentary sources, and J.D.A. Widdowson excerpting (as he had also collected) the tape recordings. All three of us contributed material from field-notes and helped solicit items from contributors specifically for the Dictionary. The familiarity with the source materials of the Dictionary thus acquired proved of particular value in the second stage of the work: the writing and editing of the entries. For obvious reasons, this was naturally the primary responsibility of the two editors residing in Newfoundland; but the successive drafts were reviewed by J.D.A. Widdowson on annual visits to Newfoundland from the United Kingdom, and although his special contribution has been the provision of the phonetic evidence in the work and the discussion of that subject in the Introduction (for which he has sole responsibility), there are few entries which have not benefited from his careful scrutiny, while he has also, of course, shared fully in all matters of editorial policy. The Dictionary is, then, a work for which in general terms we are jointly responsible; and we are conscious, now that it is completed, of the good fortune which brought us together, with our very different origins and professional training, at a particular period when an enterprise of this kind might be undertaken.

We are not less conscious of, and grateful for, the help freely given by our colleagues in the preparation of the Dictionary. Our especially warm thanks go to Robert Hilliard; when the formal editing began he offered his assistance in proof-reading the text, a service he has rendered throughout the editing process as the articles went through successive revisions in slip form. Without Joan Halley the work could scarcely have been completed in the way and time it has: she maintained the Dictionary file, typed the successive drafts of the entries through what must have seemed an interminable series of revisions, added her own lively comments, criticisms and contributions, and maintained an unfussy calm and good cheer which lightened the long task. In the final phase of our work—the production of the book by a computer assisted technology—the resident editors were ably supported by Sandra McDonald.

The list of colleagues and friends who have contributed to the work in other ways is long and their names are recorded among the more than seven hundred contributors to the Dictionary listed in the Bibliography. We have here to record our special obligation to the following: to Leslie Harris for discussions, illustrations and precise contributions to our knowledge of the regional lexicon throughout the period of preparation of the Dictionary, and Colin Story for his help over a similar length of time with the lexicon and technology of the fisheries; to F.A. Aldrich for help with problems of marine biology; to Keith Matthews for clarification of some problems in the historical evolution of the West Country-Newfoundland fishery; to Peter J. Scott for his review of all the botanical articles; to the late Leslie M. Tuck for help with the identification and nomenclature of birds; to John Hewson, H.J. Paddock and L.R. Smith of the Department of Linguistics for help with particular problems; and for special collecting in the field, Robert Hollett. Michael Staveley of the Department of Geography supervised the drawing of the map.

Specimens of the Dictionary, circulated in 1977 in an early form, were given valuable criticism by expert readers and we have to thank, most warmly, the following: A.J. Aitken, *Dictionary of the Older Scottish Tongue*, University of Edinburgh; R.W. Burchfield and Mrs Leslie Burnett, *Supplement* to *The Oxford English Dictionary*, Oxford University; Angus Cameron, *Dictionary of Old English*, University of Toronto; Frederic G. Cassidy and his colleagues, *Dictionary of American Regional English*, University of Wisconsin; Robert L. Chapman, Drew University; Leslie Harris, Memorial University; Lee Pederson, *Linguistic Atlas of the Gulf States*, Emory University; and E.R. Seary, Memorial University.

The late Walter S. Avis of The Royal Military College, Kingston, Ontario, Frederic G. Cassidy of the University of Wisconsin, the late Harold Orton of the University of Leeds, and E.R. Seary acted as our sponsors in seeking funds necessary for the preparation of the Dictionary; and The Canada Council, with a confidence in our work which we shall not easily forget, made available grants to cover many of our costs in the years between 1969-1979. Expenses incurred prior and subsequent to those years were met by Memorial University, which also provided us with the materials and space we needed, and to our colleagues and friends in their administrative capacities we are deeply indebted, especially to I.A.F. Bruce, Leslie Harris, M.O. Morgan, and D.G. Pitt.

The editors of a famous English dictionary issued in 1911 disclosed that the first letter they received after the work appeared was a demand for repayment of the book's cost on the ground that it failed to include **gal(l)iot**, to settle the spelling of which it had been bought. We are as conscious as any dictionary makers must be of the diverse expectations and demands of users of such works, and also of the improbability, despite the good company we have had along the way, that we have unfailingly avoided errors and omissions; and we shall be grateful to readers who draw our attention to the more egregious of the oversights.

G.M. STORY
W.J. KIRWIN
St John's, Newfoundland

J.D.A. WIDDOWSON
Sheffield, England

July 1982

Contents

Supplement

Introduction

SCOPE OF THE DICTIONARY

'The circle of the English language,' observed the editors of the *Oxford English Dictionary*, 'has a well-defined centre but no discernible circumference.'[1] Although this is especially true of the enormous subject to which the *OED* and its *Supplements* are addressed, any dictionary that sets out to describe the word-stock of a nation, or even of a region, within a world-wide speech-community such as that of English must also face, though of course on a much reduced scale, the practical problem of delimiting the lexicon, of marking its boundaries.

One common procedure[2] is to confine attention to words or expressions which originate in a given country; but while this focuses clearly on the central nucleus of a distinctive vocabulary it does not, perhaps, allow sufficiently for such nice problems as the overlap of that vocabulary with other English-speaking communities, consideration of special senses or high frequencies of occurrence and so on. Much closer to a solution of the problem, in our experience, is the formulation by the editors of the *Dictionary of Canadianisms on Historical Principles*[3] (*DC*) who define a 'Canadianism' as a 'word, expression, or meaning which is native to Canada or which is distinctively characteristic of Canadian usage

though not necessarily exclusive to Canada.' This definition emerges from the basic procedure of the editors who instead of focusing exclusively on a vocabulary of 'Canadianisms,' however defined, shift the emphasis to the corpus of works read in collecting for the dictionary, confining themselves 'to source materials written by persons native to or resident in Canada who were writing about Canadian life or by travellers and other visitors to Canada who were commenting on their experiences in this country.' This is an important innovation which recognizes that the English language overseas, wherever it is spoken, is not a completely different or new language. Indeed, the special contribution of each country or region in new words and expressions, though often numerically large, constitutes a relatively small proportion of the total vocabulary, and to confine attention to it as an index of national or regional usage is to ignore the subtle issues of the frequency, popularity and semantic nuance of certain lexical items otherwise common to all English speakers.

It is the purpose of the *Dictionary of Newfoundland English* to present as one such index the regional lexicon of one of the oldest overseas communities of the English-speaking world: the lexicon of Newfoundland and coastal Labrador as it is displayed

---

1 Vol. I, Oxford: The Clarendon Press, [1888] 1933, xxvii.

2 See, for example, M.M. Mathews, *A Dictionary of*

Americanisms on Historical Principles (Chicago: University of Chicago Press, 1951), v.

3 Ed Walter S. Avis et al (Toronto: W.J. Gage Ltd., 1967), xiii.

in the sources drawn upon in compiling the work, sources which range from sixteenth-century printed books to tape recordings of contemporary Newfoundland speakers. Rather than attempting to define a 'Newfoundlandism' our guiding principles in collecting have been to look for words which appear to have entered the language in Newfoundland or to have been recorded first, or solely, in books about Newfoundland; words which are characteristically Newfoundland by having continued in use here after they died out or declined elsewhere, or by having acquired a different form or developed a different meaning, or by having a distinctly higher or more general degree of use.

Thus, among the latter are articles on such words as **cod, haul, quintal, salt water**; articles on **bawn, belay, cassock, cat, dog, graple, lanch, room, strouter**, and **tilt**, for words which have been given a new form or meaning in the region; on **droke, dwy, fadge, frore, keecorn, linny, nish, still, suant**, as examples of the many survivals, or, equally common, dialectal items in use, or former use, in the British Isles; on **bawk, caplin, janny, landwash, nunny-bag, penguin, steady, sunker, ticklace** and **water-horse** among words apparently invented in Newfoundland or appearing first in books about the region. And to these are to be added a number of words which, while they are often in varying degrees part of the common English vocabulary, are nevertheless given entries in the Dictionary because they occur with important nuances in Newfoundland usage, are displayed with unusual fullness in our data, or themselves stand at the centre of semantic fields of great regional importance: **barren, bay, coast, harbour, ice, salt, ship, shore, spring, trap, water**, and so on. These take their place in the Dictionary side by side with many other words the precise regional discriminations of which have often been hard won—subtle, but critical, terms such as **in** and **out, offer** and **outside, up** and **down**, which display a people's exact sense of

place; terms such as **bank, berth, ground, fouly, ledge, shoal**, etc, which reflect a complex system of classification of water bodies according to the types of ocean floor perceived by and significant for a coastal fishing people; names for birds and plants, especially those of economic or other importance; the seemingly endless nomenclature of seals at every stage of growth and development (**bedlamer, dotard, gun seal, jar, nog-head, ragged-jacket, turner, white-coat**, and a score of others); words for conditions of ice (**ballicatter, clumper, quarr, sish, slob**); and names for familiar operations in the woods or on the water, at work or play, in the ordinary and long-established patterns of Newfoundland and Labrador life.

The Dictionary therefore has both a breadth and a detail considerably greater than we originally envisaged, and this realization has been forced upon us by the evidence at our disposal and has increased with the progress of the work. The levels and kinds of lexical record included might be displayed graphically as a series of concentric rings spreading out from a centre, these rings formed by successive stages of the historical experience of English-speakers in Newfoundland; or as a series of isoglosses marking the special lexical features shared by Newfoundland speakers with those of their principal points of origin, especially the south-west counties of England and southern Ireland, and, across the Western Ocean, with those with whom Newfoundlanders have been in language contact: the native peoples of the region (**adikey, oo-isht, sina, tabanask**), speakers in the Canadian North (**fur, stove cake, trap line**), along the Atlantic seaboard of North America from Nova Scotia to New England (**banker, dory, gangeing, scrod, trawl, tub**), and in a sea-faring world which has left a ubiquitous record of nautical terms and nautical transfers in the regional lexicon.

From a certain point of view, therefore, the work is presented as a regional parallel with the *Dictionary of American English* (1938–44), the *Dictionary of Canadianisms*, the *Dictionary of Jamaican English* (1967), and other dictionaries of branches of the language overseas planned or in progress for Australia and South Africa; but equally it supplements the *OED* itself, Wright's *English Dialect Dictionary* (1898–1905), glossaries of Anglo-Irish, and numerous specialist works on the vocabulary of fishing and logging, the language of seamen and seamanship, and the lexicons of other specific activities.

The sometimes elaborate apparatus presented in the headnotes to the Dictionary articles reflects this conception of the work: it has grown out of an attempt to display the sources and affiliations of the Newfoundland vocabulary, as well as to document and clarify the substantial core of words unique to the region. The references to other dictionaries reflect the careful winnowing process by which, over a number of years, the editors have developed and applied a collaborative sense of what the Dictionary should include and what it should omit. Important factors in our selection have been the degree of frequency of comparable usage in Great Britain or continental North America; the importance of the term in the region's main occupations and traditional culture; the amount and authenticity of our evidence; the adequacy of coverage in the major historical and encyclopaedic dictionaries against which each word considered for inclusion has been checked; and even an aesthetic sense of proportion and balance in the presentation of the regional word-stock and semantics. A final motive has been a desire to establish the lexical record for Newfoundlanders themselves and their descendants, and for readers and scholars who need to know about the speech and material culture of the region, about

The ways of lobsters and tom cod, the subtle craft of dories, the topography of the wilderness under broad flakes, the abiding places of starfish and prickly sea-eggs, the significance of squid-squalls, and the virulence of squid,[4]

4 Norman Duncan, *The Way of the Sea* (New York: McClure, Phillips, & Co.), 6–7.

and about the planting, survival and adaptation of a small group of English-speakers overseas, the lexical evidence for which spans several centuries.

That evidence is drawn from sources the nature and variety of which are described elsewhere in the Introduction (SOURCES FOR THE DICTIONARY). It is of a kind which has led us in the Dictionary articles to avoid usage labels such as 'slang,' 'dialectal,' 'colloquial,' or 'literary' in the conviction that Newfoundland usage forms a continuum of cultivated and popular speech which the use of such labels distorts. We have similarly eschewed labelling words as 'historical,' 'archaic,' or 'obsolete' not because all the words in the Dictionary are in living use but because we have been too often surprised by the occurrence of terms, long absent from the printed record, on the lips of contemporary Newfoundlanders to be confident of making definitive statements on such matters.

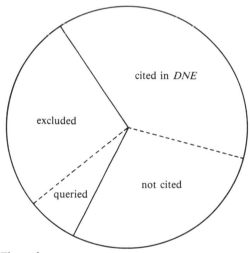

Figure 1

The file of evidence upon which the Dictionary has been built is considerably larger than that portion which is displayed in the articles and listed in the BIBLIOGRAPHY. It may be represented in the form of a diagram (Figure 1). A large number of words collected over the years have been excluded on the grounds that they seem, on balance, adequately covered in other dictionaries. Among these are certain words and idioms of considerable regional celebrity to which the recent advent of the electronic mass media has given an exaggerated currency and which, on examination, we do not find to be distinctive (*proper thing, rampike, up she comes*). Many other words have also been withheld because, on the evidence available to us, they seemed of extremely limited currency, often confined to single reports. These await the collection of further evidence. We have also, naturally, exercised judgment in selecting from our basic file of lexical material the amount of illustrative quotation for inclusion in the work. However, the complete file of material is to be preserved for the use of other students of the language.

Our judgement of the proper scope of this Dictionary will not command assent in every detail. But each decision has been made on the basis of all the evidence available to us: on our very large accumulation of field data, and on the reading and experience of the editors. Whatever the debate engaged in during the process of editorial selection, the decisions have all, in the end, been made with unanimity.

THE DICTIONARY AND ENGLISH
LANGUAGE VARIATION IN
NEWFOUNDLAND

Many words in the Newfoundland vocabulary have had a long history, and others have evolved as a resident population became established and spread around the coast of the island and to the north.[5] The earliest fishermen to live year-round, estab-

lish families and plant varieties of English permanently in Newfoundland settled along the east coast in the vicinity of St John's, the Southern Shore of the Avalon Peninsula as far as Trepassey, and in the coves and harbours of Conception Bay. English thus began its development here in the very early seventeenth century at about the time of the planting of the language in Virginia and New England in the American colonies. These early settlers were brought out by chartered companies administered from Bristol and London, and the evidence points to most of them coming, like the great numbers of transient fishermen, from the coastal ports and inland villages and hamlets of the English West Country: Devon, Dorset, Somerset, Hampshire and Wiltshire.[6] While the official plantations collapsed around the middle of the century, some of the settlers remained, and their variety of speech was reinforced annually by the thousands of West Country migratory fishermen whose seasonal voyages to the Island had long preceded the era of permanent settlement and continued down to the early nineteenth century. The English speech planted here, therefore, was the town and rural speech of the western counties of England, and varieties of cultivated speech current in England in the seventeenth century.

The second important linguistic strain in Newfoundland speech began in the late seventeenth century with the male English- and Irish-speaking helpers or 'servants' annually carried from southeastern Ireland, mainly through the port of Waterford, at the same time as the English adventurers obtained staple foods there for the fishing season in Newfoundland. Merchants from Ireland also sent trading ships to Newfoundland.[7] The numbers of Irish servants and later of

5 See G.M. Story, 'Newfoundland: Fishermen, Hunters, Planters and Merchants,' in *Christmas Mumming in Newfoundland* (Toronto: University of Toronto Press, 1969), 7–33; C. Grant Head, *Eighteenth Century Newfoundland* (Toronto: McClelland and Stewart, 1976); and *The Peopling of Newfoundland; Essays in Historical Geography*, ed John J. Mannion (St John's: Memorial University of Newfoundland, 1977).

6 See *The Peopling of Newfoundland*: W. Gordon Handcock, 'English Migration to Newfoundland,' 15–48, especially the map on p. 38.

7 See Head, 86–7.

immigrants increased enormously in the late eighteenth and early nineteenth centuries so that in some years the proportions of English to Irish in Newfoundland were about even. The mixed population at the end of the eighteenth century is well depicted by Aaron Thomas:[8]

As this Island has been inhabit'd for such a number of years and was peopled by British and Irish, you frequently meet with Familys whose Grandfathers were born in Newfoundland. These are what I call the Natives. They speak English but they have a manner perculiar to themselves—the common people Lisp. . .for [in] every Out-harbour I viseted on conversing with the people, they would on answering my enquirys say—'Yes, *dat* is the way' or 'O No, we *tant* do it so; but *den* we do it the other way, *tafter* we bring it home because it is *taffer*.'

There are occasional documentary references to monolingual and bilingual Irish-speaking fishermen working and settling in the island in the early years, but Irish seems never to have been established in Newfoundland and has had little influence on Newfoundland English independent of the development of Anglo-Irish in parts of Ireland itself.[9]

Less significant numbers from other overseas speech areas have settled in Newfoundland and Labrador, but with little effect on the two dominant systems of grammar and pronunciation. Channel Islanders came especially to the South Coast and Labrador. French-speaking settlers since the eighteenth century have come to western Newfoundland in small numbers from districts in France, from Acadian sources in the Maritime Provinces and from St Pierre and Miquelon south of Newfoundland. And the Scotch have come from two directions—as commercial and professional men from Scotland, especially to St John's and other eastern ports, and both Gaelic and English speakers from earlier settlements in Nova Scotia, to settle in western Newfoundland. Scots Gaelic is now moribund. Numerically these French and Scotch enclaves are very small.

Although it is more important for dialect geography than for the designing of a Newfoundland dictionary, it should be emphasized that until recent decades the greatest numbers of people employing folk and common speech in Newfoundland—the 'livyers' in the 'outports'—have lived in the string of settlements around the circumference of the island, along the coasts of the economically all-important bays. For most of their history, the islanders have inhabited primarily the narrow and long coastal perimeter of some 6,000 miles of deeply indented bays and inlets, and the inhabitants of Labrador a similar coast-line of well over another 1000 miles. The areas inland, beyond a few miles from the coast, are uninhabited wilderness and almost virgin territory (see Figure 2). With the advances of twentieth-century transportation and industry, it is true, a small number of routes, with accompanying dwellings and towns, have been laid out across parts of the interior. High roads such as the one from Conception Bay to Placentia were constructed in the mid-nineteenth century. The Reid Newfoundland railway, completed in 1897, was built in a wide arc through the north-central area of the island, with mining and paper-mill towns subsequently established along its route. The province's international airport has since 1940 given rise to the modern town of Gander. Roughly parallel to the railway, the Trans-Canada Highway (1965) has made possible the modernization and growth of other inland settlements, while in the inte-

8 *The Newfoundland Journal of Aaron Thomas*, ed Jean M. Murray (London: Longmans, 1968), 137.
9 A recently available study of contemporary vocabulary in Kilkenny firmly supports the view that Anglo-Irish speech in Newfoundland is actually a little changed branch of the Anglo-Irish employed in the nineteenth and twentieth centuries in south-eastern Ireland. Séamus Ó Máoláin's 'An Anglo-Irish Lexicon of County Kilkenny' (Diss. National University of Ireland, 1973) in entry after entry shows usages that are parallel or closely similar to those collected in the areas of Irish settlement in Newfoundland—in pronunciation, stress, morphology, sense or traditional customs.

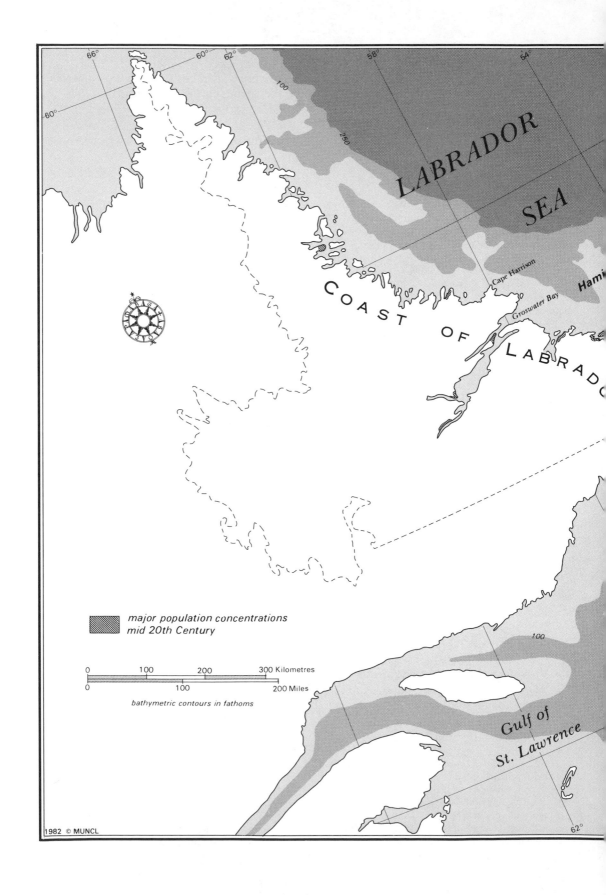

LABRADOR

SEA

COAST

OF

LABRADO

Cape Harrison

Groswater Bay

Ham

66°   60°   62°   58°   54°

60°

100

250

major population concentrations
mid 20th Century

0   100   200   300 Kilometres
0   100   200 Miles

bathymetric contours in fathoms

Gulf of
St. Lawrence

100

62°

1982 © MUNCL

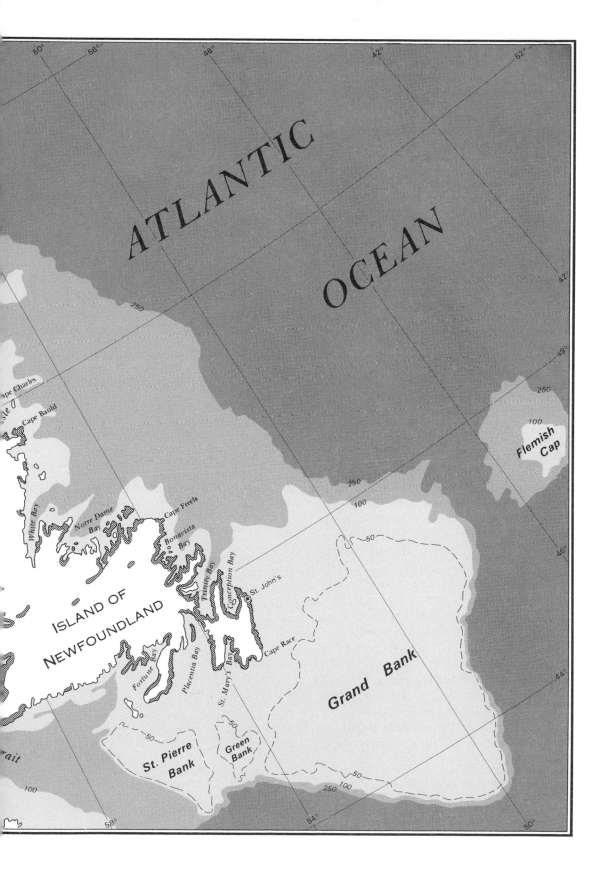

rior of Labrador several mining towns have grown up in recent years. Despite this, however, the bulk of the traditional speakers in Newfoundland still live and rear their families in the hundreds of harbours and coves of the island and Labrador.

This settlement pattern, with the populace mainly located along the coast-line, raises basic problems not simply logistical for the conduct of dialectal research in Newfoundland, and many readers who consult the Dictionary for certain kinds of dialectological data will be disappointed. Other dictionaries designed to treat dialect vocabulary have in fact listed areas, counties or other political divisions from which their quotations or glosses had been submitted; for many words the *English Dialect Dictionary* and the *American Dialect Dictionary*, for example, permit the making of rough distributional maps. But the sources on which this Dictionary has drawn have not in general allowed either the designation of areas in the region for individual words or senses or the determination of dialect areas in the manner of the word geographers elsewhere.[10] The lexical data, rich and varied though it is, is not, in our view, sufficient in quantity or dense enough in its coverage of representative settlements to enable us to describe precise patterns of geographical distribution.

For some terms, statements about areas of incidence may be cautiously made, but the designations are usually matters of geography, climate, flora and fauna, and not strictly correlated with either the ethnic origins of the speakers or with evolved dialect areas. For example, a number of words and senses can be localized on or pertain to the coast of Labrador (**floater, roomer, stationer**); sea ice, the seal hunt and associated terminology are not customary along the south coast; fishing terms of the Grand Banks differ from those of the inshore fishery; and city terms of St John's are often hardly known elsewhere (**chute, corner boy, teeveen**).

More crucially, however, close attention to all the assembled cards in our files[11]—lexical, semantic, phonological and morphological—in the process of drafting and revising the entries of the Dictionary has forced upon us a number of fresh views about the language of Newfoundland.

One of these suggests the modification of an older view that Newfoundland speech is characterized by marked differentiation of the kind generally noted by such visitors as Archdeacon Edward Wix in 1836:[12]

The difference of extraction has occasioned, as may be supposed, a marked dissimilarity between the descendants of Jersey-men, Frenchmen, Irish, Scotch, and English people. The people, too, with whom the first settlers and their immediate descendants may have had contact, or intercourse, have attributed much to the formation of the dialect, character, and habits of the present settlers. The inhabitants of Conception Bay, although a neck of land of only a few miles extent separates them from Trinity Bay, differ from the inhabitants of the latter, as much as if they were of a distant nation; the same may be said of the difference between those who live in Placentia and those who live in Fortune Bay.

The context makes it clear, however, that Wix is here thinking primarily of variation in morals and manners; but another contemporary observer noted of the North Shore men of Conception Bay that[13]

Their dialect was peculiar. It sounded particularly strange in the ears of the [neighbouring] Irish, although it was equally diverse from that of any English peasantry. One of its traits was an inability to pronounce the *th*, which became *t* or *d*. Most of them were Wesleyans, and it was amusing to hear them fervently singing in their old language: 'De ting my God dut hate / Dat I no more may do.'

10 Hans Kurath, *A Word Geography of the Eastern United States* (Ann Arbor: University of Michigan Press, 1949); Harold Orton and Nathalia Wright, *A Word Geography of England* (London: Seminar Press, 1974).

11 See below, SOURCES FOR THE DICTIONARY.

12 *Six Months of a Newfoundland Missionary's Journal*, 2nd ed (London: Smith, Elder and Co.), 143.

13 Philip Henry Gosse, c1830, in Edmund Gosse, *Life of Philip Henry Gosse* (London: Kegan Paul, 1890), 50.

A hundred years later, G. A. England remarked:[14]

It must be understood that there is no one fixed dialect for the whole island. Newfoundland was very long ago settled by at least four races—English, Irish, Scotch and French—and these races have to a large extent maintained their own peculiarities of speech, as well as of folklore and religion. . . As in ancient Greece, the deep bays and the difficulty of land-communication have tended to preserve the characteristics of the various settlements. Many of the people still consider themselves—say—Conception Bay men, or White Bay men, rather than Newfoundlanders as a whole. This has tended in some degree to preserve the various local differences of speech. Again, the lack of free public schools. . .and the resulting high degree of illiteracy, has further hindered the approach of the dialects to standard English.

The question which arises is whether such speech differentiation is a reflection of the existence of marked localized dialects within the historical speech groups who settled the region, or whether, as our own data suggests, the variation impressionistically noted by these early visitors reflects simply the two principal varieties of English which are overwhelmingly dominant, Anglo-Irish and West Country speech, the massive predominance of which will be apparent to even the casual reader of the Dictionary who observes the recurrence in the head-notes of 'Ir(e)' [= Ireland], 's w cties' [= south-west counties of England], or the specific localities of Cornwall, Devon, Dorset, Hampshire, Isle of Wight, and Somerset. For what we have begun to see more distinctly is the striking homogeneity of traditional Newfoundland culture in the twentieth century, amply demonstrated, for example, in a well-studied cultural index such as the widespread Christmas mumming activities;[15] and the linguistic counterpart of that evidence suggests that in the twentieth century, at least, too much can be made of the 'isolated communities' along the coast-line as a determinant of language variation and that, rather, numerous economic and social contacts within Newfoundland 'have exerted the most generalizing influence on the dialects, insuring that certain terms are widely known and employed, and diffusing stories, sayings, ordinary idioms, grammatical forms, specific pronunciations of words, and, possibly, phonetic qualities.'[16] It is within this general framework that such evidence as there is for language variation in Newfoundland needs to be viewed.

Along with the uneven evidence of geographical variation of terms, our files include considerable amounts of information on other sorts of variation. However, unlike Wright's *English Dialect Dictionary* and Wentworth's *American Dialect Dictionary*, the *Dictionary of Newfoundland English* does not attempt to report all the collected evidence available on variant pronunciations and recorded spellings, grammatical forms and variations in idioms. The purpose of the Dictionary is, within the general aims described in the preceding section of the Introduction, to present particularly the distinctive indigenous vernacular, with accompanying definitions that will make clear to people who have a knowledge of English the senses of these words as they are used locally. Thus the Dictionary has entries for **after, be, either** and its negative, **he** and **she, ye**, and other grammatical words which would invite misunderstanding by those unfamiliar with regional usage. At the same time, other grammatical items with non-standard forms are excluded if their senses are similar to those used elsewhere and they can easily be interpreted by a reader, e.g. *to be bet out*; past of *lie*: lid; past of *set*: sot.

Certain pronunciation variants are often recorded in the illustrative quotations, how-

14 *Dialect Notes* v, 322.
15 *Christmas Mumming in Newfoundland*, ed Herbert Halpert and G.M. Story (Toronto: University of Toronto Press, 1969), especially 5–6, 216–17, 222–9; G.M. Story, 'Notes from a Berry Patch,' *Transactions of the Royal Society of Canada*, Series IV, x (1972), 173.
16 W.J. Kirwin, 'The Dialects,' in *The Avalon Peninsula of Newfoundland; An Ethno-Linguistic Study* (Ottawa: The National Museum of Canada, Bulletin 219, 1968), 57.

ever, especially those from taped sources, but since these are widespread dialectal alternates and usually predictable, explicit detail is not usually provided in either the headnotes or in the system of cross-references. The most common variations involve [h] inserted before initial vowels of stressed syllables (or [h] omitted where educated speakers usually pronounce it); intervocalic -t- flapped or replaced by -d-; final consonant clusters ending in -t or -d often simplified (*loft* is *lof*, *sound* is *soun'*, *field* is *fiel'*); constricted *r* (i.e. [ɹ]) vocalized or omitted between vowel and consonant or in word-final position (*sca'ce, ta'n back* 'thorn back'); *th* often pronounced *t* or *d*, depending on whether [θ] or [ð] occurs in standard pronunciation; short *i* and *e* frequently interchangeable, as before -*l* or -*n* (*kellick, ven* 'fin'); short *e* frequently lowered to *a*, i.e. [æ] (*lag, zad*); *or-* plus consonant lowered to some form of *ar-* (*farty, starm*); and -*l* vocalized to a mid- or high-back vowel (*squid squall: squid squaw; tole pin: toe pin*).

A brief résumé follows of the principal grammatical features of various folk-speech types[17] to be found in Newfoundland and Labrador.

1 Nouns after numerals above *one* have no plural -*s*: 'Now a cod-trap is about sixty fathom on the round.'

2 Finite verbs in the present tense take -*(e)s* for all persons and numbers: 'I thinks this is unlawful, and as others informs me is onproper and onpossible, and this the liviers here, all could tell ye.'

3 Only one form is employed for both the past tense and past participle of strong verbs: 'She was gangboarded, fore-cuddy an' after-cuddy on her, and freeze *come* on, they got *drove* off.'

4 *Am, is*, and *are* are employed for an assertion about an event at the present moment, while *be's*, for all persons, indicates continuous or repeated activity: 'There's a sunken rock. You know when the water's high, that it be's under water.'

5 *To have (already) done (something)* is not a normal usage, the notion being expressed by *to be after doing (something)*: 'How many times am I after tellin' you?'

6 The unstressed object form for *he* is *un*: 'We'd see the sun steady for three months, never lose un.'

7 The stressed forms for the personal pronouns after verbs (including forms of *be*) and prepositions are *I, he, she, we, they*:

'[Fairies] was only little small people, they used to tell we.'
'He thought to hisself he'd a-killed the two of 'em [but] 'twasn't they now.'
'Never mind they—let 'em bite.'

(The unstressed forms, except for example 6 above, are the same as in standard colloquial English.)

8 Stressed *he* and *she* are often used as substitutes for count nouns, but *it* for mass and abstract nouns like *crookedness, fog, weather*: 'But the first hour we hauled in the log, and he registered three miles. So the next hour we hauled 'im in again, and she's got another three miles.'

9 Adjectives derived from names of materials end in -*en*: 'tinnen cup, glassen pole.'

10 For many speakers the plural demonstrative determiners are *those* with objects and events that are current, and *them* with objects and events that are past: 'Years ago, not so much those days, you'd always have a gun line.'

The distinctive inflectional and syntactic features to be heard in present-day Newfoundland, and sometimes represented in printed sketches, fiction and drama, reveal productive patterns that differ from those of educated speakers in the British Isles, continental North America and other English-speaking nations. Unfortunately, they cannot, within the framework of the Dictionary, be correlated in any direct or simple fashion with the numerous local and areal

---

17 The use of *folk, common* and *cultivated speech* in this discussion closely parallels distinctions among informants described in Kurath (1949), 7–9. See also the sketch of regional dialects by W.J. Kirwin in *The Avalon Peninsula of Newfoundland*, [54]–73.

speech-types that are being described in current scholarly investigation.[18]

Styles and accents of cultivated Newfoundland and Labrador speech have so far been little studied. They clearly tend to be like those of the principal Midland and Northern speech types of the United States and educated native speakers of the rest of anglophone Canada. A retroflex or constricted *r* is pronounced as it occurs in conventional spelling; *-ar-* tends to be more fronted toward [æɹ] than the vowel sound of most Canadian and American educated speech; *-oor*, and *-ore*, and the parallel *-eer* and *-are* (cp *poor, pour, pore, pier, pear, pare, pair* and similar groups), tend to coalesce in the lower type of vowel for many speakers; and finally usage is divided according to both birthplace and educational level in the use of one or two low-back vowels (cp *caught/cot*) and the use of the raised and shortened diphthong in words like *house, mouth* and *spout* of such high frequency in the rest of Canada. And of course educated Newfoundlanders can employ with ease and accuracy the extensive local and regional technical lexicon as it pertains to the environment, the fisheries and related industries, and local traditional customs. They can casually slip into their conversation well-known regional idioms (*some good, leff un bide, last going off, you're not easy*). When such terms and phrases are uttered by a cosmopolitan Newfoundlander, they easily bewilder the uninitiated listener.

It is easier to specify linguistically the phonemic systems and phonetic varieties of Newfoundland speech than it is to suggest in a general way distinctive qualities of stressing, intonation patterns, pitch range and, most elusively, tone of voice. Regional stress patterns of high frequency are duly indicated in the phonetic transcriptions of the Dictionary whenever, as in **stage head, Labrador** and **Newfoundland** itself, it is easy to misinterpret the placement of stress in a

printed word or word-group. The most that can be said impressionistically about intonation is that many speakers tend to use high pitch levels in much of their speech and rising intonations very frequently at ends of phrases.

SOURCES FOR THE DICTIONARY

Classified lists of the sources cited in the Dictionary articles are set forth in the Bibliography and they represent our selection from the total corpus of evidence at our disposal. But that evidence is considerably larger than the portion actually cited and, moreover, is of such discrete and varied nature as to require summary description.

Printed Sources. For more than two hundred years printed sources have formed the base upon which historical dictionaries have rested and the present work, in part, follows that tradition. Our aim was to read intensively the body of literature devoted to the island of Newfoundland and coastal Labrador from its beginning in the sixteenth and seventeenth centuries down to about 1850, and thereafter to read and excerpt more selectively as the volume of material became more extensive.

In the earlier period, the principal works were usually composed by outsiders writing about the country, and readers of the Dictionary articles will soon become familiar with the limited number of names and works which occur repeatedly in the quotations: *Gilbert's Voyages & Enterprises* (1583); James Yonge, the Devonshire surgeon, describing visits of the West Country fishing fleet in 1663, 1668 and 1670; the 1699 Act of Parliament which set down in formal terms the customary regulation of the Newfoundland fisheries which had grown up during the preceding hundred years; Joseph Banks, writing about his scientific collecting in 1766; George Cartwright with his detailed journal of sixteen years' residence

---

18 See Harold Paddock, 'Preliminary Dialect Mapping of Newfoundland: A Progress Report,' in *Languages in Newfoundland and Labrador*, Prelim.

Version, stencilled (St. John's: Memorial University of Newfoundland, 1977), 90–106.

on the coast of Labrador, beginning in 1770; Aaron Thomas, diarist and seaman (1794); the clergymen Anspach (1819) and Wix (1836); and others. These writers, and their successors Bonnycastle, Jukes, De Boilieu, Wilson, and the many twentieth-century visitors (or resident outsiders such as Grenfell) who have written about their observations and experiences, form an important and much-used resource for the Dictionary; and, as their abundant and conscious use of italics and quotation marks indicates, they contributed richly to the historical record of Newfoundland English, though in using their work we have exercised a necessary caution in distinguishing between their own use of the language and their attribution, implied or overt, of regional usage. Of course the dialogue composed by these accomplished professional writers should not be trusted as much as the grammatical evidence in the Dictionary's quotations taken from taped speech.

With native-born Newfoundland writers we are usually on more assured ground since their pamphlets, books and essays frequently tend to employ the vocabulary and idioms assimilated during childhood and youth in Newfoundland. Especially after 1807, when the printing press was introduced to the region and the settled population moved towards the status of an official colony, these writers produced works that become staple sources; Bond, Cormack, Howley, Prowse, Tocque and others are the recurring names in the quotations. In the nineteenth century, too, begins the flood of ephemeral works: pamphlets written and printed locally, Christmas annuals, magazines and trade reviews, some of them rare even in public collections and a few surviving in apparently unique copies. We have read as many of them as possible; and we have also drawn heavily on local newspapers, especially the two long-lived St John's papers, the *Daily News* and the *Evening Telegram*, together with the *Newfoundland Quarterly*.

Special care has been given to the large corpus of ballads which from about 1830 forms the principal local literary source, and we have augmented this by the plays, poems and fiction of Newfoundland and adopted Newfoundland writers ranging from Lowell and Duncan to the steadily increasing number and variety of writers of our own century: Duley, Guy, Horwood, Pratt, Russell, Scammell, and others.

One source for the documentation of the regional lexicon, place-names, perhaps needs special mention since it has not, in our experience, been much used by lexicographers. As occasion offered, we have cited these and other topographic terms from the record of their historical incidence on maps and charts in the work of E.R. Seary,[19] for they often provide the earliest authentic evidence of terms which later appear in more familiar kinds of printed sources (see **baccalao, blow-me-down, bread-and-cheese, salvage**). A specialized work of great importance for the record of the lexicon of a coastal people has been cited with particular frequency: the British Admiralty's *Newfoundland and Labrador Pilot*. We have used it mostly in the 8th edition (1951, 1953); but in its origin it reaches back through an unbroken tradition of marine surveys to the work of Cook and Lane in the eighteenth century; in its record of coastal features with lexical significance, of conditions of ice, wind and water, it has been an important source and one the very language of which is a constant reminder of the depth of the influence of nautical idiom on the speech of the region (see **brandies, ground, growler, gulch, ledge, run, sunker, tickle**).

Finally, there is a considerable number of glossarists of local words and expressions—natives and visitors alike—whose lists we have drawn upon for our evidence: Cartwright (1792), Moreton (1863), Patterson (1895–7), England

---

19 See especially his *Place Names of the Avalon Peninsula of the Island of Newfoundland* (Toronto: University of Toronto Press, 1971).

(1924–5), Devine (1937), English (1955), and others.[20] Though these writers are placed, for obvious reasons, among our printed sources, it should be borne in mind that they were almost exclusively collectors from 'oral' sources, and we do not attribute to them either more or less weight or authority over the other non-printed sources for the Dictionary simply because they achieved print. But we are deeply indebted to these predecessors for their pioneering attempt to collect and record the regional lexicon.

We have naturally made heavy demands, rarely disappointed, on the custodians of printed material related to the region, particularly the Provincial Reference Library, St John's, and the University's Centre for Newfoundland Studies, the latter also acting as intermediary in securing through inter-library loan material not available locally. In nearly every case this has enabled us to use the most authoritative text of a given work, either the earliest printed text or one available in a critical edition. But few Newfoundland texts have been edited with high standards of scholarship, and occasional problems of a special nature have been posed by the existence of some works in variant issues and editions. For example, Whitbourne's *Discourse and Discovery of Newfoundland* survives in eleven editions and issues (and one manuscript) dated variously between 1620 and 1623, two of them with considerable textual variation and all with a bibliographical relationship which has only recently been clarified.[21] Cormack's *Narrative* of his journey across the island of Newfoundland in 1822 is available in several printed editions which have not been systematically collated and critically edited. The texts of the ballads are notorious for variation introduced by the singers from whose lips (for the most part) the compositions have been collected, as well as for a lax tradition of printing and

editing. In these and other similar instances we have occasionally cited now one text of a work, now another, in illustrating a word, giving the quotation from a designated edition or editions listed in the Bibliography.

Historical Manuscripts. At an early stage of our work we decided not to attempt to read and excerpt the large collections of historical manuscripts relating to Newfoundland and Labrador such as those preserved in the Provincial Archives (assembled contemporaneously with work on the Dictionary), or abroad in the Public Record Office of Great Britain, the British Library, and elsewhere; and we have, in general, adhered to that decision for the simple and pragmatic reason that we could not afford the time it would have taken to do otherwise. But we have been led to make some exceptions to the general rule and, because they were readily available to us (in the original or in photographs) and filled important gaps in the printed record, we have systematically drawn evidence from a number of particular manuscript sources, including the *Willoughby Papers*, now located at the University of Nottingham, for the period 1610–1634; the *Pulling Manuscript* (BM Add MSS 38352) for 1792; the *Diary* of the Rev. Henry Lind from the west coast of Newfoundland (c1850); the sealing logs of Capt. Edward White for many of the years between 1854 and 1886; the manuscript *Reminiscences* of J.P. Howley, covering the years 1868–1910; the *Twillingate Minute Book* of the Fishermen's Protective Union (1912–1942); and a few other miscellaneous documents, some in private hands but most of them in public collections.

Occasionally we have found it necessary to go to microfilm copies of the original documents preserved among the papers of the British Colonial Office, especially the 194 series dealing with Newfoundland in the seventeenth and eighteenth centuries, in

20 See G.M. Story, 'A Critical History of Dialect Collecting in Newfoundland,' *Regional Language Studies. . .Newfoundland*, 6 (May, 1975), 1–4.

21 See *Short-Title Catalogue of English Books: 1475–1640*, 2nd ed (London: The Bibliographical Society, 1976) ii, 452.

order to resolve doubts about the accuracy of a published transcript or to seek corroborating evidence for the occurrence of a word (see, for example, **sud line**). But for the most part we have relied on the copious extracts from this series, and other historical manuscripts, given in such standard works as those by Reeves (1793), Pedley (1863), Prowse (1895), Innis (1940, 1954), Head (1976), etc.

Field Records. Collecting from non-printed sources specifically for the Dictionary began with the inception of the work and was both accelerated and broadened in 1959 as dialectology was formally introduced to Newfoundland.[22] Field-workers quickly discovered a richness of vocabulary similar to that documented in the British *Survey of English Dialects* (1962–8),[23] and words, pronunciations and meanings obtained in direct interviewing became part of the lexical store for the Dictionary.

Collecting for the Dictionary was also conducted by the editors in a variety of other ways as well: check-lists of words were circulated among informants for verification and information; collections were made by our students in courses taught at Memorial University; and many items were collected over several decades in the ordinary course of living, and listening, in Newfoundland. Material drawn from this body of data is cited in the Dictionary articles with the code letter P.

Folklore and Language Archive. Next to the printed sources, the largest single category of material upon which we have drawn is that contained in the Memorial University of Newfoundland Folklore and Language Archive (MUNFLA). Assembled over a period of almost a decade and a half, and still growing,[24] the Archive is the repository of materials of immense richness for, among others, the lexicographer.

In listing the Archive sources excerpted and used in the Dictionary we have set up in our Bibliography four headings: card collection, manuscript collection, questionnaire collection, and tape collection; these are cited in the Dictionary with the code letters, C, M, Q and T respectively.

The first three groups of data, from C, M and Q sources, are chiefly student collections, made as part of formal training in undergraduate courses in folklore and usually the result of investigation of the traditional life of particular home communities. At the time (1975) when we completed our excerpting of the Archive, it contained 25,000 carded items, 1000 individual manuscript collections, and 5000 questionnaire responses, each catalogued and accessioned, and recording the name of the collector, the informant, the place and date of collecting. The topics investigated range from material culture, stories, rhymes, riddles, games, ballads and songs, to accounts of the economic activities—the round of work—of the settlements, their patterns of belief and behaviour; and the submissions frequently display, in a natural and unself-conscious way, the familiar lexicon of the region. Some of the collecting instruments, especially a large and diverse questionnaire administered by 1300 student-collectors in

22 See G.M. Story, *A Newfoundland Dialect Dictionary: A Survey of the Problems* [St John's], 1956, and 'Research in the Language and Place-Names of Newfoundland,' *J Can Ling Assoc*, (1957), 47–55; J.D.A. Widdowson, 'Some Items of a Central Newfoundland Dialect,' *Can Journ Ling*, x (1964), 37–46; W.J. Kirwin, 'The Dialects,' in *The Avalon Peninsula of Newfoundland; An Ethnolinguistic Study* (Ottawa: The National Museum of Canada, 1968), 56–73; three theses directed by W.J. Kirwin: H.J. Paddock (1966), Virginia Dillon (1968), and R.G Noseworthy (1971).

23 The Newfoundland population has been so long separated from the agricultural communities of the West Country investigated for the *SED* that only a small number of useful parallels in the parts devoted to the southern counties have been recorded in our headnotes.

24 See Herbert Halpert and Neil V. Rosenberg, *Folklore Studies at Memorial University: Two Reports*, [St John's:] Folklore Reprint Series No. 4, 1978, 1–13, for an account of the origin of the Archive, the methods by which it was assembled, and an account of its accessioning and cataloguing system.

the winter of 1966–67, contained sections specifically designed by the editors of the Dictionary to elicit vocabulary.

While excerpting these collections for the lexical items, we also created a separate file of over 20,000 cards containing proverbs and proverbial comparisons which, together with a considerable store of printed reports, have been used as occasion offered in writing the Dictionary articles.

The tape collection of the Archive included by 1975 some 2000 original tapes a substantial number of which were recorded in the field by Herbert Halpert and J.D.A. Widdowson working in most of the areas of the island of Newfoundland. A considerable portion of these have been typed in running transcripts which can, like a printed book, be scanned, the lexical items marked, phonetically transcribed from the tape itself, and provided with context sentences and exact reference to collector, informant, date, and community.

For many kinds of books and articles since the mid-nineteenth century, the motives and conditions of publishing sometimes distort the vernacular speech of the people, except in the vocabulary of the gear and procedures connected with the fisheries. In this situation the taped conversations in the Archive (and indeed the student reports gleaned from grandparents and older friends and relatives) have provided a salutary corrective to the words, usages, and meanings excerpted from printed works. The recordings are most frequently of men and women born before 1900, and, as will be observed from many citations in the Dictionary, they deal with the times and activities of the older members of the speakers' families, and reach well back into the nineteenth century. The recall of these transmitters of a largely oral culture is minutely detailed and factual, and the result in the mass of the Archive sources is a splendid verbal record of the pronunciations, forms and terms of earlier generations.

We have elsewhere assessed the evidence collected from these sources from the point of view of the regional lexicon,[25] but the conventions of historical lexicography have been so heavily weighted towards an exclusive reliance on printed evidence that it is perhaps useful for us to repeat some of that discussion, for as with the data drawn from the records of trained field-workers, these Archives sources are, of course, essentially oral.

There is good reason why lexicographers have not commonly drawn upon non-printed materials for their work. For one thing, it takes much time and trouble to collect it, as Dr Johnson long ago observed:[26]

I could not visit caverns to learn the miner's language, nor take a voyage to perfect my skill in the dialect of navigation, nor visit the warehouses of merchants, and shops of artificers, to gain the names of wares, tools and operations, of which no mention is found in books. . .it had been a hopeless labour to glean up words, by courting living information. . .

Moreover, orally collected data does not, by its very nature, easily lend itself to the practice of rigorous and precise documentation of the kind essential to historical lexicography; a word heard on radio, spoken on television, or overheard in the street usually passes too quickly for verification.

Yet several dictionaries which we have habitually used in our work, and which have influenced our practice, have in one way or another gone beyond the printed record. One of the most important of these, Wright's *English Dialect Dictionary* (1898–1905), for example, drew heavily on the personal contributions of numerous correspondents, and their data is inserted among the other kinds of evidence utilized in the dictionary, identified by the initials of the informant, together with material from unprinted collections of dialect words.[27] And of course the numerous regional glos-

25 Story, Kirwin and Widdowson, 'Collecting for the Dictionary of Newfoundland English,' *Annals of the New York Academy of Sciences*, ccxi (June, 1973), 104–8.

26 *A Dictionary of the English Language* (London: J. and P. Knapton and others, 1755), vol i, C 1ᵛ.

27 *EDD*, vol. i, Preface, and xi–xiv.

saries compiled for and printed by the English Dialect Society expressly for use in the Society's dictionary which Wright undertook to edit, together with the other glossaries issued by sister organizations in the counties of England and elsewhere in the British Isles, were in many cases essentially a record of oral use. Like the *EDD*, the *Scottish National Dictionary* (begun in 1931) relied in part on a network of local informants as well as upon printed sources; and a more recent work, *The Dictionary of Jamaican English* (1967) by Cassidy and LePage, similarly rests partly on a base of non-printed evidence: questionnaire responses especially, and a limited number of tape recordings and field records. To these will soon be added the long-promised American equivalent of the *English Dialect Dictionary*, Cassidy's *Dictionary of American Regional English* (*DARE*), which is being constructed from materials assembled from varied sources over many decades by the American Dialect Society, from extensive field investigation, including tape recordings and massive questionnaire data, as well as from a reading of regional books and newspapers.[28]

What the Archive has, in effect, done is to bring together a large corpus of data from oral sources in both written and taped form and, through a careful policy of accessioning, cataloguing and transcription, turn these into documents which can be examined, verified, collated and used (like printed data) critically and precisely. In our practice, therefore, printed data, while remaining one of the staples of our work, is complemented by both manuscript and oral evidence. (See Figure 3 in which the percentages refer to the totals of specified sources, not to degree of use in citations, i.e. to 'types' not 'tokens.') Nothing less, we believe, would suffice in a work of this kind

undertaken in a region in which the local tradition of print is late and relatively weak but which displays a tenacious and robust oral culture;[29] and the reader of the majority of the articles presented in the Dictionary is invited to consider the losses and gains which would have resulted from reliance on any less broad a range of sources than we have in fact used.

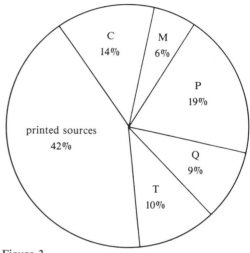

Figure 3

PRONUNCIATION AND PHONETICS

With such a large resource of oral material available for the Dictionary, a record of pronunciation in phonetic transcription, following the system of the International Phonetic Alphabet, has been included in the headnotes for certain items. Unlike many general commercial dictionaries, however, our work does not present phonetics, or respelling, for all the words which have been treated. Where certain words differ from pronunciations recorded in the principal English and North American dictionaries,

28 See Frederic G. Cassidy, 'What's New About *DARE*?' in *Papers in Language Variation*, ed David L. Shores and Carole P. Hines (University of Alabama Press, 1977), 13–17.

29 See Herbert Halpert, 'Folklore and Newfoundland,' *Papers of the Bibliographical Society of Canada*, 8 (1969), 10–22; G.M. Story, 'Notes from a Berry Patch,' *Transactions of the Royal Society of Canada*, Series IV, x (1972), 163–77.

where the word exhibits some unusual or interesting features, or where the spelling is ambiguous or a misleading guide to the local pronunciations or stress patterns, phonetic transcriptions may be given. The phonetic record in the Dictionary is therefore selective, as in such analogous dictionaries as *DA*, *DC* and *DJE*.

Further limitations on the indication of pronunciations are a result of the particular evidence which has been assembled. Certain words and phrases have been noted sporadically or in systematic field interviews by researchers and trained students. A great number have been transcribed from over 400 tape recordings in the Folklore Archive concerned with folklore topics, reminiscences, occupations and other aspects of Newfoundland cultural tradition. Tape-recorded evidence has the great advantage of immediacy and vividness, and although some of this is inevitably lost in transcribing the conventions of the spoken register into the more formal conventions of print, the quotations taken from tape are drawn from the natural context of free conversation rather than the somewhat artificial one of field interviews.

The excerpting process itself inevitably poses some problems. Each phonetic transcription cited in the headnotes represents either the pronunciation of a response to a collector perhaps using a questionnaire or of a form cited from within a segment of continuous speech. The extraction of a word from its context sometimes gives a misleading impression of its typical pronunciation and placement of stress which may differ from the specific one in the running text. The immediate phonetic environment in the utterance, for example, conditions certain features of pronunciation, especially of initial and final sounds. A similar problem arises when we wish to indicate the pronunciation of a noun in the singular and our tape recordings have it only in the plural, or when we wish to give the infinitive of a verb but have only the inflected form in our evidence. Syllable stress may also

reflect certain patterns of contrast, abbreviation or emphasis in the context which differ from those typical of the word as normally uttered in isolation.

By the very nature of human speech it is inevitable that the pronunciation of some words is very well attested in any corpus of tape recordings while other pronunciations are poorly attested or not represented at all. The pronunciations given in the headnotes are therefore not to be regarded as comprehensive or definitive.

As they represent only the information we have at our disposal in tapes and transcriptions, variants cannot be ranked in order of frequency or by other hierarchical means. In the absence of comprehensive and statistical studies of regional variation we have therefore displayed the range of phonetic evidence in as neutral a manner as possible, allowing the variants to convey a collective impression of the current pronunciations of local forms. It is important to note, however, that information concerning the individual speakers recorded on tape, together with precise reference to the location and date of each recording and other important contextual details on file in MUNFLA, enables us to identify the pronunciations of a given transcription with specific people and places. Surprisingly, however, the tape recordings reveal remarkably little variation in the distribution of forms throughout the Province. Nevertheless, the predominance of English or Irish features, for example, in the speech of individuals in specific communities sometimes indicates the preservation of pronunciations typical of regional usage in their respective parent cultures.

The phonetic transcription of the word to be exemplified is given in square brackets after the designation of the part of speech or the listing of variant spellings, where these are given. In general, pronunciations are given in the singular form for nouns and in the infinitive for verbs. Where a number of pronunciations are available, these are listed according to the vowel of the syllable under strongest stress, short vowel forms being listed first, followed by long vowel forms and diphthongs. Within each of the vowel groups, the stressed vowels are listed from high front to low and from low back to high, in the numerical order of the Cardinal Vowels,[30] followed by the central vowels, reading from high to low, in the sequence [i ɪ e ɛ æ a ɑ ɒ ʌ ɔ ɤ o ʊ u ɨ ʉ ə ɐ] (see Figure 4). In the few cases where two or more pronunciation variants have the same strongly stressed vowel, the forms are listed in the same way but based this time on the order of the vowels under secondary or minimal stress. For example ['blæstɪ ˌbaɷ] precedes ['blæstɪ ˌbɑɷ]. Occasionally, where the pronunciation of the headword itself is obvious and therefore no phonetic transcription for it is included, we indicate unusual pronunciations and stress patterns of phrases or combinations immediately after the relevant forms within the article.

PRESENTATION OF THE DICTIONARY ARTICLES

The Main Words are entered in the Dictionary in alphabetical order. Because of the complexity of a number of terms, especially some connected with the fisheries, a compound or combination may be moved from others of its kind within a massed entry and itself presented in a separate article; cross-references have been provided within such complex entries to show that the combination has in fact been treated in another place (e.g. **newfoundland dog**: see NEWFOUNDLAND DOG; **stage head**: see STAGE HEAD). Occasionally, also, a combination has been separately treated if its affiliations recorded in the historical dictionaries deserve full, specific treatment in the headnote (e.g. SALT WATER). Homographs of the same part of speech are arranged, in sometimes arbitrary order, with identifying

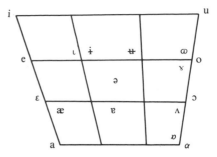

Figure 4

numerical superscripts: **cat**[1] through **cat**[7] is an extreme example.

The treatment of Main Words in this Dictionary is divided structurally into four parts: the word and accompanying technical information, presented in highly compressed form; the definitions, glosses or synonyms of the term in numbered sections arranged usually in historical order, but if early evidence is not available, then a logical order may occasionally be followed; the phrases, collocations, compounds and combinations related to the main word, also arranged in numbered sections and explained; and, in most cases, for all the definitions illustrative examples of the use of the term from printed material, speech or other identified sources. The spelling and hyphenation of all editorial matter in the Dictionary, with the exception of cited material, contractions and local vernacular, follows British practice as specified in the *Shorter Oxford English Dictionary* (3rd ed rev., 1955).

The Vocabulary Entry and Headnotes. The Main Word is printed in **bold type** and, for the sake of typographical uniformity on the page, without initial capitalization, even of proper nouns. (The supporting quotations, of course, illustrate the capitalization usually found in proper nouns, e.g. in the entries for **christmas, labrador, newfoundland**). The word is presented in a spelling supported by the printed evidence, in a spelling of the associated word in British usage, or in a spelling selected from

30 Daniel Jones, *An Outline of English Phonetics*, 8th ed (Cambridge: W. Heffer & Sons, 1956), 36.

among several available variants or even newly devised to represent the pronunciation of a form recorded only in speech. In the last situation the vocabulary entry is marked with an asterisk: **sheveen***. These shifting criteria for the choice of a spelling are necessitated by the diverse kinds of often complicated evidence that have been reviewed. In general we have tried to help readers to relate the word to the printed tradition or to speech. For most entries there was no occasion to select one spelling rather than another, but in some cases, as with **angishore, clumper, hurt, skerwink, skully, tawt** and **tolc pin**, a choice had to be made among close contenders.

The designation of the part of speech, or word-class, follows the headword; the abbreviations employed are identified in a list at the end of this Introduction. Verbs have been combined under general definitions without the separation of transitive and intransitive uses which would have excessively fragmented the articles. A small number of words present difficult problems of classification, and in such cases the designation has been arbitrary. For example, commands, calls, names and exclamations, together with idiomatic nautical usages and cures and grades of fish (e.g. **tal qual**), especially if contextual evidence is not extensive, could conceivably be analysed in other ways. The illustrative quotations in the body of the entry display the complex syntactic relations, or even outright ambiguity, of these knotty words.

Alternate forms of the headword have next been presented selectively in alphabetical order. Because of the vernacular nature of many terms, invented spellings have appeared in print and seemingly endless oral variants are found in the manuscript and taped data. All important printed variants are listed, but suspicious spellings or errors in newspapers or ballad collections have usually been omitted. Variants not recorded in print are followed by an asterisk, and are either in the spelling of a contri-

butor or in a devised spelling to suggest the approximate pronunciation. See **ballicatter** or **copy** for the abundant variations that have been noted in both print and regional speech. All printed and oral variants judged to be significant in local usage or of high frequency have been duly entered with cross-references in the alphabetical sequence of the dictionary. Exact repetition of the headword or of a form just presented is symbolized by the swung dash ~: **baccy hurt. . .backy** ~ .

The headnote includes further precise information on the pronunciation of the word in the International Phonetic Alphabet (IPA) transcription for many entries (see PRONUNCIATION AND PHONETICS above). It should be noted that these transcriptions are presented only when there is firm evidence from speech or tape, when the regional stress-pattern is distinctive (e.g. **newfoundland, tom cod, stage head**), when the spelling of the headword is misleading (e.g. **lead**; **stalk** rhyming with *talc*) or when the recorded variants are potentially useful for dialectologists. For some words the only indication of pronunciation is recorded orthographic forms, and the original pronunciations of these are unknown (e.g. **ownshook**).

The main body of the headnote is taken up with the comparative evidence presented in other pertinent historical and regional dictionaries, lexicons of other languages and a variety of published works found to be useful. The purpose of these sometimes lengthy notes citing information from the *OED* and its Supplements, the *Dictionary of Canadianisms*, Dinneen's *Irish-English Dictionary* and other specialized works is to place the Newfoundland term historically, geographically or linguistically in relation to its authenticated usage elsewhere. The data shows succinctly the chronology of the word in other speech areas; and the overlap of the word with dialect areas in the English West Country, Ireland, the Canadian Maritime Provinces, the Atlantic seaboard of the

United States, or on the high seas—in maritime usage. It shows relevant senses reported in other dictionaries, and therefore suggests origins or close semantic relationships of the term.[31] Combinations and phrases reported elsewhere are fully recorded, with the earliest dates. The Dictionary thus attempts to present in its headnotes concise but comprehensive annotation for general readers without extensive libraries as well as for specialist scholars.

Etymological information in the headnotes, in this first extensive examination of the Newfoundland lexicon, has been limited to words either traceable to foreign languages, principally Irish, standard and dialectal French,[32] Portuguese, Beothuk and Micmac, Eskimo, etc, or to terms that have long exercised local commentators and elicited numerous unsupported explanations in print and in oral speculation (e.g. **bedlamer, copy, cassock/kossa(c)k, crunnick** [*chronic*], **tickle**).[33] Familiar English forms with comprehensive derivational notes in the *OED* or in Onions's *Oxford Dictionary of English Etymology* have not been etymologized, although of course the extensive headnote references to the numbered senses and combinations in the historical and regional dictionaries imply the presumed derivational affiliations of these terms. Occasionally a word is compared to a recorded instance in another dictionary (with the direction *cp*) merely to show that the form and associated sense are extant elsewhere, even if that word is not the 'source' of the local word (e.g. **scurrifunge**). Furthermore the purpose of many cross-references in the Dictionary is in a sense etymological: they point out to the reader the standard or basic form in Newfoundland usage underlying variants in the vocabulary

(e.g. the **swale, swile, swoil** group comprehensively treated at **seal**).

Where editorial guess-work has been involved, all the discovered documentary evidence is presented as clues to the possible derivation of the term (see **catamaran, fool, ose egg, squid, touton**). Where all the sifting of data in reference works and specialized treatises has not produced any clues, no etymology is offered (see **killick, rodney**). No popular explanations or folk etymologies have been given a place in the headnotes, and the manifold explanations of terms in the citation files have been scrutinized with care before they have been considered for reprinting among the illustrative quotations. The data on spellings, pronunciations, meanings and related uses elsewhere which has been assembled in the Dictionary prepares the ground for subsequent intensive exploration into the origins of a handful of untraced words. The final information presented in a number of headnotes is cross-references, printed in small capital letters, to other Dictionary entries which contain complementing information and evidence.

The Definitions. To display the historical development of a vocabulary entry or for convenience in classifying more or less distinct senses, the definitions of the term, where there are several, are presented in numbered sections. More than in some other dictionaries of its kind, the reader will find here complicated technical words, the large number of which is a distinctive feature of the work and the defining of which, often for the first time, has been one of the greatest challenges to the editors. An effort has been made to make the definitions of these technical terms self-sufficient by indicating briefly in a defining formula the con-

31 Clarence L. Barnhart comments on the usefulness of such a practice in 'American Lexicography, 1945–1973,' *American Speech*, liii (1978), 89.
32 See William J. Kirwin, 'Selected French and English Fisheries Synonyms in Newfoundland,' *RLS* 9 (1980), 10–21.
33 See W. Kirwin, 'A Collection of Popular Etymolo-
gies in Newfoundland Vocabulary,' *RLS* 3 (1971), 16–8, and 'Folk Etymology: Remarks on Linguistic Problem-solving and Who Does it,' in *Languages in Newfoundland and Labrador*, 2nd prelim. ed, Harold J. Paddock, ed (St John's: Memorial University, 1982).

text of the word: 'in setting a cod trap,' 'in coopering,' 'at the seal hunt,' 'in the Bank fishery,' 'in the fur trade,' and so on. Some of these defining formulae also place words in their geographical setting: 'along the north-east coast,' 'at the Labrador fishery'; others place the word historically: 'in the West Country-Newfoundland migratory fishery,' 'a term formerly used in,' and so forth. Definitions also take the form of a series of near synonyms drawn from standard English. Synonyms appearing in small capital letters, however, are themselves treated separately and fully in the Dictionary, and the relevant articles contain further explanations and distinctions.

An attested sense not actually supported by a contextual quotation is followed by a reference to the glossarist or contributor set in parentheses. For flora and fauna the common or popular names, and sometimes a brief description, are given, followed by the scientific identification.

Definitions have been written with an eye to clarifying the term for the reader and to placing it in its regional and linguistic context. They are

mainly deduced from the accumulated glosses, sentences, passages and tape excerpts in the vocabulary file, but what often is ultimately produced is a definition based not only on the filed evidence but on the experience, contacts and reading of the editors. The artifact has been seen, the peculiar soggy wind has made one's clothes heavy with moisture, the operation in the home or on the fish-flake has been frequently witnessed, the tone of voice of the story-teller is still echoing. Nuances [gained] from thus living within the culture, with different vantage points for the three editors and their colleagues and critics, have frequently been incorporated in the definition, whereas in fact all the citation evidence, printed in the entry or omitted, may not always add up to the definition, written, argued over, amended and revised.[34]

The phrasing of a definition is sometimes made more direct or concise by the use of a regional term. This term should be clear from context, and it is enclosed in single quotation marks, indicating that it is local usage and is explained in its own entry (e.g. **spottedy**: of a harp seal's fur, spotted during the colour change from 'white-coat' to young adult).

Phrases and Combinations. After the main senses of some vocabulary entries, selected proverbial phrases employing the term and grammatical and idiomatic sequences are presented. In the entry for **salt**, for example, the following phrases illustrate material that is typical: *as salt as Lot's wife; spare the salt and spoil the scrod; under salt.* Where other dictionary-makers[35] and linguists struggle with decisions over classifying compounds, attributive nouns modifying noun heads, and looser combinations of two nouns in sequence (and the attendant typographical problems of hyphenation and whether or not to print two nouns solidly), editors relying heavily on manuscript sources and oral evidence are not always able to solve this thorny problem of compounds neatly and consistently. This is the principal reason why so many of these sequences in the Dictionary are labelled 'combinations.'

A number of practices have been followed in the presentation of these combinations in the large massed entries. If the principal stress is customarily on the second element, the combination is always printed as two words (e.g. **spruce beer**). Many other combinations, where the stress pattern is variable or unknown, are also printed as two words (e.g. **fish glass**). Only combinations in which the printed evidence shows a strong tendency of writers, especially in recent decades, to favour other typographical conventions are here printed with hyphens or in undivided form; unsettled usage in the printed evidence has sometimes necessitated arbitrary editorial decisions, and it follows that only the phonetic transcriptions in the entry systematically indi-

34 William Kirwin, 'Selecting and Presenting the Lexicon,' *RLS* 6 (1975), 8.

35 See *OED*, vol. I, xxxiii, 'Combinations.'

cate what the customary local stress patterns are.

Modifiers other than nouns, such as adjectives, participles and intensifiers, are separated from their headwords, unless evidence in books and newspapers shows a preference for another presentation.

With a handful of exceptions, each of these sub-entries or combinations is accompanied by a gloss or by a cross-reference to a fully defined synonym.

Quotations from Printed and Oral Sources. The organization of the articles in the Dictionary and the definitions of the vocabulary entries and any accompanying sub-entries are based upon the corpus of our collected quotations, a number of which have been selected for each article to support and illustrate the sense and usage of the word or related combinations or phrases. The usual order in any sub-section is chronological, with information for each quotation giving the year of writing (sometimes in square brackets), printing or submission by an informant. In exceptional cases, in sub-entries where a series of senses relate to one concept (such as articles of clothing, or a device used in an occupation), a general cover definition is given with the associated cluster of combinations, and the illustrative citations in these cases are arranged alphabetically (see **labrador**, sense 3 [names of animals and birds], or **spring²**, sense 4 [names of devices]).

Citations drawn from other dictionaries of material that has been otherwise unavailable to us are duly acknowledged after the quotations, although there are fewer than a score of these. Occasionally a sentence in a foreign language or background material is also cited in an entry, and if the Main Word is not employed, the quotation is set in brackets. Portuguese, for example, is quoted at **baccalao** [c1504. . .], and **spruce beer** is explained but not mentioned at **spruce** [1712. . .].

Citations from printed works are identified either by the date and the author's name in small capital letters (1861 DE BOILIEU 162) or, in the case of composite works, simply by the title (1977 *Inuit Land Use* 225) as the most efficient reference; periodical sources are given in italics (1874 *Maritime Mo* iii, 542). Authors of major manuscript sources also appear in small capitals together with title (1868 HOWLEY *MS Reminiscences* 20). Quotations from newspapers identify the year, name, date, and, for recent years when local papers have increased in size, the page number as well (1957 *Daily News* 16 Oct, p. 4). All newspapers with places of publication not specifically designated have been published in St John's (1906 *Week End* [N.Y.] Apr, p. 8). To provide further detail for interpreting the many quotations from verse, the ballad's or poem's title has been included in the identification of the illustration. Citations from printed sources are reproduced verbatim, with conventional indications of omitted words and with correction of typographical errors found in newspapers and ballad collections. Names of vessels have uniformly been italicized. The typographical practice of the Dictionary is to present all single and double quotation marks in our sources as single. This convention, however, is modified in a few cases where the source itself has potentially confusing marks of punctuation (e.g. "'and-sled," they calls it).

Quotations from the Archive card and manuscript collections, other individual contributors, returned questionnaires, and taped conversation are identified with codes beginning with C, M, P, Q, and T respectively. The wording of citations from the Archive materials and of contributions by many other individuals cited in the Dictionary has been treated more informally than the quotations from printed sources. The demands of readers perhaps unfamiliar with many aspects of the regional culture have been considered above all, and the phrasing and syntax have sometimes been rearranged and trimmed for greater clarity, at the same time preserving all the words and turns of phrase that are authentic vernacular. Naïve spellings of both standard and regional words have been altered for ease in reading, and a contributor's *ad hoc* spelling of the word being illustrated, where the form is inconsequential, has at times been adjusted to agree with the form of the headword (e.g. *stud 'n tilt: studden tilt; whitens: whitin's*).

Excerpts from taped speech have been reproduced with close attention to the original informal flow of words and the conventions of printed speech. Vernacular terms have been spelled either according to this Dictionary's selected forms or in a manner reflecting the variant pronunciations of the speakers. All the speakers' grammatical forms and syntactic patterns have been recorded faithfully. Clauses and sentences have been punctuated to indicate both sense and rhythmic units. Nevertheless, incomplete constructions, excessive repetition, habitual interrupting forms like *see, well*, and *you know*, and clauses that are extremely involved yet unessential for illustrating the Main Word have frequently been omitted to allow the speech, easily comprehensible when the informant was speaking in person, to be similarly comprehensible in the different medium of writing. To put it another way, the verbatim transcription of the tapes is often fuller than the excerpted quotations presented here. We have been conservative about replacing letters with apostrophes, as in *birdin', o'*, and *an'*, and we have avoided making the quotations appear illiterate or quaint by the overuse of spelling devices and marks of punctuation, in the manner of some writers of literary dialect. Indeed, the accurate transcriptions of many taped speeches in neutral spelling and light punctuation found scattered in the Dictionary display remarkable rhythmic patterns of delivery. A number of taped specimens are dense with local words and idioms, all of which are explained elsewhere in the Dictionary.

The work contains for many articles a greater number of illustrations than is customary in some historical dictionaries; we have not, for example, limited our quota-tions to one for each fifty-year period. Especially is this true for the sub-entries of terms that have critical economic or environmental importance in Newfoundland, for example, **fish, seal, wood**(s). Where there are large numbers of reports we have selected those which show the variety and specificity of application (e.g. **caplin, stage, trap**). At the other extreme, the Dictionary includes entries with only a small amount of exemplification. The reasons for this are various: our questionnaires, for example, may have simply elicited numerous identical responses, or the collected evidence is meagre, although we have judged it to be valid. In the main, however, the more common problem in writing this Dictionary has been to select from many worthy and informative citations in order to keep the work within bounds.

Bibliography

PRINTED SOURCES

Chronological List

Books and manuscripts from which citations have been drawn are listed with identifying date of publication (and sometimes date of the original version in square brackets) and either author's name or a short title, followed by essential bibliographical information. An index of authors' names follows in the next section, which also lists newspapers and periodicals.

[c1497–1522] 1962 *Cabot Voyages = The Cabot Voyages & Bristol Discoveries Under Henry VII*, ed J.A. Williamson (Cambridge: The Hakluyt Society, 1962)

[c1503] 1979 DUNBAR = William Dunbar, 1465–1530?, *The Poems of William Dunbar*, ed James Kinsley (Oxford: The Clarendon Press, 1979)

[1578] 1935 *Richard Hakluyt* [Parkhurst's letter] = *The Original Writings & Correspondence of the Two Richard Hakluyts*, vol. i, ed E.G.R. Taylor (London: The Hakluyt Society, 1935)

[1580] CARTIER = Jacques Cartier, 1491–1557, *Navigations and Discoueries to. . .Newe Fraunce*, tr John Florio (London: H. Bynneman, 1580)

[1583] *Gilbert's Voyages & Enterprises* [Hayes' narrative] = *The Voyages and Colonizing Enterprises of Sir Humphrey Gilbert*, 2 vols., ed D.B. Quinn (London: The Hakluyt Society, 1940)

[1583] 1972 PARMENIUS = Stephen Parmenius, d 1583, *The New Found Land of Stephen Parmenius*, ed and tr by D.B. Quinn and Neil M. Cheshire (Toronto: University of Toronto Press, 1972)

[1593–4] 1963 DONNE = John Donne, 1573–1631, *Elegies and Songs and Sonnets*, ed Helen Gardner (Oxford: The Clarendon Press, 1963)

1600 HAKLUYT = Richard Hakluyt, 1552?–1616, *Voyages, Navigations, Traffiques and Discoueries*, vol. iii (London: Imprinted by George Bishop, Ralfe Newberie and Robert Barker, 1600)

[c1610–1634] *Willoughby Papers* = a collection of inventories and letters relating to the colony at Cupids, preserved in the Middleton MSS (Mi X) at Nottingham University. We are grateful to Dr Robert Barakat for the use of his transcript of the originals and of the Lambeth Palace MS of Guy's *Journal*.

[1612] 1957 GUY *Journal* = John Guy, d 1629, 'A Journall of the voiadge of discoverie made in a barke builte in Newfoundland. . .' [printed in] *A Catalogue of an Exhibition of Books, Maps, Manuscripts and Documents* (London: Lambeth Palace Library, 1957)

[1612] 1958 SHAKESPEARE = William Shakespeare, 1564–1616, *The London Shakespeare: A new annotated and critical edition of the complete works in six volumes*, ed John Munro (London: Eyre & Spottiswoode, 1958)

[1620] 1887 MASON = John Mason, 1586–1635, *A Briefe Discovrse of the New-fovnd-land*, in *Capt. John Mason*, ed John Ward Dean (Boston: The Prince Society, 1887)

1620 WHITBOURNE = Richard Whitbourne, 1579?–1628, *A Discourse and Discovery of New-found-land* (Imprinted at London by Felix Kyngston for William Barret, 1620). This is STC² 25372. Two other editions, in 1622 [STC² 25373] and 1623 [STC² 25374], are occasionally cited.

1623 [T.C.] *A Short Discourse = A Short Discourse of the New-Found-Land, Contayning Diverse Reasons and Inducements, for the Planting of That Country* (Dublin: Printed for the Societie of Stationers, 1623)

1624 EBURNE = Richard Eburne, *A Plaine Pathway to Plantations* (London: Printed by G.P., for John Marriot, 1624)

1626 [VAUGHAN] *The Golden Fleece* = Sir William Vaughan, 1575–1641, *The Golden Fleece. . .Transported from. . .the Newfoundland, by Orpheus Iunior* (London: Printed for Francis Williams, 1626)

1628 HAYMAN[1] = Robert Hayman, 1575–1629, *Quodlibets, Lately Come Over from New Britaniola, Old Newfound-land* (London: Printed by Elizabeth All-de, for Roger Michell, 1628)

1628 HAYMAN[2] = *Certaine Epigrams Translated into English at Harbor-Grace in Bristols-Hope* (London: Imprinted for Roger Michell, 1628)

1630 VAUGHAN = William Vaughan, *The Newlanders Cure* (London: Printed by N. Okes for F. Constable, 1630)

1633 *Commission for the Well Governing of Nfld* = *A Commission for the Well Gouerning of Our People, Inhabiting in New-Found-land* (London: Robert Barker, 1633)

[1663–1670] 1963 YONGE = James Yonge, 1647–1721, *The Journal of James Yonge, Plymouth Surgeon*, ed F.N.L. Poynter (London: Longmans, 1963)

1672 [BLOME] = Richard Blome, d 1705, *A Description of the Island of Jamaica and New-Found-Land* (London: T. Milbourn, 1672)

1672 JOSSELYN = John Josselyn, *New-Englands Rarities Discovered* (London: G. Widdowes, 1672)

1682 COLLINS = John Collins, 1625–1683, *Salt and Fishery* (London: Printed by A. Godbid and J. Playford, 1682)

1687 [BLOME] = *The Present State of His Majesties Isles and Territories in America* (London: Printed by H. Clark, for D. Newman, 1687) [an expansion of the 1672 *Jamaica*]

[1698] CHILD = Sir Josiah Child, 1630–1699, *A New Discourse of Trade* [2nd ed] (London: T. Sowle [1698])

1699 *Act of Wm III*, 10 & 11 = *Act of William III*, Cap. xxv (London, 1699)

1708 GEARE = Allen Geare, *Ebenezer: or, a Monument of Thankfulness* (London: Printed for A. Bettesworth, 1708)

1708 OLDMIXON = John Oldmixon, 1673–1742, *The British Empire in America*, 2 vols. (London: J. Nickolson, B. Tooke, 1708)

[1711 THOMPSON] = Thomas Thompson, *Considerations on the Trade to Newfoundland* [London: Printed for Andrew Bell, 1711]

1712 *West-India Merchant* = *A Letter from a West-India Merchant to a Gentleman at Tunbridg* (London, 1712)

[c1720] 1910 GLEDHILL = Samuel Gledhill, b 1677, *Memoirs of Lieutenant-Colonel Samuel Gledhill, Lieutenant Governor of Placentia and Commander-in-Chief of Newfoundland from*

1719 to 1727, ed W.H. Chippindall (Kendal: Titus Wilson, 1910)

[1727] 1966 POPE = Alexander Pope, 1688–1744, *Poetical Works*, ed Herbert Davis (Oxford: Oxford University Press, 1966)

1745 [CAREW] = Bampfylde-Moore Carew, 1693–1758, *The Life and Adventures of Bampfylde-Moore Carew* (Exon: Printed for Joseph Drew, 1745)

1745 OSBORNE = Thomas Osborne, d 1767, *A Collection of Voyages and Travels* (London: T. Osborne, 1745)

1755 DOUGLASS = William Douglass, 1691?–1752, *A Summary, Historical and Political, of the First Planting, Progressive Improvements and Present State of the British Settlements in North America*, 2 vols. ([Boston, 1749–50] London: R. Baldwin, 1755)

1758 ULLOA = Antonio de Ulloa, *A Voyage to South America*, tr John Adams, 2 vols. (London: Printed for L. Davis and G. Reymers, 1758)

1765 COLE = [Thomas] Cole, *A Plan to Exclude the French from that Trade Proposed* in 1765 WILLIAMS below

1765 ROGERS = Robert Rogers, 1731–1795, *A Concise Account of North America* (London: Printed for the Author, 1765)

1765 WILLIAMS = Capt. Griffith Williams, *An Account of the Island of Newfoundland* ([London:] Printed for T. Cole, 1765)

[1766] 1971 BANKS = Sir Joseph Banks, 1743–1820, *Joseph Banks in Newfoundland and Labrador 1766: His Diary, Manuscripts and Collections*, ed A.M. Lysaght (Berkeley: University of California Press, 1971)

[1768] 1826 CARTWRIGHT = F.D. Cartwright (ed), *The Life and Correspondence of Major [John] Cartwright*, [1740–1824], 2 vols. (London: Colburn, 1826)

1768 DRAGE = Theodorus S. Drage, c1712–1774, *The Great Probability of a North West Passage* (London: Printed for T. Jefferys, 1768)

[1770–1786] 1792 CARTWRIGHT See 1792 CARTWRIGHT

1774 [LA TROBE] = Benjamin La Trobe, 1725–1786, *A Brief Account of the Mission Established among the Esquimaux Indians* (London: The Brethren's Society for the Furtherance of the Gospel, 1774)

[1775] 1955 *Journeys* (ed Harvey) = *Journeys to the Island of St John or Prince Edward Island: 1775–1832*, ed D.C. Harvey (Toronto: Macmillan Co. of Canada, 1955)

1776 COUGHLAN = Laurence Coughlan, d 1784?, *An Account of the Work of God, in*

Newfoundland (London: Printed by W. Gilbert, 1776)

1778 CASSINI = J.D. De Cassini, 1748–1845, *Voyage to Newfoundland and Sallee*, in Chappe d'Auteroche, *Voyage to California* (London: E. and C. Dilly, 1778)

1779 *N Amer Pilot = North American Pilot for Newfoundland* (London: R. Sayer and J. Bennett, 1779)

[1780–1825] c1925 *D'Alberti MS* = transcripts of Colonial Office correspondence made by A. and L. D'Alberti about 1925, copies of which are deposited in the Centre for Newfoundland Studies, Memorial University Library

[1784] 1969 BURNS = Robert Burns, 1759–1796, *Poems and Songs*, ed James Kinsley (London: Oxford University Press, 1969)

1784–5 [PENNANT] = Thomas Pennant, 1726–1798, *Arctic Zoology*, 2 vols. (London: Henry Hughs, 1784–5)

1785 SHEFFIELD = John, Lord Sheffield, 1735–1821, *Observations on the Manufactures, Trade and Present State of Ireland* (London: J. Debrett, 1785)

1787 [PENNANT] Sup = *Supplement to the Arctic Zoology* (London: Henry Hughs, 1787)

1792 CARTWRIGHT = George Cartwright, 1739–1819, *A Journal of Transactions and Events During a Residence of Nearly Sixteen Years on the Coast of Labrador*, 3 vols. (Newark: Allin and Ridge, 1792). *Gloss* = the glossary prefixed to each volume, cited from volume i. "Labrador: A Poetical Epistle" is cited from volume iii (separate pagination).

1792 *Liverpool MS* = PANL 24/A19, 1, an epitome of 1792 PULLING *MS*

1792 PULLING *MS* = George Christopher Pulling, British naval officer author of a manuscript (BM Add MSS 38352) concerning relations between settlers and Beothuks c1790. We have had the use of a photograph of the original and also a transcript provided by Dr John Hewson.

1793 PENNANT = Thomas Pennant, *History of Quadrupeds*, 3rd ed, 2 vols. (London: Printed for B. & J. White, 1793)

1793 REEVES = John Reeves, 1752?–1829, *History of the Government of the Island of Newfoundland. With an Appendix containing The Acts of Parliament made Respecting the Trade and Fishery* (London: Printed for J. Sewell, &c, 1793)

1793 *Report on Nfld Trade = Report from the Select Committee on the Newfoundland Trade* (London: The House of Commons, 1793)

1794 *Census = Census [of St John's], 1794.* Transcript by N.C. Crewe of an untraced original

[1794] 1968 THOMAS = Aaron Thomas, Able Seaman in H.M.S. *Boston*, b 1762, *The Newfoundland Journal of Aaron Thomas*, ed Jean M. Murray (London: Longmans, 1968)

[1799] 1801 [THORESBY] = *A Narrative of God's Love to William Thoresby*, 2nd ed (Redruth: Printed by J. Bennett, 1801)

[1808] 1950 BYRON = George, Lord Byron, 1788–1824, *Poetical Works* (Oxford: Oxford University Press, 1950)

1809 ANSPACH = Lewis Amadeus Anspach, 1770–1823, *A Summary of the Laws of Commerce and Navigation* (London: Printed for the Author, 1809)

[1810] 1971 ANSPACH = *Duckworth's Newfoundland: Notes from a Report to Governor Duckworth* (St John's: Provincial Archives, 1971 [mimeographed ed])

1810 STEELE = Robert Steele, *A Tour through Part of the Atlantic; or Recollections from Madeira, the Azores and Newfoundland* (London: J.J. Stockdale, 1810)

[1811] 1818 BUCHAN = David Buchan, 1780–c1837, 'Mr. Buchan's Expedition into the Interior of Newfoundand,' in John Barrow, *A Chronological History of Voyages into the Arctic Regions* (London: John Murray, 1818)

[1812] BUCHAN *MS* = handwritten journal in uncatalogued materials, Provincial Reference Library, A.C. Hunter Library, St John's

1813 CARSON — William Carson, 1770–1843, *Reasons for Colonizing the Island of Newfoundland* (Greenock: Printed by W. Scott, 1813)

1814 KOHLMEISTER & KMOCH = Benjamin Kohlmeister and George Kmoch, *Journal of a Voyage from Okkak, on the Coast of Labrador, to Ungava Bay* (London: The Brethren's Society for the Furtherance of the Gospel, 1814)

1818 CHAPPELL = Edward Chappell, 1792–1861, *Voyage of His Majesty's Ship* Rosamond *to Newfoundland and the Southern Coast of Labrador* (London: Printed for J. Mawman, 1818)

1819 ANSPACH = Lewis Amadeus Anspach, *A History of the Island of Newfoundland* (London: Printed for the Author, 1819)

[1820] 1915 BUCHAN = 'Captain Buchan's Report of 2nd Expedition,' in James P. Howley, *The Beothucks or Red Indians* (1915), 121–26

1821–24 LATHAM = John L. Latham, 1740–1837, *A General History of Birds* (Winchester: Jacob and Johnson, 1821–24)

[1822] 1928 CORMACK = William Eppes Cormack, 1796–1868, *Narrative of a Journey Across the Island of Newfoundland in 1822*, ed

F.A. Bruton (London: Longmans, Green and Co. Ltd., 1928). A text of 1856, printed at St John's, is also occasionally cited.

1823 CRABB = George Crabb, *Universal Technological Dictionary* (London: Baldwin, Cradock & Joy, 1823)

1824 [SCOTT] = Sir Walter Scott, 1771–1832, *Redgauntlet, A Tale of the Eighteenth Century*, 3 vols. (Edinburgh: Archibald Constable and Co., 1824)

1826 CARTWRIGHT See [1768] CARTWRIGHT

1826 [GLASCOCK] = William N. Glascock, 1787?–1847, *Naval Sketchbook; or, the Service Afloat and Ashore*, 2 vols. (London: Printed for the Author, 1826)

1828 MCGREGOR = John McGregor, 1797–1857, *Historical and Descriptive Sketches of the Maritime Colonies of British America* (London: Longman, Rees, Orme, Brown, and Green, 1828)

1829–1911 *Nfld Law Reports* = *Newfoundland Law Reports: Decisions of the Supreme Court of Newfoundland: 1829–1845*, ed Brian Dunfield (St John's: J.W. Withers, Queen's Printer, 1916); 1864–1874, ed E.P. Morris (1899); 1874–1884, ed E.P. Morris (1898); 1884–1896, ed E.P. Morris (1897); 1897–1903, ed E.P. Morris and D.M. Browning (1905); 1904–1911, ed D.M. Browning (1912)

[c1830] 1890 GOSSE = Philip Henry Gosse, 1810–1888, in Edmund Gosse, *The Life of Philip Henry Gosse, F.R.S.* (London: Kegan Paul, Trench, Trübner & Co., Ltd., 1890)

[1831–39] 1926 AUDUBON = John James Audubon, 1785–1851, *Delineations of American Scenery and Character* (New York: G.A. Baker, 1926)

1832 MCGREGOR = John McGregor, *British America*, 2 vols. (Edinburgh: William Blackwood, 1832)

1836 [WIX]¹ = Edward Wix, 1802–1866, *Six Months of a Newfoundland Missionary's Journal* (London: Smith, Elder and Co., 1836)

1836 [WIX]² = *Six Months of a Newfoundland Missionary's Journal*, 2nd ed (London: Smith, Elder & Co., 1836)

1837 BLUNT = Edmund M. Blunt, 1770–1862, *The American Coast Pilot*, 13th ed (New York: E. & G.W. Blunt, 1837)

[1837] 1977 DICKENS = Charles Dickens, 1812–1870, *The Posthumous Papers of the Pickwick Club* (London: Collins, 1977)

1839 MURRAY = Hugh Murray, 1779–1846, *An Historical and Descriptive Account of British America*, 3 vols. (Edinburgh: Oliver & Boyd, 1839)

1839 PRESCOTT = Henrietta Prescott, *Poems, Written in Newfoundland* (London: Saunders and Otley, 1839)

1839 TUCKER = Ephraim W. Tucker, b 1821, *Five Months in Labrador and Newfoundland* (Concord: I.S. Boyd and W. White, 1839)

1840 GOSSE = Philip Henry Gosse, *The Canadian Naturalist* (London: John Van Voorst, 1840)

1841 BONNYCASTLE = Sir Richard Henry Bonnycastle, 1791–1848, *Considerations upon the Political Position of Newfoundland* (London: The House of Commons, 1841)

1842 BONNYCASTLE = *Newfoundland in 1842*, 2 vols. (London: H. Colburn, 1842)

1842 JUKES = Joseph Beete Jukes, 1811–1869, *Excursions in and about Newfoundland, during the Years 1839 and 1840*, 2 vols. (London: John Murray, 1842)

1843 BUCKINGHAM = James S. Buckingham, 1786–1855, *Canada, Nova Scotia, New Brunswick, and the Other British Provinces in North America, with a Plan of National Colonization* (London: Fisher, Son, & Co., [1843])

1843 JUKES = J.B. Jukes, *General Report of the Geological Survey of Newfoundland* (London: John Murray, 1843)

[1844] GOSSE = Philip Henry Gosse, *An Introduction to Zoology*, 2 vols. (London: S.P.C.K. [1844])

[c1846] "Banks of Newfoundland" [broadside] = "Banks of Newfoundland"; "Afloat on the Ocean" (London [1846?])

1846 [FEILD]¹ = Edward Feild, 1801–1876, *A Journal of the Bishop's Visitation of the Missions on the Western and Southern Coast, August and September, 1845* (London: S.P.G., 1846)

1846 [FEILD]² = *A Journal of the Bishop's Visitation of the Northern Coast [in] 1846* (London: S.P.G., 1846)

1846 TOCQUE = Rev. Philip Tocque, 1814–1899, *Wandering Thoughts, or Solitary Hours* (London: Thomas Richardson and Son, 1846)

1849 MCLEAN = John McLean, 1799–1890, *Notes of a Twenty-five Years' Service in the Hudson's Bay Territory*, 2 vols. (London: Richard Bentley, 1849)

1850 [FEILD] = *Journal of a Voyage of Visitation on the Coast of Labrador, and Round Newfoundland in the year 1849* (London: S.P.G., 1850)

1850 LATHAM = Robert Gordon Latham, 1812–1888, *The Natural History of the Varieties of Man* (London: J. Van Voorst, 1850)

1850 *Nfld Almanac* = *The Newfoundland Almanac* (St John's: Henry Winton, 1850)

1851 DISNEY & GIFFORD = Rev. H.P. Disney, d

1854, and Rev. A. Gifford, *The Labrador Mission: Letters* (London: S.P.G., 1851)

1851 [FEILD] = *Journal of the Bishop of Newfoundland's Voyage on the South and West Coasts of Newfoundland and on the Labrador [in] 1848* (London: S.P.G., 1851)

1851 MELVILLE = Herman Melville, 1819–1891, *Moby Dick, Or The Whale* (London: Oxford University Press, 1963)

1852 ARCHIBALD = Samuel George Archibald, *Some Account of the Seal Fishery of Newfoundland, and the Mode of Preparing Seal Oil* (Edinburgh: Murray and Gibb, 1852)

1853 SABINE = Lorenzo Sabine, 1803–1877, *Report on the Principal Fisheries of the American Seas* (Washington: Armstrong, 1853)

1854 [FEILD] = *Journal of the Bishop of Newfoundland's Voyage of Visitation on the Coast of Labrador and the North-east Coast of Newfoundland in 1853* (London: S.P.G., 1854)

1854 MARCH = Stephen March, *The Present Condition of Newfoundland* (St John's: J.T. Burton, 1854)

[1854] 1950 THOREAU = Henry David Thoreau, 1817–1862, *Walden*, ed Brooks Atkinson (New York: Random House, 1950)

1854–1886 WHITE *MS Journal* = Capt. Edward White Sr, 1811–1888, manuscript journals and sealing logs for the years: 1854–55; 1868; 1870–71; 1874–75; 1876–86, in the possession of G.M. Story, St John's

1855 MULLALY = John Mullaly, *A Trip to Newfoundland: Its Scenery and Fisheries, with an Account of the Laying of the Submarine Telegraph Cable* (New York: T.W. Strong, 1855)

1857–1864 LIND *MS Diary* = Rev. Henry Lind, manuscript diary of residence at Sandy Point, St George's Bay, copy in the Library, Memorial University

1857 *Memo of French Fisheries* = M.H. Perley, 1804–1862, *Memorandum of French Fisheries at Newfoundland* (confidential memo, The Colonial Office, 1857)

1857 MOUNTAIN = Rev. J.G. Mountain, 1818–1856, *Some Account of a Sowing Time on the Rugged Shores of Newfoundland* (London: S.P.G., 1857)

[1858] 1877 FERLAND = Jean-Baptiste Antoine Ferland, 1805–1865, *Opuscules*. Including *Le Labrador, 1858* (Québec: Imp. A. Coté, 1877)

1858 [LOWELL] = Robert Traill Spence Lowell, 1816–1891, *The New Priest in Conception Bay*, 2 vols. (Boston: Phillips, Sampson and Company, 1858)

1860 [FEILD] = *Extracts from a Journal of a Voyage of Visitation [in] 1859* (London: S.P.G., 1860)

[1860] 1862 GOSSE = Philip Henry Gosse, *The Romance of Natural History [First Series]*, 4th ed (London: J. Nisbet, 1862)

1860 MULLOCK = Dr John Thomas Mullock, 1806–1869, *Two Lectures on Newfoundland* (New York: John Mullaly, 1860)

1860 TAYLOR = Bayard Taylor, 1825–1878, *At Home and Abroad: A Sketch-book of Life, Scenery and Men* (New York: G.P. Putnam: Sheldon & Co., 1860

1861 BEETON = Isabella Beeton, 1836–1865, *The Book of Household Management* (London: S.O. Beeton, 1861)

1861 DE BOILIEU = Lambert De Boilieu, *Recollections of Labrador Life* (London: Saunders, Otley & Co., 1861; Toronto: Ryerson Press, 1969)

1861 NOBLE = Louis L. Noble, 1813–1882, *After Icebergs with a Painter: a Summer Voyage to Labrador and around Newfoundland* (New York: D. Appleton, 1861)

1862 *Sailing Directions for the Island of Newfoundland* (London: James Imray, 1862)

1863 DURNFORD = Mary Durnford, comp., *Family Recollections of Lieut. General Elias Walker Durnford*, 1774–1850 (Montreal: Printed by J. Lovell, 1863)

1863 HIND = Henry Youle Hind, 1823–1908, *Explorations in the Interior of the Labrador Peninsula*, 2 vols. (London: Longman, Green, Longman, Roberts & Green, 1863)

1863 MORETON = Rev. Julian Moreton, b 1825, *Life and Work in Newfoundland: Reminiscences of Thirteen Years Spent There* (London: Rivingtons, 1863)

1863 PEDLEY = Rev. Charles Pedley, 1821–1872, *The History of Newfoundland from the Earliest Times to the Year 1860* (London: Longman, Green, Longman, Roberts & Green, 1863)

[1863] WINTER = James Winter, 1845–1911, *A Lecture on the Decline of the Fisheries* (St John's: J.W. McCoubrey [1863]).

[1864–1880] 1881 MURRAY & HOWLEY = Alexander Murray, 1811–1885, and James P. Howley, *Geological Survey of Newfoundland* (London: Edward Stanford, 1881)

1865 [CAMPBELL] = J.F. Campbell, 1822–1885, *A Short American Tramp in the Fall of 1864* (Edinburgh: Edmonston and Douglas, 1865)

1865 *Sailing Directions for the Island and Banks of Newfoundland* (London: Charles Wilson, 1865)

[1866] 1873 REEKS = Henry Reeks, *A List of the Flowering Plants & Ferns of Newfoundland* (Newbury [England]: Printed by Blacket and Son, 1873)

1866 WILSON = Rev. William Wilson, 1800?–1870, *Newfoundland and Its*

Missionaries (Cambridge, Mass: Dakin & Metcalf, 1866)

1867 SMYTH = Admiral W.H. Smyth, 1788–1865, *The Sailor's Word-Book: An Alphabetical Digest of Nautical Terms* (London: Blackie and Son, 1867)

[1868–1910] HOWLEY *MS Reminiscences* = James P. Howley, 1847–1918, 'Reminiscences of Forty-two Years of Exploration and Survey in and about Newfoundland, 1868–1910,' unpublished manuscript in the possession of Mr David Howley of St John's to whom we are indebted for its extended loan.

1869 MCCREA = Lieut.-Col. R.B. McCrea, *Lost Amid the Fogs: Sketches of Life in Newfoundland* (London: Sampson Low, Son, & Marston, 1869)

[1870] 1973 KELLY = Rt. Rev. James Butler Knitt Kelly, *The Voyage [of] the Church Ship Star, 1870* (St John's: Historic Resources Division of the Department of Tourism, 1973)

1871 DASHWOOD = Richard Lewes Dashwood, 1837–1905, *Chiploquorgan; or Life by the Camp Fire in Dominion of Canada and Newfoundland* (Dublin: R.T. White, 1871)

1872 SCHELE DE VERE = M. Schele De Vere, 1820–1898, *Americanisms; The English of the New World*, 2nd ed (New York: Charles Scribner & Co., 1872)

1873 CARROLL = Michael Carroll, *The Seal and Herring Fisheries of Newfoundland* (Montreal: Lovell, 1873)

1875 GRANT = James Grant, 1822–1887, *One of the Six Hundred*, 3 vols. (London: G. Routledge and Sons, 1875)

1876 HOWLEY = James P. Howley, *Geography of Newfoundland* (London: E. Stanford, 1876)

[1876] KENNEDY = David Kennedy, 1849–1885, *Kennedy's Colonial Travel; A Narrative of a Four Years' Tour through Australia, New Zealand, Canada, &c.* (Edinburgh Publishing Company [1876])

1877 ROCHFORT = John A. Rochfort, 1833?–1896, *Business and General Directory of Newfoundland* (Montreal: Lovell, 1877)

[1877] 1943 SEARS = Thomas Sears, 1824–1885, *Report of the Missions* (n.p., 1877; repr. 1943)

1877 TUCKER = H.W. Tucker, 1830–1902, *Memoir of the Life and Episcopate of Edward Feild, D.D., Bishop of Newfoundland, 1844–1876* (London: W. Wells Gardner, 1877)

1878 TOCQUE = Rev. Philip Tocque, *Newfoundland: as it was, and as it is in 1877* (Toronto: J.B. Magurn, 1878)

1879 HARVEY = Rev. Moses Harvey, 1820–1905, *Across Newfoundland with the Governor* (St John's: *Morning Chronicle* Print, 1879)

1881 KENNEDY = W.R. Kennedy, 1838–1916, *Sporting Notes in Newfoundland*, 2nd ed (St John's: J.C. Withers, Queen's Printer, 1881)

1881 RAE = W. Fraser Rae, 1835–1905, *Newfoundland to Manitoba* (London: Sampson Low, Marston, Searle, & Rivington, 1881)

1882 TALBOT = Thomas Talbot, 1818–1901, *Newfoundland; or, A Letter addressed to a Friend in Ireland* (London: Sampson Low, Marston, Searle, & Rivington, 1882)

[1883] 1971 BAKER = Capt. Julian Baker, *Newfoundland Coastal Tour 1883; Notes from the Log of H.M.S. Foam* (St John's: Provincial Archives, 1971)

1883 *Fish Exhibit Cat* = *Great International Fisheries Exhibition; Official Catalogue* (London: William Clowes and Sons, Limited, 1883)

1883 *Fish Exhibit Cat⁴* = *International Fisheries Exhibition; Official Catalogue*, 4th ed (London: William Clowes and Sons, Limited, 1883).

1883 HATTON & HARVEY = Joseph Hatton, 1841–1907, and Rev. M. Harvey, *Newfoundland: The Oldest British Colony, Its History, Its Present Condition, and Its Prospects in the Future* (London: Chapman and Hall, Limited, 1883)

1883 PILOT = Rev. William Pilot, 1841–1913, *Geography of Newfoundland* (London: William Collins, Sons, & Co., 1883)

1883 SHEA = Sir Ambrose Shea, 1817–1905, *Newfoundland, its Fisheries and General Resources* [International Fisheries Exhibition] (London: William Clowes and Sons, 1883)

1883 *Weather Proverbs* = H.H.C. Dunwoody, *Weather Proverbs* (Washington: Government Printing Office, 1883)

1884 BELL = Robert Bell, *Observations on the Geology, Mineralogy, Zoology and Botany of the Labrador Coast* (Montreal: Dawson Brothers, 1884)

1884 DEMING = Clarence Deming, 1848–1913, *By-Ways of Nature and Life* (New York: G.P. Putnam's Sons, 1884)

1884 *Fisheries Exhibit* = *International Fisheries Exhibition: Official Report*, xiii (London: William Clowes and Sons, 1884)

[1884] 1911 LINDSAY = David Moore Lindsay, b 1862, *A Voyage to the Arctic in the Whaler Aurora* (Boston: Dana Estes & Company, 1911)

1884 STEARNS = W.A. Stearns, 1852–1909, *Labrador: A Sketch of its Peoples, its Industries and its Natural History* (Boston: Lee and Shepard, 1884)

1885 KENNEDY = Capt. W.R. Kennedy, *Sport, Travel, and Adventure in Newfoundland and the West Indies* (Edinburgh and London: William Blackwood and Sons, 1885)

1886 GREGORY = J.U. Gregory, 1830–1913, *En Racontant; Recits de Voyages en Floride, au Labrador* (Québec: Typographie de C. Darveau, 1886)

[1886] LLOYD = F.E.J. Lloyd, *Two Years in the Region of Icebergs, and What I Saw There* (London: S.P.C.K. [1886])

1887 BOND = Rev. George J. Bond, 1850–1933, *Skipper George Netman: A Story of Out-port Methodism in Newfoundland* (London: T. Woolmer, 1887)

1887 *Fisheries of U S* = George Brown Goode, 1851–1896, *The Fisheries and Fishery Industries of the United States*, Section V, i (Washington: Government Printing Office, 1887)

1887 MASON See [1620] MASON

1887 *Nfld & Lab Pilot* = *Newfoundland and Labrador Pilot* (London: J.D. Potter, 1887)

1887 *Year Book* = *A Year Book and Almanac of Newfoundland* (St John's: J.W. Withers, 1887)

1888 M.F. HOWLEY = Very Rev. M.F. Howley, 1843–1914, *Ecclesiastical History of Newfoundland* (Boston: Doyle and Whittle, 1888)

1888 STEARNS = Winfrid A. Stearns, *Wrecked on Labrador* (New York: Thomas Y. Crowell, 1888)

1888 WAGHORNE = Arthur C. Waghorne, *A Summary Account of the Wild Berries and other Edible Fruits of Newfoundland and Labrador* (St John's, 1888)

1890 BAYLY = Augustus G. Bayly, d 1908, *Newfoundland; Loyal to its Mother England* (London: Gilbert & Rivington, 1890)

1890 SHIELDS = G.O. Shields (ed), 1846–1925, *Big Game in North America* (Chicago: Rand, McNally & Company, 1890)

1891 PACKARD = Alpheus Spring Packard, 1839–1905, *The Labrador Coast. A Journal of Two Summer Cruises to that Region* (New York: N.D.C. Hodges, Publisher, 1891)

1891 SKINNER = Major Thomas Skinner, 1804–1877, *Fifty Years in Ceylon: An Autobiography*, ed Annie Skinner (London: W.H. Allen, 1891)

[1891] WINSOR = See [c1977] WINSOR

1893 *Year Book* = *A Year Book and Almanac of Newfoundland* (St John's: J.W. Withers, Queen's Printer, 1893)

[1894 BURKE] = John Burke, 1851–1930, *St John's Advertiser and Fishermen's Guide* ([St John's, 1894])

1894 CHAFE = Levi G. Chafe, 1861–1942?, *Report of the Newfoundland Seal-fishery, from 1863 to 1894* (St John's: G.S. Milligan, 1894).

1894 HARVEY = Rev. M. Harvey,

Newfoundland as it is in 1894: A Hand-Book and Tourists' Guide (St John's: J.W. Withers, Queen's Printer, 1894)

1894 MORRIS = Isaac C. Morris, 1857–1937, *Sketches of Our Western Sea Coast* (St John's: George S. Milligan, Jr., 1894)

1894 MOTT = Henry Youmans Mott (ed), *Newfoundland Men. A Collection of Biographical Sketches of sons and residents of the Island who have become known in Commercial, Professional, and Political Life* (Concord, N.H.: T.W. & J.F. Cragg, Publishers, 1894)

[c1894] PANL = Rev. William Pilot, 'Newfoundland Folk Talk' MS transcript in the Provincial Archives (P4/14)

1895 BARRON = William Barron, *Old Whaling Days* (Hull: W. Andrews & Co., 1895)

1895 DAVIS = S.T. Davis, 1838-1908, *Caribou Shooting in Newfoundland* (Lancaster, Pa.: The New Era Printing House, 1895).

1895 GRENFELL = Wilfred T. Grenfell, 1868–1940, *Vikings of To-day: Or Life and Medical Work Among the Fishermen of Labrador* (London: Marshall Bros., 1895)

1895–1897 *J A Folklore* = Rev. George Patterson, 1824–1897, 'Notes on the Dialect of the People of Newfoundland,' *Journal of American Folklore*, viii, 27–40, ix, 19–37, x, 203–13

1895 PROWSE = D.W. Prowse, 1834–1914, *A History of Newfoundland from the English, Colonial, and Foreign Records* (London: Macmillan and Co., 1895)

1895 TOCQUE = Rev. Philip Tocque, *Kaleidoscope Echoes, Being Historical, Philosophical, Scientific, and Theological Sketches*, ed Annie S.W. Tocque (Toronto: The Hunter, Rose Company, Ltd., 1895)

1896 *Consolidated Statutes of Nfld* = *The Consolidated Statutes of Newfoundland*, Second Series, 1892 (St John's: J.W. Withers, Printer, 1896)

1896 LOW = A.P. Low, 1861–1942, *Report on Explorations in the Labrador Peninsula* (Ottawa: Geological Survey of Canada, 1896)

[1896] SWANSBOROUGH = W. Swansborough, *Newfoundland Months* (St John's: G.S. Milligan, Jr., [1896])

1897 HARVEY = Rev. M. Harvey, *Newfoundland in 1897* (London: S. Low, Marston & Company, Limited, 1897)

1897 WILLSON = Beckles Willson, 1869–1942, *The Tenth Island: Being Some Account of Newfoundland* (London: Grant Richards, 1897)

1898 PROWSE = D.W. Prowse, *The Justices' Manual*, 2nd ed (St John's, 1898)

1899 [ENGLISH] = Maria [Anastasia M. English,

1864–1959], *Only a Fisherman's Daughter* ([St John's:] Manning & Rabbitts, Printers, 1899)

1900 *British America* = T.B. Browning, 'Newfoundland,' 218–81 in *British America* (London: Kegan Paul, Trench, Trübner & Co., 1900)

1900 DEVINE & O'MARA = [M.A.] Devine, 1859–1915, & [M.J.] O'Mara, *Notable Events in the History of Newfoundland* (St John's: Devine & O'Mara, 1900)

1900 HARRISSE = Henry Harrisse, 1829–1910, *Découverte et évolution cartographique de Terre Neuve et des pays circonvoisins* (Paris: H. Welter, 1900)

1900 HARVEY = Rev. M. Harvey, *Newfoundland in 1900* (New York: The South Publishing Co., 1900)

[1900 OLIVER & BURKE] = [George T. Oliver & John Burke, eds], *The People's Songster* ([St John's:] Oliver and Burke, [1900])

1900 PROWSE = D.W. Prowse, *Justices' Manual, Appendix* (St John's, 1900)

1901 WILLSON = Beckles Willson, *The Truth About Newfoundland: The Tenth Island*, 2nd ed (London: Grant Richards, 1901)

1902 DELABARRE = E.B. Delabarre, *Report of the Brown-Harvard Expedition to Nachvak, Labrador, 1900* (Providence, R.I.: Preston & Rounds, 1902) = *Bulletin of the Geographical Society of Philadelphia*, vol. 3, no. 4

1902 [MURPHY] = [James Murphy, 1868–1931] *Songs and Ballads of Newfoundland, Ancient and Modern* (St John's: [James Murphy], 1902)

1903 DES VOEUX = G. William Des Voeux, 1834–1909, *My Colonial Service*, 2 vols. (London: J. Murray, 1903)

1903 DUNCAN = Norman Duncan, 1871–1916, *The Way of the Sea* (New York: McClure, Phillips, & Co., 1903)

1903 HOWLEY = The Rt. Rev. M.F. Howley, *Poems and Other Verses* (New York: J. Fischer & Bros., 1903)

1904 DUNCAN = Norman Duncan, *Doctor Luke of The Labrador* (New York: Revell, 1904)

1904 MURPHY = James Murphy, *Songs of our Land* (St John's: James Murphy, 1904)

1905 CHAFE = Levi G. Chafe, *Report of the Newfoundland Seal Fishery from 1863 to 1905* (St John's: *Evening Telegram* Job-Print, 1905)

1905 DAVEY = J.W. Davey, *The Fall of Torngak, or The Moravian Mission on the Coast of Labrador* (London: S.W. Partridge, 1905)

1905 DUNCAN = Norman Duncan, *Dr Grenfell's Parish: The Deep Sea Fishermen* (New York: F.H. Revell, 1905)

1905 GRENFELL = Wilfred T. Grenfell, *The Harvest of the Sea: A Tale of Both Sides of the Atlantic* (New York: Fleming H. Revell Company, 1905)

1905 MURPHY = James Murphy, *Murphy's Sealers' Song Book* (St John's: James Murphy, 1905)

1905 PROWSE = D.W. Prowse (ed), *The Newfoundland Guide Book* (London: Bradbury, Agnew, 1905)

1905 WALLACE = Dillon Wallace, 1863–1939, *The Lure of the Labrador Wild; The Story of the Exploring Expedition conducted by Leonidas Hubbard, Jr.* (New York: Fleming H. Revell Company, 1905)

1906 DUNCAN = Norman Duncan, *The Adventures of Billy Topsail* (New York: Revell, 1906)

[1906] GRENFELL = Wilfred T. Grenfell, *Off the Rocks: Stories of the Deep-Sea Fisherfolk of Labrador* (London: Marshall Brothers [1906])

1906 LUMSDEN = James Lumsden, 1854–1915, *The Skipper Parson; On the Bays and Barrens of Newfoundland* (Toronto: W. Briggs, 1906)

1906 MURPHY = James Murphy, compiler, *The Musty Past* (St John's: Barnes' Print, 1906)

1907 DUNCAN = Norman Duncan, *The Cruise of the* Shining Light (Toronto: H. Frowde, 1907)

1907 MILLAIS = J.G. Millais, 1865–1931, *Newfoundland and Its Untrodden Ways* (London: Longmans, Green and Co., 1907)

1907 *Nfld & Lab Pilot* = *Newfoundland and Labrador Pilot* (London: Eyre & Spottiswoode, 1907)

1907 TOWNSEND & ALLEN = Charles W. Townsend, M.D., and Glover M. Allen, *Birds of Labrador* (Boston: Printed for the Society [of Natural History], 1907) = *Proceedings of the Boston Society of Natural History*, vol. 33, no. 7, 277–428

1907 WALLACE[1] = Dillon Wallace, *The Long Labrador Trail* (London: Hodder & Stoughton, 1907)

1907 WALLACE[2] = Dillon Wallace, *Ungava Bob: A Winter's Tale* (New York: Fleming H. Revell Company, 1907)

1908 DURGIN = George Francis Durgin, *Letters from Labrador* (Concord, N.H.: Rumford Printing Co., 1908)

1908 HUBBARD = Mrs Leonidas Hubbard [Mina Ellis], *A Woman's Way Through Unknown Labrador* (Toronto: William Briggs, 1908)

1908 TOWNSEND = Charles Wendell Townsend, M.D., b 1859, *Along the Labrador Coast* (London: T. Fisher Unwin, 1908)

1909 BERNIER = J.E. Bernier, 1852–1934, *Report on the Dominion Government Expedition to Arctic Islands and the Hudson Strait 1906–1907* (Ottawa: Printed by C.H. Parmelee, 1909)

1909 BROWNE = Rev. P.W. Browne, 1864–1937, *Where the Fishers Go: The Story of Labrador* (New York: Cochrane Publishing Company, 1909)

1909 GRENFELL[1] = Wilfred Thomason Grenfell, *Adrift on an Ice-pan* (Boston: Houghton Mifflin Company, 1909)

1909 GRENFELL[2] = W.T. Grenfell and others, *Labrador, the Country and the People* (New York: Macmillan, 1909)

1909 ROBINSON = Edward Colpitts Robinson, *In an Unknown Land: A Journey through the Wastes of Labrador in Search of Gold* (London: Elliot Stock, 1909)

1909 SELOUS = F.C. Selous, 1851–1917, *Recent Hunting Trips in British North America* (London: Witherby & Co., 1909)

1910 GOSLING = W.G. Gosling, 1863–1930, *Labrador: Its Discovery, Exploration, and Development* (London: A. Rivers, 1910)

1910 GRENFELL = Wilfred T. Grenfell, *Down to the Sea; Yarns from the Labrador* (New York: Fleming H. Revell, 1910)

1910 PRICHARD = H. Hesketh Prichard, 1876–1922, *Hunting Camps in Wood and Wilderness* (London: William Heinemann, 1910)

1910 TOWNSEND = Charles Wendell Townsend, M.D., *A Labrador Spring* (Boston: Dana Estes & Company, 1910)

1911–1941 *FPU (Twillingate) Minutes* = Manuscript Minute Book of the Twillingate Council of the Fishermen's Protective Union, 1911–1941, Centre for Newfoundland Studies, Memorial University Library

1911 GOSLING = William Gilbert Gosling, *The Life of Sir Humphrey Gilbert* (London: Constable & Co., 1911)

[1911] GRENFELL = Wilfred T. Grenfell, *Down North on the Labrador* (London: James Nisbet & Co., [1911])

1911 HUTCHINSON = Horace G. Hutchinson, 1859–1932, *A Saga of the Sunbeam* (London: Longmans, Green and Co., 1911)

1911 MCGRATH = P.T. McGrath, 1868–1928, *Newfoundland in 1911* (London: Whitehead, Morris & Co., Ltd., 1911)

1911 PRICHARD = H. Hesketh Prichard, *Through Trackless Labrador* (London: William Heinemann, 1911)

1911 PROWSE = D.W. Prowse (ed), *The Newfoundland Guide Book*, 2nd ed (London: Whitehead, Morris & Co., Ltd., 1911)

1911 ROGERS = J.D. Rogers, 1857–1914, *A Historical Geography of the British Colonies: Newfoundland* (Oxford: The Clarendon Press, 1911)

1912 CABOT = William B. Cabot, 1858–1949, *In Northern Labrador* (Boston: Richard G. Badger, The Gorham Press, 1912)

1912 DUGMORE = A. Radclyffe Dugmore, 1870–1955, *Wild Life and the Camera* (London: William Heinemann, 1912)

1912 DUNCAN = Norman Duncan, *The Best of a Bad Job: A Hearty Tale of the Sea* (New York: Fleming H. Revell Company, 1912)

1912 [ENGLISH] = Maria [Anastasia English], *The Queen of Fairy Dell, and Other Tales* ([St John's:] Printed at the *Evening Herald*, 1912)

1912 HUTTON = S.K. Hutton, b 1877, *Among the Eskimos of Labrador* (London: Seeley, Service & Co. Limited, 1912)

[1912] LENCH = Charles Lench, 1860–1931, *The History of the Rise and Progress of Methodism on the Western Bay Circuit* ([St John's:] Barnes & Co., Printers, [1912])

1912 ROGERS = Sir John Rogers, b 1859, *Sport in Vancouver and Newfoundland* (London: Chapman and Hall, 1912)

1913 DUGMORE = A. Radclyffe Dugmore, *The Romance of the Newfoundland Caribou* (London: W. Heinemann, 1913)

1913 HOWLEY = James P. Howley, *Nature Studies: with Observations on the Natural History of Newfoundland* ([St John's:] 1913)

1913 THOMAS = William S. Thomas, b 1858, *Trails and Tramps in Alaska and Newfoundland* (New York: G.P. Putnam's Sons, 1913)

1914 WALLACE = Dillon Wallace, *The Gaunt Gray Wolf* (New York: Fleming H. Revell Company, 1914)

1915 *Decisions of the Supreme Court* = *Decisions of the Supreme Court of Newfoundland*, ed Brian Dunfield (St John's: J. W. Withers, 1915)

[1915–1925] 1972 GORDON = Rev. Henry Gordon, *The Labrador Parson: Journal, 1915–1925*, ed F. Burnham Gill (St John's: Provincial Archives, 1972). Also cited in an edition listed at 1918 below.

1915 HOWLEY = James P. Howley, *The Beothucks or Red Indians; The Aboriginal Inhabitants of Newfoundland* (Cambridge: Cambridge University Press, 1915)

1915 SOUTHCOTT = M. Southcott, *Some Newfoundland Wild Flowers* (St John's: Robinson and Company, 1915)

1915 WOOD = Ruth Kedzie Wood, *The Tourist's Maritime Provinces* (New York: Dodd, Mead and Company, 1915)

1916 GRENFELL = Wilfred Thomason Grenfell, *Tales of the Labrador* (Boston: Houghton Mifflin Company, 1916)

1916 HAWKES = E.W. Hawkes, b 1883, *The Labrador Eskimo*, No. 14 Anthropological

Series, Memoir 19, Geological Survey, Canada Department of Mines (Ottawa: Government Printing Bureau, 1916)

1916 LENCH = Rev. C. Lench, *An Account of the Rise and Progress of Methodism on the Grand Bank and Fortune circuits from 1816 to 1916* (St John's: Barnes & Co., 1916)

1916 MURPHY = [James Murphy], *Murphy's Old Sealing Days* ([St John's:] James Murphy, 1916)

1916 YOUNG = Arminius Young, *A Methodist Missionary in Labrador* (Toronto: Messrs. S. and A. Young, 1916)

[1918–19] GORDON = Rev. Henry Gordon, *A Winter in Labrador, 1918–1919* (n.p. [1919])

1918 KEITH (ed) = *Speeches and Documents on Colonial Policy 1763–1917*, ed Arthur Berriedale Keith, 2 vols. (London: Oxford University Press, 1918)

1918 TOWNSEND = Charles Wendell Townsend, M.D., *In Audubon's Labrador* (Boston: Houghton Mifflin Company, 1918)

1919 GRENFELL¹ = Wilfred Thomason Grenfell, *Labrador Days: Tales of the Sea Toilers* (London: Hodder and Stoughton, 1919)

1919 GRENFELL² = Wilfred Thomason Grenfell, *A Labrador Doctor: The Autobiography of Wilfred Thomason Grenfell* (Boston: Houghton Mifflin Company, 1919)

[1919] KINSELLA = P.J. Kinsella, *Some Superstitions and Traditions of Newfoundland* [St John's, 1919]

1919 LENCH = Charles Lench, *The Story of Methodism in Bonavista, and of the Settlements visited by the Early Preachers*, 2nd ed (St John's: Robinson & Company, 1919)

1920 CABOT = William B. Cabot, *Labrador* (London: Heath Cranton, [1920])

1920 GRENFELL & SPALDING = Anne Grenfell, b 1885, and Katie Spalding, *Le Petit Nord or Annals of a Labrador Harbour* (Boston: Houghton Mifflin Company, 1920)

1920 WALDO = Fullerton L. Waldo, b 1877, *With Grenfell on the Labrador* (New York: Fleming H. Revell, 1920)

[1921] CRAMM = Richard Cramm, 1889–1958, *The First Five Hundred* (Albany, N.Y.: C.F. Williams & Son, Inc., [1921])

1923 [CHAFE] = [Levi G. Chafe], *Chafe's Sealing Book*, ed H.M. Mosdell, 3rd ed (St John's: Trade Printers and Publishers, 1923)

1923 GRENFELL = Wilfred Thomason Grenfell, *Northern Neighbors: Stories of the Labrador People* (Boston: Houghton Mifflin Company, 1923)

1923 MOSDELL = H.M. Mosdell, 1883–1944, *When Was That? A Chronological Dictionary of Important Events in Newfoundland* (St

John's: Trade Printers and Publishers, Limited, 1923)

1923 PRATT = E.J. Pratt, 1882–1964, *Newfoundland Verse* (Toronto: The Ryerson Press, 1923)

1924 ENGLAND = George Allan England, 1877–1936, *Vikings of the Ice* (Garden City: Doubleday, Page & Company, 1924)

1925 CONDON = Michael E. Condon, *The Fisheries and Resources of Newfoundland* ([St John's], 1925)

1925 *Dial Notes* = G.A. England, 'Newfoundland Dialect Items,' *Dialect Notes*, v (1925), 322–46

1925 MUNN = W.A. Munn, 1864–1939, *The Cod Liver Oil Industry in Newfoundland* (St John's: W.A. Munn, Manufacturers and Exporters, [1925])

1925 MURPHY = James Murphy, *England's Oldest Possession: The Colony of Newfoundland* (St John's: James Murphy, 1925)

1926 HARVEY = Rev. Moses Harvey, *How the Fish came to Hant's Harbor Sixty Years Ago* (St John's: Robinson & Company, Limited, 1926)

1927 BURKE = John Burke [broadside] "Stoppage of Water"

1927 RULE = Rev. U.Z. Rule, *Reminiscences of My Life* (St John's: Dicks & Co., Ltd., 1927)

1928 BRUTON (ed) = *Narrative of a Journey Across the Island of Newfoundland in 1822 by W.E. Cormack*, ed F.A. Bruton (London: Longmans, Green and Co., Ltd., 1928). See also [1822] CORMACK

1928 BURKE = John Burke [broadside] "Don't You Remember the Dump, Maggie"

1928 [BURKE] = John Burke, *Burke's Popular Songs* ([St John's: John Burke], 1928)

1928 PALMER = C.H. Palmer, *The Salmon Rivers of Newfoundland* (Boston: Farrington Printing Co., 1928)

[1929] BOWEN = Frank C. Bowen, b 1894, *Sea Slang* (London: Sampson Low, Marston, [1929])

1929 BURKE = John Burke (ed), *Popular Songs* ([St John's:] Long Brothers, 1929)

[1929] [1949] ENGLISH = L.E.F. English, 1887–1971, *Newfoundland Past and Present* (Toronto: T. Nelson [?1949])

[1929] MCCAWLEY = Stuart McCawley, *Cape Breton Come-All-Ye; A Book of Songs and Rhymes of Cape Breton and Newfoundland*, 2nd ed (Glace Bay, N S [1929])

1929 MILLER = Florence Miller, b 1889, *In Caribou Land* (Toronto: The Ryerson Press, 1929)

1930 BARNES = Captain William Morris Barnes, b 1850, *When Ships Were Ships and Not Tin*

Pots (New York: Albert & Charles Boni, 1930)

1930 COAKER = W.F. Coaker, 1871–1938, *The History of the Fishermen's Protective Union of Newfoundland* (St John's: Advocate Publishing Co., 1930)

1930 DUGMORE = A. Radclyffe Dugmore, *In the Heart of the Northern Forests* (London: Chatto and Windus, 1930)

1930 RANDELL = Captain Jack Randell, b 1879, *I'm Alone* (Indianapolis: Bobbs-Merrill, 1930)

1931 BYRNES = John Maclay Byrnes, *The Paths to Yesterday* (Boston: Meador Publishing Company, 1931)

1931 SMALLWOOD = J.R. Smallwood, b. 1900, *The New Newfoundland* (New York: The Macmillan Company, 1931)

1932 BARBOUR = Job Barbour, b 1898, *Forty-Eight Days Adrift* (London: R. Clay & Sons, 1932)

1932 KEITH (ed) = *Speeches and Documents on the British Dominions 1918–1931*, ed Arthur Berriedale Keith (London: Oxford University Press, 1932)

1932 POLUNIN = Nicholas Polunin, *The Isle of Auks* (London: Edward Arnold & Co., 1932)

1933 GREENE = William Howe Greene, b 1865, *The Wooden Walls Among the Ice Floes: Telling the Romance of the Newfoundland Seal Fishery* (London: Hutchinson & Co. (Publishers) Limited, 1933)

1933 GREENLEAF (ed) = Elisabeth Bristol Greenleaf, and Grace Yarrow Mansfield, *Ballads and Sea Songs of Newfoundland* (Cambridge: Harvard University Press, 1933)

1933 GRENFELL = Wilfred Grenfell, *Forty Years for Labrador* (London: Hodder and Stoughton Company, 1933)

1933 MERRICK = Elliott Merrick, b 1905, *True North* (New York: Charles Scribner's Sons, 1933)

1933 *Nfld Royal Commission Report* = [Lord Amulree], *Newfoundland Royal Commission 1933 Report* (London: H.M. Stationery Office, 1933)

1934 BARTLETT = Captain 'Bob' Bartlett, 1875–1946, *Sails Over Ice* (New York: Charles Scribner's Sons, 1934)

[1934] KARPELES = Maud Karpeles (ed), 1885–1976, *Folk Songs from Newfoundland* ([London:] Oxford University Press [1934])

1934 LOUNSBURY = Ralph Greenlee Lounsbury, b 1896, *The British Fishery at Newfoundland: 1634–1763* (New Haven: Yale University Press, 1934)

1935 KEAN = [Captain Abram Kean, 1855–1945], *Old and Young Ahead: A Millionaire in Seals Being the Life History of Captain Abram Kean, O.B.E.* (London: Heath Cranton Limited, 1935)

1936 DEVINE = P.K. Devine, 1859–1950, *Ye Olde St John's 1750–1936* (St John's: The Newfoundland Directories, 1936)

1936 DULEY = Margaret Duley, 1894–1968, *The Eyes of the Gull* (London: Barker, 1936)

1936 SMITH = Nicholas Smith, b 1866, *Fifty-two Years at the Labrador Fishery* (London: Arthur H. Stockwell, 1936)

1937–1975 *Bk of Nfld* = *The Book of Newfoundland*, ed J.R. Smallwood, vols. i, ii (St John's: Newfoundland Book Publishers, Ltd., 1937); iii, iv (St John's: Newfoundland Book Publishers (1967) Ltd., 1967); v, vi (St John's: Newfoundland Book Publishers (1967) Ltd., 1975)

1937 DEVINE = P.K. Devine, *Devine's Folk Lore of Newfoundland in Old Words, Phrases and Expressions, Their Origin and Meaning* (St John's: Robinson & Co., Ltd., 1937)

1937 JUNEK = Oscar Waldemar Junek, *Isolated Communities: A Study of a Labrador Fishing Village* (New York: American Book Company, 1937)

1937 LUBBOCK = Basil Lubbock, 1876–1944, *The Arctic Whalers* (Glasgow: Brown, Son & Ferguson, Ltd., 1937)

1937 *Seafisheries of Nfld* = [Hon. Mr Justice Kent et al], *Report of the Commission of Enquiry Investigating the Seafisheries of Newfoundland and Labrador Other than the Sealfishery 1937* (St John's: Dicks & Co., Ltd., 1937)

[1938] AYRE = Agnes Marion Ayre, 1890–1940, *Newfoundland Names* [St John's, 1938]

1938 BRYAN = A.M. Bryan, 1893–1967, *St George's Coalfield* (St John's: Robinson & Co., Ltd., 1938)

1938 ENGLISH = Statia [Anastasia] M. English, *When the Dumb Speak* ([St John's], 1938)

1938 [MACDERMOTT] = [Hugh MacDermott], *MacDermott of Fortune Bay, Told by Himself* (London: Hodder and Stoughton, Limited, 1938)

[1939] DULEY = Margaret Duley, *Cold Pastoral* (London: Hutchinson & Company, [1939])

1939 EWBANK = R.B. Ewbank, 1883–1967, *Public Affairs in Newfoundland* (Cardiff: William Lewis, 1939)

1939 LODGE = T. Lodge, 1882–1958, *Dictatorship in Newfoundland* (London: Cassell and Company, Ltd., 1939)

1940 INNIS = 1954 INNIS

1940 SCAMMELL = A.R. Scammell, b 1913, *Songs of a Newfoundlander* (St Jerome: J.-H.-A. Labelle, 1940)

1941 DULEY = Margaret Duley, *Highway to*

Valour (Toronto: Macmillan Co. of Canada, 1941)

1941 MCLINTOCK = A.H. McLintock, *The Establishment of Constitutional Government in Newfoundland* (London: Longmans, Green and Co., 1941)

1941 SMALLWOOD = J.R. Smallwood (ed), *Hand Book, Gazetteer and Almanac* (St John's: Long Bros., [1941])

1941 WITHINGTON = Alfreda Withington, b 1860, *Mine Eyes Have Seen: A Woman Doctor's Saga* (New York: E.P. Dutton & Co., Inc., 1941)

1942 ELTON = Charles Elton, b 1900, *Voles, Mice and Lemmings* (Oxford: The Clarendon Press, 1942)

1942 *Grand Bank U C School* = *Grand Bank [Nfld] U.C. School Year-book* (1942)

1942 *Little Bay Islands* = *Past, Present, and Future. An Historical Review* ([Little Bay Islands], 1942)

[c1944] JONES = John Jones, 1904–1964, "Darn the Man that I Can Get" [undated broadside, c1944]

1944 [LAWTON & DEVINE] = [J.T. Lawton and P.K. Devine], *Old King's Cove* [St John's, 1944]

[c1945] TOBIN = Bertille Tobin, 1891?–1966, *Autumn in King's Cove* [St John's, c1945]

1946 BIRD = Will R. Bird, b 1891, *Sunrise for Peter and Other Stories* (Toronto: Ryerson Press, 1946)

1946 MACKAY (ed) = R.A. MacKay (ed), *Newfoundland: Economic, Diplomatic, and Strategic Studies* (Toronto: Oxford University Press, 1946)

1946 MUNN = W.A. Munn, *Wineland Voyages: Location of Helluland, Markland and Vineland*, 6th ed (St John's: *The Evening Telegram* Ltd., 1946)

1946 PRATT = E.J. Pratt, *Collected Poems* (Toronto: The Macmillan Company of Canada Limited, 1946)

1947 TANNER = V. Tanner, 1881–1966, *Outlines of the Geography, Life & Customs of Newfoundland-Labrador*, 2 vols. (Cambridge: At the University Press, 1947)

1948 BROSNAN = Very Rev. Michael Brosnan, 1894–1943, *Pioneer History of St George's Diocese Newfoundland* (Toronto: Mission Press, 1948)

1949 DULEY = Margaret Duley, *The Caribou Hut: The Story of a Newfoundland Hostel* (Toronto: Ryerson, 1949)

1949 FITZGERALD = Rev. Dr L.G. Fitzgerald, b 1898, *Lone Eagles of God: A Collection of Ballads* (New York: Exposition Press, 1949)

1950 HERBERT = A.P. Herbert, b 1890, *Independent Member* (London: Methuen & Co. Ltd., 1950)

1950 *Nfld: An Introduction* = *Newfoundland; An Introduction to Canada's New Province* (Ottawa: Department of External Affairs, 1950)

1950 PARKER = John Parker, b 1906, *Newfoundland: 10th Province of Canada* (London: Lincolns-Prager (Publishers), Ltd., 1950)

1951 DELDERFIELD = Eric R. Delderfield, *Torbay Story* (Exmouth: Raleigh Press, 1951)

1951–1957 *Nfld & Lab Pilot* = *Newfoundland and Labrador Pilot*, 8th ed, 2 vols. (London: Hydrographic Department, Admiralty, 1951, 1953). *Supplement No. 3* (1956); *Supplement No. 2* (1957)

1951 PETERS & BURLEIGH = Harold S. Peters and Thomas D. Burleigh, *The Birds of Newfoundland* (St John's: Department of Natural Resources, 1951)

1951 VILLIERS = Alan Villiers, *The Quest of the Schooner* Argus: *A Voyage to the Banks and Greenland* (London: Hodder and Stoughton, 1951)

1952 BANFILL = B.J. Banfill, b 1904, *Labrador Nurse* (Toronto: Ryerson Press, 1952)

1952 SMITH = J. Harry Smith, *Newfoundland Holiday* (Toronto: Ryerson Press, 1952)

1952 STANSFORD = Joshua Stansford, 1892–1961, *Fifty Years of My Life* (Ilfracombe: A.H. Stockwell, [1952])

1953 JOB = Robert John Job, b 1873, *John Job's Family* (St John's: Printed by the Telegram Printing Co., 1953)

1953 *Nfld Fish Develop Report* = [Sir Albert Walsh et al], *Newfoundland Fisheries Development Committee Report* (St John's: Guardian Limited, 1953)

1954 DISHER = T.F. Rhodes Disher, *Sixty Odd Years* (London: Clerke & Cockeran, 1954)

1954 INNIS = Harold A. Innis, 1894–1952, *The Cod Fisheries: The History of an International Economy*, 2nd ed (Toronto: University of Toronto Press, 1954)

[1954] 1972 RUSSELL = Ted Russell, 1904–1977, *The Holdin' Ground* (Toronto: McClelland and Stewart, 1972)

1955 ENGLISH = L.E.F. English, *Historic Newfoundland* (St John's: Newfoundland Tourist Development Division, 1955)

[1955] *Handbook* = *Handbook on Unemployment Insurance* (Ottawa: [1955])

1955 *Nfld Fisheries Board* = *Newfoundland Fisheries Board, General Circular No. 23* (St John's [stencilled document], August 1955)

1956 CUTTING = Charles L. Cutting, *Fish Saving; a History of Fish Processing from Ancient to Modern Times* (New York; Philosophical Library, 1956)

1956 FAY = C.R. Fay, b 1884, *Life and Labour in Newfoundland* (Toronto: University of Toronto Press, 1956)

1956 ROULEAU = Ernest Rouleau, *Studies on the Vascular Flora of the Province of Newfoundland (Canada)* (Montréal: Institut Botanique de l'Université de Montréal, 1956)

1956 STETSON = Joe Stetson, (ed), *This is The Newfoundland: Official Breed Book of The Newfoundland Club of America* (Orange, Conn.: Practical Science Pub. Co., 1956)

1956 STORY = G.M. Story, b 1927, *A Newfoundland Dialect Dictionary: A Survey of the Problems* [pamphlet] (St John's: [Memorial University], 1956)

1957–58 *Gov Arts & Letters Competition* = *Winning Entries in the 1957–1958 Competition Sponsored by the Newfoundland Government for the Encouragement of Arts and Letters* [St John's, 1958]

1957 GUY *Journal* See [1612] GUY

1957 *South Coast Commission* − [John T. Cheeseman et al], *Report of the South Coast Commission* (St John's: Province of Newfoundland, 1957)

1958 *Canadian Coins* = *Guide Book of Canadian Coins, Currency & Tokens* (Winnipeg: Canadian Numismatic Publishing Institute, 1958)

1958 HAKLUYT = *Richard Hakluyt, Voyages & Documents*, ed Janet Hampden (London: Oxford University Press, 1958). See also 1600 HAKLUYT

1958 HARRINGTON = Michael Francis Harrington, b 1916, *Sea Stories from Newfoundland* (Toronto: Ryerson Press, 1958)

1958 MOWAT = Farley Mowat, b 1921, *The Grey Seas Under* (Boston: Little, Brown, 1958)

1958 *Nfld Dishes* = *A Treasury of Newfoundland Dishes* ([St John's:] Maple Leaf Mills Ltd., 1958)

1959 MCATEE = W.L. McAtee, *Folk Names of Canadian Birds*, 2nd ed (Ottawa: National Museum of Canada, Bulletin No. 149, 1959)

1959 PERLIN = A.B. Perlin (ed), 1901–1978, *The Story of Newfoundland* [St John's, 1959]

1959 SAMSON = Solomon Samson, 1885–1957, *A Glimpse of Newfoundland (as it was and as it is) in Poetry and Picture*, ed Dr Robert Saunders (Poole: J. Looker Ltd., 1959)

[1960 BURKE] (ed White) = John Burke, *Burke's Ballads*, compiled by John White [St John's, 1960]. Augmented edition in *Songs of John Burke, Collected by John White*, ed William J. Kirwin (St John's: Cuff Publications, 1982)

1960 FUDGE = Capt. J.M. Fudge, b 1878, *His Life Story as a Fisherman and Businessman* (Moncton, N.B.: Atlas Press Limited, 1960)

1960 TUCK = Leslie M. Tuck, 1911–1979, *The Murres: their distribution, populations and biology: a study of the genus* Uria (Ottawa: Canadian Wildlife Service, 1960)

1961 FAY = C.R. Fay, *Channel Islands and Newfoundland* (Cambridge: W. Heffer & Sons, 1961)

1961 HOFFMAN = Bernard G. Hoffman, *Cabot to Cartier: Sources for a Historical Ethnography of Northeastern North America 1497–1550* (Toronto: University of Toronto Press, 1961)

1961 THOMPSON = Frederic F. Thompson, *The French Shore Problem in Newfoundland: An Imperial Study* (Toronto: University of Toronto Press, 1961)

1962 KEIR = David Keir, *The Bowring Story* (London: The Bodley Head, 1962)

1962 *Nfld Fisheries Conf* = *Newfoundland Fisheries Conference* (St John's, Sept. 24–27, 1962). Transcribed from tape recordings

1962 SPARKES = R.F. Sparkes, b 1906, *The Newfoundland Savings Bank June 12, 1834–March 31, 1962* [St John's, 1962]

1963 DIACK = Lesley Diack, 1901–1971, *Labrador Nurse* (London: Victor Gollancz Ltd., 1963)

1963 GARLAND = Joseph E. Garland, 1859–1932, *Lone Voyager* (Boston: Little, Brown and Company, 1963)

1963 HEAD = C. Grant Head, *Community Geographical Surveys* (St John's: Memorial University ISER, 1963)

1963 MANSFIELD = A.W. Mansfield, *Seals of Arctic and Eastern Canada* (Ottawa: Fisheries Research Board of Canada, 1963)

1963 MERCER = Eugene Mercer and Raymond McGrath, *A Study of a High Ptarmigan Population on Brunette Island Newfoundland in 1962* (St John's: Department of Mines, etc., 1963)

1963 PARSONS = R.A. Parsons, 1893–1981, *Sea Room* (St John's: The Newfoundland Arts Centre, 1963)

1963 TEMPLEMAN & FLEMING = Wilfred Templeman, b 1908, and A.M. Fleming, *Longlining experiments for cod off the east coast of Newfoundland and southern Labrador, 1950–1955* (Ottawa: Bulletin No. 141, Fisheries Research Board of Canada, 1963)

1963 WILLIAMS = Alan Williams, *Land Use Surveys, Part One, North East Coast* (St John's: Memorial University of Newfoundland, 1963)

1964 BLONDAHL (ed) = Omar Blondahl (ed), *Newfoundlanders, Sing!* (St John's: E.J. Bonnell, 1964)

1964 [JACKSON] = [Bernard S. Jackson], *Look for these 36 common Birds in Provincial Parks* (St John's: Newfoundland Provincial Parks Service [1964])

1964 NICHOLSON = G.W.L. Nicholson, b 1902, *The Fighting Newfoundlander: A History of The Royal Newfoundland Regiment* (St John's: The Government of Newfoundland, 1964)

1964 ROWE = Frederick W. Rowe, b 1912, *The Development of Education in Newfoundland* (Toronto: The Ryerson Press, 1964)

1964 SCOTT & CROSSMAN = W.B. Scott and E.J. Crossman, *Fishes Occurring in the Fresh Waters of Insular Newfoundland* (Ottawa: Queen's Printer, 1964)

1965 HENDERSON = Dorothy Henderson, b 1900, *The Heart of Newfoundland* (Montreal: Harvest House, 1965)

1965 LEACH (ed) = MacEdward Leach (ed), 1896–1967, *Folk Ballads and Songs of the Lower Labrador Coast* (Ottawa: National Museum of Canada, 1965)

1965 MOWAT = Farley Mowat, *Westviking: The Norse in Greenland and North America* (Toronto: McClelland & Stewart, 1965)

1965 PARSONS = R.A. Parsons, *The Rote* (Don Mills, Ont.: The Ontario Publishing Company Limited, 1965)

1965 PEACOCK (ed) = Kenneth Peacock (ed), b 1922, *Songs of the Newfoundland Outports*, 3 vols. (Ottawa: The National Museum of Canada, 1965)

1965 PETERS = Robert D. Peters, 'The Social and Economic Effects of the Transition from a System of Woods Camps to a System of Commuting in the Newfoundland Pulpwood Industry' (St John's: Memorial University M.A. Thesis, 1965). *Gloss* = the glossary of woods terms, pp. 201–7.

1965 RUSSELL = Franklin Russell, b 1922, *The Secret Islands* (Toronto: McClelland and Stewart Limited, 1965)

1965 SKELTON = R.A. Skelton, *James Cook, Surveyor of Newfoundland* (San Francisco: D. Magee, 1965)

1965 SUMMERS = William F., and Mary E. Summers, *Geography of Newfoundland* (Vancouver: Copp Clark Publishing Co., 1965)

1966 BEN-DOR = Shmuel Ben-dor, *Makkovik: Eskimos and Settlers in a Labrador Community: A Contrastive Study in Adaptation* (St John's: Memorial University ISER, 1966)

1966 FARIS = James C. Faris, *Cat Harbour: A Newfoundland Fishing Settlement* (St John's: Memorial University ISER, 1966)

1966 HORWOOD = Harold Horwood, b 1923, *Tomorrow Will Be Sunday* (New York: Doubleday & Company, Inc., 1966)

1966 PADDOCK = Harold J. Paddock, 'A Dialect Survey of Carbonear' (St John's: Memorial University M.A. Thesis, 1966). Revised form in *Publication of the American Dialect Society* No. 68 (1981)

1966 PHILBROOK = Tom Philbrook, b 1934, *Fisherman, Logger, Merchant, Miner: Social Change and Industrialism in Three Newfoundland Communities* (St John's: Memorial University ISER, 1966)

1966 PITT = David G. Pitt, b 1921, *Windows of Agates: A Short History of the Founding and Early Years of Gower Street Methodist (now United) Church in St John's, Newfoundland* (St John's: Gower Street United Church, 1966)

1966 SCAMMELL = A.R. Scammell, *My Newfoundland: Stories, Poems, Songs* (Montreal: Harvest House, 1966)

1966 SZWED = John Francis Szwed, b 1936, *Private Cultures and Public Imagery* (St John's: Memorial University ISER, 1966)

1967 BEARNS = E.R. Bearns (ed), *Native Trees of Newfoundland-Labrador* (St John's: Department of Mines, Agriculture & Resources, 1967)

1967 FIRESTONE = Melvin M. Firestone, *Brothers and Rivals: Patrilocality in Savage Cove* (St John's: Memorial University ISER, 1967)

1967 HORWOOD = Harold Horwood, *The Foxes of Beachy Cove* (Toronto: Doubleday Canada, 1967)

1967 *Nfld Education & Youth* = [Philip J. Warren et al], *Report of the Royal Commission on Education and Youth*, vol. i (St John's: Province of Newfoundland and Labrador, 1967)

1967 READER = H.J. Reader, *Newfoundland Wit, Humor and Folklore* [Corner Brook: Printed for the Author by the *Western Star*, 1967]

1968 *Avalon Penin of Nfld* = E.R. Seary, G.M. Story, W.J. Kirwin, *The Avalon Peninsula of Newfoundland: An Ethno-linguistic Study* (Ottawa: Bulletin No. 219, National Museum of Canada, 1968)

1968 DILLON = Virginia M. Dillon, 'The Anglo-Irish Element in the Speech of the Southern Shore of Newfoundland' (St John's: Memorial University M.A. Thesis, 1968)

1968 HARRIS = Leslie Harris, *Newfoundland and Labrador: A Brief History* (Don Mills, Ont.: Dent, 1968)

1968 IVERSON & MATTHEWS = Noel Iverson and D. Ralph Matthews, *Communities in Decline* (St John's: Memorial University ISER, 1968)

1968 KEATING = Bern Keating, *The Grand*

Banks (Chicago: Rand McNally & Company, 1968)

1968 MERCER = M.C. Mercer, 'Systematics and Biology of the Sepiolid Squids' (St John's: Memorial University M.Sc. Thesis, 1968)

1968 MESHER = Harvey Mesher, *The Selected Poems of an Ex-Labrador Trapper* (New York: Vantage Press, 1968)

1968 MOWAT & DE VISSER = Farley Mowat and John De Visser, *This Rock Within the Sea: A Heritage Lost* (Boston: Little, Brown, 1968)

1968 MURRAY (ed) = Jean M. Murray (ed), *The Newfoundland Journal of Aaron Thomas Able Seaman in H.M.S.* Boston (London: Longmans, 1968). See also [1794] THOMAS

1968 SCHULL = Joseph Schull, b 1910, *The Jinker: a novel* (Toronto: Macmillan of Canada, 1968)

1969 CELL = Gillian T. Cell, *English Enterprise in Newfoundland, 1577–1660* (Toronto: University of Toronto Press, 1969)

1969 *Christmas Mumming in Nfld* = Herbert Halpert and G.M. Story (eds), *Christmas Mumming in Newfoundland: Essays in Anthropology, Folklore and History* (Toronto: University of Toronto Press, 1969)

1969 DE WITT = Robert L. De Witt, *Public Policy and Community Protest: The Fogo Case* (St John's: Memorial University ISER, 1969)

1969 HORWOOD = Harold Horwood, *Newfoundland* (Toronto: Macmillan of Canada, 1969)

1969 INGSTAD = Helge Ingstad, b 1899, *Westward to Vinland: The Discovery of Pre-Columbian Norse House-sites in North America*, tr. Erik J. Friis (New York: Macmillan, 1969)

1969 MENSINKAI = S.S. Mensinkai, *Plant Location and Plant Size in the Fish Processing Industry of Newfoundland* (Ottawa: Department of Fisheries and Forestry of Canada, 1969)

1969 MOWAT = Farley Mowat, *The Boat Who Wouldn't Float* (Toronto: McClelland and Stewart, 1969)

1969 *Nfld Essays* = *Newfoundland: Introductory Essays and Excursion Guides* (St John's: Memorial University Department of Geography, 1969)

1969 WADEL = Cato Wadel, *Marginal Adaptations and Modernization in Newfoundland* (St John's: Memorial University ISER, 1969)

[c1970] *Common Butterflies* = *Common Butterflies* ([St John's:] Newfoundland Provincial Parks Service, [1970?])

1970 *Gray's Botany* = *Gray's Manual of Botany*, 8th ed, rewritten by Merritt Lyndon Fernald

(New York: Van Nostrand Reinhold Company, 1950; corrected 1970)

1970 JANES = Percy Janes, b 1922, *House of Hate* (Toronto: McClelland and Stewart, 1970)

1970 PARSONS = John Parsons, b 1939, *Labrador: Land of the North* (New York: Vantage Press, 1970)

1970 *Wooden Boats and Iron Men* = *Home of Wooden Boats and Iron Men: A Local History of Dunville, Argentia and Fox Harbour*. Women's Institutes of Newfoundland and Labrador, Dunville Branch (n.p., 1970)

1971 BOWN = Addison Bown, b 1905, *Newfoundland Journeys* (New York: Carlton Press, 1971)

1971 CASEY = George J. Casey, 'Traditions and Neighbourhoods: The Folklife of a Newfoundland Fishing Outport' (St John's: Memorial University M.A. Thesis, 1971)

1971 CHIARAMONTE = Louis J. Chiaramonte, *Craftsman-Client Contracts: Interpersonal relations in a Newfoundland fishing community* (St John's: Memorial University ISER, 1971)

[1971] GLASSIE = Henry Glassie and others, *Folksongs and Their Makers* (Bowling Green, Ohio: Bowling Green University Popular Press, [1971])

1971 HORWOOD = Andrew Horwood, *Newfoundland Ships and Men* (St John's: The Marine Researchers, 1971)

1971 JUPP = Dorothy M. Jupp, *A Journey of Wonder and Other Writings* (New York: Vantage Press, 1971)

1971 LYSAGHT = A.M. Lysaght (ed) See [1766] BANKS

1971 MANNION = John J. Mannion, 'Irish Imprints on the Landscape of Eastern Canada in the Nineteenth Century: A Study in Cultural Transfer and Adaptation' (Toronto: University of Toronto Ph.D. Thesis, 1971)

1971 NOEL = S.J.R. Noel, *Politics in Newfoundland* (Toronto: University of Toronto Press, 1971)

1971 NOSEWORTHY = Ronald G. Noseworthy, 'A Dialect Survey of Grand Bank, Newfoundland' (St John's: Memorial University M.A. Thesis, 1971)

1971 SEARY = E.R. Seary, b 1917, *Place Names of the Avalon Peninsula of the Island of Newfoundland* (Toronto: University of Toronto Press, 1971)

1972 BROWN = Cassie Brown, b 1919, *Death on the Ice: The Great Newfoundland Sealing Disaster of 1914* (Toronto: Doubleday Canada, 1972)

1972 HENDERSON = E.P. Henderson, *Surficial Geology of Avalon Peninsula, Newfoundland* (Ottawa: Geological Survey of Canada, 1972)

1972 HORWOOD = Harold Horwood, *White Eskimo: A Novel of Labrador* (Toronto: Doubleday Canada, 1972)

1972 JENSEN = Albert C. Jensen, *The Cod* (New York: Thomas Y. Crowell Company, 1972)

1972 MOWAT = Farley Mowat, *A Whale for the Killing* (Boston: Little, Brown, 1972)

1972 MURRAY = Hilda Murray, b 1934, 'The Traditional Role of Women in a Newfoundland Fishing Community' (St John's: Memorial University M.A. Thesis, 1972)

1972 NEMEC = Thomas F. Nemec, *The Origins and Development of Local Organization in Newfoundland Outport Communities: A Comparative Analysis of St Shotts and Trepassey* (St John's: Memorial University ISER, 1972)

1972 *Nfld Industrial Commission* = *Report of the Industrial Inquiry Commission* (St John's, 1972)

1972 SANGER = Chesley W. Sanger, 'Technological and Spatial adaptation in the Newfoundland seal fishery during the nineteenth century' (St John's: Memorial University M.A. Thesis, 1972)

1973 BARBOUR = Florence Grant Barbour, *Memories of Life on the Labrador and in Newfoundland* (New York: Carlton Press, 1973)

1973 COOK = Michael Cook, b 1933, *Head, Guts and Sound Bone Dance* (St John's: Breakwater Books, 1973)

1973 GOUDIE = Elizabeth Goudie, d 1982, *Woman of Labrador*, ed David Zimmerly (Toronto: Peter Martin Associates Ltd., 1973)

1973 HENRIKSEN = Georg Henriksen, *Hunters in the Barrens: The Naskapi on the Edge of the White Man's World* (St John's: Memorial University ISER, 1973)

1973 HORWOOD = Andrew Horwood, *Captain Harry Thomasen: Forty Years at Sea* [Antrim: W. & G. Baird, 1973]

1973 JELKS = Edward B. Jelks, *Archaeological Explorations at Signal Hill, Newfoundland, 1965–1966* (Ottawa: National Historic Sites Service, 1973)

1973 MOWAT = Farley Mowat and David Blackwood, *Wake of the Great Sealers* (Toronto: McClelland and Stewart, 1973)

1973 PINSENT = Gordon Pinsent, *The Rowdyman* (Toronto: McGraw-Hill Ryerson Limited, 1973)

1973 ROSE (ed) = Clyde Rose (ed), b 1937, *Baffles of Wind and Tide* (St John's: Breakwater Books, 1973)

1973 SMALLWOOD = [J.R. Smallwood], *I Chose Canada: The Memoirs of the Hon. Joseph R. 'Joey' Smallwood* (Toronto: Macmillan of Canada, 1973)

1973 WADEL = Cato Wadel, *Now, Whose Fault is That? The Struggle for Self-Esteem In the Face of Chronic Unemployment* (St John's: Memorial University ISER, 1973)

1973 WIDDOWSON = J.D.A. Widdowson, 'Aspects of Traditional Verbal Control: Threats and Threatening Figures in Newfoundland Folklore' (St John's: Memorial University Ph.D. Thesis, 1973)

1974 BRIDLE (ed) = Paul Bridle (ed), *Documents on Relations Between Canada and Newfoundland*, vol. i, 1935–1949 (Ottawa: Information Canada, 1974)

1974 CAHILL = Tom Cahill, b 1929, *As Loved Our Fathers* (St John's: Breakwater Books, 1974)

1974 *Federal Licensing Policy* = David Alexander, G.M. Story et al, *Report of the Committee on Federal Licensing Policy and its Implications for the Newfoundland Fisheries* ([St John's: Memorial University ISER], 1974)

1974 GREEN = H. Gordon Green, *Don't Have Your Baby in the Dory: A Biography of Myra Bennett* (Montreal: Harvest House, 1974)

1974 MANNION = John J. Mannion, *Irish Settlements in Eastern Canada: A Study of Cultural Transfer and Adaptation* (Toronto: University of Toronto Press, 1974)

1974 MARIN = Clive Marin, *Fogo Island* (Philadelphia: Dorrance & Company, 1974)

1974 NEARY & O'FLAHERTY (eds) = Peter Neary and Patrick O'Flaherty (eds), *By Great Waters: A Newfoundland and Labrador Anthology* (Toronto: University of Toronto Press, 1974)

1974 NORTHCOTT = Tom H. Northcott, *The Land Mammals of Insular Newfoundland* ([St John's:] Department of Tourism, 1974)

1974 PINSENT = Gordon Pinsent, *John & The Missus: a novel* (Toronto: McGraw-Hill Ryerson Limited, 1974)

1974 PITTMAN = Al Pittman, b 1940, *A Rope Against the Sun: A Play for Voices* (St John's: Breakwater Books Ltd., 1974)

1974 *Sailing Directions: Labrador and Hudson Bay* (Ottawa: Department of the Environment, 1974)

1974 SCOTT & BRASSARD = Peter J. Scott and Guy R. Brassard, *Preliminary List of the Vascular Plants of Oxen Pond Botanic Park* (St John's: Memorial University, 1974)

1974 SQUIRE = Harold Squire, *A Newfoundland Outport in the Making: The Early History of Eastport* (n.p., 1974)

1974 VIVIEN = John Vivien, *Project Homebrew: Report C* (St John's: [stencilled] 1974)

[1975] ANDREWS = C.W. Andrews, 1916–1978, *The Origin, Growth and Decline of the New-*

foundland Sealfishery [brochure] [Harbour Grace, 1975]

1975 BUTLER = Victor Butler, 1896–1981, *The Little Nord Easter: Reminiscences of a Placentia Bayman*, ed W. Wareham (St John's: Memorial University, 1975)

1975 COOK = Michael Cook, *Jacob's Wake* (Vancouver: Talonbooks, 1975)

[1975] *Fisherman's Handbook* = *Fisherman's Handbook* (St John's: Newfoundland Department of Fisheries, [1975])

1975 GUY = Ray Guy, *You May Know Them as Sea Urchins, Ma'am*, ed Eric Norman (Portugal Cove: Breakwater Books, 1975)

1975 HOLMES = Charlotte E. Holmes, *Common Insects of Oxen Pond Botanic Park* (St John's: Memorial University, 1975)

1975 LEYTON = Elliott Leyton, *Dying Hard: The Ravages of Industrial Carnage* (Toronto: McClelland and Stewart, 1975)

1975 MILLS = David B. Mills, 'The Evolution of Folk House Forms in Trinity Bay, Newfoundland' (St John's: Memorial University M.A Thesis, 1975)

1975 MOYLES (ed) = R.G. Moyles (ed), *Complaints is Many and Various, but the Odd Divil Likes it* (Toronto: Peter Martin Associates, 1975)

1975 O'NEILL = Paul O'Neill, b 1928, *The Story of St John's, Newfoundland*: vol. i *The Oldest City* (Erin, Ont.: Press Porcepic, 1975), vol. ii *A Seaport Legacy* (1976)

1975 POCIUS = Jerry Pocius, *Textile Traditions of the Avalon Peninsula* (St John's: Memorial University typescript for the National Museum of Man, 1975). See 1979 POCIUS

1975 RUSSELL = Ted Russell, *The Chronicles of Uncle Mose*, ed Elizabeth (Russell) Miller (St John's: Breakwater Books, 1975)

1975 SCOTT = Peter J. Scott, *Edible Fruits and Herbs of Newfoundland* (St John's: Memorial University Oxen Pond Botanic Park, 1975)

1975 WINTER = Keith Winter, b 1935, *Shananditti: The Last of the Beothucks* (Vancouver: J.J. Douglas Ltd., 1975)

1976 *Avifaunal Survey* = Robert D. Lamberton, *An Avifaunal Survey of L'Anse-aux-Meadows National Historic Park* (Parks Canada, Atlantic Region, 1976)

1976 BROWN = Cassie Brown, *A Winter's Tale: The Wreck of the* Florizel (Toronto: Doubleday Canada, 1976).

1976 CASHIN = Peter Cashin, 1890–1977, *My Life and Times: 1890–1919*, ed R.E. Buehler (St John's: Breakwater Books, 1976)

1976 GUY = Ray Guy, *That Far Greater Bay*, ed Eric Norman (Portugal Cove: Breakwater Books, 1976)

1976 HEAD = C. Grant Head, *Eighteenth Century Newfoundland: A Geographer's Perspective* (Toronto: McClelland and Stewart Limited, 1976)

1976 HOLLETT = Robert Hollett, 'Allegro Speech' (St John's: Memorial University M. Phil. essay, 1976)

1976 JACKSON = Bernard S. Jackson, *Butterflies of Oxen Pond Botanic Park—their Conservation and Management* (St John's: Memorial University, 1976)

1976 *Labrador Inuit* = *Labrador Inuit: Uqausingit*, ed Rose Jeddore (Nain: The Labrador Inuit Committee on Literacy, 1976)

1976 MATTHEWS = Ralph Matthews, b 1943, *There's no Better Place Than Here: Social Change in Three Newfoundland Communities* (Toronto: Peter Martin Associates Limited, 1976)

1976 MURPHY = Michael P. Murphy, b 1902, *Pathways through Yesterday* (St John's: Town Crier Publishing Company Limited, 1976)

1976 *The Newfoundland Quarterly* = *The Newfoundland Quarterly: 75th Anniversary Special Edition*, ed Harry A. Cuff, Cyril F. Poole (St John's: Creative Printers and Publishers, 1976)

1976 PINHORN = A.T. Pinhorn, *Living Marine Resources of Newfoundland-Labrador: Status and Potential* (Ottawa: Bulletin of the Fisheries Research Board of Canada 194, 1976)

1976 *St John's Heritage Conservation Area Study* ([St John's], 1976)

1976 SHEA = Hugh Shea, *Shea's Newfoundland Seduced* (New York: Vantage Press, 1976)

1976 TUCK = James A. Tuck, *Newfoundland and Labrador Prehistory* (Toronto: National Museum of Man, 1976)

1976 WINSOR = Naboth Winsor, *By Their Works: A History of the Wesleyville Congregation 1874–1974* (St John's: Printed by Newfoundland Form & Letter Duplicating, 1976)

[1977] BURSEY = W.J. Bursey, 1893–1980, *The Undaunted Pioneer: An Autobiography* [St John's, 1977]

1977 BUTLER = Victor Butler, *Sposin' I Dies in D' Dory*, ed Boyd L. Hiscock and Ivan F. Jesperson (St John's: Jesperson Printing Ltd., 1977)

1977 *Inuit Land Use* = *Our Footprints are Everywhere: Inuit Land Use and Occupancy in Labrador*, ed Carol Brice-Bennett (Nain: Labrador Inuit Association, 1977)

1977 *Lgs in Nfld* = *Languages in Newfoundland and Labrador*, Preliminary Version, ed Harold J. Paddock (St John's: Memorial University, 1977)

1977 *Peopling of Nfld* = *The Peopling of Newfoundland: Essays in Historical Geography*, ed

John J. Mannion (St John's: Memorial University ISER, 1977)

1977 QUILLIAM = Tom Quilliam (ed), *Look 'Ere Me Son!* (Grand Falls: Helme, 1977)

1977 ROWE = Frederick W. Rowe, *Extinction: The Beothuks of Newfoundland* (Toronto: McGraw-Hill Ryerson, Limited, 1977)

1977 RUSSELL = Ted Russell, *Tales from Pigeon Inlet*, ed Elizabeth (Russell) Miller (St John's: Breakwater Books, 1977)

1977 WHITELEY = Albert S. Whiteley, *A Century on Bonne Esperance: The Saga of the Whiteley Family* (Ottawa: Cheriton Graphics, 1977). One or two passages omitted from the printed book have been cited from a typescript of the Labrador diary of Capt. W.H. Whiteley, made available through the courtesy of Dr W.H. Whiteley.

1977 WIDDOWSON = J.D.A. Widdowson, *If You Don't Be Good: Verbal Social Control in Newfoundland* (St John's: Memorial University ISER, 1977) = revised version of 1973 WIDDOWSON

[c1977] WINSOR (ed) = Rev. Naboth Winsor (ed), *Three Newfoundland Stories* [n.p., stencilled book, c1977]

1978 *Beothuk Vocabularies* = John Hewson, *Beothuk Vocabularies: A Comparative Study* (St John's: Newfoundland Museum, 1978)

1978 *Haulin' Rope & Gaff* = *Haulin' Rope & Gaff: Songs and Poetry of the Newfoundland Seal Fishery*, ed Shannon Ryan and Larry Small (St John's: Breakwater Books Limited, 1978)

1978 PASTORE = Ralph T. Pastore, *Newfoundland Micmacs: A History of their Traditional Life* ([St John's:] Newfoundland Historical Society, 1978)

1978 ROULEAU = Ernest Rouleau, *List of the Vascular Plants of the Province of Newfoundland (Canada)* [2nd ed], (St John's: Oxen Pond Botanic Park, 1979)

1978 WHALLEY = George Whalley, *Birthright to the Sea: Some Poems of E.J. Pratt* (St John's: Memorial University Pratt Lecture, 1978)

1979 COOPER = Georgiana Cooper, 1885–1980, *The Deserted Island: Newfoundland Verse and Paintings*, ed Harry A. Cuff and Everard H. King (St John's: H.A. Cuff, 1979)

1979 HORWOOD = Harold Horwood, *Only the Gods Speak* (St John's: Breakwater Books, 1979)

1979 MURRAY = Hilda Murray, *More Than Fifty Percent: Woman's Life in a Newfoundland Outport, 1900–1950* (St John's: Breakwater Books, 1979) = revised version of 1972 MURRAY

1979 NEMEC = Thomas F. Nemec, 'St Shotts: The History, Ecology and Organization of an Anglo-Irish Newfoundland Outport and Its Cod Fishery' (Ann Arbor: University of Michigan Ph.D. Thesis, 1979)

1979 O'FLAHERTY = Patrick O'Flaherty, *The Rock Observed: Studies in the Literature of Newfoundland* (Toronto: University of Toronto Press, 1979)

1979 POCIUS = Gerald L. Pocius, *Textile Traditions of Eastern Newfoundland* (Ottawa: National Museums of Canada, 1979) = revised version of 1975 POCIUS

1979 POTTLE = Herbert L. Pottle, b 1907, *Newfoundland: Dawn Without Light: Politics, Power & the People in the Smallwood Era* (St John's: Breakwater Books, 1979)

1979 *Salt Water, Fresh Water* = Allan Anderson [ed], b 1915, *Salt Water, Fresh Water* (Toronto: Macmillan of Canada, 1979)

1979 TIZZARD = Aubrey Malcolm Tizzard, b 1919, *On Sloping Ground: Reminiscences of Outport Life in Notre Dame Bay, Newfoundland*, ed J.D.A. Widdowson (St John's, Memorial University, 1979)

1979 *'Twas a way of life* = *'Twas a way of life*, ed Frances Ennis, Sheilagh McMurrich Koop, Susan Shiner, Carol Baxter Wherry ([St John's:] Jesperson Press, 1979)

1980 COX = Gordon S.A. Cox, *Folk Music in a Newfoundland Outport* (Ottawa: National Museum of Canada, 1980)

1980 TAYLOR = David Taylor, 'Boatbuilding in Winterton: The Design, Construction and Use of Inshore Fishing Boats in a Newfoundland Community' (St John's: Memorial University M.A. Thesis, 1980)

1981 GUY = Ray Guy, *Beneficial Vapors*, ed Eric Norman ([St John's:] Published by Jesperson Press [1981])

1981 HUSSEY = Greta Hussey, *Our Life on Lear's Room, Labrador*, ed Susan Shiner (St John's: Robinson-Blackmore, 1981)

Alphabetical Index of Authors, Newspapers and Periodicals, and Selected Titles

This list presents an author or selected title index of written works cited in this Dictionary. The dates in parentheses following the names refer to the chronological bibliography above. The periodical publications are documented either in the Union List of Serials or in the catalogues of the Memorial University Library Centre for Newfoundland Studies and the Provincial Reference Library in the St John's Arts and Culture Centre. Periodicals followed by date refer to articles by major collectors of Newfoundland speech.

Gosse, Philip Henry (c1830); (1840); (1844); (1860)

Goudie, Elizabeth (1973)

Gov[ernment] Arts & Letters Competition (1957–8)

Grand Bank U[nited] C[hurch] School (1942)

Grant, James (1875)

Gray's Botany (1970)

Green, H. Gordon (1974)

Greene, William Howe (1933)

Greenleaf, Elisabeth Bristol, and Mansfield, Grace Yarrow (eds) (1933)

Gregory, J.U. (1886)

Grenfell, Anne, and Spalding, Katie (1920)

Grenfell, Wilfred T. (1895); (1905); (1906); (1909[1]); (1909[2]); (1910); (1911); (1912); (1916); (1919[1]); (1919[2]); (1923)

Guy, John (1612) See also *Willoughby Papers*

Guy, Ray (1975); (1976); (1981)

Habitat

Hakluyt, Richard (1600); (1958)

Halpert, H., and Story, G.M. (eds) See *Christmas Mumming in Nfld*

Handbook on Unemployment Insurance (1955)

Harbour Grace Standard

Harper's

Harrington, Michael Francis (1958)

Harris, Leslie (1968)

Harrisse, Henry (1900)

Harvey, D.C. (cd) See *Journeys*

Harvey, Moses (1879); (1894); (1897); (1900); (1926) See also HATTON

Hatton, Joseph and Harvey, M. (1883)

Haulin' Rope & Gaff (1978)

Hawkes, E.W. (1916)

Hayes, E. See *Gilbert's Voyages & Enterprises*

Hayman, Robert (1628[1,2])

Head, C. Grant (1963); (1976)

Henderson, Dorothy (1965)

Henderson, E.P. (1972)

Henriksen, Georg (1973)

Herbert, A.P. (1950)

Hind, Henry Youle (1863)

Hoffman, Bernard G. (1961)

Hollett, Robert (1976)

Holly Branch

Holly Leaves

Holmes, Charlotte E. (1975)

Horwood, Andrew (1971); (1973)

Horwood, Harold (1966); (1967); (1969); (1972); (1979)

Howley, James P. (1868-1910); (1876); (1913); (1915)

Howley, James P. See MURRAY, ALEXANDER

Howley, M.F. (1888); (1903)

Hubbard, Mrs Leonidas (1908)

Hussey, Greta (1981)

Hutchinson, Horace G. (1911)

Hutton, S.K. (1912)

Independent

Ingstad, Helge (1969)

Innis, Harold A. (1940); (1954)

Int[ernational] Journ[al] of Am[erican] Linguistics

Inuit Land Use (1977)

Inverness Scientific Society See *Transactions*

Iverson, Noel, and Matthews, D. Ralph (1968)

Jackson, Bernard S. (1964); (1976)

J[ournal of] A[merican] Folklore (1895–7)

Janes, Percy (1970)

Jeddore, Rose (ed) See *Labrador Inuit*

Jelks, Edward B. (1973)

Jensen, Albert C. (1972)

Job, Robert John (1953)

Jones, John (c1944)

Josselyn, John (1672)

Journ of Assembly = *Journal of the [Newfoundland] House of Assembly*

Journeys (ed Harvey) (1775)

Jukes, Joseph Beete (1842); (1843)

Junek, Oscar Waldemar (1937)

Jupp, Dorothy M. (1971)

Karpeles, Maud (1934)

Kean, Abram (1935)

Keating, Bern (1968)

Keir, David (1962)

Keith, Arthur Berriedale (ed) (1918); (1932)

Kelly, James Butler Knitt (1870)

Kennedy, David (1876)

Kennedy, W.R. (1881); (1885)

Kinsella, P.J. (1919)

Kirwin, W.J. See *Avalon Penin of Nfld*

Kohlmeister, Benjamin, and Kmoch, George (1814)

Labrador Inuit (1976)

Latham, John L. (1821–24)

Latham, Robert Gordon (1850)

La Trobe, Benjamin (1774)

Lawton, J.T. and Devine, P.K. (1944)

Leach, MacEdward (ed) (1965)

Leader-Post [Regina]

Leisure Hour

Lench, Charles (1912); (1916); (1919)

Leyton, Elliott (1975)

L[an]g[uage]s in Nfld (1977)

Lind, Henry (1857–1864)

Lindsay, David Moore (1884)

Literary & Historical Society of Quebec See *Transactions*

Little Bay Islands [School Magazine]

Liverpool MS (1792)

Livyere

Lloyd, F.E.J. (1886)

Lodge, T. (1939)

Lore and Language

Lounsbury, Ralph Greenlee (1934)

Lowell, Robert Traill Spence (1858)
Lubbock, Basil (1937)
Lumsden, James (1906)
Lysaght, A.M. (ed) See BANKS, JOSEPH
McAtee, W.L. (1959)
McCawley, Stuart (1929)
McCrea, R.B. (1869)
MacDermott, Hugh (1938)
McGrath, P.T. (1911)
McGregor, John (1828); (1832)
MacKay, R.A. (ed) (1946)
McLean, John (1849)
McLintock, A.H. (1941)
Mannion, John J. (1971); (1974)
Mannion, John J. (ed) See *Peopling of
  Newfoundland*
Mansfield, A.W. (1963)
Mansfield, G.Y. See GREENLEAF, ELISABETH
  BRISTOL
March, Stephen (1854)
[Maria] See ENGLISH, ANASTASIA
Marin, Clive (1974)
Maritime Mo[nthly]
Mason, John (1620)
Matthews, Ralph (1976)
Matthews, Ralph See IVERSON, NOEL
Melville, Herman (1851)
Memo of French Fisheries (1857)
Mensinkai, S.S. (1969)
Mercer, Eugene and McGrath, Raymond (1963)
Mercer, M.C. (1968)
Merrick, Elliott (1933)
Mesher, Harvey (1968)
Millais, J.G. (1907)
Miller, E. (ed) See RUSSELL, TED (1977)
Miller, Florence (1929)
Mills, David B. (1975)
Modern Christmas Number
Monthly Rev[iew]
Montreal News
Moreton, Julian (1863)
Morning Post
Morris, Isaac C. (1894)
Mosdell, H.M. (1923)
Mott, Henry Youmans (1894)
Mountain, J.G. (1857)
Mowat, Farley (1958); (1965); (1968); (1969);
  (1972); (1973)
Moyles, R. G. (ed) (1975)
Mullaly, John (1855)
Mullock, John Thomas (1860)
*MUN Gazette = Memorial University of New-
  foundland Gazette*
Munn, W.A. (1925); (1946)
Murphy, James (1902); (1904); (1905); (1906);
  (1916); (1925)
Murphy, Michael P. (1976)

Murray, Alexander, and Howley, James P.
  (1864–1880)
Murray, Hilda (1972); (1979)
Murray, Hugh (1839)
Murray, Jean M. (ed) (1968) See THOMAS,
  AARON
Muse, The [Memorial University]
Nat[ional] Geog[raphic]
Nat[ional] Mus[eum of] Can[ada] Bul[letin]
Nautical Magazine
Naval Chronicle
Neary, Peter, and O'Flaherty, Patrick (eds)
  (1974)
Nemec, Thomas F. (1972); (1979)
Newfoundlander
N[ew] Y[ork] Folklore Q[uarterly]
Nfld Almanac (1850)
Nfld & Lab[rador] Pilot (1887); (1907);
  (1951–1957)
Nfld: An Introduction (1950)
Nfld Dishes (1958)
Nfld Education & Youth (1967)
Nfld Essays (1969)
*Nfld Fish Develop Report = Newfoundland Fish-
  eries Development Committee Report* (1953)
Nfld Fisheries Board (1955)
Nfld Fisheries Conf[erence] (1962)
Nfld Herald
Nfld Illustrated Tribune
Nfld Indicator
Nfld Industrial Commission (1972)
Nfld Law Reports (1829–1911)
Nfld Magazine
Nfld Magazine & Advertiser
Nfld Pilot (1878)
Nfld Qtly = Newfoundland Quarterly
Nfld Royal Commission Report (1933)
Nfld T V Topics
[Nfld] Year Book (1887); (1893)
Nicholson, G.W.L. (1964)
Nineteenth Century
Noble, Louis L. (1861)
Noel, S.J.R. (1971)
N[orth] Amer[ican] Pilot (1779)
Northcott, Tom H. (1974)
North Star
Noseworthy, Ronald G. (1971)
*N S Inst Sci = Proceedings and Transactions of
  the Nova Scotian Institute of Science*
O'Flaherty, Patrick (1979)
O'Flaherty See NEARY, PETER
Oldmixon, John (1708)
Oliver, George T., and Burke, John (1900)
O'Mara See DEVINE
O'Neill, Paul (1975–6)
Osborne, Thomas (1745)
Our Country

Squire, Harold (1974)
Standard [Harbour Grace]
Standard [London]
Stansford, Joshua (1952)
Stearns, W.A. (1884); (1888)
Steele, Robert (1810)
Stetson, Joe (ed) (1956)
Stewart's Qtly
Story, G.M. (1956); ed (1969) See also *Avalon Penin of Nfld, Federal Licensing Policy*
Summers, William F. and Mary E. (1965)
Swansborough, W. (1896)
Szwed, John Francis (1966)
Talbot, Thomas (1882)
Tanner, V. (1947)
Taylor, Bayard (1860)
Taylor, David (1980)
T.C. (1623)
Telegram Christmas No See *Evening Telegram*
Templeman, Wilfred, and Fleming, A.M. (1963)
Them Days
Thomas, Aaron (1794)
Thomas, William S. (1913)
Thompson, Frederic F. (1961)
Thompson, Thomas (1711)
Thoreau, Henry David (1854)
Thoresby, William (1799)
Time (Canada)
Times [London]
Times [St John's]
Tizzard, Aubrey Malcolm (1979)
Tobin, Bertille (c1945)
Tocque, Philip (1846); (1878); (1895)
Townsend, Charles Wendell (1908); (1910); (1918)
Townsend, Charles Wendell, and Allen, Glover M. (1907)
Trade Review Christmas Number
Trans[actions of the] Dev[onshire] Assoc[iation]
Trans[actions of the] Geol[ogical] Soc[iety]
Trans[actions of the] Inverness Scientific Soc[iety] & Field Club
Trans[actions of the] Lit[erary] & Hist[orical] Soc[iety] of Quebec
Trans[actions of the] Phil[ological] Soc[iety]
Trans[actions of the] Roy[al] Soc[iety of] Can[ada]
Trans[actions of the] Roy[al] Soc[iety of] London]
Travel
Tribune Christmas Number
Tuck, James A. (1976)
Tuck, Leslie M. (1960)
Tucker, Ephraim W. (1839)
Tucker, H.W. (1877)
'Twas a way of life (1979)
Ulloa, Antonio de (1758)
Ulster J[ournal of] Arch[aeology]

Union Forum
Vaughan, William (1626); (1630)
Villiers, Alan (1951)
Vivien, John (1974)
Wadel, Cato (1969); (1973)
Waghorne, Arthur C. (1888)
Waldo, Fullerton L. (1920)
Wallace, Dillon (1905); (1907[1]); (1907[2]); (1914)
Walsh, A.J. See *Nfld Fisheries Development Committee Report*
Waterford Mirror [Waterford, Ire]
Weather Proverbs (1883)
Week End [New York]
Weekly Herald
Western Star [Corner Brook]
West-India Merchant (1712)
Whalley, George (1978)
What's Happening
Whitbourne, Richard (1620); (1622); (1623)
White, Edward (1854–1886)
White, John (ed) See BURKE, JOHN (1960)
Whiteley, Albert S. (1977)
Widdowson, J.D.A. (1973); (1977)
Williams, Alan (1963)
Williams, Griffith (1765)
Williamson, J.A. (ed) See *Cabot Voyages*
Willoughby Papers (c1610–1634)
Willson, Beckles (1897); (1901)
Wilson, William (1866)
Winsor, Naboth (1976); (c1977)
Winter, James (1863)
Winter, Keith (1975)
Withington, Alfreda (1941)
Wix, Edward (1836[1]); (1836[2])
Wooden Boats & Iron Men (1970)
Wood, Ruth Kedzie (1915)
Year Book (1887); (1893)
Yonge, James (1663–1670)
Young, Arminius (1916)
Yuletide Bells
Zoologist

CONTEMPORARY COLLECTIONS AND COLLECTORS

Collections

The following is a list in coded form of the collections quoted in the Dictionary and discussed above in the Introduction, SOURCES FOR THE DICTIONARY. The collections beginning with the letters C, M, Q and T are part of the Memorial University Folklore and Language Archive and refer respectively to the Card Collection, Manuscript Collection, Questionnaire Responses, and Tape Collection. The numerals following the letters C, M, and Q indicate the year of collection or accessioning, and the final numeral is that assigned to the collector; T is followed by the Archive's code for the speaker, and the final numerals indicate the date of collecting or accessioning. P = field records, and the numeral which follows in this list is that assigned to the collector, whose name and, in most cases, locality are also given; in the Dictionary itself, the citation form ends with numerals indicating the year of the field recording.

C 63–1   C. Blackwood; Wesleyville
C 63–2   G. Brooking; Deer Island
C 63–3   J. Brown; Botwood
C 63–4   H. Callahan; New Perlican
C 63–5   H. Coates; Bay Roberts
C 63–6   R. Godfrey; Trinity
C 63–7   H. Tilley; Long Pond, Manuels
C 63–8   W. Winsor; Exploits
C 64–4   I. Power; St John's
C 64–5   B. Kelleher; Brownsdale
C 64–6   R. Maunder; St John's
C 64–7   R. Penney; Seldom, N.D. Bay
C 64–8   T. Smith; Chance Cove
C 65–2   G. Casey; Conche
C 65–3   C. Decker; Roddickton
C 65–4   P. Delaney; Tor's Cove
C 65–11   F. Green; Winterton
C 65–12   C. Ollerhead; St Anthony
C 66–1   L. Ayre; St John's
C 66–2   S. Cole; Buchans
C 66–3   G. Crewe; Grand Bank
C 66–4   D. Curran; Gambo
C 66–5   J. Dawson; Bay Roberts
C 66–7   G. Hawkins; Boston
C 66–8   G. Higgins; St John's
C 66–9   W. Kennedy; Harbour Grace
C 66–10   H. Lear; Hibb's Hole
C 66–12   G. Moore; Winsor
C 66–13   R. Noseworthy; Grand Bank
C 66–18   L. Williams; Grand Bank
C 67–1   J. Adams; Upper Island Cove
C 67–4   M. Fagan; St Mary's

C 67–5   S. Fiander; Ramea
C 67–6   W. Hamlyn; St John's
C 67–7   E. Holmes; Toronto/St John's
C 67–8   S. Jackson; Vienna/St John's
C 67–9   J. Jacobs; St John's
C 67–10   R. Kendall; Ramea
C 67–12   E. Lang; Marystown
C 67–13   B. MacDonald; Scarborough
C 67–14   C. O'Brien; St John's
C 67–15   C. Sheehan; St John's
C 67–16   L. Small; Moreton's Harbour
C 67–21   J. Verge; Harbour Grace
C 67–22   J. Widdowson; Sheffield, U.K.
C 68–1   F. Burden; Shoal Brook
C 68–3   J. Dollimount; François
C 68–4   R. Drodge; Little Heart's Ease
C 68–5   G. Duggan; St John's West
C 68–7   J. Fudge; Grole
C 68–10   C. Hamlyn; Sop's Arm
C 68–12   W. Lane; Glovertown
C 68–15   J. Norman; Port Union
C 68–16   A.F. O'Brien; Cape Broyle
C 68–17   R. Park; Gillams
C 68–18   J. Pinsent; Port Nelson
C 68–19   M. Ryan; St John's
C 68–20   C. Skinner; Richard's Harbour
C 68–21   J. Stockley; Twillingate
C 68–22   B. Stratton; Corner Brook
C 68–23   H. Stroud; Glovertown South
C 68–24   B. Trask; Elliston
C 69–1   B. Bartlett; Catalina
C 69–2   C. Bishop; Wesleyville
C 69–5   W. Canning; Roddickton
C 69–6   E. Cokes; Head Bay D'Espoir
C 69–7   G. Combden; Barr'd Islands
C 69–8   W. Cooper; St John's
C 69–9   D. Courtney; Kilbride
C 69–10   D. Cox; Channel
C 69–11   M. Dobbin; St John's
C 69–12   A. Etchegary; St Lawrence
C 69–13   M. Fitzpatrick; Lord's Cove
C 69–15   E. Genge; St John's
C 69–16   J. Green; Chance Cove
C 69–17   R. Hobbs; Elliston
C 69–18   D. Legge; St John's
C 69–19   T. McCarthy; Terrenceville
C 69–20   S. Mercer; Foxtrap
C 69–21   R. Payne; Cow Head
C 69–23   Z. Sacrey; Woodstock
C 69–24   V. Sheppard; Appleton, Glenwood
C 69–25   H. Strong; Windsor
C 69–27   J. Williams; Isle Valen
C 69–28   F. Bonnell; Lamaline
C 69–29   D. Butt; Freshwater
C 69–30   R. Grant; Gaultois
C 69–31   R. Dawe; Bay Roberts
C 69–32   M. Ramsay; Thorald, Ontario
C 70–5   L. Ayre; St John's

C 70–9 L. Badcock; Shearstown
C 70–10 W. Bartlett; Dunville
C 70–11 E. Colbert; St John's
C 70–12 B. Fillier; Englee
C 70–13 P. Finney; St John's
C 70–14 C. Greene; Point Verde
C 70–15 M. Hopkins; Heart's Content
C 70–16 D. McDonald; St John's
C 70–17 J. McGrath; St John's
C 70–18 C. Matchim; Sandy Cove
C 70–20 M. Murphy; Bell Island
C 70–21 H. Murray; Elliston (Maberly)
C 70–22 S. Oliver; St John's
C 70–25 E. Peddle; Bishop's Cove
C 70–26 E. Shortall; St John's
C 70–27 K. Sullivan; Calvert
C 70–28 H. Walters; Labrador City
C 70–29 C. Wareham; Harbour Buffett
C 70–30 M. Bennett; Partick, Glasgow
C 70–34 P. Flynn; St John's
C 70–35 M. Marsh; Sarnia, Ontario
C 71–4 M. Ackerman; Centreville
C 71–5 M. Adams; St John's
C 71–6 L. Austin; St John's
C 71–7 M. Banfield; Lewisporte
C 71–8 B. Bennett; Pasadena
C 71–9 R. Bourgeois; Stephenville
C 71–14 L. Feaver; St John's
C 71–16 T. Gullage; Corner Brook
C 71–18 C. Hewitt; Corner Brook
C 71–20 E. Kipness; Atikokan, Ontario
C 71–21 J. Lane; Upper Island Cove
C 71–22 E. Leonard; Bell Island
C 71–23 M. Matheson; Burgeo
C 71–24 A. Murphy; Carbonear
C 71–26 M. Power; Branch
C 71–28 L. Roberts; St John's
C 71–30 J. Starkes; Nipper's Harbour
C 71–31 B. Stone; Bishop's Falls
C 71–32 B. Stuckless; Lewisporte
C 71–33 N. Walters; St John's
C 71–35 A. White; Point Leamington
C 71–36 S. Browne; St John's
C 71–37 V. Dalton; Little Catalina
C 71–38 R. Diamond; Corner Brook
C 71–39 R. Downey; Great Codroy
C 71–40 G. Hiscock; Winterton
C 71–42 T. Moore; Avondale
C 71–44 M. Stuckless; Badger
C 71–45 K. Vokey; Spaniard's Bay
C 71–46 E. Whalen; St John's
C 71–74 I. Mooney; Wabush
C 71–84 S. Walters; Great Paradise
C 71–86 C. Brown; St John's
C 71–87 B. Bruce; Codroy Valley
C 71–88 B. Collins; Placentia
C 71–89 M. Collins; Freshwater
C 71–90 J. Combden; Barr'd Islands

C 71–91 W. Crane; Tilton
C 71–92 M. Crotty; Topsail/St John's
C 71–93 J. Dobbin; St Joseph's
C 71–94 F. Dominie; Cape La Hune
C 71–95 G. Dwyer; Tilting
C 71–96 G. Emberley; Buchans
C 71–97 L. Harris; Glovertown
C 71–98 A. Haskvitz; Ontario/California
C 71–99 C. Hayes; Cape Broyle
C 71–100 E. Hiscock; St John's
C 71–102 I. Hynes; Port au Port
C 71–103 D. James; Corner Brook
C 71–104 J. Kean; St Anthony
C 71–105 M. Kean; Ivanhoe
C 71–106 B. Keating; Long Harbour
C 71–107 M. Kelly; Fox Harbour
C 71–108 S. Kuehn; St John's
C 71–109 F. Lamswood; Bell Island
C 71–110 W. Lodge; Deer Lake
C 71–111 M. Loveys; St John's
C 71–112 J. Parsons; St John's
C 71–113 R. Parsons; Shearstown
C 71–115 C. Perry; Daniel's Harbour
C 71–116 J. Powers; Corner Brook
C 71–117 E. Richards; Bareneed
C 71–118 E. Ricketts; Knight's Cove
C 71–119 W. Rowe; St John's
C 71–120 J. Russell; Plate Cove
C 71–121 M. Slaney; Chapel's Cove
C 71–122 E. Smith; Port-aux-Basques
C 71–123 R. Smith; Norman's Cove
C 71–124 D. Smyth; St John's
C 71–125 G. Stroud; Windsor
C 71–126 R. Tilley; Newman's Cove
C 71–127 W. Vincent; Corner Brook
C 71–128 E. Vokey; Spaniard's Bay
C 71–129 E. Walbourne; Fogo
C 71–130 L. Webber; Cupids
C 71–131 K. Welsh; Islington
C 71–132 Colin Williams; St John's
C 73–13 F. Hartery; Cape Broyle
C 73–67 J. Coldwell; Bedford, N.S.
C 73–98 W. Neville; St John's
C 73–115 M. Coady; Placentia
C 73–128 B. Moore; Avondale
C 73–164 D. Greene; Long Harbour
C 74–114 R. Lewis; Newbridge
C 74–128 J. Warren; Heart's Content
C 75–15 G. Colbert; St John's
C 75–19 G. Dicks; Mount Pearl
C 75–21 H. Doyle; Calvert
C 75–25 L. French; St John's
C 75–28 M. Gould; Port au Choix
C 75–29 G. Green; St John's
C 75–46 E. Pollard; Great Harbour Deep
C 75–48 M.L. Power; Merasheen
C 75–57 R. Strickland; Head Bay d'Espoir
C 75–61 D. Wall; Tompkins

C 75–63 R. Wells; Muddy Hole
C 75–130 F. Anderson; Mount Pearl
C 75–132 D. Colbourne; St Anthony
C 75–134 M. Healey; Grand Falls
C 75–135 G. Hynes; St Brendan's
C 75–136 M. Lewis; Conche
C 75–137 B. Loder; Harbour Deep
C 75–138 K. Loder; Harbour Deep
C 75–139 F. Murphy; Dunville
C 75–140 J. Philpott; Gander
C 75–141 M. Pittman; Harbour Deep
C 75–142 W. Rideout; Grand Bank
C 75–144 D. Smith; Mount Pearl
C 75–145 F. Douglas; Fortune
C 75–146 D. Stephenson; Victoria
M 64–1 V. Dillon; Mobile
M 64–3 C. Williams; Long Pond
M 65–1 E. Beresford; St Brendan's
M 65–5 W. McKim; St John's
M 65–9 R. Noseworthy; Grand Bank
M 66–10 H. Lear; Hibb's Hole
M 66–12 G. Moore; Windsor
M 66–18 L. Williams; Grand Bank
M 67–10 R. Kendall; Ramea
M 67–15 C. Sheehan; St John's
M 67–16 L. Small; Moreton's Harbour
M 67–17 F. Smallwood; St John's
M 68–2 E. Clarke; St Joseph's
M 68–3 J. Dollimount; François
M 68–4 R. Drodge; Little Heart's Ease
M 68–7 J. Fudge; Grole
M 68–10 C. Hamlyn; Sop's Arm
M 68–11 Z. Johnson; Renews
M 68–12 W. Lane; Glovertown
M 68–13 O. Langdon; Seal Cove, F.B.
M 68–15 J. Norman; Port Union
M 68–16 A.F. O'Brien; Cape Broyle
M 68–17 R. Park; Gillams
M 68–18 J. Pinsent; Port Nelson
M 68–20 C. Skinner; Richard's Harbour
M 68–21 J. Stockley; Twillingate
M 68–22 B. Stratton; Corner Brook
M 68–23 H. Stroud; Glovertown South
M 68–24 B. Trask; Summerville/Elliston
M 68–26 W. Wareham; Harbour Buffett
M 69–1 B. Bartlett; Catalina
M 69–2 C. Bishop; Wesleyville
M 69–5 W. Canning; Williamsport
M 69–6 E. Cokes; Head Bay d'Espoir
M 69–7 G. Combden; Barr'd Islands
M 69–9 D. Courtney; Kilbride
M 69–12 A. Etchegary; St Lawrence
M 69–13 M. Fitzpatrick; Lord's Cove, P.B.
M 69–14 B. Foote; Creston North
M 69–16 J. Green; Chance Cove
M 69–17 R. Hobbs; Elliston
M 69–23 Z. Sacrey; Woodstock
M 69–26 H. Waterman; Wareham, B.B.

M 69–27 J. Williams; Isle Valen
M 69–28 F. Bonnell; Lamaline
M 69–29 D. Butt; Freshwater, C.B.
M 70–9 L. Badcock; Shearstown
M 70–16 D. McDonald; St John's
M 70–17 J. McGrath; St John's
M 70–18 C. Matchim; Eastport
M 70–21 H. Murray; Elliston
M 70–23 V. Oliver; St John's
M 70–24 A. Parsons; Corner Brook
M 70–25 E. Peddle; Bishop's Cove
M 70–26 E. Shortall; St John's
M 70–27 K. Sullivan; Calvert
M 70–28 H. Walters; Lady Cove
M 70–29 G. Wareham; Harbour Buffett
M 71–4 M. Ackerman; Fair Island
M 71–34 J. Wheeler; St John's
M 71–35 A. White; Point Leamington
M 71–37 V. Dalton; Little Catalina
M 71–38 R. Diamond; Woods Island
M 71–39 R. Downey; Great Codroy
M 71–40 G. Hiscock; Winterton
M 71–41 C. Mooney; Buchans
M 71–42 T. Moore; Avondale
M 71–43 C. Prior; Grand Bank
M 71–44 M. Stuckless; Badger
M 71–60 G. Bursey; Old Perlican
M 71–64 J. Condon; Placentia
M 71–68 D. Gale; Great Codroy
M 71–78 E. Roche; Middle Cove
M 71–80 A. Smith; Lourdes
M 71–86 C. Brown; Joe Batt's Arm
M 71–90 J. Combden; Barr'd Islands
M 71–91 W. Crane; Tilton
M 71–94 F. Dominie; Cape La Hune
M 71–95 G. Dwyer; Tilting
M 71–97 Louise Harris; Glovertown
M 71–101 D. Hutchings; Deer Lake
M 71–103 C. James; Brigus
M 71–105 M. Kean; Ivanhoe
M 71–107 M. Kelly; Fox Harbour, P.B.
M 71–114 B. Penton; Woods Island
M 71–115 C. Perry; Daniel's Harbour
M 71–117 E. Richards; Bareneed
M 71–118 E. Ricketts; Knight's Cove
M 71–120 J. Russell; Plate Cove
M 71–122 E. Smith; Port-aux-Basques
M 71–127 W. Vincent; Shoal Harbour
M 75–61 D. Wall; Tompkins
P 1 F.A. Aldrich; New Jersey/St John's
P 2 R. Andersen; Minnesota/South Coast
P 3 A. Andrews; Point Leamington
P 4 C.W. Andrews; Wesleyville
P 5 S. Anthony; Roberts Arm
P 6 B. Antle; Grand Falls
P 7 D.M. Baird; New Brunswick
P 8 M. Barnes; Old Perlican

P 9   Ralph Barrett; Change Islands; Happy Val-
      ley, Labrador
P 10 Ray Barrett; Old Perlican
P 11 G. Barter; Mainland, Port-au-Port
P 12 B. Bartlett; Catalina
P 13 D. Bartlett; Green Bay
P 14 H. Beck; Carbonear
P 15 J. Benson; Glenwood
P 16 R. Benson; St John's
P 17 C. Bishop; Wesleyville
P 18 W.J. Blundon; Heart's Content
P 19 L.R. Brown; Joe Batt's Arm
P 20 J. Bungay; Fortune Bay
P 21 F. Burden; Woody Point
P 22 A. Burry; Baie Verte
P 23 S. Burry; Greenspond
P 24 A. Butler; St John's
P 25 P. Butler; St John's
P 26 V. Butler; Harbour Buffett
P 27 J. Byrne; Holyrood
P 28 K. Cadigan; Logy Bay
P 29 S. Canning; St John's
P 30 H. Carew; St John's
P 32 T. Carroll; St John's
P 33 G. Casey; Conche
P 34 P. Cashin; Bay Bulls
P 35 D. Clarke; St John's
P 36 H. Coates; Bay Roberts
P 37 MUC; Various localities (c1937)
P 38 R. Colbert; Bauline
P 39 D. Colbourne; St Anthony
P 40 W. Colbourne; Long Island, N.D.B.
P 41 A. Cole; Victoria
P 42 T. Cole; Englee
P 43 Maxwell Collett; Harbour Buffett
P 44 Munden Collett; Harbour Buffett
P 45 W. Collingwood; St John's
P 46 P. Collins; St John's
P 47 J. Connors; Placentia West
P 48 C. Conroy; St John's
P 49 C. Cooper; Ireland's Eye
P 50 D. L. Cooper; Nova Scotia
P 51 J. Courage; Fortune Bay
P 52 N. Cramm; St John's
P 53 G. Crewe; Grand Bank
P 54 N.C. Crewe; Elliston
P 55 B. Critch; Botwood
P 56 A. Crocker; Green's Harbour
P 57 D. Curran; Gambo
P 58 D. Dalton; Admiral's Beach
P 59 G. Dalton; Little Catalina
P 60 E. Dawe; St John's
P 61 G. Dawe; Chance Cove
P 62 L. Dawe; St John's
P 63 J. Dawson; Bay Roberts
P 64 W. Day; Trinity
P 65 C. Decker; Roddickton
P 66 G. Dicks; Mount Pearl

P 67 J. Dicks; Flat Island, P.B.
P 68 V. Dillon; Mobile
P 69 B. Dingle; St John's
P 70 J. Dodd; Torbay
P 71 K. Dollimount; Burgeo
P 72 J. Drew; St John's
P 73 G. Duggan; St John's West
P 74 F. Dunford; Burin
P 75 W. Dwyer; St John's
P 76 J.D. Eaton; St John's
P 77 P. Eddy; Little Catalina
P 78 P. Evans; Torbay
P 79 K. Farrell; St John's
P 80 M. Firestone; Arizona/Northern Peninsula
P 81 P. Flynn; St John's
P 82 B. Fong; St John's
P 83 C. Ford; St John's
P 84 G. Francis; Corner Brook
P 85 H. Frecker; Oderin
P 86 M. Frecker; St John's
P 87 C. Furlong; St John's
P 88 R.S. Furlong; St John's
P 89 H. Gardiner; St John's
P 90 J. Garland; Lower Island Cove
P 91 R. Garrett; St John's
P 92 E. Genge; St John's
P 93 S. Genge; Anchor Point
P 94 F.J. George; Bonavista
P 95 M. George; Bonavista
P 96 A. Gillis; Codroy Valley
P 97 G. Giovannini; St Lawrence
P 98 H.G. Goodridge; St John's
P 99 E. Gosse; Spaniard's Bay
P 100 M. Gosse; St John's
P 101 W. Gosse; Spaniard's Bay
P 102 S. Grant; Trinity
P 103 L. Greene; Calvert
P 104 R. Gushue; St John's
P 105 F. Hagar; Massachusetts/St John's
P 106 B. Haines; Kelligrews
P 107 D. Hallett; St John's
P 108 J. Halley; St John's
P 109 H. Halpert; New York/St John's
P 110 C. Hamlyn; Sop's Arm
P 111 W. Hamlyn; St John's
P 112 M.F. Harrington; St John's
P 113 Leslie Harris; St Joseph's, P.B.
P 114 N. Harris; St Joseph's, P.B.
P 115 L. Hatcher; Lumsden North
P 116 B. Head; Comfort Cove
P 117 B. Heale; St John's
P 118 J. Hearn; Calvert
P 119 J. Higgins; St John's
P 120 R. Hilliard; Long Island, N.Y.
P 121 H. Hillier; Fortune
P 122 R. Hillier; Corner Brook
P 123 C. Hiscock; Stone's Cove, F.B.
P 124 E. Hiscock; St John's

P 125 R. Hiscock; Badger's Quay
P 126 M. Hoben; Burin Bay Arm
P 127 R. Hollett; Spencer's Cove
P 128 W. House; Bellburns
P 129 C.K. Howse; St John's
P 130 G. Hurley; North River
P 131 J. Hutchings; Cow Head
P 132 D. Hyslop; St John's
P 133 G.W. Jeffers; Freshwater, C.B.
P 134 A. Johnson; St John's
P 135 E. Johnson; St John's
P 136 Z. Johnson; Renews
P 137 J. Jordon; Dublin/St John's
P 138 J. Kavanagh; St John's
P 139 B. Kelleher; Brownsdale
P 140 K. Kelleher; Sibley's Cove, T.B.
P 141 M. Kelly; Marystown
P 142 R. Kendall; Ramea
P 143 W. Keough; St John's
P 144 F. Kewley; Ontario
P 145 E.H. King; Kelligrews
P 146 M. King; Bauline
P 147 J. Kinsella; Fogo Island
P 148 W.J. Kirwin; Newport, Rhode Island
P 149 L. Knight; Jackson's Cove
P 150 W. Lane; Glovertown
P 151 O. Langdon; Seal Cove, F.B.
P 152 F. Lawrence; Bay L'Argent
P 153 G. Layman; Fogo
P 154 H. Lear; Hibb's Hole
P 155 R. Lebans; New Brunswick/St John's
P 156 S. Lynch; Carbonear
P 157 M. McDonald; Gander
P 158 H. McGettigan; St Mary's
P 159 A. McGrath; Harbour Grace
P 160 J.M. McGrath; St John's
P 161 B. Mctavish; St John's
P 162 J. Mannion; Ireland/St John's
P 163 J. Martin; St John's
P 164 M. Martin; Sandy Cove
P 165 W. Martin; St John's West
P 166 J. Maunder; St John's
P 167 G. Meadus; Greenspond
P 168 D. Meaney; Harbour Main
P 169 M. Mercer; Shearstown
P 170 P. Mercer; St John's
P 171 G. Moore; Anderson's Cove
P 172 J. Moore; St John's
P 173 M.O. Morgan; Salvage
P 174 J. Moss; Bonne Bay
P 175 M. Moyles; St John's
P 177 M. Mulcahy; Bay Bulls
P 178 H. Murray; Elliston
P 179 J. Murray; Pass Island
P 180 Margaret Neary; Bell Island
P 181 P. Neary; Bell Island
P 182 T. Nemec; St John's
P 183 T.C. Noel; St John's

P 184 E. Norman; Bay Roberts
P 185 L. Normore; Bell Island
P 186 H. North; St John's
P 187 R. North; Bay de Verde
P 188 H. Noseworthy; St John's
P 189 R. Noseworthy; Grand Bank
P 190 W. Nowak; Hungary/St John's
P 191 A. O'Brien; St John's
P 192 C. O'Brien; Bishop Falls
P 193 J. O'Brien; Cape Broyle
P 194 S. O'Dea; St John's
P 195 P. O'Driscoll; Conception Harbour
P 196 F. O'Flaherty; St John's
P 197 P. O'Flaherty; Long Beach, C.B.
P 198 R. O'Neill; St John's
P 199 S.L. Organ; St John's
P 200 H. Paddock; Beaumont
P 201 M. Parsons; Ochre Pit Cove
P 202 C. Patey; St Anthony
P 203 S. Payne; Fogo
P 204 F.W. Peacock; Labrador North
P 205 H. Peddle; New Perlican
P 206 C. Penney; St John's
P 207 C. Peyton; Gander
P 208 T. Peyton; St John's
P 209 C. Pickett; Centreville, B.B.
P 210 P. Pike; Victoria
P 211 J. Pinsent; Port Nelson
P 212 D.G. Pitt; St John's
P 213 S. Pittman; Old Perlican
P 214 G. Pocius; Pennsylvania/St John's
P 215 P. Power; St Kyran's, P.B.
P 216 S. Priddle; Bar Haven
P 217 S. Prior; Burin Peninsula
P 218 J. Quinton; Princeton
P 219 V. Ralph; St John's
P 220 G. Reid; Carbonear
P 221 F. Rideout; Moreton's Harbour
P 222 R. Rideout; Buchans
P 223 J. Riggs; St John's
P 224 S. Rockwood; St John's
P 225 R. Rogers; St John's
P 226 M. Rose; St John's
P 227 B. Rowe; Heart's Content
P 228 T. Russell; Coley's Point
P 229 Marilyn Ryan; St John's
P 230 Mercedes Ryan; St John's
P 231 S. Ryan; Harbour Grace
P 232 F. Samson; St John's
P 233 P. Scott; Ontario
P 234 E.R. Seary; St John's
P 235 G. Seary; St John's
P 236 A. Shea; St John's
P 237 L. Small; Moreton's Harbour
P 238 J.R. Smallwood; Gambo
P 239 W. Smeaton; St John's
P 240 D. Smith; St John's
P 241 R. Snook; Sunnyside

P 242 A. Story; St John's
P 243 C. Story; St John's
P 244 D.K. Story; St John's
P 245 G.M. Story; St John's
P 246 J. Story; St John's
P 247 B. Stratton; Valleyfield
P 248 L. Sullivan; Calvert
P 249 K. Szala-Meneok; St John's
P 250 D. Taylor; Maine
P 251 A. Templeman
P 252 M. Tobin, St John's
P 253 R. Tobin; St John's
P 254 D. Torraville; St John's
P 255 A. Trickett; St John's
P 256 J. Tuck; Syracuse, N.Y.
P 257 O. Tucker; Winterton
P 258 M. Vavasour; St John's
P 259 J. Vincent; Wesleyville
P 260 M. Walsh; Moreton's Harbour
P 261 E. White; Bonavista
P 262 J.A. White; St John's
P 263 Joan White; St John's
P 264 L. White; Buchans
P 265¹ W. White; North West River, Labrador
P 265² W. Whiteley; St John's
P 266 J.D.A. Widdowson; Sheffield, U.K./St John's
P 267 R. Wight; Deer Lake
P 268 Clarence Williams; Grand Bank
P 269 Clyde Williams; Arizona/Winterton
P 270 L. Williams; Grand Bank
P 271 A. Williamson; U.S./Labrador
P 272 P. Winter; St John's
P 273 B. Wood; Grand Bank
P 274 W. Woodford; St John's
P 275 G.B. Woodland; St John's
P 276 L. Yother; New York/Trinity
Q 67–1 L. Ackerman; Centreville
Q 67–2 F. Anderson; St John's
Q 67–3 S. Anthony; Roberts Arm
Q 67–4 L. Barbour; Newtown, B.B.
Q 67–5 G. Barnable; Bar Haven
Q 67–6 R. Bennett; Bay de Verde
Q 67–7 R. Benson; Hickman's Hr.
Q 67–8 F. Blackmore; Port Union
Q 67–9 F. Bonnell; Lamaline
Q 67–10 R. Broderick; Gambo
Q 67–11 P. Canning; St John's
Q 67–12 R. Canning; Englee
Q 67–13 B. Charles; Indian Islands
Q 67–14 S. Colbourne; St Anthony
Q 67–15 T. Cole; Victoria
Q 67–16 Maxwell Collett; Harbour Buffett
Q 67–17 C. Collins; Champney's East
Q 67–18 B. Connolly; St John's
Q 67–19 R. Conway; Colliers
Q 67–20 J. Cooper; Gander
Q 67–21 F. Crews; Grand Bank
Q 67–22 R. Crocker; Heart's Delight
Q 67–23 N. Culleton; St John's
Q 67–24 D. Dawe; Port-de-Grave
Q 67–25 G. Dawe; Upper Gullies
Q 67–26 T. Devine; St John's
Q 67–27 B. Downey; St John's
Q 67–28 J. Doyle; Gull Island, C.B.
Q 67–29 F. Dunford; Burin
Q 67–30 M. Earle; Fogo
Q 67–31 M. English; Branch
Q 67–32 M. Fagan; St Mary's
Q 67–33 S. Fiander; English Hr. West
Q 67–34 I. Gillard; Englee
Q 67–35 C. Greene; Pointe Verde
Q 67–36 C. Greenland; Coley's Point
Q 67–37 J. Guy; St John's
Q 67–38 C. Hall; Corner Brook
Q 67–39 D. Hamlyn; Lamaline
Q 67–40 B. Heffern; Salvage
Q 67–41 C. Hewitt; St John's
Q 67–42 V. Hopkins; Cartwright
Q 67–43 B. Hughes; Green Island Brook
Q 67–44 R. Hynes; Ferryland
Q 67–45 C. Jenkins; Western Bay
Q 67–46 Z. Johnson; Renews
Q 67–47 E. Jones; St John's
Q 67–48 R. Kendall; Ramea
Q 67–49 A. Kirby; Pouch Cove
Q 67–50 M. Lawless; Flower's Cove
Q 67–51 A. Lear; Hibb's Hole
Q 67–52 J. Legge; Heart's Delight
Q 67–53 L. Lewis; Fortune
Q 67–54 A. Lilly; St John's
Q 67–55 G. Loveless; Bloomfield
Q 67–56 G. Meadus; St John's
Q 67–57 M. Melbourne; Grand Bank
Q 67–59 J. Mercer; Dover
Q 67–60 L. Moores; Brigus
Q 67–61 I. Morris; Trinity
Q 67–62 S. Munro; Glenwood
Q 67–63 J. Myrick; Cape Race
Q 67–64 R. Nicholle; Grand Bank
Q 67–65 L. Norberg; St John's
Q 67–66 E. Norman; Bay Roberts
Q 67–67 A.F. O'Brien; Cape Broyle
Q 67–68 P. O'Driscoll; Conception Harbour
Q 67–69 V. Oliver; St John's
Q 67–70 F. O'Toole; St John's
Q 67–71 V. Palmer; Bay Roberts
Q 67–72 R. Park; McIver's
Q 67–73 D. Parsons; Rocky Harbour
Q 67–74 C. Peyton; Twillingate
Q 67–75 T. Philpott; St. John's
Q 67–76 K. Porter; Deer Lake
Q 67–77 Y. Powell; Lewisporte
Q 67–78 G. Randell; Harbour Deep
Q 67–79 D. Regular; Harbour Grace
Q 67–80 J. Reid; Port Blandford

Q 67–81 D. Riche; Notre Dame Bay
Q 67–82 N. Riggs; Bay de Verde
Q 67–83 P. Riggs; Glovertown
Q 67–84 C. Roche; Branch
Q 67–85 E. Rusted; Upper Island Cove
Q 67–86 E. Sheppard; St John's
Q 67–87 G. Small; Moreton's Harbour
Q 67–88 E. Sooley; Heart's Delight
Q 67–89 S. Spracklin; Brigus
Q 67–90 M. Squires; Sibley's Cove
Q 67–91 N. Starkes; Nipper's Cove
Q 67–92 S. Stead; Little Catalina
Q 67–93 E. Stockwood; Gull Island
Q 67–94 W. Sullivan; Pouch Cove
Q 67–95 J. Sutherland; Lewisporte
Q 67–96 R. Sweetland; Bonavista
Q 67–97 D. Thompson; St John's
Q 67–98 C. Tucker; Grand Falls
Q 67–99 E. Vardy; St John's
Q 67–100 J. Verge; Harbour Grace
Q 67–101 J. Vincent; St John's
Q 67–102 B. Wells; Cambellton
Q 67–103 R. Wells; St John's
Q 67–104 G. White; Twillingate
Q 67–105 J. White; St John's
Q 67–106 E. Whitten; Bay Roberts
Q 67–107 L. Winsor; St John's
Q 67–108 B. Wiseman; Newman's Cove
Q 67–109 G. Woolfrey; Moreton's Harbour
Q 71–1 A. Antle; Brigus
Q 71–2 G. Barnable; Renews
Q 71–3 L. Benoit; Burgeo
Q 71–4 J. Condon; Calvert
Q 71–5 C. Dewling; Mount Pearl
Q 71–6 E.J. Evans; St John's
Q 71–7 M. Gosse; St John's
Q 71–8 Leslie Harris; St Joseph's, P.B.
Q 71–9 R. Hillier; Corner Brook
Q 71–10 R. Hollett; St John's
Q 71–11 A. Laing; Gander
Q 71–12 E. Lear; Hibb's Hole
Q 71–13 F. Metcalfe; Manuels
Q 71–14 B. Moore; Avondale
Q 71–15 W. Smeaton; St John's
Q 71–16 G. Strong; Little Bay
Q 71–17 D. Williams; Topsail
Q 72–1 A. Hodder; Notre Dame Bay
Q 73–1 C. Barnes; St John's
Q 73–2 D. Bartlett; Green Bay
Q 73–3 D. Combden; Barr'd Islands
Q 73–4 C. Dewling; Barr'd Islands
Q 73–5 R. Hillier; Mount Pearl
Q 73–6 H. Keating; St John's
Q 73–7 E. Kennedy; Woody Point
Q 73–8 M. MacDonald; Woody Point
Q 73–9 B. Moore; Avondale
Q 74–1 C. Hiscock; Stone's Cove
T 1–63[1] C. Kelly; Avondale

T 1–63[2] T. Power; Fortune Harbour
T 9–63 P. Saunders; Botwood
T 12–64 M. Yetman; St Mary's
T 13–64 J. Harris; St Joseph's, P.B.
T 22–64 C. Parrott; Winterton
T 23–64 A. Verge; Winterton
T 25–64 C. Furey; Harbour Main
T 26–64[1] W. Babstock; St Chad's
T 26–64[2] C. Bradley; Eastport
T 26–64[3] W. Martin; St Chad's
T 27–64 M. Troke; St Chad's
T 29–64 G. Dyke; Salvage
T 30–64[1] C. Moss; Happy Adventure
T 30–64[2] H. Squire; Eastport
T 31–64 E. Squire; Eastport
T 33–64[1] C. Moss; Happy Adventure
T 33–64[2] C. Parrott; Winterton
T 33–64[3] E. Turner; Happy Adventure
T 34–64 C. Callahan; New Perlican
T 36–64 J. Harris; St Joseph's, P.B.
T 39–64 E. Brown; Baine Harbour
T 41–64 E. Rodway; Baine Harbour
T 43–64 P. Saunders; Botwood
T 45–64 N. Foley; Tilting
T 49–64 M. Aylward; Knight's Cove
T 50–64 D. Carroll; Fortune Harbour
T 52–64 W. Lyver; Fortune Harbour
T 54–64 R. Murray; Fortune Harbour
T 55–64 P. Carroll; Fortune Harbour
T 66–64 W. Quirk; Fortune Harbour
T 69–64 J. Carroll; Fortune Harbour
T 70–64[1] D. Carroll; Fortune Harbour
T 70–64[2] T. Byrne; Fortune Harbour
T 74–64 M. Foley; Tilting
T 75–64 J. Kinsella; Tilting
T 80–64 F. Hynes; Change Islands
T 84–64 E. Hynes; Change Islands
T 87–64 F. Earle, Sr.; Fogo
T 88–64 T. Farewell; Fogo
T 89–64 H. Payne; Fogo
T 90–64 G. Simms; Fogo
T 91–64 D. Miles; Herring Neck
T 92–64 Amelia Noble; Wild Cove, Twillingate
T 94–64 M. Power; Fortune Harbour
T 96–64[1] R. Barker; Mings Bight
T 96–64[2] M. Cook; Coachman's Cove
T 100–64 N. Rendell; Burnt Island Cove
T 104–64 N. Spurrell; Pool's Island
T 110–64 I. Goodyear; Musgrave Harbour
T 141–65[1] H. Bradley; Eastport
T 141–65[2] F. Hynes; Change Islands
T 143–65[1] W. Babstock; St Chad's
T 143–65[2] J. Morgan; Flat Island, B.B.
T 145–65 R. Noseworthy; Grand Bank
T 146–65 J. Melloy; Hare Harbour
T 147–65 W. Stewart; Harbour Breton
T 148–65 T. Pardy; Harbour Breton
T 154–65 W. Osborne; Grand Bank

T 156–65 B. Moss; Salvage
T 158–65 J. Collins; Dover
T 168–65 W. Earle; Change Islands
T 169–65¹ F. Earle; Change Islands
T 169–65² E. Hynes; Change Islands
T 172–65 J. Kearley; Herring Neck
T 175–65 S. Collins; Lewisporte
T 178–65 E. Elliott; Herring Neck
T 181–65 P. Miles; Herring Neck
T 183–65 D. Parsons; Herring Neck
T 184–65 H. Watkins; Herring Neck
T 185–65 G. Hamlyn; Twillingate
T 186–65 G. Watkins; Twillingate
T 187–65 J. Watkins; Twillingate
T 191–65 J. Andrews; Twillingate
T 192–65 F. Clark; Twillingate
T 194–65 A. Greenham; Twillingate
T 198–65 E. Taylor; Moreton's Harbour
T 199–65 C. Sansome; Hillgrade
T 200–65 L. Donahue; Boyd's Cove
T 203–65 J. Batstone; Jackson's Cove
T 207–65 S. Oxford; Brown's Cove
T 208–65 J. Moores; Jackson's Cove
T 210–65 D. Knight; Jackson's Cove
T 433–65 G. Cox; Harbour Breton
T 434–65 A. Snook; Harbour Breton
T 436–65 M. Snook; Sagona Island
T 437–65 S. Snook; Sagona Island
T 222–66 J. Mifflen; St John's
T 245–66 E. Bennett; St Paul's
T 246–66 C. Hutchings; Cow Head
T 250–66 D. Hutchings; Cow Head
T 253–66 A. Payne; Cow Head
T 255–66 M. Hutchings; Cow Head
T 257–66 N. Payne; Cow Head
T 258–66 J. Roberts; Sally's Cove
T 260–66 C. Decker; Rocky Harbour
T 264–66 H. Caines; Portland Creek
T 265–66¹ G. Payne; Cow Head
T 265–66² R. Payne; St Paul's
T 270–66 B. Farwell; Burin
T 271–66¹ A. Hoddinott; Brig Bay
T 271–66² H. Hoddinott; Brig Bay
T 271–66³ E. Plowman; Gargamelle
T 272–66¹ I. Caines; Port Saunders
T 272–66² L. Rumbolt; Port Saunders
T 273–66 C. Stevens; Bellburns
T 279–66 C. Bennett; St Paul's
T 283–66 F. Bennett; St Paul's
T 296–66 H. Burton; Quinton's Cove
T 301–66 T. Rideout; Beaumont
T 309–66 A. Oake; Beaumont
T 313–66 P. Hynes; Southern Head Harbour
T 325–66 J. Mansfield; Pilley's Island
T 327–66 E. Ryan; Roberts Arm
T 331–66 M. Ryan; Roberts Arm
T 342–67¹ D. Bouzan; Little Bay, N.D.B.
T 342–67² J. Hearn; Brigus

T 347–67 A. Shields; Pointe La Haye
T 353–67 H. Hillier; Brunette Island
T 354–67 F. Dunford; Burin
T 360–67 M. Hoben; Burin Bay Arm
T 361–67 G. Meadus; Greenspond
T 365–67 R. Rideout; Buchans
T 367–67 E. Buckle; St John's
T 368–67¹ A. Butler; St John's
T 368–67² B. MacDonald; St John's
T 370–67 S. Rockwood; St John's
T 375–67¹ F. Hayward; St John's
T 375–67² V. Hayward; St John's
T 377–67 G. Skinner; St John's
T 379–67 S. Skinner; Carmanville
T 380–67 M. Day; Carmanville
T 389–67¹ G. Bath; Horse Islands
T 389–67² F. Earle; Change Islands
T 390–67 D. Burton; Horse Islands
T 391–67 T. Bath; Horse Islands
T 393–67 R. Morey; La Scie
T 396–67 G. Burton; La Scie
T 398–67 J. Gray; Shoe Cove Brook
T 399–67 F. Earle; Change Islands
T 400–67 A. Noseworthy; Shoe Cove Brook
T 401–67 G. Hoddinott; Greenspond
T 406–67¹ J. Lacey; Brent's Cove
T 406–67² M. Lacey; Baie Verte
T 407–67 M. Randell; Nipper's Harbour
T 409–67 O. Starkes; Nipper's Harbour
T 410–67 Archie Noble; Nipper's Harbour
T 411–67 Maxwell Collett; Harbour Buffett
T 417–67 G. Hurley; North River
T 448–67 J. Rossiter; Ramea
T 449–67 E. Warren; Grey River
T 450–67 W. Skinner; Richards Harbour
T 453–67 K. Northcotte; White Bear Bay
T 455–67¹ W. Cooper; Pushthrough
T 455–67² A. Kendall; Round Harbour
T 458–67¹ J. Kelly; St John's
T 458–67² P. Kelly; St John's
T 459–67 L. Ayre; St John's
T 498–68 M. Kent; Cape Broyle
T 529–68 G. Molloy; St Shotts
T 543–68 A. Reardon; Croque
T 727–68 F. Clarke; St Joseph's
T 731–70 K. Jardine; St John's
T 749–70 C. Kendall; Ramea
T 868–70 A. MacArthur; Branch
T 911–71 O. Crewe; Elliston

*Alphabetical Index of Collectors and
Contributors*

This is a name index to the classified sources
listed above, excluding the Q (= Questionnaire)
lists, which are already arranged in alphabetical
order. For the codes following the names, see
the headnote on *Collections* above.

McCarthy, T.   C 69–19
MacDonald, B.   C 67–13, T 368–67
McDonald, D.   M 70–16
McDonald, M.   P
McGettigan, H.   P
McGrath, A.   P
McGrath, J.M.   P
McGrath, J.   C, M 70–17
McKim, W.   M 65–5
Mctavish, B.   P
Mannion, J.   P
Mansfield, J.   T 325–66
Marsh, M.   C 70–35
Martin, J.   P
Martin, William   T 26–64
Martin, Winnie   P
Matchim, C.   C, M 70–18
Matheson, M.   C 71–23
Maunder, J.   P
Maunder, R.   C 64–6
Meadus, G.   P, T 361–67
Meaney, D.   P
Melloy, J.   T 146–65
Mercer, M.   P
Mercer, P.   P
Mercer, S.   C 69–20
Mifflen, J.   T 222–66
Miles, D.   T 91–64
Miles, P.   T 181–65
Molloy, G.   T 529–68
Mooney, C.   M 71–41
Mooney, I.   M 71–74
Moore, B.   C 73–128
Moore, G.   C, M 66–12, P
Moore, T.   C, M 71–42
Moores, J.   T 208–65
Morey, R.   T 393–67
Morgan, J.   T 143–65
Morgan, M.O.   P
Moss, B.   T 156–65
Moss, C.   T 30–64
Moss, J.   P
Moyles, M.   P
MUC   P 37 (= c1937)
Mulcahy, M.   P
Murphy, A.   C 71–24
Murphy, B.   C 71–106
Murphy, F.   C 75–139
Murphy, M.   C 70–20
Murray, H.   C, M 70–21, P
Murray, J.   P
Murray, R.   T 54–64
Neary, M.   P
Neary, P.   P
Nemec, T.   P
Neville, W.   C 73–98
Noble, Amelia   T 92–64
Noble, Archie   T 410–67

Noel, T.C.   P
Norman, E.   P
Norman, J.   C, M 68–15
Normore, L.   P
North, H.   P
North, R.   P
Northcotte, K.   T 453–67
Noseworthy, A.   T 400–67
Noseworthy, H.   P
Noseworthy, R.   C 66–13, M 65–9, P, T 145–65
Nowak, W.   P
Oake, Allen   T 309–66
O'Brien, Aloysius   P
O'Brien, Andrew F.   C, M 68–16
O'Brien, C.   C 67–14, P
O'Brien, J.   P
O'Dea, S.   P
O'Driscoll, P.   P
O'Flaherty, F.   P
O'Flaherty, P.   P
Oliver, S.   C 70–22
Oliver, V.   M 70–23
Ollerhead, C.   C 65–12
O'Neill, R.   P
Organ, S.L.   P
Osborne, W.   T 154–65
Oxford, S.   T 207–65
Paddock, H.   P
Pardy, T.   T 148–65
Park, R.   C, M 68–17
Parrott, C.   T 22–64
Parsons, A.   M 70–24
Parsons, D.   T 183–65
Parsons, J.   C 71–112
Parsons, M.   P
Parsons, R.   C 71–113
Patey, C.   P
Payne, A.   T 253–66
Payne, G.   T 265–66
Payne, H.   T 89–64
Payne, N.   T 257–66
Payne, Richard   C 69–21
Payne, Ruth   T 265–66
Payne, S.   P
Peacock, F.W.   P
Peddle, E.   C, M 70–25
Peddle, H.   P
Penney, C.   P
Penney, R.   C 64–7
Penton, B.   M 71–114
Perry, C.   C, M 71–115
Peyton, C.   P
Peyton, T.   P
Philpott, J.   C 75–140
Pickett, C.   P
Pike, P.   P
Pinsent, J.   C, M 68–18, P
Pitt, D.G.   P

Dictionaries and
Other Works Cited

The list excludes a number of authors or works cited only once or twice; for these, specific bibliographical information is provided in the relevant headnote.

ADD — American Dialect Dictionary, ed Harold Wentworth (New York: Thomas Y. Crowell, 1944).

BARNES — A Glossary of the Dorset Dialect, comp William Barnes (Dorchester: M. & E. Case, 1886)

BERREY — The American Thesaurus of Slang, comp Lester V. Berrey and Melvin Van den Bark (New York: Thomas Y. Crowell, 1943)

BOSWORTH-TOLLER — An Anglo-Saxon Dictionary, eds Joseph Bosworth and T. Northcote Toller (London: Oxford University Press, 1898; rpt 1972).

BOWEN — Sea Slang, ed Frank C. Bowen (London: Sampson Low, Marston & Co., Ltd., [1929])

BRYANT — Ralph Clement Bryant, Logging: The Principles and General Methods of Operation in the United States, 2nd ed (New York: John Wiley & Sons, Inc., 1923)

Cent — The Century Dictionary, editor-in-chief, William Dwight Whitney, 12 vols. (New York: The Century Co., 1891; rpt 1906)

DA — A Dictionary of Americanisms on Historical Principles, ed Mitford M. Mathews (Chicago: University of Chicago Press, 1951)

DAE — A Dictionary of American English on Historical Principles, eds William A. Craigie and James R. Hulbert, 4 vols. (Chicago: University of Chicago Press, 1938–1944)

DAS — Dictionary of American Slang, 2nd supplemented ed, eds Harold Wentworth and Stuart Berg Flexner (New York: Thomas Y. Crowell Company, 1975)

DC — A Dictionary of Canadianisms on Historical Principles, editor-in-chief, Walter S. Avis (Toronto: W.J. Gage Limited, 1967)

DE LA MORANDIÈRE — Ch. De la Morandière, Histoire de la pêche française de la morue dans l'Amérique septentrionale (de la révolution a nos jours), Tome iii, 'Dictionnaire terreveuvier' (Paris: G.-P Maisonneuve et Larose, 1966)

Dict Aust Colloq — A Dictionary of Australian Colloquialisms, ed G.A. Wilkes (London: Routledge & Kegan Paul, 1978)

DINNEEN — Foclóir Gaedhilge agus

béarla; *An Irish-English Dictionary*, ed Patrick S. Dinneen (Dublin: Educational Company of Ireland, 1927; rpt 1965)

DJE   *Dictionary of Jamaican English*, eds F.G. Cassidy and R.B. Le Page (Cambridge: The University Press, 1967; 2nd ed, 1979)

EDD   *The English Dialect Dictionary*, ed Joseph Wright, 6 vols. (Oxford University Press, 1898–1905; rpt 1961)

EDD Sup   'Supplement' in vol. vi of *The English Dialect Dictionary* (Oxford University Press, 1905)

EDG   *The English Dialect Grammar*, Joseph Wright, (Oxford University Press, 1905; rpt 1961)

ELMER   Willy Elmer, *Terminology of Fishing; A Survey of English and Welsh Inshore-Fishing Things and Words* (Bern: Francke Verlag, 1973)

Fisheries of U S   *The Fisheries and Fishery Industries of the United States*, comp George Brown Goode, Sec. V, vol. i (Washington: Government Printing Office, 1887)

Glossaire   *Glossaire du parler français au Canada* (Québec: L'Action Sociale, 1930)

Gray's Botany   Merritt Lyndon Fernald, *Gray's Manual of Botany*, 8th ed (New York: Van Nostrand Reinhold Company, 1950; 1970)

GROSE   Francis Grose, *A Classical Dictionary of the Vulgar Tongue* (London: S. Hooper, 1785; rpt 1968)

HARRAP   *Harrap's New Standard French and English Dictionary*, 2 parts, 3 vols. (New York: Charles Scribner's Sons, 1972)

JOYCE   P.W. Joyce, *English as We Speak it in Ireland* (London: Longmans, Green, & Co., 1910)

Labrador Inuit   Rose Jeddore, ed *Labrador Inuit: Uqausingit* (Nain: The Labrador Inuit Committee on Literacy, 1976)

LEIM & SCOTT   A.H. Leim and W.B. Scott, *Fishes of the Atlantic Coast of Canada* (Ottawa: Fisheries Research Board of Canada, Bulletin No. 155, 1966)

LEMOINE   Geo. Lemoine, *Dictionnaire français-montagnais avec un vocabulaire montagnais-anglais* (Boston: W.B. Cabot and P. Cabot, 1901)

LEWIS & SHORT   *A Latin Dictionary*, eds Charlton T. Lewis and Charles Short (Oxford: At the Clarendon Press, 1879; rpt 1955)

Ling Atlas Scot   *The Linguistic Atlas of Scotland, Scots Section*, 2 vols., eds J.Y. Mather and H.H. Speitel (London: Croom Helm, 1975; 1977)

LUBBOCK   Basil Lubbock, *The Arctic Whalers* (Glasgow: Brown, Son & Ferguson, Ltd., 1937; rpt 1968)

MASSIGNON   Geneviève Massignon, *Les parlers français d'Acadie; enquête linguistique*, 2 vols. (Paris: C. Klincksieck [1962])

MED   *Middle English Dictionary*, eds Hans Kurath, Sherman M. Kuhn, John Reidy and others, A–O (Ann Arbor: University of Michigan Press, 1956–1980)

NID   *Webster's Third New International Dictionary*, editor-in-chief, Philip Babcock Gove (Springfield: G. & C. Merriam Company, 1961)

OED   *The Oxford English Dictionary*, ed James A.H. Murray and others, 12 vols. (Oxford: At the Clarendon Press, 1884–1928; corrected re-issue, 1933)

O Sup[1]   *The Oxford English Dic-*

	tionary; Supplement and Bibliography (Oxford: At the Clarendon Press, 1933)
O Sup²	A Supplement to the Oxford English Dictionary, ed R.W. Burchfield, 2 vols., A–N (Oxford: At the Clarendon Press, 1972; 1976)
PARTRIDGE	A Dictionary of Slang and Unconventional English, 4th ed, revised, ed Eric Partridge (London: Routledge & Kegan Paul Ltd, 1951; rpt 1956)
PEACOCK	English-Eskimo Dictionary, ed F.W. Peacock (St John's: Memorial University, [1974])
PHILLIPPS	K.C. Phillipps, Westcountry Words & Ways (Newton Abbot: David & Charles, 1976)
PIERCE	Wesley George Pierce, Goin' Fishin' The Story of the Deep-Sea Fishermen of New England (Salem: Marine Research Society, 1934)
SED	Survey of English Dialects; The Basic Material, 4 vols. in 12 parts, ed Harold Orton and others (Leeds: E.J. Arnold & Son Limited, 1962–71)
Shetland Truck System	Second Report of the Commissioners Appointed to Inquire into the Truck System (Shetland) (Edinburgh: Her Majesty's Stationery Office, 1872; rpt 1978)
SMYTH	The Sailor's Word-Book: An Alphabetical Digest of Nautical Terms, ed W.H. Smyth (London: Blackie and Son, 1867)
SND	The Scottish National Dictionary, eds William Grant and David Murison, 10 vols. (Edinburgh: The Scottish National Dictionary Association Ltd, [1931]–1976)
Trésor de la langue française	Trésor de la langue française; Dictionnaire de la langue du XIX et du XX siècle (1789–1960), [directed by] Paul Imbs (Paris: Editions du centre national de la recherche scientifique, 1971–)
WILCOCKS	J.C. Wilcocks, The Sea-fisherman, 2nd ed (London: Longmans, Green, and Co., 1868)

Abbreviations

Below are listed the abbreviations employed in the Dictionary, especially in the references found in the headnotes. For a key to the abbreviations used in quoting the sources for the Dictionary, see the BIBLIOGRAPHY.

a, adj   adjective, adjectival
A.D.   anno Domini
A-I   Anglo-Irish
arch   archaic
attrib   attributive
Austr   Australia
av   adverb
b   born
B.C.   before Christ
Brit   British
c.   approximately; century
C   item in MUNFLA Card Collection
Can   Canadian
cent   century
cm   centimetre
Co   Cornwall
CO   Colonial Office [Series]
colloq   colloquial
comb(s)   combination(s)
comp   compiler
Conn   Connecticut
cp   compare with the following term or reference
cpd   compound
CS   Colonial Series
cty, cties   county, counties
d   died
D   Devon
det   determiner
dial   dialect(al)
Do   Dorset
ed(s)   editor(s), edited by; edition
ed emend   editorial emendation
esp   especially
etym   etymology
exc   except

exclam   exclamation
ff   and the following pages
fig.   figurative
Fr   French
freq   frequent(ly)
ft   feet
gen   general
Gk   Greek
Gl   Gloucestershire
Gloss   Glossary
Ha   Hampshire
ibid   the same source
imit   imitative
imp   imperative
in.   inches
int   interjection
intens   intensifier
int pro   interrogative pronoun
Ir   Ireland, Irish
ISER   Institute of Social and Economic Research
IW   Isle of Wight
kg   kilogramme
l   litre
Lab(r)   Labrador
Lat   Latin
m   metre
M   item in MUNFLA Manuscript Collection
Mass   Massachusetts
MS(S)   manuscript(s)
m t   metric ton
MUC   Memorial University College
MUNFLA   Memorial University of Newfoundland Folklore and Language Archive
n   noun; nominal; note
naut   nautical usage
N B   New Brunswick
n d   no date
N E   New England
neg   negative
Nfld   Newfoundland
N H   New Hampshire

N I Northern Ireland
no northern
No number
N S Nova Scotia
num numeral
N Z New Zealand
obs obsolete
occas occasionally
Ork Orkney
p. page
P item submitted by a collector
PANL Provincial Archives of Newfoundland
   and Labrador
phr phrase
pl plural
poet poetical
Por Portuguese
ppl present participle
ppl a participial adjective
p ppl past participle
prcf prefix
prep preposition
pro personal pronoun
prob probably
prov proverb(ial)
Prov Provençal
Q item obtained from a questionnaire
qtl quintal 'a measure of fish'
quot quotation
rpt reprint
s southern
sb substantive
Sc Scotland
sg singular
Sh I Shetland Islands
Sh & Ork Shetland and Orkney
sig. signature
So Somerset
Span Spanish
SPCK Society for the Promotion of Christian
Knowledge
SPG Society for the Propagation of the Gospel
spp species
STC Short-Title Catalogue
subs substitute
s w southwest [counties of England: Berkshire,
   Cornwall, Devon, Dorset, Gloucestershire,
   Hampshire, Somerset]
T item in MUNFLA Tape Collection
tr translator, translation, translated by
transf transferred sense
U S United States
usu usually
v verb
v superscript verso (of a page)
var various, variant
vbl n verbal noun
vol(s) volume(s)

w west
W Wiltshire
Wxf Wexford

* a spelling not attested in printed sources; a
   spelling devised to suggest an approximate
   pronunciation: **joog***

( ) an optional spelling or inflexional ending
   occurs: **quar(r)**

= 'the preceding term means': **old king** [=
   king eider]

~ 'the word being defined'; 'the word just
   mentioned': **ochre,** ~ **pit**

~s 'the plural of the form': **sabot**. . .~s

[ ] phonetic transcription; editorial correction
   or emendation; a relevant quotation which
   does not contain the word being illustrated;
   date of first appearance, writing, or, if a
   ballad, performance

This dictionary includes some words which are or are
asserted to be proprietary names or trademarks. Their
inclusion does not imply that they have acquired for
legal purposes a non-proprietary or general significance
nor any other judgement concerning their legal status.

DICTIONARY OF NEWFOUNDLAND ENGLISH

A

aaron's rod n Roseroot (*Sedum rosea*) (1956 ROULEAU 25).

aback av *EDD* ~ prep, adv 1; *O Sup*² adv 4 arch, dial. Behind, at the back of; usu with *of, o'*.

T 96–64² I used to hide down a-back o' the chairs. T 58/65–64 There's a mine over there goes in aback o' your place. 1971 CASEY 39 We'd leave her after twelve o'clock [midnight] to go fishing. Now we'd go out aback of the Head and cast caplin. Ibid 266 And it made that much noise and the house trembled that much, that the wood was piled up aback of the stove in the box fell down.

able a *OED* ~ a 5 'strong, vigorous' obs (1375–1863) for sense 1; WASSON *Cap'n Simeon's Store* (1903), p. 149 for sense 2; *EDD* 3: able for (Ir) for sense 3.

1 Strong, muscular.

T 80/3–64 And 'twas heavy. A man heaved a cod seine was able man. T 43/4–64 Big, able man, strong man—a man that never had a thing wrong with him.

2 Of a boat or vessel, well-built, serviceable, trim.

T 194/6–65 We got a speed boat, a good one. Eighteen foot long, able boat, eighteen horsepower Johnson engine.

3 Phr *able for*: stronger than (another).

P 113–74 'Is he able for you?' Is he stronger than you are, or able to overcome you in a trial of strength?

aboard See CLOSE ABOARD.

abroad av *EDD* ~ adv 2 s w cties for sense 1; 4 So D Co for sense 2; 3 Gl Do So D Co for sense 3; *DC* (Nfld: 1909, 1916) for sense 4.

1 Spread out.

[1663] 1963 YONGE 57–8 The fish being salted, lies 3 or 4 days, sometimes (if bad weather) 8 or 10 days, and is then washed by the boys in salt or fresh water and laid in a pile skin upward on a platt of beach stones, which they call a horse. After a day or thereabout, it's laid abroad on flakes. . .and here the fish dries.

T 141/68–65 If you come in with a skiffload o' fish and there's a drash o' rain last night, sails got to go abroad—you got to look to they as well.

2 Open, apart.

[1663] 1963 YONGE 57 When the header has done his work, he thrusts the fish to the other side of the table, where sits. . .a splitter, who with a strong knife splits it abroad. 1924 ENGLAND 146 He'd be like a ole dog hood wid his narsls split abroad, an' in twenty minutes be laughin'. T 23–64 Cut un abroad, and sculp un—take the pelt off of un—and leave the carcass. 1979 TIZZARD 304 Every squid would have to be 'gone over' to pick the horns (tentacles) abroad in order that they would not hang in a bunch and therefore not dry so well.

3 In pieces, asunder.

[1775] 1792 CARTWRIGHT ii, 77 . . .when the mast,

which was very heavy, heeling to the other, I expected she would have fallen abroad. 1920 GRENFELL & SPALDING 112 Some of the goods are dropped with such a thud that the packages 'burst abroad.' 1933 MERRICK 225 He said his father, who has something of a reputation as a gunsmith, could 'take it abroad' and with the simple aid of a file and some old screws make it like new. T 50/2–64 An' they had to do that right too. If they didn't it be all no good. They had to rip it all abroad again. 1975 POCIUS 15 Picking the wool involved taking a small clump of wool into the hand, and pulling it apart, or 'abroad,' with the fingers using a teasing action.

4 Of a field of ice, separated in fragments or 'pans'; broken up; esp with *go, run* ([1907] 1979 *Nfld Qtly* Fall, p. 25).

1909 GRENFELL¹ 31 The ice was now 'all abroad,' which I was sorry for, for there was a big safe pan not twenty yards away from me. 1916 DUNCAN 130 As they say on the coast, the ice had 'gone abroad.' 1924 ENGLAND 70 That afternoon the glass took a decided turn and the sky cleared. The ice began to 'go abroad' a bit. T 78–64 The fog filled in an' the ice runned an' begin to go abroad, an' they never got to the land. 1972 BROWN 78 If that gale ye see brewin' to the south-east comes on as quick as I expect it will, and the ice stretches abroad. . .we're liable to be out here for the night.

5 In fig. senses *go abroad*: to overturn (a state of affairs).

1974 CAHILL 10 . . .if St George's electoral district is gone off half-cocked for the wrong side this early in the night, then she's liable to be all gone abroad.

be scared abroad: to be frightened to death.

P 148–71 An adult knows ghost story is not true but is based on true experience of the author, but a child would get scared abroad when he reads the part where Flora sees an apparition.

wing a cove abroad: to proceed with all sails set directly through a harbour entrance (c 67–7).

according ppl ['kɑːɹdn̩, 'kɔːɹdn̩, kɒːɹən, əˌkɒːɹdn̩ 'tʉu]. Cp *EDD* ~ adv 'in proportion to' Wo Gl So.

Phr *as according as, according as*: when; at the same time as; while; in proportion to.

1858 [LOWELL] ii, 202 The wind's like to come up here out o' Nothe-east, bum-bye, accord'n as the moon rises. T 43–64 You'd get it rough there sometimes. The fish'd wash off of the deck as 'cardin' as you throw it in. T 46–64 Nippers was that thick that they come and they used to drive their thorns down through the bark pot. 'Cardin' as they drove 'em down, he used to clench 'em [with a hammer]. T 56–64 I got that [arthritis] half a lifetime now and as 'ca'in' as I get older I'm gettin' worse. T 61–64 But as 'cordin' as the years rolled by, it still got worse. Instead of being a weekly occurrence, 'twas every night occurrence.

according to: in equal measure, in the same proportion.

1957 *Evening Telegram* 22 Aug, p. 4 And, as the Newfoundland saying goes, 'Everything else according to.' T 55–64 You have a storeful of food, nine or ten barrels of flour if you had a big family, and everything else accardin' to—nothing to worry about. 1970 JANES 78 Yes, yes. Don't be fussin'. He gives me whatever he can, accardin' to.

accordion See CARDEEN*.

adam's plaster n Lady's thumb (*Polygonum persicaria*) (1898 *J A Folklore* xi, 278).

adikey n also **adiky**. Cp *DC* atigi 2 (l934–); *Labrador Inuit* (1976), p. 24 atigik 'an Inuk parka.' Eskimo hooded outer garment or blouse made of cloth or animal skin; DICKY.
· [1868 CHIMMO 274–5 The missionary gentlemen looked very comfortable, but curious in their entire sealskin suit, the [Esquimaux] women in their 'attigeks' with their sealskin trousers and boots, many of them having their babies in their hoods]. 1907 WALLACE 219–20 The adikey, or koolutuk, of the women, has a long flap or tail, reaching nearly to the heels, and a sort of apron in front. . .[The men's] adikey. . .reaches half way to their knees, and is cut square around. . . If they wear two cloth garments at the same time, as is usually the case, the inner one only is an adikey. 1909 BROWNE 27 Over pantaloons of spacious width [the Eskimo] wear a 'Jumper' called 'Adikey' (if made of blanketing). 1916 YOUNG 76 My travelling outfit, in addition to my ordinary clothes, consisted of a pair of seal-skin pants, an adikey, [and] a pair of seal-skin mittens.

admiral n Cp *OED* ~ sb 4 'privileged commander of a fishing or merchant fleet' (1708–), *DC* (Nfld: 1620–) for sense 2; *OED* 5, SMYTH 20 for sense 3.
1 The master of an English fishing vessel, chosen weekly to exercise jurisdiction over European fishermen in a Newfoundland harbour.
[(1578) 1895 PROWSE 34–5 The English are commonly lords of the harbour where they fish, and use all strangers' help in fishing if need require, according to an old custom of the country, which thing they do willingly, so that you take nothing from them more than a boat or two of salt in respect of your protection of them against rovers or other violent intruders, who do often put them from good harbours.] [1583] 1940 *Gilbert's Voyages & Enterprises* ii, 400–1 We found also the Frigate or *Squirrill* lying at anker. Whom the English marchants (that were & alwaies be Admirals by turnes interchangeably over the fleetes of fishermen within the same harbor) would not permit to enter. . . The manner is in their fishing, every weeke to choose their Admirall a new, or rather they succeede in orderly course, and have weekely their Admirals feast solemnized.
2 The master of the first English fishing vessel to reach a cove or harbour, exercising certain privileges for the season; FISHING ADMIRAL. Freq in comb **admiral's beach**, ~ **cove**, ~ **room**, etc.
[1611] 1954 INNIS 56 The 'admiral' of each harbor was allowed only the beach and flakes needed for the

number of boats 'that he shall use with an overplus, only for one boat more than he hath.' 1620 WHITBOURNE 21 It is well knowne, that they which adventure to New-found-land a fishing, begin to dresse and provide their ships ready commonly in the moneths of December, January, and February, and are ready to set foorth at See in those voyages neare the end of February. . . And thus they doe, striving to be there first in Harbour, to obtaine the name of Admirall that yeere; and so, to have the chiefest place to make their fish on. [1663] 1963 YONGE 56 Mr Waymouth, (who is Admiral [at Renews] and always wore a flagstaff, Sundays a flag, and is called my Lord, the vice-admiral my Lady) had a chyrurgeon. [1670] ibid 132–3 We took the lower Admiral's place [in St John's] for half our boats; the other half we kept at Petty-Harbour. 1699 *Act of Wm III*, 10 & 11 That (according to the Ancient Custom there used) every such Fishing Ship from England, Wales or Berwick, or such Fishermen as shall from and after the said Twenty fifth Day of March, first enter any Harbour or Creek in Newfoundland, in behalf of his Ship, shall be Admiral of the said Harbour or Creek during that Fishing Season. [1711] 1895 PROWSE 271 One storehouse on admiral's room. 1818 CHAPPELL 111 According to a curious old custom, the sum of sixty pounds sterling is annually bestowed upon the master of that vessel which may chance to arrive first at Forteau, in the beginning of the year; and the person who receives the reward is dignified by the title *Admiral of the Fishery* for the ensuing season. Where there are no commissioned magistrates, it is the duty of this individual to take cognizance of offences. [1832] 1975 WHITELEY 42 Two days afterwards. . .the Admiral Captain Templeton entered my frame [and] kept me from taking my seals. 1837 BLUNT 19 There is however a secure place for boats within a point behind the Admiral's Stage. 1951 *Nfld & Lab Pilot* i, 192 Admiral cove, on the eastern side of Grand Bank head, affords anchorage, to vessels with local knowledge.
3 The first English fishing vessel to reach a harbour in a season.
[1766] 1971 BANKS 150 In Every harbour the First arriving Ship is admiral of the harbour her Captain administering Justice tho with Frequent Appeals to the [Governor]. 1793 REEVES 8 The ship that first entered the harbour was to be admiral. 1828 MCGREGOR 244 The English ships, however, from this period, were considered the largest and best vessels; and soon became and continued to be the *admirals*.
4 The oldest man in a community; cp SKIPPER (1896 *Dial Notes* i, 377).
[c1894] PANL P4/14, p. 197 At Heart's Ease, the *oldest man* of the settlement is called the *admiral*, and right pleased and proud he is of the title.

advent n Comb **advent wreath**: wreath of green boughs made to mark the season preceding the festival of the Nativity.
C 70–17 It has always been a custom in her family to make what they call an Advent wreath around Christmas time each year. Q 71–14 The Advent wreath is a Catholic custom. I have often helped make them in my classroom before Christmas. It would be made of

boughs to form a wreath with four candles placed on it; they would be lit each day for the three weeks of Advent. P 141–72 During Advent we would make an Advent wreath (a hoop covered with green boughs) and between the boughs we would place candles. Also on the wreath would be ribbons which would be tied to the ceiling. Before and after classes, while saying prayers, we would light all the candles and after prayers extinguish them.

adventure n also **venture**. Cp *OED* ~ 7 'commercial enterprise' (1625–). A fishing or sealing enterprise; VOYAGE.
[1548] 1895 PROWSE 53 Forasmuch as within these few Years now last past there hath been levied. . .of such Merchants and Fishermen as have used and practised the Adventures and Journeys into *Iseland*, *Newfoundland*, *Ireland* and other Places commodious for Fishing and the getting of Fish. . . [1802] 1916 MURPHY 2 I am anxious this minute that your Excellency may form some idea of the expense attending this [seal fishery] adventure, as well as of the mode in which it is conducted. P 54–63 The word venture lingered in Newfoundland usage for a trading operation until recently and the account in a firm's ledger for the cost, sale and outcome of each of its fish exportation consignments was headed up 'fish venture per (vessel's name).'

adventurer n Cp *OED* ~ 4 'one who undertakes, or shares in, a commercial enterprise' (1625–). Cp PLANTER.
1 Shareholder in an organization or company formed to establish a colony or 'plantation' in Newfoundland.
[1611] 1895 PROWSE 123 And for as much as the good and prosperous success of the plantation cannot but cheifelie depend [on] good direction of the whole enterprize by a careful and understanding counsell, and that it is not convenient, that all the adventurers shalbe soo often drawen to meete and assemble as shalbe requisite for them to have meetings and conference about their affairs. . . 1624 EBURNE 139 Sixthly, some other worthy persons there are that be adventurers in the said plantation, whose names I know not. [1639] 1895 PROWSE 149 Petition of James Marquis of Hamilton and the rest of the Adventurers of Newfoundland To the King. . .
2 A migratory English fisherman operating seasonally in Newfoundland.
[1611] 1895 PROWSE 124 And furthermore if any Adventurers or planters shall transport any moneys or merchandize out of any of our kingdomes with a pretence to land sell or otherwise dispose of them within [Newfoundland]. . . [1653] ibid 167 . . .such fit persons as you shall appoint to collect. . .the imposition of Oyle for the use of this Commonwealth, and Adventurers aforesaid. [1701] ibid 228 This was very great abuse and discouragement to the other Adventurers; besides, these bye boat keepers could afford to sell their fish cheaper than the Adventurers, which must lessen the number of fishing ships. [1766] 1976 HEAD 180 [They were engaged in] destroying the Fishing Works belonging to English Fishers there and in the North part of Newfoundland, Firing the Woods, and doing every kind of Mischief, to prevent and discourage English Adventurers from going to that Coast. [1794] 1968 THOMAS 109 Her Husband came over from England about Fifty-Five years ago as an Adventurer—what is called here a green man. [1810] 1971 ANSPACH 19 The great sums generally charged for purchases, money or yearly rents with onerous conditions for building, etc in cases which set and exceed 15 years, even of unoccupied and naked rooms, seem to indicate such a want for the adventurers who must labour under still greater inconveniences than the resident Fish Catchers.
3 A resident fisherman or settler who fishes seasonally in coastal waters distant from his home port.
[1797] 1976 HEAD 226 The great quantity of Herrings that are found [on the South Coast] at this time, encourage adventurers from most parts of Newfoundland particularly St John's and Placentia. [1803] ibid 222 [The French Shore is] a part where Fish is found in such abundance, as to have induced adventurers, for several years past, to fit out Vessels from the southern ports [of Newfoundland], and proceed thither to carry on the Fishery, in which they have always been successful, while the shore-fishery to the southward has frequently failed.

afrore See FRORE.

after prep *EDD* ~ prep 6 (2) 'completed action' Sc Ir; JOYCE 84–5; DINNEEN diaidh: i ndiaidh 'after'; éis: d'éis 'after, behind' ('he has just struck him'). In idiom *be after (doing something)*: to have (done); to have completed an action; to have already (done); to have just (done).
1897 WILLSON 38 [They were] patiently waiting until they could unfold their grievances or their demands to the 'skipper,' as Sir William is called. For they are 'afther having nothing else in the world to do.' 1910 *Nfld Qtly* Oct, p. 23 Mr Williams, sir, you're after makin' a mistake, sir, the corpse is wakin' *in the bedroom*. 1940 *Fortnightly* cliii, Apr, p. 403 Several told him, 'he was after bein' a fool.' T 43/8–64 I'm not old enough to be after doin' too much work anywhere, an' I've spent four years overseas. T 55/7–64 She come an' called me just as plain as if you called me. I knew there was something after happened her. T 75/8–64 And there was an island pan after driving along. They brought us in about half a mile of Careless Point, and dumped us out on the island pan. 1966 SZWED 66 Some poor fellers are after courting for 6 or 7 years, just trying to get a little money to buy a house. 1970 JANES 37 How many times am I after tellin' you? But it's all no good. I could talk till I'm blue in the face, and you'd still just sit there mumblin' and grumblin' like a ole nannygoat. 1977 *Nfld Qtly* Summer, p. 6 He told me the story; all hands was after leaving her, cook and all. She was an old vessel and they didn't like her. 1980 *Evening Telegram* 17 Mar, p. 3 Deputy Mayor Ray O'Neill said. . .'the provincial government is after setting up this offshore petroleum impact committee.'

after a Cp *OED* ~ 4 b 'hinder' naut.

Comb **after beam**, ~ **bunk**: stout transverse timber at the rear of a sled.

P 148–67 The after-bunk [is a cross-piece at the rear of the catamaran]. C 70–15 Sometimes a boy would help his father by using a second hauling rope fastened to the after beam.

after gunner: at the seal hunt, a marksman hunting old or mature seals, usu in a small boat; GUNNER.

1842 JUKES ii, 129 He has likewise his long sealing gun, if he is intended as a bow or after gunner, or, in other words, as an expert marksman, to shoot the animals. 1877 TOCQUE 307 One pound ten shillings for after gunner. P 213–54 The after gunner [was the] second man (less experienced) after the fore-gunner.

agent n   In the fishery (a) the manager of the operations in Newfoundland of a British or Channel Islands mercantile house; (b) the representative in a fishing settlement of a St John's fish-merchant.

[1767] 1828 CARTWRIGHT ii, 306 The list of destitute persons. . .was not put into my hands till I was on the point of sailing, and then without any other than its own evidence, though it was in the possession of Mr Street, agent to the elder White [of Poole], who was a principal sufferer, and one of the most earnest complainants. [1775] 1955 HARVEY (ed) 60 I soon heard that Mr Neave was not yet arived in the land but was Expected in a few Weeks; was informd he lived at Little Placentia about 7 miles to it Ware his Agent Capt Harrison resided. 1832 MCGREGOR i, 193 A great majority of the merchants at St John's, as well as the agents who represent the principal houses, are men who received a fair education. 1846 [FEILD] 13–14 The Bishop. . .was welcomed and entertained with the same kindness as elsewhere, by Mr Chapman, the agent of Messrs Nicolle and Co. 1868 *Royal Geog Soc* xxxviii, 263 Here the agent (Mr Bendle), for Slade and Co., came on board. He says that all the fishing-vessels are at Webeck. 1936 SMITH 42 Messrs Job Bros. & Co. owned Indian Harbour in those days, and Mr Joseph Simms was their summer agent.

airsome a   *ADD* ~ (Nfld). Cold, fresh, bracing (1863 MORETON 32).

1924 ENGLAND 66 Shrieks of storm devils shook the masts and a ravening madness smudged out the universe. 'Dirty wedder' was about all the sealers would admit. 'A bit airsome, sir.' 1933 GREENLEAF xxv 'Come in, Tammas, and hapse the door, it's a bit airsome tonight.' 1937 DEVINE 6 ~ Cold, but pleasant and bracing. [1954] 1972 RUSSELL 15 Take an oil-coat for him in case it turns wet—and the bear-skin rug. It gets airsome these evenin's.

alder n

Comb **alder berry**: fruit appearing on alder after flowering (P 245–65).

alder bird: mealy common redpoll (*Acanthis flammea flammea*).

1870 *Can Naturalist* v, 157 [The redpole] breeds early, and generally in alder bushes; hence its provincial

name of 'Alder Bird.' 1959 MCATEE 62 ~ Dusky Redpoll (Nfld., 'Labr.')

alexander n

1 Scotch lovage (*Ligusticum scothicum*), a herb used medicinally; freq pl; also attrib.

[1771] 1792 CARTWRIGHT i, 130 I named [the river] Alexander; abundance of that plant growing on its banks. 1861 DE BOILIEU 215 The only esculent (in the common sense) found on the coast fit to eat was named the 'Alexander'—a species of celery. 1920 WALDO 62 'What greens have you?' 'Alexander greens, sir.' 1930 *Am Speech* vi, 56 ~ a pot-herb growing on rocks, which can be cooked and eaten like spinage. 1975 SCOTT 31 Scotch Lovage or Alexanders is found all around the coastline and in some other places in Newfoundland. The vegetative part of the plant looks like celery except that the stalks are smaller and the leaves are larger. The taste is like that of celery and parsley.

2 Dumpling or 'duff' seasoned with the herb.

1909 BROWNE 268 'Stoggers' and 'Alexanders' are huge balls of dough. . .served with. . .'Codey.'

alix n   also **ellis***. Cp LEWIS & SHORT *alex*, var *alec* 'fish-brine.' Attrib **alix water**: the liquid residue in a cask after the rendered oil of cod livers has been drawn off in the making of 'rot(ted) oil' (1937 DEVINE 6).

P 187–73 After cod liver has been rotted the water and blood sink to the bottom; this is called ellis water.

alley-coosh* v   also **cooch***, **cush*** [kuːtʃ]. Cp *EDD* allee-couchee 'go to bed' Co. Phr *go to alley-coosh*: to go to bed.

P 229–67 It's after eleven o'clock. It's time to go to couche. Q 67–100 A friend was told at bedtime to 'go to your alley coosh.' P 41–68 When he succumbed to the Sandman, his mother put him to alley coosh. P 109–70 I'm going cush. I'm going to cush.

all quall See TAL QUAL.

amalgamated ppl *DC* ~ school Nfld (1955–). Comb **amalgamated school**: school operated by two (or more) Protestant denominations; cp PUBLIC.

1942 *Little Bay Islands* 23 For considerable time your local board in conjunction with representatives with the Salvation Army has been working to get a kind of amalgamated school service for Little Bay Islands. 1964 ROWE 94 At the present time there are forty-one amalgamated or 'common' schools in Newfoundland. . .and the movement appears to be growing among the Protestant groups. 1969 DEWITT 5 Mr Freake also said that a central amalgamated high school should be organized as a further attraction to good teachers.

american n   See *RLS* 8 (1978), 30–41, NAKED MAN and NASKAPI 2 for the same sense; possibly from an original oral form *markin' man. Comb **american man**: a marker, usu a pile of rocks prominently placed as a guide in coastal navigation, sometimes becoming a place-name; CAIRN.

1861 *Harper's* xxii, 590–1 Such caprices of the weather make it necessary to run into harbor at night; for what vessel could then run the gauntlet of hidden rocks, icebergs, and drifting ice? For these exigencies the Labrador coast is well provided [and] the securest harbors are invariably indicated by a tall pyramid of stones, piled upon the highest point of land at their entrance. These beacons are called 'American men,' from their having been erected by the Yankee fishermen, and are exceedingly useful to mariners. 1884 STEARNS 262 A pile or heap of stones [is] thrown up into some form several feet in height and usually placed on top of an island or neighbouring height to mark some position, or important spot or event. These heaps occur everywhere, and are known. . .by the name 'Nascopi,' by the natives, also 'American Man' by the sailors. 1909 BROWNE 264 These cairns, of which there are several along the coast, are called by fishermen, ''Merican men.' [They] serve as landmarks for the fishing schooners. [1951 *Nfld & Lab Pilot* i, 82 A twin summit, the southern peak of which is 816 feet high and known as American summit or Captain Orlebar's cairn, lies about three-quarters of a mile northward.] C 71–130 At the very top of the highest hill overlooking the harbour at Cupids is a sort of rock structure about four feet high and two feet across known as the merican man. 1973 WIDDOWSON 233 Jack o' Lantern was supposed to live on top of the American Man (the name given to the cairn on top of Big Island in Bay Roberts). [1977 *Inuit Land Use* 198 Pillar Islands. Inuksutoguluk. Small *inuksuk* (stone cairns). (An *inuksuk* is a pile of rocks built to resemble a man and used as a landmark.]

amper n *EDD* ~ sb 1 So. A boil or gathering (P 234–61).

amper* See HAPPER.

ampered p ppl *EDD* ~ adj Ha Do So D. Infected, purulent (1955 ENGLISH 32).

ampery a *EDD* ~ adj 1 So. Inflamed, infected. P 74–67 The cut was all red and ampery. Q 73–4 [He had] an ampry head.

and conj. Phr *and do* or *and that* occurring at the end of a sentence: and everything else; *et cetera* (P 245–56; P 54–67).

andramartins n pl also **andrew martins*** *EDD* andramartin sb Ir; *Kilkenny Lexicon* andrew martin 2. Pranks; silly tricks (1925 *Dial Notes* v, 325).

1931 BYRNES 121 How many years have passed my friends, since you heard these once familiar localisms? . . .Andramartins. 1937 DEVINE 6 ~ much the same as *gauches* [gatches]. P 88–56 Andrew martins: silly actions, usually on the part of the children. P 108–70 None of your andrew martins, now!

angish a ['æɲʃ] *EDD* ~ adj 2 'poverty-strick-

en,' 3 'sickly' Ir; cp DINNEEN aindeis 'afflicted. . .wretched, miserable.' See also ANGISHORE. Pitifully small or mean; sickly; cold (1937 DEVINE 6).

1968 DILLON 130 You looks a kind of angish today. What's the matter with you? He's an angish lookin' poor little thing.

angishore n also **angashore, angyshore, hangashore**, etc ['æŋəʃɔːɹ, 'æŋgəʃɔːɹ, 'hæɲɨʃoəɹ, 'hæŋəʃɔːɹ, æŋɪ'ʃɔːɹ, æɲɪ'ʃɔːɹ]. *EDD* angish 2: angishore 'a poverty-stricken creature' Ir (1894); JOYCE 211 ang-ishore; DINNEEN aindeiseoir 'an unfortunate person or thing, a wretch' for sense 1. An aspirate [h] is frequently pronounced initially in words beginning with vowels; therefore this Irish loan *angishore* is often pronounced and spelled *hangashore*, and this in turn has been reinterpreted by folk etymology.

1 A weak, sickly person; an unlucky person deserving pity; freq preceded by *poor*.

1914 *Cadet* Apr, p. 7 'Angyshore' a youngster who is no good, sick, weak, and unable to do his work. 1929 MILLER 44 "Big Davey's Comforting": So he kep' bathin' the place 'at's tore / An' sayin—'Pore little 'ang-ashore!' 1931 BYRNES 121 How many years have passed my friends, since you heard these once familiar localisms? . . .'The poor angashore.' 1966 HORWOOD 18 If some poor 'angshore be brought low be 'is own foolishness, maybe that be a cross an' affliction 'e can't help. P 130–67 He hasn't a coat to his back, the poor angishore. 1968 DILLON 131 You poor little angishore, are you frost-burned with the cold? P 144–77 The poor angishore! There's not flesh on her to bait a trout. 1979 *Evening Telegram* 24 Nov, p. 15 'Come in, girl,' sez the woman. 'Himself is in the kitchen with a face like black Monday on him, but I suppose the poor 'angashore is in pain.'

2 A man regarded as too lazy to fish; a worthless fellow, a sluggard; a rascal; sometimes merges with sense 3.

1924 ENGLAND 180 Know where them angyshores was to? Hidin' behind a pinnacle. They fired their pipes, an' was chewin' the fat rather 'an haulin' it in! 1964 *Evening Telegram* 17 July, p. 22 'What are you two angashores doin'?' sez he. 'I had word from a woman in Bell Island she's havin' water trouble, an' I'm going out to Portugal Cove to pick up her pump. Do you want to come along?' 1966 SCAMMELL 53–4 I got no use for that dolled-up hangashore. 1970 JANES 23 [He] grumbled that if a man was not wearing khaki people seemed to take it for granted that he was some kind of cowardly hangashore.

3 An idle, mischievous child or person; SLEEVEEN.

1956 *Daily News* 13 Aug For example, when someone (especially a child) is doing something he should not be doing one would say, 'Stop that, you angishore.' C 70–18 'You little hangashore,' my grandfather called me on a spring's day of 1956. The term was used in anger. [1973] ROSE (ed) 71 "The Hangashore": Uncle Solomon Noddy was a hangashore if ever there was one. By that I mean he was too bad to be called a good-for-nothin' and not bad enough to be called a *sleeveen*. He was just. . .a hangashore.

4 A migratory fisherman from Newfoundland who conducts a summer fishery from a fixed station on the coast of Labrador; STATIONER. Cp FLOATER.

1936 SMITH 105 [chapter title] A Freighter and a 'Hang-a-shore' at Cutthroat.

angle n Cp *EDD* ~ sb³ 'holes or runs [of] badgers, field-mice,' *DC* (Nfld: 1771, 1783) for sense 1; *EDD* ~ dog D, *DAE* (1867) for sense 4.

1 An entrance to a beaver house.

[1771] 1792 CARTWRIGHT i, 84 [They] opened the lower house in a fresh place [in the beaver house and] found the lodging with two angles to it, and tailed a trap in one of them. [1783] ibid iii, 19 From the fore part of the house, they build a projection into the pond, sloping downwards all the way, and under this they enter into their house. This entrance is called by the furriers, *the Angle*; nor do they always content themselves with one, but more commonly will have two, and sometimes three.

2 Curved inlet of a lake or pond.

T 50–64 We got into this big lake—it looked like a big angle from where we were to; gutty, and angles into it. . . He dropped a note but it fell in the water out in the angle. P 229–67 He caught a fine lot of trout in the lower angle of Burton's pond.

3 Phr *in angles*: in zig-zag fashion.

[1774] 1792 CARTWRIGHT ii, 11 I had the nets also taken up, and put out afresh in angles; the head-man. . .had set them straight across the river.

4 Comb **angle-dog**: earthworm used for freshwater fishing (1968 *Avalon Penin of Nfld* 114).

C 69–2 The man we were discussing was the seventh son of a seventh son, and my father said if you put a worm (angledog) on the palm of this man it would die. C 70–9 ~ a large fat worm, normally about a quarter of an inch in diameter and at least four inches long.

anguish n *EDD* ~ sb 1 'inflammation,' 2 'pain felt at a distance from the actual wound' Sr Ha Co. Pain; soreness; infection; suppuration or matter issuing from an inflammation; ANXIETY.

P 148–65 ~ substance which came out in your eye. Q 71–8 ~ a nagging ache. P 245–71 That misery in your arm is anguish from the boil on your neck. The anguish from me bad toe goes right up me leg. P 157–73 ~ infection in a sore.

anighst prep also **aneist, anighs*, nice*** *EDD* anighst Co Do. Near (1863 MORETON 34).

[c1894] PANL P4/14, p. 200 [I hope] he may never come aneist me. P 37 Nice: near. P 19–55 There was never birch like that growed in any droke anighst here. P 68–55 I wouldn't go nice the place. P 91–63 Don't come anighs me.

annett n *EDD* annet sb¹ Pem Co. Atlantic black-legged kittiwake (*Rissa tridactyla tridactyla*).

1959 MCATEE 37 ~ Common Kittiwake (A familiar

or 'pet' name, diminutive of 'Ann,' a transfer from British provincial usage. Nfld.)

an seery* See HAND SERRY.

ant n Comb **ant's egg**: small white globular or oval berry of capillaire or maidenhair (*Gaultheria hispidula*); CAPILLAIRE BERRY (P 245–65).

1938 MACDERMOTT 242 The capillaire or maidenhair berry. . .is a small white berry of oval shape, well described by the boys when they call it 'ants' eggs.'

anti-confederate n also **anti**. Cp *DC* ~ (1866–). An opponent of political union with Canada.

[1869] 1902 MURPHY (ed) 60 "Confederation Song of 1869": So now Confederation / A shameful death has died, / 'Tis buried up at Riverhead / Beneath the flowing tide. / O may it never rise again / To bother us I pray, / Hurrah my boy's for liberty / The Antis gained the day. 1895 *Evening Herald* 24 Apr I made enquiry all along the line, and met a great many Anti-Confederates, with very little opposition in each place. 1948 *The Confederate* No. 8, p. 2 What a sell the anti-Confederates got in that famous Bowater Report on the effects of Confederation upon Newfoundland! 1964 BLONDAHL (ed) 43 "The 'Antis' of Plate Cove": The day that the poll-booth was opened, / The 'Antis' and 'Cons' they were there. / The flag of cursed Confederation / Was gallantly marched to the rear.

anxiety n Infection; suppuration or matter issuing from an inflammation; ANGUISH.

C 71–39 When a young man had a boil on his arm, some older women said, 'You should put a poultice on that and draw the anxiety out of it.' [Another woman said] a young boy had a running ear: 'He's got a wonderful sore ear. You should see the anxiety that runs out of it.'

apast prep *EDD* ~ 1–3, *ADD*. Of time: after, past; of place: past, beyond.

1937 DEVINE 6 ~ Passed. P 148–59 You go apast a stoplight. M 83–64 Jim turned to run up the lane and the same thing was coming down the lane apast Fitzgerald's stable. T 194/6–65 And twenty minutes a-past one I seed another schooner. C 75–146 He coaxed him, but the dog wouldn't budge. . . He had to take the dog in his arms until they were apass the lights.

apple n Cp *EDD* ~ 1 (7) ~ potato 'certain kind of potato' Mayo. Home-grown potato of high quality.

C 71–24 The better quality potatoes were known as apples. These were for the rich or good potato growers.

aps n also **hapse, (h)apsen** [æps, hæps] *EDD* ~ sb s w cties. Trembling aspen (*Populus tremuloides*); also attrib.

1842 JUKES i, 160 The wood. . .they here called the 'aps.' 1907 MILLAIS 86 On each side was dense forest of good-sized birch, white pine, 'haps' [etc]. T 50/2–64 You chop up bark off o' the trees—white spruce or apse; apse was good bark. An' you dry that on a flake or a wharf. T 203/5–65 An' then you'd get those apses; you'd cut two an' you wire 'em together an' the dead stick in the centre. That's what you'd tie your trap to. 1966 FARIS 240 Apsen (aspen). . .[used for] planking for boats. C 70–21 Christ's cross was made from an aspen (hapse) and that's why the leaves always tremble. P 148–72 No woman wants it for firewood because 'aps wood is full of water.'

apse n *EDD* ~ sb So D Co. An abscess; boil.
P 148–64 [He has] an apse in gums or jaw which may need lancing. C 67–5 She has used bread poultice many times on us to draw out boils, apses, or the infection in rising fingers. M 71–44 An apse broke out and they said that everything came out of that side.

apsy a See APS. Thick with aspen trees; in place-names.
1898 *N S Inst of Sci* ix, 373 Black Knapweed [collected at] Apsey Beach [Bay of Islands].

ar, arra See E'ER: E'RA.

arch n A temporary ceremonial structure decorated with spruce or fir boughs and bunting, erected for a public procession.
1914 *FPU (Twillingate) Minutes* 6 Feb Edward White spoke about the [Army] Lads Brigade: would lend their two drums in the day of our parade. It was proposed, seconded, and carried that we ask the captain of Brigade for drums [and] that we have three arches, one at the Barracks Hill, one at Phillips place and one at Jubilee Corner. Three or four friends volunteered to haul a load of [boughs]. [1929] 1979 *Evening Telegram* 2 June, p. 16 Yesterday's gale also knocked down an arch [near] the power station at Seal Cove which we put up for the Royal visit. 1973 COOK 6 'Did you see the Bishop?' 'I didn't bother. No arches.' 'No. It's not the same.' 'I mind when we used to make 'em all along the path 'e'd come. T'ree, four arches. . .bigger'n old church door they was. And all the maids wid flowers.'

archangel n Type of seal.
1861 DE BOILIEU 92 Next comes a seal smaller in size [than the hooded seal], called the Archangel.

arctic a Comb **arctic steak**: marketing name for whale meat.
[1928] 1978 Evening Telegram 25 July, p. 7 The Newfoundland Whaling Company is putting out a new Newfoundland product, 'Arctic Steak.' The product is meat selected from choice young whales. . . It will be put on sale in stores in St John's tomorrow. 1977 BURSEY 13 "Pioneers": When you buy from us, you can buy wholesale / You can get from a caplin to a whale / I christened it just Arctic Steak, / It's the best of meat, it's no fake.

aret n Both the long-tailed and pomarine jaeger (*Stercorarius longicaudus; S. pomarinus*) (1959 MCATEE 34–5).

arg v *EDD* argue v 1: arg s w cties. To dispute verbally; to attempt to convince.
1898 *Christmas Bells* 16 'Tain't no use to *arg* with the Poor Commissioner. T 55–64 An' they get drunk an' get playin' cards an' then they get out of sorts over it, arg an' fight on the last of it lots o' times. T 253–66 My book was lost God knows how long, but Aunt Charlotte tried to arg me out of it, that I wasn't right.

arm n One of the two outer sections or wings of a seine.
1937 DEVINE 11 [The bunt is] the middle part of a fish seine with the smaller size mesh for [drawing up] when the 'arms' are hauled home. T 80/3–64 A cod seine is a huge long net with small linnet in the middle, an' as you goes on in what they call the arms is bigger linnet.

arn substitute [æːɹn, aːɹn]. See E'ER: E'ERA ONE. *EDD* ever a one (esp s w cties), *ADD* ary one; *SED* sect. vii.2.13. Any; any one; esp in well-known local joke.
1925 *Dial Notes* v, 325 Ar'ntall. Any one at all. 1955 ENGLISH 32 ~ any. P 274–65 Of course you already have that old Newfoundland chestnut— 'Arn? Narn'? Two fishermen were out in their boats, one going to and the other coming from the fishing grounds. As they passed by one said 'Arn?' and the reply came 'Narn.' 1975 GUY 168 The shortest Newfoundland conversation is well known. It occurred when one fisherman met another on the way back from the fishing grounds. The first asked: 'Arn?' To which the other replied: 'Narn.' This translates as 'Ever the one?' and 'Never the one (fish).'

around See BAY.

arse n also **ass**. *OED* ~ sb 1, 2, *EDD* 1 for sense 1; cp *O Sup²* sb 1 b arse over tip, *EDD* 2 (1) arse over head So for phr in sense 2; *O Sup²* 3 arse-end, *EDD* 3 (6) for comb in sense 3.
1 Bottom; hinder or lower part (of an object); hence **hot arse**: galvanized tin kettle; PIPER.
P 148–62 Ass of our pants. P 148–64 ~ back part of dress. T 141/65–65² 'Now put thy arse down in both of 'em,' she said, 'try 'em both out, an' whichever one thees likes best thees can have.' So anyhow he sot down in both chairs, an' had a little rock, zigzag back an' forth. 1971 *Evening Telegram* 22 Apr, p. 3 A kindly outharbor fisherman has agreed to take the visiting mainland couple for a trip in his boat. As you get aboard he may say: 'Now, sir, you can sit up in the headuver and, ma'am, you can sit back in the arsuver.' 1973 BARBOUR 94 If one wanted boiling water in a hurry for a cup of tea, one used what were called 'quicks' or 'hot asses,' made of tin by the local tinsmith. Water boiled very quickly in these kettles, which had large bottoms. 1975 BUTLER 41 Well now, when we went at the [boat] Johnny said, 'Vic, you take her arse,' he said, 'and I'll take her head.' Ibid 113 The cook woke me in the morning. He said, 'Skipper, the whole arse is gone out of your pants.' 1978 *Evening Telegram* 4 Jan, p. 4 Ontario, Canada's richest province had taken in $300 million less in income taxes this

year and 'when this happens we get kicked in the arse,' explained [Finance Minister] Doody.

2 Phr *arse foremost*: backwards, hinder part before; *arse over bottom, arse over/before kettle*: head over heels.

T l69–65² I jumped in the motor boat an' got my engine goin' ass foremost, an' Jack chopped the tow-rope. P 148–65 I'd drive him arse over kettles if he started any trouble. C 66–13 He fell arse over kettle. C 71–96 [He turned] ass over bottom. 1974 PITTMAN 25 He leapt out onto the middle of the altar and bellowed a very merry Christmas and a happy new year to ye all before he went arse before kettle over the communion rail.

3 Comb **arse bag**: capacious underclothes; ~ **end**: back part; ~ **pocket**: back pocket.

P 167–67 In cold weather he always wears ass-bags. 1979 *Salt Water, Fresh Water* 17 'Cold,' he said. 'My God, cold, boy. I'll tell you how cold it was. The kettle would be on the front part of the stove boiling like crazy, and the tea pot on the ass end froze solid.' 1974 PITTMAN 28 He liked it here when he first arrived straight from college with his 'degree in his arse pocket,' as he'd heard someone put it. 1979 POTTLE 75 Just stick it in me arse pocket, boy.

arsed p ppl Cp PARTRIDGE ragged-arse adj.

Comb **flat-arsed**: of a tin kettle, with flat bottom and bevelled sides; cp PIPER.

T 50/1–64 [They] cook their fish an' boil their kettle—pipers, they call them—little flat-arsed tin kettles with a bib on 'em.

ragged-arsed: tattered; disreputable.

1973 PINSENT 18 Why this girl, with a car of her own. . .still wanted that ragged-arsed individual I wouldn't take time to figure out. P 245–80 Mr Smallwood used to refer to his Confederate supporters with rueful affection as 'the ragged-arsed artillery.'

article n *EDD* ~ sb. Term of mild admonition; used of a member of one's family, esp child or husband, when speaking to another person.

P 80–67 (Of misbehaving children:) The young articles! P 197–76 You're an article, you are! 1978 *Evening Telegram* 24 June, p. 14 That's why I never lets my article [i.e. small son] come down to bingo with me. I'd be ashamed of me life if he started airin' his knowledge. 1979 ibid 2 June, p. 20 'Oh well,' sez the woman, 'as that article is me husband I can't run him down too much.'

ash¹ n The balsam poplar (*Populus balsamifera*) (1956 ROULEAU 26).

ash² n *EDD* ~ sb¹ 2 (6) for sense 2 (b).

1 Phr *get/take ashes*: to attend Ash Wednesday service in which ashes are marked on the forehead of the communicant by the priest (P 245–77).

2 Comb **ash-cat**: (a) member of ship's gang which hauls ashes from the boiler-room and dumps them overboard (1925 *Dial Notes* v, 325); also attrib; (b) one who hugs the fireside.

1922 *Sat Ev Post* 195, 2 Sep, p. 123 [He was] emptying ashes overside as a member of the ash-cat gang. 1924 ENGLAND 137 Coal pounds on deck kept everything a black muck. Ashes blew everywhere, as the ash-cat gang tipped their long steel buckets over the red rail and pitched ashes hissing out on ice. C 75–137 An ash-cat is a person who is always cold; when outdoors he wears a lot of clothes and when inside sits by the stove.

ashore av On board (a vessel).

1922 *Sat Ev Post* 195, 2 Sep, p. 11 'Come ashore, all hands!' Up they swarmed. . . Up the ropes they hauled themselves, over the rail. 1924 ENGLAND 92 The word 'ashore' in Newfoundland ship talk mean[s] 'aboard.'

asquish a also **squish, squish-ways**. Cp *EDD* aswish adv 'aslant,' swish adv, adj¹ 'diagonally; awry.' Askew; out of alignment; in desperate straits.

[1900] 1978 *RLS* 8, p. 25 Squish—out of plumb, all askew. T 141/59–65² [I] had to put the shelf—had to take away the bracket—an' put un a little bit squish. P 219–68 A picture which is not hanging properly is squish. 1972 MURRAY 200 But with the roses all over [the wall-paper], if 'twas a little bit asquish, you wouldn't know it. P 148–74 Squish-ways: not fair, as the frame of a window. 1979 *Evening Telegram* 9 June, p. 17 With himself all exquish so signs I got a brand new shirt and drawers up in the bottom drawer if he stops his wind [and dies].

athwart prep also **adurt, athirt, atirt, thert**, etc [ə'ðəɹt, ðəɹt, ðəɹt͡ʃ] *EDD* ~ prep 4. Of motion, across; from one side of a place to the other.

[1794] 1968 THOMAS 97 From St Mary's Bay to Cape Chapeau Rouge (which are the two angles [of Placentia Bay]) is twelve Leagues athwart. 1895 *J A Folklore* viii, 35 Atert or atort, is the same as athwart, but it is used as equivalent to across. Thus they say 'atert the road,' or 'atort the harbor.' 1901 WILLSON 19 'Aweel, sor, ye're after being athwart the rudge,' he said. l937 DEVINE 7 He's gone *athirt* the bay. T l87–65 I thought about goin' thert the harbour after dinner.

august n Comb **august flower**: fall-dandelion (*Leontodon autumnalis*) (1898 *N S Inst Sci* ix, 375).

auk See OUK.

aunt n *EDD* ~ sb 1 Gl So D Co; *DAE* 1 (1801–61) for sense 1; cp UNCLE.

1 Title of an older woman, used with first or full name; general term of respect used of an older woman in the community.

1887 *Telegram Christmas No* 9 And Aunt Betsy, as the people called her, was a fitting match for her husband. [1915] 1972 GORDON 14 And here I ought to mention that such titles as Mr & Mrs are not favoured in Labrador, being replaced by the much more homely ones of Uncle and Aunt. l930 *Am Speech* vi, 57 ~ Applied to elderly persons by those not related to them. 1949 FITZGERALD 93 ~ All old people are thus addressed by their neighbours regardless of relationship. 1977 RUSSELL 104 Aunt Sophy [is] not one of these women that you can see how to shoot gulls through. She's what you might call a comfortable armful.

2 Phr *his aunt had he/she*: used in explanation of the appearance in a family of an illegitimate child (C 71–106).

auntsary[1] n also **ansary, aunt sarah, aunt sal-(ly), nan-cary, nan-sary** (*n* is from article *an*). [æn'sɛərɩ, næn'sɛərɩ] *DC* ~ (Nfld: 1770). Prob derived from *anseres*: cp *Cent* 'in the Linnean system (1766), the third order of birds, including all "water-birds."' For the relationships between Cartwright, the earliest authority for the word, and the scientists Banks and Pennant, see LYSAGHT *Joseph Banks in Newfoundland and Labrador* (1971), esp p. 448. Greater yellowlegs (*Totanus melanoleucas*), TWILLICK; other long-legged birds frequenting shore and streams: plover.

[1770] 1792 CARTWRIGHT i, 31 In the course of the day I shot three curlews, three grouse, and an auntsary. 1792 ibid *Gloss* i, ix ~ A bird of the wading genus, resembling a redshank. 1870 *Can Naturalist* v, 295 Provincial names of this bird are 'twillick,' 'twillet' and 'nansary'—the latter name more frequently in the south of the island. 1884 STEARNS 93 I shot a bird today that has a most peculiar name in the vocabulary of the natives; it is called by them the *Nan-cary*, pronounced as if spelt *nan-sary*; it is in fact the greater yellow legs. 1907 TOWNSEND 351 Greater Yellow-legs; Winter Yellow-legs; 'Auntsary.' 1959 MCATEE 31 Greater Yellow-legs. . .Aunt Sarah (In allusion to its copious and loud crying; corrupted to ansary, lansary, nansary, and other forms.) P 113–56 Nansary: a small bird of the plover family. 1963 TODD 316 'Auntsary'—a name that has persisted in popular usage in Labrador down to the present day.

auntsary[2] See HAND SERRY.

aw int *Labrador Inuit* (1976) aa 'stop!' Command to a dog-team to stop.

1907 WALLACE 192 Edmunds. . .almost never had to use the long walrus-hide whip. They obeyed him on the instant without hesitation—'Ooisht,' and they pulled in the harness as one; 'Aw,' and they stopped.

awful a Remarkable; exceptional.

T 141/60–65[2] The arms o' the seine would be light, but the [bunt], that'd be heavy. You want two awful men, the strongest men that was about, to heave it out. T 222–66 She said, 'He sent me an awful present.' I thought that's really looking a gift horse in the face until she said, 'He sent me six hens, and they was three dollars each. My, 'twas some good of him, wasn't it?'

B

babbage See BABBISH*.

babbish* n also **babbage, babeesh** *DC* babiche 'strips of leather. . .used for laces' [Micmac] (1806–). Strips of animal hide woven to form the filling of snowshoes; cp TIBBAGE.

[1886] LLOYD 78 The space outside the bars [of the snowshoe] are filled with more finely cut skin than the middle space, the Indian term for which is *tibeesh*, while the coarser filling of the middle space is called *babeesh*. 1897 *J A Folklore* x, 203 Babbage used to the northward to denote the plaiting of a snowshoe. P 202–65 Babish: strips of goat or deer skin for snowshoes. C 75–136 Babich: long, narrow strips of cow skin used to fill homemade snowshoes.

babby n *EDD* ~ sb 1 b (4) ~ house. Comb **babby-house**: pattern of bits of china arranged by children on ground to represent rooms in a house.

1968 DILLON 133 We'd be pickin' up chainies for the 'babby house.'

baccalao n also **bacalao, baccale, bacaleau, baccalo**, etc. *OED* bacalao (Nfld: 1555–), *O Sup*[2] bacalao (1749–), *DC* ~ n 1 (1555–), *DJE* baccalow (1889–1956) for sense 1; *DC* Baccalaos n 1 (1555–) for sense 2; SEARY 171–2 'from Span. *bacallao*— cod-fish, though early navigators thought it was of native Indian origin.'

1 Cod-fish, esp dried and salted cod; FISH.

[(c1504) 1971 SEARY 171 Y dos bacalhas.] [(1558) 1962 *The Cabot Voyages* 275 . . .a kind of fish which is found in the adjacent sea, which fish [the French] name Baccales.] [1622] PURCHAS xix, 300 Especially there is a great store of those fishes which they call commonly Bacallaos. [1765] 1954 INNIS 151 Of late years the consume of Newfoundland dry'd cod fish called Baccalao has [been] greatly lessened in this province (Catalina) by the fisheries of the same kind of fish that at present carried on with success on the coast of Norway and at Knall in Russia. [1779] 1792 CARTWRIGHT ii, 497 The ship has now on board seven hundred and fifty-eight tierces of salmon, and five hundred and thirty-four quintals of bacaleau, or dried codfish. [1841] 1855 *Lit & Hist Soc Que* iv, 30 In the annals of the town of Dieppe, in France, there is authentic evidence to show, that the inhabitants of that town did carry on Baccalo fisheries, on the coast of Newfoundland and before the year 1500.

2 In pl, name given to Newfoundland and adjacent regions by early European voyagers.

[(1530) 1962 *The Cabot Voyages* 269 [tr] . . .the Bacchalaos discovered by Cabot from England sixteen years ago.] [1555] ibid 277 These regions are cauled Terra Florida and Regio Baccalearum or Bacchallaos of the which yow may reade sumwhat in this booke in the vyage of the woorthy owlde man yet lyving Sebastiane Cabote. [1576] 1940 *Gilbert's Voyages & Enterprises* i, 143 So that this Currant, being continually maintained with such force, as Jacques Cartier affirmeth it to be, who mette with the same being at Baccalaos, as he sailed alongst the coastes of America. [1583] ibid ii, 404 [Hayes' narrative] That which we doe call the Newfound land, and the Frenchmen Bacalaos, is an Iland. 1672 [BLOME] 190 About this Banck lyes dispersed several smalle *Isles*, called by. . .*Sebastian Cabot* (the first discoverer) *Los Baccaloos*, or the Isles of *Cod-fish*. 1832 MCGREGOR i, 151 Cabot, by the most undoubted authority, discovered and landed on the coast several years before, took possession of this island, which he named Baccalaos. 1895 PROWSE 23 Foreigners called these countries [The Newe-founde-lande] by the generic name of the 'Baccalaos'—the land of dried-cod-fish.

baccalieu n also **bacalao** and other variants at BACCALAO. See SEARY 171 [Baccalieu Island, a nesting place for sea fowl and a landmark for mariners off Bay de Verde]. For comb in sense 2, cp *OED* bacalao b: ~ bird (Nfld: 1865), *DC* bac-calao bird (Nfld: 1819–).

1 In navigators' proverb: *wherever you are, steer north-west for Baccalieu.*

1866 WILSON 279 Few of the masters or skippers of ice-hunters knew anything of navigation. . . Their method for calculating for their return was carefully to note the point of their departure, and the direction in which the ice drifted. When practicable, they took their departure from Bacalieu. . .from which island they steered north-east for the ice; and as the northern ice usually drifts to the south-east, in returning, they were accustomed to steer north-west for the place of their departure. Hence it became a proverb: 'Wherever you are, steer north-west for Bacalieu.' [(1929) 1933 GREENLEAF (ed), 252 "Jack was Ev'ry Inch a Sailor": He was born on board his father's ship, as she was lying to / 'Bout twenty-five or thirty miles south-east of Bacalhao.]

2 Comb **baccalieu bird**: name given to several common sea-birds: (a) Atlantic common murre or TURR (*Uria aalge aalge*); (b) Atlantic common puffin (*Fratercula arctica arctica*).

1819 ANSPACH 297 This small island is remarkable for the extraordinary number of sea-fowls which nest and lay their eggs on its rugged sides and surfaces. These are generally called Baccalao birds. [1822] 1928 CORMACK 8 Baccalieu Island. . .is famous for the numbers of sea-fowl that frequent it in the breeding season, principally the puffin, called on this coast the Baccalao or Baccalieu bird. 1842 BONNYCASTLE i, 237 The Baccaloo, or as the sailors call it Baccaloo bird, now somewhat answers the same end as the auk, or penguin, which has disappeared. It is rarely seen beyond the banks, which it frequents. 1866 WILSON 31 Baccalao Island. . .is bluff, barren, and rocky, without inhabitants, save turs, the gulls, and other sea-birds, which. . .are generally called 'Baccalao birds' by the Newfoundlanders. 1876 HOWLEY 67 *Common Puffin*. . .well known on the eastern coast as the 'Baccalieu Bird.' 1960 TUCK 34 'Baccalieu' (or Baccalo) birds is a traditional name in Newfoundland for the murres nesting on Baccalieu Island, and is usually used only when the birds are in summer plumage. C 66–10 If you and I was out gunning, and we killed so many bac-

calieu birds. . . 1967 *Bk of Nfld* iii, 265 Even today, in Conception Bay, Puffins are sometimes called 'Baccalieu Birds.'

baccalieu skiff: small decked vessel or schooner used in the fishery off Baccalieu Island; SKIFF 2.

M 71–40 Fishermen of Winterton landed their catch in small schooners every two to three weeks. These small schooners were called Baccalieu skiffs and were approximately 30 tons.

baccy* See TOBACCO.

bachelor's button n *EDD* ~ 1 (3) for 'burdock' D. One of a number of wild flowers.

1898 *N S Inst Sci* ix, 373 ~ [Ox-eye daisy] (*Chrysanthemum leucanthemum*). 1937 DEVINE 7 ~ the campion flower or that of the burdock. 1956 ROULEAU 26 ~ [chamomile] (*Matricaria maritima*).

back[1] n [= shoulders and upper dorsal area of a human being]. Cp *OED* ~ 3: ~ load (1725–), *DAE* ~ load[1] (1806–) for literal sense.

Comb **back-burn**: amount carried on shoulders, esp a load of wood; BURN[2].

1937 DEVINE 7 ~ a backload of firewood. C 67–4 [legend] A man was put in the moon as a punishment for repeatedly cutting wood on Sunday, and was made to carry a back-burn of wood for the rest of time.

back-load: an exceptionally large amount.

T 44–64 They could see these salt water ducks and all they had to do was grab their gun and go and bring home a back-load of 'em. . . You'd have to travel twenty miles by foot with a back-load of clothes in preparation for the winter. P 148–66 You've got a back-load [of sandwiches] there.

back-turn: see **back-burn**; TURN.

P 148–64 A back-turn of trout [was brought home]. Q 67–37 A back-turn of wood is as much wood as you could carry on your back.

back[2] n

1 Portion of the chimney from foundation of the house to the roof-line.

1972 MURRAY 184 The big wide chimney. . .was built of rock to the roof. However, this part of the chimney was referred to as 'the back.' Only the part projecting on the roof, built of brick, was the 'chimbly.'

2 The coast or adjacent waters on the side of an island removed from the main settlement(s); the Gulf of St Lawrence. See BACK a: BACK SIDE. Cp FRONT.

1819 ANSPACH 75 Their destination was to the island of Ramea. . .on the back of Newfoundland to the south-west. 1836 [WIX][2] 45 Went off. . .two hours' sail to Clatters' Harbour, at the back of the Isle of Valen. 1924 ENGLAND 16 One or two ships usually go 'to the back,' which means into the Gulf of St Lawrence. The others all go 'to the front,' or northeast, into the Atlantic ice pack drifting down on the Labrador current. P 167–66 Let's go over to the back of the island berry picking.

3 Area inland from a harbour or settlement; IN, INSIDE.

1842 JUKES ii, 234 The Humber. . .flows from two large ponds on the eastern flank of the 'Long Range,' and about in the latitude, or, as they expressed it, at the back of Cow Head. M 68–4 There is a good timber supply 'in on the back,' that is, on the hills surrounding the place.

4 The perpendicular section of a 'cod-trap' opposite the doors (P 127–78).

5 Phr *back foremost*: with the back of something placed in front; confused, mixed up.

T 23–64 When he gets quite excited he says things back foremost. One day he had been sick. . .he drank a whole bottle of Mickley's Buxture—which is Buckley's Mixture. P 24–67 She put her hat on back foremos'. P 108–7l He's a proper tangler, he does everything back foremost. He's a bungler.

back on: back to back.

1966 FARIS 201 People even joke about the cessation of sexual activities during the busy fishing seasons and refer to the summer as the time of 'sleeping back-on.'

back a [= located at the rear of something] DC back-tilt Labr (1770–) for comb in sense 2.

1 Phr *no back doors about*: no hesitation or shyness in speaking out.

C 69–28 People get a big kick out of the story, in that Uncle Tom had no 'backdoors about it' at all, but came right out with it. P 148–70 There are no back doors about him.

2 Comb **back cove point** and other place-names.

1951 *Nfld & Lab Pilot* i, 202 A 2-fathom. . .shoal extends about half a cable offshore from Back Cove point.

back harbour: the innermost of adjacent coves; innermost part of an inlet, bay or harbour.

1854 [FEILD] 32–3 In the afternoon I walked over to the back harbour or bight [St Francis Hr]. P 245–57 ~ That part of the harbour behind the main body of water.

back house: room in 'outport' house leading off from the kitchen and used for storage, as an entranceway, etc; cp HOUSE 2.

[1886] LLOYD 76–7 There is a small 'back house' or 'porch' built on the warmest side of the hut, in which firewood is kept. 1893 *Christmas Greeting* 15 So we whipped him off the bars agin to give him dacent burial—tho' perhaps he didn't disarve it—an' we put him in the back house. 1979 COOPER 28 "Winter": Cold Winter's sun has set, and it is night, / And from the old 'back-house' a cheerful light / Falls on the door yard snows, and wood shed near.

back junk: see JUNK.

back kitchen: see **back house**.

1979 TIZZARD 25 [I recall him building] a second storey over the back kitchen. . . This house in which I matured, measured seventeen by twenty four feet and the back kitchen part attached to it measured fourteen by sixteen feet.

back shore: innermost part of a harbour.

[1775] 1792 CARTWRIGHT ii, 115 I put some traps out for foxes, on the back-shore. 1972 NEMEC 83 [They] fish the shoals. . .off the eastern shoreline ('Back Shore') past Cape Pine into Trepassey Bay.

back side: see **back shore**.

[1663] 1963 YONGE [facing p. 81] Back side [at Ferryland]. 1858 [LOWELL] i, 138 'Sh' went right round the corner o' the house, an' down to—back part o' the place, here—' ''Is; Backside, sir, we calls it,' says a neighbor. 1953 *Nfld & Lab Pilot* ii, 127 Backside cove is entered around 1¼ miles south-westward of Southern head.

back stock: the wooden part of a shotgun, held to the shoulder when firing.

T 164–65 They picked up their guns. Some of 'em had their back-stocks broke and more of 'em didn't. T 190–65 If you was to step over the back-stock of a gun, oh my, you'd have to step right back again, backwards without turning around.

back tilt: temporary shelter in woods set up with sloping roof towards the wind and with a fire in front; a shelter or 'tilt' with back part only; BOUGH TILT.

[1770] 1792 CARTWRIGHT i, 58 We did not go far up the brook, before we constructed a back-tilt; we made a good fire in front, and passed the night there. 1792 ibid *Gloss* i, xvi A Back-tilt is a shed made of boughs, resembling the section of a roof; the back part is placed towards the wind, and a fire is generally made in the front. 1863 MORETON 80 Their only shelter for night was a shed, such as is called a back-tilt, made of a punt's sail strained along the ground on one side, and supported at an angle of about forty-five degrees from the ground by stakes. The ends are walled in with boughs, and the whole front is open; whence its name, being a back shelter only.

back av Comb **back weight**: in valuing seal 'pelts,' the number of pounds deducted from the total weight for the worthless flesh attached.

1924 ENGLAND 170 They may grouse a bit concerning the low price of fat and the extortion of 'tare,' or 'back weight,' for adherent flesh that sticks to the fat; that is always reckoned as sticking to it, no matter how clean they peel the sculps. T 84–64 The biggest one went 380—the pelt. Pelt weighed 380 pounds, clear of back weight, and back weight was fourteen pound.

backing vbl n Comb **backing-line**: long line to which a creeper is attached, threaded under the ice to retrieve seal-nets.

1861 DE BOILIEU 107 A series of holes are made in a direct line over the nets, at about twenty feet apart, say for near half-a-mile. When this is done, two long poles, tied together, are put into the first hole, and, as it were, are threaded from one hole to the other. At one end of the poles is a line called a backing-line; and at the extreme end—say where the whole length of line has been passed under the ice—a creeper or small species of anchor is let down and trailed over the nets.

bad a Phr *be not bad like*: to resemble; to be similar to.

P 133–58 ~ very much like. P 60–64 He's not bad like

his father. P 108–76 That's not bad like the carpet in Mary's dining-room.

bad scran: see SCRAN.

badness n Phr *for badness*: with mischievous intent; for devilment.

1947 TANNER ii, 712 'Just for badness,' as [the Labrador trapper] says. T 100/2–64 He'll tell that story so true, for badness, that the other feller would believe it. T 325–66 Fellers dressed up and frighten 'em. They used to do that for devilment. It was badness they used to do that for. C 71–28 [She] told me that if I stepped on a beetle we would have rain. Sometimes I would step on one for badness just to see the consequences. 1975 LEYTON 33 [He'd do it] just for devilment that's all, just for badness.

baff v Cp *EDD* ~ v¹ 'to beat, strike' Sc. To wear out by repeated use.

P 148–61 This road is baffed out. P 171–65 These files are all baffed out.

bag n *Fisheries of U S* i, 144 for sense 1.

1 A net in which cod-fish are kept in the water temporarily until they can be loaded on boat or towed ashore; COD²: COD-BAG.

[1856] 1977 WHITELEY 37 Carpenter on his first visit to the Labrador in 1856 described how the [cod] seine would be pulled to make a 'bag' of fish and then be moored, 'the modus operandi' is simply for the boats to anchor on either side of the bag. . .draw it up, fastening the ends to the thole pins of both boats and then pitch out the cod. 1898 GRENFELL 68 Large bags of net are produced and filled with the rest of the fish. These, after being buoyed, are thrown overboard to wait till they are 'wanted.' 1936 SMITH 25 When we arrived in the harbour then men with the cod seine had their boat loaded and two bags of fish moored on the west side of the Island. C 71–90 'Dad and them got the bag on' was a common and joyous remark when I went to school. P 9–73 Cod-trap fishermen carry bags of about a four-inch mesh size. In case of [catching] more than a skiff-load, including the load of the punt, the fish is put in a bag and the bag is tied fast to a mooring of the trap until next time around.

2 Part of cod-trap in which fish are contained when the trap is hauled.

T 141/67–65² He hauled up the doors, and we with the best part o' the bag o' the trap up, and took eighty barrels out of un.

bag v also **bag off, bag up**. In the inshore fishery, to moor cod in a net shaped like a bag until fish are brought ashore.

1895 GRENFELL 71 Now the weighted foot rope is 'gathered' together, the net has become one vast bag, and the prisoners are dealt with as before, i.e. dipped out and bagged off. 1925 *Dial Notes* v, 325 ~ To keep (fish) overnight in a bag. 1936 SMITH 124 Next morning, August 6th, we went out to the trap and secured another 25 quintals; we dipped in a load and bagged the remainder. P 148–63 Bag up the fish on Sunday. 1966 FARIS 221 It is occasionally the case (as when the fish 'strike') that a trap may have up to 80 quintals in it.

In such case, the trap boat is filled, and up to 25 or 30 quintals are 'bagged off'—that is, put into a large net bag which is tied to the trap and left until the boat can come back and collect the fish. M 70–29 'Bagged off'—when the trap is hauled and there are too many fish to carry in the skiff. A net in the shape of a bag is sewn onto the trap and the fish swim into it. The bag is then tied and the fish towed to the place where they are split.

baiser n Epithet for a large trout; whopper.

1896 *J A Folklore* ix, 36 ~ applied by boys fishing to a large trout. 'Oh, that's a *baiser*.'

bait n also ~ **fish**. Cp *OED* ~ sb¹ 1 b 'worms, fish, etc' [used in angling] (1496–1799), *O Sup²* ~ fish (1820–), *Fisheries of U S* i, 182–6 for sense 1; for comb in sense 3: *Fisheries of U S* i, 127 ~ board; *DAE* ~ knife (1857).

1 Caplin, herring, lance, squid and other sea creatures, formerly including birds, used in fishing for cod with baited hooks.

1620 WHITBOURNE 9 The Fishermen doe bait their hookes with the quarters of Sea-fowle on them: and therewith some ships do yeerely take a great part of their fishing voyages, with such bait, before they can get them. [1663] 1963 YONGE 60 They have divers kinds of bait. In the beginning of the year they use mussels, then come herrings and generally last all the year. The middle or end of June [come] the capling, a small sweet fish and the best bait. . . After the capling come the squids. [1693] 1793 REEVES ii–iii No alien or stranger whatsoever. . . shall at any time hereafter take any bait, or use any sort of trade or fishing whatsoever in Newfoundland. [1766] 1971 BANKS 123 Glams. . .of Peculiar use in the fishery as the fishermen depend upon them for their Baitts in their first Voyage to the Banks. [1774] 1792 CARTWRIGHT ii, 19 A skiff and six hands went to the Cape to try for baits, but they could not meet with any. [1889] 1897 *Nfld Law Reports* 379 That defendants, on or about the 8th of July last, did purchase, at or near cape St Mary's, a part of this Colony, a certain quantity of bait fishes, that is to say, caplin, for the purpose of exportation for bait purposes. [1930] 1980 *Evening Telegram* 29 Sep, p. 6 At Burgeo yesterday some boats using clams for bait secured from a quarter to half quintal of codfish. A few squid were secured at Francois and all boats are out fishing today. [1952] 1965 PEACOCK (ed) i, 143 "Skipper Tom": And down o'er the bank I steered 'er so straight, / With a whipping fine breeze and a tub of fresh bait. 1979 NEMEC 237 In late spring or early summer [the cod] shifts its habitat to the surface zone where it feeds on small 'baitfish,' such as caplin, herring, mackerel, launce and squid. 1979 *Salt Water, Fresh Water* 41 So you go out in the mornings and cut your squid for bait—a squid can make four good baits.

2 A small amount over and above quantity purchased; a present; TILLY.

P 148–63 ~ something extra given to purchaser. 1971 NOSEWORTHY 169 ~ A free gift presented to the first buyer.

3 Attrib, comb, cpd **bait bird**: sea-bird feeding on 'bait-fish' in inshore waters.

1966 SCAMMELL 130 "The Joe Batt's Arm Bully": In the summer with the trawl, with the hand-lines in the fall, / Her youthful captain ranges, braving all the weather's brunt / From Round Head to the Rock, and where the bait-birds flock / In his Joe Batt's Arm bully and the Change Island punt.

bait board: triangular piece of wood with two raised edges, used to cut up herring, squid, etc.

T 50/2–64 [We'd have] a piece o' board, bait board they call it. Take up your squid and cut it up. M 68–7 It was a pleasant sight when father began to wash the bait board, because then I knew he was going in.

bait boat: craft engaged in catching caplin, herring, squid, etc, for use as bait; BAITER.

1765 WILLIAMS 19 For the Shoremen that catch the Bait [—] Bait Boat, with Sails and sundry Materials. [1909] 1930 COAKER 4 We believe there is room for the use of motors in connection with the fisheries such as in bait boats, for supplying caplin, squid, and herring for bait, or to bait depots.

bait box: container for bait used in trawl fishing.

T 436–65 I washed un overboard in my bait box—washed out the old bait was in the box in the evenin' when I was comin' in. M 68–7 The bait box was just a common box about two feet long and one foot wide. There was a line from one end to the other for carrying purposes. 1979 TIZZARD 285 A fisherman always carried a bait box in his boat. The bait box we carried was usually a XXX Soda biscuit tin.

bait chopper: broad-bladed knife for chopping bait-fish into pieces.

1975 BUTLER 47 We said first thing we're gonna do was get that canvas chopped away. . . I got a axe and he got a big bait chopper and we used to go down under water and chop and hack as long as we could.

bait depot: facility where iced or frozen bait is stored for distribution to fishermen.

[1909] 1930 COAKER 4 [quot at **bait boat** above]. [1953] 1978 *Evening Telegram* 1 Aug, p. 5 The bait depot at Grand Bank has a good supply of caplin bait.

bait hauler: fisherman engaged in catching caplin, herring, etc, for use as bait on a 'banker.' See also HAUL v.

1975 LEYTON 102 Before Confederation [the Nova Scotia vessels] weren't allowed to take any bait in Newfoundland themselves. They hired what they called a Bait Hauler. Now Mr Lake next door, he used to be a seine man, a Bait Hauler, had his own seine net; and I'd go with him, go haul bait.

bait horn: large spiral sea-shell, blown into to announce the arrival inshore of caplin, squid, etc; CONCH.

1905 DUNCAN 113 "Tis the bait horn, Eleazar!'

bait jack: wooden tub or quarter barrel to hold bait, etc.

1942 *Grand Bank U C School* 34 He puts the liver into a baitjack. T 453/4–67 He had what was called [a] bait jack—about quarter of a barrel, sawed off, full of cod liver in the midshiproom of a small boat. 1971 NOSEWORTHY 170 ~ One quarter of a flour barrel with two *straps*, or rope handles, attached and used for storing bait.

bait knife: see **bait chopper** above.

1966 SCAMMELL 92 'Must be one of those whales,' shouted father. 'I suppose he has a turn of the rope around his tail. Stand by to cut it if it don't come clear. Here, Cecil, pass the bait knife along.' C 69–5 I can recall my father's reaction when he'd see the bait knife edge-up on the gangboards.

bait locker: covered section in bow of an undecked fishing boat; cp LOCKER (P 245–67).

bait (seine) master: man in charge of boat and nets sent from a 'banker' to secure bait (P 127–76).

1937 *Seafisheries of Nfld* 105 Each Schooner-Master must be an experienced fisherman, and bait-seine-master.

bait punt: see **bait boat** above, **baitskiff** below, and PUNT.

1976 *Decks Awash* v (5), p. 9 It was a regular chore to go in the 'bait punt.' This meant six or eight men rowing to Bonaventure Head, a distance of 8–10 miles, to haul caplin and return with the load for the fishermen to bait their trawls.

bait shed: storage place for bait on fishing premises.

T 270–66 We had flakes right along there. Our plantation used to reach from that store right over to the end o' that bait shed. That's the bait shed what they keeps their bait in now.

baitskiff: large undecked boat with 5 to 7 crewmen, propelled by oar and sail and employed to catch caplin, etc, for use in the cod-fishery; see SKIFF; also attrib.

[1770] 1792 CARTWRIGHT i, 24 Early in the morning, I took Charles and Ned with me, and sailed for Chateau in our baitskiff. 1836 [WIX]² 45 Went off on a bitter cold morning, in a bait skiff, two hours' sail to Clatters' Harbour, at the back of the Isle of Valen. 1895 *Christmas Review* 18 It was meant as the highest tribute to the boat-building capabilities of Jim Leary, whose handiwork, whether displayed in the construction of baitskiff, smack, skiff, punt or rodney, was always superior to what any other man in the settlement could turn out. 1912 DUNCAN 139–40 Well, I went down t' Jimmie Lot's stage, where the bait-skiff horn was kept, and fetched it back. 'Twas a conch shell, with a hole in it: so that if a man knowed how t'use lips an' lungs on it he could blow a blast that would wake the harbour. In the caplin season, when they uses them little fish for bait, the folk take turns at mannin' the skiff. 'Tis the bait-skiff conch that calls un t' put out; an' 'tis the bait-skiff conch that warns the harbour that the skiff is back with the bait. 1966 SCAMMELL 76 Ah, there it was, the baitskiff, just rounding the head. He could see the heap of seine-linnet in the stern of the punt that was being towed behind.

bait squadron: patrol vessels engaged in enforcement of the Newfoundland Bait Act of 1888 prohibiting the taking of bait-fish by foreign fishing vessels or unauthorized provision of bait to such vessels.

1906 *Nfld Qtly* Dec, p. 14 At one time I was district Judge, police-magistrate, by statute also police-inspector, Chairman of the Board of Health, surrogate of the

Admiralty Court, president of the Royal Marine Court of Enquiry, and, to crown all, they appointed me [Judge Prowse] Naval Commander of the Bait Squadron!

bait tub: see **bait jack** above; TUB.
[1888] 1976 *Evening Telegram* 5 Jan, p. 6 In one of those moments of peril one of the men flung over the second bait-tub which again distracted the creature's attention. 1955 DOYLE (ed) 14 "Bill Wiseman": Oh Bill rode out one morning / Just at the break of day; / He said he was sure of his bait-tub of squid / Up here in Hiscock Bay.

bait v Cp *OED* ~ v[1] 9 b (1753 quot), *Fisheries of U S* i, 185 for sense 2.
  1 In the 'bank fishery,' to supply a vessel with caplin, herring and squid for use in trawl-fishing for cod; of a vessel, to take on a supply of bait.
[1929] 1979 *Evening Telegram* 10 July, p. 26 Seventeen bankers baited at Cape Broyle yesterday and 20 more are baiting there today. Caplin are in abundance. 1960 FUDGE 4 Seining for herring to bait the French and American Vessels made up the greatest trade up until about the year 1880 [at Belleoram]. M 68–16 Everyone was baiting vessels at that time, so we never got back. P 143–74 When these [foreign] vessels were sighted, Cape Broyle fishermen raced in their motor-boats to the ships. The first man to reach each vessel 'baited it.'
  2 In fishing with trawl lines, to place bait on the hooks in preparation for setting, esp in phr *bait out/up*.
1960 FUDGE 18 'Boys, there have been fish caught here, so bait up and we will spend the day here.' We dropped our anchor and caught about four hundred quintals on our small baiting. P 148–64 [We were] down baiting up (i.e. baiting trawls with squid for the next day's fishing). M 67–10 After this first day, the night-setters will get their bait in the mornings and haul and 'bait out' their trawl as they did the first morning. 1971 CHIARAMONTE 40 Normally both men would have had equal say as to where they were going to fish, if they should 'bait up,' and whether or not they should go out.

baiter n A boat engaged in catching caplin, herring and squid for use as bait in the cod-fishery on the offshore fishing grounds; BAIT n: BAIT BOAT.
1887 HOWLEY *MS Reminiscences* 3 We steamed in amongst a crowd of bankers and baiters which literally filled the harbour.

baiting n Cp *DAE* ~ vbl n[2] 'the laying in of a supply of bait' (1881) for sense 1; *Fisheries of U S* i, 183–6 for both senses 1 and 2. See CAPLIN, HERRING, SPRING, SQUID for comb with *baiting*, which is also freq preceded by *fresh, frozen* or *first, second, third* in both senses.
  1 A quantity of caplin, herring, or squid taken aboard a 'banker' at one time for use as bait in trawl-fishing.
1895 PROWSE 478 Their full complement for their

first baiting on herring amounts to fifty-four thousand barrels. [1930] 1980 *Evening Telegram* 9 July, p. 6 Squid put in an appearance at Holyrood yesterday and bankers are expected to arrive there for baitings in a day or two. [1959] 1965 PEACOCK (ed) i, 138 "Labrador": It was on a Monday morning we got her under way, / All to look for a baiting down in Conception Bay, / We understood in Burin, we took our bait in there, / And when we arrived to Holyrood twenty thousand was our share. 1960 FUDGE 10 We secured a baiting from the netters there, and in a short while were anchored on the fishing grounds. Ibid 17 On May 20th, 1913, we took our first baiting at Great Harbour, Conniger Bay, and sailed for the Banks.
  2 A fishing voyage to the Banks, the duration fixed by the supply of bait aboard the vessel.
1960 FUDGE 11 We used all our bait in five days and caught for that baiting 180 quintals of fine cod fish. Ibid 11 We anchored on the bank close to where we fished on our previous baiting. With God's help we filled our little vessel to the hatches and made tracks again for home. M 70–27 The names of our trips [to the Banks] were as follows: the frozen baiting, fished mostly on the Western Banks and Rose Blanche Banks. . .

bake [= nose] See BEAK.

bakeapple n also **baked apple, bake(d) apple berry** [bɛɪkˈæpḷ, ˈbɛɪkapḷ, ˈbɛɪkæpḷ]. *DC* ~ (Nfld: 1775–), baked-apple berry (Nfld: 1818–). See BAKING APPLE, BOG-APPLE.
  1 A low plant growing in bogs and producing an amber berry in late summer; cloudberry (*Rubus chamaemorus*).
1792 CARTWRIGHT *Gloss* i, ix Baked Apples. The fruit of a plant so called. 1858 [LOWELL] i, 94 The sweet flower of the bake-apple, and other pretty things grow quietly upon this ground, which is scarce habitable for man. 1863 HIND [ii], 145 In favourable seasons the country is covered with many varieties of berry-bearing shrubs. . .and the bake-apple. 1902 DELABARRE 169 The bake-apple or cloudberry. . .grows thickly as far north as Hebron, but very thinly beyond. 1915 SOUTHCOTT 13 ~ Stem simple, 2 to 3 leaved, 1-flowered. Leaves 5-lobed, serrate wrinkled. Petals white. Fruit amber colored. 1916 HAWKES 35 Chief among the berries is the baked-apple (aˊkpik), also called the cloudberry. Its four-petalled white blossoms are seen covering the hillsides and swamps almost as soon as the snow is gone. 1924 ENGLAND 268 Large areas of the Vikings' land, amid pale horizons under gray skies, are just rocks, skinned over with a spongy tundra of moss where only partridge berries and baked-apple berries grow, where only caribou and ptarmigan thrive. T 175/6–65 The middle part of the island was all marsh, all bakeapples, and marsh berries, too, in the fall.
  2 The succulent amber fruit of the cloudberry, resembling a raspberry, gathered in late summer and eaten raw or cooked; also attrib.
[1775] 1792 CARTWRIGHT ii, 96 I saw the first baked apples. [1778] ibid 360 After dinner I went with all my family to Slink Point, where we picked a bowl full of baked apples. 1792 ibid *Gloss* i, ix Baked Apples. The

fruit of a plant so called, from the similarity of taste to that of the pulp of a roasted apple. 1818 CHAPPELL 138 The dry moss is variegated by innumerable clusters of. . .what is called, by the fishermen, the *baked-appleberry*. This last fruit abounds in LABRADOR. 1887 *Telegram Christmas No 5* . . .bowls of bake-apple and redberry preserve. 1947 TANNER 740 From about the middle of August the women and children are engaged in berry-picking, especially bake-apples. . .and plumboy. T 198–65 I seen places on the Labrador I was able to pick thousands of gallons of bakeapples, as far as your eye could see, in level ground, kind of a bog. 1974 PINSENT 77 They had their refreshments, which included tea-buns and bakeapple jam.

bake-pot n   also **baking-pot**. A cast-iron utensil of various sizes, used for cooking and baking.
1842 JUKES i, 20–1 The bake-pot was put in requi- sition this morning for our service, and a lot of little cakes made by our hostess for breakfast, at which she gave us also some fresh herrings. 1863 MORETON 51 [She called out] 'My gracious, girls, I forgot the loaf. Julia, go out to the next house and hang on the bake- pot.' [1870] 1973 KELLY 22 The house, or rather hut, turf-covered, with its smoke blackened rafters and open chimney, with the ever simmering kettle and bake-pot hanging over the fire of pine logs. . . 1888 HOWLEY *MS Reminiscences* 47 [We found] notches cut in the logs for various purposes, two good bakepots, a wooden dish, a pile of otter boards upon which were written with chalk or coal from the fire the names of various hunting parties who had lodged here. 1895 *Christmas Review* 9 It did not take long for these hardy fishermen to bring the bakepot and kettle from their boat, and to refresh themselves with a good meal of tea, fish, and bread. Ibid 12 [proverb] 'Up sail and down bakepot.' (The women feasting after the men have sailed away.) 1960 *Evening Telegram* 11 Aug, p. 7 The iron bake pots for baking bread, the tongs, an important item for placing live coals on the covers of the bake pots when bread was baking to give it even heat on top as well as underneath. . . T 172/3–65 In my poor grandfather's day, they had a baking pot. They make a good fire and get a lot of coals and put the cover on their pot. Put their bread in the pot and the pot on the coals. 1973 BARBOUR 73 We started out in one of the largest motor boats. We were well-supplied with cooking utensils, such as frying pan, iron bake pot, large saucepan, and a kettle, of course. 1975 GUY 96 There were rabbits in the bakepot and turrs in the oven.

baker n
Comb **baker's fog**: disparaging term for com- mercially produced bread (P 148–62). Cp FOB.
1972 MURRAY 219 Most of the menfolk refer to 'baker's bread' as 'baker's fog.' They prefer the more substantial homemade variety.
baker's loaf: name for rock or hill shaped like a 'bun' of bread; cp SUGAR-LOAF.
1953 *Nfld & Lab Pilot* ii, 102 Bakers loaf a remarka- ble peak, 546 feet high, dominates the northern side of North-West arm.

baking apple n   *DC* ~ (1771). Cloudberry; BAKEAPPLE.
[1771] 1935 *Can Hist Rev* xvi, 57 The land about is very woody. . .with some currants, raspberry, hurt 2 sorts, Partridge berrys, cranberrys, heathberrys and baking apples; both the latter are plenty all over the coast.

bald coot n   Sea duck; surf scoter (*Melanitta perspicillata*).
1870 *Can Naturalist* v, 302 Provincial names [of the surf duck are] 'Bottle-nosed diver' and 'Bald coot.' 1959 MCATEE 17 ~ Surf Scoter (The forehead and nape of the adult male are white.)

ball n
Comb **ball gun**: muzzle-loading weapon charged with power and ball.
T 29–64 He took his ball gun and hove un up 'cross the boat and he put the muzzle to the head o' the seal and ripped the ball through him.
ball mould: hollow form in which balls of lead are cast for use in muzzle-loading weapons and as weights for fish-nets; CAST-NET MOULD.
T 66/7–64 You'd have your ball-mould and you'd make your balls in the mould and drop it in the water; fill up the mould again, drop it into the water. Q 73–2 ~ used for making cast-net balls and gun balls. The inside of the mould was coated with chalk before each ball was run. This prevented the molten lead from clinging to the mould.

ballast n   Cp *OED* ~ sb 1 'gravel, sand, stones. . .placed in the hold of a ship' [for stability] for both senses 1 and 2. In sense 1, for the (accidental) ingestion of inorganic material, see the voracious feeding habits of cod in LEIM & SCOTT, pp. 197–8, and the ingestion of shell-fish in the 1766 quot; for the fisherman's weather sign developed from this, see MOORE *Anglo-Manx Dialect* (1924), p. 96, describing a cod-fish with gravel in its stomach as 'expecting a gale an' tak- ing in ballas',' and cp PLINY the Elder (A.D. 23–79) *Naturalis Historia* ix, 100 [Loeb tr] 'It is said that [sea-urchins] can forecast a rough sea and that they take the precaution of clutching stones and steadying their mobility by the weight [and] when sailors see them doing this they at once secure their vessel with more anchors.'
1 Stones, pebbles, sand, etc, (reputed to be) found in the stomach of fish, esp cod; the inges- tion of such material as a weather sign.
[1766 BANKS 123 A ship Came into harbour from which I Procurd specimens of a shell fish calld here Glams of Peculiar use in the fishery as the fishermen depend upon them for their Baitts in their first Voyage to the Banks at that time of the Year the fish feed upon them & Every fish they take has a number of them in his Stomach which the Fishermen take out & with them Bait for others.] [1794] 1968 THOMAS 173–4 A Codd has been haul'd in and when open'd a Stone has been found in him a pound in weight and sometimes more.

They are frequently catched with Stones in them. Whenever this is the case it is a sure indication of an approaching storm, as the Fish swallow the Stone for Ballast to enable them the better to encounter the jarring elements. [c1874] 1904 *Daily News* 10 June Arrah, shure your Lordship with all your larnin' ought to know that a salmon TAKES IN BALLAST, the sensible 'craythures,' when a gale is risin'. 1937 DEVINE 69 When the codfish take in ballast—small pebbles—in the stomach, 'look out for a storm.' [Ibid When caplin eat sand they are weighting their bodies and preparing for heavy seas.] [P 127–80 Placentia Bay fishermen forecast a storm if they find small pebbles or sand in a codfish. There is bad weather ahead if star fish are found to be grasping or holding on to stones when they are pulled up on trawl hooks.] P 188–80 Yes, we often find sand and rocks in 'em. The old fellers used to say 'twas ballast—the fish'd take on ballast before a storm. How big [are the stones]? Sometimes they're as big as a greengage.

2 Large rocks placed within the framework of a wharf and serving as a foundation for the upright posts; also attrib; see POUND, SUNKEN WHARF.

P 102–60 Near the mouth of the river was a large ballast wharf forty feet wide and a hundred feet long on which every spring was built a large splitting shed. Q 67–104 ~ bed—foundation of rock for stage and flake. Q 71–16 It is called a ballast bed—rocks piled into the place where the piles are driven into the ground. This keeps the wharf from being washed away. 1977 *Evening Telegram* 24 Jan, p. 2 A ballast pound—a structure of large rocks built up to add support to the wharf—was also lost [in the storm]. 1979 TIZZARD 342 I began to take apart the old wharf before it fell down on its own. I first threw the ballast out and then began to take the old wharf sticks apart.

4 Comb **ballast locker**: compartment in fishing-boat in which rocks are placed to provide stability.

1887 *Colonist Christmas No* 17 John Costello has moored his boat near that of a neighbor, with whom he is chatting; Dan—now a fine lad of seventeen—being engaged, meanwhile, in getting dinner on the ballast-locker. T 50/3–64 Small rocks—[I] placed 'em all in the midshiproom, ballast locker, an' took the few fish an' spread all over the rocks.

ballast v also **ballas, ballish***. To throw rocks or other missiles (at a person or object); BAZZ v.

P 270–66 He ballased the house [with rocks]. C 69–19 With handfuls of sand we proceeded to ballast the horse-stinger till it was knocked down. C 71–91 To balish someone means [to throw] snowballs or stones at him. C 71–117 As children we would throw a milk can or bottle in the water and ballish it with rocks, drive it off from the landwash.

ballicatter n, usu pl. Variants chronologically arranged: **ballicadoes, ballacarda, ballicater, balacadas, ballicaders, belly-carders, ballicatters, ballycatters, belly-catter, ballycadders, ballacarters, ballycater, ballaclauters, ballacaters, balla-** catters, **ballacader**; ['bɛlɪkæʈəɹ, 'bɛlɪkæʈəɹ, 'bælɪkeiʈəɹ, 'bælɪkɑːɹʈəɹ, 'bæləkɑːɹʈəɹ]. *Note*: Besides the printed forms noted above, there are manifold variants reported as single words, out of context, so that the usage actually employed by informants is often difficult to ascertain. A selection of these forms is as follows: **ballacattle, ballicabber, ballicanter, balliclamper, belliclumper** [see CLUMPER], **balliclatter, ballicutter, billicatter, cattibatter.** *DC* ballacater Nfld (1906–). See also BARRICADO, BARRICADE v, the prob source for the variants above.

1 Ice formed by the action in winter of spray and waves along the shore-line, making a fringe or band on the landward side.

1863 MORETON 29 Ballicadoes. Barricades. The banks of ice which form upon all water-washed rocks and shores in winter. 1896 *J A Folklore* ix, 36 Ballacarda—ice along the foot of a cliff touching the water. [c1900] 1978 *RLS* 8, p. 24 Ballicadre—ice formed along the fringe of the shore, or piled along the sides of a vessel. [1916] 1972 GORDON 59 Such ice-ledges, of which there are several around this district, are known by the people as 'Ballicatters,' which I imagine is a corrupted form of Barricades. The name applies also to the ice-fringe that remains glued to the edge of the shore when the bay ice breaks up and clears out to sea. 1955 ENGLISH 32 Ballycater—ice formed by spray on the shore. T 75/6–64 He landed him on Fogo Head, landed him on the ballacarter there. P 130–67 Bellycadder. A heavy shelf of ice along the shore caused by the rising and falling of the tide. 1971 NOSEWORTHY 170 Ballycatters or bellycatters. Ice on shore and rocks from waves and salt spray. C 71–129 Ballycarter. Ice around the shore-line. Usually it refers to ice around wharfs, stages and ballast beds. The ballycarter remains around the shore-line after the harbour or cove is ice-free in the spring. I also heard it used to describe [iced-up] rocks or headlands where hunters went to shoot sea birds. 1975 *Evening Telegram* 21 May, p. 6 On this day we decided to stay from school because we awoke to a silvery world of 'glitter'—the trees looked like silver filigree and the sand dunes which reached from the sea up, looked like the highway to heaven and all the beach was one shining 'ballacader.'

2 A narrow band of ice formed in winter in the salt water along the foreshore or 'landwash'; SHORE[1]: ~ ICE; large slabs, chunks and fragments of this ice after break-up.

1906 LUMSDEN 61 The rocks were covered with ice, and the shore was bespread with large pans of ice, high and dry—in local phraseology, 'balacadas.' 1924 ENGLAND 96 Instinct, for these animals [bears], seems faulty. Nature obviously does not warn them of the dangers of venturing out beyond the 'ballycatters,' or shore ice. 1931 *Am Speech* vi, 290 Belly-catter. Ice barricade: i.e. rough ice in ridges along the shore. 1949 FITZGERALD 93 Ballacarters. Ice rafted up on the fore-shore. P 114–66 He slipped on a ballyclamper, and fell in the water. 1973 BARBOUR 38 Ballacatters—this is what Newfoundlanders call the rafted pans of ice on the foreshore, unmoved by the ebb and flow of the tide.

3 A floating ice-pan.

1909 BROWNE 183 Hundreds of men were standing on the 'ballicaders' with their ropes and gaffs all in readiness. 1961 *Nfld Qtly* Spring, p. 43 It is sixty years since I lugged that old portmanteau over the ballaclauters up Clode Sound Reach and on and on. P 43–66 The boat struck a ballycanter. C 68–4 When the ice starts to break up into pans you'll see the youngsters 'ferrying.' Each one gets on a pan of ice (the old people call them belly-caters). 1976 *Daily News* 2 Mar, p. 3 Jumpin' clumpers was another favourite pasttime. In some places they call it copying on bellycaters. . . All it means is jumping from one ice pan to another without falling into the water.

4 Frozen moisture around the nose and mouth; cp BALLICATTER v.

1896 *J A Folklore* ix, 36 Ballacarda—ice about the face.

ballicatter v   also **ballicader** [baltˈkatəɹ]. See BALLICATTER n. To cover with a layer of ice.

[c1900] 1978 *RLS* 8, p. 24 A vessel or the shore is said to be ballicadered when this fringe of frozen ice attaches to her. T 31/2–64 My face was frore, my collars was frore and everything was ballicattered. . . I couldn't hear her now, way I was muffled up, 'cause I was ballicattered up—I was frore up.

ballroom n   Jocular name for crew's quarters on a sealing vessel.

1916 MURPHY 11 The 'ballroom,' so called, where the majority of the crews slept, was for-ard of the main hatch or hold of the ship. 1933 GREENE 40 The bulk of the crew were provided with double berths rigged-up in the Tween-decks over the ballast tanks of the Main Hold. The 'Ballroom' was the Forecastle, where on some ships the Masters of Watches and Engineers had their berths. C 71–94 "Preparations for the Seal Fishery": The 12th of March is drawing nigh / So we must all prepare / Our coffee pots and panikins / A sealer's life to share / And in the ballroom build the bunks. 1972 SANGER 235 ~ Forecastle of a sealing vessel used to accommodate a portion of the extra men hired on for the sealing voyage.

bam n   also **bom**. *EDD* ~ sb¹ 2. A false tale intended to deceive or hoax.

1903 *Daily News* 24 Feb "Ned the Trickster": She was picking plums and cherries / To be bought by Misther Ned, / But she's feeling now disgusted, / For she saw it was a bam. 1937 DEVINE 7 ~ a false tale, to parody or ridicule a person or sacred ceremony. 1971 NOSEWORTHY 168 A bom of a lie—a bad lie.

bang See VANG.

bangbelly n   Cp *N & Q* ([1914] 1940) 22 June, p. 434 W. A pudding, cake or pancake, originally prepared by fishermen and men in the woods, made with flour, fat pork, etc, and boiled, baked or fried, now usu served as dessert; also attrib.

1896 *J A Folklore* ix, 35 ~ a low and coarse word

denoting a boiled pudding consisting of flour, molasses, soda, etc, and not uncommonly seal-fat instead of suet. 1937 DEVINE 7 Bangbellies. Pancakes made of flour, fat and molasses, fried on a pan. 1939 DULEY 17 In the winter the stomach was frequently filled with the bulk of pea-soup floating with fat white bang-bellies. [1894–1929] [1960 BURKE] (ed White) 41 "McGinnis at the Rink": And his bullseyes were plastered all over his face / Like the whorts in a bang-belly pie. T 96–64² You can make up the bangbelly with bread soda and flour, mix it together and fat pork in it, cut it into squares; it's lovely. C 69–10 To make bangbelly you put blueberries, sugar and hot water in a pot and add a pinch of salt. When it begins to boil you drop in dough-balls and let it continue boiling until the doughballs are cooked and the blueberries are thick. Serve it hot. 1973 BARBOUR 47 [Tea] consisted of a slice of molasses bread, raisin buns, pork toutons, or bang-belly.

banger n   Cp JOYCE 213 bang-up 'frieze overcoat.' An overcoat.

1968 DILLON 313 Put on your banger.

bank n   *OED* ~ sb¹ 5 (1605–), *DAE* n¹ 1 (1635–), *DC* ~ n¹ 1 (Nfld: 1584–), banks 2 (Nfld: 1622–) for sense 1; *OED* sb¹ 2 obs (1325–1420), *EDD* sb¹ 1 for sense 2; for combs. in sense 3: *DAE* ~ cod (1814–), *OED* ~ fish (Nfld: 1666), *O Sup²* ~ fisherman (1782), ~ fishery (Nfld: 1777), ~ fishing (1797), *DC* ~ herring (Nfld: 1883). For New England background and parallels see also *Fisheries of U S* i, 123–33, 148–87.

1 An undersea elevation or area of shoal water with abundant bait-fish, plankton, etc, where fishing is successfully carried out; sometimes with specific designation GRAND, GREAT, NEWFOUNDLAND, OFFER a, WESTERN, etc; freq pl. Cp GROUND.

[1583] 1940 *Gilbert's Voyages & Enterprises* ii, 397–8 [Hayes' narrative] Before we come to Newfound land about 50 leagues on this side, we passe the banke, which are high grounds rising within the sea and under water, yet deepe enough and without danger, being commonly not lesse than 23 and 30 fadome water upon them. . . A man shall know without sounding when he is upon the banke, by the incredible multitude of sea foule hovering over the same, to pray upon the offalles & garbish of fish throwen out by fishermen, and floting upon the sea. 1612 *Willoughby Papers* [Guy's narrative] November 1 Word was broughte that theare was noe harborough, but a sandie banke for a league of a gray colour [with] not fower fadome [of] water. [1663] 1963 YONGE 54 These islands of ice infest the coast in the beginning of February, and last till June and sometimes later. They are caused by the ice breaking out of the northwest passage, which grounding on the banks, do there accumulate and by the snow and rain increase.[1693] 1793 REEVES xvi Now in order to promote these great and important purposes, and with a view, in the first place, to induce his Majesty's subjects to proceed early from the ports of *Great Britain* to the banks of *Newfoundland*, and thereby prosecute the fishery on the said banks. . . [1715] 1976 HEAD 73 This has been but lately experimented, I think last year was the first of it, that the sending of these small shalloways, sloops and other kind of vessels to the Banks for fish, and when loading is caught to come in and cure them. [1770] ibid 168 [They sailed] with Caplain for the shoals [and returned] from the Banks, or rather the Shoals with 27 [thousand] fish amongst them. [1831–9] 1926 AUDUBON 231 They all depart at once, and either by rowing or sailing, reach the banks to which the fishes are known to resort. 1842 BONNYCASTLE ii, 171 Had Newfoundland possessed a vigorous maritime population at the close of the last general war. . .we should not now see the fishery on the banks employing only a dozen or so of small island or British vessels, where a thousand formerly rode in triumph. 1933 *Nfld Royal Commission Report* 96 The Bank fishery is conducted on the Grand Bank of Newfoundland, 50–300 miles to the south-east of the Island; and on Green Bank, St Pierre Bank, Banquereau, Sable Island, Misaine and St Anne Banks. 1951 *Nfld & Lab Pilot* i, 313 Other shoals, with depths of from 6 to 9 fathoms over them, the position of which can be seen on the chart, lie between the Bank and the coast northward. [1952] 1965 PEACOCK (ed) i, 108 "The Banks of Newfoundland": The springtime of the year is come, / Once more we must away, / Out on the stormy Banks to go / In quest of fish to stay.

2 Hill, high ground or elevated 'barren'; also cpd **bank-berry.**
    [1941] 1974 BRIDLE (ed) i, 350 A raised plateau, locally known as 'The Berry Bank,' lies between the westerly end of Goose Bay and the Hamilton River. Approach in the past has been chiefly by a footpath, used for generations of berry-pickers, who frequent the bank in the fall of the year to pick cranberries. 1956 ROULEAU 26 Bank-berry: *Vaccinium macrocarpon.*

3 Attrib, comb **bank cable**: heavy 2 in. (5.1 cm) rope used aboard vessels engaged in the offshore trawl fishery (P 113–55); BANKING CABLE.

bank cod: cod-fish population frequenting offshore fishing grounds.
    1832 MCGREGOR i, 118 The bank cod (which I will take upon me to class gadus bancus) frequents the great bank of Newfoundland, and other banks at a great distance from land.

bank fish: see **bank cod**; FISH.
    [c1600] 1954 INNIS 47 [They] brought their bancke fishe, which they tooke on the bancke forty or three score leagues from Newfoundlandland. 1765 WILLIAMS 5 But from the Bank Fish you have but a small Quantity. . .which will be 645 Tuns of Train Oil. 1842 BONNYCASTLE i, 264 In this town the bank-fish, or those caught on the banks, are supposed to be superior in quality to the shore-fish, or those caught near the coast. 1969 HORWOOD 174 All the bank fish was made by the women—every cod's tail—and a hundred women might share $1,000 between them.

bank fisherman: one who engages in the cod-fishery on the offshore fishing grounds; BANKER.
    1895 GRENFELL 81 The average catch per head for 'bank' fishermen last year was 47½ quintals.

bank fishery: cod-fishery prosecuted in vessels,

or in dories carried by vessels, on the offshore fishing grounds.
    1813 CARSON 17 The frequent wars in which Great Britain has been engaged, have, by endangering, destroyed the Bank fishery; a very small proportion of the fishery carried on upon these shores, belongs to adventurers. 1839 TUCKER 80 The *Bank Fishery* is carried on in vessels generally from 60 to 100 tons burthen and manned with eight or ten men each. [1892] 1896 *Consolidated Statutes of Nfld* 257 The term 'Bank fishery' in this chapter shall be construed to mean a fishery prosecuted at a distance of at least forty miles from the coast of this colony. 1939 LODGE 50 The cod-fishery falls into three divisions. The first in point of time is the deep sea 'Bank' fishery begun in the early spring. 1975 BUTLER 65 In 1880 he outfitted two vessels for the bank fishery carrying six dories and fourteen men each.

bank fishing: fishing for cod on the offshore grounds, usu with trawls or hook and line.
    1611 GUY 414 . . .falling in the reckoning as well of the commoditie that they may make by the banke fishing, as by husbandry of the Land, besides the ordinary fishing. 1785 SHEFFIELD 92 Neither the bank fishing, nor the in-shore, or boat fishing, will admit of any other but salt provisions. 1888 *Colonist Christmas No* 19 He has lately gone largely into the bank-fishing business, and has been very successful. 1960 FUDGE 8 Fitted with four dories and single hand-lining, we went to the West Coast of the Labrador. With great disappointment I was obliged to forget the bank fishing industry for the time.

bank herring: variety of herring frequenting offshore grounds; see also HERRING.
    1883 HATTON & HARVEY 324 There are two varieties of herring taken on the shores of the island—the Bank (called also the Labrador) herring, and the Shore herring. . .the Bank being the full-grown fish, and measuring on an average thirteen and a half inches.

bank hook: type of fish-hook used in hand-line fishery for cod offshore.
    [1751–66] 1954 INNIS 181 [inventory] To 3 Dozen Bank hooks for Giggers 8s.

bank line: type of stout line or rope used in the deep-sea fishery.
    T 50/2–64 Trawl line is a big line. Bank lines is bigger again—fifty fathoms. The bankers use it. They'd be all put together—go to what they call a trawl knot; never slip. P 9–73 The ends of the doorways [of the cod-trap] are brought to like this on a bank line.

bank man: (a)see **bank fisherman**; (b) vessel prosecuting the offshore cod-fishery; BANKER.
    1907 MILLAIS 156 How many of the missing bankmen meet their end in this way can only be conjectured, but certain it is that far more are sunk than are reported to the world. 1911 MCGRATH 131 The 'bankmen' are all crewed by picked fishermen.

bank ship: see **bank man** (b); BANKING VESSEL.
    [1612] GUY 52 This night by sayling & rowing we came to Harbor de Grace, as farre in as the Pirates forte, wheare the banke shippe roade.

bank weather: damp, foggy weather.

1842 BONNYCASTLE i, 353 In 1841, there were only seventeen days and a half of thick fog at St John's, which is more exposed to the bank weather, as it is called, than any other part of the island.

banker n *OED* ~³ 1 (1666–1769), *DAE* ~¹ 1 (1704–1880), *DC* (Nfld: 1777–) for sense 1; *DAE* 1 b (1861–), *DC* 2 (Nfld: 1907–) for sense 2.

1 A vessel engaged in cod-fishing on the New-foundland offshore grounds, esp the Grand Banks.

[1749] 1755 DOUGLASS i, 292 In Newfoundland they reckon. . .200 quintals to the inhabitants boat or shal-lop, and 500 quintals to a banker. [1777] 1792 CARTWRIGHT ii, 233 The Americans had taken his Majesty's frigate *Fox* and several bankers upon the banks of Newfoundland. [1794] 1968 THOMAS 104 I afterwards gave this Garment to a Fisherman who went out on a Banker to Fish on the Grand Banks. 1832 MCGREGOR i, 226 The bankers, or vessels fishing on the banks, usually anchor where they find plenty of cod, which they catch with lines and hooks, or occa-sionally with jiggers. 1907 MILLAIS 150 During the summer the men [of the South Coast] fish, mostly in 'bankers,' off the coast. [1929] 1979 *Evening Telegram* 10 July, p. 26 Seventeen bankers baited at Cape Broyle yesterday and 20 more are baiting there today. 1933 *Nfld Royal Commission Report* 97 The fishery is con-ducted from Newfoundland by schooners of up to 150 tons, known as 'Bankers,' carrying a complement of 20–24 men and 10–12 dories. T 411–67 We call them the bankers. We've seen as high as twenty or thirty come to get ice. We would help them to take the ice out o' the ice-house and load the dories to be carried aboard the bankers. 1969 HORWOOD 174 'We didn't always have this Sunday-morning look, though,' a retired merchant confessed, 'not when we had nineteen bankers sailing out of [Grand Bank] harbour.'

2 A fisherman engaged in the offshore or 'bank' fishery.

[1794] 1968 THOMAS 174 A Banker is not a little proud of his Dog at Sea. [1839] 1916 *Nfld Law Reports* 27 The jury find that in the year 1826 the insolvents carried on business to a pretty considerable extent. . .the supplies so obtained by them were applied entirely and exclusively to the supply of bank-ers and boat-keepers, from whom they received fish in payment. 1933 GREENLEAF xxxv On the southeast coast live the 'Bankers,' who evidently have a store of chanteys as yet unrecorded. 1947 TANNER ii, 753 The floaters differentiate between the so-called Labrador-men, who fish exclusively on the coast of Labrador, and Bankers, who fish chiefly on the great fishing banks outside Newfoundland, and in the autumn make a trip to Labrador to increase their catch. T 50/2–64 [The trawl lines are] baited in the boat and then they're sot—slapped overboard, one at a time. The bankers can do it with a gaff—flick them out as fast as time. M 68–16 When the bankers used to come to Cape Broyle looking for bait, they would rent out the parish hall and have a dance.

3 The owner or operator of an offshore fishing vessel.

1979 NEMEC 254 Also prominent in the settlement

were fishery suppliers (merchants or their agents), the doctor, planters, telegraph operators, [and] 'bankers' (large vessel operators).

banking vbl n *OED* ~ vbl sb 4 (1842, 1848), *DC* n¹ (1824–) for sense 1.

1 Fishing for cod on the Newfoundland off-shore 'grounds' or shoals, esp the Grand Banks and other stretches of water off the south coast.

[1794] 1968 THOMAS 168 The [function] of the Admi-ral is very great if he goes to Sea a Banking, he having Command of all the Vessels which are employ'd on the Grand Bank a Fishing. 1937 *Seafisheries of Nfld* 34 The Deep Sea Fishery is a distinct contrast to the Shore Fishery. The fishing is usually done many miles from the Coast and a return to the land is made when the catch of fish is sufficient, or other circumstances make it necessary. This fishery is known as 'Banking.' 1971 NOSEWORTHY 11–12 There were a few spasmodic attempts at 'Banking' from Grand Bank in the 1860s and '70s but the business got its real start in 1881.

2 Attrib, comb **banking account**: financial bal-ance sheet of a deep-sea fishing enterprise.

1939 LODGE 51 It is not astonishing that when the Commission of Government had had an opportunity of investigating for themselves actual 'banking' accounts they shied at this incursion into State socialism.

banking anchor: type of ship's anchor used aboard a deep-sea fishing vessel.

Q 67–53 ~ it has a wooden stock fitted into a dia-mond-shaped hole so the anchor is sometimes called a diamond-eyed anchor. If the anchor gets caught the stock will break and the boat will be free.

banking cable: heavy 2 in. (5.1 cm) rope used aboard vessels engaged in the offshore trawl fishery; BANK CABLE.

1936 SMITH 36 We loaded freight about half for Bri-gus and the balance for Harbour Grace, comprised chiefly of rope, butter and banking cables, of which we had six on deck.

banking dory: small flat-bottomed boat with flaring sides and a sharp bow and stern, provid-ing both stability in the water and easy stowage in stacks on the deck of a deep-sea fishing vessel, used esp in fishing with hand-lines and trawls; DORY.

1971 NOSEWORTHY 170 ~ A type of dory used on the Grand Banks, from 15 to 18 feet in the bottom. 1975 RUSSELL 1 Must have been almost thirty years ago. I was just a young gaffer then—spending my third or fourth summer in the bow of the banking dory.

banking fleet: a number of **banking vessels** (see below).

1975 BUTLER 56 Dories were not used until the ban-kin' fleet. . .came about 1875 or so.

banking line: see **banking cable**; BANK LINE.

C 70–26 A young lad somehow got his neck tangled in a length of banking line.

banking outfit: fishing gear and supplies appro-priate to a vessel engaged in the offshore cod-fishery; cp FIT-OUT.

1936 SMITH 36 Capt Harry Bartlett. . .was going on

the Banks fishing in their schooner. . .which was then lying at Cupids and bound for St John's to take in his banking outfit.

banking schooner: see **banking vessel**.

[1892] 1896 *Consolidated Statutes of Nfld* 256 The owner of each banking schooner or vessel prosecuting the bank fishery. . . 1971 NOSEWORTHY 12 The average Banking schooner was eighty to one hundred twenty feet in length and carried ten dories and twenty-four men. [The catch] was split and salted on board the vessel, and was washed in the harbour upon arrival in Grand Bank.

banking vessel: deep-sea fishing craft, decked and rigged fore-and-aft or powered by engine, prosecuting the cod-fishery on the offshore 'grounds' with hand-lines and trawls operated from small open boats or 'dories.'

[1788] 1895 PROWSE 347 Under colour of the said Banking vessels taking their fish from hence when cured to be reshipped on board larger size vessels. . . [1891] 1897 *Nfld Law Reports* 580 The impression said to be prevalent that masters of banking vessels in this trade possess unlimited authority to pledge the credit of their ship-owners or out-fitters for general supplies. . . 1975 BUTLER 50 I will explain. . .the types of fishing boats used for fishing through the years including banking vessels, coastal vessels and foreign-going vessels.

banking voyage: the enterprise or period of fishing for cod on the offshore 'grounds' or 'banks'; cp BAITING, VOYAGE.

[1880] 1898 *Nfld Law Reports* 201 [The] plaintiff says he is short credited by reason of only being allowed the one-twenty-eighth part of the produce of a banking voyage in place of one-twenty-sixth.

banquese ice n Cp HARRAP *banquise* 'ice-floe.' Ice field floating south along the Labrador Coast in spring; STRING OF ICE.

1884 STEARNS 231 One of the peculiarities of a Labrador spring scene is that of drifting or 'banquese' ice. This is ice that breaks up in some northern locality, and flows, in greater or smaller masses, through the Straits towards the Gulf and open sea. . . The 'banquese' ice often lies a mile or so off shore.

bar[1] n DC ~ harbo(u)r for comb in sense 4.

1 Either of two wooden strips fastened horizontally within the oval 'bow' of a snowshoe to strengthen the frame.

[1886] LLOYD 78 The bars, of which there are two, are fitted within the bow, in order to strengthen it, and are placed about five inches from either end of the snow-shoe.

2 Wooden or metal strip forming part of the frame of a sled.

T 175/7–65 The bars went across, and a knee on both sides [of the horse slide] to keep it in position, upright. Q 67–72 ~ part of bob-sleigh which is attached to the runners by castings.

3 A net used to catch or 'bar' migrating fish.

1895 GRENFELL 125–6 'The river is not barred. It

couldn't be barred. No nets would hold against it.' It appears he was just off to destroy his 'bar.'

4 Comb **bar harbour**, ~ **haven**: bay or harbour protected, or sometimes with the entrance obstructed, by a sand-bar or shingle beach; cp BARACHOIS.

1837 BLUNT 47 The coast. . .forms a circular bay, in which the shore generally is low, with several sandy beaches, behind which are bar-harbours, fit only for boats, of which the principal is Great Garnish. 1865 *Sailing Directions* 52 The head of the bay is terminated by a low beach behind which is a large pond, or bar-harbour, fit only for boats. 1951 *Nfld & Lab Pilot* i, 161 Two peninsulas extend from the south-eastern side of [Bar Haven], the south-western of which is connected with the island by a low neck, and the northern by a narrow shingle beach near the middle.

bar-net: vertical net extending out from 'cod-trap' to obstruct passage of cod and lead them into the trap; LEADER (P 245–67).

bar tackle: rope used to constrict a 'cod-trap' when filled with fish.

M 68–16 Another rope called the bar tackle runs from the back to the leader. It is used to haul the back of the trap, bringing the front and back closer together, and bringing about a greater concentration of fish.

bar[2] n See BARLEY OVER and its variants. Home base in a game of hide-and-seek.

T 199–65 Then when he opens his eyes, there's a certain point, the bar where he starts off from, and when he's out lookin' for you, if you can sneak back there and touch it and say, 'One, two, three, the bar is free!' well, you're free. Bar over, we used to call it. C 68–21 The place where you had to 'blind' was called the bar and the object of the game was for the hidden team to get to the bar before the other team had a chance to find them.

bar[3] See BARROW[1].

bar v Cp *Fisheries of U S* i, 448 for sense 2.

1 To set the mechanism of an animal trap.

[1772] 1792 CARTWRIGHT i, 219 I visited all the traps, four of which I found robbed, and fresh tailed and barred them.

2 To place a net in a river, estuary or bay in order to trap fish.

1867 *Journ of Assembly* Appendix, p. 719 From 1000 to 1500 barrels [of herring] could be barred in a few minutes. 1870 *Stewart's Qtly* iv, 147 There is a perceptible decrease in the quantity of salmon taken yearly in Newfoundland, and that the size of the fish is declining. . . It is the natural consequence of *barring* the brooks and rivers, when the fish are about to ascend them to spawn. 1881 *Nineteenth Century* ix, 107 The rivers are persistently barred and the salmon fisheries destroyed. 1895 GRENFELL 125–6 The river is not barred. It couldn't be barred. No nets would hold against it. 1946 MACKAY (ed) 349 The American fishermen had been guilty of three distinct breaches of the Newfoundland fishery regulations: first, they had used the forbidden seine nets; second, they had 'barred' during the prohibited season; third, they had 'barred' on a Sunday, a day on which fishing was illegal.

barachois n also **barrachois, barrisois**. *DC* ~ (N B: 1760–); HARRAP ~ 'sand-bar.' For occurrence in place-names, see SEARY 48, 173–4; even in places officially named *Barachois*, the local pronunciation may be BARASWAY. A shallow river estuary, lagoon or harbour, of fresh or salt water, sheltered from the sea by a sand-bar or low strip of land; POND 2; cp COSH.

[1778 DE CASSINI 139 The fishing vessels [at St Pierre] are very safe in a pretty large *Barachois*, which answers the purpose of a harbour. What they call here *Barachois*, is a little pond near the sea, and only separated from it by a bank of pebbles.] 1842 BONNYCASTLE i, 219 Eight miles up the great Barrisois, (a corruption of Barachois, a boat-river, in the French Newfoundland dialect) near St George's Bay. . . [1873] 1971 SEARY 173 Big Barachois. 1885 KENNEDY 154 A fine salmon-river winds through the valley [near Branch] irrigating a considerable extent of land, and forcing its way by a narrow 'barachois' (a narrow gorge) to the sea. 1966 HORWOOD 120 At the end of the harborless Reach where a tiny sandspit formed a pocket-sized *barachois*. . . 1971 NOSEWORTHY 172 Barrisway (spelled 'barachois')—a large brackish-water pond opening into the sea.

barasway n also **barrasway, barrisway, barrysway** ['bærɪswɛɪ, 'baːɪswɛɪ] *DC* barrasway (Nfld: 1842–); *Glossaire*: barachois [barɑʃwe]; MASSIGNON i, 123. For occurrence in place-names, see SEARY 48, 173–4. See BARACHOIS.

1 A sand-bar.
[1766] 1976 HEAD 161 The harbor [of Grand Bank] was formed by a bay-mouth bar (a 'Barrysway' or *barrachois*, from the French), 'over which Boats can go at a [quarter] flood.'

2 A shallow river estuary, lagoon or harbour of fresh or salt water, sheltered from the sea by a sand-bar or low strip of land; cp COSH.
[1773] 1971 SEARY 48, 173 The name appears to be first recorded in Newfoundland by Lane in 1773 as G[reat] Barrysway and L[ittle] Barrysway, now BIG and LITTLE BARACHOIS (NTS Placentia), and presents an interesting example of a French name reverting to its French form after having been anglicized. 1823–4 *Edin Phil J* x, 158 There is coal of a good quality in St George's Bay, about eight miles from the sea-coast, up the South Barrasway River. 1842 JUKES i, 89 There was a shallow salt lake at the back of the harbour that filled at the rise of the tide, and was called by the people a Barrasway. This is a very common term for a shallow marshy inlet or salt lake along the south coast of Newfoundland. 1878 *Nfld Pilot* 126 Barasway point, the west point of Barasw023 bay, is a low promontory extending seaward from the slope of Father Hughes hill. 1933 GREENE 185 . . .her d'at kapes de store at wan o' d'em Barrisways. 1937 DEVINE 7 Barrasway. A small harbour where small boats may shelter, enclosed, except the shoal narrow entrance, by a sand bar. 1950 PARKER 19 The French name, Barachois, was fre-

quently given to a wide shallow river with a sandy bar across its mouth which is found in many parts of the country; it is now usually pronounced and sometimes written Barasway. 1971 NOSEWORTHY 1–2 The coast embraces a circular bay in which the shore is low with several sandy beaches, behind which are brackish water ponds, or 'barrisways,' good only for small boats.

barbarous a Bad or atrocious in quality or condition.
1924 ENGLAND 187 With our 'barbarous' coal it might take hours to get steam again. T 34–64 I seed one woman when I was in [hospital] last year and the poor woman was barbarous—she used to be in misery.

barbel See BARVEL.

barber n *O Sup*[2] ~ sb 1 c (1830–) for sense 2; *DC* n 1, 2 obs (1829–1869). See also LUBBOCK 325 (1836 Hull quot.).

1 Cold mist or vapour arising from the sea on a frosty day; frost-smoke.
1836 [WIX][2] 60 There was a great deal of thin slob ice, and the 'barber' vapor was very cutting. 'Barber' [is] a vapour of ice particles, occasioned by the temperature of the water being much warmer than the air, the caloric escaping from it forms a congealed atmosphere. 1896 *Dial Notes* i, 377 ~ the vapor rising from the water on a frosty day. 1937 DEVINE 7 ~ White fume or smoke arising from the surface of the water of the Harbour or the Bay, on a very frosty day in Winter after sunrise. P 112–57 ~ vapour off water in early morning after a cold night.

2 A sharp, stinging wind.
1879 TUCKER 62 During the heavy gales of last week people were afraid to put their faces out of their dwellings—and the Newfoundland 'barber' was never so severe. 1895 *J A Folklore* viii, 37 A very sharp, cutting wind driving small particles of ice, which strike the face in a painful manner, is expressively called a *barber*.

bare-legged a Phr *bare-legged cup of tea*: black tea offered without food; cp CUP OF TEA.
P 229–66 I'm havin' a cup of bare-legged tea. P 148–72 That's only a bare-leggèd cup of tea!

barge n Cp *Fisheries of U S* i, 138. In the Strait of Belle Isle and on the Labrador, a large boat serving as an ancillary craft in the fishery from schooners; a craft used to collect, hold and process the catch.
1856 *Trans Lit & Hist Soc of Quebec* iv, 337 American schooners coming to fish carry several of these [barges], and at the close of the season willingly sell them to the fishermen. 1860 *Atlantic Mo* vi, 443, 445 [We secured] a substantial fishing-barge, laden rather heavily in the stern with at least a cord of cod-seine, but manned by six stalwart men. . . That heavy codseine, a hundred fathoms long, sank the stern of our barge rather deeply, and made it row heavily. [1886 GREGORY 54 La morue se pêche à la ligne dans des barges.] 1888 STEARNS 181 The large ones you see,

anchored out there in the water, are the barges.
P 102–60 Twenty miles west of Blanc Sablon it was all
hook and line fishermen using a boat what they called a
barge, carrying two men with two spruce oars, about 12
to 15 feet, two spars with a mainsail and foresail and
jib. A barge looked like an English life boat, sharp at
both ends. 1979 *Evening Telegram* 21 Apr, p. 47 The
Provincial Department of Fisheries is inviting propos-
als from interested parties for operation of the barge
'Labrador No. 1' during the coming fishing season in
the Smokey area of coastal Labrador. The Barge had
been utilized in the past years as a floating salt fish
plant but it could be used as a fresh fish handling
and/or holding facility.

bargoo* See BURGOO.

bark n Cp *OED* ~ sb[1] 1 b 'rind of trees used as
material in tanning' (1565–1716); *DAE* n[1] (1694
quot); ~ tub (1662).
1 Liquid made by steeping the bark and 'buds'
of conifers to preserve fish-nets, sails, etc.
[1832] 1981 *Them Days* vi (3), p. 40 Let the two large
boats downe on their sides in order to trim them
tomorrow and got the pots in order to begin boiling
bark. [1886] LLOYD 55 [When the hair of the skins has
been removed] the denuded skins are treated to a
pickle bath over night, whence they are removed and
placed in a preparation of bark. They remain in the
bark for a week, and finally are dried in the sun. 1895 *J
A Folklore* viii, 36 The word *bark*. . .is only used as a
noun to denote the tan which the fisherman applies to
his net and sails, and as a verb to denote such an application of it. Thus he will say, 'I have been getting some
juniper or black spruce *rind* to make tan *bark*.'
T 141/67–65 You'd heave in your buds and you'd boil
them for three hours, and you dip off that bark then.
T 172/5–65 When the bark was strong enough, you'd
put your linnet into the puncheons and dip the bark out
o' the pot and put it in the puncheons.
2 Comb **bark boiling**: preparation of a preservative for nets, sails, etc, from the bark and buds
of spruce or fir trees.
1966 SCAMMELL 37 Sid nodded. 'Ours is too,' Bert
said. 'Finished bark boiling last week.' M 69–7 Another
important activity in this season was bark boiling. Here
cod traps and nets were pushed into large pots of boiling bark water that rested over open fires. The nets
were allowed to stay in the bark for perhaps half an
hour. They were then pulled out, placed on hand bars
and carried along to fences or rocks where they were
spread out to dry.
bark pot: iron cauldron in which an infusion of
'bark' is prepared; TAN POT.
[1952] 1965 PEACOCK (ed) i, 130 "For the Fish We
Must Prepare": Oh tar-mops and bark-pots, / And
fishin' caplin to the rocks. T 50/1–64 He gaffled a big
bark pot, an iron bark pot for boiling bark in, for the
twine. T 172/5–65 We had a 60-gallon bark pot. You
had to pick those buds off of the tops [of the trees] and
put those buds into this bark pot, and when he'd boil,
and that steep out, that was the way you barked your
trap. 1967 *Bk of Nfld* iv, 241 The bark pots were huge
iron pots for barking and tanning linnet. Q 67–13

[riddle] 'Four legs up cold as stone / Two legs down
flesh and bone / The head of the living and the mouth
of the dead / Tell me the riddle and I'll go to bed.' This
riddle referred to a man walking with a bark pot on his
head.
bark tub: wooden container in which nets,
sails, etc, are immersed in an infusion of conifer
'buds' as a preservative (P 148–61).

bark v *OED* ~ v[2] 2 'to steep in an infusion of
bark; to tan' (1865 quot). To immerse a fish-net,
sail, etc, in the liquid formed by boiling the bark
and buds of a conifer, as a preservative; DIP v 3.
1895 *J A Folklore* viii, 36 [A fisherman will say] 'I
have been *barking* my net or sails'. 1908 TOWNSEND 34
The nets like the sails are 'barked' a terra-cotta red.
1924 ENGLAND 264 He might see. . .a group of big-
booted, canvas-jacketed men 'barking' a sail—which is
to say, boiling it with spruce in a huge kettle. 1937
DEVINE 7 ~ To soak nets and seines or sails in tan
made from rinds of trees. T 141/67–65[2] Nowadays that
bud pickin' has gone out. Years ago we used to be at it,
of course, when we had linnet to bark. To bark an ordinary trap you wants two barrels o' buds. 1966
SCAMMELL 105 "Tommy Decker's Venture": We've
been barkin' now since Monday, but we got a berth all
right, / 'Cos we put a fleet o' codnets on a shoal just in
the bight. M 68–16 When the trap has been mended, it
must be barked. The trap is boiled to help preserve the
twine. Usually two large oil drums are set up in a fire-
place on the beach. Bark is dumped into each drum
and then they are filled with salt water. Then the fire is
lit and the mixture is boiled. The different parts of the
trap are put into large 'punchins' and the bark poured
over them. When each punchin is filled, they are covered with a sawed-off punchin and allowed to work for
a day or so. The trap is then taken and spread on the
wharf to dry. 1969 *Christmas Mumming in Nfld* 64 [The
sealskins] are worth so much now that few are 'barked'
for sealskin boots even though these are desired items.
1977 BURSEY 79 Then the cod-traps must be repaired
and barked to be ready to be put into the water before
the fish would 'strike in.'

barked p ppl also pronounced *bark*. Cp *OED* ~
ppl a 2 'tanned' obs (1430–1800).
1 Preserved by immersion in the liquid steeped
from conifer bark and 'buds'.
1895 PROWSE 404 The fishermen's clothing [in the
early nineteenth century] was made commonly of whitney and barked swanskin. P 148–63 Barked canvas.
T 141/68–65[2] The planters' schooners always had
barked sails down here. 1966 SCAMMELL 36 Sid began
filling the needle with the barked cotton twine
[already] balled off. 1975 POCIUS 56 'Barked brin' was
commonly used for the [dark brown] 'ground' of the
mat.
2 Comb **bark(ed) boot**: fine boot made from
sealskin tanned in a liquid steeped from conifer
bark.
T 389–67[1] That would be a real dress-up in the early
days. 'Twould be a pair of these bark boots. You get
'em skinned and barked, and fellers'd tan them.

They'd be a reddish colour, and you'd have a pair of short rubbers over them.

bark(ed) sail loaf: brown bread; cp LOAF.

M 70–21 A kind of bread made with molasses for colouring but containing no raisins was termed barksail loaf.

barking vbl n   *OED* ~ vbl sb² 1 (1865 quot).

1 Immersing nets, sails, etc, in the liquid steeped from the bark and buds of conifers, as a preservative.

T 141/67–65² The next thing that would turn up would be getting your barking done, your linnet barked. 1966 FARIS 139 Traps are not set until late June, but there is plenty to keep the sharemen busy—'barking,' putting in trap bottoms and general preparation. 1974 SQUIRE 17 The process called barking consisted of putting the nets and traps into huge vats. Usually these were made from rum and molasses puncheons. These containers were then filled with a solution that consisted of spruce buds and bark boiled in water for several hours in a large cast-iron or sometimes a copper pot. The dark mixture contained small amounts of myrrh and turpentine derived from the buds and bark and helped preserve the twines from the mildew and the corrosive effect of the sea water.

2 Comb **barking kettle**: large iron cauldron in which an infusion of conifer bark and buds is prepared; BARK POT.

[1842] 1944 *Yuletide Bells* They wandered past the Barking Kettle and saw a few fishermen mend and bark their nets. 1933 GREENE 46 Many of their docks and slips are still in use; while others can yet be seen, placed near to the 'barking-kettles' for the nets in many a harbour and cove. 1969 HORWOOD 144–5 On a hill above Bauline stands the huge black barking kettle. . . In spring they fill it with a tarry mixture (it used to be bark from the forests), light a fire underneath, and, while the aromatic smoke and steam drift down over the village, whole trap crews cure their nets, steeping them section by section in the hot liquid to ward off attacks by airborne fungi, bacteria, and marine organisms.

barley over int also **barl over***, **bar over***, **barrelover**. Cp *EDD* barley int 'cry for truce in a game'; *OED* barley-break 'Prisoner's Bar' [catching game] (1557–1837); I. & P. OPIE *Lore and Language of Schoolchildren* (1959), p. 150. See BAR² n. In a game similar to hide-and-seek, cry uttered by the blindfolded player as he uncovers his eyes and begins to search; the game itself.

T 169/206–65¹ Barl over was a game where one feller went blind, and he counted up to a certain number while everyone was hiding. His aim would be to try to hunt out all those that hid. T 199–65 The boys'd be playing bar over. . . If everybody gets home free, he has to do it all over again. Bar over we used to call it. 1967 *Bk of Nfld* iv, 242 . . .time lost from studies. . .playing so much 'scout' and 'barrelover' and engaging in other non-productive activities. M 68–21

Of course we played hide-and-go-seek. We called it bar-over.

barm n   [bæəɹm, baəɹm] *OED* ~ sb² 1 'used to leaven bread'; *EDD* sb¹ 'yeast.' Fermented preparation used for leavening bread; mixture of yeast and flour added to dough to induce rising; yeast; also attrib.

[1794] 1968 THOMAS 59 From the Spruce is obtain'd [yeast] or Barm that riseth Bread as well as any yeast that can be procur'd from Malt. 1895 *J A Folklore* viii, 27 [The term] barm. . .is still commonly, if not exclusively, used in Newfoundland. P 148–63 Barm is to make dough rise—used before dry yeast [came into use]. T 92/3–64 You have a proper barm bottle. You put your potato in and your hops and a little bit of sugar, and a little bit of rice, and then that had to work. T 246/7–66 To make what we call barm you'd boil your hops and then scrape some potato and then put a little bit of sugar on it. And you'd hang it up for to let it work. T 253/4–66 You'd take a cupful of [grounds] and make a barm, mix it up with flour and put it back and let it rise up. P 192–67 Sometimes there was a woman in the village called the barm woman. People would go to her to get some barm —borrow leaven or raising dough, and from this their own bread would rise. 1973 BARBOUR 81 In those days it was the old style grounds bread. . . To make what was called 'barm,' one took a cup full of the grounds, added water and flour, stirred it well, and wrapped it up warm [in a stone jar] and set it to rise.

barnacle n   *EDD* ~ sb³ 'incorrigible person.' A bad person; one despised by others.

1937 DEVINE 7 ~ A vicious man or beast. Evilly inclined. An idle waster. Q 67–107 Barnacle's breed. A bad boy or girl.

bar over* See BARLEY OVER.

barrack n   Cp *DAE* hay barrack (1807–). Structure consisting of four posts and a movable roof, designed to protect hay from rain and snow (P 245–56).

M 71–39 A barrack is composed of a square base of criss-crossed poles, to keep the hay from the ground, and at each corner a large upright pole. In each pole there are holes through which a large bolt can be passed. Resting on four large bolts, one in each pole, is a four-faced cone-shaped roof. These barracks are usually boarded in for about four feet from the ground. 1974 MANNION 176 ~ A roof sliding on four posts, under which hay is kept.

barrack head See BARRICADE n.

barred p ppl

1 Of a net, enclosing a school of fish in the water.

1960 FUDGE 51 At that time herring was very plentiful and we saw twenty American vessels tied up with scaffolds on them, waiting for frost, and dozens of seines were barred full of herring.

2 Of a fisherman's sweater or guernsey, knitted with stripes or 'cables.'

1914 *Cadet* Apr, p. 7 Rough clothing was worn in those days including swanskin drawers, moleskin trousers with an occasional change to canvas and heavy sleeved waistcoat or barred guernsey. Q 71–15 A barred guernsey [was] a rollnecked heavy dark blue wool sweater made popular by Coaker's fishermen's union. Q 71–8 Barred means knitted with ribs or 'cables.'

barrel n *DC* barrelman (Nfld: 1924) for comb in sense 4.

1 An approximate measurement of fish, esp cod, taken from net or trap; in designations of size or capacity of a fishing boat.

T 50/1–64 [Then] we runned off o' the easter bank. 'Twasn't too good. In a three-barrel punt! T 141/66–65[2] They built a boat about 23 or 24 feet long, you know, just about a ten- or twelve-barrel boat, a two-purpose boat. P 9–73 At an average of ten barrels per haul, three hauls per day, [fishermen would take] thirty barrels per day. 1977 *Peopling of Nfld* 267 Yields were sometimes measured in barrels, especially after 1850, and one barrel is taken to equal half a tierce [of salmon].

2 Protective enclosure on mast from which a man scans the sea for seals, whales, etc; crow's nest; PARLOUR.

1918 GRENFELL 76 They go up. . .in the forebarrel to 'scun' the ship. [1923] 1946 PRATT 195 "The Ice-Floes": Dawn from the Foretop! Dawn from the Barrel! / A scurry of feet with a roar overhead; / The master-watch wildly pointing to Northward, / Where the herd in front of the *Eagle* was spread! 1924 ENGLAND 46 He sent the scunner up to the 'parlour,' or barrel on the foretopmast, clambering aloft up the shrouds to the trapdoor in the bottom of the barrel. [1929] 1933 GREENLEAF (ed) 248 "The Sealing Cruise of the *Lone Flier*": It was on a Tuesday morning we made another start, / When Gordon Dove cried from the barrel, 'I can see the schooner *Harp*!' 1933 GREENE 53 [The sealing vessels] with their lofty sky-piercing masts and the 'barrels' (the Crow's-nests) set on fore and main masts. T 187–65 There was a man in the barrel for to see the whale, 'cause no trouble to see at a distance underwater.

3 Phr *have one's barrel up*: to be pregnant (P 245–57).

4 Comb **barrel-bob**: sled with runners formed by barrel-staves (M 71–115).

barrel-chair, ~ **rocker**: chair constructed from cylindrical wooden container or barrel; CHAIR BOX.

[1865 CAMPBELL 133 The old land-lady, who looked like a bolster tied in the middle, sat in an arm-chair made of an old herring-barrel.] Q 71–7 Rockers were attached to the bottom [of the barrel-chair], and the whole thing was covered, first with a padding, and then a patterned covering. 1972 MURRAY 190 'Barrel chairs' were made from a barrel, with a section cut out, the remaining section forming the back. A hinged seat was placed about halfway up the barrel, so that there was a place for storage under the seat.

barrel-heater: stove used in the construction of barrels.

T 90–64 The barrel-heater was a stove made to burn wood and with a pan [with water] on it, and you could put your barrel over that.

barrel-man: crewman sent to crow's nest to look out for seals, whales, etc; cp SCUNNER, SPY MASTER.

1917 *Christmas Bells* 1 Next we see the men leaving the ship, a patch of seals having been seen by the barrel-man a mile or two away. 1924 ENGLAND 51–2 [The *Terra-Nova's*] 1922 complement. . .comprised: Captain, second hand, barrel men (or spy masters), scunners. . . The barrel men keep watch in the main-topmast barrel, spying for seals. 1925 CONDON 245 Over the 'scunner's' head, in a large barrel slung at the top of the highest mast, is the 'barrel man.' This position is one of great importance, and is generally occupied either by the captain himself or his first officer, armed with a powerful telescope on the lookout for any and sundry indications that may point the way of the seals. T 194/5–65 Our barrelman went in the barrel and he called the captain. He said, 'Captain, there's a man comin' there on the starboard side.' 1972 BROWN 219 About 6:30 a.m. the barrelman of the *Bellaventure* had noticed some men on the ice a couple of miles or so to the south-east.

barrel stove: drum-shaped stove with a round top and bottom, sides somewhat rounded, two or three covers, and a stove-pipe which goes up through the oven on top of the stove (1971 NOSEWORTHY 172).

barrel tub: barrel sawn in two and used for various fisheries purposes; cp BARROW[1]: BARROW TUB, PUNCHEON TUB, TUB.

1931 *Nfld Magazine* 9 If you want to preserve Partridge, Curlew, Ducks or other game birds. . .clean them thoroughly, put them on end in an empty lard pail or tight barrel tub, [and] pour melted lard or any other meat fat [over them]. P 229–67 A betty murphy is a three-quarter barrel tub.

barrelover See BARLEY OVER.

barren a Of a man, childless.

[c1894] PANL P4/14, p. 193 A complaint against the Road Board of the place was thus related to me: 'The gov'ment ain't give no work to we, only *barren* men got a job out of 'em, and we got children too.'

barren n See BARRENS.

barrener n Rock ptarmigan (*Lagopus mutus*); BARRENS PARTRIDGE.

1977 *Inuit Land Use* 181 Barreners and hares are commonly found on rocky coastal islands and headlands, and barreners also occur on the plateau.

barrens n pl also **barren**. *DAE* ~ n 1 (1797–); *DC* 1 a, b (Nfld: 1770–; N B: 1832–), ~ partridge (Nfld: 1933); SEARY 102–3.

1 Elevated land or plateau with low, scrubby vegetation.

[1770] 1792 CARTWRIGHT i, 21 I landed on South
Head with Ned, and took a walk upon the barrens.
1792 ibid *Gloss* i, ix ~ elevated lands, which will not
produce timber. [1819] 1826 [GLASCOCK] i, 165 "A
Raking Broadside at Parting": Farewell to each mountain and moor, / Each desolate barren and bog. 1843
JUKES 22 The 'barrens' of Newfoundland are those districts which occupy the summits of the hills and ridges,
and other elevated and exposed tracts. They are covered with a thin and scrubby vegetation. . .and are
somewhat similar in appearance to the moorlands of
the north of England, differing only in the kind of vegetation. 1879 *Nineteenth Century* ix, 54 In Newfoundland there are barrens of many miles in extent, high,
and, comparatively speaking, dry plateaus. 1947
TANNER 348 No part is more rugged and inhospitable
than these 'barrens,' the vast rolling plateaux of the
interior, broken by stunted groups of wind-torn trees
only at the plateaus' edges. 1968 MOWAT & DE VISSER
138 Leaving the settlements in October. . .they traversed the windswept sweep of the high barrens until
they came to the southward edge of the Big Woods.

2 Uninhabited treeless stretches of wasteland,
supporting low shrubs, berries, mosses, and wild
animals; MARSH.
[1766] 1971 BANKS 121 We think it Prudent to
Return upon the Rocks & Barrens (for so they Call the
Places where Wood does not Grow). [1794] 1968
THOMAS 104 Here it was now, by the side of a Swamp
in the Barrens of Newfoundland, threadbare, wet,
dirty. 1819 ANSPACH 294 [There are] extensive plains
covered either with heath, or with rocky surfaces, more
or less extensive, where not a tree or shrub is to be
seen, and which are from thence usually called
Barrens. 1897 HARVEY 150 The 'barrens' are covered
with a rich carpet of moss of every shade and colour,
and abound in all sorts of wild berries. 1907
TOWNSEND 282 The Arctic strip extends from the
exposed coasts of the outer islands, in onto the mainland for from one to three or four miles as a practically
unbroken 'barren,' sprinkled with lichen-covered
ledges and carpeted with turf of reindeer lichen, sphagnum, Empetrum, sedges, creeping willows, and various
other species of herbaceous plants. T 175/7–65 The partridge-berry, they was on the barrens, but the marshberry was 'long wi' the bakeapples on the marsh.
M 71–97 They went out on the barrens where they usually picked berries or laid out rabbit snares or traps.
1976 JACKSON 36 Bogs, Heaths (known as 'Barrens' in
Newfoundland) and rough meadows near boglands. . .

3 Exposed, rocky areas incapable of supporting much vegetation.
1842 JUKES ii, 11 We came on some small rocky 'barrens.' 1866 WILSON 27 Passing these ravines and belts
of woods [going inland], we arrive at an open country,
called The Barrens, which are an immense waste, consisting of barren rock, or rock covered with moss. 1877
ROBINSON 279 Alternate marshes, bald granite barrens, and belts of stunted spruce and fir characterize
this [region]. 1969 *Nfld Essays* 5 The island vegetation
is coniferous forest, interspersed with barren rock
areas locally known by the colourful and descriptive
term, 'barrens.'

4 Attrib **barren(s) partridge**: rock ptarmigan
(*Lagopus mutus*); BARRENER; PARTRIDGE.
1933 MERRICK 191 In a deep gully. . .we came to a
company of barrens partridges. They are white, like
ptarmigan, only smaller. 1959 MCATEE 25 Barren
partridge—rock partridge.
barren sand: sandy patch in a treeless plateau.
[1777] 1792 CARTWRIGHT ii, 238 We passed a very
uncomfortable night at that place; for, we lay upon
barren sand, were wet to the skin with rain, and most
cruelly bit by flies.

barricade n also **barrack head**. Cp *OED* ~ 3
naut ['strong rail across the foremost part of
quarter-deck'] (1769, 1867). The short raised
deck at the fore end of a vessel; forecastle; also
attrib.
[1894–1929] [1960] BURKE (ed White) 29 "Full
Loads to the Sealers": Success to you sons of bold
Neptune, / May good luck attend you this spring /
When bound up for home and you loaded, / On the
barricade gaily will sing. 1924 ENGLAND 38 Up on the
'barricade,' or fo'c's'le head, where groups of men
stood hands in pockets. . .I penetrated to the very fore-
peak. Ibid 47 When she struck the ice full tilt, water
flew higher than the barricade rail. T 141/66–65[2] Charlie come in on the barrack 'ead. 'What a souse!' he
said. 'I'm soakin'!' 1977 *Nfld Qtly* Winter, p. 17 There
was no bowsprit on her. All you had to do was just
lower it (the jib) down to beyond the barrack head
(barricade).

barricade v Cp *OED* ~ v 1 b (1677–). See also
BALLICATTER v. To build up an obstruction (of
ice); to coat heavily (with freezing rain and ice).
[1775] 1792 CARTWRIGHT ii, 88 The shore was barricaded with ice, seven feet thick. [1786] ibid iii, 124
Their clothes were barricaded with ice in such manner,
that I was obliged to cut them off.

barricader See BARRICADO.

barricado n, often pl also **barricaders, barry catters, batty catters**, etc ['bæţɩkæţəɹ, bæţɩ'kæţəɹ,
'bædɩˌkæţəɹz, 'badɩkaţəɹs, ˌbæţɩ'kɑːɹtəɹz]. Cp
OED ~ 4 naut 'rail. . .extending, as a fence,
across the foremost part of the quarter-deck'
(1675–); *DC* (Nfld: 1775–). See BALLICATTER n,
BARRICADE n.
1 Ice formed in winter by the action of spray
and waves along the shore-line of sea, ponds or
rivers, making a barricade or band on the landward side.
[1775] 1792 CARTWRIGHT ii, 89 The scene was
greatly altered on our return, for the jam ice was not to
be seen, the barricados were fallen off from the shore,
most of the snow melted, all the harbours were open.
1792 ibid *Gloss* i, ix Barricados. That ice which is
formed upon the shore above low-water mark. 1925
Dial Notes v, 325 Batty catters, barry catters—ice frozen to the shore and hummocked up. 1937 DEVINE 9
Barricaders. The frozen sea ice on the foreshore
unmoved by the ebb and flow of the tide. T 141/63–65[2]

The ponds in the centre was thawed out, but here was the batticatter right around. . .the edge of the pond. T 194–65 When he went up, [the handle] was broke off. I suppose heavy batticatter, ice or something [did it].

2 Accumulation of masses and slabs of ice forced up on shore by tides and waves, or grounded near the shore; 'rafted' ice.

[1912 CABOT 122 Along the mainland was a line of 'barricados,' as often happens, boulders shoved up by the ice. They call them belly-carders here, in good faith.] T 84/5–64 I give un a little dart out over the battycatter. T 141/64–65² He got in and he hauled ashore—a ice claw on the heaving line, and he got a hold to the land in there somewhere, in the battycatter. Q 67–88 Battycatter: ice piled up on the beach. 1979 TIZZARD 96 This boat was painted green with yellow gunwales, and when there was enough water around the barricaders the boat was put afloat.

3 Ice-pan.

1925 *Dial Notes* v, 333 [A growler is a] small berg or large 'batty catter' floating. 1979 TIZZARD 240 It was good to get out in punt in the spring of the year and to row among the barricaders or ballycaters.

barrier n Cp *DC* ~ '[salmon] net set across a stream' obs (1793). In trapping seals in coastal waters, one of the three nets in a 'frame' which prevents seals from escaping out to sea.

[1886] LLOYD 53 [The seal net] which runs parallel with the land is known as the 'barrier'; that on the right side the 'stop-net'; that on the left as the 'heave-up net.' This last-mentioned net is the special feature of the frame. The barrier and the stop-net are always kept floating in a perpendicular position by means of the. . .floats; but the heave-up net is not so supported.

barring vbl n

1 The placing of a net in a river, estuary or bay to trap migrating fish.

1867 *Journ of Assembly* Appendix, p. 719 [We should repeal] that part of the Herring Act which refers to what is termed 'barring,' so that every man may have free access to those shoals of wealth. 1898 *Christmas Bells* 15 These questions embraced the curing of fish, appointment of inspectors, use of bultows, cod nets, barring of brooks, cure of herring, taking of bait fishes, and the observance of existing laws. 1946 MACKAY (ed) 347 Captain Erskine of the *Eclipse*, on patrol duty off the Newfoundland coast, had reported to the Admiralty concerning the injurious effects produced by the practice of 'barring' for bait.

2 Completing the knitting of a striped or 'barred' sweater.

Q 71–7 Casting off a piece of knitting was referred to as barring off. A guernsey was a man's heavy turtle-neck sweater. A barred guernsey was a sweater which had been knit and cast off, or (that is) had been knit and finished.

barrow¹ n also **bar, barry** ['bæːɹəɹ, bæːɹ, baːɹ, baˑɹ]. Cp *OED* ~ sb³ 1 (1300–1535). See also DRAFT BARROW, HAND-BARROW.

1 A flat, rectangular wooden frame with han-

dles at each end for two men to carry cod-fish, seal 'pelts' and other bulky materials; specif such a frame used in weighing seal pelts and dried cod; FISH BARROW.

1613 *Willoughby Papers* 1/10, 66 I tooke som thing Sharp unto him and have mak him cary the barry with me and Torne fishe as I have done. 1818 CHAPPELL 128 In this state the *fish* continue for a few days; when they are again taken, in barrows, to a sort of wooden box, full of holes, which is suspended from the stage in the sea. [c1830] 1890 GOSSE 58 One of the crew that has climbed up begins to lay [the seal pelts] one by one, fur downward, on the barrow; singing out, as he lays down each, 'One-two-three-four-tally.' 1904 *Nfld Qtly* Dec, p. 17 The paraphernalia of a fisherman's craft, hooks and lines, sails and twines, bultows and barrows, and nets. . . [1914] 1930 COAKER 85 The Trading Co. had prepared for storing [and] the scales, barrows, etc had been made ready. 1937 DEVINE 53 [The jig is] the swinging frame part of the scales on which a barrow of fish is placed in weighing. T 141/67–65² You take your barrer—your barrer—o' linnet—and fill in your tub about half full. T 192/3–65 They'd yaffle so much [fish] and throw [it] up to get enough for the weight to make the draft on the bar, and then there'd be, 'Yaffle at hand!' 1975 BUTLER 70 The fish was put on the barrow, weighed, packed in the drum, put under the fish screw.

2 Comb **barrow-tub**: wooden tub or half barrel with handles attached for two men to carry.

P 148–62 A barrow tub is a half barrel for salt. P 144–74 In the morning, the salt fish were brought from the stage in 'barra tubs' and were spread face-up on the flake. 1977 *Nfld Qtly* Dec, p. 37 It was more or less fun getting [the caplin], but the fun was all over when it came to carrying them in the garden in barrow tubs, and spreading them on the potatoes and covering them over.

barrow² n *EDD* ~ sb⁵ 1, 2. A child's flannel petticoat.

P 108–77 A barrow was a long flannel petticoat for a baby. It had a wide band which hugged the baby under the arms and the skirt hung well below the baby's feet. In the day-time a fine lace-trimmed petticoat was worn over it, and then the long dress.

barrow v Cp *OED* ~ v 'to cart' (1674, 1862). In curing cod, to carry an amount of fish from one place to another on a 'hand-barrow.'

1887 *Colonist Christmas No* 8 She used to barrow and split salt fish; still any one would take Mary for a real lady. 1924 ENGLAND 267 The usual burden for a couple of these Vikings' wives is a quintal of fish—112 pounds. Two men ordinarily carry twice that; 'barrow' it, as they say. T 43–64 When 'twould be dry you'd barrow it down from the shed.

barter n Attrib **barter shop**: small shop where goods can be obtained in exchange for fish and other produce.

1909 BROWNE 259 These institutions [barter shops], which are known all over the coast of Newfoundland and Labrador, are not usually very pretentious establishments, but they do considerable trade, as they are furnished with all sorts of commodities for fishing and household purposes; and you may procure anything from a puncheon of molasses to a skein of thread. [They] do little cash business, but they exchange their wares for fish, salmon, furs. 1944 LAWTON & DEVINE 12 [He] had established small barter shops in the settlements surrounding King's Cove, and it was a usual occurrence to see him start off after midnight on horseback on a tour of inspection of these barter shops. P 54–67 ~ a small shop where cash and dried fish would be exchanged, on a small scale, for goods; a chapman's shop.

barvel n　also **barbel** ['bæːɹbl̩, 'baːɹbəl] *OED* ~ (1878–83); *EDD* sb 2 K Co; *DAE* barvel² N E local (1629–), *Fisheries of U S* i, 131; cp *MED* barm 2: barm fel 'leather apron' (1450–75). A leather, canvas or oil-skin apron, reaching from breast to knees, worn when catching fish or esp when processing the catch ashore; hence a homemade domestic apron.

[(c1710) 1895 PROWSE 22 A View of a Stage & also ye manner of Fishing for, Curing & Drying Cod at Newfoundland.] [1843] *Nfld Indicator* 18 Nov, p. 3 [advertisement] English and Irish Calfskins, Kip, Cordovan, Morocco, and Patent Leather Binding and Lining Skins, Barvels, Linseed Oil. 1866 WILSON 210 The women at the splitting-table have each a leather apron, called a barvel, which fits to the neck and covers the dress. 1895 *J A Folklore* viii, 27 ~ sometimes pronounced *barbel*, a tanned sheepskin used by fishermen, and also by splitters, as an apron to keep the legs dry. 1917 *Christmas Echo* 18 Their lines are reeled up and their barvels thrown aside. 1937 DEVINE 7 Barbel. An apron of sheep's skin, used in splitting fish in the stage. Also used to keep the front of the body dry in catching fish in the early days. P 19–55 All the barbels I have seen were made of cloth which had been oiled two or three times to make it waterproof. [1959] 1965 PEACOCK (ed) i, 101 "Tom Bird's Dog": They say that you were slightly rigged with your barvel hanging slack. T 88–64 When you [used] sawdust on your floor, and your mother put on a barbel [a brin apron] and scrubbed the floor, that's not coming to pass those days, is it? T 94/5–64 The name was barbels. It's like a big apron—just went over their head like that. T 148–65 He fit me up with a barbel [to] go fishing. 1975 BUTLER 62 In these times fishermen did not wear rubber clothes, as they do today. They wore jackets made from calico and oiled with linseed oil. Instead of oil pants they wore a large apron extending below the knees. . .called a barvel.

bass See BAZZ v.

bastard a　Cp *OED* ~ a 5 'an inferior or less proper kind of.' (a) Of cod-fish, small; not large enough for sale (P 148–69); (b) of a 'dory,' medium-sized, about 14 feet (4.3 m) long (1971 NOSEWORTHY 172).

bat n
1 A stout pole, 5–8 feet (1.5–2.4 m) long with an iron hook and spike fastened to one end, used to assist a sealer on the ice and to kill seals; GAFF n 2.

1842 JUKES i, 258 [They] prepared their bats and gaffs. 1846 TOCQUE 189 They are now easily caught, being killed by a slight stroke across the nose, with a bat or gaff. 1871 *Zoologist* vi, 2549 [The hoods make] it very difficult to kill them with the ordinary 'seal-bat,' or gaff, or even with a heavy load of shot. [1896] SWANSBOROUGH 29 "The Seal Fishery": The native sons with frames so strong, / Each with his gun, or bat in hand, / And round his shoulders with a band / He lashes on his bag of clothes. 1905 CHAFE 6 The procuring of timber from the woods, building vessels, repairing those already in use, building punts, procuring firewood, gaffstems, bats, pokers, oars and other material left nobody with an excuse for being idle. 1927 DOYLE (ed) 39 "Hunting Seals": With bat and gaff and 'panning staff' / Surmounted with a flag, sir; / Away we go on the great iceflow, / And we never care to lag, sir. 1934 BARTLETT 89 He could jump from one pan to another, using the seal bats, short, gaff-like hooks, as though he'd been born a Newfoundlander. T 49–64 We went on, and went on. We killed, I don't know how much we did kill now with the bat.

2 Comb **bat(s)man**: member of sealing crew shipped to take seals with a club rather than a rifle; cp GUNNER.

1842 BONNYCASTLE ii, 129 These gunners rank before the mere batmen, and have some trifling remuneration in the way of a remission of the charge of berth money, which the sealers pay to the merchant who supplies the vessel. 1878 TOCQUE 307 The berth money had been raised by the merchants and owners of vessels to three pounds, and three pounds ten shillings currency for 'batmen,' and one pound for bow or chief gunner, who had hitherto gone free. 1924 ENGLAND 108 The other ships must h'a' got wind of it, for pretty soon I see seven smokes comin' like a terrified horse. But my batsmen an' gunners cleaned up thousands that day, before them others could get to me. 1972 SANGER 235 Batsman. A term used during the sailing vessel era and early steamer period to refer to a sealer who was not permitted to use firearms.

bat v　To kill or stun a seal by striking with a club; GAFF v 2.

1871 WHITE *MS Journal* 9 Apr At daylight saw spot old seals—batted about 5000. 1895 *Outing* xxvii, p. 22 As [hooded] seals may be approached with ease, it is considered a waste of ammunition to shoot them, and they are generally clubbed, or 'batted,' as it is locally termed. 1924 ENGLAND 16 The [seal] pups can be gaffed or batted. In many cases the wary old ones have to be shot. 1952 STANSFORD 83 Our crew succeeded in batting two young hoods, and in all twenty one seals were brought ashore. 1955 DOYLE (ed) 52 "Sealers' Song": Our boys for fat, would gaff and bat, / And make the whitecoats rattle.

batch n　Cp *OED* ~ ¹ 6 'quantity of anything coming at a time.' A fall of snow, freq in phr *batch of snow*.

[1886] LLOYD 15 It not unfrequently happens that

the heaviest falls of snow—called 'batches' by the inhabitants—are accompanied by gales of wind. T 43/4–64 In the winter there was no road at all; every batch was pilin' up and stayin' there until it would melt with the sun in the spring. T 178/9–65 And that night, sir, come on the gale o' wind to the north east, and you never saw a bigger batch o' snow in your life. T 391/3–67 Last goin' off the young fellers put out a lot o' slips; big batch o' snow come, and them slips be snowed in.

bateau n also **batteau**. Cp *DC* ~ 1 (1760–1840). Type of fishing boat rigged with a lug-sail, formerly used on the north-east coast of Newfoundland and on the Labrador.

[1773] 1792 CARTWRIGHT i, 277 After. . .buying a French batteau and two hundred weight of whalebone. . .I returned home. 1936 SMITH 33 They left Brigus about the 10th of June and arrived at Quirpon, French shore, in good time. There Mr Smith bought ten bateaux, or fishing boats, with a big round O on each bow, and a big lugger sail made in French style. T 398–67 They used to look after their salt, and their seine boats and their bateaus. 1967 READER 52 An old 'bateau' (boat) which was also unearthed, was found to be in a remarkable state of preservation.

bath n In small canning factories, the immersion in boiling water to cook and preserve lobster or salmon.

T 455/6–67[2] We'd give [tinned lobsters] two baths. We'd give 'em one bath, a hour and a quarter, and then we'd blow 'em off, let the wind out of 'em and stop 'em again. Put 'em in again and boil 'em.

bath v To immerse tinned lobsters or salmon in boiling water for a specific time.

1925 *Dial Notes* v, 325 ~ To boil (fish or lobsters) in a can. T 168/70–65 We'd bath 'em then, boil 'em three hours after they're in the tin. T 455/6–67[2] We'd put 'em in bath, and bath 'em for a couple of hours, and preserve 'em.

batten v Cp *NID* ~[2] n 5 a 'thin strip usu. of wood used in fairing a ship's lines in the mold loft.' Phr *batten out*: to secure the shaped timbers of the hull with strips of wood when building a boat.

T 183–65 You make your fore hook and your midship bend and after hook, and put up your counter, your transom. And you'd batten her out, frame her out.

batter v Cp *OED* ~ v[1] 1 'strike with repeated blows.' Of a water fowl, to flap wings while in the water and fly off; to flap wings against the water ineffectually.

T 58/65–64 They wounded the duck. They didn't kill him, but they struck un. But the duck battered up out the water, crippled duck, and he flew up over the hill. T 84–64 We picked up our birds. Never a one went to wing, never a one battered. Q 73–2 I was just about in

range when it battered off. P 127–73 He was batterin across the water when I fired at en.

battery n Cp *OED* ~ 5 'platform or fortified work. . .within which artillery is mounted.' A blind or place of concealment constructed of snow from which hunter may shoot deer; cp GAZE.

[1786] 1792 CARTWRIGHT iii, 129 Three hands were at work in building batteries in Western Tickle, for deer-shooting; the former ones being thawed away: they finished three, and brought home my double gun.

batty n Cp PARTRIDGE ~ 'wages.' A sum (of money); an amount or boat-load (of fish).

1901 *Christmas Review* 17 He came to St John's in the fall of the year; got a nice batty of money for his summer's fish, and then proceeded to buy the necessary articles for starting house-keeping. 1937 DEVINE 9 A large catch of codfish ready to be thrown up to the stage head from the boat would be called 'a fine *batty* of fish.' P 148–65 You got a batty o' it (a full boatload of fish).

batty catter See BARRICADO.

bauk, baulk See BAWK.

bautom See BOTTOM[2].

bavin n, usu pl also **babben*** ['bavin]. Cp *OED* ~ sb 1 'bundle of brushwood'; *EDD* sb[1] 1. A thin piece of wood or 'split' with end whittled and curled with a knife, used as kindling; SHAVINGS.

1925 *Dial Notes* v, 325 Bavins. Very thin kindlings. 1937 DEVINE 9 Bavins. Whittlings from a dry stick to light the fire: stiff shavings. P 212–64 Babben: whittled, split ends of wood used for kindling. T 222–66 All of you have blasty boughs and bavins in your linny, or kindling in your storehouse, and you would be able to make a quick fire in your bogie in no time. P 54–67 Bavins are sticks of wood feathered out with a knife for kindling.

bawk n also **bauk, baulk**. Greater shearwater (*Puffinus gravis*); HAGDOWN.

1924 ENGLAND 177 'Jeeze, what a big burst o' birds down on de landwash! I strick 'em down an' snick 'em down by de t'ousands! Baulks, haigdowns, scurwinks, ahl kinds.' 1940 SCAMMELL 25 "The Shooting of the Bawks": He has to watch the bawks flock 'round, upon a foggy day / And watch them rob his trawls of bait, and watch them fly away. / He's not allowed to shoot them or someone sure will squawk; / For there's a bloody law agin the killin' of a bawk. 1951 PETERS & BURLEIGH 56 The 'Bawk' is perfectly at home on the sea, visiting land only to nest upon remote islands in the South Atlantic. 1959 MCATEE 3 Bauk. Greater Shearwater. (Spelled also balk, and bawk; meaning unknown. Nfld.) C 71–119 The bawks are so thick [on the water] you can walk on them.

bawl v *OED* ~ v 'to give mouth or tongue as

an animal' obs (1440–1753); *EDD* v 1, 2 'cry out', 'low.' Of an animal or bird, esp a young seal or 'whitecoat,' to squall, cry out, wail.

1842 JUKES i, 270 [The young seal] was of a dirty white colour, with short close fur, large dark expressive eyes, and it paddled and walloped about the deck fierce and bawling. 1924 ENGLAND 6 Wouldn't dis be a big night to year a whitecoat bawl! I wish't we was pickin' up fat, by's! Pickin' up pans! 1933 GREENE 74–5 The newly born 'Cat' [is] pitiful and appealing in appearance, and curiously human in its baby crying—'bawling' as the sealers call it. 1937 DEVINE 69 [proverb] When a snipe bawls the lobster crawls. 1955 DOYLE (ed) 11 "A Noble Fleet of Sealers": When the white coats bawl, he'll risk his all. P 217–64 [proverb] The cow soon forgets her bawling calf. C 69–16 When we were almost asleep some sheep began to bawl outside the house. 'We'll have the rain tomorrow, just listen to the sheep bawlin' outside,' said my mother. 1977 *Inuit Land Use* 254 Harp seals. . .travel and feed in herds, or skulls, as they are called locally. 'They bawl to one another.'

bawn n   also **bon** [bɒːn, bɒˑən] *EDD* ~ sb 4 Ir; JOYCE 214; DINNEEN badhún for sense 1.

1 Grassy land or meadow near a house or settlement.

1897 *J A Folklore* x, 203 Bawn. . .particularly where the Irish have prevailed, is the common name for the land about the house. P 113–55 Setting spuds on the bawn (flat expanse of freshly-turned sods). 1968 DILLON 131 'We have to break up some bawn tomorrow.' 'When cattle are dry, they're out on the bawn in the spring o' the year.' M 69–29 About half-way between my house and the theatre there was a big grassy bonne (meadow) and this was a favourite place for courters to go. C 71–24 [In Calvert] a baun was an enclosed pasture which was used for the grazing of sheep. In Carbonear [it] meant ground that hadn't been ploughed before. C 75–136 ~ a plot of grass land where children play and where fishermen spread their trap when they take it up to dry or mend.

2 Expanse of rocks on which salted cod are spread for the quick-drying process of the Labrador and Bank fisheries; BEACH. Cp FLAKE.

1895 GRENFELL 66 Newfoundlanders spread [cod] on poles called 'flakes,' or on the natural rocks, called 'bournes.' [1900 OLIVER & BURKE] 34 "Fanny's Harbor Bawn": Which caused this dreadful contest on [Fanny's] Harbor Bawn. . . / So pray begone, all from the Bawn, or I'll boot you in your bloom. 1936 SMITH 17 [The fish] would then lie in the waterhorse for twenty-four hours. It was then brought out on the bawn and spread 'heads and tails.' 1937 *Seafisheries of Nfld* 47 When the fish is dried by natural means, it is placed upon flakes, beaches, rocks and bawns (i.e. artificial beaches), where the sun and wind are permitted to perform the task of extracting the moisture. 1955 DOYLE (ed) 78 "'Twas Getting Late Up in September": To spread fish on the bawn makin' wages / We went there without much sleep. T 393–67 This is where they'd make their fish—on all those small rocks about the size o' your fist. They used to call it the bawn. M 71–117 Finally the fish would be taken in hand-bar-

rows to the bawns—something like flakes except that the boughs were laid on the rocks—and spread to dry. 1977 *Inuit Land Use* 218–19 First, the cod were washed to remove the salt, then they were placed on small flat stones called *bons* to dry. The bons were loosely separated to permit air to circulate around the fish.

3 Phr *make bawn*: to prepare beach for drying salted cod by making a flat expanse of rocks.

C 70–10 Sometimes the fishermen would fill in the crevices with beach rocks, and this would be called making bawn. My grandfather said that he has made bawn down in Labrador while fishing there in the summer-time.

bay n   Cp *OED* ~ sb² 1 'indentation of the sea into the land' (1383–), *DAE* 1 (1612–) for sense 1; for proverb in sense 3 cp, among other U S sources, F BARBOUR, *Proverbs. . .of Illinois* (1965), p. 21 'you can take the boy out of the country. . .'; for comb in sense 4: *OED* sb² 5: ~ ice (1853), cp *DAE* bay man 1 (1641–) and *DC* bayman Nfld (1964), bay-noddie Nfld (1907), bay seal (Nfld: 1772, 1958); for ~ wop, see WOP¹ 'wasp' and *EDD* johnny: ~ wap, ~ wops 'simpleton.'

1 A large indentation of the sea lying between two widely-separated headlands, commonly comprising numerous harbours, coves, inlets, islands and fishing grounds; the coastal strip of such an indentation; collectively, all the bays, harbours and settlements or 'outports' of Newfoundland.

[1583] 1940 *Gilbert's Voyages & Enterprises* ii, 398 [Hayes' narrative] So againe Tuesday the 30 of July (seven weekes after) we got sight of land, being immediately embayed in the Grand bay, or some other great bay. 1620 WHITBOURNE 2–3 All along the coast of this Countrey, there are many spacious and excellent Bayes, some of them stretching into the land, one towards another, more than twenty leagues. [1770] 1866 WILSON 146 A few professors [of religion] are scattered through the different bays. [1794] 1968 THOMAS 77, 97 Capelin Bay is more properly a Harbour, being a mile and a half in length and not more than a quarter of a mile across in any part. . . Placentia Bay is one of the largest Bays in this Country. From St Mary's Bay to Cape Chapeau Rouge (which are the two angles) is twelve Leagues athwart. The Length of the Bay is more considerable. The Harbours, Creeks, Coves and Inlets in it are many. 1819 ANSPACH 295 The whole Island abounds with creeks, roads, and very fine harbours; also spaces covered with pebbles. . .vast bays, of several leagues in breadth and depth, are also very numerous on these coasts. Vessels lie in the smaller bays and harbours in perfect security, being well sheltered inside by the mountains. 1836 [WIX]² 143 The inhabitants of Conception Bay, although a neck of land of only a few miles extent separates them from Trinity Bay, differ from the inhabitants of the latter, as much as if they were of a distant nation; the same may be said of the difference between those who live in Placentia and those who live in Fortune Bay. 1866 WILSON 196 They, therefore, invited the preachers from the bay, who, on coming to St John's, were received with much kindness. 1908 DURGIN 22–3 A Newfoundland trader goes up and down the coast in a schooner, entering all the bays, their arms, coves and harbors, wherever a few fisher-folk live or there are towns. . . In White Bay, Notre Dame Bay, and many of those bays remote from St John's, there are many old people living who have never been out of the little cove they were born in. 1917 *Christmas Bells* 1 Holyrood, at the bottom of Conception Bay, had become one of our favourite summer resorts. 1946 MACKAY (ed) 336 Great Britain contended that the term 'bays'. . .must be construed in accordance with the meaning commonly assigned to 'bays' by fishermen in 1818, and it appealed to the testimony of the maps of that period, maps in which the waters in dispute were clearly designated as 'bays.' The United States [declared] that the term 'bays' referred only to small indentations and that the marine league must be measured from a line following the sinuosities of the coast [rather than from a line drawn from headland to headland]. 1973 WADEL 89 [His wife] was from the 'Bay.' 1976 HEAD 159 *The harbour* served merely as a shelter for the ocean-going ships, laid up for the fishing season, while the actual summer activities took place on *the bay.* 1979 *Salt Water, Fresh Water* 256 Different bays had different types of timber, and the waves, the tides is different, every bay is different.

2 A stretch of open water in an ice-field; LAKE; LEAD[2].

1924 ENGLAND 24 The whelping ice has to be low and more or less open, preferably with plenty of 'leads' through it—leads or bays, of course, being stretches of free water.

3 Phr *(go) around the bay*: to visit a number of coastal 'settlements.'

[1955] 1980 *Evening Telegram* 25 June, p. 6 Magistrate Trickett of Clarenville made a trip around the bay and held court at Trinity Bay and Brookfield travelling as far as Musgrave Harbour. 1979 ibid 2 June, p. 20 I minds last year me and the woman were around the bay.

[proverb] *you can take a man out of the bay, but you can't take the bay out of the man* ([1954] 1972 RUSSELL 22).

1974 *Can Forum* Mar, p. 25 Ted Russell, our leading local playwright, and a great outharbourman himself, is fond of quoting a line from the eleventh epistle of Horace, *caelum non animum, mutant; qui trans mare current* which he translates exactly in a Newfoundland proverb: 'You can take the man out of the Bay, but you can't take the Bay out of the man.'

4 Attrib, comb, cpd **bay blue**: sea blue.

[1923] 1946 PRATT 186 "The Big Fellow": A huge six-footer, / Eyes bay blue, / And as deep.

bay boat: vessel stopping at 'settlements' around Newfoundland and on the Labrador with passengers, mail and supplies; COASTAL BOAT.

1957 *Daily News* 9 Apr, p. 4 At that time Norris Arm was the terminus of the 'bay boat.'

bay boy: 'outport' lad.

1920 WALDO 163 The children cry: 'Bay boy, bay boy, come to your supper, / Two cods' heads and a lump o' butter.'

bay bun: type of baked preparation with cubes of pork fat as an ingredient; PORK BUN. Cp TOUTIN.

1979 *Salt Water, Fresh Water* 215 Now what's a bay bun? That's a molasses bun with pork in it, raw pork. It will freeze and, gee, they'll last and they won't dry up. . . You can keep it a month.

bay caplin: American smelt (*Osmerus mordax*), an inshore species found as far north as the Hamilton Inlet-Lake Melville area of Labrador.

1977 *Inuit Land Use* 265 Outside capelin are larger than bay capelin. They appear with salmon in spring and are blue-backed, unlike bay capelin, which are pale and small. Outside capelin are found mainly around outer seaward coasts, but bay caplin inhabit bays the year round.

bay crew: servants engaged in the enterprise of a 'planter' or 'merchant.' Cp CREW.

[1779] 1792 CARTWRIGHT ii, 496 n. They consumed all their provisions before the time was expired, for which they were victualled, which was more than the bay-crew did, who killed nothing of any consequence; had they done the same, all hands must have been famished.

bay girl: young woman of the 'outports.'

1975 GUY 50 Perhaps you know some young maid from home who is in service in Sin John's or going to school. However, she will cut you every time. There is nothing so stuck up as a Baygirl in Sin John's. . .or the other way around.

bay hospital: small cottage hospital serving a rural district or 'bay.'

1919 *Journ of Assembly* 314 The third suggestion, Outport Hospitals, is one that has been discussed for some time. . . I am strongly in favour of a ten-bed hospital conveniently situated in each of the principal bays. The advantages of Bay hospitals have been amply shown by the recent letters of Dr Grenfell.

bay ice: ice formed in a single winter on the surface of a harbour; HARBOUR ICE, LOCAL: *local ice.*

1865 CAMPBELL 68 Bay-ice a few feet thick, pack-ice, and broken bergs of all sorts and sizes, with anchor-ice below, all moving bodily through a rocky channel, must work notable denudation at the bottom of the sea in this strait. [1916] 1972 GORDON 94 Cracks in the bay-ice, and patches of open water off every point of land. . .made travelling a difficult business. 1977 *Them Days* ii (3), 45 When he come the bay ice was gone so he come across the brook just above the wharves. 1979 TIZZARD 98 Sometimes during late fall or early spring, when the water was rough or the bay ice had not yet thawed out, he would walk the whole distance to Summerford [with the mail].

bay man, bayman: one who lives on or near a bay or harbour; inhabitant of an 'outport'; OUT-HARBOUR: *out-harbour man*; sometimes with derogatory connotations (cp **bay wop**).

[1772] 1792 CARTWRIGHT i, 190 After breakfast the sealers went home, and the St Lewis's-Bay-men accompanied them. 1865 CAMPBELL 55 In the middle of the night there was a disturbance. A reverend 'bayman' went on deck and saw breakers, upon which he shouted, 'Breakers ahead!' [1900 OLIVER & BURKE] 34 "Fanny's Harbor Bawn": I think you are a Northern man, a bayman, I presume. 1910 GRENFELL 154 [The weather] had continued so rough that the small boats belonging to the baymen had had little chance to retrieve their fortunes with the codfish by going to the outside islands in pursuit of them. 1924 ENGLAND 171 As in all small countries where inland travel is hard and where life clusters in bays (cf ancient Greece), they cling to local attachments and think of themselves as, for example, 'White Bay men,' 'Bonavista Bay men,' 'Conception Bay men,' and so on. Ibid 250 De baymen an' de townies 'd fight, an' you couldn't stop it no ways. 1977 *Inuit Land Use* 103 The early Settlers thought of themselves as 'baymen.' They depended almost solely on the game they hunted in the confines of their bays. They rarely travelled 'outside' to hunt around the coastal islands, and they went to the 'station'—the mission village—only to trade and for religious services. 1979 POTTLE 85 So it was that bayman was set against businessman, outport against city, haves against have-nots, striking loggers and their families against everyone else.

bay noddy: mildly derogatory, or self-depreciating, term for inhabitant of an 'outport'; see NODDY 1, 2.

1901 *Christmas Review* 6 Fifty years ago, one of the expressions of contempt used by citizens of St John's, when speaking of outport men, was 'Bay-noddy.' 1903 DUNCAN 141 'I'd give you a beatin'. . .if I didn't have t' goa home an' feed the goaats.' 'You's scared, you bay-[noddie]!' Billy taunted. 1920 WALDO 163 The little boys have a mischievous way of teasing one another as 'bay noddies.' 1939 DULEY 59 'Rags to riches, and all for a little Bay-Noddy. I suppose she's as common as bog-water.' P 245–61 We bay noddies [from the Bonavista Bay islands].

bay price: price paid for fish by a local 'outport' merchant.

[1810] 1971 ANSPACH 34 The fish which they receive here in payment at the Bay-price, they sen[d] to St John's where they get the full price.

bay salmon: variety of Atlantic salmon of limited migrating range, frequenting coastal waters, estuaries and rivers; grilse.

1977 *Inuit Land Use* 137 Bay salmon migrate upriver in August and September to spawn, and they winter in ponds or in sections of rivers where there is a strong current. When they return to the bays in early July, their flesh is white and they are then called slinks. . . These bay salmon are smaller than the outside variety.

bay seal: small non-migratory seal of coastal waters (*Phoca vitulina*); HARBOUR SEAL.

[1772] 1792 CARTWRIGHT i, 210 I saw several bay-seals on the ice there, and shot at two, but missed them both. 1842 JUKES i, 309 [The] bay-seal, as its name denotes, is confined to the bays and inlets, living on the coast all the year round, and frequenting the mouths of the rivers and harbours. 1895 GRENFELL 173 When one year old the bay seal is called a 'jar seal,'. . .in the second year it is a 'doter,' and becomes speckled, in the third year, it is a 'ranger,' and is then very beauti-

ful, being checkered silver and black all over. [1929] 1933 GREENLEAF (ed) 250 "The Change Islands Song": They talked about bay seals, the mushrat, and the bear. T 391/2–67 Me and another feller killed a doter one time—a bay seal, we'll say. 1977 *Inuit Land Use* 285 Some species, such as the jar seal, referred to locally as the bay seal, are available throughout the year.

bay tilt: hut or cabin built in wooded area at the 'bottom' of a bay for winter occupancy and activities; TILT, WINTER ~ .

1924 ENGLAND 313 ~ Rough hovel in isolated place. 1966 FARIS 44 [During the winter most of the early Cat Harbour] settlers lived in sod structures in heavily wooded forests known as 'bay tilts,' which they left for the headland as soon as fishing began again each year.

bay wop: contemptuous (city) term for an 'outport' Newfoundlander (P 245–56).

1970 JANES 146 She was originally a young baywop whose family had recently moved to Milltown and settled there. 1979 O'FLAHERTY 175 'Baywops' [in Janes' novel, *House of Hate*] are generally seen. . .as semi-retarded and contemptible.

bay work: cutting wood, 'rinds,' etc, preparatory to a fishing voyage; cutting fire-wood for winter use.

T 84/5–64 We were in the bay—all our bay work was done with Uncle Sam. P 49–73 ~ After the preparation for the summer's fishing and while waiting for the squid, the men go up the bay and cut their winter's fire-wood.

bazz n *EDD* ~ sb 4. A blow, slap (Q 71–15).

P 68–56 When he said that, I gave him a bazz in the face.

bazz v also **bass, baz** [bæz, bæːz] *EDD* ~ v 1 'throw with force.' To throw (a small stone); specif in games with marbles or buttons, to pitch or toss.

1891 *Holly Branch* 19 The youth who 'bazz's' marbles, and delights in other tricks. . . 1920 WALDO 164–5 They throw marbles against a wall for a sort of carom-shot, and call it 'bazzin' marbles.' 1931 BYRNES 173 "Kenawitch's Lane": And the boys are 'bazzin'' marbles, as their fathers used to do. 1955 ENGLISH 32 Bass: to throw small stones. P 207–67 If you don't get out of here I'll bazz a rock at you. 1977 RUSSELL 124 'How *did* you baz a button?' 'Why,' said Grampa, 'you'd just bounce it off the corner post of a store out into the road, and the next fellow'd baz his button and try to make it land close to yours. If he could put it so close that he could span the distance with his thumb and finger, he kept the button and you had to find another one to baz with.'

bazzer n See BAZZ v. In child's game, the button one throws at the mark or 'dod' (P 228–64).

bazzom a *EDD* ~ 2 'purplish tint, heather-coloured' D Co. Of flesh, blue or discoloured.

Q 67–106 [He is] bazzom with cold. Q 71–12 ~ blue

colour caused by a bruise. C 75–25 Often their legs were blue with cold or bazzam as 'twas called then.

be v in form **be's**: [biˑz]. See *EDD* do III 2 (1) *to do be* 'to do habitually,' with A–I citations and O Sr Sx Co (possibly Irish labourers); *ADD* bes, bees (1898–); JOYCE 86 *do be, bees*; DINNEEN bîm and p. 1311 'habitual present'; *Fortnightly Review* O.S. xci (1909), 'The Irish Dialect of English,' p. 394. In forms *be's* and *do be*: to be in a state or situation for an unspecified duration of time; to continue; also auxiliary uses.

[c1894] PANL P4/14, p. 198 In the fall of the year, when the wind do be from the southard, it do *dismolish* the stages down to nothing all to once. Ibid 201 'Taint no use to *arg* with the Poor Commissioner though he do be giving gov'ment to some as ain't so worse off as I be. 1903 DUNCAN 112 'Iss, girl, they do be violets now t' the Needle Rock.' 1920 GRENFELL & SPALDING 177 'Nearly all the female ladies what comes aboard her do be wonderful sick.' 1924 ENGLAND 181 'I be's wake, sir. I knows me own feelin's. . . I be's ahl bet out.' P 148–62 What will you do if he don't be there? P 148–63 [In hockey] you don't be on the ice for an hour. P 148–65 Don't be talking! [i.e. You don't say!] 1968 DILLON 131 I don't know whether he's moody or whether he does be vexed with me. . . What are them little things the buds bees on? T 727–68 There's a sunker over there, a sunken rock. You know when the water's high, that it be's under water, but when the water falls down low, the kelp comes [above] the water. 1968 KEATING 55 [The Japanese] do be good fishermen. 1979 *Salt Water, Fresh Water* 92 [The fishermen] don't be scared. . . It seems like these ghost ships they see is a good omen.

beach n Cp *DC* ~ lot (1824); SEARY 90, 140, 144; cp *Shetland Truck System*, p. 13 [Restriction of fishermen by letting of beaches for curing fish] for sense 1; for comb in sense 2: *DAE* ~ bird 'sandpipers or other small birds' (1800–); cp *Shetland Truck System*, p. 35 [splitters and beach boys].

1 A level stretch of shingle or sea-worn rocks along the foreshore, convenient for spreading salted fish to dry and often belonging to a particular fishing-ship or 'planter'; freq developing into place-name; BAWN 2. Cp ROOM 1.

1613 *Willoughby Papers* 17a, 1/2 Here is a good beach and the fishinge neare, to be assured of a good place to fish and a beach, boats and stage may be worth more than one or tow hundreth pounds yearely for a shipp. [c1614] ibid 1/24 For fishing and likewise for inhabitting upon it [Bell Island is satisfactory] for ther is an exceeding good beach for the making of fish. [1693] 1895 PROWSE 233 The master of every ship shall content himself with such beach as he shall have necessary use for. [1712] ibid 273 No complaints that any admiral, vice-admiral, and rear-admiral do ingross more beach or flakes than they pitch upon at their arrival. [c1830] 1916 MURPHY 13 About daybreak it was worse. . . Ryan in the *Caledonia* got in safely. 'Native' Walsh, from the 'Beach' got in also. [c1944 JONES]

"Darn the Man that I Can Get" [broadside]: I have a few cents in the bank, / A home down by the beach, / And the very first night I am married / Hub will have a bottle of screech. 1951 *Nfld & Lab Pilot* i, 193 . . .Grand Beach point, a low wooded projection. 1971 NOSEWORTHY 12 [The catch] was split and salted on board the vessel, and was washed in the harbour upon arrival in Grand Bank. When the weather was favourable the fish was taken by cart to the 'beaches,' which were really level fields along the shore covered with the small round rocks taken from rocky beaches.

2 Attrib, comb, cpd **beach bird, beachy bird**: (a) variety of sandpiper (*Actitis macularia*) or other small bird frequenting the shore; (b) variety of plover (*Charadrius* spp) (see 1891 quot); (c) sanderling (*Crocethia alba*) (1959 quot).

[1620] 1887 MASON 151 [We saw] 2 or 3 excellent kinds of Beach Birds very fat and sweet. [1766] 1971 BANKS 122 Went with gun [and] Kill'd a small Bird. . .Call'd here Beach Bird. [1785] 1792 CARTWRIGHT iii, 76 He killed a grey-plover and five beach-birds. 1846 TOCQUE 276 Several beachbirds. . .were hopping about the rocks. 1870 *Can Naturalist* v, 292 [Each variety of plover is] a summer migrant and breeds on the coast: this and the following species are called 'beach birds.' 1891 PACKARD 427–8 Semi-palmated Plover. Occurs abundantly throughout the coast region. . . Known as 'Beach Bird' in Labrador. 1924 ENGLAND 127 Me? I can't sing no more 'an a crippled beach bird! 1957 *Daily News* 15 July, p. 2 Beachy birds, or something like them, flew and walked over the stony beach where the river ran in. 1959 MCATEE 34 Beachy bird. Sanderling (Nfld, 'Labr'). T 45/6–64 The yarn about beach-birds. They were that thick one night, this great big flock of beach-birds come, and when they flew over the place, they thought this big heavy cloud was goin' to rain. 1967 *Bk of Nfld* iii, 283 Spotted Sandpiper; Beachy Bird (because of its fondness for beaches).

beach racket: discussion concerning crews of women who will 'spread' and cure salted cod-fish in the coming summer; cp RACKET[2].

1942 *Grand Bank U C School* 37 [The] 'beach racket' begins soon after Christmas.

beach rock: large, smooth boulder rounded by the action of waves; SALT-WATER ROCK.

1909 BROWNE 281 He never kept books. . . It is said that his *standards* of weight and measurement were a 'beach-rock' and a 'flour-barrel stave.' 1937 DEVINE 63 As plentiful as beach rocks. 1975 GUY 113 A beachrock. . .heated in the oven and put into two wool socks. Sling the rock under the bedding. . .then scravel off your clothes down to the knitted undergarments.

beach room: stretch of foreshore sufficient for the activities of fishing and curing the catch; ROOM.

[1766] 1976 HEAD 192 Jerseyman's Harbour had 'convenient places for building of stages & beach room for a good many Boats.' 1976 ibid 60 Gledhill had the properties, including the all important beach room where the fish were dried, in his control.

beach woman: one employed in 'spreading'

and curing salted cod-fish on the foreshore. Cp
SHORE[1]: SHORE CREW.
   M 66–18 Beach-women would turn the fish each
morning and afternoon to dry. In the evening the fish
would be piled in 'faggots' or 'piles.'

beachy a   *OED* ~ (1597–1734); SEARY 177.
Related in a variety of ways to a level stretch of
shore-line on which waves break.
   1858 [LOWELL] i, 14 On the hill-top, near Beachy
Cove, (named from its strip of sand and shingle edging
the shore,) they stood still. 1951 *Nfld & Lab Pilot* i, 96
Beachy cove, at the head of which is a shingle beach,
lies close south-eastward of Beachy point. 1974
Evening Telegram 13 Feb, p. 13 We all knew how
sharp a cliffty rock is on the corners compared to a
round, beachy one.

beachy bird See BEACH BIRD.

be after (doing something) See AFTER prep.

beak n   also **bake** [be:k, beik] *EDD* ~ sb[1] 1;
DAS 4 (1950) for sense (a). (a) A person's nose;
face; hence (b) a nosey parker or meddlesome
busybody (1924 ENGLAND 313).
   P 148–64 I'll punch him in the bake—I'll punch him
in the gob. P 148–65 Buddy had a nose three feet long
on him. What a bake! 1976 GUY 15 It has been
recommended. . .that I take up some form of
exercise. . . I believe I'll exercise my beak. It's not too
strenuous and about my speed. I'm reading the book
'Ten Easy Steps to a More Powerful Proboscis.'

beal n   also **beel**. Cp *OED* ~ sb[3] 'mouth of a
(highland) river or valley' (1818); DINNEEN béal
'mouth.' A pass or opening between hills
through which a river flows; the mouth of a river.
   [1910] PRICHARD 200 Just before arriving at Burnt
Hill, near the 'beel of the Gander,' in Bob's phrase, we
began to pass through forests that had been destroyed
by fire. P 160–70 ~ the deep centre current of a river;
the mouth of a river.

beam [= bar of scales] See BREAK THE BEAM.

bear n   *NID* bearberry n 2 'American cranberry'; *DAE* ~ trap (1825–).
   Comb **bearberry**: (a) variety of cranberry
(*Vaccinium oxycoccos*); MARSH BERRY (1898 *N S
Inst Sci* ix, 382); (b) PARTRIDGE BERRY
(*Mitchella repens*) (P 94–57).
   1932 POLUNIN 51 There was a profusion of bearberries and other fruits not yet ripe—many, with numerous herbs, were still in flower. C 69–5 He asked him
how he had got on with the bearberries (partridge berries) when he was out on Easter Head. 1971
NOSEWORTHY 172 [Bearberries are] like cranberries.
   bear house: enclosure concealing a weapon to
dispatch a trapped bear.
   [1785] 1792 CARTWRIGHT iii, 101 Mr Collingham,
after mooring the shallop, walked to the head of Martin's Cove, and built a bear-house to tail a gun in.

bear trap: device to trap a bear.
   [1771] 1792 CARTWRIGHT i, 180 I also carried two of
the traps which were on the barrens, into the wood by
Long Pool, and tailed the beartrap at the path end, by
the river. 1977 *Inuit Land Use* 215 A bear trap is rarely
set unless certain signs of bear have been observed.

bearing vbl n Comb **bearing stick**: light pole held
at an angle over the right shoulder to balance
and distribute the weight of a log or beam carried
on the left shoulder.
   P 245–54 ~ a stick used to bear up a load of wood
when carried on the back. 1957 *Daily News* 24 Sep, p. 3
He will cut [fuel], haul it over the snow, then 'spell' it
on his shoulder with his 'bearing' stick. . .to his back
door. C 71–123 When a person was carrying a turn of
wood on his shoulder, if the load was too heavy on one
shoulder (always his left shoulder because it was considered bad luck to carry a turn on the right shoulder)
he would use a bearin' stick.

beat v   Cp *OED* ~ v[1] 19 naut 'to strive against
contrary winds or currents at sea' for sense 1; 3:
beat the streets (1375–1587), *EDD* v[2] 1 (6) So D
for phr in sense 2.
   1 Of a herd of animals, esp seals, to move
instinctively in a certain direction; to migrate.
   1866 WILSON 316 In the autumn, or near winter, [the
deer] migrate, or, as the hunters say, they 'beat to the
south,' and go near Cape Ray or the Bay of St George.
1924 ENGLAND 239 Wary at last, beating north and
ever northward, the vast herd—decimated but still
incredibly numerous—is on the trek to the far places
where men cannot pursue. 1947 TANNER 493 The
mother at last forces the remaining pups to take to the
water, a mysterious instinct at once teaches them to go
north, and by the end of May these 'beating seals' have
mostly passed along the Labrador coast. P 102–60
[They have] fresh seal meat, as early in May as the seals
beating their way north from the Gulf would trim the
shore.
   2 Phr *beat the paths/streets/roads*: to be out at
night.
   P 97–66 You're beating the paths again! 1972
MURRAY 157 Decent girls did not 'beat the roads' till
'all hours of the night.'
   bet/beaten to a snot: completely exhausted.
   1970 *Evening Telegram* 17 July, p. 2 I'm fair bet to a
snot.

beater n   For senses 1 and 2 *Kilkenny Lexicon*
~ 'a bold, aggressive individual,' *DC* ~ n Nfld
(1924–). See also BEAT v 1.
   1 A harp seal just past the 'white-coat' stage
and migrating north from the breeding grounds
on the ice floes off Newfoundland; DIPPER. Also
attrib **beater hunt,** ~ **pelt** [see PELT n], ~ **seal**.
   1893 *Trade Review Christmas No* 13 There was not a
drop of water to be seen as far as the eye could
reach—nothing but a solid jamb of ice, which was covered with seals, known as 'beaters,' in thousands. 1924
ENGLAND 102 As they start migrating, they are called
'baters,' i.e. beaters. 'Quinters' is another name for the

beating seals. 1933 GREENE 78–9 The young
seals. . .now begin naturally and fearlessly to take to
swimming and diving. . .and learning without instruc-
tion all other sea-necessities of a full seal-life. . . Now
they become 'beaters' of the Seal Hunt, and of a certain surety every little head will then be pointed for the
North. 1947 TANNER 493 By the end of May these
'beating seals' have mostly passed along the Labrador
coast. The next winter the 'beater seals' return south
again as 'bed-lamers.' T 43/4–64 After they leaves the
white coat they're called beaters because they spends
all their time in the water. 1976 *Evening Telegram* 3
Apr, p. 6 That is the importance of the late spring
'beater' hunt to the landsmen along much of our north-
east coast. Seals which are taken by these
hunters. . .have by this time doubled their weight and
value. 1978 ibid 10 Mar, p. 1 By the time the vessels
reach the whitecoats the seals may have matured to
beaters, seals 18 days of age and older and capable of
taking to the water. Ibid 9 May, p. 2 This year. . .the
company didn't receive too many beater pelts.

2 A loose woman; a tramp; cp PATH-BEATER.
1925 *Dial Notes* v, 340 ~ Vagabond; tramp. 1937
DEVINE 9 ~ A dissolute woman.

3 The final winning hand (in a game).
1977 RUSSELL 69 Then Skipper Joe and myself
played the best two out of three at cribbage, and for all
his luck, I won the beater.

beaver[1] n   [= *Castor canadensis caecator*]. For
combs. see: *OED* cod sb[1] 4 b ~ cod obs (1634,
1646); *DC* ~ cuttings (Nfld: 1770–); ~ house
(1691–); ~ root (Nfld: 1822–); ~ tail snowshoe
(1941–).

Attrib, comb **beaver cod**: inguinal or groin sac
of a beaver from which castor is obtained.
1612 GUY 55 A little peece of fleshe was broughte
away, which was fownde to be a beaver cod.

beaver cuttings: trees, saplings, branches or
stumps cut by a beaver.
[1770] 1792 CARTWRIGHT i, 22 I named it Watson
Pond, and was greatly surprised to find beaver cuttings
by the side of it: for, Mr Lucas, who lived a year at
Chateau, assured me, that there were no beavers in
this country. 1792 ibid *Gloss* i, ix Beaver-cuttings. A
furrier's term for those trees or sticks which have been
cut down by beavers. It is also used for the stumps
which are left. 1947 TANNER 418 The Labrador beaver
is a very cautious animal; yet the rich, long grass growing in the centre of the 'beaver-meadow' and the fresh
traces on the barked willows, 'beaver cuttings,' reveal
its presence.

beaver hat (man), ~ **vessel**: two-masted vessel
of 60–80 tons (54–72 m tons), rigged for the seal-
hunt with a square topsail on the foremast.
[1900 OLIVER & BURKE] 46 Topsail schooners (beaver hat men)—this last named so-called from having
only one square sail on the foremast. 1916 MURPHY
11–12 Some of the schooners carried a square sail, and
were called 'beaver hats' or 'beaver hat men,' the
majority of the vessels were brigs and brigantines. 1937
DEVINE 9 ~ vessel. A fore-topsail schooner.

beaver house: lodge or den of a beaver.

[1663] 1963 YONGE 135 I once lost myself in the
wood, and wandered to a Beaver house. . . I saw they
had cut down large branches of trees [and covered]
them with great quantities of earth, boughs, and rub-
ble. [1770] 1792 CARTWRIGHT i, 15 We took a walk to
a pond which lies upon the brook, and not far from the
mouth of it, to look at a new beaverhouse, in which the
salmoniers had killed four beavers. 1861 DE BOILIEU
81 The beaver-house consists of three room or cells.
The ground floor is (to use an Hibernianism) in the
water, the floor above is used for feeding, and the third
as a sleeping-chamber. Most of the beaver-houses have
an inlet and an outlet. 1888 HOWLEY *MS
Reminiscences* 34 We came across a fresh beaver house
but did not see the beaver themselves, though we
waited till dusk. T 203/5–65 In the winter you'll go to a
beaver's house, you'll cut a big hole in the ice and you
tie your trap so far up from the end o' the stick, and
you'd shove that in the mouth, the doorway o' the beaver house.

beaver more: yellow pond-lily (*Nuphar
variegatum*) (1893 *N S Inst Sci* viii, 364); cp
MORE n.
[c1900] 1978 *RLS* 8, p. 26 [More is] also applied to
the roots of the pond lilly, or Beaver More.

beaver(s) pride: see **beaver cod**; PRIDE.

beaver root: (a) any of several varieties of
water lily; see also **beaver more** above; (b) root
of a water lily used for medicinal purposes.
[1822] 1856 CORMACK 20 They also subsist on the
large roots of the waterlilly, Nymphea odorata; called
by the Indians beaver-root. 1846 TOCQUE 291 The
whole surface of the water was covered with the leaves
of the beaver root (*Nuphar Luteum*). 1865 CAMPBELL
138 Beaver-root—the root of the yellow lily—was nib-
bled and left about in scraps. T 172/4–65 You see those
lilies in the pond? That's beaver root. They flowers in
the summer, comes out with a big yellow bulb, and
then they turns with a white flower. C 75–132 A tonic
was made from elder berries, juniper bush, beaver
roots, bog beans, sweet mores, sasberella roots and
Indian tea. 1976 GUY 142 In their kitchen they had bottles hanging up back of the stove with beaver root in
them. 1977 *Inuit Land Use* 303 Beavers inhabit low-
lying marshy areas that have plenty of willows, birch,
poplar, aspens, spruce, and the 'beaver roots' which
grow on the bottoms of ponds and on which beavers
feed.

beaver tail(ed racquet): type of Labrador
snowshoe with an oval frame.
1884 STEARNS 149 [The beaver-tailed racquet] is a
bent bow of wood with two crossbars, the intervening
spaces being thickly woven of deerskin thong, except a
small opening where the toe goes, and which is below
the middle of the upper bar. There are great varieties
of form, called usually from some fancied resemblance
to the tail of an animal. 1910 TOWNSEND 173 The
Labrador snow-shoe or racquette is almost everywhere
tailless or nearly so. . . Some of them, however, have
short rounded tails and are appropriately called 'bea-
ver-tails.' P 118–67 I guess it's time to put on the beavertails.

beaver[2] n

1 A locally made chewing and smoking tobacco.

[1960] 1965 PEACOCK (ed) i, 123 "Fish and Brewis": And see them chew Beaver and squirt it up high, / Lie back on the [gangboards] and laugh till you die. T 55–64 Old Beaver tobacco, wonst you'd buy that for twenty-two cents or less, and now it is seventy-four cents a stick. 1972 *Evening Telegram* 24 Oct, p. 3 Imperial Tobacco's plant was located at the corner of Bond and Flavin streets. . .and it produced its own brands for the local market including cigarettes such as Wings, Royal Blend, Flag and Gems, and other tobaccos, tobacco products such as plug tobacco, marketed under the brand name Beaver. 1975 RUSSELL 43 On my way down to Levi's store for a plug of Beaver, I run into Skipper Joe.

2 Tag-man in child's chasing game.

C 71–35 There was one home base and two beavers or tag men. The object was to leave home base and tease the beavers into trying to catch you. If they did, you had to help them catch more. While running, you'd say, 'Old Billy Beaver, can't catch a weaver.'

beaver³ n Cp *EDD* ~ sb³ 'bushes' Do, beever 'a growth of brambles' So. Attrib **beaver thorn**: in children's rhyme, the name of the common garden slug.

C 69–17 Children at Elliston spent a lot of time playing with garden snails, called beaver thorns. C 70–21 We believed that if you stood over a snail and repeated the words 'Beaverthorn / Put out your horns, / The cows are in your garden,' it would put out its horns.

bed n *Cent* ~ n 8 for sense 4.

1 The foundation, floor, posts and beams of a fishing-stage; cp BALLAST n: BALLAST (BED); BEDDING.

[1675] 1976 HEAD 18 Few stages remained; at St John's in 1675 it was reported that only the bed of the admiral's stage had been left. P 148–61 Bed of [the] stage.

2 The two heavy timbers on each side of the frame of a boat, joined across the bottom by a floor (P 127–75).

T 16–64 You put a timber between each strip. You start at the forward one—the fore-hook, and you'll nail that one on the bottom. And then you will take the next one—that's the first bed aft the fore-hook.

3 Logs placed under a boat to roll it into the water (P 245–56).

4 In phr *bed of ducks*: a flock of wild fowl, densely packed in the water.

[1771] 1792 CARTWRIGHT i, 185 I went over to White-fox Island, where I got a shot at a large bed of eider-ducks, and killed seven of them. 1868 HOWLEY *MS Reminiscences* 57 We did not come across any game till we reached the pond where the traps were set. This was literally filled with Black ducks all out in the middle closely huddled together, in what Billy terms a bed of ducks; they appeared to be asleep.

5 Comb **bed cabin**: a wooden bed with interlaced rope attached to the frame to support the mattress (P 127–78).

bed fly: wingless bug infesting houses, esp beds; bed-bug; (*Cimex lectularius*).

1924 ENGLAND 313 ~s. Bedbugs; lice.

bed rock: large beach stone, heated, wrapped in a cloth and used as a bed-warmer (Q 71–7).

bed strip: decorative strip of cloth at head and foot of a bed.

1972 MURRAY 197 In the old days, no bed was properly 'made' unless it had a 'bed strip' or 'valence' attached to the bed frame and going round the front and ends of the bed. This was a strip of white material, usually shirting, which was trimmed with handmade lace.

beddamer See BEDLAMER.

bedding n

1 The floor of a fishing stage or premises.

T 43–64 This drudge barrow was made half-moon fashion so as 'twould slip along on the beddin' of the stage easy. C 75–136 Bedding is used in referring to a stage floor, particularly the outside stage where fish is cleaned. This is built of board about one to one and a half inches thick. Fishermen would tell their sons to 'throw the fish in on the bedding.'

2 Heavy timbers to which the engine of a boat or vessel is fastened.

P 200–63 Bedding is the heavy timber framework (rectangular) to which the engine is bolted. 1969 *Nfld Qtly* July, p. 19 ~ a cross keelson; or two parallel strong pieces of wood laid transverse to the keel to give support to the engine. 1979 TIZZARD 332 We then put the motor boat ashore and removed the Victor engine from the bedding and installed the Atlantic.

3 The base or floor of a lobster pot.

P 241–68 The bedding is the base or bottom of the pot; it is usually of heavier wood than the rest of the pot. The rocks are laid on the bedding to sink the pot.

bedlamer n also **beddamer, bedlemer, bedlimmer, bellamer** ['bɛdləməɹ]. Cp *OED* ~ 'lunatic' (1675, 1753); *EDD* bedlam sb¹ 1 'troublesome person or animal', *EDD* ~ 1 'Bedlam-beggar' (1742); *DC* ~ Nfld (1773–) for sense 1; *EDD* ~ 2 (Nfld: 1898) for sense 2.

1 An immature seal, esp a harp seal, approaching breeding age; also attrib.

[1766] 1971 BANKS 145 The Bedlamer Quite dusky without any mark they themselves tell you that the Bedlamer is the young harp. [1774] 1792 CARTWRIGHT ii, 35–6 We hauled some nets. . .and a couple of bedlamers. [1802] 1916 MURPHY 2–3 Our dependence rests wholly upon Harps and Bedlamers, which are driven by winds and ice from the northeast seas. 1842 JUKES i, 310 When twelve months old the males [harp-seals] are still scarcely to be distinguished from the females, and during that season they are called 'bedlamers.' 1867 SMYTH 93 ~ Young Labrador seals, which set up a dismal cry when they cannot escape their pursuers—and go madly after each other in the sea. 1905 MURPHY 21 "Seal Hunting Song": Old 'bedlamers' we often take, / Their 'pelts' being quite as good, sir, / As any 'swoil' in yield of oil / Be he 'dog harp' or 'hood,' sir. 1923

CHAFE 9 [In migrating] the Harps keep comparatively near the Shore and the Hoods a few miles off. The giddy bedlamers alone break the rules of the road. 1933 GREENE 74 These young Bedlamer seals appear to be free of the strict herd-control that comes with later days. They seem to be allowed to swim, and fish, and herd by themselves, and indeed to live as they choose; whereas some kind of an almost military discipline seems to exist amongst the adult members of these seal communities. 1937 DEVINE 9 ~ A two-year old harp seal, said to be corrupted from the French Bete de la mer, (Beast of the sea). T 80/4–64 This year they're a bellamer, small bellamer, and the next year they're a big bellamer. What we calls a turner seal is turnin' from a bellamer to a harp. 1978 *Decks Awash* vii (1) [p. ii] ~ a juvenile harp seal from about 1 to 5 years of age which has a spotted coat.

   2 A youth approaching manhood, esp in comb ~ **boy**; MANEEN.
   1896 *J A Folklore* ix, 34 Bedlamer. . .is applied rather contemptuously to young fellows between 16 and 20. 1940 SCAMMELL 8 "The Six Horse-Power Coaker": 'Twas coming on night, with the seas feather white, / When up to us rowed a small skiff, / And a bedlamer boy with a cast in his eye, / Kindly offered to give us a lift. 1959 SAMSON vii He, as a 'bedlammer' boy, entertained the notion of going to St John's. T 191–65 There would be always a crowd of bedlamer boys, and when the older people 'd be inside havin' their tea, the young fellers 'd be outside.

bedlimmer See BEDLAMER.

beel See BEAL.

beer n A flavoured, carbonated beverage; freq in phr *bottle of beer* (P 148–59).
   T 12/348–64 Any sort of soft drink we always call it bottle of beer. When we were young we used to distinguish man's beer and beer. M 70–26 Pop (we used to call it beer).

beetle n also ~ **board**, ~ **stock**, **bittle** EDD ~ sb 3. A flat board used for beating clothes.
   1891 *Holly Branch* 34 Had I been present when the Prince committed that outrage on old Foley it would have been worse for him than Mother Carter's bittle stock or old B–'s cuvvel staff. P 97–67 The bittle board [was a] long, hard spatula for beating clothes or a mat. P 191–73 The communal wash-day was held at O'Leary's River near Wickham's. The clothes were beaten by paddles or beetles.

belay v also **b'lay**. Cp SMYTH ~ 'stop' (1876) for sense 2.
   1 To row and steer with an oar from the stern of a large fishing boat, counteracting the force of the sail and other complementary oars; to scull a small boat.
   [1663] 1963 YONGE 57 The boat is 3 or 4 tons. . .but these three men will row these great boats a long way. The boat's master he rows at the stern, against the other two, who row one side; he belays against them, and so not only rows, but steers the boat. [1766] 1971

BANKS 133 They are Calld here Shallops Rigged with a main mast & foremast & Lugsail & furnishd also with 4 oars 3 of which row on one side & the other which is twice as long as any of the rest Belays as they Call it the other three by being rowed sideways over the stern by a man who stands up for that Purpose with his face towards the Rowers Counteracting them & Steering at the same time as he gives way to the boat. [(1840) 1954 INNIS 381 There was a peculiarity noticed in the French boats at Pacquet Harbour which I never observed elsewhere, namely, both oars being pulled on the larboard side, and no oar at all on the starboard; but the third person used an oar fitted into a crutch placed broad on the starboard quarter, with which he pulled the stern round against the power of the two larboard oars, and thus steers her course.] 1883 HOWLEY *MS Reminiscences* 5–6 One very curious custom is that all the [French fisher–] men row on one side of the boat, except one who stands aft and with a long wide bladed sweep keeps blaying against the rest. P 127–77 ~ to force an oar through the water, as a sculling oar or paddle.
   2 To turn a small boat by backing water with one oar and pulling with the other; SLEW v 1.
   C 64–5 To [b'lay] (turn with an oar) a boat around against the sun will bring bad luck. P 61–66 [B'lay] the punt: to turn the punt around with an oar. Q 71–6 B'lay her around, old man! Christ, I could b'lay Aunt Fanny's arse quicker than that! C 73–128 You push the oar straight down and [push] it the opposite way than before you stopped. This method is used if you want to turn the boat: you would 'b'lay' with one oar and turn with the other oar.

belk v also **bilk*** EDD ~ v¹. To belch.
   P 167–66 He bilked and said 'excuse me.'

bell n Cp OED ~ sb¹ 12: ~ roof. Comb
bell-roof: type of mansard roof with either two or four concave sides.
   M 68–17 The bell-roof house was one of the first types built [in Gillams] and was prominent until about 1925. 1974 MANNION 148 Over a dozen dwellings along the Cape Shore had a 4-sided or hipped roof, locally called a 'bell' or 'cottage' roof.

bellamer See BEDLAMER.

belly n Cp EDD ~ sb 4 (10) ~ -flapper for second comb.
   Comb **belly-cag***, ~ **-keg**: stomach; cp KEG.
   M 65–9 He got a pain in his belly-cag. M 71–104 Belly-keg: stomach of a child.
   belly-smacker: a dive flat on one's stomach into the water.
   1966 PADDOCK 124 ~ a dive in which the front of one's body hits the water horizontally. P 198–67 He did some belly-smacker that time!

bellycat(t)er See BALLICATTER.

belong v OED ~ v 4 including 'to be a member of a family. . .a native or inhabitant of a place' (quots 1485–1856). Phr *belong to*:

1 To be related by blood.

[1765] [1900 OLIVER & BURKE] 2 . . .belonging to Mr Sparks. 1858 [LOWELL] ii, 202 'Mubbe 'e belongs to 'ee, sir; do 'e?' P 148–60 Here's somebody that belongs to you.

2 To be a native of; to come from.

[c1875] 1927 DOYLE (ed) 21 "The Banks of Newfoundland": And all the rest were Irish boys, they came from Paddy's land, / Only four or five of our seamen belonged to Newfoundland. [1900 OLIVER & BURKE] 30 A boat's crew belonging to Quidi Vidi met a watery grave. 1927 DOYLE (ed) "Loss of the Schooner *Susan*": The loss of four young fishermen, / Belong to Trinity Bay. P 269–63 Where do you belong? 1965 PEACOCK (ed) i, xix One of the commonest phrases in the Newfoundland vernacular: 'he *belongs* to Rocky Harbour'—one is never *from* or even *born in* a place, one always *belongs to* it. 1975 BUTLER 65 He married a woman belong to Burin.

bend n   *OED* ~ sb⁴ 6 naut (1626–1803) for sense 1; cp sb² 1 obs 'thin flat strip adapted to bind round' for sense 2.

1 A heavy timber forming one of the principal ribs of a boat or vessel.

1913 *Nfld Qtly* July, p. 30 The following year he arrived in port with his ship leaking, pumps kept going, and five 'ben' of timbers broke in, having 500 old harps and bedlamers. T 178/9–65 Sometimes we wouldn't batten out [the boat], we'd only have three bends—fore hook, midship bend and after hook. P 13–77 ~ The very curved frames or timbers in the midships or body of a boat. Midship bend, for example.

2 A thin, flat strip of wood used to keep timbers in position when building a boat (Q 67–78).

3 A wooden strip, about 2 in. (5 cm) wide, extending from stem to stern of a boat between the binding strake and the gunwale (P 127–75).

bend v   Cp *OED* ~ naut 'to tie, fasten [a rope or cable]' (1867). To fasten a trout or salmon fly to the cast (P 245–78).

1898 *Christmas Bells* 5 With what eager haste I joined my rod, and bent my flies—a cast that had been prepared for many days before.

bender n   The spring of a rabbit snare or 'slip.'

P 148–61 ~ Small tree or alder to tie rabbit slip to. Q 71–6 I rigged a flicer or bender to catch him. P 113–72 ~ A thin flexible tree to which a wire noose or 'slip' was attached, and which, bent over a rabbit track, was released upwards when a rabbit became entangled in the trap.

bending vbl n   Cp *OED* horse sb 7 'frame or structure on which something is mounted or supported.' Comb **bending horse**: frame or structure on which a cooper bends or shapes strips of birch into hoops; HORSE n 2.

M 71–120 The hoops were not fitted on a drawing mare. When [they are shaved down, they] are bent in preparation for quiling [coiling]. This is done on a bending horse. P 127–78 'Quiling' refers to a specific procedure called 'breaking the hoop' on the bending horse.

beothuk n   also **beothic, beothick, beothuck**, etc [bi'ɒθʊk] *NID* ~; 1968 *Nfld Qtly* Fall, p. 14–15, J Hewson: /peoθuk/ 'the People.'

1 Member of a tribe of indians, now extinct, related to the Algonkian people and inhabiting Newfoundland ?–1829 A.D.; NATIVE a: *native indian*, RED INDIAN.

[1827] 1915 HOWLEY 183 The history of the original inhabitants of Newfoundland, called by themselves Beothuck, and by Europeans, the Red Indians, can only be gleaned from tradition, and that chiefly among the Micmacs. 1866 WILSON 306 They called themselves 'Boeothicks;' but the settlers called them 'Red Indians;' from the fact of their painting their bodies and their wigwams with red ochre. [1885] 1915 HOWLEY 302 [Gatschet:] The spellings of the tribal name found in the vocabularies are: Beothuk, Beothik, Béhathook, Boeothuck, and Beathook; beothuk means not only *Red Indian* of Newfoundland, but is also the generic expression for *Indian*. 1907 MILLAIS 17 The Beothicks had straight black hair, high cheek bones, small black eyes, and a copper-coloured skin. In hunting and fishing modes they also resembled the natives of the neighbouring continent, and their weapons, wigwams, and domestic interests were also similar. Ethnologists are not quite agreed as to the nature of their language, but it is generally accepted that they were probably a small branch of the warlike Algonquins, who at that time were the masters of the northeastern continent of Canada. 1923 MOSDELL 10 *Beothic*: new sealing steamer. . .arrived in Nfld for the first time, Feb 17, 1909. P 54–62 The pronunciation of the steel sealer's name, *Beothic* [was] Bo-it-ick, as I used to hear it invariably among my neighbours at Elliston when, about 1910, this ship first came to Newfoundland—said neighbours never having heard of the name Beothuck for our aborigines, using therefor the term *Red Indian*. T 25–64 And up here, about a mile from that, there was a tribe of Beothuk Indians. 1976 TUCK 76 The Beothuks slowly became extinct, because the resources of interior Newfoundland were not sufficient to provide a year-round occupation for people who had traditionally exploited the rich resources of the coast for nine or ten months of every year.

2 A language of the Algonkian type spoken by the Beothuk indians.

1850 LATHAM 330 Reasons against either of these views are supplied by a hitherto unpublished Beothuck vocabulary with which I have been kindly furnished by my friend Dr King. [1886] 1915 HOWLEY 309 The points to be gained for the morphology of Beothuk are more scanty still than what can be obtained for reconstructing its phonology, and for the inflection of its verb we are entirely in the dark. 1968 *Int Journ of Am Linguistics* xxxiv, 85 Our information on Beothuk, the language of the aboriginal inhabitants of Newfoundland, comes from four vocabularies.

berry¹ n   [= any of the principal wild berries,

esp bakeapples, blueberries, partridge berries, harvested commercially or for domestic use]. Cp *DAE* ~ 1.

Attrib, comb **berry bank**: a hill or elevated plateau bearing wild berries. See also BANK 2.

1933 MERRICK 29 The famous berry banks are just above Mininipi, and when we went ashore to boil [the kettle] we picked nearly a quart.

berry box: wooden box used by pickers to carry harvest of partridge- and blueberries.

T 1–63¹ We used to go berry picking and take berry boxes, forty or fifty, a couple of us together. We'd fill them. M 70–21 [Male] blueberry pickers often used a 'berry box' to transport their berries from the barrens to the community. This was a rectangular wooden box, fitted with a hinged cover and having two rope loops about one-third the way down, through which the man thrust his arms. Often there was an additional loop at the other side or back of the box through which he thrust a stick or pole which lodged on his shoulder and thus made the load easier to carry.

berry crop: the harvest of wild berries.

1976 *Daily News* 14 July, p. 2 Berry crops are blooming early this year and the director of the soils and crops division with the department of forestry and agriculture, is expecting a good season. 'Blueberries, partridge berries and bakeapples are already in bloom,' he said.

berry duff: a boiled or steamed pudding with wild berries as an ingredient.

1966 HORWOOD 19 Blueberry pudding, loaded with luscious fruit, boiled in a cloth, and popped open, fresh from the pot and dripping with purple juice, on the kitchen table. Mr Markady called it 'berry duff'—a term that he had brought home from his lifetime at sea.

berry ground: elevated, unwooded stretch of land or 'barren' producing wild berries. See also GROUND.

1967 HORWOOD 92 Especially on the heath above the wooded valleys—on the open back country that Newfoundlanders call. . .the berry-grounds—winter comes like a thief in the night. 1972 MURRAY 258 Women, picking blueberries for sale, went to the berry grounds or 'barrens' carrying perhaps two water buckets and a hoop, as for water. 1980 *Evening Telegram* 8 Nov, p. 6 That walk over the hills to the berry grounds was real pretty [but] we were too stunned to appreciate it.

berry hills: see **berry bank**, ~**ground**.

1938 MACDERMOTT 241 When one hears the name 'Berry Hills,' the berries referred to are partridge berries.

berry hocky: see **berry ocky** below.

berry note: buyer's receipt issued to picker for quantity of berries received.

1972 MURRAY 261 Those who sold berries were given a 'berry note' indicating the amount of berries 'shipped' and the price per gallon. The value of the note had to be 'taken up' in goods in the store where the berries were shipped.

berry ocky: home-made drink of wild berries, esp partridge berries, or jam and water; cp OCKY.

C 66–1 At home it was the grown-ups who used to go mummering [but] the young folks went too. We were always treated to cake, cookies and black-currant drinks, or partridge berry drinks which they used to call 'berryocky.' 1969 *Christmas Mumming in Nfld* 133 ~ a hot drink of berry juice, usually with rum added. Q 71–7 That's just as bitter as berryocky.

berry² n Comb **berry fish**: cod-fish suffering from a morbid condition characterised by berry-like growth on the gills; BLACKBERRY 2.

C 68–3 ~ cod with a red seedy growth under its gills. The growth is usually about the size of a partridge berry. Q 71–7 ~ a small cod with a red undergrowth under its gills. Berry fish occur where there is a shortage of food in the water.

berth n also **birth** DC ~ n 2 (Nfld: 1819–) for sense 1; 4 (Nfld: 1905) for sense 3; ~ **money** (Nfld: 1869–) for comb in sense 5.

1 A place as seal-hunter on a vessel with a share in the profits of the voyage.

1819 ANSPACH 422 The rest pay generally forty shillings each for their birth, that is, for their proportion of the provisions during the voyage; and all are to receive each half a man's share of the seals caught, or the value thereof, dividing the amount of the whole produce of the voyage into so many shares as there are men on board. 1855 WHITE *MS Journal* 1 Sep [From] Michael Hartery [for] Berth £3. 1883 HATTON & HARVEY 298 No wonder the young Newfoundlander pants for the day when he will get 'a berth for the ice,' and share in the wild joys and excitement of the hunt. 1919 GRENFELL² 174 All the wharves where there was any chance of a 'berth' to the ice were fairly in a state of siege. [1928] 1978 *Evening Telegram* 30 Jan, p. 20 The owners of Bowrings sealing fleet have instructed the captains to select their own crews on the understanding they will select experienced sealers (with perhaps a few new youths) and distribute the berths over a variety of districts. 1976 CASHIN 82 The thought struck me to ask him for a berth to the ice (the seal fishery) the coming spring in the *Florizel*.

2 A winter's job cutting timber for bed and board.

[1794] 1968 THOMAS 171 When their money is all gone some of [the fishermen] will lett themselves out for the Winter as wooders, for their Victuals and Lodgings. To get a Berth of this kind is consider'd lucky, for the Winters are long and severe.

3 A particular station on fishing grounds, and in netting seals in coastal waters, assigned by custom or lot to a vessel, boat, crew or family; freq with specifying word COD-TRAP, SALMON, TRAP¹; cp GROUND.

1905 DUNCAN 91 When he awoke at dawn there were two other schooners lying quietly at anchor near by and the berths had been 'staked.' 1921 CABOT 40 He was looking for fish, and his whole voyage, his year's fortune, might turn on his seizing upon some chance opportunity to locate in a good 'berth.' 1936 SMITH 46 On our way down from Pottles Bay I noticed that there was no trap in our berth, so I sent five men in the boat to reset ours in the old place. 1953 *Nfld Fish Develop Report* 49 The possibilities of trap-fishing in any district are determined by the number of prime 'berths' available. 1955 DOYLE (ed) 8 "A Crowd of Bold Sharemen": On the twenty-sixth of June we put out of Quirpon, / The *Morris* [bein'] lively, for the berths we were bound. 1966 BEN-DOR 45 Catching seals by nets is the primary technique employed by settlers. Nets are placed in the vicinity of the village in 'berths' which are associated with the different families. 1977 RUSSELL 16 . . .and he always fires the gun at twelve o'clock every May the tenth when the rest of us claim our berths.

4 In phr *berth free*: without any charge (for admission as hunter on a sealing vessel).

1819 ANSPACH 422 The crews of their largest craft consist of from thirteen to eighteen men; of these some are gunners, who, on finding their own guns, are admitted *birth* free; the rest pay generally forty shillings each for their birth.

5 Attrib, comb **berth money**: charge made by owner or captain for place as seal hunter on a vessel.

1842 BONNYCASTLE ii, 166 The merchant by long custom, besides the benefits derived from extra stores or clothing, had always deducted a certain varying sum for berth-money to the hands. . .for the privilege of embarking on the most hazardous and uncertain adventure which the spirit of commerce leads men to undertake. 1869 MCCREA 183 'Its the berth-money the boys is disputing. . . He's riz ten shillings. . .' The berth-money was the fee each man paid for the ticket for his chance of the voyage, including provisions put on board by the merchants. 1973 MOWAT 57 When Job Brothers brought the old *Neptune* over from Dundee, she paid for herself in fifteen years from berth money alone! In my time the owners would give out tickets for half the berths and the captain give out the other half.

berth ticket: authorization for a place as hunter on a sealing vessel. See also TICKET.

1973 MOWAT 56 But it was near as hard to get a berth-ticket as an invitation to the Governor's Ball in St John's.

best kind n phr Colloquial formula indicating general approval; in the best state or condition; FINEST KIND.

T 393/4–67 When that puncheon was gone, there'd be usually half a barrel o' sugar, molasses sugar [left] in all those puncheons. Boy, 'twas the best kind—we loved it on bread. C 73–128 Beastins was the name on the first milk from a cow when she had a calf. This was considered very good to eat. My father says it was best kind to have boiled, strained and salted. P 141–75 How are you today? Oh, the best kind.

betty n Cp *EDD* ~ sb 2 'nickname for the kettle'; 3 'instrument. . .fixed on a tub to let clothes drain through.' Comb **betty murphy**: barrel sawn to make a tub; three-quarter BARREL TUB.

P 229–67 Bring me along the betty murphy till I put some fish in it.

bever[1] n also **beaver** *EDD* ~ sb[2] 1 'slight

refreshment taken between meals' obs. Liquor taken at a specified time during working hours.

1937 DEVINE 9 Beaver. A dram at eleven in the forenoon.

bever[2] See BIVVER v, n.

bib n Cp *O Sup*[2] bib-cock 'tap with turned-down nozzle' (1797–), *NID* ~[2] 3 a for sense 1.

1 The spout of a kettle or teapot.

1928 BURKE [6] "The Scramble for the Teapots at the Fire": There was large size, small size, / And little ones for girls and boys; / Some with fancy face and eyes, / (The kind we all require); / Long bibs, short bibs; / Some for washing down spare-ribs. T 50/1–64 [They'd] cook their fish and boil their kettle—pipers, they call them—little flat-arsed tin kettles with a bib on them.

2 The peak of a cloth cap.

C 69–16 Many of the boys wore caps with a bib on them. Whenever the fishermen saw the boys put their caps on backwards they would say we [would] have the wind northern tomorrow.

3 Attrib, comb **bib cap**: flat cap with projecting brim at the front (P 83–77).

bib stage-light: oil lamp with wick placed in spout, hung in fishing stage; STAGE LAMP.

P 102–60 Two bib stage-lights using kerosene and lamp wicks and a few torch lights, piggins and spudgels.

bibber See BIVVER v, n.

bibby n See also BIB. A small tin kettle with large flat bottom tapering to the top and with a long narrow spout; PIPER.

P 9–57 ~ the kettle used for boiling water on an outdoor fire.

bibe n [baib] DINNEEN badhbh 'royston crow. . .female fairy or phantom.' Unseen supernatural creature making sound in night which signals an approaching death.

Q 67–32 ~ a spirit that attends the dead and is heard crying aloud at night round the house where someone is about to die. 1968 DILLON 132 ~ an audible omen of death, usually described as some kind of bird that cries or whistles. C 68–16 The bibe is the name applied to a strange sobbing or moaning sound which is heard by someone shortly before the death of one of his relatives. No one has ever seen the creature that makes the sound.

bide v *EDD* ~ v 1, 2; *ADD* 2 'to stay' for sense 1; *EDD* 1: let bide for sense 2.

1 To remain, stay put; to be aground.

1858 [LOWELL] ii, 262 Bide a minute. 1891 PACKARD 84 [The cow's] nautical owner informs us, in sturdy Labradorian dialect, that she had been brought up this spring. 'I made her fast to her moorings, and there let her bide to eat the grass.' 1924 ENGLAND 89–90 'Look where y're at, man! Wait, now,' as the unfortunate scrambles out on a drifting pan, 'bide where y're to. Don't jump, yet.' [1954] 1972 RUSSELL 19 If we go in there now, we'll have to bide there five or six hours till [the tide] rises again. T 80/3–64 You let hundreds [of cod-fish] bide in the linnet; you'd never haul the leader, see. T 143–65 He tied on, they bid there; a little wind come down. T 181/2–65 They runned her up the arm and that's where she bid—sunk down. But they never got her on the beach. T 187–65 And I bid up then, had my dinner 'long wi' grandfather. T 187/8–65 She bid there then till the ice all spawned abroad, and went down, and she settled down herself. T 296/7–66 They got in the punt. . .and they bid there four hours, he told me, seeing if they could see any signs of any grease floating up. T 450–67 He bided then, see, till somebody else get sick and come after him. 1972 BROWN 154 Can't take a spell, b'ys, but we'll bide a while and go fishin'.

2 In traditional phr *leff him/her/it bide*: let/ leave him alone.

1937 DEVINE 10 Let 'em bide. P 87–62 Leff 'em bide till father come, he'll chastise un. C 71–115 Better lef en bide now.

3 Comb **bide-in feast**: social gathering held shortly after baby is born at which a special cake ('groaning cake') is served to guests. Cp GROANING.

1896 *J A Folklore* ix, 22 Very soon after [a birth] occurs, with little regard to the feelings or nerves of the mother, a feast is made particularly for the elderly women, of whom all in the neighbourhood are present. This is called the *'bide-in feast'* and at it the 'groaning cake' is distributed.

biff n   Northern slate-coloured junco (*Junco hyemalis hyemalis*) (1976 *Avifaunal Survey* 157).

big a   Cp *OED* ~ a 2 'forceful, violent' obs for sense 1; cp *DC* ~ house (1910–) for comb in sense 3.

1 Of the sea, rough with heavy waves or swell.

1940 DOYLE (ed) 27 "A Great Big Sea": A great big sea hove in the Harbour, / And hove right up in Keoughs' Parlour. P 63–65 There's a big sea on today. P 187–73 Fishermen say, 'There's a big tumble up' to describe the long rolling waves that occur after a breeze from the Atlantic.

2 Phr *big lot*: most, the majority.

1977 *Inuit Land Use* 255 You only get about one of every 100 [harp seals] that goes north, that comes in here. The big lot of them going on. . . I think the big lot goes on out in the deep water.

be big in oneself: to be swollen with pride, puffed up in oneself.

P 53–68 Big in his self: proud. 1976 GUY 18 We should be down on our knees givin' tanks every minute, I says, if we wuzzen't so big in ourselves.

3 Comb **big beachy bird**: purple sandpiper (*Erolia maritima*) (1959) MCATEE 32).

big blackhead: greater scaup (*Aythya marila*) (1959) MCATEE 13).

big house: principal dwelling from which agent directs commercial operations in Labrador settlement.

1861 DE BOILIEU 108–9 Should any one of the crew absent himself from home on Christmas-eve, a deputation from the remainder is sent in search of him, and when found—even should he be enjoying himself at the big house or the cooperage—he is unceremoniously told to return to his home. 1917 *Christmas Bells* 15 One forenoon the signal was hoisted in the 'big house' window that my presence was needed.

big ice: an extensive, close-packed icefield.

1924 ENGLAND 113 If dey pans on big ice, mabbe de men has to drag de sculps fer miles.

big planter: see PLANTER 2.

1923 CHAFE 16 The principal trader of each Harbor, locally called the 'Big Planter.'

big salt water duck: American common eider (*Somateria mollissima dresseri*) (1876 HOWLEY 65).

big squid: see SQUID.

bilk* See BELK.

bill n   Cp *OED* ~ sb³ 9 b 'promissory note' obs (1613–1721).

1 The wages, or share of profit, of a fishing or sealing voyage paid to men after the deduction of expenses.

[1765] 1954 INNIS 153 The trusting the fishermen with such quantitys of strong liquors is very prejudicial to the fishery, and that [is] greatly owing to the masters themselves, for they consider that the more the servant spends in liquor, by which he [the master] gains one half by the profit he makes, he lessens the bills the servants would otherwise receive. 1887 *Colonist Christmas No 6* I went to kill seals and make a bill. . . Well, I went to Tickle Harbor, fished out of there for three years, made good wages, went to the Ice and made good bills. 1909 BROWNE 178 Enormous 'bills' were made by sealers in these days, and I have often heard old fishermen tell of the years they 'made a hundred pound' ($400.00). . .and nowadays a 'bill' of eighty dollars is regarded as something phenomenal. 1924 ENGLAND 145 If he didn't get the young fat, he'd go after de ole an' make a fine bill. 1936 SMITH 104 Owing to the old seals being less commercial value than the young, we made small 'bills,' about $30.00 per man. 1957 *Evening Telegram* 13 Aug, p. 4 Captain De Laney, hearing of the fine 'bill' his lost men had made, began to think that they only got their rights. [1894–1929] 1960 BURKE (ed White) 29 "Full Loads to the Sealers": Success to you sons of bold Neptune, / May good luck attend you this spring / When bound up for home and young loaded, / On the barricade gaily will sing. / With a bill for your wife or sweetheart, / And for your success we all pray, / And the fair maid take for a partner, / The true love you left in the Bay.

2 Total profit of a sealing voyage.

1894 CHAFE 6 The largest bill ever made at the steam seal-fishery, was that made by the crew of the s.s. *Retriever*. 1924 ENGLAND 48 As for the boys [stowaways], they are never allowed on the ice to kill seals; for should they kill, they might claim a share of the ship's 'bill.'

bill v   Of wild geese, to stretch the neck, submerge the body in water and swim with only the bill or beak visible.

1842 JUKES ii, 94 The geese 'bill' as the men call it, that is stretching out their neck, they sink themselves beneath the water, swimming away with the bill only just above the surface.

billet n   SMYTH 101 for sense 1; cp *OED* ~ sb[2] 1, *EDD* sb[1] 1 for sense 2.

1 Small wood used for dunnage on a vessel.

1877 ROCHFORT 69 Billets or Brush Wood, used for the purpose of stowage.

2 A length of birch, usu unsplit, cut for fuel; BIRCH BILLET.

1896 *Dial Notes* i, 377 ~ wood cut up for burning. 1905 DUNCAN 136 So he would continue the splitting of billets of birch wood for the winter's store. [1923] 1946 PRATT 201 "The Weather Glass": And were he now this moment at the door, / His eyes would clear the shadows from this light, / His voice put laughter in the billets' roar. T 199–65 He told my grandfather that if they wanted to get some billets, these birch billets, if they could fill the schooner full o' birch billets when they'd come down he'd buy them. 1969 HORWOOD 84 Some of the phrases are highly picturesque. . . Chunks of firewood in Newfoundland are junks, unless they happen to be *birch* junks, when they become billets.

billy n   Cp *DAE* ~ 1 (1859–) for ~ knocker; cp *OED* ~[2] 1 'applied to various machines' for ~ tub.

Comb **billy gale**: Newfoundlander.

P 104–66 Billy gale [is the term] used along the Atlantic seaboard for Newfoundlander. P 212–74 On arrival at Sydney [Nova Scotia] he was surprised to hear himself referred to as a billy gale.

billy-knocker: light wooden club carried by policeman (P 148–62).

T 367–67 I was afraid o' the policeman's billy-knocker—you know, the long stick that the policemen carry. 1975 *Daily News* 15 Apr, p. 17 [He said that they] put him in a 'small room at the police headquarters where two of the policemen pinned me over a desk and the other three jabbed their billy-knockers (nightsticks) in my ribs and chest.'

billy-tub: barrel cut down to form a tub for trawls or bait; BAIT JACK, TUB.

Q 67–84 ~ one quarter of a flour barrel used for a 10-line tub of [bultows]. Q 71–6 ~ trawl tub made of half or quarter of a barrel. Q 71–13 ~ three quarters of a flour barrel used for a 10-line tub.

bim n   also **bim fish**. Cp *O Sup*[2] ~[1] 'inhabitant of Barbadoes.' A grade or 'cull' of dried and salted cod-fish shipped to the West Indies, esp Barbados; CULLAGE, WEST a: ~ INDIA.

1955 *Nfld Fisheries Board* 23 ~ Fish showing heavy sunburnt, heavy dun, heavy slime or in pieces. P 127–75 Bim fish: the lowest cull in fish grading: sunburnt, broken, or pieces of fish.

binder n   A rope fastened around load of wood on a sled.

P 126–67 Tighten up the binder.

birch n   [= *Betula papyrifera*, white birch; *B. lutea*, yellow birch or WITCH-HAZEL] *DAE* ~ bark (1643–), ~ broom (1809–); *DC* ~ rind (1692–); *NID* birchwood n 2.

Attrib, comb, cpd **birch bark**: see **birch rind** below.

1612 *Willoughby Papers* [Guy's narrative] Theire canoaes are about 20 foote long, 4 foote [and] a halfe broad in the middle alofte, for theire keele, [and] timbers they have thinne lighte peeces of dry firre rended, as yt weare lath and in steede of boorde they vse the vtter bitche barke which is thinne [and] hath many foldes, sowed together. 1863 HIND [i] 50 I wrapped the furs in birch-bark, and tied the bundle at the end of a large branch twice as high as myself from the ground. 1873 HOWLEY *MS Reminiscences* 27 (a) John undertook to prove to me that he could [cook salmon] in a birch bark pot. He procured a large sheet of bark, folded it at the ends in such a manner as to form an oblong dish. The folded ends were kept in place by being pinned lightly with small split sticks. 1907 MILLAIS 66 . . .de men in the Bay were out that night lookin' for Noah wi' birch bark torches.

birch besom [bəːtʃ 'bɪzm̩]: broom made with birch or alder twigs.

T 43/7–64 What they swept the house with was called a birch besom. That was the name on it that the women used to have—a birch besom. C 69–17 People made their own brooms from alder branches; these brooms were called birch bisoms. You could pick the twigs to make the broom at any time and in any month with the exception of May. It was taboo to pick the alder branches in May as this would cause a death in the family.

birch billet: a length of wood cut for fuel; JUNK.

T 49–64 They used to cut stuff and take it up to St John's in the spring o' the year—birch billets—and sell them. T 14–64 One of these old Waterloo stoves would take a birch billet probably two feet long. 1977 BUTLER 86 I made a bargain with the men owing me money to cut birch billets for thirty cents per hundred.

birch broom: see **birch besom**.

1910 *Nfld Qtly* Oct, p. 19 There are no scandals now like the sale of Army commissions or flagrant jobs for Army contractors. The War Office could not at the present time send out a flagstaff for Quebec, or birch brooms at 7s. 6d. a dozen to Canada, when their price in the colonies was one-tenth of that sum. 1937 DEVINE 11 Instead of an ad. in the paper [to sell schooner], as in modern times, the old birch broom used in sweeping the deck was hoisted to the mast-head. T 43/7–64 'Twas all birch broom [then]. Ye'd go in the woods and pick the small birch and make your broom. C 67–6 A birch broom was made by cutting small alder 'gads,' binding them together by interweaving other alder gads, trimming off the bottom and driving a handle into this bundle. 1970 JANES 21 Her crinkly hair was, in the language of that time, like a birch broom in the fits.

birch drum: in the fish trade with Brazil, cylindrical wooden container in which dried cod are packed. See also DRUM n 1.

T 90–64 We made birch drums, half drums—half quintal drums—and whole quintal drums: they were for the Brazil market.

birch hoop: strip of birch fastened around barrel or fish cask.

1975 RUSSELL 52 Because after all, how was I to know that a good firm birch hoop off a five quintal fish cask wouldn't make a reasonable substitute for these crinolines?

birch junk: see **birch billet**; JUNK.

T 45/6–64 This feller empted the barrel, empted the beef out o' the brin bags and filled it up with birch junks, and took the keg and brought it out. Now when the other man went back for his beef, here he had a bag full o' birch junks. T 210–65 Couple o' year ago he was getting some o' this big birch junks in there—he'd cut them up with a chain saw, in junks, so they'd be able to handle them, heave them in the truck.

birch rind, ~ **rine**: bark or cortex of a birch tree, esp used in the fisheries as a covering, insulation, etc. See also RIND n.

1809 *Naval Chronicle* xxi, 21–2 Every night, during its process, it [the fish] is brought into round piles, covered over with birch-rinds, with weight on it, to keep the wet and damp out. [1851] 1915 HOWLEY 230 The Red Indians never wash except when a husband or wife dies, then the survivor has in some water heated by stones in a birch rind kettle. [1870] 1973 KELLY 43 The room is at present only half finished, and a smart shower, which fell during our occupation of it, found its way through the roof of birch-rind on the heads of the congregation. [1904] 1927 DOYLE (ed) 67 "The Kelligrews Soiree": There was birch rhine, Tar twine, Cherry wine and turpentine. T 55/7–64 They'd make big birch rind masks and tossel them and trim them—whiskers and everything on them. T 66–64 In the summer time when there'd be no fish, they'd go rinin' birch rine. Birch rine was a dollar a quintal. T 141/68–65[2] The birch rine would be used for [insulating cellars] and for dinnage in the schooner. If you was going to plank out a wharf, you lay birch rine over your stick [to] preserve it from the water seeping into it.

birch sheathing: protective layer of birch, esp yellow birch, on hull of a vessel.

T 141/60–65[2] He had her measured and runned her a summer fishing; [then] he had his birch sheathing sawed here, and sheathed her. And he runned her sixteen springs to the ice.

birch timber: mountain holly (*Nemopanthus mucronata*) (1956 ROULEAU 26).

birch wood: grove of birch trees.

[1778] 1792 CARTWRIGHT ii, 326 From thence I turned through the birch woods, which abound in excellent hoop-poles.

birchy a

1 Surrounded by, or thick with, birch trees; esp in place-names.

[1771] 1792 CARTWRIGHT i, 120 It was with great difficulty we regained the shore at Birchy Cascade: we hauled our skiff up and spent the night by a good fire in the woods. 1951 *Nfld & Lab Pilot* i, 224 Birchy cove is entered between a point about 6½ cables northward of the northern entrance point of Stanley cove, and a point three-quarters of a mile farther northward. 1971 SEARY 139 THE BIRCHIES [Ponds] (NTS Bay Bulls). C 75–29 Birchy rattles [is] a water area around which there was a large number of birch trees. The trees were cut for fire wood.

2 Descriptive of the flavour of the wild 'browse'-fed rabbit, etc.

P 120–76 That was a fine birchy rabbit.

bird[1] n

1 A sea-bird hunted as food or bait; SALT-WATER BIRD.

[1794] 1968 THOMAS 128 This skinning and taking the Eggs from the Funks is now prohibit'd and they are allow'd to take the Birds only for Bait to catch Fish with. 1924 ENGLAND 177 'Dat'm me life, brud—swilin', fishin', an' birdin'. I knows where to find dem birds!' 1940 SCAMMELL 25 "The Shooting of the Bawks": O Mary dear and did you hear the news I heard today? / We're only 'lowed to kill a bird up to the middle o' May. [1959] 1965 PEACOCK (ed) i, 102 "Tom Bird's Dog": And when you got down 'board your boat your tongue was hanging out, / I don't know how many birds you got, your neighbours never said, / I wish the devil had the turs and Tom Bird's dog was dead. M 69–2 The next morning they were going out 'birding'. . .the birds were never so thick. . .but fire all the guns they like and they couldn't kill a bird. The men were firmly convinced that [Tom] had 'witched' their gun. M 71–104 Birding [means] killing birds (usually turrs).

2 Attrib **bird iron**: a flat piece of iron used to singe feathers of a bird prior to cooking.

M 68–7 ~ a common iron used for swingeing birds. The iron was made red-hot in the stove.

bird island(s): island where gannets, puffins, murres, etc, nest seasonally on rocky ledges.

[1770] 1792 CARTWRIGHT i, 7 The bird-islands are so continually robbed, that the poor Indians must now find it much more difficult than before, to procure provisions in the summer. 1953 *Nfld & Lab Pilot* ii, 121 Northward from South Bird island, are the following: North Offer rock. . .Hagdown rock. . .Wall rock.

bird rock(s): see **bird island**.

1863 HIND [i] 67 Bird Rocks. These are islands of sandstone with perpendicular cliffs on all sides, in which every ledge and fissure is occupied by gannets. 1960 *Evening Telegram* 29 Feb, p. 2 I shot [the seal] near the bird rocks in the gulf.

bird[2] n Comb **bird dance, birdy** ~ : a kind of dance.

1924 ENGLAND 252 I never wants to geeze at narr nudder judy I don't know, ner have no more bird dances ner Cat Harbour reels wid 'em. No, sir! 1973 GOUDIE 15 We danced lances, cotillions and the Birdy Dance.

bird[3] See BUD[2].

bird v Cp *OED* ~ v 1 'to pursue birdcatching

or fowling' (1576–1580). To shoot sea-birds from the shore or small boats; usu in phr *go birding*.

1924 ENGLAND 177 'Dat'm me life, brud—swilin', fishin', an' birdin'. I knows were to find dem birds!' 1958 HARRINGTON 32 The boat left the vessel to go 'birding,' but oddly enough, the crew saw only a solitary seafowl. T 185–65 You'd take the [cuffs] and shove 'em on, you know, out birdin', used to have 'em out birdin', out sealin'. Used to always wear swanskin cuffs. P 148–69 The two young men had gone out in the bay the previous evening to go birding, in a dory, and had not returned.

birding vbl n Cp *OED* ~ vbl sb arch (1596–1852) for sense 1.

1 Fowling, esp shooting sea-birds from the shore or small boats; GUNNING.

M 71–37 The rodneys were left in the water a while longer as they were used till late in the fall for birding. 1974 MARIN 46 The forming of the rough ice around the island—slob ice—meant the beginning of birding. To hide the hunters, along the shore shelters, half-moon shaped, had to be built out of stones.

2 Comb **birding dart**: Inuit hunting implement; cp DART n 1.

[1772] 1792 CARTWRIGHT i, 273 We caught plenty of fish of different kinds—a few fish greatly resembling tench, (which I killed with an Esquimau birding-dart under the stern) a porpoise and a dolphin.

birding frock: protective garment, usually white, formerly worn by hunter while shooting sea-birds (P 245–69).

birth See BERTH.

bitch n

1 A female seal; also attrib **bitch harp**, ~ **hood**. Cp DOG[1].

1871 *Zoologist* vi, 2541[In spring the dogs] would have regained their lost fat, and the 'bitches' would be enlarged by pregnancy. 1897–8 *Leisure Hour* xlvii, 285 The bitches keep their blowholes open through the ice; up these they climb, and give birth on the surface of the floe. [1911] 1930 COAKER 41 We recommend that. . .the killing of bitch hoods be prohibited. 1924 ENGLAND 97 I have seen attacked bitch harps nose their whitecoats into the water [away from the hunters]. T 43/4–64 The dog hood and bitch hood, they're the biggest and the boldest, the dangerousest.

2 A cake made of flour, fat pork and molasses; also comb **bitch and dogbody**.

1924 ENGLAND 152 'Ye mind, sir,' asked Roberts, 'we used to have a kind o' cakes made o' fat pork, flour, an' molasses, called "bitch and dogbody"? An' de broken hard-bread was called "slut"?' T 156/7–65 They went aft to get some flour to bake what they calls a bitch—that's what we call a bangbelly.

bitt v Cp *OED* ~ v 'to coil or fasten (a cable) upon the bitts' [of a vessel]. Phr *bitt up*: to tighten, esp to fasten mooring lines to an object in order to warp a vessel.

T 172/5–65 We chopped grump heads enough and

got the moorin's up, and bitt 'em up on the island o' ice, and start warpin', warped tight. T 187/9–65 When the breeze was over, that one down there had a notch cut in her spar, foremast, so big around as my arm, where they had the chain come in through the hawse-pipe and bitt up around her foremast.

bitting vbl n Cp BITT. Comb **bitting stick**: piece of wood used to tighten rope holding a load of wood in place on a sled; TWISTER.

Q 67–68 ~ used for tightening up the load (of wood). Q 71–6 Bittin' sticks [are] used when hauling firewood with a hand-drawn sled. [The] stick is used in much the same manner as one would use a tourniquet. All slack in the rope is taken up and the end of the stick pushed under the standing part to secure it. Q 71–8 ~ also 'twister.' Used by inserting a stick between two parallel lines and tightening by twisting.

bivver v also **bever, bibber** ['bɪvəɹ] *EDD* bever v 3, esp s w cties, with pron. *bivver*. To shake, shiver or tremble.

1863 MORETON 34 Bibbering. Sobbing, and making noise with the lips in crying. 1897 *J A Folklore* x, 203 Bever as a noun, meaning a tremor or excitement, and as a verb, to be in such a condition. 1937 DEVINE 10 Bibber, biver. To shake with the cold (said especially of the teeth). P 222–67 He stood by the door bivvering with the cold. C 71–112 ~ To shiver or shake with the cold. It is often said [instead of] br-rr-rr. The person would say bivver-er-er-er.

bivver n also **bever, bibber** *EDD* bever sb[1] 1, 2 esp s w cties for sense 1.

1 A shiver, shake or tremor, esp a quiver of the lips.

1897 *J A Folklore* x, 203 Bever as a noun, meaning a tremor or excitement. 1975 RUSSELL 48–9 Only last night at the school concert when that "O Canada" was on the carpet again, I took special notice of Pete's lips. Not a biver in 'em!

2 A buoy or any floating object which barely breaks the surface of the water (P 245–57).

P 113–56 ~ a floating object alternately exposed and hidden by the motion of the sea.

3 Phr *all a-bivver*: shaking, moving uncertainly.

T 31/2–64 'The glass [barometer] is bottom up,' he said. 'He's broke. He's all a-bivver.'

black a *DC* ~ ice 1 for sense 1; *EDD* ~ a 5 'extreme' Sh I Ir, JOYCE 215 ~ man 'surly, vindictive, implacable fellow,' for senses 2, 3; *NID* ~ fish 2, *DC* ~ fly (1821–) for sense 4; *DAE* ~ spruce (1765–) for sense 5; *Fisheries of U S*, p. 176 ~ ball, *OED* ~ book 5 (1842), *O Sup²* ~ man 2 (1591–Nfld: 1969), *EDD* sb 1 for combs. in sense 6.

1 Of ice, thin and newly-formed on river, lake or sea; cp YOUNG: *young ice*.

1909 BERNIER 7 Black ice is thin dark looking ice with no snow on it; usually found between pans of older ice. At night or at a distance looks like open water. 1920 GRENFELL & SPALDING 143 The ice in the middle, however, which had looked so sure from the landwash, proved to be 'black'—that is, very, very thin, though being salt-water ice, it was elastic. 1924 ENGLAND 160 We was to de nardenmost flags, on de far end o' where we knocked off yesterday. I got out on de black stuff, sir, meself, an' den cut back agin. 1933 MERRICK 21 The river was covered with new black ice. Slewing around a bend, the komatik went through and they all fell in. P 245–67 Black ice [is] thin ice.

2 In designations of Protestants (cp BLACK n): atrocious, disliked (as belonging to an opposing or conflicting group); in phr *black stranger*: not of or 'belonging to' a community.

1892 HOWLEY *MS Reminiscences* 4 Poor Petrie died last month. He was a jolly whitty Irishman from the Black North. 1930 BARNES 229 If I wasn't praying at a time like that, I'd be swearing. Now, mind, I hope nobody that reads this will think I'm a black black-guard. P 148–63 Black wop (bayman). 1966 PADDOCK 121 Black Protestant: derogatory name for Protestant. 1972 *Evening Telegram* 29 Feb, p. 3 Some of those rural districts are so small in population that everybody knows everybody else and the electorate would rather go for a black stranger any day than one of their own blackguarding neighbors. 1974 CAHILL 10 We [Roman Catholics] might have changed and got broadminded, but they're still as bad as ever they were, the black bastards!

3 Touchy; moody; dangerously quarrelsome or pugnacious.

1964 *Can Journ Ling* x, 45 He's some black! 1966 FARIS 245–6 Men are, very significantly, said to be 'getting black' if they become personal and serious in their argument. Any real quarrel between persons is labelled 'black' and to be avoided in Cat Harbour at all costs. 1975 *Lore & Language* ii (3), p. 16 Looked black, he was always black you know, but he looked a little blacker this morning.

4 In names of animals, birds, fish, insects with black colouring: ~ **and white diver;** ~ **back;** ~ **bawk** [see BAWK]; **blackbird;** ~ **cap;** ~ **diver;** ~ **fish;** ~ **fly;** ~ **hagdown** [see HAGDOWN]; ~ **patch.**

1959 MCATEE 15 Black and white diver. Barrow's goldeneye (Nfld., 'Labr.') 1792 CARTWRIGHT *Gloss* i, xi Harp. An old seal of that kind called by Pennant, 'Blackback.' 1861 DE BOILIEU 92–3 The principal seal of the coast is termed the Voyage Seal, while the males are distinctively called Harps, or Blackbacks. 1925 *Dial Notes* v, 326 *Black back*, a harp seal in the fourth year. 1951 PETERS & BURLEIGH 53 Sooty Shearwater. *Puffinus griseus*. Local Names: Black Bawk, Hagdown, Hag. 1840 GOSSE 96 The American Robin is a species of thrush. In Newfoundland, where it is very common, it is always called the Blackbird. 1959 MCATEE 32 Black-cap. Knot (The crown is dark streaked) (Nfld). 1708 OLDMIXON 14 A great Flock of small black *Divers*, about the bigness of a Feldyfare, came about the Ship a little before, but all of 'em left it, and betook themselves to the Island [of ice]. [1775] 1792 CARTWRIGHT ii, 74 John Hayes, the boatsmaster, killed four ducks, a goose, a black-diver and a lord. 1959 MCATEE 18 Black diver. Black Scoter (Nfld). 1846 TOCQUE 71 Great numbers of what some call

Black-fish, and others Pot-heads, are killed during the month of September along the shores of Newfound-land. 1964 *Evening Telegram* 19 Feb, p. 2 Among fishermen there is a widespread opinion that the 'black-fish' or pothead whale, which is slaughtered in large numbers for mink meat, is a very stupid animal. [1822] 1915 HOWLEY 137 Myriads of moschetos, with black and sand flies, annoyed us. 1872 HOWLEY *MS Reminiscences* 5 I have had my eyes almost closed many a time, and streams of blood coursing down my neck and face and clotting my beard and moustache, caused by the black fly. The torment was all but unen-durable. 1975 HOLMES 41 Twenty-three species of black flies have been recorded near St John's, and of these *Simulium venustum* Say and *S. vittatus* Zetter-stedt are the commonest species that bite man. 1883 HOWLEY *MS Reminiscences* 4 With these Hagdowns are several of a rusty black colour, only the under parts of the wings being of a dirty white. . . The fishermen call them Black Hagdown. . . This is probably the Sooty Shearwater. 1967 *Bk of Nfld* iii, 282 Black Bawk or Black Hag-down. [1766] 1971 BANKS 146 The Furrs taken here are Black Patch [etc] [Black Patch is a col-our phase of the Red Fox].

5 In names of plants and shrubs: **blackberry** [see BLACKBERRY]; ~ **hurt** [see HURT]; ~ **pear;** ~ **spruce;** ~ **whort** [see HURT].

1956 ROULEAU 26 Black Hurts: *Gaylussacia baccata*. 1898 *J A Folklore* xi, 226 Black pear. *Pyrus arbutifolia*. 1967 BEARNS 44 Because of its high wood density, black spruce is the most valuable pulpwood species in the Province. 1898 *J A Folklore* xi, 273 Black whorts. *Gaylussacia* (sp).

6 Comb **black (art) book**: book believed to contain secrets enabling a person to perform supernatural acts.

C 68–10 People believed [him] to have a black-art book or to be possessed with the Devil. He could tell you your fortune just by looking into your hand. C 68–16 The black book is supposed to be a book given by the devil to someone who has given himself over to the devil. In it is information or knowledge of how to do things which ordinary men cannot do.

black ball: marker attached to trawl buoy for identification.

1921 *Nat Geog* July, p. 13 [caption:] Flying sets on the Bank / the dories are being towed by the schooner. The black disks are 'highflyers,' or 'black balls,' which are affixed to the buoys attached to the fishing lines, as markers. 1938 MACDERMOTT 170 The trawl is. . .attached to a buoy which is known as a black ball, and which marks the place where the trawl is set. The black ball is a keg strapped with rope, and with a stick as stout as a shovel handle, from four to six feet long, passed through it; the stick bears a hooped canvas about eighteen inches in diameter on which is marked the dory's number. C 71–87 ~ This flag was home-made, from calico, with a hoop sewed around the edge of it. It was then painted and the number of the dory was written on it so that each fisherman would be able to keep track of his own buoys.

black boy: (a) man with blackened face, hands and clothing, accompanying Christmas mummers; (b) charred tree remaining after a forest fire: also **black-burn, blacky-boy**.

P 133–58 ~, black burn: a stick of wood that has been seared in a forest fire. 1965 *Evening Telegram* 24 Dec The blackboys, so called because of their blackened hands and faces, were dressed in black clothes and tall hats and carried a staff. It was traditional that the blackboys should be well ahead of the mummers, for the mummers would have to try and catch them (which they always did), and having caught, would throw them in the snow and maul them about. C 70–15 Trees which had been burned over in a forest fire were much in demand [for firewood] because they were partly dry. However they were very sooty and called blacky-boys.

black jack: (a) variety of molasses from West Indies; (b) type of felt or tar paper used for waterproofing, insulation, etc.

1909 BROWNE 81 One firm did an extensive trade in 'Black Jack' (St Kitts' molasses). P 148–64 [The] roof [is] covered with black jack. 1971 NOSEWORTHY 174 ~ Black felt for placing on roofs and [in] fish boxes to hold the water.

black man: a figure invoked to terrify children into good behaviour; the devil (P 148–60).

T 301–66 They would say when children were naughty, 'Here's the bully-boo' or 'a black man.' 1961 *Christmas Mumming in Nfld* 138 The archetype stranger, the Devil, is the 'Black Man' or 'Blackie.'

black-man's bread, ~ **cap**: possibly harmful mushroom; FAIRY CAP (P 148–61).

Q 67–25 Black-man's caps [arc] mushrooms. 1971 NOSEWORTHY 174 Black-man's bread: inedible mushrooms.

black psalm: text thought to have sinister power.

M 68–17 She believed that she could put a curse on anyone by reading a certain psalm, 'the black psalm,' she called it, 'on' the person she wished to curse. The number of the psalm was secret to her.

black n   See also BLACK a. Roman Catholic term for a Protestant; freq in phr *brazen as a black, saucy as a black*, etc.

P 245–56 ~ term of opprobrium applied by Roman Catholics to Protestants, but sometimes now used humorously rather than insultingly. P 52–62 Brazen as the black: used in reference to a saucy person. 1964 *Evening Telegram* 4 May, p. 7 Some of the young ones though is as saucy as blacks. M 65–1 It is common to refer to Protestants as blacks and the Roman Catholics as micks. C 66–4 The younger generation call all Protestants blacks.

blackberry n

1 Black crowberry (*Empetrum nigrum*); CURLEW BERRY.

1908 TOWNSEND 46 The curlew berry. . .on which the curlew formerly fatted in countless numbers, is called blackberry and is also made into sauces. 1915 SOUTHCOTT 28 ~ On hills round St John's. Small prostrate spreading shrub. Leaves with margins recurved to meet at the back. Flowers small, purplish, growing in

the axils of the upper leaves. Berries edible, black. T 141/66–65[2] The blackberries, o' course you get they there in the summer. 1977 *Inuit Land Use* 205 Blackberries. . .ripen in the summer and fall on both sides of the bay and on some of the islands.

2 A parasitic growth (*Lernaeocera branchialis*) under the gills of cod-fish, resembling a crowberry; attrib ~ **fish, berry fish**. Cp BERRY[2].

Q 68–3 Berry fish—cod with a red seedy growth under its gills. The growth is usually about the size of a partridge berry. Q 71–7 Berry fish—a small cod with a red undergrowth under its gills. Berry fish occur where there is a shortage of food in the water.

3 A pteropod (*Limacina helicina*) which, when eaten by the cod, causes a parasitic growth.

T 31/2–64 There'd be things in the water for the fish, an' there was none o' them about, little blackberries flying about in the water, what the outside fish lives on. They lives on this kind o' bait—call 'em the blackberry. T 55/6–64 Labrador fish is nothin' like the fish you get here. No, different breed altogether. Hardly get one that's fit to eat smell, you know; full of what they called blackberries. Q 71–8 On the Labrador Coast blackberry fish is well known as fish that, having fed on a particular planktonic form, assumes an offensive odour and colour. 1977 *Inuit Land Use* 139 Local fishermen have noticed that, coinciding with the disappearance of cod, there has been an increase in the number of pteropods, small, round, black creatures, locally called blackberries because they are the same size as the fruit, floating near the surface of the waters around the seaward islands. . . The fish used to eat them.

4 Attrib, comb **blackberry earth**: friable soil in which black crowberry thrives, used as insulation.

M 69–2 Blackberry earth [is so-called] because black berries grow on it. It is porous and easily dries out before being used in the bins. Blackberry earth acts as an insulator, helping to keep the vegetables [in the cellar] warm in the winter and cool in the summer. It was sometimes used between the walls in houses.

blackberry heath: leaves and twigs of the black crowberry, used in home remedies.

M 71–43 I steeped some blackberry heath and gave it to her and after a while her colour began to return.

blackberry more: root of the black crowberry; cp MORE n.

1977 *Nfld Qtly* Dec, p. 37 The [herring] were cleaned, pickled, and hung up in the roof. A fire was then started and banked with sawdust and blackberry mores to put a flavour on them [when smoked].

blackberry turf: ground covering formed by the black crowberry.

T 391/2–67 That's all was on that island. No woods, only just the blackberry turf.

blackening vbl n   Comb **blackening brand**: charred piece of alder, with which a string is blackened to mark a log for sawing into planks.

P 26–72 An alder stick would be burned in the fire until well charred, then rolled in sawdust to put out the fire. This was called a blackening bran [and] this bran would be rubbed along the length of the line. Another man would raise the line between thumb and finger and let [it] snap back on the [log]. P 127–75 ~ a burnt branch of a red alder, used to blacken the measuring and plotting line used in calculating the shape of the planks.

bladder n Cp *OED* ~ sb 3, *EDD* 5 (2) for sense 1; *OED* 2 obs (1000–1607), *EDD* 4 for sense 3; *OED* ~ : 9 ~ nose for comb.

1 Inflated animal bladder used as a mock weapon by Christmas mummers; SWAB n 2.

1842 BONNYCASTLE i, 139 Some of the masks are very grotesque, and the fools or clowns are furnished with thongs, and bladders, with which they belabour the exterior mob. 1917 *Holly Leaves* 19–20 . . .the oddly garbed figures meanwhile capering in amusing fashion around the hobby-horse. . .chasing people and striking them with whips at the ends of some of which were attached inflated bladders.

2 Blister on the bark of a fir tree containing fluid resin.

1840 GOSSE 10 Its [fir or balsam] surface is covered with bladders full of a fluid resin. 1846 TOCQUE 123 The turpentine bladders of this tree [fir] are used in cases of fresh cuts and other wounds. C 68–19 People used to say that myrrh found in bladders on fir trees (sometimes called turpentine) had a healing quality. People used to say that this myrrh taken with sugar was a good tonic for T.B. 1972 MURRAY 240 They often made use of 'murre' or the turpentine 'bladders' found on the bark of fir trees to dress the cut.

3 Pimple or pustule.

C 69–2 Many of the old people in the community say one should give their blood a spring's cleaning. Many people think that if one has pimples or bladders, etc, it is because their blood is dirty.

4 Comb **bladder-nose**: large migratory seal of northern waters with a fold of loose skin on the head of the male; HOODED SEAL.

1880 *The Standard* [London] 20 May, p. 3 . . .the 'ground'. . .seal, the saddle-back. . .the bladder-nose, and the floe rat.

blank a also **blanked** *OED* ~ a 4 b, 'void of result, unsuccessful, fruitless' (1553–1832). See BLANK n. Of the cod or seal fishery, unsuccessful.

1924 ENGLAND 203 Without luck, a ship may suffer weeks of misery and come home almost blanked. 1936 DEVINE 10 Even some went to Australia, all thinking that St John's and Newfoundland generally was finished as a place to get a living in, and seeing five blank (or nearly so) cod-fisheries, good times would never come again.

blank n

1 An unsuccessful fishing season.

1901 *Christmas Review* 2 The fishery of the summer '75 is recorded as an exceptionally good one; big trips and no blanks was the universal rule. 1916 GRENFELL 6 The trouble with this particular Christmas was that it

came after such a 'total blank' in our fisheries. P 148–76 The salmon fishery was a real blank [this year].

2 Phr *make a blank*: to catch no fish or seals.

1924 ENGLAND 80 'An' if they make a blank, I'll be blamed,' the Old Man complained.

blare v also **blear** *EDD* ~ v 1, 2.

1 Of a cow, moose, etc, to low or bellow.

P 80–64 The cows blare outside to be milked. P 148–64 The blearin of the moose can be heard, even in Burgeo. C 65–3 [proverb] A blaring cow soon forgets her calf.

2 To utter prolonged complaints.

1955 ENGLISH 32 Blear—to complain loudly. P 121–67 Stop your blaring.

blast n Cp *EDD* ~ 4 So Co, and BLASTY BOUGH for sense 1; *EDD* 7 D Co Ir, JOYCE 216 for sense 2.

1 A quick-burning fire fed by dried twigs or boughs (P 9–57).

2 An infection, wound or physical injury attributed to the malignant activity of fairies; cp FAIRY SQUALL; FAIRY STRUCK.

1937 DEVINE 10 ~ A wound received from witch-craft or fairies. P 152–58 [It is believed] that if one throws water across a path or road at night, he may throw it in a ghost's face and will get a blast or rise on his finger or hand and the discharge may contain sand, fur, bones, etc. 1968 DILLON 132 That poor thing got a blast there last year in the woods—struck with a squall. . . I think she got a blast; needles used to come out of her arm. C 70–26 A traditional story in Bay Bulls tells of a lady who often crossed intersecting paths in the wood without bread in her pocket. For not carrying the bread, the fairies gave her a blast (i.e. shot needles at her and took away her voice).

blasty a ['blæstɪ]. Cp *EDD* blast v 2 'to feed a fire with furze' Do So; sb 4 'branch of dry furze, used for "blasting out" the oven' So Co. Of the branch(es) of a spruce or fir, dead and dry but with the needles, now red or brown, still adhering; esp in comb **blasty bough**, **blassy** ~ ['blæstɪ, ˌbaʊ, 'blæˈsɪ ˌbaʊ]: such a branch which, used as kindling, burns with a quick, fierce, crackling flame; cp BOUGH n, SPARCHY BOUGH.

1931 BYRNES 36 Laying the 'table' on the moss covered ground, gathering the 'blasty' boughs for the fire, boiling the 'kittle.' 1944 LAWTON & DEVINE 18 The boys made bonfires at night of tar barrels and 'blasty' boughs as a final act in the celebration [of Guy Fawkes Day]. 1966 SCAMMELL 127 "Bakeapple Jam": Uncle Isaac finds some blasty boughs and cuts a kettle stick, / Aunt Betsy brought a rounder and she shares a bit with Gran. 1972 MURRAY 246 In order to 'boil the kettle' quickly, they needed fuel that burnt easily. Most women liked to use 'blassy boughs' (dry, blasted, red branches of fir trees) for a quick, hot fire. P 245–76 Next to the fierce, crackling sound of the fire fed with blasty boughs, what I most recall is the distinct aromatic, resinous smell of the burning boughs. 1979 *Evening Telegram* 8 Feb, p. 6 Dried slash which has turned blasty is easily ignited and once alight will start the kind of fire which will destroy a large area of forest.

b'lay See BELAY.

bleacher n PARTRIDGE ~ 'maid-servant'; GROSE bleached mort 'fair complexioned wench.' A young unmarried girl or woman.

1925 ENGLAND 326 ~ A marriageable girl, esp when not attached. C 73–128 Unmarried but eligible boys were referred to as 'bedlamers'; girls were called bleachers.'

blear See BLARE.

bleater n Cp also BLEACHER. An undernourished harp seal-pup; NOG-HEAD, SCREECHER 2 (1966 FARIS 236).

blessed a Cp *EDD* ~ ppl adj 'emphatic for good'; *OED* 2 'worthy to be blessed by men'; JOYCE 196–7. *Note*: The term is of unusual frequency in the region, esp applied to natural phenomena (sun, moon, sky, stars, rain, snow, thunder, etc), or used in exclamatory phrases (e.g. 'Jesus, Mary and Joseph, look down upon us this blessed day and night!'). A few examples are given below.

Comb **blessed brand**: the remains of wood used in Ash Wednesday church ritual.

M 71–121 It was a custom on Ash Wednesday for everyone to receive a piece of Blessed Bran. Wood was burned to make the ashes [and] the wood that remained unburnt was called Blessed Bran. Each person had to clean out his stove and lay a new fire with this piece of [wood] at the bottom. This. . .would protect the house from fire for that year.

blessed bread: bread over or on which the sign of the cross is made prior to baking in order to ensure rising.

M 71–114 Home-made bread was always [made with] the sign of the cross on the dough. The bread was always referred to as blessed bread.

blessed virgin's leaf: lady's thumb (*Polygonum persicaria*).

P 85–65 ~ a common weed with the likeness of a thumb-print on the leaf. C 67–8 Any kind of bleeding can be stopped with the blessed virgin's leaf, a locally known plant.

blind a, intens Cp various games in *EDD* ~ adj: (2) ~ –bell, (8) ~ –champ, (19) ~ –harry; blind-buck-a-davy Gl Do So D Co for sense 2; cp *OED*, *O Sup*² ~ 15, as *blind-drunk* for sense 4.

1 Phr *go blind*: to close one's eyes while other players hide.

T 169/206–65 Barl over was a game also where one feller went blind, an' he counted up to a certain number while everyone was hiding.

2 In combs. in which a game involves closing eyes or turning away **blind-buck-and-davy**: blind-man's buff (1937 DEVINE 10).

P 211–68 Under the supervision of the oldest girl in the school they were allowed to play blind-buck-a-davey.

blind bulls: part of the tossing and catching game of jacks.

M 66–14 Blind Bulls follows on Last Ones.

blind hopscotch: a variety of the game of hop-scotch (T 749–70).

3 In combs. implying deficiency, inadequacy **blind look-out**: poor situation.

1968 DILLON 147 'Twas a blind look out [= outlook] anyway, to have a bridge in that condition.

blind mush: a soup of cabbage and other vegetables, but lacking the customary salt beef (C 71–121).

4 Impenetrably; extremely.

T 453/4–67 If the weather was queer, was blind thick, now he got to stand by the other end; you got to set out the trawl.

blind n also **blinder**. In the game of hide-and-seek, the player who covers his eyes (P 80–64).

C 71–130 'Keep still wherever you're at / Don't show the peak of your cap.' In the game of hide-and-go-seek this rhyme was sung out by the blinder when he was ready to begin looking for the hiders.

blind v In the game of hide-and-seck, to close one's eyes.

C 68–21 The place where you had to blind was called the bar and the object of the game was for the hidden team to get to the bar before the other team had a chance to find them.

block n In lumbering, the area to be logged or cut (1965 PETERS *Gloss*).

T 43/8–64 There'll be one man go on this road, and another man on the other road, the two o' them workin' on the same block o' timber between the two roads. You fall your timber and clean up the block as ye go.

blocked p ppl Cp *OED* block v 1 'to obstruct.' (a) Crowded; overflowing; (b) of a person eating, full to repletion.

[1904] 1940 DOYLE (ed) 16 "Kelligrews Soiree": The place was blocked with carriages / Stood waiting at the gate. C 70–10 The pond would be blocked with people [skating]. P 108–70 The church was blocked to the doors. P 181–76 'Have another cup of soup.' 'No, I'm blocked.'

blood n *ADD* for phr in sense 1.

1 Phr *blood of a bitch*: alliterative phrase expressing extreme annoyance or anger; that towards which the anger is directed.

1862 *Standard* [Harbor Grace] 26 Mar, [p. 2] If you do not clear out of Bay Roberts prepare your coffin we want no bloods of b[itche]s here but the real genuine Protestants. 1925 *Dial Notes* v, 326 ~ a term of great reproach. T 143–65² He said, 'Don't you bring over that mainsail!' And [the other fellow] said, 'I got a mind I'd bring her over and ship the blood of a bitch out.'

2 Combs. in names of plants having a red part
blood root avens; JACK[1]: JACK ROOT (*Geum macrophyllum*) (1895 *N S Inst Sci* ix, 88).

blood vine: fireweed (*Epilobium angustifolium*).

1873 REEKS 3 ~ an abundant and troublesome weed.

bloody a Phr *bloody decks to them*: traditional toast to departing sealers, wishing them a successful voyage.

[1844] 1895 PROWSE 451 Mr Brown. . .took them over to see old Billy Rabbits; of course the 'broke' sugar and the hot water and spirits were immediately produced, and a toast had to be proposed. 'Bloody decks to en,' said Billy, as he raised his glass [and] Mr Brown had to explain it was a customary toast of success to the seal fishery, and homicide was not intended. 1957 *Daily News* 16 Oct, p. 4 Oldtime seal hunters in quaffing a toast to 'Bloody Decks,' expressed the opinion that the long, hard winter, the heavy ice and the 'mauzy' weather of early March were just right for a bumper season.

blossom n *EDD* ~ sb[1] 3 'snowflake' W. Large snowflake.

P 148–64 Ne'ra blossom o' snow [on] St Patrick's Day. T 411/4–67 On a particular day when big blossoms of snow were falling, she said, 'Well, the old woman is picking her goose today.' P 121–67 The snow was falling in blossoms.

blow v Cp *OED* ~ v[1] 27, 30 'inform on' for ~ the roast; *OED* ~ hole 4, *DC* (Nfld: 1916), blowing hole (1861–) for comb.

1 Phr *blow the pudding out of the pot*: to shoot gun on Christmas at same time the 'figgy pudding' is taken from the pot (M 71–115).

blow the roast; tell the ~ : to betray, inform on; to let the secret out (1925 *Dial Notes* v, 326).

1891 *Holly Branch* 13 Thinking that he was caught, and that the indignant skipper would 'blow the roast' on him, he declared, that he never 'dealed in such a commodity.' T 245/78–66 Down he comes on the wharf. Start tellin' the roast, whole story now 'bout how he come to get this feller turned away from his house an' get his wife turned out.

2 Comb **blow hole, blowing** ~ : hole made in ice by seal to come up to breathe; BOBBING-HOLE.

1861 DE BOILIEU 132 For the purpose of obtaining this necessary element [fresh air], holes are kept open by the seals throughout the winter, and are called by the Esquimaux 'blowing-holes.' 1912 HUTTON 224 When a man finds a blow-hole—that is, a round hole in the ice that a seal has made for its occasional breath of air—he surveys it critically. 1933 GREENE 175 'Blow-holes' are made in the same manner [as the bobbing-holes], but as they are only made for the purpose of obtaining air, and for temporary use, they are allowed to freeze up again. 1947 TANNER 499 From the camp the trappers make their way to the edge of the

ocean ice, the sinâ, where the seals sport in the chilly water. . . The hunter tries to find the seal's 'blow-holes' where it comes to breathe. 1976 *Decks Awash* v (2), p. 5 As boys, when the ice came in, we would sneak off after school and spend hours waiting for a 'blowing hole' just in hope to see maybe the whisker of a seal. We would search behind all the 'clumpers' (rafted ice) to make sure there was not a live seal hidden there.

blow n Cp *OED* ~ v[1] 4 b 'to take breath'; cp *DAE* n[1] 3 'breathing space' [for horse] (1885). Short rest from work; break.

P 148–61 Take a blow! T 141/64–65[2] They wandered in on the bleak land and they got up against this big sandrock and had a blow. 1966 FARIS 98–9 [Men of Cat Harbour] spend each evening arguing, gossiping and 'telling cuffers' in the shop, and have numerous 'blows' (i.e. breaks) during the day. 1967 HORWOOD 23 [He was] trimming out sticks on the slope of Witch Hazel Road one day when, pausing for 'a blow,' he noticed a fox only ten or fifteen yards away sitting up watching him. P 41–68 There was usually a *spelling rock* where he took a *blow*.

blow-me-down n *OED* blow v[1] 29: blow me (tight), etc, 'to curse, confound' (1835–82), *0 Sup*[2] (1781–1963); BERREY blow me down, pp. 200, 749. Name given to an abrupt and isolated hill or headland rising steeply from the water and subject to sudden down-draft of wind.

[1774] 1971 SEARY 182 Blowmedown Cove (Lane). Blow-me-down (Census 1857). 1951 *Nfld & Lab Pilot* i, 273 Blow-me-down a hill 615 feet. . .high, stands at the eastern end of a range of hills.

blubber n *OED* seal sb[1] 4 ~ blubber (1773), cp *NID* ~[1] 2 'fat. . .of whales and other large marine animals' for sense 1.

1 The layer of fat cut from the skin of seals and rendered into oil; FAT[1].

1784 PENNANT 165 The oil extracted from the blubber of this Seal [the harp] is far the most valuable, being sweet, and so free from greaves as to yield a greater quantity than any other species. 1813 CARSON 14–15 A considerable quantity of excellent manure may be procured from the sea weed, cod's heads, and the refuse of the seal blubber. 1832 MCGREGOR i, 224 The fat, or seal blubber is separated from the skins, cut into pieces, and put into framework vats, through which, and the small boughs inside, the oil oozes on being exposed to the heat of the sun. 1865 CAMPBELL 60. These dogs help the men to drag blubber on the ice in sealing times, and fatten on dead seals. 1956 CAMERON 31 The hair is short, but the body is well insulated by a thick layer of fat under the skin, known as the 'blubber.' 1976 CASHIN 23 Blubber had to be landed, cod oil to be gauged, ice to be delivered and settlements of accounts to be adjusted.

2 Decomposing cod livers from which several grades of oil are obtained; COD BLUBBER.

[1794] 1968 THOMAS 182 When the oil is all drained from the Liver the remains fall under the denomination of Blubber. 1832 MCGREGOR i, 232 The livers of cod are put into vats or puncheons, exposed to the sun, the heat of which is sufficient to render them into oil, which is drained off, and put into casks for shipping. The remaining blubber is boiled to obtain the oil it contains. 1921 CABOT 129 Technically they [cod livers] are 'blubber,' as all grease-bearing things are. T 94–64 [There'd be] maybe a half the full of a barrel of blubber. Blubber is the codfish liver, and when that gets about a year old that's in good order for soap. P 229–67 Blubber is rotted cod liver and used for greasing the keel of punts and ways when hauling up the skiffs. C 75–140 When fish was being cleaned the liver was taken out and put in barrels to stand for the cod liver oil to come out. On the top of this formed a scum which was called 'blubber.' I remember a couple of times seeing some of the old fishermen putting their heads down to the barrel and drink mouthfuls of the oil.

3 In designations of types of large wooden container in which cod livers are stored or placed for the rendering of the oil: **blubber barrel, ~ butt, ~ cask, ~ puncheon, ~ tub.**

T 169/70–65[2] I dipped in the bucket in the blubber barrel and I brings un on down aboard the punt. 1979 TIZZARD 89 The first thing that came to view as you opened the stage door [was] the blubber barrel, a barrel near full of rottening cod liver. 1976 CASHIN 65 We purchased their common cod oil and old blubber. . . We emptied the blubber from the vessel's blubber butts into our own puncheons and then returned the empty butts to the vessels. [1771] 1792 CARTWRIGHT i, 182 On arriving at the stage, I perceived that [the white bear] had been there also, and overturned a blubber-cask. P 245–74 [We] were kept busy getting our blubber puncheons ready for the storage of rotten fish when the fishery began. T 96/8–64[1] I'd go down in the stage and I'd get the big blubber tub and a big bucket.

4 Comb **blubber bank**: local place-name for area where refuse from St John's seal-pelt operations was dumped (P 245–77).

blubber soap: soap made from the oil and rotted livers of cod-fish.

1925 Dial Notes v, 326 ~ Soft soap,—made from 'de hile off de livers in a barl an' de loy off de ashes.' T 141/67–65[2] The old women used to make blubber soap in [a little bark pot] years ago. 1972 MURRAY 205 Usually in the fall, Elliston women made their own 'blubber' soap or 'soft' soap, as it never really hardened properly, although they cut it into bars.

blubber v

1 To smear or coat wooden objects or structures with rendered cod livers as a preservative against the salt water.

T 96/8–64[1] I'd go down in the stage and I'd get the big blubber tub, and a bucket, and I'd blubber all the gangboards, all the tawts over with the blubber. T 169/70–65[2] Only the 'lums' o' the paddles was blubbered.

2 To hurl rotted cod livers; to assault by smearing with cod oil; cp SOD v.

1900 DEVINE & O'MARA 76 Women of Foxtrap blub-

bered and pickled the railway surveyors and made them retreat [in] 1882.

blue a   DC blueback n 1 (Nfld: 1842, 1883) for sense 1.

1 In designations of the 'hooded seal' (Cystophora cristata): ~ **back; ~ hood; ~seal.**

1842 JUKES i, 311 The young [hood seals] have whitish bellies and dark grey backs, which when wet have a bluish tinge, whence they are called 'blue-backs.' 1967 Bk of Nfld iii, 328 The young [hooded seals] are called 'bluebacks' from their first hair coat which is slate-blue coloured on the back shading to silver grey on the sides and belly. 1978 Decks Awash vii (1) [p. ii] Blueback—a new-born hooded seal which has a darkish blue fast-fur, having shed its first coat prior to being born. 1981 Evening Telegram 10 Mar, p. 2 [They] are planning to disrupt the hunt for hooded pups, known as bluebacks. T 89–64 An' we got a blue hood an' an old harp by the net last fall. 1826 Edin New Phil J i, 40 The other two kinds are the Blue Seal, so called from its colour, which is as large as the Hooded Seal; and the Jar Seal.

2 In names of birds with blue colouring: ~ **bird; ~ gull, bluey; ~ snow-bird; ~ sparrow.**

1964 Evening Telegram 28 Oct, p. 5 I am much less enthusiastic about the name 'bluebird,' locally applied to the tree swallow. It is often blue, in truth, but it is so obviously a swallow, and deserves this evocative name! 1870 Can Naturalist v, 408 [The herring gull is] abundant throughout the summer. . . It is called the 'blue gull' by the settlers. 1951 PETERS & BURLEIGH 227 American Herring Gull. Local Names: Bluey, Blue Gull. 1967 Bk of Nfld iii, 283 Junco: Blue Snow Bird (from being in flocks in the winter.) 1959 MCATEE 64 Blue sparrow. Slate-coloured Junco.

3 In names of plants, shrubs, etc, with blue flowers or berries: ~ **berry; ~ bonnet; ~ lily.**

1898 J A Folklore xi, 281 Blueberry; POISON BERRY (Clintonia borealis). 1956 ROULEAU 27 Blue-bonnet: Mertensia maritima. Ibid 27 Blue Lily: Habenaria psycodes.

4 Comb **blue bunch**: in logging, a prime stand of conifers.

1966 PHILBROOK 166 These 'woods roads' vary in respect to the terrain and timber growth, hence a 'good road of wood' or 'blue bunch' is one where a logger has an easy time cutting and makes a good day's pay. P 13–74 Blue bunch [is] a term common amongst Newfoundland lumberjacks for a stand of extremely good timber, especially balsam fir.

blue drop: the sea; an area of open water in an ice-field; CLEAR DROP.

1924 ENGLAND 154 'Way out in the blue drop, me sons, farty miles from de ice,' the Cap'n narrated. P 98–57 ~ open water in an icefield. 1973 MOWAT 78 Two days out from port we ran into a terrible storm in open water, the 'blue drop,' as the men called it.

blue note: receipt for fish sold to a merchant, used as credit for goods and provisions to be purchased.

1976 HOLLETT 8–9 If you get either dollar, you never get him [in your pocket. You'd get] what ['ee] calls blue notes. They give you a note where you had perhaps five hundred dollars coming to you. Well, they would give you a slip, blue note we call it.

blue peter: seaman's jacket.

1898 *The Record* 10 So great was his emotion, Jess expected to see the buttons fly off his 'blue-peter'. . . His manly bosom rose and fell with the regularity of a ferris-wheel.

blue puttee: member of the first contingent of the Royal Newfoundland Regiment to volunteer for service in 1914.

[1918] 1971 NOEL 139 The 'Blue Puttees' have been pushing Squires, or rather he is endeavouring to get them to push him. However, the Blue Puttees are not *all* the soldiers, and they have been badly led and advised. [1928] 1978 *Evening Telegram* 19 Sep, p. 7 A meeting of the Blue Puttees [was] held last night. 1964 NICHOLSON 110 Since no khaki woollen material suitable for making puttees was available [at St John's in August 1914], the troops at Pleasantville were issued puttees of navy blue. . . To be a 'Blue Puttee' was to be a member of the famous First Five Hundred.

bluey See BLUE GULL.

blush* See SHEILA.

boar n Comb **boar's back**: poorly formed hay-load shaped like the back of a male pig.

M 71–39 [In hauling the hay from the field] another thing to guard against was making the load too rounded before it was built high enough. This was called 'boar's back' and [was] the bane of the builder's life.

boat n Cp *OED* ~ 1 b 'small sailing vessel employed in fishing, etc'; *DAE* n 1 (1622–) for sense 1; for synonyms at different historical periods, see BULLY[1], BY-BOAT, DORY, JACK[1], PUNT, RODNEY, SHALLOP, SKIFF, WESTERN BOAT. For comb in sense 3: cp *Shetland Truck System* p. 8 boats' crew; cp *Newport [R I] History*, vol. li (3), p. 45 ship roof [= boat roof].

1 A fishing craft of variable size, design and rig, often undecked or partly decked, used in the coastal or inshore fishery, esp for cod.

1610 *Willoughby Papers* 16a/15 [inventory] small compass for the boates. 1620 WHITBOURNE 23 . . .by which unfit disorders of some first arrivers there yeerely, those which arrive after them, are sometimes twenty dayes and more to provide boords and timber, to fit their boates for fishing; and other necessary roomes to salt and dry their fish on. [1663] 1963 YONGE 55–7 The next morning we came before Renoose, and. . .entered the harbour and anchored, found no ship there, but divers possessors. . . The manner is thus: they put a man on shore at every harbour and at last, according to their turns, they take the best place they can of all their possessions. There were 4 at Renoose before us including Mr Thomas Waymouth of Dartmouth, who kept 18 boats. . . The complement of men to a boat are 5, that is 3 for to catch the fish, two to save it. . . The boat is 3 or 4 tons and will carry 1000 or 1200 cod, but these three men will row these great

boats a long way. [1705] 1895 PROWSE 251 Quantity of fish made by boats 12,000 qtls. [1766] 1971 BANKS 133 The English use boats almost twice as large as the French Some of them being 40 feet in the Keel they are Calld here Shallops Rigged with a main mast & foremast & Lugsail & furnished also with 4 oars. 1832 MCGREGOR i, 226 The boats used for the shore fishery are of different sizes; some requiring only two hands, while others have four, which is the general number. P 54–63 The word 'boat,' pronounced bwyutt, in the Bonavista-to-Catalina area did not then [c1820] mean an open fishing skiff, but always a small decked schooner, tiller-steered, about 12–20 tons, comparable to the historic Western Shore boat. 1975 BUTLER 66 He outfitted a number of fishing boats from many harbours in Placentia Bay and bought large quantities of dry codfish from boat owners.

2 In pl, blue flag, a plant of the iris group, the ovary shaped like the hull of a boat (*Iris versicolor*) (1956 ROULEAU 27).

3 Attrib, comb, cpd **boat-builder**: wood-louse or sow-bug, an isopod which swarms around rotting wood or under rocks (*Oniscus asellus*); CARPENTER.

P 189–66 ~ Little, flat, dark [creature] found under stones and wood. C 69–11 During the night a carpenter crawled across the floor and [the boy] said, 'What are boat-builders doing out this time of year?'

boat collar: anchor, chain and rope attached by means of a loop or bight to a buoy and used to moor a fishing craft in a harbour. See also COLLAR l.

1979 NEMEC 260n The 'boat collar' or 'collar' is a loop fashioned from varying sizes of rope and burlap which is secured very snugly around the bow of the boat. The collar is merely an extension above water of a mooring line which connects with a set of anchors well secured to the bottom of the Bight.

boat crew: the complement of men in an inshore fishing craft. See also CREW 1, and 1663, 1832 quots in sense 1 above.

[1777] 1792 CARTWRIGHT ii, 223 . . .two new shallops, thirty tons burthen each, built at Trinity last winter; and were brought from thence by two boats-crews, which I sent passengers from Waterford, on board one of Mr Lester's vessels. [1794] 1968 THOMAS 170 It was common for a Boat's Crew to be Fishing all Summer for a Master who supply'd them with a few necessarys, the men letting their wages remain untill the Season was over. 1893 *Trade Review Christmas No* 13 The former occurred in spring, when all the boat's crews went into the woods to get rinds off spruce and fir trees, to cover their fish piles when in process of being dried on the flakes. 1975 BUTLER 62 In the spring of the year, the boat crews which were working for the merchant would commence fishing for cod.

boat delegate: on a trawler, man elected as spokesman by the crew.

1977 *Union Forum* June, p. 15 As boat delegate Les Greene of the *Gulf Gerd* in Burgeo puts it, the delegate has to do 'a little bit of everything,' and he is the crew's key link to both the union staff and company management. . . A boat delegate holds that position until he decides to step down or until someone else wants to challenge him for the job. It takes two-thirds of a crew to call for an election and replace a delegate. In any event, the delegates are re-elected annually just before the Christmas tie-up.

boat fisherman: inshore fisherman.

1610 *Willoughby Papers* 16a/3 . . .provision for my selfe and boate fishermen for a voiage to the New-foundland.

boat fishery: cod-fishery prosecuted from small craft in inshore waters. Cp BY-BOAT FISHERY.

[1824] 1954 INNIS 320 Thus the ship fishery has diminished to little more than a name, the result of the two systems being last year the production of 750,000 quintals of fish from the boat or island fishery while that of the ships made only 34,000 quintals. 1832 MCGREGOR i, 249 The shore, or boat fishery, to which the fishermen, particularly in Newfoundland, now confine themselves, is not, strictly speaking, a nursery for seamen.

boat harbour: cove from which small craft prosecute the cod-fishery.

[1822] 1928 CORMACK 103–4 We were several days storm-stayed by winds and snow, and the inefficiency of the ice to bear us across the rivulets, at a boat-har-bour called the Barachois, six or seven miles east of the cape. 1951 *Nfld & Lab Pilot* i, 193 Between White point and the entrance to the small boat harbour of Garnish. . .the shore is fronted by Garnish rocks.

boat keeper: man who operates inshore fishing craft; BY-BOAT KEEPER. See also PLANTER 2.

[1693] 1954 INNIS 107 By the building, fitting, vict-ualling and repairing of fishing ships, multitudes of English tradesmen and artificers besides the owners and seamen, gain their subsistence; whereas by the boats which the planters and boat-keepers build or use at New-found-land, England gets nothing. [1767] 1826 CARTWRIGHT ii, 306 I expect much trouble, as I am informed that in many cases where the boat-keepers are already in debt, some of the merchants are resolved to pay no wages at all to their servants. [1793] 1954 INNIS 289 It is in the memory of several persons when the trade at St John's was in the hands of five or six merchants; these persons brought out sufficient sup-plies for the people they employed either as servants or boat-keepers to catch fish for freighting their own ships. . . At present the number of persons who can furnish supplies in the town of St John's is so increased, that all monopoly is broken, and a very active competi-tion is come in its place. [1839] 1916 *Nfld Law Reports* 27 The jury find that in the year 1826 the insolvents carried on business to a pretty considerable extent. . .the supplies so obtained by them were applied entirely and exclusively to the supply of bank-ers and boat-keepers, from whom they received fish in payment.

boat(s) kettle: metal container used for cook-ing on a fishing craft.

[1819] 1915 HOWLEY 112 [inventory] 6 Boat's Ket-tles. 1861 DE BOILIEU 121–2 'Well,' said the man, 'if the kettle is full and the boat's-kettle is full, lend me one or other of the saucepans.' [1900 OLIVER & BURKE] 46 The tinsmiths were kept busy furnishing the

cook with boats' kettles for tea and boilers to cook the celebrated 'duffs.' M 69–17 In the days of my grandfa-ther, it was quite a common thing to have cod-fish, salt meat, and potatoes cooked while on the fishing grounds. It was all cooked in a pot called a boa's kettle, a corruption of boat's kettle. 1972 MURRAY 217 Often a tin, three-quart, 'boat's kettle' was used. (This was a high, narrow pot, with a tightly fitting cover and a han-ger so the mixture might be suspended from a hook over the warm stove.) 1975 *Lore and Language* ii (3), p. 17 Sometimes a male member of a community will use an esoteric utterance as a manner of greeting another on the road. . . A passerby will say, 'What's the [price] of ya boat's kettles?'

boat master: captain of an inshore fishing craft; SKIPPER.

[1663] 1963 YONGE 57 The complement of men to a boat are 5, that is 3 for to catch the fish, two to save it. Those 3 are the boat's master, midshipman, and fore-shipman. [1771] 1792 CARTWRIGHT i, 124 I hired one of them (John Tilsed) for a boatsmaster. 1837 BLUNT 36 An able navigator, who has been 20 years employed in the fisheries, and who is a native of Newfoundland, observes, it is well understood by all the boat masters, that there is in general a strong current setting in from the eastward, along the Western Coast of Newfound-land. 1878 TOCQUE 293 . . .boat-masters, or principal men, are paid about £10 as wages. 1902 *Christmas Bells* 14 A boatsmaster, being convicted of indolence by 'ly-ing in his boat at anchor with his crew, several hours, whilst other boats around them were catching fish, and that at the time they did so they had bait in the boat,' was fined 'two guineas.'

boat path: path leading to the anchorage of a fishing craft or its winter berth on shore.

[1777] 1792 CARTWRIGHT i, 187 We tailed the trap and one slip in the boat path, for deer.

boat roof: house-roof shaped like the hull of a small fishing craft.

1975 MILLS 71–2 [There were] small houses built in the nineteenth century with 'boat roofs.' These roofs have no peak but are rounded from eave to eave.

boat's room: area of foreshore appropriated for the use of fishing craft and the cure of its catch. See also ROOM.

1711 CROWE 272 A Plantation of three boats rooms. . .in Torbay. [1804] 1954 INNIS 107 In well set-tled harbours, the ancient custom is strictly adhered to and in case of dispute is ever the standard, forty feet front being esteemed one boat's room without limita-tion backward. 1846 TOCQUE 214 In 1728 regular jus-tices of the peace were first appointed, and during this year Captain Henry Osborne, the governor, divided the island into districts, and levied a rate of a half quin-tal fish on all boat-rooms and boats.

boat v Phr *boat a net*: to haul a net into a fishing or sealing craft and reset it in the water.

[1774] 1792 CARTWRIGHT ii, 94 We put out two more nets, took up two, and boated two.

boatswain n also **boatswain bird, bo's'n, bosun bird, bo'swain**. Cp *OED* ~ 2 Arctic skua

(1835–). Pomarine jaeger, a dark, hawk-like seabird (*Stercorarius pomarinus*).

[1785] 1792 CARTWRIGHT iii, 76 I saw a curlew and killed a bird called a boatswain. 1841 BONNYCASTLE i, 15–16 We afterwards crossed a strong and noisy current, and saw many boatswain-birds, and an immense shoal of small fish. 1908 TOWNSEND 173 The jaegers, or hunters of the sea, called here 'bo'swains,' are very graceful, hawklike gulls. 1959 MCATEE 35 Bo's'n. Pomarine Jaeger.

bob n Cp *DAE* bob-sled (1848–), *DA* (1839–).

Comb **bob-cat**: small sled used for transporting wood in winter or sledding for pleasure; CAT[7], CATAMARAN.

M 68–4 These bob-cats had two runners and two boards across for seats and two sets of pins for holding onto. Sometimes the boys would tackle the dogs and have them pull the slides so they could get a better ride. P 148–76 ~ a wood-slide.

bob-sled: variety of sled supporting the forward ends of sticks, spars or logs, with the other ends dragging on the ground.

T 43/7–64 The bob-sled was used singly. They were used for pulling schooner spars out of the woods, and used a lot in the lumber woods for pulling wood on. The bob-sleds used to tail-drag the stuff. There'd be one end dragging on the ground and the other chained on the bunk of the sled, the bob-sled.

bob-slide: see **bob-sled**; SLIDE n.

M 68–10 The bob-slide is used to pull firewood or logs down steep slopes during the winter. With the butts of the wood placed on the bunk and the tops dragging over the snow, the speed at which it would go on an ordinary two-bunk sleigh is greatly decreased.

bob-stick: wooden bar in front of a sled to which horse's traces are attached; swingletree.

T 175/7–65 What we call traces come back to another stick, what we call the bob-stick, was fastened on the end of the slide and he was swung in the middle, what was pulling the slide.

bobber n Cp *OED* ~[2] 1 'float used in angling' (1837–) for sense 1.

1 Any of a variety of buoyant objects used to mark the position of a net or other type of fishing-gear, or to suspend it in the water; BUOY; also attrib.

[1785] 1792 CARTWRIGHT iii, 97 Tilsed and three hands hauled one of the [seal] nets, but both the pryor-pole and the bobber of the other being carried away, they could not find it. 1792 ibid *Gloss* i, ix ~ a small piece of wood, which is made fast by a piece of line (called the bobber-line) to that corner of a shoal-net next to the land, which, by floating upon the water, shows where the net is. T 89/90–64 We went up—everything gone. Not a grapel, n'ar a bobber, and went in 'gain the rocks where the end was tied on to, here was one cork. T 172/4–65 To take a berth, take a rope, tie a bobber on un, hang un over the slip in your trap berth. Well that was your trap berth. Every Newfoundlander 'd respect that. P 5–67 ~ float on a salmon or herring net. 1971 NOSEWORTHY 175 Bobbers.

Round balls used to hold up cod traps; pieces of cork or wood used to hold up trawls and keep the lines in the same area. C 75–63 Lobster pot swings are the line[s] connected to a pot so that it can be hauled out of the water. The swing contained a buoy at the end and a bobber in the middle. A bobber was a small buoy [that] was always under water and the purpose was to keep the swing from hooking into the bottom. 1979 TIZZARD 95 He usually put the little stove back here [in the boat], pieces of rope and a bobber or two.

2 Bull-head lily, a type of water lily (*Nuphar variegatum*) (1956 ROULEAU 27).

3 Phr *watch your bobber*: keep alert! (P 108–76).

bobbing vbl n Cp *OED* ~ vbl sb 3 fishing for eels' (1653–), *EDD* bob v[6]: bobbing for sense 1.

1 Method of catching squids with small fish as bait.

[1663] 1963 YONGE 60 They catch [squids] in nets or scaines, and sometimes by bobbing (as they call it), which is thus: they take a small cod and skin him, and hanging him a little under the water in the night, the squids will lug at it; then they pull it up softly and clap a cap-net under, and so secure them.

2 Comb **bobbing-hole**: small area in an ice floe kept open by a seal; breathing hole; BLOW HOLE.

[c1900] 1968 *RLS* 8, p. 23 ~ small hole in whelping ice, kept open by the old seals to come up or down for feeding, &c. 1916 GRENFELL 208 When the sea-ice was frozen far out from the landwash in the fall, and the big seals were no longer able to get near the land, the bay seals in plenty kept bobbing holes open quite far inshore. 1924 ENGLAND 37 'Look out fer de ole siles,' he repeated. 'I see a feller stoopin' over, killin' a whitecoat once, when de ole bitch rosen up out o' de bobbin' hole an' ketched un by de pants, an' tore 'em 'most off o' he.' 1959 SAMSON 57 Baby Harp Seals wait at a 'Bobbing Hole' for their mothers.

bobbing pole: a long, stout rod with line and baited hooks used to take cod.

1845 *Journ of Assembly* Appendix, p. 222 . . .than by our way by 'bobbing poles' from the side of the vessel; for this reason, the diameter of the circle in which our hooks play is only about sixty feet, including the breadth of the vessel. . . The Bultow mode seems to me only an extension of the same means of taking fish as that of the 'bobbing pole,' and I think the hooks of the latter named mode are allowed to lay near the bottom of the sea.

bobby-rooter n Eastern fox sparrow (*Passerella iliaca iliaca*); FOXY TOM.

1959 MCATEE 66 ~ fox sparrow (From its 'rooting', i.e. scratching among fallen leaves.)

bobtail n Comb **bobtailed racket**: snow-shoe with only a short extension at the back.

1884 STEARNS 149 The beaver, the otter, the porcupine, and the bobtailed rackets are used perhaps more frequently than any others about this coast.

bodkin n Pron **butkin***. Cp *EDD* ~ sb [2] 'bar

forming part of the harness for a plough' So. Swingletree used when harnessing an ox to a sled (M 69–6).

body n   Cp *OED* ~ 8 h; frame sb 11 d. Comb **body frame**: the part of a boat between the fore-hook and the afterhook midship bend (P 149–65).

T 43/8–64 What they call the body frame was the width of the fore-hook from the stem. You'd fasten that to the keel. P 127–75 ~ all beds of timber between and including the fore and after hook.

bog n   JOYCE 218 'what is called in England a "peat moss"' for sense 1; for comb in sense 3: *DC* bog-apple obs (N S: 1823); *DAE* bog meadow (1749).

1 Peat, esp removed from marsh-land and used for improving garden soils; also attrib.

1841 PANL GN 2/2 June-Dec, p. 7 The morass from which 'Bogstuff' is obtained. . . 1870 *Stewart's Qtly* iv (2), p. 17 With the exception of the trifling portion of this offal that is mixed with bog and applied to the land in Newfoundland, the whole is lost without utility. 1974 MANNION 62 Normally over 40 loads were hauled by slide to the 'bog pit' out on the farm. One load of [fish] offal was mixed with 5 loads of bog and clay.

2 Proverb *first in the wood, but last in the bog* [advice to travellers].

[1794] 1968 THOMAS 103 First in the wood, but always last in the Bog, Mr Thomas! Now I will lead the way if you will follow.

3 Attrib, comb **bog-apple**: cloudberry (*Rubus chamaemorus*); BAKEAPPLE.

[1822] 1856 CORMACK 13 The prevalent plants are . . .bog apple [etc]. 1966 SCAMMELL 139 Bakeapple (bog-apple). 1969 HORWOOD 102 [The expatriate] remembers. . .the bakeapples (bog apples, cloudberries) that he picked from the Witless Bay marshes.

bog lily: orchid with white flower (*Platanthera dilatata*) (1956 ROULEAU 27).

bog meadow: an open stretch of grassy marsh-land.

1895 TOCQUE 294 In some places the 'bog meadows' are very productive, producing large quantities of natural grass.

bog-nut: rush-like plant of the horsetail family, common in marshes (*Equisetum palustre*) (1956 ROULEAU 27).

bogey See BOGIE.

boggan* n   Crossbar behind horse to which traces and plough are attached; SWING (P 148–65).

bogger n   also **boggers**. Cp DINNEEN bagar 'a threat.' In children's competitions, a daring feat successfully carried out; a competition in which children try to outdo each other.

P 148–67 Boggers [is] jumping from one rock to another or from one place to another. P 35–72 ~ any

trick a kid can do that a friend cannot do. The former would say to his friend, 'I got a bogger on you.' It might be turning a somersault, jumping across a brook, etc. P 148–78 Boggers [is] follow the leader, competing [in] sometimes dangerous feats or dares.

boggering vbl n   Cp DINNEEN bagairt 'act of nodding, beckoning. . .a challenge'; bagraim 'I beckon; I threaten.' In children's pastime, competing with one another; cp COPYING.

1959 *Evening Telegram* 4 June, p. 3 The youth. . .told the court that they were playing a game of 'boggering.' It was the first time the court heard of such a game, and the youth explained that it was 'trying to see who could climb the highest.'

bogie n   also **bogey, bogy** ['bougɪ, 'bougiˑ, 'boʊgi, 'boʊgɪ, 'boʊgɪ] PARTRIDGE bogy 4 'a stove for heating'; *SND* ~ 1 'cooking galley on a fishing boat (1916); *DC* Nfld (1916–). A small stove used originally on a fishing schooner; applied generally to any small coal- or wood-burning stove.

1870 HOWLEY *MS Reminiscences* 36 We now managed to get a fire in the bogy, change our clothes and make ourselves as comfortable as possible under the circumstances. . . We set the watch for the night [on the vessel] all hands remaining up. [1894 BURKE] 11 And then drop in to Callahan's / [For] a bogie for the schooner, / Like an artist it can draw. 1897 *J A Folklore* ix, 204 ~ a small cabin stove used on board fishing schooners. 1901 *Christmas Review* 19 Our new bogie, one meeting night, refused to do duty—whether it was the fault of the funnelling or the atmosphere I cannot say. 1912 DUNCAN 86 'Grand times in the for'c's'le that night! A warm fire in the bogey-stove!' 1924 ENGLAND 29 A coal fire roared in the glowing bogey, and a certain warmth had begun to dispel the clammy cold. 1925 *Dial Notes* v, 326 Bogey—a small square stove [on sealing ship]. 1937 DEVINE 10 ~ A small stove used in schooners' cabins and forecastles, also in small houses and tilts. T 246/7–66 You'd have a little bogie made—would be a old kettle perhaps with the side out of it. 1979 TIZZARD 94 The front thwart was boarded in underneath and here was kept the bogie wood and other commodities needed to be kept from getting wet.

bogy See BOGIE.

boil v   Cp *DC* boil the kettle (1785–), boil up (1933–). Phr *boil the kettle, boil up*: to brew tea, and sometimes to take a snack, during a rest from shipboard or outdoors work; to cook a 'lunch.' Cp MUG UP.

[1663] 1963 YONGE 57 They bring the fish at the stage head, the foreshipman goes to boil their kettle; the other two throw up the fish on the stage-head. 1854 MARCH 23 In how many instances are they lounging on the beach, or hauling sticks to boil the kettle, or walking to the Government meal depot for provisions? 1869 MCCREA 260 Away you go, then, while Green and I make up the fire and boil the kettle. 1899 *Tribune Christmas No* 11 We then started on, and made such good time that we 'boiled the kettle' at the Green-woods, instead of Coxswain's Brook, and without being footsore. 1930 *Am Speech* vi, 57 Boil a kettle—Not only to boil water for tea but also with meaning of 'take lunch.' 1933 MERRICK 30 At three we boiled up again. It's wonderful how a cup of tea and a smoke and a rest picks you up. 1975 BUTLER 64 They walked across over to Chapel Arm. . .and they'd boil up the kettle on the way. 1979 TIZZARD 277 When my father boiled the kettle he usually put a couple of spruce buds in the kettle with the tea leaves and this made for a good cup of tea.

boiler n *EDD* ~ 1 'large kettle' for sense 1.
    1 A large metal cooking pot.
    [1820] 1915 HOWLEY 86 There were two iron boilers which must have been plundered from our settlers. 1887 *Telegram Christmas No* 9 The tea-kettle sang a cheery song, in perfect harmony with the hubble-bubble of a boiler, its companion, in which a big figgy pudding, rich with galores of suet and citron, was already undergoing the beginning of its long boil. [1900 OLIVER & BURKE] 46 The tinsmiths were kept busy furnishing the cook with boats' kettles for tea and boilers to cook the celebrated 'duffs.' 1932 BARBOUR 22 The boys took off the hatches, opened the barrel and took out a large piece of pork. We cut it up into small pieces and threw all into a five-gallon boiler. 1966 SCAMMELL 91 Let's have a bite of lunch before we start on our second puntload. Pass back that old boiler there in the cuddy. 1978 *Evening Telegram* 20 July, p. 16 How many children nowadays ever had the pleasure of going out in the country with their mother and father and boilin' up a boiler of corned beef and cabbage. Not only in troutin' season but in berry pickin' time especially.
    2 In hopscotch, the central square or section into which the flat stone is thrown to start the game.
    T 417/9–67 In order to start at all you had to turn backwards and put your flat rock in the boiler; it had to go in the boiler. [Then] hop in the boiler, hop in the next two, hop on one foot in the next one, stop, pick up your rock. M 68–21 If we got tired of hopping around we could jump in [the boiler] and stand on both feet for a rest before going back to the block where we left our stone.

boil-up n *O Sup*² ~ , *DC* n 2 (1933). See BOIL: *boil up*. A brew of tea, and sometimes a snack, taken during a rest from work in the country or on a vessel; cp MUG UP.
    1933 MERRICK 262 Some of the peas we save for Kay to have first thing next evening, or at one of the boil-ups during the day. P 130–67 Boil-up is used to refer to meal-time in the woods. C 69–8 One has a boil-up [when] berry-picking, hunting, fishing, etc—whenever one is out in the woods for any length of time. The boil-up is for tea of course and there may or may not be food with it.

bom See BAM.

bon See BAWN.

bond store n Cp *OED* bonded 2: bonded store. Warehouse or cellar where spiritous liquor is stored; liquor store.
    [1894–1929] 1960 BURKE (ed White) "Not Burnt Out": His face from rum would advertise / Each bond store in the town. 1936 DEVINE 156 If I mistake not, Mr Morey was also agent for Newman's and had charge of the bond store nearby where the celebrated Newman's port wine was deposited to mature. P 117–64 [Of habitual drinker] 'He keeps the bond store going.' 1976 GUY 66 She has always got something derogatory to say about the products put out by the Bond Stores at scandalous prices these days.

bone v, n *EDD* ~ v¹. To beg or solicit; solicitation.
    1904 *Daily News* 7 Mar "The Widow's Lament": In at Whitbourne you reside. . . / With no orphans or no bride. . . / There you get the pauper's bone, / In your castle all alone. C 70–21 I'll bone Mary for her help with that next time I see her. . . I think I'll bone Mr So-and-so about getting money for that project. C 71–127 ~ to beg or 'bum.'

bone n Attrib **bone finger**: inflammation and swelling of the fingers and hand caused by handling cod; cp SEAL FINGER, SQUID ~ .
    [1856] 1975 WHITELEY 123 Fine [day]—spread fifty quintals of fish—I am not well with some bone fingers. [T 47–64 Well, in headin' a lot o' fish you find that your hand gets sore here, because it take on the bone after you crack the heads].

boneen n also **bonem** *EDD* ~ Ir; DINNEEN banbh: bainbhín. See also BONNIVE. A young pig.
    [1904] 1960 BURKE (ed White) 35 "Playing for the Boneen": Let ye's bring in the pig. . .And the Boneen stretched in. 1925 *Dial Notes* v, 326 ~ a young pig. 1937 DEVINE 10 ~ a young pig. Also *bonem*.

bonfire n Cp *OED* ~ sb 4 'large fire kindled in the open air for a celebration, display or amusement': (a) on eves of St John and St Peter; (b) in celebration of some public event [see esp 1772 quot for the association with Guy Fawkes]. Comb **bonfire night**: the night of November 5th and the customary celebration of the anniversary of the Gunpowder Plot; occas various dates in midsummer celebrated by the lighting of outdoor fires; TORCH NIGHT.
    1936 SMITH 114 We opened the Club on Bonfire Night, November 5th. 1965 *Evening Telegram* 5 Nov, p. 6 Bonfire Night is an interesting carryover of an Old Country tradition, and the mere fact that it still survives in some places, is of far more significance than the name. . .of Guy Fawkes. 1966 FARIS 208 At the time of 'Bonfire Night' (5 November—though only rare individuals know the English antecedents for the celebration), barrels of any sort which are left unprotected are 'bucked.' M 68–2 November 5th was the big celebration for the Anglicans. The Catholics never took part, understandably thinking about the original

Guy Fawkes night. They tried to make really big bonfires, sometimes with full blubber barrels, to rile the Romans. 1977 *Decks Awash* vi (3), p. 54 On bonfire night he used to have a tar barrel put outside for the boys who'd be going around getting stuff for the bonfire. . . They would set the tar barrel afire then, and you could see the fire for miles around.

bonna winkie n Cp *EDD* winky-eye sb 'game played [blindfold] with eggs' Co. The game of blind-man's buff (1937 DEVINE 10).

bonnet n Comb **bonnet hop, bontop*** ['bɒntəp, 'bɔntɒp]: a public dance, a ball.
[1882] 1976 MURPHY 74 [advertisement] Excursion to conclude with a Grand Bonnet Hop in the Star of the Sea Hall. 1934 *Public Bureau Christmas No* 23 The volume of city trade was very large in Christmas week, all were in good humour anticipating the great day and making their plans for Bonnet Hops, Soirees and the big Ball at Jocelyn's. C 71–120 Bontop: a spree or social at the community hall.

bonnive n also **bonnif** ['bɒnɪf] *EDD* bonuv Ir; DINNEEN banbh. A young pig; BONEEN.
1955 ENGLISH 32 Bonnif—a young pig. T 529–68 'So,' he said, 'we took the six bonnifs and we took the pig and we brought her home. C 71–87 A piglet was called a bonnif by older people of Irish descent in Placentia.

bontop* See BONNET HOP.

boo n also **bo** *OED* bo [interjection]; bogy l 'the devil'; *EDD* ~ sb¹ 'a louse'; cp *OED* bull-beggar ['bull-bear; bogy'] (1584–1851); *NID* boogeyman, and variants 'an evil spirit'; J WIDDOWSON, *Folklore* lxxxii (Summer, 1971), 99–115; for sense 4, cp *Kilkenny Lexicon* boo-man 'bogey-man.' See also BULLY²: BULLY-BOO.
1 Imaginary figure used to terrify children into good behaviour.
1972 WIDDOWSON 74 I'm going to tell the big boo to come and carry you away if you don't stop it. Ibid 278 Bo: this was a man who lives underneath the house. Ibid 279 A small child will not go into a dark room once someone has said: 'There are boos in there.'
2 A louse.
T 361/2–67 Be careful not to sit by somebody, because she has boos in her head. P 108–70 A boo was a louse and a nit was the egg. C 71–94 It was very easy to pick up head lice (boos).
3 Nasal mucus.
P 245–64 Boos—dried mucus in nose.
4 Comb **boo-bagger**: see senses 1, 2, 3 above.
T 353–67 She would say, 'you got boo-baggers in your nose.' T 360–67 Got boo-beggers in your head! M 68–24 Boo-bagger is the name given to a supposedly evil person who chased and harmed bad little boys and girls. C 71–122 [She] used to tell us that we looked like boo-baggers when we were dressed untidily or in dirty clothes. 1973 WIDDOWSON 286 To frighten children in the dark a parent might say, 'Watch out! The Boo-Bag-

gers are in there.' 1975 GUY 158 Good luck to bad rubbish. Devil's own boo-bagger. Hope he spends the next fifty years passing through Liberal kidneys.
boo-darby: see sense 1 above; cp DARBY.
C 67–5 If you go out tonight the Boo-darby will carry you away. 1972 WIDDOWSON 84 Don't go down there! The boo-darbies are down there!
boo-man: the devil; see also senses 1, 3 above.
1887 *Colonist Christmas No* 16 No doubt, mothers sent their children to sleep by threatening to give them to the old man of St Shotts; a Booman of local growth raises the moral and social status of a district, and it is pleasant for the resident ladies to feel independent of Japanese bogies and Teutonic jotuns for the uses and purposes of child-scaring. 1903 *Daily News* 9 Sep "His Moustache": The prophet, George Gushue, man, / Oh, 'tis now he cuts a dash, / By dad he's like a 'boo man,' / Since he cut off his moustache. 1969 *Christmas Mumming in Nfld* 72 The Boo Man (or the Boo, a euphemism for the Devil) takes children 'down to his fire' if they misbehave or lie. P 148–76 ~ dried mucus in the nose.
boo-man's hat: toadstool; FAIRY CAP (P 80–64).

boogyman n *OED* bogy 1 'the devil,' *NID* boogeyman and variants 'an evil spirit.' Comb **boogyman's bread**: toadstool; BOO-MAN'S HAT, DEVIL'S CAP (1971 NOSEWORTHY 176).

book n One of a series of graded readers marking the level in the school which a child had attained to.
1972 NEMEC 171 The Chairman [of the community council], for example, has no formal education beyond the fifth 'book' (grade). 1972 MURRAY 138 One woman recalled going home and telling her father: 'I'm through me book.' 1977 RUSSELL 37 Ki is two years younger than me and we both give up school the same year. I was in number 4 book and Ki in number 3.

booshy* n *Kilkenny Lexicon* boody, booshy. A louse (P 245–81).

boot n Comb **boot stick**: length of wood held between the feet and used to knead and soften the bottom of a sealskin boot (P 130–67).

bore v *OED* ~ v¹ 2 c 'advance, push forward' (1697–); cp *OED* bear v¹ 37: bear up for, naut. To sail in a certain direction, esp to home port.
1924 ENGLAND 71 'Us goin' to bore up wid a full trip o' fat, a logger load.' Ibid 278 This meant we would have very proximately to 'bore up' for St John's. Q 73–4 Bore up, said especially of a schooner turning for home after a bad spot of weather at sea.

born v *NID* ~ v² 'dial'; *ADD* 2. (a) To act as midwife; to deliver; (b) to give birth to.
T 1–63¹ My sister was a midwife. She borned over two thousand children, my sister. T 207–65 I've borned 'bout 300 of them myself. I took [up] nursing when I was thirty-seven year old an' I finished when I was sev-

enty. P 148–66 If they can't born them, they have a cae-
sarean section. P 242–74 I don't know how she borned
the child. 1972 MURRAY 68 'Borning babies' was wom-
en's work. There might be a number of women around,
but no man.

bostoon n also **bosthoon**. *EDD* bosthoon Ir;
DINNEEN bastún. A clumsy, stupid fellow (1937
DEVINE 10).
1925 *Dial Notes* v, 326 Bosthoon—an extremely
ignorant man.

bottle n Cp *OED* bottle nose 3 'dial. name of
the puffin' obs (1678), *NID* bottle-nosed diver.
Comb **bottle-arse spider**: common spider with
bulbous body,
C 68–12 The bottle-arse spider was the type that
would bring rain if [you killed it].
bottle-arse squid: small 'squid' with shape like
a pouch.
1968 MERCER 1 Squids of this genus (*Rossia
palpebrosa*) are small. . .and have a bursiform configuration, leading to such names as 'bottleass squid' and
'purse squid' in Newfoundland. P 1–75 Bottle-ass squid
is commonly used amongst some fishermen.
bottle-brush: Canadian burnet, a perennial
herb with long club-shaped stamens
(*Sanguisorba canadensis*) (1956 ROULEAU 27).
bottle nose, ~-nosed diver, ~- nosed duck: (a)
PUFFIN¹ (*Fratercula arctica*); SEA-PARROT; (b) the
surf scoter (*Melanitta perspicillata*); (c) nickname
for resident of Bay Bulls.
[1620] 1887 MASON 151 The sea fowles, are. . . Bottle noses, with other sorts. [1771] 1792 CARTWRIGHT i,
129 Killed a shell-bird and a bottle-nosed diver. 1861
Harper's xxii, 753 Strange birds hovered
around. . .saddle-back gulls, bottle-nosed ducks, hagden, auks. 1870 *Can Naturalist* v, 302 Provincial names
[of the surf duck are] 'Bottle-nosed diver' and 'Bald
coot.' 1959 MCATEE 18 ~ Surf Scoter (The bill of the
male is enlarged basally.) C 64–1 Mobile goats, Witless
Bay gammy birds, Bay Bulls bottle noses.

bottom¹ n *OED* ~ 6 (1603–) for sense 1.
1 The innermost part of a bay, harbour or
inlet; the land adjoining the inmost part of a bay.
1612 *Willoughby Papers* [Guy's journal] Nov 5 That
Passage harbour before spoken of is in the bottome of
the bay of Placentia. 1620 WHITBOURNE 2 And here I
pray you note, that the bottomes of these Bayes do
meet together, within the compasse of a small circuit.
1630 VAUGHAN 68 I advised him to erect his Habitation in the bottome of the *Bay* at *Aquaforte*. [1770]
1792 CARTWRIGHT i, 43 My new friends intend to
spend the Winter in the bottom of the cove. 1837
BLUNT 2 At the bottom of the bay you will perceive
Petty Harbour; the entrance is to the northward of a
low point of land, which shuts the harbor in from the
sea. 1846 TOCQUE 117 . . .persons who lived a winter
in the bottom of Bonavista Bay. 1917 *Christmas Bells* 1
Holyrood, at the bottom of Conception Bay, has
become one of our favorite summer resorts. 1953 *Nfld
& Lab Pilot* ii, 230 The head of the bay, known as

South-West Bottom, is encumbered with above-water
and sunken rocks. 1964 *Evening Telegram* 1 Oct, p. 13
Most of the inhabitants fled with their valuables in shallops and schooners to the deep fjords at the bottom of
Trinity Bay where they buried or lost treasure. 1977
Nfld Qtly Winter, p. 19 For to run in Fortune Bay that
night in a sailing-schooner, in a storm of wind right in
through the bay—no radars or nothing at them times,
well, you'd be up the bottom of Fortune Bay where the
nights are long. So I knew we'd be up the bottom of
Fortune Bay before daylight.
2 A section of netting forming the floor of a
cod-trap.
1936 SMITH 19 We put the bottoms in our traps
there, and painted up our trap boat and cod seine boat.
P 9–73 Most cod traps are made in four pieces. Two
sides, the bottom and the leader.
3 Phr *bottom up*: upside down.
1924 ENGLAND 67 'De glass'm bottom up, sir. Her'm
down to 29, an' havin' awful works!' T 45/6–64 They
used to have big old bark pots then, they had for
barkin' the traps, and everything—'twas bottom up.

bottom² n also **bautom** *OED* ~ 15 obs
(1440–1754), *EDD* sb 8. A ball of wool or yarn.
1937 DEVINE 9, 10 ~ , bautom. The ball of wool or
yarn from which stockings, mitts and gloves are knitted.

bottomer n A thin, flat cake or bun.
P 103–67 ~ flat cake made with ingredients similar to
those put in tea biscuits. It is a plain cake without, for
example, nuts or raisins. P 29–74 Left-over bun batter
made into a flat bun called a bottomer.

bough n Cp *EDD* ~ sb¹ 1 So 'end of branch
terminating in twigs' for sense 1; for cpd in sense
2: *DC* ~ bed (1920–), cp *DAE* ~ house (1811–).
1 The branch of a fir or spruce tree.
[1766] 1971 BANKS 135 They take a half tub & boring
a hole Through the Bottom Press hard Down into it a
Layer of Spruce boughs upon which they Lay the Livers & place the whole apparatus in as sunny a Place as
Possible as the Livers Corrupt the Oyl runs from them
& [straining] itself clear through the Spruce Boughs is
caught by a Vessel set under the hole in the tubs bottom. [1771] 1792 CARTWRIGHT i, 87 [He had] there
broken a few boughs, upon which. . .he had lain during
the night, and gone forward again on Saturday morning. [1822] 1928 CORMACK 24–5 Boughs are broken
from the surrounding spruce trees, two or three arm-
fuls to each person, to serve to lie and sleep on; they
are laid on the ground at the windward side of the fire
to be free from smoke, tier upon tier, as feathers upon
the back of a bird, the thick or broken ends placed in
lines towards the fire, and form a kind of mat three or
four inches in thickness. 1842 BONNYCASTLE i, 292
[From the black spruce] boughs or sprays, essence
of spruce, in Canada, and spruce beer, the common
beverage here, are made. 1907 MILLAIS 278 At a distance these little spruce woods look like grass or moss,
and they are of such small stature that a passage
between them looks easy; but if you are so unfortunate
as to find your way into their midst, nothing remains

but retreat, or a short cut to the nearest hard ground, for the deceptive bush is a mass of interlaced boughs of great strength, which makes progression extremely arduous, and at times impossible. P 9–73 The [trapper's] tent is set over the pile of boughs. Inside, the boughs are scattered around the tent and tramped down. The tramping of the boughs breaks them into small pieces, the result is a draft-tight bedding. 1977 BURSEY 17 We hauled boughs and covered the flakes before spreading the fish. . . We built our own boats large and small and shipped fish to market.

2 Attrib, comb, cpd **bough bed,** ~ **bunk:** sleeping place made with the springy tips of conifer branches.

1868 HOWLEY *MS Reminiscences* 24 Our bed consisted of fir boughs spread in the inner part. There were only three occupants. . . This was my very first experience of camp life and a bough bed. T 43/7–64 The usual method was that you'd buddy up with another feller. If he had a couple o' blankets and you had a couple, and a nice bough bunk under you, you'd be fairly comfortable.

bough fence: fence made of spruce or fir branches woven into a frame of saplings (1968 *Avalon Penin of Nfld* 64).

bough house: a small, temporary shelter in the woods, constructed of conifer branches woven into a frame.

1899 ENGLISH 105 'I think you gentlemen had better set to work and build a bough house,' said Lucy. . . They selected a large tree, whose branches spread out some distance, and with the aid of a few more, which they took from other trees, they soon had a temporary though frail protection from the rain. [1902] 1976 *Evening Telegram* 9 Aug, p. 6 It got foggy around 4 p.m. so they decided to put up for the night in a bough-house. It was not very comfortable. 1978 ibid 26 Apr, p. 4 Government is reviewing the regulations [governing Crown Lands] especially regarding application of the regulations to. . .summer cabins, temporary shelters, bough-houses and the like.

bough tilt: see **bough house.** See also TILT.

1842 BONNYCASTLE ii, 143 We set to work to make a bough tilt. Cutting down a stout pole, we stretched it between two trees at a height of about eight feet from the ground. Then getting a number of smaller poles, we rested them side by side in a sloping position against the windward side of the cross-pole. Weaving a few boughs through these slanting poles, we cut a great number of branches of fir and spruce, covered with leaves, and, beginning at the bottom, laid them one over the other with the leaves outwards, in tile-like fashion. This formed a roof impervious to rain, and blocking up the sides with heaps of boughs and moss we formed a kind of weather-tight hut or shed, open only in front. On this side we made a great fire.

bough whiffen, ~ **whiffet:** see **bough house,** BACK a: BACK TILT.

P 94–57 Bough whiffen: a lean-to, temporary tent, of boughs. T 169–65[1] Bough whiffen—a little low tent, with no sides on, only a roof. C 70–18 There we made bough whiffens out of boughs. This type of crude hut was a traditional shelter hurriedly put up in an emergency. It [was] dome-shape. A fire would be built out-

side the entrance. 1980 *Evening Telegram* 19 Jan, p. 3 He comes from a part of the province 'where there isn't enough wood to build a bough-whiffin.'

bough v Cp *DAE* ~ v 'to cover [a floor] with boughs' (1861). To cover or spread a 'fish-flake' with conifer branches so that the air circulates in the fish-drying process.

1895 *Christmas Review* 18 The time selected was generally towards the end of May, when the flakes were all 'boughed,' the stage-heads finished. T 393/4–67 Now everything you saw here was all done out the best with longers, and all boughed. 1979 COOPER 20 "The Fisher Wife and Mother": Her bent form moving with a quick'ning tread / O'er the uneven ragged bough'd fish-flake.

bounty n In children's games, a prescribed place.

C 67–1 [In pitching coppers] a hole was dug in the ground and a place chosen about ten feet from it called a bounty. We took turns pitching and nicking the coppers with our thumb. M 70–25 [In frozen tag] one person (maybe two) would be the freezer. The others would try to prevent the freezer from touching them. There were two bounties which would, maybe, be poles.

bow[1] n [bou].

1 A strip of wood bent to form the frame of a snowshoe.

[1886] LLOYD 78 [Eskimo snowshoes] are composed of bow, bars, and 'filling,' as the insides are called. The bow is usually oval, and is always made of birch. 1913 *Christmas Chimes* 16 Forty years ago I saw at Wigwam Point in the Exploits River an old Micmac [woman] cutting out the bow of a snowshoe with a knife made out of a bit of iron hoop.

2 One of the curved struts forming the frame of a lobster pot (P 148–62).

T 39/40–64 First thing you got to chop three sticks and then you turn the bows, three bows, sometimes four bows, and then you [lath] it up. T 14/20–64 They'd have [three or] four of these bows. They'll make a parlour in this one, they'll put one head in this end, one in the side and one in this end—three.

bow[2] n Attrib **bow-gunner:** in the seal-hunt, principal marksman who shoots old or mature seals; see also GUNNER 1.

1842 BONNYCASTLE ii, 129 He has likewise his long sealing gun, if he is intended as a bow or after gunner, or, in other words, as an expert marksman, to shoot the animals. 1873 *Maritime Mo* i, 254 [The bow or after gunners] rank before the 'bat-men,' and obtain a trifling remuneration additional by the remission of their 'berth money.' 1878 TOCQUE 307 The bow or chief gunner. . .

bowline n Cp *OED* ~ 1 naut [rope passing from the edge of sail to bow]. A length of rope used esp to fasten a load of wood on a sled and for hauling.

box 60

[1937] 1940 DOYLE (ed) 19 "Tickle Cove Pond": Oh, lay hold William Oldford, lay hold William White, / Lay hold of the cordage and pull all your might. / Lay hold of the bow-line and pull all you can, / And give me a lift with poor Kit on the Pond. Q 67–68 ~ rope used for tying the wood on the catamaran. P 239–71 The back load of wood was tied up with a bowline, and carried on one shoulder supported by a bearing stick which went from the opposite shoulder under the load.

box n Cp *EDD* ~ sb¹ 9 (1) 'handbarrow,' *DAE* ~ cart (1890) for box-barrow in sense 2.

1 Box-shaped compartment on a 'komatik' or sled.

1905 DUNCAN 142 And he had not gone far on the way before he fell in with another komatik, provided with a box, in which lay an old woman bound to St Anthony hospital. P 153–65 She put a hooked rug on the box of the komatik. 1973 GOUDIE 79 The kamutik was down over the bank and it started slipping and Jim could not hold it. It was too heavily loaded and at last, turned over. The two eldest children fell out of the box and started rolling down the bank.

2 Comb **box-barrow, box-bar, box-bar tub**: half barrel or box with a long pole fastened to each side for carrying; see BARROW¹.

1936 SMITH 56 It was very slow work as we had to split [the fish] on the schooner deck, then pass it carefully down the boat and then bring it ashore in a boxbarrow. 1956 STORY 5 Box-bar-tub, a half barrel with two parallel handles fastened to it. T 43/7–64 You'd make the box barrow out o' this half barrel, half flour barrel, and put 'stags' on it. It came in very handy because we used to use fish manure on our potatoes and cabbage.

box-cart, ~ car: box-shaped vehicle with two wheels, drawn by horse or pony; cp CAR.

1901 *Christmas Review* 10 Some other travellers bound in the same direction came upon him later, sound asleep in a box-cart which stood at the entrance of the village in which the church was situated. [1929] [1960] BURKE (ed White) 18 "Give Her Cod Liver Oil": She'll devour at each meal / It's a sight for to see, / And a box-cart of tarts / And a puncheon of tea. M 67–17 The box cart was. . .a square box mounted on two wheels. This was the dump truck of the day. It had a removable tail-gate, and its load could be dumped by the simple expedient of removing the tail-gate, releasing the shafts from the harness and permitting the law of gravity to function. It was used around the farm, around town for delivery of coal and similar loads and in the road construction of the day. M 68–23 The caplin were cast about three or four miles out the bay from Glovertown, brought to the beach in boats, loaded on a box-cart and hauled to the potato ground by horse. 1978 *Evening Telegram* 19 Sep, p. 6 The [horse] was harnessed to a box-cart, used for delivering coal.

box stairs: stairway enclosed by a partition.

1972 MURRAY 186 Generally a small hallway separated the parlour and the kitchen, and from it the stairs, usually 'box stairs,' ascended to the four small rooms above.

box trap: box-like compartment of netting, part of a 'cod trap.'

1977 *Inuit Land Use* 261 The smaller cod that come to the coast and come right into the bays—you can stick a cod trap off from the shore. . .you have a sort of leader net and then a box trap.

boxy a also **boxey**. Descriptive of wood from certain trees, tough, gnarled.

1915 HOWLEY 212n [Beothuk bows were made] also of a species of fir called boxy fir, a hard grown, tough, springy wood, so I have been informed by the Micmacs. 1933 MERRICK 134–5 We have picked up some odd words from [man in Labrador], too, such as. . .*boxy*, which is used only of wood, and means the dark, tough wood that grows in the bend of a crooked tree. Boxy wood is the only hardwood in this country. P 94–58 'A boxy black spruce'—a log of wood difficult to saw because of irregular grain. P 148–64 Boxy timber will crack if you put a nail through it; is hard, different colour than the rest of the wood. 1965 PETERS *Gloss* ~ [describes a] type of wood, particularly spruce, which tends to make a saw bind. After being sawn lengthwise, this type of wood tends to curl. 1980 TAYLOR 385 [Boxy wood is] lumber which has the heart or center portion of a tree running through its entire length.

boy n also **b'y** [bɤi, bɑi] *OED* ~ sb¹ 2 b, 5; *EDD* sb 1 Ir Co for sense 2.

1 In the British fishery in Newfoundland, an inexperienced man on his first voyage; cp FRESH 1, GREEN MAN; YOUNGSTER.

[1785] 1792 CARTWRIGHT iii, 90 Mr Collingham took two of the boys with him in the punt, and visited the traps and ships by this harbour. [1831–39] 1926 AUDUBON 236 I have known instances of men, who, on their first voyage, ranked as 'boys,' and in ten years after were in independent circumstances, although they still continued to resort to the fishing. 1878 TOCQUE 293 Boatmasters, or principal men, are paid about £10 as wages, an ordinary fisherman £7, and boys £3 less.

2 A male of any age; a freq term of address; a marker of informality or intimacy.

1863 MORETON 9 The 'boys' in a fisherman's household are all the males, of whatever age, except the father or master. 1887 *Telegram Christmas No* 9 'I'm a younger man than you, an' ought to take the risk.' 'No, boy,' replied Uncle Joe. 'God Almighty let me hear its cry, poor little thing. . .' 'All right, Uncle Joe?' 'Yes, boy,' he said, cheerily. Have you got the child with you?' 'Yes, boy, thank God,' he answered. 1896 *J A Folklore* ix, 31 From [Ireland] also came. . .the use of the term *boys* in addressing men. . . In Newfoundland it is universal. 1905 WALLACE 171 'B'y' was a word we had picked up from the Newfoundland fishermen, who habitually use it in addressing one another, be the person addressed old or young. 1936 DEVINE 82 The late Mr John McCarthy. . .rallied the Wexford boys to his support [and] won the hard political battle. The Wexford vote was very strong in the West End. T 191–65 'If he shows there again, you put a billet o' wood at un.' An' certainly buddy said, 'There he is again.' 'Well boy,' he said, 'let go!' And he hove the junk o' wood an' he beat out glass, sash an' all! 1969 *Christmas Mumming in Nfld* 68 Males call each other 'my dear,' 'boy,' 'my son.' 1971 CASEY 168 "The Battle in Sandy Cove": Joey was no coward, but he was no Irish boy, / It was his full intention big John [Smithers] to destroy, / So with a nail drove in a stick he struck with all his might, / It was considered foul by all so Joey lost the fight. 1975 BUTLER 31 He come aboard and he said, 'Sell me this one.' I said 'Yes, boy, I'll sell her to ya.' 1977 *Inuit Land Use* 213 If you had to go in your own area for hunting now, boy, it would take a lot of time.

brachey See BREACHY.

brackety a *Kilkenny Lexicon* breac: breac-edy; DINNEEN breachtach 'spotted,' cp *EDD* braggoty 'mottled' Co D. Of domestic animals, spotted, speckled.

1968 DILLON 133 He had an old [brackety] horse. [The sheep] had [brackety] legs an' a [brackety] face.

brail v Cp *OED* ~ v 1 'to haul up (the sails) by means of the brails.' To sew or stitch carelessly (P 37).

P 243–61 ~ to tie up carelessly. Q 67–40 [They were] 'brailed up'—a type of sewing such as a man might do in mending his clothes away from home. C 70–21 If [a piece of mending] is 'just brailed' it does not have good staying qualities. [The word] might be used to indicate that you had botched a job or done it very poorly. 1975 RUSSELL 34 [The two guernseys] was more holey than righteous so she was goin' to get the darnin' needle and brail 'em up somehow.

brail n Cp *OED* ~ sb¹ 1 pl 'small ropes fastened to the edges of sails to truss them up'; b 'rope attached to a fishing net for a similar purpose' (1883–).

1 Device on ship for coiling twine (P 243–56).

2 Rough, amateurish piece of sewing; cp BRAIL v.

1972 MURRAY 108 A darn that was roughly and carelessly done was termed 'just a brail' and was the sign that the darner took no pride in her work.

brandies n pl also **brandishes**, and attrib **brandy**. Prob a re-formation based on *OED* brandise obs, *EDD* brandis(s) 'a three-legged iron stand for supporting a pan. . .over the fire'; DINNEEN brannra 'tripod,' 'a reef of rocks partly under water'; brannda 'a reef of rocks.' Group of 'sunken rocks' over which the sea breaks; BREAKER, HARRY, SUNKER; usu in place-names.

[1774] 1971 SEARY 183 Brandys (Lane 1774) [1894 BURKE] 69 "Harbour Grace Excursion": Oh, she died below the Brandies / When we were coming back. 1900 HARVEY 124 . . .its restless waves breaking upon the 'Brandies,' as the outlaying rocks are called. [1952] 1971 SEARY 90 Brandys, THE BRANDIES, 'three sunken rocks. . .and a group of sunken and above water rocks, lie about three-quarters of a mile eastward and three-quarters of a mile east-southeastward, respectively, of the light-structure on CAPE ST FRANCIS' (NTS Pouch Cove). The name occurs variously as The Brandies,

Brandies Rock(s), Brandies Shoal, Brandy Rock(s) in at least fourteen localities on the Newfoundland coast, and as The Brandies near the Saltee Islands off the southeast tip of Ireland. The name is apparently brandise—a trivet, an iron tripod for cooking over a fire, and probably referred originally to a group of three low pinnacle rocks, though subsequently it came to be applied to any low-lying rocks. 1953 *Nfld & Lab Pilot* ii, 126 The Brandishes [are] a group of above-water rocks, extending about 2 cables offshore. P 245–76 [When we docked, he said] 'You came through inside the Brandies.'

brandishes See BRANDIES.

brass-wing(ed) diver n Eastern white-winged scoter (*Melanitta deglandi deglandi*).

[1785] 1792 CARTWRIGHT iii, 56 I shot four, and a brass-winged diver. 1977 *Inuit Land Use* 212 White-winged scoter (brass-winged diver).

braych See BREACH.

brazil n also **brasile, the brazil(s)**. Cp *OED* ~ (1864 quot for pl). Esp in pl, the northern provinces of Brazil served by the seaport of Pernambuco, a market for dried and salted cod-fish; also attrib ~ **fish**, ~ **market**, ~ **trade**.

1620 WHITBOURNE 18 Sundry Portugall ships haue come thither purposely to loade fish from the *English*, and haue giuen them a good price for the same, and sailed from thence with it to *Brasile*, where that kinde of fish is in great request. 1883 *Fish Exhibit Cat*⁴ 175 Drum containing 128 lbs. Codfish, prepared for the Brazil market. 1888 *Colonist Christmas No* 2 He commanded the *Orion*, which vessel was then at Lance-au-Roi awaiting a cargo of fish for the Brazil. 1953 *Nfld Fish Develop Report* 41–2 The market for Newfoundland fish is found in the northern provinces of Brazil, where the preference is for well-cured fish of 'Madeira' quality. T 168/70–65 That madeira went to Brazil. They call that Brazil fish. 1967 *Bk of Nfld* iv, 64 [Sailing vessels] carried our salt cod to market in. . .Brazil or, to give [it] the name by which it was best known here, 'the Brazils.' 1973 HORWOOD 18 The other vessel. . .was considerably larger, and suitable for the Brazil trade.

breach v also **brach, braych** [briːtʃ] *OED* ~ v 3 'of whales' (1843–). Of cod, caplin, etc, to ruffle or break the surface of the water; of seals, to jump up in the water.

1842 JUKES i, 231 The sea was pretty still, and the fish were 'breaching,' as it is termed. For several miles around us the calm sea was alive with fish. They were sporting on the surface of the water. 1924 ENGLAND 241 In a bay of water, near at hand, a few dogs and bitches were 'braychin',' but nobody now gave them any heed. They were blowing bubbles, tossing their tails, playing with no heed whatever of the ship. 1925 *Dial Notes* v, 326 Brach [i.e. brāch]—break [the surface]. P 118–67 Look! They're breaching [said of the action of a school of fish, esp caplin, when they break the surface of the water]. 1979 NEMEC 237 Two generations ago. . .cod 'breached' in the Bight [at St Shotts] and literally filled it.

breachy a also **brachey, breechy** ['briːtʃɪ, 'brɛitʃɪ'] OED ~ a¹ obs (1662); EDD Ha Co; SMYTH 129. Of liquid, having a salt taste.

1924 ENGLAND 45 Unless one has a dash of limejuice to add thereto, the water—made of melted ice—is not only 'brachey' but also provokes distressing thirst. T 181–65 That's what we get our tea out of. Sometimes that'd be right breachy. You'd hardly drink it—come from the ice, ice [taken] aboard. P 126–67 This soup is breachy. P 33–79 The water was right breechy.

bread n OED ~ sb¹ 6 b obs (1651–1793), DAE n 1 a obs (1656–1851), EDD sb¹ 2 (Nfld: 1894) for sense 1; for combs. in sense 3: OED sb¹ 9 ~ bag (1864), DAE ~ bag (1828–1866), OED 10 ~ barge (1840).

1 Thick, coarse biscuit, baked without salt and kiln-dried; sea-biscuit; HARD BREAD. Cp CAKE.

[1677] 1976 HEAD 101 Provisions imported this yeare only in St John's Harbr. Bread (1b) 50,000 [from] England. [1742] ibid 102 Cargoes imported by 'Ships Entred in the Harbour of St John's. Bread (1b) 452,000 [from] England.' 1842 JUKES i, 17 Returning to Torbay we got a dinner of tea, eggs, and bread and butter, the latter being common ship's biscuit and salt butter. 1866 WILSON 208 Bread always means sea-biscuit. [1876] 1877 TUCKER 47 Fresh butter in many cases is almost equally scarce, and 'bread' means 'biscuit' only (there is a tub of them always standing in my dining-room). 1925 Dial Notes v, 326 ~ Hard bread. Bread when soft is called 'loaf.' 1967 READER 8 [They] would bring back [from St John's] the supplies they needed for the winter. This would be possibly 20 or 30 barrels of flour, so many bags of bread (hard tack), a puncheon of molasses, tea, sugar, beans, etc.

2 Phr *take bread for the road*: to carry bread in one's pocket to ward off the fairies; cp COMPANY BREAD.

P 108–70 Going out at night, or going into the woods, one took a bit of bread for the road, so the fairies wouldn't 'take' one.

3 In designations of containers or storage places for sea-biscuit: ~ **bag**; ~ **barge**; ~ **box**; ~ **loft**; ~ **noggin** [see NOGGIN]; ~ **sack**.

[1772] 1792 CARTWRIGHT i, 208 Leaving all my baggage except my bread-bag, we returned to Mr Hewet's, and gave up all farther thoughts of prosecuting our intended journey. T 172/4–65 Now our bread start to get soaked in a bread bag. 1930 BARNES 224 I filled out a pint mug of cocoa and hauled out what we call a bread barge and there was a pan of butter in the barge. [1786] 1792 CARTWRIGHT iii, 135 Tilsed shot a grouse, and made a bread-box. T 31/2–64 Away they goes, the crowd what was aboard the steamer, with punts, bread-boxes, kettles and everything now they could muscle up for 'em to eat, 'cause they were starvin' to death, see. 1979 TIZZARD 277 The bread box was also well packed for the trips out in the boat. [1870] 1973 KELLY 24 The agent had cleared away the sacks of biscuit in the bread loft. C 75–132 Bread noggin. A lunch box

used while fishing. T 43/7–64 Well, that's what would usually be used, or an oat sack. A oat sack is a bit coarser than a bread sack.

4 Comb **bread soda**: baking soda or sodium bicarbonate used in making soft bread or 'loaf.'

T 92/3–64 You just put that in the flour an' you'd put molasses in an' then you have bread soda for dark ones—'twas cream o' tartar an' bread soda in them days. 1975 BUTLER 80 [They'd get] margarine in tubs called firkins, bread soda and cream of tartar.

bread-and-cheese n OED bread sb¹ 2 d: bread and cheese; EDD sb 3 (1) for sense 2.

1 In feature name for a rocky, treeless hill or point.

[1772, 1840] 1971 SEARY 78 Lane recorded Bread and Cheese Islands, now Bread Island. . .in 1772 and Bread and Cheese Cove at Bay Bulls, a shift name from Thornton's Bread and Cheese Point, in 1773. Jukes 1840 also recorded Bread and Cheese (Hill) at the head of Calvert Bay. 1951 Nfld & Lab Pilot i, 82 Bread and Cheese rock. . .lies close southward of Bread and Cheese point.

2 In children's name for the opening leaf, and berry, of the hawthorn (*Crataegus oxyacantha*).

C 66–8 Children used to eat the leaves and call them the bread-and-butter leaf, or bread-and-cheese leaf. C 66–9 Bread-and-cheese nuts were small red berries or nuts that grew in little clusters on a [hawthorn] tree or bush.

break v

1 To cause water to churn or tumble; of a rock, to emerge through turbulent water.

1975 BUTLER 37 And this sunker now would break with the three big seas. When the big one would come, the last one, he'd always go in over the sunker. 1975 GUY 140–1 The water fell lower than it did at any other time, the beaches became twice as broad and rocks away out were breaking water.

2 Phr *break the beam*: in weighing dried and salted cod-fish for export, to assign more to the quantity placed on the scales than the strict weight requirement in order to make up for inadequacy of the scales or loss of weight in shipment.

P 169–80 In this fish store we are required to break the beam when packing fish for shipment.

break the bottom: to form the sort of waves induced by shallow water; of waves, to react as if the bottom were close to the surface.

1975 BUTLER 38 Sunkers was breakin' and 'twas foldin' right in the cliff and goin' up in the cliff. But I knew they wasn't breakin' the bottom because. . .I knew how much water was there. Ibid 39 'Twas just the same as you'll see pictures of it comin' down over a overfall—that's what it looked like, breakin' from side to side, that's what you'd think to look at the foam, see, but 'twasn't breakin' the bottom.

break dead amain: of a fishing ground, to be very rough.

P 187–73 Fishermen say 'it's breaking dead amain' when a big sea is causing the fishing ground to break.

break the hoop: in coopering, to bend a birch hoop into circular form.

P 127–78 The wooden hoops used around casks overlapped about ten to eighteen inches. Quiling refers to a specific procedure whereby hoops which have gone through a bending procedure called breaking the hoop, on the bending horse, are quiled on a ringer. The newly cut, split and bent birch is quiled inside pegs where it assumes a circular shape.

break one's path: to walk by another route to avoid meeting someone approaching.

C 66–13 'I was never one to break my path for anyone.' To break one's path means to attempt to avoid meeting another person by taking a different route.

break the price: to determine the price paid for fish, etc, during a given season.

[1806] 1954 INNIS 306 A custom prevails at St John's for the merchants to meet together and settle the price of fish and oil, which is termed 'breaking the price.' This is done about the beginning of August after having received advices from Europe and ascertained the state of the market.

breakage n   A gap; passageway for a boat or vessel.

P 148–59 The breakage between the islands was neither wide enough nor deep enough for the vessel to pass through. T 172/4–65 I said, 'Boys, we'll haul up our boat here and turn her up on her edge so as the wind will break her.' We propped her up and we got blackberry trees and poked that through the breakage between the stem and the stern. And that was our shelter until the storm was over. T 187/8–65 There was a breakage broke out eastern when it lightened, and the skipper said he was going to slip her now, put her out in that breakage, and let her go with the ice.

break-deck n   Cp SMYTH break 'the sudden rise of a deck'; break-beams. A raised section of the deck, fore or aft; also attrib.

P 127–73 ~ an elevated section of the deck running aft, beginning a short distance forward of the mainmast. 1977 BUTLER 7 There being a break deck-beam across the boat forward to raise the fore-castle deck. . .the heavy strain on the spar broke the fastenings in the break deck-beam and drove the planking off the bow of the boat.

breaker n   Cp OED ~ ¹ 5 'heavy ocean-wave which breaks violently into foam. . .in passing over reefs or shallows'; cp SMYTH 130. A partially submerged rock over which seas 'break' or tumble heavily; freq in coastal names; cp SUNKER.

1778 DE CASSINI 129 We suddenly perceived, at a small distance before us, the dashing of the waters, which could only be occasioned by the coast, or by rocks or breakers, which the fog concealed from our sight. 1887 *Telegram Christmas No* 4 On the northern side of the [Isle of Boys, Ferryland] are breakers and shoal waters, so that nothing except the smallest boat can enter, except through the narrows. 1913 *Christmas Chimes* 25 As the boat drifted on a breaker, 'Caplin Cove Rock,' he rose up, waved his hand as if in adieu. [1923] 1946 PRATT 201 "The Lee-Shore": 'But not to-night,' flashed the signal light / From the Cape that guarded the bay, / 'No, not to-night,' rang the foam where the white / Hard edge of the breakers lay. 1951 *Nfld & Lab Pilot* i, 318 The Breakers, rocky ledges which dry, extend a quarter of a mile offshore. 1953 ibid ii, 117 Rocky shoals extend 1¾ cables northward and southward of this island, the positions of which can best be seen on the chart, and which include on the southern side, a sunken rock, known as South-West breaker. T 58/61–64 I made Little Bay Islands that night and I also made that breaker! A breaker, you know, is a bad rock burstin'. We ran over the breaker, and she went up on a sea and she come down, and the whole bottom went out of her. 1971 NOSEWORTHY 177 ~s. Submerged rocks with water breaking over them.

break'er down n   Perhaps from break [h]er down. Cp *DAE* breakdown 'a noisy rollicking dance' (1819–). A session of lively square dancing; cp WALLOP'ER DOWN*.

T 222–66 After the concert was over, there would be a dance, and it would always be square dances, and they would be called 'break-her-downs,' which I think is a very appropriate name. M 68–11 The gang went around together and gathered at one house or another every night for a scoff, scuff, time, or breaker-down. Q 71–10 I remember the breaker-downs we used to have in the old hall.

breakfast n   Comb **breakfast fish**: caplin for household consumption; TEA FISH.

1842 BONNYCASTLE ii, 189 A keg of dried capelin, for breakfast fish 0/5/0.

breaking ppl See also BREAKER. Of partially submerged rock(s) over which seas 'break' or tumble heavily.

1953 *Nfld & Lab Pilot* ii, 384 Breaking rock, which dries 2 feet, lies about 2 cables east-north-eastward.

bream n   usu **brim, brin*** [brɪm] *NID* ~¹ 2 c. Redfish or rose-fish; ocean perch (*Sebastes marinus*).

P 245–63 Red as a brim [with] embarrassment. A brim is a rosefish. Q 71–8 Brim [was] the common South Coast usage until fish plants began calling them rose-fish, redfish or ocean perch.

breast n   Cp *NID* breastmark 'mark placed abreast of landmark in surveying.'

Comb **breast line**: (a) rope attached to bow of vessel to ease her to the wharf; (b) rope running from main buoy to the 'leader' of a 'cod-trap.'

P 148–65 The breast-line [is used] to breast [the vessel] in. P 127–76 The breast line is that rope which is attached to the centre-mooring, extending across the trap and attached to the leader.

breast mark: one of two (or more) land features or objects lined up by a fisherman in order to locate the position of a 'fishing ground'; MARK 1.

C 68–24 Fishermen, in order to be able to anchor in the same area on the fishing ground, use landmarks, sometimes called breast-marks. It could be spire of a church over a small island, the chimney of a house [in line with] the church spire, etc. Q 71–8 ~ one of the two marks used to fix a position at sea—usually the position of an underwater feature. The running mark would give the distance up or down (parallel to) the coast, the breast mark would fix the distance off shore.

breast piece: in laying out a corpse, a square cloth, with sacred inscription, placed on the chest of the deceased.

M 68–16 Accompanying the habit would be a breast-piece. This would be about eighteen inches square. There would be two strings on the upper part of this breast-piece and these strings would be used to tie this part of the habit around the neck. On [it] the letters I.H.S. would be woven or placed [and the cloth] would be trimmed with wide white silk ribbon. Above the initials would be a white cross. Beneath the letters was a white heart.

breast wharf, ~ **work**: long narrow wharf jutting out into a harbour (1971 NOSEWORTHY 178).

breastner, breastney See BRESNA.

breeches n pl also **britches, britchet(s), britchin'(s)** ['brɪtʃəz, 'brɪtʃəz] OED breech sb 6 pl 'roe of a cod-fish' obs (1688). Cod-fish roe and the ovarian membrane which contains it.

P 94–57 Britches: cod roe, so-called from shape. P 148–65 The lady fish wear the britches! 1968 Avalon Penin of Nfld 58 Britchins: cod roes. C 71–100 'Them britches, lights, and sounds are some good,' said Uncle John, 'when fresh caught and fried in scrunchions.' 1975 The Rounder Sep, p. 12 'Britches' consist of the egg sacks of the female cod, and are named for their resemblance to a pair of baggy trousers.

breechy See BREACHY.

breeder n Mammal or fish (esp seal, salmon or trout) of mature age; largest trout.

1873 CARROLL 20 It is not until the breeders [seals] leave their young. . . 1909 BROWNE 58 Notwithstanding the vigilance exercised by the Newfoundland government, the law [about barring salmon rivers] is often set at defiance, and some fishermen have no scruple in destroying the 'breeders.' 1924 ENGLAND 200 Badly enough protected as the herd is today, with slaughter of the breeders permitted, its safeguards are far better than fifty or sixty years ago. P 155–64 I like to go fishing, b'y, because I always catch the breeder! P 130–67 Quip said to a person going trouting: 'Don't catch the breeder.'

breeks n pl also **briggs** [brʊks, briːks]. Cp OED breek 1 b; EDD breek sb 1. Heavy trousers, like riding-breeches.

T 29–64 'Well now,' he says, 'he has on a curty breeks, breeches, you know, with stitching around.' T 200–65 I come home, me son, and I had a brand new suit o' clothes, winter clothes, breeks and logans. 1975 GUY 60–1 Then what is perhaps the pièce de résistance

of the whole juvenile winter ensemble was drawn on. The set of briggs. Or 'breeks' as they are called by some. . . They were reinforced at the knees with patches of the stoutest leather with slits in the legs which were snugly fitted against the juvenile calf by means of. . .lacings.

breeze n Cp SMYTH 133 'among seamen [breeze] is usually applied as synonymous with wind in general, whether weak or strong.' A strong wind, gale; cp STORM 1.

1842 JUKES ii, 162 We met a fleet of boats, large and small, with mainsails down, foresails reefed, and every sign of a heavy breeze blowing. 1861 DE BOILIEU 45 . . .or else we shall have a breeze springing up, and mayhap, lose all our nets. 1921 FPU (Twillingate) Minutes 1 Nov [He] then spoke of the big loss that some people. . .have had on account of the big gale [and] of some men belong[ing] to a Carbonear schooner which had to leave her in the breeze. 1924 ENGLAND 134 Some odd turn of thought makes many of the Newfoundlanders use diminutives. A gale becomes a 'breeze,' oars are 'paddles.' T 55/6–64 Twice lost, wrecked in the September breeze, gale—big sea, you know. T 389/90–67 Such a tremendous breeze. You'd never think anything'd live on the water— tremendous breeze o' wind. 1976 Evening Telegram 17 June, p. 3 'The lobster fishery was excellent in this area before the breeze struck!' he said. . . 'Older people say it was the biggest [wind] and sea in years. 1979 NEMEC 254 Generated in some cases by Caribbean hurricanes, 'storms of wind,' 'breezes,' or 'August Gales' as they are variously called, can create not only rough surface seas, but cause a general mixing of inshore waters such that major temperature changes take place.

breeze[1] v Cp SMYTH 133 breezing up 'the gale freshening'; DAE ~ : to breeze up (1752–). Of the wind, to increase in force markedly; to freshen to gale force; esp in phr breeze up.

[1832] 1981 Them Days vi (4), p. 34 The wind breezing up to the eastward he was obligd to go in to Fox Berry. 1888 HOWLEY MS Reminiscences 17 Made an early start with all our gear in order to get up the lake before it came on to blow, which we just succeeded in accomplishing when the wind breezed up again. 1932 BARBOUR 10 The wind began to breeze up very fast from the south. 1960 FUDGE 14 It was breezing from the southeast and spitting snow, barometer was dropping fast and all indication of a bad storm. T 50/1–64 The wind was breezin' up all the time. By and by it struck heavy. T 169–65[2] The wind was breezing to the southeast, and a big lop. 1977 Nfld Qtly Winter, p. 21 'I'll keep it on her until she blows level with the deck.' And, boy, she breezed up, and she breezed up, but when we weathered Grand Bank it was blowing.

breeze[2] v also **brieze** EDD ~ v[2] 'press, bear upon' Ha Do So, cp brize v 1 'press heavily, bear a weight on' Ha W So; BOSWORTH-TOLLER brȳsan 'to bruise.' To lean, press down on, apply pressure to.

1937 DEVINE 11 ~ To lean hard on, to press down with a lever or prise. 1955 ENGLISH 32 Brieze —to press down firmly. T 222–66 They called a doctor, and when he was examining her she said, 'For God's sake, doctor, don't breeze down on I.' T 222–67 Come here and breeze down on this plank while I nails it good. C 71–111 If we couldn't get our pencils to write dark enough my mother would say, 'You're not briezing hard enough.'

bresna n   also **breastner, breastney, bresney, brishney**. *EDD* ~ sb Ir; DINNEEN brosna 'faggot, an armful of wood.' A bundle of firewood; load of dry twigs. Cp BACK¹: BACK-BURN.

[c1894] PANL P4/14, p. 2 Who, outside of Newfoundland, would know the meaning of a 'turn,' a 'burn,' a 'breastner' of wood? [c1900] 1978 *RLS* 8, p. 25 Bresney—a small bundle of sticks for firing, carried on women's or children's backs. 1937 DEVINE 11 Breastney. A load of dry sticks or boughs that one can lift to the shoulder. 1955 ENGLISH 33 Brishney—dry twigs gathered for fuel. C 66–4 Breastney—a pile of dry bushes tied together. 1968 DILLON 133 I have to go in now for a bresney.

brew v
1 Of seals, to play sportively on the shore or in the water.
[1802] 1916 MURPHY 2 The seals upon this coast are of many species. . .[Jars], Doaters and Gunswoils and many others brew upon the rocks, in the summer season, and may be called natives. 1863 HIND ii, 203 [The seals] often stop to sport when they find a favourable place for the purpose. It is then they are seen to dive repeatedly, coming up again almost immediately, and to roll themselves about, and beat the water with their hands. The fishermen call this brewing.
2 To come down with a cold.
C 70–15 I often heard [her] say whenever somebody was getting a cold, 'I know you're brewing a cold because you are all mops and brooms.'

brewer n   Cp *OED* brew v 4 c 'bring about. . .natural phenomena' for sense 2.
1 Either the harbour seal (*Phoca vitulina*) or the grey seal (*Halichoerus grypus*), remarkable for its lively actions in the water; see BREW.
1863 HIND ii, 203 The herds of seals that frequent the Gulf of St Lawrence arrive there in the month of November. They come chiefly through the Straits of Belle Isle. They keep very close in the coasts either of Labrador or of Newfoundland, penetrating into all the bays, and not going out far from land when doubling the points and capes. They often stop to sport [and] are seen to dive repeatedly, coming up again almost immediately, and to roll themselves about, and beat the water with their hands. The fishermen call this brewing, and hence the name of 'brewer,' given to those kinds found on our coasts.
2 A period of fine weather thought to presage a storm.
1964 *Daily News* 21 Jan, p. 2 We have had one fine day so far this month, and that was what the old folk call 'a brewer' for a following storm on Friday past. . . [It] brought first very heavy snow, then torrential

rains. . .and winds gusting up to sixty miles an hour. C 75–145 A brewer is a beautiful day after a period of days which are neither really stormy, nor really fine. This beautiful day then brews the storm they believe has been in the making for some time.

brews(e) See BREWIS.

brewis n   also **brews(e), broose, bruis, bruise, bruse** [bruːz, brɒuz, brʉuz]. Cp *OED* ~ 2 '"bread soaked in boiling fat pottage, made of salted meat" [1755] (J.)'; cp *EDD* sb 2 'bread or oatcake soaked in hot water'; *DC* Nfld (c1850 [sic = 1960], 1906–). See also FISH n: FISH AND BREWIS, FISHERMAN'S BREWIS.
1 Sea-biscuit or 'hard tack' soaked in water and then boiled; such a dish cooked with salt cod and fat pork.
[(1766) 1971 BANKS 137 It is a Soup made with a small quantity of salt Pork cut into Small Slices a good deal of fish and Biscuit Boyled for about an hour.] 1858 [LOWELL] ii, 273 Putting a check upon their own curiosity, they had some tea and brewse [L's note: ship-bread soaked into a pulp in warm water] made in the best art of the ship's cook. 1895 *J A Folklore* viii, 28 Brews. . .is a dish which occupies much the same place at a Newfoundlander's breakfast-table that baked beans are supposed to do on that of a Bostonian. It consists of pieces of hard biscuit soaked over night, warmed in the morning, and then eaten with boiled codfish and butter. 1905 DUNCAN ix–x 'Broose' is a toothsome dish resembling boiled hard-tack. 1908 HUBBARD 242 'Bruise' for breakfast. Hard tack, fish, pork, boiled together—good. 'Two more early risin's, and then duff and bruise,' is said to be a Thursday remark of the fishermen. 1920 GRENFELL & SPALDING 23–4 All right-minded Newfoundlanders and Labradormen call it [brewis] 'brusc.' 1924 ENGLAND 117 'Fish an' brewis, how many youse?' It rhymed, for brewis is pronounced 'bruise.' 1933 GREENLEAF (ed) 250 "Change Islands Song": No sign of salmon on that shore; discouraging was the news; / No pirate money could be found, and not a fish for brewis. 1936 DULEY 56 Isabel had a chicken to draw, a jam tart to make, brewis to put in soak for the Sunday morning breakfast. 1937 DEVINE 5 'Brewis,' a once popular morning meal composed of broken hard biscuit soaked in water over night, boiled with small pieces of salt codfish and served up with melted fat pork, evidently came from Scotland. . . In the old days in St John's, when the merchants lived over their stores on Water Street, they all used to have brewis for breakfast on Sunday morning. It was a light meal, palatable and easy of digestion. . . The fisherman followed the merchant more from necessity than choice. . .and most days of the week, as well as Sunday, saw brewis used all over the country. 1955 DOYLE (ed) 11 "A Noble Fleet of Sealers": Tho' Newfoundland is changing fast, / Some things we must not lose, / May we always have our Flipper pie, / And Codfish for our brewis. T 75/6–64 [We'd] carry a stock o' hard bread, and [when] the soft bread'd be gone make brewis out o' the hard bread. T 43/8–64 There was no fresh meats, no baloney, no fresh fish—you'd get salt fish Fridays, salt fish and brewis and fat.

2 Phr *have a head like a brewis-bag*: to be empty-headed, forgetful.

C 67–14 'He has a head like a brewis bag' [meaning] could not 'hold' or retain anything.

stiff as brewis: dignified, unbending.

C 65–2 ~ said about a person who walks [in a] dignified [manner] and is supposed to be proud.

3 Comb **brewis bag**, ~ **net**: net-like bag in which sea-biscuit is soaked in water and then boiled.

1966 SCAMMELL 26 Mary, intimidated at last by his threat of boarding out, took down the brewis-bag and went out to fill it [with hard tack]. 1979 TIZZARD 269 The brewis was always cooked in a brewis net and lifted from the cooking pot and placed in the cullender which rested on a plate, in order that all the water would drain.

briar n Sweet gale (*Myrica gale*) (1978 ROULEAU 84).

brickle a also **breakle** *EDD* ~ adj; *ADD* 1 (1890–). Liable to break; brittle.

1862 *Atlantic Mo* ix, 370 Sech as in ships an' brickle barks / Into the seas descend. 1863 MORETON 32 Breakle. Brittle. 1937 DEVINE 11 ~ Brittle, ice or glass easily broken.

brickly a also **breakly, brockly, bruckly** *EDD* ~ (1), *ADD* adj 1 (1837–). Liable to break or shatter; brittle; BRICKLE.

1863 MORETON Breakly, brockly. P 80–64 'Boxy timber is hard—right brickly' (it will crack if you put a nail through it).

bride n *DC* bride's boys (Nfld: 1952); see also BOY; *EDD* sb¹ (1) ~ cake; *OED* sb¹ 6 (1694), *EDD* sb¹ (3) bride's knot.

Comb **bride(s) boy**: one of a number of men assisting at a wedding.

[1900 OLIVER & BURKE] 22 [They] set out for the Cathedral, with the writer as bridesboy. 1952 BANFILL 63 Wedding invitations are issued by young men and boys called 'bride's boys' who go from harbour to harbour, inviting the people. T 30–64² In the old days you weren't satisfied if you didn't have four or five sets of bridesboys and bridesmaids. The bridesboys would be expected to provide part of the drinks. M 69–2 The 'bridesboys' if possible consist of a brother of the groom, a brother of the bride, and a close friend of the groom's.

bride cake: wedding cake.

1896 *J A Folklore* ix, 22 [At the social gathering after the birth] the 'groaning cake' is distributed, bearing the same relation to the occasion that 'bride cake' does to the marriage feast. T 141/59–65² That's all we got out of the wedding—upsot the water barrels, made away with the bride-cake and hove feathers everywhere. C 68–16 She told me that if you wanted to see your future [husband] all you had to do was get a piece of bride cake and walk up the stairs backward. The bride cake had to be put under your pillow.

bride(s) girl: bridesmaid.

1933 GREENLEAF xxii Soon after my arrival at Sally's

Cove a girl was married and I was asked to be one of the 'bridesgirls' at the wedding. M 68–7 It was always the custom for the bride and groom, and all the bride-girls and bride-boys to go around the harbour to invite people to their wedding. M 69–6 The number of bride boys and bride girls varied from two to six of each. . . The 'best man' and the 'maid of honour' walked together behind the father-giver and the bride. The other bride boys and the bride girls walked in pairs behind each other.

bride knot, also **brim knot**: floral decoration worn by bridesmaid.

1933 GREENLEAF xxii Each of us bridesgirls wore her best dress and pinned on a 'bride knot' (pronounced 'brim knot') of silver leaves and flowers given her by the bride. Q 71–17 A bride knot or brim knot [was worn].

bridge n also **brudge, brudgeway** [brʊdʒ, brʌdʒ] *DC* ~ n 2 Nfld (1771–) for sense 1; *OED* sb 3 a 'gangway' obs for sense 2; *EDD* sb 3 'platform' Nfld for sense 4; JOYCE 98: brudge.

1 A stretch of ice forming a causeway across a river, harbour or strait.

[1771] 1792 CARTWRIGHT i, 182 The river was frozen over in bridges, from that place to the Narrows, but the ice was firm and good all the way home from thence. [1772] ibid i, 226 They were obliged to launch the punt across a bridge of ice in the harbour. 1916 DUNCAN 262 Archie took one step—and dropped, crashing, with a section of the bridge, which momentarily floated his weight. 1933 MERRICK 207 By bending close to the ice we could follow their track. The bridge wound. Sometimes we felt that we were surrounded by the black sliding water. 1934 LOUNSBURY 11–12 Although Cabot Strait is never completely frozen over it is often jammed with ice from the gulf to such an extent that in early spring a blockade extends from St Paul Island to Cape Ray. This blockade, known as 'the Bridge,' sometimes lasts for three weeks, holds up vessels anxious to enter the gulf, and causes wrecks on the Newfoundland coast.

2 A wooden gangway connecting the waterfront stores, sheds, 'flakes,' etc, forming 'fishing premises.'

[1778] 1792 CARTWRIGHT ii, 354 The shoremen made a bridge up the hill between the stage and the flakes. 1931 *Nfld Magazine & Advertiser* 22 A few stakes had been driven in pairs at this point and a couple of planks laid on cross-sticks nailed to the flakes. As Welter approached the 'brudge' he noticed a young woman crossing the planks. P 148–61 Brudge: wooden walkway. P 148–66 Brudgeway: ramp leading to stage. 1977 *Them Days* ii (3), p. 23 At Battle Harbour you could hardly put your foot on a rock there was so many bridges and things. 1979 TIZZARD 92 To cross the flake from the stage bridge to the wharf you walked on two pieces of two by eight inch plank placed side by side, thus there was a walkway of sixteen inches.

3 Part of the mechanism of an animal trap.

[1770] 1792 CARTWRIGHT i, 52 In the afternoon I made twenty-four bridges and tongues for deathfalls, and caught two jays on the porch, with birdlime. 1792 ibid *Gloss* i, ix Bridge of a trap. A plate of iron in the centre of a trap for the animal to tread on, which then falling down, sets the jaws [of the trap] at liberty.

4 (a) A small, uncovered platform at the door of a house to which the steps lead; (b) a similar structure at the entrance to other types of building, sometimes at more than one level.

1896 *J A Folklore* ix, 26 ~ pronounced *brudge*, is the word commonly used to denote a platform. T 139–65 They was over there on the shop brudge, and he come out and drove them off the brudge, the pop-gutted bugger. T 141/65–65² There was no bridge on [his] door. The steps went right up to the threshold o' the porch. M 69–2 The bridge is a wooden platform about 4 ft wide, with a rail around the outside, attached to the outside of the house. 1972 MURRAY 184 Every house had a 'bridge,' often two, one at the front door and one at the back, but they varied from house to house. A bridge might mean a wooden platform, extending from the doorway and ascended by a step or two, or it might simply be steps leading up to the door. Some of the 'better' homes had 'galleries' (verandas) which ran the full width of the front of the house. 1979 TIZZARD 83 I came from school at four o'clock. . .to help him put the barrels in the under store. He would have a great number lined up on the top store bridge. He would pass them down to me and I would tier them up in the under store. Ibid 271 When the dishes were washed she always threw the dishwater out over the railing that extended around the verandah, or as we always called it, the bridge.

5 Comb **bridge master**: officer aboard a sealing vessel who transmits directions for navigating the ice floes from the 'scunner' at the masthead to helmsman.

1924 ENGLAND 40 Aft was a storeroom where slept the after cooks and storekeeper; also the hellhole that bunked the carpenter, bosun, a bridge master, a scunner, the pantry steward and—for a while—myself. [1928] 1944 LAWTON & DEVINE 75 Skipper Tom Doyle, who goes [with] Capt W.C. Winsor in the S.S. *Ungava* as Bridge-Master to the Seal Fishery this Spring, has probably a longer sealing record than any man going to the ice this Spring. 1928 *Nfld Qtly* Oct, p. 31 He was spy master and I was bridge master. T 401/2–67 The bridge master was on the bridge [and] he sung out, 'Go astern!'

briggs See BREEKS.

brim See BREAM.

brim knot See BRIDE KNOT.

brin n *EDD* ~ sb² obs D 'strong linen' (1892); *DC* (1941–), ~ bag (Nfld: 1924–). Possibly from *brinded*: *OED* 'of a tawny or brownish colour'; *EDD* ppl adj¹.

1 Strong, coarse-woven sacking; burlap (P 245–56).

[c1905] P 102–60 The brin was sold by the yard double width about 36 in. wide. 1924: see **brin bag** below. 1937 DEVINE 25 Grogram [is] thick, brown brin or canvas for boat sails. T 43/7–64 Burlap is the Canadian

name for brin, but Newfoundland people call it brin. 1966 PADDOCK 109 *Brin* is the common word for the coarse sacking fabric composing the large, strong sacks for vegetables, animal feeds, and other heavy, bulky products.

2 Comb **brin apron**: capacious apron, reaching from neck to knees, made from coarse sacking material; BARVEL.

T 88–64 [The days] when you use sawdust on your floor, and your mother put on a barbel, brin apron, and scrubbed the floor—that's not coming to pass those days, is it?

brin bag: a sack made of burlap.

1924 ENGLAND 36 Atop the cabin housing lay frozen beef wrapped in dirty 'brin-bags,' which we call gunnysacks. 1933 MERRICK 18 Cecil wants a brinbag to jam some traps in and Arch is 'bringing to' a trout net. T 43/7–64 A brin bag—'twas fine, usually 'twould be an oat bag or a meal bag or a bread bag. T 45/6–64 This feller empted the beef out o' the brin bags and filled it up with birch junks. 1966 *Evening Telegram* 3 Apr You said those who voted against Confederation should put on brin bags and go about in sack cloth and ashes. P 198–67 The potatoes were in a brin bag. C 69–23 If you wish to take the broodiness out of a hen you put it in a brin bag (burlap bag) and push it wholly under salt water. 1970 JANES 16 She was put to work in the merchant's canning factory where all hands wore a stiff apron made from a material known as brin bag. 1976 CASHIN 68 He was busy at the time putting blubber into specially made brin bags to be pressed out for any oil that might remain in the rotten livers.

brin sack: see **brin bag** above.

[c1905] P 102–60 The old S.S. *Neptune*. . .would take on part of a cargo of salt in the after hold leaving enough space above the salt and below decks for the fishermen to lay out their sea-chests and brin sacks filled with shavings or straw collected from some of the crockeryware departments in the city. T 43/7–64 In them times you used to get this hard bread in a brin sack.

brindy a Cp *EDD* brinded ppl adj¹ 'red-brown' So, brinded ppl adj² 'angry' D, brindy sb 'nickname [for] person with red hair.'

1 Saucy (P 173–60).

Q 67–36 You're a brindy young thing! P 16–75 That brindy Dorothy Wyatt!

2 Comb **brindy bough**: the dry red branch of a dead spruce or fir; BLASTY BOUGH.

Q 67–74 He went to get some brindy boughs for the fire.

bring v *EDD* ~ II 2 Ir, JOYCE 225 for sense 1; cp *OED* v 25 a naut bring to 'fasten, tie,' *OED* 27 d naut bring up 'to come to anchor' for phr in sense 2.

1 To take.

P 152–58 [One says] bring something away instead of take or carry.

2 Phr *bring the land ashore*: to close with the land.

C 67–7 When you're sailing and you want to get

closer to the shore you say that you want to 'bring the land ashore.'

bring to: to knit a section of net; to fasten lengths or parts of a net together.

1861 DE BOILIEU 85 The foot of [the seal-net] is brought-to on a shallop's old rode. 1933 MERRICK 18 Cecil wants a brinbag to jam some traps in and Arch is 'bringing to' a trout net. T 141/66–65² I could bring to linnet when I was only about ten or twelve, and mend everything. T 187/90–65 On the last of it they had a 'leader' to bring to, and [the skipper] said he's going to get a man belong to Carbonear to come and bring to the leader. So I started to bring to the leader [myself]. P 9–73 [There are] two or three corks to a section and fastened solidly on each side of each section of cork to the rope to which the netting had already been fastened (brought to).

bring up: to come up against an object, stop.

T 50/1–64 She took one skitter away on the water—I allow she went as far from this down to Pad's before she brought up in big breakin' lop. T 43/8–64 When the goat would go to the fence, she'd get her head in, and the yoke would bring up on the pickets. She couldn't get any further. T 172/5–65 [The bay is] noted very much for icebergs because [of] so many shoals—icebergs brings up there.

3 Hence, cpd **bring-up**: an object which impedes; a place where one stops.

1898 *Christmas Bells* 17 This my rod would not throw satisfactorily, so after a few trials my 'fly' found the nose of one of the persons who were basking behind me—the bring-up tangling my line and breaking a joint. [1918–19]GORDON 60 One always has a most entertaining host in old Arthur Rich. It just happened that this was our bring-up for a week-end last year. 1925 *Dial Notes* v, 327 ~ The place where one stops.

brishney See BRESNA.

briss n Cp *EDD* ~ sb¹ 'little bits' Ir, sb² 2 'dust mixed with small pieces of furze, faggot-wood' D; DINNEEN brus 'dust; the lopping off of trees.' Dry conifer needles.

P 118–66 ~ the droppings of blasty boughs. P 197–76 ~ accumulated blasty needles under evergreen and spruce trees.

britaniola n also **new britaniola** SEARY 62. Short-lived name for Newfoundland in the seventeenth century.

1628 HAYMAN¹ [Al] New Britaniola, Old Newfound-land. 1628 HAYMAN² [Al] Translated into English at Harbor Grace in Bristols-Hope in Britaniola, anciently called New-found-land.

britches, britchet(s), britchin'(s) See BREECHES.

broad a *OED* ~ a 4 b for sense 1; *EDD* adj 3, 7 for sense 2; cp *OED* arrow sb 10: Broad Arrowhead 'arrow-head-shaped mark, used by British Board of Ordnance'; PHILLIPPS 52: broad fig for combs. in sense 3.

1 Of a day, fine, sunny, clear.

P 60–64 'Tis a broad day (a lovely day). Q 71–13 A broad day is a very clear day.

2 Of speech, markedly dialectal.

T 187–65 They had some old broad talk. When we'd say we was going to a place, he'd say, 'I must go thert.' And then he'd start to tell me about how 'twas over thert [in] England.

3 Comb **broad arrow**: mark placed upon a building to indicate government ownership.

T 41–64 [The] sheriff was a feller that go round and seize your house. If you couldn't pay he'd put what he called the broad arrow [on the building]. Q 67–49 When a man owed money the law confiscated his property. The broad arrow was stamped on his house and this signified that the contents of the building did not belong to its owner.

broad fig: term used to distinguish fig from raisin, which is also called fig; see FIG.

1896 *J A Folklore* ix, 35 Figs are [called] *broad figs*.

broad flake: platform built on poles and spread with boughs on which split cod are placed to dry; FLAKE.

1792 CARTWRIGHT *Gloss* i, x [Flakes] are of two sorts, viz: Broad-flakes and Hand-flakes. 1819 ANSPACH 436 The broad flakes consist of a set of beams, supported by posts and shores, or stout pieces of timber standing perpendicularly under the beams, to which similar pieces are likewise fixed in a reclined position. In some places these broad flakes are as high as twenty or thirty feet from the ground.

broad weed: knapweed (*Centaurea nigra*) (1898 *N S Inst of Sci* ix, 373).

brochet n Cp *OED* brocket, *EDD*: brocket sb So D 'two-year old stag.' A male caribou in its second year.

[1777] 1792 CARTWRIGHT ii, 234 There were three deer feeding. . . They proved to be a brochet, a knobler, and a hearse.

broken p ppl *DC* broken fish Nfld (1832, 1883).

Comb **broken fish**: dried and salted cod-fish with an irregular surface or 'face'; a defectively cured cod.

[1578] 1935 *Richard Hakluyt* [Parkhurst's letter:] 125 . . .the broken fysshe, [which] is no small quantity, at the least ii or thre thousand, [which] may be worthe xx li. or xxx li. yf yt were sale abell, and yet as good to eate as the hole. [1806] 1951 DELDERFIELD 82 An account of the sale of 1,147 Portuguese quintals of Newfoundland fish in 1806. It was listed '661 Qtls large, 208 Qtls small, 278 Qtls dumb, wet and broken.' 1832 MCGREGOR i, 232 The broken fish, dun fish, or whatever will not keep in warm countries. . .is in general equally good for domestic consumption. 1883 HATTON & HARVEY 291 [Dried cod] are weighed and 'culled,' or assorted into four different kinds, called Merchantable (the best), Madeira, West India (intended for. . .the negroes), and Dun, or broken fish, which will not keep, and is for home use. T 36–64 The broken was West India, and the thirds would be a little worse than Madeira and a little better than West Indee.

broke(n) sugar: the small fragments resulting from breaking up a sugar-loaf or cone.

1895 PROWSE 451n Mr Brown. . .took them over to see old Billy Rabbits; of course the 'broke' sugar and the hot water and spirits were immediately produced, and a toast had to be proposed.

brook n   A large stream of fresh water with such characteristics as a flat, rocky bottom, considerable width but often no great depth, and a rapid, noisy flow; a river.

1792 PULLING *MS* 8 This old man who was a salmon catcher and lived amongst the Northern brooks many years has frequently met with and parted from the Indians without offering to hurt each other. 1842 BONNYCASTLE i, 197 Rivers [are] called brooks, in Newfoundland, and lakes, ponds. 1912 CABOT 158 On this coast 'pond' and 'brook' are names for largest inland waters; 'lake' and 'river' are terms for the smaller ones. 1979 *Evening Telegram* 29 June, p. 4 [Salmon] rivers closed on the south coast are Simm's Brook, Southwest Brook, Taylor's Bay Brook and Old Bay Brook. In the Central Newfoundland area the rivers closed are: Northwest Arm Brook at New Bay, Notre Dame Bay, and Charles Brook in Bay of Exploits.

brooker n   Allen's willow ptarmigan (*Lagopus lagopus alleni*); PARTRIDGE;ROCK PARTRIDGE: ROCKER.

1977 *Inuit Land Use* 123 Spruce partridges nest on the ground near willow or spruce brush; brookers (willow ptarmigan) seek marshy areas near rivers to lay their eggs.

broom v   Cp SMYTH 139. To fasten a birch-broom to the mast-head of a vessel signifying her offer for sale.

1937 DEVINE 11 A schooner was broomed when the owner wanted to sell her. Instead of an ad. in the paper, as in modern times, the old birch broom used in sweeping the deck was hoisted to the mast-head.

broose See BREWIS.

brough a   also **brow** *EDD* brow adj 1 s w cties. Liable to break or splinter; brittle; esp of wood; BRICKLE.

1863 MORETON 32 ~ Apt to break, as rotten timber. 1937 DEVINE 11 ~ Likely to break, brittle.

brow n   also **brow of wood**. Cp BRYANT 491 (under *landing*) 'place to which logs are hauled or skidded preparatory to transportation by water or rail.' In the woods industry, a pile of logs, esp one placed at the edge of a river or lake.

1957 *Evening Telegram* 9 Nov 'What in the world is a formula?' 'I dunno. Something about how to find how many cords in a brow of wood.' 1959 ibid 4 Apr, p. 4 The haul [of logs] to the stream from the scattered piles or 'brows' left by the cutters may be a mile or more. 1965 PETERS *Gloss* A pile of sawlogs near water. The logs are piled parallel to the water, with each tier of logs resting on two or more slender poles laid across the preceding tier and the front logs resting in notches in the poles. This ties the logs together and permits the face of the brow to be nearly perpendicular. The logs are transferred to the water individually or by knocking out a bottom log and collapsing the brow.

brow v   See also BROW n. To place logs in a pile, esp on the edge of a river or lake, ready for transportation.

T 172/5–65 The timber that they was scaling was put on the lake. Usually it'd be pulled and browed; but this man was putting his timber on the lake.

brow a   See BROUGH.

browal* n   ['braɒəl]. A swelling on the head, the result of a bump.

C 70–21 A lump on the head is called a browal. Usually it is the swelling caused by bumping the head into some hard object. It only refers to a swelling on some part of the head, often the forehead or brow.

brown a   Cp *OED* brown bess 'name familiarly given in the British Army to the old flint-lock musket'; *O Sup*[2] brown a 7: brown top (Aust).

Comb **brown alder**: mountain alder (*Alnus crispa*) (1978 ROULEAU 84).

brown bobber: eastern fox sparrow (*Passerella iliaca iliaca*) (1959 MCATEE 66).

brown oil: in rendering cod-livers or seal blubber, the last oil extracted in the process.

1818 *Waterford Mirror* 28 Sep Brown seal oil. 1832 MCGREGOR i, 225 The first that runs off the seal blubber is the virgin, or pale oil, and the last the brown oil. 1888 STEARNS 186 In one corner of the platform was a big iron kettle where the men were hastening the process of oil making by boiling, and forming a different kind of oil,—the two kinds being known as the 'brown oil' and the 'straw or pale oil.' 1925 MUNN 7 Brown cod liver oil.

brown sally: a flint-lock musket.

1895 GRENFELL 225 [We left Battle Harbour] amidst the salutes from many 'Brown Sallys.'

brown top (grass): name of several varieties of wild grass: (a) woodreed grass (*Cinna latifolia*); (b) panic-grass (*Panicum lanuginosum*).

1898 *J A Folklore* xi, 283 Brown tops. 1956 ROULEAU 27 Brown-top Grass.

browse n   [braɒs, brɛɒs]. Cp *OED* ~ sb[1] 2 'fodder for cattle, consisting of young shoots and twigs' (1552–1837), *DAE* n (1721–) for sense 1; *EDD* sb[1] 1 'brushwood' Do So D Co for sense 2.

1 Birch shoots, twigs and bark as food for beaver, rabbits, etc.

[1783] 1792 CARTWRIGHT iii, 25 Those [beavers] which feed upon brouze, particularly on birch, are the most delicious eating of any animal in the known world. 1895 GRENFELL 35 The bark of these [birches] forms their winter food, and is called browse. The beaver cuts off enough for dinner, and takes it into his house. C 67–16 When the beaver's house got lots of browse around it, it's a sign of a hard, cold, snowy winter. 1979 TIZZARD 58 On sunny days such as this the cow would be let out of the stable to eat some brouse—small dogwood and small birch trees my father had hauled from the woods the day before.

2 Small branches and brushwood gathered as fuel.

1952 STANSFORD 9 I spent the remainder of the Summer carrying wood or browse on my back, until the fall of the year, when I began cutting wood, and altogether I cut 11,000 sticks of wood. M 68–17 On a good frosty night we would go out around the camp and throw out a lot of browse [on the fire]. M 69–17 [They] could be seen passing our house Winter and Summer pulling browse from Elliston Ridge. This was all they used as firewood until they got their pension when they supplemented this by purchasing a little coal.

3 Attrib **browse partridge**: Allen's willow ptarmigan (*Lagopus lagopus*).

1959 MCATEE 24 ~ Willow Ptarmigan (One that feeds on woody growth. Labr.).

browse taste: of animals feeding on twigs and bark, with a woody flavour; BROWSY.

P 127–75 'I don't like that browse taste [of moose or rabbits].'

browse v [bræuz]. Cp *DC* ~ out 'haul out logs by block and tackle' (1964) for sense 1.

1 To haul in slack rope and secure it (P 129–64).

2 To take one's time; to wander idly (Q 71–9).

1904 *Nfld Qtly* Dec, p. 4 "Topsail Stages": [In Topsail] folks go browsin' and some carousin' / From St John's town on a summer day. P 237–79 Just browsin' around in the woods (i.e. lazing around, moving around doing nothing in particular; roaming around).

browser n ['bræʊsəɹ]. See BROWSE v 2. A lethargic worker, ne'er-do-well.

P 184–67 There's a few browsers up there digging a ditch. Q 73–3 A browser is a person considered lazy. Q 73–7 ~ a wild young man who keeps late hours.

browsy a See BROWSE n 1. Of animals feeding on twigs and bark, having a woody flavour.

P 108–76 The rabbits have a nice browsy flavour.

brudge See BRIDGE.

bru(i)se See BREWIS.

brunet n also **brunette**. A person of mixed French and Micmac descent; JACKATAR.

1966 PADDOCK 120 Brunet(te): in Western Newfoundland an ethnic minority of mixed Micmac Indian-French origins. Q 71–15 [The dance] became popular with brunets or metis on the [west] coast.

brush n Cp *EDD* brash sb[1] 2 'sudden gust of wind, a spell of wet weather; a [snow] storm' Sc; G S WASSON, *Cap'n Simeon's Store* (1903), p. 36 'brush o' wind,' p. 218 [Maine]. See PATRICK'S

BRUSH, SHEILA'S ~ . A period of stormy weather; a late winter snowfall.

1866 WILSON 276 [The sealers] sailed about the twenty-first of March. They sailed thus late to avoid the equinoctial gales, or, as the saying was, 'We wait until after Saint Patrick's brush.' 1872 *Times* 20 Mar, p. 3 We may safely assert that 'St Patrick's brush, or 'Sheelah's day' if you will, was never more fully developed by the elements than on the day and night of Monday last. 1924 ENGLAND 124 Perhaps the most memorable of those occasions [for singing] was on the night of 'Sheila's Brush,' which to say the 18th of March. Newfoundland has two 'brushes,' Patrick's and Sheila's; that is to say, storms supposed to be connected with the birthday of St Patrick and that of his wife. P 148–67 A brush of weather.

brush-harrow n also **bush-** ~ *EDD* brush sb[1] 9: brush-harrow IW So; *DAE* ~ (1761, 1880). A makeshift harrow of spruce, birch or alder trees.

P 245–64 ~ small spruce or birch trees tied into long bundles and dragged by a horse to level and clear the ground. 1971 MANNION 161 In Freshwater a 'bush-harrow,' made of birch or alder branches and drawn by a horse, was used [to] spread the manure more evenly over the ground.

bubbly squall n A variety of small jelly-fish or *Medusa*; SQUID SQUALL (P 243–56).

buck n Cp BLIND-BUCK-AND-DAVY for sense 1; cp *EDD* ~ sb[3] 3 'driver used in the game of buck-stick, the game itself' for sense 2.

1 One who covers his eyes in the game hide-and-seek (P 148–64).

2 Comb **buck-cat**: game played with two sticks, one used as a bat or driver; cp CAT[4], PUSS.

C 75–139 ~ a game played with a long stick, used as a bat, and a short stick which was used to be batted. The small stick was tilted against a rock, then the batter would hook it into the air; as it fell it would be batted with the long stick.

buck v To purloin; to collect or gather surreptitiously; STING.

P 19–55 He bucked a barrel last night for the bonfire [on November 5th]. 1964 *Evening Telegram* 27 June, p. 10 I knowed her old man bucked many a bag of coal from the railway. T 181–65 When we get a chance some fellers may get a fish off the cover or buck a one, to tell the truth of it. We'd say buck was stealing [but] I don't know whether 'twas [considered] stealing or whether 'twasn't then. 1966 FARIS 207 Traditionally the ingredients for a 'scoff' are 'bucked'—that is, taken from someone else's garden or cellar. 'Bucking' for a 'scoff,' however, is sanctioned, within limits; it is not 'stealing' for a meal. 1977 RUSSELL 169 He wasn't *stealin'* carrots, he said, he was *buckin'* carrots. Accordin' to him 'twas two different things. Perhaps he's right. 'Did you ever buck anything, Uncle Mose,' he asked me. I was goin' to say 'no' when I remembered a few things. Things like the cherry tree in Uncle Zeke's garden up in Fortune Bay. Things like my trips to St Pierre. Was that stealin'? or buckin'? 1979 *Evening Telegram* 25

Aug, p. 8 'The western Canadians. . .are so well brought up that they don't even have fences anywhere.' 'My land,' sez Mrs Connors, 'that must be grand, but I suppose they wouldn't leave their wash out all night: God knows who would come along and buck that.'

buckaloon n   also **buccaloon**. Cp DINNEEN púi-cirliún 'a boorish knave.' Man of some importance; guy, fellow.
1901 *Christmas Review* 14 'I want to get back in time to see the Buckaloon coming over the side,' said Tom. 'And who may the Buckaloon be?' 'Why, the young Prince, to be sure.' 1928 BURKE "Don't You Remember the Dump, Maggie": . . .the style. . .the young buckaloons for to please. P 229–68 ~ the person with the highest authority in a given situation. In other words, a buckaloon is a 'big shot.'

buckety board See WEIGH-DE-BUCKEDY.

buckle n   *OED* - sb 1 b (1852). Comb **cover the buckle**: an intricate Irish dance (Q 71–3).
1893 *Trade Review Christmas No* 13 Gabe Ronan and John Goodall contended in the dance of 'Cover the Buckle' for the superiority of Cork or Waterford.

buckly a   also **bucklish***. Of ice, thin and liable to bend or buckle when walked on; RUBBER ICE.
1913 *Evening Telegram* 8 Aug, p. 4 "Seen at the Races": The dancing was fine, and the galleries were nice, / They were shaken and dancers like 'buckley ice.' 1937 DEVINE 11 ~ Said of ice on a pond or in a harbour that undulates when walked over. P 148–63 [The] ice is bucklish, not right safe. Q 67-2 Bucklish [ice] is thin salt-water ice.

bucky a   Of a young man, capable; aggressively self-confident.
T 194–65 He thought I was a bucky feller, and he told father, 'Skipper, that feller you've got up there is a pretty smart chap. . . He's going to get a share of fish, because he's a bucky feller.'

bud[1] n   E B WHITE *Essays* (New York, 1977), p. 11 'A spruce "bud" in Maine parlance is a spruce cone.' The cone of a spruce tree.
[1749] 1755 DOUGLASS i, 293n Spruce-leaves and buds decocted in place of hops, make an agreeable beer or drink, and is esteemed good in the scurvy. 1953 *Nfld & Lab Pilot* ii, 299 Balsam Bud cove, a small inlet, indents the coast half a mile south-westwards of Pigeon island. T 141/67–65[2] To bark an ordinary trap you wants two barrels o' buds. T 172/5–65 You had to pick those buds off of the tops [of the trees] and put those buds into this bark pot, and when he'd boil, and that steep out, that was the way you barked your trap. C 75–139 The decorations for the Christmas tree were made out of objects, e.g. reels of thread, tinsel-covered buds of trees, etc. 1979 TIZZARD 277 When my father boiled the kettle he usually put a couple of spruce buds in the kettle with the tea leaves and this made for a good cup of tea.

bud[2] n   also **bird***. DINNEEN bod. Penis.
P 148–64 His bird. P 269–64 [She said to baby boy] 'How's your little bud?' P 245–78 'I washed his [the child's] bird.'

bud[3] See HORSE'S BUD.

buddy n, proper n Cp *DAS* bud(dy) 1 'friend, fellow. Always used in direct address.'
1 Of males, that unknown or unspecified person; the youth or man one has just been discussing; CHUMMY[1].
1964 *Can Journ Ling* x, 42 [*Buddy*] means 'this man,' or 'this individual,' giving the word a pronominal function, as in the utterance [where's buddy to], meaning 'where is the person we were talking about a moment ago?' P 148–65 There was a buddy coming down the road. Ibid Buddy comes in and swipes the petty cash. T 172/4–65 When I left I had a crowd of thirty men under me, working. All because I told buddy I could do what I was told! T 191–65 Buddy was so full of devilment now, that he just bluffed the old feller off. P 266–67 He may come this afternoon. . . Who, the buddy? 1973 PINSENT 50 So the boot was sove, but poor buddy kept right on goin' [over the cliff]. 1979 *Salt Water, Fresh Water* 22 My stepson cut the engine, and when he cut the engine, our boat stopped and the rope went slack, and down went Buddy into the water. 1980 *Evening Telegram* 2 Dec, p. 3 He pulled the trigger and buddy dropped in front of him.
2 A contraption which is hard to describe; CHUMMY[1], MACHINE.
T 265–66 They used to have a buddy made, you know, with two sticks—two piece of board and a string.

bug n   Cp *DAE* bug lamp (c1849, 1924). Attrib **bug light**: kerosene lamp (P 148–63).
M 69-2 To light their homes most people used the lamp which is commonly called the 'bug light.'

bulk n   *OED* ~ sb[1] 1 'a heap, spec a pile in which fish are laid for salting' (c1440–1725), *EDD* sb[3] 1 'pile of salted pilchards' Co, *DC* n Nfld (1777–) for sense 1; *OED* 3 'hold of a ship' obs (c1470–1678) for sense 5; *OED* 1 c: in bulk (1727–1866) for sense 6.
1 A pile in which split cod-fish are placed in layers (a) during the process of curing with salt, (b) for storage or shipment when dried; SALT-BULK.
[1777] 1792 CARTWRIGHT ii, 249 We heaved a pile, piled some green fish, and washed out two bulks. 1819 ANSPACH 435 They then take up each fish separately, cleaning carefully back and belly with a woollen cloth, and next lay it in a long even bulk on the stage to drain. . . It may remain in drain-bulk no more than two days. [It is then spread on the flake]. 1883 SHEA 8 It is not more necessary that the fish should be exposed to the sun to dry than it should be piled and left in bulks to be gradually matured. 1936 SMITH 92 I lowered myself down in the hold; I landed on a bulk of fish, and from there crawled off aft. T 43–64 'Twas salted in bulks in the stage. If you were getting a big lot of fish

you'd make two or three bulks in a couple o' days. Probably about fifty quintals in a bulk. P 245–78 Fish piled mainly in a square or rectangular fashion [is] usually referred to as a bulk. A bulk is usually about 8 feet by 5 feet. A bulk might have a couple (or even more) layers in one direction and the next couple or so layers in the opposite direction. 1979 TIZZARD 88 When the salted cod was taken from the bulk and put in the water it was washed back and front with a woollen mitt.

2 A quantity of 'seal pelts' heaped in a pile on the ice; PAN n.

1860–1 *Journ of Assembly* Appendix, p. 533 A servant is entitled to his hire, and why not the killer be entitled to his bulk of Seals. 1873 CARROLL 33 The bulks [of seals] were from one quarter to one mile apart.

3 A number of caribou carcasses stored for winter use.

1861 DE BOILIEU 244 After a deer is taken out of bulk a cross-cut saw is procured, and the animal is sawed in two.

4 A large pile of logs; cp LANDING.

T 91–64 [The logs would] be piled up in the woods, and the horses'd come in [to haul it out. We'd] pile in what we call landings; probably a hundred and fifty in a bulk.

5 Ship's hold.

P 225–60 In the bulk of the ship many kinds of sea life [have] started [and] made their home in this bulk where fish were stored.

6 Phr *in bulk*: of fish, sealskins, etc, placed in layers in a pile for curing, storage or shipment.

[1712] 1895 PROWSE 273 . . .ships that fish upon the banks taking cod and sailing and carrying them in bulk to France. 1832 MCGREGOR i, 225, 229 The seal-skins are spread and salted in bulk, and afterwards packed up in bundles of five each for shipping. . . More salt is used for green fish, or fish remaining long in bulk, than for fish salted on shore, to be spread out to dry in a few days. 1860–1 *Journ of Assembly* Appendix, p. 530 Any Seals found in bulk [on the ice] and not having any person in possession, if found, should be considered as abandoned. 1863 HIND ii, 230 It is not an infrequent occurrence for the 'catch' to be salted in 'bulk'; that is to say, they are put into the hold of the vessel without washing, bleeding, or cleansing. [c1945] TOBIN 38 "A Tale of Squid": And 'cured' the squid in bulk are piled. 1979 *Evening Telegram* 24 Dec, p. 8 There are four schooners. . .waiting to load fresh herring in bulk.

7 Attrib, comb **bulk(ed) fish**: split and salted cod, (a) undried, (b) dried and stacked for shipment.

1957 *Evening Telegram* 23 Nov, p. 3 The St John's fishermen practically kept Job's going this year with bulk fish. 1976 CASHIN 71 It was part of my job to see that the windows and doors of the fish stores were open, so that the bulked fish would receive the benefit of the cool dry air created by such winds. 1977 BUTLER 68 When a ship came to Buffett to load bulk fish every man on the room would be engaged in loading.

bulk wood: timber cut into logs and piled for transportation.

T 91–64 After the A.N.D. Company started, they cut bulk wood, drove them right from Millertown to Grand Falls.

bulk v Cp *OED* ~ v¹ 4 (1822, 1881) for senses 1 and 2 (a).

1 To place 'seal pelts' in a pile on the ice for collection later; PAN v.

1860–1 *Journ of Assembly* Appendix, p. 526 No young seals should be bulked before the 24th March. . . The present mode of bulking and panning Seals before that date is ruinous to the country. 1873 CARROLL 32 No greater injury can possibly be done to seal fishery than that of bulking seals on pans of ice, by the crews of ice hunters. Thousands of seals were killed and bulked and never seen afterwards.

2 Phr *bulk up*: (a) to place split and salted codfish in piles or 'bulks' during curing process or, when dry, for storage; (b) to stack firewood, etc, in a pile.

T 175/7–65 Well, you'd bulk up a bundle o' [boughs] an' bring 'em out—bulk 'em up on the flake perhaps. T 148–65 They used to bring all their fish in [on the twentieth of] September—the salt fish, an' bulk it up in store. M 68–22 He always used to saw off and cleave enough firewood before Christmas to last for two weeks and bulk it up in the back porch.

bull n *DC* ~² n Nfld (1774–) for sense 1; *DC* ~ bird Nfld (1861–) for comb in sense 2.

1 Common dovekie (*Plautus alle alle*); ICE-BIRD. See also **bull-bird** below.

[1774] 1792 CARTWRIGHT ii, 37 I went to one of the Duck Islands in St Lewis's Bay, and killed three ducks and a bull. 1959 MCATEE 39 ~ Dovekie (Said to refer to its thick neck, but may have ironical reference also to its small size. 'Labr'.)

2 Comb **bull-bird**: see sense 1 above.

1861 DE BOILIEU 191 This year, with the mild weather, there came upon us innumerable quantities of small wild-fowl, called by the settlers 'bull-birds.' 1870 *Can Naturalist* v, 415 [It is] a very common periodical migrant arriving in October and remaining until driven farther south by ice. Provincial name 'bull-bird.' 1887 *Telegram Christmas No* 9 An appetizing odor came from the oven, where a couple of fine fat bull-birds, part proceeds of a successful day's gunning in punt, a day or two before, were yielding up their juices. 1908 TOWNSEND 18 Just as we were finishing supper, the mate put in his head and said, 'There is a bull-bird, sir, swimming close to the ship.' I rushed out, and sure enough a dovekie or little auk was swimming. . .close to the vessel. 1964 *Evening Telegram* 22 Jan, p. 5 The dovekie—called variously an ice bird and a bull bird—is the smallest of our auk-like birds, barely filling the palm of the hand as it lies dead but still feathered in the clutch of the triumphant gunner. T 143/4–65¹ Bull-birds. They'd come out o' the cliffs—you wouldn't see the sky through 'em, they was that numerous. 1977 *Evening Telegram* 17 June, p. 6 [I saw no one] except for some. . .boy with a few rabbit snares set with no licence and a 16-year-old boy with five bull birds.

bull dog: cod-fish with a blunt head; SEAL-HEAD COD (P 148–63).

bull's tongue, ~ **eye**: a shrub, rhodora
(*Rhododendron canadense*) (1956 ROULEAU 27).

bullamarue n A loud, aggressive person; a
show-off.
1937 DEVINE 11 ~ bully; a noisy, aggressive fellow
who insists on having everything go his way. Q 71–13 ~
a person. . .showing off.

bullet n Comb **bullet maker**: mould into which
lead is poured for making shot; bullet-mould.
M 68–7 The bullet maker was used for making bullets
for the muzzle-loader. Lead was melted and poured
through a little hole [and] the instrument was kept
together until the lead was hard.

bulleter n A variety of glass ally or marble.
1931 BYRNES 113 Marbles, 'bulleters' and 'glass
alleys' of rainbow hues, appeared in the shop windows,
and 'bazzing' was indulged in.

bully¹ n also **bulley**. Cp *EDD* ~ sb², ³ D Co
[applied to various short, round objects] for
sense 1.
1 A bluff, two-masted decked boat used on the
northeast coast and Labrador for fishing and carrying fish; JACK¹. See also **bully boat** below.
[1888] 1897 *Nfld Law Reports* 310 . . .and seeing the
plaintiffs come to his net in their bully. 1895 *Christmas
Review* 18 The new boats. . .were to be ordinary 'bullies,' such as all the fishermen use in pursuing their
ordinary avocation on the fishing grounds. 1913
Christmas Chimes 25 The harbor. . .of Bonavista was,
at this time, filled with schooners, some of them fishing
vessels with their full supplies for Labrador, fishing
boats of all sizes from the 20 qtl jack to the bully and
skiff of the smaller planters. 1936 SMITH 80 [At
Holton] a number of people fished from Brigus. . .each
with a cod seine and three cod traps, also four 'bulleys'
or large boats with gaff sails, expressly for fishing after
the trapping was over. T 183/5–65 Then we'd take the
fish aboard the bully and come home. 1977 *Decks
Awash* vi (3), p. 50 Before my father died I used to go
across the Bay fishing with him in a 'bully,' and after he
died my uncle took over the bully and we went across
the Bay for three summers. 1980 COX 22 They went in
"bullies," which were small fishing boats with a 20 foot
keel, rigged with a driver, a foresail and a jib.
2 Attrib, comb **bully boat**: see sense 1 above.
1904 *Nfld Qtly* Dec, p. 17 Nearly all my inspection
and visitation had to be done in bully-boats, jacks and
whale boats. 1909 GRENFELL² (ed) 306 The old two-
handed jacks, or bully boats, which, in the autumn
months, used to venture far off from the land with
hand-lines, now lie rotting on the rocks at all the harbours on the coast. 1927 DOYLE (ed) 7 "All Around
Green Island Shore": I have as staunch a bully boat /
As ever rode the ground. M 69–17 The bully boat was a
fishing craft in the early days [at Elliston]. These boats
were about 25 to 30 feet long with a capacity for about
30 quintals of fish. They had two masts and were equipped with a mainsail, foresail, topsail, and sometimes a
jib.

bully man: principal hand aboard a decked
vessel or 'bully' used in the cod-fishery.
1936 SMITH 74 When we arrived in the harbour the
bulley man was there for his second load. We discharged the bulley and finished loading her from the
bag. T 31/2–64 What they call bully man is one man in
the skiff for to do the work. [He] had to dip in all that
fish aboard to the splitters.

bully² n Cp *OED* bull-beggar obs (1584–1851).
See BOO for parallel forms and senses.
Comb **bully bagger**: imaginary figure used to
terrify children into good behaviour.
1973 WIDDOWSON 367 To get children to be quiet
and to go to sleep when put to bed parents would
sometimes say: 'Lie down before. . .the bully-bagger
come[s].'
bully-boo (a)See ~ **bagger** above; (b) a louse.
(P 155–64); (c) nasal mucus (1972 WIDDOWSON
281); (d) the fuzzy ball of a dandelion gone to
seed (C 71–36).
T 342/6–67 If the Bully Boo was mentioned, the kids
would start [to] bawl. 1972 WIDDOWSON 281 The Bully
Boo'll be here after the Boo Man, if you're not in bed
then.
bully man: see ~ **bagger** above.
1973 WIDDOWSON 93 The bullie man takes bad little
girls and boys so you'd better be good.

bully v See BULLY¹ n. In the Labrador cod-trap
fishery, to transfer the catch from net to vessel
for splitting; DIP v 1.
T 31/2–64 I had to bully that [fish]. I was bully man
now, and I had to dip [the fish] in and bring it aboard
to the splitters.

bultow n also **boulter, bultᴏ** ['bᴏltoᴜ]. Cp
OED boulter Co (1602–), bulter, bultey Co
(1769–), *EDD* boulter, bultys Co; *OED* bultow
Nfld (1858–), *DC* Nfld (1849–); WILCOCKS, pp.
147–9: bulter, trot or spiller (s w England);
Fisheries of U S, p. 79: bull-tow, boulter (Nfld);
NANCE, pp. 42, 50: boulter, bolter; bulter(-stick)
Co. In the cod-fishery, a long, buoyed fishing-
line with closely-placed and baited hooks
attached at intervals; set line; TRAWL. Also
attrib.
1845 *Journ of Assembly* Appendix, p. 209 [The
French] have adopted what is called the *Bultow* system, by which means they extend lines and hooks miles
round a ship. 1850 [FEILD] 91 The French at Quirpon
fish with the bulto, and with enormous seines. 1855
WARREN 13 The bultow fishing is carried on in the following manner:— The vessel is provided with three or
four large boats [which] carry out from 5 to 8000
fathoms of rope, to which are fastened leads, with
baited hooks at certain distances from each other;
these are placed out from the vessel in different directions, let down, and secured with suitable moorings, to
prevent their being carried away by the strong currents
which usually prevail on the Banks. They are laid out
at stated distances from each other, with several thou-

sand hooks well baited, and frequently occupying several miles of ground. 1868 HOWLEY *MS Reminiscences* 8 The people of this place. . .use nothing but bultows and codnets. 1886 *Colonist Christmas No* 15 In the summer she ran a ferry-boat from Gallows Harbor to Ram Islands, and attended to a bultow. 1905 GRENFELL 124 We have other methods also for catching 'fish,' for we use nets in which they will mesh, and also 'bultos,' or long lines fitted with thousands of hooks. 1937 DEVINE 75 This might be codnet fish or bultow fish. T 187/90–65 Bultows is what you call trawls, and the twentieth of October, that's when you'd be allowed to put [them] out. 1972 NEMEC 57 'Bultows' or 'trawls' [were introduced at St Shotts] sometime after 1850.

bumblebee n
   Comb **bumblebee flower**: flower of the dandelion (P 148–63).
   C 68–12 Bumblebee-flower [is] the name given to the dandelion [on which] bumblebees are seen flitting from one flower to the next.
   bumblebee-spit: white frothy secretion on the stems or leaves of plants, enclosing larvae of spittle bugs; SPIT (P 148–68).

bumbleberry n   Cp *EDD* bumble sb[5] 'bramble'; 2 bumble-berry. Small cranberry; MARSH BERRY (*Vaccinium oxycoccos*) (1971 NOSEWORTHY 179).

bumper n   Cp *OED* ~ sb[1] 2 'anything unusually large' for sense 1; cp *OED* 1 'cup. . .filled to the brim'; 2 'anything unusually abundant' for sense 4.
   1 A large mass or chunk of snow.
   P 148–65 Snow bumpers [are] large, hard chunks of snow–the sort that might get jammed underneath car in a driveway. 1966 *Evening Telegram* 8 Feb, p. 15 You never see them makin' bumpers or snowmen. P 25–73 Bumpers are the large blocks of snow [lifted] when shovelling.
   2 In sledding, a hump followed by a sudden dip; a bump.
   [c1945] TOBIN 38 "Coasting on Stretton's Hill, Hr. Grace": There was no place in Town / Could give such breathless pleasure. . . / Especially when a 'bumper' made it more thrilling still.
   3 Home-grown potato of inferior quality.
   C 71–24 The better quality potatoes were known as apples. The bumpers were an inferior quality.
   4 Attrib in designations of a fishing or sealing season, vessel or 'voyage' resulting in a full catch or load.
   1872 *Newfoundlander* 2 Apr There were several bumper trips at the wharves. 1905 MURPHY 10 May [The sealers] return with bumper trips. 1922 *Sat Ev Post* 2 Sep, p. 123 The Dominion's prosperity hangs largely on the annual hunt. A bumper fishery—for these people still insist that seals are fish—feeds thousands of hungry mouths ashore. 1924 ENGLAND 243 'Now den, me sons,' directed the Cap'n, 'let's see how quick ye can get a bumper trip o' fat.' [1926] 1946

PRATT 173 "The Cachalot": She had three thousand barrels stowed / Under the hatches, though she could, / Below and on her deck, have stood / Four thousand as her bumper load. [1929] 1933 GREENLEAF (ed) 282 "The *Southern Cross*": 'No doubt it is the *Southern Cross*,' the operator said, / 'And looking to have a bumper trip, and well down by the head.' T 342–67[1] A bumper trip is a full load. 1972 BROWN 47 They needed almost twice that number [of seals] for a 'bumper trip.'

bumps n pl Cp *EDD* bump v[1] 1; I & P OPIE *Lore and Language of Schoolchildren* (1959), 199-200, 301. Phr *give one the bumps*: to hold a person horizontally by arms and legs on his birthday and bounce him on the floor.
   M 70–17 At school, after telling everybody that it was your birthday, a bunch of the fellows would usually gang up on you and give you the 'bumps.' They would grab you by the arms and legs and bounce your backside off the floor, once for every year of your age, and always an extra one for good luck.

bun n   Cp *OED* ~ sb[2] 1 'in north of Ireland. . .round loaf of ordinary bread'; *ADD* 'loaf of soft bread' Nfld for sense 1.
   1 A loaf of soft bread; one of the sections of a loaf of home-made bread; LOAF.
   [1918–19] GORDON 41 The gang arrived at daylight, bringing some welcome buns of bread with them. 1924 ENGLAND 220 'Gi's nudder bun o' bread, yar, b'y,' one day a master watch called out at tea. C 66–12 Bread was home-baked and each loaf was divided into several buns. When a person went to borrow bread he always asked for a 'bun o' loaf.' 1979 TIZZARD 278 The bread was now carried in a bun and the butter in a bottle so the bread was cut and buttered out in punt.
   2 Phr *like the bun*: simple-minded (C 75–46).

bunchy-berry n   also **bunchy**. Cp *DAE* bunch-berry (1845–), *O Sup*[2] (1969). The red fruit of the dwarf cornel (*Cornus canadensis*); CRACKER BERRY.
   P 145–61 Bunchies: a kind of berry with stones in them. C 70–28 ~ a type of red berry found in the woods which grows in clumps with a bunch of a half-dozen or so berries per stalk.

bungalow n
   1 A loose dress worn by pregnant mother.
   C 71–128 [The statement], 'She is wearing a bungalow these days' was sufficient information that a new member of the family would soon be added.
   2 Comb **bungalow apron**: cuckoo-flower, a type of cress; lady's smock (*Cardamine pratensis*) (P 233–78).

bung-your-eye n   Cp PARTRIDGE bung one's eye 'drink heartily.' Strong alcoholic beverage.
   [1958] 1965 PEACOCK (ed) iii, 896 "Young Bung-'er-eye": When I was out walking, my sea stock to buy, / Got tricked in the liquor and bought Bung-'er-eye. [Note:] 'Bung-'er-eye' is usually pronounced 'bung-yer-eye' or 'bung-your-eye.' Mr Willis uses a hard 'g.'

It is an old sailing term for strong rum or any hard liquor.

bunk n [= heavy timber or cross-beam on a sled].

Attrib **bunk chain**: length of chain to secure a load of wood to the cross-beams of a sled.

P 128–56 A good bunk chain is necessary to keep the wood from falling [off]. T 43/8–64 You throw a bunch o' wood on this bob-sled, and you chain it up with a bunk chain, and bind it up tight.

bunk sled: sled with stout transverse timbers on which the logs rest between the runners.

T 96/7–64[1] That was a bunk sled. Wagon sleds, some called them.

buoy n Cp *OED* ~ sb 1 'floating object fastened to a particular place to point out position of things under water'; NID ~[2] 1 'float.'

1 Any of a variety of buoyant objects used to mark the position of a fish-net, trap or trawl and to suspend it in the water; BOBBER.

P 241–68 This boat-hook is used for pushing the boat off from the shore or for hooking the buoy of a cod net. 1971 NOSEWORTHY 179–80 ~ A cylinder of wood with a stick down through it and a long flag on the stick. It is used to keep fishing lines in the same area. [Also] a small barrel used to float a cod-trap.

2 Attrib **buoy line**: rope leading from float to net; STRAP 4 (Q 67–33).

buoy pole: stick of wood fastened to float to indicate the position of a net at a distance; MARK(ER) BUOY, SPOT BUOY.

[1776] 1792 CARTWRIGHT ii, 166 Some firewood was cut, and buoy-poles prepared to lay on the Tyrconnel Shoal.

burgoo n also **bargoo*** [bəˑɹˈguː, bəːɹˈguː, bəɹˈgɵu]. Cp *OED* ~ 'oatmeal gruel. . .used chiefly by seamen' (1750–); *O Sup*[2] 2 'soup or stew' N Amer (1743–). Left-over vegetables prepared in a hash; thick liquid preparation (Q 67–38).

T 12–64 Thick as burgoo. Burgoo is a word we use for anything liquid which is rather thick. Q 71–10 We made bargoo from a hashed-up meal.

burn v Cp *OED* ~ v[1] 13 d 'to produce on (anything) an effect resembling that of burning' for senses 1 (a), 2, 3; 4 c (1667) and burning vbl sb (1667, 1753) for sense 4.

1 Of a seal's skin, (a) to make tender or sore by exposure to the sun; (b) to spoil for processing through failure to bleed the animal quickly.

1924 ENGLAND 100–1 Sometimes a seal. . .is unwilling to take the water because its pelt gets sunburned and so tender that it tears. I have seen 'burned' skins that could be ripped with the finger. 1978 *Decks Awash* vii (1), p. 29 It's difficult to get rid of 'burned' pelts. Pelts 'burn' when the seal is not bled immediately after being shot. The skin becomes rotten and is totally valueless.

2 In the curing of cod-fish, to spoil the texture of the dried fish by using too much salt or by excessive exposure to sun: SALT n: SALT BURN, SUNBURNT.

[1663] 1963 YONGE 57 A salter is a skilful officer, for too much salt burns the fish and makes it break. 1778 DE CASSINI 147 A different depth of salt is requisite for different fishes. Too much salt burns up the fish, and makes it brittle when it comes to dry, and too little makes it greasy, and difficult to dry. P 245–55 Burnt fish [is] codfish over-exposed to the sun while drying.

3 To freeze a part of the body in extreme cold; to experience discomfort in the cold; FROSTBURN n.

1708 GEARE 20 Several of those that died in the Boat were so burnt in their Feet. . .we should pull off their Toes with their Stockings. [1772] 1792 CARTWRIGHT i, 214 John Tilsed having burnt his toes again, on the twenty-second of January, in returning home from hence, and having thawed them by the fire, they mortified so far that he lost both nails, and bared the ends of the bones. [1776] ibid ii, 136 Stopping to fresh tail a trap was at the risk of fingers and toes: for the instant a bare hand came in contact with a cold trap, it was burnt almost equal to what it would have been by a red hot iron. [1794] 1968 THOMAS 125 They lighted a fire and continued rambling along the shore for three days in a deplorable condition, all of their fingers being burnt (as it is called) with the Frost. 1924 ENGLAND 39 A sailor [was] holding snow to his 'burned' (frozen) cheeks to keep them from freezing more. T 222–66 Sometimes in early spring the slob ice comes in an' it's enough to burn 'ee on the land, or in other words enough to freeze you. 1972 BROWN 231 [of members of a sealing crew rescued from the ice floes] They're all burned to some degree, Cap'n, but there's some pretty bad cases that need a doctor.

4 Of the salt water, to be phosphorescent.

1861 NOBLE 91 At every dip of the oars it was like unraking the sparkling embers, so brilliant was that beautiful light of the sea. The boatmen called it the burning of the water. 'When the water burnt,' they said 'it was a sure sign of south wind and a plenty of fish.' 1900 *J A Folklore* xiii, 299 The sea 'burning' is a sign of a northwest wind.

5 Phr *burn down*: to bank down the fires on a steam-powered sealing vessel and stop in one place.

1924 ENGLAND 66 The tired old ship, unable to advance in the teeth of such frenzy, 'burned down' for the night; which is to say, stopped and reduced steam. 1972 BROWN 29 Far off, but still in sight, the steel fleet had run into heavy ice and was forced to burn down also.

6 Comb **burned ocky, burnt** ~ [bəːɪnd ˈɒkɪ]: boiled molasses, or a candy prepared from this molasses; cp OCKY and BERRY OCKY.

C 71–117 To make burned ocky, molasses is boiled in a saucepan. After it cools a little but is still soft, the stuff is pulled, twisted, cut into short sticks and eaten as candy.

burn¹ n   Blister or scar on a seal from a bullet wound.

1924 ENGLAND 23 The dog [seal] looked spotted, mottled with black and gray. It showed a 'last year's burn,' or the scar of a bullet wound from the previous spring.

burn² n   *OED* ~ sb² obs exc dial 'contracted form of *burden*'; *EDD* sb² 'burden. . .esp a load of sticks.' See also BACK¹: BACK-BURN. Phr *burn of wood, ~ of boughs*, etc: the amount carried on one's shoulders.

[c1894] PANL P4/14, p. 2 Who, outside of Newfoundland, would know the meaning of a 'turn,' a 'burn,' a 'breastner' of wood. P 48–60 [He went for] a burn of boughs. Q 67–5 One goes into the woods for a burn of wood. Q 71–15 A burn was a back-load of wood, usually young birch or alders. This was tied up with a bowline, and carried on one shoulder supported by a bearing stick.

burney* n   In the game of marbles, two alleys or marbles touching each other at rest (P 188–78).

P 275–76 [The players cried] It's a burney!

bush n
     Comb **bush-born**: resident of Newfoundland born and bred on the island; COUNTRY BORN, NATIVE n.

1931 BYRNES 125 The 'Bush Borns' and the 'Old Country' people had a difference of opinion as to which had the larger load [of wood for the Bishop]. 1937 DEVINE 12 ~ A term of contempt for one born in Newfoundland used when the majority of the population was Irish and English born. When the 'bushborns' became the majority they silenced the immigrants and made them respect the new name, Native.
     bush-rake: bundle of small trees and branches dragged along the ground to rake plowed area and break up clods; BRUSH-HARROW (P 148–3).

busk n   Cp *OED* ~ sb¹ 'strip of wood, etc to stiffen corset'; *DC* 'beaver stretcher' (Nfld: 1792). A strip of wood used to stretch a beaver skin in drying process.

1792 CARTWRIGHT *Gloss* i, ix ~ A piece of board which is pointed at one end and broad at the other. When a furboard is not broad enough to spread a skin properly, the busk is introduced on the belly side to stretch it completely.

busk v   *OED* ~ v² 2 'to go about seeking for' (1734–); *EDD* v³ 5 'to hurry, hustle.' To go about begging (for food).

1897 *J A Folklore* x, 204 The poor man was badly off last winter and got his living by *busking* round among his neighbors. 1937 DEVINE 12 ~ To hustle around and get food, etc for nothing. P 147–56 He's coming again to busk his supper. P 191–73 ~ to beg, seek out in difficult places.

busker n   See BUSK.

1 A vigorous, energetic man.

1897 *J A Folklore* x, 204 So a good *busker* is one who moves about briskly. P 18–56 ~ an assertive, energetic, able person.
     2 One who hustles about, begging for food (1925 *Dial Notes* v, 327).

P 191–73 ~ one who begs.

buskin n   Cp *OED* ~ 1 'covering for the foot and leg' (1503–1860); *EDD* buskins 'leather gaiters' Ir Do So D. A cloth or woollen gaiter or legging worn to keep snow out of boot.

[1774] 1792 CARTWRIGHT ii, 28 We engaged the master and three of his men to serve us the winter, for their provisions, buskins, and cuffs. 1866 WILSON 214 The buskin is for the leg, to keep out the snow. It is. . .made of swanskin. 1914 *Cadet* Apr, p. 7 Hamburg boots and bluchers were all the go and the swanskin or buskin when worn over the latter made a tidy, warm and comfortable footwear, except in wet weather. Q 67–5 Buskins were a homemade addition to winterized boots made of canvas 'duck' wrapped around the leg above a boot. Waterproofed by dipping in turpentine. 1971 NOSEWORTHY 180 Buzkins. A type of leggings used in the 'olden days' made of thick cloth, pulled on over boots, and buttoned around the legs under the pants. 1979 POCIUS 26, 28 Several women on the Southern Shore claimed that they knitted a type of oversock that was worn over the boot and extended up almost to the knee on the outside of the pants. These were also worn by men when they went into the forest to gather fire wood. They were commonly called 'buskins.'

busy a   Comb **busy bee**, ~ **wop**: bumblebee; cp WOP¹.

P 184–67 You can smell the busy-bee flowers all over the garden. M 69–1 Busywop: bumblebee. 1970 *Evening Telegram* 21 May, p. 3 Now and then a dumbledore or 'busy bee' as they are called by some, propelled itself across our path, they being extremely large and heavy this year.

butt v   *OED* ~ v¹ 1 'thrust, shove.' To strike with prow repeatedly to force a passage through the ice.

[1899] 1905 *Nfld Law Reports* 292 Some of the crew of the *Kite* assisted to turn the *Gaspesia* round by a rope from her bow to the ice. The *Kite* then went ahead 'butting' the pans of ice and making a track as well as she could, and the *Gaspesia* followed. 1909 BERNIER 7 Butting—is backing off and running the ship at ice in order to force or head a way through it. 1979 *Evening Telegram* 24 Dec, p. 8 The ship was in Jackson's Arm and had butted three miles of ice on the way to Hampden.

butt¹ n   *OED* ~ sb² 1 b 'cask for fish, fruit' obs (1423–1753). A type of cask for dried cod-fish or other goods.

P 102–60 In the fall of the year before closing up the shop, dry goods left over from the summer [were] stowed] away for the winter in tin-lined wood cases. This we did every fall and put a sugar butt with its head on a swivel so as it would tip every time a rat passed over it and down he would go never to return. T 90–64 The donkey was a inch shorter, with a 24-inch head, and the butt had a 28-inch head and it was 32 inches long. . . The butt, from 18 inches up, would take the larger fish. M 71–94 I was the first one to carr' a butt of sugar out of Fair Island Tickle. [It was] 385 pounds and I had sugar to last us till December when we knocked off. P 127–73 ~ bigger round but not as high as a cask.

butt² n　Cp *OED* ~ sb³ 1 'thicker end of anything.'
　1 Comb **butt-end**: part of the 'sound-bone' closest to the head of a cod-fish (P 127–76).
　M 69–27 Sounds were the film covering the sound bones of the fish. In some homes, the sound bones were also cooked—referred to as butt-ends.
　2 In av phr *butt-end foremost, butt first*: fiercely, powerfully.
　P 245–56 The north-east wind came up butt end foremost. 1961 *Nfld Qtly* Spring, p. 27 The squall came down 'butt first.'

butter n　Cp *NID* butternose; cp *OED* ~ sb¹ 4: ~ pot (1693), SEARY 61, 63; *OED* ~ tooth obs (1571–1782), *EDD* 1 (34).
　Attrib, comb **butter bitch**: man in charge of ship's stores.
　1924 ENGLAND 52 The storekeeper, because he has charge of the butter, rejoices in the euphonious title of 'butter bitch.'
　buttercup: marsh marigold (*Caltha palustris*) (1956 ROULEAU 27).
　butter-nosed diver: American black scoter (*Oidemia nigra americana*) (1959 MCATEE 18).
　butter plant, ~ **root**: cinnamon fern (*Osmunda cinnamomea*) (1956 ROULEAU 27).
　P 113–73 Butter root [is] a fern with crisp, carrotty-like root [which] was eaten.
　butter pot: in place-names, prominent rounded hill; TOLT.
　1626 [VAUGHAN] *The Golden Fleece* [alᵛ] Butter pots [Mason's map]. [1663] 1963 YONGE 55 The land we saw [near Renews] was two hommitts, or craggy hills which (before the land near the sea appeared) seemed like islands, and these they call the Butter Pots. 1951 *Nfld & Lab Pilot* i, 88 Butterpot hill rises to an elevation of 955 feet.
　butter tooth: either of the two broad front teeth.
　P 151–68 The words 'front teeth' [are] never used, it is always 'butter teeth.'

button n　Cp *OED* ~ sb 4 for sense 1.
　1 Wooden device to fasten the door of a lobster trap.
　T 246/7–66 You'd unbutton your button, swing your door down, put your hand in an' pick your lobster out. T 250–66 That'd be the button there; you'd turn that crossways and it [would] come down over the other lat'.

　2 Comb **button berry**: squashberry, from its large flat seed (*Viburnum edule*); also attrib.
　P 84–71 Squashberries are called button berries.
　P 212–74 Button berry jam [is] made from squashberries.

buzaglo proper n　Cp British Museum *Catalogue*: Abraham Buzaglo, *A Treatise on the Gout* (1778); *Assoc for the Preservation of Technology* iii, Nos. 2–3 (1971), pp. 48, 60 and references [Williamsburg, Va, 1771]. Attrib **buzaglo stove**: heating stove named for the English manufacturer.
　[1770] 1792 CARTWRIGHT i, 38 We finished the roof of the East end of the house to-day, and set up a Buzaglo stove in the dining-room.

by-boat n　also **bye-boat** *OED* ~ obs (Nfld: 1698–1796), cp *OED* by a 2 fig 'away from the main purpose,' 'of secondary importance'; *DC* by(e)-boat Nfld (1806), by(e)-boat keeper (1765–1842). See also BOAT.
　1 A fishing craft, usually undecked, of variable size, design and rig, owned and used in the inshore cod-fishery by men migrating annually as passengers to Newfoundland, the craft being left on the island on their return to the West Country of England.
　[1677] 1976 HEAD 78 *By-boats*. Besides the Inhabitants and the Adventurers, there are other Persons, that not being willing or able to buy a Share in the fishing ships hire Servants in the West of England and carry them as Passengers to Newfoundland where they employ them in private Boats to catch and cure fish, and after the Season is over bring them back to England, or permit them to take Service with the Planters, or on board the Ship. [1693] 1793 REEVES viii And be it further enacted. . .That every master of a by-boat or by-boats shall carry with him at least two fresh men in six, (viz.) one man that hath made no more than one voyage, and one man who hath never been at sea before. [1714] 1895 PROWSE 274 Fishing ships 441, Boats 441, Bye-boats 133, Inhabitants Boats 362. 1956 FAY 43 The by-boat belonged to a merchant or fisherman in England, who employed a crew to operate his boat—the word 'by' may refer to its being laid 'by' for the winter, or to its being an 'extra' to the fishing ship. It represented a break from the fishing ship, inasmuch as the merchant concerned came out independently of the ship or bought his passage and worked with the crew during the season. At first the crews returned to their home base at the end of the fishing season, but increasingly they remained in the island and became resident fishermen.
　2 Attrib, comb **by-boat fishery**: cod-fishery prosecuted from small craft in coastal waters; BOAT FISHERY.
　[1792] 1954 INNIS 295 Every merchant is become a boatkeeper, and where one bye boat is lost many are kept by the merchants, so that on the whole the bye boat fishery is increased. [1806] 1956 FAY 135 Bye boat fishery wholly laid aside; formerly employed several thousands.

by-boat keeper: man who operates inshore fishing craft; BOAT KEEPER. See also PLANTER 2.

[1693] 1793 REEVES viii Every inhabitant shall be obliged to employ two such fresh men, as the by-boat keepers are obliged for every boat kept by them. [1701] 1954 INNIS 109 These byeboatkeepers can afford to sell their fish cheaper than the Adventurers which must lessen the number of fishing ships. 1793 REEVES 28 The private boat-keepers here spoken of, or *bye boat-keepers*, as they otherwise were called. [1794] 1968 THOMAS 172 The persons [Holdsworth] brought out with him were mostly Bye Boat Keepers, which are people who possess a Boat and leave her all the year in Newfoundland. 1819 ANSPACH 265 . . .bye-boat-keepers, who were supplied by the merchants to whom they sold the produce of their voyage; these by-boat-keepers kept also a certain number of servants; and, in process of time, became resident planters. 1895 PROWSE 297 Bye-boat keepers were what we should now call planters or middle-men. They were not possessed of fishing ships, but they generally either had fishing establishments or hired them; they fitted out a number of men and boats; all who were independent sold their fish for the best price to sack-ships, traders, &c.

by-boatman: fisherman engaged in the inshore cod-fishery in small craft.

[1738] 1901 *Christmas Bells* 5 16 boats of inhabitants, 130 bye boatmen, 12,000 quintals fish. 1934 LOUNSBURY 112 The byeboatmen paid for 40s. to 50s. for a passage. Most of the men were able seamen, although from a fifth to a quarter were green. The bye-boatkeepers made the voyage in small vessels, which carried enough men to provide crews for four or five of the larger ships operated by the adventurers.

C

cabin n See *Kilkenny Lexicon* cabin-hunting, DINNEEN botthántaidheacht ['cabin stealing'], *Ireland and Newfoundland* (St John's, 1977), p. 97.

Comb **cabin house**: deck cabin on a fishing vessel; HOUSE.

1960 FUDGE 54 'If we had been baiting up at 3 o'clock, as the watch was set, there would have been a terrible mess.' Over half of the crew may have been killed because the main rigging came down on each side of the cabin house as the mast came down right over and on the middle of her stern.

cabin-hunting: going idly from house to house to chat (Q 67–32).

Q 71–7 ~ Going from house to house looking for someone with whom to have a chat; especially to exchange gossip.

cable n Cp *OED* ~ sb 2 naut 'strong thick [anchor] rope.' Attrib **cable anchor**: heavy ship's anchor.

1960 FUDGE 15 We left for St John's where we arrived and took on a part cargo of cable anchors, which proved to be good ballast.

cable v Cp *EDD* capeling sb 'outer nets of a trammel' Co. To entangle or twist (a net).

[1802] 1916 MURPHY 2 The seals in their efforts to free themselves, cable the nets at the bottom and none but experienced sealers can disengage them without cutting the net.

cacorne See KEECORN.

cad n Cp *DAE* cad(d)y (1883–). A large box of tobacco (1924 ENGLAND 314).

cadder n also **catter**
['kædəɹ, 'kætəɹ]. Cp *OED* caddow[2] obs (1579–1860); *EDD* caddow 'a quilt, coverlet'; *DAE* cadder (1789–). A quilt (P 234–57).

M 71–103 Accommodation for fishermen and their families on the *Kyle* was in the steerage and very third class. We had to pick our bunks and hold them while the fishermen poured aboard from the various ports of call. Since no sheets or blankets were provided, we brought our own cadders. The men slept in the holds of the ship on sacks they brought with them. C 71–130 Cadders [are] heavy quilts or a number of lighter quilts sewn together. Each bed, especially on the Labrador in summer, would have one cadder. 1979 POCIUS 33 A special type of quilt called a 'catter' was constructed to be used on the boats going to Labrador. They were smaller than a normal quilt used for a single bed, fitting the small bunks aboard ship. Catters were thicker than normal quilts and only one or two were needed for warmth.

cadge, cadgy See KEDGY.

cafner* See CARPENTER.

cag See KEG v.

cage n Wooden trap with slatted sides to catch lobster; lobster-pot (P 148–61).

cairn n Cp *NID* ~ n 'landmark for explorers.' A marker, usu a pile of rocks prominently placed as a guide in coastal navigation, sometimes becoming a place-name; AMERICAN MAN, NAKED MAN.

1888 HOWLEY *MS Reminiscences* 48 But the highest and most rugged looking land was towards the seacoast near the head of Bay de Lievre. . . After taking all the bearings I required, and erecting a cairn on the summit with a flag staff set in the centre and a piece of birch bark for a flag we left a record of our visit and then descended to our canoe. 1909 BROWNE 264 These cairns, of which there are several along the coast [of Labrador], are called by fishermen, "'Merican men." These cairns serve as landmarks for the fishing schooners. 1951 *Nfld & Lab Pilot* i, 107 Cairn head, on the opposite shore, is situated half a mile south-westward of Broad Cove point. 1953 ibid ii, 85 Butter Pot, 991 feet high, on the summit of which is a cairn, stands about 3 miles southward of the eastern entrance point.

cake n   Esp in phr *cake of bread*: hard, rounded, dry ship's biscuit; BREAD, HARD TACK.

[1772] 1792 CARTWRIGHT i, 212 I put the dogs to an allowance of one cake of bread each. 1937 DEVINE 65 If you're only going to the well for a turn of water 'twill do no harm to take a cake of bread in your pocket. 1955 DOYLE (ed) 30 "I'se the B'y": Sods and rinds to cover yer flake, / Cake and tea for supper, / Codfish in the spring o' the year / Fried in maggoty butter. T 34–64 I was always home—don't know what [it was] to go in service or to work for a cake of bread.

calabogus See CALLIBOGUS.

calavance n   also **callivance, cavalance** *OED* ~ obs (1620–1880); *DAE* (1682–); *DJE* sb (1634–1794). Type of small bean used esp for soup (*Dolichos barbadensis, D. sinensis*).

1895 *J A Folklore* viii, 38 Callivances: a species of white bean. . .in contrast with the broad English bean. [c1904] 1927 DOYLE (ed) 67 "The Kelligrews Soiree": There was birch rhine, tar twine, / Cherry wine and turpentine; / Jowls and cavalances. P 245–61 ~ small bean.

calebogus, calibogus See CALLIBOGUS.

calk See CARK*[2].

callabogus See CALLIBOGUS.

calli See CALLIBOGUS.

callibogus n   also **calabogus, calebogus, calibogus, callabogus; calli**. Apparently a maritime beverage of eastern North America: *DAE* calibogus (1758 [Dedham, Mass]–), *DC* callibogus (Nfld: 1771–); see also *OED* purl sb[3] b 'hot beer with gin'; switchel (1840 quot Haliburton: purl talabogus). A drink made by mixing spruce beer, rum or other liquor and molasses; formerly also in clipped form *calli* with specifying word *egg, king*, etc.

[1766] 1971 BANKS 140 From this [spruce] Liquor in itself Very Weak are made three Kinds of Flip Cald here Callibogus, Egg Calli & King Calli the first Simply by adding Rum Brandy or Gin If you cannot get Either of the First as much as is agreable The second by heating the first with the Addition of an Egg & Some Sugar the third King Calli By adding spirit to the Contents of the Copper as soon as it is ready to Put into the Cask & Drinking it hot. [1771] 1792 CARTWRIGHT i, 139 They supped with me, and afterwards smoked a few whiffs of tobacco and drank a little callibogus. [1826] 1866 WILSON 350 You had better take a drop of calebogus to keep out the cold. 1861 DE BOILIEU 161–2 Then we take copious draughts of drink, christened on the [Labrador] coast 'callibogus,'—a mixture of rum and spruce-beer, 'more of the former and less of the latter,'—when the meal is over. 1886 *Colonist Christmas No* 11 On the Goulds Road the following very suggestive advertisement dangled from a fir tree, near a tilt, 'Spruce Beer & Co.' It is easy to imagine the sleep-

ing partners in the firm who might be classed under the generic title of 'Calibogus.' 1901 *Christmas Review* 6 The social side of the club life consisted of story-telling and a discussion of that favourite outport brew, Calabogus. 1937 DEVINE 13 Callabogus. A drink of spruce beer and rum mixed. 1964 *Evening Telegram* 7 Feb, p. 3 Calabogus, a drink popular in Newfoundland for more than 200 years, is now being made available to tourists at Canadian National's Newfoundland Hotel. The drink, a mixture of spruce beer, molasses and dark rum, is now among the cocktails available.

callivance See CALAVANCE.

calms n pl   Cp SMYTH calm latitudes. The horse latitudes, esp the region of the Atlantic around 30° N. latitude.

1977 *Nfld Qtly* Sum, p. 7 We went on and we got in the Calms; this is a place where there's no wind. You could be into them a day, you could be into them a week, or you could be into them a month. But we were fortunate we were only into them a week; very hot weather there too. Then we took the Northeast Trades.

cam a   also **cam-crooked** *OED* ~ obs exc dial (1600–1642); *EDD* 1; DINNEEN 'twisted, awry.' Crooked or bent (1925 *Dial Notes* v, 327).

1937 DEVINE 13 Cam-crooked. Awry, as shoe heel.

cambriola n   also **cambrioll**. Short-lived name in the seventeenth century for the southern part of the Avalon Peninsula.

[1620] 1626 [VAUGHAN] *The Golden Fleece* [map facing sig. a 1] Cambriola. 1626 ibid [a 1] Cambrioll Colchos, out of the Southermost Part of the Iland, commonly called the Newfoundland. 1842 BONNYCASTLE i, 74 [Vaughan's] settlement was called Cambriol, and was on that part of the south coast, now named Little Britain, and was expressly planned on such a scale as to make agricultural pursuits and the fishery mutually depend upon each other. 1971 SEARY 61 Names first recorded by Mason [include] Cambriola—Little Wales or Little Britain, as that part of the south coast of the Peninsula was known. . .as late as 1842.

cambrioll See CAMBRIOLA.

camp n   Cp *DAE* ~ n e 'one or more buildings. . .forming a temporary residence' (1881–). A shelter set up in the woods; tent; in lumbering operations, a bunk-house (P 65–64).

1870 *Can Naturalist* v, 158 I had the hearts of three caribou hanging to the 'tilt,' or camp, within four feet of my head. 1888 HOWLEY *MS Reminiscences* 11 We then carried the two canoes and our camps and reached the outlet of Soulis Pond. Ibid 15 We had much difficulty in procuring sufficient green boughs to just cover the floors of our camps. P 65–64 After a camp has been built there is sometimes a need for extra space. This space is secured by building a lean-to, which is a small camp leaning against a bigger camp. 1979 TIZZARD 361

My bunk was next to Gerald Gidge's and it was built of board and one end fastened to the wall of the camp.

canada n also **canady**. Cp *DC* ~ n 1–5 for sense 1.

1 The areas of mainland North America located esp near the St Lawrence River; the Dominion of Canada excluding Newfoundland and Labrador; the MAINLAND.
[1583] 1940 *Gilbert's Voyages & Enterprises* ii, 404 [Hayes' narrative] That which we doe call the New-found land, and the Frenchmen Bacalaos, is an Iland, or rather (after the opinion of some) it consisteth of sundry Ilands and broken lands, situate in the North regions of America, upon the gulfe and entrance of the great river called S Laurence in Canada. 1708 OLDMIXON 6 Thus they who are Intruders, by their Industry, and the Convenience of their Neighbourhood with *Canada*, the Counry, such as it is, of the French Dominions in *America*, have got the better Part of this Island, and have a more numerous Colony and better Fortifications than the English. 1793 REEVES 132 Mr Palliser carried into execution upon the coast of *Labrador* (which by proclamation, the 7th of October 1763, had been separated from *Canada*, and annexed to the government of Newfoundland) that plan of a free fishery, to be carried on by ships from Great Britain. 1842 BONNYCASTLE i, 142 [In 1809 there was a] scarcity of fresh provisions, in consequence of the prohibition of export from Canada, Nova Scotia and Prince Edward's Island. 1850 [FEILD] 63 Here the government is divided from that of Canada by a small stream. . .which I [as Bishop] may not. . .pass. [c1880] 1933 GREENLEAF (ed) 314 My dear, I'm bound for Canady; / Love Sally, we must part. / I'm forced to leave my blue-eyed girl, / All with an aching heart, / To face cold-hearted strangers / All in some foreign land. 1916 GRENFELL 44 They say blind Pat is going to Canady to get his sight cured t' fall. 1950 *Nfld: An Introduction* 3 On December 11, 1948, representatives of Canada and Newfoundland, in an historic ceremony in the Senate Chamber at Ottawa, signed final Terms of Union between the two countries. 1974 *Evening Telegram* 12 Jan, p. 3 And there was a news report that a 'frigid air mass' was moving down on us from Canada—leaving us to wonder just what sort of tropical weather we've been having here for the past few weeks.
2 Attrib **canada board**: type of building material made of compacted chips; wallboard.
1973 WADEL 62 Inside the house, he put new 'canvas' on the kitchen floor, boarded the walls with 'Canada boards,' and painted various things.

canadian a Cp *DC* ~ Labrador (1918–). Comb **canadian-labrador**: the north shore of the Gulf of St Lawrence west from Blanc Sablon.
1894 MOTT 105 [Whiteley] proceeded to Bonne Esperance, Straits of Belle Isle, Canadian Labrador, intending to remain there a year. 1919 GRENFELL[2] 139 At Blanc Sablon, on the north coast in the Straits of Belle Isle, the Canadian Labrador begins, so far as the coast-line is concerned. 1942 *Little Bay Islands* 14 Some skippers went in the Straits, Canadian Labrador,

in the vicinity of Greenly Island, in the early summer, and if they got sufficient fish would come home and then go to Northern Labrador. 1946 MACKAY (ed) 181 The terms *Canadian-Labrador* and *Newfoundland-Labrador* were once very common and are still frequently used in Newfoundland. The Canadian-Labrador, a stretch of coastline from the St John River in the Province of Quebec (later from Mt Joli) to Blanc Sablon, is now part of the Province of Quebec, and the term *Labrador*. . .is officially restricted to the Newfoundland territory on the mainland.

canadian n An indian from eastern North America who has migrated to Newfoundland; cp MICMAC, MOUNTAINEER.
[1776] BANKS 133 [The Newfoundland indians'] Canoes are made like the Canadians of Birch Bark sewed together with Deer sinews or some other material. [1768] 1828 CARTWRIGHT ii, 316 The Canadians have generally a pretty strong hunt that range the western coast of Newfoundland, between whom and these natives reigns so mortal an enmity. [1811] 1818 BUCHAN 5 On the south side we discovered a canoe, which I observed to be one belonging to the Canadian who resided at Wigwam Point. 1872 HOWLEY *MS Reminiscences* 2 John was not a pure blooded micmac. His father, also John, was a Canadian belonging to some of the tribes along the St Lawrence.

canady See CANADA.

candlemas n Comb **candlemas cake**: type of sweetened bread baked for party on 2 February or Candlemas Day; the party itself.
T 33–64[1] The people play [cards] for what they call the Candlemas cake. You get a cake baked and whoever bid [i.e. be'd] the loser would have to find a cake. When Candlemas Day come they all come to this house and eat the cake and drink the rum. 1971 CASEY 101 The social gathering held on this day was known as 'the Candlemas Cake.' There was dancing, singing, drinking and a meal at these parties. However, there was no actual 'Candlemas Cake,' the term referred only to the party.

can hook n Cp *OED* cant-hook pl, north dial 'the fingers.' Hand, fist.
[1894 BURKE] 78 [jest:] 'The plate Miss,' shouted Harry, shoving out his canhooks for the ten cents. [1929] 1933 GREENLEAF (ed) 161 "Maurice Kelly": By this time old Kelly was feeling half sober; / The ghost left and right his two can-hooks did fly.

canker n *NID* ~[1] 4 c 'potato wart'; cp *EDD* sb[2] 3 'kind of dry rot in turnips.' A disease attacking potato tubers caused by *Phytophthora infestans*.
1911 *Tribune Christmas No* The canker in the potato is a very serious thing, and too much care cannot be taken to exterminate it. 1964 *Can Dept of Agri* [pamphlet] A serious disease of potatoes commonly known as potato wart, canker or black wart occurs at several points in Newfoundland but is not known to be in any other province. T 411/4–67 After using the land

for so long, we had what we called canker would grow on the potato.

canoe n *DC* ~ rest (Nfld: 1883). Comb **canoe rest**: frame or platform to support a canoe.

[1829] 1915 HOWLEY 190 A canoe-rest, is simply a few beams supported horizontally about five feet from the ground, by perpendicular posts. A party with two canoes. . .leave one canoe resting, bottom up, on this kind of frame, to protect it from injury by the weather, until their return.

cantal See QUINTAL.

canterbury n Comb **canterbury bells**: twinflower (*Linnaea borealis*) (1956 ROULEAU 27).

canting vbl n Gossiping, telling merry tales or sayings.

[c1945] TOBIN 34 "Gleams on the Squid Ground": That's [on squid grounds] where you hear the comical sayings! / 'Canting' 'twas called, to be perfectly true.

canvas n From painted ship's canvas, or from the heavy fabric used in manufacturing floor covering. Commercial floor covering; linoleum; freq with defining word *floor*.

1877 ROCHFORT 57 Canvas, for the manufacture of floor oil cloth, not less than 18 feet wide, and not pressed or calendered. 1944 LAWTON & DEVINE 22–3 Stoves, floor-canvas and lucifer matches came into use about [1870]. The sand was swept off the floor and the gayly-flowered canvas put down. T 39–64 [You'd] have some dances in their houses and have some sport. There's nothing now, too much canvas on the house floors. 1976 *Evening Telegram* 21 Feb, p. 2 There was no canvas on the wooden floor, she recalled. 1979 TIZZARD 36 The floors in the dining room, living room and hall downstairs were all covered with floor canvas and on top of that, of course, were many hooked mats. 1981 *Evening Telegram* 4 Apr, p. 12 I see [what's under my feet] every time I go in the kitchen and walk on canvas we bought from Henry Blair and that wasn't yesterday.

cap n For usage with specifying word, see DEAD-MAN'S CAP, DEVIL'S ~ , FAIRY ~ .

1 Inflatable pouch on the snout of the hooded seal; HOOD.

T 104–64 They had what we used to call a cap, and they'd toss about from side to side, and you can pound all you like [with a gaff] and it wouldn't make a bit o' difference at all.

2 Comb **cap-knee boot**: fisherman's leather boot reaching above the knee.

T 50/2–64 The leather'd come on up over the knee—cap-knee boots. They were built good.

cap v Cp *NID* ~ v2 4. Of fog, to close in, forming a dense cover.

T 194–65 In capped the fog, and about three o'clock in the evening I seed Cape John, Gull Island.

cap Comb **cap net** See KEEP NET.

capderace See CAPE RACE.

cape n [= projecting headland or promontory].

1 Proverb **cape st mary's will pay for all** (1895 *Christmas Review* 12).

1937 DEVINE 62 ~ A saying of the large number of fishermen who frequented this favourite fishing ground, including men from Conception Bay, 80 to 100 years ago.

2 Attrib, comb **cape ann**: see CAPE ANN.

cape boat: large fishing boat, rigged fore and aft, used to fish the inshore banks, esp Cape St Mary's grounds, on the south coast.

1975 BUTLER 56 The larger boats being used [about 1870] were from fifteen tons to about thirty tons. . . A thirty ton boat would be classed as a three dory boat with a crew of seven men. All those boats would use four six line tubs of trawls. They would fish up the Southern Shore of Placentia Bay to Cape St Mary's and sometimes beyond. The largest of these boats were called Cape boats. 1977 ibid 39 On the island of Iona, the fishermen fished in open fishing boats around the year 1930. A few years earlier they discontinued the use of Cape boats.

cape race: see CAPE RACE.

cape shore: (a) the stretch of coast on the east side of Placentia Bay from Point Verde to Cape St Mary's; (b) the east coast of Bonavista Bay, stretching to Cape Bonavista (see 1895, 1919 quots).

1895 *J A Folklore* viii, 288 At Bonavista, somewhere down the Cape Shore, there is an immense treasure [said to be buried]. 1910 *Nfld Qtly* Dec, p. 30 The Cape Shore—in the district of Placentia and St Mary's—has always had the reputation of being an 'eerie' locality. 1919 LENCH 67 The late Joseph Fisher of Cape Shore, was always busy in the service of his Lord and Methodism. 1964 *Evening Telegram* 25 Sep, p. 6 If the people of Cape Shore, Colinet, Salmonier and Placentia area would organize the present petitions to their respective members, as people from other areas do, then the government. . .might consider that this road needs to be paved. 1974 MANNION 19 The migration to the Cape Shore was but a small part of the wave of southern Irish immigration that reached the shores of the Avalon during the first two decades of the nineteenth century.

cape ann n *DC* ~ (hat) (Nfld: 1894–); see *Fish Exhibit Cat* (1883), p. 333 [Boston, Mass company]. After Cape Ann, Mass. A fisherman's oilskin cap with broad brim, sloping at the back, and side flaps tied under the chin; SOU'WESTER.

[1894 BURKE] 57 [mock rules for regatta] None but the coxwains allowed Cape-Anns. 1898 *Record* 9 He wiped the salt water from off his face with his 'cape Ann,' and looked again. 1936 DEVINE 115 He sold. . .oil clothing, which was a specialty and included south-westers, Cape Anns and 'Lincolns.' 1940 SCAMMELL 9 "Squid Jiggin' Ground": O this is the place where the fishermen gather / With oilskins, boots and cape-anns battened down. T 141/66–65² He tricked her with this old cape ann. Red flannel lining in un. A kind of a greenish colour, they was. T 194/6–65 My sling hooked in the tolepin, old man, and I hauled hard and broke the string o' my cape ann, lost my cape ann. 1967 *Bk of Nfld* iv, 242 Soon the oiled calico would become chafed and worn (especially the pants), but that first yellow robing, together with the black Cape Ann, is a highlight in my memory.

capelan, capelin, capeling See CAPLIN.

cape race n   also **capderace, cape racer, ?carbrace, ?corbrace**. From Cape Race, Nfld. *DA* cape (11) ~ racer (1835); *DAE* (1875–); *DC* cape-race(r) (1956) for sense 1.
  1 Red-throated loon (*Gavia stellata*) WHABBY.
  1623 WHITBOURNE [sig R 2ᵛ] Those of the Sea, are Goose, Duckes of foure sorts, Capderace, Teale, Snipes, Penguyns, Murres, Hounds. 1959 MCATEE 2 Capderace, cape-race, corbrace. Red-throated Loon. 1967 *Bk of Nfld* iii, 282 Cape racer.
  2 Eastern turkey vulture (*Cathartes aura septentrionalis*).
  1876 HOWLEY 67 This bird is called here 'Carbrace.'

cape racer See CAPE RACE.

capillaire n   Cp *OED* ~ 'syrup or infusion of maidenhair fern' (1745–); HARRAP *capillaire* 'maidenhair fern.'
  1 Creeping snowberry (*Gaultheria hispidula*); the berry of this plant; MAIDENHAIR; also attrib.
  [(1766) 1971 BANKS 122 Gatherd in very shady Places the Plant from the Berries of which Syrup of Capillare is made.] 1894 MOTT 155 [Davidson] was the first to commence the preserving of native fruits, notably capillaire, squash, marsh, and glowberries. 1915 SOUTHCOTT 22 ~ a trailing evergreen, sometimes mistaken for Linnaea, but leaves are much smaller. Flowers are very small one in the axils of the leaves. Plants aromatic. Berries bright white. Grows in the shade of firs. 1933 GREENE 295 'Capillaire' berry (a small white berry rather difficult to find as it grows on a sort of vine amongst the grasses, but has a wonderfully delicate and scented flavour) [is] scattered all over the interior. 1953 *Nfld & Lab Pilot* ii, 341 White Hills (Capillaire Mountains) within [the bay's] northern shore have a remarkable summit.
  2 Attrib **capillaire tea**: tea made from creeping snowberries.
  1884 HOWLEY *MS Reminiscences* 24 Had spruce beer for breakfast varied with cappillaire tea for dinner and spruce again at night. Sick that evening.

caplain See CAPLIN.

caplin n   also **capelan, capelin, capeling, caplain, capline, capling, capon*, ceaplin** ['keɪplɪn, 'keɪpɔlɪn, 'keɪplən, 'keəplən, 'kɛɪpəlɪn, 'kɛɪplən, 'kɛʊpʉln] *OED* capelin (Nfld: 1620–), *DAE* capelin 1 (Nfld: 1620–), *DC* ~ (Nfld: 1620–), and cp *Trésor de la langue*

française capelan, from Prov (1558–) for sense 1; for combs. in sense 2: *Fisheries of U S* (1887), p. 184 ~ seine, p. 141 ~ sick, *DC* ~ weather (1869). *DAE* kib(b)lings is a rare variant: see [1843] quot.
  1 A small, iridescent deep-water fish (*Mallotus villosus*) like a smelt which, followed by the cod, appears inshore during June and July to spawn along the beaches, and is netted for bait, for manuring the fields, or dried, salted, smoked or frozen for eating; freq in coastal place-names.
  [1600 HAKLUYT iii, 133 (Hakluyt's note) (a fish like a Smelt) Called by the Spaniards Anchovas, and by the Portugals Capelinas.] 1620 WHITBOURNE 10 The Rivers also and Harbours are generally stored with delicate Fish, as Salmons, Peales, Eeles, Herring, Mackerell, Flounders, Launce, Capelin, Cod, and Troutes. [1663] 1963 YONGE 60 The middle or end of June come the capling, a small sweet fish and the best bait. [1766] 1971 BANKS 137 But their greatest Delicacy in the fish way is a small Fish calld here Capelin in appearance not unlike a smelt tho scarce half as Large they Come in Very Large Shoals From the southward to Deposite their spawn. [1770] 1976 HEAD 168 [Three vessels sailed] with Caplain for the shoals [fishing]. [1810] 1971 ANSPACH 20 About the latter end of June, the *Capelines* make their appearance, going up the Bay along the south Shore, and down again along the north shore, in such abundance as almost to exceed credibility. 1839 TUCKER 85 There is no prey of which the cod seems to be so fond as the capling. . . According to the plenty or scarcity of those capling do the fishermen prognosticate the result of their labors. 1842 BONNYCASTLE i, 266 This fish, the capelin, rarely exceeds seven inches in length; its colour is a very pale green, with a tinge of brown above the abdomen, and its sides are silvery. [1843] 1887 *Fisheries of U S* 160–1 On these a small cork is placed at every 12 feet [by the French]. . .while metal hooks, baited with parts of small fish (by us called kiblings) [capelins are no doubt meant], are alternately fastened by snoods of 3 feet long, 6 feet apart. [1907] 1912 *Nfld Law Reports* 296 No person shall (4) take, ship, or put or haul on board. . .any herring, caplin, squid or other bait-fishes. 1912 CABOT 84 Dense schools of caplin (cápe-lin) sometimes wrinkled the surface. They are much like smelts, and may be dipped up readily with a hand net. Cod disgorge them on the stage and in the boats, and so do sea trout. 1953 *Nfld & Lab Pilot* ii, 342 Capelan bay indents the eastern side of North-East island. 1969 HORWOOD 165 [Caplin] are smoked not only in smoke houses or smokers improvised out of barrels or puncheons, but even in the tops of chimneys. C 71–105 When the taties came up through the ground we used to put caplin on for fertilizer. 1979 TIZZARD 285 Everyone in the area kept dogs, therefore everyone must dry a certain amount of caplin for dog food. . .during the winter.
  2 Attrib, comb **caplin bait**: caplin netted for use as bait, esp in trawl-fishing for cod; see BAIT (FISH).
  [1953] 1978 *Evening Telegram* 1 Aug, p. 5 The bait depot at Grand Bank has a good supply of caplin bait.

1976 CASHIN 65 Fishermen with their own caplin seines generally hauled the caplin bait and it was our business to sell them the necessary ice.

caplin baiting: (a) in the Bank fishery, a quantity of caplin taken aboard a vessel in port at one time; (b) a fishing voyage to the Banks, the duration of which is fixed by the supply of caplin bait aboard; see BAITING.

1960 FUDGE 17, 19 After about three caplin baitings we returned to Belleoram. . . After using three caplin baitings we had secured a fair trip. P 34–74 Another of our scheduled jobs was to give ice to the Banking Vessels to ice down their caplin or squid baiting. P 113–74 ~ a voyage to the Banks.

caplin bunting: grade of net, with very fine mesh, for catching caplin.

1957 *Evening Telegram* 28 Sep, p. 11 [The Colonial Cordage Co] manufactures all types of netting, one of which is Caplin Bunting.

caplin cart: two-wheeled, horse-drawn cart used to carry caplin from the shore to the fields for fertilizer; CAR (P 148–61).

caplin fishery: the organized catching of caplin on a large scale for processing.

1965 *Evening Telegram* 3 Nov, p. 4 At the present time the caplin fishery is carried out in a limited way on the Southern Shore.

caplin mesh: small mesh of the 'cast-net' used to catch caplin.

T 66/7–64 That needle's too big for [making] a caplin mash.

caplin pit: hole in the ground into which caplin are thrown to be used as fertilizer.

1975 GUY 9 The caplin pit, moving with little white maggots, or the fishes guts pit in a like condition, was a useful source of nutrient for the potatoes.

caplin run: migration of caplin to the shore to spawn; see RUN n.

1967 HORWOOD 42–3 With the dawn of July came the annual miracle of the caplin run, when any meat-eater could pick up his fill on almost any Newfoundland beach.

caplin scull: see CAPLIN SCULL.

caplin season: June-July, when caplin appear inshore.

1842 BONNYCASTLE i, 267 [The caplin] migrates to Newfoundland about the middle of June, when it is so numerous as to cause the week or two after the 20th of that month to be called the 'caplin season,' the wind being then easterly.

caplin seine: vertical net with small meshes, the ends being hauled together to catch caplin; see SEINE.

[1742] 1954 INNIS 182 [inventory] Ceaplin Sean 30 foot deep and 40 fathom Long. [1775] 1792 CARTWRIGHT ii, 89 A skiff came up from our stage, which was built since I left this place on Great Caribou, for a caplin-sein, and reported that there was plenty of caplin, but no cod. 1866 WILSON 209 The caplin is sometimes taken by hand with a dip-net; at other times, it is hauled in a caplin seine. 1936 SMITH 16 We had the arm of a caplin seine for a leader. T 80/3–64 You've seen a caplin seine used, well the cod seine was the same thing, only he was that much bigger.

caplin sick: of cod-fish, glutted with caplin.

[1820] 1897 *Fisheries of U S* 141 After the capelan had finished spawning the fish slacked off, and we used to say the cod were 'capelan sick.'

caplin spawn.

[1778] 1792 CARTWRIGHT ii, 318 On opening the ground, I observed that the kelp which I laid on the garden last year, had now bred an infinite number of those small worms, which I saw among the caplin-spawn. [1889] 1897 *Nfld Law Reports* 380 The rail and side of the schooner were covered with caplin spawn, quite fresh, and caplin and salt were scattered about the deck.

caplin time: see **caplin season** above.

[c1945] TOBIN 16 "Caplin and Lilacs": He was an old man nigh past his toil / . . .He said he was born in caplin time. 1977 *Nfld Qtly* Dec, p. 37 One time of the year would be hard to forget was caplin time around the first week in July.

caplin trap: type of fixed fishing-gear used in inshore waters to take caplin; see TRAP[1].

M 70–18 Each June month saw the same activity. Large caplin traps decked along the beach showed the black contrast to the sandy bottom as boat loads of caplin were trapped inside. Several boats would then haul it and fill each [craft]. 1974 SQUIRES 21 A caplin trap patterned after the cod-trap was also devised.

caplin trip: in the Bank fishery, a voyage using caplin as bait; TRIP.

1960 FUDGE 25 The caplin trip came next, and on June 12th we were baiting caplin for the Grand Banks. After using three baitings of Caplin, we secured a fair trip, returned home around the first week in August, stored it all and washed out all our medium and small fish.

caplin voyage: in the inshore fishery, the taking of cod in traps during the period June to July when the fish follow caplin inshore; cp VOYAGE.

T 396–67 The caplin voyage [is] when the traps would be in use. After caplin voyage over [it would] be all trawls or hook and line.

caplin weather: foggy, wet, and sometimes cold weather which usu coincides with the appearance inshore of caplin to spawn in early summer; CAPLIN-SCULL WEATHER.

1933 GREENE 297 'Caplin weather' is generally warm and humid, with Southerly winds and sea-fog as the accompaniment. 1957 *Evening Telegram* 2 May, p. 3 The ice is back along most of Newfoundland's east coast, and the 'caplin weather' which has settled over St John's and its vicinity will probably remain until it moves off. C 66–3 If the weather during the month of June is foggy, dull and damp, this is a sign that the caplin are in and this is said to be caplin weather. 1979 *Evening Telegram* 3 May, p. 3 Foggy weather, often referred to as caplin weather in Newfoundland, grounded all flights in and out of St John's Wednesday.

capline, capling See CAPLIN.

caplin school, ~ **schule,** ~ **shoal** See CAPLIN SCULL.

caplin scull n also ~ **school,** ~ **schule,** ~ **shoal**. Cp *OED* shoal sb[1] 1 (1579–), school sb[2] 1 (1400–), scull spellings 15th–19th c; *DC* ~ Nfld (1964) for senses 1, 2; see also SCULL n 2.
1 The migration of the caplin from the deep sea to inshore waters to spawn along the beaches.
1819 ANSPACH 414 [The seal-fishery] was found to interfere at the most important period, that of the herring and capelin-sculls. 1842 BONNYCASTLE i, 267 A capelin school, schule, or shoal, is eagerly looked for as the real commencement of the cod fishery. 1866 WILSON 208 This small fish. . .comes to the shore to spawn. . .in the most inconceivable shoals. This is called the 'caplin scull.' 1933 GREENE 189 Just as de rum gives out, de caplin-scull happens along an' d'ey fergits arl about it! 1952 STANSFORD 109 On June 29th the caplin school came in. T 36/8–64 And when the caplin scull would be over [the] squid would be in. 1969 HORWOOD 163 Along the east coast of Newfoundland, summer begins with the Caplin Scull. At Outer Cove and Middle Cove, at Torbay and Beachy Cove, at Northern Bay and Spillers Cove, as June begins to mellow towards July men slip down to cliffs and beaches every day at dawn to inspect the landwash and the green waters heaving restlessly beyond. Then one morning word runs like wildfire through the villages, 'The caplin are in!'
2 The period, usu June and July, when caplin spawn along the shore.
[1810] 1971 ANSPACH 29 Whales come here in the capelin-scull, that is during the time that the capelins remain in the Bay. 1857 MOUNTAIN 8 ~ This period, so called from a small fish of that name making its appearance in such astonishing quantities. 1887 *Telegram Christmas No* 8 It is sweet at the close of a summer's day to behold maidens out from the cool shadows of the forest, raking up sweet-scented hay, and there is gruff music in the deep voices of tired fishermen as they climb the lamp-lit stage-head on a foggy night in the caplin-school. 1902 *Nfld Qtly* Sep, p. 26 It being the month of June when codfish was plenty, or, what is commonly called by my brother baymen, the 'caplin school.' 1929 MILLER 44 An' wunst, one day, in the Caplin-scull. . . 1975 BUTLER 41 [We] went to Merasheen and before about half the caplin scull was over we had her loaded—forty five quintals [of cod].
3 The shoals of cod-fish which appear in coastal waters in pursuit of the migrating caplin.
[1820] 1887 *Fisheries of U S* 141 On our arrival on the coast of Labrador very few could be caught until the capelan came in, and then the capelan schools of cod came in also.
4 Attrib **caplin-scull fishery**: cod-fishery during and after the spawning season of the caplin; SUMMER FISHERY; TRAP[1]: ~ FISHERY.
T 169–65[2] If we lost our caplin scull fishery, if that was bad, look out for a fall's fishery; we'm going to have the booming fall. But if we have a big summer, we have a poor fall.

caplin-scull salmon: smaller salmon migrating to fresh water during June and July (P 148–65).
caplin-scull season: June and July; CAPLIN SEASON.
T 169–65[2] We fishermen always looked at the fishery as two seasons: there's the caplin scull season and the fall's fishery.
caplin-scull weather: wet, foggy weather which often coincides with the spawning season of caplin in June and July; CAPLIN WEATHER (P 245–57).
1964 *Nfld Herald* 2 Aug Something strange has happened this year with our caplin scull weather.

capon* See CAPLIN.

capse* See CAPSIZE.

capsize v also **capse***. Cp SMYTH 160. To overturn; to tip over and empty (a container).
P 148–63 The whole thing capsed over. T 50/2–64 'Twas broke bad. Sledload o' wood capsized on it. All spalled up. P 80–64 You capsizes the potatoes in [the pounds of a vegetable cellar]. 1980 *Nfld Qtly* Fall, p. 58 When [the children] reached the bonfire [dragging the boat], the man was forceably removed and the boat capsized and set ablaze.

captain n Cp SMYTH 162 captain of the head 'man appointed to keep ship's head clean.' Cook on a fishing boat.
1861 DE BOILIEU 25–6 The cargo unloaded and stored, the crews are divided in parties of three or four men, each being titled according to the position he holds in the boat. For instance, 'skipper,' 'second hand,' 'midshipman': last comes the 'captain,' who has the least to do—merely, indeed, to cook for the rest and to keep the boat clean. 1866 WILSON 207 The foreshipman is sometimes called captain; but the captain of a fishing-boat is the cook. [He] is frequently a youngster.

car n also **cart**. Cp *EDD* ~ sb[1] 1 'a common cart' for sense 1; *OED* sb[1] 3 obs 'sleigh or hurdle without wheels' for sense 2. See also LONG CAR(T).
1 Horse-drawn vehicle.
[1867] 1899 *Nfld Law Reports* 210 [He was] maintained by the produce of the farm and the monies earned by the hire of defendant's horse and car. 1972 NEMEC 85 In the pre-Confederation era it was not unusual for upwards of 1,500 horse 'car' (cart) loads of kelp to be taken each spring from local beaches for use as fertilizer in gardens and meadows and as feed for sheep and cattle.
2 Sledge.
1937 DEVINE 13 Cart—used for *slide* in Herring Neck, and neighbourhood. P 205–55 'He tackled the horse to the car.' Horse-car and hand-car both mean a slide used for hauling wood. P 266–67 Cart—used to haul wood across ice and over fairly level ground.
3 Comb **car-driver,** ~ **man**: carter.
[1867] 1899 *Nfld Law Reports* 210 The

plaintiff. . .abandoned a fishery in which he was engaged at Brigus South to come and live with his father and serve him on the farm and as a car-driver in the town. 1978 *Evening Telegram* 19 Sep, p. 6 He [took down] the name of the carman.

carawat* v   also **corawat*** ['kɔərəwɔt] JOYCE 231 caravat and shanavest 'names of two hostile factions'; DINNEEN carabhat 'cravat.' To gossip, talk idly; argue.
    P 24–67 He thought we were corawatting together about it when he found the line busy. Q 67–41 A bunch of old women carawattin' over the back fence.

carbuckle* v   To collect (kelp) for use as fertilizer.
    M 68–2 "When Summer Comes": When the summer comes you'll see the women down in the beach, / Carbucklin up the kelp, / They'll haul so much ashore, / And look 'ere, Jane, there's more, / And Uncle Johnny started haulin with his nag.

card n   In 'knitting' a net, a thin wooden oblong, four or more inches long and of varying width, used as a guide to the size of mesh required.
    1873 CARROLL 35 The twine [seal nets] are made of is about three times the size of salmon net twine; it will require sixty pounds weight of such description of twine to make a seal net. The net is made on an 8½ inch card. 1888 STEARNS 287 The working instruments were a needle and a card. . . The card was a simple flat piece of wood, as wide as the meshes were to be long, and long enough to overlap the last mesh by about half an inch. T 43/8–64 You had a card the size of the [mesh] that you were going to knit, and you just go over it with a clove hitch and bring it back over the card. Go over again and put on another one, and put on until you get one hundred [meshes]. Then you'd slip that off o' your card. 1980 *Nfld Qtly* Fall, p. 60 [In the kitchen] my two older brothers, my sister and myself were expected to do our daily share of knitting, using special handmade wooden needles and mesh measuring card.

cardeen* n   also **carjel***, **carjo** [kæːɹ'diːn, 'kaːɹdʒɨn, 'kæːɹdʒou]. Cp *ADD* accordion for *a-cordeen* etc. Accordion.
    P 8–55 Allan played the carjal for the dance. T 1–63[1] I learned that day to play the 'cordion. M 68–26 [They] could also play the carjel and on slack days one or the other could be found in the forecastle playing a few jigs. 1979 *MUN Gazette* 13 Dec, p. 13 Skipper John Hewlett still up at that late hour, relaxed for the first time, that fall, I 'llows stretched out on the couch with his feet up on the woodbox playing his old button accordian or 'carjo' as he called it.

carey See CAREY'S CHICKEN.

carey's chicken n   also **carey's chick, carey chick**. Cp *OED* chicken 4: Mother Carey's chicken (1767–); *DC* Carey: Carey's chick (Nfld: 1953–); see also PALL CAREY for sense 1.

1 Variety of petrel, esp northern Leach's petrel (*Oceanodroma leucorhoa*).
    [1937] 1940 DOYLE (ed) 11 "Two Jinkers": They went battin' Carey's chicks / And said that they were puffins. 1959 MCATEE 4 Carey chick—Leach's petrel. (Nfld, Que.) C 69–7 The kerry-chicken, which lives away out at sea, shows signs of a storm if it is seen near land. P 127–73 Carey chick is a small bird that walks on water.
    2 In clipped form **carey**: in coastal features, esp shallow waters of an inshore fishing ground identified by the habitual presence of Leach's petrel.
    1953 *Nfld & Lab Pilot* ii, 550 These include North Carey island. . .and Bingham island. . . 2⅔ miles north-eastward. . .of Carey island. 1966 SCAMMELL 139 ~ [name] of fishing grounds [off Fogo Island]. Q 71–3 ~ shoal on a fishing ground [on the South Coast].
    3 Cpd **carey-church**: large square lantern at the masthead of a fishing schooner, a lure to the seabird in foggy weather (P 90–69).

caribou n   also **cariboo, carribou, ~ deer, karaboo**. Developed from *caribou* [= North American reindeer]; *OED* ~ (1774–); *O Sup*[2] (1672–); *DAE* [1610–]; *DC* (1665–) for sense 1; *DC* ~ fly Nfld (1835) for cpd in sense 2.
    1 The species of deer native to Newfoundland (*Rangifer tarandus*); DEER.
    1823–4 *Edin Phil J* x, 160 The western division being nearly destitute of wood, affords pasture to numerous herds of deer (the *Carribou*). Of these animals there are here many thousands; indeed, the country seems covered with them. They migrate eastward to the woody districts in winter, and return westward very early in spring. Their flesh forms almost the sole subsistence of the Indians. [1831–9] 1926 AUDUBON 144 At that period [when winter approaches] the karaboos come towards the shore. 1875 GRANT 217 We met no traces of Red, or of Micmac Indians, or of the wild cariboo deer. 1897 WILLSON 136 The *caribou* or reindeer are finer than the similar breed of Norway. 1913 DUGMORE 13 Before going into the life of the Newfoundland Caribou let us glance at the animal itself, for he is a stranger to most people. He is known scientifically as *Rangifer tarandus*, or perhaps more specifically as *Rangifer terrae novae*. By the general public who know the animal at all, he is called a Woodland Caribou, the name being derived from the Indian 'maccarib,' or 'maccaribo,' or 'caribo,' and not as Sir John Richardson would have us believe from the French 'Quarré boeuf.' The spelling that is now used—'caribou'—dates at least as far back as 1609, when it was used by Les Cabot. T 417/20–67 The only time you can travel for caribou is in the wintertime.
    2 Attrib, cpd **caribou berry**: fruit of the white and rose mandarin (*Streptopus amplexifolius, S. roseus*) (1956 ROULEAU 27).
    caribou feed: Canadian burnet (*Sanguisorba canadensis*) (1956 ROULEAU 27).
    caribou fly: deer fly (*Chrysops excitans*).
    [1831–9] 1926 AUDUBON 344 How different from a

camp on the shores of the Mississippi. . .where musqui-toes, although plentiful enough, are not accompanied by carraboo flies. 1911 PROWSE 43 During the summer the skin is simply riddled with the pupae of the small caribou fly, which gives the animal no little discomfort. Another pest is the great caribou fly, which lives in the nostrils, the palate and the throat until August.

caribou v To hunt the native deer of New-foundland.
T 398/9–67 Our people here always went down cari-bouing.

carjel*, carjo See CARDEEN*.

cark*[1] n [kæːɹk]. From *OED* caulk, calk v 1.
1 Oakum used to fill the seams of a boat or other wooden structure to be made watertight.
M 68–13 He would pitch the seams so that they wouldn't leak. He would put cark in the seams also. He would do the same job with the coffin as with a dory so that it wouldn't leak.
2 Comb **cark iron** ['kæːɹk ˌaiəɹn]: metal chisel used to wedge oakum in seams of a boat or ves-sel; caulking iron.
T 141/66–65[2] I never seed a'r cark iron. And I went back up and I said, 'He isn't there.'

cark*[2] n [kɑːɹk]. Cp *OED* calk sb[1] 1, 2. Pro-truding metal point on a sled to hold logs in place.
P 65–64 Carks are driven into the bunks to keep the bottom logs from rolling around [on the sled]. Carks are spikes with the sharp part up.

cark* v also **cork*** [kɑːɹk, kɔːɹk]. Cp *OED* caulk v 1. To wedge oakum in seams of a boat or other wooden structure.
T 58–64 The coffin was leaky. And I hauled it ashore and I corked it and I tarred it. T 203–65 They roll it till they gets a little thread about a half inch big. Then they'll lay it along the seam and cark it in with the car-kin' iron.

carpenter n also **cafner*** ['kæːɹpəntəɹ, 'kæːɹpᶿmtəɹ] *EDD* ~ sb 2 Wa Sa; cafender sb 2 D Co. Wood-louse or sow-bug, an isopod which swarms around rotting wood and under rocks (*Oniscus asellus*); BOAT-BUILDER.
1964 *Evening Telegram* 25 Mar, p. 5 The first I noticed were the wood lice (or 'carpenters' as they are commonly called in Newfoundland). T 370–67 We call them carpenters. I think they're woodlice. 1970 *Evening Telegram* 17 July, p. 2 From a carpenter, to be more accurate, which was busy crawling up the right string of my left bootlace.

car pot See CAR TRAP.

carry v *OED* ~ v 5 arch or dial for senses 1, 2; *EDD* v 1 for sense 2.
1 To navigate or sail (a vessel); to drive (a vehicle).

1745 CAREW 26–7 One Ship they took laden with Fish, which they afterwards manned, and put a Mid-ship-man Captain of her, giving him Orders to carry her round to *St John's*; instead of which he carried her into *Lisbon*, and there disposed of both Ship and Car-go. [1771] 1792 CARTWRIGHT i, 151 I went down to the schooner and carried her to Stage Cove, moored her there. . . After making a short stay at the stage, I went on board and piloted her up the river. C 71–87 'I'm going to carry the truck over to the harbour now.' This was in St Albans and I soon learned that old and young in that area use the verb 'carry' in the same manner that we use the verb 'drive' and 'bring.'
2 To escort, guide, conduct (a person).
1891 *Holly Branch* 9 ['The road is] a mighty wet one just now, although it would be no trouble to carry yer honor over the bad spots.' P 148–62 Did you carry him over the place?
3 Phr *carry the key*: at the seal hunt, to be the last vessel to leave the ice or return to port (1925 *Dial Notes* v, 327).

cart See CAR.

cartail*, carteel See CARTEL.

cartel n also **cartail*, carteel**. Cp *OED* ~ sb 3 b, 5 ~ ship [vessel used to exchange prisoners]. Attrib **cartel boat** ['kæːɹteil ˌboˑt], ~ **bully**: large boat serving as an ancillary craft in the fishery, esp in carrying fish; cp BARGE.
1909 BROWNE 218 'Carteel-boats' (fish-barges) were arriving hourly, laden to the gunwales with fish. 1937 DEVINE 13 ~ A lighter used to take fish to a loading vessel. T 80/3–64 You always have a cartail boat, and the man that go into her, that was his work, bring fish from the cod-bag. He would have two splitters to keep going on two tables. A cartail boat come from the cod-seine boat. Of course a cod-seine would be hauled in one boat, and the other boat would dip the fish. They'd go [away] with the fish in that boat. P 245–70 Another boat used for transporting fish from seine to shore or schooner was a cartail bully. 1974 SQUIRE 73 One of the toughest jobs in cod-seine fishing is to operate the cartel bully which is what we called the boat used to bring fish from the seine to the schooner. This boat was about twenty-five feet long, fitted with sails; but when there was no wind, it would have to be propelled with a long sweep pushed through a hole in the stern.

carter n *DC* ~ 2 Nfld (1918). The driver of a dog-team.
1918 GRENFELL 138 I have enjoyed the luxury of a driver, or a 'carter' as we call them. P 80–63 ~ dog-team driver.

car trap n also **car pot**. Cp *NID* car n 4 'live-box for fish or lobsters.' Wooden crate placed in sea-water to hold live lobsters (P 94–57).
1971 NOSEWORTHY 181 Car pot. A large box anchored offshore where lobsters are stored to keep them fresh. Q 71–17 ~ a crate for storing lobster, also called a car-pot.

cartwheel n   Cp *NID* ~ n 1 c 'twopenny copper coin issued in England in 1797.' Attrib **cartwheel penny**: large Newfoundland copper coin of the nineteenth century; two-penny piece.

1957 *Daily News* 10 Aug, p. 2 With a penny (we used to call it a cent then for a cartwheel penny was worth two cents) we could buy two all-day suckers. Q 71–13 ~ worth two cents. It is often referred to as a big penny.

carver n   Cp *DAE* ~ 2 'one who splits fish in preparing them for market' (1765). Member of a fishing crew who slices open the belly of a codfish before passing it to the 'splitter.'

[1794] 1968 THOMAS 181 The names of Header, Cutt Throat, Carver, Splitter and Salter are the appellations given to the Fishermen who perform the various offices in the stages or in the Rooms.

case n   Comb **case-pipe**: meerschaum, from the protective case enclosing it.

[c1880] 1933 GREENLEAF (ed) 267 "The Ryans and the Pittmans": I bought me a case pipe—they call it a meerschum,— / It melted like butter upon a hot day.

case v   To re-cover, as a chair, quilt, etc; esp in phr *case up* (1969 *Nfld Qtly* July, p. 19).

P 148–64 'Case up an old barber's chair'—to upholster or re-upholster. Q 71–7 I'm going to get that piece of cotton and case up my old quilt.

casing n   Protective pieces of wood fastened along the gunwale of a boat.

T 48–64 From your counter knees you'd run along what was called a casing over the top of your gunnel, and then after that come your rowlocks.

cassock n   also **cossack, cossock, cozzock, kossack, kossak, kossok** ['kazak, 'kɑzɑk, kɑ'zɑk, 'kɒsɒk, 'kɒzɛk, 'kɑ'zɑk]. Cp *OED* ~ sb 2 b 'long loose coat or gown worn by rustics [and] sailors' obs (1590–1628) for sense 1; cp *O Sup²* kossak n 'jacket' (Nfld: 1919), *DC* kossack n 1, 2 'short [animal] skin jacket of pullover type' (Nfld-Labr: 1884; 1939) for sense 2.

1 Name given by English visitors and settlers to a loose coat of caribou skin or purloined ship's canvas worn by the Beothuk indians.

1612 *Willoughby Papers* [Guy's journal] 8 [The Beothuks wore] a sheete gowne or cassocke made of stag skinnes the moste that came downe to the middle of theire leg, with sleves to the middle of theire arme, [and] a beaver skinne about theire necke was all theire apparell. 1792 PULLING *MS* 12.2 Mr Clark who I've before mentioned as residing at Fogo told me Hooper does not say he killed the Indian but that he saw his cossock fall. [1811] BUCHAN *MS* 86 Their dress consisted of a loose cossack, without sleeves, but puckered at the collar to prevent it falling off the shoulders, and made so long that when fastened up around the haunches it became triple, forming a good security against accident happening to the abdomen. This is fringed round with cutting of the same substance. The only discernible difference between the dress of the

sexes, was the addition of a hood attached to the back of the cossack of the female for the reception of their children. [1820] 1915 HOWLEY 124 [describing body of Beothuk woman at a burial site] In her cossack were placed all such articles as belonged to her that could not be contained in the coffin. 1846 TOCQUE 285 After travelling nearly a day, they espied them on a distant hill, shaking their cassocks at them in defiance, which were made out of the boat's sails, and daubed with red ochre. 1860 MULLOCK 11 A person told me there some time ago, that a party of mountaineer Indians saw at some distance (about fifty miles from the seacoast) a party of strange Indians, clothed in long robes or cassocks of skin, who fled from them.

2 A loosely-fitting pull-over garment of animal skin, swanskin, canvas or calico, with a hood attached, worn in northern Newfoundland and Labrador; the Inuit ADIKEY, DICKY².

1861 DE BOILIEU 138 As fashion is not studied, a suit of clothes or a cassock and trousers are supposed to last ten or fifteen years. 1861 *Harper's* xxii, 751 The Ungava Esquimaux inhabit houses of ice, dress wholly in furs, carry their children in their boot-legs, or cradle them in the hoods of their kossoks. 1884 STEARNS 168 A cossack is a loose short jacket. It is made of swanskin, and the long sleeves reach to the hand while the robe or hood for the head is cornucopia-shaped, and fastened to the collar behind. The binding is of calico. 1895 GRENFELL 190–1 At one time, with their skin kossack or coat, laced over the opening, and fast around their wrists and face, they could upset with impunity, for with a couple of deft strokes with their paddles they were soon right way up again. 1923 GRENFELL 69 He showed me his second and last covering, a shoddy border with a split open 'kossak' or outside dickey, regularly crucified into the middle of the so-called 'blanket.' 1937 JUNEK 103 Eskimo dog culture with all of its associated traits. . .sealing and sealskin curing, seal oil; other traits are the making of sealskin boots (*pacs*), and 'cossacks' (fur-trimmed winter garments). T 178–65 He was a loose jacket, come down across here. There'd be lots of them would have a bit of fur around the tails and round the faces. And they'd have loose sleeves. Cozzock is the name of them. And they'd have they for summer and winter—made out of calico for summertime, and this heavy material [like swanskin] for winter. T 181–65 Had on their cozzocks; skin cozzock, skin pants, and [what] we'd call skin boots. C 70–12 [At Englee] the sweater was worn inside a cozzock, a coat made from sailing canvas, when it was very cold.

3 A garment worn over head and shoulders in winter; NORTH-WESTER.

1972 MURRAY 270 'Cossocks' (a sort of helmet which covered the whole head and most of the face except the eyes), especially welcomed by those who went in the country ten to twelve miles for wood on snowy, frosty days in winter.

cast v   Cp *OED* ~ v 6 'throw forth. . .a net.' In fishing for caplin, to secure a catch with the use of a 'cast-net'; TUCK v.

[1954] 1979 *Evening Telegram* 22 June, p. 9 The harbour at Holyrood was literally alive with fishermen and

boats—some jiggin' cod and others castin' caplin.
T 190–65 The first of June we cast our first caplin.
M 68–23 The caplin were cast about three or four miles
out the bay from Glovertown, brought to the beach in
boats, loaded on a box-cart and hauled to the potato
ground by horse. 1971 CASEY 39 We'd leave here after
twelve o'clock [midnight] to go fishing. Now we'd go
out aback of the Head and cast caplin. 1979 TIZZARD
283 We would go to Tizzard's Cove, Broad Cove or
some other sandy beach on Trump Island and there
father would cast the caplin with the castnet he made
himself. Ibid 285 On the way to the fishing grounds in
the early morning the fisherman would stop into some
cove and cast his bait box full of caplin.

cast-net n   Cp *O Sup*² cast sb 42: ~ net (1647–)
for sense 1.
   1 An open-mouthed, circular and weighted net
thrown by hand among schooling caplin and
drawn ashore or to the boat as the net is closed
on the catch.
   [1810] 1971 ANSPACH 20 When [caplin are] in the
greatest plenty near the shore, they use *cast-nets* which
cost from 15 to 17 shillings. These are cylindrical nets
open at both ends the upper end being gathered by a
running ball; the catcher holding the upper end in his
mouth, opens this lower as wide as possible with his
hands, and throws it over the shoal of capeline; then
draws it up quickly by the upper end with his hands,
the balls forming a bottom to the net which makes it
impossible to the capelin to escape. 1895 GRENFELL 74
Caplin. . .are taken in fine meshed seine nets or in cast
nets thrown from the shoulder like the 'retiarius' of old
threw his. T 203/6–65 When the cast net is spread out
he's so much as six feet across, or five feet. 1966
SCAMMELL 26 ['The doctor] can have 'em all except
the one I nips the castnet with,' chuckled Bill. 'I got
two letters inked on that one so the doctor can see it.
C.T. Stands for Castnet Tooth.' 1974 SQUIRE 21 People who required only small amounts of caplin used a
device called a cast-net. This net, threaded with lead
balls at the foot to promote fast sinking, was operated
by a man taking one of these weights in his teeth.
Holding the net with both hands, he threw it in a circular motion over the fish. Tucking lines affixed to the
bottom and top would close the net.
   2 Comb **cast-net ball**: spherical lead weight
used to sink net thrown to catch caplin.
   1929 MILLER 44 "Big Davey's Comforting": Black
Jarge, he see' some caplin come by / An' throwed his
net, an' I wuz too nigh / An' got a clout f'm a cas'net
ball. T 14–64 A castnet ball is about the size of a
musket-ball. . .with a hole bored through. You run the
line through the hole, and you'd have these [balls]
about one inch from another. You'll fasten it all along
by the head of your net.
   cast-net mould: hollow form in which balls of
lead are cast for use as weights for a net; BALL
MOULD.
   T 66/7–64 You have the castnet mould. You get the
sheet-lead (usen't to get much o' pig-lead round here),
or get if off o' the tea-chests.

cat¹ n   [= the common domesticated animal].

   1 Comb **cat berry**: wild lily-of-the valley
(*Maianthemum canadense*) (1974 SCOTT &
BRASSARD 4).
   2 Phr *cat's gale*: heavy winds presaged by skit-
tery cats; cp GALE v.
   P 148–62 Cats' gales can blow any time of year.
   turn cat out of skin: to turn head over heels.
   1977 BURSEY 31 I was on the beach receiving the
sticks of wood as they were thrown over the bank. One
of them stood on end, turned 'cat o'er the skin' and fell
on top of my head. P 108–78 He gave me such a fright I
nearly jumped cat out of skin.

cat² n   Cp *OED* marten 4: marten cat (1798–)
for sense 1; *DC* ~ house (Nfld: 1770–), ~ killer
(Nfld: 1819), ~ path (Nfld: 1775–) for combs. in
sense 2.
   1 Pine marten (*Martes americana*).
   [1759] 1976 HEAD 173 There are here the furz of
Badgers, Foxes, Deer sometimes, the two first are
much prized in this Country, & also what they Call Cat
or Marten Furz. [1778] 1792 CARTWRIGHT ii, 304 A cat
had robbed a couple of [my traps], and a brace of
wolves, two of his. [1886] LLOYD 82 Of the above, the
beaver, otter, musk-rat, cat, bear, and porcupine, are
eaten by the inhabitants.
   2 Comb **cat-house**: covering placed over a trap
set for marten or lynx.
   [1770] 1792 CARTWRIGHT i, 70 The furriers took
four traps out of cat-houses near home. 1792 ibid *Gloss*
i, x ~ A hut of boughs erected over a trap, to defend it
from snow. 1819 PANL CS 1 [He found] an Indians
Arrow drawn through the roof of the Cat House at the
end of the Path.
   cat-killer: deadfall trap for taking marten and
lynx.
   1792 CARTWRIGHT *Gloss* i, x The Cat-killer, one
end of which turns upon a nail which is driven into a
strong stake, and the other is supported high up by a
line which passes over a crutch on the top of a stake
and then comes down to another at the bottom, under
which one end of the tongue is fixed, while the other
supports the bridge; which being pressed by the animal, disengages the point of the tongue, that sets the
cat-killer at liberty and it falls down upon the ground-
killer.
   cat-path: trail prepared for the trapping of
marten or lynx.
   [1775] 1792 CARTWRIGHT ii, 130 Two others were
cutting cat-paths from the south side of the harbour.
   cat-trap: device for snaring marten or lynx.
   [1777] 1792 CARTWRIGHT ii, 276 Jack went to the
cat-traps, but they were so covered with snow, that
they could not strike up. 1819 PANL CS 1 I found five
of my Cat Traps set as I supposed to protect their Venison from the Cats. 1894 *Evening Herald* 13 Dec I have
been. . .to some of my rabbit snares and [steel] traps,
cat traps and mink traps.

cat³ n   Newly-born seal; pup; WHITE-COAT.
Also attrib ~ **harp** [see HARP]; ~ **hood** [see
HOOD]; ~ **seal**.
   1842 JUKES i, 292 Stuwitz made. . .several interest-

ing observations today on both old and young. . .as also on the still-born young, which the men call cats, and of which we found several lying on the ice. 1846 TOCQUE 190 These 'cats' are highly prized by the seal-hunters, as the skin when dressed makes excellent caps for them to wear while engaged in this perilous and dangerous voyage. 1866 WILSON 275 Sometimes these young 'whitecoats,' when weakly, will be found frozen in the ice, when the hunters call them 'cats.' 1874 WHITE *MS Journal* 19 Mar Several sailing and steam vessels around us shooting old and taking cat seals. Shot old [seals] 1170 young cats 940. 1879 ibid May Cat harps £168/1/10. 1882 ibid May 5 cat hoods 3/19. 1896 *J A Folklore* ix, 34 When the pelt, that is the skin and fat together, does not weigh more than twenty-five pounds, [the seal] is called a *cat*. [1929] 1933 GREENLEAF (ed) 247 "Sealing Cruise of the *Lone Flier*": We motored until three o'clock, and then we struck the fat, / Herbert Legge picked up a seal, Claude Hawkins got a cat. T 141/65–65[2] [He] had a stuffed seal, just a cat cut out o' the old ones in the fall.

cat[4] n also **cat-stick**. A game similar to hurley, played with sticks on the ice.
    1901 *Christmas Bells* 11 During the days of Christmas, the 'boys' assembled on the pond or in the meadow for a game of football, or a game of 'cat.' 1937 DEVINE 13 ~ A game played with flat-end sticks and a ball on the ice in winter. T 141/66–65[2] There was another game where you try to keep the ball out of the hole. Cut a hole in the ice, or in the frozen ground—'cat.' P 245–75 Cat-stick—game played by sealers 'at the ice.'

cat[5] n Alder bush which in spring bears clusters of soft spikes like a cat's tail (*Alnus crispa, A. rugosa*) (P 245–56).

cat[6] See CATFISH.

cat[7] See CATAMARAN.

catalina n [= settlement in Trinity Bay]. Comb **catalina stone**: pyrite.
    [1810] 1971 ANSPACH 31 In *Catalina* Harbour is a high rock intersected with veins or pieces of a shining pale-yellow metallic substance: it is compact and brittle; like flint it emits fire when struck with the steel or a piece of its own kind, and at the same time a strong sulphurous smell. I beg to transmit as a specimen, the largest piece of Catalina Stone. . .that I have been able to find. 1869 MURRAY & HOWLEY 199 The pyritiferous character of the slates [of Catalina] has long been known; the cubical crystals of large size and brilliant aspect having attracted attention, and acquired a local reputation as *Catalina stone*. 1937 *Bk of Nfld* i, 202 The rocks along the sea-shore contain what is called 'Catalina Stone.' This is iron pyrites.

catamaran n also **cat** [kætəmə'ræn, kætəmə'ræn] *DC* ~ n 2 a, b Nfld (1819–); cp *OED* catamountain 2 'wild man' (1616–); catamaran 1 'raft' (from Tamil; quots from East and West Indies, South America [STANFORD 1673–]),

3 'cross-grained person' [STANFORD 1779–]; catmarant 'wooden box set on a plank used for hauling fish on mudflats' (Guyana, reported by S R R Allsopp, personal commun., 1979). See also DOG[1] n: DOG-CAT, HAND-CAT.
    1 Sled with stout wooden runners curved up in front and with a vertical stick, or 'horn,' at each corner, hauled in the winter by dogs, horse or man, used esp for carting wood and other heavy loads, but also for pleasure; SLIDE n.
    1810 *Gazette* 12 July For sale. . .3 catamarans. 1819 ANSPACH 383 [Sledges, or *catamarans*] are formed of two pieces of plank shoed underneath with hoops of iron or of hard wood, joined by thick pieces from two feet to two and a half feet in length, and supporting four strong long knees, two at each end, fastened in an opposite direction. [1820] 1915 HOWLEY 122 We were until the 29th employed repairing the sledges which had become much shattered, and others totally useless were replaced with catamarans. 1846 TOCQUE 128 The firewood is drawn from the interior over the snow in slides and catamarans or sledges. 1868 HOWLEY *MS Reminiscences* 52 He comes up here every fall cuts and makes the hay and then piles it in stacks till the river freezes over, when he hauls it down on [catamaran]. 1879 TUCKER 63 The absence of snow. . .prevents their going into the woods with their 'cats' and dogs to procure fuel. [1892] 1896 *Consolidated Statutes of Nfld* 282 All carriages, carts, waggons, catamarans, sleighs, and other vehicles, shall, by the person in charge of same. . . 1900 *Evening Telegram* 29 Jan [The boy who] lived with his grandmother in Hoylestown, was accidentally killed near the Herald office on Saturday evening last. He was playing around the office while waiting for his newspapers. A large slide or catamaran ran him over. 1931 BYRNES 99 In making a sharp turn, the catamaran upsets, and you and your crew are shot into a bank of fleecy snow, from which all emerge, unhurt and happy, for your good old Newfoundland 'Cat' has licked the arrogant 'Yankee Clipper.' T 43/7–64 The hand slide, or the dog slide, as some people would refer to it, was also called a catamaran, and there's another type called a komatik. C 70–15 The men fastened a rope called a 'hauling rope' to the front or 'forward' beam of the catamaran and guided the load of wood with a stick jutting out called a 'steering stick.' C 71–120 Cat shoes are the [metal] runners under a catamaran. 1973 PINSENT 138 That's one, two, three, four, five trees. The catamaran won't hold any more than that.
    2 Horse-drawn sleigh for winter use, passengers facing the side of the vehicle; SIDE SLEIGH.
    1895 *J A Folklore* viii, 38 ~ When side sleighs were first introduced, [this term was] applied to them. M 71–78 Social outings were by express, a wagon with a raised seat, and by a catamaran in winter.

catch v For phr in sense 1: *OED* ~ v 31 b (1886); *EDD* v 5 W So D; *DC* ~ v (Nfld: 1920), ~ over Nfld (1878–).
    1 Phr *catch out*: to deplete the fish stock of a pond or stream; fish out.
    T 58/64–64 How much trout was there? Never caught

out, never fished out—thousands, I'd say. 1977 RUSSELL 74 'I lost interest in troutin' years ago.' 'How come?' said I. 'They all got caught out,' said he.

catch (over): of a body of water: to begin to freeze; to form a thin layer of ice; by extension, to freeze (the flesh) or be frozen.

1878 *North Star* 30 Mar The bay here was caught over last week, and a string of 'slob' made its appearance across the mouth, but the heavy sea of Thursday broke it all up.[*DC*] 1895 PROWSE 452–3 There was a channel just caught over, which the Canadian did not see, and down he went; as he rose the boys, seven in number, came to the edge [of the ice] and successfully copied over the Canadian's head and shoulders. 1920 GRENFELL & SPALDING 125 I 'caught' both my cheeks on the way, or in common parlance I froze them. 1963 *Daily News* 8 Jan, p. 3 Walking ahead of the others [they] stepped on a 'spring hole' which had caught over in Sunday night's frost. T 141/68–65[2] Sometimes you couldn't cross [the river]. The lop'd break up the ice, the wind would, but she'd catch over again. P 127–76 One could not say 'the water is starting to catch,' rather one says 'starting to catch over.'

2 Comb **catching thirds**: children's chasing game.

T 168–65 They run after that third one, and if they catch him before he gets to another third, he's still out in the middle. But if they can't catch him, the other feller gets the third and that one gets in the middle. Catchin' thirds.

catch n Cp *OED* ~ sb[1] 2 b 'number of fish caught.' The number of animals taken at the 'seal fishery' for their 'pelts'; TRIP, VOYAGE.

1852 ARCHIBALD 3 Although it was a disastrous season, in respect to loss of vessels, yet the catch of seals upon the whole was above an average one, there being from half to three-quarters of a million seals captured. 1891 PACKARD 122 A successful 'catch' of seals is 'better than 9000.' 1978 *Evening Telegram* 13 Feb, p. 6 As long as this surplus stock [of seal meat] is unsold they won't be buying any of this year's catch. . .from the landsmen.

catchy See KEDGY.

catfish n also **cat** *OED* ~ [1] (Nfld: 1620–), cat sb[1] (1796–); *DC* (Nfld: 1620). Atlantic wolffish; spotted wolffish; (*Anarhichas lupus, A. minor*).

[1578] 1935 *Richard Hakluyt* 129 [Parkhurst's letter:] As touching the kindes of fish beside Cod, there are Herrings, Salmons, Thornebacke, Plase, or rather wee should call them Flounders, Dog fish, and another most excellent of taste called of us a Cat, Oisters, and Muskles. [1620] 1887 MASON 152 . . .a kinde of fish [called] Catfish. 1628 HAYMAN[1] 37 Dogs and Cats are fishes so call'd. [1886] LLOYD 62 Although trawls are set for cod alone, they gather of every kind—halibut, haddock, catfish, dogfish, and other varieties. 1972 NEMEC 83 Besides cod, the sea also provides several other useful or valuable species, including flounder or sole, wolf or cat fish.

catnaghene See CATTAGENA.

cat-stick See CAT[4].

cattagena n also **catnaghene**. Possibly a misunderstanding of *châtaigne de mer* 'sea urchin,' found in early works by voyagers. See *Trésor de la langue française* châtaigne and cp 1909 *Trans Roy Soc Can* iii (II), 229 'Thwaites' Jesuit Relations (I, 69) wrongly. . .translates [Chatagne de Mer] Porpoises.' Small fur-bearing animal.

[1620] 1887 MASON 150 The Beastes are. . .Wolues, Foxes, Beauers, Catnaghenes excellent, Otteres. 1623 WHITBOURNE [sig R 2] We coozened many of [the foxes] of their rich coates, which our worthy Governour keepes carefully, as also of Cattagenas and Otters.

catter See CADDER.

cattibatter* See BALLICATTER.

caubeen n *OED* caubeen, DINNEEN cáibín. A cap or hat (1937 DEVINE 13).

P 69–80 ~ any cap or hat, but in the fish plant refers to the paper head-dress worn by the workers. 'I lost my caubeen over the whaft when I was out by the boats.'

caudle v *EDD* ~ v 'to do household work in an untidy manner' Co.

1 To do carelessly; to prepare in an off-hand fashion.

T 141/59–65[2] She'd have to caudle up something else for he now, or warm up—kept this warm what they had cooking. C 73–128 To caudle it up—to make a poor attempt at anything, whether it be a plan or a cake.

2 To litter; to confuse.

Q 71–7 The room was all caudled up with ornaments. C 73–128 I'm so caudled up now, I don't know what I'm doing.

caudler n *EDD* caudle: caudler Co. A person who muddles up any activity (C 73–128).

caulcannon See COLCANNON.

caulk See CARK* n[1], v.

caulker n also **corker**. American bittern (*Botaurus lentiginosus*).

1870 *Can Naturalist* v, 292 The American bittern makes a curious thumping noise, very much resembling the noise made by fishermen when driving oakum into the seams of their boats; hence. . .'corker' (?caulker) in Newfoundland. 1967 *Bk of Nfld* iii, 282 ~ (from the notes likened to the sounds made by pounding caulkings into the seams of a boat.)

cause n Outcome; result.

1863 MORETON 30 ~ Used for consequences, and vice versa. A person lamenting some adverse state of things will say, 'I don't know what will be the cause of it,' i.e. what will come of it.

cavalance See CALAVANCE.

cay See KEY.

ceaplin See CAPLIN.

centre n   In a 'cod trap,' the middle area of the top ropes, in line with the 'leader'; also attrib.
  P 9–73 The spanline is fastened to the offshore end of the leader and it in turn is fastened to the centre buoy and mooring. The mooring is then run out and the anchor or grapnel is dropped overboard. Q 67–34 The centre line is the rope that spans the trap from the leader to the back.

chafe n   Cp *OED* ~ sb 1 arch (1551–1825). A prolonged, wearisome experience; vexation (1924 ENGLAND 314).
  Q 71–8 We left Oporto on the 25th of January, ran into a big norwester and then got jammed in the ice for fifty odd days. We got into Louisborg by and by but I tell you, 'twas a long chafe.

chaff n   Bits of wood shavings and chips useful for starting fires (P 207–67).
  M 71–117 . . .a load of kindling chaff (chips), obtainable at any sawmill at 2¢ per oat-bag 'chinched' full.

chair n   Attrib **chair box**: kitchen chair made out of a box or barrel; BARREL-CHAIR.
  1887 *Colonist Christmas No* 17 Mary is sitting in her 'chair-box,' knitting. Q 71–6 A chair made from an empty flour barrel was often referred to as a chair-box. Q 71–7 A chair box consisted of a wooden biscuit box to which a back had been nailed.

champkin n   Cp *EDD* championing 'going round as mummers' K; *EDD Sup* ~ 'champion' K. One of the combatants in the mummers' play.
  1969 *Trans Dev Assoc* ci, 193 The plays recorded so far are of the St George type and include at least one combat between such champkins (champions) as King George, Prince Valentine and the Turkish Knight.

chapel n   Comb **chapel servant**: at Moravian Mission stations in Labrador, layman appointed to assist the missionary.
  1947 TANNER 560 The organist is mostly a native and the native 'chapel-servant' frequently leads the service and can invariably preach and pray with fluency. 1966 BEN-DOR 88 This governing body in each of the Moravian Mission posts is composed of the missionary, and the so-called 'chapel servants' and 'elders.' A chapel servant, 'Kixak,' is appointed by the missionary and installed in a public service. P 204–73 Male chapel servants acted as lay readers, and were responsible for the physical structure of the church. Female chapel servants oversaw and arranged for the cleaning of the church, care of the church silverware, drapes, and clergy gowns.

charm v   *EDD* ~ v¹ 3 for sense 1; *EDD* v² 3 Gl Do for sense 2.
  1 To cure an ailment by para-medical means.
  1895 *J A Folklore* viii, 286 Toothache is charmed away. 1910 GRENFELL 22–3 'But, you know, I don't

charm people, Skipper.' 1966 FARIS 178 Those possessing this quality are able to 'charm' (stop) blood, cure warts, toothache, stomach upset. M 69–7 In our community there still are two old gentlemen who are considered mighty powerful in charming an aching tooth or ear. [One of them] is also able to charm blood, that is to make it stop. 1971 CASEY 115 The sufferer of a major toothache went outside the family and sought specialized treatment from a male member of the settlement who 'charmed' teeth.
  2 To chatter or talk idly (P 118–67).

charm n   also **cherm*** *OED* ~ sb² b obs (1633) for sense 1; *EDD* sb² 2: cherm D for sense 2.
  1 A chant or song.
  1863 MORETON 30 ~ Pronounced *cherm*. A chant or song.
  2 Confused noise or sound (of voices); talking noisily.
  1940 SCAMMELL 37 "Squarin' Up": Skipper Harry his brother was next to go in, / With the backy juice dribblin' down over his chin, / And when he went home he was all in a charm, / With a box of black Jumbo tucked under each arm. 1975 GUY 149 But it is still a mystery why everything seemed to the outharbor juvenile with all this dreadful charm and racket constantly going on—why everything then seemed so quiet, so damned quiet, for all that.

charmer n   Cp *EDD* charm v¹ 3: charmer Co. A person, often male, able to cure ailments by apparently supernatural or sometimes para-medical means.
  T 172/5–65 I heard talk of a man was down there treating a man that was deaf. He was a charmer. 1971 CASEY 115–6 [The] afflicted person went to the specialist and expressed his desire to have his tooth 'charmed.' Something was then written on paper and given to the suffering person by the 'charmer.' C 75–146 [They believed him] to be a charmer and sent for him whenever they were seriously bleeding.

charming vbl n   The curing of ailments by para-medical means.
  1910 GRENFELL 20 I showed him that his life was at stake, and that I could painlessly open the deep wound. He absolutely refused, as he had already sent a messenger to an old lady up the bay who was given to 'charming.'

chastise v   Cp *OED* ~ v 1 obs (1330–1579); *EDD* v 1 'scold, rebuke.' To teach, instruct or correct by admonition.
  1863 MORETON 36 ~ To rebuke, to admonish. It never means to punish. 1896 *J A Folklore* ix, 27 Chastise is used not as particularly meaning to punish either corporally or otherwise, but to train for good. A father will ask the person to whom he is intrusting his son to chastise him well, meaning merely bring him up in a good way. 1937 DEVINE 13 ~ To rebuke. P 93–73 ~ to lecture child about wrongdoing.

chaw n   Cp *EDD* ~ v 1 'to chew.'
  1 Talk; a talkative person.

1904 *Daily News* 17 Aug "Bond the 'Curled Darling' and 'Paddy McGraw'": Give me Bond and good pickins'—I'll laugh at their 'chaw'; / They may go to the 'dickens,' said Paddy McGraw. [1927 BURKE] "Cadwell the Chaw": In the paper Digest, one Cy Cadwell the Chaw, / Writes a lot of old thrash of the queer sights he saw, / And in the same paper the Chaw makes a boast / Of the strange lot of dwellers around the West Coast. 1927 DOYLE (ed) 65 "Captain Bill Ryan Left Terry Behind": Terry is a fine young man, / But he has a lot of 'chaw,' / He thought to do the devil and all, / When he got the *Esquimaux*. P 110–68 'More chaw than a sheep's head' refers to one who talks too much.

2 Phr *chaw and glutch*: a meal of bread and tea.

P 74–67 We got a feed of chaw and glutch (bread and tea). C 69–17 During the Depression bread and tea became a standard meal of many people and became known as chaw and glutch (chew and swallow). From this came the grace: For this bit of chaw and glutch / We thank thee Lord so very much.

3 Comb **chaw bag**, ~ **mouth**: a gossip (P 148–65).

1904 *Daily News* 3 Oct "The Shan Van Vought": There's 'big Tom' the Jader's chum. . . / He's another 'chaw mouth' bum. 1930 BARNES 350 'Aw, go on, you're only a chaw-mouth.' That was a great word them days.

cheek n Cp *OED* ~ sb 10 'side-pieces of a pike-head' (1598–1635) for sense 2.

1 Fleshy part of cod's head; FACE.

1962 *Nfld Fisheries Conf* 219 [Using a splitting machine] there is a little loss of flesh on the cheek of the fish, not on the bone, it cleans the bone cleaner than a knife. Q 71–15 The cheeks of the cod [are] also known as sculps. 1975 *The Rounder* Sep, p. 12 Cheeks have a taste and texture all their own but are almost impossible to buy.

2 Notch in a sealer's 'gaff' in which the iron hook is fastened.

T 80/3–64 One end [of the plank is] jammed between the rising and the plank o' the boat; and t'other end, he'd be cut out like a cheek of a gaff so as your boat-hook'd bide unto un.

3 Attrib **cheek music**: humming or singing non-sense syllables by one person to provide lively, rhythmic accompaniment for others to dance; CHIN MUSIC, MOUTH MUSIC.

[1900 OLIVER & BURKE] 58 Cheek music, song for you, / Our repertory through. 1906 *Nfld Qtly* Dec, p. 4 The more lively lilt of the wordless songs, the jigging or cheek-music in which the airs of 'The pigeon on the gate' or the 'Wind that shakes the barley,' were very melodiously turned round the tongue while the younger folks danced jigs, reels, cotillions and 'setts.' 1924 ENGLAND 264 If instrumental music lacked, some old livyere might hold quid in hand and furnish 'cheek music' with a lively refrain of 'Tra-la-la, Toora-loo!' or of 'Ty-de-lit-lit-de! Do-de-do! Tiddle-do-do-dum!' 1968 DILLON 144 Someone there had [i.e. knew or used] cheek music.

cherm* See CHARM n.

chickling n Cp *Cent* ~ n[1] 2. American ruddy turnstone or chicaric; FAT a: FAT OX (*Arenaria interpres morinella*) (1959 MCATEE 28).

chiddles* See CHITLINGS.

chime n Cp *OED* ~ sb[2] 1 'projecting rim at the ends of a cask'; *EDD* sb 2: chine-hoops D So.

In comb **chime-built**: of a boat or vessel, built with overlapping planks; clinker-built.

P 48–60 ~ like clapboard, as life-boats are built. Q 71–6 Chime built or clinker built refers to 'lapped plank' boat.

chime-hoop: hoop placed around the ends of a wooden barrel or cask.

[1772] 1792 CARTWRIGHT i, 214 The cask was made of strong oak staves, well secured by thick, broad hoops of birch; yet this creature [bear] with one stroke of his tremendous paw, had snapped off the four chime-hoops, and broken the staves short off. M 71–40 [In the making of a barrel] The first hoop (the runner) is taken off, which is replaced by another hoop called a chime hoop. P 127–75 ~ The smallest of all coopering trusses used right on both ends of the barrel.

chin n Cp *EDD* ~ sb 1 (3): ~ music 'crying,' 'chattering'; *DAE* ~ music 'chatter' (1836–); *O Sup*[2] sb[1] 2 (1834 quot). Attrib **chin music**: humming or singing nonsense syllables by one person to provide lively, rhythmic accompaniment for others to dance; occas a song, esp a hymn, sung without musical accompaniment; CHEEK MUSIC, MOUTH ~ .

[1861 DE BOILIEU 119–20 After supper there is generally a dance, the music of which (lacking ordinary instruments) is played upon the chin.] [1879] 1887 *Fisheries of U S* iv, 79 One of the favorite pastimes of a crew, while 'in baitin,' is a dance. . . There was no fiddler, but only a boy who sang for them, or, according to the Newfoundland vernacular, made 'chin-music.'. . .When I entered, the host was leading off with an opening break-down. . . The orchestra furnished 'chin-music.' The musician was a young man who hummed in a sort of grunting nasal tone various tunes of proper time for square dances. . .it was a succession of nasal tones in the key of C. . . Their dances were all the square dances, and generally the well-known lancers. The various figures were called off by one of the crew. 1896 *J A Folklore* ix, 35 ~ singing at dances, where they have no fiddle or accordion. 1933 GREENLEAF xxiii When there is no one to play even on a jews-harp, some man has to furnish 'chin-music.' 1964 *Evening Telegram* 2 June, p. 17 . . .an Marty givin' chin music—you know, singin' f'r the skaters. C 70–15 The expression chin-music was given to a form of singing or humming by one or more persons to provide the rhythm for dancing when a musical instrument, such as a fiddle or an accordion, was not available, e.g. 'diddely-diddely-diddely-do, diddely-diddely-dumpty. 1971 CASEY 149 In the old days at garden parties and other 'times,' chin music and/or the 'fiddle' were the only music for the square dances, reels and jigs, which were held on all occasions.

chinch See CHINSE.

chinker n *EDD* chinkers sb pl IW; *OED* ~[1] obs (1581–1616). Crack, crevice or slit; chink.

1937 DEVINE 13 Chinkers. Interstices between logs or boards of a house. T 437–65 What goes round and round and peeps in every chinker? P 61–67 ~ anal slit.

chinse v also **chinch, chintz** [tʃʊnʃ, tʃʊŋks]. Cp *OED* ~ v 2 'to caulk'; chynchinge (1513), chincing (1748) for sense 1; *O Sup*[2] ~ (Nfld: 1770) for sense 2.

1 To caulk the seams of a boat; CARK* v.

1920 GRENFELL & SPALDING 151 To stop a boat leaking you 'chinch' the seams with oakum. T 139/40–65 They found a old punt there. And he cut up his jacket [and] chinksed the seams as well as he could. C 71–32 Chinch—to caulk the seams of a boat [with] oakum.

2 To fill the interstices of a log house with moss; STOG.

[1770] 1792 CARTWRIGHT i, 24 Fogarty chinsed the storehouse with moss. 1863 MORETON 82 The chinks between the sticks of which the walls [of the tilt] are made are caulked, or as these people say, chintzed, with moss. P 65–64 Studded camps have seams between the studs. These seams are 'chinched' with moss. A chinched camp is a camp whose seams have been filled in. 1972 MURRAY 181 These [studs] were placed upright, side by side, to form the walls. The narrow spaces between were 'chinched' with moss or wood shavings—anything that would keep out draughts.

3 To stow, stuff or pack tightly; cp BLOCKED.

1920 GRENFELL & SPALDING 151 Our fisherman sexton has just told me that 'the church was right chinched last night'. T 141/66–65[2] My son, she was chinched! M 71–117 . . .to haul a load of kindling chaff (chips), obtainable at any sawmill at 2¢ per oat-bag 'chinched' full. P 209–73 Chinch—to stow fish tightly.

chinsing vbl n See CHINSE. The process of filling the interstices of a log house with moss.

[1770] 1792 CARTWRIGHT i, 20 [The house] might easily be made proof against the weather, by chinsing between the studs with moss, and giving it an additional covering. 1792 ibid *Gloss* i, x ~ Filling with moss, the vacancies between the studs of houses, to keep out the wind and frost.

chintz See CHINSE.

chip echoic syllable.

Comb **chip-bird**: Labrador savannah sparrow (*Passerculus sandwichensis labradorius*).

[1951 PETERS & BURLEIGH 385 (The sparrow's) song is a lisping *tsip-tsip-tsip*. . .] 1959 MCATEE 64 ~ white-crowned sparrow (Labr.).

chip-chip: children's game in which players guess the number of marbles (or other objects) hidden in hand or bag (P 245–57).

P 148–71 When ally season began everyone tried to get as many allies as possible. Each had his bag or sock of allies [and we played chip-chip]. P 108–76 We used to say also 'Chip, chip, how many men aboard?'

chipple v Cp *EDD* chibble v 1 'break off in small pieces, chip.' To whittle.

M 70–28 The workhouse, or, as some people called it, the storehouse, was where the family kept its barrel of beef or pork and where a man did the carpenter work that is found around the home: mending a chair, building a stool, or just 'chippling' (whittling) out a boat for his son.

chirper n Blue flag (*Iris versicolor*); CONCH 2.

P 233–78 Peel the leaf [of chirpers] and blow between your hands.

chisel[1] n

1 Thin metal strip driven into heel or sole of sealer's boot to prevent slipping on the ice.

1842 JUKES i, 275 I had not got my boots properly fitted [for walking on the ice] with 'sparables' and 'chisels.' 1924 ENGLAND 6 I marvelled at the thick soles of these waterproof boots: soles studded with 'sparables,' 'chisels,' or 'frosters,' as various kinds of nails are called. 1933 GREENE 166 [The sealer's] knee-boots need to be studded all round the soles and heels with a neat row of projecting hobnails; three 'chisels' being always placed in each heel in addition to the nails—two across and one lengthwise—so as to prevent a forward or side slip, with the consequent possibility of falling into the ice water when travelling on open pans.

2 Comb **chisel-bar**: ice chisel.

1924 ENGLAND 78 Men brought 'chisel-bars,' inspected them on deck, in preparation for possible blasting. . . Uncle Edgar told me sometimes the cold is so intense up here that solid steel bars snap short.

chisel[2] n Cp *DAE* ~ 2: full chisel 'at headlong speed' (1835–). A vigorously danced variation of the lancers.

1974 SQUIRE 41 Dancing invariably consisted of two types, the square dance with the accent on step-dancing, and, when sufficient space was available, an adaptation of the lancers called the Chisel was performed. A minimum of eight couples took part in the latter. It was an exhilarating experience to dance to the fast music which continued for approximately an hour. The men stripped to their shirts. Even then they would be entirely saturated with perspiration by the time the turn was completed.

chistlings See CHITLINGS.

chitlings n pl also **chiddles*, chidlins, chistlings** ['tʃɪtlʊnz]. Cp *EDD* chitterling sb 1 'small intestines of animals dressed and cooked for food.' Small portion of the viscera of a cod-fish, cooked and eaten as a delicacy; FISH'S PEA.

1897 *J A Folklore* x, 204 In Newfoundland [chitterlings] is generally pronounced *chistlings*, and is applied to the roe of a cod as well. Q 67–51 Chiddles: testes of codfish. 1971 NOSEWORTHY 182 Chidlins or chitlins. Small, pink or red, edible viscera in the stomach of a codfish, shaped like a pair of pants. 1975 *The*

Rounder Sep, p. 12 'Chitlins' contain the milt from the male [cod] fish.

choby* See CHOVY*.

chocolate root n   *Cent* ~ (1890); *DC* ~ (Nfld: 1822–). Water avens (*Geum rivale*) (1956 ROULEAU 28).
  [1822] 1856 CORMACK 13 At and in the running waters are the willow-leaved meadow-sweet, water aven or chocolate root. 1895 *N S Inst Sci* ix, 88 Chocolate root.

choice a   Cp *NID* ~ 4 a 'of meat and other products' for sense 1.
  1 In designation of a quality, cure or 'cull' of dried and salted cod-fish.
  1937 *Seafisheries of Nfld* 56 The standards of cull for Labrador codfish are: Choice or Number One. Prime or Number Two. Cullage. 1962 *Nfld Fisheries Conf* 50 We could have good Madeira or good Choice, in other words the expensive fish. Ibid 207 $17.00 for small choice, to $18.50 for large choice. T 36–64 When you sell this fish for market there used to be choice, large and small, and extra large. 1977 *Decks Awash* vi (3), p. 29 I'll leave here, and in an hour I can have my two traps hauled and I'm back again; give me another half an hour and the fish is in the plants. That's why we can deliver choice quality fish.
  2 Of a fishing 'berth' or 'ground,' prolific in cod-fish; PRIME 3.
  1936 SMITH 149 There were fifteen trap-berths in all, but only two real choice ones, Fox Borough being the favourite.

chook int also **chooky, chuck, chucky** [tʃɒk, tʃʌkʔ, 'tʃʌkɪ] *EDD* ~ int D So, chuck 2. A call to pigs.
  T 255/6–66 O, chook, chook, chook. P 167–67 Come chucky, chucky, chucky. C 71–113 Here chuck, chuck, chuck, chucky, chucky, here pig.

chop v
  1 Of cod-fish, to slap the surface of the water with the tail and back extremities when swimming in schools or enclosed in a net.
  1927 DOYLE (ed) 65 "Three Devils for Fish": She steers like a rigger, she mounts the big lop, / But hark, Skipper Harry, I heard a fish chop. P 148–67 To hear fish chopping is a sign of plenty. Q 71–7 The fisherman could hear the fish chopping when he rowed near the trap.
  2 Phr *chop the beam*: to express surprise or amazement about something; see also NOTCH v.
  P 207–67 Well, chop the beam! Aunt Sally is coming to visit us. C 67–10 If someone visits your home who hasn't been there for a long time the saying when he comes in is 'Chop the beam!' This means to make a mark somewhere so as to remember it. It is said in an exclamatory voice.

chop n   Phr *have one's chop in*: to have cut one's allotted quantity of wood.

1979 TIZZARD 263 I continued as first cookie until the camp closed on May 19th, Peter Rowsell 'had his chop in'—he had cut his quota of wood that was allotted for his camp.

chopper See HORSE CHOPPER.

chopy* See CHOVY*.

chouder beer See CHOWDER BEER.

chovy* n   also **choby*, chopy*, chuffy*, shovy*** ['tʃoɒbiˑ, 'tʃoɒvɪ, 'ʃoɒvɪ].
  1 Piece of kindling wood shaved with a knife so that the wood curls at the sides; MOP¹: MOP-HEAD; SHAVINGS.
  [c1900] 1978 *RLS* 8, p. 22 Chuffies—dry shavings made to kindle fires. P 245–57 Chovee—a split sliced into shavings which are accumulated at one end, leaving a part of the split intact. P 133–58 Chopies—shavings. 1964 *Can Journ Ling* x, 41 When a thin piece of kindling wood is shaved along half its length so that the shavings stick out from it but are still attached, the pieces are called [chovis] or [shovis]. C 68–10 Before going to bed, my father would first cut out some chobies to light the fire with next morning. 1977 RUSSELL 118 Makin' chovies was a skillful piece of business, and a man with a good sharp knife and some dry kindlin' could make 'em right bushy and fancy like.
  2 Sulphur match.
  [c1900] 1978 *RLS* 8, p. 22 Chuffies—also the sulphur match used with old tinder box.

chowder n   *OED* ~ sb: ~ beer (1828). Attrib **chowder beer, chouder** ~ ; also **chowder**: a concoction of black-spruce boughs, molasses, etc, drunk to prevent scurvy; SPRUCE BEER.
  1745 CAREW 100 . . .and applying to Lady *Mules* in the Character of a *Newfoundland* man; she particularly enquired of the Drink made Use of in that Country, and he being able to give an Account of their Method of making their Chouder-Beer, and the ingredients whereof it is made, this whimsical Gentlewoman generously relieved and entertained him, and brought him a Cup of that Country Liquor which was of her own brewing. 1823 CRABB Chowder (med.) an antiscorbutic used on the Newfoundland station.

christian n   *EDD* ~ sb 1; *OED* sb 5 'now only colloq or humorous.' A human being as distinguished from an animal.
  [1783] 1792 CARTWRIGHT iii, 24 It is an actual truth however, that a late servant of mine. . .could never be prevailed upon to taste the flesh of beavers, because he was sure, he said, 'They were enchanted Christians.' P 245–56 The dog eats like a Christian. T 49–64 When I was going to the seal fishery 'twas dogs then; you were not Christians, but all dogs. 1968 DILLON 134 Some animals, girl, are as cute as a Christian. . . He was working up there for three or four years, an' he didn't know a Christian.

christmas n   Cp *EDD* ~ sb 1, sb 3 Co for senses

1, 2; for combs. in sense 4: *EDD* sb 4 ~ block D, *OED* sb 4 ~ log obs (1648), *DC* ~ tree (1882–).

1 The twelve days of Christmas, 25 Dec to 6 Jan; the Christmas season.

[(1770) 1792 CARTWRIGHT i, 74 At sun-set the people ushered in Christmas, according to the Newfoundland custom. In the first place, they built up a prodigious large fire in their house; all hands then assembled before the door, and one of them fired a gun, loaded with powder only; afterwards each of them drank a dram of rum; concluding the ceremony with three cheers. These formalities being performed with great solemnity, they retired into their house, got drunk as fast as they could, and spent the whole night in drinking, quarrelling, and fighting.] [1888] 1936 SMITH 45 We moored the schooner in winter quarters and had a few holidays during Christmas enjoying ourselves. . .mummering and dancing. 1901 *Christmas Bells* 11 During the days of Christmas, the 'boys' assembled on the pond or in the meadow for a game of football, or a game of 'cat.' T 172–65 I had to have wood enough sawed off that I wouldn't have to saw no wood in Christmas. I'd have it bulked in the porch. Q 67–51 A saying during summer when fish are scarce: 'Poor Christmas, boys.' 1976 HOLLETT 14 Would not escape, every night of Christmas, twelve nights.

2 Food and drink served to visitors at Christmas.

C 67–16 What would a bit of Christmas consist of? It was a glass of syrup, a piece of dark cake, sometimes a piece of light cake, and a piece of cheese. 1969 *Christmas Mumming in Nfld* 133 After the mummers are identified and have unmasked, a 'lunch' or 'some Christmas' is served. This usually consists of pastries, cakes, cookies, pies, and tea. Drinks are then offered, chiefly to the men. 1972 MURRAY 230 No visitor could leave the house without a 'bit of Christmas'—a sampling of the Christmas cake. . .and a drink.

3 Phr *blow the christmas pudding*: to celebrate with gun-fire the lifting of the Christmas pudding.

C 67–16 On Christmas Day I was astonished to hear so many gun shots and ran quickly about to see what was wrong. There they have a fashion of blowin' the Christmas puddin' out of the pot. As the wife or woman of the house is lifting the pudding from the pot, the husband or man of the house is standing outside the back door with the gun. As soon as the pudding rises out, the shot is fired into the air.

4 Attrib, comb **christmas apple**: variety of Canadian apple, Red Delicious, imported esp for the Christmas season (P 245–75).

christmas back-junk: see JUNK.

christmas block: Yule log.

[See 1770 quot in sense 1.] 1819 ANSPACH 475 The ancient British custom of the *Yule*, or Christmas log or block, is universally observed by the inhabitants of Newfoundland. On Christmas-eve, at sun-set, an immense block. . .is laid across on the back of the fireplace, to be left there till it is entirely consumed: the ceremony of lighting it is announced by the firing of muskets or seal guns before the door of each dwelling

house. This, among them, is the prelude to a season of joy and merriment.

christmas box: see CHRISTMAS-BOX.

christmas fish: dried and salted cod-fish eaten on St Stephen's Day, 26 Dec.

1957 *Atlantic Advocate* Dec, p. 23 It is said that no family with any pretensions to 'quality,' or with deep-rooted religious convictions, would eat any kind of meat on St Stephen's Day. Fish was required eating, especially salt codfish, and elaborate recipes were in existence for the preparation of the so-called 'Christmas Fish.'

christmas log: see **christmas block**.

[See 1819 quot at **christmas block**]. C 70–27 Birch wood was always used in open fireplaces during Christmas. Those smooth white logs were called Christmas logs.

christmas masque: mummers' play.

[1952] 1969 *Christmas Mumming in Nfld* 184 [She] reported that 'A Christmas Masque' used to be performed at Herring Neck.

christmas time: communal gathering with refreshments, dancing, etc; TIME.

1950 *Newfoundlander* Jan, p. 15 There's no play today can come up to the old-fashioned mumming play, because at Christmas times everyone is into it. 1969 *Christmas Mumming in Nfld* 154 Well, your Christmas times. . . Some people they rig up.

christmas tree: communal Christmas party.

1891 *Holly Branch* 4 The goat sprang through the window, and landed on the shoulders of Mr O'Grady's eldest boy, who was coming home from a Christmas Tree. 1971 CASEY 100 On St Stephen's night (December 26) a concert. . .usually was performed by the school children. The following night a community social gathering with supper and dancing known as 'the Christmas tree' was held in the parish hall.

christmas-box n *OED* ~ 1 obs (1611–1802) for sense 1; *DAE* (1810, 1823) for sense 2; JOYCE 298 for sense 3.

1 A box in which money is collected by soliciting at Christmas.

1937 DEVINE 13 Christmas boxes. Carried around by poor people at Christmas soliciting money.

2 A gift of food, money, etc, given at Christmas.

1819 ANSPACH 476–7 Men and women exchange clothes with each other, and go from house to house singing and dancing, on which occasion Christmas-boxes are expected, and generally granted previous to the performance. [The Christmas boxes are] presents, not in coin. . .but in eatables, from a turkey or a quarter of veal or mutton, or a piece of beef just killed for the occasion, down to a nicely smoked salmon. 1887 *Telegram Christmas No* 9 'I've brought a Christmas Box for 'ee, my maid,' said her husband, with a strange quiver in his voice, placing the [baby] in her motherly arms. 1893 *J A Folklore* vi, 63 Christmas presents or boxes. P 148–62 ~ a gift of money. C 71–86 He would never say to us 'I have to get a Christmas present for your mother'; he would say, 'I'll soon have to get your mother's Christmas box.' 1976 GUY 66 'Was that a

Christmas box, I dare say?' It was a gilt frame under a glass and nicely done out with dicky birds and old fashioned roses.

3 Phr *christmas box on you*: Christmas greeting.

1931 BYRNES 100–1 Your heart is singing in blissful anticipation, as you plow through the snow drifted streets, and everyone you meet, even the most casual acquaintance. . .you greet with 'Christmas Box on you,' and indeed you receive a goodly response to your obviously implied request. C 71–107 ~ This is a Christmas greeting meaning Merry Christmas and I hope you get lots of good things.

chuck See CHUCKLEY PEAR.

chuckle v Cp *OED* chuck v[2] 1 'to give a gentle blow under the chin'; perhaps influenced by *throttle*. To grasp (someone) by the throat.

1927 *Chr Messenger* 47 'Chuckle' has another meaning besides to laugh: namely, to catch a person under the throat with the open hand and violent[ly] push back the head. P 108–74 'You let go of that slide or I'll chuckle you.' I heard this often and thought it meant to catch by the throat and to shake.

chuckle-de-muck* See TRUCKLY-MUCK.

chuckley a Cp various astringent fruit in *OED* and *DAE*: choke cherry (1796–), choke plum (1556), choke pear (1530–1672); *EDD* chuckley 'of bread: gritty, badly made' Ha.

Comb **chuckley pear**, also **chuck**: a flowering shrub; the sweet purple berries of this shrub; Juneberry; INDIAN PEAR, WILD ~ (*Amelanchier* spp) (1956 ROULEAU 28).

P 245–56 [Berries called] chucks are chuckley pears. 1966 HORWOOD 19 Among the former were the purple chuckley pears. 1975 SCOTT 45 The Chuckley Pears appeal most to the palate in the autumn but it is in the spring when they are most beautiful.

chuckley-plum, also **chucky** ~: a small tree; the dark fruit of this tree; choke-cherry (*Prunus virginiana*) (1895 *N S Inst Sci* ix, 89).

1883 HOWLEY *MS Reminiscences* 27 Cherry of two varieties, the ordinary Wild Cherry and the Choke cherry, which latter is known to the Northern people as Chockly plum. 1972 MURRAY 235 'Chucky plums'. . . and 'sasprilla berries' (*Aralia hispida*) were both mentioned as cures for eczema. 1975 SCOTT 49 The Choke Cherry or Chuckley Plum is not as common as the Pin Cherry.

chucky-plum See CHUCKLEY-PLUM.

chuffed p ppl *OED* chuff a[1] 1 'puffed out (with fat)' obs exc dial (1609–1821); *EDD* chuff adj[2] 1: chuffed. Puffed out, chubby.

1971 *Evening Telegram* 17 June, p. 3 'Fallin' into flesh, isn't you? All chuffed out like a dick with the mites.'

chuffy* See CHOVY*.

chum n also **chummy** Cp *EDD* champ v 2 'to chop, mash; to crush, bruise,' sb 5 'potatoes boiled and mashed' NI; cham v 'to chew, bite; to nibble into small fragments'; *Kilkenny Lexicon* chomp; *DAE* ~ n 1 'remains of menhaden after the oil has been pressed out' (1859–), 2 'fish chopped up and used as bait' (1872–). A formless mass (of vegetables) from over-boiling; cp COLCANNON.

P 269–63 The potatoes are gone to a chum. Q 71–7 I dare say the potatoes are cooked to a chum now. P 148–77 Chummy—left-over dinner consisting of cabbage, turnip, ham, potatoes, carrots.

chummy[1] n, proper n ['tʃʌmɪ]. Cp *O Sup[2]* ~ 'chum' naut (1849–) for sense 1.

1 That person; unnamed person, usu male; BUDDY.

P 54–61 ~ refers to anyone, acquaintance or not. P 148–62 When chummy came up to the corner [he stopped]. T 54–64 So he played some card and chummy couldn't beat him. C 71–92 ~ refers to a person whose name one does not know. C 71–107 Where is chummy going?

2 Gadget, device; object; thing with an unknown name; MACHINE.

T 89/90–64 A feller had a chummy, you know, on his ear, a phone—chummy for when he want to come up now. C 68–10 He can't remember off-hand, the correct name of an object. He may call it a ting-a-bob, wossnim, chummy, chummy thing, etc. C 71–107 When repairing his motor, he may say, 'Get me the chummy,' meaning wrench. In cards, a person who goes in the hole may say, 'If I had the five and chummy (meaning the jack), I would have made it.'

3 Cpd **chummy-fella**: person one cannot call by name (C 71–95).

chummy-call, ~ **-jigger,** ~ **-thing**: thing one does not specifically name (P 126–67; P 273–70).

chummy[2] See CHUM.

church n Comb **church ship**: vessel in which episcopal visitation is made to coastal settlements; cp PARISH BOAT.

1846 [FEILD] 14 The good Church ship rolls in this open Bay, so that I can hardly write. 1895 TOCQUE 265 Another great loss was the church ship *Havelock*—the 'Floating Cathedral,' by which the bishop visited the remote parts of his diocese, and in which he held services. 1902 *Christmas Bells* 1 These two pictures show the Church ship while on her visitation voyage this summer with the Bishop of Newfoundland and his Chaplain to the North West Portion of the Island and the Labrador.

chute n also **shoot, shute**. Cp *OED* ~ 1 [1725–], *DAE* n 1 (1806–), *DC* 1 (1793) [shoot obs (Nfld: 1772–)] for sense 1; *EDD* shoot sb 11 for sense 2; *OED* shute[3] 1 dial for sense 3.

1 A narrow declivity in a river.

[1770] 1792 CARTWRIGHT i, 12 The rest of the bed of

the river runs more on a level, but is incommoded by many rocky obstructions, which form falls, shoots, and rapids. 1792 ibid *Gloss* i, xiv Shoot in a river. A place where the stream, being confined by rocks which appear above water, is shot through the aperture with great force. 1842 JUKES ii, 93 A narrow foaming channel and up a 'shute,' or small fall of a foot or two. 1868 HOWLEY *MS Reminiscences* 29 There are two long smooth reaches on the river above, called 'Steadies. . . Between the latter and the steady the river is very rugged and broken by falls, chutes and rapids. 1879 HARVEY 20 When the stream is collected into a narrow channel, and rushes along one bank with great rapidity, it forms a 'chute,' and it is often hard work to pole a boat against such a current. [1900 OLIVER & BURKE] 42 The west end had Carroll's well, Apple-Tree well. . .with Mullins' river and Waterford river to fall back on when the wells ran dry. The east end had Bell Shute, Garrett's well, Garrison hill well, Bray's well, and Rennie's river to depend on. 1969 HORWOOD 2 The river forked above, and there was a whisper of a rapids below—a 'chute' leading to a 'rattle,' as our woodsmen describe it.

2 Hence, a St John's place-name for a steep path by a stream.

1931 BYRNES 93 How many can recall the old streets and lanes of our youth?. . .Bell Shoot. . .The Barking Kettle. 1937 DEVINE 13, 43 Chute, shoot, shute—a declivity. A narrow, inclined street or lane, e.g. Bell Shoot, Sheen Shoot, hill-streets in old St John's. 1944 LAWTON & DEVINE 70 When [the mailman] came to the 'Chute' (the rising ground at which you catch the first sight of the town) he blew a tin horn about two feet long.

3 Eaves-gutter of a house (1966 PADDOCK 126).

cillick See KILLICK.

circle n   Attrib **circle line**: spiral effect created by turbulent cross-currents.

1965 LEACH (ed) 204 "George's Banks": The hardships of those Georgie's Banks no mortal can pen down, / With circle lines, and shifting sands and breakers all around. Q 71–7 ~ whirling waves. I don't like the look of the water. I'm not putting the boat out—there's too many circle lines.

cive n   also **scyve, sieve** *EDD* ~(s) 'small leek' Co. A variety of small onion or onion-sprout.

1937 DEVINE 45 Sieves—small kind of onion or sprouts of same. 1975 GUY 6 A few other plants were found in the front garden such as. . .chives (pronounced scyves) which were employed in cooking.

civil a   *DC* ~ Nfld (1905–) for sense 1; *NID* 6 c obs for sense 3.

1 Of the weather, with no wind; still.

1887 *Telegram Christmas No* 9 You know it looked civil enough this mornin', an' I'm sure 'twas as mild as October yesterday. 1895 *J A Folklore* viii, 37 A calm day is *civil*. 1905 DUNCAN 109 It was a mere 'puff' on a civil evening—but a swift, wicked little puff, sweeping round Breakheart Head. 1924 ENGLAND 229 De sun's

risin' troo a bank fer a fine day, me son. . . We may 'ave a civil spring, from now out. 1933 GREENLEAF xxii Please God, we'll have civil weather for ou-er toime. C 66–2 When there is a star behind the moon there will be wind. When there is a star in front of the moon there will be civil weather.

2 Of the sea, calm, placid.

1937 DEVINE 14 The water is civil now. 1968 KEATING 58 'It's a handsome day,' said a wrinkled old fisherman, 'but the water be too civil for the tuna, *cruel* civil. C 71–120 When the water in the harbour is very calm and still, elderly people say, 'How civil it is!'

3 Of persons, orderly, restrained, quiet.

T 264–66 They were civil and orderly; they kept order. P 74–67 If you don't be civil you'll go to bed! C 71–44 He was a civil man (quiet, mannerly fellow).

clamper See CLUMPER.

clampet* See CLUMPET.

clap-dish n   *OED* ~ 'wooden dish. . .carried by lepers' (1577–); *EDD* ~: 'his tongue moves like a beggar's clap-dish.' Noisy, rattling object; esp in prov phr.

P 167–67 Applied to a gossipy woman— [She's like] old mother's clap-dish. M 68–24 Your tongue never stops. It's like a miller's clap-dish.

clarenville n   [= settlement in Trinity Bay]. Comb **clarenville boat**, ~ **fleet**: one of a number of small wooden vessels built at Clarenville, c1945 by Newfoundland government; SPLINTER BOAT.

1950 PARKER 57 At the end of the war some of the 'Clarenville' wooden motor boats, which the Government built during the war, were fitted out as refrigerator ships. 1973 HORWOOD 93 His position included supervision of a fleet of boats known locally as the Splinter Fleet, but officially as the Clarenville Fleet.

clave* v   also **cleave** [kleɨv, klɛɨv, klɛʊv, kliːv] *OED* cleave v¹ 1.

1 Of kindling, to cut or split; esp *clave splits*.

[1786] 1792 CARTWRIGHT iii, 121 Tilsed was employed on carpenter's work, and the rest of the people in sawing and cleaving firewood. 1920 GRENFELL & SPALDING 35 [I had commanded one] to attend to this matter, and he had promptly departed, as I thought, to 'cleave the splits.' 1936 DULEY 194 With difficulty Joe Perry had cleaved some splits, and because they had no paper Uncle Seth had whittled some shavings with his knife. T 12–64 The piece of wood was clev. T 185–65 In the spring when they gave 'em wood to cleave, they used to break off the axe helves as fast as they'd mind to. P 245–67 Clavin' splits. P 245–67 'Cleave some junks.' This is the usual way of saying 'chop some wood.' C 68–21 Parents used to tell their children that they should not clave splits on Sunday. C 71–126 Clave un up—chop a piece of wood in half.

2 To threaten to do someone harm.

C 66–16 So help me, I'll cleave you in two. C 66–13 I'll cleave 'ee open.

3 To peel or slip off neatly.

T 34/8–64 You take [the shim] and shove it, with the sap in the tree; you'd shove it around the rine, and the rine'd all cleave off o' the tree.

clavy n ['kleɪvɪ]. Cp *EDD* clavel: clavvy, clavy s w cties 'mantelpiece.' Shelf or recess in chimney used for storage.

1896 *J A Folklore* ix, 20 ~ a shelf over the mantelpiece. 1925 *Dial Notes* v, 328 Clavies—square holes in chimneys for odds and ends. 1937 DEVINE 14 Clavey. A square hole in the chimney in a kitchen, on each side of the fireplace to put odds and ends in; one for father and one for mother. 1969 *Trans Dev Assoc* ci, 187 ~ small hole or shelf for oddments in the chimney breast.

clay n Loose stony soil; also attrib.

[1772] 1792 CARTWRIGHT i, 217 After which I went to the stage with a load of clay. 1915 *Christmas Greeting* 23 We knew 'twas no live man, but we kept on clearing the clay off the chest and from the ends so that we could lift it. P 148–65 ~ soil, rocky soil, loosely whatever can be dug up out of the ground. C 71–106 Clay scrape [is] a height of land on which no trees or other vegetation grew. It was usually a steep piece of land, very difficult to climb because there was no vegetation to use as a foothold.

clean a Cp *EDD* clever av 13: clever and clean Ir for sense 3.

1 Of the sea-water, containing abundant plankton for the fish but lacking the organisms which cause 'slub' to form on nets; hence, descriptive of an area good for fishing. Antonyms are DIRTY, SLUBBY.

1966 FARIS 30 'Good water,' water that is 'clean' is in essence much less clear and much more full of opaque organisms and miniscule organic life than is the crystal-clear, absolutely transparent 'dirty' or 'bad' water. P 245–80 'Clean' water has very poor visibility, and although it is murky due to phytoplankton and zooplankton, there are no *Oikopleura* present [to cause slub].

2 Of the several strakes or planks forming the sides of a boat, the first or top one, technically called the *sheer strake*; ['klein straik]; cp RAGGED (strake).

T 43/8–64 You had her pretty solid then. You had your gunwales on, and then you'd put on the clane strike, and the one under that was the binding strike, that's in plankin', you know. P 13–74 In a vessel's hull, the clean strake is the first plank below the rail or gunwale.

3 Phr *clean and clever*: completely.

P 54–67 'E done it clayn 'n' cliver.

clean v In logging, to fell the trees in a given cutting area.

T 48–64 If there's a man on the other side o' that block, he's cutting towards me and I'm cutting towards him so you have to clean every tree as you go along, and clean your block between the two roads.

clear a Cp *Limerick Reporter and Tipperary Indicator* (1867) 23 June 'the west gate [of Carrick-on-Suir] facing "the clear air" of Tipperary'; *ADD* clear of (Nfld); *DAE* a 3 clear thing.

Phr *clear air*: epithet for person originally from Tipperary; member of Newfoundland-Irish faction.

1863 PEDLEY 294 Two great Irish factions established themselves [c1815] in St John's. They had various names denoting the different parts of Ireland from which they came. The watchword of those from the county of Tipperary was 'Clear Air.' 1895 PROWSE 402 The Tipperary 'clear airs'. . .and a number of other names for the [St John's Irish factions].

clear drop: the open sea; BLUE DROP.

1924 ENGLAND 165 An' de mudder o' he—her'll come an' find un, ahl rate, even if him out in de cl'ar drop.

clear of: except for, apart from; in addition to.

1924 ENGLAND 51 Well, clear o' Levi, ye got thirty an' thirty-one apiece. Can't get it nigher 'n that! 1962 *Nfld Fisheries Conf* 240 There's not too much facilities for keeping fish making, clear of those community stages. Ibid 268 We salt quite a bit of our fish in the summer, clear of what we sell green. T 43/4–64 They were fierce to a stranger. In fact, they were fierce to everybody, clear o' the owner. P 245–74 [Young men] knows there's some things in life clear o' fishin'. 1977 *Them Days* ii (3), p. 6 I killed two more [polar bears] clear of that one.

clear thing: ideal material or solution.

1971 CASEY 117 Bakeapples are the clear thing [for stomach cramp]. P 13–74 ~ ideal, perfect (substance).

cleave See CLAVE*.

clergy n An ordained priest or minister; clergyman.

[1900 OLIVER & BURKE] 54 Me own clergy at home will do it four dollars cheaper. 1909 BROWNE 233 Our arrival was the source of much speculation. . .but when they discovered ''twas the clargy's boat,' their curiosity was intensified. 1964 BLONDAHL (ed) 15 "The Man from Newfoundland": They sailed the Mediterranean, I've heard the clergy tell, / They went out into Egypt, from that to Jacob's Well. T 58–64 They went right up in the upper pew in the church. When they went in, the clergy was preaching—sermon. M 68–24 The Anglican clergy usually comes one Sunday, the United the next. 1973 WIDDOWSON 461 The clergy will come with his 'cat an' nine tails.'

clever a Cp *EDD* ~ adj for most senses.

1 Of persons, esp men, and beasts, large, fine, handsome in appearance.

[1845] 1927 DOYLE (ed) 25 "The John Martin": Good luck to Skipper Nick Ash for he is a clever man. 1863 MORETON 32 ~ Large, stout. A 'clever man' is a large strong man. So is a baby [or] a cow. 1895 *J A Folklore* viii, 34 In Newfoundland [clever] means large and handsome. It is applied not only to men but to animals. [1900 OLIVER & BURKE] 36 "Lines on the Sad Drownings": And hear of two fine, clever young men, /

[Were] lost in Witless Bay. 1924 ENGLAND 143 Standin' dere on de ship's brudge, sir, barehanded an' in a green split-tail coat. Ah, what a clever lookin' man he was, too! T 222–66 A clever woman is a handsome woman. She might be a complete dimwit, but if she is good-looking she is said to be a clever woman. 1974 *Evening Telegram* 23 Mar, p. 3 The people in Barbados are, compared to us, remarkably handsome. . . They are smartly dressed. . . Especially clever looking are the long lines of children going and coming to school in perfectly neat uniforms after the English fashion.

2 Well; in good health.

1937 DEVINE 14 'How's you mother?' 'Oh, she's *clever*.' 1975 GUY 64 We didn't use the word 'clever' to mean smart. But on second thought, we did. . . We would say, 'My, what a clever baby'. . .meaning. . .that the baby was healthy looking.

3 Of inanimate objects, neatly or well designed, shaped or built.

1863 MORETON 32 A house, a boat [or anything inanimate] is called clever. 1895 *J A Folklore* viii, 34 A fisherman will speak of a 'clever-built boat,' meaning that it is large and shapely. 1907 DUNCAN 143 'Twas a brave prospect. Beyond the tickle in a gale o' wind! 'Twas irresistible—to be accomplished with the fool of Twist Tickle and his clever punt. T 69–64 Had you been here last year you'd seed our old school-house. Clever big house, I suppose 'twas sixty or seventy feet long. T 141/59–65[2] We had a clever camp there, and there was only four of us into un, two more bunks left. 1971 CASEY 176 The *L. and M. Rudolph*, a vessel staunch and clever seaboat too, / Her skipper's name was Blackwood and he composed her crew. 1972 *Evening Telegram* 18 May, p. 3 When I was small our house had a clever latch on the door. It was made of wood and you could lift it up on the outside.

4 Successful; large (in amount or quantity).

[1894–1929] 1960 BURKE (ed White) 16 "Brave Colloway": The best of seals the ships brought in, / And clever bills laid down, / A year to be remembered / When the strike was in the town.

5 Of weather, fine, pleasant; CIVIL.

1962 *Nfld Fisheries Conf* 206 As I look out the window here I see a very nice clever day.

clew n Cp *OED* ~ sb 7 'corner of a sail' for sense 1.

1 The corner of a fish-net (P 243–57).

1792 CARTWRIGHT *Gloss* i, xiv The Pryor-pole at the outer clew (corner) [of the shoal-net] and the bobber at the inner one, shew where the net is.

2 Comb **clew rock**: stone fastened to end of a herring, salmon or cod-trap as an anchor (P 190–77).

clew v Cp *OED* ~ v 4 b fig 'wind up' (1867) from naut usage. Phr *clew up*: to cease (doing something); to complete or finish (an action, task, etc).

[1923] 1946 PRATT 175 "The Cachalot": 'Clew up you gab!' / 'Let go that mast! / 'There'll be row enough when you get him fast.' 1938 MACDERMOTT 143 When the fishery was over, and the men had 'clewed up' with their merchant. . . [1952] 1965 PEACOCK (ed) i, 136 "High Times in Our Ship": He clewed up the voyage and went to get more. T 100–64 You had to be on the road seven o'clock in the morning and be on till six in the evening before you'd clew up to come back to where your camp was. 1972 MURRAY 256 Working like this. . .when we clues up we won't have a copper to put on our eyes.

click n *EDD* ~ sb[1] for sense 2.

1 A stiff piece of leather on the inside part of the heel of a shoe (1925 *Dial Notes* v, 328).

1937 DEVINE 14 ~ The stiff inner leather of the heel of a shoe or boot.

2 A smart blow; CLINK n.

T 171–65 If their teacher touches 'em in school, next thing you know their parents are into 'em because they gave 'em a click in the head or something. C 68–24 We played the game called 'Click for Uncle John.' One person would be 'it.' He would have a stick (piece of an alder tree). This 'it' character would chase a whole group of kids and as he caught one he could hit him across the legs with the stick, saying 'Click for Uncle John.'

3 Pace, speed.

1924 ENGLAND 70 We got great goin', now [at the seal hunt]. Got a fine click on 'er. A good tune on this one; she's shakin' her tail some, now!

cliff n Cp *EDD* ~ sb 1 (2) ~ hawk 'peregrine falcon' Ir D Co.

Comb **cliff-hawk**: sparrow hawk (*Falco sparverius*) (1959 MCATEE 23).

cliff rock, clifty ~ : slab of rock from face of a cliff; rock with sharp, jagged edges.

1966 PHILBROOK 121 The soil cover is so thin and overlays great masses of flat rock—locally called 'cliff rock.' 1974 *Evening Telegram* 13 Feb, p. 3 'I'm puttin' a cliffty rock in this one [snowball]!' he would shout. We all knew how sharp a clifty rock is on the corners compared to a round, beachy one. But, generally, everyone would heave snowballs at each other.

clinch n Cp *OED* ~ sb[1] 2 'method of fastening large ropes by a half hitch' naut. Comb **clinch keg**: wooden float attached at the point where the anchor-chain of a 'collar' or boat mooring is clinched to the cable which leads to a buoy (C 68–26).

cling See CLINGY.

clingy n also **cling**. Sweet, fruit-flavoured drink; occas refreshments including this drink; SYRUP (P 94–57).

M 69–20 The people whom the janneys visited treated them to Christmas cake and clingy. M 70–9 If there is any food custom that is strictly typical of Newfoundland it is the giving and eating of clingy. Clingy is a snack of Christmas cake and syrup. Syrup is a sweet, concentrated, fruit-flavoured drink manufactured. . .in St John's.

clink v *EDD* ~ v¹ 9 for sense 1; *EDD* v² 1 for
sense 2.

1 To beat or slap (a person).
1955 ENGLISH 33 ~ To beat another with the fists.
P 148–67 ~ to beat someone over the head.

2 To clinch, fasten or secure (a nail); CLINT.
T 94/5–64 'Twas stuck on the end of it to clink the
sprig [i.e. nail used in making or repairing shoes].

clink n *EDD* ~ sb¹ 2. A blow or slap.
1937 DEVINE 14 ~ A smart stroke. C 71–44 ~ a hard
blow given with the fist, usually in the face.

clint v *OED* ~ v obs exc dial (1575, 1655);
EDD v 1 Do So D. To fasten firmly by bending
the protruding point of a nail; CLINK.
[1917] 1972 GORDON 97 *St Helen* made good headway under her engine, but she got such a thumping that
the engine-bed bolts were started, and we were only
able to keep going by 'clinting' six-inch nails along the
bedding plate. C 68–24 Shaving was an every day affair
if I wanted to have a clean face. I was discussing my
problem with my friend. . .[he said]: 'I don't know
what you can do, b'y, unless you hammers it in and
clints it.' P 113–69 ~ To turn over the end of a nail protruding through a board, so that it holds firmly and
does not stick out.

clip v *EDD* ~ v¹ 2 for sense 1; *EDD* v² 20 for
sense 2.

1 To freeze; (literally, to seize).
T 398/9–67 Jesus, down there with the wind up northern, on the battycatters, and that cold (enough) to clip
you.

2 To take first choice of players in a game.
P 228–64 When leaders of teams discuss choosing of
team members the following exchange takes place: A:
I'll clip (that is, I'll choose first man). B: I'll call. A: I'll
take Tom. B: I'll take Dick. C: I'll take Harry.

clit n *EDD* ~ sb 4 Ha W. A tangle or knot (of
hair, twine); a confused heap.
1937 DEVINE 14 ~ A tangle of the hair, lines and
twines, or chains and anchors on the bottom of the harbour. In general confusion. C 67–13 You've got a clit in
your hair. C 69–1 My hair is full of clits because it's so
windy outside.

clitchin' n, usu pl Cp *OED* clitch v 2 'to crook,
bend a joint'; *EDD* clitch sb² 1 'groin; the fork
part of the leg or arm' Gl W Do. Groin; that part
of the leg behind the knee.
1937 DEVINE 14 ~ That point on the side of the body
indicating the right length of a shirt. T 222–66 This
friend was one day admiring a woman's hair as she was
brushing it, a patient. And the patient said, 'Oh that's
nothing now. You should have seen first when I was
married it came right down to my clitchin's. C 66–12
Wet in the clitchin's—used when someone got wet to
their knee joints either by rain or snow. P 229–66 The
thigh rubbers comes right up to his clitchin's.

clitty a *EDD* clit v 1 (3) ~ W. Of hair, etc, tangled, knotted or matted (P 48–60).

clobber n ['klæbəɹ, 'klɒbəɹ, 'klɔbəɹ]. Cp
DINNEEN clábar 'filth, mire, mud.' Untidy state;
sloppy or cluttered remains of some activity.
1955 ENGLISH 33 ~ An untidy state of things.
T 222–66 After such hearty meals your kitchen would
really be in a reeraw and you'd have to turn to and
clean up the clobber. 1968 KEATING 55–6 Sailors
jumped into the hold to spear strays on long-handled
fish forks and throw them back into the squirming mass
of cod. When they had tidied up the 'clobber,' all
hands stripped off the work gloves and threw them into
the sea.

clom See CLUM.

close a *EDD* ~ adj 4 for sense 1; SMYTH 192
close-aboard 'alongside' for phr in sense 2.

1 Of bread, heavy, close-textured; cp DUNCH¹.
T 80/2–64 They'd have this old-fashioned bakepot,
and the cover will be down and the bread will rise up to
the cover and [can't] expand any more, and it'd be a little bit close, but the taste of it was beautiful. 1971
NOSEWORTHY 184 Close bread [is] bread with too
much salt which has been kneaded too hard, and does
not rise very well.

2 Of sea-ice, packed in a dense floe.
[1907] 1979 *Nfld Qtly* Fall, p. 22 It would be impossible for them to get ahead unless we made a track for
them, ice is very close and heavy and we [in the
Adventure] can only make slow progress.

3 Phr *close aboard*: near, alongside.
1924 ENGLAND 314 Close aburd to dat. P 54–67 ~
Near to. 'Close aboard of the church.'
    close-reef breeze: stiff breeze.
1909 BROWNE 231 We left Chimney Tickle with a
flowing tide and a 'close-reef' breeze.
    close-rigged gear: in long-line fishing, lines
with hooks set closely together.
1963 TEMPLEMAN & FLEMING 7 The gear used in
[long-lining] experiments was of the same type, standard gear (50–52 hooks per line). . .some 'close rigged'
gear (80–82 hooks per line) and 'far-away' gear (33–34
hooks per line).

cloth n Comb **cloth pudding**: pudding made of
flour and water, sometimes with suet and raisins
added, boiled in a cloth bag; DUFF¹.
M 71–41 Dessert was usually a cloth pudding or duff,
served with molasses.

cloud n *OED* ~ 8 (1877); *DAE* (1875). Woman's woollen shawl or head-covering.
1893 *Christmas Greeting* 19 I next got into a 'boiled
shirt,' which the girls had decorated with ribbons and
rosettes, and with a large red and white 'cloud' tied
about my neck and then brought sash-wise about my
waist, my bodily 'rig' was complete. 1912 [ENGLISH] 62
Why did you not put that cloud about your neck and
shoulders, instead of round your arm? 1931 BYRNES 114
[These] were their staple purchases, supplemented by a

brightly colored 'cloud' for the 'missus.' 1937 DEVINE 14 ~ A woolen knitted scarf or shawl worn by women and girls. The corresponding thing worn by men is a *muffler*. P 24–67 Wrap this cloud around you to cover up your head. Q 67–64 ~ large wool scarf. 1972 MURRAY 155 In recent years 'bandanas' have been the standard head covering for girls and women during inclement weather. Prior to that older women wore 'the cloud' (a heavy square scarf).

club n A new or extra sole added to a boot or shoe (1937 DEVINE 14).

club v To put a new or extra sole on a boot or shoe.
1937 DEVINE 14 ~ To put an extra sole on a boot, which is then called 'club-soled.' T 199–65 Everybody had his iron last and his cobblin' box, and when the tap'd go on the shoe, out'd come the iron last and the hammer and the sprigs, going to club the shoes, they'd say, going to get 'em clubbed—that's a new sole put on 'em.

clum v also **clom** *EDD* ~ v 1 'to handle clumsily. . .to paw' Ha W Do D; cp GLAUM v. To grapple, grab with hands.
1937 DEVINE 14 ~ To close or tackle, as in a fight. 'They clum together.' Ibid 14 Clom. To clutch. 1955 ENGLISH 33 ~ to grapple with an adversary. C 71–38 Clummin'—used to describe playful wrestling, boxing or mock-fighting.

clum n also **clom**. Cp GLAUM n. Scuffle; physical grappling; fight.
1937 DEVINE 14 Clom. A tight embrace in wrestling. Ibid 14 They were in a clum. P 269–63 Let's have a clum—a little wrestling. P 109–70 No good comes out of carrying on. It usually leads to a clum, a little bit of a row.

clumber See CLUMPER.

clumper n also **clamper, clumber**. Cp *OED* ~ sb 1 'lump, mass' obs exc dial; *EDD* sb 1 'lump' W Do So; see also CLUMPET.
1 A small ice-berg; floating pan of ice; GROWLER.
1933 GREENE 61 This fine brig struck a heavy clumper of ice one stormy night with a big sea, and foundered at once with all hands. 1937 DEVINE 14 ~ A small floating ice-berg. [1954] 1972 RUSSELL 25 Our pan had broke up a lot durin' the night, and by daylight twas no more than a clumper—likely to roll over any minute. P 213–55 The boy fell in the water while hopping clampers. 1967 *Evening Telegram* 13 Mar, p. 3 Clumber: submerged, waterlogged ice that shows above the surface when the water is disturbed. M 69–14 Then with the approach of spring and thaw there would be a breaking up of the ice in the coves with ice pans which we called clampers. The boys of the community, sometimes half a dozen to each 'clamper,' depending on the size, would get on these 'clampers' and with a long stick manoeuvre them along the shoreline. 1976 *Daily News* 2 Mar, p. 3 Jumpin' clumpers was another

favourite pastime. In some places they call it copying on the bellycaters, and its known as fackying in parts of Conception Bay. All it means is jumping from one ice pan to another without falling into the water.
2 A hummock of ice in an ice-field.
1924 ENGLAND 54 'If you'm caught in a starm on de ice,' said bridge master Llewellen White, 'an' a lake breaks between you an' de ship so you can't get aburd, you build up a barricade o' clumpers an' make a fire.' 1944 LAWTON & DEVINE 93 Down the steep slippery sides and away, half running, half walking, each man making his own trail amongst the frozen clumpers. T 31/2–64 We come to the clumper, come to the [rifts] there now, where ice come together in the night [because of] that storm. 1976 *Decks Awash* v, 2 As boys, when the ice came in, we would sneak off after school and spend hours waiting for a 'blowing hole' just in hope to see maybe the whisker of a seal. We would search behind all the 'clumpers' (rafted ice) to make sure there was not a live seal hidden there.
3 A slab of ice forced up along the shoreline; formation of ice frozen on shore from action of waves and wind; cp BALLICATTER, esp variant BALLICLAMPER, etc.
C 67–13 Clumpers [are] chunks of hard ice found along the shore. P 207–67 We could see clumpers along the shore. 1971 NOSEWORTHY 184 Clumpers. Ice on shore and rocks from waves and salt spray.
4 A small chunk of ice or snow.
T 82/4–64 There's clumpers—about the size o' dumplin's. T 389–67[2] [You] get up on a big rafter an' heave clumpers at them. P 148–72 I was drivin' down the road, mindin' me own business, when these two fellers fired clumpers of snow at my car. So I went down the road, slewed around, came back and got in a ger|t| clum.
5 Attrib **clumper anchor**: iron chain with 'jigs' protruding at intervals, used to moor a boat to a small iceberg; ICE CLAW (P 243–65).

clumpet n also **clampet***. Cp *EDD* ~ sb 'clod of earth' Ha; *DC* Nfld (1835). See also CLUMPER. A large chunk of ice; a 'pan' of ice floating in a bay or harbour.
1836 [WIX][2] 51 I came. . .down a rapid brook, which had a fall of water in it, and marks of a recent freshet in immense 'clumpets' of ice, a yard and a half thick, which had been carried a hundred yards into the woods on each side. P 37 ~ large floating lump of ice. P 48–60 Clampet: ice-pan. P 118–67 In the spring the ice sometimes breaks up to form pans or sections which become free and floating. These are called clumpids. M 71–41 'Clumpet riding' was leaping from one ice pan to another, or rowing oneself along on one of them with a stick.

coach n Comb **coach box**: box for passenger, fastened on a 'komatik'; WOMAN BOX; KOMATIK ~ .
1887 *Telegram Christmas No* 5 Dinner is served, the dogs are harnessed, the 'komatik' brought to the door, and, enveloped in buffalo, bear, and other skins, with many injunctions to the drivers to take care of the rap-

ids, the rosy, laughing crowd are tucked in the coach-box, and, with one crack of the whip and signal to the head dog, they are gone. C 71–124 When komatiks were drawn by dogs, a wooden box, large enough for a man to lie down in, was put on the komatik especially to carry a sick person. This was called a coach box. 1973 GOUDIE 77 We loaded up the kamutik. The coachbox Jim built for me and the children was about six feet long. It was wider at the top than at the bottom to give me room to hold the children. . . The coachbox was covered over with canvas, something like those that were used for a horse and wagon. 1975 WHITELEY 268 The coach box was fastened to the komatik by cords and in it were placed a feather bed, pillows and rugs. The traveller was carefully tucked into the box.

coady n also **cody, codey, coly*** ['koʊdɪ, 'koʊdɪ, 'koˑədɪ]. *ADD* cody Nfld for sense 1.

1 A sweet sauce, often boiled molasses, served with 'duff' or boiled pudding.
1909 BROWNE 268 The 'sauce' served with the paste-ball is known as 'Codey.' 1925 *Dial Notes* v, 328 Cody—boiled molasses. 1933 GREENLEAF xxiv There would be steamed pudding—and molasses 'cody' (sauce). 1937 DEVINE 14 ~ Sauce, usually of boiled molasses to spread over puddings or dumplings. T 43/7–64 The coady is made from molasses with a bit of butter in, then a bit of flavouring. T 175/7–65 Then coady over the doughboys on the last—dessert. 1972 MURRAY 226 My mother used to make it with sugar, butter, water and vinegar. She'd cook it until it got thick. That was the cody she used to make. . . I make cody now, on times. And I make it with milk and sug-ar, a little water, vanilla and cornstarch. Other possi-bilities were vinegar and sugar mixed on the plate. In early days, molasses was frequently used.

2 Comb **coady dipper** ['koʊdɪ ˌdɪpəɹ]: metal container in which a sweet sauce is boiled and served; DIPPER.
T 80/2–64 The coady dipper was there, with lassie into un, and they took the coady dipper and lassied [the duff] right over.

coady duff [ˌkoʊdɪ 'dʌf, ˌkoʊdɪ 'dʌf, 'koʊdɪ ˌdʌf]: boiled pudding served with molasses; DUFF[1] (1924 ENGLAND 314).
T 178/9–65 Of course you'd have your coady duff.

coadys See COALIES.

coaker n Attrib **coaker engine, coaker**: gasoline fuelled engine used in fishing boats c1920, and named for Sir William Coaker, president of the Fishermen's Protective Union.
1940 SCAMMELL 6 "The Six Horse-Power Coaker": Now they cost quite a lot, so when she got hot, / We cooled off that Coaker by hand. C 69–2 Before the coaker engine was used in motor boats, the engines which were used were quite noisy and one could hear it for miles. With the introduction of the coaker engine the engine was a quiet 'chuck, chuck, chuck.' 1978 *Evening Telegram* 6 May, p. 6 I heard the doctor's boat leave the harbour. We kids knew the sound of all the engines in the place, especially the old 'Coaker.'

coalies n pl also **coadys** *ADD* ~ Nfld. Playing cards, esp the court cards (P 108–69).
1924 ENGLAND 179 Ahl he do is go sick, an' lay in bunk wid his hocks [boots] on, workin' de coaleys.

coarse a *EDD* ~ a 2. Of the weather, rough, stormy; DIRTY (P 98–57).
1895 *J A Folklore* viii, 37 A stormy day is *coarse*. 1909 BROWNE 64 The day is too 'coarse' (unfit) for fishing. 1924 ENGLAND 65 Black clouds of ill augury began to stream across the sky. The wind grew 'coarse'; presently deluges of rain drowned the world.

coast n *DC* ~ n 2 (1861–) for sense 1.
1 The shore-line of North America from Blanc Sablon to Cape Chidley, esp the areas of settle-ment and fishing; shortened form of *coast of Labrador* (see LABRADOR 1).
[1771] 1935 *Can Hist Rev* xvi, 57 Heathberrys and baking apples. . .are plenty all over the coast. 1774 *Trans Roy Soc* lxiv, 373 With a small vessel, and having an Indian with me, who knew of every rock and shoal upon the coast, I was enabled to be accurate in my observations. 1861 DE BOILIEU 58 [I was one day] in conversation with an old man who had resided on the coast fifty years. 1952 BANFILL 151 Coast mothers and wives have to face many stern realities with fortitude and calmness.
2 Attrib **coast fishery**: cod-fishery carried out in coastal waters; SHORE[1]: ~ FISHERY.
1839 TUCKER 83–4 The *Coast* and *Labrador Fisheries* are prosecuted in vessels of from 40 to 120 tons burthen, carrying a number of men, according to their respective sizes, in about the same proportion as the vessels on the Banks. 1870 *Stewart's Qtly* iv, 10–11 [France] does not care nearly so much for the coast fishery as for the bank fishery. . . It is probable that the quantity of fish caught by the French on *the shores* of Newfoundland, as distinct from the *banks*, does not exceed 100,000 quintals annually.

coast v To ship or transport (cargoes) between settlements in a 'coasting vessel.'
1936 SMITH 20 While coasting [around Conception Bay communities] we took on board 1,100 quintals of shore fish and a deck load of herring, and sailed for St John's and discharged our cargo at Baine Johnston & Co. 1975 BUTLER 70 He operated coasting vessels, pas-senger boats and he had some vessels of one hundred and twenty tons to one hundred and forty tons in the foreign coasting trade coasting salt bulk fish to Lunen-berg and Halifax and bringing back coal and produce from Sydney and Prince Edward Island. 1978 *Evening Telegram* 8 Sep, p. 2 After its construction at Port Union, the *Swile* spent about a dozen years at the seal hunt. . .and then went 'coasting' with a crew of six men, bringing supplies to various parts of Newfound-land and Labrador.

coastal a Phr *coastal boat*, ~ *steamer*: a vessel carrying passengers, mail and supplies to desig-nated settlements around Newfoundland and on the Labrador; BAY BOAT.

1869 HOWLEY *MS Reminiscences* 1 We left St John's [in June] in the old steamer *Ariel*, the first coastal steamer employed to convey mails and passengers around the island. . . She made alternate trips north and south about once every month, during summer. 1906 LUMSDEN 165 But the most frequent, as by far the most prized, ripples of excitement were occasioned by the regular weekly call of the coastal boat. T 43/4–64 We brought this man to Hopedale [Labrador] to have him ready for the coastal boat (that) came down from St John's. 1976 *Evening Telegram* 23 Mar, p. 1 The [Canadian National] coastal boat *Petit Forte* was towed into St John's harbor last night after the vessel's steering jammed and her rear compartment flooded.

coasting vbl n *OED* ~ vbl sb 1 (1679–1796) for sense 1; *DAE* ~ schooner (1775–), ~ trade (1802–), ~ vessel (1794–) for combs. in sense 2.
1 Sailing between settlements around the coast for trading purposes.
1861 DE BOILIEU 174 The summer of this year I was much employed in coasting, and mixed much with the Irish. 1944 LAWTON & DEVINE 74 He had his own schooner, and after a few voyages to Labrador, took up coasting, in which he was actively engaged for nearly half a century. 1953 *Nfld Fish Develop Report* 21 Over half the families obtained income averaging about $250 a year, from a variety of other kinds of work; in fish and wood-product plants, boat-building, carpentry, road construction, 'coasting,' trucking, making handicraft articles and providing rooms or board. T 141/67–65 There was no coasting to be done because nearly all the mercantile businesses had coasters of their own to keep their trade going.
2 Attrib, comb **coasting crew**: seamen shipped aboard a coastal trading vessel.
1977 *Nfld Qtly* Winter, p. 17 A 'coastin' crew' of five men were busy in Grand Bank cleaning, painting and fumigating the *Conrad* while he was in St John's.
coasting schooner: see **coasting vessel**.
1872 DASHWOOD 247 At that season the traffic is carried on by coasting schooners, with the exception of one steamer, which makes two or three trips during the year. 1973 HORWOOD 60 Had he not accepted the position of Master of the *Marie Spindler*, which was in fact a coasting schooner, he might have been Mate of the *General Gough* on that voyage from which she never returned.
coasting skipper: master of a coastal trading vessel; SKIPPER.
1942 *Little Bay Islands* 20 George, son of John—Fish Culler; Son of John—Coasting Skipper.
coasting trip: see **coasting voyage**.
1944 LAWTON & DEVINE 74 He was well known all over the country, as his coasting trips took him to all parts of Newfoundland.
coasting vessel: a vessel, usu a schooner, engaged in trading between coastal settlements.
1832 MCGREGOR i, 184 In this number, neither the coasting nor sealing vessels, about 350, are taken into account. 1881 *Nineteenth Century* ix, 88 The regular fortnightly steamer did not call in anywhere near our destination, and day after day passed without any coasting vessel sailing in that direction. 1932 BARBOUR

13 In the case of the *Neptune II*, unlike many, in fact most of our coasting vessels, the hull was, even with the hold full of freight, well out of water. 1975 BUTLER 50 All my father's years at sea were spent as mate and sometimes cook on various banking and coasting vessels.
coasting voyage: a passage between settlements for trading purposes.
1861 DE BOILIEU 176 While afloat on a coasting and trading voyage, I visited some old friends in St Michael's Bay.

cobbler n Comb **cobbler's house**: point of intersection of arcs of a boat-builder's compasses as he plots the shape of timbers or planks (P 127–75).

cobblestone n *OED* ~ 'water-worn rounded stone.' Attrib **cobblestone wall**: the wall of a dwelling or other structure built with round stones collected from a beach.
1897 *J A Folklore* x, 204 *Cob* or *cob-wall*, in Devonshire and Cornwall, denotes a wall built of a mixture of clay and straw, but in Newfoundland one built with round stones and clay, which, however, is more frequently spoken of as a cobble stone.

cobby (house) n also **cob, cobs, coopy house, copy (house)**. Cp *OED* cubby: ~ hole, ~ house 'little house built by children.' See also COOPY 'to squat.' A small building; a place on the ground outlined with rocks. Cp also COPY v, another children's activity.
P 163–63 The girls there would ask me if I wanted to cobby with them in their cobby-house. 1966 PHILBROOK 141 A very popular diversion is 'playing copy house.' P 210–69 Let's play copy. C 71–5 A cob is a playhouse in the woods, roughly built. C 71–45 Whenever the girls played house they would refer to it as 'playin' cobbies' or 'playin' cobs.' 1972 MURRAY 120 Girls often held their 'copyhouses,' '[cobby] houses' (i.e. playhouses) in the rocks just above the dash of the sea.

cock n Cp *OED* sb[1] 21 b 'male'; *DC* cock and hen (Nfld: 1842); phr prob an extension of *OED* hen sb 6 (1603–).
1 Phr *cock and hen*: soft-shell clam, used as bait (*Mya arenaria*); fresh-water clam; GLAM.
1842 JUKES ii, 190 The animals of this species. . .are called 'cocks and hens' by the fishermen, who sometimes use them as bait for the cod. 1895 *J A Folklore* viii, 34 Freshwater clams, *cocks and hens*. 1977 RUSSELL 173 We dug up clams and cocks and hens till even these were gone. But still no squids, so in despair we give it up for good. 1979 TIZZARD 290 I would be sent in the bottom when the water was low to dig 'cocks and hens,' a small clam, or to pick mussels along the shoreline.
2 Comb **cock caplin**: male 'caplin.'
1861 NOBLE 157 The males and females of these delicate fishes, (capelin) are called here, very comically, cocks and hens. 1966 SCAMMELL 45 My brother

hooked a cock-caplin out of one ear and a small thole-pin out of the other.

cock indian: male 'Beothuk' indian.

1792 PULLING MS Aug The Indian men are as often called *Cock Indians* by those gentlemen salmon catchers and furriers as they are called anything else.

cockabaloo n Cp *OED* cock sb[1] 7 'leader, head,' as cock of the school. A bully.

1924 ENGLAND 251 'But be glory, ye're goin' to hell, de day!' says de feller as chased me, comin' up. De cockabaloo o' de whole settlement, he was.

cocket n Haycock; POOK.

1622 PURCHAS xix, 444 Meadow of about three Acres: it flourished lately with many cockets of good Hay.

cocksel* See COXSWAIN.

cock shot n also **cod shot*** *OED* ~ (1842, 1884). A target at which to throw a missile; a shot at the target.

1875 HOWLEY MS Reminiscences 69 I saw the bottle so placed and by way of a joke, took up a stone and calling out to the others, 'boys, there's a fine cock shot,' pretended I was going to have a shy at it. C 71–86 [The cod-shot] is placed at a distance for the purpose of throwing stones at it. It is sometimes a tin can, placed on a post or left on the ground. Also, if a worker was standing around, wasting his time, his boss might say to him, 'Stop standing there like a cod shot.' P 245–76 I took a cock shot at the tin can on the fence.

cocksiddle v also **cocksettle***, **cocksdiddle**, etc. *EDD* cock sb[1] (58) cock-steddling Ha; cockshed-dle, cocksettle IW So. To turn a somersault; to fall down and over.

P 131–70 A woman watching boys turn somersaults said, 'Oh look at them cockstiddle!' 1971 NOSEWORTHY 185 Cocksdiddle, cocksettle, cocksid-dle. To jump head over heels; to somersault. Q 71–8 Cocksiddle—to turn somersaults, usually used in the form 'cocksiddly over.' Q 71–17 Cockstiddle. To turn suddenly or fall down.

cod[1] n A football.

1898 *The Record* 14 The name Rugby Football is known here as 'Kicking the Cod' and 'Rushing the Waddock.' M 71–91 [In] 'kick the cod,' the cod was a ball about the size of a football, though of a different shape. It was made of pieces of old cloth and covered with a piece of tarpaulin or any other type of strong and durable material.

cod[2] n also **codd, codde; cod-fish**. See *MED* ~ (2) (b) (1273; 1399); *OED* sb[3] 1 (1357–), cod-fish (1565–), *DAE* (1616–), codfish (1630–) for sense 1; for combs. in sense 3: *OED* sb[3] 4: ~ fishery (1753–), *DAE* (1735–); *O Sup*[2] ~ fishing (1632–); *DC* ~ flake (Nfld: 1907); PARTRIDGE ~ hauler (19c Nfld); *DC* ~ jigger Nfld (1958); ~ jigging Nfld (1964); *OED* sb[3] 4 ~ line (Nfld:

1794); ~ oil (1868); *OED* cod's head 1 for sense (a); *DC* ~ stage Nfld (1861).

1 The common North Atlantic salt-water fish (*Gadus morhua*), since the sixteenth century the principal object of the commercial fishery in Newfoundland, where the common synonym is FISH n; freq with defining word BANK, RED, ROCK, SHORE[1], TOM COD, etc.

[1583] 1940 *Gilbert's Voyages & Enterprises* ii, 406 [Hayes' narrative] With incredible quantities, and no lesse varietie of kindes of fish in the sea and fresh waters, as Trouts, Salmons and. . .also Cod, which alone draweth many nations thither, and is become the most famous fishing of the world. 1620 WHITBOURNE 38 And it is well approved by all those that yeerely fish for Ling, Codde, and Herrings. . .that salt orderly boyled in such manner, doth much better preserve fish. [1663] 1963 YONGE 60 The middle or end of June came the capling, a small sweet fish and the best bait, and when they come we have the best fishing, the cods pursuing them so eager that both have run ashore. [1786] 1792 CARTWRIGHT iii [sig A 2ᵛ] "Labrador: A Poetical Epistle": The codfish now in shoals come on the coast, / (A Fish'ry this, our Nation's chiefest boast). 1875 JEVONS 27 Dried codfish have acted as currency in. . .Newfoundland [*OED*]. 1911 ROGERS 209 The central object in an allegorical picture which symbolized Newfoundland would be the cod-fish, and around it would be grouped its favourite bait the herring, the caplin. . .and the squid. 1955 DOYLE (ed) 30 "I'se The B'y": Codfish in the spring o' the year / Fried in mag-goty butter. 1972 JENSEN 4 Cod are winter spawners and each female sheds between 3 and 9 million eggs, depending on the size of the fish.

2 Proverb, prov phr *as cold as a cod's nose* (1937 DEVINE 63); *cod-fish is cod by name and by nature* (Q 67–9); *no cod, no cash* (1895 *Christmas Review* 12).

3 Attrib, comb, cpd **cod-bag**: net in which cod are kept in the water until they can be loaded on vessel or towed ashore for processing; BAG.

1872 *Times* 13 Mar, p. 3 [American Net and Twine Co ad] Cod Bags. [1886] LLOYD 62 The catch of fish is removed from the seine and placed in the boat. . . If a larger number is enclosed than can be taken ashore in the seine boat at once, the remaining fish are placed in what are known as 'cod bags,' which resemble cabbage nets in all but the size, and safely moored until they can be taken ashore to be dressed and cured. 1936 SMITH 124 We loaded our boat and put the balance [of the trap catch] in the cod bag, which we tied fast to our friends' stage-head. 1953 *Nfld & Lab Pilot* ii, 425 Cod-bag or Tinker Share island is situated about three-quarters of a mile north-eastward of Murr island. T 82/3–64 That was his work—bring in fish from the cod-bag. You'd bag your fish in the morning and that man'd bring in the fish. 1977 BURSEY 193 Our men came in with two boatloads of fish from that trap and had left another two boatloads in a cod-bag tied onto the trap. 1979 *Evening Telegram* 5 Mar, p. 4 The project. . .is aimed at producing cod bags for fish unloading purposes, which will serve to improve the quality of landed fish.

cod blubber: cod livers, rendered for their oil; BLUBBER.

[1771] 1792 CARTWRIGHT i, 90 I baited the traps and deathfalls with salt-fish and seal's flesh fried in cod-blubber. 1832 MCGREGOR i, 225 Whatever water is mixed with the cod blubber, is afterwards allowed to run out by a plug-hole at the bottom, while the oil, floating on the top, runs off at different holes, and is guided into casks by leather spouts. 1885 *Harper's* lxxi, 657 A hogshead of herrings. . .[is] protected from the flies and the air by a layer of cod blubber—the livers after the oil has been extracted. P 9–73 The boiler was filled about one-third full with the lye and codfish blubber enough added to bring it up to about two-thirds full. The blubber would be a year or more old.

cod-fish: to engage in the fishery for cod.

T 270–66 An' then soon as [the lobster fishery is over] they cod-fishes. . .and the money's always coming in.

cod-fishery: principal commercial fishery in which cod are taken by various means according to season and types of available bait; FISHERY.

[1810] 1971 ANSPACH 20 In the cod-fishery, which, in this Bay begins about the 10th June, and ends between the 20th and the last of October, fish is taken either with jiggers, or with hooks furnished with Bait. 1837 BLUNT 59 The Bay of Islands was formerly much frequented by vessels in the cod fishery, and stages were erected at Small Bay. 1898 *Christmas Bells* 14 Skipper Tom. . .and three other hardy fishers were 'fit-out,' as usual, by Mr Hardfist, to prosecute the codfishery.

cod-fishing: the prosecution of the chief commercial fishery of Newfoundland.

1620 WHITBOURNE 11 But the chiefe commodity of *New-found-land*. . .is the Cod-fishing upon that Coast, by which our Nation and many other Countries are enrich. [1876] 1977 WHITELEY 38 On August 15, 1876 Whiteley made application to the Department of Fisheries 'For leave to set a pound net for cod fishing at Bonne Espérance Harbour.' 1978 *Evening Telegram* 4 Mar, p. 2 The Fortune trawlers were returning with more than 300,000 pounds of cod a trip until cod fishing was closed in the Gulf of St Lawrence.

cod-fish weather: foggy, chill weather associated with the appearance of cod in coastal waters in June and July; CAPLIN WEATHER.

1912 CABOT 81 It was true 'codfish weather,'—fog, the wind on the shore, the air rawness itself.

cod flake: platform built on poles and spread with boughs for drying split and salted cod-fish; FLAKE.

1845 *Fraser's Mag* xxxii, 740 The 'breath of the sweet south,' blowing fresh from the waters, passes over the 'cod-flakes,' and becomes tainted with the sickening odour. 1907 MILLAIS 5 On one side of the beautiful harbour are endless cod-flakes and a few sealing vessels.

cod hauler: fisherman; epithet for a man engaged in the Newfoundland cod-fishery.

[1794] 1968 THOMAS 155–6 In her early days she had been much used to the Bon Ton, altho now the Wife of a Newfoundland Codd Hauler. 1924 ENGLAND 258 'Gi' lang wid ye!' the old man retorted. 'Ye lang, slinky cod

hauler, wid legs crooked as a rainbow an' I dare say webbed feet on ye.' 1952 *Atlantic Advocate* Mar, p. 49 He remembers too, when Newfoundlanders began to sneer good-humoredly at Nova Scotians as 'bluenoses' and the Scotians retaliated with 'cod haulers' for the Newfoundlanders.

cod jigger: unbaited hook set in lead sinker, pulled up sharply to take cod; JIGGER.

[1810] 1971 ANSPACH 21 [Squids are taken with] a lead in the shape of a small inverted cone, having round the thickest end six or eight pieces of iron bent and sharpened in the form of fish hooks, and used in the same manner as the cod-jigger. 1877 ROCHFORT 101 [advertisement] Richard Neyle, 234 Water Street, Sign of Kettle and Cod Jigger. Q 67–46 ~ unbaited piece of lead with two hooks used to [take fish].

cod-jigging: fishing for cod with a weighted, unbaited hook attached to a line and jerked sharply upward; JIGGING.

1965 RUSSELL 152 I knew that cod-jigging was an archaic method of catching fish.

cod-line: stout 18-thread line used in the fishery for cod.

[1775] 1792 CARTWRIGHT ii, 127–8 On searching my pockets, I found a fathom of cod-line, one end of which I tied to a small birch tree, which grew close to the top [of the cliff and] eased myself down over the edge. [1828] 1956 FAY 101 I send a newspaper by John Louis, a cod line and £18.

cod-net: twine net placed vertically in the water to enmesh cod by the head and gills ; gill-net.

1868 HOWLEY *MS Reminiscences* 8 The people of this place. . .use nothing but bultows and codnets. [1892] 1896 *Consolidated Statutes of Nfld* 918 No cod-net shall be set on any of the fishing grounds of this Colony or its dependencies at a less distance than fifty fathoms from the nearest point of any cod-trap or cod-net previously set. 1907 MILLAIS 152 Cod-nets are of somewhat different construction, the mesh being small, only 6 inches. They are about 100 fathoms long, and are about 20 feet deep. Weights are attached to the bottom, and they are sunk in from 18 to 20 fathoms of water. The cod run their heads into the net, and get their gills entangled. These nets are hauled once a day, and contain from a few fish to 10 quintals. 1937 DEVINE 75 This might be codnet fish or bultow fish. T 25–64 Cod-nets are just a straight net put out like a salmon net or a herring net. 1975 BUTLER 58 Fishermen [in Placentia Bay] commenced using cod nets about 1875. They knit their own nets with hemp twine fifty or sixty fathoms long, thirty or forty meshes deep, a rope on both edges with lead weights on the foot and corks on the head. These nets were set with one end attached to a stake driven in the crevice of the land and the other end attached to an anchor with corks to keep the head of the net afloat. As time went on fishermen sank their nets to the bottom on the fishing grounds.

cod oil: oil obtained from cod livers by natural or artificial processes and used for curing leather, illumination and medicinal purposes; cod-liver oil.

[1776] 1792 CARTWRIGHT ii, 214 We trimmed and

finished the cod-oil, and landed goods. [1794] 1968
THOMAS 173 From Ten to Forty pounds is given, with a
free Passage out, and some petty gratuitys are sometimes admit'd, such as a Cask of Codd Sounds, a Cask
of Codd Oil, a few Quintals of Fish. [1812] 1895
PROWSE 403 Price of cod oil. . .£38 sterling per ton.
1900 *Tribune Christmas No* 7 Suddenly a weird screech
seemed to fill the air, the dogs growled and whined, the
cod-oil gave a flicker and went out, leaving the room in
darkness, excepting for the firelight. 1904 *Daily News*
18 July . . .our Knight of the realm, / With a *cod* on his
crest, that the *cod oil* light showed, / And a 'cowld storage' steamer with Ned at her helm. 1937 JUNEK 33 Left
exposed to the sun and air the liver eventually decom-
poses; the stroma sinks to the bottom; and the oil rises
to the surface. This is essentially what we know as cod-
liver oil, though in an unrefined state; the folk, however, refer to it simply as cod oil. 1944 LAWTON &
DEVINE 16 Cod-oil and candles were the illuminants till
the introduction of the kerosene lamp in the year 1870.
T 34/8–64 In the morning you'd have to dip [the frostbitten fingers] in the cod-oil and put fresh liver on your
hands. 1975 BUTLER 63 Grandfather had a cooper shop
with coopers making herring barrels, cod oil casks and
other barrels.

cod seine: see COD-SEINE.

cod's head: (a) the head of a cod-fish, esp used
as fertilizer; the fleshy part of the head eaten as a
delicacy; cp CHEEK, FACE, JOWL, SCULP(S); (b) a
type of woollen mitten.
1626 [VAUGHAN] *The Golden Fleece* 20 Some of the
Dunkirkes may take their progresse into your
Britanniol, to. . .glut their greedy throats with cods-
heads. [1771] 1935 *Can Hist Rev* xvi, 56 [The Eskimo]
liked the scalps of the raw cods heads best. 1813
CARSON 14–15 In the neighbourhood of all the fishing
harbours, a considerable quantity of excellent manure
may be procured from the sea weed, cods' heads, and
the refuse of the seal blubber. 1846 TOCQUE 60 On
going into a stage after night, I have often seen it
appear as if being on fire, from the luminosity of the
cods-heads. 1883 HATTON & HARVEY 271 [exports:]
300 barrels cods'-heads, at $1. 1929 BURKE [7] "The
Wedding in Renews": The men will make the table
groan, / And everything in style, / They'll have Cod's
Heads / And Oatmeal, Fat Pork and Castor Oil.
P 224–66 My mother is knitting me some cod's heads.
C 70–28 A type of mitt that has only one digit on it (for
the thumb) is called a cod's head. 1977 *Evening
Telegram* 25 Jan, p. 5 [advertisement] Salt Cod Heads.

cod sound: air-bladder, or gelatinous sac
attached to the backbone of cod-fish, removed
during splitting and salted as a delicacy; SOUND.
[1794] 1968 THOMAS 173 Some petty gratuitys are
sometimes admit'd, such as a Cask of Codd Sounds.
1861 (Mrs) BEETON 119–20 Cod sounds. These are the
air or swimming bladders, by means of which the fishes
are enabled to ascend or descend in the water. In the
Newfoundland fishery they are taken out previous to
incipient putrefaction, washed from their slime and
salted for exportation. 1977 *Evening Telegram* 25 Jan,
p. 5 [advertisement] Salt Cod Sounds.

cod stage: elevated platform on shore on which

cod are landed and processed before drying;
STAGE.
[1774] 1792 CARTWRIGHT ii, 17 I went to Great Caribou and fixed on a spot for building a cod-stage next
spring. 1792 ibid *Gloss* i, x ~ a covered platform,
which is built, projecting over the water, to split and
salt codfish in. 1861 DE BOILIEU 29 In large establishments the cod-stage is usually a permanent building
built over the water, with generally a good depth of
water in front, in which is cast the offal of the fish.

cod(s) tongue: the tongue or hyoid apparatus
of the cod-fish, much prized for its glutinous
jelly-like consistency and delicate flavour when
lightly fried; TONGUE.
[1771] 1792 CARTWRIGHT i, 170 In the morning Condon came up and brought some cod tongues and
sounds. 1842 BONNYCASTLE ii, 179 Cod, mackerel,
herrings, caplin, cods' tongues and
sounds. . .constitute the chief items of export. 1854
[FEILD] 26 He provided us with an excellent repast of
Labrador delicacies, fried salmon and cod's tongues.
1941 SMALLWOOD 272 [list of exports] Cod Tongues,
Fresh 1,740 lbs. . . Salted 1,728 lbs. 1977 *Evening
Telegram* 25 Jan, p. 5 [advertisement] Fresh Frozen
Cod Tongues.

cod trap: see COD TRAP.

codey See COADY.

codge n *EDD* ~ sb 3 'muddle.' A tangle; CLIT
(Q 67–48).
P 243–56 ~ A tangle in fishing lines.

cod-seine n See also SEINE.
1 A large net, up to 600 feet (182.8 m) in
length, set around a school of cod, the 'foots'
drawn together to form a bag, and hauled at sea
or in shallow water near the shore; freq in place-
names.
[1775] 1792 CARTWRIGHT ii, 92 We had fish for the
haul this morning, and I never saw so fine a place for a
cod-sein; the bottom being smooth, white sand, with
an extensive beach of the same. [1775] 1895 PROWSE
342 Codd Seans we deem a great nuizance as by them
we destroy a great quantity of small fish. 1861 NOBLE
48 That heavy cod-seine, a hundred fathoms long, sank
the stern of our barge rather deeply, and made it row
heavily. [1885] 1897 *Nfld Law Reports* 100 [He] was
engaged. . .in the capacity of master of cod-seine, and
as such delivered to two ship masters, who collected
fish for defendants at Labrador, a large quantity of fish.
1907 MILLAIS 152 A cod-seine is a long net 102 to 130
fathoms of still smaller mesh, 4 inches in the centre and
5 at both ends. It is coiled in the stern of a small boat,
and two men cast it out as the boat is rowed in a circle.
The men, by means of a water-glass, see the school of
fish before casting their net, and are sometimes very
successful at this method of fishing. The cod-seine can
be cast several times during the day. 1937 *Seafisheries
of Nfld* 33 A cod-seine is a net about 120 fathoms long
and about ten or twelve fathoms deep with ropes and
corks at the head and ropes and leads at the foot. It is
used to encircle a shoal of fish, and when closed forms

a bag net, from which the fish are taken. This type of net is not in use today for cod, but smaller types are used for catching bait fishes. 1953 *Nfld & Lab Pilot* ii, 354 A shoal bank, with a depth of 15 feet over it, extends half a cable offshore from Cod Seine cove. T 25–64 They used what they called cod-seines. They was a huge affair. Go where the fish were plentiful and they'd shoot the seine. They'd have two boats at this and they'd shoot the seine right round, then pull it in till they'd get it nearly into the beach and draw it up by pulling up the foot ropes. T 82/3–64 A cod-seine is a huge long net with small linnet in the middle, and as you goes on in what they call the arms is bigger linnet [or mesh]. T 75/6–64 When a man would haul the fish with a cod-seine, he'd haul the seine in the stern of his boat. P 9–73 The cod-seine. . .was a straight net. It was set from an oar-propelled boat, into the stern of which it had been piled. It was used in shallow water about five or six fathom deep. It was shot (set) in a circular shape, so that the last end overboard could be brought near enough to the first end, so that both ends would be on board for hauling purposes.

2 Attrib **cod-seine boat**: see **cod-seine skiff**.

[1877] 1898 *Nfld Law Reports* 147 [The men were] distributed by the defendant, seven with himself to a cod-seine boat, and five under plaintiff. . .in a hook-and-line boat. 1936 SMITH 19 We put the bottoms in our traps there, and painted up our trap boat and cod seine boat. T 82/3–64 A cartail boat would come from the cod-seine boat [and deliver the fish to shore].

cod-seine crew: six or more men engaged to fish with a cod-seine under the direction of a 'seine master.'

1877 TOCQUE 293 [The catch] of a cod seine crew amounted, for the season. . .to 1,200 quintals. 1976 CASHIN 1 My father. . .was one of the trap crew or cod seine crew with his father.

cod-seine fishery: the prosecution of the cod-fishery with seines.

[1863] 1954 INNIS 397 We, the undersigned memorialists in our time have carried on a hook-and-line fishery for such a great number of years and for want of fish to pay the expense of such fishery were compelled to abandon the same and adopt the cod seine fishery.

cod-seine fishing: prosecuting the cod-fishery with seines.

1975 BUTLER 50 At the age of fourteen, he went to sea in a vessel cod-seine fishing at Golden Bay near Cape St Mary's.

cod-seine skiff: large, undecked fishing boat used to set and haul cod-seines in the coastal fishery; see also SKIFF.

[1832] 1981 *Them Days* vi (4), p. 37 Got 2 cod seine skifts in order & took in the seines, bent the new boats sails. 1854 [FEILD] 93 As it would have been impossible to have clambered over the rocks and through the woods in the dark, we were rowed back by six stout fishermen in a cod-seine skiff. 1887 BOND 73 Anyhow, I've got a couple of cod-seine skiffs myself, and there are four other boats from the harbour, and we're going to try. . .if we can find any tidings of them. [1900 OLIVER & BURKE] 69 "An Outharbour Merchant Writes for a Wife": He wants a girl. . . / Can take her seat in a codseine [skiff], / When the fish is on the

ground. 1906 LUMSDEN 55 If confined to the Arm and when the day was fine, a punt (in Newfoundland a keeled rowboat of peculiar native construction) and one man sufficed; if out in the bay to Deer Harbor, a 'cod-seine skiff' and half a dozen men might be needed. T 210–65 He used to build those big cod-seine skiffs [for] working cod seine. And this skiff would be around thirty feet long, and probably eight feet wide.

cod-sock See COSSOCK*.

cod trap n *DC* ~ n Nfld (1904–). See also TRAP[1].

1 A type of fixed fishing-gear used in inshore waters, box-shaped with a length of net stretching from shore to entrance through which cod enter and are trapped.

1868 HOWLEY *MS Reminiscences* 12 A man named Doyle, of Gooseberry, found a large whale dead in his cod trap. [1875] 1936 SMITH 15 The month of May, 1875, soon arrived and Labrador time. It was not a matter of choice, for I was compelled to go to try and earn something for my mother and family, so I went again with my brother-in-law, and this summer we had a cod-trap, the first coming of cod-traps. [1883] 1898 *Nfld Law Reports* 494 [They] were engaged in hauling their own cod-trap, when they discovered another cod-trap. . .afloat, adrift from its moorings. [1892] 1896 *Consolidated Statutes of Nfld* 918 No cod-trap shall be set on any of the fishing grounds of this Colony or its dependencies at a less distance than eighty fathoms from the nearest point of any cod-trap previously set. [1899] 1977 WHITELEY 40 Looking over my records I find that 1871 was the year that I first fished 'the cod trap.' For three years previous I had used Salmon Nets (6 inch mesh) reaching the bottom for the purpose of meshing codfish when schooling—finding this worked well the bottom or 'trap' was first tried in 1871 with great success. 1907 MILLAIS 152 In shape a cod-trap is very like a house, with a large door at which the fish can enter. In the water it is 15 fathoms square on the ground plan, and 10 to 12 fathoms deep, the mesh of the net being 7 inches. The trap is set in 10 to 12 fathoms of water, and a long net stretching landwards, and called a 'leader,' guides the fish in at the front door. Once they go in they seldom return. This effective trap is hauled up twice a day. [1929] 1933 GREENLEAF (ed) 251 "Change Islands Song": The weather still got hotter, plenty nippers, flies and stout; / A decision they arrived at and a cod-trap was put out. 1937 *Seafisheries of Nfld* 29 The gear most favoured by the Shore fishermen are cod-traps, cod-nets, hand lines, trawls and jiggers. T 25–64 Then fish became scarcer and the cod-trap was invented—a square affair with a twine bottom in it and a doorway where the fish go in, and when they get in they can't get out. 1980 *Evening Telegram* 20 Sep, p. 1 Catches are still very good and fishermen are still using cod traps in places such as Black Tickle.

2 Attrib, comb **cod-trap berth**: position on inshore fishing grounds, assigned by custom or lot; BERTH.

P 102–60 The *Tommie* proceeded around the island to the next codtrap berth and repeated the same operation. 1977 *Inuit Land Use* 169 Fishermen used the same cod trap berths every year. A berth belonged to the man who had first set his trap there and had continually used it since.

cod-trap crew: three to six men engaged on the share system to fish under a 'skipper' with cod-traps; CREW.

1953 *Nfld Fisheries Develop Report* 15 The cod-trap crews in the areas surveyed have capital assets valued at nearly $3,000, on the average, while the assets of line-fishing crews are well under $800.

cod-trap fishery: prosecution of the inshore fishery for cod using a stationary net or trap.

1979 *Evening Telegram* 6 Mar, p. 2 The federal department indicates that persons who have traditionally fished as operators in the codtrap fishery, even though they may have small businesses such as trucking. . .and the like, and are considered fishermen, provided they operate the boat and gear themselves, 'should be given a draw.'

cod-trap linnet: twine 'knitted' into meshes to form a trap; cp LINNET.

1977 *Evening Telegram* 28 Apr, p. 42 Tenders are invited for the purchase. . .of approximately 1000 lbs. of Cod Trap linnet.

cod-trap season: summer months when cod appear in schools in inshore water.

1979 *Evening Telegram* 6 Mar, p. 2 To be eligible for a draw, a cod-trap operator must 'not be employed outside the fishery during the cod-trap season.'

cod-trap twine: hemp, cotton or nylon thread used in 'knitting' cod-trap; TWINE.

P 9–73 A leaf of cod trap twine is set up at ninety-eight meshes and knit long enough to reach the required depth or width as the case may be.

cogrovice* v ['kɑgrə‚vɐis]. To gossip, yarn.

P 27–80 To young people: 'What are ye cogrovicing about?'

coish See COSH.

colcannon n also **caulcannon** [kɑl'kænən, kɑl'kænə, kɒl'kænən, kɔl'kænən, 'kɒ‧lkænən]. Cp *OED* ~ 'an Irish dish' (1774–); DINNEEN cál ceannfhionn 'cabbage, etc, dressed up with butter, etc.' A mixture or hash of various vegetables, and sometimes meat, eaten on Hallowe'en; hence attrib **colcannon night**; SNAP-APPLE NIGHT.

1896 *Dial Notes* i, 378 Colcannon night: almost universal in St John's, Nfld, for Hallowe'en. The name is used by those who eat colcannon on that night. Others speak of it as 'snap-apple night.' The term Hallowe'en is not generally used. 1931 BYRNES 120 Remember how on Hallowe'en you ate 'caulcannon' till you nearly burst, in the fond hope, if you were a maid, of finding the button, or if you were a youth, in constant fear of finding the button, which doomed you to irrevocable bachelorhood? 1937 DEVINE 14 ~ The seven kinds of vegetables boiled in one pot and served on Hallowe'en. T 34–64 We had colcannon. We used to have our bit of cabbage, have our big feed of pork and cabbage, you know, and rabbit and perhaps a piece of fresh pork.

T 347/50–67 Hallowe'en, or snap-apple night, or colcannon night.

collar n Cp *OED* ~ sb 12 'eye in the end or bight of a shroud or stay' naut (1626–) for sense 1; *OED* sb 8: out of collar (1862) and v 2 'to break in to work' (1750–), PARTRIDGE collar, in—out of; collared up (1850–) for phr in sense 3.

1 An anchor, chain and rope attached by means of a loop or bight to a buoy and to bow of boat and used to moor the craft in a harbour; freq with defining word BOAT, *mooring*, etc. Cp RODE.

[1894] P 265²–75 Rainy—landed salt—hauled up boats—took up collars. 1895 *Christmas Review* 18 The larger boats [were] tarred and cleaned up, swinging from their 'collars,' ready to start to the fishing grounds. 1957 *Daily News* 19 July, p. 4 Fifty or more trap skiffs may be seen at the collars in the little harbour. T 14–64 I have mooring, an anchor, out for my boat, see, that runs off from the wharf on a piece of larger rope, tied on the main rope for to go over the stem-head. The piece you put over the stem-head you generally [call] the collar. 1966 FARIS 235 During the summer, boats (especially trap vessels) are moored on a 'collar' (a heavy chain anchored to the bottom by large schooner anchors—the chain being raised by means of an attached buoyed rope) just off shore. C 65–10 Collar is used when referring to the means used to moor a boat off shore in the harbour. This is usually a killick with one end of a rope or chain fastened to it. This is thrown into the water about thirty yards from shore. The other end of the chain or rope stays afloat by means of a large stick or buoy. Collar refers to all three items, killick, rope and stick. 1979 TIZZARD 96 But during the fall of the year we put out a mooring collar in the bottom of the cove and moored the boat there until freeze up time, around the end of December.

2 Location where a boat is anchored; BERTH; usu in phr *on the collar*.

[c1900] 1978 *RLS* 8, p. 25 ~ a place near shore where boats are moored for safety. A boat is said then to be on the collar. 1915 HOWLEY 269 Several of the then oldest inhabitants remembered the depredations committed by the Indians as late as 1775. They came at night and stole the sails and other articles from a boat on the collar, as well as all the gear they could lay hands upon. 1937 DEVINE 14 The place where a fishing boat is anchored for the night or Sunday, just a few yards from the stage, is called the *collar*, from the bight of rope or chain that goes over the stem-head. 'Putting the boat on the collar' is really 'putting the collar on the boat.' P 69–63 ~ a place where a fisherman anchors his boat, chosen for holding ground, waves breaking, tide, etc. T 186–65 The biggest [boat] ever I build, she's out there now, down the tickle on the collar; 28 feet long she is. 1977 BURSEY 136 Our boats were on the collar.

3 Phr *go in collar, come to collar*, etc: to sign on or 'ship' as member of a fishing or sealing crew; esp to engage in the kinds of work prepara-

tory to the 'voyage.' Also *break collar*: to come
to the end of one's period of employment.

[1830] 1890 GOSSE 49 In the spring. . .when the
crews 'came to collar,' as their arrival was called. . .
1866 WILSON 208 The crew shipped, the first thing is to
'come in collar,' that is, to commence the spring work.
Ibid 278 About the last of February, hundreds of ice-
hunters might be seen toiling up the sculping highlands
[ed emend: Sculpin Islands], with their gaffs, and long
swaling guns on their shoulders, and bearing packs on
their backs, in order to join their respective vessels on
the first of March, when every man was expected to be
in collar for the ice. [1888] 1897 *Nfld Law Reports* 307
The plaintiff was a hired shareman of one Charles Parsons, a dealer and freighter of the defendant's, and was
engaged to proceed with Parsons to the Labrador
fishery. The plaintiff 'entered into collar' with Parsons,
and worked in his service prior to the intended voyage
to Labrador. 1896 *J A Folklore* ix, 37 Getting into collar [means] working on a ship preparatory to sailing
either for seal or cod fishing. 1901 *Christmas Bells* 11
Going into service on the 1st of May was termed to 'go
into collar'; the end of October was 'out of collar.' 1924
ENGLAND 3 'Goin' swilin,' is ye, sir?' 'I'd like to be
goin' in collar meself, agin, wid me rope an' gaff an'
sculpin' knife!' 1953 *Nfld Fish Develop Report* 19 In the
floater enterprise, the men usually go 'in collar'
between the 1st and 10th of May, and are first
employed in readying vessels and gear for the expedition. T 36/8–64 You were supposed to build your flakes
when you had the collar on; build your flakes, build
your stage heads, tar your roof, go in the woods and
cut rines for to cover up your fish. T 43–64 Usually the
first of May you'd go in collar. You'd sign on for the
summer and you'd work around until everything was
ready and the schooner was ready, and you'd go on
again [fishing]. T 31/4–64 A man was swearing in the
spring o' the year when he'd go in collar the first o'
May. 1974 SQUIRE 17–18 Preparations for the Labrador fishery generally began around May 1 each year.
That was when the various crews came in collar. . .
Fishermen broke collar about the end of October and
the schooner was moored for the winter.

4 Attrib, comb **collar boat**: small row-boat; cp
RODNEY.

P 127–73 ~ twelve to fourteen foot row-boat, flat
bottom, used to go from boat to shore, or from boat to
boat. 1974 *Daily News* 11 Dec, p. 11 In addition to
licensing fishermen, the program also requires that vessels from which fish are sold must be registered.
Included in that category are the longliner, trap skiff or
dory, if those vessels are primary fishing craft. 'Collar
boats' or support boats are excluded.

collar buoy: float attached to the anchor and
rope used to moor small craft in a harbour;
BUOY.

1966 SCAMMELL 90 The splash of a collar buoy and
the sharp stutter of a seven horse-power, mufflerless
Fairbanks hit my ears as I stepped outside the shack
door.

collar chain: length of chain joining anchor
and rope to form the mooring of a boat.

[1894] 1975 WHITELEY *MS* 170 Men fixing collar
chains. 1936 SMITH 133 In looking around the deck I
saw a lot of small chain that would be very suitable for
collar chains and shore-fasts.

collar day: date on which sharemen and fisheries 'servants' commence their 'voyage.'

C 67–6 [proverbial rhyme] The first of May is Collar
Day. / When you're shipped you must obey. / When
you're tied you can't run away.

collar punt: see **collar boat**; PUNT.

T 43/7–64 The skiff would be on the collar and you'd
[use this collar punt] for going off to the skiff in.

collar time: spring; period of preparation for
the summer fishery.

Q 73–9 Collar time refers to the period before and
after a crew goes to Labrador fishing for the summer
months. The five or six people prepare for the trip and
they are said to be in collar. 'It's spring again and it's
collar time for a lot of folks.'

collecting vbl n Attrib **collecting boat**: COLLEC-
TOR.

1846 [FEILD] 13 Sailed early for Pinchard's Island in
a collecting boat, and arrived by ten o'clock. 1933 *Nfld
Royal Commission Report* 111 They operate in connection with fast collecting boats, which in turn collect the
salmon from the fishermen, bring it in ice to the
mother vessel.

collector n A vessel which sails from one
coastal settlement or fishing station to another to
take aboard the catch for shipment to a larger
centre; also attrib; COLLECTING BOAT.

1909 BROWNE 292 [A boat from Long Tickle
arrived.] The boat was a decked sloop, the *collector* of
the 'Room' at Long Tickle. 1953 *Nfld Fish Develop
Report* 87 The [salmon] catch is now generally sold by
the fishermen in the dressed form, i.e. with gut and
head removed, directly to collector-boats which call at
the fishermen's premises daily and bring the fish to central assembly points. M 69–5 The cod was taken from
the fishermen and iced into boxes to await the arrival
of the collector, which came every evening and took
the cod back to the cold storage for processing. 1975
Evening Telegram 8 July, p. 2 The Government should
have planned to ship the salmon out sooner last
year. . . Mr Doyle said the division operates five or six
collector boats along the northern coast for picking up
fishermen's catches. 1977 BUTLER 28 A herring collector came from Buffett. 1980 *Evening Telegram* 20 Sep,
p. 1 He cannot accept the corporation's reasons that it
is unable to find boats to be used as collectors in buying
fish from fishermen [on the Labrador].

collop n Cp *OED* ~[2] ['four or five sheep';
'number of animals'] (1672–) A-I. A herd of
goats (P 205–54).

colly n *EDD* ~ 'term of endearment for a cow.'
A cow.

1968 DILLON 134 'Come collie, come collie, come
collie.' 'Go out in the meda [meadow] an' drive home
the collie.' P 108–70 Collie-cow—a cow.

colony n

1 A seventeenth-century English settlement in Newfoundland authorized by royal charter; PLANTATION.

[1611] 1895 PROWSE 99 [Guy's laws] No master of any ship to receive into his ship any person of the Colony, that are already planted by virtue of His Majesty's gracious Patent without speciall warrant under the handwriting of the Governor of the Colony or Colonies in the Newfoundlande aforesaide. [1620] ibid 108 Grant of a Commission from George, Duke of Buckingham, Lord Admiral to the Treasurer & Company of the Colony of Newfoundland. 1626 [VAUGHAN] *The Golden Fleece* [sig 3 C¹] The *Lord Baltimore* is likewise busie in supplying his Colony at *Feriland*. [1640] 1895 PROWSE 151 We doubt not but you shall find a sufficient quantity of provisions to maintain you, and the Colony all the winter.

2 The *de facto* English settlements in the eighteenth century; esp the Island of Newfoundland, including the jurisdiction of Labrador, as formally recognized by the granting of representative government in 1832; freq in phr *the old-(est) colony*.

[1814] 1895 PROWSE 398 [Instructions to Sir Richard Keats] Directed his attention to the propriety of authorising the cultivation of those lands of the colony which might be applicable to that purpose. 1842 BONNYCASTLE i, 157 The year 1831 is remarkable from the numerous petitions and memorials to the home government for constituting a permanent colony, by the institution of a 'Local Legislature' for the island. These petitions were vehemently opposed by the principal mercantile houses at home connected with the fisheries; and after long and patient discussion, a 'Representative Assembly' was granted in 1832, which placed Newfoundland on a par with the neighbouring provinces of Great Britain. 1845 *Journ of Assembly* Appendix, p. 223 This colony can hardly be supposed to raise such a sum as above for bounties, and. . .it seems too much to expect the Mother country will advance the amount. 1897 HARVEY 55 England's oldest Colony has shared in this great boon of self-government; and, in common with the others, has profited thereby. 1924 ENGLAND 56 Captain Westbury Kean had 119 men caught on ice by an immense blind whiteness that raged for two days. . . Again the Colony was plunged in woe.

colours n pl Children's game in which each player is assigned a colour (P 246–56).

T 375–67 I know another game: colours. You have eight boys or girls, and one'll stay out and give them colours. Then another one go over in the corner while they wait, and the feller says: 'Come back. Got any colours today?'

coly* See COADY.

comatick n See KOMATIK.

comb n A number of sulphur-tipped matches fastened together in a comb-like arrangement; also attrib.

1870 HOWLEY *MS Reminiscences* 19 I had in my pocket some of those old fashioned comb matches with plenty of brimstone on them. 1906 *Nfld Qtly* Dec, p. 3 I remember the days of the flint and steel and the 'tinder box,' made of a cow's horn. I remember when lucifer matches were first introduced and were made in single stems (the 'comb' is quite a modern invention) and sold in little cylindrical wooden boxes. P 102–60 Every fisherman received. . .a few pounds of Home Rule Tobacco. . .not forgetting the brimstone tipped matches in combs, about one dozen combs to the package folded in tissue paper, made by the Horwood Lumber Co. T 80/2–64 A comb would be twelve matches, and there was a bunch, see, would be twelve—a lot of matches, gross, 144 matches. T 147–65 I don't know whether you seen any o' those comb matches wi' the brimstone on 'em—stink like the devil. 1978 *Evening Telegram* 9 Sep, p. 14 They weren't sold as a package at all, you'd ask for a comb of stinkers.

come v

Phr *come against*: to affect adversely.

1924 ENGLAND 225–6 It is this running to oil that sometimes puts an end to seal hunts, as in time the process begins to 'come agin' the cargo so that further labour is fruitless. 1968 DILLON 13 'Girl, don't worry about it; that might never come against you.' 'It was in his hip two year before it come against 'im.'

come to collar: see COLLAR 3.

commeteck See KOMATIK.

commission n Rule by governor and six commissioners appointed by the Crown which replaced self-government between 1934 and 1949; esp in phr *commission of government*.

1933 *Nfld Royal Commission Report* 224 We therefore recommend that the Newfoundland Government, recognising that it is impossible for the Island to surmount unaided the unprecedented difficulties that now confront it, should make an immediate appeal for the sympathetic co-operation of Your Majesty's Government in the United Kingdom in the adoption and execution of a joint plan of reconstruction, of which the following would be the main features:– (a) The existing form of government would be suspended until such time as the Island may become self-supporting again. (b) A special Commission of Government would be created which would be presided over by His Excellency the Governor, would be vested with full legislative and executive authority, and would take the place of the existing Legislature and Executive Council. (c) The Commission of Government would be composed of six members, exclusive of the Governor, three of whom would be drawn from Newfoundland and three from the United Kingdom. [c1934] [1960] BURKE (ed White) 51 "We Must Close Our Little Store on Sunday Morning": And since 'Commission' took a notion / For to cross the briny ocean / We must close our little store / On Sunday mornin'. [1939] 1974 BRIDLE (ed) i, 57 In view of all these circumstances the Commission of Government have felt that it would not be inappropriate to ascertain from the Government of the Dominion of Canada whether they would be prepared to make provision for this coastal defence of Bell Island.

1974 CAHILL 14 You voted for Commission of Government! Merciful Christ, you must be out of your mind!. . . A bloody crowd of civil servants brought over from England together with a bunch of lounge lizards from St John's all put in charge of this island by a clique of anti-Christs in London, and you vote to keep them there!

commodore n The senior naval officer in Newfoundland having jurisdiction over the fisheries.

[1753] 1902 *Christmas Bells* 14 Justices, constables, commodores, nor all the commodores in [hell] should have a man off his room. 1765 WILLIAMS 3 The Commodores or Governors of Newfoundland always send them a just State of the Fishery.

community n Attrib **community stage**: waterfront facilities to serve the common needs of fishermen in a settlement for the landing and handling of the catch; STAGE.

1963 WILLIAMS 17 Some fishing communities may see fit to seek the benefit of a government-provided community stage. This is shoreline modification which perhaps makes fishing more attracive, not necessarily more productive. T 175/7–65 Where a community stage is to, there's no shortage o' water for gettin' in to the wharf. 1979 NEMEC 257 The St Shotts' 'community stage' is a relatively large (180 feet long, 26 feet wide) wooden structure which is employed by the great majority of crews each summer in storing 'saltbulk fish.' 1976 *Decks Awash* Aug, p. 32 All fish from the community stage goes to the plant in La Scie.

company n Cp *OED* ~ sb 3 (1393 quot).
  1 A number or group (of birds or animals).
[1832] 1980 *Them Days* vi (2), p. 37 Seen a very large company of ducks at the back of the island in the afternoon. 1861 DE BOILIEU 239–40 [The watch-dog] will instantly lie down and crawl out of their sight, then immediately rise and run towards you, when by his actions you may be sure he has sighted a company. 1881 KENNEDY 53–4 The quick sight of the Indian at once pronounced them to be a herd of deer, or 'company' of them, as he called them. P 130–67 I see a company of ducks going over this morning. 1973 GOUDIE 34 We saw lots of seals, too. They were in companies of about fifty to a hundred in one lot. 1977 *Inuit Land Use* 225 Caribou herds, called companies, are small in winter, usually consisting of 15 to 25 animals but sometimes of as many as 40.
  2 Comb **company bread**: bread carried when travelling alone to ward off fairies; FAIRY BUN.
1924 ENGLAND 220 Bread, called 'comp'ny bread,' in one's pocket, will keep the fairies away.

complete a also **complate**. Cp *OED* ~ a 5 'of persons: fully equipped or endowed;
. . .accomplished' (1526–1822). Ideal; thoroughly good; accomplished; freq in phr *a complete hand*.
1887 BOND 60 [It was] a complete place for spyin'. 1902 *Christmas Bells* 2 When [the singer] had finished, Joe Doyle of the *Ellen Munn* remarked to Bill McGrath, 'Bill, that's a complate song and I'd like to

have it. I don't believe there's a new song in our place for the winter.' 1924 ENGLAND 190 Bear a hand, dere. . . Ah, dat's it! I'll call *ye* complete hands! 1937 DEVINE 15 He's a *complete hand* to sing a song or play the fiddle (or to make a sail, etc.) T 31/2–64 Every steamer [that] used to go out to the seal fishery, he had this put into the song, and 'tis a complate song what he had put together. 1973 BARBOUR 93 My Uncle Burnell was what some folks called 'a complete hand' at playing either the violin or accordion.

concern n also **kinsarn** [kɪn'sæɹn]. Cp PARTRIDGE ~ 'genitals' (1840–). Scrotum of an animal, inflated for use as a football.
T 33–64[1] A kinsarn would be the sack of a buck sheep, or a bull, skinned out and a bladder put into it and blowed up, like a football. All hands would be out kicking that on a Christmas. 1974 SQUIRE 39 Another favourite pastime for boys and young men was 'kicking the concern,' (in the dialect of the day it was 'kickin the kin-sarn'). . . The scrotum was taken from a large bullhide, the skin stretched and dried. Into this was placed a pig's bladder which had been immersed in a salt brine for several days to toughen it. It was blown up tight and the pouch drawn together tightly with strong twine.

concert n A miscellaneous public performance of songs, recitations, skits, etc.
1966 PHILBROOK 155 Traditionally, Orangemen raise money by a variety of means: variety programs, dances, and community suppers. The programs are locally called 'Times' and 'Concerts' and are presented with enthusiasm by men who have thoroughly enjoyed their creation. They consist of songs, usually Newfoundland ballads, recitations, and skits of a slap-stick nature. 1969 *Christmas Mumming in Nfld* 82 A 'concert' resembles a variety show—with or without a theme—and might include one-act plays, skits of various kinds and individual acts, or a three act play by itself. 1975 RUSSELL 47 And that night last fall when the Women's Association had their concert, and we were all doin' our best with that song, the one that starts off 'O Canada'. . .

conch n also **conk*** [kɔŋk]. Cp *DAE* ~[2] 'a fungus. . .that grows on. . .trees' for sense 3.
  1 A variety of large, spiral sea-shell, used for sounding a boat's signal in foggy weather, or for announcing the arrival of bait-fish in coastal waters.
1870 HOWLEY *MS Reminiscences* 1 There were a number of fishing boats on the ground about [Cape St Mary's] and they greeted us with blowing of conchs, yelling and shouting. 1886 *Colonist Christmas No* 15 She always referred to him as the 'old man,' and sometimes when asked concerning him she gave vent to a laugh like the silvery ripple of a baitskiff's conch and said, 'Oh, the old man's busy at home.' 1912 DUNCAN 139–40 Well, I sent down t' Jimmie Lot's stage, where the baitskiff horn was kept, and fetched it back. 'Twas a conch shell, with a hole in it: so that if a man knowed how t' use lips an' lungs on it he could blow a blast that would wake the harbour. In the caplin season, when

they uses them little fish for bait, the folk take turns at mannin' the skiff. 'Tis the bait-skiff conch that calls un t' put out; an' 'tis the bait-skiff conch that warns the harbour that the skiff is back with the bait. P 9–73 The opening of the conch shell was oblong and a man's hand could be inserted into it with the thumb on the outside as a grip when blowing into its top end. As the skiff was returning in the evening with the bait, a man in the bow blew into the conch shell as a signal.

2 Blue flag, the stalks of which produce noise when blown upon; CHIRPER.

T 400/1–67 Conch, it grew up from the ground. It was right green, and oh, it was hollow, yes—purple flower. Poison, they used to call it.

3 Large knot cut from a tree.

P 65–64 Some old trees have large knots in them, called *conks*. Many times a lumberman who found an entire big conk has brought it to the camp for an ornament.

condemn v To discard, cast aside, get rid of.

[1774] 1792 CARTWRIGHT ii, 4 Such [goods] as were not spoiled, were dried; and the rest were condemned. P 80–64 We condemned dogs around here. T 43/7–64 'Twas hooked with rags, condemned rags, and they had a proper mat hook. P 148–64 [It was ruined] so they condemned it.

confederate n Cp *DC* ~ n. An advocate of the political union of Newfoundland and Canada.

1895 PROWSE 495 The result was an overwhelming defeat for the Confederate party; they were simply annihilated [in 1869]. 1948 *The Independent* No 14, p. 1 Things are being whispered around to try and set one sect against another, and so give the Confederates a few more votes. 1953 JOB 12 In spite of the local slogan of the 'confederates'—that it was always the 'merchant-princes' who prevented union with Canada, it can be safely asserted that opinion was varied among them. 1974 CAHILL 26 And that's what you get for backing the Confederates, bad luck.

confederation n Cp *DC* ~ n. The political union of Newfoundland and Canada.

1895 PROWSE 495 From [1869] to this [day] Confederation has never been put forward before the country as a practical political question. 1895 *Evening Herald* 24 Apr Promptly at 4 o'clock yesterday the House opened, and an immense crowd had assembled. Inside the bar were gathered notables of Church and State, and every point of vantage was occupied. All were intensely interested, for the announcement of the terms for Confederation was expected, and the audience were not disappointed. 1948 *The Confederate* No 8, p. 1 Mr Smallwood addressed the great crowd [at Twillingate]. The ladies cheered him specially many of them exclaiming: 'God bless you!' and 'God bless Confederation!' 1948 *The Independent* No 14, p. 1 Mr Gushue. . .says the position of our fisheries under Confederation has not been investigated and views with 'grave disquietude,' in other words with fear, the impact of Confederation on our salt fish industry particularly. 1953 JOB 12 Over the old cobble-paved street has rattled the island's provisions, and now, curiously

enough, in 1949, since the advent of Confederation, old Water Street is paved, and one hears a less dominant note, which seems to indicate that Newfoundland has settled down to become part of a greater whole.

confloption n *EDD* ~ 'flurry, confusion' Co. State of confusion; mishap, misfortune.

P 167–66 That was a terrible confloption. Q 73–3 If the children had messed up the house by throwing around the toys and other things this would be known as a confloption by the parents.

conkerbell See CONKERBILL.

conkerbill n also **conkerbell**. Cp *OED* cock-bell 3 'an icicle' obs exc dial; *EDD* clinker sb³: clinker-bell; cock-bell; conkerbell D Co. (a) Icicle; ICE-CANDLE; (b) something hanging down from an object, as mucus from the nose, balls of dung in animal fur.

[c1894] PANL P4/14, pp. 197–8 An icicle, hanging from the eaves of a house, or from a horse's nose, is a conkerbill. 1924 ENGLAND 137 Seal flesh in the lifeboats made long lines of red 'conkerbills' [icicles] festoon the boats' keels with fringes of frozen blood. 1937 DEVINE 15 ~s. Icicles depending from the eaves of a house. T 12–64 The conkerbells were the balls of manure that stuck to the wool in a sheep and didn't fall off. P 182–77 Conkerbells: [streams] hanging from nose, usually of small child playing outdoors, especially in winter.

conner n also **cunner** ['kɑnəɹ, 'kɒnəɹ] *OED* cunner b (Nfld: 1620–); *DAE* cunner (1672–), conner (1685–). The blue perch (*Tautogolabrus adspersus*), a bottom-feeding fish of inshore waters, esp common around wharves and 'stages'; with defining word *sly*, and in phr *sly as a conner*; JACKY CONNER, TOM(MY) CONNER.

[1620] 1887 MASON 152 What should I speake of Flownders, Crabbes, Cunners, Catfish, Millers, thunnes &c. 1907 MILLAIS 149 There are many other excellent fish. . .such as. . .wrasse (conors). 1965 *Evening Telegram* 5 May, p. 8 In addition to well rotted compost, I have added from time to time a little 6-12-12 fertilizer to my rhubarb bed. . .and occasionally when I had a few conners or flat fish too small to be filletted, I have buried them whole. P 126–67 ~ an orange and green coloured salt water fish—similar in size to a rose fish—caught by boys around old wharves, etc. C 70–10 One fish that we would always catch had a thorny bone running down its back and we called this fish a conner. We would never eat this fish. C 71–127 He's as sly as a conner (describing a person you couldn't trust). P 40–78 Sly conners.

conner v To fish for 'conners.'

M 70–28 Most youngsters took their bamboos or hooks-and-lines and went connerin' down on the wharf.

conniver n Schemer; sly person; SLEEVEEN n (Q 67–67).

Q 71–7 My grandfather called me a conniver when I
was teasing him: 'You conniver, what did you do with
my tobacco?'

control See CONTROLLER.

controller n also **control**. The government-ap-
pointed Board of Liquor Control or one of its
retail stores.

1929 BURKE [21] "Three Bottles a Week": You must
go to the Control / In sun shine or rain / And wait for
three weeks / For to take down your name. T 257–66
They didn't buy beer them days; there was no controller's beer. They always brewed their own. P 245–76 I'll
try to get down to the controller's and pick up a bottle
of rum.

conversation n *EDD Sup* ~ : ~ sweet; *O Sup²*
~ lozenge. A flat sweet or candy with an
inscribed motto or legend; also attrib **conversation sweet**.

P 108–72 Conversations were—and probably they
exist still—cheap candies, flat and heart-shaped, on
which were 'Be Mine,' 'I Love You,' etc. I think they
were of different colours—white, pink, yellow. 'Five
cents worth of Conversations, please.' 1973 BARBOUR
32–3 [At the annual Sunday school picnic] scrambling
for candy took place. . . Some of the candy would be
what was called 'conversation Sweets,' round and flat
and of various colours. On these would be printed 'I
love you,' 'Be my sweetheart' and 'You're my pal.'

coochee n See CROOCHY*. American knot, a
shore-bird (*Calidris canutus rufa*).

1959 MCATEE 32 ~ knot. . . (From dial., 'cooch,' to
crouch, hence croucher. Nfld.)

coochy See CROOCHY*.

cook room n Cp *OED* ~ 'on board a ship, the
galley; a separate building or outhouse' (chiefly
naut quots 1553–); cp *DJE* 'room or building
used as a kitchen' (1707–); *DC* Nfld (1633–). A
large building forming part of fishing premises or
'room' in which food is prepared and the 'crew'
accommodated.

[1611] 1895 PROWSE 99 [Guy's laws] No person to
destroy, deface, or spoile any stage cooke room flakes
&c. Penalty £10. [1663] 1963 YONGE 56 With this
[timber] they built stages, flakes, cookroom, and houses. [1693] 1793 REEVES vi Several inhabitants in
Newfoundland. . .have. . .ingrossed and detained in
their own hands, and for their own private benefit, several stages, cook rooms, beeches, and other places in
the said harbours and creeks. [1718] ibid 88 I have
given out several orders for the admirals and the oldest
masters and planters to survey the stages and cook-
rooms, etc to know what belong to ship-rooms and
what was boat-rooms. [1778] 1792 CARTWRIGHT ii, 387
I built a deathfall for wolves, near the cook-room. 1888
M F HOWLEY 208 In the winter men lived in 'cook-
rooms' attached to the stages, and boarded themselves
or 'ate themselves,' as they said. 1893 *Trade Review
Christmas No* 13 The size of the ancient cookrooms

depended entirely on the extent of the planter's fishery
business, but in general they were about fifty feet long
and thirty wide. Along the sides, a few feet from the
floor, were the sleeping berths for the men, and a place
underneath for each man's chest. The open space in
the middle was devoted to the use of the tables where
sometimes fifty men sat down together at meal-time.
The bill of fare consisted of pork and duff, Hamburg
bread and butter, tea, and oftimes spruce beer, a large
cask of which was always on draft. 1895 PROWSE 450
On every large mercantile establishment the cook-
room was a necessary institution. All the planters and
servants were boarded and lodged on the premises during their stay in the capital; the men slept in bunks
ranged round the cook-room like the berths in a ship.
1953 *Nfld & Lab Pilot* ii, 78 A small inlet [near Harbour Grace], known as Cook Room, indents the shore
close southward of Old Sow point. T 147–65 They got
into this fight Christmas morning; they had a cook-
room down there—that's where the Jerseymen used to
stay.

cooler n also **cooling tub**. A wooden container
or half-barrel used for washing fish. Cp TUB.

P 147–56 Coolin' tub—a tub made from either end of
a puncheon sawed in half. P 10–57 ~ puncheon cut in
two, used for washing fish in on the stage.

coopy v also **croop*** ['kupɪ, 'kɒˑpɪ, 'kɒˑpɪˑ,
'kuːpɪ]. Cp *EDD* croopy 'crouch' Gl W Do So
Co; *EDD Sup* coopey down Do. See also
CROOCHY*. To squat; to bend down close to the
ground, crouch.

P 269–63 Coopy down! P 148–65 Coopy down, so he
won't see you. M 71–90 When a 'shot of ducks' was
coming you had to coopy down, or bend your back so
the birds would not be able to see you. C 71–122 We
would coopy down to draw a picture on the ground, or
hide away.

copper n Cp *OED* ~ sb¹ 11: copper-fastened
'fastened with copper bolts to prevent corrosion';
Dial Notes v (1923), 239 copper-toes boots;
EDD sb¹ (4): ~-topt 'red-haired.'

Comb **copper-fasten** v: to nail down or secure;
to reach a clear and firm understanding or agreement without loop-holes or ambiguity.

1962 *Nfld Fisheries Conf* 54 We'd asked him a few
questions to clarify it and copper fasten it. M 70–21 A
deal completed, one you were very sure of, was considered to be copper-fastened, a reminder of the days
when wooden ships were sheeted in copper. 1974
Evening Telegram 23 Apr, p. 3 In some areas, there
seem to have been some wildcatters sprung up to throw
a monkey wrench into the works the good old mercantile boys had so long established and copper-fastened.

copperhead: small biting fly with a metallic
sheen.

P 148–76 Fishing includes long, tiring hikes. . .and
the torment from insects, since mosquitoes, black flies,
wasps and copperheads swarm around the river.

copper-nose(d): of boy's boots, strengthened
with copper at the toe.

T 141/66–65[2] You'd have a pair for Sundays—they was copper-nosed, you see. There was a strip of copper put in there somehow in the tap. And after you had 'em beat about, he was so shiny. 1976 *Daily News* 15 Mar, p. 4 [Do you remember when] a young man owned a pair of copper nose boots?

coppertop: person with red hair; cp FOXY.

P 53–62 Mind your coppertops! An exclamation used to warn someone to get out of the way, e.g. working in the hold of a ship. P 134–81 [Of several children] Look at the coppertops—except for the little one.

copy v also **cockey**; and such oral variants as **cobby, conky, coody, cooking, coony**, etc, and numerous synonyms treated alphabetically. Cp *EDD* ~ sb 3 (3): shedding copies 'children's game of "follow my leader" La [1837–]; *DC* Nfld (1933–). See also COPYING (1889–) and COPY PAN.

1 To jump from one floating pan of ice to another in a children's game or pastime of following or copying a leader when the ice is breaking up in spring in a cove or harbour.

1905 DUNCAN 138 'Come on copyin', Billy,' said Ezekiel Sevior. That is a game of follow-my-leader over the broken ice, every cake of which, it may be, sinks under the weight of a lad. It is a training for the perilous work of seal hunting, which comes later in the life of a Newfoundlander. 1933 GREENE 38 You will see the merry young lads 'copying' as they call it—jumping from pan to pan till far out in the Cove in fearless rivalry. 1945 *Atlantic Guardian* i (5), p. 13 We were so busy catching tomcods, 'copying' pans in the Spring, doing chores, sailing boats, etc, that we didn't have time to chase all our vitamins. 1964 *Can Journ Ling* x, 40 The game which the children play of jumping from one pan of ice to another is called 'copyin' the pans.' 1973 BARBOUR 25 The minute school was out, we ran helter-skelter to one of the coves to 'copy pans.' 1976 *Daily News* 2 Mar, p. 3 Jumpin' clumpers was another favourite [pastime]. In some places they call it copying on the bellycaters.

2 To jump across loose or floating ice while pursuing seals on the ice-floes.

1895 PROWSE 452–3 There was a channel just caught over, which the Canadian did not see, and down he went; as he rose the boys, seven in number, came to the edge, and successfully copied over the Canadian's head and shoulders. 1905 MURPHY 4 "The Spring Maurice Crotty Fought the Old Dog Hood": With his bat and his gaff on his shoulder, / All copying from ice pan to pan. 1919 GRENFELL[1] 279 The young men were 'copying,' as we say, over the ice, that is, jumping from pan to pan as they ventured far out from the land. 1924 ENGLAND 274 All at once a string of ice floated along. Taking desperate chance they leaped for it, landed, 'copied' from cake to rocking cake. By incredible skill, agility, and speed they reached the ship. 1933 GREENE 32 'Intervals' of all widths and shapes—these dividing spaces [are] filled deep with the crushed ice and snow of the spurting 'sish.' And it is over these intervals, which are often several yards across, that the sealers must step, or jump, or 'copy' when they are travelling

on foot over the Floe. T 80/1–64 The ice was all loose, where the ice was together, but not enough for to copy about. You have to do a lot of punt work, see.

3 To run over a series of logs floating in the water (P 65–64).

copying vbl n also **cobbying***, **cockeying**, **conkying***, **coodying***, **coonying*** *DC* ~ Nfld (1933–). See COPY.

1 In a children's pastime, the action of leaping from one piece of floating ice to another as the participants follow or copy the leader.

1889 *Nineteenth Cent* xxv, 513–14 The youth of Newfoundland look forward to the arrival of the ice for their spring pastime of 'copying'. . . It is not every pan that will bear any weight; a plucky and experienced leader is therefore desirable. The youths follow in the single file, jumping from pan to pan in the fashion of the old game of 'follow-my-leader.' 1895 *J A Folklore* viii, 38 . . .*cockeying* at Harbor Grace, *copying* in St John's, describing an amusement of boys in spring, when the ice is breaking up, of jumping from cake to cake, in supposed imitation of the sealers. 1895 *Dial Notes* i, 378 ~ jumping from piece to piece. . .of floating ice that is not large enough to bear, until you reach one that is. 1937 DEVINE 39 Randy—any noisy fun: 'Copying' over buckly ice, snow sliding, etc. 1967 READER 1 Arctic ice fills all bays and harbours on the N.E. Coast during the spring, and the boys jumping from pan to pan call this copying or quibbing. 1969 MOWAT 39 The woman made her way on foot ('copying,' they call it) across the floe-ice to the land. C 70–12 If you were jumping from one *big* pan of ice to another, it was not considered copyin'. It was only copyin' where there was danger. M 71–91 Cockying was played during the spring thaw. Several blocks of ice about four feet square were cut and left floating. The boys. . .dared each other to run the length of them.

2 The action of running over ice-pans, esp during the seal-hunt.

1883 *Fish Exhibit Cat*[4] 175 ~ i.e., running across Channel over small pans of ice. 1889 *Nineteenth Century* xxv, 514 The term 'copying,'. . .is now applied to the mere act of progressing from pan to pan of ice where no game is in question, so that one may often hear a man announce that he is going 'to copy out' to such and such a vessel or point.

copy pan n also **cocky pan***. See also COPY. Small piece of floating ice; PAN.

P 19–55 Cocky-pans: small pans of ice. 1964 *Can Journ Ling* x, 40 Small pieces of floating ice called 'copy pans.' Q 67–71 Copying the cocky pans. C 71–119 Copy pans: pans of ice too little to take weight of a person. Skipping across these was called 'copying.'

corker See CAULKER.

corner n Cp *EDD* catch v 2 (3) ~ corner So for sense 2; cp *O Sup*[2] sb[1] 16 ~ boy 'loafer' esp Ir (1855–), *ADD* Nfld for sense 3.

1 The angle formed by any two walls of a cod-trap; also attrib in names of attachments to this part of the net.

Q 67–34 Each square that turns the walls or bottoms [of the trap is called a corner]. Ibid Corner ropes [are] ropes fastened to the corner v's and fastened to the end of the doorway, when the doorway is pulled to the side of the boat and the doorway is released. The doorlines passed around the head and stern of the boat and slacked away as required to be assured that the trap is re-set in a fishing position again. P 9–73 From the middle of the spanline four ropes are laid out, one for each corner, long enough so that each corner buoy is far enough away that when it is hauled back and fastened to its respective corner and let out again the trap will be in the shape it should be when set. Ibid At the top, ropes are fastened at each corner as straps to fasten the corner floats that keep the corners of the trap and mooring from sinking.

2 In pl, children's game of puss-in-the-corner.

T 375–67 Another game in corners. They had four people in corners and the one who is 'it.' They trade over corners, and if the feller runs [and never gets] there, he's 'it.'

3 Comb **corner boy**: 'outport' term for a St John's-man; street-corner lout.

1862 *Daily News* 21 Apr, [p. 2] He met with a crowd of corner boys at the foot of Cochrane Street, a spot that has now an unenviable [notoriety], as being the *nucleus* of rowdies. 1924 ENGLAND 6 By the men's glances at the city dwellers or 'corner boys,' no love seemed lost between them. T 141/166–65[2] One time he was up there [in St John's] and the corner boys they'd get down aboard the schooner. 1976 *Evening Telegram* 9 Mar, p. 12 And now everything is changed. You can't tell a bayman from a corner boy, they all talk alike.

cor(r)e fish n Cp *OED* corved ppl a 'corved herring' obs (1641–). Undried salted cod-fish; GREEN FISH, SALT-BULK.

[1583] 1940 *Gilbert's Voyages & Enterprises* ii, 398 [Hayes' narrative] The Portugals, and French chiefly. . .who commonly beginne the fishing in Apriell, and have ended by July. That fish is large, always wet, having no land neere to drie, and is called Corre fish. 1610 *Willoughby Papers* 13a/101 Dry fish 7s or 7s 4d must needs yeeld Proffitt Corrfishe beinge good and resenable bought will bee heer vented For both dry and Corrfishe beginnes heere to be in use. 1631 ibid 1/58 Fortie Fower men to Load a ship with drie Fish in the Countrie off Fishing besids Cor Fish. 1842 BONNYCASTLE ii, 204 Fish (core) quintals 966. Fish (dry cod) quintals 915,795

cosh n also **coish** [kɑʃ] *DC* ~ Nfld (1842); SEARY 112, 119; DINNEEN cos 'a leg, a foot'; P W JOYCE *Irish Names of Places* (1901) i, 527. Part of a river estuary cut off from the sea at low tide; place-name for such a lagoon; cp BARASWAY 2.

1842 JUKES i, 42 Here a brook empties itself into the sea, having run for about three miles through a narrow pond, or 'cosh,' as my men called it. 1858 [LOWELL] i, 138 There's the summer w'y and the winter w'y, by Cub's Cove, and the Cosh, and so into the woods. M 69–20 There is a section of Bay Roberts harbour in

the west called the Coish (kosh). . . Within the coish there is a smaller coish formed in the extreme west end during low tide. This second coish is also formed by a causeway but this causeway is natural. 1973 WIDDOWSON 517 He was a gnarled man with a twisted face who lived beside the Coish, or river-head.

cossock* n also **cod-sock, cossack*, cozzock** pl ['kazaks]. Cp *DAE* cossack 1 'a kind of shoe or boot' (1805, 1806); *EDD* cossicks 'boots without loose tongues; bluchers' Y. Cp also similar var forms under CASSOCK. Footwear made by cutting the legs off a pair of old rubber boots at the ankle.

P 148–65 At the end of the fishing season the father would come home and cut off his boots. These cut-off boots would be worn over the winter, called kazakses. P 126–67 ~ a kind of footwear made by cutting the top part off a pair of rubber boots. 1971 NOSEWORTHY 16 Cozzocks. A pair of knee rubbers cut away, with only the foot portion left, so that they look like shoes.

cossock See CASSOCK.

cosy egg* See OSE EGG.

cottage n

Attrib, comb **cottage meeting**: Salvation Army service held in a private home.

M 69–16 In 1915 the few families of Salvation Army there began to hold cottage meetings. A few years later, 1917, they built a church.

cottage range: cheaply-built row of small adjoined wooden houses.

1936 DEVINE 87 Galleghy's range and beyond Vail's bakery breaking in on the isolation of the cottage ranges of the Kerrymen, who had fled there 'out in the woods' in the early days to live in peace out of the way, with a little house of their own, and to be clear of the hated landlord. A few of those cottages remain to-day.

cottage roof: hip roof.

[1911] LENCH 5 [The church was built on the old fashioned plan and] had a cottage roof like John Stretton's Meeting House in Harbour Grace, and the greater Methodist Church in Carbonear. 1972 MURRAY 181–2 Another type mentioned was the 'cottage roofed' house. This was also two-stories, but the roof had four equally sloping sides. 1974 MANNION 148 Over a dozen dwellings along the Cape Shore had a 4-sided or hipped roof, locally called a 'bell' or 'cottage' roof.

cotterall n also **cottle*, crottle** *EDD* cotterel sb 2 s w cties. A metal bar with notches on which pot is hung in fire-place; one of the notches on a pot-hook; POT BAR.

1866 WILSON 353 On this pot-bar was hung the cotterall and pot-hooks, which sustained the vessels. 1883 HOWLEY *MS Reminiscences* 6 [Crémaillère] referred to a toothed or notched piece of iron to be seen suspended from a beam in the old fashioned chimneys of country houses. I believe the English term for this article is coterel. 1903 *Nfld Qtly* Dec, p. 5 Hanging over the fire, on the cottrel and hangers, were a large three-legged pot. . .a flat bake-pot. . .and finally a large 'piper.' T 156–65 They bake un, see. But you can't bake in they ovens like you'd bake on cottles. You've seen the cottles. There's notches for risin' up the pot if 'tis too hot, put un up on t'other notch. 1972 MURRAY 183–4 'I remember the open fireplace,' he said, 'the flue with the crooks and crottles for hanging pots on.' The 'crook and crottles' was shaped not unlike a walking stick with a hook which went over the iron bar that stretched across the open fireplace. It had one straight side and the other side was notched. The whole hung down from the horizontal iron bar and could be slid along it. Pots could be raised or lowered on the crottles according to the housewife's desires.

cottle* See COTTERALL.

country n   Cp *DAE* ~ 1 'part of Atlantic coast settled by English' obs (1633–1693) for sense 1; *DAE* 4 'region remote from a town' (1841–) for sense 2; for comb in sense 3: *DC* ~ tea 2 obs (1887).

1 Newfoundland; esp the thin line of coastal 'settlements'; LABRADOR (COAST); SHORE[1].

[1583] 1940 *Gilbert's Voyages & Enterprises* ii, 402 [Hayes' narrative] Munday following, the General had his tent set up, who being accompanied with his own followers, sommoned the marchants and masters, both English and strangers to be present at his taking possession of those Countries. Before whom openly was read & interpreted unto the strangers his Commission: by vertue whereof he tooke possession in the same harbour of S John, and 200 leagues every way. 1620 WHITBOURNE 1 I shall not much neede to commend the wholesome temperature of that Countrey, seeing the greatest part thereof lieth above 3 degrees neerer to the South, then any part of *England* doth. 1775 CURTIS 64 The beginning of December the Country is thinly inhabitanted and the time nearly fixt for the last Vessel departure in which was to go my Relation. 1813 CARSON 7 The numbers of those opposing colonization are rapidly decreasing. . . They principally reside in England, migrating to this country during the summer months. 1900 *Tribune Christmas No* 3 Of Father Kyran Walsh we may truly say that his name has been a household word all over the country. 1962 *Nfld Fisheries Conf* 203 There's no more molasses coming in the country in tubs.

2 The uninhabited interior of Newfoundland and Labrador beyond the thin line of coastal 'settlements.'

1623 WHITBOURNE [sig. R 2] I. . .did coast some ten miles into the Country, Westward from our Plantation to make some discovery of the country and to kill a Deere. 1775 CURTIS 63 When the Fishing Season was allmost over it was Proposed to me to make one of three to go in the Country Shooting for the Family. 1819 PANL CS 1 J Peyton 28 May In April 1814 John Morris a furrier of mine, came out from one of my Furrier's Tilts in the Country on business to me, leaving in the Tilt his Provisions some Fur, and his Cloths. 1870 HOWLEY *MS Reminiscences* 25 Spent all day examining both sides of the Cove and the country inside. T 34–64

He'd go away in March. Take his bag on a anseery, kind of a slide, and haul un through the country till they get to Carbonear to go on the train. 1972 MURRAY 263 If [the men] were at home, they were mainly responsible for getting the year's supply of firewood from the 'country.' 1979 TIZZARD 183 We travelled quite a distance in the country and searched many a hill and valley, finally finding a pine tree.

3 Attrib, comb **country born**: native-born inhabitant(s) of Newfoundland; BUSH-BORN, NATIVE n.

1857 MOUNTAIN 3–5 This shore is inhabited by fishermen of the English and Irish race who have either themselves come out to settle, or have been born in the country; these last are called 'Shumachs' or 'the country-born'. . .the 'country-born,' and the non-residents.

country deer: Newfoundland caribou (*Rangifer tarandus*); DEER.

[1766] 1971 BANKS 131 I Picked up the Horn of one of the Country Deer Shed Probably on the Spot as they are remarkable for swimming from the main to Islands sometimes to those that are far out at sea.

country man: (a) trapper or hunter; (b) person from another 'settlement' or 'outport.'

1968 MOWAT & DE VISSER 138 Most outports held a few men who preferred the stark tundra to the rolling plains of ocean. . . Leaving the settlements in October, accompanied by their dogs and laden with all the supplies they could carry, they traversed the windswept sweep of the high barrens until they came to the southward edge of the Big Woods. . . Here they would build tiny cabins called tilts, and spend the winters trapping. They were seldom seen again until late February. . . They were called 'the country-men.' 1971 NOSEWORTHY 187 ~ An outsider from a small settlement.

country meat: see **country deer**.

1972 MOWAT 15 'Niver did see such a toime for caribou. I tell ye, me son, they's thicker'n flies on a fish flake, and coming right down to the landwash to pick away at the kelp. Oh, yiss bye, they's lots o' country meat on the go!'

country sled: sledge with wooden runners used to haul firewood; SLIDE n (P 148–60).

country spruce: large spruce tree cut in the interior.

1979 TIZZARD 85 My father sold it. . .for one hundred sticks of good country spruce.

country tea: LABRADOR TEA (*Ledum groenlandicum*).

1908 HUBBARD 79 The 'country,' or 'Indian,' tea which grew in abundance was in blossom, and the air was filled with fragrance.

courier n   also **currier**. Cp *OED* ~ 1 'a running messenger.' Hooded seal on the periphery of a seal herd; hooded seal in its third year. Also attrib **courier hood**.

1924 ENGLAND 3 Sure enough, there they were, six or seven huge, fat fellows resting on pans, off our port bow. The Captain called them 'currier hoods,' or scattered outscouts of the hood nation, and added that it

was most unusual to find seals in this latitude. Ibid 103
The hoods, for their first four years, are 'young hoods,'
'bedlamers,' 'curriers' and 'old hoods.' 1925 *Dial Notes*
v, 329 Courier hoods. Scattering guards outside the
harp seals.

course n Cp *OED* ~ sb 12 b 'points' of the
compass. Comb **course-bag**: in the Bank fishery,
container from which lots are drawn assigning
areas for dories to fish.
1942 *Grand Bank U C School* 34 [A] course bag is a
canvas cylinder with a wooden bottom. [There are]
eleven square wooden blocks, with eleven points of the
compass on them. A man from each dory put in his
hand and drew out a block. The course that was on that
block was the course that man's dory had to go from
the ship, to put out its trawls.

court n Attrib **court work**, **law work**: legal proceedings (1925 *Dial Notes* v, 328).
1902 *Nfld Qtly* Mar, p. 9 On arrival at the port of
sailing, law-work was the order of the day, but, in nine
cases out of ten, no conviction could be had. 1975
RUSSELL 9 About ten years ago, just before King
David [the goat] give up jumpin' fences, he destroyed
Grampa Walcott's cabbage garden and they had court
work over it. 1976 *Culture & Tradition* 70 We had law
work you know, for something he'd done, see, for badness you know.

cove n Cp *OED* ~ sb¹ 4 'sheltered recess in a
coast' (1590–), *DAE* 1 (1616–) for sense 1; *DC* 2
Nfld (1958) for sense 2.
1 A small bay or inlet of the sea affording shelter to small craft; the inhabited coastal strip of
such an indentation; SETTLEMENT.
1610 *Willoughby Papers* 17a, 1/2 We arrived (God be
praised) all in safetie in the bay of Conception, in Newfoundland [in the] Harbour here called Cuperrs Cove.
[1663] 1963 YONGE 55 Coming near the shore, we saw
a large cove, called Glam cove, a little kind of harbour
where the Renoose boats, when put to leeward, use to
shelter. [1712] 1895 PROWSE 273 Orders sent to admirals and chief planters of every little cove, to give
account of boats and fish and of inhabitants. 1906
DUNCAN 86 He was a sturdy, fearless giant, was Eli
Zitt, of Ruddy Cove. And for this the Cove very properly called him a 'hard' man. 1951 *Nfld & Lab Pilot* i,
322 Flowers cove is entered between Capstan point and
a point about a quarter of a mile southward. . . It is
much frequented by fishing craft, and has regular
steamer communication with other Newfoundland
ports.
2 In a seaport town, esp St John's, a short side
street, built on the site of a filled-in stream or
cove, running from the main business street
towards the harbour; usu in place-names.
[(1846) 1965 *Am Speech* xl, 169 Beck's Cove
fire-break.] 1887 *Telegram Christmas No* 10 One touch
of his strong hand on her bowed head and he was gone
with quick step across the street, down the passageway, or 'cove,' as the people of Jacksonville call the
entrance to their wharves. [1898] 1905 *Nfld Law*

Reports 69 . . .the convenience and security afforded
by the making, opening, widening or altering of the
said street, cross-street, fire-break, cove, road or lane.
1907 *Tribune Christmas No* 12 [In Harbour Grace]
across the cove we find Mr Thomas Ross, who is conducting a general business on the premises formerly C
W Ross and Company, which in the 'good old times' to
pass without giving a call was almost considered a
crime. 1929 BURKE [9] "A Hearty Welcome to General
Higgins": And in the coves in rain or storm / Those
Soldiers do their part, / For small donations in the pot /
To cheer some lonely heart. 1936 DEVINE 47 As an
example of. . .the backwardness of the system of
domestic water supply, he kept a man in winter and a
boy in summer to bring water from the pump in the
public cove. 1953 JOB 11 Water Street is saturated with
Newfoundland history. From its buildings, its coves
leading down to the wharves. . . T 731–70 A truckman
meant a man that had a horse an' long cart an' stood in
the coves until he was hired.
3 Comb **cove net**: small 'seal net' placed in the
water near the shore to enmesh migrating seals.
1977 *Inuit Land Use* 140 In early fall, jars and lassies
(young square-flipper seals) travel into the bays to feed
before freeze-up. The men hunted them around the
coastal islands and in the bays or they set short 'cove'
nets, 25 fathoms long, after fishing was over.

covel n also **coufle** ['kʌvl]. Cp *OED* cowl sb² 1
cuvel, etc (c1400–); *EDD* ~ sb 1 K Do for sense
1; *EDD* sb 2 ~ stick Do for sense 2.
1 A half-barrel or tub, freq with handles or
rope affixed to the sides or with holes for insert-
ing a staff for two men to carry; cp GULLY² 1.
1866 WILSON 347 ~ A barrel with a strong stake pas-
sel through or near the upper hoops. 1896 *J A Folklore*
ix, 36 ~ A tub made to hold blubber oil. 1925 *Dial
Notes* v, 328 ~ a three-quarter flour barrel, used in fish
cleaning. 1937 DEVINE 15 ~ A sawn-off barrel with
two handles attached to the sides, used for carrying fish
or fish offal. T 36/8 64 There's a hole in the table about
three inches in diameter, and a tub or a barrel—covel,
they calls it, liver covel. You'd pull out the gut, separate the liver and let the liver go down in the barrel.
M 71–117 A quick flick of the left hand ripped out the
liver which was deposited through a hole in the table to
a tub called a covel.
2 Comb **covel staff**: pole put through holes in a
tub to support it on men's shoulders.
1891 *Holly Branch* 34 Had I been present when the
Prince committed that outrage on old Foley it would
have been worse for him than Mother Carter's bittle
stock or old B's cuvvel staff.

covey a ['koɒvɪ]. Phr *covey fellow*, etc: native-
born resident of a coastal settlement.
1924 ENGLAND 33 One of the master watches woke
up in time to reprove me for throwing away this water
after I'd washed in it. 'Yare [there], now, sir, ye wasted
good water!. . .Us covey fellers don't mind water like
dat, whatever.' P 243–76 'Us covey ducks'— (Portugal
Cove man speaking of natives of the cove).

cow n Cp *EDD* ~ sb¹ 1 (11) ~ belly 'a quicksand'; *DAE* 6 ~ fly (1879); DINNEEN riabhach: laetheanta na riaibhche 'the days of the brindled cow' for cow's days; *EDD* sb[1] 1 (85) ~ plat.

Attrib, comb **cow bee**: fly attracted to cows and other large animals.

[1970] 1976 GUY 117 In the course of an hour I had upset the ecology of the region to the tune of thirty-eight nippers, sixteen cowbees and six others of a nasty sort. Q 71–3 Cow bees are the kind of insects you find on a moose's skin. They don't bite you.

cow belly: bog-land.

1958 *Evening Telegram* 18 Mar, p. 4 This is peat land, or commonly known to Newfoundlanders as 'cowbelly' and is highly acid and required ample cultivation by skilled farmers.

cow(s) days: period from April 1–13.

C 68–16 The first of April to the thirteenth are known as 'the cow days.' These days are usually cold and windy. The old folk years ago used to say that those were the days for skinning the cow. C 71–26 'Old cows days' referred to the first thirteen days of April, which were always supposed to be days of bad weather. The old people never counted on doing any outdoor work during this weather for 'the old cows days are coming up,' they'd say.

cow flock: marsh marigold (*Caltha palustris*) (1956 ROULEAU 28).

cow fly: see **cow bee** (Q 71–8).

cow platter, ~ plat(e): cow dung.

P 206–69 Cow's plate: the round dried cow droppings. 1973 PINSENT 9 Ruth Lowe and a downtown girl friend stop to help Roger to his feet after he falls to his knees in a cow platter.

cow(s) tail: (a) in coopering, a mop-like device used to shape a barrel; (b) cirrus cloud or mare's tail.

T 90–64 [The barrel would be] tressed over a fire and steamed with a cow's tail—a stick with a piece of brin on it, stuck down in a barrel, and you give it a swish around on the hot wood and then hammer your level best, and you'd bring that barrel to a shape. 1965 PEACOCK (ed) i, 141 "On the Schooner *John Joe*": But now we're bound home and our wings they are spread, / And the cow-tails are flying all over our heads. Q 71–7 ~ a cloud formation predicting strong winds.

cow v Phr **cow out**: to tire, exhaust physically.

1924 ENGLAND 16 We'm ahl rate 'cept fer bein' a little cowed out. 1937 DEVINE 15 I'm cowed out. T 70/1–64 One feller caught a big salmon that day, and he lost him there in the harbour. His line busted. Ten pound he 'lowed he was. He'd cow him out after a spell, but he reeled too hard and [the salmon] busted clear. T 222–66 By the time you had that finished you would be all cowed out, and you'd need to keel out for a spell on the settle.

coxswain n also **cocksel***. Transverse bar at the rear of a sled on which the driver stands.

P 101–71 Cocksel. Bar to stand on at back of slide. C 75–146 A man went up the country one morning in the winter for a load of wood when a strange man

jumped on behind the slide on the cocksuns. The man was so big the horse had a difficult time pulling the slide.

crabbed a also **crabit** ['krabɪt] *EDD* crab sb[3] 1 (1) (b): crabbed. Of a child, clever, shrewd, smart.

1863 MORETON 31 ~ Precociously knowing. [1900 OLIVER & BURKE] 58 "Kissing Duett": Will you teach me if you please, / I believe I'm quick and crabit, / If you show me thus the habit. P 207–67 What a crabbit child little Johnny is!

crabit See CRABBED.

crack[1] v *OED* ~ v 22 naut (1840, 1867) for sense 1.

1 To clap sail on a vessel and proceed at full speed.

1842 JUKES i, 264 We accordingly crowded all sail, and cracked on with a fresh breeze, urging our way through slowly yielding pans, now sailing gallantly through an open lake of water. 1916 MURPHY 46 At length, well on in April, the wind changed and the ice slackened off and let them clear. All the ships then started north and cracked on northward for all they were worth. 1924 ENGLAND 153 One watch to work de canvas an' one to kill swiles. Crack evvery stich o' canvas on 'er, an' wear round. T 178–65 [We] cracked the mainsail on her, single reef mainsail, and come on. 1977 *Nfld Qtly* Winter, p. 17 The wind was around easter. Still a big swell in the water. . .and we put the big mains'le on her again, and took the storm sail we had here and put (it) there for a fores'le, and put the jib and jumbo on her and cracked it to her right for Burin.

2 To provide liberally; apply vigorously.

T 156–65 They cracked on a big fire o' birch, and he begin to thaw, and the water begin to run out of un. T 172/3–65 They'd starve their own dogs [but] in the spring o' the year they'd crack the food to them and get them back in working condition. 1975 BUTLER 31 But anyway, by gar, 'twas goin' pretty good, big square dance, crackin' right to it.

crack[2] v *EDD* ~ v 25 (1) Wxf (1869–), *Kilkenny Lexicon* cry crack, *O Sup*[2] 25 (Austr: 1888–). Phr *cry crack*: to give up an action; to cease.

1875 HOWLEY *MS Reminiscences* 68 I knew from experience that if let alone he would never cry crack till he had emptied the bottle, and consequently would not be able to travel for several days after. P 222–67 I went to sleep as soon as I went to bed, and I never cried crack until 7:30 this morning. P 113–69 ~ to give in or give up. 'Crack' is the highest bid in 45's. C 70–21 [He] never cried crack till the job was finished.

cracker n *NID* crackerberry.

Comb **cracker berry, cracker**: dwarf cornel (*Cornus canadensis*); PIGEON BERRY.

[1822] 1928 CORMACK 21–2 The surface is bespangled. . .by. . .the one-sided wintergreen, the crackerberry bearing a cluster of wholesome red berries, sometimes called pigeon-berries. 1858 [LOWELL] i, 94 Crackers, partridge-berries, horts, and others enrich the barrenness, and make it worth while for women and children to come and gather them. 1908 TOWNSEND 46 The fruit of the northern dwarf cornel or bunchberry is sometimes gathered and cooked. It is called 'cracker.' 1915 SOUTHCOTT 15 Crackerberry. Leaves in a whorl. Flowers greenish, surrounded by a 4-leaved white or pinkish involucre. Fruit bright red. Woods everywhere. 1939 DULEY 19 Then there was the little plant that was a white star in spring and four red berries in autumn. They were holding her worse than the Little People. All at once the Priest made her forget the whorts and the cracker-berries. 1966 HORWOOD 19 Fat, red crackerberries, which snapped and cracked between your teeth. 1975 SCOTT 57 The Crackerberry, Crackers, or Bunchberry is familiar to everyone throughout the island. . . It grows in woods and some open spots.

cracker bone, **crack bone**: forked bone between the neck and breast of a fowl; wishbone.
C 69–28 A common practice among children is to crack the cracker bone of a chicken or any fowl to see who's going to [be] married first. 1971 NOSEWORTHY 188 Crack-bone: breastbone.

cracker jack: see **cracker berry**.
C 70–28 [There is] a type of red berry found in the woods near Lady Cove, grow in clumps, with a bunch of a half-dozen or so berries per stalk. They are called bunchy-berries or crackerjacks.

cracky a ADD ~ 3 Nfld. Saucy, pert (1925 *Dial Notes* v, 328).
P 148–62 He's some cracky!

cracky n also **cracky dog, krackie** EDD ~ sb[1] 1 'wren,' 2 'little person or thing' D; DC crackie Nfld (1895–). A small, noisy mongrel dog; freq in phr *saucy as a cracky*.
1858 [LOWELL] ii, 293 A 'cracky,' in Newfoundland, is a little dog. [1894 BURKE] 83 He can bite off horse shoe nails and twist crackeys by the tails. 1895 *J A Folklore* viii, 38 ~ a little dog. 1917 *Christmas Echo* 14 There was nothing particular about him any more than any other dog. He was larger than an ordinary crackie, but not so large as a sporting dog. 1937 DEVINE 15 Crackie—A small dog. A lap dog, lively, frisking and barking. 1966 FARIS 97 People today only keep small 'krakies,' and have killed or sold most of the part-Husky sled dogs which once abounded. C 66–8 'Saucy as a cracky.' This is applied to a person who usually has a saucy tongue or a person who will answer back.

craft[1] n OED ~ sb[1] 10 (1688–1704 quots). Fishing paraphernalia used in the sea-fisheries; GEAR; also attrib.
[1736–39] 1954 INNIS 148 Craft, Cloathing, Provisions, Sail Cloth, Cordage, Ironwork, and other fishing Utensils necessary for fitting out the Fishing Boats. [1775] 1792 CARTWRIGHT ii, 121 The sealers were mending their nets, and cutting killick-claws. . . I selected a net, to have under my own management, and mended it. . . The sealers worked on their craft.

[c1780] 1966 *Evening Telegram* 14 Nov, p. 6 'Craft house' was a store on a fishing room for storing [fishing equipment exclusive of boats and vessels]. 1792 CARTWRIGHT *Gloss* i, x ~ A fisherman's term, signifying the whole of the implements they use; such as nets, hooks, lines, etc. 1792 PULLING *MS* Aug Mr Clark also told me as did all the principal people who reside at Fogo that I conversed with on the subject, that scarce a year passes that they don't lose more or less of their fishing craft [by theft to the Beothuks]. 1813 *Gazette* 4 Nov For Sale, on moderate terms, Fishing Craft of every description. 1839 TUCKER 82–3 An old fisherman perceiving the awkward manner in which I was proceeding [to tie on my hooks] told me the 'cod would laugh at such a craft as I was fixing.' I threw it aside. . .and told him. . .that if they wanted me to work, they must fix me out with a craft. I was told, however, that it was the duty of each one to provide his own fishing gear. P 245–82 We used to get our craft for the Labrador [fishery] at Earle's in Carbonear.

craft[2] n Phr *fresh craft*: recently killed game or birds.
1861 DE BOILIEU 120 I forgot to mention one person who generally figures high in the woodman's crew I mean the gunner, or the man who provides the crew with fresh craft—the term 'fresh craft' signifying fresh provisions. [1886] LLOYD 95 Feasting becomes general; and the horrors of perpetual salt pork are forgotten in the delight with which 'fresh craft' is devoured. For days a fierce cannonade is continued, until 'birds enough' have been obtained.

cram v Cp EDD ~ v[1] 1 'to squeeze, hold fast'; scram v[2] 1 'to crush; to squeeze' D. To squeeze or fondle (an animal) excessively.
C 66–10 Don't cram the cat too much, sure it'll never grow [if] you cram it to death.

cramp a also **cramped** EDD ~ adj 3 (1) cramp-hand, (2) ~ -word.
1 Of a person, difficult to understand, amusing, because of clever or humorous speech.
T 22–64 They gets into this house, and there's a woman here—she's a kind of a cramp hand; she was liable to say anything. . . My uncle he was a cramp hand in dressing-up, mummering—talk, all kinds of talk.
2 Of words or speech, old-fashioned, dialectal, difficult to understand.
1933 GREENLEAF 62 [She] called it 'a cramped song,' and the imperfections in the lines show how hard it was for her to remember and sing it. . . Newfoundlanders use 'cramped' in much the same sense that we say 'tongue-twister.' T 22–64 [The mummers] used to have some awful cramp talk. T 31/4–64 He was wonderful [at] all them old cramp songs, all them old-fashioned ones about steamers, etc. 1971 NOSEWORTHY 188 Cramp words, cramp names—unusual dialect words or pronunciations, which the local people think peculiar.

cramp n Attrib **cramp knot**: small knot cut from a tree and worn as a charm against muscular contractions.

M 68–5 Cramp was believed to be prevented by a 'cramp knot' worn on the person. A cramp knot is a small round knob of wood varying in size from one to two inches in diameter and larger. It grows mainly on fir trees. C 69–23 It was a belief that by wearing a cramp knot (a node cut from a tree) around your neck you would have no cramps.

cran n See CRUNNICK: CRANNICK. Dead twisted piece of wood; SCRAG.
P 41–68 Even the tangled burnt-over undergrowth had a name but it had to wait a few years till it turned white, then it became crans. C 75–146 Crans are thin crooked sticks. 'She found a good spot of berries among the crans somewhere in the woods.'

crannick See CRUNNICK.

crap See CROP n.

crape* See CREEP.

cravat n Cp *OED* ~ sb 1 (1688). Long woollen scarf worn by men.
Q 67–45 Most of the men used to wear woollen scarfs around their necks especially when they went in the woods. They called them cravats. 1970 *Wooden Boats and Iron Men* 70 ~ A long woollen scarf tied around the neck.

craw n *EDD* ~ sb² 'breast; bosom of a shirt.' Upper part of chest; collar of a garment, esp in phr *button your craw.*
P 118–67 If you go out, be sure and button up your craw. M 71–95 To avoid the croup [he] would tell us to 'button your craw' which meant to button your coat under the chin. C 71–111 Often when it was cold [she] would say 'put something around your craw.'

creak-cold a Of weather, extremely cold.
[1959] 1965 PEACOCK (ed) iii, 942 "The Loss of the *Danny Goodwin*": It was on a Monday morning they got her under way, / The sixth day of December, a creak-cold winter's day.

crease n
1 The depression, containing the backbone, left in a cod-fish when it is 'split.'
P 80–64 If the crease is taken out, the fish goes out of shape. Q 71–6 He put a perfect crease in the fish he split.
2 Parting of the hair when combed.
C 71–119 Many people refer to a parting of the hair at the side as a crease. P 181–78 Where do you want the crease?

'crease v [= increase]. Cp *EDD* ~ sb³, v² D. Comb **'crease mesh**: in a fish-net, esp a 'cast net,' a section with mesh of a larger size than the rest.
T 198–65 There's about eight or ten crease meshes into a cast net. You'll knit just so many meshes down, and then you start making crease meshes to make un wider and wider.

credit n Cp *OED* ~ sb 14: ~ system (1880).
Comb **credit system**: arrangement by which a fisherman is supplied by a merchant with provisions, gear, etc, against the season's catch; TRUCK¹ (SYSTEM).
1846 TOCQUE 137 The merchants seeing the great improbability of receiving any immediate returns for their goods [because of the 1817 disasters], circumscribed the accustomed credit system. 1863 PEDLEY 204–5 It is difficult to trace to its origin what is well known in the colony by the name of the credit system. . . In fitting out his servants in the fishing ships. . .what was so furnished to them was charged by the merchant on credit, to be repaid in fish when the voyage was over. 1906 LUMSDEN 71–2 They are not, however, as provident and independent as one might wish, and if we are correct in this estimate we are sure that the greatest cause is the 'credit system,' by which a large portion of the population have been all their lives in debt, with no better prospect for the future. 1933 *Nfld Royal Commission Report* 102 Emerging from the old feudal practice under which the merchant, who was at once a store-keeper and an exporter of fish, employed a number of fishermen to catch fish for him and provided them in return with sufficient necessaries to maintain themselves and their families throughout the year, the fishery in all its branches. . .has been conducted during the last century on what is known as the credit system. [1959] 1966 FARIS 20 Several factors led to the inception and development of this 'credit system.' In the first place, the uncertainty of the fishery—the hope of a good season encouraged the fishermen to borrow. In the second place, there were numerous small settlements with only one merchant, which eliminated the need for cash as the fishermen could only trade at the local store.

credit time: period of preparation for the summer fishery.
1977 RUSSELL 32 'Twas then Liz reminded him of his two swileskins. True, one of 'em had some shotholes in it, but the other was perfect and between 'em they ought to fetch enough molasses to tide 'em over till credit time.

creep v also **crape*** [krɛip] *OED* ~ v 7 naut (1813–). To drag the sea bottom for submerged nets, etc, with a grapnel or creeper.
[1772] 1792 CARTWRIGHT i, 234 By the way we crept for a grapnel and road, which captain Lane had lost last year, but could not find them. 1919 GRENFELL² 170 Yet an extended period of 'creeping' the bottom with drags and grapples had revealed nothing. P 19–55 Crape. To drag the sea bottom with a hook, jigger or grapnel. P 245–70 We craped [the drowned fisherman] in. 1971 CHIARAMONTE 36 George 'creeped' for his gear for a couple of hours and then gave up the search, deciding to wait until the tide shifted.

creeper¹ n *DAE* ~ 1 c (1859); *DC* (c1820–). Metal device with sharp points, fastened to boot for walking on ice; cp CHISEL¹.
1801 [THORESBY] 50 I was obliged to walk on creepers, (two pieces of iron made to fit the feet, having prods to pierce the ice to prevent the foot from slip-

ping). 1861 DE BOILEU 155 We generally wear what on the coast are called 'creepers,' which are much the same as cricketers wear in England. P 207–67 Before he went out on the ice he put on his creepers. 1971 NOSEWORTHY 188 Creepers. Small, flat pieces of iron with the four corners bent outward which were strapped onto shoes to provide support when a person walked on ice.

creeper² n Cp *OED* ~ 5 'a kind of grapnel used for dragging the bottom of the sea.' A grapnel attaching an animal trap to the ground, with a length of chain to permit various placements.

[1771] 1792 CARTWRIGHT i, 198 [The wolverine] got into a trap which was not far off, and carried it to some distance where the creeper caught hold of a bush, and he escaped after a very long struggle.

creeping vbl n *OED* ~ 4 (1886). Dragging the sea bottom with a grapnel or 'creeper' to recover a lost object; attrib **creeping gear**.

1895 GRENFELL 169 Sometimes the buoys [of seal nets] are under the ice, and the process known as 'creeping' has to be undertaken to find the nets at all, for it will not do to lose these most valuable possessions. . . Often hours may be spent 'creeping.' P 90–69 ~ dragging the ocean bottom with a hook for the body of a person drowned. 1971 CHIARAMONTE 36 When a man loses his gear, he hauls a small grapple-type anchor across the ocean floor attempting to hook the grapple on the line of his gear. This is called 'creeping.' 1976 *Evening Telegram* 27 Mar, p. 4 Various types of creeping gear were designed and used during the operation and these devices were dragged over the sea bottom in areas where 'ghost nets' were suspected to be located.

crew n Cp *OED* ~ ¹ 6 'men belonging to and manning a ship, boat or other vessel' naut for sense 1; 3 b 'an assembly of animals,' *DC* (Nfld: 1770) for sense 4. See also CROWD.

1 A group (of persons) engaged or 'shipped' by a merchant, 'planter,' or 'skipper' to conduct afloat and on shore the various branches and operations of fishing and sealing, usu on the share system.

[1771] 1792 CARTWRIGHT i, 173 At noon the shallop *Dispatch* arrived from Fogo with dry provisions; also brought a calf, some fowls, and a crew of hands for St Lewis's Bay. 1792 PULLING *MS* Aug [The indians] are seldom seen by any of Miller's people though they must pass very near several houses inhabited by Miller and his crew. [1802] 1916 MURPHY 2 Four or five men constitute a crew to tend about twenty [sealing] nets. 1849 [FEILD] 63 [There is] a small 'crew' here; that is, a few men dwelling together to prosecute the fishing in the summer and kill seals in the winter. 1882 TALBOT 22 The vessel contained the principal portion of his own family. . .these, with his fishing crew of seven or eight men, constituted his portion of the passengers [to Labrador fishery]. But there was another planter with his crew on board, so that the whole number of passengers amounted to twenty-five or twenty-six. 1895

GRENFELL 59 Some Newfoundland planters and agents provide boarded huts for their 'crowd'. . . Each 'crew' has a fish stage, alongside which the fish are brought in the boats. [1915] 1960 FUDGE 52 In the spring of 1915, while fishing on Scaierie Banks with a crew of eleven dories, we made up a total of 25 [souls] onboard the *Harry A Nickerson*. [1955] 1980 *Evening Telegram* 16 June, p. 8 Four crews of fishermen left Carbonear for Labrador this week.

2 A number of people functioning as a unit.

[1918–19] GORDON 26 There is some very heavy work ahead of us, for we are such a small and weak crew. P 148–62 What a crew [of children]! P 80–63 Crew and crowd are used for groups of people, or associated cooperating individuals. C 71–96 [There was] the biggest kind of crew in [the house].

3 Members of a family.

P 262–58 A Newfoundlander often uses the word crew in reference to a man's family, as, 'Tom Shears' crew will be along for dinner tomorrow.' P 121–67 Our crew is not in from fishing yet.

4 A family of beavers.

[1770] 1792 CARTWRIGHT i, 58 I had the satisfaction of finding a large new beaverhouse; which appeared to be inhabited by a numerous crew. 1792 ibid *Gloss* i, x Crew of beavers. The two old beavers, and all their young ones which have not yet begun to breed. If there are more breeding pairs than one in the same house, it is said, to be inhabited by a double or treble crew.

5 Phr **call crews**: of two people, to choose the players for one's team.

T 141/65–65² Stew and Evelyn called crews on the cricket ground, where you chuck your bat back and forth, catch un six times, and then put your hand one over the other till you get up to the top.

cribby n Cp GROSE (1785) cribbeys 'blind allies, courts or bye ways'; PARTRIDGE Cribbeys or Cribby Islands [Caribee Islands].

1 In pl, a dense and cheaply-built part of St John's.

[1856] 1906 MURPHY 11 Several houses burnt at 'cubeers' [= cribbies] St John's. 1862 *Daily News* 13 May, [p. 2] The scene of these Bacchanalian peace disturbers was that poetic place ycleped cribbies. 1892 *Evening Herald* 21 Nov, p. 4 An assault case, brought by a woman from Brennan's Lane against a man from 'the Cribbies,' was dismissed. [1900 OLIVER & BURKE] 42 In parts of the town were crowded places like Tarehin's town, the Cribbies, Dogstown and Maggotty Cove. 1973 *Evening Telegram* 26 May, p. 8 'Oh no thank you' sez Mag, 'and another thing Edward, if you want to discuss that relict of the cribbies I hope you refer to it as a cuspidor.' 1981 ibid 2 May How often have I asked you never to use the word grub, people will think you came from the cribbies, always refer to food as sustenance.

2 A resident of St John's; TOWNY; also attrib; (P 76–67).

P 63–99 ~s. A slightly derogatory term for St John's-men (or townspeople). 1979 *Evening Telegram* 23 June, p. 15 'Of course, you wouldn't say body [instead of rames],' sez Mag. 'You got to bring cribbie talk into it.'

cribby* v also **quib**. To jump from one ice-pan to another; COPY (P 245–67).

Q 67–69 Cribbying on the ballycatters. 1967 READER 1 Arctic ice fills all bays and harbours on the N.E. Coast during the spring, and boys jumping from pan to pan call this copying or quibbing.

crinkly a Comb **crinkly dick**: rock gunnel; radiated shanny, an invertebrate fish (*Ulvaria subbifurcata*) (P 63–63).

cripsy See CRISPY.

crispy a also **cripsy**. Cp *EDD* crips (cripsy Co) 2 'brittle, easily broken.' Brittle; liable to fragment or crumble; crinkly.

1933 MERRICK 134 Crispy. . .means brittle. P 80–63 A piece of rusty iron is cripsy. T 36/8–64 In a good many cases when the fish had been finished the [bark] wouldn't be much good for the next year because he'd be cripsy, right dry. T 169–65² Around here [the ground] is wonderful crispy, and the same way at Fogo Islands. All those spots o' ground, 'tis right over a cliff. 1979 *Evening Telegram* 24 Nov, p. 15 'Not buttin' in,' sez Ned, 'but how did Bill look? He's not a bad lookin' fella and he got grand cripsy hair.'

crit n JOYCE 242 crith; DINNEEN 276 cruit 'hump on the back.' A stoop; hump; esp in phr *in a crit*: stooped, bent over; in a cramped position.

1925 *Dial Notes* v, 328 In a crit. Squatting. 1937 DEVINE 15 I was all in a *crit*, sitting in that chair. 1968 DILLON 134 Haven't he got a shockin' crit on 'im? C 73–13 [tall tale] Ould Tim ya know was found dead sittin' on the hole in his out-house. Naturally he was in a crit. Unfortunately rigor mortis had set in and when they tried to lay him out they couldn't keep him from sitting up. 1976 *Evening Telegram* 9 Mar, p. 12 The poor women of them days were bent over in a crit after a day workin' over the washboard.

crit v from CRIT n. To stoop or slump so as to appear shorter; QUAT.

1968 DILLON 135 There's girls here and they're tryin' to crit down.

critch¹ n *EDD* ~ sb¹ 1 Do W So. Small earthenware jar.

1937 DEVINE 15 ~ A small covered china bowl used for keeping molasses in on the kitchen dresser. P 96–72 [They] always called the butter dish a critch.

critch² See CRUTCH.

cronnick See CRUNNICK.

croochy* v also **cooch*, coochy, coojy*** ['kruːtʃɪ, 'krʉutʃɨ, 'krʉutʃiˑ, 'kuːtʃɪ]. Cp *EDD* couch v 2, crouch, crouging; *ADD* scrouge, etc, with similar senses. See also COOPY. To squat; to bend down close to the ground, crouch; QUAT; esp in phr *croochy down*.

P 113–56 If you croochy down you won't hit your head on the beam. T 141/2–65² My gar, 'tis croochy down now, and get back now. T 158–65 There was three black ducks coming over, and he see 'em coming, and he coochy down. P 184–67 When I let him go, he's sure to coochy down. 1972 MURRAY 132 Someone else crouched in the middle of the slide, feet on the runners and holding on the front 'horns' (i.e., in the 'coocheying down' position).

croodle v *EDD* ~ v¹ 2. To stoop, squat; COOPY; esp in phr *croodle down*.

1937 DEVINE 17 Croodle down. To stoop or lie low so as not to be seen. P 127–73 To croodle down: to squat down on heels.

crooked a ['krʌkɪd, 'krɵkəd] *EDD* ~ ppl a 4; *Kilkenny Lexicon* 'bad-tempered.' Ill-tempered, cross, cranky; DIRTY 4.

P 68–54 He's a crooked old man. 1966 *Evening Telegram* 30 June, p. 19 Sure that crooked look is not his way though. 1970 JANES 84 'How crooked is you!' she countered, trying to divert him. The word 'crooked' in our family meant cantankerous, not dishonest.

croost* v JOYCE 242; cp DINNEEN crústa 'clod, missile.' To throw; pelt, hurl stones at.

P 108–70 Croostin' rocks. P 148–70 Croos'in' old black cats.

crop n also **crap** *DC* ~ Nfld (1906); cp *OED* crap sb¹ 5 'money' obs or dial (1700–1787) for sense 1.

1 In sealing and fishing, the personal equipment or supplies issued against the profits of the 'voyage.'

[1854] P 197–77 I propose leaving [Bay de Verde] on Tuesday for New Perlican to issue the sealers their crop. 1897 *J A Folklore* x, 204 Crop, usually pronounced *crap*, the personal equipment of a man going on a sealing voyage, supplied by the merchants, but distinct from the provisions of the ship. It includes provisions for his family, if he receives any advance of that kind. 1906 LUMSDEN 116 The voyage had been a failure; the men had hardly earned enough to pay for their 'crop,' or outfit, and had nothing coming to them. [1918–19] GORDON 32 Went out to Porter's Post and got Mr Haviland to give me a 'crop.' [1929] 1933 GREENLEAF (ed) 246 "The Sealing Cruise of the *Lone Flier*": It was on a Tuesday morning when our captain came from ship, / Says he, 'My boys, you'll sign on, and then you'll get the crop.' / Our crop composed of boots and clothes, likewise a fork and pan. / 'If there's anything else you want, my boys, you must get it how you can.' 1936 SMITH 12 I shall never forget my first crop that I had—one pair of long-tongued fishing boots and a suit of oilskins, including a sou'wester. T 36–64 When you starts in the spring you'd want, say, twenty-five or thirty or forty dollars of a fit-out—bit o' grub, rubber boots an' rubber clothes and so on. They call that your crop. T 141/68–65 In the event you made a poor voyage, the difference between what you did get an' the price o' your crop [would] be wiped off. 1976

CASHIN 54 This 'crop' or advance consisted mainly of sealskin boots for each of the crew, some tobacco, oatmeal, sugar and raisins and some other necessities of comfort. The actual cost was nine dollars, and in view of the fact that the firm was taking a gamble on the venture, the sealers were charged twelve dollars or 33% more than the actual cost.

2 Comb **crop note**: merchant's chit entitling sealer to his personal equipment.

1929 *Nat Geog* July, p. 130 The only guarantee a sealer gets is food and a crop note, equivalent to $9. 1936 SMITH 49 Job's premises were filled with men, as there were four ships, as well as the *Neptune*, taking on supplies for the seal-fishery. There was over a thousand men along all the ships. The next morning we signed articles and got our ticket and crop note.

crop[1] v also **crap***. Cp *OED* ~ v 8. To clip one wing of a domestic fowl.

C 66–10 'We'll have to crap the wings of the fowls. They'm gettin' into Aunt Callie's garden and eating her plant seed.' The wings of the hens are crapped to keep them from flying in over the fences and getting in and ruining people's early plants. Only one wing is crapped. This keeps the hen off balance and she can't fly. If you crapped her two wings she'd fly.

crop[2] v from CROP n. To supply a sealer or fisherman with personal equipment, and sometimes supplies, against the profits of the 'voyage.'

1924 ENGLAND 248 De strikers got cropped [supplied] an' jumped out of 'er in de deed hour o' de night. 1936 SMITH 70 We arrived at Brigus on June the first, where we discharged some of our supplies, and started in 'cropping' the hundred men and boys.

cropping vbl n

Comb **cropping shed**: store on a merchant's premises in which items of personal equipment for sealing voyage are distributed.

1924 ENGLAND 11 Some were drawing water at an icicled faucet near the cropping shed, bringing 'sluts' (kettles) aboard, and brewing tea.

cropping time: period when sealers (or fishermen) are provided with personal equipment for the 'voyage'.

[1900 OLIVER & BURKE] 46 . . .when cropping time arrived.

cross a *OED* ~ bar sb 1 (1856 quot) for sense (a); cp *OED* cross-beak (1688, 1789).

Comb **cross-bar**: (a) one of the heavy timbers fastened on top of the runners of a sled; also attrib; (b) horizontal timber nailed to the side of a fishing 'stage'; RAIL.

1874 *Maritime Mo* iii, 552 They reached the little stage before their cottage and fastened their boat to the cross-bars, leaving the herrings on board. T 100/1–64 The bob-sled behind was pulled with a cross-bar chain, going from that runner—that side of the bunk of the first sleigh—and this way, forming a cross in the centre. Whichever way the front bob-sled slewed, he'd pull on this chain and slew the back one same way. T 175/7–65

Your crooked piece for a runner, what your shoes go on, and then the cross-bars and knees—more crooked pieces of stuff to strengthen the cross-bars.

cross-beak(ed) linnet: white-winged crossbill (*Loxia leucoptera leucoptera*).

[1776] 1792 CARTWRIGHT ii, 151 I was pleasingly entertained with the melodious singing of the cross-beaked linnets; they remain all winter with us, and feed on the seeds of black spruce. 1959 MCATEE 63 Cross-beak linnet, cross-billed linnet—white-winged crossbill.

cross-buoy, ~ **bobber**: float with rod inserted at right angles, used to prevent the twisting of the mooring ropes of a net (Q 67–91; P 127–76).

cross-handed: see CROSS-HANDED.

cross av *OED* ~ hackle v (1826); *EDD* ~ 11 (3) ~ hopple (a), (b); *OED* ~ hackling vbl n (1886).

Comb **cross-hackle, cross 'ackle, cross-heckle** [krɑˈsak], ˈkrɑsækəl, ˈkruˈsæk], ˈkrɒˈsæk]]: to cross-examine vexatiously; to question; to argue with, contradict; by opposing someone, to annoy.

1896 *J A Folklore* ix, 22 In Newfoundland *hackle* and *cross hackle* are especially applied to the questioning of a witness by a lawyer, when carried to a worrying degree. 1937 DEVINE 17 Cross 'ackle. To contradict. To ask difficult questions. T 222–66 I wonder how you vent your spleen on your husbands when they cross-hackle you; that is, if they ever do argue with you. 1966 SCAMMELL 36 Sid never got the courage to talk to his father about it. He knew it would only crosshackle him. 1975 RUSSELL 66 And they cross-hackled over it until Matty remembered something.

cross-hackling: vexatious questioning, cross-examining; arguing.

1966 *Nfld Qtly* Dec, p. 16 After two days of cross-heckling and every kind of pressure, nothing was discovered, and all the witnesses with the exception of Jacquard, were allowed to return home to Miquelon.

cross pile v: to make a rectangular pile (of logs, dried cod, etc) with successive layers placed at right angles to the ones beneath.

T 66/7–64 They'd got the fir rines for their fish—covering for their fish—they'd bring home what they think they'd need, pile 'em and cross pile 'em, shift 'em again, try them again. They'd stay flat. P 245–78 ~ Usually refers to piling sticks of firewood; one layer, say, east-west, the other north-south, keeping edges as square as possible. The term is also applied to fish piled in a square or bulk about 8 ft by 5 ft. A bulk might have a couple or more layers in one direction and the next couple or so in the opposite direction. Cross piling in this way is supposed to bind the fish and keep the bulk from falling over.

cross n

Comb **cross(-fox)**: red fox (*Vulpes fulvus*) in a colour variation with cross-like marking on back.

[1771] 1792 CARTWRIGHT i, 82 I examined the traps and death-falls near Fox Pond, and upon the river, and had a good cross fox. [1778] ibid ii, 305 There was a fox in one of my traps; it proved a cross; was a little trace-galled, and smelt strong. 1908 HUBBARD 7 In 1907 there were brought in at one point seventeen silvers, twenty 'cross' foxes, and one hundred and thirteen of the common red ones. T 203/5–65 And the cross fox, some of him is grey on the sides, mixed with dark and a form of a cross on his back. It goes across from his forelegs across his shoulders, and right up the back of his neck [and] down.

cross-patch: see **cross-fox**; PATCH FOX.

1888 STEARNS 347 They are now said to be of one species, and the common red fox [is] the father of them all. . . We have the variety known as the patch fox, which is only a darker and blacker form of the red; after that the cross or cross-patch, with a lighter area in the center of the back, in the form of a bar down the back and another across the fore-shoulders.

cross v Phr *cross off*: to intercept, cut off.

T 70–64 She was going fast, he says, and they had to pull hard to cross her off. And they crossed her off [and] towed her in.

cross-handed av Cp *DAE* ~ 'in a manner which involves crossing one's hands, esp in rowing' (1838); *ADD* ~ 'alone' (Nfld: 1938).

1 With a man handling two oars instead of one to propel a boat.

1871 HOWLEY *MS Reminiscences* 10 All row cross handed using two oars or paddles. There are no rollocks of the usual kind seen further south. There is but one thole pin set in the gunwale, the oars being kept in place by a ring usually made of withe or twisted spruce roots, slipped over the oar and the pin. [1911] GRENFELL 131 His four stalwart boys were already able to help with the trap net. . .though the youngest could scarcely yet row 'cross handed,' *i.e.*, handle two oars at once.

2 Rowing a boat alone, esp for purpose of catching fish; (fishing) alone, doing one's own rowing; esp in phr *fish cross-handed, go* ~ .

1849 [FEILD] 94 [He is] a person who, though eighty-five years of age, can row himself over the bay cross-handed. 1901 *Christmas Review* 6 He himself fully appreciated his ignorance of the fisherman's calling, and, instead of going as a shoreman or servant in the regular crew, he decided to go cross-handed, and try his luck on the grounds within a half mile from the harbor. [1906] GRENFELL 184 'I've got as much as I used to get all summer cross-handed,' he said to me. 1937 DEVINE 17 'He goes cross-handed.' Used particularly of one carrying on the hand-line fishery alone. 1953 *Nfld Fish Develop Report* 18 [The skipper's] partners and sharemen, however, may fish with other crews or on their own ('cross-handed') during the course of the season. T 449–67 Lots o' times I went cross handed, sir, and lobster fishin' I done that a lot o' years cross handed. That was hard going. 1981 *Evening Telegram* 13 July, p. 6 He rowed and fished 'crosshanded' (alone) after [his sons] died.

3 Carrying out any activity alone rather than in a co-operative group.

1924 ENGLAND 117 I made me own livin' iver since I could work cross-handed [alone], an' 'spects to till I

straighten rate up fer Cap'n Jones [Davy Jones]. T 222–66 Up on the south coast, if a person is going to do anything by himself it is said that he is going to do it cross-handed. . . She asked the young man if he would sing a solo, and he said, 'Oh no, miss; I couldn't sing cross-handed.' P 131–70 He built his barn cross-handed. C 71–94 If he went in the woods alone he was 'in the woods cross-handed.'

4 Comb **cross-handed dory**: dory rigged for rowing by one man; DORY.

1940 SCAMMELL 7 "The Six Horse-Power Coaker": One evenin' last fall we went out to our trawl / Though it looked like 'twas going to blow. / We turned to go in, in the teeth of the wind / With a cross-handed dory in tow.

cross-hand(ed) skiff: boat operated by one man; SKIFF.

[1906] GRENFELL 52 No man can't be sure o' getting a winter's diet with only a cross-hand skiff to work in.

crottle See COTTERALL.

crousty a ['kræʊstɪ, 'kræʊsti, 'krɐʊstɪ] *EDD* ~ s w cties. Cantankerous; easily annoyed; CROOKED.

1964 *Can Journ Ling* x, 41 *Crousty* and *crooked* meaning 'crabby' or 'ill-tempered.' P 54–65 ~ having a sour, nasty, penurious disposition. T 417–67 Certainly the croustiest people'd have the worst tricks played on 'em. . . Crowsty people, more or less. Take now my aunt, she don't want anybody in messing up her floor. C 70–21 ~ applied to a very crotchety person, someone glum and grumpy.

crow n

1 Local nickname for resident of a nearby community.

P 53–66 Grand Bank shags, Fortune goats, Garnish crows. P 245–69 Heart's Delight 'bright buttons' / Heart's Content 'beaus', / Perlican 'cockies,' / Scilly Cove 'crows.'

2 Comb **crow blackbird**: Newfoundland rusty blackbird (*Euphagus carolinus nigrans*) (1959 MCATEE 60).

crow's bread, ~ food, ~ pork: variety of toadstool; DEVIL'S CAP.

P 47–66 Crow's pork—large mushroom not fit to eat. P 148–69 ~ like a big mushroom, the size of a saucer. It grows among trees, in wet marshes. 1971 NOSEWORTHY 189 Crowfood—inedible mushrooms.

crowd n Cp *DAE* ~ 'set, clique, or "ring"' (1840–); *DA* b [party of cowboys]. See also CREW.

1 An organized, integrated group of people, esp a fishing or sealing crew.

1895 GRENFELL 59 Some Newfoundland planters and agents provide boarded huts for their 'crowd'. . . Each 'crew' has a fish stage, alongside which the fish are brought in the boats. 1924 ENGLAND 240 'Master watches, call up ahl y'r crowds. Get ahl y'r men ready to go away. Take plenty flags. Evvery man that can drag a seal, get ready! Evvery man out o' them castles.'

[1961] 1965 PEACOCK (ed) i, 114 "A Crowd of Bold Sharemen": 'You'll go home again, sir, but that's not the thing, / There's seven of our boys you brought down here this spring, / You said you were going fishing in the Straits of Belle Isle, / And if you don't do it we'll have you on trial' [Said] a crowd of bold sharemen. T 141/66–65[2] I said, 'Billy got his crowd?' 'Yes, he got men enough, but he got n'ar a splitter. He's leaving a berth for a splitter.' T 187/90–65 [When the house is to be moved] the man that owns the house he'd have to go around then and look for a crowd. 1966 FARIS 138 Only the actual male fishing crew members of the effective 'crowd' share the voyage, although the share of each will be largely determined by the number of persons he contributes to the 'shore crowd,' that is, those helping to 'put away the fish'—sons, daughters, wife or brothers. 1967 FIRESTONE 45 When the brothers' children grow up there will in most cases be a split and each brother will fish with his sons. This group is referred to as a *crowd* or *crew*. 1979 *Salt Water, Fresh Water* 319 I could have went into St Anthony, but somehow I was young and wanted to get home; and I had this crowd [of stationers] aboard.

2 All or most of the people (of another community or group).

T 141/2–65[2] Nobody sove [= saved] the crowd. 1966 FARIS 86 'Crowd' is an extremely flexible term [and can mean] a group of young children playing together, a group of people at a 'time,' a group of men gathered to talk, move a boat or watch something on the sea, or one entire half of the community (as in the 'Dog Cove crowd' or the 'Upper Harbour crowd'). 1975 BUTLER 39 There was about twenty-five men in on the point watchin' [the tight squeeze]. . . But anyway, they were a pretty good crowd in Merasheen. . .the women come down when they found out the trouble. 1977 *Inuit Land Use* 335 And over around Flowers Bay, the other crowd were trapping all this area.

3 Members of a family; relatives.

[1918–19] GORDON 34 Called in at [Burnt] Harbor to visit the Lethbridges, and tell them the unpleasant news that four of their crowd were dead. M 67–4 She's none o' your crowd anyway. P 41–68 The parents referred to the children as my crowd. 1969 DE WITT 32 My crowd (sons) want nothing to do with the fishing.

crozing n Cp *OED* croze v: crozing. Point near the croze of a barrel; the top.

P 243–55 Crozin'—the top of a barrel. P 113–56 The puncheon was filled to the crozin'.

crubeen n also **crube** *O Sup*[2] ~ (1847–); DINNEEN crúibín. Pig's trotter; esp the hock prepared for food by pickling.

[1894 BURKE] 76 He eat everything was in the house, pig's head and boiled crubeens. [1904] [1960] BURKE (ed White) 35 "Playing for the Boneen": But Fogarty fisted his pig by the tail, / And struck right and left, where a head could be seen, / And Murphy, poor feller, was knocked into the cellar, / From a lick of the crube of the little Boneen. 1937 DEVINE 17 ~ Pig's feet salted and prepared for cooking. P 108–70 Crubeens are pig's feet or hocks, pickled like salt pork. 1979 *Evening Telegram* 12 Nov, p. 6 Every pupil was

expected to be sent down to the cove for. . .a watered crubeen, a head of cabbage, a bucket of coal, or a turn of water from Gaden's stream.

crud n *EDD* ~ sb 1. Curd; coagulated milk.

1937 DEVINE 17 ~s. Curds; sediment. P 148–62 ~s. Thick milk, boiled on stove. 1979 *Evening Telegram* 25 Aug, p. 8 Sure the cows are as fat as butter. They are mostly tan colour with white faces, and they are as clean as a crud.

cruddy a also **crudly** *O Sup*[2] ~ 1 obs exc dial (1509–1678); *EDD* crud sb 1: cruddy, crudly adj 1, 2.

1 Having a curdled appearance or texture; softened, disintegrating.

1874 HOWLEY *MS Reminiscences* 47 [The salmon] was almost black outside from long sojourn in the fresh water, had lost all its silvery sheen and when boiled next day the flesh was found to be colourless and cruddy. P 245–55 Poached eggs will run away all cruddy unless you put a drop of vinegar in the water. P 148–64 Ice cream gets right cruddy after it's been frozen again. T 253/4–66 [In making fat soap with lye] you'd salt it, separate it, because when you salt it, it'd get right cruddly. P 148–67 Crudly ice or snow crunches underfoot after a mild or rain. C 71–127 Cruddy was used to describe milk that had turned sour, especially [when added to] coffee or tea.

2 Crispy and dry; crumbling.

1964 *Evening Telegram* 4 June, p. 13 Talkin' about fish, though, ever notice how fish is nice an' cruddy around August? When they gets that way they're better stuffed and roasted. P 148–64 The fish is right cruddy [dry and well cooked]. C 69–2 When our fathers came with a load of wood, we would cut off the frankum. We would warm it so as to make it soft, and then chew [it] for gum. After a while, however, it became crudly and hard.

crudly See CRUDDY.

cruel a, intens *EDD* ~ adj 1, adv 2 esp Ir and s w cties; JOYCE 89. See also SOME, WONDERFUL.

1 Of inanimate objects, terrible, dreadful.

1836 [WIX][2] 53 My eyes. . .are further tried within the houses by the quantity of smoke, or 'cruel steam,' as the people emphatically and correctly designate it, with which every tilt is filled. 1887 *Colonist Christmas No* 8 I did not grudge Pugsley the drink, after his yarn; but it was a cruel waste of good liquor to give it to those common fishermen. P 148–63 You're a cruel sight. T 222–66 A Girl Guide Commissioner visited a village where I was working at the time. She had a great many medals and so on, and it was said of her that she had 'a cruel mess of gear on her.' P 245–67 Cruel weather [means] stormy or unpleasant weather. 1976 *Evening Telegram* 3 Aug, p. 6 I think this would be a real service to the people [of Harbour Grace] if the minister would do something about this cruel odor [from the fish-meal plant].

2 Very, extremely.

1924 ENGLAND 132 "Johnny Burke": Till crool sad misfartune, which caused 'im to sleep / On a cold bed o' sand where de water run deep! Ibid 257 An' I know one cap'n, too, as runs a store; an' one year when de men was paid off de swiler, he took a canvas bag an' stood on de w'arf, an' as de men come off, he collected ahl as was owed him. Yes, he had de right to, but a lot of 'em went home bare. An' dat was crool hard, me son. 1937 DEVINE 50 [Master,] that's a cruel stun boy. 1968 DILLON 135 Boy, 'tis a cruel stormy day, isn't it? C 71–93 It's a cruel wonderful day.

cruise n [kruːs, krʉus]. Cp *OED* ~ sb b transf.
    1 A walk, ramble, trip on foot.
    [1794] 1968 THOMAS 155 I had a cruize to myself around this Bay. In my perambulations I met with a few Mushrooms on the borders of a Bog. [c1894] PANL P4/14, p. 200 'I ain't had a cruise to-year.' 1925 *Dial Notes* v, 329 ~ a long walk. P 191–73 Let's go for a cruce.
    2 A trip or drive in a vehicle.
    1906 LUMSDEN 53 Every trip was a cruise, whether by sea or by land, and there was no commoner question than this: 'Bound for a cruise to-day, sir?' P 262–58 ~ often used for a drive in a car.
    3 An excursion or journey on dog-sled.
    1894 *Evening Herald* 12 Dec I thought about the time. . .my poor John and me went up for a cruise to my sister Hannah's house. 1920 GRENFELL & SPALDING 136 Last week I had a three days' 'cruise' while the doctor considerately sent a nurse up here to try her hand at my family. This time the cruise was 'on the dogs' instead of the rolling sea. P 245–67 [Labrador 'livyers'] would go for a cruise on their dog-teams.
    4 A visit with relatives or friends; pleasurable journey (P 152–58).
    1933 MERRICK 16 Like the few others who have ever been 'outside' from here he'd like to go again some day for 'a cruise' just to see the movies and the lights and all the incomprehensible things people do, but never to live.
    5 Hunting expedition.
    [1770] 1792 CARTWRIGHT i, 59 Ned and Milmouth returned on Saturday, with a brace of spruce-game. . . I sent them out again on another cruise. [1775] ibid ii, 62 I took a cruise over Lyon Head and Eyre Island and. . .killed a yellow fox with a greyhound. 1889 HOWLEY *MS Reminiscences* 42 After dinner I went for a long cruise taking my gun with me. Travelled in on our path nearly a mile and then took a lead of marshes running eastward. 1914 WALLACE 187 'Tisn't th' havin' a poor cruise now an' again's what's botherin' me.

cruise v [krʉus]. Cp *OED* ~ v b transf (1698–).
    1 To go around on foot; to look for game or some object.
    [1819] 1915 HOWLEY 108 Should I be appointed to cruise the summer for them. . .I have not the least doubt but that I shall, through the medium of the woman I now have, be enabled to open an intercourse with [the indians]. 1894 *Evening Herald* 13 Dec I have been what people calls cruising about here. I have been visiting some of my friends. . .with my snow-shoes and axe. 1907 WALLACE 88 Th' Nascaupees are back here a bit t' th' west'ard. I saw some of 'em one day when I was cruisin' that way an' I made tracks back fer I didn't

want t' die so quick. 1933 GREENE xv Cruising the Floe—denotes the search for the seals on foot, often over many miles of ice. T 58/64–64 This morning I took my two dogs, and lunch, went in about three miles, four miles, and cruised round a bit, and I got shapes of a keel for a boat.
    2 (a) Of animals, to wander about in a particular area; (b) of marine creatures, to swim.
    [1775] 1792 CARTWRIGHT ii, 126 Great numbers of foxes had cruised about last night; they struck up three traps; which is the first time I had been certain of their touching the baits. T 58/64–64 [The whale] wasn't used to cold water. Now he cruised round here all the summer. 1979 TIZZARD 310 If the salmon saw the net and cruised along by it he would surely be caught by the [hawk].
    3 To float timber by water or transport it on vessels; to carry supplies.
    P 54–63 [This firm was] sending logging crews into the wooded parts of the bays. . .and cutting timber. Some of it would be 'cruised' down to the firm's place of business in the spring. T 141/2–65² They'd cruise up—go up and bring down their own supplies. T 141/67–65² If you was up the bay and cut some wood for the winter to cruise down in the spring, you got to make another trip. T 175/6–65 Bulk 'em up on the flake perhaps in the spring. He'd cruise them home just the same as he would his firewood. 1979 *Salt Water, Fresh Water* 55 Now when the ice would move off in March or April, we'd launch out the boat, get the engine in, steam up there nine or ten miles, and load the stuff aboard the boat and bring it back. We call this cruising the wood back.

cruiser n See CRUISE v for sense 2 and 3.
    1 Crewman of a vessel engaged in coastal trade.
    [1819] P 54–63 Cruiser [named] John Eagan.
    2 A migratory fisherman prosecuting the cod-fishery in a schooner on the Labrador coast.
    1895 *Outing* xxvii, p. 20 These [floaters] are the 'cruisers,' who live on board their craft, shifting about from place to place in search of fish, which, when caught, are cleaned upon the decks, salted 'green.'
    3 One who visits friends and neighbours.
    M 69–5 Since there was no fishing carried on on Sunday, a favourite custom of the fisherfolk was to exchange visits between neighbouring communities on that day. [This photo shows] three 'cruisers' (visitors) returning home on Sunday evening after making a visit to our community.

cruising vbl n Visiting friends or relatives.
    1894 *Evening Telegram* 13 Dec, p. 3 Since I wrote last on this book I have been what people calls cruising about here. I have been visiting some of my friends, all though scattered far apart, with my snow-shoes on and axe on my shoulders. The nearest house to this place is about 5 miles up a beautiful river. 1910 GRENFELL 198 Cruising [by dog-team] can be carried on in perfect safety, and one can cover hundreds of miles without ever seeing the open water at all, as the outlying islands are so numerous. [1915] GORDON 18 Visiting friends and relatives en masse was, I found, a common

practice on the part of some of the Labrador people. They called it 'cruising,' and as they had very few other forms of recreation, one could quite understand its popularity.

crump¹ n *EDD* ~ sb³ 3 s w cties. Stooped, hunched position; CRIT.

P 232–64 There's a crump you're in—peculiar sitting position. C 71–38 When sitting at the table in a slouched position or standing droop shouldered, my father would tell me to get out of the crump I was in.

crump² n Cp DINNEEN 1331 crompa 'a gnarled branch.' Small twisted tree or trunk; CRAN, CRUNNICK.

P 126–67 To cut crump, that is, small, crooked trees sometimes used for firewood. C 75–19 Crumps are old stumps and crooked pieces of wood. Usually found in an area that has been burnt over by a forest fire. 1976 *Daily News* 15 Jan, p. 3 How about 'chucking hoops' or 'cuttin' crump.'

cruncheons See SCRUNCHINS.

crunnick n also **crannick, chronic, cronnick, crunnock, scronnick***, etc; **cranny*, croony*** ['krænɪk, 'krʌnɪk] *EDD* crannock 'root of furze; the stem of a furze-brush, which has been burnt' Pem Do; cp *EDD* crank sb² 'dead branch' Gl; *DC* ~ (Nfld: 1895–). See also CRAN. Tree or root killed or much weathered by wind, water or fire; piece of such wood gathered as fuel; small twisted fir or spruce. Also attrib.

[c1894] PANL P4/14, p. 198 Dry wood is *staragons* or *crunnocks*. 'To *spell* a *yafful* of *crunnocks*' is to [carry] an armful of dry wood for kindling purposes. 1896 *J A Folklore* ix, 36 Crannocks on the west coast, crunnocks to the north, small pieces of wood for kindling. [c1900] 1978 *RLS* 8, p. 22 Crawnick. Small dry or withered timber, trunk, etc. Crawnick grove, patch of same. 1937 DEVINE 15 Cronic—the stump or bole of a tree, also the roots with bark all gone and whitened by the sun and weather for many years. P 4–59 Cronic. A root of tree washed out on shore of lake or ocean. 1963 HEAD 141 Crunicks (the twisted trunks of stunted trees) and in some areas peat, are the only local fuel resources [in extreme south of Avalon Peninsula]. T 33–64 You might see a scattered old crannick [old dead tree] sticking up. T 194–65 Up in the bottom of Harbour Deep was all burned, the forest fire. And we'd go there to get our summer's wood, cause 'twas all crunnicks—dry wood. Q 67–15 Crannies. Burnt-over wood that has turned white after a long period of time. 1968 DILLON 135 You wouldn't cut cronnicks, you'd just haul 'em up out o' the ground. . . Cronnicks is old stuff bent down on the ground; on the small side, no growth in 'em. 1969 *Nfld Essays* 33 The only vegetation, other than grass, is made up of small, stunted dwarf-trees, usually blasted on their seaward sides. . .cronnick.

crutch n usu pron **critch*** [krʊtʃ, krʌtʃ]. Cp *OED* ~ sb 4 'various contrivances of a forked

shape in a ship or boat.' In hauling a cod-trap, a forked device fastened to side of boat to hold the 'head' of the net above water.

T 43/7–64 You put a boat hook in a crutch in the side o' the skiff, and you hook the boat hook into the head of the trap. T 80/3–64 A critch is a stick cut out something like the gaff of a sail, and you stick one end down the risin's o' the boat and [on] the other end your boat hook'll lodge into un and keep up the offer end o' codbag. P 187–73 ~ a stick of wood about 3 ft long with a V-shaped piece of iron on top. It is used to suspend a gaff which keeps the heads of a cod-trap above the water level while it is being hauled.

cry crack See CRACK².

crystal n *NID* ~ tea 1, 2.

Comb **crystal berry**: bog rosemary (*Andromeda glaucophylla*) (1956 ROULEAU 28).

crystal tea: (a) three-toothed cinquefoil (*Potentilla tridentata*) (1898 *J A Folklore* xi, 226); (b) LABRADOR TEA (*Ledum palustre; L. groenlandicum*) (1898 *N S Inst Sci* ix, 386; 1956 ROULEAU 28); (c) bog rosemary (1898 *J A Folklore* ix, 273).

cuckoo n LA MORANDIÈRE, p. 1333 '[sea-snail, called] coucou à St Malo.' Whelk or large snail (P 39–75).

cucumber See WILD CUCUMBER.

cuddy n Cp *OED* ~ ² 'room or cabin [aft] in a large ship' naut (1660–1845); SMYTH 227 'sort of cabin or cook-room, gen. in the fore-part. . .of lighters and barges'; cp *DC* cud NS (1945, 1960) for sense 1.

1 A cabin at bow or stern of a small vessel or large boat for accommodation and provisions, usu with defining word *aft(er)*, FORE; esp in an undecked fishing boat, a small enclosed space forward or aft. Also attrib: ~ **hole,** ~ **house,** ~ **room.**

[1766] 1971 BANKS 128 At 3 o'clock came to the ship very compleatly tired as we had not Pulld off our Cloaths since we came out nor lodgd any where but in the aft Cuddy of our boat. [1779] 1792 CARTWRIGHT ii, 484 James Gready and his crew calked the cuddies of the *Beaver*, examined her rigging and prepared her for sea. 1842 JUKES i, 220 [It was] an open boat, with a little cuddy at each end, in which it was just possible to stow a bed, leaving barely room enough to sit or lie down. [c1875] 1927 DOYLE (ed) 53 "Huntingdon Shore": 'Twas early next morning, just at break of day, / We arose from our slumber and got underway, / Put bread in the 'cuddy' and pork on the floor, / And shaped her for fishing on Huntingdon Shore. [1879] TUCKER 78 [The craft's] accommodation was limited to a small cuddy, fore and aft. 'I slipped,' wrote the Bishop, 'into the after cuddy, and made myself contented, if not comfortable.' 1910 TOWNSEND 105 In the cuddy of our boat was a tiny iron stove, which, however, took up so much of the little room that there was but space for one man to lie out at length on that side. 1927 DOYLE (ed) 63 "Three Devils for Fish": O crawl into the cuddy, crawl in my old cock, / Haul out me oil trousers, likewise me oil frock. T 96/9–64[1] My father used to take me up in his arms in the night, carry me down and put me into the cuddy o' the boat. T 45/6–64 In the fall o' the year she left to go to St John's in an open boat—she was gangboarded, fore cuddy and after cuddy on her—and breeze come on, they got drove off. 1966 SCAMMELL 91 Let's have a bite of lunch before we start on our second puntload. Pass back that old boiler there in the cuddy. I'll boil the kettle on the after-room while you fellows tend to your lines. T 394/5–67 We never put any fish in what we call the cuddy o' the boat, no fish there [but that time] we had ninety-seven large fish laid down there. We filled her up. 1967 *Bk of Nfld* iv, 246 Up forward [the *Dasher*] had a cuddy, which means she was decked over so that a man could crawl and lay down if they were out all night. M 71–95 In [his] day, schooners, or bulleys were common, characterized by their [size], cuddy house and spar or mast.

2 Bed (in a house).

P 245–67 [parent to child] Go to your cuddy.

3 Comb **cuddy oar**: bow oar (1925 *Dial Notes* v, 328).

cuddy sweep: see **cuddy oar**.

1949 FITZGERALD 93 ~ Foreward oar, dilldom, etc. Position of oars used in a trap skiff.

cue n *EDD* ~ sb[1] 1, 2 s w cties.

1 Shoe for an ox.

M 69–6 Locally made 'cues' were nailed to an ox's cloven hoofs to keep him from slipping during the winter. One cue was placed on each part of a hoof.

2 Small piece of metal, shaped like a half-moon, fastened to heel of boot or shoe.

T 141/66–65[2] Cues was a little ring o' iron to go [in] the heel.

cue v *EDD* ~ v[1] 3 s w cties. To shoe an ox.

Q 67–39 Cued [is] used for 'shod' when referring to oxen which were used in hauling wood. 1971 NOSEWORTHY 189 [Cueing]. Placing special metal 'shoes,' or *cues*, on the [hooves] of oxen.

cuff[1] n *OED* ~ sb[1] obs (1362–1467); cp *EDD* hedge v 5 (4): hedging-cuffs; *DAE* Newfoundland 2: Newfoundland cuff (1884).

1 A thick usu fingerless mitten, made of wool, swanskin or leather, worn in winter; cp MITT.

[1771] 1792 CARTWRIGHT i, 78 After this disaster, I found, that besides being so wet, I had lost one of my cuffs in the water. 1792 ibid *Gloss* i, x ~s. Mittens to wear upon the hands. They resemble those made use of by hedgers in England. [1811] 1818 BUCHAN 4 Spare snow shoes, buskins, vamps, cuffs, and twenty-eight knapsacks. 1836 [WIX][2] 51 I was glad to procure a pair of 'cuffs' or mittens, made in this bay, of a kind of thick woollen or swan-skin. 1866 WILSON 214 The cuff is for the hand, made like a mitten, but the substance is a stout, white cloth, called 'swanskin.' It is doubled on the back of the hand, and stitched until it is almost

impervious to water. [1894 BURKE] 53 'There's one thing about blanketing cuffs,' said a Harbour Main man, 'let them be ever so wet and cold, they're always warm and dry.' [1904] 1927 DOYLE (ed) 67 "The Kelligrews Soiree": We had boiled duffs, cold duffs, / And sugar boiled in knitted cuffs. 1914 *Cadet* Apr, p. 7 Swanskin cuffs, with a separate place for the thumb only, were worn on the hands and the headgear in winter was a warm, if awkward-looking cap made of fur. T 50/2–64 They'd have black wool, too, to mix with [the white] to make grey, for cuffs and socks. T 185–65 You'd always wear swanskin cuffs out birdin', out sealin'; 'twas white, they'd have that doubled. I've made hundreds o' pair, cuffs. 1975 POCIUS 31 A mit contains no partitions between three or four of the fingers, though the thumb is always separate. A mit is commonly referred to as a 'cuff.'

2 A fisherman's heavy mitten, often with fingers cut off, used to protect the hand in hauling lines or splitting fish; HAUL v: HAUL-ON; SPLITTING CUFF.

1895 GRENFELL 228 Hence the distribution of woollens, cuffs, etc, comes as a great boon to many a poor fisherman whose hands are cut by the lines. T 203–65 We'd have what we call a cuff; that is just a palm and a thumb. We'd use them when we'd be haulin' the nets. 1971 NOSEWORTHY 190 ~ A type of glove used for splitting fish. It may be a full glove or may have the fingers cut out. Often made of calico or flour bags. 1979 NEMEC 275 Using the same woolen 'cuff' (mitt) which he used to hold onto the fish while it was being split. . .

3 Strap on horse's harness into which cart-shafts fit.

T 100/1–64 There was what they used to call breechin'—a big double machine [of] heavy leather, to go right around from the back pad, and there was cuffs on the back pad, strap for the shafts to go in.

4 Phr *lick one's cuff*: to submit to any humiliation in order to secure an object (1896 *J A Folklore* ix, 37).

cuff[2] See CUFFER n.

cuffer n also **cuff** *EDD* cuff v 4 (2): cuffer 'a tale, a yarn' (Austr); 6 sb 'a lie'; *O Sup[2]* ~ sb[2] (1887).

1 A tale or yarn.

1924 ENGLAND 314 ~ A lie; a tall story. 1961 *Evening Telegram* 28 Apr, p. 7 My conversations frequently (from lifelong habit) 'slewed into cuffers' on family and local traditions. T 31/5–64 I'm going to tell you a little cuffer now about un. T 70–64 That's a great cuffer, isn't it? That's a great story. 1966 FARIS 28 The 'cuffers' (items of exaggeration on past common knowledge). . .are most commonly about the sea, sea exploits and sea storms. 1966 SCAMMELL 105–6 "Tommy Decker's Venture": I chats with Tom a minute, he likes a 'cuffer' too. / And then he ups and tells me what's makin' of him blue.

2 A friendly chat; an exchange of reminiscences; a gathering for this purpose; freq in phr *have a cuffer*.

1937 DEVINE 17 ~ a meeting of fishermen or sea-men, generally aboard a ship, to have a friendly chat or 'swap yarns.' P 10–57 ~ conversation, usually recalling old times. T 194/7–65 Every night there'd be a cuffer going off, in the saloon. P 207–66 The two truck drivers stopped to have a cuffer. P 103–67 A cuff [is] a chat. 1972 BROWN 137 They'll have a chance to exchange 'cuffers' with the men on the *Stephano*.

cuffer v also **cuff** *EDD* cuff v 4: cuff over, to cuff a tale D; *O Sup*[2] cuff v[1] 4 (1746–). See CUFFER n.

1 To exchange tales.

P 10–57 ~ to converse, usually about old times. C 66–18 He is o.k. now he has someone to cuffer with. C 69–2 A whole bunch of us were sitting around cuffer-ing at a friend's house.

2 To vie or compete with others in telling tales.

1966 FARIS 245 When I pointed out to him that some men were not acknowledged, that some men could not, in essence, 'cuffer,' he replied, 'Only certain fellers can cuffer—some hands make a good story sound like a lie.' T 410–67 Three or four of we fellers gets down there on the wharf and we cuffs her off; some tells lies and whoever can tell the biggest one. . .

cull n Cp *OED* ~ sb[3] 1 'a selection' obs (1618–1692), *O Sup*[2] (1958–) for sense 1; cp *EDD* sb[3] 4 'inferior articles. . .picked out from others' for sense 2. See CULL v.

1 Of dried and salted cod-fish, herring, etc, the act of sorting, or the product of sorting, into grades; the criteria by which fish are sorted; the grades into which fish are divided.

[1911] 1930 COAKER 33 The cull of herring, which the Board of Trade established in the early spring, caused great dissatisfaction amongst the packers. 1920 *FPU (Twillingate) Minutes* 11 Mar Then quite a discus-sion arose concerning fish, about different qualities of fish and also the different prices paid for fish and the standard cull of fish. 1962 *Nfld Fisheries Conf* 251 A man has to secure a bulk of fish to light-cure it, and when he gets it dried he has to stand the cull, and if the sub-sidy is only on the high quality. . .no advantage to him at all. T 168/70–65 That used to be all the cull in my day, but now today there's more culls than that on it. 1965 *Evening Telegram* 4 Nov, p. 3 [Mr Antle] also called on the federation to press for the return of the salt fish cull. 1966 SCAMMELL 82 You'll have to watch that temper of yours. Chaps like Bill Pratt can be pretty ugly if they don't like the cull. 1979 TIZZARD 90 Wherever he thought he'd get the best price or the best cull that is where he would take the fish.

2 The lowest commercial grade of salted cod-fish, lobsters, etc; CULLAGE.

1934 LOUNSBURY 58 Each producer culled his own fish, the 'refuse' fish or 'culls' being set aside and sold to less discriminating buyers than those who took 'mer-chantable' fish. 1953 *Nfld Fish Develop Report* 88 On the average, about five per cent of the total number of lobsters shipped are condemned. Rather less than 15 per cent are 'weaks' and somewhat over 5 per cent are 'culls.'

cull v Cp *DAE* culling v 1 (1721, 1891). To sort dried and salted cod-fish into grades by quality, size and 'cure.'

[1739] 1954 INNIS 150 All the fish buyers have the lib-erty of culling for themselves; it must be their own faults if they take what is bad and it often happens for cheapness they load green fish not thoroughly cured. 1832 MCGREGOR i, 231 Previous to exportation, the fish is again spread out to dry, when it is culled, or sort-ed, into four qualities. 1881 *Nineteenth Century* ix, 87 There [the fish] are culled over, sorted into three or four piles according to their quality by experienced cul-lers. 1898 PROWSE 113 No person shall cull codfish as between vendor and vendee in place or places under the operation of this Act. [1952] 1965 PEACOCK (ed) i, 118 "Culling Fish": We tied up to the pier when the weather changed dull, / There were men standing idle and no one to cull. T 43–64 There'd be a special culler, a man authorized to cull the fish for the firm. He'd cull your fish and whatever decision he came to on it you had to put up with. 1975 BUTLER 69 The fish would be culled by a licensed fish culler keeping the different grades separate. 1980 *Evening Telegram* 22 Nov, p. 24 All the fish I culled [would be] enough to keep you in fish and brewis for ages and ages.

cullage n Cp *NID* ~ n 'material eliminated in culling.' An inferior commercial grade or 'cure' of dried and salted cod-fish; also attrib. Cp BIM, REFUSE FISH.

1845 *Journ of Assembly* Appendix, p. 221 Our Brig *Triumvirate* took a cargo of fish of 4100 qtls. to Naples early in January last, it turned out well, scarcely any cullage. 1928 *FPU (Twillingate) Minutes* 5 Oct [He] said that tal qual fish was $8.20 and Spanish $9 and cul-lage $5 in Port Union today. 1937 *Seafisheries of Nfld* 56 The standards of cull for Labrador codfish are:– Choice or Number One. Prime or Number Two. Cul-lage. The class termed 'Cullage' includes all fish not up to the standard of Number Two. T 36–64 Now the fish is maggoty and it's slimy, an' I got to get out on the flake again with small tubs an' pickle an' wash it, and rewash it an' perhaps the weather'll continue on for a fortnight, an' when 'tis all over I got nothing only cul-lage fish. T 43–64 The way we knew the fish was num-ber one, number two an' West India. West India now was supposed to be cullage. So that's the way it was graded. T 168/70–65 And then, tomcods—under twelve inches; an' then cullage—broken or sunburnt. That used to be all the cull in my day, but now today there's more culls than that on it. 1966 SCAMMELL 83 He threw fish after fish into the cullage pile, hardly bother-ing to look at the faces. 1979 TIZZARD 296 The ship-ment [included] 21 pounds of cullage at $7.00 per quin-tal.

culler n *DC* ~ obs (Nfld: 1907, 1957); cp *DAE* 'official appointed to inspect fish, staves, etc' obs (1663–1832). One employed to sort dried and salted cod-fish into grades by quality, size and 'cure'; sometimes with designation *government; sworn(-in)*.

[1810] 1971 ANSPACH 28 There are in Harbour Grace experienced Cullers who have been sworn in our

Court, against whom I have heard of no complaint made. 1866 WILSON 212 A culler usually goes in the [galloper] to select the mercantile fish. 1881 *Nineteenth Century* ix, 87. There they are culled over, sorted into three or four piles according to their quality by experienced cullers, who separate the good from the indifferent, and the indifferent from the bad, with great rapidity and unerring skill. [1892] 1896 *Consolidated Statutes of Nfld* 824 No person shall be licensed as a culler to cull codfish, as between vendor and vendee, in any of the places that come under the operation of this chapter. 1933 *Nfld Royal Commission Report* 80 In cases where fish was valued according to quality, the quality of the fish tendered by the fisherman was determined by a 'culler' or valuer. 1939 LODGE 53 When made [the fish] is divided by expert 'cullers' into a dozen categories according to the market for which it is most suitable. [1952] 1965 PEACOCK (ed) i, 118 "Culling Fish": We went to the super when arrangements were made, / To send for the culler to test out the grade, / We got the bars ready, the board and the stand, / When Alfred appeared, a sworn-in man. 1953 *Nfld Fish Develop Report* 79 Cullers are licensed by the Government but employed by the fish buyers. T 43–64 There'd be a special culler, a man authorized to cull the fish for the firm, an' in later years a sworn-in culler, a government culler. 1979 TIZZARD 295 My father knew a great deal about culling fish, because he was a sworn-in culler for some years while he worked with the firm of George J Carter Ltd., Herring Neck, but it was not permissible for him to cull his own codfish.

culling vbl n See CULL v. Comb **culling board**, ~ **table**: plank, or wooden table, on which dried and salted cod-fish is placed for sorting and grading; cp TALLY[1] n: TALLY BOARD.
1890 BAYLY 27 Great 'drays' of dry cod are being unloaded, and put in 'yaffels' on to the culling tables, where each fish is carefully examined, passed thence to hand-barrows, and next to the scales. [1929] 1933 GREENLEAF (ed) 304 "The Merchants of Fogo": Let you go down to the staple room, and there you will see fun. / When he stands to the culling board, his neighbours do him shun; / When he stands to the culling board, he'll say it is no use, / And when they go to bring back the fish, gets nothing but abuse. T 43–64 When you go to ship your fish, there'd be a cullin board put out, and a culler to cull the fish for the firm. 1966 SCAMMELL 84 The old man was flipping fish into the different grade piles with expert wrist, at the same time keeping up a steady flow of conversation with the owner who stood at the culling board, catching the yaffels thrown to him by the men in the boat and putting them on the board back up at the speed that the culler could judge and grade them. T 394–67 They'd go down to the culling board and they'd put that thumb on un and press and tip him a little bit and see if he was sunburned. C 75–142 Culling board. A four-legged table, approximately eight [feet] long, ten inches wide and four feet high, with markings on it in various lengths, for culling dried fish.

cunner See CONNER.

cup n

Phr *cup of tea*: refreshment consisting of tea with bread, cake or cookies.
1910 GRENFELL 158 No, I know a cup of tea isn't much to give you—just bread and butter and tea. [1927] 1971 *Inuit Land Use* 315 At each house we make a halt for a cup of tea, a chat, and a short service. 1972 MURRAY 284 So the group giving the picnic had to be very sure they had lots of food baked (cakes, cookies etc.) so that everyone who came might be given a 'cup of tea.'
See READ CUPS.

cure n *DAE* ~ n 2 (1846); *O Sup*[2] sb[1] 9 (Nfld: 1883–). A method of preserving fish by salting, drying or pickling.
1883 SHEA 7 The cure of the fish requires much care and judgment. . .the best cure is effected when the weather is variable. [1911] 1930 COAKER 33 The cure of shore fish the past season could not be much worse. 1962 *Nfld Fisheries Conf* 195 I suggest that there can be an improvement in the cure and that we can make more Spanish fish, high price fish. 1969 MENSINKAI 13 Between these two types [light-salted dried and heavy-salted wet or salt bulk] there are various types of 'cures,' mostly of the heavy-salted dried variety.

curing vbl n Cp *OED* ~ 2 (1791 quot); *Shetland Truck System* (1872), p. 7 for sense 1.
1 The process of preserving fish by salting, drying, etc; MAKING.
[1693] 1793 REEVES ii . . .and liberty to go on shore or any part of *Newfoundland*, or any of the said islands, for the curing, salting, drying, and husbanding of their fish. [1898] 1905 *Nfld Law Reports* 23 From. . .the method of curing and sending [fish] to market, it is the common practice of the island to take it off the rooms at different times.
2 The processing of cod-liver oil.
1931 *Nfld Mag & Advertiser* 13 He has done more to educate our people in the curing of refined cod liver oil and up-to-date methods of packing herring, than any other person in Newfoundland.

curlew n *OED* ~ 3 (1766 quot), *DAE* 2 (1813, 1839) for sense 1; *Cent* curlewberry (Labr: 1890) for comb in sense 2.
1 Either of two birds of the genus *Numenius*: (a) Hudsonian whimbrel (*N. phaeopus hudsonicus*); (b) Eskimo curlew (*N. borealis*); also in Labr place-names.
1623 *Short Discourse* [sig. B3] There are also infinite numbers of Geese, Duckes, Pigeons, Gulls, Penguins, Godwits, Curlewes, Swanns, &c. [1766] 1971 BANKS 130 But particularly at this season with a Bird of Passage Calld here a Curlew from the Great Likeness to the smaller sort of that Bird found in England. [1770] 1792 CARTWRIGHT i, 23 I sent Ned and Charles to South Head where they killed a brace of curlews and three grouse. 1774 *Trans Roy Soc* lxiv, 377 In the autumn, there come a prodigious quantity of birds, which are called CURLEWS. They are about the size of a wood-cock, shaped like them, and nearly of the same colour; extremely fat, and most delicious eating. 1951

PETERS & BURLEIGH 182–3 Hudsonian Whimbrel. Local name: Curlew. . . The Hudsonian Whimbrel is the only species of curlew which frequents Newfoundland, since the smaller Eskimo Curlew is now only a memory. Ibid 183–4 Eskimo Curlew. Local name: Curlew. . .The Eskimo curlew was formerly one of the most abundant birds in North America. 'It was said to have visited Newfoundland in autumn in millions that darkened the sky.' 1953 *Nfld & Lab Pilot* ii, 439 Curlew harbour is entered between Curlew head. . .and a point about three-quarters of a mile south-westward. . . Curlew island. . .is situated close westward.

2 Proverb *no curlew, no herring*.
1909 BROWNE 201 It is rather surprising to find Sportsmen who contend that the curlew feeds on fish; and they allege as proof of their contention the Labrador adage, 'No curlew, no herring.'

3 Comb **curlew berry**: black crowberry (*Empetrum nigrum*); BLACKBERRY (1891 PACKARD 63).
1918 TOWNSEND 23 On this day, August 3, the Eskimo curlew, now almost extinct, appeared from the north. This species here takes the place of the Migratory Pigeon (alas, now entirely extinct). . . They fly in compact bodies. . .covering a great extent of country ere they make choice of a spot on which to alight; this is done where-ever a certain berry called the 'Curlew berry' proves to be abundant. 1941 WITHINGTON 139 The country produced various berries—huckleberries, curlew, and bear berries, but the one peculiar to Labrador was the 'bake-apple,' a fruit growing above a stalk of crumpled green leavs. 1951 PETERS & BURLEIGH 185 In Newfoundland [the Eskimo curlew] fed mainly upon crowberry. . .which is sometimes called 'curlew berry.'

curlew net: device used to enmesh the Eskimo curlew when flocking.
[1771] 1792 CARTWRIGHT i, 179 I was making a curlew net.

curvy See KIRBY*.

curwibble n JOYCE 244 curwhibbles, etc; *Kilkenny Lexicon* ~ v. A sudden lurch; unsteady or teetering motion.
1937 DEVINE 17 ~ Unsteady or fantastic motions (of man or beast), such as those caused by too many glasses. 'He was cuttin' the curwibbles alright.' P 178–72 ~ a sudden change of direction.

cushy n ['kʌʃi, 'kɔʃi]. Labrador term for a small, freshwater fish (P 236–57).
Q 67–82 Cushies are seen in winter time when one fishes through holes in the ice. Many appear at once, and when larger fish come, they scatter.

cut v *DC* cut throat 1 (Nfld: 1818–), *DAE* 2 (1842) for comb in sense 3.
1 At the seal hunt, to kill seals and load them on a vessel, the term being from the practice of cutting the pelt and fat from the carcass.
1937 DEVINE 17 The patch of seals is 'cut' when nearly all in sight are killed and hauled on board. T 80/1–64 They left Twillingate and come out here, and cut a patch o' seals, and captured a load of seals.

2 Phr *cut off (the linnet/twine)*: when hauling a cod-trap, to draw up certain ropes so as to entrap the fish in one section of the net.
P 9–73 Cutting off is where the expert is required at either end of the boat. If the cut linnet is not handled properly a loop [of the net] can be let down and the fish lost.

cut out (a young seal): to select and kill a young 'white-coat' from among a patch of seals.
1873 CARROLL 27–8 When the young ones were cut out of them they were much larger than the run of young harps cut out of female harps on the 10th March. T 141/65–65² Billy had a stuffed seal, just a cat cut out o' the old ones in the fall.

cut tails: to cut a notch in the tail of a cod-fish to indicate the fisherman who caught it. See **cut-tail** below.
1866 WILSON 212 Some of the fishermen are not engaged for wages, but are on shares, and are said to *cut their tails*; which means that they cut a piece from the tail of the fish as soon as it is taken out of the water, by which the man's fish is known from the rest. Of this fish one half is his, as wages, and the other half belongs to the planter for the supplies. 1936 SMITH 13 I went with Uncle Harry, as he was commonly called, in the 'highrat'; three hands and I cut the tails of my fish to know them when they dried. 1955 ENGLISH 36 [proverb] Don't cut tails. Don't be too particular. Fish tails were cut as a mark. P 211–68 Bellamer boys were usually recruited to go afloat and cut their tails. 1976 *Decks Awash* v (4), p. 19 I started fishing in 1916 when I was eleven, at Cut Throat Islands. I was supposed to cut tails and go jigging.

cut throats: in preparing cod for salting and drying, to cut the throat of the fish and slit the belly open to the vent. See **cut-throat** below.
T 175/6–65 I cut throats for two splitters, two fast splitters.

3 Comb **cut-off**: a make-shift shoe made by cutting down a long rubber boot.
P 113–65 ~ rubber boot cut down into slipper size, and used for house wear or for short excursions out of doors (e.g. to get an armful of wood). P 118–66 ~ hip rubbers cut off just below the knees usually because the knees are worn out.

cut pole: a slender fir no more than one inch in diameter, with branches removed, used when fishing for trout.
P 27–80 If you come across a cut pole, there was a fellow there [at the river] before you.

cut-tail: a cod-fish identified by a notch in the tail made by an apprentice fisherman or supernumerary on the boat who caught it; also attrib.
T 96/9–64¹ When they go splitting the fish, my mother'd [be] picking out the ones with the tails cut, the cut-tails. 1974 SQUIRE 71 I went to the Labrador as a cut-tail man which meant that the only share of the voyage I got was what I caught myself and marked by cutting a corner off the tail of the fish—hence the term cut-tail man.

cut-throat(er): (a) fisherman who cuts the throat of the cod-fish and slits the belly open from gills to vent in preparation for salting; (b) two-edged knife used in this process; also in place-names.

(a) [1794] 1968 THOMAS 181 The names of Header, Cutt Throat, Carver, Splitter and Salter are the appellations given the Fishermen who perform the various offices in the stages or in the Rooms. [1810] 1971 ANSPACH 21 On the forepart of the stage is a table on one side of which is the *cut-throat*, and on his right, the *Header*. . . The *cut-throat* takes the fish upon the table, cuts with a knife the throat down to the nave[l], then [pushes] it to the *Header*. 1863 HIND i, 304 The cut-throat, armed with a two-edged knife, seizes the fish by the eyes, cuts his throat, and, having opened it down to the vent with a single stroke of his knife, passes it to the header. 1926 HARVEY 11 Day and night for several weeks 'headers,' 'cut-throats,' 'splitters,' 'salters,' were at work. T 43–64 The cut-throater would dive over and pick up two fish, cut them and pass them along to the header. (b) 1878 *Nfld Pilot* 433 Splitting Knife bight. . .lies on the north-east shore. . . Cut-throat harbour is a narrow creek running in from the west side. 1909 BROWNE 279 ~ a double-bladed weapon, not unlike a stiletto. T 183–65 Then somebody'd jump down with a cut throat and stick a gaff into him, and cut him open. P 148–68 The table once smooth is now all humps and hollows, worn down by the scraping of the cut throats and splitting knives.

cutwater: one of the projecting edges of a caribou horn.

1892 HOWLEY *MS Reminiscences* 11 He has a nice set of horns just peeled, indeed some fragments of the velvet are still hanging on. They have three frontal tines or cutwaters as the lads call them.

cut n Cp *O Sup*² ~ 23 c 'a number of sheep or cattle cut out from flock or herd' (1888–) for sense 1.

1 The number of walruses, seals, etc, taken from a herd for killing; a slaughter; cp CUT v 1.

[1766] 1971 BANKS 148 [The walruses] Continue Landing for some time Tumbling one over the other & the hinder ones still driving forward those that are before them till a quantity sufficient for a Cut as [the Magdalen Island hunters] call it are Drove far Enough from the water the People then Begin with Clubs to beat the hindermost of those they chuse to take who imagining the Blows to Proceed from the teeth of those who come after still continue to drive those who lie before them. 1924 ENGLAND 92 All seal life has vanished. The first 'whitecoat cut' has been made.

2 The course of a sealing vessel through the ice-floes.

1924 ENGLAND 80 The *Thetis* and *Diana* dogged our every 'jife' and 'cut.' They spied on us. 1933 GREENE xv *Cut* is the course selected, by each Captain, as the best or shortest ice passage to the Patch.

3 In hauling a cod trap, a portion of netting raised by ropes so as to force the fish back toward the end of the net; TUCK v.

P 80–64 ~s. Intersects of linnet formed when cod trap is tucked. T 43/7–64 Then you get another cut o' linnet and you gather up again the top linnet and you push that out underneath. 1967 FIRESTONE 92 The punt then moves along that end of the trap and the men aboard it and those aboard the motor boat proceed to haul netting out of the trap and stretch it between the boats forming *cuts* [ridges] of linnet which restricts the fish. These *cuts* continue to be made as the punt proceeds towards and then along the seaward side of the trap and accordingly the fish are forced into the end of the trap. P 9–73 The second hand hooks up the spanline buoy and lifts the line over the boat's head and passes it back to her middle. A point here is that the second hand attends to the forward cuts and the skipper to the stern cuts. The cuts or double linnet is a particular job and requires an expert to handle.

cutter n A pointed steel bar projecting down from a sledge onto ice to prevent it from sliding sideways (C 63–16).

cutting ppl Comb **cutting out**: the sawing of a channel through ice for sealing vessels to reach open water.

[1884] GOSSE 111 ~ [picture caption. The crews of all the vessels in the port unite to cut with ice-saws a broad channel through the midst of the harbour to the open sea.]

D

d– See note at TH –.

da n [dæ:] *OED* ~ ['father'], *EDD* ~ ; *Trans Phil Soc* (1895–8), 377 Ulster. Father; grandfather; respected elderly man.

[1880] 1927 DOYLE (ed) "The Ryans and the Pittmans": Farewell and adieu to ye girls of St Kyran's, / Of Paradise and Presque, Big and Little Bona, / I'm bound unto Toslow to marry sweet Biddy, / And if I don't do so, I'm afraid of her da. [1894 BURKE] 55 No crying out 'go in da' is allowed, 'Go in grand-pa' strictly prohibited. [c1894] PANL P4/14, p. 199 Greenspond is a purty place / And so is Pincher's Island; / Ma shall have a new silk Dress, / When Da comes home from swoiling. 1902 *Christmas Bells* 14 One of the very few inhabitants of this lonely cove. . .introduced us to 'Da,' the patriarch of the settlement. T 70–64¹ He says to the father, he said, 'Da, there's a punt there.'

dab See SMOKED.

dabber* See DAPPER.

daddle n also **dattle***. Cp *OED* ~ sb dial 'the hand' (1785–). The hind flipper or paw of a seal; SCUTTER (1955 ENGLISH 33).

1929 *Nat Geog* July, p. 125 [He] then cuts off the hinder daddles (back flippers). T 104–64 We would play with the dattles or scutters [as] we used to call [them].

daddle v *EDD* ~ v[1] 1, 6 for senses 1, 2.
    1 To approach (slowly).
    C 70–12 When [he] was hunting and was telling the story to some friends he would say, 'We daddled right up along side o' the birds, then I fired.'
    2 To dandle (a child).
    1934 KARPELES (ed) 55 She has a baby for herself to daddle upon her knee.

dadyeens n pl Epithet for members of a group of settlers originally from Cork; cp YELLOW-BELLY.
    1863 PEDLEY 295 Two great Irish factions had established themselves [c1815] in St John's. . . Those of the country of Cork were designated 'Dadyeens.' 1895 PROWSE 402 [There were] the Cork 'dadyeens'. . .and a number of other names for the [St John's Irish factions].

dagger n   A tapered whetstone used to sharpen scythe, etc; NORWAY (P 94–58).
    T 437–65 So he took [the scythe] an' he give un the dagger an' away they goes down the field. M 70–21 The mower always carried with him a dagger or whetstone with which he periodically sharpened the scythe.

dale n   [= deal] *OED* deal sb[3] 2 'the wood of. . .pine.' Attrib **dale pine**: red pine (*Pinus resinoso*) (1978 ROULEAU 86).

dally n, v (a) Sudden lull or slackening of wind; (b) of the wind, to turn or shift in direction.
    P 205–55 I expect the wind will dally around any moment. P 245–57 ~ A decrease in the force of the wind during a snow-storm. P 218–68 The wind kept dallying about.

damp a   Descriptive of a low grade of dried and salted cod; SLIMY.
    1909 BROWNE 75 He is content with a reasonable profit on his goods; he does not 'cull' the fisherman's 'voyage' as 'Madeira' and 'damp,' and recull it when it enters his fish store.

damper n
    1 A round lid or cover placed over aperture on the cooking surface of a wood, coal or oil stove; also attrib (P 269–63).
    T 12–64 'Feet like dampers.' Describes very large feet. Dampers are the covers on a stove. P 130–67 ~ One of several covers or lids situated on the top of the stove. 1973 BARBOUR 94 Water boiled very quickly in these kettles, which had large bottoms that fitted the hole of the stove when the lid or damper was removed. 1973 PINSENT 5 He. . .almost rammed his red hands into the damper hole on the top of the woodstove. 1979 HORWOOD 94 Beside the iron-and-nickel range, which was stuffed to the dampers with blazing logs, a huge woodbox spilled cloven lengths of spruce and fir upon the floor.
    2 In names of breadstuffs originally fried on stove lids: **damper boy, ~ cake, ~ devil, ~ dog**.
    P 224–67 Damper boys are made from fried dough. 1976 GUY 61 Home made bread, pork buns, figgy duff. . .damper cakes. 1969 HORWOOD 84 And my old grandmother, running short of bread with the new batch not yet ready to bake, often made damper devils by cooking small pieces of risen dough like pancakes on top of the stove. 1958 *Nfld Dishes* 19 Flacoons or damper dogs—pan-cakes. Pan-cakes made of a flour and water mixture and cooked on top of the stove.

damper* See DAPPER.

damsel n   *EDD* ~ sb[2]. Damson plum (*Prunus insititia*); also attrib (P 148–64).
    1974 VIVIEN 3 Types of homebrew: . . .Black Currant Wine, Damsel Wine, Plum Wine.

dancers See MERRY.

dancing-master n   Wooden puppet set in motion by vibrating a pliable board under its feet.
    T 22–64 The first dancing-master I made, I made un for the first feller that we had, and I danced it for him.

dand n   *EDD* ~ sb Do. A dandy, fop.
    P 51–67 On Saturday night when he's dressed in his best clothes, he's a real dand.

dandelion n   Comb **dandelion look**: a hard stare; bold look.
    P 148–65 He gave me a dandelion look.

dandy n   Cp *DAE* daddy longlegs. Comb **dandy longlegs**: (a) crane fly, an insect of the family *Tipulidae*; (b) a tall thin person.
    P 148–64 ~ very large, long flying insect, late August and September, with a drooping tail, transparent wings. M 71–101 The skinny person was prone to name-calling as fat boys and girls were. We were frequent users of several names. . .dandy long legs, scarecrow, scraggy, sparrow, skinflint and tubby.

danger n
    Comb **danger bell**: ship's bell rung as warning at night or in fog.
    [1822] 1891 SKINNER 55 We could carry but little sail [in the dense fog], and had to keep the danger bell going continually to prevent, if possible, our being run into. Q 71–7 ~ bell rung on a boat when out in fog as thick as pea soup. The danger bell serves as a warning for other boats in the area to avoid a collision.
    danger flag: flag hoisted on vessel to recall sealers from the ice.
    1924 ENGLAND 276 [caption under photo] Danger-flag going up, to warn men far on ice of approaching blizzard.

dap v   Cp *OED* ~ v 1; see also DAPPER. To fish for cod with hand-line and weighted hook and bait near the surface of the water (1937 DEVINE 17); cp JIG v.

dapper n   also **dabber*, damper***. A weighted hook used with bait in hand-line fishing for cod

near the surface of the water; FLICKER, FLOAT n.
Cp JIGGER. Also attrib.
1937 DEVINE 17 ~ A hook weighted with a lead haft
for quick sinking in codfishing. 1937 *Seafisheries of Nfld*
31–2 ~ This is about the same size as the Float, except
that there is a small portion of melted lead fastened to
the end of the hook to which the line is attached.
P 102–60 Spare dipnets, prongs, jiggers and dappers
[were] all under lock and key. T 50/2–64 Take up your
squid an' cut it up, or your herring—whatever [the
bait] might be. They use dabbers for caplin—snake
that onto your line an' skiver your caplin on. T 76/6–64
They'd catch the fish on dappers—they'd have only
couple o' fathoms o' line out, first o' the fishin'.
P 171–66 Dabber. This is a hook which is enclosed in a
piece of lead, baited, and thrown out about the boat to
catch surface fish. It is used in the early part of spring
when the fish are 'up' after caplin, i.e. the fish swim
near the surface of the water to catch the caplin which
habitually swim near the surface. T 272/3–66² [You]
catch 'em on floats—some people calls 'em flickers,
some more calls 'em dampers; made about that long
an' a hook into it. You just put the caplin onto that an'
throw 'em out an' the fish take hold to it. 1967
FIRESTONE 96 The dapper hook was smaller than a jigger hook. It was baited and put overboard on an eight
to ten fathom line. 1977 *Evening Telegram* 7 Oct, p. 6
We heard familiar phrases such as 'I caught my fish
today on the rock or on the shoal with dabber and
ground lead.' 1979 TIZZARD 290 Each fisherman had
two dappers and lines so that he could fish from both
sides of the boat.

daps* n pl *EDD* dap sb 12 pl s w cties. Likeness;
image.
P 227–72 He is the very daps of someone.

darby n Cp *EDD* dabby sb² 'apparition';
dobby-horse 1 'hobby-horse' [in Soulers' play].
Disguised person who participates in various
group activities, esp visiting from house to
house, during the twelve days of Christmas;
MUMMER; a mischievous person or prankster;
Hallow-e'en spectre.
M 71–42 Some people use the expression darbies
[for] groups of people dressing up in disguise and going
around the community janneying. C 71–26 At that time
they had a word for fellows like him—scoundrel, sly or
cunning fellow. They used to call such a fellow a darby.
Q 73–6 Get out o' here, you little darby, 'fore I gets a
broom to you! This word [was also used of] the Halloween darby or spook. 1978 *MUN Gazette* 21 Dec, p.
24 You and your brothers and father now begin to
make your rounds. You go from house to house, singing, dancing, dressing up as the darbies, frightening
children and little old ladies with your masks and the
hobby-horse, and you have a wonderful time chasing,
finding and blackening your friends, particularly the
ones who showed any sign of fear of the darbies.

dark a Comb **dark angel harp**: type of harp seal
with black fur.
1909 ROBINSON 75 Some of [the harps] will get black
as jet, and these are known as dark angel harps.

dark one: disguised mummer or janny.
1966 FARIS 182 Mummers. The disguised individuals
who come from house to house during Christmastide
are sometimes called 'the Dark Ones.'

dart n Cp PARTRIDGE ~, *Kilkenny Lexicon* for
sense 2; *OED* sb 6 for sense 3.
1 A type of harpoon used by Inuit in killing
seals, birds and salmon; also attrib.
[1771] 1792 CARTWRIGHT i, 139–40 The other six
[Esquimaux] attended in their kyacks, and threw their
different kinds of darts as they went along; an art at
which they are amazingly dexterous. 1839 TUCKER 113
Advancing near enough, for he is sure to measure his
distance with accuracy, he flings the dart, and scarcely
ever fails to strike. The seal, terrified and wounded,
dives in the greatest terror; but a float being attached
to the dart by a leathern line, he is soon forced up
again, and despatched. 1866 WILSON 297 The canoe,
darts, kettles, and other utensils are buried with [the
Eskimo], supposing he will need them in another
world. 1916 GRENFELL 231 The remaining dog-traces,
and every square inch of skin, including the dart-line,
had to be split for thongs to fasten the little pieces of
wood together. 1916 HAWKES 33 Small birds, particularly the little sea-pigeon. . .and 'Tinker' duck are
secured in summer with the bird dart or net and added
to the winter store. 1977 *Inuit Land Use* 168 And the
men weren't allowed to fire any guns—or anything like
that. They were allowed to use the dart.
2 A quick blow; a teasing rebuke.
1846 TOCQUE 196 Here you behold a heap of seals
which have only received a slight dart from the gaff.
[1929] 1933 GREENLEAF (ed) 161 "Maurice Kelly": His
lower and top teeth tumbled out on the street / With
the wonderful dart that he got from the ghost. 1964
Evening Telegram 2 Apr, p. 9 One night last Lent we
saw a big man in our Church havin' a little snooze
durin' the sermon. When we came out Ned sez, 'I'm
goin' to give him a little dart about that.'
3 Phr *take/make a dart*: to make a quick visit, a
sudden movement.
1933 GREENE 171 Even the Engineers and stokers
take 'a dart up on deck' to see for themselves. T 31–64 I
made a dart now to go along under the other one. And
as I did, sling goes the other one an' took me, an' away
I goes out in the water. C 71–89 Make a dart over to
Mrs Smith's for some sugar.

dart v To spear salmon, seals or birds.
[1771] 1792 CARTWRIGHT i, 142 Shuglawina and
Attuiock employed themselves in darting some salmon. 1973 GOUDIE 67 When the seals came up to their
breathing holes, the men would dart them with a long
wooden handle and a piece of iron at the end about
two feet long. At the end of the rod was a detachable
spear point on a tarry line made from sealskin. 1977
Inuit Land Use 128 Mostly the old people used to dart
the seals, and then when they dart them, they'd kill
right quick.

dasher n A device used to drive fish in a desired
direction by thrashing the water; DOUSER,
TROUNCER.

Q 71–8 ~ a steel barrel-head, painted white and tied to a string; thrown into the water it flashes and glances hither and yon frightening fish and driving them into the bunt of a seine or into a gill net.

dattle* See DADDLE.

daughter See DOTARD.

dawn n Cp ELEVENER. A drink of rum.

1907 DUNCAN 324 'Here I is—havin' a little [dawn] o' rum with Nature!' 'Twas a draught of salt air he meant. 1924 ENGLAND 315 A [dawn] o' rum. 1937 DEVINE 17 'He gid'me a good [dawn] of rum.'

dawnies* n pl ['dɒːnɪ'z]. Cp EDD dawny 'sickly' Ir, JOYCE 248 donny, DINNEEN donaidhe 'miserable; in low health.'

1 The nightmare; DIDDIES; HAG¹ (P 94–57).

C 71–99 In previous years many people used dawnies to mean a 'nightmare' or 'to be hagged.' It suggests that the person is between consciousness and unconsciousness, a sort of dream.

2 Phr *have the dawnies/be in the ~* : to be harried or tired; to be hung-over (C 71 106).

dawning n *OED* ~ poetic; *EDD* dawnin Wex, Nfld. Sunrise.

[1891 (1977)] WINSOR (ed) 48 When mornin' came, the second dawnin' I'd seen on the rock, I saw that it was goin' to be a fine day. 1914 *Cadet* Apr, p. 7 For instance. . .'betwixt' for between, 'dawnin' for daybreak. . .all those are found in Chaucer. 1918 *FPU (Twillingate) Minutes* 21 Mar The majority of members were in favour of stopping work from dawning until dark hauling nets and also from dark Saturday until Monday morning dawning. 1932 BARBOUR 60 After my watch was off, which was just before dawning, I went to the cabin. 1975 COX 65 "The *Ella M Rudolph*": They searched with all endeavours, / but no creature could be found, / And as the dawning broke again, / a sadly sight did see.

day n Cp *OED* day-dawn 'daybreak' poetic (1813–) for cpd in sense 2.

1 See TO: *the day*.

2 Cpd **day-dawn**: layer of clouds over horizon at break of day.

1900 *J A Folklore* xiii, 298 The higher the day-dawn the more wind, the lower, the less wind.

day-set: see SET n.

de*: de once See TO.

dead a Cp *OED* ~ D 2 ~ cart 'during pestilence' (1722–).

Comb **dead car(t)**: hearse.

1930 BARNES 185 They were dying that quick that they couldn't get coffins—couldn't get anything to bury them in. They had what they called the 'dead carts' and Joe Bell, he was an old captain but he used to drive one of them. 1931 BYRNES 89 [We hid] our frightened

heads under the blankets, as we heard, oh so distinctly, the 'Dead Car' go rumbling by our window.

dead-eye: sore or callus on hand (P 148–60).

C 69–23 One type of dead eye is the boil without a head. The second type is a callus that forms on a fisherman's palms after continuous hauling of trawls or cod-traps. These are little white heads which appear in the centre of the galls and can be picked off periodically.

dead-man: see DEAD-MAN.

dead moss: beard moss (*Usnea barbata*); DEER MOSS.

1971 NOSEWORTHY 191 ~ Whitish moss hanging on fir trees, usually on dead branches. It can be used for making yellow, brown, and green dye for wool.

dead snow: loosely packed snow without firm surface.

[1811] 1915 HOWLEY 74 Most of this day's travelling smooth, with dead snow, the sledges consequently hauled heavy.

dead n See ON.

dead-man n Cp *EDD* ~ sb 1 (13) ~ plunge; (12) ~ pinches Ir.

Comb **dead-man's cap**: toadstool; mushroom; DEVIL'S CAP, FAIRY ~ .

C 69–20 The few times I have seen them I always heard them referred to as dead-man's caps.

dead-man's daisy, **~ posy**: common yarrow (*Achillea millefolium*) (1898 *N S Inst Sci* ix, 369).

M 68–16 Deadman's posy was a good cure for piles. Some people called it yarrow.

dead-man's dive: method of throwing a stone into the water without making a splash (P 148–60).

dead-man's flower: meadow-sweet (*Spiraea latifolia*) (1956 ROULEAU 29).

1970 *Daily News* 9 Sep, p. 8 Our own lovely Spirea. . .nicknamed 'Deadman's Flowers.' C 71–86 There is a very common, white-coloured field flower which was called dead men's flowers by the children. They believed that if you picked such flowers your father would die.

dead-man's pinch: small mark or bruise appearing without apparent cause (C 69–32).

dead-man's share: small portion (Q 71–3); cp SHARE n.

dealer n Cp *OED* ~ 3 'one who deals in merchandise, a trader' for sense 1; *DC* Nfld (1918) for sense 2.

1 Businessman operating as middleman between the fishermen of a locality and a fish-merchant in a central community; cp AGENT.

[1770] 1894 HARVEY 281 Another stone [in the Placentia graveyard] records the departure of a certain Richard Walsh in 1770, 'who carried on a most extensive trade in this harbour with the greatest credit, and died in the 53rd year of his age feelingly lamented by his Planters and Dealers.' 1850 [FEILD] 92 They depend for other supplies upon dealers from St John's and Harbour Grace. 1923 PRATT 48 "Overheard in a

Cove":. . .no dealer born could take 'em in. . . / or show them any solid reason / Why number one prime cod might any season / Drop in price. 1936 SMITH 18 [We] brought up two loads of codfish from Jigger Tickle for Capt William Pumphrey, a large dealer of John Munn & Co., 1,060 quintals each trip, and shipped it on board the fish steamer at Emily Harbour. We also brought up another load from Mr George Smith from Edwards Harbor, another large dealer of John Munn & Co., and shipped it on board the second steamer. 1975 BUTLER 66 This barter business sounds very, very bad. But, if you were a good dealer and the merchant was carryin' ya, 'tis not so bad as it sounds. 1977 BUTLER 67 [We visited] all the harbours around the Bay, selling goods and collecting fish from the firm's dealers.

2 Fisherman operating under the CREDIT or TRUCK SYSTEM (see TRUCK[1]).

[1888] 1897 *Nfld Law Reports* 307 The plaintiff was a hired shareman of one Charles Parsons, a dealer and freighter of the defendant's, and was engaged to proceed with Parsons to the Labrador fishery. The plaintiff 'entered into collar' with Parsons, and worked in his service prior to the intended voyage to Labrador. 1900 BROWNING 270 It was observed that [the merchant] held the lever at both ends, and could, at least where he had many 'dealers,' recoup from one the losses he may have suffered from another. 1909 BROWNE 284 *Horse Harbor*, another large fishing centre, is situated near *Holton*; and it is settled chiefly by 'dealers' of the concern which operates so largely in Holton.

death n DC deathfall (Nfld: 1770) for comb in sense 2.

1 Proverb *the death of a horse is the life of a crow* (1937 DEVINE 63).

2 Comb **death clock**: clicking sound thought to presage death.
C 71–103 ~ The sound of ticking (as of a clock) in the woodwork of a house foretold death.

deathfall: variety of animal trap; deadfall; also attrib.
[1770] 1792 CARTWRIGHT i, 46 In our return we found two old furriers' tilts, and snow deathfalls; which appeared to be of Canadian construction. [1786] ibid iii, 145 Crane walked the deathfall-path and brought a marten.

death kit: candles, holy water, and other items kept in a household for the laying-out of the dead (M 69–9).

death plant: cabbage with distinctive cup-shaped leaves.
C 64–5 Oftentimes among a bed of cabbage plants you will find one of the leaves of a plant shaped like a cup. This is called a death plant. This means that someone will die in the family within twelve months.

death wagon: hearse; DEAD CAR (P 148–62).

deck n
1 Clipped form of *deck-load* (of fish).
1863 HIND ii, 233 After a 'deck' of mackerel is obtained, all hands prepare to put them in salt.

2 In mining, ground level, surface (P 148–63); also attrib.
P 222–67 Deckhead. A tall, tapering, tower-like structure erected over the shaft. Its principal purpose is as a mount for the bull wheels.

3 Attrib, comb **deck boot**: heavy boot worn by fishermen.
1967 *Bk of Nfld* iv, 248 [Father] got me the deck boots. They were made of all leather, the hardest kind. They were called quarter boots and came about halfway up to the knee. C 75–19 ~ Made of leather for fishing.

deck broom: heavy broom or brush used to sweep decks and fishing-stages (1975 BUTLER 180).
M 68–26 The guts were thrown overboard and the deck hosed off with the water pump and brushed off with deck brooms.

deck engine: mechanical contrivance to hoist sails on a vessel.
T 43–64 You hoist by hand or by deck engine. You'd use the deck engine because a schooner [of] a hundred tons would have a thousand yards of canvas in the mainsail—a heavy hoist by hand.

deck glass: piece of heavy glass let into the bottom of a boat for underwater observation of fish; cp FISH GLASS.
T 80/3–64 He had a fish-glass and he had a proper deck glass, cut round, about one and five eight [inches] thick.

deck router: in a sealing crew, second in command of a WATCH (1972 SANGER 236).
1924 ENGLAND 52 In case a master watch is killed or disabled, his second master watch, or 'deck-router,' (pronounced 'rowter') replaces him. 1925 *Dial Notes* v, 329 ~ One of the four assistant master watches.

deck weight: deck-load.
1975 BUTLER 113 It was now early September and we had a load of fish and a deck weight of cod oil.

dee-dee n NEWFOUNDLAND BLACK-CAPPED CHICKADEE (*Parus atricapillus bartletti*).
1964 *Evening Telegram* 28 Oct, p. 5 Where I live both species of chickadee are universally called 'dee-dees,' never chickadees.

deep a Cp *OED* a 2 'having a (specified) dimension downward.' Signifying the number of meshes in one dimension of a net.
T 43/8–64 If you were knittin' trap linnet you'd put up your linnet one hundred meshes deep. P 229–67 How many meeshes deep is your salmon net? 1979 TIZZARD 317 [I bought] a forty rand two and three-quarter mesh herring net. It cost me $34.00. The net was of Gold Medal Brand and was two hundred meshes deep.

deep(s) n, n pl Cp *OED* deep sb 2 b pl 'the deep sea' obs (1598–1725). Area(s) of deep water, esp between 'grounds,' shoals, 'ledges' or 'banks' where fish congregate.
[1772] 1792 CARTWRIGHT i, 231 In the afternoon I took up both nets, and put them out afresh below the

deeps, and had two slinks in them. 1951 *Nfld & Lab Pilot* i, 73 Cordelia deeps, with depths of from 90 to 99 fathoms, extend northward parallel with the coast. 1953 ibid ii, 70 Whale deep, extensive and irregular in shape, with depths of from 50 to 65 fathoms in it, lies between the eastern side of Green banks and the Great Bank of Newfoundland.

deer n Cp *DC* ~ 'caribou' for sense 1; for combs. in sense 2: *DC* ~ fence (Nfld: 1832), ~ pass (1836); *DAE* ~ path (1823), ~ trap (1634).

1 The species of deer native to Newfoundland (*Rangifer tarandus*); CARIBOU, NEWFOUNDLAND DEER.

[1583] 1940 *Gilbert's Voyages & Enterprises* ii, 407 [Hayes' narrative] Beasts of sundry kindes, red deare. . . 1620 WHITBOURNE 52 There are yeerely neere unto the said Harbour of Renouze, great store of Deere seene; and sometimes divers of them have been taken. [1698] 1975 ANDREWS [2] In the winter time the Planters both to the northward and southward of St John's hunt for Deer, Beaver, Otter, Bear, Martin, Fox, and Seales, on which flesh they feed for the greater part of the [winter] season. [1794] 1968 THOMAS 129 There is a Noble Animal to be found in the Woods in this Country which far surpasses anything of its species in Europe. This is a remarkable large Deer. They are very numerous, go in Herds, are of a cream colour, and some of them so large as to vie with an English Ox. 1823–4 *Edin Phil J* x, 160 The western division being nearly destitute of wood, affords pasture to numerous herds of deer (the Carribou). Of these animals there are here many thousands; indeed, the country seems covered with them. They migrate eastward to the woody districts in winter, and return westward very early in spring. 1871 HOWLEY *MS Reminiscences* 15 We had hoped to see some deer or game of some kind but were disappointed and had to retreat empty handed as we came. 1966 BEN-DOR 39 Caribou. . .is plain 'deer' to the settlers. 1977 *Inuit Land Use* 245 We always used to be able to get deer south of here every winter.

2 Comb **deer bush**: dwarf birch (*Betula* spp).

1912 CABOT 46 There was a little scrub spruce in the pass, and dwarf birch, the 'deerbush' which caribou like so well in summer. It is an agreeable bush to the eye, with shiny, roundish leaves, neatly scalloped, and the size of a dime.

deer fence: barrier to corral migrating caribou; cp SEWELL.

[1768] 1828 CARTWRIGHT ii, 309–10 The deer fences we found erected on the banks of the Exploits, are situated in places the most proper for intercepting herds of those animals, as they cross the river in their route to the southward, on the approach of winter, and again at the return of mild weather when they wander back again. . . [These] fences and our plashed hedges are formed on the same principle, differing only in their magnitude. They are raised to the height of six, eight or ten feet. 1866 WILSON 316 The labor the Red Indians performed, in order to catch deer for their subsistence, was very great, as is evident from the remains of the deer-fences, which were standing only a few years ago. 1913 *Christmas Chimes* 16 But to return to my

subject, the last station of the [Beothuks] was in the Exploits River, I myself have seen some of the deer fences they erected there.

deer moss: beard-moss (*Usnea barbata*); DEAD MOSS.

1933 GREENE 120 Juniper and the spruce trunks bent in the direction of the prevailing winds, with their boughs snow-laden, and fringed and bearded with the 'deer-moss' that the Caribou will eat in winter. 1977 *Inuit Land Use* 295 The caribou feed mainly on Cladonia lichens, referred to locally as deer moss, and on other lichens, grasses, sedges, leaves and bark.

deer pass: point on the migration route of caribou.

[1829] 1915 HOWLEY 191 They might be at that time stationed about the borders of the low tract of country before us, at the deer-passes, or were employed somewhere else in the interior, killing deer for winter provision. At these passes, which are particular places in the migration lines of path, such as the extreme ends of and straits in, many of the larger lakes,—the foot of valleys between high or rugged mountains,—fords in the large rivers, and the like,—the Indians kill great numbers of deer with very little trouble, during their migrations. 1953 *Nfld & Lab Pilot* ii, 407 Caplin bay is connected with Hawke bay. . .by Deer pass. This channel, known locally as Squasho run, separates Hawke island from the mainland westward.

deer path: passage habitually used by caribou; cp LEAD[2].

[1771] 1792 CARTWRIGHT i, 164 At the head of the harbour a pretty brook runs in, and there are some deerpaths, in which we tailed five slips. [1822] 1928 CORMACK 45 The way through the woods elsewhere, except by the deer-paths, is obstructed by wind-fallen trees and brushwood. 1842 JUKES ii, 98 A deer-path is like a sheep-walk on a common—a narrow winding track about six inches wide. . . .a herd of some hundreds had been seen to pass along it the preceding winter.

deer pound: enclosure to capture caribou; cp POUND.

[1779] 1792 CARTWRIGHT ii, 496 I set them to work to erect a pound of my own invention for catching any number of deer alive. . . I am certain that the. . .deer-pound would have answered my expectation, and caught a great number of deer, had it been properly executed.

deer skin: caribou hide.

1823–4 *Edin Phil J* x, 160 The canoes used on the lakes are partly from necessity, and partly for the sake of convenience, made of basket-work, covered over outside with deer-skins; the latter requiring to be renewed commonly once in six weeks. 1842 JUKES i, 147 At dawn this morning we stowed our meat and baggage in the boat, covering it with the deer skin.

deer slide: sled with vertical posts or 'horns'; CATAMARAN, SLIDE n.

Q 74–1 A large slide with horns for hauling wood and meat out of the interior was called a deer slide in the Long Harbour, Fortune Bay area.

deer slip: snare, arranged like a noose, to catch caribou; SLIP[2].

[1772] 1792 CARTWRIGHT i, 253–4 I sent one of the *Otter's* people in my kyack to the *Coleroon*, to bring some deer-slips.

deer trap: device, sprung by a bent tree, to catch caribou.

[1776] 1792 CARTWRIGHT ii, 200 Two hands brought the deer-trap.

delco n Trade name applied to any make of gasoline generator.

1976 *Culture & Tradition* i, 109 A gasoline generator. . .was commonly referred to as a 'delco' no matter what its actual brand.

dell See DILL[1].

dennage See DINNAGE.

desert n Comb **desert flower**: sea thrift (*Armeria maritima*) (1956 ROULEAU 29).

desperate a Cp *OED* ~ a 7 'hopelessly or extremely bad' (1604–1814). Disturbing; shocking; beyond description.

1888 HOWLEY *MS Reminiscences* 35 About noon we had two or three desperate showers of rain accompanied by a few very loud claps of thunder. [1959] P 245–76 [He said] 'How dare these outsiders come into this decent Christian province and by such desperate, such terrible methods try to seize control of our province's main industry!' P 148–63 The desperate sight of the light in the lodge [saddened the college]. P 78–76 The weather is desperate! P 108–76 The road is in a desperate state after all that rain. P 148–76 [The people are upset about] the desperate lack of medical care in the region.

destroy v Cp *OED* ~ v 4 'to put out of existence.' Phr *destroy oneself*: to take one's own life.

1888 *Colonist Christmas No* 2 He disappeared mysteriously, no one knew how. Some say that in an hour or moment of mental derangement he destroyed himself; more say he was drowned accidentally. 1971 CASEY 263–4 'That was a man,' he said, 'that destroyed himself down in the woods years ago. And that's what he destroyed himself with, his handkerchief was on his neck. Hung himself they said down there in the woods.' Q 71–6 'He destroyed himself' was the euphemism used to break the news of a suicide.

devil n *EDD* ~ sb 3 (10) Ir for sense 1; for combs. in sense 3: *NID* devil's claw 2, cp *EDD* 1 (32) devil's racket 'noise or commotion,' *EDD* devilskin '[from] devil's kin.'

1 Phr *the devil's cure to you*: mild imprecation, expression of ill will or lack of sympathy.

1931 BYRNES 121 The devil skewered to ye. C 71–118 When a person whom one does not like has a stroke of bad luck, one may say 'The devil's cure to him!' It may also be used when a person is warned not to do something because it may hurt or injure him, and then does it despite the warning and brings bad luck to himself. C 71–124 ~ if something happened to a person through carelessness or through impetuosity this was said.

play with the devil: see PLAY.

2 Comb **devil-ma-click**: adroit, versatile worker; jack of all trades.

C 71–115 Any person who could turn his hand to a number of tasks with more or less equal success was referred to as a devil-ma-click.

devil-ma-jig: device, implement or utensil capable of varied use; thingamajig (C 71–115).

3 Combs. with the possessive *devil's*:

devil's angel: small biting winged insect (*Simulium* spp).

1907 WALLACE 29 And the black-flies—the 'devil's angels' some one called them—came in thousands to feast upon the newcomers and make life miserable for us all. 1947 TANNER i, 435 Not until the end of August are the mosquitoes and black-flies less numerous and no longer a nuisance in Labrador. The swamp is the home of these 'devil's angels.'

devil's birthday: day on which pea soup is served; Saturday (C 75–145).

C 71–110 It was quite common for people to say, when pea soup was being served, 'It's the Devil's birthday again.'

devil's blanket, ~ **feathers**: snowfall which hinders habitual work (P 151–68).

devil's cap: toadstool; mushroom thought to be poisonous; DEAD-MAN'S CAP, FAIRY ~ (P 148–68).

devil's claw: grapnel to anchor vessel to ice.

1925 *Dial Notes* v, 329 ~ An ice anchor. Its two tines are bent in the same direction at right angles to the shank. 1930 BARNES 222 Everything was there, chain hooks, devil's claws. . .fish tackle, block and fall, all but the cat block.

devil's fashion: the manner of giving something and then taking it back (C 69–12); cp FASHION.

P 148–64 That's devil's fashion to give something and take it back.

devil's laughter: Wilson's common snipe (*Capella gallinago delicata*) (P 133–69).

devil's match: (a) British soldier, a type of lichen (*Cladonia* spp); (b) type of bulrush (*Scirpus cespitosus*) (1978 ROULEAU 86).

C 69–19 We used to pick a tiny plant [called] the devil's matches. C 71–38 We used to eat a plant that looked like matches, a long stem—2 inches—with a small head on top of them. They had a sweetish taste and we used to call them devil's matches.

devil's pelt: mischievous child or boy; PELT (P 269–64).

devil's pipe: PITCHER PLANT (*Sarracenia purpurea*); INDIAN PIPE (C 71–4).

devil's racket: hard bout of drinking; cp RACKET.

1929 BURKE [4] "Mary Joe Slip on your Bloomers": For father always took a smile, / But only just in spurts, / Now he's on the Devil's racket / Since the rush came on the whorts.

devilskin: mischievous, prankish boy or man; see **devil's pelt** above.

T 367–67 Actually, 'twould be some devilskin, some funny man around the camp or town. P 260–68 Come here you devilskin and finish your breakfast!

devil's spit: white, foam-like deposit secreted by the larvae of insects; SPIT n (C 71–124).

devil's thumb-print: black marks on haddock's back—from a belief that the devil once grabbed the fish, which then got away (C 66–12).

devil's umbrella: see **devil's cap** above (C 69–12).

dewberry n Dwarf raspberry; PLUMBOY.

[1578] 1935 *Richard Hakluyt* [Parkhurst's letter:] 129 Strawberries, Dewberies, and Raspis, as common as grasse. 1849 [FEILD] 78 Wild fruits are abundant; gooseberries, strawberries, currants, bake-apples, and dewberries. 1911 *Rhodora* xiii, 123 Here were the common plants of the granitic barrens of Newfoundland. . .Dewberry or Plumboy (*Rubus arcticus*), Partridge-berry or Red Berry. 1916 HAWKES 36 The dewberry (*Rubus ar[c]ticus*) is found in large quantities on the islands off the east coast of Hudson Bay, also in Northern Labrador along the rivers. 1956 ROULEAU 29 ~ *Rubus acaulis*. 1971 NOSEWORTHY 191 ~s. Like raspberries, but juicier. 1975 SCOTT 57 The Plumboy is also called the Ground Raspberry or Dewberry (*Rubus pubescens*).

dialogue n Cp *Cent* ~ n 2 (b) 'part of a play to be acted.' A play or act performed or spoken as part of a concert.

[1906] 1976 WINSOR 62 A very interesting program was prepared consisting of solos, duets, readings and recitations, and a dialogue. . . The dialogue, 'How Aunt Polly Blodkins joined the Missionary Society' won the admiration of all. 1916 *FPU (Twillingate) Minutes* 1 Mar The Chairman then announced that those members of the entertainment committee who had parts in the dialogue not perfected may come back to the Hall to practice. M 70–28 A staged production, in a Christmas concert for example, would be called a dialogue.

diamond n In names of objects resembling a rhombus in shape: **diamond-eyed anchor, diamond point**.

P 148–64 Diamond point [is] a type of lobster trap resembling a diamond. Q 71–8 Diamond-eyed anchor: an anchor with a wooden stock. The diamond eye (actually square) allowed the use of square timber for the stock and this was more easily wedged and held in place than a round stock would be.

dick n Cp *EDD* ~ sb¹ 1 (2) ~ bird 'a cock bird.'

1 A rooster; also attrib; DICKY¹.

M 65–1 "Betsy's Cock": Now to conclude and finish, / I hope you will agree, / And never go cock stealing, / Above the sparrow tree. / And remember the dark September night, / They stole poor Betsy's dick. T 139/40–65 Here's to the dick that treads the hen. C 68–19 On Fogo Island they used to say 'May chicks brings all dicks.' 1971 *Evening Telegram* 17

June, p. 3 Fallin' into flesh, isn't you? All chuffed out like a dick with the mites. C 75–140 Dick spraddle: how far a rooster could go in one leap.

2 Phr *as dead as a dick*: quite dead.

1924 ENGLAND 90 'Go on; more seals!' . . .Along the rail: 'Dey ahl deed, now, cl'ar o' one young un, a-dere. Deed as a dick.'

dickey See DICKY².

dicky¹ n A rooster; DICK. Also attrib.

C 68–7 Billy had a dickey for an alarm clock. C 69–7 [They] used to use the blood from dicky-birds' combs [as] one of the best cures for canker of the mouth. 1971 CASEY 134 We're goin' to have rain, listen to that dickie-bird (rooster) crowin'.

dicky² n also **dickey**. Cp *OED* ~ sb 8 'covering worn to protect the dress or upper part of it during work' (1847–); *EDD* sb² 1, 3; *DC* dickey (1916–) for sense 1; cp *EDD* dick sb² 'apron and bib worn by children' for sense 2.

1 Hooded outer garment or blouse made of cloth; ADIKEY.

1894 *Evening Herald* 4 Dec In came her husband in size and shape with a dicky on his body—hood up over his head. 1907 WALLACE 33 The adikey or 'dikey,' as Bob called it, was a seamless garment to be drawn on over the head and worn instead of a coat. 1912 CABOT 231 He was a silent boy, and a little shy. . .his little white 'dickey' held most of the good qualities of dog, boy, and man. 1916 GRENFELL 130 Yet real men, indeed, they looked, when, on their removing their simple but effective canvas 'dickeys,' I got a view of their keen tanned faces. 1933 MERRICK 265 We had our dickies belted tight and the fur hoods up. 1941 DULEY 196 She wants to be photographed, but she wants you to wait until she changes her dicky—probably for the one she wears to church. 1966 BEN-DOR 35 The two-part frock is known to the settlers as a 'dickey.' 1973 GOUDIE 57 I was all dressed up in my boots and dickie.

2 A woollen bib worn by children.

Q 71–8 A dicky was a sort of woollen bib attached to a collar—used to keep the neck and chest warm and protected without the weight of a regular sweater or guernsey.

diddies n pl also **ditties***. Cp *EDD* dither v: var didder 'to tremble, shiver'; 4 sb pl 'shivering fit. . .horrors.' Nightmare; restlessness in one's sleep; cp HAG¹, HAG-RODE.

1896 *J A Folklore* ix, 36 ~ nightmare. P 205–54 ~ nightmare; walking in your sleep crying and bawling. C 70–25 The person hagged is said to be in the ditties. C 75–146 You were up with the ditties again last night.

diet n *OED* ~ sb¹ 5 obs (1533–1671); *EDD* sb¹ 2 Ir. Board, keep, esp for fishing servant or 'shareman' or member of a sealing crew. Cp WINTER DIET.

1613 *Willoughby Papers* 16a/28 12 pounds of bred one hogged full of pease 3 tonnes of beere 6 hundred of dry fish 2 [gallons] of butter more for vittells p[ai]d in Plymoth for there dyett £3/8s/10d. [1822] 1856 CORMACK 51 . . .the employer providing diet. 1857 *Courier* 6 May [p. 2] . . .for his diet [on sealing vessel].

dieter n also **diter**. Cp *OED* ~ b obs (1603, 1617 quots) for sense 1.
1 (a) One who receives winter board and accommodation against the promise of cash or service in the next fishing season; (b) one engaged, in return for board, in the preparatory work of the fishing season; cp COLLAR 3. Also attrib.
[1789] 1895 PROWSE 695 No. of inhabitants: Dieters 1,378. [1789] 1954 INNIS 310 In 1789 a proclamation was issued 'against fishermen coming from the out harbours to winter at St John's. . .' Any person during the winter season harboring or entertaining 'dieters' was subject to deportation. 1793 *Report on Nfld Trade* Appendix. Dieters. Men who remain in the Island during the winter (living upon their Summers wages) without engaging as Winter Servants. [1794] 1968 THOMAS 172 Some of these poor Fellows are less fortunate. They are forc'd to beome Dieters [*boarders*] with some Housekeeper, for which they promize to Fish for them the next season or pay them in cash at the next Fall. T 36/8–64 When the tenth of October [would] come the voyage was over, fish was sold an' the collar was taken off an' every man was at liberty. Whoever had homes then would go to them, an' [those] who had no homes [would] go back with the same man, or he'd ship with someone else; an' then he was a dieter. P 191–67 When the spring came those who had cod traps would ship a few men for the fishing voyage. The men would be called dieters because the man who shipped them would have to feed them for a few months. 1978 *Evening Telegram* 9 Sep, p. 14 'What was their diter walls?' 'That's the rock walls they had around their property. They were made by men who left their ships. . . They weren't paid any money, just given their bed and diet, as meals were called in them times.'
2 Prov phr *out dogs and in dieters*.
1895 *Christmas Review* 12 ~ (an old proverb of the 'youngsters' days, signifying the return of the fishermen to their winter houses, of which the dogs had possession during the summer). 1937 DEVINE 62 ~ Slogan for the first of May to get ready for fishing preparations. The dogs were useful all the Winter in hauling firewood and roomstuff and were well and regularly fed at the cookrooms. Now they must go at large and forage for themselves while the Summer crews of fishermen are shipped on for the voyage and their meals supplied at the cookroom. P 108–68 One time when a mother was hurrying her children from the table after a meal, so that she could set it again for the grown-ups, she said 'Out dogs, and in diters!'
The man who brags with dieter's knees, / Is not the first to face the breeze (1895 *Christmas Review* 12).

dill¹ n also **dell** *OED* ~ sb³ naut (1882); cp *OED* dell¹ 1 'deep hole,' *EDD* dell sb 3 'low, hollow place' Ha for sense 1.

1 Space in bottom of a fishing boat in which bilge-water collects; in a decked boat, the opening which leads to such a space.
1897 *J A Folklore* x, 204 ~ a space under the floor of a boat, either open or with a movable covering, from which the water is bailed out. 1937 DEVINE 18 ~ The opening in the floor boards of a boat for bailing. It is made over the place where the bilge water collects. P 102–60 The man using [the spudgel] did not have to stoop down to bail out water from the dill in the after part of the boat. C 70–18 Many times I remember [him] boiling [the mussels] in the piggin, a tin container used to throw bilge water from the dell in the boat. C 71–94 The dell is the hole left in the floor boards of a motor boat. This hole is left in front of the engineroom because this is the deepest part of the boat [in which] the piggin may be used to dip the water out of the boat.
2 Attrib, comb **dill board**: movable wooden cover placed over aperture in floor-boards of a boat (P 187–73).
dill room: the well or deepest inside part of a boat; ROOM.
[1774] 1792 CARTWRIGHT ii, 23 The boat worked up, took me on board there, and soon after we ran upon a rock near Bettres Island. The shock started a timber, and staved a plank in the dillroom. 1949 FITZGERALD 32 "The Ballad of Pious Pad": The cuddy sweep was pulled by Black Jim Flynn, / I had the bow, Aunt Mary's Tom, the stroke; / The midship oar was manned by John Joe Greene; / The [dillroom] oar by Skipper Peter Croke. T 80/3–64 He had a glass put in the skiff, in the bottom o' the skiff. An' he had a funnel made, an' he was rowin' along, he'd be down in the dell room lookin' down through. T 31/2–64 I had boards up to keep [the fish] from comin' down in the dell room where you used to heave the water out. T 172/5–65 He could handle hisself in the water, an' when he came up he grabbed the boat at the dellroom.
dill water: bilge-water.
P 148–59 The stench from the dell water was sickening.

dill² n *EDD* ~ int 1. Call to domestic geese or ducks.
C 67–20 He always called domestic geese and ducks 'Dill-dill-dill-dill-dill' in groups of five with a break between each group. The call was in the same high pitch with each 'dill' running almost on top of the other so it almost sounded like 'diddle.'

dill-cup n *EDD* ~ sb Ha W Do. Buttercup (*Ranunculus* spp); GILLCUP.
P 197–73 Yellow as a dill cup.

dinnage n also **dennage, dynnage** *OED* dunnage sb naut [in 17th cent *dynnage, dinnage*] (Nfld: 1623–). Twigs, brushwood, bark, etc, placed as a mat on which a cargo of dried fish, seal pelts, etc, is laid in a vessel's hold or spread on a fish-flake; dunnage.
1623 WHITBOURNE 75 Mats and dynnage under the Salt, and Salt Shovels. [1674–7] 1976 HEAD 50 Dinnage or Dinadge: small birchen rods cut down to lay

between the fish and the sides of the ship to keep them from bruising. [1777] 1792 CARTWRIGHT ii, 252 The *Otter* came down, and brought forty tierces of salmon, some spars, and dennage; I put some provisions into her for the stage. T 141/68–65² The birch rine would be used for collars, the same way for dinnage in the schooner. They'd put birch rines up to the sides o' the schooner. C 67–6 ~ Slight, twig-like branches of birch and alder trees. This was used by merchants in St John's to spread their fish on to dry. Most merchants had flakes on the roofs of their stores on which they placed dinnage. P 148–78 Dennage on which seal pelts or fat were placed [aboard sealing vessels]. P 254–78 ~ Dry boughs placed on the bottom and up the sides of the hold of a schooner, on which the cured fish was packed for the trip from the home port to St John's.

dip v   Cp *OED* ~ v 5 (1602 Co quot) for sense 1; cp *DAE* 2, 4 for sense 2; cp *OED* for sense 3 and *EDD* ~ sb 7 ~ net for sense 5 (a).

1 To transfer fish from one holding area to another with a net, esp cod from a seine or cod-trap to another net, a boat or a 'fishing-stage.'

1792 PULLING MS Aug Rowsell went one morning as usual to dip the salmon out of an adjacent pond where he was shot in several places and afterwards beheaded by the Indians. 1936 SMITH 83 They loaded their boat and then put the head of the trap on board my boat and began dipping in the fish; when all was dipped in I found my boat more than half loaded. T 80/3–64 I was the very feller that dipped all that in a boat and brought it in and pronged it on deck. T 43–64 A couple o' men would get back in the boat then an' go on an' dip in what was in the cod bags. T 31–64 I was bullyman in the skiff, and I had to dip [the fish] in and bring it aboard to the splitters. 1971 *Them Days* ii (3), p. 29 Johnny Straw was a salter, Jack Morris used to dip the fish with the dip-net, Bill Dyson was cut-throat.

2 To remove (cod-oil, tanning liquid, etc) from one container to another.

T 14–64 You'll take your spudgel and you'll dip out your tan out of the boiler and throw it on your twine and let it remain there all night. T 141/67–65² You'd heave in your buds an' you'd boil them now for three hours, an' you dip off that bark then. T 175–65 When the bark was strong enough, you'd put your linnet into the puncheons an' dip the bark out o' the pot an' put it in the puncheons.

3 To immerse nets, sails, etc, in tanning liquid as a preservative; BARK v.

[1794] 1968 THOMAS 62 In every Harbour, Creek and Cove there is what may be called a Parish Pott, this holds about 20 Gallons, and it is filled with water and Spruce Bark, which is boiled together; they then dip the netts of the Fishermen in to it, and the Sails of their Boats to which it is a great preservative. . . T 141/67–65² You take your [barrow] o' linnet an' you fill in your tub about half full. An' the feller on the other side'll haul it out—one feller dippin' it down, an' the other feller haul it out.

4 Of young harp and hooded seals, to leave the ice-floes and take to open water.

1873 CARROLL 28 The first rain after young seals are some twelve days old, they begin to 'dip' in the water.

When young seals first begin to dabble in the water they require at least five days amusing themselves before they are able to get out of danger. 1895 *Christmas Review* 12 When the whitecoat commences to dip, he commences to change his coat. [1898] 1905 *Nfld Law Reports* 295 As a general rule seals will 'dip' (that is, take to the water) about the first of April, but if the sheets of ice hold solid they may remain on the ice for a few days longer. 1909 ROBINSON 74 As soon as they lose the white fur they take to the water, and once they begin to 'dip' the seal-hunter is unable to catch them, as they will take to the water, and are away in no time. 1924 ENGLAND 25 The young harps, better outfitted for life, keep their snowy dress for about a month, till nearly ready to 'dip' and go on their own. 1957 *Evening Telegram* 1 Apr, p. 3 Thousands of seals will soon be 'dipping' and will be lost to seal hunters, unless the ships can get out of ice in time.

5 Cpd **dip-net**: (a) a circular net with a long handle used to scoop up caplin, herring, etc, in shallow water; KEEP NET; a net used to transfer fish from a seine or cod-trap into a boat or to handle it in the fishing-stage; (b) dandelion flower (see 1971 quot).

1861 *Harper's* xxii, 595 The caplin swarm in millions, swimming so densely that often a dip net can be filled from a passing school. 1873 CARROLL 38 If not prevented by ice when spawning time arrives, the Herrings will swarm to the beach, always selecting a sandy one for such purpose, where they can be taken in seines, herring nets, cast or dip nets, in large quantities, so numerous are they in spawning time. [1889] 1897 *Nfld Law Reports* 382 This quantity so obtained was not more than six dip-nets full. 1899 *Tribune Christmas No* 15 A large boat is moored to one corner of the trap and the work of [underrunning] begun, the object being to force the fish into one corner that they may the more easily be transferred to the boat by the dip-net. T 194/6–65 An' he wi' the dip net was right up forrard. 1971 NOSEWORTHY 192 ~s. The yellow flowers of 'dandelions' which grow in gardens and back yards all spring and summer. P 122–73 ~ A net used for taking fish from the large splitting tub. This is made of twine and has a rounded metal portion connected to long wooden handle. 1974 SQUIRE 21 The caplin were taken from the seine by a small net with a handle attached. This was called a dip-net. 1979 *Salt Water, Fresh Water* 40 Then the dip-net is lowered, and you dip the net into the fish that's out in the trap out beside the boat.

dip n   Cp *OED* ~ 1 c. The act of transferring fish from one holding area to another with a net; the quantity of fish so moved.

1979 *Salt Water, Fresh Water* 46 And I just sit there countin' the dips, that's one dip, two dips, how many pounds is in a dip? Two hundred pounds in a dip, well that is four hundred pounds [of cod].

dipper n   Cp *DAE* ~ 2 'utensil for dipping up water' for sense 1; see DIP v 4 for sense 2.

1 A small saucepan, a variety of cooking-pot.

T 80/2–64 We had peas duff and potatoes, you know, and the coady dipper was there with lassy into un.

T 407/8–67 I took [the moose meat] and put it in the dipper and put it on the stove, and 'twas cooking on that stove until dinner time Monday. C 69–29 Get a small dipper and fill it up with molasses and put it on the stove. C 69–18 Cooking pots are referred to as dippers. 1976 GUY 131 By and by out comes this miserable little dribble [of water] which takes five minutes to top off a small dipper.

2 Harp seal in its first year, when it takes to the water; BEATER (1972 SANGER 236).

dipping vbl n See DIP v.

Comb **dipping time**: period in March-April when young seals take to the water (1925 *Dial Notes* v, 329).

1924 ENGLAND 97 As the hoods pup anywhere from the 10th to the 20th of March, or two to three weeks later than the harps, dipping time for them is later than for the harps.

dipping tub: wooden container in which cod are immersed in water after being headed, gutted and split; WASHING VAT.

T 178–65 Just as well for them to have a dippin' tub up there with a scullin' oar out through un as that thing there!

directly av also **d'rackly*, rackly*, treckly**, etc. *EDD* ~ adv 2 D, *O Sup*[2] ~ 6 c dial and U S. Right away; soon.

1924 ENGLAND 68 'It'd wet the canvas,' judged Cap'n Abraham. 'But we'll get the stays'ls on her, 'rectly. Don't want to putt 'em on too soon, though, fear they'll tear to pieces.' Ibid 79 'Look like we'm handy to young fat,' said Kelloway. 'Look like de first spurt comin', 'treckly.' P 69–63 I'll be there d'rackly. T 141/64–65[2] They wandered in on the bleak land, and directly they come to a big sandrock, and they got up against this rock and had a blow. T 194/6–65 But I'm goin' to catch un again therackly, you know, 'cause I could sail faster than he. P 136–68 Da-rackley means 'after a while' or 'when I'm ready.' C 71–87 'Leaving?' 'Rackly.' 1975 BUTLER 44 'You'll go to Buffett,' I said, 'faster than ever you went directly.'

dirt n Minute marine animals (*Ascidiacea*) covered with a sticky substance and growing on fishnets; SLUB[1].

1979 NEMEC 266 Since monofilament did not have the same tendency as nylon to collect 'dirt' ('slub,' seaweed or crustacea), less time was needed to clear it.

dirty a *OED* ~ a 4 (esp 1745, 1836 quots) for sense 2.

1 Of transparent sea-water, abounding in marine organsims which cling to the nets, but lacking plankton which attract fish and make the water itself murky; SLUBBY. The antonym is CLEAN.

1966 FARIS 30 'Good water,' water that is 'clean' is in essence much less clear and much more full of opaque organisms and miniscule organic life than is the crystal-clear, absolutely transparent 'dirty' or 'bad' water. But it is 'dirty water' or 'bad water,' regardless of its appearance to an outsider, because most sea creatures cannot be caught in such water. 1975 *Evening Telegram* 3 July, p. 4 At the beginning of the season. . .lobster fishermen were doing fairly well, but a heavy storm and the subsequent 'dirty' water had apparently caused the lobster to be scarce. 1979 ibid 8 June, p. 1 A number of other explanations have been put forward to explain the lack of salmon this year: dirty water, slub on salmon nets, the fact that caplin haven't begun rolling on the beaches. P 245–80 When the visibility is good, the water is loaded with *Oikopleura*, the organism which produces the mucus which is called 'slub.' Thus, clean water is 'dirty,' that is, contains slub.

2 Of the weather, marked by squalls and precipitation.

[1779] 1792 CARTWRIGHT ii, 481 A clear morning, a hazy day, and dirty evening and night. 1887 BOND 121 [We are] in for a breeze from the north-east, and some real dirty weather. 1891 *Holly Branch* 12 [They] would examine the chart or peruse the American Coast Pilot Book to make themselves familiar with the rocks and shoals, in case they'd be caught out of a 'dirty' night, and have to 'lie to' or 'run' for a harbor. 1924 ENGLAND 66 Shrieks of storm devils shook the masts and a ravening madness smudged all the universe. 'Dirty wedder' was about all the sealers would admit. 'A bit airsome, sir.' Airsome, indeed! [1954] 1972 RUSSELL 37 It wasn't too bad goin' home. Just a dirty wind lop and a drop of spr'y back in the stern. 1960 FUDGE 19 [We left] for Rose Blanche February 22 in a dirty southerly. T 245/80–66 An' shortly after he leaved it never come [so] dirty ever since the world was made—rough, black rough. 1977 *Nfld Qtly* Winter, p. 18 And the wind come up to easter(ly) just a little after dark, by the time we got out to Green Island, so it became dirty pretty quick.

3 Of various objects, etc, hazardous, threatening.

1919 GRENFELL[2] 174 Now it is 'slob' mixed with snow born on the Newfoundland coast. This is called 'dirty ice' by the sealers. Even it at times packs very thick and is hard to get through. P 47–66 A boat is dirty if it ships much water in rough weather. T 453–67 That's when we took the dirty one, an' the same [wave] took the works—three dories, binnacle, log, broke the jib-boom off, cable went up in the middle o' the foresail, broke the fore boom off. C 70–21 [She] mentioned that we had a dirty moon that evening—an indication of dirty weather. 1975 BUTLER 113 Late in the evening, just before night, we were abreast the Dirty Rocks—an island rock situated near the southern part of Merasheen Head.

4 Of persons, angry, ill-humoured, vindictive (P 148–60); CROOKED.

T 54/9–64 She said, 'He got saucy an' dirty and rose a row here,' she said, 'an' he got beat up, an' he took to his scrapers.' T 55–64 A crowd of Irishmen come here an' one'd stay a little way down the tickle, another feller lived somewhere else, an' they couldn't agree any handier than that, they were that jealous an' dirty. T 84/5–64 'Cause I never gets dirty over a trick, never gets crooked like that. 1977 *Evening Telegram* 13 June, p. 3 I was on the picket line last night and the workers said they were dirty with those individuals [who crossed the picket line] but they just accepted the fact that the people have elected to go back to work.

discourse v   *OED* ~ v 5, 6 obs, arch; *EDD* v 3 Ir. To talk to or confer with (another).

1891 *Holly Branch* 9 'Don't be butting me,' interrupted Paddy, 'and your betthers waiting to discoorse me.'

disgusted p ppl Sorry, grieved (1924 ENGLAND 315).

1937 DEVINE 18 In Bonavista Bay means pained, disappointed, grieved. 'I was disgusted when they tole me he was dead.'

dishy a   Cp *DAE* dishwatery (1890). Of a person, pale or sickly in complexion, esp in phr *dishy looking*.

C 66–13 'You knows you'm not goin' de have dat dishy lookin' creature fer a husbin.' Q 71–7 [of someone in poor health] She was really dishy lookin'.

ditties See DIDDIES.

diver See BLACK a: BLACK DIVER, SLEEPY DIVER.

doater See DOTARD.

dob n   Cp *EDD* ~ v¹ 1 'to fall suddenly and roughly; to bob down.' The dip or movement of the bow of a vessel into a wave (1925 *Dial Notes* v, 329).

do be See BE.

dock n   Cow-parsnip (*Heracleum maximum*) (1956 ROULEAU 29).

P 80–64 ~ A plant whose leaves are used for greens. 1972 MURRAY 235 The roots of the 'dock'. . .were steeped out and taken as a cure for boils.

doctor¹ n   *NID* ~ 2 d, *EDD* So D for sense 1; *EDD* sb 7 for sense 4.

1 A man with power to charm or cure ailments; WIZARD.

1966 FARIS 178 'Wizards' or 'doctors' (both terms are used in Cat Harbour) are always men. This is an *all good* category, and those possessing this quality are able to 'charm' (stop) blood, cure warts, toothache, stomach upset, and find lost objects. C 69–5 The seventh son in a family was always hailed as the 'doctor.' The residents always said that the proof of his ability to cure was that an earthworm would die if it was put into the palm of his hand.

2 A minute aquatic form or copepod which attaches itself to the wound of a fish; also attrib.

1912 CABOT 127 When a fish is hurt he hurries away for the 'doctor,' a beetlish bug which fastens to the wound until it heals. This doctor and his mission are told of seriously on all the fishing coast. There is no questioning the doctor's existence and activity, though the motives for his attentions may well be suspected.

P 1–69 Doctor fish: found in sores on fish and believed by fishermen to be cleaning the wound or abrasion.

3 Water strider of the family *Gerridae*; WATER DOCTOR.

1970 *Evening Telegram* 22 Apr, p. 18 We drank from small pools where water-striders freckled the surface: 'Doctors' we called them, and believed that they cured trout of leech-marks. P 70–34 Doctors were queer hopping water spiders. They flitted about on top of the streams and brooks. We caught them in our bare hands. They were easier to catch than pricklies.

4 Stickleback; PRICKLY: PRICKLEY (P 183–73).

5 Comb **doctor's box**: ship's medicine chest.

T 194–65 So I took the pneumonia pills out of the doctor's box, took this bottle o' medicine and went ashore.

doctor² See GREEN DOCTOR.

doctor v   To emasculate male animals (1966 PADDOCK 104).

dod n   *ADD* ~ n 2 Nfld for sense (a). (a) A ship's course; (b) mark or target in the game of pitching buttons (see PITCH) (P 228–64).

1925 *Dial Notes* v, 329 Make a straight *dod* [course].

dodge v   *EDD* ~ v 1 for sense 1; *OED* 5 for sense 2.

1 To stroll casually and slowly along, to saunter.

1937 DEVINE 18 ~ To walk along leisurely. A person invited to a house in the suburbs said, 'I may dodge in that way some evening.' T 313–66 So I was dodgin' on, happy as a lark. 1970 *Evening Telegram* 17 July, p. 2 So we said we'd dodge over here [to Come-by-Chance from Dildo] and see what was the chances [of work]. 1976 GUY 95 The grandfather angel dodged along puffing on an imaginary pipe.

2 To follow or pursue other people stealthily; DOG v.

1937 DEVINE 18 ~ To trail somebody. C 68–24 Boys dodging them said that all they talked about was the fast horse her father had, the weather, and how the crops turned out.

3 Of a vessel, to stand up or down under easy sail.

1887 BOND 121 We kept on, just dodging along nearly head to wind. 1930 BARNES 272 If we don't keep off the Cape we'll have to put her head around to the westward again and dodge away up the Gulf. 1977 *Nfld Qtly* Summer, p. 7 We had a sail on her then and just let her dodge on before the wind to see if we could see anything coming behind us.

dodger n   Large horn button on overcoat (1937 DEVINE 14).

C 70–25 The term used for big buttons, usually on men's overcoats, was dodgers.

dodtrel See DOTTEREL.

dog¹ n   Cp *OED* ~ sb 2 'male hound. . .male

fox'; *DC* ~ bear (1910–), ~ hood (1883–) for sense 1.

1 Hunter's term for male animal, esp seal, usu with second specifying element: **dog bear,** ~ **harp** [see HARP], ~ **hood** [see HOOD], etc; cp BITCH.

[1772] 1792 CARTWRIGHT i, 216 [I] saw the fresh tracks of three white-bears; a dog, a bitch, and her cub. [1778] ibid ii, 346 [I turned] to an enormous, old, dog bear which came out of some alder-bushes on my right and was walking slowly towards me, with his eyes fixed on the ground, and his nose not far from it. 1842 JUKES i, 314 If they can once kill the female [hooded-seal], they are sure of the rest, as the young one does not stir, and the dog will not go far from the spot. [1896] SWANSBOROUGH 33 "The Seal Fishery": . . .for I am told / An 'old dog hood' is very bold, / That he will break the sealers bats. 1922 *Sat Ev Post* 195, 2 Sep, p. 10 It was a fat dog. It faced him, raised its head, flashed sharp teeth—sometimes such teeth work havoc on incautious hunters. 1936 SMITH 105 Some of the boys indulged rather too freely, and got top heavy, and the result was a running fight in the after hold, while they enjoyed the reward of their old dog harps. T 43/4–64 The dog hood an' bitch hood, they're the biggest an' the boldest, the dangerousest. T 141/68–65[2] An' I said, 'Was there a'r young one into her, Uncle Bill?' 'No, boy. No, boy. She was a dog [seal].' 1975 RUSSELL 54 Uncle Sol told Skipper Lige right to his face that he was uglier lookin' than an old dog hood.

2 In designations of dog-drawn sleds: **dog cat** [see CAT(AMARAN)], ~ **killer,** ~ **slide** [see SLIDE n].

[1900 OLIVER & BURKE] 46 Troops of men with their dog-cats—coming in from the outports. . . Those that had no dog and slide had runners on their boxes to pull them along. 1920 WALDO 158 Dog-cat is a dog-sledge. Cat is short for catamaran, which is not a sea-boat but a land-sledge, so that when you hear it said: 'He's taken his dog and his cat and gone to the woods' you may know that it means 'He's taken his dog and his sledge.' T 264–66 [Other people use sleds] with machines up forrard—they sit there. That's what we call 'dog-killers,' that sled. One man all the heavier up there sitting in that seat than three would be on the stern. P 167–67 We used the dog-cat when hauling the wood. 1931 BYRNES 72 It was customary for the people to bring firewood from the surrounding wooded country by dog slide during the winter. 1972 MURRAY 131 Lucky children. . .had slides tailored to their size, especially for riding on. Others had to use 'dog slides' (bigger, heavier slides on which firewood was hauled).

3 At the seal-hunt, gunner's assistant who carries the ammunition; also in phr *go dog for*: to accompany as a helper (1925 *Dial Notes* v, 332).

1895 GRENFELL 161–2 Sometimes they work in pairs, one man shooting the seals, and his chum, who is called 'the dog,' following up, cutting off the tail from the dead seal to 'mark it,' and then gathering them in heaps, and putting up a pole with a flag or a piece of liver as a claim. 1922 *Sat Ev Post* 195, 2 Sep, p. 126 Dogs, by the way, are the riflemen's attendants, who carry cartridges in a canvas bag not slung over the shoulder. No, indeed! The cartridge bags are borne

carefully in the hand, and there's a very good reason for that. . .with the bag in your hand you can let go of it [if you fall between two ice pans], and so you can scramble out on the pan with nothing worse than a sea bath in a temperature of zero. 1924 ENGLAND 39 One time a 'dog,' or gunner's attendant, dropped a bag [of cartridges] and a lot went off; but as nobody happened to get shot, 'what odds?' 1972 SANGER 237 Dogs. Ordinary sealers who carried cartridges for the fore-gunners. 1978 *Haulin' Rope & Gaff* 5 These men were called 'dogs' and they were also required to cut off the tails of the seals shot by the gunner and bring them back to the captain as evidence of the kill.

4 Proverb *out dogs and in dieters*: see DIETER.

5 Comb **dog hold**: hatchway in a 'jack-boat' from which a man fishes.

1975 BUTLER 55 Next to the aft part of the forecastle and in forward part of the fish hold there was two small hatchways about two feet by two feet square where the fishermen used to stand when fishing. These hatchways were called dog holds.

dog pup: see WATER PUP, ~ WHELP.

dog[2] n Cp *OED* ~ sb 7 'name given to various mechanical devices'; *EDD* 12 for sense 4.

1 Improvised sled made for transporting wood.

[1770] 1792 CARTWRIGHT i, 67 Two men sawed spruce and fir on Nescaupick Ridge; two sawed larch by Watson Brook; one squared timber; and two made dogs to haul home the boards upon.

2 Iron hook used to haul 'seal pelts' aboard vessel; SEAL DOG.

1933 GREENE 172 The steam is already on the winches, so on coming close the whip is thrown, the hook of the 'dog' replaces that of the gaff and up onto the deck the stubby white body [white-coat] goes.

3 A piece of wood with hooks in it for retrieving a shot bird from the water; TODGER.

1966 HORWOOD 42–3 He had a wooden dog—a cross made out of wood, with rows of large fish hooks fastened to both sides of its beam, and a light heaving line attached to the upright. You spin a wooden dog around your head until it achieves a great velocity, then let it go so that the line flies out before you. You can throw it pretty well the distance a normal gunshot travels, and use it to retrieve birds from open water. C 75–135 ~ a small piece of wood with a lot of hooks on it. If you kill a bird you heave out the dog and hook it in the bird and haul it in.

4 Piece of wood placed in a rope during sawing with a pit-saw to prevent timber from tipping.

T 196/9–64[1] You get up there and you put a dog—that was a big piece of wood—you put it in the rope so as he wouldn't tip on that end.

dog v Cp *OED* ~ v 1 'follow pertinaciously. . .track.'

1 At the seal hunt, to follow another vessel thought to be approaching the herd.

1924 ENGLAND 70 He [was] vexed at the other ships so closely tagging. 'They ahl want to dog in the same road!' he grumbled. . . He hated to admit the Newfoundland icefields were free for all.

2 To follow and spy on young lovers; DODGE, SKIM.

C 69–27 When we were kids we would get a real kick out of dogging people. Usually we would hide somewhere along a dark road and wait for a couple to come along. Then we would follow them around all night—however always keeping out of their sight. 1972 MURRAY 162 Courting couples were apt to be 'dogged.' That is, younger people, usually young boys, would attempt to spy on their activities. Sometimes. . .the boys simply tagged along a few feet behind, teasing and tormenting the courting couple, giving them no privacy.

dogberry n   *Cent* ~ 2 'in Nova Scotia, the mountain ash.' Mountain ash (*Pyrus americana*); the berries of this tree; DOGWOOD. Also attrib.

[1779] 1792 CARTWRIGHT ii, 438 I saw some dogberry-bushes in bud. 1836 [WIX]² 164 [He suddenly came] upon a bear, which [had] been in the upper branches of a dog-berry or mountain ash, deliberately bending and breaking the boughs, that he might eat the berries. 1846 TOCQUE 307 The berries [of mountain ash] are generally called 'dog berries'; by some, however, in Newfoundland, they are called 'pig-berries.' 1886 HOWLEY *MS Reminiscences* 4 All along shore clusters of Dogberry and Wild pear blossoms peeped out through the woods or hung gracefully over the banks. T 158–65 I went an' got a big pan o' dog-berries, an' I brought 'em in, washed 'em an' put on the stove an' cooked 'em. 1967 HORWOOD 116 The rowans, a group of mountain ashes locally called 'dog-berries,' are large trees that produce massive crops of fruit. They not only grow plentifully in Newfoundland forests, but are cultivated for windbreaks, hedges, and as ornamental specimens.

dogger n   Cp DOG v. Youth who follows and spies on young lovers; SKIMMER.

M 69–29 Young boys between the ages of eleven to fourteen are the traditional doggers. They follow the courters to their rendezvous and observe the proceedings.

dogging vbl n   Cp DOG v 2. Following surreptitiously a pair of lovers, esp at night out of doors (P 53–65).

C 66–18 ~ Secretly following young lovers at night—usually walking behind them to where they hide themselves. M 69–21 One of the favourite pastimes of young people, especially the young men, is 'dogging.' This was more common before cars came on the scene. Dogging simply meant following the couple without being noticed by them until they came to a spot where the courting was to take place. C 71–130 ~ Boys in our area would follow a young couple as they walked along the roads of the community making sure they were never left alone.

dog rose n   Wild rose (*Rosa nitida; R. virginiana*) (1956 ROULEAU 29).

dogwood n   Mountain ash (*Pyrus americana*); DOGBERRY. Also attrib.

[1819] 1978 *Beothuk Vocabularies* 41 Dogwood—emoethook. 1929 *Nat Geog* July, p. 124 In Newfoundland we had mountain ash, and from the young saplings we cut the bats or clubs. We call them dogwood bats. 1937 DEVINE 77 Dogwood Tree: It was quite common practice to pass a child through limbs of a dogberry tree to secure its future good health. 1971 CASEY 99 The form of a belief about what is known locally as 'the dogwood tree'. . .varies from individual to individual.

dole n

Attrib **dole bread**: bread made from unrefined flour containing bran, distributed to needy families during the Depression.

[1948] P 148–76 And how do you go about giving Ches a chance? By voting for Responsible Government as it existed in 1933, with all the dole and the dole bread?

dole days: the Depression.

1972 NEMEC 125 During the 'dole days' (Depression) [the Priest] served. . .in the capacity of surrogate, social worker or welfare officer.

dolly n   Cp *EDD* ~ sb¹: ~ douccy 'child's doll'; *OED* ~ Varden b 'a large hat'; *ADD* doozy 2 'fine specimen.'

Comb **dolly blaster**: child's china doll.

1937 DEVINE 18 ~ A doll made of porcelain or alabaster, of which latter name it is likely a corruption.

dolly bodger: piece of bread dough fried; DAMPER DOG, TOUTIN (C 75–132).

doll(y) doucer [ˌdɒlʊ ˈduːsəɹ]: child's doll; attractive baby (P 108–70).

P 148–66 'You're a doll doucer' (a lovely little baby). Q 71–7 'Oh, what a sweet baby—a real doll doucer.'

dolly varden: capacious earthenware crock used by fisherman to drink tea (P 213–56).

dominion n   Cp *O Sup²* ~ 2 b (c) esp 1912, 1931 quots. Newfoundland as a self-governing part of the British Empire and Commonwealth. Cp COLONY.

[1917] 1918 KEITH (ed) ii, 399 [Sir Edward Morris] But in all other matters the Colonies, as they have been termed [before the Colonial Conference of 1907], the Dominions, have enjoyed the full benefits and advantages of responsible Government, and that has been year after year broadened out. [1918] 1971 NOEL 131n The first official assumption of the title Dominion was in the Speech from the Throne on 23rd April last. 1922 *Sat Ev Post* 2 Sep, p. 123 The Dominion's prosperity hangs largely on the annual hunt. [1931] 1932 KEITH (ed) 304 [*Statute of Westminster*] In this Act the expression 'Dominion' means any of the following Dominions, that is to say, the Dominion of Canada, the Commonwealth of Australia, the Dominion of New Zealand, the Union of South Africa, the Irish Free State and Newfoundland. 1933 *Nfld Royal Commission Report* 202 It is fully present to our minds that, in view of Newfoundland's status as a Dominion, neither part of the plan can be put into effect except on the initiative of the Newfoundland Government and Legislature.

donkey n W C RUSSELL *Sailor's Language* (1883), p. 42 'a sailor's chest' for sense 2.

1 A wooden barrel or cask for the export of dried and salted cod-fish.

T 90–64 We had local names for the fish cask. The donkey was the one you put the large small fish in, the eighteen or twenty inches. [It had] a twenty-four inch head. P 127–76 ~ a four-quintal fish cask.

2 A home-made wooden chest for storing clothes.

C 68–1 The donkey, as it is commonly called, is about 2½ feet long, 2 feet wide and 1½ feet high. It is made out of boards and has a cover on hinges.

3 A frame on which logs are placed to be sawn (P 148–64).

doodle-laddle* See LOODLE-LADDLE*.

doone n also **doonaneen, doonee**. Epithet for member of a group of settlers originally from Kilkenny.

1863 PEDLEY 295 Two great Irish factions had established themselves [c1815] in St John's [one of which] was composed of 'Doonees,' or Kilkenny boys. 1895 PROWSE 402 The Tipperary 'clear airs,' the Waterford 'whey bellies' and the Cork 'dadyeens' were arrayed against the 'yellow belly' faction—the 'Doones' or Kilkenny boys, and the Wexford 'yellow-bellies.' 1976 MURPHY 30 The 'Daydeens' from Cork [were always] ready to fight at the drop of a hat against the 'doonaneens' from Kilkenny and the 'Yellow Bellies' from Wexford.

door n

1 In various types of fixed or stationary fishing-gear, the entrance; esp in a 'cod-trap,' a section of the box-like net structure placed to permit fish to enter. Also attrib.

1895 GRENFELL 67 A long telescope, with a plain glass bottom—the fish glass—is pushed down into the room, through which the trap-master is peering to see how many finny prisoners there are. Now the door is pulled up, and now the floor is rising—rising—rising, being passed right over the boat, until all the frightened captives are huddled together in one seething mass near the surface. 1936 SMITH 16 The doors of the [cod] trap were nine inches open, the rim of the trap eight fathoms deep and the leader of the trap four and a half fathoms. P 148–61 ~ Slatted entrance at one side of lobster trap. T 43–64 When you lets go your first lot o' linnet in underneath, you also let go your doors. Now your trap is goin' down in the same shape it was in when you pulled it up. 1966 SCAMMELL 38 'I s'pose your father got his moorings out all ready?' Mr Blanchard said casually, coiling two Manilla door-ropes on the splitting table. Q 67–34 Door lines are lines fastened to the bottom of the mouth of the trap (sometimes this opening is called doorways) and comes to the surface of the water; by these the trap is raised, closing the doorway as the trap rises to the surface. T 141/67–65[2]

An' I said, 'We can handle what we got, but haul up the doors—there's enough in un for you.' An' he hauled up the doors, an' we with the best part o' the bag o' the trap up, an' took eighty barrels out of un. 1979 *Salt Water, Fresh Water* 46 And when you go to haul the trap, the first thing you do is lift up your rope and close the door off, so that the fish cannot get out of the trap.

2 Comb **door box**: porch or shelter at the entrance of a house, 'fishing-stage,' etc.

T 80–64 He put in a night or two hangin' round the station, an' sleepin' out in the door box—anywhere out o' the weather. P 55–68 In the front of the stage there was a fairly large door which was kept closed by a piece of rope tied to the door-box.

door place: open space near usual entrance to a house.

Q 67–109 ~ area where wood is sawed and split. Q 71–8 One of the things I likes about St John's is the beautiful door-places what you calls 'lawns.' P 122–71 Clean the door place! (area directly adjacent to back door of a home).

doorway: see sense 1 above. Also attrib.

T 43–64 This leader would guide the fish to the mouth of the trap, what the old fishermen used to call doorways. The fish would go in the doorways and now it couldn't come back. Q 67–91 Doorway float [used to suspend section of the net in the water]. P 9–73 The doorway is about two to three fathoms wide, and the leader fastens in the middle, both bottom and top. An iron rod is sometimes used, as a sinker for the doorway; it is about one inch in diameter. 1977 *Inuit Land Use* 132 Care had to be taken in setting the traps. . . However, if properly set, the cod would follow the leader net into the doorway of the trap and be caught.

dory n *DAE* ~[2] (1709–), *Fisheries of U S* (1887), p. 173 for sense 1; for comb in sense 2: *O Sup*[2] b ~ man (1962), ~ mate (1890).

1 A small flat-bottomed boat with flaring sides and a sharp bow and stern, providing both stability in the water and easy stowage in stacks on deck, used esp in fishing with hand-lines and trawls; freq in designations of various sizes of vessel employing such craft: *four-dory vessel*, etc.

[1895 PROWSE 571 Fishing for Cod on the Banks from a Doris.] 1933 *Nfld Royal Commission Report* 97 The fishery is conducted from Newfoundland by schooners of up to 150 tons, known as 'Bankers,' carrying a complement of 20–24 men and 10–12 dories. 1937 *Seafisheries of Nfld* 29 The gear favoured by the Shore fishermen are cod-traps, cod-nets, hand lines, trawls and jigger and the boats used are schooners, trap skiffs, jack-boats, dories and punts; many of these are now propelled by motor engines. 1940 SCAMMELL 9 "Squid Jiggin' Ground": There's a red rantin' Tory out here in a dory, / A-runnin' down Squires on the squid-jiggin' ground. 1960 FUDGE 10 We made tracks for home with 280 quintals onboard, a fair trip for our little four dory vessel. 1972 NEMEC 57 A slightly larger, open, two-man boat, the 'dory,' was also frequently employed. 1975 BUTLER 56 About 1870 to 1875 fishermen began to build larger boats to enable them to fish farther from home. At about the same time, dories were being used by the owners of fishing boats in place of punts, which formerly were used for tending trawls on the fishing ground.

2 Attrib, comb: **dory banker** [see BANKER], **~ banking**, **~ boat** [see BOAT], **~ buff**, **~ hat**, **~ hook**, **~ man**, **~ master**, **~ mate**, **~ piggin**, [see PIGGIN], **~ pin** [see TOLE PIN], **~ schooner**, **~ scoop** [see SCOOP], **~ skipper** [see SKIPPER], **~ strap** [cp PLUG STRAP].

P 148–62 Dory banker. 1963 TEMPLEMAN & FLEMING 53 The best longlining, particularly from August onward, could be obtained in the inshore area where the dory banking schooners had previously obtained autumn catches. M 68–17 The fishermen [c1940] began to put gasoline engines in their dories, ranging from 3–5 h.p. Dories used for these salmon and lobster fisheries were built larger than the row-dory and [were] much more sturdy. [Later] the dory-boat gave way to the out-board motor boat. M 68–26 The four dories were made ready. They were painted (the colour was dory buff [yellow] and the gunwales were green) and equipped with a good supply of 'toe' pins. 1971 NOSEWORTHY 192 Dory hat. A waterproof hat worn by fishermen with the brim the same size all around. M 68–26 The dory was always kept on deck except during the day when she might be used. She was hoisted in and out by block and tackle using dory hooks. 1958 MOWAT 33 They came to see [the *Foundation Franklin*]: old dory-men who had given their years to the Grand Banks. 1972 NEMEC 57 In a few instances, 'dory men' employed cotton nets in addition to bultows and jiggers. P 127–76 Dory master. At the fishing grounds, the person who assumes control of a dory, its other occupants and the general fishing activities, while away from the main ship. [1905] 1960 FUDGE 9 The year 1905 found me and my Brother Edward on board the 90 ton vessel *Mattie*, dorymates. C 148–65 He would have neither dory mate. 'Dory mate or no,' I said, 'stay where you're to.' 1973 BARBOUR 51 A dory piggin is made of wood and shaped very much like the dust-pan one uses around the house. It has a short handle and is used to dip water from the bottom of a dory. 1971 NOSEWORTHY 192 Dory pins. Small, round pegs in the sides of a dory to keep the oars from slipping back and forth. 1953 *Nfld Fish Develop Report* 57 The importance of the dory-schooner for a properly balanced deep-sea fishery in this region has been emphasized. [c1900] 1978 *RLS* 8, p. 26 Dory scoop. 1971 NOSEWORTHY 192 Dory Scoop. *Bailer.* 1971 CHIARAMONTE 39 The obligation felt by Samson became evident in his relationship toward George as a 'dory-mate.' Traditionally the man who owns the dory is referred to as the 'dory-skipper.' T 145–65 Fortunately they each found themselves clinging to the dory straps. P 113–76 The dory strap is secured to the counter by a knot at each end on the inside of each hole.

dose of shot See SHOT.

dotard n also **daughter, doater, doter**, etc ['dɑtəɹd, 'dɔːtəɹ, 'doɯtəɹ, 'doutəɹ] *O Sup*[2] ~ 3

(Nfld: 1884); *DC* doter (Nfld: 1771, 1963). Common seal, esp in its second or third year (*Phoca vitulina*); BAY SEAL, HARBOUR ~ , RANGER. Also attrib.

[1766] 1971 BANKS 393 Incolis Harbour seal or Dotard. [1770] 1792 CARTWRIGHT i, 30 After breakfast I went up the river again; looked at the traps; got a tub of fine sand; and killed a doater with my rifle. 1792 ibid *Gloss* i, x Doater. An old, common seal. [1802] 1916 MURPHY 2 The seals upon this coast are of many species, they are classed and distinguished by names only to be found in the Newfoundland nomenclature, and only understood by the Newfoundland naturalists, Tars [ed emend: Jars], Doaters and Gunswoils and many others brew upon the rocks, in the summer season, and may be called natives. 1873 CARROLL 10 The native seal never leaves the island. When three years old they are called dotards. 1895 GRENFELL 173 When one year old the bay seal is called a 'jar seal,' and its skin is poor; in the second year it is a 'doter' and becoming speckled, in the third year, it is a 'ranger,' and is then very beautiful, being checkered silver and black all over. 1911 HUTCHINSON 111 Those [seals] that we see in the Exploits River are what they locally call 'dotter' seals—I cannot be responsible for the spelling—and look very much like the common seal about our own coasts. 1924 ENGLAND 103 Once in a while a 'jar' seal is sighted, and even a 'daughter,' as the dotard is called. 1953 *Nfld & Lab Pilot* ii, 253 Doater point. . .the northern extremity of Alcock island. T 391/2–67 We killed one one time, me an' another feller—a doter, you know, a bay seal, we'll say. M 71–44 The seal skins used to be in great demand, the doter skins (the old seal). 1976 *Evening Telegram* 18 Mar, p. 6 He made reference to the appearance of seals in the Exploits estuary and the Humber River many years ago. . . This is a different species known as the dotar seal. They are still found in our rivers and lakes. 1977 *Inuit Land Use* 128 In early or mid-June, ranger and grey seals migrate north to shallow areas near rocky shores, where they haul out to bask in the sun or hide from hunters among the rocks. Old rangers (dotters) are especially clever at concealing themselves. Unlike other seals, rangers breed late (mid-June) and moult late (mid-August).

dote v Cp *OED* ~ 'to be weak-minded from old age'; cp also *doze off*. In phr *dote off*: to drift off into sleep.

P 148–63 He was dotin' off to sleep.

doter See DOTARD.

dotterel n also **dodtrel** *EDD* ~ sb[1] for sense 1; cp *OED* 1 'a species of [European] plover' for sense 2.

1 A stupid or feeble-minded person.

1896 *J A Folklore* ix, 21 Dodtrel: an old fool in his dotage, or indeed a silly person of any age. It is usually spelled *dotterel*.

2 Marbled godwit; Hudsonian godwit (*Limosa fedoa; L. haemastica*) (1959 MCATEE 33–4).

1870 *Can Naturalist* v, 296 [The dotterel is] only a periodical visitor; most common in the fall. 1896 *J A*

Folklore ix, 21 Dodtrel. . .is usually spelled *dotterel*, and primarily denoted a bird, a species of plover. From its assumed stupidity, it being alleged to be so fond of imitation that it suffers itself to be caught while intent on mimicking the actions of the fowler.

double a Cp *DC* ~ sleigh 2 for **double sled**.
Comb **double-ball mitt**: heavy mitten made by knitting with two balls of wool.
1979 POCIUS 26 In some instances, however, a heavy-duty mitt was fabricated using two balls of yarn. This technique was called double-knitting, and mitts that were constructed by this method were called 'double-ball' mitts.
double bitter: axe with two cutting edges.
T 43/7–64 When you'd go up to the camp and sign on, the company would issue a double bitter—a blade on each side of the axe. 1977 RUSSELL 114 So out he darted into the back yard and come back with an axe, and a good job it was, said Grampa, that it wasn't a double bitter.
double crew: see CREW 4.
double-handed: see DOUBLE-HANDED.
double Irish chain: see IRISH CHAIN.
double jar: common seal after its first year; JAR².
1792 CARTWRIGHT *Gloss* i, xi Jar. The young of the smallest kind of seal [are called Jars]; the old ones are called Double Jars.
double linnet: overlap of netting formed when a cod-trap is drawn to the surface; cp CUT n, LINNET.
P 9–73 The second hand attends to the forward cuts and the skipper to the stern cuts. The cuts or double linnet is a particular job and requires an expert to handle.
double sled, ~ **sleigh**: heavy sled drawn by two horses; a sled in two linked sections used to haul wood; cp WAGON SLED.
[1920] 1933 GREENLEAF (ed) "The Lumber Camp Song": I sit upon my double sleigh as happy as a king. / My horse is always ready, and I am never sad; / There's no one else so happy as the double-sleigher lad.
T 43/8–64 My job was loadin' double sleds—a feller drivin' a pair of horses an' I was loader for him. M 68–10 [The double sled] is pulled by a horse [and is] used to pull logs for long distances. The roller bunk allows the sled to turn under the load of logs. If the land is very steep, then only the front sled is used.
double-spring trap: animal trap with two rods placed under tension to secure the prey.
[1770] 1792 CARTWRIGHT i, 52 I caught a marten near the river side, and tailed two double-spring traps on the north shore.
double-team cart: see **double sled** above.
T 101–64 [They used to use] a double team cart—that's two horses. That was a big machine with four wheels on it, and the wheels I daresay might be five or six feet in diameter; big working carts for handling heavy material like timber.
double wagon sled: see WAGON SLED.

double-handed av Rowing or fishing in a boat with another man rather than alone; cp CROSS HANDED.
T 449–67 Yes, sir. Lots o' times I went cross-handed. An' other times been double-handed.

dough n *EDD* ~ fig 'a Turkey fig' So D Co. Attrib **dough fig**: term used to distinguish fig from raisin, also called FIG, preserved in local place-names.
1953 *Nfld & Lab Pilot* ii, 116 Dough-fig point lies about half a mile north-eastward of Low Point, and Oarblade point.

douse v Cp *OED* ~ v¹ 2 'to lower or slacken suddenly' naut for sense 2.
1 To throw away or discard (P 209–73).
P 148–68 Of scraps of paper, 'Douse 'em after.'
2 In command *douse the killick*! Heave out the small anchor. See KILLICK.
1955 ENGLISH 38 ~ Throw the grapnel overboard.

douser n ['daɯsəɹ]. Cp DOUSE v. A device used to drive fish in a desired direction by thrashing the water; DASHER, THRASHER, TROUNCER (Q 71–8).
1971 CASEY 63 A 'doucer' was a twelve or fourteen inch bolt of iron with four iron rings fastened through the bolt at three or four inch intervals. When four or five 'doucers' were lowered overboard and pulled up and down by a line or were allowed to strike the ocean floor, they produced a loud noise which drove the cod into the 'bunt' or the loose bag of netting of the seine.

dout v *OED* ~ v (1526–1841) now dial; *EDD* 1. To extinguish a fire; turn off an electric light.
1896 *J A Folklore* ix, 21 ~ a contraction of 'do out,' to extinguish. 1907 MILLAIS 339 ~ the fire, to put out. 1937 DEVINE 18 ~ To put out. . .a fire or light. [1926] 1946 PRATT 176 "The Cachalot": The second oarsman snatched and shot / The piggin like a shuttlecock, / Bailing the swamping torrent out, / Or throwing sidelong spurts to dout / The flame. P 222–66 I'll go and dout [the electric light] now. T 391/2–67 The first thing hè done then was hauled off his boot for to dout it, you know, full o' water—plenty of water there. 1979 POTTLE 95 But the fires of slander were not so handily 'douted,' and more fanning of the flames was soon to come from a new direction.

douter n *EDD* dout v 1 (1) ~ . An extinguisher (1896 *J A Folklore* ix, 21).

down av, prep *DC* ~ north 1 Nfld (1905) for sense 1; JOYCE 71 for sense 3 *(give) down the banks*; cp *EDD* ~ 2 (1), (2) ~ along (folk) for sense 4. Cp UP.
1 Northward along the coast of Newfoundland and Labrador, esp in phr *down along*, ~ *north*, ~ *the shore*, ~ *to the Labrador*.
1862 NOBLE 27–8 *Down* the northern sea! . . .This calling north *down*. . .instead of *up*, appears to me to be reversing the right order of things. It is against the stream, which, inshore, sets from Baffin's Bay south;

and, in respect of latitude, it is *up-hill*; the nearer the pole, the higher the latitude. And besides, it is *up* on the map, and was *up* all through my boyhood, when geography was a favourite study. But as down seems to be the direction settled upon in common parlance, *down* it shall be in all these pages. [1870] 1973 KELLY 18 Her husband and sons were 'down the shore,' i.e. further north, in search of the best fishing-ground. 1888 STEARNS 9–10 'You've been there [Labrador] before, I suppose?' '. . .I lived down there for three years! . . .That was about 1870, and since that time I've been *'down along,'* as they call it. . .nearly every year and two or three parties have been down with me almost every time.' 1909 BROWNE 295 My grandfather, if not the pioneer of fishing this little nook, was the first to make it headquarters for 'the down-the-shore trip.' 1919 GRENFELL¹ 61 December days are short, anyhow, 'down north' and every moment warned them that the chances of getting out before dark were rapidly diminishing. 1936 SMITH 47 Fish wasn't plentiful the remainder of that week, and most of the schooners left for down the shore. 1964 BLONDAHL (ed) 45 "Lukey's Boat": Oh, Lukey he sailed her down the shore, / To catch the fish on the Labrador. 1973 BARBOUR 9 Newfoundlanders have always said 'down to the Labrador,' or 'down' to any place north of where they were living; or 'up to St John's' or 'up to New York,' when they were really going in a southerly direction. 1979 *Salt Water, Fresh Water* 53 You'd only have to go down here about thirty or forty miles north of the Funk Islands. Usually the ships would get down twenty-five or thirty miles north of that island and would strike the seals.

2 A little distance off along a shore-line or road near the water.

T 158/63–65 There was livye[rs]. . .people lived down on the easter part o' the island. T 264–66 To the left was 'hold in' always when you was goin' [by dog-team] down the shore; you sing out 'hold in' an' he turn towards the water. 1968 DILLON 137 I believe old Tom Brophy down uses it, 'the rack' [directly]. 1977 RUSSELL 61 A fellow from down the shore come to Pigeon Inlet to take the census.

Comb **down alongs**: residents of the east end of St John's.

1976 MURPHY 32 But the clashes between the 'Down-Alongs,' the boys of the East End, and the 'Up-Alongs,' the boys of the West End, that were in being in the sixties, seventies and eighties were reminders of the old faction fight days.

down dru me's (pron of down through me's): diarrhoea (1937 DEVINE 18; M 68–18).

down shaft: in mining, a vertical shaft or tunnel.

1974 PINSENT 6 They had drilled and blasted into a down shaft of the old mine, according to bad information from inaccurate and outdated blue-prints. A down shaft now filled with water.

down the banks: a reprimand; TONGUE-BANGING.

P 108–76 I'll give him down the banks when I catch him, the young sleeveen!

down the Labrador: part of the movement of a cotillion.

C 75–141 'Goat. . .is a dance which in some areas of the province is known as the cotillion. It consists of eight people, four girls and four boys. It includes (i) through the bushes; (ii) figure eight; (iii) down the Labrador; (iv) threading the needle.

downs n pl Cp *OED* down sb¹ 2. Applied variously to stretches of open, rolling country, elevated barrens or treeless marsh land; SAVANNA.

1842 JUKES ii, 220–1 He distinguished. . .'eminences of nearly equal altitude. . .at several parts of the range to which the local names of Bold Face, Bread and Cheese, the Drop, the Flakey Downs, &c., have been attached.' 1901 *Christmas Bells* 13 During its height, the *Mercade* was driven on shore at the back of the Downs. 1904 MURPHY (ed) 23 "Dear Old Ferryland": Oh! the Downs of dear old Ferryland / How the pictures come and go. 1960 *Nfld Qtly* Summer, p. 17 In Berry Season I did a lot of berry-picking and I remember once we all went on a glorious picnic on to the Downs after bakeapples. 1963 *Evening Telegram* 17 Dec, p. 6 When I was a young man I'd go deer-hunting 50 or 60 miles in the country, 'In on the Downs' we used to say.

down-scent* n, av [daun 'sɛnt, dɑun 'sɛnt]. A blend of *descent* and *downhill*: a downward slope, declivity or descent; downhill.

T 70/2–64¹ Wonderful brook, too, down-cent, you know; big power o' water. T 393–67 There'd be force enough and weight enough, you know, and there's a little downsent. Q 73–9 ~ downhill.

dows'y poll* n also ~ **po*** Cp *EDD* dusty sb: dowsty poll 'a head covered with flour'; 'Miller, O miller, O dowsty poll!' D. A moth, miller.

P 94–57 Dousy poles: large moths attracted to lamp. C 71–105 Dousy-po—name we gave to the little white flying moths.

draft n also **draught**. Cp *OED* draught sb 2 b 'a quantity drawn: used as a specific measure of something'; *NID* ~ n 10 c 'measures of weight of fish' *Brit* for sense 1.

1 Amount of dried and salted cod-fish carried on a 'barrow' by two men; two quintals or 224 lbs (101.6 kg); various other weights of dry fish.

1896 *J A Folklore* ix, 28 Draft or *draught*. . .a load for two men to carry, hence two quintals of codfish. 1902 *Christmas Bells* 15 We packed our baskets and 'gadded' the balance of our catch—seventeen dozen all told, and equal in weight to a good 'draft' of fish (two quintals). 1954 INNIS 426 After catching, splitting, and washing, the fish were put into three-quintal tubs along with two gallons of salt per draft. (A 'draft' and a half of fresh fish, or 238 pounds, made about one quintal of fish, or 108 pounds of dried). T 192/3–65 The men down in the hold'd be yafflin' up the fish, an' they'd yaffle so much to get enough for the weight to make the draft on the bar, and then there'd be, 'Yaffle at hand. Yaffle at hand.' T 194–65 They come in the punt, sir, an' we take out ten quintals, ten drafts a man a day—that's our take-out always since I've been on a schooner. T 393/4–67 We used to ship our fish a draft a time—that's two quintals, that's 224 lbs. 1979 NEMEC 276 Fish are arranged in even rows and laid down in such a way as to form a 'bulk' or pile (usually no more than waist high) consisting of an estimated number of 'draughts' (224 pounds each).

2 Comb **draft bar(row)**: flat, rectangular wooden frame with handles at each end for two men to carry dried cod-fish; such a frame used in weighing fish; BARROW¹, FISH BARROW (P 8–55).

T 433–65 An' I'd be carryin' draft bar from six o'clock to six in th' evenin' for twenty-five cents a hour. M 68–26 The draft bar was heavier [than the Johnnie bar], weighing about twenty pounds, it could carry a draft of fish (two quintals) which weighed 224 pounds. 1977 BUTLER 68 When a ship came to Buffett to load bulk fish every man on the room would be engaged in loading. John Manning and I usually worked together carrying the draft barrow.

drag v Comb **drag-twine**: twine of a certain size used in making animal snares.
[1785] 1792 CARTWRIGHT iii, 73 I made three deer-slips of drag-twine.

drag n See DRUG.

drain n Cp *OED* ~ sb 1 'artificial conduit or channel for carrying off water, sewage, etc.' Ditch at side of road or gutter of a street to carry off rain-water; drain-pipe laid across road to prevent flooding (P 148–62).
1837 *Journ of Assembly* 451 Our reason for opening the road twenty-four feet was that the road when finished might be twenty feet wide, allowing two feet upon each side for drains. 1869 *Stewart's Qtly* iii, 55 The rock-fragment, enclosing our *Oldhamia*, was broken off by some of these forces from the original mass; tossed about; rounded by friction. . .till at length the casual blow of a pick axe, in cutting a drain, laid open the venerable forms. 1887 *Daily Colonist Christmas No* 5 In the Spring when the side drains were choked, he told the chairman 'that the sinuosities of the aqueducts had impeded the flow of the aqueous fluid, and caused it to permeate through the viaducts.' [1927 BURKE] [broadside] "Stoppage of Water": So we might scoop an egg cup [of water] outside in the drain.

drain v
1 Phr *drain one's words*: in singing, to hold the syllables of words for an unusually long time.
T 265/6–66 He did drain his words. Oh, my, he'd go off. You could go out of doors and come back and he be still drainin' his words. Lot of breath.
2 Comb **drain-bulk**: a stage in the curing of cod-fish in which the split and salted fish are laid in piles to drain before being moved to the 'flake' to dry; cp BULK n, SALT-BULK.
1819 ANSPACH 435 They then take up each fish separately, cleaning carefully back and belly with a woollen cloth, and next lay it in a long even bulk on the stage to drain. . . It may remain in drain-bulk no more than two days.

drain hole: opening in the ice used by seals; BOBBING-HOLE; SWATCH n.
1977 *Inuit Land Use* 218 [The arrival of the harp seals] coincided with the first appearance of drain holes, or openings in the ice cover.

drainings n pl The small residue of molasses adhering to container in measuring a quantity for a customer. Cp TILLY.
1957 *Evening Telegram* 27 Nov 'Don't forget a extra drop of 'lassey to allow for drainin's.' 1971 NOSEWORTHY 193 ~ A small amount of molasses over and above the quantity purchased.

drang See DRUNG.

drash v also **dresh**. Cp *EDD* thresh, *OED* thresh v 8 'to throw oneself. . .to and fro with violence' for sense (a). (a) To go around in lively fashion visiting; cp CRUISE v; (b) to inundate, pour over; to exhaust (someone).
1895 *J A Folklore* viii, 28 Dresh: to go round visiting. A man said of a minister, 'He's na'ar a bit of good for dreshing round.' 1971 CASEY 182 The women and the children stood on the quarter deck, / A heavy sea drashed over them, and swept them from the wreck. C 71–90 If a boy was late for supper, his mother would say on his coming home, 'Ah, you're drashed to pieces.' This meant running till you were very tired and hungry.

drash n Cp *OED* thrash sb¹ 2 'a beat or beating [of rain]' (1899–); cp *EDD* ~ v 'to thrash'; 'to thresh corn.' A heavy shower esp in phr *a drash of rain*.
T 141/68–65² If you come in with a skiffload o' fish an' there's a drash o' rain last night, sails got to go abroad—you got to look out to they as well. C 70–15 [He was] caught in the biggest kind of a drash of rain.

drashel* n *EDD* ~ sb² W Do So D Co. Threshold.
T 437/8–65 An' Jack come out next morn, the very first thing he opened the door an' jumped down on the drash o' the door. P 171–66 [You won't put your] foot over the drashel of that door till you gets all that wood clove up. M 68–24 Be careful, don't trip over the drashel.

draught See DRAFT.

draw v [drɑ:]. Cp *OED* ~ v 34 b 'to obtain or select by lot' for sense 1; for cpd in sense 4: *EDD* draw-latch v 3; *EDD* draw 3: drying (So) for the pronunciation *dry up* common in several localities; for comb in sense 4: *EDD* draw v 28 (11) ~ bucket Co.
1 In the inshore fishery, to secure a fishing location or 'berth' by lot in competition with others.
[(1862)] 1877 TOCQUE 294 The proprietors of the vessels of these various classes draw lots every five years for the right of occupying the various fishing set-

tlements on the coast; the best numbers select the best fishing posts, and so on to the least advantageous. 1936 SMITH 148 The other men knew all this, and were in a great hurry so that I couldn't secure the berths; the excitement ran very high, and finally they came to me and asked if I were satisfied to draw for the trap-berths. 1979 *Evening Telegram* 6 Mar, p. 2 With regard to the trap berth drawing, noting that the fishermen must draw for their berths in accordance with guidelines drawn up by the federal fisheries department. . .

2 Proverb: *you can draw [fish] by the head, but you must drag by the tail* (1895 *Christmas Review* 12).

3 Phr *draw a blank*: see BLANK n.

draw the spile: to imbibe.

1891 *Holly Branch* 15 Spruce beer, free to all who cared to *draw the spile*, and calabogus the universal beverage.

draw/dry up ['drai ʌp]: to pull fish to the surface in a net or trap; HAUL v.

1927 *Christmas Messenger* 48 The 'Bunt' of seine is the more closely and strong-knitted part where the fish are collected [when] the seine is 'dried up.' T 43–64 If the fish was runnin' good, you'd dry up thirty, forty, fifty quintals. T 158–65 Look down an' see the fish, an' you take the bunt an' heave [him] overboard an' go on round, sweep it, then dry un up. M 68–16 When the skiff gets to the trap, the haul-up ropes are hooked and the doorways shut off. After this the back of the trap is pulled closer to the boat and the crew begins drying up the twine. By drying up is meant that the bottom is brought nearer the surface by hauling the twine into the boat. In this way the fish are brought to the surface also.

4 Comb **draw-bucket, drawing- ~** : container to draw water from a well, or from the salt-water to boat or stage; also attrib.

1936 SMITH 77 After a meal all hands seemed refreshed, and we started off again for Drawbucket Tickle. 1944 *Yuletide Bells* 'Fetch the pumps,' commanded the skipper. Someone already had the draw-bucket over the side when he spoke. T 146–65 He was drawin' up water for 'em in the hold [to] wash out the locker. He hove the drawbucket an' the drawbucket took un overboard. C 70–15 Every household had a well which was equipped with a draw-bucket (a bucket with a long rope attached to the handle) . . .The water was poured from the draw-bucket into a pair of galvanized water buckets used for carrying the water from the well to the house. 1979 *Salt Water, Fresh Water* 21 They finally got a drawing bucket, hauled up some salt water, and threw it in his face and brought him around.

draw-latch v: to loiter (1937 DEVINE 19).

C 71–31 Oftentimes when we are taking our time in doing something that we should do more quickly my grandmother says 'Don't be draw-latchin'.' By this she means that we should make more haste and avoid killing time.

draw n Cp *OED* ~ sb 4 'drawing of lots'; see also DRAW v 1. In the inshore fishery, the selection by lot of a fishing location or 'berth.'

1969 WADEL 49 The antagonism has become espe-cially great where there is a 'draw' for salmon berths. M 70–27 In the late 1920's the 'draw' came into the cod-trap fishery. At this time, due to the large number of codtraps in the area fishermen had to draw for their berths. The fishermen assembled before the codtrap season started to decide who would set his codtrap in the better berths. The names of all the skippers were put in one bag and the names of the codtrap berths in another bag. A man's name and the name of a berth were drawn with the fisherman getting the berth which was drawn with his name. Berths were good for one year. A crew entitled a man to one draw; a first draw. If a fisherman had two traps he had to take a second draw—those berths being second class berths. 1971 CASEY 166 "Drawing of the Berths": About one hour did pass since first we did begin, / And every man had a draw except Uncle Cyril Flynn. 1979 *Evening Telegram* 6 Mar, p. 2 The federal department indicates that persons who have traditionally fished as operators in the codtrap fishery, even though they may have small businesses such as trucking. . .and the like, and are considered fishermen, provided they operate the boat and gear themselves, 'should be given a draw.'

drawing n, vbl n also **dryin'** * in sense 2.

1 The selection of a fishing location by lot; DRAW n.

1936 SMITH 149 All hands signed the agreement, and then Capt Randall made the tickets and put them all in a bag, each ticket bearing the name of a trap-berth. The drawing then began, Capt Randall calling each man by name. 1977 RUSSELL 16 He always supervises the drawing for our salmon and net berths every spring in April. 1979 *Evening Telegram* Mar 6, p. 2 [She] outlined difficulties being experienced in the areas of trap berth drawing, fisher-women and unemployment insurance benefits, boat subsidies. . .

2 Comb **drawing twine, drying ~** : in a cod-trap, the small mesh of the bunt in which the fish collect when the trap is hauled to the surface (Q 67–24).

P 127–73 Dryin' twine. A 'leaf' of small-meshed netting located in the back of a cod trap, towards one or both of the back corners, used for the 'drying up' of cod, to prevent the smaller fish from being caught in the meshes.

dreadful a *OED* ~ a 1 obs (1225–1659). Fearful, full of dread.

T 74–64 She didn't recognize any of 'em. She was dreadful [and] thought the best to come home.

dreadful intens *EDD* ~ adv 1 So Do; *ADD* 2. Very, extremely.

1975 GUY 63 We, in turn, were amused by the way the people from Mussel Harbour (later, Kingwell after Parson Kingwell) on Long Island used the word 'dread-ful.' Everything with them seemed to be dreadful. 'I'm dread-ful fond of them polar bars,' or ''Tis a dread-ful nice day' or 'The weather is a dread-ful kind of poor.' Things could also be a dread-ful kind of good.

dredge See DRUDGE n, v.

drenty a *EDD* drent sb (1) ~ Ha W. Of badly washed linen, stained, streaked.

P 212–65 ~ of the streaking of clothes when imperfectly or unevenly dried after washing. 1972 MURRAY 206 Many women felt that clothes dried in the house dried 'drenty' (not a bright clean white).

dresh See DRASH v.

dress v Cp *OED* ~ v 13 'to prepare for use as food' for sense 1; cp *OED* 11 'to subject to process [of] trimming, smoothing' for sense 2; for phr in sense 4: cp *OED* 7 d ~ up 'to attire. . .in a manner appropriate. . .to a part which one aspires to play.'

1 To head, gut and split fish preparatory to any further 'curing' process; freq in phr *dress down*.

[1583] 1940 *Gilbert's Voyages & Enterprises* ii, 403 [Hayes' narrative] The Generall granted in fee farme divers parcells of land lying by the water side, both in this harbor of S John, and elsewhere, which was to the owners a great commoditie, being thereby assured (by their proper inheritance) of grounds convenient to dresse and to drie their fish. [1620] 1887 MASON 151–2 Of these, three men to sea in a boate with some on Shoare to dresse and dry them in 30. dayes will kill commonlie betwixte 25. and thirty thousand worth. 1839 TUCKER 119 At the fish stands, while the cod fishery is in the full tide of operation, the women are seen among the most constant and dextrous in dressing the fish, thrown up by the fishermen. 1861 *Harper's* xxii, 459–60 Then the order was given by the skipper to 'haul in gear,' and fall to splitting and salting. This operation, which is known as 'dressing down,' is performed on hogshead tubs or boards placed between two barrels. 1936 SMITH 89 We dressed down our fish and had it all split and salted before dark. 1953 *Nfld Fish Develop Report* 87 The catch is now generally sold by the fishermen in the dressed form, i.e. with gut and head removed. T 141/67–65² Where the fish is scarce of course it pays to dress [it] an' get that an' salt it light cured an' get the most out of it. 1977 BUTLER 14 We would dress our fish and herring. We had a canvas shed among the trees to dress and pack our herring. We had no heat in the shed for frosty weather. This was a real ordeal, dressing, washing and packing in barrels.

2 To trim branches from a felled tree; LIMB; in constructing a boat, to smooth down timber and planks; freq in phr *dress down, ~ off, ~ up*.

[1874] 1881 MURRAY & HOWLEY 361 He cuts down. . .*three* trees (frequently, however, many more) and, after fixing upon his quarry he retires for that day. On the next or some future day he returns to dress up the selected tree. T 43/8–64 You'd have a day or two dressin' her off then outside, wherever you could plane a bit off without strikin' a nail. You'd dress [the boat] off an' get ready for caulkin'. T 183–65 An' then you'd dress up your keel, you scarf your boat an' build her. P 148–68 To the right of the lumber is the keel of a small motor boat all dressed and cut ready for construction.

3 To make a bed (P 78–76).

1888 *Colonist Christmas No* 16 I see the chamber-maid (when she comes up each morning to dress the beds) attire herself in her mistress's new bonnet and cloak.

4 Phr *dress off/out*: to attire in one's best clothes.

1916 *Evening Telegram* 28 Aug "Humby's Balloon": It is thought that the Kaiser was takin' a gambol, / Dressed out in a murderous aeroplane garb. P 102–60 [He] brought me out an [Eton] suit consisting of a pair of long gray pants, a vest, hammer-tail coat and a silk hat, and Sundays my mother had to dress me off. P 148–61 [In this club] you have to be dressed off after seven. P 54–67 He was all dressed off in his Sunday clothes.

dress up: in Christmas 'mummering,' to put on a fantastic disguise or costume and visit various houses.

1893 *Christmas Greeting* 20 However I enjoyed myself thoroughly, and went out after, every night that the boys 'dressed up.' 1973 PINSENT 53 I never cared much for jannying or mummering or dressing up or whatever the hell it was.

5 Comb **dress-up**: (a) man disguised as a ghost; (b) the act of donning a disguise at Christmas in order to go 'jannying.'

1966 PADDOCK 122 A less ethereal, but no less frightening, apparition was the *dress-up*. . .a person disguised as a ghost to frighten or even assault others at night. T 361–67 There is a dress-up at Greenspond. Somebody around February or March month dresses up and goes around and steals clothes off lines, frightens people and is a weird-looking character. 1979 TIZZARD 175 The dress up meant you would don some old wearing apparel that you felt sure no one knew, and put on a mask, usually of cotton cloth, over your face.

drew* n

1 In 'knitting' a fish-net, a certain number of meshes formed in a row.

T 43/8–64 Then you'd slip that off o' your card—'twas a bit tedious first until you get three or four drews, they called it, knit up; that was three or four back an' forth—the hundred meshes. Q 73–1 [There are] ninety-eight meshes in a drew.

2 A quantity of dried and salted cod-fish equal to the length of a storage pound.

T 395–67 [We'd] turn over the fish what was there, turn over one drew, right the length o' that pound; instead of face up, they'd be back up.

dribble n also **driddle***. Cp *OED* ~ sb 1 'small trickling and barely continuous stream.' The head water of a river; a small stream flowing into a river or pond; a spring.

1938 BRYAN 7 North side of Middle Barachois Brook and West Bank of Joe McKay's Dribble. 1957 *Evening Telegram* 13 July, p. 4 The [salmon] pools from the mouth of the Dribble are not many and the large numbers [of fishermen] occupying them appear to make it apparent that the fishing water is thronged. P 245–59 ~ The headwater of a river; a small brook forming headwater. T 50/2–64 Up there in those ponds, in the dribbles, in the brooks, you know, when the water'd be runnin', the fresh water, an' that'd be as warm as milk. P 118–67 ~ a small brook or stream of water running into a pond. 1971 NOSEWORTHY 194 Driddle brook. Same as a spring, which is a thin stream of water flowing out of the ground.

driddle* See DRIBBLE.

driet n See DRITE.

drift n Cp *OED* ~ sb 2, 2b for senses 1 and 2; cp *OED* 9 'floating matter' for 4; *OED* drift-ice (1600–), *DC* (1829–) for comb in sense 7.

1 Sea-room.
[1783] 1792 CARTWRIGHT iii, 34 I am decidedly for setting more sail immediately, and endeavouring to get outside of Funk Island, where we shall have drift enough.

2 The slow passage of a boat over a fishing-ground, with men using hand-lines and jiggers; vessel's course.
1955 DOYLE (ed) 28 "Hard, Hard Times": Go out in the morning go on a drift still; / It's over the side you will hear the line nell; / For out flows the jigger and freeze with the cold, / And as to for starting, all gone in the hole. T 194/6–65 I kept away—south by west, half west, an' run chances, an' run her back a hour an' twenty minutes, an' I considered now she was 'bout on her same drift, wasn't she?

3 Spray, esp freezing spray at sea.
[1907] 1979 *Nfld Qtly* Fall, p. 22 Can scarcely see the length of the ship for drift. 1933 GREENE 64 In addition to the loss of the *Southern Cross*, the *Newfoundland* lost 77 of her crew in the blinding, freezing snow—the icy, choking, impenetrable veil of 'drift' in which none may live for long. T 194/5–65 An' this drift was high as her spars, up th' upper part o' Belle Isle.

4 Rubbish; odds and ends.
[1902] 1909 *Tribune Christmas No* 23 No person shall, within the City limits, cast or throw drift, dung, rubbish, or other offensive matter in or upon any grating.

5 A spree; TIME.
T 141/65–65² [At Christmas] whatever 'twould cost for that night's drift, that night's entertainment, he'd have to [pay].

6 Phr *drift of fish*: concentration of cod-fish; SCULL, SPOT.
1979 NEMEC 277 If the tide is 'running' strong a crew may 'hit' or run into a 'drift of fish' and 'jig' hundreds of pounds of large cod in a matter of minutes.
in the drift of: in a particular ocean current or flow.
1866 WILSON 275 From the twentieth to the last of February is the whelping time; and the ice about that time is generally in the drift of White Bay, or the Bay of Exploits. 1873 CARROLL 18 As long as white fish are in with the land, so sure will seals of every description be there, as white fish are swarming along from the Labrador coast, when in drift of the straits of Belle Isle, provided the winds hang at the time they are swarming along from the south from the E. or N.E.

7 Comb **drift-bank**: snow-bank.
[1778] 1792 CARTWRIGHT ii, 294 I took a turn round the island; and was near breaking my neck by a fall over a drift-bank.
drift-ice: floating masses or fragments of ice, driven by wind and current; ICE; ROUGH ICE.
1610 *Willoughby Papers* 17a, 1/2 The worst time [for shipping] is when the fishermen come to fishinge, because the drifts Ice from the northern Countries, at that time only troubleth them. [1768] 1826 CARTWRIGHT i, 33 After very deep snows are dissolved by a hasty thaw, this river swells above banks of twenty feet high, as appears by the wounds made by drift ice in the trunks of the standing trees. [1775] 1792 CARTWRIGHT ii, 75 Observing the drift ice to draw nearer in shore, and it being calm, I went out to the shalloway and towed her into this harbour. 1837 *Journ of Assembly* 451 The immense fields of drift ice from the northern regions so completely blocks and fills up Conception Bay that the communication with the capital by water is impeded. 1895 *Christmas Review* 12 The tow of an iceberg is better than none. (Vessels caught in drift ice are often made fast to an iceberg, in order to prevent their driving south, and also in order to enable them to wait for an opening in the ice). [1917] 1972 GORDON 95 There is always a risk that an in-shore wind may send a consignment of drift-ice well up into the bay again. 1936 SMITH 71 I said that we had a good chance of getting there, and securing the berths, as our vessel was a good sailor, and sheathed with greenheart, a good thing should we meet any drift ice. 1977 *Inuit Land Use* 167 White fox travel south in the fall on the drift ice, and they are sometimes plentiful on the seaward islands and interior plateau.

drill v To subject (one) to hard manual labour (1925 *Dial Notes* v, 329).
1924 ENGLAND 165 He'll drill [work] ye to death.

drilling n See DRILL. Rough, strained experience; difficult passage.
T 141/67–65² I've often heard [him] talking about when they used to go down there, the drillin's they got comin' up out of it in October month. T 194/5–65 Give her a hard drillin', and that's what we done; we put the three reef foresail on her, sir, and every chance in the world that she could live, we'd cut her in.

drite* n also **driet, dryth** [dræɪt] *OED* dryth now dial (1533–); *EDD* dryth 1 s cties. Dryness in the air, low humidity; little dampness or fog, consequently a condition suitable for drying salted cod; hence the degree of dryness of the various grades or 'culls' of fish (see 1962 quot).
1897 *J A Folklore* x, 205 Driet or dryth, dryness or dryingness. 'It's no use spreading out the fish, there is no driet in the weather.' 1924 ENGLAND 221–2 Such wind an' rain, me sons! Dere was no let-up, an' no driet [clearing up] in de wedder, a week on end. 1937 DEVINE 19 Driet, dryth. Drying power in the weather prevailing. 1962 *Nfld Fisheries Conf* 202 He don't feel like selling a draft of light cured fish say for $13.00 which is a problem which must arise owing to the drieth of the fish, there is so much moisture in the heavy

cured fish. 1966 HORWOOD 266 But this early in the morning the day had almost perfect 'dryth.' P 157–73 There's no dryth for the fish today.

drive v   *OED* ~ v 26 for sense 1; cp *EDD* II 1 (8) drive a noise Ha, (12) drive works Ha Do So for sense 2.

1 Of a boat, vessel, etc, to drift or move rapidly impelled by wind or current; freq in phr *drive away,* ~ *off,* etc.

[1862] 1916 MURPHY 30 We are now off Cape St Francis and expect to drive to Cape Race before getting clear. [1891] (c1977) WINSOR (ed) 46 We was drivin' along, every man of us anxiously lookin' out into the darkness. 1932 BARBOUR 44 We had never been 'driven to sea' before and we had won so far with the elements, and wanted to see the game played out and who would win the last trick. T 45/6–64 So he left, 'twas in the fall o' the year, to go to St John's in an open boat—she was gangboarded, fore cuddy an' after cuddy on her, an' breeze come on, they got drove off. T 54–64 I threw him overboard an' I suppose he went on, or went to the bottom, or drove to sea. T 186–65 An' we had to leave our schooner—she drove away, a wrack. P 245–74 She druv out to sea and they was drownded. 1977 *Nfld Qtly* Winter, p. 21 He said 'This is the *Allan F Rose,* this schooner. We left St John's about seven or eight days ago,' and he drove off in the storms I was off in, and his vessel sprung a leak.

2 Phr *drive works*: to engage in rough, boisterous play; to romp, skylark (P 245–56).

T 208–65 There was a couple o' fellers, young fellers, that pulled through [their night on the ice-floes]. They was drivin' works all night—skylarkin', keepin' theirselves warm. C 70–15 Whenever people, young or old, are engaged in playful activities such as chasing each other, tickling, pinching, twisting arms, they are said to be drivin' works. P 182–75 Drive works [is used] when referring to kids, drunks, or angry individuals creating disorder by spilling things or dumping or tipping food, drink or furniture over.

3 Comb **drive-screw**: screwdriver (C 70–30).

driver n   Cp *OED* ~ 5 a obs. Square sail hoisted at stern of a small boat.

1896 *J A Folklore* ix, 28 ~ used in Newfoundland to denote a small sail at the stern of their fishing punts or boats. 1902 *Christmas Bells* 14 After another 'bilin' of the kettle, we hoisted the driver on the punt and set forth for our rendezvous of the previous evening. 1969 *Nfld Qtly* July, p. 19 ~ a small quadrilateral sail at the stern of a boat.

driving vbl n Comb **driving shack**: woods shelter for lumbermen engaged in driving or floating logs down-stream.

T 50–64 When I started to go into Bishop Falls first I slept on the ice [in] an old drivin' shack.

droch See DROKE.

drogue See DROKE.

drogue* n   See DRUG.

droke n   also **droch, drogue, drook**. Cp *EDD* drock sb[2] 'a small watercourse' s w cties, droke 'a furrow; a passage, groove' Co; *DC* ~ 'a copse' Nfld (1772–); SEARY 146.

1 A valley with steep sides, sometimes wooded and with a stream; freq in place-names. Cp GULCH n.

[1771] 1792 CARTWRIGHT i, 210 I sent Fogarty forward to Foul-weather Droke to prepare for the night; while I walked to Condon Tickle and measured the breadth of it. I then went over Lower Table to the Droke. 1848 *Journ of Assembly* Appendix, p. 299 Job's Cove Droke [Western Bay]. 1895 *J A Folklore* viii, 288 I tooked her [the gun] and the powder-harn and shot-bag and starts up yander through the droke. You know the little pond at the top of the hill. When I cumed in sigh' o' un, the first thing I see is a loo' (loon) sitting about the middle uv un. 1907 DUNCAN 269 Across the droch, lifted high above the maid and me, his slender figure black against the pale-green sky, stood John Cather on the brink of Tom Tulk's cliff. 1937 DEVINE 5 Mr Munn's identification of 'droke' as a Devonshire usage is 'a valley with sides so steep as to be extremely difficult of ascent.' 1953 *Nfld & Lab Pilot* ii, 112 Ben Droke. . .rises to an elevation of 713 feet. [1954] 1972 RUSSELL 21 'And where did they live?' 'Just up the droke a piece.' M 71–103 We sometimes went berry picking in nearby areas, but we were cautioned not to wander too far because in certain drokes, small valleys, lived fairies who might spirit us away.

2 A thick grove of trees (in a valley); a belt or patch of trees; cp HAT, TUCK[2]. Freq in phr *droke of woods.*

[1822] 1866 WILSON 330–1 On our right hand, in looking along the ridge of the land, it was an extended barren covered with its mantle of snow; numerous ponds were to be seen in every direction, with here and there a 'droke' of woods; and the thick forest skirting the seashore. 1881 KENNEDY 92 The country hereabouts was marshy, with belts or 'drogues' of woods scattered about exactly like groups of islands in a sea. 1890 HOWLEY *MS Reminiscences* 28 Got in to end of our line and camped a short distance below in a droke of woods. 1895 *J A Folklore* viii, 39 Droke of wood, denoting a wood extending from one side of a valley to the other. 1910 PRICHARD 89 These barrens show great spreads of sulphur-coloured reindeer moss, and a loose scattering of trees, which gather here and there into clumps, or 'drogues,' of spruce, of juniper, or of birch. 1937 DEVINE 19 ~ A thick grove of trees; also pronounced *drook.* T 89–64 An' there's a droke o' woods down the back of our camp, an' now the next mornin' everything was all altered. 1980 *Evening Telegram* 8 Nov, p. 6 What happens of course is that the moose are driven from the tucks and drokes far back into the country into the thick woods.

droll a   *EDD* ~ a 8. Strange or unusual in manner or state.

1863 MORETON 32 ~ Odd, unusual. The idea of humour is not attached to the word. A sick person describing his feelings will say, 'I seems terrible droll.' When trying to show a servant some proper method of doing work, she will tell you she is 'not used to them droll ways.' 1925 *Dial Notes* v, 329 ~ Queer feeling. 'A *droll* head' (when ill). 1937 DEVINE 19 ~ Unusual; odd. A sick person may say 'I feel *droll* to-day.' P 5–67 ~ Peculiar. 'He's a droll old soul.'

drong See DRUNG.

drook See DROKE.

drudge v   also **dredge**. Cp *OED* dredge v¹ 1 'bring up [oysters]' for sense 1; dredge v² 2 'to sprinkle (any powdered substance)' for sense 2; *OED* ~ v 1 'to work hard or slavishly' for comb in sense 3.

   1 To catch herring.
   T 141/67–65² Catch a lot of fish like you would herring years ago, drudge it in. Course we used to drudge in herring then, go down to Green Bay.
   2 To sprinkle salt on herring as a preservative.
   1896 *J A Folklore* ix, 28 Dredge, pronounced in Newfoundland *drudge*, is used to denote the sprinkling of salt over herring when caught, and mixing them together to preserve them in the mean time. 1937 DEVINE 19 ~ To sprinkle salt on a deck load of fresh herring; also to 'rouse' them. 1977 BUTLER 16 We dressed and dredged the herring ourselves in the boat. Dredging herring is sprinkling salt through them.
   3 Comb **drudge bar(row), dredge** ~ : a rectangular wooden frame, often with a tub fitted on top, with handles at each end enabling two men to pull, carry or slide fish, etc; cp BARROW¹, FISH BARROW, HAND- ~ .
   [1663] 1963 YONGE 57 When the fish is split, he falls into a drooge barrow, which, when full, is drawn to one side of the stage, where boys lay it one on top of another. 1819 ANSPACH 431 [The splitter] pushes the fish into the *drudge-barrow*. 1866 WILSON 210 The splitter. . .slides the fish into a drudge-barrow. . . When. . .full, it is dragged to the upper end of the stage, where the fish is taken out and salted. 1909 BROWNE 68 The fish is then slapped into a dredge barrow and borne to the end of the stage to the salt bulk. 1924 ENGLAND 267 There they labour all day, making up the fish, carrying it on dredge barrows, spreading and turning it. T 43–64 The stage would have to be a big place because there was so much stuff in it, like drudge barrows—what they used to pull the fish along in to the salt bulk. This drudge barrow was made half-moon fashion so as 'twould slip along on the beddin' of the stage easy. M 71–117 When split, the fish went into a puncheon partly filled with salt water. From there it went by means of a 'drudgebarrow'—a square barrow on runners with a rope strap at the head for hauling—to the salter whose job was to salt the fish and stack it into a saltbulk pile which was the width of two fish and in length stretched across the back end of the stage.
   drudge horn: cow's horn used for administering medicine to cow or other large farm animal (P 245–58).

drudge n   also **dredge**. Cp *OED* dredge sb¹ a var drudge 'drag-net for taking oysters' (1561–); *DAE* (1879–). Drag-net used in fishing.
   1613 *Willoughby Papers* 1/3, 45 It[em] ii dredges. [1777] 1792 CARTWRIGHT ii, 256 The whole bay seems extremely fit to use both a trall and a drudge in, but with what success, experience must prove.

drug n   also **drag, drogue***. Cp *OED* drag sb 3 'something that drags. . .so as to impede motion'; *EDD* drug sb¹ 5 'a drag or shoe placed under a wheel to prevent it from turning' So D Co. A device serving as a brake on a sled; TOW²; a dog's clog. Also attrib.
   1910 GRENFELL 91 We were now racing down a series of steep hillsides, so steep that in spite of the 'drugs' or drags, it took all our attention to keep from running over the dogs. P 65–64 The brake to slow a komatic down is the drug. A drug is an endless chain six or seven feet long. When not in use the drug is hung on the nose rope. When applied it slips down over the nose and under the runner. 1966 BEN-DOR 128 A rifle shot sends the 'kamotiks' on their way. Whips and sticks are absent, but the sound of the 'drag,' the shouts and swears, and the skillful use of snowballs are sufficient to get the best performance from the dogs. T 264–66 Over rough country you had to have drugs. I never used two, though, for all I seed people with two—one on each runner. We always had a chain drug—a chain wrapped around the nose o' the sled. An' that was a great help sometimes when the dogs'd want to go where you didn't want 'em to go. You drop that drug an' they'd understand you wanted them to stop. T 417/8–67 She opened up the door an' here is the dog. The dog had the drogue on, you see, as they call it in Labrador: a drug. P 207–67 He tried to slow down the sled with a drag chain. T 409–67 'How d'you ever do it, hold on the steerin' stick one hand?' 'One hand, one hand; put me drugs on inside here on the level, and let her come! Hold on the steerin' stick [of the sled].' M 69–6 To help the ox keep the load from going down a hill too fast, a drug was placed under a runner of the 'fard slide' and the end held by the logger on the load.

drugs n pl   *EDD* ~ sb pl So D; *ADD*. Dregs (P 94–57).
   P 148–61 ~ in home-brew the stuff settling to bottom of bottle or barrel. P 61–67 This wine is good, right to the drugs. P 167–67 There's lots o' drugs in me tea.

drum n   *OED* ~ sb¹ 9 b (1858). Cylindrical wooden container in which dried and salted codfish are packed for export esp to South America; a quantity of fish so packed; also attrib **drum fish**: the quality, 'cure,' or 'cull' of fish prepared for that market; SCREWED FISH.
   [1869] 1899 *Nfld Law Reports* 291 For the preservation of the vessel and the remainder of the cargo it was necessary to lighten her, and for this purpose there were 556 drums of fish, part of the cargo, thrown overboard. 1883 *Fish Exhibit Cat*⁴ 175 [exhibit] Screw Press for pressing dried Fish into drums. 1894 HARVEY 251 A glance at one of the large fish-stores—such as Baine

Johnstone's, Job's, Monroe's or Thorburn and Tessier's—is interesting as showing how the dried cod-fish are sorted, stacked in huge piles, and made up in 'drums' for foreign markets. 1925 *Dial Notes* v, 330 ~ Four quintals (of fish). 1937 *Seafisheries of Nfld* 23 The original method of shipping dried codfish from New-foundland was in bulk by sailing vessels. The next method was the use of barrels, to which reference is made in the very early records of the Newfoundland fishery. With the opening up of trade between New-foundland and Brazil there came the introduction of the packages known as drums and half-drums. 1953 JOB 58 Though as indicated the firm's experiments with the converted steel ships were not satisfactory, the *Earlshall* and the *Madeleine Constance* both made suc-cessful trips to Brazil with full loads of drum fish. T 90–64 We made birch drums, half drums—half quin-tal drums—and whole quintal drums: they were for the Brazil market. 1973 HORWOOD 40–1 This time the *Olive Moore* was not long delayed. There was another load of fish prepared for her and already screwed into drums and half drums, and this time consigned to dif-ferent dealers. One in Maceio and the other in Bahia. 1975 BUTLER 69 The making of those casks and drums for packing fish was itself an industry. . . For the quin-tal and half quintal drums, the staves would be three eights of an inch thick sawn from birch and the bottom and heads one half an inch thick.

drum v
1 To pack dried and salted cod-fish into a cy-lindrical wooden container or DRUM n; SCREW v.
1942 *Grand Bank U C School* 37 [Fish] is drummed and boxed. 1977 BUTLER 78–80 'I want you to go to Spencer's Cove and bring up a load of drummed fish.'
2 To place empty oil-barrels under a house in order to float it across a stretch of water; cp LANCH v.
P 148–60 Before the house could be pulled to the sea shore where it was drummed before being put into the water. . . P 245–62 I drummed me house an' floated 'er across the bay.

drung n also **drang, drong** *EDD* drang sb 1 s w cties . . .'same word as OE [*thrang*], a throng, crowd.' A narrow lane or passage between hous-es, fenced gardens, etc.
[c1830] 1890 GOSSE 41 This 'drong,' or lane, was reputed to be haunted. 1858 [LOWELL] i, 176 The con-stable passed the drung that led up to his forge and dwelling, and keeping on. . .knocked at the door. 1895 *J A Folklore* viii, 28 ~ a narrow lane. [1929] 1949 ENGLISH 115 A rocky lane may still be called a 'drong' and a canyon is a 'drook.' 1937 DEVINE 19 Drang. A narrow path or lane. 1965 PARSONS 53 "The Rote": the meadow (where the land was dry) / 'Bout where they'd lodged the foremast that had sprung / Hardby 'poor Martin's,' off the Balsam drung. 1972 MURRAY 29 There are 'drungs' (lanes) and roads shooting off in all directions from the main artery.

dry a Cp *OED* ~ a 2 (esp Nfld 1677 quot 'dry fish'); *DAE* dry fish (1616–); *DC* ~ fish (Nfld: 1905).

Comb **dry bulk**: dried and salted cod-fish stacked in layers; BULK n.
1909 GRENFELL[2] (ed) 284 The fish can be preserved in wet bulk all winter by putting enough salt between adjacent layers to prevent them from touching one another. It may also be preserved as dry bulk in piles covered over and well pressed down.

dry-cure v: to preserve cod-fish by light appli-cations of salt and through exposure to sun and wind; the method of doing this; cp CURE, HARD-DRIED.
1977 BUTLER 20 At the time, merchants were paying the men washing and dry-curing fish on their premises the hourly pay of eight to ten cents per hour.

dry diet: habitual fare of ship biscuit, dried and salted fish and meat, etc (1925 *Dial Notes* v, 330); cp WINTER DIET.
1919 GRENFELL[1] 119 The poor fellow was a skeleton, with the characteristic sunken face and fallen skin with which we are familiar in those living on what we know as 'dry diet.'

dry fish: cod-fish preserved by exposure to sun and wind after application of salt; FISH, SALT FISH.
[1577–8] 1935 *Richard Hakluyt* [Parkhurst's letter:] 124 We might not only sell thynges better chepe, but mighte make grete store of dry fysshe. 1613 *Willoughby Papers* 16a, 25 [inventory] 6 hundred of dry fish. . .for there dyett. [1712] 1895 PROWSE 273 They load with dry fish bound to several ports as Spain and Portugal. [1766] 1971 BANKS 135 Their Dry Fish are only opend Down to the navel. [1786] 1792 CARTWRIGHT iii, 211 A good deal of dry-fish was spoiled on Durant's Island, where the Jersey fishery is carried on. 1866 WILSON 212 In the month of August, the merchant's large boat, or galloper, goes to the planter's fishing-room, to select the first 'dry fish.' 1936 SMITH 17 After the next time spread [the cured cod-fish] would be shipped on board the dry fish vessel and the supercargo would inspect it and pass his ver-dict. T 192/3–65 Two falls I went to St John's with our fish, our dry fish; carried it up to sell it there. 1975 BUTLER 63 My grandfather was in the dry fish business [and] had two schooners to freight dry fish, salmon, herring and mackerel to St John's and bring back sup-plies.

dry moss: beard moss (*Usnea barbata*); DEAD MOSS, DEER ~ (1971 NOSEWORTHY 195).

dry pile: split and salted cod-fish placed in a stack towards the end of the curing process; PILE n.
[1663] 1963 YONGE 58 After [the pressed pile process the fish is] dried one day on the ground and then put up in dry pile, as they call it, that is a pile big-ger than the prest pile by 3 times.

dry-salt v: to prepare split cod-fish, or seal pelts, for curing by placing them in layers with applications of salt.
1854 *Chambers's Journ* xxi, 76 As soon as the pelts reach St John's, they are unshipped, and immediately

begin to undergo a series of manipulations. The first operation after being landed, is that of separating the fat from the skin: a dexterous hand can manage 400 a day. The pelts are dry-salted for a month, and are then sufficiently cured for shipment. 1937 *Seafisheries of Nfld* 45 In the dry salting method, the fish, having been split, are placed with the flesh upwards side by side, usually head to tail alternately, until a space in the curing stage about three feet in width and varying from four to twelve feet in length is covered; dry salt is then spread over the surface of the fish; another layer of fish is placed upon the first, and so on, until the pile or bulk reaches the height that the curers deem advisable.

dry set: the placing of an animal trap on land rather than in the water; SET n.
P 9–73 Mink, otter, muskrat and beaver. . .could be caught in dry sets or on the land if the set was properly arranged in the right place.

semi-dry: a grade of cod-fish involving a quick drying operation.
1958 *Evening Telegram* 11 Feb, p. 19 I know large Madeira, small Madeira, West India, semi-dry, ordinary cure, Labrador cure, large and small merchantable, and cullage, and more recently the new cull known as thirds.

dry¹ v Cp *DAE* ~ v 1 'to cure (meat or fish) by expelling moisture' (1622–). To expose a split and gutted cod-fish to sun and wind as part of a curing process involving diminution of its natural moisture and corning by prior application of salt; cp MAKE, SAVE, SPREAD v.
[1583] 1940 *Gilbert's Voyages & Enterprises* ii, 403 [Hayes' narrative] The Generall granted. . .divers parcells of land lying by the water side, both in this harbor of S John, and elsewhere, which was to the owners a great commoditie, being thereby assured. . .of grounds convenient to dresse and to drie their fish. 1620 WHITBOURNE 24 In some of those necessary houses or roomes they may put their fish when it is dried, which fish now standeth after such time it is dried, untill it is shipped, which is commonly above two moneths. [1663] 1963 YONGE 58 When well dried, it's made up into prest pile, where it sweats; that is, the salt sweats out, and corning, makes the fish look white. [1766] 1971 BANKS 134–5 They are Carried to the Last operation of Drying them which the English Do upon Standing flakes. . .in some Places as high as twenty feet from the ground here they are Exposd with the open side to the sun & every night or when it is bad weather Piled up five or 6 on a heap. 1819 ANSPACH 435 The next day, or as soon as the weather permits, the fish is spread out on boughs in the open air to dry, head to tail, the open side being exposed to the sun. 1907 MILLAIS 158 After this they are spread out to dry in the sun on the fir-branched trestles or flakes. It takes about five fine days to dry a cod. 1937 *Seafisheries of Nfld* 49 The uncertainty as to the length of the voyage, and the time that the fish must remain under salt before it can be dried makes [it] almost essential [to heavily salt the Labrador catch]. [1952] 1965 PEACOCK (ed) i, 118 "Culling Fish": He stood to his post like a soldier on guard, / While Stewart kept saying its dried fine and hard, / 'Oh yes' he replied, pressing finger and thumb, /

'In Jim Rose's day this would pass "number one."'
1953 *Nfld Fish Develop Report* 59 In good drying weather, the fish may be dried with about eight days' exposure to wind and sun; in poor weather, a month or even two months may be required. Sometimes a quantity of fish has to be carried over the winter and finished the following spring. 1954 INNIS 486 [In the sixteenth century] in place of the Spanish, who made their fish 'all wet and do drie it when they come home,' the English and French dried it in the New World and carried it to Spain. . . The fishing industry in Newfoundland provided a new frontier; and in its development, with the increase in ships, seamen, and trade, it broke the rigid chains of centralized control.

dry² See DRAW v: DRAW (UP).

drying vbl n See DRY¹ v. *DC* ~ stage 1 Nfld (1907). The process of removing natural moisture from a split and salted cod-fish by exposure to sun and wind. Attrib in designations of structures where the process takes place: ~ **flake** [see FLAKE], ~ **stage** [see STAGE].
[1693] 1793 REEVES ii . . .and liberty to go on shore on any part of *Newfoundland*, or any of the said islands, for the curing, salting, drying, and husbanding of their fish, and for making of oil, and to cut down wood and trees there for building and making or repairing of stages. 1861 DE BOILIEU 31 The cod is now placed in what is called salt-bulk, where it may remain any period of time; for, so long as fish is being caught in the bay, so long will the 'drying' and 'washing'—which constitute the final process—be delayed. 1904 DUNCAN 17 . . .the little shop and storehouse and the broad drying-flakes and the wharf. 1907 MILLAIS 148 The women work on the drying stages as well as the men, laying out the fish whenever the sun shines, and piling into heaps under layers of bark whenever it threatened to rain. 1937 *Seafisheries of Nfld* 49 The extra quantity of salt used in curing drives out additional moisture and obviates the necessity of prolonged drying. 1953 *Nfld Fish Develop Report* 62 With 80 drying days and giving each lot of fish eight spreads, a total of 10 lots of fish can be dried. 1979 COOPER 20 "The Fish Wife": The women plant and cultivate their gardens, / And tend the fish upon the drying-flakes.

dryth See DRITE*.

dub n Cp *EDD* dab v¹ 4 'to dibble [holes in furrow].' A small plow pushed by hand (P 273–70).
P 191–73 ~ A small hand plough, used on freshly cleared ground.

duck¹ n *DAE* ~ gun (1834–); cp *O Sup²* ~ sb¹ 12 ~ dive 'a vertical dive' (1942–).
Comb **duckberry**: bog bilberry (*Vaccinium uliginosum*).
1916 HAWKES 35 The creeper and plant varieties are legion: Shrub blueberry (Duckberry).
duck's dive: boy's pastime of throwing a stone

into the water without making a splash;
DEAD-MAN'S DIVE (1971 NOSEWORTHY 196).

duck gull: a variety of gull (*Larus glaucoides;
Pagophila eburnea*); ICE-PARTRIDGE.

1959 MCATEE 37 ~ Ivory Gull (From robbing ducks
of their food. Labr.) 1976 *Avifaunal Survey* 131 The
name 'duck gull' seems to be reserved for [the Iceland
gull] by the fishermen, and it would seem that Iceland
Gulls often sit on the water with flocks of ducks.

duck gun: large-bore fowling-piece.

1842 BONNYCASTLE ii, 261 Mr Cormack told Mr
McGregor, in 1827, that if Cull could catch the author
of that book within reach of his long duck-gun, he
would be as dead as any of the Red Indians that Cull
had often shot. 1870 *Can Naturalist* v, 298 Such is not
generally the case among the settlers, who chiefly use
the old-fashioned long duck guns, single barrelled, of
ten or twelve bore.

duck snare: device to capture wild fowl.

[1785] 1792 CARTWRIGHT iii, 73 At noon I sent William to put out some duck-snares, by the pond under
Berry Hill.

duck² n   Cp *OED* ~ sb³ 1 'strong untwilled
linen. . .used for small sails and men's outer
clothing.' Ship's sail; canvas.

1977 *Nfld Qtly* Winter, p. 20 And there was the fore-
gaff up, and the foreboom all up. The duck was gone,
but that was still up, swinging back and forth.

duckedy-mud n   Cp *EDD* dunduckity [mud] N
I, dunduckytimur; *O Sup²* dunducketty
[mud-coloured] (1818–). Yellow; tan or brownish; an indeterminate shade; attrib.

1909 BROWNE 274 The Esquimaux dog is usually of a
mottled black and white colour; but sometimes of a
tawny yellowish hue (duckedy-mud colour, it is termed
by Newfoundland fishermen). C 71–107 ~ a dark
brown colour. P 108–76 Duckety-mud was a favourite
colour used by children when they played games such
as Colours, etc, and also used facetiously: 'What colour
is your new coat?' 'Oh, duckety-mud.'

duckies See DUCKISH n.

duckish n   also **duckies** pl. *EDD* duck sb⁴ ['a
form of dusk'] var duckest, duckish IW Do D;
ADD ~ n 2 Nfld. Dusk, twilight. Some uses may
be interpreted as adjectival.

1896 *J A Folklore* ix, 28 Twilight is expressed as 'between the *duckies*.' 1909 BROWNE xxii During the day
we kept the land aboard; and between 'dark and duckish' (the fishermen's term for twilight), another light
peered out of the gloom. 1919 GRENFELL¹ 85 The wind
veered as the sun sank, and 'headed' us continually.
The northern current was running strong, and it was
just 'duckish' when at last we entered the creek. 1924
ENGLAND 160 When it come duckish [dusk], de wind
chopped to de nar-narwest, wonnerful sharp. T 89–64
'Twas in fall o' the year, in duckish, th' evening. 1970
Evening Telegram 17 June, p. 2 Perchance I took
myself to the top of Signal Hill yesterday just at duckish. 1975 ibid 23 Aug, p. 14 Coming on duckish, I

looked up over the hill and swore I could see someone
rooting in the potato patch.

duckish a   *ADD* ~ a 1 (1895). Dark, gloomy,
esp at end of day.

1863 MORETON 34 ~ Dusky. 1895 *Dial Notes* i, 378
~ dark, gloomy. P 74–67 It's getting duckish. 1980
Evening Telegram 12 Jan, p. 11 I might rather have
seen you in the duckish light. At least your suit won't
look so shiny.

dudee See DUDEEN.

dudeen n   also **dudee** *EDD* ~ sb Ir; *OED*
(1841–); *DAE* (1850–); DINNEEN dúidin. Short-
stemmed tobacco pipe.

1836 [WIX]² 145 The girls among the rest, are also
smoking tobacco in short pipes, blackened with constant use, like what the Irish here call 'dudees,' all day
long. 1863 MORETON 95 The man then offered me the
little black dudeen which he was himself smoking. 1902
Christmas Bells 15 Feeling perfectly satisfied with my
catch, I filled my 'dudeen' and sat down on the bank to
enjoy a quiet smoke. 1931 BYRNES 89 He liked to relax
in a big rocking chair, contentedly puffing his 'dudh-
deen.' [1951] 1965 PEACOCK (ed) ii, 377 "My Old
Dudeen": He might have been a jinker it's plainly to
be seen, / And if it weren't for him I wouldn't be smoking my old dudeen. 1968 DILLON 137 A spell ago, a
pipe was a dudeen.

duff¹ n   *EDD* ~ sb¹ 1 esp Co quot; *DAE* 1
(1838–) for sense 1; for comb in sense 2: *Cent*
duff-day 'on board ship, Sunday.'

1 A pudding made of flour and water, sometimes with suet and raisins added, boiled in a
cloth bag; CLOTH PUDDING, FIGGY DUFF,
STOGGER.

[1856] 1975 WHITELEY 56 Today we have chowder
(cod) breakfast, duff (flour pudding) for dinner (with
W.I. Molasses). 1883 HATTON & HARVEY 305 On
three days of the week dinner consists of pork and
'duff,' the latter item consisting of flour and water with
a little fatty substance intermixed 'to lighten it.' When
boiled it is almost as hard as a cannon-ball. [1886]
LLOYD 36 The fare usually consists of salt pork, duff,
molasses, tea, and codfish; on which the changes are
rung from January to December in each year. 1924
ENGLAND 151 Then they got pork an' duff three times
a week, an' hard biscuit an' tea. [1926] 1946 PRATT 174
"The Cachalot": The weather fair, the weather
rough, / With watch and sleep, with tack and reef, /
With swab and holystone, salt beef / And its eternal
partner, duff. 1936 SMITH 52 Ready or raw give the
men their 'duffs' and let us get on the ice. [1960] 1965
PEACOCK (ed) i, 141 "On the Schooner *John Joe*": We
ate a bang-belly, we had sure enough, / We made a
good meal of the fat pork and duff. T 178/9–65 A duff
and a pudding is two different things. A pudding is
cooked into a pudding cloth and tied up; a duff is
[made in] a bag about so long, and you put your dough
in the bag, and he's small down under and big on top.
When you'd take un out of the pot, you would untie
him and take hold by the end and the duff would shoot

out in the pan. That was the rig of a duff! 1977 BURSEY 24 The duff was made of water and flour and a generous addition of raisins and all saturated with molassses. We called it a figged duff and it was indeed a luxury.

2 Comb **duff bag**: cloth bag in which pudding is boiled (1924 ENGLAND 315).

duff day: day of the week when a boiled pudding is customarily served at the main meal.

C 70–15 Dinner was at 1 p.m. and again there was a heavy meal designed for a particular day; Tuesday and Thursday were 'duff' days when the meal was vegetables of different kinds, salt beef or salt pork, and pease pudding. M 71–103 Sundays, Tuesdays and Thursdays were 'duff days.' 1977 BURSEY 24 Tuesday was 'duff day' and we must buy the necessaries.

duff² n *EDD* ~ sb⁴. A blow, esp a kick in the backside.

[1968] 1976 *Culture & Tradition* 37 [He] comes up and gives him a good swift duff in the hole. P 148–79 He's so stubborn that I want to give him a duff.

duffy a *EDD* duffie 'round-headed' Ork. Of a cod-fish, with a rounded, blunt head or snout; SNUB¹, SNUBBY.

1891 PACKARD 179 . . .variety of cod, called 'duffy' which may be the same as Professor Wyman's 'bull-dog cod.' Its head is blunter, the under-jaw is shorter, while the fish is darker than ordinary cod; the fishermen pronounce them 'no good'; it is possible that such as are taken are simply deformed individuals of the common species.

dullifare* n also **dulliver*** ['dʌlɪfɛəɹ]. Cp *DAE* thorough-fare 'a strait or. . .passage' (1699–). Channel; TICKLE n (Q 67–2).

P 126–67 Some sea in the dullifare today!

dumb a *EDD* ~ 1 (2) ~ cake.

Comb **dumb arrow**: arrow pointed at the tip but without a barbed head.

1915 HOWLEY 270 [The Beothuks] sometimes used 'dumb arrows,' all of wood, without any iron point, which by reason of their lightness fell short when fired off, thus leading the fishermen to believe they could approach nearer without running any risk, but when they did so they were met with a shower of well pointed and heavier arrows.

dumb cake: cake mixed, baked and eaten in silence by young unmarried women wishing for a vision of future husbands.

P 127–75 As a form of community entertainment unmarried females, young or old, would gather at an individual's home to assist in baking a cake. During the making of the cake and until it was completely consumed (this could be a matter of hours or days) the participants could not speak—hence a dumb cake.

dumb line: one of the ropes used to raise the cod-trap 'door' before the trap is hauled to the surface.

T 194/5–65 The boys put the dumb lines to the capstans and hove 'em out.

dum(b) See DUN a: DUN FISH.

dumbledore n also **dumbledor** *EDD* ~ sb 1 s w cties for sense 1.

1 Bumble-bee.

P 51–67 Dumbledores make honey. 1970 *Evening Telegram* 21 May, p. 3 Now and then a dumbledore or 'busy bee' as they are called by some, propelled itself across our path, they being extremely large and heavy this year. 1975 GUY 168 About the best time to visit the Awlin is in June when the dumbledores is buzzin' around the pissabeds, or as they would say upalong where the language has been watered down to a shocking extent, 'when the bees are buzzing around the dandelions.'

2 Common dandelion (*Taraxacum officinale*); PISS-A-BED (1898 *J A Folklore* xi, 230).

1975 SCOTT 39 The Dandelion has a number of common names in Newfoundland. These include Dumbledor, Faceclock, and Piss-a-beds.

dun a also **dum(b)**. Cp *OED* ~ a 1 'of a dull or dingy colour' for sense 1; for comb in sense 2: cp *DC* dun n Nfld (1819); *DAE* dumbfish (1746–), dunfish (1818–) [an excellent type of cure].

1 Of dried cod-fish, brown, discoloured through faulty drying and curing. Merges in some contexts with sense 2.

[1806] 1951 DELDERFIELD 82 Most interesting is an account of the sale of 1,147 Portuguese quintals of Newfoundland fish in 1806. It was listed:– '661 Qtls large, 208 Qtls small, 278 Qtls dumb, wet and broken.' 1819 ANSPACH 440 To mention one defect more, [cod] may become *dun*, if left too long in the pile. . .the weather beating into those piles softens the fish and gives it a black, snuffy, or dun colour. 1895 GRENFELL 60 If the fish has lain too long, it will be sodden, and go grey or dun. 1937 DEVINE 19 ~ Applied to a certain (bad) quality of dried codfish which has turned reddish in colour, due to insufficient salt, or on account of having been kept too long in a store away from the open air. M 71–103 Four or five good drying days of sun and wind would be sufficient to make (dry or cure) the fish. If as was often the case, the weather turned wet, and the partly dried fish had to remain in bulk too long, it would become dun, brown spots would appear on it. The fish would then have to be washed and scrubbed again to get rid of the brown spots.

2 Comb **dun fish, dum(b) fish**: a grade or 'cull' of cod-fish exhibiting discoloration as a result of faulty drying and curing and hence unsuitable for the export market; cp CULLAGE, MUD FISH, SCRUFF.

[1799] 1954 INNIS 300–1 'Dumb fish' or fish which had been kept too long on the flakes were seldom sent to market, being preferred by the Newfoundland people, and 'in most use at the first tables.' 1840 MURRAY ii, 127 There remain the dunfish and others discoloured, broken, and otherwise damaged, which nevertheless may be as fit as others for immediate consumption, to which they are therefore applied. [1895] 1897 *Nfld Law Reports* 835 The plaintiffs should have the privilege of rejecting the 'dunn' fish. 1939 EWBANK 61

It has been proved that stores where pink or dun fish has been kept become infected and unless treated will carry forward the germ to the following year. 1951 *Nfld & Lab Pilot* i, 207 Dun Fish shoal, with a depth of 9 fathoms over it. C 66–13 That's the third piece of dun fish I been culled in five minutes.

dun n Cp DUN a. The mould or fungus which develops on imperfectly cured cod-fish.

1937 *Seafisheries of Nfld* 113 The attention of the Fisheries Research Division [should be] directed to the study of the causes of deterioration of Salt Codfish whilst in store awaiting shipment, particularly as to the growth of what is locally described as 'Dun.' P 113–64 'Go dun' means not merely 'spoiled' but spoiled by a particular fungus known as dun. P 127–73 ~ A dusty yellowish mould which grows on damp fish.

dunch¹ a *EDD* ~ a 2 'dull, heavy,' hence (1) dunch v 'to get stiff with long waiting' K for sense 1, 4 'heavy. . .doughy' W for sense 2.

1 Stiff; cramped or numbed from sitting in one position.

P 10–57 Dunch. To be cramped in the legs, arms, etc. T 222–66 You wouldn't be able to stay keeled out on the settle very long because it would be quite hard an' you would get dunch, I'm sure. P 192–67 Dunch is also used to explain that your foot has gone to sleep. C 71–97 My leg is dunch from sitting on it.

2 Doughy, heavy, soggy; cp CLOSE. Also a noun.

1896 *Dial Notes* i, 378 ~ : bread not properly baked. 1896 *J A Folklore* ix, 21 Dunch cake or bread, unleavened bread, composed of flour mixed with water and baked at once. 1925 ENGLAND v, 330 ~ Heavy; soggy;—of bread, etc. 1941 *Beaver* 37 ~ Said of bread when it fails to rise and is heavy. P 60–64 I make good bread, though these [loaves] are dunch. C 71–113 Dunch bread is bread that doesn't rise as bread with leaven normally does.

dunch² a also **dunce**. Cp *EDD* ~ a 2 (4) ~ nettle. Comb **dunch-nettle**: swamp thistle (*Cirsium muticum*) (1956 ROULEAU 29).

Q 72–1 Dunch nettles [are] an edible kind of wild nettle.

duncher n Cp DUNCH¹. Small cake sweetened with molasses and containing cubes of fat-back pork; MOLASSES/LASSY BUN.

C 71–120 A duncher is a soggy cake. M 71–60 For a mug up, beside the usual cup of tea, you would have a lassy duncher, which was really a molasses bun with fat pork and raisins in it.

dung n Cp *EDD* ~ sb¹ 1 (21) ~ pot (a), (b) IW So D Co for comb in sense 1; for combs. in sense 2: *EDD* ~ sb¹ (18) ~ mixen 'dung-hill' IW So; cp *OED* sink sb¹ 1 a now rare.

1 In designations of various containers, carts, etc, for moving fertilizers to planted 'grounds': ~ **bar(row)** [see BARROW¹], ~ **box**, ~ **pot**.

P 9–73 We had a flour barrel sawed off in the middle

and a framework with handles built around it. It was called the dung tub or dung barrow. When filled to the top [with manure] it was a carrying load for two men. P 40–78 The dung-bar was a round or square container with two long poles attached half way up the sides, one on each side so that it can be carried by two men; used for transporting manure, caplin and so on. T 187–65 I bid up then, had my dinner 'long with grandfather for the sake o' gettin' into a old dumb [i.e. dung] box [or cart]. P 126–67 Dung pot: sleigh used with horse to haul caplin, manure, etc. 1979 TIZZARD 192 With this dung barrow we carried loads of stable manure up on the hill, boatloads of caplin and rockweed to the potato ground in bottom and on Big Island. . .

2 Comb **dung bird**: parasitic jaeger (*Stercorarius parasiticus*).

1870 *Can Naturalist* v, 407 . . .called 'dung birds' by the settlers, evidently from the manner in which they persecute the smaller species of *Laridae*, and devour. . .their feces.

dung mixen: snow.

P 151–68 The old people have nicknames put on almost everything, and snow is no exception. I have heard [it called] 'dung-mixen,' 'the devil's blanket,' 'devil's feathers,' etc.

dung sink: drain or pit where garbage, waste, etc, are deposited.

C 69–2 Dumsink refers particularly to a hole dug in the ground near the house. Into this hole is thrown all the garbage such as potato scraps, left-over food, etc. The water from the kitchen sink also flows into this hole. Every now and again mud was thrown into the hole because this keeps it from smelling too much. In the spring the dumsink was dug out and all the garbage put on the gardens for manure. C 71–37 Dunksink [i.e. dung sink], a drain usually just outside the back door where slop water is thrown, (also things like tea leaves, pot liquor, etc).

dungeon n On a sealing vessel, the often makeshift quarters below decks for the accommodation of the seal-hunters.

1924 ENGLAND 59 Shouts, raw laughter echo; and laughter too from the 'tweendecks, even from the 'dungeon,' or under-fo'c's'le, vastly filthier than the 'tweendecks. How can men laugh in such places? 1933 GREENE 40 The 'Dungeon' on board of an old-time Sealer was the name often given to a space bulkheaded off under the main deck where the cooks and servers slept. The bulk of the crew were provided with double berths rigged-up in the Tween-decks over the ballast tanks of the Main Hold. T 181–65 But we was down into a place called the dungeon—all dark. We had our candles—that's all our light; and your rope to haul on. Four of us in one berth.

dwall n also **drool**, **dwoll** *MED* dwāle n 'dazed or unconscious condition' (c1400–1450); *EDD* dwal(l) sb 1 'light slumber' Sh I Nfld. The state of being half-asleep; a slumber.

1858 [LOWELL] i, 84 Once or twice I falled into a kind of dwall [i.e. doze]. 1895 *J A Folklore* viii, 28 Dwoll: a state between sleeping and walking, a dozing. A man will say, 'I got no sleep last night, I had only a dwoll.' 1937 DEVINE 19 Drool. A state between sleeping and waking. 'I was asleep, surely, but I 'urd what was goin' on: I was only in a drool.'

dwall v   also **dawl, drole** [dwɒl] *EDD* dwal(l) v 2 'to slumber' Sh I Ork. To fall asleep; to doze; to become unconscious; esp in phr *dwall off* (P 113–73).

[c1894] PANL P4/14, p. 199 What are the precise meaning and application of to *dwall*, to *glutch*, to *hackle*. . .? 1909 GRENFELL¹ 67 'E said 'e droled off once or twice, but th' night seemed wonderfu' long. 1920 GRENFELL & SPALDING 193 'Oh! I does [give the baby the bottle] ma'm,' Mira replied. 'If he dwalls off, I gives him a scattered jolt.' 1941 WITHINGTON 157 Dr Grenfell had warned me to have him lie down for even the slightest surgical incision, because they fainted easily. So I discovered one day when I forgot this injunction and my patient 'dawled' over. P 14–72 The old man dwalled off.

dwigh See DWY.

dwoll See DWALL n.

dwoy See DWY.

dwy n   also **dwey, dwigh, dwoi, dwoy, dwye**, etc [dwai, dwɑɪ, dwɒi, dwɔi, dwʌi] *EDD* dwyes sb pl 'eddies' IW (1863–); cp SMYTH 704 twy 'meteor squall on the coasts' W Ha. Eddy, gust, flurry; squall; brief shower or storm. Freq in phr *dwy of rain*, ~ *of snow*, and comb **snow** ~ .

1863 MORETON 30 Dwigh. A short shower or storm, whether of rain, hail or snow. 1866 WILSON 344 When they reached the barrens, it became foggy; then a '*snow-dwie*,' that is, a slight snow-shower, came on; another 'dwie' followed, until it became a heavy snowstorm. 1895 *J A Folklore* viii, 39 ~ A mist or slight shower. 'Is it going to rain to-day?' 'No, it is only a dwy,' a Newfoundlander may reply. [c1900] 1978 *RLS* 8, p. 26 Dwye. A squall of wind accompanied by rain, hail or snow. 1919 GRENFELL¹ 61 They supposed that surely between the worst snow 'dweys' they would catch sight of some familiar leading mark. 1927 *Christmas Messenger* 47 Dwye, or dwigh. A sudden shower of rain or snow. . . This word. . .is not known or used on the coastline south of St John's. . . I have heard Placentia Bay men using the word as a joke on northern men. 1932 BARBOUR 3 What was in the store was safe from 'dwighs' (sudden short local showers of rain or snow) which might come up. P 19–55 A snow dwigh usually stops as quick as it comes. P 148–63 The snow comes in dwies. T 70/1–64 Used to be dwies o' snow, late November, last a couple of hours, an' frosty, an' then the blue sky'd shine out again, clear again for a spell, an' then dwies again—wind northern, see. T 75/8–64 But we started to haul in; little dwy of snow come, an' fog. 1979 *Evening Telegram* 9 June, p. 17 He knows he'll be lucky to last until the first dwigh of the winter.

dynnage See DINNAGE.

E

eagle n   Cp *Cent* ~ n 2. American osprey or fish-hawk (*Pandion haliaetus carolinensis*) (1959 MCATEE 22).

1908 HUBBARD 87 Some fish eagles, circling high above us, screamed their disapproval of our presence there. [1932] 1971 LYSAGHT 172 To add to the confusion the Osprey *Pandion haliaetus* (L.) also occurs in Labrador and O L Austin, writing in 1932, stated that the natives of Sandwich Bay called it eagle then.

ear n   Cp *OED* ~ sb¹ 9 'projection on a tool' for sense 1; the comb in sense 2 is from *OED* winker 3 'blinker.'
   1 The forked part of a claw-hammer.
   T 172/4–65 He's a ordinary hammer, you know, made with the car for pulling nails.
   2 Comb **ear winker**: type of ear-muff.
   1896 *J A Folklore* ix, 35 ~s. Flannel coverings for the cars in winter.

earache* See EARWIG.

earwig n   also **earache*** *Cent* ~ 2. A variety of centipede (*Lithicolus centipede*) (P 1–69).
   P 148–67 ~ , earache, an insect like a centipede. 1972 MURRAY 114 15 The beneficial reddish centipede was feared also [by children]. It was called an 'earwig' or 'yurwig' and no child liked to lie down for a nap outdoors in case one of these crawled in his ear. 1975 HOLMES 15 In Newfoundland centipedes are often called 'earwigs.'

easter a   *OED* ~ a obs (1387–1816); *EDD* 1 D. (a) Eastern; freq in place-names; (b) from the east (1977 quot).
   [1900] OLIVER & BURKE] 76 "Old Salvage": No other mark can equal it; / Long Harry and Easter Rock. T 58/62–64 Th' easter side an' the wester side was blocked off by a cliff. T 74–64 They used to go out on the easter grounds in the fall of the year. T 175/6–65 People living down on the easter part o' the island. 1977 *Nfld Qtly* Winter, p. 18 We was in pretty close to land. I was hugging the shoreline because the wind was blowing off the land—easter, and the sea was smooth.

easy a   Phr *not easy*: alert, competent, successful.
   T 12–64 When we succeed in some small feat we say, 'I'm not too easy, am I?' M 71–104 'You're not too easy'—said to a person who is on the ball.

eat v   Cp *DAE* ~ v 1 'to provide (a person) with food' (1837–); R M NANCE *Glossary of Cornish Sea-words* (1963), p. 77 'When the corn is in the shock, / Then the fish is to the rock' Co.
   Phr *eat oneself*: to provide oneself with food.
   1888 M F HOWLEY 208 In the winter men lived in 'cook-rooms' attached to the stages, and boarded themselves or 'ate themselves,' as they said.
   eat one's path: to eat while walking along a trail or road (M 68–3).

eat the rocks: of cod-fish, to school in large numbers close to shore, esp in pursuit of caplin.

[(1786) 1792 CARTWRIGHT iii "Labrador: A Poetical Epistle" [4] The Codfish now in shoals come on the coast, / (A Fish'ry this, our Nation's chiefest boast) / Now numerous Caplin croud along the shore; / Tho' great their numbers, yet their Foes seem more; / Whilst Birds of rapine, hover o'er their Heads, / Voracious Fish in myriads throng their Beds. / With these our Hooks we artfully disguise, / And soon the glutton Cod becomes our Prise.] 1909 BROWNE 281 At the time of our visit 'the fish was eating the rocks' (this is a fisherman's term for plentifulness). 1966 HORWOOD 17 The codfish crowd towards shore behind [the caplin] until they are 'eating the rocks.'

eating vbl n Comb **eating fish**: salted cod kept for home consumption (P 148–78).

1966 HORWOOD 101 The fish they caught that fall were the biggest. . .that they had ever seen. Split and cleaned and put into salt bulk, they ran to fifteen or twenty pounds each. . . They were the best 'eating fish' that had ever been landed in the Bight—an eating fish being one that you saved for your own table.

eddy n Cp *OED* ~ sb 2, flaw sb² 1. Comb **eddy flaw**: a deflection of the movement of the wind.

[1771] 1792 CARTWRIGHT i, 147 Before I got within shot, an eddy flaw gave [the deer] the wind of me, and he went off. 1792 ibid *Gloss* i, x Where the current of wind is interrupted by a hill or any other body, short puffs will often strike in a contrary direction; those are called Eddy Flaws.

e'er det also **ar, arra, e'er a, e'ra**, etc ['eɹ ə, ɛɹ, æːɹ, 'æːɹ ə, aəɹ] *OED* ever adv 8 a (1597–); *EDD* ever a esp s cties; *ADD* ary; *SED* section VII.2.13; for sense 2 *OED* ever 8 a (1598–), *EDD* ever a one w and s cties, *ADD* ary one. See NE'ER.

1 A; a single; any; EITHER.

1858 [LOWELL] i, 139 I'm sarten sure my Lucy would never have agrowed to e'er a body, knowunly, about my knowun it, as well. 1907 DUNCAN 24 'They isn't ar another man in Newf'un'land would take that basket t' sea!' 1916 GRENFELL 168 There was nothin' but the open water left—not a whelpin'-pan to hold e'er an old harp to have her young on. 1937 DEVINE 7 Arra—either [i.e. 'any']. T 36–64 Then with the weight of so much fish on, if there's a'r drop o' pickle in it, ['t]would press out. T 50–64 He said he could pass as much seals as e'er three men was there! T 82/3–64 I don't suppose there's ar a man on Change Islands got a fish-glass. T 398–67 I wouldn't say there's ar trap here got over fifty quintals. 1977 QUILLIAM 4 'Then how come. . .we never gets arr Christmas card from 'em?'

2 Phr *e'er (a) bit*: a little bit; somewhat.

T 34–64 Blubber soap. I made some fat soap, old-fashioned. Get ar a bit of fat, if we had sheep to kill and the fat of the sheep, we'd put that on and fry it out and put the fat for soap. T 55/6–64 Pick a load of soft fir boughs, and then it is up to yourself if you want to keep it e'er a bit soft, and all right to sleep on. P 47–66 If 'tis e'er bit good atall, 'tis good enough for that.

e'er (a) one: a single one; any one; ARN.

1858 [LOWELL] ii, 141 We don't want to mistrust e'er a one; we wants only just to know ef Lucy's there, that's all. 1863 MORETON 95 'Boys, have yez a pipe?'. . .'Uncle Billy, have ye e'er a one?' P 148–64 [He couldn't pass] without e'ra one of those seein' him. C 71–109 I not gonna give you ar one, 'cause I won't have nar one left for meself.

egg v *OED* ~ v² c (1887). To collect eggs from the nests of sea-birds.

[1775] 1792 CARTWRIGHT ii, 91 I sent the Indians out a shooting and egging.

eggdown See HAGDOWN.

egger n *O Sup²* ~ sb² (1834–); *NID* n². Person who plunders the nests of sea-birds for the eggs.

[1822] 1928 CORMACK 8 Baccalieu Island. . .is visited by men in boats and small schooners called Eggers, who carry off cargoes of new-laid eggs. [1833] 1848 *Nautical Magazine* 667 These men, the eggers, combine together and form a strong company. They suffer no one to interfere with their business, driving away the fishermen, or any one else that attempts to collect eggs near where they happen to be. [1834] 1926 AUDUBON 253 "The Eggers of Labrador." 1863 HIND [ii], 190 It was formerly the custom for Americans called 'eggers' to take possession of the islands on which innumerable sea-birds laid their eggs, and drive the inhabitants of the coast away when they ventured to take any. 1902 DELABARRE 202 Murre. Common, but much less so than formerly, owing to eggers.

either det, subs also **either a** ['iːðəɹ, 'iːðə, 'aiðəɹ, 'aiðə, 'aidəɹ, 'aidə]. Cp *EDD* other adj¹ 2, 3, So D for parallel usage; RLS 1 (1968), 8–10. See also NEITHER.

1 Determiner: a; any; a single; a formal variant of E'ER. No quotations imply 'one out of two.'

P 148–60 Either a game tonight? T 43/7–64 An' if you weredn't up to the standard, if you couldn't do either job reasonably, they'd send you down. P 148–65 Either dry cloth around. P 148–65 I don't have either class this year that I don't like. T 172/5–65 And they didn't have either cook. P 148–68 He could not go home because he never had either home to go to. P 245–75 This year there was a man there by himself and he didn't have either radio. 1977 RUSSELL 120 [He] couldn't find either comic book scuffled around on the kitchen floor.

2 Substitute: any; a single one.

P 148–60 Either of the forms have their own formation and all are interesting to read. P 148–65 'Why don't you speak to Dr Smith?' 'I didn't do either [any course] with him.'

3 Phr *either bit*, ~ *one*; cp E'ER (A) ONE.

P 148–61 There isn't either one out near university. P 148–63 If he had been either bit smart at all [that wouldn't have happened]. P 148–66 If the waves were either bit high. . . T 394/403–67 You didn't see 'em either, 'cause you didn't kill either one.

elder-blossom n also **elder-bloom**. Cow-parsnip

(*Heracleum maximum*) (1956 ROULEAU 29);
ELTROT (of which this *elder* may be a re-interpretation or corruption).
　　c 63–1 Elderblossom is supposed to cure sores.
M 70–24 Elderbloom or elderblossom. . .had to be
boiled and steeped on the stove. It was very bitter to
take.

elevener n　also **eleven, levener** *EDD* ~ D Co:
levener. A drink of liquor, or a light snack, taken
at 11 a.m.; LUNCH, MUG UP.
　　1866 WILSON 348 If a tradesman were employed, he
must have *three drinks* a day; or what he called his
morning, his *eleven*, and his *evening*. [c1894] PANL
P4/14, p. 194 I know of what [callibogus] is compounded, and that *rum* and *spruce beer* is becoming a far less
common 'elevener' than it used to be. 1896 *J A
Folklore* ix, 35 ~ a glass of grog taken at eleven
o'clock, when the sun is over the fore yard. 1914 *Cadet*
Apr, p. 7 The skipper is ['crooked'] this mornin' and
will be till he gets his 'levener' (glass of rum) at 11
o'clock. 1937 DEVINE 31 Levener. A drink of rum or
other spirits taken around eleven a.m. Also a lunch at
that time. C 70–15 Besides the three basic meals, there
was a lunch at 11 a.m. called the levener, usually a cup
of tea and a biscuit or bun. C 71–111 'Come in now and
we'll have our elevener.' Then all the girls would go in
for a snack.

elevenses n pl Neck muscles; splenius.
　　P 108–70 'Oh, poor man, his elevenses are up.' This
means a person is fading, not long for this world,
because the two muscles in the back of the neck stick
out like two bones [resembling *11*].

ellan n　*OED* ~ Nova Francia (1613–); HARRAP
élan 'Euroasiatic moose.' A deer erroneously
interpreted to be hunted in Newfoundland.
　　1613 PURCHAS i, viii, iv, p. 630 [Champlain, writing
of North American Indians:] The Ellan, Deare, Stag-
ge, and Beare, are their game.[*OED*] [1620] 1887
MASON 150 The Beasts are Ellans, Follow-deare,
Hares, Beares harmeles, Wolues, Foxes. 1626
[VAUGHAN] *The Golden Fleece* 23 It abounds with
Deere, as well fallow Deere, as Ellans, which are as
bigge as our Oxen. 1682 COLLINS 99 Deer called Ellans
as big as Oxen.

ellis water* See ALIX.

elsinore n　also **elsanor, elsinor, elson**. A cap,
often made of leather, with ear flaps; also attrib.
　　1904 MURPHY (ed) 52 "The Low-backed Car": My
cap was the Elson—my coat plainly made. 1913
Christmas Post 12 The fisherman wanted a macintosh
instead of his old oil skins, and a cloth cap instead of
the old elsinore. 1929 BURKE [17] "Vote for Bride
McGinnis": But in the fall and winter / She must wear
an Elsanor. 1933 GREENLEAF 238 The elsinor cap was
the common headgear of the Newfoundland boy. It is
shaped like a teamster's cap, with a string around the
bottom to protect the neck and ears. T 58/64–64 I had a
skin cap, what they call an elsinore. They were leather

and there was flaps come down and a string come
down, tied under your chin.

elson See ELSINORE.

elt n　Cp *EDD* ~ sb[1] 'young pig' So Do D.
Scoundrel; wag.
　　P 108–70 An elt is a real nothing. 'There's another elt
in the harbour / John Mitchell is his name / And when
the wind is at its height / He'll say it's getting calm.'

eltrot n　also **health root, hell-trot, heltrope**, etc.
OED ~ (1878–); *EDD* 1 Ha W Do So; *Gray's
Botany* 1104. Cow-parsnip (*Heracleum maximum; H. Sphondylium*); ELDER-BLOSSOM.
　　1894 *N S Inst Sci* ix, 99 Health root or Hell trot. 1956
ROULEAU 31 Hell-trot. . .Heltrope. M 69–5 A common
cure for headache was a poultice made from the roots
of an illtrot plant. An illtrot plant is a wild plant with
broad green leaves similar to rhubarb leaves.

embloch See HEMLOCK.

emper* See EMPTER.

empt v　[ɛmpt, ɛmp, hɛmp] *OED* ~ v obs exc
dial; *EDD* s w cties. See *Som & Dor N & Q* vi
(1899), 105 for Dorset infinitives with and without -*y*. *Empt* has generalized the alternate without -*y*. Cp LIVYER. To empty or pour out (1925
Dial Notes v, 330).
　　T 33–64[1] When the Eskimau come to sell his furs
[they] emp their bags—all the fur out the one time.
T 80–64 And it gets too tough, he's goin' a hemp she
out! [empty charge in gun by firing it]. T 141/68–65[2]
You enjoy a chew moreso than you would smoke; your
pipe'd emp out anyhow.

empter* n　also **emper***. See EMPT. A container
used during berry-picking, emptied frequently
into a larger container near the pickers.
　　P 128–56 Have you got your empter full yet?
P 140–70 Emper. Small tin or dipper used to fill a larger
one. M 70–21 Each berry picker also had a smaller container, a quart can, saucepan, perhaps even a gallon
can. As this 'emptier' or 'emper' as we called it was
filled, its contents were transferred to the buckets till
these were filled to the brim.

en [= him] See UN.

english a　*DC* ~ 3 rare (1898–) for sense 1.
　　1 Related to the Church of England.
　　1887 HOWLEY *MS Reminiscences* 1 There is to be a
grand Jubilee Service at the English Cathedral.
P 148–64 English Board: the Church of England
[School] Board. T 43/4–64 It's an English mission at
Hopedale, a mission from the Church of England. 1966
PADDOCK 121 English Church: The Anglican Church.
　　2 In designations of birds and plants identified
with England, esp in contrast with other indigenous varieties: **english blackberry, ~ blackbird,
~ blueberry, ~ fern, ~ gull, ~ woodpecker**.

1895 *N S Inst of Sci* ix, 92 English blackberry—local term for Thimbleberry or Bramble. 1964 *Evening Telegram* 28 Oct, p. 5 Thus, in my part of the country starlings are universally described as 'English blackbirds.' And that is exactly what they are—blackbirds which immigrated from England—though how the people who gave them their local name knew this escapes me. 1956 ROULEAU 29 English Blueberry [dwarf bilberry]: *Vaccinium cespitosum.* Ibid 29 English Fern: *Tanacetum vulgare.* 1959 MCATEE 36 English gull. Great Black-backed Gull (*Larus marinus*). As a distinctive kind; it does, however, occur in England. 'Labr.') 1870 *Can Naturalist* v, 152 [The flicker] is called the 'English Woodpecker,' and is fairly common. It has a peculiar note, which bears a fancied resemblance to that of the green Woodpecker.

enter v Comb **enter net**: movable net forming the entrance or 'door' of a seal-net.
1967 FIRESTONE 103 One of the side nets is so arranged that it can be lowered to the bottom to be raised when a seal swims over it to enter the enclosure. The latter, the *enter net*, is operated by means of a capstan on shore.

equal a *OED* ~ 4 c obs; JOYCE 43. Immaterial, indifferent.
P 192–66 If someone says to you, 'Would you like tea or coffee?' and you liked them both, you would say, 'it's all equal to me.'

escopic See NASKAPI.

eskimo n also **esquimau**, etc. *DC* ~ boot (1768–); *O Sup*[2] ~ curlew (1813–); *DC* ~ dog (Nfld: 1774–); ~ indian (1742–); ~ sled (Nfld: 1770–). See also HUSKIMAW, INDIAN.
Attrib **eskimo boot**: sealskin boot reaching to the knee; SKINNY-WOPPER.
1861 DE BOILIEU 104 The Esquimaux boots are very differently made from [mocassins] and shield the leg right over the knee; and are generally so large as to admit of the wearer having on three thick flannel socks and a good large 'boot-stocking' over these. 1877 SEARS 25 What was still worse the Esquimaux boots worn to suit the snow-shoe were as slippery as the ice itself.
eskimo cold: influenza.
1942 ELTON 306 Old mission diaries speak of deaths from the prevalent 'Eskimo cold,' and this is the disease which we know as Influenza. . . The pandemics arise annually in February and August.
eskimo curlew: a shore-bird (*Numenius borealis*); CURLEW; MOUNTAIN CURLEW.
1774 PENNANT 461 Esquimaux curlew. 1902 DELABARRE 204 ~ Barely a remnant of their former numbers. Nearly exterminated. 1951 PETERS & BURLEIGH 184 The Eskimo Curlew was formerly one of the most abundant birds in North America. . . Now it is extinct, or very nearly so.
eskimo dog: strongly-built dog, native to Greenland and Labrador, used to haul sleds or 'komatiks' (*Canis familiaris borealis*); husky; LABRADOR DOG 2.
[1772] 1792 CARTWRIGHT i, 267 [The London people were] attracted not only by the uncommon appearance of the Indians who were in their seal-skin dresses, but also by a beautiful eagle, and an Esquimau dog; which had much the resemblance of a wolf, and a remarkable wildness of look. 1774 [LA TROBE] 29 The great number of Esquimaux dogs, that must seek their own maintenance, prevent the success they might have in catching fish, as these half-starved dogs, at low water, run into the nets, tear out and devour the fish, and moreover tear the nets to pieces. 1839 TUCKER 121 The Esquimaux dog does not bark. His ears are short and erect, and his bushy tail curves over his back. His average stature is one foot ten inches, and the length of his body, from the back of the head to the commencement of the tail, is two feet three inches. His coat is long and furry, and is sometimes brindled, sometimes of a dingy red, black and white, or wholly black. Some naturalists consider this race of dogs as descended from the wolf and fox. 1863 HIND [ii], 158 The Esquimaux dog of pure breed, with his strong-built frame, long white fur, pointed ears, and bushy tail, is capable of enduring hunger to a far greater extent than the mixed breed.
eskimo duck: American common eider (*Somateria mollissima dresseri*).
1918 TOWNSEND 301 [The eider] which is locally known as. . .Eskimo duck. . .is everywhere diminishing in numbers.
eskimo fiddle: stringed instrument made by Inuit.
1916 HAWKES 122 A characteristic specimen of an Eskimo 'fiddle' was obtained on this trip. It consists of a rude box, with a square hole in the top, three sinew strings with bridge and tail-piece, and a short bow with a whalebone strip for hair. It must be a rude imitation of 'fiddles' seen on whaling ships, as the drum is the only indigenous musical instrument of the Eskimo. Most Eskimo fiddles have only one string. When I asked an Eskimo musician once about this he said, 'One string is plenty for an Eskimo song.'
eskimo indian: Inuit.
1765 COLE 28 The *French*. . .carry on a great Trade with the *Esquameau Indians* that inhabit the vast Coast of *Labradore*. [1766] 1971 BANKS 128 We had intelligence during this Voyage that the French Carreid on an illicit trade with the Esquimaux indians tho Probably not Countenancd by Government. 1839 TUCKER 120 One mode of travelling during winter prevails throughout the country, both amongst the white population and the Esquimaux Indians.
eskimo sled: long wooden sledge used by Inuit for transporting people and goods in winter; KOMATIK.
[1770] 1792 CARTWRIGHT i, 71 As the construction of an Esquimau sled differs so widely, and is, I think, so much superior to all others which have yet come to my knowledge; a particular description may not be unworthy of notice. [(1786) ibid iii, 235 The Esquimaux make use of a long sled, about twenty-one feet by fourteen inches, the sides of which are made of two-inch plank, about a foot broad; the under edges are

shod with the jaw-bone of a whale, a quarter of an inch thick, fastened on with pegs made out of the teeth of the sea-cow; across the upper edges, are placed broad, thin battens to sit and stow their baggage upon. They yoke a number of stout dogs to this sled, and travel at the rate of six or seven miles an hour upon ice, or barren hills: but they cannot go into the woods, for the dogs would not only bog in the snow there, but the sled would sink too deep, and be always getting foul of the young trees.]

establishment n   Cp *DAE* ~ 2 'place of business' (1805–). The business of a fish merchant, usu the branch of a firm with headquarters in St John's or Britain, comprising the 'premises,' employees and the operations of taking and shipping the catch; cp ROOM.

[1822] 1928 CORMACK 112 . . .in sight of the whaling and cod-fishery establishment of Messrs Newman, Hunt & Company of London. 1837 BLUNT 23 Keels. This is another establishment for the fisheries. 1857 MOUNTAIN 11 A merchant's establishment [Gaultois and Hr Breton], each consisting of an agent and family, storekeepers, and other officers, and about 200 men. 1861 DE BOILIEU 44 The Labrador Fishing Establishment is also a general store, and when any one requires supplies the mode of dealing is entirely by barter. 1870 HOWLEY *MS Reminiscences* 8 Newman and Company an old English firm have extensive establishments both here and at Harbour Britain. The fishery is carried on by them on a real old time plan. Every year they bring out in their vessels a number of English boys or youngsters who are apprenticed for 3 or 4 years on small wages. 1895 PROWSE 602 Thirty years ago Mr Nathan Norman's establishment at Indian Harbour, now owned by Job Brothers, was the most northern of the Newfoundland establishments. 1957 JOB 87 During the whole existence of Job Brothers & Co Ltd and its predecessors the main interest of the Company has been much more intimately connected with production and development of the fisheries than with trading, and in this connection a passing reference should be made to the Company's fishery establishments at Blanc Sablon, Lance-au-Loup and Forteau in the Straits of Belle Isle.

eunchuck n   See OWNSHOOK.

evening n   *EDD* ~ sb 1; *DAE* 2 (1790–) for sense 1.

1 The time between noon, or the midday meal, and twilight or dark; afternoon.

1874 WHITE *MS Journal* 1 Apr Took 2 young Harps this evening. 1920 GRENFELL & SPALDING 14 They jerk their heads and remark, 'Good morning,' or, 'Good evening,' according as it is before or after midday. This is an afternoonless country. The day is divided into morning, evening, and night. [1929] 1964 BLONDAHL (ed) 76 "The Sealing Cruise of the *Lone Flier*": At four o'clock that evening we put her in the ice. 1936 SMITH 29 [We] arrived at Ramah at dark on Saturday evening. T 12–64 Mug-up was usually a light snack around four o'clock in the evening. 1966 FARIS 197 On the third day, the funeral is held. . .usually in

the early afternoon (or 'evening,' as the day past 12 is termed).

2 A drink of liquor at the end of the working day.

1866 WILSON 348 If a tradesman were employed, he must have *three drinks* a day; or what he called his *morning*, his *eleven*, and his *evening*. 1937 DEVINE 21 ~ A glass of grog after the day's work.

evergreen n   Variety of club-moss (*Lycopodium* spp) (1898 *J A Folklore* xi, 283).

everlasting n   (a) Variety of the herb thrift (*Armeria maritima*) (1956 ROULEAU 30); (b) variety of club-moss (*Lycopodium* spp); EVERGREEN (1898 *J A Folklore* xi, 283).

every a   Phr *every way's likely*: stock phr, anything can happen, even the unexpected.

C 69–10 Such-a-one [an old maid] got married this morning. Every way's likely!

excursion n   Comb **excursion bread**, ~ **biscuit**: dry, sweet biscuit, shaped like a cake of 'hard tack.'

P 184–67 Let's go in the house and get some 'scursion bread. P 108 70 Trouters, hikers, picnickers, school children would generally have a cake of excursion biscuit in the pocket to eat between meals. 1975 *Evening Telegram* 28 June, p. 16 How I minds comin' down here in the long ago, on your way to the blockhouse, and goin' into Billy Brophy's for a cake of excursion bread.

extra a   In designations of grades of dried and salted cod: **extra large**, ~ **small**.

1955 *Nfld Fisheries Board* 39 Extra large fish 26'' and over. Ibid 39 Extra small fish under 12'' in length. T 36–64 Extra large [is] from twenty-one to twenty-four [inches long].

eye n   Cpd **eyeberry**: variety of plumboy (*Rubus pubescens*).

1916 HAWKES 36 The dewberry (*Rubus arcticus*) is found in large quantities on the islands off the east coast of Hudson bay. . . A smaller species, the eyeberry, *Rubus triflorus*, is found on Hamilton river.

F

fab n   *OED* ~ obs var of fob sb¹ 2 (1622–1852); PARTRIDGE fob obs. A trick.

T 80–64 When they used to catch a feller out Christmas Day to his dinner, they always sell un. That was a kind of Christmas fab that they'd work on fellers.

face n   *EDD* face sb 2 (10) K; PHILLIPPS, p. 66 for *face and eyes*.

1 The fleshy part of a cod's head eaten as a delicacy; CHEEK, JOWL, SCULP (P 133–58).

1979 NEMEC 275n Besides tongues, hearts and faces or 'jowls,' as well as the membrane ('sound'). . .

2 The inner or split side of a dried and salted cod-fish (1925 *Dial Notes* v, 330).

1955 *Nfld Fisheries Board* 23 Merchantable [is] sound quality fish, thoroughly clean on back and face, not sour or showing blood stains, clots, liver, gut or excessive salt on face. T 168/70–65 The next grade, madeira—that'd be touched with salt, showing the salt on the face, and thinner quality.

3 A mask worn by mummer; FALSE FACE.

T 26–64³ One party of mummers would attack another party, or sometimes people who weren't mummers would try to get the face off the mummers. T 169/70–65² We had beautiful faces, sir, beautiful masks. T 210/11–65 They'd be trying to guess who it was; a scattered time you'd get your face pulled off. T 272–66² After they talked a while they would rise their face and let 'em see who he was. 1973 WIDDOWSON 424 Well the first thing you'd open the door and a big man [was] coming in with a nasty-looking face on.

2 Comb, phr *face and eyes*: the face.

P 54–61 I told him to his face and eyes. T 94/106–64 He started to run and I went face and eyes in the mud. 1971 CASEY 285 They'd have served him barbarous. But they used to try to drag him on his face and eyes and everything.

the face and eyes of (someone): the exact likeness of.

P 108–70 He's the face and eyes of his father.

face-and-eye berry: juniper berry (*Juniperus horizontalis*); SAFFRON (1898 *J A Folklore* xi, 280).

face clock: dandelion (*Taraxacum officinale*) (1956 ROULEAU 30).

1975 SCOTT 39 The Dandelion has a number of common names in Newfoundland. These include Dumbledor, Faceclock, and Piss-a-beds.

have the face of a robber's horse: to be brazen, without shame or pity.

1981 *Evening Telegram* 6 May, p. 2 'What gall the minister of finance must have,' said [Steve] Neary. 'He must have the face of a robber's horse to come into the House [of Assembly] and ask for tax increases.'

faction n *OED* ~ 3 c (1880–); 5 faction-fight (1841). One of several Irish groups in St John's which in the nineteenth century frequently joined in pitched battles.

1863 PEDLEY 294 Two great Irish factions had established themselves [c1815] in St John's. They had various names, denoting the different parts of Ireland from which they came. The watchword of those from the county of Tipperary was 'Clear Air.' 1895 PROWSE 402 The faction fights went on for many years after Colclough left [in 1815]. . . The Tipperary 'clear airs,' the Waterford 'whey bellies,' and the Cork 'dadyeens' were arrayed against the 'yellow belly' faction—the 'Doones' or Kilkenny boys, and the Wexford 'yellow bellies.' There were besides the 'young colts' and a number of other names for the factions. They fought

with one another 'out of pure devilment and divarsion,' as an old Irishman explained it to me.

factory n A building or plant with facilities for the processing of fish, lobster, whales, 'seal oil,' etc.

1883 *Fish Exhibit Cat⁴* 176 Model of Seal Factory. New process of manufacture, whereby the Oil is expressed free from odour. 1895 PROWSE 539 This was all a trick, for the captain of the French man-of-war schooner *Perle*, which came into port just after, allowed the factory to go on again. 1904 *Daily News* 28 Sep Bond told you that the French Shore question was settled. The closing down of the Lark Harbor whale factory doesn't show as if that were the case. 1912 *Nfld Qtly* Christmas, p. 11 In Hawke's Bay is a whaling factory and when I was there it seemed to be doing well. 1936 SMITH 189 After a while the merchants and fishermen lodged a protest with the manager, saying that the old whale carcasses and dirt from the factory were polluting both the drinking water and the sea water. 1941 SMALLWOOD 39 [advertisement for herring and herring products] Factories [at the following harbours]. 1977 BUTLER 84 I asked Mr Wareham if I could go to work in the factory dressing herring that night to try and earn a couple of extra dollars.

faddle n *EDD* fardel: var faddle Do. A bundle of fire-wood.

[1929] 1949 ENGLISH 117 'Fardel' or 'faddle' is a bundle of firewood. C 71–120 A faddle of wood is a load either carried on one's back or on a slide drawn by a horse, dog, or even by a person with a haulin' rope.

fade v Cp *OED* ~ v¹ 1 for sense 1.

1 Of a tree, to wither and die.

T 54/62–64 I spoiled the tree because it's going to fade now. It was blowed out of root. Well, 'twould fade in any case.

2 Phr *fade it out*: to last, survive.

1944 LAWTON & DEVINE 96 And though by no means did we live in luxury, we faded it out until Spring.

fadge v also **fodge***, **fudge** *OED* ~ 5 obs (1611–1789); *EDD* ~ v³. To do things for oneself; to manage (on one's own).

1937 DEVINE 21 ~ To bustle about; to manage. 'I got to *fadge* for meself now.' C 71–99 When [the husband] finds himself suddenly living alone, now he has to fodge for himself. . . To a guest: 'Fodge for yourself. Make yourself at home.' 1976 GUY 65 Me here all alone, a poor old widow woman, fudgin' along for myself through a hardish winter.

faffering v ppl also **farferin'***. Cp *EDD* faff v 1 'to blow in sudden gusts'; SMYTH faff 'to blow in flaws.' Of the wind, blowing with cold, chilly gusts (P 95–55).

P 127–76 Boy, 'tis farferin' today.

faggot n also **fagot**. Cp *OED* ~ 3 (1489–1854), *DAE* fagot 2 (1800, 1889), *DC* ~ Nfld (1777–) for sense 1; *EDD* 4 for sense 2. See also PILE n.

1 A stack of split and salted cod-fish at various stages of the drying process.

[1663] 1963 YONGE 58 By night, or in wet weather, [the drying fish is] made up in faggots (as they call it), that is, 4 or five fishes with the skin upwards, and a broad fish on top. [1726] 1976 HEAD 74 Some time after this they lay them together in small heaps, about a dozen or 14 of them, what they call faggots, this they doe always in the evenings or when it Rains, & Spread them again in the mornings. [1777] 1792 CARTWRIGHT ii, 368 The green fish being in a state of taking damage, we spread it all; also, the half-cured fish which the Americans had thrown out of pile; the latter we piled again, and made up the former into faggots. 1861 DE BOILIEU 37 The fish having been 'turned' each evening, about the third day they are put in faggots, about a dozen fish being laid one upon the other, their backs upwards, as a defence from wet or the dampness of the night. 1866 WILSON 211 And as evening approaches, the fish spread in the morning has to be taken up and put in fagot, or little heaps, and left on the flake until next day. 1936 SMITH 17 After the first day's sun it would be made up in small faggots, not more than a half-quintal to each faggot. On the second day it would be spread out, all the one way, and made up in the evening in large faggots of two quintals or more. When spread again it would be made up in twenty-quintal piles. T 36–64 Providing the next day is fine and the next day is fine you'll always enlarge on your faggots, and when the fish gets half-made you got it in quintal faggots. C 69–17 When codfish [were] spread on the flake for the first few days it was taken up and placed in little piles or heaps called faggots. After each day's spread it was made a little larger till it reached the stage called pile containing over 5 quintals in a circular stack. 1977 BURSEY 196–7 Every fisherman at the Battery had a long face for they had fish in different stages of making, from waterhorse through fagots to fish wanting but one day's sun. 1979 TIZZARD 295 [The cod-fish were] packed in the store in either round or square faggots.

2 A naughty or mischievous child.

1899 ENGLISH 15 What's that, ye saucy little faggot, if I don't complain ye to yer uncle. . . 1937 DEVINE 21 ~ A mild term of reproach used towards a small girl. 'You little *Faggot*.' [1960] 1965 LEACH (ed) 130 "Stowaway": One day he came up from below decks, / And seizing a lad by the hand, / Some little half-wornout faggot, / Who ought to be home with his dad. T 222–66 And when your small fry aggravate you, do you call them bad narders or young gommels or brazen faggots or bedlamer boys or noggyheads?

faggot v also **faggot up**. Cp *OED* ~ 1 (1598–1786); *DC* ~ (Nfld: 1779). See also FAGGOT n. To place split and salted cod in piles during the process of curing; PILE v.

[1779] 1792 CARTWRIGHT ii, 469 We heaved part of the fish that was re-packed last; but were obliged to faggot it upon the flakes immediately, on account of rain coming on. 1977 RUSSELL 42 King David'd have 'em [the goats] all out to the brow of the hill long before the rain started. . .and before the rain did come

every quintal of fish on every flake in Pigeon Inlet'd be faggoted up and safe.

fainaigue v [fə'neig] *EDD* ~ s w cties. To play a card of another suit, against the rules of a game.

P 167–66 You're not allowed to fainaigue the jack of hearts.

fairity n *EDD* ~ Ir. Fairness (1896 *Dial Notes* i, 379).

T 43–64 Somebody would look at the fish and average it, or just estimate what you had—there was nothing too accurate about fairity in them times. P 148–75 I believe in fairity [in political discussions—recognizing when the opponents have done well].

fairy n Cp JOYCE 255: fairy breeze, for ~ squall, 303 pookapyle, and DINNEEN púca 'fairy' for 'toadstool' terms in sense 1; *Kilkenny Lexicon* fairy blast, ~ struck, *EDD* ~ II (41) (b): fairy-stricken, ~ struck Ir for cpd in sense 2.

Attrib, comb **fairy('s) bread**: wild mushroom; toadstool.

C 65–4 In Fogo the mushrooms that are found growing around trees are called fairy's bread. C 71–120 The toadstool was called fairy caps by older people; also fairy bread.

fairy bun: bread carried when travelling alone to ward off the fairies; COMPANY BREAD; cp BUN.

1966 FARIS 40 Many of the more traditional men carry small buns (called 'fairy buns') into the woods with them to drop along the trail at intervals in order to satisfy the mischievous [fairies] and bribe them into not disguising the trail.

fairy cap: toadstool; mushroom; DEAD-MAN'S CAP, DEVIL'S ~ .

1939 DULEY 23 Running ahead, Mary Immaculate had kicked over a fairy-cap. Large and flat, like the crust of new bread, it lay spilled from its stalk. T 175/6–65 The wild mushrooms, you know—we call it fairy caps. C 71–92 As children we were told not to touch the 'fairy caps' because the fairies would take us if we did.

fairy hand-bar: variety of kelp, shaped like a miniature hand-barrow.

1972 MURRAY 119 [She] said that when she was a child in the early 1900s she used to pick up 'fairy handbars.' These were sections of seaweed tossed up on the beach which, when dry, resembled the handbar used for carrying fish.

fairy-led: led astray by fairies; lost in familiar surroundings; dazed.

T 34–64 She went into the woods and couldn't find her way out, and they said she was fairy-led. C 66–1 This girl down on the Cape Shore was fairy led. . .gone from home for seven or eight days. The fairies took her off in the woods and when she came home she was crazy. C 66–9 Persons who are alone in the woods at night are likely to be fairy-led. T 271–66[3] [If people] lose their way in the country they thought they were fairyled. C 67–12 'You are going around fairy led.' This expression was often used of anyone going around in a daze.

fairy man: changeling.

1931 BYRNES 76 Stuart Taylor, known to the small boys as the 'fairy man' or 'changeling' who played incesssantly on a tin whistle.

fairy path: a clear but little-used woods path.

C 64–1 A fairy path is. . .a path which never becomes overgrown by shrubs or bushes, even though it is little used by humans. It is believed that such paths are used by the fairies who keep them beaten down.

fairy pipe: the immature frond of a variety of fern; fiddle-head.

C 69–15 We always referred to what are known in Nova Soctia as fiddle-heads as fairy pipes. We were not afraid of them, but often picked them and pretended to smoke them.

fairy squall: a strong, sudden gust of wind on an otherwise calm day (C 64–1).

1968 DILLON 137 A fairy squall blows up kind o' sudden, but there's no lasting to it. M 71–42 He told me about a fairy squall, which consisted of a little whirlwind, and when these came around early fall the old people would say the fairies were dancing.

fairy stool: see **fairy cap** above.

C 69–24 Toadstools were also called fairy stools.

fairy stroke: ailment inflicted by fairies; paralysis thought to be caused supernaturally; BLAST. Cp **fairy struck**.

M 71–42 Fairy stroke is paralysis of any limbs due to the power of the fairies, who could cause this effect at will.

fairy-struck: mentally or physically harmed by the fairies; afflicted by paralysis. Cp BLAST 2.

C 64–1 If a child or even an adult strays into such a [fairy] path he is likely to be taken away by fairies. If not actually taken away, he may be fairy-struck or queer in some way. C 66–2 If you went too far in the woods the fairies would lead you astray—you would get fairy-struck.

fairy tune: song supposedly learned supernaturally.

C 71–26 This Irishman knew many unfamiliar songs, for the people believed that he learned these songs from the fairies. His songs came to be called fairy tunes. People requested the fiddlers of the place to play fairy tunes, that were passed down from father to son but had been first learned from Dick, the Irishman.

fairy v Phr *fairy away*: to misdirect or mislead (by enchantment).

C 67–7 There was a man who would never cut wood alone. He was afraid of being 'fairied away' if he went into the woods alone.

faitour n also **futter** *OED* ~ 'imposter, vagrant' obs (1340–1828); *Kilkenny Lexicon* futter 'clumsy, fussy, inefficient worker.' A lazy fellow (1925 *Dialect Notes* v, 330).

1914 *Cadet* Apr, p. 7 ~ for idle fellow (pronounced futter).

fall v *OED* ~ 80 d fall back 'fall into arrear'

obs (1786); *OED* 100 a 'of the eyes: to close' obs (1300).

In phr *fall back*: to go into debt.

1924 ENGLAND 257 The merchants, if so disposed, have everything all their own way. Once the men 'fall back,' they are sometimes never again able to 'put up money' or to 'straighten up,' i.e., pay their bills.

fall together: of one's eyes, to close drowsily.

C 66–10 I heard this said when John was leaning on the table and his eyes were falling together because of sleep.

fall n *OED* ~ sb[1] 2 for *fall of the year; DAE* ~ 3 b; cp SPRING[2]: *spring of the year*.

1 Phr *fall of the year*: autumn, esp the fishing season between the end of the spring and summer fishery and Christmas.

[1776 (1792) CARTWRIGHT ii, 177 I sent five hands in a skiff. . .to look for the nets, which we lost there last fall.] [1794] 1968 THOMAS 171 Numbers of Fishermen, at the Fall of the year (the 25th of October) on their terms of serving being expired are paid the residue of their wages. [1822] 1928 CORMACK 106 The fishery may be commenced here six weeks or a month earlier than at any other part of the coast, and continued in the fall of the year until Christmas. T 45/6–64 'Twas in the fall 'o the year, she left to go to St John's in an open boat. . .and they got—breeze come on, they got drove off. T 43/4–64 They got no boats, only flats or a canoe—kayak they call it. That's what they run the rivers with and go back up the country in the fall o' the year. 1971 CASEY 233 When the evening would begin to get long, or sometimes now a stormy day in the fall of the year when they wouldn't be able to get out in boat and the weather would be too bad for spreading fish. . . 1975 LEYTON 21 We used to keep sheep and three or four cows. We'd sell one of them right late in the fall of the year, try to get a pair of boots for all hands.

2 Attrib, comb **fall baiting**: a quantity of baitfish used in the autumn cod-fishery. See BAITING.

fall fish: cod-fish, large and fat, caught in the autumn with hook-and-line (1966 FARIS 236).

1842 BONNYCASTLE ii, 189 A quintal of fall fish, or best cod £0/12/6. 1850 [FEILD] 87 Nor the 'fall-fish' with autumn's showers await. . .

fall fishery: the cod-fishery prosecuted between the end of the spring and summer fishery and Christmas.

1916 LENCH 15 We have. . .the Fall fishery which [lasts for seven or eight weeks and is] not over till close near Christmas. 1933 *Nfld Royal Commission Report* 99 The fishery in the fall is not conducted by means of traps (since the fish do not run quite so close to shore, and in any case the weather is too stormy for traps) but by motor-boats using bultows, long lines with hooks set at intervals in the sea-flow. This fishery produces the best fish, since in the fall the fish have recovered from the effects of the spawning season and have been fattened by their summer diet. Their texture is firm and thick and their livers are rich in oil. T 141/69–65[2] We fishermen always looked at the fishery as two seasons: there's the caplin scull season and the fall's fishery. If we lose our caplin scull fishery, if that was bad, look out for a fall's fishery: we'm going to have a booming fall. But if we have a big summer, we have a poor fall. 1980 *Evening Telegram* 6 Aug, p. 6 It depends on how the fall fishery will go and if there is more salt required then we can get it.

fall fishing: the autumn cod-fishery.

1973 HORWOOD 9 And so it was not long before he could speak the Lambert tongue. Mr Lambert was an inshore fisherman, he owned boats and fishing gear and was just about to begin the fall fishing.

fall herring: herring taken in coastal waters in the autumn.

1842 JUKES i, 228 These are succeeded by the 'fall herrings,' as they are called, or the autumnal herring-shoals. 1873 CARROLL 38 Many and various were the opinions given. . .as to the best possible mode of pre-serving the Spring, Summer, and Fall Herrings that resort to this Island. 1883 HATTON & HARVEY 324 The Fall herring is the marketable fish, and it is then that they are taken on the Labrador coast, where they appear early in September. P 243–56 ~ Particularly fat [Labrador] herring of the late fishing season.

fall run: autumn migration of seals in coastal waters. See also RUN n.

1909 BROWNE 56 This [seal] fishery is carried on from May to June 10 (spring 'Run'), and from 20th November to 10th December (fall 'run').

fall trip: in the Bank fishery, autumn fishing voyage for cod.

1845 *Journ of Assembly* Appendix, p. 231 [The English Bankers proceeded] to the Labrador the summer months, and upon their return, again went on the Banks for the fall trip. 1960 FUDGE 18 All of my men went home for a few days, after which we prepared for the fall trip.

fall voyage: see **fall fishery** above. See also VOYAGE.

1964 *Daily News* 22 July, p. 4 The fall voyage can compensate for a poor trapping season. 1966 FARIS 34–5 The fishery further offshore—with nets, trawls and hand lines—is called the 'fall voyage.'

fall tucker* See POLTOGUE*.

false a *OED* ~ III 13 e (1818, 1833); *EDD* adj 5 (5) (a) 'a mask' [worn by Christmas guisards] Sc. Comb **false face**: a mask, usu home-made, worn by a Christmas mummer; also a Hallowe'en mask; FACE.

1928 *Nfld Qtly* Dec, p. 15 The merry party of 'Jannies,' or 'Mummers,' made the welkin ring with their weird shouts and cries, and their 'false faces' sent many a frightened child in haste to its mother's knee. T 22–64 Some more would make them out of cardboard, the false faces, and whiskers—put the whiskers on, and a moustache and all of it; trim it all up. M 68–22 We went mummering every night, clear of Sunday, for two weeks. We made our false faces and firked out all the old clothes we could find. 1969 *Christmas Mumming in Nfld* 131 Anything which disguises the head is called a 'false face.' C 71–113 ~ A mask either home-made or store bought. The mask would be used by children at

Halloween [and] by adults during the Christmas holidays when [they] would go out for a night jannying. 1979 TIZZARD 175 Each one with a 'false face' disguised his or her voice, but in the event that they were guessed the 'false face' was generally removed.

family n Cp *DAE* mess beef for first comb.
Comb **family-mess (pork)**: superior grade of barrelled, salted pork.

[1894 BURKE] 2, 5 Hearn & Co always keep in stock Family mess. . . T J Edens is remarkable for keeping first-class flour. . . Family mess and good molasses. [1911] GRENFELL 65 'Figgy Duff,' a big boiling of family-mess pork, [etc].

family room: see ROOM 1.

famish gut n SEARY 84. Cp PINCHGUT. A narrow strait, sound or 'tickle.'

[1772] 1971 SEARY 210 Famishgut (Lane 1772). 1951 *Nfld & Lab Pilot* i, 145 Red Cove head, about one mile farther northward, forms the southern entrance point of Red cove and Famish gut.

fance n Female dog, bitch.
P 229–67 The fance is going to have pups.

far av
1 In phr *as far as*: to (with no comparison implied); cp FARFORTH.

1930 BARNES 83 'Come into Lasher's with me'—a bar was there at the time. He said, 'Come in as far as Lasher's with me and we'll have a drink.' P 148–65 Dad has gone over as far as Henry's. 1979 TIZZARD 45 He. . .would get Hiram and some other young fellow to row him up as far as Thomas Mehaney's in punt, a distance of a mile and a half.

2 Comb **far-away gear**: trawl-line with lines and hooks spaced well apart.

1963 TEMPLEMAN & FLEMING 7 The gear used in [long-lining] experiments was of the same type, standard gear (50–52 hooks per line). . .some 'close rigged' gear (80–82 hooks per line) and 'far-away' gear (33–34 hooks per line). Q 67–48 Far-away gear [has] suds far apart, about forty hooks to a line.

farferin'* See FAFFERING.

farforth av *OED* ~ 2 b (1297–1827). In phr *as/so farforth as*: to a certain extent; as far as, as much as.

P 148–61 I'll enlighten you as farforth as I can. T 54–64 He was no good as far forth as a man was concerned. He hadn't sense enough to fish. 1972 *Evening Telegram* 25 Feb, p. 3 There's blasting going on here you know and you can't be too careful so far forth as what dynamite is concerned, can you? 1975 GUY 159 So far forth as hair is concerned I found it economical in years past to get it all mowed down, smack smooth, in what was called in those faroff times a 'brush cut.'

farl See FOREL.

farm n A parcel of land away from the waterfront; a wood-lot.

[1825] 1882 *Nfld Law Reports* 368–9 A deed of that date is put in, and shews a conveyance to these parties of half Martin Mahoney's 'farm or plantation'. . . If the term 'plantation' had stood alone, I should have felt no difficulty in holding that it embraced waterside as well as inside land. 1972 MURRAY 118–19 A play area used chiefly in spring and fall was a grassy clearing among trees in a 'farm' (i.e., a woodlot).

farrell See FOREL.

fart See HORSE(S) FART.

fashion n 1904 *Ulster J Arch* x, 126 ~ 'habit.' Custom, habit or practice (1925 *Dial Notes* v, 330).
1930 BARNES 172, 276 I had a fashion always of going in a bar there called Jimmie McKay's. . . He had a great fashion of saying that when he was doing anything of consequence. T 54–64 The door to our fishin' room [in] the little shack place we had built, had a fashion when the door'd go to an' lots o' times the button we had on it'd turn. P 54–69 It used to be a fashion to frame and glass vaccination certificates. 1975 GUY 145 I always had the fashion of sleeping with my head as handy to the window as possible.

fast a *O Sup*[2] ~ 2 c 'frozen' N Amer ?obs (1706–1854) for sense 1.
1 Of a body of water, frozen.
[1771] 1792 CARTWRIGHT i, 176 [I] sent him to Atkinson Pond for the traps, but he found the pond fast. 1861 DE BOILIEU 101 'Now, boys, bear a hand!' cries the old skipper. 'Where are the dogs? Everything is getting fast, and we must have them whilst the weather is calm.' 1919 GRENFELL[1] 224 It was getting late in the year. . . The ponds were all 'fast,' and the fall deer hunt which follows the fishery was over.
2 Of sealskin, not liable to shed its hair.
1924 ENGLAND 14 Their pelts, save in the case of the 'cat' or still-born harp seal, are usually valueless as fur, the hair not being 'fast.'

fasten v *DAE* ~ (1784). Of a river, to freeze.
[1820] 1915 HOWLEY 122 The frost had been very severe for three days which fastened the river above.

fasting vbl n *OED* ~ vbl sb[2] 3 (1460–1818); *EDD* ~ -spittle 'spittle of a fasting man.' Comb **fasting spit(tle)**: one's spit in the morning before breakfast, thought to have curative powers.
C 68–19 If a child is born with any birthmark, the mother must make the sign of the cross on the mark of the child with a finger wet with fasting spit. C 68–22 To cure a wart, 'Use your fastin' spittle.' This meant you would have to spit on it before eating in the morning.

fat a For combs. in sense 2, *NID* ~ back 3.
1 Of a sealing season, prosperous; see also var senses of FAT[1] n.
1934 *Nfld Qtly* Summer, p. 30 In speaking of the seal fishery I quoted an old adage: 'A frosty winter for a fat spring.'

2 Comb **fatback (pork)**: salt-cured fat from a hog.
T 75/7–64 They never saw a bit o' meat for a long time. Them days there used to be ham butt pork, you know, an' fat back. C 64–5 A sure cure for warts is fatback pork. It must be rubbed on the area briefly, once a day for three consecutive days, each time the pork being thrown over the left shoulder, and then discarded. T 178/9–65 No, not fat back, not then; mostly what you call heavy mess. 1972 MURRAY 222 'Hambutt' pork differed from 'fat back' pork used for frying purposes in that 'it had a bone in it.'

fat oxen: the ruddy turnstone, a distinctively marked shore-bird (*Arenaria interpres*).
1870 *Can Naturalist* v, 292 [The turnstone is] abundant on the seashore in the fall of the year, and generally so fat that the settlers have bestowed on it the appropriate name of 'fat oxen.' 1967 *Bk of Nfld* iii, 283 Ruddy Turnstone: Fat Oxen (it is a common name in Newfoundland but the origin is unknown).

fat pork: see **fatback** above; also attrib.
[1794] 1968 THOMAS 140 People who go into the Woods in hott weather smear their faces over with Fatt Pork or some severe acid which the Muscatoos dislike and then they do not follow. 1927 DOYLE (ed) 5 "Wedding in Renews": They'll have sweet cake and turnip tops, / Fat pork and castor oil. 1937 DEVINE 55 [Vang is] melted fat pork served on fresh codfish. C 68–4 You might get hit with a fat-pork bun. C 70–15 Another favourite outport item of diet was the fat-pork touton. These were buns made with molasses and dotted with little chunks of fat pork. They were nearly always put in the lunch box on fishing trips, or especially when cutting firewood.

fat[1] n *DC* ~ 1 a Nfld ([1960]–1965) for sense 1, b (1925, 1933) for sense 2; 2 a, b (1918–1964) for sense 3; *OED* a II 8 fat-oil (1875) for comb in sense 5.
1 The layer of fatty tissue cut from the skin of seals for rendering into oil; BLUBBER.
1708 GEARE 17–18 . . .[flour] mixt with Water and boiled upon the fat of the Seal. [1771] 1792 CARTWRIGHT i, 89 I had the fat of two harps melted, which produced eighteen gallons of oil. 1832 MCGREGOR i, 224 The fat, or seal blubber, is separated from the skins, cut into pieces, and put into framework vats, through which, and small boughs inside, the oil oozes on being exposed to the heat of the sun. [1896] SWANSBOROUGH 4 "The Seal Fishery": But hope is active, all now chat / Of sealing fleets, and seals, and 'fat.' 1955 DOYLE (ed) 10 "A Noble Fleet of Sealers": There's a noble fleet of sealers, / Being fitted for the 'ice.' / They'll take a chance again this year / Tho' fat's gone down in price. T 50–64 Bill went down an' she was up to the floor then, trying to get the pumps cleaned—choked up with fat, see. 1978 *Decks Awash* vii (1), 19 Out of the $27 which is top price, we were getting $23 or $24. We were also getting 4 cents for the fat.
2 A collection of the skins of seals with fatty tissue attached. See PELT n, SCULP n.
1894 MOTT 25 [Captain Dawe] brought a big lot of 'fat into the country.' 1906 DUNCAN 280 Two pennant

bearers, carrying flags to mark the heaps of 'fat,' as they should be formed, led the file. 1933 GREENE 47 The bunting was only hoisted when the holds were filled to the hatch-coamings and over—and indeed wherever else (no matter where!) that seal-pelts could be 'stowed'—or the 'fat' as the sealers term it. 1936 DEVINE 122 His son, a fine young lad of 12 years of age, was killed by falling over Signal Hill on the harbour [side] in 1880, the spring the *Walrus* brought in three loads of fat. 1977 *Evening Telegram* 8 Mar, p. 4 [At the seal-hunt in 1960] we had to sleep in the [hold]. . .and when there was so much fat aboard, we had to buddy up.

3 Seals; the seal herds; esp in phr *in the fat, strike the fat.*

1895 *Christmas Review* 12 [proverb] Out of the fog and into the 'fat.' [1900 OLIVER & BURKE] 12 "Local Poet on Harbor Grace": For fat and fish you stand alone— / Unequall'd—Harbor Grace. 1916 GRENFELL 8 As long as you have enough flour not to starve, and can get some fat, you'll be all right, Jake, till the ducks come south. 1924 ENGLAND 47 'We got a grand shot on us now,' cried the Cap'n. 'We'll be into the fat afore lang, me sons!' P 245–55 To strike the fat, i.e. the seal herds. 1964 BLONDAHL (ed) 77 "Sealing Cruise of the *Lone Flier*": We motored until three o'clock, and then we struck the fat, / Herbert Legge picked up a seal, Claude Hawkins got a 'cat.' 1972 BROWN 28 An' when we reach the swiles I'll let ye know be raisin' the after derrick. Now when ye see the after derrick ris, ye'll know we're in the fat.

4 Comb **fat-oil**: oil rendered from the blubber of whales or seals.

[1766] 1971 BANKS 135 Let us remember their Train Oyl for by that name they distinguish it from Whale or Seal oyle which they Call Fat Oyle Which is sold at a Lower Price. 1819 ANSPACH 446 [Oil] which is extracted from whales and seals. . .is there designated by the appellation of *fat-oil.*

fat-soap: soap made from the fatty tissue of sheep or cows.

T 34–64 Some people used to make their own soap out of blubber in days gone by, or make it in fat, the fat of the sheep, if we had sheep to kill. T 94–64 So the fat soap is the same, you know. You'd save up fat—you kill a cow, you'd have a lot o' fat.

fat² [= vat]. See TRAIN²: TRAIN-FAT; VAT.

father-giver n Cp *EDD* father II 1 (4) father-in-church. The man who gives the bride away.

1967 FIRESTONE 76 If the father does not perform [as father-giver] the bride may choose any man, but usually this is an uncle or older brother. 1972 MURRAY 171 The 'father-giver' was a cross between the 'father' and the 'best man'; he performed both duties. . .when the minister asked 'who giveth this woman' he responded, but he still stayed in his position and 'supported' the groom.

feared a *OED* ~ 1 obs exc dial; *EDD* ~ 1. Afraid, frightened.

1842 JUKES i, 73 Oh, by God, sir, I'm feared to go after that! 1924 ENGLAND 315 ~ Afraid. T 100/2–64

When I stepped on the bridge I felt my hair stood on my head—I was frightened, see, feared. T 301–66 There's some youngsters feared o' people [i.e. mummers] goes into a house with nothing on their face.

feather n *EDD* ~ : feather-bed Co, cp ~ -bog (1810).

1 In phr *not a feather out*: unruffled, unweary.

1888 HOWLEY *MS Reminiscences* 59 They had a great blaze going and other indications told us our long lost voyageurs had returned. Sure enough there they were. . .and not a feather out of them. P 108–70 After footing it all that way, she didn't have a feather out of her. . . She walked all the way home, and not a feather out of her.

2 Comb **feather bed**: bog (P 154–78).

feather-sewell: line with feathers attached to guide the movement of caribou. See also SEWELL.

[1771] 1792 CARTWRIGHT i, 118 I gave them a feather-sewel to run on that side.

feature v *OED* ~ 1 now dial; *EDD* ~ for sense 1.

1 To resemble.

1925 *Dial Notes* v, 330 ~ look like; favor. 'It'd hardly *feature* her.'

2 To remember, call to mind, picture.

P 54–67 'I fatures all dem places now' he said, speaking of the Labrador where he had fished in schooners for many years.

feck n A fine goose feather used in oiling the works of a clock. (1927 *Christmas Messenger* 47).

feed v Cp FARMER & HENLEY ~ the fishes (1884).

In phr *feed the gulls*: to vomit (from sea-sickness).

C 70–27 Young children who get sick at sea are often teased by the fishermen. When they throw up, this is called feeding the gulls.

feeder n *OED* ~ 8 b (1844, 1875). The pitcher in the game of rounders.

T 181–65 We have our feeder, the man in the centre, and so many on the outside and so many on the inside; if the man in the centre, the feeder, would heave that ball and strike you. . .you were out.

feeting n *EDD* footing, var featin, feeten, feeting; *DAE* ~ 1 'track or trail' (1663). The footprints or tracks of animals.

[1778] 1792 CARTWRIGHT ii, [328] [We] took up the traps; nothing had been on them: but we saw the fresh feeting of beavers, on the sands below the stint. M 69–6 Rabbits were so plentiful that on winter nights when a little snow fell rabbits feeten. . .could be seen all over our garden.

fegary n also **vagary** [fəˈgɛˈəri] *OED* ~ dial var of vagary (1724–1823); *EDD* ~ 3. Excessive

ornament; too elaborate fastenings (on clothing).
P 180–72 I don't want to get your fegary tangled up.

fellow n also **fella, feller** *ADD* ~ 1 (Nfld: 1921).
Young boy; son.
1899 ENGLISH 68 The little fellow had called some of
the neighbours. 1924 ENGLAND 166 'My feller. . .bring
dat from de wahr.' T 22–64 The first dancing-master I
made, I made un for the first feller that we had, and I
danced it for him. 1973 WIDDOWSON 467 Her 'little
fellow'. . .aged six, had just been down in the 'cove'
and walked out in the water up to his knees.

felt n Cp *NID* ~¹ 3 a, b. A heavy, fibrous material placed in sheets as a roof covering and tarred.
[1918–19] GORDON 17 By the evening, we had the
building completely covered round and on top, and the
felt nailed onto the roof. T 35/8–64 When the fish had
been finished the [birch] rind wouldn't be much good
for the next year, so some fellers would keep it for felt
[to] rine the roofs. T 158–65 All that ridge burned in
there; flankers come out [and] pitch on the felt. 1976
GUY 141 On the roof there was tarred felt and on warm
days in the summer you could smell the tar upstairs.

fence n
1 An obstruction built to guide and entrap wild
animals. See also SEWELL for 1811 quot.
[1811] 1915 HOWLEY 75 On either side of the
river. . .fences were thrown up to prevent the deer
from landing, after taking to the water. M 68–23 When
the area being snared was on the side of a bog or a
'droke' (heavily wooded area) we would build a fence
along the side. Openings were made in the fence every
ten yards or so in order for the rabbits to get from one
type of terrain to the other; they had to go through the
openings in which snares were set.
2 Comb **fence-longer**: horizontal rail in one
type of fence. See also LONGER.
1896 *J A Folklore* ix, 32 Fence-longers: . . .the fence
rails. T 43/7–64 [There'd be] a nail through the
rail—longers they used to call them, fence-longers.

feraun n Cp DINNEEN *feorán curraigh* (*Lycopus
europaeus*). Weed with yellow flowers and strong
unpleasant odour; pineapple-weed (*Matricaria
matricarioides*) (P 160–56).

fern n Common yarrow (*Achillea millefolium*)
(1956 ROULEAU 30).

ferry v To jump from one pan of ice to another; to propel an ice-pan with a pole; COPY.
P 148–60 ~ run from one pan of ice to another.
C 68–4 You'll see all the youngsters ferrying. The kids
get a long stick and each one gets on a pan of ice and
pushes it around the water with the stick.

fess a *EDD* ~ 2 Bk D for sense 1, 4 'over-
zealous, officious, meddlesome; fussy' Do So for
sense 2.

1 Bright, lively, alert; intently busy or active.
Q 71–7 If Aunt Polly was almost too busy [making a
mat] to talk, she would be said to be fain fess at that
mat. Q 71–8 That maiden, she's some fess.
2 Odd, peculiar, abnormal or unusual.
P 75–113 [They are] fess people (for putting out their
cod-traps in that manner, for living off welfare, etc).

fetch n *OED* ~ sb² 1 (1787–1871), *EDD* sb¹ for
sense 1; cp *EDD* 13 'quantity fetched or carried
at one time' for sense 3.
1 An apparition or double of a living person,
the appearance of which often portends death or
disaster; ghost; TOKEN.
1924 ENGLAND 219 'Fetches,' or spirits, are annoy-
ingly familiar at sea. They wander about vessels and try
to get the crew to chat with them; also with ghostly
hands they essay to remove human ones from the
wheel. If the living steersman will only keep cool and
quiet and hold fast, the fetch will presently disappear;
if not, and the fetch gets possession of the wheel, woe
to that ship! 1937 DEVINE 21 ~ An apparition of an
acquaintance that the observer knew to be in a distant
locality. 1968 DILLON 138 If I didn't meet you on the
road last night, 'twas your fetch. C 68–16 A fetch is
something seen which resembles a human person. It
may be seen at night or day usually before or after a
person dies. A person may see his own fetch. C 71–95
To see someone's fetch from midnight to noon was a
sign that person would soon die, but to see a fetch from
noon to midnight was a sign that person still had a long
life.
2 A phantom ship.
T 55/7–64 Lots o' people see her beating in here
under sail, you know, this schooner—the fetch or
whatever you call it.
3 A cargo (of seals) (1925 *Dial Notes* v, 330).

fetch v *OED* ~ 10 naut; *EDD* ~ 11 esp s w
cties. To reach, arrive at.
1937 DEVINE 21 ~ To reach a point steered for in a
boat. P 113–56 We should fetch the point on this tack.
1966 SCAMMELL 78 Not hardly, grandpa, with this
wind I think we can just about fetch to the nets.
P 108–70 He didn't fetch home till dark. 1971
HORWOOD 22 The wind hauled farther ahead and the
schooner could not fetch Baccalieu Tickle.

fettle See QUEEN'S FETTLE.

fib* n Cp *EDD* phibbie 'the Phoebe, an old
country dance' Co. A dance in which each person tries to participate until accompanying verse
is completed.
C 70–24 The fib is very difficult and this verse is sung
to accompany it: Won't you come dancing, dancing,
dancing, / Won't you come dance the Fib with me? /
Can't you see my elbows shaking, / Can't you see my
knees so weak, / Don't you see the trouble I take, / To
dance the Fib with you, and I so weak?

fiddle v To play (the accordion) for a dance.

c 71–39 I was told to ask [him] to fiddle for the time, i.e. the dance.

fiddler n
1 Musician who performs for a dance (on an accordion).

1966 SCAMMELL 85–6 In the center of the floor on a raised platform sat the fiddler, who was really an accordion player. 1967 *Bk of Nfld* iv, 236 A fiddler would perch himself on a chair on top of a table in the centre of the hall and for $5 play all night, beating time with his feet and bathed in perspiration. The instrument was not a fiddle but an accordion but nevertheless he was called the fiddler. T 411/12–67 We had to head up socials, and on several occasions I acted as fiddler for them—I played the accordion. 1973 ROSE (ed) 31 Before many more years had passed I had put two and two together and figured out that this noise was coming from the fiddler who was playing an accordion. He was always called the fiddler regardless of what he played upon. Even a rack comb and tissue paper.

2 Phr *have the fiddlers*: to stagger.
M 68–26 Sometimes after carrying the bar [barrow] for possibly an hour, a person might begin to stagger with the weight. The men said that man had the fiddlers. This meant that he couldn't carry the loaded bar with a steady walk.

field n *OED* ~ 12 b (1813, 1818) for sense 1; *DC* field ice (1850–) for comb in sense 3.

1 Esp in phr *field of ice*: an extensive area of floating ice, usu stretching farther than the eye can see; a large ice-floe.
1774 [LA TROBE] 18 After sailing three days, they were stopt by a field of ice, which extended beyond the bounds of their sight, and were obliged to run with contrary wind, and in a storm, into the bay Notre-Dame. 1832 MCGREGOR i, 222 It is little more than thirty years since the first vessels ventured among those formidable fields of ice that float from the northern regions, during the months of March, April, and May, down to the coast of Newfoundland. 1887 *Colonist Christmas No* 12 In a short time we reach a field of ice, like a polished mirror. 1909 BERNIER 7 ~ A large body of ice that may be seen around. 1957 *Nfld & Lab Pilot* Supplement No 2, p. 6 ~ Area of pack-ice/drift ice, consisting of any size of floes, of such extent that its limits cannot be seen from the crow's nest.

2 Occas in name of underwater feature or shoal.
1953 *Nfld & Lab Pilot* ii, 225 Several shoals, with depths of from 10 to 20 fathoms over them. . .lie. . .in order from east to west, The Field, Gull Island ground, Friday ledge, and Gruffy ground.

3 Comb **field-bunk**: in the bunk-house of fishing premises, a large platform running the length of the building, on which the men slept (c 75–19).

field-ice: see *field of ice* above; ice from such a field.
[1766] 1971 BANKS 119 [The island of ice] is accompanied by several small flat Pieces of Ice which the seamen call field Ice which drives very near us & is Easily

seen by its white appearance not unlike the Breaking of a wave into foam. 1832 MCGREGOR i, 223 The vessels then proceed to the field ice, pushing their way through the openings, or working to windward of it, until they meet with the herds of seals that accompany the ice. 1846 TOCQUE 67 In the month of March the field ice passes along the northern and eastern shores of Newfoundland. 1887 BOND 28 We could see nothing but open water all around us, as far as the eye could reach, with here and there a bit of field ice floating about; no sign of the main body of ice anywhere to be seen. 1924 ENGLAND 70 We made the field ice, now; got down to the reg'lar sheet ice, now, an' no more slob.

fierce a, av used intensively. To the extreme.
T 141/62–65² He had cut his foot that much that he was bleedin' fierce when he would go to put a bit o' weight on un. P 184–67 She's a fierce size! P 204–73 After a number of religious services, a lay reader commented, 'that was fierce ugly.'

fig n *OED* ~ sb¹ 5 dial, *EDD* ~ 2 s w cties for sense 1; for combs. in sense 2: *EDD* 2 (10) ~ duff, (14) ~ pudding. See also FIGGY.

1 A raisin.
1858 [LOWELL] i, 128 [I] get a marsel o' figs, or sech-like, for my poor, dear maid; hopin, mayhap the faver m'y take a turn. 1896 *J A Folklore* ix, 35 Raisins are universally known as figs. 1933 GREENLEAF xxiv There would be. . .steamed pudding with 'figs' as they called raisins. T 169–65² And I went over there and got the pound o' figs and he filled up me two little hands.

2 Comb **fig duff**: boiled pudding containing raisins.
1923 CHAFE 23 [Under a law of 1916] 'Fig Duff' was to be served three times a week [to sealers]. 1952 SMITH 169 Items called for included fresh vegetables, soft bread now and again, 'fig duff' three times weekly.

fig pudding: see **fig duff**.
1869 MCCREA 84 For the Gordian knot of the first course was cut only to be once reravelled with gooseberry-tart and clotted cream—actually clotted cream, as good as Devonshire ever boasted of—fig-pudding, jellies, and tipsy-cake.

fig tit: raisins wrapped in a thin cloth and given to older babies to suck (M 68–18).

figged See FIGGY.

figgity See FIGGY.

figgy a also **figged, figgity** ['fʊɡɪd]. *Note*: figged duff/figgy duff are prob pron the same; figgity is the spelling of figged + y. *OED* figged ppl a (1720), figgy a 2 (1846, 1867); *EDD* fig sb¹ 2: figged, figgedy, figgy in comb with cake, duff, pudding s w cties. See also FIG.

Attrib, comb, cpd **figgy bread**: bread made with raisins as an ingredient; SWEET BREAD.
1931 BYRNES 101 Apples, oranges, generous slices of 'figgy' bread. T 141–65¹ Yes, sir, watered fish, and figged bread, and plain bread, and we'd enjoy ourselves. M 70–9 Another typical food is figgy bread, also

called sweet bread. It is simply ordinary home-made white bread, but with raisins, extra sugar, and sometimes molasses added. P 188–78 Some of the old people still come into the store and ask for a loaf of figgity bread.

figgy bun: small bread bun with raisins in it. See also BUN 1.

P 102–60 Around 1900 the [rum] puncheons faded out and the mug up of tea or coffee with a figged bun came into use. P 207–67 We'll throw out the figgy buns (in welcome) when the boat comes in the harbour.

figgy cake: unrisen dough and raisins fried as a small bun.

1933 MERRICK 281 Kay made some 'figgy cake,' which is simply the eternal bannock with a few raisins baked into it.

figgy duff: a boiled pudding containing raisins.

[1900] 1975 WHITELEY 57 Dinner—salt meat, turnip, and potatoes, figged duff (boiled in a cloth). [1911] GRENFELL 65 'Figgy duff,' a big boiling of family-mess pork, some crackers, a tin of condensed milk, a pot of real jam (not Labrador berries), and some apples. [1894–1929] 1960 BURKE (ed White) 35 "The Terra Nova Regatta": Where the figgy duffs are seen, / That would sink a brigantine. T 181/2–65 You'd have figgy duff, boy; all the figs go down to the bottom o' your bag; when they cut the duff he'd cut off [the bottom]—the other fellers'd get none o' the figs. 1977 BURSEY 24 Tuesday was 'duff day' and we must buy the necessaries. The duff was made of water and flour and a generous addition of raisins and all saturated with molasses. We called it a figged duff and it was indeed a luxury.

figgy loaf: see **figgy bread**. See also LOAF.

1931 BYRNES 110 . . .the Argus eyed raisin pudding, and the luscious white grapes, and the 'figgy' loaf, and all the other good things. P 207–67 A figgy loaf was put on the table for supper. M 70–21 Raisin bread (figged loaf), fruit breads and cookies would not be made until nearly Christmas, for freshness was the key to the former's goodness.

figgy pudding: plum pudding; see also **figgy duff**.

[1886] LLOYD 88 Plum puddings, which are known as 'figgy pudden,' are in great demand, as is also what is called 'sweetcake,' a concoction of flour, yeast, and molasses. 1887 *Telegram Christmas No* 9 A boiler. . .in which a big figgy pudding, rich with galores of suet and citron, was already undergoing the beginning of its long boil for to-morrow's [Christmas] dinner. 1937 DEVINE 21 Figgity-pudding. Raisin or plum pudding. T 141–65[1] Oh, yes, [we'd have] a figged pudding, yes. M 69–17 As a dessert there was sure to be a figged pudding with coady made of milk, sugar, and butter boiled in a pan.

figgy tit: raisins wrapped in a thin cloth and given to older babies to suck; FIG TIT (P 167–67).

figged toutin: see **figgy cake**. See also TOUTIN.

P 102–60 If the cook had any spare time a few figged toutons [were added] as a special treat.

figure n *EDD* ~ 2 Ir. In phr *go out in one's figure*: to go out in one's indoor clothing.

1941 DULEY 106 'Cold? Stuff and nonsense,' contra-

dicted her father. 'There's days you can go out in your figger.' P 108–74 It was warm enough yesterday to go out in your figure.

file n Cp *OED* foil sb[5]. A game in which players flick a knife.

T 255–66 'Charlie, you remembers that, play file?' 'Play file? Oh, yes.' [A game in which a knife or other sharp object is flicked or dropped from various positions. A sequence of throws in which the knife sticks in some surface three times wins the game.]

fill v *DC* ~ v (1954) for sense 1; *OED* v 18 fill-dike, ~ ditch (1611, 1869), *Weather Proverbs* (1883), pp. 93–4 'January fill dyke. . .February fill dike' for sense 4.

1 See variant at FULL v.

2 To weave strips of animal hide to form the webbing of a snowshoe.

[1886] LLOYD 78 The spaces outside the bars [of the snowshoe] are filled with more finely cut skin than the middle space, the Indian term for which is *tibeesh*. C 75–136 Babich: long, narrow strips of cow skin used to fill home-made snowshoes. 1979 *'Twas a way of life* 27 Once the racquets are garnished, they have to be filled—a mesh has to be woven in.

3 To wind twine on the implement used to knit a fish-net.

T 43/8–64 Then you could knit [a net] as fast as you like. If there was somebody there to fill the needles for you, you could knit out a needle in ten minutes. 1979 *'Twas a way of life* 130 Filling the needle.

4 Comb **fill-dike**: the month of February.

C 68–16 Around the last of January you will often hear people saying, 'Filldyke will soon be here.' [It] is a term used to mean the month of February [or] up until the middle of February. Q 71–4 ~ cold harsh weather of February. 'February always fills the dykes,' i.e. ditches or hollows.

filler n The last strake or plank to be placed on the hull of a boat or vessel.

T 43/8–64 You get on your garbets, the first [strake] along the keel, and the next one and the next one, and you wouldn't put on any more on top until you'd put in what was called the filler. That means the complete plank. C 66–5 The filler is the middle board between the binding strake and the clean strake. 1969 *Nfld Qtly* July, p. 19 ~ the last strake [or] plank, on either side of a boat, to be fastened.

filliday n also **fillady, phillida** *OED* fillady, filliday 'some bird in Nfld' obs (1622–1674). A small song-bird; cp the imitative name TICKLACE.

[1620] 1887 MASON 151 The Fowles are. . .Butters, blacke Birds with redd breastes, Phillidas, Wrens, Swallowes, Jayes, with other small Birds. [1622] 1623 WHITBOURNE [N.H. letter] The Fowles and Birds of the Land are Partriges, Curlues, Fillidaies, Blackbirds, Bulfinches, Larks, Sparrowes, and such like. Ibid 7 As also Filladies, Nightingales and such like small birds that sing most pleasantly.

filling n See also FILL. The skin webbing which forms the centre of a snowshoe (P 113–78).

[1886] LLOYD 78 The coarser filling of the middle space [of the snowshoe] is called *babeesh*.

fimble* n *OED* ~ sb² 'ring for fastening gate' obs (1597); cp *EDD* thimble 5. See also GIMBLE. Door hinge (P 37).

fin [= appendage on a fish] See VEN.

find v *OED* ~ 18, 19, *EDD* ~ 6 for sense 1; *OED* 7 b colloq or dial, *EDD* 4, *DAE* b for sense 2.

1 To provide or furnish (for oneself); to equip, maintain or supply with provisions or materials.

[1770] 1792 CARTWRIGHT i, 46 These men are engaged on, what is called, the shares: that is, they find their own provisions, and we furnish them with nets, &c, for the loan of which, we receive one half the produce of their labour; and, the other half, they engage to sell us at a stipulated price. 1819 ANSPACH 422 The crews of their largest craft consist of from thirteen to eighteen men; of these some are gunners, who, on finding their own guns, are admitted *birth* free; the rest pay generally forty shillings each for their birth. 1842 BONNYCASTLE ii, 162 The merchant finds the ship or vessel, the nets, and the provisions, in fact, the means of carrying on the fishery, which he supplies to the planter. 1923 GRENFELL 282 The generous advance of supplies given him enabled him to take in a less fortunate friend for the winter, and to 'feed and find' him in return for his labor. 1936 SMITH 13 Half the catches went to the skipper for finding and supporting the crew for the summer. P 148–64 [When they hire local guides] the sports find us in food.

2 To feel a sensation (of discomfort or pain); to suffer from.

1895 *Christmas Review* 12 [proverb] If you squeeze the sculpion, you'll find his thorns. 1924 ENGLAND 162 The doctor came along with an ice-blinded man following him, hands on the doctor's shoulders, eyes bandaged. 'Studdy [steady] me alang, sir,' said the victim. 'I find [feel] it like sand in me eyes.' 1940 SCAMMELL 7 "The Six Horse-power Coaker": Tom hove up the wheel, and he cussed a good deal / He cranked till he found of his heart. T 148–61 I finds me back. T 49–64 I walked on crutches for a spell—got on alright. Never found it after. T 75/6–64 I don't find anything—don't find the effects of the man being on my back, only back part of my legs are sore. 1970 JANES 25 [They] reached the point where Saul was telling her all about his bodily complaints. He 'found' his stomach, it seemed, and could get no satisfaction in his diet.

3 To act as midwife.

1933 MERRICK 320 Meanwhile we have visited every house in the village. The women all know Kay very well as she has treated many of their children when they were sick. She even 'found' some of them, that is, was midwife at their birth.

fine¹ v *OED* ~ v³ 7 rare (1888), *EDD* 11 for

sense 1. In phr *fine off*, ~ *out*: of the weather, to clear up, to become fine.

P 245–63 It's going to fine off later today. C 71–95 If it looked as if the sun would come out later, the people would say, 'It's going to fine out.'

fine² v past, p ppl: found. *ADD* found 2 (1903–). In court decision, to exact a payment.

P 148–61 I got found, but they got free.

finest kind n phr Colloquial formula indicating general approval; in the best state or condition; BEST KIND.

T 141/69–65² Anyway next day, yes, she's finest kind. Got in, put our salt back, put our salt aboard, put our traps back. Yes, she's pretty good. P 108–70 'How are you feeling now?' 'The finest kind.' P 157–73 'Have a good summer?' 'Finest kind.'

finger n *OED* ~ 5 (c1400–1850) for sense 1; finger-stall for cpd in sense 2.

1 The width of a finger used as a measure; a finger's length.

1842 JUKES i, 284 5 The scaling-gun is an immense affair. . . The men put in a great charge of powder and shot—frequently ten fingers' breadth. 1895 *J A Folklore* viii, 288 The gun kicked pow'ful an' I loads her agen, a light load not more'n six fingers. 1938 MACDERMOTT 60 The charge was gauged by testing with the ramrod, measuring by the breadth of the hand how many fingers' width the ramrod protruded from the muzzle. This was spoken of as 'measuring the fingers,' or 'the number of fingers.' T 43/4–64 You'd pour out the powder in your hand, you'd pour out so much and judge what was enough to make about five fingers in the gun. 1972 MURRAY 270 I recall my mother using her middle finger as a measure and giving the length of a stocking leg as being so many 'fingers' long instead of inches.

2 In names of infections: see BONE FINGER, SEAL ~ , SQUID ~ .

3 Comb **finger mitt**: woollen mitten with sheaths for the index finger and thumb (1971 NOSEWORTHY 198).

finger-stall: covering for an injured finger; STALL.

[1952] 1964 PEACOCK (ed) i, 130 "For the Fish We Must Prepare": Oh traps and trawls and finger-stalls, / Rubber boots and killick claws, / Some lines and twines and rope and coils, / You get sore hands and full of boils. P 167–67 ~ finger or thumb of glove removed and used as shield for wounded member of the hand. 1973 HORWOOD 10 He was knitting leaves for a cod-trap. Harry watched and wanted to learn. . . Now he was becoming familiar with the knitting needle and the finger stall.

fippar, fipper See FLIPPER.

fir See SNOTTY VAR, VAR.

fire n

1 A supply of cartridges or ammunition.

1924 ENGLAND 278 An arresting piece of news ran through the ship—a report that only one week's 'fire' was left. By this the hunters meant that only cartridges enough remained for a week more of shooting. 'Dey been wastin' fire,' claimed Bosun Mike, 'an' when de cattidges away, you'm done!'

2 Cpd fire-break: wide thoroughfare designed to impede the spread of fire.

[1820] 1895 PROWSE 410 Four Cross Streets or open spaces [sixty feet wide] to serve as Fire-breaks. [1846] 1965 *Am Speech* xl, 169–70 King's Beach fire-break, Hill of Chips fire-break. 1966 PADDOCK 86 In Carbonear only three exceptionally wide transverse roads are regularly called firebreaks.

fire-fight: fire-fighting operation.

T 100/1–64 [I] was on a fire-fight one time and we got caught in the fire.

fire-pot: heavy iron pot in which fire was made for cooking aboard a fishing-craft.

M 68–7 [The fire-pot] was a big iron pot with a hole in the side of it for ventilation.

fire-weed: spotted touch-me-not (*Impatiens capensis*) (1893 *N S Inst Sci* viii, 371).

firk v *OED* ~ 3 b obs for sense 1; *EDD* ~ 1 'move in a jerking manner; to scratch.'

1 To move about quickly, aimlessly.

1937 DEVINE 21 ~ to bustle about. 'What's the old man *firkin*' about there?' P 245–57 Firking around—pottering about.

2 Esp of fowl and other birds, to scratch, dig, stir up (something).

P 148–63 To cool off in the grass: 'The hens are firkin.' P 10–64 Get the besom and firk the dirt. M 68–22 We made our false faces and firked out all the old clothes we could find for mummering. C 70–21 If someone is nosy or is known to be always poking in where's he's not wanted he is said to 'be firking around.' C 71–16 He came upon a big flock of crows ferkin' in the dust.

first num Cp *EDD* go v 1 (6) the first go-off 'beginning, outset.' Phr *first along/first going off*: in the beginning; at first; cp LAST a: *last going off*.

1858 [LOWELL] i, 199 'Izik,' I says, as soon as ever I could speak—for I was dumb-foundered entirely, first goun off. . . 1924 ENGLAND 63 I'll get ye a rope an' gaff, me son, an ye can go on ice alang o' me, killin' swiles. . . Ye mightn't like dat, first-alang, an' it might putt ye in a fluster. T 181/2–65 An' first along, when there was no wheels—I was never into one (without wheels).

fish n [fiʃ, fʊʃ, vʊʃ] *Cent* ~ [1] n 5 'codfish: so called by Cape Cod and Cape Ann fishermen' (1890), *DC* esp Nfld (1861–) for sense 1; for combs. in sense 3: cp *DAE* ~ box; *Cent* ~ book; *OED* ~ flake (1837–), *DC* (1818–); *NID* ~ fly; *Cent* ~ fork; *OED* ~ house (a) obs (1485, 1701), *DAE* (1651–), *DC* 1 (1934–); *DC* ~ pile (Nfld: 1861); *Cent* ~ prong; cp *OED* ~ room naut (1815, 1850); *Cent* ~ stage, *DC* 2 Nfld (1910–);

Cent ~ store. *Fish* combinations expressing condition, cure, seasonal or geographical occurrence, etc, are listed alphabetically: cp BANK, FALL, GREEN, SALT FISH, SUMMER. See also FISHING and its combs.

1 Cod (*Gadus morhua*).

[(1497) 1962 *Cabot Voyages* 210 [tr] They assert that the sea there is swarming with fish, which can be taken not only with the net, but in baskets let down with a stone, so that it sinks in the water.] [1583] 1940 *Gilbert's Voyages & Enterprises* ii, 392 [Hayes' narrative] Where being usually at that time of the yere, and untill the fine of August, a multitude of ships repairing thither for fish, we should be relieved abundantly with many necessaries. 1610 *Willoughby Papers* 9a/330 . . .and allso Five pounds p[er] Cent upon all goods by them shipped oute from thence other then fishe and other necessaries requesite to fishinge. [1663] 1963 YONGE 57 They bring the fish at the stage head, the foreshipman goes to boil their kettle, the other two throw up the fish on the stage-head by pears [pews]. [1786] 1792 CARTWRIGHT iii, 199 A very poor voyage of fish has been killed at this place. 1842 *Monthly Rev* 107 At dinner, the Newfoundlanders will ask you whether you will take 'herring or fish?'—'salmon or fish?' meaning by the latter nothing more, and nothing less than cod. [1848] 1915 *Decisions of the Supreme Court of Newfoundland* 22–5 The word 'fish' without further addition means in the Newfoundland trade cod-fish. . . Verdict for the plaintiff. 1858 [LOWELL] i, 74 She had given her lesson to her little sister, who was no great proficient at learning, and who was, by degrees, (like some other children, with other words,) getting broken of making 'c - o - d' spell 'fish.' 1887 *Colonist Christmas No* 17 As you lay with your head over the gunwale, thinking yourself the most miserable of human beings, you hated the [vocation] that could give you—fish plenty and price good—your ten pounds a day. 1912 CABOT 78 The Spracklins had fish; namely, cod. Nothing is fish to a Newfoundlander but cod,—cod alone. Salmon are salmon, trout are trout, the same with herring, caplin, and the rest; but to him cod only is Fish. [1930] 1980 *Evening Telegram* 14 June, p. 6 Fish and bait are scarce at Port aux Basques, a few fish were taken at Sagona yesterday. [1952] 1965 PEACOCK (ed) i, 130 "For the Fish We Must Prepare": The winter will soon be past b'ys, / Look out for maggots and flies, / Summer time is drawing near, / For the fish we must prepare. T 194/5–65 I went over and pulled my trap, and he was right full of herring—they was meshed in the vees, meshed in the skirts. I never witnessed the like; that's herring, not fish. T 210/12–65 When we speak about fish 'tis always cod-fish; that's what we calls fish. 1974 SQUIRE 28 Shortly after the war. . .the price of fish fell to a low ebb. 1981 *Evening Telegram* 9 Mar, p. 6 'Fish,' said the local chap in answer to a visitor's question, 'fish is fish'. . .that is to say, codfish.

2 In var collocations and phr *a big fish day*: a successful day's cod-fishing.

1909 BROWNE 251 It was very dark when we entered *Francis Harbor*, but every stage was aglow, as it had been 'a big fish day.'

fish and brewis [fʊʃ n̩ 'bruːz]: cod-fish cooked

with hard tack or sea biscuit. See also BREWIS,
FISHERMAN'S ~ .

[1785 SHEFFIELD 92 The fishermen live on fish and
fat pork, of which with hard biscuit, they make a dish
that is preferred by them to fresh provisions; neither
the bank fishing, nor the in-shore, or boat fishing, will
admit of any other but salt provisions.] [1900] 1975
WHITELEY 57 Breakfast—Porridge or fish and brewis
(hard tack). 1924 ENGLAND 117 'Fish an' brewis, how
many youse?' It rhymed, for brewis is pronounced
'bruise.' [1960] 1965 PEACOCK (ed) i, 123 "Fish and
Brewis": When springtime come round we'll go cutting
spruce, / We'll make just enough to have fish and
brewis, / If the cutting is bad then we'll go in the hole, /
There's no other redemption but live on the dole.
T 75/6–64 [We'd] carry a stock o' hard bread, and make
brewis out o' the hard bread. You often heard of brewis, fish an' brewis. 1975 COOK 10 He's jest like one of
the family. Eats his bit of fish and brewis. Jest loves a
salt pork dinner. 1979 POTTLE v I was a child of that
Canadian province-to-be where the attachment of the
word 'dirty' to politics was as natural as the affinity of
fish and brewis.

fish-and-fog-land: jocular name for Newfoundland.
1869 MCCREA 124 Fish-and-fog-land was, about this
time, in a denser fog than usual.

fish and vang: cod cooked with fat pork. See
also VANG.
1842 JUKES ii, 68 We dined on 'fish and vang,' which
being interpreted means cod-fish and salt pork cut into
'junks' and boiled together, and with a mealy potato it
is really a most excellent dish. 1909 BROWNE 294 We
dined. . .off 'fish and vang'. . .a delicacy known only to
Labrador fishermen. P 245–55 ~ Codfish and fatback
pork.

fish or no fish: an expression of determination:
regardless of circumstances.
P 108–70 Please god, we'll be married in the fall, fish
or no fish!

fish upon the gang-boards: fully loaded with
cod.
1792 CARTWRIGHT *Gloss* i, x [There are] fish upon
the gangboards. An expression used by fishermen to
denote, a boat being completely laden with fish; to
shew which, they bring in two or three upon the Gang-
boards.

3 Attrib, comb, cpd **fish barrel**: wooden container for a designated quantity of cod-fish; cp
BARREL.
1979 TIZZARD 81 Here my father made fish barrels
of different sizes: four quintals, two quintals and one
quintal.

fish barrow: a flat, rectangular wooden frame
with handles at each end for two men to carry
cod-fish; BARROW[1].
1897 *J A Folklore* x, 212 [A] *tommy nogger* [is] a
frame usually of wood, but sometimes of iron, on
which to rest the fish-barrow when the fish is being
weighed. 1936 SMITH 38 Mr Apsey gave me orders to
get the schooner ready for dry fish, and we began ballasting her and putting dunnage on board, also rinds,
fish barrows, fish beams and weights. M 71–103 Fish

barrows, two shafts with a boarded mid-section, were
used by two men to carry fish long distances. 1976
CASHIN 61 I was put to work at varied jobs such as carrying the fish barrow and stowing dry fish in the holds
of boats.

fish beach: an expanse of beach levelled for the
drying of salt cod; BAWN.
1971 NOSEWORTHY 198 ~ A rocky beach on which
fish is spread to dry.

fish-beam: a scale for weighing dried cod (see
1936 quot at **fish barrow**).

fish beetle: rove beetle (*Staphylinus villosus*).
See **fish-fly** below.
1840 GOSSE 136 There were numbers of Staphylini-
dae, the Fish-beetle of Newfoundland.

fish bird: Atlantic black-legged kittiwake or
the northern common tern, the appearance of
which in coastal waters heralds the commencement of fishing. See also STEARIN, TICKLACE.
T 31–64 Soon as [we] see the first tickleace, first little
bird come yer in the spring—you would see 'em round
the rocks—that'd be our mark, see, tickleace or a sarun
[stearin] is a fish-bird. Time to get away now! Time to
go on now!

fish board: wooden platform serving as a table
on a fishing boat.
M 69–17 [Cod-fish, salt meat and potatoes were] all
cooked while on the fishing grounds. It was all cooked
in a pot called a bo's kettle, a corruption of boat's kettle, and thrown out on the gang boards, or a properly
made board called a fish board. Each fisherman took
his spot on the board and ate away until it was all
finished.

fish boil: blister, sore or inflammation common
among fishermen, whose skin is often in contact
with salt water; WATER PUP.
1912 CABOT 80 Poor Spracklin, his arms and wrists
set with fish boils, 'pups' in the vernacular, slept with
his bandaged arms raised clear of all touch.

fish book: ledger in which a fish-dealer records
quantity of cod received from a fisherman.
1976 CASHIN 50 First the fish had to be landed from
the several vessels, schooners or boats, culled by specially sworn cullers, tallied by a special tallyman and
each evening the tallyman came to the office and gave
in his returns to Jim Foley, who had charge of the large
fish book. This book gave the names, the quantities in
quintals of the various qualities of fish received from
each dealer or fisherman.

fish-box: wooden receptacle in fishing stage
where cod are placed for washing and salting
after being headed, gutted and split.
T 43–64 There'd be what they call a cut-throat and a
header and two splitters, and possibly you'd have
somebody keepin' what they call a fish box full, to the
end of the splittin' table. T 141/67–65[2] Now you rigs out
and makes your swabs and makes your fish boxes an'
splittin' tables. 1971 NOSEWORTHY 198 ~ A square
box, open on one side and closed on three sides. Those
boxes are kept. . .on a stage, in rows by the walls,
where fishermen salt down each successive day's fish
and keep them through various stages of drying. 1975
BUTLER 32 So we landed my stuff and Charlie's down

there by Man-of-War Brook where he lived. [We] puts it on the wharf and turned a fish box over it.

fish breeches: cod-fish roe; BREECHES.

C 71–116 Fish britches is the name given to fish roe or spawn—quite a delicacy.

fish-cask: a type of wooden barrel for the export of dried and salted cod.

T 90–64 The fish cask: we had local names for these. The donkey was the one you put the large small fish [in]. 1975 RUSSELL 52 How was I to know that a good firm birch hoop off a five quintal fish cask wouldn't make a reasonable substitute for these crinolines? 1977 *Decks Awash* vi (3), p. 50 I've come home in the fall and gotten a job across the Bay cutting fish cask hoops. We'd have two bundles of 24 hoops at a time and you'd bring them out, land them, cleave them, draw them, ring them, put them together, and after all that, you'd get 20¢ a bundle, about 5¢ an hour.

fish colony: Newfoundland; see COLONY.

1869 MCCREA 119 So for this time the authority of the Fish colony was handled ostensibly with success.

fish culler: one employed to sort dried and salted cod into grades by cure, quality and size; CULLER.

[1870] 1899 *Nfld Law Reports* 363 John Cuddihy, late of St John's, fish culler, who died at that place in the year 1841. . . 1977 BURSEY 184 A fish culler joined her to cull the fish on the Labrador.

fish doctor: crustacean parasite on cod (*Aega psora*).

1925 *Dial Notes* v, 331 ~ A small marine animal with hard shell. M 69–7 Fish doctors are [like] shrimps and are the colour of bright orange. They average about an inch long [and] are found on codfish who are wounded.

fish dog: a skilled, experienced fisherman.

T 43/4–64 I moved to Fogo when I was eleven years old and went with an old sea captain there, an old fisherman, fish dog. T 148–65 Now the next year I used to go fishin' again with some other man, [and] another feller next year, old fish dog.

fish drier: see **fish flake**.

P 214–74 They used to sit down in under the fish driers all along the shore. You walk along the shore under the fish driers we used to call them.

fish drum: a cylindrical wooden container in which dried cod are packed for shipment; DRUM n.

1936 DEVINE 104–5 Michael Lawlor, an apprentice cooper at Frank Boggan's cooperage, was coming down to Harvey's premises with a cart load of fish drums. 1978 *Evening Telegram* 7 Aug, p. 6 [The arch] was constructed entirely of fish drums (i.e. barrels for shipping codfish) to a height of thirty feet.

fish('s) face: the fleshy part of a cod's head eaten as a delicacy; CHEEK, FACE, JOWL, SCULP.

1924 ENGLAND 315 Fishes' faces. Cod heads. T 178–65 And they had cods' heads cooked, fishes' faces; that's what they had cooked. 1971 *Daily News* 9 Nov, p. 4 I had tended to confuse cod cheeks with the meat in the jawbone which bears the curious local name of 'fishes faces.'

fish-flake: elevated platform for drying salted cod; FLAKE.

[1766] 1971 BANKS 147 [St John's] is Built upon the side of a hill facing the Harbour Containing two or three hundred houses & near as many fish Flakes interspersed. [1794] 1968 THOMAS 70 Here are about Twenty Fishermen's Hutts, a Fish Room and a Fish Flake. 1818 CHAPPELL 45 Numerous supporters, exactly resembling *Kentish* hop-poles, are first fixed in the ground; over these is placed a horizontal platform of similar poles; and the whole is finally overspread with a covering of dry fern. This sort of structure is called, by the fishermen, a *Fish Flake*. 1873 *Maritime Mo* i, p. 435 In almost every spot where a fishing boat can find shelter, the rough stage and 'fish-flake,' for the landing and drying of cod, may be seen. 1912 *Nfld Qtly* Christmas, p. 26 Another feature of the place, striking to me, was the low fish flake, which seems a very sensible idea. 1938 MACDERMOTT 36 The men were expert at walking on such 'fish-flakes.'

fish('s) float: the air bladder of a cod-fish; SOUND.

1895 *J A Folklore* viii, 289 It looks just like a vish's float.

fish-fly: rove beetle (*Staphylinus villosus*).

1846 TOCQUE 278 Rove-beetles are now swarming every fishing establishment; they are generally called fish-flies. T 370–67 This was a cloud, like the locusts in the bible, a cloud of what we call fish flies. 1979 NEMEC 274 The resulting stench and 'fish flies' can, with a southerly wind, become a vexatious nuisance to the entire community.

fish-fork: a sharp metal implement with one or two tines attached to a wooden handle and used to throw cod from a boat to a 'stage'; PEW[1].

1942 *Grand Bank U C School* 35 Fish fork. T 14/20–64 He stuck the fork in the bottom of the boat, the fish fork, and lay and rest on un, and fell down in the skiff asleep. 1971 NOSEWORTHY 199 ~ A large steel fork with one [or] two prongs.

fish glass: tube-shaped device with glass in bottom for viewing fish underwater.

1895 GRENFELL 71 The seine master stands, fish-glass in hand, high on the bow of the seine skiff. 1956 *Evening Telegram* 12 Dec, p. 4 An important ancillary piece of equipment in fishing the codseine was the 'fish glass,' more commonly known today as the water glass, which was employed in peering under the surface to locate shoals of cod. T 80/3–64 A fish-glass, sir, is like a length o' stove-pipe, an' he have a eye-piece soldered on the top part of un so as he'd fit around your face. You'd see over the bottom when you be lookin' down through un. 1971 CASEY 62–3 The cod seine was shot from the skiff around a school of fish which had been located with a 'fish glass.'

fish halfpenny: a small nineteenth-century halfpenny piece.

1937 DEVINE 21 ~ A coin current in the sixties with the figure of a split codfish on one side.

fish hawk: see **fish dog**.

1904 *Nfld Qtly* Dec, p. 18 He had in his day been a successful fish-hawk and sealing skipper.

fish-house: (a) a small building for storing dried and salted cod; (b) a movable box-like structure to cover piled cod-fish.

[1812] 1966 *Evening Telegram* 27 May, p. 6 Fish house. 1832 MCGREGOR i, 171 The sea broke in upon the lands where fish-houses, flakes &c., were erected, and occasioned vast loss and destruction. 1891 PACKARD 132 The fish-houses were rude structures of one low shed, roofed with turf and built on piles, reminding us somewhat of pictures of the ancient pile-dwellings of prehistoric Switzerland. T 36–64 Some people haves fish-houses, little small houses made right square and turned down over these faggots, with handles on 'em where you can lift 'em off an' on. M 69–27 As the fish dried, it was gradually made up in larger piles, and fish houses (wooden boxes made with a steep roof so the rain would run off) placed over them to prevent rain from wetting the fish again. 1970 PARSONS 40 Most of the fish houses at The Point were all built in the last few years with new lumber, and the whole place had a texture far ahead of many other places on the coast.

fish killer: a fisherman, esp a 'skipper,' known for catching great quantities of fish.

1909 *Tribune Christmas No* 15 Even when the 'jowlers'—the big fish-killers—were successful, and had money on the merchants' hands, they were no better off. 1928 *Nfld Qtly* Oct, p. 31 His early life was first spent with his brother at the cod fishery until he became Master himself and for a number of years took a foremost place among the big fish killers of this country. 1936 SMITH 29 [We] arrived at Ramah at dark on Saturday evening. There were some six or seven vessels there from Bonavista Bay, mostly Barbours, thorough fishermen and fish-killers. T 141–65[2] He was a real fish killer. 1975 BUTLER 51 George Rodway was the biggest fish killer in Placentia Bay in his day.

fish-lead: lead weight used in hook-and-line fishing for cod; LEAD[1].

T 203–65 That's a fish lead for weight—droppin' to bottom.

fish-locker: compartment in a boat for stowing the catch; LOCKER.

1866 WILSON 338 In removing to our stations, our conveyance was a fishing-boat, our luggage would be stowed in the fish-lockers, and covered with a tarpaulin to keep it from the wet.

fish-loft: area of a fishing-stage for storing dried cod; cp LOFT.

[1870] 1973 KELLY 27 Our morning congregation assembled in the fish-loft of the Messrs Hunt. M 68–24 The men gather in fish-lofts, wood-stores, etc, to hear and tell their famous tall tales or work interests. 1972 MURRAY 249 When fish had dried to a certain stage, it was stored in the 'fish store' or 'fish loft' for a few days, 'to work.'

fish-maker: person engaged in curing cod on the flakes.

T 43–64 The old people used to say two for one—that was the way they'd weigh it out to the fish-makers. T 194/7–65 I had to wire the merchant and ask if he would be good enough to go around to the fish-makers and pay 'em in advance for so many quintals. M 71–94 We used to have so high as twenty-five or thirty fish-makers.

fish-making: the process of curing cod-fish; cp MAKE.

1891 *Holly Branch* 12 The crew were mostly on the shares—half their fish—and paid so much for fishmaking. 1936 SMITH 128 We spread our first fish, the weather being fairly good for fish-making. T 141/68–65[2] You wouldn't use birch rine, not for fish-makin' very much. 1977 BUTLER 60 When men were too old to continue fishing, the only way they could earn a few dollars was fish-making (washing and drying codfish) for merchants on their own private fishing rooms, at twenty-five cents per quintal.

fish merchant: see MERCHANT.

fish-mouth cap: a knitted cap covering most of the head.

T 94–64 They used to make caps, fish-mouth caps for the winter-time, and a big piece goin' down here make a scarf and all, for the woods.

fish('s) pea(s): small portion of the viscera of a cod-fish, eaten as a delicacy; CHITLINGS.

1971 NOSEWORTHY 199 Fishes pea, fish pea, fishy pea. Small, pink or red, edible viscera in the stomach of a codfish, shaped like a pair of pants.

fish-pen: wooden bin for salting cod in a fishing-stage.

M 68–20 The day's catch was brought in and taken to the stage |and| gutted, split and washed. Then it was spread out in the fish-pen and salted.

fish-pile: a stack of split and salted cod at various stages of the drying process; FAGGOT n, PILE n.

1861 DE BOILIEU 37 When sufficiently dry, a fine warm day is chosen to lay the fish out, singly, on a large stage; and during the hottest hours they are made up into a 'fish pile,'—which is a large quantity of dry fish, built up in the form of a round haystack. [1910] 1930 COAKER 26 We respectfully contend that rinding trees to provide covering for fish piles or other uses should be prohibited.

fish-pipe: oesophagus of a seal.

1873 CARROLL 35 I procured several of these and sent the same to Scotland to have them dressed, and ascertained that the gullet or fish pipes of all seals would make beautiful gloves, &c.

fish pound: wooden compartment, or container, in which cod are placed during the curing process; POUND.

P 102–60 If fine they were spread out again and in the evening taken to the fish pound. M 65–9 ~ A large square wooden container used by the bank fishermen in which to wash their salted fish. Q 67–11 ~ area of stage divided by boards for salting fish.

fish prong: see **fish-fork** above; PRONG n.

P 102–60 A shore crew would unload [the lighters] with fish prongs on top of the stage-head. T 84–64 I had a gaff that was made out of a fish prong; he was a nice slender gaff, and the start on it was exactly the same as a fish prong. 1975 *Evening Telegram* 2 July, p. 3 Normally, one good-sized cod would fill this fish prong, but Petty Harbour fisherman Richard Clements shows just how many small fish are being caught in the traps.

fish-proud: self-satisfied because of a large catch of cod or good profits from the fishery.

1936 SMITH 84 I was beginning to feel lively, and 'fish proud,' having secured 20 quintals in two days. C 75–28

'Fish proud' is applied to a man who has made a good season of fishing, and he praises himself on a job well done.

fish room: (a) see **fish-house** (a) above; (b) see FISHING ROOM; ROOM.

[1775] 1976 O'NEILL ii, 724 The Justice of the Peace for Harbour Main, Charles Garland, was ordered to fine Katem 'the sum of fifty pounds, and to demolish the said fish-room or store-room where mass was said, and I do likewise order the said Michael Katem to sell all the possessions he had or holds in this harbour.' 1765 WILLIAMS 9 [The Irish] were in Possession of above three Quarters of the Fish Rooms and Harbours of the Island. 1924 ENGLAND 255 'The planter's eye spreads the water horse.' (The boss of a fish room gets the fish quickly spread.)

fish scale: a diminutive five-cent silver coin minted 1865–1947 (P 133–58).

fish-screw: a device for packing dried cod in 'drums' tightly before shipment (1883 *Fish Exhibit Cat*[4] 174).

1975 BUTLER 70 A fish screw was an iron stand set up on the floor of the fish store. A large screw was placed in the center of the metal stand with four handles. The drum of fish would be placed under the screw and four men would turn the handles.

fish stage: an elevated structure at the water's edge comprising wharf and rooms for the reception and processing of fish, storage of gear, etc; STAGE.

1842 BONNYCASTLE ii, 165 It is impossible in so scattered a population, with such amazing extent of fishing bank and shore, that he whose establishment is in St John's, or in one of the out-harbours or settlements, could attend to the large import and export trade upon which he subsists, and at the same time employ himself or his clerks on a fish stage in twenty different places, or in perhaps a hundred boats at sea. [1870] 1973 KELLY 17 We were, therefore, kept prisoners in our unsavoury mooring-place, between two fish-stages, in this narrow harbour. [c1900] 1978 RLS 8, p. 25 ~ a shed near waters edge covered usually with sticks & rinds or bows where fish is landed from the boats, & then split & headed at Splitting table, before being salted into bulk in the stage.

fish store: a structure or area of a fishing-stage or merchant's premises in which dried cod is placed ready for collection or export; STORE.

[1812] 1966 *Evening Telegram* 27 May, p. 6 [To be sold:] dry goods store, net loft. . .cook room, fisherman's house, fish store, salt store, small salmon plantation. 1904 *Nfld Qtly* Dec, p. 17 Not infrequently a sail loft, or the upper storey of a fish store was dubbed with the exalted name of a school. 1942 *Little Bay Islands* 12 James built a new store where the Company's fish store now is. 1975 BUTLER 70 A fish screw was an iron stand set up on the floor of the fish store. 1977 BURSEY 95 The gallery of the fish-store a two story structure was lined by a cheering crowd.

fish ticket: record of a fisherman's landings, given him by dealer as a receipt for later payment; WEIGHT NOTE.

M 67–10 When their turn came the fish were hoisted, weighed and fishermen given a fish-ticket. On this ticket the number of pounds, the kind of fish and the value were marked.

fish-top: see **fish-house** (b).

1979 TIZZARD 88 When [the drying cod-fish] was taken up in the evening it would be covered with a tarpaulin. . . Some [fishermen] used fish tops, a little house to cover two or three quintals of fish when in a pile.

fish trade: collectively, the commercial enterprise of the fishery; the fish merchants; TRADE.

[1694]1895 PROWSE 188 Amongst the Trades not yet lost is the Newfoundland fish trade. 1765 WILLIAMS 11 Even some went so far as to think *Boston* in *New England* a very convenient Place to carry on the Fish Trade. 1972 NEMEC 164 The potential threat posed by 'the Union,' as it is called, to the traditional control of 'the fish trade' over prices. . .

fish tub: a 'puncheon,' sawn in half, used to hold split cod in salt; cp TUB.

T 36/8–64 Puncheon tubs, anywhere from eighty to one hundred and ten gallons, would be sawed in two halves for fish tubs. 1979 TIZZARD 291 The fish tub was a half of a beef or pork barrel. The fish tub full meant that we would have caught a half a quintal of codfish when dried, fifty six pounds.

fish weather: overcast, damp and chill weather; cp CAPLIN SCULL.

1906 DUNCAN 15 It was 'fish weather,' as the Ruddy Cove men say—gray, cold and misty.

fish weight: one of the iron objects used in the weighing of dried cod (P 245–71).

P 188–78 The fish-weights would also be used by the drivers to tether the horse and box-car to.

fish v

1 To engage in the sea-fishery, esp for cod, as opposed to angling in fresh water for trout.

[1583] 1940 *Gilbert's Voyages & Enterprises* ii, 328 [Hayes' narrative] At Sea towards the East there is nothing els but perpetuall mists, and in the Sea it selfe, about the Banke (for so they call the place where they find ground fourty leagues distant from the shore, and where they beginne to fish) there is no day without raine. 1620 WHITBOURNE 51 Yet there are many other excellent good Harbors where our nation useth to fish, lying betweene them both, which are very good for ships to moore fast at anchor. [1663] 1963 YONGE 60 Nor are the fishermen better to pass, who row hard and fish all day, and every second night take nets and drive to catch herrings for bait. [1794] 1968 THOMAS 170 It was common for a Boat's Crew to be Fishing all Summer for a Master who supply'd them with a few necessarys, the men letting their Wages remain until the Season was over. [1886 LLOYD 72 On Stormy days when the cod fishery cannot be prosecuted. . .the fishermen go 'trouting,' as they say.] 1895 PROWSE 21 The bank or deep sea codfishery was carried on very differently. . . The men all fished from the ship, each in a sort of gangway hung over the side of the vessel. [1951] 1965 PEACOCK (ed) i, 54 "Feller From Fortune": Oh—Sally got a bouncin' new baby, / Father said that he didn't care, / 'Cause she got that from the feller from Fortune / What was down here fishin' the year. T 54–64 That summer I fished ashore [inshore] on the easter side o' Hilliard's Harbour.

2 Phr *fish cross-handed*: see CROSS HANDED.

fish for stamps: to engage in the fishery for a period sufficient to qualify one for unemployment insurance; cp STAMP.

1979 POTTLE 63 It is a far cry from. . .seeing with mature insight our condition in terms of its hazards and its opportunities—to be looking always for our salvation to government dollars or 'fishing for stamps.'

fisherman n

Attrib, comb **fisherman's basket**: (a) pitcher-plant (*Sarracenia purpurea*) (1956 ROULEAU 30); (b) slipperwort (*Calceolaria*) (Q 72–1).

fisherman's brewis: cod-fish cooked with hard tack or sea biscuit and pork fat. See also BREWIS, FISH AND BREWIS.

T 80/2–64 He keeps up the old tradition. Every Sunday morning—fisherman's brewis, just as regular as the mornin's comes. P 9–73 A recipe for fisherman's brewis, schooner-style, for five or six hungry men: two cakes of hard bread per man, two plump codfish with head off and entrails removed, one piece of fatback pork. 1978 *Evening Telegram* 7 Aug, p. 4 [Hc] promises [visitors to Bonavista] a parade, races and feeds of fisherman's brewis. 1979 TIZZARD 278 In the boat sometimes my father carried a cooking pot and a frying pan, and with that a piece of fat back pork in the bread box. This meant that he could have fish and brewis or fisherman's brewis, whichever was preferable. . . The pork would be fried out in the frying pan. When the codfish was cooked the brewis and pork fat would all be thrown in the pot together and mashed up, thus making fisherman's brewis.

fisherman's holiday: (a) a holiday to mark the end of the fishing season in the autumn and the return of the migratory vessels to England; (b) enforced cessation from fishing because of storms.

1888 *Colonist Christmas No* 10 In this capacity [the naval officer] erected in that harbour four forts and mounted one of them. . .with six cannon. Here [c1770] on Fishermen's Holiday, Coughlan drilled his men. 1909 BROWNE 252 [After the gale there] was a 'fishermen's holiday.' 1917 *Christmas Echo* 19 . . .regret for the prosperous fisheries and good old times gone bye; for the rude but hearty cheer that enlivened the walls of a cookroom on a fisherman's holiday, and above all for the chorus and song of the blithe Corkman. 1933 GREENLEAF (ed) 243 "The Crowd of Bold Sharemen" is said to have been composed about fifteen years ago by a group of young fellows from Little Bay Islands on the East Coast, while they were having fisherman's holidays, i.e. were storm-bound, down on the French Shore. 1971 CASEY 233 When the evening would begin to get long, or sometimes now a stormy day in the fall of the year when they wouldn't be able to get out in boat and the weather would be too bad for spreading fish, and all that sort of thing. It would be more or less what they call a fisherman's holiday.

fisherman-planter: a fisherman and owner of fishing premises, boat or small vessel who, sup-

plied by a merchant, engages a crew to work on the share system; PLANTER.

1888 *Colonist Christmas No* 10 Sims himself. . .was a fine specimen of the fisherman-planter. 1976 CASHIN 1 Grandfather Richard Cashin was a fisherman planter in his settlement, and Grandfather Pierre Mullowney was also a fisherman planter, as well as being one of the most successful sealing skippers of his time. 1977 BURSEY 87 The *Lobelia* must be brought so near as possible to the small harbours where the fishermen planters were.

fisherman's room: see ROOM.

fisherman's trawl: see **fisherman's basket** above (Q 72–1).

fishery n   *OED* ~ 1, 2 (1677–; 1699–); *DAE* ~ 1 a, b, (1677–; 1699–; 1682–); *DC* ~ 1, 2, 3 (1765–; 1807–). See also FISHING.

1 The marine fishing industry; freq qualified by the location where fish are caught, the season of the operation, the technology used, and the species caught. See also BANK, BOAT, COAST, COD, FALL, INSHORE, LABRADOR, NORTHERN, SEAL, SHIP, SHORE, SUMMER, TRAP[1], WESTERN, WINTER.

[1637] 1895 PROWSE 143 And also shall have full power and liberty to build any fort or forts for defence of said Country and fishing and shall have timber where it may be spared to the least prejudice to the fishery. [1653] ibid 167 You are upon the close of this sumers fishery to returne back into England. [1732] 1976 HEAD 57 Many People from Bonavista being removed to Fogo, a Harbour 30 or 40 Leagues to ye Northward. . .& being very Successful in the Fishery there, tis Expected yt Many More will soon follow. 1792 CARTWRIGHT iii "Labrador: A Poetical Epistle" [4] The Codfish now in shoals come on the coast, / (A Fish'ry this, our Nation's chiefest boast) / Now numerous Caplin croud along the Shore; / Tho' great their numbers, yet their Foes seem more. 1839 MURRAY ii, 186 The fishery. . .decidedly rivals the timber-trade, especially when we include the capture of seals, which in mercantile language is considered a branch of it. 1852 ARCHIBALD 3 In the year 1850, the outfit for this [seal] fishery from Newfoundland consisted of 229 vessels, of 20,581 tons, employing 7919 men. 1873 CARROLL 39–40 If it is a winter fishery, very little salt is used. 1883 *Our Country* 23 Nov, p. 2 The fishing [in the herring fishery] was attended to by the cod fishermen as an adjunct to 'the fishery,' as codfishing was termed. 1907 ibid 24 May, p. 2 A considerable number of men were employed in the prosecution of these salmon fisheries, which were at first very lucrative. 1902 *Christmas Bells* 14, 19 On a lovely morning in August, just after the close of the lobster fishery three summers ago. . . A schooner, bound to Fortune Bay to engage in the herring fishery, happened to call into the harbour. 1912 *Christmas Chimes* 11 They had a hard time of it for the first few years, but eventually became the most important firm carrying on the seal, codfishery and also herring fishery in Newfoundland. 1924 ENGLAND 15 A bumper 'fishery,' as they call it— for Newfoundlanders insist that seals are fish!—feeds thousands of hungry mouths ashore. 1954 INNIS 496 The extension of trade in the outports and the development of industries subordinate to the cod fishery. . .have offset the trend toward centralization. P 82–72 'How's the fishery this year?' 'Not so good. Them that get ar'n, ain't no better than them that get nar'n.'

2 Attrib **fishery servant**: a man or woman indentured or engaged on 'shares' or wages for a period in the fishery.

1887 *Colonist Christmas No* 7 The merchants of St John's memorialized the Governor, expressing their sorrow that the number of public houses had been reduced from twenty-four to twelve, 'which has considerably decreased the strength of civil power in this place, as every publican served the office of constable,' and fishery servants waiting their passage 'home' cannot find houses enough for their entertainment, and lie about the streets and under flakes, 'endangering the town to fire and continued broils.' P 102–60 Two of the firm's sealers would be at Blanc Sablon for the summer and if a poor fishery around the first of August would be fitted with cod traps, boats, splitting tables, etc, and a number of fishery servants with sufficient supplies for a month or two.

fishing vbl n Cp *OED* ~ sb¹ 1 b (c1300–1814), *DAE* (1622–) for sense 1; for combs. in sense 2: *OED* admiral: ~ admiral (1708), *DC* Nfld (1718–); *DAE* ~ bank(s) (1789–), *DC* (1765–); *DC* ~ berth (Nfld: 1916); *OED* ~ boat (1732–), *DAE* (1705–); *DAE* ~ boot (1894); *OED* ~ ground (1641), *DAE* (1668–); *DAE* ~ lead (1661); *DC* ~ post (1807–); *OED* ~ room (1879), *DC* Nfld (1713–); *OED* ~ season (1699), *DAE* (1656–); *DAE* ~ shallop (1704–26); *OED* ~ ship (1785), *DAE* (1637–1708); *OED* ~ smack (1876–), *DAE* (1819–); *DAE* ~ stage (1705–), *DC* Nfld (1715–); *DAE* ~ station (1828–), *DC* (1832–); *OED* ~ trade (1662–), *DAE* (1636–); *DAE* ~ vessel (1684–); *DAE* ~ voyage (1682–).

1 The action or occupation of prosecuting the marine fishing industry, specif the cod-fishery.

[1578] 1895 PROWSE 34 The English are commonly lords of the harbour where they fish, and use all strangers' help in fishing if need require, according to an old custom of the country. [1583] 1940 *Gilbert's Voyages & Enterprises* ii, 406 Also Cod, which alone draweth many nations thither, and is become the most famous fishing of the world. 1620 WHITBOURNE 34 . . .those Ships and men so sent, may be so fitted and provided with Salt, Nets, Hooks, Lines and such like provisions, as those Ships and men are, which yeerely saile thither a fishing. [1653] 1895 PROWSE 168 That all provisions imported for sale necessarye for fishing be free for any person to buy. [1715] 1976 HEAD 79 It is almost entirely different from ye common way of fishing in other places. There must be large Boats to carry off ye fish taken by ye Little Ones. [1877] 1895 PROWSE 505 In return Great Britain had conceded to the United States the right of fishing in. . .Newfoundland waters in common with British subjects. [1929] 1933 GREENLEAF (ed) 241 "The Crowd of Bold Sharemen": For we were bound fishing in the Strait of Belle Isle / Our skipper wouldn't give us one stain of our ile. [1951] 1965

PEACOCK (ed) i, 105 "The Banks of Newfoundland": 'Twas east-be-south we steered, me b'ys, the Grand Banks for to find, / To prosecute the fishing there we all felt well-inclined. [1952] ibid i, 58 "Hard Times": Oh now comes the merchant to see your supply: / 'The fine side of fishing we'll have bye and bye, / Seven dollars for large and six-fifty for small.' / Pick out your West Indie, you got nothing at all, / And it's hard, hard times. C 71–98 When you ask someone how the fishing is (in reference to trouting in a pond or stream), they won't understand. To them fishing is strictly from the ocean.

2 Attrib, comb, cpd **fishing admiral**: the master of the first English migratory fishing vessel to reach a harbour in Newfoundland, exercising certain privileges for the season; ADMIRAL.

[1693] 1793 REEVES xii Any difference or controversy. . .shall be judged and determined by the fishing admirals. [1706] 1895 PROWSE 267 Fishing Admirals and masters of ships do not exactly observe the Rules of the Act. [1810] 1971 ANSPACH 7 With respect to the provisions in the 10th and 11th, of Wm. the 3rd. relative to the fishing Admirals, which, it is represented have long since. . . 1895 PROWSE 226 Mr Pearce, of Twillingate, who died not long ago, remembered as a boy seeing a man triangled—tied by the outstretched arms—and whipped by order of a fishing admiral.

fishing bank: an underseas elevation or shoal forming a fishing ground; BANK.

[1766] 1973 *Can Hist Rev* liv, 268 One of Cook's major discoveries was 'a fishing bank (hitherto unknown by fishermen),' located between the Penguin and Ramea Islands, and 'abounding with very large cod and at a time when they were very scarce on every other part of the coast.' 1818 CHAPPELL 51 In the fishing season, it is resorted to by at least 10,000 people, on account of the fishing banks. 1837 BLUNT 58 The whole bay and the adjacent coasts abound with cod, and extensive fishing banks lie all along the coasts. 1865 *Sailing Directions* 57 Off this point is a fishing bank. . .having from 20 to 36 fathoms over it. P 102–60 [The vessel] would steam out to the fishing bank and heading the tide at a very low speed. . .the twine would follow of its own accord.

fishing berth: a particular station on the fishing grounds assigned to or claimed by a vessel, boat, crew, or family; BERTH 3.

1916 DUNCAN 175 It is a long way for fame to carry—north to the uttermost fishing-berths of the Labrador.

fishing boat: a fishing craft of variable size, design and rig, used in the inshore fishery; BOAT.

1613 *Willoughby Papers* 17a, 1/2 We maye serve the fishinge fleete with boords to make fishinge boats whereof they bring good store yearely from England. 1620 WHITBOURNE 63 There are many men, yeerly, who unlawfully convey away other mens fishing boates, from the Harbour & place where they were left ye yeere before. 1819 ANSPACH 300 They even now, with evident signs of dread and horror, show a cove where upwards of two hundred fishing-boats perished, with all their crews. 1866 WILSON 287 The boats that used to be employed in this hazardous voyage [sealing] were open fishing-boats. 1954 INNIS 155–6 The fishing industry depended upon the initiative of the individual fisherman, and for the old incentive of profit sharing in the fishing ships, new devices were found. The fishing boat became the basic unit, and the wage or truck system was in part an adaptation to this unit. 1960 FUDGE 2 [The merchant] had one large fishing boat. . .of 20 tons.

fishing boot: a high leather boot formerly worn by fishermen. See also SMALLWOOD BOOT.

1936 SMITH 12 I shall never forget my first crop that I had—one pair of long-tongued fishing boots and a suit of oilskins, including a sou'wester. 1975 BUTLER 88 My son, you are going on a rough trip. Put on your knee high leather fishing boots and your heavy woolen cap, and strap your oilskins on your suitcase.

fishing crew: a group (of persons) engaged or 'shipped' by a merchant, planter or skipper to conduct the various branches and operations of fishing, usu on the share system. See also CREW.

1882 TALBOT 22 The vessel contained the principal portion of his own family. . .there, with his fishing crew of seven to eight men. 1966 PHILBROOK 60 Nipper's Harbour crews engaged in catching and curing fish are of two types: the trap crew made up of a skipper and three to five crew men; and the fishing crew, usually two men and formed by pairing of trap crew members. 1973 HORWOOD 11 The fishing crew, with the exception of Harry, abandoned the voyage and went home.

fishing establishment: in a coastal settlement, the business of a fish merchant, usu the branch of a firm with headquarters in St John's or Britain, comprising the premises and the operations of taking and shipping the catch in exchange for supplies to the fishermen; ESTABLISHMENT.

1846 TOCQUE 278 Rove-beetles are now swarming every fishing establishment. 1861 DE BOILIEU 44 The Labrador Fishing Establishment is also a general store, and when any one requires supplies the mode of dealing is entirely by barter. 1895 PROWSE 598 Cartwright and Darby had a fishing establishment at Cape Charles, beginning 1767. 1951 Nfld & Lab Pilot i, 318 Job's room, consisting of a fishing establishment with several prominent white houses and a flagstaff, stands on the eastern entrance point of the Rivière Blanc Sablon, on each side of which are wharves.

fishing fleet: the West Country-Newfoundland migratory fishing vessels. See also **fishing ship**.

[1583] 1940 Gilbert's Voyages & Enterprises ii, 401 [Hayes' narrative] Whither also came immediately the Masters and owners of the fishing fleete of Englishmen, to understand the Generals intent and cause of our arrival there. 1610 Willoughby Papers 17a, 1/2 When a saw-mill is rected here we maye serve the fishinge fleete with boords to make fishing boats whereof they bringe food store yearely from England. 1626 [VAUGHAN] The Golden Fleece 26 After the Fishing Fleetes are returned homewards, we are safe, for the windes are commonly from August out Westerly, whereby none can come to us.

fishing ground: an area of shoal water with abundant bait-fish, plankton, etc, where fishing is successfully carried out; GROUND.

[1683] 1976 HEAD 35 Though there be Harbours and conveniences on shoare for the making of Fish there is not fishing ground or can constantly be fish enough for so many Boates as they have kept. [1763] 1973 Can Hist Rev liv, 252 The island of St Pierre was 'as subject to fogs as any part of Newfoundland, yet if we may credit the late planters it is very convenient for catching and curing of cod fish, there being good fishing ground all round the Island.' 1819 ANSPACH 285 [There] is an elevated space giving from ten to twenty-five fathoms, which is designated by the appellation of Rough Fishing-ground. 1861 DE BOILIEU 27 You may observe some two hundred boats or more on the Fishing Ground, the occupants sitting, still and dark, against the clear, sparkling atmosphere. 1898 PROWSE 316 Any one who shall throw overboard or deposit upon any fishing ground or ledges in or near the coasts of Newfoundland or Labrador, any heads, entrails, bones or offal of codfish. Penalty, not exceeding $200, or in default of payment, imprisonment not exceeding 60 days. [1900 OLIVER & BURKE] 36 "Lines on the Sad Drowning": They left home Saturday morning, / On the fishing ground to go. 1937 DEVINE 62 'Cape St Mary's will pay for all.' A saying of the large number of fishermen who frequented this favourite fishing ground. 1960 FUDGE 10 We secured a baiting from the netters there, and in a short while were anchored on the fishing grounds. 1975 BUTLER 105 The island, situated out in the bay as it was, was much the same as a vessel anchored on the fishing grounds.

fishing jack: schooner-rigged decked vessel of from five to twenty-five tons; JACK[1].

[1883] 1898 Nfld Law Reports 516 This was a case of collision in which the plaintiff's fishing jack was run down by the defendant's schooner, and her hull damaged, and mainsail carried away &c. 1916 GRENFELL 137 It were only a fishing-jack, t' old Dayspring, us had. 1944 LAWTON & DEVINE 14 [Sealers could] tell how fast a vessel was going by listening to the swish of the log line over the taffrel. They could handle a brig like a fishing jack. P 243–56 ~ Boat next in size to the bully boat, usually about 10 tons, rigged with fore and aft sails.

fishing lead: a lead weight used in hook-and-line fishing; LEAD[1].

[1751–66] 1954 INNIS 181 [inventory] To fishing Leads 56 pounds. [1771] 1792 CARTWRIGHT i, 94 The woodmen were employed in new-casting, and ganging fishing leads. M 68–7 The fishing lead is used to sink the line and bait when you are fishing with a hand line. The lead varies in weight. If you are fishing in deep water a heavy lead would be used but in shallow water a lead half its size would be used.

fishing ledge: an underwater elevation, steep-to, frequented by cod; LEDGE.

[1778] 1863 PEDLEY 132 We. . .inform you of the dangerous situation which we at this time are in, as the enemy (say a brig of twelve guns) has been on the fishing ledge, and destroyed eight large shallops and craft. [1863] 1954 INNIS 397 We attribute the cause mainly to the custom adopted, of using Cod seines along the shore here, which runs almost in close proximity with our fishing ledges, impeding and proving a complete obstacle to our mode of fishing.

fishing plantation: area of foreshore and buildings upon it for the landing and curing of fish; PLANTATION, ROOM.

1828 MCGREGOR 209 [The Newfoundland dogs] are very serviceable in all the fishing plantations, and are yoked in pairs and used to haul the winter fuel home.

fishing post: see **fishing station**.

[1785] 1792 CARTWRIGHT iii, 72 I had informed my assignees, that the fishing-posts and the buildings thereon, were well worth a thousand pounds. [1862] 1878 TOCQUE 294 The proprietors of the vessels of these various classes draw lots every five years for the right of occupying the various fishing settlements on the coast; the best numbers select the best fishing posts, and so on to the least advantageous.

fishing premises: the waterfront stores, sheds, wharf and other facilities of a merchant or planter; PREMISES, ROOM.

1895 PROWSE 183 [He] thus put an end to the constant fighting that went on about the debateable subject of fishing premises, known in Newfoundland as *rooms*. 1938 *FPU (Twillingate) Minutes* 29 Dec It is impossible for fishermen to exist under present conditions and keep fishing premises, boats and gear in repair. 1975 BUTLER 60 Most were employed as fishermen while three or four worked on the room or the fishing premises as the merchant's premises were called in those early days.

fishing punt: an undecked boat, 20–25 ft. (6.096–7.62 m) in length, round-bottomed and keeled, driven by oars or sail; PUNT.

1849 [FEILD] 98 At St Jacques we found a fishing-punt waiting for us. 1871 HOWLEY *MS Reminiscences* 9 In running up the Tickle we passed a fishing punt in which a man and his wife were trying for cod. [1952] 1965 PEACOCK (ed) i, 137 "High Times in Our Ship": We started to scrape down the last of the month, / We hoist Joe aloft in the big fishing punt.

fishing room: a tract or parcel of land on the waterfront of a cove or harbour from which a fishery is conducted; the stores, sheds, flakes, wharves and other facilities where the catch is landed and processed, and the crew housed; ROOM.

[1652] 1954 INNIS 96 Every planter in each harbour may take their stages and fishing room together in one part of the harbour. [1713–14] 1793 REEVES 76 In such case should the ships fishing rooms of that harbour be taken up before he arrives, they often remove some planter or other for him [an acquaintance], pretending that the planter's title is not good to the room he possesses, when the commanders of men of war, some years before, adjudged it to be the said planter's right. [1785] 1792 CARTWRIGHT iii, 49 This harbour was formerly full of fishing-rooms, but the very frequent depredations of the American privateers in the last war caused every merchant and planter to abandon it. [1810] 1971 ANSPACH 5 But a spot of ground of a limited extent might be annexed to each fishing room, for potatoes and cabbage gardens to be held by lease from a yearly rent and in every other respect to be held on the same tenure as the fishing room. 1870 HOWLEY *MS Reminiscences* 26 How Spanish Room came by its

name I could not ascertain but in all probability in olden days during the earlier prosecution of the fisheries by foreigners some Spaniards may have located here and established what was called a fishing room. 1916 GRENFELL 35 Once the die is cast, a house built, a fishing-room established, a fur path secured, the settler here, like the limpet on our rocks, finds moving to a distance almost an impossibility. 1936 SMITH 33 Mr Smith himself was on board to supervise the building of the different fishing rooms at Edwards Harbour. 1960 *Evening Telegram* 11 Aug, p. 7 Eighty years ago in summer there would be a regular exodus of families from Conception Bay to Labrador. They had fishing room at the various harbours all down the coast from Battle Harbour to Turnavik. T 54–64 That summer I fished ashore on th' easter side o' Hilliard's Harbour, where th' only fishin' room was on th' easter side o' the harbour. T 192/3–65 There's only one or two fishin' rooms in this arm now.

fishing salt: a kind of coarse salt used to cure fish; fishery salt; SALT n.

1977 BURSEY 32 He was sailing toward Labrador with his traps and fishing salt aboard with supplies for six months.

fishing season: the period of the principal fishery for cod from spring to early autumn; SEASON.

[1652] 1895 PROWSE 153 These were. . .young men who came over as Servants. . .divers of whom were brought from Newfoundland for the fishing season. [1693] 1793 REEVES iv That (according to the ancient custom there used) every such fishing ship from England, Wales, or Berwick, or such fisherman as shall, from and after the said twenty-fifth day of March shall enter any harbour or creek in *Newfoundland*, in behalf of his ship, shall be admiral of the said harbour or creek during that fishing season. 1708 OLDMIXON 14 The Fishing-season is from *Spring* to *September*. [1794] 1968 THOMAS 33 There were many Passengers on board, men who engaged themselves in the fishing season at Newfoundland for a certain price. 1837 BLUNT 3 This is a snug and secure harbor, though small, and generally filled with vessels, during the fishing season, considerable fisheries being carried on in its vicinity. 1895 PROWSE 602 Planters, with their families and household belongings, including their dogs and goats, used annually to transport themselves to the Labrador for the fishing season.

fishing servant: a person indentured, or engaged on 'shares' or wages, for a period in the fishery; FISHERY SERVANT, SERVANT[1].

[1794] 1968 THOMAS 113 My Friends are my Irish Fishing Servants now in the Kitchen who, I am confident, will be as noisy and as merry and as *friendly* with you as your best *Friends* in England, providing you pay for the *Liquor*. [1867] 1899 *Nfld Law Reports* 215 If it were the law that a fishing servant would not be bound by an agreement he should make with a merchant to accept an immediate settlement of his wages in any particular mode agreed upon. [1896] SWANSBOROUGH 7 "May": The fishing servants are shipped now [in May].

fishing shallop: a large partly-decked boat used in the inshore cod and seal-fisheries; SHALLOP.

1837 BLUNT 46 On its western side there is a small creek admitting fishing shallops.

fishing ship: a British vessel engaged seasonally in the Newfoundland cod-fishery; a large decked vessel.

1613 *Willoughby Papers* 17a, 35 Att our arrivall here we found the fishinge shipps not departed, having ended there fishinge and expectinge a faire wind, kept in by easterlie winds. [1676] 1895 PROWSE 206 English fishing ships commonly all gone in September or quickly in October—not to sail out of England till 1st March. [1693] 1793 REEVES iv (quot at **fishing season**). [1701] 1895 PROWSE 228 These bye boat keepers could afford to sell their fish cheaper than the Adventurers, which must lessen the number of fishing ships. 1903 *Nfld Qtly* Mar, p. 17 There were spaces set apart or specially reserved for the purpose, and known as the fishing ships' rooms. 1953 *Nfld & Lab Pilot* ii, 386 Fishing Ship harbour, which has regular communication by sea with other Labrador and Newfoundland ports, is a small sound, with depths of from 4 to 16 fathoms.

fishing skiff: a large undecked boat of up to thirty feet (9.14 m) in length, used to set and haul nets or traps; SKIFF.

1923 GRENFELL 153 So in b'tween times I hauled out the wood to build a fishin' skiff on my own. T 455–67[2] Small skiffs or fishin' skiffs. We've a-build them, I've a-build them. What we always used here, sir, was a fifteen- and sixteen-foot keel.

fishing smack: small decked vessel used esp to collect fish from fishermen for shipment; SMACK[2].

1886 *Colonist Christmas No* 9 The labor of the week is o'er, the fishing-smacks are securely moored at the stage-heads, while the smaller skiffs are hauled upon the beach. [1900 OLIVER & BURKE] 20 [He was] nothing the worse after his night under the fishing smack. M 68–20 Every two days the fishing smack from Gaultois used to come and bring ice and take the fish.

fishing stage: an elevated platform on the shore with working tables, sheds, etc, at which fish are landed and processed for salting and drying; STAGE.

1765 ROGERS 5–6 [This Act] proved a poor bulwark against the French, who, in 1705, laid siege to, and demolished the town of St John's, with all the fishing stages, &c. but could not reduce the fort. 1866 WILSON 205 ~ a long shed, built out sufficiently far in the water for the fishing-boats to lie at the stage-head. The stage is supported by posts fixed in crevices of the rocks, against which the sea often beats. 1937 DEVINE 40 [Strouters are] the perpendicular posts at the front end of a fishing stage.

fishing stamp: government form administered by a fish-dealer recording amount of unemployment benefits due a fisherman; STAMP.

1972 NEMEC 92–3 Most St Shotts fishermen depended heavily each winter on unemployment benefits accrued in the preceding summer while fishing. Now. . .an individual can earn more on the plant than from 'fishing stamps.'

fishing stand: see **fishing station**.
1839 TUCKER 106–7 The shore inhabitants [of

Labrador], in some instances, amass a small property, by fortunately obtaining possession of some good sealing post, or fishing stand.

fishing station: a harbour or other sheltered place on the coast from which the fishery is conducted seasonally; STATION.

[1788] 1975 *Evening Telegram* 22 Dec, p. 6 Vessels were sent to Quirpon, Bay of Islands and [Croque] and other fishing stations for spare supplies of 'bay' or rock salt. [1831–39] AUDUBON 236 The fishes taken along the coast, or on fishing-stations only a few miles off, are of small dimensions. 1832 MCGREGOR i, 207 During the fishing season, from 280 to 300 schooners proceed from Newfoundland to the different fishing-stations on the coast of Labrador. 1866 WILSON 28 . . .a spacious inlet. . .yet not a good fishing station. 1912 *Nfld Qtly* Christmas, pp. 26–8 [He] resides in the little fishing station of Boat Harbour just below Cape Norman.

fishing trade: the comprehensive activity of the Newfoundland cod-fishery, catching, processing and shipping.

1620 WHITBOURNE 37 And withall it is to be considered, that whereas now there are yeerely at *New-found-land* of your Maiesties Subiects ships in the fishing trade, at least 15000. tunne burthen of shipping. [1653] 1895 PROWSE 168 That noe person doe deminish take away perloyne or steale. . .any other provisions belonginge to ye fishinge Trade or to ye ships. [1667] ibid 157 . . .at which time there was noe Governour there, or above two or three poor people inhabited there, and such salt, boates, staiges and other materialls for ye Fishing trade left by ye shippes the Former year. 1863 PEDLEY 206 This system of credit is that which still prevails in the fishing trade of Newfoundland, one of those legacies from the past, which, from being interwoven in the habits of the people, is so difficult to remove.

fishing vessel: a large decked fishing craft. Cp **fishing ship**.

[1649] 1895 PROWSE 161 Desire that two ships may be sent thither if they can be spared to defend the fishing vessels. [1766] 1976 HEAD 182 A small snug commodious Harbour for Fishing Vessels. 1960 FUDGE 2 He commanded several fishing vessels [at the Bank fishery]. 1978 *Evening Telegram* 21 Sep, p. 2 [The] federal government plans to scrap its fishing vessel insurance program. . .'under the guise of austerity.'

fishing voyage: enterprise or period of fishing; VOYAGE.

1611 *Willoughby Papers* 17a, 1/10 I have put my help in hand: to Further the Fishing Voige with the Master. 1620 WHITBOURNE [sig. C1[v]] We likewise then did set forth another Ship, for a fishing Voyage, which also carried some victuals for those people which had been formerly sent to inhabite there [in Newfoundland]. [1693] 1793 REEVES viii That all and every person or persons whatsoever, that shall go over with their servants to *Newfoundland*, to keep boats on a fishing voyage, commonly called *By-boat keepers*, shall not pretend to or meddle with any house, stage. . .

fishocracy n *DC* ~ Nfld 1, 2 (1878, 1940). The mercantile class, esp the merchants of St John's engaged in the export of cod-fish and the supplying of fishermen.

1878 TOCQUE 86 The mercantile class is the only one who accumulate wealth in large amounts, hence, like the 'Colonocracy' [i.e. cod-fish aristocracy] of Boston, the 'Fishocracy' of St John's exert a great influence over all the other classes of the community. 1954 INNIS 387 The 'fishocracy' comprised, in descending order: (1) the principal merchants, high officials, and some lawyers, and medical men; (2) small merchants, important shopkeepers, lawyers, doctors and secondary officials; (3) grocers, master mechanics, and schooner holders; and (4) fishermen. 1971 NOEL 21 There was still [c1870] no substantial middle class: a gross inequality of wealth continued to separate the upper class of merchants, the 'fishocracy,' from the lower class of fishermen. The credit structure of the fishery was unchanged: the city of St John's was still the financial as well as the political capital, its relationship to the outports being that of creditor to debtor.

fit v In phr *fit out*. *OED* fit v[1] 11 obs when object is a person (1591–), *DAE* 1 naut (1704–) for sense 1.

1 To equip a vessel or man with gear (for fishing, sealing); to furnish with supplies or provisions.

[1667] 1963 YONGE 111 By this time the ship Mr Martyn owned was returned and he fitting her out for Newfoundland. [1711] THOMPSON 2 And now instead of Fifty, they [in Barnstaple and Bideford] do not fit out of late above Six or Eight small Ships, and find it very difficult to Man these few. [1775] 1792 CARTWRIGHT ii, 120 I was fitting out the crews for the winter. 1898 *Christmas Bells* 14 Skipper Tom. . .and three other hardy fishers were 'fit-out,' as usual, by Mr Hardfist, to prosecute the codfishery. T 43–64 Your supplier in the Spring would fit out the owner, an' he'd fit also any men that was goin' with him. T 31/2–64 He fitted every man out for the winter; 'give un all they wants' he said, 'to go wi' me again next summer.' 1967 FIRESTONE 47 At the present time even those crews that have sufficient cash to pay for their own fishing supplies at the beginning of the season continue to be fitted out by a merchant because it provides a convenient accounting system. . . Few families are now fitted out with food.

2 To prepare, get ready (for the seal hunt).

1873 CARROLL 27 Such seals are seldom seen by the ice hunters that fit out from the east side.

3 To make netting into the size and shape of a fish-net or trap.

1976 *Evening Telegram* 21 Jan, p. 4 One thousand pounds of knitted fish net are for sale by tender at the Waterford Hospital. The fish net, which needs to be 'fitted out' before it can actually be used in the water, was knitted by about a dozen patients at the hospital.

fit-out n ['fɪtæut, 'fɪtæut] *OED* fit sb[4] 4 (1836, 1844), *DAE* (1840–), *DC* 1, 2 (1829–; 1955) for senses 1, 3. See also FIT: *fit out*, RIG n.

1 An outfit; clothing, supplies and equipment (for a fishing voyage, sealing, etc); gear.

1887 HOWLEY *MS Reminiscences* 5 We got them out as soon as possible and then of course they each wanted a fit out [to accompany me into the interior]. 1924 ENGLAND 30 I have just dumped my 'fit-out' and myself into a kind of little hellhole aft of the main cabin. T 36–64 That's your crop, you see; when you starts in the spring you'd want, say, twenty-five or thirty or forty dollars of a fit-out—bit o' grub, rubber boots an' rubber clothes an' so on. T 31/2–64 We had to leave the Straits and got us fit-out to Job Brothers there to lanch 'em along. He had a room by that time—got us a fit-out there for the Labrador, so much of everything: baccy an' some grub. T 396/7–67 When you're goin' to fish in the spring o' the year you go an' take out a fit-out. You take your salt. . . Well, if you had traps you'd get twine an' rope an' stuff from the merchant, see; all charged up to you. 1967 FIRESTONE 57 The implication when a man marries into his wife's community is that he hadn't enough substance, in capital goods or personality, not to have to rely upon her or her people. There are, however, men who have married into their own 'fit outs' of gear and who are in no way considered in this light.

2 The costume, face disguise and appurtenances of a Christmas mummer; odd or bizarre apparel.

1893 *Christmas Greeting* 19 A rapidly improvised canvas mask with an enormous nose, like the flying jib of a schooner turned upside down, and an old 'beaver hat,' with a red band around it, gave the finishing touch to my somewhat mongrel fit-out. T 26–64[2] I once saw a young fellow dressed up in a barrel. He had the head cut out and a piece of brin or some material like that, put [it] in the bottom and a hole cut out for his arm. He just poked his head up into it and went on! Of course he didn't get in anybody's house with that fit-out on! 1976 GUY 27 . . .sitting on his back wearing a fitout all done out with lumps of gold as big as hens eggs.

3 Habitual wearing apparel; suit of clothes.

T 139/40–65 He was in poor circumstances—he didn't have any fit-out, see. So she [was] goin' to give him a fit-out o' clothes. M 70–21 A person receiving a new outfit (or fit-out) of clothes might be considered all 'rigged-out' for the coming season, be it winter or summer.

4 A group (of persons).

1892 *Christmas Review* 26 . . .to say that a Red Indian, from the wild hills, was able to do for us what the whole fit-out of us, who hailed from the middle of civilization, couldn't do for ourselves.

5 A technical device for a specified purpose; contraption; MACHINE.

P 148–60 ~ A term applied to any object or instrument, when proper name is unknown or too burdensome [to use]. T 26–64[3] [The brigs] used to have yards across them, see. They had the same kind of a fit-out, but they had yards besides up the topsail. T 92/3–64 Then when this got worked, they'd have to get their fit-out an' runned it off—moonshine.

fitting ppl Phr *fitting out*: the equipping of a vessel or man with gear and provisions (for fishing, sealing).

1832 MCGREGOR i, 247 There are two or more modes of fitting out for the fisheries followed by [the

Americans]. [1892] 1897 *Nfld Law Reports* 644 We are aware the fitting out for the seal fishery involves a large outlay, the voyage occupies a short period.

five-leg n In a net, a mesh erroneously made with five sides (P 127–78).

flacoon n [flə'kuːnz]. A type of pancake; a cake that does not rise.
C 13–71 Flacoons were made from flour and water and cooked on the top of the stove.

flag n The pennant of a sealing vessel used to mark the ownership and position on the ice of a pile of seal 'pelts'; PAN n: PAN FLAG.
1873 *Maritime Mo* i, 259 [The sealers] kill and 'sculp' all the seals within two or three miles of the ship, and then, piling them in heaps marked with the flag of the vessel, they are left to be hauled in at a favorable moment. 1924 ENGLAND 245, 282 With the decks a bristle of gaffs and flags, and in as near silence as the engine permitted, the *Terra Nova* rapidly bore down on the herd. . . The long monotony was broken by our chancing on a huge pan of sculps with a Job Brothers flag on it. 1936 SMITH 52 At 12.30 the order was given, and all hands were out with the flagpoles and flags. You could jump on a whitecoat from the ship's side-sticks if you wished to do so. It was snowing a little, and we could not see very far, but all hands started panning and, in a short while the ice was red with blood, and the *Neptune* steaming around picking up the pans. 1972 BROWN 33 The pelts would be collected together on ice pans big enough to keep them safe, and a flag stuck on each pan to mark ownership. The flags had distinctive colours and were also numbered.

flag v
1 To set vessel's pennant over a pile of seal 'pelts' on the ice.
[1870] 1899 *Nfld Law Reports* 348 The seals. . .killed by the plaintiff's crew, were reduced into possession by them by their afterwards sculping, cutting open, piling, flagging and executing all the rights of ownership over them. [1907] 1964 BLONDAHL (ed) 82 "The Master Watch": I see afar 'gainst the sinking sun, / The flagged-pans lift on the line. 1972 BROWN 59 The Old Man, leaning over the rail, yelled, 'Flag yer seals, me son, we're headin' west'ard.'
2 Phr *flag in*: to quarantine.
C 71–103 When diphtheria and scarlet fever were prevalent people were isolated from the public. A sign was nailed on the house and people kept their distance. The older people refer to quarantine as flagged in.
flag off, ~ out: to decorate a sealing vessel with pennants at the start and (successful) conclusion of a voyage.
1924 ENGLAND 243 A full ship an' ahl flagged out, that's my motto! . . .Go get evveryt'ing with hair on it. Ibid 316 Flagged off. Decorated with flags.

flahoolach a also **flahoola, flooholic** [flə'huːlɪk] JOYCE flahoolagh, cp DINNEEN flaitheamhlach

'generous.' Lavish; generous; wasteful; sometimes ironic.
1937 DEVINE 22 Flooholic—lavish. P 108–70 ~ overly generous. C 71–89 He was very flahoolic with his money. . . Go down to flahoolic John Joe's for some tobacco. 1975 *Evening Telegram* 28 June, p. 16 If you were flahoola with the money you could buy a slice of baloney there, and a cake of hardbread all for five cents. 1982 ibid 16 Feb, p. 17 I heard of one man who came from England [without a stitch of spare clothing] when things were not too flahoola over there.

flake n *OED* ~ sb[1] 2 b (Nfld: 1623–1876), orig 'a wattled hurdle'; *EDD* sb[1] 7 (Nfld: 1892); *DAE* (1635–1886); *DC* (Nfld: 1620–). See also BROAD FLAKE, HAND- ~ .
1 A platform built on poles and spread with boughs for drying cod-fish on the foreshore; FISH-FLAKE.
[1578] 1935 *Richard Hakluyt* 124 [Parkurst's letter:] In makyng of flakes and other dryinge places. 1620 WHITBOURNE 63 There are also some, who arriving first in Harbor, take away other mens Salt that they had left there the yeare before, and also rip and spoile the Fats wherein they make their Traine; and some teare down the Flakes, whereon men yeerely dry their fish. [1663] 1963 YONGE 57–8 After a day or thereabouts [in the horse the fish is] laid abroad on flakes, that is boughs thinly laid upon a frame, like that of a table, and here the fish dries. 1699 *Act of William III*, 10 & 11, Cap. xxv And be it further enacted by the authority aforesaid, That no person or persons whatsoever shall (at his departure out of the said country, or at any other time) destroy, deface, or do any detriment to any such stage or cook room, or to the flakes, spikes, nails, or any other thing whatsoever thereto belonging. [1712] 1895 PROWSE 273 No complaints that any admiral, vice-admiral, and rear-admiral do ingross more beach or flakes than they pitch upon at their arrival. [1766] 1971 BANKS 134 [The fish] are Carried to the Last operation of Drying them which the English Do upon Standing flakes made by a slight Wattle Just strong enough to support the men who Lay on the fish supported upon Poles in some Places as high as twenty feet from the ground. [1771] 1792 CARTWRIGHT i, 133 At nine I went myself with three hands in the skiff to Stage Cove, and carried all the rinds which were below the house. We got one raft on shore there, and I fixed on the places for the stage, flakes, and the shoremen's house. 1832 MCGREGOR i, 171 The sea broke in upon the lands where fish-houses, flakes, &c., were erected, and occasioned vast loss and destruction. 1863 HIND i, 306 The hurdles on which cod are stretched to dry are called flakes; they are placed parallel to each other, with spaces of four feet between to enable the men in charge of the fish to move round them. 1883 HATTON & HARVEY 291 The flake consists of a horizontal framework of small poles, covered with spruce boughs and supported by upright poles, the air having free access beneath. Here the cod are spread out to bleach in the sun and air, and during the process require constant attention. [1905] 1912 *Nfld Law Reports* 158 [The agreement] shows the property to be of considerable value, consisting of land at Brigus and Labrador,

goods, wares, merchandize, houses, stores, flakes, boats, fishing gear, fourteen traps, salt, several schooners, and other fishing property. [1929] 1933 GREENLEAF (ed) 255 "Lukey's Boat": And when he was coming around the cape, / He spied old Jennie all on the flake. 1937 JUNEK 34 [The washed fish] is then carried to the 'flakes'—framework raised a short distance above the ground and covered with old nets. 1964 *Daily News* 3 Feb, p. 4 Today few fishermen are prepared to devote the time to the proper sun-drying of fish and it is a rare place today where women and children toil on the 'flakes.' T 36/8–64 You were supposed to build your flakes, when you had the collar on; build your flakes, build your stage heads, tar your roof, go in the woods and cut rines for to cover up your fish. T 43–64 The flakes was usually built up in [on] the beach by the stage— beams shored up, handy about level, and he probably cover over three, four, five hundred feet square.

2 Phr *flakes of money*: lots of money (1924 ENGLAND 316).

P 108–74 'I see you're putting another piece on to the house. You must have money to burn!' 'Yes, boy, flakes of it.'

leaky as a flake: very leaky.

M 65–2 ~ used when talking about a boat which is not watertight. C 71–93 So for something to be as leaky as a flake means to be very leaky indeed.

go on the flake: to work on the flake curing fish, spreading, turning and piling it (Q 67–69).

3 Attrib, comb, cpd **flake bar**: length of wood used in the construction of a drying-platform for cod.

P 102–60 Two saw mill operators using two benches sawed all the flake bars and laths used for making our fish flakes.

flake beam: wooden pole placed vertically to support the platform of a drying-flake.

T 14/21–64 We'd have what we call a flake-beam, a stick, say, he'd be thirty feet long, about 2 inches in diameter in the top and about 5 in the butt. 1977 BURSEY 28 During the winter he went into the forest to cut flake beams.

flake bough: the branch of a spruce or fir tree spread on the flake to permit air to circulate under the drying fish. See also BOUGH n.

[1832] 1981 *Them Days* vi (4), p. 35 Capt Quinton retd from St Francis Harb and the *Plover* from Shole Cove with flake bows. T 43–64 So every spring, 'twould be handy about the last woodswork would be done, [you'd] get the flake boughs, you'd pull them out and you'd pile 'em in a big pile, and then you'd put a terrific weight on 'em to flatten 'em out so as when you put 'em on your flake, they'd be handy about flat. And you cover them boughs over with your fish. 1975 BUTLER 60 Flake boughs were straight sticks about one and one half inches in the butt with the limbs and twigs left on. 1979 TIZZARD 242 I suppose the last thing my father hauled out of the woods. . .was flake boughs. He would select the best branches from the fir and spruce trees, and a few white spruce boughs mixed in with them. These he would haul to the fish flakes and spread them out. These would be pressed out by placing large

sticks or logs on them, so that they would be quite flat by the time the caplin were ready to be spread on them.

flake-longer, ~ **lunger**: a long pole placed horizontally on uprights to form the elevated surface of a drying-platform for cod-fish. See also LONGER.

1896 *J A Folklore* ix, 32 ~ [one of] the horizontal pieces in flakes, on which boughs are laid to form the bed on which fish are placed to dry. T 169/70–65[2] I had a flake longer hooked onto the strap I had in my bucket. T 43–64 A flake longer is a small tree about three inches in the butt and it'll go right away to the top. You'd cover over these beams with these longers. 1977 RUSSELL 107 You cut two holes eight or ten foot apart, tie a rope to one end of a flake longer, poke it down through one hole and hook it up through the other with a hand gaff.

flake-room: an allotment near the shore for building a drying-platform for cod-fish. See also ROOM.

[1763] 1954 INNIS 181 Allowed to a single boat. Flake room 50 yards long & 40 yards wide. [1882] 1898 *Nfld Law Reports* 369 The very strip or dock now the subject of litigation, or at all events the flake room immediately adjoining at the back of it, was held by Father Murphy to form part of the plaintiff's property. T 141/67–65[2] Of course there'd be a flake room to keep up, there'd be a stage to repair, or boats to repair.

flake-work: the activities connected with curing and drying cod-fish.

1972 MURRAY 248 The skipper's wife took charge of the 'flake work' if the men were away fishing.

flaking vbl n Attrib **flaking stick**: wooden pole used in the construction of a drying platform for cod-fish; cp STICK.

T 12/348–64 Back about thirty years ago, when you were building your flakes for drying fish, you could walk up from the beach with an axe, an' cut down your flaking sticks and carry 'em on your back down to where you were goin' to build your flake.

flan-dadolin* n [flæn'dædəlɨnz]. Bread dough rolled very thin and fried in pork fat (C 71–130).

flangey* See PHILANDY*.

flang-tile n A type of pancake.

P 79–73 I don't want any of your old flang-tiles, give me a bun.

flanker n *OED* ~ sb[2] (?Nfld 1840–); *EDD* ~ sb[2] Do So Nfld; *DC* Nfld (1835–). A live spark from a wood fire; a burning ember.

1836 [WIX][2] 49 'Flankers,' or bright sparks. . .flew up his chimney to some height in the clear star-lit sky, from his brisk birch fire. 1840 GOSSE 11 Even when dry, they consume so quickly, and so continually throw out lighted fragments, 'flankers,' as they are called, that they are confined to our close stoves. 1939 DULEY 67 Flankers flew ahead. . .while heat blistered the new white paint. T 158–65 All that ridge burned in there—flames used to come out, flankers come out, pitch on the felt. 1976 O'NEILL ii, 629 A number of ships in the harbour were burned to the waterline by 'flankers' (flaming embers) carried on board by the high wind.

flapper n   Cp *OED* ~ 3 (1773–), *EDD* ~ 2 'young wild duck.' Comb **flapper-jack**: a cage for catching wild birds (P 94–57).

flare-up n   also **flirrup**. Cp *OED* ~ 3 naut 'a night-signal' (1858–); *EDD* flare sb 5 (3) flare-up 'a lighted torch.' A torch; an oil-lamp, esp one used on a 'fishing-stage' when handling and processing fish at night; STAGE LAMP.
[1865 CAMPBELL 88 The stage, a long low building of fir poles and branches, is perched on the rocks, so as to project over the sea. . . In this long room a number of double-beaked tin lamps hung flaring from the roof.] 1937 DEVINE 22 Flirrup—A stage lamp of large size; a torch.

flash[1] n   Cp *EDD* ~ v 'to lash' for sense 2.
   1 A brief opportunity or chance (to take seals).
1924 ENGLAND 183 [He] 'wished to de Lard we'd get a flash at de rusties in a jam.' No 'hard rowt' was now too tough for Jonas.
   2 A flexible strip of animal hide at the end of a dog-whip, six feet long and tightly bound with twine (P 80–64).

flash[2] n   See FLASHET.

flash v   *OED* ~ v[1] 2 obs (c1460–1813). To splash (water) about (1971 NOSEWORTHY 200).

flashet n   also **flash** *OED* flash sb[1] 1 'pool, marshy place' obs exc local (1440–1870); *EDD* flash sb[1] 1 'pool. . .marshy pond.' A small pond in a marshy area.
[c1900] 1978 *RLS* 8, p. 23 ~ Small pond of water usually such as occur in bogs or marshes. 1912 CABOT 5 Its lakes are Labrador's glory. . . Nowhere are such lakes,—from the tiny 'flashets' of the Newfoundlanders, their mission only to reflect the sky, to great Michikamau and Mistassini, with their far water horizons. 1937 DEVINE 22 ~ a small pond or puddle, especially in a marsh. P 113–56 A flash does not usually have a brook running in or out. 'Watch the flashes for black ducks.' P 184–67 'He's in on the flashet skating.' In this case it was frozen.

flask n   Inner tube (of a tire); rubber bladder.
M 71–97 Children out home learn to swim on flasses (usually the discarded inner tubes of car tires). P 13–74 The flask [is] inside the leather case of a football. P 32–74 We used to call the inflatable interior of a football the bladder or flask. When deflated it looks like a flask.

flat a

Cpd, comb: **flat boat,** ~ **punt**: small boat with flat bottom; FLAT n.
[1819] 1915 HOWLEY 180 They lived in a hut outside our door until Peyton gave them their liberty and furnished them with a small flat boat for the summer. P 148–75 Everyone built his own trapboat or rodney or flat punt, jack or dory as the case may be.
   flatform, also **frafferm*** ['fræfəɹm]: (a) a raised wooden structure at the door of a house; BRIDGE; (b) a teacher's dais.
1896 *J A Folklore* ix, 27 Platform. . .is known or coming into use [for bridge] but they generally pronounce it *flatform*. T 172–65 So we had a rumpus one day [in school], an' I was chasing somebody round this flatform. T 181–65 But we didn't mind seein' the [teacher's] cane comin' down from the flatform, firin' at you. T 203/4–65 Somebody'd make a desk for her or perhaps a table, an' she'd sit up there on a little higher flatform built up. P 229–67 Sweep the snow off the flatform.
   flatjack: pancake; turnover; flapjack.
T 96–64[2] This is the one, the flatjacks. You'd roll out the flour and put dried apples or apricots between 'em—jam, then turn 'em over. 1973 GOUDIE 49 We only had a camp stove. I had to make flat cakes of flour and salt and baking powder. . . One day I said to Jim, 'I am tired of eating flat cakes.' Jim called them *flat jacks*.

flat n   Cp *DC* ~ 2 (1954). A small flat-bottomed boat, ten feet long and with a square stern, rowed with a pair of oars and used chiefly by fishermen as a tender in a cove or harbour, occas for fishing in sheltered coastal waters.
[1774] 1792 CARTWRIGHT ii, 17 I took two hands in a punt, with a flat in tow. 1842 JUKES ii, 133 . . .two small 'flats,' these latter being little flat-bottomed boats with square ends, about the shape of a common knife-tray. 1912 CABOT 73 Presently came three or four women with a good catch of sea trout in a 'flat,' a little dory-like skiff. T 210/11–65 When I was fifteen, or fourteen, I'm not sure which—it would depend on when I built the flat, flat boat—I built another one—a rodney boat. My father just marked out an' showed me how to do it. M 68–17 A flat was used mostly within the cove itself, for going to the collar, etc. 1977 *Inuit Land Use* 132 The common method of fishing among the Inuit and Settler families was jigging with a hand-line from a flat or a punt.

flatty n   *O Sup*[2] ~[2] (1892–); *EDD* ~ 1. A flatfish.
P 229–67 He took a tub of flatties off the trawl. 1976 GUY 108 It's all very easy to catch a conner or even a flatty, but an eel is something else.

flaus See FLOUSE.

fleece n   Cp *OED* fleece 3 e. Comb **fleece calico**: a soft fabric used for linings.
T 94–64 And then you'd line 'em with this fleece calico; one side is smooth and the other side was soft and, you know, soft and silky like. 1972 MURRAY 269 Many men wore knitted underwear in the early days. This

was lined with 'fleece calico' which kept it from being itchy and irritable next to the skin.

fleet n *OED* ~ sb¹ 3 (1879–1892); *EDD* ~ sb¹ 5 'a number of fishing lines or nets'; *Cent* ~ ¹ n 3 (Nfld: 1846) for sense 2.

1 Two or more nets strung or tied together.
[1770] 1792 CARTWRIGHT i, 14 When the salmoniers visited their nets this morning, they found that the Indians had stolen one fleet. 1792 ibid *Gloss* i, x Fleet of nets. A number of nets, which are fastened to each other, in such manner as to form a pound, or pounds. A fleet of salmon-nets, commonly speaking, is but three. But there is no determined number for a fleet of Stopper-nets for seals. 1861 DE BOILIEU 41 Besides the cod, Labrador is rich in salmon. The mode of catching these is with a 'fleet' of three nets, which are fastened to each other so as to form a pound; the fish in striking the first and even the second of these may not be meshed, but he cannot escape the third, as, when once there, it is impossible for it to retrace its swim. 1925 *Dial Notes* v, 331 Fleet of nets. Two nets. T 54/60–64 Well, I dreamt I was a killick, an' I was on a fleet o' nets up in Hall's Bay, moorin' for a fleet o' nets. 1975 *Evening Telegram* 24 May, p. 6 He put the salmon nets up from $75 per fleet to approximately $300 per fleet. 1979 NEMEC 232 Nets are reset and 'fleets' (four nets strung together) of nets straightened out only when tidal conditions permit.

2 In trawl-fishing for cod, a single line with one hundred hooks attached at intervals.
1891 *Cent* ~ In *fishing*, a single line of 100 hooks: so called when the bultow was introduced in Newfoundland (1846). T 41–64 We take about twenty-eight hemp lines. We'd have four tubs o' lines, seven line tubs. Four sevens are twenty-eight, an' that's what we'd use for a dory. We'd have one fleet for to set [as] all-night gear, an' another set in the morning.

flice* v Perhaps a local var pron of FLOUSE v. To make a sudden, quick gesture or movement; to engage in rough and tumble play.
P 245–59 ~ to chase hens away (by moving arms). Q 71–5 ~ to kick, as a horse, while still in harness. Q 71–8 Kicking and flicing with arms, legs or both. P 148–75 Flicing [is] the carrying on of youngsters; horse-play.

flicer n also **flicer-stick**. Cp FLICE*. The spring of a rabbit snare; BENDER.
P 94–57 ~ flexible sprig used as a spring to catch rabbits in a wire or string noose. P 227–71 I rigged a flicer (also referred to as a bender) to catch him. P 183–75 The flicer-stick is a small stick or twig holding the noose of a rabbit snare in place and which flies or flicks up when the rabbit is caught.

flick v
In phr *flick the stick*: a children's game in which a stick is placed on rocks and flicked up into air with another piece of wood; PIDDLY, TIDDLY.
1973 BARBOUR 26 Spring also meant the playing of different games, once the snow had disappeared. . .

Hop-scotch was the first on our list. . . After that came 'Flick the Stick.' . . .for 'flick the stick,' nothing, just nothing, took the place of the nice rounded broom which had been sawed into two pieces.

flicker n A lead weight forming part of a hook, used when fishing with a hand-line for cod near the surface of the water; DAPPER, FLOAT n.
[1856] 1975 WHITELEY 148 Float line [refers] to fishing with a 'flicker'—that is, a single hook around which a small amount of lead has been run. 1937 *Seafisheries of Nfld* 32 The Flicker. . .is the same as the Float, with a piece of lead between one and two ounces in weight, about 18 inches from the hook. T 272/3–66² [You] catch 'em on floats—some people calls 'em flickers. You just put the caplin onto that an' throw 'em out an' the fish take hold to it. 1975 BUTLER 57 A flicker was a small piece of lead weighing half a pound with one hook embedded in the lead. A line was attached to the other end of the lead. In the caplin scull fishermen would bait the hook with caplin and throw it out on the water. When a fish took the bait, the fisherman would flick the fish on board the boat. Hence the name flicker.

flicy* a Cp FLOUSE v. Fidgety, restless.
P 269–63 ~ throwing [things] around, not settling down (said of a baby who is restless and whiny).

flier n Cp *OED* fly sb¹ 7 b 'head-dress' obs (1773, 1774). A white band fastened to the cap of a pall-bearer.
1971 CASEY 302 The pall-bearers would have white fliers, a white band around their caps, and the women [mourners] they'd have a veil, a black veil come right down to their waist, right over their head.

flight n Cp *OED* ~ sb¹ 1 e, 8, 9; *EDD* 7: flighting-time.
Comb **flight-duck**: a migratory duck in a flock.
[1783] 1792 CARTWRIGHT iii, 32 Edwards killed seven flight-ducks, and got three of them.
flight-time: migration period of wildfowl.
[1770] 1792 CARTWRIGHT i, 19 In the flight-time, which commences about the middle of April, and commonly ends with the month of May, he said, they had killed above fifteen hundred ducks, which appeared probable enough, from the bags of feathers he shewed me. 1792 ibid *Gloss* i, x ~ The periodical migration of ducks.

flincher n Cp SMYTH flinch v 'in ship-carpentry, to hance or bevel the end of anything.' In coopering, a kind of plane used to smooth the rough edge of a stave (P 127–76).

flint n Attrib **flint biscuit**: sea biscuit; HARD TACK.
[1794] 1968 THOMAS 114 How hard the times was, how slow the Fish bite at present and that there was nothing to be got but Flint Biscuits in Newfoundland.

flinter n *EDD* ~ 'a term of reproach, used of a

drunken woman' (1862). A mischievous or saucy girl.
P 108–71 She's a saucy flinter, a hard case. C 75–28 Old people when referring to a mischievous child would address them as flinters.

flipper n also **fippar, fipper, phripper** *OED* ~ sb² 1 (1822) for sense 1; *DC* flipper dinner or supper Nfld (1933, 1958) for comb in sense 2.
1 The fore-limb of a seal, used to propel the animal in the water or on the ice; esp as prepared for eating.
[1770] 1792 CARTWRIGHT i, 55 [The skinbag] had been filled with phrippers, pieces of flesh, and rands of seals' fur. [1822] 1866 WILSON 341 Each man had a nunny-bag, which is a kind of knapsack, made of seal-skin, with the two fore-fippers passing over the shoulders, and tied across the breast with a piece of cod-line. 1846 TOCQUE 212 [Penguin's] wings were short, resembling the fippars of the seal, and its feet broad and webbed. 1861 DE BOILIEU 133 Finding himself disturbed and the means of retreat cut off, he stands as it were on his head, and, using the fore-fins or phrippers as a motive power, whirls himself round at an inconceivable speed. 1891 PACKARD 81 Seal's flippers we also found not to be distasteful, though never to be regarded as a delicacy. 1916 MURPHY 24 [He] used seal, covered with herb sauce, he was very fond of seal, or 'flippers,' and we pray that the coming voyage may be prosperous, and that our wishes may be gratified for a 'good square feed of flippers.' [1926] 1946 PRATT 242 "The Witches' Brew": Five sea-lion cubs were then thrown in, / Shot by the Cretan's javelin / In a wild fight off Uruguay; / With flippers fresh from the Azores, / Fijian kidneys by the scores. . . 1957 *Daily News* 16 Oct, p. 4 The men's earnings were supplemented by the sale of 'flippers,' the seals' front paws, which in Newfoundland are a gourmet's delight. T 84–64 It's like his fippers; his scutters is like his fippers. He uses 'em for scullin'! C 67–12 Flippers are classed as fish, not meat [and were exempted from the Roman Catholic prohibition of meat during Lent which coincided with the seal-hunt]. 1969 HORWOOD 95–6 Canadians (and other foreigners) often make the mistake of supposing that this famous Newfoundland delicacy consists of the animals' paws. Not at all. The paws are called pads, and are usually discarded. The flipper is the front shoulder, corresponding to a shoulder of lamb or a shoulder of pork, except that it is much tastier than either. It is heavy with rich, lean meat, the colour of red mahogany, so tender that you can cut it with a fork, and of a hearty, gamy flavour like that of wild duck. 1981 *Evening Telegram* 27 Mar, p. 3 Some of the sealers. . .said most people buy a dozen or a half-dozen flippers.
2 In designations of container for the storage of flippers and in various dishes prepared from the meat: ~ **barrel**, ~ **pie**, ~ **stew**, etc.
C 71–119 [He often referred] to a group of ladies at a sale as being 'like hungry dogs around a flipper barrel.' 1955 DOYLE (ed) 11 "A Noble Fleet of Sealers": Tho' Newfoundland is changing fast / Some things we must not lose, / May we always have our Flipper pie, / And Codfish for our brewis. [1894–1929] 1960 BURKE (ed White) 49 "Mrs Mullowney": For her friends had no

fault [finding] / At this famous fipper stew. 1933 GREENE 49 Endless are the stories of the Wooden Walls. . .once heard in the days gone-by at 'F'ipper Suppers' on board the early arrivals.

flipsy v To jump from one ice pan to another; COPY.
M 68–12 When the ice was right we would [play] dinner time and after school. The ice would have to be broken in ice pans near the shore. We used to flipsy most in the mouth of the river, usually where the water was about up to our necks.

flirrup See FLARE-UP.

float n
1 A lead weight forming part of a hook, used when fishing with a hand-line for cod near the surface of the water; DAPPER, FLICKER.
1937 *Seafisheries of Nfld* 31 The Float. . .is an ordinary straight or twisted hook, to which the bait is applied and which is at the end of the fishing line. T 272/3–66 [You] catch 'em on floats—some people calls 'em flickers, some more calls 'em dampers. That's a little thing made about that long an' a hook into it. You just put the caplin onto that and throw 'em out an' the fish take hold to it.
2 Comb **float line**: hand-line used in fishing with a weighted hook.
[1856] 1975 WHITELEY 148 [refers] to fishing with a 'flicker'—that is, a single hook around which a small amount of lead has been run—this type of fishing hook is only used when the fish are on the surface—schooling—sometimes bait was used—sometimes not . . . The method of fishing was to hold about a fathom of line in one hand and whirl the hook at the end of the line around one's head and then let go—the line would snake 20 or 30 feet—and then the hook would be hauled in—surface fishing, the hook would not sink very far down in the water.

float v To kill a seal by shooting it in the throat so that it will not submerge.
T 84–64 I had five shots and I killed the five of 'em. And I floated the five of 'em—never lost one.

floater n *DC* ~ 2 a, b Nfld (1909–; 1930) for senses 1 and 3.
1 A migratory fisherman prosecuting the cod-fishery in a schooner along the north-east coast and esp on the Labrador Coast; GREEN FISHERMAN.
1895 *Outing* xxvii, p. 20 The remaining fishermen who visit Labrador are designated 'green-fishers' or 'floaters.' 1908 HUBBARD 11 [The fishermen] sooner or later either scatter for the short season among the shore stations of the southerly coast, or, fishing as 'floaters,' enliven the littoral to the latitudes of the walrus and white bear at Nachvack and Chidley. 1924 ENGLAND 261 Thousands of outport men migrate almost as regularly as the seals themselves. With small, home-built schooners—these ingenious people can turn their hands to making almost everything they need—they take up the sea trek every summer and go

down the Labrador. If they pick some berth and settle down, they're called 'stationers,' 'squatters,' or 'roomers.' If they keep on the move, they're 'floaters.' 1947 TANNER 753 The schooner fishers are termed floaters, meaning they are not generally attached to fishing establishments on the Labrador, but catch their fish wherever they can get it, and take it direct to Newfoundland ports, where it is cured. T 75/7–64 Sometimes the floaters'd come here [to Tilting] an' they'd have nowhere to split their fish. T 141/63–65² [Change Islands] is a rough place, but it used to be used a good bit by our floaters. 1970 PARSONS 71 We came to the small harbour of Fish Cove where we met some fishing boats. These were some floaters (large fishing vessel whose crew stays on board all during the summer and stores their fish on their vessel as they catch and clean it) from Newfoundland.

2 A fishing schooner working northern coastal waters for cod.

1902 *Christmas Bells* 1 This shows one of the many 'floaters' working their way north in pursuit of fish, from Southern to Northern Labrador. 1925 *Dial Notes* v, 331 ~ A schooner that goes north every summer to fish. 1937 *Seafisheries of Nfld* 35 The units of production in the Shore Fishery range from the man who fishes by himself, to the crew of the largest Labrador Floater, which usually numbers fifteen men. 1970 PARSONS 55 There were two 'floaters' at Batteau when we arrived. Both had secured a load of fish, and were working their way down the coast towards Newfoundland.

3 On Bell Island, a man who travelled by boat from his home in Conception Bay to work during the week in the mines.

1931 SMALLWOOD 148 Hundreds of [the men] live in the various towns around Conception Bay. These, coming from their homes to work in and about the mines, and returning each week-end, are called 'floaters.'

4 A buoy or float.

1971 NOSEWORTHY 201 ~ Floating objects used to hold up cod-traps. P 190–77 Floaters [are] glass buoys used on a fish trap.

5 Attrib, comb **floater-crew**: crew of up to fifteen who man a migratory fishing schooner.

1953 *Nfld Fish Develop Report* 20 While almost 90 per cent of the floater crews and about 70 per cent of the stationer crews fish for cod only 60 per cent of the livyer crews fish for both salmon and cod.

floater(s) fish: cod taken in Labrador waters and shipped in 'salt-bulk' to be dried in Newfoundland.

[1912] 1930 COAKER 47 The great bulk of floaters fish was made dry in compliance with our instructions.

floater fishery: cod-fishery in Labrador waters prosecuted by migratory fishing schooners from Newfoundland.

1968 *Avalon Penin of Nfld* 30 The Newfoundland Labrador fishery was of two kinds. . . The second [the floater fishery] was prosecuted by the crews of the Labrador schooners, not always attached to particular shore establishments, catching their fish wherever they could get it and often taking it direct to Newfoundland

ports to be cured. 1970 PARSONS 295 The floater fishery became popular because it had the advantage of being able to search for the schools of fish. If a floater (skipper) anchored in a certain harbour and found that cod was scarce he could always move to another location and, if necessary, keep moving until he found enough fish to launch his fishing operation.

floater trader: itinerant buyer of cod who deals with the migratory schooner-fishermen.

1953 *Nfld Fish Develop Report* 79 Much of it [price competition] is provided by itinerant buyers of fish, i.e. 'floater' traders.

floating ppl *DC* ~ surrogate Nfld (1819, 1964).

In comb **floating governor**: naval officer in command of the convoy of English migratory fishing ships, exercising powers of civil jurisdiction during the fishing season.

1895 PROWSE 254 Sir John Leake, Rodney, Duckworth, Graves, Lord Radstock, &c., are amongst the honoured names of Newfoundland's floating governors [between 1728 and 1817].

floating stage: a buoyant platform for working on the hull of a vessel.

P 94–57 ~ platform made of casks for working on the hull of schooner. 1966 PADDOCK 98 ~ A wooden platform supported by empty oil drums or logs [which] is a fairly common sight on both salt and fresh water in the Carbonear area.

floating surrogate: naval officer empowered to hold courts in civil cases on authority delegated by the naval governor; SURROGATE.

[1811] 1957 *Nfld Qtly* Mar, p. 21 Floating Surrogate Court opened in Trinity. 1842 BONNYCASTLE i, 137 These officers were called 'floating surrogates,' and, as may be imagined, administered the law after the naval code. 1915 HOWLEY 178 During the year 1820 Buchan acted as floating Surrogate in the *Egeria* at Harbour Grace, and administered justice in conjunction with the Rev Mr Leigh.

floating trawl: a type of trawl with an anchor at each end and the trawl-line stretched horizontal under the surface of the water (1971 NOSEWORTHY 201).

1979 *Salt Water, Fresh Water* 30 The floating trawl would have floats on it to keep it up in the water so the fish, if they were moving, would get the bait that way and get caught.

flobber n Cp *EDD* ~ 'anything loose and flabby.' The soft lap of a wave (on rocks); usu in phr *not a flobber*; WAG.

1937 DEVINE 22 ~ The gentlest possible motion of waves striking the rocks. 'Not a flobber,' is a dead calm. 'Not a *wag* of sea.' 1951 *Nfld & Lab Pilot* i, 219 Flobber Cove islet, 15 feet high, with two drying rocks close east-north-eastward. P 187–73 [There's] not a flobber. A phrase which means the sea is very calm.

flobber v To lap against; to flow against; to wash or splash over; hence vbl n.

1888 HOWLEY *MS Reminiscences* Oct 24 But it was ticklesome work and several times we shipped a lot of water which flobbered in over the bows of our canoes. T 70–64¹ So he said, the flobberin' o' the wind in again the bow o' the boat woke him.

flog v *OED* ~ 1 d (1894) for sense 2.

1 To carry dried cod in a barrow on a merchant's premises as an occupation (1937 DEVINE 22).

2 Phr *flog the clock*: to move the hands of a clock.

1924 ENGLAND 274 I niver trusts dat clock, whatever. Somet'ing always floggin' dat clock a'eed or astarn.

flood n Attrib **flood-gate**: one of a number of openings on each side of a vessel permitting water to drain overboard from the deck; scupper.

T 194–65 I had a job to get her foot up in the floodgate, you know, the waterway. An' after we'd lifted up enough, [she] got in deck. P 209–73 ~s [are] holes on each side of a vessel at deck level, which is a means of letting water off the deck.

floor n also **flooring** for sense 1. For sense 3, *EDD Sup* ~ Sc, *Kilkenny Lexicon*.

1 In boat-building, a straight piece of wood used to join the body-frame timbers across the bottom of the craft.

T 43/8–64 The rule was that your fore-hook now was put together, an' the bottom piece we'd call the floor, an' the two pieces that come up an' shaped the side o' the boat was called the timbers. 1969 *Nfld Qtly* July, p. 19 Floors [are] curved wooden timbers joining two stuttles and extending transverse along the flat part of a boat's bottom. 1973 *Decks Awash* May, p. 28 The 'Flooring' is used to fasten the ends of the timbers.

2 The horizontal surface of a 'fish-flake,' esp the thin poles resting on the vertical 'shores' and covered with boughs.

P 143–74 The flake was a long table-like structure on which the fish were dried. Its foundation was made of longers. The 'floor', or bottom layer of the flake, was made of planks and covered with boughs. Longers were placed on the boughs at intervals of two feet, serving to prevent the boughs from blowing away as well as to mark off the 'lists' (spaces for drying the fish).

3 Phr *on the floor*: in one's home.

P 148–63 Only one child was allowed on the floor, a baby in the crawling stage. T 222–60 People use the expression 'on my floor' when they mean 'in my house.' I remember one time a woman telling me that her daughter's child was born on her floor.

floption n also **flopshion** *ADD* ~ [Nfld: 1896]. In phr *all in/of a floption*: in confusion, in a fluster.

1896 *Dial Notes* i, 379 To catch one all of a floption—to take one unawares. 1896 *J A Folklore* ix, 30 All in a floption, confusion or disorder. 1925 *Dial Notes* v, 331 Flopshion. Agitation.

flour-barrel n

1 Phr *eat out of one flour barrel*: to share a single account at a merchant's store.

1967 FIRESTONE 48 In the past there were many extended families that had no household accounts. There was but the company account and to this were charged all the food, clothing and other articles purchased by the father for the group. . . They would all 'eat out of one flour barrel,' both in the sense that they shared what had been purchased for all and, literally, in that the family head would open a barrel of flour which all would use until the contents were consumed.

2 Comb **flour-barrel chair**: a home-made chair fashioned from a flour-barrel; BARREL-CHAIR.

T 96/9–64¹ That was a flour-barrel chair, sawed off. They had a flour-barrel chair, sawed off. They had a flop here in 'em, see, used to rise up, cover. Rise up the cover and that's where they put all their sewin' and knittin'. 1966 SCAMMELL 50 Uncle Neddie leaned back in his flour-barrel chair, lit his pipe and expatiated on his favourite subject. T 409–67 That's all I had then—the flour-barrel chair.

flouse v also **flaus** [flæuz] *OED* ~ v 1 dial; *EDD* flosh: flouse, flowse in Ha Do W. Of a vessel, to come down heavily in a running sea; to thrash about in the water (while swimming).

1924 ENGLAND 221–2 Such wind an' rain, me sons! Dere was no let-up, an' no driet [clearing up] in de wedder, a week on end. De schooner flaus down in de trock o' de sea, like she goin' to de bottom, evvery minute. Q 67–30 ~ To thrash around in the water like one who cannot swim. P 167–67 ~ To jump into the water (with a splash).

flouse n also **flaus** *ADD* flaus Nfld; see FLICY*. Splash.

1924 ENGLAND 249–50 My darlin' man, such a muckery! *Flaus*, evveryt'ing was goin'. 1925 *Dial Notes* v, 331 Flaus. interj. An exclamation denoting sudden or violent action. T 194/6–65 I never tried to swim in my life, not before then. An' I was lookin' over my shoulder at Fred an' I made one flouse wi' my right hand like that, an' I slewed around an' I come out of water breast high.

flowers n pl Cp HARRAP *fleur: rocher à f. d'eau* 'rock that is awash.' Rocks or ledges over which the sea breaks; see SUNKEN ROCK.

1708 OLDMIXON 9 The Bay of *Flowers* near Greenspond is dangerous for shelves. 1745 CAREW 25 The Vessels were all that Night in danger of being lost off a Rock called the *Flower's* especially the *Kingsale*. [1929] 1933 GREENLEAF (ed) 288 "The *Nordfeld* and the *Raleigh*": He put her ashore on Flower's Ledge at four in the afternoon; / He put her ashore on Flower's Ledge, she was in her full bloom. 1951 *Nfld & Lab Pilot* i, 322 A vessel entering Flowers cove should steer to pass at least a quarter of a mile northward of Seal islands.

fluking v, ppl

1 Very drunk.

[1894 BURKE] 53 "Challenge Walking Match": You'll beat out Druken, says I half fluken, [drunk] /

With heat near cookin', I thought I'd boil. P 148–60
That man is flukin'.

2 Moving rapidly, twitching.

P 148–60 We say a cow was flukin' when she waved
her tail around.

flummy n also **flummy dum** ['flʌmi]. A kind of
bread made by hunters and trappers. Cp FUNNEL
BUN.

P 130–67 The bread is all gone, we'll have to make
some flummies. C 71–27 A common dish among hunters is known as flummy dum. It consists of a dough
made of flour, bread soda and water which is wrapped
on a stick and then toasted over an open fire in the
woods, [and] when cooked is somewhat like unleavened bread. C 74–94 In North West River I heard of a
concoction made up by trappers called a flummedum, a
mixture of flour, salt, butter and sugar. It was mixed in
the morning, rolled up in a long string, wrapped
around the funnel of a stove and left to bake.

flunky n also **flunkey**. Cp *DC* flunkey 2 (1923)
for sense 1.

1 An unspecialized helper aboard a fishing vessel (P 245–55).

1936 SMITH 85 I will give you the carpenter, a good
man, Skipper Samuel Bonnell, and Willie Campbell,
also the kitchen flunkey, Robert Spracklin, who was on
all calls. 1976 *Decks Awash* Aug, p. 19 When we went
trapping the fish, I went flunky, pronging the fish out of
the boat. When I would fill the box, they would give
me a fish and this was my pay.

2 An anchor fixing a trawl-line in place.

1938 MACDERMOTT 170 The trawl is anchored to the
bottom by a small anchor called a 'flunkey' on either
end.

3 Comb **flunky buoy**, ~ **keg**: a float.

1942 *Grand Bank U C School* 39 ~ On the bank
fishery, this is used at any point of the trawl to tell
fisherman how far he has removed fish from the hooks.
P 113–79 ~ keg: small keg kept aboard dory and used
to temporarily support a trawl with a heavy catch of
fish while taking the catch off the hooks.

flute n *ADD* ~ 2 Nfld; cp *Dict Aust Colloq*
fluter 'incessant talker.' A man's mouth (1925
Dial Notes v, 331).

flux v *EDD* ~ Ha IW W. To snatch or steal; to
beat or thrash; to move, shake or pluck violently.

P 118–67 We used to flux apples [from neighbour's
trees]. P 148–71 If I disobeyed when I was younger,
[she] would say, 'You're going to get a good fluxing.'
C 71–37 [At] any light fall of snow [she] would mus-
ingly look through the window and say, 'Well, the old
woman [Sheila] is fluxing her geese again.' Q 71–5 He
was fluxing the furniture around. Q 71–13 ~ to shake in
a violent manner.

fly v *EDD* fly-by-night 3 Co for sense 2.

1 Phr *fly a drop of water*: of a boat, to run
before a squall.

[1954] 1972 RUSSELL 37 And we'll fly a drop of water
gettin' back home. Nothin' to hurt, but a wettin'
wouldn't do you any good. I think we'd better run
before it to Hartley's Harbour.

2 Comb **fly and set***: see FLYING SET.

fly-by-night: a young female gadabout;
PATH-BEATER.

C 66–4 A fly-by-night is a girl who is always out
flirting around with the boys.

fly¹ n Cp *DAE* ~² (1708–) for sense 1.

1 A small, biting winged insect, appearing in
the summer months (*Simulium* spp); BLACK FLY.

[1620] 1895 PROWSE 117–18 Those flies seeme to
have a greate power and authority upon all loytering
people that come to the Newfoundland; for they have
the property, that when they find any such lying lazily,
or sleeping in the Woods, they will presently bee more
nimble to seize on them, than any Sargeant will bee to
arrest a man for debt; neither will they leave stinging
or sucking out the blood of such sluggards, untill like a
beadle they bring him to his Master. [1663] 1963
YONGE 60 In July, the muscetos (a little biting fly) and
garnippers (a larger one) will much vex us. 1774 *Trans
Roy Soc* lxiv, 377 A venomous reptile, or insect, is not
to be found. . . The whole country is filled with very
small flies, which are exceedingly tormenting.
[1831–1839] 1926 AUDUBON 344 We found that camping out at night was extremely uncomfortable, on
account of the annoyance caused by flies and musqui-
toes, which attacked the hunters in swarms at all times,
but more especially when they lay down, unless they
enveloped themselves in thick smoke. 1933
GREENLEAF (ed) 251 "Change Islands Song": The
weather still got hotter, plenty nippers, flies and stout.
1971 CASEY 134 The flies are some thick or the flies are
mad, so you can watch out for the northeast wind.

2 Comb **fly-catcher**: (a) round-leaved sundew,
a bog plant that attracts and traps small insects
(*Drosera rotundiflora*) (1956 ROULEAU 30); (b)
red-breasted nuthatch (*Sitta canadensis*) (1976
Avifaunal Survey 145).

fly-oil: an insect repellent, esp for 'black flies.'

P 65–64 Fly oil is insect repellent. T 55/7–64 And the
flies in ten thousands. They eats me now but then they
wouldn't eat me because I used to keep the fly dope
on, you know, oil, fly oil.

fly spit: see SPIT n.

fly² n A triangular flag flown at the top of the
foremast (Q 67–75).

1925 *Dial Notes* v, 331 ~ A small flag on the mast
denoting a good catch.

flying ppl Cp *Fisheries of U S*, p. 14. Attrib **flying
set**, **fly and set***: in Bank fishing, the dropping of
dories in rapid succession to set their trawl-lines;
see SET n.

1921 *Nat Geog* July, p. 28 The method of fishing by
'flying sets'—towing the dories and dropping them over
the Bank—is carried on [to] some extent by salt fishermen, but these craft usually anchor on the Bank, and
the dories row away from the vessel, take up their posi-

tion, and set the gear. 1942 *Grand Bank U C School* 36
A 'flying set'—dropping dories while schooner sails in a
circle. M 70–27 Each vessel carried from four to twelve
dories with two men in each using from forty-eight to
sixty lines, when we would fly and set. What I mean by
fly and set is that in the early part of the season we
would fish under sail. The vessel would get underway,
take up anchor, hoist the sails, and the Captain would
drop his dories, with two men and all the gear in each,
in rotation; when the gear was set, he would sail back
and pick up all his men. Each man would quickly eat
his meal and the Captain would drop them all by their
gear. After the gear was taken back, the Captain would
again take them all aboard. P 113–74 A flying set is the
lowering of dories one at a time as the banking vessel
sails in a circle. When the last dory is away the vessel
would pick up the first one, and so on.

fob n also **fobber** *OED* ~ sb[3] dial; *EDD* 1 Gl
Ha So D. Foam, froth; something unsubstantial.
   P 104–60 ~ Froth on sea-shore after the water
recedes; something with no substance to it. T 50–64
They had lots o' tinned meat, an cottage beef, an' stuff
like that. An' baker's bread—nothing you get tired of
quicker. Baker's bread—it is only a fob. C 71–21 Fobber. Foam which settles on the top of water. Q 71–17 ~
froth on sea-shore after water recedes or froth around
ponds.

fodge n Cp *EDD* fadge sb[5] 'a thick cake or
loaf.' Cp FADGE. A free meal.
   1888 HOWLEY *MS Reminiscences* 7 [They] all come
to have a feast at our expense. They are a most shame-
faced crowd and will hang around as long as we are
within reach or they see a chance of getting a fodge.

fodge v See FADGE.

fog n For combs. in sense 2: *OED* ~ sb[2] 6 b ~
gun (n.d.); *EDD* ~ v 'to eat heartily', 3 ~ meal
'a hearty meal' Ir, JOYCE 257.
   1 Commercially-produced food, esp bread, as
opposed to home-made product; BAKER'S FOG.
   P 130–67 Get two loaves of fog. 1971 NOSEWORTHY
202 ~ Bread which is bought in a store. Often soft.
   2 Comb **fog-bird**: sooty shearwater (*Puffinus
griseus*), or greater shearwater (*P. gravis*);
HAGDOWN.
   1908 DURGIN 25 On every berg and piece of pan ice
were perched groups of curious birds, called by the
natives [hagdowns] or fog-birds, and countless numbers flew about the ship uttering strange cries.
   fog-gun: fire-arm or cannon discharged as a
warning-signal to vessels in foggy weather.
   [1794] 1968 THOMAS 45 Our Ship was enveloped in
one of those fogs which eternally hover over the
Banks. Fog guns were constantly fir'd, and a horn continually kept sounding to warn other Vessels of our situation. 1820 *Waterford Mirror* [Ireland] 26 Jan . . .was
in the act of loading a Gun, that he had just discharged, as a fog-gun, at the Battery at Fort Amherst.
1839 PRESCOTT 147 "The Fog-gun": Again! again the
welcome sound, / Nearer and nearer still! / It cometh
from their native ground, / The steep and well-known

hill / Frowns through the evening's darkening glooms /
As once again the Fog-gun booms.
   fog-loom: distorted appearance of an object in
foggy weather.
   1861 DE BOILIEU 164 One of the most remarkable
phenomena of the coast is the mirage, or fog-loom,
when objects take monstrous sizes, and when mere
cockboats expand to three-deckers!
   fog man: supposed supernatural creator of fog.
   T 453/4–67 Some people used to call it the fog man,
but as far as I know there's no fog man. . . The feller
[who] makes the fog makes the sunshine.
   fog-meal: a big meal; SCOFF.
   C 75–19 ~ A term which means the same as a big
meal. 1978 *Evening Telegram* 20 May, p. 14 Poor Jack
was gettin' ready to have a fog meal, he opened the tin
of Armour's [beans] and then went to pour out a cup of
tea.

follow v also **folly** ['fɒlɪ, 'vɒlɪ] *EDD* folly v Ir, s
w cties, *ADD* follow, var folly for sense 1; *OED*
follow 1 c, *EDD* 2 for phr in sense 2.
   1 In the form *folly*: to follow.
   1862 *Atlantic Mo* ix, 368 In course I wanted to folly
the schooner; so I runned up along, a little ways from
the edge, and then I runned down along. T 50/3–64 My
father used to often come after us when it be stormy
over the harbour. They couldn't folly the road 'cause it
be drifted in. T 208/9–65 So he follied the strake and
come to the moose. C 71–92 I heard my father say,
'folly me.'
   2 Phr *follow a horse*: to work as a teamster or
carter.
   1838 *Gazette* 20 May Deserted—James Walsh, a
hired servant—generally employed in following a
Horse and Cart. 1925 *Dial Notes* v, 331 ~ [To] work as
a teamster or coachman. 1937 DEVINE 22 'What does
he do now?' 'Oh, he *follows a horse*.' 1978 *Evening
Telegram* 19 Sep, p. 6 The driver, a man named Power,
used to 'follow' a horse for Charlie Lester.

folly See FOLLOW.

fong n also **fung*** *Kilkenny Lexicon* fong. A
long leather boot- or shoe-lace; thong.
   1897 *J A Folklore* x, 205 ~ a leather or deer[skin]
string or strap. 1925 *Dial Notes* v, 331 ~ The string of a
boot. 1937 DEVINE 22 ~ A leather or deerskin bootlace. P 148–65 Fungs [are] shoe-laces—in common use
around fifty years ago. P 103–67 Fung—long leather
shoe lace.

fool n Prob a loan-translation of OWNSHOOK,
'foolish woman, female fool' in Irish, recorded in
Nfld after 1885 with the sense of a mummer, esp
one dressed as a woman.
   1 One of the men, usu elaborately dressed,
who participated in a mummers' parade; a
Christmas 'mummer' or 'janny.'
   1842 BONNYCASTLE ii, 139–40 Some of the masks
are very grotesque, and the fools or clowns are furnished with thongs and bladders, with which they
belabour the exterior mob. 1842 JUKES i, 221 Men,

dressed in all kinds of fantastic disguises. . .called themselves Fools and Mummers. [1886] 1893 *J A Folklore* vi, 64 [I remember] one of my brothers, who was quite a genius in that line, making a full-rigged brig, and giving it to a person who was to be a 'fool' on New Year's Day, to be used in the decoration of his cap. [1900 OLIVER & BURKE] 47 The mummers ceased to appear in the latter part of the [eighteen] fifties, and a new party known as the Fools came in their place—the juniors from Xmas day to New Year, and the seniors from New Year to Old Xmas. All kinds of fancy costumes were worn by the Fools, and great amusement was afforded to the people. 1937 *Bk of Nfld* ii, 259 The Fools were one of the great Christmas institutions in the city, as persistently perennial as the season itself. For the time being they held right of way on Water Street, Middle Street, and the streets uniting them. In processions and in detachments they made things lively for other pedestrians, whom they banged over the head and shoulders with inflated bladders. The fools wore masks or thick veils. Their heads were crowned with triangular hats made of cardboard and covered with wallpaper, or gigantic cocked hats adorned with a profusion of glittering metallic spangles and gaily coloured ribbons, and terminated at the top in two or three points from which issued plumes. T 74–64 But then they used to have a bunch of what they call fools, dressed out an' mat rags an' everything sewed onto their clothes. They were a rough bunch. Everyone used to be afraid o' them. T 75–64 An' there were so many masked men then, you know, they were called fools. An' they were to protect the flag while the mummers were in reciting in the dwelling houses. C 71–124 [The women] spent weeks sewing ribbons all over the shirts. They had their own music and used to dance on the snow until they were invited in for a dance in the kitchen. Where the fools went everyone went. They would ask 'Where are the fools tonight?' They would be served cake and ginger wine.

2 Phr *dress in the fools; go out in the fools*: to dress in the disguise and costume of a Christmas mummer or janny.

1893 *Christmas Greeting* 18 I think it was on St Stephen's Day, that my friend. . .first showed me his 'rig,' and told me that I should get one too as they were all 'going out in the fools' that night. C 67–39 As a child he and his friends used [the] greyish-green hair-like substance which grows on dead branches of trees to make whiskers and eyebrows, very often for cloth or brown paper masks, when they 'dressed up in the fools' at Christmas and went from house to house much as children do now at Halloween.

foolish a *NID* ~ 1 a. Feeble-minded, simple or retarded.

T 70/1–64[1] 'Twas a foolish feller on shore, what they call a foolish—silly feller, used to tell the people that he used to see a light. T 54/62–64 Everybody there knew him. The foolish feller, we used to call him. 1973 WIDDOWSON 510 [He] was supposed to be foolish or mentally retarded.

foot n pl [vuɥts]. Cp HEAD n 3.

1 The bottom or lower part of a seal-net, fish-net, etc, weighted to sink the device in the water.

1792 CARTWRIGHT *Gloss* i, xiv The foot of [the shoal-net] is brought to, on a shallop's old rode, and the head, on two fishing-lines; with corks between. [1886] LLOYD 51–2 The [seal] nets are heavily leaded on the foot or bottom, and are placed in a perpendicular position on the bottom of the sea, the head or upper side of the net being supported by floats. 1937 DEVINE 22 Foots. The bottom of nets, where the leads are attached. In hauling home the linnet, so as to lose no fish, the frequent orders of the skipper would be heard: 'Pull on (or easy on) the *foots*.' T 80/3–64 You heave the edge clear; well now, the feller that heave the voots had to heave linnet an' all, an' an awful weight to pick up. M 69–23 [Parts of a cod-trap include:] back foots, leader foots, side-wall foots. P 90–73 The leader is the same depth as the trap [and] is brought to along the head rope at about the thirds or slightly under, and along the foot rope of full thirds or slightly over. This is so that the foots will be longer than the heads. All straight nets are brought to, so that the foots are longer than the heads.

2 Comb **foot rope**: a weighted line attached to the bottom of a net; foot-line.

[1776] 1792 CARTWRIGHT ii, 177 I sent five hands in a skiff to Laar Cove to look for the nets, which we lost there last fall; they found the foot-ropes of two, with the killicks and moorings, but the lennet was all rotted off. [1802] 1895 PROWSE 419 About fifty pounds weight of strong twine will be required to make a [seal] net, the half worn small hawsers, which the boats have used in the summer fishery, serve for foot ropes. 1861 DE BOILIEU 85 [The seal-net] is set to any depth of water not exceeding fifteen fathoms nor less than three, and is moored by a couple of killicks, fastened by eight or ten fathoms of rope to the ends of the foot-rope, which, by its weight, keeps the end of the net close to the bottom of the water, while the corks make it stand perpendicular. 1895 GRENFELL 71 Thus the whole school are enclosed. Now the weighted foot rope is 'gathered' together, the net has become one vast bag, and the prisoners are dealt with as before, i.e. dipped out and bagged off. T 25–64 They'd shoot the seine right around, then pull it in till they'd get it nearly into the beach and they draw it by pulling up the footropes. They get huge catches of fish like this. T 187/90–65 When you'm bringing to a net you put on perhaps a ball here and a ball there, a couple o' fathom apart [so they] don't tangle up the linnet; your foot rope'd just about fit that, and 'cordin' as you heaves away your net he'd sink to the bottom. 1977 *Evening Telegram* 28 Apr, p. 42 Tenders are invited for the purchase of. . .approximately 600 lbs of seine leads, complete with footrope and leadrope.

footing n *OED* ~ 2 (1572–1847), *EDD* 2 for sense 1; *OED* 9, *EDD* 6 for sense 2. See also FEETING.

1 Footprint (of a man, animal or bird); track; a path indicated by such signs; TRACKINGS.

[1776] 1792 CARTWRIGHT ii, 114 [The wolf] took [i.e. followed] my footing, and robbed six of my traps in succession, by digging at the backs of them. 1819

PANL CS 1 29 May After travelling about 1 Mile I discovered the footing of two or more Indians quite fresh. 1842 JUKES ii, 141 I could follow a 'footing' of a man, or detect that of a deer. [1886] LLOYD 87 'Oh! there's no trouble to find her; show me the footin' and I'll soon show you the hare!' 1914 WALLACE 187 ''Tisn't th' havin' a poor cruise now an' again's what's botherin' me,' began Ed, 'but they ain't no footin'; and where they ain't no footin', they ain't nothin'.' [1916] 1972 GORDON 87 We had a well-marked track over the snow-crusted marshes, but soon after leaving here it came on to snow, and all sign of footing was quickly obliterated. P 245–63 Footins [are] tracks left by partridge. T 453/4–67 We walked down along by the side o' the snow. By an' by we sees the footin', gone across the snow, man's footin'. 1972 *Evening Telegram* 19 May, p. 3 By the size of his footing he is not a small one either. I have never seen a moose's footing that size before.

2 Phr *pay one's footing, ~ footery*: of a person new to a job, to stand a treat for the other workmen.

1842 JUKES i, 263 Every fresh hand, they said, has to pay his footing for his first dip [i.e. fall into the water]: so I was obliged not only to lose my footing in water myself, but give it afterwards in rum to the crew. 1902 *Christmas Bells* 19 Now that this is your first winter's visit, you'll have to pay your footing by telling us a yarn. 1937 DEVINE 71 A custom prevailed in Newfoundland amongst fishermen, labourers and men of trades, especially those paid by the day, to wipe the boots and shoes of those who visited the scene of their work for the first time. It was called 'paying their footery,' which usually meant standing drinks for the crowd. The writer first saw this ceremony performed on the visiting member for the district of Bonavista in the sixties.

for prep JOYCE 29, DINNEEN *mar* 'for'; *OED* ~ 11 for to 'now arch or vulgar'; *EDD* 7.

1 As a satisfactory member of (its class or kind).

1968 DILLON 138 That's the smallest thing ever I see for a woman. . . Them tulips, they're no good for flowers. . . The last one we had, she was no good for a cow.

2 Phr *for to*: in order to; for the purpose of.

T 1–63¹ [The oxen] used to pull out their logs and stuff for to build their rooms. T 36/8–64 You were supposed to build your flakes, when you had the collar on; build your flakes, build your stage-heads, tar your roof, go in the woods and cut rines for to cover up your fish. T 31/2–64 You want a good memory for to mind all this kind o' stuff.

fore- prefix Cp *OED* fore-peak naut 'extreme end of the forehold'; forerunner 3 'prognostic, sign.'

Comb **fore-cuddy**: cabin at the bow of a small vessel; esp on an undecked fishing-boat, a small enclosed space forward; CUDDY.

1842 JUKES ii, 53 I went and lay down in the fore cuddy, a place about the size of a dog-kennel, and stinking of salt butter and fish, and was dreadfully sea-

sick. 1887 *Colonist Christmas No* 5 I had just settled this in my mind, when who should I see coming up out of the fore-cuddy but Tom Pugsley, in his go-ashore clothes, like myself. [1929] 1933 GREENLEAF (ed) 254 "Lukey's Boat": O, Lukey's boat got a fine fore cutty, / And every seam is chinked with putty. T 45/6–64 'Twas in the fall o' the year, she left to go to St John's in an open boat—she was gangboarded, you know, fore cuddy an' after cuddy on her, an' breeze come on, they got drove off. C 71–127 ~ bow of a small boat where the ropes and anchor were kept. 1974 SQUIRE 20 A crew for such boats would normally be five men. The skipper stood on the forecuddy to guide the boat.

forelay: see FORELAY.

fore-peak ['fɔɹpiːk, 'foɹpʊk]: in a lumber camp, the living quarters and store-room of the foreman or 'skipper.'

[1958] 1965 PEACOCK (ed) iii, 762 "Twin Lakes": I awoke in the morning in very good humour, / Straightway to the forepeak my bucksaw to take. T 96/7–64¹ So the foreman went then into the fore-peak an' got a new suit of clothes and put on un. P 65–64 The living quarters for the skipper and the second hand is called the fore peak. The fore peak is always situated at the extreme end of the cook-house. T 187/90–65 He'd go to the fore peak then; the boss'd have clothes in there to deliver, an' take it from your wages. 1977 *Park Interpret Pub No* 15 . . .a full-scale reconstruction of an old-time logging camp, complete with bunkhouse, cookhouse, forepeak, filing-shack and barn. . . The forepeak contains instruments for scaling or measuring wood. 1979 TIZZARD 362 The foreman, cook and cookies slept in the 'fore peak,' one end of the cookhouse. No-one went to the 'fore peak' except on special business. This was the office for the camp and was sort of private.

forerunner: premonition; cp FETCH.

T 55/7–64 She come and called me just as plain as if you called me. I knew there was something after happened her. Forerunner of death. . .I got forerunner of death myself. C 71–87 On the eve of a death in the family it was said that sounds of boards being sawed could be heard from [the carpenter's] workshop, although he was not then at work. Such happenings were called 'fore-runners.'

foreshipman: in the 'boat-fishery,' member of the crew stationed forward.

[1663] 1963 YONGE 57 The boats' masters, generally, are able men, the midshipmen next, and the foreshipmen are generally striplings. They bring the fish at the stage head, the foreshipman goes to boil the kettle, the other two throw up the fish on the stage-head. 1866 WILSON 207 [The planter] requires two men with him. One is called midshipman, because his station is the middle of the boat; the other man is called the foreshipman, because his station is forward. The fore-shipman is sometimes called captain; but the captain of a fishing-boat is the cook.

fore standing-room also **foreroom, forward standing room** [ˌfoɹ ˌstændʊŋ 'rʉum]: in a fishing boat, a compartment between the 'tawts' [seats] of the craft; see also ROOM, STANDING ROOM.

T 43/8–64 Now, from the bow tawt to the stem is the

fore standing room and from that to the after tawt is the midship room. T 172/5–65 I came down, pitched on the cuddy on my crown, on my head, like that, but I fell down in the fore standing room. Q 67–18 Forward standing room: section in small fishing boat for standing. Q 67–86 Foreroom for standing [in a boat]. 1977 BURSEY 126 He was steaming out the narrows in his motor boat with two goats in the fore standing room that were looking ashore and bewildered. 1979 TIZZARD 200 Rowena's grandfather. . .fished in the front of the boat from the fore standing room, I fished by the engine room [and] Thomas Watkins fished from 'back aft.'

foreign av   *OED* ~ 13 naut colloq (1844) for sense 1; *OED* 14 (1863) for sense 2.

1 Phr *go foreign/use foreign*, etc: to sail overseas; to employ a vessel in overseas trade.

T 141/64–65² I suppose he didn't go foreign, but he used to drive away on a foreign ocean, an' pick hisself up an' get back to Newfoundland again. 1975 BUTLER 51 Wakely got the *Jean Wakely* built two years after that up in Nova Scotia to use foreign.

2 Comb **foreign-going**.

1845 *Journ of Assembly* Appendix, p. 233 The colliers in the coasting trade employ a large number of sailors; which, together with all our Foreign going ships, give. . .a supply of seamen for the navy. 1894 MOTT 171 [Duder] owns over two hundred sail of fishing and foreign going vessels, besides a large number of boats and skiffs. 1900 PROWSE 100 The Merchant Shipping Act of 1894. . .consolidates the law relating to merchant shipping and becomes the law of this colony with reference to our foreign-going ships. [1929] 1933 GREENLEAF 235 Mr Noftall said that the maid of Newfoundland came from Conception Bay, and that the composer was Captain Duer of St John's a 'foreign-going' captain, who ought to know what he's talking about when he mentions all the other girls of the world! 1936 SMITH 152 Mr Hiscock loaded three foreign-going vessels, which sailed direct from the coast. 1960 *Evening Telegram* 11 Aug, p. 7 John Rourke had three foreign-going vessels, one of these was the brigantine *Shamrock* built at Carbonear by the master ship-builder of his day, Michael Kearney. 1973 HORWOOD 14 Now the owners planned to send her back into coasting again. Harry didn't want to go, paid off and looked around for a foreign-going berth. P 245–74 They might go to Liverpool and get their foreign-going tickets. 1977 BURSEY 85 [He] had been a foreign going seaman.

foreigner n   A vessel engaged in carrying dried cod to overseas markets; informal development of FOREIGN-GOING (vessel).

1895 PROWSE 153 The sack ships or freighters, now generally known in Newfoundland as 'Foreigners.' 1909 BROWNE 68 When the fish is 'made' it is shipped on board a 'foreigner,' or to the collector of the 'firm' with which the fisherman 'deals.' 1920 WALDO 80 [That store] had three ships in the summer of 1919 carrying fish abroad—'foreigners.' 1936 SMITH 34 All that Mr Smith had were his ten crews around Edward's Harbour, and two schooners green-fish catching. . .; both

schooners got a saving voyage, and John Munn & Co sent a foreigner to Edwards Harbour for their voyage.

forel n   also **farel, farrell, farrow*, furl*, varl** ['færəl, 'farəl, 'fərəl] *OED* ~ 1 c (1393–); *EDD* forrel s w cties. Cover of a book.

1897 *J A Folklore* x, 205 Farl or varl—the cover of a book. 1937 DEVINE 21 Farrell—the cover of a book. T 141–65¹ He brought un and give un to me, a blue farrell with gold letters around. P 229–67 He tore the farrell off the book. M 69–2 [on autograph book:] 'Be it ever so narrow / You can write on the farrow.'

forelay v   *EDD* fore (69) ~ lay 'to get ahead. . .of anything' K; *ADD* 1; G S WASSON *Cap'n Simeon's Store* (1903), pp. 225–6 [Maine]. To get ahead or in front of (a person).

T 58/64–64 Well how much trout was there? I mean, if you were rigged for gettin' trout. . .thousands, I'd say. One trying to forelay the other as you landed it; they were that plenty. T 148–65 She knowed a place they used to go every night. So this night she forelaid him and she got in a tree. 1966 SCAMMELL 91 If I don't be forelaid by one of them Easter Tickle pirates. 1977 RUSSELL 122 I noticed these two barrels there, gettin' in our way, but Jethro forelaid me whenever I went to shift one of 'em, so I didn't much heed to 'em first along.

foreright a   *OED* ~ 3 a dial; *EDD* 5 s w cties; *ADD* (Nfld). Careless; heedless; reckless.

1887 BOND 67 [He was] venturesome and foreright. 1897 *J A Folklore* x, 205 ~ But in Newfoundland it means reckless or foolhardy. 1924 ENGLAND 179 He'm foreright [careless], an' don't 'eed to nothin'. He do not one livin' tap, dat feller!

fork n   Cp *EDD* ~ 4 'bifurcation of. . .human body' So D for sense 1.

1 Crotch.

P 256–66 [said of a woman disguised as a man during mummers' visit] I know he's a maid, sure—he got a soft fork. M 71–104 The fork of a pair of pants or the fork of a person's legs. 1975 GUY 53 I had up a pair of them 93 cent panty hose on the five-minute super special and I had half a mind to have 'em but this other streel, she grabbed hold of one leg and we took 'em in two at the fork. P 141–77 Ferks or firks: the crotch of a pair of trousers.

2 Comb **fork (and kissing) kin**: close blood relations; cousins.

1972 *Evening Telegram* 28 June, p. 3 There are three separate spider webs holding St John's together. One is lawyers. Two is fork and kissin' kin. And three is the fraternity of captains of commerce. P 188–75 [With hiring practice] in the old days, 'twas a lot of father and son and what we used to call fork relations.

fork v   Cp *OED* ~ 4. To transfer fish from a boat to a vessel or fishing-stage with a long-handled pronged implement; PEW v, PRONG v.

1842 JUKES i, 226–7 Here the fish are forked out of the boat with a kind of boat-hook or [pike], the prong being stuck into the head, and the fish thrown up on to the stage much in the same manner as hay is thrown into a cart. 1960 FUDGE 12 We forked our load of haddock onboard, passed our forks to the Captain. 1977 *Evening Telegram* 10 Nov, p. 6 I heard one fisherman say this summer when he was forking the lovely fish overboard with no market for it he said the old fork comes in handy today and he also said I wonder if Father Neptune would object to me using this two prong fork to fork the fish overboard on account of no markets.

forward a   Comb **forward boat**: a light boat used at the seal-hunt, capable of being hauled over the ice when the floes are too heavy to sail through.

1895 *Xmas Review* 19 The forward boat now rounded Suther Point and, pulling her sheets home taut, stood well in the harbor. 'She'll fotch Little Beach,' said the light-keeper. T 29–64 Years gone by the men of the place used to go out seal-hunting into what we call a forward boat. That will be a boat sixteen feet long [used] hunting the bellamer and the harp seals. T 172/5–65 Well, 'tis get the boat out—we had a forward boat—an' take her in tow.

foss v   Cp FARMER & HENLEY fossed ppl adj 'thrown.' To play around with; to throw roughly.

[1894–1929] 1960 BURKE (ed White) 9 "Why Don't the Men Propose?": I am fossed 'round like a crackie / And my head is sore from blows. P 148–67 [It is] so easy to foss around [with a small alarm clock].

foss n   [fɔs]. A kick.

P 245–62 He gave him a foss in the arse. P 259–67 Come on, boys, let's have a foss (with the football). P 145–73 I'll give you a foss right up the arse.

fouly a   Cp *OED* foul 6 c foul bottom naut; *EDD* 11 (3) foul-ground. Rough or rocky condition of the sea-bed, harmful to fishing nets.

T 80/3–64 You couldn't haul trap there—tear un up, see; fouly bottom. He had a spurt first heavin' down th' rocks; he hove down tons an' tons o' ballast: made it a bit better but 'twas still hooky an' fouly. P 13–74 We can't set out nets 'ere, b'y, the bottom is too fouly.

found [past tense] See FINE².

founder v   Cp *OED* ~ 3 'to fall down, give way.' To crumble, capsize, let fall, to cause to collapse.

1891 PACKARD 147–8 A man told me, an iceberg 'as tall as a steeple' floated in as if to make a safe harbor, and became anchored within fifty yards of his 'stage.' Just after he and his family had gone to bed, the berg broke to pieces—'foundered.' M 68–24 We decided to founder [a pile of firewood] against the side of the house facing the cemetery. Q 71–3 The wall foundered last Friday killing three people. 1975 GUY 17 There are two methods for the proper foundering of cliffs. One is where you get down on the beach and keep chucking up rocks at a piece of cliff that is loose and almost ready to fall. Presently, it is dislodged and crashes down with quite an amusing roar and in a cloud of

dust. The other method is to get up on top of the cliff and dislodge a loose piece either by chucking rocks at it, poking it with a stick, or, most trepid of all, getting someone to hold on to your arm while you reach down and kick it with your foot.

fourer n   Cp *O Sup²* four 3 d fourses; *EDD* fours 1. A drink of liquor or a light snack taken at 4 p.m.

P 133–58 ~ A drink [of spirits] at four o'clock. C 70–15 Besides the three basic meals there was. . .another [light refreshment] at 4 p.m. called the 'fourer' and again a cup of tea and a biscuit.

foust n   also **fowst**. Cp *EDD* fust v: foust Ha. See FOUSTY. Mould.

1966 SCAMMELL 127 "Bakeapple Jam": But when my mom with reverent hands removed the outer seal, / There was 'fowst' on the top of her Bakeapple jam.

fousty a   also **fausty** ['fæɵstɩ, 'fæustɩ·, 'faustɩ, 'faustɩ, 'fɵɵstɩ] *EDD* fusty; fousty Gl Ha W So D. Mouldy; musty; gone sour; having a bad smell. Cp SMATCHY.

1925 *Dial Notes* v, 330 Fausty—musty or mouldy; of tea or bread. 1937 DEVINE 22 ~ Sour, decaying. P 148–61 Look at the fousty clothes on him. T 141/66–65² [This old cape ann] was fousty. He was one of them old timers, red flannel linin's in un, see. A kind of greenish colour, they was. T 222–66 [The other kind of jam] often has [foust] on it after a few months. . .in other words it's fousty. C 69–31 My mother called a dress she found in an old trunk fousty   having a stale, bad odour. C 24 71 [The soup is] rather smatchy and I was going to give it to the cow, but you can have it if you want it. (Smatchy means sour or fousty).

fox a   Cp *OED* fox v 6 'to repair (boots) by renewing the upper leather.' Comb **fox boot** [fɒks 'buut]: a boot with a renewed foot; a foxed boot.

T 199–65 In the spring o' the year, when the weather'd start to get wet, they had the same legs but they'd cut the bottom part off of 'em an' they'd put a leather bottom an' a leather sole an' heel on 'em, and they'd have what they call fox boots. P 207–67 He put on his fox boots to go out in the storm.

fox n   *Cent* fox-trap (1890) for cpd.

   1 Red fox (*Vulpes fulvus*). See CROSS n: CROSS-FOX, PATCH (FOX).

   2 Attrib, comb, cpd **fox-board**: wooden board on which a fox-pelt is stretched to dry; FUR n: FUR-BOARD.

[1776] 1792 CARTWRIGHT ii, 133 Two hands sawing a stock for foxboards, and two others were at work on the ice about the shalloway. The eastern furriers went round their walk.

   fox dog: local variety of mongrel dog.

[1823] 1977 *Evening Telegram* 30 May, p. 6 It was hauled on sledges by a small breed of dogs which appeared to be a cross between the collie and the fox, called the 'fox dog.'

fox-eye: a circle around the moon, indicative of bad weather.

Q 71–11 ~ a sign of weather. If it's a big ring round the moon then the weather is far away and if it's a small ring then the weather is handy.

fox-flower: thrift (*Armeria labradorica*) (1956 ROULEAU 30).

fox-hook: a device to capture a fox.

[1775] 1792 CARTWRIGHT ii, 121 I set a fox-hook, baited with a small bird.

fox-trap: a device to snare foxes.

[1785] 1792 CARTWRIGHT iii, 56 At four this morning I went on shore [at Fogo] and bought seventeen foxtraps of captain Cheater. 1792 PULLING *MS* Aug William Elliott who resides at Ragged Harbor was going along near the seaside with another man and a boy to set some fox traps and coming to a pond fired at some ducks. 1836 [WIX]² 124–5 . . .the distribution of a south-wester, a fox-trap, or a pair of mokasins, was not a. . .matter for Divine interference. 1914 WALLACE 182 Fox traps were set upon the marshes, and baited with rabbits which had been hung in the tilt until they began to smell badly, or with other scraps of flesh. The trap securely fastened by its chain to a block of wood or the base of willow brush, was carefully concealed under a thin crust of snow. P 9–73 In winter fox traps are set on humps on open ground so that the wind blows the snow away. 1977 *Them Days* ii (3), 6 That was in the spring when we was out to the islands checkin' our fox traps.

foxy a   also **foxey** *OED* ~ 2 (1850, 1879), *Cent* ~ 2 (1890) for sense 1.

1 Reddish-coloured; sandy-haired; rufous.

1895 *Outing* 94 His luxuriant, reddish beard [has] earned for him the sobriquet of 'the foxy man,' contracted to simple 'Fox' in familiar intercourse. [1897] 1927 DOYLE (ed) 72 "The Landfall of Cabot": With a scattered foxey whisker. 1901 *Christmas Review* 8 The crowning glory of Con's makeup was a foxy wig, and never did Sampson have more strength in his locks than did Chas B Hawkins in his red head-covering. 1910 PRICHARD 86 He was able to secure his brother Frank—a 'foxy man,' as Jack described him, meaning red-haired and bearded, a man with as genial a temper and as broad a back as ever added to the gaiety of a camp. 1924 ENGLAND 147 Den Hickson call un ahl de foxy sons o' guns, an' start to make fast to un. . . Can't strike de cap'n of a ship, ye know. 1941 DULEY 263–4 But he had an amazing skipper. His navigation was something to write home about. He never looked at a sextant. He searched for a 'foxy rock' and turned north. 1953 *Nfld & Lab Pilot* ii, 483 Foxey islands. . .both have conical mounds, composed of reddish rocks covered with grass.

2 Faded in colour from a dark to a lighter hue.

[c1904] 1927 DOYLE (ed) 67 "The Kelligrews Soiree": And a swallow-tail from Hogan / That was foxy on the tail. 1925 *Dial Notes* v, 331 Foxey. Discoloured through age; faded. M 65–9 He turns a foxy colour (pale). 1982 *Evening Telegram* 16 Feb, p. 17 [He] said

it would be better if she had a bottle of ammonia to take the foxy colour out of her husband's gansey.

3 Attrib, comb **foxy chub**: eastern ruby-crowned kinglet (*Regulus calendula calendula*) (1959 MCATEE 56).

foxy rogue, ~ **ruler**, ~ **tom**: fox sparrow (*Passerella iliaca*); BOBBY-ROOTER, HEDGE SPARROW, RUSTY TOM ROOTER (1959 MCATEE 66; 1976 *Avifaunal Survey* 159).

1913 HOWLEY 8 Later on the loud harmonious note of the fox sparrow, as we call him the 'Foxy Tom' [enlivens] the woods.

foxy rum: a light-coloured or amber rum.

[1927 BURKE] "Who Put the Herring on the Booze?": And Herrings saturated, boys, / With Old Tom and foxy Rum, / While us poor devils in the town / A drink is trying to bum. 1933 GREENE 99 There might be seen a black bottle of 'foxy' St Pierre rum (that has more than likely never paid its duty) being passed from hand to hand. Q 71–13 When light rum first appeared on the Newfoundland market, it was referred to as foxy rum.

foxy tom: see **foxy rogue** above.

foxy tom-cod: a small cod-fish.

P 148–63 ~ Small tom cod sold at door, 10–12 in. long. Q 71–6 ~ used to describe a small reddish-brown cod usually caught close to shore.

frafferm* See FLAT a: FLATFORM.

frame n   Cp *OED* ~ 7 'structure. . .constructed of parts fitted together' obs or arch for sense 1; *EDD* sb¹ 1, *ADD* 2 (Maine) for sense 2.

1 A number of nets strung together from the shore to catch migrating seals in coastal waters; STOPPER.

1818 CHAPPELL 197 There are two modes of catching the *seals*: the one is, by mooring strong nets at the bottom of the sea; and the other, by constructing what is called '*a frame of nets*,' near the shore of some small bay. The latter is the most-approved method. [1832] 1975 WHITELEY 42 Two days afterwards the American schooner. . .entered my frame. [1886] LLOYD 52 Immediately they begin to 'run' the 'frames' are put out. A frame consists of three nets of the same depth as the water in which they are placed. They vary in length according to the distance the seals run from the shore. They are often eighty and a hundred fathoms in length. The frame is placed in the run of the seals in the form of a square, the two side nets being safely secured to the shore by means of a ring bolt. 1923 CHAFE 15 A trap or a 'frame of nets' which was the most approved [method of catching seals] in the Straits of Belle Isle one hundred years ago. Strong nets were moored, running from the beach into the sea, reaching from the bottom to the surface of the water, and smaller nets sunk to the bottom. The fishermen then used their best efforts to drive the seals between the outer net and the beach. On a given signal the people on the shore hove up the small nets and the seals became enclosed on all sides. 1972 SANGER 237 ~ A trap used to catch seals on their coastal migration.

2 A skeleton; RAMES.

P 269–63 ~ skeleton, whether man, beast or fowl.
P 63–70 ~ left-over [rib cage] of a cooked chicken.

frankincense n   *OED* ~ 2 (1577, Nfld: 1620; 1866). The resin of a spruce tree.

1613 *Willoughby Papers* 16, 1/2 The turpentine that commeth from the firr and pine and frankincense of the spruce is likewise sent. [1620] 1887 MASON 157 Tarre, Tirpintine, Frank-Incense. 1682 COLLINS 98 And out of these Woods may be had, Pitch, Tar, Rosin, Turpentine, Frankincense.

frankintine* n   blend of *frankincense* and *turpentine*. The resin exuding from a fir tree or other conifer; MYRRH (Q 67–83).

frankum n   also **frankgum**. Clipped form of *OED* frankincense: var franc(k)umsence. See FRANKINCENSE. The hardened resin of a spruce tree, often used for chewing; GUM.

[c1880] 1927 DOYLE (ed) 33 "The Ryans and the Pittmans": There was one pretty maiden a-chawing of frankgum, / Just like a young kitten a-gnawing fresh fish. 1892 *Christmas Review* 25 After he was through, he got some 'frankum' off a tree near at hand, doubled up the rind and sealed it as complete as you please. 1903 *Daily News* 8 July "He's Not the Man for Green Bay": So let the old boy thank him, / If he possessed the entire sway / He'd have you "pickin" frankum. 1937 DEVINE 22 ~ Hardened gum of spruce tree, used as chewing gum. 1966 HORWOOD 134 . . .a large wad of spruce gum—which the boys called 'frankum'—chewed to a soft, stringy consistency. . . C 69–8 Spruce trees, through various gashes, excrete a sap which hardens into a whitish or honey-coloured substance of a dry brittle texture. We called [it] frankum. If pried off the tree with a knife, usually in lumps about the size of marbles, and put into the mouth, one can chew it into a fine, dry powder. This dry powder all over one's mouth is rather disagreeable, but after about two minutes, saliva apparently begins to work on it and it grows sticky and lumps together. Eventually it will be just like chewing gum. C 70–15 This hardened resin or frankum was pink in colour and when softened in the mouth produced a gum for chewing. It was tougher than the commercial chewing gum, but it was claimed by older people to have some medicinal properties for the protection of the teeth. 1970 *Evening Telegram* 18 Apr, p. 22 But we knew the taste of frankum from an old spruce.

frape n   [freɪp]. Cp *OED* frape² ['ropes which our Seamen call Fraping' (1703)]. A rope forming part of the 'collar' or mooring of a boat.

1955 ENGLISH 34 ~ a rope with blocks to moor a boat. P 113–56 Go down and put the punt on the frape. 1963 HEAD 161 The boats. . .are moored on a collar from which a frape, or tight rope, extends inland to a mooring on the beach. P 13–73 ~ A form of mooring with a pulley fixed in the end of an anchor buoy. A rope fitted into this pulley allows a means of pulling a boat to shore for embarking.

frape v, n   also **frapse*** [freɪps]. Cp *OED* frap v 2 naut 'to bind tightly'; *EDD* ~ v¹ 1 So, D Co for sense 1.

1 To draw or haul (a rope, etc).

1937 DEVINE 22 ~ To drag the sea bottom with a hook, jigger or grapnel. P 94–57 ~ To draw the line over the gunwale of a boat.

2 To fasten (a line) carelessly; to dress in an untidy fashion.

P 203–56 Frapse. To bind or tie in a careless or haphazard way. P 210–69 When she sees anybody who is dressed untidily, she says that their clothes is fraped around 'em. C 71–111 When we were small, if she didn't like the way we were dressed, she would say, 'How have they got that fraped around them?'

3 Phr *be in a frapse*: to be carelessly attired (P 207–67).

frapse* See FRAPE v.

fraw See FRORE.

frawsy n   ['frɑːzi·]. Cp *EDD* ~ 'a treat; a dainty' Ha D Co. A sweet cake or biscuit with an added or special ingredient.

P 103–67 A frozie [is] a molasses pork-cake. P 29–74 A froozie [is] a gingerbread with scruncheons added to the batter.

free v   Cp *OED* free 3 b naut (1627–). Phr *free out*: to bail water from a boat.

1936 SMITH 91 The gunwales of the boat were broken, and she was three-parts full of water. I tied the log line around the second hand. . .and he jumped on board the boat and began freeing her out. T 50/1–64 He gaffed that un overboard and the two of them dumped her—they hove her to—dumped the bread boxes and freed her out.

freely n   Local name in Cape Freels area for a syrupy drink made from the berry of the 'bakeapple' or cloudberry (*Rubus chamaemorus*).

P 259–67 Freely is bakeapple juice, served like syrup to mummers at Xmas time, and was only referred to as freely during this time of the year. C 75–29 ~ a drink made from bakeapple berries.

freighter n   Cp *DC* ~ 2 Nfld 'passenger or crew member on a coastal vessel' (1905–).

1 Member of a fishing-crew transported by vessel to his fishing station; esp one sailing to his 'station' or 'room' on the Labrador; STATIONER.

[1701] 1954 INNIS 109 Captain Arthur Holdsworth from Dartmouth, had brought 236 passengers, 'all or great part of which are byeboat-keepers and under a pretence of being freighters aboard his ship, which is only for some few provisions for their necessary use, he had put and continued them in the most convenient stages. . .' 1871 HOWLEY *MS Reminiscences* 22 I was aboard the Labradorman coming home and saw the little schooner during a flash of lightening. . . Our vessel was the *William* from Brigus filled with freighters coming home after the voyage was over. [1888] 1897 *Nfld Law Reports* 307 The plaintiff was a hired shareman of one Charles Parsons, a dealer and freighter of the defendant's, and was engaged to proceed with Parsons to the Labrador fishery. 1895 GRENFELL 52 Each Newfoundland vessel brings a number of people called 'freighters.' These are landed at various harbours, where they have left mud huts and boats the previous year, and where they will fish all summer. 1908 TOWNSEND 123 Besides their own crew of five or six men and a woman and girls to cook and help at the splitting tables, the vessels are often burdened with 'freighters,'—fishermen and their families with no schooners of their own. 1936 SMITH 138 On the 12th the *Ruby* arrived. She discharged the freighters and Labrador gear. 1977 *Inuit Land Use* 314 The freighters were the men and women who did not own their own schooners, but were left on the shore for the summer months. During this time, they fished for the cod in bays and safer inshore waters, where a small rowboat could be used.

2 Phr *go freighter*: to sail as a passenger to one's summer fishing-station.

1936 SMITH 106 I went freighter again with Mr Jerrett in the schooner.

french a *DC* ~ shore 1 (Nfld: 1806–); cp *EDD* ~ a 1 (7) ~ tobacco 'a weed smoked by boys.'

Attrib **french clover**: see **french tobacco** below.

french hen: the ruffed grouse (*Bonasa umbellus*).

1891 PACKARD 426 Ruffed Grouse [occur] rarely at the head of Hamilton Inlet, but only on the south side; rather common at Paradise River, flowing into Sandwich Bay, and abundantly in the valleys to the southward, where birch grows plentifully. These birds are known as 'French Hens.' 1909 BROWNE 208 The 'Ruffed' Grouse. . .is known to settlers as 'French Hen,' or 'Birch Partridge.' 1959 MCATEE 24 ~ Ruffed Grouse (Nfld., 'Labr.').

french shore: the coast of the island of Newfoundland where the French held fishing and curing rights until 1904, defined by the Treaty of Utrecht (1713) as north from Cape Bonavista on the east coast to Point Riche on the west, and amended by the Treaty of Versailles (1783) to extend from Cape St John to Cape Ray; TREATY SHORE.

[1822] 1928 CORMACK 93 The French shore of Newfoundland is one of the most valuable on the globe for fisheries. 1886 HOWLEY *MS Reminiscences* 44 Had a visit last evening from some French shore men named Noseworthy and Taylor about taking up land. They want to settle down in North Arm on some of the lots we laid off sometime ago. They come from Griquet. 1902 *Christmas Bells* 3 However that be, she had fished the Labrador seas, traded the French Shore, smuggled red liquor from St Pierre. 1936 SMITH 33 Mr Smith himself was on board to supervise the building of the different fishing rooms at Edwards Harbour, and they left Brigus about the 10th of June and arrived at Quirpon, French shore, in good time. 1942 *Little Bay Islands* 12 It also sent a trader to the French shore. [1952] 1965 PEACOCK (ed) i, 136 "High Times in Our Ship": He got the yacht ready, / Went on the French

Shore. 1979 TIZZARD 200 Her father was half owner of an eighteen ton schooner, and after a little while going there he persuaded me to make the trip to the French shore with them in the spring for a load of codfish.

french tobacco, ~ **clover**: knapweed (*Centaurea nigra*).

1898 *J A Folklore* xi, 229 ~ *Centaurea nigra*. 1898 *N S Inst Sci* ix, 373 French clover.

fresh a Cp *OED* ~ a 3 'raw, inexperienced, green' (1724–) for sense 1.

1 Of a fisherman in his first or second season at the West Country-Newfoundland fishery; cp GREEN MAN, YOUNGSTER.

1699 *Act of Wm III*, 10 & 11, Cap. xxv Every Master of a By-Boat, or By-Boats, shall Carry with him at least Two Fresh Men in six (viz.) one Man that hath made no more than one Voyage, and one Man who hath never been at Sea before. [1701] 1895 PROWSE 228 These Bye boat keepers. . .were most of them able fishermen and there was not one fresh man or green man amongst them as the Act requires.

2 Comb **fresh water**: esp in coastal placenames signifying the availability of fresh water in a cove or harbour for replenishing ship's supplies and for fisheries purposes. Cp WATERING.

1620 WHITBOURNE 9 The fresh waters and Springs of that Countrey, are many in number, and withall very pleasant. [1675] 1971 SEARY 215 Freshwater Bay. [1772] 1792 CARTWRIGHT i, 249 In the evening, twenty geese came into the fresh-water pond, which empties itself into the Cove. [1775] 1955 *Journeys* (ed Harvey) 62 The first harbour we made and got up near the fresh Water we proposed to fix our Nets. [1794] 1968 THOMAS 123 Every Harbour, every Bay and every Inlet you enter it is surprizing to see the many fresh water streams that rush down with heedless violence to be swallowed up in the boundless Ocean. 1823–4 *Edin Phil J* x, 157 The primitive rocks extend onwards to Gower's Lake. The shores of this lake bear a strong resemblance to the shores of Fresh-water Bay near St John's. 1951 *Nfld & Lab Pilot* i, 103 Freshwater cove, the landing place for telegraph cables, indents the northern shore. 1971 SEARY 71 Freshwater occurs at least eight times as a specific on the Avalon Peninsula, signifying a source of fresh water for ships.

fresh av *OED* ~ av B 1 'newly.'

In v phr *fresh cork*: to renew the cork floats on a net.

[1772] 1792 CARTWRIGHT i, 231 At day-light we hauled the nets, and had two spring fish and a slink: we afterwards tightened the moorings, and fresh corked part of one of the nets.

fresh tail: to reset or bait an animal trap or snare; cp TAIL².

[1771] 1792 CARTWRIGHT i, 175 I then crossed the river, and fresh tailed all the traps and deathfalls in Prospect Hill Path.

fresh n *OED* ~ a 4; cp *DAE* n 4 (1849, 1883). The unsalted flesh of birds or animals eaten fresh. See also CRAFT².

[1906] GRENFELL 182 The old gun, six foot in the barrel, was deadly for ducks or even with ball for deer. Of this he was always very fond, so that a sigh of joy escaped him when she was once more brought down, cleaned up and loaded—more especially as he got a bit of 'fresh' for all hands during the winter. 1940 SCAMMELL 24 "The Shooting of the Bawks": No doubt our wise Commissioners will formulate a plan, / To furnish fresh for everyone who lives in Newfoundland. T 92/3–64 I nearly always kept boarders and they had all they could eat—plenty of fresh. Birds, you know, they have the salt water birds, turrs, these beautiful birds. So there'd be plenty o' fresh. We'd bottle for the summer, we'd can and bottle them. 1973 WADEL 25 George also engages in various subsistence activities: fishing, hunting, and some gardening, and is thus able to supply his household with fresh food or just 'fresh' as he calls it. 1979 TIZZARD 226 No-one ever complained about the beef or pork given away because when the neighbours butchered, we got a good meal of fresh.

friend n Comb **friend-girl**: a girl's girl-friend.
P 269–63 ~ A girl's girl-friend [contrasting] with a boy's girl-friend, sweetheart. T 34–64 [She] was my friend-girl because we was old pals and she was my age. P 25–67 George's wife and a friend-girl went to Chicago.

frightish a Timid, nervous, easily frightened.
P 269–64 [The horse is] not frightish. P 100–71 She's pretty frightish when it comes to strangers.

fritten a Comb **fritten bread**: ship's biscuit or bread fried, for example in pork fat (P 212–81).
1932 BARBOUR 35 We were all very hungry and decided to make some 'fritten bread.' We got the frying-pan and put in some butter and hard tack and fried it. 1937 DEVINE 23 Fritters—small cakes or soaked hard biscuit, fried with bits of pork; [are also called] fritten bread.

front n Cp *OED* ~ 7 e for sense 1; *DC* 3 (Nfld: 1933–) for sense 2.
1 A stretch of coast facing the sea.
1901 *Christmas Bells* 14 The inhabitants all along that part of the north west coast, known as the Newfoundland side of the Straits of Belle Isle, leave their dwellings on the front, at the first appearance of winter, and in a body repair some five or six miles inland. 1942 *Little Bay Islands* 13 The men living on the front of the Island in Northern and Southern harbours fished with hook and line on the fishing grounds off the Island, such as Offer Ground, Parker's to the Cross, Salmon Rock, etc.
2 The seas east and north-east of Newfoundland, esp the area covered by the leading edge of the ice which moves south in the spring and on which the seal-herds whelp; the seal-hunt; cp BACK².
1924 ENGLAND 16 One or two ships usually go 'to the back,' which means into the Gulf of St Lawrence. The others all go 'to the front,' or northeast, into the Atlantic ice pack drifting down on the Labrador cur-

rent. 1925 *Dial Notes* v, 331 ~ The region east of Newfoundland. 1933 GREENE 9–10 . . .The 'Front'—as the Seal Fishery on the east coast of Newfoundland is termed (in contradistinction to that of the 'Gulf,' which is the smaller west-coast Seal Fishery). 1972 BROWN 7 The wooden steamers were allowed to leave their final ports. . .a day earlier [than the steel ships]. These dates applied to ships killing seals at The Front, north and east of Newfoundland. 1981 *Evening Telegram* 27 Mar, p. 3 All three captains said the slob ice experienced during mild temperatures after the first four days at the Front off the coast of Labrador was one of the main reasons why they returned.

frore p ppl, a also **fraw, ?froke, vrore**, and forms with *a-*: **afrore**, etc. [froəɹ, froəɹ] *EDD* freeze 3, var frore Ha W Gl D etc, vrore So IW W. Many observers note *(a)frore* in isolation, but it has been rarely recorded in unselfconscious speech. Frozen solid, esp in phr *frore over*: very cold.
1863 MORETON 34 Hard a fraw. Frozen, hard frozen. 1895 *J A Folklore* VIII, 29 ~ for froze or frozen. 1907 MILLAIS 339 Frore and froke, for frozen. [1927] 1946 PRATT 213 "The Iron Door": To dim-illumined reaches where the frore, / Dumb faces of despair / Gazed at their natural mirror in the door. 1937 DEVINE 23 The brook is frore over. T 31/2–64 I wasn't frost-burned. My mitts were frore onto my hands. My face was frore, my collars was frore an' everything was balli-cattered. C 71–112 Frore over is a term used to describe water that has frozen over on the top.

frost n Cp *OED* ~ 7 b frostburnt (1770); cp *DAE* frost 2 (1718) for frost-shoe.
Cpd **frostburn**: an injury of the flesh caused by exposure to freezing temperatures; frostbite.
1792 CARTWRIGHT *Gloss* i, x ~ A deep and serious penetration of frost on any animal substance. The effect of severe frost on animal substances being equal with that of fire, is the reason of that term. [1820] 1915 HOWLEY 122 On the 31st many of the party with myself fell in, precautionary measures were instantly taken to prevent frostburn, and we put up on the South side of the river. 1861 DE BOILIEU 104–5 I leave the reader to conclude which of the two poor fellows had the best chance of being preserved from frost-burns. [1916] 1972 GORDON 45 In cases where a lonely traveller may enter a house unaware that he has been touched [by the frost], the effect is like the application of a red-hot poker! That is why the term 'frost-burn' is used rather than that of 'frost-bite.'
Hence **frostburn** v: (a) to injure the flesh by exposure to freezing temperatures; (b) to spoil the quality (of fish, fur, etc) by exposure to cold or ice (see 1873 quot).
[1770] 1792 CARTWRIGHT i, 70 Three of the men were slightly frostburnt, and most of them seared. . . Frostburnt is a term used in this part of the world, to signify that the flesh is amazingly benumbed with cold, so as to render it callous. It has not unfrequently happened, that people have lost the use of their limbs, by the severity of the frost. [1794] 1968 THOMAS 125 All were *frost burnt* in March and April, but with good Treatment none of them have lost as much as a Finger.

1836 [WIX]² 55 I was in more danger to-day than probably at any other period of my journey, of being frost-burned. 1873 CARROLL 33 The first evil is, that if the weather is severe, many of the [seal] skins are sure to be frost burnt. [1929] MCCAWLEY 44 "The Newfoundland Fishermen": What a brave set of men are the sealers, / Who venture each spring to the ice, / Whose sufferings 'tis hard to describe. / For they're often frost burnt and crushed in the ice. T 84–64 You'll have some frostburned fingers if you'd take four or five minutes to load a gun! T 88–64 We left Boyds Cove the next morning, an' we frostburned ourself before we got home. We got frostbitten—our faces, noses an' the whole thing: a bitter day. 1972 BROWN 39 Others was out all the next night, and they was all froze, all but six or seven that were picked up next day, frost-burned somethin' cruel an' their minds gone wanderin'.

frost-shoe: boot or shoe with studs or nails in the sole to prevent slipping on ice.

[1794] 1968 THOMAS 52 [Newfoundland dogs] have gearing the same as horses; the wood is put into Sledges which they draw, and sometimes they drag a single stick only, attended by one man who wears frost shoes.

frost v Cp OED ~ 4 'to treat (a horse's shoes) by the insertion of frost-nails.' To fasten nails or cleats to a (sealer's) boot.

1976 CASHIN 86 I had not been accustomed to walking on slippery ice for any length of time and the soles of my sealskin boots were not properly 'frosted.'

froster n Cp OED frost sb 7 c frost-nail (1874); *Kilkenny Lexicon* froster. A nail or cleat on horse's hoof to prevent slipping on the ice; a similar device fastened to a man's boot.

1785 PANL [engineers' report] Frosters [on horses' hooves]. [1900 OLIVER & BURKE] 63 "Wedding Cake at Betsy's Marriage in Fogo": And frosters from sealer's skin boots. 1924 ENGLAND 6 I marvelled at the thick soles of these waterproof boots: soles studded with 'sparables,' 'chisels,' or 'frosters,' as various kinds of nails are called. 1968 DILLON 159 They used to put frosters in the heels o' the boots. They'd leave 'em down so far, the way you wouldn't slip of a frosty day.

froth n Comb **froth-berry**: BUNCHY-BERRY, CRACKER ~ (*Cornus canadensis*).

1916 HAWKES 35 The creeper and plant varieties are legion: cracker berry or froth-berry.

frounge* v [fraɒndʒ]. To have reason to complain.

T 437–65 'There'll be no terms on nar side now. You can't frounge 'gain me,' he said, 'an' I won't be able to frounge 'gain you.'

fruz v OED ~ obs exc dial 'to spread out (hair) in a frizzy mass; tangle'; EDD 1. To prepare or arrange (one's) hair.

1924 ENGLAND 74 'Wash y'r 'ands, an' you'm fit fer church,' Uncle Edgar bade me. 'Just fruz up y'r hair, an' dat'm well enough!'

fruz n ADD ~ Nfld. Phr *in a fruz*: in a state of excitement, confusion.

1924 ENGLAND 4 Gales and snowstorms soon swallowed us; ice blocked us; we had 'de devil's own fruz' for some three lively days. Ibid 155 One night we came near to having what the Old Man called 'a very miserable affair.' Long after tea, presages of serious trouble threw the ship 'rate in a fruz.'

fudge See FADGE.

full a

Comb **full breed**: a pure-bred horse (P 245–74).

1955 DOYLE (ed) 85 "When the Caplin Come In": Oh, here comes the horses backed out in their breeches, / Bedecked in gay colours, red, white, black and gray, / There's Macks and Maloney's with full breeds and ponies.

full mounting: see MOUNTING.

full av Comb **full studded**: (a) of a sealing vessel, strengthened with studs or timbers as protection against ice; (b) of a house or building, studded with upright timbers abutting each other and covered with siding. See also STUD¹ v.

T 141/60–65² He had she built, see, full studded for ice. T 181–65 You can look at the building, a hundred years old, [and] tell where they are. They're all full studded right around, all pine.

full n OED ~ B 2 b obs (1799), EDD 15. The quantity or content that fills (a receptacle) or completes a series.

1910 *Daily News* 23 Feb, p. 3 "The Price of Food": I often for a shilling got, / The 'full up' of a bag. / To-day we got to take it, / With the price marked on the stump. 1925 *Dial Notes* v, 331 ~ A good load or cargo [of seals]. T 54–64 Lots o' squid summer evenings. He'd jig the full of the boat again before he'd leave. T 94–64 Maybe a half the full of a barrel of blubber. M 68–16 He told me to go back any time I felt like it and he would sing the full of a dozen tapes if I wanted. P 108–74 The child is the full of his clothes.

full v EDD ~ v¹ 19; ADD 2. To fill.

1924 ENGLAND 79 'Safer out nigh the selvage, me son,' the Cap'n declared. 'A no'd-east wind'd full evvery bay out the Front an' might jam us.' [1929] 1933 GREENLEAF (ed) 242 "The Crowd of Bold Sharemen": We says to our skipper, 'What do you expect? / For we to go fulling all the puncheons on deck, / Go home in the fall, lift them out on your wharf, / And you then tell we sharemen we can't claim our part.' T 50/2–64 'Cordin' as the needle o' twine'd be used they'd full another one, see, with a ball. T 54/8–64 Pat stood guard, Mike went in the orchard. He got up in the orange trees an' he started pickin' the oranges, fullin' his pockets. T 75/7–64 But he had a cook. He told him to get rice for dinner. He fulled an oval boiler wi' rice, cover on the stove, an' it begin to plim. T 143–65 While we was fullin' the boat with water they killed three water bears. They was right up on the hill an' they never stopped till [they] tumbled right down alongside

of us. 1977 RUSSELL 33 When Liz, his missus,
(Grandma she is now), tipped up the keg that night to
full the molasses dish, she noticed there wasn't much in
it, so she wormed the story out of Grampa.

fungy a ['fʌndʒɪ] *OED* ~ obs (1578, 1721).
Spongy; full of air-holes.
P 224–67 Fungy bread has risen a lot, and the holes
are quite large. It is not considered good bread. 'That
bread is some fungy.'

funk n   *OED* ~ sb² obs [exc U S] 'strong smell
or stink' (1623–1725); *ADD* now rare for sense
1; for cpd in sense 2, cp Funk Island, a nesting
colony for sea-birds.
1 Evil-smelling odour or smoke (P 133–58).
1955 ENGLISH 34 ~ Smoke or vapour of evil odour.
2 Cpd **funk-bird**: sea-bird which nests on
coastal island.
Q 67–47 To smell like a funk bird; stink like a funk
bird.

funnel n   Cp *OED* ~ sb¹ 2, 2 b for sense 1.
1 A stove-pipe; also the chimney of a lamp.
[1770] 1792 CARTWRIGHT i, 38 The kitchen chimney, being a wooden one, and the roof of the dining-
room, (which the funnel of the stove almost touched)
took fire to-day; but it was extinguished before they
had received much damage. 1842 BONNYCASTLE ii,
125 [A] habitation which often contains the poor fisherman, and his generally numerous family, the smoke
escaping always from an old barrel, or a square funnel
of boards placed over the fire. 1895 *J A Folklore* viii,
35–6 *Funnel* and *funnelling* are used in Newfoundland,
and also in some parts of the United States, for stove-
pipe. 1921 *FPU (Twillingate) Minutes* 13 Jan Also a
bill. . .for funnels for stove and other repairs. 1937
DEVINE 23 ~s. An outport word for both stove pipes,
and lamp chimneys. T 141/64–65² An' here's the funnel, with smoke comin' out of un, an' down over the
weather edge was the end o' the house.
2 Jocular term for a top hat.
[c1904] 1927 DOYLE (ed) 67 "The Kelligrews Soiree": Oh, when I arrived at Betsey Snook's / That
night at half past eight, / The place was blocked with
carriages / Stood waiting at the gate. / With Cluney's
funnel on my pate, / The first words Betsey said: /
'Here comes a local preacher / With the pulpit on his
head.'
3 A narrow neck of land or isthmus; a passage
between steep hills (P 148–61; Q 71–9).
4 Comb **funnel bun**, ~ **cake**: bread-dough
baked on a hot stove-pipe or stove lid; STOVE
CAKE.
P 148–67 Funnel buns consist of ordinary dough,
wrapped around the funnel of the stove. C 71–97 Funnel cakes. Instead of putting dough in pans to make
bread, she just slapped it onto the funnel of the stove
and let it bake there.

funnelling n   The metal tubing of a stove-pipe.
1895 *J A Folklore* viii, 36 He bought so many feet of
funnelling. 1901 *Christmas Review* 19 Whether it was

the fault of the funnelling or the atmosphere I cannot
say, but said bogie became unmanageable, and fumi-
gated the club unmercifully. T 169/70–65² There was a
lot of fellers, had chimleys, but it's nearly all funnelling
[now]. 1972 MURRAY 139 Heat came from a big pot-
bellied stove situated toward the front of the room,
with several lengths of funnelling going from there to
the chimney at the back; the funnelling helped heat up
the room, hence placement of the stove away from the
chimney.

fur n   *OED* ~ sb¹ 5 (1827–), *DC* 2 (1928–) for
sense 1; for combs. in sense 2: *DC* ~ board
(Nfld: 1771–), ~ path 1 (1921–), ~ trade
(1743–).
1 An animal hunted or trapped for its fur.
[1771] 1792 CARTWRIGHT i, 189 No furs stirring
since the fine weather set in. [1777] ibid ii, 274 Jack and
I visited our traps in the home walks; no sign of furs
about mine, but many foxes had been near his. 1973
GOUDIE 56, 64 In January 1926, Jim got home with his
first catch of fur. . . He trapped a few fox while he was
waiting for the river to freeze up so he could get into
the country to trap the inland furs. 1977 *Inuit Land Use*
107 It was a hard life, you had to do a lot of walking.
Wasn't too hard when you got the fur, but the year you
got no fur, then it used to be hard—hard to get a thing
to eat.
2 Comb **fur board**: wooden board on which
animal pelt is spread to dry.
[1771] 1792 CARTWRIGHT i, 106 Charles and I were
engaged all day in altering the furboards, and making
new ones after the Canadian form. Those used in Newfoundland, being too short and too broad, do not make
the skins look near so well as the furboards of Canada.
1933 MERRICK 185 Since arriving, Harvey has built the
new cabin. . .and a whole set of new fur boards.
    fur catcher: trapper.
[1819] 1915 HOWLEY 118 I am informed by those
that live there that they do a great deal of injury to the
fur catchers in that quarter.
    fur path: hunting territory claimed by a trap-
per; TRAP²: TRAP LINE.
[1906] GRENFELL 182 So Uncle Rube could tend his
fur-path again, as he used to do before. 1947 TANNER
ii, 702 A tacit agreement has developed with regard to
individual rights to use certain fur-paths, i.e. certain
stretches in the forests where a trapper may lay out his
traps to the exclusion of all others.
    fur trade: the pursuit of and commerce in ani-
mal furs.
[1725] 1975 ANDREWS [3] The masters say they do
not connive at nor encourage their men to remain in
the Land, except such as come to carry on the Seale
and Furr Trade to the Northward. 1765 WILLIAMS 6–7
I shall make no Calculation on the Fur Trade, which
was very considerable before the French had such vast
Possessions to the Northward. 1936 DEVINE 50 His
specialty was the fur trade, but he also had general dry
goods.
    fur trap line: see **fur path**; TRAP²: TRAP LINE.
1976 *Evening Telegram* 3 July, p. 2 [The Advisory
Council] is preparing its case against the method and
location of. . .woodcutting in the Goose Bay area as

the Company's loggers bear down on valuable fur trap lines.

fur v *DC* ~ Nfld (1799–) for sense 1.

1 To hunt seals for their fur pelts; esp to trap fur-bearing land animals.

[1698] 1975 ANDREWS [2] The number of boats that are Furring this winter is 20. 1792 PULLING *MS* Aug He furred at two brooks called the Northern and Peter's Brooks (that is he placed traps on and near both those brooks last winter to catch the beaver, foxes etc that frequented those parts.) [1849] [FEILD] 60 Two Englishmen are also with them this summer fishing, as sharemen; in the winter they go afurring. 1881 *Nineteenth Century* ix, p. 92 Fur was pretty plentiful in those days, and a man could make a good income out of a couple of months' hard work, furring in the fall. 1907 MILLAIS 53 I was in furrin' (trapping) wi' him. 1933 MERRICK 71 He used to fur the path that cuts in over the hills from Grand Lake, near Cotter's Point, some twelve miles from North West River. T 203/5–65 He was furrin' in on that country. C 70–15 Although he was a logger he also did some hunting and furring as a sideline.

2 Phr *fur together*: to share a trapping area with another.

1916 GRENFELL 11 These two men were furring together—that is, they shared the same fur path and halved all they caught. 1925 *Dial Notes* v, 331 ~ Share the same fur path.

furrier n *DC* ~ 1 esp Nfld (1770–). A fur hunter or trapper.

[1766] 1971 BANKS 140 An old Furrier we spoke with told us he rememberd a skin sold for five Guineas which was taken somewhere in Canada bay. [1775] 1792 CARTWRIGHT ii, 43 I appointed two men to look after the traps, whom I shall henceforth distinguish by the name of furriers. 1811 BUCHAN *MS* 25 Several Furriers had called. 1871 HOWLEY *MS Reminiscences* 6 With the exception of Mr Peyton and a few of his furriers, there was no one living who had ever penetrated as far as Red Indian Lake and the whole territory was a veritable terra incognita. 1919 GRENFELL[2] 137 One day a Northern furrier came to me as a magistrate to insist that a trading company keep its bargain by paying him in cash for a valuable fox skin. T 178/9–65 He was furrin'; he was a furrier.

furriery n *DC* ~ Nfld (1770). The activity of hunting and trapping fur-animals.

[1770] 1792 CARTWRIGHT i, 72 The furriers began to build a tilt of boards, which is to be sent to Eyre Island, for the convenience of furriery and shooting.

furring vbl n *DC* ~ esp Nfld (1778–); *O Sup*[2] 4 (Nfld: 1778–) for sense 1.

1 The occupation or business of hunting or trapping fur-bearing animals.

[1766] 1971 BANKS 146 For the Prosecuting of this Fishery many hands are Left every year in the different Harbours who by this & furring give a very good account of their time to their Employers. [1785] 1792 CARTWRIGHT iii, 21–2 As the killing of beavers is an art appertaining to the science of furring. . .I shall say no more on that head, except that they are always killed by staking their houses, by guns, or by traps. [1822] 1928 CORMACK 100 They exist by furring and a small cod-fishery. 1871 HOWLEY *MS Reminscences* 5 They live by salmon fishing in summer; lumbering and furring in winter. 1909 GRENFELL[2] (ed) 195 Their winter method is to take what supplies can be hauled on sleds by hand, set traps along their route, the length of which is determined somewhat by snow conditions, and take up the catch of fur on their return march. They are known as 'planters'; their occupation is 'furring.'

2 Attrib **furring land**: hunting or trapping territory yielding fur-bearing animals; FUR PATH, TRAP[2]: TRAP LINE.

1977 *Inuit Land Use* 285 You had a place for the summer and a place in the winter in regards to making a living. You'd have to go in a bay where there is good furring land—get lots of fur. . . In the summer you had to come out on the coast after the fish.

furring voyage: an enterprise or period of hunting or trapping animals for their fur pelts. See VOYAGE.

[1778] 1792 CARTWRIGHT ii, 373 I fitted out Joseph Tero for a furring voyage to White-bear River, at which place he is to reside by himself during the winter.

futter See FAITOUR.

fuzz* n, v *EDD* ~ v[2], sb 2. An effervescent mixture; to fizz.

T 33–64[3] I knowed a feller put a bottle o' Eno's fruit-salts in the chamber upstairs, where there's no toilet. When they'd [piss] in the chamber it would all go to fuzz. T 36/9–64 The cook would mix up fuzz—a water-bucket full of vinegar and half a pack of bakin' soda. After it was made and stirred up, the fuzz would all go out of it, but there's a nice sharp taste to it. P 148–71 [Of a bottle of spruce beer that is shaken] It's fuzz up.

G

gache See GATCH n.

gad n Cp *OED* ~ sb[1] 5 'rod or wand' dial (1535–) for sense 1; *OED* ~ sb[4] (1728–), DINNEEN ~ 'withe, a twisted twig or osier; a tie or cord' for sense 2; *ADD* 1 'a whip' for sense 3; JOYCE 259 for sense 4.

1 A pliable branch, often forked, passed through the gills of a trout or the toes of a seal's 'flipper' for ease in carrying; the quantity of trout or flippers so carried.

[1894 BURKE] 43 "The Trouters' Yarn": Last week a crowd of sporting lads / Went off to string them on the gads. 1898 *Christmas Bells* 5 We gathered our fish in baskets and on 'gads' and made our way down to the beach. 1924 ENGLAND 53 Some of the men growl that more than once they had 'got home wid not'in'' but a bundle o' dirty clo'es an' a gad o' smatchy [tainted] flippers!' [1894–1929] 1960 BURKE (ed White) 49 "Mrs Mullowney": Sure she worked him like a hoss, / Till his back got in a double / Lugging gads each day across; / Till he nearly filled a puncheon / And to feed a steamer's crew— / For her friends had no fault finding / At this famous fipper stew. 1937 DEVINE 23 ~ A witherod to carry trout or flippers. [1954] 1972 RUSSELL 12 Look at the fine gad of trout I've got. P 108–70 A gad for trout is made by breaking off a small branch of a tree below the V and peeling it, and you string the trout through the gills.

2 A slender, flexible twig used like a rope for fastening; WITHE.

1913 THOMAS 187 We cut down four or five old tree stubs, bone dry from years and years of exposure to the elements. Lashing them together with redwood twisted into a 'gad' and propelling the impromptu raft with a pole, we landed safely on the island. 1925 *Dial Notes* v, 331 ~ A withe for a wattled fence. 1968 DILLON 139 Fences were always tied with gads, a spell ago. There was no such thing as a nail, them times. M 71–120 Six hoops are fitted to make a 'ring.' A ring is then taken off and another started. Six rings make a bundle of hoops and two bundles make a nitch. Each nitch is tied together with 'gads' or 'ritrods' [withe-rods] which are twigs cut from trees.

3 A stick or rod used for whipping (P 269–64).

M 68–16 Although the horses were by no stretch of the imagination race horses, with a cut of a gad across the hind quarters we could get quite a bit of speed out of them. M 71–91 Girls also liked 'lacing the top.' Their fathers would carve large tops for them to spin. They also needed a small stick (or gad) with a piece of string attached to the end. The top was spun and then whipped or laced. M 71–34 The gad was a stick of about three or four feet long used for instilling discipline into the school-master's charges. C 75–144 [He] told me that a gad was a very tough and flexible stick [that] he used when he was a boy to beat the cows home.

4 Phr *as tough as a gad* (1937 DEVINE 63).

P 230–67 That piece of meat is as tough as a gad. 1979 *Salt Water, Fresh Water* 83 Well, I was as tough as a gad—that's an expression in Newfoundland to say you're tough—and with big thick hands, fisherman's hands.

5 Comb **gadberry**: the shrub, northern wild raisin (*Viburnum cassinoides*); THRASHBERRY; WITHE-ROD.

1970 *Daily News* 9 Sep, p. 8 Among our local shrubs and trees [is] our Withe Rod or 'Gadberry.'

gad v See GAD n. To string a catch of trout on a pliable branch passed through the gills.

1902 *Christmas Bells* 15 We packed our baskets and 'gadded' the balance of our catch—seventeen dozen all told.

gaff n also **gaft**. Cp *OED* ~ sb¹ 1 b (1656–), *DAE* 2 (1832–), *EDD* sb¹ 2 for sense 1; *DC* Nfld (1883–) for sense 2; *OED* sb¹ 5 ~ hook (1844–) for comb in sense 3.

1 A type of boat-hook with a (usu short)

wooden handle, used for various fisheries purposes; HAND-GAFF.

1745 OSBORNE 822 [They] drew [porpoises] aboard, with the help of the other sailors, which, with iron hooks, which they call *Gaffes*, tied at the end of a long pole, pulled them up. 1819 ANSPACH 429 If [the cod] is of large size, it is seized, as soon as raised to the surface of the water, with a gaff or large hook fixed to the end of a pole. 1832 MCGREGOR i, 227 The cod. . .is lifted into the boat. . .by a strong iron hook fixed on the end of a short pole, called a gaft. 1911 LINDSAY 50 Each man carried a spruce pole, on the end of which was a sort of boat hook called a 'gaff.' 1967 *Bk of Nfld* iv, 246 And then there was a gaff; that is a stick with a hook in one end of it. It is used to pull fish in over the boat with. C 67–14 When a man who is a member of the Society of United Fishermen is buried, a gaff is broken in two pieces and placed in the grave. The gaff is used (as well as to pick up fish) also for guiding a boat into the wharf or reaching things almost out of reach. M 68–7 Gaft. Used on board a punt to pick up the buoys or the salmon nets. There are gafts of all sizes; some handles are short while others are long. There is a hook fastened to the end of the stick with some service around it. 1971 NOSEWORTHY 203 ~ A stick placed in the side of a dory and used to guide the hauling of trawls.

2 A stout pole, 5–8 feet (1.5–2.4 m) long with an iron hook and spike fastened to one end, used to assist a sealer on the ice and to kill seals; BAT n.

1842 JUKES i, 260 Every man prepared his 'gaff,' by firmly fastening a spiked hook like a boat-hook, with strong line, to the head of a stout pole, about six or eight feet long. 1873 *Maritime Mo* i, 254 He carries. . .a stick six or eight feet long, which is called a 'gaff,' and serves as a bat or club to strike the seal on the nose, where it is vulnerable, and also as an ice-pole in leaping from 'pan' to 'pan,' as well as for dragging the skin and fat of the seal over the fields and hummocks of ice, to the side of the vessel. To answer these purposes, the gaff is armed with an iron hook at one end and bound with iron. [1884] 1897 *Nfld Law Reports* 35 For the purpose of preventing competition and anticipating the arrival and active participation of others in the fruits of the ice-fields, kill as they go with a blow of a gaff, taking no heed to collect and pan and mark their spoil. . . [c1900] 1978 *RLS* 8, p. 25 ~ small stick used by the seal hunter for killing or stunning the seals, usually Dogwood or spruce. 1906 DUNCAN 134 Billy's father led me down to the landing-stage, put a gaff in my hand, and warned me to be careful—warned me particularly not to take a step without sounding the ice ahead with my gaff. 1916 MURPHY 28 The men had to use a sealing gaff to beat off the dog. 1924 ENGLAND 54 An' de odders'll haul ye out wid dey gaves [gaffs]—if ye don't get too far away from de gang. 1927 DOYLE (ed) 39 "Hunting Seals": With bat and gaff and 'panning staff' / Surmounted with a flag, sir; / Away we go on the great iceflow, / And we never care to lag, sir. T 43–64 If the ice was in, you'd walk off from the land, an' you'd have your gaff with you and your sealing rope, and probably you get the chance to kill one, two, or three or four. 1979 *Salt Water, Fresh Water* 53 We'd have a gaff you know, with a hook into her. The gaff was long enough to take you from one pan [of ice] to another, about seven or eight feet in length.

3 In designations of various parts and uses of 'gaffs' in senses 1, 2 above: ~ **head**, ~ **hook**, ~ **point**, ~ **stem**, ~ **stick**, ~ **work**.

1892 *Christmas Review* 11 Fires were blazing in the forges; sharp and clear rang out the sound of anvils, re-echoing to the stroke of the sturdy smith as he fashioned the iron 'gaff-heads' for the impatient sealing captains. [1771] 1792 CARTWRIGHT i, 141 I caught one [salmon] with a gaff-hook. 1924 ENGLAND 304 At the critical moment the gaff hook tore through the seal's fat and hide, and away his sealship surged with a mighty splash, leaving the man empty handed and agape. Ibid 87 An' you, there, don't putt y'r gaff p'int down! Remember, arr hole in a skin, aft o' the fippers, is ten cents out o' y'r pocket. 1905 CHAFE 6 The procuring of timber from the woods, building vessels, repairing those already in use, building punts, procuring firewood, gaffstems, bats, pokers, oars and other material left nobody with an excuse for being idle. 1924 ENGLAND 44 Some fell to work seizing cruel points on gaff sticks with a kind of tarred cord known as 'spun yarn.' Ibid 239 The season is over when many of the young can be taken. They have gone, either into the fleet's reeking holds or into the Atlantic. Gaff-work recedes; Winchesters come to the fore.

gaff v *OED* ~ v¹ (1844–); *EDD* v¹ 6 for sense 1.

1 To pull a fish, etc, from the water with a hook fastened to a short stick.

[1786] 1792 CARTWRIGHT iii, 208 We gaffed up a few lobsters. 1924 ENGLAND 153 'I've fired a ship to port, when coal run out, with sharks' livers,' affirmed the Cap'n. . . 'We got thousands of livers; gaffed the sharks on pans, where they come attracted by fippers for bait, an' by tarchlights too.' 1928 PALMER 159 After I worked [the salmon] in to the shore and was ready to gaff I told the man to brace himself and gaff him near the gills. 1979 *Salt Water, Fresh Water* 83 No gurdies in those days to do the hauling for you—and the fish was on the hooks, you see. . .four feet long, big. I would just get the hook in them and get them aboard, gaff them in.

2 To kill or stun a seal with a blow from the sealer's iron-shod club or 'gaff'; BAT v.

1924 ENGLAND 16 The pups can be gaffed or batted. In many cases the wary old ones have to be shot, and ammunition costs money. 1955 DOYLE (ed) 52 "Sealers' Song": Our boys for fat, would gaff and bat, / And make the whitecoats rattle.

3 To steal or pilfer; BUCK v, STING (P 148–64).

gaffer n JOYCE 259. A boy, young fellow, esp one capable of assisting older men at work.

1896 *J A Folklore* ix, 31 ~ as applied to children only, must have been derived from Ireland. 1937 DEVINE 23 ~ A boy, between ten and fifteen, able to help at the fishery. 1966 SCAMMELL 106 "Tommy Decker's Venture": Three smart young gaffers right enough, I know it for a fact, / Or else they'd never have the nerve to start the like o' that. / And we old codgers

wish 'em luck and all the folks around / Will feel right glad if lots o' fish strikes on the handy ground. M 68–24 ~ This was the name given to any young boy who could pick berries fast, could catch fish fast, could split wood fast, who really could work fast. 1975 RUSSELL 1 Must have been almost thirty years ago. I was just a young gaffer then—spending my third or fourth summer in the bow of the banking dory. 1979 *Salt Water, Fresh Water* 83 The wind had come down and was blowing us hard and we two young gaffers were sayin': 'Let's go in.'

gaffle v Cp *ADD* v (1940–). See GAFF v, perhaps influenced by *grapple*. To set to (something) with force and vigour; seize hold of; HEAVE.

P 94–57 ~ To attack something or somebody with physical force. T 50/1–64 He gaffled a big bark pot, an iron pot, out o' the after room, an' he gaffled that un overboard, an' the two of 'em hove her head to, dumped the bread boxes an' freed her out. P 140–70 ~ pitch into, go at eagerly.

gaft See GAFF n.

gale n
    Comb **gale bird, gill** ~ : red phalarope (*Phalaropus fulicarius*); northern phalarope (*Lobipes lobatus*).

1870 *Can Naturalist* v, 293 Called by the settlers the 'gale bird.' It is wonderful to watch these pretty and delicate-looking little birds swimming and taking their tiny food from the crests of waves that would swamp any boat. [1886] LLOYD 93 . . .bull-bird, gannet, hound, harlequin duck, gale bird, twillick, and several other varieties of whose names I am ignorant. 1908 TOWNSEND 62 It was evidently a phalarope. . .'gale-birds' [they are called] by the Labradorians. 1951 PETERS & BURLEIGH 212 Commonly called 'Gill Bird' or 'Gale Bird' by fishermen, it easily rides the waves, swimming well with its lobed toes. 1967 *Bk of Nfld* iii, 283 Northern Phalarope: Gale Bird (because it was frequently seen inshore after northeasterlies). T 389/92–67² Do these little gale birds breed around here?

    gale rose: dog rose (*Rosa nitida*).
[1822] 1856 CORMACK 12 On the skirts of the forest, and of the marshes are found. . .gale Roses.

gale v *Weather Proverbs* (1883), p. 30 '[When a cat] happens to be more frisky than usual [sailors] have a popular saying that the cat has a gale of wind in her tail'; cp *EDD* ~ v² 'of birds: to circle about as before a storm'; *DAE* ~ ¹ n 'a high-spirited mood' (1838–). (a) Of animals, to scamper about with irrepressible spirits, freq taken to presage high winds; (b) of persons, esp children, to be hilarious, noisy, lively. Common in phr *gale for a storm*, etc.

1955 ENGLISH 41 When cats are very playful, they are said to 'gale up the weather.' C 65–2 When any of the animals (cows, horses or dogs) started running around and jumping wildly in a playful manner, one would hear the older people make the following remark: 'The cows are gailin' for wind.' P 207–67 We could hear the youngsters galin' in the kitchen. C 69–19 Whenever some of the youngsters would get exceptionally playful and make a lot of noise my mother would always say, 'You're galing for wind tonight. You can look out for the storm tomorrow.' By this she meant that the youngsters were brewing for a storm—that is they were laughing now but later probably would be crying for something. 1976 *Evening Telegram* 22 May, p. 3 Newfoundland grannies all knew this when they shook heads and warned, 'Ah, you're goin' to cry for this!' whenever the little tykes in their charge were especially gay and exuberant—what was called 'gailing.' Horses 'gailed,' too, and that was a sign of a storm coming.

galefilero* n [gæːlifəˈlɛərou, galifəˈlɛəro]. Jaunt; rambling walk or ride just for the sake of breaking restraint (P 24–67).

gallery n Cp *DAE* ~ 3 'porch or piazza of a house' (1784–) for sense 1.
   1 Platform at the entrance to a building or a house; BRIDGE.
   [1780] P 148–81 [*Colonial Records*] Sullivans gallery to come down. . .Clues Gallery to be taken down. [1900 OLIVER & BURKE] 55 Coming down the gallery one day [collecting dues], his companion priest had moved ahead of him. 1944 LAWTON & DEVINE 25 The gay dancers came out on the long front gallery to cool off. T 375–67² They can just shovel away the snow like on the gallery an' they can play there. 1972 MURRAY 184 Some of the 'better' homes had 'galleries' (verandas) which ran the full width of the front of the house. P 127–76 A gallery is a floor-like structure constructed of spaced or closely set boards, located at the outside front or back doors of a house. The structure may be located at, or raised above, ground level, depending upon the distance of the door-step above ground. The length may range from a couple of feet on either side of the door-way to a structure extending the whole width of the house. The gallery is usually enclosed by a rail.
   2 Part of a 'fishing stage' where the catch is landed on its way to the STAGE HEAD (P 148–62); GAZEBO.
   1975 *Bk of Nfld* vi, 494 The fish had to be handled three times before reaching the splitting table. It was first pronged from the boat to the gallery, which was halfway to the stage [head], there to the top of the stage head, and thence to the splitting table.

galley n Cp *OED* ~ sb 4 'ship's cooking-range'; SMYTH 332 'ship's hearth, where the grates are put up.' Makeshift stove used in cooking in a boat; also attrib.
   1951 *Nfld & Lab Pilot* i, 265 Gallyboy head projects. . .westward from the eastern shore. T 50/1–64 He gaffled a big iron bark pot out o' th' after room. They had it for a galley—put kindlin' in, cook their fish an' boil their kettle. T 393/5–67 I had the galley up on the gang-boards, boilin' the kettle. A galley is a piece of iron, a bottom of a old stove or something, not too big; an' you put a couple of junks o' wood under this.

An' now you got your birch wood all split up short, small an' dried. Put your wood on, put the kettle on. 1973 MOWAT 68 The tea was made up in the morning by the galley-bitch—one of the sealers serving as cook—in ten-gallon coppers. 1979 TIZZARD 94 On top of the gangboards many things could be kept such as the galley or bogie stove, an old water bucket or suchlike.

gallinipper See GARNIPPER.

gallon n *EDD* ~ sb¹ 1 'dry measure for corn, flour, bread, potatoes, fruit.' Cp PINT. A dry measure for berries, oats and potatoes.
   [1840] 1842 BONNYCASTLE ii, 204 Exports in 1840. Berries. . .gallons 2,850. [1872] 1877 ROCHFORT 72 [exports] Berries. . .4,436 gals. T 158–65 Berries are good now. A woman told me she picked two gallons [of] hurts. 1977 *Nfld Qtly* Dec, p. 36 A family of four or five, picking berries at ten cents a gallon, which was usually the price, could put in a winter's diet of flour. P 188–77 Some of the older people still come into the store and ask for a gallon of potatoes. 1979 TIZZARD 169 It came just as natural [for some merchants] to sell dry goods by the pound as it did for them to sell peas, beans, rice and so on by the gallon, half gallon, quart or pint.

gallop v *OED* ~ v² 'to boil' obs exc dial (1605–), *EDD* v²: potatoes are boiling galloping Sf. To boil; to be turbulent.
   1951 *Nfld & Lab Pilot* i, 250 Galloping Moll, a rock which dries one foot, is situated 6 cables westward. P 103–67 The water is boiling gallops. . .boiling stretch gallops. P 108–78 The potatoes are galloping.

galloper n A type of small vessel used in the cod-fishery, the seal hunt, and coastal trade.
   [c1790–1830] 1902 *Nfld Qtly* Mar, p. 9 The sealing fleet consisted of a number of pink-stern crafts, that is, whale boat shape. . . These crafts, or, gallopers (from thirty to forty tons), as they were more generally styled, would leave the various ports in Conception Bay. . .and would hunt the seals as far north as Cape Bonavista. 1866 WILSON 212 In the month of August, the merchant's large boat, or galloper, goes to the planter's fishing-room, to select the first 'dry fish.' 1901 *Christmas Review* 7 About the time that the schooner (for there were no steamers in those days) was to leave St John's with the bridal party, the 'galloper'— *Evening Star*—was preparing to leave the village in which the festivities were about to be held, to sail for the Capital with a load of dry fish.

gallows n Cp *EDD* ~ sb 5 Ha quot for sense 2.
   1 Frame on which nets are spread to dry; NET n: NET-GALLOWS, SEINE ~ ; freq in place-names.
   1878 *Nfld Pilot* 49 Gallows Harbour separates Little and Great Gallows harbours. 1907 *Nfld Qtly* Dec, p. 2 The Canon thinks the name [Gallows Cove] is derived from a sort of erection which was, until recent years, to be seen in many settlements. . .a sort of 'horse' or trestle made of rough rails or *starrigans*, and was used for drying nets on. 1966 SCAMMELL 133

"The Caplin Haul": Put the seine on the 'gallis,' one hand share the bait, / Hurry up there, my lads, for 'tis now getting late. P 13–77 ~ usually pronounced gallis: a frame of cleanly peeled poles erected 12–15 feet high and used to drape nets and ropes over for drying or repairing.

2 Framework used to support vertically placed 'sticks' to be dried and used for firewood; WOOD GALLOWS.

1976 GUY 142 There was gravel from the beach in the yard by the door and sticks of wood stuck up on a gallows like a teepee.

gally n Cp *EDD* gally-bagger sb 1 'scare-crow' Ha IW W Do So D. Epithet applied locally to residents of Fortune, on the Burin Peninsula.

C 66–13 Fortune gallies and the Grand Bank shags, / All tied up in wrapper bags, / When the bags began to bust / The Fortune gallies began to cuss. Grand Bankers are called shags by those from Fortune, but we always call them goats.

gally v *EDD* ~ v 1 s w cties; *ADD* gallied for sense 1.

1 To frighten; to exhaust through alarm or exertion (P 54–67).

1937 DEVINE 23 ~ To tire, to frighten; to exhaust one's strength on a work or a journey. P 37 Gallied. [Descriptive of] state of excitement or exhaustion, usually caused by some sort of compulsion; state of desperation.

2 Comb **gallygee** vbl n: ['gælɪgiːən], **gallygolt**: in children's pastime, to jump from one pan of floating ice to another; COPY (C 71–131; Q 67–88).

galore n *OED* ~ sb (1863 quot); *EDD* 2. Phr *in galore*: in abundance.

[c1880] 1927 DOYLE (ed) 53 "Huntingdon Shore": And we got thirty shillings to find our own gear, / 'Thirty shillings in hand' and good tea in galore / And four meals a day on the Huntingdon Shore. 1901 *Christmas Bells* 14 He had seen writing materials in galore with other good things of his. [1926] 1933 GREENLEAF (ed) 251 "Change Islands Song": A lot of men lived in that place had nets out in galore; / They could not see there what to do, nor room for any more. 1968 DILLON 139 The berries were there in galore.

gam n Comb **gam bird**, ~ **drake, gammy bird**: American common eider (*Somateria mollissima dresseri*); SHORE[1]: ~ DUCK, SHOREYER.

1821–8 LATHAM 265 In Newfoundland [the eider duck is called] Gam Drake. C 64–1 [nicknames] Mobile goats, Witless Bay gammy birds, Bay Bulls bottle noses. 1967 *Bk of Nfld* iii, 282 Common Eider: Gam-birds (from the social meeting of whalers at sea and because this species gathers in large flocks).

gammett* n Cp *EDD* gammock sb 'prank; rough play.' An instance of noise-making; a period of carrying on.

C 71–109 He would say to the children, 'You are getting on with your gammetts.'

gandy n *ADD* ~ Nfld. Pancake, or piece of bread dough, fried and served with molasses and other garnish.

1895 *J A Folklore* viii, 38 ~ the fisherman's name for a pancake. 1903 *Nfld Qtly* Dec, p. 5 A good hot cup of tea with plenty of milk and honest molasses, hot gandies off the frying pan, and a print of golden butter. 1924 ENGLAND 261 Lassy loaf and 'gandies' (pancakes made with pork fat and molasses). 1966 HORWOOD 24 I'd have dumplings every day for dinner, and candy afterward, and gandies with lassy coady. P 108–73 Gandies: a sort of pancakes of flour and water.

gang n Cp *OED* ~ sb[1] 9; SMYTH 334 'selected number of a ship's crew appointed on any particular service.' A group of seal-hunters; WATCH.

1924 ENGLAND 271 The ship was thrusting onward, grinding through heavy ice, and every quarter mile or so the Old Man ordered a gang out; and all these gangs trailed away toward the herd, advancing like troops *en échelon*.

gang-board n Cp *OED* ~ naut. In an undecked fishing-boat, wooden plank(s) placed over the compartment or 'room' in which fish are stowed. Hence **gang-boarded** p ppl.

1792 CARTWRIGHT *Gloss* i, x ['Fish upon the gang-boards' is] an expression used by fishermen to denote, a boat being completely laden with fish; to shew which, they bring in three or more upon the *gangboards*. 1863 MORETON 88 ~s. A partial deck covering the fish lockers [in a boat]. 1914 *Cadet* 23 From leaning against a gangboard put up on end to rest his back the Bishop had the sleeve of his coat well saturated with fish and vang (pork), for when the meal was cooked it was thrown out of the kettle on to the gangboards. 1937 DEVINE 23 ~ The movable covering boards of the compartments ('rooms') of a fishing boat. T 1–63[2] When they puts the fish in they puts the gang-boards down to keep the sun [off]. T 45/6–64 'Twas in the fall o' the year [he] left to go to St John's in an open boat—she was gang-boarded, fore cuddy an' after cuddy on her, an' a breeze come on, they got drove off. T 141/69–65[2] We slept aboard the boat, on the gang-boards. 1975 BUTLER 54 Gang boards were loose boards of no special size laid down on the tawts fore and aft and unfastened. . .in lieu of a deck but not watertight. They were just to keep the sun off the fish.

gange v also **genge, ginge*** *DAE* ~ v (1854, 1877); *Fisheries of U S* (1887), p. 175; cp *EDD* 1 'to twist fine. . .wire around a fishing-line to prevent the hook from being bitten off' Co (1871). To fasten an eyeless fish-hook or lead weight to a line.

[1771] 1792 CARTWRIGHT i, 94 The woodmen were employed in new-casting, and ganging fishing leads. [1785] ibid iii, 76 I ganged a set of hooks for a boat's crew. 1792 ibid *Gloss* i, x Ganging hooks and leads. To fix fine twine in a particular manner to fish-hooks, and small straps of line to leads, that they may be ready for immediate use. [1856] 1975 WHITELEY 111 Fine day—in the house gauging [ganging] hooks. 1877 ROCHFORT 101 [advertisement] Tinned [Bultow] Hooks genged and ungenged. 1909 BROWNE 67 The traps is a lazy way of gettin' a voyage, and you can hardly find a man goin' to the fishery now who is able to 'genge a hook.' 1937 DEVINE 23 ~ To attach a fish hook permanently to a line. Q 67–61 A term used to describe the method of fastening a hook without an eye to a line is to ginge on the hooks. M 69–17 A piece of black sewing cotton about 2 yds. in length was doubled twice and then the hook was slipped on this thread. Next a pair of scissors was hung on the hook and two persons began to twist in opposite directions, one on each end of the thread. This would make the scissors turn and this turning and twisting would result in the braiding of the four strands of thread into one piece of about a foot in length. This process is called 'ganging' the hook, and when completed it was attached to the line already on the pole.

gangeing n also **gengeing, gingeing*** ['gendʒɨn] *DAE* ganging (1884, 1889); *Fisheries of U S* (1887), pp. 10, 175; cp *EDD* gange sb 2 'fine wire [twisted round a fishing-line].' See also GANGE v. The braiding which fastens an eyeless fish-hook to a line; the hook and line fastened to a trawl. Also attrib: ~ **line,** ~ **twine**; cp SUD LINE.
   [1819] 1915 HOWLEY 112 [inventory] 1 Rand of Ganging Twine. 1925 *Dial Notes* v, 332 Ganging line. A strong, small cotton line, like herring net twine. 1937 DEVINE 23 The part of the line so fastened is generally strengthened with overlaid twine, and the whole set-up is a *Gengeing.* T 41–64 We'd have to take a piece o' line about that long, an' you'd bend it on around the end o' the hook here. The end o' the hook was flat—have your gengein' on there somehow—an' then we tie it onto the lines. P 121–67 Gingein. This is a piece of line about three feet long which is attached to a fisherman's trawl at the end of which there is a hook. 1975 BUTLER 56 The jack boat used one tub of trawls for fishing. Each tub contained twelve hemp lines, each line thirty fathoms in length. Each line was fitted with hooks and gangens about one fathom apart. . . Gangen is a short fishin' line. . . Sud line was the smallest line to make gangens. C 75–63 When the cod was going strong, I have seen my father making gingens on the back of the chair. Gingens were short lines with a small loop at the end where the fish hook was connected; sometimes he would bring an old line of gear in the kitchen and repair it, by putting gingens on a line. 1979 TIZZARD 288 A trawl is a fifty fathom line with gingens and hooks spaced four feet apart.

gansey n also **garnsey** ['gæˑnzɪ, 'gæːɹnzɪ, 'gaːɹnzɪ]. Cp *OED* guernsey 2 a (1851–); *O Sup²* 2 a (1839–); *EDD* ~ (1896–); SMYTH 410 gearn-sey, ganzee. Heavy, closely-knit pull-over sweater worn by fishermen and sealers.
   [1843] 1957 *Daily News* 26 Feb [merchandise] gan-seys. [1901] 1927 DOYLE (ed) 9 "The Outharbour Planter": He's gon' with gansy and corduroy pants; with Hamburg boots and ne'er collar. 1924 ENGLAND 63 'T'ink of a feller layvin' a fine place like de States

an' goin' to de ice to write books about dat, just!' put in another, huge-shouldered in a blue 'gansey' (jersey), as he squatted down before the bogey and toasted bread on a knife point. 1933 GREENE 98 Then with thick woollen 'g'arnseys,' oilskins, sou'westers, and stout canvas jumpers, the outfit is complete and the men are ready—and more than willing too. 1937 DEVINE 23 Gansey. A heavy woolen knitted man's gar-ment with no opening back or front, pulled on over the head and reaching just below the waist. T 141–65² He would haul off his pants and his garnsey perhaps, but nothing else. 1982 *Evening Telegram* 16 Feb, p. 17 [He] said it would be better if she had a bottle of ammonia to take the foxy colour out of her husband's gansey.

gap n *EDD* ~ sb 1; *ADD* 5. An opening in a fence; gate.
   1929 BURKE [8] "When your Old Woman Takes a Cramp": My mind so tormented / I'll cut through the gap / What the neighbours might say / Sure I don't care a snap. P 148–60 ~ space in fence for gate, and gate itself. Q 67–5 [riddle] Twenty sick sheep went through a gap. / One died. How many came back? C 71–131 I heard her tell someone to take down the gap.

garagee n also **garagy, garricky, garrickty***, **garrity*** ['gærɪkɪ, 'gærɪkʊˑ, 'gærədʒɪ, 'gærɨktɪ, 'garɨtɪ]. Street urchins' scramble for coins; cp GEARY; boisterous, rough-and-tumble beha-viour; fun, devilment.
   1914 *Cadet* Apr, p. 7 [Local words include] 'leggies,' 'barbel,' 'lobscouse,' 'garagee.' 1924 ENGLAND 71–2 If 'twasn't Sunday, us wouldn't bide yere aburd o' dis-un. 'Twould be a bloody garagee [free-for-all scramble]! 1937 DEVINE 23 Garagy. Fun. A scramble to be first to pick up coins. T 191–65 They got the horse, an' they got a bough an' just give her a few tickles under the belly, an' she of course give the big kick, put the door in an' upset the barrel o' water. It was all those things they do for garrickty. Ibid 'Twas nothing but garrity. They upset barrels o' water, an' they blew the glass out, firin' so many guns. C 71–95 He would say [of the children] 'They are havin' some garagy in there now!'

garagy See GARAGEE.

garden n *EDD* ~ sb 2 So; *ADD* 2; A BLISS *Spoken English in Ireland 1600–1740*, p. 280 'small field [for] vegetables' for sense 1; *OED* ~ -party 'party held on a lawn' (1869–) for comb in sense 4.
   1 A piece of land belonging to a family, some-times fenced; an area enclosed for the cultivation of hay or vegetables; GROUND.
   [1766] 1971 BANKS 146 After this short stay at Cro-que intended only for filling Water & getting on board the Produce of the Gardens & Poultry we Saild for St John's. [1776] 1792 CARTWRIGHT ii, 170 I had part of the garden manured and dug over again. I then sowed some radishes, turnips, carrots, onions, cresses, and fennel. 1819 ANSPACH 374 Swine are likewise extremely common, to the frequent annoyance of the gardens and potatoe-grounds. 1848 *Journ of Assembly*

426 I commenced my line at the western end of Patterson's Garden, and continued from thence to Little Barrisway Bridge. 1888 STEARNS 98 Then they all went out to the barn and saw the cows and the goat; into the garden and saw the young potatoes, cabbage, lettuce, and turnip heads. 1934 BARTLETT 150 Of course all the people who came here (Wadham Islands) had gardens on the mainland. They would set out their gardens, bring their families to the islands, and from time to time go back to see to it that weeds were kept within bounds, and that the gardens were growing well. 1938 MACDERMOTT 158 Fish offal, herring, squid, caplin, dogfish, indeed any kind of unsaleable fish was thrown into the small garden, or spread on the land to produce hay. 1942 *Grand Bank U C School* 37 [There were] smooth, clean beach stones in level gardens away from the flying spray. T 43/7–64 [You'd have] your garden in that garden, where you'd sow your vegetables. You'd have a fence around that and that would be referred to as a potato garden or the cabbage garden an' those places. . .inside of the big field. M 67–16 There are from two to six houses in a garden. If several houses are in a garden, they still have front yards and some have front and back yards. Some houses stand alone in a garden that could accommodate ten to twenty more houses. C 71–22 He was in his garden raking hay. 1977 BURSEY 39 To a great extent Old Perlican was left to the women from Spring to late Fall but the gardens were never neglected up to the time when Newfoundland joined in Confederation with Canada, the men might be seen in the gardens in May plowing the ground and setting potatoes, digging in the cabbage gardens and making agriculture easier for the women to do. 1979 TIZZARD 77 The two dwelling houses were in the same garden.

2 Ice-floe where seals give birth to their young; SEAL MEADOW, WHELPING GROUND.

1938 MACDERMOTT 201 Generally speaking, the ice is rough. . .but it is not for this kind of ice that the sealer is looking, but for what he calls the 'garden'—the smooth whelping ice of the harp seal.

3 Small area cleared and enclosed to lure rabbits.

M 68–23 In an area where there was plenty of sign, we would set a garden. This was a circular area fenced off with boughs and small trees. Inside the garden we would place browse. . .in order for the rabbits to get the browse they had to go through one of several openings in the fence in which we had placed snares. This garden was only about ten or twelve feet in diameter.

4 Attrib, comb **garden beer**: beer brewed from locally-grown hops.

[1890] 1900 DEVINE & O'MARA 41 Over one thousand bottles of garden beer seized this day, in stores around town.

garden-party: communal social gathering held each summer on grounds surrounding the local church or in another field at which games and contests are held, food served, and funds raised for parish activities.

1909 *Tribune Christmas No* 6 The same runner also carrying off the road race from Torbay to Mount Cashel in connection with the annual garden party at the latter place. 1937 *Bk of Nfld* i, 27 [In St John's]

dozens and dozens of amateur plays, concerts, recitals, garden-parties, regattas and all possible kinds of similar events take place every year, and are attended by practically the whole body of citizens. [c1940] 1979 TIZZARD 256 The picnic in the early forties gave way to the garden party. . .It was not as enjoyable perhaps as the picnic but I am sure everyone had a good time and a little money was made for the Ladies Aid. 1966 SCAMMELL 127 "Bakeapple Jam": When garden party time rolls round to swell the church's funds, / There's food galore for one and all and little boys can cram. 1972 MURRAY 284–5 The old-type Sunday school picnics, involving the whole community, were replaced in the late 1930's by the Garden Party which the Anglican and United Churches held annually until the 1960's. Here patrons paid for their meals and for the entertainments. There were different games and competitions. . .with prizes. 1976 CASHIN 93 When the annual fancy fair (garden party, today) for the church came around about the middle of August, I was given two or three dollars to spend.

garden rod, ~ **fence**: slender, peeled stick used in fence construction; the fence itself. See RIDDLE n.

1858 [LOWELL] ii, 13–14 The horse. . .began to go. . .but down hill, though keeping the side near the garden-rod fence. 1944 LAWTON & DEVINE 15 There was a summer's supply of firewood to be hauled from the woods, garden-rods, rails, posts and 'shores' for the spring fencing. 1966 PADDOCK 105 *The garden rod fence*. . .consisted of three horizontal rails. . .interlaced. . .with very slender, peeled rods.

garnipper n also **gallinipper** *DAE* gurnipper (1634–47), gallinipper: ganniper (1709–); cp *DC* gadnipper (1829); perhaps from *EDD* great: gert, girt, gurt. A large biting mosquito; NIPPER[1].

[1663] 1963 YONGE 60 In July, the muscetos (a little biting fly) and garnippers (a larger one) will much vex us. 1842 JUKES ii, 4 These mosquitoes were of the kind called in Newfoundland *gallinippers*: they are a species of gnat, with long thin legs and a slender body, having a long trunk or proboscis, the end of which they insert into the skin, and suck blood till their bodies increase to three or four times their original size, becoming quite red and bloated. . .the gallinipper with his sonorous hum hovers over you both by day and night, sailing about, banishing all sleep. P 108–70 Gallynippers [are] mosquitoes.

garnsey See GANSEY.

garricky See GARAGEE.

gary See GEARY.

gasher n *DC* ~ Nfld (1895). A small fishing boat with sharp prow and stern.

1895 *St Nicholas* [New York] Apr, p. 448 Here [at Blanc Sablon, Labr], too, I saw for the first time the dapper little Labrador gasher—a small fishing craft not much longer than a dory, but with a sharp prow and stern, and two masts fitted with reddish-brown sails. [*DC*] P 102–60 They had other [boats] called gashers about the same shape as the barge but smaller. Instead of rock ballast these had an iron centre-board which they let down through a slot in the keel. If they turned over, all the men could do was to hold on until someone came and rescued them.

gatch n   also **gache, gauch**. Cp DINNEEN gaisch 'hero, a champion,' gaisceadh 'boasting'; JOYCE 259 gaatch 'affected gesture.' Swaggering type of behaviour; pompous gait or strut; a person behaving in such a manner; GATCHER.

1937 DEVINE 23 Gauches. Similar to the word *gags* on the modern stage; funny words and tricks. P 48–60 ~ A show-off. 1964 *Evening Telegram* 23 June, p. 2 Them houses will be still good when half the new ones have fallen down. Built by tradesmen, not young know all gaches. 1968 DILLON 139 The gatch o' that one makes me sick.

gatch v   See ~ n. To behave in a boastful, boisterous fashion; to show off (P 245–55).

P 148–61 What are you gatchin about tonight? P 54–66 However, it's nothing we Liberals want to gatch about. 1968 DILLON 139 All she does is gatchin' around, showin' herself off. P 191–75 ~ To put on airs, to boast.

gatcher n   A person who behaves in a swaggering manner; show-off (C 75–15).

P 148–61 [I could tell by] the way the gatcher come in. 1966 *Evening Telegram* 8 Feb, p. 15 The rest of the crowd wouldn't get on with him, but I had to go, a gatcher, that's what I was. 1968 DILLON 139 Look at that fella now; he's the proper gatchcr, he is.

gate n   *EDD* ~ sb² 15 also pl 'whims, crotchets' Ha W So D. Habit, peculiarity.

C 66–13 When a child is crying and will not say why, someone will say, 'Oh, that's gates out of him,' meaning he doesn't know what he's crying about. Q 71–8 Smoking is a dirty gate.

gather v

1 To draw together the open end of a net in order to enclose fish; TUCK v.

1895 GRENFELL 71 Thus the whole school are enclosed. Now the weighted foot rope is 'gathered' together, the net has become one vast bag, and the prisoners are dealt with as before, i.e. dipped out and bagged off.

2 Phr *gather in*: to become overcast.

1883 HOWLEY *MS Reminiscences* 12 Fine morning but gathered in cloudy.

gauch See GATCH n.

gawmoge n, usu pl also **gamogue, gomogue** [gæ'moꭓg] DINNEEN gamóg 'clown, a simpleton'; JOYCE 261 'soft foolish fellow.' A silly, mischievous person; cp GOMMEL; the action or conduct of such a person.

1937 DEVINE 25 Gomogues. Clownish tricks and play. 1964 *Evening Telegram* 4 June, p. 13 It costs

more to catch fish now than in the old days. Remember, they got nylon nets an' everything now. 'That's only the fishermen's gaumogues,' sez Ned. 1968 DILLON 140 She's a real gawmogue, she is; she haven't got the sense she was born with. . . The gawmogues o' him now'd set you cracked. C 75–139 Look at the gawmoges of him!

gawmoge v   See ~ n. To deceive.

1895 PROWSE 390 He had, however, shrewd mother wit, and the true Hibernian faculty of 'gammoging the Saxons.' C 71–21 A person is [gawmogin'] when he is pretending to be sick. . .to get away from doing something.

gaze n

1 A hunter's blind or place of concealment.

[1768] 1828 CARTWRIGHT ii, 310 At certain convenient stations they have small breast works half the height of a man (by the furriers called gazes), over which it may be presumed they shoot the dccr passing between the waterside and the bank. 1792 PULLING *MS* Aug The natives knowing his usual morning's employment, had built up what the Newfoundlanders call a gaze; which is a wall made of stones, turf, bushes, etc to [hide] behind, and is often made use of to get a shot at birds as they pass over a projecting point of land. 1861 DE BOILIEU 160 At early dawn about the middle of May four or five men repair to some small island near the mainland, and there erect what is termed a Gaze, which is like a small fort cut out of the solid ice close to the landwash. 1912 DUGMORE 28 My blind, or gaze, as the Newfoundlanders call it, is a simple affair composed of about a dozen small fir trees stuck securely into the bog, arranged in a circle open at the southern end; on the north side, facing the leads, the branches are cut away, leaving an opening through which the camera protrudes. 1924 ENGLAND 177 I load up me ole birdin' gun wid a span o' two fingers powder an' more 'an a t'ousand shot, an' wad 'em wid tarry oakum, an' go down to me gaze [shelter], an' de birds pitch [come down] by t'ousands just after de sun risin'. 1966 SCAMMELL 59 At last we were ready and soon found ourselves stumbling around shore to the blind or 'gaze' on the point. T 89/90–64 We went back to the gaze again, an' when we looked in, sir, here was the old dog hood just leavin' th' ice with the old bitch; dragged her out an' carried her away. 1979 TIZZARD 260 A gaze was built out on Salton's Head, out of branches of trees, and so on, a kind of camouflage. There was a small opening in order that one inside could see the birds as they flew along the shore.

2 An elevated point or look-out, esp one commanding the approach to a bay or harbour; common in local place-names.

[1774] 1792 CARTWRIGHT ii, 28 I went in the punt to Gaze Point. 1901 *Christmas Bells* 13 "Ferryland": On the Gaze of dear old Ferryland, / By the spreading boughs of green, / Where I often roved in boyhood. 1969 MOWAT 31 [He] took me. . .up to the high places like the Gaze, a long hill crest from which, for centuries, women watched for the returning ships, or men stood guard to cry the alarm when pirate sails hove over the horizon. 1972 MURRAY 292 On Sunday mornings, during the late spring, summer, and early fall, even during the forties, all the men of the community gathered in a group. Maberly and Neck men generally got together in Maberly 'over on the Gaze'; some others might gather together on the 'Bum Rocks' upon the Hill.

3 Man assigned to mast-head to scan the ice for seals; BARREL-MAN, SPY MASTER (1925 *Dial Notes* v, 332).

gazebo n also **gizaboo*** ['gæzə,bu, 'gɪzə,bu]. Cp *OED* ~ 2 'projecting window, balcony'; *EDD* 1 'tall building'; 3 'any object which attracts attention' Ir; JOYCE 261 'any tall object.'

1 Strange object; person wearing odd clothes.

P 148–66 [Look at] that gazeboo over there! Q 71–7 She described someone dressed in outlandish garb as a gizaboo.

2 Part of a 'fishing-stage' where the catch is landed on its way to the 'stage head'; GALLERY 2.

C 71–108 Gizzieboo. An intermediate level like a natural shelf or a built-on shelf onto which the fishermen [un]loaded the fish. From the gizzieboo the fish were then flipped up to the [stage head]. P 135–74 Gizaboo. The outside part of the wharf where the fish are [landed].

gear n Cp *OED* ~ sb 5 'apparatus. . .tackle' (1885 quot), *EDD* 4 for sense 1; *EDD* 13 'food' for phr in sense 2.

1 Fishing paraphernalia used in the sea-fisheries, esp nets, lines, and buoys; CRAFT[1].

1909 GRENFELL[2] 298 The salt, nets and puncheons for oil are bulky; spare canvas and gear, if the crew is fortunate enough to be able to afford any, fill much of the remaining space [on the Labrador schooners]. 1936 SMITH 24 On the 21st of July we took all gear out of the water and left Bluff Head for down the shore. 1953 *Nfld Fish Develop Report* 50 In general, the fishing craft in use with these several kinds of gear are comparatively small in size. 1975 *Fisherman's Handbook* 16 The Department of Fisheries has inaugurated a new program designed to assist the fishermen in the purchase of new gear. . . Under the program, fishermen will be able to receive subsidization up to about 60 percent on the webbing content of certain types of gear. 1976 *Evening Telegram* 2 Mar, p. 24 Fishermen here are now busy preparing for this year's fishery. Salmon traps, and nets and cod traps, trawls, herring nets, lobster traps and other gear are being overhauled in stores. 1977 ibid 30 Dec, p. 6 The freak waves that hit the coast took away their stages, their stores, their nets and the thousand and one items which go to make up the gear of an inshore fisherman.

2 Phr *best of gear*: perfect, all right.

P 148–65 'How's everything?' 'The best o' gear.'

plate of gear: helping of food.

P 126–67 Come and get your plate of gear.

3 Comb **gear bank**: a store of fishing equipment from which items are leased to fishermen.

1977 *Evening Telegram* 21 Mar, p. 4 In the area of

the fishery, resolutions call for. . .a gear bank [for the inshore fishermen].

gear-tub: wooden container in which trawl-lines are coiled in dory-fishing; TUB (1971 NOSEWORTHY 203).

geary v also **gary** ['gɛˑri 'gɛˑri]. Cp *OED* gare 'a cry of warning: Look out! beware!' (1653–1896); *EDD* gar int. obs 'a word of admonition to a child' [Fr *garre*, as *garre, garre!* an interjection betokennyng warnyng, of a daunger, PALSGR, (1530) 888]; cp *EDD* gar(e) 'ready': I'll say 'gar gar' for it. Y. To snatch someone's marbles; possibly 'watch out!' 'I got 'em.' See GARAGEE.

1931 BYRNES 174 When I 'gearied' Billy's 'ally' in Kenawitch's Lane. C 71–18 Sometimes a person would come along and try to steal some of the marbles [in a game]. He would sneak up, grab a few marbles, shout 'Geary, Geary' and run away as fast as he could. 1981 *Evening Telegram* 15 May, p. 6 And what oldtimer, never experienced the shock of having some boy (usually a bigger one) come running towards your little group, shouting at the top of his lungs, 'gary, gary, gary,' then calmly stooping down and pocketing all the marbles for himself, as if this were his divine right.

genge See GANGE.

gengeing See GANGEING.

gentles n pl *OED* ~ n 1 b obs; *EDD* 7. People of high status and leisure.

1912 ROGERS 179 John Denny at once told me he had signed on as cook, but added quaintly: 'I have never cooked for gentles.'

george martin n Cp DINNEEN máirtín 'vampless stocking.' Ankle-high rubber boot with lacings; LUMP.

C 67–16 During the week we wore a short rubber boot, a little higher than today's shoes. These were called 'rubber lumps.' We wore a woollen sock and these boots used to lace up. At another place these boots were called george martins.

get v Phr *get a hide*: see HIDE; ~ *along*: to succeed, prosper; ~ *in*: to light (the fire); ~ *in go with*: to court; ~ *in young*: of seals, to become pregnant; ~ *one's anchor*: to depart.

1863 MORETON 39 How d'ye get along? Common [form] of inquiring how you do. . .no doubt [originating] in the sympathy of poor people with their brethren whom they knew to be struggling with poverty. P 148–61 Has Mary got in the fire? T 187/90–65 He left the ship. I suppose he got in go with a girl, an' he wanted to hang wi' she if he could. 1873 CARROLL 21 Seals generally whelp some 3 feet apart, and frequently at the same time, consequently they get in young at the same period. 1920 GRENFELL & SPALDING 154 'And one day, miss,' he explained, 'the whole crew of them gets their anchors and leaves in a body.'

ghost n *DAE* ~ flower (1892–).

Attrib, comb **ghost-fish**: of a 'ghost-net,' to entrap fish while drifting untended and unmoored.

1975 *Evening Telegram* 28 Oct, p. 6 The number of lost nets is estimated to run as high as 80,000. . . If there is anything like that number of nets ghost fishing it must mount up to quite a lot of wasted fish every year.

ghost-flower, ~ **plant**: indian pipe; corpse plant (*Monotropa uniflora*) (1898 *J A Folklore* xi, 273).

ghost net: fish-net lost through storms or neglect, one which continues to entrap fish.

1975 *Evening Telegram* 1 Feb, p. 11 All fishermen interviewed felt gill nets were a factor in the decline of the stocks, contending that 'ghost nets' continue to catch fish long after they have been lost or abandoned by their owners. 1976 *The Rounder* Mar, p. 3 [They feel] that 'ghost-nets,' whether lost as a result of ice, wind, tides, etc. continue to fish at a declining rate until either the headrope and footrope are twisted together or where in areas of high crab concentration the net becomes infested with crab, until it is eventually covered with bottom debris. Where these conditions do not occur, however, 'nets continue to fish effectively, for at least one or two years.'

ghost ship: apparition of a vessel seen at the time the actual ship is sinking.

1924 ENGLAND 217–18 Ghost ships—some with skeleton crews—are well known. . . The sealing steamer *Newfoundland* was seen sailing in Quidi Vidi gut at the very hour she was lost in the ice. An old man whose son perished in the disaster clearly perceived her and knew trouble had befallen.

gib v also **gip** [gɪb]. Cp *OED* ~ v² 'to disembowel (fish') (1883, 1893); gip (1603–); *Fisheries of U S* (1887), p. 433; DINNEEN giobaim 'I prick, peck, pluck, pull, tear.' To remove the gills and entrails of a herring; SPLIT v.

1862 LIND *MS Diary* 18 June Very small attendance at Singing this evening as nearly all are gipping or packing herrings. 1863 HIND ii, 233 After a 'deck' of mackerel is obtained, all hands prepare to put them in salt. The operations of 'passing up,' 'splitting,' and 'gibbing,' are gone through, and they are packed in salt in the barrels. P 148–61 Gibbing: taking the gill out of the herring. T 185–65 First I was workin' in Matthews' factory, gibbin herring and packin' herring.

gib n [gɪb]. The gills and entrails of a herring: PIP¹ (P 245–75).

T 110–64 They caught a lot of herring in that time. They used to save the gibs, that's the inside of the herring, for fertiliser to put on their fields for their hay.

gibbing vbl n Cp *OED* gip: gipping knife (1615–1641); GIB v. Comb **gibbing knife**: knife with a short blade, used to remove the gills and entrails of herring (P 243–75).

1855 WHITE *MS Journal* 1 Aug 1 gibbing knife 4/s.

gig* n [gɪg]. Cp DINNEEN giog 'a very slight sound'; *Kilkenny Lexicon* giog: gig.

1 Slight sound; usu after negative.

P 269–63 There's not a gig out of her.

2 Slight sign of life; tremor, movement; JOOG.

T 141/64–65² He's dead, isn't her, Line? Goes back certainly to look at un—not a gig of life into un! P 41–68 [After death] there was not a gig left in you.

gigger See JIGGER.

gilguy* n also **gilgoy***. Cp SMYTH ~ 'guy for tracing up, or bearing a boom'; *O Sup²* 2 naval slang 'thingummy' (1886–). Gaudy trinket; showy attire; cp gewgaw.

C 70–21 Should see a woman loaded down with jewellery, several rings, brooches, bangles—in other words wearing far more ornamentation than good taste demanded—they would say she was wearing a lot of gilgoys. C 71–121 ~ something purchased or something treasured that is of no possible value. Often applied to decoration and ornaments. C 75–19 Of one wearing good clothes: 'He is all gilguys.'

gill n

Comb **gillcap**, ~ **cup**, **gilly** ~ : crowfoot, buttercup (*Ranunculus* spp) (1893 *N S Instit Sci* viii, 363); freq in phr *yellow as a gillcup* (P 189–66).

gillflower: bladderwort (*Utricularia cornuta*) (1956 ROULEAU 30).

gill bird See GALE n: GALE BIRD.

gilly n Common dovekie (*Plautus alle alle*); BULL-BIRD, ICE- ~ .

1959 MCATEE 39 ~ dovekie (Shortening of guillemot. . .Nfld.).

gimble n *OED* gimmal 3 obs (1605); *EDD* gimmal 2 Gl So. A hinge; FIMBLE* (P 37).

ginge* See GANGE.

gingeing* See GANGEING.

ginny See JINNY*.

girl n Affectionate term of address by one woman to another.

P 148–65 ~ form of address used by salespeople in stores. 'Girl dear, I don't know.' 1974 CAHILL 33 He was only sporting you, Mother, girl. Don't mind him.

give v Phr *give it*: to say to, assure; ~ *it out*: to reprimand, scold; ~ *one the breeze*: to get married; ~ *out*: to give birth; ~ *tea in a mug*: to scold, berate.

T 253–66 Some of 'em was frightened, some wasn't. I wasn't frightened, I'll give it you. P 136–68 'What are you givin' it out about now?' 'Don't do that or she'll give it out to you.' P 148–64 There are two midwives playing with me, just in case I give out down at bingo. 1937 DEVINE 25 Give us the breeze. To get married.

1905 DUNCAN 118 An' if you don't put my spinnin' wheel t' rights this night I'll give you your tea in a mug (a scolding) t'morrow.

gizaboo* See GAZEBO.

glab v [glæb, glɒb, glæˑb]. Cp DINNEEN gláib 'dirty water, mud.' To coat, cake; to become gummed up.

T 141/67–65² You don't put this linnet in and pour that tar, because the tar'll glab on your linnet. C 71–105 A rubber stamp was donated to the museum. At the time it was brought in it was all glabbed up, meaning there was too much old ink left in it.

gladger n also **gladyer**. Cp *OED* gledge v 'to look asquint. . .to look cunningly on one side.' One who jokes or takes a rise out of his neighbour (1897 *J A Folklore* x, 205).

1937 DEVINE 25 ~ A joker who pretends to be in earnest. P 191–73 ~ A person quick at repartee.

glam n *OED* ~ ³ (1797 D quot). Soft-shelled clam, used as bait (*Mya arenaria*); fresh-water shell-fish; COCK: COCK AND HEN.

[1662] 1963 YONGE 55 Coming near the shore, we saw a large cove, called Glam cove. [1766] 1971 BANKS 123 A ship Came into harbour from which I Procurd specimens of a shell fish calld here Glams. . .of Peculiar use in the fishery as the fishermen depend upon them for their Baitts in their first Voyage to the Banks. 1842 JUKES ii, 190 Species of fresh-water mussel, or Unio, may be found in some of the ponds and brooks. These are also used by the fishermen as bait, and called likewise 'clams' or 'glams.' P 77–74 ~ A big clam found usually near a brook.

glander n Cp *OED* ~ 2 pl 'contagious disease in horses [accompanied by] discharge of mucous matter from the nostrils.' Phlegm which one coughs up; nasal mucus.

P 189–65 ~ the mucus that a person spits out. P 222–67 He had a bad cold and coughed up a glander. P 275–74 ~ Mucus substance coughed ('hawked') from lungs.

glass n Attrib **glass eel**: American eel (*Anguilla rostrata*).

1971 *RLS* 3, p. 2 The young eels, or elvers, which are transparent are known as glass eels.

glassen a *OED* ~ 1 obs (971–1765); *EDD* esp Gl Do So. Made of glass.

T 34–64 We had a washboard, a glassen washboard. T 279/80–66 [folk tale] He come to a glassen hill, an' he wouldn't climb over the hill because glass is slippery. C 66–13 You better not drop that glassen dish. 1971 NOSEWORTHY 79 Glassen bobbers: glass floats for trawls. P 11–79 Glassen jar.

glaum n DINNEEN glám 'a clutch, a snatch'; *Kilkenny Lexicon* glaum: make a glaum at. Phr

make a glaum: to snatch; to make a grabbing motion.

1927 *Christmas Messenger* 47 I made a 'glaum' at him. Meaning a violent open-hand attempt to catch a person by the upper part of the body, head, neck or breast. 1965 *Evening Telegram* 21 Dec, p. 28 'Did your wife lend you them sharp scidders? She said she would.' 'Deed she did,' sez I, makin' a glaum for me inside pocket. 1968 DILLON 140 He made a glaum at me when I passed him.

glaum v [glɔːm]. Cp DINNEEN glámaim 'pull about, maul,' *EDD, NID*. To grab; to scoop up shoaling fish (with a net). Cp CLUM v: clom.

1937 DEVINE 25 ~ To snatch suddenly with the hand. 1968 DILLON 140 They're always there to glawm up anything they can get their hands on. P 157–73 Glom—to grab with vigour. P 27–81 [The caplin—we] glaum em all up!

glavaun n also **glabaun, glawvawn** DINNEEN glámhán 'a murmuring, complaining'; *Kilkenny Lexicon* glámhán. Continuous complaining; one who grumbles.

1968 DILLON 140 'Tis the one glawvawn with him all the time. That's all that one is, a glawvawn. C 71–95 A person who is always worrying about something, usually a trivial matter, is a glabaun.

glauvaun v also **glawvawn** [ˌglɒˈvɔːn]. To complain about trifles (1937 DEVINE 25).

1968 DILLON 140 He's always glawvawnin' about something. There's hardly a day but he have a different complaint. P 108–70 She always has the poor mouth; she's always glauvauning. C 75–139 When a person is said to be glauvauning it is indicative that he has troubles.

glean v *EDD* ~ v¹ 'to leer; sneer' Do So. To laugh covertly; to grin, jeer (P 54–68).

gleaner n Cp GLEAN. One who jeers or laughs covertly at another.

C 66–4 A gleaner is a person who makes fun of other people; a back-biter who laughs at them.

glidder* See GLITTER.

glim n also **glin, glynn**. Glow or brightness seen over a distant ice-field; shimmer over ice; ice-blink; ICE-GLIM.

[1668] 1963 YONGE 116 The wind springing up, make sail; see no sign of ice, only a glynn in the N.N.W. 1861 *Harper's* xxii, 598 He predicts the weather by the moaning of the sea, or by the 'loam' or 'glin' in the atmosphere. 1866 WILSON 275 Some days before the ice is actually seen, its approach can be descried from the shore by its glim, or the reflection of light which it throws into the atmosphere when the night is dark. 1925 *Dial Notes* v, 332 Glin. Dazzle of the ice.

glin See GLIM.

glitter n also **glidder***. Cp *OED* glidder v 'to

glaze over' obs exc dial (1616–); *EDD* glidder sb 'frosted or glazed surface,' gliddering 'slippery' D Co; *DC* ~ Nfld (1868–). See also SILVER THAW.

1 The coating of ice deposited on exposed objects by freezing rain; in some contexts overlaps with sense 2.

1840 GOSSE 42 The wetness running from their bodies freezes on the surface of the [otter] slide, and so the snow becomes a smooth glitter of ice. 1855 WHITE *MS Journal* 12 Mar All hands employed clearing the rigging from glitter. [1896] SWANSBOROUGH 7 "May": Easterly winds, which glitter brings, / And silver trees, and other things. 1897 *J A Folklore* x, 206 ~ used on the west coast to denote that peculiar phenomenon known generally through the northern part of America as 'a silver thaw'; that is, when fine rain falling meets near the earth a colder stratum of air and becomes congealed, forming a covering of ice upon every object. [1906] GRENFELL 89 The 'glitter,' however, most effectually concealed the blazings, and we were at last driven to try to force a way on our own. 1924 ENGLAND 69 The barrelman had gone aloft, careless of the 'glitter' on shrouds and ratlines, indifferent to the shrieking zero gale. T 54/65–64 They were froze in th' ice—glitter enough in the whole winter; quarried over, an' snow. They chopped 'em out, the bodies out th' ice. 1975 *Evening Telegram* 21 May, p. 6 On this day we decided to stay from school because we awoke to a silvery world of 'glitter'—the trees looked like silver filigree.

2 A condition of the weather in which freezing rain deposits a coating of ice on exposed objects. Attrib **glitter storm**.

1855 WHITE *MS Journal* 11 Mar Strong breeze with glitter. [1868] 1873 REEKS 8 ~ rain freezing and coating everything with a layer of ice. 1893 *Trade Review Christmas No* 15 After a heavy glitter-storm, I went with my man Walter Hearn. 1913 DUGMORE 40 [The caribou] are obliged to make forced marches owing to a 'glitter' or ice storm, which will imprison all the food, both on the ground and on the trees, in its icy grip. 1917 *Christmas Bells* 12 On our way a 'glitter,' or as it is termed 'silver thaw,' had set in. We were cased in Nature's armour. C 71–42 A girl got astray in a glidder storm and her name was Sheila.

glory n *DC* ~ fit Nfld (1905–).
Comb **glory fit**: lively show of religious enthusiasm.

1905 DUNCAN 107 He was a cheerful Methodist, too, and subject to 'glory-fits.' 1946 BIRD 5 He had not the religion of the outport Newfoundlanders who were subject to 'glory fits' and loud repentances.

glory-in-the-morning: speedwell (*Veronica persica*) (1956 ROULEAU 31).

glory roll: see **glory fit** above.

1973 BARBOUR 63 Such was the setting for any service, during which one often heard a hand clap. This was not the hand-clapping of the 'Glory Roll,' however, but the sound of someone trying to catch a wily mosquito.

glum a *EDD* ~ adj 1; SMYTH 342. Of the weather, gloomy, overcast; GRUM (P 133–58).

C 63–1 [proverb] If Candlemas Day [Feb 2nd] is fair and fine, the worst of winter is left behind. / If Candlemas Day is rough and glum, the worst of winter is to come.

glut n Cp *OED* ~ sb³ 2 'supply. . .greatly in excess of the demand.' A catch of fish in excess of the capacity to handle or process; esp in phr *glut of fish*. Also attrib.

1939 LODGE 107 With English trawlers a practice is developing of catching cod with the definite intention of selling to the salt-fish curers. When this is done the fish is gutted and split at sea and the resultant product is of so much better a quality as to warrant a definitely higher price being paid than for 'glut' fish. M 70–21 If there were a 'glut' of fish there might be four or five boatloads, that is, about fifty quintals to 'put away' during a working period from eight in the morning till after midnight. 1978 *Evening Telegram* 4 Mar, p. 19 We have never learned how to take full advantage of the summer glut of fish.

glutch v *EDD* ~ v 1 s w cties. To swallow; to gulp down (with difficulty).

1895 *J A Folklore* viii, 29 My throat is so sore that I cannot *glutch* anything. [c1900] 1978 *RLS* 8, p. 23 Gluch—to swallow. 1924 ENGLAND 125 Uncle Edgar Tucker, being called upon, protested that he was so hoarse he could "ardly glutch.' 1952 BANFILL 98 I went from one patient to another, easing a gasping pain, softening and freshening the pillows of men and women, preparing gargles for kinkorns that would not glutch. T 80/2–64 An' the once I get sick. Smokin' I suppose, an' glutchin' the smoke. 1973 *Evening Telegram* 10 Oct, p. 3 They may say the Newfoundland people are sheepish and easily led and will glutch down more than a saddleback gull without gagging but only wait, I say, wait.

glutch n *EDD* ~ sb 3 Do So. A gulp or swallow; the act of swallowing.

1920 GRENFELL & SPALDING 191 The next case was a young girl with a 'kink in her glutch.' 1924 ENGLAND 54 I know lots o' fellers fall in on purpose, to get a glutch o' rum. C 68–17 If a person has hiccups and wants to get rid of them he can do so by taking nine glutches of water. 1973 MOWAT 122 A few had bottles of Radway's Ready Relief—supposed to be a pain killer but, if the truth was out, only flavoured alcohol—good enough stuff, but there wasn't more than a glutch for every man.

glutted p ppl Cp *EDD* glut v 2 'fill to satiety' D Co. Of fish, esp cod, filled to satiety with caplin or squid.

1861 NOBLE 69 Fish were so glutted with capelin that they would not bite well. [1896] SWANSBOROUGH 9 "July": Fish may upon the bottom lie, / But won't eat bait, in vain we try; / They're glutted, that is fat with bait. T 43–64 The fish would be glutted with caplin.

gly n   A device with baited hooks to catch sea-
birds; DOG[2] 3; TODGER.

1896 *J A Folklore* ix, 36 ~ a sort of trap made with a
barrel-hoop with net interwoven, and hook and bait
attached, set afloat to catch gulls, and other marine
birds. 1909 BROWNE 207 During the sealing voyage
[the ivory gull] frequents the 'pans,' and sealers capture it by laying a 'gly' or bait on the ice. 1925 *Dial
Notes* v, 332 ~ A trap having a hook attached to a
float. It is baited and used for catching gulls. C 70–15
The method of trapping the gulls was to use a gly. A
piece of cylindrical cork into which a number of small
fish hooks were embedded was attached to a line and
'anchored' with a rock in a place where the gulls frequent. The cork and hooks were encased in bait, usually squid. The cork would keep the bait afloat, and
when the gull seized the bait, it would be caught by the
beak with one of the hooks. M 71–103 They would set
glies to catch gulls. This consisted of a fish hook
inserted into a piece of cork. A fish liver was used as
bait and fish puddick (stomach) was gloved over the
cork. This was left to float on the water anchored by a
rock off from shore.

go v   For phr in sense 3: *EDD* ~ v 2 (1) go awa'
'exclamation of impatience, disbelief'; *OED* 83 f
go off (1795–).

1 Of fish, esp salmon, to migrate; run.

[1774] 1792 CARTWRIGHT ii, 14 At night a punt
arrived from the lodge with the tools, and brought a
report that few fish were going; so that I am afraid the
salmon season is nearly over.

2 To challenge, defy; cp MANUS.

1924 ENGLAND 181 Do you think you can go [defy]
Skipper Abram Best? An' *me*? What ye got to say fer
y'rself, now?

3 Phr *go away*: (a) to leave vessel in search of
seals; (b) exclamation of incredulity (1964 quot),
~ *off*: of cured cod-fish, to deteriorate in quality;
~ *on*: to take up or resume decisively an activity
which has been interrupted; ~ *to wing*: to
become a spendthrift; become uncontrollable; ~
(up) for: to approach a certain point in time.

1924 ENGLAND 52 The master watches are in charge
of gangs both on the ship and when the men 'go away,'
on ice, and have to be responsible for the lives and
safety of the hunters. 1964 *Can Journ Ling* x, 45 If a
young woman is reproached, the speaker may say: Go
away maid [I don't believe you]. [1674–77] 1976 HEAD
40 This would make fish better cured; it would not
other wise go off, at least not in a plentiful year. 1855
WHITE *MS Journal* 9 Mar Ice rented in one Place succeeded in getting Ship in the lake which was not more
than 15 feet Ship went on in this lake 5 miles NW.
T 54/64–64 Got him handy to shore, an' got a rope
around him, an' tied him onto some trees. An' he come
to life again an' he took a whole lot o' the trees out o'
roots an' went on with the whole works. T 31–64 Soon
as [we] see the first tickleace, first little bird come yer
in the spring, that'd be our mark. 'Time to get away
now! Time to go on now!' P 108–71 Since he came into
a bit of money he's gone to wing. 1916 MURPHY 7
About 14 years ago Mr David King, of the Southside,

who was then going up for ninety years of age, gave [a]
description of the first sealers' strike. P 148–60 It
should be goin' up for three o'clock.

4 Comb **go-by**: (a) navigation mark; (b) pattern or model.

1951 *Nfld & Lab Pilot* i, 116 Go By point. . .lies
about 2 cables northward of the eastern entrance point
of Beaubois cove. C 67–13 ~ pattern for making a
dress.

go n   A division of a sealing crew; GANG,
WATCH (1925 *Dial Notes* v, 332).

1924 ENGLAND 83 They seemed now to have no
organization. There was no gathering of 'goes,' or
gangs, under command of master watches, as later in
the old-fat kill. This was just a free-for-all scramble.

goat n

1 Epithet for resident of a neighbouring community.

C 66–3 Fortune 'goats' / Grand Bank 'shags' / All
tied up in wrapper bags. C 69–15 Billy goat, nanny
goat: nicknames for people born on the Southside, St
John's. 1976 CASHIN 52 The saying goes at one time a
'goat spoke in Mobile.' From that time onwards the
people in that settlement were called Mobile goats.
1977 *Evening Telegram* 24 Aug, p. 6 [letter signed] A
[Upper] gullie Goat and a Newfie forever.

2 One of the figures of a cotillion; a dance.

C 75–138 An old fashioned square dance done in
some outport communities is the 'Goat.' In this dance
there are parts called 'going on the Labrador,' 'through
the bushes,' etc. C 75–46 Today the young people only
dance the rock and roll type of dance, as opposed to
their parents, who only danced the cotillion or the goat
as they called it.

3 Weather proverb.

1937 DEVINE 67 If the goats come home in files, /
Get your fish in covered piles.

4 Attrib, comb **goat rubber**; also **sheep chaser,
~ rubber**: knee-length rubber boot; RUBBER (P
65–64).

P 148–66 'Get your sheep chasers on today.' This was
often said to anyone wearing knee-high rubber boots,
whether bought that length or cut down from hip rubbers which had cracked above the knee. It is usually
said jokingly. C 71–118 Sheep chasers are rubber boots
cut off at the knee. It would be too warm to wear the
long boots in the spring and even if turned down, they
would be very heavy and bulky. P 148–80 They are
called goat rubbers because the men used to put the
rubbers on the back legs of the goat, or of a sheep.

goat sculpin: scavenger fish (*Myoxocephalus
octodecemspinosus; M. scorpius*); SCULPIN.

1967 *Nfld Qtly* June, p. 10 Occasionally there was
the thrill of spearing a 'goat' sculpin, so named, presumably, because of its extraordinarily long horns, and
of feeling, as the spear pierced its flesh, a strong vibration run through the shaft of the spear and through the
arm to the very shoulder, being sensed almost as a
minor electric shock.

goat shoe: winter foot covering for goat hauling sled (C 70–15).

goat's house: quarter hatch on sealing vessel (1925 *Dial Notes* v, 332).

1924 ENGLAND 116 Another grinned from the 'goat's house' or 'lobby,' near the aft winch.

gob¹ n Cp *EDD* ~ sb¹ 1, 6. A certain unspecified amount (of fish); SIGN.

1891 *Holly Branch* 12 Skipper Tom and crew began to get careless when they saw the 'summer' go 'agen' 'em, slept late in the mornings right 'under the nose' of old 'Hardy,' remained longer at home whenever they came with a little 'gob.' C 70–20 When a fisherman doesn't want to tell how much fish he's got, he is likely to put off questions by answering that he's got 'a gob of fish.' My informant says she always thought it meant an unusually large catch.

gob² n Cp *OED* ~ sb² 'mouth' for sense 1; *OED* gob sb² b (b) ~ stick (1883), *Fisheries of U S* (1887), p. 153 for comb (a) in sense 2.

1 Cod's tongue and lips; cp SCULP(S), TONGUE.

[1960] 1965 LEACH (ed) 191 "Big Sam": The *Danny R* is comin' with cods heads and gobs. / He says I'll get down cause she haven't got much.

2 Comb **gob-stick**: (a) stick with notch in the end to pry hook from fish's gullet; cp GAFF; (b) lollipop.

1924 ENGLAND 141 Men dragged the cold sculps away, some using 'gobsticks' to carry them. 1937 DEVINE 25 ~ A stick about two feet long and half an inch in diameter kept at hand when fishing, to remove the hook from its hold when swallowed by the fish. 1967 *Bk of Nfld* iv, 246 Then there was a gob-stick, that's a piece of board with a notch in one end with a rod across the opening. It is used to unhook the fish with. P 90–69 ~ all-day sucker.

gob v To remove hook from gullet of a cod-fish with a 'gob-stick.'

1968 DILLON 141 Then the hook comes out; that's gobbin' 'em.

god n *OED* mark sb¹ 18: (God) bless the mark (1591–1625), JOYCE 195 for phr in sense 2; *EDD* 3 (2) god's cow, 1 (15) ~ stone for combs. in sense 3.

1 In fisherman's proverb.

1895 *Christmas Review* 12 God makes the ocean narrow, the devil makes the river broad. Ibid With God on the lookout, it's easy to steer.

2 In phr of greeting or supplication: *god between us and all harm, ~ bless the mark, ~ look down on us, ~ rest you, ~ save all here.*

P 108–70 God between us and all harm: an expression said hopefully to avert misfortune. P 108–70 As a child I remember that when passing anyone lame, blind or disfigured in some way, we were told to whisper to ourselves 'God bless the mark.' 1977 *Evening Telegram* 3 Dec, p. 46 'Well gentlemen,' sez I, 'God bless the mark, but this is really a chilly day.' P 191–73 God look down on us. Said when things are going badly or when evil is impending. P 148–64 God rest you: a greeting in a Catholic household given to a group of visitors on Christmas night. 1869 MCCREA 112 'God save all here!' says he, with the sign of the cross, and a pleasant look around. 1931 BYRNES 103 'A Merry Christmas! God save all here!'

3 Comb **god-be-merciful pipe and tobacco**: smoking equipment supplied at a wake.

1971 CASEY 296 Until 1897 or later, clay pipes and tobacco were also spread out on a table near the coffin. These 'God be merciful pipes and tobacco' were smoked by visitors and could be taken when leaving the 'wake house.'

god's cow: lady-bird beetle (*Anatis ocellata malis; Adalia bipunctata*).

C 69–2 One of the cures for a toothache is to get an insect which is called God's cow, put [it] in a bag and hang it around the neck. C 71–4 Residents of Fair Island always referred to the lady bug as God's cow.

god's rock: white stone, thought to be lucky.

C 69–19 A white rock, which we always called a God's rock, was supposed to be lucky. If you fire [it] at a target you were supposed never to miss.

god walkers: new pair of boots or shoes (worn to church); cp SCROOPY (BOOTS).

C 71–111 Whenever he buys a new pair of boots he says proudly, 'There's a fine pair of god-walkers.'

goggy n *EDD* ~ 'child's name for an egg' for sense (a). Comb **goggy-egg**: (a) hen's egg (1968 DILLON 143); (b) small white berry of the creeping snowberry; CAPILLAIRE (1968 DILLON 143).

C 71–93 ~ This is a small white berry found on miniature leaves on mossy hills under fir trees anywhere in St Mary's Bay. It has a sweet taste.

gold n also **goold, gould**. Cp *EDD* ~ sb² 'sweet willow' So for sense 1; *OED* ~² 1 a obs exc dial; SEARY 112, 218 for sense 2.

1 Sheep laurel (*Kalmia angustifolia*); similar low shrub; in place-names. Also attrib ~ **bush**, ~ **leaf**; GOLD-WITHY.

1840 GOSSE 300 [In Newfoundland sheep laurel and swamp laurel are]. . .called Gould; they bear bunches of pretty little pink flowers, nearly circular. 1858 [LOWELL] i, 143 And there he's coming now, sir, over the gool'-bushes yonder. Ibid ii, 208 . . .and the shadows in the abyss below them, and the little thickets of 'goold,' and other bushes and small trees. 1938 AYRE 30 Someone telephoned me to ask for information about a plant named 'goole' for his local broadcast. 1951 *Nfld & Lab Pilot* i, 117 Gould head. . .Gould cove. C 70–10 Indian tea was made by steeping out the tops and flowers of the gools. Q 71–4 [Gold-withy] called goldleaf.

2 Marsh-marigold (*Caltha palustris*); pl in place-names (1971 SEARY 218).

1842 JUKES i, 42 [The farm called the Golds is] so called from a yellow flower which grows abundantly on the banks of some of the brooks. 1904 MURPHY (ed) 52 "Old Low-Back-Car": Again at the Goulds, with my basket quite heavy, / I spent happy hours with no trouble to mar, / And listened to many a trout-catcher's story, / As told by some friend of the Old Low-Back-Car.

3 Comb **gold bird**: Wilson's pileolated warbler (*Wilsonia pusilla pusilla*).

[1766] 1971 BANKS 123 Killed a very small but beautiful bird called here a Gold Bird.

goldfinch: North American redstart (*Setophaga ruticilla tricolora*).

1870 *Can Naturalist* v, 154 [The redstart is] a summer migrant, but rare in the north of Newfoundland. It is called 'Goldfinch' by the English settlers.

golden a Comb **golden-root** (*Coptis groenlandica*) (1893 *N S Inst Sci* viii, 362).

gold-withy n also **goowiddy, gould withy, ~ woody, gowithy**, etc ['guːlwɪtɪ, 'ɡʉulwɪdɪ, 'guˑɪdɪ, 'guːwədɪ, 'gouwɪtɪ]. Cp *EDD* gold sb¹ 2 (11) ~ withy 'bog myrtle' Ha IW. See also GOLD, WITHY. Sheep laurel (*Kalmia angustifolia*); similar sort of low shrub; also attrib.

1846 TOCQUE 124 Swamp laurel. . .called in Newfoundland Gould Withy, (when boiled with tobacco and sprinkled over the parts affected, it is an infallible remedy to cure dogs of the mange). 1887 HOWLEY *MS Reminiscences* 38 I was particularly struck with the beauty of the Goldworthy flowers and examined them very minutely. This beautiful plume-like flower looked into closely is extremely lovely. . . The colour of the flowerlets generally is yellowish white with a faint pinkish tinge. 1907 MILLAIS 32 About midday we emerged on to beautiful undulating high ground covered with blueberries and a short bush called locally 'goudie.' 1953 *Nfld & Labrador Pilot* ii, 151 Goodwithy harbour indents the northern shore of the bay about half a mile. 1956 ROULEAU 31 Gold-withy. Although I believe that this application should be restricted to *Kalmia angustifolia* L., it is in fact applied to any shrubby species occurring in the 'barrens.' [e.g.] *Andromeda glaucophylla, Chamaedaphne calyculata, Cornus stolonifera. . .Kalmia polifolia, Myrica gale, Potentilla fruticosa, Rhododendron canadense.* T 208/9–65 They made a smoke but it wouldn't burn; 'twas goolwiddy, an' 'twas in the fall o' the year, and snow down. C 67–13 Gowiddy means a certain type of vegetative cover. It consists of a barren-like site covered with such things as lichen, Labrador tea, alders or stunted larch. C 68–12 He drinks a bit and she saw him the other day when he was going into his home, falling around like a lamb with the goo-widdy. I asked her what that meant and she told me that lambs, when they eat the goo-widdy bush, act like they were drunk. 1982 *Evening Telegram* 9 Jan, p. 2 About 20 head of the cattle brought to St Bride's from western Canada earlier this year [are said to have] died after eating a local poisonous weed. . .known as 'lambkill,' in the books, and known locally as 'gouldwoody'.

gom n *O Sup²* ~ 4 Ir (1834–); *EDD* gaum sb³ 2 'lout; gaping, idle fellow' Ir; JOYCE 264. A stupid clumsy fellow; GOMMEL. Also phr *act the gom*: to play the fool (P 148–61).

P 132–64 ~ a stupid person.

gombeen n also **gumbean, gumbeen** ['gʌmbiːn,

gʌm'biːn] DINNEEN gaimbín tobac 'morsel of tobacco.' Small lump of tobacco, esp when used as stakes in a card game.

1896 *J A Folklore* ix, 35 Gum bean: a chew of tobacco. 1909 BROWNE 64 Others are playing a game of 'five and forty' with 'gumbeens' for stakes. 1924 ENGLAND 119 Dey was ahl gamblin' fer baccy, fer gumbeans. Gumbeans? Dem's small little pellets o' baccy. 1937 DEVINE 25 Gombeen—small cubes of tobacco. 1968 DILLON 143 Gumbeens. Small pieces of tobacco used as stakes in playing cards; tobacco chewed for a time, then saved and dried for smoking in a pipe. 1976 CASHIN 95 Frequently we had the nightly game of cards, the old game of forty-fives, which we played at a couple of private homes, the stakes generally being small 'gumbeens.'

gommel n also **gommil** JOYCE 264 gommul 'simple-minded fellow'; DINNEEN gamal 'stupid looking fellow.' Epithet for a stupid person; freq with *foolish*, etc; GOM.

1924 ENGLAND 221 'He must of went off his 'eed, to curse on de lightnin',' put in Arthur Roberts. 'Ondly a gommel [fool] 'd take a chance like dat.' 1937 DEVINE 25 ~ A stupid or foolish person. 1968 DILLON 143 That poor gommil, sure he don't know what you're talkin' about. C 70–11 When slightly irritated with him she calls him a foolish gommil. 1975 RUSSELL 51 'Come here,' said she, 'you foolish gommil, and help me.'

gommer v, n To grumble; a grumbler.

[1929] 1933 GREENLEAF 232 [The crew of the schooner] had to draw lots as to which dory they were to go in all the voyage, and as to which of the six seats in the dory they should occupy, and it was no use to 'gommer' (grumble); for whatever they drew, they had to abide by the lot. P 94–57 ~ One who grumbles or complains.

goold See GOLD.

goolo* n also **gooloze*, goolos***, etc ['guːlə, 'guːlɐ, 'gʉʉlə, 'guloz, 'guːlouz, 'gʉʉlouz 'guːldouz, gʉʉlz, gʉʉls]. Cp *OED* goal sb 3 b 'used (also pl) as the name of certain games' (1884); *Ling Atlas Scot* (1975) i, pp. 220 ff. Home or base in playing certain games; such a game. Freq pl; also attrib.

P 199–55 ~ game of tag in which one cannot be tagged if one exclaims 'goolos!' M 65–4 In Fogo during the winter, football is played and called goolo. When a player scores, the team yells 'goolo!' T 75/6–64 We used to play gools. A ball on the ice, just like you play hockey now. T 417/9–67 There was another [game in which] you had to move back towards a certain point behind rocks, an' if you were seen—goola. [We] used to call that one goola; goola rock, the home rock. C 67–9 There were many kinds of hide-and-go-seek we used to play but home base was always goolos. P 245–75 You can't touch me—I'm on goolos.

goose n Cpd **goose-grass**: bur-reed, a plant of the muddy shores of ponds and streams

(*Sparganium* spp); eel-grass, a marine herb of salt-water shoals (*Zostera marina*).

[1783] 1792 CARTWRIGHT iii, 17 We found the lake to be very shoaly in general, particularly the upper part; the bottom of it is mostly fine sand, covered with long weed, called goose-grass. 1836 [WIX]² 92 [The wild geese] had been attracted to this arm by the quantity of goose-grass. 1861 DE BOILIEU 242 The neighbourhood of a small wood, with goose-grass in the foreground, is [the favourite resort of the geese]. T 250–66 All down around this harbour, all eel grass, we call it—goose grass. 1976 GUY 60 The potatoes were kept in cellars made of mounds of earth lined with sawdust or goose-grass. 1977 *Inuit Land Use* 293 In summer, the geese feed on coarse grasses known as goose grass, and in shallow waters.

goowiddy See GOLD-WITHY.

gossard See GOZZARD.

gould withy See GOLD-WITHY.

government n Designating a facility, service, etc, provided by the central governing authority in Newfoundland: **government appointment, ~ bull, ~ culler** [see CULLER], **~ relief, ~ road, ~ store, ~ wharf**.

1895 GRENFELL 79 The recipients [of government relief] are frequently able-bodied men, and they have no shame in accepting it, looking on the government as an independent source of wealth, and calling their annual six to twenty-four dollars 'a government appointment.' 1937 DEVINE 73 A government bull has no friends in November and d—n few at any other time. T 43–64 There'd be a special culler, a man authorized to cull the fish for the firm, and in later years a sworn-in culler, a government culler. [1826] 1924 MURPHY 1 Archdeacon Coaster, writing from Bonavista, April 26th [1826], said that times were very poor there; scarcely any food in stores; only for Government relief, conditions would be bad. P 262–60 I find everywhere a tendency to refer to roads in settlements which were built in days long gone as 'Government roads.' This is separate from those that have more or less been formed through use. 1977 *Inuit Land Use* 137 Fishermen then turned to netting char in the bays and, after 1969, when the government store began to purchase salmon, to the salmon fishery. 1883 HOWLEY *MS Reminiscences* 7 He is now Telegraph operator [in Harbour Breton] and is also in charge of the Government wharf and store. 1932 BARBOUR 91 Do you see the wharf? It looks like a government wharf. 1951 *Nfld & Lab Pilot* i, 282 A wharf—known as Government wharf, is situated about half a cable westward of Point Pleasant [Port aux Basques]. 1979 *Evening Telegram* 14 July, p. 16 Since the destruction of the government wharf [at Elliston] last spring, fishermen have been faced with limited space for landing their catches.

governor n Cp SMYTH 345 'officer placed by royal commission in command of a. . .colony.'

1 One in charge of a seventeenth-century 'plantation' authorized under royal charter; a deputy in charge of a 'settlement.'

[1611] 1895 PROWSE 123 And for divers reasons and considerations that immediately from and after such tyme as any governour soe to be nominated shall arive in Newfoundland and give notice of his commission in that behalfe. [1622] ibid 130 The Land where on our Governour hath planted, is so good and commodious, that for the quantity, I think there is no better in many parts of England. 1628 HAYMAN [sig. A1] Epigrams. . .Composed and done at *Harbor-Grace Britaniola*, anciently called *Newfound-land* By R.H. Sometimes Governour of the Plantation there.

2 The master of the first English fishing vessel to reach a harbour, exercising certain prerogatives for the season; ADMIRAL, FISHING ~ .

[1698] CHILD 229 A Governor there is already of antient custom among the masters of the fishing Ships, to whom the fishermen are inured and that free from oppression.

3 A British naval officer in command of the ships on the Newfoundland station, with civil jurisdiction.

[1669] 1793 REEVES 13 Captain *Robert Robinson* petitioned for the settlement of a governor; and, on a reference of this question to the lords of the committee for trade and plantations, their lordships reported, after hearing several merchants and others concerned in the trade, 'that they did not think fit to recommend the petition and proposal of *Mr Robinson* for making him governor of Newfoundland; but, for keeping people living there in Christianity, they proposed that his Majesty should send a chaplain in the convoy-ships; and *that the captains of the said ships should have power to regulate abuses there.* [1766] 1971 BANKS 150 Newfoundland has always been Defended by a Squadron of Ships the Commodore of which for the Time being is Governor & administers Civil Justice Returning home in the winter & Leaving to a Deputy whose title is no more than Justice the Power of Regulating small disputes in his absence. 1813 CARSON 11 A Governor of Newfoundland holds his commission for three years, and during that period he resides in the island nine months. It is not probable that during that short space, he can become acquainted with our laws, customs, characters, or interests.

4 One appointed to represent the Crown in the colony of Newfoundland.

[1819] 1915 HOWLEY 119 Despatch from Governor Hamilton to Earl Bathurst. Fort Townsend, St John's, Newfoundland. Sept 27th, 1819. With reference to the 11th article of the general instructions of His Royal Highness the Prince Regent to me as Governor of Newfoundland. . . 1842 BONNYCASTLE i, 149 Sir Charles [Hamilton] was the first permanently resident civil governor, and occupied the old wooden government house, since pulled down, in Fort Townsend. 1933 *Nfld Royal Commission Report* 224 We therefore recommend that. . .(a) The existing form of government would be suspended until such time as the Island may become self-supporting again. (b) A special Commission of Government would be created which would be presided over by His Excellency the Governor, would be vested with full legislative and executive authority, and would take the place of the existing Legislature and Executive Council. 1941 SMALLWOOD 156 Chairman: His Excellency the Governor, Vice Admiral Sir Humphrey T Walwyn.

gowithy See GOLD-WITHY.

gozzard n also **gossard, gosset**. Cp *OED* ~ 'gooseherd.' American common merganser (*Mergus merganser americanus*).

[1776] 1792 CARTWRIGHT ii, 185 I killed a gozzard, gathered a few eggs on Diver Island, and got home at seven in the evening. 1870 *Can Naturalist* v, 303 [The gossander] breeds on the margins of lakes and rivers. . .called the 'gozzard' by the settlers. 1951 PETERS & BURLEIGH 128 The 'Gossard' is heavy-bodied and often has considerable difficulty in rising from the water, running along the surface to gain speed for flight. 1967 *Bk of Nfld* iii, 283 American Merganser: Gozzard (a variation of goosander, of Norse origin, which means goose-duck).

grain n also **grains** *OED* ~ sb² 5, 5 b grains; *EDD* sb¹ 5. The prong or tine of a 'fish fork'; cp PEW¹.

1930 BARNES 14 Sometimes I would catch [a dolphin] with a grains—that is an iron with four prongs like a fork with a beard on the end of each so that it will hold on to the fish when you drive it in. T 141/67–65² I've seen it when the schooners would come up empty—ain't shook a grain.

grand a *DC* grand banks (1935–); *Fisheries of U S* (1887), pp. 129 ff.

Comb **grand bank(s)**: large area of shoal water southeast of Newfoundland forming a rich fishing-ground; BANK, GREAT ~ . Also attrib.

[1794] 1968 THOMAS 173 A Fisherman who works in a Banker on the Grand Bank has a most laborous life of it. . . I can find none bad enough for comparison. 1909 GRENFELL² (ed) 294 There is little doubt that the cod does not travel far in its annual migration. After spawning, the school simply moves out into deeper water on the slopes of the continental plateau or on the Grand Banks. 1960 FUDGE 36 I have been fishing in small boats since I was eleven years of age, and in the large Grand Bank vessels since I was seventeen years of age. 1969 *Christmas Mumming in Nfld* 10 [The Labrador Current] brushes the northeast coast of the Island, and then turns in a gigantic clockwise motion around the eastern tip. As it turns, it meets the warm waters of the eastward-bound Gulf Stream, and their union occurs over the shoal waters of the Grand Banks. 1978 *Evening Telegram* 27 Apr, p. 1 The most damaging overfishing would be on the eastern reaches of the Grand Banks off Newfoundland.

grand banker: fisherman engaged in the offshore or 'bank fishery'; BANKER 2; BANK FISHERMAN.

1971 NOSEWORTHY 16 The erection of a Fishermen's Museum on Marine Drive will ensure that the lives and achievements of the 'Grand Bankers' of the past will not be forgotten and the heritage they have passed on to their descendants will never be lost.

grand bay: the waters of the Gulf of St Lawrence and the Strait of Belle Isle.

[1583] 1940 *Gilbert's Voyages & Enterprises* i, 398 [Hayes' narrative] So again Tuesday the 30 of July (seven weekes after) we got sight of land, being immediately embayed in the Grand Bay, or some other great bay. [1708 OLDMIXON 9 There are abundance of other Bays round about the Western Shore, as far as the *Great Bay*, and many more between that and *Trinity Bay*.] 1895 PROWSE 43 [The headquarters of the Basque whale fishery] were in the gulf and straits known in those ancient times as the Grand Bay. 1937 LUBBOCK 128 The first Greenland whale is said to have been killed in Grand Bay, Newfoundland, hence the name of Grand Bay Whale.

grand goose: great skua (*Catharacta skua skua*) (1951 PETERS & BURLEIGH 219).

granny n *DAE* ~ (1794–), *ADD* for sense 1.
  1 Midwife; also attrib.
  1858 [LOWELL] i, 117 The title 'Granny,' common to them both, is as well a medical and professional distinction, in Newfoundland, as one implying age. 1888 WAGHORNE 10 [Juniper berries] are much in request by our 'grannies' for their 'sick' women. [1927 BURKE] "Hold Your Water": As you hammer down doors and no Granny can find, / The rush is now on, and the contracts are signed, / When one of God's creatures is reeking with pain, / After beating the town up to Haggerty's Lane. T 450–67 [One] o' the old granny womans'd do that up, sir. You wouldn't want to get n'ar doctor, get n'ar cut done up. M 70–28 She was a midwife and whenever she was seen carrying her old green granny bag (designed something like the shopping bags with handles one sees in stores today, and made of some straw-like fibre) everyone knew she was going to visit one of the pregnant women in the settlement.

  2 An anchor made of an elongated stone encased in pliable sticks bound at the top and fixed in two curved cross-pieces; KILLICK; freq with *old*.
  1924 ENGLAND 263 Buoys, 'old grannies' (kellock anchors), and all manner of strange gear. . .lie scattered everywhere. P 148–61 ~ home-made anchor. 1971 NOSEWORTHY 205 ~ A wooden anchor for fishing lines, with two sticks at the bottom, crossed and sharpened at both ends, and four, or more, longer, thinner sticks holding a long, heavy rock.

  3 Part of the inner organs of a lobster, discarded in eating; HAG, OLD WOMAN (P 154–78).

grapelin*, grapenel See GRAPLE.

graple n also **grapelin*, grapenel, graypnel** ['greɪpəl, 'greɪpɫ, 'greɪb, 'greˑɪpɫ, 'greəpɫ, 'grɛʊpɫ, 'grɛʊpʉl, 'grɛʊpəl, 'greɪplɪn, 'grɛʊplən, 'greɪpnəl]. Cp *OED* grapple sb 2, grappling 3 b, grapnel 2, cp *NID* tackle¹ 'by seamen often 'tā-k-'; *ADD* grapnel (Nfld: 1921). Light anchor to moor small boats and fixed or stationary fishing gear; also attrib.

[1923] 1946 PRATT 182 "The Drag Irons": But with his Captain's blood he did resent, / With livid silence and with glassy look, / This fishy treatment when his years were spent— / To come up dead upon a grapnel hook. 1924 ENGLAND 237 Here I been workin' ahl me life, draggin' and 'aulin', mucklin' up grayples, sometimes bloody gert 'auls two hundred an' fifty viddum [fathom] lang on a gurdy. 1925 *Dial Notes* v, 333 Grappels. . . Also *grapenel.* P 147–55 Throw out the graple. P 113–56 Grapelin. A small anchor having four or more 'claws.' T 58/60–64 Most fishermen uses killicks instead of grapelin. You can make 'em yourself, where a grapelin cost a whole lot of money. T 89/90–64 We went up—everything gone! Not a grapel, n'ar a bobber, an' went in 'gain the rocks where the end was tied on to, here was one cork. T 187–65 They use a harpoon 'bout that long, like a big double shank graple. An' four claws onto un, double back 'longside. T 194/5–65 I hoist in the trap boat, the graple punt on top of that one. I filled she right full o' split fish. T 141/68–65[2] Put a piece o' board on an' a rock or piece of old iron, whatever you had picked up, graple-shank or whatever it might be. 1966 SCAMMELL 21 Skipper Joe Caines moved the small graple out of his way and sat down on the stage-head. M 67–16 This pole was placed in a berth and would have a rope tied to one end of it with a graple or killick attached to the pole. P 110–68 *Rode* at my home is a rope that has one end tied to a graple or kellick and the other end to the risin' of the boat. P 127–77 The purpose of the tailing is to ensure the retrieval of the grapelin if its claws become hooked in the sea-bed. 1977 *Inuit Land Use* 274 Grapelin Island.

grass n Cp SCOTT *Rob Roy* (1818) iii, 35 grass-ground, *NID* ~ mouse 'meadow mouse' for combs. in sense 2.

1 Mature hay ready to be dried for fodder.

T 43/7–64 You're goin' in the woods [and] you'd carry a bag o' grass. They wouldn't use the word 'hay.' They'd say, 'Fill up a bag o' grass for the horse.' 1972 MURRAY 254 The men cut the grass with long-handled scythes (sives). . .'making grass' was frequently a family affair. 1979 POTTLE 74 A veteran fisherman, 'Uncle' John Vey, who had just come in from his trawl, was mowing grass in his garden.

2 Comb **grass bag**: bag of dry hay carried to feed horse (P 130–67).

1979 TIZZARD 56 The hay would be carried down over the hill in grass-bags which were made from large mesh fish nets and would hold anywhere from fifty to a hundred pounds of hay.

grass bird, grassy ~ : type of sparrow.

1870 *Can Naturalist* v, 157 [The savannah sparrow] frequents grassy places, building its nest on the ground. Provincial name, 'Grass Bird.' 1959 MCATEE 66 Grass bird. Song Sparrow. 1964 *Evening Telegram* 28 Oct, p. 5 'Grassy bird' is applied exclusively to the savannah sparrow, and means the same thing as the more widely-accepted name, for 'savannah' is, of course, just a fancy word for meadow or grassland.

grass garden: pasture land; hayfield; GARDEN (P 269–64).

1972 MURRAY 250 Families had pieces of land, of varying shapes and sizes in different parts of the community. Some of these might be entirely in grass and

within the main 'grass garden,' there might be plots about 18' by 20' for carrots or turnips, and a 200' by 500' plot for potatoes.

grass ground: see **grass garden**; GROUND (P 102–60).

1972 MURRAY 114 Grass ground, enclosed by fences was forbidden territory in summer. 1975 GUY 9 Horse manure. . .was useful in hotbeds if anyone wanted to go to that trouble but otherwise would be scattered around the grass ground just to get rid of it.

grass house: small building for storing hay (C 75–19).

1966 FARIS 45 Grass is cut with scythe in the 'fall,' dried in the open, and stored in barns and 'grass houses' to be used for winter feed.

grass mouse: field-mouse.

[1785] 1971 BANKS 448 The Field or Grasssmice of Labrador, migrate also, I believe, for at the end of the summer of 1785 few or none were to be found even where they used to be in the greatest plenty. . . For these mice keep underground in the Summer, but after the snow falls come on the surface, where they collect grass and form a nest like the Dormice and by means of galleries which they work under the snow go out among the grass and seek their food.

grass net: net made of heavy cotton fishing 'twine' to carry hay to barn; LINNET 2 (P 148–63).

grass v Of young couples, to pet and engage in sexual play in a grassy location; GULCH v.

M 69–29 On summer nights it was very pleasant out of doors and the ground was dry, so the courters would lie down on the grass. This latter custom was called 'grassing.' Q 71–6 I caught two young [people] grassing out behind the barn.

grave v also **gravy**, with infinitive *-y* freq in s w cties: *EDG* (1905), p. 298. In repairing broken planking, to insert snugly a piece of new wood; scarf.

T 31/4–64 He got [to] grave two more pieces in there, gravy two more pieces like [those that] come out. He carried pine down there in [the] locker for that. He had [the skiff] carried ashore, and they had to gravy two more pieces in the plank.

gravel n Esp in pl, a pebble-strewn isthmus or sea-bottom; also attrib.

1836 [WIX][2] 136 On looking at the chart, it will be seen that the walk from the Middle Point, which separates West Bay and East Bay in this Port-au-Port, to the Isthmus, or 'Gravel,' as it is termed, which is at the bottom of St George's Bay, is no great distance. 1883 PILOT 10 'The Gravels,' which joins the peninsula of Port au Port to the mainland of the Island, not more than a quarter of a mile. 1951 *Nfld & Lab Pilot* i, 389 Gravels bank. . .extends. . .southward from the head of Isthmus bay.

graypnel See GRAPLE.

grease n also **graice, grase**. Cp *OED* ~ sb 2, d; *O Sup*[2] 2 d. Used variously of herring oil, fat rendered from salt pork, gravy and margarine; also attrib.

1873 CARROLL 43 If the hole is in the bilge, you cannot see if the cask leaks without taking out the bung; and if the herring oil, or grease, rise from the fish, it remains in the cask to the [great] injury of the herring, for it will be sure to turn them rusty, and of course injure them. 1924 ENGLAND 117 The cooks slopped out the famous dish [fish and brewis] renowned in Newfoundland lore: hard bread boiled with cod. 'Putt a little grase on un, b'ys. . .' Liberally the cooks drenched the fish and brewis with liquid pork grease and bits of crackling. 1931 BYRNES 115 It might be but a 'mug o' tay' sweetened with molasses and thick slices of home made bread and 'oleo' (or 'grease' as it was termed by some in the more remote districts). 1933 GREENE 182 On the Captain's side, is a cracked small tureen with a piece out of its upper edge through which you can see the 'graice' (or gravy) with lots and lots of onions floating in it. 1966 PADDOCK 115 Grease-cakes: fried homemade bread dough.

greasy a
1 Of the balsam-fir (*Abies balsamea*) in spring, full of sap; cp SNOTTY VAR.
P 148–65 Snotty var is too greasy to be good for cutting for winter's fires.
2 Comb **greasy-cake**: piece of dough dipped in fat, used to grease pan in which bread is baked, then left in corner of pan and baked (P 244–55).
greasy-jacket: seal hunter, with coat impregnated with seal's fat.
1924 ENGLAND 36 Along our rails the 'greasy-jackets' jammed, roaring back messages and cheers.

great a   Cp *OED* auk (1796 quot), *DAE* (1883), PENNANT ii, 509 (1785); *DC* Great Banks (1955–).
Comb **great ant**: variety of large ant.
1840 GOSSE 279 I saw a winged specimen of the Great Ant of Newfoundland (*Formica Pubescens*), and the Falcate Crane-fly. . .so common in that country.
great auk: large, flightless bird (*Pinguinus impennis*) once living in large numbers on Funk Island, extinct since the nineteenth century; PENGUIN (1918 TOWNSEND 341).
1947 TANNER 430 During the last hundred years two species have become extinct; the flightless great auk. . .in 1852 and the Labrador duck. 1951 PETERS & BURLEIGH 247 Men camped on Funk Island throughout the summer to kill and pluck the Great Auks. 1970 PARSONS 173 The great auk, in size larger than a goose, was a true native of the northern waters.
great bank: large area of shoal water southeast of Newfoundland forming a rich fishing ground; BANK(S); GRAND BANK(S).
1708 OLDMIXON 13 The Great Bank is about 20 Leagues from *Cape de Raz*, the nearest Point of Land to it; 'tis 300 Miles long, and 75 broad; the Sea that runs over it is, when 'tis Flood, several Fathom deep. 1778 DE CASSINI 115 We were sailing westward at a season when the winds generally blow from that quarter, yet, notwithstanding their obstinate opposition, in

twenty-eight days we reached the eastern skirts of the bank of Newfoundland, commonly called the Great Bank. 1819 ANSPACH 284 The Great Bank is five degrees wide in its broadest part, from east to west, including Jacquet-Bank, the southern extremity of which forms its outer edge, and upwards of nine degress in length from north to south. 1955 *Western Star* 14 Mar, p. 5 For 400 years its menfolk have gone down to the sea in small ships to snatch a bare and uncertain living from the famous Great Banks and to market their catches as best they could. [*DC*]
great grey gull: great black-backed gull (*Larus marinus*) (1959 MCATEE 36).

grebe See GREPE.

green a   Cp *OED* ~ a 9 b, *EDD* 6, *DC* (1965) for sense 1; *OED* 9 c for sense 2; for combs. in sense 4: *OED* green-fish obs, *DC* 1 Nfld (1777–); *EDD* 1 (24) ~ gravel; *OED* ~ man 2 obs (Nfld: 1682–1867), *DC* Nfld (1832–); *NID* ~ wood¹ n 3.
1 Of cod-fish, split, salted but not dried; SALT-BULK.
[1810] 1971 ANSPACH 23 In those fisheries. . .the fish is brought home *green*. 1819 ibid 433 When the fish is to be brought *green* from the place of catching, that is, cured as far as salting, but not dried, more salt is used in proportion to the distance, than when it undergoes all the operations of curing and drying without any considerable delay. 1836 [WIX]² 37 They are constrained to part with their fish to the supplying merchant in a 'green' state. 1898 PROWSE 112 Stealing codfish, green or cured, to a value not exceeding $20, may be tried summarily before a Stipendiary Magistrate. [1909] 1930 COAKER 7 When sold as green Labrador, No. 1 should consist of all sound fish over 17 inches. 1933 *Nfld Royal Commission Report* 118 A certain amount of codfish is exported 'green' from the south-west coast to Canada. P 230–67 The fish is too green to take up [off the flake]. T 203/5–65 Leave it there, back up—a big fish on top. If it come to rain on it, [it] wouldn't hurt it because 'tis green anyway. 1977 BURSEY 167 While the fish was still green, the Monroe Company sent some vessels to our wharf that took the fish and carried it to Valleyfield. The salt was shaken off at our premises.
2 Of an animal skin, in the state before tanning.
[1770] 1792 CARTWRIGHT i, 45 Ickcongogue (the youngest wife) was dressing a green seal skin. 1880 HOWLEY *MS Reminiscences* 68 Mike and Joe spent the best part of the day skinning the heads and legs of the deer [caribou]. . . I intend bringing the skins out green and when we reach the shore get some coarse salt to preserve them. 1895 GRENFELL 168 The skins are salted without being stretched, and are then exported 'green,' for making into leather for boot tops, gloves, etc. 1952 BANFILL 151 Mrs Tole agreed to put new feet on the legs [of the boots] but, said she, 'Theyse are green so Is'll has to soak theys overnight before Ise can sew theys.'
3 Phr *too green to burn*: of fir and spruce cut for fire-wood, full of sap, undried; hence of persons, very gullible.

[1866 WILSON 353 The wood was sometimes quite green, and hence making a fire was quite an art. . .and the fishermen would sometimes say whoever can build a good fire with green fir can build a boat.] 1904 *Daily News* "A Song for Fishermen": Bond is too green to burn theres no doubt about that / Whilst a shoe horn he'll turn for to get on his hat. 1974 CAHILL 12 Somebody said us crowd was too green to burn, and you two is the living proof of it. 1976 *Evening Telegram* 10 Jan, p. 3 But the Newfoundlander remains too green to burn even if he was first marinated in all the oil in Arabia.

4 Comb **green doctor**: fir with the sap running, the dried stick used as fuel, the resin applied to cuts by woodsmen; SPRING[2]: SPRING VAR, VAR. Cp LICKERY.

M 65–9 I wants some dry wood; you got green doctor, it won't burn. 1971 NOSEWORTHY 206 ~ Young fir trees full of sap which does not run out, which are driest in the winter. They do not have as much sap as *licky-doctor*.

green fish: see sense 1 above; also attrib.

1623 WHITBOURNE 82 Likewise [a price] may bee gotten vpon the Traine Oyle and greene Fish, if it be not sold in *Newfoundland*, but brought home. 1682 COLLINS 94 The Bank. . .abounds with Fish all the year, by curing rendred Green-Fish, worth [£5 or £6] the hundred. [1777] 1792 CARTWRIGHT ii, 241 The men did not come out of the stage till seven o'clock this morning; they then spread the water-horse and green fish, before they went to bed. 1868 HOWLEY *MS Reminiscences* 8 One man brought me through his stage to see the fish and I must confess I never saw so much green fish together before. 1895 GRENFELL 121 He turned out to be a green-fish catcher, who was 'making' his fish on his vessel. [1911] 1930 COAKER 33 The future of the Colony depends upon the sale of green fish in bulk, and I hope the whole fall's catch will be purchased green before five years pass away. 1936 SMITH 34 All that Mr Smith had were his ten crews around Edward's Harbour, and two schooners greenfish catching. T 175/7–65 But you wouldn't want too good [a drying day] for the first day, 'cause that's what we called water-horse—we call the first an' green fish.

green-fisher, ~ **fisherman**: migrating fisherman prosecuting the cod-fishery in a schooner on the Labrador, salting the catch aboard the vessel; FLOATER; cp **green fish**.

1895 *Outing* xxvii, p. 20 The remaining fishermen who visit Labrador are designated 'green-fishers' or 'floaters,' though it must not be inferred from this that they are novices, or in any way inferior in skill. 1908 TOWNSEND 123 [The stationers], like the liveyers, are more or less fixed, and the fish must come to them, while the fleet of 'green fishermen,' as they are called, are here to-day and gone to-morrow. 1977 *Inuit Land Use* 314 The green fishermen were the schoonermen who travelled in fleets of boats that came and went as the fishing took them. They went ashore only for supplies, emergencies, or visits.

green-gravel: child's ring game.

M 67–15 ~ A ring, with hands joined, was formed, and circled while the song was sung. At the last line, someone in the ring would turn around, and the ring would continue to circle, with that person facing outside the ring. 'Green Gravel, Green Gravel, your grass is so green / And all the young ladies so fair to be seen. / O [name], O [name], your true love is dead. / He sends you a letter to turn back your head.'

green hand: see **green man**.

[1886] 1897 *Nfld Law Reports* 132 One Ruthven, employed by defendants, was, in the forenoon of that day, as a 'green hand,' engaged in running the engine on board the scow. [1929] 1949 ENGLISH 51 Immigrants from England and Ireland who generally came out as helpers for the summer fishery were called 'green hands' or 'youngsters.'

green lick: newly-cut fir or spruce with the sap still running.

[c1900] 1978 *RLS* 8, p. 26 Starigan [is] a green stick, especially a var of small dimension Also called a green lick. C 71–40 ~ Firewood just being cut. Usually left in woods for a season before becoming dry enough to bring home to burn.

green man: on a British migratory fishing vessel, one of a specified number of inexperienced men required by regulations to be carried on the voyage; a novice; cp FRESH 1, YOUNGSTER.

[1661] 1954 INNIS 99 It was commanded that every fifth man taken [out on a West Country fishing boat] must be a 'green man.' [1693] 1793 REEVES ix That every master or owner of any fishing ship going to *Newfoundland* (after the said twenty-fifth day of March), shall have in his ship's company every fifth man a green man (that is to say) not a seaman, or having been ever at sea before. [1701] 1895 PROWSE 228 These bye boat keepers. . .were most of them able fishermen and there was not one fresh man or green man amongst them as the Act requires. 1712 *West-India Merchant* 7 That will amount at a medium to 16000 Men employ'd annually in this Trade; and one fourth of those being usually green Men, it proves a Nursery of 4000 Seamen *per ann.* for their Men of War and Privateers. [1794] 1968 THOMAS 109 Her Husband came over from England about Fifty-Five years ago as an Adventurer—what is called here a green man, which means a man that has never been in a Fishing Boat on this Coast before. 1934 LOUNSBURY 130 In order to provide a more continuous supply of sailors, the proposed rules required that one out of every five men engaged for the Newfoundland voyage should be a green man, 'that is to say not a Seaman.'

greenwood: mountain holly (*Nemopanthus mucronata*) (1898 *J A Folklore* xi, 224).

greenhouse n Underground, or partly sunken, cellar for winter storage of vegetables, esp cabbage; root cellar. Also attrib.

T 92/3–64 When you go into your greenhouse an' take out so much cabbage you make sure that you shovel in so much snow an' keep your door from the draught and frost going in again. T 94/5–64 You keep your greenhouse cabbage there the whole winter. M 69–2 Besides the cellar there was sometimes a greenhouse or cabbage house as some people call it. The greenhouse was a small cellar used for the storing of cabbage.

greenland n *NID* ~ halibut. Attrib ~ **cod** (*Gadus ogac*); ~ **halibut**: turbot (*Reinhardtius hippoglossoides*).

1899 *Tribune Christmas No* 15 The Labrador cod are much smaller in size than those obtained by the fishermen on the Grand Banks and in addition to the rock species a variety of the Greenland cod is caught, much the same in size, but with a mottled skin. 1953 *Nfld Fish Develop Report* 31 The Greenland halibut or turbot inhabit deep and moderately cold water in Trinity Bay, White Bay, Fortune Bay, Placentia Bay and the various deep arms of Notre Dame Bay, the deep water area between Bonavista and Cape Bauld and the deep water off Labrador.

greep See GREPE.

grepe n also **grebe, greep, gripe**. Cp *OED* grebe 1 'diving birds of the genus *Podiceps*' (1766–). Used variously of the bald eagle (*Haliaeetus leucocephalus washingtonii*), golden eagle (*Aquila chrysaëtos*), and osprey (*Pandion haliaetus carolinensis*); freq in names of coastal features.

1620 WHITBOURNE 9 There are also birds that live by prey, as Ravens, Gripes, Crowes, etc. 1842 JUKES ii, 78 . . .a fine 'gripe,' or eagle, who had just killed, and was eating a shelldrake. Ibid 182 There is at least one large species of hawk or eagle, the bird called the gripe, which has a white head, brownish body, and yellow legs. 1870 *Can Naturalist* v, 42 [Baldheaded eagle] is called the 'grepe' in Newfoundland. It is tolerably common, but as the settlers increase, this noble bird gradually, but surely, decreases. 1895 *J A Folklore* viii, 34 Thus *grepe* seems unquestionably the same word as *grebe*; but it is used in Newfoundland to denote the sea eagle. 1951 *Nfld & Lab Pilot* i, 144 Between Greep head and a point one mile north-north-eastward, there is a considerable bight. Ibid 215 Grip Head rock, awash, lies one cable west-south-westward. 1953 ibid ii, 434 Cape Greep rises to a dark conical mound. 1966 HORWOOD 252 I always admired the eagles. . . I remember 'em when I was a boy, an' they were called 'grepes' hereabouts. C 70–28 'Greedy as a greep'—the comparison is with a seabird.

grey a, n LEIM & SCOTT, p. 388 gray sole.

1 The red fox (*Vulpes fulvus*), in a colour variation with black fur interspersed with silver-grey ends; SILVER.

1888 STEARNS 347 The gray or silver gray has, according as it is a poor, a medium, or a fine skin, each hair alternating.

2 Comb **grey man's beard**: type of lichen which grows on trees (*Usnea barbata*); MOLDOW, OLD MAN'S WHISKER.

1880 *Journ of Assembly* 48 The road from Piccott's Pond to the Prince's Mount called the Grey Man's Beard road.

grey-sole: flounder (*Glyptocephalus cynoglossus*).

1971 NOSEWORTHY 206 ~ type of flatfish obtained by fishing draggers and used as food.

grey sparrow: slate-coloured junco (*Junco hyemalis hyemalis*).

1964 *Evening Telegram*) 28 Oct, p. 5 The slate-colored junco is locally called a 'grey sparrow.'

grin n Cp *OED* ~ sb¹ 2 a 'noose,' b 'halter' obs; *EDD* sb¹ 'noose.' Noose used by blacksmith on horse's mouth to control the animal while shoeing it.

P 65–64 In a grin, a piece of rope with a loop (bight) in it is fastened to a stick about a foot and a half long. The loop is put around the horse's bottom lip. The harder the blacksmith twists the grin—the more peaceful the horse becomes until it is quite simple to take off and put on horse-shoes. Q 71–13 A grin consists of a stick and a loop of rope attached to one end. The loop is placed over the horse's nose and then the stick is twisted, cutting off the horse's breathing.

griny a ['græni]. Dirty, foul.

T 84/5–64 I dipped the bucket overboard an' dipped up the real griny salt water, an' placed my dipper back in the salt-water bucket.

gripe See GREPE.

grist n [grɪs] *EDD* ~ sb¹ 3 'dust, sand' Ha Do. Bits of sand, fine gravel, broken sea-shells; granules of salt, etc, on fish.

P 148–61 ~ salt and accumulation that must be washed from fish. P 229–67 Look at all the griss you brought in on your boots. M 69–6 Bringing sea shells and sand from the beach to put in the hens' yard was nearly always the job for boys. Hens were given this griss to keep them from eating their eggs and also make the egg shells hard.

groaner n *O Sup*² ~ b local U S for sense a. (a) A bell-buoy; whistling buoy; (b) water spout which blows through aperture in a coastal cave.

P 7–55 ~ Water spout in rock because of compression of air in cave caused by advancing water. 1966 SCAMMELL 74 Criticizing the Fishery estimates, one of our opponents wanted to know if there was anything in them provided for a 'groaner' (bell-buoy) on Jerry's Rock just around the point of the harbour.

groaning n *EDD* ~ sb 'child-birth; lying-in' 2 (4) ~ cake Co. Comb **groaning cake**: sweet-cake served in the house of a woman who has given birth, or at a christening; cp BIDE-IN FEAST.

1896 *J A Folklore* ix, 22 When a birth is expected, a cake is prepared called the *groaning cake*. Very soon after it occurs, with little regard to the feelings or nerves of the mother, a feast is made, particularly for the elderly women, of whom all in the neighbourhood are present. 1925 *Dial Notes* v, 333 ~ A cake for the first birthday and christening.

grog n Cp *OED* ~ sb 'a drink' (1770–) for sense 1.

1 A quantity, a sup; a shot (of liquor).

T 141/2–65² We got a bottle o' Captain Morgan rum

left. An' we had a drink o' rum apiece—a little small one. Well, we go down to Li's now and we give he a grog. T 187/8–65 They was licensed to [sell] it, and they'd call it a drink or a grog or whatever. Some fellers 'd go in an' ask for a little toddy an' more to ask for a grog.

2 Attrib, comb **grog bag**: toper (1924 ENGLAND 316).

grog bit: small amount of food; snack accompanying a drink.

1929 BURKE [4] "Mary Jo": We will bust ourselves on pastry, / Basses Ale and cuts of meat; / And the turkeys have for grog bits, / And the best of grub you bet. 1964 *Evening Telegram* 24 Dec, p. 29 On the other side we had a man who lived alone. He would have a piece of pork about three or four pounds boiled. This pork would be skewered on a sharp stick. When he came to the house all hands would have the drink and a bit of pork for the grog bit. 1975 GUY 58 In a frantic grab to save myself I thrust several fingers of one hand into the cheesy grog bits.

grog fish: first cod-fish of the season.

C 71–105 ~ When the first haul of fish was brought on board the schooner at the beginning of the fishing season at Labrador one fish was split, gutted, and head left on. It was put in the hold of the schooner with the other fish. The member of the crew who later took this fish out of the hold had to buy 'grogs' (drinks) for all the crew when they went to St John's to sell the fish.

ground n Cp *OED* ~ sb 2 now naut, 12 a (1872 quot) for sense 1; *DC* grounds n pl (1913–) for sense 2; *OED* 12 b, *EDD* sb 4, *DJE* (1873–) for sense 3; cp *OED* 3 pl 'dregs, lees' for sense 5; for sense 6: *DC* ~ hemlock (Nfld: (1822–), ~ juniper (1793–). See also SEALING GROUND, WHELPING ~ .

1 An area of shoal water with abundant bait-fish, plankton, etc, where fishing is successfully carried out; freq in names of underwater coastal features with designations of customary use or ownership, etc; BANK(S), FISHING GROUND; cp BERTH. Also attrib.

[1583] 1940 *Gilbert's Voyages & Enterprises* ii, 397–8 [Hayes' narrative] Before we come to Newfound land about 50 leagues on this side, we passe the banke, which are high grounds rising within the sea and under water. [1715] 1976 HEAD 63 In 1715, it was observed that the cod were so glutted with food that 'tho you shall see the ground cover'd with them, yet they'l hardly touch the bait.' [1770] ibid 168 [The arrival of these vessels with small catches] affords us but an Extremely bad prospect all through means of not being soon enough on the Grounds, as its evident [per] them who was there in due season. 1837 BLUNT 51 On the W.S.W. side of the large island, which is the highest, is a small cove, fit for shallops, and convenient for the fisheries, and the ground about it is considered to be good for fishing. 1898 *Christmas Bells* 14 With what feeling they'd discuss the weather, bait, how they got on the 'ground,' how bravely they rode out such a breeze. 1927 DOYLE (ed) 7 "Green Island Shore": I have as staunch a bully boat / As ever rode the ground.

1953 *Nfld & Lab Pilot* ii, 225 Several shoals, with depths of from 10 to 20 fathoms over them. . .lie. . .in order from east to west, The Field, Gull Island ground, Friday ledge, and Gruffy ground. Ibid 263 Budgell's ground and Parsons ground [lie] eastward. P 245–79 You fix Wester ledge by two ground-marks (i.e. recognisable features on land). 1979 *Salt Water, Fresh Water* 3 In the fall when you're fishing with handlines on the ground, on the ledges, there's only certain spots where you catch the fish. 1979 TIZZARD 301 My father sometimes threw the [cod] heads into the sea as he was leaving the fishing grounds and would say, 'We'll bait the grounds for the morning,' in other words, keep the fish around until we get back in the morning.

2 A stretch of country, wooded or barren, producing edible berries, game-birds, or animals trapped for their fur; sometimes preceded by defining word; cp BERRY[1] ~ .

1869 MCCREA 231 Hark to 'em, sir! That's the Doctor's party; they must have camped out on the Cody's Well ground, and they'll take the Indian-meal Barrens. 1969 HORWOOD 102 The hunting trips with dog and gun and kettles of boiled tea on the partridge grounds to the west. . . 1972 MURRAY 258 Women, picking blueberries for sale, went to the berry grounds or 'barrens' carrying perhaps two water buckets and a hoop, as for water. 1977 *Inuit Land Use* 335 Every man had his own place [for trapping furs], his own ground, you know. I guess it came right up from my grandfather's time up till now. P 245–77 When my father took me shooting we used to try to get out on the grounds as early in the morning as we could while the [partridge] were at their early feeding.

3 A parcel of land, often enclosed, appropriated for a specific purpose indicated sometimes by defining word; see also GRASS ~ , POTATO ~ .

[1583] 1940 *Gilbert's Voyages & Enterprises* ii, 403 [Hayes' narrative] The Generall granted in fee farme divers parcells of land lying by the water side. . .which was to owners a great commoditie, being thereby assured. . .of grounds convenient to dresse and to drie their fish. P 245–79 I had a bit of ground in Maddox Cove, but they wouldn't let me build on it. If you can't build on it, what's the use of a bit of ground?

4 The plain background in the spaces between the decorative design of a hooked rag-mat.

T 43/7–64 They'd trace out their mat first, an' then they'd fill whatever kind of a ground they liked best. 1975 POCIUS 51 When a mat was hooked, the major design motif, or the outline of the geometric pattern would be hooked first. The background, or 'ground,' of the mat would be finished last.

5 In pl, the lees or sediment of 'spruce beer' used as yeast.

[1766] 1971 BANKS 140 Take a half hogshead & Put in nineteen Gallons of water & fill it up with the Essence, work it with Barm or Beergrounds. 1832 MCGREGOR i, 221 A part of the grounds of the last brewing, and a few hops, if at hand, are also put in. 1937 DEVINE 25 ~ Sediment of liquid in a cup or other vessel, that of spruce beer being often used as yeast or barm in making bread. T 207–65 You make a hole in your flour an' heave your grounds in, let it work, rise up; then you mix it. P 143–74 Hops were picked from the kitchen garden in September and were 'put in to dry' in sugar bags. They were made into 'barm' or 'grounds'—a yeast-like substance used in making bread.

6 In names of plants, birds: **ground blueberry** [see ~ **hurt** below], ~ **hemlock** [see HEMLOCK], ~ **hurt** (also ~ **whort,** ~ **whortle,** ~ **whortleberry**) [see HURT], ~ **ivory flower,** ~ **ivy,** ~ **juniper** [see JUNIPER], ~ **palm,** ~ **plover,** ~ **raspberry,** ~ **spruce.**

1916 HAWKES 35 Ground blueberry (*Vaccinium boreale*). 1956 ROULEAU 31 Ground hemlock (*Heracleum maximum*). 1931 *Am Speech* vi (4), 291 Ground hurts. Small, round, blue berries on a low, small-leafed shrub. 1956 ROULEAU 31 Ground Hurts. *Vaccinium angustifolium, V. uliginosum.* 1898 *J A Folklore* xi, 274 Ground ivory flower. *Diapensia lapponica.* Ibid 228 Ground ivy. *Linnaea borealis.* 1898 *J A Folklore* xi, 280 Ground juniper. *Juniperus communis.* M 68–16 Ground juniper was used for water trouble. You'd put it in a pot with water and steep it just like tea. 1843 *Journ of Assembly* Appendix, p. 463 There are also Mountain Ash or Dogwood, White-wood, and Ground Palm, very luxuriant; these always indicate good soil. 1956 ROULEAU 31 Ground Palm: *Taxus canadensis.* 1959 MCATEE 28 Ground plover. American Golden Plover (Nfld). 1975 SCOTT 55 The Plumboy is also called the Ground Raspberry or Dew-berry. It is found throughout the island and I have generally found it in grassy open areas. *Rubus pubescens.* [1822] 1856 CORMACK 48 The ground spruce (Taxus canadensis) bearing its red berries, constitutes the chief underwood. [1770] 1792 CARTWRIGHT i, 29 [There are] some delicious blue berries which grow on a small shrubby plant, called Ground Whortle,. . .which are now ripe. . .what the curlews delight to feed on. [1786] ibid iii, 227 The only vegetables which I found fit to eat, were alexander (or wild celery,) fathen, scurvy-grass, the young leaves of the osier, and of the ground-whortleberry. 1898 *J A Folklore* xi, 274 Ground whorts.

7 Attrib, comb **ground flake**: poles or 'longers' placed on the beach for the drying of cod-fish; FLAKE.

1891 PACKARD 141 On the shores of the harbor was a narrow margin of grass enriched by the drippings of years from the fish-flakes which, supported on stakes like those on the Maine coast, ran down in parallel rows to near the water's edge, where were ground-flakes, or floors of poles lying on the ground.

ground killer: part of an animal trap.

1792 CARTWRIGHT *Gloss* i, xi The Ground-killer; which lies upon the ground, across the front of the Deathfall.

ground lead: weight used to sink a fishing-line; LEAD[1].

1967 FIRESTONE 95–6 Here a groundlead (a piece of lead six to seven inches long) is attached to the end of a line. There are two hooks attached to the lead, one on each end. 1977 *Evening Telegram* 7 Oct, p. 6 We heard familiar phrases such as 'I caught my fish today on the rock or on the shoal with dabber and ground lead.'

ground line: single fishing-line with hooks attached; BULTOW.

1845 *Journ of Assembly* Appendix, p. 216 Ground lines, commonly called Bultows. 1927 DOYLE (ed) 71 "The Newfoundland Fishermen": For early and late they are moving / From one fishing place to another, / And jiggers and ground lines are using. T 250–66 But then we used to do a lot o' fishin' wi' what we called ground lines, you know—two hooks, bait two hooks.

ground pinion: sill of a house (P 233–78).

grounder a Rock or shoal over which the sea breaks; SUNKER (P 148–60).

Q 71–9 ~ Shoal or breaker.

groundy a *OED* ~ b rare (1892). (a) Of vegetables, tasting of the earth; (b) of home-brewed beer, etc, containing or tasting of lees or sediment.

P 148–63 [The beer] tastiz groundy to what the other was. P 245–64 The carrots tasted groun'y. 1981 HUSSEY 22 Water from the Bottom had a sort of groundy taste.

grouse n Allen's willow ptarmigan (*Lagopus lagopus alleni*); PARTRIDGE n. Also attrib.

[1773] 1792 CARTWRIGHT i, 278 This morning. . .I killed seven brace of grouse. These birds are exactly the same with those of the same name in Europe, save only in the colour of their feathers, which are speckled with white in summer, and perfectly white in winter, (fourteen black ones in the tail excepted) which always remain the same. [1777] ibid ii, 274 I began a grouse-net, and worked upon it most of the day. 1959 MCATEE 25 ~ Willow Ptarmigan (Labr).

grout n Cp *OED* ~ sb[1] 4 'sediment; dregs.'

1 Detritus left after snow or ice melts.

1909 BROWNE 216 Large quantities of silt (fishermen call it *grout*) and small boulders are sometimes seen on these [ice] floes in early spring.

2 Small stunted wood suitable only for firewood; CRUMP[2], CRUNNICK.

P 113–56 He spent the winter cutting grout. P 130–67 I'm just burning some old grout. C 70–15 When the supply of firewood ran low the men would go into the woods and 'make up' a slide (catamaran) load to tide them over. It usually consisted of small birches, alders, dry windfalls, and any other trees that might burn easily. These loads were called 'a load of grout.' C 71–21 I'm going in the woods to get a turn of grout.

growl n Card game; auction forty-fives (P 148–65).

P 127–77 The game of growl is widespread.

growler n *DC* ~ esp Nfld (1920–); *O Sup*[2] 5 (1912–). Piece of floating ice esp hazardous to vessels because of its instability or indeterminate size.

1865 CAMPBELL 97 Passed a berg near Greedy Harbour. . . It was aground in 90 feet of water (15 fathoms), the height was about 18 feet, and the shape out of water was very irregular. A progeny of small 'growlers' were bobbing about near the parent berg. Got alongside one and tried to capsize him, but he was too much for us. The surface was barely a foot out of water, and the mass was larger than our boat. 1870 HOWLEY *MS Reminiscences* 1 There was some loose ice about and one small growler struck us on the bilge but fortunately it was a slanting blow and did no damage. 1896 *J A Folklore* ix, 33 ~ Through the melting of the part under water they lose their equilibrium, and sometimes even a little noise will cause them to turn over with a sound like a growl. 1906 DUNCAN 249 A growler is a berg which trembles on the verge of toppling over. 1923 GRENFELL 154 In the dark you can't see one of them northern growlers when them's just level wi' the water. 1936 SMITH 155 We met a jam of ice and in trying to force our way through it the Captain struck the schooner against a large 'growler.' 1940 DOYLE (ed) 11 "Two Jinkers": Our water line a growler rives, / And through the seam comes seivin' / The ocean roaring for the lives. T 141/60–65[2] He dismast her out there one time, and made her leak. Tied up to a big growler, an' he broke his rudder post.

grub n Cp *DC* ~ bag (1913–). In designations of containers for food carried into the woods, fishing or at the seal hunt: ~ **bag**, ~ **keg**, ~ **tub**.

1907 WALLACE 74 Their 'grub bag' received several of the [ptarmigan], which were very tame and easily shot. 1936 SMITH 51 In the meantime Mr Mac had our grub bags filled with food for our day's travel, and he included the best that the ship possessed, oranges, raisins, cold meat, cheese and fancy biscuits. P 269–57 Grub tub: a 221 lb. butter tub for storing food when at sea. T 92/3–64 The men never go out on the ice without that—always want [food] in the grub bag. Q 67–64 The cuddy [is] a cupboard in the front of the boat where the grub-keg was kept.

grum a Cp *OED* ~ a 'of persons. . .gloomy, morose.' Overcast; stormy; GLUM.

C 65–2 Candlemas Day is fair and fine / Half the winter is left behind. / Candlemas Day is rough and grum / The worst of the winter is yet to come.

grummet n Cp *OED* ~[2] 'ring or wreath of rope.' Sheath or thick, narrow band of cloth or knitted wool worn around the fingers or palms by fisherman to protect the hand in line-fishing; NIPPER[2].

C 71–131 ~ finger stall with no top in it, made out of a piece of soft leather. It was used on the index finger of the right hand while hauling lines so that the finger would not be chafed. Sometimes they were used on the little finger of the left hand when a person was knitting twine. 1975 POCIUS 33 Small tubular coverings were knitted to slip over each of the fingers. These coverings. . .were frequently called 'nippers' or 'grummets.'

grump (head) See GUMP.

guardian n also **gardien**.
1 In the French-Newfoundland migratory fishery, a resident placed in charge of fishing gear and premises during the winter.

1857 *Memo of French Fisheries* 8 Before this [French] family came, a British settler on the mainland had charge of the island in winter, and acted as 'gardien.' [1859] 1971 CASEY 32 The French captains change every five years their places on the coast, if they do not like the Gardien whom they find on the spot, they bring another man and his family to act as Gardien. [1863] 1977 *Evening Telegram* 24 May, p. 6 From La Scie, Hamilton went to Fleur de Lys [on the French Shore] where he talked to two Englishmen, Robert and Joseph Walsh (actually two Newfoundlanders). They were 'gardiens,' i.e. residents who 'minded' or looked after the French establishments after they returned to France. 1895 PROWSE 479 Let the French have exclusive possession for the fishing season within the three-mile limit around each harbour which they actually occupied with their fishing ships and crews last season, one or two guardians to be allowed in each harbour to protect their property.

2 Warden of a salmon river.

1963 SCOTT & CROSSMAN 60 Mr Lane, Department of Fisheries Guardian at Gambo Lake. 1977 *Evening Telegram* 8 June, p. 8 The protective force is made up of river wardens and guardians. The wardens are regulars who work every year for about eight months while the guardians are seasonal employees who work for about two and a half months.

gud n Northern razor-bill (*Alca torda*); TINKER.

1884 STEARNS 235–6 I have often seen the water covered with a clustered flock [of puffins], all engaged in making a hoarse, rasping sound, not unlike the filing of a saw; this is also done both by the 'murre,' and the 'turre,' and at such times, which ever species is present, they receive from the sailors the name of 'guds,' from a fancied resemblance to that sound.

guess n Comb **guess cake**: cake with object hidden inside.

1933 GREENLEAF xvii A feature of the fair which brought in a substantial sum was that of the 'guess cake.' Each unmarried girl in a village made a cake, in which she concealed some object. At intervals during the day, an auctioneer would hold up a guess cake, announce the name of the fair baker, and call for guesses as to what it contained. The men and boys paid five cents for each guess, and the one who guessed correctly got the cake.

guffy n A scavenger fish (*Myoxocephalus octodecemspinosus; M. scorpius*); SCULPIN (P 37).

C 67–13 ~ This is another word for the sculpin, which usually lies near the shore of fishing villages in harbours. It has a long head and is quite ugly. C 71–45 Before I was ever allowed out in boat I would spend a lot of time down on the beach. One bit of fun we'd have down on the beach was jiggin' guffies. 'Guffy' was our local terminology for sculpin, an ugly spring fish which lives around the shores.

guggle v *EDD* ~ v¹ 'drink with gurgling sound.' To swallow noisily; to make a gurgling noise.

[1929] 1933 GREENLEAF (ed) 257 "Greedy Harbour": I picked it up, I thought it was wine, / I guggled it down, 'twas turkentine. T 245–66 One of 'em jumped in, an' he was gugglin'—the water was in his throat.

guide v Comb **guide-stick**: short stick used by dory-fishermen as an aid in hauling trawls (1971 NOSEWORTHY 207).

guider n A long pole jutting out from the front of a sled-load of wood, held by the man hauling the load so as to control the movement of the vehicle over the snow; STEERING STICK.

Q 71–15 When a handslide was loaded with wood, which was firmly lashed to the fore and aft stanchions, one stick on the top of the load projected out in front, for the purpose of steering the slide around irregularities in the path, roots, trees, etc. The hauler rope extended from the rear left stanchion over the man's left shoulder, and he walked slightly in front of the slide with his right hand on the guider or steerin' stick.

gulch n also **gulsh**. Cp *O Sup*² ~ sb³ (N Z 1832–); *DAE* 1 'ravine, canyon' (Nfld: 1835–); *DC* 1 (Nfld: 1835–) for senses 1, 2; *Cent* n³ 2 for sense 3.

1 A narrow, precipitous break in a cliff leading inland; a small, steep-sided cove; freq in coastal names.

1836 [WIX]² 14 I have met with places in Fortune Bay, two or three miles only from each other, to visit which by land in winter, it might be necessary to make a circuit of fifteen miles, to get round the deep precipitous chasms or 'gulshes' and ravines which cross from the coast into the interior. 1842 JUKES i, 21 I then found a deep narrow 'gulch' or crevice in the rocks still separated us from the point of the cove, and that it would cost another hour at least to reach it. [1867] 1934 *Public Bureau Christmas No* 11 We ran into a gulch on the Island on the morning of Thursday, the 12th inst., about six o'clock. 1873 HOWLEY *MS Reminiscences* 12 Great gulches cut into the land and ran up the mountain side, through which flowed and tumbled tumultuously, beautiful cataracts. 1895 GRENFELL 197 Helped by their companions, [they] staggered feebly ashore, and tried to crawl up the steep gulch from their landing place. 1936 SMITH 59 When daylight broke we caught sight of Biscayan Island, and we knew then our position; we had drifted into the same gulch where Capt Samuel Spracklin of Cupids had lost his schooner, the *Waterwitch*, a few years previously. Most of his crew too were lost. We could almost touch the spars of our schooner from the cliff. 1951 *Nfld & Lab Pilot* i, 317 Pointe au Diable. . .is situated at the eastern entrance to Gulch Cove, a creek between two granite spurs, which is frequented by fishermen during the summer; the narrowness of this cove makes it difficult to approach, and fishing vessels are hauled in stern first and moored by chains to the rocks on either side. T 54–64 They knew nothing till they struck this land in the night—a big sea runnin'—but they were in a kind

of a cove or gulch. 1979 NEMEC 231 A distance of approximately 18 miles along the coast, there are literally dozens of gulches and small coves which have been named by the local 'livyers.'

2 A valley between hills; a depression permitting passage.

1836 [WIX]² 119 I was put across La Hune Bay in a boat, and walked about two miles, across some mountainous ridges, in the 'gulshes,' between which the hardened snow was still thirty or forty feet high, to Western Cul de Sac. 1858 [LOWELL] ii, 27 Mr Wellon, who followed, was going thoughtfully up the side of the first 'gulch,' when he was suddenly overtaken. 1863 MORETON 29 ~ A mountain gorge, or ravine. 1912 *Nfld Qtly* Sum, p. 14 The summit reached, a mile or two of barren, broken limestone lay before us. This was followed by a descent into a swampy valley known as Wallace's Gulch. T 54/62–64 Do you remember taking a short cut to see was your cows in a certain gulch, or a certain bog? T 184–65 We had fifty ducks hung up. We caught 'em in a gulch, got 'em pinned in the gulch. P 121–67 We shot the moose in the gulch.

3 A narrow depression in the sea-bottom.

1937 DEVINE 54 [The trouncer is] used to thrash the water in order to drive fish into a net or narrow gulch. 1952 STANSFORD 21 We put out our trap (moorings in the gulch called 'Kits Gulsh'). T 80/3–64 There was a gulch under the leader, twelve fathom o' water into un. Nine fathom at the mouth o' the trap. 1966 SCAMMELL 41 I bet the fish goes through that gulch under his leader of a rush.

4 Deep ruts in snow or ice.

1917 *Daily News* 27 Feb, p. 5 A heavy fall of snow brings its trouble to the horse traffic on our streets which are filled with gulches. 1975 *Evening Telegram* 25 Jan, p. 12 When you think of the old days, do you people mind the terrible gulches we had years ago?

gulch v See GULCH n. To frequent a sheltered hollow for sexual intimacy; cp GRASS v.

1895 *J A Folklore* viii, 29 [Gulch] has come, on the Labrador coast, to have a meaning peculiar to that region and to those who frequent it. In summer, men, women, and children from Newfoundland spend some weeks there at the fishing, living in a very promiscuous way. As there is no tree for shelter for hundreds of miles of islands and shores, parties resort to the hollows for secret indulgence. Hence gulching has, among them, become a synonym for living a wanton life. P 99–69 I saw [them] gulching Sunday. C 71–128 ~ a term used by fishermen who went to Labrador in summer, to denote courting. Sunday afternoons were good gulching days.

gulf n [= Gulf of St Lawrence]. Attrib: **gulf ice**, ~ **seal**, ~ **shore**.

1868 HOWLEY *MS Reminiscences* 15 It is of course an unusual occurrence for this bay to become ice-blocked but such has occurred occasionally, especially when a large body of the Gulf ice has been driven along the southern coast [to Placentia Bay]. 1924 ENGLAND 22–3 Some of the Gulf seals apparently go no farther south, and whelp near the Magdalene Islands. Others, seldom hunted, whelp around Anticosti. But the major portion seem to keep on down, passing through Cabot Strait. 1842 BONNYCASTLE i, 196 After passing Cape Ray, the gulf shore of Newfoundland exhibits ranges of mountains.

gull n
1 Epithet for resident of Burgeo (C 67–10).
2 Proverb: *it is hard to tell the mind of a gull* (1937 DEVINE 61).

gully¹ n   also **gulley**. Cp *OED* ~ sb¹ 2 'channel or ravine worn in the earth by the action of water'; *EDD* sb² 1 'a narrow brook or stream' for sense 1.
1 A small pond or series of linked ponds forming the head waters of a stream, or adjacent to a larger body of water; a pond-like body of water where a stream moves slowly through marshland; cp STEADY.
[1836] 1971 SEARY 117 Lower Gullies. 1842 JUKES ii, 215 Numerous small holes and pools of water, and in the lower parts small sluggish brooks or gullies, are also met with in these tracts [of moss]. 1846 TOCQUE 291 A few hundred yards from the Cove is a gulley or small pond. 1848 *Journ of Assembly* 438 Passing Black Duck Gully and crossing the now opened road to the ferry. . . 1888 HOWLEY *MS Reminiscences* 52 We got up to the head of this long pond by dinner-time, then made another short portage to a small gully where we camped in a nice place, near the river on an old otter rub. 1903 M F HOWLEY 84 "Dear Old South-side Hill": I love each nook, each darkling drook, / Each copse of russet brown: / Each gully, pond, and laughing brook / That tumbles rattling down. 1905 *Nfld Qtly* July, p. 1 A little intelligent care now in preserving our rivers, will keep the Island, the greatest game fish country in the world, bar none, till some cataclysm changes its formation, and the countless lakes, ponds, gullies, rivers and streams cease to be. 1931 BYRNES 22 [We discussed] . . .the 'gullies,' and ponds that promised the best trouting, and the summer crop of potatoes and cabbages. T 43/7–64 A small pond in this country is referred to as a gully. . .it can also be a stream. P 240–75 [She spoke of] the small weeds and grasses that grew around the small gullies where the frogs and eels used to breed.
2 Phr *leave/leff* her go for the gullies*: to get underway.
P 125–72 'Now me son, wind 'er up and leff 'er go fer the gullies.' This means to start the car and drive as fast as possible.

gully² n   Cp *EDD* gurry sb⁴ var gully 'hand-barrow' D for sense 1.
1 A barrel or tub, freq with handles or rope affixed to the sides, used as a receptacle for salt, cod livers, etc; COVEL.
[1774] 1792 CARTWRIGHT ii, 22 In the evening I sailed for the Colleroon, in the *Otter*, with a hundred and fifty gullies of salt. 1792 ibid *Gloss* i, xi ~ A Barrel with only one head in it, and a couple of large holes bored under the chime hoops of the other end, to introduce a stang to carry it upon. They are used

chiefly to carry salt in. 1866 WILSON 213 The liver of the fish, as said above, is dropped through a hole in the splitting-table, into the gully or barrel beneath; when the gully is full of liver it is emptied into a vat or hogshead outside, and exposed to the weather. 1937 DEVINE 26 ~ a covel or half barrel with handles. P 148–60 ~ a tub with side handles, made out of a half-barrel and used for washing fish. 1971 NOSEWORTHY 207 ~ A tub made of a half-barrel and carried by a rope and a long stick.
2 A water barrel (P 261–55).
T 141/62–65² He went back to the gully back o' the foremast, an' got the mug o' water. 1972 MURRAY 187 The 'gully' (water barrel) and the water buckets would be placed there [in the porch] both winter and summer.
3 Comb **gully stick**: stick placed through tub or barrel for two men to carry.
M 71–4 There was also an unwritten law that anyone who entered your house during supper [on Christmas Eve] had to be taken home on the 'gully stick.' The gully stick was merely a straight pole which fitted through two holes of a water barrel and was used to carry the water barrel home.

gulsh See GULCH n.

gulvin n   also **gulbin**. The curved sac of a cod's alimentary canal; stomach; PUDDICK.
1955 ENGLISH 34 ~ the stomach of a codfish. C 71–44 ~ used when speaking of a person who had a big stomach or great capacity for holding food. 1979 NEMEC 274 The stomach and intestinal tract or 'gulbin,' as it is called, was saved frequently prior to Confederation for use as garden fertilizer.

gum n   Cp *OED* ~ sb² 1 'viscid secretion from certain trees' (esp 1631, 1894 quots); *DAE* n¹ 1 (1612–), *DC* 1 (1749–) for sense 1. Cp ROBERT FROST, "The Gum-Gatherer" (1916).
1 The resin of a fir or esp a spruce tree used for various purposes including, when hardened, chewing; FRANKUM.
[1583] 1940 *Gilbert's Voyages & Enterprises* ii, 406 [Hayes' narrative] The trees for the most part in those South parts, are Firre-trees, pine and Cypresse, all yielding Gumme and Turpentine. [1811] 1915 HOWLEY 86 [Their canoes are] covered over with that bark cut into sheets, and neatly sewn together and lackered over with the gum of the spruce tree. 1888 STEARNS 403 [They] soon caught Max, who was cutting off several small, roundish balls of a dark substance from one of the trees, and putting it into a piece of paper which he held in his hand. 'Spruce gum. My jimmy!' exclaimed Fred; a moment later all the boys were at work scraping and cutting. 1937 DEVINE 22 [Frankum is the] hardened gum of spruce trees, used as chewing gum. 1966 HORWOOD 134 . . .a large wad of spruce gum—which the boys called 'frankum' chewed to a soft, stringy consistency. T 255–66 Bread poultice an' juniper water, an' gum plasters—turkumtine [from] the bladders—fir gum.
2 Comb **gum-box**: receptacle for human waste.
1931 BYRNES 75 The 'gum box' was in institution

which pre-dated the advent of the more advanced (!) 'soil cart.'

gum-bucket: receptacle for kitchen garbage, etc.

M 67–16 Near the washstand there used to be a bucket, called a gum-bucket, where the dirty water was thrown. This bucket would be emptied two or three times each day. P 17–69 ~ garbage pail aboard a schooner.

gumbean, gumbeen See GOMBEEN.

gump n also **grump, grump head, gump ~** [gʌmp, grʌmp, grɤmp, grɔ'mp]. Cp *DAE* gump-headed (1722); *EDD* gump(h) 'stupid person' Sc Ir Ha D: gumphead. Stout wooden pile protruding above a wharf to which vessels may be moored; similar mooring-post aboard a vessel; bollard, cleat. Also attrib.

1895 PROWSE 388 [They] spent their Sunday afternoons firing at champagne bottles on a gumphead at the end of the wharf. 1910 GRENFELL 218 But the iron mooring chains are fast to the great gump heads of the wharf—the sails are already unreeved—the ship dismantled—the very funnel covered in. 1929 BURKE [8] "When your Old Woman Takes a Cramp": She's in bed half the day, / And the floor never scrub, / And legs like gump heads / From the bare force of grub. 1937 DEVINE 26 Grump heads. Posts on a wharf for making fast lines and warps from vessels, etc. Corresponds to the *Bitts* on a vessel. T 200–65 To slacken her grumps though, boy, there's four bolts in each grump on the deck. T 194/5–65 An' my brother was back wi' the downhaul round the grump, as they was giggin' her up the mainsail. T 175–65 An' then we chopped three grump heads in the island o' ice. 1975 BUTLER 44 If you thinks anything about your new wedded wife, you sit down back be that gump there on the win'ard quarter. 1975 *Evening Telegram* 28 June, p. 16 God be with the old days when fellas our age could lean on a gump and take a spell. 1977 RUSSELL 131 What about when I want a big stick like a grump stick for my wharf and I've got to go away inside?

gun n [= muzzle-loading fowling-piece, musket, etc]. Cp POOLE GUN, SEALING ~ .

Attrib, comb, cpd **gun ball**: spherical lead projectile.

T 272–66[1] They used to use these muzzle-loaders [loaded with] the gun ball. T 453/4–67 He had one bullet left, old number ten—that's gun balls.

gun cap: primer for a muzzle-loading weapon.

T 96/9–64[1] He put up the gun [but] couldn't get her to go. He was after losing his gun-caps, old-time gun-caps [that] used to be on [the musket].

gun line: length of line fastened to the stock of a weapon as a precaution against loss.

T 141/64–65[2] Years ago you'd always have a gun line [fastened through a hole] in the back stock, and the gun line hitched around your foot or something.

gunman: marksman who shoots old or mature seals; GUNNER.

1972 SANGER 238 ~ A term used during the sailing vessel era and early steamer period referring to a sealer who enjoyed special status due to his prowess with firearms.

gun seal, ~ swail: old or mature seal hunted with a gun rather than a club or 'gaff.'

[1802] 1895 PROWSE 420 Seals. . .distinguished. . .in the Newfoundland nomenclature [as] *Gunswails*. T 390–67 That's in old seals, you know, gun seals, mostly.

gunshot: as a measure of distance, the range of a muzzle-loading fire-arm; also attrib **gunshot growth**: rapid growth (see 1949 quot).

[1771] 1792 CARTWRIGHT i, 118 I soon discovered, that we had passed each other by the way, within gunshot; the inequality of the ground having hid them from my sight. [1794] 1968 THOMAS 187 He was pursued by a Flock of Wolves and in imminent danger of his life. They were within Gunshot of him and no hope left of escaping, except that of firing amongst them. 1909 *Christmas Annual* 15 The term 'gun-shot,' to indicate a distance, was quite common. A person would say, 'How far is it?' The answer would be, 'Oh! about a gun-shot,' or two gun-shots as the case may be. 1924 ENGLAND 189 We got open water not half a gunshot away. 1949 DULEY 9 Yet the old island can manifest a splendour unknown to temperate places. Its stayed bud and blossom can leap into what the native calls 'gun-shot growth.' T 89–64 I got right as handy as a gunshot of the brook, an' the slide stopped, brought up, on her side. 1975 BUTLER 36 Went out and went down and I see something moving, comin' up off about a gunshot.

gunner n Cp *EDD* ~ sb[1] 1 'one who gets his living by shooting wildfowl' for sense 2.

1 At the seal-hunt, marksman who shoots old or mature seals; cp AFTER a: AFTER GUNNER; BOW[2]: BOW-GUNNER.

1819 ANSPACH 422 The crews of their largest craft consist of from thirteen to eighteen men; of these some are gunners, who on finding their own guns, are admitted *birth* free. 1882 TALBOT 20 Here the old seals began to show themselves, here and there in the open spaces, and the gunners began to prepare their weapons for action. A certain proportion of every sealing crew are shipped as gunners, whose business is to shoot and capture the old seals. 1924 ENGLAND 248 Dey took deir gaves [gaffs] one time in de *Ranger*, an' paraded in St John's, an' de Cap'n took gunners an' dogs an' got after 'em. [1929] 1979 *Evening Telegram* 6 Apr, p. 14 Messages received from the sealing ships last night report that a few hundred old seals were shot by gunners yesterday. 1933 GREENE 45 The 'gunner' carrying an enormous muzzle-loading hammer-and-flint-lock gun that was about eight feet long, while his 'dog' (as his mate was called) carried the powder-horn, and bullets or slugs. 1967 *Evening Telegram* 11 Jan, p. 6 As for shooting seals, yes, that should have been put away forty years ago as in the case of a poor gunner there are lots of seals that get away to perish.

2 One who hunts sea-birds for food in a small boat or from a station or 'gaze' on the shore.

[1886] LLOYD 95 As soon as the ice breaks up and water appears. . .sea birds literally cover its surface. . . Boats are out in all directions, each containing from three to seven 'gunners,' who wage war with the unlucky birds. [1929] 1979 *Evening Telegram* 15 Jan, p. 17 Gunners on shore and in boats took a heavy toll of salt water birds which flocked into the harbor yesterday during an easterly storm. Ducks were selling in local stores today at 50 cents each and the smaller birds were 40 and 50 cents a pair. 1951 *Nfld & Lab Pilot* i, 75 From the western entrance point of Gunner's cove steep precipitous cliffs extend about one mile northward to Fort Amherst. M 70–21 There was no path even; just a tiny trail meandering among the rocks, worn down by goats, berry-pickers, gunners, and children.

3 Comb **gunner's cuff**: woollen mitten with forefinger and thumb separated; CUFF[1].

1933 GREENE 98 Each [sealer] will have a pair or two of plain woollen cuffs to serve the same purpose for his hands [to save them from frostbite]. These cover all the fingers together, or are of the kind called 'gunners'-cuffs,' which leave the trigger-finger free for use with a gun.

gunning ppl, vbl n also **a-gunning**. Cp *DAE* ~ 1 (1678–).

1 Shooting sea-birds for food from small boats or from a 'gaze' on the shore; attrib in names of coastal features; BIRDING.

[1832] 1981 *Them Days* vi (4), p. 34 Capt Quinton [returned] from guning with 2 ducks. 1858 [LOWELL] i, 82 Our poor boys were out agunnun. 1884 STEARNS 224 The birds. . .have a certain course which they pursue, and the shoals over which they fly are called the 'gunning points.' Here the men and boys congregate, and, lying low, behind some rock or cake of ice, await the flight. 1887 *Telegram Christmas No* 9 An appetizing odor came from the oven, where a couple of fine fat bull-birds, part proceeds of a successful day's gunning in punt, a day or two before, were yielding up their juices. 1909 BROWNE xxii In April of the following year, while a man and a boy were gunning in the direction of the island, their attention was attracted to the peculiar movements of a bird. 1951 *Nfld & Lab Pilot* i, 155 Clatise Harbour is entered between [the head] and Gunning point. [1952] 1965 PEACOCK (ed) i, 89 "Our Island is Covered with Fog": Some are out gunning, the rivers are running / And Uncle is towing a log / More are scoffing, while others are coughing, / Our island is covered with fog. 1953 *Nfld & Lab Pilot* ii, 196 [The coast trends] to Gunning head. T 66–64 There was a feller he was out gunnin' we called it, after birds. He fired at a bird; he didn't kill it, but the bird swam in this cove. T 141/68–65[2] We went down [in] the spring o' the year, went down th' islands gunnin'. 1965 PEACOCK (ed) i, 101 "Tom Bird's Dog": It was on a Monday morning as far as we all know / When you and Freeman Pink decided a-gunning for to go.

2 Comb **gunning gaff**: pole with metal crook used to retrieve birds from the water; GAFF.

1861 DE BOILIEU 240–1 It constantly arises that the spot from whence the ducks are shot is, at least, ten feet perpendicular from the water; sportsmen provide themselves in such instances with what is termed a 'gunning gaff,' some twelve feet long, with an iron crook at the end, made in the shape of a shepherd's crook. The dog brings a duck at a time under the rock; you place the crook round its neck, and draw it up or land it.

gunning punt: small open boat used to hunt sea-birds and seals in inshore waters (P 237–81).

gunning rodney: see **gunning punt**; RODNEY.

T 399–67 We used to row them times in what we called gunnin' rodney. 1979 TIZZARD 259 I always did the rowing back aft in the punt or gunnin' rodney, whichever the case may be. . . Chasing after a flock of bullbirds floating on the water, and then just as we get within gunshot they all dive was sort of frustrating.

gunny v *EDD* ~ v 'to cast one's eye over anything' Ha Co. To look (P 223–72).

gurdy n Cp *NID* ~ n 'spool used in hauling nets aboard'; *DC* (1936–); cp *OED* hurdy-gurdy 'trawl winch' (1883). Winch for hauling a load of sealskins aboard a vessel; similar device for hauling fish-nets and lines.

1924 ENGLAND 237 Here I been workin' ahl me life, draggin' and 'aulin, mucklin' up grayples, sometimes bloody gert 'auls two hundurd an' fifty viddum [fathom] lang on a gurdy. 1971 NOSEWORTHY 204 ~ A machine with two handles used to free trawls caught on the bottom and to wind them up. This was used mainly on the Grand Banks. P 237–77 ~ small winch 'made up' either by fishermen or someone who can weld; used only in boat, not in stage, etc. Used to haul trawls (or gill-nets on long-liners).

gurry n Cp *OED* ~ 'refuse from "cutting-in" a whale; fish offal' (1850–); *DAE* 'offal' (1838–); *DC* (1791–).

1 Blood, slime, refuse from splitting cod-fish and handling fish-offal; SLUB[1].

1861 *Harper's* xxii, 595 After remaining thus [in 'kenches'] for three weeks the water and 'gurry' are absorbed, and they are then placed upon 'flakes' to dry. 1908 TOWNSEND 88 I go ashore in the mail-boat, and clamber up a fish-stage dripping with fish 'gurry.' 1937 DEVINE 26 ~ Same as *slub*, except that the offal is more liquified. P 229–67 Take the draw bucket and wash down the gurry from under the splittin' table. 1971 *Evening Telegram* 21 May, p. 7 Mr Delaney said he could probably have rented some old building steeped with the smell of 50 years of urine and fish gurry.

2 Oil running out from 'seal pelts' or cod livers.

1888 STEARNS 185 The boys would not at first believe that all those huge barrels or puncheons that they saw were full of anything but slime and gurry, but Mr Godard took a stick and, pushing away the top, showed them that beneath the gurry was clear, brown oil. 1924 ENGLAND 297 Our starboard quarter pound began to 'run to ile' very badly, and an overpowering stench invaded the cabin. 'Gurry,' they call such seal oil, and the name fits. 1969 MOWAT 9 Devil a seam can ye keep tight wit' corkin (caulking). But dey seals dersel's, ye might say, wit' gurry and blood, and dat's what keeps dey tight.

gut n *OED* gut sb 8 ~ foundered now dial. Cpd **gut-foundered**: very hungry, famished
(P 133–58).
  C 71–125 I wish the food was ready because I'm gut-foundered. 1975 GUY 48 You had better ask for two hot turkey sandwiches if you don't want to be gut-foundered before supper.

guttle n Cp *EDD* ~ v 'to eat or drink greedily.' A large mouthful.
  P 245–57 After being offered a sip only, he said, 'Give me a guttle of water.'

guttle v In the game of marbles, to win a number from opponent; HAWK v.
  M 66–12 If a person pitched three marbles and ended up with five, then he had guttled two marbles off the other players. C 71–125 When one player captures all of the marbles, he is said to have guttled the other player.

guzzle v *EDD* ~ v 2 'to throttle.' To grasp someone with the arm around the neck
(P 140–70).

H

habit n A garment in which the dead are dressed to be waked and buried.
  M 67–15 The [dead] lady, prepared for 'wake' and burial, was dressed in a 'habit'—resembling those of a religious order. M 68–16 The habit was brown or black. Women wore brown, men, black. This habit was full length, from shoulders to the feet. The habit had long sleeves. Accompanying the habit would be a breast-piece. This would be about eighteen inches square. There would be two strings on the upper part of this breast-piece and these strings would be used to tie this part of the habit around the neck. On this breast-piece the letters I.H.S. would be woven or placed. This piece of clothing would be trimmed with wide white silk ribbon. Above the initials I.H.S. would be a white cross. Beneath the letters was a white heart. Another piece of clothing was a face covering. 1971 CASEY 295 Until twenty years ago, many of the dead were dressed in an additional outer garment known as a 'habit.' This habit was prepared prior to death, especially if the person was old or had an extensive period of illness. The habit was a dark brown monk-like robe which reached the toes and had long sleeves. On the chest of the habit was a white or red shaped heart made of ribbon and the letters I.H.S. (In Hoc Signo), but explained locally as 'I have suffered.'

hacker v *EDD* ~ 2, 4, 5.
  1 To stammer.
  T 168/7–65 He used to stammer: 'Here comes I B–, Beelzebub,' an' his two knees'd go down. He'd hacker at it.
  2 To shiver or chatter (with cold).
  Q 71–6 He was so cold his teeth were hackering.
  Q 71–10 He was hackering with the cold.

3 To cough in a dry, chesty manner (Q 71–8).

hackle See CROSS-HACKLE.

haddock n Comb **haddock-whale** ['ædɪk wɛil]: harbour porpoise (*Phocoena phocoena*).
  T 1–63[1] 'Haddock-whale' they is called. They's just the same as fresh meat. You never ate better.

hag[1] n [ould 'hæg, ould 'hæ·g, ould 'æ·g, oul 'æ·g, oʉld 'hæ·ɨg]. Cp *OED* ~[1] 1 c obs (1632, 1696) for sense 1; *OED* hag-ridden 1, *EDD* hag sb[1] 2 (4) hag-ride esp Do So D Co for comb in sense 3. See D Hufford, 'A New Approach to the "Old Hag" [Nfld],' in WAYLAND D HAND *American Folk Medicine* (1976), pp. 73–85.
  1 The nightmare; freq in form **old hag**. Cp DIDDIES.
  1896 *J A Folklore* ix, 222 A man. . .told me he had been ridden to death by an old hag, until a knowledge-able old man advised him to drive nails through a shingle, and lash it to his breast when he went to bed. [1929] BURKE [6] "No Short Skirts": For her skirts are so tight round the hips, Jennie, / It's no wonder she got the old hag. 1924 ENGLAND 216 A sufferer from night-mare is supposed to be ridden by something called 'the old hag,' and the only way to free him from torment is to call his name backward. 1937 *Bk of Nfld* i, 230 Nightmare is called by fishermen the 'Old Hag.' T 222–66 Well, by this time it would be bedtime, and perhaps after such an exciting day you would probably have bad dreams; in fact you might have the old hag, or a nightmare. C 69–22 He often gets the hag. Usually he is dreaming that someone is chasing him [or] he may be falling from somewhere. C 70–23 If you sleep on your back you'll have hags. 1975 *Evening Telegram* 20 Dec, p. 3 Christmas for many has moved beyond the yearly sufferable nightmare to the realm of that particularly exquisite nocturnal terror called, in Newfoundland, 'The Old Hag.'
  2 Part of inner organs of a lobster, discarded in eating (P 127–73); OLD WOMAN.
  3 Comb **hag-rode**: (a) troubled by nightmare; (b) bewitched (see P 51–67 quot).
  P 213–55 Hagorid: [afflicted by] a nightmare, especially one in which the victim feels someone sitting on his chest. P 51–67 When he couldn't catch any fish, he said he was hagrode. C 67–10 ~ [Hagrode is when] she awakes in a sweat and feels pinned to the bed by some unseen force.

hag[2] See HAGDOWN.

hag v Cp HAG n: HAG-RODE. To torment (in a nightmare).
  C 70–25 If you think or talk badly of someone who is dead, the dead person will hag you. The person hagged will become light headed and will talk in his sleep. The way to get him out is to slap him across the face. C 71–6 As a young girl she got hagged. That night she woke up screaming, she had felt the young man's hands around her throat but she couldn't scream or move.

hagden, hagdon See HAGDOWN.

hagdown n also **eggdown, hag, hagden, hagdon, haigdown, hegdown, hogdown** ['hægdæɵn] *OED* hagden local (1843–1885); *O Sup*[2] (1832–); *EDD* ~ I Ma; *DAE* hagdel (1813, 1832) for sense 1.

1 Greater shearwater (*Puffinus gravis*); sooty shearwater (*P. griseus*); BAWK.

[1670] 1963 YONGE 127 The weather warm, can see no birds but hagdens. [1794] 1968 THOMAS 144 Penguins, Hegdowns, Muirs and Tuirs, Ice Birds, Mother Carey's Chickens, Loons, Noddys, Sea Parrots, Sea Pigeons and a number of other Sea Fowl. [c1830] 1890 GOSSE 31 . . .'hog-downs, and other birds.' 1861 *Harper's* xxii, 753 Strange birds hovered around. . .saddle-back gulls, bottle-nosed ducks, hagden, auks, puffins, sea-pigeons, eiders, and gannets. 1883 HOWLEY *MS Reminiscences* 4 The Hagdowns are very bold birds would scarcely move out of the steamers way until she almost touched them with her prow. 1907 TOWNSEND 319–20 Greater Shearwater; 'Hag'; 'Hagdon.' Sooty Shearwater; 'Black Hag or Hagdon.' 1909 BROWNE 207 'Hagdons'. . .are found plentifully along the southern coast of Labrador; and fishermen consider them harbingers of 'bad' weather. 1921 CABOT 25 Not many gulls appeared, but beds of shearwaters, locally 'hagdowns,' and other kinds, stretched along on both sides [of the ship]. 1951 PETERS & BURLEIGH 54 The 'Hagdown,' known to all fishermen, soars gracefully over the waves, dropping into the troughs, seemingly always in danger of being swallowed by the next wave, but swinging up just enough to slide over the crest without wetting even a wing-tip. . . It is a greedy bird and very bold in securing food, often following dories to seize bait from trawls. 1955 DOYLE (ed) 39 "Let Me Fish Off Cape St Mary's": Cape St Mary's / Where the hag-downs sail. 1959 MCATEE 3, 4 Eggdown. 1966 HORWOOD 329 Bawks. . .which are sometimes called eggdowns, or hagdons.

2 Nickname for a man from Placentia Bay.

T 66/8–64 All three fellers going around to put down dogs: a pig-headed Irishman, a flat-footed Englishman and a hagdown from the west'ard! This is an Irishman, and an Englishman, and a man from Placentia.

haigdown See HAGDOWN.

hail v Cp *Cent* ~[3]. Phr *hail for*: to report number of fish or seals taken by a vessel (1925 *Dial Notes* v, 333).

[1930 *Am Speech* v, 390 ~ The total number of pounds of fish which a vessel may *have* in her hold at the time a declaration is made.] 1952 *Atlantic Guardian* Mar, p. 26 The *St Filian*. . .was outfitted by Hunter and Company and hailed for five thousand pelts.

hair n *OED* ~ sb 10: ~ seal (1865–); *DAE* (1824–); *DC* (1872) for comb in sense 2.

1 Phr *hair of the head*: hair.

T 36/7–64 An' then she grabbed o' this woman—got her hold by the hair o' the head an' hauled her down through the church an' throwed her out. T 191–65 An' they took him right hold by the head, by the hair o' the head, an' give a big jig.

2 Comb **hair-seal**: seal valued chiefly for its oil rather than fur; the type of seal hunted in Newfoundland waters; HARP, HOOD.

1872 DASHWOOD 255 But these are the hair seals; the fur species, which are made into jackets, inhabit the South Seas, as many of my readers are doubtless aware. 1888 STEARNS 206 He brought with him two very prettily spotted sealskins. . . Freddie was quite disappointed when we found that they were the hair and not the fur seal, and that he could not take home a cloak to Eva and his mother. 1908 DURGIN 20 These are the hair seals, the young of which have a beautifully mottled coat, used now for automobile garments. 1924 ENGLAND 103 The hoods, for their first four years, are 'young hoods,' 'bedlamers,' 'curriers' and 'old hoods.' And 'old dog hoods' or 'old bitch hoods' they remain. Like the harps, they are hair seals, not fur seals.

hairy See NEWFOUNDLAND HAIRY WOODPECKER, PALMER.

half n Cp *OED* ~ n 7 f *on the halves*, *DAE* now dial.

Phr *half one's hand*: one half a 'share' of the catch of fish due to a crew-member, the other half-share going to owner, 'planter' or skipper.

1866 WILSON 212 Of this fish one half is his, as wages, and the other half belongs to the planter for the supplies. Such a person is said to 'have half his hand.' [1877] 1898 *Nfld Law Reports* 148 The evidence, as I understand its effect, also established, that the men regularly engaged in a cod-seine boat as its permanent crew shared half the catch of the boat in proportion to their numbers. . . That except in the way of bounty, as above mentioned, no shareman ever received more than half his hand, or received fish which he did not participate in taking. 1920 WALDO 156 If a man goes 'half his hand' then he gets half his catch for his labour. 1937 *Bk of Nfld* i, 14 There is a uniform method of division. . .called 'having half your hand.' There are four men in the crew, including the skipper-owner. Say, for the sake of simplicity, that the boat gets a hundred quintals for the season: that is, four shares of twenty-five quintals each. The skipper takes one of them. He also takes as his further share one-half of the twenty-five quintal share of each of the three sharemen. This giving him an additional twelve and a half quintals from each shareman or thirty-seven and a half quintals from the three, he now has a grand total of sixty-two and a half quintals out of the hundred, and each shareman has twelve and a half quintals 'to his own hand.' 1957 *Evening Telegram* 13 Aug, p. 4 Then, as they had shipped with him, that he had the same rights as they did, for they had signed on for half their 'hand,' he sued. T 36–64 When you'd go in collar in the spring your pay would be a half your hand, they used to call it; that will be half a share. 1967 FIRESTONE 53 People have heard of rare instances where a man, upon retiring, claims 'one half of his hand,' that is, one-half of the income derived from his share. This would be what he would obtain if he employed a shareman to fish his part.

on the halves: (a) sharing equally with another;

(b) of the fastening of a fish net, in a certain traditional fashion.

1887 *Fisheries of U S* 146 The crews. . .fished at the halves, counting their fish as they were thrown aboard the vessel. [1900] 1905 *Nfld Law Reports* 342 Q. Did the captain ask you what was the usual amount to pay for salvage? A. He did; I told him on the halves, that was the arrangement on that side of the country for every wreck. Q. You were asking him for 70 per cent? A. I had nothing to do with it; I heard Mr Condon and himself settling it; he put me into it. 1937 *Seafisheries of Nfld* 102 Three years ago, a large purchase of frozen herring was made for stocking the cold storage plants [but] a considerable quantity of those purchased could not be used, and had to be destroyed. The present system of freezing, on the halves, has been found to be more satisfactory than straight purchase and sale. 1938 MACDERMOTT 82 As we were not paying cash at the mill for the sawing of our logs into the required sizes of timber and beams, we cut double the number of logs needed, and paid one log for every log sawn. This is known as 'sawing on the halves.' M 69–5 The owners had a scheme called 'sawing on the halves.' Under this scheme they got half the lumber they sawed. . .if a fisherman got 1000 board feet of lumber sawed, the sawmill owner got 500 board feet and the fisherman got 500 board feet. In the spring the sawmill operators sold their surplus lumber to some firm outside. 1975 RUSSELL 81 But a sadder case still is the case of Lige Bartle's will and his tool chest that he left 'on the halves' to his two sons. P 9–73 The number of feet or fathoms covered by ninety-eight meshes would depend on whether the linnet was brought to (fastened to) on the halves, the thirds, a bit under or over the halves or thirds. So, two inches along the rope and two inches each side of a half-mesh is halves. The linnet edge forms a half-mesh with the rope only. Thirds are two thirds of four inches along the rope and two inches each side of a half-mesh. 1979 NEMEC 263 Each net in a 'fleet' when 'roped on the halves' has a mesh of either [6, 6½, or 7 inches].

half a *EDD* ~ a 6, *Kilkenny Lexicon*, pp. 189–90 half-fool; cp *DAE* half-leg.

Comb **half-bend**: a set of two timbers which do not require a 'floor,' located anywhere in the body-frame of a boat; see also BEND n (P 127–78).

half door: an outside door protecting the main door of a house; storm door.

1929 BURKE [6] "No Short Skirts to their Knees": And their dresses as large as a tent, Jennie, / They wouldn't come through a half door.

half drum: in the fish trade with Brazil, a cylindrical wooden container in which dried cod are packed; see also DRUM n.

T 90–64 We made birch drums, half drums. . .and whole quintal drums: they were for the Brazil market. 1973 HORWOOD 40–1 This time the *Olive Moore* was not long delayed. There was another load of fish prepared for her and already screwed into drums and half drums, and this time consigned to different dealers. One in Maceio and the other in Bahia. 1977 BURSEY 154 [The staves] were of birchwood, sawn to the size to make drums and half drums, the drums to hold little more than a quintal of dry codfish, half drums, half the quantity.

half fool: a mentally deficient person.

1955 ENGLISH 34 A moron, a half fool. C 75–139 [Gommil was applied] to a person who was as foolish as a hen, or a half-fool.

half gallon: a rubber boot cut off at the ankle.

1977 *Nfld Qtly* Dec, p. 36 Half gallons. . .were rubber boots knee high that had seen several years service in the fishing boat, and the bush, had become leaky, and were cut off at the ankles, then to finish them off, were worn in the gardens, and around the beaches.

half gommel: see **half fool**; GOMMEL (Q 67–23).

half-hitcher: (a) half-hitch, a type of knot; (b) untrustworthy person.

P 101–64 [proverb] Two half-hitchers lost a longboat. Q 71–6 Two half-hitchers were commonly used to tie a boat to a grump.

half-leg (boot): a boot reaching half-way to the knee.

T 191–65 They'd wear the half-leg boots, they're hard leather boots. That was before the Smallwood boots came out. They were well fitted, could stand up to a pretty good storm. P 189–65 On both sides of each half-leg were loops to aid in pulling them on. The women would wear them drying fish or around the house. They were worn on land and while fishing. T 187/8–65 [The rocks] was out of the water this high; could walk out across 'em with a pair of half-leg rubber boots on.

half-moon seal: HARP-SEAL (*Phoca groenlandica*).

1846 TOCQUE 189 Naturalists describe no less than fifteen species of seals. The kind most plentiful, and which pass along the coast of Newfoundland with the ice, are the harps or half-moon seals. 1866 WILSON 274 The seal most frequent upon the coast is the harp, sometimes called the half-moon. It receives the name harp from a large black or dark spot on the back of the old dog-seal; but the female has no such mark. 1924 ENGLAND 102 Sometimes harps are called 'half-moon seals.' The marking looks like a broad curved line of connected dark spots, starting from each shoulder and meeting on the back, above the tail. Only the dogs have this marking, and then not till their second year.

half puncheon: large wooden cask cut down and adapted for various uses; see also PUNCHEON (TUB).

1916 MURPHY 11 These cabooses stood on the deck of the vessels [to make a fire in], sometimes a half puncheon was used, around which a number of bricks were placed.

half intens *EDD* ~ 8 half-saved. Comb **half-saved**: (a) of cod-fish, only partially cured; (b) of a person, mentally deficient. See SAVE for sense (a).

1920 WALDO 154 Fish when half-cured are said to be 'half-saved,' and a man who is 'not all there' is likely to be styled 'half-saved.' P 108–71 O, don't mind him, he's only half-saved.

halifax [= Halifax, N S]. Attrib **halifax job**: job done for oneself or another on company time.

c 69–15 ~ An expression used in almost every workshop in St John's [meaning] doing a job for yourself or a friend on company time, usually with company tools and materials, for which the company will not be paid. P 148–76 I'm having some friends put the lock in. It's a halifax job.

hambro See HAMBURG.

hamburg n also **hambro** *DC* ~ bread Nfld (1906–).

Attrib, from nineteenth-century trade between Newfoundland and Hamburg, the city of north Germany.

hamburg boot: fisherman's long leather boot.

1901 *Christmas Bells* 11 Aye, indeed!—the good old days of homespun, Hamburg boots, bread and butter, are gone, and with it much that went to make the outport fisherman's life a veritable recreation indeed. 1914 *Cadet* Apr., p. 7 Hamburg boots and bluchers were all the go and the swanskin or buskin when worn over the latter made a tidy, warm and comfortable footwear. 1927 DOYLE (ed) 9 "The Outharbour Planter": He's gon' with gansy and corduroy pants; with Hamburg boots and ne'er collar. 1936 DEVINE 41 An old fisherman once said to me, in praise of the Hamburg boot: 'We never claimed 'em to be waterproof, but I tell you, me son, they "obliged" the foot of men in every other way.'

hamburg bread: hard thick biscuit; HARD BREAD.

1852 *Morning Post* 12 Feb., p. 4 800 bags No. 1, 2, and 3, Hambro' Bread. [1879] 1898 *Nfld Law Reports* 185 [The plaintiff] being dissatisfied with the quality of the machine-made biscuit of Newfoundland, as compared with that imported from Hamburg, he introduced into his establishment a process known amongst bakers as hand rolling. . .and a biscuit is thus produced which. . .in the words of one of the witnesses, has driven Hamburg bread out of the market. 1906 LUMSDEN 68 'Hamburg bread,' or hard biscuit (not to be confounded with pilot or sailor biscuit as popularly known, being thick and cake-like in shape and extraordinarily hard), is in constant use on the vessels and in the houses of the fishermen. 1936 DEVINE 92 He laid his plans to get the formula or recipe for making Hamburg bread and succeeded [in making hard bread]. 1964 BLONDAHL (ed) 97 "Red Cap's Hole": When they came to dine at dinner-time, / Some joyful words were said. . . / Of days of yore when the pots boiled o'er, / With brewis from hamburg's made.

hamburg butter

1897 WILLSON x Fifty years ago, when the hardest ship's-biscuit, fish, Hamburg butter, and pork was the food. . .

hamburg pork

1916 MURPHY 11 Hamburg bread and butter, and Hamburg pork, contributed to a portion of their fare.

hammer n Phr *hammer and tiss*: from the vocabulary of muzzle-loading fire-arms, a violent argument or dispute. See also TISS.

T 178/80–65 Well we has hammer an' tiss about it, an' he put it in Supreme Court. An' I went to St John's. Well that's where we had this hammer an' tiss, sir—his lawyers.

hand n Cp *OED* ~ sb 8 b, c naut 'each of the sailors belonging to a ship's crew'; *all hands*: 'the whole crew' (1699–) for sense 1; *OED* 45 *make a hand* for phr in sense 2; for combs. in sense 3: *OED* ~ barrow (14..-1854), *EDD* hand sb 1 (2): ~ barrow; *ADD* handsignment; *EDD* sb 1 (111): ~ wrist s w cties.

1 Each of the persons engaged or 'shipped' by a merchant, planter or skipper to conduct afloat and on shore the various branches and operations of fishing and sealing; *all hands*: the whole CREW, everybody.

[1766] 1971 BANKS 134 [The splitter] then Shoves the Fish off the table which fall into a kind of hand barrow set there to receive it which as soon as it [is] full is wheeld off to the Salt Pile by another hand. [1770] 1792 CARTWRIGHT i, 74 In the first place, they built up a prodigious large fire in their house; all hands then assembled before the door, and one of them fired a gun, loaded with powder only. [1794] 1968 THOMAS 173 The Countys of Devonshire and Dorsetshire supply the greatest number of hands for the Newfoundland Fisherys yearly then all the rest put together. [1916] 1972 GORDON 49 And to round off a busy and happy day, all hands re-collected at Porcupine in the evening for the rare but exciting event of a wedding. 1936 SMITH 14 After discharging the winter's supplies and mooring the vessel for the winter, all hands settled down. . .and I returned to school again. T 49–64 There'd be the well to shovel out, an' there'd be the barn to shovel, because all hands kept cattle.

2 Phr *hand (over) going*: rapidly.

P 64–65 Yesterday I could do that hand over going, but today I can't do it. Q 71–8 Hand going [is] extremely common for hand over fist.

make a hand: to have success.

1924 ENGLAND 189 Stop chin-waggin', now an' get to work. Ye won't make arr hand, just talking'! C 68–10 I can remember several times I tried to spin some wool on the old spinning wheel, but I never could make any hand at it. 1975 BUTLER 61 [The saw] would be pushed and pulled. They had to coordinate because if they didn't they'd make no hand of it at all, 'twould drag on the wood.

on the hand of: nearly.

P 148–61 When she's on the hand of coming. . . 1975 GUY 111 Come into the kitchen from outdoors on the hand of being frozen. 1977 RUSSELL 155 Here was poor Luke with over a hundred quintals of medium salted fish in his stage on the hand of spoilin'.

to (one's) hand: to one's share (1925 *Dial Notes* v, 333).

3 Attrib, comb, cpd **hand-barrel**: tub with side handles for two men to carry (c 71–123). See **hand-tub** below.

hand-barrow, ~ **bar** ['hænbærou, 'hænbærə, 'hændbæːɹ, 'ændbæːɹ]: flat rectangular wooden frame with handles at each end for two men to carry cod-fish, seal 'pelts' and other bulky materials; DRUDGE V: DRUDGE BARROW. Also attrib.

[See 1766 quot in sense 1 above.] 1778 DE CASSINI 147 The cod is left in salt two days at least, and sometimes above a fortnight; then it is washed. For this purpose they load it on hand barrows, and empty it out into a laver not unlike a great cage, by the sea-side. [c1830] 1890 GOSSE 57 Before me is a wide hand-barrow. A boat loaded to the water's edge with seal-pelts is being slowly pulled from one of the schooners. 1866 WILSON 210 The females have to carry the last water-horse from the stage to the flake, a distance of some fifty yards, in a hand-barrow. The hand-barrow is made by nailing a few short pieces of board on two small poles, about eight feet long; and is carried between two persons. 1920 CABOT 96 Water being scarce, it had to be brought from the hill in a hand-barrow tank. 1924 ENGLAND 264 Two oldsters toiling up a lane with a hand barrow of rocks. T 43–64 The hand-barrow was the thing you used to carry the fish on the flake with an' carry it back to the boat if you were shippin' fish. A crew of fishermen'd have up to a dozen hand-barrows. 1966 *Evening Telegram* 10 Oct, p. 4 The cargo was carried from the wharf to the fish plant in what were known as handbars, a box with handles attached which was carried by two men. 1979 TIZZARD 87 If it was late in the afternoon the washed fish was either put out on the flake, back up, or piled on the hand bar in the stage ready to put out in the morning.

hand carder: flat implement with wire teeth, used in pairs to comb wool for spinning; card.

T 175/7–65 We had the old-time carders, the two hand-carders. But now they got the carders what you turned around, revolved.

hand-cart: (a) see **hand-cat**, ~ **slide** below; (b) see **hand-barrow** above.

Q 67–3 [The] 'ancart [is] used in hauling firewood, pulpwood, etc. 1971 NOSEWORTHY 209 ~ same as hand-bar(row).

hand-cat: (a) small sledge used for transporting wood in winter and hauled or pushed by a man (see also CAT[7], CATAMARAN, DOG[1] n: DOG-CAT); (b) to transport wood with such a sledge.

P 128–56 I hand-catted twenty cords of wood last spring. 1971 NOSEWORTHY 209 ~ A small slide, about three to four feet long, with two runners, two *knees* (curved pieces of wood) attached to the runners in front, two beams going across the runners, and four *harns* (vertical sticks) to support a load of wood.

hand-flake: lightly-constructed platform, about four feet above ground level, used to spread and dry cod-fish; FLAKE.

1792 CARTWRIGHT *Gloss* i, x [Flakes] are of two sorts, viz: Broad-flakes and Hand-flakes. 1832 MCGREGOR i, 230 They are spread, heads and tails. . .on hand-flakes, which are about breast-high from the ground. P 80–64 Hand-flakes are narrow enough so that you can reach across them.

hand-gaff: iron hook attached to a three-foot (7.6 cm) stick and used for various (fisheries) purposes; see also GAFF n.

1966 SCAMMELL 79 Here's another handgaff in case the dogfish are in the nets. 1977 RUSSELL 107 You cut two holes eight or ten foot apart, tie a rope to one end of a flake longer, poke it down through one hole and hook it up through the other with a hand gaff.

hand serry: see HAND SERRY.

handsignment: written and signed agreement; signature.

1896 *Dial Notes* i, 379 ~ signature. 1896 *J A Folklore* ix, 37 Put your handsignment to it: to sign your name to it.

hand-slide: (a) small sled used for transporting wood in winter and hauled or pushed by hand or dog; (b) to transport (wood, etc) with such a sled. See **hand-cat** above.

P 65–64 Some branch roads are very short. In such a case a man may hand-slide logs to the main road. To hand-slide logs a man has a komatic and hauls it himself without the help of dogs or horse. T 175/7–65 Just a knee slide, sir, proper wood slide—the same that they use for pulling wood; just a hand-slide, not a horse-slide. T 393/6–67 We were all hand-slidin', what we call hand-slide. We'd pull our rope on our back. 1976 *Decks Awash* Aug, p. 19 Then around the first of March we'd take off with the hand slide up the bay again after the rabbits.

hand-tub: wooden container with side handles for two men to carry, often made by sawing a barrel in half. See TUB.

M 68–7 ~ Used mainly for carrying green fish, salt and sometimes used for carrying manure to the gardens. Apple barrels are cut off and two sticks put on the sides for carrying it. 1971 NOSEWORTHY 209 ~ A tub made of a half-barrel and carried by a rope and a long stick.

hand-wrist pl ['ænd ˌrɪsəz]: the wrist.

1858 [LOWELL] i, 82, 88 Jesse an' his crew made straight for Back-Cove an' got in, though they were weak-handed, for one had hurted his hand-wrist. . . His hand-wristès were all worn aw'y wi' workun at the oar. 1863 MORETON 37 Terminal [s] after a consonant, is changed to a syllable es; as askes, ghostes, priestes, hand-wristes. T 141/67–65[2] You got to grease your arms over unless you puts on arm sleeves; but then they gets around your hand wris'es. T 172/5–65 So he reached down with his boathook, he drove the boathook down to his hand wrist, and he hooked un there in his shirt an' he hauled un up.

hand serry n also ad **serry***, an **seery***, an **serry***, **auntsary**, **nansarey**, **nansernie***, **nants-a-nerry***, etc [æd'sɪərɪ, æn'sɪərɪ, hæn'sɪərɪ]. See SKERRY* n 'sledge'; cp AUNTSARY[1] 'the greater yellowlegs' (1770–). Small sledge with wooden runners, hauled by hand or by horse and used for moving heavy objects.

[c1894] PANL P4/14, p. 193 I heard a man say he was going to 'car' home a barrel of flour on his 'Aunt Sarah' [but I learned] his *auntsary* was no other than a kind of catamaran turned up at both ends. 1937 DEVINE 34

Nansarey—a small hand sledge with runners of staves, suitable for hauling over the snow crust, and used especially by sealers and loggers for their clothes bags and chests. P 37 Handsery, ansery, nansery—sledge with wooden runners, used on fish-stage. P 10–57 Aunt-sary—hand-slide made of pork barrel staves. T 34–64 He'd. . .take his bag on a adserry. That's what they used to call a old slide, so many barrel staves we used to put [on it] and they'd put their canvas bag on that slide and haul un through the country till they get to Carbonear. P 269–64 An serry—device with two wooden runners for hauling wood over rocks, bushes, and rough paths. 1966 PADDOCK 101 Nants-a-nerry—a low vehicle pulled by a horse in dragging stones off a field. C 71–131 Han serry—a slide, sometimes called a bob-sled, used to haul wood when there is no snow on the ground. . .just a single sled with a beam laid on the runners. P 227–77 The an serry was used primarily if not solely for hauling heavy logs to the main road, where the large sled was left. The teamster would unhitch the horse from the main sled, harness him to the an serry and proceed up a narrow, steep woodpath to the heavy timber, place a number of logs on [the an serry] and return to the main sled.

handy a, av From *OED* ~ 2 'ready to hand; near at hand'; *EDD* 4, 5, 6 esp s w cties; JOYCE 271; *O Sup*[2] 2 b handy by.

1 Near by; close.

1792 PULLING *MS* Aug Says I here they are handy for I see their canocs just to the side of that point. Presently down comes an Indian and calls out Yoho three times. [1794] 1968 THOMAS 62 It also serves for the necessary purpose of Fish Flakes, both in building and covering, which yearly want repair. The Spruce growing handy, it is got with little trouble. 1849 [FEILD] 79 One of the men [opposite Anchor Point, St Barbe], as his wife reported, came from 'handy Bath, *or* Somersetshire.' [1870] 1973 KELLY 23 One fine old man, from Stoke Gabriel, 'handy Plymouth,' who narrowly escaped being enlisted in the 'King's Guards,' some forty-five years ago, could tell us the names of the two Clergymen who were with the Bishop. 1932 BARBOUR 92 Keep a good look-out for sand bars, or rocks. We must go quite handy. 1953 *Nfld & Lab Pilot* ii, 449 Handy Harbour islands, a group of four principal islands. . .lies about half a mile westward of Ragged rocks. Within this group there is a good boat harbour, with numerous passages into it between the various islands. T 49–64 After so many pitches, well the handiest'd be to the peg, he tossed the buttons. T 55–64 One'd stay a little way down the tickle, another feller lived somewhere else, and they couldn't agree any handier than that. T 29/30–64 'Don't come no handier to me,' she says, 'I'm afraid of you.' T 313/5–66 I went on down through the woods, and handier I got—what do you allow that was? 'Twas a darn big horse. 1977 *Nfld Qtly* Summer, p. 7 Anyway it blowed so hard we had to run off the land and hove her to. We was eight days running on that one side. It drove her across the Virgin Banks; we were handier to them than he thought she was.

2 Almost, nearly, just about.

P 245–64 [The trawlers are] handy all sold off. C 71–95 I'm handy gone. I'm exhausted.

3 Phr *handy about*.

1924 ENGLAND 36 Wind's nor'-be-east; 'andy 'bout dat. T 43/4–64 Beams shored up, handy about level. . . I remember one summer we were down the Labrador. 'Twas handy about the last summer I was down there. M 71–39 On first of cold November or handy thereabout / This family barred up their home to ramble to the South.

handy by

1868 *Royal Geog Soc* xxxviii, 270 A term he often used was 'handy-by,' meaning close to. 1908 TOWNSEND 118 The water is smooth, for, as a sailor says, the ice is 'handy-by.'

handy to

1905 DUNCAN 117 'Twere handy t' dark when I seed the merman rise from the water. 1911 PRICHARD 56 He added that at one time among the alders he was 'so handy' to the bear, that he might have struck it with the axe but did not do so—wisely, I think. P 148 61 Rover would not go handy to the bear and beaver. T 31/4–64 We got pretty handy to the island. T 43/4–64 I was too much afraid of the dogs to go handy to 'em. P 148–66 Where is that 50-degree temperature? It's not handy to it. 1972 BROWN 175 He clumsily backed down off the ice pinnacle, reluctant to look into their burning eyes. 'B'ys, I gotta tell ye, there's no ship handy to us at all.'

4 Comb **handy buoy**: in Bank fishery, the buoy or float marking the end of trawl nearest to the vessel.

1942 *Grand Bank U C School* 34 ~ The three buoys on each dory; this one for nearest the ship, *faraway buoy* for the other end, *flunky buoy* used at any spot to tell fisherman how far he has removed fish from trawl.

handy gear: in trawl-fishing, a close setting of the hooks; about 60 hooks to a line (Q 67–48).

handy-jan, ~ **(h)an**: a woollen wristband, worn by fisherman to prevent 'water-pups' (inflammation from salt water) (P 37).

1937 DEVINE 26 ~s. Woollen wristlets worn in winter. P 83–77 Handy (h)an—wrist band worn to prevent boils.

hangashore See ANGISHORE.

hanger n The handle of a bucket.

T 43/7–64 You'd dip up your two buckets out of the well or pond, and then put your hoop on, on the buckets, inside of the hangers. . .so as when you'd take up your buckets they'd be pushing against your hoop.

hanker n A hand reel for yarn; niddy noddy.

T 43/8–64 The hanker was. . .the same thing that we used to use for ballin' off twine to knit traps. [It] was made like a cross and you'd have small holes, see, an' pegs down in these holes. 1979 POCIUS 21 A much simpler device [for the winding of yarn into skeins] consists merely of a pole fastened to each end, at ninety degrees to the pole and each other; this device was called a niddy-noddy. . . A woman from Cape Broyle said she often used a device which she called a 'hanker' to make skeins of wool. This device was placed on the table, and was probably a type of niddy-noddy.

happer v also **amper*** *EDD* ~ Ha W Do So. To crackle or sputter (as a wood fire).

P 148–64 ~ to make a sputtering, crackling noise, said of a fire. Q 71–7 A fire fed by dry wood would amper, not a fire of coal.

hapse¹ n also **apse, haps** *EDD* hasp: var apse, haps s w cties. A latch or fastening (on a door or gate); snap-button (on clothing).

1924 *Dial Notes* v, 333 ~ latch; hasp. 1937 DEVINE 26 Haps. The hasp of a door. P 266–67 Apse also applies to a fastening which is closed by pressing one part into the other.

hapse² n See APS.

hapse v also **haps.** See HAPSE¹ n. To fasten or latch (a door or gate); to button up or fasten (clothing).

1896 *J A Folklore* ix, 22 Haps. To hasp or fasten a door. 1924 ENGLAND 252 I run in a house, an' hapsed de door, an' dey broke in an' took after me. 1933 GREENLEAF xxv Come in, Tammas, and hapse the door, it's a bit airsome tonight. P 148–61 The hood [of the jacket] hapses on.

harbour n also **harbor, harborough.** Cp *OED* ~ sb¹ 3, *DAE* 1 for sense 1; *DC* harbo(u)r seal (1832–), *O Sup²* (Nfld: 1766–) for cpd in sense 3. Cp BAY.

1 An indentation of the sea affording shelter to boats and vessels, commonly comprising numerous coves and inlets, shore space for curing fish and fishing grounds or access to such grounds; the inhabited coastal strip of such an indentation; SETTLEMENT.

[1583] 1940 *Gilbert's Voyages and Enterprises* ii, 406 [Hayes' narrative] . . .the English marchants (that were & alwaies be Admirals by turnes interchangeably over the fleets of fishermen within the same harbor). . . 1612 GUY 413 Three peeces of Ordnance are planted there to command the Harboroughs upon a platforme made of great posts, and railes, and great Poles sixteene foot long set upright round about, with two Flankers to scoure the quarters. [1663] 1963 YONGE 56 The harbour we were in was very much esteemed for a good fishing place—the Barnstaple men prefer it above any. 1708 OLDMIXON 12 But they make use still of their old Harbours also, as their small Settlements here were termed, and not *Towns*, a Name indeed which they did not deserve. [1749] 1755 DOUGLASS i, 289 At present there are nine or ten settlements called harbours, not towns, where they cure and ship off their dry cod-fish. [1794] 1968 THOMAS 77 Capelin Bay is more properly a Harbour, being a mile and a half in length and not more than a quarter of a mile across in any part. 1887 BOND 73 Anyhow, I've got a couple of cod-seine skiffs myself, and there are four other boats from the harbour, and we're going to try. . .if we can find any tidings of them. [1911] 1930 COAKER 35 We desire to see

every harbor which is qualified possessing a Union Cash Store. 1937 DEVINE 45 I'll take a *slew* around the harbour before going to bed. 1971 SEARY 141 Harbour occurs thirty-five times [in Avalon place-names]. 1977 BUTLER 67–8 The building of this vessel gave a lot of employment to residents of the Harbour.

2 Phr *a harbour grace gentleman*: a man of genteel poverty or pretensions, after the town in Conception Bay.

Q 67–41 ~ a person putting on airs. P 157–74 ~ a man who can still look dignified with backside, knees and elbows out.

3 Comb, cpd **harbour ice**: ice formed during the winter in a bay or harbour; LOCAL: *local ice*.

[1706–7] 1745 OSBORNE 789 At four in the afternoon we saw some shattered ice, which we all supposed to be the harbour ice broken up. 1936 SMITH 65 When we arrived there we could not get in the harbour again for ice, so we tied fast to the harbour ice and began discharging cargo on the ice. 1975 RUSSELL 88 And [he] made for home—all the way across the harbour ice to his own stage head. 1977 *Evening Telegram* 18 Feb, p. 4 [caption] these two children slide on the harbor ice of Colinet.

harbour man: inhabitant of a coastal settlement; BAYMAN, OUT-HARBOUR: *out-harbour man*.

[c1897] 1965 PEACOCK (ed) iii, 976 "The Spring of '97": 'Twas bad enough till death it came, / Made our condition worse, / For one of our brave harbour men, / Died on the twenty-first.

harbour price: price paid for fish by a local merchant; BAY PRICE.

P 54–63 The harbor price or current price of codfish, to be paid at a particular place and time to a fishermen-producer. . .has long had a customary formula for its calculation, which, on proof of the custom, is given legal force in the Newfoundland courts.

harbour seal: common seal, inhabiting Atlantic coastal waters (*Phoca vitulina*); BAY SEAL.

[1766] 1971 BANKS 145 The Fishermen. . .divide them into five sorts which they call Square Phipper Hooded Seal Heart or houke Bedlamer & harbour seal which Last stays in the Countrey all the year & is the Common in Europe the *Phoca Vitulina* of Linnaeus. 1832 MCGREGOR i, 107 There are apparently five or six varieties of seals that frequent the coasts of America, but with the exception of the harbour seal (phoca vitulina), which does not seem to be migratory, it is probable that age and accident produce the difference in size, shape, and colour. 1871 HOWLEY *MS Reminiscences* 11 Bay or harbour seals are quite common in this quiet place. 1895 TOCQUE 195 The harbor seal frequent the harbors of Newfoundland summer and winter. 1947 TANNER 426–7 The next most important is the small bay seal or harbour seal, the Eskimo's *kasigiak*, it lives apart and is to be met with in the same places at all seasons. Of all seals this one is the most adaptable to different environments.

harbour tom-cod: small immature cod-fish, esp in prov phr *foolish as a* ~ ; see also TOM COD.

P 108–63 'He has as much brains as a harbour tom cod.' P 148–65 He's as foolish as a harbour tom cod.

hard a For combs. in sense 4: *O Sup*[2] ~ a 22: ~ bread (1781–); *Cent* hard-dried; *OED* ~ tack (1841–), *DAE* (1836–). Cp SOFT.

1 Of cod-fish, cured by drying in the sun after salting; **hard-dried**.

1909 BROWNE 68 Labrador fish is not cured 'hard,' such as the catch on the Newfoundland coast; hence the great difference in the price received in foreign markets.

2 Of a stretch of ice, too thick and solid for a vessel to penetrate.

1924 ENGLAND 78, 108 'Wonnerful 'ummocky ice, Cap'n,' judged the master watch. 'But not too 'ard,' averred the Old Man, putting his gold-rimmed glasses into their case. . . 'The very instant we broke that last key pan, it ahl raftered together, but we got through. . . I had me squares'ls on her, an' evverythin' topped aloft, an' jammed through a hard knot.'

3 Of a man, hardy.

1906 DUNCAN 86 Ruddy Cove called Eli Zitt a 'hard' man. In Newfoundland, that means 'hardy'—not 'bad.'

4 Comb **hard afrore**: see FRORE.

hard berry: bearberry (*Arctostaphylos Uva-ursi*) (1898 *J A Folklore* xi, 273).

hard biscuit: see **hard bread**.

1907 *Our Country* 24 May, p. 15 The work carried on includes the baking of hard biscuit, fancy biscuits of different varieties, and soft cakes. 1933 GREENE 117 Now, while drinking your tea and soaking your 'hard biscuit' in it to save your teeth. . .

hard bread [hæːɹd 'brɛd]: thick, oval-shaped coarse biscuit, baked without salt and kiln-dried; ship-biscuit.

[1856] P 265²–75 Breakfast—hard bread and molasses. 1905 DUNCAN 116 We had disposed of Aunt Ruth's watered fish and soaked hard-bread. 1924 ENGLAND 55 Some [sealers] had died while crawling; others still clutched hard bread in their frozen hands. [1931] 1981 *Evening Telegram* 13 July, p. 6 Dealers and purchasers of hard bread. . .complain of present prices [of] three dollars a half-bag. T 141/68–65² But all you get in your scrawn bag clear o' that, clear o' hard bread, would be rolled oats. 1975 *Evening Telegram* 28 June, p. 16 If you were flahoola with the money you could buy a slice of baloney there, and a cake of hardbread all for five cents.

hard-dried, ~ dry: thoroughly dried after salting so that the cod-fish has a firm texture suitable for export to warmer countries.

1937 *Seafisheries of Nfld* 47 Light Salted, Hard Dry Fish, known as Shore Fish. . . The Hard Dry Shore fish must be sound with an even surface, thoroughly clean, not showing salt, well split and thoroughly hard dry. 1977 BURSEY 152 We caught a fine lot of fish and made it 'Hard Dried' to prepare it for the Brazil Market.

hard hat [hæːɹd 'hæt, hæːɹd 'æt]: top-hat.

T 31/5–64 Rich old people used to have [a] big hard hat on. T 168/71–65 [The Doctor in the mummers' play] had a clawed hammer coat on, an' a hard hat.

hard-tack [hæːɹd 'tæk, 'hæːɹd tæk, 'haːɹd tak]: see **hard bread** above.

1869 HOWLEY *MS Reminiscences* 26 Their diet consisted of hard tack and spruce beer to drink.

[1894–1929] 1960 BURKE (ed White) 28 "Full Loads to the Sealers": In stormy or sunshiny weather, / The sealer must face the wild floe / With a cake of hard tack in his jumper, / And three fathoms for hauling his tow. 1941 WITHINGTON 140–1 Always on Sunday morning we had brewis, a national dish of hardtack soaked in water overnight, boiled down in the morning with fish added, and served with butter. 1977 RUSSELL 30–1 One bit of good news give us hope. Aunt Polly told us that Lige had plenty of hard tack with him, but no tobaccy.

hard ticket [ˌhæːɹd 'tikɪt, ˌhæːɹd 'tɪkɪt, 'æːɹd ˌtɪkɪt]: intractable person; hard case.

T 74/5–64 They were two old Irishmen, you know, two old hard tickets. T 194/6–65 We knows just what we're up 'longside of—one o' the hardest tickets that's ever come to Millertown. C 71–101 Anyone who was constantly getting into trouble, fighting frequently, or playing practical jokes was referred to as a 'ard ticket.

hardy a Cp *OED* ~ 4, *Kilkenny Lexicon* 'a hardy child, pig.' Young and active.

[1764] 1976 HEAD 173 The Families that remain During Winter being Store-Keepers, contain about fifty People in Each of Hardy Men without either a woman or child among them; While Men Women and Children are got into the Woods where they reside in little Hutts untill Seasonable Weather. 1937 DEVINE 46 [A spalpeen is] a hardy boy, satisfied to do chores for small pay or his meals. P 99–69 A pucklin is a hardy boy making his first voyage to the fisheries. P 108–70 When wild dogs get a couple of months old, they gets hardy then. You will never catch them. They gets saucy. They stay hardy then. Before then, they were only pups. 1975 GUY 3 For coarse language of any sort was frowned upon greatly. I was a hardy boy before I would risk a 'heck' or 'darn' within parental earshot.

hare n *EDD* ~ sb² 1 Ir for sense 1.

1 The last sheaf of harvest.

1974 MANNION 113 Both in Avalon and Miramichi the last sheaf of harvest was referred to as the 'hare' or 'rabbit,' but there were no end-of-harvest Irish ceremonies within living memory. In Irish folk-tradition, the last handful of standing corn in a field was twisted into a three-stranded plait and the reapers threw their sickles at it until it was severed. The triumphant slayer was then feted and made guest of honour at the harvest supper, where the last sheaf (*cailleach* or 'hare') would be waked, like a corpse. It was unusual in Miramichi and Avalon for a reaper to say 'we'll get the hare out of it to-day' to hasten the last day's reaping.

2 Comb **hare-net**: a device for snaring rabbits.

[1785] 1792 CARTWRIGHT iii, 72 In the evening I placed a hare-net across this end of Slink Point, and had it beat by two of the boys and three dogs, but found nothing.

hare rabbit: arctic hare (*Lepus arcticus*).

T 868–70 And the other kind we call the hare rabbit, they was twice as big as the normal ones.

hare's-ears, hazures: a pair of pointed rocks protruding above the surface of the water; twin peaks (of a hill).

[1773] 1971 SEARY 224 Two rocks, known as Hare's

Ears, 40 feet high, lie close eastward of [Branch] head. 1909 *Nfld Qtly* Mar, p. 3 Now at our Ferryland, we have an excellent specimen of a *Forillon*, in the well known rock called *The Hazures*. 1951 *Nfld & Lab Pilot* i, 159 Two smaller peaks, about 350 feet high, in the southern part of the island are known as Hare's ears. Q 67–84 Hasures [is the name given to] a rock split in the middle looking like hare's ears. 1971 SEARY 87 Hare's Ears. . .is a descriptive which occurs in at least seven localities in Newfoundland to describe two steep, adjacent, pinnacle-like rocks, standing offshore.

harp n   *OED* ~ sb¹ 7: harp-seal (1784–), *DC* ~ (seal) (Nfld: 1771–) for sense 1 and cpd in sense 3; *EDD* sb¹ 2 Ir, PARTRIDGE 376, cp *OED* sb¹ 4 'Irish coins bearing figure of a harp' obs (1542–1606) for sense 2.

1 Migratory seal of northern waters, hunted for its fur and oil; Greenland seal (*Phoca groenlandica*). See also **harp-seal** below.

[1771] 1792 CARTWRIGHT i, 89 I had the fat of two harps melted, which produced eighteen gallons of oil. [1802] 1916 MURPHY 2–3 Our dependence rests wholly upon Harps and Bedlamers, which are driven by winds and ice from the northeast seas. 1846 TOCQUE 189 The kind most plentiful, and which pass along the coast of Newfoundland with the ice, are the harps or half-moon seals. 1924 ENGLAND 101 'Harps' are so called because they have a patch of brown hair on the shoulders roughly resembling a harp. T 84–64 What we calls a turner seal is turnin' from a bellamer to a harp. Now next year he'll be a harp, a breedin' seal. T 210/11–65 When they'll be four year old in the spring, that winter they're a harp; there's plain harp on their back.

2 Phr *heads and/or harps*: head or tail, a call in the game of tossing coins or buttons.

T 75/6–64 They'd put all the buttons on his hand an' he'd toss them in height. And the buttons fall on the ground, heads and harps. If the button was front up, it'd be a head; 'twas back up, 'twould be a harp. P 245–74 ~ The reverse side of a coin, the head of which bears the monarch's likeness. As children we used to toss a coin to decide who would have first chance at anything and call out 'Heads or harps?'

3 Comb **harp-ice**: ice-floe on which the migratory Greenland seal whelps; see also ICE.

1933 GREENE 206 'Sheer moonlight madness fer April-Fool's Day I calls it—' says the Loquacious One—'lavin' d'at fine Harp Ice in de sout' ter go ter de likes o' d'is!'

harp-patch: a concentration of Greenland seals on the ice-floes; PATCH.

1933 GREENE 177 As regards the Patches as a whole: 'Ye may say'—says Zeb—'dat arl Harp-patches on Field-ice is de same as de next wan. Only, wan will contain t'ousands, an' de udder wan hunnerds-o'-t'ousands.'

harp-seal or **heart-** ~ : see sense 1 above.

[1766] 1971 BANKS 145 The Heart or Possibly Harp Seal is markd over the Shoulders with a brown figure rudely resembling a harp which they Call the Saddle. 1793 PENNANT ii, 280 Inhabits Greenland and Newfoundland [etc]; is the most valuable kind; the skin the

thickest and best, and its produce of oil the greatest: grows to the length of nine feet. Our Fishers call this the *Harp*, or *Heart Seal*. 1852 ARCHIBALD 4 The principal species captured are the hood and harp seal. The bulk of the catch consists of the young hood and harp in nearly equal proportions. The best and most productive seal taken is the young harp. [c1900] 1978 *RLS* 8, p. 24 ~ So called from a peculiar black mark on back of mature seal, resembling a harp in shape. 1981 *Evening Telegram* 10 Mar, p. 2 A large herd of harp seals has been spotted off the Labrador coast.

harper n   Cp *NID* harp¹ 5 'Irish person'; *O Sup²* harp 1 f (1904–). An Irish Roman Catholic.

C 70–18 I had asked him how did the old people [c1890] feel towards Catholics. His reply was: 'There was never no Catholics in Sandy Cove, but I can remember when my mother used to tell me not to go down on the beach, 'fraid the Harpers will come after ya.'

harrat n   Cp ARET. Rough-legged hawk (*Buteo lagopus*) (1976 *Avifaunal Survey* 119).

harrish* v   ['harɪʃ], i.e. harass *EDD* ~ v; JOYCE 96. To torment, pester, annoy.

P 126–67 Don't harrish me. Q 71–7 You're doing your best to harrish me, aren't you? C 73–128 I'm fair harrished. P 188–77 You'll harrish the heart out o' me if you keep on.

harry n   Cp SEARY 254 '. . .southeast of Poole [Dorset]. . .are two chalk rocks, Old Harry and Old Harry's Wife.' A barely submerged rock on which the sea breaks; SUNKER.

[1675] 1971 SEARY 253 Old Harry (Rock). 1953 *Nfld & Lab Pilot* ii, 122 Middle rock, with a depth of 3 fathoms over it, and Kelp rock with a depth of 2½ over it, lie between Old Harry and Young Harry. The sea breaks on all these dangers. T 70/1–64 You hear the skiff goin' ashore and the oars rattlin'. By an' by it would all go away to nothing. I suppose [they were] comin' to let 'em know they were gone. But. . .I often hear her sayin' that—she was a young woman then—she heared the old people sayin'—'twas a voice come to the door that evenin' they were lost and sung out, a voice sung out 'We're all lost on the harries this evenin''—that's breakin' ground off Bonavist Bay, way off about thirty miles in the ocean. P 75–70 ~ General term for a rock along coast. [The waves are] 'breakin' on the harry.'

hart See HURT.

hartle n   *OED* hurtle sb² obs, rare (1597, 1630); cp *EDD* hurtleberry So D. A variety of blueberry; HURT.

1682 COLLINS 99 [Fruits in Newfoundland] As Vines. . .Strawberries, Hartles, Cherries, Wild Pease. . .

hat n   *EDD* ~ sb² Bk Ha Nfld; *MED* 2 (esp c1410 quot). Esp phr *hat of woods*, etc: a clump of woods (on a hill or barren); TUCK².

1866 WILSON 340 A hat of woods meant a small, isolated patch of woods in a barren; a droke of woods
meant a piece of wood, whether large or small, on the
sides of two opposite hills, with a valley between them.
1895 *J A Folklore* viii, 29 A hat of trees means a clump
of trees. [c1900] 1978 *RLS* 8, 23 ~ Small island or
patch of low green wood. 1937 DEVINE 26 ~ A low
growth of trees on the top of a small hill. 1971 SEARY
224 Hat Pond.

hatch v *EDD* ~ v[2] Ha IW for sense 1; *OED* v[3]
obs (1581, 1608), *NID* ~[2] Brit dial for sense 2.
    1 To catch; to become entangled; to tear.
1920 WALDO 157 If something 'hatches' in your
'glutch,' it catches in your throat. 1937 DEVINE 26 ~ to
be caught by some obstruction when a net, rope or line
is being hauled. T 80/3–64 Then he made a gert sail,
made un here in the winter, an' had un barked. An' he
carried he down an' he spread he out on the bottom [of
the water], moored he out first. Then he put his trap
down an' never hatched [on the rocks] afterwards.
T 141/64–65[2] O' course anybody wasn't used to a gun
line, see, perhaps, he'd go to haul her up, look, an' the
gun line hatched up around your foot or something.
    2 To fasten (a door) with a 'hapse' (1937
DEVINE 26).

hatchet n Comb **hatchet-face**, ~ **bill**: the common puffin (*Fratercula arctica arctica*).
1959 MCATEE 40 Hatchet-bill,
hatchet face Common Puffin (The beak is laterally
compressed). P 38–77 Puffin is a bird sometimes called
hatchet face.

haul v Cp *OED* ~ 1; *EDD* 1 esp Gl Do So;
DAE 1; *NID* 2 a with naut use influencing nearly
all senses; cp P KEMP *Oxford Companion to Ships
and the Sea* (1976), p. 378 *Haul* 'the seaman's
word to pull'; *DC* haul-off for cpd (b) in sense 8.
Cp HEAVE.
    1 To draw (a seine, caplin-net, etc) through
the water so as to enclose fish for capture; to pull
up fish (or seals) in a net or on a line to the surface; cp OVERHAUL.
[1699] 1895 PROWSE 233 No person shall cast anchor
or do anything to hinder the haling of sayns in the
accustomed baiting places. [1775] ibid 342 Codd Seans
we deem a great nuizance as by them we destroy a
great quantity of small fish, which after being inclosed
in the sean (and not worth the attention of the person
who hauls them) are left to rot. [1777] 1792
CARTWRIGHT ii, 248 I went in a skiff with two hands,
to the head of this bay to look at a pond, and see if it
were practicable to get a skiff into it, to haul for trouts.
1792 ibid *Gloss* i, xi Such nets as are constantly moored
in the water are hauled by going out to them in a boat,
laying hold of one end, and hauling the boat along the
head-rope to the other end, taking the fish out into
the boat; the meshes being made large enough for the
fish to entangle themselves in them. A seine is hauled,
by shooting it, by degrees, out of a boat into the water,
and hauling it on shore again by the two ends. [1818]
1974 NEARY & O'FLAHERTY (eds) 67 Landergan was

summoned to appear before them, and being found in
the act of hauling a little fish for the present use of the
family, he apologized. [1856] 1975 WHITELEY 117 This
day got eleven salmon and made up fifty seals—a few
capelin hauled at Salmon Bay. 1896 HOWLEY *MS
Reminiscences* 15 [They] went off in the boat to amuse
themselves hauling lobster pots. 1902 *Nfld Qtly* Sep, p.
26 I sat down to rest on a mossy bank that overlooked
the sea and to watch the fishermen hauling their traps
while others came or went to the fishing ground. 1918
FPU (Twillingate) Minutes 21 Mar The majority of
members were in favour stopping work from dawning
until dark hauling nets and also from dark Saturday
until Monday morning dawning cutting out Sundays
work hauling nets. 1936 SMITH 47 We hauled that trap
at 4 p.m., and had a boat-load of fish. 1955 DOYLE (ed)
63 "The Banks of Newfoundland": It's early every
morning our cook all up and bawls, / Get up and eat
your breakfast, b'ys, and then go haul your trawls.
1973 GOUDIE 83 The first of June came and the men
started setting the seal nets. They had to go about
fifteen miles twice a week to haul the nets. 1975
Evening Telegram 21 June, p. 2 The traps were not
hauled yesterday and [the plant does not expect] to
purchase trap fish until Monday. 1977 BUTLER 13 I
would haul the trawls and Billy would sit on the after
thwart to bait the hooks as I passed them back.
    2 To drag a quantity of seal 'pelts' over the ice
to vessel, using a 'hauling-rope'; TOW v.
1845 *Fraser's Magazine* xxxii, 740 Their talk is of
seals and cod-fish, of *hauling* and *jigging*; and their jargon generally betrays an Irish origin. 1855 WHITE *MS
Journal* 19 Mar Spyed some men from vessels on lee
Bow hauling Seals. 1924 ENGLAND 149 But a iceberg
come alang, an' we hauled lots o' tows to that. The
wind come up, an' the berg floated to land, an' we got
'em ahl. 1976 CASHIN 88 We continued working at the
seals on the ice, killing and hauling, then loading.
    3 To pull or drag fire-wood by sled in winter.
[1771] 1792 CARTWRIGHT i, 95 They afterwards
assisted my people to haul wood home upon their sled.
1949 FITZGERALD 93 Hauling. When snow paths permit, firewood is brought in by dog team and horse slide
from the near-by woods. 1964 BLONDAHL (ed) 16
"Tickle Cove Pond": The hard and the easy we take as
it comes, / And when ponds freeze over we shorten our
runs. / To hurry my haulin', the spring comin' on, /
Near lost me my mare on the Tickle Cove Pond.
    4 To travel by sled.
[1772] 1792 CARTWRIGHT i, 218 It was very good
hauling down, but on my return the dogs and sled
broke in several times. [1811] 1915 HOWLEY 83 The
day proved pleasant and mild, and hauling good.
    5 To pull a house (on rollers); to float a dwell-
ing (on empty oil-barrels); LANCH v.
P 245–74 All we did was haul houses [after the 1929
tidal wave]. 1976 MATTHEWS 113 'Well,' he says, 'she's
[i.e. the house] going to be hard to haul.' I says, 'Hard
to haul? What do you mean by that?' 'Well,' he says,
'you got to shift from Grande Terre.' 1979 TIZZARD
208 George was to haul his house to his father-in-law's
property on Ings' Point, and when the time came I
helped haul that house.
    6 To extract a tooth.

1920 WALDO 57 The first woman had a 'bad stummick'; the second wanted 'turble bad' to have her tooth
'hauled.' 1950 HERBERT 281 Our Captain told us that
she had had half a dozen men all looking for a doctor
to 'haul' a tooth (they talk of 'hauling' a tooth as they
do of 'hauling' a trawl). 1974 GREEN 86 'Will you haul
a tooth, m'am?' Which was his indigenous way of asking if he could please have a tooth extracted!

7 Phr *haul the cod off*: to deceive, fool, trick.
1924 ENGLAND 290 Oh, ain't narr gunner can haul
the cod off *me*!

the devil haul you: a mild imprecation.
[c1904] 1960 BURKE (ed White) 23 "Kelligrews Soiree": Oh! says I, the devil haul ye / And your Kelligrews Soiree. P 138–72 A familiar expression is the
devil haul ya. This is said when they want to say, 'it's
too *bad* about you.'

haul home (something): to close the opening of
a fish-net; cp BRING TO.
1937 DEVINE 22 In hauling home the linnet, so as to
lose no fish, the frequent orders of the skipper would
be heard: 'Pull on (or easy on) the *foots*.'

haul in: (a) of a vessel, to tie up at a wharf; (b)
to arrest a person.
1936 SMITH 43 We hauled in to Munn's wharf and
began discharging fish and oil. P 245–75 The Mountie
hauled him in and he bawled like a baby.

haul on: of a vessel, to go forward (1925 *Dial
Notes* v, 333).

haul together: to work together, cooperate.
P 80–63 Brothers should haul together.

haul up: to take a boat or vessel out of the
water for the winter; hence the derived cpd in
the final quot.
[1918–19] GORDON 16 A great crowd had gathered
in to haul up the Company's schooner *Thistle*. This is
always the first of our hauls, and everybody turns out
to assist. 1936 SMITH 34 A great many people visited
Edwards Harbour for the express purpose of seeing
these boats hauled up. T 29–64 I ran the ferry that fall,
and when she was hauled up she was never lanched no
more. P 148–73 This place is for boat haul-up.

8 Cpd **haul hand**: see **haul-on** below.
P 127–73 ~s [are] knitted gloves, without tops in the
fingers.

haul-off: (a) rope forming part of the 'collar'
or mooring of a boat by which the craft is kept in
station off the wharf; (b) the hauling of logs in
winter to the shores of a lake or river for floating
to the mill in spring.
1955 *Western Star* 12 Mar The pulpwood haul-off, in
the Deer Lake jurisdiction. . .has now reached an
interesting stage, and it is beginning to look as though
very little wood will be left to haul at the end of the
present month.[*DC*] T 191–65 They'd have the boats,
the small boats, on what they call the haul-off. They'd
pull the boat off an' they'd pull it in, just slip in the
block [i.e. pulley] you know. 1973 WADEL 5 The 'haul-
off' involved the hauling of the pulp wood along frozen
ground to rivers and other collecting places; this took
place from early January to early or mid-March.
P 135–74 ~ A rope used to haul the boat off from the
wharf when it is supposed to be anchored. The rope

goes from the wharf to an anchor and works on the
same principle as a pulley.

haul-on: knitted woollen glove covering palm,
with opening for the fingers to protrude, used in
handling fishing-lines; HANDY-JAN.
1971 NOSEWORTHY 211 ~ a part of a glove, with or
without a thumb, but never any fingers. The palms are
padded to keep the lines from cutting them.

haul-tub: half-barrel on wooden runners.
M 71–103 The salter using a dip net transferred the
fish from the puncheon tub to the haul tub. This was
merely a half barrel on wooden runners and could be
easily hauled by an attached rope over the lungers, or
longers, of the stage floor.

haul-up (line/rope): rope used to raise a cod-
trap to the surface; UP av: UPHAUL.
1971 NOSEWORTHY 211 Haulups. Ropes used to
haul up nets. P 9–73 The trap is made and set, now
comes the hauling of it for the first time. The haul up
lines are fastened to the top and bottom, two, one on
each side of the doorway. The boat comes up to the
trap and the second hand (mate) stands by with the
boathook. P 10–76 ~ One of the ropes used to haul a
codtrap. Also called a V-rope, it is fastened to one of
the corners of the trap and is hauled diagonally. 1979
Evening Telegram 20 Aug, p. 3 [He] says the whales
usually get tangled in the haul-up ropes on the nets.

haul n *OED* ~ 1, 2 (1670–; 1854–) for sense 1.
Cp HAUL v.

1 The act of drawing a net through the water
so as to enclose fish for capture; the pulling of a
catch of netted fish to the surface; the quantity of
fish so taken; cp PUT(T).
[1775] 1792 CARTWRIGHT ii, 92 We had fish for the
haul this morning, and I never saw so fine a place for a
cod-sein; the bottom being smooth, white sand, with
an extensive beach of the same. 1849 [FEILD] 40 The
quantity [of herring] taken at one haul is sometimes
prodigious—a hundred barrels at a time. 1861 DE
BOILIEU 30 The fish being all landed, the operation of
salting commences, and no one ever thinks of leaving
off work until the whole haul of fish is cleared and
salted in bulk. 1874 *Maritime Mo* iii, 549 He had set
some herring nets the day previous: outside the
'heads,' and from certain signs and tokens, he felt confident that he would obtain a fine 'haul' of herrings.
[1929] 1979 *Evening Telegram* 9 July, p. 11 There is a
good sign of fish with trawls between Fortune and Carmel and traps are averaging five quintals a haul. P 9–73
At an average of ten barrels per haul, three hauls a
day, thirty barrels [of cod] per day. A forty or fifty
quintal haul is no guarantee of that much next time.
Next time could perhaps be a water haul, that is no fish
at all. 1975 *Evening Telegram* 3 July, p. 4 During the
first days of the [salmon-fishing season] the men were
taking in good hauls, but this was really the last of the
salmon run. 1977 BURSEY 115 Our first great haul
came as the result of that anchor being dropped from
our boat. When Charlie threw it over it frightened a
school of salmon that happened to be swimming by and
they darted in their fright right into our net.

2 A quantity of seal pelts pulled over the ice

and raised aboard the vessel; TOW[2]; the catch of seals taken.

1842 PANL GN 2/2 (May), p. 45 A haul of seals which is a circumstance of frequent occurrence within this Bay in. . .March. . . 1866 WILSON 285 Sometimes the drift-ice will come into the harbors with thousands of seals, when men, women, and children will go to get a haul. 1924 ENGLAND 237 Sometimes bloody gert 'auls two hundred and fifty viddum [fathom] lang on a gurdy [are hoisted aboard]. 1937 DEVINE 42 I heard an old timer say: 'The spring of the big haul of seals, you couldn't hear your ears in church with *scroopy* boots.' 1949 *Evening Telegram* 12 Feb, p. 3 With the date of the annual sailing for the icefields drawing near, it is interesting to recall that the year 1843 was known as the Spring of the Big Haul. In that year there were 40,000 seals killed and landed by shoremen in Bonavista Bay. They made wages as high as £120 and women made £40.

3 Phr *a haul of wood*: a co-operative gathering of fuel for a clergyman or school.

1828 *Newfoundlander* 5 Mar [The editor notes] the alacrity and promptitude manifested by all classes of this community, at the late appeal made to them, by the Committee for conducting the affairs of the *Orphan Asylum School*, for a Haul of Wood, in aid of its funds. . . Some of the loads of wood were, certainly, the largest ever seen in this town, at any haul. . . The haul of wood. . .will be sold, on Saturday next, at 12 o'clock. 1866 WILSON 215 The preacher, some time during winter, would have a 'haul of wood,' when all the men in the village would turn out, double man the slides, and take four dogs to each slide, and bring, in one day, wood enough for the whole year.

hauler n Member of a sealing crew assigned to drag seal 'pelts' across the ice to vessel.

1860–1 *Journ of Assembly* Appendix, p. 533 . . .never to send my men after old seals before ten o'clock in the forenoon; even at that hour they were wary enough for the sharpest shooters, haulers would not be allowed to go within a considerable distance of the gunners.

hauling vbl n Cp *DAE* frolic 2 for hauling frolic; *EDD* hauling-home Ir, JOYCE 273.

1 The activity of pulling or dragging fire-wood by sled in winter.

1863 LIND *MS Diary* 24 Mar Cold, but fine, no hauling across the ice.

2 Attrib, comb **hauling chantey**: working song. Cp WARPING CHANTEY.

1927 *Christmas Messenger* i (1), 29 A great favourite with Newfoundland sailors was the song "Across the Western Ocean". It was a great hauling chantey.

hauling frolic: the co-operative gathering of firewood for one person in turn, followed by food and entertainment.

C 63–1 A frolic is an occasion for work and celebration. Usually about 6 to 10 men go into the woods for a day cutting wood. This would be called a 'cutting frolic.' Later on, the wood is hauled out with horses and is given to one particular man in the group. This would

be called the 'hauling frolic.' Each of these frolics is followed up at night by a 'get together' at the home of the man who received the wood. This would be repeated for each member of the group until all had their supply of wood.

hauling home: bringing home of the bride to husband's house after the wedding; celebration of the occasion.

1887 *Colonist Christmas No* 2 The near friends of the couple [just married], and a few of the more privileged neighbors, will assemble again in a few days, when what is called the 'hauling home' takes place—that is, the installation of the bride in her new home, when, of course, a dance must take place. C 71–128 ~ The last of several nights (and days) on which a wedding feast and celebrations are held.

hauling line: length of rope fastened to a 'komatik' with which the driver assists the dogs to pull. Cp **hauling-rope** (b) below.

P 9–73 I turned my komatik around, rested its heel against a tree root, straightened out my hauling line.

hauling-rope: (a) a short length of rope, carried coiled over the shoulder, and used by sealers to drag seal pelts over the ice; TOW v: TOW LINE, ~ ROPE; (b) a stout line fastened to a sled and used by driver to pull, or assist in pulling, a heavy load; WOODS ROPE.

1842 JUKES i, 260 Several yards of strong cord were also selected, which were prepared with a noose, for a 'hauling rope' [for hauling seal pelts]. 1866 WILSON 214–15 The catamaran was made like a hand-sled. To these carriages two dogs were harnessed in tandem, and a man on the left side, to guide the carriage and its load with his right arm, while a 'hauling rope' would pass over his left shoulder, with which he would assist the dogs in dragging their burden. Ibid 282 The pelt of the white-coat will weigh about fifty pounds; and when the hunter has taken three pelts, it is a load; which he ties in his hauling-rope, and then returns to the vessel. 1924 ENGLAND 233 De time is drawin' near me b'ys, / De narthern floe to face, / So we must get out 'aulin' rope, / De whitecoats fer to lace! T 84–64 I takes off my haulin' rope an' I throws that down, an' I puts down my nunny bag. I got it all stowed away. C 70–15 The men fastened a rope called a hauling rope to the front or forward beam of the catamaran and guided the load of wood with one stick of wood jutting out from the other sticks and called a steering stick. Sometimes a boy would help his father by using a second hauling rope fastened to the after beam. 1976 CASHIN 85 We had been issued with our gaffs and hauling ropes and were all ready to take to the frozen pans immediately we would strike the seals.

hauling (down) song: chantey; HEAVE v: HEAVE-UP SONG.

C 71–5 A group of about 25 to 30 men and school-boys would work together pulling and singing a hauling-down song: 'Haul on the bowline; / The bugger must come this time; / Haul on the bowline; / Haul, boys, haul.'

hawk n Cp *OED* ~ sb[2] 'a kind of fish-trap' obs (1669–1705) for senses 1, 2; cp *OED* sb[1] 3 fig for sense 3; hawkbill 2 [pliers with curved nose] for sense 4.

1 A net set at an angle to lead salmon into the centre of the meshes.

P 243–55 ~ That part of a [salmon] net which is set so as to form a V-shape. T 80/3–64 You'll put a bottom in this hawk end, and what salmon is disturbed up in the hawk end'll mesh down in this bottom, and it's the means o' gettin' a lot more salmon than you would otherwise with a straight net. And they haves them now too with a hawk in the side. M 69–26 At one time it was common to have an hawk on the outside end of the [salmon] net to catch those salmon that detected the net's presence and swam along by it to escape. When the net was set with an hawk, it took the form or shape of the letter 'L,' but formed an angle of about 45°. 1979 TIZZARD 310 When the net was set in the water about four or five fathoms was turned at a right angle to the net making the 'auk' of the net. If the salmon saw the net and cruised along by it he would surely be caught by the 'auk.'

2 A long fence arranged to lead deer into a central enclosure or trap; WING n: WING FENCE.

[1785] 1792 CARTWRIGHT iii, 92 Tilsed finished the hawks of the deer-pound, then covered the shed with loose boards.

3 An expert player (of the game of marbles).

T 458–67[1] There were all kinds of terms used playing alleys. For instance if, say, in alleys, he hawked me—that meant he won all the alleys. . . 'Don't play with him—he's a hawk.'

4 Comb **hawk-door**: entrance to a deer enclosure.

[1785] 1792 CARTWRIGHT iii, 91 Tilsed began the hawk-doors for the deer-pound.

hawk-end: see sense 1 above.

hawk-fence: see sense 2 above.

[1770] 1792 CARTWRIGHT i, 8–9 From their house, which is always situated by the side of the river, they erect two high, and very strong fences, parallel to each other, forming a narrow lane of some length, and stretching into the country. From the farther end of each, they extend two very long wing-fences, the extremities of which are from one mile to two, or more, asunder. The deer travel in small companies, few of them exceeding a dozen head, and when they meet with these hawk, or wing-fences, they walk along them, until they are insensibly drawn into the pound, as partridges are into a tunnel net.

hawksbill: part of a cutting tool used by a cooper.

T 90–64 The croze was a piece of metal and in that piece of metal was two cutters, and behind these two there was another cutter—we call it the hawksbill. And that'd make a nice square cut.

hawk-setting: arrangement of a net to lead salmon into central mesh; see sense 1 above.

M 69–26 The introduction of the nylon net has done away with this old-fashioned hawk-setting.

hawk v To win all the marbles of an opponent; GUTTLE v.

T 458–67[1] There were all kinds of terms used playing

alleys. For instance if, say, in alleys, he hawked me—that meant he won all your alleys.

hawser n Cp *OED* ~ naut 'large rope. . .used in warping and mooring.'

1 A length of stout rope used ashore for various hauling operations.

1955 DOYLE (ed) 76 "Tickle Cove Pond": 'Lay hold William Oldford, lay hold William White, / Lay hold of the hawser and pull all your might. / Lay hold to the bowline and pull all you can' / And with that we brought Kit out of Tickle Cove Pond.

2 A line attached to the 'tucking-line' and 'horn' of a caplin-net to keep the horn in place (P 127–76).

hay n *OED* hay-house (1000–1611); *OED* pick sb[1] 4 b dial for hay-pick; *EDD* ~ sb[1] (35) hay-pook So D; cp *EDD* prong 2 s w cties, Nfld for hay-prong; cp *OED* hay sb[1] 5 hay-tea (1826) for hay-water.

Attrib, comb, cpd **hay cloth**: burlap or 'brin' bag used to carry hay from the field.

P 143–74 Hay from the meadows close to the stable was carried in hay-cloths (made of brin bags by the women in the winter) slung over the back.

hay barrack: see BARRACK.

hay frame: a flat rectangular wooden frame used for dragging hay from field to barn; travois.

1963 *Evening Telegram* 26 July, p. 6 . . .hauled in anything tighter than a hay frame. P 143–74 The hay from the meadows further in was brought on hay-frames (trellis-like structures drawn by horse and cart) to the stable.

hay garden: see GARDEN.

hay-house: a farm out-building for storing hay; the upper floor of a stable.

[1900] 1905 *Nfld Law Reports* 370 Award to build hay-house and cellar, not to be paid until erected, $800. T 12–64 The upper part of the stable where the hay is kept is known as the hay-house.

hay-net: fish-net adapted for use in gathering hay in the fields (P 243–57).

Q 71–8 ~ grass-net, usually a piece of discarded linnet with tie strings attached to the corners.

hay-pick: pitchfork.

1971 NOSEWORTHY 211 ~ A fork with two prongs for pitching hay.

hay-pook: hay piled in a heap for later transfer to barn; POOK n.

1868 HOWLEY *MS Reminiscences* 34 In the far distance some high hills or tolts are visible rising like gigantic hay pooks above the tree tops. [1886] LLOYD 126 'Hay-pook' (a small stack of hay). 1920 GRENFELL & SPALDING 165 I knew my cattle had plenty of food, but something forced me to go to the hay-pook. 1953 *Nfld & Lab Pilot* ii, 448 Farmer ledge. . .is. . .situated. . .westward of Haypook island. C 71–111 ~ a pile of hay.

hay-prong: pitchfork, PRONG n.

1899 ENGLISH 16 We smothered him with hay and tripped him with our hay prongs, every time he came near us. T 13/9–64 So he goes out in the porch and he gets a hay-prong.

hay-stack: in feature names, a hill or rock shaped like a hay-stack.

1951 *Nfld & Lab Pilot* i, 144 Haystack harbour is formed westward of a wedge-shaped peninsula, 256 feet high. 1970 PARSONS 65 The most conspicuous little island is the Haystack (Haypook), so named because it resembles a pile of hay.

hay-stick: one of the two sticks carried horizontally by two people supporting a load of hay; cp **hay-frame** above.

M 68–17 Hay sticks are simply two straight pieces of wood about 12'–16' long and ranging in diameter from two inches on smaller end to four or five inches on bigger end. They are used to carry hay to the barn with one person on each end of the sticks.

hay-water: a decoction of hay used for goats, sheep, etc; also fig.

P 210–69 He refers to weak tea as hay-water. C 70–21 All new mother goats were given 'haywater.' This was obtained by steeping a [bundle] of dry hay in a bucket of boiling water and very dark and aromatic it was. They were given this liquid for at least a month to help them get their strength back and to ensure lots of milk for the baby goats. The first smell of haywater in the kitchen was a signal to us children that new kids had arrived. Q 71–7 ~ boiled hay liquid. After the hay was boiled, the liquid was cooled and given to young animals in order to encourage them to acquire a taste for hay. Haywater was often given to orphan lambs. Q 71–8 To make haywater for weak or ailing animals was a common practice.

hazures* See HARE'S EARS.

he pro *EDD* ~ 3 'of inanimate objects. . .it'; his: he's, etc D. See also UN 'unstressed *he*.'

1 Of count nouns, it.

1861 *Harper's* xxii, 744 Where's the dish-cloth? No, that beant *he*, blockhead. 1895 *J A Folklore* viii, 32 Entering the court-house, I heard a witness asked to describe a cod-trap that was in dispute. He immediately replied, '*He* was about seventy-five fathoms long.' 1947 TANNER 730 I left he [the rifle]; put he [the kettle] on; he's [the wind] come right across. P 148–63 Man speaking of a killick: 'He can be used for a small boat.' T 1065–72 I learned he [a story] from that old man that's up there to Sally's Cove. C 75–135 They put a potato in the pickle and if he floats, then the pickle is good. 1977 *Nfld Qtly* Winter, p. 19 But the first hour we hauled in the log, and he registered three miles.

2 In the form *he's* [hiːz], i.e. 'his.'

1858 [LOWELL] ii, 256 'And this is *'e's* punt; and was n' there *fourteen went over the bow?* an' was n' that a visage [vision]?' 1913 *Christmas Chimes* 5 He'm 's 'ard 's nails an' tar'ble sot in 'e's ways. M 71–94 Man speaking of the moon: 'If he's on he's back like that, he's a bad moon, bad 'nough.' 1976 GUY 18 I gets me check, John get hees check, the two boys gets dere checks.

3 Cpd **he-moon**: the moon in its first quarter (P 80–63).

head n Cp *OED* ~ 15 (esp 1862 quot) for sense

1, 18 b 'end of a pier' (Co: 1758) for sense 2; for phr in sense 6, cp R BREATNACH *Studies in. . .Déise Irish* (1961), pp. 82–3 *ceann* 'head'. . . 'He's an extraordinary character,' *OED* 46 heads and points, *EDD* 2 (15) heads and tails, 2 (7) head or harp Ir and JOYCE 273; for combs. in sense 7, *Cent* headlight 2 rare, *OED* head-man 'in var contextual applications'; head-rope 3 (1883) influenced by *OED* 1 naut.

1 The innermost part of a bay, harbour or inlet; the land adjoining the inmost part of a bay; BOTTOM[1].

[1772] 1792 CARTWRIGHT i, 233 The head of Cutter Harbour is full of small coves. 1846 TOCQUE 112 Since that time he has been ranging about from the neighbourhood of St John's to the head of Conception Bay. 1870 HOWLEY *MS Reminiscences* 11 He was very kind, invited me to dinner and gave me much information about the bay up towards its head. 1901 *Christmas Review* 5 This will be more particularly the case in the settlements at the heads of the bays, which, before the advent of the railway, were considered 'up in the woods.' 1951 *Nfld & Lab Pilot* i, 382–3 Inner Part of Port au Port. . .Head Harbour.

2 The seaward end of a 'fishing-stage' or wharf; STAGE HEAD.

1792 CARTWRIGHT *Gloss* i, xv [Stouters are] very strong shores, which are placed round the head of a stage or wharf, to prevent them from being damaged by ships or boats. 1818 *Waterford Mirror* [Ire.] 26 Dec [He] took hold of Mullaly by the collar to shove him away from the head of the stage. 1842 JUKES i, 233–4 At the head of the stage are generally two or three poles, nailed horizontally against the upright posts, forming a rude ladder, up which it is necessary to climb from a boat in order to get on the stage. These are frequently the only landing-places in a harbour. Q 67–87 ~ the end of the wharf farthest from shore.

3 The top portion of a (seal or fish) net.

1792 CARTWRIGHT *Gloss* i, xiv The sealers lay hold of either [buoy], and by their means bring the head of the net to the boat. 1861 DE BOILIEU 85 The foot of [the seal net] is brought-to on a shallop's old rode, and the head on two fishing-lines with corks between. [1886] LLOYD 52 The head or upper side of the [seal] net [is] supported by floats. T 43/7–64 You hook the boat-hook into the head of the [cod] trap. Well, then you can dry [i.e. draw] away. P 9–73 One rope is right-hand twist, the other is left-hand. This is to keep the twine (netting) from being rolled around the heads (the top). 1975 BUTLER 58 These nets were set with one end attached to a stake driven in the crevice of the land and the other end attached to an anchor with corks to keep the head of the net afloat.

4 Funnel-shaped netting through which lobster enters trap; HEADING n.

T 250–66 This'd be the end head, and that'd be a head across there. Then they'd have a side head to go in through here, an' the lobsters'd crawl in through here, an' crawl in through there, an' when they get in they slide down to this parlour, you understand. P 40–78 Heads refers to the linnet used in a lobster pot which serves as an entrance for the lobster into the pot where hopefully he will not find his way back out through.

5 Part of spinning wheel.

T 50/2–64 They'd make the head. There had to be a band on that, a little band, a pulley we'll call it, an' a band on the big wheel—fishin' line. 1975 POCIUS 22–3 The portion of the spinning wheel that contained the spindle was commonly known as the 'head' of the wheel. A special type of head was used in many areas of Newfoundland.

6 Phr *(be) the head*, and var other collocations expressing admiration, surprise, wonder; first, hence chief; finest, greatest, etc.

1924 ENGLAND 249 'De spring dat So-and-so went first [chief engineer] in de *Kite*,' or 'De head [first] spring Such-a-one had de *Osprey*.' P 167–67 Well, boy, dat's de ederal! Well boy, that's the head of all. 1968 DILLON 144 Oh, 'tis the head place for the winter; ye'll be in out o' the cold. C 70–20 Whenever she does something unusual, surprising or strange, she is sure to say, 'Well, that's the head out, that is!' M 71–95 One would not be too long in Tilting before getting used to hearing: the head load of fish, the head thing, the head storm last night, etc. P 181–75 Old Tom got himself another woman. Well, that's the head yet!

heads and points: with the head of one by the feet of the next, and so on.

1842 JUKES i, 123 [They] lay down to sleep, there being just room enough for six people lying 'heads and points,' as the men called it, meaning heads and feet alternately. 1863 HIND [ii] 87 'Lie, man—why, at full length, to be sure,' was the reply. 'Did they? Where did they put their heads?' 'Why, they slept heads and points, to be sure.'

heads and tails: see *heads and points*.

1832 MCGREGOR i, 230 They are spread, heads and tails, . . .on hand-flakes, which are about breast high from the ground, and slightly constructed. 1938 *Nfld Qtly* Dec, p. 12 When he was a boy watching some workmen tearing up old boards on Steer's wharf, St John's, he saw a curious sight, a number of rats' skeletons were packed like sardines. Other rats perhaps had laid them thus 'heads and tails.'

heads or harps: heads or tails; the game of flipping a coin (P 148–64); see also HARP.

7 Attrib, comb, cpd **head dog**: the leading dog of a sled-team.

[1886] LLOYD 124 'Black' was the 'head dog' of the kammutik team, and as such was the more valued and valuable.

head lead: an open stretch of water in an ice-field; LEAD².

1925 *Dial Notes* v, 333 ~ An opening of water in front of a ship.

head-light: a light carried at the mast-head of a vessel (P 148–67).

head-man: hired supervisor of a fishing or trading station, esp on the Labrador Coast; man in charge of a fishing crew.

[1771] 1792 CARTWRIGHT i, 88 Being exceedingly weak and out of condition, and he a stout, robust young fellow, I should have had the worst of it, had not my head-man interfered. [1772] ibid i, 243 Coghlan's

head-man brought me some letters from England and Fogo. 1849 [FEILD] 18 It appeared that Archdeacon Wix had called at the Venison Islands seventeen years ago—or, as an old fisherman told me, 'the head man of St John's.' 1868 *Roy Geog Soc* xxxviii, 271 I visited the place in charge of Mr E A Goldston (formerly Mr Bright), with his head man 'Rennie Labbie,' who had been thirty-five years in the place. P 102–60 This rope was kept taut until the headman of the crew saw some seals showing their heads above water coming east. When they dived he had to estimate how long it would take for them to reach the net.

head-pin: small pin used in dress-making.

C 71–94 ~ A safety-pin or stick-pin.

head-rope: (a) rope attached to the upper part of a (seal or fish) net, often with floats or buoys to suspend the device in the water; (b) rope fastened to the bow of a small boat; painter (1971 NOSEWORTHY 211).

[1770] 1792 CARTWRIGHT i, 64 The whole consist of twelve shoal nets, of forty fathoms by two; and three stoppers, of a hundred and thirty fathoms by six. The latter are made fast at one end to White-Fox Island; and at the other, to capstans, which are fixed on this island; by these means, the headropes are either lowered to the bottom, or raised to the surface of the water, at pleasure; and, being placed about forty yards behind each other, form two pounds. [1802] 1895 PROWSE 419 The half worn small hawsers, which the boats have used in the summer fishery serve for foot ropes; new ratline is necessary for head ropes. 1819 PANL CS 1 28 May [They] were sent by me to put out a new fleet of Salmon Nets. . . On going the following Morning to haul them, they were cut from the Moorings and nothing but a small part of the Head Rope left. 1873 CARROLL 35 The net is made on an 8½ inch card; they require 20 lbs. of good cork cut up in pieces 7 inches long and 2½ inches in the middle and sharp at both ends, and placed one fathom apart on the head rope. 1924 ENGLAND 196 The nets are hung vertically, with corks on the 'head ropes' and with two long poles fastened to the upper corners of each net. T 43/8–64 Now, in makin' the trap, that would be brought to. Here's your head-rope here. Well, you take up your mesh here. 1976 *Evening Telegram* 17 June, p. 3 One fisherman reported that he had a 720-foot leader to his cod trap and there is nothing left [after the storm] but the corks and the headropes.

head v *OED* ~ 1 b (1800 quot). To remove the head of a cod-fish.

[1749] 1755 DOUGLASS i, 293 After the fish are headed, boned, split, and salted, the shoremen deliver one half the weight. 1861 *Harper's* xxii, 595 Woman, too, hath part in this business. . .her voice may be often heard singing gayly as she 'heads,' while the unceasing splash of the water beneath fitly chimes in unison. T 43/7–64 Well, in headin' a lot o' fish you find that your hand gets sore here, because it take on the bone after you crack the heads. 1977 BURSEY 188 We were still buying fresh fish weighed after being headed and split at one cent a pound and the fishermen were satisfied.

header n *OED* ~ 1 b (Nfld: 1623, 1809), *DC* (Nfld: 1777–) for sense 1.

1 Member of a fishing crew who removes the heads and entrails of cod-fish brought ashore to be dressed.

1623 WHITBOURNE 82 Skilfull headders, and splitters of fish. [1663] 1963 YONGE 57 Then a boy takes [the fish from the stage-head] and lays them on a table on the stage, on one side of which stands a header, who opens the belly, takes out the liver and twines off the head and guts. [1766] 1971 BANKS 134 The header. . .stands on the side of the table nearest to the water End whose business it is to gut the Fish & cut off its head which he does by Pressing the Back of the head with Both hands against the side of the table made sharp for the Purpose when both head and Guts fall through a hole in the Floor into the water. [1794] 1968 THOMAS 181 The process of Curing Fish is curious. The names of Header, Cutt Throat, Carver, Splitter and Salter are the appellations given to the Fishermen who perform the various offices in the stages or in the Rooms. 1863 HIND i, 304 The header detaches the liver, which he throws into a barrel placed near him, and with the same hand tears out the entrails; after which, with his left hand, he cuts off the fish's head. 1895 GRENFELL 59 The green fish are hove up on to the stage with pitchforks, seized by a woman who cuts off the head—'the header,' and passed on to one who opens the throat—'the throater.' 1918 TOWNSEND 85 I was particularly attracted by a pale salmon-colored waist worn by a woman in a big apron, the 'header' at a splitting table. T 43–64 The cut throater would dive over an' pick up two fish an' cut them an' pass 'em along to the header. He'd take the liver out and the gut an' the head off. And he was the busiest person, the header, because he had to keep two splitters goin'. T 175/7–65 He was cut-throater an' header, both of it. He worked that knife—there's a certain way you can cut the head off a fish that you won't cut a bone. M 68–11 A typical day at the fish plant would begin at 8:00 a.m. [when] the headers (who take the head off the fish, if it has been bought head-on), cutters (who cut the fish in packable-size pieces), skinners (who remove the skin before it can be packed) begin to get fish ready for the packers.

2 A low barricade at the edges of a wharf.

1976 *Evening Telegram* 18 Nov, p. 3 A header on a wharf. . .at Upper Gullies has been missing since early fall. The barricade. . .has been gone since early fall.

3 Comb **header's mitt,** ~ **palm**: fingerless mitten worn on one hand when removing the head of a cod-fish; HEADING-PALM, PALM².

Q 67–68 Header's palm [is] a cuff with no fingers. 1979 POCIUS 23 One type was constructed which covered only the palm of the hand. This mitt was used in the splitting of fish, and protected the palm from injury when it was pressed against the backbone of the fish during splitting. This covering for the palm was frequently called a 'header's mitt.'

heading vbl n *OED* ~ -knife b (n.d.).

In comb **heading-knife**: a knife used to cut the throat of a cod-fish, slit the belly open and remove the head; cp CUT-THROAT.

[1622] 1954 INNIS 58 [inventory] Heading and splitting knives.

heading-palm: a fingerless glove worn on one hand for protection when removing the head of a cod-fish; HEADER'S MITT, ~ PALM.

1924 ENGLAND 267 . . .while along the stages 'headers' and 'splitters' are busily at work with 'heading palms' on hands, with keen knives never still. T 26–64³ When he was goin' on the Labrador I'd have twelve, fifteen an' sixteen splittin' mitts, an' so many headin' palms, an' mitts an' stockin's an' everything for un. T 43/7–64 In headin' a lot o' fish you find that your hand gets sore here, because it [takes] on the bone after you crack the heads, you know, so they invented these heading palms. 1965 LEACH 5 The header, wearing a 'headin' palm' (pam), grasps the fish by the dangling head, pulls out the liver and throws it in the bucket. P 254–78 The headen pam [is] a mitten knit to cover the hand only to the first joints of fingers and thumb. The thumb and first finger protrude through individual holes but the other three fingers protrude through the one hole. Only one such mitten is worn (on the right hand if the user is right handed or on the left if left handed).

heading n See also HEAD n 4. Netting through which lobster enters trap.

P 241–68 The headin' is knit of cod-net twine. In the centre of the headin' is the wit [withe] which is the hole that the lobster crawls in through. There are also three of these.

health root See ELTROT.

heart n

1 The instep of a boot or shoe.

T 50/2–64 Cap knee boots were built good; good leather in 'em and pegged. Pegged, and under the heart there'd be some sort of steel sprigs. T 94/5–64 Anything happened to the shoe in the heart o' the foot or the heel, you could fix it on this [heelstick].

2 Comb **heart seal**: see HARP-SEAL.

heat n also **heat-up** *OED* ~ 4 d obs. With *a*, a warming.

1925 *Dial Notes* v, 333 A warming after cold. 'Go get a *hate* for yerself.' P 148–62 Are you coming in to get a heat-up?

heatable a Heated, angry.

T 194/7–65 And I said, 'Pray on, ma'am; you pray now that I won't heat.' I got that heatable. 'Pray that I won't heat.' And every word a oath, too, sir.

heath See BLACKBERRY.

heave v [(h)iːv, (h)eiv], past forms heaved, hev, hove, hoven [(h)ev, (h)ʌv, (h)ouv]. Of uncommon frequency in regional speech esp in naut senses and their extensions (cp HAUL v). Cp *OED* ~ 1 arch, b, 9 naut; *EDD* 1 for sense 1.

1 To lift, bring, move, throw, etc (freq with *down, into, on, up*).

1895 GRENFELL 59 The green fish are hove up on to the stage with pitchforks, seized by a woman who cuts off the head—the 'header,' and passed on to one who opens the throat—'the throater.' 1940 *Dal Rev* xx, 65 Do you want your tea hove up now? T 12–64 He hev the rock. T 50–64 Keep the water huv on them they keep wet, see. T 80/3–64 An' that's what I done single-handed one time: brought in a hundred an' fifteen barrels o' fish an' 'ove it up on deck. T 283/4–66 By an' by they come an' they 'ove down their turns an' they all sot down around. T 391–67 An' [a seal] 'ove his hinder scutters; he struck me in the back. P 245–67 It's just as well to have hoven (the fish) in the sea.

2 To turn (over).

[1777] 1792 CARTWRIGHT ii, 249 The water-horse was spread, and a pile heaved. . . We heaved a pile, piled some green fish, and washed out two bulks. 1924 ENGLAND 232 Hayve over the seal dog! *Kill* y'r seal! Turn him belly up an' putt the seal dog through his lower jaw!

3 Phr *heave in*: of heavy seas, to roll in on the shore.

1870 HOWLEY *MS Reminiscences* 22 A heavy swell hove in all night [as we lay anchored in the harbour]. 1940 DOYLE (ed) 27 "A Great Big Sea Hove in Long Beach": A great big sea hove in the Harbour. . . /And hove right up in Keoughs' Parlour. T 50–64 The ground [was] bet away by the side o' the lake, where the lop, you know, [kept] heavin' in.

heave out: of a vessel, to capsize or roll over.

1873 CARROLL 21 Some vessels will 'heave out' on the ice and not injure, owing no doubt to the form of the vessel's bottom. [1946] 1976 *Evening Telegram* 12 Jan, p. 6 The *Lavinia Bride* was caught [on the stern by a rock] and before the anchors could be secured and the crew get back on board, the vessel began to 'heave out.' C 71–117 He was asked to go out with his crew to look for bodies or signs of the ill-fated ship. When he got back, I asked him what caused the ship to sink. 'Well b'y,' he said, 'we all thinks she hove out.'

heave up: (a) command to Christmas mummers to remove or lift their face disguise; (b) to settle down, heave to.

P 245–66 Heave up!—the order given to jannies to remove their face covering and reveal their identity. C 71–8 After they were married they went to New Hampshire and that's where they hove up.

4 Comb **heave-up net**: part of a seal-net manoeuvred so as to impound seals.

[1886] LLOYD 53 That [net] on the left [is] the 'heave-up net.' . . .The barrier and stop-net are always kept floating in a perpendicular position by means of the above-mentioned floats; but the heave-up net is not so supported. . . It is attached to a capstan by means of a thick rope or 'road' which runs along the entire length of the head; it meanwhile rests on the bottom, ready to be lifted at a moment's notice.

heave-up song: chantey.

1938 MACDERMOTT 93 . . .the singing of sea shanties and 'heave-up' songs. T 39/41–64 [When we] use the windlass, you know—heave-up songs, any kind of song. There was six or seven men aboard, everybody would do the singing, when they'd be pumping up the anchor.

heaven See *as near to heaven by sea* at SEA.

heavy a Cp *OED* ~ 14 'overcast' for sense 1; *DC* (1850–) for sense 2.

1 Stormy.

[1848] 1975 MOYLES (ed) 173 The poor men have been prevented fishing for several weeks by the heavy weather. [1857] 1916 MURPHY 28 We made Brigus, it was very thick and heavy with snow, and sea, and in wearing her around, they unhooked the throat halyards of the mainsail. T 12–64 'It blew hard enough last night to blow the horns out of a cow.' A humorous way to describe a heavy wind.

2 Of an ice-floe, close-packed, thick.

[1862] 1916 MURPHY 30 While I am writing there is so much sea and the ice is so heavy that I cannot tell the moment the sides of my own vessel will be driven in. 1982 *Evening Telegram* 6 Mar, p. 4 Heavy ice is causing problems for shipping in the Bay of Exploits. . . There is approximately two feet of ice in the Botwood harbor, the thickest in 30 years.

3 Comb **heavy fish**: see **heavy salted** below.

P 143–75 No green fish (cod) were sent to market from Cape Broyle, although some 'heavy fish,' that is fish that were heavily salted but not dried, were shipped from the harbour.

heavy mess (pork): large chunks of salted pork; mess pork.

T 178/9–65 No, not fat back; mostly what you call heavy mess: great pieces of pork, half around the barrel, that weigh twenty pounds in the one piece. T 194–65 I never seed a bit o' salt meat, let alone fresh. I seed heavy mess pork. 1975 BUTLER 63 This was called heavy mess pork [and] was in large pieces as much as 20 and 25 pounds in one piece.

heavy salt(ed): (a) a type of salted and partially dried cod: GREEN FISH, SALT-BULK; (b) to cure or 'make' cod.

1937 *Seafisheries of Nfld* 47 The Heavy Salted class should be sound, well-split, thoroughly clean, fully salted, with a firm, clear surface, not wet but not hard dry. [1953] 1978 *Evening Telegram* 13 Nov, p. 13 The federation resolved not to engage in the production of. . .heavy salted, unless saltbulk prices are set on or before March 15 of each year. T 175/7–65 There's different cures: what they call the shore cure, light salted—that had to be fairly good and hard. But the heavy salted—perhaps two or three days' sun is enough for that, because the salt was into it and the moisture was into it and 'twouldn't spoil. T 141/67–65² Even when they heavy salts it, 'tis better to dry the fish than to sell salt bulk, 'cause there's a big margin between [them in price]. 1969 MENSINKAI 8 The salt fish takes four different forms, viz., light-salted, heavy-salted, pickled-split and ordinary cure. 1979 *'Twas a way of life* 95 We heavy salted any fish over fifteen inches.

heavy trip: a full load of seals; see also TRIP.

1873 CARROLL 36 Three fourths of the heavy trips of seals' fat that were brought heretofore into port as well as the heavy trips of seals' fat brought into port at the present day were got also by chance.

heck v *EDD* ~ v² 'hop' So. To walk or jump quickly.

[1900 OLIVER & BURKE] 59 For first he hecks with his run-te-tun. 1925 *Dial Notes* v, 333 To heck it. Walk quickly.

hedge sparrow n   Eastern fox sparrow (*Passerella iliaca*); FOXY TOM.
1870 *Can Naturalist* v, 157 It is called the 'Hedge Sparrow' by the settlers, and is very troublesome in gardens, scratching up fine seeds. 1876 HOWLEY 59 *Fox-coloured Sparrow* . . .a very common summer migrant; called here the 'Hedge Sparrow.'

heel n
1 Curved projection at the rear of the runners of a sled; see also **heel-stick** in sense 3 below.
P 141–72 The backs of slide runners are referred to as the heels. While sliding, one person would normally steer the sled, and stand on the heels when in an open space which was good for sliding. P 9–73 I turned my komatik around, rested its heel against a tree root, straightened out my hauling line.
2 Phr *the heel of* in var collocations: the end or conclusion of.
1924 ENGLAND 316 On the heel of it. As a result of it. 1937 DEVINE 26 Heel of the day. Evening; about sunset. P 108–74 Well, in the heel of the hunt we had to pack up and go home.
3 Comb **heel-stick**: (a) wooden last used in making or repairing shoes or mending socks; (b) see sense 1 above.
T 54/9–64 Piece o' wood about three foot long, about two and a half inches in diameter. . .stood on the floor and put up into the shoe for to make it solid for nailing the heel of the shoe on—that'd be a heelstick.
T 94/5–64 A round stick so it fit into the shoe: they call that a heelstick. Anything happened to the shoe in the heart of the foot or the heel, you could fix it on this thing. Q 71–7 Heelsticks were made from bent wood, and were placed at the back of the catamaran so that the driver could stand on them and control the horse's reins. Q 71–13 ~ A device women used in mending a heel of a sock. You place it on the floor and pull the sock over its round head.
heel-tap: the end piece of a loaf of bread; heel.
C 69–22 When I was small, I always referred to the first and last slices of bread (or the crusty part) as the heel-tap. C 71–101 Every loaf has two heel taps.

hegdown See HAGDOWN.

height n   Cp *O Sup*[2] ~ 14; *DC* 2 (Nfld: 1887–); *DC* height of lander (1933). Phr *height of land*: the highest stretch of land in an area; esp the elevated plateau of western Labrador forming the head of the Atlantic drainage system. Hence **height of lander**: trapper working the interior of Labrador.
1861 *Harper's* xxii, 760 The *voyageurs* are preparing for their arduous journey to Fort Nascopie, at the 'Heights of Land,' 300 miles in the interior. 1879 HARVEY 32 This is the water-shed, or, in the vernacular, the 'height of land,' but is only one hundred feet above the level of the sea. 1888 HOWLEY *MS*

Reminiscences 54 The country up here on the height of land [in the interior of the island of Newfoundland] is rugged and barren with very little wood of any kind. 1905 DUNCAN 68 The interior [of Labrador] is forbidding; few explorers have essayed adventure there; but the Indians—an expiring tribe—and trappers who have caught sight of the 'height of land' say that it is for the most part a vast table-land, barren. . .a sullen, forsaken waste. 1933 MERRICK 17 Tomorrow the first bunch of Height of Landers leaves and I hope we will not be too far behind to catch them. 1947 TANNER ii, 705 The Hamilton River trappers usually divide themselves into two groups: valley trappers and Height of Landers (= trappers working near the water-divide in the west). The boundary between the two lies at the Big Hill Portage where the Grand Falls must be avoided. C 71–106 A height of land in which no trees or vegetation grew [is called a scrape]. P 245–78 Temperatures on the Height of Land [Labrador] are expected to be in the low 20's.

hell-trot See ELTROT.

hemlock n   also **embloch, ground hemlock**.
1 Angelica, alexanders (*Angelica atropurpurea*).
1956 ROULEAU 29 Embloch.
2 Cow parsnip (*Heracleum maximum*).
1956 ROULEAU 29, 31 Embloch. . .ground hemlock.

hen n
Comb **hen and dick**: spruce grouse (*Canachites canadensis*) (1959 MCATEE 24). See DICK.
hen bird: northern slate-coloured junco (*Junco hyemalis hyemalis*).
1959 MCATEE 24 ~ slate-coloured Junco (perhaps from its call being deemed a 'cluck.' 'Labr.')
hen hawk: a variety of hawk (*Accipiter gentilis atricapillus; Circus cyaneus hudsonius*).
1870 *Can Naturalist* v, 42 Some of the settlers knew the bird by its white rump, and distinguished it by the name of 'hen hawk.' 1951 PETERS & BURLEIGH 133 It. . .sometimes robs a chicken yard, whereupon it is known as 'hen hawk' and in such instances it can cause considerable damage.
hen-skin: fisherman's waterproofed clothing.
P 127–73 ~ oiled calico. P 43–74 You buy hen-skin, yellow oil-clothes.

hermit n   also **hermit-beaver**. Cp *OED* ~ sb 3 'applied to var animals of solitary habits.' A beaver which has lost its mate.
[1783] 1792 CARTWRIGHT iii, 22–3 It oftentimes happens, that a single beaver lies retired, and is then stiled by furriers, a hermit: they say, it is turned out from the family, because it is lazy and will not work; and what is very singular (for be the cause what it will, the fact is certain) all hermit beavers have a black mark on the inside of the skin upon their backs, called a saddle, which distinguishes them. I rather think the cause of hermit beavers to be fidelity; as they are very faithful creatures to their mate; and by some accident or other, loosing that mate, they either will not pair again, or remain single until they can find another hermit of the

contrary sex; and that the saddle proceeds from the want of a partner to keep their back warm. I am sure that supposition is more natural, than, that it should be turned out because it is lazy; for many of those hermit beavers do so much work, that good furriers have sometimes been deceived and imagined, they had found a small crew. [1784–7] 1971 BANKS 446 Mr Graham is mistaken; he supposes the Hermit-beaver to be the drone but these are only such as have lost their mates and, like swans not being inclined to pair again, live by themselves.

herring n also **hern***, **herning***, **herron** ['hɛrʊŋ, 'ɛrin, 'hærʊŋ] *OED* ~ 1, *DAE* 1 (1588–) for sense 1; for combs. in sense 2: *OED* 3: herring barrel (1420–1818), 3 b herring hog (1640, 1674), *EDD* 1 (11) (b) herring-hog D, *OED* 3: herring-net (1535, 1615). *Herring* with qualifications expressing condition, cure and seasonal occurrence are listed elsewhere alphabetically: cp FALL n ~ , LABRADOR ~, SPRING² ~ , SPAWN ~ , SUMMER ~ .

1 Atlantic herring (*Clupea harengus harengus*); one of the principal fish used as bait in the cod-fishery, and, in modern times, pickled for export as food; freq in place-names.

[1583] 1940 *Gilbert's Voyages & Enterprises* ii, 406 [Hayes' narrative] Herring the largest that have bene heard of, and exceeding the Malstrond herring of Norway. 1620 WHITBOURNE 10 The. . .Harbours are generally stored with delicate Fish, as Salmons, Peales, Eeles, Herring, Mackerell. [1663] 1963 YONGE 60 They have divers kinds of bait. In the beginning of the year they use mussels, then come herrings and generally last all the year. 1819 ANSPACH 407 In Conception-Bay the shoals of herrings arrive generally about the beginning of May, and continue until the latter end of June: their first appearance is anxiously expected, because they are the first fish used there as bait in the cod-fishery. 1911 ROGERS 209 The central object in an allegorical picture which symbolized Newfoundland would be the cod-fish, and around it would be grouped its favourite bait the herring, the caplin. . .and the squid. 1925 *Dial Notes* v, 334 Herden. Herring. Also *herron*. 1933 *Nfld Royal Commission Report* 123 Herring is used in the spring, caplin in the summer, and squid in the fall [as bait]. [1952] 1965 PEACOCK (ed) i, 125 "The Fisherman's Alphabet": 'G' stands for grapnel, five hooks and a ring, / 'H' is for herring the first bait in spring. 1953 *Nfld & Lab Pilot* ii, 397 Herring cove. . .extends about 2 cables westward to its head, which is shoal. 1960 FUDGE 5 The first work that I started after leaving school was at the herring. P 148–65 Herning is used for bait when it is in season. P 229–67 We had a meal of salt hern for dinner. 1976 PINHORN 27 Prior to 1965 the Newfoundland herring fishery was associated largely with the demand for herring as bait for the cod fishery and with the periodic demand for pickled herring products as food, especially during and just after World War I and II.

2 Attrib, comb, cpd **herring bait**: see sense 1 above.

[1896] SWANSBOROUGH 11 "September": With her-

ring bait some fish is caught, / And some from Labrador is brought. 1963 TEMPLEMAN & FLEMING 56 Thus a cod catch of 10,000 or 5000 pounds with squid bait would be less than 6000 and 3000 pounds, respectively, with herring bait. . .

herring baiting: the quantity of herring taken aboard a vessel for use as bait in trawl-fishing for cod on the Grand Banks; see also BAITING.

1973 HORWOOD 11 Before they were ready to sail the men went to work making ready for the herring baiting.

herring barrel: wooden container made from birch or other hard wood for the export of pickled herring.

1868 HOWLEY *MS Reminiscences* 39 Some of them are expert coopers and can make first class herring barrels with only an axe and this crooked knife. 1873 CARROLL 42 Herring catchers ought to take the herring barrels with them, so that the herrings would be secured after being removed from the Vats. T 90–64 The herring barrels were twenty-nine inches long and a seventeen-inch head. . . 'Twas all birch.

herring bone: to sail through an ice-field in a zigzag pattern to locate seals (1937 DEVINE 27).

herring catcher: knitted woollen glove having two sheaths for thumb and first finger.

P 118–67 See my herring catchers anywhere?

herring gib(b): the gills and intestinal tract of a herring; GIB n.

1960 FUDGE 30 On dumping my barrel of herring gibbs my oil clothes were found in the bottom of the barrel.

herring gibber: man who guts a herring.

[1958] 1965 PEACOCK (ed) i, 133 "The Herring Gibbers": Sandy Royal our second hand is plainly to be seen, / He looks all over these herring gibbers for they is sort of green.

herring hog: harbour porpoise (*Phocoena phocoena*).

1620 MASON 152 . . .kind of Whales called Gibberts, Dogfish, Porposes, Herring-Hogges, Squides. 1883 HATTON & HARVEY 233 Another variety. . .is called puffing-pig and herring-hog by the fishermen. 1966 *Evening Telegram* 24 May, p. 13 The last line you had wouldn't land a prickley, let alone one of them herring hogs, as we used to call them in my days. P 148–68 To eat like a hern-hog.

herring jack: American shad (*Alosa sapidissima*) (P 1–69).

herring net: (a) seine-like net used to enclose schooling herring; (b) type of stationary net in which herring mesh themselves; freq in place-names.

1765 WILLIAMS 20 Six Herring Nets. [1771] 1792 CARTWRIGHT i, 153 I sent the *Poegie* shallop with a herring-net to Chateau, to try for baits and fish. 1953 *Nfld & Lab Pilot* ii, 380 Herring-net island [lies] between it and the coast. 1967 *Bk of Nfld* iv, 240 Not a winter passed that there was not linnet to be knitted in our house. Some was for ourselves—the odd codnet, herring net, seal net or perhaps a caplin seine. Q 67–52 A herring net has meshes 2¾ in. in diameter. 1973 HORWOOD 67 The harbour had a difficult approach.

To make it the more difficult, fishermen had herring nets set near the entrance.

herring scull, ~ **school**: the appearance in inshore waters of schools of herring; see also SCULL.

1819 ANSPACH 414 [The seal-fishery] was found to interfere at the most important period, that of the herring and capelin-sculls. [1953 *Nfld Fish Develop Report* 33 The spawning schools [of herring] which are presently being fished are made up chiefly of very large and very old fish, most of which have already spawned several times. Except for the fishery along the Labrador coast, catches are made from pre-spawning and spawning schools which are found close inshore.] 1972 MOWAT 22 Like always. First part o' December. . .along of the herring scull. They's five. . .maybe six cruising midst the islands, and they's the biggest kind.

herring station: a harbour from which the herring fishery is prosecuted and where the catch is processed for export; see also STATION.

1873 CARROLL 41 For some days five barrels may be taken, and some days one hundred; and such Vats to be placed in the hold of the vessel until her arrival at the Herring station, and there united together and properly arranged along the deck, or on shore and to be furnished with tight covers.

herring store: part of fishing premises where herring are processed for storage and export; see also STORE.

1960 FUDGE 49 We were forced to tie our boat to the wharf and pay off the crew, including the laborers in the herring store.

herring trip: voyage to the fishing banks using herring as bait in trawl-fishing for cod.

1977 *Nfld Qtly* Winter, p. 22 The banking schooner cod fishing year for most vessels operating from Grand Bank was organized in three phases, each according to the main bait species used, viz. herring in the Spring, caplin in the Summer, and squid in the Fall. Thus men spoke of the 'herring trip,' 'caplin trip,' and 'squid trip,' though each bait phase might embrace several journeys between ports and fishing grounds before actual completion.

herring tub: an 18-gallon (68.1 l) wooden container (1977 BUTLER 16).

hert See HURT.

he's = 'his' See HE.

hicker n Cp *EDD* hick v[3] 'hitch.'
1 A tangle (in a fishing-line or net) (P 243–56).
2 Phr *without a hicker*: smoothly, without difficulty (P 113–74).

hickory n Serviceberry (*Amelanchier* spp.) (1898 *J A Folklore* xi, 226).

hide n
1 Euphemism for service of cow by a bull.
T 141/60–65[2] He said 'That's where Bobby's keeping his bull, and she's gone there to get her hide.'

2 Phr *get a hide; on the hide*, etc: to conceal oneself; secretly.

[1900 OLIVER & BURKE] 58 "We Are Going to Call": Let us quietly slide, / Away on the hide. 1910 *Daily News* 10 Mar, p. 3 "The Sealers!": I assure you 'tis seldom or never, / That they from the prize ran ahide. P 253–68 'She'd get a hide on her'—hiding in the game of hide-and-seek. 'He's got a hide on him'—said when a shy horse moves behind some trees so as to get out of sight of watchers.

hidey n *EDD* 1 (9) hide-hoop; *EDD* hidy a (2) hidy-hole (a) for combs. in sense 2.
1 Children's game in which one player must find the others (P 148–63).
2 Comb **hidey-bunk**: hide-and-seek.
1971 NOSEWORTHY 212 ~ A game for children where everyone hides except one, who is 'it' and must find the others.

hidey-hole: small space for storage and concealment.
P 148–65 ~ place to store things in a house, out of the way. Q 71–7 ~ a secret place, used for hiding valuables. [She] recalls a patient who, when being admitted to hospital, was extremely anxious to confide about her hidy-hole. The patient had hidden all her savings behind a loose brick in her chimney. Q 71–8 ~ [A place] on a schooner [to conceal] small contraband. Q 71–9 ~ pantry.

hidey-hoop: see **hidey-bunk**.
P 124–71 Hideyhoop was a children's game and was the same as Hide & Seek is today.

hidey-over: game in which a ball is thrown over a building, the catcher tagging the other players (M 69–12).

high a Cp *O Sup*[2] ~ a 21 high line (a) (1856–), *DAE* high line 2 (1885–); *EDD* ~ 1 (26) high-learned; cp *OED* trap-ball for high-trap.

Attrib, comb, cpd **high back(s)**: a sport like leap-frog.
1965 *Evening Telegram* 16 Nov, p. 16 We used to play high backs on the hydrant. 1975 ibid 22 Dec, p. 6A Hydrants also were never passed in a walk. Make a jump and over. Highbacks that was called.

high dory: the dory crew with the largest catch of cod; high liner.
1960 FUDGE 37 We were fishing for high dory. That is, all were counting fish. We were the highest dory and shared the grand sum of $204.00 each.

high flyer: pole buoyed in the water with a flag to mark trawl-line.
P 148–65 These high-flyers are about nine feet long and float about six feet out of the water. They are tied onto each end of the trawl by a long piece of rope and thus show the fisherman where his line is running and also warn anyone who is sailing by to keep away from the trawl. P 127–78 ~ Flag on a trawl line.

high-learned: scholarly, learned.
1836 [WIX][2] 55 Here I met. . .an old man from. . .Dorset who begged of me to send him a supply of plain sermons, or, as he expressed it, 'not too high learnt.'

high pear: Juneberry (*Amelanchier* spp); CHUCKLEY PEAR (1898 *J A Folklore* xi, 226).

high-rat: large undecked boat with high bulwarks.

1895 *J A Folklore* viii, 39 ~ a boat with a board along the edge to prevent the water coming over, called a *washboard*. 1907 *Nfld & Lab Pilot* 684 High Rat rock. . .lies S.E.. . .from the southern point of Green island. 1936 SMITH 13 The next job was building out stage-heads and repairing boats. We had two standing boats and a 'highrat.' I went with Uncle Harry, as he was commonly called, in the 'highrat.' 1967 *Evening Telegram* 19 July, p. 41 [Highrats] were about the size of a four-oared punt and could carry six or seven barrels of round cod. They were fitted with a moveable mast which carried a mainsail and a jib. A small mizzen or spanker was carried at the sterns. The boat was steered by means of a rudder or a sculling oar and had a crew of two men or a man and a boy. The distinguishing feature of the highrat was the plank, about four inches high, which ran along the top side of each gunnel from stem to stern. These planks were called wash-boards and served to increase the height of the gunnels above the water line, thus making it possible for the boat to carry a heavier load.

high-trap: boys' game in which a ball is hit into the air from a stick on which it rests.

T 272–66¹ Hightrap was another game they used to play. You get a ball and put a stick across this way, another one here, and you put the ball on the end.

hind, hinder See SCUTTER.

hinder a

1 Phr *hinder part before, ~ to fore*: backwards.

C 71–95 Hinder part before is used when you put on a garment back to front. P 212–71 Hinder part to fore: backwards.

2 Comb **hinder flipper**: the rear limb of a seal.

1842 JUKES i, 317 It swam like a fish. . .closing and spreading out its hinder flippers into the exact form of the tail of a fish. 1873 CARROLL 24 Whilst swimming they are sent headlong by the power of their hinder flippers.

hindersome a *EDD* ~ 1. Troublesome, esp of the weather.

[c1894] PANL P4/14, pp. 200–1 [The fisherman] is sure to find either that there has been too little bait or too much *hindersome* weather.

hip v In dancing the lancers, to bump (one's partner) lightly with the hip.

1955 DOYLE (ed) 30 "I'se the B'y": Hip yer partner, Sally Tibbo! / Hip yer partner, Sally Brown! / Fogo, Twillingate, Mor'ton's Harbour, / All around the circle.

hipper n A bent nail used as a makeshift suspender button or trouser fastening.

1924 ENGLAND 6 Open-coated, with rough trousers held up by 'hippers,' or nails doing duty for suspender buttons, groups of these hardy Vikings gathered at cor-

ners. 1925 *Dial Notes* v, 334 ~s. Nails used to fasten trousers to a shirt.

hirt See HURT.

hit v Past tense *hot. EDD* hit 2.

1 To strike (1924 ENGLAND 317 hot).

P 68–54 He hot the dog with a stick. P 88–56 I riz up an' hot 'en right among the eyes. C 71–88 I hot him.

2 Phr *hit on the lee side*: to catch unawares, to surprise (1925 *Dial Notes* v, 334).

hit the patch: of a sealing vessel, to reach the seal herds on the ice-floes; STRIKE 1.

1924 ENGLAND 272 'If us could ondly hit de patch wid a hot sun, de swiles'd stay up an' us could almost bat a load, to say nothin' of shootin' one!'

hobble n Cp *EDD* ~ sb² 3 'sum of money received by a "hobbler"' Co, 4 'casual piece of work' Gmg. See HOBBLER.

1 A casual piece of work (a St John's localism).

1960 *Daily News* 31 May, p. 17 The professional ranks of the longshoremen in St John's. . .might be watered down by the forced acceptance of every unemployed labourer with the chance of a 'hobble' on the waterfront. P 245–63 'Do you want a hobble, mister?'—asked by small boy offering to shovel snow. 1964 *Evening Telegram* 4 May, p. 7 Them old truckmen were great sports too. I knowed a few of them only had one hobble for the day. C 71–119 The word 'hobble' is used to describe an odd job—piece work done on an hourly basis. 1973 SMALLWOOD 31 One could see in every cove eight or ten horses and carts lined up with their drivers near them, waiting for a 'hobble.' 1980 *Evening Telegram* 8 Nov, p. 18 How often do I hope himself would run into an extra hobble.

2 In phr *be on the hobbles*: to look for odd jobs.

P 97–67 ~ making the rounds during the winter to see if other people wanted their driveways cleared [of snow].

hobbler n Cp *OED* ~² 3, c 'casual labourer employed at quays, docks' (1885–); 'hoveller'; *EDD* hobble v²: hobbler 'boatman. . .employed to assist in bringing a vessel into or out of harbour' s cties. Casual labourer.

P 244–56 ~ a handy-man.

hobbling ppl, vbl n See HOBBLER. Offering one's services for temporary or casual work.

P 73–67 After a big snow storm all of us would go hobblin' to earn some pocket money. . . 'I earned two dollars yesterday hobblin'.' 1973 SMALLWOOD 30 The second kind of the carting trade was 'hobbling.' The driver would stand around with his horse in one of the various coves leading from Water Street, and wait for an individual order to cart something to some destination in the city.

hobby horse n also **hobby horse and bull**. Cp

OED ~ 2 'in the morris-dance, and on the stage. . .a figure of a horse. . .fastened about the waist of one of the performers' (1557–1821); EDD ~ 1: 'a hobby-horse is carried through the streets [of Padstow]' Co. See also HORSY-HOPS. A figure of a horse carried by mummers during Christmas festivities.

[1583 (1940) *Gilbert's Voyages and Enterprises* ii, 396 Besides for solace of our people, and allurement of the Savages, we were provided of Musike in good variety: not omitting the least toyes, as Morris dancers, Hobby horsse, and Maylike conceits to delight the Savage people.] 1893 *Christmas Greetings* 19 There were hobby horses, men, women, and I don't know what else, with the most outrageous masks and costumes I have ever seen. 1895 PROWSE 402 Each company [of fools or mummers] had one or more hobby-horses, with gaping jaws to snap at people. [1917] 1969 *Christmas Mumming in Nfld* 175 A weird figure bearing the head of a horse, nodding and gesticulating wildly to his companions. . .paraded Water Street. . .the oddly garbed figures meanwhile capering in amusing fashion around the hobby-horse—as I found the centre figure was called. M 65–5 In St Philips people sometimes dress up as a hobby-horse, one in front and one in the back. The one in front puts on a horse's head and the one behind has a blanket. The head is carved out of wood and the jaws work on strings. These hobby-horses chase everyone who is not a janny and are considered to be a nuisance. They frighten children and if you let them in the house they would turn the place upside down, turning over chairs, etc. These hobby-horses were ugly creatures and they had horns on their heads to make them look like the devil. When they had horns they were called hobby-horse-and-bull. T 265–66[2] Hobby horse they used to call it. There'd be two people stoop down, and they put a big blanket over them, and they'd be walking off like an animal. C 71–116 The jannies make what they call a 'hobby horse.' They have the head of a horse, cow, or moose with a piece of canvas attached to it. About six men get under the canvas. They put nails or something like that in the mouth to make a clacking noise. They put sticks or something in the head so that they can turn it and open and close the mouth. Then this fierce looking thing goes around to the different houses.

hodge n One of the heavy beams used as a support in constructing a 'stage' or wharf.
1967 FIRESTONE 97 Another form of support for stages is called *hodges* or *cross wharves*. Here the wharf is laid upon beams which are held in the angles formed by crossed supports. This is used usually in temporary structures.

hog n Comb **hog's nose**: a water-spout; a freak whirlwind at sea.
1957 *Evening Telegram* 30 May, p. 4 The tornadoes in Kansas and Missouri are the same as used to be known to Newfoundland fishermen and coasters as a 'Hog's Nose'—a dreaded and sudden eruption of nature that was very frequent around our coasts up to about 50 years ago, but which seems to have disappeared in this part of the world.

hogdown See HAGDOWN.

hoist v Comb **hoist-your-sails-and-run**: cry by player in children's game of hide-and-seek before going to find the other players hiding; the game itself.
1905 DUNCAN 136 When spring came, with the ice still clinging to the coast. . .the lads played at 'h'ist-your-sails-an'-run' among the boulders of the hillside. 1929 MILLER 28 '"Long To'des Dark": . . .to join the shoutin' / 'Hoist yer sails an' run, boys!' P 199–56 The signal to begin is the cry from the seeker: Hi, ho wherever you're at, / Don't show the brim of your hat, / Hoist your sails and run. T 459–67[1] They'd yell out, 'Hoist your sails an' run!' an' everybody'd take off. 1975 *Evening Telegram* 21 June, p. 17 We always seemed to have lots to do. Like rollin' hoops, playing hoist your sails and run, over troutin' in the landwash.

hoist n also **hoister** for sense 1; *ADD* ~ 'fall, jolt' for sense 3.
1 A small flexible tree or branch bent to activate an animal snare.
[1894] 1977 *Them Days* ii (3), p. 53 After breakfast I, old Lydia Campbell, seventy-five years old, will put on my out-door clothes and take my game bag, axe and matches (in case they are needed) and off I goes to my snares. It looks pretty to see the rabbits hanging in, what we calls, histys (hoists). T 203/5–65 You'd hook it out what we call a hoister—a tree [bent] down in the marsh, because if you didn't [the animal would] perhaps break the slip off.
2 A postponement, deferral.
1901 *Christmas Review* 19 The book was artistically manufactured by Mr Thomas Grace. . . However, after a very warm debate, this emblem of literature got a 999 year hoist, and the writer has since thought such action a very wise and prudent one.
3 Phr *take a hoist*: to fall down (from a height).
P 245–56 Trying to jump the fence, he took a hoist.

hoister* See HOIST n 1.

hold v SMYTH 385 for sense 1.
1 Of a boat or vessel, to maintain a position (in relation to something else, as land, course, etc).
T 80/1–64 An' o' course they couldn't hold th' island any longer in the schooner. T 43–64 You'd often leave the schooner an' come up one way an' haul your traps an' have to go the other way back to the schooner, go right around the isle to hold a bit o' smooth water, so as you could nurse your boat along with the load of fish.
2 Phr *hold in*: command to dog-team to turn left; RA.
1920 WALDO 144 In Labrador 'ouk, ouk!' turns the team to the right. . .and 'urrah, urrah!' swerves it to the left. The corresponding directions in Newfoundland are 'keep off!' and 'hold in.' No reins are used—some drivers use no whip. T 271–66[2] Your leader had to get that, an' to your left was 'hold in,' an' to your right 'keep off.'

holder n   Cp *OED* ~ 4 a 'canine tooth,' *EDD* 9
Gl So. A long, pointed (animal) tooth.

1971 NOSEWORTHY 212 Land animals have holders,
sea animals have 'tusks.'

holly* n   Cp *EDD* hollo v 'to call loudly': var
hollie W So Do. See also OLD HOLLY. In pl,
ghost noises; cries of dead fishermen heard on
stormy nights (C 71–98).

C 68–4 The hollies is the word these people use when
the wind is in this direction [and] they hear the echoes
of the hollering or crying [of] the drowning crew.
C 71–40 It is a community belief that on any stormy day
or night from Legg's Point, a jut of land outside the
harbour [at L'Anse aux Meadows], can be heard the
cries of seamen who lost their lives off that coast.
These cries are referred to as hollies.

home n   Cp *OED* ~ sb¹ 6 'used. . .for Great
Britain.'

1 Attrib **home boat**: a ship from the 'old country.'

1953 JOB 48 He also became a partner in the Liverpool firm, and in the Newfoundland tradition spent
many weeks of his life in going and coming from one
country to another—from Newfoundland to England
and back to Newfoundland again on what used to be
called 'the home boat.' P 108–70 A gun was fired on
Signal Hill when the home boat hove in sight, and if it
belonged to one of the mercantile houses here, the
house flag of that house was raised on the flag-pole on
the hill.

home soldier: see MAHONE SOLDIER.

homely a   Cp *EDD* ~ 1 'at home.' Satisfied in
the home; 'at home.'

1937 DEVINE 27 ~ Inclined to stay at home, seldom
seen out visiting; 'Mrs Smith is got very *homely*.'
P 148–63 Of cat left with relatives: 'She's very homely
now.'

honke See HOWK.

hood n   *OED* ~ 6 (1854) for sense 2; *DC* hood
seal (1883–) for cpd in sense 3. See also OLD ~ ,
YOUNG ~ .

1 A fold of loose skin on head of mature male
seal which can be inflated to protect the animal;
CAP.

[1766] 1971 BANKS 145 [This seal] differs from the
rest by a white hood or peice of Moveable Skin upon
his head which he can at Pleasure throw over his nose
& with it defend himself from the Blows of the Fishermen. 1842 JUKES i, 293 This is the hood which, when
angry or excited, can be blown out to a considerable
size. 1846 TOCQUE 191–2 When they inflate their
hoods it seems almost impossible to kill one of them.

2 See **hood seal** in sense 3.

1849 [FEILD] 50 The Hood is still larger [than square
fipper], the skin twelve feet in length. 1852
ARCHIBALD 4 The bulk of the catch consists of the
young hood and harp in nearly equal proportions. 1924
ENGLAND 22 It cannot be that the hoods stay farther at

sea because of greater timidity. . .the hood is rough,
surly, pugnacious, very different from the peaceful and
confiding harp. 1927 DOYLE (ed) 39 "Hunting Seals":
Of bedlamers we often take, / Their 'pelts' being quite
as good, sir, / As any 'swoils' in yield of oil / Be he 'dog
harp' or hood, sir. T 43/4–64 There's the hood,
now—they're the biggest an' the boldest, the dangerousest.

3 Comb, cpd **hood ice**: heavy pack-ice on
which the hooded seals breed.

1925 CONDON 238 The rugged 'Hood ice' is in comparatively small pans, so that the Hoods do not require
blow-holes, but scramble over the edge when they
want to get into the water, and it is much harder for
men to work upon it.

hood pup: the young of the hooded seal.

1924 ENGLAND 25 The hood pups are considerably
larger than the harps and show a dark slatey blue colour. In a foetal condition they also have a white coat;
but they lose this before birth.

hood seal: large migratory seal (*Cystophora
cristata*); HOODED SEAL.

1842 JUKES i, 302 Among them was the pelt of a
female hood-seal and two young hoods, one of which
had not long been whelped. 1873 *Maritime Mo* i, 262
The third species is the hood-seal, which is much larger
than the harp. 1907 WALLACE 263 There are five varieties of them, the largest of which is the hood seal and
the smallest the doter or harbour seal. 1976 *Decks
Awash* v (2), p. 6 Very little is known of the hood seal.
It appears the Newfoundland population which is east
of the harps, has a few that wander off from some
unknown herd—maybe from Davis Inlet. The hoods
do not congregate closely like the harp seals, but are
found scattered and in families.

hood season: March-April; SPRING².

T 141/68–65² If you struck a family o' hoods in the
hood season, the best thing to do is try to capture th'
ol' dog, because he's pretty treacherous.

hooded p ppl *OED* ~ a 2: hooded seal (1820),
DC hood seal (1784 quot). Comb **hooded seal**:
large migratory seal (*Cystophora cristata*) of
northern waters which breeds on the ice-floe in
spring and is hunted for its skin and oil; HOOD
(SEAL).

[1766] 1971 BANKS 145 The hooded Seal differs from
the rest by a white hood or peice of Moveable Skin
upon his head which he can at Pleasure throw over his
nose & with it defend himself from the Blows of the
Fishermen until we can't Kill him till they remove it.
1842 JUKES i, 288–9 An old hooded seal made his
appearance alongside. 1863 HIND ii, 202 . . .and the
Hooded Seal. . .which is sometimes nine feet long.
1981 *Evening Telegram* 10 Mar, p. 2 [He] said some
hooded seals also were sighted.

hoo-eet See OO-ISHT.

hook n   Cp *DAE* hook-and-line (1709–); *DC*
hook-and-line man Nfld (1905, 1916) for sense 1.

Comb **hook-and-line**: a single fishing line with
hook attached, used manually in the cod-fishery,

esp from small boats in coastal waters; hand-line. Also attrib.

1620 WHITBOURNE 62–3 Some men presuming to goe to Sea, and to fish with hooke and lyne, upon the Sabbath day, as usually as upon the weeke dayes. [1712] 1895 PROWSE 273 Go out of harbours in shallops, seven men and five men in a boat; catch fish with hook and line. 1842 JUKES i, 229 I do not know the [largest] amount ever caught by a man with a hook and line in a single day, but it must sometimes be enormous. [1877] 1898 *Nfld Law Reports* 147 . . .the defendant, seven with himself to a cod-seine boat, and five under plaintiff, who received a bounty as skipper in a hook-and-line boat. 1883 HATTON & HARVEY 292 The hook-and-line men do best when the fish is thin and towards the end of the season. 1909 GRENFELL[2] (ed) 79 September. Hooks and lines replace the large trap nets, as the cod are now only to be taken in deep water. 1966 SCAMMELL 40 You might be a good trawl and hook-and-line man, but you don't know the first thing about traps! T 49–64 There was three brothers with my father [and] we used to go in the one boat, with the hook an' line. 1975 *Evening Telegram* 12 Apr, p. 22 Longliner, trap, hook and line crews are busy preparing for this year's fishery.

hook-maker: artisan making fish-hooks for use in the cod-fishery.

1620 WHITBOURNE 13–14 The trade thither. . .doth yeerly set on worke and relieve many numbers of people, as. . .Line-makers, Hooke-makers, Pully-makers, and many other trades.

hook-set: device for bending fish-hooks into proper shape; TRAWL HOOK-SET.

M 67–10 The trawl tub was laid on the floor with a hook-set fastened to its brim. In the baiting process the fisherman has to be always on the look-out for straightened hooks.

hook v

1 To get along amiably with another; usu in neg.

P 262–59 They couldn't hook, in other words they couldn't get on together.

2 Phr *hook out*: to trim the wick (of a lamp).

1863 MORETON 51 My predecessor was once interrupted, in the midst of his sermon I believe, by the mistress of the house exclaiming to her grandchildren, 'Lotte, hook out the lamp.'

hooking vbl n Cp *OED* ~ (esp 1430 quot) for sense 1.

1 Fishing for cod with hand-lines; cp HOOK n: HOOK-AND-LINE.

[1857] 1975 WHITELEY 229 If there was any hooking this month they would soon get some.

2 Comb **hooking-boat**: small, single-masted fishing vessel; hooker.

[1883] 1971 BAKER 1 12 schooners belonging to [Burgeo], and about 100 small hooking boats.

hooky a   Liable to snag or hook (an object).

1933 MERRICK 219 Sometimes the crust bears you up on snowshoes, sometimes the crust will not bear up

under the racquets. Then each step is a delayed happening, for the hard surface goes down slowly and unwillingly. Another kind of crust is brittle. It trips you every step. The men call it 'hookey.' T 80/3–64 You couldn't haul trap there—tear un up, see; fouly bottom. He hove down tons and tons of ballast; made it a bit better but 'twas still hooky and fouly.

hoosing vbl n Cp *EDD* hoosh int 1 'cry used to. . .drive away fowls, pigs.' Comb **hoosing stick**: short piece of wood used in child's pastime of catching sticklebacks.

M 70–23 ~ This was an ordinary stick or branch about 2½ ft. long. We used to tie the piece of string around the mouth of the empty bottle and lower it slowly under the water. Then we would quietly wait until we saw some pricklies and use our 'hoosing stick' to guide the pricklies into the bottle. Then the bottle would be yanked upright suddenly to capture the prickly. P 275–73 ~ A stick used to guide pricklies into a bottle or tin can.

hopper n

1 A short stick which is struck at one of its tapered ends to make it hop in the air; the children's game played with this stick, somewhat similar to tip-cat (M 69–2).

1976 *Daily News* 15 Jan, p. 3 The only equipment. . .required was two sticks—one short and the other long. In hopper, the short stick was pointed at both ends, thus making it possible to hop by striking either end with the longer stick.

2 A seal in its second year, remarkable for its liveliness; see BEDLAMER.

[1899] *OED* ~[1] 2 'in Newfoundland. . .a seal of the second year,' 10 ~ -hood 'a hooded seal in its second year.' T 210/11–65 First 'tis called the young one, young harp and the next year it's called hopper, and the next year, two-yeared seal. T 410–67 They canned all what they got the year there, that's clear o' the old harps, they wouldn't can them. The bedlamers and hoppers, you can all that stuff.

hoppy a   Cp *EDD* hopper sb[2] 4 'crackling coal' So. Comb **hoppy wood**: fire-wood which burns noisily, emitting sparks (P 234–62).

horn n [hɑːɹn, ɑːɹn, hɒːɹn]. Cp *OED* ~ 5 'tentacles of gastropods' for sense 1; cp *OED* naut for sense 4; *OED* 12, *EDD* 3 for sense 6; for comb in sense 7: cp *DAE* horn ail (for hornbound), *EDD* hornie sb 2: hoorniman.

1 Tentacle or arm of the giant 'squid' or devilfish (*Architeuthis dux*), and the short-finned 'squid' (*Illex illecebrosus*).

[1794] 1968 THOMAS 183 I have heard storys at St John's of [a giant squid] being caught on the Grand Banks—and also of the horn of one being found cast ashore in Freshwater Bay which Two men with difficulty could carry. 1874 *Maritime Mo* iii, 554 He had often laughed at the stories of the older fishermen about the 'big squids,' with 'horns' forty feet in length, which they had seen on 'the Labrador.' 1898 HOWLEY

MS Reminiscences 2 Our informant also stated that some of the squids this season had ten horns or tentacles. T 54/64–64 I never saw the squid, but you know those suckers be on the horns. 1979 *Daily News* 9 Aug, p. 10 [He] knew he had caught a giant squid in his nets. 'I knowed en be his harns.' 1979 TIZZARD 304 After the squid had been cleaned and put on the lines to dry. . .every squid would have to be 'gone over' to pick the horns (tentacles) abroad in order that they would not hang in a bunch and therefore not dry so well.

2 A piece of wood projecting from the quarters of a fishing vessel to secure the mainsail boom.

1896 *J A Folklore* ix, 34 [She was] a fishing-boat. . .from seven to fifteen tons' burden. The deck has open standing spaces forward and aft for the fishermen to stand in while they fish. The deck is formed of movable boards. It is schooner-rigged, but without either fore or main boom. The foresail is trimmed aft by a sheet, and the mainsail trimmed aft to horns or pieces of wood projecting from the quarters. It thus avoids the danger of either of the booms knocking the fishermen overboard.

3 One of four vertical sticks placed at the corners of a sled (or on the deck of a vessel) to secure a load of wood.

1897 *J A Folklore* x, 206 [On the west coast] the stakes placed in the ends of the crossbars of their sleds to prevent the load sliding off are called the *horns*. [c1928] [BURKE] "Dump on the Old South Side": For the corn is still on my back. . . / From the horn of a catamaran. 1936 SMITH 116 We then started putting the wood on board, and by daylight she was piled over the horns. 1937 JUNEK 36 [They convey] the wood from the mountains down to the village. The roots are placed lengthwise between the horns of the *cométique*. . .and roped tightly down. 1959 *Daily News* 13 Feb, p. 20 Mind's eye recalls slide 'horns' festooned, each with a pair of [swanskin mitts] as the wearers shed them [since] running to keep up with the dog team made them over warm to wear. 1974 *Evening Telegram* 29 Jan, p. 8 [The] catamarans, as they were mostly called, had the Union Jack and the Red Ensign on a stick and tied to a front horn of the leading sled. 1979 TIZZARD 65 The dog cart was made of wood: there were twelve knees, two wooden runners and two iron shoes, two beams and four cart horns.

4 An upright pole bracing the side of a logging chute.

T 43/8–64 The landing was made of three skids goin' down to the edge of the river bank, and there was horns comin' down at the front o' the river.

5 A ring, often made of cross-section of a cow's horn, forming apex of a caplin-net.

1955 DOYLE (ed) 86 "When the Caplin Come In": Me net is all tangled and tattered and torn, / A tuck full o' caplin got hitched in a grapnel, / And now me old net is gone right from the horn. P 127–78 ~ The ring attached to the top of a cast-net.

6 A drink or swallow (of liquor, etc).

1866 WILSON 348 He must take a *horn* [i.e. a drink of liquor] for joy. [1894 BURKE] 33 [He] remarked how merry the cows were. 'Why wouldn't they,' said Tom, 'when they all got a couple of *horns* in.' 1895 TOCQUE

143 I was travelling with a preacher in Conception Bay, Newfoundland, when we came to a brook, he took a cocoa-nut shell out of his pocket, filled with rum, from which he took a good 'horn.' 1925 *Dial Notes* v, 334 Five *horns* of beer. 1931 BYRNES 73 Someone was sure to suggest a stiff 'horn' of Jamaica rum, or Old Tom, (according to their personal preference) as a sovereign remedy for 'fits.' T 208–65 We'd get up in the morning, we'd have a cup o' coffee, ol' black coffee, boiled in an iron kettle. An' you get a horn o' that an' a crumb o' hard bread for an appetite. 1976 CASHIN 68 He never missed a Sunday morning coming down to the house before Mass to get his usual good 'horn of rum.'

7 Comb **horn-bound**: of cattle, afflicted by an ailment caused by, or attributed to, its horns.

1910 GRENFELL 188 He had already, with a long gimlet, bored holes into its head through to the root of its horns, as he was told it was 'horn-bound,' by much the same reasoning process that some of our people attribute the squalling of their babies to being 'tongue-tied.'

horn bowsprit: a straight, unsheered bowsprit.

1973 HORWOOD 126 Newfoundland vessels, that mostly used horn bowsprits, had a single stick stand straight out of their stems. However, some were rigged with the addition of a jibboom that followed the sheer of the deck.

horn man: the devil.

P 51–67 The horn man takes bad people.

horn-slide: a wood-sled or 'catamaran' rigged with four vertical sticks or 'horns.' See sense 3 above (Q 74–1).

horny a, n also **hornie**.

1 A small marine invertebrate; the creature's shell.

C 71–35 When I was ten years old I used to fish off the government wharf. We used the bodies of small sea shells for bait. These shells were called 'harnies.'

2 Comb **horny whore**: sculpin (*Myoxocephalus scorpius*).

1979 NEMEC 242 Because of their unaesthetic appearance, allegedly poisonous horns, the considerable effort required at times to remove them from gill-nets, and the lack of any redeeming commercial value, sculpins have earned a variety of names ('horny whore,' e.g.).

horse n Cp *OED* ~ sb 7 for sense 2; for combs. in sense 3: cp *OED* chop sb[2] 1 b 'jaw,' 4 b 'entrance to channel' for horse chop(s) (a), (b); *Kilkenny Lexicon* bull-fart, sheep-fart for horse(s) fart; *DC* horse-head (1965); *EDD* 1 (89) horse Protestant Ir; *OED* 27 (b) horse-stinger (1772), *EDD* 1 (104) (a) esp s w cties.

1 A platform (of stones or boards) on which split and salted cod-fish are placed in layers after washing in order to drain during the curing process; the pile of fish so placed; WATER-HORSE. See also BULK n, FAGGOT, PILE n.

[1663] 1963 YONGE 57 The fish being salted, lies 3 or

4 days, sometimes (if bad weather) 8 or 10 days, and is then washed by the boys in salt or fresh water and laid in a pile skin upward on a platt of beach stones, which they call a horse. [1758 (1807) ULLOA ii, 408 When the salt appears to have sufficiently penetrated, they wash them, and take them in pairs by the tails, then shake them in the water in order to carry off the scum extracted by the salt: afterwards, that the water may run off, they are piled up on little boards; then they are stretched out one by one, with the skin upwards, in order for drying, where they are turned three or four times.] Q 67–65 Salt horse: salt [cod] fish in bulk.

2 A frame in which a cooper places the head of a barrel for shaping; cp BENDING HORSE.

T 90–64 Make your mark around the head, stick your head in the horse an' chop it around with your axe and take your drawing knife and do the finery.

3 Attrib, comb, cpd **horse(s) bud**: seed pod of the wild iris.

P 189–66 We usually called those buds harses' buds, or just buds, and used them for throwing at each other.

horse car: see **horse-cat** below; CAR.

P 205–55 This larger type [of sled] was called the horse-car [to distinguish it from] the smaller type used by the man alone—the hand-car.

horse-cat: a heavy sled or 'catamaran' drawn by a horse; CAT[7] (P 148–61).

P 254–78 ~ A horse-drawn sled used for carrying tree-length (10'–15') sticks of wood home from the forest. They can be of varying size, although generally any horsecat is large enough to carry tree-length wood. The runners are made of 2" x 4" wood of varying length. The 2" running surface is covered by steel (not barrel hoops except in the case of very small horsecats, which are meant to be drawn by hand and are called man-cats).

horse chop(s), ~ chopper: (a) the figure of a horse's head, with movable jaws, carried by a Christmas mummer; HOBBY HORSE; (b) the entrance to a cove, esp in place-names, indicative of shape.

1953 *Nfld & Lab Pilot* ii, 193 Horse Chop cove is situated about 2 cables southward of the south-western extremity of Powell island. T 327–66 They haul a bag over their heads, and they'd have a pole to go up through this bag and have it rigged on a mouth. It had nails for teeth and it come open. It was made like a horse's head. That's why it was called a horse-chopper. T 354–67 They pronounce it horse-chops.

horse-cock: large freshwater mussel; horse mussel (P 77–74). See also COCK AND HEN, HEN.

horse-dandelion: fall dandelion (*Leontodon autumnalis*) (1898 *N S Inst Sci* ix, 375).

horse(s) fart: puffball (*Lycoperdon gemmatum*); SMOKY JACK.

P 189–65 Harse's fart is the local term for the common puffball when it is in a ripe condition and bursts, freely giving off brown spores into the air, upon bursting. P 126–67 Don't squeeze that horse's fart! C 70–28 We called them horse's farts and would squeeze them in each other's face in a playful manner.

horse(s) flower: wild iris (*Iris versicolor*) (P 189–66).

horse-fly: see **horse-stinger** below.

C 66–2 There is an insect that we call a horse-fly and its bite is supposed to be dangerous. C 69–20 We always called dragon flies horse flies because we used to see them around horses.

horse-haul: a small catch (of fish); WATER HAUL.

M 71–95 It was exciting to see the men return, the boats 'swamped,' or discouraging if their work resulted in a horse-haul.

horse-head: grey seal (*Halichoerus grypus*).

1871 *Zoologist* vi, 2550 Another species of seal is mentioned by the settlers under the local name of the 'horse-headed seal,' but I was unable to identify it. 1884 BELL 52 Grey or Horse-head Seal. . .is not uncommon along the East-main Coast. 1929 *Nat Geog* July, p. 108 The horsehead or gray seal. 1960 *Evening Telegram* 29 Feb, p. 2 The alien of all the seal species is the horsehead. Many people in Newfoundland have never seen or heard tell of one. I have only seen one such seal in many years of the seal hunt. In fact, I could not name it until an old Port aux Basques seal hunter named it for me. . . It has a long head exactly like a horse, and the nails on its flippers are more than twice as big as those of a harp seal. The hair on its body is more than twice as long as that of a harp or hood. They pup about the middle of February, and have never been known or seen in large numbers.

horse protestant: derogatory name (among Roman Catholics) for Protestant, esp one lax in attendance at church.

P 108–75 She said a horse Protestant was one who didn't go to church or went only occasionally.

horse-slide: see **horse-cat** above.

T 43/7–64 The hand-slide was small, you'd usually use dogs on that, but the horse-slide, you had to build that strong and sturdy—that's what she'd pull her load on. T 175/7–65 Just a hand slide, sir, what a man'd pull hisself—not a horse slide.

horse-stinger: dragon-fly.

1846 TOCQUE 269 In Newfoundland these [dragon] flies are generally called horse-stingers, though they do not possess the power of stinging. [1900 OLIVER & BURKE] 58 "The Amorous Tomcod": Then his heart gave away / To the horsestinger gay, / Or the birds that twit, twit, twitter. 1966 SCAMMELL 31 I remember, among the small-fry, when we heard that a certain merchant was offering the grand sum of two cents each for horsestingers' wings. We knew them as 'hosstingers' and I understand the modern name is dragonflies. Years later I found out the wings were used for cleaning the delicate insides of watches. 1975 HOLMES 8 Dragonflies are called devil's darning needles by some people because of the belief that they sew up the lips and ears of naughty children. In Newfoundland they are called horse stingers, but they do not bite or sting and are in no way harmful to man. On the contrary, they are beneficial as they eat large quantities of mosquitoes and black flies.

horse-tops: swamp thistle (*Cirsium muticum*) (1898 *N S Inst Sci* ix, 373).

horse-work: heavy manual labour.

1887 *Telegram Christmas No* 12 But on account of the three great prevailing evils, namely, poverty, horse-work, which thousands of men have to do in order to obtain fuel and lumber for domestic purposes, and the ordinary cooking-stoves in chimney-less houses. . .

horse v Cp HORSE n 1, WATER-HORSE. Phr *horse (something) up*: to place split cod-fish, taken from the salt, to drain in a 'pile' during curing process.

1936 SMITH 17 In horsing the fish up, any fish not perfectly clean would be washed over again, then put in the waterhorse, back up, with a slight sprinkling of salt; it would then lie in the waterhorse for twenty-four hours. C 75–136 ~ This is used by Conche fishermen in referring to making a pile of fish on a flake. Usually this fish has only [had] one or two days drying in the sun.

horsy-hops n A figure of a horse carried by mummers during Christmas festivities; HOBBY HORSE.

P 245–65 Then we'd get out the old horsy-hops and go jannyin'. 1969 *Christmas Mumming in Nfld* 66 There was until recently a 'hobby horse' or 'horsey-hops' in Sandy Cove. . . This is a frightening mask in the shape of a horse's head with a movable jaw controlled by a string. The jaws contain teeth of nails. 'You could tell that it was a horsey-hops outside by his jaws snocking [knocking] together.'

hort See HURT.

hose egg* See OSE EGG.

hot a
Comb **hot ass**: a tin kettle with a large flat bottom and sides tapering to the top; PIPER.
1973 BARBOUR 94 There were large iron [kettles] for heating water to wash dishes, but if one wanted boiling water in a hurry for a cup of tea, one used what were called 'quicks' or 'hot asses,' made of tin by the local tinsmith. Water boiled very quickly in these kettles, which had large bottoms that fitted the hole of the stove when the lid or damper was removed.
hot seal: a freshly killed seal (1924 ENGLAND 317).

hot = past See HIT.

hotten v Cp ADD ~ . To heat.
P 148–62 When the lock is frozen, people hotten their key and put it in. T 36/7–64 Now they got nothing to open this barrel with, so they picked up an old bolt and they lit a fire and hottened the bolt. M 68–16 She put salt in the frying pan and hottened it and put it in a wool sock. She told me to hold it against my back for as long as I could. 1971 CASEY . . .and he hottened the shovel.

hound n OED ~ sb¹ 6 (Nfld: 1623); O Sup² (Nfld: 1779–); DC (Nfld: 1779–). Oldsquaw or long-tailed duck (*Clangula hyemalis*).
1623 WHITBOURNE 114 The Fowles and Birds. . .of the Sea are. . .Teale, Snipes, Penguyns, Murres,

Hounds. . .and others. 1628 HAYMAN¹ 37 Hounds a kind of Fowle. [1779] 1792 CARTWRIGHT ii, 440 There were several hounds and gulls, with some pigeons and black-divers among them. 1819 ANSPACH 391 The most remarkable of the sea-birds which frequent these coasts [include] the hounds, rather larger than the teal, which migrate to the north in the spring in large flocks, and as they fly, make a continual noise resembling that of a pack of beagles when in chase. 1842 JUKES ii, 185 [A] kind of sea-bird, abundant on the south coast in the summer, called the 'hound' from its cry. 1884 STEARNS 92 Another name for the [cau-cau-wee] is that of 'hounds.' 1910 TOWNSEND 51–2 Many flocks of old squaws or long-tailed ducks flew about us. . . On the eastern Labrador coast they are called 'hounds.' 1976 *The Rounder* Mar, p. 20 Shortly after, an old cock hound, all alone, approached the decoys. There was the sound of one single shot and the duck hit the water.

house n Cp OED ~ sb¹ 4 f 'a business establishment' (1582–) for sense 1; EDD sb¹ 7 for sense 2; *Fisheries of U S* (1887), p. 154 for sense 3 (a); for combs. in sense 4: OED sb¹ 23: ~ -flag (1884), EDD sb¹ 7 (1) (a) ~ -place.
1 A merchant firm engaged in the Newfoundland seal hunt and fish trade, esp in the purchase and export of salt cod, and the financing of the fishing operation through the advance of supplies and credit.
1819 ANSPACH 427–8 Thus, in the spring of the year 1811, a principal house in Harbour-Grace, and the inhabitants of the North Shore, in Conception-Bay, reaped a most plentiful harvest [of seals]. 1832 MCGREGOR i, 193 A great majority of the merchants at St John's, as well as the agents who represent the principal houses, are men who received a fair education. 1849 [FEILD] 13–14 [It is] desirable to have a Clergyman here who can speak the French language, as many of the men at the Jersey house understand but little English. One house here brings upwards of seventy men. . .and at L'Anse-à-Loup which I visited on Monday. . .the merchant's house has 130 hands. 1905 *Nfld Qtly* July, p. 13 The mails from Europe generally came out in care of the captains of the merchant vessels, and were consigned to the Mercantile House to which the ship itself was consigned. The Head of the House or chief agent, became, on the arrival of the vessel, Postmaster for the time being, and distributed the letters and papers to their addresses. 1937 DEVINE 27 ~ Also denotes a mercantile house, i.e. 'Bowring's House.'
2 A kitchen, regarded as the principal living-room of a dwelling. See also **house-place** in sense 4 below.
[1886] LLOYD 76–7 The hut usually consists of four apartments, two downstairs and a similar number upstairs. These apartments are severally known as 'the house' (kitchen), 'room' (which may for sake of distinction be called a parlour), 'outside loft' (room over kitchen), and 'inside loft' (over parlour); in addition to which there is a small 'back house' or 'porch,' built on the warmest side of the hut, in which firewood is kept. 1937 DEVINE 27 ~ Used specifically to denote the kitchen or living room. For instance, one may ask in an

upstairs bedroom: 'Where are my boots?' Answer: 'They're down in the *house*.' T 222–66 The kitchen, of course, is the all-purpose room, and the kitchen is called 'the house.' C 69–5 I recall [her] usual comment when flankers popped out of the stove and unto the floor when she was putting in wood: My goodness, there must be a stranger coming, by the looks of the 'fire' going all over the 'house.'

3 (a) Deck cabin on a vessel; (b) wheel house.

1905 DUNCAN 32 The falling ice made great havoc with the deck-works; the boats were crushed; the 'house' was stove in; the deck was littered with ice. 1932 BARBOUR 73 Pearce Barbour, the mate, was on the cabin house counting the flashes on Wolf Rock light. T 187/8–65 I told the skipper he'd better take the wheel now, handle her better than what [I could]; I'd get up on the house an' watch the time for un to heave her to. T 194/5–65 An' when she fell under, the corner of her house went under water. T 203/6–65 He was a passenger boat, you know. He had one o' those housed in [places], a house built on her, but open in the stern an' ahead.

4 Attrib, comb, cpd **house-flag**: the distinctive flag or pennant of a firm engaged in the fisheries, seal hunt, etc.

1836 [WIX]² 65 Two full services in the sail-room of Messrs Newman and Hunt, which had been fitted up with house-flags for the occasion. 1842 JUKES i, 253 We saw over the roofs of the houses the topsails of a vessel loose, with the house-flag of my companion at the mast-head. 1858 [LOWELL] ii, 247 The *Ice-Blink* got herself ready to start, with sails filling and flapping, and streamer, and pennon, and house-flag, and union-jack, all flaunting gayly in the wind. [1872] 1899 *Nfld Law Reports* 446 On arriving at the flag, they found it to be a house-flag of Messrs Job Brothers placed apparently, with another flag and with pieces of canvas marked 'Nimrod, E White,' for the purpose of distinguishing three pans of piled and sculped seals. 1913 SHORTIS 11 John Munn of Buteshire and Wm. Punton of Perthshire. . .founded the firm of Punton & Munn, and built up the premises, where the firm still flies the blue and white flag, the same house flag as Baine Johnston. [1929] 1979 *Evening Telegram* 14 Feb, p. 9 The S.S. *Silvia*, flying the Furness Withy Company house flag, and with her funnels painted black and red, arrived in St John's harbour this morning on her first trip since being taken over from the Red Cross Line. P 108–70 Every mercantile house had its own flag, which was called its house flag.

house-haul(ing): the shift(ing) of a house from one site to another by dragging on rollers or by floating.

T 141/68–65² If you go house-hauling, you pick up wads enough to carry it home and dry it and make 'baccy enough to smoke for a month. P 245–74 The minister would announce that there would be a house-haul on a certain day and men would be supposed to gather and help haul the house to a new site.

houseleek: type of stonecrop; roseroot (1895 *N S Inst Sci* ix, 95).

house-paper: wall-paper.

T 55–64 The old house got damp an' there were so many tiers of house paper then on had let go from the boards. T 100/01–64 In them days you get house paper with old pictures—faces o' people an' big roses an' stuff like that.

house-place: kitchen. See sense 2 above.

1895 *J A Folklore* viii, 29 ~ the kitchen.

house standard: the quality or 'cull' of dried and salted cod specified by a mercantile firm as the basis for payment to a fisherman (P 245–55).

housetop: the covering of a vessel's deckhouse.

T 194/6–65 I had a two-inch mooring out over her housetop, rolled the nets around un; a hundred-pound grapel tied on, and he was on her cabin house.

hove, hoven See HEAVE.

hovel n Cp *EDD* ~ 1 'shed for cattle or pigs; out-house of any kind.' Subsidiary beaver-house or place of retreat.

[1777] 1792 CARTWRIGHT ii, 250 We found four dams and a hovel as we went up the brook. [1783] ibid iii, 25 If [the beaver] house is disturbed much before the pond is frozen, they commonly quit it. . .or they will go into an old house in the same pond, or a small one of their own there, which they generally have besides the one they live in, and it is termed the *hovel*. 1895 GRENFELL 36 When surprised [the beaver] retreat to holes in the bank, of which the entrances are hidden under water. These are called 'hovels.'

howden n Lesser scaup (*Aythya affinis*).

1884 BELL 55 Lesser Scaup Duck, Little Blue-bill. Howden of the people of Labrador and Newfoundland.

howk n also **houke**. A variety of seal.

[1766] 1971 BANKS 145 [The fishermen] divide them into five sorts which they Call Square Phipper Hooded Seal Heart or houke Bedlamer & harbour seal. 1855 MULLALY 60 The principal varieties are the harps, the hoods, the howks, the bedlamers, and square flippers.

hulder v *EDD* ~ v² 'conceal, harbour.' To shield, protect (a person) (P 9–55).

P 133–58 Don't go huldering that person around here. 1970 JANES 88 'I'm tired tellin' you about the way you goes on wit 'em. Hulderin' 'em and takin' up for 'em when you should be givin' 'em some discipleen. They're saucy as blacks, every one.'

hungered p ppl *EDD* hunger v 3 (1). Hungry, starved for food.

T 187/9–65 'No,' he said, 'we baint a bit hungered. We had our breakfast before we left this morning.'

hungry a Cp *OED* ~ 6 for sense 1; *EDD* 1 (1) hungry-grass Ir (1881–) for comb in sense 3.

1 Descriptive of a vessel without (a catch of) fish or seals.

1925 *Dial Notes* v, 334 ~ Without fish or seals; of a ship. 1937 DEVINE 27 ~ schooner. A schooner returning from the voyage with little or no fish. 'That schooner looks *hungry* alright.'

2 Phr *the hungry month of March*.

1924 ENGLAND 66 Morning again, the eleventh of 'de lang, hungry March month.' T 246/7–66 That's what the sayin' was: 'the hungry month o' March.'

3 Comb hungry grass

1842 JUKES i, 25 ~ a kind of grass they called hungry grass, and whoever passed over it immediately became so faint for want of food, that unless they could shortly obtain it they would drop and perish by the way. C 67–15 If someone came home very hungry, after walking about most of the day, someone might say to him, 'You must have walked on hungry grass.'

hungry wave: one wave following so quickly on another that it overwhelms a craft before it rides the first (P 243–57).

hunk v To cut, divide or place in large chunks.

T 347/50–67 Lumps of butter which Grandma used to hunk in, the big fresh butter in, and pepper and salt. . . You hunk off your leg of lamb, you hunk off your piece of corn beef.

hunt v Cp *OED* ~ v 4 b 'persecute, pester, worry.'

1 To tease jokingly.

1925 *Dial Notes* v, 334 ~ To jolly or josh (a person). 1937 DEVINE 27 ~ To joke, to 'take a rise' out of one and get him to believe a lie. T 141/68–65² I knowed he was tryin' to hunt me, see, and I said, 'She started gawkin'.'

2 Phr *hunt the wren*: see WREN.

hunt See SEAL HUNT.

hupper See UPPER.

hurdle-foot See HURL-FOOT.

hurl-foot n also **hurdle-foot**. Cp [John Walsh] *Ireland Ninety Years Ago* 77 'Maher, called Hurlfoot Bill'; *EDD* hurl v², sb⁴ 2 hurl-bat, 4 hurl 'crooked stick used in. . ."hurling"' Ir; hurdle sb 1 (2) hurdle-footed 'club-footed' W. A club-foot, esp in fanciful comparisons.

P 207–67 He's got feet like an earl-footed turnip (said of someone who walks with his feet turned out). Q 73–8 Turnips with a twisted root are called earl-footed. Q 154–78 'Url-footed—with deformed feet. P 127–79 Hurl-footed turnip—it never grew, just went to root.

hurry-up n A small, flat-bottomed tin kettle; PIPER, QUICK.

C 67–13 ~ small kettle usually used for cooking outdoors. Q 71–7 ~ small tin kettle, used for boiling water in a hurry.

hurt n also **hart, hert, hirt, hort, whort** [həːɹt, əːɹt, æːɹt, aːɹt] *OED* ~ sb³ now dial (1542–), whort (1578–), hurtleberry (1460–), whortleberry (1578–), *EDD* hurts, whort s w cties. See also BLACK HURT, GROUND ~ , INDIAN ~ , LOWBUSH ~ , STONE ~ .

1 Any of a variety of low bushes, producing blue or blue-black berries; the fruit of these bushes harvested commercially or for domestic use; bilberry, blueberry, huckleberry (*Vaccinium* spp).

[1578] 1935 *Richard Hakluyt* [Parkhurst's letter] 126 There groweth. . .hurtes, strawberryes. . . [1583] 1940 *Gilbert's Voyages & Enterprises* ii, 406–7 [Hayes' narrative] The soyle along the coast is not deepe of earth, bringing foorth abundantly. . .a berry which we call Hurts, good and holesome to eat. 1620 WHITBOURNE 6 Then have you there. . .multitudes of Bilberries, which are called by some, Whortes. [1794] 1968 THOMAS 140 The Berry which is to be found in the greatest quantitys is Hurts, they are called Whimberrys in England. 1842 JUKES i, 112 Whortle-berries, which the men called 'hirts.' 1858 [LOWELL] i, 94 Crackers, partridge-berries, horts, and others enrich the barrenness, and make it worth while for women and children to come and gather them. 1895 DAVIS 32 Berry-bearing plants are found distributed over the whole of the island. . .among which may be mentioned strawberries, raspberries, capillaire, partridge berries, bakeapple and 'hurtz' or blueberries. 1915 SOUTHCOTT 21 *V. Pennsylvanicum*. Whort, 6 to 15 inches high. Leaves oblong with bristle-pointed teeth, smooth and shining both sides. Branches angled, green, warty. Berries abundant blue or black, with a bloom, sweet. . . *V. Uliginosum*. Whorts, low and spreading. 4 to 18 inches high. 1920 WALDO 157 The berries called 'harts' (whorts) are, I presume, the 'hurts' of Surrey. 1929 BURKE [4] "Mary Joe Slip on your Bloomers": There's a pair of shoes for Benjamin, / The girls they want short skirts, / It's better than the [Klondike] / Since the rush came on the whorts. 1938 MACDERMOTT 239 In the summer the blueberry or 'hert' is probably more widely used than any other berry in Newfoundland. 1956 ROULEAU 32 Hurts: *Chamaedaphne calyculata*. . .*V. angustifolium*. T 158–65 She told me she picked two gallons [of] 'urts, but there's lots of 'em yet, you know, an' when they gets ripe they be thousands. 1970 PARSONS 156 Billberries, known to the livyers as 'herts,' are also widespread as well as strawberries and partridgeberries. 1981 *Evening Telegram* 16 May, p. 20 Sure everyone knows Topsail herts can't be jammed.

2 Comb hurt cake: a sweet cake made with blueberries as an ingredient (P 245–55).

hurt pie

1907 MILLAIS 6 At every meal you get 'hert pie.'

hurt mash: an area producing blueberries. See also MARSH: MASH.

M 69–12 The 'hurt mash' used to be the best blueberry-picking grounds around St Lawrence.

hurt pudding, hurty ~ : a boiled or steamed pudding with blueberries as an ingredient.

P 148–60 Hurty pudding: blueberry pudding. C 68–11 We had a hurt puddin' on Sunday.

hurt wine: home-made wine brewed from blueberries.

[1900 OLIVER & BURKE] 58 "If You Will Come to Tea": We'll do it fine / On strong whort wine, / Out on a Topsail spree. M 68–11 They got into the cupboard and stole her hurt wine. M 71–37 [The mummers] would then get a piece of Christmas cake and a glass of syrup or something stronger. There was usually an ample supply of dogberry and eart (blueberry) wine.

husk See HUSKY.

huskimaw n [ˈʌskɨmɑ:, ʌskəˈmɒə, ʌskɨˈmɒˈə] *DC* ~ Nfld (1921, 1924); cp *DC* eskimo: Ehuskemay (1743). See also HUSKY. Coastal Eskimo or Inuit of Labrador; the Eskimo language.

1895 PROWSE 591 The old English voyagers called them 'Huskimaws,' or shorter, 'Huskies.' 1910 PRICHARD 86 On our return he, fresh from desolations compared with which his native outport of Glovertown, Alexander Bay, was a populous centre, rejoiced to set foot again in a land where, as he said, 'a man might see a body now and again what wasn't a Huskimaw.' 1924 ENGLAND 176 Summers, I go down de Labrador. Oh, yes, I knows de Huskimaws, good. . .I can talk Huskimaw, some. [1929] 1933 GREENLEAF (ed) 310 "The Franklin Expedition": And the Huskimaw in his skin canoe, / That was the only living soul. T 1–63¹ They were all colours and all sizes: great big Newfoundland dogs they used to call them; but the Uskimaws used to have them, you know. T 31–64 In walks a fine-lookin' maid, Uskimaw maid, in through the door, and she had on a swanskin coat, jacket.

husky n also **husk** *DC* ~ ([Ehuskemay: 1743] 1830–). See also HUSKIMAW. Coastal Eskimo or Inuit of Labrador; attrib.

1849 MCLEAN 54 Myself and two men, along with my 'husky' interpreter, followed next morning. 1907 WALLACE 216 [The Eskimos] are pretty generally known as 'Huskies,' a contraction of 'Huskimos,' the pronunciation given to the word *Eskimos* by the English sailors of the trading vessels. 1911 PRICHARD 47 The next morning, Porter woke me with the words: 'Well, Husky Boaz has gone all right.' T 54/63–64 The old husk, he took the brand and he threw this one out in the water. C 69–23 When I was a child the other children called me 'husky' (my mother is an Eskimo).

huss v [hɒs] *EDD* ~ v² Gl So. To incite, or urge on, a dog; SISS.

P 148–69 I'll huss the dog after you. 1969 *Trans Dev Assoc* ci, 187 ~ call to urge on a dog. P 245–73 ~ A cry to dog, either to chase something or to pull a slide.

hyacinth n
1 False Solomon's seal (*Smilacina trifolia*) (1956 ROULEAU 32).
2 See WILD HYACINTH.

hypocrite n *EDD* ~ sb 2 'a lame person.' A cripple.

T 543–68 [folktale] And before they left to go down aboard, down comes this hypocrite on two critches.

I

I pro Cp *OED* ~ III I AM (1611, 1722). In n comb **I am**: the outstanding thing; excellent one.

T 169/70–65² Oh my God [for our mummers' disguises] we had the real I ams. And we had beautiful faces, sir, beautiful masks.

ice n *DC* ~ n 1 a, b Nfld (1819–; 1964) for sense 1; for combs. in sense 2: *OED* ~ bird 1 (Nfld: 1620); *EDD* ice sb 1 (2) ~ candle; cp *OED* chock sb¹ 5 naut for ~ -chock; *DC* ~ clamper (1945); cp *EDD* gall sb² 6 [spot] 'through which springs of water constantly ooze up' Do So D; cp *DC* ~ master (1853–) for sense (a); *DC* ~ pan (1918–), *O Sup²* (1901–); *DC* ~ pilot (1934–); ~ pole (1850–), *O Sup²* (Nfld: 1906–); cp *Cent* ~ saw (1890). Numerous other combinations, and many synonyms, are listed alphabetically elsewhere.

1 The ice-cover formed by the southward drift of the arctic ice-floes off Labrador, the northeast coast of Newfoundland, and the Gulf of St Lawrence; these floes as the breeding ground of the harp and hooded seal-herds, the objects of the annual seal hunt; esp in phr with *at, for, to*, etc.

1819 ANSPACH 428 In the same spring [1811], an unusual number of schooners and boats belonging to [Conception Bay] were totally lost at the ice, several of the mariners perished, some were carried away on the fields of ice in sight of their more fortunate companions. [c1845] 1978 *Haulin' Rope & Gaff* 21 "The John Martin (2)": Come all ye jolly fishermen agoing to the ice, / Oh, beware of the *John Martin* and don't go in her twice. 1850 *Weekly Herald* [Hr Grace] 15 May [p. 2] . . .the disheartening truthfulness of the old local proverb, —'In the long run no one's the better for what's got at the ice.' 1862 *Atlantic Mo* ix, 366 ''T was one time I goed to th' Ice, Sir. I never goed but once.' [1870] 1899 *Nfld Law Reports* 336 In an action of trover for seals taken at the ice, it is in law no defence to say that if not taken by the defendants the plaintiff in all probability could not have secured them. 1895 GRENFELL 157 But it is to the spring sealing, or 'going to the ice,' as they call it, that most look for the extra few dollars to help fill the children's mouths. 1918 *FPU (Twillingate) Minutes* 18 Apr [He] made remarks if Mr Coaker sent a seaman down here to take men to the ice for to get the benefit of the seal fishery he would get more shares for the Trading Company. 1933 GREENE xv The Ice. The name by which the great Ice Floe is always referred to in Newfoundland. 1936 SMITH 49 By the middle of February I had my own traps practically repaired and ready, so I thought of going to the Ice, or Seal-fishery, again. 1977 *Nfld Qtly* Summer, p. 6 The first time I was shipwrecked I was twenty-four; that was the first spring I was to the ice.

2 Attrib, comb, cpd **ice-bird**: the common dovekie (*Plautus alle alle*), winter resident and esp common in newly-formed ice; BULL-BIRD.
[1620] 1887 MASON 151 The sea fowles, are Sea Pigeons, Ice Birds, Bottle noses. [1668–9] 1963 YONGE

116 The wind freshning, we make the sail we can; see no ice but many noddies, ice birds, and one gull. 1784–5 PENNANT 512 [This bird] is called in *Newfoundland* the *Ice Bird*, being the *harbinger* of ice. [1794] 1968 THOMAS 47 . . .a bird called Ice Birds. . .about the size of crows, all white, except their Bills and Feet which are yellow. 1819 ANSPACH 391 The most remarkable of the sea-birds which frequent these coasts are. . .the tinker, or razor-bill; the loon and whabby, both of the diving genus; and the bull, a smaller bird, also called ice-bird. 1951 PETERS & BURLEIGH 258–9 ~ The smallest of our sea birds, with black upper parts and white under parts. . . Common winter resident and sometimes a summer straggler. Generally arrives in October and most depart by late May. They often occur in countless numbers in the slob ice.

ice-blind(ness): temporary loss of sight caused by the glare of light on an ice-field.
[c1860] 1916 MURPHY 12 As a rule, each man carries with him a little salve, in case of a cut, a little Friar's Balsam for strains, and a small phial containing a solution of sulphate of zinc to counteract ice blindness. 1924 ENGLAND 55 'Yes, an' look out fer de ice blind, too,' warned master-watch Roberts. . . 'De sun on de ice 'm enough to scald de bloody eyes out o' y'r 'id. An' travellin' fer de day's len'th, you'm liable to get a dose o' ice blind, even if you'm got smoked glasses. Dat feel like sand in y'r eyes.' 1929 *Nat Geog* July, p. 127 Landsmen call it snow blindness, but we call it ice blindness.

ice-block: ice blockade of coast during winter.
1916 GRENFELL 209 Then came the winter ice block again, and its life of more or less enforced idleness.

ice-boat: see **ice-skiff** below.
1935 KEAN 127 As late as 1795 the total catch of seals for Newfoundland only amounted to 4,900. In these days the mode of prosecuting was by ice-boats.

ice-candle [ˌɐis ˈkændl̩, ˈɐis ˌkænl̩]: icicle; CONKERBELL.
[1906] GRENFELL 196 Yes, and there were plenty o' ice candles a-hanging from our bows, too, before us left for home again. 1910 ibid 80–1 The precipitous faces of the cliffs are hung with the most exquisite ice candles forty feet in length. 1924 ENGLAND 207 I believe he could allocate any individual 'ice candle' (icicle) on any clumper in all the North! 1937 DEVINE 27 ~s. Icicles on the eaves of a building. T 141/63–65² But now in August again we'd have the frost, see, 'cause you see those great ice candles where the water was runnin' from the hills—'twould form in ice candles. C 68–24 [tall tale] When he went to feed his sheep one morning in January it seemed that the roof of the barn was supported by ice candles that hung from the eaves. He took them down, about a hundred of them and used them for longers for his fish flake. C 71–104 A riddle in which ice candles is the answer is 'What grows with its roots upward?' 1974 MARIN 45 'Cold enough to freeze ice-candles on your liver,' Mrs W—would tell us. At any rate, cold enough to freeze the harbour that year.

ice-cat: sled used to haul fire-wood in winter (P 148–61); CAT⁷, CATAMARAN.

ice-chock: heavy timber used to strengthen the hull of a sealing-vessel.
1895 GRENFELL 160–1 These are queer-looking craft to the unaccustomed eye, these steam sealers of about 300 to 400 tons burden, with their outside thick sheathing of hard wood, called 'ice chocks,' and their huge double stems, filled between with from nine to twelve feet of solid oak, built for charging through floe ice.

ice-claw: grapnel attached to a line and used to anchor a boat or vessel to the ice; CLUMPER ANCHOR.
1924 ENGLAND 138 'Bosun,' the Cap'n that night ordered, 'get the ice claw an' hold her 'ere to-night. An' when you get the claw out, tell the engineers to start ahead, easy.' We often, by the way, anchored to ice with a claw, or sometimes even to a pinnacle with a 'score' cut deep, casting a wire cable around it. T 141/64–65² He got in an' he hauled ashore a ice claw on th' heavin' line, an' he got a hold to the land in there in the battycatter.

ice clumper: floating pan of ice; CLUMPER, CLUMPET.
C 71–122 Ice clumpers is the name given to [pieces of] drift ice. To go jumping ice-clumpers was the pastime of the boys and some girls during the winter.

ice-fishing: seal hunting.
1907 MILLAIS 9 Twenty years at the 'ice fishing' (seal hunting). . .will try the strongest man.

ice-gall: patch of bare, slippery (melting) ice.
T 50/3–64 Travelled Exploits Bay with a clothes bag on our backs—sometimes in the clifts—ice gall—bad ice.

ice gaze: hunter's blind constructed from ice found in the vicinity; GAZE.
1870 *Can Naturalist* v, 298 Ice-gazes and false geese are also employed on the ice for killing these beautiful birds in the spring of the year.

ice-glim: glow or brightness seen over a distant ice field; ice-blink. See also GLIM and **ice-loom** below.
1887 BOND 64 The dreamy light of the 'ice-glim' in the sky showed that the white field was just beyond its rim.

ice-grip: metal device used to carry a large piece of ice; ice-tongs.
T 411–67 They cut it in square blocks about two feet by two feet. They would stick the ice grips into the ice and bring it through the ice house and put sawdust on it. They would have a rope over their shoulders and they would haul it over the ice. M 68–7 ~s. These grips were used and are still used for taking ice from the ice house or for carrying the ice to the water for to wash it. They are made of all iron, and weigh approximately eight pounds.

ice-hunter: (a) man who engages in the hunt or fishery for seals; (b) vessel so engaged.
[c1833] 1927 DOYLE (ed) 15 "Come All Ye Jolly Ice-Hunters": Come all ye jolly ice-hunters and listen to my song; / I hope I won't offend you, I don't mean to keep you long; / 'Tis concerning an ice-hunter from Tilton Harbour sailed away, / On the fourteenth day of March, eighteen hundred and thirty-three. [1837] 1906 MURPHY 3 [They were] trying to reach the land in a

boat after their vessel, an ice Hunter, was driven on the rocks. 1861 DE BOILIEU 198 One of the ship-wrecked men saved from the schooner had been an ice-hunter, and whiled away many an hour relating the mode of catching seals in the spring of the year on the coast of Newfoundland. 1866 WILSON 278 Few of the masters or skippers of ice-hunters knew anything of navigation. 1887 HOWLEY *MS Reminiscences* 3 No one but an experienced ice hunter, used to treading his devious way through the ice floe and taking advantage of every small opening and lead of water would attempt it. 1928 *FPU (Twillingate) Minutes* 5 Oct There was quite a talk over Mr Ashbourne buying a new ice hunter and having a Bonavista Bay man for captain. T 80/1–64 Now grandfather, he always runned a ice-hunter, you know—his own schooner, see. T 183–64 The ice hunters used to moor up there winter time an' go to th' ice. 1972 BROWN 119 Even in fine weather ice hunters never went anywhere alone.

ice-hunting: hunting seals amid the ice-floes; also attrib.
1861 DE BOILIEU 201 I knew a skipper who had a famous dog for ice-hunting, and this would kill from thirty to forty old seals in the course of a day. 1873 CARROLL 20 The great object is when ice hunting mas-ters come up with old seals on loose ice to keep by them and remain quiet until the ice runs together. 1877 TUCKER 229–30 In February the steamers were ready to start for the ice-fields in search of seals; the accus-tomed 'Ice-hunting Sermons' were preached. [1900 OLIVER & BURKE] 12 It was his first spring out ice-hunting. 1905 GRENFELL 120 Though we made very lit-tle by it, somehow we all looked forward to the 'ice-hunting,' as we called it. T 187/9–65 'This here ice hunt-ing racket,' he said, '(is) a hell of a hard racket.' T 401/2–67 Fifteen year old an' when I went ice huntin', took a man's share.

ice-island: see ISLAND OF ICE.

ice-jam: see JAM n: JAM (OF ICE).

ice-line: rope with grapnel attached, used to anchor a vessel to the ice; cp **ice-claw** above.
1935 KEAN 20 The trip was knocked away and the big ice line that my uncle trusted to stop the schooner snapped like a thread that was burnt by fire.

ice-loom: see **ice-glim** above; LOOM.
1891 PACKARD 136 We pass Battle Island, a compar-atively low island, with the 'ice-loom' or mirage resting over it.

ice-master: (a) captain of a sealing vessel; (b) experienced sealer in charge of a group of men hunting seals on the ice-floes; MASTER.
1895 PROWSE 452 And the great army of sealing skippers and great planters, where are they? . . .Their descendants. . .are still the most skilful ice masters, and their crews of Newfoundlanders the best sealers in the world. 1924 ENGLAND 4 The Cap'n looked a splen-did type of seaman and a famous ice master. . .the vig-our of a man of fifty, for all his seventy years, and a full half-century of seal killing to his credit. 1972 BROWN 34 The watches were divided, in turn, into ice parties, each party in charge of an experienced sealer known as an ice master, who, unlike the master watch, had no authority on board ship, only on the ice.

ice-pan: loose piece of floating ice with a flat surface; PAN n.
1861 DE BOILIEU 12–13 Almost at one breath the words were shouted to the man at the helm, 'hard up,' 'hard down,' and in less than another minute all hands had jumped out on the ice-pans to clear the ice from the brig's bow. 1891 *Holly Branch* 39 To the time when oil-clothes were not worn at the fishery, and feather beds were not carried to the Labrador. To the time when men hauled seals in bluchers, and slept on ice-pans. 1912 HUTTON 220 He felt the ice-pan rolling over; he heard the shout of 'Stay where you are,' and saw his brother leap into the waves.

ice-partridge: ivory gull (*Pagophila eburnea*), which frequents the edges of pack-ice and adja-cent coasts.
1907 TOWNSEND 311 [They] told us of shooting 'Ice Partridges' which came with the ice and seals in November or December. 1959 MCATEE 37 ~ Ivory gull (Especially the spotted young, which has a vague resemblance to a partridge or ptarmigan. Nfld., 'Labr.'). 1972 BROWN 35 Among [the gulls] hovered the pure white, pigeon-sized birds that the sealers called ice partridges. Ivory gulls from the Polar Pack, the world's most northerly sea birds, they were almost never seen on shore.

ice-party: group of sealers on the ice-floes.
1972 BROWN 34 The watches were divided, in turn, into ice parties, each party in charge of an experienced sealer known as an ice master.

ice-pilot: seaman skilled and experienced in navigating a vessel through ice-infested seas.
1916 MURPHY 13 The fame of [Brigus] captains [has] become world wide for their skill as ice pilots, so much so that they have been sought for by all our great Arc-tic explorers during the past fifty years or more. 1944 LAWTON & DEVINE 75 He missed two Springs from the Seal Fishery, during which time he was in the Arctic regions with Capt Bernier, as Ice Pilot, in the Canadian Government steamer *Arctic*. 1972 BROWN 17 [Newfoundland's] was the only sealing fleet in the world, commanded by captains who were national heroes, and in great demand as ice pilots for polar expeditions.

ice pinnacle: peak of ice, usu glacial or fresh-water ice, projecting above a surrounding field of ice; PINNACLE n.
1924 ENGLAND 56 Some were found crouched dead behind ice pinnacles, while a few had tried to build rude shelters of ice. 1972 BROWN 118 [He] directed some of the men to take up a zig-zag course, reporting flagpoles or blackened ice pinnacles whenever they saw them.

ice-plant: sea lungwort (*Mertensia maritima*), a spreading plant with oval leaves and pink-blue flowers, common near the sea-coast; BLUE BONNET (1898 *J A Folklore* xi, 275).

ice-poker: stout pole used to break a channel through the ice and push ice-pans away from the bow of a vessel; POKER[1]; POLE.
1892 *Christmas Review* 11 'Slides,' piled high with the clothes-bags of the seamen, were arriving at the

wharves, and loads of ice-pokers were being put on board the vessels.

ice-pole: wooden stick used as a club to kill seals and as a pole to assist sealer moving over floating ice; BAT n, GAFF.

1873 *Maritime Mo* i, 254 [The sealer carries] a stick six or eight feet long, which is called a 'gaff,' and serves as a bat or club to strike the seal on the nose, where it is vulnerable, and also as an ice-pole in leaping from 'pan' to 'pan.' 1906 LUMSDEN 107 This useful instrument also serves as an ice pole, enabling the daring sealer, amid the dangers of floating ice, to leap from 'pan to pan.'

ice-pounder: wooden mallet used to break a channel through the ice.

1836 [WIX]² 12 We took a heavy mallet, with a long handle, which the people call an ice-pounder, and escaped some hours of very laborious walking, by crossing in a boat to Bay Roberts.

ice-quar(r): ice formed from water seeping from or over the ground in freezing temperatures; see QUAR(R).

P 184–67 The water in the rock when freezing, squeezes out through the cracks and runs down the face of the rock where it freezes on. Ice quars are formed on the ground where the water cannot penetrate downwards.

ice-rind: thin layer of ice on water recently frozen or 'caught' over.

1946 MACKAY (ed) 490 The Newfoundlander has developed a wide vocabulary to describe ice conditions. To him, slush, ice-rind, pancake, sludge, slob, brash, and young ice each has its own characteristic. 1956 *Nfld & Lab Pilot* Supplement No 3, p. 8 ~ A thin, elastic, shining crust of ice, formed by the freezing of slush/sludge on a quiet sea surface. Thickness less than 2 inches. It is easily broken by wind or swell, and makes a tinkling noise when passed through by a ship.

ice saw: long saw used to cut a channel through the ice for a vessel.

1842 JUKES i, 262 If a large and strong pan was met with, the ice-saw was got out. [1844] GOSSE 111 The crews of all the vessels in the port unite to cut with ice-saws a broad channel through the midst of the harbour to the open sea. 1873 *Maritime Mo* i, 256 At times [the steamer] is arrested by the heavy ice, seven feet in thickness, and then, perhaps, the ice-saws are called into requisition to cut a pathway to the nearest 'lead' of clear water. T 14/20–64 Well, [an] ice-saw is about four feet long and a long handle on her, and we could take her up like this and shove her down through the ice; and teeth about an inch long, or two inches.

ice-seal: any of the species of seal frequenting the ice-floes.

[1749] 1755 DOUGLASS i, 298 The other sort called the Ice-seal, hath a large black patch, runs slow, and is killed by a small blow on the head. 1826 *Edin New Phil J* i, 40 [The jar seal] keeps more in the water than the other ice-seals. These all differ from the shore or harbour-seal. . . of these coasts. The ice-seals are alike migratory, and promiscuously gregarious.

ice skiff: large (usu undecked) boat, from

thirty to forty feet long, used in the seal hunt in coastal waters; SKIFF.

[1802] 1895 PROWSE 419 This adventurous and perilous pursuit is prosecuted in two different ways—during the winter months by nets, and from March to June in ice-skiffs and decked boats, or schooners. 1924 ENGLAND 197 And their next development of the 'fishery' was a gradual abandonment of netting in favour of going to the icefields in small boats—'ice skiffs' and open craft; incredibly small affairs with which to buck the arctic ice.

ice skipper: see ICE-MASTER; SKIPPER.

1972 BROWN 23 [He] was an experienced ice skipper, who had spent many years in the Arctic.

ice voyage: a sealing trip.

[1863] 1975 MOYLES (ed) 39 When I reached Lockyer's Bay several young men at that place were preparing to start for Greenspond and join their vessels for the ice voyage.

ice-work: the seal hunt.

T 141/66–65² In the winter months we still went gunnin', and by and by in March month come ice work.

idle a *EDD* ~ 2 Ha IW W Do. Mischievous; thoughtless; foolish in behaviour.

1857 LIND *MS Diary* 23 Nov I found some idle boys had been cutting down some trees near the Church & Parsonage. 1863 MORETON 32 ~ Full of mischievous tricks. It never is used as meaning simply without occupation. 1897 *J A Folklore* x, 206 *Idle* is used to mean wicked, expressing the full force of Watt's line, that 'Satan finds some mischief still for idle hands to do.' 1937 DEVINE 27 ~ Full of tricks; mischievous. T 264–66 Lots o' times this idle feller, you know, half drunk, go along an' try to tear it off o' their head. T 255–66 He was idle, you know, an' runnin' around, an' he fell on a drink bottle, an' he split his eye open. P 54–67 ~ lazy, non-serious; endearingly said of a small child.

idleness n *EDD* idle a 2: hence *idleness* 'mischief.' Enjoyable, trivial or light-hearted fun.

T 253/4–66 All sorts o' idleness one time, but you don't see no fun now like that, no fun hardly those days.

ignorant a *EDD* ~ 1, *O Sup*² 5 'dial and colloq.' Exhibiting bad manners.

P 108–70 He's an ignorant bostoon. 1973 PINSENT 71 He got the window down on my shirt sleeve and laughed. . . It worked out in his favour again. The ignorant thing, I thought. P 127–79 She was as ig'rint as a pig.

improve v Cp *OED* ~ v² 4 obs; *EDD* 2 'to grow larger.' Of a pregnant woman, to increase in size.

C 71–94 As the woman's stomach became bigger it was always said that 'so and so, she's improving.'

in av, prep *OED* in-draft 3 'an inward passage' obs (1570–1706) for sense 4.

1 Close to, approaching (the shore).

1873 CARROLL 18 As long as white fish are in with the land, so sure will seals of every description be

there. P 245–55 The wind is east—in from the sea.
T 43–64 If the ice was in, you'd walk off from the land,
an' you'd have your gaff with you and your sealing
rope, and probably you get the chance to kill one, two,
or three or four.

2 Toward the interior; away from the coast or
settled area.

P 148–64 I went in the road [toward the Goulds].
C 71–113 He went in the road [away from the coastal
highway]. 1976 GUY 38 [The Americans] put up some
camps in at the Station which was three miles in the
road. 1977 QUILLIAM 36 In this sea-girt isle, one 'goes
out' fishing and 'goes in' trouting; goes out to the salt
water bay or harbour to fish and goes into the fresh
water ponds and brooks to trout. 1979 TIZZARD 277 So
my father and later myself enjoyed a good meal of food
when we were cutting firewood in over Indian Hill or in
toward the Ridge.

3 Phr *in bulk*: see BULK n.

4 Comb **in-draft** ['ʊn ˌdræft, 'ʊndræf]: (a) narrow passage from the sea deep into the land; also
attrib (Q 71–8); (b) length of a bay or passage to
its innermost point (see Q 71 and 1974 quots).

T 70/1–64 Takes a big sea to hurt you there, a big
sea; like it is an in-draught place, see. T 33–64[1] We
brought up in Nain, it's a long in-draught you see, and
when they saw us we had our flag up. They knew we
were coming with provisions. Q 71–6 The bay has a
deep in-draft. It is a long bay. Q 71–8 What is the in-
draft of Cape Roger Bay? How far is it from the mouth
to the bottom? 1974 SQUIRE 9 Eastport. . .has an open-
mouth bay facing northeast toward the Atlantic Ocean.
It has an indraft of about four miles, with a shoreline of
little over seven miles.

in-wind: wind blowing from sea to shore.

1918 GORDON 79 Wind still in from the sea, keeping
everything back. . . Everybody has had to knock off
boat work as these in-winds are too chilly. C 67–162
[saying] 'Bubbles on the water during rain, sure to have
in-wind.'

increase mesh See 'CREASE MESH.

indian n Cp *OED* ~ 2 'original inhabitants of
America' (1618–); *DAE* 1 (1602–), *DC* 1 a
(1576–) for sense 1; for combs. in sense 2: *DC* ~
cup (1823–), *DAE* ~ meal (1635–), *DC* ~ pear 2
(1822–), *DC* ~ racket (1779); *DC* ~ salad (Nfld:
1778), *O Sup*[2] ~ tea (1709–), *DC* (1771–). See
also RED INDIAN.

1 Any of the non-European native people of
Newfoundland and Labrador; BEOTHUK, MIC-
MAC, MONTAGNAIS, NASKAPI, and occas ESKIMO;
freq in place-names.

[1617] 1915 HOWLEY 19 We shall visit the Naturalls
(Indians) of the country, with whom I propose to
trade. [1766] 1971 BANKS 132 This Subject Leads me to
say Something (tho I have as yet been able to Learn
Very little about them) of the Indians that inhabit the
interior Parts of Newfoundland and are supposed to be
the original inhabitants of that Countrey they are in
general thought to be very few as I have been told not
Exceeding 500 in number. [1771] 1792 CARTWRIGHT i,

156 Most of the inhabitants of this place [Fogo] came
to see the Indian; for none of them had ever seen an
Esquimau before. 1819 ANSPACH 180–1 Attempts had
been made, at various times, by the Governors of Newfoundland, to open a communication and establish an
intercourse with the native Indians of the island; but
hitherto without success. 1868 HOWLEY *MS
Reminiscences* 24 Sent the two Indians on in the canoe
to put up camps and have all ready by the time we
reached there. 1907 WALLACE 206 The Indians of the
Ungava district are chiefly Nascaupees, with occasionally a few Crees from the West. 1953 *Nfld & Lab Pilot*
ii, 372 Indian island, flat, 75 feet high, and covered
with turf, is situated. . .eastward.

2 In names of plants **indian cup**: PITCHER
PLANT (*Sarracenia purpurea*); ~ **hurt**: bearberry
(*Arctostaphylos Uva-ursi*) (1898 *N S Inst Sci* ix,
384) [see also HURT]; ~ **jug**: see **indian cup**
(1956 ROULEAU 32); ~ **pea**: beach-pea
(*Lathyrus japonicus*) (1956 ROULEAU 35); ~
pear: Juneberry; CHUCKLEY PEAR (*Amelanchier*
spp); ~ **pipe**: see **indian cup**; ~ **salad**: an edible
perennial of the Labrador coast; **india(n) tea**:
LABRADOR TEA (*Ledum groenlandicum*; also
Rhododendron canadense); ~ **tobacco**: Cana-
dian burnet (*Sanguisorba canadensis*) (1956
ROULEAU 32); ~ **vervine**: shining club-moss
(*Lycopodium lucidulum*) (1898 *J A Folklore* xi,
283); ~ **whort**: see **indian hurt** (1898 *J A
Folklore* xi, 273).

[1819] 1978 *Beothuk Vocabularies* 64 Indian
Cup—shucodidimit. [1822] 1856 CORMACK 13 The
prevalent plants are. . .Indian cup. . .marsh berry. 1840
GOSSE 300 The Indian Cup, or Pitcher Plant. . . the
leaves of this plant have their edges united together,
each one forming a deep and capacious cup, always
filled with water. 1865 CAMPBELL 61 Found a curious
plant, Indian cup by name. It has a yellow flower like a
waterlily, and the leaves are like small pitchers. These
fill with water, and nourish the plant in dry weather.
The root is said to be a cure for small-pox. 1968
THOMAS (ed Murray) 143 n. [Thomas's] description
undoubtedly refers to the Pitcher Plant or Indian
Dipper. . .which is the floral emblem of Newfoundland. [1822] 1856 CORMACK 12 On the skirts of the forest, and of the marshes are found. . .Indian Pear. 1895
N S Inst Sci ix, 87 Indian pear. 1846 TOCQUE 309 Pursuing my course round the edge of the pond, I
observed all the banks studded with snake-root. . . The
Indian pipe or Indian cup. . .grew in all directions.
1893 *N S Inst Sci* viii, 365 Indian pipe. 1963 MERCER 54
'Indian Pipe,' Pitcher plant. [1778] 1792 CARTWRIGHT
ii, 319 I went upon the hill this morning, but could not
perceive much ice gone since yesterday. Indian salad is
now [14 May] springing up. [1786] ibid iii, 227 The only
vegetables which I found fit to eat, were alexander (or
wild celery), fathen, scurvy-grass, the young leaves of
the osier, and of the ground-whortleberry; Indian-sal-
lad, red-docks, and an alpine plant, which the reindeer are very fond of. [1771] 1792 ibid i, 100 Being destitute of medicine which Dr Brookes prescribes in such
cases. . .I judged, that Indian tea was of the same
nature with the herbs which are recommended by that

author, I had some gathered from under the snow in the woods, and gave her a pint of the strong infusion of that plant sweetened with sugar; repeating the same three hours after. [1783] ibid iii, 16 Here we found bad walking in general (for the country had been burnt some years ago, and is now over-grown with strong Indian tea, with many large cubical rocks among it. . .). [1794] 1968 THOMAS 141 The Indian Tea grows on a Bush which riseth to the size of a Gooseberry Bush. Its Sprays shoot out trifoliated, pointed Leaves—the upper part green, the under part a beautiful Orange Colour. 1840 GOSSE 300 The ground was covered with the same spongy moss, with shrubs of Indian Tea. 1916 HAWKES 37 Indian tea. . .makes a good poultice for chills. 1937 DEVINE 29 ~ A substitute for tea, brewed from the wisha capucoa. In the old days when tea was scarce its consumption was general over Newfoundland. 1951 *Nfld & Lab Pilot* i, 209 Indian tea island lies close off the eastern shore. 1973 GOUDIE 26–7 We have a lot of Indian Tea in our country and it bears little white flowers.

3 Attrib, comb **indian lock**: notching cut into the ends of beams to secure the corners of log structures.

M 69–6 After the hole had been dug, the walls of the cellar would be built. A few cellars were built with logs fitted together at the ends with the Ingin Lock (Indian lock).

indian meal: corn-meal, a staple on shore and aboard ship, esp distributed through dole.

1843 *Nfld Indicator* 18 Nov, p. 3 10 barrels Indian meal. 1848 [FEILD] 103 Many families were entirely supported on Indian meal supplied by the Government. [1867] 1899 *Nfld Law Reports* 184 The board, by a majority of one, attempted through a resolution to extract from the plaintiff a particular description of Indian meal, or an abatement in the stipulated price, whilst his contract enabled him to supply any description of meal, whether white or yellow, provided it was sound and good, at the same price. 1869 HOWLEY *MS Reminiscences* 30 Their only sustenance seemed to be Indian meal bread a little tea and molasses but very little else. [1959] 1965 PEACOCK (ed) iii, 898 "Young Chambers": We'll lock you now in jail, my boys, for four long months or more / To feed you well on Injun meal and bread out of the store. T 448–67 They give some o' that them days, when you couldn't get nothin' else; indian meal they used to call it—dark stuff. 'Twas hard eatin'.

indian papoose: porcupine.

1884 STEARNS 215 [The porcupine] occasionally utters a sort of plaintive cry, and this, with many other circumstances, has won for it, by the whites along the coast, the name of 'Indian papoose.'

indian racket: a type of snowshoe.

[1771] 1792 CARTWRIGHT i, 92 The snow is exceedingly deep; but it was good walking with Indian rackets. 1792 PULLING *MS* Aug I hastened back to my tilt as fast as I could then pulled off my *pot-lid* rackets (which are round, about the size of the rim of a man's hat) and put on my Indian rackets (which are the shape nearly of a boy's paper kite). . .and set out in pursuit of the Indians.

indian spear: type of Inuit fish-spear.

[1771] 1792 CARTWRIGHT i, 139 Killed three brace of fine trout, but had the misfortune to break my rod. I then took up an Indian spear, and killed two salmon with it.

indulgence n A box placed beside the splitting-table and constantly replenished with cod to be processed.

M 71–117 From [the stage head] the cutthroater carried them inside to the splitting table. In later years one of the crew hands would do this carrying job, keeping a box called an 'indulgence' (for the old hands this was a luxury) filled for the cutthroater.

inflammation n Pneumonia.

T 207–65 The pneumonia they calls it now—used to call it inflammation in them days.

inshore a *OED* ~ B 'situated or carried on near. . .the shore' (1855); *DAE* ~ cod (1884–).

Comb **inshore cod**: cod-fish migrating to, and taken in, waters adjacent to the coast; SHORE[1]: ~ COD, ~ FISH.

1965 *Daily News* 15 Nov, p. 3 Large inshore cod are fetching from [4 to 4.75] at selected fish plants. 1969 MENSINKAI 42 The most extensive incidence of settlement in small and scattered communities coincides with the whole of the east coast, where the density of raw material production (inshore cod) is highest.

inshore fisherman: fisherman who operates (with small boat or traps) in coastal waters; SHORE[1]: ~ FISHERMAN.

1957 *South Coast Commission* 108 The plight of the inshore fisherman on the South Coast is not unlike that of the fishermen of some other parts of the Province, except that it is more pronounced. 1973 HORWOOD 9 Lambert was an inshore fisherman, he owned boats and fishing gear and was just about to begin the fall fishing. 1974 *Federal Licensing Policy* 28 One concern that we have is that an effort to increase Canada's share of the catch will redound solely to the benefit of the integrated offshore fishing corporation and to the detriment of the inshore and nearshore fishermen. 1977 BUTLER 57 The purpose of this late trip was to collect fish from some inshore fishermen.

inshore fishery: all the branches of the fishery, but esp the cod-fishery, conducted in small boats in coastal waters; SHORE[1]: ~ FISHERY.

[1841] 1954 INNIS 405 The inhabitants complain of the Fishermen of Fortune Bay coming to the Harbour of St Laurence, with large Schooners, (which they cannot afford to procure for themselves,) each having two or three punts with them, for the purpose of the inshore Fishery, while the Schooners are employed in the offing. 1845 *Journ of Assembly* Appendix, p. 208 The British Fishery is now confined to an in-shore fishery prosecuted in punts and small craft, leaving the deep sea fishery on the Great Bank and other valuable Banks and fishing grounds altogether in the hands of the French and Americans. 1953 *Nfld Fish Develop Report* 91 Historically, the fishery of Newfoundland, exclusive of the whale and seal fishery, has been mainly an inshore fishery and has been prosecuted by fishing with trap, trawl-line and hand-line for cod that follow

baitfishes to the shore. 1969 MENSINKAI 59 We accept
the official definitions which regard an 'offshore'
fishery as one where boats weighing 25 tons and over
are used and an 'inshore' fishery as one where boats of
less than 25 tons are used. 1981 *Evening Telegram* 15
July, p. 2 The province's inshore fishery has been 'disastrous' in most areas this year.

inshore fishing: see **inshore fishery**; SHORE[1]: ~
FISHING.

1785 SHEFFIELD 92 The fishermen live on fish and fat
pork, of which with hard biscuit, they make a dish that
is preferred by them to fresh provisions; neither the
bank fishing nor the in-shore, or boat fishing, will
admit of any other but salt provisions. 1975 BUTLER 50
He was in a position to learn at first hand all the
types. . .of boats used in the inshore fishing industry of
the nineteenth and first part of the twentieth centuries.

inshore seal: the 'harp' seal during its migration.

1924 ENGLAND 21 The harps cling to land as much as
possible, if they can manage to escape heavy ice during
the early part of their voyaging. They keep a quarter to
half a mile at sea, and are called 'inshore' seals; but if
any danger or obstacle threatens, they beat away
promptly from land.

inside n

1 Interior of the country, away from the sea-
coast. See IN av, sense 1.

T 33–64[1] The agent for the Hudson Bay Company he
told me now the Eskimo wasn't as 'telligent as the
Indian on the inside, the Mountaineer.

2 The coast, or mainland, of Labrador; the
protected inlets of the Labrador coast. Cp
OUTSIDE.

1977 *Inuit Land Use* 337 The Settlers, then, lived on
the 'inside,' and they regarded their homesteads, trapping areas, and fishing spots as their own. When they
refer to the 'outside,' they mean the islands, sea, and
ice that lie off shore, beyond the mouths of the bays,
estuaries, and islands that make up 'inside.'

inside av

1 Located in the interior, away from the settled coast.

1870 HOWLEY *MS Reminiscences* 25 Spent all day
examining both sides of the Cove and the country
inside. T 58/62–64 We had meadows inside over the hill
there. T 69–64 All of them people they all wanted to
settle right out on the seashore—fish after fish. There's
none of 'em never went inside now; they always stayed
out to the salt water. T 186–65 There was some inside,
but not very big. . .the people used to get most of their
firin' then off o' this land.

2 Located on the landward side of an ice-field,
or between an ice-field and land.

[1907] 1979 *Nfld Qtly* Fall, p. 22 Three steamers can
be seen steaming south of Cabot Island, they evidently
cannot get down [north] inside and are afraid of getting
jammed on the land. T 84–64 When I gets there,
there's good many seals outside—more seals outside
than was inside.

3 In the Labrador mainland away from the
open sea.

1977 *Inuit Land Use* 167 Settlers had different rules
for trapping 'inside,' at their places in the bays, and for
activities 'outside,' around the coastal islands and in
the interior.

4 Attrib in var combs. **inside cut**: passage of
open water between an ice-floe and the land.

[1907] 1979 *Nfld Qtly* Fall, p. 22 All these steamers
took the inside cut through Baccalieu Tickle and were
in open water all day. 1933 GREENE 35 Generally the
Floe will rift some little distance east of the shores,
thus leaving broad or narrow that ice-clear passage by
the Island's coast that the sealers know so well as the
'Inside Cut.'

inside door: the entrance to a cod-trap situated
nearest to the land.

T 82/3–64 I asked this feller how the fish was workin',
was it comin' down—where he was gettin' it, in his
inside door or outside door. Didn't know!

inside garden: an area cleared for growing vegetables in the country away from dwellings (P 148–
76).

inside place, ~ **room**: the room in the house
used only for formal occasions, special visitors,
etc.

T 222–66 It is called simply the room, which is an
indication of its exalted status; or sometimes it is called
the inside place. It is used very infrequently. M 69–6
The room in which the body was kept was in most cases
small since it was not made for a living room and was
always referred to as the inside place. This room had
very little use. . . [There were four kerosene lamps,] a
big one for the kitchen and small ones for the bed-
rooms or inside room. M 71–44 We have the mats off
the inside place (what we would call a parlour) on
Christmas Eve. They never went back no more until
after Old Twelfth. 1972 MURRAY 68 In some cases the
birth might take place in the 'inside place' (i.e., the
parlor), or even in the kitchen.

inside run: see **inside cut**.

1972 BROWN 28 He didn't need wireless to tell him
that the ice was tight to the land, and that there was no
chance of taking the 'inside run' where the water was
often clear.

inside stage: shed on a fishing 'stage' where
split cod-fish are salted and piled.

1967 FIRESTONE 97 The split fish are carried to the
inside stage, at the other end of the wharf in a wheel
barrow. There they are salted and stacked in tiers
(made into salt bulk). C 75–136 [There's a] bridge
between the outside stage where the fish is cleaned and
the inside stage where the fish is salted.

inside water: see **inside cut**.

1924 ENGLAND 25 Both the [hoods] and the harps,
after abandoning their pups, strike for land, they take
'the inside water' and work north as rapidly as possible.

inside of prep phr Between (ice-field, a boat, etc)
and the land.

1873 CARROLL 14 When the ice hunters come across
the whelping bags containing lumps of white fur or hair
they know at once that it belongs to the hood seal, and

believe that the harp seals are to the north-west of them or in other words inside of them. [1896] SWANSBOROUGH 32 "The Seal Fishery": But you must not suppose that all / The vessels are within a call; / For some skippers keep the outside, / Others the centre, some inside / Of the ice. [1907] 1979 *Nfld Qtly* Fall, p. 22 We are now off Cabot Island, the steamers inside of us are in bad position as shoals abound near the land. 1975 BUTLER 42 There was a couple of small [boats], Walt Dicks and Tom Upshall they were inside of us.

into prep In.

1896 *J A Folklore* ix, 30 There is nothing into the man. T 41–64 Now the hook you get those days has a little eye into it, a little hole in it, you see, put on with the gengin'. 1964 *Can Journ Ling* x, 45 He was born into it, lived into it and died into it. 1971 CASEY 257 The hole was there then but whatever was into it was gone. 1979 *Evening Telegram* 2 June, p. 6 I have often remarked 'What's into the cat is into the kitten.'

irish a

1 In phr *go into an irish sulk*: to become morose esp after an interlude of high-spirited gaiety (P 243–64).

2 In comb **irish chain**: a decorative pattern used in making quilts or in knitting.

P 255–65 ~ quilt. Home-made quilt with rows of little coloured squares. Q 71–7 Homemade quilt with a solid white back-ground; small squares (all of the same colour) are sewn together to form a chain pattern against the white background. Grandmother had always heard it called double Irish chain quilt. 1975 POCIUS 32 [knitting of mitts and gloves] In Conception Harbour, a type of block pattern was used that was called a 'double Irish Chain'. . . This pattern consisted of blocks arranged in a chain-like pattern, and was identical to the pattern used on quilts.

irish lord: type of sea-bird.

[1794] 1968 THOMAS 34–5 The next day, May the Second, I saw a brace of Birds called Irish Lords. How they came by this ludicrous name I cannot learn, they always being found some hundreds of Leagues from the Land.

irish toothache: pregnancy (P 175–67).

iron n

Comb **iron-house**: blacksmith's shop.

T 195–65 Put them in, old man, and went up in the iron house and got two keys made for to put through the pins again, and took my hammer and rivet the shaft.

iron spruce: red spruce (P 27–81).

ironwood: Juneberry (*Amelanchier* spp); CHUCKLEY PEAR (1898 *J A Folklore* xi, 226). Also **iron-wood berry**: fruit of the highbush-cranberry (*Viburnum trilobum*) (1956 ROULEAU 32).

island n *OED* ~ 1 c *island of ice* obs (1613–1769), SMYTH 405 for sense 1.

1 Phr *island of ice*: iceberg; ice-island.

[c1545] 1895 PROWSE 40 We met with all the Ilands of ice; that was the first day of July at night and there

arose a great and marvallous great storme. 1612 GUY 414 No Ice had bin seene fleeting in any of the Bayes of this Countrey all this yeare, (notwithstanding that [they] met one hundred and fifty leagues off in the Sea great store of Ilands of Ice). 1620 WHITBOURNE 56 Those Ilands of Ice are not dangerous unto Ships being once descried, as by their whitnes they may in a dark night when men looke out for them. [1663] 1963 YONGE 54 Next morning we saw many great islands of ice, of divers shapes, and many smaller pieces of different forms. . . These islands of ice infest the coast in the beginning of February, and last till June and sometimes later. [1766] 1971 BANKS 119 At ten tonight for the first time we see an Island of Ice the night is Hazy but the Sky clear no moon the Ice itself appears like a body of whitish light the Waves Dashing against it appear much more Luminous. [1771] 1792 CARTWRIGHT i, 157 A light air springing up at north in the afternoon, we got an offing of four miles by night; but, in affecting that, we narrowly escaped getting foul of a large island of ice. [1794] 1968 THOMAS 47 These Islands of Ice, altho seen floating here in the month of May, are not masses of Ice frozen last Winter, but were frozen about a year ago in the Greenland Sea or the Labrador Coast, which on the Sun assuming its powers, separates these immense Seas of Ice into large fields and islands and is then drifted about by the winds and currents for fifteen or sixteen months before the Sun totally dissolves them. 1861 NOBLE 47 Even the hardy fishermen, no lovers of 'islands-of-ice,' as they call the bergs, felt for us. 1895 TOCQUE 198 The islands of ice or icebergs are dreadful engines of destruction. 1924 ENGLAND 114 'Dem islands of ice looms more 'an what dem is,' he asserted. 1936 SMITH 26 To make matters worse an island of ice came in the harbour at noon and headed straight for our schooner. T 172/5–65 So when he got there, there was a island o' ice right in the berth—tide took un there, I suppose; right where the trap would go, this island o' ice was right there—had the berth took. 1981 HUSSEY 9 These were never referred to as icebergs. We always used the term 'Islands of Ice.'

2 Comb **island pan**: a flat piece of (floating) ice; PAN n.

T 75/8–64 And there was an island pan after driving along. They brought us in about half a mile of Careless Point, and dumped us out on the island pan.

island rock: a small rocky islet near the shore.

[1778] 1792 CARTWRIGHT ii, 334 I brought all the traps away from thence, and saw two otters on the island rock at the mouth of the river. 1873 CARROLL 10 They repair to the different Island rocks off the shore. 1953 *Nfld & Lab Pilot* ii, 243 Island rock, 6 feet high, lies on this shoal bank half a cable eastward. 1975 BUTLER 113 Late in the evening, just before night, we were abreast the Dirty Rocks—an island rock situated near the southern part of Merasheen Head.

iss See YESS.

italian n A grade or cull of dried and salted cod-fish prepared for the Mediterranean, esp the Italian, market.

1955 *Nfld Fisheries Board* No 23 Choice Italian. Sound quality fish, reasonably thick, hard-dried, well-split, clean on back and face, slightly yellowish cast, not sour or showing liver or gut, or excessive blood stains or clots, or excessive salt on face, not to include round or lap tails. Prime Italian. Sound quality fish, hard-dried, not up to the standard of Choice but excluding oversalted, round and lap tails, sunburnt, broken, slimy and dun. T 410–67 There was small madeira, large madeira; small thirds an' large thirds; small West Indee; tomcods. . .Italian—too many grades for me!

i tally-o n   also **tally-(h)o** [æi 'tælɪ oʉ]. Cp *OED* tally-ho 1 b [huntsman's cry]; see also TALLY¹ n: the cries of men piling or counting fish, seals, etc. Noise, racket; state or condition of excitement.

P 198–66 They're making a lot of tally-o. T 257–66 They get up, the whole lot of them in the middle of the house for a big step-dance then, a real I tally-o. P 167–67 What a party! We had I tally-o.

J

jack¹ n   *O Sup²* ~ sb¹ 25 (1891–), *DC* 3 Nfld (1895–) for sense 1; *EDD* 1 (6) jack-blunt, (35) (a) jack's alive for phr in sense 2; *DC* jackboat Nfld (1951–) for comb in sense 3.

1 A bluff, two-masted decked vessel, schooner-rigged and varying from 5 to 20 tons (4.5–18.1 m t), used for various fisheries purposes; see also **jack-boat** in sense 3 below. Cp BULLY¹.

1845 *Journ of Assembly* Appendix, p. 215 Is it not chiefly an in-shore fishery, prosecuted in what are called Jacks, with two [or] three hands, and in Punts? 1861 DE BOILIEU 28–9 A boat from the fishing establishment or depôt having arrived alongside one of these, the work of loading the jack (by which name all boats attending the seine are called) is soon completed, and the fish are brought home and unloaded. 1891 PACKARD 132 The fisherman's sail-boat is a ponderous, clumsy affair called a 'jack.' It is twenty-five or thirty feet long, with not much breadth of beam, rudely built, with short masts, and small sails stained red or black, or with both colors; the oars are of spruce, and very large and heavy, and the stern of the boat is provided with two stakes, such as whalemen use for sculling. 1896 *J A Folklore* ix, 34 ~ a fishing-boat. . .from seven to fifteen tons' burden. The deck has open standing spaces forward and aft for the fishermen to stand in while they fish. The deck is formed of movable boards. It is schooner-rigged, but without either fore or main boom. The foresail is trimmed aft by a sheet, and the mainsail trimmed aft to horns or pieces of wood projecting from the quarters. 1913 *Christmas Chimes* 25 The harbor—so called—of Bonavista was, at this time, filled with schooners, some of them fishing vessels with their full supplies for Labrador, fishing boats of all sizes from the 20 qtl. jack to the bully and skiff of the smaller planters. T 25–64 And then the fishing schooners, the small ones, they call them jacks. They would be about five or six tons, decked in, good enough to cross the Atlantic if they were handled right. 1975

BUTLER 30 He bought an old jack down in Woody Island and we had a wonderful summer. . . She was about eighteen ton.

2 Phr *jack-blunt*: outspoken, forthright.

P 24–67 She was very jack-blunt in telling me what she thought of it.

jack-easy: unworried, happy-go-lucky.

P 56–63 He's jack-easy about it all. 1975 *Evening Telegram* 19 June, p. 6 The need at Goose is too critical to allow a jack-easy attitude to prevail in government.

jack's alive: game in which a burning object is handed round a circle, the player in whose hand the brand expires paying forefeit.

1937 DEVINE 29 ~ A game with a lighted stick.

3 Attrib, comb **jack-boat**: see 'jack' (sense 1 above).

1937 *Seafisheries of Nfld* 29 The gear most favoured by the Shore fishermen are cod-traps, cod-nets, hand lines, trawls and jiggers, and the boats used are schooners, trap skiffs, jack-boats, dories and punts; many of these are now propelled by motor engines. 1957 *South Coast Commission* 154 In the area from Cape La Hune to Codroy there are some 30 fishing communities with approximately 800 fishermen using 300 small open boats and about 50 jack boats and long-liners. T 39/40–64 They used to have jack-boats, you know, boats around perhaps fifteen, twenty ton. 1975 BUTLER 53 A jack boat was a small boat which carried one dory [and] had three men for crew. . .about thirteen to fifteen tons with rudder outside.

jack curlew: hudsonian whimbrel (*Numenius phaeopus hudsonicus*); CURLEW.

1870 *Can Naturalist* v, 296 [The jack curlew] visits Newfoundland in its migrations.

jack fisherman: man fishing with a seine in a 'jack-boat.'

1909 BROWNE 225 [These islands] were formerly important fishing places, but are now rarely visited except by 'jack' fishermen.

jack-jump-up-and-kiss-me: snapweed (*Impatiens capensis*) (1898 *J A Folklore* xi, 224).

jack root: avens; BLOOD ROOT (*Geum macrophyllum*) (1895 *N S Inst Sci* ix, 88).

jack² See BAIT JACK.

jack³ See POOR JACK.

jackabaun* n   also **jockabaun***. Cp *OED* Jacobin 2 b 'nickname for any political reformer' (1793–); *EDD* jacobines ?obs 'loose, disorderly persons.' A mischievous, untrustworthy person.

P 41–68 A person not wholly trustworthy was called a jockabaun. C 75–144 ~ A saucy, deceitful person. My aunt caught a young man picking her berries. Next time she saw him she referred to him as an ugly jackabaun.

jackass n   SMYTH 406 'heavy rough boats used in Newfoundland'; cp *O Sup²* jackass 5. A two-masted vessel rigged for the seal hunt with square, rather than fore-and-aft, sails on the

mainmast; attrib in **jackass brig**; BEAVER¹: BEA-
VER HAT MAN.

1826 [GLASCOCK] i, 140 It was notorious that a considerable part of the property plundered was secreted
and carried away in boats, called 'jack-
asses,' to the
outports. 1892 *Christmas Bells* 14 Our skipper could
not read or write, so to make matters clear and intelli-
gible for him, I drew all the different vessels as he
described them—one was a brig; another a jackass
brig; another a schooner with a square main-topsail
(common rig in those days); every spar and sail was
minutely drawn out from his description. 1933 GREENE
45–6 Some [of the sealing schooners] were of special
and local design, and so original in rig and suits of sail
for the Ice, as to earn such quaint names as the 'Jack-
Ass-Brigs' or the 'Beaver-Hat-Men'; and almost all of
these craft were built by the handy sealers themselves.
1961 *Evening Telegram* 23 May, p. 6 The type of two-
masted craft on whose mainmast upper square sails
would be fitted temporarily, to make a jackass brig,
was the vessel that regularly was all square-rigged on
the foremast and all fore-and-aft-rigged on the
mainmast. . . They were numerous in the Newfoundland trade.

jackatar n   also **jackie tar, jackitar, jack-o-tar,
jackotaw, jacky tar** ['dʒækətɑːɹ, dʒækə'tɑːɹ,
'dʒækɪtɑːɹ]. Cp *OED* jack-tar 'appellation for
common sailor' (1781–); *EDD* jacky (17) ~ tar 'a
sailor's hornpipe' (1873) Sc; LA MORANDIÈRE iii,
1380 jacotars [Nfld]. A Newfoundlander of
mixed French and Micmac indian descent; the
speech of such a person.

1857 LIND *MS Diary* 23 May [I] went to see a poor
man who has been very ill for 7 months, he & all his
family belong to a much despised & neglected race
called 'Jack a Tars,' they speak an impure dialect of
French & Indian, R.C.'s and of almost lawless habits.
1873 HOWLEY *MS Reminiscences* 15 Intermixed with
all these [Highland Scotch, the French Acadians and
the English in Bay St George] were a number of Micmacs and half-breeds, known locally as Jack-o-Tars.
1925 *Dial Notes* v, 334 Jack-o-tar. A west coast Newfoundlander of half French or Indian extraction. 1927
RULE 25–6 The population of the Bay of Islands consisted [in 1865, apart from English settlers, of] a few
mixed French and Indian blood—jackotaws they were
called; though I don't know how the word should be
spelt. 1933 GREENLEAF xxv The French
inhabitants. . .speak. . .in a mixed dialect of French,
English, and Indian called 'Jack-a-tar.' T 189/90–65
An' we used to have some jackatars from over across
the island. T 273–66 Jackatar belonged to Stephenville
[area]. 1966 SZWED 31 Here, the Scots remained resis-
tant to intermarriage with the French for many years
(although marriage occurred in increasing numbers),
labelling the French 'Jack-o-tars,' a synonym for half-
breeds. [1971] GLASSIE (ed) 164 He stops at Journois
Brook, Shallop's Cove, and Bank Head, settlements
known on the West Coast of Newfoundland as the
homes of the 'Jack-o-Tars,' or 'dark people'—the
French-Indians. 1975 BUTLER 89 We met two Jackie
Tar hunters from the West Coast and they told us we
would need a boat to cross the Humber River.

jacket n   Cp *OED* ~ 3 d 'a young seal' Nfld;
SND jack n³ 'the skin of a seal' Ork (1795).
From RAGGED-JACKET and, indirectly,
WHITE-COAT.

1 The skin of a harp or hooded seal with the
fat or blubber attached; PELT n, SCULP n.

1880 *Standard* [London] 20 May, p. 3 As fast as one
[seal] is clubbed or shot the skinner with the sharp
knife turns it out of its 'jacket,' as the skin with the
attached blubber is styled.[*OED*] 1936 SMITH 199 In
my sixteen springs at the Seal fishery I sculped, or took
the jackets off (that is, the fat from the carcass) about
one thousand seals.

2 Phr *a jacket colder*: rather colder.

1863 MORETON 37 The climate of the lower end of
Greenspond harbour was said to be 'a jacket colder'
than the upper end, being more exposed. It was common, also, to indicate the degree of change in weather
by this phrase. 1937 DEVINE 29 It's a jacket colder tonight than last night. P 118–67 Yeah boy, it's a jacket
colder today.

3 Comb **jacket warmer**: a warm place (on a
vessel).

1924 ENGLAND 317 I had off and on to retreat to the
'jacketwarmer' (warm place) of the cabin.

jacky n   *EDD* ~ 1 (10) ~ long-legs 'a large
gnat' Ha D.

Comb **jacky conner**: blue perch
(*Tautogolabrus adspersus*); CONNER (P 17–69).

jacky longlegs: crane fly (*Tipula oloracea*).

C 69–19 When we were young we had a rhyme which
we would say whenever we saw a jackie long-legs.

jader n   Person who is disliked; nuisance;
jonah.

[1894 BURKE] 13 [joke:] Close the door till that one
in the lower berth smothers with the asthma, and
then. . .open the door till the other Jader freezes to
death. 1904 *Daily News* 2 Sep "Haul on the Plunder":
Tom Murphy is a 'soaker,' oh; / Ned Jackman is a
jader, / And John Scott a mailbag trader. 1925 *Dial
Notes* v, 334 ~ jinker.

jam v   *DC* ~ 1 (1771–) for sense 1; *OED* v¹ 1
(1753 quot), *DC* 2 (1784–) for sense 2.

1 Of ice, to become packed into a solid field.

[1771] 1792 CARTWRIGHT i, 120 Early in the morning we launched the boat, and rowed along shore to
Foulweather Droke, but could get no farther; the ice
being firmly jammed quite across, from Table Point to
Belle Isle. 1846 TOCQUE 107 Sometimes, when the ice
has been jammed close on one side of the promontory
of Cape Bonavista, the seals, during the night, have
crawled over the land. . .to the water on the other side.
1855 WHITE *MS Journal* 15 Mar Before the Ship gets
that distance the water Closes & the Ice Jams. 1861 DE
BOILIEU 103 With the change in the weather the seals
made their appearance on the ice, which was so thick,
and jammed or packed so tightly, that—once on—it
was impossible for them to penetrate through to reach
the water, and they thus became an easy prize. [1902]
1976 *Evening Telegram* 9 Apr, p. 6 She just managed

to clear Grey Islands and the ice jammed with the land and then 'rafted.'

2 Of a vessel, to become caught in tightly-packed field-ice.

[c1840] 1978 *Haulin' Rope & Gaff* 16 "We Will Not Go to White Bay': The poor man was mistaken / Upon that very day / Which left us jammed in White Bay / Until the last of May. [1870] 1899 *Nfld Law Reports* 327 On Saturday the 17th of April last plaintiffs' vessel. . .lay jammed in the ice in Green Bay. 1871 WHITE *MS Journal* 3 Mar Passed between Cape Bonavista & Gull Island at 2 p.m. at 3 p.m. met some sheet ice—at 7 p.m. got jammed. 1893 *Trade Review Christmas No* 13 As the vessel was jammed a short distance from the land, it was suggested by the captain that they might leave her and land what seals they could. 1913 *Nfld Qtly* July, p. 30 His first voyage to the ice-fields as master was unsuccessful, due to the ship having been jammed at Pool's Island. 1936 SMITH 49 That night we met the ice and made slow progress; some of the ships got almost jammed, as the ice was very heavy.

3 Phr *not be jammed*, etc: to succeed, get through (difficulties); to be clever, efficient.

1924 ENGLAND 165 You can't jam an ole swile, sir, when it comes to findin' de young un, not no ways in dis martal world! 1937 DEVINE 65 Can't be jammed. Clever and efficient in overcoming difficulties—smart, proficient—when such a man is referred to by an admirer who will say, 'He can't be jammed.' The expression got its [land] usage from the sealers at the seal fishery in their admiration of the first steel-built steamers, owing to the way they sped through the ice-floes as compared with the old wooden whalers. I have even heard a sealer referring to his girl in these terms: 'A fine girl. Why, she can't be jammed.' 1973 BARBOUR 100 Secondly, there was the imitation fireplace. For the latter we were grateful to Mr William Sullivan, who, to use a good old Newfoundland expression 'couldn't be jammed' (meaning he could do anything).

4 Comb **jam-block**: a wooden support with a notch in which a length of wood is placed to be cut or split (P 8–55).

T 255–66 He'd always say he was going to put [the children] in his jam block. Oh that's a stick of wood with a natch sawed into un. Well, the old people one time used to use these sticks. They saw out a square natch, saw down so far in the log like that, and split it out, and jam that in, wedge it in, keep it in place. C 66–12 A jam-block is a wooden block specially designed for chopping rails. There is a hole in the block and the stick being cut is put in this hole.

jam n also **jamb** *DC* ~ 1 (1771–) for sense 1; jam ice obs (Nfld: 1775, 1792) for sense 3.

1 An impenetrable, tightly-packed field of salt-water floe-ice; esp in phr *jam of ice*.

[1771] 1792 CARTWRIGHT i, 120 We had clear water till we passed Camp Islands; but on observing a jam of ice which extended from Table Point towards Belle Isle, we endeavoured to go on the outside of it. 1812 BUCHAN *MS* 27 June Even at this protracted period it was with difficulty that the Schooner penetrated the

field ice to Trinity bay, when finding heavy ice forming a complete Jam to Cape Bonavista, I bore up for Trinity. [c1845] 1927 DOYLE (ed) 25 "The John Martin": Sure he spied the 'Laddioes' ten miles in on the jam. 1855 WHITE *MS Journal* 13 Mar All Sails in a Close Jam of Ice. 1861 DE BOILIEU 12 After passing the iceberg we encountered some rough weather, which the master attributed—rightly enough, as we subsequently found—to our being in the vicinity of the main jam of ice. A 'jam of ice' was his own expressive phrase. 1895 *Christmas Review* 19 As soon as the northern 'jam' cleared out of the Bay, they were launched, and moored off the stage-heads of their respective owners. 1936 SMITH 102 We forced away through the jam, steering south, but the ice was heavy, and we made poor progress. [1894–1929] 1960 BURKE (ed White) 29 "Full Loads to the Sealers": To tread the frozen pans of ice, / The sealer tough and strong, / Well able on a jamb of ice, / To haul a tow along. [1954] 1979 *Evening Telegram* 30 May, p. 15 A solid jam of Arctic ice still blockades the northeast coast from Cape St John to Battle Harbor.

2 A herd of seals on the ice-floes; PATCH.

1882 TALBOT 19 We wandered about for some time in search of what Devereux called the main jam or body, that is, one of those multitudinous groups of seals lying in large fields of ice, where the old ones, assembled in large numbers, have delivered their young. 1924 ENGLAND 183 More than any other he longed for 'a gert rally,' with infinite work, and 'wished to de Lard we'd get a flash at de rusties in a jam.'

3 Comb **jam ice**: floe-ice packed into an impenetrable field.

[1775] 1792 CARTWRIGHT ii, 89 The scene was greatly altered on our return, for the jam ice was not to be seen, the barricados were fallen off from the shore, most of the snow melted, all the harbours were open. 1792 ibid *Gloss* i, xi ~ The low ice with which the whole face of the ocean is covered every winter, and until late in the summer. 1855 WHITE *MS Journal* 6 Mar Ship entering a large jam Ice strong breeze ship making good way *Sarah* with two Brigs in sight men all employed Breaking the Ice before the Boats with hand spikes.

jamming n The condition of (a vessel) being caught in tightly-packed ice.

1873 *Maritime Mo* i, 257 There is, of course, room for considerable skill and sagacity in taking advantage of winds, and currents, and openings in the ice, and in avoiding 'jammings' and other mishaps [in searching for the seal 'whelping grounds']; still, whether any particular vessel will reach 'patches' of young seals, scattered, perhaps, very widely, is very largely a lottery. 1933 GREENE xv ~ : Occurs when the ship has been immovably imprisoned by the Floe.

janney See JANNY.

janny n, usu pl also **janney, jenny, johnny** ['dʒænɪ, 'dʒanɪ, 'dʒɛnɪ, 'dʒanɪ, 'dʒɒnɪ]. Cp *OED* johnny 1 'a fellow, chap'; *EDD* john 2 (6 a) 'the mummers used to be called John Jacks' (1875–) W; *O Sup²* janney Nfld (1896–).

1 Elaborately costumed person who participates in various group activities at Christmas;
FOOL, MUMMER n.

1896 *J A Folklore* ix, 36 *Old teaks* and *jannies*, boys
and men who turn out in various disguises and carry on
various pranks during the Christmas holidays, which
last from 25th December to Old Christmas day, 6th
January. [c1900] 1978 *RLS* 8, p. 27 ~ a mummer. 1925
Dial Notes v, 335 Johnnies—Christmas mummers.
Also jennies. 1928 *Nfld Qtly* Dec, p. 15 The merry
party of 'Jannies,' or 'Mummers' made the welkin ring
with their weird shouts and cries and their 'false faces'
sent many [a] frightened child in haste to its mother's
knee. 1937 DEVINE 29 ~ies. Mummers; persons
dressed in disguise at Christmas for visiting. 1957
Atlantic Advocate xlviii, 23 . . .extra large kitchens that
served as the stage for the 'Fools' or 'Mummers' or
'Janneys,' to give them their peculiar local names.
T 45–64 You had no rhyme or nothing goin' out in
these janneys. We usen't. Only get in [a house] and try
and talk way they wouldn't understand you or get out
and waltz or dance. T 172/3–65 Same thing, janney.
Since that, we're not known as mummers today,
they're janneys today. T 181–65 They have those johnnies, they calls 'em now. So many boys and girls
around, but they got no recitations, see, nothing to say.
1969 *Christmas Mumming in Nfld* 65–6 There are 'big
janneys,' adults, and 'little janneys,' children. . . Some
are able to 'talk like a janney'—ingressive utterances at
a high pitch. 1973 PINSENT 55 Apparently this janny
had been making the rounds for years and not once
had anyone guessed him—till this night. 1973
WIDDOWSON 424 'Now they big Janneys is comin' in!
They'll take you tonight if yous don't be good!'

2 Phr *go out in the jannies*: to dress in the disguise and costume of a Christmas mummer; cp
FOOL 2.

T 45–64 Oh yes, we went out in the janneys several
times down home before we left.

3 Comb **janny-night**: any night during Christmas season on which jannies go around visiting
at people's houses.

C 67–2 On janny-night they used to get dressed up
and go from house to house. Would dance and get
something to eat. Usually had a harmonica or a jews
harp. . . Would go out most nights from Christmas Eve
to New Year.

janny-talk: distorted or ingressive speech of a
mummer used as a means of disguising one's
identity.

1969 *Christmas Mumming in Nfld* 211 When the janneys come to a house they wish to visit, they open,
without knocking, the storm-door, stick their heads
inside the 'porch' and 'sing out': 'Any janneys in
tonight?' in the high-pitched, squeaky voice that janneys always use—'janney-talk.' T 257–66 Oh yes, 'twas
queer talk—janney talk. Some people can't talk and
some of 'em can, you know. Some of them make a
queer talk, draw in their voice, and make a queer
sound.

janny v

1 To participate in various group activities by
disguised figures during Christmas; MUMMER v.

T 168/71–65 They called 'johnnies' up there.
'Janneying—Going janneying tonight?' But 'twas all
'mummers' in my day, twenty years ago. T 196–65 I
never went what you call mummin', you know, jannin'.
T 246–66 We knocked his teapot off of the stove and
broke it up. He got kind of dirty went it and I hasn't
janneyed since. Promised myself I wouldn't janney any
more. T 253–66 They don't janney very much now.
They janneys some; all the old stuff you can get, you
put on, so they wouldn't know your clothes.

2 In phr *janny up*: to dress up in a fantastic
costume and mask for mummering at Christmas;
RIG (UP) v; also fig. (1964 *Can Journ Ling* x, 44).

T 246–66 'Tis only fun at that time, see. When people janney up, they only janney up for sport. T 253–66
Two or three of us'd janney up with all sorts of old rags
on; perhaps one with a big hump on his back, another
one [with a] big hump on their belly, so you wouldn't
know 'em, see. 1980 COX 36 You had a scarf on your
neck, and big pair of mits on, and a coat on, you'd say,
'Boy, where are you going all janneyed up?' 1981
Evening Telegram 24 Jan, p. 6 The project was to 'janney up' and visit my brother which I did.

jannying vbl n The practice of visiting houses disguised as a mummer at Christmas ([c1900] 1978
RLS 8, p. 27).

1951 *N Y Folk Q* vii, 272 The most fun for the children, and even for the grownups, was 'janneying' at
Christmas time. 1963 DIACK 70–1 From Christmas Day
to Twelfth Night. . .was the season for 'Mummering' or
'Janny-ing.' There was much dressing up and disguising, and parties went round from house to house to
entertain and have fun. As soon as the identity of the
'Janny' is guessed he is supposed to unmask; meantime
there's endless fun to be had trying to guess who it is
under grandma's best quilt. 1973 PINSENT 53 I never
cared much for jannying or mummering or dressing up
or whatever the hell it was.

jar¹ n Cp *EDD* ~ 2 'a stone bottle' So; *O Sup²*
sb² 2 c 'a drink (of beer, etc)' (1925–); JOYCE *Old
Irish Folk Music* (1909) p. 345 "There's Whiskey
in the Jar." Container or crock for spirits.

1893 *Christmas Greetings* 15 While some of the boys
were makin' coffins two other of the boys came in with
two jars of whiskey. 1901 *Christmas Bells* 11 The father
of the family broached a jar of spirits, and every member of the household should take a drop of punch. 1902
ibid 2 The sound of the saws and hatchets cutting up
the Christmas back-junks re-echoed on the frosty air,
and a 'scattered' man from the 'Coves' was met going
home with his jar. 1917 ibid 15 Go and fill these jars
from the cask, and begin whistling the moment you put
key to lock. 1930 BARNES 206 [So they went down and
brought up the two demijohns.] I took one of the jars
and set it up on the cabin table. 1978 *MUN Gazette* 21
Dec, p. 4 Mr Nolan has made his last run to St Peter's
and every man-boy around has a jar or two under
water in his own bog pond.

jar² n also **jar-seal**

(1832–). A small non-migratory seal of coastal waters; ringed seal (*Phoca hispida*); DOUBLE JAR.

[1771] 1792 CARTWRIGHT i, 113 [A white bear] had eaten a round jar. 1792 ibid *Gloss* i, xi ~ The young of the smallest kind of seal; the old ones are called Double Jars. 1826 *Edin New Phil J* 39–40 The Jar Seal [is] so named from its form resembling that of a jar, thick at the shoulders, and tapering off suddenly towards the tail; head small, body 4 or 5 feet long, the fur spotted, and it keeps more in the water than the other ice-seals. 1861 DE BOILIEU 97 The 'Jar' is a seal of social habits, like the beaver, living in large communities under the ice in winter, and in the numerous bays along the coast in summer. 1886 HOWLEY *MS Reminiscences* 7 There is a round, fat seal called a Jar, a distinct species. This is the ringed seal. 1906 DUNCAN 281 Archie and Billy came upon a family of four [seals], lying at some distance from their blow-hole—two grown harps, a 'jar,' which is a one year old seal, and a ranger, which is three years old and spotted like a leopard. 1933 MERRICK 108 To fit right [sealskin boots] have to be cut out with the utmost skill. The bottoms are made of an old 'harp' whose skin is thick, and the legs of a thin-skinned 'jar.' T 143/4–65[1] I don't know [whether] they was harps or jars or what they were. 1977 *Inuit Land Use* 112 Jar seals travel along the floe edge in winter, and they have their young in dens in the ice during spring. When the ice breaks up in late spring and summer, they move into the bays.

jaw n Cp Daniel 5:13 for sense 1; for combs. in sense 2: *EDD* ~ sb[1] (7) jaw-lock, (8) jaw-locked; *OED* jaw-tooth 'cheek-tooth' (1601–).

1 Phr *jaws of Jewry*: extreme danger or hazard.

C 66–18 [He] was coming from Sydney, N S with a load of coal in his schooner. This schooner began to settle in the water and sink so the man went and got his Bible and began to read. The schooner settled back to normal and returned from the Jaws of Jewry. Q 71–7 When one says 'the dory escaped the Jaws of Jewry,' he means how close the boat came to disaster.

2 Comb **jaw bones**: forward timbers of a boat.

T 14/28–64 Two [boats] broke up—jawbones broke, and there was one boat in particular hove out on a shoal.

jaw-lock, ~ **locked**: (a) lock-jaw; (b) with jaw muscles cramped.

1916 *Evening Telegram* 28 Aug "Humby's Balloon": [as nickname] The genial 'John R,' when he read the despatch / 'Tis said that he didn't see anything in it, / It looked like a story which 'Jaw-lock' would 'hatch.' T 731–70 And at that time there was Dandy Cakes on the go. Those were little cakes, ten cents each. . . He said, 'By God,' he said, 'if I wasn't jaw-locked from Dandy Cakes you wouldn't have won it!' C 75–141 If you drive a nail in your foot you should take the nail and file the tip of it and drive it into a piece of pine so that you will not get blood poisoning, or tetanus, called jaw-lock.

jaw-tooth: molar.

P 245–56 ~ teeth other than the front ones. T 362–67

And so first thing he said, 'Now open your mouth,' an' he put his dirty finger on my jaw tooth.

jay n
1 Newfoundland grey jay (*Perisoreus canadensis sanfordi*).

[1771] 1792 CARTWRIGHT i, 174 Going up Watson Brook, I found most of the traps had been robbed by jays. 1840 GOSSE 345–6 These birds, from their carnivorous habits are here [in Canada] called by the common people 'Carrion-birds'; in Newfoundland, it is known as 'the Jay.' 1959 MCATEE 50 ~ Grey Jay (Nfld., 'Labr.').

2 Comb **jay killer**: shrike (*Lanius excubitor borealis*).

1912 CABOT 219 Hereabouts a pine grosbeak is a 'mope,' a shrike a 'jay killer' or 'shreek.'

jenny[1] n Female harlequin duck (*Histrionicus histrionicus*); LADY[2] (1870 *Can Naturalist* v, 301).

jenny[2] See JANNY n.

jenny[3] See JINNY*.

jersey n [= Channel Islands, esp Jersey]. See C R FAY *The Channel Islands and Newfoundland* (1961).

Attrib **jersey fish**: cod-fish caught and cured in Newfoundland and Labrador by entrepreneurs from the Channel Islands.

1892 *Christmas Review* 18 In the old days he was the owner's right-hand man, looked after his cargo and its quality (Jersey fish always had a good reputation), attended well to his sales abroad, a bold navigator, splendid sailor, honest, upright servant.

jersey house: a mercantile firm of the Channel Islands engaged in fishing operations in Newfoundland. See also HOUSE.

1832 MCGREGOR i, 208 There are six or seven English houses, and four or five Jersey houses, established at Labrador. 1891 *Holly Branch* 20 Fortunately, a cannon was on the premises, used by the 'Jersey house' on state occasions.

jersey man: Channel Islands migratory fisherman or settler.

1832 MCGREGOR i, 208 Half of these people [living year-round on the Labrador] are Jerseymen and Canadians, most of whom have families. 1895 PROWSE 451 A large number of English and Irish went home every autumn, and returned in the spring; Jersey men always left. 1941 WITHINGTON 138 My first day 'On the Rock' Mr Thomas Morel paid a call. He was the last representative of the Jerseymen who had controlled the fisheries for over a hundred years. T 147–65 They got into this fight Christmas morning; the Jerseymen used to stay in the cook-room. 1975 *Evening Telegram* 14 July, p. 6 The name 'Jerseymen' is given to all the fishermen from the Channel Islands who frequented Newfoundland.

jersey room: a tract of land on the waterfront of a cove or harbour, together with its facilities, from which the fishery is conducted by Channel Islanders; ROOM.

1891 *Holly Branch* 20 Very soon a light was seen in the upper-hall of 'Jersey-room.' 1916 *Geog Rev* ii, 454 These fishing establishments were called 'rooms,' and it was quite usual in this country to speak of them as 'Jersey rooms,' no matter whether the proprietors belonged to Jersey or Guernsey. 1919 GRENFELL[1] 157 All t' Government did was to offer Captain Fordland, who fished t' big Jersey rooms across near Isle au Loup on Labrador, another hundred dollars. 1941 WITHINGTON 138 He was the last representative of the Jerseymen who had controlled the fisheries for over a hundred years, and the proprietor of the only remaining Isle of Jersey Room on the coast.

jersey ship: Channel Islands fishing vessel.

[1702] 1895 PROWSE 239 [They] carried him and his goods aboard a Jersey ship laden with fish and sailed northwards.

jerseyside: part of a bay or harbour customarily used or frequented by Channel Islands' fishermen.

1971 SEARY 144 'Side,' in the sense 'A region, district, or the inhabitants of this,' occurs in Jerseyside.

jib n PARTRIDGE 438 naut colloq for sense 2.

1 A small parcel of land, irregular in shape.

1960 *Daily News* 31 Mar, p. 11 The site is rather small to provide sufficient manoeuvring space for a Bus, and in order to obtain the minimum requirements it will be necessary to acquire an additional jib of land.

2 Phr *long may your big jib draw*: good luck.

1937 DEVINE 65 ~ A salutation of good will and good wishes when a free drink of Jamaica is about to be lowered down by the recipient. A schooner can get out of almost any difficulty if the big jib holds out. 1957 *Evening Telegram* 6 May, p. 4 Long may your big jib draw.

jibs n pl Cp *EDD* ~ 'small, waste pieces of cloth' Co. Scattered articles of clothing.

C 71–128 Pick up your jibs and put them where they belong.

jife n Cp *OED* gybe v naut 2 'to put about or alter course,' *NID* jibe[1] v 2 '[to] tack.' A course or direction (through the ice-floes).

1924 ENGLAND 69 'I'll try if I can see the 'orizon, an' get a sight,' said he. 'Then I'll know if we're on the right jife.' Ibid 80 The *Thetis* and *Diana* dogged our every 'jife' and 'cut.' They spied on us. Not if they could help it should Cap'n Kean steal a march on them. He, 'admiral of the fleet,' should not be allowed to strike fat and leave them out of it.

jig v also **jigg** past tense **jigged, jug, jugged**. *OED* ~ v 2 'to move up and down with a jerky motion' (esp 1886 quot); *EDD* v[1] 12 N Ir; *DC* 1 Nfld (1859–) for sense 1.

1 To fish by jerking an unbaited, weighted hook sharply upwards through the water where cod, squid, etc, are swarming.

[1794] 1968 THOMAS 181 Codd Fish are the Sover-

eign specie and are so numerous as to be jigged. This is letting a Line down with Hooks on it, and then pulling it up quickly and on each Hook will be catched a Codd. 1842 JUKES i, 231 There will always be enough to hook, enough to jigg, enough to net, and more than enough to go away. [1896] SWANSBOROUGH 9 "July": The fish called 'squid,' its visit pays, / And hundreds may be jigged some days. 1924 ENGLAND 129 Uncle Bill Teller died las' fall, / Young maiden, where ye bound to? / We jigged t'ree days an' niver got one, / Acrost de Western Ocean. 1947 TANNER 491 Day after day men and boys 'jig' from morning to night. Patiently they jerk the bright leaden lure up and down within a couple of meters of the sea bottom. 1965 *Daily News* 5 Nov, p. 4 There has always been fish to be jigged from these so-called 'offer' shoals and rocks. T 172/5–65 I'm goin' up in Chronicle Tickle to see if I can jig a fish. It's a good place to jig a fish up there. M 71–97 I jug a twenty-three pound cod four day ago. 1976 GUY 108 Catching flatfish is great sport. They're brown on the back and almost as hard to see as sculpins but they won't take bait. They must be jug. 1979 *Evening Telegram* 21 Dec, p. 3 In summer, he finds other things to go away from the mosquitos, like jigging cod from a small boat. 1979 NEMEC 249–51 Ordinarily, cod are 'jug' close to the surface.

2 Of cod-fish, squid, etc, to be lured and hooked by a 'jigger.'

[1928] 1978 *Evening Telegram* 1 Sep, p. 7 Fish are reported plentiful around the Southern Shore but fishermen cannot get bait. On Saturday more than 70 men sat in their boats hour after hour jigging for squid in Bay Bulls harbor. Squid were there but they would not jig. [1930] 1980 ibid 11 Aug, p. 6 Squid have been seen [at Burgeo] but will not jig. There is a good sign of codfish and dogfish are numerous.

3 Of an unmarried woman, to secure or hook a husband.

1929 BURKE [7] "Mary Ann Hoolligan Takes in the Circus": And some old maids and pretty girls / That's trying to jig a man.

jig n *OED* ~ 6 c (1858–), *DAE* 2 (1846–), *EDD* sb[1] 2 N Ir, *DC* (1956–) for sense 1; cp *OED* 6 'mechanical contrivance' for sense 3.

1 An unbaited, weighted hook used with a line to catch cod (or squid) by a sharp, upward jerk; JIGGER.

[1766] 1971 BANKS 136 These Jiggs are fastened to the ends of their Lines and Let Down to the bottom. 1861 *Harper's* xxii, 458 Lines were wound upon reels; hooks were spread out upon deck, and carefully examined and assorted; sinkers, gaffs, and jigs got ready for action; and a barrel of bait prepared. 1918 TOWNSEND 267–8 The 'jig' is a bright piece of lead, somewhat of the shape of fish, about six inches long, terminating in two cod-hooks placed back to back. The fisherman lets this down until it touches the bottom, withdraws it a foot or two, and then proceeds to 'jig.' 1925 *Dial Notes* v, 334 [Men] catch fish with a jig. P 243–75 Any fish on the jig?

2 A jerk (upwards); a tug.

T 54/63–64 I took ahold to the end o' the rope an' I made the jig. An' I brought [the corpse] out an' I threw him in the boat. T 191–65 An' they took him right hold by the hair o' the head, an' give a big jig.

3 The portable balance or steelyard used to weigh dried cod, seal-pelts, etc; the platform on which these are placed to be weighed; TOMMY NOGGIN.

1924 ENGLAND 91 Men bring a 'jig,' or steelyard, up on deck, and weigh four of the old-fat sculps. 1937 DEVINE 53 [The jig is] the swinging frame part of the scales on which a fish is placed in weighing. P 54–67 ~ the part of a fish-weighing machine on which the barrow of fish is put; the whole machine. P 231–76 The men had to discharge [the seals] when they come in, they had to throw them in a gig, an old fashioned gig, and they were weighed on a swinging beam, and they weighed them and the tally man would tally it down.

4 An engagement or date with someone of the opposite sex.

C 69–13 If anyone had a ravel (a piece of thread or string) on his or her clothes, people would say this was the sign of a jig for him or her. C 70–21 If you happened to pick a ravel or thread, locally called a 'jig,' off your clothes, it could be used to determine the initial of your next date or boyfriend. P 108–74 Have you got a jig for tomorrow night?

5 Phr *between the jigs and the reels*: in one way or another; somehow.

1937 DEVINE 10 ~ During odd times. Has another meaning akin to the expression 'what with one thing and another.' 'So, *between the jigs and the reels*, poor Tom lost all his money.' In an expression of determination, the phrase may mean *somehow*. P 184–67 I got all my work done between the jigs and the reels. P 108–74 Well, between the jigs and the reels, we made it home by dark.

jigamaree n   Cp *OED* ~ 2 'a fanciful contrivance.' A Y-shaped wooden fixture set up in a boat with an iron bar on the top across which a hooked fish is jerked in order to unhook it quickly (1937 DEVINE 29); MACHINE.

jigger n   also **gigger** *OED* ~ sb[1] 4 (1815, 1884), *DC* 1 Nfld (1778–).

1 Unbaited, weighted hook(s) used with a line to catch cod (or squid) by giving a sharp, upward jerk; JIG n.

[1751–66] 1954 INNIS 181 [inventory] To 3 Dozen Bank hooks for Giggers. . . [1778] 1792 CARTWRIGHT ii, 340 The *Stag* brought in seven quintals of fish this evening which were killed with jiggers. 1792 ibid *Gloss* i, xi Gigger or Jigger. A pair of large hooks fixed back to back with some lead run upon the shanks, in the shape of a fish. The Gigger being let down to the bottom, is played by sharp jerks, and such fish are hooked by it, as are enticed by the resemblance of the lead to a real fish. 1842 JUKES i, 29 A jigger is a plummet of lead, with two or three hooks stuck at the bottom, projecting on every side, and quite bare. This is let down by the line to the proper depth, and then a man, taking a hitch of the line in his hand, jerks it smartly in, the full length of his arm, then lets it down slowly and jerks

it in again. 1884 DEMING 87 The 'jigger' is a red stick of wood circled with sharp but barbless hooks. The hook is let down, the squid, which enters the Newfoundland bays by myriads for food, is attracted by the red color, clasps its arms over the hooks, and is drawn up to its death. 1906 DUNCAN 66 It struck me that I might do something with my line and jigger. 1937 *Seafisheries of Nfld* 32 Jiggers are made by fastening two hooks together so that their barbs are as far apart as possible. Lead of various weight, usually half-a-pound, is melted round them in the shape of a fish. 1940 SCAMMELL 9 "The Squid Jiggin' Ground": All sizes of figures, with squid lines and jiggers, / They congregate here on the squid jiggin' ground. T 191–65 They didn't have much equipment to catch fish with, apart from a jigger or probably a dabber to catch a few, but lots of 'em didn't even have a trawl or a net. T 198–65 Two hooks in 'em, see. A little hole here in the ass o' the jigger for [to] tie your line on; two hooks for jigging fish. But now they got 'em [with] three or four hooks. 1965 HENDERSON 96 After being shown the box of squid, we were shown a jigger, a small circular piece of lead with about fifty fine prongs around its base. This jigger is attached to a short line. The squid are not caught on a hook, as is a fish, but rather flipped into the boats.

2 Comb **jigger fish**: cod-fish caught with an unbaited hook.

1979 NEMEC 251 As a rule, 'jigger fish' tend to be fairly small (under 18 inches).

jigging vbl n *DC* ~ 1 (1859–) for sense 1. See also JIG v.

1 Fishing for cod (or squid) with a weighted, unbaited hook attached to a line and jerked sharply upward.

[1766] 1971 BANKS 135 Jigging Done by 2 large hooks Each of them twice as large as those used for bait these hooks are fastened together back to back and a heavy Lead Plac'd upon their shanks which the french whither out of whim or from any use they find in it I do not Know Cast in the Shape of a fish these Jiggs are fastened to the Ends of their Lines & Let Down to the bottom from whence they are raised Every half minute or their abouts by a strong Jerk of the Fishermans arm in hopes of striking them into the fish who are accidentaly swimming by. [1810] 1971 ANSPACH 20 The fish caught by jigging is immediately opened, and a herring is generally found in the [body], which serves as bait. 1845 *Fraser's Magazine* xxxii, 740 Their talk is of seals and cod-fish, of *hauling* and *jigging*; and their jargon generally betrays an Irish origin. 1868 *Royal Geog Soc* xxxviii, 267 [We] found numerous fishing-boats 'jigging,' that is, with two hooks backed and a lead between resembling a small fish, in which manner they are caught by all parts of the body, head, tail, fins, &c. 1912 HUTTON 253 'Jigging,' as it is called among the fishermen, is horribly cold work on dull, bleak days. 1972 JENSEN 28 But in order to catch the cod, the fishermen first have to catch the bait. This they do by 'jigging' for squid with a multihooked artificial lure.

2 Comb **jigging ground**: in the coastal fishery, shoal area with abundant bait-fish. See also GROUND, SQUID(JIGGING).

T 49–64 But now perhaps sometimes you might have

to go on the jiggin' ground, jig squids. 1977 *Inuit Land Use* 132 The best jigging grounds were shallow areas along the shores of the coastal islands, but the cod in deep water tended to be larger.

jigging veil: widow's veil.

C 66–1 A widow's veil [was] known as a jiggin' veil because it is considered an obvious method of showing men you are now available for marriage.

jig-house n   also **jig-loft**. Cp *OED* jigger sb¹ 7 'illicit distillery.' A boarding house for seamen, flop-house; esp one at which liquor is sold illegally.

1887 *Colonist Christmas No* 5 A woman came aboard one day with a basket on her arm, selling spruce beer, and rum. . . 'Come to my house, honey,' says she, 'and I will get you a good master and lots of money'. . . I went to mother Gilhooly's jig-house; before day she sent me off in a cart somewhere in the country, and I stayed there three days planting potatoes. 1937 *Bk of Nfld* ii, 27 He had to put up in a 'Jig loft,' as the boarding-houses frequented by sailors were known, and very often he was stripped of his clothes and money.

jillick v   *EDD* jellick Do; cp *EDD* jelt 1. To throw a (flat) stone across the surface of a body of water, using an underhand motion; SKIM.

1937 DEVINE 29 ~ To throw a stone underhand using the side of the body as a fulcrum. P 99–69 ~ To skim flat stones over water, saying: 'A duck and a drake / And a salt-water cake / And a bottle of brandy.'

jimmy-jar n   Cp *DAE* jimmy-john, and JAR¹. Demijohn.

1977 BURSEY 87 We sampled the jimmie-jar [of rum] and the sampling steadied our nerves.

jingle n   *EDD* ~ sb² 4 'covered two-wheeled cart' Ir. A two-wheeled cart (1974 MANNION 176).

P 70–61 ~ cart with two wheels, more fancier than a caplin-cart. There were many on the Torbay road. It seats three. 'A jingle with a nag like a shingle.'

jink n   See JINKER.

1 A failure (esp in the catch of fish or seals).

1924 ENGLAND 156 'Dere'm a gert way, wherever dem to,' pessimized a bridge master. '*I* t'ink dem made a jink of it, dat time!' T 194/5–65 An' he said, 'Pap, we're goin' to make a jink this summer' [said of a voyage to the Labrador]. 1966 FARIS 175 A 'jink' is simply an unexpected and usually annoying outcome or happening, thought to be due to the unwitting influence of a 'jinker.' P 245–72 This year you could have a full trap, and next year you could have a jink.

2 One who brings bad luck, jinx; cp LINK for *lynx*.

C 66–3 At Grand Bank if a stranger goes fishing with a group who may be used to get a good catch and on this particular voyage gets a poor catch then that stranger is classed as a 'jink' or 'jinker.' C 66–13 ~ same as jinker, but used more by the younger people.

jink¹ v   Cp *DA* jinx v 'to cast a spell on someone' (1917–1928), *O Sup²* (1912–). To affect adversely, to spoil; to cause subsequent bad luck.

1899 ENGLISH 104 Do give us a rest about your judgment, and don't holler 'till you're out of the woods, or you'll jink the fine day. 1924 ENGLAND 12 It's the worst of bad luck for a sealing vessel to get away without at least one stowaway—it is 'jinked' or 'hoodooed' from the start; yet when such are found, they are always heaved off the vessel, if possible. 1966 FARIS 175 In contrast to witchcraft, any normal endeavour can be 'jinked' (i.e., jinxed). 1972 BROWN 43 'We'm jinked,' the men muttered among themselves, blaming the two stowaways who were thought to be 'jinkers.'

jink² v   Cp *EDD* ~ v¹ 3 'to frolic; to be gay and thoughtless.' To compliment or praise (sportively).

P 29–73 The grandmother was commenting on the fact that when she was young she had long, thick lovely hair. She noted 'They jinked me about my hair'—meaning they continuously noted and praised her beautiful hair or frequently remarked how lovely it was.

jinker n   *EDD* jink¹ v 3 'to play tricks; to frolic.' Hence (1) jinker [Nfld: an unlucky fellow]; *DC* ~ Nfld 1 (1953, 1962); cp *O Sup²* jinx 'a Jonah' (1911–); cp *OED* jynx [= a bird, the wryneck, used in witchcraft, hence] 2 'a charm or spell' (1693).

1 A person (on a vessel) bringing bad luck; a Jonah.

1896 *J A Folklore* ix, 36 ~ an unlucky fellow, one who cannot or does not succeed in fishing. 1924 ENGLAND 220 'Jinkers' are common enough; men who always carry bad winds and weather with them. Such men usually acquire nicknames like 'Foggy Bill,' 'Heavy-weather Jack,' or 'Squally Jim.' 1927 DOYLE (ed) [72] "The Landfall of Cabot": In the schooner called the *Blinker*, / That's the spring the crew turned manus / They said Cabot was a jinker. 1932 BARBOUR 5 A 'Jinker,' in Newfoundland, is a member of a ship's crew or a passenger who is believed always to bring bad luck. 1933 GREENE 170 There is a 'jinx' on the ship, or a 'jinker' aboard; and then the hands may settle that this jinker is some unfortunate who has a cast in his eye, or who was born with 'foxy-coloured' hair, or a stammer—anything of the most foolish. But, foolish or not, Heaven help the miserable one on whom they may decide as the guilty one. His life will be a burden to him till the seals are struck and the Voyage is over—for all sorts of tricks, painful and otherwise, will be played on him when either sleeping or waking. 1934 BARTLETT 172 I knew his father was always out of luck, and was known among the fishermen as a 'jinker.' Carrying a man with that reputation, or even taking his son, on a sealer or a [fishing craft], would be an invitation to trouble, and I refused. 1964 BLONDAHL (ed) 34 "Two Jinkers": Two jinkers in our harbour dwell, / Adventuresome and plucky. / The plans they make all promise well, / But always turn unlucky. T 12–64 A jinker is a person who just seems to bring bad luck. For instance, if a fellow comes to a town and it rains straight afterwards, well they'll say, 'He's a jinker. He brings the bad weather.' 1966 FARIS 96 The more traditional men would not consider going out if a woman had set foot in the boat that day—they are 'jinkers.' 1971 CASEY 280 The term 'jinker' [was part of] a joking technique used by people for younger children and outsiders who were not familiar with the specifics of fishing. . . A child or a visitor might be accused of being a 'jinker' if no salmon or codfish were obtained when he accompanied the fishermen to their nets or traps. 1976 CASHIN 91 They all commented on the fact that the cargo [of seals] we had procured was the biggest on record and that certainly I was no 'jinker.'

2 Comb **jinker-fish**: a cod-fish left in a fishing boat overnight.

C 71–105 ~ the fish left in the boat by mistake and carried back to sea the next day. It was considered a jinker (bad luck) and the belief was that no fish would be caught that day.

jinny* n also **ginny, jenny**. Seal believed to act as a sentinel for the herd; cp COURIER.

1886 HOWLEY *MS Reminiscences* 7 [Winsor says] the young harp of the second year is a bedlamer and the third year, a jinney. 1889 *Nineteenth Century* xxv, 517 At each seal meadow the sealers affirm that a small seal, called by them a 'Jenny,' takes up its position on a block of ice and acts as a sentinel, warning its companions of the approach of danger. . .as the sealers have a superstitious aversion to killing a 'jenny,' so no specimen has ever been procured. 1913 HOWLEY 28 [This] is known to our sealers as the Jar, presumably from the resemblance it bears in outline to that article. . . Another seal is called the Ginny by our people, but whether it is a variety of the last, or a different species, I do not know. Some say the Ginny is a deformed or [half] grown Harp, one that has lost its mother and is not properly nourished, but this appears to be merely conjecture.

jit v also **jut** [dʒʌtʔ] *EDD* jet v 2 W Do So D Co for sense 1; cp *EDD* jot v² 2 'jolt' So for sense 2.

1 To nudge, jog, jar (a person).
1937 DEVINE 29 ~ to nudge. 1955 ENGLISH 35 Jut—to hit the elbow of another. P 74–67 Jut me when it's time to go. C 71–30 I was sitting next to my mother who jutted me and told me to jut the next person to me to ask them something.

2 To jiggle or rock (a cradle).
P 148–63 Jittin' the baby [to sleep]. C 70–28 Jit the bed and get the baby to sleep.

jiver n Cp *NID* jibe² n 'the swing of a sail or its boom in jibing'; see also **jife**. The ropes and blocks which secure a fore-and-aft sail in place while a vessel is on a given tack.
1977 *Nfld Qtly* Winter, p. 20 We got up and put that big mains'le on. And just as we had it on her she give a surge in a swell, (and) just where the sheet goes in, what we calls the jiver—the blocks and everything, burst.

joanie n ['dʒounı]. Cp *EDD* joan (8) Miss Joan 'a card game' Co for comb in sense 2.

1 Bread dough cooked on stove-lid; DAMPER DOG.
T 12–64 The joanie is not made from a mixture. It's just leftover dough which is rolled in a ball and placed on the stove and hardened.

2 Comb **joanie-come-tickle-me, johnny ~** : children's card game.
P 113–73 Johnny-come-tickle-me. [A game in which the] object is to get rid of all your cards first. P 141–74 ~ a card game with 26 cards each: Here's a very good ace for thee / Here's another as good as he / Here's the best of all the three / And here's Joanie-come-tickle-me.

jockabaun See JACKABAUN*.

jockey club n One-flowered pyrola (*Moneses uniflora*) (1956 ROULEAU 32).

jog v also **jug** *OED* ~ 4 b (1697, 1758 quots); PIERCE 279. Of a vessel, to sail slowly; to heave to into the wind.
[1929] BOWEN 76 On the Grand Banks a schooner is said to be *Jogging* when the fore-staysail is hauled to windward and the main sheet is paid off, the wheel being lashed a few spokes from hard down. In this condition she makes little headway; useful when most of the hands are out in the dories. Of a vessel, to sail slowly; to heave into the wind. 1960 FUDGE 52 After getting all our dories, I would run her in towards Flint Island as the weather still looked Easterly, and give our vessel room to jog all night and be close to our fishing spot in the morning. I sent two men aloft to stow the gaff topsail, which had been loose since leaving home, and, after jugging our vessel far enough, I put her in the port tack where we could spend the night, reaching along quietly with the jib. T 453–67 We hove her around on the other tack and let her go up. We jogged Sunday night, all day Monday. Tuesday dinnertime we tried her again [to] see if we could make any headway. M 71–86 Joggin' along—sailing along at sea in a boat.

john¹ n *O Sup²* John Down 'fulmar' Nfld (1852–), *DC* Nfld (1852–).
Comb **john bull**: common dovekie (*Plautus alle alle*); BULL-BIRD, ICE- ~ .
1959 MCATEE 39 ~ Dovekie (Elaboration of 'bull'. . .Nfld; 'Labr.').
john casey: blueberry pudding; HURT PUDDING.
1958 *Nfld Dishes* 55 Blueberry pudding was usually referred to as 'John Casey,' especially if it was served with molasses 'coady' or sauce. C 75–145 ~ Blueberry pudding.
john down: Atlantic fulmar; NODDY (*Fulmarus glacialis glacialis*).
1852 *Arctic Miscel* 10 On the banks of Newfoundland where this bird is known by the name of 'John Down'. . .[*DC*] 1959 MCATEE 4 ~ Fulmar . . .John Down (Sailor's name, significance unknown. Nfld.).

john² See POOR JOHN.

johnny¹ n Cp *EDD* johnny sb 1 (17) ~ Magory Ir for sense (a); DINNEEN mucóir etc 'a haw.'

Comb **johnny barrow**: a flat, rectangular wooden frame with handles at each end for two boys to carry light loads; BARROW¹.

M 68–26 There were two other kinds of hand barrows used around the 'room' [premises] for bringing fish—the 'Johnnie barra' and the Draft Barra. The Johnnie 'bar' weighed about 12–14 pounds and was suitable for boys to use. It could carry about a quintal and one half of fish (168 lbs). 1975 BUTLER 183 John-nie 'Barra' [barrow] first made for use of boys and thus called Johnnie barra.

johnny-come-tickle-me: see JOANIE -COME-TICKLE-ME.

johnny magorey [ˌdʒɒnɪ məˈgoʊɹɪ]: (a) fruit or hip of wild rose; (b) subject of various nonsense verses with sudden, unexpected ending for child's amusement.

1968 DILLON 145 ~ part of the flower [of the wild rose] left when petals fall off, gathered by children and strung as beads. C 69–12 There was a young man named Johnny Maggorie, / Went into the woods to build a new dory, / When he came back his mother was dead, / And three little niggers sat up in the bed. P 108–70 I'll tell you a story / 'Bout Johnny Magorey. / Shall I begin it? / That's all that's in it. C 71–14 I'll tell you a story 'bout Johnny McGory, / Now I'll begin it, that's all that's in it. / I'll tell you another about his brother, / 'E 'ad an awl an' 'e nailed it to the wall—that's all.

johnny miller: (a) a small moth or DOWS'Y POLL*; (b) ring-dance and song.

M 69–22 An Orangemen's Parade was always held on [St Stephen's Day]. . . In the night a Johnny Miller was held in the Orange Hall. The members' wives made and served salads, etc. After this meal, games were played and songs were sung. It was a time where they had a meal and played games and sang songs. M 71–103 Everyone, young and old alike, formed a ring with a few people in the centre. Then they began to go around in a clockwise direction singing to the top of their voices the Johnny Brown song. Note the game was called Johnny Miller, but the song was called Johnny Brown. It was sung to the accompaniment of much stamping of feet. There was no music. The song went like this: 'Wallop her down,' says Johnny Brown. P 148–72 ~ a young miller; a small, light-coloured moth.

johnny poker: see JOLLY.

johnny² See JANNY.

join v In quilt-making, to sew patches on sheet or blanket to form coverlet.

1972 MURRAY 273 Quilt making or 'joining quilts' was also considered a 'winter' job. They chose an old flannelette sheet or blanket to 'join the quilt on.' Ibid 308 Some women still hook an occasional rag rug, or join a quilt.

jolly a also **johnny**. See GREENLEAF (1933), p. 339 n. Comb **jolly poker**, **johnny boker**, ~ **coak-er**, ~ **poker**, etc. A person or object mentioned in a 'hauling song'; hence, the song itself; a particular chantey; HEAVE-UP SONG; POKER².

1904 *Daily News* 2 Sep "Haul on the Plunder": Oh, 'tis my Johnnie Poker, / Sure Ned Morris is a joker. 1924 ENGLAND 44 Tailed on, in a long line, they gave way with a will to the rough-chanted strains of "Johnny Boker", led by a 'shanty man': We'll do our Johnny Boker, / We will 'aul an' 'eave togedder, / An' we'll do our Johnny Boker, / Do! T 43–64 I often heard a crowd haulin' up a boat, an' they'd be yellin', 'Come me jolly pokers!' That's when they get all ready now to pull; you'd have tackles to her. 'Now boys, give her the jolly poker!' T 379–67 Just runners. . .on the ice or under the house, pulled along on the ice. That's when the Johnny Poker'd be singin', when they come to a hard nip.

jone* v Cp *OED* Jonah v (1887–). To put a spell on (a person); JINK¹.

P 141–75 A woman went around to houses begging for food, clothing, etc. She would tell the householders if they didn't give what she wanted she would jone them, meaning she would put a spell or curse on them.

jonnick a *EDD* jannock (var jonnick IW W Do So Co) 1, 3 for senses 1 and 2.

1 Fair, equitable, honest.

1895 *J A Folklore* viii, 29 ~ honest. 1937 DEVINE 29 'That's not jonnick,' one will say in a raw deal. P 173–57 ~ Not just right.

2 Ready, fit, in proper condition.

1920 WALDO 156 'The big spuds are not jonnick yet,' means that the potatoes are not well done. C 71–27 'I am quite jonnick today' meaning I am in fit condition and am feeling well.

3 An asseveration, 'I swear.'

1924 ENGLAND 71 'Dem de outscouts o' de patch, by's! Dis-un goin' rate di-rect fer de patch, jonnick [I swear]!'

joog n also **jook***, **jug** [dʒuːg, dʒuːk] DINNEEN diúg 'a drop, a drain.' See also GIG*.

1 A drop.

1968 DILLON 146 When he put the bottle back on the table, there wasn't a joog in it.

2 Slight sign of force, energy, life; usu after a negative.

1937 DEVINE 30 Jug—motion, palpitation or any sign that life exists. 'Not a *jug* out of (or in) him.' P 148–61 There's not a juke in [the battery]. P 148–64 [After a small boy was hit by a car, he said] 'Not a juke in him.' No sign of life in him. P 193–74 A man who has been knocked out or is dead drunk might have someone say of him 'there's not a joog in him look.' The man is out cold, still and silent. A dead or dying horse on the road could also be described thus. 1976 GUY 20 They should be hung up, yes, and cut down before the last joog goes out of them and brought to and hung up again.

joog* v DINNEEN diúgaim 'I drink off.' To drink or drain completely.

1968 DILLON 146 He jooged the bottle right to the last drop.

jook* See JOOG.

jostler n ['dʒɔsləɹ]. Cp *EDD* jossler (a) 'a big person of rude manners.' Old fellow; codger.

T 208–65 There was an old jostler there—call him an old feller—he had a whisker and a home-knit guernsey on, a little T.D. pipe stuck in his face, not saying nothing.

jowl n also **jole** [dʒoɵl, 'dʒoɵəl] *EDD* ~ sb¹ 1 for sense 1; *NID* ~³ n 2 for sense 2.

1 Meat from the jaw-bone of a pig.

[1894 BURKE] 27 "The July Fire": With the *Herald* on my knee, / And a piece of cold pig's jole upon a plate. [c1904] 1927 DOYLE (ed) 67 "The Kelligrews Soiree": There was birch rhine, tar twine, / Cherry wine and turpentine; / Jowls and cavalances. 1925 *Dial Notes* v, 335 ~ A pig's jawbone, cleaned and boiled. P 148–67 ~ salt [pork] which must be watered before cooking.

2 The fleshy part of a cod's head; CHEEK, FACE.

P 126–67 [There's nothing like] a meal of joles. P 148–78 Jowls and tongues [of a cod]. 1979 NEMEC 275 Besides tongues, hearts and faces or 'jowls,' as well as the membrane ('sound'). . .

3 Comb **jowl-man**: one of the men engaged in processing cod in a fishing-stage.

T 36/8–64 When you'd start to gut the fish, of course, one man will cut the throat an' the jowl-man, we'll call him, cut the sides o' the head, see, an' push it along on the table.

jowl v also **jole***.

1 To seize (a person) by the throat.

M 64–5 To jole a person would be to take him by the throat. Q 73–9 People often threaten to joul you, meaning to take you by the throat.

2 Phr *jowl down* [dʒæɵl 'dæun]: to force (another) to the ground; to hold down.

P 61–67 Jowl 'em down! (meaning wrestle him to the ground). P 127–73 He jowled him down on the floor.

jowler¹ n A hard slap on the side of the face (P 148–63).

jowler² n *DC* ~ Nfld (1924–); cp *EDD* 'a heavy-jawed dog,' *OED* obs exc dial (1679–1826). 1819 ANSPACH 380 employs 'jowler' as name for a Newfoundland dog; for the animal's agility in catching fish, see 1794 THOMAS 52–3. See also FISH DOG, ~ KILLER. A skilled and energetic fisherman or sealer; esp the habitually successful master of a fishing boat or sealing vessel.

1898 *Christmas Bells* 14 Skipper Tom ranked high in the estimation of all who knew him, as he was a recognized 'jowler.' 1909 *Tribune Christmas No* 15 Even when the 'jowlers'—the big fish-killers—were successful, and had money on the merchant's hands, they were no better off. 1924 ENGLAND 114 Cap'n Kean appeared a 'jowler,' indeed, to judge by the anxiety of the others [sealing ships] to keep an eye on him. 1937 DEVINE 30 ~ A term applied to a sealing skipper who in time has brought in many loads of seals; an able man, physically. 1955 DOYLE (ed) 11 "A Noble Fleet of Sealers": Her crew worked with a will, / Led by that modern Jowler / The Sealer's friend—Sid Hill. 1964 *Evening Telegram* 25 Sep, 6 But, long before that tragedy happened, the *Newfoundland* had some exciting adventures under one of the old sealing 'jowlers,' Captain Farquhar.

jubilee n Comb **jubilee guild**: women's organization formed in 1935 (the jubilee of George V) to encourage home handicraft work, gardening, etc.

1946 MACKAY (ed) 176 The Jubilee Guilds. . .were modelled on the Women's Institutes of Canada and the United Kingdom. The Rotary Club of St John's sponsored the movement. 1952 SMITH 21 'Jubilee Guilds of Newfoundland and Labrador,' somewhat more cultural in purpose [than Nonia] and fostering home handicrafts throughout the Island. It also has a sales organization at St John's and, like 'Nonia,' supplies looms and materials to a large number of workers.

jug See JOOG.

july n Cp *O Sup²* drive 1 j 'a forceful advance or attack' (1911, 1918). Attrib **july drive**: in the Great War, the July offensive opening the first battle of the Somme in 1916; esp the engagement of the Newfoundland Regiment at Beaumont Hamel.

M 68–24 There was the celebration of the July Drive. All the fishermen took the afternoon off. They bedecked their boats with flags and took their wives and families out for a picnic. P 245–76 ~ Remembered as the 'big push' of the British Army in which, on July 1, the Newfoundland Regiment suffered casualties at Beaumont Hamel which have made it ever since a day of national mourning. 1977 *Evening Telegram* 2 July, p. 1 A couple of older men. . .asked what the significance of July 1 was to them, didn't say either Dominion Day or Memorial Day, but simply, 'July Drive.'

jump v

1 To hop from one floating pan of ice to another, esp in phr *jump 'ballicatters,'* ~ *'clumpers,'* ~ *pans*; COPY.

[1896] SWANSBOROUGH 31 "The Seal Fishery": Then watching each other they go, / Jumping the pans, up high, down low. Q 67–50 The process of jumping from one ice pan to another is known as jumping ballycatters. 1976 *Daily News* 2 Mar, p. 3 Jumpin' clumpers was another favorite pastime. In some places they call it copying on the bellycaters. . . All it means is jumping from one ice pan to another without falling into the water.

2 Phr *jump rocks*: to throw flat stones across the surface of a body of water; SKIM.

P 127–75 Jumping rocks was a children's game, also called 'skipping rocks,' in which the children selected flat stones and jumped or skipped them across the flat surface of the water.

jumper n Name given to several marine animals, esp the northern pilot whale, the porpoise and tuna, which leap out of the water; cp SQUID HOUND.

[1794] 1968 THOMAS 183 Whenever Squids are found is also found a Fish called Jumpers, or Squid Hounds, from the avidity with which they pursue and eat Squids. 1956 STORY 12 The obvious appropriateness of many words makes it easy to see how they have come about: *jumpers*, porpoises. 1971 *RLS* 3, p. 3 ~ Bluefin tuna. 1977 *Inuit Land Use* 140 In late August and September, jumpers, harbour porpoise, and grumpus appeared around the coastal islands where families were camped. 'If people saw a jumper while they were cod fishing, there would be excited screams and yells. Fishing was abandoned and everyone hunted the jumper.' Jumpers, as the bottlenose dolphin is called locally, usually travel in herds of ten or more together.

jump-stay n Wire or rope stay forming a brace at the top of a mast; jumper-stay.

T 194/5–65 Had to chop that jump-stay. 'Get the jump-stay slipped,' I said, 'Jack. Safe game, boy. We'll put the foremast out of her in a hurry.' 1975 BUTLER 114 Everything was fine until about eleven o'clock at night, when bang, the jumpstay burst—that is the stay between the mainmast head and foremast.

june n Cpd **june-flower**: soldier's-plume, a variety of rein-orchis (*Platanthera psycodes*) (1956 ROULEAU 32).

juniper n *OED* ~ 1 for sense 1; b (1748, 1866) for sense 2.

1 Low-growing evergreen shrub (*Juniperus communis*); GROUND JUNIPER.

[1822] 1856 CORMACK 8 Juniper *J. communis*. 1881 *Nineteenth Century* ix, 100 We got among the junipers growing horizontally like creepers along the ground, not rising more than three or four feet above the surface, but with stems as thick as your leg, and interlacing branches as hard and springy as steel. C 70–10 You get an old kettle, put a small amount of water in it and boil some 'juniper limbs' in that water. This was a ground juniper which grew on the rocky ground and spread out over a large area.

2 Larch or tamarack (*Larix laricina*).

[1766] 1971 BANKS 121 The Larch. . .which is here Calld Juniper & which is said to make better timber for shipping especially masts than any tree this Countrey affords. . . 1898 *J A Folklore* xi, 280 ~ Larix Americana. 1967 BEARNS 40 Tamarack [also called] larch, hackmatack, juniper. . .is the heaviest and strongest of the Newfoundland softwoods. C 70–15 Juniper grew sparsely and nobody used it to any extent [for firewood] because it would take too long to cut and load.

3 Comb **juniper beer**: a fermented beverage made from the boughs of the tamarack (P 148–75).

P 11–79 Juniper beer is also known as hop beer.

juniper salve: a medication prepared from the bark of the tamarack.

C 71–103 Juniper salve was made from the bark of the juniper tree. The soft pulpy layer was scraped from the inside of the bark and boiled. It was then whipped to make a creamy salve. This was a very good cure for frostbite among other things for the older folk felt it could cure almost any type of sore.

juniper tea: an effusion of the berries of the ground juniper.

1960 *Nat Mus Can*, Bul No 190, p. 218 "The Dance to Jim McBride's": Rabbit jam, juniper tea, / Fresh cod roes from Englee. M 70–15 He had to go for some juniper berries to make some juniper tea for the new mother. I afterwards learned that the juniper had some special medicinal qualities found to be very beneficial to the mother after childbirth.

juniper water: see **juniper salve** above.

T 255–66 [We'd use] bread poultice, you know, an' juniper water, an' gum plasters—turcumtine [from] the bladders, you know.

junk n Cp *OED* ~ sb² 2 'a piece or lump of anything' for all senses; *DC* (1827–) for sense 1; *OED* sb² 3 naut (1762–) for sense 2; *Kilkenny Lexicon* 'short, thick-set man' for sense 5.

1 A short log to fit a wood-burning stove or fire-place, often with *back, fore* or *middle* as qualifying word; BILLET.

[c1845] 1927 DOYLE (ed) 27 "The John Martin": Now when we got into the jam the swoiles were very thick, / And the skipper he came forward with a junk of a stick. 1866 WILSON 353 The wood was sometimes quite green, and hence making a fire was quite an art, and required back-junks, fore-junks, middle-junks, triggers, splits, and brands; and the fishermen would sometimes say whoever can build a good fire with green fir can build a boat. 1893 *Christmas Greeting* 18 It was then I discovered the purpose for which the large 'back junk' had been provided, as it occupied an important position in the huge fire, being to it what the foundation stone is to a building. 1903 *Nfld Qtly* Dec, p. 56 He went to the wood-pile and selected a nice handy looking whiting and cut it up into junks about two feet long, just sufficient to lay nicely across the dog-irons. T 12–64 If it's a short piece of wood long enough for the firebox of a stove it's called a junk. T 185–65 When they gave 'em wood to cleave, they used to strike the helve instead o' the junk o' wood with the axe, see, purpose, to break 'em off, for devilment. T 191–65 'If he shows there again, you put a billet o' wood at un.' An' certainly buddy said, 'There he is again. Well boy,' he said, 'let go!' And he hove the junk o' wood an' he beat out glass, sash an' all! C 75–136 Junks: small pieces of wood about one foot long used as firewood.

2 A piece of salt beef or pork, etc.

1842 JUKES ii, 68 Salt pork cut into 'junks'. . . 1964 *Evening Telegram* 24 Dec, p. 29 'I forgot to say,' sez the skipper, 'on the way home we'd call in to Mike O'Regan's, and he usually gave us a junk to take home with us.' 'What's a junk?' sez Ned. 'Don't get them nowadays,' sez the skipper. 'A junk was a sheep's head with the neck and liver on it. We'd bring that home and all hands would have a big scoff.' T 203/4–65 It was those big bakin' pans, so long, an' they'd have he full of turrs or rabbits, perhaps a piece o' pork. You'd have your junk o' pork, perhaps in one end o' the pan, and perhaps something else over in the other.

3 A piece of ice or lump of snow.

[1771] 1935 *Can Hist Rev* xvi, 57 . . .hardened snow. . .in long square junks. 1858 [LOWELL] i, 295 Say ye've got a junk o' pure ice, in water 'taint altogether clean. . . 1971 NOSEWORTHY 214 ~ Small, floating iceberg.

4 A large chunk of ore.

T 393–67 [The ore] come out in junk, we'd say, big pieces, thirty pounds, forty pounds, fifty pounds and less. That's how it was shipped out.

5 Phr *junk of a boy*: physical specimen.

[c1894] PANL P4/14, p. 200 A *terrible* fine junk of a boy *entirely*.

6 Comb **junk-buoy**: wooden float used with a lobster trap or fish-net (P 127–76).

junk v also **junk up** *OED* ~ b (1803–1847). To cut (wood or meat) into pieces.

[1776] 1792 CARTWRIGHT ii, 170 The rest of the people were employed in cutting the ice round the shalloway, and in junking up the fire-wood. P 245–55 ~ to cut up into pieces (esp of a carcass). Q 67–77 Junkin' 'em up: a favourite term among woodsmen as they cut the wood.

junky a *EDD* junk sb[1] 1: junky. Thick, chunky.

T 178/80–65 I believe he gave me the stick for sixteen dollars—he [was] fifty feet long, but he was big; he was too big, almost—junky, Labrador spruce. T 187/90–65 They was short, like the Frenchmen is, short, junky fellows—black, black hair.

justice n A large, heavy wooden hammer used to drive fence-posts into the ground.

P 267–58 ~ Heavy hammer made from tree-trunk (also stake mall). P 245–66 ~ Heavy section of a tree-trunk, with handle inserted, used to hammer in posts. Q 71–8 A beetle [is] known as a justice at St Joseph's.

jut See JIT.

K

kag See KEG n, v.

kanat See KENAT.

karaboo See CARIBOU.

kechhorn See KEECORN.

kedgy n also **cadge***, **cadgy***, **catchy**, **kedge**. Cp *EDD* cadger sb[1] [var occupational senses] esp 5 'one who does odd jobs'; SMYTH kedger 'mean fellow; fisherman.' In the Bank fishery, boy who helps with various tasks aboard the vessel; LUMPER.

P 258–64 ~ Young boy, 12–13, on board a schooner who stays aboard with cookee and the captain. His main job is to catch the lines from the fishing dories and tie them up when they comes alongsides. P 189–65 Tom's going kedgy this trip. P 126–67 Catch the painter, cadgy. 1977 BURSEY 27 [Tom's] job was to work about the deck, blow the fog-horn and catch the line when the dories would come alongside. The latter is the origin of the word 'catchy.' This is usually the job of a boy who goes to the Banks for the first time.

kee chorn See KEECORN.

keecorn n also **cacorne**, **kechhorn**, **kee chorn**, **kilcorn**, **kingcorn**, **kinkhorn**, **kinkorn** [ˈkʊŋkæːɹn, ˈkʊŋkaːɹn]. Cp *OED* kech v 1 'to retch'; *EDD* kecker sb 1 'gullet, windpipe'; cacorne D Do, keacorn, kiakeharn Do, keckorn w cy, keckhorn IW, kyeckhorn So. The windpipe; Adam's apple; throat.

1863 MORETON 30 Kechhorn. The swallow. Eve's apple. 1897 *J A Folklore* x, 206 Keecorn—the windpipe or Adam's apple. [c1900] 1978 *RLS* 8, p. 23 Kinkhorn—the wind pipe. 1914 *Cadet* Apr, p. 7 Kee chorn—the Adam's apple. 1920 WALDO 160 'I find my kinkhorn and I can't glutch' means 'I have a pain in my throat and I can't swallow.' The kinkhorn is the Adam's apple. A man at Chimney Cove remarked: 'I have a pain in my kinkhorn and it has gone to my wizen (chest).' 1940 *Dal Rev* xx, 67 Kilcorn—larynx. T 84–64 That blood clots in the seal's kingcarn and the blood don't flow out. P 167–67 Your kinkarn is sticking out.

keel v Phr *keel off*, ~ *out*: to lie down to rest or sleep.

1937 DEVINE 30 Keel out. To lie down; to go to bed. T 222–66 By the time you had that finished I expect you would be all cowed out, an' you'd need to keel out for a spell on the settle. You wouldn't be able to stay keeled out on the settle very long because it would be quite hard an' you would get dunch. P 118–67 He keeled out on the daybed. 1976 GUY 120 There is the cherubic Infant Guy keeled off in a wheel-barrow for want of a baby carriage, taking the sun in the garden.

keels n pl *OED* kayles 'skittles' now dial or hist (c1325–1737), b sg 'one of the pins used in the game' rare (1652); *EDD* kails esp Ir Co So D. The game of ninepins, skittles or ball and hurley; one of the wooden pins used in the game; attrib **keel ball**.

P 228–64 Keels. Short sticks knocked down in [the game of] puckin' keels. M 66–10 The ball used to knock down the pins and called a keel ball was a hard knot or bump found in the trunk of a tree. 1977 RUSSELL 125–6 'About what?' said I. 'About puckin' keels,' said Grampa. 'The day that clergyman saw us puckin' keels, he was overjoyed. In fact, he took off his clergyman's jacket, hung it on the fence, rolled up his sleeves and joined in the game. He was good at it too,' said Grampa, 'and he showed us things about puckin' keels that we'd never heard about before. And he could knock the middle man out of the pack while standin' almost half a gunshot away.'

keen a Cp *NID* ~ ¹ adj 6 slang 'wonderful.' (a) Of the weather, perfect of its kind and season; (b) of a meal, tasty.

Q 67–31 Boy, this is a keen day. Q 67–101 A real cold, crisp, clear winter day is a keen day. C 68–15 The moose meat was some keen. C 71–26 They had a keen scoff at Joe's last night.

keep v Cp *OED* off adj C 2 'of horses and vehicles: right, as opposed to the *near* or left side' for sense 1; *OED* ~ v 58: keep-net (Nfld: 1623) for comb in sense 2.

1 Imp phr *keep off*: command to dog-team to turn right; OUK.

1910 GRENFELL 113–14 A reply our knowing little leader seemed to have anticipated, for she needed but a single shout of 'kp orf!' —which is dog lingo for 'keep off'—and our komatik, swinging to the right, was flying down the decline. [1929] 1933 GREENLEAF (ed) 301 "The Dog Song": 'Keep off!' the carter sings / . . .'Hold in! you barking things!' T 271–66² Your leader had to get that, and to your left was 'hold in,' and to your right 'keep off.'

2 Comb **keep a goin's**: small pieces of firewood that burn readily; KIPPIN.

P 94–57 Kippy goins—stunted spruce or fir, cut into small junks, and used as a substitute for large junks. C 70–15 When the supply of firewood ran low the men would go into the woods and make up a slide load to tide them over. It usually consisted of small birches, alders, dry windfalls, and any other trees that might burn easily. These loads were called a load of 'keep e goins.'

keep net, also **cap** ~ , **keip** ~ , **kipp** ~ : net used to keep or hold fish; cp BAG n, DIP v: DIP NET; also attrib **keep-net irons**.

1611 *Willoughby Papers* 1/3 It[e]m 6 newe boates [and] one skiffe. It[e]m 1 dozen of kipp nett irons. 1622 WHITBOURNE 75, 81 Ten keipnet irons. . .twine to make keipnets etc. [1663] 1963 YONGE 60 After the capling come the squids. . . They catch them in nets or scaines, and sometimes by bobbing (as they call it), which is thus: they take a small cod and skin him, and hanging him a little under the water in the night, the squids will lug at it; then they pull it up softly and clap a cap-net under, and so secure them.

keg n also **kag** [kæg]. Cp *OED* ~ sb 2: ~ buoy; *EDD Sup* sb⁴ Co for sense 1.

1 A small wooden cask used as a 'buoy' or float for fish-net, cod-trap,etc.

[1888] 1897 *Nfld Law Reports* 310 He was of the opinion from the look of the end of rope saved by defendant from one of the kegs of his salmon-moorings, and of the rope of the moorings delivered up by

him, that they were the same. 1930 *Am Speech* vi, 57 ~ (pronounced *kag*)—Small barrel used as a buoy to float the outside end of a salmon net. 1936 SMITH 125 We then spanned our kegs with new 18-thread manilla rope, and I never seen bags or moorings from that day to this. T 43/7–64 There's a kag on each corner [of the cod-trap] and a kag in the centre. P 9–73 The old time wooden floats and wood kegs are giving way to plastic floats.

2 Proverb: *when the rum is in the 'kag,' the tongue doesn't wag* (1895 *Christmas Review* 12).

keg v also **cag** GROSE cagg (1785); *DAE* ~ (1789–) for sense 1.

1 To swear off liquor for a specified period.

1819 ANSPACH 465 It is not, however, uncommon to see a servant, who finds that his drink has a violent effect on his passions. . .*swear against liquor*, that is, swear before his clergyman that he will not drink any kind of spirits for one year, sometimes for a longer period, or during his stay on shore: this is *cagging* or *kegging*. [c1894] PANL P4/14, p. 194 [To hear] that 'So-and-So is cagged,' suggests the idea that possibly he has been *barrelled* up. . . It simply means the *cagged* man *has taken the pledge*, and has sworn against the *cag*.

2 Phr *keg/cag out*: (a) to become unconscious from intoxication; to pass out; (b) to lie down; to collapse (with exhaustion); KEEL OUT.

1937 DEVINE 30 ~ To lie down; to go to bed. P 41–68 Finally, but maintaining his sobriety to the bitter end, he would cag out, i.e. succumb to demon rum. 1976 GUY 54 To make a long story short I rallied [the rat] around the bedroom for the better part of thirty minutes until he was pretty much kegged out. Then I saw my chance, grabbed him by the tail and soused him into a small plastic bag.

keipnet See KEEP NET.

kellick See KILLICK.

kenat n also **kanat** [kə'næt] JOYCE 281 kinnatt; DINNEEN cnat 'selfish, niggardly person.' Sly, tricky youth; insignificant object.

1883 *Our Country* 23 Nov, p. 4 'What am I going to land him with, is it a *kanat* of a cabbage net?' said Mihel; 'sure his tail wouldn't go into it.' 1904 *Daily News* 29 June "Brave Alfred Morine": For Bond has 'swelled head' he's a 'bumptious kanat' / That's true for you 'Paddy boy,' true for you, 'Pat.' 1924 ENGLAND 227 'Bring dat jib [nose] o' yours yere, ye kenat!' he said. 'Layve me sove y'r miserable life fer ye. My glorianna, well, ye *are* an affliction case, ain't ye?' 1937 DEVINE 30 Kenat—a contemptible young fellow. P 108–70 'That little kenat!'—a fellow with a lot of talk.

kental See QUINTAL.

kettle n *DC* ~ stick (Nfld: 1933).

1 Phr *boil the kettle*: see BOIL.

2 Comb **kettle-stick**: stick used to suspend a kettle of water over a camp-fire.

1897 *J A Folklore* x, 215 It is very unlucky to burn your kettle-stick when on a journey either on land or water. If this occurs on the water, you will have head winds and a tedious time; if on land, you will kill no game, or perhaps meet with a serious accident. 1933 MERRICK 289 John had left us some warm tea hanging on the blackened kettle-stick over the fire. 1966 SCAMMELL 127 "Bakeapple Jam": Uncle Isaac finds some blasty boughs and cuts a kettle stick. / Aunt Bessy brought a rounder and she shares a bit with Gran.

kettle tea: brew of tea with all the ingredients added in the kettle.

1977 BURSEY 36 'Kettle tea' [was] tea, hot and sweet and ready to be poured into a mug . . . No milk or sugar needed to be added. Everything was in the kettle.

key n   also **cay**. Cp *OED* ~ sb³ 'low island, sandbank, or reef' (1697–), *DJE* Cay (1683–), *DAE* kay (1761–), key³ (1772–). A rock protruding above the surface of the ocean.

[1772] 1971 SEARY 84 Lane also first records the generic in the form Keys at St Mary's [for] the two small rocks. . .southward of Cape St Mary's. 1951 *Nfld & Lab Pilot* i, 100, 141 False cay, a rock with a depth of 2 fathoms. . .over it, lies about 1½ miles northward of Saint Mary's cays. . . A sharp point, with an above-water rock close north-westward of it, and known as The Key, lies about 1½ miles east-north-eastwards.

kick v   Cp *EDD* ~ v¹ 2 (5) (a) Co. Phr *kick it out*: to dance in lively fashion.

1870 HOWLEY *MS Reminiscences* 25 When they heard me playing my flute aboard they were off at once to get me ashore for a dance, and didn't they kick it out in style.

kid n   Cp *DAE* kid² (1848), PARTRIDGE kid's eye for combs. in sense 2.

1 A piece of leather in which the missile of a sling-shot is placed.

M 71–80 One slingshot is made of an alder stalk, with rubber attached to the stalk and the 'kidd.' The 'kidd' is usually made of leather, preferably the tongue of an old boot.

2 Comb **kid-board**: one of the movable boards separating compartments of a fish 'pound' on a vessel (1969 *Nfld Qtly* July, p. 20).

kid's eye: diminutive Newfoundland five-cent silver coin first minted in 1865 (P 133–58).

kilcorn See KEECORN.

kill v

1 To catch fish, esp cod or salmon; see FISH n: FISH KILLER.

[c1711] *Considerations on the Trade to Newfoundland* 2 [The French] kill One or Two Hundred Quintals *per* Boat more than the *English* kill. [1775] 1792 CARTWRIGHT ii, 116 This day I had a haunch of venison roasted for the people, and gave them as much porter as they would drink, (having promised the salmoniers a treat;) and intend to do the same every year that they kill a good voyage. 1895

GRENFELL 82 But a still more vicious circle is established when, to procure food for this winter, a settler has to part with his means of 'killing a voyage' next summer.

2 To fell (a tree).

T 91–64 There were the choppers, fellers that kill the trees. They used to chop down the trees.

killer n   *DC* ~ (Nfld: 1771). See also DEATHFALL. One of the three timbers arranged in an animal trap so as to kill the animal which trips them.

[1771] 1792 CARTWRIGHT i, 176 We then went to Wolf Cove where we finished the deathfall except fixing the killers. 1792 ibid *Gloss* i, xi Killers of a Deathfall, are three, viz. The Ground-killer; which lies upon the ground, across the front of the Deathfall. The Cat-killer; one end of which turns upon a nail which is driven into a strong stake, and the other is supported high up by a line which passes over a crutch on the top of a stake and then comes down to another at the bottom, under which one end of the tongue is fixed, while the other supports the bridge; which being pressed by the animal, disengages the point of the tongue, that sets the cat-killer at liberty and it falls down upon the ground-killer; consequently falls down upon the back of any animal, which may be standing across the latter. And the Main-killer; one end of which rests upon the ground and the other upon the elevated end of the Cat-killer, and falls with it; serving to keep the latter down.

killick n   also **cillick**, **kellick**, **killock**, etc ['kɪlɪk, 'kɪlɒk, 'kʊlɪk, 'kɛlɪk, 'kɛlɪk] *OED* ~ naut (N E: 1630–); *DAE* killock (N E: 1649–); *DC* (Nfld: 1774–); cp *EDD* kelk sb² 'a large detached stone' for sense 1.

1 An anchor made up of an elongated stone encased in pliable sticks bound at the top and fixed in two curved cross-pieces, used in mooring nets and small boats; GRANNY 2.

1760 CO 194: 15 To 1 Small Anchor of 40 lb & 1 Cillick. [1785] 1792 CARTWRIGHT iii, 96 Mr Collingham and two hands finished the shortest seal-net, and the people then carried them both, as also the killicks, &c. to the yawl; but the wind being too high to put them out, they left them there. 1792 ibid *Gloss* i, xii ~ A wooden anchor, made by nailing a pair of claws across each other, and fixing three rods to each claw; within which a large stone is placed to give it weight, and the ends of all the rods are tied together above the stone to secure it in its place. [1802] 1895 PROWSE 419 The [seal net] is extended at the bottom by a mooring and killock fixed to each end. 1857 MOUNTAIN 7 Arrived on the spot, they cast out a home-made anchor called a 'killock,' composed of a long shaped stone encircled with pliant strips of wood, bound tightly at one end. 1878 TOCQUE 192 He lets go his grapnel, or more commonly his kellick, and commences fishing in from 80 to 120 fathoms of water. 1896 *J A Folklore* ix, 23 Killock. . .a small anchor, partly of stone and partly of wood, still used by fishermen, but going out of use in favor of iron grapnels. 1937 DEVINE 30 Killock. A home made anchor, consisting of a frame of witherods enclosing one or two oblong stones, settled on a base of four wooden claws: used to moor small boats and nets. [1952] 1965 PEACOCK (ed) i, 125 "The Fisherman's Alphabet": "K" stands for killick, wood, rock and nails. T 47–64 You'd put your mooring around the claws of the killick and then take a turn around the back end of the killick so as 'twill be layin' on the bottom. 1969 HORWOOD 81 Cod traps are set to moorings, in rather shallow water. . . The traps are. . .often moored to the bottom with killicks.

2 Proverb *lose your killick, and [you'll] find it in the fall.*

C 71–102 ~ If you lose your boat anchor, you'll find it [charged on the merchant's bill in the fall].

3 Phr *have a rock in one's killick*: of a woman, to be pregnant (P 148–75).

4 Attrib **killick-claw**: one of the four arms formed by the two cross-pieces of a killick.

[1774] 1792 CARTWRIGHT ii, 32 Four hands. . .cut some killick-claws. [1952] 1965 PEACOCK (ed) i, 130 "For the Fish We Must Prepare": Oh traps and trawls and fingerstalls, / Rubber boots and killick claws.

killick-rod: one of the pliable sticks encasing the 'killick stone'; RUNG.

[1774] 1792 CARTWRIGHT ii, 29 Having filled up the boat with whitings, pryor-poles and killick-rods, at high water we sailed home.

killick-stone: elongated stone suitable for providing the ballast of home-made anchor.

[1776] 1792 CARTWRIGHT ii, 178 Five hands were at work on the shalloway, and the rest were gathering killick stones, cutting longers, and rinding birch. 1953 *Nfld & Lab Pilot* ii, 211 Killick Stone islands [are located] 6 cables northwestward. . .of Bridgeport Harbour head.

killock See KILLICK.

kind See BEST KIND, FINEST ~ .

king n *DC* ~ n 2 (Nfld: 1965) for sense 1; for combs. in sense 2: *DC* ~ duck (Nfld: 1775–), *DAE* (1785–), *DC* ~ hair Nfld obs (1776, 1819), *NID* for sense (a).

1 The senior migratory fisherman from England in a harbour; ADMIRAL, LORD[1].

1858 [LOWELL] i, 203 The King (ef 'twas the king 'isself that doned it) might as well take a squid or a tomcod for a magistrate, as some 'e'd amade. 1895 PROWSE 226 The oldest ship fisherman in each harbour was called the 'king.'

2 Comb **king bird**, ~ **drake**, ~ **duck**, **old king**: king eider (*Somateria spectabilis*).

[1775] 1792 CARTWRIGHT ii, 61 The water being open, I saw many winter-ducks; also one flock of king-ducks, which are the first I have ever heard of this year. [1832] 1981 *Them Days* vi (3), p. 35 Mr Simon killd the first King Drake for the spring. 1870 *Can Naturalist* v, 303 The king eider. . .is called the 'king bird' in Newfoundland. 1951 PETERS & BURLEIGH 118 King Eider. . .Local Names: King Drake, King Bird. T 389–67[1] Was that kings or shore ducks? That was shore ducks, sir. There might have been a scattered king bird among them. C 69–7 During the St Stephen's

night a group of men went around the community with a relatively small spruce or fir tree. On the top they placed a head of a male eider duck, called a king drake.

king calli: see CALLI(BOGUS).

king hair: (a) long coarse hair covering the underfur of an animal; guard hair; (b) woman's pubic hair (P 113–74 quot).

[1776] 1792 CARTWRIGHT ii, 148 On examining [the rabbit] I find the white coat is an additional one which it got in autumn, and will lose it again in spring; it is composed of long, coarse, king-hairs: the summer furcoat remaining underneath, and retaining its colour. 1792 ibid *Gloss* i, xii ~s. The long, glossy hairs in the skin of a beast, which cover the thick coat of fur. 1819 ANSPACH 376 This coat [of wild animals in winter] is covered with long white glossy hairs, known there by the name of king-hairs, and in the spring fall off in large flocks. 1909 GRENFELL[2] (ed) 77 Traps are all taken in by the first day, as the [fox] fur is now losing colour and the long 'king' hairs fall. P 113–74 ~ Hair of female genitalia.

king hand: surprising or unusual person.

P 184–67 You're the king hand!

king hoop: in coopering, the final hoop placed on a cask or barrel.

T 90–64 And then we would put on a king hoop on the end, iron hoop, and that would fasten everything tight, and then 'twould be ready for shipment.

king's arm: long, muzzle-loading gun.

1858 [LOWELL] ii, 22 Jesse. . .bore, beside his parcel containing food, a huge king's-arm, fired off. . .his cumbrous piece.

king trap: large cod-trap.

M 68–26 One of the traps was called the king trap because it was a bit higher than the others. It was 13 fathoms deep, 2 fathoms on the square, and had a leader 8 fathoms long.

kingcorn, kinkhorn, kinkorn See KEECORN.

kinsarn See CONCERN.

kintal See QUINTAL.

kippin n *OED* kippeen, kippin 'short thin stick' Ir (1830); DINNEEN cipín.

1 Small, slender stick; piece of kindling; cp KEEP A GOIN'S.

1878 *Nfld Pilot* 191 The coast [is] indented by three coves, Cape, Kippin, and Wild coves. Q 71–13 ~s. Small chips of wood that will make a fire burn quickly. P 191–73 ~s. Immature trees or rods; pickets.

2 An insignificant thing or amount.

1968 DILLON 146 I haven't got a kippin to give you. Q 71–7 Give me more to eat, b'y, this is only kippens.

kirby* n also **curvy** ['kəːɹbɪ]. Cp *ADD* curby Nfld. Sealer's quilt; on shore, a heavy blanket or bed-covering.

1924 ENGLAND 66 Morning, after a night spent in fitfully trying to keep the 'curvey' and my rug over me. T 141/59–65[2] Here he comes with his kirby. He hauled off his boots, fixed 'em under his head for a pillow and spreads his kirby out and got in on un. C 69–2 Grandfather told me to go over and get the kirby for him. C 75–28 Cover up in the curbies.

kirlogue n A slap; POLTOGUE*.
Q 67–63 ~ a slap with the left hand. 1972 WIDDOWSON 67 Adults threaten him directly with. . .'claps' under the ear, a 'pholtague' (slap) or a 'kirlogue' (slap).

kissing ring See RING.

klondike n ['klɒndɐik] from the Klondike gold rush of the 1890's. A period of good income; a time of plenty.
[1894–1929] 1960 BURKE (ed White) 44 "Mary Joe": It's better than the Klondike / Since the rush came on the whorts. T 187/90–65 'Tis a klondike here now. The year is so bad as any year, but 'tis what you call pure klondike—gold-digging, the year—to what there was some years back in my day. T 207–65 Heavens, man, it is klondyke now, sure.

knap n also **nap** OED ~ sb¹ 1 chief dial (c1000–); EDD sb¹ 2 esp s w cties for sense 1.
1 A raised portion of land, often with a round top; crest of a hill; KNOB; cp TOLT.
[1786] 1792 CARTWRIGHT iii, 124 He met with some deer in the vale beyond Burnt Knap, and surrounded them. 1836 [WIX]² 81 These bare spots upon the hills, from which the snow had melted. . .are called 'naps.' 1843 Journ of Assembly Appendix, p. 467 But in consequence of the Knaps and Ponds being so numerous, parts of it are rather curved. 1868 HOWLEY MS Reminiscences 37 In the evening Mr Murray and Joe walked to a knap about a mile from camp on the south side of the river to take bearings on the surrounding hills and fix the position of our camp. 1907 MILLAIS 278 Here and there are little rocky eminences, locally designated as 'knaps,' from which miles of country may be easily spied. 1937 DEVINE 30 Knapp. A rising ground; the upper end of a slope. 1966 SCAMMELL 127 "Bakeapple Jam": I picked a pint around that knap, I'll shuck 'em later on, / I'm the fastest picker here I'm pretty sure I am; / We're going to lose a lot of sweat afore the day is gone, / And have to pay with nipper bites for Bakeapple jam. 1971 NOSEWORTHY 160 Gravelly Knap—a small, rocky hill approximately one-half mile south of Maloney's Hill.
2 A shoal or 'bank' on the fishing grounds.
[1929] 1933 GREENLEAF (ed) 370 "The Roving Newfoundlanders": They've fished the Northern and Grand Banks from every hole and knap, / They are the tyrants of the sea, they fished the Flemish Cap.

knee n Cp OED ~ sb 6 c (b) 'piece framed into. . .sled' (1875) for knee-slide.
Comb **knee-cap boot**: fisherman's leather boot of medium height; CAP n: CAP-KNEE BOOT.
P 102–60 All the local shoemakers would be working overtime to fill orders for long knee-cap boots mostly worn by the skipper men and the three-quarter length by the ordinary fisherman. T 84–64 The first of the

Smallwood boots, what they call knee-cap boots, they come on around here and turn up, and the leather come up here for kneeling down.
knee-knocked: with legs bent in so that the knees touch; knock-kneed (P 252–69).
knee knockers: men's trousers gathered in at the knees; knickerbockers (Q 71–1).
knee-slide: sled strengthened with wooden knees or angular pieces of timber.
T 175/7–65 A knee-slide, sir, proper wood slide, the same slide as they use for pulling wood, just a hand-slide. . . The knee-slide, she was stronger slide, anyway.

knit v also ~ **up**; **net***. Both [nɪt] and [nɛt] are widespread; it is assumed that knit is the basic form, with net as a variant pronunciation. OED ~ v 2 a 'to knot string in open meshes so as to form (a net); to net' obs (1290, 1687 quots) for sense 1.
1 To make or repair a net; to knot 'twine' into meshes to form a fish-net.
P 102–60 Stormy days [we] engaged some of the native men to come to the shore and knit salmon twine and I would instruct them how to make up the twine into nets. P 148–60 [You would] knit the twine. T 43/7–64 The name for the twine when 'tis net up is linnet. You'd slip that off o' your card—'twas a bit tedious first until you get three or four drews, they call it, knit up—that was three of four back and forth. M 69–7 [Mending nets] is done usually in fishing stores, although much twine is still netted in the kitchen. 1975 BUTLER 58 They knit their own nets with hemp twine. 1979 TIZZARD 187 January 7th saw men and women back again to the usual routine of the everyday chores: working. . .woodcutting and hauling, gossiping, mending nets and knitting twine. 1981 Livyere Fall, p. 38 The art of 'knitting' a cast net requires considerable skill due to both the small mesh size [and] the circular shape of the net.
2 Phr **knit out**: to empty a needleful of 'twine' when making a fish-net.
T 43/8–64 If there was somebody there to fill the needles for you, you could knit out a needle in ten minutes, which would be two or three rounds on the hundred meshes.

knitch n also **nitch** OED ~ now dial (13..–); EDD 'bundle of. . .straw, corn, or wood.' A number of pieces of bark removed from spruce, birch or fir trees and carried on the shoulder; esp a bundle of ten pieces.
[1771] 1792 CARTWRIGHT i, 129 The rinders took off twenty-seven nitches; and found an old, double-spring, french trap. 1792 ibid Gloss i, xii Nitch of rinds—ten in number, or as many large ones, as a man can conveniently carry under his arm. 1937 DEVINE 30 ~ a bundle or backload, especially of ten spruce or fir tree rinds, rolled up as taken off the standing trees. T 31/4–64 I had to go and get three knitches—two knitches o' rines. T 141/68–65² You do them up in tens, ten rines; that would be a knitch. A knitch of boughs is ten, of course. A knitch of anything, I suppose, is ten. . . And

ten rinds would be so heavy as a big turn of wood. Boy, you'd never believe the weight is in rind. M 69–17 The rinders counted their rinds [by this rhyme]: Two and two is four, / And two is a couple of more. / This one and that one, / And the two in the road is a knitch.

knitting vbl n also **netting**. Cp *EDD* needle sb 3 'shuttle. . .with which nets are made'; *NID* needle[1] [illust:] netting needle for sense 2.

1 The activity of making or repairing a fish-net.

1888 STEARNS 4 In netting, the needle was thrust through the loop above, the twine brought over the card, to which it was tightly drawn, and a knot made by drawing the needle between the threads and through a loop in its own thread, and the whole drawn tightly.

2 Attrib **knitting-needle**, **needle**: implement designed to hold a quantity of 'twine' and used to knot meshes in a fish-net.

1888 STEARNS 287 The working instruments were a needle and a card. The needle was flat, eight inches long, conical at the top, and the bottom concave for about an inch; the inside of the upper third was also hollow, saving a small needle shaped piece, running up in the center to within half an inch of the top. . . Each needle, and there were several for each person, was wound full of twine, the turns running around the inner point of the needle, and over the concave end. T 43/8–64 You'd put up your netting—you had proper netting needles. P 9–73 The fishermen made their own needles from birch woods. Now, they can be bought in the stores and are made from plastic. They are from 8 to 9 inches long and from one to one and one-eighth inches wide. A smaller needle, about half or a little over half the size given was used for nets with a mesh of two inches or less.

knob n also **nob** *OED* ~ sb 2 esp U S (1650–), *EDD* sb 2, *DAE* (1796–) for sense 1; cp *OED* 3 'a small lump' for senses 3, 4, 5. See also KNAP.

1 A prominent rounded hill; cp TOLT.

[1766] 1971 BANKS 450 All the Land to the West-ward of it is high, of a Uniform even figure Sloping away to nothing to the Westward & terminating to the Eastward over this Bay with a conspicuous Nobb from which it is a steep Cliff. This Nobb or hillock is on the West Side of Temple Bay. 1821 *D'Alberti MS* 13 Sep Remarkably high peaked hills situated on the western side of Connaigre Bay commonly called among the fishermen 'the Devil's Nob.' 1842 JUKES ii, 229 [The country is] grooved in every direction by small valleys or ravines, and covered with round hummocky knobs and hills with rocky and precipitous sides. 1971 NOSEWORTHY 215 ~ A small hill, round and not very high, and water runs off it quickly.

2 A submerged rock.

1955 *Nfld & Lab Pilot* ii, 365, 398 Saunders Knob, with a depth of 15 fathoms over it, lies about half a mile farther south-westward. . . The Knob, a small rock with a depth of 5¼ fathoms over it, lies one cable north-westward.

3 A piece of floating ice.

1920 WALDO 151 A little piece of ice is called a knob, and a larger piece is a pan. A pan is the same

thing as a floe, but the latter expression is not in common usage.

4 Small ball or knot of lint.

C 71–102 She remarked to me that there were a 'lot of knobs on my slacks which came off the bed.' . . .She said the knobs were tiny particles which came off onto her slacks while she was sitting on the bed. I had always referred to this as 'woolies' or 'lint' from the blankets.

5 A piece of hard, usu spherical, candy; cube sugar. Also attrib.

[1894 BURKE] 58 Coco Nut Candy, Knobs, Sticks, Butter Rocks. T 199–65 [At Christmas] you'd probably get an apple right in the toe o' your stocking, and prob-ably a couple o' big Gibraltar candy; they're pepper-mint knobs—great big uns. P 126–67 'This is my knob night' (night to go out to see the girlfriend). T 410–67 If anybody come in on a Sunday, the knob sugar was on the table—little square knobs.

knobbly a also **knobby, nobbly, nobby**. Cp *OED* ~ knobby. Of a surface, rough, choppy; lumpy.

[c1905] DEVINE P 148–74 [He] went on the ice to hunt seals, / But he fell once or twice, on the knobbly ice. 1924 ENGLAND 59 Irregular gusts of tumult from ice-ramming shuddered the cabin. 'Gettin' pretty knobbly in de water, dat time.' 1930 BARNES 386 He says, 'Pretty nobby, now.' 'Yes,' says I, 'dangerous sea running.' P 207–67 The sea is knobbly this morning. C 75–46 'Tis a bit knobby out there this morning. 1979 POTTLE 132 The Newfoundland House [of Assembly] was not a sea of tranquility for long. In fact, it soon became much more than a trifle ruffled or 'nobbly,' in the fishermen's language, and before many sessions had passed, it was rocked by verbal storms.

knobby See KNOBBLY.

knot n A hard, densely-packed stretch of ice in an ice-floe (1925 *Dial Notes* v, 335).

1924 ENGLAND 167 We tried to reach the seals indi-cated. Alas, impenetrable 'knots' of ice reared them-selves in our way.

knotty a also **noddy** Of the weather, rough, stormy; cp **knobbly**: (1924 ENGLAND 317, 318).

P 250–80 You only gets a little wind lop, more or less, up here, but down there you gets the ocean swell and the water is really tumbly, noddy water, we'll say.

know v *OED* ~ 17 obs rare (1597); *EDD* II 1 (2) ~ for. Phr *know for*: to know of or concern-ing (something).

Q 67–98 Do you know for a pen? (Where can I get a pen?).

knuck n also **knuckle** *OED* knuckle sb 3 'pro-jection of carpal or tarsal joint of quadruped'; *Cent* ~ 'knuckle' N E. The knee, esp of animals that kneel (Q 71–8); hence the knee of a human being.

1964 *Evening Telegram* 9 June, p. 7 [To scrub the

floor] down on yer knucks men! C 68–19 According to
an old tradition, on Old Christmas Day the cows kneel
down on their knucks to pray. Q 71–7 She got down on
her knucks and scrubbed the floor. P 9–73 When I
looked up, the wounded deer. . .reared up on his hind
legs again. She falls down on her fore knuckles.

komatik n also **comatic, comatick, commeteck,
kamutik, kometik,** etc ['kɑmətɪk] *DC* ~ n
([1824], 1853–) for sense 1; *NID*; *Labrador Inuit*
qamutik 'sled.'

1 A long sled, adopted in northern Newfoundland and esp Labrador for winter travel and
hauled by dogs or sometimes men; sledge for
hauling wood; ESKIMO SLED.
[1832] 1980 *Them Days* vi (2), p. 35 4 Indians arrivd
here from St Francis Harbour with a comatic and 13
dogs after seals [carcasses]. 1861 *Harper's* xxii, 744
Lamps of sputtering seal-oil emitted a feeble light,
barely visible through the smoke of their burning, yet
revealing seal-skins pendent from the rafters, komme-
tiks (dog-sleds) stowed overhead. 1884 STEARNS 145
The komatik. . .is a sort of sledge or sled. . .from nine
to thirteen feet in length, from two to three feet in
width, and it stands about eight inches from the
ground. 1887 *Evening Telegram Christmas No* 5 The
dogs are harnessed, the 'komatik' brought to the door,
and, enveloped in buffalo, bear, and other skins, with
many injunctions to the drivers to take care of the rapids, the rosy, laughing crowd are tucked in the coach-
box. 1907 WALLACE 229 Crossbars extending about an
inch over the outer runner on either side are lashed
across the runners by means of thongs of sealskin or
heavy twine, which is passed through holes bored into
the crossbars and the runners. The use of lashings
instead of nails or screws permits the komatik to yield
readily in passing over rough places, where metal fastenings would be pulled out, or be snapped off by the
frost. P 236–59 [The white man's] komatik is shorter
than the Eskimo komatik, and usually has a sea chest
lashed to it, for stores and as a seat. T 43/6–64 If [the
sled is] loaded you stand behind and just guide your
komatik with your two stags behind. P 130–67 We'll
take the wood komatik, a sled used for carrying wood.
In the wood-path the komatik is not turned around; the
dogs are harnessed to the other end. 1977 *Inuit Land
Use* 332 We had to do it all by dog team. Sometimes we
had to walk beside the komatik when the going was
bad.
2 Attrib **komatik-box**: compartment on komatik for passenger or load; COACH BOX.
[1916] 1972 GORDON 62 He filled his big komatik
box with rocks and Steve couldn't make out why his
dogs were so sluggish—until he reached home.
P 148–64 ~ a box strapped on a komatik in which
women and children are carried. It is oblong, has vertical sides and a sloping rear against which the back may
lean. 1973 GOUDIE 79 The kamutik. . .was too heavily
loaded and at last turned over. . . I landed standing on
my head in the kamutik box with the baby under my
arm.
komatik-dog: husky; ESKIMO DOG.
1938 MACDERMOTT 52 William Caines had his Car-
lo, the fastest komatik-dog I have ever seen.

kometic See KOMATIK.

kossa(c)k See CASSOCK.

L

labrador n also **laborador, labradore,
larbadore** [læbrə'dɔɹ, 'læbrədɔɹ, 'laəbədɔɹ].
Cp *Dicionário Português-Inglês*: lavrador 'tiller,
one who farms. . .ploughman. . .landowner.' For
combs. in sense 3: *OED* ~ duck (1884–5), *DAE*
(1869); *NID* ~ jay; in sense 4: *OED* ~ feldspar
(1794–), *DC* (1824–), *OED* ~ hornblende
(1794), *OED* ~ spar (1799), *DC* (1887–), *OED*
~ stone (1778); in sense 5: *DAE* ~ pine (1803–),
DC ~ herring (1866).

1 The north-eastern peninsula of North America, lying between Hudson Bay and the Gulf of
St Lawrence, which forms part of the Province of
Newfoundland; the Atlantic coast of the peninsula from Cape Chidley to the Strait of Belle
Isle; freq preceded by *the*; in var phrases: *coast
of Labrador, Labrador coast, (down) on (the)
Labrador.* Cp CANADIAN-LABRADOR.
[c1516 (1962) *Cabot Voyages* 310 Terra noua de pes-
caria inuenta de laboradore de re de anglitera tera
frigida.] [c1525 ibid 311 TIERA DEL LABRADOR laqual
fue descubierta por los Yngleses dela uila de bristol e
por q̃ el q̃ dio el lauiso della era labrador de las islas de
los acares le quido este nõbre]. [1580] ibid 210 Sebastian Caboto, sent by King Henry the seventh, did dis
cover from Newfownd Land so far along and abowt the
Coaste next to Labrador. [1693] 1793 REEVES xxii
. . .and shall take and kill one whale at least in the
Gulph of Saint Lawrence, or on the coasts of
Labrador, Newfoundland, or in any other seas. [1766]
1976 HEAD 180 When the King's Ships arriv'd on their
Stations this year, upon the Coast of Labradore, they
found between two and three hundred Whaling Vessels
from ye Plantations. [1770] 1792 CARTWRIGHT i, 3 I
found [at Fogo] Messrs Coghlan and Lucas, who had
been employed in getting ready our schooner called the
Enterprise, for the purpose of landing me upon some
part of Labrador, and Mr Lucas was afterwards to
explore the Coast to the Northward. [1794] 1968
THOMAS 47 These Islands of Ice. . .were frozen about a
year ago in the Greenland Sea or the Labrador Coast.
1819 ANSPACH 443 What is called the *northern-fishery*,
is carried on on the northern coasts of the island and
the adjoining parts of Labrador by planters from Conception-Bay, Trinity-Bay, and Saint John's. 1842
JUKES ii, 130–1 The total disappearance of the Red
Indians. . .is not due to their utter destruction, but to
their having passed over to the Labrador. [1851] 1963
MELVILLE 33 Had it not been for us whalemen, that
tract of land [New Bedford] would this day perhaps
have been in as howling condition as the coast of
Labrador. 1858 [LOWELL] i, 90 He would one day have
manned his schooner for 'the Larbadore.' 1920
GRENFELL 24 You go 'down North'; and your friend is
not bound for Labrador. She is going to 'the Labra-

dor,' or, to be more of a purist still, 'the Larbadore.'
1924 ENGLAND 261 With small, home-built
schooners—this ingenious people can turn their hands
to making almost everything they need—they take up
the sea trek every summer and go down the Labrador.
1942 *Little Bay Islands* 14 These fishermen made very
good catches of fish, but spent a longer time on the
Labrador coast (sometimes from July to November)
than they usually do now. 1955 DOYLE (ed) 11 "A
Noble Fleet of Sealers": The 'Viking' blood was in his
veins, / As in the days of yore / When the Barbours
fought the seal and whale / And fished the Labrador.
1981 *Them Days* vi (4), p. 47 "My Home": For we are
two composers that never composed before, / We live
at St Mary's River down here in Labrador.

2 A variety of heavily salted, semi-dried cod
produced in the Labrador fishery; often attrib
with designations of 'cure' or grade.
[1811] 1954 INNIS 237–8 The shore fish are so dry and
horney that we get only 8 ct. into a common hhd. 6½
into the second size and 6. [Labrador fish are] very lim-
ber and [we] get 10 ct. in hhd. 1845 *Journ of Assembly*
217 . . .the best and largest fish. . .worth several shillings per Qtl. more than the Labrador or Shore fish. . .
[1909] 1930 COAKER 5 We must not forget that
although this season's catch of fish is small, yet the
prices are now below $5 for No. 1 small and Labrador
only $3.50 per qtl. [1912] 1930 ibid 47 Some merchants
were working for all they were worth to bring about a
slump in prices—they failed, although at that time
some 50,000 qtls. of Labrador shore was afloat at St
John's. . .Labrador slop was sold at $4.30 to $4.40 up
to the time of the war breaking out. 1925 *Journ of
Assembly* 448 As the season advanced fish gradually
advanced in price from $5.00 to $8.00 per quintal for
Labrador. 1933 *Nfld Royal Commission Report* 106
The fish, when culled or valued according to quality are
divided into the following grades:– Labrador (heavy
salted, soft cured). (a) Quality No. 1. (b) Quality No.
2. (c) Cullage. 1937 *Seafisheries of Nfld* 47 Heavy
Salted partially dried fish, [is] known as Labrador. 1955
Nfld Fisheries Board 23 Labrador, Ordinary Cure.
Sound quality fish, having a moisture content of over
44% up to and including 50%, well pressed, firm and
heavily salted; nearly or quite white, with clear surface,
clean on face and back, well split, not showing blood
stains, clots, liver, gut or slime. P 243–55 Labrador
cure [is] codfish caught on the Labrador; also fish
caught north of Goose Cape on the NE Coast, and N
of Flower's Cove on the NW Coast and cured in the
Labrador style. There are two kinds: 1) ordinary cure,
2) semi-dry cure. 1970 PARSONS 303 A [fisherman] in
Labrador today can get around twenty dollars for a
quintal of dried fish which is referred to as 'Labrador
cure.' A quintal of salt bulk sells for around eight dollars to twelve dollars. 1979 TIZZARD 375 I shipped
twelve quintals, two quarters and fourteen pounds of
merchantable Labrador.

3 In names of animals and birds: **labrador curlew,** ~ **deer-mouse,** ~ **duck,** ~ **flying squirrel,** ~
herring (see sense 5), ~ **horned owl,** ~ **jay,** ~
jumping mouse, ~ **martin,** ~ **muskrat,** ~ **polar
bear,** ~ **porcupine,** ~ **red fox,** ~ **sable,** ~ **savan-**
nah sparrow, ~ **seal,** ~ **shrew,** ~ **vole,** ~ **white
fox,** ~ **woodchuck.**
1970 PARSONS 173 The two most important of these
[extinct birds] were the great auk and the Labrador
curlew [Eskimo curlew: *Numenius borealis*]. [1845]
1909 GRENFELL[2] (ed) 461 Labrador deer-mouse.
Hesperomys maniculatus. . . Common throughout the
peninsula south at least to Hamilton Inlet. The Labrador deer-mouse, like many of its congeners, is apt to
take up its abode in buildings and huts like the house
mouse, and in Labrador seems to be much more abundant in such places than in the woods and among rocks.
1918 TOWNSEND 22 [Audubon] makes a tantalizing
record of the now extinct pied or Labrador duck as follows: 'The Pied Duck breeds here.' 1947 TANNER 430
During the last hundred years two species have become
extinct, the flightless great auk (Plautus impennis) in
1852 and the Labrador duck (Camptorhynchus labradorius) in 1874. 1977 *Them Days* ii (3), p. 13 The
Labrador Duck, known also as the 'pied duck' and the
'skunk duck' was common on the Labrador coast until
about 1842. [1900] 1909 GRENFELL[2] (ed) 461 Labrador
flying squirrel. *Sciuropterus sabrinus makkovikensis*. . .
Rather generally distributed throughout the wooded
region, though apparently not common anywhere. The
Labrador form is a very well-marked subspecies. 1909
ibid 475 Labrador horned owl [*Bubo virginianus
heterocnemis*]. Common permanent resident. 1907
TOWNSEND 385 Labrador jay. *Perisoreus canadensis
nigricapillus*. 1947 TANNER i, 429 One of the most
amusing of Labrador's animals is the extremely curious
Labrador jay. . .resembling in all its behaviour and
especially its pilfering habits his cousin in Lapland.
[1899] 1909 GRENFELL[2] (ed) 463 Labrador jumping
mouse. *Zapus hudsonius ladas*. . . Abundant in the
southern wooded region, about Black Bay, etc., and
extending northward, along the coast, to beyond Hamilton Inlet. [1897] ibid 466–7 Labrador marten. *Mustela
brumalis*. . . The Labrador subspecies is a fine large,
dark-coloured marten, and is generally distributed
throughout the wooded regions. [1899] ibid 463 Labrador muskrat. *Fiber zibethicus aquilonius*. Known only
from Black Bay, where Doane secured a good series.
[1899] ibid 464 Labrador polar bear. *Lepus
labradorius*. . . Of general distribution in the barrens
and semi-barrens of Labrador, occasionally reaching so
far south as Hamilton Inlet. [1900] ibid 464 Labrador
porcupine. *Erethizon dorsatus picinus*. . . Common and
generally distributed from the St Lawrence, north to
the semi-barrens. [1900] ibid 465 Labrador red fox.
Vulpes rubricosa bangsi. . . Common throughout the
whole of Labrador from the St Lawrence to Hudson
Strait. [1897] ibid 466–7 Labrador sable. *Mustela
brumalis*. 1947 TANNER i, 418–19 The darker and
thicker the black spruce woods are, the darker and
richer are the skins of the marten living there—the so-
called 'Labrador sable.' 1951 PETERS & BURLEIGH
384–5 Labrador savannah sparrow. *Passerculus sandwichensis labradorius*. A small striped sparrow with a
yellowish line over the eye and with a rather short and
slightly notched tail, found in open country and grassy
fields. The Labrador race breeds in Labrador and Newfoundland. 1911 PRICHARD 44 It was the Labrador bay
or harbour seal, an animal identical with our British
common seal (*Phoca vitulina*). [1899] 1909 GRENFELL[2]

(ed) 468 Labrador shrew. *Sorex personatus miscix*. . .
Common throughout the Labrador peninsula from
Fort Chimo south. 1942 ELTON 321 Authorities (as
Anderson) consider that the chief actor is the large
Labrador vole (*Microtus enixus*). But other species of
small rodents live in Northern Labrador, the following
being recorded. . .: at least two voles or meadow-mice
(*Microtus enixus* and *M. pennsylvanicus labradorius*),
two red-backed voles (*Clethrionomys gapperi ungava*
and *C. g. proteus*), a false lemming-mouse
(*Phenacomys ungava ungava*), a lemming-mouse
(*Synaptomys borealis innuitus*), a banded lemming
(*Dicrostonyx hudsonius*), and a white-footed deer-
mouse (*Peromyscus maniculatus maniculatus*). [1902]
1909 GRENFELL[2] (ed) 465 Labrador white fox. *Vulpes
lagopus ungava*. . . The Arctic fox is abundant in the
barren-grounds and extends south to about Lake
Michikamaw and to Nichicum. [On the coast] it pushes
rather farther south; on the Atlantic to Hamilton Inlet,
and rarely even to the Strait of Belle Isle. [1899] ibid
460 Labrador woodchuck. *Arctomys ignavus*. . . Low
speaks of a woodchuck as common in the country
between Lake St John and the East Main River; this
may possibly be another form.

4 In names of various crystalline minerals:
**labrador fel(d)spar, ~ hornblende, ~ spar, ~
stone**. See also LABRADORITE.
1814 *Trans Geol Soc* ii, 49 To the south of this chain
the district commences, where the Labrador felspar is
found. 1839 MURRAY iii, 343 The well-known Labrador felspar is found south of Kiglapyed, but is chiefly
brought to us from the vicinity of Nain, especially from
a lagoon in which the river of Nain terminates, where it
is associated with hyperstene. 1814 *Trans Geol Soc* ii,
49 The same district produces also the Labrador hornblende, (hyperstene) and a white stone striped with
green. [1786] 1792 CARTWRIGHT iii, 228 White spar is
very common; and several samples of that beautiful
one called Labrador spar, has been picked up by the
Esquimaux, of which there is one large piece in the
Leverian Museum. 1787 PENNANT 44 That curious
body the *Labrador* stone, which reflects all the colors
of the peacock, is found there in loose masses. The late
Mr *La Trobe* shewed me a piece of exquisite beauty,
finely polished, which he procured from the laudable
missions in that country. 1819 ANSPACH 373 The only
article of any interest that the coast of Labrador presents to the mineralogist, is known by the name of the
Labrador-stone, or 'spatum rutilum versicolor.'

5 Attrib, comb **labrador current**: cold ocean
current flowing from the arctic past Labrador
and eastern Newfoundland.
1837 BLUNT 666 I have long since become satisfied
that the current in question is neither more nor less
than a direct continuation of the polar or Labrador current, which bears southward the great stream of drift
ice from Davis' Strait. 1953 *Nfld & Lab Pilot* ii, 7
Northward of Hudson Strait, the current flowing down
the Canadian shore of Baffin bay is known as the
Baffin Land current. Its continuation, southward of
Hudson strait is called the Labrador current. The
Labrador current widens as it proceeds southward,
and, after passing Belle Isle strait and the eastern coast
of Newfoundland, it floods the whole of the Grand

Bank of Newfoundland, with the exception, during the
summer months, of the extreme southern part. 1975
COOK 41–2 All those brave boys. . . Iced down. . .
Rolling in the Labrador current. 1981 *Evening
Telegram* 15 Aug, p. 3 It might take several months for
the southbound Labrador current to be warmed a bit
by the. . .Gulf Stream [this year].

labrador dance: see NEWFOUNDLAND DANCE.

labrador dog: see LABRADOR DOG.

labrador fishery: a branch of the inshore cod-
fishery, esp that prosecuted from early summer
to fall by migratory Newfoundland fishermen in
schooners or from shore stations; NORTHERN
FISHERY.
1819 ANSPACH 433–4 In the Labrador fishery, the
usual proportion for every hundred quintal of fish is
between thirteen and fourteen hogsheads of Lisbon
salt, which is always preferred where the strongest
pickle is required. 1846 TOCQUE 216 Trade is now at its
full height; all is bustle and activity preparing for the
fishery. About the tenth of June the vessels sail for the
Labrador fishery: the Newfoundland fishery commences at some places in May, and at other places not
until the last of June. [1905] 1912 *Nfld Law Reports* 158
It was alleged and not denied that this was one of the
most valuable fishing properties in connection with the
Labrador fishery. 1936 SMITH 11–12 Brigus was a very
prominent outport in those days, with about forty vessels all engaged in the Labrador fishery, from a 200-ton
brig down to a 30-ton fore and aft schooner, employing
about one thousand men and girls, besides the squatters who fished on the land in stages. 1965 *Daily News*
18 Oct, p. 16 From then until the fall of 1926 he successfully prosecuted the Labrador fishery.

labrador floater: a fishing schooner; FLOATER
2.
1937 *Seafisheries of Nfld* 35 The units of production
in the Shore Fishery range from the man who fishes by
himself, to the crew of the largest Labrador Floater,
which usually numbers fifteen men.

labrador herring: part of the Newfoundland
population of the Atlantic herring (*Clupea harengus harengus*); see also HERRING.
1863 HIND i, 330 Owing to the thick coating of fat
which covers the flesh of these Labrador herrings, they
must be salted immediately, and with great care, to
prevent their turning yellow and spoiling. 1883
HATTON & HARVEY 324 There are two varieties of herring taken on the shores of the island—the Bank
(called also the Labrador) herring, and the Shore
herring. . .the Bank being the full-grown fish, and
measuring on an average thirteen and a half inches.
1909 BROWNE 58 The herring of the Labrador coast are
reputed to be the richest and finest as regards quality in
the world. . . When Labrador herring were exported in
large quantities little care was taken of either the cure
or packing. 1976 PINHORN 30 Little information is
available on the Labrador herring except that they are
predominately late summer spawners and consist
mainly of large, old, slow-growing fish. Large catches
were taken in the Labrador area in the late 1800's.

labrador indian: MONTAGNAIS, NASKAPI.
1866 WILSON 294 About two years before [1821],

considerable excitement had been produced by the baptism of six Labrador Indians by our missionary, Mr Ellis, at Bearneed. 1872 DASHWOOD 195 The Labrador Indians make the most beautifully finished bark canoes of any of the Indian tribes. 1915 HOWLEY 270 Peyton also told Jukes that the Red Indians were on good terms with the Labrador Indians (Mountaineers)? whom they called Shudamunks, or Shaunamuncks, meaning 'good Indians.'

labrador livyer: see LIVYER.

labradorman: see LABRADORMAN.

labrador (scrub) pine: jack pine (*Pinus banksiana*).

1839 MURRAY iii, 326 *Pinus Banksiana* (Labrador scrub, or gray pine) inhabits cold, barren, and rocky situations in Nova Scotia, Canada, and Hudson's Bay. 1908 HUBBARD 6 The river levels of the south-western districts are widely timbered with the small Banksian or Labrador pine.

labrador planter: see PLANTER.

labrador room: see ROOM.

labrador schooner: Newfoundland migratory fishing vessel of from 30–200 tons prosecuting the Labrador coastal cod-fishery during the summer; FLOATER. Also attrib.

1902 HOWLEY *MS Reminiscences* 45 The Labrador schooners on their homeward voyages every Autumn are in the habit of hugging the shores pretty closely so as to avail if necessary of the shelter of some of the numerous harbours along this northern Peninsula. [1915] 1930 COAKER 101 We are fully in accord with your suggestions respecting the prohibition of motor power in connection with the Labrador schooner fishery. 1974 SQUIRE 29 All these little [Labrador schooners] rarely reaching forty tons in size had two masts, foremast and mainmast together with a bowsprit to the under side of which a cutwater was attached, the latter giving the bow a curved rakish appearance. All of them carried a main topmast. There were four sails: mainsail, foresail, jib and jumbo, with sometimes a gaff topsail.

labrador station(er): see STATION, STATIONER.

labrador tea: see LABRADOR TEA.

labrador voyage: the enterprise or period of fishing by Newfoundland migratory cod-fishermen in Labrador waters; see also VOYAGE.

1887 *Colonist Christmas No* 14 They determined to leave it till a more favorable opportunity offered. This did not occur until the following Autumn, after the winding up of the Labrador voyage. 1939 LODGE 103 According to the Commission of Enquiry the Labrador voyages analysed gave the owner a resultant average profit of $430, out of which he would have to meet the cost of repairs to his ship and his gear.

labrador dog n *DC* ~ 1, 2 (1842–; 1957). See also NEWFOUNDLAND DOG.

1 A strong, short-haired dog from which the Labrador Retriever has been bred; WATER DOG.

1842 BONNYCASTLE ii, 24–5 There are, however, still some splendid water dogs to be found. . . They are of two kinds; the short, wiry-haired Labrador dog, and the long, curly-haired Newfoundland species. 1861 DE

BOILIEU 172–3 The Labrador dog, let me remark, is a bold fellow, and, when well taught, understands, almost as well as any Christian biped, what you say to him.

2 Sled-dog of the Labrador coast; husky.

1863 HIND ii, 155 The Labrador dogs are excessively quarrelsome, and, wolf-like, always attack the weaker. 1909 GRENFELL[2] (ed) 272 The real Labrador dog is a very slightly modified wolf. A good specimen stands two feet six inches, or even two feet eight inches high at the shoulder, measures over six feet six inches from the tip of the nose to the tip of the tail, and will scale a hundred pounds. The hair is thick and straight; on the neck it may be six inches in length. The ears are pointed and stand directly up. T 43/4–64 The thing that I used to be most afraid of down there was the Labrador dogs, Eskimo dogs.

labradorian a *O Sup*[2] ~ (1888–). Of or pertaining to Labrador or its people.

1891 PACKARD 84 [The cow's] nautical owner informs us, in sturdy Labradorian dialect, that she had been brought up this spring. 'I made her fast to her moorings, and there let her bide to eat the grass.' Ibid 125 The lumber for these shanties had evidently. . .been sawn upon the spot and taken from the Labradorian forest of firs near at hand, which measured twelve inches through at the butt, and were about twenty feet high. 1908 TOWNSEND 81 Going down north,—it is with a wrench that I use this Labradorian phraseology instead of up north as the maps would seem to indicate. 1947 TANNER 730 A particularity of some of the Labradorean liveyers is to give sex to all the ordinary objects of daily life; I left he [the rifle]; put he [the kettle] on; he's [the wind] come right across.

labradorian n *O Sup*[2] ~ (1863–). A person born or resident in Labrador.

1863 HIND ii, 135 The residents on the coast, or Labradorians as they may well be termed, frequent the St Augustine in the winter and travel towards its source. 1884 STEARNS 184 The walking would have been called good by a native Labradorian; to me it was terrible. 1918 TOWNSEND 79 All the names of Labradorians mentioned by Audubon in his Journal were familiar to the captain. The descendants of most of them were still living on the coast. 1947 TANNER 527 The heavy, clumsy *tupek* of the Labradoreans, the skin tent, is said to have never given complete protection from rain or wind. 1970 *Evening Telegram* 12 May, p. 1 EPA subsidy restricted to Labradorians. The Eastern Provincial Airways subsidy has been restricted to permanent residents of Labrador.

labradorite n *OED* ~ (1814–); *DC* (1864–) for sense 1.

1 An iridescent crystalline mineral prized for its shifting colours of blue, green, grey, etc; LABRADOR FELSPAR.

1863 HIND i, 115 Labradorite is a lime felspar, which, upon decomposition, yields a very fertile soil. 1895 GRENFELL 11 Near Hopedale a beautiful blue and bronze iridescent felspar is found. It is called labradorite, and polished glistens in the sunlight like a peacock's feather. It is used for brooches, and occasionally for ornamenting buildings. 1947 TANNER 90 The universally known, blue, green, bronze schillerizing labradorite is found in the Nain district in limited bands in the anorthosite, also the pale green amazonite. The ordinary biotite gneiss underlies the eastern part of Paul's Island, but a few miles west of Ford Harbour it comes in contact with the famous anorthosite and allied gabbro whence is derived the labradorite. . .the Labradorite is called 'fire-rock' by the Indians. 1970 PARSONS 100 The colour of the rock is unique and beautiful in appearance. Each time a small rock containing the colourful labradorite is turned to a different angle, a new splendor of gorgeous colour is seen.

2 Inhabitant of Labrador; LABRADORIAN n.

1895 GRENFELL 226 . . .and the hope that they would grow and increase, bringing health, happiness, and much comfort to these Labradorites. 1908 TOWNSEND 44 The hard bare rocks are for the most part covered with lichens, black and gray, yellow and orange. Everywhere it can get a foothold is the fir-like creeping empetrum, the 'blackberry' of the Labradorites, the well-known curlew berry or crowberry.

labradorman n   DC ~ 1, 2, 3 (1905; 1918–; 1905–).

1 A person born or resident in Labrador; LABRADORIAN n.

1895 GRENFELL 83 The Newfoundlanders are too often only little better off than Labradormen. [1919] 1972 GORDON 163 There I was able to get one of our Labrador-men to take me on to Cartwright. 1933 MERRICK 89 Perhaps it is wrong to say Labradormen are afraid. They're not, they're merely respectful. They understand old Dame Nature, read her warnings, know she's kind and at the same time merciless. 1968 MESHER 34 "The Gals from Newfoundland": Though I am a Labrador man, / Have I held a lassie's hand / While honouring the company, of / The gals from Newfoundland.

2 Migratory fisherman prosecuting the cod-fishery in Labrador coastal waters; FLOATER, STATIONER.

1907 DUNCAN 87 What with the Labradormen an' the woman t' Thunder Arm an' the heathen 'tis fair awful. 1947 TANNER 753–4 The floaters differentiate between the so-called Labradormen, who fish exclusively on the coast of Labrador, and Bankers, who fish chiefly on the great fishing banks outside Newfoundland, and in the autumn make a trip to Labrador to increase their catch. Among [them] Labradormen are the most numerous.

3 Vessel from Newfoundland engaged in the Labrador cod-fishery.

1871 HOWLEY MS Reminiscences 13 Many a fine sealing vessel or Labradorman has come to grief on those awful rocks and shoals. 1891 Holly Branch 37 So brilliant was the electric discharge that we could make out the stranger to be a Labradorman, bound home with her living freight of human beings. 1907 DUNCAN 307 She would ship on a Labradorman.

labrador tea n   DC ~ 1 b (1822–; 1833–). See also INDIAN TEA.

1 A low-growing evergreen of the genus *Ledum* (*L. groenlandicum*).

[1822] 1856 CORMACK 12 On the skirts of the forest, and of the [marshes] are found. . .Indian or Labrador tea [etc]. 1842 BONNYCASTLE i, 301 Of the evergreens there are many kinds. . .the most celebrated being the Labrador tea plant. 1863 HIND i, 130 The Labrador tea-plant is in bloom and casts a faint but delicious fragrance around. 1908 TOWNSEND 97 In the shelter of the depression caused by the erosion of the dikes, fir and spruce, Labrador tea and laurel, manage to exist, while all around is wind-swept rock, naked except for the lichen growth which stains its rugged sides. 1947 TANNER 397 The surface, where not burnt, is covered with patches of caribou moss with 'Labrador tea' and bilberry bushes between the maze of boulders. 1973 GOUDIE 26 We have a lot of Indian Tea [also called Labrador Tea] in our country and it bears little white flowers.

2 An infusion of the bruised leaves of the Labrador tea plant, used as a substitute for tea.

[1872 SCHELE DE VERE 396 Even distant Labrador is called upon to aid in furnishing a variety of the favorite beverage; at least in the Northwest they have a tea called *Mash*-tea, and another called *Labrador*-tea, made from two plants. . .the leaves of which possess moderate narcotic qualities, and are said to furnish a pleasant infusion]. 1895 GRENFELL 13 The tips of the young spruce branches are used for making a non-intoxicating beer, being boiled with molasses. When other tea gives out, the leaves of *uva ursi* are used. These are known as Labrador tea.

labry* n   also **lavry*** ['læbrɪ, 'lævrɪ] HARRAP *abri* 'shelter.' A narrow wooden covered walkway, often forming part of a network of passages, connecting different parts of a fishing stage.

P 126–67 To walk on the labrey; to fall off the labrey. Q 67–78 ~ the walk around a stage. P 245–75 Lavery—the bridge between the outside stage where the fish is cleaned and the inside stage where the fish is salted. This bridge is built with longers.

lace v   To fasten a number of seal pelts together at the edge, forming a 'tow' for hauling over the ice by rope.

1882 TALBOT 16 The [hauling] rope is used for lacing two or more of these skulps or skins, and hauling them. . .to the vessel. [1923] 1946 PRATT 196 "To Angelina": With three fathoms of rope we laced them fast, / With their skins to the ice to be easy to drag, / With our shoulders galled we drew them, and cast / Them in thousands around the watch's flag. 1924 ENGLAND 86 Now some of the hunters, having slain all they could make shift to get aboard, were returning. Open came the loops of the lines; swiftly the nimrods laced their 'tows.' They cut holes in the edges of the sculps, passed the ropes back and forth through these, and made a peculiar complicated knot. A turn of rope served as a grip for the left hand. The long end was passed over the right shoulder, wrapped round the arm, and firmly held by the right hand. Lacing a tow is something of a trick in itself. 1927 DOYLE (ed) 49

"Maurice Crotty": Not a rope in the ship did he know, / Not even to fold up the bunting, / And awkward to lace up a tow. T 187/90–65 When you'd got three or four, you'd have 'em all laced together.

lace-line n Cp *NID* lacing (line) n 5 a naut 'rope or line on edge of sail,' etc. A length of rope used to fasten seal pelts together at the edge into a 'tow.'
   T 187/90–65 You'd start with that lace line, and you'd lace up one down so far as his fore flippers, then you'd stick the head of he in there, and tie un, and then lace on down till you get to the lower part of un. . . You'd take the pelt off of un. . .and lace un together with that line, and then joined onto that one, your haulin' rope, [which] you put on your shoulder.

lad n *EDD* ~ sb¹ (7) lad's love.
   Comb **lad-in-a-bag**: a boiled pudding; DUFF¹.
   C 71–87 ~ name given to a boiled pudding which was cooked in a pudding bag. P 197–76 ~ another name for a figgy duff.
   lad's love: southernwood (*Artemisia abrotanum*) (1897 *J A Folklore* x, 206).

ladder* See TOUGH LADDER*.

laddie-sucker n Sheep sorrel (*Rumex acetosella*); SALLY².
   1975 SCOTT 15 Most children in Newfoundland have enjoyed the refreshing taste of the Sheep Sorrel and it is too bad that this habit is lost with childhood. The Sheep Sorrel is known as Sweet Leaf or Laddie Suckers or Sally Suckers.

laddio n Cp *O Sup²* laddo 'lad' (1870; 1939–).
   1 A (mischievous) boy or fellow; cp BEDLAMER (BOY).
   1937 DEVINE 30 ~ A diminutive of 'laddy,' especially used of a prankish fellow. 'He's a laddio.' M 69–1 You behave yourself, laddio. C 71–127 ~ Especially applicable to young boys who had misbehaved.
   2 A young harp seal; WHITE-COAT. Cp BEDLAMER.
   [c1845] 1927 DOYLE (ed) 25 "The John Martin": Good luck to skipper Nick Ash for he is a clever man. / Sure he spied the 'laddioes' ten miles in on the jam / And following his [counsel] we struck a heavy patch. / And it wasn't very long before we filled our the hatch. 1937 DEVINE 30 [Laddios] may also be applied to. . .whitecoats. 1976 *Evening Telegram* 10 May, p. 6 The 'laddio,' by the way, was a local name or one of the local names for the whitecoat.

lady¹ n Cp LORD¹. Title of the masters of the second and third English fishing vessels to reach a harbour in Newfoundland, exercising certain privileges for the season; REAR-ADMIRAL, VICE-~ .
   [1663] 1963 YONGE 56 Mr Waymouth, (who is Admiral and always wore a flagstaff, Sundays a flag, and is called my Lord, the vice-admiral my Lady) had a chyrurgeon. [1794] 1968 THOMAS 168 The Rear Admi-

ral has the Appellation of Lady. 1975 O'NEILL 43 The presence of these ship's rooms retarded the orderly growth of the St John's waterfront until the end of the eighteenth century. There were nine of them located on the north slopes of the harbour [including] Lady's. . .Admiral's, and Isle of Chips.

lady² n also **lady bird**, ~ **duck** *O Sup²* ~ (Nfld: 1792), *DC* (Nfld: 1770, 1771), see also LORD²: *lord and lady* for sense 1; cp *EDD* sb 3 (1) ~ bird 'pintail duck' for sense 3.
   1 Female harlequin duck (*Histrionicus histrionicus*); JENNY¹.
   [1770] 1792 CARTWRIGHT i, 42 I shot a bird called a lady. 1792 ibid *Gloss* i, xii ~ A water-fowl of the duck genus, and the hen of the lord. 1967 *Bk of Nfld* iii, 282 Harlequin Duck: Lord and Ladies (in allusion to their beautiful plumage); Old Lord (a fully mature male); and Lady or Jenny (the female or immature).
   2 Atlantic black-legged kittiwake (*Rissa tridactyla*); TICKLACE.
   1945 *Can Field-Naturalist* lix, 141 In some localities the kittiwake is also known as the lady or the lady-bird possibly from the snow white breast and the general clean and dainty appearance of the bird. 1951 PETERS & BURLEIGH 235 Kittiwake. . . Local Names: Tickle-lace. . .Lady-bird, Lady.
   3 American common goldeneye (*Bucephala clangula americana*); PIED DUCK.
   1887 HOWLEY *MS Reminiscences* 15 I shot what the men called a Lady Duck, a small plump little bird of a dusky brownish black colour with a white spot behind each eye. It is the golden eye.

lady³ n Cp *OED* ~ 10 (1704–1804); *OED* side-saddle flower.
   Comb **lady in the chair**: part of lobster, esp inner calcareous structure; cp OLD WOMAN.
   1899 *Tribune Christmas No* 19 The stomach [of lobster] is fitted with a series of rough, bony plates to masticate the food, and when opened shows a fanciful figure called 'the lady in the chair.'
   lady's side-saddle: PITCHER PLANT (*Sarracenia purpurea*) (1866 WILSON 57).
   lady's twist: type of chewing tobacco.
   T 66/7–64 You get the real chewing tobacco. One kind they used to call 'lady's twist.' 'Twas twisted up around like a plait.

lady day n Attrib **lady day fish**: catch of cod brought in at the end of the summer fishery, 15 Aug, Lady Day.
   1900 *Tribune Christmas No* 3 When the sealers came in from the ice every spring, Father Kyran would go aboard, and get two dollars at least, from every man. . . In the same way he would collect the St Peter and Paul's and Lady Day fish in the summer, and so raised the thousands of pounds that were needful to complete the Cathedral. [1979 NEMEC 251 By 'Lady's Day,' the fifteenth of August [the Feast of the Assumption], it is not unusual for some fishermen to 'give it up'—in other words to discontinue fishing for the remainder of the summer.]

laggy See LEGGY.

lake n A stretch of salt water in a field of ice, esp in phr *lake of water*; BAY 2.

1826 *Edin New Phil J* 38 These fields of ice. . .are so extensive, that their interior parts, with the openings or lakes interspersed. . .remain serene and unbroken. [1842] 1905 MURPHY 21 "Old Time Sealers' Song": Yon iceberg's wake has formed a lake that lies our course along. 1846 TOCQUE 197 Before eight o'clock a lake of water broke away immediately under the bows [of an ice-locked sealer]. 1855 WHITE *MS Journal* 14 Mar The Ship under way Beating to windward in lakes of water. [1862] 1916 MURPHY 31 I ran over slob, I know not how, and got on a pan of ice in the lake with 21 men and one woman and several dogs. 1924 ENGLAND 54 'If you'm caught in a starm on de ice,' said bridge master Llewellen White, 'an' a lake breaks between you an' de ship so you can't get aburd, you build up a barricade o' clumpers an' make a fire.' 1944 LAWTON & DEVINE 94 Lakes of water appeared everywhere. Men and women could be seen running here and there on the pans of ice. T 49–64 We got in about a mile of [the vessel], I suppose, an' we couldn't get no further—lake of water broke between us an' her, and now she couldn't get [out] because she was jammed. 1972 BROWN 29 The *Newfoundland* found herself, shortly after dawn, steaming through 'lakes' of clear water. But by 10:30 a.m. the ice closed, and brought her to a halt.

lallik* n also **lollik***. A children's chasing game, tag; the person who is 'it' in this game.

P 148–63 You're lallik! Q 71–12 [In] a game called lallik, the child who is lallik tries to get near enough to another to touch him/her who then becomes lallik.

lally See LOLLY.

lamb n EDD ~ 1 (13) lamb's legs Suf Co.

Comb **lamb's legs**: string(s) of mucus hanging from the nose; CONKERBILL.

M 68–24 ~ refers to the long strings of mucus which persistently hang from the noses of people, especially kids.

lamb's tails: lamb's quarters; white goosefoot (*Chenopodium album*).

1974 GREEN 81 We would make delicious greens from the young dock weeds and another plant commonly known on the mainland as 'lamb's quarters.' To Daniel's Harbour this plant was known simply as 'lamb's tails.'

lammocken* n Cp EDD lammock v 'to lounge lazily' Do. A lively insect of the family *Gerridae* that darts along surface of fresh water; water strider (Q 71–12). See also DOCTOR[1], LAMP-LIGHTER.

lammy n OED lammie naut (1886). A short, heavy coat or jacket.

C 75–25 Men had no parkas but did have what was known as a 'sheepskin lammy.' This was a short or three-quarter-length denim or leather coat, lined with sheep's or lamb's wool.

lamp-lighter n Cp EDD lamp sb[1] 1 (2) phr *like a lamp-lighter* 'very quickly' for senses 2, 3.

1 A variety of large moth with dusty wings; miller (Q 71–12).

2 An agile, nimble person.

Q 67–109 ~ a nimble person especially when running or getting away. Q 71–6 He skipped around like a lamp-lighter.

3 A lively insect of the family *Gerridae* that darts along surface of fresh water; water strider (Q 73–17); DOCTOR[1].

lamwash* See LANDWASH.

lance n also **lant(s), launce, lawnce** OED lant sb[2] (Nfld: 1620, 1880–4 Co); launce[2] (Nfld: 1623–).

1 A small, elongate fish, used as bait; sand eel, sand lance (*Ammodytes hexapterus, A. dubius*); also in place-names of shelving, sandy coves frequented by the fish.

[1620] 1887 MASON 151 May hath Herings, on[e] equall to 2 of ours, Lants and Cods in good quantity. 1620 WHITBOURNE 10 The Rivers also and Harbours are generally stored with delicate Fish, as Salmons, Peales, Eeles, Herring, Mackerell, Flounders, Launce, Capelin, Cod, and Troutes. 1623 ibid 89 A sufficient quantity of Herrings, Mackerel, Capeling, & Lawnce, to bait their hooks withal. [1712] 1895 PROWSE 273 Go out of harbours in shallops, seven and five men in a boat; catch fish with hook and line, first part of year their bait is muscles and lances. [1778] 1792 CARTWRIGHT ii, 354 The *Caplin* returned at ten o'clock at night, with twenty buckets of good lance, which they hauled in Sandhill Cove. [1810] 1971 ANSPACH 20 Lance [bait used for taking the cod-fish] which in the latter part of that perview, is ashore in *very small meshed nets*. 1863 HIND i, 300 [Cod] are generally fished for with hemped lines and hooks baited with pieces of fresh fish, or even with small fishes whole, as caplin and launce. 1921 CABOT 222 A cloud of lance, eel-like fish five or six inches long. . . 1955 *Nfld & Lab Pilot* ii, 101 Between Lance Cove head and Bluff point. . .the southern side of the second forms a bight known as Britannia cove. [1958] 1964 PEACOCK (ed) i, 192 "George Bunker": We runned her into Forteau to get what bait we could, / The lants they did not care about or the squids they were no good.

2 Comb **lance seine**: a net with fine meshes, the ends of which are hauled together to enclose schooling lance; see also SEINE.

[1751–66] 1954 INNIS 182 [inventory] To 1 Lance Seain 22 foot deep and 75 fathom Long. 1765 WILLIAMS 20 A Lance Swaine. . . Three hundred Weight of Swaine Line.

lanch v also **launch** [lænʃ] OED lanch obs form of launch. Cp OED launch v 4 'to cause a vessel to move or slide from the land. . .into the water'; 7 b naut 'to move (heavy goods) by pushing'

(1711, 1753); LUBBOCK *Arctic Whalers* (1937), pp. 304–5 [1835] for first gloss in sense 1.

1 To haul or push (a boat or vessel) over the ice; to move (a house) over the ground or across a body of water; DRUM v 2.

[1772] 1792 CARTWRIGHT i, 226 They were obliged to launch the punt across a bridge of ice in the harbour; the rest was open. [1856] 1966 PITT 65 The spacious old wooden Chapel in Gower Street,. . .which the Wesleyans of this city have worshipped in for nearly the last half-century, was yesterday launched to the opposite side of the street. T 33–64¹ Some of 'em brought their houses, lanched their houses off o' the islands an' towed 'em by motor-boats. T 203/6–65 They all work together, an' you know in them days if you wanted a boat pulled, wanted a house lanched—if you wanted to move your house to anywhere—well, 'tis only go around, 'Boys, I'm goin' to lanch my house tomorrow; how about comin'?' T 172/4–65 Aboard o' the boat, sometimes we'd have to lanch, more times we'd have to slophaul. When [the ice] was not strong enough to lanch over it and 'twouldn't bear the boat [then we'd] haul the boat through. 1969 MOWAT 49 Scores of houses were 'launched off,' and one of the most remarkable sights I have ever seen was a flotilla of such houses being towed by a gaggle of little motor-boats.

2 To transfer (something) from one vessel to another by boat.

T 26–64¹ We picked up eighteen men, dead men, an' had 'em in the boats an' lanched 'em aboard Captain Barber—lanched aboard the *Greenland*.

lanch* n also **launch**. See LANCH v. Organized operation to move a house from one location to another; HOUSE-HAUL.

C 64–31 After Uncle's death, Peter decided to have the house moved up to the road about a hundred yards away from the garden. In order to move a house a lanch had to be organized. Finally the house was moved up to the road. About two months later another lanch and the house was moved back down to the garden.

lanching vbl n Attrib **lanching song**: chantey; HAULING SONG.

C 70–15 To get the house moving the men from the two communities attached the blocks and tackle and when everything was ready one man with a good voice started the 'lanchin' song.' . . .It was also used in pulling up the boats for the winter.

land n Cp *OED* stand 11 c through lands and stands (1380) for sense 2.

1 With *the*, Newfoundland; cp NEWFOUNDLAND, NEWLAND.

1708 OLDMIXON i, 14, 20 Under, the Name of *Newfoundland*, call'd, as I have said already, *The Land* by Sea-men. . .when the Masters sail directly to the *Land* to purchase Cargoes of Fish. . .

2 Phr *land nor stand*: any human habitation; a station.

T 187/9–65 One feller said, 'Well,' he said, 'we shall never see land nor stand no more.'

3 Comb **land-bear**: the black bear (*Ursus americanus*) (P 80–63). Contrast WATER BEAR.

land-crab: a person who is not a fisherman (M 68–24).

land-head: headland.

1858 [LOWELL] i, 199 . . .an' comed right home round the land-head.

land-sealing: hunting seals near the shore on foot or in small boats.

1975 *Evening Telegram* 12 Apr, p. 2 Although many of the fishermen in the area were out land-sealing, a good-sized crowd of men gathered at the Fogo Island Motel to inform the committee of the state of the fishery in the area.

landsman: see LANDSMAN.

landwash: see LANDWASH.

lander v Cp *EDD* ~ sb 'a heavy blow.' To hit or strike (a person or animal).

Q 71–8 Lander means to hit hard. One would lander only a person or animal, never an inanimate object.

landing n Cp *DAE* ~ 2 b; R C BRYANT *Logging* (1923), p. 491 'place to which logs are hauled preparatory to transportation by water or rail.' A pile of logs placed together for scaling, transportaion, etc. Cp BULK n 4.

P 65–64 A large pile of logs waiting to be sawed [makes] up a landing of logs. T 91–64 An' 'twould be piled up in the woods, an' the horses'd come in, pile in what we call landings, see; probably hundred, a hundred an' fifty in a bulk. 1965 PETERS *Gloss* ~ A pile of logs or, especially, pulpwood. Contrasts with 'brow,' which is normally a pile of saw-logs. Q 67–74 Landing of wood: wood piled up ready for scaling (measuring).

landsman n also **landman** *DC* ~ Nfld (1958–) for sense 3. Cp SHOREMAN.

1 Member of a fishing crew who processes the catch on shore.

1613 *Willoughby Papers* 17a, 1/2 There are here already eight that are fishermen, and one spilter, and the rest here will serve for land men.

2 Migratory fisherman from Newfoundland who fishes from a shore station on the Labrador coast; STATIONER.

1915 WOOD 361 Those who live on the schooners during the summer are 'floaters,' the men who hire out to no one, but provision themselves and fish from the shore in dories are 'landsmen.' 1947 TANNER 749 Planters or 'stationers,' also called 'landsmen,' are as already pointed out seasonal visitors to Labrador. T 141/63–65² O' course that's inhabited now by the landsmen.

3 Man who prosecutes the seal hunt on foot or in a small boat or vessel from a land base near his community.

1889 *Nineteenth Century* xxv, 521 Occasionally the whelping ice approaches so close to the shore that the landsmen come in for their share of the spoil, and then even the women and children eagerly join the scene of carnage. 1933 GREENE 12 In this same Green Bay

Spring of 1880, thirty-three thousand pelts were taken by landsmen from Cape St John to Cape Race. 1966 PHILBROOK 32 During this period, if the winds are right, seals enter the bay in large numbers, close enough to the shore to be hunted from small boats. The Nippers Harbour landsmen who hunt these seals from small boats are thus able to add three or four hundred dollars to their year's earnings. 1978 *Evening Telegram* 10 Mar, p. 2 Land[s]men operating in small vessels out of fishing ports along Notre Dame Bay and White Bay have taken about 14,000 seals so far this winter. 1982 ibid 22 Jan, p. 3 Landsmen with vessels between 35 feet and 65 feet can take 1,100 harp seals on the North Front [this year].

landwash n   also **lamwash*** by assimilation, **lan' awash*** ['lænwɒʃ, 'lændwɒʃ, 'lænəwɒʃ]. Cp *OED* land sb 12 (1891 quot), wash sb 7, 7 b. The sea-shore between high and low tide marks, washed by the sea; occas the shore of a pond or river; foreshore. Also attrib.
[1770] 1792 CARTWRIGHT i, 48–9 They had tailed a trap on the landwash at the head of Niger Sound. 1792 ibid *Gloss* i, xii -- That part of the shore which is within the reach of the water in heavy gales of wind. 1792 PULLING *MS* Aug We saw the tracks of Indians in the snow on an island in the brook. But a short time after we saw a great many Indians in the landwash where they had some skins spread. They went to their wigwams which were a very little way from the side of the brook. [c1830] 1890 GOSSE 41 . . .coming up from the 'landwash' with a 'turn' of sand for her mother's kitchen floor. 1842 JUKES ii, 37 ~ This term is always used in Newfoundland for the margin of the sea, meaning that strip of land washed by the water. 1861 DE BOILIEU 34 On a clear day, when there is a light ripple on the beach, you may see thousands of these beautiful small female fishes swimming towards the shore or landwash, each accompanied by two males, one on each side of her; nearing the sand, the males press against the female, when the spawn is rapidly deposited. [1862] 1975 WHITELEY 135 [The Mountaineer indians] 'come out to landwash' for the purpose of trafficking their furs. 1887 *Telegram Christmas No* 5 . . .and that strange silence, broken only by the sound of the aurora borealis flashing through the still night air, or the ice cracking in the landwash, settles down over the scene. 1895 GRENFELL 81 Often the winter's diet that can be laid in is all too small for the needs of the family; and before the breaking up of the ice once more allows cod-fishing to commence, and the planters to return from Newfoundland, the poor Livyeres are reduced to living on 'the landwash.' 1921 *Evening Telegram* 20 July, p. 4 Last evening boys playing in the landwash at low tide discovered six kegs containing about 50 gallons of rum under a premises in the West End of the city. T 436–64 He was always goin' down round the landwash, you know, an' he used to bring up all kinds o' old stuff what was no use for nothing. 1967 FIRESTONE 7 When travelling the wood paths on foot when the ice is gone you skirt the shorelines of the ponds [landwashes] to return to where the path goes overland between the little lakes. C 68–3 Don't go down landwash, or the mermaids will get you! C 71–122

My mother would always warn us when we were kids to stay away from the landowash because we might get drowned. 1977 RUSSELL 29 They started to run their lines from the landwash road and by dinnertime when they knocked off for a mug-up they were just disappearin' over the brow of the hill. 1979 POTTLE 2 The people, who for generations saw their politics no farther afield than the 'landwash'. . .

lant(s) See LANCE.

lap n   Cp *NID* lap seam; cp *OED* ~ sb³ 2 for lap tail.
   Comb **lap rock**: a heated rock used as a bed warmer.
c 70–10 During the cold winters the people would keep warm in bed by means of a lap rock. This would be a big, oval-shaped beach rock. The women would heat it in the oven, wrap it in a towel and place it in the bed.
   lap seam: the placing of the exterior planks of a vessel so that one overlaps another; lapstrake.
1967 *Bk of Nfld* iv, 246 [The *Dasher*] was built with what they called a lap seam, that is, she was clap-boarded like a house.
   lap stone: see **lap rock** above.
1977 BURSEY 80 'I've got old Mr Howel's rock that he put at his feet when he went to bed. I heat it and get a warm reception when I lie down for the night.' This was a large beach-rock weighing about ten pounds often called a lapstone. It would be warm all night.
   lap tail: a dried and salted cod-fish split too far towards the tail, leaving a small flap of flesh.
1955 *Nfld Fisheries Board* 23 Choice Italian. . .not to include round or lap tails.

lap v   *EDD* ~ v³ 1 'flog, beat' So Co; *ADD* 3 'whip' for sense 1.
   1 To slap.
P 121–67 Be quiet or I'll lap you across the face!
   2 Phr *lap back*: to talk back (saucily).
P 121–67 Don't you dare lap back at me.

large a
   1 In various grades or culls of dried and salted cod: fish of a certain specified size and quality or 'cure.'
[1909] 1930 COAKER 7 No. 1 large should be dry, sound, smooth, well salted fish, over. . .18 inches. 1955 *Nfld Fisheries Board* 39 Large fish 22 in. to 26 in. T 36–64 Extra large from twenty-one to twenty-four [inches long], large from eighteen to twenty-one. . . And when you sell this fish for market there used to be choice, large and small; and extra large; large; small; small madeira; small west indee; small thirds; large thirds; large west indee; large choice and large madeira. T 410–67 There was small madeira, large madeira; small thirds, an' large thirds; small west indee; tomcods, italian—too many grades for me!
   2 In animal and bird names: **large ice gull,** ~ **medler,** [see MIDDLER], ~ **spruce bird**.
1870 *Can Naturalist* v, 407–8 Tolerably common in its periodical migrations, especially in the fall of the

year. . .the 'large ice gull.' [1783] 1792 CARTWRIGHT iii, 22 The third [year beavers are called] *large* medlers. 1870 *Can Naturalist* v, 156 Feeds on the seeds of Coniferae, and is called by the settlers the 'large spruce bird.'

lark n American water pipit (*Anthus spinoletta rubescens*) (1959 MCATEE 56).

larrigan n ['lærɪgɪn, 'lærɪgən]. Cp *O Sup²* ~ 'a long boot' (1886–). Jocular term for leg, from the knee-boot worn by woodsmen and fishermen.
    P 43–67 Stretch your larrigans [to the fire]. C 71–103 ~s: legs. It was commonly used by the fishermen when I was a child.

larry* n Home base in children's chasing game; GOOLO*.
    M 71–64 The aim [in hoist-your-sails-and-run] is to have the ones hidden get back to the beginning place—larry—without the other team seeing them.

lash v *EDD* ~ v 16; *DC* ~ -line (Nfld: 1933) for cpd.
    1 Phr *lash into*: to eat with gusto.
    1976 *Daily News* 15 Jan, p. 3 Did you ever. . .lash into a 'blueberry grunt'?
    2 Cpd **lash-line**: a length of rope used to secure a load on a sled or 'komatik'; cp BOWLINE.
    [1916] 1972 GORDON 61 We soon had our lash-line round the stump of a tree and hauled Tom up. P 130–67 What are [you] going to use for a lash-line?

lasses See MOLASSES.

lassy¹ n See MOLASSES.

lassy² n Comb **lassy-berry**: wild lily-of-the-valley (*Maianthemum canadense*) (1978 ROULEAU 89).

lassy v To spread (food) with molasses.
    T 80/2–64 [They] shares this dinner was left, see, an' they took the coady dipper an' lassied her right over; cleaned out the lot! 'Twas some feed now—lassy on praties! 1977 QUILLIAM 22 To this she added a billy can of good strong tea and on the side placed six hefty rounds of thick home made bread, buttered and lassied.

lassy-bug n See also MOLASSES: LASSY. Ladybird beetle (*Anatis ocellata male; Adalia bipunctata*).
    C 71–98 Lady bugs are called lassy bugs. M 71–118 We used to pick them up in our hands and say, 'lassy bug, lassy bug, give me some lassy. If you don't I'll kill your mother and father.' One expected to find a little brown spot on his hand if the lassy bug obeyed.

last a Phr *last going off, on the last of it*: finally, in the end, at last.
    T 55–64 They get drunk and get out of sorts, and arg and fight on the last of it. T 66/7–64 On the last of it he

seemed to get puzzled. T 148–65 But they had to banish all that. Last going off the customs got after them and made them make away with that old stuff. T 391/3–67 In the fall o' the year, last going off the young fellows put out a lot of slips. P 54–69 He got saved on the last going off of the revival meetings.

last n Cp *EDD* lace sb¹ 2 'the round stick used to form the mesh in netting fishing-nets.' Do. A wire frame or pattern used in knitting a cast-net.
    T 66/7–64 You'd have your needle an' mesh, an' last, round last made out of a piece o' copper wire; that's a last.

lat See LATH n.

late a Cp *OED* ~ a¹ 6 'recent in date.' Of a woman, recently married.
    1896 *J A Folklore* ix, 27 'The late Mrs Prince visited us,' meaning the lady who had recently become Mrs Prince.

lath n also **lat** [læt]. Cp *OED* ~ sb 2 'thin, narrow, flat piece of wood used for any purpose.'
    1 One of the thin strips of wood nailed on a frame to form a lobster trap.
    P 148–65 A small lat is used as a fastening to keep the door of lobster trap closed; it doesn't slip out; placed under tension perpendicular to the lats of the trap. Q 67–28 Lats are one inch wide and spaced one and a half inches apart.
    2 A strip of wood with bark attached sawn off a log when producing planks, used for fuel, fencing, etc.
    P 148–62 Lats (in a wooden fence). P 65–64 The strips which the edger cuts off live plank are called lats.
    3 One of two narrow boards forming crosspieces of a quilt- or mat-frame.
    T 43/7–64 [Women would] zig-zag their stitches and when they get that frameful done they'd take out their lats and roll back and continue from where they left off. 1975 POCIUS 38 The quilting frame (and the mat frame) in Newfoundland consisted of four boards, two long pieces and two shorter pieces or 'lats.'

lath v also **lat*** [læt]. To fasten thin strips of wood, or laths, on the frame of a lobster-trap.
    T 39/40–64 You got to turn the bows; there's three bows, sometimes four bows, an' then you lat it up.

launce See LANCE.

launch See LANCH n, v.

lavry* See LABRY*.

lawnce See LANCE.

lawnya vawnya* n also **lawnya**. Cp JOYCE 283 launa-vaula; DINNEEN lán: l[án] an mhála 'the full of the bag.' A good time at a dance or party; plenty to eat.

1968 DILLON 147 We had lawnya vawnya last night. P 245–79 Lawnya—having a grand old time.

law work See COURT WORK.

lay v *OED* ~ v¹ 22 ~ hold (up)on; cp KEMP *Oxford Companion to Ships & the Sea* 470 ~ 'a verb much used by seamen.'

Comb **lay chase**: to pursue; to attempt to capture.

C 67–21 They laid chase after him, and they had great big long arms and legs, and they kept waving their arms at him. Q 71–7 She laid chase and finally brought him to the altar.

lay hold: to take in hand; to prepare oneself.

[1940] 1964 BLONDAHL (ed) 16 "Tickle Cove Pond": Oh, lay hold William Oldford, lay hold William White, / Lay hold of the cordage and pull all your might! C 75–139 The woman who gave the reception said aloud, 'lay-hold,' meaning to dig in.

layer n [leəɹ]. Cp *EDD* lay v 6 ~ 'the piece of wood cut and laid in a hedge.' A small pliable rod, often interlaced to form a fence; RIDDLE n; WITHE-ROD.

[1878] 1944 LAWTON & DEVINE 88 P. K. had been accused by John Holland Sr, of stealing some of his fence layers and accompanied the accusation with a severe ear-cuffing. 1937 DEVINE 30 ~s Pieces of whit-rod or young firs to make a fence. P 268–64 ~s riggles in a riggle-fence. T 194–65 Our bunk was longers in the bunk house, round; our bunk was layers, and fir boughs put on top. 1973 *Evening Telegram* 25 May, p. 13 [The] layer or 'Ring Rod' fence. . .is made from three rails the top and bottom ones being nailed to stakes some 10–12 feet apart while small fir and spruce trees called 'layers' about four or five feet long are woven in and out through the middle rail holding it in place.

laying ppl, vbl n *NID* ~ duck.

Comb **laying duck**: common eider (*Somateria mollissima dresseri*).

1918 TOWNSEND 301 The treatment of that magnificent duck the eider. . .along our Atlantic coast is rapidly leading to its extermination. This duck which is locally known as *sea duck, laying duck, shoreyer, Eskimo duck, maynak,* and *metic,* is everywhere diminishing in numbers.

laying-room: area where cod-fish are spread to dry.

[1774] 1792 CARTWRIGHT ii, 19 The people were employed on both houses, and in making laying-rooms. 1792 ibid *Gloss* i, xii ~ Boughs spread upon the ground to dry fish upon. They are seldom made use of, except on the first establishing of a cod-fishery before there has been time to erect flakes.

lazarus n *DC* ~ Nfld (1774, 1861). A variety of seal.

[1774] 1792 CARTWRIGHT ii, 34 At noon I went in a skiff and hauled the nets under the Lyon Head, and had a lazarus in one of them. [1775] ibid ii, 49 We found five seals in it, one of which was intirely eaten by the lice, but the others were fresh struck in; and two of them were lazaruses. 1861 DE BOILIEU 97 The next seal I have to catalogue (there is nothing special in it to describe) generally loiters on the coast later than the Harp, and frequents it sooner in the spring: it is called the Lazarus.

lazy a JOYCE 283 lazy man's load.

1 Phr *lazy man's load*: a (foolishly) heavy load.

C 69–19 When someone is carrying a large turn on their back [it is said], 'Look, he's carrying a lazy man's load.' It is supposed to be a lazy man's load because he wanted to carry it all the once so he wouldn't have to make two trips. C 75–140 Very often my mother would send me out for to fill the woodbox with wood. Instead of making four trips I would pile my arms as high as I could with as much as I could lift and go for two trips—she termed these as 'lazy man's loads.'

2 Comb **lazy-stick**: a game in which two contestants try to raise each other from a sitting position by pulling on a stick; the stick used in this game.

P 227–61 ~ a game in which two people sit and pull a broomstick in opposite directions as a test of strength. T 49–64 We used to see who could run the fastest, and who could jump the farthest, and hauling down the tug-of-war, and lazy stick. Lazy stick: You take a broomstick or anything that size, and two hands would get down and put their feet up again one another. M 68–24 To decide who was the stronger, two men would sit on the floor or the ground facing each other. Each would place the soles of his feet against the soles of the feet of his opponent. Some other person would place a round stick, about two inches in diameter, and three feet long, midway between them. The contestants would catch hold of the stick, and at the word 'go,' they would pull as hard as they were able. This stick was called a 'lazy-stick.' 1981 HUSSEY 71 We would also try games that the adults played. We learned how to 'go through the broom handle' and 'haul on the lazy stick.'

lead¹ n [lɛd] *OED* ~ sb¹ 6 obs (1657), *EDD* sb¹ 1 (10) ~ stone Sh I Ork for sense 1.

1 Lead weight used to sink a fishing-line or net.

1611 *Willoughby Papers* 1/3, 67 [inventory: Cuper's Cove] Hookes, Leades, lynes. [1751–66] 1954 INNIS 182 [inventory] To Fishing Leads 3 hund[red] weight. 1843 *Trans Lit & Hist Soc Que* iv, 35–6 When a seal fishery is to be established, houses and stores are built, fixtures erected; craft, with nets, hawsers, leads, anchors, &c, to be procured; these, with tools, utensils, and provisions, cost several hundred pounds, sometimes thousands. 1937 *Seafisheries of Nfld* 32 The Leads. This is the same as the Float, with a piece of lead of standard shape and over a pound in weight, about three feet from the hook. Sometimes two hooks are used, attached to the lead by lines three and four feet long known as 'nostles.' Q 67–93 ~ (for keeping net down).

2 Comb **lead rope**: rope at the bottom of fish-net to which lead sinkers are attached.

1975 BUTLER 59 These nets were fifty fathoms long and twenty five meshes deep and they were made of nylon twine with a lead rope on the foot and plastic floats on the head.

lead² n [li:d] *OED* ~ sb² 3 b (1835–), *DC* (1850–) for sense 1.

1 A channel or lane of open water (for a vessel) in an ice-field; a stretch of open water frequented by sea-birds. Cp CUT n, LAKE.

1873 *Maritime Mo* i, 256 At times [the steamer] is arrested by the heavy ice, seven feet in thickness, and then, perhaps, the ice-saws are called into requisition to cut a pathway to the nearest 'lead' of clear water, and the stout vessel then dashes through the crashing and grinding masses, where the ice is looser. 1891 PACKARD 150 From this high elevation the ice was everywhere in view with leads between the floes. [1921] 1972 GORDON 181 We were lucky enough to find a lead which brought us outside Spotted Islands and into a stretch of clear sea as far as Batteau. 1924 ENGLAND 80 [The turrs] laboured to rise from open leads or took fearful slides as they tried to land on new ice. 1933 GREENE 146 These are what the sealers call the 'lanes' or 'leads' of the Floe, whose presence the scunner will always take advantage of just as he will do with the lakes; selecting from afar only those which will result in the Captain's cut being maintained on its proper course. 1957 *Evening Telegram* 11 Mar, p. 3 The aircraft guided the ship to a lead that led to open water. . . 1972 BROWN 44 They worked the *Newfoundland* northward, pitting their puny strength against the pressures of the Ice-field, levering the pans aside, hauling on hawsers to help drag the ship through tight 'leads' as their fathers had done in the days of sail.

2 A stretch of low, open country affording passage through an area thickly interspersed with lakes, clumps of trees and hills; such a passageway frequented by migrating caribou; an animal trail; DEER PATH.

1865 CAMPBELL 135 I shouldered my rod, and we marched off into 'the country.' Our way lay through 'leads,' marshy land overgrown with rein-moss, multiberries, and such-like. 1889 HOWLEY *MS Reminiscences* 36 A lead of barrens between the ponds seemed to offer the best route as a ravine [led] from thence out towards the main river. . . We descended to the valley and took the lead of barrens between the ponds. 1907 MILLAIS 37 A broad series of 'leads' converged and led sharply to the right at this point, for [the caribou] determined to adopt this route. 1909 SELOUS 61–2 On migration, certain tracts of country are annually traversed, through which well-defined paths are made. These deer paths are known in Newfoundland as 'leads,' and during the autumn migration the usual method of securing caribou was (at the time of which I am writing) by watching a 'lead' and shooting the animals from an ambush as they passed. 1912 DUGMORE 27 I circled around the river to my blind so as to leave no scent along the Caribou leads, for unless pressed by bad weather, these animals will not cross a fresh human trail. T 393/403–67 They had their leads, an' they'd come through in those leads. You'd wait for [the caribou] there, see. M 70–28 They found some

fresh rabbit's buttons and this was the lead they needed. Then they tailed a slip. The slip was camouflaged with boughs. Running along the lead a rabbit would stick its neck in the slip.

lead³ n [li:d]. Cp *EDD* leader sb 3; *ADD*. Tendon.

P 148–62 The leads in your arms.

leader n *DC* ~ n 2 (Nfld: 1818–) for sense 1; *DC* 2 (Nfld: 1907–), *OED* ~ ¹ 6 b (1884), cp *Fisheries of U S*, Sec V, i, pp. 599, 606, etc, for sense 2.

1 The dog placed at the head of a sled or 'komatik' team.

1818 CHAPPELL 143 Two of the most sagacious and best-trained dogs are placed in front, as leaders; no reins being necessary; for the animals will naturally follow a beaten track through the snow; and they are easily guided by a long whip, the lash of which extends to the foremost dogs. 1849 [FEILD] 49 He drives from six to twelve dogs, with a leader. 1895 GRENFELL 146 He once put a young dog in front of his old leader, a magnificent old fellow on whom he always could rely in danger. Before he had, however, mounted the komatik, he found the pup scampering away loose—the leader had bitten through the traces. 1909 *Nfld Qtly* Mar, p. 14 It is the mail on dog sleds. . .now I make out one dog a good bit ahead of the first, and another ahead of the second streak. These are the leaders. . . I can make out now three men in charge of the first team and two in charge of the second. How well the dogs all pull together, following the leaders and urged on by the drivers. P 65–64 The head dog of a dog team—the dog that leads—is called the 'leader.' The leader knows the meaning of the signal words 'keep off' and 'hold in.'

2 A length of net stretching from the shore to a cod-trap to guide fish into the entrance; LEADING NET.

1895 GRENFELL 68 Some men were landed with 'leaders' on one station late at night. 1905 GRENFELL 124 There is also a long straight net running to the rocks. This is called the 'leader,' because as the shoals of cod swim along past the rocks, it leads them right into the door. 1921 *FPU (Twillingate) Minutes* 24 Feb In reference to trap berths [the letter recommended] leader and moorings on the rock instead of in the water until sign of fish. 1936 SMITH 16 The doors of the [cod] trap were nine inches open, the rim of the trap eight fathoms and the leader of the trap four and a half fathoms. 1946 MACKAY (ed) 86 The trap is a box-shaped net with a bottom and an opening at one end. From the opening a *leader* (a long net) is stretched from the shore to the trap. The fish, finding the leader, cannot get through it and follow it along to the opening of the trap. T 43–64 The leader used to go so far in the trap so as when the fish will swim round the trap they'd strike up against the linnet every time, but the fish trimmin' the leader an' goin' for the trap had an open doorway. 1976 *Evening Telegram* 17 June, p. 3 One fisherman reported that he had a 720-foot leader to his cod trap and there is nothing left [after the storm] but the corks and the headropes.

3 Comb **leader backer**: length of rope securing the 'leader' of a cod-trap to the shore.

1967 FIRESTONE 89 The doorway or opening [of a cod-trap] in which the fish enter is held apart by an iron bar or chain. The leader runs from this towards the shore and is held in place by short rodes called leader *backers*.

leader buoy: float (Q 67–34); BUOY.

leader foot(s): bottom or lower part of 'leader'; FOOT(S) (M 69–23).

leader head: length of rope forming the top part of 'leader' (P 9–73).

leader linnet: length of netting forming the 'leader' of a cod-trap; LINNET.

P 9–73 About four or five fathoms back from the doorway, the leader linnet along the head is stretched to over the thirds to take up any slack. Slack linnet here can close the doorway and keep the fish out.

leader net: see sense 2 above.

1969 MOWAT 35 Stretching out from a 'door' on one side is a long, vertically hung leader-net to guide the slow moving cod into the trap. 1977 *Inuit Land Use* 132 Care had to be taken in setting the traps. . . However, if properly set, the cod would follow the leader net into the doorway of the trap and be caught.

leading ppl

Comb **leading dog**: dog placed at the head of a sled or komatik team; LEADER.

1909 *Nfld Qtly* Mar, p. 15 We couldn't help remarking these dogs, what noble animals for hauling they are; every one with his own name which he knows well and to which he responds at the call of the guide. The leading dogs were very handsome animals and seemed to be proud of their position away off by themselves, without tackling, and acting simply as leaders.

leading man: principal inhabitant of a settlement.

1887 BOND 37 [IIe] was the 'leadin' man' of the harbour. 1887 *Telegram Christmas No* 9 Uncle Joe, kindly, shrewd and blunt, was, by sheer force of personal character, a 'leadin' man' in the little settlement.

leading net: length of net stretching from the shore to a cod-trap to guide fish into the entrance; LEADER (NET).

1895 GRENFELL 68 The law does not allow traps to be set till a certain day, and the leading net must be put out to secure the berth. . .and unless within four days the whole trap is set, the claim becomes void.

leading tickle: in coastal nomenclature, a channel providing passage or route between islands or between islands and a mainland; TICKLE.

1845 [FEILD] 61 At eight o'clock the captain pointed out to me, very confidently, Fortune Island and the leading Tickles, close on one quarter. 1953 *Nfld & Lab Pilot* ii, 545 Leading or Ladle tickles. This name is given to the passage between the islands. . .and between them and the mainland.

leaf n pl **leafs, leaves** [liːfs, leifs, liːifs]. In net-making, an oblong section which is joined to other sections of netting.

1908 DURGIN 27 The net is laid in leaves, one hundred meshes in a leaf. 1937 DEVINE 31 Leaves. The unit quantities of rands in knitting a trap or seine etc. 1956 *Evening Telegram* 12 Dec, p. 11 The walls of the trap are made of panels of mesh, somewhat like a panel of wallboard, called 'leaves.' Each leaf is 99 meshes wide. . . Reason for the leaf construction is that if any part of the trap is badly damaged, the entire leaf can be taken out and a new one quickly installed. T 50/2–64 Leafs o' twine, big leaf perhaps four, five fathoms wide, an' as long as they mind to knit it. . . Now he's a great hand at the twine. He put a lot o' leafs o' twine in their trap the spring. T 52–64 No, [you knit it] in leafs. Ye put that together on the meadows in the spring o' the year with a needle o' twine. P 9–73 The trap is made up of sections called leaves and the leaves are scunned together. Scunning is done by taking two edges of netting, pulling them tight and passing twine from a especially made needle around and around through the edge meshes, making a solid fastening every foot or so. The bottom is scunned unto the walls in the same way. 1973 HORWOOD 10 He was knitting leaves for a cod-trap. Harry watched and wanted to learn. . . Now he was becoming familiar with the knitting needle and the finger stall.

leaky a Phr *leaky paw*: inflammation of hand or wrist caused by exposure to salt water (P 45–61); WATER PUP, ~ WHELP.

lean v Phr *lean on*: (a) to injure (another); (b) to row (a boat) vigorously.

1897 *J A Folklore* x, 206 ~ to abuse or do personal injury to one. [A boy complained] that another boy *leaned on him*. 'Yes,' said his mother, 'he leaned on him too hard, sir.' 'What do you mean?' asked the judge. 'He leaned on him with rocks and one of them struck him on the head and cut his head open.' T 70–64[1] They were goin' down for caplin, an' they were leanin' on her, afraid the wind'd come in.

lean-in n A cow-shed.

1971 NOSEWORTHY 216 ~ A place in a field built as a shelter for cows.

lean-to n Cp *OED* ~ sb; *DAE* 1; *DC* 1 (1872–). A temporary shelter in the woods with a single sloping roof; TILT.

1836 [WIX][2] 91 I. . .walked on to the winter crew's tilt. . . There throwing myself into a dark linny, or 'lean-to,' I sought some repose. 1914 WALLACE 142 A comfortable lean-to under the lee of the hill, with back and ends enclosed, and closely thatched with bough and moss, was considered sufficient. A thick, springy bed of spruce boughs was then arranged. P 245–55 ~ A temporary shelter constructed for an overnight stay in the country, and consisting of a few uprights covered with boughs. It is rarely more than four feet high at the peak, and often leans against a tree, large rock, or other fixed object. P 148–61 ~ a one-side camp (in the woods).

leap v Phr *leaping pans, leap the* ~ , *lipping** ~

: in children's pastime, to jump from one floating pan of ice to another; COPY.

Q 67–40 Lippin' the pans: jumping from one ice pan to another. Q 67–99 Leap the pan: jumping from one ice pan to another. M 70–18 Lippin' pans [means] leaping pans. It is an activity that children engaged in while walking on pans of ice that come to the shore.

leary a also **leery** ['liərɪ, 'liərɨi, 'lɪːərʉi] *EDD* lear adj[1] 2 (2) ~ Co Ha Do So D Ir Nfld. Hungry; weak with hunger.

1863 MORETON 35 ~ Sinking with hunger and exhaustion. The feeling of a traveller who needs refreshment. 1887 BOND 20 I was pretty well tired and leary, as we say. 1896 *J A Folklore* ix, 23 ~ hungry, faint. 1937 DEVINE 31 ~ Exhausted; tired; hungry. Not inclined to work. T 222–66 Well, by the middle of the afternoon you would probably be getting leary, an' would like to have a mug up. C 70–21 A person might say: 'Get me a cup of tea quick, I feel leary.' Or, if you were going on a long trip in the woods you'd be urged to take some food along in case you 'got leary.'

leave See LEFF*.

leaven n Cp *EDD* leaven 2 (3) ~ tub. Attrib **leaven tub, leven** ~ : a wooden container for bread dough.

[1772] 1792 CARTWRIGHT i, 215 Fogarty employed in squaring whitings, and the cooper in making a leaven-tub and a pail. [1786] ibid iii, 135 William and Tom were felling firewood. Tilsed made a leven-tub. Mr Collingham was making a clothes-horse.

ledge n Cp *OED* ~ sb 4 'ridge of rocks, esp. . .near the shore beneath the surface of the sea.' An underwater rock formation, steep-to, forming an area of shoal water which cod and bait-fish frequent; GROUND.

[1715] 1976 HEAD 80 The ledges of that port lying 8 or 10 leagues off, the French were obliged to build. . .shalloways, fitted with a deck, that can keep the sea five or six days for a loading. [1778] 1792 CARTWRIGHT ii, 354 The boats brought in but one quintal of fish to-day; owing, I hope to the bad weather: but I fear the want of baits has made them quit these ledges. 1792 ibid *Gloss* i, xii ~ Sunken rocks, and shoaly places in the sea, where the codfish resort. 1819 ANSPACH 429 The boat having taken her station on a ledge, or other shoally ground, each line being fastened on the inside of the boat, and the hooks baited, the man [operates the lines]. P 66–69 [The] jigging ledge [is] where bait was jigged.

lee n Cp *OED* ~ sb[1] 2 naut b (b) at lee 'under shelter'; *O Sup*[2] 5 lee ho, lee o.

1 Phr *at lee*: of a wild animal, hiding.

T 203/5–65 The secret was slips, wire slips. You'd find the fox at lee in the marshes, when he crossed the marsh. You'd tail a slip in that.

lee hello: hard a lee (on the helm).

T 181/2–65 They'll say 'leehello' then, 'leehello.' That would be 'hard up.'

on (his) lee ends: in Bank fishing, situated near the most distant of a number of dories launched from a vessel.

1960 FUDGE 26 My Brother Kenneth was away on his lee ends picking up his dories.

2 Comb **lee-cloth**: section of mainsail furthest from the mast.

T 453–67 The lee-cloth come out of his mainsail when he lowered un.

leery* n A fantastic, improbable tale (P 94–56); BAM, CUFFER n.

Q 71–7 ~ a false story or tall tale. Q 71–13 ~ a short story told in great [circumstantial] detail.

leeward See LEWERDLY, LOOARD.

leff* v [lɛf] *EDD* leave v[1] 1 (14) (15) ~ So D; *DJE* 1 for sense 1.

1 To leave.

1924 ENGLAND 317 Liff. Leave. T 187/90–65 He got in go with a girl an' I suppose he didn't want to leff she. T 194/6–65 I'd tell the young feller [to] leff the wheel. I thought she was comin' aboard. 1977 *Them Days* ii (3), p. 24 I said, 'I wants grub and I'll have grub before I lefs this. I got me hatchet out here and if I don't get grub I'm going to chop the store out.'

2 Phr *leff him bide*: see BIDE.

leggy n also **laggy** ['læɡɪ, 'læˈɡɪ]. A small codfish, gutted, headed, salted and dried without being split, usu for home consumption; ROUNDER, TOM COD.

1908 TOWNSEND 132 The very small cod are not boned, but are salted whole. These are called 'leggies' or 'rounders.' 1909 BROWNE 259 These barter shops do little cash business, but they exchange their wares for fish, salmon, furs and even 'rounders' and 'laggies.' P 261–56 The leggies are small salted unsplit codfish. 'The leggies were salted for the winter.' 1964 *Can Journ Ling* x, 140 A cod which is too small to split is called a [tomcod] or a [rounder] and a fish even younger than this is the [leggy]. C 71–129 Laggy. A small cod fish which has been salted round and then dried. It is important to remember that a 'laggy' is not split as are larger fish. When dried it is not sold but consumed locally. Most fishermen salt a stock of them for the winter. 1973 BARBOUR 74 There was also the rounder or leggy.

length n *EDD* ~ sb 2. Height (of a person).

P 148–60 He's an awful length of a man. T 54/63–64 He was a man six foot long in his life, and I bet you he was eight foot long, stretched. You talk about a length of a man!

lennet See LINNET.

leopard n Comb **leopard-plant**: slipperwort (*Calceolaria*) (Q 71–10); FISHERMAN'S BASKET.

lesser newfoundland See NEWFOUNDLAND (DOG).

letter n Phr *letter of tobacco*: a portion cut from a stick of tobacco, containing part of the impression of the brand name.
C 68–7 When the evening come they would go in to get paid, and for the day's work they would get a letter of tobacco. Q 71–8 ~ used in poor times [when] tobacco sold for 25 cents a stick, which divided evenly into five letters at 5 cents each. 1976 GUY 95 . . .and three letters of a plug of Beaver still left in his Guernsey pocket.

letter of jesus christ See SAVIOUR'S LETTER.

levener See ELEVENER.

lew See LOO.

lewerdly a also **looardly** *OED* leewardly a 'of a ship: apt to fall to leeward'; *ADD* Nfld. Unlucky; awkward, clumsy.
1914 *Cadet* Apr, p. 7 Lewerdly, a lewerdly fellow, one subject to constant ill luck or misfortune. 1924 ENGLAND 182 You're nothin' but a lewerdly slinger as won't hold up the harm [acknowledge it].

lick v Phr *lick(ed) out*: (a) tired, exhausted; (b) to stick out one's tongue.
T 139/40–65 'Twas a long song too. By the time 'twas over he was just about licked out. P 130–67 Lick out your tongue [so that I can see it]. P 245–75 Don't lick your tongue out at me!

lickery a also **licky**. Cp *OED* liquorice; *ADD* lick 1 'syrup.' Of a conifer, esp fir, exuding resin or sap; MYRRHY, SNOTTY.
1929 MILLER 31 Chops up two-three sticks o' lickery var with turkumtimy han's. P 269–64 Licky-wood: green wood, not dry. 1971 NOSEWORTHY 217 Licky doctor. Young fir trees, always full of sap, especially in the spring when it runs out of big bladders on the trunks. Always has more sap than *green-doctor*. 1977 *Decks Awash* vi (6), p. 64 "Uncle Josh": For planken 'e would cut some sticks, Myrrhy pine and licky vir.

lick for smatter See SMATTER.

licky See LICKERY.

liddick* See LITTOCKS.

light a
Comb **light-cure(d)**: dried cod-fish prepared for market with application of minimum amount of salt (P 245–62); SHORE[1]: ~ CURE.
T 141/67–65[2] Where the fish is scarce of course it pays to dress and salt it light cured and get the most out of it [by way of price].
light-fished: of a vessel, with a small catch.
1923 GRENFELL 4 Nearly every craft was 'light-fished,' the season was almost gone, and 't' merchants' had fixed a low price for fish.
light-salted: see **light cure(d)** above.
1873 CARROLL 44 As they fill up the cask [when

pickling cod-fish], they increase the quantity on each line of the fish, and on the top fish, better than one half of an inch is put on it. Notwithstanding which, the top fish are often light salted, and the bottom fish in the puncheon, are salt-burned, and often must be watered before being exposed to the sun for making. T 175/7–65 There's different cures: what they call the shore cure, light salted—that had to be fairly good and hard. But the heavy salted, perhaps two or three days' sun is enough for that, because the salt was into it and 'twouldn't spoil anyway. 1969 MENSINKAI 8 The salt fish takes four different forms, viz., light-salted, heavy-split, pickled-split and ordinary cure.
Hence **light-salt** v [lɤitʔ 'sɒ·lt]: to process cod-fish with moderate application of salt over an extended drying period; SALT v.
T 175/7–65 But the feller getting a fair amount of trap fish couldn't afford to light-salt it, because it had to stay in salt a long time; he had to put a lot of salt on it, and you couldn't get number one fish out of that.

light n Phr *a light of wood*: a load of fire-wood, esp as much as can be carried by a person at one time; TURN n.
C 71–22 ~ As much wood as you can bring on your back. Q 73–9 I was in the woods [today] and got a light o' wood.

lily n Wild lily-of-the valley (*Maianthemum canadense*) (1956 ROULEAU 33); SCENT-BOTTLE. Also in names of other plants: BLUE LILY, BOG ~ , MARSH ~ , MOSS ~ , ST JOSEPH'S ~ , WHITE ~ .

limb v Cp *O Sup*[2] ~ v 1 b; *EDD* 11 So. Phr *limb out*: to remove the branches and top from a tree.
1937 DEVINE 31 ~ To strip a tree of its branches. T 96/8–64[1] A big white spruce he was. They cut un down, and begar when they cut un down he fell on the ground, and they start to limb un out. 1979 TIZZARD 204 [The wood] would lie just as he cut it all through the summer and then in the fall of the year he would go and 'limb it out,' cut the branches off.

lincoln n also **linkum**. A fisherman's oilskin hat with elongated flap at the back; CAPE ANN, SOU'WESTER.
1936 DEVINE 115 He sold. . .oil clothing, which was a specialty and included south-westers, Cape Anns and 'Lincolns.' 1937 ibid 31 Linkum. An oiled hat (sou'-wester) worn by fishermen. 1970 *Wooden Boats* 20 Those three shipwrecked men clung to the rock from Saturday to Tuesday, without food and the only water they had to drink was rain water they caught in a lincoln. 1971 NOSEWORTHY 217 Linkum. A large waterproof hat worn by fishermen with a strap under the chin, a small rim in front, and a flap on the back to keep the neck dry. 1978 *Evening Telegram* 9 Sep, p. 14 A linkum is an oil hat with a long back on it to protect your shoulders.

line[1] n *OED* ~ sb[2] 2, *DAE* 1 (1634–) for sense

1; cp *EDD* 6 'reins' I Ma So [Amer], *DAE* 2 dial for sense 2 (b).

1 A single fishing line with hook(s)attached used esp in fishing for cod (and squid); handline; HOOK-AND-LINE.

1612 *Willoughby Papers* 16a, 10 For our fishing voiage one Seane 6 neats 7 dosen of Lynes. 1620 WHITBOURNE 13 . . .native commodities, or other adventure (then of necessary provisions for the fishing) as Salt, Nets, Leads, Hookes, Lines, and the like. [1766] 1971 BANKS 133 Each of the men in this Boat is furnished with two Lines one at Each side of the boat Each of which Lines are furnished with two hooks so here are 16 hooks Constantly Employed which are thought to make a tolerably good Days work if they bring in from 5 to ten Quintals of fish. 1819 ANSPACH 429 Most boats have four men, each with one line on each side of him, and these lines have two hooks. . . The man sits at an equal distance from the two lines which are committed to his care, moving them from time to time: as soon as the least tightness or motion is observed in the line, it is drawn up with all possible speed, and the fish thrown into the boat. [1952] 1964 PEACOCK (ed) i, 130 "For the Fish We Must Prepare": Oh traps and trawls and finger-stalls, / Rubber boots and killick claws, / Some lines and twines and ropes and coils, / You get sore hands and full of boils. T 437–65 So we [outed] the lines an' we catched away and catched away. We had half a locker full [of fish], I suppose. 1975 BUTLER 56 At that time [trawl] lines were hemp and they measured thirty fathoms in length.

2 In pl: (a) ropes arranged to lead caribou into a 'pound' or enclosure; (b) long leather straps used to guide oxen.

[1785] 1792 CARTWRIGHT iii, 95 Mr Collingham and five hands went this morning to set up the deer-pound, and fixed one pair of hawkdoors, and some of the lines. 1971 NOSEWORTHY 217 ~ The long straps with which one guides oxen, usually attached to their horns.

3 Phr *line of water*: unit for measuring depth of water; the length of a trawl-line.

c 69–5 She thought that the doctor said 'a line of water' (i.e. 50 fathoms). Q 71–8 A line of water is a measure of depth related to the length of a cotton trawl line, i.e. 60 fathoms. The other commonly used trawl line was of hemp but these were only 30 fathoms in length & were never used as a standard of measure.

4 Attrib, comb **line gear**: hand-lines, trawl lines, etc.

1953 *Nfld Fish Develop Report* 49 The most successful crews are those that rely principally on the trap and use *line gear* to bolster their catch in seasons when trapping yields relatively poor results.

line maker: artisan engaged in the making of fishing-lines.

1620 WHITBOURNE 13 . . .many numbers of people, as. . .Coopers, Ship-Carpenters, Smiths, Net-makers, Rope-makers, Line-makers, Hooke-makers.

line² n Cp *OED* ~ sb² 26 'track, course, direction; route: e.g. line of communication'; SMITH *County of Kerry* (1756), p. 169 [They have greatly improved this estate, by cutting a new

road from *Abbey-feal*. . .to *Castle-Island*. . .which roads are carried in direct lines, over mountains, through bogs, and morasses. . .]. MASON *Survey of Ireland* (1814–19) i, 298 'a great line of road. . .has been long projected.' W SCOTT *Rob Roy* (1818) i, 57 I should have been glad if I had journeyed upon a line of road better calculated to afford reasonable objects of curiosity. LEWIS *Disturbances in Ireland* (1836), p. 289 '[They] mostly reside on the line of road between Kilcommon and Borrisaleigh.' *O Sup²* ~ 26 e Chiefly Canada and N Z 'a settlement road, a bush road'; cp *DC* ~ 3 b, c 'a settlement road in Upper Canada' (1828–), 'a road, esp one built through the bush' (1830–) and other listed senses; 1880 *EDS* No. 7, p. 63 ~ 'the new roads are so called' N I; SEARY 147–8.

1 In phr *line of road*, ~ *of street*: a way or path planned and cut through rough country by surveyors and crews.

1835 *Journ of Assembly* 147 [This forms] part of a main line of road, which [extends] from Topsail along the Southern Shore of Conception Bay. 1836 [WIX]² 193 [From Petty Harbour] I walked. . .by the new line of road through the woods to St John's, on which the road commissioners have lately expended [£52]. [c1837] 1882 TALBOT 2 [In St John's] there were some good shops and stores in the line of street along the water's edge, and some few detached private residences. . .along the side of the hill. 1846 TOCQUE 125 This clearly points out the necessity of having a line of road between these places. 1887 *Colonist Christmas No* 16 The opening of the main lines of road is also worthy of notice, as they not only afforded necessary employment during the season of depression, but opened communication for traffic.

2 A road planned and cut across rough country by surveyors, often between coastal settlements; freq in road-names.

1835 *Journ of Assembly* 147 Brookfield road. . .would form part of a new line to Topsail. [1843] 1846 TOCQUE 148 [They opened] up its interior by means of good roads and communications upon lines carefully surveyed and carried through lands. [1848] 1971 SEARY 227 Indian Meal Line. 1850 *Nfld Almanac* 43 Road Commissioners: Tickle Cove to Main Line from King's Cove. 1901 *Christmas Review* 10 The charred skeleton of the horse was found the next summer four miles in on the Holyrood line. 1911 *Tribune Christmas No* You can take a horse and carriage and drive into the village over the Salmonier line, through beautiful scenery that well repays you for your visit. P 148–65 Where do you belong to, the back line? P 148–65 The road from Old Perlican to Lead Cove was built in the 1920's to replace the path along Trinity Bay, which was hard on the horses. Mr A tracked it out; there were no surveyors for a job like that [at that time]. It is still called the new line. 1977 RUSSELL 26 Almost half the men in Pigeon Inlet used to go in over the line every fall as soon as fishin' was over, and come back just in time to get ready for fishin' again.

line v *DC* ~ down, for first phr (Nfld: 1907–).
Phr *line down*: to guide a canoe through rapids,
keeping the craft, not broadside, but in the direction of the current.

1888 HOWLEY *MS Reminiscences* 57 We made good
headway notwithstanding encountering frequent bad
places, where we were obliged to get out and line down
the canoe. 1907 MILLAIS 305 Several times they packed
everything for a mile or two, but negotiated most of
the worst rapids by 'lining' down them, whilst one man
kept the nose of the canoe straight with a long spruce
pole.

line off: of persons, to stand in a line on or
alongside (something).

P 148–61 When we see five or six people lining off
the sidewalks, we can say that they are out-port people. Q 71–15 Lined off the sidewalk—in a line facing
outwards.

line out: to make a line or mark on a log prior
to sawing it into boards.

T 393/4–67 Now this stick was all lined out. If you
were goin' to saw inch board, say, [and] say that [log]
made six boards, there's seven lines struck on that.

liner n Cp *DAE* line storm N E. A high wind or
gale at the time of the equinox.

1957 *Evening Telegram* 20 Oct In the days when 600
fishing vessel crews put out their gear around the coasts
of Newfoundland and Labrador and when 400 of them
went to the ice, the sailors, fishermen and sealers all
looked for the 'liner breeze' about the time of the fall
equinox and 'Sheila's brush' about the time the sun
crossed the Equator coming towards us. T 141/63–65²
At that time when there was all canvas [on vessels] you
had a dread o' the liners. When the sun was crossin' the
line you'd get a storm, see, an' it was not good to be
caught out 'cause you got a gale o' wind. An' you
either be ahead o' the liners or behind 'em, see. 1971
HORWOOD 154 The tropical hurricane that struck Newfoundland on September 17th [1907] might have been
known to the world by some other name but in Twillingate it was the Liner Breeze.

linhay See LINNY.

link n also **lynx** *DC* ~ (1896–) for sense 1.
    1 Lynx (*Lynx canadensis*).
1964 *Evening Telegram* 28 Oct, p. 5 There is no such
thing as a lynx, unless there are two. A single one is a
'link.' 1977 *Decks Awash* vi (6), p. 64 Me Uncle Josh,
as smart a man / As ever trod shoe ledder, / Afeard of
no man in de world, / Nor starmy wind nor wedder, /
'E feared no bear nor wolf nor lynk, / Not one nor alto-
gedder.
    2 Comb **link-house**: type of trap used to catch
lynx.
1910 GRENFELL 76 A delicious scent issuing from a
cave covered with boughs attracted [the dog] in. Even
as he crossed the doorway there was a loud snap, and
he was fast caught in the cruel teeth of an iron trap. It
was a lynx house of a neighboring trapper. P 245–74 A
link-house is a log structure, about three feet high,
shaped like a hut, with baited trap or noose inside to
snare links.

link v *EDD* ~ v¹ 14. To take (another) by the
arm, escort.

P 29–73 The policeman linked her home.

linkum See LINCOLN.

linnet n also **lennet** ['lɪnət, 'lɛnət]. Cp *EDD* lin-
et: linnet, linnit sb 1 'flax dressed, but not twisted
into thread' Gl W Do; *EDD* lint sb 5 'a fishing-
net'; *OED* lint 4 a 'netting for fishing-nets' now
dial or U S (1615; 1874–92).
    1 Twine for knitting fish-nets; the sections of
netting forming the several parts of such nets;
the complete net, seine, trap or all of these collectively; TWINE.
[1776] 1792 CARTWRIGHT ii, 177 I sent five hands in
a skiff. . .to look for the nets, which we lost there last
fall. . .but the lennet was all rotted off. 1913 *Christmas
Chimes* 25 Every stage was down, the broken timber of
all these washing about in the beaches, mixed with
pieces of broken up skiffs and boats, masts, oars, trap
buoys, corks, linnet. . . 1936 SMITH 110 I put the twine
out in small lots to be knit up into linnet of different
size meshes. 1937 DEVINE 31 Twine made up into nets,
seines or traps, all of which are called collectively *linnet*
by the fishermen. T 43–64 When the fish will swim
round the trap they'd strike up against the linnet every
time. . . The name for the twine when 'tis knit up is linnet. T 80/3–64 An' you let hundreds [of fish] bide in the
linnet; you'd never haul the leader. T 172/5–65 And
you had your puncheons then; when the bark was
strong enough, you'd put your linnet into the puncheons. 1966 FARIS 36 Moving a cod trap is no small
task, as the 'linnet' (net portions) may weigh over 2000
pounds. P 229–67 We got all our linnet in the water.
1975 BUTLER 58n Now if you go in a store, you won't
ask for twine but for linnet—linnet for a cod trap, linnet for a salmon net, linnet for a gill net—'tis all called
linnet. 1977 *Evening Telegram* 28 Apr, p. 42 Tenders
are invited for the purchase. . .of approximately 1000
lbs of Cod Trap linnet, the majority of this material is
3½ inch mesh.
    2 A section of netting used for various pur-
poses on land.
P 167–67 ~ net placed over an enclosure to keep the
hens from flying out. C 70–12 We would put some
bread out on the snow to attract the birds, over which
would be a hoop covered with old linnet. C 71–95
When the hay was dry enough it was taken off the
pooks with a prong and put into the linets making a
bundle of hay. There was a special art to tying up the
bundles.
    3 Attrib, comb **linnet edge**: in a cod-trap, the
part of a section of netting attached to a line or
rope forming the frame of the device.
P 9–73 So, two inches along the rope and two inches
each side of a half-mesh is halves. The linnet edge
forms a half-mesh with the rope only.
    linnet pole: a stick from which a fish-net is sus-
pended to dry.
T 169–65 An' I had a stick, see, a linnet pole [there
on the hill].

linny n also **linhay, linney** ['lɪnɪ, 'lɪnïi, 'lɛnɪ]. Cp *OED* linhay, linn(e)y (1695–); *EDD* linhay, linney 'shed with lean-to roof and an open front' s w cties Ir Nfld; JOYCE 287 linnie.

1 A storage shed or room attached to the back of a dwelling; PORCH.

1819 ANSPACH 468 Tilt-backs, or linneys, are sheds made of studs, and covered either with boards or with boughs, resembling the section of a roof, fixed to the back of their dwellings towards the wind. 1836 [WIX]² 91 I. . .walked on to the winter crew's tilt. . . There throwing myself into a dark linny, or 'lean-to,' I sought some repose. 1894 BURKE 79 "The Men on the Linnie": We had to add two stories, / And a linnie to the [Advertisers'] Howl. 1907 MILLAIS 339 Linhay: a lean-to, attached to the main building; pronounced by the natives *linney*. 1937 DEVINE 31 ~ A one-storey room built on to a residence. An annex to a house, one storey high. 1972 MURRAY 186 The back of the house was usually taken up with a long entrance porch and a walk-in pantry or storeroom often referred to as the 'linney' or 'linnay.' This storeroom might be half as big as the kitchen itself. 1974 MANNION 130 Whether the 'linhay' in the St John's study areas is based on Irish antecedents or was borrowed from a Devonshire tradition there remains a vexed question, but it is certain that the placing of this building along the rear of the farmhouse does not have any Irish, or indeed English, antecedents. 1976 *St John's Heritage Conservation Area Study* 41 In addition, most houses have additions (called linhays) built on the back. These linhays, usually containing kitchens, are generally in fairly poor condition, crowding the available back yard space and cutting out light.

2 Comb **linny-hole**.

C 69–2 The word linneyhole is used sometimes to refer to a small room in the porch where various things were put such as water buckets, the gallon of kerosene, etc.

lippin* pans See LEAP v.

lirippy* a Cp *EDD* lerrup sb 1 'a rent, tear' So D Co. Of a hem-line, uneven; ragged (P 245–55).

list n One of the sections into which the horizontal surface of a 'fish-flake' is divided (Q 67–11).

little a *OED* ~ 1 e (1542 quot) for sense 1.

1 Phr *little small*: very small.

T 36–64 But some people haves fish-houses, little small houses made right square and turned down over these faggots [of fish]. T 33–64¹ A feed o' toutons would be dough, mixed up with pork cut up in little small pieces, an' put in the oven an' baked. T 194/7–65 An' the little girl, baby, want to know if I was goin' [to the] barracks, see; a little small maid.

2 Comb in the names of var birds **little auk**: common dovekie (*Plautus alle alle*); BULL-BIRD, ICE- ~ (1876 HOWLEY 68).

1908 TOWNSEND 18 Just as we were finishing supper, the mate put in his head and said, 'There is a bull-bird,

sir, swimming close to the ship.' I rushed out, and sure enough a dovekie or little auk was swimming. . .close to the vessel.

little black diver: American black scoter (*Oidemia nigra americana*) (1870 *Can Naturalist* v, 302).

little bull: see **little auk** (1959 MCATEE 39).

little crow: bird of the family *Corvidae*.

1964 *Evening Telegram* 28 Oct, p. 5 When it comes to that larger blackbird, the grackle, our local name-givers are a little less accurate, but just as descriptive. They call it the 'little crow.'

little curlew: Eskimo curlew (*Numenius borealis*) (1959 MCATEE 34).

little diver: northern razor-bill (*Alca torda torda*); TINKER (1959 MCATEE 39).

little noddy: see **little auk** (1959 MCATEE 39).

little turr: see **little auk**. (1959 MCATEE 39).

littocks n pl also **liddick*** ['lɪdɪks] *EDD* ~ 'rags and tatters' Bk (1790–). Scraps (of clothing); a small portion.

P 37 Liddick. A very small portion. C 68–19 You won't have a liddick—you'll be left with nothing. C 71–128 Liddocks. Any garment of clothing. P 107–78 He left us not a liddick.

live a [laiv]. Cp *EDD* ~ 3 'fresh' So for sense 2.

1 Real, actual.

T 70–64¹ They all pulled up their graplins an' pulled out, an' went with him to see if 'twas a live boat. 1979 POTTLE 70 A very large proportion of the people existed on little or no live cash from January to June. . . .They were dependent upon 'credit' by the local merchant and, in the case of the very dependent, a mere pittance of government 'relief.'

2 Freshly made or prepared, esp **live jam**, ~ **tea**.

1941 DULEY 54 'Thank you, my maid,' said Mrs Slater, as if she missed no spark of life. 'Soon we'll hearten all hands with a drop of strong tea.' 'I could do with a live-drop,' muttered a voice from an outer room. ''Tis a tragical day! A tragical day!" T 222–66 Live tea is made just by putting the leaves in a cup an' pouring the boiling water over it, an' drunk right off the leaves. T 222–66 Now live jam is jam that's made up to be eaten right away and not preserved like sometimes people put up jam that they were not going to use for four or five months. C 70–34 She was telling him about the grand live jam she had made from raspberries. Any jam which is not preserved with pectin is live jam.

3 Of seal pelts, recently removed from the animal.

1924 ENGLAND 141 Still others were 'tallying down' sculps cold enough for stowage. The fresh ones, though dead enough (God wot!) are called 'live seals.' 1978 *Evening Telegram* 15 Apr, p. 6 The old sealers and fishermen said that [the *Southern Cross*] possibly went around the cape that evening getting into the big heavy rollers with a top load of 'live' fat (i.e. that which is not frozen or settled down.) The seals' live fat slid forward, broke the bulkheads.

4 Of a slab of timber, with bark on both edges.

P 65–64 The plank from the re-saw has bark on both edges. This plank is called 'live plank.' P 222–67 The ribs [of a stope from which all the ore has been extracted] are lined with live edge—long pieces of timber with two slabs taken off, leaving two edges with the bark still on them. The pieces of live edge are erected vertically all around the ribs of the stope. Q 71–9 The carpenter ordered live plank from the yard.

5 Of a road, covered with loose gravel.

C 71–132 When the road has a lot of gravel on top, it is dangerous driving and people say the road is live.

6 Comb **live rock**: coral-like seaweed; nullipore (*Corallina officinalis*).

1884 STEARNS 291 Natural grottoes, and varieties of rock-work, all were there [on the sea-bottom at Dead Island], and all covered with 'red rock,' or 'live rock' as the people call this peculiar growth. P 148–62 ~ local variety of coral. 1981 GUY 101 Shells from the bigger [clams] that are a light purple or dark blue and white, or that have live rock (or 'coral'. . .) on them.

liver¹ n

1 Cod liver from which a commercially valuable oil is produced; cp COD OIL, TRAIN²: TRAIN-OIL.

[1663] 1963 YONGE 57, 59 A train fatt [vat] is a great square chest the corners of which are frythed athwart; the liver is thrown into the middle, which melting, the train leaks through this fryth and is by tappe drawn out and put into cask. . . In the midst of the season, men are apt to have vexatious hemorrhages of the nose, which they are sensible proceeds from eating much of the liver of the cods, which is here very delicious. [1758] 1807 ULLOA ii, 408 I shall not enter into an account of the disproportion of its head comparatively with the other fishes, or the quantity of oil made from it and the livers, which are also very large. [1794] 1968 THOMAS 182 The Livers is thrown into large Casks with Spruce Branches placed about the Bung Hole, the head of the Cask being out. They are exposed to the Sun to rott. 1866 WILSON 210 [Another] female. . .takes out the liver, and drops that into the gully. 1924 ENGLAND 264 . . .a grandame making soap from 'de hile off de livers, sir, an' de loy of ashes.' [1952] 1964 PEACOCK (ed) i, 130 "For the Fish We Must Prepare": Your bit of old clothes all torn in rags, / Yoke your goats and fix your fence, / A gallon of liver is twenty cents. T 36/8–64 [From] every finger there'd be a drop o' blood droppin' out of un—never a bit o' skin left on the tops. And in the morning you'd have to go dip 'em in the cod-oil, and some people used to have cotton mitts made purposely for to put fresh liver on your hands an' tie the mitts on your wristes before you'd go to sleep.

2 In names of var containers for cod livers and their natural processing into oil: **liver butt, ~ covel, ~ maund** [= basket], **~ puncheon.**

T 146–65 She [was] full o' water on deck an' [her] liver butts was loose. T 36/8–64 There's a hole in the table about three inches wide, an' a tub or a barrel—covel, they calls it, liver covel. And you'd pull out the gut, separate the liver an' let the liver go down through this hole, in the barrel. [1622] 1954 INNIS 58

[inventory] for pots and liver mands. . . 1909 BROWNE 68 The liver is thrown into a receptacle known as 'the liver puncheon.'

3 Comb **liver factory**: a building or plant with facilities for the processing of cod-liver oil; FACTORY.

P 102–60 As well as spare dipnets, prongs, jiggers, and dappers all under lock and key nearby and south was a liver factory where we manufactured refined cod liver oil. 1977 BURSEY 16 There may have been other liver factories that I have forgotten. He bought the raw cod livers and manufactured them into Cod Liver Oil.

liver note: a token given to fisherman for the value of cod livers sold to merchant.

C 70–35 I recall the use of liver notes in Bay de Verde. These were small tokens with a hole in the centre which were paid to the fisherman when he sold the fish liver. It had a particular value that I do not recall, but dollars and cents were never paid to the fisherman. These 'notes' could be used as currency in the community store but change was never given. . . The liver note was used in the exact same manner as true currency but the merchant controlled the spending of it completely.

liver² See LIVYER.

livere See LIVYER.

liveyer See LIVYER.

liveyere See LIVYER.

livier See LIVYER.

living ppl *OED* ~ ppl a 5 naut (1883 quot) for sense 1.

1 Of the wind or weather, strong, stormy.

1922 *Sat Ev Post* 195, 2 Sep, p. 133 At six in the evening darkness fell, with a high wind and a blinding snowstorm—'a living starm,' as those folk say. Only one watch could get aboard. Forty-eight men perished miserably, and Newfoundland wept. 1958 HARRINGTON 82 By afternoon the southwest wind had chopped to east-northeast and was blowing 'a livin' starm.' T 96/7–64¹ Come across the lake; blowed a livin' storm o' wind. Well, in the evening we eat the last bit o' grub we had, an' it blowed a livin' gale—we couldn't get across now. 1977 RUSSELL 153 I remember one October day we were all out fishin', when all of a sudden a gale struck from the west'ard, smack offshore. All of us managed to buck in against it and get home except Skipper Jonathan. He was fishin' out of Offer Ledge and we didn't miss him until we got back home. By that time, 'twas blowin' a livin' hurricane and 'twas too late to do anything about him anyway.

2 Phr *by the living man*: by the living God.

[1843] 1944 LAWTON & DEVINE 33 Father Scanlan: 'Ha, you old rascal, you never sent me the paint you promised me to paint the church.' 'Well, then' agreed William, 'by the living man you'll have it to-morrow.' 'By the livin' man' was his familiar expletive. T 156/7–65 'By the livin' man,' that was his cuss word—'by the livin' man,' he says to Devine, 'if you can put down five thousand pound on that end o' table, see,' he says, 'I'll put down five thousand an' half.'

livyer n also **liver, livere, liveyer, liveyere, livier** ['lɪvjəɹ, 'livjəɹ]. Cp *DAE* liver 'inhabitant, resident' (1678–1850), *EDD* liver sb[1] 1 'dweller' s w cties: var livier Do So D, livyer D; *O Sup*[2] liveyere (Nfld: 1863–); *DC* liveyere Nfld 2 (1946–) for sense 1, 1 (1905–) for sense 2. See *OED* -ier. Cp LOVYER, MILLIER, SHOREYER.

1 A permanent settler of coastal Newfoundland (as opposed to migratory fisherman from England).

1745 CAREW 30 Bampfylde. . .this Trip visited *St John's, Torbay, Kitty-Vitty* Harbour and *Bay Bulls*, very industriously remarking their Situations and Anchorage, and making himself fully acquainted with the Names, Circumstances and Characters of all the Inhabitants and Livers of any Account therein. [1759] 1895 PROWSE 295–6 The men mentioned in the margin [are] to repair to work on the said church from the date hereof to the 4th day of November next, as it appears that they are livers in this place and have not subscribed towards the building of the same. 1850 [FEILD] 27 The whole settlement [of Burnt Islands, S W coast] has sprung up within ten years, and now there are nearly one hundred 'livers' or settled inhabitants. 1863 MORETON 34 Livier. An inhabitant or liver. One who lives in any place. It is said of any uninhabited place that there are no *liviers* in it. 1868 HOWLEY *MS Reminiscences* 7 On our way from Ship Cove to Patrick's Cove by water we passed Gooseberry, where a few liviers reside. 1895 PROWSE 279 Some of the first 'liviers,' in Old Newfoundland parlance, had by this time built their huts and fishing stages as far north as Twillingate. 1932 BARBOUR 17 I also allowed for the possibility of our drifting to land on some island where no 'liviers' (small communities of original settlers) would be. 1937 DEVINE 31 Livier. An inhabitant. Originally, it was probably applied to settlers in a new or unfrequented place, but it has come to apply to population generally. 1949 DULEY 13 It was definitely laid down that local labour must be used in ordinary construction. The fisherman knew he could beach his boat and take a rest from the sea. The 'livvyer' understood construction. Was he not a natural Jack-of-all-trades, accustomed to entering the virgin forest to cut wood for his house, his boat, his oars? T 70/1–64[1] I often said to myself it'd make a wonderful place for livyers. T 54/62–64 It was a forsaken place over on the other side o' the harbour here. I mean, there was no liviers or no nothing there. T 272/3–66[2] An' there was no bridges, no roads an' no livyers, an' that man walked from Bonne Bay to Flowers Cove. 1975 BUTLER 80 [In the early days at Buffett] with a homemade table and stools for seats, those livyers would be as proud of their homes as wealthy people would be of a mansion.

2 A settler on the coast of Labrador (as opposed to migratory summer fisherman from Newfoundland). Also attrib.

1895 *J A Folklore* viii, 36 Liveyers. A name applied by the Newfoundland fishermen to those who permanently reside on the Labrador coast, in contrast with those who came there during summer. It seems simply the word *livers*, but curiously altered in the pronunciation. [1906] GRENFELL 146 They once more dropped me over the rail that I might visit a tiny, out-of-the-world settlement of liveyeres (or residents) of Labrador. 1908 TOWNSEND 120 The permanent inhabitants of the Labrador coast, the 'livyers,' are about three thousand in number, while between twenty and thirty thousand fishermen spend the short summer there. [1918–19] GORDON 5–6 The true Labradorman, or 'Livyere,' as he is called, is a mixture of white and dark. British servants, sailors, carpenters, coopers, tinsmiths, or shipwrights, who came out in the employ of trading companies of a century ago, these were the progenitors of the Labrador race. 1946 MACKAY (ed) 79 There are three classes of fishermen [in Labrador fishery]: the *liviers*, who live the year round on the Labrador; the *stationers*, who come to the Labrador each season as passengers on the coastal steamers or on the schooners, and return to Newfoundland in the autumn; and the *floaters*, who come from Newfoundland as members of crews of fishing vessels, and who operate with the vessel throughout the season. 1950 PARKER 15 Over 3,000 'Liviers' are now in residence along this coast between Hamilton Inlet and Blanc Sablon at the Quebec border. Most of these came from Newfoundland although a number of Channel Islanders settled directly along the north shore of the straits of Belle Isle. 1953 *Nfld Fish Develop Report* 20 While almost 90 per cent of the floater crews and about 70 per cent of the stationer crews fish for cod only 60 per cent of the livyer crews fish for both salmon and cod. T 141/64–65[2] An' everybody had a suggestion which way they'd go, 'cause I mean there was livyers somewhere. 1970 *Daily News* 2 June, p. 9 The *Dingo* will discharge supplies to fishermen in White Bay and ports along the Labrador coast. These fishermen are 'liviers.' 1973 GOUDIE 37 There were no liveyers around that part of the bay.

loader n *DAE* ~ 2 (1851–), *DC* (1942–) for sense 1.

1 In the lumber woods, man who piles logs on a sled.

[1920] 1933 GREENLEAF (ed) 321 "The Lumber Camp Song": The next comes is the loader, all at the break of day, / 'Load up my slide, five hundred feet; to the river drive away.' T 66/8–64 So many [men] for a team, horse team. Two choppers, a loader, an' a chainer, they call it, an' a swamper, you know—the feller that would make the roads. Q 67–95 Loaders. Two men at the brow who loaded the double-sled and then chained up the load.

2 Cod-fish with a blunt head, believed to be sign of a large catch to follow; BULL DOG, SEAL-HEAD COD.

P 148–63 Bull-dog or loader, a fish with turned up nose (supposed to give owner loads of fish). C 68–1 He told me that the old skippers of schooners going outside to fish, always used to say they would be sure of getting a full load of fish, if someone caught a loader. They would even take the head of the fish and hang it up in the schooner. In other words, it was a sign of good luck. P 135–77 ~ A fish with a broken nose. If you catch one of them you are supposed to have a full load of fish when you haul the trap the next day.

loaf n *EDD* ~ 2, 1 (1) ~ bread.

1 Soft, home-baked bread, as opposed to sea-biscuit or BREAD; BUN 1.

1863 MORETON 51 'My gracious, girls, I forgot the loaf. Julia, go out to the next house and hang on the bakepot.' 1895 *J A Folklore* viii, 35 Soft-baked bread is called *loaf*. 1916 GRENFELL 6 Christmas. . .came after such a 'total blank' in our fisheries that, far from expecting Santa Claus, it was absolutely that some of our folk would be looking for 'a bit of loaf.' 1920 WALDO 65 Mrs Grenfell visited White Bay in July and in two villages found a number of people all but utterly destitute. They were living on 'loaf' (bread) and tea. C 66–10 She just took the last slice of loaf off of the plate. She must be goin' to be a old maid. C 70–15 Instead of saying, 'have another slice of bread,' a person would say, have another slice of loaf.'

2 Comb **loaf-bread**; also attrib.

1967 READER 28 The lady at this particular boarding house had baked some 'loaf bread' buns. M 71–86 A boil could also be treated by applying a 'loaf bread poultice.' This consisted of chewed up bread or a piece of bread soaked in boiling water, being placed on the boil and secured with a bandage or tape.

lobster n

Comb **lobster box**: large box or crate anchored in shallow water and used to store live lobster (1971 NOSEWORTHY 217).

lobster buoy: float used to mark the position of a lobster pot; BUOY.

M 70–18 Secured to a rope this lobster trap was complete except for a marker called a lobster buoy tied on at the opposite end of the rope.

lobster factory: building or plant for the commercial processing of lobster, esp cooking and canning; FACTORY.

1892 VINCENT 7, 16 Far below us is a cluster of houses, a fishing settlement, with a lobster factory and some flakes. . . The [lobster] factory, it appears, only consists of an open shed and a stove. 1896 HOWLEY *MS Reminiscences* 4 This is where the Bay of Islands men come to fish. There is also a lobster factory here belonging to Anguin.

lobster-fish: to engage in the lobster fishery.

T 270–66 An' then soon as that's over they lobster fishes; an' then soon as that's over they cod fishes, an' what don't lobster fish they cod fishes, an' the money is always coming in.

lobster float: see **lobster box**.

1975 BUTLER 72 They moved the live lobster-floats near this plant.

lobster head: funnel-shaped netting through which lobster enters trap; HEAD.

T 39–64 They got a net inside. . .what they call the lobster head. M 70–18 A specially knitted 'lobster head' had to be fitted in place to allow the lobster in and yet preventing him from escaping.

lobster lath: thin wooden strip used to construct a lobster-trap; LATH n.

M 70–18 Lobster pots require a fair amount of wood and it was in the winter months, small pieces of logs were hauled home to be split into 'lobster lats.'

lobster pole: pole with hook attached, used to catch lobsters.

1979 TIZZARD 305 [We would] be out along the shore in punt, with a long pole and a large fish hook in the end of it to hook the lobsters from off the bottom. This pole was called a 'lobster pole.'

local a Of ice formed in the bays and harbours, or in the 'leads' between masses of drift ice from arctic or Labrador waters; cp BAY ICE, HARBOUR ~ .

1972 BROWN 3 Newfoundlanders distinguish between 'local slob,' usually too small to bear a man's weight, even when he is 'copying,' or jumping from pan to pan, and 'northern slob,' formed off Labrador. 1972 SANGER 238 ~ ice [is] formed locally either onshore or in open water and between pans of ice.

locker n Cp *NID* ~ n 1 b 'chest or compartment on shipboard' for sense 1; *OED* sb[1] 5 for sense 3.

1 A storage area for fish or gear in a boat.

P 148–65 ~s. Spaces in dory about a foot wide, separated by removable wooden spacers. T 437–65 An' when we got up, they all had their lockers packed full o' fish, an' we still n'er a one yet. So we [outed] the lines an' we catched away an' catched away. We had half a locker full, I suppose. Q 67–87 ~ a place in the cuddy where jigger lines and similar types of gear are stored. 1969 *Nfld Qtly* July, p. 20 ~ a chest or compartment in a boat usually found amidship. 1975 BUTLER 68 When they hauled their bait, they would ice it down in the holds of their boats in the lockers and get the boats under way to go to the fishing grounds.

2 A wooden receptacle in fishing-stage where cod are placed for washing and salting after being headed, gutted and split; FISH-BOX (1971 NOSEWORTHY 218).

3 A storage area in a house; esp a kitchen seat with space underneath for stowing objects.

M 69–6 Potatoes had to be brought from the cellar every day except Sundays. . .carried to the 'locker' (small room) under the stairs in the house. 1969 *Christmas Mumming in Nfld* 64 There are also practices which reflect this [nautical] orientation, such as the storing of clothes in chests rather than in closets and the use of 'lockers' like those on boats, which run the length of the kitchen wall and also serve as benches.

4 In collocations describing foods prepared from materials kept in a storage compartment in the house.

C 71–28 Cold locker is salt beef, pork, vegetables, etc, served cold from remnants of a previous meal. C 70–10 When they had a pease pudding or scald water duff, they would call this dinner a locker feed.

lodge v *EDD* ~ v 8 'to place, lay' Gl Nfld. To place (an object) in a position; to set down on a surface.

1863 HIND i, 156 I had not seen him for several weeks, and met him at the mouth of a creek leading into the Matawan, as I was passing down in a canoe, picking up the lodged sticks. 1895 *J A Folklore* viii, 36 ~ to place or put, as 'I lodged the book on the shelf.' 'She lodged the dish in the closet.' C 71–46 When a boy came in with groceries she would point to the table where she wished them to be placed and say 'lodge them here.' P 96–72 I lodged the cup on the table. 1973 ROSE (ed) 31 I can mind, when I was small, being lodged off down on the coats down in the back of the school at dances.

loft n *EDD* ~ sb 1 for sense 1; cp *DAE* for sense 2; *OED* 5 c obs for sense 3.

1 Floor or platform built to form an upper level in a house.

[1785] 1792 CARTWRIGHT iii, 75–6 In the course of the day I had the partition between my bed-room and the dining-room pulled down, and a loft made of it over the other bed-room, on which I stowed many small things. 1842 JUKES ii, 55 I slept with several of the male branches of the family in a long, low loft, extending the whole length of the house, with a range of narrow beds, or berths, along the wall on one side, and stores and provisions on the other. [1918–19] GORDON 28 Three bodies lay on the floor, the other was upstairs on the loft, and necessitated the removing of the floor before we could get it down. P 12–69 We'll put the trunk in the loft. P 127–73 George, you go up over loft now [to bed]. 1975 MILLS 41 Children and unmarried males slept in the loft which was reached by a wooden ladder or by a small enclosed stairway leading from the kitchen.

2 Upper room in building, esp on fishing premises, for the storage and repair of gear; STAGE LOFT.

1936 SMITH 43 [He] gave us a dance that night on the loft of the store, and we all greatly enjoyed it. 1966 FARIS 185 Men will know by an open window or a 'fire in' (smoke coming from the store loft chimney) that a man is 'on the loft,' usually 'mending twine.' 1975 BUTLER 173 [diagram of a merchant's premises] Dory Loft.

3 Ceiling.

P 148–72 The older people would say 'wash the loft'. . .whereas now the younger people say 'wash the ceiling.' 1976 GUY 132 There's vile green spatters over everything from the floor to the loft.

log n

Comb **log-path**: (a) man's customary path or right-of-way to an area to cut and haul wood; WINTER PATH; (b) path surfaced with logs; logroad.

C 69–6 If one logger has a log path broken through the snow for hauling logs, another man who wants to go with his animal into that path has to ask the owner of the path for permission to do so. The second fellow would only be allowed to cut fire wood in there and no logs because the area is the first man's logging place for that winter. Q 71–7 ~ a path made in a short time using unpeeled logs laid side to side. Q 71–8 ~ A winter path (usually across bogs and ponds, where possible, to take advantage of level ground and ice to make hauling easier) on which by hand-slide and horse-slide wood was hauled to the bank.

log tilt: a small log hut used seasonally by woodsmen; TILT.

1869 HOWLEY *MS Reminiscences* 3 Here Mr Carroll had erected a log tilt in which he and his men resided. 1895 ibid 7 Before the weather became too cold and stormy we constructed a very substantial log tilt composed of old sleepers stood upright and well stogged with moss. [1917] 1972 GORDON 112 On our way, we stopped at a small log tilt, put up for the benefit of travellers. 1973 GOUDIE xvi Pitching their tents and log tilts first on Otter Creek near the new base, the settlers were soon ordered to move to an area no closer than five miles from the military reserve.

log v Cp *DAE* ~ v 2 'to protect a structure with logs' (1786–) for sense 2.

1 To fetter (a dog) with a clog.

1900 PROWSE 108 All dogs found at large to be logged or to be effectually muzzled. If not may be shot by any person.

2 To build (a structure) with logs; esp with *up*.

T 43/7–64 The men would build the camps, and these camps were logged lengthwise, one on top o' the other. T 55/7–64 My mother reared lots o' pigs out there in a big pen, logged up. My father logged it up.

logan n also **luggin*** ['lougən].

1 A leather boot with rubber foot, reaching below the knee, and used for woods or winter wear; LARRIGAN.

P 215–63 A logan is a big knee-boot with a long tongue. People who talk a lot are said to have as much tongue as a logan. P 65–64 Luggins are factory-made and have rubber bottoms and leather legs [with laces]. T 200–65 An' I come home, my son, an' I had a brand new suit o' clothes, new pair breeks an' logans. 1973 PINSENT 80 You could hear the dry twigs crackling under his logans as he walked the country, and feel flushed in the face by his night fires. 1975 GUY 133 Another piece of footwear much favored by the outharbor juvenile was the logan which consists, essentially, of two refined rubber lumps attached to the knee-length leather uppers. They are secured by means of great yellow laces, six feet or more in length which are crisscrossed through numerous eye-holes and then hitched back and forth through rows of hooks near the top.

2 Comb **logan sock**: long, heavy woollen sock.

M 69–1 Before they went to bed [on Christmas Eve] they would hang up a logan sock behind the stove.

loging ppl ['lougn̩]. Cp LOGY. Of cod-fish, moving in a sluggish fashion.

T 80/3–64 Anyhow, we got out this time with the fishglass, lookin' at the fish. An' 'tis login' around, 'twon't do nothing. An' we started in trouncin' then.

log-load n also **logger load** *DC* ~ Nfld (1933). A full cargo (of fish or seals).

1904 *Nfld Qtly* iv (3), p. 5 The description of the 'drive' for the first load of mackerel, with a little alteration, would describe the struggle for the 'log load' enacted every spring in our waters by our local vikings. 1924 ENGLAND 71 Us goin' to bore up wid a full trip o' fat, a logger load. 1933 GREENE 43 Owners and crews alike would always look. . .with implicit confidence in their skill and intuition to set the course aright, and to bring a log-load home. C 71–86 ~ He remembers this expression being used in Joe Batt's Arm to refer to a boat that was coming into harbour with a full load of fish. 1971 NOSEWORTHY 218 ~ A good boat-load of fish.

log-loaded p ppl [lɒg 'loudəd].
1 Of a boat or vessel, fully laden (with fish or seals, etc); heavily laden; DEEP a 1.
1906 *Week End* [N Y] 8 Apr, p. 8 The floes spread over the North Atlantic, and it requires the keenest judgment to locate the seal herds among them, the least error frequently resulting in a ship returning empty, while a more fortunate one may come back log-loaded. [1926] 1946 PRATT 240 "The Witches' Brew": So to the distant isles there sailed, / In honour of the ivy god, / Scores of log-loaded ships that hailed / From Christiania to Cape Cod. 1931 BYRNES 114 Then the crowds rushing down to the wharves, and the wild cheers, as the grimy, blackened vessel, log loaded, and flying its house flag, steamed up the harbour. 1955 DOYLE (ed) 11 "A Noble Fleet of Sealers": And on March the twenty-ninth / Bore-up log loaded to the hatches. T 50/3–64 Then he wanted some beef, he wanted a gallon o' molasses an' a bit o' butter an' so on. Got it all down the punt anyway. She was log loaded comin' home. 1966 SCAMMELL 11 Our people fished for cod, lobsters and herring; they grew potatoes and cabbages, built their own houses and their own schooners which they sailed, log-loaded with salt cod, to Europe through the autumn gales. 1976 *Daily News* 6 Oct, p. 1 Every dogberry tree in the city is log-loaded with berries.
2 Drunk, loaded.
P 148–63 He come home log-loaded. C 71–105 If a person got very drunk he was said to be log-loaded. P 13–75 ~ Quite drunk, barely able to stagger around.

logy a also **loggy** ['lougɪ]. Cp *EDD* loggy a 2 var logey, logy 'heavy, slow-moving' Ha IW Amer Nfld, JOYCE 287 logey 'heavy or fat,' *OED, O Sup²* loggy, logy N Amer (1859–) for senses 1, 2. Cp SEARY 73 for occurrence as place-name Logy Bay (Lugy Bay 1675).
1 Of persons (animals, fish, etc), heavy, sluggish, in poor condition; dull.
1863 MORETON 33 Loggy. Often applied in reproachful metaphor to a dull slow person. 1928 PALMER 159 The fish weighed not less than 70 lbs. I say he must have weighed 60 lbs, for he was as long as my other big one and that one was half logy and the meat was white, whereas this one was round and in best possible condition. P 148–61 I feel right logy. P 54–67 ~ torpid, sluggish, lazy. C 71–130 A person complained of feeling 'logy' when he lacked energy or felt partly sick. 1979 *Evening Telegram* 6 Aug, p. 1 If you felt a bit logy on Saturday, there was good reason. The Tor-

bay weather office said the mercury climbed to 29.6 [celsius].
2 Of a vessel, slow-moving, deep-laden and heavy in sailing.
1896 *J A Folklore* ix, 23 In Newfoundland. . .they will speak of a *logy* vessel, a slow sailer. 1905 DUNCAN 115 The punt was too low for a lop—too loggy; a ripple would threaten her with swamping, and new ice was continuously forcing her deeper. 1922 *Sat Ev Post* 195, 2 Sep, p. 126 Fifteen. . .twenty miles a day the *Terra Nova* must win, every day hitting the herd, hoping always for some luck that will bring wind, weather, ice conditions, seals and all into such happy accord as will full her up logy and bring her richly to port.
3 Of the weather, (a) heavy (with moisture); (b) oppressively hot.
1863 MORETON 31 Loggy. Saturated and heavy with moisture. 1904 *Nfld Qtly* Dec, p. 17 It was a glorious day, and so was the Sunday, but on Monday when we started it was foggy and logy, and we were just one week going about seventy miles. 1907 MILLAIS 339 ~ heavy, dull. Thus a logy day. 1924 ENGLAND 258 Ah, dat was a fine, logy [hot] summer, last summer twelve month. P 148–63 Foggy, mauzy, logy days.

logy n *OED* ~ a b (1897); CLAPIN (1902) ~ fish of inferior quality. A large cod-fish; SOAKER (P 148–65).
P 106–79 ~ a cod-fish about five feet long. It lives on the bottom.

lollik* See LALLIK*.

lolly n Cp *OED* loblolly 1 'thick gruel,' *EDD* ~ sb³ 'broth, soup' D (1777–), *DC* ~ Nfld (1771–); *NID* ~ 2. Soft ice forming in water; loose ice or snow floating in water.
[1771] 1792 CARTWRIGHT i, 180 There being much lolly in the river, it was with great difficulty that I could cross it in a punt. 1792 ibid *Gloss* i, xii ~ Soft ice, or congealed snow floating in the water when it first begins to freeze. 1842 JUKES i, 256 ~ . . .soft, half-frozen snow, floating on the surface of the water, not more than five or six inches in thickness, and yielding readily to pressure. 1887 BOND 65 I got out of my reach of the solid ice, an' among the soft slob an' lolly in the middle of the swatch. 1896 *J A Folklore* ix, 28 ~ ice broken up into small pieces. 1896 *Dial Notes* i, 379 ~ ice and snow in the water along the shore. 1927 *Christmas Messenger* 47 [Devine:] ~ the first effect of frost on the surface of the sea, giving it a dark oily colour like the face of a mirror. 1947 TANNER 495 When the anchor ice, or 'lolly,' began to form the nets must be taken in. 1955 ENGLISH 35 ~ soft ice beginning to form in harbours. C 37–71 ~ ice which has been crushed by the action of wind and wave. It has an appearance somewhat like froth on the water. It usually appeared and was formed from ice being churned through wave action close to shore.

london n Cp *OED* London: ~ smoke 'shade of grey' (1883); PARTRIDGE (1860–90). Attrib **london smoke**: type of flannelette used for making clothes.

[1905] 1974 SQUIRE 83 Four yds. london smoke. T 39–64 Pink London smoke. Women used to use it for making underwear; pink London smoke, and dark. Now that was a good item. You wouldn't use it for a tarmop now! T 168/70–65 Flannelette, London smoke and shirting—they'd make everything. You couldn't buy ready-mades for women. . . This London smoke, for making shirts, would be fifteen cents a yard. 1976 *Evening Telegram* 9 Mar, p. 12 We'd bring a warm brick to bed, and tuck it under the tail of your London smoke nightdress down around your heels to keep warm.

lonesome a   Cp *OED* ~ 1 'solitary.' Apprehensive, fearful, because alone.
   T 70–64[1] His mother made him take the stuff what belonged to the boat [from which someone drowned] and bring it up on the stable loft, because she was lonesome, see, to have it in the house.

long a   *EDD* ~ 4 for sense 1; *O Sup*[2] a[1] 1 c make a long arm (1854–), JOYCE 114 putting on the long finger for phr in sense 2; for combs. in sense 3: *EDD* ~ adj 1 (2) ~ cart D So; cp *O Sup*[2] ~ -liner 'fishing vessel which uses long-lines' N Amer (1909–), *DC* (1955); cp *DAE* ~ sugar 'molasses' obs (1729). See also LONGER.
   1 Tall.
   1929 BURKE [19] "The Night We Played Cards for the Little Boneen": The partners were Kielley / And long Denis Doyle. T 54–64 He was a man six foot long in his life, and I bet you he was eight foot long, stretched.
   2 Phr *long in the water*: of a vessel, sunk deep (1924 ENGLAND 317).
   make a long arm: to reach (one's arm) for food.
   1887 BOND 42 . . .injunctions to 'make a long arm,' and help yourself, and 'not wait for compliments.' Q 67–102 ~ reach for anything you want on the table.
   not be the longest: to be very quick.
   T 54/9–64 'You go over there,' he said, 'and there's a bottle of rum there.' Certainly I wasn't the longest before I was to that cupboard.
   put on the long finger: to delay, procrastinate.
   1968 DILLON 147 I don't believe in puttin' things on the long finger; I likes to get a thing done. P 108–70 You should get to work painting the house, and don't keep putting if off on the long finger.
   3 Comb **long-billed mouse**: LABRADOR SHREW (*Sorex personatus miscix*).
   1964 *Evening Telegram* 28 Oct, p. 5 In Labrador I have heard a shrew referred to as 'a long-billed mouse,' which, though totally inaccurate, is at least descriptive.
   long boot: fisherman's leather thigh-boot.
   1881 *Nineteenth Century* ix, 89 To see eminent counsel staggering about the slippery deck in long boots and guernsey frocks. . .produced [in me] a feeling of somewhat irreverent amusement. 1906 LUMSDEN 48 The hat chosen was not the best fit, neither was it in the latest fashion; the coat evidently was not made for me, and now I boasted a brand-new pair of long boots. 1931 BYRNES 98 [There was] joy in store for you when the

morning dawns, plowing gaily and pantingly through the soft, yielding snow banks, testing the merits of your new 'long boots' for the first time, and the warmth of your new 'Elsinore.'

long car, ~ **cart** ['lɔŋkɑːɹt]: horse-drawn cart with a long body on two wheels; CAR.
   [1930] 1980 *Evening Telegram* 15 Mar, p. 6 A horse owned by Steers Limited, attached to a long cart, bolted from Hamilton Street yesterday and dashed at a wild pace along New Gower Street. 1931 BYRNES 112 The accumulated water in the 'ruts' caused by the heavy wheels of the 'long carts' from the country, froze lightly. 1953 *Christmas Greeting* 21 Some twenty years passed and one sunny August day Bill went with a long cart into St John's to sell a load of hay. 1960 *Daily News* 29 Aug, p. 60 A complete museum should have on display not only a catamaran but also a side sleigh, an old-fashioned dog-sled if one is to be found, a long cart, and although a few may still be found in use, a box-cart. M 64–1 A longcar is the local form of longcart which is a sort of flat cart often used with a horse for hauling things. M 67–17 For heavier work, the long cart was favoured. This was little more than a heavy, rack-like frame, balanced on a pair of iron-tired wheels. It was an all-purpose vehicle, useful for hauling loads of logs, sacks of feed or barrels of beef. . . The driver sat on the load, or on a wooden box, usually covered with a piece of brin bag. T 731–70 A truckman meant a man that had a horse an' long cart an' stood in the coves until he was hired. 1973 *Daily News* 1 May, p. 4 At the turn of the century. . .horse-drawn long carts, box carts and slovens, transported goods between the wooden finger wharves and the warehouses. 1974 MANNION 104 Near St John's this vehicle was called a 'long cart,' a 'long car' or 'dray-car' on the Cape Shore.

long gun: jocular name for telescope (on a sealing vessel).
   1924 ENGLAND 277 Skipper Abe polished the lenses of the 'long gun.' This master telescope, by the way, was always an object of vast solicitude.

long-liner [lɔŋ 'lainəɹ, lɔŋ 'lɛinəɹ]: a vessel of up to 60 feet (18.28 m) in length adapted for various types of fishing in waters intermediate between the coastal and offshore 'grounds,' but chiefly using fleets of gill-nets; such a vessel used by 'landsmen' at the seal-hunt (1953 *Nfld Fish Develop Report* 50).
   1975 BUTLER 59–60 When long liners came to be used [in Placentia Bay in 1962] as many as from twenty to one hundred nets per boat were being used. 1982 *Evening Telegram* 20 Mar, p. 7 Longliner fishermen [at Catalina] are eagerly preparing for this year's fishery. They are busy in their stores getting nets and other gear ready.

long live: roseroot (*Sedum rosea*) (P 233–78).

long rubber: flexible boot reaching to the thigh; RUBBER.
   1931 *Nfld Magazine* 11 He. . .used to wear a long coat, belted at the waist, and a pair of long rubbers. P 102–60 Every fisherman received free board; his only expense was his personal account which was generally small consisting of a pair of long rubbers, a suit of oil skin clothes, homespun mitts, a sou-wester, homespun

socks. . . 1975 GUY 61 Alas, it was never the author's privilege to own a pair of logans, the most dashing sort of footwear next to the long rubber.

long-shanks: long-legged person.

P 41–68 If you were tall, you were [called] long shanks; if you were short you were a muzzle. Q 71-7 ~ a person who has long legs.

long sweetness: molasses.

[c1894] PANL P4/14, p. 197 *Long sweetness* is molasses, as opposed to sugar which is *short sweetness*. 1895 *St Nicholas* [N Y] Apr, p. 451 With it they buy their clothes, their flour, . . .their 'long sweetness' (molasses), which are about the only edibles you will find.

long-tail: a type of narrow, elongated snow-shoe.

1908 TOWNSEND 108 The 'long tails' are apparently not so commonly used as the oval tailless racquettes.

long-tail account: fisherman's account (with a merchant) extending from one fall season to the next (1957 *Evening Telegram* 22 Mar, p. 4).

long-tailed duck: American pintail (*Anas acuta tzitzihoa*) (1870 *Can Naturalist* v, 229).

long-tail(ed) sugar: molasses (P 98–57).

longer n   also **lunger** ['lɒŋɡəɹ, 'lʌŋɡəɹ] *O Sup*[2] ~ sb[3] (Nfld: 1772–); *DC* ~ (1772–), ~ fence (1842). Cp STROUTER: STOUTER.

1 A long tapering pole, usu a conifer with bark left on, used in constructing roofs, floors, surfaces of stages and flakes, etc; fence rail.

[1772] 1792 CARTWRIGHT i, 216 At noon I went round the traps, and searched the woods by the south side of Hare Hill, where I found some good longers and boat-hook staffs. [1786] ibid iii, 224 Where the soil is pretty good [the trees] run clear and tall, and attain substance sufficient for shallop's-oars, skiff's-oars, stage-beams, rafters, longers, and other purposes, for which length is principally required. 1792 ibid *Gloss* i, xii ~s. Poles, which, by being nailed top to but[t], are made use of for floors, instead of boards. 1842 BONNYCASTLE i, 292 The other mode [of making fences] is to set up a strong stick every eight or ten feet, and then to nail three or four longer ones of less diameter to them. This is called a longer fence, and the poles of spruce are called 'longers.' 1846 [FEILD] 7–8 The road is merely an opening cut through the woods, and the marshy places covered with the corduroy or longers of the country. 1848 *Journ of Assembly* 120 . . .new longers on said bridge [at New Harbour]. 1861 DE BOILIEU 118 The floor of the house is composed of the same material as the sides—small trees cut and squared, and placed side by side. These are called 'longers,' which, I suppose, is an abbreviation for 'long-layers.' 1863 MORETON 82 A longer is extended from one to the other of these trees, and seized to them at the proper height for the roof ridge [of the tilt]. 1920 WALDO 158–9 The scaffolding [of a flake] is made of poles called longers. 1935 KEAN 100 In my early days I was never taught to spread water-horse fish on lungers or rocks until it had first been spread on flakes for two or three days. T 43–64 You get what they call flake longers, that's a small tree about three inches in the butt and it'll go right away to the top. You'd cover over these beams with these longers. 1966 FARIS 38 Many slide-loads of 'lungers' (small straight poles) are needed for 'bridges' and wharves, and timber is always needed for house and shed construction. C 68–24 [tall tale] When he went to feed his sheep one morning in January it seemed that the roof of the barn was supported by ice candles that hung from the eaves. He took them down, about a hundred of them and used them for longers for his fish flake. M 69–6 If hard frosts did not come before the snow to freeze the bogs, lungers had to be laid across them to keep the animals from getting 'stogged' (stuck in the bog). P 146–63 'A tongue as long as a longer' refers to a person who talks a lot. P 197–74 [The man in his will left his son a piece of land measuring] three longers' length. 1975 BUTLER 60 The servants were therefore sent in the woods to cut wharf beams, wharf shores, flake beams, flake longers and flake boughs.

2 Attrib **longer fence**: (see 1842 quot above).

1835 PANL GN 2/2 Sep, p. 103 A longer fence shall be composed of four longers at one foot apart in height and a post every six feet distance to which the longers are to be strongly nailed and the longer no less than two inches at the smallest end in diameter. [1900 OLIVER & BURKE] 68 I took off my monkey jacket, coat, pants, bloomers and socks, and hung them on the longer fence. 1964 *Evening Telegram* 4 May, p. 7 He had to bring that water three hundred feet from Healey's well, get through a three-longer fence, and he never once spilled a drop. 1981 ibid 16 May, p. 20 All they had to do was get under the longer fence, and make their way to the first marshy place and there they were, lovely smell bottles with a scent fit for a queen.

longer v   *DC* ~ (Nfld: 1775). See LONGER n. To fasten sticks or 'longers' in position.

[1771] 1792 CARTWRIGHT i, 173 The east end of the storehouse was longered, and the provisions stowed in it. 1964 *Can Journ Ling* x, 40 The flake is said to be [longered over] when the rails or [longers] are in position. P 173–75 Get down there and longer that fence!

longshoreman n   *DC* ~ (1891–). A permanent resident of coastal Labrador; LIVYER.

1891 PACKARD 141 The houses of the 'long-shoremen,' or those of the permanent residents, were clapboarded and a little better looking than the tilts. 1947 TANNER 748 *Liveyeres* or *Long-shore men* (white or Eskimo half-breeds).

loo n   also **lew** [luː]. Common loon or great northern diver (*Gavia immer*).

[1794] 1968 THOMAS 135 Having shot some Lews which fell in the Lake, they thought of making use of the Canoe to fetch them on Shore. 1812 BUCHAN *MS* 27 June Farmers Islands, Loo bay, Indian Arm, Burnt bay, Comfort Islands. 1842 JUKES i, 106 I was awoke at daybreak this morning by the cry of the 'Loo,' or great northern diver, a very handsome dark bird with white spots, and almost as large as a goose. Its cry is a wild unearthly yell, with a rather musical cadence, and sometimes a sharp termination. 1858 [LOWELL] ii, 24 ~s. So called because they cry 'Loo!' 1895 *J A Folklore* viii, 288 I tooked her [the gun] and the powder-harn and shot-bag and starts up yander through the droke. You know the little pond at the top of the hill. When I cumed in sigh' o' un, the first thing I see is a loo' (loon) sitting about the middle uv un. 1931 *Nfld Magazine* 113 He was born the year Jimmy (the father) built the punt or Tommy was born, sir, the year uncle John shot the loo. 1959 MCATEE 2 ~ Common Loon (Sonic. Nfld., 'Labr.' Hawker 1826 records Tommy loo for Great Britain). C 69–30 If you hear a loo making a noise after night it is a sign of a breeze of wind. C 71–126 He's as silly as a loo.

looard a also **leeward, looward** ['luˈəɹd] *EDD* leeward phr *to go to* ~ 'go to the bad' IW for sense 2.
  1 Stormy, threatening.
  1955 ENGLISH 35 Lourd—dark, gloomy. P 120–67 It was a louard day and we was in port. This means a stormy day; too stormy for boats to leave port, or if the boats are on the Banks it is blowing too much to fish. Q 67–73 Sun dogs on each side of sun call for a windy leeward day. 1969 *Christmas Mumming in Nfld* 80 Even on a 'looard [leeward] day' (that is a stormy one) when men cannot fish, there is always the net to repair.
  2 Phr *go to leeward*: to decline in fortune.
  1863 MORETON 40 Going to leeward: to be in declining circumstances. 1924 ENGLAND 318 Come to looard; get into trouble.

loodle-laddle* n also **doodle-laddle*,** **oodle-addle*** ['udḷ ˌædḷ] *Kilkenny Lexicon* loodle laddle. A contraption; esp a deliberately humorous or evasive name given to an object in order to puzzle a child.
  C 71–94 When a man was making something and some curious boy asked him what he was making the man always told him that he was making a oodle-addle. P 245–77 Do you know what we call that drain pipe? We call it the oodle-addle. P 30–79 My mother used to tease me by saying that a doodle laddle was a machine for catching wild ducks.

look-out n Cp *OED* ~ 2 a 'station or building from which a look-out can be kept' orig naut (1700–) for sense 1; *OED* 2 b 'prospective condition,' *EDD* look 2 (6) ~ up for sense 2.
  1 In coastal nomenclature, a high, naked hill near a cove or harbour from which a seaward watch is kept.
  1951 *Nfld & Lab Pilot* i, 158 Tacks Lookout, a bare-topped hill, 212 feet high, falls almost perpendicularly to the northern side of the cove. 1953 ibid ii, 184 Lane's Lookout, a rocky hill, 383 feet high, the highest on Fogo Island, stands on the eastern side of the harbour. 1971 SEARY 144 Lookout occurs six times [as a coastal topographic generic on the Avalon Peninsula alone].
  2 Prospect, outlook. Also **look-up.**
  1924 ENGLAND 285 De *Ranger* do a strange t'ing if she come out agin. She'm a mystery if she do. If she don't, us got a good look-up to see de Notch wonnerful soon, now. 1968 DILLON 147 Girl, the fishery wasn't good this year. 'Tis a blue look out for the winter.

'Twas a blind look out anyway, to have a bridge in that condition.

looper n Pine grosbeak (*Pinicola enucleator*) (1976 *Avifaunal Survey* 155).

loose a *OED* ~ 9 (1774, 1835) for sense 1.
  1 Of ice, broken or separated into floating pieces which afford passage for a vessel; cp DRIFT-ICE.
  1870 HOWLEY *MS Reminiscences* (1) There was some loose ice about and one small growler struck us on the bilge. [1915] 1972 GORDON 15 To while away the time I got out my .22 rifle and had some target practice on bits of loose ice. 1924 ENGLAND 44 We got into loose ice almost at once, and there began that quivering and cruel battering which for long weeks was to companion all my days and nights. Q 71–7 Loose ice, generally seen in the spring, is very dangerous for walking on. 1972 BROWN 65 The *Bellaventure* was steaming through loose ice.
  2 Of persons, agile, supple.
  T 222–66 [She] was complimented on her agility by an elderly gentleman who said to her, 'My, miss, you'm a loose woman.' P 54–67 [He's a] loose man on ice.

lop¹ n *OED* ~ sb² now dial (c1460–); *EDD* sb¹. A flea.
  1895 *J A Folklore* viii, 33 Then they call a flea a *lop*, the Anglo-Saxon *loppe*, from *lope*, to leap. 1940 *Dal Rev* xx, 66 ~ A flea. C 71–98 [overheard at a dog show in St John's] This one has lops.

lop² n *OED* ~ sb⁶ naut 'a state of the sea in which the waves are short and lumpy' (1829–).
  1 The rough surface of the sea (or a pond) caused by a stiff wind and marked by a quick succession of short breaking waves; cp TUMBLE.
  1850 [FEILD] 111 I was very anxious to proceed to Greenspond today—but. . .no wind, and a very heavy lop outside. 1862 NOBLE 204 We are having a long ground-swell, roughened with a 'lop' or short sea, and the promise of high wind. 1887 BOND 26 To leeward of us was the open sea, ugly-looking enough. . .with a short lop which the wind had stirred up. 1912 CABOT 48 His two stout masts, unstayed, were ready to be jerked from their sockets and laid down if the 'lop' became too sharp. 1927 DOYLE (ed) 65 "Three Devils for Fish": She steers like a rigger, she mounts the big lop, / But hark, Skipper Harry, I heard a fish chop. [1952] 1965 PEACOCK (ed) i, 136 "High Times in Our Ship": In crossing the White Bay met up with the lop, / Ran into a puncheon and thought 'twas a rock. T 50/1–64 The ground [was] bet away by the side o' the lake, where the lop [was] heavin' in. Ibid An' she took one skitter away on the water—I allow she went as far from this down to Pad's before she brought up in big breakin' lop. T 194/5–65 I seed more lop one look than I seed all my life. T 397–67 You'll get northerly wind right in the harbour. It makes a big lop, what we call a wind lop.
  2 A choppy wave.
  1910 *Nfld Qtly* Oct, p. 22 'We'll have to get square with the Mate for this,' said the Commodore, severely,

next morning—and they did one morning coming out of Fischot by sticking the *Comet's* nose into a 'lop' while the mate was hoisting the jib. 1937 DEVINE 33 ~s. Waves thrown up in a stiff breeze or shortly after the subsidence of a storm. P 147–56 The lops came aboard and drenched everyone. T 50/1–64 Thunder an' lightnin' you know, out to the north, an' they could hear the big lops rushin' an' breakin' away outside of 'em. T 43–64 You get out in th' old boat and she beatin' down the lops. T 194/6–65 An' just as I turned astarn, I reached wi' my hand to take hold o' the skig, the keel; another lop struck me on the breast an' knocked me away about nine feet, clean clear of her again. P 245–64 The ship went into the lop till you couldn't see her spars.

3 Phr *have a lop on*: of the sea, to be rough, choppy (1925 *Dial Notes* v, 335).

stir up a lop in a piggin: to make much ado about nothing; to cause a tempest in a teapot.

1964 *Evening Telegram* 3 June, p. 6 Mr Smallwood's recent utterances concerning the state of church affairs in Newfoundland seem to have stirred up a Lop in a Piggin.

lop v *OED* ~ v³ 'to break' (1897). Of rough water, to break in swift, tumbling waves.

T 50/1–64 Sometimes they have a bit o' the mains'l on her, an' sometimes a bit o' the fores'l on her, comin' through the water, loppin' mountains. Had a load o' fish in.

lopchops n Figure of an animal head with movable jaws; cp HOBBY HORSE, HORSY-HOPS.

C 67–2 He used to make [it] to entertain the children. Two sticks together, lopchops; just like a jaw. 1973 WIDDOWSON 428 ~ It resembled a gert cow with horns, and jaws that snapped.

lopper n Northern short-eared owl (*Asio flammeus flammeus*) (1976 *Avifaunal Survey* 140).

loppy a *OED* ~ a³ (1883–), *EDD* Co. Of the water, rough from wind or storm; choppy, lumpy; KNOBBLY.

1905 DUNCAN 3 The enviable achievement in his sight was a gunwale load snatched from a loppy sea. 1925 *Dial Notes* v, 335 The bay'll be *loppier* the marnin'. 1966 PHILBROOK 61 When the sea is 'loppy' or rough the skipper takes part in all operations, maintaining the routine and coordinating all phases. P 148–67 It was loppy out in the bay (with small breaking seas).

lord¹ n also **lord of the harbour**. Cp *OED* ~ sb 2. See also LADY¹. The master of the first English fishing vessel to reach a harbour in Newfoundland, exercising certain privileges for the season; ADMIRAL, FISHING ~ . Cp KING 1.

[(1578) 1935 *Richard Hakluyt* 128 [Parkhurst's letter:] The Englishmen, who commonly are lordes of the harbors where they fish, and do use all strangers helpe in fishing if need require.] [1663] 1963 YONGE 56

Mr Waymouth, (who is Admiral and. . .is called my Lord, the vice-admiral my Lady) had a chyrurgeon. 1708 OLDMIXON 11 The first Master of a Ship that arrives there, tho he commands a Bark but of 30 or 40 Tuns, is Chief Governour for that Fishing Season with the Stile of, *Lord of the Harbour*. 1745 CAREW 88 After a Passage of about three Weeks the *Robert* arrives at *St John's* in *Newfoundland*, of which Harbour Capt *John Masters* of *Bristol* was then Lord. [1788] 1977 *Peopling of Nfld* 35 Until the mid-18th century, missionary contact with Newfoundland inhabitants was scant and irregular, so that '. . .the custom with respect to marriages there is for the Lord of the Harbour. . .to perform the ceremony in the same way as it is performed in England by clergymen, and that in the Winter when they have no Lord of the Harbour, it is performed by any common man that can read.'

lord² n also **lady, lord and lady bird** *O Sup²* ~ (Nfld: 1770–); *DC* (Nfld: 1771–). Phr *lord and lady*: a pair of harlequin ducks, the male regal in its colour (*Histrionicus histrionicus*).

[1766] 1971 BANKS 139 The People here tell a remarkable Fact if it is a true one of a Kind of duck Cald here Lords & Ladies who they say at times Pursue the Gulls whom they Persecute till they make them Dung which they catch with great dexterity before it reaches the water & immediately Leave off the Chace. [1770] 1792 CARTWRIGHT i, 20 I shot four eider ducks, and seven lords and ladies; the latter being in full moult could not fly, but they were very fat. 1792 ibid *Gloss* i, xii Lord. A water-fowl of the teal kind. 1836 [WIX]² 138 I had a fine view of. . .some of those very beautiful birds, called by the people of Newfoundland 'lords and ladies.' 1870 *Can Naturalist* v, 301 The male of this species, which is called a 'lord' in Newfoundland, is decidedly the handsomest little duck inhabiting those cold regions, and is a most expert diver. 1907 TOWNSEND 330 Harlequin Duck, 'Lord and Lady.' 1951 PETERS & BURLEIGH 111–12 Eastern Harlequin Duck. . .Local name: Lord and Lady. A rather small duck. . . Nests in the interior, along fast flowing streams or on islands in rivers. . . Uncommon winter resident and occasional in summer. 1959 MCATEE 16 ~ Harlequin Duck (Usually in the plural, 'Lords and ladies.' In allusion to the handsome plumage. While these terms refer basically to the sexes, they are customarily used together to indicate the species.) 1967 *Bk of Nfld* iii, 282 Harlequin Duck: Lord and Ladies (in allusion to their beautiful plumage); Old Lord (a fully mature male); and Lady or Jenny (the female or immature). 1977 *Inuit Land Use* 176 Species commonly found nesting and feeding at the head of the coastal bays [include] harlequin ducks (lords and ladies).

lord-fish n also **lord**. Cp *OED* ~ (1836). A fish with a dorsal deformity or hump (P 252–67).

1981 *Evening Telegram* 15 May, p. 6 [Later] I will relate how as a very small boy, I once caught a 'Lord' or humpbacked trout, in Waterford River.

lose v also **loss*** [las, lɒˑs] *EDD* loss v 1 Ir So D Co for sense 1.

1 In form *loss*: to lose

T 222–66 She asked [the wife] how he was and the woman said he was 'quite rough today.' And she sympathised with her, and said she hoped her husband would get better. And the woman said, 'I hope so too. I wouldn't want to loss un 'cause he's so harmless.' P 222–67 Don't loss it.

2 Phr *lose the bottle*: to be obliged to stand a treat for others.

1893 *Trade Review Christmas No* 13 And on that day happened also what was termed 'losing the bottle,' which accident fell to the lot of the man who happened to catch the last fish on the first wetting of the lines. 1937 DEVINE 33 On the first day fishing, in the old time, the member of the crew who caught the third fish, if there were three hands, or the fourth, if there were four, and so on, would have to stand treat in a bottle of rum and would be hailed as having *lost the bottle*.

lose one's spring/summer: see SPRING², SUMMER.

lose one's vote: to have one's candidate defeated in an election (P 108–75).

losing vbl n Phr *losing of the moon*: the period of waning.

C 75–135 It is not good to cut timber on the losing of the moon because it will sink because the timber will shrink. 1979 TIZZARD 55 The questions were sent in at a time when my father killed a pig at the losing of the moon and when mother would cook it.

loss* v See LOSE.

lovyer n also **loveyer, lovier** ['lʌvjəɹ, 'lɒvjəɹ] *OED* lovyer obs form of lover; *EDD* lovier Do So Nfld; *ADD* lover (1815–). Cp LIVYER. Lover, true-love, esp in ballad usage.

[c1894] PANL P4/14, p. 198 We see at a glance the meaning of *livier* or *lovier*. 1896 *J A Folklore* ix, 23 For lover they say *loveyer*, as is done in some English provincial dialects. [1920] 1933 GREENLEAF (ed) 115 "Thomas and Nancy": Come all you young maids that goes courting, / That never object any grief, / Be like Nancy, that I'yal true lovyer, / That died with her Thomas so brave. [1929] 1933 ibid 332 "Young Monroe": Down in the mill-shade all around, true lovyers now lie low,— / One is Miss Clara Dennis, and her true-love, young Monroe. T 156–65 There's one thing I don't remember an' that is "The Lost Lovyer." T 222–66 Following the dance, or even during it, as everywhere, young people would get together an' go off in couples, and their elders would say to them, to the girl, 'I bound now you an your lovyer's goin' courtin'.'

low a Cp *EDD* ~ II (1) ~ backed car 'car without any back' Ir, JOYCE 288–9; II (13) for low-lifed [lou 'lɐifɨd].

Comb **low-back(ed) car**: St John's feature name.

1904 MURPHY 52 The 'Low-Back-Car'. . .was a high mound of earth situated on Duckworth Street; a part of it was taken down after the great fire of July, '92, and a more imposing structure substituted. Ibid 52 "The Low-Back Car": Fond recollections thy name brings unto me, / I sigh for my home near the old Low-Back-Car.

low-bush hurt: variety of blueberry (*Vaccinium* spp) (1898 *J A Folklore* xi, 274); HURT.

low-lifed: of unpleasant, mean habits or disposition.

T 175/6–65 But there was always a kind of low-lifed fellow, you know, an' everyone more or less playin' tricks on he.

low-minded: feeble-minded; depressed.

T 436–65 But he was all the time foolin' around 'cause he wasn't all there. No, sir, sometimes he was kind o' low-minded.

low pear: purple chokeberry (*Aronia prunifolia*) (1956 ROULEAU 33).

lowers n pl ['louəɹz]. The lower sails of a schooner (1964 *Can Journ Ling* x, 39).

loyal n Cp *OED* ~ 4 b 'of goods: of the legal standard of quality' obs (1690 quot). Of high quality, splendid.

1924 ENGLAND 150 In four days they had new masts in her an' topped her again. 'Twas all a loyal fitout.

lucky a Cp *EDD* ~ 1 (11) ~ stone. Comb **lucky-rock**: stone with a hole worn through it by a natural force.

C 67–5 I came across about 10 or 12 on a string. I asked why she had the rocks on a string. She answered, 'Don't take them out of it; they're lucky rocks. As long as they are in there, the house will not burn.' C 68–17 In my community, a rock that has a hole worn through it by the forces of nature is 'a lucky rock.'

lum n [lʌm]. Cp *OED* loom sb¹ 5; *EDD* lum sb⁵ 1 (1855). The handle or shaft of an oar (1925 *Dial Notes* v, 336).

1937 DEVINE 33 The *lum* (loom) of an oar is the end held in rowing. The old ones used to have a thole pin stuck in them for the inside hand to grasp. T 169/70–65 Only the lums of the paddles was blubbered [with oil].

lumber n *DC* lumber-woods (1896–).

Comb **lumber-skiff**: flat, shallow-draught boat used to carry lumber.

C 66–10 they took him off the train at Clarke's Beach and brought him home in a lumber skiff.

lumber-woods, lumbering ~ : forest area for the commercial cutting of timber.

[1930] 1933 GREENLEAF (ed) 329 "Harry Dunn": A boy was killed in the lumbering woods. His body they will send home. T 43/7–64 A shim is used for stoggin' moss in a winter house. They use 'em in the lumber woods. Q 67–73 Come on, Bill, let's (get) in the lumber woods handcatting. 1976 GUY 86. . . cracking and popping in the forest like the sound of a distant lumber-woods operation.

lume n On the west coast of Newfoundland, a lighthouse (1897 *J A Folklore* x, 206).

lump n *OED* ~ sb² 2 (1545–1828), *O Sup²* (1844–) for sense 1; *OED* sb¹ 4 b naut (1857–1872), *EDD* 7 Sh I for sense 2.

1 Lumpfish (*Cyclopterus lumpus*) (P 148–63).

P 171–66 Lumps are black fish, shaped like big round blimps. When they die, they float. . . They are quite often caught in traps with cod fish and brought in the boats. M 70–21 Someone could be 'as ugly as a lump' (a black, stubby fish). 1979 TIZZARD 322 The most stupid fish of all we called the lump. They were given this name because of their short thick body. They were called stupid because they would just rest by the side of the wharf, or rock, or net seemingly for hours without even moving a fin.

2 A heavy, choppy sea; LOP², TUMBLE.

C 75–28 When fishermen talk of heavy seas and high waves, they say there is a 'big lump on.'

3 A heavy, ankle-high rubber boot.

P 167–67 ~s. Pair of thick rubber boots which come as far as the ankles. M 70–15 [During the Depression] I vividly remember children coming to school in September in their bare feet and continuing to do so until late October. At that time they were outfitted with knee-rubbers, both boys and girls, or supplied by the government with ankle-high rubber boots. Those boots were known locally as 'lumps' because of their clumsy-looking appearance. 1975 GUY 132 Lumps [were made] with little eye to the differences in foot size or the shape of the right foot compared to the left. The main virtue of lumps is that they 'stood up.' Which is to say that even the most ambitious and active outport juvenile could not hope to wear out his lumps inside of five years.

lumper n Cp *OED* ~ 1 a 'labourer employed in loading and unloading cargoes' (1785–), *NID* ~ ² 1 b 'one who unloads fish' for sense 1.

1 In the Bank fishery, a helper aboard vessel or ashore (P 245–58); KEDGY.

[1663] 1963 YONGE 58 . . .foreshipman 3 pounds, or half a share and ten shillings, boys, lurgens, [?lumpers Eds.], and such, 20 d., 30 d., or 40 d. M 65–9 ~ Helper or substitute. Used in the days of the Banking Fleet. When a fisherman wished to go home to see his family he would hire someone to work for him washing the fish, which was stored in the hold of the vessel. Q 71–4 ~ His special job is to unload the fish off the boat, in place of one of the crew. He is not employed on the boat himself, strictly an on-the-shore man. Q 71–8 ~ A person employed to throw fish from dories to deck, from deck to crates, etc, while fishing crew were 'mugging up' or otherwise engaged. A sort of helper in a banker as was a 'kedgy.'

2 A heavy, sluggish wave; LUMP.

1934 BARTLETT 143 I had lowered sail and everything was secured, but conditions were so bad that we made practically no headway in the dead lumper, or backwash, and could barely maintain steerage way.

lumpus av ['lʌmpəs] *EDD* ~ esp s w cties. Heavily; hard; all in a heap.

[c1860] C 69–5 [local legend on naming of Lumpus Pond, White Bay, a crossing-point for migrating caribou] One of the hunters put up his gun, took aim, fired and killed the deer. One of his friends said, 'Boy, did he come down lumpus!' P 167–67 I fell down lumpus! 1969 *Trans Dev Assoc* ci, 187 Lumpus (as in 'He fell *lumpus*,' i.e., he fell in a heap).

lun n also **lund** [lɔn, lʌn] *EDD* lown sb¹ 6: lun GROSE w cty, 1790), lunn Ha; cp *OED* lown sb Sc; *DC* ~ Nfld (1933–). A sheltered location; lee.

1896 *J A Folklore* ix, 23 ~ a calm. 1924 ENGLAND 318 ~ the lee of anything. 1933 MERRICK 42 When Harvey gets across, there will be the dog, sitting behind a point or under the trees waiting 'in the lun.' 1937 DEVINE 33 ~ absence of wind; calm. Also a spot sheltered from the wind. Also *lund*. P 147–55 Come over in the lun of the shed. P 148–63 I'm in the lund [behind the house]. T 80/1–64 They went in, they hove up the schooner in the lun of this island. 1965 *Can Nurse* lxi (9), 737 Outside, oxen, huge cumbersome beasts with wicked looking horns, shelter in the [lune] of the building when the wind blows from the north. C 70–12 In the lun of the land, that is to say, if the wind was blowing off from the shore, boats would come home from the fishing grounds keeping close to the land.

lun a also **lund** [lʌn]. See LUN n; cp *OED*, *EDD* lown a Sc. Calm; sheltered.

1931 *Am Sp* vi, 290 'A right lund place,' meaning a quiet, protected place. P 148–61 You'll have it lund [sleeping in the room on that side of the house]. T 70/1–64¹ There's one place in there I 'lows you can place three hundred houses, a lovely, beautiful place, too—lun in the winter, you know. P 12–69 The sea was very lund yesterday.

lun v [lʌn]. See LUN n; cp *OED*, *EDD* lown v Sc (1400–); *DC* ~ v (Labr: 1946). Of the wind, to die down, abate.

[1663] 1963 YONGE 54 [The storm] lasted almost a day, but that night it lunned and continued at east. [1669] ibid 121 The wind lunns this morning, and comes at West, a moderate gale, and fair sunshine. T 70–64¹ There's eight or nine boats there with their graplins out, waiting for the wind to lun; the wind was in a strong breeze then. T 194/5–65 And about nine o'clock the wind lunned.

lunch n *EDD* ~ sb 2 'light repast'; *DAE* 1 c.

1 A snack or light meal taken between any of the three main meals; MUG UP. Also attrib.

[1916] 1972 GORDON 59 I soon had a fire going in the stove and fortunately still had my parcel of lunch which Mrs Chaulk had put up for me. 1937 DEVINE 31 [A levener is] a lunch [taken] around eleven a.m. T 64–64 An' then I went to boil my kettle, get a lunch before I come out. T 84–64 Five miles from land now, an' still no breakfast. An' no nunny bag, never had no grub aboard o' boat, 'cause I was comin' back for my breakfast, you see, an' I never took any lunch. T 394–67 One feller took up a lunch bag forrard, an' th' other feller says, 'There you are,' he said, 'that's the first comin' o' poverty.' P 198–67 We can't wait till lunch time (10:30 a.m. recess in school). 1975 BUTLER 90 For the next two weeks [snaring rabbits in the woods] our routine was breakfast of pancakes and tea, leave the camp by daylight, take along hard bread and soak it in water for lunch, look at our snares and set some more every day, and return to camp. 1979 *Salt Water, Fresh Water* 30 When we'd go on the ice, for our lunch we'd carry some raisins with us, and dry rolled oats, we carried that in a knapsack.

2 A late evening meal.

P 148–63 Will you have a lunch? (11 p.m. meal of tea, cheese, crackers, bread, jam). 1969 *Christmas Mumming in Nfld* 109 A cow or a pig is usually slaughtered so that all visitors can be given a meal or a 'lunch'—a late evening meal—of the highest quality. 1972 MURRAY 215 In winter, there were fewer meals per day than during a busy fishing season. Four meals—breakfast, dinner, tea, and a 'mug-up' or 'lunch' before bedtime—were standard in most homes. 1974 MARIN 4 Finally, before bedtime, the table would be laid for a 'lunch': Depending on the appetite, this could mean almost anything. 1979 TIZZARD 189 The first thing after the parents had gone to bed. . .was to get a lunch. A lunch would be bread and tea and raisin buns or sweet molasses cake.

lund See LUN n, a.

lunger See LONGER.

lungy a ['lʌndʒɩ] *EDD* ~ 'lumberingly awkward.' Clumsy, awkward.

C 70–21 You're so lungie you'd trip up in a pencil mark!

lunny a also **lundy**. See LUN n. Calm, sheltered (P 147–55).

P 269–64 It's more lundy here—out of the wind.

lynx See LINK.

M

machine n Cp *OED* ~ sb 3 'apparatus, appliance, instrument' obs (1650–1741). A device, contrivance or contraption, esp one without a specific name; an object or phenomenon; thingumajig; CHUMMY[1] 2.

1956 *Evening Telegram* 12 Dec, p. 5 He wrestled with the problem of designing a machine that would consistently catch fish while he slept [—the cod-trap]. P 148–60 A [cod] sound is a flat machine which comes off the bone. T 1–63[1] [When] anybody dies [and must be brought home for burial] they put them in a machine—some kind of canvas and put salt around [the corpse]. T 94/5–64 In the summer when [the well-water was low] they'd have a spudgell, a big can on a wooden machine they made. A long stick went right through from side to side and you'd fill up your buckets with

that. T 203–65 There's a mat-hook here somewhere—a little machine like a sewing awl. T 264–66 [Some] people use sleds that they walk behind and use two handles; and some more use them with machines up forrard—they sit in there. T 272–66[2] Some people call [the weather sign] milk vein—it's white, just an opening, and this machine is steady, and wherever that opens that's the way the wind is going to blow. P 260–68 This word *machine* is used when referring to something the name of which temporarily escapes you. P 181–78 [Patient to doctor] Look at the big machine I've got on my hand.

mackerel n Attrib

mackerel-bird, ~ **gull**: caspian tern (*Hydroprogne caspia*) (1870 *Can Naturalist* v, 409).

1951 PETERS & BURLEIGH 246 This large tern does not occur in many parts of our area, but is known as the 'Mackerel Gull' at some points on the southeast coast. P 245–71 Mackerelbird Island is southwest of Isle aux Morts.

mad a, intens Cp *OED* ~ a 7 b 'of storm, wind: wild, violent' (1836–) for sense 1 (a).

1 (a) Of the sea, wind or weather, stormy, rough; (b) of sunken rocks over which the sea breaks, dangerous, threatening; freq in names of coastal features.

[1774] 1971 SEARY 241 Mad Rock. 1862 *Sailing Directions for the Island of Newfoundland* 49 Mad rocks are so called 'from the circumstance that the sea breaks upon them with considerable violence when the wind sends in a swell from eastward.' 1940 *Fortnightly* 653 (147), p. 401 Joel hated Mad Moll. Snaky and slimy with sea-weed hair, she slobbered all day with the water going over her head. 1951 *Nfld & Lab Pilot* i, 213 [At Picarre harbour] a 16-foot patch lies 1½ cables southward of the eastern entrance point, with Mad Moll, a rock which dries 2 feet, midway between them. Crazy Betty, a rock which dries 1½ feet, three-quarters of a cable north-westward of the eastern entrance point, lies on a rocky spit. P 148–64 [The weather] was mad. P 148–65 It's snowing mad. P 113–67 There's a mad sea on.

2 Of fish, mosquitoes, etc, gathering in large numbers; NUMEROUS.

P 68–54 The flies are mad. P 245–55 ~ plentiful (of fish).

3 Very.

T 54/63–64 After he died the dogs got mad hungry, an' they turned to an' they eat him after he died. There was nothing left in the bed only his boots. P 11–79 It's mad rough today.

madeira n *DC* ~ (fish) Nfld (1818–). A grade or 'cull' of dried and salted cod-fish; also attrib. Cp WEST a: ~ INDIA.

[c1720] (1954) INNIS 145 The fish were sold to sack ships in return for bills, or, if they were refuse fish, they were sold in the Madeiras and the West Indies.] [1786] ibid 288 In 1786 prices quoted were: 'Large merchantable' cod, 15 shillings. . .'Small merchantable,' 13

shillings. . .'Madeira'. . .10 to 11 shillings. 1818
CHAPPELL 130 *Madeira fish*: which are nearly as valuable as [Merchantable]. This sort is chiefly exported
to supply the *Spanish* and *Portuguese* markets. 1819
ANSPACH 442 The common distinction, in Newfoundland, of the fish when completely dried, is not according to its size, but according to its degree of perfection,
both in appearance and in quality, into *merchantable*,
Madeira, and *West Indian*. 1866 WILSON 212 Halifax
and the United States are markets for the madeira.
[c1894] PANL P4/14, p. 197 Madeira, a term applied to
the second best class of fish, recalls the name of a market now never heard of, and abandoned long ago. 1909
BROWNE 75 He does not 'cull' the fisherman's 'voyage'
as 'Madeira' and 'damp.' [1929] 1933 GREENLEAF (ed)
304 "The Merchants of Fogo": For fish they'll give half
value, they will sacrifice it sore, / If it's under eleven
inches, for Madeira it will go. 1953 *Nfld Fish Develop
Report* 41 The market for [this] Newfoundland fish [in
Brazil] is found in the northern provinces of Brazil,
where the preference is for well-cured fish of 'Madeira'
quality. 1955 *Nfld Fisheries Board* No 23 ~ Sound
quality fish, hard dried, not up to the standard of Merchantable, but not over-salted, broken, sunburnt,
slimy, sour, dun or otherwise defective. May be slightly
rough in appearance. T 168/70–65 The next grade,
madeira—that'd be touched with salt, showin' the salt
on the face, an' thinner quality.

mag n   also **meg** *EDD* ~ sb² var meg. Stick used
as target in pitching-game; cp MOT.
    1937 DEVINE 33 Meg. The mark aimed at in pitching
quoits. Also mag. T 75/6–64 A meg. . .that was the
name for the stick you pitched [the button] at. M 69–17
The first thing to do was to stick a small piece of wood,
called a 'meg' or 'mag,' in the ground. The earth
around this 'meg' was made moist so that the buttons
would stick when tossed towards it.

maggoty a   Cp *OED* ~ a 1 'full of maggots'
(1727–). Of cod-fish, improperly cured and
infested with the larvae of blow-flies; spoiled,
unsavoury; freq in names of small coves where
fish are landed and offal discarded.
    [1773] 1971 SEARY 241 Maggotty Cove (Lane 1773).
[1810] 1971 ANSPACH 25 ~ When the smallest quantity
of fresh or rain water is suffered to lodge in any part of
the fish. . .or when the splitter has left too many joints
of the bone, so that any quantity of blood has
remained, or where there is too great a quantity
of fish in the water horse. . .the flies will gather about
it, and leave on it fly-blows, which will [soon turn] into
maggots. 1905 DUNCAN 125–6 'Way down on Pigeon
Pond Island, / When daddy comes home from swilin', /
(Maggoty fish hung up in the air, / Fried in maggoty
butter)! 1953 *Nfld & Lab Pilot* ii, 106 [At Hickmans
harbour] Maggotty cove indents the southern shore of
the arm. . . A large stream discharges into this cove.
1955 DOYLE (ed) 30 "I'se the B'y": I don't want your
maggoty fish, / That's no good for winter.

magorey See JOHNNY¹.

mahone soldier n   Cp PARTRIDGE Port Mahon

sailor 'inferior seaman.' In prov comparison,
person well-known for his laziness.
    C 70–26 Lazy as a mahone soldier.

maid n   *OED* sb¹ 1, 3 arch exc dial; *EDD* sb 1, 4
for sense 1.
    1 A woman; a young unmarried girl or daugh-
ter; freq as term of address; MAIDEN.
    1858 [LOWELL] i, 15 I'll carry this bit of a thing to my
maid. 1887 *Evening Telegram Christmas* No 9 [to wife:]
Pray for us, maid; we're in God's hands. . . 'I've
brought a Christmas Box for 'ee, Bets, my maid,' said
her husband. 1907 DUNCAN 150 'Who is this person?
Man or woman?' 'Maid,' said Parson Stump. 1933
GREENLEAF xxv So, too. . .'maid' [is used] for
'girl'—or rather for 'woman,' as I have heard a grandmother addressed as 'maid.' T 80/2–64 If you get caught
up there wi' a maid, 'twas murder! Snowballed an' sodded or whatever time o' the year 'twas! T 194/7–65 An'
the little girl want to know if I was goin' [to the] barracks; a little small maid. C 68–5 It is very common in
[Bonavista] to hear a person say, 'I met Jack Smith's
maid at the store today'; reference is being made either
to his wife or his daughter. 1975 COOK 12 He wor jest
somebody dying and I wor just a slip of a maid.
    2 Attrib, comb **maid racket**: courting; see
RACKET².
    T 141/68–65² An' we'd go down practically every
night on the maid racket.
    maid teacher: unmarried female schoolteach-
er.
    T 169/206–65¹ We had two [teachers]; there was
always a maid teacher in lower part an' a man teacher
in upper part.

maiden n   *OED* ~ sb 1 obs exc dial; *EDD* 3b 3
D for sense 1; cp *OED* B 5 b (a)(b) for sense 2;
for comb in sense 3: *EDD* ~ 13 ~ skate.
    1 Girl; young woman; daughter; MAID.
    [1906] 1976 WINSOR 10 When I arrived in July I
found all the men, excepting of course, the aged or
decrepit, and all the boys as well as many of the maidens, were away on the Labrador. P 245–61 I had eleven
children—four maidens and five b'ys. T 158–65 We'd
all get together and dress up, maidens and boys together. T 169/206–65¹ The boys an' the maidens would get
together an' we would [play] rings. There were three or
four songs we'd sing, about taking a maid or kissing a
maid. And the maiden[s] naturally, they sort of refrain
from the kiss first, but nevertheless they always stood
fire when they come to the test, see. T 449–67 Her
maidens, her girls, daughters will wash all clothes for
her now. 1977 RUSSELL 96 Skipper Phineas had fourteen children and you might be sure he give 'em all
(boys and maidens alike) good solid names straight
from the scriptures.
    2 In designations of trees associated with
beliefs and remedies attributed to their manner
of growth, pruning, or sex: ~ **dog-berry (tree)**;
~ **fir** [see SHE VAR].
    1896 *J A Folklore* ix, 222–3 I'd as lief cut my right
hand off. . .as cut down a maiden dog-berry tree; a
man is sure to die as does it. C 69–23 He called his cure

for eczema maiden-fir. He made it by steeping out fir tree tops. The tree tops had to have seven branches or the maiden-fir wouldn't work. He would boil these tree tops and the substance left was known as maiden-fir.

3 Comb **maidenhair**: see MAIDENHAIR.

maiden ray: skate (*Raja radiata*).

1876 HOWLEY 69 *Rays* (called here *Maiden Ray*) are pretty plentiful. 1976 GUY 109 There is tons more stuff that can be caught from a wharf on a summer day. Tomcods, maidenrays (skates). . .

maiden's tresses: MAIDENHAIR (*Gaultheria hispidula*).

1939 DULEY 26 'There,' she said regretfully. 'I wish I was in the woods. Do you know about the wild roses there, and the scentbottles and the maiden's tresses?'

maiden vein: Milky Way.

1933 GREENLEAF xxv Besides the usual signs of [weather] forecast, they consulted the Milky Way, called 'Maiden Vein' (or Vane or Vain), saying of the fork at the southern end, 'Well, we must see where the Maiden Vein opens tonight, so we'll see where the wind will come from in the marnin'.' C 66–7 The milky way is called either the maiden vein or the milky vein. The wind will blow either in or out of where it forks. 1971 NOSEWORTHY 219 Maiden-vane. A thick band of stars across the sky.

maidenhair n Cp *OED* ~ 1 a [fern] 'formerly much used in medicine' for sense 1; *DC* teaberry for sense 2.

1 (a) Wintergreen, teaberry (*Gaultheria procumbens*); (b) creeping snowberry (*G. hispidula*) (1898 *J A Folklore* xi, 273); also attrib; CAPILLAIRE.

[1766] 1971 BANKS 122 Gatherd in very shady Places the Plant from the Berries of which Syrup of Capillare is made. . .it is Calld here Maidinhair & drank by way of substitute for tea. [1794] 1968 THOMAS 141 The Maidenhair Plant is a humble but insinuating production, creeping through the Moss and just showing its head. 1858 [LOWELL] i, 94 The graceful maidenhair, with its pretty, spicy fruit. . .and others enrich the barrenness. 1866 WILSON 57 A beautiful little trailing-plant, called 'maiden hair,' is found in abundance. It bears a small white fruit, like the egg of an ant. 1909 ROBINSON 103 It was a beautiful little fruit about the size of a large pea, but creamy in colour, like an egg, and very much of the same shape. Like the others, it grew along the ground, and the plant is locally known as the maiden-hair. *Nfld & Lab Pilot* ii, 129 Maiden Hair cove indents the western shore of the bay.

2 Comb **maidenhair tea (berry)**, **magna-tea (berry)***, **maidner tea (berry)**, **manna-tea (berry)***, and prob MOUNTAINEER TEA: see sense 1.

[1794] 1968 THOMAS 140–1 The Berry of the Maidenhair Tea is one of the richest to be met with in this Country. 1861 DE BOILIEU 214–15 I saw one fine shrub, and was told that it was called the 'maiden-hair tea-shrub,' used, when it could be found, as a substitute for our China tea. 1938 MACDERMOTT 242 The capillaire or maidenhair berry; often called Maiden-a-tea, because it is said that from the leaves of this berry

the Micmacs and the early settlers made a tea. T 14/19–64 Did you ever see the maidener tea berries? It's white, the shape of an ant's egg and very little larger. T 43/7–64 They're a good berry, maiden tea berries. 1966 HORWOOD 19 . . .and delicate little maidner tea-berries, greenish-white and hidden securely from prying eyes by glossy leaves tasting faintly of winter-green. 1975 SCOTT 59 This plant has a number of local names: Manna-tea Berry, Magna-tea Berry, and Maidenhair Berry. Capillaire is the name most commonly used in the St John's area. . . The leaves can be picked and used to make tea when they are fresh or dried.

main a *DC* main patch Nfld (1933).

Comb **main patch**: principal concentration of harp and hooded seals on the ice-floes for whelping; PATCH.

1907 *Tribune Christmas No* 16 Funk-Islets, off Bonavista, where the sealing steamers often strike the 'Main Patch' of seals. 1923 CHAFE 7 The 'Main patch' is supposed to be the principal body of seals, which have left the Southern fishing banks first, and have mounted the whelping ice about the 20th of February. [1929] 1979 *Evening Telegram* 10 Mar, p. 19 A message received last night from airman Caldwell at St Anthony reported that he had located the main patch of seals northeast of Fogo. 1972 BROWN 59 For there on the smooth ice ahead was the Main Patch he had so diligently sought for more than a week. They lay in a string of at least half a mile wide, extending for miles to the north-north-west on his starboard bow, and to the south-south-east on his port. The ice was alive with them!

main road: in logging, a road cut through a stand of timber with short side-roads at right angles to it.

T 100/1–64 We had a road going up through it and short roads in, what they call swampin' roads, short roads into the main road. T 43/8–64 The first thing they do was blaze in their main road through the centre of their block. You pull [the logs] out to the edge of the main road, and pile it so the loaders could load it on the double wagon-sleds.

mainland n

1 The provinces of Canada, singly or collectively, other than Newfoundland and Labrador; CANADA, UPALONG. Hence **mainlander**.

1881 *Nineteenth Century* ix, 106 [The French Shore] is inhabited by refugees from other parts of the island, and emigrants from Cape Breton or Prince Edward's Island, and from Nova Scotia and other portions of the mainland. [c1920] 1975 BUTLER 51 Rum from St Pierre, smuggled rum. They were going up to the mainland with it but she got froze in. 1973 WADEL 91 The only alternative open to them, said John, would be to move to the mainland (Canada). 1977 RUSSELL 81 We. . .are nothin' if not democratic and that means givin' every man the right to talk—even a mainlander. . . Yes, he said, he was a mainlander. Growed up among snakes and got to be real fond of 'em. 1980 *Evening Telegram* 1 Mar, p. 4 The government has rejected about 30 applications from individuals on the mainland who are interested in developing farmland on the west coast of the province.

2 To dwellers of the coastal islands, the island of Newfoundland, the coast of Labrador; INSIDE n 2.

1792 *Liverpool MS* July 30 They will go to the Funk Island, which is 15 leagues from the Main Land, and return from it in the thickest weather. [1920] 1976 WINSOR 7 Captain George Hann, and his brothers Peter and Charles, moved from Cape Freels, in 1870, and obtained a grant for eleven acres of land, located at 'the mainland opposite Swain's Island.' P 124–71 These people moved to the mainland in search of work but I have not mentioned where on the mainland they did eventually settle. Of the residents who left prior to 1956, the majority settled at nearby communities around Bonavista Bay. 1977 *Inuit Land Use* 334 On the 'outside,' however, on and around the outer islands as well as on the sea ice, trapping was more of a free-for-all. Similarly, caribou hunting on the mainland was not confined to personal or family areas: anyone went where he thought the hunting would be good.

make v *OED* ~ v¹ 39 obs (1555–1690), *O Sup²* (1856–), *DAE* 1 (1623–1828), *DC* ~ fish (Nfld: 1620–) for sense 1; *O Sup²* v¹ 72 b (1784–), *DC* 1 (1817–) for sense 2; *OED* 72 naut, *EDD* 20 for sense 3(a); for phr in sense 4: *EDD* ~ v¹ II (3)(b) ~ away with, *OED* 88 b ~ in, *EDD* (15) ~ out 'extinguish' D.

1 To preserve cod-fish by drying and the application of salt; DRY¹ v.

[(1578) 1935 *Richard Hakluyt* 124 [Parkhurst's letter:] We shold. . .kepe people fysshynge halfe the yere and busyed in the makynge thereof.] 1620 WHITBOURNE 24 And for the want of such fit houses, some mens voyages (to my knowledge) have been greatly overthrowne; and then a meane place to make fish on, will be made more commodious then the best place is now, that men so dangerously and desperately runne for every yeere. [1714] 1976 HEAD 59 Fish made by Fishing Ships (qtls.) 3300. . . Fish made by Inhabitants 2800. 1842 JUKES i, 229–30 Lastly, many families in some of the outports, instead of '*making*,' or curing, their own fish, bring it as it is caught to the merchant's stores and stages. [1906] GRENFELL 53 Now, Tom was always careful to 'make' his fish well. He knew that it meant a deal of difference to the price that it was worth if it was white and hard, carefully cleaned and dried. 1936 SMITH 31 Anyway we didn't have any fish to make, only about one spreading for our crew. T 43–64 It wasn't a big problem to get the fish made. You put out so much to one person, so much to another an' usually women used to make the fish. 1966 SCAMMELL 30 We were clothed, fed and sent to school without our hardly becoming aware of any medium of exchange except the cod that father caught and that we helped to 'make.' 1977 *Inuit Land Use* 132 The fish had then to be split, cleaned, salted, and stored until the end of August or early September, when the fish were 'made'—that is, washed and spread out on the rocks until they were thoroughly dried by the sun and wind.

2 Of ice, to form.

[1774] 1792 CARTWRIGHT ii, 39 Lolly beginning to make. [1896] SWANSBOROUGH 31 "The Seal Fishery": (I mean the bergs,) 'tis on the coast / Bays and straits, the field ice makes most. 1916 GRENFELL 98 Day after day, and almost night after night, till the slob ice made, and the 'sish' actually cut holes through the skin covering of his borrowed kayak, he unflaggingly maintained his quest. 1933 GREENE 28 The varying local severity of each winter's frost also greatly affects its composition, especially as regards the extent of the Field-ice that 'makes' on the waters approaching to the latitudes of Northern Labrador. M 68–10 We'll leave out Brown's Cove and won't go there a-tall / The slob it is making and it's late in the fall. 1977 *Inuit Land Use* 144 [Slob ice] starts moving in November, making more all the time. Last part of October and first part of November, it starts making.

3 (a) Of the tide, to rise; (b) of the sea, to become rough, heave with a big swell.

[1785] 1792 CARTWRIGHT iii, 93 But the tide did not make high enough to get [the ship] upon the proper place. [1929] 1933 GREENLEAF (ed) 288 "The *Nordfeld* and the *Raleigh*": It must have been a dreadful day, for the seas were making high. 1930 BARNES 272 We're shortening sail all the time, the breeze is increasing and the sea is making. 1936 SMITH 59 [We] crawled into the cliff to see if there was any sea making. The slob was rising and falling by the cliff about a foot or eighteen inches, so we decided to get our clothes and a bit of food and get on shore while we could. 1975 GUY 13 The tide made higher—as was the saying—and the tide made lower a couple of times each twenty-four hours within half a gunshot of his house.

4 Phr *make a blank*: see BLANK n; ~ *away with*: to discard, stop using; - *battle*: to attack; ~ *bawn*: to fill crevices in a rocky shore for spreading cod-fish to dry [cp BAWN]; ~ *berth*: to heave to in preparation for throwing out fishing lines [cp BERTH]; ~ *in*: (a) to approach land from the sea, (b) to attack; ~ *out*: (a) to extinguish a light, (b) of oil, to render or form from cod livers; ~ *pancakes*: to skim rocks over the water [cp PANCAKE]; ~ *the spring/summer/fall voyage*, etc: to carry out or prosecute a fishing enterprise; ~ *strange*: see STRANGE.

T 148–65 The customs got after 'em an' made 'em make away wi' that old stuff. P 108–76 We made away with the lamps as soon as we got the [electric] lights in. T 54/9–64 'You can have the heelstick,' I said, 'but I'm holdin' on to this. Now, you make battle with the stick and you get that iron in the head.' C 70–10 My grandfather has often made bawn down in Labrador. The fishermen would fill in the crevices with beach rocks and this was called making bawn. 1966 SCAMMELL 91 Most of them were too far away to tell accurately how the fishing was, but as far as we could make out none of them was shifting position or 'making berths,' and that was a pretty good sign that they were yanking cod aboard. 1932 BARBOUR 38 If we ever 'made in' (approached) on land we would want canvas and ropes to get us off again unless we struck some inhabited harbour. T 70/1–64¹ They said she passed there. Well, if she did, she was lost—shoal ground. Made in there—thick, see. T 54/60–64 The two pigs made into

me, and I scuffled out o' that and got out of it. 1896 *J A
Folklore* ix, 21 Newfoundlanders also express the [idea
of extinguishing] by the phrase, *'make out* the light.'
1956 CUTTING 150 The livers putrified in the heat of
the sun and as the oil begins to make its appearance at
the top of the casks, or 'makes out,' it is dipped out
into water barrels and stowed away in the hold,' in barrels, and more livers added. P 127–74 Some calls it
making pan cakes (i.e. skipping flat rocks over the surface of the water). [1766] 1971 BANKS 146 The French
not being allowd to Leave a man here in the winter or
to benefit themselves in any Degree by the Produce of
the Countrey Except merely the Codfish notwithstanding which we have reason to beleive that some of the
French this Year (who in general made very bad fishing
Voyages) made up their freights by Carrying home timber. 1937 DEVINE 33 Make one's spring (summer, fall,
or winter). Used in the opposite sense of *lose one's
spring* etc. 1960 FUDGE 16 By offering wages we picked
up a crew [and] made up the summer in three trips.
1975 BUTLER 41 I fished from home in the fall months
and made a very bad voyage.

making vbl n See MAKE v 1, 2.
  1 The process of preserving fish by salting and
drying; CURING.
  [1578] 1935 *Richard Hakluyt* 124 [Parkhurst's letter:]
We shold. . .kepe people fysshynge halfe the yere and
busyed in the makynge thereof. [1683] 1976 HEAD 35
Though there be Harbours and conveniences on shoare
for the making of Fish there is not fishing ground or
can constantly be fish enough for so many Boates as
they have kept. [1810] 1971 ANSPACH 22 The same
process is continued until the end of about six weeks,
when, if the weather has been favourable (at certain
times damp weather is useful in *making* of fish) the fish
is perfectly dry, and [ready] for market. 1873 CARROLL
44 Notwithstanding which, the top fish are often light
salted, and the bottom fish in the puncheon, are salt-
burned and often must be watered before being exposed to the sun for making.
  2 The formation of ice during winter.
  1924 ENGLAND 20 As autumn begins to nip the seas
to ice in Baffin Bay, the gigantic herds heave into
motion. The 'making' of the young ice is their dispossess notice, evicting them from their summer home.

maldow See MOLDOW.

mamateek n *Beothuk Vocabularies*, p. 83 mammateek (1818); *DC* mamateek Nfld (1832–).
Beothuk winter wigwam.
  [1829] 1915 HOWLEY 190 Here are the remains of
one of their villages, where the vestiges of eight or ten
winter *mamateeks* or wigwams, each intended to contain from six to eighteen or twenty people, are distinctly seen close together. [1829] ibid 211 The sides of
these mamateeks were covered with arms, that is,
bows, arrows, clubs, stone hatchets, arrow heads, &c.
and all these were arranged in the neatest manner.
[1829] ibid 306 Mammatik *house*,
mammateek. . .*winter wigwam*.

mampus* n   also **mompus*** *EDD* ~ 'crowd' Do.
A crowd; a numerous group (P 37).
  P 167–66 The fish were mompus today.

man n   *EDD* ~ sb¹ 2 (11) ~ above; JOYCE 291;
appears as second element in AMERICAN ~ ,
NAKED ~ .
  Comb **man above**: God (1924 ENGLAND 318).
  T 50–64 I said, ''Twas never nothing got out of Sunday's work yet. It may be all right for this one and that
one, but 'tis not all right for the man above.' T 448–67
Who put him there? The man above, I suppose.
  man-and-woman: yellow mountain saxifrage
(*Saxifraga aizoides*) (1978 ROULEAU 90).
  man-cat: small sled used in winter for transporting wood and hauled by a man;
CAT(AMARAN) (Q 67–5).

maneen n   [mæ'niːn] *NID* ~ Ir; JOYCE 90 ~ 'a
boy who apes to be a man'; JAMES JOYCE *Portrait
of the Artist* (1916), Ch 2. Bold youth; adolescent
boy trying to act the part of a man; BEDLAMER 2.
  [1894–1929] 1960 BURKE (ed White) 34 "The Terra
Nova Regatta": And it's many a cute maneen / Got
well oiled off on the green, / The morning of the Terra
Nova Races. 1964 *Evening Telegram* 14 Feb, p. 5 It is
reasonable to think that most of the depredations are
carried out by maneens. 1968 DILLON 147 Go way you
little maneen; you'd think you were an old man the
way you're talkin'.

mang v, n   *EDD* ~ v¹ 1, sb¹ 3.
  1 To mix together, esp food; to mangle or
crush.
  P 245–56 Mang it all together! P 269–63 A manged
finger—cut or bruised with a hammer. P 130–67 She's
mangin' up something out there [in the kitchen].
  2 A mixture.
  P 148–65 That's a real mang!

mantel n   Cp *OED* ~ tree (1482–1811); *EDD*
mantel sb 1 (2) ~ tree. Attrib **mantel beam**:
heavy wooden beam, or sometimes two, supporting the upper masonry into which the opening of
a second-floor fire-place or stove leads.
  T 187/8–65 The mantel beam they used to call it—a
big beam across the house where the chimley hole'd be
to.

manus v   *21 Victoria*, c. 9, 78 (1858) 'Any sealer
who, by refusing to work. . .shall wilfully compel
any master of a sealing vessel. . .to give up the
voyage. . .' Of one or more sealers, to refuse to
work in order to force the captain to return to
port; MUTINIZE. Hence **manus** n (1937 quot).
  1862 *Standard* [Harbor Grace] 30 Apr, p. 2 [They
were] disobeying orders and obliging him to bring his
vessel into port, or in other words 'Manusing.' This is
what may be called a coined word to express the act of
mutiny of sealing crews who refuse [to continue a
voyage]. Ibid 7 May, p. 2 What! manus and ruin a person who has fed you. . . 1891 *Holly Branch* 38 [John

Halley] was before the time of *Manus*, or the Strong Hand—before the time:—'When the father of Manus, by name Tom Keough, / Led the crew of the brig against Skipper John Snow.' 1902 *Nfld Qtly* Mar, p. 9 The most reliable authorities in the old days place its origin to a row between some Irish youngsters, led by one Mickey McManus and the captain of a pink-stern schooner of about one hundred years ago. 1916 MURPHY 44 'Manusing' was a thing which was a very serious performance in the days of the sailing vessels. . .it was becoming a continual practice among the sealers. Men shipped from the 1st or 15th of March till the 20th of May. If there were no seals seen by them after the 10th or 15th of April they 'struck' or 'manused.' They refused to obey the captain's orders and all hands would go below, the ship would be then 'headed' for home. [c1897] 1927 DOYLE (ed) 72 "The Landfall of Cabot": In a schooner called the *Blinker*, / That's the spring the crew turned manus / They said Cabot was a jinker. 1924 ENGLAND 246 Night brought news of the final scene in the crippled *Diana's* career, a message that her crew had 'manused' in good earnest, had abandoned her in a sinking condition, and burned her with all her thousands of sculps still aboard. 1937 DEVINE 33 ~ To mutiny on board a vessel; also used as a noun. A *manus* may be for better grub or to compel the skipper to bear up for home.

marconi n [= G M Marconi (1874–1937), inventor of a system of wireless telegraphy successfully demonstrated in trans-Atlantic communication at Signal Hill, St John's, 12 Dec 1901]. *OED* ~ 'used attrib' (1897–). Used familiarly for a wireless set, the operator, or the message; attrib in designations of various installations connected with wireless telegraphy.
1909 BROWNE 137 [account of destructive gale of 1867] We had no Marconi conveniences in these days; and we depended on passing schooners for means of transportation. 1917 *Christmas Bells* 4 The Marconi poles at the different harbors [on the Labrador], where the stations are placed, have become the recognized marks for the fishermen, and they deprecate the case of a station being dismantled and changed. 1924 ENGLAND 39–40 'If a man die,' the carpenter informed me, 'us builds un a coffin out o' pound boards, an' salt un down [ice him], an' putt un [in] de Marconi house or the fo'c's'le 'eed.' 1929 *National Geog* July, p. 123 The chief engineer, 'Marconi' (radio man), second hand, barrelman, and doctor dine with the captain. 1930 BARNES 434 I have just received a marconi that there is a fellow about forty miles off here trying to sink a steamer. 1941 WITHINGTON 175 I was called down to Forteau and to the lighthouse at L'Anse Amour, which served the double purpose of beacon and wireless station. From it the Marconi messages went out to the North. 1977 *Them Days* ii (3), p. 24 Brazil was there keepin' Marconi and he was the Justice of the Peace. He wouldn't send no messages about a man with no grub.

mare n Comb **mare-browed**: of a man whose eyebrows meet in a continuous line of hair; beetle-browed.

1895 *J A Folklore* viii, 285 Above all, a mare-browed man, one whose eyebrows meet and extend continuously across his forehead, is unlucky and is supposed to have the power of casting a spell upon a person. Hence he is always dreaded in the community, and believes as firmly as his neighbours in his power to cast a spell or cause ill luck.

mar falten* See VALENTINE.

marish See MARSH.

mark n Cp *OED* ~ sb[1] 9 for sense 1, 10 for sense 2, 18 for sense 3.
  1 One of two (or more) land features or objects lined up by a fisherman in order to locate the position of a fishing ground; BREAST MARK (P 113–79).
  [1837 BLUNT 20 Keep this mark on, until you are half way over to the Neddick.] 1966 FARIS 35 'Spots of ground' are found by a system of triangulation with shore 'marks.' 1979 TIZZARD 329 We were up quite early and steamed down the main tickle so that we were on Scrub by the time it was light enough to see the marks: low land in Paradise opened in Burnt Island Tickle and a ridge of high land in Little Harbour Bight opened by the Gunnin' Head. We caught two barrels of fish that day.
  2 A sign, portent.
  T 31–64 Soon as we see the first tickleace or a [steerin] (a fish-bird), first little bird come yer in the spring (you would see 'em round the rocks), that'd be our mark. Time to get away now! Time to go on [fishing].
  3 Phr *God bless the mark*: see GOD.
  4 Comb **mark(er) buoy**: float to fix the location of stationary fishing-gear, a channel, etc (P 148–61); SPOT BUOY.

marked ppl Comb **marked ground**: fishing ground located by observing certain landmarks from the sea (P 148–65).

marl* v To stroll, meander.
  P 37 ~ to walk around aimlessly. P 104–58 I thought I'd marl along to see you. P 71–64 He's always marreling down the road somewhere. C 69–17 I had to marl down here [to school] this marnin' and now I got to traipse back.

marling vbl n Cp *OED* ~ vbl sb[2] naut. Comb **marling machine**: device used to fasten or hitch marline or small line tightly around a spar, boom, etc; cp MACHINE.
  P 245–71 ~ A wooden handle with holes bored at intervals, and with metal angles at the top. A spool of line with a rod running through the centre was placed between the metal arms, turning on the rod which was inserted in two holes. The line was then drawn through a hole in the handle, and used in repairing, for example, a broken spar.

marry v Phr *marry too far*: to wed (a girl) from a distant community.

1969 *Christmas Mumming in Nfld* 138 Men formerly admonished their sons, 'You don't want to marry too far; you can't trust them,' that is, do not marry a girl from too far away, too much of a stranger.

marsh n also **marish, mash, mesh, mish** [mɪʃ, mæʃ, mæːɪʃ, maːɪʃ]. Cp *OED* ~ 1 'tract of low-lying land. . .more or less watery throughout the year'; *EDD* sb¹: mash esp IW So D, meesh Sr, mesh esp Ha D; 3 'name given locally to particular marshes,' 4 'low-lying land liable to be flooded; grass lands' for sense 1; for comb in sense 2: *NID* marshberry 'European cranberry.'

1 Bog or marshland, freq a specific named area of wet ground; expanse of land producing grass, often suitable for grazing: BOG MEADOW; stretch of wasteland supporting low shrubs, wild berries, mosses and game: BARRENS, SAVANNA.

[1620] 1887 MASON 156 . . .the marish and Boggie groundes. 1843 JUKES 20 Embosomed in the woods, and covering the valleys and lower lands, are found open tracts, which are called 'marshes.' These marshes are not necessarily low, or even level land, but are frequently at a considerable height above the sea, and have often an undulated surface. They are open tracts, covered with moss to a depth sometimes of several feet. 1869 MCCREA 256 A miserable walk through driving mist, guns under arm, and head to ground, brought us to the edge of the 'yellow mash,' a great inland bog covered with a short jaundiced grass. [1886] LLOYD 11 The marshes, or 'meshes' of the inhabitants, abound. 1895 DAVIS 197 Scattered deer in sight all day. 'Deer on the ma'sh' causes no excitement now; three weeks ago things were different. [1900 OLIVER & BURKE] 59 "Toy Duett": The swinging boats in Bob Cole's mash, / Molly.—Of course I know the sort you mean, / Them swinging boats I'se often seen. 1912 ROGERS 190 A bright yellow grass showed where the marshes, locally called 'mishes,' which we had to cross, lay. 1933 GREENE 186 So the woodland talk went on with its tales of deer, and of 'pa'tridge,' and of snipe-shooting in the 'ma'shes.' T 158–65 There's two mishes down there an' my wife picked half a gallon [of berries] off o' one. T 436–65 [We] cut some wood in 'cross the mish, an' drag it out with a slide. P 118–67 I found the cow down on the mash. P 207–67 They were picking bake-apples on the mish. 1975 RUSSELL 70 'And what,' said Grampa, 'did you call it before they had dictionaries? Do you think' said Grampa, 'that generations of people lived for thousands of years alongside a mish, and even tumblin' into the mish, and pickin' berries off the mish, and then had to wait until two or three hundred years ago for some fellow to write a dictionary to tell 'em what to call it?'

2 Comb **marsh berry**: small cranberry (*Vaccinium oxycoccos*) (1956 ROULEAU 34).

[1822] 1856 CORMACK 13 The prevalent plants are Indian [cup]. . .marsh berry. . .bog apple. 1894 MOTT 155 [He] was the first to commence the preserving of native fruits, notably capillaire, squash, marsh, and glowberries. 1960 *Nfld Qtly* Summer, p. 17 Cranber-

ries, or what we Newfoundlanders called Marshberries, were here in plenty. 1964 *Can Journ Ling* x, 43 Marsh berries. T 169/206–65¹ There were plenty o' berries all around us. We eat partridge berries, an' mish berries. 1966 SCAMMELL 32 He even shook his head at bake-apple jam, squashberry jelly and 'meshberries.' He had to have the hard cash.

marsh birch: white birch (*Betula papyrifera*).

T 296/7–66 Right at the lower end of the cemetery where the road was, with the golewitty and the mish birch—a few trees was there.

marsh blackbird: Newfoundland rusty black-bird (*Euphagus carolinus nigrans*) (1959 MCATEE 60).

marsh lily: (a) leafy white orchid (*Platanthera dilatata*) (1898 *J A Folklore* xi, 280); (b) Canadian burnet (*Sanguisorba canadensis*) (1956 ROULEAU 34).

marsh moss: sphagnum moss.

1916 *Daily News* 10 Oct, p. 5 Sphagnum moss under various local names, one of which was 'marsh moss,' has been used in Newfoundland as a dressing for wounds and sores, especially old running sores that are difficult to heal.

marsh peat: thick underlay of decomposed mosses found in marshes.

[1822] 1856 CORMACK 12 The marshes consist of what is termed marsh peat, formed chiefly of the mosses, sphagnum [capillifolium].

marsh tea: an infusion of the bruised leaves of the 'Labrador tea' plant (*Ledum* spp), used as a substitute for tea.

1872 SCHELE DE VERE 396 Even distant Labrador is called upon to aid in furnishing a variety of the favorite beverage; at least in the Northwest they have a tea called *Mash*-tea, and another called *Labrador*-tea, made from two plants. . .the leaves of which possess moderate narcotic qualitites, and are said to furnish a pleasant infusion.

mash See MARSH.

master n Cp *DAE* ~ 1 'one who has the oversight or direction of others' for sense 1; for comb in sense 2: *OED* ~ builder 3 naut (1799).

1 Man in charge of a fishing crew and the operation of catching and processing the fish; freq in phr *master of the fishery,* ~ *(of) voyage*; BOAT MASTER, SKIPPER n 1.

[1663] 1963 YONGE 57 The boat's master he rows at the stern. . .and. . .steers the boat. The boats' masters, generally, are able men. [1771] 1792 CARTWRIGHT i, 160 Having sent the skiff home with my baggage, Macgraith, our master of voyage, and I, walked over the hills and met the boat at Bare Point. [1793] 1954 INNIS 315 [Some] hire their own servants, and plan out their own voyages, independent of the merchant (except being supplied by him) which is not the case in many parts where master and crew are in fact servants to the merchant. 1832 MCGREGOR i, 228 The splitter is next in rank to the foreman of the fishing-rooms, who is called master-voyage, and under him, receives most wages; the next in precedence and wages is the salter.

1861 DE BOILIEU 38 One or more of the masters in port generally accompanied the party,—if not to shoot, to cook for the rest. [1887] 1897 *Nfld Law Reports* 239 Three men (sharemen) being in custody on the magistrate's commitment for larceny in forcibly taking fish which they claimed to be their share of the voyage, and the Crown officer considering it inexpedient to prosecute them, as it appeared the master-voyage (as he said from fear) had weighed out the fish to them, and the value of the fish taken was not very great. 1902 *Christmas Bells* 19 The only occupants then of the servants quarters were the chiefs of the room, that is to say, the 'master-of-voyage,' cooper, splitter, salter, gardener, and cook. 1953 *Nfld Fish Develop Report* 13 Originally, the industry seems to have been well organized for its period, fishing crews being divided into separate groups: one specializing in operations on the fishing grounds and the other in work ashore, i.e., dressing, curing and storing the catch—all under the direction of a 'master of the fisheries.'

2 Comb **master builder**: man experienced and skilled in building boats and vessels.

T 66/7–64 First thing they'd have to get the timber—[send men] in the woods. Then you have to get a master builder.

master (of) watch: man placed in charge of one of the groups aboard a sealing vessel organized to hunt seals on the ice-floes; cp WATCH.

1842 JUKES i, 259 The crew consisted of thirty-six men, who were divided into three watches, each under an appointed master of watch, specifically engaged under that designation, and receiving something more than the rest of the crew. 1868 WHITE *MS Journal* 7 Apr At 6 p.m. . . .a fatal accident occurs to the master of watch Mr Alexander Hudson which fell from Ships rail into a boat and so damaged himself that he expired 12 hours after the fall. 1907 *Nfld Qtly* Dec, p. 12 "The Master-Watch": The master-watch of the fearless heart, / Who shall tread the 'pans' no more. 1924 ENGLAND 42 Master watches, usually four, are petty officers in charge of 'goes,' or gangs, for work both aboard ship and on the ice. 1944 LAWTON & DEVINE 74 When quite a young man he was made a 'Master of Watch,' at the Ice, in which capacity he sailed for many years with some of the leading Captains. 1979 *Salt Water, Fresh Water* 53 Say I was appointed as a master watch, I would have thirty or forty men under me, and another master watch would have thirty or forty men, and we would have different directions to go to kill the seals, and we would have to look after the men. If the weather got bad we would have to know when to go aboard that ship. The captain would give us orders what to do.

master a *EDD* ~ adj 16; *ADD* 2. Large; remarkable.

1912 CABOT 192 The sea trout are holding out, also the fresh water trout that now and then come with them; these are known as 'hard head' trout here. Whitefish are coming in too, of about two pounds; are found in all the neighbouring lakes. They are not quite up to the southern-slope ones, but sometimes they get large ones, the 'master fish,' which are better. T 88–64 They had lobster cages out, an' one morning they got a master lobster. Oh he was that large. T 90–64 You'd ply it out, an' slide down your nice piece o' rush on each side an' you had a master job done.

mat n Hooked rug; also attrib in names of implements and materials used in making the rugs.

T 43/7–64 'Twas hooked with rags, condemned rags, and they had a proper mat hook. Some o' them could go as fast as the wind. T 70–64[2] We done it with a mat-hooker, we used to call it, an' nice coloured rags. T 74–64 [At Christmas] they used to have what they call fools, dressed out, an' mat rags an' everything sewed onto their clothes. M 68–10 [She] hooked her own mats. I can still see in my mind, the wooden mat frame as it stood in one corner of the kitchen with a heap of old rags of assorted colours and the mat hook lying on top. My father made the frames himself, and to them he stretched and tied the brin—material from an empty oat sack or potato bag. 1975 POCIUS 41 Of all the textile crafts practised in Newfoundland, the most creative was the making of hooked rugs, or 'mats.' Mat hooking was practised in almost every household.

mathers n pl Type of bilberry; MAZZARD (*Vaccinium ovalifolium*) (1950 *Gray's Botany* 1132: Nfld).

matting vbl n

Comb **matting needle**: implement for making hooked rugs; MAT n: *mat hook* (T 1–63[1]).

matting party: gathering of women engaged in hooking rugs.

1944 LAWTON & DEVINE 23 Prospective weddings [were] a delightful theme for the women and girls at the quilting and matting parties.

mauzy a also **maus(e)y, mawzy** ['mɑːzɪ, 'mɒːzɪ]. Cp *EDD* mosey adj[1] 3 'damp and warm, muggy, close; foggy.' Of the weather, damp, foggy, misty or close, sometimes with very light rain or condensation on objects and a cool, gentle wind off the sea; cp CAPLIN (SCULL) WEATHER.

1897 *J A Folklore* x, 207 Mausey day, one dull and heavy, with no wind and thick mist. 1937 DEVINE 33 A *mausey* day is a cloudy, foggy day with no wind and a little rain at times. 1957 *Daily News* 16 Oct, p. 4 Old-time seal hunters. . .expressed the opinion that the long, hard winter, the heavy ice and the 'mauzy' weather of early March were just right for a bumper season. P 105–63 It's a mauzy old day, sir. 1968 KEATING 13–14 'Breeze comin' from duh suddard,' the skipper said. 'Always blows up mauzy weather.' And the fog did indeed roll over the deep as the warm south wind hit the chill air of the bank. 1969 HORWOOD 166 The Caplin Scull is not just a phenomenon of nature, but also a period of the year, and even a special kind of weather—'mausy' weather, with high humidity, frequent fogs or drizzles, easterly winds.

mawk n *EDD* ~ sb[1] 1 'maggot,' 3 (4) silly as a mawk. A silly, foolish fellow (P 94–56).

P 218–68 Go on, you foolish mawk.

maw-mouth n Cp *DAE* ~ 'fish with large mouth' (1840–); *Kilkenny Lexicon* 'a mouth wide open'; [person with open mouth]. A braggart; a loud, talkative fellow (P 189–65).

1975 GUY 157 I was fit to be tied when this maw-mouth is bragging about all the places he has been into.

may n See K DANAHER *The Year in Ireland* (1972) 88–95 ~ bush; *EDD* ~ sb¹ 1 (36) ~ water 'May-dew' D.

Comb **mayflower**: name of several plants which flower in May; cuckoo flower (*Cardamine pratensis*); ground laurel (*Epigaea repens*); alpine azalea (*Loiseleuria procumbens*); saxifrage (*Saxifraga oppositifolia*); violet (*Viola pallens*) (1956 ROULEAU 34).

[1886] LLOYD 101 In May, a modest little pink flower may be seen peeping timidly above the ground in all directions. It resembles the primrose in form, differing only in size and colour. It is known by the inhabitants as the May flower.

may tree, ~ **pole**: tree with branches removed, decorated and placed near entrance to a property in May.

C 64–4 I noticed a long sapling which had been stripped of all its boughs except for a plume on top, standing upright to the front of the gate-post. He explained that this was his May pole which he put there the first of May for luck. C 70–13 In Paradise about thirty years ago it was a frequent practice to cut a tree and prop it up on the gate post near their homes in May. It was called a May Tree and it was decorated by ribbons and bits of paper. It was supposed to bring good luck for planting.

may water: May snow, melted and used for medicinal purposes.

C 71–9 Snow from the first snowfall in May would be collected because it was supposed to have healing powers. It would be used to cure sore eyes. It was called May water.

maze v *OED* ~ sb 3 obs (1430–1819); *EDD* ~ v, sb, adj; 6 (2) ~ headed So D.

1 To confuse, bewilder.

1897 *J A Folklore* x, 207 ~ as a verb, transitive, to bewilder, and as intransitive, to be bewildered, to wander in mind. 1937 DEVINE 63 As foolish as a mazed caplin. M 71–114 She often told us to stop rompsin' and roarin'. She would tell us, 'You got me head mazed.'

2 Comb **maze-headed**: confused.

P 148–64 Turn off that radio. I get maze headed.
P 155–64 He's maze 'ided this marnin'.

mazzard n (a) Bilberry (*Vaccinium ovalifolium*) (1898 *N S Inst Sci* ix, 384); (b) choke cherry (*Prunus virginiana*) (1895 ibid ix, 89).

meadow n Comb **meadow-sweet**: Canadian burnet (*Sanguisorba canadensis*) (1956 ROULEAU 34).

medicine n Cp *EDD* ~ sb 1 So. Medicinal preparation in liquid form.

P 136–68 He handed me a prescription and I said, 'What is it for? Pills or medicine?' He started to laugh and said 'You're rather old-fashioned, aren't you? That's what the old people used to say—anything liquid was medicine, pills were just pills.'

medium a In various grades or 'culls' of dried and salted cod: fish of a certain specified size between 'large' and 'small,' freq with designation of quality or cure.

1937 *Seafisheries of Nfld* 47 Medium Salted Dry Fish. 1953 *Nfld Fish Develop Report* 81 The average price per quintal obtained by fishermen for their 1950 production of shore-cure fish ranged from $10.55 for large and medium 'Merchantable' grade down to $4.80 for small 'West India.' 1955 *Nfld Fisheries Board* No 39 Medium fish. 18 in to 22 in. T 202/5–65 Now if you could get number one—merchantable fish, the large, would be the best price, certainly. Medium ['d] be the next.

meg See MAG.

memory n

1 Embroidered cloth bearing name of deceased relative, displayed on wall as a memorial.

P 108–72 Memories [were] usually done in cross-stitch. 1972 NEMEC 212 Southern Avalon informants occasionally employ 'memory' to mean an embroidered wall-hanging upon which is inscribed the vital statistics of deceased kin.

2 Comb **memory card**: printed card requesting prayers for the deceased (C 71–26).

merchant n also **marchant**.

1 An entrepreneur engaged in the Newfoundland fish trade, esp in the purchase and export of salt cod-fish, and the financing of the fishing operation through the advance of supplies and credit.

[1583] 1940 *Gilbert's Voyages & Enterprises* ii, 401 [Hayes' narrative] It was further determined that every ship of our fleete should deliver unto the marchants and Masters of that harbour a note of all their wants. . . And besides, Commissioners were appointed. . .to go into other harbours adjoyning (for our English marchants command all there) to leavie our provision. 1620 WHITBOURNE 41 Those which hire ships, are bound by conditions under hand and seale, which we call Charter parties; wherein it is expressed, in how many daies the owners of the ships are to make them ready, & how many daies she must stay there, to attend the Marchant, and such like conditions. 1793 REEVES 43–4 It is a remarkable circumstance in the history of this trade, that many of the papers relating to it, whether coming from the commanders, or from the merchants and adventurers, in the times of king William and Queen Anne, would apply to later times, as well as to those in which they originated. 1818 CHAPPELL 220 Every merchant, and master of a *fishery*, is the *huckster* of his whole establishment; and the servants are compelled to purchase their supplies of food, raiment, and every trifling necessary, of the person in whose service they may chance to be engaged. No money passes between them; but the account of every article that is supplied to the fishermen is entered in the books of their masters. 1842 BONNYCASTLE ii, 162 The merchant finds the ship or vessel, the nets, and the provisions, in fact, the means of carrying on the fishery which he supplies to the planter. 1895 GRENFELL 80 The various firms agreed at one time not to buy fish from another merchant's planters. [1929] 1933 GREENLEAF (ed) 304 "The Merchants of Fogo": Come all ye toil-worn fishermen, combine and lend an ear; / Beware of those cursed merchants,—in their dealings they're not fair; / For fish they'll give half value, they will sacrifice it sore, / If it's under eleven inches, for Madeira it will go. 1933 *Nfld Royal Commission Report* 102 It has been the almost universal practice for each fisherman in the spring to approach either a local merchant or one of the large mercantile houses in St John's with a view to obtaining, on credit, sufficient supplies of gear, salt and provisions to enable him to conduct his fishery operations and to maintain himself and his family during the fishing season. Having obtained these 'supplies,' or 'outfit' as it is called, he is then in a position to start fishing. At the conclusion of the season, he takes his fish, dried and cured, to the merchant as a set off against his account. 1966 FARIS 151 If the voyage is good, the merchant's accounts are covered; if not, the merchant is commonly left holding the deficit and the fishery of a subsequent year must pay the expense. This is, of course, where the merchant stands to lose and several successive years of bad fishing can ruin him. 1977 BURSEY 36 The fish merchants in St John's expected to do some trade with the men from whom they bought the fish. 1980 *Evening Telegram* 16 July, p. 1 The battle lines were drawn [yesterday] as a major confrontation between Newfoundland's inshore fishermen and the province's fish merchants began to come to a head.

2 Proverbs: *a fisherman is one rogue, a merchant is many* (1924 ENGLAND 255); *a good merchant is better than a godfather* (1937 DEVINE 62).

3 Attrib, comb **merchant brig**, ~ **man**, ~ **party**, ~ **prince**, ~ **room** [see ROOM], ~ **scrip**, ~ **store** [see STORE], ~ **talk**.
1842 JUKES ii, 183 The judge's vessel was a merchant-brig hired for the purpose, and fitted up fore and aft with cabins and apartments for the various law-officers. [1784] 1895 PROWSE 357 The Judges who compose the Court of Oyer and Terminer are usually, the Judge of the Admiralty who presides, two or three justices, one or two Merchant men not the least acquainted with law or the form of it. 1882 TALBOT 34 Even at this early stage of their parliamentary government the population had divided themselves into two political parties, the one called Tory or Conservative, the other Liberal. Derisively they were called respectively, the Merchants' Party and the Priests' Party. 1953 JOB 11 In local language, the old firms that handled the Island's economy stemming from the cod fishery, the seal fishery, the extract of cod liver oil, the cold-storage products, etc., are called the 'merchant-

princes' and they must of necessity be bound up with Newfoundland history. 1895 *J A Folklore* viii, 37 One of the most singular peculiarities, however, of the dialect of Newfoundlanders is the use of the word *room* to denote the whole premises of a merchant, planter, or fisherman. On the principal harbors, the land on the shore was granted in small sections, measuring so many yards in front, and running back two or three hundred yards, with a lane between. Each of these allotments was called a *room*, and according to the way in which it was employed, was known as a merchant's room, a planter's room, or a fisherman's room. . . 1953 *Nfld Fish Develop Report* 14 About 90 per cent of all fishermen still operate on credit—and in a few of the more isolated districts the merchants' scrip is still current. 1907 MILLAIS 54 There was a. . .feller that kept a merchant store down Bonava' Bay. P 243–55 Merchant talk [means] attempts to explain why the price of fish is low.

merchantable a, n also **merchable*** ['mɜ.tʃntəb],
'mɜːtʃtəb], 'mɜːtʃəb]] *OED* ~ a 1 (1769 quot),
DAE (1674 quot), *EDD* merchant sb 2 ~ 'fit for sale' So D for sense (a); for sense (b): *OED* 1 b (Nfld: 1883), *DC* esp Nfld (1837 quots). (a) Of cod-fish, split, salted and dried in a manner suitable for sale or marketing; becoming in some contexts (b) a specific and superior grade or 'cull' of 'dry fish' (see 1786– quots).
[1580] 1895 PROWSE 84 It is agreed this day betwixt Wm Massie and Thomas Tetlow, merchants of city of Chester, of the one part, and Wm Dale, master of ye good ship called *ye William of London*, of the other part, and doth bargain and sell 34,000 Newland fish, merchantable at 10s. the 100, current money in England. . . [1663] 1963 YONGE 57 Too much salt burns the fish and makes it break, and wet, too little makes it redshanks, that is, look red when dried, and so is not merchantable. [1711] 1895 PROWSE 272 Minister to have subscription for ensuing year from shollups, three, the two men boats, two, and the ship one quintol of dry merchandable fish to be levied. [1749] 1755 DOUGLASS i, 302 No sun-burnt, salt-burnt, or that have been a considerable time pickled before dried, are to be deemed merchantable fish. [1786] 1954 INNIS 288 'Large merchantable' cod, 15 shillings. . . 'Small merchantable,' 13 shillings. . .'Madeira'. . .10 to 11 shillings. 1819 ANSPACH 442 The common distinction, in Newfoundland, of the fish when completely dried, is not according to its size, but according to its degree of perfection, both in appearance and in quality, into *merchantable, Madeira*, and *West Indian*. 1866 WILSON 212 The culler makes three qualities of fish,—merchantable, madeira, and West Indian. The merchantable goes up the Mediterranean, to Roman Catholic countries; Halifax and the United States are markets for the madeira, and the inferior fish find sale in the West India Islands. [1906] GRENFELL 55 'But the fish were every bit merchantable,' he insisted, 'and you only gives me credit for ten quintals o' merchantables.' 1955 *Nfld Fisheries Board* No 23 ~ Sound quality fish, reasonably thick, hard-dried smooth surface, well split, thoroughly clean on back and face, not sour or showing blood stains, clots, liver, gut, or excessive salt on face. T 168/70–65 Shore fish, for to be merchable fish, had to

be reasonably t'ick, and show no signs of salt. Yellow cast. 1966 SCAMMELL 84 Durned old fool got lippy about the cull. Trying to tell me his sunburned fish should have gone merchantable. 1977 RUSSELL 104 She's what you might call a comfortable armful or to put it in good fishermen's language, she's medium merchantable.

merr See MURRE[1].

merry a   *OED* ~ a B adv b ~ begot (1785, 1890), *EDD* (2) (a); *OED* dancer n 5, *EDD* ~ a 1 (6) ~ dancers, *DC* (1946).
    Comb **merry-begot**, ~ **me-got**: bastard; MOSS CHILD.
    1924 ENGLAND 183 'The merry-me-got!' exclaimed the Cap'n, wrathfully. To call a man a merry-me-got seriously reflects on the legitimacy of his entrance into this sorry world. T 222–66 This child is not simply an illegitimate child, but a 'moss child' or a 'moonlight child' or a child that is 'merry begot.' 1968 *Nfld Qtly* Christmas, pp. 5–6 They often lived together without benefit of clergy and children born out of wedlock were called by the delightful name of 'merrybegots.'
    merry dancers, dancers: northern lights, aurora borealis (1937 DEVINE 33).
    C 65–2 The northern dancers or merry dancers are really going it tonight. We're going to have a nice day tomorrow. C 66–18 Extra brilliant light of the northern lights is a sign of good weather. They are called dancers in Bonavista. 1981 HUSSEY 62 The merry dancers were northern lights but they looked a bit different and were a bit more lively. . .always in motion and continually dancing.

mesh[1] n   *OED* ~ sb 6 ~ net (Nfld: 1883).
    Comb **mesh herring**: small herring up to 6 in. (15.2 cm) long (P 127–73).
    1977 BUTLER 8 In October month some small herring began to appear in some of the coves. Small herring, or 'mesh herring' as referred to by the fishermen, was an excellent bait to catch codfish.
    mesh net: gill-net.
    1883 SHEA 12 Herrings are taken in mesh nets and in seines.

mesh[2] See MARSH.

mesh v   See TRAP[1]. To 'knit' the sides, bottom and 'leader' of a 'cod trap.'
    1909 BROWNE 75 He doesn't need 'to call the head clerk' to know how many bundles of linnet are required to mesh a trap.

methodist n   Cp WESLEYAN. Comb **methodist bread**, ~ **feet**, ~ **hatchet**.
    1937 DEVINE 33 Methodist bread. Raisin bread. 1972 MURRAY 280 A common saying which referred to a person who couldn't dance was 'He's got Methodist (or Wesleyan) feet.' Because they did not permit dancing. P 212–60 Methodist hatchet: two-edged (i.e. faced) axe.

methody a   Cp *OED* ~ dial (1847, 1848); *EDD* sb 1. Of or pertaining to Methodism.
    1887 *Colonist Christmas No* 8 I am all for the Queen and the English Constitution, and I stand by the good old Church of England, though they are getting very Methody in this country now.

micmac n   also **mickmack** *O Sup*[2] ~ sb a. (1830–), b. (1911–). (a) Indian of a branch of the Algonkian people settled in Newfoundland; (b) the language of these indians.
    [(1705) 1978 PASTORE 6 Vingt ou Vingt Cinq familles des Sauvages Miquemacs du Cap Breton sont passez dans cette Isle.] [1767] 1965 SKELTON 17 Found here a tribe of the Mickmack Indians. 1819 ANSPACH 182 He was cruising, in September, 1763, as Surrogate, along the south-west part of Newfoundland, when he observed a large party of the Indians, called Mickmacks. [1822] 1928 CORMACK 1 To accompany me in the performance, I engaged in my service first, a Micmac Indian, a noted hunter from the south-west of the island. [1886] 1915 HOWLEY 314 The first of these, Micmac, was spoken also upon the isle itself. 1907 MILLAIS 217 The Micmac Indians, who are a branch of the Great Algonquin race of Eastern Canada, first arrived in Newfoundland about the middle of the eighteenth century. 1972 *RLS* 4, p. 2 As far as concerns the Micmac spoken in Newfoundland, [there is] occasional free alternation of [k] and [x].

middleman n   *Cent* ~ n 3. A fisherman and owner of fishing premises, boat or vessel who, supplied by a merchant, engages a crew on the share system; PLANTER.
    1842 BONNYCASTLE ii, 165 Why does [the merchant] employ a middle-man, or planter? Because it is impossible in so scattered a population, with such amazing extent of fishing bank and shore, that he whose establishment is in St John's, or in one of the out-harbours or settlements, could attend to the large import and export trade upon which he subsists, and at the same time employ himself or his clerks on a fish stage in twenty different places, or in perhaps a hundred boats at sea. He therefore uses at his need the planter, and as the fisherman must supply himself from his warehouses with winter food, and with clothing, he retains both planter and fisherman as his constant clients. 1888 *Colonist Christmas No* 19 Mr Power is of a naturally diffident disposition, but he possesses sound, common sense, together with excellent qualitites of head and heart which make him one of the most representative middle men of the West end.

middler n   also **medler**. Beaver in its second and third years.
    [1783] 1792 CARTWRIGHT iii, 22 The first year, they are called *pappooses*; the second, *small medlers*; the third, *large medlers*; the fourth, *beaver*; and after that, *old* or *great beaver*. 1967 FIRESTONE 121 But he said,—'One time I got a big middler' [middle-sized beaver], and, he said, 'I cooked 'n and I ate every cursed bit of 'n myself at one time.'

midship n Cp *OED* midships sb 'the middle part of a vessel' (1626–), b ~ man (1626–).

Comb **midshipman**: fisherman occupying the midship position in an undecked boat.

[1663] 1963 YONGE 57 The complement of men to a boat are 5, that is 3 for to catch the fish, two to save it. Those 3 are the boat's master, midshipman, and fore-shipman. The boat is 3 or 4 tons and will carry 1000 or 1200 cod, but these three men will row these great boats a long way. 1861 DE BOILIEU 25–6 The cargo unloaded and stored, the crews are divided in parties of three or four men, each being titled according to the position he holds in the boat. For instance, 'skipper,' 'second hand,' 'midshipman'; last comes the 'captain,' who has the least to do,—merely, indeed, to cook for the rest and to keep the boat clean. 1866 WILSON 207 [The skipper] requires two men with him. One is called midshipman, because his station is the middle of the boat.

midship-room: ['mɪdʃɪprɵm, 'mɪdʃɪbrɵm, 'mɪdtʃɪprɵm, 'mɪdʃɪp ˌrʉum, ˌmɪdʃɪp 'ruːm, ˌmɪdʃɪp 'rʉum, ˌmɪdʃɪp 'ruːm, ˌmɪtʃən 'bruːm]: the middle compartment between the 'tawts' [tʰwɑrts] of an undecked or partly decked fishing boat; ROOM, STANDING ~ .

1842 JUKES ii, 74 The 'midship-room,' or hold of the boat, was covered with loose plank, and contained our stores. 1915 *Cadet* July, p. [9] Note the blissful poise of his better half as she gazes intently from the stage head on the well filled midship-room of the trap boat. 1957 *Nfld Qtly* Sep, p. 5 Seated on the fish bulk in the midshiproom they roared assent. T 1–63² The other fellow would be heaving [the fish] down in the midship-room, right in the middle of her. T 50/3 64 Packed 'em all in the midshiproom—ballast locker, an' took the few fish an' spread all over the rocks. T 199–65 The room in the middle of the boat [is] what they call the midship room—full o' lobsters, in their boat.

midship tawt: see TAWT.

midsummer n Comb **midsummer men**: stonecrop; roseroot (*Sedum roseum*) (1956 ROULEAU 34).

C 71–33 If the two flowers [of the midsummer men] grow together and intertwine it is true love between that couple. If, however, they grow apart the love will not last.

mild n *DC* ~ Labr (1933); *ADD* Nfld. A period of mild weather in winter; thaw.

[1906] GRENFELL 86 But a 'mild' or 'warm flaw' in the weather had set in. [1918–19] GORDON 56–7 Froze just enough to ruin the going utterly. A partially-bearing crust everywhere, guaranteed to cut the dogs' legs to pieces. . . Another mild is the only remedy for this shell, and that may not be for months. 1924 ENGLAND 65–6 In consonance with the 'wedderish' barometer, and with the men's opinion that 'de kind of a moil [mild spell] is over now,' a roaring blizzard that night screamed furiously out of the northern dark. 1933 MERRICK 219 Generally in January or February each winter there comes a two or three day 'mild' when the snow thaws. C 71–39 The sound of the train blowing

was always a sign of rain in Codroy Valley. If we heard the train blow in winter, it meant a 'mild' was coming.

mile n Comb **mile-a-minute**: Japanese knotweed (*Polygonum cuspidatum*) (1978 ROULEAU 90).

milk n *EDD* ~ sb 1 (25) ~ maid's path. Cp *Weather Proverbs* (1883), p. 73 'The edge of the Milky Way, which is the brightest, indicates the direction from which the approaching storm will come.' In combs **milk-maid's path, milk(y) vein**, and variations MAIDEN VEIN, **old-maid's path**: the Milky Way (P 148–60); a streak in the night sky.

C 66–7 The Milky Way is called either the 'maiden vein' or the 'milky vein.' The wind will blow either in or out of where it forks. T 272–66² There's a vein comes in the sky, milk vein people calls it. Yeah, vein in the sky, just like the Northern Lights last night. 'Tis a shape, 'tis a opening, but not a cloud just the same. It's white, you see. Just a opening, an' 'tis steady, this machine is steady, an' wherever it opens, well, that's the way the wind is goin' to blow the next day.

mill n Comb **mill blanket**: blanket made from the heavy fabric used in the paper-rolling process at a paper mill.

1967 *Bk of Nfld* iv, 251 Then it was up to bed early and my wife recalls 'mill blankets,' thick, heavy, and warm, that were in every home on the west coast.

miller n Cp *OED* ~ 3 a 'a ray' (1836). The thorny skate (*Raja radiata*).

[1620] 1887 MASON 152 What should I speake of. . .Cunners, Catfish, Millers, thunnes, &c of al which there are innumerable in the Summer season. [*OED*]

millyer n Cp LIVYER headnote. In various ball games, the pitcher.

M 69–2 The millyer and the nipper were similar to what is today the pitcher and the catcher.

mind v *OED* ~ v 2 dial; *EDD* 1; *ADD* 2; *SED* iv, 3, pp. 970–1. To remember.

1792 PULLING *MS* Aug It was on the 17th of March last (I mind the day because it was Patrick's Day). 1858 [LOWELL] i, 80 'Do 'ee mind about ten years ago, in Newfoundland, sir?' began Skipper George. T 49–64 I mind the time the seventh [of] April batch, that was some batch of snow. T 50/5–64 My people come from Ireland, my old grandmother did. County Carlow, my old grandmother. I can mind her. I'm goin' on seventy-five year old an' I can mind a long time now. 1977 *Them Days* ii (3), 28 Poor Mother took sick and almost died after we moved to Spotted Islands. That was in March. I can mind (remember) that good enough.

minister n Cp *EDD* parson gull [Sx 1849].

1 American smelt (*Osmerus mordax*).

1895 *J A Folklore* viii, 34 The westward smelts are known as *ministers*.

2 Comb **minister gull**: eastern glaucous gull (*Larus hyperboreus hyperboreus*) (1959 MCATEE 36).

miserable a, intens *OED* ~ a 6 now dial, *EDD* 1 for sense 1; *EDD* 3 IW for sense 2.

1 Miserly, mean, stingy.

T 54/8–64 He'd give them twenty-five cents in the night to go to bed without their supper. He was pretty miserable, wasn't he?

2 Very.

1895 *J A Folklore* viii, 40 Thus a person will speak of 'a miserable fine day.' T 187/9–65 She was as good [a gun] as ever was put to your face, and she could kill anywhere. All you had to do was hold her straight. But she was miserable saucy. She've had me [shoulder] beat all to pieces.

mish See MARSH.

misk n *EDD* ~ sb[1] 'mist, fog' So D. Light rain or mist; vapour rising from the sea after a cold night; BARBER 1 (1971 NOSEWORTHY 222).

misky a *EDD* misk sb[1]: misky So D. Misty.

P 148–64 'Is it fine out?' '[No], misky rain.' P 122–67 The weather is some misky today? 1971 NOSEWORTHY 222 ~ Wet and foggy.

missus n Cp *EDD* mistress 5: missis 'term of address.' Term of respect or affection for a mature woman.

T 54/9–64 There was an old lady sot in a rocking chair 'cross the kitchen from where I was at, and I said 'Missus, where's my friend that came here with me?' P 210–69 I have never heard my father call my mother anything but 'Missus,' but she always calls him by his first name. 1973 PINSENT 55 'Hello dere Missus,' said Will, swaggering up to Mrs Lowe's chair.

mitt n also **mit** *OED* ~ 2 (esp 1856, 1867 quots); *NID* 1 b; cp *Ling Atlas Scot* (1975) i, 169–71. Knitted woollen glove with separate sheaths for thumb and forefinger or for thumb alone; CUFF[1].

1901 *Christmas Review* 14 Yarn for one pair of mitts. 1908 HUBBARD 213 They gave George a piece of deer-skin dressed without the hair, 'to line a pair of mits,' they said. [1923] 1946 PRATT 207 "Reverie on a Dog": Blindfolded you could tell / The folk from one another by their smell, / Identifying the owner by a sniff / At a shoe-lace or a mitt, and when your tail / Began to wag, we knew it without fail. T 203–65 They have another one with three fingers—a palm there was would take three fingers an' a thumb. That'd be the mitt. 1975 POCIUS 31 A mit contains no partitions between three or four of the fingers, though the thumb is always separate. 1979 *Salt Water, Fresh Water* 54 The [sealers] usually wore mitts, what you call woollen mitts.

mitten n Comb **mitten flower**: cotton grass (*Eriophorum* spp).

1921 CABOT 118 About the islands the cotton-flower

grows to a fine size, with its great white boll. It is 'Mitten flower' here.

mog n Cp *DC* moccasin (esp 1825–7 quots for spelling with g). Clipped form of *moccasin*; SKIN BOOT.

T 191–65 They got into this sish and it could hardly bear the boat, so 'twas so slippery with their boots on that they used to wear skin boots—some people call them mogs, you know, Usquimaux skin boots.

molasses n also **lasses, lassy, molassy*** *OED* ~ 1 'now rare in Brit usage' (1582–); *DAE* 1 a (1666–), lasses (1775–) for sense 1; for combs. in sense 3: *OED* ~ beer (1742), *O Sup*[2] ~ candy (1809), *DAE* ~ cake (1836–), lasses candy (1807–).

1 Thick dark or light brown syrup produced in the manufacture of sugar.

[1677] 1976 HEAD 101 Provisions imported this yeare only in St John's Harbr: . . .Molasses (tuns) 14 [from West Indies]. [1766] 1971 BANKS 139–40 [Add to the spruce boughs and water] one Gallon of Melasses Let the whole Boil till the Melasses are disolvd. [c1845] 1927 DOYLE (ed) 27 "The John Martin": He said you burned all my lasses and you roasted all my pork. [1869] 1964 BLONDAHL (ed) 42 "Anti-Confederation Song": Cheap tea and molasses they say they will give; / All taxes take off that a poor man may live. 1902 *Daily News* 19 Dec My coal is getting low, John, / And the 'lasses in my can. 1924 ENGLAND 119 I turned to an' smoked. . .'lassy an' tea, an' spruce bark an' coffee. 1927 DOYLE (ed) 39 "Hunting Seals": And we take our tea with 'lasses.' T 80/2–64 And there was a bit o' everything—perhaps we had peas duff an' potatoes an' stuff like that left, you know, an' the coady dipper was there, see, with lassie into un. 1973 PINSENT 124 He lumbered, stiff-legged and stone-like, up the path and on towards his house and a big bowl of Mary's porridge, with lassey all over it, and a big cup of tea.

2 In designations of containers for storing or measuring molasses: **molasses critch, ~ dish, ~ keg, ~ monkey, ~ puncheon, ~ spile, ~ tub.**

1937 *Bk of Nfld* i, 232 . . .the sugar-basin or the molasses 'critch.' P 94–56 [The] lassy critch [was a] crock containing molasses. 1977 RUSSELL 33 When Liz, his missus, (Grandma she is now), tipped up the keg that night to full the molasses dish, she noticed there wasn't much in it. T 391/2–67 He lost it all except the molassy keg, an' that's where the molassy keg come up there now in the brook. That's where he stayed to. 1977 RUSSELL 117 It's years since I've used my molasses keg, for molasses, that is, 'cause I get my molasses at a lot higher price in what they call handy, convenient tin cans. P 128–56 A lassy monkey [was] a small keg for keeping molasses in. 1932 BARBOUR 138 'Johnnie,' I said, 'they are like flies around a 'lassy' puncheon, one before the other. T 187–65 One o' 'em was as big around as a molasses puncheon. 1973 HORWOOD 102 It didn't matter which part of the island the ship discharged, the flies followed the 'Lassie puncheon.' P 245–71 A lassie spile was a triangular piece of leather nailed over the bung-hole of a barrel of molasses in the merchant's store, off which the molasses dripped into the customer's jar. T 391/2–67 We always pickle our fish in tubs, puncheon tubs—you know, molassy tubs they was one time.

3 Designating food, drink, etc, in which molasses is a principal ingredient: **molasses beer, ~ bread, ~ (pork) bun, ~ cake, ~ candy, ~ coady** [see COADY], **~ knob** [see KNOB], **~ loaf** [see LOAF], **~ mog, ~ sauce, ~ sugar, ~ tea, ~ tit, ~ toutin** [see TOUTIN], **~ water.**

P 148–74 Types of homebrew [include] Juniper Beer, Molasses Beer. T 406–67[2] I never had no ear [for music]. I must 'a broke my ear when I was cryin' for lassy bread! T 410–67 Molasses bread you'd have to get; no buyin' jam [to] put on your bread. 1973 PINSENT 13 Mom, can I have a slice of lassey bread? 1964 *Daily News* 5 May, p. 5 'Lassey buns' were a favourite of the fisherman when he went to the fishing grounds or into the woods in winter. They are a sort of cookie containing generous flavoring of molasses and man-sized shares of pork or fat drippings and are still made in many homes. T 92/3–64 Molasses pork buns. You get so much flour, so much pork, an' so much molasses, an' you cut your pork right fine. M 68–10 [märchen] Jack and Tom and Bill were brothers. One spring they decided to go fishing but they never had nar punt. So Tom said to his mudder one day, 'mudder bake me up some molasses buns 'cause I'm goin' in the country the mar to cut some timbers fer a boat.' 1933 MERRICK 308 In the morning when it's time to shove off on the long haul, Martha has a loaf of bread or a bun of 'lasses cake tucked in the sled load somewhere. T 92–64 Molasses candy [was] much better than what you gets now. 1972 MURRAY 205 [In making blubber soap] blubber and wood ashes were boiled together in a pot until stringy like 'lassy candy.' C 71–112 Molasses coaty is served on the figgy duff. 1951 *N Y Folklore Qtly* vii, 272 Molasses knobs, a kind of Christmas candy, were also made. [1911] GRENFELL 64–5 Our cook, who had gone ashore to forage for some fresh food supplies, had discovered his wife mixing a few spoonfuls of the ever-scarce molasses into the loaf she was baking, that the family might, in 'lassie loaf,' have the nearest approach to a birthday cake they could afford. M 70–9 Weiners and beans. That's what I'm taking. And lots of lassie loaf. M 65–9 Lassy mogs [are] small round cakes made from a mixture of flour, baking powder and molasses, etc. 1979 *Salt Water, Fresh Water* 28 We had a mug-up, home-made bread, strawberry jam, molasses mogs, hard molasses cookies. 1939 DULEY 36 I'm going to make boiled pudding with lassey sauce. T 393/4–67 Now when that puncheon tea was gone, there'd be usually a half a barrel o' sugar, molasses sugar [left]. An' 'twas the best kind—we loved it on bread. 1842 JUKES i, 49 Molasses-tea [is] common tea, *boiled* in a tea-kettle, with a spoonful of molasses for sweetening, and often drunk, in default of a better cup, out of the tea-kettle lid. 1897 HOWLEY *MS Reminiscences* 29 When I got up they were just boiling their kettle so I came in for a cup of molasses tea. 1909 BROWNE 179 The fare of these sealers. . .was solid and substantial, consisting of biscuit, pork, butter and 'lassey-tea.' T 187/8–65 I never drinked a cup o' sugar tea, not for forty years, I suppose. An' I never drinked [a] cup o' molasses tea for forty years or over. M 71–84 They used

to make a molasses tit and give the children of two and three years of age, even younger sometimes. They would take a piece of rag and pour molasses in it, roll it up and tie it off at the end. 1979 *Evening Telegram* 21 July, p. 14 [She] sent over some molasses toutens and all I got to do is heat them up in the oven. 1975 ibid 2 Aug, p. 17 [They'd] be delivering ice in the neighbourhood [and] you'd bum a bit from the expressman and then go in the house and make molasses water, then put the ice in.

4 Attrib **lassy-bug**: in children's rhyme, ladybird beetle; ladybug.

M 71–118 We used to pick them up in our hands and say, 'lassy bug, lassy bug, give me some lassy. If you don't I'll kill your mother and father.' One expected to find a little brown spot on his hand if the lassy bug obeyed.

moldow n   also **maldow, moldown, moldow**, etc. ['mɒldɐu, mɒˑɔl'dɐu, maːl'daɷ, 'maːldɐu, 'mɒldɒl, mɔl'dɔəl].

1 Any of several species of beard-moss (*Usnea* spp; *Alectoria* spp); OLD MAN'S BEARD.

1846 TOCQUE 123 [There was a] small stunted woods, which was covered with a litchen, Negrohair. . .called in Newfoundland Molldow. . .cows are very fond of it. 1861 DE BOILIEU 116 The whole of the sides are caulked, or clinched, with a species of moss called on the coast 'molldow.' 1866 WILSON 56 The branches of the stunted spruce, on the verge of the barrens. . .arc usually fringed with a yellow parasite, called in the island, *molldow*. . . This lichen is the chief food of the deer during the winter season. 1897 *J A Folklore* x, 207 *Moldow* or *moldown*, the lichen on fir-trees. 1907 MILLAIS 321 The long-bearded tree moss, known to the Newfoundlander as 'maldow,' is a favourite food in winter [of caribou]. P 65–64 Mall dow is greenish-black hair-like substance [hanging down] on trees. Mall dow burns easily if it is dry. It is a second best to birch rind to get a fire started. T 33–64[2] [They made false moustaches out of] black sheep's wool, and black malldow what comes off of the wood. T 100/1–64 They used to go in the woods an' get the malldow off o' the trees—you could see it on trees, just like hair, like whiskers.

2 Jocular name for beard or hair.

[1927 BURKE] "A Wink and a Nod": A grand crop of whiskers with plenty of rain, / Every man in St George's has his face in a frame, / The soil must be fertile, well used to the plough, / The pride of the place is the foxy moldow. P 148–60 He's got a bit of moll dow. C 71–88 The bit of fuzz that one finds on one's chin [in late adolescence] is referred to as moll doll by some adults. 1979 *Evening Telegram* 24 Nov, p. 15 'Well now,' sez Mag to the woman, 'what did you wear? And you got your hair done. Looks pretty good too. Seein' as you are like meself, only got a bit of moldow left.'

3 Type of lichen used to make a dye; MOLLYFODGE.

C 69–28 Years ago the housewife had to make her own dye as well as many other things. Since they had to spin their own wool, it needed dyeing. This dye was obtained by boiling 'mow-dow' (lichens gotten off rocks) in water for two or three days. The result was a rusty colored water. After the water was sufficiently colored the mow-dow was strained out of it and a handful of salt was added to the colored water for every gallon. This water was then used to dye the wool used for knitting all sorts of clothes for the family.

4 Used variously for mildew, mould, dust.

P 148–62 Molldow [is] mildew on any object, caused by dampness. T 222–66 The live jam is eaten almost immediately. It's sometimes better than the other kind of jam, because that often has fise on it after a few months, or maldow; in other words it's fousty. Q 67–100 ~ dust (under a bed, etc).

mollyfodge n Lichen on rocks (and trees) used to make a dye; MOLDOW 3, ROCK DYE.

C 63–1 Molly fudge is picked off rocks or trees and used by women of Summerville to dye materials. P 192–67 Molly vodge—type of lichen which grows on a rock. It is a green and yellow colour used to dye mats and hooked rugs. C 71–118 Molly fodge—soft spongy material usually green or brown which grows on rocks. It used to be smoked in a pipe. 1976 *What's Happening* i (6), p. 22 One of her [favourite dyes], and now one of mine, is 'mollyfodge,' a grey rock lichen which produces a deep rich chocolate brown that she used on rags which were then hooked into rugs.

molly-fo-ster* v also **mollfooster*** *Kilkenny Lexicon* mallafooster 'to scuffle or frolic with a girl. . .attempt to take liberties.' To fool around (P 245–55).

P 108–71 Mollfoostering—poking around aimlessly; fussing around.

montagnais n also **montagnard, montagnet**. Cree indian of the Algonkian people, resident in southern Labrador; MOUNTAINEER.

1863 HIND 12 The leading object was. . .to obtain as much information as possible respecting the general features and resources of that portion of the Labrador Peninsula, and of the Montagnais who now hunt chiefly on the coast, as well as of the Nasquapees who roam throughout the interior. 1884 STEARNS 261 The 'Montagnards,' or 'Montagnet,' or 'Montagnais' are found in abundance chiefly along the shores of the lower St Lawrence. 1908 HUBBARD 10 The southern half of the country is occupied by the Montagnais or Mountaineers, a branch of the Cree family. 1970 PARSONS 258 The two branches of the Algonquin tribe referred to are the Montagnais (called Mountaineers by the English), and the Naskapi. . . Today the two tribes are divided socially and geographically, though there is little difference between them otherwise.

month n *OED* May sb[3] 5 ~ month, September 1 c ~ month; *EDD* March sb[1] (5) ~ month, May sb[1] 1 (27) ~ month. Season (of the year); period; with the specifying month of the year added.

1861 DE BOILIEU 197 The mild November month threatens a severe frost for December, with little or no prospect for a 'voyage of seals' for this year. 1873 CARROLL 18 After November month, white fish are sure to pass through. 1900 DEVINE & O'MARA 33 These two events crept into January month; they rightly belong to the dates given in February. 1960 FUDGE 12 But March month came on and we fished tub racket. 1964 BLONDAHL (ed) 15 "The Roving Newfoundlander": His age had scarce been twenty-one, just entered in full bloom / On the eighteenth day of June-month he was summoned to his tomb. C 67–16 I saw a fellow from Black Island (Notre Dame Bay) gettin' ready in September month. 1973 WIDDOWSON 547 In September month we go berry-picking.

monument n A marker, usu a pile of rocks prominently placed as a guide to mark a road or path in winter; cp CAIRN.

1872 *Times* [St John's] 16 Mar, p. 2 A few cairns or monuments, as they are here more generally named, similar to those on the Perlican barrens, are much required for directing the traveller in the winter over the part of the road.

mooch v [muːtʃ] *OED* ~ 2, 3 (1622–; 1851–); *EDD* mitch v 3, meech v[2], mooch v[2] esp s w cties for all forms. To play truant from school; to loaf or idle. See PIP[2]: *on the pip*.

1895 *J A Folklore* viii, 30 Mouch: to play truant, and also applied to one shirking work or duty. 1924 ENGLAND 180 But you got to watch these fellers that [mouches], an' that goes out an' comes in with one seal when other people's gettin' two! 1931 BYRNES 161 "The Old Picket Fence": When I 'mooched' from Tom Foster, and hid many mornings, / The one book I owned, near the old picket fence. 1937 DEVINE 34 Miche. To sulk, hide away or play truant. Mouch. To play truant from school. 1970 JANES 178 'Why haven't that youngster been goin' to Sunday School?' the old man demanded. . . 'I didn't really know he was moochin',' said Mom without much conviction.

moocher n *OED* ~ 2 dial (1870, 1876); *EDD* mooch v[2] 2: ~ s w cties. A truant from school (P 148–60).

P 247–68 When we went to school, if anyone cut out going for a day we used to call the person who mooched a moocher.

moonlight n Comb **moonlight child**: illegitimate child; MERRY-BEGOT.

T 169/212–65[1] They were sometimes called love childs or moonlight childs. C 70–34 She has always been self-conscious about being a moonlight child.

moonshine n Comb **moonshine can**: container in which illegal alcohol is distilled; still.

[1959] 1965 PEACOCK (ed) i, 75 "The Moonshine Can": He did come down to me, my boys, and put me on the stand / Saying, 'Pat there is a big kick up about your moonshine can.' T 200–65 An' then, if you want to, you can get un out in the can, or the moonshine can; run it off an' make the shine, moonshine.

mooring vbl n Cp *OED* ~ vbl sb 2 a 'something to which a floating object is made fast; the object to which it is moored' somewhat rare [in sg] (1775–). A line by which various types of fixed or stationary fish-nets or traps are held in place in the water, fastened to an anchor, float or the shore; cp RODE. Also attrib.

[1785] 1792 CARTWRIGHT iii, 99 The inner mooring of the old net being parted, they brought it home, fixed another mooring and killick, and then put it out again. 1936 SMITH 84 The next morning I was on the job again at sunrise, and out, tied fast to the main mooring keg of the cod-trap, waiting for the men to come out and haul the trap. M 68–7 On a rode there were two morin's one on the inside (near the shore) and one on the outside. These morin's were of six-thread rope. P 9–73 The improvement to a larger size mesh has many advantages. Less twine is required reducing the cost, a lighter mooring gear can be used, less strain on the trap when strong currents are running and a reduction in the amount of labour required in handling the gear. 1977 BUTLER 22 If a fisherman had to take out a supply of nets and mooring rope from his merchant, this bill would be deducted from his earnings.

moot* n [muːt]. See MOOT* v.
1 One of the roots in the skin of a plucked bird; pin-feather; down (P 269–64; P 127–77).
P 40–78 Dere's some moots left in that turr.
2 A (human) hair (P 145–72).
C 71–128 [You'll recognize him, because he has] nar moot on 'e's 'id.

moot* v Cp OED moult v. Of chickens, to shed feathers, moult (O 71–8).

mootie a Having pin-feathers.
1980 Nfld TV Topics 12 Apr, p. 25 "This bird is 'mootie.'" Mootie meant that the picked bird looked like a man's face that hadn't been shaved for a day or two. Even now when my husband is on holiday and he skips a day without shaving I'm reminded of a mootie bird.

mop¹ n EDD ~ sb¹ 2 Do D for sense 1; cp OED sb² 4 (a) ~ head 'the head of a mop' for sense 2.
1 Phr mops and brooms: out of sorts, not well.
1897 J A Folklore x, 212 Neither mops nor brooms: used to express a man's condition as neither sick enough to be in bed nor well enough to work. 1937 DEVINE 34 ~ Sick or in a disordered condition. P 51–67 Since I had the flu, I just feel mops and brooms. C 70–15 I often heard [her] say whenever somebody was getting a cold, 'I know you're brewing a cold because you are all mops and brooms.'
2 Comb **mop-head**: piece of kindling wood shaved with a knife so that the wood curls at end or the sides; CHOVY* (P 148–63).
Q 73–4 ~s: split ends of wood, for kindling.

mop² n A draw at a pipe.
T 141/60–65² He'd get up his pipe, and then he wouldn't have suction enough to hardly draw the flame down into un. There'd be a smack, and a mop at un.

mop* v also **smop*** [mɒp, smɒp]. Cp EDD

mapse, var: mopse 'to make a smacking noise with the lips when eating or talking' So D. To take a draw or puff on a pipe.
T 194/7–65 [I'd] lie down, moppin' my pipe, an' spend my Sundays. T 437/8–65 Anyhow Jack smopped and smopped away when it come just about dark an' couldn't get no smoke. P 154–78 The old man is mopping at his old pipe.

mope n
1 Newfoundland pine grosbeak; (Pinicola enucleator eschatosus).
1870 Can Naturalist v, 156 [The mope feeds] on the buds only of Pinus Abies, Larix, &c, and [is] very tame, being often killed with sticks. [1886] LLOYD 100 The mope is very like the British bullfinch, only he is larger. He whistles very prettily on fine days in Winter. 1912 CABOT 219 Hereabouts a pine grosbeak is a 'mope,' a shrike, a 'jay killer' or a 'shreek.' 1951 PETERS & BURLEIGH 374 The Pine Grosbeak is known by all Newfoundlanders as the 'Mope.' Indeed, it does appear to mope, for it sits around on stunted spruces and will often allow very close approach, or will even approach an observer. 1964 Evening Telegram 28 Oct, p. 5 All the local names of the beautiful pine grosbeak are more or less misfortunes. In most parts of the country—including Labrador—it is called the 'mope,' although it doesn't mope, and is abused solely for its comparative tameness and its interest in human affairs.
2 Prov phr stun(ned) as a mope: dense, stupid.
P 22–63 Stun as a mope. Used of persons who are slow to understand a point.

more n OED ~ sb¹ 1 obs exc dial (c1000–1725); EDD 1 s w cties. Cp BEAVER¹: BEAVER MORE, TUCKAMORE. Large root of a tree; fibrous root.
1792 PULLING MS Aug They sew all their fine work with deer sinews and for their coarse make use of the moors of trees. 1863 MORETON 31 ~ A root. [c1900] 1978 RLS 8, p. 26 More or mores. The long roots of a tree spread out under the ground, also applied to the roots of the pond lily or Beaver More. 1937 DEVINE 34 ~ A root of a tree. P 148–62 ~ The tiny roots. T 14/6–64 Then you will go and cut knees. You know what a knee is. Cut down a tree and you will look until you find one with a square more or a flaring more. T 54/62–64 An' I took th' axe off my back an' I shoved along to the moor. The tree was blown out o' roots. T 331–66 Here was this big juniper right alongside the camp. And the moors of this juniper stick runned across under [the camp]. 1977 Nfld Qtly Dec, p. 37 The [herring] were cleaned, picked, and hung up in the roof. A fire was then started and banked with sawdust and blackberry mores to put a flavour on them.

more v OED ~ v¹ 3 obs exc dial (1279, 1890); EDD 8 Gl. To dig up the base and root of a tree, esp one with a curve suitable to form the timber of a vessel.
1977 Decks Awash vi (6), p. 64 'E'd moor out timber in de fall.

more det, substitute See G P R PULMAN Rustic

Sketches (1853) [Devon], pp. 16, 54; JOYCE 296 moretimes.

1 Other; some; others.

[c1833] 1927 DOYLE (ed) "Come All Ye Jolly Ice-Hunters": All hands were called on deck, / Some to rig up jury masts, and more to clear the wreck. 1858 [LOWELL] i, 81 Some wanted food, and more agen got broken in spirit, (and that's bad for a man,) and some got lawless like. [c1880] 1927 DOYLE (ed) 53 "Hunting-don Shore": Men, women and children they lay on their backs, / While more in their bunks, they were straightened like sacks, / And more lay on boxes their sides they were sore. 1888 *Colonist Christmas No* 2 Some say that in an hour or moment of mental derangement he destroyed himself; more say he was drowned accidentally. [(1891) 1977] WINSOR (ed) 467 Some four or five men jumped from the weather bow. . .more took to the riggin'. 1930 BARNES 48 We used to play games, checkers, cards. More of us would play follow the leader. 1944 *Yuletide Bells* A certain missionary Bishop from a faraway spot called New-foundland (or as some more called it 'the Wild Planta-tion') had visited the convent. P 148–64 Some poetry is written for humour and more poetry produces sadness. T 246/8–66 Some would warm the water and chuck on the bark, and some more would [put] it in cold. 1972 MURRAY 199 Some people liked striped [wall] paper. A stripe 'd go down the roses and some more wouldn't get that 'fraid their homes wouldn't fair [i.e. weren't plumb]. 1973 WIDDOWSON 421 Their parents would tell 'em, well, 'The mummers will be here tonight. They're not going to hurt you' or something like that. But more fellers you know, more parents, would try to, well. . .'The Mummer is comin' to take you tonight!'

2 In sequence **sometimes. . .more times**.

1858 [LOWELL] i, 147 'Sometimes we sid it, an' more times agin we didn' see it.' 1862 *Atlantic Mo* ix, 370 [I set out] keepun up mostly a Nor-norwest, so well as I could: sometimes away, round th' open, an' more times round a lump of ice, and more times, agen, off from one an' on to another, every minute. T 1–63[1] Sometimes we'd have black masks, you know, do them black; more times we'd put veils on our faces. 1975 RUSSELL 18 And so sometimes he'd just glower at the fellow that was braggin' and get up and walk away. More times, he'd try another remedy.

more av In comb **more so**: to a greater extent; rather.

P 54–67 A trout'll go after a red fly more so than a green one. T 360–67 [Boo-man is used] in a sort of playful sense more so than [as] a serious threat. T 417–67 [We use] boos more so than anything else.

morgan n An adult Christmas mummer or 'jan-ny' (P 148–61).

M 71–99 [Around Christmas] it was customary for the 'morgans' to pay a visit to the people of the com-munity. No one knows why they were called morgans. Adults, usually three in number, would come and pay a visit to almost every house in the harbour. Their visit-ing would end in some house with a dance and a 'scoff.'

moryeen* n Cp DINNEEN múrach

'slab-mud. . .from the sea-shore used for manure.' Fertilizer prepared from fish offal mixed with peat or 'bog.'

1968 DILLON 148 They're makin' moryeen down by the flake.

mosquito n A small, biting, winged insect, esp *Simulium venustum, S. vittatum*; BLACK FLY (1975 HOLMES 41).

[1819] 1978 *Beothuk Vocabularies* 45 Mosquito—shema bogosthue. 1842 JUKES ii, 4 Another kind, which in Newfoundland is always distin-guished as the mosquito, is a little black fly with white thighs, and is more like a small house-fly than a gnat: and this insect seems to bite off a piece of the skin, as the wound bleeds copiously. 1895 *J A Folklore* viii, 34 The black fly is known as the *mosquito*.

moss n

Comb **moss berry**: black crowberry (*Empetrum nigrum*) (1894 *Evening Herald* 3 Dec).

1908 HUBBARD 225 There is a big bed of moss ber-ries (a small black berry, which grows on a species of moss and is quite palatable) right at my tent door tonight.

moss child: illegitimate child; MOONLIGHT CHILD.

T 222–66 Sometimes as a result there is a child born out of wedlock. This child is not simply an illegitimate child, but a 'moss child' or a 'moonlight child' or a child that is 'merry begot.'

moss lily: low evergreen plant (*Diapensia lapponica*) (1898 *J A Folklore* xi, 274).

mot n Cp *EDD* ~ sb[2] 1 'mark in the game of quoits, etc.' Shallow depression in the ground providing target in game of marbles; cp MAG.

P 245–55 ~ Hole in the ground, made by heel of shoe in spring, into which marbles are 'bazzed.' T 458–67[1] You had a mot which you dug with your heel in the mud, and you stood so far away. C 71–14 You rolled the marble towards the mot and if you were the closest, you shot first and had the chance to collect everyone else's marbles by flicking them into the mot. 1981 *Evening Telegram* 15 May, p. 6 A boy was the envy of his peers if he was lucky enough to be able to shoot a marble anywhere he wanted around the rim of the mot or into it.

mote n Also **mot**. Cp *EDD* ~ sb[1] 3 'a single straw or stalk of hay; a twig' D Do So Co Wxf. A thin sliver used as a spill.

1937 DEVINE 34 Mot. A roll of paper or other inflammable stuff to light a pipe or fire.

mother n Cp *OED* ~ sb 13 a (1630 quot). Comb **mother fish**: large cod-fish of breeding age; BREEDER.

1845 *Journ of Assembly* Appendix, p. 222 The latter named mode [bobbing pole is] allowed to lay near the bottom of the sea, and probably as liable to take what is called the mother fish with the spawn as the other [the Bultow]. 1975 *Evening Telegram* 2 July, p. 3 Fishermen in the area were blaming the small size of fish on the gill nets, which they maintained were scooping up all the large or 'mother' cod. P 245–75 The gill nets destroy the mother fish—the breedin' fish.

motion n A stretch of water the turbulent movement of which is caused by the meeting of heavy cross-currents; freq in coastal names.

1837 BLUNT 29 Having passed Little Motion, keep the extreme point of the head over the Narrows Point. 1848 *Journ of Assembly* 263 Road from Catholic Chapel towards Motion Bridge. [1902] 1916 MURPHY 13 Picco missed the Cape, ran in, and took the land near Petty Harbour Motion. A blinding snowstorm was raging and not a soul was saved. 1951 *Nfld and Lab Pilot* i, 80 A conspicuous rock stands close southward of Motion head. Motion rocks, on which the sea always breaks, are 4 feet high, and lie three-quarters of a cable north-eastward of the head. The irregular and broken ground extending off the head causes a heavy cross sea and should be given a wide berth.

mould v To shape the frame or skeleton of a boat or vessel by the use of thin strips of wood formed in the intended shape and proportions of the craft, or by a model; freq in phr *mould out*.

T 43/8–64 You had your mould to go by—you couldn't make any mistake. You mould out your frame by your mould and a rising-board, or a model if you prefer. T 178/9–65 We'd have a mould, and he was marked; and then another board, a risin' board. We only mould all the midship timbers, but then we'd batten her out.

mountain n Cp *OED* ~ 9 c ~ hare 'alpine hare' (1785). *DC* ~ ptarmigan (1883–).

Comb **mountain curlew**: ESKIMO CURLEW (*Numenius borealis*) (1959 MCATEE 30).

mountain hare: Arctic hare (*Lepus arcticus*).

[1785] 1792 CARTWRIGHT iii, 109 This being Christmas-day, we gave the people roasted venison for dinner, and had for ourselves a mountain hare, an excellent venison pasty, and a berry pie. 1956 CAMERON 53 Very little is known about the life-history of the 'Mountain hare' in Newfoundland, but it is assumed that it does not differ greatly in habits from the Arctic hares of Northern Canada.

mountain partridge, ~ ptarmigan: Welch's rock ptarmigan (*Lagopus mutus welchi*) (1959 MCATEE 25); PARTRIDGE.

1870 *Can Naturalist* v, 291 A truly alpine species in Newfoundland; rarely found below the line of stunted black spruce. . .called by the settlers the 'mountain partridge.' 1891 PACKARD 104 There were four varieties of partridge: the spruce partridge, and the white or ptarmigan, of which they distinguish the mountain ptarmigan and the river ptarmigan, the latter the rarest; the fourth kind they call the pheasant.

mountain turnip: white lettuce (*Prenanthes trifoliolata*) (1898 *N S Inst Sci* ix, 376).

mountaineer n [mæunt‿ŋˈiəɹ, ˈmɑuntənɛɹ, ˈmɑuntˀŋɛɹ, ˈmɑuntˀŋɛɹ] *DC* ~ 1 (1770–) for sense 1.

1 Cree indian of the Algonkian people, resident in southern Labrador; MONTAGNAIS. Also attrib.

[1770] 1792 CARTWRIGHT i, 5 Although [the Beothuks are] beyond a doubt descendants from some of the tribes upon the continent of America, and most probably from the Mountaineers of Labrador, yet it will be very difficult to trace their origin. [1776] ibid ii, 191 At the head of the bay we found a mountaineer whigwham of last year. . .and on the east side there were two old ones. [1822] 1928 CORMACK 61 The Red Indians' country, or the waters which they frequented, we were told by the mountaineer, lay six or seven miles to the north of us. 1842 JUKES ii, 130–1 [The Beothuks] were acquainted with another tribe of Indians, whom they called Shaunamunc, and with whom they were very friendly. . . They answer, I believe, to the Indians called Mountaineers, on the Labrador shore. 1861 DE BOILIEU 82 A small species of dog, called the Mountaineer dog, is very useful in directing the trapper to the beaver-houses. 1907 WALLACE 68 No, 'twere no Mountaineers—*them* don't steal. No un ever heard o' a Mountaineer takin' things as belongs to *other* folks. T 178–65 Mountaineer, Mountaineer. I saw one o' they. They're more of our growth [than the Eskimo].

2 Comb **mountaineer sled**: type of sled used by Montagnais indians for winter travel.

[1786] 1792 CARTWRIGHT iii, 150 At two o'clock one of the Canadians came here from Muddy Bay, with a new Mountaineer sled, a pair of rackets, and a pair of racket-bows. Ibid 235–6 Their sleds are made of two thin boards of birch; each about six inches broad, a quarter of an inch thick, and six feet long: these are fastened parallel to each other by slight battens, sewed on with thongs of deer-skin; and the foremost end is curved up to rise over the inequalities of the snow. Each individual who is able to walk, is furnished with one of these; but those for the children are proportionably less. On them they stow all their goods, and also their infants; which they bundle up very warm in deer-skins. The two ends of a leather thong are tied to the corners of the sled; the bright [ed emend: bight], or double part of which is placed against the breast, and in that manner it is drawn along. 1977 *Them Days* ii (3), 57 Hannah and me would slide on the Mountaineer sleds father would buy for us. We were thought a great deal of by the Mountaineers and they would bring us pretty snowshoes and deer skin shoes for wearing indoors or out, all painted pretty.

mountaineer tea: prob a distorted form of MAIDENHAIR TEA or its variants; creeping snowberry (*Gaultheria hispidula*) (1898 *N S Inst Sci* ix, 386).

mounting n Cp *Cent* ~ n 4 'that which is mounted for use or ornament.' Decorative strip of metallic ribbon fastened on rim of coffin.

M 71–42 When the lid [of the coffin] was put on, a tinny metallic substance called 'mountin,' like ribbon, an inch or two wide, was tacked around the coffin every foot or so. This was white or silvery. The breast-

plate was of the same substance. 1972 MURRAY 297 All
coffins were lined inside with shirting or sateen.
Around the rim, where the cover was thrown back, it
was trimmed with 'full mountain,' a gold or black
material, heavier than present day tinfoil. . . Children's
coffins were often trimmed with lace instead of full
mountain.

mouth n *EDD* ~ sb 2 (7) for sense 1; for comb
in sense 2: *EDD* 1 (14) ~ speech So D Co;
Kilkenny Lexicon pus music.

1 Phr *have a mouth on one*: to be hungry or
thirsty.
1901 *Trade Review Christmas No* 10 When I had it
on this morning the fellows took it for the badge of the
Total Abstinence Society, and didn't ask if I had as
much as a mouth on me. P 148–68 They wouldn't even
ask ya if you got a mout' on ya. 1974 CAHILL 46 I'm
gone with starvation. And that crowd down at Bennett's wouldn't know you had a mouth on you.

2 Comb **mouth music**: humming or singing of
nonsense syllables by one person to provide lively, rhythmic accompaniment for others to dance;
CHEEK MUSIC, CHIN ~ .
1965 PEACOCK (ed) i, 61 'Chin' or 'mouth' music is a
vocal imitation of instrumental music and is used for
dancing when a fiddle or accordion is not handy.

mouth speech: utterance (1897 *J A Folklore* xi,
208).

mouze* v [mɐʊz]. Cp *OED* mow 1 'to make
mouths,' *EDD* mouth v 9 'to make faces.' To
make faces (P 167–67).
C 69–2 Children sometimes make faces at their parents and other children or 'mouse' as they say. Parents
tell their children that if the direction of the wind
changes, their faces will remain in this position.

muckle v To tug or strenuously pull up (something).
1924 ENGLAND 237 Here I been workin' ahl me life,
draggin' and 'aulin, mucklin' up grayples. 1975
RUSSELL 20 'Did you get 'em all dug up?' said I. 'Yes,
Paddy,' said she, 'every blessed one of 'em, exceptin'
one. . .one of 'em was a bit too big for me to muckle.
So I left it bide for you and the crew to handle.'

mud n *DC* ~ fish esp Nfld (1762–1832); *O Sup*²
~ 5 b ~ trout (Nfld: 1917–).
Comb **mud fish**: cod-fish partially split, salted
and placed in pickle; cp DUN a: DUN FISH; GREEN
~ .
[1745] 1954 INNIS 169 The green fish, or 'mud' fish,
at 9 pence each. [1766] 1971 BANKS 135 They Prepare
[for England] another kind of fish Cured wet & calld by
them mud Fish which instead of Being split quite open
as their Dry Fish are only opend Down to the navel
They are salted & Lie in salt & the Salt is washd out of
them in the Same manner as the others but instead of
Being Laid out to Dry they are Barrelld up in a Pickle
of Salt Boild in water. 1819 ANSPACH 441 It frequently
happens that some of the fish, taken towards the close
of the fishing season, is not fit to be put on-board for

exportation. In this case it is either put into stores, the
fishermen taking advantage of every favourable opportunity to complete its drying, and to keep it in a proper
state of readiness for the first vessels that will be able to
take it in, late in the fall or early in the spring; or else it
is reserved for use in the island: it eats better than
other kinds, but cannot be kept so long. It is called
mud-fish. 1861 *Harper's* xxii, 457 They remain at home
to assist in gathering their crops, and proceed again for
another cargo, which is salted down and not afterward
dried. This is termed mud-fish, and is kept for home
consumption. 1937 DEVINE 34 ~ Codfish caught in the
autumn too late to cure and kept in the store in salt all
the winter for spring curing.

mud puck: mud hole or puddle.
1938 MACDERMOTT 57 The small body of water usually called Pond in England is a 'mud puck' to a real
outport man. C 71–23 A pothole filled with muddy
water is called a mud puck.

mud rubber: a low waterproof overshoe.
P 148–64 ~s: low rubbers around the soles, but not
coming up to the laces.

mud sucker: (a) PITCHER PLANT (*Sarracenia
purpurea*); (b) boggy area in which the plant
grows.
C 69–23 To us the pitcher plant was known as a mudsucker which would take us bodily under the mud if we
went too near. C 71–104 Children were warned to stay
away from the meshes (marshes) because the mudsuck-
ers would get them. The mudsucker was supposed to
be a creature down below the soft wet places. P 40–78 I
was always 'fraid of puttin' my foot down in the mud-
suckers.

mud trout: eastern brook trout (*Salvelinus
fontinalis*); TROUT.
1842 BONNYCASTLE i, 269 The salmo trutta, salmon
trout, and salmon fario, common trout, with a variety
called mud trout, are also plentiful in rivers and ponds.
1888 HOWLEY *MS Reminiscences* 12 I caught one large
mud trout, the finest I ever saw. He was as big as a
small codfish. [1896] 1906 FRASER 185 They are sweet
eating, red-fleshed, and firm, run about three or four to
the pound, more or less, and rise freely. . . The natives
(colonists) call them mud trout. 1921 CABOT 21 They
were what the St John's trouters call mud trout, which
curiously is their most complimentary term. 'They
were real mud trout!' a fisherman would say in climax,
when describing his catch. 1969 HORWOOD 224 Newfoundland's only native trout. . .is the speckled brook
trout (known locally. . .as a 'mud trout'). 1982 *Evening
Telegram* 9 Jan, p. 12 They used sticklebacks or 'pricklies' for these initial experiments and found that. . .our
'mud trout' (local name for eastern brook trout)
weren't crazy about the fare.

mug v *OED* ~ v⁷ (1897, 1901); *DC* ~ up
(1936–); *Fisheries of U S* (1887), p. 75 [Grand
Banks]. Phr *mug up*: to have a cup or mug of tea
and a snack between main meals.
1912 CABOT 38 Once during the forenoon, while
most of the men were below, 'mugging up' on hard
bread and tea. . . 1925 *Dial Notes* v, 336 Mug-up—to
feed; entertain with food or drink. 'I'll *mug* you up.'
1966 PHILBROOK 50 Between the meal and evening

lunches, 'mug-ups' are always served. . . All [the family] 'mug up' before retiring. P 148–69 He's always mugging up.

mug up n [mʌg 'ʌp, 'mʌg ʌp, mɔg 'ɔp] *O Sup²* ~ (1933–); *DC* (1933–). (a) A cup or mug of tea and a snack taken between any of the main meals, esp in a pause from work; (b) a repast in late evening; LUNCH; also attrib.

1869 HOWLEY *MS Reminiscences* 17 Had a mug up at the Skipper's house, after which he and one of his men took me in their punt and rowed me up to the head of the Arm. 1909 BROWNE 268 We arrived at our destination. . .just in time for the 'mug-up.' This is the eleven o'clock collation which precedes the fishermen's dinner. [1922] 1972 GORDON 193 During a short break for what is locally known as a 'Mug-up,' he confided to us that he had caught a very fine black fox and was taking the skin to North West River. 1924 ENGLAND 42 First mess goin' now. Putt a good wahrm mug-up into y'r body, alang o' y'r soul, an' it'll be wonnerful fine fer ye! 1941 WITHINGTON 141 For breakfast they had tea, bread, and oleo; mid-morning and afternoon a 'Mug-up' of bread and tea; for dinner cod and potatoes three times a week. T 1/8/9–65 I'd have my mug up in the morning 'fore I'd leave up home, an' go to work, an' [at] nine we have breakfast. T 436–65 [We] put our little kettle on the bucket till he boiled, an' then we take un off an' we have a mug up out in dory. 1975 *Evening Telegram* 28 June, p. 16 What about dodging along, it's gettin' near mug-up time. 1975 RUSSELL 20 So, after we'd had a mugup, me and the crew took a flake [longer] each and went up the side of the hill to where this potato was lyin'. 1979 *Salt Water, Fresh Water* 17 He came in this night and we had our game and we had our mug-up, and he said, 'Wonderful cold tonight.'

muir See MURRE¹.

mummer n Cp *OED* ~ 2 'one who takes part in a mumming' (esp 1829 quot); *EDD* mum v¹ 1: mummer (a). An elaborately costumed and disguised person who participates in various group activities at Christmas; FOOL, JANNY, OWNSHOOK. Also attrib in designations of apparel, behaviour, etc, of mummers.

1812 *Gazette* 23 Jan Mr Michael Wall, who took an active part in forming and practising the *mummers* that assembled on last twelfth day, appeared in the character of a General Officer, with his Lady. 1842 BONNYCASTLE ii, 139 There was, and still is, a sort of saturnalia amongst the lower classes, in St John's particularly, and which lasts three days, commencing at Christmas, with boys only. The mummers prepare, before the New Year, dresses of all possible shapes and hues. . .but the general colour is white, with sundry bedaubments of tinsel and paint. 1842 JUKES i, 221 Men, dressed in all kinds of fantastic disguises paraded the streets. . . They called themselves Fools and Mummers. [1861] 1892 *Consolidated Statutes of Nfld* 281 Any Person who shall be found, at any Season of the Year, in any Town or Settlement in this Colony, without a written Licence from a Magistrate, dressed as a Mummer, masked, or otherwise disguised, shall be deemed guilty of a Public Nuisance. 1886 *Colonist Christmas No* 9, 12 Here they come! the mummers! Such are the exclamations that are heard, as a number of young men and maidens—[their] fantastic disguises trimmed with ribbons of various hues—pass along, and stop before a long low house in the centre of the villages. 1902 MURPHY 37 "Terra Novean Exile's Song": How oft' some of us here to-night / Have seen the 'mummers out,' / As thro' the fields by pale moonlight / They came with merry shout, / In costumes quaint, with mask or paint. 1928 *Nfld Qtly* Dec, p. 15 The merry party of 'Jannies,' or 'Mummers,' made the welkin ring with their weird shouts and cries, and their 'false faces' sent many a frightened child in haste to its mother's knee. T 45–64 An' the last house you go into, you'd have a mummer's ball there—have a big time. T 184–65 Leg of a old pair o' oil pants—that's what they'd make the mummer caps of. Chop the leg off, cut the eyes, an' cut the mouth. 1969 *Christmas Mumming in Nfld* 82–3 Both the 'little mummers' and 'big mummers' give the same cue before entering a house: they knock on the door, and give an ingressive shout (that is, they draw in their breath) while saying, 'Mummers allowed in?' Ibid 110 Once inside, they begin a jogging, half-dance, half-shake that is the 'mummer's walk.' 1982 *Evening Telegram* 6 Jan, p. 2 The Mummers of old visited in neighborhoods throughout the Christmas season, but 12th night was their time for a community concert.

mummer v *O Sup²* ~ v (1884; Nfld: 1964–). To participate in various group activities of disguised persons during Christmas; esp in phr *go mummering*; JANNY V.

1901 *Christmas Bells* 11 At night they went 'mummering,' or had a dance. [1904] 1968 *Nfld Qtly* Christmas, p. 28 Christmas night ushered in a gay social season, which continued until January 6th. During that time many of the grownups went 'jannying' or 'mummering' every night. 1905 DUNCAN 136 . . .when the lads and maids decked themselves out in fantastic fashion and went mummering from cottage to cottage at Christmas tide. M 65–1 We mummered from Saint Stephen's Day which is December 26 until the 12th day which we called Old Christmas Day (Jan 6). Everyone, old and young, mummered. 1967 *Bk of Nfld* iv, 236 After a non-stop day outdoors we would dress-up at night and go mummering (or mumming).

mummering vbl n also **mumming** *OED* mumming vbl sb 2 (esp 1546 quot); *O Sup²* mummer v: mummering (1884–). The practice of visiting houses disguised as a mummer at Christmas; JANNYING; also attrib.

1860 *Times* [St John's] 22 Dec Every well-disposed citizen must be gratified at the proclamation issued by the Police Magistrates to suppress 'mumming' with its disgusting attendants,—rioting, drunkenness, and profane swearing. 1887 *Evening Telegram Christmas No* 10 [The] city has 'done away with' mummering. 1895 PROWSE 451 There was always, however, a carnival of dancing, mumming, and, of course, drinking, from Christmas to Twelfth day. 1917 *Holly Leaves* 19 One of the most popular amusements incidental to the Christmas holidays. . .was the carnival, locally known as 'mumming' or 'mummering.' 1950 *Newfoundlander* Jan, p. 14 This is an account of the mumming play that was used on Christmas times in the early days. . . I have seen the old fellows at Christmas time acting it, all dressed in uniform. T 168/71–65 You got out to the door—they knock at the door, got a stick for mummering—johnnies, they call 'em. T 194/6–65 I only dressed up twice in my life for mumming, but I've had 'em in the house by the galores—thirty, forty, fifty of a night, in my house. 1973 PINSENT 53 I never cared much for jannying or mummering or dressing up or whatever the hell it was. 1975 RUSSELL 63 Right now I'm overhaulin' my old duds pickin' out something to wear tonight mummerin'—something people are not likely to recognize. Yes, I'm goin' mummerin'—playin' the fool like everybody else and havin' a good time for myself.

mumming See MUMMERING.

mundle n also **mundel** *OED* ~ dial; *EDD* sb 1. Wooden utensil used for stirring various mixtures; SHIM, SLICE.
1896 *J A Folklore* ix, 23 Mundel: a stick with a flat end for stirring meal when boiling for porridge.
P 118–67 There's an old mundel out in the pantry now.
C 75–144 ~ a wooden utensil used for stirring large amounts of dough, soup or batter. [It] is the shape of a miniature shovel. C 75–146 ~ a flat, wooden stick about 12 in. long, pared at the top with the bottom flat. It was used to stir up mixtures of paint, paste, batters, limestone, etc.

munge v, n also **monge** [mʌndʒ] *EDD* ~ v¹, sb¹.
1 To munch, chew.
1903 *Daily News* 24 Feb As I sat down upon a flake / . . .to munge a piece of oaten cake, / A steamer passed that way, sir. 1937 DEVINE 34 Monge. To eat, to munch. P 41–68 ~ to eat slowly. P 108–70 He was munging on a carrot.
2 Mouth; mouthful (P 205–54).
P 264–79 A dry munge [is] a bite to eat with nothing to drink—bread or biscuits consumed without liquids.

murre¹ n also **merr, muir, mur(r)** [məɹ, məːɹ] *OED* ~ (1602–); *DAE* (1674–); *EDD* murr(e) sb 1 'common guillemot' D Co, 2 'razor-bill' Sh I Co, 3 'puffin' So D Co. (a) Sea-bird resembling the penguin in coloration and posture (*Uria aalge; U. lomvia*); (b) other sea-bird (*Cepphus grylle atlantis; Alca torda torda*); BACCALIEU BIRD, TURR n; also attrib.
[1578] 1935 *Richard Hakluyt* 131 [Parkhurst's letter:] There are Sea Guls, Murres, Duckes, wild geese, and many other kind of birdes store. [1777] 1792 CARTWRIGHT ii, 264 At noon, Jack returned, and brought only a grouse and a mur. [1794] 1968 THOMAS 144 Penguins, Hegdowns, Muirs and Tuirs, Ice Birds. . .and a number of other Sea Fowl. 1842 BONNYCASTLE i, 234 The guillemot. . .or merr of Newfoundland. 1842 JUKES i, 265 I shot a sea-bird, called in Newfoundland a mur, which is, I believe, some species of mergulus. 1951 PETERS & BURLEIGH 251 Atlantic

Common Murre. . . Local Names: Turr, Murre, Baccalieu Bird. 1953 *Nfld & Lab Pilot* ii, 425 Cod-bag or Tinker Share island is situated about three-quarters of a mile north-eastward of Murr island. 1960 TUCK 13 There are two species; the common murre (*Uria aalge*), with some tolerance for warmish water, and the thick-billed murre (*Uria lomvia*), largely restricted to arctic waters.

murre², **murr** See MYRRH.

muskrat n Comb **muskrat flower**: round-leaved sundew (*Drosera rotundifolia*) (1956 ROULEAU 34).

mutinize v *OED* ~ v a. obs (1605–1841). Of a sealing crew, to mutiny; cp MANUS.
[1896] SWANSBOROUGH 37 "The Seal Fishery": The men will sometimes mutinize, / That is against the skipper rise. / If kept at sea after this date, / Anxiety for home is great. 1924 ENGLAND 248 An' I was on a ship as mutinized at de hice, too.

muzzle n Comb **muzzle rope**: length of rope securing the gaff or 'spread' on which the sail of a craft is hoisted; cp SPREAD v: SPREAD-SAIL PUNT.
1975 BUTLER 54–5 Since there were no gaffs or booms on those sails, a long stick called a spread from fourteen to fifteen feet long was used to hoist sail. This spread would be put in a loop in the peak of the sail and pushed up until the sail came tight, and a piece of rope called a muzzle rope put in a groove in the lower end of the spread was made fast to a cleat on the spread.

myrrh n also **murr(e)**, etc. Possibly from the biblical association of myrrh and frankincense. Cp *OED* ~¹ 1 (esp 1672 medical quot); see also FRANKINCENSE, FRANKINTINE*, FRANKUM, GUM, TURPENTINE. The resin of a fir or spruce tree, freq in home remedies; also attrib (P 133–58).
P 65–64 Turpentine on trees is called 'mur.' Mur is put on cuts to cause a cure. T 396/7–67 There was a myrrh you could use, what you get out o' the woods—a good medicine for inside use and outside use. . . I've drink molasses an' myrrh. C 67–16 Go to the wood-pile and get some murr; then we won't need any stitches to keep the cut together. C 68–10 He hurried into the nearby woods and in a few moments came back with a handful of mur bladders. These he squeezed out and mixed with molasses. The cut (about ½ inch deep) was covered with this mixture and wrapped with white cloth. In just one week my leg was completely healed. C 70–15 [He] went out into the garden where there was an abundance of balsam fir, and he brought back a strip of rind on which there were a number of 'myrrh bladders.' He cut open the bladders and squeezed the 'myrrh' on the cut. Of course the bleeding stopped, and within a few days the cut had healed nicely. 1972 MURRAY 240 They often made use of 'murre' or the turpentine 'bladders' found on the bark of fir trees to dress the cut. 1976 *Decks Awash* v (5), p. 16 I know of a man who believed that turpentine (murr) from the fir

tree was a cure for TB. He went about with a teaspoon bursting the bladders on the trees and swallowing the stuff. He died at the beginning of an elderly age, but not from TB. The murr was supposed to be good for cuts and to stop bleeding. Whether it had any healing qualitites is a matter of conjecture, but one thing is certain, if a wound was clean and bandaged and plastered with murr, it was not possible for any outside bacteria to infect the wound.

myrrhy a Sticky with resin or turpentine (P 94–57); LICKERY.

1977 *Decks Awash* vi (6), p. 64 "Uncle Josh": For planken 'e would cut some sticks / Myrrhy pine and licky vir.

N

nag n The target in child's game of 'pitching buttons.'

C 70–15 A stick, about the size of a lead pencil, called a nag, was stuck into the ground and a hole was scuffed with your boot about 12 or 14 feet away from the nag. The object of the game was to pitch a button from the hole in the ground so that the button touched the nag.

nag v *EDD* ~ v 2. To chip, nick or chop with a blunt axe (1937 DEVINE 34).

naggin See NOGGIN.

naggle v Cp *EDD* ~ v[1] 'to fret'; gnaggle 'grumble.' To live frugally, skimp.

1966 SZWED 156 ["Squarin' Up":] If I've got to naggle on six cents a day, / I'll be wanting the Doctor by the end of next May; / And maybe the Parson will have to come round, / To help me square up 'fore I goes underground.

nail v To set a vessel or vehicle on a fixed course.

T 194/6–65 'Now,' I said, 'Jack, nail her south.' And he nailed her south and she come across the bay. P 148–79 [waiting at corner to enter heavy traffic:] After this one, nail 'er!

nailbag n Attrib **nailbag gansey**: rough, durable canvas jacket worn by fishermen and sealers; cp GANSEY.

1916 MURPHY 12 Comfortable, though not attractive clothing. . .were worn by the sealers. The 'nail bag,' or strong rough guernsey (gansey) so called, was a favourite attire. T 296–66 He seen Uncle Tom, when Uncle Tom dashed out of this hole, and he appeared to be like a man with a nailbag garnsey on.

naked a Cp *EDD* naked 1 (a) ~ man 'old, decayed, leafless tree' Ha; SEARY 115; *RLS* 8 (1978), 30–41; *Labrador Inuit* inutsuk 'a pile of rocks erected on a hillside'; cp *DC* inukshuk (1939–); PEACOCK persons: inuit. Comb **naked**

man: a marker, usu a pile of rocks prominently placed as a guide in coastal navigation; sometimes becomes a place-name; AMERICAN MAN, CAIRN, ROCKY MAN. Also attrib.

1842 JUKES ii, 54 . . .a spot called from a tall pile of stones, 'the Naked Man.' 1879 HARVEY 88–9 A wealthy London Company have leased from Messrs Browning and White a mine which has got the queer name of 'Naked Man.' 1953 *Nfld & Lab Pilot* ii, 574 Skynner cove indents the northern shore, about 1¾ miles westward of Naked Man point. 1974 PITTMAN 62 For a moment she is stirred by a compulsion to go to the Naked Man, to bring one more rock from the beach in supplication.

naluyuk n *Labrador Inuit* 77 nalujuk 'janny.' Inuit name for a Christmas mummer.

1969 *Christmas Mumming in Nfld* 121 The Eskimo mummers, the 'naluyuks. . .'

nan[1] n also **nanny** *O Sup*[2] ·· (1940–). Children's name for grandmother; granny.

P 148–64 'Nanny's' is grandmother's place. T 12–64 Cuck-a-doodle-doo, / Nanny lost her shoe; / Grandy lost his walking stick, / Cuck-a-doodle-doo. 1971 NOSEWORTHY 224 ~ or nanny—Grandmother. 1980 *Evening Telegram* 15 Nov, p. 1 [caption] Mrs Hannah Peyton, known as Nanny Peyton, blows out the candle on her 100th [birthday] cake Friday at St Luke's Anglican home.

nan[2] n also **nanny**. Sheep; call to sheep.

T 145–65 An' the usual way of getting the sheep would be to go out with a leaf of cabbage, and hear the mother o' the family, late in the afternoon. 'Come nan, nan, nan, nan, nan, nan. . . Come on nanny, come on nan.' T 255/6–66 We always call a sheep 'nanny.' 1971 NOSEWORTHY 224 Nanny. Call to sheep to get them from the pasture.

nan-cary See AUNTSARY[1].

nansarey See HAND SERRY.

nan-sary See AUNTSARY[1].

nan-slide* See HAND-SLIDE.

nap See KNAP.

nape n *OED* ~ sb[1] 2 a obs (1482); cp *OED* 2 b 'part of a fish near the head' rare (1656), *O Sup*[2] (1884). Fleshy ridge or flap at the end of cod's backbone after the head is removed and the fish split.

1936 SMITH 17 When spread again [the fish] would be made up in twenty-quintal piles, and well covered with rinds on top and tarpaulins around the napes to keep it thoroughly dry; it would remain there for a few days to press and work in pile. T 175/7–65 An' then, when it got perhaps two or three days' sun on it, good days, you put it in what they call a pile. You go around, all yaffle around, around. All tails inside, all the napes o' the fish out around. P 229–67 Napes are the protruding bits of fish on dry cod where the head was torn off. Youngsters have the habit of taking them off the dry fish and eating them. 1971 NOSEWORTHY 224 ~ The top part of a piece of dried codfish.

nar See NE'ER.

narder* See ORDER.

narn neg substitute. See NE'ER and ARN. None; not a single one.

1937 DEVINE 34 ~ never a one, e.g. 'I got narn.' P 148–64 I ain't got narn. P 274–65 Of course you already have that old Newfoundland chestnut—'Arn? Narn'? Two fishermen were out in their boats, one going to and the other from the fishing grounds. As they passed by one said 'Arn?' and the reply came 'Narn.' Translated it meant *arn* 'ar a one, or either one'; *narn* 'nar a one, or neither one.' C 74–128 [local rhyme] John Antle got a quintal, / John Pew got a few. / John War'n got narn, / That was all was got this mar'n. 1979 *Salt Water, Fresh Water* 3 'Any fish?' 'No. . .nar'n. . .very scarce.' And the fish would be down drowning on your lines, and you wouldn't haul up, no way. You'd get a smoke. . .or pretend to cook a feed, and he'd say: 'Well, nothing here,' and be gone.

narrow a also **narry***. Comb **narrow-face**: a caplin.

P 184–67 Did you see either narry-face this morning? M 71–97 Narry-faces are caplin, a name descriptive of the tiny fish. P 13–79 ~ an affectionate term for fish, especially caplin, and most often used when fishing is good and one is excited.

naskapi n also **escopic, nascapee, nascaupee, nascopi, naskupi, nasquapee, nescaupick.** *O Sup*[2] ~ (Nfld: 1774–) for senses 1, 2; *RLS* 8 (1978), 30 for sense 3; *DC* naskapi sled (Nfld: 1779).

1 Member of a nomadic branch of the Algonkian people who migrate seasonally from the interior of Labrador to the coast; LABRADOR INDIAN.

1774 *Trans Roy Soc* lxiv, 379–80 Next to the Mountaineers, and still farther westward, you come to a nation called the ESCOPICS. We know not much of this people: and beyond them, are the Hudson Bay Indians, with whom the world is but little better acquainted. 1863 HIND 12 The leading object was. . .to obtain as much information as possible respecting the general features and resources of that portion of the Labrador Peninsula, and of the Montagnais who now hunt chiefly on the coast, as well as of the Nasquapees who roam throughout the interior. 1884 STEARNS 262 The 'Ounadcapis,' 'Ounascapis,' 'Naskapis,' 'Nascapees,' 'Nascopi,' 'Naskupi,' or 'Nasquapee,' as they have been variously called, speak a dialect of the Cree language, nearly like, but not identical with, that of the Montagnais Indians, of the same stock. The word 'Nascopi' is properly the name for an 'Indian man' (i.e., *vir*) in their dialect, and that, in all Algonquin languages, the name for 'man' and the verb 'to stand erect' are nearly related. 1908 HUBBARD 10 The Nascaupees, who hunt northward into the barrens, are properly Swampy

Crees, who very possibly left their ancient home southwest of Hudson Bay to escape the Iroquois incursions of two or three centuries ago. 1973 HENRIKSEN ix The Naskapi live in two different worlds: in the winter, they roam the interior of Labrador, hunting caribou; in the summer, they live in or around the village of Davis Inlet on the coast of Labrador.

2 The language of the Naskapi indians.

1973 HENRIKSEN 21 They write in Naskapi using the English alphabet.

3 A pile of rocks placed on a prominent coastal eminence; AMERICAN MAN, CAIRN, NAKED MAN.

1884 STEARNS 262 In relation to the name Nascopi, I found it in common use all along the coast for a pile or heap of stones thrown up into some form several feet in height and usually placed on top of an island or neighboring height to mark some position, or important spot or event. These heaps occur everywhere, and are known, as I have said, by the name 'Nascopi.'

4 Comb **naskapi path**: track habitually used by Naskapi indians either for passage or trapping; PATH.

[1770] 1792 CARTWRIGHT i, 62 Early in the morning, I took Charles and Ned with me to Nescaupick path; where we found the slot of the deer which they saw yesterday. After continuing the path to North Head we returned back; knowing that the furriers must cross the slot in their way back home.

naskapi sled: type of sled used in winter by Labrador indians.

[1775] 1792 CARTWRIGHT ii, 53 At eleven o'clock, taking Edward Croke and Jack with me, together with our provisions, upon a Nescaupick sled drawn by two dogs, we set off for Young's Droke.

natch See NOTCH n.

native a

1 Indigenous (to Newfoundland); see BEOTHUK, RED INDIAN.

1672 [BLOME] 187 The North and West part of this *Countrey* the *Native-Indians* Inhabit. 1792 PULLING *MS* 30 July Richard Richmond supposes that there are about 5 or 6 hundred of the Native Indians on the Island of Newfoundland, but this is only a wild conjecture. 1819 PANL CS 1 28 May I beg leave to lay before your Excellency the following Statements by which it will appear to what extent I have been a sufferer by depredations committed on my property by the Native Indians.

2 Living and breeding in Newfoundland waters, as distinguished from migrating; see HARBOUR SEAL.

1873 CARROLL 10 The different kinds of seals that frequent the coast of Newfoundland. . .are classed as follows: The square flipper seal, the hood seal, the harp seal and dotard or native seal of Newfoundland. The native seal never leaves the island.

native n

1 European of British or Irish descent born in Newfoundland and distinguished from seasonal migratory fishermen and planters; also attrib.

[1794] 1968 THOMAS 137 As this Island has been inhabit'd for such a number of years and was peopled by British and Irish, you frequently meet with Familys whose Grandfathers were born in Newfoundland. These are what I call the Natives. 1813 CARSON 9 The natives [of Newfoundland] while young possess as strong an attachment for their native harbours, as the Scotch and Swiss do for their native mountains. 1852 *Morning Post* [St John's] 12 Feb, p. 2 Then, he pointed at Mr William Thomas, whom he represented as a native (in this, however, the hon. member was mistaken, for William Thomas was not a native). [He] was the son of old Bevel Thomas, a Fishing Admiral. 1892 HOWLEY *MS Reminiscences* 1 Dr Mike Howley was duly consecrated. . .by Rgt Revd Dr Power. There was great rejoicing amongst the Roman Catholic people at the elevation of a native priest to this dignity. He being the first Native of the Island so honoured. 1931 BYRNES 126 A few of the founders stuck to the plain Pink for two or three years, but after the death of Barnes, and the blowing down of the Native Hall in 1846, the Pink, White and Green, became the recognized Native Flag.

2 Inhabitant of Labrador, often one of mixed European and indian or Inuit descent.

T 25–64 What they call the natives on the Labrador might be English, Irish or Scotch settlers who came out and left vessels down there and married Eskimo women, say, three or four generations ago. And their descendants are called natives.

3 Harbour seal (*Phoca vitulina*) as distinguished from the migratory 'harp' and 'hooded seal.'

[1802] 1916 MURPHY 2 The seals upon this coast are of many species. . . [J]ars, Doaters and Gunswoils and many others brew upon the rocks, in the summer season, and may be called natives.

nature n *EDD* ~ sb 4 for sense 1; cp *OED* 6, 6 b, *ADD* 2 for sense 2.

1 Good nature, kindliness.

P 54–67 'E an't got no more nature 'n a picket.

2 Sexual drive.

P 131–70 If a man gets impotent, he'll say to the nurse, 'I've lost my nature.' Of a married woman who went off with another man: 'Her nature got the better of her.' 1975 LEYTON 16–17 You know what that does with you? That'll even take away your nature. You won't want women or nothing. P 40–78 He got more nature than he needs.

nawpoll* n ['nɒ:poʉl]. Cp *EDD* nauphead; knaw-post 'fool' So. Stupid person; stunpoll (see STUN a).

T 222–66 I wonder how you vent your spleen on your husbands when they cross-hackle you; that is, if they ever do argue with you. Do you call them angishores, or nawpolls or ninnyhammers?

nearshore See INSHORE, SHORE¹.

neck n *OED* ~ sb¹ 10 c for sense 1; 11 b (1780 quot) for sense 2.

1 The narrow entrance to a harbour.

1953 *Nfld & Lab Pilot* ii, 191 Herring Neck is the name given to the entrance to Goldson arm.

2 A narrow strip of woods.

[1820] 1915 HOWLEY 122 The frost had been very severe for three days which fastened the river above, where we reached by passing over two necks of burnt woods for three miles.

neddick See NUDDICK.

needle See KNITTING.

ne'er neg determiner also **naar a, nair a, nar a, nera, norra** [næəɹ, neəɹ, nɑəɹ, næˈɹ ə, næəɹ ə, nɛəɹ ə, nɑɹ ə] *OED* never adv 3: never a (1250–), ne'er a (1420–); *EDD* never a 'gen dial use.' See E'ER, NARN, (N)EITHER. No; not a; not one.

1895 *J A Folklore* viii, 32 'Naar a bit' [is] a favourite expression to denote a strong negative. 1899 ENGLISH 11 'Nera wan o' ye id fire a snow-ball at her.' 1901 *Christmas Review* 5 "The Outport Planter": He's gon' wid gansy and coatin' pants; with Hamburg boots and ne'e'r a collar. 1904 MURPHY 74 "Hawco, the Hero": For there's nair a man from Topsail / Clear up the whole South Shore, / Who has not heard of Hawco, the last two months or more. 1924 ENGLAND 62 'Him a gert man, my son!' 'Ain't narr nudder man like dat un,' murmured a third. P 148–63 We didn't take nar copper from him. T 31/4–64 'I don't want nar a glass [telescope]. I can see the line.' 'No,' they says, 'you won't see nar a line there; you can't.' T 284–66 I used to know that [story]. That's a man with ne'er soul, and he had his soul on a island, see? 1975 LEYTON 66–7 Me own two fellows; one fellow works on the surface in there. The other guy, he won't even go over the hill. There's ne'er one of them going underground while I'm alive. 1977 *Nfld Qtly* Summer, pp. 11–12 When we got in St John's it was frosty. We never had ne'er bit of clothes on us. . . 'This is a bit of clothes,' I said, 'we put on about three months ago and,' I said, 'it's still on us, half the time,' I said, 'soaking in salt water.'

neither neg determiner, substitute also **nother*** ['niːðəɹ, 'niːdəɹ, 'nɐiðəɹ, 'nɐidə]. Cp *OED* nother a²; neither nother (1530–1640); *EDD* nowther adj 1 'no, not any,' 3 nother-nother, nother-one D So; J REEVES *Idiom of the People*, p. 62 Nor neither young man in this place [1906 So]. See EITHER. No; not any; none; NE'ER.

1902 *Christmas Bells* 3 But I tells you, b'y, that there's neither maid in Green Bay. . .I'd trade that old craft for. 1940 SCAMMELL 26 "Shooting of the Bawks": As yet there's neither law agin' the killin of a hen! P 148–60 The twins looked at each other, neither word had to be spoken, the pair just headed for the wharf where father's boat was tied. P 148–62 'Did you watch television?' 'Neither one upstairs.' P 148–63 We hadn't had neither letter since. T 45–64 By and by you got wise to that and you knew there were neither one. T 49–64 Not very much sleep. Many's a night neither wink, you wouldn't close your eyes. T 141/64–65² I looked right back through the whole history o' the lodge, an' we never had five deaths in neither one year. P 148–67 [people looking for a church:] There's neither 'nother church here. P 148–67 [riddle:] North, south, east, west / 300 teeth and neither mouth. . . A wool carder. 1971 CASEY 41 And he ran in the old stable there and got the broom, there was neither old gun around.

nelson n Phr *drink it off dead Nelson, ~ the one-eyed hero*: of indiscriminate and copious consumption of alcohol.

1930 BARNES 317 So that's what the saying means, 'He'd drink the rum off Nelson's corpse.' P 181–75 Why, he'd drink it off dead Nelson. He'd drink it off the one-eyed hero.

nesh See NISH.

net v Cp *OED* netting vbl sb 1 'making a net' (1872–). To make a net for catching animals, birds, etc; hence **netting**.

[1772] 1792 CARTWRIGHT i, 196 This being another bad day, I employed myself in netting. [1777] 1792 ibid ii, 278 I was netting all day, and finished my grouse-net at night.

net* v [= to knit a net]. See KNIT.

net n *OED* ~ sb¹ 5 a (Nfld: 1883). Also occurring in other combs: COD-NET, HERRING ~ , SEAL ~ , etc.

Attrib, comb **net-bag**: in the inshore fishery, a large net, shaped like a bag, in which surplus cod are temporarily moored until brought ashore; BAG, COD- ~ .

1972 MURRAY 243 If the trap contained more than one boatload of fish, the remainder was 'bagged,' that is, channelled into a 'net bag' which was then attached to the stern of the small boat or 'rodney.' This was left at the trap site.

net-fishery: cod-fishery using gear other than hook-and-line.

[1863] 1954 INNIS 397 The net fishery is conducted by fishermen who have rooms [on the Labrador], the seine fishery mostly by those who follow it in vessels.

net-fishing: the taking of cod by various means using nets.

1832 MCGREGOR i, 245 The net fishing, which, by the limits of three miles, was intended to be secured to our people, the Americans are daring enough to persevere in prosecuting, while their ingenuity ensures them success.

net-gallows: frame used to spread fish-net for drying; GALLOWS.

1937 DEVINE 34 ~ A framework of longers with two sides and a ridge-pole, for spreading nets to dry. P 127–76 ~ A single pole, slung between four supporting poles, two on each end, used for drying newly tanned 'twine,' i.e. fish nets.

net-ground: area of foreshore on which fish-nets are spread to dry.

T 185–65 That strip that runs up through, that's reserved for net-ground, spread nets on. [Nobody allowed] to build there.

net-hook: wooden angle or fork cut from a tree

and used to stretch a fish-net when drying it (P 245–71).

net-horse: see net-gallows.

1905 DUNCAN 12 . . .past the skipper's stage and net-horse, where the cod-trap was spread to dry in the sun.

net-loft: area of a fishing-stage or premises for the storing and mending of nets; LOFT, TWINE ~ .

[1812] 1966 *Evening Telegram* 27 May, p. 6 [to be sold] Dry goods store, net loft. . .cook room, fisherman's house, fish store, salt store, small salmon plantation. [1918] 1972 GORDON 121 The noise of the fiddles and the thumping of feet in the Company's net-loft were still in evidence when, at dawn next day, we set off for our next port of call at Ticoralak. T 192–65 He had it bought for a net loft, for mendin' traps, but he uses it now for oil storage, an' salt. 1967 *Bk of Nfld* iv, 236 The net-loft was reserved for older folk and admittance was a privilege rarely granted to the child. 1977 RUSSELL 48 A crowd of us with nothing better to do at the time, were sittin' around in Grampa Walcott's net loft.

net-mender: man employed to oversee and repair fishing-gear.

[1775] *Journeys* (ed Harvey) 61 He said they had many Nets to mend, their Net mender was Ill, and if I would by Choise go to Work he would engage to give me after the rate of thirty Pounds pʳ year till Mʳ Neave came. 1836 [WIX]² 31 Assembled a very attentive congregation of twenty-one, in the net-menders' room on Mr Tucker's wharf.

netting n *OED* ~ sb² 2 (1883 quot). Fish-net or particular section knitted to form the several parts of such a net; LINNET.

[1693] 1793 REEVES xxiv That it shall be lawful for any of his Majesty's subjects residing in *Ireland* to ship and lade there, and to transport directly from thence to *Newfoundland*. . .on board any ship or vessel which may lawfully trade or fish there, any provisions, and also any hooks, lines, netting, or other tools or implements necessary for and used in the fishery. P 9–73 [The cod-trap together with] the heads and linnet (netting) going with it.

netting vbl n See KNITTING.

never

1 A negative modifying the past of the verb; did not.

T 141/64–65² And I looked back through the whole history of the Lodge, and we never had five deaths in neither one year. P 148–69 I never had nother [any] sports coat on. 1977 *Nfld Qtly* Winter, p. 17 I never looked up. I took off me oil clothes. I knowed (that if) she never struck the rocks, she wasn't going to strike it then.

2 In phr *be the nevers*: to be full of mischief, the limit.

P 272–60 You're the nevers: you are the limit, mischievous. P 207–66 Tommy, you're the nevers!—a hard case.

new a   Of ice, recently formed as the water freezes or 'catches over'; LOCAL: *local ice*.

1924 ENGLAND 21–2 On the southern way they hunt and fish, till ousted by the 'slob' or new ice. 1929 *Nat Geog* July, p. 117 . . .new ice—that is, ice a few inches thick that forms in the open leads between the heavier ice. Only in new ice can the harp bore bobbing holes. [1964 BLONDAHL (ed) 84 "The Loss of the *Ellen Munn*": And now to close, take this advice: Don't ever trust the new-made ice.]

new britaniola See BRITANIOLA.

newfie n   also **newf, newfy** BERREY (1942) 52, 385, 734 ~ 'New Foundland,' 'a Newfoundlander,' 'a Newfoundland seaman'; *DC* 1, 2 (1945–; 1958); *O Sup²* (1942–). A native-born inhabitant of Newfoundland; NEWFOUNDLANDER; sometimes used locally in imitation of Americans and mainland Canadians. Also attrib, and comb **newfyjohn(s)**: St John's.

1945 *Atlantic Guardian* Jan, p. 16 Then he found out that the 'Newfies,' as the islanders are sometimes called by one another and by the Americans, refer to supper as 'tea.' 1949 DULEY 11 Now he felt dispossessed, crowded on his own streets, mowed down by the ever-increasing numbers of dun-coloured, army-vehicles. The strangers were strutting, becoming the 'big-shots.' They looked down their noses at the natives. They were disdainful of a hard old heritage. They began to call the towns-folk 'the Newfies' and like Queen Victoria, the Newfoundlanders were not amused. 1952 *Atlantic Advocate* Mar, p. 49 He is a strong advocate of the horse and waggon, home-made bread and 'Newfie screech.' 1976 *Daily News* 22 Jan, p. 3 Anyone who knows anything might be inclined to the conclusion that [he] is just another stunned Newf. 1976 WHALLEY 4 St John's, a mean ironbound slot for a navigator to find in foul weather or in bad visibility, yet a snug haven for so many ships in the long struggle with the dangers of the North Atlantic and 'the violence of the enemy' that 'Newfy-John's' was a name as much to be conjured with as the Murmansk Run or the Rose Garden. 1977 *Evening Telegram* 24 Nov, p. 8 The Crowsnest is mentioned often. . .as an officers' club where the men spent many happy hours while docked in 'Newfyjohn,' the name [used] to refer to St John's.

newfoundland n   also **new founde lande, new-found land**, etc. [ˌnjufənˈlænd, ˌnufənˈlænd, ˌnufənˈlæn, ˌnufaˑʊnˈlæn] *OED* Newfound a: ~ land (1527, 1626 quots) for sense 1; *OED* ~ b (1845–), *O Sup²* (1773–), *DC* (1880–) for sense 2. For comb in sense 3: *NID* ~ caribou; for sense 4: *DAE* bank n¹ 1 ~ bank (1635–), *OED* coffin sb 3 e naut (1833–) for ~ coffin, *DC* ~ Ranger Force (1965). See also BACCALAO, NEWLAND.

1 The north-east coast of North America and its adjacent islands; esp the large island situated at the entrance to the Gulf of St Lawrence; that island and the territory of Labrador comprising the Colony and Dominion of Newfoundland; since 1949, the tenth province of Canada.

[1502] 1962 *Cabot Voyages* 216 Item to the merchauntes of bristoll that have bene in the newe founde launde £20. [c1503] 1979 DUNBAR 120 ["To the King"] It micht have cuming in schortar quhyll / Fra [Calyecot] and the new fund Yle, / The partis of Transmeridiane. [1583] 1940 *Gilbert's Voyages & Enterprises* ii, 404 [Hayes' narrative] That which we doe call the New-found land, and the Frenchmen Bacalaos, is an Iland, or rather (after the opinion of some) it consistenth of sundry Ilands and broken lands, situate in the North Regions of America, upon the gulfe and entrance of the great river called S Laurence in Canada. [1611] 1895 PROWSE 122 [London and Bristol Company's Charter] . . .to inhabite and establish a Colony or Colonies in the Southerne and easterne p'tes of the country and Islande commonlie called Newfoundland. 1620 WHITBOURNE [sig. B1] Among my undertakings and imployments in Seafaring, the most part have been to an Iland, called *New-found-land*. 1628 HAYMAN¹ 31 The Aire, in *Newfound-Land* is wholesome good; / The fire, as sweet as any made of wood; / The Waters, very rich, both salt and fresh; / The Earth more rich, you know it is no lesse. / Where all are good, *Fire, Water, Earth*, and *Aire*, / What man made of these foure would not live there? [1662] 1963 YONGE 53–4 In February, my father shipped me to go Chyrurgeon of the *Reformation*. . .bound for Newfoundland, to make a voyage. [1727] 1966 POPE 678 "The Lamentation of Glumdalclitch": O! squander not thy Grief; those Tears command / To weep upon our Cod in *Newfound-Land*: / The plenteous Pickle shall preserve the Fish, / And *Europe* taste thy Sorrows in her Dish. [1794] 1968 THOMAS 63 Newfoundland being in all parts intersected with Bogs, Barrens, Lakes, Morasses, Hills, Rivulets and Woods we find all places are plaster'd or thickly scatter'd with stones of all shapes and all sizes. [1869] 1966 DOYLE (ed) 64 "Anti-Confederation Song": Hurrah for our own native Isle, Newfoundland, / Not a stranger shall hold one inch of its strand, / Her face turns to Britain, her back to the Gulf, / Come near at your peril Canadian Wolf. 1869 MCCREA 6 She laughed at my calling it New-fōūnd-land, and said: 'Newfunlan'.' 1887 *Colonist Christmas No* 5 [On the quay at Poole] I axed him, 'Where be these goin' to, Mister?' 'You fule!' said he, 'these be for Newfunland.' 1911 HUTCHINSON 78–9 Newfoundland—accent on the last syllable, please, for this is the only way of speaking of it that can please a native. 1949 DULEY 4 But the basic characteristic of Newfoundland is drama. Climatically the country is deranged, flouting the calendar most of the year. Sometimes it likes a touch of spring in January, and frequently winter in June. . . One has to be tough to be a resident. 1951 *Nfld & Lab Pilot* i, 1 Newfoundland is a large island situated at the mouth of the Gulf of St Lawrence; it contains an area of 42,734 square miles [and] is of roughly triangular shape; its coasts are indented with deep bays and harbours, many of which are very fine and nearly all afford shelter to vessels during summer. [1959] 1965 PEACOCK (ed) i, 138 "Labrador": The *Carey* being our schooner's name as you may understand, / With a crowd of brave young fishermen brought up in Newfoundland.

2 NEWFOUNDLAND DOG; also attrib.

1745 CAREW 134 A fine bitch of the *Newfoundland*-Breed he enticed away by the Art which had rendered him so famous. [1771] 1792 CARTWRIGHT i, 87 He found the unfortunate Mr Jones frozen to death, with his faithful Newfoundland bitch by his side! He gave the poor creature what bread he had about him, but could not prevail on her to leave her master. 1863 HIND ii, 156 He soon missed the pet Newfoundland, and after a few hours discovered the mangled body of his favourite [dog] lying on the beach. 1883 HATTON & HARVEY 232 Landseer, as is well known, has immortalized one of the Newfoundland dogs in his celebrated picture entitled 'A Distinguished Member of the Humane Society,' and the breed to which he belonged is known as the 'Landseer New-foundland.' [1923] 1946 PRATT 187 "The Big Fellow": And I thought of the big Newfoundland / I saw, asleep by a rock / The day before. 1969 HORWOOD 191 The other native Canadian breed, the Newfoundland, origi-nated on the east coast, at or near St John's. It is a huge, sweet-tempered animal, also with a natural affi-nity for water, and also with webbed feet, developed by natural selection over many generations. The New-foundland is bigger, much more heavily furred, and with a larger, kinder-looking head than the water dogs. It is the greatest of all life-savers.

3 In names of animals and birds: **newfoundland beaver**, ~ **black-capped chicka-dee**, ~ **boreal chickadee**, ~ **caribou** [see also CARIBOU], ~ **deer** [see also DEER], ~ **grey jay**, ~ **hairy woodpecker**, ~ **hermit thrush**, ~ **lynx** [see also LINK], ~ **ovenbird**, ~ **pine grosbeak**, ~ **purple finch**, ~ **red crossbill**, ~ **robin** [see also ROBIN REDBREAST], ~ **small-billed water-thrush**, ~ **thrush**, ~ **veery**, ~ **winter wren**, ~ **wolf**, ~ **yellow warbler**.

1967 *Bk of Nfld* iii, 326 The Newfoundland beaver (*Castor canadensis caecator*) shows an excellent exam-ple of animal adaption to habitat which would be termed unsuitable in mainland areas. 1951 PETERS & BURLEIGH 310–11 Newfoundland Black-Capped Chickadee. *Parus atricapillus bartletti*. . . A small bird with black cap and throat, white cheeks and ashy upper parts. Resident in Newfoundland. . . This bird was named for the well known Arctic explorer and New-foundlander, the late Captain R A Bartlett. 1951 ibid 311 Newfoundland Boreal Chickadee. *Parus hudsoni-cus rabbittsi*. A small bird with a brown cap, black throat and general brownish-gray appearance. Resi-dent in Newfoundland. We named this race in honour of the late Gower Rabbitts, former clerk of Game and Inland Fisheries, St John's. 1905 PROWSE 34 As a gen-eral rule, island races of wild animals are inferior to those of the great continents, but with the Newfound-land caribou. . .this cannot be said to be the case. Far surpassing the European reindeer, of which it is now considered a sub-species, it is equal in size to the cari-bou of Eastern Canada, but distinctly finer in the mat-ter of horn growth. [1822] 1928 CORMACK 32 The Newfoundland deer—and there is only one species in the Island—is a variety of the reindeer, or caribou; and like that animal, in every other country, it is migratory, always changing place with the seasons for the sake of

its favourite kinds of food. Although they migrate in herds, they travel in files, with their heads in some degree to windward. 1951 PETERS & BURLEIGH 303 Newfoundland Gray Jay. *Perisoreus canadensis sanfordi*. . . A gray bird, larger than a Robin, with white forehead, cheeks, throat and ring around neck; with fluffy plumage and no crest on head. Comes near campers and woods workers. Common resident. Ibid 287 Newfoundland Hairy Woodpecker. . .*Dendrocopos villosus terraenovae*. Found throughout the province but usually restricted to heavier woods with a sprinkling of deciduous trees. . . It is more shy and retiring than its smaller rel-ative, the Downy, but is more active and noisier. Ibid 320–1 Newfoundland Hermit Thrush. *Hylocichla gut-tata crymophila*. . . A brown-backed bird with a spot-ted breast and rufous tail. Breeds in Newfoundland. Common summer resident. Like other thrushes [it] inhabits the dense woods; so is more frequently heard than seen. 1967 *Bk of Nfld* iii, 326 The Newfoundland Lynx (*Lynx canadensis subsolanus*) has about the same size and proportions as the mainland species but is darker. It is easily recognized by the cat-like face top-ped by tufted sharp-pointed ears, a black tipped tail and excessively large paws well suited for travel over soft ground and snow. 1951 PETERS & BURLEIGH 352 Newfoundland Ovenbird. *Seiurus aurocapillus furvior*. . . An olive-brown bird with a light breast streaked with black. The nest is usually sunken in the moss or soil, is arched over like an old-fashioned brick oven. Ibid 373 Newfoundland Pine Grosbeak. *Pinicola enucleator eschatosus*. . . A Robin-sized finch; the males mostly rose-red, and the females gray with a yel-lowish tinge to head and rump. Breeds in Newfound-land. Common summer resident and fairly common winter resident. The Pine Grosbeak is known by all Newfoundlanders as the 'Mope.' Indeed, it does appear to mope, for it sits around on stunted spruces and will often allow very close approach. Ibid 372 New-foundland Purple Finch. *Carpodacus purpureus nesophilus*. . . A sparrow-sized bird mostly rosy-red, distinguished by the rather heavy bill. Breeds only in Newfoundland. Ibid 379–80 Newfoundland Red Cross-bill. *Loxia curvirostra pusilla*. . . Adult males are brick-red; young males are yellow and females are yellow-gray. This parrot-like finch is unmistakable if you are close enough to see its crossed bill. This race breeds in Newfoundland and Nova Scotia. The local name [Spruce Mope] refers to their slow movements while feeding in the spruce tops. Ibid 317 Newfoundland Robin. *Turdus migratorius nigrideus*. . . Familiar to all persons, with its dark black and red breast. Breeds in Newfoundland, Labrador and Ungava. Abundant sum-mer resident. Ibid 366 Newfoundland Rusty Blackbird. . . A rather short-tailed bird, slightly smaller than a Robin. In fall it becomes rusty above and brownish below. Breeds in Newfoundland. Ibid 353 Newfoundland Small-billed Water-thrush. *Seiurus noveboracensis uliginosus*. . . A brown-backed bird, with yellow underneath, which walks along banks of streams and ponds, constantly teetering. Breeds in Newfoundland. Common summer resident. [1766] 1971 BANKS 392 Robin or Newfoundland Thrush: *Turdus migratorius nigrideus*. 1951 PETERS & BURLEIGH 325 Newfoundland veery. *Hylocichla fus-*

cescens fuliginosa. . . The most reddish-backed of our thrushes and with the smallest spots on the breast. Breeds in Newfoundland. Uncommon summer resident. Ibid 315–16 Newfoundland Winter Wren. *Troglodytes troglodytes aquilonaris*. . . A very small, dark-brown bird, which holds its stubby tail erect over its back. Breeds in Newfoundland. Uncommon summer resident and rare winter resident. 1974 NORTHCOTT 49 *Canis lupus beothucus*, the extinct Newfoundland wolf was closely related to the wolf which still occupies Labrador. From what is known about this species, it appears to have resembled the tundra wolf of the north more closely than the timber wolf familiar in southern Canada. It was reported to have been light in color. 1951 PETERS & BURLEIGH 342 Newfoundland Yellow Warbler. *Dendroica petechia amnicola*. . . Our only all-yellow bird. Abundant summer resident. This all-yellow bird is locally known as 'yellow-hammer,' but this name seems to be applied also to all small birds showing yellow in their plumage.

4 Attrib, comb **newfoundland banks**: areas of shoal water forming the offshore fishing grounds; BANK, GRAND BANK(S).

[1794] 1968 THOMAS 181 The Newfoundland Banks are the most celebrated in the World for Fish. 1934 LOUNSBURY 8 The Newfoundland Banks are separated from those of Nova Scotia by a great submarine channel, the Laurentian Valley, which is from fifty to seventy miles wide. It is broader near the edge of the continental shelf and attains a depth of 15,000 feet. The banks which lie north and east of the great channel and south and southeast of Newfoundland are Burgeo, St Pierre, Green, the Grand Bank proper, and Flemish Cap. [1941] 1974 BRIDLE (ed) i, 193 Problems relating to the operation of foreign trawlers off the Newfoundland Banks. . .

newfoundland brewis [ˌnjuufənd'lænd bruuz]: see BREWIS, FISHERMAN'S BREWIS.

newfoundland coffin: early sea-going vessel locally constructed.

1819 ANSPACH 364 The few attempts that have hitherto [1812] been made to build in that island ships or brigs, intended for long voyages, have ended in the production of vessels that might perhaps live *seven* years at the most, and which were designated there by the ominous appellation of Newfoundland coffins.

newfoundland company: in the seventeenth century, a group authorized by charter to establish a plantation in Newfoundland.

1628 HAYMAN[1] 31 To the right worshipfull Iohn Slany, Treasurer to the Newfound-land Company, and to all the rest of that Honorable Corporation. 1708 OLDMIXON 5 He therefore resolv'd to retire to *America*, and finding the *Newfoundland* Company made no use of their Grant, he thought of this Place for his Retreat.

newfoundland dance: a lively, vigorous group step-dance.

1884 STEARNS 293 [At Bonne Espérance] Monday night, for our benefit, the natives performed a Labrador, or rather Newfoundland dance, at one of the native cabins near by. A crowd of about thirty assembled and danced till nearly morning. Their main object seemed to be to 'start the sweat, and see who could

make the most noise.' It seemed as if the very house would come down over our heads as they hammered on the floor with their top-legged boots pounding with the full force of their powers.

newfoundland dialect: any of the varieties of English spoken by native Newfoundlanders; Newfoundland English.

[1836 [WIX][2] 143 The difference of extraction has occasioned, as may be supposed, a marked dissimilarity between the descendants of Jersey-men, Frenchmen, Irish, Scotch, and English people. The people, too, with whom the first settlers and their immediate descendants may have had contact, or intercourse, have attributed much to the formation of the dialect, character, and habits of the present settlers.] 1922 *Sat Ev Post* 195, 2 Sep, p. 129 . . .a babel of loud talk, in the half-comprehensible Newfoundland dialect, troubled that dim, stifling air. 1967 *Bk of Nfld* iii, 560 It must not be thought that Newfoundland dialects can be described purely in terms of their British and Irish origins, or of the elements of those origins which have been retained in the new land. In many respects local speech has been conservative; but in others it has been immensely creative and innovating.

newfoundland dog: see NEWFOUNDLAND DOG.

newfoundland dwarf birch: *Betula michauxii* (1970 *Gray's Botany* 536).

newfoundland fish: cod-fish; FISH.

1623 [T C] *A Short Discourse* [sig. B1ᵛ] Lastly, there can no reason be given to the contrary, why the forraine vent of the *Newfoundland* fish. . .may not yearly return great quantities of mony. [1943] 1974 BRIDLE (ed) i, 1247 Dunn tells me that when he was in Washington, the American authorities with whom he was in discussion concerning the purchase of Newfoundland fish, told him that Newfoundland must control the export price or the United States would not continue to deal with them. 1973 HORWOOD 45–6 The *Sunner* was chartered to take another load of drums and half drums of Newfoundland fish, the whole cargo to be delivered in Maceio, Brazil.

newfoundland fish-box: jocular term for a sailing vessel engaged in transporting dried cod to foreign markets.

1930 BARNES 64 Them days every one knew that the China Tea Clippers and the Newfoundland Fish Boxes, as they were called, were the hardest driven ships afloat because they had to run for markets.

newfoundland fishery: the marine fishing industry in Newfoundland waters, esp the cod-fishery. See also FISHERY.

[1693] 1793 REEVES xx That for the better accommodation of the persons belonging to vessels employed in the *Newfoundland* fishery, it shall be made lawful for the masters and crews belonging to any vessels fitted out and employed in that fishery. . . 1712 *West-India Merchant* 7 Nor are we to wonder at this, for of late years they have imploy'd in the *Newfoundland* fishery 4 or 500 Sail of Ships *per ann.* of good Burden. 1846 TOCQUE 216 The Newfoundland fishery commences at some places in May. 1954 INNIS 31 The English advanced from a position of minor importance in the Newfoundland fishery at the beginning of the second half of the [16th] century to one of major importance at the end.

newfoundland hardwood ['nuːfənlænd ˌhæəɹdwʊd]: birch (*Betula papyrifera; B. lutea*).

T 54/60–64 Now my claws was made out of birch, Newfoundland birch, which was called Newfoundland hardwood.

newfoundland indian: see INDIAN.

newfoundland-labrador: the north-eastern peninsula of North America, lying between Hudson Bay and the Gulf of St Lawrence, which forms part of the Province of Newfoundland; LABRADOR. Cp CANADIAN-LABRADOR.

1909 BROWNE 104 The Labrador missions [became part of the parish of Fortune Harbour in 1834]. From that date Newfoundland priests have visited the coast regularly, though Canadian priests still have jurisdiction on Newfoundland-Labrador. 1946 MACKAY (ed) 181 The terms *Canadian-Labrador* and *Newfoundland-Labrador* were once very common and are still frequently used in Newfoundland. The Canadian-Labrador, a stretch of coastline from the St John river in the Province of Quebec (later from Mt Joli) to Blanc Sablon, is now part of the Province of Quebec, and the term *Labrador*, as mentioned later, is officially restricted to the Newfoundland territory on the mainland. 1947 TANNER 42 Newfoundland's share is called Newfoundland-Labrador.

newfoundland-man: see NEWFOUNDLAND-MAN.

newfoundland oak: yellow or grey birch (*Betula lutea*); WITCH-HAZEL (1956 ROULEAU 34).

1938 MACDERMOTT 251 . . .a strip of Witch Hazel or 'Newfoundland Oak.'

newfoundland ranger: officer in an early twentieth-century force (1935–49) engaged in police and other duties in parts of Newfoundland and Labrador outside the jurisdiction of the St John's constabulary; RANGER.

[1941] 1974 BRIDLE (ed) i, 450 Passes for admission to the area have been issued by the Department of Public Utilities or Department of Justice. Passes have also been issued by the Newfoundland Rangers. 1966 BEN-DOR 192 In 1934 the first policemen were stationed on the coast and in [1935], when the new body of the Newfoundland Rangers was formed, it took over the police duties in Labrador. 1977 *Inuit Land Use* 107 After 1934, they might obtain relief from the Newfoundland Rangers, who were responsible for enforcing the game laws, which prohibited the hunting of caribou after Easter.

newfoundland regiment: any of several volunteer military units formed in Newfoundland; see also BLUE PUTTEE.

[1781] 1964 NICHOLSON 20 The Newfoundland Regiment is completed, in good order, and very well disciplined. [1812] 1954 SAUNDERS 14 In consequence of the nature of the service required from the Royal Newfoundland Regiment necessarily subdividing that corps into small detachments, Major Heathcote is directed to leave the colours of the Regiment in this Garrison. 1964 NICHOLSON 112 The first commissions for the offi-

cers of the Newfoundland Regiment were granted by His Excellency on September 21 [1914] when ten captains and two lieutenants were appointed.

newfoundland spell: a rest from the tedium of one type of work by a change to another (P 148–64). See also SPELL n.

newfoundland trade: the fishery in Newfoundland, esp the supplying of men engaged in the cod-fishery and the marketing of the dried and salted product overseas; see also FISH TRADE, TRADE.

1765 WILLIAMS 8 Unfortunately for the Government, as well as those concerned in the Newfoundland Trade. . .several of the Forts were dismantled. [1769] 1961 FAY 22 A winter of bread riots in Jersey—official emphasis on 'the great disadvantages agriculture is reduced to, by the great number of hands yearly employed in the Newfoundland trade.' [1770] 1792 CARTWRIGHT i, 2 In consequence of our partnership it was resolved, that we should purchase from Messrs Perkins and Coghlan (who are in the Newfoundland trade) a schooner of eighty tons, then lying in the harbour of Poole. [1817] 1953 JOB 24 Have you a large capital employed in the Newfoundland trade at present? 1953 *Nfld Fish Develop Report* 39 The losses of the Newfoundland trade in European countries—both shore-cure and Labrador fish—were affected but the latter, perhaps especially.

newfoundland turbot: see TURBOT.

newfoundland voyage: see VOYAGE.

newfoundland dog n *OED* Newfoundland b (1845–), *O Sup*[2] (1773–), *DC* (1766–) for sense 1.

1 A large, strong dog with heavy black or black-and-white coat and webbed feet; Landseer Newfoundland; NEWFOUNDLAND(ER).

[1745 CAREW 29 This Dog was very remarkable on account of his great Size, Strength and unconquerable Fierceness, as also for his particular Aptness for the Water; which is a Qualification common and natural to the Dogs of that Country.] [1766] 1971 BANKS 149–50 Those I met with were mostly Curs with a Cross of the Mastiff in them Some took the water well others not at all the thing they are valued for here is strength as they are employed in winter time to Draw in Sledges whatever is wanted from the woods I was told indeed that at trepassy Livd a man who had a distinct breed which he called the original Newfoundland Dogs. [1779] 1792 CARTWRIGHT ii, 448 Both the weather and water were so cold, that my greyhound, who has learnt from the Newfoundland dogs to fetch birds out of the water, would go in but once. [(1784) 1969 BURNS 110 "The Twa Dogs": His hair, his size, his mouth, his lugs, / Show'd he was nane o' Scotland's dogs; / But whalpet some place far abroad, / Whare sailors gang to fish for cod.] [1794] 1968 THOMAS 52 The celebrity of Newfoundland dogs in England is so notorious that the value of them needs no comment, but their usefulness in Britain cannot be put in competition with the great utility they are to the people of this cold Country. . . This wood [in winter] is sometimes cut seven or ten miles in the woods and is drawn home by Dogs. They have gearing the same as Horses. [1822] 1856

CORMACK 33 A large Newfoundland dog, her only companion in her husband's absence, had welcomed us at the landing-place with signs of the greatest joy. 1824 SCOTT i, 64 My companion's loud whistle. . .speedily brought to the door of the principal cottage. . .two large Newfoundland dogs. [1854] 1950 THOREAU 67 A man is not a good *man* to me because he will feed me if I should be starving, or warm me if I should be freezing, or pull me out of a ditch if I should ever fall into one. I can find you a Newfoundland dog that will do as much. 1865 CAMPBELL 59 Everyone has heard of Newfoundland dogs, and everybody wants to get one. They ought to be pretty large, quite black, with rough waving shiny hair, black roofs to their mouths, mild wise faces, and long tails, with a slight curl at the end. 1956 STETSON 20 Dr Heim believes that many of these dogs were the large white or brown-and-white Butcher dogs sometimes known as Estate dogs. They were apparently even bigger than the Newfoundland dog himself. Whatever the dog was, he did breed with the smaller black native dog, producing what we know today as the Landseer.

2 A strong, short-haired dog from which the Labrador retriever has been bred; LABRADOR DOG, WATER ~ .

1832 MCGREGOR i, 149 The smooth short-haired dog, so much admired in England as a Newfoundland dog, though an useful and sagacious animal, and nearly as hardy and fond of the water, is a cross breed. 1842 BONNYCASTLE ii, 24–5 I have said nothing of the Newfoundland dog in the natural history section of this work. . . They are of two kinds; the short, wiry-haired Labrador dog, and the long, curly-haired Newfoundland species, generally black, with a white cross upon the breast. 1906 DUNCAN 12 Skipper was a Newfoundland dog, born of reputable parents at Back Arm and decently bred in Ruddy Cove. He had black hair, short, straight and wiry—the curly-haired breed has failed on the Island—and broad, ample shoulders, which his forebears transmitted to him from generations of hauling wood. 1911 HUTCHINSON 69 One sees very few of that type which the mind associates with the name [Newfoundland dog], but there are many large black dogs, some with shaggy coats and some of the smoother wave, that we think of as appropriate to the Labrador retrievers.

newfoundlander n [ˌnufən'lændəɹ, ˌnʉufæɵn-'lændəɹ] *OED* ~ 1, 2, 3 ([1611] 1817–; 1801; 1806–); *DC* (1779–) for sense 3.

1 A permanent inhabitant or native of Newfoundland.

1765 WILLIAMS 9 So at the Time the *French* took the country, the *Irish* were above six Times the Number of the West Country and *Newfoundlanders*. [1770] 1792 CARTWRIGHT i, 14 A Newfoundlander will seldom fire at a deer or a bear, without putting seven to fourteen balls into his piece, which so overweights the powder, that it loses great part of its effect. 1819 ANSPACH 464 The advocates of the use of *tea* have, no doubt, been struck with the remark just made, that this vegetable forms a considerable article in the diet of the Newfoundlanders. 1858 [LOWELL] ii, 268 He was no Newfoundlander, though trading for so many years into and

out of Newfoundland. [1900 OLIVER & BURKE] 45 "Kelly and His Slide": Young Kelly had a splendid slide, the smartest ever seen, / A regular Newfoundlander—painted colors pink, white and green. [1941] 1974 BRIDLE (ed) i, 115 An essential preliminary step [to the question of Newfoundland entering the Canadian Confederation] is the re-education of Newfoundlanders about Canada and Canadians. 1982 *Evening Telegram* 26 Jan, p. 6 It is the traditional right of Newfoundlanders to stop along the roadside, to boil the kettle or to camp overnight.

2 A vessel from, or engaged in the fish trade with, Newfoundland; NEWFOUNDLAND-MAN, NEWLANDER.

[1786] 1792 CARTWRIGHT iii, 218 Here I learned that great numbers of vessels, particularly Newfoundlanders, had been lost, and others greatly damaged in the late gales. 1962 KEIR 132 The loss of *C T Bowring* [a schooner sailing in the 1880's between Newfoundland and the West Country] is noted in an article entitled 'The Story of the West Country Newfoundlanders.'

3 A large dog with heavy black or black-and-white coat and webbed feet; NEWFOUNDLAND (DOG).

[1779] 1792 CARTWRIGHT ii, 423 The bloodhound and Newfoundlander, which were in the shed, ran vehemently at the deer. [1786] ibid iii, 127 Mr Collingham returned at three, with both the dogs; the Newfoundlander was lying by Alexander's gun. 1952 SMITH 75 It is said the Norwegians had dogs not unlike the Newfoundlander, and it may be that a few of these found their way to add their bit to the outstanding physique, courage and intelligence marking the Newfoundlander today.

newfoundlandiana n also **newfoundlandia**. Materials relating to the culture, history and life of Newfoundland.

1957 *Nfld Qtly* Dec, p. 3 [editorial] Newfoundlandiana. 1975 *English Qtly* viii, 87 'Newfoundlandia'. . . The question posed by this unit is simply: What aspects of Newfoundland environment, language, life, and literature lend themselves to individual and small group activities, and projects through which one can focus on English skills and at the same time develop an awareness of Newfoundland?

newfoundland-man n

1 An English West Country migratory fishing vessel; crew-member of such a vessel; NEWLANDER.

[1663] 1963 YONGE 54 Those mad Newfoundland men are so greedy of a good [fishing] place they ventured in [towards land] strangely. 1682 COLLINS 17 The Isle of *May*, one of the Islands of *Cape Verd*, where whole Fleets of *Newfoundland-Men*, and *New Englanders* use yearly to Lade. . . 1745 CAREW 116–17 But Bampfylde. . .was discovered. . .by one *Brown* a Watchmaker, who. . .knew this poor distressed *Newfoundland*-Man, this *Aaron Cock*, to be the famous *Bampfylde-Moore Carew*. 1765 WILLIAMS 8 An *Irishman* can't catch as much Fish as a West Country or *Newfoundland* man. . .the one manned by People of the West Country and *Newfoundland*, the other by

Irish. 1895 PROWSE 297–8 The late Hon Stephen Rendell has often told me that even when he came to the Colony in 1834, hundreds of sturdy Devonshire lads came out every spring. . . Mr Rendell said nearly every labouring man about Coffinwell had been a servant in Newfoundland. . . The coming and going of the Newfoundland men was an event in Devonshire. The rurals reckoned the time by the old Church of England lectionary: 'Jan! the Parson be in Pruverbs, the Newfanlan men will soon be a coming whome.'

2 Inhabitant of Newfoundland; NEWFOUNDLANDER 1.

1863 MORETON 58 The liberality of most monied men at home is a far easier virtue than that of these poor Newfoundlandmen.

newing ppl, vbl n Cp *OED* ~ vbl sb 1 obs. Waxing; the waxing of the moon.

C 68–21 Never cut wood when the moon is newing. It will not dry. Q 73–7 ~ between new moon and full moon.

newland n *OED* ~ 1: newland fish obs (1550–1591). See also LAND, NEWFOUNDLAND. The north-east coast of North America, esp the island of Newfoundland and the coast of Labrador. Also attrib.

[1542] 1895 PROWSE 33 Provided furthermore that this Act or any thing therin conteyned shall not extende to any person whiche shall bye eny fisshe in any parties of Iseland Scotlands Orkeney, Shotlande, Irelande, or *Newland*. [1564–5] 1954 INNIS 44 There goeth out of Fraunce commonly five hundreth saile of shippes yearely in Marche to Neuve-foundlande, to fishe for Newlande fish and comes home again in August. [1583] 1940 *Gilbert's Voyages and Enterprises* ii, 392 [Hayes' narrative] Not staying long upon that Newland coast, we might proceed Southward, and follow still the Sunne, untill we arrived at places more temperate to our content. 1630 VAUGHAN [p. 10] Let me intreate you to conceiue charitably of our *New-Land* Plantation. 1934 LOUNSBURY 34 During Elizabethan times there does not seem to have been any extensive demand for Newfoundland fish in England. 'Newland' fish was sometimes used to provision the fleet and the army in Ireland or to feed the poor in England. The greater part of the annual catch of 'Poor John' or 'Poor Jack' was sold to foreigners for shipment to southern Europe.

newlander n See also NEWFOUNDLANDER.

1 English vessel fishing seasonally in Newfoundland.

[1583] 1940 *Gilbert's Voyages and Enterprises* ii, 399 [Hayes' narrative] This company met with a barke returning home. . .they besought the captaine they might go aboord this Newlander, only to borrow what might be spared, the rather because the same was bound homeward.

2 Inhabitant of Newfoundland.

1630 VAUGHAN [p. 6] I tooke her for my *Gossip* to this Pigmey infant, which now is named *the New-Landers Cure*.

nib v Cp *EDD* nip v 13. In rounders, to strike the ball offside with edge of bat.

T 66/7–64 One bat, one feller ahead o' ya throwin' up the ball to the feller behind ya. Certainly if you nibbed it three times you were out.

nice a Cp *EDD* ~ 6 (1): ~ few. In various phrases expressing distance, quantity, etc: considerable.

1924 ENGLAND 240 The spy master brushed in the distances with his winking brass telescope. 'Big jag o' fat, a nice bit off, sir. A good spurt.' C 75–134 When asked how far you would have to go to shoot duck, the answer would be 'a nice piece away.'

nice* [= nighst] See ANIGHST.

nickel n Adapted from 'The Nickel,' a movie hall in the centre of St John's; cp *DAE* nickelodeon (1888–). A motion picture.

[1916 *Evening Telegram* 23 May "McGuire's Bread": There's hundreds go home with their wives from the Nickel, / At night time and then they will sit round their fires.] 1924 ENGLAND 108 I 'spects I'll go down town dis evenin' an' go to a nickel [movie]. 1973 PINSENT 5 I asked him what he was going to do with his dime. 'Goin' to the Nickel, Saturday.' P 148–76 (Listening to the old timers telling yarns) is as good as a nickel.

nicodemus n Cp John 7:50; 19:39 [the Pharisee who came to Jesus by night]. A person who changes from one denomination to another; turn-coat (1971 NOSEWORTHY 225).

night n Comb **night-set**: see SET n.
  night-worm: earthworm.

P 148–62 [Night-worms are] big, fat worms for fishing. 1966 PADDOCK 93 ~ Slender, round sliding creatures.

nine num In phr indicating a limited but unspecified number of days.

1888 *Colonist Christmas No* 2 We have every reason to believe that he employed this short time given him judiciously, for in less than a month from that the marriage was announced between Guy Ashton and Amy Forbes, a circumstance which furnished the village with nine days' food, in the shape of gossip. 1965 MOWAT 91 A stiff northeaster is a rare wind in summer in the southern reaches of the Labrador Sea. . . In Newfoundland it is known as the 'nine-day wind' because, when it does blow, it tends to hold for several days with undiminished force and unchanged direction.

nineteen See NUMBER.

ninny bag See NUNNY-BAG.

nip n *EDD* ~ sb³. A difficult or awkward place in a path or passage.

1937 DEVINE 34 ~ A hard place to get over in the road when hauling a load. T 379–67 Just runners on the ice or under the house, pulled along on the ice. That's when the "Johnny Poker" 'd be singing, when they come to a hard nip. P 211–68 The nips (uphill sections of the path).

nip v   Cp *OED* ~ v¹ d naut 'of ice, to squeeze or crush (a vessel).' Phr *nip to/on/with the land*: of a field of ice, to drift right to the coast; to be forced up on the shore; RAFT¹.

1924 ENGLAND 80, 189 The ice grew formidable, 'nippin' to de land,' a sealer told me. . . 'De h'ice settled in on de land!' someone shouts. 'It'm nipped on de land!' P 148–62 [The ice was] nipped with the land. Q 67–51 This happens when ice is moving [and] is forced to rise up, and one end of floe gets nipped, as on a tongue of land.

nipper¹ n

1 A large biting mosquito; GARNIPPER: gally-nipper.

[(1663) 1963 YONGE 60 In July, the muscetos (a little biting fly) and garnippers (a larger one) will much vex us.] [1819] 1978 *Beothuk Vocabularies* 46 Nipper—bebadrook. 1854 [FEILD] 70 The title or name [Nipper's Harbour] is rather an alarming one, particularly to thin skinned Southerners, as the Nipper is the largest and most formidable of the mosquitoes. 1861 *Harper's* xxii, 744 Mercy! who ever saw the flies and nippers so bad as they! 1893 *Trade Review Christmas No* 14 The operator in charge waged a daily and [nightly] war against insect life, viz.:—black flies, [mosquitoes], nippers, horse and sand flies. 1913 THOMAS 191 All day long the black flies made our lives miserable, and as night approached the 'nippers' took their place. [1926] 1933 GREENLEAF (ed) 251 "Change Islands Song": The weather still got hotter, plenty nippers, flies and stout. T 45/6–64 [tall tale] Nippers was that thick that they come and used to drive their thorns down through the bark-pot. According as they drove them down, he used to clench them, and by and by they got that thick on it that they rose the bark-pot and went away with it. C 68–23 We didn't want [the frog] to die because we were told that frogs used to eat nippers (mosquitoes) and we didn't want to hurt anything that helped to destroy the nippers. 1973 PINSENT 56 All Ruth could seem to do was point to the door, which made about as much impression as a nipper's bite on an elephant's arse.

2 In various ball games, the catcher.

M 69–2 The millyer and the nipper were similar to what is today the pitcher and the catcher.

nipper² n   Cp *DAE* ~ 2 (1840–); *DC* ~¹ (1955). A thick, narrow band of cloth or knitted wool worn around the fingers or palm by fisherman to protect the hand in line-fishing; cp GRUMMET.

1895 *Christmas Review* 18 Throughout the winter, Sam Holland, who, though as good a fellow as ever donned a 'nipper' or threw a line from a 'standing room,' had done considerable bragging. 1937 DEVINE 34 ~s. Swanskin bands, fitting tightly around the hand to protect the fingers from being chafed by the friction of the lines in cod fishing. 1961 *Evening Telegram* 30 May, p. 6 That kind of 'nipper' consisted of a ring of wool, two rings in fact, large enough to slip over the

palm of a man's hand. The two rings were joined in such a way that the part that slips on over the palm of the hand was flat, while the outer side had a deep groove between the two rings of wool where they were sewed or knitted together—[it] thus caught a fisherman's line in the groove between the two rings of wool, and the line was 'nipped' tightly when the fisherman closed his hand. T 43/7–64 Nippers [are] made of wool, they're knitted like a stall. You just slip it on over your finger and it takes the line. Instead o' the line rubbin' on your finger it's rubbin' on this nipper. 1971 NOSEWORTHY 225 ~s. Circular bands of knitted wool with heavier material sewn inside and folded over for thickness. They are worn across the palm of the hand and the base of the fingers to prevent the fishing lines from cutting the hands. Some nippers are also made of rubber.

nipper³ See WATER NIPPER.

nish a   also **nesh** [nɪʃ]. Cp *EDD* nesh: var neesh Do, nish D, 1 'soft, tender' for sense 1; 2 'brittle' for sense 2; 4 'delicate' for sense 3.

1 Soft or tender; sore or inflamed; delicate.

1863 MORETON 35 ~ Tender, delicate. 1955 ENGLISH 35 ~ tender, easily injured. P 3–63 That's the best bit of meat I've had for a long time. It's very nish. T 203/5–65 You can haul all you like on a otter skin, but a fox skin, when you put un on the board you'd have to be very careful, because it's a very nish fur, a very nish skin. 1966 *Evening Telegram* 12 July, p. 8 I always burn red and blisters, my skin is very nish. C 70–21 A person's hands might be neash if he has ncash skin, thin skin, easily bruised. 1974 *Evening Telegram* 28 Dec, p. 4 It is hoped that the report will have a wide circulation as a guideline to asking sharp and pertinent questions that strip away the nish outer flesh and get right to the bone of the problem. 1980 ibid 5 Jan, p. 11 She had a very nish skin which ran in families with refined blood in their veins.

2 Brittle, easily broken; of ice, very thin.

1958 *Nfld Dishes* 46 ~ applied to ice or even to pastry. P 210–69 Be careful with that cup—it's very nish. C 71–125 ~ Anything thin or frail, easily broken. New ice, very thin, is very often referred to as 'nish.'

3 Of persons, delicate, lacking in hardiness.

1896 *J A Folklore* ix, 23 Nesh. Tender and delicate, used to describe one who cannot stand much cold or hard work. [1906] GRENFELL 168 So Pete has to depend more and more on his knowledge of boiling springs, for he never yet was 'nish' (tender) enough to stop and boil the kettle when he could melt snow for water. 1925 *Dial Notes* v, 337 ~ Delicate; of a person. M 71–114 A person who is sensitive to pain is said to be nish.

nitch See KNITCH.

noax See NOKES.

nob See KNOB.

nobble v   To drag a heavy object on the ground.

1866 WILSON 215 The slide, or catamaran, can only

be used on the snow. If wood be wanted before the snow fall, it must be 'spelled out,' that is, carried on men's shoulders; and when some snow has fallen, but not sufficient to make a good path, the stick of wood is nobbled out. To nobble is to drag on the ground.

nobby See KNOBBLY.

noddy n Cp *DAE* ~ b (1917 quot).
  1 Atlantic fulmar, a seabird of northern waters (*Fulmarus glacialis glacialis*).
  [1663] 1963 YONGE 54 Here are divers particular animals which I saw, as a noddy, a bird by which they know they are near Newfoundland. It's less than a gull, of a blunt head and short bill. [1785] 1792 CARTWRIGHT iii, 44 We saw some noddies to-day. . .We saw a tern, with great plenty of noddies and peterels. [1794] 1968 THOMAS 144 Loons, Noddys, Sea Parrots, Sea Pigeons and a number of other Sea Fowl. 1902 DELABARRE 203 ~ Rather common off shore with the shearwaters. 1925 *Dial Notes* v, 337 ~ A bird that likes rough water. 1940 SCAMMELL 26 "The Shooting of the Bawks": But if they keep this law that's passed, they will not get a taste / Of bawk or noddy, tinker, tur, and not a tickleace. 1945 *Can Field-Naturalist* lix, 138 Several local observers say that the reason for this name [noddies] is that they constantly nod their heads while flying. Most fishermen do not eat noddys but some say that they do and that noddy makes a delicious meal. 1951 PETERS & BURLEIGH 57–9 ~ A gliding seabird [of] North Atlantic and Arctic [found in Newfoundland waters throughout the year]. . . In former years the fishermen caught hundreds for use as bait.
  2 Mildly derogatory term for inhabitant of a coastal settlement; BAY NODDY.
  1901 *Christmas Review* 6 The outcome of this resolution was the formation of a club which was known as the Noddy Club. At first this club contained about twenty members. 1912 DUNCAN 144 'Have done, ye noddie!'

noddy a See KNOTTY.

noggin n also **naggin** *DAE* ~ 1 b local (1890 quot) for sense 1.
  1 A small wooden cask; esp such a cask sawn in half; TUB.
  [1836] 1944 LAWTON & DEVINE 61 He kept a general goods store and sold rum. It does not seem that any less than a naggin of rum was bought at a time. . .1 naggin rum. 1925 *Dial Notes* v, 337 ~ A flat tub. 1937 DEVINE 35 ~ a small tub formerly used on a sealer for taking food from the galley. Q 67–46 ~ a wooden tub usually holding 10 lb of butter. M 68–10 ~ sawed-off 10-lb tub. Used for mixing horses' feed in.
  2 Phr *a noggin of scrape, ~ to scrape*: a chore or a difficulty (1940 *Dal Rev* xx, 62; P 148–64).

noggin* See NOG-HEAD.

noggy-head* See NOG-HEAD.

nog-head n also **noggin***, **noggy-head*** *EDD*

nog sb[1] 1 'small log or block' for sense 1; *EDD* 1 (1) ~ head, (4) noggy 'block-head' for sense 2.
  1 Small chunk of wood; NUG.
  P 126–67 Make some nog-heads for the morning [fire]. P 148–67 The fire needs some noggins.
  2 Blockhead.
  T 222–66 Noggyheads is the [name] with which I am most familiar, because when I was a small child and tormented her she was apt to call me that. P 148–67 [Go away], ya old noghead!
  3 An undernourished seal-pup; BLEATER.
  1924 ENGLAND 193 Far from the ship, alone, deserted, we found a 'nogg-head.' That is to say, a motherless whitecoat, 'wid narr pick o' fat on he.' 1925 *Dial Notes* v, 337 ~ A young seal with the mother killed;—all head and no body.

nointer n ['nɑintəɹ] *EDD* ~ sb 1. A mischievous child.
  T 12–64 ~ a term used [of] young children when they are a source of distraction. 'Go [a]way, you little nointer.'

nokes n also **noax** *OED* ~ obs (1700). A simpleton.
  1937 DEVINE 35 Noax, nokes. A simple minded fellow. P 205–55 Noax [a fool]. P 74–67 He's some nox. P 127–79 Boy, you're a noakes, you are.

nonia n ['noɵniə]. Acronym for Newfoundland Outport Nursing and Industrial Association; also attrib.
  [1924] 1946 MACKAY (ed) 174 The Newfoundland Outport Nursing and Industrial Association, known as Nonia, did pioneer work in providing nursing services for the outports and in improving the household economy in many Newfoundland settlements. 1933 *Nfld Royal Commission Report* 212 The present system under which 'Nonia' nurses are appointed in the outports is based on the salutary doctrine of self-help. 1950 PARKER 99 Some attempts have been made by Nonia and other societies working among women in the island to build up the home manufacture of carpets, rugs, blankets, dresses and other woollen products. 1974 *Daily News* 9 Sep, p. 3 Wednesday, Mrs Winter will be hostess to directors of Nonia, who will hold their monthly meeting at 10:30 am.

nonny bag See NUNNY-BAG.

non-plush n also **on plush*** *EDD* ~ 1 'non plus, dilemma' Ha for this phr. Phr *on a non-plush*: by surprise.
  1924 ENGLAND 127 I can't make much of a hand at singin'. You took me too much on a nonplush. C 70–21 'Oh, you took me on the on plush!' This used to be a common expression in our area and may still be heard among the older folk. It means that I've been taken unawares or unprepared.

nonsical a *EDD* ~ He Gl So D. Nonsensical (1896 *J A Folklore* ix, 36).

noody nawdy a, n DINNEEN niúdar neádar 'indecision, trifling'; *Kilkenny Lexicon* núdaí nádaí 'listless. . .unambitious individual.' Indolent, fair and easy; also a person with these characteristics (P 191–73).

P 108–75 ~ A slow-moving, possibly slow-thinking person; maybe lazy, lackadaisical.

nopper n ['nɒpəɹ]. Cp *EDD* napper. Head.

C 71–118 I'll beat the nopper offa you!

nor'ard n also **nor'ad, nor'id** ['næɹəd, 'nɑɹəd] *EDD* norward, var norad, norrud So. The north; also attrib.

1891 PACKARD 222 We learned that the weather here had been pleasanter than 'to the nor'ard,' and that though the cod fishery had been 'bad,' it was now beginning to 'look up.' 1902 MURPHY 8 "Petty Harbour Bait Skiff": When we came to the 'Nor'ad' head, / A rainbow did appear. 1924 ENGLAND 130 "Betsy Brennan's Blue Hen": May two girls from the Nor'id / Stick pins in his forehead. T 141/60–65[2] They estimated ice to be twenty miles off an' with the glass goin' down. An' she chopped in around that night, that evenin', chopped in around to the norrard, blowed a gale wi' a snow blizzard. M 68–11 The mouth of the harbour [of Renews] is flanked by two points of land—Suddard Head and Norrad Head. 1977 RUSSELL 30 Only the night before he must've been dreamin' he and Jonas were swile huntin' because he'd bawled out in his sleep, 'Jonas boy, you take this swatch. I'll take the one further to the nor'ard.'

north a Comb **north shore**: the western side of Conception Bay stretching north of Carbonear from Salmon Cove to Bay de Verde; also attrib.

1776 COUGHLAN 18 A Proof of the great Zeal, which filled those dear Souls in one Part of the Bay, called *Black Head*, upon the *North Shore*, was this: They proposed to me, to point out a Place where I would choose to build a Church, which was agreed upon; accordingly all Hands went into the Wood, and cut down as much of it as they wanted, which they hauled out upon what they call Slides. 1819 ANSPACH 428 The inhabitants of the North Shore, in Conception-Bay, reaped a most plentiful harvest [of seals in 1811]. [c1830] 1890 GOSSE 49 Many of the North Shore men [inhabitants of the coast of Conception Bay from Carbonear to Point Baccalao] were tall, well-made, handsome fellows, singularly simple and guileless. 1866 WILSON 141 The ministrations of Mr Coughlan were mostly confined to Harbor Grace, or within the radius of a few miles, yet the benefit was felt all down the north shore. [1896] SWANSBOROUGH 18 "Lines on Topsail": Seaward a charming view / Of Isles, and the North Shore! / Where live a hardy race, / Who fish at Labrador. 1975 RUSSELL 84 He swallered that hunk of salt pork like a real north-shoreman.

norther n Cp *DAE* ~ 'a furious cold wind from the north, esp one blowing over Texas, the plains, or Gulf of Mexico.' A sudden, violent winter gale from the north.

1895 *Christmas Review* 9 Oft times, when anchored in 100 fathoms of water, some miles from shore, the cruel 'norther' suddenly blows in fearful squalls off the land, driving before it a blinding storm of snow, and covering the little crafts with a mantle of ice. 1934 LOUNSBURY 17 During the period from November to April the island and surrounding seas are disturbed by a series of cyclonic storms, called either 'southers' or 'northers,' which bring rain, snow, and sleet, and which are often so violent that they cause the loss of ships and men.

norther a *OED* ~ a 1 'situated to the north' obs (901–1497). Esp in place-names, the more northerly of two places or coastal features.

[1864] 1971 SEARY 251 Norther Head. 1953 *Nfld & Lab Pilot* ii, 116 Norther cove is entered between Green point and Norther point. . . These hills back the tableland forming the coast between Norther point and South head. T 313–66 But they rowed down there in Little Norther Harbour, 'cause they was goin' out the run, summer fishin'.

northern a

Comb **northern coast**: north-east coast of Newfoundland. Cp FRENCH SHORE.

1846 TOCQUE 318 The next bait for catching the codfish which the fishermen resort to after the departure of the squids, are the lance (*Am[m]odytes Tobianus*); these fish also form the earliest bait in the spring on the northern coast.

northern cod: cod-fish stocks of the waters adjacent to the north-east coast and Labrador; esp those of the Hamilton Banks.

1977 *Union Forum* Sep, p. 5 The union feels there should be no further such ventures involving northern cod. . . One of the great concerns the union has had about these ventures is that landings of foreign-caught fish from the northern cod stocks might be contrary to the best interests of the inshore fishermen on the north-east coast. 1981 *Evening Telegram* 24 Feb, p. 1 The northern cod—actually the Labrador-Northeast Newfoundland stock—differs from other cod stocks in its migration and associated behaviour. In winter the fish migrate offshore into northern waters and come inshore, following the caplin, in summer.

northern dancers: aurora borealis or northern lights; MERRY DANCERS.

C 65–2 The Northern Lights (also Northern Dancers and Merry Dancers) are really going it tonight. We're going to have a nice day tomorrow. Q 73–9 Look at the northern dancers shining tonight.

northern fishery: cod-fishery prosecuted by eastern Newfoundland fishermen in waters of the north-east coast and Labrador; LABRADOR FISHERY.

[1736–9] 1954 INNIS 148 Fogo & Twillingate, the Northern Fisheries. 1819 ANSPACH 443 What is called the *northern-fishery*, is carried on on the northern coasts of the island and the adjoining parts of Labrador by planters from Conception Bay, Trinity Bay and Saint John's, who go there early in the season in large schooners carrying several skiffs, a numerous crew, and provisions for the whole fishing season. 1832 MCGREGOR i, 232–3 The northern fishery, now enjoyed by France, was carried on by the planters, by proceeding in schooners, with necessary stores and skiffs, to the northern harbours of Newfoundland, much in the same way as the fishery is at present conducted at Labrador, and the schooners sent back with the fish to the respective merchants.

northern indian: Montagnais or Naskapi indian of Labrador (1839 TUCKER 126).

northern man: inhabitant of the north-east coast of Newfoundland.

1894 HOWLEY *MS Reminiscences* 30 Harbour Main District in particular supplies the bulk of the labourers [on the railway] and they are the only ones who appear to stick to the work. . . The Northern men hate pick and shovel work. 1902 MURPHY 72 "Fanny's Harbour Bawn": I did address this young man, and unto him did say, / Are you from Bonavista or are you from the bay? / I think you are a Northern man, a bayman I presume. 1927 *Christmas Messenger* 47 The remarkable thing about this word [Dwye, or Dwigh] is that it is not known or used on the coast line south of St John's. From Cape Spear north to Belle Isle every one knows what it means; but from Cape Race west it is Greek to the people. I have heard Placentia Bay men using the word as a joke on northern men. 1964 BLONDAHL (ed) 75 "A Noble Fleet of Sealers": His crew of bully northern men / Can handle gaff or gun. P 245–72 [speaker in Placentia Bay] You are from Bonavista? You are a northern man then.

northern patch: a concentration of harp or hooded seals breeding on the ice-floes off Labrador and the north-east coast of Newfoundland; PATCH.

1905 CHAFE 7 It is generally believed that these seals belonged to the 'northern patch' which had not been disturbed. 1924 ENGLAND 24 Some of the seals are scattered; some lie in immense patches. The patches, especially 'the main patch,' form the seal hunters' goal. There is supposed to be a 'northern patch' and a 'southern patch,' but discussion about this is endless and sterile. 1933 GREENE 16–17 The 'Northern Patch' of Harps would not cover one-fifth of this area of the Main Patch; while the biggest Patches of Newfoundland Hoods—in spite of their 'Families' being so widely separate—would be considerably less in area still. [c1920] [1960] BURKE (ed White) 15 "Cotton's Patch": And soon was cutting through the gap / For the Northern patch that day.

northern shore: see **northern coast**.

[1802] 1916 MURPHY 3 The ports on the coast of Labrador, on the northern shore, now possessed by the French. . .

northern slob: heavy, slushy, densely-packed mass of ice fragments and snow and water formed in winter each year off Labrador and the north-east coast; SLOB.

1934 LOUNSBURY 12 The first field ice to appear is 'white' or 'northern slob' formed off Labrador in the early winter, but it is followed almost immediately by 'sheet' ice which is more dense and solid though not as thick. T 50/1–64 That was somewhere round her last trip, see, 'fore the northern slob would come. 1966 FARIS 29 There is slush, sludge, ice rind, pancake ice,

brash, pack ice, northern slob, Arctic slob, string ice. T 398–67 First we'd get what we call northern slob, an' then we'd get th' Arctic ice. 1972 BROWN 3 Northern slob still consists of rounded pans, but larger, thicker ones that you can safely cross by copying, provided you are careful to jump from each pan as it begins to sink under your weight.

northern turr: thick-billed murre (*Uria lomvia lomvia*); TURR n.

1954 *Can Field-Naturalist* lix, 144 This is the bird which the fishermen call the 'northern turr' which they say is larger than the 'southern turr.'

north-wester n Cp *O Sup*[2] nor'wester 3 'strong oilskin coat' U S (1689–90). A garment worn over the head and shoulders in winter; CASSOCK; PIN v: PINOVER.

1792 CARTWRIGHT *Gloss* i, xii ~ A hood to cover the head and shoulders in severe weather. It is intended chiefly to defend the cheeks and neck. 1819 ANSPACH 375 The hunter's head is sheltered by a north-wester, or hood, which covers his head and shoulders, and is fastened by pinovers, or pieces of flannel tacked to one side of the north-wester and pinned to the other, the one covering the nose, and the other the chin.

norway n *EDD* ~ sb 3 So D. A fine-grained, tapering stone used dry to sharpen knives and other implements; DAGGER; ROUGHSTONE.

[1834] P 54–63 In the crediting entries, for goods returned to [Slade's] store from sealing voyage outfits, May 27, 1834, there are listed. . .two Norways. 1937 DEVINE 35 ~ A whetstone.

nose n

1 The front of a sled or 'komatik.'

1910 GRENFELL 88 . . .while he trotted on beside, his good hand on the upturned nose of the komatik. T 50/2–64 Lots of it hauled by shoulder—a biggish rope to the nose of the slide [or] on the side.

2 Comb **nose-rope**: (a) transverse rope at the front of a sled or 'komatik'; (b) short rope attached to the bow of a boat; painter.

P 65–64 The rope in the nose of a komatic joining the two runners is the 'nose rope.' The driver can sit in the nose rope and steer the komatic. If it is too hard going he can haul on the nose rope and help the dogs. T 145–65 So one fisherman found himself with his arm in around the plug strap, while the other was clinging to the nose rope or painter of the dory.

not bad like See BAD.

notch n also **natch, netch*** [nɛtʃ, nætʃ, nɒtʃ]. Cp *EDD* natch sb[1] 1 'a notch,' *OED* natch now dial (1570–1659; 1878–); cp *DAE* ~ 3 'narrow defile' (1718–) for sense 1; *OED* ~ 1 for sense 2.

1 A break in cliffs; an inlet or harbour; GULCH n.

1924 ENGLAND 285 De *Ranger* do a strange t'ing if she come out agin. She'm a mystery if she do. If she don't, us got a good look-up to see de Notch wonnerful soon, now. 1925 *Dial Notes* v, 337 ~ A split in the coast; harbour entrance, esp to St John's. T 50/1–64 An' they run for the harbour—a bad natch to run for here, you know. . . . A stranger he might make a mess of it. There's only a notch comin' in through when you comes to the tickle. They made in on the bill o' Snook's Head somewhere; right in the clift she went, in a notch, an' hung there, and they all left her. T 393/4–67 In Shoe Cove it's only a notch, there's no harbour. They had to hoist their boats when [they have] any sea at all worthwhile. It's just a little notch, boy. 1974 SQUIRE 36 Uncle Joe came where I was and said, 'Chris, what are you listening for?' I replied, 'For the sea around the rocks.' He said, 'There is no sea but keep looking up. You should see two saddles in the fog.' I immediately did as he suggested, and before he reached the after deck, I shouted that I could see two notches in the fog. He said, 'Yes, that one to port is the Narrows,' and before long we were entering St John's harbour.

2 A gash around a tree-trunk; a piece sawn or chopped from a log.

T 36/8–64 A tree would be about anywhere from five to ten inches in diameter, so however far up you could reach you'll cut a notch around the tree an' a slit down to the bottom, an' cut it around down there again [to strip the bark off]. T 246/55–66 He'd always say he was goin' to put 'em in his jam block, see. That's a stick o' wood with a natch sawed out into un. When the ol' people used to use sticks, they saw out a square notch, split it out, an' jam that in, wedge it in.

3 Pleat in a petticoat.

T 70–64[2] [They] used to knit lovely underskirts, big natches in 'em, frills around 'em, right round, an' done with all colours.

4 Comb **notch-block**: piece of timber with a notch in it to secure log in place when cutting; JAM v: JAM-BLOCK.

1977 BUTLER 70 He was intending to chop some timber. He set up a piece of timber in a notch-block, secured with wedges.

notch v also **natch***, **netch*** [nɑtʃ, nɒtʃ]. Cp *OED* natch, notch v 2 for sense 1.

1 To cut notches in; to gash.

P 269–63 I netched the tree. T 43/8–64 There was your stanchion, we used to call it, that would keep your wood from fallin' out over, was notched in an' you were also notched in [at] the end of your skid. P 148–65 To bake a good cod-fish, natch his back and put the fatback pork in.

2 Phr *notch the beam*: to express surprise or amazement about something.

C 68–17 'I'll have to notch the beam.' This saying is used to indicate that something unusual or unexpected has happened. C 71–92 'Natch the beam' is used when someone does something he does not normally do.

notchy a *OED* ~ (1883 quot). With sharp indentations; serrated.

1955 DOYLE (ed) 22 "Down by Jim Long's Stage": And I'll build a fairy bower / For her on notchy hill. T 393–67 The hills was kind o' notchy around, you

know; a bunch o' woods stickin' up here an' then a little hollow an' another bunch.

note n Supplier's chit entitling a person to specified items of clothing, equipment, etc. Cp CROP n: CROP NOTE.

[c1830] 1890 GOSSE 47–8 The names of the crew having been registered at the counting-house, each man was allowed to take up goods on the credit of the voyage, to a certain amount, perhaps one-third, or even one-half, of his probable earnings. The clerks were the judges of the amount. For these goods both planter and crew applied at the office, in order, and received tickets, or 'notes,' for the several articles. 1894 [BURKE] 25 "The July Fire": Oh, he then gave me a note / For to get a soldier's coat.

nother* See NEITHER.

not(t) n Cp *EDD* ~ a, sb[3] 1, 3 s w cties for sense 2.

1 Hornless male caribou.

1907 MILLAIS 292 . . .a 'hummel,' or 'nott,' as these hornless stags are called in Newfoundland.

2 Comb **not-cow**: hornless cow.

1971 NOSEWORTHY 226 It can freeze hard enough to freeze the horns of a not-cow.

novie n A Nova Scotia fishing craft.

1888 STEARNS 181 Yes; that's a 'novie.' We have two kinds of boats in our fishing: the 'novies' and the 'American barges'; this one is a novie; it is painted red, inside and out: the large ones you see, anchored out there in the water, are the barges.

nuddick n also **neddick** ['nʌdɪk]. Cp *EDD* niddick So D Co, var neddick, nuddick Co 'head or skull.' A small, bare, rounded hill; KNOB, TOLT.

1837 BLUNT 20 Keep this mark on, until you are half way over to the Neddick. 1937 DEVINE 35 ~ A hillock, generally with a level top of sufficient space for a house or small garden. 1951 *Nfld & Lab Pilot* i, 251 Another promontory, known as the Nuddick, is situated. . .farther westward. M 68–24 Elliston has its 'Nuddock' so-called because the marks assuring the fisherman that he's got on the exact spot are two small ridges (nuddocks). C 71–115 Nuddik: small knob or hill; any interruption in an otherwise even surface. 1973 BARBOUR 37 After a silver thaw we gathered in a field below the 'Nuddick.' Using a barrel stave or a heavy piece of cardboard, we slid over the slippery, frozen, drifted banks of snow.

nug n [nʌg] *EDD* ~ sb[1] 1 D, 2 So D. A chunk of wood cut or sawn off a log for fuel; JUNK; cp NOG-HEAD.

1937 DEVINE 35 ~ A rude, unshapely piece of timber, a block. P 205–55 He has birch nugs stored for firewood. P 245–60 ~s. Irregular-sized billets. P 130–67 We used to burn nugs of birch. 1973 PINSENT 25 The river [was] roaring by, bringing with it the discarded logs and 'nugs' from the Anglo-Newfoundland Development Company and depositing some of them in the cove ahead of us. 1980 COX 136 Sometimes [skylarking] they would fill a man's rubbers with 'nugs' of wood, or take some food off the kitchen stove and hide it away.

nuisance n Human waste, excrement.

[1874] 1974 *Daily News* 5 June, p. 4 It could hardly have been a pleasant place for a box had to be placed on the north side of the street 'for the accommodation of the people of the locality to deposit their nuisance in.' [c1928] BURKE [broadside] "Don't You Remember the Dump, Maggie": For they're going to find out the man, Maggie, / That dumped all the nuisance out there. P 245–54 I used to empty your father's nuisance. P 148–64 [sign] Nuisance must be dumped in the Salt Water.

number n Cp *OED* ~ 5 for sense 1.

1 Prefixed to numeral *one, two* or *three* in designations of various grades or 'culls' of dried and salted cod.

1923 PRATT 48 "Overheard in a Cove": No dealer born could take 'em in, / . . .or show them any solid reason / Why number one prime cod might any season / Drop in price. 1928 *FPU (Twillingate) Minutes* 5 Oct Ask him. . .if they are buying number one and number two fish, also the price of each quality. 1937 *Seafisheries of Nfld* 55 In those localities where the fishermen are accustomed to the production of the class of fish known as Spanish, the standard of cull may include: Number One Spanish Fish, of two sizes, Number Two Spanish Fish, of two sizes, Number Three Spanish Fish, of two sizes. Ibid 56 The standards of cull for Labrador codfish are: Choice or Number One. Prime or Number Two. T 43–64 That's the way it was graded. Number one, number two and number three. Well, the number three we knew what that was: they threw that on the floor. 1977 RUSSELL 42 There's been no quintal of Prime Madeira Codfish or No. 1 Spanish produced in Pigeon Inlet since.

2 Phr *number nineteen*: out-door privy (P 245–55).

1966 PADDOCK 111 ~ outdoor toilet. C 69–6 The most common name for the outdoor toilet was number nineteen.

numerous a *OED* ~ 3. In large numbers, plentiful; freq in colloq usage with very informal connotation. Cp SCATTERED; THOUSAND.

1863 MORETON 35 ~ Filled with a large number; as 'the room is numerous with people;' 'the pantry is numerous with flies.' [1930] 1980 *Evening Telegram* 11 Aug, p. 6 Squid have been seen [at Burgeo] but will not jig. There is a good sign of codfish and dogfish are numerous. T 143/4–65[1] Bull-birds, yes. They'd come out o' the cliffs—you wouldn't see the sky through 'em, they was that numerous. T 141/2–65[2] Crowd o' goats in there, an' goats was supposed to be numerous on Change Islands. 1977 BUTLER 63 We had to haul them three miles. Some undertaking!. . .the flies were numerous! 1979 *Evening Telegram* 21 Nov, p. 6 The fish are numerous along the shore right now. . . I made 200 dollars with a cod-jigger Nov. 16.

nunch n *EDD* ~ sb[1] 2 So for sense 1; cp *EDD* nuncheon 2: ~ bag for sense 2.

1 Snack taken between any of the main meals, esp in the woods or while fishing or sealing; LUNCH.

1896 *J A Folklore* ix, 30 ~ the refreshment men take with them on going to the woods. P 212–57 ~ lunch; a snack.

2 Comb **nunch-bag, nunchy**: small canvas bag used to carry food, etc; NUNNY-BAG.

[c1900] 1978 *RLS* 8, p. 26 Nunny or nunchy bag. Made of seal-skin, usually skinned round, used for carrying grub on back when travelling. 1924 ENGLAND 241 The dogs (gunners' attendants) were meanwhile getting gaffs, belts, knives, and canvas nunch bags. In those bags, along with the cartridges, they stowed hard-bread; for who could tell what swift blizzard might cut off hunters miles from the ship?

nunchie n Common dovekie (*Plautus alle alle*); BULL-BIRD.

1959 MCATEE 39 ~ Dovekie (Possibly in allusion to its small size, enough for 'nunch' = lunch. Nfld.) P 126–67 Look at the nunchie out there in the bay!

nunny-bag n also **ninny bag, nonny** ~ ['nʌnɪ bæg, 'nʌnɪ bɛɪg] *DC* ~ Nfld (1842–1961); *O Sup*[2] Nfld; cp NUNCH. A sealskin, burlap or canvas knapsack used to carry food and personal equipment esp when hunting, sealing or travelling long distances on foot; a hunting bag.

[1822] 1866 WILSON 341 Each man had a nunny-bag, which is a kind of knapsack, made of seal-skin, with the two fore-flippers passing over the shoulders, and tied across the breast with a piece of cod-line. In our nunny-bag, we carried dry stockings, a change of linen, with any papers we might require. . .also. . .two days' provisions; and, as lucifer matches were not then known, we carried the old-fashioned tinder-box, with flint and steel, also an extinguished firebrand, so as to facilitate the kindling of a fire if necessary. 1842 JUKES ii, 146 We hung up in the tilt a 'nunny bag' full of bread. . . This is a bag made of seal-skin converted into a knapsack: what the origin of the word 'nunny' is I cannot tell, but it is in universal use in the country. 1886 *Colonist Christmas No* 8 Our guides profiting by the delay, open their 'nunny-bags,' (to use a local term) large seal-skin pouches, from which they draw forth a very good lunch. 1896 *J A Folklore* ix, 24 ~ originally meaning a lunch-bag, but now used in the general sense of a bag to carry all the articles deemed necessary in travelling. 1919 GRENFELL[1] 204 Our sealers carry dry oatmeal and sugar in their 'nonny bags,' which, mixed with snow, assuage their thirst and hunger as well. 1925 *Dial Notes* v, 337 Nonny bag. A small knapsack to carry out on the ice; ditty bag. 1937 DEVINE 35 ~ A small skin or canvas bag for holding provisions on a journey. T 84–64 Five mile from land now, an' still no breakfast. An' no nunny bag, never had no grub aboard o' boat. C 71–103 A nunny bag could be like a knapsack or it could be a drawstring bag. It had only one strap which went over the two shoulders and behind the neck. 1975 LEYTON 21 I got in the copse, in the thick woods right around the road, and I hauled the nonny bag off me back. 1976 CASHIN 86 We carried certain emergency food with us. This generally consisted of oatmeal, sugar and raisins all mixed together and carried in what is called a 'ninny bag' attached to your belt.

nunny-fudger n   Cp *EDD* ninny sb¹ 2 (3) ~ fudgy. Idler, shirker.
1897 *J A Folklore* x, 208 ~ denoting primarily a man who is thinking more of his dinner than of his work, hence generally a man who, from selfish regard to his own interest or comfort, shirks his duty.

nuzzle-tripe* n   also ~ **trite**. Cp *OED* nestletripe (1616–), *EDD* nestle 6 -ripe, -trip(e) 'smallest and weakest of a brood' etc. A misbehaving child.
Q 73–4 A nuzzle tripe is someone who has been fooling you. P 237–79 ~ contemptuous term for a youngster. 'You young nuzzle trite!'

O

obedience n   *OED* ~ 3 arch, dial; *EDD*. Phr *make one's obedience*: to bow or curtsy.
1863 MORETON 31 Children are enjoined to 'make their obedience,' which they do by making a bow. 1937 DEVINE 35 ~ For 'obeisance.'

oblige v   Cp *OED* ~ v 6 obs. To be of service to; to fit.
1936 DEVINE 41 An old fisherman once said to me, in praise of the Hamburg boot: 'We never claimed 'em to be waterproof, but I tell you, me son, they "obliged" the foot of men in every other way.'

ochre n   also **oker** *OED* ~ sb 4: ~ pit (1839).
Comb **ochre-box**: container in which ochre and water are mixed and a length of string dipped to mark timber for sawing; REDDENING BOX.
T 393/6–67 We used to call it a reddening box, you know, an' some people call it a ochre box. Q 67–109 ~ device used [in marking] a straight line on a log. Ochre is red stuff inside box in water. The string gets saturated.
ochre pit: ochre-working used by Beothuk indians to secure pigment; esp in place-names.
[1774] 1971 SEARY 253 Oker Pit Cove (Lane 1774). Ochre Pit Brook (1946). 1953 *Nfld & Lab Pilot* ii, 131 Ochre Pit hill. . .stands about three-quarters of a mile westward of the head of Bread cove and is prominent from seaward.

ocky n   ['ɒːkɪ, 'hɒːkɪ]. Cp *EDD* ~ adj 1 'dirty, nasty.' Human or animal excrement (P 245–62). See BERRY¹.
M 71–104 ~ polite word for excrement. P 127–76 ~ a children's term for the excrement of humans or animals.

odds n pl *EDD* ~ 1 for sense 1; *EDD* 4 (5) So D for sense 2.
1 Difference, consequences, esp in phr *what odds*.
1895 *Xmas Review* 7 Besmirch, defame, each honored name, for that's the proper caper; / You might blast the lives of some husbands and wives—what odds, if you sell the paper. 1937 DEVINE 35 'What odds is it to you?' Equivalent to 'Mind your own business.' P 62–64 Your kettle's boiled, it's no odds to me though.
2 Phr *odds of*: about, approximately.
1887 *Colonist Christmas No* 5 Tom and I went to kill seals and make a bill; odds of sixty pounds we had one time with Harry Andrews, only three weeks at sea. . .and I am in this country now odds of forty years.

of prep *EDD* ~ 3. Descended from; son of.
1911 HUTCHINSON 84–5 Thus in a village where the name of Frost prevails, it is only natural, perhaps, that Jack Frosts should be many, and they have become so numerous that it has been found necessary to distinguish by calling the one 'Jack Frost of Charley,' and another 'Jack Frost of William,' to say nothing of 'Jack Frost of Jack'—the said Charley, William, and Jack being names of the respective fathers. 1938 MACDERMOTT 117 The common or accepted way to distinguish similar Christian names in the outports, where so many people of the same surname live, is to refer to a person as 'John Smith of James.' P 245–64 ~ Son of, e.g. John of John [Brown].

offal(s) n, n pl ['ɔfl] *OED* ~ 1 b obs for sense 2; *EDD* sb¹ 4 for sense 3.
1 Part(s) of fish, esp cod-fish, discarded as waste or used to manure a garden.
[1583] 1940 *Gilbert's Voyages and Enterprises* ii, 398 [Hayes' narrative] . . .the incredible multitude of sea foule hovering over the same [banke] to prey upon the offalles & garbish of fish throwen out by fishermen, and floting upon the sea. 1758 ULLOA 407 The fish. . .are opened with one cut lengthwise, their backbone, and all their entrails are taken out. . .and the offals thrown into the sea. While some open, others salt, and others again pile up. [1766] 1971 BANKS 147 The Very Cows Eat the Fish offal & thus milk is Fishy. [1786] 1792 CARTWRIGHT iii, 193 Mr Collingham split and salted the fish this morning; the offals, he spread round the cabbages for manure. 1898 PROWSE 316 . . .any heads, entrails, bones or offal of codfish. P 148–63 Rotting fish offals.
2 Leavings from a meal.
T 145–65 An' the ordinary [feed for chickens] would be offals from the table and breadcrumbs, dry breadcrumbs.
3 Waste wood.
1971 NOSEWORTHY 226 ~ Short pieces of sawn wood and ends of boards which are only good for burning.

off-and-on phr Comb **off-and-on boat**, ~ **punt**: small boat (P 187–73); COLLAR BOAT.
M 71–40 To get to their motor boats in the morning and from them in the evening, the crowd had a small

row boat which was called 'the off-and-on punt.' This
little boat was hauled up on the slipway each night.

offer n *EDD* ~ 7 Ir for sense 1; *EDD* 6 Ir So
for sense 2.

1 Chance, opportunity.

1924 ENGLAND 63 'I'll get ye a rope an' gaff, me son,
and ye can go on ice alang o' me, killin' swiles. I'll get
ye some good offers [chances] as'll putt ye up in glee.'
1925 *Dial Notes* v, 337 ~ A chance (at seals).

2 Attempt.

1937 DEVINE 35 I'm going to make an *offer* towards
building a punt in the spring. 1968 DILLON 149 He med
an offer to ket [catch] me, but I hauled clear of him. . .
He never med no offer to get out o' the car.

offer a compar of *OED* off adj 1 b naut 'seaward' (1666–1745). Offshore, away from the
land; the further seaward of two (or more)
objects or features; OUTER.

1837 BLUNT 26 A cluster of large islands extends off
the frontage of this bay, full 20 miles, or so far as Offer
Gooseberry Island. [1906] GRENFELL 53 He saw himself seated in it, going out farther than ever, right to
the 'offer banks,' and then coming home loaded, and
the surprise and joy of his dear wife as he tied up to the
stage. 1910 *Nfld Qtly* Oct, p. 23 . . .one of the fishermen whom we espied as we neared St Julien's on the
'offer-ground.' 1924 ENGLAND 265 Other names of
romantic connotation are: Wild Bight, Sunday
Cove. . .Joe Batt's Arm, Offer Wadhams, The Rat,
Squib Tickle, Oarblade. 1937 DEVINE 35 Offer ground.
The distant fishing ledges. 1942 *Little Bay Islands* 13
The men living on the front of the Island in Northern
and Southern harbours fished with hook and line on
the fishing grounds off the Island, such as Offer
Ground, Parker's to the Cross, Salmon Rock, etc. 1951
Nfld & Lab Pilot i, 114 Cooper bank, with a depth of
18 fathoms over it, and Offer bank, with a depth of 16
fathoms over it, lie about 1¾ miles and 5 miles farther
eastward, respectively. 1953 ibid ii, 142 Gooseberry
islands are a group consisting of Inner and Offer
Gooseberry islands, and a number of islets and dangers
lying between them. 1964 BLONDAHL (ed) 34 "Two
Jinkers": To offer-ground you'd see them bound, /
Look out for squalls that even'! T 80/3–64 Keep up the
offer end, outside end, o' your cod-bag. 1966 FARIS 35
Trap berths are referred to as 'inshore' or 'inner'
grounds, and the most distant 'grounds' of the 'fall voyage' are 'offer grounds.' 1969 HORWOOD 83 Beyond
the headlands lie the offer islands, threaded by tickles
of narrow water.

offshore n attrib *OED* ~ b 'situated, existing, or
operating at a distance from the shore' (1883–).
Relating to the fishery in large vessels on the
'grounds' and 'banks' distant from the shore.

1964 *Daily News* 8 July, p. 5 In the offshore fishery,
greater quantities of cod and plaice were landed. 1969
MENSINKAI 59 We accept the official definitions which
regard an 'offshore' fishery as one where boats weighing 25 tons and over are used and an 'inshore' fishery as
one where boats of less than 25 tons are used. 1974
Federal Licensing Policy 37 If the Canadian groundfish

quota is increased in years to come, it will probably be
easier to generate the capacity to fill that quota through
a build-up of off-shore vessels rather than by arranging
for some of that quota to reach the independent fishermen and nurturing among them an effective entrepre-
neurial response. 1977 BUTLER 16 My boat was old and
not fit to fish on the offshore ground.

oil n [ɑil, ɑil, 'hɑiəl, ɒil, ɔul, ɔil]. For combs. in
sense 3: *DAE* ~ factory (1841–), ~ house 1
(1678), *OED* ~ sb[1] 5 ~ tank (n.d.); for sense 4:
DAE ~ II 3 a ~ case (1744), oilcloth 2 b pl
(1884), ~ 3 a ~ jacket (1851).

1 Viscous liquid extracted from the livers of
cod-fish; COD OIL, TRAIN[2].

[1693] 1793 REEVES ii . . .and liberty to go on shore
on any part of *Newfoundland*, or any of the said
islands, for the curing, salting, drying, and husbanding
of their fish, and for making of oil. [1712] 1895 PROWSE
273 Broken fish which they call refuse sold for twenty
ryalls per quintal, and carried to Spain and Portugal
and oyl made of livers carried to England. 1765
WILLIAMS 6 So that the whole Produce of Fish and Oil,
for any of the aforesaid Years, will be (exclusive of the
Whale and Seal Oil), Fish, 1,032,000 Quintals; Oil,
5,160 Tuns. 1882 TALBOT 22 . . .summer's produce of
fish and oil. 1902 MURPHY 65 "A Dialogue": For
Croucher, said Hoyles, why that fellow is always
engaged in some broil, / I cannot forget how he acted
in that famous case of the oil. [1911] 1930 COAKER 30 I
stated plainly that fish would advance to six dollars in
October and that oil would advance to $110. P 102–60
On the back of the factory half the roof was covered
with glass facing the sun and on the inside underneath
the glass roof was a large steel tank into which was
placed the fat that came from the bottom of other
tanks after being steamed which the sun's rays melted
into oil, the oil that came from the steamed tanks was
pale and No. 1, but from the sun rays tank brown in
colour and No. 2.

2 Oleaginous or thick liquid rendered from the
fat of seals; SEAL OIL.

[1715] 1975 ANDREWS [2] . . .these last two winters
by less than 200 persons belonging to Bonavista there
was made 130 tun of oyl. [1776] 1895 PROWSE 344 Seal
skins and oil to be free of duty. 1888 STEARNS 202 We
git five or six gallons of ile from the passing seal, and
they weigh four to five hundred pounds apiece. 1925
Dial Notes v, 332 [Of seal pelts] To go to oil. To
become valueless.

3 In designation of facilities for the storage and
processing of cod and seal oil: **oil factory** [see
FACTORY], ~ **gully** [see GULLY[2]], ~ **house**, ~
store, ~ **tank**, ~ **tub** [see TUB].

1909 BROWNE 259 There *was* a factory in the vicinity
[of Webber's Cove], but it was an *oil factory*. 1977
BURSEY 81 We had several oil factories to operate.
The cod-liver-oil was medicinal and was much in
demand as a food supplement. [1775] 1792
CARTWRIGHT ii, 53–4 We looked into the old sealing-
house on Round Island, and observed that it had been
much frequented by foxes, there being some oil-gullies
left there. 1860 *Harper's* xxii, 755 Each of the fourteen
buildings belonging to the post, comprising houses for

the officers and servants, store-houses for furs and other goods, a sale shop, coopers' shop, oil-house, fish-house, packing-house, oven-house, etc, excited a degree of interest. 1866 WILSON 31 A line of fishing-stages, fishing-flakes, and oil-houses is erected along the shore. 1894 MORRIS 24 By the kindness of Mr LeMercier we were taken over to the oil house, where was moored a large whale, sixty-nine feet long, and already undergoing the process of sculping. 1861 DE BOILIEU 233 On inquiry I found the open stock was expended, so, sending for the carpenter and his mate, we proceeded to the oil-store, and selected a butt, and cut it in two with a saw. 1977 BURSEY 117 I had to make presses and fifty press boards for each press. The oil tanks must be washed out and painted and the building made thoroughly clean and the inside walls limed. 1971 NOSEWORTHY 227 Oil tub. A tub made of a half-barrel with two side shafts for two men to carry.

4 In names of var articles of clothing or fabrics waterproofed with oil and worn while fishing or handling fish: **oil bag**, **~ case**, **~ clothes** or **~ clothing**, **~ frock**, **~ hat** [see CAPE ANN, LINCOLN, SOU'WESTER], **~ jacket**, **~ pants**, **~ petticoat**.

1910 GRENFELL 138 Our second axe was donated to their impoverished equipment, and indeed, a heterogeneous collection, which included some needles and thread, soap, and other trifles in a couple of oil bags that had been sent us for sailors' use. T 194–65 'Th' only board,' I said, 'gentlemen, that was in our camp was a table an' the doors, an' no oil-case onto un.' C 66–13 She heard the hall door open three times and the rattling of oil case (oil clothes). The next day she heard that her husband was drowned. 1855 WHITE MS Journal 30 May 1 suit oil clothes. [1910] 1930 COAKER 16 Purchase wholesale from the factories such articles as butter, tobacco, boots, oil-clothes, in order to secure the discounts that go into Union funds. 1913 Christmas Chimes 6 Sounded like a man wearin' fishin' boots, it did, an' I could ye'r he's oil-clo'es a-scrubbin'. 1937 DEVINE 115 He sold. . .oil clothing, which was a specialty and included south-westers, Cape Anns and 'Lincolns.' 1977 Nfld Qtly Winter, p. 17 They all had their oil clothes on. [1906] GRENFELL 25–6 But just then an extra big sea came along and washed us both off, me still holding on to Arch's oil frock. 1927 DOYLE (ed) 65 "Three Devils for Fish": O crawl into the cuddy, crawl in my old cock, / Haul out me oil trousers, likewise me oil frock. 1971 NOSEWORTHY 226 Oil hat. A waterproof hat worn by fishermen with the brim the same size all around. 1855 WHITE MS Journal 31 May 1 oil Jacket 6/. 1895 Xmas Review 12 [proverb] When the weather is fair, your oil jacket bear. 1936 SMITH 126 After all just debts were paid I had a nice fat cheque remaining to my credit, which wasn't so bad for an 'Oil Jacket Planter.' T 70/2–64[2] He used to bring a pound [of tobacco] in the fishin' punt, wrapped up in a piece of oil-jacket—plug a day, he used to chew. C 68–24 [tall tale] I took off me Cape ann and me oil-jacket and put them on the [tawt]; the skitties (mosquitoes) was so tick that when I slooed around they was lugging away me clothes; one bunch had the Cape Ann, and another had me oil-jacket. 1974 SQUIRE 79 After a while I pulled my oil jacket right up round my head just leav-

ing my eyes, nose, and mouth exposed. T 184–65 Leg of a old pair of oil pants, fishermen's oil pants—that's what they'd make the mummer caps of. Chop the leg off, lace un up behind, cut the eyes, and cut the mouth. P 143–74 The women always made their own oil-petticoats for wearing at the stage and the flake. The oil-petticoat was made from flour sacks or 'bought calico,' cut in the shape of an apron with a bib that tied around the neck and waist. The apron underwent the same waterproofing process as did the oilskins.

5 Comb **oil rat**: one engaged in processing cod and seal oil, esp transferring it from one container to another.

T 12–64 [He] looked like an oil-rat. Q 73–4 [An oil rat was] a person who was dirty from dipping the rendered cod-liver oil out of the blubber barrels.

oil v EDD ~ v 7; cp Kilkenny Lexicon oiling. To beat or thrash.

[1927] BURKE "Cadwell the Chaw": If a flyweight or bantam that's looking for fight, / You will get well oiled before you fly for Detroit. P 216–72 He once told me about a stubborn horse his father used to own. This is the way he described the horse's stubbornness. 'Me father iled her, I iled her and Jack iled her but the jases ting still never moved.'

old a For combs. in sense 2: EDD ~ 1 (21) ~ Christmas; (38) ~ fellow Ir; ~ man; NID old-man's beard 2 b 'beard lichen'; EDD (125)(b) ~ soldier 'red herring'; (143) ~ Tom 'gin.'

1 Of var species of seal, designating a mature animal of breeding age contrasted with the young of the species (cp CAT[3], WHITE-COAT, YOUNG); usu in comb with BEDLAMER, DOG[1], FAT[1], HARP, HOOD, SEAL, etc, and in other sealing collocations.

[1802] 1895 PROWSE 420 The old [hoods] yielded about fourteen shillings and the young seven. 1846 TOCQUE 191 An old dog hood is a very formidable animal. 1852 ARCHIBALD 4–5 There are generally four different qualities in a cargo of seals,—namely, the young harp, young hood, old harp and bedlamer (the latter is the year old hood), and the old hood. 1862 Atlantic Mo ix, 367 They laved two old uns an' a young whelp to me, as they runned by. 1873 Maritime Mo i, 254 Some of the [sealers], in addition, carry a long sealing-gun on their shoulders. These are the 'bow' or 'after gunners,' who are marksmen to shoot old seals, or others that cannot be reached with the 'gaff.' 1888 STEARNS 109 'Well, you've got an old saddler now,' said Mason. [1895] 1923 CHAFE 62 Price of Seals per cwt: Old Harps, $2.45. Old Hoods, $2.45. 1923 ibid 23 Another law was passed [c1895] to prevent Steamers going on 'Second Trips' as it was considered only a slaughter of the 'Old Seals,' and this was believed to be exterminating the herds. 1924 ENGLAND 37 'Dem whiteycoats is wonnerful azy to kill, sir, but ye'll have to look out fer de old dogs an' bitches. . . Look out fer de old siles,' he repeated. Ibid 71 Us 'andy to de fat now, me sons! Dis de rale ole-hood ice, now. Ibid 91 Men bring a 'jig,' or steelyard, up on deck, and weigh four of the old-fat sculps. One tips the yard at ninety pounds. Ibid 234 A few more days, an' ahl will sail, / Doze steamboats strong an' good, / To face de harp an' bellamer, / Whitecoats an' ole dog hood. [1929] 1979 *Evening Telegram* 9 Mar, p. 5 One buyer has already quoted his prices as $19 for old harp pelts. 1936 SMITH 102–3 He also had missed the young fat, and was looking for the old seals. 1937 DEVINE 67 Old seals jumping and making for the water is a sign of wind and snow. 1947 TANNER 493 The next winter the 'beater seals' return south again as 'bed-lamers,' the second winter as 'young harps,' in the fourth year having the dignity of 'old harps.' [1954] 1979 *Evening Telegram* 22 Feb, p. 12 The price [for fat] will be the same as last year and will be as follows. . .old harps, $4. T 89/90–64 We hauled un out, a old bitch hood. We went back to the gaze again, an' when we looked in, sir, here was the old dog hood just leavin' the ice with the old bitch; dragged her out and carried her away. T 141/68–65² If you struck a family o' hoods, the best thing to do is to try to capture th' ol' dog, because he's pretty treacherous. T 172/3–65 An' they'd have their seal bottles, made out of sealskin, dried, and they'd have their old fat, old seal oil, in certain bags, an' they'd have their young seal oil, what they had for mixin' their bread an' their flour, in other. 1976 *Decks Awash* v (2), p. 6 Right now with the old seals in the water you have to chase them all over the place which is expensive. But in heavy ice you can stop the boat on the ice and bring back the seals.

2 Comb **old christmas**: Twelfth Day, or Epiphany, as reckoned by the old style.

1937 *Bk of Nfld* ii, 259 From before Christmas till Old Christmas Day, called Twelfth Day, they held high carnival. C 67–6 A Christmas tree should be taken down on Old Christmas Night, January 6, because it is bad luck to leave it up after that. 1982 *Evening Telegram* 6 Jan, p. 2 Today is the 12th day of Christmas or Old Christmas Day [traditionally] in Newfoundland. . .an important occasion for celebration.

old cows' days: see COW DAYS.

old cow path: course between Newfoundland and the ice-floe usu taken by vessels on their way to the seal hunt; INSIDE CUT.

1929 *Nat Geog* July, p. 102 The other fleet, going down the 'old cow path' on the front of the island, clears from St John's.

old fellow: (a) [= husband; father. See FELLOW]; (b) the devil.

T 22–64 Never scared in my life. But I did one time see th' Old Feller, and heard un, with his chain, comin' rattlin' his chain! C 68–15 She would say, 'Now you get home before 10 o'clock or the old feller'll have you for sure.' 1973 WIDDOWSON 203 When I was young, about four or five years old, one way my mother used to frighten me from doing something she did not want me to do was by saying that the Old Fellow would come after me.

old granny: see GRANNY².

old hag: see HAG.

old harry: reef or rock hazardous to vessels.

1951 *Nfld & Lab Pilot* i, 233 Old Harry, one of three high pinnacle rocks, lies close offshore. 1953 ibid ii, 122 [They] lie between Old Harry and Young Harry. The sea breaks on all these dangers.

old holly: strange cry or noise, an omen of danger or of the devil. See HOLLY*.

T 370–67 This frightening noise [of the loon] is about the old holly; he is going to come aboard the boat after you. C 70–29 Old holly is a warning that a storm is coming. It is always some sort of weird noise that cannot be explained or identified.

old king: [= king eider] see KING 2.

old link: the devil.

1924 ENGLAND 179 Ye ought to give us Ole Link, sir, de martal son of a scaldy!

old lord: mature male eastern harlequin duck (*Histrionicus histrionicus*) (1959 MCATEE 16); LORD².

1967 *Bk of Nfld* iii, 282 Harlequin Duck: Lord and Ladies (in allusion to their beautiful plumage); Old Lord (a fully mature male); and Lady or Jenny (the female or immature).

old maid: see **old woman** below.

old maid's path: see MILK.

old man's beard, ~ **whisker**: (a) lichen which grows on conifers; beard-moss (*Usnea barbata*); MOLDOW; (b) lingering patch of snow in summer.

[1898 *J A Folklore* xi, 283 Old man's beard (prob confused with another species).] 1903 M F HOWLEY 3 The 'Old Man's Beard' is a patch of snow on the 'Southside Hill,' which from its position in a deep ravine is protected from the sun's rays, and remains long after all the other ice and snow have disappeared and the trees have put on their summer's verdure. 1907 MILLAIS 338 Maldow (Old man's beard moss). 1913 DUGMORE 39 During the very heavy falls of snow all ground food is hidden, they must then turn to the tree-growing mosses, such as *Sticla pulmonaria* and the common Usnea, or Old Man's Beard, which hangs from the trees in graceful wind-blown festoons. P 245–55 Old man's whiskers. Moldow, or long stringy substance growing from trees.

old man's bread: mushroom (C 66–3); FAIRY BREAD.

1971 NOSEWORTHY 227 ~ Edible mushroom.

old man's cap: see **old man's bread** (P 17–69); FAIRY CAP.

old moll: imaginary figure invoked to frighten children into good behaviour.

T 434–65 I don't know whether 'twas the old feller of all [but they'd say], 'Old Moll is coming if you don't look out, if you don't get quiet, you'll see Old Moll directly; he'll be in here. An old black man.'

old saddler: great black-backed gull (*Larus marinus*); SADDLEBACK, SADDLER.

1870 *Can Naturalist* v, 408 Should [the dead bird] prove to be a goose or duck, or even one of their own species, the 'old saddler' usually commences operations [devouring it]. 1888 STEARNS 109 'Well, you've got an old saddler now,' said Mason. . .an immense bird of the gull tribe. P 131–70 That's an old saddler.

old scripture cake: Christmas cake made from recipe drawn from biblical texts.

M 69–7 Here is a recipe for an Old Scripture Cake

used [at Christmas]: 1 cup Judges 5:25 milk, 2 cups Jeremiah 6:20 sugar, 3½ cups 1st Kings 4:22 flour, 3 cups Samuel 30:12 raisins, 1 cup Genesis 43:11 nuts, 1 cup Exodus 3:8 honey, 5 Isaiah 10:14 eggs, a little Leviticus 2:13 salt, a few kinds of 1st Kings 10:2 spices, 1 large spoon Genesis 24:20 water. Follow Solomon's advice for making a good boy, Proverbs 23:14, and you will have a good cake.

old soaker: see SOAKER.

old soldier, soldier: squid bait, beginning to go stale.

[c1869] 1927 DOYLE (ed) "The Antis of Plate Cove": The gang got a full tub of 'soldiers' / And pelted him down to his door, / His mother did not know her son / 'Till she washed him a dozen times o'er. 1937 DEVINE 35 ~s. Squid that are becoming stale and unfit for codfish bait. P 234–57 ~ A squid that has been on the beach for a few days (?so-called from its reddish colour: red-coat). P 229–67 I got some old soldiers for fishin' tomorrow.

old trout: familiar form of address to a male.

1975 Evening Telegram 6 June, p. 1 The defence witness brought down the house when, in replying affirmatively to questions by Magistrate Hugh O'Neill, he said:- 'That's right, me old trout.'. . . His final reply was: 'That's right, your honor, me old trout.'

old twelfth: see **old christmas** above.

C 67–21 Old Christmas Day is sometimes called Old Twelfth Day. On this day the Christmas tree is taken down, and Christmas is over.

old wife

1870 Can Naturalist v, 302 'Old Wife' is another provincial name for [the long-tailed duck].

old woman, ~ maid: (a) part of inner organs of a lobster, discarded in eating; HAG[1]; (b) variety of small shell-fish (see 1972 quot).

P 148–65 There is an old woman in a rockin' chair in the lobster. 1971 NOSEWORTHY 227 Old maid. The part in the head of a lobster which is not normally eaten. 1972 MURRAY 119 [Children] also pried small shells less than an inch in diameter loose from the rocks at high water mark. These were shaped very much like Chinese pointed peasant hats, and were called 'ol'domans.' P 78–75 The old woman in the rocking chair [is] part of the lobster which one shouldn't eat. 1976 GUY 60 When eating the lobster bodies you must be careful to stay away from the 'old woman,' a lump of bitter black stuff up near the head which is said to be poisonous.

old year: New Year's Eve.

C 62–2 It took place from Christmas to Old Year.

olderly a Elderly.

T 187/9–65 He was a olderly man then, you know, gettin' up in years.

oldster n See YOUNGSTER. In the British migratory fishery in Newfoundland, a man who has served his time for two summers and one winter; a sealer after one season at the 'hunt.'

1866 WILSON 207 When [the youngsters'] full time of service is expired, they receive the honourable appellation of *oldsters*. 1925 Dial Notes v, 337 ~ One who has made former trips on the ice.

omadhaun n also **omadaun, omadawn, omaudaun** ['ɑmədaun, ɔmə'dɔːn] OED ~ Ir (1818–1895); EDD ~ var omadhawn, omadaun, etc, Ir I Ma; DINNEEN amadán. A stupid, idle, foolish fellow; fool.

1925 Dial Notes v, 337 Omadaun. A lazy, good-for-nothing fellow; fool. 1937 DEVINE 35 Omadawn. A clown. T 12–64 We use 'dumb-bell,' meaning a stupid person, and an omadhaun is much the same thing. 1968 DILLON 149 Omadawn. A simple or foolish person. C 71–89 'You stupid omagon' simply means a fool or a very ill-witted soul. 1974 CAHILL 15 Do you know why we went broke in 1932 and England took our own government away from us, and sent over that clique of mouldy omaudauns in the first place? Do you? 1978 Evening Telegram 29 July, p. 16 'Oh, come on now,' sez Mr English, 'sure I thought every omadhaun knew that.'

omaloor n DINNEEN amalóir. A clumsy, stupid, simple-minded fellow.

1925 Dial Notes v, 337 ~ An ungainly fellow with big feet. 1937 DEVINE 35 ~ A half wit. 1968 DILLON 149 Omalore. A simple, foolish person; one to be pitied.

on prep

1 Phr *on the dead*: (a) simply, directly; without equipment; (b) without guarantee of success or profit.

1819 ANSPACH 383 The principal use of [the Newfoundland dog], in addition to his quality of a good watch-dog, is to assist in fetching from the woods the lumber intended either for repairing the stages, or for fuel, which has been there cut and laid up in piles; and this is done. . .by dragging it *on the dead*, that is, on the bare snow and ice, the ends being fastened together with a rope fixed to the tackling of the dog. P 108–70 The dogs haul the wood in the winter, but we have to keep them on the dead in the summer. They don't earn their keep in the summer and are then a dead loss. P 148–74 I had to take that boat [from the builders] on the dead.

on light: afire.

P 269–64 Catch the house on light.

2 Comb **on-rope**: rope used to pull a sled; HAULING-ROPE.

M 69–6 The animal then started to run with the wood still between his horns so Jack grabbed his 'on-rope' (hauling rope) and chased him.

once: the once, to ~ See TO.

one num, n Cp OED ~ 13 b for sense 1; EDD 7, *Kilkenny Lexicon* for sense 3; for combs. in sense 5: cp OED one-handed a; NID one-lunger.

1 The same; identical.

[1900 OLIVER & BURKE] 62 Both squadrons arrived off St John's the wan time. T 43/7–64 Oh, it's the one thing, but some people call 'em scythestone an' others call 'em roughstone. P 148–66 The children with the one father.

2 Vessel, ship.

1924 ENGLAND 12 Us'll soon be gadderin' de pans now, b'ys! Soon 'aulin' 'em aburd o' dis un! 1925 *Dial Notes* v, 337 ~ Used in referring to the ship. T 187/9–65 When the breeze was over, that one down there had a notch cut in her spar, foremast, so big around as my arm, where they had the chain come in through the hawse-pipe and bitt up around her foremast.

3 Girl, woman; wife.

P 48–60 ~ Refers to the wife of someone. 'Mr Johnson's one.' 1973 PINSENT 86 [The old man] then looked at the letters. 'But 'ere, now—dis one could 'ave given me da kind of life I never 'ad. Dey're sweet letters, Will.'

4 Phr *one day under*: nearly, almost (of a certain age).

C 70–12 These three words, *one day under*, meant that you were not quite a certain age but you would be in the very near future. It did not mean that one more day and you would be ten years old or whatever the age may be, but that within the month you would reach this age people were referring to.

5 Comb **one-claw jigger**: type of fishing-hook with a single barb, used without bait.

[1929] 1933 GREENLEAF (ed) 254 "Lukey's Boat": 'I think,' said Lukey, 'I'll maker her bigger; / I'll load her down with a one-claw jigger.'

one-eyed hero: see NELSON.

one-handed boat: small two-oared boat.

P 102–60 Capt Jos Blandford. . .was one of the old hardy Newfoundlanders who previous to his passing was always the first man in his one handed boat to be seen on the fishing ground.

one-lunger: boat with a single-cylinder engine.

1956 *Evening Telegram* 12 Dec, p. 11 A graduate from the days of sail and oar, most boats are 'one lungers' (equipped with single cylinder make-and-break gasoline engines), but a fair number have had multiple-cylinder engines installed. 1969 MOWAT 35 She was a broad-beamed skiff powered by a five-horsepower, 'jump spark,' single-cylinder engine. It was calm and cold as we puttered out of the harbour accompanied in darkness by the muted reverberations from a score of other 'one-lungers' pushing unseen boats toward the open sea.

one-poler: sailing vessel with a single topmast (P 209–73).

one-room: school in which all the grades are accommodated in a single room with one teacher.

1976 *Daily News* 24 Feb, p. 3 The one-room where I began teaching in Fortune Bay was heated by a black, pot-bellied stove.

one-tub set: in trawl-fishing, a single tub of line set out to fish; see also SET n, TUB.

1924 ENGLAND 262 Sometimes these Vikings work all night, fishing, with flares. Days and nights on end they're never dry. In ugly weather they snatch one-tub sets between squalls, fairly pulling the whiskers of death.

one-twenty: variety of the card-game, auction, in which the winning score is one hundred and twenty points (P 108–75).

M 69–6 During winter nights. . .many men played cards when they weren't tired. The two popular games were five-hundreds and one-twenty or auction.

oodle-addle* See LOODLE-LADDLE*.

oo-isht int also **hoo-eet, puit, twet** *Labrador Inuit* huit 'go.' Command to dog-team to pull ahead.

1861 *Harper's* xxii, 756 The driver [was] half-reclining, with the whip over his shoulder trailing behind, five fathoms long! *'Twet! Twet!'* on! on!—'ouk! ouk!' to the right! 1885 ibid lxxi, 658 The words of command are 'Ra-ra,' haw; 'Ak,' gee; 'Ha,' ho; 'Puit,' get up. 1907 WALLACE 231 To start his team the driver calls 'oo-isht,' (in the south this becomes 'hoo-eet') to turn to the right 'ouk,' to the left 'ra-der, ra-der' and to stop 'aw-aw.' The leader responds to the shouted directions and the pack follow. 1916 YOUNG 77 In the morning there would be some difficulty in getting all the dogs harnessed and fastened to the komatik. . . As soon as we were ready for a start, Charlie gave the command 'ooisht' and instantly they were off at a gallop.

oonchook See OWNSHOOK.

open a *DC* open spring Nfld (1933).

Comb **open-mouthed (skiff)**: type of large, undecked fishing-boat.

T 50/1–64 Boats [would be] brought around there 'fore th' ice'd come in. Big boats, skiffs, open mouthed skiffs.

open spring: year in which the ice-floes are off shore.

1933 GREENE 35 Again, in what the Newfoundlanders call an 'Open Spring,' the ice will be swept so far east into the broad Atlantic, that the thankful land will be seen rejoicing in its early garb of green.

open v Cp *Cent* ~ 2. To build (a road).

1837 *Journ of Assembly* 451, 458 . . .to open a narrow road through wooded country. . .to open the whole line of road. P 245–79 The Government has promised to open a new road to the community during the next fiscal year.

opening vbl n Comb **opening medicine**: a laxative.

P 269–63 Give her some op'n medicine. C 71–7 [Senna leaves] had to be steeped and the liquid would then be drunk to cure colds or taken as opening medicine.

ordain v *EDD* ~ 3 Sh I Co. To intend (something) for a particular purpose.

1896 *J A Folklore* ix, 29 ~ in common use, and is applied to matters in ordinary business of life. Thus a man will say, 'I *ordained* that piece of wood for an axe helve.'

order n *OED* ~ sb 20 (1568–); regionally of high frequency in nautical usage: see 1832 quot.

In phr *in order*, pron as *narder** ['næːɹdəɹ, 'naːɹdəɹ]: ready, prepared (P 37).

[(1832) 1981 *Them Days* vi (4), p. 44 Put the seine in the boat in order for tomorrow to see if there is any lance to be got.] P 121–68 I'll be narder in a minute. P 245–67 It takes him some time to get narder. P 179–73 How long will they women take to get narder?

ordinary a Comb **ordinary cure**: cod-fish salted and dried in a manner intermediate between light- and heavy-salted grades.

1958 *Evening Telegram* 11 Feb, p. 19 I know. . .ordinary cure, Labrador cure, etc. 1969 MENSINKAI 8 The salt fish takes four different forms, viz., light-salted, heavy-salted, pickled-split and ordinary cure.

ore n
Comb **ore mine**: hard layer of soil immediately below surface soil.

P 229–67 After we got through the ore mine, the grave wasn't too hard to dig.

ore pass: passage or chute from one level of a mine to another.

P 222–67 The muck is transferred to an ore pass [which] leads to a hopper where it is stored until raised to the surface via the bucket.

oreweed n ['oɹɹwɪ] *EDD* ore sb²: ~ weed D Co. Sea-weed, sea-wrack; kelp.

T 498–68 An' he drifted in right in to a beach. An' there was a big pile of orewee'. An' the cows, you could hear them coming down.

ornament n A remarkable sight.

P 148–74 If you want to see an ornament [when you see things caught in nets, you should see a polar bear in a fish net].

ose egg n also **cosy-egg*, oar's-egg, osy-egg*, whore's egg** ['hɔɹɹ ɛg, 'hoɹɹ ɛg, 'hoɹɹ lɛɨg] *Cent* whore's egg; 1930 *Am Sp* v, 393 whore's egg [?Nfld]; [1948] 1963 *PADS* No 40, p. 10 whore's egg [Florida]. Possibly developed from URSENA and *sea-egg*. Sea-urchin; sea-egg (*Strongylocentrolus drobachiensis*); URSENA.

1846 TOCQUE 107 I observed the margin of the beach strewed with sea-urchins (*Echinidae*), usually called in Newfoundland, ose eggs. 1878 ibid 497 The Sea Urchin, Hedgehog, or Sea Egg. . .usually called in Newfoundland Ox eggs [ed emend: ose eggs], are found on all parts of the coast, clinging, by the suckers which they possess, to the rocks, and to the wharves and stays. . . They are frequently eaten in Newfoundland. P 243–56 Whore's egg—a spiny shell-fish. P 148–65 Ozy-eggs. C 66–10 Ozz-egg. T 391/2–67 [The seal would] get a whore's egg and break 'em up and eat 'em, you know. 1970 *Evening Telegram* 17 July, p. 2 Meditating, I was, on the wondrous oil refineries, the great paper mills and the magnificent hose eggs works that would soon sprout from the bogs behind me. C 71–120 Cosy-eggs—local name for sea urchins. 1972 MURRAY 119 In the thirties and forties children picked

up 'oar's eggs,' the prickly sea urchin which, when dry, lost its spines and made a nice round coracle-type boat.

other a Specified; (the one) being thought of; intimately related.

P 148–63 The other one (i.e. his girl-friend) has gone away. T 195–65 The other feller is making [a net] next winter fourteen fathom deep. P 148–67 What about the other fella (i.e. an infant son)?

otter n *DC* otterboard (Nfld: 1771); *OED* ~ 7 ~ path (1864); *DC* otter rub (1933).
Comb **otterboard**: flat board on which otter skin is stretched to dry.

[1771] 1792 CARTWRIGHT i, 123 The sawyers were picking oakum, and the furriers making otterboards.

otter crow [i.e. other crow]: eastern common crow (*Corvus brachyrhynchos brachyrhynchos*).

1870 *Can Naturalist* v, 158 [The otter crow] frequents the sea coast, breeds in trees, and lays four or five eggs.

otter-path: well-marked trail made by otters.

[1772] 1792 CARTWRIGHT i, 253 From the head of the pond, a good otter-path led into Twelve-o'clock Harbour.

otter racquet: narrow, elongated snowshoe.

1884 STEARNS 149 There are great varieties of form, called usually from some fancied resemblance to the tail of an animal. The beaver, the otter, the porcupine, and the bobtailed rackets are used perhaps more frequently than any others about this coast.

otter rub, also **rub**: spot of ground, vegetation, etc, worn smooth by otters rubbing there repeatedly; a slope where otters playfully slide down; RUBBING-PLACE.

1842 JUKES i, 66 Among the roots of these trees numerous otters have formed their burrows. These are called 'otter rubs,' from the smooth and beaten path leading to them, or from the polished stems and roots of the trees, against which the animals apparently rub themselves. 1907 WALLACE 131 Several otter rubs were noted, and we saw some of the animals, but did not disturb them. 1933 MERRICK 76 A rub is a smooth, worn shoot-the-chute down the side of a bank where the otters play, running up and sliding down like children. T 253/67–66 I was lookin' for a spot where there was a otter rub. 1974 NORTHCOTT 71 Otter slides or 'rubs' on inland bodies of water and at the seaside are familiar to all observant travellers in the country.

otter slide: see **otter rub**.

1840 GOSSE 42 The old furrier, who acted as my guide, showed me many 'otter slides.' These were always on a steep sloping bank of a pond or stream, where the water remained unfrozen. They were as smooth and slippery, as glass, caused by the otters sliding on them in play. T 253/67–66 You understand the otter rub? Otter slide.

ouananiche n also **ouinanish, winnish**, etc. [ˌwɪˌnɪ'nɪʃ, 'wɪnənɪʃ, ˌwɒnə'nɪʃ] *OED* ~ (1896–7), *DC* (1808–). Landlocked Atlantic salmon (*Salmo salar*).

1907 MILLAIS 202 Here we took out our rods and fished, although the worst time of the day for such an operation, and soon had enough ouananiche to feed our men for another day. 1908 HUBBARD 9 The fish are of peculiar excellence, from the ouinanish, trout and lake trout to the less valued pike and red and white suckers. 1928 PALMER 250 I have fished in many. . .lakes. . .for Rainbow and Ouananiche. 1964 SCOTT & CROSSMAN 36 Ouananiche. . .inhabit lakes that are distributed along the fringe of the presumed maximum extent of Pleistocene glaciation in North America. . .occurring in Newfoundland in Red Indian Lake, Terra Nova Lake, and the lakes at the head of Gambo River.

ouk int also **ak, auk**. Cp *Labrador Inuit* auk 1; *DC* Lab (1924). Command to dog-team to turn right; KEEP OFF.
1861 *Harper's* xxii, 756 The driver half-reclining, with the whip over his shoulder trailing behind, five fathoms long! *'Twet! twet!'* on! on!—*'ouk! ouk!'* to the right! 1895 GRENFELL 146 As there are no reins, the leading dog is trained to obey the voice. At the shout 'Auk' he goes to the right, and at 'Ra' to the left, and so on, the others following him. 1907 WALLACE 160 Tom got off the komatik and ran by its side, guiding the team by calling out 'ouk' when he wanted to turn to the right and 'rudder' to turn to the left, repeating the words many times in rapid succession as though trying to see how fast he could say them. 1920 WALDO 144 In Labrador 'ouk, ouk!' turns the team to the right. . .and 'urrah urrah!' swerves it to the left. The corresponding directions in Newfoundland are 'keep off!' and 'hold in!' No reins are used—some drivers use no whip.

out av, prep Cp *OED* ~ av 2 for senses 1, 2.
1 To Newfoundland from Great Britain or Ireland.
[1794] 1968 THOMAS 172 He reported that, in the year before his arrival, Captain Holdsworth of Dartmouth had brought out from England no less than Two Hundred and Thirty-Six Passengers. 1888 *Colonist Christmas No* 4 If she had 'come out' here as a young person, which is more than probable, her memory would have gone back to the commencement of the previous century. 1901 *Christmas Review* 8 He had come out on a health trip at the suggestion of his doctors. 1912 *Nfld Qtly* Dec, p. 28 Joe Woodford, who resides in the little fishing station of Boat Harbour just below Cape Norman. Joe Woodford is an Englishman 'out of England' as they are termed on the shore. P 108–71 He came out as a draper to Bowring's.
2 Towards the sea-coast; seaward.
1964 *Evening Telegram* 30 Oct, p. 6 Carried by the tide the *Sierstad* drifted out Conception Bay to within two miles of Cape St Francis when she suddenly went down. C 71–113 'He went out the road,' meaning towards the east [and the sea].
3 Phr *out of collar*: see COLLAR.
out (of) doors: attached to the stern of a boat rather than in-board.
T 43/7–64 But these wester shore boats had the rudder out o' doors, hung down by the stern, an' a big tiller. P 241–68 Some ships had a transom and the rudder came up through the stern, but if the boat had a counter stern like the one I am describing it will be

referred to as a rudder out of doors or counter stern. 1977 BUTLER 34 Many of the fishermen residing at Kingwell were experienced boat builders. All the fishing boats were the same type with the rudder outdoors.
out of one barrel: living closely together; sharing.
1958 HARRINGTON 116 The families lived as we say 'out of one barrel, and one purse.'

out v *EDD* ~ 3 IW; *ADD* 2. To extinguish a fire, put out; DOUT.
T 50–64 There had to be so many stopped for another week in case the [forest] fire'd [pop] up again an' get hot. But the big storm outed the works—the power o' the Almighty God. That's the only one outs the fire.

outer a Offshore, away from the land; the further seaward of two (or more) objects or features; OFFER; OUTSIDE.
1832 MCGREGOR i, 196 The outer bank, or Flemish Cap, appears to be a continuation of the grand bank, at a lower elevation. 1951 *Nfld & Lab Pilot* i, 72 The promontory separating Middle and Outer coves rises to an elevation of 202 feet about 2½ cables from its seaward extremity. Ibid 370 A rock. . .is situated about midway between The Hat and Outer Shag rock, and the passage between them must not be attempted.

outfit n Cp *DC* ~ 3 a (esp 1822 quot) for sense 1. See also FIT-OUT.
1 Supplies and gear for a man or vessel to prosecute the fishery or seal-hunt.
[1739] 1954 INNIS 148 Craft. . .necessary for fitting out the Fishing Boats as also the [outfits] of the several fishing Ships & others employed in that Trade & Fishery. [1822] 1928 CORMACK 109 The fishermen, or planters, as they are called, obtain their outfits. . .from the merchants at Fortune Bay. 1852 *Morning Post* 12 Feb, p. 3 Outfits for the seal fishery. [1896] SWANSBOROUGH 35 "The Seal Fishery": This is the way that many crews / Must get their trip, or else must lose / For the out-fits are very high; / So both skippers and men must try / To get at least a saving trip. 1966 SZWED 41 Each spring a man approached a merchant in order to obtain an 'outfit' on credit—the necessary supplies to begin fishing or farming.
2 A technical device for a specified purpose; contraption; MACHINE.
P 102–60 Then fasten that much line to a tolepin, then rebait the hooks and throw them from the side of the boat. The hooks and lead would sink the measured depth to where they catch the last fish, and sit and await another jerk on the line and then haul it back again. They generally used two of these outfits, one each side of the boat. 1972 MURRAY 245 Her husband had an outfit made so that she could 'carry out' his fish. It was a frame [fitting over the shoulders] and two containers. 1975 BUTLER 69 I was never able to find out why those outfits were named ram's horn to throw the fish in when washed.

outfit v Cp *Cent* ~ (1886). To prepare a boat or

vessel for fishing or the fish trade; to equip with supplies and gear; FIT: *fit out*.

[1739] 1954 INNIS 148 Craft, Cloathing, Provisions, Sail Cloth, Cordage, Ironwork, and other fishing Utensils necessary for fitting out the Fishing Boats. . . 1975 BUTLER 67 Around the first of July, I would outfit one of Wareham's schooners for trading and buying dried codfish from his dealers in all the harbours around the bay. 1973 WADEL 2 Some merchants could own a great number of schooners themselves and 'outfit' an even larger number owned by local skippers. 1975 *Evening Telegram* 26 Apr, p. 7 These fishermen are preparing and outfitting for the salmon fishery which is less than a month away.

out-harbour n ['ɑuthæːɹbəɹ] *DC* ~ (Nfld: 1818–). See also HARBOUR. A bay or harbour other than the chief port of St John's; the inhabited coastal strip or settlement of such an inlet of the sea; OUTPORT. Also attrib.

[1764] 1976 HEAD 169 Dark Corners of the Out Harbours [of Trinity Bay]. . . [1789] 1954 INNIS 310 [A proclamation was issued] against fishermen coming from the out harbours to winter at St John's. [1794] 1968 THOMAS 77 We are on a Coasting Cruize, Captain Morris meaning to viset St Pierre. . .and some of the principal out-harbours. 1818 CHAPPELL 27 All the ports of *Newfoundland*, except that of the Capital, *St John's*, are called *Out-harbours*. [1831] 1916 *Nfld Law Reports* 38 I am aware, from personal observation, at some of the outharbours, planters of good character, and having the reputation of skilful and industrious fishermen, procure at St John's, without difficulty an advance of necessary supplies. 1869 HOWLEY *MS Reminiscences* 10 [At British Harbour we were] treated. . .with the proverbial outharbour hospitality. 1895 PROWSE 114 A lady sent her servant—an out-harbour man—to ask a friend to go calling with her. The message delivered was: 'The Mistress wants to know, "Mam," if you will go *cruizing* with her this afternoon.' 1898 *Record Christmas No* 10 About this time a dark looking man came to the outharbour on some kind of business. [1900 OLIVER & BURKE] 69 I'm wild to get a rich outharbour merchant from the bay. 1955 DOYLE (ed) 53 "Sealers' Song": So here's success to Susie Bess, / And girls from all outharbours, / For a kiss set in on a sealer's chin, / Which never saw the barber. 1970 *Evening Telegram* 11 May, p. 3 They could have seen it coming long ago if they had paid more attention to what was going on in the outharbours. Now there's a big buzz and a stir as they find it can happen in the great metropolis too.

outport n ['æutˌpoəɹt, 'ɑutpɔːɹt]. Cp *OED* ~ [1] 1 'term including all ports other than that of London' (1642–); *DC* 1 Nfld (1820–). A coastal settlement other than the chief port of St John's; OUT-HARBOUR. Also attrib.

1810 STEELE 94 Some few years since, four or five [native Indians] were discovered in a wigwam, by persons who were on the search for them, from an outport. 1842 JUKES i, 25 . . .the recent establishment of schools in the outports. 1863 PEDLEY 257 The systematic encroachment on the ships' fishing-rooms, so much

complained of by the authorities in St John's, were still more rife in the outports, the innovators being probably encouraged by their distance from the notice and correction of the government. 1887 *Colonist Christmas No* 2 And, after all, there is nothing but what is quite natural in this great love of Christmas among our outport people, for it is only then that the fisherman can safely say that his summer's toil is over. 1900 PROWSE 116 Outport pilots demanding a greater sum than rate, or accepting a lesser sum. 1907 DUNCAN 113 I'd be a Newfoundlander, outport born, outport bred, of outport strength and tenderness of heart, of outport sincerity, had I my birth to choose. [1909] 1930 COAKER 8 The Inspector of Cullers to be appointed by and responsible to the Department of Marine and Fisheries, and should be an Outport Planter. 1919 *Journ of Assembly* 314 The third suggestion, Outport Hospitals, is one that has been discussed for some time. . . I am strongly in favour of a ten-bed hospital conveniently situated in each of the principal bays. 1941 DULEY 74 One of the larger outports, Ship Haven looked as if the sea had bitten the land with a horse-shoe mouth. Scattered widely, the settlement seemed lifted to stare at the sea. 1950 HERBERT 255–6 But if you come in from the sea to any of the innumerable fishing villages (or 'outports') on a sunny day, you would say you were in Norway, or Cornwall. T 43/7–64 But in the outports now, if you're goin' into a house, in the back entrance, the first thing you'll see is a birch broom. 1976 CASHIN 48 Also many of the outport dealers, planters or merchants operated their own coastal schooners or boats, which were continually coming to St John's for additional supplies of all kinds.

outporter n *DC* ~ Nfld (1905–). See OUTPORT. A native or inhabitant of a coastal settlement; an outsider's term for BAY MAN, *out-harbour man* (see OUT-HARBOUR).

1905 DUNCAN 67 There is the Newfoundland 'outporter'—the small fisherman of the remoter coast. 1963 WILLIAMS 21 Perhaps a quarter of all houses in the study-area is situated on the Coast Road. The proportion is increasing as many outporters have moved in to enjoy the freedom of mobility it affords. 1973 WADEL 108 Outporters do not evaluate a man according to his occupation to the extent that this is done in an urban industrial culture.

outside n, av *OED* ~ adj 1 (1872 quot) for sense 2. See also OUT, OUTER.

1 Towards the coast from the interior; the settled coast-line.

1891 PACKARD 68 The otter frequents the brooks at the head of Salmon and Esquimaux rivers. In winter they rarely come outside, i.e., to the coast. 1902 HOWLEY *MS Reminiscences* 28 There are several houses scattered around in coves and outside near the Northern Head there is quite a large settlement in Seal Cove. [1918–19] GORDON 77 Everything looks like the advent of spring at last, although the folk from the outside say that the ocean ice is just as solid as in midwinter.

2 Beyond a harbour, seaward.

1812 BUCHAN *MS* 10 July At midnight having made

a considerable run amongst Islands and shoals, we at [length] got outside. 1865 CAMPBELL 64–5 They all got safe to land at last, but there were hundreds outside, and the whole sea was opening. 1894 *Evening Herald* 10 Dec [In Labrador] another. . .started for to go outside with his wife. . .her husband got knocked overboard while steering with an oar. 1924 ENGLAND 104 Seals are also said to move offshore in a gale that urges the fish 'outside.' 1953 *Nfld & Lab Pilot* ii, 244 These include the following in approximate order from east to west: Gull Island ground. . .Shoal Ground; Paddy Spot; Paddy Outside Spot; and Outside Spot. Ibid 520 Kidlit or Outside islands. . .lie about 3½ miles eastward of Ukallik. T 84–64 An' when I gets there oh there's good many seals outside—more seals outside than was inside. 1969 WADEL 7 The area might be divided into two broad ecological zones; the outer islands, locally referred to as 'the outside,' relying mainly on the exploitation of marine resources, particularly cod but also lobster and salmon, and the inner 'bay' area. 1975 BUTLER 42 And Joe Coady was outside of us, but we took him with us certainly, took his anchor and chain, took the anchor we had ashore, we slacked away chain on that. She went off and she dragged down so far through the reach. Couldn't stand up on deck. 'Twas a typhoon, that's all.

3 On the seaward side of the Arctic ice-floes.
[1771] 1792 CARTWRIGHT i, 120 On observing a jamb of ice which extended from Table Point towards Belle Isle, we endeavoured to go on the outside of it. In this attempt we got so far out to sea. . .that it was with great difficulty we regained the shore at Birchy Cascade. 1887 BOND 63 . . .the real breedin' ice from outside. [1896] SWANSBOROUGH 32 "The Seal Fishery": But you must not suppose that all / The vessels are within a call; / For some skippers keep the outside, / Others the centre, some inside / Of the ice.

4 Comb **outside cut**: course of a sealing vessel seaward or to the east of the Arctic ice-floe; see CUT n.
1905 CHAFE 7 The S.S. *Eagle*, Captain Arthur Jackman, took an outside cut from St John's and struck the seals on the 16th of March.
outside door: the seaward entrance to a cod-trap; DOOR.
T 80/3–64 I asked this feller here the other day how the fish was workin'—[whether] he was gettin' it in his inside door or outside door. Didn't know! I said, 'You still use two doors in a trap?' 'Oh, yes.'
outside edge: seaward, or eastward, side of the Arctic ice-floe; FRONT, STRAIGHT EDGE.
1855 WHITE *MS Journal* 4 Mar Passing along the outside edge of the Ice in large lakes at 4 p.m.
outside loft: upper room in a building; LOFT.
[1886] LLOYD 76 These apartments are severally known as 'outside loft' (room over kitchen). . .
outside stage: part of the elevated platform on the shore at which fish are landed and prepared for salting (Q 67–92). Cp STAGE, STAGE HEAD.
C 75–136 The bridge between the outside stage where the fish is cleaned and the inside stage where the fish is salted.

out-wind n Wind blowing off the land seaward.

1860 MULLOCK 40 How surprised they are then when you tell them that, for ten months at least in the year, all the fog and damp of the banks goes over to their side and descends in rain there with the south-westerly winds, while we never have the benefit of it, unless when what we call the out-winds blow. 1887 BOND 15–16 The best time for sealers is when there is just enough out-winds to keep the ice together, but not driving it together too tight [on the land] for the vessels [to navigate]. C 66–2 If the wind is out on the first of April, you'll have out-winds for the rest of the month.

overbearer n One who carries the pall in a funeral procession; pall-bearer; TOPBEARER.
1967 FIRESTONE 78 The overbearers, or topbearers, are an equal number who hold the pall, a large white sheet upon which a black cross has been sewn, over the coffin.

overest a Farthest away or over.
T 70/1–64[1] In that big flat-roof house over there, th' overest one—he'd tell you a good yarn about that.

overfall n *OED* ~ sb 3 obs (1596–1613). A waterfall in a river. Also attrib.
1811 BUCHAN 6 They convey their Canoe's into the River above the overfall. 1912 CABOT 158 On this coast. . . Rapids are 'rattles'; the reaches between are 'steadies'; falls are 'overfalls.' 1951 *Nfld & Lab Pilot* i, 315 Overfall brook, a waterfall 118 feet high, is situated 4½ cables northward of the patch of sunken rocks. 1977 BUTLER 64 We anchored the boat in Sandy Harbour and went to the overfall at the mouth of the river in the skiff.

overhaul v Cp *OED* ~ v 2 naut 'to investigate or examine with a view to repairs'; WILCOCKS *Sea-Fisherman* (1868) 138 'overhauled the remaining [mackerel] line.' To pull to the surface a fishing-line or net in order to determine one's catch. Cp HAUL v.
[1856] 1975 WHITELEY 132 Overhauled—had one seal—put out more net. 1861 DE BOILIEU 93–4 On one occasion I had charge of a boat's crew, and, on overhauling the nets, I heard the exclamation, 'A Harp! a Harp, by George!' 1874 *Maritime Mo* iii, 208 The fisherman informed me that in overhauling his herring net, he found the creature entangled in the meshes. 1878 TOCQUE 289 On the next day [the bultows] are taken up and overhauled—the fish taken off—and, if the berth is approved, the hooks fresh baited and let down again, and thus successively during the voyage. 1896 HOWLEY *MS Reminiscences* 24 Only yesterday a heavy sea hove up quite suddenly when the boats were all out in the morning overhauling their traps, and some of them had narrow escapes getting back. 1925 MUNN 7 These traps are overhauled twice a day. [1959] 1965 PEACOCK (ed) iii, 969 "Peter's Banks": We'll go out on St Peter's Banks, myself and Goddard went, / To overhaul our trawls that day it was our full intent.

over-head n In fishing premises, storage space where nets, sails, masts, oars, etc, are stored.
P 116–68 Another important section of the stage is

called the over-head, a section where all the poles and the sail are kept. This place is full of trap poles and nets, and comprises a very essential part of the fishing stage.

overing vbl n Breaking a channel through the ice by rocking vessel from side to side; cp SALLY v.

1937 LUBBOCK 41, 56 No present day seaman, unless he belongs to the Newfoundland sealing fleet, has probably ever heard of 'overing'. . . [It] consisted of the crew running in a body from one side of the ship to the other in order to give her a rolling movement and break the ice around her.

overlong *EDD* over 12 (8) ~ long Co. Over along, to.

P 148–66 You going overlong [to Water Street] today?

overright prep *EDD* over 12 (10) ~ right s w cties. Opposite; in front of.

[c1894] PANL P4/14, p. 200 *Over-right* [is used] for *opposite*, or *over against*. P 142–67 Each man who participates in the square dance must get a partner. At Ramea we say, 'Will you [stand] fore me in the next dance?' At Pass Island they say, 'Will you [stand] over-right me in the next dance?' P 108–70 Don't be cursing and swearing overright the child!

overtop v Cp *OED* ~ v 3 'to render top-heavy' obs. To overburden with care or worry.

1920 WALDO 57 She couldn't do her work and it overcast her. She overtopped her mind, sir.

owenshook See OWNSHOOK.

owl See PUT: *put the owl*.

own v Cp *EDD* ~ v[2] 2 'to acknowledge an acquaintanceship'; cp VALENTINE. To claim as one's own in Valentine's Day greeting.

P 167–67 The first person to say, 'Good mornin', fautin,' says, 'I own 'ee,' and then he 'owns' the other person. M 70–21 On Valentine's Day if the person owned happened to like you, you might be given a small gift. All 'owning' had to be over by noon; ridicule was your lot if you went past that deadline.

ownshook n also **eunchuck, oanshick, onshook, oonchook, oonshik, owenshook**. Cp DINNEEN óinseach 'a fool, *esp* a female fool'; JOYCE oanshagh 'a female fool'; *EDD* oonshugh Ir; *O Sup*[2] oonchook Nfld (1885–); *Kilkenny Lexicon* óinseach ['uːnʃək]. See FOOL 1 'Christmas mummer,' as in sense 2.

1 Foolish, ignorant person.

1924 ENGLAND 318 Onshook—[a fool]. 1937 DEVINE 35 Ownshook—an ignorant, stupid fellow. 1968 DILLON 149 Boy, Mike is the real oanshik, isn't he? C 71–99 If she saw someone swimming on a cold day, he would be referred to as an oonshick of a thing.

2 One of the men, usually elaborately dressed,

who participated in a mummers' parade; a Christmas mummer; FOOL.

[1885] 1962 *Evening Telegram* 21 Dec, p. 22 Davey Foley was always the owner of a stylish rig, while his friend, Masey Murphy, appeared, I think, as an 'Owenshook.' The 'Owenshook' was always a terror to encounter, for he rarely was merciful to any one who made him draw upon his wind, and woe to the man who disputed his right of giving a sound castigation for the trouble incurred. 1895 PROWSE 402 Some [of the fools or mummers] were dressed as women, with long garments, known as 'eunchucks.' 1937 *Bk of Nfld* ii, 259 Joined with these gaily bedecked Fools were a smaller number of veiled men in women's garments. They bore the appellation of Oonchooks, and were perhaps more persistent and punishing in their thrashing of people than their more spectacular companions.

ox n Cp *OED* ox 6: ~ (1602 Co, 1623 Nfld). Phr *oxen and kine*: Atlantic fulmar; NODDY (*Fulmar glacialis glacialis*).

1620 WHITBOURNE 9 There are also Godwits, Curlewes, and a certain kinde of fowle that are called Oxen and Kine.

P

pack n *Cent* ~ 3 (e) 'staves. . .of a cask secured in a compact bundle.'

1 Cask staves tied in a bundle; cp PACKAGE.

[1777] 1792 CARTWRIGHT ii, 231 [The skiff] was laden with slops, provisions, salt, and cask-packs. 1792 ibid *Gloss* i, xii Pack of casks. A cask which is taken to pieces, first marking the staves, bundled up together and secured by four hoops.

2 A bundle of preserved caribou flesh.

1792 PULLING *MS* Aug We then began to *cook a kettle* and opened a pack of venison. The Indians had preserved forty or fifty packs (by the frost) which we found in wigwams. All the bones of the deer was taken out and the flesh pressed together in packs nearly square of four or five the longest way.

package n See PACK. Any type of barrel for shipping dried fish.

1909 BROWNE 58 [Salmon] are exported, usually in tierces of three hundred pounds weight, but sometimes in smaller packages. 1937 *Seafisheries of Nfld* 23 With the opening up of trade between Newfoundland and Brazil there came the introduction of the [fish] packages known as drums and half-drums. T 90–64 There'd be about twenty staves in a package. The larger cask and the smaller drums. The smaller ones, the stock would be narrower. The larger the package, the easier [the stave] would be to ply. So you could use a wider stave in a larger package. We used to make 'em for squid, a squid barrel; that's only another package about the size of the barrels we pack tom-cods in. 1975 BUTLER 69 When the method of packing dried codfish in wooden packages commenced, there were a number of [saw] mills located in different parts of Placentia Bay.

paddle n Cp *OED* ~ sb[1] 2 'short oar used without rowlock.'

1 One of the two oars used to propel a small boat; also attrib (1925 *Dial Notes* v, 338).

1894 *Evening Herald* 4 Dec I. . .shot one of [the deer] and my eldest daughter came to me with a paddle to strike it on the head. 1907 DUNCAN 127 A paddle-punt is patrimony enough for the like of him. P 102–60 More crews mostly planters were taken on board with dozens of sticks of wood with a large flat end rough chopped to be made into oars and paddles after arriving at their stations. T 70–64[1] By an' by she hove in sight again. A man sot forrard, facin' forrard, sheavin' the paddles. T 141–65[2] They would haul up on th' ice because their paddles was under the thawts. M 68–7 ~ an instrument for propelling a punt or dory. Two of these are used by one person.

2 Phr *row paddles*: to row a small boat with oars.

T 55/7–64 [I] didn't think nothing about rowing paddles. I rowed paddles out o' this place way down off o' Waldron's Cove night after night, day after day; get very little fish, too.

paddler n Two-week-old seal, just able to swim.

1907 WALLACE 263 When [the young seal] is old enough to take to the water, which is within a fortnight after birth, it becomes a 'paddler,'. . .a little later a 'bedlamer,' then a 'young harp' and finally a harp.

paddy See PATRICK.

paddy keefe a, av phr Near; almost to the point of doing; 'purty close.'

1937 DEVINE 35 If you didn't lose her, you went *Paddy Keefe* to it. C 70–14 He didn't lose the boat, but he came paddy keefe to it.

palace n Cp *OED* ~ 1 b 'episcopal residence' [in England]. Residence of the Roman Catholic bishop or archbishop; in some rural communities, the dwelling of the parish priest.

1882 TALBOT 45–6 Even the Old Palace, as it was called—that is, the former residence of the Roman Catholic bishop—was converted into a place of meeting for the. . .opposition. 1887 *Colonist Christmas No* 15 [The Star of the Sea Hall] also covers the ground on which formerly stood the 'Old Palace,' the residence of the early Roman Catholic clergy. The old structures which were erected in 1754, were standing till 1873, in which year the Palace, having [been] destroyed by fire, the Chapel, had become dilapidated by age, was removed. 1888 M F HOWLEY 351 The line of road, instead of running in a straight line, curved suddenly westwards at the corner of the Palace. 1968 *Avalon Penin of Nfld* 64 ~ priest's house.

pale a Comb **pale (seal) oil**: the first oil yielded by seal blubber in the process of repeated rendering; SEAL OIL (1925 MUNN 8).

1818 *Waterford Mirror* [Ire.] [for sale] Pale [seal oil]. 1832 MCGREGOR i, 225 The first that runs off the seal

blubber is the virgin, or pale oil, and the last, the brown oil. 1852 ARCHIBALD 5, 7 The first running, which is caused by compression from its own weight, begins about the 10th of May, and will continue to yield what is termed *pale seal oil* from two to three months, until 50 to 70 per cent. of the quantity is drawn off, according to the season, or in proportion to the quantity of old seal fat being put into the vats. . . A uniform quality of oil is produced, superior to the best *pale* by the old process, and free from smell;. . .a considerable per-centage is saved in the yield, and what is termed *pale seal*, produced from the old as well as from the young seal. 1873 CARROLL 31 When seal oil is drawn off out of tank all the oil rendered out of the young seal fat is sure to come first, which is called pale seal.

pall n Comb **pall carey**: Leach's petrel (*Oceanodroma leucorhoa*); CAREY'S CHICKEN (Q 71–9).

1959 MCATEE 4 ~ The adjective refers to the birds' dark coloration. Nfld.

palm[1] n American yew or ground hemlock; a sprig of this bush worn on Palm Sunday; (*Taxus canadensis*); GROUND PALM (1956 ROULEAU 35).

1967 *Bk of Nfld* iv, 251 On Palm Sunday everyone had to go off and pick what they called 'palm,' a low growing bush, and her father says they used this to feed the cattle when the hay was low. Then everyone would wear the palm in their coat and it would be off to church. M 69–8 On the Saturday [before Palm Sunday] 'palm' (a low evergreen, similar to fir but with a sweet smell growing in the area) was picked and put on the walls of the kitchen. Everyone wore a piece of palm, which was in the shape of a cross, for the day. C 71–74 He told me he has no worries about industrial accidents for he always carries a piece of palm in his pocket from one Palm Sunday to the next.

palm[2] n A fisherman's heavy mitten, with fingers cut off, used to protect the hand in splitting fish or hauling lines; CUFF[1].

1819 ANSPACH 431 [The header] presses upon the [cod's] neck with his left hand to which a thick piece of leather, called the *palm*, is fastened for that purpose. 1852 *Morning Post* 12 Feb, p. 4 [advertisement] oiled clothing, covered hats and south-westers for the world. . .also palms, sheaths, and belts, sheath knives, etc. P 143–75 The women began spinning in September. . . Throughout the fall and winter they produced such items as sweaters, 'buskins,' stockings, 'vamps,' caps, scarves, 'palms' and petticoats for their families.

palm v Phr *palm out*: to renew a woollen glove or mitten by picking up the stitches from the back and wrist and knitting a new palm (P 108–77).

T 96–64[2] Thousands and thousands of pairs of gloves out of wool, home-made wool. I even palmed them out, took the backs and the wrist and knit palms in them.

palmer n *OED* ~ sb¹ 2; *EDD* sb¹ So. Esp in form **hairy palmer,** ~ **pammer***: palmer-worm, a destructive hairy caterpillar (*Ypsilophus pometellus*).

C 69–12 One day when I was a child I happened to notice a big fuzzy looking object on an alder bush. [Dad] told me it was a hairy-pammer. Q 71–8 Hairy palmer: large yellow, hairy caterpillar, the same as is sometimes called the woolly bear caterpillar.

pampooty n [pæm'puːtɪ] JOYCE 300 'shoe made of untanned hide'; DINNEEN pampúta. A sock or soft shoe (P 191–73).

P 108–70 Said to a child: 'Put on your little pampooties.'

pan n also **pen**. Cp *OED* ~ sb¹ 2 for sense 1 (a); *OED* 9 (1863–), *DC* 1 (1771–) for sense 2; *DC* 2 Nfld (1907–) for sense 3; *OED* sb¹ 10 b ~ ice (Labr: 1878–), *DC* pan-ice (1916–) for comb in sense 4. The children's activity of jumping or 'copying' from pan to pan of floating ice in the spring has produced a complex cluster of terms and phrases, and these are treated alphabetically under the simple verb form: COPY, JUMP, SKIP, etc.

1 (a) A shallow circular container or vessel used in rendering fish or seal oil; (b) makeshift stove used for cooking in a boat; GALLEY.

1682 COLLINS 96 Our planters [in 1670 did] remove and carry away the Boats, Rayles, Cask, Salt, Nets, and Pans for Boyling of Oyle. 1852 ARCHIBALD 5 The pan [of the seal vat] is about three feet deep, and tightly caulked. A small quantity of water is kept on the bottom of the pan, for the double purpose of saving the oil in case of a leak, and for purifying it from the blood and any other animal matter of superior gravity. M 71–103 Fishermen always carried a gun, bread box, kettle, water jar and pan when they went out for a day's fishing. . . The pan was. . .the bottom part of an old stove which served the purpose of a stove in the boat.

2 A piece of flat ice, varying in size and shape but roughly circular.

[1771] 1792 CARTWRIGHT i, 78 I attempted to cross over at a place where the ice lay in small pans, and appeared to be firm. 1792 ibid *Gloss* i, xii Pan of ice. A piece of ice of no determined size, but not very large; the large ones are called sheets of ice. [1822] 1866 WILSON 330 The ice did not reach the shore, so that, with our gaffs, we had each to get a pan of ice for himself and push himself, toward the land. But no pan of ice would bear a second person. 1836 [WIX]² 93 Started over the rotten ice, which let me through once, as I leaped from pen to pen. 1887 *Colonist Christmas No* 12 Once on the floating ice you may expect to have a lively time in leaping from one pan to another. [1899] 1905 *Nfld Law Reports* 292 Some of the crew of the *Kite* assisted to turn the *Gaspesia* round by a rope from her bow to the ice. The *Kite* then went ahead 'butting' the pans of ice and making a track as well as she could, and the *Gaspesia* followed. 1906 DUNCAN 71 Some of the 'pans' were acres in size; others were not big

enough to bear the weight of a man; all were floating free, rising and falling with the ground swell. 1916 HAWKES 113 When the 'young ice' forms on the shore-line, the boys delight in making a [miniature] boat out of one of the cakes and paddle around with a little oar, or leap from cake to cake, following the leader, or perform an impromptu song and dance on a shifting 'pan.' 1927 DOYLE (ed) 39 "Hunting Seals": For we are swoilers fearless, bold, / As we copy from pan to pan, sir; / With pelts astern we shipward go— / Nor yield to any man, sir. 1972 BROWN 33 The pelts would be collected together on ice pans big enough to keep them safe, and a flag stuck on each pan to mark ownership.

3 A quantity of sealskins with blubber attached piled on the ice to be picked up by a sealing vessel; BULK n.

[1872] 1899 *Nfld Law Reports* 446 On arriving at the flag they found it to be a house-flag of Messrs Job Brothers, placed apparently, with another flag and with pieces of canvas marked '*Nimrod*, E White,' for the purpose of distinguishing three pans of piled and sculped seals, several of which were similarly marked. [1907] 1979 *Nfld Qtly* Fall, p. 25 A number of pans of seals which we killed on Saturday have been stolen. . . Some of our men say they saw them take one pan. 1924 ENGLAND 142 When the pan was all aboard the last hunters on the ice at the ship's side swarmed up, black-faced and red-handed in the torch glares. [1929] 1933 GREENLEAF (ed) 247 "The Sealing Cruise of the *Lone Flier*": We picked up all our seals that day, but minus of one pan. 1936 SMITH 51 The crew of the *Wolf* were very busy hoisting pans of seals, and the donkey winch was going all night. 1968 *Nfld Qtly* Christmas, pp. 21–2 Each man then hauls as many as he can manage, usually three, to a spot chosen by the master watchman making what is called a 'pan,' and then after leaving a flag with the ship's name on it, to denote to whom the seals belong.

4 Comb **pan flag**: pennant of a sealing vessel used to mark the ownership and position on the ice of a pile of seal pelts; FLAG n.

1911 LINDSAY 52 I went aloft again and saw our pan flags flying in great numbers, while the men were very busy several miles away. 1933 GREENE 178–9 [The sealers] lace the sculps to their tow-ropes, and being all selected men, each one can drag five or six sculps in his tow to where the 'Pan-flags' are set up in the ice to mark the gathering places. 1968 SCHULL 115 By tomorrow sunrise there would be two hundred men on the ice, broken up into four hunting-watches, loaded down with gaffs and pan-flags and tow-ropes and sculping-knives.

pan-ice: a variety of ice cover consisting of flat floating pieces of ice.

1865 CAMPBELL 92 The mouth of Hamilton Inlet. . .was full of heavy drift, 'pan-ice.' 1916 DUNCAN 139 When he was within two fathoms of the pan-ice a foot broke through and tripped him flat on his face. [1961 *Evening Telegram* 12 May, p. 6 What was even more interesting was the appearance of the ice pans farther out from shore. Almost without exception they were uniform in shape, small, almost round, and for all the world like Shrove Tuesday pancakes, on an enormous frying pan, arranged in an endless pattern of symmetry. Indeed, I am under the impression gained from some source that that is how such ice was named.]

pan v Cp *OED* ~ v[1] 3 b (1887); *DC* 2 Nfld (1916–). To pile a quantity of seal pelts on the ice with a marker; BULK v.

1860–1 *Journ of Assembly* Appendix, p. 531 Young seals may be panned and bulked after 20th March. 1868 WHITE *MS Journal* 31 Mar All hands on ice panning Seals. 1873 *Maritime Mo* i, 259 [The sealers] kill and 'sculp' all the seals within two or three miles of the ship, and then, piling them in heaps marked with the flag of the vessel, they are left to be hauled in at a favourable moment. This is called 'panning' seals. [1884] 1897 *Nfld Law Reports* 35 For the purpose of preventing competition and anticipating the arrival and active participation of others in the fruits of the icefields, [they] kill as they go with a blow of a gaff, taking no heed to collect and pan and mark their spoil. 1895 *J A Folklore* viii, 40 To pan is to gather at one place a quantity say of seals. 1924 ENGLAND 113 De master watch. . .He got to go to de hindermost end o' de flags, an' got to see de men placed out rate. . .an' wait till de swell come an' break up de ice. If dey pans on big ice, mabbe de men has to drag sculps fer miles. 1937 LUBBOCK 436 From the 18th, when the wind eased, to the 22nd, the *Neptune* and the *Newfoundland* managed to *pan* 41,000 seals, but, with the resumption of the gale, the ice containing many of the pans was broken up on the Funks. [1951] 1965 PEACOCK (ed) iii, 926 "The *Greenland* Disaster": They struck the seals St Patrick's day and then the work began, / With thirteen thousand hoist on board, seven thousand more did pan. 1979 *Salt Water, Fresh Water* 54 I know in the *Imogene* with my uncle that was captain he had over two hundred men, I know they killed and panned fourteen thousand seals one day.

pancake n *OED* ~ sb 3 ~ day; *EDD* 1 (2) ~ day for sense 3.

1 A flat rock or shoal over which the sea breaks.

[1775] 1971 SEARY 255 Pancake (Shoal) (St John's Harbour). 1951 *Nfld & Lab Pilot* i, 77 Pancake shoal, rocks which dry about 4 feet, lies close to the southern shore of the channel. 1953 ibid ii, 422 The Pancake, a flat rock which dries 3 feet, lies half a cable southward of it.

2 In pl, the game of ducks and drakes.

P 245–67 Making pancakes on the water—throwing those flat stones. 1968 *Avalon Penin of Nfld* 112 ~ shying flat stones over the surface of the water.

3 Comb **pancake day**, ~ **night**: Shrove Tuesday.

1912 [ENGLISH] 4 . . .and the time of the year early in the month of March, the day Shrove Tuesday, or, commonly called, Pancake Day. 1924 ENGLAND 215 Shrove Tuesday night, otherwise 'pancake night,' is sometimes celebrated in the outports by baking a cake containing a white horn button, a dime or a nickel, and a ring. T 45–64 An' you'd have pancakes, pancake night down there—day before Lent comes in.

pank v *EDD* ~ v 2 'pant' s w cties. To pant, breathe heavily.

1937 DEVINE 37 ~ To pant as a dog on a warm day. P 148–69 'Around, around,' he said, panking for breath. C 71–128 When I walks uphill I panks like the devil. I got ne'er bit of wind like I used to.

panned p ppl *DC* ~ adj 1 Nfld (1878–). Of seal pelts, gathered in piles on the ice and marked for later collection by a sealing vessel.

1860–1 *Journ of Assembly* Appendix, p. 526 If part of crew was left in charge of panned Seals, it would cause great loss of life. 1878 *North Star* 13 Apr, p. 2 When she left the ice the *Tiger*, with 2,000 on board, was alongside a sufficient number of panned seals to fill her.[*DC*] 1887 BOND 17 [They] left a couple of hundred more, panned. [1927] 1933 GREENLEAF (ed) 281 "The *Southern Cross*": She reached the Gulf in early March, the whitecoats for to slew, / When seventeen thousand prime young harps killed by her hardy crew, / All panned and safely stowed below. 1972 BROWN 66 [He] steamed slowly north-west picking up panned seals.

panning vbl n

1 The process or activity of placing seal pelts in a pile on the ice and marking them for collection by a sealing vessel; also attrib.

1860–1 *Journ of Assembly* 528 The system of panning, which is a necessity some times in April and May, should not entitle any crew to the Seals they have killed. [1911] 1930 COAKER 41 We recommend. . .that the panning of seals. . .be prohibited. 1927 DOYLE (ed) 39 "Hunting Seals": With bat and gaff and 'panning staff' / Surmounted with a flag, sir; / Away we go to the great iceflow, / And we never care to lag, sir. 1972 SANGER 239 ~ The gathering of seal pelts to a central location on the ice so as to facilitate collection by the sealing vessels.

2 In children's pastime, the action of leaping from one piece of floating ice to another; COPYING (c 65–4).

panshard n *EDD* ~ sb 1 Ha W Do So D. Fragment of broken glass or crockery; potsherd (P 245–56).

T 253/4–66 We used to have little pieces of panshard, broke[n] dishes, an' have it all washed an' put on our shelves an' play like that when we was youngsters. P 207–67 ~ pieces of glass that have been washed up on the shore and that have been made smooth by the waves. . .collected mostly by children and used for playing 'coppy house.' 1969 *Trans Dev Assoc* ci, 187 ~ small pieces of broken pottery.

pant v *OED* ~ v 1 b fig 'of wind or waves' (1666, 1819). Of the sea, to heave with a swell; of a field of ice, to rise and fall with the movement of the water.

1924 ENGLAND 114 The air shimmered over the ice that gleamed above the slow swells and opening breadths of sea. The ocean, as Newfoundlanders say, was 'panting.' 1925 *Dial Notes* v, 338 Panting. Said of ice moved by a long swell.

pantry n Comb **pantry stall**: a sale of home-made preserves, etc.
M 69–23 ~ This is a gathering in which mostly women take part, and is usually sponsored by some church group. The women gather in some public place around 2 p.m. and they have a sale of home-made goods. Included in the sale are some cooked foods usually bottled, such as home-made pickles or jam. During and after the sale a lunch is served, and men may go there to buy their supper.

papoose n *DC* ~ n 2 (1680, 1861). A beaver in its first year.
[1783] 1792 CARTWRIGHT iii, 22 The first year, they are called *pappooses*; the second, *small medlers*. 1861 DE BOILIEU 82 The beaver is a social kind of animal, living in communities or families, generally consisting of five—father, mother, and three 'papouses' (so the young beavers are called). 1887 HOWLEY *MS Reminiscences* 39 Went to look for the beaver. They were all young. I succeeded in killing two papooses with the only two cartridges I had left.

paps n pl *OED* pap sb[1] 2 b pl 'formerly, a name for two conical hill summits, rising side by side; still retained in local nomenclature.' A pair of prominent rounded hills.
1951 *Nfld & Lab Pilot* i, 305 The Paps, twin summits, 890 feet high, stand about three-quarters of a mile inland from the head of the bay.

parakeet n also **per(r)oque(e)t**, etc. LAROUSSE perroquet de mer 'sea parrot' (17..–). Atlantic common puffin (*Fratercula arctica arctica*).
1884 STEARNS 233 They commenced to appear, flying around the boat or resting on the water; all were 'parrakeets,' and 'tinkers,' except now and then a solitary 'turre.' 1907 TOWNSEND 302 The Puffin or 'Paroqueet' as it is universally called in Labrador breeds in colonies on islands along the southern and eastern coasts. 1959 MCATEE 41 Perroquet—common Puffin (Parakeet. From its high, curved, and coloured beak. Nfld., 'Labr.').

paralyse n Paralysis.
1910 GRENFELL 89 An attack of 'the paralyze' in his boyhood had left him a hard struggle. P 191–73 He got a touch of paralyse.

parish n Comb **parish boat**: large boat or small vessel in which a clergyman visits coastal parishioners or which brings members of congregation to church (P 113–76); cp CHURCH SHIP.
1924 ENGLAND 224 Remote settlements may lack nearly everything, but they always have a church. If they cannot afford a resident clergyman, circuit clergy and laymen officiate. 'Parish boats' bring in people for services, from inaccessible places.

parley n *OED* ~ sb[2] Sc & dial (1825–); *EDD* sb[1] 1 Sc Ir. Comb **parley cake**: a kind of sweet cake.
C 70–27 In addition to the traditional light and dark fruitcakes usually reserved for Christmas my grandmother said that they also had a parley cake. It was described as a go-between, a dark cake with a fine texture.

parlour n Cp *EDD* pudge sb[2] 1 'a puddle' for comb in sense 3.
1 Protective enclosure on mast from which a man scans the sea for seals, whales, etc; crow's nest; BARREL (1925 *Dial Notes* v, 338).
1924 ENGLAND 46 He sent the scunner up to the 'parlour,' or barrel on the foretopmast, clambering aloft up the shrouds to the trapdoor in the bottom of the barrel.
2 The innermost section of a type of lobster pot; also attrib **parlour door, ~ pot, ~ trap** (P 148–65).
1964 *Can Journ Ling* x, 40 In lobster fishing the area in the pot where the bait is placed and which is at a lower level than the entrance to the pot is called the 'parlour.' T 14/20–64 In other pots they'd have four of these bows. On the inside bow here they put a head in the pot and the lobster'll go in through the parlour door and get his food. There's only one special pot and that would be the parlour pot. M 70–18 Some traps called parlor traps had two 'heads' to make doubly sure the lobster wouldn't escape when it entered the trap.
3 Comb **parlour pudge**: in the game of hopscotch, any of the two large spaces adjoining one another in the pattern of squares marked on the ground (1971 NOSEWORTHY 229).

parrot See SEA PARROT.

parson n *OED* ~ 3 'from the black coat of a clergyman, applied. . .to birds with black feathers' for sense 1.
1 Atlantic common puffin (*Fratercula arctica*); SEA PARROT.
1941 WITHINGTON 165 Scattered on other islands were tinkers flying off and on the ledges, while the puffins (called 'parsons') with their spectacled eyes, white shirt bosoms, and red bills, sat on the cliffs dictating and chattering to their kind.
2 Comb **parson harvey**: piece of fried dough; also a slice of bread heavily soaked with molasses.
P 207–67 Mother is making parson harveys for supper (fried dough). P 41–68 A parson harvey was a molasses cake made of soaked bread.

parting n Wall or partition separating adjacent rooms.
P 68–54 She hung the picture on the partin'. 1971 CASEY 266 And the two doors came open and shut, and the kitchen door came open, went back and hit against the partin' and went to again and shut. C 71–118 ~ This word was used to mean a partition—a wall separating one room from another. When some-

body said 'Don't beat down the partin',' they simply meant don't beat down the wall.

partinged p ppl [ˌpæəɹdṇd 'ɒˑf]. See PARTING. Closed in by a partition.

T 178–65 They had their own room. They had a room partined off, you see, and a lock and key on the door.

partridge n   also **patridge** ['pædrɨdʒ] DC ~ 2 (1696–) for sense 1; for comb in sense 2: DC ~ hawk 2 (1959).

1 Allen's willow ptarmigan (*Lagopus lagopus alleni*); Welch's rock ptarmigan (*L. mutus welchi*); GROUSE. Also attrib.

[1583] 1940 *Gilbert's Voyages & Enterprises* ii, 407 [Hayes' narrative] Partridges most plentifull larger than ours, gray and white of colour, and rough footed like doves, which our men after one flight did kill with cudgels, they were so fat and unable to flie. 1613 *Willoughby Papers* 1/21 A kind of partridges their is which. . .bee white in the winter [and] browne speckeled in the summer somwhat bigger then the partriges bee in England. 1626 [VAUGHAN] *Golden Fleece* pt 3, p. 24 I knew one Fowler in a winter, which killed above 700 Partridges himself at *Renoos*. 1687 [BLOME] 241 They had. . .*Foxes* in the Winter, *White Patridges* in the Summer, larger than ours, who are much afraid of *Ravens*. [1766] 1971 BANKS 138 Here are Partrides also of two Kinds brown and white for so they Call those Distinguished by a white spot upon their wings they are like our heath fowl but near as Large as the Black game. 1868 HOWLEY *MS Reminiscences* 12 We stopped at one pond to try for trout and boil our kettle. Saw a couple of old partridge and some young ones. 1870 *Can Naturalist* v, 291 If I had been there I should have walked round and round them *pattridges* till I got 'em all in a heap, and then I should have killed nearly all at a shot. 1885 KENNEDY 153 These people [of St Mary's] all spoke with a foreign accent, declaring the 'patterridges' to be jostling each other on the barrens. [1892] 1896 *Consolidated Statutes of Nfld* 980 No person shall hunt, kill, take, sell, barter, purchase. . .any ptarmigan or willow grouse (commonly called partridge). 1914 WALLACE 70–1 'Them trout makes me think,' says Ed, as he cut some tobacco from a plug and filled his pipe after dinner, 'of onct I were out huntin' pa'tridges.' 1933 GREENE 294–5 In 'Partridge Season' it is quite true that in many spots on the barrens where you will rest, especially when out shooting in early October, there are more 'whorts' (blueberries) within reach of your hand than you can eat. 1967 *Bk of Nfld* iii, 271 Willow ptarmigan (*Lagopus lagopus*): The 'partridge' of the barrens. Widely distributed in Newfoundland.

2 Comb **partridge berry**: see PARTRIDGE BERRY.

partridge bird: fox sparrow (*Passerella iliaca iliaca*).

1959 MCATEE 66 ~ Fox Sparrow (From its rufescent coloration. Nfld., 'Labr.').

partridge hawk: eastern goshawk (*Accipiter gentilis atricapillus*) (1959 MCATEE 20).

1892 PACKARD 424–5 American Goshawk. Resident in Ungava district. Winter specimen obtained in early December, 1882. Breeds at the 'Chapel' near Fort Chimo. Specimen obtained from Rigolet. Known as 'Partridge Hawk.'

partridge v   Cp *OED* ~ 5: partridging vbl sb. To shoot or snare partridges; cp BIRDING.

1975 LEYTON 21 If you had older brothers, perhaps they'd be out partridging, and they'd get a lot of partridges.

partridge berry n   also **patridge** ~ , etc. ['pæəɹtrɪdʒ ˌberɪ, 'pæəɹtrɪdʒ ˌbərɪ, 'pætɔrɪdʒ ˌberɪ, 'pædrɨdʒ ˌberi]. Cp *DC* ~ (1748–; 1770–). A low creeping plant producing small tart red berries; the berry of this plant harvested on the 'barrens' in the autumn; mountain cranberry (*Vaccinium vitis-idaea*); BERRY[1]. Also attrib.

[1770] 1792 CARTWRIGHT i, 30 We landed opposite Grove Island, and walked upon the low hills, where we found plenty of partridge berries. [1794] 1968 THOMAS 140 Partridge Berrys are form'd like a large Pea and coloured like the finest Vermillion when ripe. They make good Tarts. 1836 [WIX][1] 97 The partridge, or ptarmigan were also very numerous upon these hills, searching for a species of cranberry, which is called here, the partridge-berry. 1858 [LOWELL] i, 94 Crackers, partridge-berries, horts, and others enrich the barrenness, and make it worth while for women and children to come and gather them. 1868 HOWLEY *MS Reminiscences* 49 There are lots of Partridge berries over the barrens all ripe at this season. 1909 SELOUS 90 [We made a halt] to eat some delicious berries which we found growing in profusion on a mossy 'barren,'. . .[which] are known in Newfoundland as partridge berries. 1933 MERRICK 66 These redberries, or partridge berries, are a Labrador staple that takes the place of fruit and vegetables in many a home. T 175/7–65 The partridge berry, they was on the barrens, but the marshberry was 'long wi' the bakeapples on the marsh. 1977 BURSEY 42 [He] would sometimes come to Old Perlican in the partridge berry season.

pass v   Phr *pass oneself*: to behave confidently.

T 458–67 He can pass himself in company. In other words he'll behave. He won't make a holy show of you, and can talk enough to join in a conversation. P 108–70 He can pass himself anywhere.

pass n   Cp *OED* ~ sb[1] 3 d 'passage across a river,' e 'navigable channel.' (a) Particular point on migration route of caribou, esp across a river or lake; DEER PASS; (b) narrow channel between islands, or islands and mainland, through which seals migrate.

[1772] 1976 HEAD 76 A certain number of nets remarkable for strength, and of a particular contexture fitted to the depth of water and the width of the respective Passes ['. . .formed by the Contiguity of small Islands or Rocks to the main Land, which occasion strong Currents. . .'] are fixed to strong Cables or hawsers, & placed in the Pass at certain distances. [1829] 1915 HOWLEY 191 At these passes which are particular places in the migration lines of path, such as the extreme ends of and straits in, many of the larger lakes. . .fords in the large rivers, and the like [the Beothuk] Indians kill great numbers of deer with very little trouble, during their migrations. 1866 WILSON 316 A number of men now got within the fence, and from the wider enclosure they drove them to the narrower part, or to passes of the river where others were stationed, and thus killed the deer at their leisure. 1888 STEARNS 191 The net was made of stout twine, and was nearly three hundred feet long and about twenty deep, of meshes six inches wide. The bottom was kept down by heavy stone sinkers at both ends and in the middle, while the top was fastened to a long rope, which stretched from point to point, across the pass, and was buoyed up with large pieces of cork.

passage n   *EDD* ~ sb 1 D Co, *OED* 4 for sense 1; 11 for sense 2.

1 Transportation by water; a lift.

1930 *Am Speech* vi, 57 [Used] when asking to be carried even a short distance in an open boat: e.g. 'Can you give me a passage to Battle Harbour?' P 133–58 ~ a lift in a boat, however short.

2 A narrow salt-water strait between islands or other land masses; cp DULLIFARE*, REACH, RUN, TICKLE.

1850 [FEILD] 24 Two fishermen and a boy. . .offered to take us into a neighbouring harbour, which they called Grundy's Passage. 1876 HOWLEY 19 Passage merely indicates any place in a difficult or dangerous locality where vessels or boats are in the habit of passing [through a narrow passageway]. 1951 *Nfld & Lab Pilot* i, 217 Riches island is separated from Dawson point. . .by Dawson passage, 2½ cables wide. 1977 BUTLER 48 One fine evening they were sailing through the entrance to Presque and, taking the wrong passage, ran the schooner on a shoal.

passing ppl Designating animals or birds which habitually migrate and the season of the year: **passing duck, ~ seal, ~ time**.

1959 MCATEE 17 Passing duck. King Eider (That is a migrant. Nfld., 'Labr.') 1888 STEARNS 202 We call the Harp and Hood seal, 'passing seal,' as they only come in the spring and fall and pass down and up the coast, according to the season. We git five or six gallons of ile from the passing seal, and they weigh four to five hundred pounds apiece. [1778] 1792 CARTWRIGHT ii, 307 The marshes are exceedingly well situated for intercepting deer at the passing times.

patch n   *DC* ~ n 2 esp Nfld (1878–) for sense 1; *DC* ~ fox (1861–) for comb in sense 3.

1 A concentration of harp or hood seals on the ice-floes, usu for purposes of breeding, whelping or moulting; freq in phr *patch of seals*; SPOT. See also MAIN ~ , NORTHERN ~ , SOUTHERN ~ .

1873 *Maritime Mo* i, 257 There is, of course, room for considerable skill and sagacity in taking advantage of winds, and currents, and openings in the ice, and in avoiding 'jammings' and other mishaps [in searching for the seal 'whelping grounds']; still, whether any particular vessel will reach 'patches' of young seals, scattered, perhaps, very widely, is very largely a lottery. 1886 HOWLEY *MS Reminiscences* 7 He believes in

three distinct patches of seals. 1916 DUNCAN 234 Next day Cap'n Saul found the herds—a patch of harps and new-whelped young. 1925 *Journ of Assembly* 451 The Aeroplane took a flight before the ice was broken and only reported a patch of Seals four miles long and eight miles wide, which Capt George Barbour estimated about 50,000 Seals. 1936 SMITH 52 We steamed into another nice little patch and secured another 7,000 [seals]; the patch was now getting cut up, as practically all the fleet was working there. 1955 DOYLE (ed) 52 "Sealers' Song": But Job's are wishing Blandford first who never missed the patches, / He struck them on the twenty-third and filled her to the hatches. 1975 COOK 85 Big patch of swiles to the sout' east. Barrelman spotted anudder herd to the north.

2 A shoal or reef.

1951 *Nfld & Lab Pilot* i, 336 Cornish patch, with a least depth of 6 fathoms over it, lies about 2 cables south-eastward of Horn island. 1953 ibid ii, 544 Petch's patch, with a depth of less than 6 feet over it, lies in the middle of the fairway.

3 Comb **patch-bag**: container for small personal effects, esp used by sealers (1925 *Dial Notes* v, 338).

1924 ENGLAND 119 I turned to an' smoked every pocket out o' me pants an' coat an' vest, an' smoked ahl de plaster rags out o' me patch bag. T 64–64 I got my patch bag out, got my scissors an' I goin' to patch my overhaul. C 71–94 ~ a bag carried by sealers in which they had 'rag,' buttons, needle & thread, finger stalls, etc.

patch (fox): red fox (*Vulpes fulvus*) in a colour variation with cross-like marking on back; CROSS-FOX.

1836 [WIX][2] 138 I had a fine view of a patch fox in my walk, saw several seals. 1879 HOWLEY *MS Reminiscences* 9 They were both young patch foxes and at this season were poorly furred. 1888 STEARNS 347 Then we have the variety known as the patch fox, which is only a darker and blacker form of the red; after that the cross or cross-patch, with a lighter area in the center of the black, in the form of a bar down the back and another across the fore-shoulders. 1919 GRENFELL[1] 209 T' Company gave he over four hundred dollars for a dark silver he got, and as much more, some say, for a batch o' reds and patches. T 203/5–65 A patch then is [a] patch fox—perhaps he got a patch of grey or a patch o' dark and a patch o' red, mixed.

patent n   [ˌpeitn̩ ˈæŋkəɹ, ˌpɛit?n̩t? ˈbæːɹk].

Comb **patent anchor**: a type of folding anchor.

P 127–77 A patent anchor is an anchor the flukes of which fold in toward the stock when it is stored on deck.

patent bark: commercially marketed tanning extract; cutch.

T 14/18–64 So you hear the women going around, 'Mother, have you got bit of cutch? Got either bit of patent bark? Got e'er a bit of catechu?' Now, there's three names for the one item. P 124–71 If sails were white they were dipped in a solution of lime and pickle but if they were dark they were put in a special substance known as patenbark. This was bought in St John's each previous spring, and was in solid form, and the men melted it down in large barkpots and put it on the sails. This solution was also put on twine and on traps used by the fishermen.

path n Cp *OED* ~ sb 1, *DAE* 1 for sense 1; *DC Labr* (1933) for sense 3.

1 One of the principal roads or streets in a town or 'settlement,' or between settlements, formed incidentally by habitual passage rather than expressly planned; also cpd **path-road**.

[(1766) 1971 BANKS 110 Here is no regular Street the houses being built in rows immediately adjoining to the Flakes Consequently no Pavement.] [1794] 1968 THOMAS 56 The distance from St John's to Portugal Cove is suppos'd to be fourteen miles. I had engag'd one Thomas Murphy, a poor but honest old Irishman, who knew the Path perfectly well. 1832 MCGREGOR i, 195 There is now a tolerable road from St John's to Portugal Cove in Conception Bay, and a path-road to a few other places. 1882 TALBOT 2–3 The streets, which were not called streets then but *paths*, were dirty, narrow, and crooked. 1893 *Christmas Greeting* 17 I set out for a distant outport. . . The day was very frosty, but the 'paths' were in splendid condition, and, muffled up as I was in the sleigh, I enjoyed the bracing air and the music of the jingling bells. 1896 *J A Folklore* ix, 31 ~ Pronounced with the hard Irish *th*, was applied to a road or even the streets of a town. Not long ago one might hear in St John's of the 'lower *pat-h*' or the 'upper *pat-h*.'

2 A track used in winter and leading to good stands of timber for fuel; WOOD PATH.

1866 WILSON 215 The slide, or catamaran, can only be used on the snow. . .and when some snow has fallen, but not sufficient to make a good path, the stick of wood is nobbled out. . . When the snow has fallen sufficiently deep, the snow path is formed. This is done by a number of men walking with pot-lid rackets.

3 Hunting territory claimed by a trapper; FUR PATH, TRAP LINE.

1916 GRENFELL 11 It had come Tom Marvin's turn to visit the 'path.' 1977 *Inuit Land Use* 280 Each 'planter' had a 'path,' or line of traps, often extending fifty miles or more inland, and as these paths cannot be covered in one day, he has small 'shacks,' or log houses referred to as tilts, at convenient intervals along them. . . Some of the paths are so long that they require a week to go over and to attend to the traps on the way.

4 Comb **path-beater**: young woman frequently out of doors at night; BEATER 2.

C 71–26 She would call me a path-beater—always out.

path-walloper: see **path-beater**.

P 108–70 ~ A girl or woman who is seen frequently walking along the roads or streets with different 'followers,' or on the look-out for them.

patrick n also **paddy, st patrick** [= patron saint of Ireland]. Cp *OED* paddy sb² 1 'nickname for an Irishman' (1780–) for sense 1; for combs. in sense 2, *NID* saint patrick's day, *Kilkenny Lexicon* patrick's pot 'a drink on the house'; see

H HALPERT 'Ireland, Sheila and Newfoundland,' in *Ireland and Nfld* (1977), pp. 147–72 for the folk legend of St Patrick and Sheila, and SHEILA 2 for weather combs. in sense 3.

1 Fisherman, esp an Irish fisheries 'servant.'

1826 [GLASCOCK] i, 131 Indeed, for three years successively, upon the close of the fishery for the season, or rather upon the return of the *Paddies* into port, an annual fire was as regularly looked for as the coming of the frost. 1955 DOYLE (ed) 85 "When the Caplin Come In": There's Dick's, Jim's and Billy's, Joe's, George's and Jack's, / From wee little laddies to big-headed paddy's / All coming along with their nets on their backs.

2 Comb **patrick's day**, ~ **night**: 17 March.

1924 ENGLAND 234 On Patrick's Day, wid colours gay, / When in de narthern floe, / We hopes ye'll have your steamer full, / An' safely stowed below. C 69–2 The men when they used to go in the woods on Paddy's Day would always get a green bough, preferably a pine, and put [it] at the top of the sail on the slide. 1971 CASEY 150 They use to sing mostly at weddings and parties which were held in someone's house, and during Christmas and Easter and Patrick's night, Candlemas, Lady Day [August 15] and at the garden party time.

patrick's pot: a windfall.

1936 SMITH 22 The ice was very heavy and in large sheets; consequently slow progress was made for the first few days, but on March 17th, St Patrick's Day, Capt William, who was second hand with his father, came to the fo'castle and fore and main hatchway and called everybody at daylight to get out to their 'Patrick's Pot' as we were among the seals, and plenty of them. C 64–4 Silver coins given to children on St Patrick's Day when they visited relatives. 'And here's a Paddy's Pot for ye, me little colleens.'

3 Designating weather conditions around 18 March, esp comb **patrick's batch** [see BATCH], ~ **broom**, ~ **brush** [see BRUSH], ~ **snap**.

C 69–28 It is believed that we have an annual snowstorm, known as paddy's batch on or near St Patrick's Day. This 'batch' is expected every year and quite often we may have it weeks after or before St Patrick's Day. C 66–8 [She] asked me if I'd heard of Sheilah's Brush and before I could answer, said, 'That's the storm that comes just before or after St Patrick's Day, and the other one is Paddy's Broom, but Paddy's Broom comes after Sheilah's Brush. 1866 WILSON 276 They sailed about the twenty-first of March. They sailed thus late to avoid the equinoctial gales, or, as the saying was, 'We wait until after Saint Patrick's brush.' M 69–5 [He] told me that you could expect a big snow storm either on, or immediately following, Calamas Day. This snow storm was always called Paddy's brush. Q 67–35 Paddy's snap: frosty weather around St Patrick's Day.

paytrick n also **pietrie**. Cp *EDD* partridge: variants paetrick, paitrick. Variety of tern (*Sterna hirundo hirundo; S. paradisaea*); STEARIN (1959 MCATEE 37–8).

1951 PETERS & BURLEIGH 240 Northern Common Tern. . . Local Names: Stearin, Paytrick.

pea n   *OED* ~ sb¹ 4; *EDD* sb¹ 3 D Co; *Fisheries of U S* (1887), pp. 167–8 for sense 1; for comb in sense 2: cp *DAE* 3 b ~ blower (1821).
   1 Freq pl, fish spawn; roe (P 152–58).
   [1812] 1956 FAY 20 The roes should be broken to pieces into a tub of water and stirred round with a stick till every particle or pea be separated from each other. 1971 NOSEWORTHY 229 Peas. The eggs of a codfish.
   2 Comb **pea blower**: hollow-stemmed weed improvised as a pea-shooter (P 148–60).
   pea top: herbaceous plant, skullcap (*Scuttelaria epilobiifolia*) (1898 *J A Folklore* xi, 277).

pear n
   1 Juneberry (*Amelanchier* spp); CHUCKLEY PEAR.
   [1620] 1887 MASON 149 The Countrie fruites wild, are cherries small, whole groaues of them, Filberds good, a small pleasant fruite, called a Peare. [1886] LLOYD 103 The pear, so-called, is a small spongy fruit, as unlike a real pear as possible in every respect. It is almost worthless.
   2 Attrib **pear tree**: the flowering shrub, Juneberry (1956 ROULEAU 35).

pease n   Comb **pease duff**: pease pudding; cp DUFF.
   T 80/2–64 There was a bit o' everything left—pease duff and potatoes and stuff like that. T 184–65 They used to have three duffs—a figgy one, a plain one and pease duff.

pease v   *EDD* ~ v Ha Do So D. To ooze; to leak through (a surface).
   1955 ENGLISH 35 Peeze: to leak in small bubbles. T 50–64 When [the canvas] would be dry, the water'd be peasin' through this canvas. P 155–64 The sweat started to pease out of me. C 69–11 The tar is peasin' out through the crack. P 135–77 Peasin'—when water comes in through the planks of a boat very slowly.

peck v   also **pick***. To begin to rain; to precipitate in small drops or flakes.
   P 148–63 It's pecking. It's a drizzle, just beginning to rain, in scattered drops. T 26–64¹ It just began to come picking snow. Q 67–57 When we have a heavy fog, the people don't say it is foggy, they will say it is pecking rain.

peck n   Speck; tiny spot (P 54–68).
   T 141/64–65² Directly they could see a little black peck.

peddle v   ['pæd] ‚æus]. Cp BERREY 472 peddle one's hips,—butt. Comb **peddle-house**: brothel.
   T 455–67¹ [She] had to go to the whorehouse—to a paddle-house, I suppose it'd be.

pedlar n   *DC* ~ n 3 Nfld (1964) for sense 2. Cp TRADER.
   1 Entrepreneur and vessel owner who purchases fish from fishermen in exchange for cash or supplies, operating outside the established merchant structure and 'truck system.'
   [1810] 1971 ANSPACH 334 There is here, among these who wish to come under the denomination of Planters, a numerous class of what we may call *Resident Pedlers*, people who get their supplies from merchants in St John's at reduced prices, and dispose of them here *at the broken price of the Bay*, which of course it is their interest to keep as high as possible. The fish which they receive here in payment at the Bay-price, they send to St John's where they get the full price.
   2 Vessel engaged in collecting fish from fishermen and in carrying supplies.
   [1832] 1981 *Them Days* vi (4), pp. 39–40 People left the stage abt 3 o'clock this morning, they may have finishd before but some of them got wine from the Pedlars got drunk & whent fighting for abt an hour. 1964 *Nfld Qtly* Summer, p. 25 The 'peddler'—not a man with a pack, but a trading schooner, from St John's, the American mainland, or even England—became in the 18th century, a competitive nuisance to the regular supplying merchant in Newfoundland harbours.[*DC*]

peggin See PIGGIN.

pelm n   *EDD* pilm sb 1 s w cties. Light ashes; dust.
   1896 *J A Folklore* ix, 36 ⋅ any light ashes such as those from burnt cotton, cardboard, also the light dust that rises from wood, and some kinds of coal-ashes.

pelt n   Cp *OED* ~ sb¹ 'skin of a sheep or goat'; cp *EDD* sb³ for sense 2; *OED* sb¹ 3 (1903 quot), *EDD* sb¹ 3 (2) for sense 3.
   1 The skin of a seal with the fat or blubber attached; SCULP n; occas the seal itself (see 1891 quot); FAT¹ 2.
   1792 CARTWRIGHT *Gloss* i, xii–xiii ~ The skin of an animal with the fat adhering to it. That term is made use of for the skins of seals, and other such animals, the fat of which lies between the skin and the flesh. [1799] 1976 HEAD 224–5 The ice. . .affords the inhabitants an opportunity of going off and killing the seals in great numbers, bringing their pelts on shore. 1842 JUKES i, 273 The skin is laid out flat and entire, with the layer of fat or blubber firmly adhering to it, and the skin in this state is called the 'pelt,' and sometimes the 'sculp.' [1870] 1899 *Nfld Law Reports* 338 The action was brought to recover damages for the wrongful conversion of the pelts of certain seals which the plaintiffs allege they had killed, and sculped, and left on the ice several miles from their vessel during the last seal fishery. 1891 PACKARD 444 The Hooded Seal is not uncommonly, during the spring, killed in considerable numbers by the sealers. The young 'pelt' weighs 70–80 pounds, while the old male or 'dog hood,' weighs 400 pounds. 1933 GREENE 72 Size of hide or weight of fat—both of which together, after being cut away from

the carcase, form what the sealer terms the 'sculps' or 'pelts' that he gathers when in the Patches. T 43/4–64 The pelt is the fat an' the skin. 1976 *Evening Telegram* 19 Mar, p. 6 You don't skin a seal, you sculp them! You take the seal's pelt, fat, and hide off.

2 Mischievous boy or youth, freq in phr *pelt of a tripe*; DEVIL'S PELT. Cp NUZZLE-TRIPE*.

1937 DEVINE 37 Pelt of a tripe. A rascal. P 118–67 You brazen little pelts!

3 Phr *in bare pelt*: stark naked (P 108–70).

pelt v Cp *OED* ~ v² 'to skin' obs (1596, 1641); cp *NID* ~ ² v. To remove the skin and the attached fat from a seal carcass; SCULP¹ 1.

[1771] 1792 CARTWRIGHT i, 181 I pelted ten harps. 1819 ANSPACH 423 The dead seals are dragged on the ice to the schooner or boat; they are then *pelted*, that is, the skin with the coat of fat adhering to it is separated from the carcase. 1895 GRENFELL 200 I had two seals in my boat, and we pelted (i.e. skinned) them to burn the fat, breaking up one of the smaller boats, also, to use as fuel. 1924 ENGLAND 88 Lusty toilers are meantime, with 'seal-dog' hooks and ropes, hauling the round-seals up and in. Once on board, the men pelt these in a jiffy. T 43–64 On the ice you crack 'em on the head with your gaff, an' then you pelt 'em. 1976 *Evening Telegram* 19 Mar, p. 6 The seals were 'pelted' by the sealers and skinned by seal skinners.

pen¹ n Cp *Cent* ~ ¹ n 3 'movable receptacle on board ship where fish are. . .iced.' Wooden enclosure in which cod-fish are salted in fishing premises; section of the hold of a boat in which fish are placed. Attrib ~ **board**: partition used to divide sections of the fish-hold. Cp POUND.

P 148–64 Pen-boards [are] used on draggers out of Burgeo. They are placed in slots as separators. Q 67–10 Part of the stage [is the] pen for salting fish. M 67–10 The old fellow pulled one of the 'pin-boards' across the built-in engine to the side of the boat. T 453–67 We chopped down the windward pen-boards an' we threw the rocks an' salt together.

pen² See PAN n.

penguin n also **pinwing** *OED* ~ 1 (Nfld: 1578–); *DAE* (1674–); *DC* (Nfld: 1578–). For a summary discussion of the obscure origin, see the *OED* note and W B LOCKWOOD *Zeits für Ang und Amer* xvii (1969), 262–4. A large, flightless bird once living in large numbers on Funk Island, extinct since the nineteenth century (*Pinguinus impennis*); attrib in coastal names; GREAT AUK.

[1536] 1600 HAKLUYT iii, 130 They came to part of the West Indies about Cape Briton, shaping their course thence Northeastwardes, vntill they came to the Island of Penguin, which is very full of rockes and stones, whereon they went and found it full of great foules white and gray, as big as geese, and they saw infinite numbers of their egges. They draue a great number of the foules into their boats vpon their sayles. [1578] 1935 *Richard Hakluyt* [Parkhurst's letter:] 131–2 There are. . .many other kind of birdes store, too long

to write, especially at one Island named Penguin, where wee may drive them on a planke into our ship as many as shall lade her. These birds are also called Penguins, and cannot flie, there is more meate in one of these then in a goose. [1583] 1940 *Gilbert's Voyages & Enterprises* ii, 398 [Hayes' narrative] We had sight of an Iland named Penguin, of a foule there breeding in abundance, almost incredible, which cannot flie, their wings not able to carry their body, being very large. . .which the French men use to take without difficulty upon that Iland, and to barrell them up with salt. 1613 *Willoughby Papers* 1/24 [They] wear gone all abroad acoastinge all the [islands] for Eeggs and birds agaynst the [winter] which in one Iland [to] the northwards the may fill [the boats] with penn gwynes. 1620 WHITBOURNE 9 These Penguins are as bigge as Geese, and flye not, for they have but a little short wing. [1663] 1963 YONGE 55 Here are also strange coloured gulls, penguins; a bird with a great bill and no wings but such as goslings have. They can not fly, but when pursued, take their yong on their back. [1766] 1971 BANKS 119 A number of Birds are about the ship which the seamen call Penguins. [1785] 1792 CARTWRIGHT iii, 55 A boat came in from Funk Island with birds, chiefly penguins. [1822] 1928 CORMACK 8 Penguins, once numerous on this coast, may be considered as now extirpated, for none have been seen for many years past. 1870 *Can Naturalist* v, 411–12 Almost the sole object of my visiting the island was to collect further information [about] this bird,—which is called 'Pinwing' by the settlers, and *not* Penguin, as Audubon informs us. . . [I was informed] 'a living pinwing was caught by one Captain Stirling about twelve years ago.' 1913 HOWLEY 10 Owing to its peculiar flipper-like wings, with short thick pinfeathers thereon, it was called the Penguin (pin or pen-wing). 1951 *Nfld & Lab Pilot* i, 233 Penguin islands. . .south-south-westward of Cape La Hune, are a group of numerous islands and rocks.

pep See PIP¹.

pepper n Comb **pepper tops**: sweet gale (*Myrica gale*).

1898 *J A Folklore* xi, 279 ~ . . .referring to the pollen.

perfume n Comb **perfume-willow**: bog candle; SCENT-BOTTLE (*Platanthera dilatata*) (1956 ROULEAU 35).

pet n *EDD* ~ sb 2 ~ day Sc Ir; DINNEEN peata: 'a pet. . .day in bad weather.' Comb **pet day**: an exceptionally fine day, esp during a normally inclement season (P 113–72).

1933 GREENE 24–5 What the sealer terms 'Pet-days' are rare—but generally in every Spring will come to all parts within the Ice Floe's boundaries some one or two of these delicious sun-filled days when the cold bracing air is just crystal-bright. P 148–65 A good day in April: 'They call it a pet day; a storm tomorrow!' M 70–21 Had they begun to dig the grave on Monday, the grave would have been ready for Wednesday, which in local terms was a 'pet' day (a calm, sunny, cloudless day) one not often experienced at that time of the year (mid-winter).

pew[1] n also **?pears, pue** *OED* ~ sb[2] Fr *pieu* (Nfld: 1861), *DC* esp Nfld (1835–). See W KIRWIN 'Selected French and English Fisheries Synonyms,' *RLS* 9 (1980), pp. 10–21. The Fr equivalent of *pew* was *piquois*, not *pieu*. A long stick with a sharp prong or tine affixed to the end, used in moving fish from boat to fishing-stage, etc; cp FORK n, PRONG n.

[(1663) 1963 YONGE 57 [They] throw up the fish on the stage-head by pears, that is, a staff with a prong of iron in him, which they stick in the fish and throw them up.] 1765 WILLIAMS 19 Pewes and Gafts. 1818 *Waterford Mirror* [Ire] 26 Dec The latter then went up the stage. . .when Tott was passing, gave him a violent stab in the side with a pew. 1836 [WIX][2] 17 A large species of fish. . .had been killed here last summer, by a girl with a 'pew,' or fork used for throwing fish from the boats on to the 'stages.' 1866 WILSON 210 The pue is an instrument having a long handle like a hay-fork, with only one prong, which is fixed in the centre of the stick. This prong is stuck in the head of the fish, and thus, with great ease and rapidity, it is thrown from the boat to the stage-head. 1919 GRENFELL[7] 196 The great plum puddings which served for wedding cakes were pulled out of the same boiling froth tightly wrapped in their cloth jackets, with long fish 'pews' or forks. T 41–64 I'd catch the dory painter, tie her on and hand down the pew, and [he'd] throw the fish up on deck. 1977 *Evening Telegram* 10 Nov, p. 6 But, mostly [the fishermen] use what is called a 'pew' which has only one prong. Most fishermen stab the fish in the head near the skull with this 'pew.' In handling small fish they use the two-pronged fork.

pew[2] n A sealer's bunk or berth; SYNAGOGUE.
1924 ENGLAND 64 He who had lain on a hard board to give me his 'pew' (bunk)—now busied himself with hammer and nails and tinkered up for me a berth in the cubbyhole mentioned.

pew v To transfer cod from boat to fishing-stage with a long-handled pronged implement; FORK v, PRONG v.
1895 *J A Folklore* viii, 39 . . .hence the verb *to pew*, to cast [cod-fish from the boats on to the stages]. 1909 BROWNE 68 [Fish] is 'pewed' to the 'stage head,' and then passed on to the 'cutthroat.' 1923 GRENFELL 43 . . .the surprise and joy of his dear wife as he tied up to the stage, while he began to 'pew' it up with the sharp hoe to where it could be split and salted. C 69–17 It was always thought to be unlucky for a fish to be left in the boat after the others had been taken out. Therefore the man pewing the fish from the boat would make certain that he did not leave a fish. P 143–74 The men pronged the fish from the boat onto the stagehead. From there, the women 'pewed' (a 'pew' was a prong with only one tine) the cod through the open windows onto the cutting table, always being careful to stab the fish in the head for 'broken fish' brought a low price.

pewer n One who moves cod from boat to

fishing-stage, etc, with a long-handled pronged implement or 'pew' (P 97–67).

philandy* v, n also **flangey*, phlandy*** [fɪˈlændɪ, fəˈlændɪ, ˈflændʒɪ]. Cp *EDD* philander v 'prance, caper' (1828); *Kilkenny Lexicon* ~ 'a heavy blow; a kick.' (a) To caper, jump about; (b) a blow, an act of striking; lively action for the fun of it.
P 94–57 When the cow came out of the woods / She began to philandy / 'Get out of the way,' says Martha Jane, / 'O she's all right,' says Andy. T 33–64[3] When the cow got in the slip [snare] / She began to philandy, / 'Why didn't you kill her?' says Becky Dyke / 'So I did, madam,' said Sandy. P 113–74 There was a wild phlandy. P 266–78 (Driving posts in the ground) I'll have a flangey at it.

phillida See FILLIDAY.

phripper See FLIPPER.

pick n DINNEEN pioc 'a bit, a peck, a jot; with *neg.* nothing.' Slightest piece, bit; small amount.
1924 ENGLAND 119 But after me gumbeans was ahl gone, I had narr pick o' baccy an' couldn't get none. C 69–12 We trouted all day long and never got a pick. 1977 BURSEY 23 We started to get the other anchor and hoisted it up short a pick and it was caught in a rock.

picket n Cp *DAE* ~ 5 'thin, narrow strip of wood used as a lath or as a paling for a fence' (1800–), ~ fence [open fence] (1800–). A tall, slender, uniform, round stick of fir or spruce, with or without bark, placed vertically for fencing. Attrib ~ **fence**.
1842 BONNYCASTLE i, 292 Fences here are made. . .by placing pickets, or small sticks, close alongside of each other, with the ends in the ground, and then nailing a riband over the whole, at about two feet, or so from the top; these fences are called, in the 'vernacular,' picket fences. 1946 MACKAY (ed) 153 There is a picturesqueness about the Newfoundland settlement with its houses huddled together without rhyme or reason, its narrow roadways, and its distinctive 'picket' fences of tiny, trimmed trees. T 43/7–64 If you had a bit of a front garden you'd get palings for that, but the pasture fields or the gardens were fenced with pickets. 1971 NOSEWORTHY 230 Pickets. Small, 'green,' round sticks with the *rind* removed. Made from small trees. 1979 *Evening Telegram* 25 Aug, p. 8 'Diter Walls' were rock walls. The farmers of long ago, when clearing land, put all their boulders in straight lines. In that way you didn't have to go in the woods and cut pickets.

pickle n Cp *OED* ~ sb[1] 1 'salt or acid liquor. . .in which flesh, vegetables, etc, are preserved' (1440–); *DAE* 2 (1761–). A mixture of fisheries salt and water used principally in the preservation of fish, esp cod, herring and mackerel, either as a type of cure for the finished product, or as a stage in the production of dried and salted fish; freq in phr *in pickle*. Cp SALT n.

[1766] 1971 BANKS 135 Instead of Being Laid out to Dry they are Barrelld up in a Pickle of Salt Boild in water. 1819 ANSPACH 412 [Cod] may be kept long in a frozen state, or else it is immediately split and put in pickle, where it remains until the weather will allow it to be spread on the flakes or beaches for drying. 1932 BARBOUR 23 After I had dished out the soup. . .he tasted it, spat it out, twisted his face and said, 'The soup's no good; 'tis salt as pickle.' 1957 *Daily News* 19 July, p. 4 He had a few barrels of fish in pickle. 1960 FUDGE 22 We were about all loaded together, and, in spite of the pleadings of the other captains to wait over until Monday morning to pump out some of the pickle and lighten our vessel. . . T 36–64 Then with the weight of so much fish on, if there's a'r drop o' pickle in it [it] would press out. T 43–64 You couldn't spread salt fish on the ground because. . .the dampness from the ground would take the pickle out of the fish. T 391/2–67 [They uses] salt [to make] their own pickle. 1975 BUTLER 75 We would leave the mackerel for fourteen days in pickle. We would then wash them and pack them in barrels with a sprinkle of salt. We would head up the barrels and fill them with one hundred test pickle. 1979 POCIUS 52 Yes, salt, cup of salt, or cup of pickle to every bit of dye she'd boil. That don't let it fade, see.

pickle v Cp *OED* ~ v[1] 1 'to put into or steep in pickle' (1552–). To treat cod-fish, sealskins, etc, with brine, or sometimes with applications of salt, in the curing process.

[1745] 1976 HEAD 125 Truck our Goods for Skins, feathers and fish, and be sure you Gitt all the Sile Skins both dry and Pickled. T 50/2–64 They'll bring [the skin] down then an' put it in pickle again, pickle it in. T 36–64 Now the fish is maggoty and it's slimy, an' I got to get out on the flake again with small tubs an' pickle an' wash it. T 391/2–67 We always pickles our fish, you know, in tubs, in puncheon tubs. 1976 *Decks Awash* Aug, p. 31 When he returned each year around September 1, he would salt and pickle his fish and then take it into St John's. 1977 *Inuit Land Use* 289 Furs and pickled (salted) salmon were traded at the Hudson's Bay Company stores for food and supplies.

piddly n One of several varieties of children's game which opposing sides play with sticks, variously sized and named, one of which is flicked into the air from a base or goal; TIDDLY (1980 *Daily News* 18 Mar, p. 4). Cp CAT[4]. Also attrib.

T 14/21–64 We used to play piddly. We put down two large-size stones, we'll say about eight inches from the ground. Then we got two sticks: one short stick about a foot long and one about two foot long. Well then I put this short stick across these stones I'd push it with the. . .long one, you see. Well, perhaps that would go eight or ten and twelve feet. Then I'd lay my long stick across the same stones. And if you could throw this short one and hit this off, well I'm out. T 169/206–65[1] When you had 120 stick lengths, the long stick, that was the game. And so that was piddly. 1967 READER 47 There was also 'Piddley' a game we used to play

with a long stick and a small short stick, putting this between two large stones. This was played with another person. 1976 *Daily News* 15 Jan, p. 3 The only equipment. . .required was two sticks—one short and the other long. . . In piddly, both ends of the short stick were blunt, for the idea was to flick it for the other team to catch if they could, and this was done with bare hands. 1982 *Evening Telegram* 6 Mar, p. 14 In those days we had a sloppy spring it is true, then the brilliant warm sun and the games of hide and seek for girls and boys and Pidley Sticks for boys only.

pie See PIED.

pied p ppl *OED* ~ [1] d (1899 quot), *DAE* ~ duck (1637–) for sense 1. Comb **pied duck**, ~ **bird, pie bird**.

1 Labrador duck, a bird now extinct (*Camptorhynchus labradorius*).

[1770] 1792 CARTWRIGHT i, 48 Ned and the furriers returned in the evening, having killed only a pied-duck. [1773] ibid 280 One of my people killed a pair of pied-birds, which afforded us an excellent supper.

2 Variety of golden-eye (*Bucephala clangula americana; B. islandica*).

1870 *Can Naturalist* v, 300 [The pie duck] breeds in holes in trees, sometimes near the ground, but very frequently fifteen or twenty feet high. [1918–19] GORDON 73 We have seen two pie-birds so far, by way of spring birds. 1951 PETERS & BURLEIGH 104 The 'Pie Duck' is familiar to most Newfoundlanders, for it is found on streams and wooded ponds throughout the province. T 272–66[2] There's a pie bird'll fly around here once in a while, an' the house that bird visits. . .somebody'll die in that house shortly after. 1977 *Inuit Land Use* 176 Species commonly found nesting and feeding at the head of the coastal bays are black ducks, harlequin ducks (lords and ladies), goldeneye ducks (pie ducks).

3 Other sea-bird (*Histrionicus histrionicus histrionicus; Melanitta perspicillata*).

1959 MCATEE 16 Pie bird. Harlequin duck (That is, pied, Nfld., 'Labr.'). Ibid 18 Pied duck. Surf scoter (Only the head of the male is pied or particoloured. Nfld., 'Labr.').

pietrie See PAYTRICK.

pig n *EDD* ~ sb[1] 3 (8) Ir for sense 1.

1 Phr *be on the pig's back*: to be prosperous.

1925 *Dial Notes* v, 338 ~ As one wants to be; all hunky dory; on easy street. P 108–74 They're on the pig's back now, since the young fellow got a job.

2 Comb **pig-a-wee**: Newfoundland black-capped chickadee (*Parus atricapillus bartletti*); TOM: TOM-TEE (1959 MCATEE 52).

1967 *Bk of Nfld* iii, 283 Black-capped Chickadee: Pig-a-wee (from its calls); Tom-tit or Tom-tee (many small land birds were called tom-tits).

pig berry: fruit or berry of the mountain ash (*Sorbus* spp); DOGBERRY (1895 *N S Inst Sci* ix, 90).

1846 TOCQUE 307 The berries [of mountain ash] are

generally called 'dog-berries'; by some, however, in Newfoundland, they are called 'pig-berries.'

pig-fish: a scavenger fish (*Myoxocephalus octodecemspinosus; M. scorpius*); SCULPIN.

1895 GRENFELL 17–18 The only other common fish is the sculpin, pig-fish, or grubby. He is a voracious scavenger, and, in foul companionship with his friend the flounder, may be seen sweltering on the rotting heaps of offal which surround every Labrador fish-stage.

pigeon n   *OED* ~ sb 2 b (1694 quot), *DC* n 2 (1959) for sense 1; for comb in sense 2: cp *DC* pigeonberry 1.

1 Black guillemot (*Cepphus grylle atlantis*); SEA-PIGEON; also attrib in coastal names.

[1774] 1792 CARTWRIGHT ii, 15 I killed a pigeon with my rifle. [1819] 1978 *Beothuk Vocabularies* 68 Pigeon—Bobbodish. 1870 *Can Naturalist* v, 415 A very common periodical migrant, breeding plentifully on islands on the north coast of Newfoundland. . .[the] 'pigeon.' 1902 DELABARRE 202 Black Guillemot. Pigeon. Very abundant all along the coast. The most numerous of all the water fowl, after the kittiwakes. . . Much used by the settlers as an article of food. 1953 *Nfld & Lab Pilot* ii, 324 Pigeon cove is entered about 3 miles farther north-eastward. 1977 *Inuit Land Use* 123 Soon after the pigeons and saddlers arrive, the first harp seals begin to migrate north along the floe edge.

2 Comb **pigeon berry**: dwarf cornel (*Cornus canadensis*); CRACKER BERRY (1956 ROULEAU 35).

[1822] 1856 CORMACK 13 Cornus Canadensis [bears] a cluster of wholesome red berries called pigeon berries. 1869 HARDY 267 On the 18th [of July] I observed various Vaccineae, the purple iris, the pigeon-berry, and Smilacina bifolia in flower.

pigeon diver: common dovekie (*Plautus alle alle*); BULL-BIRD, ICE- ~ (1959 MCATEE 39).

piggin n   also **peggin**. Cp *OED* ~ 'small pail or tub' chief dial (1554–), *EDD* sb 1, *DAE* (1653–); SMYTH 527 'a little pail having a long stave, for a handle; used to bale water out of a boat.' Small wooden bucket made of staves, one of which protrudes to form a handle, used to bail water from a deep-keeled boat; SPUDGEL.

[1870] 1973 *Evening Telegram* 25 Oct, p. 3 Then you hear the splashing where they were bailing her out with the piggin if it rained the night before. 1897 *J A Folklore* x, 210 ~ a small bucket used for dipping water out of the dill and bailing their boats. [c1900] 1978 *RLS* 8, p. 24 Peggin: a bale bucket for a punt. [1926] 1946 PRATT 176 "The Cachalot": The second oarsman snatched and shot / The piggin like a shuttlecock, / Bailing the swamping torrent out, / Or throwing side-long spurts to dout / The flame. T 90–64 And there's the piggin, the round little keg with the one handle. C 71–128 ~ a wooden tub used to bail bilge water from a fishing boat. The piggin was made from staves one of which was longer than all of the others, and used as a handle. Piggins were hand made after the fashion of a small barrel (except of course, it had no cover), the

staves being held together by two hoops. 1977 RUSSELL 153 One of us asked him how far off he drove. He said he didn't rightly know, because he had no way of measurin' the mileage, but on the mornin' the wind died out, he took his piggin and baled the boat out, then took his last cake of hard tack out of his bread box and ate it.

pile n   A stack of split and salted cod-fish at various stages of the drying and curing process, often with defining word DRY a, FISH, PRESS(ED), SALT, etc; freq in phr *in pile*. Cp FAGGOT n.

[1663] 1963 YONGE 57 The fish being salted, lies 3 or 4 days, sometimes (if bad weather) 8 or 10 days, and is then washed by the boys in salt or fresh water and laid in a pile skin upward on a platt of beach stones, which they call a horse. [1766] 1971 BANKS 135 I had almost Forgot that when the Fish are tolerably dry they Put them in Round Piles of 8 or ten Quintals Each Covering them on the top with bark in these Piles they remain 3 or 4 days or a week to sweat after which they are again Spread. [1777] 1792 CARTWRIGHT ii, 241 We made those fish into pile, which were spread on Friday; washed out forty quintals, and spread the fish which were carried out yesterday. 1809 *Naval Chronicle* xxi, 21–2 Every night, during its process, it [the fish] is brought into round piles, covered over with birch-rinds, with weight on it, to keep the wet and damp out. 1888 STEARNS 184 The fish were arranged in layers built up, one above the other, and out, from a common center of fish-tails, until the pile was about as deep as it was high. Those the boys saw were about six feet in diameter and three feet high. 1936 SMITH 17 When spread again [the fish] would be made up in twenty-quintal piles, and well covered with rinds on top and tarpaulins around the napes to keep it thoroughly dry; it would remain there for a few days to press and work in pile. 1937 DEVINE 67 [proverb] If the goats come home in files, / Get your fish in covered piles.
T 175/7–65 An' then the next thing, when it got perhaps two or three days sun on it, you put it in what they call a pile. You go around, all yaffle around, around. All tails inside, all the napes o' the fish out around. C 69–17 When codfish [was] spread on the flake for the first few days it was taken up and placed in little piles or heaps called faggots. After each day's spread it was made a little larger till it reached the stage called pile containing over 5 quintals in a circular stack. 1977 BURSEY 197 My waterhorse fish was left in the pile all that day and our crew went where they would.

pile v   To place split and salted cod-fish in a stack at various stages of the drying and curing process; cp FAGGOT v, PRESS.

1888 STEARNS 184 That is the way we pile our fish over night and when we have bad weather. [1894] 1975 WHITELEY 175 Fine day—carried out and piled fish. Ibid 178 Spread fish and piled waterhorse.

pin n, v   SMYTH 528 pin-maul.

Comb **pin bough(s)**: needle of a conifer, esp dried and heaped on the ground; SPRINKLE[1] (1971 NOSEWORTHY 231).

pin hole: hole in which 'tolepin' is placed; hole

at stern of a boat in which a sculling-oar is placed.

T 54/8–64 So I lanched out the coffin and 'twas leaky. An' I hauled it ashore an' I caulked it an' tarred it, an' I put two pinholes in the foot of the coffin an' put an oar on an' got into it an' sculled down the length of the harbour.

pin man: ship's carpenter, esp one who repairs small boats.

T 141/69–65² We got a pin man there for to repair the side of our motor boat, put some plank in she and some timber into her.

pin-maul: hammer with iron head opposite the face (P 148–74).

pinover: piece of cloth or flap protecting the nose and chin from severe cold. Cp NORTH-WESTER.

[1779] 1792 CARTWRIGHT ii, 416 Yet my eye-brows were never free from ice, and the pinover on my chin, was frozen an inch thick. 1792 ibid *Gloss* i, xiii ~s. Bits of flannel, which are tacked to one side of the North-wester, and pinned to the other; one covering the nose, and the other, the chin.

pinch n *DAE* ~ n 'steep or difficult part of a road' (1754–); *EDD* sb⁴ 9 'short, steep hill' Ir D. Steep incline on a path or road; section of road as it passes over crest of a hill; freq in local place-names.

1937 DEVINE 37 ~ a hill or upgrade on a country road or woods path. 1938 MACDERMOTT 250 John Henry's Pinch is a heart-breaking pinch to pull up a komatik or catamaran load of wood. P 61–67 Old Ned's Pinch—a short but very steep hill. C 71–128 The load of wood had to be hauled up Jackie's Pinch, and to do this several men were needed, until every load reached the top. 1973 WIDDOWSON 220 In my mother's day. . .you could not pass the Stand (the little level place in Brigus where the church stands) or the Forge. . .or the Pinch (the high point on the road just before you come down into Brigus) after dark because these were the places the fairies lived. 1978 *Evening Telegram* 9 Sep, p. 14 We would have missed a lot of lovin' sessions sittin' on Crimps diter walls on Hennebury's Pinch.

pinchgut n SEARY 84; cp *OED* gut sb 5 a 'channel or run of water'; *OED* pinch-gut sb 1 'one who stints himself or others of food' obs. Cp FAMISH GUT. In place-names, a narrow 'tickle,' strait, sound or passage; also attrib.

[1772] 1971 SEARY 258 ~ (Lane 1772). 1951 *Nfld & Lab Pilot* i, 99 Pinchgut tickle is formed between the eastern side of Pinchgut island, which lies with Pinchgut point, its southern extremity, 7 cables west-south-westward of Tickle point, and the mainland eastward. . . The entrance, less than half a cable wide, lies between a spit of shingle and sand. . .and the eastern shore.

pink a

1 Of dried and salted cod-fish, pinkish in colour through impurities in the salt and faulty dry-ing. Shifts in some contexts to noun use. Cp DUN a.

1953 *Nfld Fish Develop Report* 65–6 Solar salt. . .contains varying proportions of impurities. . . This affects the curing process and the appearance and taste of the product and may result in the infection known as 'pink.' 1971 NOSEWORTHY 231 ~ Describing a condition of spoiled fish which is pinkish in colour and slimy. 1977 BURSEY 167 Then the fish makers at Valleyfield went on strike and the fish lay there till it turned pink.

2 Comb **pink bells**: twin-flower (*Linnaea borealis*) (1956 ROULEAU 35); PINKY 2.

pink fish: see sense 1 above.

T 175/7–65 An' not only that, we just about had the voyage turned down. We had what we call pink, what they call the pink fish. M 69–17 The weather had to be just right for the spreading of water horse fish: not too hot, for the fish could boil; not too dull, for it might rain, and rain on such fish could wash the salt from it, making it into pink fish. 1977 RUSSELL 39 'You remember the fellow in the fisheries Lab in St John's that used to give me all the information about salt and pink fish and things like that?

pink tops: fireweeds (*Epilobium angustifolium*) (1956 ROULEAU 35).

pinky n *DC* pinkie (Nfld: 1958), *DAC* pinkie 'cheap wine' (1935–) for sense 1.

1 Cheap port wine; wine mixed with other spirits.

P 245–55 ~ Two parts cheap port wine, one part screech. A waterfront drink. 1964 *Daily News* 7 May, p. 4 "Down the Hatch": Even 'Pinky' now is high brow / For a fellow with the shakes, / As he pays an extra quarter / For the juice from a pound of grapes.

2 In pl, twin-flower (*Linnaea borealis*); PINK BELLS (1956 ROULEAU 35).

pinnacle n Cp *OED* ~ sb 2 'any natural peaked formation; esp a lofty rock or stone.' See *Sailing Directions: Labrador and Hudson Bay* (1974), p. 52: *iceberg*.

1 A peak of ice projecting from an iceberg or 'rafted' up in an ice-floe.

1842 JUKES i, 298 [The berg] was full of hollows at the top and sides, having a pinnacle at one end thirty-five feet high, with a perpendicular wall or cliff, and at the other a round hummock. [c1900] 1978 *RLS* 8, p. 24 Pinacle of ice: rough ice or pans turned up on end and so frozen as to form pinacles. 1910 GRENFELL 168 There was one about sixty feet or more high as we was driving by, and there were two grand pinnacles on it. 1933 GREENE 165 As no water was carried, ice had to be melted every day for drinking-water and for cooking. This, if possible, was chopped with axes from some berg or selected 'blue-pinnacle' of fresh-water ice, for the water thus obtained would be of the best and purest. 1937 DEVINE 37 ~ A conical piece of ice standing out prominently. Sealers use them as marks when they wish to leave any of their impedimenta or seals, so that they can be located easily on return. They were also used to tie vessels onto, for warping through the ice.

1972 BROWN 56 The fleet was scouting the edges of the heavy Arctic ice-field, with its rafters and pinnacles and pressure ridges.

2 Attrib, comb **pinnacle ice**: see sense 1 above.
1929 *Nat Geog* July, p. 108 The captain sends men overboard to cut pinnacle ice.

pinnacle tank: water tank aboard sealing vessel in which fresh-water or glacial ice is melted; TOP TANK (1924 ENGLAND 319).

pinnacle tea: tea brewed at sea from melted fragments of glacial ice.
1924 ENGLAND 129 Our duff was hard, our pork was bad, / We had to drink pinnacle tea! 1940 *Dal Rev* xx, 66 When the cook on a schooner runs out of fresh water, he rows over to the berg, chips off a piece (which is, of course, not salt) and brings it back to fill the kettle for a pot of 'pinnacle tea.'

pinnacle v Of floating ice, to become forced upwards by the pressure of the floe; RAFTER.
1873 CARROLL 21 It is well understood, that after young seals are whelped that their 'whereabouts' depends on wind and tide, the smoother the ice the more it will raft or pinnacle up in heavy weather. 1972 BROWN 31 They found that heavy Arctic ice, rafted and pinnacled, had been thrust up into a great series of pressure ridges.

pinny owl See PINYOLE.

pint n A dry measure used by both pickers and sellers of such wild berries as bakeapples, blueberries, partridge berries, etc (P 245–77). Cp GALLON.
1966 SCAMMELL 127 "Bakeapple Jam": I picked a pint around that knap, I'll shuck 'em later on, / I'm the fastest picker here I'm pretty sure I am.

pinwing See PENGUIN.

pinyole n also **pinny owl**. Atlantic black-legged kittiwake; TICKLACE (*Rissa tridactyla tridactyla*).
1959 MCATEE 37 ~ common kittiwake ('Northeastern Banks,' Nfld.).

pip¹ n also **pep**. The entrails of a fish or squid; cp GIB n.
1924 ENGLAND 320 ~ Salmon guts. P 261–55 The pip of the squid is good bait. T 90/1–64 The squid would be taken fresh, and you'd take un by the horns an' pop out the two eyes, an' take your knife and slit un down the belly, and cut off the pip, leave the horns on, and wash it clean. T 192–65 Anyhow we got some salmon and took the salmon pips, me an' a boy, the other boy, an' we went across th' harbour, across about half a mile, an' we caught three barrel, two barrel o' fish with the hook an' line. 1976 HOLLETT 1 They would take one pound for the pip out of every each one of the salmon. . .that was a racket they had had. . .say the salmon weigh ten pound, you only get paid for nine. And if he weigh twenty pound you get paid for nineteen, always doed that. 1979 TIZZARD 302 The [squid] entrails or pep were all saved in blubber barrels to rot out, as there was a lot of oil contained in those peps.

pip² n Phr *on the pip*: purposely absent from school; truant; cp MOOCH (P 148–61).
P 198–67 He went on the pip yesterday. 1979 *Evening Telegram* 12 Nov, p. 6 It was no use to go on the pip [from school].

pip v To remove the gills and entrails of a herring; GIB v; to gut and head a squid (P 148–74).
[1886] LLOYD 69 When taken ashore the herring are 'pipped'—i.e. the entrails and gills are removed. T 141/67–65² You go down there late as Christmas an' catch herring an' bring 'em up here, an' be pippin' herrin' an' packin' herrin' all the winter. 1977 *Nfld Qtly* Dec, p. 37 The [herring] were cleaned, [pipped], and hung up in the roof [for smoking].

piper n *ADD* ~ Nfld (1921). Locally made galvanized tin kettle with bevelled sides, flat bottom and a long narrow spout or 'bib' emitting a piping sound when it boils; BIBBY, QUICK, SLUT.
[c1845] 1927 DOYLE (ed) 27 "The John Martin": He took the kettle by the hangers, and he threw it on the ice; / I never felt so scalded since the day that I was born, / When I saw my little piper and it floating off astern. [1894 BURKE] 8 [advertisement] And William Malcolm's is the place, / For pipers, pans, or pot. 1906 *Nfld Qtly* Dec, p. 4 The friendly old three-legged pot and the cheerful 'piper' soon followed the bake-pot. 1909 BROWNE 255 Here we landed to 'boil the piper' (a tin kettle used by fishing boats). 1939 DULEY 11 Its whole ceiling was hidden with clusters of hanging kettles, enamel mugs, earthenware tea-pots, pipers, skillets, pots and pans. T 50/1–64 [They'd] cook their fish an' boil their kettle—pipers, they call them—little flat-arsed tin kettles with a bib on 'em. 1980 *Evening Telegram* 5 Jan, p. 11 They roasted [the fish] when the piper was boilin'.

pippy* n One of several variations of a children's game which opposing sides play with sticks, one of which is flicked into the air from a base or goal; PIDDLY, TIDDLY. Also attrib.
P 167–67 Let's have a game of pippy! M 71–39 Pippy is playing outdoors in a field of any size—but preferably rectangular shaped. The contestant plays from one end of the field where a small hole has been dug in the ground. This hole [is] called the pippy hole. The children brought their own pippy sticks to school. M 71–68 ~ This game could be played by two teams or two people. You needed one stick about three feet long and another one about ten inches long. . . The short stick was placed across two small logs to form an H. Then the first player hooked the short stick out as far as he could with the longer stick to the opposing team in the field. If an outfielder caught the stick, then the player was out, and the next person on the team was up.

pipsi n also **pipsey, pipshy** *DC* pipshi (Labr: 1771–); PEACOCK *English-Eskimo Dictionary* 225 Fish, dried: *pipsi;* Labrador Inuit 101 *pitsik* 'dried fish.' Cod-fish and trout preserved by drying in the sun and wind without salt.

[1771] 1792 CARTWRIGHT i, 138 I was greatly pleased with [the Eskimo] method of curing codfish without salt; which, in that state, they call *pipshy.* The fish is split down the back, the bone taken out, and the thick parts scored down to the skin, an inch asunder; two of them are then fastened together by their tails, and hung across a pole to dry in the open air. 1895 GRENFELL 63 To prevent scurvy in winter, when fresh fish is not attainable, salt meat must be avoided, even if they can afford to buy it. The following recipe is invented with that end: 'Dry the cod in the sun till it is so hard none can go bad. In winter powder this, rub it up with fresh seal oil, and add cranberries if you have any.' This dainty is known as 'Pipsey.' 1966 BEN-DOR 50 Dried fish, 'pipsi,' is the Eskimo technique of preserving cod and trout for future use. 1977 *Inuit Land Use* 123 Char caught in the spring make the best dried fish (pipsi); later in summer, their flesh is more oily, and it quickly becomes rancid if left long in the sun.

pishogue n, usu pl also **pisherogue, fizoge*,** etc [fʊˈʃoːg, ˈfʊʃərog] *EDD* ~ Ir; JOYCE 302; DINNEEN piseog 'witchcraft, sorcery,' pl, 'superstitious acts.' Incredible story, foolish talk; complaint.
1931 BYRNES 121 How many years have passed my friends, since you heard these once familiar localisms?. . . 'Sure it's all pisherogues.' 1937 DEVINE 37 ~s Superstitions. Gossipy yarns and incredible stories. 1968 DILLON 138 Fishogues, pisharogues—superstitions about ghosts, fairies, etc; matters a person complains about. 'Them are only some of your old fishogues.'

piss v *OED* pissabed obs exc dial (1597–1822); *EDD* piss-a-bed sb 1, 2.
Comb **piss-a-bed,** ~ **t' bed**: dandelion (*Taraxacum officinale*); DUMBLEDORE.
1937 DEVINE 37 ~ The dandelion flower. 'Pied-the-bed.' M 70–16 In April generally the dandelion comes out. This is a sort of a green—not a vegetable really such as turnip or potato—and it grows along with a little yellow flower which was often referred to as a piss t' bed. 1975 SCOTT 39 The Dandelion has a number of common names in Newfoundland. These include Dumbledor, Faceclock, and Piss-a-beds. 1976 *Evening Telegram* 22 May, p. 3 Some little pissabeds already out. Horse chestnut buds sticky and about to break.
piss quick, ~ **pump**: boot cut off at the ankle and used as a slipper; cp LUMP.
P 54–65 I got into me piss-quicks and went up on deck [to] piss over the side of the vessel. C 71–97 Piss pumps are short ankle-length rubber boots which are made by cutting off the knee-length rubber boots. 1981 HUSSEY 25 These cut-off rubbers were known as piss-quicks and were very handy.
pisswig: mildly opprobrious term for a small child (P 148–67).
P 29–74 You little pisswig (a little rascal who would come and mess up your work when you had everything laid out).

pit n Cp *EDD* ~ sb¹ 5 So. Comb **pit hole**: saw-pit.

C 71–52 ~ hole in the loft floor of a store, where pit saw is used. One man stands downstairs, at one end of the saw, the other is upstairs; they push the saw up and down through the log which is laid on the loft floor, protruding over the hole.

pitch v *OED* ~ v 8 'settle, alight' rare or arch (1623–1900) for sense 1; *EDD* v¹ 12 Do So for sense 3; *EDD* 1 (2) ~ button for sense 4.
1 To alight, land; to fall (from a height).
1924 ENGLAND 177 An' de birds pitch [come down] by t'ousands just after de sun risin'. T 50–64 'Is that where we have to pitch?' 'Oh, that's a big lake when we get down.' And by and by [the plane] pitched on the water. T 31/2–64 I don't know which way I pitched, on my head or on my hands, or how I pitched. I jumped. T 139/40–65 He used to have a puncheon in the marsh, have a few trees put around the puncheon. And then the geese come and pitch. T 158–65 All that ridge burned in there, flames used to come out, flankers come out, pitch on the felt. T 172/5–65 An' I come down, I pitched on the cuddy on my crown, on my head—nearly knocked the life out o' me. M 71–95 When a plane circled the harbour we knew it was going to pitch.
2 Of a storm, to blow up suddenly from a certain direction; to strike.
T 39/2–67 An' a storm pitched to the north-east, they thought, or nor'west. T 398/9–67 The wind pitched from the southeast, but they got clear of it.
3 Of a swelling, to reduce, lessen.
T 187/8–65 My mother had my throat and everything all done up with tansy poultice for to pitch the swelling.
4 Phr *pitch buttons*: in a child's game, to throw buttons at a target (P 228–64).
T 49–64 You stand away so far, an' you pitch your button. The handiest to the peg, after so many pitches [would win]. C 70–15 The object of the game was to pitch a button from the hole [where you stood] so that the button touched the 'nag' (or stick). C 71–22 Make a mot in the ground with your heel. Stand at a distance from the hole and pitch the buttons. 1975 LEYTON 34 I was down the beach, a little boy in me bare feet pitching buttons, five or six of us.

pitcher n One of the timbers or ribs of a boat, set in raked or slanted fashion in the frame of the forward and after sections of the craft.
1937 DEVINE 37 ~s. The ribs in the fore and after sections of a boat's frame. T 43/8–64 You'd ribbon her out then, an' you'd make these pitchers—after pitchers an' forrard pitchers—and finish timberin' her out. 1969 *Nfld Qtly* July, p. 19 After pitchers: slightly curved timbers fastened to the chalks. P 13–76 ~s. Crooked timbers in a vessel that are located forward of the fore-hook and aft of the after-hook.

pitcher plant n *OED* ~ (1835–); *DAE* (1857–); *DC* (Nfld: 1819–). Bronze or green perennial of boggy areas with a single tall capsuled stem growing out of a cluster of curved pitcher-shaped leaves which trap water and insects, the floral emblem of Newfoundland (*Sarracenia purpurea*); INDIAN CUP.

[(1766) 1971 BANKS 301 [plant catalogue] Sarracenia purpurea 1 Bogs Croque St John's Hare Bay.] 1810 STEELE 99 The most frequent and beautiful wild roses have been observed here; as, likewise, a remarkable production called the pitcher-plant. 1819 ANSPACH 362 Another still more remarkable plant, found in the woods of Newfoundland, is the *Saracenia*, commonly called side-saddle-flower, or pitcher-plant. Its flowers, shaped like a lady's saddle, are surrounded with a vast number of pitchers along with the leaves, to receive the rain-water. 1866 WILSON 57 The 'pitcher plant'. . .is the natural production of the swamps. 1910 TOWNSEND 15 Clumps of pitcher-plant leaves were everywhere in the bogs, looking often as fresh and intact as if they had been preserved in a green-house, instead of lying buried under the snow for seven long months. 1965 *Can Geog J* lxx (4), p. 127 The floral emblem of Newfoundland is the Pitcher Plant. . .a sturdy, lonely plant which grows in boggy, barren areas, produces no fragrant flower, and lives carnivorously on insects. It is a hunter.

pitchy-paw n   Cp *EDD* pitch-poll v: pitchipoll Gl 'turn head over heels,' pitch v[1] 2 (5) pitch pitch, butterfly. Common butterfly most often noticed by children (1937 DEVINE 37).

C 69 1 Whenever she saw a pitchy-paw—(brown-winged butterfly) she would say, 'Pitchy, pitchy butterfly, / If you don't your mother will cry.' A pitchy-paw is a butterfly that is generally dark-coloured and pitches (lands, alights) on the ground often.

pitnagen n   Purple-stemmed aster (*Aster puniceus*); TEA-FLOWER (1956 ROULEAU 35).

1978 *Decks Awash* vii (2), p. 48 We'd put potato peelings in the oven, dry them and crumb them up. Then we'd dig petnoggin—that's a white root that grows in boggy land—hang them up to dry, break them up and put them amongst our potato peels. Enough tobacco to last a week.

pitty n   Cp *OED* pit-hole sb b 'a grave' (1621–1768); *EDD* pit sb[1] 1 (19) (b): pittee-'awl D. Comb **pitty-hole**: grave, esp as used in threats to naughty children.

M 70–9 As my mother used to say when I was very young, 'You'll go down into the pitty-hole.' 1973 WIDDOWSON 231 If you don't be good, the hob-goblin will get you and throw you down the pity-hole.

planch v   *OED* ~ v obs (1516–1723); *EDD* 2 D Co. To put down floor-boards.

T 414–67 [The shores] were put in apparently before the place was planched. But once the place was planched it was virtually impossible to get at [the shores] any more. P 127–78 A house may be planched, then covered with tar-paper and planched again, to give a double-planchin.

planchen, plancheon, planchion See PLANCHING.

planching n   also **planchen, plancheon, planchion**, etc ['plænʃən]. Cp *OED* ~ vbl sb b 'flooring' dial (1600–1886); *EDD* 'planking' So D Co. (a) Floor-boards; the floor of a dwelling; (b) planks laid down to form the floor of a barn, fishing-stage, or the cabin or engine-room of a vessel.

1901 *Christmas Review* 5 "The Outharbour Planter": His house the village meetin' place, tho' it not always was a mansion; / Its carpet was a sanded floor, with sometimes sawdust on the planchin'. 1906 *Nfld Qtly* Dec, p. 4 The floor or 'planchion,' as it is called, is well scrubbed and sprinkled with sand. P 152–58 Planchion—the first flooring of a house. P 148–62 Planchin: a wooden floor or walk-way [in a fishing stage]. P 148–66 ~ wooden floor in stable, strong enough to support cows. M 70–29 They were about to take up the planchin (floorboards) around the engine when the skipper told them that they would have to put every plank back just as it was and that they would pay for any they broke. 1972 MURRAY 188–9 Some early kitchens had the 'planchen' (floor) covered with tar paper, except for about a foot around each side which was left bare. 1975 BUTLER 41 There was about a ton of coal under the forecastle floor. . . There was about half a ton under her cabin planchin'.

plant n

1 Specific area of foreshore with structures upon it for the landing and curing of fish; PLANTATION; ROOM.

[1817] 1953 JOB 24 I have been many years in Newfoundland and from my experience of conditions am persuaded that it would take a long time and large outlay to put in order a plant that had been neglected even for three years. In point of fact the whole property value lies in the erections that stand upon it. T 270–66 We had flakes right along there. All our plantation is gone [now]. Our plant used to reach from that store right over to the end o' that baitshed there.

2 Phr *go on the plant*: to fish on one's own account (1895 *J A Folklore* viii, 34).

1878 TOCQUE 147 Half the fishermen [of Bonavista], in consequence of their having no water-side premises, cannot 'go on the plant,' as it is called (all the fishermen who keep a boat and employ men, or even keep a skiff and fish alone, are called 'planters' in Newfoundland), they are therefore obliged to go as sharemen.

plantation n   Cp *OED* ~ 4 'a colony' (1614–), *DAE* 1 (1606–), *DC* 1 (Nfld: 1620–) for sense 1.

1 The houses, structures and ground on or adjacent to the foreshore of a cove, bay or harbour; COLONY, SETTLEMENT; merges in some contexts with sense 2. Also attrib.

[1611] 1895 PROWSE 99 [Guy's laws] A Plantation and Government is begun to be settled within this Country of Newfoundland and whereas among those persons that use the trade of fishing in these parts many disorders abuses and bad customs are crept in. . . 1620 WHITBOURNE 17 And it may be feared, that such a Plantation, growing to have strength, your subjects shall be (if not prohibited) yet at least hindred of their free trading and fishing there. [1622] 1895 PROWSE 130 At the *Bristow Plantation*, there is as goodly Rue now growing as can be in any part of England. 1626 [VAUGHAN] *Golden Fleece* Pt 3, p. 15 The *Plantations* well and orderly there once erected, will helpe us to settle our *Fishing Trade* farre more commodiously, then now it is. For whereas our Fisher-men set out at the end of February, they may choose to set out before the end of March, if every man hath his stages there ready against their coming. 1631 *Willoughby Papers* 1/57 If you please to send any men you may Send them by waye of bristoll if you Cane in the plantation ship that doth come. [1711] 1895 PROWSE 272 A plantation of three boats rooms in possession of Abraham Barrot and Richard Sutton in Torbay. Being ships rooms, they are dispossessed in right of ships that have occasion for them next year. 1944 *Yuletide Bells* . . .and how a certain missionary Bishop from a faraway spot called Newfoundland (or as some more called it 'the Wild Plantation') had visited the convent.

2 A tract or parcel of land on the waterfront from which a fishery is conducted; the buildings and structures on such ground where the fish is landed and cured; ROOM.

[1714] 1976 HEAD 185 Went in a Boat and Survey'd the Plantations at Fortune which is also a Tide harbour for small vessels. Beech for 30 Boats but not water [deep] enough for Ships. 1765 WILLIAMS 14 Why don't our Fishermen extend their Fisheries Northward? The Reason is very clear: The Expense of building Storehouses, clearing of Plantations, and building Fishing Rooms, Stages, Etc. Etc. are very expensive. [1794] 1968 THOMAS 116 We call it Jerseyman's Plantation because a Jerseyman was the last person who Resid'd here; but it is now deserted, the man, having failed, became a Wreck in point of property, with the rest of the Settlers in this Bay. This little Plantation forms one of the charmingest scenes I have yet beheld in Newfoundland. [1812] 1966 *Evening Telegram* 27 May, p. 6 [for sale] A small salmon plantation at Trinity without buildings. 1896 *Dial Notes* i, 380 ~ ground with buildings and improvements for fishing purposes. T 25–64 He was engaged in general fishery, principally codfish. And he had a little plantation on the Labrador. He used to send crews down there.

planter n *OED* ~ 3 'a colonist' (1620–), *DAE* 1 (1618–), *DC* 1 a (Nfld: 1620–) for sense 1; *OED* 7 Nfld (1860–), *DC* 1 b (1841–), 2 a, b (1771–; 1875–) for sense 2; *DC* 2 e (1944–) for sense 3; *DC* 2 d (1905–) for sense 4. See also LIVYER, SETTLER.

1 A settler in Newfoundland as opposed to a migratory English fisherman; merges in certain contexts with sense 2.

1610 *Willoughby Papers* 5a [They] shall bee the counsell of the said Companie of adventures and planters in the said teritories and Countryes. 1626 [VAUGHAN] *Golden Fleece* Pt 3, p. 15 And likewise the *Planters* themselves may fish for Cod there a moneth before our *English men* can arrive thither, and also after they are gone they may fish almost all the yeare after. [1663] 1963 YONGE 55 We presently hired a sloop from a planter and sent the mate with divers men

alongshore to get possessions, as they call it. [1680] 1976 HEAD 19 There is Store of wood in all places for many [st]ages and generally Neer at hand except in some particular places farr to fetch as at St John's, by reason of ye Many plantrs Residing and many ffishers resorting thither. [1718] 1793 REEVES 89 These things are done by masters of ships, when the admiral has been in harbour, without his order. By this irregular proceeding the strongest man gets all, and the rest of the creditors nothing; so that the next year a planter is forced to hire himself out for a servant. [1794] 1968 THOMAS 165 The Planters, as they were called, grew jealous of the Fishermen and discord and contention was evident in every little Settlement. 1819 ANSPACH 265 These bye-boat keepers kept also a certain number of servants; and, in process of time, became resident planters. 1969 HORWOOD 171 [They] landed here as planters and sharemen in the great days of the shore fishery and the transatlantic fish trade.

2 A fisherman and owner of fishing premises, boat or small vessel who, supplied by a merchant, engages a crew to work on the share system; SKIPPER.

[1771] 1792 CARTWRIGHT i, 156 I sent Shuglawina on shore there, with a letter to Guy's father, who is a planter. 1792 PULLING *MS* Aug While we were gone up the Exploits, Mr Slade, a merchant at Fogo, lost four salmon nets, and one of Mr Clark's planters lost the major part of a herring net. [1805] 1976 HEAD 234 [There is] anxiety expressed among the Planters at the Out Harbours to avail themselves whenever their circumstances will admit, of the Saint John's market, where they come in great numbers and dispose of their fish and oil, and purchase their supplies on much better terms than at their respective homes, owing to the competition. [1822] 1928 CORMACK 109 The fishermen, or planters, as they are called, obtain their outfits, to enable them to carry on the fisheries, from the merchants at Fortune Bay. 1861 DE BOILIEU 32 The man who prosecutes, or speculates in, the fishery, is called the Planter; and his mode is generally to hire his men by the voyage, giving them food and lodging, with the use of a boat, for half their labour, retaining, however, the cod-livers for himself. [1898] 1905 *Nfld Law Reports* 29 In the case of Ridley & Sons there was a number of large planters, such as Messrs Henry Thomey, John Pumphrey, John Ryan and others who supplied other planters, whose servants claimed on Ridley & Sons as receivers of the voyage. 1924 ENGLAND 255 [proverb] 'The planter's eye spreads the water horse.' (The boss of a fish room gets the fish quickly spread.) 1953 *Nfld Fish Develop Report* 15 Most Newfoundland fishing enterprises consist of crews numbering three or four men under the charge of a skipper, or 'planter' as he is called in some districts. 1976 CASHIN 48 Also many of the outport dealers, planters or merchants operated their own coastal schooners or boats, which were continually coming to St John's for additional supplies of all kinds.

3 Migratory fisherman from Newfoundland who conducts summer fishery from a 'station,' 'room' or harbour on the coast of Labrador; ROOMER, STATIONER.

1947 TANNER 748 *Planters* or *Stationers* (white shore

fishers mostly from Newfoundland). T 141–65[2] That would be right in the height of the floaters, planters and the schooners that run [for] the firms. 1970 *Daily News* 2 June, p. 9 The 'planters' are fishermen who have summer premises along the coast (of Labrador).

4 On the coast of Labrador, a settler of European or mixed European and Inuit descent engaged in fishing and trapping for furs.

1849 MCLEAN 161 The planters, as they are designated, live in houses which they call 'tilts,' varying in shape and size according to the taste or circumstances of the owner. 1896 LOW 42 Northward of Sandwich Bay, the white inhabitants are, for the most part, descended from Hudson's Bay Company servants, who married Eskimo women and remained on the coast after their services had expired. They are known along the coast as 'planters.' 1907 WALLACE 30 In the year I had spent in Labrador I had never before heard a planter or native of Groswater Bay swear. 1947 TANNER 720 He had for years followed the life of a 'planter'; that is, had engaged in the fisheries during the summer and trapped in the winter, trading with the Hudson's Bay Company and drawing his supplies from them.

5 Attrib, comb **planter fisherman**: see sense 3.

1979 *Evening Telegram* 15 Oct, p. 6 Captain Burden's father was a planter-fisherman with a 'room' at Merchantman's Harbour in the mouth of Alexis River, Labrador.

planter fishery: fishery for cod conducted by migratory fishermen from Newfoundland operating from a 'station' or 'room' on shore (P 245–67).

planter man: see sense 2.

T 141/67–65[2] A lot o' we fellers in our generations [have] become planter men and got ahead better than what the sharemen did.

planting vbl n See PLANTER. Comb **planting business**: the operation of a fishing enterprise by a 'planter' who employs a crew usu on the share system.

[1889] 1897 *Nfld Law Reports* 395 For fully thirty years her deceased husband carried on a 'general planting business' in the fisheries on the Labrador, and had during that time John Munn & Co as his supplying merchants.

play v Phr *play with the devil*: to play solitaire.

C 69–1 Whenever she saw me playing cards by myself she would tell me I was playing with the devil. P 108–75 'Playing with the devil again!'—said to someone playing patience.

plim v Cp *EDD* ~ v[2] 'to swell out' esp s w cties.

1 To expand or swell from absorption of liquid.

1920 WALDO 160 A man who ate hard bread and drank water said 'it plimmed up inside and nearly killed me.' T 75/7–64 He fulled an oval boiler with rice, cover on the stove, and it began to plim. T 194/5–65 We had a half bag of bread down there. He was plimmed so tight as he could plim. P 148–65 During the thaw, a

gravel road is soft. It plims up, then goes down. 1979 POCIUS 36 One woman described how she boiled a particular brin bag with coarse mesh to make the strands 'plim right together' in order to use it for a mat.

2 Of a boat, cask or barrel, to absorb water so as to become watertight.

[c1900] 1978 *RLS* 8, p. 25 A vessel's or boat's planks when [they are] drawn apart by heat [are] then put in the water to plim or swell and close up. 1920 GRENFELL & SPALDING 151 When a boat is not 'plymmed,' it leaks in all its seams. 1937 DEVINE 37 ~ To make a barrel or keg tight by filling it with water or standing it in running water to soak. P 99–69 The boat plimmed up as soon as she went in the water. 1981 *Evening Telegram* 4 July, p. 18 He left [his boat in the pond] for a few days to 'plim up'. . .prior to a fishing trip.

plover n Comb **plover curlew**: black-bellied plover (*Squatarola squatarola*) (1959 MCATEE 28).

plug n See *Fisheries of U S* 173.

1 Wooden stopper or peg for the drainage-hole in the bottom of a dory (P 113–73).

Q 67–53 There is a plug in the bottom of the boat with a piece of rope through it and a loop on the outside. If the boat turns over, the men will have something to hang on to. This has saved the lives of many men.

2 Attrib **plug hole**: see sense 1 above.

1971 NOSEWORTHY 232 ~ The hole in the bottom of a dory to let the water run out when the dory is pulled up on the beach.

plug strap: length of line securing dory 'plug' to the craft; DORY STRAP.

T 145–65 The other one [had] his arm around the plug strap—that would be the strap that kept the plug in the dory when they want to let the water out.

plug-eye n SCULPIN, a scavenger fish (*Myoxocephalus octodecemspinosus*) (P 11–79).

plumboy n *Gray's Botany*, p. 819. Fruit of the dwarf raspberry (*Rubus pubescens; R. acaulis*) (1956 ROULEAU 35); DEWBERRY.

1858 [LOWELL] i, 94 Some simple flowers grow here among the stones and shrubs, and berries in their season. . .plumboys, bake-apples, crackers, partridge-berries, horts, and others. 1947 TANNER 740 From about the middle of August the women and children are engaged in berry-picking, especially bake-apples. . .and plumboy. 1970 *Evening Telegram* 22 Apr, p. 18 But we knew the taste of. . .plumboys plucked purple black from a thorn thicket. C 71–130 ~ an edible berry very similar to the raspberry but darker in colour when ripe. A mature berry is deep purple or black. It appears to be a number of small, round berries joined together. The plant looks much like a raspberry plant and is usually found around the edges of rocks.

plunder n also **plundering**. In phr *second*

plunder: goods stolen from a person who had previously plundered or stolen them.

1966 FARIS 208 Action taken if someone is victimized by those taking from his garden or store for a 'scoff' is to attempt to get it back after it is cooked, by 'second plundering' (i.e. taking it, when ready to eat, from those who 'bucked'—or 'plundered'—it the first time). . .also applies to goods plundered from ship wrecks, for 'bucking' goods initially plundered is regarded as legitimate, and it is said 'second plunder is the sweetest.'

ply v *OED* ~ v¹ 2 obs (c1386–1753); *EDD* v 1 esp s w cties. To bend or be bent; twist.

P 245–55 After the ship was pulled off the rocks, it was found that her propeller was plied. T 90–64 The smaller [barrels], the stock would be narrower. The larger the package, the easier [the stave] would be to ply. T 96/7–64¹ But now he couldn't ply, see, couldn't take un off his back, and he brought un down again and the crowd took un off of his back. P 148–68 One of [the anchor's claws] is plied and one is broken off. P 148–70 The iron barrel was plied in a U-shape.

pod auger n also **pat auger***, **pot auger***, etc [pɒt̮ 'ɒːɡəɹ, pɒt̮ 'ɒːɡəɹd, 'pat̮ ˌɑːɹɡəɹ ˌdɛɪz, 'pɒt̮ ˌɒːɡəɹ ˌdeiz, pɒt̮ 'ɒːɡəɹ ˌdeiz, pɒt̮ 'ɒːɡəɹ ˌdɛɪz, pæt 'ɒːɡəɹz ˌdɛɪ, 'pɒt ˌɒːɡəɹ ˌtɛɪm]. Cp *OED* pad sb³ 8 'socket of a brace,' pod sb 1; *DAE* pod auger (1833–1878); *Am Speech* xxiii, 114: pod auger days (1887: Maine). Phr *pod auger days, ~ time(s)*: bygone days, olden times.

P 37 Pat auger times. A very remote period before modern inventions. T 208–65 That come from Spain away back in pot auger time. T 250–66 In them times, back in pot auger days, very few families [were] here; probably six, seven families. P 167–67 They dressed like that in podogger days. 1970 *Evening Telegram* 16 July, p. 2 Me father's father had a tiff with a lord of the realm back in podauger days. C 71–92 Pot auger—a term meaning hard, difficult, or poor times [long ago]. 1976 GUY 59 What feeds we used to have. Not way back in the pod auger days, mind you. That was before my time. P 245–77 Pot hook and hanger days or pot auger days (the old days). P 148–79 That's one of the old ones—way back in pothogger time.

pod auger v *Dial Notes* iii, 585 ~ 'to live. . .aimlessly' Indiana. To act in a carefree manner.

P 152–58 Pot augering—fooling around.

poegie n also **poojy*** ['pɒˑdʒɪˑ] *Labrador Inuit puijik* 'seal.' A seal.

[1771] 1792 CARTWRIGHT i, 153 I sent the *Poegie* shallop with a herring-net to Chateau. T 172/3–65 Their dogs was kingmik, and a seal was a poojy.

poison n

Comb **poison berry**: one of a variety of plants thought to produce poisonous or harmful berries; BLUE BERRY.

1898 *J A Folklore* xi, 281 Poison berries. *Clintonia*

borealis. 1956 ROULEAU 35 ~ *Actaea rubra*. *Arctostaphylos alpina*. T 207–65 This [blueberry]—you've seen it in the woods perhaps; poison berries some calls 'em.

poison eel: conger eel (*Conger oceanicus*).

1976 GUY 108 Pizen eels (conger) are grey and rough and have wavy fins the whole length.

poison flower: blue flag (*Iris versicolor*) (P 148–63).

poison snake: variety of eelpout (*Lycodes reticulatus; L. vahlii*) (1971 *RLS* 3, p. 3).

poison turnip: cow-parsnip (*Heracleum maximum*) (1956 ROULEAU 39).

poison v Cp DINNEEN neimh 'poison,' neimhneach 'peevish, passionate, spiteful.' To cause to be annoyed, irritated, disappointed or completely disgusted.

1924 ENGLAND 115 We'm havin' a fine, smooth time alang. Most gen'ly it'd poison ye wid frost, out yere. . .but now we'm havin' it pretty moild. P 148–60 [The hat] would poison me if I saw it on someone else. T 55/6–64 They come aboard for a piece of fat pork from you, bumming hard bread. And crowds of 'em aboard, women and men—poisoned with 'em. P 245–64 'I'm poisoned,' usually said in a tone of deep resignation, with no suggestion of doing anything about it. P 148–76 There's crowds of people goes to work every day and poisons theirselves so they can live a half-decent life and get something for their families. 1980 *Daily News* 29 May, p. 3 [The St John's City] Council is also 'poisoned' with the possibility CN's recent announcement about plans to add 350 rooms to the Hotel Newfoundland, may jeopardize the plans of local [entrepreneurs] for the development of land adjacent to city hall.

poker¹ n Stout pole used to break ice and push ice-pans away from the bow of a vessel.

1842 JUKES i, 261 The pokers were large poles of light wood, six or eight inches in circumference, and twelve or fifteen feet long: pounding with these. . .the men would split the pans near the bows of the vessel, and then, inserting the ends of the pokers, use them as large levers, lifting up one side of the broken piece and depressing the other. [c1900] 1978 *RLS* 8, p. 25 ~s: sticks used on board a sealer to fend off loose pieces of ice. 1916 MURPHY 11 Pokers, made of firewood with a stout rim of iron around one end of the poker from which protruded an iron dart about four or five inches long, used in shoving the ice pans from before the bows of the stout ships. 1936 SMITH 62 In less than an hour there were two boats alongside with twenty men in them, armed with pokers and hatchets. They all got going, chopping ice and pushing it away, and in less than an hour we had the schooner clear. 1972 SANGER 239 ~s. Twelve- to fifteen-foot wooden poles used to warp sailing vessels through loose ice.

poker² n Cp GREENLEAF (1933), p. 339 "Jolly Poker" and n. A chantey; HAULING SONG, HEAVE V: HEAVE-UP SONG; also attrib.

C 151–61 The following are a list of "Johnny Pokers"

or "Jolly Pokers" sung when men are hauling boats at Port-de-Grave. The custom was always for to get a poker-man to sing the pokers and he used to sit in the boat and be hauled along. C 43–71 One fellow was so good at singing The Poker that none of the men would really be hauling until he came to the final word *haul* in these final lines: Oh me Jolly Poker / What the hell's the matter / Oh me Jolly Poker, haul!

pole n
    1 (a) A long, stout stick of wood, shod with iron, used to fend ice-pans from bow of sealing vessel; POKER[1]; (b) 5–8 ft (1.5–2.4 m) stick with an iron hook and spike fastened to one end, used to assist sealer on the ice and to kill seals; BAT n, GAFF n.
    1832 MCGREGOR i, 223 They are always prepared for sea with necessary stores and fire-arms, poles to defend them from the ice, &c., before the Feast of St Patrick. [1867] 1978 *Haulin' Rope & Gaff* 27 "Terra Nova Seal Fishing": The young, ye see, we manage fine— / [They] differ frae the alder kin'— / As ae stroke frae a batsman's pole / Puts them at once into control.
    2 Attrib, comb **pole birch**: tall, straight birch suitable for building purposes.
    [1783] 1792 CARTWRIGHT iii, 14 We descended this hill on the east side, and there found the finest spot of pole-birch I ever saw, both for goodness and quantity.
    pole buoy: float with an upright stick to mark the position of stationary fishing-gear; PRYOR, SPOT BUOY.
    1937 DEVINE 38 [A prior is] a pole-buoy attached to a net or trawl. Its rope is hauled taut at the moorings, so that the *prior* stands out of the water on end and can be seen from a distance.
    poleman: one who propels a boat or canoe using a pole.
    1842 JUKES ii, 147 In passing these it requires the poleman to look out carefully, for as you dart along you have. . .to decide on which side of the rock it is best to pass.

poll n   also **pow** [poɒl, poʉl, po·ʉl]. Cp *EDD* ~ sb[1] 1 'head, esp the human head.' Top and back of a person's head; area of loose skin at the back of an animal's head; scruff.
    1895 *J A Folklore* viii, 30 A Newfoundlander speaks of his head as his *poll*. 1904 *Daily News* 28 Sep "A Song for Fishermen": Bond must have his eyes, in the back of his 'pow' / So make him arise, with his bundle to go. T 169–65[1] I lost my grip on the fox's poll and I told Esau for to hold [his tail]. T 391/3–67 They'd bite you, but there's a way to catch 'em, right by the poll. Once you gets 'em back there in the poll, they're finished then.

pollard n   Cp *OED* ~ sb[2] 'tree which has been polled or cut back.' A dead tree still standing; WHITING.
    [c1900] 1978 *RLS* 8, p. 22 ~ A dry stick in a green woods, kindling wood. P 191–73 ~ A dead tree, usually hollow.

polly pitchum* n   also **polly peach***, polypudjum, etc. Type of fern prescribed in folk remedies; rock polypody (*Polypodium vulgare*) (1898 *J A Folklore* xi, 283).
    C 63–1 A woman gave this to her [pregnant] daughter. It was a home brew concoction, the ingredients picked off the rocks or trees. 'Her mother gave her polly pitchum; she'll be all right.' C 75–132 A cure for fever of pregnant women: take a polly peach [lichen] from a crevice of a rock. The polly peach was steeped and given to the mothers after the baby was born to clean the blood and bring back their strength.

poltogue* n   also **fall tucker*** JOYCE 303 polt-hogue; DINNEEN palltóg, falltóg. A smack; a kick (1968 DILLON 150). Cp KIRLOGUE.
    T 139–65 'Here, Josiah,' he said, 'take my cuffs an' if he comes another inch further I'll give un the fall tucker.' P 79–73 What a poltogue Bill gave John on the side of the jaw!

pompey n   Cp *EDD* ~ sb 2 'tea-kettle.' A small broad-bottomed tin kettle with bevelled sides; PIPER (P 113–55).
    1925 *Dial Notes* v, 338 ~ A small sloping tea kettle.

pond n   *OED* ~ sb 1 b 'local' (1480–), *DAE* 1 'esp New England' (1622–), *DC* 2 esp Nfld (1693–) for sense 1; *DC* 1 (1760, 1954) for sense 2; *DC* 4 a obs (1832, 1849) for sense 3.
    1 A natural body of still water of any size; lake.
    1612 *Willoughby Papers* 1/20 We found great store of paunds [on] every side as we passed, and in every paund great store of beavers nestes. 1620 WHITBOURNE 10 And likewise the Bevers, Otters and such like, that seeke their food in the Ponds and fresh Rivers. [1794] 1968 THOMAS 57 Twenty Mile Pond, so call'd from its being that space in circumference, from its magnitude properly is a Lake. [1811] 1818 BUCHAN 22 The lakes and ponds abound with trout, and flocks of wild geese annually visit them. 1842 BONNYCASTLE i, 197 There is, therefore, water communication, with few interruptions, both from St George's Bay and the Bay of Islands, to the northward and eastward, through St George's River, the Great Humber River, the Grand Pond, and Red Indian Pond, and other series of extensive lakes (rivers being called brooks, in Newfoundland, and lakes, ponds,) to the Bay of Nôtre Dame. 1872 DASHWOOD 268–9 Having paddled through a series of long lakes, connected by short streams, towards sundown we reached a large lake or 'pond' as they are termed by the natives, fifteen miles long and five broad. 1927 RULE 11 I was much struck with the amazing number of small 'ponds'—tarns as they would be called in the North of England. 1950 PARKER 17 More of the sheets of water are in fact known as ponds than the maps would suggest; I found that Lake St John was mainly spoken of by loggers as 'John's Pond.'
    2 A shallow river estuary, lagoon or harbour of fresh or salt water, sheltered from the sea by a sand-bar or low strip of land; BARACHOIS.

[1772] 1971 SEARY 260 The Pond. . .Argentia. 1870
HOWLEY *MS Reminiscences* 15 Fortune. . .like Grand
Bank is a barred harbour with a narrow entrance
between two breakwaters. The Pond inside is fairly
large and affords shelter for the fishing schooners, but
they can only get in and out at the full tide. When it
runs out most of the pond is quite dry and the schooners lay down on their sides in the mud. 1951
Nfld & Lab Pilot i, 104 The Pond, which lies about 3
cables eastward of Latine point, is a small salt water
lagoon to which there are at present two narrow openings, available for boats at high water.
  3 An area of still water in a river; GULLY[1],
STEADY, STILL.
  1792 CARTWRIGHT *Gloss* i, xv Steady in a river. A
part where the bed widens, inclining to a pond, and
there is no perceptible stream. 1874 MURRAY &
HOWLEY 369 Long stretches of still water, commonly
called ponds by the trappers, constitute the greater
part of the river's course, and these are connected by
gentle currents.
  4 Attrib, comb **pond diver**: shoveller (*Spatula
clypeata*).
  1870 *Can Naturalist* v, 299 A summer migrant, and
generally distributed over the island. . .[the 'Pond
diver'].
  pond gull: ring-billed gull (*Larus delawarensis*).
  1951 PETERS & BURLEIGH 231 It is well named 'Pond
Gull' for it frequents fresh-water ponds during the
nesting season in many parts of its range. 1967
HORWOOD 190 The boys told me of a colony of 'pond
gulls' that had established itself away up-country near
the head of the brook. They had discovered what
turned out to be the second large colony of ring-bills
ever known in Newfoundland.
  pond hockey: loosely organized ice hockey
played on a frozen pond without referee (M 70–
9).
  pond hopper: small aircraft equipped with
pontoons (P 148–66).
  pond ice: smooth, uniform freshwater ice (Q 67–
51).
  1846 TOCQUE 199 Our pond ice has now become an
article of exportation. . .being sent to the United States
and the West Indies, where it usually sells at forty shillings per ton.
  pond poppy: a variety of yellow pond-lily
(*Nuphar variegatum*) (1956 ROULEAU 35).

poodler n ['pɒdləɹ]. Cp *EDD* ~ 'immature
coal-fish.' Ocean pout (*Macrozoarces
americanus*) (1971 *RLS* 3, p. 3).

pook n [puk, pɒk, puˑk, puːk] *OED* ~ sb 1
local (1718–); *EDD* sb[1] 1 s w cties for sense 1.
  1 Haycock; freq in phr *in pook, pook of hay*.
  1895 *J A Folklore* viii, 30 ~ a haycock. 1957 *Daily
News* 10 Aug, p. 2 Spreading the new mown hay in the
morning, tossing it on the hayfork at noon, and raking
it together in 'Pooks' before sundown made a lot of
work; but it was also lots of fun. T 145–65 We didn't
call 'em mows or piles of hay. We call 'em pooks of

hay. P 118–67 You can leave [hay] in pooks for the winter. 1972 MURRAY 254 The next evening, it was placed
in tiny 'pooks' (i.e., stacks) all over the garden; next
day larger 'pooks' were made, and finally one large
'pook.'
  2 Protruding crest in the top of a hat.
  T 87–64 Their hats had a kind o' notches; they stick
up [into a] little pook. C 71–124 I have a pook in my
hat.

pook v [puːk] *OED* ~ v[1] 1 local (1587–); *EDD*
v[1] 1 s w cties. To place hay in a stack (P 13–74).
  1964 *Can Journ Ling* x, 43 ~ To pile hay around the
centre stick of the stack.

pooked off ppl phr Of ears, stuck out, protruding
(P 141–75).

pooking vbl n Comb **pooking rod**: one of the two
long sticks with a net in between, the whole
forming a rack on which hay is carried to the
'pook' or stack (1971 NOSEWORTHY 232).

pooky a Shaped like a haycock.
  T 92/3–64 The head of the hat, the crown [was] kind
of oval, round—not up too high, not pooky.

poole n [= Poole, Dorset]. Attrib **poole gun**: a
long, muzzle-loading gun; GUN; POWDER ~ .
  1895 PROWSE 62 The long single barrel gun—known
as the Poole gun. 1910 *Nfld Qtly* Dec, p. 30 Every
house possessed one or more six foot Poole guns, and
every man was skillful in the use of firearms. 1927
DOYLE (ed) 7 "All Around Green Island Shore":
Besides, I have a big Poole gun / About five feet barrel
or more. 1973 MOWAT 33 They had them old Poole
guns, as some calls them, swile guns eight feet long and
firing a charge would kick you clean out of the boat if
you didn't mind.

pooler n A salmon which has lain a long time in
a river but not yet spawned (1792 CARTWRIGHT
Gloss i, xiii).
  [1770] 1792 CARTWRIGHT i, 21 In the course of this
day, we killed about thirty salmon, but they were all
poolers; which shews, that the season for their coming
fresh from sea is past.

poor a *OED* Poor Jack obs (Nfld: 1682, 1775),
Poor John 1 obs (c1585–1841), *EDD* ~ a 1 (9) ~
john 'cod found in poor condition in shoal water'
Sh I Ork for comb in sense 2.
  Comb **poor jack**: see **poor john**.
  [1663] 1963 YONGE 58 [The surgeon of a fishing vessel receives payment in cash] besides which he has one
hundred poor Jack from the whole [catch]. 1682
COLLINS 93 That sort of Cod that is caught near the
Shore, and on the Coast of Newfoundland and dried,
is called *Poor-Jack*. 1720 FISHER 52 We may easily
catch our Cod ashoar, and dry them after the manner
of the Poor-Jack of *Newfoundland*, which it's impossible the *Dutch* can do. 1934 LOUNSBURY 34 During Elizabethan times there does not seem to have been any

extensive demand for Newfoundland fish in England. 'Newland' fish was sometimes used to provision the fleet and the army in Ireland or to feed the poor in England. The greater part of the annual catch of 'Poor John' or 'Poor Jack' was sold to foreigners for shipment to southern Europe.

poor john: dried and salted cod-fish; HARD DRY.

[1585] 1905 HAKLUYT x, 100 In this ship was great store of dry New land fish, commonly called with us Poore John. [1612] 1958 SHAKESPEARE *The Tempest* II, ii, 23–6 A fish: he smells like a fish: a very ancient and fishlike smell; a kind of not-of-the-newest Poor-John. 1628 HAYMAN[1] 37 Yet let me tell you, Sir, what I love best / Its a *Poore John* thats cleane, and neatly drest / There's not a meat found in the Land, or Seas, / Can Stomacks better please, or lesse displease. 1672 [BLOME] 189–90 But the whole *Coast* of the *Island*, affords infinite plenty of Codd, and *Poor John*, which is the chief *Commodity* of the *Isle*. 1720 FISHER 62 And besides this Fishing upon the Coasts for dry Fish, or *Poor-John*, as they call them, there is a most lucrative Fishing for Green Fish. 1940 INNIS 11 Cod taken in winter in Iceland and dried in the frost were known as 'stockfish'; when taken in summer and dried they became the 'poor john' of Newfoundland.

poor man's cows: goats.

T 14/21–64 Goats—we used to call them poor man's cows.

pop n also **poppy**. Children's name for grandfather (P 148–64).

P 148–65 ~ intimate name for grandfather, on mother's side. P 245–80 I saw poppy this morning—at nan's house.

poppy n An extract of the buds of the yellow pond-lily (*Nuphar variegatum*) used as a home remedy.

M 69–7 [He had] more than his share of headaches and sinus trouble [and] used to use poppy [made from] water-lily buds. These buds were collected in the spring before flowering and then boiled in a pot. With his head covered by a blanket [he] bent over the boiling water and inhaled the steam.

porch n Cp *ADD* stoop, etc, esp Maine quots for porch. A room attached to a house, usu at the back, often adjoining the kitchen and used for various storage purposes; cp LINNY.

1878 WHITE *MS Journal* 10 Sep 2 porches Back of House [£10]. [1886] LLOYD 76–7 In addition to which there is a small 'back house' or 'porch' built on the warmest side of the hut, in which firewood is kept. 1887 *Evening Telegram* Christmas No 9 A sudden, hurried scuffling in the back porch and a loud rap at the door, startled them from the quiet in which they had been working. [1918–19] GORDON 47 The local dogs started in on Turk, so I brought him into the porch for the night. P 121–67 ~ This is a small room one must pass through to enter the kitchen; the chamber between the back door and the kitchen door. M 69–7 Each house usually had another large room called the porch, which held water barrel, fire wood, outside

clothing, guns, etc. It was the custom during the summer time for the whole family to eat in the porch, except Sundays, or when guests came. 1972 MURRAY 187 The porch which occupied approximately half of the back section of the house, was, in wintertime, a cold cheerless place, and little better in summer. Here the snow would be swept off outer garments and footwear, or muddy feet would be wiped clean in a rough mat. 1977 RUSSELL 167 When he went out to his back porch for a dipper of water to put in his kettle, what should he find in the back porch but King David, Jethro Noddy's billy goat.

porcupine n Comb **porcupine racket**: type of Labrador snowshoe.

1884 STEARNS 149 There are great varieties of form, called usually from some fancied resemblance to the tail of an animal. The beaver, the otter, the porcupine, and the bobtailed rackets are used perhaps more frequently than any others along this coast, though the long racket is used throughout many of the Canadian provinces.

pork n [= salt-cured fat from a hog; see FATBACK, FAT-PORK]. For comb in sense 2: *OED* ~[1] 3 ~ fat (1856).

1 In designations of food, esp baked preparations, with cubes of pork fat as an ingredient: **pork bun, ~ cake, ~ joe, ~ toutin** [see TOUTIN].

1916 GRENFELL 40 With a good bag of non-freezable pork buns from our cook, and a large sack of dry capelin for their dogs at night. . .the friends left. 1966 SCAMMELL 64 An' I told her it looked to me like a few pork buns and a couple tomcods. 'Tother boys laughed at me and so did the teacher. They looked just like the pork buns we haves, Sattidy night, mom! T 398–67 Well, in our days in Christmas, all we'd get'd be a pork bun, a molasses bun. 1918 TOWNSEND 269 Tea and trout, pie and 'pork cake,' made a good supper. [1960] 1965 PEACOCK (ed) i, 141 "On the Schooner *John Joe*": 'Make us a pork cake,' old George he did jaw / To the cook in the fo'c'sle a-mixin' the dough. T 347/9–67 You made pork cake, which was a wonderful thing. Fat pork, cut in little squares, and you mix it with bakin' powder an' milk, and you bake cakes, because it didn't crumble up, it didn't go scrappy, didn't dry, an' they could warm it over the fires. T 246/7–66 Good old-fashioned pork joe. I don't see none of 'em now. You make that out o' molasses an' flour an' a bit of pork; cut up big junks o' pork, about half inch big. 1973 BARBOUR 47 [The snack] usually consisted of a slice of molasses bread, raisin buns, pork toutons, or bang-belly.

2 Attrib **pork fat**: FAT a: FAT-PORK.

[1770] 1792 CARTWRIGHT i, 53 [The jays] even suffered me to stroke them with one hand, while they were eating some pork fat out of the other. [1811] 1915 BUCHAN 82 [All had the parts affected] rubbed with rum and pork fat. P 148–64 ~ salt pork.

pork rind: 'fatback' pork; cp SCRUNCHINS 2 (C 69–6).

pork tit: child's pacifier (M 68–18).

porpoise n Cp *DC* ~ 'beluga. . .whale' (1897–).

Attrib **porpoise hide**: skin of the beluga or white whale (*Delphinapterus leucas*).

1909 GRENFELL[2] (ed) 356 The white whale is a slender, graceful animal about twenty feet long. His skin forms excellent leather, called 'porpoise hide'; it is very impervious to water.

post n Cp *DC* ~ n [fur] 'trading post' (1789–). A cove or harbour with space on the foreshore for the erection of facilities for the conduct of the fishery in adjacent coastal waters; STATION.

[1774] 1792 CARTWRIGHT ii, 40 As the lower part only of the harbour is open, I do not expect any seals coming near us till our whole post is entirely frozen up. 1792 ibid *Gloss* i, xiii ~ A station from whence a fishery is carried on.

posy n Cp *EDD* ~ 4 'any single flower.' A flower of a dandelion, buttercup, etc.

c 65–2 The posies (buttercups) are closed up so we're goin' to have rain. M 68–16 Deadman's posy was a good cure for piles. Some people call it yarrow. P 29–74 On the hops was a little posy, rosette flower, pale green in colour.

pot n For combs. in sense 3: *DC* ~ cover Nfld (1906); cp *EDD* ~ sb[1] 17 (22) ~ day 'day on which broth is made in the kale-pot.'

1 A large iron cauldron in which an infusion of spruce bark is prepared; BARK POT, BARKING KETTLE.

[1794] 1968 THOMAS 62 In every Harbour, Creek and Cove there is what may be called a Parish Pott, this holds about 20 gallons, and it is filled with water and Spruce Bark, which is boiled together; they then dip the netts of the Fishermen in to it, and the Sails of their Boats to which it is a great preservative. This Pott is generally the property of one person, and it is seldom that you will find more than one of these Potts in a Creek or Cove. For dipping a set of Boat Sails they pay 3/6d. [1832] 1981 *Them Days* vi (3), p. 40 Let the two large boats downe on their sides. . .and got the pots in order to begin boiling bark.

2 Phr *pot or brim*: heads or tails, played with a hat or cap.

c 69–2 To see who would have the first choice we would throw up our cap. Before throwing up the cap we would ask 'Pot' or 'Brim'? One boy would then take pot or brim and depending on which he took the other boy would of course have to take the other. The cap was then thrown in the air. If the cap came down bottom up it would be 'pot' and the boy who said pot would have the first pick of the players. If it came down top up then the boy who said 'brim' would have first choice. If the cap came down on its side it was 'snigs' and the cap had to be thrown up again.

3 Comb pot bar: pot-hook; COTTERALL.

1960 *Evening Telegram* 11 Aug, p. 7 I remember grandfather's old home, with the large, open fireplace, the flagstones surrounding it, the dog irons, the pot bars and hangers from which pots and kettles were suspended over the open fire.

pot cover: see **pot lid**.

1906 LUMSDEN 57 There was a clumsy imitation in use, made of wood, called 'pot-covers,' which they wore with long boots.

pot day: day of the week on which meat and vegetables, cooked together in a 'boiler' or pot, are served; cp SOLOMON GOSSE.

P 245–55 ~s. Days when pots of salt beef, pork, spare ribs, turnips, carrots, potatoes, and cabbage are cooked and served hot. M 68–24 Tomorrow [Thursday] is pot day.

pot-head: see POT-HEAD.

pot-lid (racket): type of snow-shoe.

1792 PULLING *MS* Aug I hastened back to my tilt as fast as I could then pulled off my *pot-lid* rackets (which are round, about the size of the rim of a man's hat) and put on my Indian rackets (which are the shape nearly of a boy's paper kite). 1866 WILSON 215 When the snow has fallen sufficiently deep, the snow path is formed. This is done by a number of men walking with pot-lid rackets. 1937 DEVINE 38 ~ The circular snow shoes or rackets worn by woodsmen and hunters: home made, of thin pieces of board nailed to a frame of birch bent to shape. T 55–64 I had a pair o' pot lids on me—something like a racket. C 75–146 ~s. They were made of a birch stick which was rounded and the two ends fastened together. Several other birch sticks were nailed across the rounded one. A rope was brought up through the snowshoe and fastened to the instep of the foot. P 13–77 ~s. Round snowshoes about 12 in. in diameter, made of 2 in. plank, or else of wooden frames 'filled' with small rope. These snowshoes were strapped unto horses' hooves when the snow was too deep and heavy for the horses to wade through. Used especially when breaking new roads or picking up scattered timber in such conditions.

potato n See also PRATIE, TATIE. *OED* ~ 6 ~ garden (1778), ~ ground (1753).

Attrib, comb **potato cellar**: detached structure built below, or partly below, ground level for winter storage of potatoes, etc.

[1794] 1968 THOMAS 156 A few days ago a person in Ferryland had opened a Potato Cellar, the door of which was only pushed to. C 71–98 ~ Use slate rock piled about 8 feet high and supported by wood beams. Fill in cracks with moss and cover with dirt. Inside, in separate bins, potatoes are kept all year.

potato garden: area enclosed for the cultivation of vegetables; GARDEN.

1869 MCCREA 246 I knew there'd be a sprinkling in that old potato-garden. T 43/7–64 You'd have a fence around that and that would be referred to as a potato garden or the cabbage garden.

potato ground: parcel of land, enclosed and cleared of rocks, used for the growing of potatoes, etc; GROUND.

1819 ANSPACH 374 Swine are likewise extremely common, to the frequent annoyance of the gardens and potatoe-grounds. 1842 JUKES ii, 37 They had abundance of good potato-ground cleared, and excellent potatoes. 1976 GUY 16 For there is not much of the smell of land in Newfoundland. Only a bit from the bakeapple bogs at the end of July and the steam flying out of the potato ground on the first warm days in June. 1979 TIZZARD 282 Caplin [had to be obtained] and put on the potato ground. By the time we got caplin to put on the potatoes they were usually through the ground, but the caplin were put on just the same and then they were 'hilled.'

potato grounds: yeast made from potatoes.
1972 MURRAY 217 Potato grounds were also used for leavening when the house-wife was short of regular yeast.

pot-head n   *DC* ~¹ (Nfld: 1863–). Northern pilot whale (*Globicephala melaena*); also attrib.
1853 PANL GN 2/2, July, p. 370 About New Harbour the failure of the codfishery has been amply made up by their success in taking above 950 'pot Heads,' giving about a Tun of oil to each person employed. 1878 TOCQUE 482 Great numbers of what some call Black-fish, and others Pot-heads, are killed during the autumn along the shores. 1937 DEVINE 37 ~s. Small whales. . .known by American fishermen as 'Black-fish.' 1976 PINHORN 49 ~ This toothed whale is easily recognized by the prominent bulbous head which is the source of the local vernacular appellation 'pothead' and by its broad-based dorsal fin. Small numbers were harpooned in 1947–50 and the first large landings (3100 in 1951) began when the practice of driving the animals ashore was initiated. P 148–75 Pot-head drive: practice of chasing pot-head whales into shore around Dildo by banging on metal, making great deal of noise.

pound n   *OED* ~ sb² 5 c (1873), *DAE* ~² 2 (1870) for sense 1; *OED* 5 a, b (Nfld: 1809, 1867), *DC* 3 obs (1784) for senses 2, 3; *OED* 1 c (1877 quot), *DC* 1 (Nfld: 1770–) for sense 8 (a), *EDD* sb² 1 Sh I Ork D for 8 (b).
1 A net-trap to catch fish, esp migratory salmon; pound-net; TRAP¹.
[1771] 1792 CARTWRIGHT i, 141 Shuglawina. . .advised me to make a pound to catch salmon, and shewed me where to place it. [1774] ibid ii, 14 We had a hundred and seventy fish in the nets, and twenty-seven in the pound. 1861 DE BOILIEU 41 Besides the cod, Labrador is rich in salmon. The mode of catching these is with a 'fleet' of three nets, which are fastened to each other so as to form a [pound]; the fish in striking the first and even the second of these may not be meshed, but he cannot escape the third, as, when once there, it is impossible for it to retrace its swim. 1915 HOWLEY 270 He. . .was killed by them while taking salmon out of his pound (weir) in New Bay River.
2 Variety of enclosure used for the temporary holding of fish for or during processing; PEN¹; RAM'S HORN.
[1766] 1971 BANKS 134 [The fish] are then Carried From [the Salt Pile] & the Salt washd out of them in sea water by towing them off from shore in a Kind of float made for that Purpose calld by them a Pound. P 148–65 ~ wooden vessel, filled with fish, taken into the salt water to wash them. P 248–67 ~ part of stage used for salting fish. 1971 NOSEWORTHY 233 ~ A large box anchored offshore where lobsters are stored to keep them fresh. 1975 BUTLER 74 First we would hoist

the mackerel from the boat to the wharf. Then we would take them in the store and put them in pounds. We would then rip them down the back, take out the gill and gut, scrape the blood from the fish, throw them in vats of clean water and let them soak again.
3 Section of a fishing-boat in which the catch is stowed; ROOM.
1809 *Naval Chronicle* xxi, 21 There are pounds or enclosures made on the deck, for each fisherman to throw in what he catches. 1882 TALBOT 25 The fishes were quickly unhooked and cast into the pounds—square spaces in the boat set apart for their reception. P 102–60 In the centre half (of boat) between stem and stern they had a pound filled up to within 10 inches of thwart with large rocks.
4 On a sealing vessel, a section of the hold or a structure erected on deck for stowing seal 'pelts.'
1842 JUKES i, 279 The hold is divided by stout partitions into several compartments or 'pounds' to prevent too much motion among the seal-skins and keep each in its place. 1894 CHAFE 5 The S. S. *Commodore*. . .towed a quantity of seals from Baccalieu up Conception Bay on her tow rope, as far as Western Bay, where they were taken on board, and placed along with others in pounds on the deck. 1924 ENGLAND 137 Down there, at the aft end, weltered a 'pound' of sculps. 1972 BROWN 35 The piles of pelts were hoisted aboard with tackle rigged from the masts. It was slippery, unstable cargo, and was stowed in wooden pounds in the holds to keep it from shifting too much. 1972 SANGER 239 ~s. Smaller holding units, temporarily installed in the cargo holds, which were designed to reduce the danger of fat rendering during the sealing voyage.
5 In processing seal oil, one of the compartments into which the framework or crib of the vat is divided.
1852 ARCHIBALD 6 The crib [of the seal-vat is] generally divided into nine apartments or pounds.
6 A storage compartment for various dry materials.
1924 ENGLAND 10 Everything was a gorgeous confusion of screaming winches, of shouts and orders, of coal in deck pounds. 1975 BUTLER 46 But we had a top weight of coal, big mainsail over her and we had a coal pound on the for'ard hatch. P 245–77 We always had two pounds in the coal cellar, one for soft coal and one for the hard, long burning coal. 1979 TIZZARD 86 There were two pounds on the easterly side of the store in which the dried caplin for the dogs were stored.
7 A framework of heavy logs or beams, filled with rocks, forming the crib of a wharf or breakwater; BALLAST: *ballast bed*, SUNKEN POUND (P 148–65).
8 (a) Enclosure to capture wild animals; (b) enclosure for domestic animals.
1823–4 *Edin Phil J* 161 The Micmacs say, among other things, of the Red Indians, that they catch deer in the *pound*, and kill them with spears, and that they dry great quantities of their flesh in autumn, as provision for winter. P 148–63 We'd build a pound for a pig. 1974 MANNION 68 After the milking each evening cows were folded in a 'pound' by the farmstead for the night

and were driven out after the morning's milking to graze unfenced land around the settlement. P 143–75 Women and children gathered eggs from the henhouse in the morning, and both were assigned the task of catching any escapees from the hen pound before they reached the kitchen gardens.

9 Small enclosed space off kitchen in which utensils are stored.

P 108–71 In our house we had a 'pot pound' off the kitchen where were hung along the walls pots and pans and sundry kitchen aids. You could push aside a sliding door and walk into it.

10 Attrib **pound board**: plank used to construct wooden partitions or enclosures; PEN BOARD.

1924 ENGLAND 39 'If a man die,' the carpenter informed me, 'us builds un a coffin out o' pound boards, an' salt un down [ice him].' P 169–80 The pound boards is some slimy sometimes.

pound v *OED* ~ v² 4 (Nfld: 1887). To divide an enclosed space into compartments for storage; to partition.

1873 CARROLL 9 Sailing vessels as well as [steamships] are pounded off in the hold to prevent the seals' pelts from shifting. P 181–77 My father had our basement pounded off.

pourdown n *ADD* ~ n. Downpour (of rain).

T 50–64 But the big storm outed the works—the power o' the Almighty God. That's the only one outs the [forest] fire. . .the pourdown o' rain.

pow See POLL.

powder n *EDD* ~ sb 1 (2) ~ devil; *OED* sb¹ 5 b (b) ~ gun.

Comb **powder-devil**: small charge of gunpowder in a cloth or paper container.

1924 ENGLAND 319 ~ A rag enclosing charge of powder. P 244–55 To celebrate the Relief of Ladysmith [during the Boer War] your grandfather placed several hundred powder-devils along the board fence and fired them off.

powder gun: muzzle-loading weapon; GUN.

1913 *Christmas Chimes* 5 But the prolific display of flags and salvoes of 'powder guns' [in connection with the wedding] had no reference whatever to his prominence or his wealth. C 68–10 The young fellows got a great kick out of firing powder guns at a wedding. It was common to see men buying in powder a day or two before the wedding and to hear them talk about the 'big loadin'' that so and so fired one time at such and such a person's wedding. M 69–5 At noon on Christmas day a series of shots rang out, as many of the men had their powder guns (muskets) to welcome in Christmas. 1976 *Decks Awash* Aug, p. 28 There was a big night parade, the ever popular shooting off of powder guns.

prate v Cp *EDD* ~ 1 (1) ~ -apace esp s w cties. Comb **prate-box**: chatterbox.

[1900 OLIVER & BURKE] 61 "Interfering Prate Box": Prate box gäve a sigh and praty winked her eye, / And praty took her best hat down. 1937 DEVINE 49 [A

stage-head clerk is a] prate-box who knows how to do everything except work. M 65–9 He is a regular prate-box!

pratie n Cp *OED* potato 2 d: pratie A-I (1832–); *EDD* I (32) Ir; DINNEEN práta, préata. See also TATIE. Potato; also attrib.

1904 *Daily News* 19 Aug "This Is the Place to Live and Die": For he didn't know 'green fish from dry,' / Yet, he knows the Poor House 'praytees.' T 80/1–64 He sowed some praties one time, see; it was frosty. T 158–65 I'm goin' to put on a meal of duff tonight—meat an' duff an' praties. C 66–10 A person might accidentally pick up a small rock and put it in the sack with the potatoes. This [pratie rock] would be boiled with the potatoes and then kept as a charm to cure toothache. 1972 MURRAY 251 Potatoes were sown by both men and women. The seeds were set in raised 'beds' separated by deep trenches. Each sower wore a 'pratie' (potato) bag, a sort of pouch, tied around his middle, containing a supply of seed. 1979 *Evening Telegram* 12 Nov, p. 6 The taste of Old Ireland, was either 'pratie oatens' or 'boxty bread'. . . The 'pratie oatens' were mashed potatoes mixed with oatmeal, made into cakes and fried with a mixture of sausage fat and bacon.

preacher n A dissenting clergyman.

[1886] LLOYD 37 The clergyman of the Church of England is known as the 'Minister'; of the Church of Rome as the 'Priest,' and of the Wesleyan or any of the dissenting bodies as the 'Preacher.' [c1904] 1955 DOYLE (ed) 36 "The Kelligrews Soiree": With Cluney's funnel on my pate, / The first words Betsey said: / Here comes a local preacher / With the pulpit on his head.'

preliminary n Familiar name for a division of the school system corresponding to grades 7 and 8.

[1905] 1976 WINSOR 35–6 Five obtained passes last year in the Council of Higher Education examinations: one in Intermediate, three in Preliminary and one in Primary. . . (Probably should explain for our young readers, that Intermediate corresponded to our present Grades Nine and Ten; Preliminary to Grades Seven and Eight, and Primary to Grade Six.) P 124–71 22 Having successfully completed primary, you moved into the preliminary grades for two years, where you would hopefully emerge with your preliminary two grade. 1975 BUTLER 28 And then we were supposed to go to the school in Buffett; that was to study for Primary. . . I sat for Primary and I passed and I was studying for Preliminary [at the age of fourteen].

premises n sg or pl The waterfront property, esp the stores, wharf, 'flakes,' and other facilities, of a merchant, 'planter,' or fisherman; ROOM.

[1748] 1888 HOWLEY 400 The water formerly flowed [so as to] damage the . . .plantation or grounds [and I find that] the aforesaid Gutt was the property of the aforesaid premises. 1842 JUKES i, 6 The merchants' wharfs and premises were crowded with their men unloading the vessels, and preparing the seals for the

oil vats. 1887 *Colonist Christmas No* 11 The stores and
dwellings extended from there about as far westward as
Newman's premises. 1901 *Christmas Review* 5 The traveller, who visited our principal outports twenty years
ago, will look in vain today for the big premises of the
big planter. As in Feudal times, the castle of the lord
was the centre from which all immediate social life
radiated, so in the Newfoundland outports the adjacent village drew its supplies and existed only thro the
premises of the principal planter. 1936 SMITH 106 At
last I had premises [a fishing stage, small hold. . .a
dwelling-house, puncheons and a good bawn for
spreading about 300 quintals fish] at Cutthroat of my
own, which I could improve on as circumstances permitted. 1975 BUTLER 62 Individual fishermen fishing
from their own premises would either sell the fish fresh
to the merchant or cure it on their own premises and
sell it dried to the merchant. 1977 BUTLER 31 Another
man and I on Wareham's premises commenced work
on the vessel *Annie Francis*, and repaired all the dories
of the fishing fleet and did all other carpentry jobs
needed to be done on the fleet of boats and vessels.

press v To place split and salted cod-fish in a
'pile' or 'faggot' at various stages of the curing
and drying process.
[1726] 1976 HEAD 73–4 Then they take [the split and
salted fish] out & Spread them upon the Fleakes,
where they lay for a day or two if the Weather will
allow, only at Night they turn them back up, & if they
need it, press them twice or thrice, in the time that they
are lying after this manner. 1954 INNIS 56 He said that
the men fished with hook and line on Sundays [and]
that they dumped very large stones used to press dry
fish, into the harbors, thus spoiling the anchorage.

pressed p ppl also **press**. Cp *OED* ~ , prest 'subjected to pressure'; *Cent* press-pile 'a. . .kench of
fish' (Canada). Of split and salted cod-fish,
placed in a pile and weighed down, sometimes by
stones, so as to aid in the curing process; hence
comb **press(ed) pile**, and phr *in press, under* ~ .
Cp FAGGOT n.
[1620 WHITBOURNE 51 The Harbor of *Renouze* [is]
in danger to be spoiled by the stones and ballast that
are throwne into the same, which are to be seene in
great heapes when the water is cleare.] [1653] 1895
PROWSE 167 That noe Ballast, Prest stones nor anything else hurtfull to the Harbours bee throwne out to
the prejudice of said Harbours, but that it be carryed
ashore and layd where it may not doe annoyance.
[1663] 1963 YONGE 58 When well dried, it's made up
into prest pile, where it sweats; that is, the salt sweats
out, and corning, makes the fish look white. 1896 *J A
Folklore* ix, 34 A *press pile* is fish piled up to make, and
a *press pile compass* is a trick played on a green hand of
sending him to the next neighbour to borrow the press
pile compass. The party applied to has not one to spare
and sends him to the next, and so on as on April fool's
day. T 175/7–65 'Tis leaved in salt bulk for so long; and
then it's took out and in press so long; washed out, and
then in press—perhaps a day or a couple o' days. 1979
TIZZARD 295 The bark about six or seven feet from
around the butt part of the tree was peeled off in the

spring of the year and put under press so that by the
time the pieces were to be used they would lie very flat
and covered the fish without any difficulty.

prickle n Needle of spruce or fir; SPRINKLE[1].
T 30/3–64[1] They'd put spruce boughs, prickles, those
prickles, down under the bed. When they get in bed
they stick right into 'em.

prickly a Cp *OED* prickle-back (1746–). Comb
prickly back, also **prickley**: any of a variety of
sticklebacks (*Gasterosteus* spp); small fish found
in fresh or brackish water; SPANTICKLE.
1883 *Fisheries Exhibit Cat*[4] 174 [Nfld:]
Mussels. . .Prickly Backs. . .Cat Fish. . .Dog
Fish.[*OED*] 1899 ENGLISH 19 'Let us go down to that
little river,' she said, 'and catch some prickleys.'
[(c1904) 1960] BURKE (ed White) 23 "The Kelligrews
Soiree": We had pork fat and stuffed rat, / And pricklies in a beaver hat. 1966 *Evening Telegram* 24 May, p.
13 Sure you haven't got any gear strong enough to
catch a tuna on. The last line you had wouldn't land a
prickley, let alone one of them herring hogs, as we
used to call them in my day. P 198–67 ~ Small freshwater fish, about 2 inches long, some with small thorn-like
fins on their backs. C 70–34 My cousins and I used to
take great sport in catching 'pricklies' and 'doctors.'
1982 *Evening Telegram* 9 Jan, p. 12 They used sticklebacks or 'pricklies' for these initial experiments and
found that. . .our 'mud trout' (local name for eastern
brook trout) weren't crazy about the fare.

pride n Cp *NID* ~ n 7 pl 'male genitals.' A beaver's testicle; comb **beaver's pride**: a specific for
male potency.
[1783] 1792 CARTWRIGHT iii, 22 Nor do they ever
castrate themselves to escape their pursuers, for that
part is not only of no use, but both those, their prides,
and oil-bags (the two latter vessels being common to
both sexes, and the prides only used in medicine,
known by the name of castoreum) lie so completely
within them, that the operation must be performed by
a very skilful hand indeed, and with the greatest care
not to kill them. C 75–141 For potency a man should
steep out beavers' testicles and drink the liquid. This is
called beaver's pride. 1976 *Decks Awash* v (5), Oct, p.
16 Beaver castor, locally called beaver pride, is the
scent glands of the beaver. It is supposed to be able to
relieve stoppage of water and it is good for an aching
back. It was soaked in warm water and the liquid
drunk.

prime a
1 Of harp or hooded seals, perfect with respect
to condition of fur and 'fat.'
1873 CARROLL 15–16 Forty-six years ago sealing vessels did not leave the different ports in the Island until
the 17th of March, or thereabouts, for the prosecution
of the sealing voyage, at which date the different kinds
of young seals were not considered prime until the 20th
or 25th of March. 1916 MURPHY 35 A few days later
the *Echo* got clear, and very soon ran into the prime
young harps. 1924 ENGLAND 242 Prime-cut harps, dem
is, an' wonnerful fine!—De nothren patch, I'm

sayin'!—We'm goin into de blood of 'em, now! [1960] 1965 LEACH (ed) 208 "*Neptune*": 'Twas over the rail you cou!d wash your hands; she was so deep in fat, / With thirty thousand prime young harps got slaughtered with their bat.

2 In designations of a quality, cure or 'cull' of dried and salted cod-fish; cp MERCHANTABLE.

[1890] 1897 *Nfld Law Reports* 430 Words merely descriptive cannot be registered so as to give an exclusive right to the use of the words, and if such had got on the register the court would, on application, remove them; such as in this case the words 'prime dry codfish,' which are common to the trade. 1937 *Seafisheries of Nfld* 56 The standards of cull for Labrador codfish are:- Choice or Number One. Prime or Number Two. Cullage. 1977 RUSSELL 42 There's been no quintal of Prime Madeira Codfish or No. 1 Spanish produced in Pigeon Inlet since.

3 Of a specific area in inshore waters, habitually prolific in cod-fish; CHOICE 2.

1913 *FPU (Twillingate) Minutes* 19 Dec Friend Fred Newman spoke about the fishing ground from lower head to long point re cod nets saying the prime grounds was taken up with cod nets. He says it should be stopped in the future. 1953 *Nfld Fish Develop Report* 49 In some instances, the number of crews exceeds the number of prime berths by more than four to one. 1975 BUTLER 54 As one might expect for an island community situated on prime fishing grounds, the principal occupation of most male residents was fishing. 1977 BURSEY 132 The next year all the prime berths were claimed again before we got here from Old Perlican.

primer n   Cp *OED* ~ sb[1] 'school-book for teaching children to read.' See also BOOK. The first or primary school level, in which children learn letters and reading.

M 69–14 My mother's first cousin was teaching 'primer,' as the primitive kindergarten was then called. P 124–71 At that time, you went to school and took primer, which I feel must have been similar to what [kindergarten] is today. [1977 RUSSELL 86 [His] mother sent him off to school for the first time. . . He had a slate, a Primer and a slate pencil which was standard equipment in those days.] 1979 TIZZARD 112 My sister Eleanor continued her studies from Primer to Grade XI Matriculation without a break.

principal a   Comb **principal man**: in a fishing crew, the man in charge of the boat; BOAT MASTER; a member of the crew with skill and experience in fishing and related activities.

1878 TOCQUE 293 Boat masters, or principal men, are paid about £10 as wages. 1975 BUTLER 62 A man who was a good splitter was a principal man in a boat's crew.

prinkle See SPRINKLE[1].

prior See PRYOR.

prog n   also **proggin's*** *OED* ~ sb[2] 1; *EDD* 11. Food (for a meal or 'lunch'); victuals, grub or winter supplies. Also attrib.

1869 MCCREA 237 Our little baskets of prog—hard-boiled eggs, cold tongue, fowl, and sandwiches, with a screw of salt—lay ready open. [1891] 1981 *Evening Telegram* 28 Sep, p. 6 The hunters began to 'make our prog' (i.e. putting their pork, flour and tea, etc into loads). 1933 MERRICK 103 A progbag is to a trapper what a dittybox is to a sailor. In it he carries a few matches, a few candles and cartridges, a spare pair of sox, his pencil, an awl and crooked-knife, a snowshoe needle, sewing materials, deerskin and sealskin patches and other cherished encumbrances. 1955 DOYLE (ed) 52 "Sealers' Song": Though short of grog still lots of prog / To bring us home quite hearty. P 126–67 Bring along the prog tub [for the fishing boat]. P 184–67 Tell the missus I won't be home prog time. 1971 *Evening Telegram* 22 Apr, p. 3 Don't forget the prog bag [for the picnic]. C 71–38 At supper time she would call, 'Come in to your proggins.'

prog v   To feed (another); provide food and accommodation.

P 189–66 'Prog the clergy'—a common phrase meaning that the clergyman would stay for a week in each parishioner's house while waiting for his residence to be built. 1979 *Daily News* 9 Aug, p. 10 I'm going to prog you this week and somebody else will do it next week.

proggin's* See PROG n.

prong n   Cp *OED* ~ sb[2] 1 'instrument or implement with two, three or more. . .tines'; *EDD* sb 2 'a pitchfork' s w cties.

1 Hayfork (1895 *J A Folklore* viii, 30).

[c1945] TOBIN 8 "Hay-making in Brown's Garden": Maidens are matrons with homes of their own / . . .in bright days gone by / As prong or rake they did duly ply. T 26–64[3] I cut twenty-nine hundred [pounds] o' grass one year, I an' my daughter, an' put it in, lugged every bit of it in, an' stowed every bit away. He never had to put a prong in it when he come home from Labrador.

2 A long-handled implement with one or sometimes two sharp tines used to transfer fish from one place to another; FISH-FORK, PEW[1], SPRONG.

[1819] 1826 [GLASCOCK] i, 164 "For the *Royal Gazette*": 'T appears in you a disease, / For you *cut-up* whom *ye* please. / Careless of your *ranc'rous* prong / Is saucy 'OLD GO-ALONG'. [1831–39] 1926 AUDUBON 232 Arrived at the vessel, each man employs a pole armed with a bent iron, resembling the prong of a hay-fork, with which he pierces the fish, and throws it with a jerk on deck, counting the number thus discharged with a loud voice. 1842 JUKES i, 226 Here the fish are forked out of the boat with a kind of boat-hook or pike, the prong being stuck into the head [of the fish]. 1925 *Dial Notes* v, 339 ~ A large two-tined fork for tossing fish. T 361/2–67 For us in Greenspond it would be the traditional fisherman's prong with the two tines on it. 1979 *Evening Telegram* 8 June, p. 6 Among them is the tradition of using a prong as a tool for handling fish.

prong v   Cp *OED* ~ v 1 'to pierce or stab with a

prong' (1840–). To transfer (fish) from one place to another with a long-handled tined implement; to fork (hay); PEW v, SPRONG v.

1963 *Daily News* 8 July, p. 4 After throwing the fish to the stage head, a man has then to prong it into a crate, then from the crate to a table to gut it. T 43–64 You'd be back again to the schooner with a skiff load o' fish. Prong that in on the deck an' go for another one. M 71–117 From the trapskiff the fish was pronged onto the stagehead. P 143–75 Another man inside the loft pronged the hay to the further end where children jumped on the piles to press the hay more firmly together. 1977 *Decks Awash* vi (3), 28 It's a lot easier to handle our fish on our own stages. I can prong the fish from the boat to the truck when the water is high.

prosecute v Cp *OED* ~ v 2 'to engage in, carry on' (1576–, esp 1883 quot). To engage in the pursuit of fishing and sealing.

[1693] 1793 REEVES xvi Now in order to promote these great and important purposes, and with a view. . .to induce his Majesty's subjects to proceed early from the ports of *Great Britain* to the banks of *Newfoundland*, and thereby prosecute the fishery on the said banks. . . [1766] 1971 BANKS 146 For the Prosecuting of this Fishery many hands are Left every year in the different Harbours who by this & furring give a very good account of their time to their Employers. 1809 *Naval Chronicle* xxI, p. 22 The vessels generally stay but three days in the harbour, before they go out again on the banks to prosecute their voyage. 1866 WILSON 33 From its harbor, every spring, hundreds of vessels sail for the ice in quest of seals; and, on their returning from their sealing voyage, sail again in the month of June to prosecute the cod-fishery on the coast of Labrador. 1873 CARROLL 27 . . .90 sailing vessels prosecuting the seal fishery on the west side. [1920] 1933 GREENLEAF (ed) 285 "The Fishermen of Nfld": They lived to prosecute their v'yage / On Grand Banks' stormy shore, / Where's many a hardy fisherman / That never returns no more. [1951] 1965 PEACOCK (ed) i, 105 "The Banks of Nfld": 'Twas east-be-south we steered, me b'ys, the Grand Banks for to find, / To prosecute the fishing there we all felt well-inclined.

prosecution n Cp *OED* ~ 2 'plying of a pursuit, occupation' (1631–). The activity of fishing and sealing.

1846 TOCQUE 196 In the prosecution of the seal fishery the sabbath is violated to an awful extent. 1870 HOWLEY *MS Reminiscences* 26 How Spanish Room came by its name I could not ascertain but in all probability in olden days during the earlier prosecution of the fisheries by foreigners some Spaniards may have located here and established what was called a fishing room. 1882 TALBOT 5 Their sole business, it may be said, was the prosecution of the fisheries.

protestant n JOYCE 307–8 for sense 1.
1 Salt herring (1903 *Nfld Qtly* June, p. 4).
P 131–70 We got good old protestants for dinner.
2 Comb **protestant deal**: method of dealing cards in the game of forty-fives.
P 108–70 Playing 45's, the usual deal is two cards to

each player and then three. Sometimes to vary it, or change the luck, the dealer will give out a 'Protestant Deal'—three at first and then two.

protestant whisker: side-burns and beard under the chin; cp WHISKER[1].
1930 BARNES 207 He wore a big whisker that came down to his middle. . . Them days, anybody the sailors would see with a great big whisker like that—they used to call it Protestant whiskers. 1937 DEVINE 38 ~ Whiskers under the throat. P 212–60 There he sat in his top hat and his Protestant whiskers.

proud a *EDD* ~ adj 3, *ADD* 2 for sense 1; *OED* 8 b obs, *ADD* 3 for sense 2.
1 Pleased.
1858 [LOWELL] i, 159 'Ef 'ee'll plase to take me an' Izik,' said Jesse Hill, 'we'll be proud to go along wi' 'ee, sir.' 1909 GRENFELL[1] 67–8 'E said 'e was proud to see us comin' for un, and so 'e might, for it grew wonderfu' cold in th' day and th' sea so 'igh the pan could n' 'a' lived outside. 1924 ENGLAND 30 'Ain't got narr bunk, is it?' he kindly asked. 'Well, sir, I'm ondly too proud to gi' ye mine!' 1932 BARBOUR 61 That old 'saddle back' certainly cheered us up. In a few hours we saw several and we were very proud to see them, but we could not kill one. T 54/63–64 An' after a week there was nothing at all about him. They were just proud he was gone, his people.
2 Of a bitch, in heat (P 13–73).

pryor n also **prior** DC ~ pole (Nfld: 1774–). A wooden pole fixed vertically to a net or buoy; SPOT BUOY. Also comb ~ **line**, ~ **pole**.
[1774] 1792 CARTWRIGHT ii, 29 Having filled up the boat with whitings, pryor-poles and killick-rods, at high water we sailed home. 1792 ibid *Gloss* i, xiii Pryor-pole. A long pole, which is fastened to that end of a shoal-net that is farthest from the land, by a piece of rat-line; which, not being long enough to reach to the surface of the water, causes the top of the pole to appear, when the water is covered with ice or lolly. 1861 DE BOILIEU 85–6 A long pole fastened to one corner of the net and a short one on the other corner (the former called a 'pryor' and the latter a 'bobber') show where the net is. 1937 DEVINE 38 Prior. A pole-buoy attached to a net or trawl. Its rope is hauled taut at the moorings, so that the *prior* stands out of the water on end and can be seen from a distance. C 66–5 Prior is a pole about 30 feet long which is fastened to the buoy rope (strayline) in winter time. This makes the buoy rope easy to find when the ice goes out the bay and it also prevents the ice from towing the buoy line away. 1971 NOSEWORTHY 234 Pryor-line. Rope used to haul up nets.

ptarmigan n also **pattermegan, ptharmakin**. Cp *OED* ~ b (1893–), *DAE* 1 (1872–). Applied variously to Allen's willow ptarmigan (*Lagopus lagopus alleni*) and Welch's rock ptarmigan (*L. mutus welchi*); GROUSE, PARTRIDGE.
[1770] 1792 CARTWRIGHT i, 44 I killed a pair of eider ducks, a grouse, and a ptharmakin. 1792 ibid *Gloss* i, xiii ~ A bird of the grouse kind; it generally weighs about a pound, but seldom more. 1872 DASHWOOD

275 Flocks of wild geese soared over head, and packs of the Newfoundland grouse were frequently met with in the open places. These birds, misnamed ptarmigan by the settlers, are apparently the same species as the Norwegian grouse. 1959 MCATEE 25 Pattermegan. Rock Ptarmigan (Labr).

public n, usu pl Pupil of an amalgamated or non-denominational school.

C 68–22 There were battles over school games, etc [between us and the Catholic pupils] and I remember one chant we used: 'Publics, publics, ring the bell, / Catholics, Catholics, go to hell.' M 71–41 We used to call the Protestants 'publics.' I don't know why, but the two main divisions in the town were 'publics' and 'catlics.'

puck v   EDD ~ v[1] 'hit or strike sharply' Ir. To butt; to strike.

1902 MURPHY (ed) 73 "Fanny's Harbour Bawn": He stood no hesitating, but struck immediately; / This damsel mild, stood like a child, to witness the fray. / A pain all in my chest there struck before 'twas very long, / My person pucked and darling took on Fanny's Harbour 'Bawn.' P 198–67 Teacher, he pucked me. 1968 DILLON 150 Mind that cow, she pucks you know.

puck n   EDD ~ sb[2] 'a blow, esp a blow with the horns of a goat' Ir; DINNEEN poc 'a prod. . .of the horn.' A blow; a butt (1896 Dial Notes i, 380).

1968 DILLON 150 Boy, the cow gave me some puck, that time. I wouldn't like to get a puck o' her horns. P 76–70 I'll give you a puck in the belly.

puckawn n   EDD ~ sb 1 'he-goat' Ir; JOYCE 308; DINNEEN pocán. A goat.

C 73–164 A person having an unpleasant odor was said to stink like a puckawn. P 27–80 Puckawn rock is a hill of massive rocks where the goats hang out.

pucklin n   A boy.

1957 Daily News 7 Mar, p. 7 My two boys Haig and Hadow, were 'pucklins' then. P 184–67 Run along, you young pucklin! P 99–69 ~ a hardy boy making his first voyage to the fisheries.

pud n   EDD ~ sb[1] Ha W Do So Co. Hand.

P 40–78 Puds. Common name for a person's hands; used informally when referring to children.

puddick n   also **puttick, puttock** ['pʌdɪk, 'pʌdɨk]. Cp OED puttock[1] [= a bird of prey] b 'applied. . .to a person, as having some attribute of the kite' obs (1605–1631); EDD puddock 'kite or buzzard'; SMYTH 551 'a cormorant; a ravenous fellow'; DINNEEN patóg 'intestine; an animal's intestine stuffed and cooked.' (a) The intestinal tract of a seal, whale, or cod-fish (see GULVIN), esp the walls of the main sac or paunch of the alimentary canal; stomach; (b) figuratively, a glutton. Also attrib.

1792 PULLING MS Aug They keep the seal's fat in the puttooks of those animals. 1920 WALDO 161 'Pud-

dick' is a common name for the stomach. 1937 DEVINE 38 ~ A codfish's stomach. 1953 Nfld & Lab Pilot ii, 132 Puttick rock, with a depth of 4 fathoms over it, lies. . .northward of the northern extremity of the eastern island. T 54–64 They were wondering what was in [the whale's] inside, in his puddick or bowels. M 65–9 Used when referring to a person with an enormous appetite: 'He is a real puddick!' C 66–2 If you catch a cod and his puddick is up in his throat, there's a storm coming on. 1966 FARIS 223 He (or she) then takes the anal end of the fish's intestine ('puttick') and pulls it toward the head, grabbing the head with the same hand and in the same motion, and holding the back down with the other hand breaks off the fish's head on the edge of the table. 1971 Evening Telegram 29 Apr, p. 3 Ye'll get none of that Budget baloney here today. Perhaps some other day when our puddicks settle down again. M 71–103 A fish liver was used as bait and fish puddick (stomach) was gloved over the cork.

pue See PEW[1].

puerto rico n   Attrib **puerto rico fish**: a grade or 'cull' of dried and salted cod-fish prepared for the market in Puerto Rico (M 71–117).

1937 Seafisheries of Nfld 47–8 Medium Salted Dry Fish [is] known as Porto Rico Fish. . .must be well dried and show a dry, white, salty surface on the face.

puffin[1] n   OED ~[1] (1337–); DAE 1 (1835–) for sense 1.

1 Atlantic common puffin (Fratercula arctica); SEA-PARROT; also attrib.

[1766] 1971 BANKS 119 A number of Birds are about the ship which the seamen call Penguins Gulls Shearwaters one species of them with sharpe tails. Puffins & Sea Pigeons. . .we could not get any of them tho we took Pains. [1783] 1792 CARTWRIGHT iii, 53 I then went out a shooting in my yawl to Shag Rock, where I killed ten tinkers and five puffins. [1794] 1968 THOMAS 90 They make holes in the ground like Rabbits, in which they breed. People who go after their Eggs take Pick-axes and Spades to get at their nests, this is called Puffin digging. 1868 Royal Geog Soc xxxviii, 261 The first [iceberg] seen was 80 feet high, perfectly white, with a streak of ultramarine here and there, aground. Around it were whales, ducks, Arctic puffin, divers and tern of nearly every description. 1909 BROWNE 206 Puffins, or, as they are called in the Strait of Belle Isle, 'Paroqueets'. . .abound. 1951 Nfld & Lab Pilot i, 189 Duck island, the northernmost of the groups, is 296 feet high. Puffin bank, with a depth of 3½ fathoms over it, is situated about 7 cables east-north-eastward of Puffin island.

2 Local nickname for resident of Ramea (C 67–10).

3 Phr as far as ever a puffin flew: a very long distance (1937 DEVINE 21).

puffin[2] n

1 Harbour porpoise (Phocaena phocaena); PUFFING-PIG.

1964 Evening Telegram 28 Oct, p. 5 At least from Cape St Francis to Cape John, if not further, fishermen describe the small dolphins as 'puffins.' Fairly easy to see how this arose, too, since the dolphin breathes air, or 'puffs' when it comes to the surface. 1979 NEMEC 268 [From the nets, sharks, jellyfish, maiden ray, herring hog or puffin, and runner] are removed, whenever possible at the side of the boat or in the water itself.

2 A scavenger fish (*Myoxocephalus octodecemspinosus; M. scorpius*); PIG-FISH, SCULPIN.

1971 NOSEWORTHY 235 ~ A large type of sculpin, usually reddish in colour, and found around wharves. It is often jigged by boys who 'blow it up' by hitting the fish across the stomach with a stick.

puffing-pig n also **puff-pig** *OED* puff sb 9 b (Nfld: 1861); cp *DAE* ~ (1884). Name given to (a) harbour porpoise (*Phocaena phocaena*); (b) northern pilot whale (*Globicephala melaena*); HERRING HOG, PUFFIN[2].

1861 NOBLE 91 At the mention of the puff-pig, the local name for the common porpoise, we indulged ourselves in a childish laugh. A more ludicrous, and at the same time a more descriptive name could not be hit upon. 1883 HATTON & HARVEY 233 Another variety [of whale] is called puffing-pig and herring hog by the fishermen. [1900 OLIVER & BURKE] 24 Richard spied a lot of puffing pigs. 1976 GUY 60 We ate. . .puffin' pig (a sort of porpoise that had black meat).

puff-up n A pregnancy; birth (P 133–58).

1930 *Am Speech* vi, 57 I hear you are expecting a *puff up* at your house.

puit See OO-ISHT.

pull v Cp *EDD* ~ v 4 'to pull up by the roots' for sense 1. Cp HAUL v.

1 To collect flexible roots or pliable shoots suitable for use as fastenings or 'withes.'

[1774] 1792 CARTWRIGHT ii, 32 Four hands brought the traps from Atkinson Pond, hauled up the flat which is there, cut some killick-claws, and pulled rods.

2 Phr *pull oneself*: to masturbate; also as expletive (P 269–63).

3 Comb **pull-line**: rope used to raise a fishing-line or net to the surface; HAUL v: HAUL-UP (LINE) (1971 NOSEWORTHY 235).

pull-rope: length of line forming part of a cast-net and used to draw the 'tucks' together, closing the net; TUTTLE LINE*.

C 71–128 Attached to the circumference [of the cast-net] at regular intervals are lines which pass through the horn and are joined to a rope of about three fathoms, called the pull-rope.

pull-up box: wooden box or frame holding the propeller in a motor dory (1971 NOSEWORTHY 235).

pull-up dory: type of motorized 'dory' which, lacking a keel, has the engine-shaft in two sections permitting easy raising or lowering in shallow water (M 68–3).

pumbly a also **pommelly, pumly**, etc. Cp *EDD*

pumple 2 (2) ~ stone 'pebble-stone,' *ADD* pumble 'bit of hard rock embedded in soft limestone' Bermuda. Of rocks, large and coarse; fragmented; boulder-like; ragged.

1878 *Nfld Pilot* 166 Pomley Cove. 1951 *Nfld & Lab Pilot* i, 258 Pumbly Cove. 1953 ibid ii, 321 Pumbley and Clay coves. Ibid ii, 371 Pommelly Cove. P 213–55 ~ rock is broken, ragged rock, spread thickly. P 226–72 Get out of here with all that stuff. You'll have the garden gone to all pumbly little rocks. P 148–73 Of huge boulders worn by the waves: those are some pumbly rocks! 1977 *Inuit Land Use* 331 I came to another hill. There were a lot of pumly rocks on the lower side of that hill. That's where the fox went, right under the pumly rocks.

pumly See PUMBLY.

pummy n Cp *EDD* pomace sb 2: all to a pummy 'anything crushed to a pulp' W Do So D. A pulpy, squashed mass; phr *go/reduce to pummy*.

1924 ENGLAND 70 She began to shove through the ice, grinding it to 'pummy.' Ibid 225 The [seal] skins now began 'running to oil,' and the fat 'goin' to pummy,' which is to say, getting very ripe and degenerating to a nauseous mess. 1925 *Dial Notes* v, 332 To go to pummy: disintegrate. P 200–77 ~ mixture of chunks of ice and slush on the sea. P 2–80 Worthless potatoes are sometimes used to make pummy, 'mashed up' as one stage in preparing starch. It is also used in pranks, when children throw pummy at house windows at night.

pump n, v Cp PARTRIDGE pump ship 'to make water' naut for sense 1.

1 Phr *have a pump*: to urinate.

T 53/4–64 An' I said to myself, 'Now that's father or my other brother, see, went out to have a pump.'

2 Comb **pump-house**: men's urinal (P 148–61).

pump-trolley: railway trolley propelled by a manually-operated pumping-lever; hand-car.

T 100–64 That was in the Reid-Newfoundland Company time when we had those old pump-trolleys and there was no speeders.

puncheon n also **punch***. Cp *OED* ~[2] 'a large cask for liquids, fish, etc' now rare exc hist (1479–1833); *DAE* ~[2] (1760–1855) for sense 1.

1 The largest of the wooden casks used as containers in the fisheries; a molasses cask with a capacity of 44–140 gallons (166.5–530 l); MOLASSES PUNCHEON. Also attrib.

[1775] 1792 CARTWRIGHT ii, 94 Packed five tierces of fish, (a puncheon contains two tierces and a half; a hogshead, one and a quarter). 1873 CARROLL 44 Notwithstanding which, the top fish are often light salted, and the bottom fish in the puncheon, are salt-burned and often must be watered before being exposed to the sun for making. T 50/2–64 Some o' the puncheons'd gauge a hundred an' twenty an' a hundred an' thirty an' a hundred an' forty gallons, an' more of 'em ninety six. T 43/7–64 [It was] a leather thing tacked on to the puncheon's head. T 141/67–65[2] The biggest bark pots that we used to use around here—there's one up there in cove now—about a hundred gallons; about a puncheon o' water into un to fill un up. T 172/5–65 When the bark was strong enough, you'd put your linnet into the puncheons and dip the bark out o' the pot and put it in the puncheons. T 214–65 So he jumped in a punch o' molasses, an' then out of the punch o' molasses into a feather bed. C 70–11 ~ A large wooden container which was used for storing molasses imported from Barbados. The barrel was made of oak and bound with large steel hoops. It was about 4 feet high and 3 feet wide. It was too large to be lifted and had to be rolled.

2 Proverb *don't get into a puncheon when a barrel can hold you*: don't make a fuss about trifles (P 131–70).

3 Comb **puncheon tub**: puncheon sawn in half and used for various fisheries activities and processes; cp RAM'S HORN, TUB.

1936 SMITH 17 We would wash our fish from the knife before salting; when washing out we would use a swab and a cloth, using two puncheon tubs filled with sea water. T 43/7–64 You saw your puncheon in half an' you have two puncheon tubs [each] about five feet in diameter, and that'd hold a couple o' quintals o' fish. Then you'd dip up your water from the sea an' throw it in on that and wash out your tub of fish. T 141/65–65[2] I never rigged a puncheon tub [as a boy], but [you could] take a puncheon tub out of a feller's stage, put un overboard, put the spile into un, put a rock into un; take a piece o' board, an' get a stalligan or something an' paddle across the tickle. P 9–73 A puncheon tub is approximately one half of a puncheon, the puncheon being sawed in two pieces crosswise at the middle. It will hold forty-five or more gallons. It is used to wash codfish before putting them under salt and to wash them again before putting them under the sun to dry. 1973 HORWOOD 50 Then a puncheon tub was placed on deck and a dozen draw-bucketfulls of sea-water put in it. P 143–74 Small fish were pickled in a puncheon tub.

punt n   Cp *OED* ~ sb[1] 1 'flat-bottomed shallow boat, broad and square at both ends'; *DC* Nfld (1792–) for sense 1.

1 An undecked boat up to 25 ft (7.6 m) in length, round-bottomed and keeled, driven by oars, sail or engine and used variously in the inshore or coastal fishery; cp BOAT, RODNEY, SKIFF.

[1770] 1792 CARTWRIGHT i, 25 We got a punt of mine, and their small boat, into a winding pond, which lies between this river and Niger Sound. 1792 PULLING *MS* July About nine years since in the summer season he then taking up his boat in Gander Bay was out in his punt (or small boat) accompanied only by a boy. 1842 JUKES i, 28 Punt is the term usually given to a small row-boat. 1857 MOUNTAIN 6 [She had] one mast, a low, snug mainsail, jib and driver at the stern, though occasionally two masts, and foresail as well as mainsail. The latter is called a skiff, the former a 'punt and driver,' to distinguish it from a punt without that appendage. 1906 LUMSDEN 55 If confined to the Arm and

when the day was fine, a punt (in Newfoundland a keeled rowboat of peculiar native construction) and one man sufficed; if out in the bay to Deer Harbour, a 'cod-seine skiff' and half a dozen men might be needed. [1926] 1946 PRATT 169 "The Cachalot": And the islands of his pancreas / Were so tremendous that between 'em / A punt would sink; while a cart might pass / Without a peristaltic quiver. 1937 *Seafisheries of Nfld* 29 The gear most favoured by the Shore fishermen are cod-traps, cod-nets, hand lines, trawls and jiggers, and the boats used are schooners, trap skiffs, jack-boats, dories and punts; many of these are now propelled by motor engines. T 25–64 They called them punts. These would be about sixteen or eighteen feet long: two-men boats these were. T 43/7–64 A flat is flat-bottomed but a punt is moulded, you know—she's built by scale. Well, rodney is the other name for a punt. T 50/1–64 [Then] we runned off o' the easter bank. 'Twasn't too good. In a three barrel punt! 1975 BUTLER 54 Up until about 1880 the boats used by the first settlers [in Placentia Bay] were from five to seven quintals capacity. They were called punts and were manned by two men. They were open boats with the center part of the boat covered with boards called gang boards laid on the thwarts. There was a place in the aft and forward part of the boat called standing rooms for the fishermen to stand in when fishing. The boats were equipped with three sails, mainsail and jib.

2 In phr and proverb: *a pig, a punt and a potato patch; a fish in the punt is worth two in the water* (1895 *Christmas Review* 12); *fish in the punt, pork in the pot* (ibid); *in a leaky punt, with a broken oar, / It's always best to hug the shore* (ibid).

1905 DUNCAN 105 'Still and all, they's no country in the world like this!' said the old skipper. 'Sure, a man's set up in life when he haves a pig an' a punt an' a potato patch.'

3 Attrib, comb **punt crew** [see CREW], ~ **fisherman**, ~ **fishing**, ~ **load**, ~ **man**, ~ **master** [cp MASTER WATCH], ~**(s) piggin** [see PIGGIN], ~ **race**, ~ **skiff** [see SKIFF].

1842 JUKES i, 258 This evening the crew were divided into watches and punts-crews, and prepared their bats and gaffs. 1909 BROWNE 67 One still finds the 'hook and line' amongst the class of fishermen who are known as 'punt fishermen.' These are the class who are unable to purchase a trap or cod seine. 1864 *Times* [St John's] 2 Jan, p. 1 [Ballard Bank] will, no doubt, prove good fishing-ground and be of much advantage to the different stations along the coast, where, mostly punt-fishing prevails close to the shore. 1966 SCAMMELL 23 Mary was down on the stage-head that evening when her father came in with a half a punt-load of cod. She watched him pitch-fork the big ones up on the stage-head. 1937 *Seafisheries of Nfld* 35 The units of production in the Shore Fishery range from the man who fishes by himself, to the crew of the largest Labrador Floater, which usually numbers fifteen men. Between these limits are, the Punt Man who with another fisherman fishes with hand-lines, jiggers, trawls and cod-nets; the small skiffs that operate the winter fishery with crews of three men; the trap crews of from three to six men. 1842 JUKES i, 260 These punt-masters then drew lots [for position on the sealing vessel]. Each punt had. . .three men and a master attached to it. 1973 BARBOUR 51 A dory piggin is made of wood and shaped very much like the dust-pan one uses around the house. It has a short handle and is used to dip water from the bottom of a dory. A punt's piggin is also made of wood and shaped like a small bucket. It has a short handle, and is used to dip water from any boat other than a dory. 1917 *Christmas Echo* 12 A punt race took place in 1881; a dory race in 1886. . .a canoe race in 1888. 1964 *Daily News* 26 May, p. 8 One fisherman last week is reported to have filled a punt skiff out of nine of the fifteen nets he had in the water.

pup n   A blister, sore or inflammation common among fishermen whose skin is often in contact with salt-water; clipped form of WATER PUP.
1912 CABOT 80 Poor Spracklin, his arms and wrists set with fish boils, 'pups' in the vernacular, slept with his bandaged arms raised clear of all touch, in his face the look of the overworn. C 71–93 Pups [are] septic lumps which appear on the wrists due to chafing of oil-clothes when salt-water fishing. 1979 NEMEC 279 [Wet oilskins] induce 'pups' or boils which resist most cures.

puppy n   Phr *sleep in puppy's parlour*: to sleep on the floor in one's clothes.
[1771] 1792 CARTWRIGHT i, 181–2 Having caught a severe cold, by sleeping in puppy's parlour for the three last nights, I determined to return home. [1775] ibid ii, 53 Killed a porcupine, which we found in possession of the house, if it is worthy to be called one; for it has neither sides nor roof: however, we made a good fire on the hearth, and lay in puppy's parlour.

pure a, av, intens. *OED* ~ a 3 c 'true, real, genuine' obs for sense 1; *EDD* 6 'very' for sense 3.
   1 Real, actual; proper.
P 148–61 It's pure stone, not brick. P 148–63 This practice is a pure sign of an 'Informal' essay. 1977 *Inuit Land Use* 332 We'd steep out some bark off a juniper tree. That was real good for a bad cold, if you got it on your chest. You'd keep drinking that, and it's pure medicine for all that kind of sickness you know.
   2 Absolutely, utterly.
T 54/8–64 They passed along by this orange tree and orchard, an' their mouth was pure waterin' to get at th' oranges. P 148–66 [That drink will] pure kill you.
   3 Very.
1964 *Can Journ Ling* x, 45 ['Tis pure sad].

purse n   Comb **purse squid**: small squid with shape like a pouch.
1968 MERCER 1 Squids of this genus (*Rossia palpebrosa*) are small. . .and have a bursiform configuration, leading to such names as 'bottleass squid' and 'purse squid' in Newfoundland.

puss n   Cp *EDD* cat sb¹ 9 'game of "tip-cat".'
One of several varieties of children's game which opposing sides play with sticks, variously sized and named, one of which is flicked into the air from a base or goal; PIDDLY, TIDDLY. Cp CAT⁴. Also attrib.
T 246/9–66 Puss an' duck I know was played. C 69–19 Puss is the game for the spring. It is played with two sticks; one is a long one used for flicking the other. C 71–115 No one caught you if you put your puss-stick across the hole; if the person who picked up your tiddley-stick could throw it and hit your puss-stick, you were out.

pussel n   Cent ~ n Labr. Giant or deep sea scallop (*Placopecten magellanicus*).
1909 GRENFELL² (ed) 454 The great scallop. . .locally known by the name of 'pussel,' is found in the Strait of Belle Isle. It is excellent eating. . .and fried in lard or butter. 1925 *Dial Notes* v, 339 ~ A kind of shell fish. C 71–40 Pussels [is a word] used by fishermen of Winterton, Trinity Bay when talking of the shellfish scallops.

put v   Cp *OED* ~ v¹ 2 'to propel (a stone or weight)' for sense 1; for phr in sense 2: cp GROSE (1785) owl: to catch the owl, *EDD* catching, and owl 2 (3).
   1 To throw (an object); HEAVE.
T 191–65 'If he shows there again, you put a billet o' wood at un.' An' certainly buddy said, 'There he is again.' 'Well boy,' he said, 'let go!' And he hove the junk o' wood.
   2 Phr *put it on one's head*: to take a drink out of a bottle.
T 54/9–64 By and by he got hold to that. When he had a dirty drink out of it, 'Now,' he said, 'you put it on your head and have another one.'
   put the owl to roost: game or trick in which a barrel of water is poured from above on victim.
T 169/70–65 And we'd get a feller among us now that never put the owl to roost; he don't know nothing about putting the owl to roost. [And then we'd play the trick].
   put the towny on: see TOWNY.
   3 In comb with av **put along**: to transport (a person) to the next destination along his route.
[1916] 1972 GORDON 86 I had decided to rely on being what is locally known as 'Put along,' on this present trip. Will Martin, my next-door neighbour, was there to take me on for the first two days, as far as Roach's Brook. From there it would be a simple matter to be relayed on to Reid's Pond, [etc].
   put away: (a) to remove warts by a charm; (b) to process cod-fish by unloading, splitting and salting the catch.
[1832] 1981 *Them Days* vi (4), p. 40 Seines haul abt 100 qtls, all brought home and put away by 10 o'clock in the evening. 1937 DEVINE 71 *Put away warts*: He could get rid of them by tying up in a piece of rag a number of pebbles corresponding to the warts on his hand. [1954] 1972 RUSSELL 17 He and his crew were puttin' away their fish. T 26–64² I know people who can put away warts. . . They're not witches, either, and actually I had my own put away when I was livin' at Sop's Island. 1979 COOPER 5 "The Old Stagehead": There when the night came down, sped the fish-wife, /

Her man will be coming in from the bay, / And she must be there to help 'put away' / His 'catch,' it may be a quintal or more, / A soft shining heap upon the stage floor.

put down: to sow, plant.

P 197–73 I put down everything but the potatoes.

put in: (a) to turn over (a catch of cod-fish) to one's supplying merchant for credit; (b) of fish, to appear in inshore waters.

[1885] 1897 *Nfld Law Reports* 99–100 Their contention is that they are entitled to be paid in full; that the defendants, as supplying merchants of Ellis and receivers of the voyage, are liable to them for the full amount, as the fish 'put in' to the merchant during the season was much more than sufficient to meet all their claims. 1891 PACKARD 184 The cod had not yet 'put in.' Last year on the 26th they took a hundred quintals the first day they appeared.

put off: (a) see **put in** (a); (b) to produce an entertainment or social event.

1909 *Tribune Christmas Number* 9 It is the object. . .to establish practices. . .which will be alike satisfactory to the man who puts his fish off to the merchant, and to the man who buys the fish from the merchant in a foreign country. T 29–64 There was another time we were going to put off that play over in the Orange Hall. M 69–2 The women put off their duck suppers, soup suppers, pork and cabbage suppers, their concerts and plays.

put up: to spread split cod-fish between layers of salt; see **put away** (b).

1979 NEMEC 259 [They] serve as platforms upon which fish is gutted, headed, split and washed at a 'splitting table' prior to being 'put up in salt' in an adjacent stage.

put(t) n Cp C SMITH *Present State. . .of Waterford* (1746) 266 '[with the beam trawl the] ground is swept clean. . .at every put, as they call it'; DINNEEN pat 'a short space (of distance or time), amount done at a time.' A quantity of fish taken at one setting of a net or trap; such an amount brought ashore; cp DIP n, HAUL n, TUCK¹ 2.

[1817] P 54–67 On 17 June 1817 there is this entry in the Gaylor Occurrences Book, Bonavista, at Nfld. Archives: 'Many birds killed, and some puts of fish caught by them for bait.' [1829] P 265¹–67 [Slade papers] Thursday 16th June 1829, Pleasant breeze from the S.W. at M. Day. Fine Weather inshore but foggy in the offing and very warm. Some capelin was hauled in Robinhoods Bay yesterday and a few small puts of fish were obtained from it by several boats in the bight and principally brought from about Baccalao. 1866 WILSON 211 The quantity of fish in the water-horse is indefinite; it simply means one put or trip of fish, that had been washed from the salt the day before, and left to drain; sometimes it is not more than two or three quintals, sometimes it is ten or twelve. 1924 ENGLAND 260 What *do* chafe we, dough, is when some angyshore [worthless fellow] carries off a putt o' fish at night an' den in de marn come round an' sell 'em to we agin! 1937 DEVINE 38 A 'putt' of fish means a catch of fish,

generally it is used in a complimentary way. 'A fine *putt* of fish you've got in that punt.' P 54–67 I have heard of *put* in Elliston, as meaning the quantity of fish got in a single trip to the grounds. C 68–18 'That's a fine put.' A fisherman fairly well satisfied with his day's catch could use the above sentence when we had completed cleaning and salting the catch.

puttick See PUDDICK.

puttock See PUDDICK.

Q

quar(r) v also **quarry, quor** ['kwɔrɪ] *OED* ~ v¹ 'to choke or block up (a channel)' (1542–1628), v² 'to curdle, coagulate' (1578–1591); *EDD* v 1 'of milk in the breast, to coagulate' So, 2 'to become choked' Wo D. Of water, to coagulate or freeze; of flowing water, to become blocked with slush and, hence, frozen; cp SLOB v.

[c1900] 1978 *RLS* 8, p. 24 Quard or quarry ice. Ice formed on a road or around a pump from successive overfloes of water then frozen. T 54/65–64 They were froze in the ice, glitter enough in the whole winter—quarried over and snow. They chopped them out, the bodies out [of] the ice. P 9–73 The water had come up through the snow from the easing of the frost in the snowfalls. The brook had quarred. The local name in places that set in this way, in Labrador, in winter, is quarr. The brook had quarred or the brook is quarring or the quarr is heaving out of the land. P 13–74 ~ [to form heavy ice] where water runs over a cliff or seeps out of the ground. . .[during] intense or prolonged periods of frost. It is often followed by *out* or *up*.

quarter n Cp *OED* ~ sb 2 c 'haunch' for sense 1.

1 Back and side of upper part of the leg; hip.

T 222–66 One of her most frequent complaints was that she had a shocking pain in her quarter. 1975 GUY 161 As I came abreast of a little old lady in front of the Court House steps she gave me a nasty cut across the quarters with her umbrella which, fortunately, was furled.

2 Attrib **quarter-boot**: fisherman's leather boot.

1967 *Bk of Nfld* iv, 248 [Father] got me the deck boots. They were made of all leather, the hardest kind. They were called quarter boots and came about half-way up to the knee.

quat v also **quot** [kwɑt, kwɑʧ, kwɒt, kwɒʧ] *EDD* ~ v 1 'to squat. . .to crouch down' s w cties. To crouch down on heels, often bowing the head as if to hide; CROOCHY*.

1863 MORETON 36 ~ to squat. T 250–66 'I got short taken, I got to run.' 'No you don't,' he said. 'If you're short taken,' he said, 'quat right down where you're to.' P 130–67 Quat down so he won't see you. C 70–18 Child imitating a hen sitting on nest: In I come / Down

I quot / Laid a egg / And up I got. 1974 *Evening Telegram* 6 Feb, p. 3 Mr — spoke of people having to wade through snow drifts to get to outdoor privies and 'quot down' with the wind and snow howling around them.

queak n   *EDD* ~ sb 2 'gentle squeak of the young of small animals.' The slightest sound or squeak.

T 100/2–64 Then o' course the children [would] go to bed, and they'd say, 'Now don't make a queak, don't one of you get out of bed. Go to sleep.'

queen n
   Comb **queen bird**: northern double-crested cormorant (*Phalacrocorax auritus*).
   1959 MCATEE 5 ~ double-crested cormorant (Possibly in allusion to the crest or 'crown.' Nfld.)
   queen's fettle: garden monkshood (*Aconitum Napellus*).
   1907 MILLAIS 144 Neglected as a weed, and most beautiful of all, were great clumps of the blue monks-hood, locally [St Lawrence] known as 'Queen's fettle.'

quib v   See CRIBBY* v.

quick n   also **quicknie, quicky**. Locally made galvanized tin kettle with bevelled sides and flat bottom, coming in several sizes convenient for boiling water rapidly; HURRY-UP, PIPER.
   P 245–55 Quicknie. Small boat's kettle with a flange about ¼ ways up from the bottom to prevent its passing through into the fire, and also to divert the heat onto its sides. P 148 69 ~ A small, wide-bottomed kettle for boiling up. Because of its narrow top and wide bottom it boils very fast. 1973 BARBOUR 94 [One] used what were called 'quicks' or 'hot asses,' made of tin by the local tinsmith. Water boiled very quickly in these kettles, which had large bottoms that fitted the hole of the stove when the lid or damper was removed. The sides sloped inwards to the comparatively small cover.

quiff n   [kwɪf]. Cp E FRASER & J GIBBONS *Soldier and Sailor Words* (1925) 243 ~ 'smartly got up. . .of a man carefully dressed for some special occasion.' Man's soft felt hat with brim; fedora. Also comb **quiff hat**
   1930 BARNES x When I buy a new felt hat I take it and put two portholes in it the size of my middle finger, one on each side of the quiff inside, so the wind will go through. [1952] 1965 PEACOCK (ed) i, 46 "Brown Flour": If you want to get fat, and wear a quiff hat, / Just try a sack of brown flour. T 29–64 He has on a curty breeks, breeches, you know, with stitching around, and he wears a quiff hat and glasses. C 66–8 When ordering a quiff hat in a store one would ask for a 'quiff.' T 367–67 I remember that year I had my father's old quiff hat and an old plaid shirt.

quintal n   also **cantal, kental, kintal(l)** [ˈkʊntl̩], [ˈkɛntl̩], [ˈkæntl̩]] *OED* ~ a. 'a hundredweight (112 lbs.)' (c1470–); *DAE* 'esp in measuring fish' (1651–); *DC* 1 esp Nfld (1712–) for senses 1, 2.

1 A measure of cod-fish caught by fishermen.
   [1664] 1963 YONGE 67 Having sold our salt, and caught about 130 kentals of fish, for our 5 boats, we took aboard our trade and sailed for Torbay. [1676] 1895 PROWSE 206 300 kintalls for each boat one year with another accounted with them an ordinary voyage. [1711] 1745 OSBORNE 794 [The French] have also salt, and some fishing craft, cheaper than us; and generally kill one or two hundred quintals *per* boat more than the *English* kill. 1787 PENNANT *Sup* 45 A banking vessel of ten thousand fish ought to be filled in three weeks, and so in proportion; and eighty quintals (112 lb. each) for a boat in the same time. 1888 STEARNS 185 'How much is a quintal?' asked Allie. 'Oh, a quintal is different, according,' laughed Mr Godard. 'It's 212 pounds of wet fish, just out of the water, and, as fish shrink one-half in drying, it's 112 pounds of dry fish. We measure all our fish, dry or wet, by quintals, because that's the way we sell it. 1912 CABOT 79 The Spracklins had a few hundred quintals (said 'kintle') of fish, taken in the last few days. 1966 FARIS 221 The amount of catch each time is measured roughly in 'drafts' or 'quintals,' simply by visual judgment. Fishermen can see a boat approaching, and judge by the amount of water the boat is drawing how far down it is in the water the number of drafts (or quintals) of fish caught.

2 A measure of dried and salted cod-fish ready for the market; 112 lbs (50.8 kg); cp DRAFT.
   1623 WHITBOURNE 79 The foresaid two hundred thousand of Fish, loading the said ship, it will then make at Marseiles aboue two and twenty hundred Kentalls of that waight. [1698] CHILD 222 The current price of our Fish in that Country, was. . .seventeen *Rials* which is eight shillings six pence *per* Quintal. 1787 PENNANT *Sup* 46 A heap of dried fish twenty feet long, and ten wide, and four deep, contains three hundred quintals. Such an heap settles, in the course of forty-eight hours after it is made, about 1/12th. [1806] 1951 DELDERFIELD 82 Most interesting is an account of the sale of 1,147 Portuguese quintals of Newfoundland fish in 1806. It was listed:– '661 Qtls large, 208 Qtls small, 278 Qtls dumb, wet and broken.' 1882 TALBOT 13 About one hundred twenty fishes of fair size go to make up a hundredweight [or quintal] of dry or cured fish. T 36/8–64 And when the tub was full they'd have an idea how much fish they had—a tub would hold about a kantal; that would be a hundred and twelve pounds. T 41–64 A hundred and twelve pounds [would be] a quintal o' fish, dried fish. 1977 *Inuit Land Use* 332 [Fish] would be about $1.50 a quintal then. A quintal used to be 112 pounds. We worked hard for that.

3 A measure (of bread, flour, seal 'pelts', bark, etc); 100 or 112 pounds of a commodity.
   1813 CARSON 15 One hundred and forty thousand quintals of bread and flour, are required for the support of the people in this island. 1895 *Outing* xxvii, p. 23 The values [of the sculps] range from $2.75 to $5.50 per quintal, the old hoods bringing the lowest and the pups the highest prices. 1916 MURPHY 19 [In 1859] the crew of the *Zambesi* made £40 19s a man, seals fetched 27 shillings per quintal and the rise. 1924 ENGLAND 248 Not so many years ago—three thousand sealers struck for a minimum of $5 a quintal for their fat. 1944

LAWTON & DEVINE 79 This Company paid the sealers one dollar and twenty-five cents per quintal more than was offered by Bowring Brothers. T 66–64 In the summer time when there'd be no fish, they'd go rining. Birch rine was a dollar a quintal.

4 Attrib **quintal drum**, ~ **fish drum**: wooden container holding 112 lbs of dried and salted codfish; DRUM.

T 90–64 There was the quintal drum with twenty inches and the sixteen-inch head. 1977 RUSSELL 51 He was goin' to earn a few cents with it, by making it into a quintal fish-drum like they used to use in those days for the Brazil market.

quintal faggot: 'pile' of dried cod-fish weighing 112 lbs; FAGGOT.

T 36–64 Providing the next day was fine, you'll enlarge on your faggot [till] you got it in quintal faggots.

quinter n Cp *SND* ~ 'ewe in her third year.' [Scottish sealers in Newfoundland waters in 1860's.] A harp seal just past the 'white-coat' stage and migrating north from the breeding grounds on the ice floes off Newfoundland; BEATER.

1924 ENGLAND 102 As [the seals] start migrating, they are called 'baters,' i.e., beaters. 'Quinters' is another name for the beating seals.

quinter v *DC* quintering Nfld (1937–); from QUINTER n. To hunt scattered migrating seals, esp from a vessel moving slowly through the icefloes.

1925 *Dial Notes* v, 339 ~ to pursue or hunt scattered beaters. 1937 DEVINE 39 Quinterin'—killing scattered seals while the ship is moving through loose ice, the men going over the side for the purpose. P 54–69 Quinter'n—jumping from the bowsprit of a vessel (steamer or sailing ship) to kill a seal as she (vessel) slowly moves through the ice.

quism n *EDD* ~ 'an odd or witty saying or quip' So. A quaint saying; a remark felt to be foolish or silly.

[c1894] PANL P4/14, pp. 198–9 A *quism* is a quaint saying or conundrum. C 71–46 If a black cat crossed in front of you and [you said] you wanted to detour, my grandmother would promptly retort that she was not having anything to do with your 'old quisms' and continue in the same direction.

quoit n [kweɪt]. Newfoundland and English two-penny piece.

1976 HOLLETT 12 What was kwaits? That was what they call old fashion [pennies], see. That was what we call them, see, pitching kwaits.

quoit v also **kite***. Cp *OED* ~ 2 'to throw like a quoit' (1597–). To skip flat stones over the surface of the water.

P 148–61 Kiting is shying flat stones.

quot See QUAT.

R

ra int also **ra-der, rudder, urrah**. Cp *Labrador Inuit* hara, F W PEACOCK *English-Eskimo Dict* [1974] 263 arra! Command to dog-team to turn left; HOLD v 2.

1861 *Harper's* xxii, 756 'Twet! twet!' on! on!—'ouk! ouk!' to the right!—'urrah! urrah!' to the left! Trees and shrubs whirl past with dizzy speed, the crisp snow sparkles as it flies from the bone-shod runners. 1895 GRENFELL 146 As there are no reins the leading dog is trained to obey the voice. At the shout 'Auk' he goes to the right, and at 'Ra' to the left, and so on, the others all following him. 1907 WALLACE 231 To start his team the driver calls 'oo-isht,'. . .to turn to the right 'ouk,' to the left 'ra-der, ra-der.' Ibid 160 . . .'rudder' to turn to the left. 1920 WALDO 144 In Labrador 'ouk-ouk!' turns the team to the right. . .and 'urrah urrah!' swerves it to the left.

rabbit n In designations of places where the snowshoe hare (*Lepus americanus*) is snared and the devices to capture the animal as food: **rabbit garden** [see GARDEN 3], ~ **run** [= ~ **garden**], ~ **slip** [see SLIP² 1], ~ **slipping**, ~ **wire**: fine flexible wire used to make snares.

P 19–55 A rabbit garden is a small enclosure of brush, stones, etc, with 'runs' leading into it, along which 'slips' are set. P 221–67 Wire snares [are] tied to a small strong stick in a rabbit run for the purpose of catching the rabbit. 1960 *Nfld Qtly* Summer, p. 19 A few times I went with Uriah Stead when he went to his rabbit slips. 1979 *Evening Telegram* 27 Aug, p. 6 In my youth after school I used to traverse the hills on the north-western side of Leamey's Gullies, tending my rabbit slips. C 70–15 When I was about eight years old my father used to take me with him into the woods, rabbit slipping (snaring) and cutting firewood. 1920 WALDO 21 Around these fresh-air cases the verandah was netted with rabbit-wire. 1966 SCAMMELL 55 When they'd get excited over something they was puttin' down they'd press so hard their pen-nibs'd just cut through the paper or crumple up like a piece of rabbit wire.

race¹ n Comb **race-pipe**: hawse-hole (P 209–73).

P 148–59 The rusty chains stretched from the race-pipe into the shallow, foaming water.

race² n Cp *OED* ~ sb² 1 c obs. A generation.

1929 BURKE [6] "No Short Skirts to Their Knees": For the old stock is fast dying out, Jennie, / And a young race is taking their place. T 158–65 Now when they had to leave the island—the young race, what was livin'—they shift in there. 1975 GUY 123 You can ask any of the older race out there about it and they will tell you the same thing. 1979 NEMEC 280 For as the 'older race' of St Shotts' fishermen used to say: 'Fish carry no bells; it can come overnight.'

rack n also **rack-comb** *EDD* ~ sb⁴ 9 Ir; JOYCE 310. A comb.

[1819] 1915 HOWLEY 112 [inventory] 1 Doz. Rack
Combs. 1924 ENGLAND 33–4 'Ain't got a rack, is you?'
'What, Uncle?' 'A rack, fer y'r hair, o' course.' 1973
ROSE (ed) 31 Before many more years had passed I
had put two and two together and figured out that this
noise was coming from the fiddler who was playing an
accordian. He was always called the fiddler regardless
of what he played upon. Even a rack comb and tissue
paper.

rack v EDD ~ v¹ 22 for sense 1.
  1 To comb (1968 DILLON 151).
  P 28–63 It would be common to say 'rack your hair'
for comb your hair.
  2 Phr *rack together*: to be close companions.
  T 80/2–64 He was about my age and we used to rack
together a good bit.

racket¹ n Comb **racket bow**: the wooden frame
of a snowshoe.
  [1786] 1792 CARTWRIGHT iii, 150 At two o'clock one
of the Canadians came here from Muddy Bay, with a
new Mountaineer sled, a pair of rackets, and a pair of
racket-bows; being presents [from] captain Gabourit to
me.

racket² n OED ~ sb³ 2 b (1745–) for sense 1;
DAS 3 for sense 2.
  1 A social gathering, party; TIME; freq with
defining word *kitchen* (1924 ENGLAND 319).
  P 245–66 Kitchen racket [is] an impromptu house-
party. P 121–67 We had a kitchen racket last night.
M 71–39 They gathered at the homes of more liberal
hosts and had what was most likely a very innocent
party. These illicit gatherings were called by the more
pious parishioners 'kitchen rackets.'. . . The host of the
party, or 'racket,' was named and branded as the Devil's Advocate.
  2 Habitual activity or occupation, freq with
defining word *fish, sealing, wood*, etc.
  1924 ENGLAND 30 'T'ings is ahl in a fruz, now,' he
added, 'but you'm goin' to like dis racket.' Ibid 262
One who knows how poor their food resources are at
home and during the cod fishery can perhaps understand why the 'swilin' racket' attracts so many. 1960
FUDGE 12 March month came on and we fished tub
racket. We took two tubs of gear baited and sat one
tub at a time, lay on the end and fish until a dory load
of Haddock was secured, then go on board.
T 141/60–65² They got it renamed since that woods
racket was started up there. T 187/9–65 He said 'This
swilin' racket is a hell of a hard racket.' T 410–67 That's
something is goin' out—the wood racket. Most people
use oil now.

rackly* See DIRECTLY.

raft¹ v also var pronunciation **rift***. Cp OED ~
sb 3 'a flat structure. . .for the conveyance. . .of
things on water'; O Sup¹ v¹ 5 'to pass above other
ice' (1919); DC v̇ b (1883–) and derivatives; 1957
Nfld & Lab Pilot Sup. No. 2, p. 7 'Rafted

ice.—Type of pressure-ice/screw-ice formed by
one floe overriding another.'
  1 Of a sheet of ice, to override another sheet
of ice; to be forced up on shore; extended also to
vessels; to RAFTER v; cp PINNACLE v.
  1843 *Journ of Assembly* Appendix, p. 465 From the
rhinding of the Trees, by the Ice, along the banks of
this River, it would appear that the ice rafts to an
almost incredible height. [1862] 1916 MURPHY 31 I
took four [white-coats] in tow being so far off. I found
it killing work to drag them over the rafted ice. 1871
WHITE *MS Journal* 21 Apr Strong breeze with snow,
SE at 2 pm. ice commenced rafting very much. Ice running very fast & rafting. 1873 CARROLL 21 No doubt
ice hunters have many dangers to contend with
amongst the many, none so great as when the ice
begins to raft. 1883 HATTON & HARVEY 95 When they
are in danger from 'rafting' ice, or fragments of
floes. . .the self-sacrificing affection of the mothers
leads them to brave all dangers. Ibid 301 Or, under
pressure of the storms, it frequently happens that the
ice is 'rafted,' as the sealers call it; that is, the fragments are piled in layers one over the other, to the
height of thirty or forty feet, being lifted by the swell
and hurled forward, as if from large catapults. 1895 *J A*
Folklore viii, 40 When, by the pressure of sea and
storm, the ice is piled in layers one upon the other, it is
said to be *rafted*. [1902] 1976 *Evening Telegram* 9 Apr,
p. 6 She just managed to clear with the land and then
the ice jammed with the land and then 'rafted.' It hove
the ship on her side and then went over her. [1904]
1968 *Nfld Qtly* Christmas, p. 21 Went on deck again
enjoying the novel sight of the masses of ice piled block
upon block, 'rafted ice' is the technical term, with occasional rifts of water between, of a deep green colour.
1906 DUNCAN 274 Raftin' ice. . .a floe of pans so forcibly driven by the wind as to be crowded into layers.
1910 GRENFELL 165 She were driven back by a huge
pan more'n a mile long, which went rafting along over
the standing edge. 1913 *Daily News* 17 Mar, p. 1 Yesterday afternoon the Long Bridge was swept away by
rafting ice which was carried by the overflow of Waterford River, caused by the free thaw and rain of the previous 24 hours. [1916] 1972 GORDON 67 At first the floe
moved through steadily but as the pressure increased,
great sheets of ice were rafted up over the rocky shore
and piled high and dry up to the very edge of the
woods. 1929 *Nat Geog* July, p. 107 The ice, rafting (tel-
escoping) under the force of the gale, threw down our
markers. 1937 DEVINE 39 Rafted. . .Said of ice piled
up after a stormy sea. [1955] 1980 *Evening Telegram* 24
Apr, p. 6 Ice in Conception Bay has rafted to a thickness where even an icebreaker couldn't help to get
through [to Bell Island]. 1959 SAMSON 78 Rafting ice
means the piling up of ice brought about mainly by a
shift in the wind, carrying great masses of ice against
the solid land. T 49–64 You had to cut the ice up, the
pinnacles on the ice through where the ice'd be rafted.
Then you get the pinnacles and [heave them] into a
tank. P 148–65 . . .ice raftin' five storeys high. T 186–65
We got jammed an' we was rifted out then all night.
After we got jammed she rifted right out on ice, an' she
was drove down on Fogo. 1972 BROWN 31 Then the ice
buckled and began to raft. Huge fragments went skid-

ding over the surface to pile up with a thunderous noise against the ships' sides. The *Nascopie* was nipped by the rafting ice and held fast. 1978 *Evening Telegram* 19 Jan, p. 3 The new bridge will temporarily take the place of a 52 year-old concrete structure which partially collapsed Sunday due to ice rafting in the swollen river.

2 Hence, derivative **rafter, rifter*** n: large sheet of ice tilted or forced up by pressure of the sea.

1909 BERNIER 7 [A decker is] a rafter at a pressure ridge. 1935 KEAN 140–1 The next day we were held in the rafter, the ice broke about a mile from us and my men could not cross. . . After that we could not reach the seals and were still held in the rafter, being driven fifteen miles from our pans. P 148–60 Rafter, rafting, running ice; ice pushed on shore by wind. P 148–63 Rifter—ice pile up on shore. T 194/5–65 I walked over the rifter on another sheet, an' when I did, over there in the lun o' the rifter there was eight men. T 389¹–67 [We] get up on a big rifter now and heave clumpers at 'em. Q 67–80 Rifters—large blocks of ice. 1972 BROWN 208 'I want to get to that rafter there,' Mouland told the men, pointing ahead. 'Come on, George, we can signal from the rafter.' With help, Tuff made it to the foot of the rafter, and Mouland climbed it. P 13–75 Rifter—formed from two sheets of ice which come together under pressure, and splinter and raft into rough ridges.

3 Vbl n **rafting**: the forcing of sheets of ice into tumbled masses.

1909 BERNIER 7 Rafting. . .occurs when two pans meet with force either by the action of the winds or currents—the edges are broken off and either rise on top of or pass under the body of the pans. 1933 GREENE 235 As the Floe is at present drifting well clear of the land no 'rafting' need be feared till the turn of the tide! Q 67–27 When strong onshore winds cause the slob and pan ice to be jammed tightly together, some pieces of ice will be forced into an almost vertical position and then come crashing down upon another piece, creating the condition known as rafting.

raft² v   *EDD* ~ v 'to disturb. . .irritate' Ha Do So. To upset, irritate (a person).

M 69–12 A dying person who was rafted by any member of the family would be sure to live for an extra nine days. For example if a dying person was transferred from one bed to another, or taken out of bed for any reason [he might be rafted]. P 197–75 ~ to upset, torment.

raft n   See RAFT¹ v. The action of thick sheets of ice being forced to buckle and override other ice.

1913 *Daily News* 17 Mar, p. 1 Yesterday afternoon the Long Bridge was swept away by rafting ice which was carried by the overflow of Waterford River. . . The raft caused the Reid Co's private yacht *Fife* to be torn from her moorings. [1955] 1980 *Evening Telegram* 24 Apr, p. 6 A raft of ice 50 feet thick has Bell Island in its grip.

rafter v   also a var pronunciation **rifter***. Cp *OED* ~ v 2 'to plough (land) in a certain way' (1733–); *EDD* v Gl Ha W 'they. . .turn the grass

side of the ploughed furrow on the land that is left unploughed'; *DC* v Nfld (1861–), *NID* ~²; *NID* rifter 'crack in sea ice.' Cp RAFT¹ v 2: RAFTER.

1 Of sheets of ice, to buckle from the pressure of wind, wave and tide; to override another sheet of ice; cp PINNACLE v; to be forced up on the shore; by extension, applied to vessels in the ice-floes.

1792 CARTWRIGHT *Gloss* i, xiii Ice is said to rafter, when, by being stopped in its passage, one piece is forced under another, until the uppermost ones rise to a great height. 1861 DE BOILIEU 100 It is a sad sight to see a ship on the weather edge of ice not enabled to work off; for when the ice begins to rafter she is thrown up, falls over, and becomes like corn between two mill-stones, and is literally ground up. 1916 DUNCAN 130 It was six miles from the edge of the raftered ice to the first island. 1924 ENGLAND 233 It raftered formidably; and before long, despite all our churning, we were jammed again. 1925 *Dial Notes* v, 339 ~ to rise up in hummocks;—of ice. T 50/1–64 They're e'er bit handy to the land when th' ice rafters. . .then it rafters back out in th' ocean. Ibid The schooner raftered out of the water altogether, out on her beam ends, and they had [to unload her] where she wouldn't beat up. 1964 *Nfld Qtly* Spring, p. 16 Evidently, just like frozen masses of ice raftered, one layer rising above the other by pressure, the crust of the earth broke and travelled southward. Q 67–64 Riftered—what the brook did every spring. P 156–73 The water riz and the brook is raftered.

2 Hence vbl n **raftering**: the forcing of sheets of ice into tumbled masses or onto the shore.

[1770] 1792 CARTWRIGHT i, 30 We perceive that the adjacent land was liable to high floods, and raftering of the ice in the Spring. 1935 KEAN 137–8 Large sheets of ice, larger and thicker ice driven by the force of the current and wind will double up and smash smaller sheets. When this takes place, it is called 'raftering.' It is especially dangerous when the ice is in large sheets and comes in contact with land; when the ice is broken in small pans by the lift of a swell, there will be no raftering.

rafter n   See RAFT¹ v 2.

ragged a   Cp *OED* ~ 2 b 'of stones, rocks, cliffs' (1400–) for sense 1; *OED* 7 ~ jacket (Nfld: 1884 quot), *DC* Nfld (1880, 1883) for comb in sense 2; by analogy with WHITE-COAT.

1 In coastal names, denoting features encumbered with shoals, 'sunkers,' and other hazards; cp SALVAGE, TICKLE (1971 SEARY 35).

1675 SOUTHWOOD (map) Ragged harbour. 1895 GRENFELL 103 [We] found ourselves suddenly amidst numbers of ragged rocks and small islands. Our chart book described on the north side of Trinity Bay some 'Ragged Islands.' 1951 *Nfld & Lab Pilot* i, 169 Ragged head is the southern extremity of a promontory, rising to an elevation of 140 feet. . . A reef of low rocks extends nearly 2 cables east-south-eastward of Ragged head. 1953 ibid ii, 164 Ragged harbour is entered between the western entrance point of Muddy Hole and Ragged point. . .two sunken rocks lie within half a mile north-westward, and another one cable south-westward. 1971 CASEY 183 [On] the ragged shores of Labrador this fearful deed was done.

2 Comb **ragged-jacket**, **ragajack**, **raggy jack** [ˈrægɨd ˌdʒækɨt]: young harp seal undergoing colour change from 'white-coat' to 'bedlamer' stage; RAGGEDY COAT, ~ JACKET; cp TURN v: TURNCOAT, TURNER.

1873 CARROLL 16 Once they begin to turn they are called 'ragged jackets,' the skins are then not of as much value. 1883 HATTON & HARVEY 311 At the end of six weeks the young shed their white woolly robe, which has a yellowish or golden lustre, and a smooth spotted skin appears, having a rough, darkish fur. They have now ceased to be 'white coats,' and become 'rag-ged-jackets.' 1925 *Dial Notes* v, 339 ~ A seal when half white and half brown, as when moulting. T 43/4–64 As soon as they starts taking to the water this white coat starts to come off, and they're called a ragged-jacket, because there's the new fur coming on. 'Tis old dark fur, and their beautiful white coat is falling off. 1967 FIRESTONE 102 Ragajack—(from 'ragged jacket') skin buyers call it a *shedder*; has black spots on belly. P 157–73 Raggy jack is a seal losing his coat, sometimes called a beater. 1978 *Decks Awash* viii (1), [p. ii] ~ a young harp seal undergoing its first moult from a white-coat to a beater, beginning at an age of about 12 days to 2 weeks.

ragged strake: the second strake or plank below the gunwale of a boat, so-called from its roughness caused by rubbing against wharf (P 127–77).

raggedy a

1 Of imperfectly dried cod-fish, with rough, slightly cracked surface.

T 43–64 You couldn't spread salt fish on the ground because 'twould go right soft. The dampness would take the pickle out of the fish and turn it. . .right rag-gedy.

2 Comb **raggedy coat**, ~ **jacket**: young harp seal undergoing change from 'white-coat' to 'bedlamer' stage.

1933 GREENE 78 With the arrival of April, yellowish and grey patches will have begun to appear among the white hair of the baby pelts of the now deserted Whitecoats. . . As these first grey patches become prominent, the youngsters are no longer called 'White-coats' by the men but 'Raggedy-coats.' 1976 *Decks Awash* v (2), p. 7 Those seals that have some white and some blue-black (known as raggedy jackets) only bring in about $5.00. In early April there are many raggedy jacket seals. They are not valuable because the white fur has to be hand combed before the pelt is usable.

raggedy-jack, ~ **mat**: home-made pile rug.

1979 POCIUS 54 This mat was made in a similar manner to a regular mat, but the loops were pulled up higher when they were hooked, perhaps to an inch in length. When the mat was completed, the tops of all the loops were cut off, and a type of pile rug was the result. This mat was commonly called a 'raggedy jack,' 'rag-a-jack,' and 'raggedy mat.'

rag-moll n   also **rag-maw*** [ˈræg mɒl]. Cp *EDD* rag sb[1] 2 (14) ~ mag 'a ragged beggar; a woman all in tatters' W. A slovenly, untidy person; cp STREEL.

P 19–55 That boy is actually a rag-maw (because of his carelessness his clothes are torn and he wears them that way). 1972 MURRAY 209 Women had to [mend] unless they wanted their children to be referred to as 'rag molls' (children whose clothes were often getting torn and were left in that condition, unmended).

rail n   A long tapering pole, undressed or trimmed on two sides, used in the construction of 'fish-flakes,' etc; esp the poles fastened horizontally on the seaward side of a 'stage head'; LONGER, STAGE-HEAD RAIL.

1626 [VAUGHAN] *The Golden Fleece* Pt 3, p. 17 [A plantation] will bridle their thefts, which filch at their departure all the railes of other mens stages, together with their salt, which being full laden with fish, they are forced oftentimes to leave behind them. [1819 ANSPACH 430 (The stage head) is fortified with stouters, or very strong shores, to prevent the stage from receiving any damage from ships or boats; it has also longers fixed horizontally at intervals, like so many steps, to facilitate the ascent to the stage]. 1937 DEVINE 50 Strouters [are] perpendicular posts at the front end of a fishing stage, jammed firmly into the sea bottom, and having rails nailed across to make the ladder for getting into and out of boats. 1944 LAWTON & DEVINE 31 You were given your third degree [in swimming] when you showed courage enough to dive off the lower rail of a stage head. 1979 *Salt Water, Fresh Water* 55 This would be stuff thirty feet long, garden rails, garden stakes, and beams for flakes for drying the fish on, and beams for our stagehead or our wharf.

rain n   Comb **rain spider**: type of spider which, if killed by a person, is thought to cause it to rain or otherwise bring misfortune.

C 69–28 If you kill a rain spider, it will rain. This rain spider is grey and is found in grass and under logs usually. C 70–27 If you step on a rain spider you will be stung by a bee.

raise v   *EDD* ~ v 6 'to start or lead a tune'; *ADD* raising 1 Nfld for sense 2.

1 To begin singing (a hymn).

M 68–2 [She] usually had the job of raising the hymns, that is, starting them when the minister announced the hymn.

2 Phr *raising for*: eager for.

1925 *Dial Notes* v, 339 ~ Very desirous; as, *raisin'* for baccy.

rake* n   In phr *rake for run*: in disarray, untidy; in an uproar.

C 70–21 If someone were to come into a house and see all doors open and the furniture not in its usual place, he might say the place is all rake for run. [Similarly] if someone's hair were in disarray, a shirt not tucked in, a stocking wrinkled. P 154–78 It's been rake for run here all day—a free-for-all, unruly behaviour.

ral n *DC* ~ Nfld [1954–]; *Kilkenny Lexicon* raille; DINNEEN raille 'vagabond. . .trickster.' A rowdy; esp in historical allusion *the winter of the rals*, 1817–18; also attrib (1955 ENGLISH 35).
1846 TOCQUE 137 Numbers of the inhabitants [of St John's], rendered desperate by want, began to break open the stores. . . This winter [1817] is universally designated by the old inhabitants of Conception Bay as the 'Winter of the Rals.' 1858 [LOWELL] i, 123 The schoolmaster, who had been in the island for a good many years, said that the [tumultuous] scene 'reminded him of the "Ralls" they had years ago.' 1862 *Daily News* 2 May . . .a true specimen of the ral crowd. Ibid 13 May raldom. [1863] 1963 *Evening Telegram* 28 Oct, p. 6 Notwithstanding the number of his assailants, he arrested one of them, a notorious 'ral' who had been in the lockup and the jail several times. It is hoped this fellow's comrades will be caught and punished. 1866 WILSON 91 The people wanted food. . .but they committed other depredations besides their search for food, and generally would use the word *Ral*, as a watch-word to their companions in crime. 1895 PROWSE 406 Many more incidents could be related about the winter of the 'Rals,' or 'Rowdies.' 1924 ENGLAND 236 'Ah, gi' lang, ye ral!' another retorted. 'Ral' is a mild term of reproach.

rally n
1 Foray on the ice (after seals); an attempt, a go; TRAVEL n.
1924 ENGLAND 77 Whitecoats still were bawling not far off; not enough, perhaps, for a 'rally,' but harbingers of 'de t'ick patch.' Ibid 120 The *Terra Nova* stopped for another rally at the seals, and I arrived on the bridge just in time to see the hunters going over again. [1960] 1965 PEACOCK (ed) i, 120 "Ferryland Sealer": We had vittles for to last more than two months at the least, / And plenty of good rum, boys, stowed away in our chest, / We will give her a rally for to praise all our fancy, / All our seals will be collected by the *William* and the *Nancy*.
2 Street fight between neighbourhood groups.
1976 MURPHY 32 [These clashes] were reminders of the old faction fight days. And so were the 'rallies' between different streets of St John's that took place in the days just before the First World War, when it was hardly safe for a boy from the Higher Levels to appear on New Gower Street or in the East End.

ram-cat n also **ram** *OED* ~ now dial (1672–1809); *EDD* ram sb[1] 1 (2) ~(s)-cat Ir So D Co. A tom cat.
1863 MORETON 30 Ram. A male cat. 1937 DEVINE 39 Ram. A male cat. 1973 WIDDOWSON 380 If you don't go to sleep I'll give you to the Ram Cats. 1977 *Inuit Land Use* 278 Ram Cat Island.

rames n pl also **reims** [reɪmz, rɛɪmz] *OED* rame sb[1] a, b dial; *EDD* s w cties. (a) The bones or skeleton; fig., the keel and ribs of a boat or vessel, derelict on the shore; (b) a very thin person or creature; freq in prov phr *thin as the rames*, etc.
1920 WALDO 157 The remains of birds or of animals are the 'rames.' 1937 DEVINE 39 ~ A skeleton—the bare bones. Applied to a thin man or woman. 1964 *Evening Telegram* 9 June, p. 10 I never see such a skinny thing in all my life [said of a turkey]. Just a reims, that's all. T 80/3–64 An' you let hundreds bide in the linnet; you'd never haul the leader o' the trap. Never trouble about 'em. Nothing there only the rames an' heads when you haul in your linnet. P 198–67 He is as thin as the rames. P 207–67 He was as thin as the rames of mercy. P 245–67 The rames of the schooner [were left on the shore]. P 246–69 When me wife came home from the hospital she was some thin. Only the rames came home. Wasn't enough of her left to bait a trout-hook. 1979 *Evening Telegram* 23 June, p. 15 This is a hardy Newfoundlander quaffing [medicine] to ease his labor-torn rhaymes.

ramey a Cp *EDD* raimsy adj W So. See RAMES. Thin; like a skeleton (P 157–70).

ramlatch n Cp *Kilkenny Lexicon* ~ v 'talk meaninglessly or incoherently.' An example of foolishness or nonsense.
1931 BYRNES 121 How many years have passed my friends, since you heard these once familiar localisms? 'A ramlatch of a song.' 'The devil skewered to ye' (meaning the devil's cure to you).

rampse* See ROMPSE.

rams n pl Stout timbers fastened under the bowsprit of a sealing vessel to support men pushing ice-pans to clear a passage for the ship; SHEARS (1972 SANGER 240).
1923 CHAFE 16 The crew were continually at the 'Rams' that is sticks fastened under the Jib-boom for the men to hold on to when forcing the pans of ice under the vessel's bow to enable her to get ahead. [1929] 1933 GREENLEAF (ed) 247 "The Lone Flier": At four o'clock that evening we put her in the ice; / We had to get her back again, and that did not look nice. / On the following morning the captain called all hands; / He thought it a good suggestion to put us on the rams. 1936 SMITH 58 Tuesday was just the same, and we rigged out rams over the bows of the schooner so that the men could get down on those sticks and break the ice ahead of the schooner. 1937 DEVINE 39 ~ Long sticks extending from the bow of a sealing vessel lashed under the bowsprit, to afford a footing to the sealers for poking pans of ice out of the ship's way.

ram's horn n *OED* ~ 4 (Nfld: 1809, 1883); b 'a winding-net supported by stakes, to inclose fish that come in with the tide' So [1847] for sense 1. See also CH DE LA MORANDIÈRE *Histoire de la pêche de la morue* iii, 1383 *timbre* for a similar washing vat.

1 A wooden trough with slatted sides, submerged in the salt water and used to scrub and wash cod-fish at various stages in the process of salting and curing; cp PEN[1], POUND, WASHING VAT.

[(1710) 1895 PROWSE 22 [illust] The Cleansing y[e] Cod.] [1766 (1971) BANKS 136 (The French) Method of washing their Fish out of the Salt is very Different & much worse then ours they do it in a square trough the sides of which are securd with Lattice work this is set between 4 poles raised up in the water always where I have seen it close by the side of the stages on the tops of these poles are blocks by which the Trough is easily hoisted up or Let Down into the water into this they Put their Fish & Letting it down into the water Poke them about with Sticks till they are Sufficiently washd some of the People also getting into the trough & moving them about with their hands & feet.] [1778 DE CASSINI 147 (For washing) they load it on hand barrows, and empty it out into a laver not unlike a great cage, by the sea-side.] 1809 *Naval Chronicle* xxi, 21 The fish are thrown into what is called a ram's-horn (a square wooden thing, perforated with holes, to admit the water to pass), when the fish are tumbled about and well washed, afterwards thrown up on a stage or wharf, and laid out again by men employed in the fishery on the shore.[*OED*] 1819 ANSPACH 444 As soon as the boat arrives, she is fixed close to an oblong square low vessel of boards, so loosely joined at the bottom as to let the sea water run through it. This vessel, called *Ram's horn*, probably a corruption of the French *Rinçoir*, is fastened to the wharf's or stage's head. The fish is thrown, one by one, into the Ram's horn, where there are three men standing up to their knees in the water, two of whom rub, shake, and clean the fish with mops; this is afterwards thrown up by the third man on a kind of scaffold. 1895 *J A Folklore* viii, 31 ~ a wooden pound for washing fish in. [c1900] 1978 *RLS* 8, p. 24 Ramshorn—a sort of box with holes bored through bottom, used for washing the fish in. 1937 DEVINE 39 ~ A box with slatted sides, about eight feet long, three feet wide and three feet deep, used in washing fish. It is lashed by falls to the schooner discharging green fish and the men stand in it. 1975 BUTLER 69 The fish would be washed in ram's horns. A ram's horn was made. . .about twelve feet long and eight feet wide and two feet deep. The boards would be one inch apart and there was a bottom in the contraption. There were rope straps in both ends. This ram's horn would be placed in the water with the rope straps tied to the wharf. Four men would throw the fish down in this ram's horn and get down and sit on the boards around the edge and wash the fish with scrub brushes. P 127–80 I dumped bars of fish times out o' number into the ram's horn.

2 Wooden crate, suspended in the water, for the storage of live lobster; CAR TRAP (P 94–57).

P 254–78 ~ large box anchored off a wharf where lobsters are stored to keep them alive and fresh.

ran n also **rand** *OED* ~ 1 'a certain length of twine' (1794–); *EDD* sb[1] 1 'hank of string' IW Do. A hank of twine (for fish-nets, etc); also as a measure of net size; attrib.

1765 WILLIAMS 19 Six [dozen] Rand Twine. [1933] 1964 BLONDAHL (ed) 35 "Squarin' Up": Skipper John Wilkins strolled in to [divine] / If his credit was good for a few slips of twine; / He got such a fright when they gave him a 'ran'; / He bought a baloney for Aunt Mary Ann. 1937 DEVINE 31 Leaves. The unit quantities or rands in knitting a trap or seine etc. C 70–15 First we bought a ran of sail twine, and rolled it up into balls such as women do when knitting. 1979 TIZZARD 317 [I bought] a forty rand two and three quarter mesh herring net.

rand[1] n Cp *OED* ~ sb 2 'strip or long slice. . .of meat' now dial (1394–); *EDD* sb[1] 6 'piece of beef.' A strip of fat cut from an animal.

[1770] 1792 CARTWRIGHT i, 55 [The skinbag] had been filled with phrippers, pieces of flesh, and rands of seals' fat. 1792 ibid *Gloss* i, xiii Rand of fat. A sealer's term for a large piece of fat, just as it happens to be cut off the animal. 1861 DE BOILIEU 156–7 The operation is thus performed: a man takes what is termed a 'rand,' or a large piece of fat. 1971 NOSEWORTHY 237 Rans. Strips of pork from the back-bone (of the pig) to the belly.

rand[2] See RAN.

randy n Cp *EDD* ~ sb 1 'a frolic. . .a drunken carousal.' (a) Boisterous play, esp a ride on a sled or in a vehicle or boat; a boisterous spree or celebration, esp in phr *go on a randy*; (b) sexual intercourse (P 269–64 quot).

1895 *J A Folklore* viii, 31 Give us a randy [a ride]. 1919 GRENFELL[1] 31 There is no better fun than a 'randy' over the snow on a light komatik. 1937 DEVINE 39 ~ Any noisy fun: 'Copying' over buckly ice, snow-sliding, etc. P 269–64 You tell her: 'How about a randy?' T 141/64–65[2] Well come over now, boy, I goin' to kill my sheep now, an' we'll have another little randy. C 70–22 Come up a randy in our car. 1974 *Evening Telegram* 13 Feb, p. 3 Or you could catch hold to the sticks of wood sticking off the horses and slides in the evening and get a free randy along on your coaster.

randy v Cp *EDD* ~ v 12 'to frolic; to enjoy oneself.' To play boisterously, esp to ride on a sled; to ride in a vehicle.

1895 *J A Folklore* viii, 31 The boys are randying [coasting]. 1907 *Tribune Christmas No* 12 In the early seventies we were wont to 'randy' over the incline. 1910 GRENFELL 82–3 This meant, however, that we tramped till we came to a decline where we sat on [the komatik] and 'randied.' C 71–131 ~ To go riding on a sled in the wintertime or to ride on anything at any time. 1975 GUY 100 You could randy on anything. Bits of old floor canvas and pieces of cardboard boxes. Stave slides which your father made out of old barrels. Made slides and coasters, hand slides and catamarans, toboggans and even a person's plain stomach.

ranger n *OED* ~[1] 1 b (Nfld: 1884 quot), *DC* 1 Nfld (1771–) for sense 1; *DC* 2 b (1954–) for sense 2.

1 The common seal (*Phoca vitulina*), esp in its

third year; BAY SEAL, DOTARD, HARBOUR SEAL. Also attrib.

[1771] 1792 CARTWRIGHT i, 140 [He] gave me a ranger-skin. 1861 DE BOILIEU 97 The next kind [of seal] is a small and beautiful animal, called the Ranger, which remains on the coast all the winter, and is sometimes found about the bays during the summer months. This species is very interesting, as they may be tamed and sent out fishing, which they will do readily. They are beautifully marked, and the skin is much esteemed by the natives. 1873 CARROLL 10 When three years old they are called dotards, and their young rangers, which they have when 3 years old on the different island rocks in the different bays, all round the island, but more particularly in the northern bays. 1906 DUNCAN 281 Archie and Billy came upon a family of four, lying at some distance from their blow-hole—two grown harps, a 'jar,' which is a one year old seal, and a ranger, which is three years old and spotted like a leopard. 1977 *Inuit Land Use* 128 In early or mid-June, ranger and grey seals migrate north to shallow areas near rocky shores, where they haul out to bask in the sun or hide from hunters among the rocks. Old rangers (dotters) are especially clever at concealing themselves. Unlike other seals, rangers breed late (mid-June) and moult late (mid-August).

2 Officer of an early twentieth-century force (1935–49) engaged in police and other duties in parts of Newfoundland and Labrador outside jurisdiction of the St John's constabulary; NEWFOUNDLAND RANGER.

[1933 *Nfld Royal Commission Report* 218–19 We have suggested that the force [of 30–40] should be modelled on the Royal Canadian Mounted Police [and might] eventually take over all public work not only in the interior but in the outports as well, might collect the Customs and other revenue at all but the most important ports, might act as the representatives of the various Departments of Government. . .and generally might undertake duties, excluding those assigned to the Magistrates and Fishery Inspectors, which are at present distributed among a number of minor officials.] 1939 EWBANK 96 Throughout the greater part of the Island and in Labrador, the Rangers are responsible for maintaining the law and for prosecuting offenders. [1960] 1965 LEACH (ed) 211 "Game Warden Song": And dat was Judge Hodge and a gruff spoken ranger, / Sure dey was a bringin' a summons for me. M 69–6 He then got angry and said he was going to tell the Ranger on us. That was in 1950, and we still called Mounties Rangers since we had always been told about Rangers up to 1949. 1975 RUSSELL 9 The Ranger (that was before the Mounties) measured the height of Grampa Walcott's fence and even brought the goat into court and measured his yoke. 1977 *Them Days* ii (3), 7 The Ranger. . .was also the Welfare Officer at that time.

rat n Comb **rat's tail**: club moss (*Lycopodium selago*) (1898 *J A Folklore* xi, 283).

rattle[1] n *DC* ~ n Nfld (1770, 1861) for sense 1; see also RATTLING.

1 A shallow, rocky declivity in a stream; rapid; a waterfall.

[1768] 1828 CARTWRIGHT i, 33 Were it not for the several rattles on this river, and the great falls, it would be navigable for flat boats up to the lake. At every one of them except Flat Rattle, which is a shingle bank, the bed is an entire rock, with ragged prominences that make so many small cascades. 1792 CARTWRIGHT *Gloss* i, xiii Rattle in a river. Where there is a succession of falls in a river (which are frequently to be met with in mountainous countries) the falling water makes a great noise; such a place is called a *Rattle*. [1811] 1818 BUCHAN 4 A mile above these [islands] occurs the first rattle or small waterfall. 1842 JUKES ii, 136 *Rattle* [is] the term used in Newfoundland for *rapid*. 1888 HOWLEY *MS Reminiscences* 71 We got over and down to the head of the long rapid or rattle as it is called. . . Met several more hunters below the falls going down. 1909 SELOUS 110 Saunders and Wells had a very hard day hauling the canoes through innumerable rapids, or 'rattles,' as they called them, and our progress was necessarily very slow. 1969 HORWOOD 2 The river forked above, and there was a whisper of a rapids below—a 'chute' leading to a 'rattle,' as our woodsmen describe it. 1970 *Evening Telegram* 20 July, p. 6 This was caused by a combination of sharp rocks in the 'rattle,' or rapids, and the lack of skilled men.

2 (a) A narrow passage, inlet or arm of the sea, swept by strong tides; TICKLE n; (b) a spot of unfrozen water in such an area in winter, used as a breathing-hole by seals (see 1977 quot); BOBBING-HOLE, SWATCH.

1895 GRENFELL 135 Whilst endeavouring one night to navigate a narrow passage known as 'the Rattle,' the *Princess Mary* had been suddenly caught by the current, and at full speed taken a rocky bottom. 1947 TANNER i, 285 The 'rattles' are of particular interest. . .they are narrow passages, in which the tide runs so fast that it makes a noise. . . In the channels in the Nain Archipelago numerous eddies with 'rattles' are formed. 1953 *Nfld & Lab Pilot* ii, 54 The shores of Second rattle are steep and rocky, and the tidal stream runs strongly through it. 1966 HORWOOD 137 [We set] out to try for one last sea trout in the rattle at Lattice Harbour Run. 1977 *Inuit Land Use* 52 As long as there was new ice, the people hunted seals either at their breathing-holes or at rattles, the local name for areas of water kept open by currents.

3 Phr **rattle on the stomach**: a cough.

1966 FARIS 209 Any complaint from the 'neck to the knees,' as it is expressed, centres on the stomach; a cough, for example, is a 'rattle on the stomach.'

4 Comb **rattle-box**, ~ **seed**: yellow rattle (*Rhinanthus Christa-galli*) (1956 ROULEAU 36).

rattle[2] n Cp *EDD* ~ sb[2], raddle sb[1] K Sr Sx. Wattle; cp RIDDLE n.

P 126–67 Rattle fence, to cut rattles, etc. [A rattle is] a piece of wood for fence similar to a picket but small enough to be flexible. Used to build a closed fence.

rattler n Attrib **rattler brook**: a stream marked by numerous shallow, rocky declivities or rapids; cp RATTLING.

1951 *Nfld & Lab Pilot* i, 371 Skeleton cove lies close

southward, and Rattler brook forms a prominent waterfall about 3 cables northward.

rattling ppl See also RATTLE[1]. Of a river or stream, noisy, clattering, swift.

[1783] 1792 CARTWRIGHT iii, 15 We rowed along [the lake] for a mile and an half, when we arrived at the mouth of a strong, rattling brook. [1811] 1818 BUCHAN 5 [It lay a] mile above the rattling Brook. 1842 JUKES ii, 136 We soon reached the mouth of the Great Rattling Brook, a considerable stream coming down from the north. 1953 *Nfld & Lab Pilot* ii, 294 Rattling brook descends in a waterfall into Corner Brook cove.

ravel n also **revel*, rivel***, etc. *NID* ~[2] b 'a loose thread.' A short piece of thread clinging to one's clothing.

P 61–66 Reevel—a short thread. P 165–72 Finding a ravel on someone's clothes means a jig (a date or boyfriend) for the person finding it. P 148–75 A revel is a thread sticking to clothes. The old people say that you take it off and twirl it around your finger saying A, B, C, D. . .at each circle. The letter where the revel ends is the initial of the one you will marry.

rawler See ROLLER[2].

rawny a *EDD* ~ adj[2] 1 'thin,' 2 'of cloth, thin' W So; DINNEEN ránaidhe 'thin'; JOYCE 311.

1 Thin, gaunt, bony (1937 DEVINE 39).

P 207–67 I never saw such a rawny horse. 1968 DILLON 151 He was a big rawney-boned fella.

2 Of cloth, flimsy, threadbare.

P 113–56 His coat must have been cheap. It became rawny after only one winter. P 245–61 His shirt cuffs are rawny (frayed). P 184–67 That material is rawny. 1979 *'Twas a way of life* 45 If the [sweater] was poorly done, comment was passed on it, 'Some rawny! You could shoot gulls through that!'

reach n [retʃ, rɛtʃ]. Cp *OED* ~ sb[1] 13 b 'a bay' obs (1526–1736); *NID* n[2] a (4) 'an arm of the sea' for sense 1.

1 An inlet of the sea; an expanse of salt-water adjacent to the land; run, sound; a channel between islands or an island and the mainland; TICKLE n; freq in coastal names.

1612 *Willoughby Papers* [Guy's Journal] [November] The 4 we put forward in the sound. The firste reach lieth. . .westerlie one league [from where] the sound did end. 1842 JUKES ii, 101 We then sailed to 'the Beaches,' a small cove at the mouth of Bloody Reach. 1871 HOWLEY *MS Reminiscences* 15 Next day I took the boat and two of the men with some provisions and went up the Reach visiting several of the islands. 1876 HOWLEY 19 Reach appears to mean a wider channel [than a tickle] with not such a force of tide. 1902 *Christmas Bells* 15 We felt very confident of making a good run home, but alas, were doomed to disappointment, for we got becalmed till sunset in the 'reach,' between Barron and Merasheen Island. 1940 DOYLE (ed) 6 "The Loss of the *Ellen Munn*": And Barrow Harbour we could not fetch, / The gale grew blustering down the 'retch.' 1951 *Nfld & Lab Pilot* i, 244 Grandy

island. . .is separated from the mainland westward of Richards head by Long reach, a narrow strait, the eastern end of which is shallow. T 143–65[2] There was a little wind. Soaked on down the reach an' about, oh, four mile from our place there's an island called Hunch Island. C 71–87 A long retch of water, as in a harbour. 1976 WINSOR 7 Most of the people before 1870, lived on a cluster of islands, across a narrow body of water, called 'The Reach.'

2 Phr *the reach of the year*: high point, peak of a season.

P 245–66 I n'er heard tell of a man findin' seals in the reach of the year as we used to. Q 73–7 ~ high summer.

have the forward reach: to be ahead of (another).

T 12–64 He has the forward reach on him now.

read v Cp *EDD* cup sb 3 (6): reading cups. Phr *read cups*: to tell one's future by inspecting tea-leaves in a cup.

C 70–12 To be able to read cups was considered a great [gift] and was often done to entertain guests. The cup could only be read if one had drunk all the tea, but had kept the tea leaves.

rear v Cp *OED* ~ v[1] 8 b 'to make (a noise) by shouting' rare (13..-1500); *EDD* v[2] 11 'to mock, gibe; to scold.' Phr *rear out*: to yell.

T 313/4–66 If I was to go up along and show you where [this woman] is and you walk in the house where she's to, she liable to rear out the biggest kind right down on top of you. But don't you get across her forefoot or you'll hear some large ones. P 108–70 I was that taken aback when she reared out at me!

rear-admiral n *DC* ~ Nfld (1765, 1883). The master of the third English fishing vessel to reach a harbour in Newfoundland, exercising certain privileges for the season under the 'admiral' and 'vice-admiral'; FISHING ADMIRAL, LADY[1].

[1693] 1793 REEVES iv–v . . .and that the master of every such fishing ship next coming, as shall enter any such harbour or creek, shall be rear admiral of such harbour or creek during the fishing season. 1883 HATTON & HARVEY 44 The masters of the second and third following vessels were to be vice-admiral and rear-admiral.

red a For combs. in sense 2: *DC* redberry Lab (1933–), *DAE* red rod (1785–); for sense 3: *EDD* sb[1] 1 (2) ~ cap 'a sprite or elf,' *DC* Red Indian 1 (1819–).

1 In names of birds with red or reddish colouring: **red game, ~ headed sparrow, ~ leg, ~ singer, ~ thrush**.

1774 *Trans Roy Soc* lxiv, 377 Here are. . .the *Red-Game*, with a smaller sort which resemble them, called the *Spruce-Partridge*: these we may call the constant inhabitants of the feathered kind. 1959 MCATEE 62 Red-headed sparrow. Dusky Redpoll [*Acanthis flammea flammea*]. Ibid 27 Redleg. Semipalmated ringed plover; [*Charadrius hiaticula semipalmatus*].

Ibid 66 Red singer. Eastern fox sparrow [*Passerella iliaca iliaca*]. Ibid 66 Red thrush. Eastern fox sparrow.

2 In names of plants, shrubs and trees with red or reddish flowers, berries, bark, wood, etc: **red berry** (a) red crowberry; (b) PARTRIDGE BERRY, ~ **heath**, ~ **pear** [see CHUCKLEY PEAR], ~ **rock**, ~ **rod**, ~ **tops**, ~ **wood** [= ~ **rod**].

1898 *J A Folklore* xi, 279 ~ Red Crowberry (*Empetrum Eamesii*). 1933 MERRICK 306 Last came the redberry pie and the fourth cup of tea. 1977 *Inuit Land Use* 205 Many berries, such as bake apples. . .blueberries, redberries or partridge berries. . .ripen in the summer and fall. 1898 *J A Folklore* xi, 279 Red heath (*Empetrum Eamesii*). Ibid 226 Red pear [Serviceberry; CHUCKLEY PEAR] [*Amelanchier* spp]. 1884 STEARNS 291 Natural grottoes, and varieties of rock-work, all were there, and all covered with 'red rock (*Corallina officinalis*), or 'live rock' as the people call this peculiar growth. [1822] 1856 CORMACK 8 On the acclivities are. . .C. Strica or red rod. 1956 ROULEAU 36 Red Rod: *Cornus stolonifera*. Ibid 36 Red-tops: *Scutellaria epilobiifolia*. 1913 THOMAS 187 We cut down four or five old tree stubs, bone dry from years and years of exposure to the elements. Lashing them together with redwood twisted into a 'gad' and propelling the impromptu raft with a pole, we landed safely on the island.

3 Cpd, comb **red-cap**: (a) fairy; (b) toadstool.

1971 CASEY 283 As fairies did not like to be referred to by name, various euphemistic terms were used:. . .'red caps' and 'the good people.' 1973 WIDDOWSON 216 'Fairy cap' and 'red cap' are also the names given to species of poisonous fungi.

red-cod: red-coloured variation of the common cod.

1826 *Edin New Phil J* 33 The third [variety] is the *red-cod* (Gadus callarias), resembling the rock-cod or red-ware codling of Scotland, caught near the shores.

red indian: member of a tribe of indians, now extinct, related to the Algonkian people and inhabiting Newfoundland ?–1829 A.D., distinctive because of the red ochre used on their bodies; BEOTHUK, INDIAN, NATIVE a: *native indian*. Also attrib.

[1768] 1828 CARTWRIGHT ii, 307 [We wished] to acquire a more certain knowledge of the settlements of the natives or Red Indians. The epithet of 'red' is given to these Indians, from their universal practice of coloring their garments, their canoes, bows, arrows, and every other utensil belonging to them, with red ochre. 1819 ANSPACH 14 It is a somewhat striking coincidence, that these presumed descendants of the family of Eric Roude, or Red-head, should have been to this day distinguished by the name of *Red Indians*. 1888 HOWLEY *MS Reminiscences* 67 About two miles below Noel Paul's, we stopped at a point to look at the remains of several Red Indian wigwams, or rather the circular hollows where they once had stood. 1891 *Trans Roy Soc Can* ix (2), 124 The name Red Indians. . .is the translation of the Micmac name for them, Maquajik, which means red men or red people. 1947 TANNER 579 On the basis of archeological facts [Jennes] suggested that eastern Labrador was inhabited in prehis-

toric times by Beothuks, an Indian tribe who are mostly known to ethnology under the name of Newfoundland's Red Indians.

red jack: fisherman's leather boot reaching to below the knee.

P 97–66 Here are your red-jacks (three-quarter length boots [treated with] cod-liver oil or linseed oil).

red raw: see REE-RAW.

redshanks: fig., with reddened flesh; PINK FISH.

[1663] 1963 YONGE 57 Too much salt burns the fish and makes it break, and wet, too little makes it redshanks, that is, look red when dried, and so is not merchantable.

reddening n   also **redding**. Cp *OED* redding sb[1] 'red ochre'; *EDD* redding sb 'red ochre' So D. Attrib in designations of container for ochre and water used to mark timber to be cut, and line used to make the mark: ~ **box**, ~ **line**.

T 393/6–67 A red'ning box, you know, but some people call it a ochre box. This is a old red'ning line I was telling about lining the sticks. You use ochre in there and a drop of water. T 91–64 They'd have the reddin' lines, they used to call it. They used to strike the [log] with a marking line, with red ochre on it. That would leave the mark on the log where he wanted to come along and saw.

redding See REDDENING.

ree-raw n, a also **red raw**, **reerah** ['riːrɑː, 'riːrɑːə] *EDD* ~ N I Wxf Nfld, under reel-ral(l) Sc; DINNEEN rí-rá; cp *OED* ~ a (1842–).

1 A state of disorder, confusion; uproar, racket, hullabaloo.

1863 MORETON 30 Reerah. Any uproarious noise. 1896 *J A Folklore* ix, 30 All in a reeraw, confusion or disorder. 1937 DEVINE 41 Ree raw. Disorder; an upset condition of affairs. T 12–64 The place was in a ree-raw. P 167–67 After the time there was a ree-raw. C 70–12 To have a ree-for-raw means to have a good time, as at a Christmas party where everybody was feeling their drinks and were engaged in a step dance.

2 By folk-etymology, eager to begin (1937 DEVINE 41).

1936 SMITH 114 We opened the Club. . .all members being present, and 'red raw' for a game of billiards.

3 Phr *on the ree-raw*: quickly, without preparation.

1937 DEVINE 41 I had to take up the job right on the *ree raw*.

reeve[1] v   *OED* ~ v[1] naut 1 'to pass (a rope) through a hole,' b 'to thrust or pass (a rod, etc) *through* any aperture,' for sense 1; cp *OED* reave v[3] [unravel] 1643 quot, *EDD* ~ v[2] 4 'unwind' Gl for sense 2.

1 To tie, attach; to interweave (a fish) on a sharp stick; GAD v.

T 14/21–64 And directly you put a line or reeve off something where you stand [the corpse] up. She wouldn't ply, buckle, because she was stiff. M 69–6 I was so overjoyed that I stopped trouting, got a skiver and reeved the trout and the salmon on it.

2 To unravel (a knitted garment) (P 24–66).

reeve² v Cp *OED* rave v² n dial and Sc 'wander, stray, rove' (13..-1841). To wander about.

1907 MILLAIS 56 They reeves around all day now in de woods, now on de meshes. P 113–56 She's never home, she's forever reevin' around. P 54–61 ~ to rove about, as in anger.

reeves* n pl In phr *by the reeves*: of heavy rain or snow, in great swirls and drifts.

P 37 It was raining by the reeves. C 63–1 It's snowing by the reeves.

reeving vbl n See REEVE¹ v, *EDD* reeve v² 1 (3): reeving-string 'string put in to gather up a hem.' Wa Gl. Comb **reeving rope**, ~ **string**: drawstring laced in edge of a bag or net.

T 100/2–64 They used to pull in the bottom of the trap with some kind of a reevin' rope, and pull in the trap. . . When you throw [the cast net] out among the caplin, he's spread abroad and he'll go down right to the bottom, and whatever caplin is in the bag, when you hauls the reevin' string, you got un all, see. P 118–67 Reevin' string—the string in the top of a food or clothes bag.

refuse n attrib *DAE* ~ fish (1654–1710). Comb **refuse fish**: dried and salted cod-fish well below 'merchantable' standard or 'cull'; CULLAGE, WEST a: *West india*.

[1698] 1954 INNIS 104 [They] generally sell their cargo for money and bills which makes 25 per cent to them in New England; but if they cannot get them they buy refuse fish and go to the West Indies. [1712] 1895 PROWSE 273 Broken fish which they call refuse fish sold for twenty ryalls per quintal, and carried to Spain and Portugal. 1934 LOUNSBURY 192 These [colonial] vessels brought ladings of bread, peas, flour, beef, pork, butter, tar, boards, brown sugar, and molasses, and received in exchange brandy, clothing, fishing gear, hard money in the form of Spanish pieces of eight, if they were obtainable, French and Spanish wines, as well as 'some red stinking fish' otherwise known as 'refuse' fish which they took to Barbados to serve as food for the negro slaves.

relieving ppl *OED* ~ 2 ~ officer (1851–1876). Comb **relieving officer**: person appointed to administer poor-relief.

1940 *Fortnightly* cliii (Apr), p. 406 If this summer's fishery failed, the disgrace of the dole, and the dreaded spectre of the relieving-officer lay heavily on their minds. 1944 LAWTON & DEVINE 51 In [Fr Veitch's] position as relieving officer he had many calls upon his generosity and he never failed to make some provision for the destitute. T 145–65 These men in many cases would have to go directly to the relieving officer to get enough food to sustain their families during the winter months. 1977 *Them Days* ii (3), 24 I can remember one time we had a relievin' officer come there (Battle Harbour) givin' out grub.

revel* See RAVEL.

rhind See RIND n.

rhode See RODE.

rhyme n Phr *rhyme of oaths*: a sustained string of oaths; a fit of cursing.

1930 BARNES 379 I grabbed [the mirror] before it fell on the floor and I swore a rhyme of oaths at him. P 148–65 I was in a rhyme of oat's.

rhyme v Phr *rhyme off*: to recite poetry; WORD (1925 *Dial Notes* v, 339).

1924 ENGLAND 126 But I can word out a piece for ye, I can just mind "Willy March," an' I'll rhyme it off.

ribband v Cp *OED* ~ sb 1 'flexible piece of timber. . .bolted externally to ribs of ship' (1711–). Phr *ribband out*: in boat-building, to secure the frame with a piece of timber running lengthwise until the outside planking is put on.

T 43/8–64 The next thing you'd put on after timbering out the boat is your counter—your stern. You'd ribban' her out then, and you'd make these pitchers—after pitchers and forrard pitchers.

ribbon n Cp RIBBAND. Piece of wood fastened lengthwise to the cross-bars of a sledge.

1897 *J A Folklore* x, 206 [Newfoundlanders] also use the term ribbon, properly *rib-band*, to denote. . .the bar of wood in [sleds] placed lengthwise, resting on the ends of the crossbars, the whole being kept in place by pins alongside the latter, with their lower ends inserted in the runner, and the upper in the ribband.

riddle n also **riddling, riggle, riggling, roddle, wriggle, wriggling**, etc. *EDD* ~ sb² 'strip of wood split like a lath to make a wall'; riddling 'thin piece of wood'; cp *EDD* raddle sb¹ 1 'sticks twisted between upright stakes'; 'wattle or hurdle.' Small pliable wooden rod interwoven between horizontal rails in making a fence; GARDEN ROD; RATTLE²; also attrib, comb for a fence so constructed.

1835 PANL GN 2/2 Sep, p. 103 A roddle fence shall have three longers in height and a post at the distance of every six feet the rods to be as close as possible. P 37 Ringle-rod fence. A picket fence made without using nails to fasten the pickets in place. The top of one picket is on one side of the rail and the top of the next one is on the other side. T 14/9–64 One rail [with three posts] would take a hundred and twenty riddles. . . I imagine it's good for ten, fifteen years, a riddling fence. T 43/7–64 Your riddles would cross on [the centre one], one goin' one way, the next one could come up the other way—the riddles criss-crossed in the centre. P 269–64 Riggle-fence. A fence with three horizontal rails and pliable branches to form the vertical members. C 70–15 They were called wriggle-rod fences and

were constructed almost entirely without nails. Three
rails were fastened between the posts, and saplings,
usually spruce for toughness, called wriggle rods were
twisted alternately between the rails. 1971 *Daily News*
15 May, p. 9 The riddle fence was made by weaving
slender sticks onto three main bars. . . The riddle fence
was commonly used years ago because there was no
need for nails. Pickets, slim enough to be springy were
woven onto three main bars. 1978 *Evening Telegram* 23
Mar, p. 2 [The film] *Wrigglin' Fence* demonstrates a
particular style of fence-making which uses few man-
made materials. 1979 TIZZARD 233, 236 Some of the
fence was made of pickets, some of rails, and some of
wriggling rods. . . A wriggling rod was a little slender
tree too small for a picket.

riddle v also **riggle**. See RIDDLE n.
  1 To shake.
  1929 BURKE [3] "The Trinity Cake": While Flanni-
gan grabbed the Melodian, / And there he did riddle
and shake.
  2 To interlace vertical rods between rails to
make a fence.
  1835 PANL GN 2/2 Sep, p. 104 A riddled fence [has]
three longers, and not less than five feet high. P 269–64
You riggle [the riggle] through the fence. T 43/7–64
These riddles were smaller than pickets. You had to
use three rails, and riddle your fence, one on one side
of the centre one, one would come up the other way.
1966 PADDOCK 105 [The fence] consisted of three horizontal rails. . .interlaced (*riddled*) with very slender,
peeled rods. . .which alternated in their directions of
curvature so that the second opposed the first, the third
the second, and so on.

ride v Phr *ride the ice*: of seals, to frequent the
drifting ice-floes (1922 *Sat Ev Post* 195, p. 126).
  1924 ENGLAND 24 The young and their
mothers. . .with the dog seals more or less in attendance, 'ride the ice' for a month or so. 1980 *Evening
Telegram* 22 Nov, p. 24 I wish I had a shilling for every
seal that rode the ice [floes] passing the Groais Islands.

rider n Small triangular sail sheeted down at
the stern of a boat or vessel to steady the craft
into the wind; riding sail; cp DRIVER.
  T 453–67 Then we decided to chance it, try to get the
rider on her. We went down the stern locker and we
got the rider out.

riding vbl n The act of sledding down slopes.
  1972 MURRAY 130–1 In winter. . .'Riding' or 'sliding'
topped the list of play activities. Every section of the
community had its favourite 'riding spot' or spots.

rift* See RAFT[1] v.

rifter* n See RAFT[1] v 2.

rifter* v See RAFTER v.

rig n also **rig-out**. Cp *OED* ~ sb[6] 2 (1857–), rig-
out (1823–) for sense 1. See FIT-OUT.
  1 Habitual wearing apparel.

1874 *Maritime Mo* iii, 555 It was sold in St John's for
a handsome sum, out of which Job purchased a new
'rig-out' for Mary and Zek. 1887 BOND 37 He was a
goodly man to look at. . .even in his homely fisherman's 'rig.' 1900 DEVINE & O'MARA 239 First time
policemen wore uniform in this island. The rigout was
plain blue coat, with stand-up collar, figured white.
1924 ENGLAND 250 Dem Scotchmen'd walk round in
full rig [best clothes], an' de Newf'un'landers'd come
on to 'em wid guns. T 222–66 They would usually dress
up in their Sunday rig, perhaps put on their new
scroopy boots or shoes, and take the whole family with
them.
  2 The costume, face-disguise and appurtenances of a Christmas mummer or 'janny.'
  1893 *Christmas Greetings* 18 I think it was on St
Stephen's Day, that my friend Will J— first showed me
his 'rig,' and told me that I should get one too as they
were all 'going out in the fools' that night. 1895
PROWSE 402 A good 'rig-out' [for the fools or
mummers] cost both time and money. 1944 LAWTON &
DEVINE 23 Christmas was anticipated keenly by young
and old. It was mummering time. Long before Christmas, considerable time was spent on designing costumes and fantastic rigs. T 55/7–64 You would know
'em if they weren't masked. That's why they'd have a
false rig on an' a mask. 1969 *Christmas Mumming in
Nfld* 155 In this section we shall describe how mummers deliberately distort their normal physical appearance by the use of costumes and 'rig-outs.'
  3 A technical device contrived for a specified
purpose; contraption.
  1910 *Nfld Qtly* Oct, p. 23 Where ye goin with that
'rig-out'? D'ye want to frighten all the fish wid yer
puffin? T 178/9–65 A duff is [made in] a bag about so
long, and you put your dough in the bag. And when
you'd take un out of the pot you would untie him—he
had a drawing-string in the mouth of un, and tied over;
and you'd untie that and take hold by the end and the
duff'd shoot out in the pan. That was the rig of a duff!
P 243–66 [The Japanese automatic squid-jigger is] a
grand rig-out.

rig v also ~ **out**, ~ **up**. *OED* ~ v[2] 6, 6 b for
sense 1; cp *OED* 3 for sense 2. See FIT: *fit out*.
  1 To prepare, equip, put into order (something); esp to improvise in an impromptu or
ingenious manner.
  [c1875] 1977 *Evening Telegram* 14 Feb, p. 6 It was
the old lady who discovered what was wrong. It seems
she had forgotten to 'rig' the lamp. Her husband, in his
anxiety to keep the lamp burning, had applied the
genge hook too vigorously and drawn the last inch of
the 'rigging' [i.e. the makeshift wick]. 1884 STEARNS
193 It is a matter of no small difficulty to 'rig' a komatik
for a trip, getting all the lashings and the ropes in
proper order. 1897 HOWLEY *MS Reminiscences* 15 Had
to give up for the night and try to rig up a shelter.
T 54/64–64 But the Waterloo stove was perfect. Even
the oven was on the stove, rigged up, and a stove-pipe
on it. T 96–64[1] He had this hobby-horse rigged out with
a string [and] two pieces o' wood for a mouth.
T 100/2–64 A cast-net is a bigger thing than that. 'Tis a
big thing perhaps hold a barrel o' salmon, and he's rig-

ged with a reevin' string in the mouth. T 141/65–65¹ I never rigged a puncheon tub, but [boys might] take a puncheon tub out of a feller's stage, put un overboard, put the spile into un; put a rock into un, take a piece o' board and get a stalligan or something and paddle across the tickle. P 245–66 Sometimes we'd rig up a kitchen-scoff. C 71–37 Can't get VOCM on me radio at all, but be Jesus I could rig up a tar can and get the government station. 1977 BURSEY 43 First when he got the [radio] set he rigged it up and heard a man speak. 'Here shove this on your head and just listen,' he shouted to Aunt Millie Ann, 'I heard a man speak.'

2 To put on one's clothes; dress.

1893 *Christmas Greetings* 19 'Come Jack,' said he, 'we must rig you up now. Get those duds girls.' P 269–63 I was going to rig up for Mass. T 169–65² We boys used to wear petticoats till we was about three or four year old. Just the same as a girl. That's how we was rigged. 1971 HORWOOD 148 The captain and mate took off their oil-skins and rigged out the girls. 1979 NEMEC 257–8 After 'riggin' up,' the men will cluster together in one of the 'shacks,' if it appears likely that they will be unable to go fishing.

3 To disguise one's body and face to take the part of a Christmas mummer; JANNY v: *janny up*.

T 45–64 If a feller rigged out as a girl he'd get girl's clothes an' put on, an' put a veil over your face then, that they wouldn't know you. T 154–65 [The mummer] would rig up [in] all kinds of faces.

rigging(s) n Cp *DAE* rigging 1 'equipment, apparatus' (1849–) for sense 1.

1 An improvised part of an apparatus.

[See (c1875) 1977 quot at **rig** v.]

2 Supply of tea, sugar, etc, to 'boil the kettle', fixings (P 37).

Q 67–8 The old folks getting ready to go in the woods fishing or berry picking, etc, used such sayings as 'got the riggins for the kettle.'

riggle, riggling See RIDDLE n.

right int *OED* ~ adv 9 a, b arch; *EDD* 11 'thoroughly, completely'; *ADD* 3 a. Cp SOME. Thoroughly; absolutely, 'really'; excessively; very.

[c1833] 1927 DOYLE (ed) 15 "Come all ye Jolly Ice-Hunters": 'Twas on the fourth of April, right well I mind the day. 1861 DE BOILIEU 191 We had two visits from the mountaineers, but they conducted themselves so savagely that I was right glad to see their backs. 1895 *Christmas Review* 18 Sam Holland *was* a bit of a builder, and no mistake, and a number of fishermen did believe, that if he put his mind to work, 'right hard,' he would succeed. 1924 ENGLAND 120 "Tis a martal hard t'ing to be cut off right-a shart from de stuff. Well, me son, 'ere's to ye!' P 148–63 The coffee's not right done yet. T 36–64 Some people haves fish-houses, little small houses made right square and. . .turned down over these faggots. T 43–64 [the fish. . .] 'Twould go like grass, right soft. The dampness from the ground would take the pickle out of the fish and turn it right raggety. T 92/3–64 You get so much flour, so much pork, and so much molasses, and you cut your pork right fine. T 141/67–65² Now seine tar will mix with the hot

water—hot, perhaps right boiling, but [not] the coal tar. T 194/5–65 I went over and pulled my trap, and he was right full of herring—they was meshed in the vees, meshed in the skirts. 1977 *Inuit Land Use* 254 Just at break-up when the ice is moving, the water is right thick; you can't see the bottom.

rightify v *EDD* ~ v Ir, *ADD*. To correct, rectify; put right (1924 ENGLAND 319).

P 148–61 Make a mistake. . .rightify it. T 253/4–66 If I'd go wrong I'd rightify myself, but he's a long song. P 245–82 The drains on the Arterial is wrong in some places. And the Government will have to rightify them—the flooding in the fall showed that.

rind n also **rhind, rine*** [rɛind, rain, raɪn, rein] *OED* ~ sb¹ 1 'bark of a tree or plant' (888–1845); *EDD* sb¹ 3 esp s w cties; *DC* Nfld (1620–) for sense 1.

1 The bark or cortex of a tree, specif a 6-ft (1.8 m) length of bark removed in one piece from a standing spruce or fir and used for various fisheries and building purposes.

1620 WHITBOURNE 30 The rindes of these trees serve to cover their Stages, and necessary roomes, with turfes on them; so that in a few yeares, I feare, that most of the good timber trees neere the Sea-side, where men use to fish, will be either felled, spoyled or burned. [1663] 1963 YONGE 56 The houses are made of a frythe of boughs, sealed inside with rinds. . .and covered with the same. 1792 CARTWRIGHT i, xii Each rind must be six feet long, and as wide as the circumference of the tree on which it grew. [1822] 1856 CORMACK 9 Fishermen of the neighbouring parts came hither in spring for the rinds of the fir tree. 1840 GOSSE 25 A rind is the whole bark, for about five feet in length, of a young fir, or spruce, which, (an incision all round at each end, and a longitudinal division, having been made,) is at that season easily stripped off: when pressed flat, they are used as a covering for piles of fish in wet weather. [1894] 1975 WHITELEY 169 Men went for Rinds—two boats. 1927 DOYLE (ed) 59 "One Summer in 'Bonay'": 'Twas Banbary River where we were consigned, / We had one boat for wood, and another for rhind. 1932 BARBOUR 1 We then spread rinds all over the hold, and the ship was ready for the fish the next day. 1955 DOYLE (ed) 30 "I'se the B'y": Sods and rinds to cover yer flake, / Cake and tea for supper, / Codfish in the spring o' the year / Fried in maggoty butter. T 14/20–64 Before the men would start to go fishing, they'd go away in the woods where there was timber, let's say six to ten inches in diameter. As far as they could reach, they'd cut the rine off and come right down through and cleave the rine off. With sap in the tree the rine would come off. . . You'd have what we used to call a shim, something like a slice. You take that and you shove it around the rine. T 141/68–65² You do 'em up in tens, ten rines—that'd be a nitch. . .you'd never believe the weight is in rind—enough for an ordinary man to lug, a nitch o' rines is. 1973 GOUDIE 40 Every spare moment I had I peeled the rind (bark) off the logs and helped lay the floor.

2 Phr *as near as rind on a tree*: very close
(P 148–63).

rind v   also **rend, rine*** [rɛind, ræin, rain, rɛin,
'rainən, 'raindɨd] *OED* ~ v¹ (Nfld: 1623–); *EDD*
v¹ 8 So; *DC* Nfld (1620–1793) for sense 1.

1 To decorticate or peel the bark from a tree
or log; specif to strip the bark from a standing
spruce or fir in fixed lengths for various fisheries
or building purposes.

1612 *Willoughby Papers* [Guy's Journal] Theire
canoaes are about 20 foote long [and] they have thinne
lighte peeces of dry firre rended, as yt weare lath and in
steede of boorde they use the utter [birch] barke which
is thinne [and] hath many foldes, sowed togeather.
1620 WHITBOURNE 30 For our Nation, upon their arrivall yeerly to that Countrey, doe cut downe many of
the best trees they can finde, to build their stages and
roomes withall for their necessary occasions; hewing,
rinding, and destroying many others that grow within a
mile of the Sea, where they use to fish. [1676] 1895
PROWSE 205 Trees are rinded, the shipps doing it most,
and the comers out of England—done. . .to cover
whole stages and lodging houses. [1693] 1793 REEVES x
That no person whatsoever shall, at any time after the
said twenty-fifth of March, rind any of the trees there
standing or growing upon any occasion whatsoever.
1895 *J A Folklore* viii, 36 ~ to strip [the bark] off [a
tree]. 1901 *Christmas Review* 13 We cut a dogwood
stick, about twelve feet long; rinded it, sharpened it at
the ends with our knives; drove it thro the molasses.
[1910] 1930 COAKER 26 Every tree rinded becomes
valueless and useless, and as the prime young fir tree is
generally the victim, every rind means the waste of 100
feet of prime lumber. T 50–64 Logs [were] cut in the
woods, an' when they'd come out they'd be rinded.
C 70–35 In the spring of the year, the men go into the
woods to 'rine the trees'. . . The bark is removed from
the tree with an axe in six or seven foot lengths. The
width would depend on the diameter of the tree being
rined. This is dried out by placing it flat on the floor of
the flake, store, or stage and covered with rocks to
weight it down. M 71–115 She went in the wood to rind
birch rinds (inner bark) for tanning sealskins.

2 To spread strips of bark on the roof and
walls of a house as insulation and waterproofing.

T 36/8–64 When the fish had been finished the [birch]
rind wouldn't be much good for the next year, so some
fellers would keep it for felt [to] rine the roofs.

3 Phr *rind out, ~ over*: to scrape the skin off (a
person's limb).

P 269–63 You're going to rind over your leg. 1973
PINSENT 9 He didn't show the damage to the others but
from what I could see I knew goddam well he should
have wrapped the rope around his hands before his
famous flight. 'Dey're all rined out! Dey're all rined
out!' was what I thought he kept saying all along the
pipeline to Fourth Avenue.

rinded p ppl also **rined***. See RIND v. Of a tree,
with the bark or 'rind' removed (P 266–64).

M 69–6 A twister [tightening rope] was made from a
rinned fir tree.

rinder n   also **rhynder**. One engaged to remove
sections of bark from spruce or fir trees.

[1771] 1792 CARTWRIGHT i, 129 [Two of the hands]
then joined the rinders, and the other two ground
hatchets. [1774] ibid ii, 21 I sailed this morning. . .to
bring home the rinds and rinders. 1876 MURRAY &
HOWLEY 449 The more recent destruction [of the
forest] is in many cases clearly traceable to the most
culpable neglect, on the part of the trappers, lumber
explorers or '*rhynders*,' in omitting to extinguish their
camp fires, or smoke heaps, which they had used to
drive off flies. M 69–17 My father told me how the
rinders counted their rinds. . . This is the rhyme they
used: Two and two is four, / And two is a couple of
more. / This one and that one, / And the two in the
road is a nitch.

rinding vbl n   also **a-rinding, rining** ['ræinɨn]. Cp
OED ~ (1580–); *DC* Nfld (1633, 1792) for sense
1.

1 The action of stripping the bark from standing spruce or fir trees in sheets for use in the
fisheries and in building.

[1633] 1745 OSBORNE 785 That no person set fire in
any of the woods of the country, or work any detriment
or destruction to the same, by rinding of the trees,
either for the seeling of ships holds, or for rooms on
shore. [1676] 1895 PROWSE 205 [Inhabitants'] stages
and houses are most covered with New England and
the country's boards, so have little occasion of rinding.
[1771] 1792 CARTWRIGHT i, 129 At day-light I sent
three hands [a-]rinding. 1792 ibid *Gloss* i, xiii ~ The
action of taking the bark from trees. In this part of the
world, one length only, of six feet, is taken off the
lower part of the trunk of a tree. The chief use of rinds
is, to cover the roofs of houses and piles of fish. 1861
DE BOILIEU 168 A few [men] are left for a week or two
longer to procure the rinds, or bark of trees. Their
work is called 'rinding.' 1919 *Journ of Assembly* 482
The rinding of trees should be prohibited. . . This is too
great a destruction of green timber to be allowed.
T 141/67–65² Then there was rinin'. You had to go up
and rind your white-ends, rind your rind, sir.

2 Comb **rinding party**: members of a fishing
crew designated to strip sheets of bark from conifers.

1866 WILSON 208 About the tenth of May, the rinding parties go into the woods and strip the rind or bark
from the spruce-trees for about four feet of their
height, tie it in bundles, and bring it out on their
backs. . .to the fishing-room, where it is used for covering the fish when nearly dry, and also for covering their
stages and small houses.

rinding shim: wooden implement like a spatula, used to strip the bark off trees in sheets; SHIM
(P 243–71).

rinding time: early spring period of preparation for the fishing season; COLLAR TIME; May,
when the sap runs in fir trees, and bark is easy to
remove.

1893 *Trade Review Christmas No* 13 Two other
events were tacitly claimed by the fishermen as occasions for merry-making, such as 'Rinding time' and

'Wetting the lines.' The former occurred in spring, when all the boats' crews went into the woods to get rinds off spruce and fir trees, to cover their fish piles when in process of being dried on the flakes.

rine* See RIND n, v.

ring n   Cp *OED* kiss-in-the-ring (1825–) for sense 1.

1 Esp in pl, game in which boys and girls form a circle, act out parts and often kiss.

T 92/3–64 Yes, always a dance an' rings, you know. All kinds o' fun. T 169/206–65² The boys an' the maidens would get together an' we would have rings. There were three or four songs we'd sing there; an' they were all about takin' a maid or kissin' a maid—you always do that; and the maiden, they sort of refrain from the kiss first but nevertheless they always stood fire when they come to the test. T 172/5–65 If 'twas time enough we'd be playin' rings—"King William was King George's Son" and all that. 1972 MURRAY 159–60 At the picnics. . .the chief entertainment for the older boys and girls was the 'rings'—the closest most of them came to dancing—for most elderly Methodists considered dancing a sin.

2 Phr *rings around*: noisy row, rumpus.

1937 DEVINE 63 There was rings around at Blank's last night.

3 Comb **ring-billed diver**: ring-necked duck (*Aythya collaris*).

1964 *Evening Telegram* 28 Oct, p. 5 But the much rarer ring-necked duck is called a 'ring-billed diver,' a better and more accurate description than its accepted name—for the ringed bill is common to both sexes and to all plumages, whereas the ring on the neck is only occasionally to be seen.

ring(a)rod See RIDDLE n.

ringer n

1 Circular plank table used in shaping cask hoops from birch rods; RINGING TABLE.

P 127–78 Hoops which have gone through a bending procedure called 'breaking the hoop' on the 'bendin horse' are quiled on a 'ringer.' The ringer is circular like the head of a barrel, with pegs, usually four, around the outside edges. The newly cut, split, and bent birch is quiled inside the pegs, where it assumes a circular shape. When twelve hoops are quiled they are removed and tied into a circular bundle.

2 Semipalmated ringed plover (*Charadrius hiaticula semipalmatus*) (1959 MCATEE 27).

ringing vbl n Comb **ringing table**: circular plank table used in shaping cask hoops from birch rods; RINGER.

1937 DEVINE 41 The birch hoop-poles (young saplings) are split from end to end and [coiled] round the wooden spikes set into [the ringing table]. Afterwards they are tied in bundles and left to soak for some days in a brook. M 71–120 They then go to the ringin' table on which wooden pegs formed a circle which was to be the desired circumference of the hoops.

rip v   To remove the gills and intestinal tract of herring or mackerel; GIB v.

[1892] 1896 *Consolidated Statutes of Nfld* 829 All herrings that are not gibbed or ripped, shall be branded or marked with the word 'round,' in addition to other brands or marks. 1960 FUDGE 5, 6 The pay was small, being twenty-four cents per barrel [of herring], ripped and packed, with all bellies filled. . . I was very quick at ripping herring and became nicknamed 'Jack the Ripper.' 1975 BUTLER 74 First we would hoist the mackerel from the boat to the wharf. Then we would take them in the store and put them in pounds. We would then rip them down the back, take out the gill and gut, scrape the blood from the fish, throw them in vats of clean water and let them soak again.

rise v   Cp *OED* ~ v 10 c 'to work or swell under leaven' [intrans] for sense 1.

1 To cause (dough) to swell up by the use of yeast; to cause to ferment.

1887 *Telegram Christmas No* 9 [There were] bull-birds. . .supported on the one side by an overflowing plate of mealy potatoes and, on the other, by an equally generous plate of 'riz' bread and butter. 1888 STEARNS 98 'What do you make your beer of?' said Mr Benton. 'Of spruce steeped in water, and molasses, and water, and rise it with some of the last mixing,' replied Mason. 1933 MERRICK 304 And John told me you was a proper trapper now and how you baked rose bread fer'n when you was way up there. T 92/3–64 That was the barm to put in your bread. That's what had to rise the bread. T 94/5–64 Toutons is rose dough.

2 Of a cod-net, to add to the number of meshes as one knits row after row.

T 66/7–64 We'll knit around perhaps six or seven rounds. Now [they are all] the one size. Now you have to rise on that, and you have to make the net large.

rise n

1 In knitting a cod-net, an increase in the number of meshes per row; cp RISE v 2.

T 66/7–64 What they had in a rise, you make eight parts. You'd put two meshes into one—you'd go twice in a hole.

2 The ascending curvature at the bow and stern of a boat's deck viewed broadside on; a boat's sheer.

T 43/8–64 Sheerin' her meant that there was so much rise to give her forrards, to bring her in proportion, and so much rise to give her aft down the counter.

3 The difference between the market price of seals or fish, estimated when a crew is engaged, and the (higher) price actually obtained at the end of the season.

1898 *Record* 10 When the merchants give the rise in fish. . . 1916 MURPHY 19 The crew of the *Zambesi* made £40 19s a man, seals fetched 27 shillings per quintal and the rise.

4 Phr *in rise*: of dough, placed in a warm place to rise (P 148–65).

5 Comb **rise deck**: elevated section of a ship's

deck aft of the wheel-house; BREAK-DECK
(P 148–67).

P 127–77 The rise deck [is] an elevated section of a
ship's deck running aft from a short distance behind the
wheel-house.

rise end [ˌreɪz ˈɪn]: rear portion of a cod's
backbone, curving slightly upwards near the tail
(P 127–76).

rise line: rope attached to the bottom of the
'doors' of a cod-trap and used to close the
entrance before the net is hauled to the surface
(P 127–73).

rising ppl, vbl n. Cp *OED* ~ vbl sb 13 naut,
SMYTH 576; cp *OED* rise v 10 b 'to swell up,'
EDD ~ sb 5 'boil, a swelling' So.

Comb **rising board**: a form used as a guide in
determining the sheer of a boat or vessel during
construction; rising-square.

T 43/8–64 You had your mould to go by. You would
cut your frame by a mould and a rising board.
T 178/9–65 We'd have a mould for the timber, and he
was marked. And then another board, a risin'-board to
[hold] her, 'cordin as you go forrard and aft. We only
mould all the midship timbers.

rising finger, ~ **hand**: an extremity swollen
from infection; galled finger.

1952 BANFILL 137 On a sweltering First of July a boy
came to the Station and said he had a 'rizin finger.'
. . .One glance at the finger and I recalled these 'galled
fingers.'. . .In other words, one of those over-ripe
infected fingers which require immediate operation.
T 255–66 If you had a risin' sometimes, like you get a
risin' hand, and people believe that he could charm
that and stop it, so, well. . .he did. C 69–7 The best
thing he finds for a rising finger, hand, etc, or for any
sore or cut that gets full of pus and won't heal is a small
piece of salt pork.

rising pan: container in which bread dough is
placed to rise.

T 50/2–64 You know what a risin' pan is? Tin pan—it
is a small one.

rising n *Cent* ~ n 6. Amount of dough set by to
rise; batch (P 97–67).

1976 GUY 66 There was a good coat of blackening on
her Waterloo and she had in a rising of bread.

rittick n Cp *EDD* rittoch 'greater tern' Ork
(1805–). Arctic tern (*Sterna paradisaea*);
STEARIN.

1891 PACKARD 438 Arctic Tern. Breeds plentifully
on islets in Ungava Bay; young of the year and adults
and eggs were procured there. Abundant on the other
coasts of the country. Known as the 'Rittick' at Ungava.

rivel* n See RAVEL.

rivel* v [ˈrɪvl]. Cp RAVEL. To unweave, unravel.

T 14/18–64 They're continually boiling and dyeing

rags for these mats, and rivelling out brin bags; rivel
out the bags, and take two or three strands and take it
on the spinning-wheel and twist together like worsted.

river n Comb **river head** [ˌrɪvəɹ ˈhɛd]: the
confluence of a river and the sea; river mouth or
estuary and the area adjacent to it; esp in place-
names, a settlement or neighbourhood at the
'head' or innermost part of an inhabited bay,
cove or harbour; also attrib.

[1663] 1963 YONGE [map facing p. 81] Riverhead.
1850 [FEILD] 44 I determined to proceed at once to
River Head [Bay of Islands]. 1858 [LOWELL] i, 128 [I]
travelled afoot the [best] part o' the w'y, and got the
trifle o' things, and came round by Castle B'y riverhead. 1861 DE BOILIEU 141 I had gone about five
miles, when crossing the river-head, or extreme end of
a small cove, I found the sea had increased in violence,
and the ice had commenced breaking adrift; with some
risk I crossed to the opposite side. 1909 BROWNE 263
Griffin's Harbor, which is situated on the northeast
corner of *Spotted Island*, was originally settled by Irishmen from St John's—'The Riverhead men,' as they
were usually called. 1953 *Nfld & Lab Pilot* ii, 79 From
Point of Beach the. . .shore trends
south-westward. . .to Riverhead at the head of the harbour. 1971 SEARY 68 In Newfoundland usage
[riverhead] denotes the mouth of a river. . .at the place
where it enters what again in Newfoundland usage is
indiscriminately and contradictorily called the head or
bottom of a harbour. 1975 *Evening Telegram* 28 June,
p. 16 That was for east end people. . .but the riverhead
crowd, as we called the westenders, went in the Jensen
camp way. There were lovely grassy spots there for
courtin'.

roach a *EDD* ~ adj 8 'rough, coarse' Do. (a)
Of wood or vegetation, coarse or rough in texture; (b) of a voice, deep, rasping, hoarse; distorted.

1863 MORETON 32 ~ Coarse. Of large gross growth.
Spoken of timber, it seems generally to be meant in
disparagement, signifying that it is too free and open
grained to be long serviceable: a stunted growth producing harder wood. To whatever it is applied, coarseness
of quality is usually intended. 1937 DEVINE 41 ~
Coarse, rough, applied to the voice or person, generally. C 67–14 ~ This word is used to describe a voice that
is deeper or more rasping than usual. My grandfather
says that smoking gives you a roach voice. My mother
also uses this word to mean hoarse. C 69–23 Soon she
saw him coming so she got up close to the fence and
when he was opposite her she said in a roach voice,
'I'm the devil.' Her husband looked at her and replied
in his drunken voice, 'Shake hands, brother, I'm married to your sister.'

road¹ n

1 One of a number of intersecting paths used
in cutting pulp-wood in a stand of timber; logging road; WOODS ROAD. Also in phr *road of
wood*: a quantity of pulp-wood.

T 43/8–64 There'll be one man on this road, an'
another man on the other road, the two o' them work-

ing on the same block o' timber between the two roads. 1966 PHILBROOK 166 These 'woods roads' vary in respect to the terrain and timber growth, hence a 'good road of wood' or 'blue bunch' is one where a logger has an easy time cutting and makes a good day's pay. C 68–17 [He] was always careful not to start a new phase of this work on a Friday. If he finished cutting a road of wood at dark on a Thursday, he would begin a new road, after dark, so as not to have to start a new road the next morning, Friday. 1979 TIZZARD 362 I continued cutting wood, and seemingly getting better every day, until the 21st. I cut out that road and had gone to another.

2 Comb road board: body responsible for the maintenance of local roads.

1853 *Journ of Assembly* Appendix, p. 195 Harbor Grace Road Board. [1897] 1911 ROGERS 186 Nominee road-boards were appointed in the electoral districts to distribute appropriations voted by the Legislature for local roads. The new Divisional Local Boards of 1897–8 are elective. 1914 *FPU (Twillingate) Minutes* 15 Jan The Chairman gave a little information regarding election of road board. 1980 *Nfld Qtly* Winter, p. 17 With their lists of planters and merchants, road boards and colonial office-holders. . . [these books] rarely fail us as handy guides to Newfoundland.

road² See RODE.

roaration n A deep and prolonged noise.

P 245–74 [describing the 1929 tidal wave] There was a roaration—a great noise [and then the sea struck].

roast See BLOW v.

robber n Comb **robber-bird**: Newfoundland grey jay (*Perisoreus canadensis sanfordi*).

1912 ROGERS 213 Our camp was simply infested with grey jays, generally known as robber-birds.

robin redbreast n also **robin** Cp *OED* ~ 1 a 'European redbreast' (1450–1862); *DAE* 'thrush' (1761–). Red-breasted migrating thrush of North America (*Turdus migratorius nigrideus*); NEWFOUNDLAND ROBIN.

[1766] 1971 BANKS 382 *Turdus ferrungineus*. . .Vernacular name Robin. . .Common in weeds, very abundant about St John's. [1779] 1792 CARTWRIGHT ii, 454 I shot a loon, took a duck's nest. . .and found a robin's nest. These birds are somewhat bigger than a thrush, are like that bird in shape, but of a more beautiful plumage. They build the same sort of nest, but their note is like the blackbird's; their eggs also, of which they seldom lay more than three, are very like those of the blackbird's. 1842 BONNYCASTLE i, 227 The Newfoundland blackbird is, perhaps, the rose-coloured ouzel (turdus roseus), called a robin here, although as large as a blackbird. [1930] 1980 *Evening Telegram* 2 Apr, p. 6 The robin red breast, harbinger of spring, is finally here. A flock of eighteen or twenty of the beautiful little birds was observed yesterday near Long Pond woods. 1967 *Bk of Nfld* iii, 280 ROBIN (*Turdus migratorius*): Arrives in large flocks in late March. More and more in recent

years, it has been overwintering. P 245–77 We'd always say, 'I saw a robin redbreast on the tree'—never 'I saw a robin.'

robustic a *OED* ~ a obs (1683–1719). Robust, strong (Q 67–91).

1895 *J A Folklore* viii, 31 But the Newfoundlanders still use [robustious], or the similar word *robustic*. 1937 DEVINE 41 ~ Vigorous, strong.

rock n Cp *OED* ~ cod (1634–), *DAE* (1634–); *DC* ~ partridge obs (1743–1795), rocker² (1883–).

Attrib, comb **rock bun**: small, plain bun.

P 148–60 Old salt-fish, old salt-pork, buns and rock-buns—that is what they gave him up here.

rock cod: variety of cod-fish; FISH.

[1785] 1792 CARTWRIGHT iii, 84 I sent four hands a fishing in the sealing-skiff, but they could catch only one rock-cod. 1832 MCGREGOR i, 118 The rock or red cod (gadus callarias) resembles, but is generally somewhat larger than, the rock cod or red-ware codling of Scotland. [1918–19] GORDON 55 I had bought a hundred rock cod for Turk's feed, and rode home sitting on top of them. 1932 POLUNIN 52 . . .calling them 'rock cod' and swearing they were 'no meat for no man'—if not actually poison. He said they were darker than ordinary cod, especially the lining of the stomach wall, and he split one open to show how black they were before throwing them overboard in disgust. 1953 *Nfld & Lab Pilot* ii, 273 Rock Cod islet. . .lies close northward. . .of Indian head. T 141/63–65² And somebody hove over the jigger, jig a rock cod. 1979 TIZZARD 323 My father sometimes caught a rock cod, so named because it stayed very close to the shoreline. These were never eaten but dried and sold, and when sold they were always classed as cullage, the lowest grade of fish.

rock dye: natural colouring matter made from lichens growing on rocks (P 13–80); MOLLY-FODGE.

1979 TIZZARD 62 Often we would gather a certain scale from rocks and when steeped, this would make a beautiful yellow color. I wore many a sweater dyed with rock dye.

rock flower: fireweed (*Epilobium angustifolium*) (1956 ROULEAU 36).

rock partridge, rocker: Welch's rock ptarmigan (*Lagopus mutus welchi*); GROUSE, PARTRIDGE.

1876 HOWLEY 60 *Rock Ptarmigan*. . .inhabiting only the highest and barest mountain ridges; it is called here 'Rock' or 'Mountain Partridge.' 1884 BELL 55 Rock Ptarmigan or Rocker. . .abundant on both sides of Hudson's Strait. 1908 HUBBARD 257 I shot three [rockers] with pistol, old one, two young, but could fly. 1910 *Nfld Qtly* Oct, p. 18 The ptarmigan, locally the 'rock partridge,' is like its congener of the high moors of old Scotia, the only difference being that our willow grouse turns white in winter. 1951 PETERS & BURLEIGH 152 Local names: Partridge, Ptarmigan, Rock Partridge, Rocker. . . Distinguished at all seasons by decided smaller size than the Willow Ptarmigan, and also by different habitat, the present species preferring the higher and rockier ridges and hills.

rocker¹ n Comb **rocker-tail lark**: spotted sand-piper (*Actitis macularia*); BEACH BIRD (1959 MCATEE 30).

rocker² See ROCK PARTRIDGE.

rocky a
Comb **rocky bone**: breastbone (of a fowl); wish-bone; CRACKER BONE.
C 69–2 The rocky bone was taken and placed on the stove to make it dry and easy to break. Each person then takes hold of it on each end. Whoever gets the longest part will be married first.
  rocky man: a marker, usu a pile of rocks prominently placed as a guide in coastal navigation; AMERICAN MAN, NAKED ~ .
P 256–79 The only term I have heard for those things is rocky man. There are a number of these off southern Labrador which may be navigational markers although one such cairn contained the broken bones of a caribou and a bright red pigment, perhaps a vermillion. In northern Labrador, of course, there may be *inukshuks* and I know there are small stone piles that mark old Inuit overland winter trails.

rod n Cp *OED* ~ sb¹ 1 (esp 1885 quot). A slender, pliable tree or shoot used for fencing, etc; cp RIDDLE: *riddle rod*, WITHE-ROD. Also attrib.
[1774] 1792 CARTWRIGHT ii, 32 Four hands. . .cut some killick-claws, and pulled rods. 1835 PANL GN 2/2, p. 103 A roddle fence shall have three longers in height and a post at the distance of every six feet the rods to be as close as possible. 1971 NOSEWORTHY 238 Rod fence. Same as *picket fence*. P 141–72 Rod broom. Limbs of trees, or twigs, tied to a stick to make a broom, commonly used to sweep out barns, etc. 1979 TIZZARD 236 In order to fence with those rods three garden rails were used. . .so that these little rods could twist easily around them.

rode n also **rhode, road** *DAE* ~ 'a rope for securing an anchor' (1643–1726); *Cent* ~⁵ [Bay of Fundy]; 1883 *Fish Exhibit Cat* 14 [Plymouth, England]; cp *OED* cable-laid for sense 2. From *OED* road sb 3 'sheltered piece of water near the shore where vessel may lie at anchor' (1320–1850): see *OED* 3 b at road 'riding at anchor' obs (1439–1641); see also *Mariner's Mirror* li (May, 1965), 115–16 and lii (1966), 87–9, with citations by Bertil Sandahl of rodrope, roderope (1294–1364).
  1 A strong, tightly woven rope used esp to secure an anchor or grapnel by which a small boat is moored in the harbour or on the inshore fishing-grounds; a line used to secure a fishing- or seal-net in place, etc. Attrib in coastal names. Cp COLLAR 1.
1612 *Willoughby Papers* 16 a [inventory for a voyage to Newfoundland] small coyle of ropes. . .for boates

hallers and roades. 1762 CO 194:15 [inventory for Northern fishery] To 20 Roades [for boat] £40. [1777] 1792 CARTWRIGHT ii, 261 The *Hautboy*, riding at the stage head, parted her road and drove on shore near the salt-house. 1792 ibid *Gloss* i, xiii ~ A small tow-line, of four inches and an half; made use of by shallops, by way of a cable. 1792 PULLING *MS* Aug We were nine of us in the boat, and had come too, about a roads length from the shore in Shoal Bay, two miles from Fogo Harbor, and went into the punt to go a-shore in a little cove. 1843 *Nfld Indicator* 18 Nov, p. 3 Cordage—viz. Hawsers, Roads, Ratlin, Bolt-rope, Houseline, Marline, Hambroline, and Spunyarn. 1861 DE BOILIEU 85 The foot of [the seal-net] is brought-to on a shallop's old rode, and the head on two fishing-lines with corks between. 1895 *Christmas Review* 12 [proverb] When the 'rode' cuts the liar comes in. (Rode is the rope attached to grapnel.) 1937 DEVINE 71 It was extremely unlucky to coil a rope, line or rhode against the sun. 1953 *Nfld & Lab Pilot* ii, 540 Rhodes island lies close westward of Bennet island and is separated from it by Shoal tickle, a narrow channel only navigable by boats. 1967 FIRESTONE 89 The trap is held up by five water tight kegs or some times by plastic buoys. *Five rodes* [lines running to grapnels] hold the trap in place. 1971 SEARY 87–8 The specific in Double Road Point, DOUBLE ROAD POINT (NTS St Mary's), variously spelled rode, road or rhode, is a term current in Newfoundland for a rope, especially one attached to a boat anchor or trawl. 1975 BUTLER 55 A rhode was a rope used for mooring [the boat]. [It was] a piece of hemp rope, the size depended on the size of boat—from one half to three quarters of an inch in diameter. 1979 TIZZARD 94 The punt was fitted with a little cuddy at the front, the rode—the rope on the grapnel—was always coiled here.
  2 Comb **rode-laid**: distinguishing a rope composed of a certain number of strands.
1852 *Morning Post* 12 Feb, p. 4 P & L Tessier 200 coils shroud and rode laid cordage at a low figure. . . Rendell 200 coils prime Russian and English, shroud and rode laid *Cordage*.

rodney n also **rondey*** *DC* ~ n Nfld (1916–). A small round-bottomed boat with square stern, used chiefly as a tender; a small 'punt'; cp COLLAR BOAT; attrib, esp in coastal names. Fig. term of endearment for a girl or child.
1887 *Nfld & Lab Pilot* (2nd ed) 213 Bluff head cove lies southward of Rodney cove. 1896 *Christmas Review* 18 It was meant as the highest tribute to the boat-building capabilities of Jim Leary, whose handiwork, whether displayed in the construction of baitskiff, smack, skiff, punt or rodney, was always superior to what any other man in the settlement could turn out. [1900 OLIVER & BURKE] 57 "Dear Little Tommy": . . .he turned her young head, / When he gallantly said, / You're a trim little rodney, my hearty. 1906 DUNCAN 71 The punt and the rodney, the latter far in the lead, ran quietly out from the harbour, with their little sails all spread. [1929] 1933 GREENLEAF (ed) 248 "The Sealing Cruise of the *Lone Flier*": On the twenty-fifth of April, as we were near our town, / Four rodneys we then put out to tow her to the town. 1953 *Nfld*

& *Lab Pilot* ii, 203 Rodney rock, with a depth of less than 6 feet over it, is situated in the entrance to Rodney cove. T 210/11–65 When I was fifteen, or fourteen, I'm not sure which—it would depend on when I built the flat. . .flat-boat—I built another one—a rodney boat. My father just marked out an' showed me how to do it. . . She turned out to be a good rodney boat; about fourteen feet long, say four foot wide an' 'bout twenty inches deep. T 198–65 I dare say we built eight or ten, you know. . .boats; an' what they called rodneys—small ones, you know, for sealin' in. M 68–15 The length of the rodney ranges from fourteen to eighteen feet. It is used most often in the lobster fishery and the catching of cod. When employed in the cod fishery it is generally towed behind a motor boat, which resembles a rodney, being approximately twice as large and propelled by an engine. C 71–105 If a child followed his parents wherever they went, they [might] comment: ''E goes wherever I goes. 'E's me rodney, 'e is.' C 71–123 A type of small boat used to go to the collar to get the big boat was called a rondey [and it was sculled not rowed]. 1974 SQUIRE 15 Each would build his own small boat or rodney as they were more often called. This was a boat varying from ten to fifteen feet in length, usually operated by one man, or sometimes a man and a boy. 1975 BUTLER 37 He had this punt and he had a hole down in her aft. . . We were in a rodney, a punt, built right light a purpose for that [easy lanching], see.

roke n   Cp *OED* ~ sb 'smoke, steam; vapour'; *EDD* roak(e) sb 1, 2. Smoke, vapour; perspiring state; anger; esp in phr *be all of a roke, be in a roke* (1896 *J A Folklore* ix, 24).
    1937 DEVINE 41 I'm all of a *roke* of sweat. The stove is giving out a great *roke*. P 37 ~ State of uncontrolled anger. To be 'in a roke.'

roll v
    1 Of caplin, to school in inshore waters; during spring spawning time, to be swept on the beaches at high tide.
    C 68–17 In the spring when the caplin come in and rolls, most men get some to salt and dry. 1977 BURSEY 13 ''Pioneering'': Caplin is a fish in great demand / They roll in millions on the sand. 1977 *Inuit Land Use* 264 [The caplin] come into the shore and spawn right up to the shore. They roll up by the thousands on the beach. 1978 *Evening Telegram* 4 Mar, p. 2 Although it is March, caplin are rolling in on the beaches of the Trinity Bay community of Random Island. Caplin usually don't roll in on the province's beaches until mid-June. 1979 TIZZARD 285 After spending considerable time at the shore or rolling on the beaches the caplin would move off to about five or six fathoms of water and rest on the bottom there before disappearing altogether.
    2 Phr *roll out. . .roll in*.
    1901 *Christmas Review* 9 [In] those days, so we have been told by our grandfathers, the principle of the supply trade, was 'roll out in the spring and roll in in the fall'; in other words, the merchant gave the fisherman all his household supplies, and took all his fish and oil in return.

roller[1] n   *Fisheries of U S*, p. 15 for sense 3.
    1 A small iceberg that tips over easily; ROLLING PAN.
    1846 TOCQUE 195 Sometimes vessels are crushed between large masses of ice called 'rollers,' when all are consigned to one common destruction.
    2 Male caplin at spawning time; cp ROLL.
    P 245–67 The fishermen calls 'em rollers—they rolls in ahead of the females.
    3 Wheel or rotating wooden cylinder used on a small boat to handle or haul fishing-lines, nets, ropes, etc.
    P 148–65 The trawl line goes over [the roller], with one man baiting the hooks. M 68–7 A roller is used to pull in the rode or moorings. 1971 NOSEWORTHY 238 ~ A wheel used to aid in bringing up trawls.
    4 Transverse bar forming part of a bob-sled.
    T 100/1–64 Bob-sled is a little sleigh about five feet long. There's just one bulk going across the middle, with a bar across the front of it, what they used to call a roller, roller bar.

roller[2] n   also **rawler** *EDD* ~ sb 3 'roll of carded wool,' BARNES 94 'has the sound of "o" in collar' Do. Carded wool formed into rolls and ready for spinning.
    P 154–78 *Rollers* rhymes with *hollers*. 1979 POCIUS 14 [In Conception Bay] her mother frequently [commented] 'I probably made one hundred and fifty rawlers today.'

rolling ppl Comb **rolling pan**: small iceberg rocking in the sea water (1966 FARIS 29).
    1842 JUKES i, 297–8 We discovered the noise we heard last night to proceed from what is called a 'rolling' pan. This was a small iceberg of very irregular shape, about sixty yards across, and its average height above the water about twenty-five feet. . .[and] swinging to and fro in the water. . .producing a noise and motion exactly like that of breakers.

rompse v   also **rampse***. Cp DINNEEN ramsach adj 'romping. . .noisy,' n 'jumping, hopping. . .uproar.' To fight playfully and noisily; to skylark.
    1955 ENGLISH 35 ~ to wrestle. P 251–65 I've already told them not to rompse in the classroom. C 71–95 ~ used by my parents when two or more of us were carrying on, tormenting one another, throwing light cracks or punches, but with no intent to quarrel. P 191–73 ~ to romp or wrestle.

rookery n   *EDD* ~ sb[2] 'a heap of disorder' Gl. A state of confusion; litter, disorder.
    1896 *J A Folklore* ix, 30 ~ all in a rookery, confusion or disorder. 1925 *Dial Notes* v, 340 ~ Confusion; ruckus. 1969 *Trans Dev Assoc* ci, 187 *Rookery* (as in the phrase 'All in a *rookery*' meaning 'in confusion or uproar').

room n   *OED* ~ sb[1] 6 c 'fishing station in BNA Provinces' (1858), 2 'sufficient space,' *DC* 1, 2 Nfld (1620–; 1948) for sense 1; *EDD* sb[1] 5 Sh I

Co, *OED* 9 d for sense 2; *EDD* 3, JOYCE 315 for sense 3.

1 A tract or parcel of land on the waterfront of a cove or harbour from which a fishery is conducted; the stores, sheds, 'flakes,' wharves and other facilities where the catch is landed and processed, and the crew housed; often with specifying word: ADMIRAL, BOAT, COOK, FISH(ING), FLAKE, SHIP(S), STAGE, etc, or the name or nationality of the original user; common in phr *on the room*; sometimes in place-names indicating the whole of a cove, harbour or settlement. Cp PLANTATION, PREMISES, STATION.

1620 WHITBOURNE 30 The rindes of these trees serve to cover their Stages, and necessary rooms, with turfes on them. [1676] 1895 PROWSE 205 Their Stages and Roomes were for the most part well left. [1786] 1792 CARTWRIGHT iii, 199 A brig belonging to Mr Tory, of Poole; who has established a codfishery here, on the room which was formerly mine. [1804] 1954 INNIS 106 These byeboatkeepers in England generally choose the best sailing ships so as to gain their passage sooner, and if they reach the country early they place themselves in the best and most convenient places by the water side, whereby later ships are often obliged to hire both stage and room from them. 1857 MOUNTAIN 4 They went out to fish. . .receiving in return a regular amount of wages, and living in the 'Rooms' or merchant's establishment. 1895 *J A Folklore* viii, 37 One of the most singular peculiarities, however, of the dialect of Newfoundlanders is the use of the word *room* to denote the whole premises of a merchant, planter, or fisherman. On the principal harbors, the land on the shore was granted in small sections, measuring so many yards in front, and running back two or three hundred yards, with a lane between. Each of these allotments was called a *room*, and according to the way in which it was employed, was known as a merchant's room, a planter's room, or a fisherman's room. [1898] 1905 *Nfld Law Reports* 24 If the servant is to lose his lien by the removal of the fish, he must arrest it upon the room. 1902 *Christmas Bells* 19 I had to take old Skipper Ben, as he was supposed to be a good pilot, and also Jim Rogers, who was a hand on the room, and Tom Sparks, who was a fine rigger. 1909 BROWNE 62 'Room'. . .is difficult to describe, as it may consist of a substantial dwelling house, commodious stores, substantial wharves and landings; or, as is the case in the recently settled places in the far North, it may consist of an 8x10 shanty, a 'bunkhouse' and a 'stage'. . .and a 'stagehead,' or landing place, built of 'longers.' 1936 SMITH 205–6 My next business was to buy a room at Cutthroat. . . I asked Mr Ryan what property he had there, and what price he wanted for it. He named what he had there, a fishing-stage, small hold (about 300 quintals fish), a bulley, or fishing boat, to carry about 16 quintals, a dwelling-house, puncheons and a good bawn for spreading about 300 quintals fish. 1951 *Nfld & Lab Pilot* i, 117 Spanish Room is situated on the eastern side of a peninsula the south-western extremity of which, known as Spanish Room point, lies about one mile northward of Big head. 1953 ibid ii, 200 Duder's Room and Slade's Room, two small inlets,

lies. . .southward. . .of Carters head. T 192–65 Grandfather bought half of his room, Walsh's room, and he gave the other half of his room [to] two more sons for to look after him as long as he lived. 1966 SCAMMELL 30 As we got old enough to work on the 'room' at ten or twelve cents an hour, 'yaffling fish' we got a huge kick out of taking up the value of our earnings in those little personal necessities which meant to us gracious living. T 411–67 Fish was brought there in a semi-dry state and it was taken in and dried. We referred to their premises as the rooms. These were a large group of stores with flakes all around and so high as sixty and seventy men working there. 1975 BUTLER 65 When he first went in operation in Buffett, he operated along much the same lines as Thomas Hann; that is, he had fishermen fishing off his room.

2 In a fishing craft, the division between the several thwarts of an undecked, or partly decked, boat; freq with specifying word *after, forward*, MIDSHIP, STANDING. Cp POUND.

[1857 MOUNTAIN 6 (The punt) is about six feet keel. . .with 'standing rooms' to row in, and the midship and stern, where the fish is stowed.] 1937 DEVINE 23 . . .the compartments ('rooms') of a fishing boat. 1952 STANSFORD 8 They had their small schooners there also, and we were fortunate in hauling aboard a good catch, putting the fish in the rooms (that is the pounds). . .we put some in the midships rooms. T 43/8–64 From the bow tawt which is the forrard tawt, to the stem is the fore-standing-room, an' from that to the after tawt is the midship room, an' from the after tawt to the counter is the after room. T 455/6–67[2] You'd stand in those little rooms across her—there'd be three o' they into her. M 69–17 When the fish is caught it is thrown in a room in the boat. These rooms are covered with gang-boards to keep the sun off the fish. Gang-boards are movable boards made to fit the different rooms in a fishing boat. 1979 TIZZARD 94 This room was covered with gangboards. During fishing one or two of these gangboards would be removed so that when fish was put in there the sun would not shine directly on them.

3 The living-room or parlour (of a dwelling).

[1886] LLOYD 76–7 The hut usually consists of four apartments, two downstairs and a similar number upstairs. These apartments are severally known as 'the house' (kitchen), 'room' (which may for sake of distinction be called a parlour), 'outside loft' (room over kitchen), and 'inside loft' (over parlour). [1906] GRENFELL 147–8 'The room' is that part of a fisherman's house where all the best furniture is kept, and into which the children are only permitted to peep when the schoolmaster or the chance preacher comes along. T 222–66 There is no such word in the vocabulary of many Newfoundlanders as 'living room.' It is called simply 'the room,' which is an indication of its exalted status; or sometimes it's called 'the inside place.'

4 The central section of a 'seal net'; POUND.

1895 GRENFELL 170–1 The easier way of catching the 'old harps' is with the submerged room of net, resembling the cod trap, with the difference that the wall which is on the side the seals enter from is lowered to the bottom. A watch is kept from the shore, and as soon as the seals enter the room a rope attached to this wall is wound up on a capstan on the land, and the seals are thus imprisoned.

5 Attrib, comb **room berth**: a place as seal-hunter on a vessel given by the merchant firm owning the craft; BERTH.

1924 ENGLAND 7 The captains 'give out tickets' and so do the officers; and these tickets, entitling men to berths, are. . .eagerly sought. . . 'Room berths' are berths given out by the firms. These are greatly desired; firms and captains alike keep their retainers in true feudal style by judicious distribution.

room holder: occupier of fishing premises or 'station.'

1909 BROWNE 258 England paid an indemnity to French 'roomholders' on the French shore.

room keeper: see **room holder**; cp BY-BOAT KEEPER, PLANTER.

[1863] 1954 INNIS 397 [petition of] the roomkeepers of Bay Bulls.

room stuff: timber, the bark or 'rinds' of trees, and other materials for the construction and maintenance of buildings on a fishing premises.

1866 WILSON 214 The men in general do little else during winter, than get 'room-stuff' and firewood. 1937 DEVINE 41 ~ Timber cut in the woods for stage, flakes and stores, etc.

roomer n   Cp *OED* room sb¹ 3 b to make room, E K CHAMBERS *The English Folk-Play* (1933), pp. 16 ff for sense 1; for sense 2, see ROOM.

1 In Christmas mummers' play, the presenter of the action, speaker of the induction.

[c1900] 1969 *Christmas Mumming in Nfld* 197 *Roomer (Introduction Officer)*. Room, room, gallant room, room required here tonight / For some of my bold champions are coming forth to fight; / Old act, new act, acts you never saw before, / For I am the very champion that brings old Father Christmas to your door, / And if you don't believe these words I say, step in Father Christmas and boldly declare thy way.

2 Migratory fisherman from the island of New-foundland who conducts summer fishery from a 'station' or 'room' on the coast of Labrador; STATIONER.

1909 BROWNE 62 'Stationers' (sometimes called. . .'Roomers'). 1924 ENGLAND 261 Thousands of outport men migrate almost as regularly as the seals themselves. With small, home-built schooners—these ingenious people can turn their hands to making almost everything they need—they take up the sea trek every summer and go down the Labrador. If they pick some berth and settle down, they're called 'stationers,' 'squatters,' or 'roomers.'

roost n   Cp *OED* ~ sb¹ 1 'perch for domestic fowls.' A wooden bar serving as a foot support for one using a seat-less privy.

1979 TIZZARD 361 The bathroom was a small shed and roost. . . [This was] a three-inch diameter rod in the small shed approximately four feet by five. The roost was fastened to the side walls about eighteen inches from the floor and one foot from the back wall.

With your feet on this roost and your back resting against the back wall of the shed you let nature have her way.

rooster n   Attrib **rooster chicken**: a cock.

1979 TIZZARD 343 I made arrangements. . .to buy our calf and also a few chicken, because all the rooster chicken would be killed off in the fall of the year and just one rooster kept through the winter months.

root n   *ADD* 2 'a drink' Nfld (1921). A stiff drink; a shot.

1925 *Dial Notes* v, 340 Nar *root* aroun'? 1929 BURKE [7] "Mary Ann Hooligan": I'd knock the Devil out of the Circus man / With a couple of Roots of Booze.

rope n

1 Phr *look at both ropes*: to consider both sides of a question (P 148–69).

2 Attrib **rope-strap**: length of stout cordage forming one of the 'corners' of a 'cod-trap.'

T 43/7–64 You make your rope straps, when you get her measured up, to make a corner.

rose n   *DJE* ~ sb 'generic term for flower.' The blossom of a cultivated plant.

1938 AYRE 22 Very often we hear people who do not know the name of a flower speak of it in a general way as 'lily' or 'rose.' T 222–66 Women. . .call them all by their right names until they come in bloom, when the blooms automatically become 'roses.' And so you are asked to admire 'the nice red rose' on the geranium, or 'the pretty blue rose' on the petunia.

rot v   Of ice, to become honeycombed and soft-ened in the course of melting.

1862 LIND *MS Diary* 6 Mar I am sorry to find the ice is rotting away before the people can haul their wood over from the opposite side.

rot n

Comb **rot hole**: soft place in a field of ice or snow, hazardous to walk on (1925 *Dial Notes* v, 340).

1924 ENGLAND 149 Me an' a whitecoat fell in togeth-er, down a rot-hole, an' I went clean under, but I got me seal!

rot oil: oil of cod livers, rendered by the process of decomposition in a vat or barrel; ROTTED: *rotted oil*.

P 54–63 The oil in this book [of Slade papers, c1820] is, of course, 'cod oil' formerly 'train oil' or just 'train.' Later, this two-word name distinguished it from the mechanically rendered 'medicinal cod-liver oil,' and it was often further differentiated as 'rotted cod oil' or 'rot oil,' indicative of its method of manufacture, which was to merely store the cod livers in casks or vats, and allow them to rot into blubber, the oil collecting on top.

rote n   also **rut** *OED* ~ sb⁶ (1610–), rut sb³ (1633–); *DAE* (1855–); *ADD* rut 2 obs (1892); *EDD* rut sb² 2 'friction' Co, rute sb 4 'dashing of the waves' Ch; and cp the 3rd c. Greek poet ARATUS *Phaenomena*, 11.909–10: μακρὸν ἐπ' αἰγιαλοὶ βοόωντεσ 'the far sounding beach' [as a sign of wind to come]. The sound of the sea, esp the noise of waves breaking on the shore; freq in phr *rote of the sea*; a weather sign.

1612 *Willoughby Papers* 1/62, 17 [Guy's Journal] We went N.W. [and] weare within hearing of the rut of the shoare before we could see yt. 1887 *Telegram Christmas No* 9 It was not more than half a mile to the gulch, and. . .they could hear the hoarse 'rote' of the breakers and the boom of the waves, as they were hurled into the chasm. 1908 TOWNSEND 80 The 'rote' or sound of the surf on the rocks, or the echo of the whistle from a cliff unseen in the fog, give him the needed clue to his position. 1909 *Nfld Qtly* Dec, p. 9 The fishermen are accustomed, in foggy weather, to find their bearings by carefully listening to the rout of the sea on the shore, which they (very correctly) call rote, or rut. According to the nature of the shore, whether, sandy beach, gravel, rocky caves, and so forth, a different rote is made, and the fishermen are wonderfully expert in detecting their whereabouts by this sign. 1924 ENGLAND 167 An' her ingine sound like de rote [roar] o' de sea. 1937 DEVINE 41 ~ A faint sound made by waves on the shore. P 147–56 When the sea is 'rough,' the rote can be heard quite plainly, especially in the night-time. It always comes from a particular direction and fishermen say that the wind will come from that same direction the next day. C 69–28 I have heard it said that a rote (also known as a roach) is a sure sign of a storm the next day. A rote is the roaring of the sea as the waves break along the shore. This roaring can only be heard during a calm. If this rote is heard when there is no apparent cause for a big sea (no strong winds within the past twenty-four hours) you can be sure of a storm on the next day. This rote is most commonly heard in the late evening and night. C 75–142 Rote from the shore on a calm night indicates wind from that direction the following day. 1979 NEMEC 256 The sound of the 'rote' (waves against the shore).

rotted p ppl Of cod-liver oil, rendered by the process of decomposition of the livers in vat or barrel.

1938 MACDERMOTT 165 The cod livers are thrown into butts for the crude oil to render itself out in the sun, and the oil thus extracted is known as 'rotted oil.'

rotten a *DC* ~ adj (1665–); *Nfld & Lab Pilot* (1950), *Supplement* No 3, p. 9. Of ice or snow, made soft by the process of melting.

[1670] 1963 YONGE 128 With our mainsail close hauled, [we] lay all night, having several small bits of rotten ice by us. [1771] 1792 CARTWRIGHT i, 119 I arrived home exceedingly fatigued, and my feet were much inflamed by the wet; the snow being full of water and rotten to the bottom. 1819 ANSPACH 344 The melting of the snow is much more rapid in its lower parts, which, in the most severe winters, are found, by digging, to consist of a soft substance, called in Newfoundland *rotten* snow. 1836 [WIX]² 93 Started over the rotten ice, which let me through once, as I leaped from pen to pen. 1933 GREENE 153 There may be seen in the

sealing waters the 'foundering' of a mighty berg. This happens when the vast foundations have been so rudely sapped by the sea below, whilst sun and frost combined have been so hard at work above the waters—melting, cracking, and rending—that it becomes what Newfoundland fishermen call 'rotten,' and then anything may happen.

rough a Cp *OED* ~ a 4 b, *EDD* 5 'of weather, rainy' IW for sense 1; *EDD* 7 IW Do So for sense 2; for combs. in sense 3: cp *DC* ~ ice (1963); cp *EDD* shop sb 3 'place where any business is carried on'; *OED* shop sb 4 colloq; PARTRIDGE shop; *OED* rough-spun 'rough-mannered' (1822, 1828).

1 Of the weather, turbulent with high winds and heavy, drifting snow.

[1832] 1980 *Them Days* vi (2), p. 34 Strong gale with heavy drift of snow, very cold rough day. Walked to the cook room in the morning but could scarcely stand it. [1886] LLOYD 15 It not infrequently happens that the heaviest falls of snow—called 'batches' by the inhabitants—are accompanied by gales of wind. The weather at such times is said to be 'rough,' a word which strikes terror into the stoutest heart. C 67–14 It was a 'rough' night in winter and the girl lost her way and froze to death. 1975 BUTLER 91 I had experience enough to know we were in for a rough day [with the weather].

2 Gravely ill.

T 222–66 A friend of mine once went to see a woman whose husband was very ill, and she was amazed when she asked how he was an' the woman said he was 'quite rough today.' Q 67–85 If a person was very sick he was pretty rough or rough.

3 Comb **rough ice**: ice formed by the southward drift of the arctic ice-floes; DRIFT-ICE, ICE (Q 67–51).

1979 TIZZARD 130 Spring. . .posed many problems, that is when the ice was not firm enough to go on, or when the bay ice had gone out and the rough ice had come in. Ibid 318 A few harp seals came to land almost every spring, especially when the rough ice was close to land.

rough shop: a strait, channel or harbour difficult to navigate; a hazardous fishing ground.

1909 BROWNE 284 *Horse Harbor*, another large fishing centre, is situated near *Holton*; and it is settled chiefly by 'dealers' of the concern which operates so largely in *Holton*. It is known to fishermen as 'a rough shop' (not the firm, but the Harbor); and it has an evil reputation for wrecks and storms. Ibid 309 These islands are dubbed 'rough-shop' by fishermen; and from reports they deserve this appellation, as terrible storms have visited the islands. T 55/6–64 I was shipwrecked twice to Belle Isle in the Straits. That's a rough shop. Lost all I had.

rough-spun: rough-mannered.

1792 PULLING *MS* Aug The aforementioned John Hodder who is a *rough spun* tar lived many years to the Northward but is now one of Mr Lester's boats-masters.

roughstone: whetstone; SIVE STONE.

T 43/7–64 Some people call 'em a scythestone an'
others call 'em roughstone. 1979 TIZZARD 90 There
was always a piece of 'rough-stone' on the splitting
table for sharpening knives and putting on them a good
keen edge. With the rough-stone which was part of a
scythe-stone, there was a piece of brick; both would
put a good edge on a knife.

rough av Cpd **rough-handle**: to treat roughly.
T 342–67[2] He said they didn't molest him any other
way; never rough-handled him, only took the ears off
of him.

roughery n A heavy sea or swell (1896 *J A
Folklore* ix, 33).
1937 DEVINE ~ A heavy sea.

round a *Fisheries of U S*, p. 465 'round herring'
for sense 2.
1 Of a seal, killed but not skinned or 'sculped.'
[1771] 1792 CARTWRIGHT i, 93 Two of the Indians
came here in the evening with a couple of round seals.
1792 ibid *Gloss* i, xiv Round seal. A seal which has not
yet been either skinned or pelted. 1842 JUKES i, 291
Thirty old or 'round seals,' are as many
as the boat will carry with four men. [1870] 1899 *Nfld
Law Reports* 327 Plaintiff's crew killed, as they computed, about 3,000 seals, of which some were sculped
and piled, some were cut open, and others were left
round. 1924 ENGLAND 88 Lusty toilers are meantime,
with 'seal-dog' hooks and ropes, hauling the round-
seals up and in.
2 Of cod-fish, etc, not gutted or 'split'; cp
ROUNDER.
1893 *Christmas Bells* 14 Well, when we got home
with a full load of about thirty qtls. round fish, it was
nearly evening and I said we'd commence to split after
tea. [1892] 1896 *Consolidated Statutes of Nfld* 829 All
herrings that are not gibbed or ripped, shall be branded
or marked with the word 'round,' in addition to other
brands or marks. T 36/8–64 You wouldn't split any fish.
You'd simply throw the fish down round. 1976
HOLLETT 2 But then they always take a pound off for
the pip. Even if he was gutted? You would not, you
would sell him round, see. 1979 TIZZARD 263 There
were also. . .cod too small to split, which were salted
and dried round.
3 Comb **round-bower, round-bow vessel**:
schooner with a blunt, rather than a sharp, cutwater.
T 183–65 I rebuilt the *Scarlet Knight* for my own,
made she a lot bigger, an' she was a round-bower after
I repaired her. 1975 BUTLER 53 The old time schooner
had a cutwater stem and a figurehead and probably a
transom. The Americans commenced to change to the
round stem called round bows—round bow vessel with
no bowsprit.
round-tail: small cod-fish gutted, headed,
salted but not split; ROUNDER; dried and salted
cod-fish 'split' insufficiently towards the tail.
1853 WARREN 17 The last trip [the Bankers] split
round tails, and took them in salt to England, without
being dried, and there sold them in that state. 1955
Nfld Fisheries Board No 23 Choice Italian—not to

include round or lap tails. 1957 *Nfld Qtly* Sep, p. 49
The splitter you got now is no good either. Look at this
round-tail. See what I mean? M 69–17 The splitter also
must cut the tail part of the fish open in the correct
way: if it is not 'laid' open properly, it is known as a
'round tail,' and such fish, however well cured, could
never become a Grade One product.

round n
1 In a fish-net, (a) a single row of netting going
the full extent of the device; (b) the sides of a
'cod-trap' knitted in one continuous piece.
T 66/7–64 [In making a caplin net] we'll knit around
six or seven rounds. Now you have to rise on that to
make the net large. T 141/67–65[2] I uses cutch [as a
preservative] for the trunks and leader of a cod-trap.
1967 FIRESTONE 91 The trap proper is in three parts:
the leader, the *round*, and the *bottom*. . .the round
makes up the sides of the trap and is of one piece. The
top line of the round, to which the linnet [netting] is
attached, has corks attached to it to keep the linnet up
in the water.
2 Phr *in the round*: (a) describing undressed
timber or logs trimmed or 'quatted' on only two
sides; (b) of small cod-fish or 'rounders,' headed
and gutted but not 'split.'
P 243–57 ~ Tree trunks slightly trimmed on opposite
sides. 1963 HEAD 152 [Fish] which cannot be handled
by the settlement is sold in the round to the fish plants
at Tor's Cove and Witless Bay. 1969 MOWAT 121
[Rounders] are very small cod that have been sun-dried
'in the round,' rather than split, as are larger fish.

on the round: describing the measurement
around an object, esp the size of a cod-trap.
1956 *Evening Telegram* 12 Dec, p. 5 In size [the
cod-traps] range from a very rare small one of thirty-
five fathoms 'on the round' to giants of 84 fathoms.
P 9–73 The Newfoundland fisherman in talking of the
cod-trap size says 60 or 40 or what have you on the
round (not around). Not many cod-traps are more than
60 or 40 fathoms on the round. 1975 RUSSELL 18
There's always bound to be one or two among 'em
who'll be inclined to brag a bit—you know—about how
their codtrap is a few more fathoms on the round than
anybody else's.

rounder n See ROUND a 2, 3: ROUND TAIL.
1 A small cod-fish or 'tom cod,' gutted, headed, salted and dried without being split; LEGGY.
1908 TOWNSEND 132 The very small cod are not
boned, but are salted whole. These are called 'leggies'
or 'rounders.' 1966 HORWOOD 254 The rounders came
smoking from the fireplace—small cured fish, not split,
but dried round, for roasting or broiling. 1977 *Nfld
Qtly* Dec, p. 37 What could one ask for more than to
build a fire by a stream amongst the rocks, suspend the
tin kettle on a stick over the blaze, and roast dried caplin, or a rounder? 1979 TIZZARD 263 There were also a
few rounders, cod too small to split, which were salted
and dried round. There were three different ways to
prepare those for eating: roast them in the oven, roast
them in the stove or cook them on the stove.

2 A long tapering pole of undressed timber; LONGER.

1895 GRENFELL 59 These [fish] stages are built out on piles driven into the mud. Long poles, known as 'rounders,' are laid side by side across the tops of these, and form a kind of flooring. The whole is then roofed in. 1908 DURGIN 112 Inside the sod-roofed stage, we found it floored with round poles called 'rounders' laid closely, side by side.

roundy a *OED* ~ a 1 now dial (1586, 1821); *EDD* 2 So. Rounded.

1972 MURRAY 266 [in carding wool] You'd take them off 'roundy.' Some'd take 'um off flat, but they're not so good.

rouse v [rɑʊs, 'ræusɨn]. Cp *OED* ~ v[1] 11 'to move with violence; rush' rare (1582, 1818). To throw oneself with vigour and energy into an activity; cp SLOUSE, SOUSE v. Shifts to exclamation in some contexts.

P 113–56 Though the water was cold, he rowsed in. T 258–66 He's tipped the boards an' down comes the horse collars, chains, breechin'; an' hisself rouse! on the floor. T 398/9–67 Twelve of us up in the side o' the hill, rowsin' right to 'em. 1975 GUY 91 If two people swinging happened to rouse into two more [in a Reel] some bad injuries were likely to result. If you let go at top speed you would clear the floor like an oblong bowling ball and probably have to be dug out of the wall.

rouse n [rɛus]. A ship's cable. Hence **rouse-chock**: metal casting at bow and stern through which mooring or towing cable passes.

1924 ENGLAND 187 Vague forms rig lines out through rouse-chocks and make them fast to thumb-cleats; lead them to winches. M 68–26 The service is a piece of brin or canvas which was wrapped around the rope at the point where it passes through the 'rouse chocks.' P 148–74 Rouse. [A] line [which] rests on cleats on the gunwale of a 30-ton boat. P 40–78 When you're tyin' up you got to make sure the ropes are in the rouse-chocks so the boat won't drift around.

row v Comb **row dory**: a small flat-bottomed boat propelled by oars; DORY.

M 68–3 With the change from the barque to the big skiff by the fishermen that used the larger boats these fishermen began to use row-dories. 1975 LEYTON 23 I knows two men did it a couple of times in a row dory [i.e. rowed to St Pierre with a load of caplin]. 1977 BUTLER 9 Men I contacted would rather live on dole than face the hardship which would be encountered fishing from a rough shore in a row dory.

row punt: undecked, round-bottomed boat propelled by oars; PUNT.

1975 BUTLER 61 [The old timers] used to use [witrod oarlocks] in row punts, the old time row punts.

rowt n [rɛut]. Phr *hard rowt*: unpleasant experience; difficult, exhausting employment.

1924 ENGLAND 29 Why the devil should anybody want to write—or read—anything about 'de hard rowt o' swilin'? Ibid 156 'They'd have a hard rowt,' judged the Cap'n, 'if they was to bide on ice to-night. A murderin' time!' P 127–80 That was a hard rowt to have to come down like that. The wind fled up from the nor-wes' an' I was leavin' in the dawnin'.

royal a The comb is perhaps from the celebrated flag-ship of Admiral Kempenfelt sunk at anchor 29 Aug 1782 (see G WHITE *The Naturalist's Journal* [1979], p. 61: 'On this day the Royal George, a 100 gun ship, was unfortunately overset at Spithead, as she was heaving down'), a vessel made famous by Cowper's poem "Loss of the *Royal George*." Comb **royal george**: sermon by a Methodist clergyman prepared for a special occasion; one's best sermon.

P 212–73 [Invited] to be considered as the clergyman of a congregation, a minister might say, 'I'll give them my Royal George.'

rub n

1 A barely formed or discernible passage through dense woods.

C 71–106 ~ a passage through dense woods which has not been used long [or often] enough to be called a path. In our community the rub was always named for the person who was believed to have used it first, for example Michael's Rub where a man named Michael long ago hauled wood to the seashore.

2 See OTTER RUB.

rubber n *NID* ~ n 1 c (1) for sense 1; *DC* ~ ice (1916–) for comb in sense 3.

1 A strip of wood fastened on the outside of the gunwale of a boat or vessel; SCRUBBER.

T 141/66–65[2] On the side o' Ray's schooner she got a rubber around her, piece o' greenheart; an' 'tis tapered off round the edges. P 127–75 ~ a protective wooden strip extending from stem to stern, attached to the top outside of the binding-strake.

2 A long, flexible boot worn by fishermen, freq with defining word *hip, thigh*, etc.

[1900 OLIVER & BURKE] 59 "Topsail Geisha": And for sailors and land lubbers, / I can dance it in my rubbers. 1955 DOYLE (ed) 85 "When the Caplin Come In": Oh, now is the time when the men are all ready, / With oil skins and rubbers their work to begin. T 84–64 There was no rubbers around here then. There was all Smallwood boots then, for fishin' boots, no rubbers. T 145–65 The kids had to go with what we call rubbers, thigh rubbers or hip rubbers, cut off, just enough left. . .to put their feet into. 1973 WIDDOWSON 191 I [was] always having a problem of getting my feet wet, because I used to have short rubbers an' I used to always get my feet wet. 1975 BUTLER 38 I said to Jack, 'I'm goin' to Buffett, come with me, get your oilclothes and rubbers and come down with me.'

3 Attrib, comb **rubber gun**: sling-shot (M 71–80).

rubber ice: newly-formed sea-ice which bends under weight; see BUCKLY.

1916 DUNCAN 120 What the frost had accomplished

since dusk could be determined only upon trial. 'Soft as cheese!' Doctor Luke concluded. 'Rubber ice,' said Billy. C 65–4 [Bendying] is used when referring to the sport of playing on rubber ice. The ice is not very firm and bends easily under the weight of a person's body. It moves up and down as a body runs across.

rubber lump: heavy, ankle-high rubber boot; LUMP.

C 67–16 During the week we wore a short rubber boot, a little higher than today's shoes. These were called rubber lumps. P 154–78 ~s. These were cut off rubber boots—cut off just above the ankles.

rubbing vbl n *DC* ~ place (Nfld: 1770–). Attrib **rubbing-place**: spot of ground worn smooth by otters rubbing there repeatedly; a slope where otters playfully slide; OTTER RUB.

[1770] 1792 CARTWRIGHT i, 28 The shores on each side are hilly, and we observed many signs of porcupines and several rubbing places. 1792 ibid *Gloss* i, xiv ~ A place by the water-side, which otters have frequently made use of to rub themselves on after fishing. 1861 DE BOILIEU 79 The mode of trapping the otter is exceedingly simple. Being of most cleanly habits, and liking to repose at early dawn (wild animals mostly feed at night) he selects a smooth spot on the bank of the river, which on the coast is called a 'rubbing-place.'

rubbish n   Any species of salt-water fish other than salmon and cod. Cp FISH.

1842 JUKES ii, 68 Everything [in the fish category] but cod and salmon is frequently spoken of by the fishermen as rubbish.

ruckle v   Cp *EDD* truckle v 1 'to trundle, roll' W Do So D Co. See also CHUCKLE, TRUCKLE. To trundle or roll (a wheeled toy).

C 68–22 To ruckle the hoops they'd take the metal hoops off barrels and use a stick to see if they could roll it along. C 71–21 The most important thing in rucklin' hoops was to find a stiff piece of wire [to use as a brake]. 1976 *Daily News* 9 Mar, p. 3 Then there were lielow (a hide and seek game), ruckling or chuckling hoops, and a host of others.

ruckler n   See RUCKLE, TRUCKLY-MUCK. A child's toy.

C 71–21 [There's] a piece of stiff wire bent at one end just the width of an [evaporated] milk can. Then you put one milk can [on the end] and another four milk cans on the handle and you ruckle this gadget along the road making a lot of noise—the more noise, the better ruckler you had.

rudder   See RA.

rummage v   *DC* ~ v Nfld (1770–1835); cp *EDD* 1 'ransack' So D Co; *OED* 2 naut 'search thoroughly.' To search for game, esp for fur-bearing animals; to gather firewood.

[1770] 1792 CARTWRIGHT i, 56 The other furrier accompanied me in rummaging for beavers. 1792 ibid *Gloss* i, xiv ~ A furrier's term for searching a country; particularly for beaver-houses, when nothing else is mentioned. 1819 ANSPACH 376 Thus prepared [the hunter] fearlessly ranges about, or, according to the technical term, *rummages* in search of his game. 1836 [WIX][2] 49 . . .persons who have been 'rummaging,' or searching for fire-sticks of timber in the woods. 1888 HOWLEY *MS Reminiscences* 68[v] In rummaging about here near our camp I came across a pile of large pine logs almost [hidden] in earth & overgrown with moss.

rummage n   *DC* ~ n Nfld (1770) for sense 1; cp *OED* sb 1 c 'place of stowage' obs (1598–1639) for sense 2.

1 A search for game, etc.

[1770] 1792 CARTWRIGHT i, 56 . . .leaving my attendant behind, to join the other man, and pass the night in the woods; in order that they might finish the rummage of that brook tomorrow.

2 Comb **rummage house**: small building for firewood, goats, etc (1971 NOSEWORTHY 239).

rumper n   Turnip (1971 NOSEWORTHY 239).

P 20–55 Rumpers [are] small turnips, especially locally grown [by a family]. T 36–64 You'd pack fir boughs down in the bottom, throw in your spuds and your rumpers, and pack [turf] all over 'em again.

run v   Cp *DAE* ~ v 16 [esp of ice] 'to float down a stream' (1805–) for sense 1; *DAE* 2 (1748–1852) for sense 3.

1 Of sea-ice, to move impelled by wind or current; cp RUNNING ICE. Also in phr *run abroad*: to break up into loose 'pans'; see ABROAD; *run out*: to move offshore; see OUT[2]; *run together*: to form a close-packed floe.

1871 WHITE *MS Journal* 21 Apr Ice running very fast & rafting. 1873 CARROLL 20 The great object is when ice hunting masters come up with old seals on loose ice to keep by them and remain quiet until the ice runs together, for if the seals are once disturbed it is a difficult task to fall in with them again. 1887 BOND 73 Please God, we may find the poor fellows; but the ice ran out so fast that I'm terribly afraid they went too far and are driven off. 1909 GRENFELL[1] 6–7 So quickly did the wind now come off shore, and so quickly did the packed 'slob,' relieved of the wind pressure, 'run abroad,' that already I could not see one pan larger than ten feet square; moreover, the ice was loosening so rapidly that I saw that retreat was absolutely impossible. 1975 BUTLER 94 We kept the boat as far to the windward as the wind would let us, as the heavy ice was runnning the shore at about half a mile an hour.

2 Of oil from seal 'fat' or blubber, to ooze forth prematurely while in storage. Also in phr *run away, ~ (into) oil*; cp GURRY, PUMMY.

1842 JUKES i, 320 Meanwhile our seals began to run, the pumps brought up. . .the mixture of seal-oil and salt bilge-water. [1902] 1916 MURPHY 8 Tobin brought up all the skippers, who proved that it was a custom of the fishery to leave one seal in the vessel to be run into oil for her use during the summer. 1916 ibid 30 A heavy gale of north-east wind sprang up on Good Friday, which drove the ice and vessels up in Green Bay where some of them remained until June; their seals 'ran into oil.' 1924 ENGLAND 226 We got jammed, an' had to live on bread dust an' fipper, an' ahl our skins runned away. We ondly got four dollars apiece, dat spring! Ibid 297 This rolling, by next day, had ground up the fat so thoroughly that our starboard quarter pound began to 'run to ile' very badly, and an overpowering stench invaded the cabin. 'Gurry,' they call such seal oil.

3 To mould bullets, etc.

Q 73–2 [The ball mould was used] for making cast-net balls and gun balls. The inside of the mould was coated with chalk, before each ball was run (made). This prevented the molten lead from clinging to the mould.

4 Phr *run boomed out*: to sail before the wind under reduced canvas.

1932 BARBOUR 42 The wind grew more steady; the log was set again and we lowered the mainsail, as we had to run boomed out. We ran before the wind all that evening.

run chances: to take risks while sailing.

T 194/7–65 I lowered my foresail, double reef foresail, tied un up; put a reef in the jumbo, and put her under double reef mainsail and reef jumbo, and runned south for Twillingate; run chances. . .but I'm goin' to run chances; I'll trust in the Lord.

run out: to sail a vessel to the ice-fields to hunt seals.

1944 LAWTON & DEVINE 75 [In 1869] Mr Doyle sailed from his native place, King's Cove, in the *Goldfinder*, with Skipper Jim Martin. . . Their plan was to run out when the seals came along and drift South with them.

run n Cp *OED* ~ sb¹ 14 b 'shoal of fish in motion, esp ascending a river to spawn' (1820–), *DAE* 5 (1832–), *DC* 6 'of animals, a period of abundance' (1937) for sense 1; cp *OED* 9 b 'a flow or current of water; a strong rush or sweep of the tide' (1814–), *DC* 5 (Nfld: 1918–) for sense 2.

1 Of fur animals, and fish in coastal waters and estuaries, a large number migrating or in motion; the period of their availability or abundance to trappers and fishermen; cp SCULL.

[1771] 1792 CARTWRIGHT i, 180 Found all the traps and deathfalls robbed; and a great run of martens. [1772] ibid i, 234 The run of slinks abates, and that of the spring fish increases. [1775] ibid ii, 48 There was a great run of foxes, but they would not touch the baits. 1903 DES VOEUX ii, 151 I. . .fished a river which we were told had a 'run' of sea-trout. [1929] 1979 *Evening Telegram* 27 June, p. 40 Only a small run of fish was had for the morning haul. 1977 *Inuit Land Use* 218 With spring come the first runs of fish. Freshwater smelts are first, and they abound at the head of the bay during their spawning season around the last two weeks in May. Ibid 266 They used to go from here to Cape Harrison in the speedboat, and sometimes a 50 horsepower would slow right down in a run of caplin. 1979 TIZZARD 310 By the time the salmon run was over we would have near half a barrel of salted salmon.

2 A narrow salt-water strait or extended navigable passage between the coast and an island or series of islands; a passage between islands; cp REACH, TICKLE n.

1842 JUKES ii, 155 [We] then tried to beat up for Dildo Run, hoping to get through into Exploits Bay in that direction. 1871 HOWLEY *MS Reminiscences* 15 Next day I took the boat and two of the men with some provisions and went up the Reach visiting several of the islands and inspecting the rocks, thence around the Run to New World Island. 1908 DURGIN 37 What the natives call a 'run' is a channel of water between the mainland and a chain of islands or between two chains of islands. Almost the entire coast of Labrador can be made through 'runs.' A 'tickle' is a narrow space of water between land and is smaller and shorter than a 'run.' 1947 TANNER 285 As has been said the tides are of no great size at the Atlantic coast, but they are sufficient to produce strong tidal currents in the archipelagos and channels of different orders: runs, tickles and rattles. 1953 *Nfld & Lab Pilot* ii, 426 Domino run is the passage, about 4½ cables wide, between the northern coast of the Island of Ponds, and the coasts of Spotted island and those of the north-westward of it. T 396/7–67 An' sometimes you get the big sea, an' the sea comes in—one sea after the other, an' breaks clear o' the stages outside the runs. 1979 TIZZARD 323 One winter when I was very young some fishermen were going to the ships' run, the waters between New World Island and Black Island, to fish for turbot.

3 Phr *on the run*: of animals, on the loose for summer pasturage.

M 68–10 During the summer the animals were driven outside the fences to roam the public grass areas and paths. Except for the hens, the other animals remained 'on the run' until late in the fall.

run of the year: course of the year.

M 69–6 In the run of the year, there were many red, blue, or even blistered hands in the classroom.

rung n [rɒŋ]. Cp *OED* ~ sb 1 'stout stick. . .used as a rail, cross-bar, or spoke.' One of the pliable vertical sticks encasing the elongated stone in a home-made anchor or 'killick'; KILLICK-ROD.

T 13–64 Bore a hole in each of these claws. Put your rung down into it, and when you have your rung in each claw, you have a round, long rock and you put un down on the claw. You bring the two rungs together and tie them two.

runner n

1 A stick placed in the side of a dory and used to guide the hauling of trawls; RUNNING STICK (1971 NOSEWORTHY 236).

2 In coopering, a metal or wooden truss or hoop to secure the staves at the widest part of the cask or barrel.

M 71–40 The next step [in making a barrel] is to put on a hoop called a 'runner' which is placed on the barrel down as far as possible and holds the staves in place. P 127–75 ~ The largest of all iron trusses—a kind of measuring hoop. When the barrel is made properly, the runner will just hang on the widest part of the barrel.

running vbl n, ppl *DC* ~ ice (1913–) for comb in sense 2.

1 The process of oil oozing from the blubber or 'fat' of a seal 'pelt' kept too long in storage. See RUN v.

1873 CARROLL 9 Pelts stowed carefully, hair to fat, so as to prevent the fat from 'running.'

2 Attrib, comb **running ice**: ice, usu separated in fragments or pans, carried along by sea currents or wind; cp STANDING ICE.

1846 TOCQUE 196 All these vessels were forced in upon the land by the running ice, the crews of which were all saved. [1886] LLOYD 48–9 The Northern Newfoundlanders often run great risks in seal hunting. They walk out over the 'standing ice' which lies along the coast to a distance of three, four, or more miles, to what is known as the 'running ice,' i.e. that which lies in the current of the Strait, and which is always in motion. This running ice does not, like the standing ice, consist of an extensive unbroken field, but is split up into small floes, or 'pans,' as they are called, of all sizes and shapes. 1916 GRENFELL 168 The wind had pinned the runnin' ice ag'in' the standin' edge. 1924 ENGLAND 239–40 The *Ranger* seemed to have discovered the huge herd afar, about the same time we did; and now she came fiercely straining through the 'running ice.' T 185–65 This would be all solid ice in here but that would be runnin' ice out there. 1982 *Evening Telegram* 19 Apr, p. 6 The strength of the gale and the force of the ocean currents began to heave the ice; it creaked, growled, and began to move, what the sealers called the 'running ice.'

running line: one of the vertical ropes fastened to the head and foot of a 'cast-net.'

T 13/4–64 Then you puts twelve, or thirteen or fourteen running-lines—fasten them to the head of your net about a foot asunder. You'll put all the ends together and shove them up through the small end.

running mark: one of the land features or objects lined up by fisherman in order to locate the position of a fishing ground; cp BREAST MARK.

Q 71–8 The running mark would give the distance up or down (parallel to) the coast, the breast mark would fix the distance off shore.

running mesh: one of the alternate meshes of a 'cod-trap' left unfastened to head- or foot-ropes (Q 67–87).

running stick: wooden device placed in the side of a dory and used to guide the hauling of trawls; TRAVELLER (P 243–57).

P 40–78 ~ A stick about two feet long used to handle a trawl when it is being put overboard with the boat moving and the trawl running out of a round container in which it is coiled up. The stick is used to avoid getting one's hands caught in the hooks on the trawl.

running tap: a second sole fastened to the bottom of a sealskin boot.

T 50/2–64 An' when that bottom'd get a bit thin then they'd put what they call runnin' taps over 'em. They stand all the winter then.

running trap: a type of animal trap.

1909 ROBINSON 148–9 The way in which the bears are generally caught in Labrador is by what is called a 'running trap.' Two upright sticks are placed one each side of the bear's run. . . But his weight on the centre of the platform drags out the two wedges, and down falls the heavy log on the bear's back and breaks it.

rusty a, n Cp *OED* ~ a[1] 8 '[disagreeable] light reddish brown.' Cp also WHITE-COAT, RAGGED-JACKET for sense 1.

1 A young harp seal in a phase following 'white-coat' and 'bedlamer' stages; TURNER. Also comb **rusty jacket, ~ ranger**.

1924 ENGLAND 102 Second-year harps are 'rusties,' or 'rusty jackets.' A 'rusty ranger' is a second-year seal with rounded spots that have not yet opened into the harp shape. 1933 GREENE 73–4 On the backs of all adult Harp Seals. . .there appears that curious well-defined saddle of brown hair. . .when distinctly visible on the pelt, the saddle seems to become the outward sign of full tribal initiation; and until it is complete all these unmarked seals, when in the returning herds of the succeeding Springs, are known to the sealers first as 'Rusties'—and then, after a couple of years and until maturity, as 'Bedlamers.' 1952 STANSFORD 54 We killed and secured for our day's work two turning seals (called 'Rusties'). 1961 *Atlantic Advocate* li (7), p. 45 Our young female was now a yearling, or a 'rusty' to the sealers whom she had not yet met. T 104–64 The young harp was the white one, in the Spring o' the year, before the coat comes off. Then they becomes rusties after that, an' then there's the bedlamers.

2 Comb **rusty tom rooter**: eastern fox sparrow (*Passerella iliaca iliaca*); FOXY TOM (P 113–66).

rut See ROTE.

S

sabine See SAFFRON.

sabot n   also **sawboo*** ['sɑ·bou]. Big, clumsy shoe or boot; rubber boot cut off at the ankle (P 245–56).

T 145–65 The kids had to go with what we call today thigh rubbers or hip rubbers, cut off, just enough left for them to put their feet into. The old name of that time would be sawboos. C 67–6 ~s. A pair of boots (shoes, rubbers, sneakers, etc) which look rather odd on the person's feet, usually by being too big for him.

sack[1] n   Scrotum of male animal; CONCERN.

T 33–64[1] And then they used to have the sack of a buck sheep, or a buck goat, or a bull, skinned out and a bladder put into this and blowed up and made like a football, you know.

sack[2] n   *DC* ~ ship (1957–). Comb **sack ship**, also **sack**: a vessel engaged in carrying supplies and migratory fishermen from Britain to New-foundland, dried cod from the island to Mediter-ranean markets, and wine or sack, etc, thence to British ports; a cargo as opposed to a fishing vessel.

[1610] *Willoughby Papers* 17a 1/2 If lead be sent hether in the sacke, for a smale matter it maye be sent hence to any part of Spaine, or Italy, servinge so fitt for ballaste vnder the fishe. [1620] 1887 MASON 154 . . .shippes that goe sackes at ten shilling pertunne, and thirtie shillings home. [1650] 1954 INNIS 52 Ships called sacks being commonly in great number every year. . .carry fish from Newfoundland into the Straits, France, Portugal and Spain and. . .bring in their return into England bullion and other native commodities of those countries. [1749] 1755 DOUGLASS i, 293 Their fish-ships are distinguished into, fishing-ships. . .and sack-ships, which purchase their fish from the inhabitants. [1810] 1971 ANSPACH 29 The reason for which the St John's merchant did not like *sack* or *net-ships*, was that they *raised the price* of fish. 1895 PROWSE 22 From the very earliest period the English had a carrying fleet (sack ships). 1934 LOUNSBURY 80 Among the disputed points was the proposal of the new patentees to levy an impost of five fish per quintal upon foreigners buying from either the fishermen or the planters. The West Country merchants felt that this would discourage foreign 'sack ships,' as the carriers were called, from touching at Newfoundland.

saddle n   *OED* ~ sb 7 a (Nfld: 1784–) for sense 1.

1 Saddle-shaped marking on the back of a harp seal.

[1766] 1971 BANKS 145 The Heart or Possibly Harp Seal is markd over the Shoulders with a brown figure rudely resembling a harp which they Call the Saddle. 1793 PENNANT ii, 280 Our Fishers call this the *Harp*, or *Heart Seal*, and style the marks on the sides the saddle. 1873 CARROLL 15 The harp seals have the black stripes, which is called the 'saddle.'

2 Mark on the flesh side of the skin of a 'hermit beaver.'

[1783] 1792 CARTWRIGHT iii, 22 It often-times happens, that a single beaver lies retired, and it is then stiled by furriers, a hermit: they say, it is turned out from the family, because it is lazy and will not work; and what is very singular (for be the cause what it will, the fact is certain) all hermit beavers have a black mark on the inside of the skin upon their backs, called a saddle, which distinguishes them.

3 Comb **saddle-dog**: mature male harp seal; DOG[1], SADDLEBACK.

1924 ENGLAND 102 The fourth-year harps are 'black backs,' 'saddle backs,' or 'saddlers'—'de saddle dogs an' de rale ole bitches, de rale ole 'ers.' From that time onward, they are all 'old harps.'

saddleback n   also attrib *OED* ~ 4 c (1856) for sense 1; *OED* 4 b (1847–) for sense 2.

1 Mature harp seal (*Phoca groenlandica*); SADDLER. Cp SADDLE.

1923 CHAFE 3 *The Harp or Saddle Back.* 1924

ENGLAND 102 The fourth-year harps are 'black backs,' 'saddle backs,' or 'saddlers.' 1937 LUBBOCK 422 At Greenland, the main pack of saddle-backs was missed. 1966 BEN-DOR 38 The saddleback seal. . .is commonly known to the sealers as a 'bedlamer' in its young stage and 'harp' in its later years.

2 Great black-backed gull (*Larus marinus*); SADDLER.

[1776] 1792 CARTWRIGHT ii, 161 Several saddle-backs and a pair of eagles were seen today. 1819 ANSPACH 391 The most remarkable of the sea-birds which frequent these coasts are. . .the saddle-back, called also blackback, the largest species of gulls. 1891 PACKARD 90 . . .a pair of saddle-back gulls sailing aloft. 1932 BARBOUR 61 In the evening Ephraim Blackmore called out: 'I can see a "saddle back" coming towards us,' which was a good sign we were getting near the land. That old 'saddle back' certainly cheered us up. In a few hours we saw several and we were very proud to see them, but we could not kill one. 1967 *Bk of Nfld* iii, 283 Great Black-backed Gull: Saddle Back (from its colouring).

3 Variety of louse (1924 ENGLAND 319).

C 71–113 Graybacks and saddlebacks refer to lice that are spotted and light in colour.

saddler n   *OED* ~ 4 (Nfld: 1873–) for sense 1.

1 A mature harp seal (*Phoca groenlandica*); SADDLEBACK.

1873 CARROLL 15 The reason they are called harp seals or 'sadlers' is, the male as well as the female has a dark stripe on each side from the shoulders to the tail, leaving a muddy white stripe down the back. 1924 ENGLAND 163 A huge saddler emerges! Startled, it tries to plunge. But—Crack! Swifter speaks the rifle.

2 Great black-backed gull (*Larus marinus*); SADDLEBACK; also attrib.

1870 *Can Naturalist* v, 408 A common summer migrant, arriving towards the last of April and remaining until the drift-ice appears. . .[the] 'Saddler Gull.' 1891 PACKARD 237 [The] Great Black-backed Gull [is] known as the 'Saddler' or 'Saddle-back' on the coast. 1959 MCATEE 36 ~ Great Black-backed Gull (Nfld., 'Labr.', N.S.). 1977 *Inuit Land Use* 123 Soon after the pigeons and saddlers arrive, the first harp seals begin to migrate north along the floe edge.

3 Any large creature.

C 71–120 ~ Something of unusual size. C 71–128 ~ jumbo-size fish, animal, bird, person.

sadogue n   DINNEEN sodóg 'cake.' Bread; cake.

1968 DILLON 152 ~ soggy cake, bread that does not rise. They'd say, 'That's a real sadogue,' if it was soggy. P 191–73 ~ inexpensive but [delicious] cake.

saffron n   also **sabine, safran** for sense 2. DINNEEN cróch na mbánta 'juice of sheep's droppings [for] measles'; cp *OED* savin 1 'juniperus,' *NID* savin 'used in folk medicine' for sense 2.

1 The dung of sheep, used in folk remedies.

M 68–11 To drive out measles saffron was used. This was sheep's manure steeped in milk. . . The manure was placed in a little cloth bag and steeped in the milk, and the mixture was drunk. C 69–25 Cure for yellow jaunders with the following ingredients: spring water, sheep's safferin, epsom salts and syrup. C 71–21 For yellow jaundice, you steep sheep saphrines and strain in spring water. Pineapple cubes are then strained and added to the mixture, which is taken internally.

2 A low-growing juniper; creeping savin; FACE-AND-EYE BERRY (*Juniperus horizontalis*).

1898 *J A Folklore* xi, 280 *Juniperus sabina*. . .sabine, saffron. 1956 ROULEAU 37 Safran—*Juniperus communis*. C 68–23 Saffron is not very common. The old people used to use it for young girls who got pregnant before they were married. They used to steep the roots and have the girls drink the tea.

sagger n   A good boat-load of 'fish' (P 148–62); SWAMPER.

sagwa n   Cp *DJE* ~ 'a medicine show' (1943–).

1 A patented medicine.

1891 *Holly Branch* 24 [The folk practice performed on the children] produced much less mischief, perhaps, than would an application of *Minard* or a dose of *Kickapoo Sagwa*. [1894 BURKE] 65 [Gave her] Mrs Winslow's Soothing Syrup, / Thinking 'twould do her good, / Then a couple bottles of Sagwa, / And a mug of Buchanan's best.

2 Rum, whisky (P 227–72).

sail n   For combs. in sense 2: *DAE* sail loft (1759–); cp *OED* ~ sb¹ 10 ~ room 'room (in a ship) for storing sails' (1805).

1 A piece of canvas using wind power to propel sled over ice or snow.

C 69–2 The men when they used to go in the woods on Paddy's Day would always get a green bough, preferably a pine, and put it at the top of the sail on the slide. The sails were usually square or triangular in shape.

2 Comb **sail-loft**: room on a fishing premises in which sails are stored and repaired; LOFT.

[1900 OLIVER & BURKE] 45 He hauled her along proudly, past Shambler's old sail loft. 1904 *Nfld Qtly* Dec, p. 17 Not infrequently a sail loft, or the upper storey of a fish store was dubbed with the exalted name of a school. T 141/69–65² We put our mainsail in the sail loft—a feller there doin' canvas. 1977 BUTLER 81 The next day. . .we unloaded the boat, unbent the sails, put them in the sail loft, moored the boat for the winter.

sail-palm: in sail-making, leather device worn on hand to push needle through the canvas; palm.

1972 MURRAY 276 For working by hand, there was a special 'sailneedle' (triangular instead of round) and a 'sail palm' made of leather with a round metal section for forcing the needle through the heavy material. T 187/90–65 Oh I know what he is—a sail palm.

sail-room: see **sail-loft**.

1836 [WIX]² 65 Two full services in the sail-room of Messrs Newman and Hunt.

sail-skiff: small vessel or large boat driven by sail and oar; SKIFF.

T 191–65 An' they were rowing down the ol' sail skiffs, you know. They used to go up the bay them

times about fifteen, twenty miles, for a load o' wood, firewood. T 185–65 I used to be goin' around here in the sail skiff with 'em when they'd be carrying round loads o' fish.

sailing vbl n Comb **sailing pan**: floating piece of ice on which children leap in the sport of COPYING.

1973 *Evening Telegram* 26 May, p. 8 'I always liked him,' sez Ned, 'in his younger days he was a great hand on the sailing pans over on the landwash.'

saine See SEINE.

st john's n   [= capital of Newfoundland].

1 Phr *how do times govern in st john's*: what is the situation in the capital, esp the cost of goods and the price of fish.

1863 MORETON 39 ~ This question, always asked of any man lately returned from the capital, is answered by recounting the prices which fish and oil realized, and those at which food and clothing were got in return.

2 Comb **st john's dog**: strong, short-haired black dog popular with fishermen (P 243–56); WATER DOG.

1967 *Bk of Nfld* iii, 337 The Flat Coated Retriever, once called the St John's dog, was originally from Newfoundland.

st john's slate: rock formation found in the vicinity of St John's.

1869 *Stewart's Qtly* iii, 54 The rock formation, named the St John's Slate, in which they [*Oldhamia*] are thus buried, is 3,000 feet in thickness.

st joseph n   Comb **st joseph's lily**: bog candle (*Platanthera dilatata*) (1956 ROULEAU 37).

st patrick See PATRICK.

st peter's n   [= islands of St Pierre and Miquelon]. Cp Dorset County Record Office, 1799 Gundry inventory (D203/A6) Lines. . .St Peters.

Comb **st peter's gin**, ~ **rum**: liquor procured or smuggled from St Pierre.

1892 *Christmas Review* 17 To secure the votes of five leading planters, I had to gulp down five glasses of hot St Peter's gin, with loaf sugar, before breakfast. [1900 OLIVER & BURKE] 62 I'll have you unsated and disqualified. . .for bribery and corruption, by manes of sellin' yer chape Sin Peter rum.

st peter's line: stout twine or rope used for var fisheries purposes.

T 66/7–64 You'll have the ball [of the caplin-net] strung on a piece o' heavy twine, heavy line, St Peter's line we used to call it, larger than a fishin' line, hard too.

st stephen n   Comb **st stephen's day**, stevenses ~ : December 26, a traditional holiday.

1901 *Christmas Review* 8 During Christmas day and St Stephen's Day, the theatre closed down. 1909 BROWNE 178 In my early years 'getting a berth' or 'signing' for the seal-fishery was one of the great annual events; and the day set apart by custom for this important function was St Stephen's Day (the fishermen termed it 'Stephenses Day'). 1937 *Bk of Nfld* ii, 259 St Stephen's Day—Boxing Day as they call it in England: the day after Christmas.

st tib See TIB'S EVE.

salad See INDIAN SALAD.

sally[1] n   *OED* sallow: sally; *EDD* ~ sb[2] 'willow' for sense 1.
   1 Willow tree; willow branch (*Salix* spp).
   1883 HOWLEY *MS Reminiscneces* 27 Willow or Sally and Wild pear trees, with an abundance of Hazel-nut trees grow on these flats. 1898 *J A Folklore* xi, 279 ~s. Salix (sp.). 1931 BYRNES 28 From the time when he is big enough to cut a 'pole' from the twig of a 'sally' tree, and equip it with a length of common twine. . . 1937 DEVINE 41 ~ a willow tree or sprig from it. P 37–63 A gad is a green twig from 2–6 feet in length cut from a sally tree.
   2 Sweet gale (*Myrica gale*) (P 233–78).
   3 Cpd **sallywood**: mountain holly (*Nemopanthus mucronata*) (1898 *J A Folklore* xi, 224).

sally[2] n, usu pl also ~ **cives**, ~ **saucers**, ~ **sours**, ~ **suckers**. Cp *EDD* salad, salary 'common sorrel.' A weed with sour leaves chewed by children; sheep sorrel (*Rumex acetosella*); LADDIE-SUCKER.
   1915 SOUTHCOTT 27 Sally sours. A common weed growing abundantly in waste places and fields. The fertile panicles of flowers usually turn reddish in summer. Stems juicy, very acid. 1956 ROULEAU 37 Sally Cives. C 66–7 They didn't swallow the sallies but just chewed them up until the taste was out. 1975 SCOTT 15 The Sheep Sorrel is known as Sweet Leaf or Laddie Suckers or Sally Suckers.

sally v   also **solly*** *EDD* ~ v[2] 1. To move from side to side; to sway a boat. Cp OVERING.
   1937 DEVINE 41 ~ To run from side to side. T 31/2–64 I started my sculling-oar now, hauled on my grapel to start the sculling-oar. I couldn't solly her nothing. Q 67–22 The boat sallied against the wind. P 27–80 ~ to rock (a boat).

salmon n   *OED* ~ sb[1] 1 (13..–), *DAE* 1 (1616–) for sense 1; for combs. in sense 2: cp *NID* ~ boat; *OED* crib sb 10 'wickerwork contrivance for catching salmon' (1873); *OED* leap sb 2 b ~ leap (1387, 1661); *DAE* ~ 4 b ~ net (1828 quot); *DC* ~ post (1770); *DAE* rack 3 (1735) for ~ rack; *Cent* ~ twine (1890). *Salmon* with words denoting condition, cure and seasonal occurrence are listed alphabetically: cp FALL n, SPRING[2].
   1 The Atlantic salmon (*Salmo salar*), object of an important commercial fishery conducted in inshore waters and river estuaries; freq in place-names.
   [1555] 1915 HOWLEY 2 [The inhabitants] eate fysshe more than any other thynge, and especially salmons, although they have fowles and fruits. [1583] 1940 *Gilbert's Voyages & Enterprises* ii, 406 [Hayes' narrative] [There are] no lesse varietie of kindes of fish in the sea and fresh waters, as Trouts, Salmons and other fish to us unknown, 1620 WHITBOURNE 10 The Rivers also and Harbours are generally stored with delicate Fish, as Salmons, Peales. . . [1663] 1963 YONGE 56 At the head of this river are many salmon; we caught abundance and our master saved several hogsheads and dried abundance in the smoke. [1771] 1792 CARTWRIGHT i, 135 We had five salmon to-day, and I killed one with a fly. 1819 ANSPACH 401 The salmon here is excellent, and in great abundance from June to August; it is taken in nets, placed along the sea shores in bays and large harbours. 1925 *Dial Notes* v, 340 ~ The stages of growth have names running from *fry* through *parr* and *grilse* to *kelt* or *slinks*. 1936 SMITH 131 We landed our Labrador gear and crews, took on board more cod oil and salmon and left for St John's. 1976 PINHORN 34 Atlantic salmon landings from Newfoundland and Labrador [in] 1973 indicated a total catch of 2019 t, the highest since 1940. The fishery is conducted mainly by surface gillnets set out from shore.
   2 Attrib, comb, cpd: **salmon barrel**: wooden container for the export of dried, salted or smoked salmon.
   [1891] 1897 *Nfld Law Reports* 540 Upon further questioning the plaintiff yet added to the list, dry goods, boots and shoes, salmon barrels and salt, oil-clothes and twine.
   salmon berth: particular station on inshore fishing grounds assigned by custom or lot to salmon fisherman; BERTH.
   1969 HORWOOD 65 'How does he get his salmon berth, if he isn't home?' 'I draw for his berth, sir. The teacher lets me off from school, and I go to the store and draw for a berth with the men.' There was more than a touch of pride in his voice as he said it. 1977 BURSEY 14 We knew where there was a good salmon berth and we were aware that more than one fisherman would try to get his nets into it.
   salmon boat: undecked boat used in the commercial salmon fishery.
   [1888] 1897 *Nfld Law Reports* 310 Part of the salmon-boat crew of the defendant deposed to their having been at the nets early in the morning, of having overhauled them, and having left them moored all straight.
   salmon box: shallow wooden container for the export of dried, salted or smoked salmon.
   1849 [FEILD] 53–4 The seats on this occasion were salmon-boxes, i.e. oblong boxes, about fourteen inches deep and wide, and six feet long, in which the preserved salmon is packed for exportation.
   salmon catcher: commercial salmon fisherman; SALMONIER.
   1792 PULLING *MS* 8 This old man who was a salmon catcher and lived amongst the Northern brooks many

years has frequently met with and parted from the Indians without offering to hurt each other. 1854 [FEILD] 88 One very respectable planter, a salmon-catcher, had come from his residence [near Flat Islands]. [1888] 1907 *Our Country* 3 [He was] a typical specimen of the old English salmon catcher and furrier, and one of the few of that class surviving.

salmon collector: buyer of salmon in the commercial fishery. Cp COLLECTOR, TRADER.

T 80/3–64 Well, there was a salmon collector then, an' we was told there was a salmon collector gone in the bay. Q 73–3 ~ This was a person who came around in a truck or a boat to collect the salmon from the fishermen.

salmon crew: group of persons engaged or 'shipped' to conduct afloat and on shore the various operations of the commercial salmon fishery; CREW.

[1777] 1792 CARTWRIGHT ii, 229 The *Fox* was then laden with salt, and sailed for White-Bear River, with a salmon crew. . . I sent off a salmon-crew to Paradise in two skiffs.

salmon crib: wickerwork contrivance to trap salmon migrating up a river.

[1771] 1792 CARTWRIGHT i, 139 Milmouth cut staves for a salmon-crib until the evening, when he and I brought the net on shore to shift it.

salmon flower: primrose, cowslip (*Primula laurentiana*) (1895 *N S Inst Sci* ix, 390).

1836 [WIX]² 162 There is a flower here resembling the English auricula, but smaller; it is the precursor of the salmon, and is, in consequence, called the salmon-flower.

salmon house: structure in which salmon are split, salted and stored for export.

[1771] 1792 CARTWRIGHT i, 99 The sawyers were cutting beams and other timber, for a salmon-house. [1774] ibid ii, 11 I went down to the salmon-house. . .and found the fish were very badly split, and not properly salted. [1783] ibid iii, 9 My houses. . .now consist of a dwelling-house and store-house in one, sixty feet by twenty-five, and two stories high; a house for the servants, thirty feet by seventeen; three salmon-houses, ninety feet by twenty each; and a smith's shop, sixteen feet by twelve.

salmon leap: natural declivity or fall in a river up which migrating salmon jump.

[1776] 1792 CARTWRIGHT ii, 182 [I] was going up to the salmon-leap myself, in the other skiff. . . I afterwards went up to the salmon-leap, which I found to be the most magnificent and beautiful cascade I ever saw.

salmon net: type of net moored in inshore waters or river estuaries to trap salmon; cp **salmon trap** below. Also attrib.

1792 PULLING *MS* 8 He. . .sent eight of his men the latter end of February to go up the Main Brook in pursuit of some Indians who had the preceding summer taken away some of his salmon nets, traps and many other things. [1866] 1975 WHITELEY 117 Fine—got three seals—Got the salmon nets. 1873 CARROLL 35 The twine they are made of is about three times the size of salmon net twine. 1941 SMALLWOOD 258 [statistics] Salmon Nets. . .11,415. Q 67–94 The first

thing done in making the [salmon] net is that the linnet is roped onto the headrope. Then the floats are put onto the float rope about ½ fathom apart. They are kept in place by pieces of twine that are wound around the head and float ropes at each end of the float. The skirt ropes are then put on each end of the net and then the lead line is roped onto the bottom of the net. This line sinks the net and keeps it in fishing order. 1979 *Evening Telegram* 8 June, p. 1 A number of other explanations have been put forward to explain the lack of salmon this year: dirty water, slub on salmon nets, the fact that caplin haven't begun rolling on the beaches.

salmon peel: OUANANICHE; a variety of trout. Also attrib.

1846 TOCQUE 128 Angling is now pursued, as our ponds at this season abound with myriads of trout (*Salmo fario*) and salmon peel. 1888 HOWLEY *MS Reminiscences* 31 [The lake] is well stocked also with fine trout, mostly salmon peel. I caught one very large one. 1902 *Christmas Bells* 14 As the morning advanced the big ones got mighty shy and nothing could be procured but small, trashy salmon peel which appeared in galore wherever and however we tried. 1929 BURKE [15] "Damm the Ever": I married a girl called Ann Steer, / She had a face like a man on the Beer, / When she opened her mouth, / Like a Salmon peel trout, / I thought her a duck of a deer. T 80/3–64 You had containers to bring 'em in for the winter, all these four-pound salmon—what they call salmon peel. 1964 SCOTT & CROSSMAN 26 Atlantic Salmon *Salmo salar* (thought by some to be trout and called 'salmon peel'). P 127–79 ~ A five- to ten-inch fish which has the coloration and form of a full grown salmon. They are sometimes called land-locked salmon.

salmon pip: see PIP¹.

salmon plantation: area of foreshore with or without buildings upon it for the prosecution of the commercial salmon fishery; PLANTATION, ROOM.

[1812] 1966 *Evening Telegram* 27 May, p. 6 [To be sold] dry goods store, net loft. . .cook room, fisherman's house, fish store, salt store, small salmon plantation [at Trinity] without buildings.

salmon post: see **salmon station** below.

[1770] 1792 CARTWRIGHT i, 14 Upon landing at the salmon-post, I found the crew to consist of three men. [1865] 1971 CASEY 36 [Conche] is the only place I have visited where. . .ill-feeling exists between the English and French, owing in a great measure to the English being prevented from putting down salmon nets, it being an excellent salmon post.

salmon pound: enclosure to trap salmon in a river.

[1771] 1792 CARTWRIGHT i, 168 This morning, we discovered that the salmon pound was carried away by the current; the river being much higher now than at any time since I came to the place.

salmon punt: see **salmon boat** above; PUNT.

[1771] 1792 CARTWRIGHT i, 106 I accompanied them to Seal Island; and the Indians carried their provisions, traps, and a salmon-punt upon their sled.

salmon rack: type of obstruction to trap salmon migrating up a river.

[1779] 1792 CARTWRIGHT ii, 485 I. . .made him a present, by a written deed of gift, of my houses and all my interest in that place and Deer Harbour, which is an appendage to it, and also of what salmon-racks and cribs I had at Charles Harbour.

salmon station: area on the foreshore, or on the banks of a river, often with buildings, from which the commercial salmon fishery is prosecuted; STATION.

[1811] 1818 BUCHAN 4 Mr Miller's upper Salmon station. [1888] 1907 *Our Country* 2 The Gander, the Exploits, and the Indian Brook of Hall's Bay were the three most important salmon stations of the Island.

salmon tierce: wooden cask for the export of split and cured salmon.

T 90–64 We would get our stock from the sawmills, and we would make herring barrels and salmon tierces.

salmon trap: type of fixed fishing gear used in inshore water, box-shaped with a length of net stretching from shore to entrance through which migrating salmon enter and are trapped; TRAP[1].

1941 SMALLWOOD 258 [statistics] Salmon Traps. . .543. T 250–66 We had salmon nets, and an old man to Norris Point, he was in the salmon business and he recommended the salmon trap. Where you'd get one in the net, you'd get three or four or five in the trap. 1976 *Evening Telegram* 2 Mar, p. 24 Fishermen here are now busy preparing for this year's fishery. Salmon traps, and nets, cod traps, trawls, herring nets, lobster traps and other gear are being overhauled in stores.

salmon twine: stout linen line used in the knitting of salmon nets, seines and traps. Also attrib.

[1785] 1792 CARTWRIGHT iii, 96 Mr Collingham and two hands finished the shortest seal-net, and the people then carried them both, as also the killicks, &c. to the yawl; but the wind being too high to put them out, they left them there, and two hands began to mend the old net with salmon-twine. 1874 MURRAY & HOWLEY 353–4 I have received a coil of salmon twine, 90 fathoms in length, which I assume to be the depth found by a trapper I engaged to try the soundings. 1910 *Nfld Qtly* Oct, p. 23 You speak of salmon, and we have nothing to catch them with except a withered bamboo[,] a John Winter cast with three flies and a ball of salmon twine. P 102–60 In the fall we order a quantity of salmon twine and stormy days engaged some of the native men to come to the store and knit salmon twine. In the spring we had completed 100 nets and three salmon traps. T 80/3–64 An' at that time 'twas all salmon twine, salmon twine linnet, see, 'cause there was no cotton then; an' 'twas heavy, boy. A man heaved a cod seine was a able man.

salmonier n also **salmoneer** DC ~ (Nfld: 1770). A commercial salmon fisherman; freq in place-names.

[1723 (1971) SEARY 82 John Masters and Phill Wattson are to be allowed to prosecute their salmon fishery on Great and Little Salmonier. . .Rivers.] [1766] 1971 BANKS 140 We were told by the Old Salmoneer that

there were Owls there as big as Turkies. [1770] 1792 CARTWRIGHT i, 14 When the salmoniers visited their nets this morning, they found that the Indians had stolen one fleet. 1951 *Nfld & Lab Pilot* i, 107 No. 13 black can buoy is moored close north-north-westward of Salmonier point, about half a mile south-westward of Travers Cove point. Salmonier cove is situated between these two points.

salmonry n The rights to the salmon fishery at a specified stretch of coast or on a 'room'; SALMON STATION.

[1727] 1976 HEAD 60 Gledhill further had one salmonry which he kept for himself, another he rented out, 'which he calls his royalty.'

salt n Cp *OED* ~ sb[1] (c1000–), *DAE* 1 (1641–) for sense 1; cp Genesis 19:26 for phr in sense 3 *as salt as Lot's wife*; for combs. in sense 4: *DAE* ~ beef (1779–); cp *DC* ~ burnt adj Nfld (1832); cp *OED* salt a[1] 2 (c1460 quot); *DJE* ~ fish 1 (1774–); *OED* ~ house obs (1000–1730), *DAE* obs (1638–1846), *DC* Nfld (1832); *DAE* ~ junk (1792–); *DC* ~ pile 1 Nfld (1784); *Fisheries of U S* 156 for ~ trip.

1 Common salt or sodium chloride, esp the heavy coarse salt used in the preservation of codfish; fishery salt.

[1578] 1895 PROWSE 35 . . .so that you take nothing from [European fishermen] more than a boat or two of salt. [1612] 1957 GUY *Journal* 7 Oct We did bring the banke shippe a shoare, land the salt vpon the hyheste parte of the ground thereaboutes, putting yt vp in a round hoope, [and] burning of yt to preserve yt. 1620 WHITBOURNE 34 . . .and those Ships and men so sent, may be so fitted and provided with Salt, Nets, Hooks, Lines and such like provisions, as those Ships and men are, which yeerely saile thither a fishing. [1663] 1963 YONGE 57 When the fish is split, he falls into a drooge barrow, which, when full, is drawn to one side of the stage, where boys lay it one on top of another. The salter comes with salt on a wooden shovel and with a little brush strews the salt on it. [1712] 1895 PROWSE 272 Inhabitants have most salt provisions from Ireland; fresh provisions. . .from New England. . .salt from Lisbon and Isle of May. 1819 ANSPACH 433 It is generally said that ten hogsheads of salt will cure one hundred quintals of fish. This, however, depends upon the quality of the salt, and other circumstances. The Newfoundland fishermen say that there is a difference in weight between the same bulk of Liverpool and of Lisbon salt of four to five. [1856] 1975 WHITELEY 119 The Jersey vessel came with salt—landed twelve hogsheads. 1936 SMITH 83 He told me to take her out when the men were hauling their traps, as they all were getting more than they wanted, and would give me a few quintals each; it would be all my own, except that I would have to pay for the salt. 1945 INNIS 475 Cadiz salt, matured by a year's storage, was regarded as most satisfactory for Straits fish shore-cured, but was not sufficiently strong for Labrador, for which Santa Pola salt was required. 1980 *Evening Telegram* 6 Aug, p. 4 He said however his company will not be caught short of salt for the fishermen or fish plants, since a cargo of fishery salt is due sometime this weekend from Spain.

2 Chipped ice spread on layers of seal pelts as a preservative; esp with *fresh*.

1924 ENGLAND 141 'Ice, dere, b'ys! Come 'eed de salt!' 'Salt,' they called the ice; 'fresh salt.' Down it rained, to be sprinkled between the layers of sculps, laid fat-to-fat. The empty baskets flew up, spinning. 'Dat's enough on de salt, me sons! Dat's ice enough, b'ys!'

3 Phr *as salt as Lot's wife*: very salt.

1932 BARBOUR 49 I hope he knows how to make pea soup and not stuff that's as salt as Lot's wife.

spare the salt and spoil the scrod [= small cod-fish]: proverb cautioning against false economy (1895 *Christmas Review* 12).

under salt: of split cod-fish, sprinkled with salt and placed in layers; SALT-BULK.

1873 CARROLL 39 The difference is, that those taken out of a seine, if not under salt in four hours will be of little value. P 102–60 The final mugup [was] between 10 and midnight according to the amount of cod to be dressed and under salt before retiring for the night.

4 Attrib, comb **salt beef**: beef cured in brine as a preservative; corned beef.

[1794] 1968 THOMAS 171 Salt Pork and Salt Beefe comes within the denomination of good living. [1900] 1975 WHITELEY 58 Sunday—cook's day off—salt beef and vegetables with raisin pudding. [1926] 1946 PRATT 174 "The Cachalot": Thither he sailed; but many a day / Passed by in its unending way, / The weather fair, the weather rough, / With watch and sleep, with tack and reef, / With swab and holystone, salt beef / And its eternal partner, duff.

salt-bulk: see SALT-BULK.

salt burn v: to spoil cod-fish by the application of too much salt; BURN v.

[1663 (1954)] INNIS 117 The second sort they call [in New England] refuse fish, that is such as is salt burnt, spotted, rotten and carelessly ordered.] [1749] 1755 DOUGLASS i, 302 No sun-burnt, salt-burnt, or that have been a considerable time pickled before dried, are to be deemed merchantable fish. 1819 ANSPACH 433 The defect [in dried cod] occasioned by an excess of salt is in Newfoundland known by the name of *salt-burnt*. 1832 MCGREGOR i, 231 If too much salt have been used, the fibres break in drying, and the fish easily falls to pieces. In this state, it is called salt-burnt, and is unfit for market. 1873 CARROLL 44 The top fish are often lightly salted, and the bottom fish in the puncheon, are salt-burned and often must be watered before being exposed to the sun for making. 1895 GRENFELL 60 The washed fish is next laid in pile and salted. The 'salter' is also a skilled mechanic. It is easy to undersalt and easy to 'saltburn,' or oversalt, whereby much valuable salt is wasted. 1937 DEVINE 50 Both terms [i.e. sunburnt and saltburnt] applied to deterioration of codfish in process of cure, from too much exposure to the sun, and excessive use of salt, respectively. 1942 *Grand Bank U C School* 37 [Cullage] is fish perhaps sun burned or salt burned. T 43–64 If [the salter] gave it too much [salt] he'd salt-burn the fish and it wouldn't be fit to eat.

salt(ed) cabbage: cabbage pickled in brine.

P 131–70 Salt cabbage plims when you boil it. 1972 MURRAY 262–3 Usually the best [cabbage] heads were 'pickled,' that is, salted in a barrel in a manner similar to the way fish were treated. A layer of cabbage was laid down and then a layer of coarse salt. Sometimes a little beef pickle was added to give a special flavour. Kept tightly covered 'salted cabbage' could last a long time.

salt cart: small wooden cart with two wheels and high sides, open at one end, used on fishing premises to move salt (M 68–26).

salt fish: cod-fish, split, salted and dried; DRY a: DRY FISH; FISH. Also attrib.

[1771] 1792 CARTWRIGHT i, 90 I baited the traps and deathfalls with salt-fish and seal's flesh fried in cod-blubber. [1794] 1968 THOMAS 171 The living of the poor people is, of course, in the extreme, Salt Fish and Potatoes is the common Fare. 1861 Mrs BEETON 119 Salt cod, commonly called 'salt-fish.' 1862 LIND *MS Diary* 8 July The rain is falling fast & thick, beautiful for the gardens, but bad for Salt fish. 1937 *Seafisheries of Nfld* 123 Competition in business is by no means unusual and its absence from the Salt Fish trade of Newfoundland would call for just as much comment. 1965 *Evening Telegram* 4 Nov, p. 3 He also called on the federation to press for the return of the salt fish cull. 1979 *Salt Water, Fresh Water* 32 He still. . .goes out and jigs enough codfish to keep himself for the winter, salt fish. 1982 *Evening Telegram* 30 Jan, p. 6 [Someone] must be getting rich on the shoulders of our poor, hardworking exploited fishermen according to the prices some consumers have to pay for salt fish. . .$2.39 a pound.

salt fisherman: in the Bank and Labrador fisheries, a vessel whose catch of cod is salted wet on board and taken to port to be dried.

[1892] 1960 FUDGE 36 In the spring of 1892 I found myself onboard the Gloucester vessel with my Father, the *Lawrence A Monroe*. . . She was a salt fisherman, fitted for three months.

salt fishing vessel: see **salt fisherman**.

1960 FUDGE 7 It was a customary thing for salt fishing vessels to come to NFLD and pick up their crews in the spring of the year.

salt-house: structure forming part of fishing premises in which salt is stored and applied to fish.

1626 [VAUGHAN] *The Golden Fleece* pt 3, p. 16 They may erect salt houses there, having woods sufficient for that purpose. [1779] 1792 CARTWRIGHT ii, 429 Three men were throwing the snow out of the salt-house. 1832 MCGREGOR i, 228 Generally covered over and attached to [the stage], or rather on the same platform, is the salt-house, in which there are one or more tables, with strong wooden stools for four important personages among the shoremen. 1964 *Evening Telegram* 24 Dec, p. 29 'I saw waves wash right across the road and over that salt house on the opposite side,' sez he.

salt junk: see **salt beef** above; JUNK.

1865 CAMPBELL 116 One man tired of salt junk went to a dozen houses knocking up the natives. When the sleepy mortals came to their windows the question was,

'Have you any lamb?' 1924 ENGLAND 170 Oh, they may grumble a little because there is too much salt junk, too little tobacco, and practically no adequate rum. T 55/6–64 [We'd] get salt junk an' doughboys an' duff an' that's about all. Not much vegebles in the winter.

salt lake: sea-inlet narrowly separated from the ocean; SALT-WATER POND.

1884 STEARNS 154 Again long open stretches of water would compel us to go by the land, either around some island pond or *lac salé* (salt lake, as the people call these inlets of the sea, and of which there are so many all along the coastline), or over some low and narrow, or high strip of land to the river again.

salt pen: wooden enclosure in which salt for curing fish is stored in fishing premises or on a vessel (Q 108–67); PEN.

salt pile: a quantity of split and washed cod-fish, salted and placed in layers during the curing process; PILE n, SALT-BULK, WATER-HORSE.

[1766] 1971 BANKS 134 In the Salt Pile the fish are Placd spread open one upon another & between Each Layer of fish a layer of salt is thrown here they remain an uncertain time till they have taken salt.

salt pound: see **salt pen**; POUND.

P 9–73 Roll the wet fish in the salt in the schooner's salt pound.

salt-room: area of fishing-stage in which salt is stored and applied to fish.

[1775] 1792 CARTWRIGHT ii, 85 In the course of the day we studded the salt-room, made four killicks, started most of the salt, altered the nets.

salt ship: see **salt vessel**.

[1706] 1895 PROWSE 267 Salt for fishery chiefly supplied from Portugal; ordered convoy's for salt ships from Lisbon to Newfoundland.

salt shovel: wooden implement used in handling salt on a fishing-stage.

[1622] 1954 INNIS 58 [inventory] Salt shovels. . .£2/10. [See 1663 quot at SALTER.] P 102–60 Most of these men were capable of making wheel barrows, hand barrows, salt shovels and any kind of tool required for the fish business.

salt skid: wooden sledge on runners used to move salt on fishing premises (M 68–26).

salt stage: see **salt-room**.

Q 67–43 Then the fish is wheeled [fom the splitting stage] into the salt stage where it is salted.

salt store: storage area for salt on fishing premises; STORE.

[1812] 1966 *Evening Telegram* 27 May, p. 6 [To be sold] dry goods store, net loft. . .cook room, fisherman's house, fish store, salt store, small salmon plantation [at Trinity]. 1866 WILSON 204 On their wharves are fish stores, salt stores, and provision stores. 1936 SMITH 42 Our next course was for Pigeon Island, at the mouth of Indian Harbour, and we made that also, and a few minutes later we were safely anchored off the salt store at Indian Harbour, all well. T 191–65 He went down between the old stage and another old building that was partly down—it used to be an old salt-store. 1975 BUTLER 173 [diagram of Wareham's premises] Salt store.

salt-struck: see STRIKE.

salt trip: a fishing voyage in which the catch is salted on board the ship; TRIP.

1960 FUDGE 31, 36 The next spring Father and myself shipped onboard an American fishing vessel and made two salt trips, returning home December 15th. . . Each year fishing I usually made five thousand dollars, including the winter salt herring trip.

salt trough: container for salt or brine on fishing stage.

[1779] 1792 CARTWRIGHT ii, 491 I had the sides of the stage, over the two outer beams, pulled down, and the splitting-table and outer salt-trough taken up.

salt tub: puncheon sawn in half, containing salt to apply to cod-fish; TUB.

P 102–60 A row of salt tubs [were placed] up and down the whole length of the building spaced about twelve feet apart and it was one man's job to keep these tubs filled by wheeling salt from the salt store nearby.

salt vessel: cargo-vessel for the shipment of fisheries salt.

1911 *FPU (Twillingate) Minutes* 2 June Also the salt vessel was then spoken of and proposed, seconded and carried that we wait until the last of June for said vessel.

salt water: see SALT WATER.

salt v *OED* ~ v¹ 1 (1634 quot) for sense 1.

1 To apply salt to split cod-fish as a preservative. See also HEAVY SALT, LIGHT a: LIGHT-SALT.

[1581] 1895 PROWSE 56 This Act. . .shall not extend or be prejudicial to any providing or bringing of fish in or out of the country of Iceland, Shetland or Newfoundland or any parts or seas thereto adjoining. . .nor to any fish that shall be killed taken and salted by the Queen's Natural Subjects. 1620 WHITBOURNE 38–9 And I am well assured, that such fish as is salted with the finest white salt, will sell farre better in *Sivill*, and other places of *Spaine* and *Italie*, then that which is preserved with any other kinde of muddie salt. 1758 ULLOA 407 The fish. . .are opened with one cut lengthwise, their back-bone, and all their entrails are taken out. . .and the offals thrown into the sea. While some open, others salt, and others again pile up. 1819 ANSPACH 433 Fish properly salted, when dry, will be firm and may be handled without breaking. 1866 WILSON 210 When the drudge-barrow is full, it is dragged to the upper end of the stage, where the fish is taken out and salted. 1936 SMITH 83 I asked him if he would undertake to split, salt, dry and ship whatever fish I might get, at so much per quintal. T 43–64 Whether 'tis in the stage or if 'tis in the schooner. . .the salter would come. . .an' salt it. 1975 *Evening Telegram* 2 July, p. 3 'I've never had to salt for the past couple of years,' the young man said, 'but otherwise I'd have to throw the fish away.' 1981 ibid 5 Sep, p. 7 Men and women [on the Labrador side of the Strait of Belle Isle] are employed salting the fish, after which it is transported by truck or boat.

2 To apply salt to a corpse, or immerse the body in brine, for later burial; sometimes with *in.* Cp naval practice implied at NELSON phr *drink [rum] off the one-eyed hero.*

P 243–56 In 1948 one of the crew on the Labrador died and I salted him in a box the boys made, then shipped him home on the coastal boat. T 1–63[1] If they died very far out at sea, you know, they'd be long getting home; they salt them in. If 'twas in the summer they'd have to. 1977 *Decks Awash* vi (3), p. 55 [He] succumbed [to typhoid fever] and died there. . . I went over and made a box with a little help and we salted Martin in his box.

3 To apply chipped ice to (a) seal pelts, (b) a corpse, as a preservative; often with *down.*

1924 ENGLAND 39–40 'If a man die,' the carpenter informed me, 'us builds un a coffin out o' pound boards, an' salt un down [ice him], an' putt un de Marconi house or the fo'c's'le 'eed.' He said it as if mentioning a side of beef. Ibid 320 Salt down. To ice [seal pelts].

4 *salt for labrador*: to apply salt liberally, as in the production of LABRADOR fish.

P 59–64 We say that people who put a lot of salt on food are salting for Labrador.

salt bulk n ['sɑltʔ bʌlk, 'sɒltʔ bʌlk]. Cp *DC* ~ Nfld [1861–]. Freq in phr *in salt-bulk.* Cp BULK n.

1 A quantity of salt, esp when heaped in the hold of a boat or vessel.

1870 HOWLEY *MS Reminiscences* 23 It is amusing to watch them loading salt aboard their vessels. They come alongside with a large boat full of salt. A sail is let down from the ship's gunwale to that of the boat to prevent the salt being lost overboard. A number of men with large wooden shovels throw the salt up on to the vessel's deck singing all the while in a sort of measured sing song tone. At every bar they dig their shovels into the salt bulk then at a given moment all heave up together and so on till the cargo is aboard.

2 A pile of split, washed and salted cod-fish placed not yet dried in a fishing stage or aboard a vessel; cp FAGGOT n, HORSE, PILE n, WATER-HORSE. This use merges in some contexts with sense 3.

1925 *Dial Notes* v, 340 ~ Fish in its storing vat. 1955 *Nfld Fisheries Board* No 23 ~ Fish which has been not less than three weeks in the original saltbulk in store and then repiled in store for a period of not less than 10 days; fish which has been not less than three weeks in the original saltbulk in vessel and then repiled in store for a period of not less than 10 days; fish which has been heavily salted on board a vessel for a period of less than three weeks and then repiled and resalted in store in bulk for a period not less than 20 days. T 43–64 The fish had to be laid out perfect, you know, in the salt bulk, an' salted. 1977 BURSEY 166 The premises must be made strong enough to take the fish that we would pile in salt bulk. 1979 NEMEC 248 Any fish. . .which was salted and stored in 'saltbulks' in local stages for sale later in the summer or fall, was not included.

3 A stage of preserving cod-fish temporarily in salted piles; the fish itself, wet and salted but not yet dried; GREEN FISH.

1861 DE BOILIEU 31 The cod is now placed in what is called salt-bulk, where it may remain any period of time; for, so long as fish is being caught in the bay, so long will the 'drying' and 'washing'—which constitute the final process—be delayed. 1933 *Nfld Royal Commission Report* 97 The fish caught on the Banks are gutted, washed and split on the vessels and then put into what is known as 'salt-bulk,' viz., they are stowed in the hold in a heavily salted condition without being dried or cured, the salt acting as a dehydrating preservative. 1946 MACKAY (ed) 82 By far the larger part of the Labrador catch is carried back to Newfoundland in salt bulk (after it has been salted but before it has been exposed to the sun), where the curing process is completed by the fishermen and their families. 1954 INNIS 462 In 1910, American firms were engaged in purchasing green fish—now known as salt bulk, i.e. fish wet-salted in piles—in Newfoundland. T 175/7–65 'Tis leaved in salt bulk for so long, washed out and then in press perhaps a day or a couple o' days. 1972 MURRAY 247 Trapping crews usually put most of their fish in 'salt bulk' (i.e., dry salted in big rectangular piles) and worked as a unit—men and women—to 'wash out' the salted fish. This was put in 'water horse' (the washed fish, back up, in rectangular piles) overnight till the water pressed out of it. 1973 HORWOOD 75 It was in the spring of the year 1940 that a group of Greek merchants came to Grand Bank and bought twelve thousand quintals of fish in salt bulk to be delivered by Newfoundland vessels to Patras, the port that serves Athens.

4 Phr *sell salt-bulk*: to sell cod-fish in its salted but undried condition.

T 139–65 There was none sold salt-bulk, like they sells now, at them times. They had to dry it all.

5 Attrib.

[1953] 1978 *Evening Telegram* 8 Nov, p. 13 Advance prices for saltbulk and fresh fish were demanded in a key resolution. 1960 FUDGE 16 [The vessel] was loaded with salt bulk cod fish. 1975 BUTLER 69 The salt bulk fish would be packed in bulks in the stores. 1976 CASHIN 81 In a few cases we even bought salt-bulk fish from the Nova Scotia banking vessels and cured it ourselves on our flakes at Cape Broyle. 1981 *Evening Telegram* 5 Sep, p. 7 Boat loads of saltbulk fish continue to arrive regularly [at Catalina] from the Labrador.

salter n Cp *OED* ~[1] 3 'one who salts meat or fish' (1714 quot), *DAE* 1 b (1800 quot); *EDD* 3 Sh I, *DC* (1760–). Member of a fishing crew who applies salt in the processing of dried cod.

[1663] 1963 YONGE 57 [When the fish is split] the salter comes with salt on a wooden shovel and with a little brush strews the salt on it. [1751–66] 1954 INNIS 182 To 3 Salters. . .£48. 1778 DE CASSINI 122 [After the fish is cleaned] the salter crams as much salt as he can into the belly of the fish, lays it down, the tail end lowest, rubs the skin all over with salt, and then covers it with more salt; then goes through the same process with the rest of the cod, which he heaps one upon another till the whole is laid up. 1819 ANSPACH 432 At the opposite end of the stage stands the *salter*, who, as soon as the drudge-barrow is brought to him, takes out the fish, one by one, and placing it in layers on one side of the stage, spreads on each with his hand some salt. 1866 WILSON 210 The mistress is generally the salter. 1957 *Nfld Qtly* Sep, p. 49 'What's wrong with that one?' demanded Pratt. Jim spoke quietly. 'Burned up with salt. Who's your salter?' [1961] 1965 PEACOCK (ed) i, 127 "The Fisher Who Died in His Bed": There was never such a salter this side of the water, / There was never such a glutton for eatin' cods' heads. T 43–64 And your fish would go through the water an' go to the salter. Now the salter was the main man in handlin' a load o' fish. A salter was a man that was depended on because he couldn't give it too much an' he couldn't give it too little. T 175/7–65 Whether 'tis in the stage or if 'tis in the schooner, 'twill drop down [in] the tub, an' perhaps the salter would come up from the hold an' pull along and prong it down the hold. Well he got to go back again an' salt it.

salting vbl n Cp *OED* ~ 4 ~ house (1682).
    Attrib **salting cask**: barrel-shaped wooden container for cured fish.
    [1777] 1792 CARTWRIGHT ii, 237 I delivered all the empty casks, and then took on board some salting casks, and twenty-one coils of cordage.
    salting house: area of fishing premises in which cod-fish are processed for drying; SALT-HOUSE.
    1818 CHAPPELL 127 Each *salting-house* is provided with one or more tables, around which are placed wooden chairs and leathern aprons, for the *cut-throats, headers*, and *splitters*.
    salting scoop: wooden implement for spreading salt on split cod-fish (P 243–61); cp SALT SHOVEL.
    salting stage: see **salting store**; STAGE.
    1966 FARIS 224 From here [the cod are] wheeled up a narrow track on the long wharf to a more substantial building. . .the 'salting stage' where the fish are spread in rows and salted.
    salting store: see **salting house**; SALT STORE.
    P 102–60 The salting store [is] where the salters laid [the fish] flat all face up and covered them, [using] a salt shovel which was home-made of wood.

salt water n Cp *OED* ~ sb 'sea-water' (esp 1440 quot), c. 'applied to the sea' (1843 quot), *DAE* 1 (1684 quot), *EDD* salt 9 (7) ~ water 'sea side' for sense 1. Cp FRESH a: FRESH WATER.
    1 The sea, esp near the shore; inshore fishing grounds; the WATER.
    1620 WHITBOURNE 38 [The fishing trade will profit] if those which yeerely adventure thither, will settle people in every harbor where they use to fish, and provide pannes in every such harbor to boyle salt to preserve their fish withall [for] one panne will make aboue twentie bushels of good salt in every four and twentie houres for that purpose, onely with mans labour and the salt water. [1822] 1928 CORMACK28 We discovered that under the cover of the forest we had been uniformly ascending ever since we left the salt water at Random Bar. 1868 HOWLEY *MS Reminiscences* 31 They come up [the river] in winter cut all they want, drag it out to the river deposit it on the ice, and await

the spring thaws to float it out to the salt water. 1912 *Nfld Qtly* July, p. 16 We see in great splendour the majestic range of mountains that run along the coast at an average distance of some ten miles from the salt water. T 178–65 And he was stopped, an' he said he saw he was to the salt water because he seen the kelp. 1975 BUTLER 117 That was, I think, the worst night I ever put in on salt water. P 245–75 'Don't go near the salt water' [Portugal Cove mother to small child on its way down to the wharf]. 1977 BUTLER 26 The night was a dreadful night on salt water, with the howling of the wind in the rigging. There were white smokes of wind as high as the hills and water blew over the vessel in sheets. 1977 COOK 56 Fish. Who cares about fish. Oh, they are necessary. On account o' them, we took to the salt water. 1978 WHALLEY 5 What gives definition and force to poems is not simply the subject-matter. . .but something intrinsic, with its root in what has been experienced to the bone, its fibre in the taste of the words and names caught up in events. For Pratt, that was the sea—or, as a Newfoundlander would say, salt-water. 1981 *Evening Telegram* 10 Oct, p. 1 The young moose took to the salt water off Portugal Cove about 5 a.m. yesterday and. . .kept going for 4 kilometres until it reached the beach at Bell Island.
    2 Attrib **salt-water bird**: sea-bird, esp one hunted as food or bait; BIRD[1].
    [1831–9] 1863 HIND i, 17 The 'Brent Goose' may be considered as a salt-water bird, for it never ascends our rivers beyond the influence of the tides, nor is found in inland lakes or ponds, unless it be wounded, and happens to alight accidentally in such places. [1929] 1979 *Evening Telegram* 6 Mar, p. 5 Salt water birds are very scarce in Bonavista Bay this winter. 1975 GUY 96 There were ducks and geese and venison and salt water birds. 1977 *Evening Telegram* 17 June, p. 6 [The bull bird] is a salt water bird, weighs approximately four ounces. . . It used to be a great dish (still is).
    salt-water cake, ~ **pancake**: in children's rhyme when playing ducks and drakes.
    Q 67–42 Ducks and drakes / And salt water cakes / A bottle of brandy, O. Q 67–62 A duck and a drake and a salt water cake / And a penny all over the water. Q 67–79 A duck, a drake, a salt water cake and a bottle of Brandy O. A riddle used when rocks are skimmed across the water. When the rock hits the water the first time the thrower would say 'a duck.' At the second hitting in the water he would say 'a drake' and so on until the rock stopped skimming. If it skimmed more than four or five times then you would begin from the beginning of your riddle. Q 67–92 [In] skimming rocks on water we made salt water pancakes.
    salt-water duck: see **salt-water bird**.
    1959 MCATEE 17 ~ White-winged Scoter (Nfld.). T 43/4–64 In the winter they could look out an' see these salt water ducks, birds of all description, an' all they had to do was grab their gun an' go an' bring home [a] backload of 'em. T 398/9–67 I was out an' killed a good many sea ducks though, salt water ducks. C 70–21 When we had salt water duck for dinner we always kept the wishbone and put it away to dry. 1977 *Evening Telegram* 18 Feb, p. 1 On the lookout for salt water ducks, the prospective hunters were spotted on the weekend.

salt-water ice: sea ice formed in coastal waters as opposed to the arctic ice-floe; BAY ICE, HARBOUR ICE, LOCAL: *local ice*.

1836 [WIX]² 98–9 The women and children cut holes in the salt-water ice, and catch great quantities of codfish all through the winter. 1910 GRENFELL 89 We were crossing a large arm of the sea, and the salt water ice being a bit sticky I attempted to get off and walk. [1918–19] 1972 GORDON 47 Left Black Bear about 9.0 and struck in across the country for several miles. . . At last we came out onto the salt-water ice, and soon reached Long Pond. T 43–64 You had to travel. . .over salt water ice, and then take the train at Lewisporte.

salt-water lake: see **salt-water pond**.

1849 [FEILD] 109 Just before the house is a salt-water lake, which rises and falls with the tide, though its connexion with the sea is not visible.

salt-water otter: variety of otter frequenting sea-coast.

1868 HOWLEY *MS Reminiscences* 43 It was a very fine salt water otter as large as two of the freshwater species.

salt-water pancake: see **salt-water cake**.

salt-water pigeon: sea pigeon or southern black guillemot (*Cepphus grylle atlantis*) (P 148–69). See WATER PIGEON.

1860 TAYLOR 271 A herring net was set inside of the cove, and two or three youths in a boat with a gun, were endeavouring to shoot a salt-water pigeon.

salt-water pond: small body of sea-water barely linked to the ocean.

[1774] 1792 CARTWRIGHT ii, 22 I killed a pair of black-ducks in a salt-water pond. 1979 O'FLAHERTY 179 A large female finback whale stranded itself by pursuing bait fish into a deep salt water pond near Burgeo.

salt-water rock: beach stone, worn round and smooth by the sea.

M 69–28 They kept the sick man warm by wrapping him in 'salt water rocks' since there was no central heating. These salt water rocks gotten from the seashore, were heated in the oven of the kitchen stove, and wrapped in old clothes to keep from burning the sick person. The rocks had to be from the sea-shore, because they hold the heat longer, and they have smooth surfaces. C 70–15 [In winter] every night about an hour before going to bed, salt-water rocks which had been heated in the oven were placed in the bed. Those rocks were shaped much like a curling-stone and were very smooth. Those used in our house had been given to my mother by her mother, and presumably had been obtained somewhere where heavy seas would roll the rocks on the beaches and in time they were worn smooth. Of course after the rocks were removed from the oven they were wrapped in old clothing such as sweaters so as not to burn the feet.

salt-water shore: heavy log used in wharf construction; SHORE².

P 245–74 ~ 7–10 in. [thick] log, driven into ground below tide-level to support a wharf or other heavy water-front structure.

salt-water snake: rock gunnel (*Pholis gunnellus*) (P 77–74); TANSY.

salt-water soap: home-made lye soap.

1932 BARBOUR 48 If we had some salt-water soap we would have been able to wash our faces, but there was nothing like that on board.

salt-water trout: sea-trout, esp arctic char (*Salvelinus alpinus*).

[1775] 1792 CARTWRIGHT ii, 95–6 Killed two hundred and twenty-five salmon, and a trout; such a one as neither I nor any of our people had ever seen before;. . .the Indian boy called it a 'salt-water trout,' and said, the rivers to the northward had plenty of them.

salt-water worm: sea-worm; a marine annelid (*Nereis* spp) (P 154–78).

salvage a, n [sæl'veɪdʒ] *OED* Savage: salvage a 2 b 'horribly wild and rugged.' Cp H GARDNER *Composition of Four Quartets* (1978), p. 51 'The Dry Salvages and the Little Salvages lie about a mile east-north-easterly. . .of the northern point of Cape Ann [Mass.].' In place-names, rugged, treacherous; cp RAGGED.

1613 *Willoughby Papers* 1/23 We ankered in Sollvagg baye: so-called because ther we had the first sight of [the indians]. [?1677] 1971 SEARY 21 Salvage Point. [1689] ibid Salvage. [1689] ibid 275 Salvages. [1900 OLIVER & BURKE] 76 "Old Salvage": Grim stands the well-known sea-mark. . . / So well known to Harbor Gracians, / The triangular Salvage. 1953 *Nfld & Lab Pilot* ii, 78–9 Salvage rock. . .stands on a shoal bank near the middle of the fairway [near Harbour Grace].

salvationer n *OED* ~ rare (1889). Member of the Salvation Army; also attrib.

1971 NOSEWORTHY 240 ~ An old word meaning 'Salvationist,' and used when talking about a member of the Salvation Army. P 257–79 Church of England people on Change Islands when I was a Corps Officer there would refer to us Army people as Salvationers [and also] as an adjective: 'He's a Salvationer man.'

sand n Cp *DAE* sand peep (1872–); *OED* ~ sb² 10 ~ rock.

Comb **sand-crown**: sand-dollar, a type of sea-urchin (*Echinarachnius parma*) (1966 FARIS 238).

sand-hill grass: sand-sedge (*Carex arenaria*) ([1822] 1928 CORMACK 120).

sand-peep: least sandpiper (*Erolia minutilla*) (1959 MCATEE 33).

sand-plover: black-bellied plover (*Squatarola squatarola*) (1959 MCATEE 28).

sand-rock: sandstone.

T 141/64–65² An' they wandered in on the bleak land, an' directly they come to a big sand-rock, an' they got up against this big rock an' had a blow. C 70–12 She always used the sand rock to clean up the floors. The women would use a large rock to break up the sand-rock so that the remains could be used to put on the floor when cleaning.

sapper n A full boat-load of cod; SWAMPER.

1968 *Avalon Penin of Nfld* 112 ~ a good boat-load of

fish. C 70–12 When the fishermen would come in with a full load of fish, that is to say only the gunnels were out of the water, my uncle would say, 'they have got a full sapper,' which meant they had a full load of codfish. P 135–74 ~ The term describes a boat when there is a load of fish in it.

saucy a ['sɑːsɪ, 'sɒːsɪ, 'sɒˈsɪ, 'sɒəsɪ] *EDD* ~ 2 IW. Skittish, belligerent; unpredictable, dangerous.

1925 *Dial Notes* v, 340 ~ Pugnacious; esp of seals. 1929 *Nat Geog* July, p. 125 Young seals are saucy and will come for a man until he snogs them with his bat. T 50/2–64 You wouldn't be allowed to let 'em run, if you had a bull, especially if he got saucy—[wouldn't] let a saucy bull or saucy horse run. But them days the bulls used to be as saucy as mischief. T 187/9–65 [The gun] could kill anywhere at all. All you had to do was hold her straight. But she was miserable saucy. She've had me beat all to pieces.

savanna n Cp *DAE* ~ 1; *DC* (1849–). Uninhabited treeless stretches of wasteland in the interior of the island of Newfoundland, supporting low shrubs, berries, mosses and grass; BARRENS, DOWNS. Also attrib.

[1822] 1856 CORMACK 18–19 The plains which shone so brilliantly are steppes or savannas. . . They are in the form of extensive gently undulating beds stretching northward and southward. . . The savannas are continually moist or wet on the surface, even in the middle of summer, but hard underneath. 1846 TOCQUE 123 All the rest of the country through which we passed was one vast savanna. 1866 WILSON 37 Passing these ravines and belts of woods, we arrive at an open country, called The Barrens, which are an immense waste, consisting of barren rock, or rock covered with moss. Also extensive marshes or savannas, and ponds of all sizes and figures, around which patches of woods vary the scene. 1868 HOWLEY *MS Reminiscences* 34 To the west only, beyond the head of the steady we caught glimpses of a level prairie land of vast green tracts like cultivated fields. This is the Savanna country so enthusiastically described by W E Cormack in his itinerary of 1822.

save v *OED* ~ v 11 obs (1602 quot Co) for sense 1; *EDD* 3 D for sense 2.

1 To preserve cod, etc, by salting and drying; cure; DRY, MAKE.

1620 WHITBOURNE 37 These shippes yeerely carrie thither, neere halfe their lading of salt, to save their fish withall. [1653] 1956 CUTTING 136 [That] no planter be permitted to. . .keep any pigs or other cattle upon or near the ground where fish is saved or dried. [1663] 1963 YONGE 57 The complement of men to a boat are 5, that is 3 for to catch the [cod] fish, two to save it. 1873 CARROLL 38 I always endeavoured to make myself thoroughly acquainted with the best and surest way of saving Herring, so as to make them a good and profitable article of Trade.

2 To harvest and store hay.

1974 MANNION 93 Traditionally, the settlers near St John's began mowing on 'the day after the races in Quidi Vidi,' in early August, and by Lady Day (August 15) most of the hay was usually 'saved.'

3 Phr *save one's spring*: to show a moderate profit at the end of a fishing season. Cp SPRING².

1960 FUDGE 51 . . .my Seine Master George Pauls, who saved his spring to the amazement of himself and his crew.

save-cock n A large mound of hay in a field; POOK n.

1971 MANNION 247 These rows were then converted into small heaps—'smallcocks' in Mirimichi and Avalon. . .from three to five feet in diameter at the base. In the Avalon these cocks were merged next day into larger 'save-cocks' out in the meadow.

saving ppl Cp *OED* ~ 5 'not turning to loss, though not gainful' obs (1614–1832). See also SAVE.

Comb **saving trip**: moderately profitable fishing or sealing venture; cp TRIP.

1873 CARROLL 36 Nine tenths of [the ice-hunting masters] when they first took charge of ice-hunting vessels generally brought into port what is usually termed 'good saving trips.' [1896] SWANSBOROUGH 35 "The Seal Fishery": This is the way that many crews / Must get their trip, or else must lose / For the out-fits are very high; / So both skippers and men must try / To get at least a saving trip. [1929] 1933 GREENLEAF (ed) 299 "The *Greenland* Disaster": From that until the twenty-first all seemed bright and gay, / And for to get a saving trip they killed and panned away.

saving voyage: see **saving trip**; cp VOYAGE.

[1766] 1971 BANKS 134 200 Quintals a boat is Calld a saving Voyage, but not under. [1786] 1792 CARTWRIGHT iii, 198 The codfish also had been so scarce this summer, that few people were likely to kill a saving voyage. 1936 SMITH 130 There was a sign of fish; all hands then set the traps, but the fish was not so plentiful. Everyone secured a saving voyage with traps and hooks combined. 1941 WITHINGTON 129–30 All were eagerly going north on the chance of a 'savin vige,' as the season's work was called. The year before and for several years, the haul had been light; but the men were always buoyed up by hope in the great gamble of the Labrador, the gamble for their very existence—cod being practically their only means of livelihood. 1977 BURSEY 132 We both had made a saving voyage by keeping our traps in the berths.

saviour's letter n also **letter of Jesus Christ**. A letter, usu printed, purporting to be by Christ, kept as a moral guide and as a charm.

1836 [WIX]² 114 There is, among the poor, in many parts of this island, a superstitious respect paid to a piece of printed paper, which is called the 'Letter of Jesus Christ.' This, in addition to Lentulus's well-known epistle to the Senate of Rome, contains many absurd superstitions, such as the promise of safe delivery in child-bed, and freedom from bodily hurt to those who may possess a copy of it. M 69–5 When she knew that her neighbour's house was burning she went, got her copy of the Saviour's Letter and pinned it up on the end of her [house] nearest the burning house. M 69–7

Some families have two copies of the letter; one in their house and one in their fishing boat. . . The granny woman about 1910–20 always carried the Saviour's Letter with her when she went to deliver a baby.

saw n *EDD* ~ sb 1 (4) ~ box So D.
Comb **saw-box**: detachable handle at lower end of a pit-saw.
1975 BUTLER 60 The men were kept busy all winter long using a pit saw to saw logs. Those two men were considered principal men. They were called sawyers. A pit saw was six to seven feet long with a stationary handle on the top end and a handle called a saw box that could be detached from the lower end of the saw.
saw-dog: frame on which plank is laid to be sawn (1971 NOSEWORTHY 240).
saw-gallows: frame against which newly-sawn planks are laid to dry; GALLOWS, WOOD ~ .
[1771] 1792 CARTWRIGHT i, 86 The sawyers were occupied in hauling home some boards, and making fresh pits, or more properly speaking, saw-gallows.

saw v See HALF n: *on the halves*.

sawboo* See SABOT.

say v *OED* ~ v¹ 5 now dial (1588–1643); *EDD* v¹ 4. Phr *be said by*: to be guided by, to be advised.
1937 DEVINE 59 Had right to be said-by. Should have taken his advice. Q 67–32 'Be said by me'—take my advice.

scab v To steal trifles.
P 148–66 The baby scabs every pin I lay down.
P 184–67 I think I'll scab one of her cookies.

scad n also **scat, skad** [skæd, skæ·d] *EDD* ~ sb³ 'sudden and brief shower of rain' So D; scat sb² 1 w cty (1790–); cp *OED* scud sb¹ 2 b (1687–).
1 Flurry, snow-shower; DWY.
1910 *Nfld Qtly* Dec, p. 30 The evening was calm, and there was a light scad of snow falling. 1924 ENGLAND 225 Came 'scats o' snow' when the fog fanned away and all grew sheeted with blowing drifts. 1933 GREENE 230–1 The heavy 'scats' of snow-crystals that now are occasionally sweeping over the Floe, so sting all faces in the gusts with the temperature rapidly falling, that ear-flaps are pulled down on every cap. P 148–66 Is this the first snow? We had a little scad. P 111–67 Sheila's brush, a scad of snow on March 18, is called after St Sheila. 1973 *Evening Telegram* 29 Dec, p. 4 I was looking out of my office window on Duckworth Street recently when the first scad of December snow suddenly covered the ground.
2 Thin layer of snow on the ground.
1897 *J A Folklore* x, 209 Skad of snow, a fall of a few inches covering the ground. 1907 MILLAIS 339 Scat of snow, just a light fall. 1925 *Dial Notes* v, 340 ~ a light, thin coating of snow. P 118–66 A light fall of snow is referred to as a scad. P 13–74 ~ up to an inch in depth. A hunter might wish for a scad of snow to cover up the old tracks.

scaffold n Cp *DAE* ~ 1 (1634–). An elevated platform on which nets are placed to dry or for storage; such a platform used for the safe-keeping of fish, meat, etc.
[1782] 1792 CARTWRIGHT i, 276 I had the sealnets taken out of the dwelling-house here, stowed them on a scaffold out of doors, and covered them with sealskins. 1876 HOWLEY *MS Reminiscences* 5 This is a place where in the late autumn the people of Conne River collect the deer carcasses killed in the vicinity, which they placed upon scaffolds, to freeze, and when the snow comes they haul them out the coast on sleds. 1910 GRENFELL 91 I often treat dogs, for my thoughts flew to the scaffold at the hospital on which the best part of a ton of whale meat still reposed. 1973 GOUDIE 24 I built a scaffold and put my trout up where the little animals could not get at them.

scaffold v *DAE* ~ v 2 (1799–1808). To place game on an elevated platform for safe-keeping.
1895 DAVIS 166 As Indian Jim desired to complete the 'scaffling' of the two fat does killed by the Kid yesterday, the writer went with him. [1913] GRENFELL 153 We found Harry had come in a hurry to get help from the village to bring out two stags he had killed, and as he had not 'scaffolded' them out of the reach of animals, he simply must go right back in the morning.

scaine See SEINE.

scalp¹ See SCULP v.

scalp² See SCULP n.

scarlet a Comb **scarlet runner**: ground-ivy, gill-over-the-ground (*Glechoma hederacea*) (1898 *N S Inst Sci* ix, 400).

scat See SCAD.

scath* a [skæ·əθ]. Cp *EDD* scathe sb 1 'danger.' Dangerous, risky.
T 141/66–65² 'Twas a little bit scath, see, comin' down. An' the green squalls, my son, comin' down out o' Salt Pond.

scatter See SCATTERED.

scattered p ppl also **scatter**. Cp *OED* ~ 2 'widely separated one from another. . .spread over a wide area.' For sealing uses see 1933 GREENE 16 . . .in an area of about 60 to 80 square miles, according as the seals are close or 'scattering.' See SCATTERING; cp NUMEROUS.
1 Located here and there; in the seal fishery, so widely dispersed as to be difficult to hunt successfully.
[1783] 1792 CARTWRIGHT iii, 7 I met with some scattered curlews, and killed six of them. [1785] ibid iii, 45 In crossing the bay we saw several grampuses, and seals, also birds pursuing some scattered caplin. 1851 [FEILD] 60 Mr Hoyles visited five or six different islands and harbours in which were scattered settlers.

[1856] 1975 WHITELEY 116 Put out the seal nets—saw a great many scattered seals. 1882 TALBOT 20 For a day or two we passed in and out through skirts of ice, picking up scattered seals as we passed along, until at length we got into a large plain of loose ice, interspersed with lakes of clear blue water. [1894 BURKE] 21 'Don't be picking up the scattered ones [shillings found among the silver thaw],' cried one of them [hard cases]; 'wait till you get on Water Street, in the thick of them.' 1895 GRENFELL 164 Work proceeds during the night by torchlight, and the scattered fires, with their ruddy glow on the heaps of dead seals and uncouth-looking figures at work, must present indeed a weird sight. [1900 OLIVER & BURKE] 10 Seals were fairly plentiful but scattered. 1924 ENGLAND 276 Men were out, running through drifts after a few scattered seals. 1937 DEVINE 39 Quintern' [is] killing scattered seals while the ship is moving through loose ice, the men going over the side for the purpose.

2 Sporadic; isolated; single; occasional.

1887 BOND 16 We crept along slowly for several days, picking up a scattered seal here and there, but not many. [1897] 1927 DOYLE (ed) 72 "The Landfall of Cabot": And a devil for tobaccy, / With a scattered foxey whisker / Like an Upper Island cracky. 1902 *Christmas Bells* 2 A 'scattered' man from the 'Coves' was met going home with his jar. 1936 SMITH 45 During Christmas [we enjoyed] ourselves with the boys mummering and dancing, and a scattered game of 'forty-fives.' Ibid 85 We hauled [the trap] in good time, a scattered fish coming in 'meshed.' T 49–64 Course they used to have a scattered row, you know, a scattered fight—one crowd [with] the other. T 36/8–64 The roof would be covered with rines, and 'twould be tight apart from a scattered knothole in the rine. 1973 BARBOUR 92 At that time one would frequently hear the remark, 'It was an old time Bonnieventer weddin', a scatter gun all night.' 1981 *Evening Telegram* 24 Mar, p. 1 Men from seven. . .vessels were picking up scattered hooded seals Monday.

3 Phr *scattered bit*.

[1906] GRENFELL 199 There was still more'n a scattered bit o' ice about. P 148–62 I used to box scatter bit.

scattered few

[c1894] PANL P4/14, p. 200 A *scattered few* is a very few, while a *smart* few is a *great many*. 1973 WADEL 85 [There are] other neighbourhoods where only 'a scattered few' are on welfare.

scattered one

1924 ENGLAND 89 You two men, there's a scattered one off to winnard. Get 'em! 1937 DEVINE 42 A fisherman, wishing to minimise the report of a good day's fishing may use the word in a deprecatory sense: 'There was a *scattered* one going, you know.' T 66/7–64 You would get [fish] sunburned, spite o' ya. Not very often, though. Might get scatter one sunburnt. C 70–12 Were the birds very thick? No, boy, but there was a scattered one. I killed four.

scattered time

1854 [FEILD] 57 [I asked] whether the inhabitants of Fortune and Griquet attended this service. . . I was told, 'scattered times,' and 'scattered' is the common term, or expression, in Newfoundland for 'few and far

between.' 1863 HIND [ii] 196 The poor English people on this part of the coast attend the service of their fisherman 'minister' at 'scattered times' during the winter months. 1920 WALDO 57 'Do you wash the children?' 'Scattered times, sir.' T 22–64 They always had the string on the goat coming behind them, see, to get them in. Scattered time they start milking him [in] a scattered place. T 50–64 You could haul a joint most anywhere, through the stumps and through the woods. Very scattered time I'd hitch up. T 210/11–65 They'd be tryin' to guess who it was, and a scattered time you'd get your [false] face pulled off, but not many times that'd happen.

scattering ppl Cp *EDD* ~ : ~ few Y. See SCATTERED. A few; a small number of things.

1924 ENGLAND 250 Used to be men stabbed, when de Dundee swilers come out. Scatterin' men got stabbed. 1925 *Dial Notes* v, 340 Scatterin' times—now and then.

scent n *Gray's Botany* 472. Cpd **scent-bottle**: leafy white orchid, bog-candle (*Platanthera dilatata*) (1898 *J A Folklore* xi, 273); LILY; MARSH-LILY; PERFUME-WILLOW.

1939 DULEY 17 She grew tall and slender like the delicate scent-bottles growing at the edge of the forests. 1974 SCOTT & BRASSARD 3 Scent-bottle.

school See SCULL.

schooner n Cp *DAE* ~ 1 (1716–); PARTRIDGE schooner-rigged 'destitute.'

Comb **schooner boat**: small decked vessel, rigged fore-and aft like a schooner.

[1766] 1971 BANKS 149 I take this opportunity of setting down the dimensions of a schooner Boat we had with us for a tender as it appears to me the most rational Plan of a Pleasure boat I have met with our People all agreeing that when her hatches were shut down it was scarcely in the Power of wind or water to sink she swimming upon the surface like a corkd bottle her schooner sails also allowing her to be workd by fewer hands than any other Kind she had 42 feet Keel 12 feet Beam & was 5½ feet Deep Pink stern deckd flush fore & aft. . . She Carried mainsail Foresail Fore stay sail & Gib with a square sail to go before the wind. [1829] P 265¹–67 [Slade papers] Thursday 24th Sept., 1829, Mr Graham in his Schooner Boat from New Harbour and off for St John's this afternoon.

schooner-rigged: possessing only the clothes one stands in (P 85–66).

scithers n pl also **scidders*** ['sɨðəɹz, 'sɪdəɹz] *EDD* ~ . Scissors; shears.

1965 *Evening Telegram* 21 Dec, p. 28 'Did your wife lend you them sharp scidders? She said she would.' P 148–65 He said that he had always heard [scissors] as if it were scithers. T 437/8–65 He chopped off so much with that and so much with the scithers. 1971 NOSEWORTHY 240 ~ Shears used for cutting the wool from a sheep.

scoff n *OED* ~ sb² 'food; a meal' (1879–); cp

EDD scaff sb[1] **1** Sc. A cooked meal at sea or ashore, esp at night and often part of an impromptu party; such a repast prepared with 'bucked' or stolen ingredients (1966 FARIS 207).

[c1894] PANL P4/14, p. 200 You may find a *large* spread; *lashings* of pork and duff, indeed a veritable *scoff*. 1896 *J A Folklore* ix, 33 To [scouse or lobscouse] they give the name *scoff*. 1898 *Christmas Bells* 14 In the nights there'd be nothing but 'scoffs' aboard, while the housekeepers of the place frequently complained of the loss of a fine fat hen, or a half dozen o' cabbages. 1932 BARBOUR 59 We will have a 'scoff' (a meal of boiled salt pork, cabbage, potatoes and turnips served hurriedly on board ship) cooked. T 34–64 In years gone by we used to. . .on the last of October we'd all get together, and we'd get our bit of cabbage and go to one or t'other of the houses, and we have our scoff cooked, and have a big time then. T 246–66 We all meet together an' have a few songs, an' we put on a big feed, you know—scoff, we'd always call it. C 68–7 The young people and sometimes the older people would have a scoff every two or three weeks during the winter months. A scoff was a big feed of potatoes, cabbage, pork and other things. While this scoff was cooking they would have a game of cards. Each person involved in the scoff would carry his share of the vegetables. 1974 SQUIRE 40 The scoff was another form of entertainment, taken part in chiefly by the younger men. (The older people frowned on it, especially the name.) This pastime was not so widely known in the early days, as in the latter part of the 1800's and the early part of the 20th century. The event usually took place in the period between October and Christmas. A group of young men secured a supply of fresh meat, usually sea birds. When these were not procureable, a hen or duck would be gotten from a neighbour's supply, this chiefly by stealth. . . Young men then congregated at one of the homes and together with their girl friends cooked a large meal of meat and vegetables. . . The party would normally end with a dance, and a card game.

scolly See SKULLY.

scoop n Cp *EDD* ~ sb 1 for sense 1.
1 A flat-bottomed wooden container with short handle used to bail water from a boat.
1938 MACDERMOTT 173 I dropped the scoop and tried to row. C 66–19 It would be a terrible thing for an old fisherman to see his scoop bottom up in his dory. It is a sure sign of bad luck. The scoop is normally kept stuck in the side of the gunwale and fishermen dislike to see it anyplace else. M 67–10 The seine, dip-net, trawl-tub, scoop, and oars are the main things in the flat.
2 A length of slack rope kept in reserve when hauling a hand-line.
T 393/5–67 You'd have that for a case of a tide, you know; you'd have what we call scoop—slack, see; you'd pick up your bobber quicker.

scoopy a Sharply angled, with concave sides. Cp SCOOP.
T 100–64 [The snow-plough] was just like a scoop—like a box-car in shape, only the front of it went away scoopy, sharp, like the head of a boat.

scoot n Cp *DAE* ~ 2 'sled for drawing logs,' ~ v 1 'to slide.' A child's makeshift snow-sled.
P 220–78 ~ Small vehicle used by children for sliding on snow. It consists of one 'runner' made from a barrel stave with a flat piece of board for a seat.

scooter n also **scouter*** ['skuutəɹ]. A clay pipe.
T 169/70–65[2] You could get clay pipes then for a cent a pipe, a clay pipe—the old scooters. M 71–71 Scouter; clay pipe.

scopin*, **scopy*** See SCULPIN.

score n Cp *OED* ~ sb 1 b naut.
1 A groove cut in the stern of a boat in which sculling oar is placed (1969 *Nfld Qtly* July, p. 20).
2 Comb **score-hole**: hole in stern of boat through which oar is worked in sculling or steering the craft.
T 70–64[1] An' they claims that he was steerin' the boat with a paddle on the quarter—no score-hole, a hole for to shove th' oar through. C 71–40 ~ a hole in the stern of a small boat or punt through [which] an oar is placed to scull or row.

scotch a See *Fisheries of U S* 427 ff for herring combs.
Comb **scotch apple**: (a) juneberry; CHUCKLEY PEAR (*Amelanchier* spp) (1978 ROULEAU 93); (b) potato; see APPLE.
[1894–1929] 1960 BURKE (ed White) 36 "Sly Jackeen Sailor": Some stayed up all night for the order to fill, / Filling sacks with Scotch apples and worked with a will.
scotch barrel: locally-made wooden container for export of herring processed as 'scotch cure' (see below).
1918 *FPU (Twillingate) Minutes* 21 Mar The question was asked [whether] you could make scotch herring barrels on local trusses. His reply was that on scotch barrels he would have steel trusses.
scotch cure: a process, adopted from Scottish practice, employed to preserve herring by gutting and packing directly in barrels with salt; the herring so processed.
[1915] 1930 COAKER 103 The dimensions of packages for Scotch cure shall be. . . [1929] 1979 *Evening Telegram* 14 Dec, p. 5 The SS *Sambro* sailed from Lark Harbour yesterday for Halifax, taking. . .500 barrels of scotch cure and 530 barrels of split herring. 1953 *Nfld Fish Develop Report* 46 In the United States, and generally throughout North America. . .the market for the traditional splits and 'Scotch'-cure has all but disappeared. 1966 PHILBROOK 48 We took on a number of different fish. . .and used different kinds of processing: salt, drying, pickling and tinning. Herring, for instance, we used a scotch cure, local cure, kippering and pickling. P 243–75 In scotch cure the gills and intestinal tract of the herring are removed with a gibbing knife without splitting the belly; blood, milt and roe

are left in. Then the herring are packed in barrels with less salt than in other cures. It's a slow cure.

scotch dumpling: kind of haggis made with cod-livers.

1975 *The Rounder* Sep, p. 12 It was common for fishermen on the Labrador to bake and eat the fresh livers [of cod] as a cure for night blindness. Livers form the main ingredient for 'Scotch Dumplings' which consist of cods' stomachs stuffed with chopped liver and cornmeal.

scotch herring: see **scotch cure**.

T 185–65 I went away from here when I was sixteen years of age, went to Halls Bay packin' Scotch herring.

scotch pack(ed): see **scotch cure**.

T 185–65 First I was workin' in Matthews' factory, [gibbin'] herring an' packin' herring—Scotch pack. 1977 BUTLER 23 Scotch packed herring were in good demand for the coming winter catch.

scotch poke: in shuffling cards, dealer's device to change luck of the draw.

P 108–70 When dealing cards, to change the luck the dealer sometimes gives the deck a poke from the end, pushing up the middle cards which he puts on top of the pack and then deals. This is a 'Scotch poke.'

scote v also **skote** [skoːt, skout, skoʉt, skoːət, sko·ət]. Cp *EDD* ~ 2 'to put a drag on a wheel' Ha IW W for sense 2.

1 To drag, haul or tow a heavy object.

1924 ENGLAND 86 Through ice defiles and around pinnacles they toiled, each 'scotin' his tow,' bending far forward with the weight of the load. P 65–64 To skote a log is to drag it, bring it, roll it, or to use any means to bring the log from one place to another. T 30/1–64² I've seen men workin' away an' hauling an' pushing an' skoting—that's when you're pulling very hard. T 141/2–65² Lin is comin' in the road scotin' away at this sheep. T 194/5–65 But the other fellers mak[ing] one next winter fourteen fathom deep, an' he's goin' to scote his out in sixteen fathom o' water. C 71–125 ~ To half drag, half carry a heavy load.

2 To struggle against, resist; to brake a sled using one's feet as a drag.

T 141/64–65² An' when he's comin' back an' he's draggin' this sheep—sometimes [the animal will] get up an' make a run, more times he won't; more times he's down scotin' his two forelegs out. P 54–67 I had t' skot wid d' big load o' wood. 1967 READER 49 A man would go in the woods for a load of wood and when he had to come down a steep hill with this loaded sled and his dogs keeping up the pressure, he needed something to act as a brake, and the brake he used was himself and his boots, and this was called 'skotin'.' 1972 MURRAY 132 He or she sat on the rear seat and guided the slide on its run down the slope by the pressure of feet only. This 'skoating' was very hard on the footwear.

3 To strain, toil, work hard.

1940 DOYLE (ed) 74 "The Six Horse-Power Coaker": So we lashed her with wire and a motor car tire; / O how we did labour and scote; / And with posts on each side we earnestly tried / To keep her from leaving the boat. P 184–67 He scotes his heart out at it. C 70–12 If you were returning from the fishing ground after a hard day's work, you were rowing and the wind was

blowing against you making it almost impossible to make any headway, when you finally reached the shore you would say, 'B'y, I had a hard time scotin' in.'

scote n *EDD* ~ sb 5 Ha IW for sense 2. See also SCOTE v.

1 A task, struggle; something dragged or towed.

1924 ENGLAND 320 ~ a tow [of seals]. 1925 *Dial Notes* v, 340 ~ A job; task. P 54–67 She had a main scote to maintain the children after he died.

2 A diagonal buttress placed against an upright timber to support a pile of wood.

1965 PETERS *Gloss* ~ A stick placed at an angle to an 'upstand' in order to support the pile of wood. One end is driven into the earth and the other is placed in a notch in the upstand.

3 Comb **scote-shore**: see sense 2 above, and SHORE².

1965 PETERS *Gloss* ~ From 'shore' meaning a pillar, and 'scote' meaning, in the vernacular, to push or work hard. P 13–75 ~ A brace or span or stay having one end fastened to a peg and the other to a vertical wall, post, or shore.

scout n also ~ **out, scouty out** [skæut 'æut, ˌskɛɒʈi 'æɒt]. Children's chasing game.

P 148–63 Scouty out—a game that the boys play on the road. T 75/6–64 We used to play skating and scout out. [In] scout out we'd get out on the ice and I'd take so many men out from the fellows over here. And another fellow'd take charge o' same amount o' fellows over there. And one feller'd run, and there'd be another feller run from that crowd, and if you could catch him he's a prisoner. 1967 *Bk of Nfld* iv, 242 Time lost from studies. . .playing so much 'scout' and 'barrel-over' and engaging in other non-productive activities. P 108–73 [He said] that when the [Great] Fire broke out in 1892 he was playing Scout Out with some other boys, and he related his memories of that day.

scow* v [skɑu]. See SCOW-WAYS. To slant; to move, put or make something slantwise.

P 148–63 [In shuffle-board] you got to scow 'em each way. T 43/8–64 They'd cross these sticks—the holes were bored scowed [so] that the horns they put through the yoke would cross up on the back of the goat's neck.

scow-ways a, av also **scowish*** ['skɑɒɪʃ]. Cp DINNEEN sceabha 'a skew, slant or slope,' BERREY 43 sky-west. See SCOW. On a slant, askew; untidy.

P 121–67 Her hat was all scowish. C 70–20 A skirt that is twisted or pulled sideways is said to be 'all scow-ways,' and a slide is also scow-ways if it does not run smoothly and is jerked along on the edge of the runner. People who look upon others with leery eyes are told 'not to be looking scow-ways.' 1973 BARBOUR 52 A long handle goes through the bucket slantwise, or as a fisherman would say, 'scow ways.' 1975 GUY 50 Don't take any nonsense from motor cars or you will be pegged for a Bayman right away. Walk scow-ways across the street as slow as you can and dare them to hit you.

scrabble See SCRAVEL n.

scrad* See SCROD.

scrag n   *OED* ~ sb[2] 'stump of a tree' now dial;
EDD sb[1] 3 'broken bough' Gl Do. Tree stump;
small burnt or broken tree or bush; CRAN,
CRUNNICK.

T 5/9–63 'Twas a burnt-over country too, you know,
and scrags of trees, and windfalls that he had to go
through. Q 67–29 ~s. Alders and small birch. 1971
NOSEWORTHY 241 ~s. Small burned bushes on the
barrens.

scram See SCRAWN*.

scrammed a   also **schrammed, scrammy**. Cp
EDD scram v[3] 1 'to benumb; to paralyze' Do So
D, 2 adj 'benumbed' W So, hence scrammy D;
ADD (Nfld: 1895–); *DAC* scrammy 'man with
defective. . .arm' (1822–).

1 Stiff, benumbed with cold; chilled.

1863 MORETON 34 Schram'd. Cramped, and clammy
cold. 1890 HOWLEY *MS Reminiscences* 50 They could
not rest nor light a fire. They were nearly scrammed
with cold. 1896 *Dial Notes* i, 380 'Are you very cold?'
'Yes, I am just *scrammed*.' (Nfld). [1922] 1960 BURKE
(ed White) 14 "Cotton's Patch": If you want to find out
you must pay through the nose; / And we scrammed
with the cold and our fists nearly froze, / After flying all
day over oceans of ice, / If you want information you
must pay the price. 1932 BARBOUR 15 When the job
was completed and the spanker gaff topsail tied up
securely, we slid to the deck, our hands 'scrammed'
(benumbed) with the cold. 1953 *Nfld & Lab Pilot* ii,
390 Persons with this [local] knowledge are usually
available at Square Island harbour, Pinsent arm, or
Scrammy bay, during the summer months. White Bear
arm freezes over about the 25th of December, and the
ice breaks up about the 10th of May. T 222–66 And you
should certainly wear cuffs—or mittens—otherwise
your hands would surely be scrammed, especially if
they are nish—or tender. 1975 RUSSELL 87 Grandma is
losin' hope that me and her daughter Aunt Sophy'll
make a match, and she said one time how some men
were so slow blooded 'tis a wonder they didn't get
scrammed with the cold in August.

2 Cramped, paralyzed or stiff from disease or
injury.

1910 GRENFELL 84, 88 Bill is a strange figure to look
at, limping on the left leg, and with the corresponding
hand 'scrammed' or partly paralyzed. . . You sees, he's
a bit scrammed just now, and he can't cut up his firewood. P 245–57 A scrammed arm—withered, shrunk.

scran[1] n   also **scram*** *EDD* ~ 6: *bad scran to*;
JOYCE 318; DINNEEN screain.

Phr *bad scran to*: mild imprecation; bad luck
to (you) (1896 *Dial Notes* i, 380).

C 70–28 If a pot boils over on the stove, for example,
a person might say, 'Well, bad-scram to that!'

scran[2] See SCRAWN*.

scrape[1] n   Cp *EDD* ~ 15 'bare place on a steep
hillside' Do. A bare patch, often caused by erosion or a landslide, on a steep bank or hill, freq
in place-names; a pathway worn on a hillside.

1867 MURRAY & HOWLEY 128 . . .the point called
'the Scrape,' on the western side of Tilt Cove. 1895 *J A
Folklore* viii, 38 ~ a rough road down the face of a
bank or steep hill, used specially in regard to such as
are formed by sliding or hauling logs down. 1905 *Geog
J* xxvi, 188 We. . .ascended to the high plateau that lies
to the north of the bay by a landslide, or 'scrape,' to
use the local expression, of over 1000 feet in height.
1937 DEVINE 42 ~ A narrow path down the side of a
hill, worn by passing cattle; or made by an avalanche of
the soil. 1951 *Nfld & Lab Pilot* i, 152 Scrape Cove
head. . .westward of Big Bald head, is 419 feet high,
and shows dark against the lighter background.
P 238–59 Scrape has two usages—to describe the result
of glacial movement, and to describe the collapsing of
the side of a hill caused by inundation or the building
of a railway or road at the base (very commonly used
by railroaders: 'Connors' Scrape,' etc). T 13/17–64
Cape Broyle Head is a very high head, roughly five
hundred, four hundred feet. And there's a big scrape,
bare ground, down through a grove of woods, which
was after being a landslide. And there's footin's, cliffs
you [can] walk up there. Q 67–6 ~ a rough road or path
in the hills. Q 67–109 ~ a bare trench about 40 feet
wide down the side of a steep hill where wood has been
thrown down for generations. 1971 CASEY 245 Only a
few days after that, there was one of the fellows, they
were heavin' down the wood over the scrape and a
rock rolled down and crippled him up. 1979 TIZZARD
330 We went to fish on Bullock's Rock with the marks:
a white scrape in Little Harbour Bight overright the
Clam Rocks and the Dead Man. . .opened in Spiller's
Tickle.

scrape[2] See NOGGIN.

scrapers n pl   *OED* scraper 8 A-I (1824, 1842);
EDD sb 10 Ir. Phr *take to one's scrapers*: to take
to one's heels, run away quickly.

1888 HOWLEY *MS Reminiscences* 21 Before we could
get near [the black fox] he took to his scrapers and was
off in the woods. T 54/9–64 'He got saucy an' dirty and
rose a row here,' she said, 'an' he got beat up, an' he
took to his scrapers.' P 108–70 She took to her scrapers
and never cried crack till she got home. C 71–117 I tell
you, I took to me scrapers when I got half up the hill
and seen that black dog.

scraub See SCROB v.

scraud See SCROD.

scravel v   ['skrævl, 'skravl]. Cp *OED* scrabble v
3 'to scramble on hands and feet,' 4 'to obtain by
scratching'; *EDD* scravvle 'to scramble' Sh &
Ork.

1 To crawl, scramble, move hurriedly; to hurry
in a task.

P 245–59 'Scravel ashore' was shouted to someone in
a small boat. T 54/65–64 They scravelled ashore on the

clift anyway. They scravelled up the clift as good as they could. Everything was iced up and slippery. M 67–16 The fellow would quickly bid good-night and scravel as fast as he could. C 71–110 We scravel to get the work finished. They scravel to the store before it closes. 1973 ROSE (ed) 24 Well, I'm scravellin aft to see if the Skipper's gone crazy when I sees two shapes be the wheel instead a one. 1977 RUSSELL 120 Jethro scraveled down stairs just as Soos was strikin' the match.

2 To scratch, claw; hence, to grab, pick up (something).

P 245–56 ~ to go around picking up chips of wood for burning. P 148–65 He obliged by rummagin' and scravelin' t'rough his pockets and comes out with a piece of newsprint. C 71–22 [Playing jack-stones] you had to catch the stone in the air and also scravel the others on the ground at the same time. P 13–74 Let's scravel up the fish before the shower comes.

scravel n also **scrabble**. See SCRAVEL v.

1 A rapid movement; dash.

1924 ENGLAND 16 One old sealer told me: 'De landsmen made a scrabble from shore, an' got about of ten t'ousand, w'iles dey was passin' alang.' 1976 GUY 55 [The rat] leaped about three feet straight up in the air and when his feet struck the concrete he made the mad scravell straight at me.

2 Attrib **scravel day**: final work-day of the week, a time of hectic activity.

C 70–20 Friday was known to the Bell Island miners as scravel day. The term was used to describe the flurry of activity which invariably characterized the last work-day of the week.

scrawb See SCROB v.

scrawd See SCROD.

scrawl v [skrɒəl] EDD ~ v[1] 'move slowly or with difficulty.' To walk in a clumsy, awkward manner.

T 141/66–65[2] While we were in the chat, looked through the window, and here's Lionel going down the road, scrawling along, swinging his arms, and going down the road.

scrawm v EDD ~ v 3 'to gather'; DINNEEN scramaim 'I snatch, snap, grab.' To reach (for something); to grope.

[1897] [1960] BURKE (ed White) 32 "The Landfall of Cabot": Then up spoke old Bill Furlong, / Saying this thing it is a joke / While a scramin of his pocket, / For to try and get a smoke.

scrawn* n also **scram, scran*** ['skrɒːn bæˑg, 'skrɒˑn beɨg, 'skrɑən bɛɨg] EDD scran 1 'food, provisions,' 2 (1) ~ bag.

Comb **scrawn-bag**: canvas bag in which sealer or fisherman carries his day's food; NUNCH-BAG.

T 141/68–65[2] Carry figs on ice in your scrawn bag. But all you get in your scrawn bag clear o' that, clear o' hard bread, would be rolled oats, see. T 181–65 We

carry our own sugar, our own figs, and have a little bag onto us—scrawn bag what we have made 'fore we go away. P 207–67 He always took the scrawn bag out in boat with him.

scrawn-box: lunch-box.

1967 Bk of Nfld iv, 246 And there was a scram box or a grub box, as it was called. This was a box to carry food in. P 135–74 ~ A fisherman's lunch-box. M 79–504 When breakfast was finished, Dad would take the 'scram-box' (a small box of food to carry in the dory) and go down to the stage.

scred See SCREED.

screech n DC ~ Nfld (1957–). Popular name for a variety of cheap, dark Demerara rum bottled in Newfoundland; trade-name of a type of rum marketed with the label 'Screech.'

[1904 Daily News 21 Sep "A Razzle-dazzle": The great unwashed, if he's not squashed, / Where rotten rum does flow, boys, / 'Tis he will screech upon the beach / To join this Wild West show, boys.] [1944 JONES broadside] "Darn the Man that I Can Get": I have a few cents in the bank, / A home down by the beach, / And the very first night I am married / Hub will have a bottle of screech. 1964 Daily News 11 May, p. 4 But those were the days when what is now known as 'screech' could be purchased for two dollars a bottle or less. T 141/68–65[2] Course, a bottle o' rum—you get a bottle o' screech then for about a dollar fifty. 1973 PINSENT 35 If I'm old enough to slug me guts out in a paper mill, I'm old enough to drink screech. 1979 Evening Telegram 21 Apr, p. 14 God help me with my plebian tastes, but I loves [a] drop of Screech and Pepsi.

screecher n

1 A howling storm.

1877 HOWLEY MS Reminiscences 32 As we had anticipated it came to blow a regular screecher which soon caused a big sea.

2 An undernourished harp seal-pup; BLEATER.

1924 ENGLAND 193–4 I saw several nogg-heads in different scouting trips away from the ship, but not one would the men ever kill. One day a fireman brought in a nogg-head—alias a 'screecher,' though why so called I do not know. C 70–12 ~ This is the name given to a baby seal which has lost its mother and has survived by eating snow and ice. The seal is only about half the size of the regular harp seal when it is a month old. It changes its coat taking on the appearance of the regular harp seal but does not grow mainly because of lack of nourishment.

screed n also **scred** OED ~ 1 obs exc dial; EDD 3 (2) neither script nor screed 'no particle' D (1880). A piece of something, esp cloth or clothing.

1858 [LOWELL] i, 159 But there wasn't a scred nor a scrap to be found. 1895 J A Folklore viii, 31 Scred. A piece or fragment. 1937 DEVINE 42 ~ A bit of clothing. 'Not a screed on him.' Naked.

screedless a Without a stitch of clothing; fig, without possessions. Cp SCREED.

1937 DEVINE 42 ~ Poorly off, generally, or having nothing of some particular thing. A man, well off otherwise, may say, after losing his nets in a storm, 'I'm left *screedless*.' P 148–62 The boy is screedless. T 50–64 An' we got burned out after that again. We were left screedless—lost all our clothes, everything. C 71–129 Screedless means that a person hasn't got anything to wear. Usually it is used as an exaggeration.

screw n Cp *OED* ~ sb¹ 22: ~-press [bookbinding] (1688, 1864).

Comb **screw press**: a device for pressing dried cod-fish into casks or 'drums'; FISH-SCREW (1883 *Fish Exhibit Cat*⁴ 175).

screw store: area in merchant's premises in which cod-fish are pressed in casks for export; SCREWING ROOM (1829 *Newfoundlander* 23 July).

screw v Cp *Cent* screw-fish for comb.

1 To press dried cod-fish tightly into a cask using mechanical pressure; DRUM v.

[1799] 1954 INNIS 300 [The salt cod] was 'screw'd in casks in order for its better preservation.' [1814] 1956 FAY 20 During the winter you will have time to pack and screw the fish properly. 1973 HORWOOD 40–1 This time the *Olive Moore* was not long delayed. There was another load of fish prepared for her and already screwed into drums and half drums, and this time consigned to different dealers.

2 Comb **screwed fish**: dried cod-fish pressed tightly in a cask or drum for export; DRUM FISH.

1846 TOCQUE 122 The fir is used mostly for the frame-work of dwelling houses and stores. . .casks for screwed fish.

screwing vbl n Comb **screwing room**: area in merchant's premises in which cod-fish are pressed in casks for export (P 245–64).

scribbler n A soft-covered note-book with ruled pages used in school for class exercise.

P 124–71 By 1930 however the use of slates and the long type seat, had disappeared from the educational scene and they were replaced by seats seating two people and by cheap scribblers. 1972 MURRAY 147 The slates were replaced by 'scribblers' and 'exercise books' (i.e., lined writing pads), and lead pencils. 1973 PINSENT 34 So if they lost their buttons [on their fly] they'd have to wear a scribbler down in front, lashed in place by their belts. 1978 *Sat Night* Dec, p. 22 Her book, *Woman of Labrador*, [was] composed in scribblers at her kitchen table.

script n also **scrip**. Doctor's prescription, esp to obtain alcohol for medicinal purposes during the Prohibition era.

1917 *Daily News* 19 Oct "The Trouble a Scrip Gave": A man called on a Doctor / A scrip to write him down. / 'A bottle full of whisky,' / So wrote the kindly D. 1925 *Dial Notes* v, 341 Scrip. Prescription.

1964 *Daily News* 11 May, p. 4 Doctors would give them a 'script' (short for prescription) to enable them to obtain a bottle for medicinal purposes.

scrob v also **scraub, scrawb** JOYCE 318 Scrab; scraub; DINNEEN scrábaim, scrabhaim 'scrape, scrawl or tear.' To scratch; to tear the flesh with claws or nails (1955 ENGLISH 36).

1924 ENGLAND 225 Days passed, each crammed with colour. The whitecoats kept getting rustier, 'scrobbin' off de hair' as the time approached for the gun hunt after old fat. 1937 DEVINE 42 If my name's on that petition, you *scraub* me off. P 148–63 The cat might scrob ya. C 66–8 I'll scrob your eyes out. T 375/6–67¹ He grabbed me by the coat [and ripped it]. But I grabbed his hand and scrabbed it. 1968 DILLON 152 She scrobbed the face off o' me. 1977 *Evening Telegram* 17 Sep, p. 18 When we tell those yarns we don't use the word old or some of the women would scrawb the eyes out of you. 1982 *The Muse* 15 Jan, p. 8 She sat up and scrawbed his chin.

scrob n DINNEEN scráib 'a scrape or scratch'; cp *EDD* scrab sb³ NI. A scratch in one's flesh.

1968 DILLON 152 Just look at the scrob the cat gave me.

scrod n also **schrod*, scrad*, scraud, scrawd** [skrɒd] *DAE* ~ (1856–), *Cent* 1 [New England]. Cp JOYCE 318 scraddhin 'anything small—smaller than usual [as a potato]; applied to a very small man'; DINNEEN scráidín 'small portion or article of food. . .small herring.'

1 A small cod-fish or codling, esp for home consumption, fresh or lightly salted and partly dried; TOM COD. Also attrib.

1858 [LOWELL] i, 161 [She] urged him, modestly, to 'plase to make use o' the milk,' (which is quite a luxury among planters of the out harbors,) and of the 'scrod' and all her simple dainties. 1895 *Christmas Review* 12 [proverb] Spare the salt and spoil the 'scraud.' 1895 *J A Folklore* viii, 38 ~ in New England *escrod*, a fresh young codfish broiled. [c1900] 1978 *RLS* 8, p. 25 Scrawd—small fish split & corned and partly dried. 1909 BROWNE 259 [Barter Shops] even have a 'candy department,' to attract the younger members of the fishing community who deal in 'scrawds.' 1953 *Nfld Fish Develop Report* 53 It is suggested that a suitable differential be instituted between the price paid for green or raw fish of large size and that paid for scrod fish, i.e. fish 2½ pounds or less in weight on a drawn or 'gutted, head-on' basis. P 243–57 ~ , also scrad, scrawd, small cod-fish, slightly salted and dried. P 133–58 Schrod. Very small split cod. 1963 TEMPLEMAN & FLEMING 47 Offshore cod or scrod and smaller sizes made up 6% of the total weight of cod caught in June but less than 1% in September. T 36–64 That's only a tom cod. An' now, th'other one is a scrod, see—the right small [cod]. M 71–103 Tea on Sunday had a specialty of its own—fried scrawds (small partly dried cod), or fried salmon. 1972 MURRAY 226 Scrod was a name given a cod prepared in a special way. It was sprinkled with a little salt and left overnight. In the morning, it was washed and dried and perhaps hung on the line to dry. When it was ready for cooking, it was put in a pan in the oven with salt pork over it.

2 A child small for its age; a small person.

1968 DILLON 152 What a little scrawd he is! 1978 *Evening Telegram* 8 July, p. 30 She's only a scraud, but as the old people said, the nearer the bone the sweeter the meat.

scroll n Decorative pattern in a hooked mat.

T 43/7–64 If a woman had a stamped mat, and another woman wanted the design, they'd trace out the pattern of the scroll they'd call it, and the woman would hook it. When the mat would be finished your scroll would be showing up. Would be black and yellow and red and blue or whatever. T 94–64 You'd have scrolls on them. You'd mark out a big scroll, or maybe your father'd take the scissors and double up a piece o' paper, double it, keep doubling it, and then he take the scissors and cut it. When he'd opened it up he'd have a nice scroll.

scroop v *EDD* ~ v¹ 1 s w cties (esp Do quot). To squeak; to make a grating sound.

1937 DEVINE 42 ~ To creak like new shoes or boots. T 191–65 [The door] had a wooden latch, and a hole underneath that you shove your finger in. And when you shove the door open he would drag on the floor of the stage—he'd scroop quite a bit. T 200/2–65 By an' by you hear the old stage door scroopin'.

scroople* v Cp *EDD* scruple v¹ 'to grudge money' Bk, v² 'to squeak or creak' W. See also SCROOP. To squeak; fig., to object to spending money.

P 221–63 Anything tight makes a squeaking sound when moved. A tight person would be referred to as scroopling when he spends money. 'He's so tight he scrooples.' P 42–68 To the fisherman launching his boat, when the sheave of the block and tackle scruples, he must add a lubricant.

scroopy a See also SCROOP. Squeaking, esp of new boots or shoes.

1937 DEVINE 42 In the old days the scrooping of new, 'Sunday' boots gave a great pleasure to the wearers while walking into church. It indicated a degree of prosperity. I heard an old timer say: 'The spring of the big haul of seals, you couldn't hear your ears in church with *scroopy* boots. T 222–66 They would usually dress up in their Sunday rig, perhaps put on their new scroopy boots or shoes, and take the whole family with them. P 79–73 I wish you take off those scroopy boots.

scrub v Cp *NID* ~ 1 b 'to subject to friction.'

1 (a) To make a squeaking, rubbing sound; (b) of a boat or vessel, to scrape or rub against wharf.

1913 *Christmas Chimes* 6 Sounded like a man wearin' fishin' boots it did, an' I could ye'r he's oil-clo'es a-scrubbin.' M 70–29 Scrubber tires are old [rubber] tires fastened over the sides of a boat to prevent [them] from scrubbing against the wharf.

2 Comb **scrub board**: a board or fender bar

along the side of a boat or vessel to protect hull from scraping against wharf or another craft (P 245–75); SCRUBBER.

scrubber n

1 A board or fender bar along the side of a boat or vessel to protect hull from scraping; RUBBER, SCRUB BOARD.

1969 *Nfld Qtly* July, p. 20 ~ a protecting board along the top outside edge of a boat. Q 71–8 [They are] what we would call scrubbers, strips of wood fastened to the plank of a boat, running fore and aft along the bilge to protect her from damage when they pulled up on a beach.

2 Comb **scrubber tire**: boat's fender; RUBBER.

M 70–29 Scrubber tires are old car, truck or airplane tires fastened over the side of a boat to prevent the sides of the boat from scrubbing against the wharf.

scruff n Cp E HOLDSWORTH *Deep-Sea Fishing* (1874), p. 81 ~ 'marine productions. . .of no value to the fishermen.' An inferior grade of codfish; DUN.

[1870] 1951 PARTRIDGE (ed) *Dict of Slang* 739–40 The best society is called 'merchantable,' that being the term for fish of the best quality; while the lowest stratum is 'scruff' or 'dun.'

scrugility* n also **scrutility*** [skruː'dʒɪlətɪ, skruː'tɪlətɪ]. Careful scrutiny; extreme care, esp in playing cards (P 40–78).

P 245–55 We must play this hand of cards with scrugility. P 108–70 Play 'em with scrutility, now!

scrump v *EDD* ~ v¹ 3 'overbake' So D. Phr *scrump up*: to overcook.

P 207–67 The roast was all scrumped up when we took it out of the oven.

scrunch v *EDD* ~ v 2, 3.

1 To produce a crunching, grating sound.

1941 WITHINGTON 141–2 Among [the patients] was a girl from the cook-rooms holding up one badly swollen arm with the hand of the other. 'Rheumatism,' she said, and as I examined it she observed, 'He scrunches.' And indeed he did 'scrunch,' for the arm was broken. P 40–78 ~ To grind with the teeth; to grind teeth together when angry or while sleeping.

2 To crush, crumble; to collapse, to be crushed.

T 50/1–64 Little soft-wood vessel, see—Newfoundland wood. Well, if 'twas in [these] days, they'd be lost 'cause the big ones scrunches up now with the ice. T 158–65 I couldn't get no baccy [so] I get this hard stuff, like comed off trees, an' cut her up an' scrunch up, put in pipe, smoke un.

scrunch n Phr *burnt to a scrunch*: spoiled; burnt to a worthless state.

P 97–67 Food on the stove or clothes under the iron could be burnt to a scrunch.

scrunchins n pl also **cruncheons, scrunche(o)ns,**

scrunchings, scrunchions [ˈskrʌnʃənz, ˈskrʌnʃəns]. Cp *EDD* scrunching(s) 1 'the remains of a feast; remnants of food, broken meat, scraps,' 2 'refuse of any kind' Y, and also crunch Sc Lei Gl, crunshon Y Ha, scrunch 7 Ox, 8.

1 Bits of animal fat or fish liver, esp after its oil has been rendered out.

1792 PULLING *MS* 8 The only substitute I can find they have for bread is eggs, mixed up with deer's and *swile's cruncheons* which forms a kind of paste. [1844] GOSSE 114–15 The advancing heat of spring melts the fat from the cellular tissue, which, when the oil has been drawn off, is rejected under the name of *scruncheons*. 1861 DE BOILIEU 158 After taking out as much oil as possible, and placing it in a tank, the remainder in the boiler, called 'scrunchens,' is collected, and undergoes the process of being pressed with a strong screw. 1897 *J A Folklore* x, 208 Scrunchings, the fibrous part of seal blubber and cods' livers, after they have been boiled or tried out and the oil pressed out of them. 1937 DEVINE 43 ~ the residue in a cask or boiler of cod livers or seal fat after the oil has been drawn off. P 218–68 ~ squares of whale fat after the oil has been rendered from them. Often used as fuel to keep the fires going under the oil vats. 1981 HUSSEY 21 When the cod oil was all rendered out and sold, we used to go over across the harbour to the factory and get the scruncheons (the residue that remained after all the [cod liver] oil was pressed out. . .and although it didn't burn quite so well as the cod livers. . .it helped. . .to keep us warm in the fall.

2 Fatback pork, cut into cubes, often fried and served as a garnish, esp over FISH AND BREWIS.

1920 WALDO 160 'Bruise' is a very popular dish of hard bread boiled with fish, and with 'scrunchins' (pork) fried and put over it. P 245–55 ~ small, finely cut bits of fat pork, fried and eaten with fish and bruise. They are in the form of little cubes, ⅛ in. thick or smaller, and crisp on the top. T 92/3–64 And cut it real fine. What we used to call scrunchins, the little chunks. You cut them up and you put that in the flour. P 207–66 We're having scrunchins with our fish and potatoes. 1966 SCAMMELL 23 'Fish and brewis?' Uncle Jasper's tone was reverent. 'And scruncheons?' 'And scruncheons. Mary needn't know. And if she does, what odds?'

scrunchy a See also SCRUNCH v. Producing a crunching, grating sound.

P 167–67 The snow is scrunchy under foot.

scrutility* See SCRUGILITY.

scuddling vbl n

Comb **scuddling hole**: hole at stern of boat through which oar is worked to steer or propel craft (Q 67–33); SCORE-HOLE, SCULLING HOLE.

scuddling oar, scuddle ~ : scull; SCULLING OAR.

Q 67–1 Scuddle oar—the oar used to steer the punt with. One person sits or stands in the stern of the punt

and steers it with a scuddle oar. P 209–73 ~ an oar used to propel a punt through a hole in the stern.

scuddy a Cp *EDD* scud sb¹ 11: ~ 'misty, showery.' Of the weather, uncertain, liable to sudden scuds or gusts of wind.

1924 ENGLAND 156, 225 It might be a hard fuss to get in, if de ice go abroad, an' *I* t'ink us going to have scuddy wedder, too. . . 'Scuddy weather' of uncertain winds sometimes set the ice 'ahl in a whirl.'

scuff n A dance held at someone's house.

M 68–11 [They all] went around together and gathered at one house or another every night for a scoff, scuff, time, or breaker-down. C 71–106 ~ a dance, usually held in somebody's house, barn or stage.

scull n also **school, skull** *OED* school sb²: obs var scull, skull (c1400–) for sense 1.

1 A large number of fish (esp cod) or seals swimming in company while feeding or migrating.

[1586] 1954 INNIS 38 [Davis reported] wee saw an incredible number of birds; having divers fishermen aboord their barke, they all concluded that there was a great skull of fish. [1598] 1958 HAKLUYT 231 A skull of fish appeared on the shore. 1819 ANSPACH 391 Gulls and mews, with large bodies and remarkably strong pinions, fly in flocks over the surface of the water where there is a scull or shoal of capelins, or other fish. 1842 JUKES i, 230 Shoals, or, as they are called, 'schools' of fish, may sometimes be seen sweeping alongshore. [1856] 1975 WHITELEY 116 Rainy—saw two schools of seals out one road and anchor. 1861 *Harper's* xxii, 598 He predicts the weather by the moaning of the sea, or by the 'loam' or 'glin' in the atmosphere, and never mistakes a 'cat's-paw' that ruffles the water for a 'skull' of fish briching (breaking) the surface. 1924 ENGLAND 272 We kept running through small 'sculls' of old fat, and picking up odd lots of a few. T 80/3–64 Four days wi' thousands an' millions o' fish! Fin an' fin an' dry on the water, like we see a scull o' dogfish. Cod-fish right up like that. 1979 TIZZARD 319 The seals were quite plentiful that day and there were schools of them everywhere in the cove.

2 The migration of 'caplin' from the deep sea to inshore waters to spawn along the beaches; CAPLIN SCULL.

1842 BONNYCASTLE i, 267 A capelin school, schule, or shoal, is eagerly looked for as the real commencement of the cod fishery. 1955 DOYLE (ed) 86 "When the Caplin Come In": When the school is all over an old fellow bellows / As he tosses his net on his back with a grin. 1969 *Christmas Mumming in Nfld* 10 And the cod, in a unique phenomenon, detach enormous numbers of their deep-sea populations each spring and summer, turning in pursuit of the tiny silvery caplin and other 'baitfish' on their annual roll, or 'scull,' towards the shore.

sculling vbl n *OED* ~ b: ~ hole (1874), ~ oar (1833).

1 Of a seal, swimming.

T 84–64 [A seal's] scutters is like his fippers. He uses 'em for scullin'.

2 Comb **sculling hole**: hole at rear of boat through which oar is worked in steering or propelling the craft (Q 67–33); SCORE-HOLE, SCUDDLING HOLE.

sculling oar: long oar used to steer or propel a boat; SCUDDLING OAR.

[1894 BURKE] 90 As he'll caper with his scullin' oar behind. . . T 172–65 I took a oar an' the other feller took the scullin' oar, and my brother-in-law he stood on the cuddy with the boathook. 1969 *Nfld Qtly* July, p. 20 ~ a long oar having a pin at one end to enable a twisting motion to propel a boat. 1972 NEMEC 58 The crew [of a skiff] typically numbered seven men, six at the oars and one 'aft' on the 'sculling oar.'

scully* See SCULPIN.

sculp n also **scalp, skulp** *OED* ~ sb² (Nfld: 1840–), *DC* Nfld (1832–). Cp DINNEEN scealp 'a splinter, a piece, a slice, a layer'; *EDD* ~s. 'remains of turnips,' scallop sb² 'residue after lard is melted.'

1 The skin of a harp or hooded seal with the blubber attached; PELT n.

1826 *Edin New Phil J* 39 When the vessels are loaded with these scalps. . .they return to their respective ports. 1832 MCGREGOR i, 224 The pelts, or scalps, are carried to the vessel, and packed closely in the hold. 1842 JUKES i, 273 In skinning, a cut is made through the fat to the flesh, a thickness generally of about three inches, along the whole length of the belly, from the throat to the tail. The legs, or 'fippers,' and also the head, are then drawn out from the inside and the skin is laid out flat and entire, with the layer of fat or blubber firmly adhering to it, and the skin in this state is called the 'pelt,' and sometimes the 'sculp.' It is generally about 3 feet long and 2½ wide, and weighs from 30 to 50 pounds. 1905 MURPHY 13 "Died on the Ice Floe": While the keen, glittering sheath knives soon gave / Them the 'sculp' they required for their 'tows.' 1924 ENGLAND 14 The great value of the sculps, or pelts, is due to the thick layer of pure white fat, and to the extremely high grade of leather manufactured from the skin. T 187/90–65 An' then all th' ol' sculps an' odds an' ends was hove in an' boiled, and that'd be number three oil. But now still they had use for it all, see. 1973 MOWAT 33 Put 206 sculps in that little boat, and she loaded down till every slop come over her gunwales.

2 The fleshy part of a cod's head, cut off and eaten as a delicacy; CHEEK(S), FACE, JOWL(S).

[1771] 1935 *Can Hist Rev* xvi, 56 [The Eskimos] liked the scalps of the raw cods heads best. P 68–54 I had a fine meal of sculps today. C 71–99 ~ A name given to fishes heads and faces. After the cod fish have been headed, the heads are saved and cooked, either fried or boiled, to make a very tasty meal. P 143–74 The tongues and sculps were later cut from the heads [of the fish] and were either eaten shortly after or were salted in butter tubs for the winter. 1975 *The Rounder* Sep, p. 12 By and large when people speak of heads they are actually referring to 'skulps.' These are the

two side flaps cut from the sides of the head proper and joined by the bottom jaw. . . Skulps provide hours of sticky pleasure for those who enjoy picking [cod] bones.

3 A fragment gouged from an object.

P 194–65 Noticing a mark in a table which had a lacquered surface, her words were 'There's a sculp been taken out of it.'

sculp v also **scalp, skulp** *OED* ~ v² (Nfld: 1840–), *DC* Nfld (1832–) for sense 1.

1 To cut the skin and attached blubber from a harp or hooded seal; flense; PELT v.

1819 ANSPACH 427 It has been said that the seals are generally *sculped* at sea; but sometimes, from want of leisure, stress of weather, or some damage received by the vessel, this operation of sculping, or separating the pelt from the carcase, is performed on land. 1832 MCGREGOR i, 224 But the weather often is such as to leave no time to scalp the seals on the ice, and the carcasses are then carried whole to the vessel. [1844] GOSSE 113 As soon as a Seal is killed. . .a circular cut is made with a sharp knife around the neck, and a longitudinal one down the belly to the tail: the skin with the surface fat is then 'scalped' off, forming altogether 'a pelt.' [1870] 1899 *Nfld Law Reports* 327 Plaintiffs' crew killed, as they computed, about 3,000 seals, of which some were sculped and piled, some were cut open, and others were left round. [1896] SWANSBOROUGH 33 "The Seal Fishery": Then with his knife from nose to stern, / He sculps it, this as you must learn / Is to cut the fat from the flesh. 1911 LINDSAY 50 He would pull them together [seals which had been killed] and sculp them, that is, with his sculping knife he would make an incision on the under surface of the body, its entire length, through the skin and fat. . .with a very few sweeps of the knife the body was separated and thrown away. T 23–64 Cut un abroad, and sculp un—take the pelt off of un—and leave the carcass. 1976 *Evening Telegram* 19 Mar, p. 6 It makes my 'townie' blood boil to hear people talk about skinning seals. You don't skin a seal, you sculp them! You take the seal's pelt, fat, and hide off. Of all the seals that were killed there wasn't one skinned out to the ice. They were all skinned when they were landed on Bowring's wharf or Job's and hoisted up to the skinning loft.

2 To skin and quarter a beaver or deer.

1872 HOWLEY *MS Reminiscences* 6 Having first sculped the [beaver] in a somewhat similar manner to sculping a seal, except that instead of merely taking off the skin and fat, he took the flesh with the skin, cutting right into the bone. T 208/9–65 An' while [the moose] was hot we sculped un, all we could get off of un, an' we shared it when we got out here, myself an' my buddy, an' we had six hundred pound o' meat.

3 To cut off the fleshy parts of a cod's head.

1934 *Nfld Qtly* Apr, p. 12 "Jenkins the Fisherman": Cut out the tongues from the heads of the fishes, / Or sculp out the cod-heads. 1975 *The Rounder* Sep, p. 12 A woman on the South Coast is reputed to have been able to 'skulp a head' with her two thumbs but it is much easier to do it with a knife.

sculpin n also **scolping, scopin*, scopy*,**

scully*, scummy, scumpy*, etc. *OED* ~ (1672–);
1672 JOSSELYN 30 Sculpin; *DAE* (1761–). A scavenger fish (*Myoxocephalus octodecemspinosus;
M. scorpius*); PIG-FISH, PLUG-EYE; also attrib.

1767 tr *Cranz' Greenland* i, 95 The Ulkes, *scorpius
marinus*, which we call Toadfish, or in Newfoundland
Scolping.[*OED*] [1770] 1792 CARTWRIGHT i, 45 She
sometimes indulged the child with the tail of a raw sculpin to suck. 1792 PULLING *MS* Aug In the [Beothuk]
wigwam were some salmon and sculpin lately caught
with some English fishing gear. . . The sculpin were
split like codfish. [c1830] 1890 GOSSE 114 The large,
richly coloured sculpen (Cottus) so common in the
clear water round the wharves of Carbonear. 1842
JUKES i, 192 . . .three or four heavy clumsy-looking
fish, called in Newfoundland 'sculpins,' with great
heads and mouths, and many spines about them, and
generally about a foot long. 1895 *Christmas Review* 12
If you squeeze the sculpion, you'll find his thorns.
T 70/1–64[1] [Talk of] hunger—if they had a few o' those
old sculpins I eat then. P 189–65 Scopy gob is a derisive
term for anyone who talks too much. A scopy's mouth
is large and gaping. It also means big mouth. M 71–107
Skullies are fairly big fish with a large head and an
enormous mouth. They also have sharp fins. They also
eat the entrails of fish at the head of wharfs and usually
stay on the sea bottom. 1971 *RLS* 3, p. 4 Longhorn
sculpin. . .scummy.

sculping vbl n *DC* ~ 1 (Nfld: 1883–) for sense 1,
2 (1894–) for sense 2; for combs. in sense 3 see
dolphin and rabbit dances, *Inuit Land Use*
(1977), p. 132, *DC* ~ knife (1842).

1 The process of removing the skin and blubber from a seal.

1819 ANSPACH 427 Sometimes, from want of leisure,
stress of weather, or some damage received by the vessel, this operation of sculping, or separating the pelt
from the carcase, is performed on land. [1870] 1899
Nfld Law Reports 328 Taking measures to identify and
recover them by the use of flags, by sculping, piling,
cutting, marking, or such like means, had reduced
them into possession. 1895 *J A Folklore* viii, 40 The
process of separating the skin with the fat adhering to it
from the rest of the carcass is called *sculping*. 1933
GREENE 229 The sculping and panning starts afresh,
and all proceeds exactly as before but on new and
untouched ice.

2 Flensing a whale.

1894 MORRIS 24 By the kindness of Mr LeMercier
we were taken over to the oil house, where was
moored a large whale, sixty-nine feet long, and already
undergoing the process of sculping.

3 Comb **sculping dance**: an Eskimo dance in
which two men act out the 'sculping' of a seal
(P 245–72). Cp SPLIT v: *come split the fish.*

sculping knife: stout knife with a broad, thin,
rounded blade five or six inches (12.7–15.2 cm)
in length, used to remove the skin and blubber
from a seal.

1842 JUKES i, 274 They 'sculp' [the seals] with a
broad clasp-knife, called a sculping-knife. 1873
Maritime Mo i, 257 The sealers are armed with a 'gaff,'

'sculping knife,' and 'towing-line.' . . .A blow on the
nose from the 'gaff' stuns or kills the young seal.
Instantly the knife is at work; the skin and adhering fat
are detached with amazing rapidity from the
carcase. . .while the fat and skin alone are carried off.
1924 ENGLAND 37 At a primitive little grindstone, a
couple of hunters were already putting a keen edge to
their sculping knives. 1973 MOWAT 95 Just the same, a
number got 'seal finger' and had to come to me. That
was some kind of infection they'd get when they nicked
a finger with their bloodstained old sculping knives.

scummy See SCULPIN.

scumshy* n also **scrumpshy*, scumpsion*.** A
fool; epithet for clumsy, incompetent person
(P 37).

C 71–90 If a father told his son to put the boat on the
collar and the boy had some difficulty due to wind and
tide, the father would say, 'Come here, ya scumpshy.'
P 127–79 'Well, what a scumpsion Eli Tallyo was!'

scun[1] v [skʌn]. Cp *OED* con, conne, cun v[2] 'to
direct the steering of (a ship)' (1626–), and cond,
cund 2, 3; *DC* Nfld (1918–) for sense 1.

1 To direct, or conn, a sealing vessel through
the ice-floes.

1897 *J A Folklore* x, 208 [Scun 'er through the ice
floes *ed emend*] used in the peculiar sense of guiding a
vessel through the ice on a sealing voyage. It is almost
equivalent to the nautical term *to con*. . . But [scun 'er]
is limited in its application to steering a vessel through
the ice. 1918 GRENFELL 76 [They] go up. . .in the forebarrel to 'scun' the ship—that is, to find the way or
leads through the ice. 1924 ENGLAND 239–40 The
Ranger seemed to have discovered the huge herd afar,
about the same time we did. . . We beat her to a rift
that fortune opened in the barrier. . . 'Scun 'er up to
'em, Jacob!' the Old Man shouted from the bridge.
'How them bear?' 'Two p'ints on de starburd bow!'
1933 GREENE 143 A laughing shout comes from a head
leaning over the barrel of the foremast—and this is followed by a hail from its occupant to the deck
below—for Ben to fetch you up the mainmast 'to help
scun' the ship! 1937 DEVINE 43 To scun a sealing
steamer is to direct her course by observation from the
crow's nest or barrel at the masthead, where the best
leads through the ice are picked out and signalled to
the bridge. 1972 BROWN 136 All the master watches
are gone, so in the mornin' ye'll have to go to the barrel to scun her through the ice.

2 To keep a look-out for fish, seals, etc.

1972 MOWAT 41 'Scunnin' for whales?' He lowered
the glass and gave me his slow smile.

scun[2] v also **skun.** Cp *EDD* ~ v[1] 1 'to run swiftly,' 2 'to throw with quick and hasty effort' for
sense 1.

1 To swim, sail, move, haul or snatch swiftly.

P 148–65 Tuna scun along just below the surface of
the water. 1963 PARSONS 19 "My Little Town": Of
vessels too, that skunned their way to hunt / For seals
in March out on the Gulf and Front. 1968 SCHULL 112
The ship was scunning easily through one of the rare

patches of open water. M 68–24 We jest scunned up the anchor and wez about to 'ead fer lan' when a big brute turned belly up right gin the boat. C 71–18 Look at the marbles I scunned off Tom! C 71–118 Scunning about refers to persons who are always going from one place to another [idly]. C 75–140 [The old man often used to say] 'scun that old punt up on the beach and scrape her.' They also had to scun water and wood into the house.

2 To fasten parts of a fish-net together; to repair a net, often in temporary fashion.

1937 DEVINE 43 ~ To join nets or linnet together by stitching the edges with twine. 1956 *Evening Telegram* 12 Dec, p. 11 The leaves [of the cod-trap] are 'scunned' (fastened by twine) together to form the wall. Reason for the leaf construction is that if any part of the trap is badly damaged, the entire leaf can be taken out and a new one quickly installed. T 66/8–64 No, he didn't knit that. That's an old piece o' net I had. An' he scunned it all together, see. T 250–66 Oh, you knit the head, an' then you scun it in those loops after. C 71–20 After a storm, when the nets would be in disrepair and need mending [he would say] 'I have to go scun the nets.' P 9–73 After the bottom has been scunned in, it is taken by the middle of the back and stretched length-wise. C 75–132 To scun a net [is] to draw the sides of the cut or hole in net together instead of mending every mesh. P 127–77 ~ To attach two nets of a differ-ent mesh-size. P 237–77 ~ To repair a net by taking up broken meshes and knotting these together at inter-vals.

3 To sew or stitch clothing rapidly (P 245–56).

P 207–67 She cut out the dress and I scunned it up. P 157–73 ~ To sew up carelessly. P 178–73 The missus jest scunned up the hole in me garnsey.

scun n A searching glance.

P 245–57 I took a little scun around the house [before locking up].

scunner n *DC* ~ n Nfld (1924–). See also SCUN[1]. Member of crew who directs or conns sealing vessel through the ice-floes; look-out on a vessel; BARREL-MAN.

1906 DUNCAN 311 The scunner in the foretop was near blinded by the driven snow. 1919 GRENFELL[2] 174–5 The masters of watches are also called 'scunners'—they go up night and day in the forebarrel to 'scun' the ship—that is, to find the way through the ice. 1924 ENGLAND 42 The duty of the scunners is going aloft to spy out ways through the ice, leads and ways; bridge masters transmit orders from the scunners to the men at the wheel. 1933 GREENE 132 [The barrel] on the foremast holds the 'Scunner,' whose job it is to work the ship on the correct line, and in the most eas-ily-negotiated ice, through the Floe. 1940 DOYLE (ed) 11 "Two Jinkers": We found that Stephen was at the wheel, / And Jimmie was the scunner; / That we still lived 'twas good to feel / When two such craytures run 'er. 1973 MOWAT 73 Not a sign of a patch of young seals had we seen when the scunner, up in the foremast barrel, lets out a whoop: 'Young fat to star-r-r-r-b'ard!'

scunning[1] vbl n See SCUN[1]. Directing a sealing vessel through the ice-floes; conning.

1933 GREENE xv ~ means the guiding of the ship, from the Barrel, through the great Ice-fields and pans.

scunning[2] vbl n See SCUN[2]. Fastening the parts of a fish-net together; mending a net.

P 9–73 Scunning is done by taking two edges of net-ting, pulling them tight and passing twine from a espe-cially made needle around and around through the edge meshes, making a solid fastening every foot or so.

scurrifunge* v [skʌrəˈfʌndʒ]. Cp *EDD* ~ v 'to lash tightly, coïre'; fung v 3 'to do anything briskly. . .to work or walk hurriedly' Sc; *Kilkenny Lexicon* scurryfunge 'to scrounge, cadge or wheedle.'

1 To clean thoroughly, scour (P 108–70).

P 272–57 ~ as to clean out a dirty sink.

2 To scold, reprove.

P 108–79 To scurravunge someone.

scurrifungeing* vbl n [skʌrəˈfʌndʒən]. See SCURRIFUNGE*. Cp *EDD* fung 1 'to strike, beat, kick' Sc for sense 2.

1 A thorough cleaning.

P 194–65 The charwoman gave an instance of this word when she was about to clean a table—she gave it a good scurrifunshin. C 71–118 If a child comes into the house with a dirty face or dirty hands his mother may say to him 'You need a good scurrafungin'—a good washing or cleaning up. It may also be giving a good scrubbing or cleaning to anything that is dirty.

2 A trouncing; decisive defeat in a game.

P 43–66 We received a scurrafungin'. We were beaten in playing cards many times in succession. C 71–95 In a fight, the man who received the most marks or took the most punches was said to get 'some scurrifungen.'

scurry* See SKERRY n.

scurwink See SKERWINK.

scut v Cp *EDD* scud v[1] 8 'to scrape or cleanse.' To scrape or clean the hull of a boat or vessel.

[1774] 1792 CARTWRIGHT ii, 38 All hands were employed in thwarting up the *Otter*; that done, we scut-ted and blocked her up for the winter.

scut n See SCUTTER.

scutter n ['skʌtɚ, 'skʌtɚ]. Also hind ~, hinder ~, scut. Cp *EDD* scut v[2] 'make short, hurried runs,' scutter v 'to hurry off.' The rear webbed flipper of a seal, used for swimming; usu pl; DADDLE n.

1924 ENGLAND 320 ~s. Hind flippers of seal. 1933 GREENE 72 The slender flexible flippers, both hind and fore, have small inoffensive claws at the extremities—the hind flippers (or 'scutters') alone being used for propulsion while swimming, the fore flippers serving to help in its ice or land progression.

T 84–64 We don't call it hind flippers, we calls it hind scutters; it's what he swims wi', you see. . . He uses 'em for scullin'. T 104–64 We would play with the dattles, or scutters we used to call [them]. T 391–67 An' he hove his hinder scutters; he struck me in the back. 1973 MOWAT 51 'Twarn't long afore our own skippers took hole of the steamers, and when they did, my dear man, didn't they make the seal scutters fly!

scutter v Cp *EDD* ~ v 1 'to hurry off.' To sail swiftly before the wind.
T 31/4–64 A storm, a pure storm, wi' rain an' wind. Never such day you ever see [in] ever your life. An' I had to scutter under two goose-wing sails; took the spreads out an' run un round through among the rocks, down to Poole's Island an' Wesleyville.

scutters n pl *EDD* scutter sb 13. Diarrhoea.
P 148–62 ~ The runs, diarrhoea. M 71–38 If the tails [of the sheep] weren't cut down, big chunks of the stuff would cling to them, especially if the sheep had, as they sometimes did have, 'scudders.'

scutty a
1 Angry; irritable, mean-tempered (P 99–64).
P 148–64 I'm some scutty now!
2 Miserly; skimpy (P 184–67).
P 24–67 She liked to see the dinner plates well filled, otherwise she commented, 'that looks too scutty for me.'

scythe See SIVE.

scyve See CIVE.

sea n [= SALT WATER, WATER]. For first proverb in sense 1, cp MORE *Utopia* [1518], ed J H Lupton (Oxford, 1895), p. 28 Vndique ad superos tantundem esse uiae [tr R Robinson 1551] 'the way to heauen owte of all places is of like length and distance' (cp ERASMUS *Apophthegmata* lib. viii Bono animo idem undelibet ad inferos descensus est, itself adapted from a saying of CICERO *Quaestiones Tusculum* I. 104). For combs. in sense 2: *DC* sea boil (Nfld: 1905–); cp *OED* 18 j ~ boot (1851), ~ owl 2 (Nfld: 1842), ~ ox 2 (Nfld: 1613), ~ parrot 1 (1664); *Cent* ~ pea; *OED* ~ pheasant 2 (1672–); *OED* ~ 23: ~ stick (1618–1813); cp *NID* ~ stock 'ship's stores.'
1 Proverb *as near to heaven by sea as by land*
[1583] 1940 *Gilbert's Voyages & Enterprises* ii, 420 [Hayes' narrative] Munday the ninth of September, in the afternoone, the Frigat was neere cast away, oppressed by waves, yet at that time recovered: and giving foorth signes of joy, the Generall sitting abaft with a booke in his hand, cried out unto us in the *Hind* (so oft as we did approch within hearing) We are as neere to heauen by sea as by land.
the sea is made of mothers' tears [proverb] (1895 *Christmas Review* 12).
2 Attrib, comb **sea-bird**: any of the species of birds frequenting inshore or coastal waters, esp those taken as food or bait; BIRD[1], SALT-WATER ~ .
[1766] 1971 BANKS 134 When Small Fish is not to be got [for bait] as in some situations it cannot they use sea birds [*Oceanodroma leucorhoa leucorhoa*]. 1842 JUKES i, 307 The flesh [of seal] was rather dark and strong, but by no means disagreeable as that of some sea-birds I have eaten. 1866 WILSON 31 It is bluff, barren, and rocky, without inhabitants, save the turs, the gulls, and other sea-birds which build their nests in its clefts. 1915 HOWLEY 268–9 Fishermen relate that on several occasions the Indians were seen in their canoes coming from the Funk Islands where they had been in search of eggs and sea birds. 1937 DEVINE 67 Sea birds keeping near the land, / Tell a storm is near at hand. / But flying seaward out of sight, / You may stay and fish all night. 1977 BUTLER 40 Those people suffered unbelievable hardships and privation through the [Depression] years. If it had not been for the seabirds they shot, they would have starved completely.
sea-boil: blister, sore or inflammation caused by excessive exposure to salt water; WATER PUP.
1905 DUNCAN 39 [There are also] sea-boils—with which the fishermen are cruelly afflicted upon the hands and wrists in raw weather. 1919 GRENFELL[2] 143 'I never gets sea boils,' one old chap told me the other day. 'How is that?' I asked. 'Oh! I always cuts my nails on a Monday, so I never has any.'
sea boot: knee-length leather boot worn by fishermen and sealers.
1887 BOND 37 Then, indeed he looked his best, his fine figure set off to advantage in the tight-fitting blue guernsey, with the appropriate accompaniment of heavy sea-boots, and yellow oil-cloth sou'-wester. 1898 *The Record* 9 Jones, who was splitting fish on the stage-head, saw the accident, and in less time than it takes to write it, threw off his sea-boots and plunged into the water to her rescue. 1924 ENGLAND 288 A sober, serious-minded man is the bosun; wears a sou'wester, a stiff canvas jacket that has gradually changed from white to black; is belted with a knife, and has vast canvas trousers over enormous sea boots.
sea-cherry: variety of sea-cucumber; holothurian.
1884 DEMING 85–6 What lures the cod from the ocean depths to which he goes in winter is not certainly known, but it is surmised that he either follows up the small shore fish or seeks the sea cherry—a small red berry that grows on the weedy bottoms where the cod is found. 1888 STEARNS 147 Mr Murphy had picked up a quantity of star-fish, and several species of holothurian, like the sea-cucumber, only they were red, and one of the fishermen, he said, called them sea-cherries. They were small, round, and red, and had a sort of bud on one end of them, from which they extended their feelers or tentacles, when in the water and undisturbed.
sea-dab: variety of jelly-fish (1971 NOSEWORTHY 241).
1975 GUY 66 There's a shockin' sight of sea dabs (jelly fish) out there today.
sea duck: eider duck.
1870 *Can Naturalist* v, 303 The common eider does

not breed or assume the adult plumage until the third year: it is called the 'sea duck.'

sea hen: (a) great skua (*Catharacta skua skua*); (b) pomarine jaeger (*Stercorarius pomarinus*).

1951 PETERS & BURLEIGH 219 Great skua. . . Local names: Sea Hen, Grand Goose. . . Uncommon summer visitant off our coasts. 1959 MCATEE 34 ~ Pomarine jaeger (A sizable bird seen at sea).

sea-owl: see **sea-parrot**.

1842 BONNYCASTLE ii, 234 The puffin. . .which may be called the sea-owl, from its extraordinary head and wise look.

sea-ox: walrus.

1613 PURCHAS 626 Neere to New-found-land in 47 deg. is great killing of the Morse or Sea-oxe. [*OED*]

sea-parrot, also **parrot**: Atlantic common puffin; PARSON, PUFFIN[1].

[1778] 1792 CARTWRIGHT ii, 351 Shot twenty-two terns, an eider-duck, and a sea-parrot. [1794] 1968 THOMAS 90 These Birds were all of one kind and are called Puffins or Sea Parrots. Their heads are exactly alike Parrots in point of shape, much about their size, the bodys of them black and white. 1869 HARDY 265 The puffin is termed a parrot, and the little auk, the bull-bird. 1964 *Evening Telegram* 28 Oct, p. 5 And the worst of it is that the same people who call a dolphin a puffin also call a bird a puffin (unless, rarely, they call it a sea parrot).

sea-pea: variety of wild pea (*Lathyrus japonicus*).

[1822] 1856 CORMACK 7 On the sea beaches the common plants are the sea plantain, *Plantago Maritima*, the sea pea, *Pisum Maritimum*.

sea-pheasant: pintail duck (*Anas acuta*).

1842 BONNYCASTLE ii, 236 The pintail duck. . .from its plumage and the shape of its tail is called the sea pheasant. 1959 MCATEE 11 ~ Pintail (The long tail and decorative plumage of the male suggest the latter part of this name. . .)

sea-pigeon: see SEA-PIGEON.

sea-pup: see **sea-boil** above; WATER PUP.

T 145–65 They say they used [a brass chain] as a cure for the sea pups or another term for water whelps. It was sort of pimple that would get infected by the clothing and the hands in salt water.

sea rat: see **sea-cherry** above (P 154–78).

sea stick: herring salted at sea immediately after being caught.

1960 FUDGE 51 We had taken all the herring from Mr Paul's seine and had secured them in pickle or in sea sticks, as we call it, and about one hundred barrels of dressed and fillet herring.

sea stock: rum carried on vessel for medicinal purposes.

[1952] 1965 PEACOCK (ed) iii, 896 "Young Bung-'er-eye": When I was out walking, my sea stock to buy, / Got tricked in the liquor and bought Bung-'er-eye. P 102–60 Around 1900 the puncheons [of rum] faded out and the mugup of tea or coffee with a figged bun came into use. The only rum used was what they called sea stock in case a man became ill or contracted a heavy cold.

seal n also **sile, soil, swale, swile, swoil(e)**, etc [swail, swaɨl, swɑul, swɛɨl, swɔil]. Cp *OED* ~ sb[1] (c1000–), *DAE* n[1] (1622–) for sense 1, and for var forms: *OED* soile 'common seal' Co (1602–; esp 1672 quot), *O Sup*[1] swile (Nfld: 1877–), *EDD* soil sb[3] var soile, soyle Co. See *EDG* 58 for added -*w*- developed before a back vowel (s w cties). Cp *OED* ~ 3 'sealskin' for sense 2. For combs. in sense 4: *OED* 5 ~ fish (1661); 4 d ~ fishery (Nfld: 1785), *DC* Nfld (1808–); *NID* ~ finger; *DC* ~ gun (1942); *OED* 4 d ~ hunt (1886); *DC* (1883–); *OED* 4 d ~ hunter (Nfld: 1781), *DC* 1, 2 (1832–; 1889–); *DC* ~ meadow (1819); *OED* 4 ~ oil (1839), *DC* (1829); *DC* ~ patch (1883); *OED* 4 b ~ shot (Nfld: 1842); *OED* 5 ~ vat (1853).

Seal with defining word is entered alphabetically, e.g. BAY, HARBOUR, HARP, HOOD, OLD, SQUARE FLIPPER (at SQUARE a), YOUNG; the many regional designations of the mammal in its various stages of growth are also listed separately, e.g. BEDLAMER, DOTARD, RAGGED-JACKET, SADDLEBACK, TURNER, WHITE-COAT.

1 Any of the North Atlantic hair seals (family *Phocidae*) taken for the skin, used as leather, and the fat, rendered as oil; esp the harp seal (*Phoca groenlandica*) and the hooded seal (*Cystophora cristata*); freq in place-names.

[1549 (1915) HOWLEY 2 (tr) The country is sterile and uncultivated [but] it yields plenty of fish, and these very large; such as seals and salmon.] 1610 *Willoughby Papers* 12a/13 The oportunitie for fishinge For Codd Salmon Seales not Lett. 1620 WHITBOURNE 44 In process of time, they may also settle a traffike with the Savages for their Furres of Beaver, Martons, Seale, Otters, and what else is of worth amongst them. [1663] 1963 YONGE 55 Here are also seals, an amphibious animal like a dog. I have seen them abundantly on the ice, 30 leagues off the shore. [1675] 1971 SEARY 276 Seal Cove. Freshwater B (Southwood 1675). [1712] 1976 HEAD 129 In the winter, the planters both to the northward and southward of St John's hunt for deer, beaver, otter, bear, martin, fox and seales, on whose flesh they feed for the greatest part of that season. 1745 CAREW 25–6 They that Night anchored in a fine Bay, where was a most beautiful and commodious Harbour, which was fished in neither by *French* nor *English*, that was covered with prodigious Numbers of all Sorts of Wild-Fowl, Otters and Soils. [1802] 1916 MURPHY 2 The seals upon this coast are of many species, they are classed and distinguished by names only to be found in the Newfoundland nomenclature, and only understood by the Newfoundland naturalists. [J]ars, Doaters and Gunswoils and many others brew upon the rocks, in the summer season, and may be called natives. 1837 BLUNT 24 The eastern island [and the two western ones] form the northern boundary to Swale Tickle and Newman's Sound. [c1845] 1927 DOYLE (ed) 27 "The John Martin": Now when we got into the jam the swoiles were very thick, / And the skipper he came forward with a junk of a stick. 1863 HIND ii, 201 The fishermen and Indians who live on the coasts of the gulf or estuary of the St Lawrence, and on the shores of Newfoundland, watch for the coming of the seals in November and December with as much anxiety as the Swampy Crees of Hudson's Bay or the Nasquapees of Ungava listen for the first note of the Canada goose. 1866 WILSON 278 The men themselves do not call the animal. . .a seal, but a swale, or a soil. 1907 MILLAIS 40 We sealers say, too, that man'll go for a swile where gold won't drag 'un. 1923 CHAFE 3 In the North Atlantic we have the *hair seals*, which are not nearly so valuable [as the fur seals of the Pacific], the skin being utilized wholly for leather, but the fat or blubber attached to the skin is its most valuable product. 1936 SMITH 54 My God, men, it is like picking up two-dollar bills off the ice; every half-hour you can get a tow of seals worth eight dollars, every seal weighing fifty pounds. . . I have 150 men as good as ever salt water wet, and I also know that I got 100 naughty boys who don't care a damn whether they get a 'swile' or not. 1964 BLONDAHL (ed) 70 "The Bird Rocks": One day these three brave men went out / As they did wont to do, / On rugged sheets of frozen ice, / To capture seals a few. / But as they lingered o'er the swile, / At length they failed to see / The wind had veered from south to east, / And drove the ice to sea. T 141/2–65² 'Take thy gun,' he said, 'take thy gun an' come on; there's a swile out there on the pan, a young harp.' T 141/68–65² An' there's a thunderin' fine sile into her, boy, in the net. T 398–67 A seal is twice as good shot as what he is net. 1975 RUSSELL 69 [The teacher] told him it ought to be spelled SEAL instead of SWILE. Pete said maybe so. She was the teacher and she ought to know, but to him SEAL was an awful foolish way to spell swile. 1976 PINHORN 50–1 Seals of the western [arctic] population. . .migrate southward in autumn reaching eastern Newfoundland and the Gulf of St Lawrence by late December and early January. Nearly all whelping occurs in the first 2 weeks of March.

2 The skin of a seal with the blubber attached; PELT n, SCULP n.

1866 WILSON 282 By the word pelt is meant the skin and the fat. . .when, therefore, it is said that such a vessel brought home so many seals, the reader must understand, those were only seals' pelts, for the carcass, which scarcely contains a particle of fat, is left upon the ice. 1878 TOCQUE 304 What is called the seal is the skin with the fat or blubber attached, the carcase being thrown away. 1923 CHAFE 32 He stands for the greatest number of seals ever brought in by one ship, the greatest weight ever brought in one ship and the greatest value.

3 Short for 'seal oil.'

1929 BURKE [8] "When Your Old Woman": He told me to give her / A cup of old swoil / And a cupful of fly hooks / On Cod Liver Oil.

4 Attrib, comb **seal bait**: American smelt (*Osmerus mordax*).

1977 *Inuit Land Use* 254 There's another kind of fish—we calls white fish. Some of us calls it seal bait—seal food. They're almost like a capelin, only they're smaller. . . They stay around the rocks. . . The seal really likes them.

seal bat: see BAT.

seal bottle: sealskin bag with wooden plug,

used by men hunting on the ice-floes to carry seal oil as a substitute for butter or lard.

T 172/3–65 They'd have their seal bottles, made out of sealskin, dried; and they'd have their old fat (old seal oil) in certain bags, and they'd have their young seal oil, what they had for mixing their bread and their flour, in [the] other.

seal cat: newly-born seal; pup; CAT³.

1860–1 *Journ of Assembly*: Appendix, p. 527 I think no Seals should be killed under 26 lbs, and that any Vessel bringing in over 100 Seal Cats should be subject to a penalty.

seal catcher: trapper who takes seals with nets near the shore.

[1770] 1792 CARTWRIGHT i, 47 In Furriers' Cove, we met with some of the seal-catchers, cutting firewood. 1832 MCGREGOR i, 208 The other two-thirds live constantly at Labrador, as furriers and seal-catchers, on their own account, but chiefly in the former capacity, during winter; and all are engaged in the fisheries during summer.

seal dart: see DART n.

seal dog: iron hook used with rope or chain to hoist seal pelts and carcasses aboard vessel. Cp DOG².

[1834] P 54–63 In the crediting entries, for goods returned to store from sealing voyage outfits, May 27, 1834, there are listed. . .two seal dogs. 1924 ENGLAND 88 Lusty toilers are meantime, with 'seal-dog' hooks and ropes, hauling the round-seals up and in.

seal fat: (a) skin of harp or hooded seal with blubber attached; (b) the blubber adhering to the skin, rendered for oil. See also FAT¹.

1792 PULLING MS The seal's fat they melt down and keep in the stomach of that animal. 1896 *J A Folklore* ix, 35 *Bangbelly*, a low and coarse word denoting a boiled pudding consisting of flour, molasses, soda, etc, and not uncommonly seal-fat instead of suet. 1915 *FPU (Twillingate) Minutes* 9 Apr The Chairman then read circular number 11 and 12 referring to fish, shares, price of seal fats, salt, opening of stores, and other important items. 1924 ENGLAND 54 If you'm caught in a starm on de ice. . .you build up a barricade o' clumpers an' make a fire. . . De ropes gets grasey-like [greasy], draggin' swiles, an' you make shavin's off y'r gaff sticks, an' cut strips o' swile-fat an' let 'em drip on de shavin's. Dem burns like de hobs o' hell. 1965 RUSSELL 83 Half a century before, the islanders had used large cast-metal cauldrons for boiling down seal fat and extracting oil. 1972 BROWN 57 Fog closed around them, and they lit a fire, cutting the flagpoles into shavings with their sculping knives, then adding a little seal fat until it was blazing brightly.

seal finger: inflammation and swelling of fingers and hand caused by an infection acquired by sealers handling seal pelts and carcasses. Cp SQUID FINGER, WATER PUP.

1924 ENGLAND 39 Some of these wounds, on account (it is said) of the seal fat, develop terrific infections. 'Seal fingers' are such infections of the hands. 1957 *Can Med Assoc J* lxxvi, 455 Seal finger or speck finger. . .is the idiomatic name for a severe type of finger infection found in seal hunters and workers in the seal fishery. T 377–67 When the men'd go out to the seal fishery in the spring o' the year, if they cut their finger or anything, an' the oil of the seal got into it, 'twould cause what they call a seal finger. C 70–11 At the seal fishery, a finger infected from blubber from the seal is known as 'swoiles finger.' 1979 *Salt Water, Fresh Water* 157 Your finger would get like a seal. . .it would be a seal finger. . .crooked, right red and glassy, swollen.

seal fish: seal.
[1872] 1878 TOCQUE 313 [list of exports] 119,539 cwt Seal-fish.

seal fisher: vessel prosecuting the seal hunt.
[1875] 1904 GRANT 227 We remained till the ice broke up, when we were taken to St John's in a seal-fisher.

seal fishery: the taking of seals in nets or from boats near the shore or on the ice-floes from vessels; cp **seal hunt**.
[1763] 1973 *Can Hist Rev* liv, 252 Henley Harbour seems to be the most convenient place for curing of fish and Seal Islands for catching of seals, where there appears to have been a considerable seal fishery. [1766] 1971 BANKS 144 The Seal Fishery is Carried on all over this Countrey. [1802] 1916 MURPHY 2 On the Labrador Coast the sealfishery begins in November, and ends about Christmas, when the nets are taken up. 1819 ANSPACH 421 Soon after Candlemas-day, they begin their preparations for the *seal-fishery*, fixing their craft and afterwards laying in their stock of provisions. They employ. . .schooners measuring from forty to seventy-five tuns, and large decked boats, from twenty-five to thirty-five tuns, strongly built. [1885] 1979 *Evening Telegram* 6 Apr, p. 14 The brig *Mary*. . .lost seven punts with four men in each. . .while prosecuting the seal fishery. 1891 PACKARD 184 Add to the lack of cod-fish, the failure of the spring's 'swile,' 'sile,' or seal fishery, and they were doomed to fare pretty hard that winter. [1900] 1905 *Nfld Law Reports* 396 The plaintiff was the master of the steamer *Newfoundland* at the seal fishery in the month of March, 1899. [1929] 1979 *Evening Telegram* 10 Mar, p. 19 An address on the seal fishery was given by Hon R B Job. 1978 *Decks Awash* vii (1), p. 10 [They] said that Newfoundlanders didn't depend on the seal fishery because they were only at it three weeks, but all they knew about were the big boats which went to the ice for approximately a month. But. . .I'm at it two months. I start about 3 o'clock in the morning and spend 16–17 hours a day at it, every day until the sealing is over. 1982 *Evening Telegram* 28 Jan, p. 6 [The ruling of the Supreme Court] should have considerable impact on a vital sector of the economy, the Newfoundland sealfishery.

seal fishing: see **seal fishery**.
1907 MILLAIS 40 Young fellers that's bin once or twice to the swoile fishin'.

seal flipper: see FLIPPER.

seal frame: an arrangement of nets forming an enclosure to catch seals; FRAME.
[1832] 1975 WHITELEY 42 I laid out my seal frames this spring in the hopes of doing the fishery. 1871 *Zoologist* vi, 2541–2 Large quantities are also captured in nets, which are called 'seal-frames.' Three long nets of strong seal-twine are required to construct a frame.

1909 BROWNE 56 The Labrador seal fishery is carried on along the coast; it is known as an 'inshore' fishery; and is prosecuted by means of nets, or 'seal frames.' 1967 FIRESTONE 102 Seals are also taken in *seal frames* which are anchored immediately off shore. . . The seal frame is a more elaborate affair than the net. It consists of three nets set at right angles so as to form a three sided enclosure with the shore making up the fourth side. One of the side nets is so arranged that it can be lowered to the bottom to be raised when a seal swims over it to enter the enclosure.

seal gun: long, muzzle-loading weapon used to shoot seals; SEALING GUN.
1819 ANSPACH 475 The ceremony of lighting [the Christmas log] is announced by the firing of muskets or seal guns before the door of each dwelling house. This, among them, is the prelude to a season of joy and merriment. 1966 HORWOOD 42 Unlike most of the fishermen's swile guns, which were used for all purposes, from hunting little bull-birds to celebrating elections and marriages, and which were loaded by pouring powder and shot into the barrel. . . 1971 BOWN 23 Loading their seal guns, which had a barrel about five feet long with a bore from 7/8 to 1¼ inches, they rowed silently up on them and opened fire.

seal hand: see **seal finger**.
C 69–23 He had what people call a seal hand. He had cut a finger while pelting a seal and had gotten it infected with the result that he lost use of the hand.

seal head: selfheal, a type of mint (*Prunella vulgaris*) (1895 *N S Inst Sci* 398).

seal-head cod: cod-fish with deformed head; SNUB[1].
1826 *Edin New Phil J* 33 The seal-headed cod, is of the same colour and size as the shore-cod, and its head is, in like manner, covered with skin; and it is comparatively rare. C 68–17 Fishermen on Flat Island, Placentia Bay, believe that a swile-head codfish left on the stage-head for any length of time is a Joner. A swile-head (seal-head) codfish is one having a deformed head—possibly from being bitten by a larger fish.

seal hole: small area in an ice-floe kept open by a seal; breathing-hole; BLOW HOLE, BOBBING ~ .
1977 *Inuit Land Use* 169 There was a rule about seal holes. The first person to get to a seal hole could have the hole. He would put his white shield by the hole to show that it was his.

seal hunt: the pursuit of seals, esp from a vessel on the ice-floes; cp **seal fishery**.
1854 *Chambers's Journ* xxi, 76 Breeding-season is deemed the best time for the seal-hunt, as the animals are then in the best condition. 1897 HARVEY 180 Formerly the seal-hunt was carried on in stout schooners, but these have been, in late years, almost superseded by steamers. 1923 CHAFE iii Soon these sealers learned from experience the advantages of making an earlier start on the sealhunt in order to reach the sealherds before the young took to the water. The first of March at length became the usual time of starting 'for the ice.' 1979 *Evening Telegram* 28 Apr, p. 6 It is now apparent that organized mainland seal hunt protestors are writing letters to Newfoundland newspapers above nom de plume signatures.

seal hunter: (a) man who prosecutes the seal

fishery from a land base near his community, or from a vessel on the ice-floes; (b) vessel; SEALER[1].

1793 PENNANT ii, 278 Rough Seal. Perhaps what our Newfoundland Seal-hunters call *Square Phipper*. 1819 ANSPACH 416 It is during their sleep that the seal-hunters chiefly contrive to attack them with bludgeons, a very slight blow on the nose immediately destroying them. 1874 *Maritime Mo* iii, 544–5 And even Captain Rideout, who has been 'forty springs to the ice,' and caused the death of more seals than any other seal-hunter within a hundred miles, admits that the parson is 'a wonderful knowin' man about soils.' 1882 TALBOT 20 It was long after midnight when we came into contact with another vessel—a seal-hunter like our own—and then ensued a state of confusion. . .in the efforts to separate the vessels, that was frightful to witness. 1924 ENGLAND 53 Sometimes a seal hunter, after his travelling expenses are paid, will clear only $15 or $20 for his 'spring.' 1936 SMITH 14 My father was now engaged repairing a brigantine named *The Herald*, 160 tons, a seal-hunter belonging to Capt Joseph Bartlett. 1978 *Evening Telegram* 10 Mar, p. 2 [They] released the name of the seal hunter who drowned Wednesday in Bonavista Bay.

seal hunting: the pursuit of seals.

1883 HATTON & HARVEY 305 The food of the men is none of the daintiest and no one who is at all squeamish about what he 'eats, drinks, and avoids' need attempt to go 'swile huntin'.' 1895 *J A Folklore* viii, 32 Seal hunting is *swile* hunting. 1906 LUMSDEN 110 'The seal-hunting sermon,' as it was called, was an institution, being a discourse specially adapted to the men and the hour, preached the Sabbath before sailing. 1977 RUSSELL 30 Only the night before he must've been dreamin' he and Jonas were swile hunting because he'd bawled out in his sleep, 'Jonas boy, you take this swatch. I'll take the one further to the n-or'ard.' 1982 *Evening Telegram* 27 Jan, p. 1 The Supreme Court of Canada has ruled that seal hunting can be legally carried out on Sundays.

seal killer: habitually successful captain of a sealing vessel. Cp FISH KILLER.

1869 HOWLEY *MS Reminiscences* 8 I met. . .Capt James Murphy, the noted seal killer and his wife. 1874 *Maritime Mo* iii, 545 The ancient seal-killer comforted himself by saying, that 'such beastesses hadn't no souls.' 1887 BOND 38 Didn't he know. . .the path from his 'thrastle' to his stage? Wasn't he the greatest 'sile killer' on the shore? [1902] 1916 MURPHY 13 The gales drove them south fifty miles or more, to the outer edge of the Banks in the strain of Cape Broyle. Picco, of the Cove, was out in the *True Blue*. He was a great 'swoil' killer and had 5,500 that year on March 29. 1936 DEVINE 139 After him, Capt Wm Ryan, the seal-killer. . .had a grocery business in this store. 1978 *Haulin Rope & Gaff* 79 "The Sealer's Song": Joe Barbour sails the *Iceland* / A bold seal killer too.

seal meadow: ice-floe where migratory harp and hooded seals gather to give birth to and wean their young; usu pl.

1819 ANSPACH 416 [The seals] sleep principally during the day; and for that purpose fix themselves upon fields of ice, hence called seal-meadows, where they

are frequently found collected in immense multitudes, either basking or sleeping in the sun. 1832 MCGREGOR i, 223 The vessels then proceed to the field ice, pushing their way through the openings, or working to windward of it, until they meet with the herds of seals that accompany the ice. Where these occur, the part on which they are, is called seal meadows. 1873 *Maritime Mo* i, 257 The steamer has surmounted all obstacles, and is at length approaching the 'seal-meadows.' Suddenly the welcome whimpering of the young harps is heard.

seal man: see **seal hunter** (a) above.

[1929] 1933 GREENLEAF (ed) 246 "The Lone Flier": Come all ye jolly seal-men and listen to my song; / I don't mean to offend you, and won't delay you long; / It's all about our sealing trip from Twillingate to St John's.

seal net: large net, often joined with others to form a 'frame,' set in water near the shore to catch seals.

[1785] 1792 CARTWRIGHT iii, 91 The people having finished the seal-net, began another this morning, and worked on it till noon. 1863 HIND ii, 207–8 Seal nets are made of very strong hempen cord, although not more than the twelfth part of an inch thick. The meshes are eight inches square, and will admit the head and neck of the seal. Some nets are more than 100 fathoms long, by 10 fathoms wide; and several nets, placed together as advantageously as possible for the purpose of taking seals when they are migrating in herds in the spring or in the autumn, form what the fishermen call a set of nets. 1895 TOCQUE 195 The harbor seal. . .frequent the harbors of Newfoundland summer and winter. Numbers are taken during the winter and spring in seal nets. [1932] 1982 *Evening Telegram* 26 Jan, p. 6 One morning's haul from several fleets of seal nets in the Bight [at Twillingate] made up over 20 [seals]. T 43/4–64 An' there's another way we used to get seals—in nets, seal nets; about a twelve-inch mesh would be in that net. You put them out in the winter when the seals are goin' north, an' you'd get so many, an' then again when they're goin' south in the spring. T 141/66–65[2] [He's] out there puttin' out a swile net by hisself. 1967 *Bk of Nfld* iv, 240 Not a winter passed that there was not linnet to be knitted in our home. Some was for ourselves—the odd codnet, herring net, seal net or perhaps a caplin net. 1977 *Inuit Land Use* 168 Every man had his own seal net berths. Nobody would set a net at someone else's seal net berth. 1979 TIZZARD 317 There were two ways to get the seals; one was by using seal nets and the other was by shooting them with the big sealing gun.

seal oil: oil extracted from the blubber of seals, esp harp and hooded seals.

[1582 (1915) HOWLEY 11 [tr] They drink seal oil, but this is at their great feasts.] [1672 JOSSELYN *New-Englands Rarities* 34 She annointed the Playster with *Soyles Oyl*, and the Sore, likewise, then she laid it on warm.] [1775] 1792 CARTWRIGHT ii, 125 We fresh baited, and poured some seal oil about them [traps]. 1810 STEELE 100–1 The town forms one line, a mile in length, in which the smell of fish, and the stink of seal oil, is inconceivably disgusting. 1861 DE BOILIEU 156 The fat is then removed and placed in a store for the purpose of being cut up into small pieces, so as to be easily melted and converted into seal-oil. 1889 *Nineteenth Century* xxv, 524 In some of the outports seal oil is used to trim the lamps, and a picturesque substitute for lamp or candle is sometimes resorted to in a large scallop-shell holding a piece of blubber with a wick fastened in it. 1901 *Christmas Bells* 5 12,000 quintals fish, £440 worth of seal oil. 1924 ENGLAND 15 A good sculp will often have three inches of solid white fat adhering to it. Many are the uses of the seal oil derived therefrom. My Lady Dainty's costliest soaps and perfumes often contain seal oil; and by chance her purest Italian olive oil holds a good percentage that came from the frozen North. The finest illuminating and lubricating oil, too, is a seal product. T 172/3–65 They'd simply mix their flour with seal oil until it come to a batter, and they'd put that to rise.

seal pan: seal skins with blubber attached, heaped in a pile on the ice and marked for later collection; PAN n.

1933 GREENE 219 There are also a few men to work the seal-pans from the ice, or to help to stow the pelts below when once they are hoisted on deck by the winch.

seal pass: habitual route of seals migrating near the shore.

[1783] 1961 FAY 23–4 He built a fishing room where he did intend to keep 2 vessels this year to pursue the cod and salmon fishery. There are 2 seal passes in the said Bay near the fishing room we occupy. One Collard. . .has possession of the said passes.

seal patch: concentration of harp or hooded seals on the ice-floes; PATCH.

1873 *Maritime Mo* i, 257 At other times the vessel, two or three days after leaving the harbor, finds herself in the midst of a 'seal patch' sufficient to load the *Great Eastern*. 1897 WILLSON 112 On the third or fourth day a seal-patch is sighted. 1916 GRENFELL 57 But Ben was like the master watch who cannot find the seal-patch in March. [1979 *Salt Water, Fresh Water* 103 I'm going to take you back a couple of miles and put you on to a patch of seal, and when you kill the seal, you can go back to your own ship.]

seal pelt: skin of a harp or hooded seal with the blubber attached; PELT n, SCULP n.

1866 WILSON 285 When the seal-pelts are landed, the skinners scrape the fat from the skin, and put it into large vats. [1900] 1905 *Nfld Law Reports* 397 The crew of the *Newfoundland* killed a large number of seals and panned and marked the seal pelts and reduced them into possession. 1978 *Evening Telegram* 9 May, p. 2 There is 'no comparison' between the quality of seal pelts purchased this year and those purchased five years ago.

seal shot: lead shot of large size, used to load gun employed at the seal hunt.

1842 JUKES i, 285, 289 [The shot is] larger than buckshot, consisting, in fact, rather of small bullets than shot, being cast, and not dropped. . . I went with one punt, taking my double-barrelled gun and some seal-shot.

seal skin: see SEALSKIN.

seal skinner: man employed on shore to separate skin and blubber of harp and hooded seals.

[1900 OLIVER & BURKE] 42 The seal-skinners fifty years ago were just as expert as they are now. 1937 *Bk of Nfld* ii, 100 An average seal-skinner would skin from 300 to 350 skins in nine or nine and a half hours. 1976 *Evening Telegram* 19 Mar, p. 6 The seals were 'pelted' by the sealers and skinned by the seal skinners. They were 'townies' who could skin a seal pelt with three cuts of their big knives. . .separating the fat from the skin with two swipes of their knives.

seal soap: soap made with seal oil as an ingredient.

1897 WILLSON 110–11 [The fat of the seal] furnishes an oil very much in demand for illuminating and lubricating purposes, and also for the manufacture of 'seal soap.'

seal twine: strong line used to make net to catch seals, etc.

[1779] 1792 CARTWRIGHT ii, 428 I made a beaver-net to-day of seal-twine. 1871 *Zoologist* vi, 2542 Three long nets of strong seal-twine are required to construct a [seal] frame. 1909 BROWNE 56 [Seal nets] are made from a large twine (commonly known as 'swile twine'), and they vary from twenty-five to forty fathoms in length, with a mesh of fourteen or sixteen inches. 1924 ENGLAND 196 The nets. . .are made of very strong cord, called 'seal twine,' with a mesh of eleven to fifteen inches.

seal vat: wooden structure used to render oil from seal blubber; VAT.

1852 ARCHIBALD 5 The seal-vat consists of what are termed the crib and the pan. The crib is a strong wooden erection, from twenty to thirty feet square, and twenty to twenty-five feet in height. It is firmly secured with iron clamps, and the interstices between the upright posts are filled in with small round poles. It has a strong timber floor, capable of sustaining 300 or 400 tons. The crib stands in a strong wooden pan, three or four feet larger than the square of the crib, so as to catch all the drippings. 1865 CAMPBELL 149 Planted amongst these flakes are the seal-vats, into which blubber is tossed to melt into oil by natural chemistry. 1936 DEVINE 48 There was a seal vat in the rear of the store, near the wharf, for converting seal fat into oil. 1944 LAWTON & DEVINE 14 McBraire's and William Brown's firms each had a seal vat on the south side of the harbor where Jas Ryan Co's premises was built in later years and ran off their own seal oil for export.

seal v also **swile**, **swoil** *OED* ~ v[3] (1828–). To hunt seals, esp from a vessel in the ice-floes.

1896 *Dial Notes* i, 381 To go swoiling. 1905 DUNCAN 40 You'll know more about packs nex' spring, me b'y.—I been swilin'. . .in these seas every spring for fifty-seven years. [1952] 1978 *Haulin' Rope & Gaff* 142 "Last of the Wooden Walls": Withstood the northern elements of many a whitecoat season / To 'swoile' the crusted swell. T 185–65 You hear talk o' [swanskin cuffs]? Made out of swanskin; they'd come to your elbow, and a thumb in 'em. You'd shove 'em on out birdin', out sealin'. 1977 *Inuit Land Use* 211 They'd always come [and set their net in the bight] and seal alongside of us.

sealer¹ n   also **siler, soiler, swiler, swoiler** *OED*
~ sb² 1 (1820–), 2 (Nfld: 1842–); *DC* ~¹ 1 Nfld
(1770–), 2 (1829–), swiler Nfld (1883–).

1 Man who prosecutes the seal fishery from a
land base near his community, LANDSMAN; one
engaged to hunt seals from a vessel in the ice-
floes off Newfoundland and Labrador or in the
Gulf of St Lawrence.

[1766] 1971 BANKS 104 This Time is Carefully
watch'd for by the Sealers who are Prepard according
to their Situation to secure as many of them as the
Shortness of their Stay will Permit. 1792 CARTWRIGHT
Gloss i, xiv Shoal-net. The sealers lay hold of either
[corner], and by their means bring the head of the net
to the boat; they then haul their boat to the other end,
and take the seals out as they go. 1873 *Maritime Mo* i,
254 As the first of March, the time of starting for the
seal hunt, approaches, the roads leading from the various outports to St John's begin to be enlivened by the
appearance of the sealers, or 'soilers,' as they are
called in the vernacular, marching towards the capital,
each with a bundle of spare clothing over his shoulders.
1900 PROWSE 190 Sealer shall mean any one who signs
agreement for sealing voyage under sec. 12, cap. 134,
CS. 1919 GRENFELL¹ 259–60 Us found t' seals early
that year, and panned a voyage of as fine young fat as
ever a 'swiler' wished for. 1924 ENGLAND 9–10 More
sealers kept piling into town, with bags and battered
blue sea chests. Some, having no tickets, were coming
'on prospect,' with the hope of picking up a berth at
the last moment. 1927 DOYLE (ed) 39 "Hunting Seals":
For we are swoilers fearless, bold, / As we copy from
pan to pan, sir; / With pelts astern we shipward go.
1950 *Daily News* 25 July One could imagine 'Swoilers'
going over the rail with gaff and hauling rope. 1976
WINSOR 18 The most important Service held during the
Winter was the Sealer's Service, held on Sunday night
before about three hundred men of the community left
for the icefields. 1978 *Haulin' Rope & Gaff* 57 "The
Greenland Disaster": We now relate the mournful fate
of gallant sealers dead, / Whose Frost-burnt hands and
faces paid the price of daily bread; / A vanished race of
experts on the rafting Arctic floe: / The victims of disaster in a wilderness of snow. 1981 *Evening Telegram*
27 March, p. 3 Some of the sealers (or swilers as they
are also known). . .said most people buy a dozen or a
half-dozen flippers.

2 Vessel engaged in hunting seals in the ice-
floes.

1842 BONNYCASTLE ii, 128 The fitments of the seal
fishing vessels, or *soilers*, as they are vernacularly
called. . . [1864] 1975 MOYLES (ed) 122 We sail
through a fleet of Newfoundland fishermen, whose
low, thick masts, strong clumsy rigging, and ironed and
planked hulks—for they were sealers, and had not
stopped to doff their ice-armor—contrasted with the
beautiful model, slender, tapering masts and spars of
our fleeter craft. 1895 *Christmas Review* 12 [proverb]
Before you leave the sealer's side, the ice or slob must
first be tried. 1897 WILLSON 110 And so when the
'swiler' came to start I give my place to another man. I
knew after that I was no good for 'swilin'' any more.
[1900 OLIVER & BURKE] 46 The interest of all the people was centred on the 'swoilers.' 1924 ENGLAND 257

An' I knows one cap'n, too, as runs a store; an' one
year when de men was paid off de swiler, he took a
canvas bag an' stood on de w'arf, an' as de men come
off, he collected ahl as was owed him. [1955] 1978
Haulin' Rope & Gaff 115 "A Noble Fleet of Sealers":
There's a noble fleet of sealers, / Being fitted for the
'ice' / They'll take a chance again this year / Tho' fat's
gone down in price. [1959] 1978 ibid 70 "When the
Flippers Strike the Town": In the morning you'll rise
early / And you'll need no Daylight Bill / When a
'swiler' first is sighted / From the tower upon the 'Hill.'
1972 BROWN 58 [The] *Southern Cross* would be the
first sealer into port that year.

sealer² n   (a) Device for fastening lid on a tin
can; (b) person who operates the device.

[1926] 1933 GREENLEAF (ed) 251 "Change Islands
Song": They got three cases of berries, minus of one
can. / They had a patent sealer, driven by the second
hand; / Torreville turned the handle; 'twas he who
spoiled the can. 1975 BUTLER 71 When this [lobster]
factory was in full production, Oates employed thirty
men and women. He brought his own tinsmiths and
sealers with him. . .to seal the tins. . . The sealers
would then seal the tins by hand.

sealing vbl n   also **swaling, swiling, swoiling**
['siːlin, 'swɑilən] *OED* ~ vbl sb² (1848, 1870),
DAE (1839–), *DC* (Nfld: 1777–) for sense 1; for
combs. in sense 2: *DC* ~ dog Nfld (1916); ~ fleet
(Nfld: 1906–); ~ grounds (1921–); *OED* ~ gun
(1842 quot), *DC* swiling gun Nfld (1906); ~ post
(Nfld: 1775–); *OED* ~ vessel (1860 quot); *DAE*
~ voyage (1807 quot).

1 The taking of seals, esp harp and hooded
seals, by net, gun or 'gaff' near the shore, or the
hunt for them from a vessel on the ice-floes.

[1777] 1792 CARTWRIGHT ii, 256 It is rather too
shoal for sealing, yet I must try it, since there is not
better hereabouts. [1798] 1863 PEDLEY 194–5 If the
Government could be induced to grant a small bounty
to each boat or vessel carrying ten hands, three of
which should be green men, such as never were sealing, it would be an extraordinary nursery for seamen. 1839 TUCKER 107 The more common mode of
sealing of late years, however, is to fit out vessels, and
search for these amphibia in the straits and along the
Gulf. [c1894] PANL P4/14, p. 199 Greenspond is a purty
place / And so is Pincher's Island; / Ma shall have a
new silk dress, / When Da comes home from swoiling.
1897 WILLSON 110 I give my place to another man. I
knew after that I was no good for 'swilin'' any more.
1933 GREENE 166 And everything of all sorts must be
made ready for any one of the emergencies that may
arise at the Ice—not only for 'swilin'' in the Patch, or
'swatching' in the lanes of the Floe—but for the off-
chance of the ship being nipped, or of some other bad
accident or jamming. 1952 SMITH 119 [He] was master
of his own ship at eighteen and as daring and successful
a sealing skipper as any in this town, where sealing, or
'swoiling,' as oldtimers still call it, made many wealthy
and not a few famous. T 398/9–67 He was one man that
loved swilin'. 1972 BROWN 1 The father. . .now forty-

nine, had sworn off seal hunting ('swiling') three years before after a harrowing experience at the ice.

2 Attrib, comb **sealing adventure**: commercial sealing enterprise; ADVENTURE, VOYAGE.

[1802] 1895 PROWSE 420 The sealing-adventure by large boats, which sail about the middle of March, has not been general longer than nine years.

sealing bat: see BAT.

sealing berth: see BERTH.

sealing capstan: device for hauling seal nets ashore.

[1774] 1792 CARTWRIGHT ii, 32 The carpenter and four hands carried the sealing-capstans to the head of the sound.

sealing captain: see **sealing master**.

1906 LUMSDEN 106 Each steamer, besides its own navigating captain and crew, carried a sealing captain and from one hundred and fifty to three hundred of a sealing crew. 1912 DUNCAN 71 An' the Giant-Killer scowled like a swilein (sealing) captain on his bridge. 1924 ENGLAND 9 Both were huge-shouldered and hard-fisted sealing cap'ns. 1982 *Evening Telegram* 27 Jan, p. 1 [He] had alleged that three sealing captains. . .violated an old statute prohibiting the killing of seals on Sunday.

sealing craft: (a) implements, gear and other requisites for capturing seals; CRAFT; (b) vessel.

[1773] 1792 CARTWRIGHT i, 285 I went down in the boat to Stage Cove, and there had the satisfaction to find almost all the sealing-craft in order, and four nets out. 1907 DUNCAN 323 We were picked up by the steamer *Fortune*, a sealing-craft commissioned by the government for rescue when surmise of the disaster grew.

sealing crew: (a) organized group of men engaged in taking seals with nets near the shore; (b) group of men aboard a vessel, engaged to hunt seals on the ice-floes; CREW.

[1771] 1792 CARTWRIGHT i, 124 Two of the people belonging to the sealing crew came here this morning, to engage with me for the summer's fishing. 1861 DE BOILIEU 84 A sealing crew consists of not less than six men. [1891] 1978 *Haulin' Rope & Gaff* 35 Please pay attention for a while / And I will sing to you / A song about the *Greenland* / And her hardy sealing crew. [See 1906 quot at **sealing captain**.] 1924 ENGLAND 234 "Success to Every Man": De warriors o' de wooden fleet, / Dey soon will sail away, / In charge of 'ardy swilin' crews, / Wid colours flyin' gay! [1954] 1979 *Evening Telegram* 14 Mar, p. 8 He says the reason for this is that the sealing crews begin killing seals too early.

sealing dog: (a) experienced seal hunter; (b) gunner's assistant at the seal hunt; DOG[1].

1916 DUNCAN 218 It was even held by some old sealing dogs that the floes had gone to the east in a spurt of westerly weather.[*DC*] C 71–37 First swilin' dog: man who carried the cartridges for the gunner. Second swilin' dog: [man who] carried extra amount of cartridges. Cut tails off the swiles to check the number killed.

sealing flag: see FLAG n.

sealing fleet: collectively, all the vessels prosecuting the seal hunt among the ice-floes.

1873 *Maritime Mo* ii, 135 At daylight, on the morning of April 30th, 1873, a steamer named the *Tigress*, one of the Newfoundland sealing fleet, was ploughing her way in pursuit of seals, amid the ice-laden sea. [1896] SWANSBOROUGH 4 "The Seal Fishery": But hope is active, all now chat / Of sealing fleets, and seals, and 'fat.' 1909 *Tribune Christmas No* 11 At that time our sealing fleet was the proudest feature in the trade of the colony. [1929] 1979 *Evening Telegram* 10 Mar, p. 19 A message received last night from airman Caldwell at St Anthony reported that he had located the main patch of seals northeast of Fogo. Most of the sealing fleet are in the vicinity and news of a considerable kill is expected tonight. 1981 *Evening Telegram* 9 Mar, p. 3 Greenpeace protest activity was absent from this year's blessing of the sealing fleet.

sealing gaff: see GAFF n.

sealing ground: ice-floes where harp and hooded seals gather to breed; cp GROUND.

1936 SMITH 101 On the 20th of March we were jammed for a day about ten miles west-north-west of Point Riche, on good sealing ground, where many a load in previous years was killed, but there wasn't a seal to be seen. 1953 JOB 10 Other members of the family also visited the sealing grounds off Newfoundland. 1982 *Evening Telegram* 24 Mar, p. 1 All the large hunting vessels were gone Tuesday from the sealing grounds known as the Front.

sealing gun: long, muzzle-loading gun formerly used at the seal hunt.

1842 JUKES i, 284 The sealing-gun is an immense affair, as long as a duck-gun, but with a much wider bore. . . The men put in a great charge of powder and shot—frequently ten fingers' breadth. . . It was as much as I could do to hold one of these guns straight out. 1866 WILSON 278 About the last of February, hundreds of ice-hunters might be seen. . .with their gaffs, and long swaling guns on their backs, in order to join their respective vessels on the first of March. 1886 *Colonist Christmas No* 9 As the evening advances, the report of a gun is heard,—another answers it—then bang! bang!! bang!!! go the sealing guns from all parts of the village, sounding forth a welcome to the 'Good Old Christmas time.' 1906 LUMSDEN 90 If the Canadians come down here to take our country I'll get down my 'swiling gun,' and we'll go out to meet 'em. 1909 *Christmas Annual* 12 But the old sealing gun had its day, and held a proud position in the planter's house before the breech-loader and modern rifle supplanted it. . . It was usually from six to seven feet long, and required 'a man' to hold it out straight when using it. 1973 MOWAT 19 The banging of them swiling guns was something for to hear, and the smell of the black powder sticks in me nostrils yet.

sealing house: dwelling for men engaged in catching seals with nets near the shore.

[1775] 1792 CARTWRIGHT ii, 53–4 We looked into the old sealing-house on Round Island, and observed that it had been much frequented by foxes there being some oil-gullies left there. [1786] ibid iii, 198 Came to anchor in Venison Harbour: where we found a very good sealing-house, which had been built last fall, by a crew belonging to Mr Hyde of Poole; a new adventurer on this coast. 1977 *Inuit Land Use* 209 John and his wife moved into Abe's sealing house at Rapid Point.

sealing ice: ice-floe frequented by harp and hooded seals.

1916 GRENFELL 168 The wind had pinned the runnin' ice ag'in the standin' edge, and it looked good swilin' ice, too. I thought it was as well to die one way as another, and so here goes—and we started out across the floe.

sealing master: person in charge of a vessel and of men engaged in the hunt for seals.

[1870] 1899 *Nfld Law Reports* 329 That a seal abandoned at the ice might be taken possession of by the finder, only went to show the illegal and conflicting practice of two or three sealing masters. 1923 CHAFE 28 It is clear that occasions will arise when this may happen, but the sealing master will be in possession of definite information, and at the first slackening can proceed direct to the patch, without any loss of time. 1976 CASHIN 44 Two sealing masters stand out prominently in my mind. . . The first, and I would say the most colourful of Newfoundland sealing skippers, was the then well-known Captain Arthur Jackman.

sealing net: net, often joined with others to form a 'frame,' set in water near the shore to catch migrating seals; SEAL NET.

1854 [FEILD] 16 . . .when men leave their sealingnets, which require continued watching and attendance.

sealing owner: merchant or entrepreneur engaged in the various activities of the sealing industry; ship-owner.

1923 CHAFE 28 In the latter end of 1920, the Sealing owners made arrangements for the assistance of aeroplanes and airships to be given to the ships in the seal fishery of 1921.

sealing plane: aircraft used to locate seal herds and report position to vessels engaged in the seal hunt; SPOTTER.

[1928] 1964 *Evening Telegram* 21 June, p. 6 The new sealing plane 'Avro Avian' arrived this morning by S.S. *Newfoundland*. [1954] 1979 ibid 14 Mar, p. 8 Captain Ken Barbour, official spotter on the sealing plane, says Newfoundland is going to lose her sealing industry.

sealing post: coastal station from which seals are captured by means of nets; POST.

[1775] 1792 CARTWRIGHT ii, 52 Mr Lymburner is a merchant at Quebec, who keeps sealing-posts. 1778 ibid ii, 309 At four this morning I sent Patrick to the sealing-post, to examine the condition of the provisions and craft; and to secure them from taking damage by the thawing weather. 1839 TUCKER 107 A good sealing post is ranked as of the most valuable species of property, and is transmitted from one family to another; and sold, sometimes for a round price.

sealing pound: enclosure formed by placing three seal nets together in the water; cp POUND.

[1775] 1792 CARTWRIGHT ii, 52 I went round Little Caribou, and afterwards measured the Little Tickle, and marked out a sealing-pound upon the ice; in order to ascertain the dimensions of the nets.

sealing punt: undecked boat used to capture seals with nets close to shore and at the hunt among the ice-floes; PUNT.

1878 TOCQUE 123 Some are employed. . .preparing the sealing-punts or skiffs.

sealing racket: see RACKET[2].

sealing rope ['si:lin ,roup]: length of stout line used to haul seal carcasses and 'pelts' over the ice; HAULING-ROPE, TOW v: ~ ROPE.

[1900 OLIVER & BURKE] 45 'Twas a heavy, stout manilla, greasy enough to fry, / And in the centre of that sealing rope was placed a hook-and-eye. 1944 LAWTON & DEVINE 93 Excited crowds,—the women with tea-kettles and bundles of bread, the men with their gaffs and sealing ropes—scaled the jagged cliff sides. T 43–64 You'd walk off from the land, you know, on the ice, an' you'd have your gaff with you and your rope, sealing rope, and you get the chance to kill one, two, or three or four probably.

sealing schooner: see **sealing vessel**.

1895 PROWSE 450–1 The work required for fitting out the vessels, building punts, repairing and strengthening the sealing schooners, kept masters and crews at work all through the winter.

sealing season: period when harp and hooded seals migrate past Newfoundland and Labrador and are taken by hunters.

[1771] 1792 CARTWRIGHT i, 181 They have now not more than half a load, nor can they spare time to get more, before the sealing season is over.

sealing ship: see **sealing vessel**.

[1951] 1978 *Haulin' Rope & Gaff* 85 "Ballad of Capt Bob Bartlett": The sealing ships whose bloody decks betokened paying trips, / As ev'ry Spring they wriggled through the ice-field's crushing grips. 1982 *Evening Telegram* 24 Mar, p. 1 Sealing ships returned to port Tuesday amid indications the proposed European ban on seal products has already shaken the market.

sealing skiff: large undecked boat used to set and haul seal nets; SKIFF.

[1771] 1792 CARTWRIGHT i, 177 I carried three of the sealing crew to the stage, from whence they went to Seal Island in a sealing skiff. [1786] ibid iii, 173 After breakfast I sent four hands in the sealing-skiff to get the *Fox* off, which they did, by making the largest raft of wood fast to a rock, and taking her anchor; with which. . .they moored her in deep water.

sealing skipper: see **sealing master**.

1895 PROWSE 452 And the great army of sealing skippers and great planters, where are they? . . .the Ashes, Dawes, Delaneys, Blandfords, Kanes, Knees, Jackmans, Bartletts, and others. 1923 CHAFE 23 The other sealing skippers ridiculed the idea and their argument was that a large vessel could never be turned in the ice. 1976 CASHIN 44 The first, and I would say the most colourful of Newfoundland sealing skippers, was the then well-known Captain Arthur Jackman. 1981 *Evening Telegram* 27 Mar, p. 3 The first three sealing skippers back from this year's hunt all complained yesterday about ice conditions their crews worked under.

sealing spring: period when harp and hooded seals, having whelped on the floes, are hunted; cp SPRING[2].

1933 GREENE xv A Sealing Spring: Lasts from the middle of February to the middle or end of May.

sealing steamer: large vessel, powered by

steam, engaged in the seal hunt among the ice-floes.

1895 PROWSE 453 When Mr Walter Grieve sent the first sealing steamer to the ice it was a poor day for Newfoundland. 1923 CHAFE [iii] In 1866, there were five sealing steamers engaged, while the number of sailing vessels was one hundred and seventy seven. . . At present the total of sealing steamers is but eight, while the sailing fleet has disappeared altogether. 1950 *Daily News* 23 July, p. 3 [The S.S. *Eagle*] the last of the old wooden sealing steamships. . .made her final voyage yesterday.

sealing ticket: see TICKET.

sealing time: see **sealing season, ~ spring**.

1901 *Christmas Bells* 14 The good people. . .started in a body for the forest, there to remain until March, or as the male sex would have it, 'until swoilin' time,' when in truth good work would be done in that line.

sealing vessel: sailing craft or engine-driven ship of varying size engaged in the seal hunt among the ice-floes.

1826 *Edin New Phil J* i, 37 The capelin is also sometimes taken in the month of April, by the sealing vessels, among the ice on the banks. 1866 WILSON 277 The swearing. . .drinking, and general profanity, in the sealing-vessels are truly fearful. 1871 HOWLEY *MS Reminiscences* 13 Many a fine sealing vessel or Labradorman has come to grief on those awful rocks and shoals. 1978 *Evening Telegram* 10 Mar, p. 1 The four Newfoundland. . .sealing vessels have been unable to penetrate the standing ice.

sealing voyage: enterprise or period of prosecuting the seal hunt among the ice-floes; trip; VOYAGE.

1840 GOSSE 25 In the latter part of May [in Newfoundland], after the sealing voyage is closed, among other preparations for the cod-fishery, the crews are sent into the woods to cut rinds. 1855 WHITE *MS Journal* Mar 'Journal of a Sealing Voyage on board Brig *Evanthes*.' 1866 WILSON 276 The length of time spent in sealing-voyages is from three to eight weeks. [1882] 1898 *Nfld Law Reports* 441 The fishery mainly and almost exclusively contemplated by the Act is the sealing voyage, which for all purposes of local construction and intendment is one of the *fisheries* of the colony. 1900 PROWSE 70 No intoxicating liquors shall be carried in any ship, vessel or boat engaged in any fishing or trading voyage, except vessels engaged on a sealing voyage, beyond such quantity (not exceeding four gallons) as may be *bona fide* required or necessary for ship's stores. 1964 BLONDAHL (ed) 75 "The Sealers' Song": And the owners will supply them as they did in days of old, / For in Newfoundland the sealing voyage means something more than gold.

sealskin n also **sileskin, swileskin**. Cp *OED* ~ 1 'skin of any of the Fur Seals' (1325–), *DAE* 1 (1790–) for sense 1.

1 The skin, with blubber removed, of any of the hair seals, esp harp and hooded seals.

1612 *Willoughby Papers* [Guy's Journal] 21 Oct We fownd theare a cupper kettle kepte very brighte, a furre gowne, some seale skinnes ane old sayle. [1693]

1793 REEVES xxix That nothing in this act shall extend, or be construed to extend, to give liberty of importing any such seal skins duty-free. [1745] 1976 HEAD 125 Truck our Goods for Skins, feathers and fish, and be sure you Gitt all the Sile Skins both dry and Pickled. 1792 PULLING *MS* Aug We got about a hundred deer skins made up in eight bundles and put each bundle on a swile's skin which served as a sledge to haul them on. 1810 STEELE 148 We recaptured the brig *Bellona*, laden with fish-oil and seal-skin, from Newfoundland. 1883 SHEA 11 Several descriptions of leather have been produced, which meet the wants of bookbinders and upholsterers as well as the former purpose of shoe-leather, to which, until recently, the Newfoundland sealskin was exclusively applied. 1933 *Nfld Royal Commission Report* 95 Value of seal oil and seal skins exported: 1933 $328,371. 1957 *Evening Telegram* 6 July Like the feller that come here last spring bringin' swile skins.

2 Attrib **sealskin boot** [see SKINNY-WOPPER], **~ cap, ~ dicky** [see DICKY[2]], **~ dress, ~ mantle, ~ slipper**.

1842 JUKES i, 266 I had heavy seal-skin boots on, coming half way up the thigh, which [were] now full of lolly [ice]. 1873 *Maritime Mo* i, 254 Seal-skin boots reaching to the knee, having a thick, leather sole, well nailed, to enable them to walk over the ice, protect the feet. . . Seal-skin caps, and tweed or moleskin trousers complete the costume. 1899 *Tribune Christmas No* 11 On our arrival at St John's we each supplied ourselves with a pair of those horrible, ill-smelling seal-skin boots, nasty things, but for which I know of no substitute. 1975 BUTLER 91 I was wet from above the knees to my waist, and I was wearing sealskin boots tied below the knees, so my feet were dry. 1912 HUTTON 187 Little Johannes pulled off his sealskin dicky. [1772] 1792 CARTWRIGHT i, 267 On landing at Westminster Bridge, we were immediately surrounded by a great concourse of people; attracted not only by the uncommon appearance of the Indians who were in their seal-skin dresses, but also by a beautiful eagle, and an Esquimau dog. 1923 CHAFE 30 Auxiliary Industries to preserve the skins and manufacture them into seal skin mantles. 1977 *Inuit Land Use* 221 During the winter, the women made sealskin mitts and boots to sell to traders on the fishing schooners the next summer. 1977 RUSSELL 32 He tells this story about how he got the pair of swileskin slippers that he's been wearin' now for nigh on thirty years.

seam n Comb **seam boat**: boat or vessel with exterior planks which abut rather than overlap. Cp LAP SEAM.

T 250–66 They were all seam boats [in those days], and my poor old dad and a man from Nova Scotia built the first clinker boat, lap one plank over the other.

seane See SEINE.

sea-pigeon n *OED* ~ 1 (Nfld: 1620–) for sense 1; cp 1870 quot for sense 2.

1 Black guillemot (*Cepphus grylle atlantis*); PIGEON.

[1620] 1887 MASON 151 The sea fowles are. . .Sea

Pigeons, Ice Birds, Bottle noses. . . [1766] 1971 BANKS 119 A number of Birds are about the ship which the seamen call Penguins [auks] Gulls Shearwaters one species of them with sharpe tails. . .Puffins & Sea Pigeons. [1794] 1968 THOMAS 87 They were the size of a Blackbird, the shape of a Pigeon, had white under their Wings, their Tails tipt with white, red Feet, and other parts of the Back. They are call'd Sea Pigeons and are very numerous. 1842 JUKES ii, 185 Eider ducks, sheldrakes, cormorants called 'shags,' puffins, a kind of auk called 'sea pigeon,' and several species of petrel, with many other birds, abound. 1861 *Harper's* xxii, 746 The day following they ran down to a small island tenanted by sea-pigeons. 1891 PACKARD 90 People here call the guillemots sea-pigeons, though more like crows than pigeons in size and color. 1964 *Evening Telegram* 22 Jan, p. 5 Guillemots (sea pigeons) are much bigger than pigeons, and respectable pot birds. Black, with very large white wing patches, they have no colors in the plumage, but seem more colorful than most sea birds because of the bright red feet and scarlet lining to the mouth and beak.

2 Ivory gull (*Pagophila eburnea*); ICE-PARTRIDGE.

[c1830] 1890 GOSSE 64 One day a fisherman brought him a pretty bird, of dense, soft, spotless white plumage, calling it a sea-pigeon. It was a kittiwake gull.

season n The period of the principal fishery for cod from spring to early autumn; FISHING SEASON.

[1663] 1963 YONGE 56 Now the manner of this country is, for those that have no chyrurgeon to agree with one, and give 18d., 20d., or 2s. per man for the season to look after their men, which the masters pay in fish at the end of the summer. 1708 OLDMIXON 14 The 20th of *August* some years ago us'd to be the last day of the Season, and kept as a Holiday; but lately the Fishers stay longer; and. . .they now seldom sail till *October*. [1794] 1968 THOMAS 98 The French should evacuate Placentia and all their Settlements, but that they should retain a Right to come and fish here in the Season, and dry it ashore, but that they should not remain there during the winter. [1909] 1930 COAKER 5 We must not forget that although this season's catch of fish is small, yet the prices are now below $5. . .per qtl.

second num Comb **second hand** [ˌsɛkən 'hænd, ˌsʊkn̩ 'ænd]. See also HAND.

1 One in command of a fishing or sealing vessel under the captain or 'skipper.'

1924 ENGLAND 51 Her 1922 complement. . .comprised: Captain, second hand, barrel men (or spy masters), scunners. 1936 SMITH 91 I tied the log line around the second hand. . .and he jumped on board the boat and began freeing her out. T 43–64 But usually the skipper and second hand, or mate—whichever you mind to call him—would sleep aft in the cabin. P 9–73 The trap is made and set, now comes the hauling of it for the first time. The haul up lines are fastened to the top and bottom, two, one on each side of the doorway. The boat comes up to the trap and the second hand (mate) stands by with the boathook. 1976 CASHIN 91 Captain Kean's son, Wes-

ley, who was second hand with his father, was much more popular with the crew.

2 Junior officer in command of a group working ashore, as in lumbering or railway maintenance.

1861 DE BOILIEU 25–6 The cargo unloaded and stored, the crews are divided in parties of three or four men, each being titled according to the position he holds in the boat. For instance, 'skipper,' 'second hand,' 'midshipman'; last comes the 'captain,' who has the least to do—merely, indeed, to cook for the rest and to keep the boat clean. P 65–64 Although the skipper has the authority to hire whom he wishes, he usually hires only one man. This man is the 'second hand.' The second hand hires all the other men required for the year's work. The second hand is actually the personnel manager. T 100–64 The man on one side o' the old pump-trolley, an' the foreman on another side. Well, he'd watch his side an' this man'd watch his, what they used to call second hand, you know, right on the front o' the car wi' the foreman.

section n In western Newfoundland, a community; SETTLEMENT.

1966 SZWED 20 The Codroy Valley is divided into 14 settlements or 'sections' as they are called. Ibid 70 You always tried to marry girls from outside the section. After your family had lived in the place for awhile you were related to everyone. We always tried to know girls from other sections.

sed See SUD LINE.

sedentary a Cp *OED* 3 'not migratory' (esp 1891 quot); from terminology of the French fisheries: DE LA MORANDIÈRE iii, 1381 pêche sédentaire, and ~ errante. Of the fisheries, prosecuted in coastal waters in boats stationed in convenient harbours and coves; conducted by residents, not migratory fishermen; see SHORE[2]: SHORE FISHERY.

[1762 (1895)] PROWSE 322 At the breaking out of this war we had. . .fishermen, who carried on most successfully in shoal waters the *pêche sedentaire*—[shore fishery.] 1793 REEVES 134 [The regulations] were calculated only for a cod, or whale fishery, whereas the seal fishery, which was most pursued [in Labrador], was a sedentary fishery. [1831] 1916 *Nfld Law Reports* 39–40 In the early condition of the sedentary fisheries of this Island, there were I apprehend, at most but three classes of persons engaged in them: viz. the merchant who provided capital—the planter or resident boatkeeper, who supplied skill—and the servant who contributed labour—for their prosecution. 1863 PEDLEY 278 On one point, there was a general concurrence, viz. that the fisheries of Newfoundland had become decidedly sedentary—i.e. chiefly confined to the resident population. 1976 HEAD 39 The sedentary fishery was more efficient. . .because the settlers specialized in the taking of fish, not the transporting of it or of men—the shipping trade could be left to the West Country.

seedy a *EDD* ~ 3 (2) ~ wart Co. Comb **seedy**

wart: large wart with irregular, seed-like surface (P 148–66).

seeny-sawney n ['siːnɪ 'sɑnɪ]. Silly person; one slightly deranged (P 43–66).

seine n also **saine, scaine, seane** [sein, sɛin, sɛin] *OED* ~ sb[1] (c950– esp 1602 quot Co), *DAE* (1634–) for sense 1; see also CAPLIN ~, COD ~, LANCE ~. For combs. in sense 2: *OED* c ~ line (1794–), ~ man (1876–).

1 A large vertical net placed in position around a school of fish, the 'foots' drawn together to form a bag, and hauled at sea or in shallow water near the shore.

1612 *Willoughby Papers* 16a/9 For our fishing voiage [to the Newfoundland] one Seane 6 neats 7 dosen of Lynes. [1622] 1954 INNIS 58 2 saines, a greater and a less. [1663] 1963 YONGE 60 They catch [caplin and squid] in nets or scaines. 1699 *Act of Wm III*, 10 & 11 [It is forbidden to] Shoot his or their Sayn or Sayns within or upon the Sayn or Sayns of any other Person. [1775] 1895 PROWSE 342 We destroy a great quantity of small fish, which after being inclosed in the sean (and not worth the attention of the person who hauls them) are left to rot. [1778] 1792 CARTWRIGHT ii, 354 The seine was hauled to day by the stage, and took some small lance. [1863] 1954 INNIS 397 Large seines must be used in Bay Bulls, or none, in consequence of the depth of water in that locality. 1884 DEMING 90 The 'seine,' so called locally, is a net of great length and depth, so arranged as to 'purse' at the bottom by a drawn cord, and secure the fish in the same manner that menhaden are caught on our [U S] coasts. 1975 BUTLER 58 The bottom had to be smooth in order to use those seines since the seine had to be hauled over the bottom to catch the fish.

2 Comb **seine ball**: lead sinker attached to the foot of a seine to suspend it vertically in the water (M 68–7).

seine barrow: flat, rectangular wooden frame with handles at each end for two men to carry a cod-seine (1975 BUTLER 181); BARROW[1].

seine gallows: wooden frame on which seine is placed to dry (C 75–130); GALLOWS.

1907 *Nfld Qtly* Dec, p. 2 The Canon thinks the name [Gallows Cove] is derived from a sort of erection which was, until recent years, to be seen in many settlements, and which was known as a 'SEINE GALLOWS.' It was a sort of 'horse' or trestle made of rough rails or *starrigans*, and was used for drying nets on. P 127–76 ~ A slanted flake-like construction used to dry newly barked nets.

seine lead: see **seine ball**; LEAD[1].

1977 *Evening Telegram* 28 Apr, p. 42 Tenders are invited for the purchase. . .of approximately 600 lbs. of seine leads, complete with footrope and [headrope].

seine line: type of stout rope to which the netting of a seine is fastened at top and bottom.

[1751–66] 1954 INNIS 182 Ropes for Sean Lines.

seine linnet: netting which forms a seine; LINNET.

1966 SCAMMELL 76 Ah, there it was, the baitskiff, just rounding the head. He could see the heap of seine-linnet in the stern of the punt that was being towed behind.

seine man: one engaged in fishing with a seine, esp for bait to supply banking vessel.

1975 LEYTON 102 Before Confederation [the Nova Scotia vessels] weren't allowed to take any bait in Newfoundland themselves. They hired what they called a Bait Hauler. Now Mr Lake next door, he used to be a seine man, a Bait Hauler, had his own seine net; and I'd go with him, go haul bait.

seine master, master of the seine: man in charge of a boat and crew fishing with seines.

[1886] LLOYD 62 A seine-boat crew usually numbers from four to eight hands, including the 'master of the seine,' who is also the coxswain of the boat. 1895 GRENFELL 71 The seine master stands, fish-glass in hand, high on the bow of the seine skiff. 1960 FUDGE 19 It had been a herring famine for twenty years, but a Enos Davidge, a big seine master, happened to haul herring in St Keels, and about twenty sails rushed to the scene.

seine skiff: large open boat, propelled by oars, used to fish with seines.

1895 GRENFELL 71 [He stood] high on the bow of the seine skiff, as his stalwart crew, with eight huge pine oars, drive the boat along. T 100/2–64 Well, a seine skiff was something like the trap skiff, but she mightn't be hardly so big in width and length, she'd be a lighter built boat. 1975 BUTLER 68 The fishermen owned herring seines and seine skiffs which they rowed with long oars.

seine tar: kind of cutch used to tan fish-nets.

T 178–65 After we started usin' this patent bark we used to use two three gallons o' tar, of seine tar, used to call it. And that didn't use to bide in 'em then, sir, not like the spruce bark. T 141/67–65[2] But now seine tar, seine tar will mix with the hot water, perhaps right boiling.

semi-dry See DRY a.

send v Phr *send down*: (a) to imprison; (b) to dismiss from a woods or lumber camp.

1887 *Colonist Christmas No* 5 He asked me where I came from. I told him the place (in Dorset), and I think he wanted to let me off; but Martin, the Irishman, swore so against me that I was sent down. This was my first and last visit to Court. T 43/7–64 An' if you weren't up to the standard, if you couldn't do either [any] job reasonably, they'd send you down.

send n *OED* ~ sb[2] naut (1726–). Swell; force or movement of sea waves.

1873 CARROLL 20 Old seals know the more northern the more safety for their young, as there is less danger of a southern send or sea that would wash their young off the ice. P 113–56 Though it's calm, there's a heavy send in the water. P 243–57 ~ Sea lop when wind is absent; gentle swell.

sennet n *OED* sennit b naut 'plaited straw. . .of which grass hats are made' (1769, 1858). Attrib

sennet hat: fisherman's home-made summer hat, woven with strips of birch bark (1937 DEVINE 43).

sermon n *OED* ~ 4 ~ book (1772). Attrib **sermon book**: collection of published sermons used by lay reader in absence of clergyman.

1906 LUMSDEN 77 Now there is heard a simple, earnest prayer, after which the 'sermon book' is produced, and the congregation of sea-toilers listen with becoming attention and interest to the reading of the words of some noted preacher, great in his simplicity. P 212–75 The sermon book was a familiar piece of essential equipment in the Newfoundland outport. Without [sermon books], usually provided by the minister, the lay reader who 'took the service' in the absence of the minister, preaching at the other churches on his circuit, would not have been able to provide a sermon for his congregation.

servant[1] n *OED* ~ 2; cp *DC* 'employee of the Hudson's Bay Company' (1690–). Man or woman indentured or engaged on wages or shares for a period in the fishery; FISHERY SERVANT, FISHING ~. Cp DIETER.

[1652 (1895) PROWSE 153 These were for the most part, either young men who came over as Servants and never had over much shew of religion in them, or fishermen of Marblehead feared to be profane persons, divers of whom were brought from Newfoundland for the fishing season.] 1699 *Act of Wm III*, 10 & 11 . . .and other Necessaries for themselves and their Servants. [1712] 1895 PROWSE 273 No wine nor brandy brought from New England, only rum and molasses, which is the liquor drunk by servants. 1793 *Report on Nfld Trade* [Appendix] Winter Inhabitants [of Newfoundland]: Men Servants—Men who do engage as Servants in the Fishery [and] Women. [1772] 1792 CARTWRIGHT i, 265 At daylight we found ourselves between Youghall and Dungarvon, and hauled close up to the mouth of the latter place in hopes of a boat coming off to take the servant passengers on shore. [1794] 1968 THOMAS 170 If any Master becomes insolvent the Servants he has employ'd in the Fisherys have a prior claim to the Oil, Blubber and Fish to satisfy their Wages. [1810] 1971 ANSPACH 3 It would be advisable that the passage-money. . .to be deducted out of the wages of every servant hired or employed in the fisheries should, according to the current prices of a Man's passage from or to His Majesty's European Dominions, be deducted out of the Servant's wages or earnings and paid. . .into the hands of persons appointed for that purpose. [1880] 1898 *Nfld Law Reports* 218 It is said that the wages-servant in the fishery runs no such risk as the shareman; that he has certain wages, and the result of the voyage is immaterial to him. I cannot go the whole length with this argument, seeing that all servants in the fishery are as a rule very much dependent upon the success of the voyage as security for their earnings. [1896] SWANSBOROUGH 12 "October": The summer servants get their pay, / Their time is up on the last day. 1898 PROWSE 304 Females engaged as servants in the fishery or as Passengers between Newfoundland and Labrador must have sepa-rate cabin accommodation. 1937 *Seafisheries of Nfld* 75 All the men engaged in the fishery are not fishing on their own account; some are in the service of persons who own, or operate vessels, boats, traps or gear. This type of fisherman is usually described as a servant or shareman. The servants are paid a fixed wage for the season, or a monthly wage, with or without board and lodging. 1954 INNIS 296 After 1789 servants on ships became fewer, dropping from 4,799 to 2,438 in 1792; servants in boats from 7,323 in 1789 to 7,138 in 1792; and servants on shore from 6,152 in 1789 to 4,465 in 1792. 1969 HORWOOD 171 They are the men of the south coast, whose ancestors were expelled from Placentia when the English took it from the French, hired as servants in the Channel Islands when the great Newman Company went out to trade in fish and oil. 1975 BUTLER 60 A [merchant] who employed a large number of servants usually had a cook and a bunkhouse for the servants to live in. . . The servants were usually paid a very low wage.

servant[2] See CHAPEL SERVANT.

serve v *EDD* ~ v[1] 5. To feed and water domestic animals.

P 54–67 I got up and served the sheep.

service v Cp *OED* ~ n[1] 35 naut 'small cord wound about a rope to protect.' To wind rope or other material tightly around a cable to protect it; STRAD v.

1855 WARREN 16 This cable [on the Banking vessels] was serviced or covered with a small rope to prevent it chafing, or being cut on the bottom. M 68–26 The hawser is 'stradded,' while the skiff collar is 'serviced.' P 40–78 We'll have to service that rope or the once it will chafe off.

sess See SISS.

set n *Fisheries of U S*, p. 176: setting trawl, day set, night set on Grand Banks.

1 The placement of a trawl-line when fishing for cod, often with defining word *day, night*; length of trawl-line set out. See also FLYING SET.

1955 DOYLE (ed) 63 "The Banks of Nfld": We scarce get time to light our pipes when our dories go, / We've got to make three sets a day, let the wind blow high or low. 1960 FUDGE 17 She had a half set of trawl gear. 1963 *Nfld Record* ii (3), p. 15 The hooks were baited, the trawl line paid out and marked by buoys, and the set periodically taken up to remove the fish and re-bait the hooks for another setting. 1963 TEMPLEMAN & FLEMING 11 Sets were made in the shallow to intermediate depths on some occasions. T 41–64 We use one [group of] twenty-eight [lines] for all-day fishing, an' then we bait up another twenty-eight in the nights for a night-set. Take that back in the morning an' leave it on board. M 71–94 The men would leave the islands at about 3 a.m., set their trawl which would consist of five or six ten line tubs. They would wait for two or three hours and then haul it back. This was referred to as a 'day set.' 1973 HORWOOD 11 She was a vessel of considerable size and carried a crew of twenty-five, and eleven dories. . . But before they had time to make a 'set,' a gale of wind and a choppy sea overtook them and two masts broke off and went over the side.

2 Phr *set of harness*: assembled straps of horse's gear.

1917 *Christmas Bells* 16 Such was the price of learning how to make a pair of boots, or a suit of clothes; or to make a sail or an anchor, or to build a house, or make a set of harness.

set of nets: number of nets placed together to trap seals; FLEET, FRAME.

1863 HIND ii, 207–8 Some nets are more than 100 fathoms long, by 10 fathoms wide; and several nets, placed together as advantageously as possible for the purpose of taking seals when they are migrating in herds in the spring or in the autumn, form what the fishermen call a set of nets.

3 See WATER n: WATER SET.

set p ppl Cp *EDD* ~ v 2 (8) (c) 'to make stiff and cramped' for sense 1.

1 Phr *set fast*: solidly frozen; FAST.

1842 JUKES i, 148 He had never seen the southern part near the island 'set fast,' or sufficiently frozen over to enable him to cross.

2 Comb **set wood**: wood which is just starting to dry out (P 195–67).

settle n Cp *OED* ~ sb¹ 3, *EDD* sb² 1; *DAE*. A long, home-made wooden bench with arms and high back; an unupholstered couch; STRETCHER.

1869 HOWLEY *MS Reminiscences* 24 The main or living room was a space of some 10 or 12 feet square with an open fire-place at one end, on either side of which were rough benches or settles made of squatted sticks. [c1880] 1927 DOYLE (ed) 31 "The Ryans and the Pittmans": I'll get me a settle, a pot and a kettle. 1887 *Colonist Christmas No* 7 On a bench, or settle, by a fire, we observe a man in a half-sitting, half recumbent position. [1897] 1927 DOYLE (ed) [72] "The Landfall of Cabot": Sure I turned a coat for Cabot / Says a woman on the settle, / By the same he drank that evening / What cold tea was in the kettle. [1906] GRENFELL 154 The child was lying on a wooden settle when I entered. T 43/7–64 But the settle had two arms on it, was handmade, but no cushions or anything like that. C 71–106 ~ a couch kept in the kitchen, also called a day-bed. Most settles were made of wood with a raised headboard. 1979 HORWOOD 94 [He] sprawled on the wooden settle, puffing quietly at his pipe, feet propped before the fire whose front drafters cast dancing red images across his face and chest.

settlement n Cp *OED* ~ 15 'a small village' (1827–), *DAE* 2 a (1711–), *DC* 1 (1769–). The houses and other buildings often clustering around a freshwater stream on a cove, bay, harbour, beach or shore along the coast; a similar small community established inland: cp OUTPORT, PLANTATION.

1708 OLDMIXON 12 But they make use still of their old Harbours also, as their small Settlements here were termed, and not *Towns*, a Name indeed which they did not deserve. [1749] 1755 DOUGLASS i, 289 At present there are nine or ten settlements called harbours, not towns, where they cure and ship off their dry cod-fish. [1794] 1968 THOMAS 125 Our man. . .kept advancing along the shore in the hope of coming to some Settlement. 1842 BONNYCASTLE ii, 165 It is impossible in so scattered a population, with such amazing extent to fishing bank and shore, that he whose establishment is in St John's, or in one of the out-harbours or settlements, could attend to the large import and export trade upon which he subsists, and at the same time employ himself or his clerks on a fish stage in twenty different places, or in perhaps a hundred boats at sea. 1881 *Nineteenth Century* ix, 91 There was quite a settlement in those parts, consisting of a small saw-mill and house adjoining inhabited by the white man who ran the mill, and of two or three families of Indians, all rejoicing in the name of Joe. 1898 PROWSE 31 . . .setting forth the limits or boundaries within which such area or district is comprised, and the names of the towns, harbours, or settlements included therein. 1902 HOWLEY *MS Reminiscences* 28 There are several houses scattered around in coves and outside near the Northern Head there is quite a large settlement in Seal Cove. 1933 *Nfld Royal Commission Report* 4 The remainder of the people are distributed among some 1,300 settlements, spread for the most part over the 6,000 miles of coast, with populations ranging from 50 to 5,000. [1964] 1979 *Evening Telegram* 27 June, p. 40 The motor vessel *Catalina Trader*. . .is now visiting Newfoundland settlements collecting seal pelts from landsmen. 1973 SMALLWOOD 66 I was taken about the settlement by the local boys, and in a small boat about the harbour, jigging sculpins and tom-cods.

settler n Cp *OED* ~ 2 'colonist' (1788–), *DAE* 1 (1739–). A permanent resident of coastal Newfoundland and Labrador as distinguished from a seasonal migratory fisherman; LIVYER, PLANTER.

1795 REEVES 67 They say, that heretofore much encouragement had not been given the settlers, to continue in the island, and therefore regular governors, as in other colonies, had very seldom been appointed to them. 1836 [WIX]¹ 168 The people, too, with whom the first settlers and their immediate descendants may have had contact, or intercourse, have attributed much to the formation of the dialect, character, and habits of the present settlers. 1861 DE BOILIEU 222 I have already remarked that the settlers in Labrador were hospitable in the extreme. 1869 HOWLEY *MS Reminiscences* 4 The only settler at this time near the mouth of the Terra Nova was an old man named Stroud. . . He was one of that type of old Englishman originally brought out as a youngster by some of the mercantile firms. 1883 ibid 1 The settlers, or rather squatters, on the West Coast particularly in the Codroy Valley and Bay St George, had up to this time no legal claim to the lands they occupied. 1912 *Nfld Qtly* Dec, p. 26 I visited the churchyard in which the 'rude forefathers of the hamlet sleep' for the purpose of witnessing among the tombs that of the late Mr Steer, the first settler of the place and the grandfather of the well known merchants of the capital. Leaving Anchor Point we journey through Deadman's Cove, where I met an old settler named Chambers who told me that in the old days partridges were very numerous in that part of the country. 1916 GRENFELL 35 Once the die is cast, a house built, a fishing-room established, a fur path secured, the settler here, like the limpet on our rocks, finds moving to a distance almost an impossibility. 1974 CAHILL 22 They figured settlers were nothing but trouble, wanting land grants and concessions and finally to run the show themselves.

settling vbl n In designations of the date when a fisherman pays his account with the merchant who has advanced credit for the fishing enterprise or 'voyage': **settling day, ~ season, ~ time.**

1849 [FEILD] 98 Nearly all the men of the settlement had sailed this day [20 Sept] for Harbour Briton, the place we had just left, this being the great settling day of the yearly accounts at the merchants' establishment. 1891 *Holly Branch* 20 The 'settling season' was the proper time for marriages. This came in September. [1877] 1898 *Nfld Law Reports* 148 No objection seems to have been made as to this being the proper mode of settlement at settling time, but afterwards the plaintiff preferred a claim for a man's share of the whole fish taken by the cod-seine. 1981 *Evening Telegram* 19 Sep, p. 6 Christmas at Gaultois in its prime is something to recall: a four day trip in Garland's Trader at 'Settlin Time.'

seven num Comb **seven-years grass**: variety of hairgrass (*Deschampsia caespitosa*) (1898 *J A Folklore* xi, 283).

sevens n also **sevenses** *OED* seven sb 2 (1868). Children's game in which a ball is thrown against a wall.

T 459–67 As younger children [we] played 'sevens,' where you threw [the ball] against the wall. M 68–21 Sevenses—played with a ball by children.

sevenses See SEVENS.

sewell n also **sewel** *OED* shewell, var sewell, etc 'something hung up to keep a deer from going in a particular direction' obs exc dial (c1250–1688); *DC* sewel (Nfld: 1770–); cp *EDD* sewell, shewell Ox Bk for sense 1.

1 A fence placed to herd caribou in a desired direction; DEER FENCE.
[1768] 1828 CARTWRIGHT ii, 310 [The fences are] only discontinued here and there for short distances, where the ill growth of the wood does not favour such works. The Indians are here at no loss; for their knowledge of the use of sewels supplies the deficiency, and completes their toils. [1770] 1792 CARTWRIGHT i, 7–8 Where any open place intervened, they made use of a sort of sewell, made of narrow strips of birch rind, tied together in the form of the wing of a paper kite; each of these was suspended from the end of a stick, stuck into the ground in an oblique position, that it might play with every breeze of wind. These sewells were placed at no great distance from each other, and the effect produced by their motion, was considerably heightened by the noise of the strips, when they struck

against each other. By these means, the deer were deterred by the sewells from attempting to enter the woods at the open places, and the fences were too high to be overleaped, and too strong to be forced. 1896 *J A Folklore* ix, 24 ~ in old English a scarecrow, especially in order to turn deer. It generally consisted of feathers hung up, which by their fluttering scared those timid animals. The Red Indians of Newfoundland suspended from poles streamers of birch-bark for the same purpose. 1915 HOWLEY 31 ~ This word is probably compounded from see and well; another example is Semore (Mt See-more) near Birchy Lake, Upper Humber River.

2 Comb **sewell stick**: slender pole, six feet long, forming with other similar poles a fence to herd caribou.
[1771] 1792 CARTWRIGHT i, 108 I likewise placed sewel-sticks across the river, ready for fixing up. [1786] ibid iii, 137 Tilsed was at cooper's work, and three hands were felling firewood: at night, they brought home another sled-load of sewel-sticks.

sewell twine: line used in the construction of barrier to herd caribou.
[1771] 1792 CARTWRIGHT i, 111 Milmouth returned at night, and brought me two dogs from home; also some sewel-twine and other things.

sewell v also **sewel**. To erect barriers or fences in order to herd caribou; also vbl n.
[1768] 1828 CARTWRIGHT ii, 320 Their habitations are soon put in order, their deer-fences repaired, the necessary sewelling completed, and every preparation made for the ensuing slaughter. [1771] 1792 CARTWRIGHT i, 111 Milmouth and I were employed all the rest of the day in cutting boughs to sewel the harbour, in order to cause the deer to come close to a point of Eyre Island, where I intend to watch for them. . . Early in the morning the men began to sewel the harbour with boughs.

shack n A simple dwelling built by a pond or in another location away from a town for week-end or holiday use; cabin.
P 74–66 Any cottage, no matter how beautiful or what size, built in the 'country' and used primarily during the summer months. 'We're going in to the shack for the holiday.' 1975 GUY 19 Newfoundlanders have a great fondness for shacks. A great profusion of them is maintained in all parts. Those with grander notions call them summer cottages or even lodges but the most common term is still 'a shack in the country.'

shack[1] v also **~ oneself.** Cp *NID* ~[5] 'live,' with sawmill quot. In lumbering operations, to live in a small, roughly made dwelling; to cook and care for oneself in the 'lumber woods' or in a cheap dwelling.
P 65–64 Not all lumbermen eat in the skipper's cook house. Some have their own little camps and 'shack for themselves.' They do their own cooking, wash their own dishes, clean their own camp, etc. T 172/4–65 We had to shack ourselves now. Find ourselves a little ol' shack. We got to get up an' boil our kettle in the morning an' have our breakfast. 1965 PETERS *Gloss* Shack-

ing [is] living in a small and usually very rough private camp. Shacks are used by commuting loggers whose homes are not within commuting distance. 'Shackers' provide for themselves. . . Usually used in the phrase 'shacking and batching.' P 148–65 By shacking himself and working in his spare time [he got his education].

2 Comb **shack locker**: a compartment on a ship used for placing snacks; see also LOCKER.

1921 *Nat Geog* July, p. 25 A fisherman is always hungry, and in addition to three square meals per diem, he indulges in a 'mug-up' between times from the 'shack-locker,' or quick-lunch cupboard in the forecastle. [1929] BOWEN 121 ~ On the Grand Banks, the forecastle locker in which left-over food is left for future use.

shack² v

1 Of trawl-lines and hooks, to clean and repair.

Q 67–48 Shacking gear is cleaning the trawl, putting on new hooks, suds, or gingins, and checking all knots. 1971 NOSEWORTHY 241 To shack gear is to mend trawls. C 75–28 The repairing of trawls was known as 'shackin' trawl.'

2 In phr *shack in, ~ down*: to coil trawl-lines in a tub.

P 113–79 One man hauls, the other shacks. [When shacking in,] the hooks on the suds are placed in spiral fashion.

shade* See SHEATH.

shader* See SHEETER.

shag n   also shaig *DAE* ~² (1737–).

1 Large black sea-bird of the cormorant family (*Phalacro-coracidae* spp); freq in place-names.

[1773] 1971 SEARY 278 Shag Rocks. [1775] 1792 CARTWRIGHT ii, 92 We saw great plenty of cod and caplin round the Dismal Islands; and observed that plenty of shaggs and tinkers breed on them. 1842 JUKES ii, 185 Eider-ducks, sheldrakes, cormorants called 'shags,' puffins. . .abound at various parts of the coast. 1891 PACKARD 102 We also saw a king eider flying with a small flock of eiders, as well as several 'shags' and a northern [phalarope]. [1923] 1946 PRATT 202 "The Ritual": . . .the cries / Of the curlews issuing from dark caves, / Accompanied by the thud of wings from shags / That veered down from their nests upon the crags / To pounce on bulwarks shattered by the waves. 1951 PETERS & BURLEIGH 67–8 Atlantic Common Cormorant, *Phalacrocorax carbo carbo*. . . Local name: Shag. . .a black bird, the size of a small goose, with long neck and long tail. . . Nests in colonies on rocky islands or isolated cliffs. . . The flesh and eggs of cormorants are so fishy that they are seldom killed or taken for human food. Ibid 69–70 Northern Double-crested Cormorant. *Phalacrocorax auritus auritus*. . . Local Name: Shag. . . This species is slightly smaller than the preceding one and is more commonly seen about the coasts. . . A very offensive bird, especially around the nesting area which is slimy and white from excrement and reeks with the odor of dead fish. 1951 *Nfld & Lab Pilot* i, 145 Shag Roost, with a depth of 18 fathoms. . .over it, lies about one mile west-north-

westward. 1959 MCATEE 5 ~ Common Cormorant (This name, referring to the shaggy crest, is a transfer from Great Britain where it has long been on record.)

2 Nickname for resident of Grand Bank.

C 47–66 Fortune gallies and the Grand Bank shags, / All tied up in wrapper bags, / When the bags began to bust, / The Fortune gallies began to cuss.

shaig See SHAG.

shaky-bog n   [ˈʃɛikɪbɒg] *OED* shake sb¹ 13 shake-bog (1815), *EDD* shake v 1 (13) ~ bog; *Kilkenny Lexicon* ~. A stretch of marshland or bog with springy surface.

1869 HOWLEY *MS Reminiscences* 3 Though quite dry when we pitched our camp [the swampy hollow] soon became a perfect shakybog in which one would sink to the knees in wet muck. P 148–62 ~ low-lying piece of land, wet, with grass and weeds. C 71–93 ~ Ground above a spring, thus called because when one walks upon it it shakes. P 141–73 As one walks over the wet bog, it shakes under one's feet, and this kind of bog we called shaky-bog.

shall See SHAUL n, v.

shallop n   also **shalloppe, shollup**. Cp *OED* ~ sb 1 (1578–), *DAE* (1611–); SMYTH 610 'small light fishing vessel' for sense 1.

1 A large, partly-decked boat, rigged with lug-sails and used in the cod and seal fisheries.

1612 *Willoughby Papers* 7 Oct [Guy's Journal] We departed from Harbor de Grace, [and] that nighte came to Greene bay, both the barke [and] the shalloppe. 1682 COLLINS 93 When the Shallops or Fishing Boats are full, they carry the Fish on Shore. [1711] 1895 PROWSE 272 Minister to have subscription for ensuing year from shollups, three, the two men boats, two, and the ship one quintol of dry merchandable fish to be levied. [1757] 1902 *Christmas Bells* 12 Petition of John Barrett, relating to six French prisoners running away with his shallop. [1766] 1971 BANKS 133 First then of the English method they use boats almost twice as large as the French Some of them being 40 feet in the Keel they are Calld here Shallops Rigged with a main mast & foremast & Lugsail & furnishd also with 4 oars 3 of which row on one side & the other which is twice as long as any of the rest Belays as they call it the other three. [1797] 1976 HEAD 222 Some of the Merchants from St John's and Trinity, had sent a few large Shallops [to Croque] in preference to the Banks; those that I met with had five Men in each Boat, and caught not less than forty Quintals, in less than twelve hours, fishing near the entrance of the Harbours. [1856] 1975 WHITELEY 126 Uncle John's shallop came up and went up the river. 1895 PROWSE 404 The shallop was a large boat, decked at both ends and open in the centre, with moveable deck boards and pounds; there were cuddies both fore and aft where the fishermen could sleep. There were never less than three men in a shallop; their dimensions were—30 to 40 feet keel, 10 to 40 feet beam; many of the larger shallops had five men, and would carry 200 qtls. dry fish. 1935 KEAN 128 The shallops appear to have all disappeared by 1806, and the seal fishery was then prosecuted in decked schooners.

2 Comb **shallop(s) tub**: wooden container, often a barrel sawn in half, used to hoist cod from boat to wharf, or, on runners, to haul fish in the 'stage'; TUB.

P 54–67 Shallop's tub [is] a flour barrel with about ⅓ its height cut off, used to receive split fish from the splitting table—2 of 'em roughly yield a quintal of fish when dried. Q 67–96 Shallop tub of fish: half barrel of fish. M 68–24 Shallop's tub: an ordinary pork barrel sawed off about two-thirds of its usual height, and used for hauling fish from the splitting table to the salt-pound. This type had wooden runners on it. It was also used, without runners, to hoist fish up the stage-head from the boat. Two of these tubs made one quintal (112 lbs) of fish.

shalloway n   also **sherway**. Cp DE LA MORANDIÈRE iii, 1377 charroy 'chaloupe de service servant. . .à assurer le transport des hommes et du matériel d'un endroit à l'autre dans le havre'; DC ~ (Nfld: 1774–). A type of vessel used originally by the French and then by the English in the offshore fishery, esp in collecting fish from smaller craft and transporting it to shore for curing.

[1676] 1895 PROWSE 206 No Indians come [to Placentia] but some Canida Indians from the forts of Canida in french shallowayes. [17..] 1976 HEAD 185 [Grand Bank's] Tide harbour very good for Shalloways and Beech enough for 30 boats fishing. [1715] ibid 73 This has been but lately experimented, I think last year was the first of it, that the sending these small shallow-ways, sloops and other kind of vessels to the Banks for fish, and when loading is caught to come in and cure them. [1715] ibid 80 Our boats are not sizeable for that service, for our fishing ledges, not lying above a mile or two, from our harbours' mouth, our boats are built accordingly, but the ledges of that port lying 8 or 10 leagues off [Placentia] the French were obliged to build a larger sort called shalloways, fitted with a deck, that can keep the sea five or six days for a loading. [1727] 1910 GLEDHILL 120–1 By Sherways Boats & Skifts. . . To the Hire of a Sherway, Sholloops &c Licenses. [1772] 1971 SEARY 278 Shalloway Point. [1774] 1792 CARTWRIGHT ii, 14 Hooper's shalloway having sprung her foremast, when she was out with Captain Scott, I sent the boat-builder to make her a new one. 1937 *Seafisheries of Nfld* 22 The shalloways were open boats that are now called punts. 1951 *Nfld & Lab Pilot* i, 111 Herring cove is entered between Cat and Shalloway islands but affords no shelter.

shard n   EDD ~ sb² Gl W So. Dent or notch in an edged tool.

1937 DEVINE 43 ~ A nick or gap in an edged tool. P 65–64 If the blade of an axe strikes anything harder than its own metal, there will be a dent put in the metal. This dent is a 'shard.' C 71–123 When a knife, an axe or other cutting utensil had a piece taken out of the edge (probably accidentally) it was said to have a shard in it and thus needed to be ground and sharpened.

share n   Cp *OED* ~ sb³ 1 (1372–; esp 1544 quot), *DC* Nfld (1877, 1964) for sense 1; *OED* 3 d *on shares* (1792–), *DAE* ~¹ 3 (1656–) for sense 2.

1 One of the specified proportions assigned to owner and crew of the value of the catch taken in a fishing or sealing voyage after deducting the expenses of the enterprise, i.e. the 'boats's share.'

[1577–8] 1935 *Richard Hakluyt* 125 [Parkhurst's letter:] For ther is given out of every mans share, and of the shippes parte, and also the vytellers at the least xiid. upon every syngell share. 1620 WHITBOURNE 29 The better sort of men [are yeerely hired by the Owners] for small wages, who have the benefit of their shares. [1663] 1963 YONGE 58 The men in these voyages have no wages but are paid after this manner: the owners have two thirds and the men one third; this one is divided into so many shares as there are men in the ship. [1723] 1954 INNIS 152 One or two ships from Barnstaple and Bideford continue to allow their company's [crew's] shares. 1881 RAE 19–20 It is found that by such means they are debauched, neglecting their labor, and poor ill-governed men not only spend most part of their *shares* before they come home upon which the life and maintenance of their wives and children depend. 1927 DOYLE (ed) 65 "Three Devils for Fish": Saying this is the summer we'll all get our share. 1933 *Nfld Royal Commission Report* 103 In cases where the vessel is owned and operated by an individual fisherman, the latter is responsible for obtaining the necessary outfit from the merchant, including salt for the entire catch and provisions for the crew. The value of the catch is then divided into two, one half being allotted to the vessel (i.e. to the captain, or owner), the other half being equally distributed among the crew. In the latter half, one share goes to the captain. Thus, in the case of a vessel carrying 20 men, exclusive of the captain, the latter received ½ + 1/42 of the total value of the catch, out of which he must square accounts with the merchant, while each of the men receives 1/42 of the value of the catch. 1937 *Seafisheries of Nfld* 75–6 The voyages are shared in almost every conceivable way, but the system for shore fishermen is usually two-thirds. . .of the voyage between the sharemen and one-third for the owner. In some cases everyone shares alike and assumes proportionate responsibility for the cost of the outfit. In such case the owner of the fishing gear, i.e. traps, boats, engines, fishing rooms, etc., is allowed a full share or may be a share and a quarter, or half, for the use of his property [etc, etc]. 1964 BLONDAHL (ed) 75 "The Sealers' Song": His crew of bully northern men can handle gaff or gun, / To get their 'share' they'll risk and dare and think it all great fun. T 100/2–64 If the voyage, we'll say, turned out a thousand dollars, well the skipper took his share an' a share for the ship, an' the other seven or eight shares was divided up with the men. Now whatever that come to for each man, that's what they got for the summer. If they got no fish they got nothing. 1975 LEYTON 35 I went trapping after that, fishing with the Farrells. . . When you'd get up to man's age you'd get a full share.

2 Phr *on shares*: arrangement by which member of a fishing or trapping crew receives a proportion of the value of the catch rather than wages.

[1749] 1954 INNIS 152 All ships and boats. . .are upon certain wages and not upon shares. . . Some give a premium upon every thousand of fish to encourage their men to industry, who keep an account of every fish they catch. [1770] 1792 CARTWRIGHT i, 46 These men are engaged on, what is called, the shares; that is, they find their own provisions, and we furnish them with nets, &c. for the loan of which, we receive one half the produce of their labour; and, the other half, they engage to sell us at a stipulated price. [1771] ibid 146 Guy and his crew (who had engaged to fish for us this summer on the shares) having already suffered extremely for want of baits. . .I proposed to them to cancel the former agreement, and to engage them on wages. 1866 WILSON 212 Some of the fishermen are not engaged for wages, but are on shares, and are said to *cut their tails*; which means that they cut a piece from the tail of the fish as soon as it is taken out of the water, by which the man's fish is known from the rest. Of this fish one half is his, as wages, and the other half belongs to the planter for the supplies. 1914 WALLACE 19 Bob thinks a wonderful lot o' Emily. He be only sixteen then, but a rare big an' stalwart lad for his years, an' unbeknown t' Richard an' his ma he goes t' Douglas Campbell, an' says t' Douglas, an' he lets he work th' Big Hill trail on shares th' winter. 1975 BUTLER 33 We then proceeded to Paradise and engaged in the cod-trap fishery on a full share basis as I had my own trap skiff and engine.

3 Comb **share man**: see SHAREMAN.

share money: cash earned from shared profits of a fishing voyage.

1853 SABINE 40 The vessels commonly left England in March and returned in September; the fishermen passing their winters at home, idly spending their summer's earnings, or 'share-money.'

share v *DC* ~ esp Nfld (1964). See also SHARE n. To divide among owner and crew the value of the catch taken in a fishing or sealing voyage after deducting the expenses of the enterprise.

[1877] 1898 *Nfld Law Reports* 148 The evidence, as I understand its effect, also established, that the men regularly engaged in a cod-seine boat as its permanent crew shared half the catch of the boat in proportion to their number. 1936 SMITH 67 The Captain and men were in good spirits, homeward bound with 26,000 prime young harps on board, and we arrived at Job Bros all well, where we discharged our cargo and shared $67.00 a man for the voyage. 1955 DOYLE (ed) 11 "A Noble Fleet of Sealers": And now they're back in old St John's, / A-sharing out the Flippers. 1960 FUDGE 7 About fourteen hundred quintals were shared by [me and my] dory mate, about $220 each, being the highest dory in the share.

shareman n *OED* share sb³ 6 ~ man (1901), *DAE* ~¹ 4 (1687), *DC* esp Nfld (1820–) for sense 1.

1 Member of a fishing crew who receives a stipulated proportion of the profits of a voyage rather than wages.

[1810] 1971 ANSPACH 32 Among the servants employed in this Bay, the number of sharemen is considerable. 1849 [FEILD] 60 Two Englishmen are also with them this summer [in Labrador], as sharemen; in the winter they go a-furring. [1851] 1954 INNIS 402 The men who come from Jersey are found everything, and a free passage out and home again. Six boats and twelve men are employed as sharemen, and get one third of the fish they take, and one third of the oil. [1888] 1897 *Nfld Law Reports* 371 The plaintiff in the court below, was really not engaged as a servant on wages, but as a shareman in the fishing voyage. 1900 PROWSE [Appendix] 92 Any person who shall enter into a contract in writing, to be signed by both parties or their agents. . .for the performance of any duty within colony of Newfoundland as fisherman, shoreman, or shareman, and shall fail or refuse to perform such duty without showing sufficient cause. Penalty. . . 1937 *Seafisheries of Nfld* 75 Sharemen are usually paid with a proportional part of the realized value of the fish and oil secured. The shareman's part of the proceeds of the voyage varies according to the terms of his engagement and the class of fishing in which he is employed. [1959] 1965 PEACOCK (ed) iii, 937 "The Loss of the *Barbara Ann [Rodney]*": Five sharemen were on board of the boat and fished out from the bay, / And when the season ended they prepared to sail away. [1961] 1965 ibid i, 114 "A Crowd of Bold Sharemen": We said to our skipper, 'What do you expect, / For us to go fulling all the puncheons on deck, / Go home in the fall, hoist 'em out on your wharf, / And then you will tell us we can't claim our part / As a crowd of bold sharemen.' T 40/1–64 He was what they call a shareman, gettin' this ten [quintals] out o' the hundred. Very hard to live in them days. Get nothing but the fish, you know. T 43–64 The merchants used to supply the owner, and we used to be sharemen, see, an' the owner takes half an' gives us half. That would leave you with half a share, of course. T 175/7–65 But that's how she was—half went for the traps, an' the schooner, an' then the other half was divided up among the sharemen. Ibid Some fellers just never considered the skipper man—what he was up against; how much time he put in in the twine loft, when perhaps the shareman, when he was finished he was free to go on an' make another dollar. 1975 BUTLER 60 Servants who went fishing for the merchant were sharemen. That is, the owner supplied the boat, equipment and food and the men were paid shares of the fish caught. The value of the fish caught was divided between the owner of the boat and the crew. The owner would take half and the crew half; hence the name sharemen.

2 Phr *come/go shareman*: to sign on as member of a fishing crew in return for a share in the profits of the voyage.

1957 *Evening Telegram* 6 Aug I wonder would he come shareman with me? T 100/2–64 When you go fishin' you go shareman—you get your share o' fish. 1966 SCAMMELL 39 Lige lived in a nearby house with his old mother and went shareman with them every year.

sharoosed p ppl also **sharooshed, sharoused**. Cp DINNEEN searbhas 'disgust. . .thoroughly displeased with.' Disgusted, surprised.

1925 *Dial Notes* v, 341 Sharooshed—taken aback; surprised; also disappointed; disgusted. 1955 ENGLISH 36 Sharoused—nonplussed. 1968 DILLON 152 His wife must be some sharoosed when it all come out.

shaugraun n DINNEEN seachrán 'wandering, straying,' JOYCE ~ n: be on the shaugraun. Wandering condition; drifting state; a drinking spree. Cp WALK (AROUND).

1955 ENGLISH 36 ~ a vagabond state. P 159–75 ~ a drunk. 1968 DILLON 153 Out of work, doing nothing: Girl, he's gone on the shogarawn. [They] are all now on the shogarawn.

shaul n also **shall, shawl** *EDD* ~ sb 'husk' D. Shell or husk.

1895 *J A Folklore* viii, 37 Shall—a husk, the case of seeds. 1971 NOSEWORTHY 242 Shawls—the outer covering of oats.

shaul v also **shall, shaw*** [ʃɑː] *EDD* ~ v 'to shell' W So Ir. To remove a husk.

1895 *J A Folklore* viii, 37 Shall—[to hull] strawberries and such fruit. P 97–67 To shaw the bakeapples.

shaves* n pl also **shavs*** *EDD* shav(e)s. The shafts of a horse-drawn sled or other vehicle.

P 269–64 Shavs—shafts, as on a wagon. P 5–67 [When using a horse with the hand-slide] the steerin' stick, haulin' rope, traces and bridle gave way to shaves between which was the horse with its harness attached to them.

shavings n pl Thin pieces of kindling wood or 'splits' shaved with a knife so that curls of wood remain attached to the side; CHOVY*.

1924 ENGLAND 54 De ropes gets grasey-like, draggin' swiles, an' you make shavin's off y'r gaff sticks, an' cut strips o' swile-fat an' let 'em drip on de shavin's. Dem burns like de hobs o' hell. P 130–67 ~ A split, a small piece of wood, that has shavings attached to one side. C 71–126 ~ A small piece of wood about a foot long and ½ in. thick. On this stick bristles are cut with a knife. 1975 GUY 95 The kitchen stove was the only source of heat in the house. It was allowed to die out at night and was relit each morning with splits and shavings.

shayt See SHEATH.

she pro *EDD* ~ 3 s cties and *So & Do Notes & Queries* vi, for sense 2. See also HE.

1 A substitute word, under strong stress, for various objects and mechanical contrivances.

1895 *J A Folklore* viii, 32 Every object is spoken of as either masculine or feminine, and has either 'he' or 'she' applied to it. [1929] MCCAWLEY 24 "My Son Jarge": And now the wind she's blowing strong, / And I wonder what's keeping my son Jarge so long. 1931 *Am Speech* vi, 291 'She' is as often used in the same

indefinite sense [as 'he'], for example: 'Put she in a bag,' referring to a struggling fish. P 148–64 Of a stopped watch: 'I'll break she up one of these days.' P 148–75 After completing a difficult repair job, an expression of satisfaction: 'That's she.' 1977 *Nfld Qtly* Winter, p. 17 But the first hour we hauled in the log, and he registered three miles. So the next hour we hauled him in again, and she's got another three miles. . . We done that for three hours.

2 A feminine substitute word uttered with strong stress after any verb (including *be*) or preposition.

[1875] 1887 *Fisheries of U S* Sec iv, p. 19 'I's took no notice to she.' 1904 *Harper's* cviii, 858 'I 'low *I'd* know where she were to, an *I* were skipper o' she!' 1964 BLONDAHL (ed) 111 "Down by Jim Long's Stage": Young man you wants me daughter / But you never will have she! T 22–64 And that girl, they never found—we never found she that night. 1965 LEACH (ed) 75 "Bold Princess Royal": She ripped him and she stripped him till she tore him in three, / Because he had murdered her baby and she. 1979 POTTLE 14 'Don't vote for she. She's not for he.'

3 Comb **she-moon**: crescent-shaped moon in a horizontal position, believed to be a weather sign; cp HE-MOON.

C 75–132 A moon upside down was called a 'she' moon which was a sign of fine weather. P 123–75 When it was lyin 'flat on its back' the moon was called a 'she-moon.'

she var: balsam fir. See also MAIDEN FIR and VAR.

C 66–10 In the spring of the year you need a cleaning out. The best thing is to get the tops of the 'she var' or female fir tree and boil them and drink the juice.

shears n pl Cp *OED* shear sb[1] 4 'device used. . .for raising heavy gear, consisting of two (or more) sloping poles fastened at top.'

1 Sloping poles on which nets are hung to dry; cp GALLOWS.

[1774] 1792 CARTWRIGHT ii, 42 The nets which were on shore were put upon shears. [1776] ibid ii, 159 I went to the tickle and tried for fish, but could not catch any. Sheers were set up for the nets, and the snow thrown off them.

2 Heavy logs or 'shores' placed crosswise as support for elevated platform or 'flake' on which fish are dried.

P 269–64 ~ pieces of wood four inches in diameter upon which are set the beams when building a flake. They are crossed like an *X*, and set in the ground.

3 Stout timbers fastened under the bowsprit of a sealing vessel to support men pushing ice-pans to clear a passage for the ship (1972 SANGER 240); RAMS, **shearstick**.

1937 DEVINE 39 ~ Long sticks extending from the bow of a sealing vessel lashed under the bowsprit, to afford a footing to the sealers for poking pans of ice out of the ship's way.

4 Comb **shearstick**: see sense 3 above.

1924 ENGLAND 153 Shearsticks an' rams at de bows!

sheath n also **shade***, **shayt**, **sheet**. Cp *OED* ~
1 'case or covering of sword, dagger, knife, etc,'
7 ~ -knife 'dagger-like knife.'

1 An eight-inch (20.3 cm) leather case in which
sealer keeps his knife, hung at the side by a
leather strap slung crosswise over the shoulder or
fastened around the waist (P 245–79).

1905 MURPHY (ed) 18 "The Fisherman's Son": His
belt and sheath he has girded on, / And his tow rope
slung behind him.

2 Comb **sheath knife, shade*** ~ , **shayt*** ~ ,
shaything ~ , **sheet** ~ ['ʃɛɪdn̩ naɪf]: stout knife
with a broad, thin, curved blade five or six inches
(12.7–15.2 cm) in length, used to remove the
skin and blubber of seals; SCULPING KNIFE.

1871 *Zoologist* vi, 2546 A knife called a *sheath*-knife,
and carried in the waist-belt, is generally used for
sculping seals. 1905 MURPHY (ed) 13 "Died on the Ice
Floe": While the keen, glittering sheath knives soon
gave / Them the 'scurp' they required for their 'tows.'
1924 ENGLAND 185 At times, when no killing offered,
some of the men would drive a couple of 'sheet knives'
a few paces apart in the filthy, splintered deck, and
with little circlets of rope would play ring toss. Ibid 233
Our belt, skin boots an' shaythin' knife, / Our piper
and our pan. P 130–67 Shadin' knife. Wooden handled
knife having a six-inch blade carried to the ice by sealers. This knife was carried in a sheath. Also any knife
worn in a sheath. P 148–67 A big shade knife.

sheathe v [ʃeɪð] *OED* ~ 5 a (often sheath) 'to
cover (a ship) with a sheathing of metal.' To
strengthen the hull of a sealing vessel against
pressure of ice with a protective layer of hard
wood.

1883 SHEA 10 The steamers are from three to six
hundred tons burthen—wood built, full timbered, with
hold beams, heavily planked, sheathed, and thoroughly equipped to endure severe trials in the ice floes.
1936 SMITH 71 I said that we had a good chance of getting there, and securing the berths, as our vessel was a
good sailor, and sheathed with greenheart, a good
thing should we meet any drift ice. T 141/60–65² He had
her measured and runned her a summer fishing, and he
had his birch sheathin' sawed here, and sheathed her.
And he runned her sixteen springs to the ice.

sheathing vbl n Cp *OED* ~ 2 'protective layer on
the outside of the bottom of a wooden ship.' Casing of hard wood placed on the hull of a sealing
vessel as protection against pressure of ice.

1873 *Maritime Mo* i, 249 The sheathing of the ships,
which has to stand the grinding of the ice floes, is carefully looked to. 1933 GREENE 54 Inside there were
great oak beams, bulkheads, and frames; the thick
sheathing of the sides was of the hardest, toughest
greenheart. The bows were solid, and all was bolted,
stiffened, and strengthened everywhere.

sheave v also **sheeve** [ʃiːv, ʃeˑɪv] *OED* ~ v²
(1611–); *EDD* v² D. (a) In rowing a boat, to hold
one or both oars in the water to stop, turn or

reverse direction; to back water; BELAY; (b) to
reverse (ship's) engines; to row backwards.

1896 *Dial Notes* i, 381 ~ : to hold water with the oar
to stop the boat or turn more quickly. 1924 ENGLAND
147 Still de engineer try to sheeve [back-water]. Can't
strike de cap'n of a ship, ye know. 1937 DEVINE 43 ~
To 'back water' in rowing a boat. T 70–64¹ An' by an'
by she hove in sight again. A man sot forrard, facin'
forrard, sheavin' the paddles. T 393/5–67 Not my first
time goin' down the shore in the morning, an' by an' by
I'd be sheavin' instead o' rowin'. A yell 'd come out o'
my father: 'Keep your paddles out o' the water, an'
row! Never mind sheavin' astern!' Q 71–10 Sheeve: to
turn a boat by holding one oar firmly in the water or
lifting it out and pulling on the other oar. P 29–74 ~ To
row backwards, but not turn the boat around in the
process.

shebeen n also **sheebeen, sheveen*** [ʃiːˈbiːn,
ʃiːˈviːn] DINNEEN síbín, JOYCE ~ 320, *EDD* 1 Sc
Ir I Ma, hence ~ keeper Ir.

1 Unlicensed place where illicit liquor is sold.

1886 *Colonist Christmas No* 11 Peggy Rose kept a
snug sheebeen at Twenty-mile Pond, on which was
read the following: 'I've trusted many to my sorrow. /
Pay to-day and trust tomorrow.' 1891 *Holly Branch* 19
But shebeens, and they are plenty, should be rooted
out pell mell. [1900 OLIVER & BURKE] 61 "Topsail
Volunteers": And we have the proper bugles boys, /
To smell out a shebeen. 1909 BROWNE 260 Batteau in
former years had an unsavory reputation for 'Shee-
beens' (places where liquor was sold surreptitiously).
[1929] 1949 ENGLISH 115 'Sheebeen' is an unlicensed
liquor tavern. T 342/6–67² You had five
shebeens—that's the place where they get a drink early
in the morning—forty water grog they used to call it.
1968 DILLON 153 Mag had a sheebeen up there for
years. C 71–93 ~ , sheveen—a word used by the older
residents of Salmonier to mean a house which contained smuggled liquor.

2 Comb **shebeen keeper**: owner of a 'shebeen';
SHEBEENER.

1975 *Globe & Mail* 22 Nov, p. 35 But the selection
[of St John's subjects treated in the book] seems arbitrary. Why not, instead, lawyers and shebeen-keepers?

sheebeener n Owner of an unlicensed place
where illicit liquor is sold; boot-legger; SHEBEEN
KEEPER.

[1929] 1979 *Evening Telegram* 14 Feb, p. 9 Sergeant
Stapleton of the local Constabulary, during the past
week, made a raid on a suspected sheebeener in St
John's and seized over 100 bottles of liquor.

sheebeen See SHEBEEN.

sheep n See GOAT RUBBER.

sheer¹ v Cp *OED* ~ v² naut for all senses, esp 2
(1816 quot) for sense 1.

1 To swing a boat (by a length of rope) into a
desired position.

1977 BUTLER 28 When the rope was all out we could

shear the dories in the shelter of a little point of land and reach shore.

2 To direct one's way around an obstacle.

1792 PULLING *MS* Aug Wells landed and sheered round the cliffs where the poor wounded Indians were hid and when he caught sight of them fired at them again and increased their wounds sufficiently even in his opinion.

3 To throw a 'cast-net' for caplin with a sweeping circular motion.

T 202/6–65 You take the ball an' put it in your mouth like that an' nip un, see. Take one hand on this side an' one hand on that side. An' you take them like that—sheer 'em; a big swing.

sheer² v   *OED* ~ v³ (1711 quot). In building a boat or vessel, to give the craft the correct curvature, or sheer, from bow to stern as measured in the side elevation.

T 43/8–64 Then you'd get what you call your gunnels put on, an' you sheer her. . . Sheerin' her meant that there was so much rise to give her forrards to bring her into proportion, and so much rise to give her aft down the counter, an' you'd bring that along suent on the timbers an' make sure that you had it equally alike on both sides. P 241–68 After the boat is timbered it is planked up from the garbits to the top plank. Now the boat is sheered.

sheering vbl n In fishing for caplin, throwing the 'cast-net' outwards with a sweeping, circular motion.

T 203/6–65 Take one hand on this side an' one hand on that side. An' you take them like that—sheer 'em; a big swing—we all call [it] sheerin'.

shee-shee See SISHY.

sheet¹ n   *NID* ~ ice. Attrib **sheet ice**: a stretch of flat, thin ice formed locally in an ice-floe, frequented by seals.

[1792 CARTWRIGHT *Gloss* i, xii Pan. A piece of ice of no determined size, but not very large; the large ones are called sheets of ice.] 1868 WHITE *MS Journal* 18 Apr Ship in sheet ice. 1873 CARROLL 21 When seals whelp they select sheet ice, they keep holes open through it to get to their young. [c1900] 1978 *RLS* 8, p. 24 ~ thin ice of one or two nights frost. 1922 *Sat Ev Post* 195, 2 Sep, p. 10 You'll see somethin' like seal runnin' now we've got down to the reg'lar sheet ice and no more slob! 1934 LOUNSBURY 12 The first field ice to appear is 'white' or 'northern slob' formed off Labrador in the early winter, but it is followed almost immediately by 'sheet' ice which is more dense and solid though not as thick. 1972 BROWN 57 Wes told Joe of his belief that the seals lay to the west on the sheet ice, and of his ill luck so far.

sheet² See SHEATH.

sheeter n   also **shader*** [ˈʃiˑətəɹ, ˈʃeˑitəɹ]. Young seal on 'sheet ice.'

T 398/9–67 An' they come down here in the evening an' want to know where they should see any shaders.

'Yes,' he says, 'there's thousands of 'em.' T 393/6–67 An' now this was the sheeters on th' ice in spring o' the year.

sheeve See SHEAVE.

sheila n   also **sheelagh, sheiler**. H HALPERT 'Ireland, Sheila and Newfoundland,' in *Ireland and Nfld* (1977), 147–72; W HONE *Every-Day Book* (1827) ii, 194–5: Sheelah, ~'s day; see BRUSH and PATRICK'S BRUSH for sense 2.

1 In folk legend, the wife, sister, housekeeper or acquaintance of St Patrick, patron saint of Ireland.

1819 ANSPACH 473 It is hardly in the power of any priest in the world to hinder an Irishman from getting gloriously drunk, if he is so inclined, on the whole of the 17th of March, as well as the next day in honour of Sheelagh, Saint Patrick's wife. 1829 *Newfoundlander* 26 Mar, pp. 2–3 Members of Benevolent Irish Society had dinner on March 17th. The company continued to retire, successively, until six o'clock on Sheelah's morning, at which hour, we understand, a few of the campaigners might have been seen, as usual, piously and patriotically employed in 'drowning the shamrock.' 1901 *Christmas Bells* 13 [The crew brought] her safe into the harbour of Placentia, after a thrilling experience, having been driven by the celebrated storm of Sheelah's Day to Indian Harbour, and just getting to anchorage before the veer of the wind to the northwest. C 68–20 Sheila's day is the day after St Patrick's Day, the eighteenth of March. C 73–98 Patty walks the shores around and Sheila follows in a long white gown. . . Sheila's gown apparently is a blanket of snow.

2 Comb **sheila's blush***, ~ **brush**; also **sheila**: fierce storm and heavy snowfall about the eighteenth of March; LINER; see also PATRICK'S BATCH, ~ BROOM, ~ BRUSH.

1923 CHAFE 21 About St Patrick's Day [the sealers] start, most of them waiting until after Sheilah's brush or the equinoxial gale has passed. 1924 ENGLAND 124 Perhaps the most memorable of those occasions was on the night of 'Sheila's Brush,' which is to say the 18th of March. Newfoundland has two 'brushes,' Patrick's and Sheila's; that is to say, storms supposed to be connected with the birthday of St Patrick and that of his wife. . . The word 'brush' is not always used, however; you will hear Newfoundlanders say: 'We have our Sheila dis time o' year.' 1957 *Evening Telegram* 20 Oct In the days when 600 fishing vessel crews put out their gear around the coasts of Newfoundland and Labrador and when 400 of them went to the ice, the sailors, fishermen and sealers all looked for. . .'Sheila's brush' about the time the sun crossed the Equator coming towards us. 1966 FARIS 48 These storms are termed 'St Patrick's Storms' until St Patrick's Day in March. The much less violent storms after that are called 'Sheila's Blush.' 1969 *Daily News* 12 Mar, p. 1 Don't worry, it's only Sheilagh's Brush. Nothing to worry about, that is. It doesn't mean another long extension of winter. C 69–2 When I was growing up and we didn't have a storm on or before Paddy's Day (called around home 'Patrick and Sheila') someone was sure to say 'Ha boy, we got it coming yet.' 1982 *Evening Telegram* 3 Apr, p.

33 You seem glad to be alive even if you have to wait for Sheila's Brush before we can safely say summer is just around the corner.

shell-bird n *DC* ~ (Nfld: 1770–). Merganser, esp lesser red-breasted merganser; shell-duck (*Mergus serrator serrator*).

[1770] 1792 CARTWRIGHT i, 4 Nor could I kill any thing but a single shellbird. 1842 JUKES ii, 78 There were several broods of shell-birds, of which we shot some. 1870 *Can Naturalist* v, 304 At early morning the [shell birds] fly out to sea in large flocks, but return to fresh water in the evening. 1907 TOWNSEND 324 'Shelldrake'; 'Shell-bird'. . .common summer resident along the coast and in the interior; more common transient visitor. 1937 DEVINE 62 [proverb] 'You can get only one shot at a Shell bird.' Meaning that if a Shell duck escapes your first attempt you will never see it more. Fishermen who have been stung by a merchant, and whose dealings are invited again, I have heard them say this. 1951 *Nfld & Lab Pilot* i, 220 Shellbird islet, 6 feet high, lies close northward of the southern entrance point of this cove. 1951 PETERS & BURLEIGH 129–30 Lesser Red-breasted Merganser. . . Local names: Shell Duck, Shell Bird. . . The 'Shell Duck' feeds mainly upon fish, but also upon various molluscs, crustaceans and aquatic insects. 1967 *Bk of Nfld* iii, 283 Shell bird (probably from its habit of feeding in shallow waters offshore or on mussel beds).

shem See SHIM.

shepherd n Comb **shepherd's purse**: pink lady's slipper (*Cypripedium acaule*) (1978 ROULEAU 93).

sherway See SHALLOWAY.

sheveen* See SHEBEEN.

shift v *OED* ~ v 6, 12; *EDD* 2, 1.
  1 To change one's clothing, boots, etc.
  1964 *Can Journ Ling* x, 42 Like Cloten they still shift clothes. T 84–64 I'm up there now—this is Saturday night, an' I was after shiftin', an' I had a hell of a job to get my clothes. T 253–66 Dress up in oil clothes or somethin' like that, an' shift your boots. T 398–67 He hauled his clothes in an' got shift an' dried.
  P 148–74[The hunting was so wet] I had to shift my tack. 1975 BUTLER 43 I empt out me rubbers, wrung out me socks—soakin' wet. Anyway, about twelve o'clock that night it moderated and we went aboard again. I never took off no clothes, never shifted.
  2 To move one's residence from one place to another.
  C 66–25 We shift down here, we lived down here alone, not one other soul in the place. C 71–90 She was born the year Uncle George shifted to Fogo. 1976 MATTHEWS 113 [He] was going all over saying this one wants to shift, that one wants to shift. All the time it was lies.

shift n *OED* ~ sb 9 obs exc dial; *EDD* 12 for sense 1.

  1 A change of clothing.
  T 187/90–65 The boss'd have clothes in there to deliver, an' take it from your wages. Every Saturday night he'd take this old [suit of clothes] an' carry it around the dump and heave it over, an' go in the fore-peak an' get another shift an' put on. C 71–122 She'd always say, make sure you take a clean shift of clothes with you.
  2 Phr *take a shift*: to move from one location to another; SHIFT v.
  1910 PRICHARD 110 No doubt in that year the herds 'took a shift,' as my men called it, as neither before nor since, within their experience, had there been such an invasion [by caribou] of the Terra Nova country.

shilling n Cp *DAE* ~ . In pre-Confederate Newfoundland, a silver coin worth twenty cents (P 245–54).
  P 167–67 She paid a shillin' for the package. 1978 *Evening Telegram* 29 July, p. 16 'I'm glad you said shillin',' said Mr English, 'there were no quarters in them times. That kind of money came in after Confederation. . . .a shillin' was 20 cents. . . God be with them times, if you had a shillin' you could get two packages of Gem cigarettes for a shillin'.' 1980 *Evening Telegram* 22 Nov, p. 24 I wish I had a shilling for every seal that rode the ice [floes] passing the Groais Islands.

shim n also **shem**. Cp *OED* ~ sb² 2 [sort of hoe or plough] local (1723–); 5 'thin slip used to fill up a space' U S (1864–).
  1 A wooden implement like a spatula, used to strip the bark off trees in sheets.
  [1776] 1792 CARTWRIGHT ii, 183 This morning I manned four shims, and sent off two skiffs crews a rinding; they found but few, and got only thirty nitches. 1792 ibid *Gloss* i, xiv Shin [i.e. shim]. An instrument of wood, to take rinds off the trees. 1897 *J A Folklore* x, 209 ~ a bat-like instrument for taking the bark off trees. [c1900] 1978 *RLS* 8, 26 ~ chisel shaped piece of wood for taking off rinds. 1937 DEVINE 43 ~ A wooden sliver for peeling rinds off trees. T 36/8–64 You'd have what we used to call a shim, something like a slice, cut straight on the top side an' roundin' on the lower side—it would come right up to an edge, an' a handle on it about eight or nine inches long. You take that an' you shove it, with the sap in the tree, you'd shove it around the rine, an' the rine'd all cleave off o' the tree. T 141/68–65² You'd have a pork barrel stave called a shim, an' he'd be cut out like a little coal shovel; an' tapered away, an' he was a little bit rounding, see, so as the ends wouldn't hook, see, tear your rine. T 347/9–67 They made some sort of shims they used to call 'em, an' they took the rines off the big trees which they used for putting in store, spread out on the floor, when the fish was dry in the fall. C 75–146 ~ a handmade wooden tool [about] two feet long with a flat end. The bark on the tree was split first and then the shim inserted. The bark was then pried off.
  2 A pointed wooden implement used to pack moss in the chinks of a log-house.
  T 43/7–64 If you build a log house, winter house, they'd stop them with moss. You have to make a shim to stog the moss in—a thin piece of wood, you usually use a barrel stave, oak stave, that would take more

wear than soft wood. They use 'em in the lumber woods. 1974 MANNION 147 The abutting edges of the studs were 'stogged' or 'chintzed' with moss using a sharply pointed wooden implement called a 'shem.'

3 A wooden utensil for stirring or eating food; MUNDLE, SLICE.

P 148–65 A pine shim [was used] on ship to prepare and stir fish chowder made in big iron pot. M 68–16 The pot of stewed fish is placed in the center of the boat on the gang-plank. The crew sit around the pot and begin. Their spoons are called shims, which are wooden and made by the fishermen. P 143–74 The grub box [or bread box] was packed by one of the women. . .and contained gingerbread, a crock of molasses, sweet-bread, milk, butter, tea, sugar, flour, fatback for frying the fish, and hardbread, as well as certain utensils such as shims (wooden spoons for eating fish) and mugs for drinking tea.

4 A wedge.

1897 *J A Folklore* x, 209 Shem. In Newfoundland it is employed to denote a thin piece of wood placed between the timber and plank of a vessel, where the plank does not fit solidly. P 148–65 [He went to a shoemaker] when he wanted a shim or wedge inserted between the inner and outer sole of his shoe. P 241–68 The door [of the lobster pot] is kept in place by a small wooden stick called a shim. P 122–73 A shim [is] a piece of wood used by carpenter for purposes of blocking and levelling.

shimmick n Cp *EDD* shimmickar 'mean fellow' So. A despised person; a dissembler.

1895 *J A Folklore* viii, 39 ~ used on the west coast as a term of contempt for one who, born of English parents, attempts to conceal or deny his birth in Newfoundland. P 152–58 ~ coward.

shinnicked* p ppl Benumbed, paralysed with the cold, esp when accompanied by contraction of the muscles and a violent shivering (P 37); SCRAMMED.

P 115–56 'Are you cold?' 'Yes, I'm shinnicked.'

shinny v To jump from one ice-pan to another; COPY (P 213–55).

ship n Cp *OED* ~ sb[1] 1 (1622–) for sense 1; for combs. in sense 2: *DC* ~ fishery (1963), ~ room (1829–). See also FISHING SHIP; cp BOAT.

1 A vessel engaged in the English migratory fishery in Newfoundland, esp in the carrying of men and supplies for the season's enterprise and their shipment home with the catch; freq in place-names deriving from customary rights and practices of the migratory fishermen.

[1583] 1940 *Gilbert's Voyages & Enterprises* ii, 400 [Hayes' narrative] [As] they tooke their cocke boate to go aboord their own ship, it was overwhelmed in the sea. . . What became afterward of the poore Newlander, perhaps destitute of sayles and furniture sufficient to carry them home. . .God alone knoweth. 1613 *Willoughby Papers* 17a, 1/2 Here is a good beach and the fishing neare, to be assured of a good place to fish

and a beach, boats and stage may be worth more than one or two hundreth pounds yearely for a shipp. [1663] 1963 YONGE 58 The men in these voyages have no wages but are paid after this manner: The owners have two thirds and the men one third; this one third is divided into so many shares as there are men in the ship. [1705] 1895 PROWSE 251 Quantity of fish made by ships 18,000 qtls. [1794] 1968 THOMAS 174 I have heard of a Dog who was absent from a Ship on the Grand Bank for Two days, on the Third he return'd with a Hegdown in his mouth. [1811] 1965 *Am Speech* xl, 169 Precaution against the dreadful event of a fire in this Town requires that a facility of access to the Ships Coves should be preserved in the utmost possible degree. This is to give notice that all obstructions are expected to be removed. 1951 *Nfld & Lab Pilot* i, 109 Ship harbour is entered between Isaac point and Ship Harbour point. 1979 TIZZARD 323 One winter when I was very young some fishermen were going to the ships' run, the waters between New World Island and Black Island, to fish for turbot.

2 Comb **ship fisherman**: English fisherman engaged for a specified period in the migratory fishery in Newfoundland; cp SERVANT[1], SHAREMAN, WEST-COUNTRY(MAN).

[1674] 1895 PROWSE 191 [They argued that] the Trade could not support the charge of forts and a Governor; and that in winter the colony was defended by ice and in summer by the ship fishermen. 1895 ibid 275 In 1711 and 1712 the common danger had united the ship fishermen and the planters in arrangements for orderly government.

ship fishery: English migratory fishery in Newfoundland.

[1764] 1969 *Can Hist Rev* l, 152 The ship fishery is in a manner dropped or excluded, the country crowded with poor, idle, and the most disorderly people, who are neither good fishermen nor seamen. [1824] 1954 INNIS 320 Thus the ship fishery has diminished to little more than a name, the result of the two systems being last year the production of 750,000 quintals from the boat or island fishery while that of the ships made only 34,000 quintals. 1870 *Stewart's Qtly* iv, 137 But its main object was to perpetuate the old system of a ship-fishery from England, as a means of strengthening the navy of the kingdom.

ship(s) room: tract or parcel of land on the water-front of a cove or harbour from which English migratory fishermen conducted the cod-fishery; structures erected in such a place; ADMIRAL'S ROOM, FISHING ~ , ROOM.

[1693] 1793 REEVES ii [They shall have] liberty to go on shore on any part of *Newfoundland*, or any of the said islands, for the curing, salting, drying, and husbanding of their fish, and for making of oil, and to cut down wood and trees there for building and making or repairing of stages, ship-rooms. [1726] 1976 HEAD 73 The Ships that come here to fish upon the Banks, generally leave England in ffeb. & are in the Country some time in March, the first thing they doe is to Land their Stores, & make choice of a Stage & Flakes belonging to it, what they call a Ships Room. [1765] 1973 *Can Hist Rev* liv, 267 There are, or might be made, twenty convenient ship's rooms, and above that

number of ships have been known fishing there in one
summer. [1820] 1895 PROWSE 409 . . .extending from
the house and stores occupied. . .at the East end [of
Water Street, St John's] to the public Ships Room,
commonly called the *Western Ships Room*, at the West
end thereof. [1839] 1916 *Nfld Law Reports* 20 Thus all
those parts of the country which had at any time been
used as 'Ships-rooms' since the year 1685, were for
ever appropriated to the use of the fishing-ships; but a
permission to occupy and possess all the sea-coast, not
included in any of these ships-rooms, was distinctly
conceded to the resident inhabitants.

ship v   Cp *OED* ~ v 12 'to engage for service on
a ship' (1643–).

1 To engage a person for service as member of
a fishing or sealing crew; to agree to serve in a
crew.
[1791] 1902 *Christmas Bells* 12 [He was sentenced] to
leave the district, and all persons were forbidden from
shipping him. [1810] 1971 ANSPACH 2 This would make
the regulations more general and extend it to such persons though not *shipped* or *actually employed* in the
fishery, at the time of their desertion. 1842
BONNYCASTLE ii, 216 The farm-servants frequently go
to the seal-fishery, and are, with the other classes,
except amongst the higher grades, shipped, as it is
called; or in other words, have a paper to sign mutually
with the master, for the agreement as to time and wages. [1880] 1898 *Nfld Law Reports* 372 I as agent for the
plaintiffs agreed that the defendant and his brother
should be engaged as in previous years, the one as a
shipped servant on wages and the other as a shareman.
1895 PROWSE 278 All these 'youngsters' were shipped
for two summers and a winter. 1919 GRENFELL[2] 419
There's a girl down North I fancies, but I'm shipped to
a man here for the summer, and can't get away.
Wouldn't you just propose to her for me, and bring her
along as you comes South? 1936 SMITH 106 Having all
my crew [for the Labrador] agreed and shipped, eight
men and two girls. . . 1944 LAWTON & DEVINE 65 The
first summer he was married, he and his wife shipped
to a planter for that summer. [1951] 1965 PEACOCK
(ed) i, 105 "The Banks of Newfoundland": Most sad
was my misfortune in the year of 'sixty-three / When I
shipped on board for fishing there caught on a drunken
spree, / I shipped on board the *Eastern Light* as you
might understand / For to go out on the salty sea to the
Banks of Newfoundland. C 67–6 [of girls hired to cook
for a Labrador fishing crew] The first of May is Collar
Day. / When you're shipped you must obey. / When
you're tied you can't run away. P 72–74 The other three
men were known as 'shipped men' and their wages
were paid by the three sharemen regardless if the
fishing season was a success or not. 1976 CASHIN 64 A
trap crew came into service around the middle of May.
They were hired, or as we called it in those days, 'shipped,' for a period of two months or until August 5th or
10th.

2 To engage for domestic or other employment on land or in activities other than the
fishing enterprise; to agree to such service.
1842 JUKES i, 13–14 I engaged, or in his own language 'shipped' [him]. All domestic servants come to

be 'shipped.' Families are applied to to know whether
they want to 'ship' a housemaid or a cook. 1875
HOWLEY *MS Reminiscences* 61 He told me he had just
arrived from a foreign voyage as the men were being
shipped for the survey, and he concluded he would like
to try a trip ashore, so applied and was accepted. 1880
WHITE *MS Journal* 15 Nov [John Moore] shipped to E
White for 12 Months wages £23–0–0. 1896 *J A Folklore*
ix, 35 Girls coming to the mainland to hire as servants
will talk of shipping for three months, or whatever time
they propose to engage. 1937 DEVINE 43 ~ To employ
or be employed. From being used in connection with
employment at the fishery, the word has passed into
general use for any capacity, where a written agreement of service is made. P 266–64 ~ To sign contract to
work in woods for specified length of time. P 141–73 A
girl employed for household work was said to be 'shipped' to her employer.

3 To sell produce of the fishery, etc, to a merchant.
1846 TOCQUE 322 The cured cod-fish. . .are now
being shipped off to the merchants by the fishermen.
1957 *Nfld Qtly* Sep, p. 5 Ned Perry owes a big bill here
and if he ships all his fish to Penny's, Mr Stone'll stand
a poor chance of getting paid. P 54–63 The verb has
also been used for generations meaning to sell produce
of the country, e.g. 'Skipper Mark Chard shipped his
fish' (oil, seals, berries, etc) to Slade's. C 75–136 Ship is
used by Conche fishermen in referring to the selling of
salt fish to the merchant. The process involves taking
the dry fish from the store and bringing it to the merchant's store or to a schooner collecting fish for the
merchant. 1976 CASHIN 70 [He] was generally able to
obtain special prices from Bowring's, to whom we
nearly always shipped our fish. 1979 TIZZARD 295–6
[We] went to Twillingate to ship the following list of
codfish at Arthur Manuel Ltd. . .

4 Phr *ship green*: to stow cod-fish aboard a vessel salted but not dried (1925 *Dial Notes* v, 341).
See GREEN.
ship out: to cut branches off a tree or log;
LIMB, SHIVE*.
1937 DEVINE 43 ~ To *limb out* a tree. P 54–61 ~ to
cut off all its branches with an axe.

shipping vbl n Cp *DC* ~ paper Nfld (1964); see
also SHIP v. Attrib **shipping paper**: written agreement specifying terms of service of member of a
fishing crew or other person with whom a contract is made.
[1776] 1895 PROWSE 344 Agreement in writing with
fishermen obligatory. No advance to fishermen to be
more than half their wages—other half on return
home. Master must produce Shipping paper. 1866
WILSON 207–8 A written agreement is made which defines the work each [member of the shore crew] is to
perform. This agreement is called the shipping-paper.
[1885] 1897 *Nfld Law Reports* 100 Some of them were
employed in St John's and entered into their agreements or 'shipping papers' with Ellis on the premises of
the defendants. . .and there, upon the printed forms
supplied by the defendants, Ellis and these servants
executed their agreements. 1893 *Trade Review Christmas No* 13 A case is on record where the planter and

youngster could not, for a long time, agree on the usual terms, where the shipping paper stipulates £18 a year and *one* boot. 1937 DEVINE 43 In the old days, a 'Shipping Paper' was used for practically all seasonal employment by the planter or merchant: for fishermen, shipbuilders, maids, etc. 1977 BURSEY 57 [He] gave each of us a shipping paper, very similar to the shipping paper used for engaging men to work at the Labrador fishery.

shive* v To trim off (limbs of a conifer); LIMB (OUT).
P 41–68 The starrigans must be shived. C 75–146 Wattles are fence-rails—small trees shived out for fence-rails.

shivery a Comb **shivery aps**: aspen (*Populus tremuloides*) (P 94–57); APS.

shoal¹ n Cp *OED* ~ sb¹ 'a shallow' for sense 1; *DAE* ~ cod (1838–), cp *OED* ~ ground (1712) for combs. in sense 2.
1 Area of shallow water where fish (esp cod) and bait-fish frequent; BANK, GROUND, LEDGE.
1953 *Nfld & Lab Pilot* ii, 244 A number of shoals, with depths of from 12 to 20 fathoms over them. . .lie. . .offshore [including] Gull Island ground; Little Harbour bank, Ice ledge [etc]. M 69–6 Once in a while when it was calm, my older brother and I used to go off on the 'shoals' to fish for flat fish. The water was only about four or five feet deep, so we could see the fish on the bottom.
2 Comb **shoal cod**: cod-fish frequenting inshore waters; SHORE¹; ~ FISH.
1842 BONNYCASTLE i, 264 Gadus arenosus, shoal cod, are also inhabitants of these seas.
shoal ground: see sense 1 above.
1953 *Nfld & Lab Pilot* ii, 172 Shoal ground, with a depth of 7 fathoms over it, Creeper ledge, with a least depth of 11 fathoms over it, and Sly ledge, with a depth of 14 fathoms over it. T 70/1–64¹ [She] went right in the shoal ground gulch.

shoal² n *OED* ~ sb² 1 (1601–) for sense 1; 4 ~ net (Nfld: 1792).
1 A large number of fish (esp cod) or seals swimming in company while feeding or migrating; the migration of the fish or seals to inshore water; SCULL.
1620 WHITBOURNE 35 They may imploy themselves all the time that there is good to be done in fishing in that trade onely, and betweene the faile of the Shoales of fish, they may build houses and other necessarie things. [1766] 1971 BANKS 145 The Seals who Come in Shoals finding themselves Stopd by the tight net Crowd to it trying to find some way of getting on in the mean time the fishermen Draw tight the second net by which they are inclosd in a pound the Second Shoal of Seals are stopd by the second net & securd by the third & so they Proceed till they have filld all their nets or taken all the Seals that Come through that Passage which are Easily Drawn ashore from the Pounds by a little Seine made for the Purpose. 1792 CARTWRIGHT *Gloss* i, xiv

A number of seals or fish being in company, are called a *shoal*. I presume the term arose, from the breaking of the water among them, appearing like the rippling of shoaly ground. 1792 ibid iii, [4] "Labrador: A Poetical Epistle": The Codfish now in shoals come on the coast, / (A Fish'ry this, our Nation's chiefest boast). 1842 BONNYCASTLE i, 267 A capelin school, schule, or shoal, is eagerly looked for as the real commencement of the cod fishery. 1863 HIND ii, 224 The fish which supply the Straits and the Labrador fisheries consist for the most part of two large shoals, one of which, entering the Gulf off Cape Ray in April or May, passes through the Straits down the Labrador shore.
2 A mass of floating ice.
1712 *West-India Merchant* 8 For lying furthest S as I hinted already, their Seas are clear of Ice at least six Weeks before ours, where the Shoals of Ice continue many times till the beginning of *May*. 1814 KOHLMEISTER & KMOCH 46 The ice being drawn towards them with great force, the largest shoals are carried under water, and thrown up again, broken into numerous fragments.
3 Comb **shoal net**: number of nets placed together to trap seals swimming near the shore; FRAME, STOPPER.
[1770] 1792 CARTWRIGHT i, 64 The people could not visit more than half their nets. The whole consist of twelve shoal nets, of forty fathoms by two; and three stoppers, of a hundred and thirty fathoms by six. [1774] ibid ii, 30 The sealers put out a shoal-net at the head of White-Bear Sound.

shoal a Of a vessel, having a shallow draught.
T 455–67² She measured twenty tons, but she was a shoal boat, understand; she didn't measure like a schooner because she's not deep.

shoar See SHORE².

shocking intens *OED* ~ ppl a 4 b (1831–); *EDD* 2. Very; extremely.
1850 [FEILD] 47 [The wolves] are shocking fierce and dangerous entirely. 1863 MORETON 33 ~ used as [superlative], as 'a shocking fine day.' 1920 GRENFELL & SPALDING 62 They do be shockin' hard on us poor sailors. 1924 ENGLAND 225 Again it would be 'man-murderin' wid starm,' and 'freezin' gert guns, shockin' cold, b'y.' 1938 ENGLISH 118 The women of the house were somewhat surprised at seeing Mr Thorne around at such an early hour, and thought he must be 'Shocking fond of salmon and trout.' C 75–134 Shockin' dear: very expensive.

shoe v Cp *EDD* ~ sb 10 (4) shoe the old mare Ir for sense 2.
1 To fit strips of leather or sinew to frame of snowshoe.
[1918–19] GORDON 46 It was quite impossible to think of stirring out, so George and I set to work on various little jobs that needed to be done, such as shoeing snow-shoes, mending clothes, etc.
2 Comb **shoe the horse**: balancing game (1937 DEVINE 43).

shoo n Cp *OED* ~ int[1]. Person who orders people aside to clear space for performance of Christmas mumming play; cp ROOMER.

1973 WIDDOWSON 419 Even those mummers who perform the mumming plays behave as strangers in that they are usually preceded by 'fools' or 'the shoo' or other functionaries who have authority to clear the houses where the play is to be acted.

shoot[1] v *Cent* ~ 11; *Fisheries of U S* (1887), p. 448.

1 To place or set a net or fishing line in position in the water.

1792 CARTWRIGHT *Gloss* i, xi A seine is hauled, by shooting it, by degrees, out of a boat into the water, and hauling it on shore again by the two ends. 1865 CAMPBELL 86 Scrambled up again, and got down on the other side at a place where a boat was hauling caplin. They shot a seine in a rocky bay, and hauled it into the boat. P 9–73 The cod-seine. . .was used in shallow water about five or six fathom deep. It was shot (set) in a circular shape, so that the last end overboard could be brought near enough to the first end, so that both ends would be on board for hauling purposes. 1977 *Peopling of Nfld* 142 We'd use the nets—seal nets. They were pretty common, most everyone had them. We'd use them up in the bight in anywhere from 20 to 60 fathom of water. They were right on the bottom. Two nets (a fleet) and they would be shot out from shore straight. 1979 TIZZARD 289 Then the trawl was 'shot out,' with myself in the front of the boat, when I was big enough, rowing in whatever direction my father said; it didn't matter much just so long as it was 'shot' across the bight. Ibid 312 There was only one thing to do: pull the herring net with the herring in it into the punt. . .then carry it back and shoot it out.

2 Phr *shoot the witch's heart*: see WITCH.

shoot[2] v In boat-building, to put floor-boards in the forward and after parts of the craft (1969 *Nfld Qtly* July, p. 20).

T 396/7–67 He bulkheaded the boat—I can't say he put the ceiling in her, but he bulkheaded her, he shooted her, an' he done out the gangboards, put 'em all down, in one day.

shoot[1] n, usu pl Cp *OED* ~ sb[2] 'sheet' naut obs (1495–1633); ELMER 136 shoots 'floorboards' Sf. Flooring board in the forward and after parts of a boat (Q 67–78).

1969 *Nfld Qtly* July, p. 19 After shoots: boards nailed flat to permit standing in the rear of a boat. Ibid 20 Fore shoots: the boards nailed flat across the inside front part of a boat to permit standing.

shoot[2] n See CHUTE.

shooting vbl n Attrib **shooting stand**: in hunting for game, hiding place for marksman; GAZE.

[1771] 1792 CARTWRIGHT i, 111 We made a shooting-stand of snow at the South West point of this island.

shop See ROUGH SHOP.

shore[1] n Cp *OED* ~ sb[1] 1 'land bordering on the sea' etc (13..) for sense 1; for combs. in sense 2: cp *OED* 5 ~ fast naut (1867), *DC* ~ ice (1752–). Cp COAST n, INSHORE, LANDWASH.

1 The perimeter of the island of Newfoundland and Labrador marking the juncture of the marine resources of the region (birds, fish, seals, etc) with the coastal strip and its hinterland bordering the bays, coves, harbours and inlets, comprising the area of aboriginal and European settlement and fishery enterprise; particular stretches of coast-line, often with defining words: EASTER, FRENCH, NORTH(ERN), SOUTH(ERN), STRAIGHT, TREATY, WESTERN.

[1583] 1940 *Gilbert's Voyages & Enterprises* ii, 400 [Hayes' narrative] The Admirall fell upon a rocke on the larboord side by great oversight, in that the weather was faire, the rocke muche above water fast by the shore. [1663] 1963 YONGE 56 As soon as we resolve to fish here, the ship is all unrigged, and in the snow and cold all the men go into the woods to cut timber, fir, spruce, and birch being here plentiful. With this they build stages, flakes, cookroom, and houses. . . The stages are begun on the edge of the shore, and built out into the sea. [1675] 1895 PROWSE 192 That no Planter cut down any wood or inhabit within six miles of the shore. [c1756] 1933 GREENLEAF (ed) 236 "Wadham's Song": Then nor'west by west twelve miles or more, / There lies Round Head on Fogo's shore. 1863 PEDLEY 48 But the French were recognized as having the right of fishing concurrently with the English along certain portions of the shore, and the use of the shore so far as was needed for the prosecution of their fishery. 1866 WILSON 280 'I never was at St John's,' said our friend; 'but you must steer north-east seven leagues to Cape Chapeau Rouge, then east half south twenty-three leagues to Cape St Mary, then south-east about twenty-two leagues, and you will come to Cape Race, and St John's is on that shore.' 1912 *Nfld Qtly* Dec, p. 28 Although the shore is for the most part barren along this portion of the coast, the seas are full of cod-fish and thousands of men come annually to these parts to engage in the summer fishery. [1920] 1933 GREENLEAF (ed) 291 "The *Thorwaldsen*": The wreck is all that is left of you, / Washed high on a foreign strand, / That tells the fate of the gallant crew / On the shore of Newfoundland. [1929] ibid 250 "Change Islands Song": No sign of salmon on that shore; discouraging was the news; / No pirate money could be found, and not a fish for brewis. 1969 *Christmas Mumming in Nfld* 3 And the cod, in a unique phenomenon, detach enormous numbers of their deep sea populations each spring and summer, turning in pursuit of the tiny silvery caplin and other 'baitfish' on their annual roll, or 'scull,' towards the shore. 1976 WINSOR 95 As the woman at the head of the grave bent down to place her shovel of earth in the grave, the tall plume of her hat would fall over her face, as she exclaimed, 'This was never known before'; and as the woman at the foot of the grave placed her shovel of earth, the plume of her hat falling over her face, she would say, 'On this shore.' So they continued until the grave was filled, all the time repeating, 'This was never known before,' 'On this shore.'

2 Proverb *In a leaky punt, with a broken oar, / It's always best to hug the shore* (1895 *Christmas Review* 12).

the shore eats up the fog
1860 MULLOCK 41 Though in general [the fog] does not penetrate far inland, as the people say, 'the shore eats up the fog.'

3 Attrib, comb **shore boat**: any of the small undecked craft used in the coastal fishery; SKIFF, TRAP¹: ~ BOAT.
1842 BONNYCASTLE ii, 161 The little shore boat, with its simple apparatus, has settled the question already, as to whether a native and resident population cannot carry on the cod-fishery with less expenditure and more success than vessels from a distance, tossing and tumbling on the foggy and uneasy swells of the great banks.

shore boss: man (or woman) in charge of the processing of cod ashore (M 70–27).

shore cod(fish): see **shore fish**.
1826 *Edin New Phil J* i, 33 The shore-cod resembles most the cod in a healthy state on the coasts of Britain, and is that of which the greatest quantity is caught, owing to its being most conveniently taken: the back is of a dusky brown colour; the belly, silvery or yellowish, and the spots in general not remarkably distinct. 1941 SMALLWOOD 18 [advertisement] Exporters Shore and Labrador Codfish.

shore cod-fishery: see **shore fishery**.
1895 PROWSE 21 The shore codfishery, known amongst the French as '*La pêche sedentaire*,' was pursued [in the 17th c] very much in the same manner as it is carried on to-day. The boats went out before dawn, returned with their loads, the fish were thrown up at the stage heads, split, and salted.

shore crew: (a) members of a fishing crew who process the catch as it is landed; see SHOREMAN; (b) at the seal hunt, crewmen remaining aboard to work the vessel while the sealers are on the ice.
1866 WILSON 207 The shore crew are mostly females. The planter's wife is generally skipper of the shore crew. 1882 TALBOT 24 There were four or five persons, including one or two women, kept about the house and stage; these were called the shore crew, whose business it was to receive the fish at the stage-head from the boats, and put it through its various stages. 1924 ENGLAND 189 Pans heave and grumble apart. . . Yelling, the stabber-pole crew come running back and fall to work. Cooks, stewards, all the shore crew line the rails, shout advice. P 102–60 A shore crew would unload them with fish prongs on top of the stage head while the two lighter men called at the bunk house for breakfast. 1972 NEMEC 8 Each boat which was 20 to 30 feet in length carried a crew of four and in addition required a 'shorecrew' of two.

shore cure(d fish): cod-fish prepared for market with light application of salt and extended drying period. See also CURE, MERCHANTABLE, SPANISH FISH.

1947 TANNER ii, 758 The best cure is obtained from fish dried on the flakes when the weather has been fine enough to dry them thoroughly but not so fine as to burn them. The produce is known as 'shore-cured Labrador fish' and will be sold to the Newfoundland merchants for export. 1953 *Nfld Fish Develop Report* 59 The predominance of the 'shore-cure,' i.e. dried light-salted codfish, is evident. This. . .is the principal product of the traditional industry. T 175/7–65 There's different cures: what they call the shore cure, light salted—that had to be fairly good an' hard. 1969 HORWOOD 82 The traditional Newfoundland way of making fish inherited from the Bristol men, to whom salt was an expensive commodity, requires light salting, very careful handling, washing, pressing, and prolonged sun-drying to achieve the aromatic, amber perfection of a good 'shore cure.'

shore duck: (a) American common eider (*Somateria mollissima dresseri*); SHOREYER; (b) black guillemot (*Cepphus grylle atlantis*); PIGEON, SEA- ~ .
[1918–19] GORDON 75 Had a good feed of two shore ducks, sent down by Miss Bright from Spotted Islands. 1951 PETERS & BURLEIGH 115 This eider is the common 'shore duck,' and is the race which nests in our territory. . . When inhabitants of the outports speak of 'ducks' they usually mean eiders, for it is the most common duck on the coast. 1959 MCATEE 40 ~ Black Guillemot (Nfld., 'Labr.'). T 389–67² Was that kings or shore ducks? That was shore ducks, sir. There might have been a scattered king bird among 'em.

shore-fast: line and mooring attaching cod-trap or seal-net to the land.
[1772] 1792 CARTWRIGHT i, 231 We hauled the nets. . .we afterwards tightened the moorings, and fresh corked part of one of the nets. On the ebb the upper killick came home, which obliged me to cast off the shore-fast of the southernmost one, to prevent its being torn. 1936 SMITH 125 This was some job for two men, but we went out and started from the shorefast to take it in; the sweat was streaming from our foreheads as we hauled the trap in the boat. 1937 *Seafisheries of Nfld* 33 In the centre of one side there is an opening about six feet wide through which the leader passes into the [cod] trap for several feet. These traps are usually set with the free end of the leader fastened to the land by a line, known as a shore-fast. C 63–1 As soon as they could make their way through the ice in the late spring, the fishing schooners would race for Labrador to get the best trap berths. The first crew to put down their shorefast (a post that the trap leader was tied to) and fasten the leader to it was the crew that had that berth for the summer. 1967 FIRESTONE 89 The leader [of a cod trap]. . .its end is marked with a buoy and it is held to the landwash by a *shore fast*.

shore fish: (a) Atlantic cod (*Gadus morhua*) frequenting or migrating to coastal waters; (b) cod-fish prepared for market with light application of salt and extended drying period; see **shore cure** above.
1765 WILLIAMS 5 From the Shore Fish, you have Three Hogsheads of Oil to an Hundred Quintals: But from the Bank Fish you have but a small Quantity. [1811] 1954 INNIS 237 The shore fish are so dry and hor-

ney that we get only 8 ct. into a common hhd. 1842 BONNYCASTLE i, 264 In this town the bank-fish, or those caught on the banks, are supposed to be superior in quality to the shore-fish, or those caught near the coast. 1870 *Stewart's Qtly* iv (2), p. 15 So, too, the vast fish colonies of the Great Banks, at a considerable distance from the shores, differ from shore fish, being larger and finer. 1907 *Parson's Christmas Annual* 7 In the early part of the past century, the splendid new ship *General Wolfe*, owned by the above firm of George and James Kemp, of Poole, England and Carbonear, left the latter port. . .with a full cargo of shore fish. 1919 *FPU (Twillingate) Minutes* 27 Nov The Chairman remarked that Mr Ashbourne was paying eight and a quarter for Labrador fish and also saying that shore fish was on the move up. 1933 *Nfld Royal Commission Report* 106 The fish, when culled or valued according to quality, are divided into the following grades:- (1) Shore Fish (including Bank Fish), dry salted. (a) Choice. (b) Merchantable. (c) Madeira. (d) West India. 1937 *Seafisheries of Nfld* 47–8 Light Salted, Hard Dry Fish, known as Shore Fish. . . The Hard Dry Shore fish must be sound, with an even surface, thoroughly clean, not showing salt, well split and thoroughly hard dry. T 168/70–65 Shore fish, for to be merchable fish, it had to be reasonably thick, and show no signs of salt. Yellow cast. T 141–65[2] I ended up wi' six quintals o' fish. An' I remember it was six dollars a quintal, 'twas shore fish, too. 1976 CASHIN 69 We had to rely on our own judgment as to whether or not it would be a good day for the curing of shore fish.

shore fisherman: fisherman who operates in coastal waters near his community using nets, hook-and-line or traps.

1937 *Seafisheries of Nfld* 29 The gear most favoured by the Shore fishermen are cod-traps, cod-nets, hand lines, trawls and jiggers. 1960 FUDGE 42 [I] am now trying to influence our Government to build a fisherman's Bait Cooler here in Belleoram to supply our shore fishermen with sufficient bait supply all the year around. 1975 BUTLER 65 He supplied fishermen, boat owners and shore fishermen in a number of harbours in Placentia Bay.

shore fishery: fishery, esp for cod, prosecuted in inshore or coastal waters in small boats; SEDENTARY (FISHERY).

[1803] 1976 HEAD 222 They have always been successful [in the northern fishery] while the shore-fishery to the southward has frequently failed. 1809 *Naval Chron* xxi, 23 There is what is called the shore fishery; which is carried on by large open boats, called shallops, which go out and return nearly every day, and fish very near the shores: the fish which these boats take are small in size, well cured, and are, in general, the best. 1853 SABINE 32 Thus, as in all shore-fisheries, the fishermen always sleep at their own homes. 1882 TALBOT 30 This [price] applies, however, to the shore fishery, as the fishery in the bays and along the coast of Newfoundland is called. 1911 MCGRATH 129 The principal branch of the cod industry is what is known as the 'shore' fishery, that prosecuted directly from the coast of the Island by the thousands of seafarers settled in its countless coves and creeks. 1933 *Nfld Royal Commission Report* 99 The shore-fishery accounts on the aver-

age for three-quarters of the entire catch of Newfoundland. [Its] distinguishing features. . .are that it is an 'individual' fishery, i.e. that it is prosecuted by individual fishermen spread round the Island's 6,000 miles of coastline. 1978 *Evening Telegram* 2 Feb, p. 6 Over the past two decades [foreign fleets have fished] off our coastal waters to the point of nearly wiping out our shore fishery.

shore fishing: see **shore fishery**.

1868 *Royal Geog Soc* xxxviii, 263 All the fishing was 'shore fishing,' no such thing as 'bank fishing.' T 455–67[1] I fished then. Oh, shore fishing—handline. 1977 RUSSELL 18 Anyway, he's finished with the Labrador fishery and he's settled down to shore fishin' like the rest of us.

shore gang: see **shore crew** (b).

1925 *Dial Notes* v, 341 ~ Those of the crew left aboard.

shore herring: variety of the Atlantic herring (*Clupea harengus harengus*) which migrates periodically to coastal waters; see HERRING.

1883 HATTON & HARVEY 324 There are two varieties of herring taken on the shores of the island—the Bank (called also the Labrador) herring, and the Shore herring. . .the Bank being the full-grown fish, and measuring on an average thirteen and a half inches, while the Shore is eleven inches long.

shore ice: sea-ice which adheres to the coastline.

1887 *Colonist Christmas No* 13 When safely landed on the shore-ice, no time is lost in shifting the mails to the sleighs in waiting. 1916 HAWKES 27 The 'shore' ice, or ice which adheres to the land, and is often seen in spring after the ocean is clear of pack ice, is called *qai naq*. 1969 HORWOOD 84 When you travel by hopping from pan to pan over ice so small that the individual pieces will not bear your weight, you are 'copying over the ballycaters,' but only if it's shore ice, because a ballycater has to make along shore.

shore labrador: cod-fish caught in Labrador waters and prepared for market with light application of salt and extended drying period; see **shore cure** above, and cp LABRADOR.

1920 *FPU (Twillingate) Minutes* 18 Nov The Chairman read circular letter no. 12. . .stating shore Labrador was practically unsaleable.

shoreman: see SHOREMAN.

shore net: net used in coastal waters.

1974 *Federal Licensing Policy* 41 The [salmon] drift-net fishery started in the 1930's, when small 'skiffs' (single dory schooners) using cotton nets began stringing shore-nets together and 'drifting' through the inshore areas as much as 15 miles out during night hours.

shore plantation: water-front buildings and structures where fish are landed and cured; PLANTATION 2, ROOM.

1979 *Salt Water, Fresh Water* 56 He was the boss of the shore plantation, he stayed ashore and looked after the women.

shore punt: see **shore boat** above; PUNT.

1857 MOUNTAIN 6 They have other punts, called

'shore punts,' merely for the purpose of hauling the nets and bringing wood, &c.

shore seal: small non-migratory seal of coastal waters (*Phoca vitulina*); BAY SEAL (1826 *Edin New Phil J* 40).

1913 HOWLEY 27 The common Bay or shore seal. . .is that prettily marked or spotted animal. . .which frequents the bays and estuaries.

shore season: period when the cod-fishery in inshore or coastal waters is prosecuted in small craft; cp SEASON.

1787 PENNANT 45 The fishery is divided into two seasons: that on the shore, or the shore season, commences about the 20th of *April*, and ends about the 10th of *October*; the boats fish in from four to twenty fathoms water.

shore skipper: jocular term for a retired fisherman.

1979 NEMEC 271 Retired fishermen (or 'shore skippers' as they are sometimes occasionally referred to).

shore work: all the operations of processing and curing cod.

1972 MURRAY 51 Thus a skipper's wife had to have a keen weather sense for when the men were away, she was responsible for the direction of the 'shore work.'

shore² n   also **shoar**. Cp *OED* ~ sb³ 1 'prop or strut'; *EDD* sb² 'a support.'

1 A stout post set vertically or slanted in the ground to support a 'fishing-stage' or wharf.

[1663] 1963 YONGE 56 The stages are begun on the edge of the shore, and built out into the sea, a floor of round timber, supported with posts, and shores of great timber. [1711] 1895 PROWSE 272 [Regulations against] removing raffters, rinds, floorings, shoars, stakes. . . [1771] 1792 CARTWRIGHT i, 132 We loaded the shallop with posts and shores. 1819 ANSPACH 436 The broad flakes consist of a set of beams, supported by posts and shores, or stout pieces of timber standing perpendicularly under the beams. 1866 WILSON 205 These stage-posts are of different lengths, but usually from ten to fifteen feet, and are braced with shorter posts or shores. 1895 *J A Folklore* viii, 31 The inner [piles of a wharf], which are called *shores*. . . T 14/6–64 The main front of the wharf are strouters. The inside part of what they put on are generally shores. 1975 BUTLER 61 For the shores there'd be strouters. They'd be shorter, probably eight feet long, twelve feet long shores.

2 An upright post which supports house above ground level.

[1711] 1975 O'NEILL 56 In 1711 Capt Jos Crowe mentions Capt Arthur Holdsworth's house as 'standing upon stakes and shores.' 1853 *Ecclesiologist* xiv, 157 Sills are laid down consisting of chopped sticks, about eight inches at the small end, which, when chopped square, brings them about eight inches cube throughout; they are levelled, and kept there by shores driven well down in the ground. 1966 PHILBROOK 34 The houses [of Nippers Harbour] are on a foundation of wooden poles or 'shores' resting on bedrock, and occasionally must be replaced. T 411/4–67 Older people built their houses so close to the ground that this back

sill was never very easy to replace. An' indeed when the shores rotted off it [was] almost impossible to get them put back new. C 69–6 When I was diggin' holes for the shores (pillars) fer me new house, in the one place only two feet down, I felt hollow ground an' wouldn't dig no more. 1975 BUTLER 79 [To build a house] four straight logs would be laid in place as level as possible on wood shores or posts in the ground.

shoreman n   *OED* ~ 2 (Nfld: 169[8]–); *DAE* (1670–); *DC* Nfld (1771–) for sense 1, 1958 quot for sense 2.

1 Member of a fishing-crew who processes the catch on shore; cp CUT v: ~ -THROAT, HEADER, SALTER, SPLITTER; SHORE¹: ~ CREW.

[1663] 1963 YONGE 60 When the fishermen lade, or sometimes moor in the day, it's hard work for the shore men, so as they rest not above two hours in a night. [1698] CHILD 227 . . .there being employed in that Trade two hundred and fifty ships, which might carry about ten thousand seamen, fishermen and shoremen, as they usually call the younger persons, who were never before at Sea. [1749] 1755 DOUGLASS i, 293 After the fish are headed, boned, split, and salted, the shoremen deliver one half the weight. [1767] 1954 INNIS 186 I pay for my part of the shoremen, the rest of the crew [are] on the common lay of this place. [1777] 1976 HEAD 89 [advertisement] For Harbor-Grace in Newfoundland. The *Hannah and Lydia* of Cork, John Collins will be ready to sail the 10th of April. For passage apply to said Master at Cove. Fishermen, Shoremen, and Youngsters. 1792 CARTWRIGHT *Gloss* i, xiv Shoremen. The people who are employed on shore, to head, split, and salt the codfish. [1810] 1971 ANSPACH 21 [The fish] is brought home and immediately landed on their respective stages, after which they return to their fishing, leaving the curing of it to the Shore-men or people, generally the wives, children and other inmates of the owner of the craft. 1832 MCGREGOR i, 228 On the same platform, is the salt-house, in which there are one or more tables, with strong wooden stools for four important personages among the shoremen, distinguished by the expressive cognomens of cut-throat, header, splitter, and salter. [1892] 1896 *Consolidated Statutes of Nfld* 955 Any fisherman, shareman, shoreman, mechanical or other servant, who shall absent himself from his employer's service without leave. . . P 54–63 Shoreman. A fishing establishment employing about twelve or more producers would divide them in a fishing crew and a smaller shore crew, the latter remaining on the 'room' to 'put away' (split and salt) the 'voyage of fish' and, later, to 'make' (sun-dry) it.

2 Resident fisherman who prosecutes the fishery in coastal waters, usu adjacent to his community; cp LANDSMAN.

1895 PROWSE 492 All along our northern coast the catch of seals by shore men was the largest on record. 1924 ENGLAND 150 Now, sealin's a pure luxury, with engines to do ahl the work, an' with bunks, an' hot food. Pooh! It ain't a man's game at ahl, now! Why, even the shore men thinks they got to have motor boats. 1947 TANNER 748 'Shore-men' are thus either resident or transient. The floaters and planters never penetrate the interior or even pass out of sight of sea-water as do the liveyeres, T 169/70–65 [There'd be] schooners for the Labrador. An' then we'd have the shoremen besides, see, an' codtraps home here, an' the hook-and-line-men. T 141/67–65[2] A lot o' we fellers in our generations, we've become plantermen, and got ahead in good many cases better than what the shore-men did.

shoreyer n also **shorier** *DC* ~ Nfld (1958–); for the form, cp LIVYER. American common eider (*Somateria mollissima dresseri*); SHORE[1]: ~ DUCK.

1918 TOWNSEND 301 This duck which is locally known as *sea duck, laying duck, shoreyer, Eskimo duck, maynak*, and *metic*, is everywhere diminishing in numbers. 1958 HARRINGTON 167 [They] immediately loaded their guns and went after the saltwater ducks or 'shoriers.' 1967 *Bk of Nfld* iii, 282 Common Eider: Gam-birds (from the social meeting of whalers at sea and because this species gathers in large flocks); Shore-yer (because they frequent the shore).

shorier See SHOREYER.

short a
  Comb **short leader**: section of netting fastened to the landward side of the 'leader' of a cod-trap and fixed to the shore (Q 67–56).
  P 127–77 ~ When a trap leader is anchored to the shore, sometimes a piece of old netting is used between the landwash end of the leader and the shore. While this seems to save the main leader from being torn by the rough seas and the rocks, it also guides the fish to the main leader and thus into the trap.

shorten v Phr *shorten the baby*: to dress an infant in clothes coming down to the feet.
  P 108–80 'When are you going to shorten the baby?' Babies used to be dressed in long clothes, well beyond their feet. Then at a certain age it was shortened, that is, dressed in clothes which came only to the ankle.

shot n Cp *OED* ~ sb[1] 15 b [Pellets] 'used. . .as a dose to give a horse a temporary appearance of sound-windedness.' Phr *dose of shot*: pellets taken for an ailment.
  P 54–67 He was awakened by someone knocking on the outside door after he had gone to bed. Coming downstairs, he was confronted by a man. . .from 'The Big Hill,' who asked him 'ver a dose o' shot, t'kip me lights down—dey'm cum'n up.'
  3 Comb **shot box**: container for ammunition.
  1888 HOWLEY *MS Reminiscences* 25 After dinner Noel and I went down to our cache to leave some of our clothes and my shot box.

shoulder n
  Comb **shoulder bag**: bag carried when travel-ling in the woods and 'barrens.' (P 9–73).
  shoulder spell: (a) the distance a man can carry a burden without resting; (b) the burden carried; SPELL n.

1863 MORETON 30 'Two shoulder spells' is the dis-tance a man would ordinarily carry a burden on his shoulders, resting once in the midst. 1896 *J A Folklore* ix, 25 'How far did you carry that load?' 'Three shoul-der spells,' meaning as far as one could carry without resting more than three times. 1937 DEVINE 45 ~ As far as one can carry a load on the shoulder without stopping to rest. Also, the quantity that can be carried thus. 1971 NOSEWORTHY 242 ~ A load on the back. 1977 QUILLIAM 70 A shoulder-spell is the distance a man can carry a backload of wood without taking a spell.
  shoulder turn: the amount, esp of wood, a man can carry on his back; TURN n.
  1966 PADDOCK 109 A shoulder turn of lumber [is the] amount of wood one can carry. Q 73–9 ~ As much wood as you can bring on your back.

shove n [ʃʌv]. Cooper's tool with sharp edge for making groove inside of barrel before insert-ing head (P 127–75).
  T 90–64 If the timber was uneven we would use a shove. He'd go around after champering, then with the shove, then with the croze an' you had her ready for the head. M 68–10 The shove is used to plane the inside edge of the newly-made barrel to a smooth, even sur-face before crosing can be done.

shovel n Secondary horn, shaped like a curved spade, on caribou antler.
  1909 SELOUS 123 This stag carried a truly magnifi-cent head of forty points. The number of points, though high, was, however, not its strongest claim to excellence, as the horns were palmated from base to tops, and the secondary 'shovels' above the brow ant-lers were extraordinarily broad and strong, as were all the points on the upper portion of the horns.

shovings n pl ['ʃʌvɨnz]. Cp *EDD* shove v[2] 2 'of plants: to germinate, to shoot.' Potato tubers as they come up through the soil, esp with *second* (Q 73–4).
  T 69–64 Our potatoes are only just beginnin' to come up through the ground now—the second shovins, we call it.

shovy* See CHOVY*.

show v imp JOYCE 37–8. Surrender an object to another person for inspection.
  1863 MORETON 36 ~ (Imperative) Give. 1937 DEVINE 45 ~ Used in the sense of 'Give it to me.' 'Let me see.' T 245/51–66 'I got a hard sum to do tonight,' she said. 'I don't know how I'm goin' a do un.' 'Show,' he said. 'Let me see un.' 1968 DILLON 153 Show me that knife, show. That's an awful thing to be foolin' around with. 1976 GUY 97 What old trash and rubbitch there do be washin' up on the beaches these days. . . Show here.

shroud n, usu pl also **shrouder**. Cp *OED* shroud 'part of the standing rigging of a ship,' and STROUTER. One of the vertical poles fixed to side of a fishing stage or wharf.

P 37 Shrouders. Bars on the side of a wharf by means of which one can climb up. P 195–67 ~s. Sticks placed at an angle from the floor of the ocean to the top of the stage head on which were fastened horizontal sticks to enable men to climb from the boat to the stage. 1979 TIZZARD 92–3 Railings were nailed across the shrouders—upright posts at the head of the wharf.

shuck n Cp *EDD* ~ sb² 1 'a husk, shell.'
1 The cloth covering or case of a feather mattress.
M 69–5 [To prepare for the wake] the room was cleaned from top to bottom. Even the feathers were thrown out of the bed 'shuck.' These feathers were washed and dried, then put back again into the 'shuck.'
2 The bottom or foot of a long rubber boot with the leg cut off; LUMP.
1972 MURRAY 112 For rough playing, especially 'in the beach,' 'shucks' (rubber waders cut off at the ankle) were favoured by many girls and boys.
3 Lumberman's leather mitten.
P 65–64 Skin shucks are skin mitts worn over woollen 'cuffs.' M 69–5 [He] is dressed in an old pair of lumberjack's pants, a lumberman's jacket, and he has skin shucks on his hands.
4 A shawl.
Q 73–4 Shawls [were] known as shucks.

shuck v Cp *EDD* ~ v¹ 2 'to slip. . .wriggle' esp s w cties. Of seals, to slip into the water or under the ice.
1924 ENGLAND 230 The bitch turned, slithered away. . .ducked into a rifter—'drawed de 'atch over 'er, an' shucked unner de pan.' 1925 *Dial Notes* v, 341 ~ To slip down in the water.

shuck int *EDD* ~ Bk, Do. Call to pigs.
1937 DEVINE 45 ~ A call to pigs repeated quickly and often.

shuff v [ʃʌf]. Cp *OED* shove, var shuff (16–18th c); *EDD* ~ v. To push, shove (1924 ENGLAND 320).
T 185–65 You take 'em an' shuff ['em] on, out birdin', out sealin'; used to always wear swanskin cuffs. T 141/59–65² There's a ladder there, an' we sticks up the ladder an' shuffed up the trap hatch an' gets up in the top loft. T 143–65² So he shuffed alongside and hove aboard a line. 1966 SCAMMELL 39 Lige, hold your prate and shuff her off. Heave the wheel, Andrew. Take the tiller, Sid, I've got to whip them new buoy ropes.

shuff n [ʃʌf]. Cp *EDD* ~ sb¹ 'gust of wind.' Breaking of the sea on the shore; a rough sea.
P 61–67 There's just a little shuff on tonight. P 187–73 [There's a] big shuff on—big sea around the shore. P 148–77 They had a rough time. There's a shuff on.

shute See CHUTE.

sick a *Cent* ~ 6 for sense 1; *EDD* turn sb 5 for comb ~ turn.

1 Pregnant; with child.
P 148–62 She's sick four months. T 245–66 'If our two women,' he said, 'are sick when we gets back,' he said, 'an they got a. . .one a boy an' th' other a girl,' he said, 'we'll marry 'em.'
2 Comb **sick turn**: an illness.
[1954] 1972 RUSSELL 12 I get so worried with you in there by yourself. Supposin' you had an accident, or a sick turn—or something?

sid* See SUD LINE.

side n For combs. in sense 2: *EDD* ~ sb¹ 1 (19) ~ lichts Sh I; *DC* ~ sleigh Nfld (1964).
1 Either of two vertical sections of netting forming the 'walls' of a cod-trap.
P 9–73 Most cod traps are made in four pieces. Two sides, the bottom and the leader. . . Side here means from the middle of the back to the side of the mouth.
2 Comb **side camp**: temporary shelter in the woods with a sloping roof and open front (P 148–60); BACK a: ~ TILT, LEAN-TO.
1971 CASEY 238 We had to build camps, side camps with a big fire lit between 'em.
side head: see HEAD n 4.
side lights: whiskers on side of face.
1893 *Trade Review Christmas No* 15 We arrived at LaManche at 8 p.m., and were boarded by twenty Cornish miners, in full forehead and side-lights, and giving off a full perfume of genuine Jamaica. 1925 *Dial Notes* v, 342 ~s. Hair on either cheek extending down to the lobe of the ear.
side rope, ~ **line**: length of rope along the top of each runner of a 'komatik,' used to secure load (P 80–78).
side sleigh: horse-drawn sled for winter use, occupants facing the side of the road; CATAMARAN.
1895 *J A Folklore* viii, 38 Catamaran [is used] in Newfoundland. . .to denote a wood-sled, and, when side sleighs were first introduced, applied to them. [1896] 1906 FRASER 181 But the Newfoundlanders have a conveyance of their own for winter—the side sleigh—which a Canadian described to me as anything but a comfortable vehicle, it being quite impossible to keep one's feet warm in it, though it had its advantages in the ease with which one can get off and on. 1960 *Daily News* 29 Aug, p. 4 A complete museum should have on display not only a catamaran but also a side sleigh, an old-fashioned dog-sled if one is to be found, a long cart, and although a few may still be found in use, a box-cart. M 67–17 Established 'cabmen,' who, with their horse-drawn 'victorias' and 'side-sleighs,' had enjoyed up to then, a monopoly in the field of hired transportation.
side stick: one of a number of beams fastened to sides of a sealing vessel to enable sealers to leave or re-join the ship in the ice-floes.
1922 *Sat Ev Post* 195, 2 Sep, p. 10 They had slid down the ropes to the side sticks, or horizontal rope-hung timbers, and were ready to spring. 1924 ENGLAND 159 Soon the skins were loaded, ghastly under torch flames; and the black-faced men came

swarming up the side sticks. 1936 SMITH 52 At 12.30 the order was given, and all hands were out with flagpoles and flags. You could jump on a whitecoat from the ship's sidesticks if you wished to do so. 1972 BROWN 35 'Side sticks'—the sort of primitive ladders that sealers used when going up and down over the sides.

side tilt: see **side camp** above; TILT.

1883 HOWLEY *MS Reminiscences* 30 We built two fine side tilts facing each other covered with birch bark and made a fire between which sufficed for both.

sideling a *EDD* ~ a 1. Of ground, sloping, inclining steeply.

M 71–39 A horse and cart was used to haul hay from the field. . . The thing to guard against was making the load 'lop-sided'—it would surely tip over at the 'sideling' places or on the rough spots.

siding vbl n Comb **siding axe**: axe used to chop or 'squat' two flat surfaces on a log.

T 393/6–67 This is what we call a siding axe; all those uprights is chopped—bevelled on that side, straight on this side.

sieve See CIVE.

sign n Cp *OED* ~ sb 7 'a token or indication'; *DAE* 1 b (1804–) for sense 1; JOYCE 323 for sense 3; *EDD* 2 (2) *signs on it* Ir, JOYCE 323 for phr in sense 4.

1 Evidence of the recent presence of an animal.

[1771] 1792 CARTWRIGHT i, 131 We saw but few signs of deer or black-bears; nor were there any vestiges of Indians. 1868 WHITE *MS Journal* 23 Apr 52 Men on ice returned no Sign of Seals. 1924 ENGLAND 320 ~ Indication of seals. 1968 DILLON 153 You'd never see a sign on 'im. 1972 BROWN 46 By March 26, there was just a 'sign' of seals. Scouting groups brought in fifteen pelts that day. P 13–74 A hunter might complain about the scarcity of rabbit-sign.

2 Quantity, number or amount of fish; appearance of migrating fish in coastal waters.

[1832] 1981 *Them Days* vi (4), p. 38 [Two seines out]. . .there appeared to be some signs this evening. 1895 *J A Folklore* viii, 35 This I have no doubt originated in the use of the term on the fishing grounds in something of its proper meaning. When, on reaching them and seeking spots where the fish were to be found, they first caught some, it afforded a sign of their presence. . . When they caught them in greater abundance, they spoke of it as 'a *good* sign of fish.' 1920 WALDO 161–2 'Poor sign fish' means that fish are scarce. 1921 *FPU (Twillingate) Minutes* 24 Feb In reference to trap berths [the letter recommended] leader and moorings on the rock instead of in the water until sign of fish. [1929] 1933 GREENLEAF (ed) 251 "Change Islands Song": The sign of fish got better, they thought it would be thick, / And they'd get it a great deal quicker, if they anchored in the Creek. 1936 SMITH 130 The ice cleared away on the 20th, and there was a sign of fish; all hands then set the traps, but the fish was not so plentiful. 1937 DEVINE 45 Sign of fish. Nothing is more

indirect than the ways of using this expression. A crew, just returned from quickly loading a boat where there was in fact plenty of fish to be caught, may report, 'Oh, yes, there was a *nice sign* of fish.' 1976 *Evening Telegram* 10 May, p. 4 A lobster fisherman in Manuels says there is 'a good sign of lobsters' this season. 1980 *Evening Telegram* 18 June, p. 6 Reports from around the province indicate few signs of cod, perhaps because the cod follow the caplin and the caplin haven't shown up yet, except on the Burin peninsula.

3 Portion of food; a small serving or quantity.

1895 *J A Folklore* viii, 35 One at table, being asked if he would have any more of a dish, replied 'Just a sign.' 1937 DEVINE 45 'Give me a *sign* of pudding,' might mean a plate full. C 70–10 An old gentleman told me recently a cure he said was sure for boils. You would just take a sign of soft soap and black molasses in the palm of your hand and mix it up. This mixture you would put on the boil by means of a cloth, to keep it in place. C 75–145 ~ Refers to a small quantity of tobacco, food, etc.

4 Phr *signs on, so signs*: consequently.

1968 DILLON 153 He bet the divil for the drink, signs on, he lived no time. . . She always tended on 'em hand and foot, so signs, they can't do a hand's turn for themselves. P 108–70 He was out late last night, and so signs he's sleepy this morning. 1979 *Evening Telegram* 9 June, p. 17 . . .now with himself all [asquish], so signs I got a brand new shirt and drawers up in the bottom drawer if he stops his wind [dies]. 1981 ibid 18 July, p. 10 So signs, when I die, all my close relatives will have a pot or two [of Southside Hills' clay] to pass on down to posterity.

sile See SEAL.

silk n

Comb **silk jay, silken** ~ : northern blue jay (*Cyanocitta cristata bromia*).

1870 *Can Naturalist* v, 158 A summer migrant, but not common. . .[the] 'Silken Jay.'

silk thread: fireweed (*Epilobium angustifolium*) (1956 ROULEAU 37).

silky a Comb **silky jay**: northern great grey shrike (*Lanius excubitor borealis*) (1959 MCATEE 57).

1891 PACKARD 415–16 Great Northern Shrike. Not common at Fort Chimo. Breeds there. Young, unable to fly more than a few rods, were taken by the hand at that place, June 30, 1884. Said to be common in the more southern portions, and there known as the 'Silky Jay.'

silver n *DC* ~ (Nfld: 1771, 1956) for sense 1; for combs. in sense 2: *DC* ~ fir 1 (1775–); fox 1 (1770–); ~ frost Maritimes (1828–), ~ hair (1861).

1 The red fox (*Vulpes fulvus*), in a colour variation with black fur interspersed with silver-grey ends.

[1771] 1792 CARTWRIGHT i, 91 I went down the river, where I observed. . .a brace of silvers. 1907

WALLACE 15 Good silvers are worth five hundred dollars cash in St John's. 1916 GRENFELL 27 Before night the whole three were safely home, and all the village knew that Tom Marvin had caught a silver. P 148–64 Silvers [are] grey foxes—we gets lots of money for these furs.

2 Comb **silver fir**: balsam fir (*Abies balsamea*). [1775] 1792 CARTWRIGHT ii, 58 [Porcupine] feed on nothing but rinds the whole winter. . .they prefer the silver-fir to all others. [1784] 1971 BANKS 444 Almost all kinds of garden stuff will grow there [Nain, or Nuninock] in very great perfection, but corn, I believe, will not ripen though it grows and ears well and no Pines, but Spruces, Silver Fir, Larch, Birch and Aspin. All grow large. 1861 DE BOILIEU 214 The trees I mostly observed were the black, white, and red spruce, larch, silver-fir, birch and aspen.

silver fox: see sense 1 above. [1770] 1792 CARTWRIGHT i, 76 On Niger Sound we saw a good silver fox. 1792 ibid *Gloss* i, xv ~ A black-fox, with white king-hairs dispersed on the back of it. 1905 DAVEY 42 The white, red, blue, and so-called 'silver' foxes are hunted for their skins, which command a good price in the European Market. 1956 CAMERON 27 The 'silver fox' is black with a white-tipped tail and a sprinkling of white hairs along the middle of the back.

silver frost: coating of ground, vegetation, etc, with ice, owing to precipitation at the freezing point; GLITTER, SILVER THAW. 1832 MCGREGOR i, 129 A phenomenon appears frequently during winter, known by the appellation of silver frost. When a fine misty rain takes place. . .the moment it rests on any substance, it adheres and freezes, incrusting every tree, shrub, or whatever else is exposed to the weather, with ice.

silver hair (fox): see sense 1 above. 1861 DE BOILIEU 76 Of the fox there are several species on the coast, but the valuable breed known as 'silver-hairs' are scarce. T 100/2–64 You get nine an' ten hundred dollars for a black fox. An' get about the same for a silver hair. T 391/3–67 But no ice foxes comes up now. Never see ne'er one. 'Tis all dark foxes now, red an' silver hairs. M 71–44 He was a wonderful man for catching fox, and he wanted to catch this fox one time, silver haired fox.

silver jar: ringed seal (*Phoca hispida*); see JAR[2]. 1977 *Inuit Land Use* 255 Then there's another lot of jar; they're all small, same ring—silver jars. They're way out—you get a lot at the *sina* [floe edge].

silver thaw: see SILVER THAW.

silver thaw n *OED* silver sb 21 ~ thaw (Nfld: 1860–); *DC* Atlantic Prov, B C 1, 2 (Nfld: 1770–; 1842–); SMYTH 626 'term for ice falling in large flakes from the sails and rigging, consequent on a frost followed suddenly by a thaw.' See also GLITTER, SILVER FROST.

1 A condition of the weather in which freezing rain deposits a coating of ice on exposed objects; the gradual deposit of ice on countryside, trees, etc, during a freezing rain. [1770] 1792 CARTWRIGHT i, 73 There was a silver

thaw in the morning, and it rained freely; very mild weather all the rest of the day. 1792 ibid *Gloss* i, xv ~ When it rains and freezes at the same time. [1822] 1928 CORMACK 83 While in this situation a silver thaw sometimes comes on, and the incrustation of the surface becomes too thick. 1893 *Trade Review Christmas No* 13 There is a tradition that our ancestors, who flocked to this country in such numbers in the beginning of the century, were induced to emigrate by the prospect of becoming immensely rich in a short time, by simply gathering money after a 'silver thaw.' It is very probable that this witticism originated in the humorous imagination of some droll Irishman when describing the country to his newly-arrived and uninitiated fellow-countrymen. 1897 *J A Folklore* x, 206 Glitter [is] used on the west coast to denote that peculiar phenomenon known generally through the northern part of America as 'a silver thaw'; that is, when fine rain falling meets near the earth a colder stratum of air and becomes congealed, forming a covering of ice upon every object. 1949 *Evening Telegram* 26 Feb, p. 3 Last night's silver thaw created slippery conditions and havoc in the pedestrian ranks this morning as early walkers skidded, slithered and went up-ended on their way to work. T 368/9–67 An' we had the silver thaw for a week from the first day we arrived.

2 The coating of ice deposited on exposed objects by freezing rain; in some contexts overlapping with sense 1. 1836 [WIX][2] 20 The country at this time presented an appearance quite different from that produced by the vegetation when affected by a moistness of the atmosphere which is afterwards operated upon by sudden frosts, and is improperly denominated here, a silver *thaw*. 1840 GOSSE 21 In Newfoundland it is by no means rare, where it is known by the name of 'silver thaw.' It is caused by rain descending when the stratum of air nearest the earth is below the temperature of 32°, and consequently freezing the instant it touches any object; the ice accumulates with every drop, until a thick transparent coating is formed. 1842 BONNYCASTLE i, 338 Another phenomenon, seldom seen in Canada, is the silver thaw, as it is called in Newfoundland. Rain in heavy torrents in February, accompanied by a low state of the thermometer near the earth, causes a regular deposition of ice round all the branches and twigs of the plants and trees. 1846 TOCQUE 101 'Silver thaw'. . .is produced by a shower of rain falling during a frost, and freezing the instant it comes in contact with any object. [1894 BURKE] 21 'Don't be picking up the scattered ones [shillings found among the silver thaw],' cried one of them [hard cases]; 'wait till you get on Water Street, in the thick of them.' 1903 HOWLEY 55 ~ This is the name given by Newfoundlanders to that brilliant ice-garment with which the trees, houses, bushes, etc., are clothed when the Spring showers are frozen in the act of falling. 1919 GRENFELL[1] 201 Wind and t' weight of t' silver thaw. 1939 DULEY 30 It had rained in the night, frozen lightly in the morning, leaving a magical silver thaw. Enchanted, dazzling, glittering, the village stood covered in a cellophane coating of ice. C 68–16 [He] used to tell me the following story. When the first Irish immigrants came to Newfoundland they came expecting to find silver growing on trees. . . When they came however the silver on the trees was nothing more than silver thaw, an ice coating which covers the trees when the temperature suddenly falls on a country-side which is covered with a dense fog. 1970 *Evening Telegram* 11 May, p. 3 A mild winter it was here on the east coast with next to no snow but a lot of glitter and silver thaw around March.

simon-saw* n A long, two-handled cross-cut saw (Q 67–76).
P 276–71 ~ Two-man saw, five feet long. P 143–74 In the early lumbering years, the simon-saw, which was six feet long and required two men to operate, and the double-bitter axe were used to cut wood.

simple n Perhaps from cinquefoil. Comb **simple tea**: three-toothed cinquefoil (*Potentilla tridentata*) (1978 ROULEAU 93).

sin n *OED* ~ 3 a (c1300–1470), still in colloq use, esp Sc; PARTRIDGE ~ . A cause for regret, 'a shame,' usu said in reproach for a cruel or thoughtless deed (P 148–61).
1905 DUNCAN 121 ''Tis a sin,' said he, 't' waste good hay like that.' [1960] 1965 PEACOCK (ed) iii, 780 ''Downey's Our Member'': And then in the spring, oh what a darn sin, / When they'll cull out those ties and they'll steal them again. 1964 BLONDAHL (ed) 36 ''Squarin' Up'': The way that old ruffian took on was a sin. . . / And just at that moment the Parson walked in. P 148–65 'It's a sin.' Equivalent to 'It's a shame!' but not to 'Shockin'!' Often said when dogs or cats might be tormented by children. 1973 PINSENT 3 They'll never taste that way again. Anyway. You don't change. . . Don't ask me if that's a sin. I can't keep up with it myself.

sina n *Labrador Inuit, sinaa* 'edge of ice.' The edge of the floating field of ice off the Labrador coast; floe-edge.
1947 TANNER 499 From the camp the trappers make their way to the edge of the ocean ice, the sinâ, where the seals sport in the chilly water or clamber up on the ice to rest. 1977 *Inuit Land Use* 255 Then there's another lot of jar [seals]; they're all small, same ring—silver jars. They're way out—you get a lot at the *sina* [floe edge].

sing v *OED* ~ v[1] 12 d (1833–); *EDD* 5. Phr *sing out*: to call loudly, yell; hail.
1861 *Harper's* xxii, 470 'Did you make out the name?' asked some one, as the voice, borne away by the wind, came faintly to us. 'No. Sing out again!' 1930 *Am Speech* vi, 57 [Sing] out. To call loudly; halloo. T 13–64 He cut two or three sticks and he got all shaky and shivery and finally he had to sing out to the other feller [who] was cuttin' down below him for to come and take him down, and take him home. T 172/5–65 An' he said, 'All right, boy, go forrard an' tell the—she'll do it.' So I went forrard an' sung out to 'em. I said, 'All right, boys, skipper said she'll do it.' P 108–70 Mary, sing out to Tom to come in.

single a Cp *OED* single-handed 1 a, 2 a. Comb

single-handed: with only one man involved; carried out by one person; cp CROSS-HANDED, HAND.
1936 SMITH 51 It was a big job to provide three meals and sleeping quarters for 125 [sealers]. There certainly were no 'single-handed' beds that night. 1971 NOSEWORTHY 243 Single-handed dance. A dance by only one person. (Probably a step-dance). Ibid Single-handed dory. A small dory, about 13 feet long in the bottom. 1975 BUTLER 48 We used to fish singlehanded up till last of caplin.

single-step: step-dance performed alone by a person.
1944 LAWTON & DEVINE 24–5 After the cotillion was finished, it was an unwritten law that each couple should dance a single step. . . In the single-step dancing every dancer danced to his own favorite air; and the fiddler was expected to respond to the individual demands made upon his musical repertoire.

single trace: method of harnessing an ox.
M 69–6 Single trace was a way of harnessing an ox without using a slide. The collar with a butkin tied to the end of its [traces] along with a chain tied to the middle of the butkin was used.

sinker n A rock hazardous to boats and vessels (P 148–66); SUNKER.
1979 NEMEC 277 Offshore 'sinkers' or rocks are particularly productive jigging areas.

sinks n pl Cp *OED* sink sb[1] 12 b (1865 angling quot). The lead weights attached to the bottom of a fish-net; sinker (Q 67–91).
P 127–76 ~ The weights used on the bottom of a cod-trap leader.

sintiffin* See TIFFIN*.

sir samuel n A game in which players are tricked to carry out wrong command.
1861 DE BOILIEU 109–10 A favourite Christmas game amongst the men, enacted nearly every night during the holidays, is—or was—one called 'Sir Samuel and his Man Samuel,' in which you are to obey the orders of the first, but not of the second. Consequently, when Sir Samuel gives an order, his man contradicts it; and whoever obeys the latter becomes the object of 'after-consideration,' which means that he is physically punished, fined, or given some laborious task to perform.

sish n, imit also **swish** [sʊʃ, siˑʃ, sɨiʃ] *DC* ~ (ice) Nfld (1887–), swish ice Nfld (1835); cp *OED* swish sb 2 'dash of water' for sense 3.
1 Fine, granulated ice floating on the surface of the sea; brash ice; attrib in **sish ice, swish** ~ ; cp SLOB ICE.
1836 [WIX][2] 18 [The bay] was full of a species of ice, significantly called by the people, 'swish-ice,' which, when struck with the oar, makes a sound similar to that of straw when thrashed with a stick. 1873 CARROLL 19 No matter how thin the ice is during whelping time, seals are sure to whelp on it as long as it will bear their

weight, as every moment it will be getting stronger as the 'slob' or 'sish' ice drifts off the land, or drifts in from the sea against the shore, pressing such ice together. 1887 BOND 116 [There was] a slight coating of 'sish' or ice-scum on the harbour. 1895 *J A Folklore* viii, 40 Swish ice—ice ground fine. [c1900] 1978 *RLS* 8, p. 24 ~ broken up ice between pans from action of sea knocking them together. 1909 GRENFELL[1] 7 The sish ice consists of the tiny fragments where the large pans have been pounding together on the heaving sea, like the stone of Freya's grinding mill. 1937 DEVINE 33 Lolly—said of the sea surface on a calm day just before it freezes into 'sish.' T 191–65 An' they got into this sish, an' it could hardly bear the boat, so 'twas so slippery with their boots on, they hauled [them] off.

2 A thin layer of ice newly formed on the surface of the sea; ICE-RIND, LOCAL: *local ice*.

1909 BERNIER 7 ~ thin new ice just formed in thin sheets. P 245–76 What I call sish—overnight ice.

3 Sound of rushing water.

1960 FUDGE 33 The sish, sish of the rushing sea passing swiftly by her lee as she pulls her sleek hull through the [water] brought dreams of home and loved ones.

sish v   Phr *sish over* [si:ʃ 'oɵvəɪ]: of the surface of a body of water, to form a thin layer of ice; CATCH V: ~ OVER.

1964 *Can Journ Ling* x, 43 If a pond freezes over they say it seized over or sished over. P 127–73 The pond sished over during the night.

sishy a   also **shee-shee, shishy*** ['sɪʃɪ]. Composed of loose fragments of floating ice; cp SISH (ICE).

1884 STEARNS 222 Though the ice had broken up, leaving water visible, there were still large masses of drift, or as it is called *shee-shee* ice floating up or down with the current or drifting about at the mercy of wind and tide. Q 67–29 Shishy ice. Q 67–64 Sishy ice.

siss v   also **sess** *EDD* ~ v 2. To urge dog to run, attack or threaten (someone); HUSS.

1937 DEVINE 45 ~ To set the dogs onto someone or something. An instance of onomatopoeia, from the sound made in urging them on. Also *sess*. P 12–69 I'll siss the dog on you! 1971 NOSEWORTHY 243 ~ A call to a dog to attack a person or another dog. C 75–28 When a man has a harness of dogs he will 'siss' them after something in order to get them to move.

sive n   also **sy** [saɪv, saɪ] *EDD* ~ s w cties, var sy(e) D Co for sense 1; (3) ~ stone So.

1 Scythe (P 148–63).

P 61–67 Sharpen the sive! M 69–6 Hay cutting started on July twentieth most years. The bulk of it was cut in the morning as the sive cut through the dew-wet grass much easier than when dry. M 70–21 Everyone cut grass by means of a scythe; locally it was called a 'sive.' C 71–123 A sy is used to cut grass. It has a long crooked handle with a single-edged curved blade. P 40–78 The sive is up in the barn if you wants to cut some grass.

2 Comb **sive-stone, sy-** ~ : portable, finely-

grained stone used for sharpening scythes or knives (1971 NOSEWORTHY 253).

skad See SCAD.

skate v   also **skeet***. To throw flat stones over the surface of water; to play ducks-and-drakes; SKITTER V.

P 148–61 Skeeting [is] shying flat rocks over the surface of the water. C 69–7 I often had the habit of skating rocks on water. The idea was to see who could make a rock skate or hop the most times. 1971 NOSEWORTHY 243 Skating a rock—a game where a flat stone is thrown to bounce several times on top of the water.

skeety See SKITTY[2].

skeg n   Cp *OED* ~ sb[1] 2 after part of ship's keel. Comb **skeg bone**: tailbone.

P 229–67 He fell on his backside and hurt his 'skig' bone.

skein n   Cp *OED* ~ sb[1] 2 b 'flight of wild fowl' (1851–) for sense 1. See also STRING.

1 A long line of migrating seals.

1922 *Sat Ev Post* 195, 2 Sep, p. 10 'Dere'm de fat, sir!'. . . 'Only a little skein of swiles, but dat'm a beginnin'!' 1924 ENGLAND 239–40 The *Ranger* seemed to have discovered the huge herd afar, about the same time we did. . . 'Scun 'er up to 'em, Jacob!' the Old Man shouted from the bridge. 'How them bear?' 'Two p'ints on de starburd bow!' 'Good skein?' 'Big jag o' fat, a nice bit off, sir.'

2 A narrow strip of floating ice (1925 *Dial Notes* v, 342).

skeleton n   Comb **skeleton skate**: light metal skate fastened to boot by clamps; club skate.

1973 BARBOUR 55 If there were any ice formed on the 'steady' of Gotts Cove Pond, father would suggest that we take our skates, and walk the mile and a half to the 'steady.' I remember how well my father skated, in the old-fashioned skeleton skates, which clamped on over his ordinary boots.

skents n pl   also **skints*** *EDD* skent v[2], sb IW Do So. Diarrhoea (in animals); SCUTTERS.

P 61–66 The skints [are] run-outs suffered by sheep, or other animals, in spring as a result of eating new grass or new spring plants.

skerries n pl   *OED* skerry sb[2] Sc (1612–); *EDD* sb[1] 1, 2 Sh I, Ork. In place-names, small islets; underwater shoals or rocks on which seas break.

1878 *Nfld Pilot* 232 The Skerries with 6 fathoms, lies E.¼S. 6 miles. 1909 BROWNE 257 After leaving *Venison Island* we passed close by the 'Skerries' and 'Eddystone' islands. 1951 *Nfld & Lab Pilot* i, 73 Small point is rounded and 318 feet high; close southward of it is Skerries bight. 1953 ibid ii, 383 The Skerries, a bank with depths of 8 fathoms over it, lies about three-quarters of a mile north-eastward of Flat island; the sea

is reported to break on it during heavy gales. 1971
SEARY 76 The current local name [of islets in Trinity
Bay] is The Skerries, found also in Skerrys Bight.

skerry* n also **scurry*** ['skɛəri, 'skʌrɨi]. Cp
OED ~ sb¹ 'small boat' obs (1540–1861). See
also SKIRR. Small sled on wooden runners used
for hauling objects on fishing premises or in the
woods (P 245–56).
  P 148–65 ~ kind of slide four feet wide, with two
straight runners and two traces going out to the horse;
holds two cord of wood, pieces fourteen feet long.
C 71–95 A scurry was used for clearing the land of
rocks and sods. It was made simply by splitting a tree,
rinding it and using [the halves] for runners, and nailing a few slats across to put the rocks and sods on. It
was then tackled to the horse or hauled by hand.
P 148–74 ~ A box on runners used to haul rocks,
wood, caplin on the shore. P 245–78 ~ A couple of barrel staves, joined, and used to haul firewood.

skerry* v To drag or haul (a load) on a sled.
  P 106–76 It would be a slide. They'd use it for skerry-
ing rocks, or they could skerry caplin from the beach.

skerwink n also **scurwink, spurwink**. Cp *OED*
skirwingle 'bird' (1610). See SEARY 280 for var
spellings. Shearwater, esp in place-names;
HAGDOWN (*Puffinus* spp).
  [1689] 1971 SEARY 280 Sherwink Point. [1873] ibid
286 Spurwink Island. 1925 *Dial Notes* v, 341
Scurwink—a kind of seabird. . .haigdown. 1953 *Nfld &
Lab Pilot* ii, 94 Skerwink rocks. . .lie about 2½ cables
eastward of Skerwink head.

sketch n
  1 A slight bit (of something); smattering.
  1937 DEVINE 45 ~ A slight touch, contact, acquire-
ment or experience. 'Bill had a sketch of paralysis last
fall.' 'He's a good sailor and he got a sketch of navigation, too.'
  2 A photograph.
  C 71–100 'Would ye take me sketch?' Skipper—
asked as I was taking a snap-shot of what turned out to
be his western boat moored in Salmonier.

sketch v To photograph, esp in phr *sketch off*.
  1920 WALDO 157 To be photographed is to be
'skitched off.' 1924 ENGLAND 109 The word 'sketch,'
by the way, they didn't know, save as applied to pho-
tography. Drawing was always 'markin' out,' and taking photographs was 'sketchin' off.' 1941 WITHINGTON
142–3 A fisherman suddenly looking up at me in this
costume started to laugh, but restrained himself. A second one standing by could not control his expression.
His efforts to do so made me burst out laughing, a privilege they both then exercised; and the first exclaimed,
'Oh, Miss, youse ought to be sketched off.' 1973
MOWAT 9 Jacob never got clear of the time the doctor
on the S.S. *Terra Nova* sketched him off with a camera. He kept that picture by him till he died.

skid n Cp *EDD* ~ 1 c 'plank or roller,' ELMER
149–52 for sense 3.

1 Projection of keel to which rudder is
attached; skeg (Q 67–17).
  [1918–19] GORDON 26 Devoted the whole day to
hauling up boats. First of all we tackled the *St Helen*,
who taxed our utmost strength. When halfway up the
bank, her ropes snapped and she slid back onto the
mud, breaking off her keel-projection (locally termed
the 'skid'). [1928] MCCAWLEY 10 "Lukie's Boat": Lukie's boat got a fine new jib, / And a nice little rudder
hung to her skid.
  2 Gangway.
  [1960] BURKE (ed White) 11 "The Little Bunch of
Whiskers": A lady then got on the skids / To try and
hail a cab / When soon the gangway broke / And down
in the water, dab. T 141/66–65² There was a skid off
from the rail o' the schooner to the wharf, and I was up
on the skid going ashore.
  3 Boat's slipway.
  C 75–132 A skid is a place for hauling up
boats—made with long round logs—easy for rolling
boat in and out of the water.

skier n Prob from *sky*. Small islet in inshore
waters; SKERRIES.
  1891 PACKARD 142 The transformed light falling
bronzed and red upon the broad bay dotted with 'ski-
ers,' or small low islets. . .

skiff n Cp *OED* ~ sb¹ 1 'a small sea-going boat,
adapted to rowing and sailing; esp one attached
to a ship; hence a small light boat of any kind'
(1575–); *DAE* (1638–). See also BAITSKIFF,
BOAT, ICE SKIFF, TRAP¹: ~ SKIFF.
  1 A large partly-decked fishing boat, propelled
by oars or small sail and used in the coastal
fishery to set and haul nets and traps and for
other purposes; freq merges with sense 2.
  1611 *Willoughby Papers* 1/3 It[e]m 6 newe boates
[and] one skiffe. [1712] 1895 PROWSE 272 Confirmed
last year. . .that Mr Jacob Rice, minister of St John's,
should have as follows: From shallops three quintals of
dry merchandable fish, From two-men boat two
[quintals], From the skiffs one [quintal]. [1774] 1792
CARTWRIGHT ii, 34 At noon I went in a skiff and
hauled the nets. [1822] 1928 CORMACK 97 A light skiff
or punt is therefore the safest mode of conveyance
along this horrific coast. 1842 JUKES ii, 30 The boat was
a small unpainted skiff. T 43/7–64 The skiff would be
on the collar an' you'd put this collar punt on when
you'd take [the skiff off] an' go on. M 68–3 Around
1890, however, the fishery underwent a slump and it
became increasingly difficult to obtain fish close to
home. This caused a change in the boat type and the
barque gave way to the 'big skiff' (about twenty feet in
the keel and carried a four man crew). 1972 NEMEC
57–8 A 'skiff' was a large boat which could handle
upwards of several thousand pounds of cod at one
time. P 9–73 ~ One or two-men fisherman skiff, used
for handlining in Fall time fishing in early 1900's. It had
three sails.
  2 A small vessel of up to twenty tons (18.1
mt).
  [1808] 1976 O'NEILL ii, 504 [advertisement] Packet

Boat—For Harbour Grace, Carbonear or any of the Out-Harbours. The subscriber respectfully informs the public that he has provided a New Skiff that rows six oars for the purpose of conveying passengers etc. to any of the Out-Harbours. 1957 MOUNTAIN 6 [They have] one mast, a low, snug mainsail, jib and driver at the stern, though occasionally two masts, and foresail as well as mainsail. The latter is called a skiff, the former a 'punt and driver,' to distinguish it from a punt without that appendage. 1925 *Dial Notes* v, 342 ~ A small, two-masted boat. [1923] 1946 PRATT 182 "The Drag-Irons": He who had learned for thirty years to ride / The seas and storms in punt and skiff and brig, / Would hardly scorn to take before he died / His final lap in Neptune's whirligig. T 455/6–67² Fishing boats, well, we used to build them, skiffs we call 'em. They'd be 'bout fifteen, sixteen feet keel, rigged with four sails. 1967 *Bk of Nfld* iv, 248 [We had a boat] about twenty tons with three sails; there were bunks and a place to cook. . . This boat was called a skiff. . . She had two spars with three large sails. We had a little five horsepower engine in her. 1974 *Federal Licensing Policy* 41 The [salmon] drift-net fishery started in the 1930's, when small 'skiffs' (single dory schooners) using cotton nets began stringing shore-nets together and 'drifting' through the inshore areas as much as 15 miles out during night hours. 1975 BUTLER 55 A larger type boat from seven to fifteen quintal capacity was named a skiff. These boats had a fore cuddy. The skiff was decked over from the forward part to about eight feet from the stern. . . They had gaff sails and booms on the lower part of the sail and they carried oars for rowing when calm.

3 Attrib, comb **skiff collar**: anchor, chain and rope attached by means of a loop or bight to a buoy and used to moor craft in a harbour; COLLAR (M 68–26).

skiff(s) crew: from two to six men ([1774] 1792 CARTWRIGHT ii, 35).

skiff-load: the number or quantity of fish, etc, the craft can carry.

[1774] 1792 CARTWRIGHT ii, 37 A skiff-load of wood was brought out of the sound. [1870] 1973 KELLY 44 After prayers a large skiff load of people pushed off from the stage before us. 1902 *Christmas Bells* 4 'Twould be a pity, skipper,' he said, 't' goa hoame 'ithout runnin' a cargo—a skiff load now, zur—just t' smuggle a bit of a skiff load.' 1957 *Nfld Qtly* Sep, p. 6 I'm shipping a skiffload of fish your way tomorrow, and I want you to be able to see straight if it comes to your culling board. T 43–64 An' you'd be back again to the schooner with a skiff load o' fish. 1966 SCAMMELL 23 There you are skipper. Not a vitamin in a skiff-load. And we got doughboys an' 'lasses sauce comin' up.

skiff-oar

[1786] 1792 CARTWRIGHT iii, 142 Tilsed hewed out another set of skiff-oars.

skiffsail: in local place-names.

1951 *Nfld & Lab Pilot* i, 116 Skiffsail rock, with a depth of less than 6 feet over it, is situated 3¾ cables [eastward] and 2 cables southward of Skiffsail point.

skig n *EDD* skeeg sb¹, squig 'smallest portion' Ir. Remnant of food.

P 37 Skeeg. Breastbone of a bird. 1957 *Evening Telegram* 13 Dec 'There's another skig left, Mose. Pass your plate.' 'No, thankee, grampa. I couldn't hold another morsel.' Q 73–9 There's another skig left.

skim v *OED* ~ v 8 for sense 1; cp *EDD* skime v¹ 4 'to leer, ogle' for sense 2.

1 In the game of ducks and drakes, to throw a flat stone so that it skitters lightly over the surface of the water; SKIP.

P 148–63 [He] can skim [a rock] 16 times. 1964 *Can Journ Ling* x, 43 Skimming—shying flat stones over the water.

2 To pursue a woman or courting couple furtively; to peep at; DOG v (P 48–60).

skimmer n *EDD* ~ sb¹ 3 for sense 1; cp *EDD* v 9 'to peep' for sense 2. See also SKIM.

1 A small, flat stone used in the game of ducks and drakes (P 148–63).

C 69–8 ~ Small stone, which is held by resting on the thumb and middle finger, with the index finger curled around it. They are thrown out over a body of water so that when it lands, it does so on a flat side and skips up off the water surface and is again airborne. Then hopefully it will repeat the performance again and as often as possible.

2 Voyeur, peeping tom; DOGGER (P 148–64).

1970 *Evening Telegram* 17 June, p. 2 If I don't push off soon I'll get the reputation of being a voyeur which is what they call a skimmer in the Boston States.

skimmy n The game of ducks and drakes (P 148–66).

skimo n also pl **skimaux** ['ski:mou] *DC* ~ (1817–). Eskimo; Inuit. Also attrib.

1817 CHAPPELL 92 *Esquimaux*, or *Skimaux*, is an expression of the Cree and other inland *Indians*, signifying 'eaters of raw flesh.' T 377–67 I heard one tale about this Skimo woman: this guy went ashore with a seal finger, and he went to this Skimo woman, and she went down the beach and picked up a handful o' sea lice and put it in a cloth and wrapped it around his finger.

skin n [= SEALSKIN] *DC* ~ boot (1940).

Attrib **skin bag**: sealskin container used to hold oil rendered from seal blubber; SEAL BOTTLE.

[1770] 1792 CARTWRIGHT i, 55 I gave them a skinbag of oil.

skin boot: boot made of sealskin, reaching almost to the knee; SKINNY-WOPPER.

1887 BOND 45–7 The minister's skin-boots and 'vamps' lying by the fender were steaming with heat. [1894 BURKE] 47 She put on my skin boots for to keep her warm sure. 1910 GRENFELL 195 My former patient came aboard tendering me a splendid pair of skin boots. T 50/2–64 Give him [i.e. the sealskin] a couple or three coats o' cod oil, take her down, roll it up. You could make away at your skin boots then—fine ones! T 141/66–65² [We] had skin boots, you know, with a pair o' vamps in 'em an' a pair o' socks. All skin boots them times, 'cause they used to make 'em, see. T 178/9–65 [I would]n't be dressed till I was fifty years old without a pair o' skin boots on in winter. 1967 FIRESTONE 37 This church is known locally as 'skin boot' church, because the money to erect it was obtained by the sale of seal skin boots made by the women of the mission. P 207–67 She's got a fine leg for a skin boot (said of someone with a shapely leg). C 75–25 All autumn would be spent working skin boots for the men going to the icefields. The [taps] of these had to be pegged with wooden pegs so as to provide traction on the ice.

skin v Cp *OED* ~ v 4 'to flay, peel' for sense 1.

1 To separate the skin of a seal from the attached layer of blubber. Cp PELT v, SCULP v.

[1832] 1981 *Them Days* vi (3), p. 36 . . .the weather still to cold to skin out the seals. [1844] GOSSE 114 He seizes a pelt with his left hand, the fur being downward, then, with a sharp knife, edge outward, he boldly and dexterously cuts between the fat and the skin, the former rolling down in large and long masses, while the latter, though shaved clean, rarely receives a gash. A very expert hand will skin five hundred a day. 1852 ARCHIBALD 5 The first operation after landing and weighing is the. . .separating the fat from the skin; this is speedily done, for an expert skinner will skin from 300 to 400 young pelts a day. 1976 *Evening Telegram* 19 Mar, p. 6 The seals were 'pelted' by the sealers and skinned by seal skinners.

2 Phr *skin out*: to escape.

T 309–66 An' then we'll say it come to the rooster. He was goin' to have his head chopped off, probably for dinner next day. Well 'twas skin out too, an' join the crowd.

skin up: to roll up (one's sleeves).

1924 ENGLAND 258 Her was sarnly a fine-looking woman. An' couldn't her split fish, dough? When her'd skin up her sleeve, her arm look like de mainmast o' dis one.

skinner n Cp *OED* ~ 2 'one who removes the skin' (1699, 1884).

1 Man employed ashore to separate the skin of a harp or hooded seal from the attached layer of blubber; SEAL SKINNER.

1852 ARCHIBALD 5 . . .an expert skinner will skin from 300 to 400 young pelts a day. [1909] 1930 COAKER 5 If Sailors, Labourers, Carpenters. . .Coopers, Firemen, Printers, Skinners. . .can form Unions, and derive great benefits through them, why should not the Fishermen[?] 1924 ENGLAND 226 The only really respectable pay made by any workers in the sealing industry is cleared by the skinners, at St John's. The skinners are tremendously deft. With long knives they peel away the fat in two or three slashes, never leaving a shred of fat on the skins or cutting the hides. 1931 BYRNES 114 The South Side, became a bee hive of feverish activity, as an army of 'skinners' worked day and night, with deft knives, separating the fat from the 'pelt.' [1960] 1965 LEACH (ed) 190 "Big Sam": He was covered with grease from cutting loose fat, / And he said to the skinners I'm fed up on that.

2 In preparation of cod fillets, plant worker who removes the skin.

M 68–11 A typical day at the fish plant would begin at 8:00 a.m. [when] the 'headers' (who take the head off the fish, if it has been bought head-on), 'cutters' (who cut the fish in packable-size pieces), 'skinners' (who remove the skin before it can be packed) begin to get fish ready for the packers.

skinning vbl n Cp *OED* ~ 2 'the removal or stripping off, of skin,' 3 ~ knife (1884).

1 In processing seal 'pelts' or 'sculps,' the separation of the skin from the attached blubber.

1883 SHEA 10 When successful, the sealers sometimes return in two or three weeks. The seals—or rather the skin and fat, the carcase being left on the ice—are quickly landed, and the one separated from the other by a process termed skinning.

2 Attrib **skinning knife**: long, slightly curved knife used to separate the blubber from the skin of a seal.

[1795–6] 1974 SQUIRE 84 [inventory] 1 skinning knife 1s. 6d. [1862] 1916 MURPHY 32 One man offered me a pelt worth twelve shillings for the skinning knife. 1873 CARROLL 9 The skinner stands holding the skin and fat in his left hand, removing the fat with a skinning knife in his right hand. 1924 ENGLAND 62 [He] was chipping tobacco from a plug with his skinning knife.

skinning loft: area of merchant's premises where seal 'pelts' are processed by the separation of the skin from the blubber; LOFT.

1976 *Evening Telegram* 19 Mar, p. 6 The seals were all skinned when they were landed on Bowring's wharf or Job's and hoisted up to the skinning loft.

skinning table: platform on which the fat is cut away from a sealskin.

[1844] GOSSE 114 [The pelts] are now skinned; for this purpose a man stands before the *skinning-table*, an inclined plane reaching from his middle to the ground.

skinny a Hazardous; dangerously close (1925 *Dial Notes* v, 342).

1924 ENGLAND 80 An' de ice is wonnerful tight, in spots. Dat was skinny, las' night, 'bout two o'clock.

skinny-wopper n also ~ **hopper**, ~ **wapper**, ~ **whopper**, ~ **wop** ['skɪnɪ ˌwɒpəɪ]. Sealskin boot reaching to below the knee; SKIN BOOT.

1922 *Sat Ev Post* 195, 2 Sep, p. 10 [The yelling crowd] scrambled with goatlike agility to solid ice, and in their heavily spiked Eskimo skinnywoppers, or skin boots, ran like madmen across its fantastic and tumbled-up confusions. 1924 ENGLAND 6 The pavements clicked under the tread of their huge 'skinny woppers,' made of sealskin which had been tanned by Esquimau women—tanned in the primitive way, by being chewed. I marvelled at the thick soles of these waterproof boots: soles studded with 'sparables,' 'chisels,' or 'frosters,' as various kinds of nails are called. 1958 HARRINGTON 119 The captain sat on his bunk and pulled off his 'skinny-whopper' boots. 1967 FIRESTONE 34 Men from the Straits wearing seal skin boots in Corner Brook find that children call *skinny-hoppers* after them. C 71–113 ~ a pair of sealskin boots, very light and comfortable [but] they had to be greased each night or they would become as hard as iron. 1977 BURSEY 93 The engineer bought a pair of sealskin [moccasins] and I bought a pair of skinny hoppers for my small son.

skip v *EDD* ~ v[1] 2 for sense 2.

1 In children's pastime, to jump from one pan of floating ice to another; COPY.

C 65–4 Skippin' pans; jumping from one pan of ice to another. M 62–23 Skipping pans or flipsying over the pans of ice.

2 To throw a flat stone over the surface of the water; of such a stone, to bounce a number of times on the surface (Q 67–59); SKATE, SKITTER v.

C 67–22 A counting rhyme is used in Change Islands to count the number of times a rock skips when it is skimmed over the water in the game called 'skippin' rocks.'

skipper n Cp *OED* ~ sb[2] 1 'master of a small. . .vessel' (1300–), *EDD* sb[2] 1 'head man on board a fishing-boat,' *Fisheries of U S* 149 'skipper of the dory' for sense 1; BERREY 401 'father' for sense 4.

1 The master of a fishing boat, vessel or crew; BOAT MASTER. Cp PLANTER.

1861 DE BOILIEU 25–6 The cargo unloaded and stored, the crews are divided in parties of three or four men, each being titled according to the position he holds in the boat. For instance, 'skipper,' 'second hand,' 'midshipman'; last comes the 'captain,' who has the least to do—merely, indeed, to cook for the rest and to keep the boat clean. 1866 WILSON 207 [The planter] generally commands the boat himself, and his title is skipper. . . The planter's wife is generally skipper of the shore crew. [1877] 1898 *Nfld Law Reports* 147 The defendant, seven with himself to a cod-seine boat, and five under plaintiff, who received a bounty as skipper in a hook-and-line boat. 1898 *Christmas Bells* 14 Skipper Tom (skipper being the especial title of boat-masters at that time) and three other hardy fishers were 'fit-out.' 1936 SMITH 31 When Sunday came Skipper Garland came over, a distance of five miles, to know how we were getting on, and was delighted to hear of our good luck. He had met with the same luck himself, and had got fish in the first haul after setting his trap. 1953 *Nfld Fish Develop Report* 18 In most 'lay' arrangements, the owner of the fishing enterprise, i.e., the skipper (and his partners, if any), bears the full extent of these costs as well as capital costs. 1974 SQUIRE 18 The skipper of the schooner took half the catch of fish. The other half was shared equally among the crew. . . The skipper provided everything for the voyage, the schooner, boats and gear, food for his crew up to six months of the year. 1976 *Decks Awash* v (2), p. 4 The license, which is slated to go to all fishermen, skippers and crewmembers, must be granted before any other fishing license can be given to the fisherman.

2 Term of respect for a person of high status or esteem; in some contexts a familiar form of address; UNCLE.

[c1830] 1890 GOSSE 53 During the first summer, while the skipper (our representative for the modern term 'governor') was in England. . . 1858 [LOWELL] i, 90 They called him 'Skipper' as a token of respect. 1895 *J A Folklore* viii, 37 The word *skipper* is in universal use, and so commonly applied as almost to have lost its original meaning of the master of a small vessel. It is used toward every person whom one wishes to address with respect, and is almost as common as 'Mr' is elsewhere. Generally the Christian name is used after it, as Skipper Jan, Skipper Kish. 1897 WILLSON 38 . . .patiently waiting until they could unfold their grievances or their demands to the 'skipper,' as Sir William is called. [1915] 1972 GORDON 3 As was the case with most of the little communities one finds along the coast, this one had its leader or 'skipper,' as he was generally called. 1924 ENGLAND 46 Everybody aboard a sealing vessel is 'skipper.' T 406–67[2] What do you say, skipper?

3 Principal of a merchant house or his delegate in shore operations on fishing premises.

1836 [WIX][2] 42–3 While I was thus engaged [in sermon], Mr John Cosens, who had been absent, returned, and heard with much satisfaction, of the very hospitable reception which his 'skipper' had given me on my arrival. [1870] 1973 KELLY 19 We got into harbour about 8 a.m. 'Skipper George,' alias George Reynolds, the man in charge of the merchant's rooms, coming out. . .with a crew, to pilot us in through the narrow entrance. 1909 BROWNE 70 The merchant, in the fisherman's vocabulary, is the outfitter who provides the supplies for the fishing industry. . .and the principal of the 'firm' is known as 'The Skipper.' M 71–95 'Skipper' was used for the head of a household, firm or any employer.

4 Husband; head of the household.

1874 *Maritime Mo* iii, 547 Jerusha Biddicomb. . .observed that 'she should have to wait long before her "skipper" took out the baby for an airing.' P 102–60 As a young man I had a rifle which the skipper gave me permission to use and any seal that I shot from the bank would sink to the bottom this was my share of the catch. P 210–70 Older married people in Carbonear don't call each other by their first names. The man is always 'Skipper' and the lady is always 'Missus.' 1973 WADEL 55 An outport wife is supposed to admit, at least in public, that the husband is in charge—in the local language, that the husband is 'the skipper.' 1977 QUILLIAM 1 The son told the skipper if their old mutt could be taught it would be a wonderful companion when he was away. 1982 *Evening Telegram* 2 Jan, p. 13 The poor old skipper spoke to everyone [even] to the family rooster, here you are son, dig in your heels, there's lots [of food] for everyone.

5 In the woods industry, contractor for a logging operation.

[1952] 1965 PEACOCK (ed) iii, 746 "The Boys at 'Ninety-Five'": Herb Porter is our skipper, with him we did go way, / He is a good old lumberjack raised up in Trinity Bay. / Herb Baker is some foreman as you may understand, / No bigger sport can be found on the shores of Newfoundland. P 65–64 The man in charge of a lumber camp is the 'skipper.' He owns the camp, some tractors, horses, sleds, etc.

6 Attrib **skipper man**: see sense 1 above. Cp PLANTER MAN.

1909 GRENFELL[1] 63–4 George Read was skipper-man an' th' rest was just youngsters. 1916 *FPU (Twillingate) Minutes* 1 Mar The Chairman then asked all the skipper men and old members to come forward and take seats on the platform. 1953 *Nfld Fish Develop Report* 21 Moreover, the conclusion is based on an investigation of families of skipper men—and it is possible that among sharemen, who belong probably to a younger age-group than skippers, some of the more strenuous alternative occupations contribute more significantly to family incomes. T 50/2–64 Every oar in the water at one time, and a man scullin'—mostly the skipper man, with a big oar. 1975 *Evening Telegram* 1 Feb, p. 11 In 1968. . .there were 68 skippermen in trap boats, while last year only 23 drew berths and only 14 traps were fished. 1979 *Salt Water, Fresh Water* 65 And the captain of a dragger today represents the restoration of the Newfoundland aristocracy, which always was the skipper man, the master of his own vessel.

skipper v *OED* ~ v[1] (1893); *EDD* 2 Sh I (1898). To act as master of a boat or vessel.

1960 FUDGE 4 In those early days. . .[they] owned a boat or schooner built and skippered by the same man. 1971 HORWOOD 39 She was skippered by Captain Douglas Burden of Carbonear. M 71–117 My grandfather's schooner, *The Brisk* (he skippered her around 1870), had two masts, with a mainsail, a foresail and a full jib-boom carrying two jibs. 1972 BROWN 56 At eight o'clock in the morning, with the sun at his back, Wes Kean sighted the ships skippered by his father and his brother.

skirr v [skəɹ] *OED* ~ v 3 (1605–), *EDD* 6 for sense 1; *OED* 2, *EDD* 5, 8 s w cties for sense 2; *OED* 4, *EDD* 1 for sense 3.

1 To hurry about in search of something; scour.

1914 *Cadet* Apr, p. 7 The word 'skir' used by the fishermen is pure English. Shakespeare makes Macbeth say 'Send out horses, skir the country round.' 1925 *Dial Notes* v, 342 ~ To take a short walk. 1937 DEVINE 45 ~ To scour the country; to hike.

2 To fly or glide rapidly.

1924 ENGLAND 167 Dem hairyplane can skirr, sarnly. T 437/8–65 [*märchen*] John got up, put his two arms around [the eagle's] neck, an' he gives two deep flaps an' he went out around th' house an' he skirred back again, an' he dropped. Wasn't enough, see. Wasn't strong enough yet [i.e. to fly with heavy load on his back].

3 To throw flat stones across the surface of the water in the game of ducks and drakes; SKATE, SKITTER v (Q 67–90).

skirt n

1 A long, narrow stretch of floating ice-pans; SKEIN, STRING.

1842 JUKES i, 318 There was no ice to windward of us but this thin skirt about a mile broad, which was marked into small round pieces about a foot wide, forming a perfect mosaic pavement on a gigantic scale. 1882 TALBOT 20 We passed in and out through skirts of ice.

2 The vertical 'wall' or 'side' of a cod-trap.

T 194/5–65 There couldn't be no more herring into un than what was into un. An' they was meshed in the vees, meshed in the skirts. There was nobody reached over to take hold the skirts o' the trap.

3 Attrib **skirt line**, ~ **rope**: rope forming the edge of sections of netting on each side of the entrance to a cod-trap or salmon-net (Q 67–34).

skit v *EDD* ~ v[1] 6 'to taunt; joke'; JOYCE 325–6. To laugh, giggle.

P 171–67 You'll be there [at the wedding] skittin' and carrying on. P 108–75 The childer were laughin' and skittin' behind his back.

skit*[1] n Cp DINNEEN scitheach 'left-handed.' Nickname for left-handed man.

P 76–80 'This is Skit —.' 'So you're left-handed.' Everybody named Skit is left-handed.' 'That's right.' P 188–80 Oh, I remember that one—Skit — used to work with us.

skit*[2] See SKITTY[2].

skitter v ['skɪtəɹ] *EDD* ~ v 4 Co, *NID* 2 for sense 1; *EDD* 3 for sense 2.

1 To throw a flat stone across the surface of the water (Q 67–42); SKATE, SKIRR.

P 148–60 ~ To shy flat stones over surface of water.

2 To slip or slide, esp of a boat moving over the water.

T 141/66–65[2] An' he skittered [it] in on the kitchen table, this old cape ann in this paper bag. 'There's a hat there for 'ee, maid,' he said. An' she went along an' hauled un out, see, an' this is a cape ann! P 40–78 The boat skittered across the water.

skitter n Cp SKITTER v. A sudden movement across surface, esp of a boat over the water.

T 50/1–64 I was stood up, ready to let go o' the spread, give her the shoulder o' mutton, an' she took one skitter away on the water— I allow she went as far from this down to Pad's before she brought up. Q 73–4 ~ sudden movement of boat over water.

skitty[1] n Cp SKITTER v. Comb **skitty rock**: flat stone used in game of ducks and drakes (Q 67–81).

C 71–32 ~ flat rock used by children to skip over surface of water.

skitty[2] n also **skeety**, **skit***. A biting fly; MOSQUITO, NIPPER[1].

[1894 BURKE] 45 Oh their [trouters'] faces were all raw, / Where the 'skeety' had his chaw. P 126–67 The skits are biting me. C 68–24 [tall tale] I took off me cape ann and me oil-jacket and put them on the dought [thwart]. The skitties was so tick that when I slewed around they was lugging away me clothes. One bunch had the cape ann, and another had me oil-jacket.

skiver n [ˈskɪvəɹ] *OED* ~ sb[1] chief dial (1664–1746); *EDD* 1 esp s w cties for sense 1.

1 A skewer, esp a forked stick on which fish are impaled or strung through the gills in carrying; the load of trout so carried; GAD n (1896 *Dial Notes* i, 381).

1894 *Evening Herald* 12 Dec All [in the tent] looking so happy with deers meat stuck up on scivers made of wood. P 126–67 [That's a fine] skiver of trout. M 69–6 I was so overjoyed that I stopped trouting, got a skiver (a Y-shaped section of an alder) and reeved the trout and the salmon on it. M 70–9 'Have you got e'ra troutin' bag, Aubrey?' 'Na, I'm going to string mine on a skiver.' 1974 SQUIRE 67 'Now,' he said, 'you will need a skivver (skewer) to bring home your squid.' The skivver is actually a forked stick, pointed at the ends on which the squid were impaled to promote carrying. He handed me the hook and the skivver, and I started to run down the hill toward the sea-shore.

2 Pointed peg on which bait is impaled in a lobster-trap.

T 13/20–64 Now in the centre of the pot there's a skiver, a little stick about six inches long, right small in the end. Well now, I'll put my bait on this skiver. P 148–65 The skiver [is] the pointed peg where bait is stuck. Then a rubber ring [is] slid down to lock bait and hold skiver upright to a vertical line.

3 Knitting needle (1940 *Dal Rev* xv, 65).

P 171–65 A skiver is a knitting needle with a knob on one end so that only the other end is free for knitting. P 160–70 ~ One of a set of two knitting needles; those making up a set of four will not be called skivers. 1979 POCIUS 23 Some women also stated that wooden needles were often made by local men. These needles were called 'skivvers,' and this term now often refers to any type of knitting needle.

4 A thin person; a small child (1971 NOSEWORTHY 243).

P 229–67 He's only a skiver (i.e. very thin). P 170–70 She's been sick so long that she's just a skiver. 1975 *Them Days* i (1), p. 21 I used to tend her best I could, but I was just a little skivver.

5 Comb **skiver line**: (a) in a lobster-trap, line hanging from top of trap to hold baited 'skiver' in place; (b) rope with wire hangers used for landing fish when boat is prevented from coming alongside the stage (P 186–73).

P 241–68 In the centre of the [lobster] pot there is a skiver line which hangs down from the top of the pot. About half way down the line there is a stick tied onto the line. On this stick the bait is placed. P 127–76 The skiver is attached to a line strung between the top and bottom of the trap. It is pushed through the bait and then secured in place by pushing it through a loop of leather or twine which is also attached to the skiver line.

skiver v [ˈskɪvəɹ] *OED* ~ v[1] (1832–); *EDD* 5 esp Ir, s w cties. To pierce or impale; esp to bait

a fish-hook, 'fork' a fish, string a trout to a withe, etc; to slip (something) on.

1891 *Holly Branch* 15 You know zur, there was nobody to take that there needle but the dawgs, and we had three o' 'em, so I ups with my knife and skivers the first dawg I sees—sarched he, no needle—then I rips up another one, no sign, the other dawg runned away. T 50/2–64 Take up your squid an' cut it up, or your herring—whatever it might be. But they use dabbers for caplin—snake that onto your line and skiver your caplin on. C 69–17 [tall tale] He once killed twenty-one ducks by skivering them through the eyes with the ramrod of his musket. 1970 *Evening Telegram* 12 May, p. 2 He threatens to skivver the first government feller what comes along with the fish prong. C 71–104 He skivered the stocking over his head.

skolly* See SKULLY.

skully n also **scolly, scully, skolly*** [ˈskɒlɪ]. A cotton sun-bonnet worn by women for outdoors work; occas a fisherman's home-made sou'wester.

1897 *J A Folklore* x, 209 Scully—a loose cotton hood worn by the women when fish-making. 1937 DEVINE 42 Scolly or scully A wide rimmed cotton head dress, with drooping peak in front, used by women and girls. An exaggerated sun bonnet or 'Dolly Varden.' P 54–65 Skolly. Rhymes with jolly. A large kind of sun-bonnet, made of cotton or shirting, worn by women while haymaking, fishmaking, working in gardens, etc, having a very wide brim covering the neck. It also means a large kind of home-made sou'wester, made of calico & treated with linseed oil, to make it waterproof, used by men out fishing, having the same kind of very wide brim over the neck, & buttoning in front under the chin, so that the hat almost covers the entire skull, except for the face & eyes. C 71–118 ~ This was a sunbonnet tied under the chin. C 71–130 Skolly. A sunbonnet covering the head and shoulders. Worn by women while working outdoors in summer.

skulp See SCULP v, n.

skun See SCUN[2].

skunk n Comb **skunk duck**: Labrador duck, now extinct (*Camptorhynchus labradorius*); PIED DUCK.

1977 *Them Days* ii (3), p. 13 The Labrador Duck, known also as the 'pied duck' and the 'skunk duck' was common on the Labrador coast until about 1842. It measured approximately twenty-nine inches long. The males were black with white heads and markings and the females were greyish-brown above and greyish-white below.

slack a Cp *EDD* ~ a[1] 11 (7) ~ handed for sense 3.

1 Of fish, slow in appearing; scarce.

[1772] 1792 CARTWRIGHT i, 241 The salmon have been slack these four days past. P 102–60 In his young days as a boy he was partly self taught taking his books out in the fishing boat to study when the fishing was slack.

2 Not firm; loose; flabby.

[1879] 1956 CUTTING 149 [It treats] how much salt each fish requires and on what part the most is needed. Otherwise the fish either come out 'slack' and strongly smelling for want of salt, or 'dry as a chip' from over salting. 1940 SCAMMELL 7 "The Six Horse-Power Coaker": She was easy on fuel, but she kicked like a mule, / For the screws on the beddin' were slack. P 148–69 Your [car] tire is slack. 1973 WIDDOWSON 354 Anyway you could deduce from the story what happened to him and that made you a good boy for the next few weeks anyway (until your memory started to get slack again).

3 Of the tide, not running; motionless.

1979 NEMEC 277 Few fish are 'jug' when the tide is 'slack.' On the other hand, if the tide is 'running' strong a crew may 'hit' or run into a 'drift of fish' and 'jig' hundreds of pounds of large cod in a matter of minutes.

4 Comb **slack-fisted**: lazy, without ambition.

T 194–65 There was a good girl, industrious girl, had married a slack-fisted feller, and consequently both of them were down. . . The industrious feller, he'd give he a good girl, and the slack-fisted feller, he'd give him the slack-fisted girl.

slack v also **slacken (off)**. Cp OED ~ v 12 (1820 quot). Of an ice-field, to break up into loose pieces.

[1856] 1975 WHITELEY 112 Strong breeze offshore— Ice began to slack. 1866 WILSON 393 Just then a light north-west wind slacked the ice from the north shore of Trinity Bay, by which a boat got from Trinity to Catalina. . .and in less than half an hour after the arrival of the boat, the ice again came in and stopped all navigation for ten days more. 1873 Maritime Mo ii, 140 Here the ice slackened; steam was got up. 1901 Christmas Bells 13 As these men worked together they soon carried the instrument to safety, just arriving at the store before the ice commenced to slack. 1916 MURPHY 46 At length, well on in April, the wind changed and the ice slackened off and let them clear. All the ships then started north and cracked on northward for all they were worth. T 43–64 I've seen as high as three hundred schooners huddled together in a harbour waitin' for the ice to slack.

slam n

1 Phr all of a slam: in a hurry; violently (1925 Dial Notes v, 342).

2 Comb **slam bang**, **~ gut**: heavy pudding, cake or pancake; cp BANGBELLY (1971 NOSEWORTHY 244).

C 66–3 Slam-gut. A steamed bread pudding containing raisins, molasses and other ingredients. It gets such a name because of its sogginess or heaviness as a result of being steamed in a cloth. P 25–67 Slam bang. A cake which fell in the process of being baked.

slapper n OED ~¹ 3 (1886). A wooden stick used to beat school-children.

[1897] 1927 DOYLE (ed) 72 "The Landfall of Cabot":

And his tongue was like a clapper / And his fingers were all broken / From the master's hardwood slapper. 1931 BYRNES 74 You would always tell a pupil of Mrs Walsh, by merely looking at the palm of his or her hand, which was invariably stained a rich purple, from the continued use of the 'slapper.' 1938 ENGLISH 121 Though keeping her little charges under control, Agatha never—as was the custom in those days—used a 'slapper.' C 65–4 When we were in school in [the] early fifties the teacher would have a long wooden pointer, a 'slapper,' for punishing the children. We usually got five to eight cracks on the palm of the hands.

slat v Cp EDD ~ v³ 1 'to throw violently. . .dash down'; Fisheries of U S 153. To remove a fish from hook with a quick, dexterous jerk.

1861 Harper's xxii, 598 Fish after fish came floundering over the sides of the boats, were dexterously 'slatted' off upon the 'crotch irons,' and the hooks, quickly baited, were tossed into the water again. M 67–10 We find [the fishermen] 'slatting' the fish off the hooks and at intervals 'fark' them back into a pen.

slatch n Cp OED ~ 2 'brief respite or interval' naut obs (1625–1769). See also SWATCH n. An expanse of open water in an ice-field.

[1882] P 54–69 I have seen [swatch] in a news item in the Harbour Grace Standard, 25 Mar, written as slatch, about old seals off Cape Spear in slatches. 1909 BERNIER 7 Slatches are considerable pools of open water in the ice.

slatchy a Of a stretch of water, covered with scattered pieces of floating ice; LOOSE.

1925 Dial Notes v, 342 ~ Descriptive of water containing loose ice.

slatter n Cp EDD slatter-cum-drash sb D Co 'uproar, confusion,' slatterly a 2 'slovenly.' Phr slatter and sling, slatterly sling, slatter to sling, etc: untidy, chaotic; SLING: in slings.

1863 MORETON 32 Slattery-sling. Perhaps meaning slatternly sling. An expressive nautical substitute for the English 'sixes and sevens,' or 'hither and thither.' 1937 DEVINE 45 Slatterly-sling. In disorder. The Irish youngsters used their own word in the early days, viz. Train-ah-Kalia. P 57–65 Everything's all slatter and sling. P 266–66 When a room or other place is in a state of disorder it is said to be all slatter to sling.

slawm* n DINNEEN slám. Roll of wool slightly carded to remove the matted parts.

1968 DILLON 154 I was all night makin' slawms.

slawmeen* n DINNEEN sláimín. Dirty, untidy person. Cp SLOMMOCKY.

1968 DILLON 154 She's the real slawmeen that one. Her house is not fit to go into.

sleepy a Cp EDD ~ 3 'having a kind of white,

dry rot' Co for sense 1; *EDD* 1 (3) ~ dust for comb in sense 2.

1 Of snow, soft, melting; ROTTEN.

1910 PRICHARD 95 For some time after this the weather alternated between frost and 'sleepy' snow.

2 Comb **sleepy diver**: American black scoter (*Oidemia nigra americana*) (1959 MCATEE 18).

1870 *Can Naturalist* v, 302 [The scoter] is called the 'sleepy diver'. . .when adult, by the settlers. 1884 STEARNS 92 . . .a bird called the dipper or buffle head, sometimes the butter ball and spirit duck, but which is here called 'sleepy diver,' from the slowness of its movements in the water. 1951 PETERS & BURLEIGH 124 ~ When noted from the land, they appear to sink into the water, but are really rising and falling with the waves.

sleepy dust: matter in corners of eye after sleeping.

P 41–68 A small child who was fighting a losing battle against sleep, was told the sandman was coming, sprinkling sleepy dust. Finally, when he succumbed to the sandman, his mother put him to alley coosh (bed). By the way, sleepy dust is that which you wash from your eyes every morning.

sleeveen n   also **sleiveen, sleveen, slieveen** [sliː'viːn, 'sliːviːn] *EDD* slieveen, var sleeveen, sleiveen sb 1 'rogue, rascal' Ir; JOYCE 326–7 'guileful fellow'; DINNEEN slighbhín 'a schemer, a trickster.' A sly deceitful man; a mean fellow; rascal; a mischievous child.

[1929] 1949 ENGLISH 115 'Sleiveen' is a mean character. 1937 DEVINE 45 Sleveen. A sly fellow; a hypocrite; a bad man generally. T 54/8–64 'Pretty tough,' he said, 'my wife in bed with [another man]. I always knew he was a sleeveen.' 1968 DILLON 154 He's a real sleeveen, that fella. He'd steal the two eyes out o' your head. C 68–5 Some of those businessmen on Water Street are real sleeveens! C 71–127 (of a misbehaving child) You young sleeveen! 1977 RUSSELL 112 Those sleveens in Hartley's Harbour were just as bad then as they are now. 1981 GUY 15 This sleveen [of a doctor] we got now told me right to me face that three kinds of pills was enough for me.

sleeveen v   To steal, purloin.

P 27–80 I'm sure someone sleeveened a rabbit out of that slip.

sleiveen See SLEEVEEN.

slether See SLITHER.

sleveen See SLEEVEEN.

slew v   also **sloo, slue**. Cp *OED* ~ v 2 'to turn about' for senses 1 and 3; *EDD* 3 'to edge around; avoid' Co for sense 4.

1 To turn a boat, esp by backing water with one oar and pulling with the other; BELAY.

P 229–67 Slue around the punt! C 70–10 [He] told me that he would never slew his boat against the sun because it would be a sign of bad luck. He said that he

would always slew it towards the sun [and] the people I went out with this summer used to always slew the boat that way. Q 71–16 To turn with an oar or just to turn is called slew around in Little Bay and Little Bay Islands.

2 To force ice to one side with the bow of a vessel; BUTT v.

1909 BERNIER 7 Slew, slewing is forcing the vessel ahead against the corner of a piece of ice, with the intention of causing it to slew or swing out of the way, so as to force a passage by it.

3 To avoid; veer off.

1955 ENGLISH 36 Sloo. To get out of the way. 1968 KEATING 57 But when the English laddies come ashore, byes, look out. A wise man'll sloo, for it's takin' the drop of drink and clinkin' and cloutin' and ballyraggin' the town to a clobber.

4 To shift; take another direction.

1961 *Evening Telegram* 28 Apr, p. 7 My conversations frequently (from lifelong habit) 'slewed into cuffers' on family and local traditions.

slew n   Cp SLEW v.

1 A short walk or stroll; turn (1897 *J A Folklore* x, 209); CRUISE n.

1925 *Dial Notes* v, 342 [A] slew around. A short walk. 1937 DEVINE 45 I'll take a *slew* around the harbour before going to bed.

2 Phr *slew of your eye*: a glance; hence, a very short time (1925 *Dial Notes* v, 342).

1924 ENGLAND 320 One slew o' y'r hcyc. Onc look.

3 A drink (of liquor); swig (P 152–58).

C 71–115 ~ small drink of beer or wine.

slewed p ppl Cp *EDD* slew 8 slewed a 'twisted.' Bent; crooked; at an angle.

[1894–1927] 1960 BURKE (ed White) 7 "Mrs Brookin's Cat": And her nose was slewed all crooked, / Dodging boot-jacks in the night. [1946] 1976 *Evening Telegram* 12 Jan, p. 6 With the tide down so much, and the vessel all slewed and down by the head [as a result of running her stern on a rock] she was taking water in through a dozen places. P 148–62 That house is slewed.

slice n   Cp *OED* ~ sb¹ 4 'spatula used for stirring and mixing' obs for sense 1; *EDD* 4, *OED* 5 for sense 2.

1 A flat wooden implement used in various operations for stirring and mixing.

1861 DE BOILIEU 108 I say rough, because the forfeits, beginning with rum, invariably end in what is termed a 'cobbing'; which means a dozen strokes across the soles of the feet with a wooden slice. M 69–5 [They used] a wooden slice, eighteen inches long to stir the blubber while it was boiling or melting. 1971 NOSEWORTHY 244 ~ Wooden stick used for stirring oil or paint.

2 A wooden utensil used in cooking.

T 43/7–64 A slice [is] made straight an' something in the manner of a oar, boat's oar. It was for stirrin' the soap or soup or anything that the women would be cookin'. 1971 NOSEWORTHY 246 Soup-slice. Stick used for stirring soup.

slicker n   A lead weight forming part of a hook, used when fishing with a hand-line for cod near the surface of the water; DAPPER, FLICKER.

1937 DEVINE 46 ~ A hook with lead around it for quick sinking.

slide v   Cp *DC* sliding 2 'coasting' (1805, 1923). See also SLIDE n 2. To coast over snow or ice on a sled, esp in children's pastime.

[c1894] PANL P4/14, p. 196 [The local meaning of coast] is to *skim* or *slide* over a hill of snow on a sled or slide. 1900 PROWSE [Appendix] 144 [offence:] Sliding down hills or highways, or streets. 1904 *Nfld Qtly* Oct, p. 21 "Sliding": 'Twas winter, we were sliding adown the Poor House Lane, / My slide she was a dandy, and 'Rover' was her name. 1937 DEVINE 39 [Randy means] any noisy fun: 'Copying' over buckly ice, snow-sliding, etc. P 124–71 Sliding was a sport in which practically everyone took part (much like tobogganing is today) and the slides were made out of pork barrel staves.

slide n   *DC* ~ n 4 Nfld ([1665]; 1906–); cp *OED* 4 a 'a kind of sledge' (1685–1896), *EDD* 'a sledge' (1796; Nfld: 1895), *DAE* 'dray' (1858–96) for sense 1.

1 A sled with stout wooden runners curved up in front, hauled in the winter by dogs, horse or man, used esp for carting wood and other heavy loads; often with defining word DOG[1], HAND, HORSE, WOOD; CATAMARAN.

1776 COUGHLAN 18 They proposed to me, to point out a Place where I would choose to build a Church, which was agreed upon; accordingly all Hands went into the Wood, and cut down as much of it as they wanted, which they hauled out upon what they call Slides. 1828 *Newfoundlander* 27 Feb [Death of Thomas Power who] was crushed to death by the upsetting of his slide of wood. 1846 TOCQUE 118 Men hauling wood at the time thought the sound came out of the ground immediately under the slide or sledge. 1887 *Telegram Christmas No* 12 In this particular they are of great service, although it is a most unusual thing to see a loaded slide coming from the woods with dogs attached, to which some man is not bound by an equally strong attachment. 1895 *J A Folklore* viii, 31 In Newfoundland the sled or sleigh of the Continent, the sledge of the English, is called a *slide*. 1900 PROWSE [Appendix] 142 *Sledges, Slides, Sleighs* Horse attached thereto must have person leading or driving with reins, and two good bells attached to horse's harness. 1909 *Nfld Qtly* Mar, p. 15 The [funeral] procession was on snow shoes. The coffin was on a slide which was drawn by four men holding the shafts. A numerous company of mourners followed behind, two and two. 1964 *Evening Telegram* 25 Sep, p. 18 He recalled that when Dr Harris came to Marystown, there were very few roads. Many visits to the sick took him over stormy waters in open boats and in winter a catamaran or horse and slide was the only means of conveyance. T 43/7–64 Apart from the wagon sleds now for winter work there was the slide. Well, it could be a horse slide or a hand slide. T 89–64 I got right as handy as a gunshot of the brook, an' the slide stopped, brought up, on her side. T 436–65 [We'd go]

an' cut some wood in 'cross the mish, you see, an' take the ropes on our back an' drag it out with a slide on the bank.

2 A light sled on runners, or a home-made substitute, used by children in winter.

See [c1894] quot above at SLIDE v. 1902 MURPHY (ed) 77 "Granny Bates's Hill": I see the hillside white, / I see the moonlight bright, / I see the slides on Granny Bates's Hill. 1931 BYRNES 99 Sleighs with flat runners, slides with half round runners, and the humble home made affairs with runners made from pieces of tin hoop. 1971 NOSEWORTHY 244 ~ A device with two metal runners for children to coast in the snow; a sled.

3 Attrib, comb **slide load**: quantity of wood, etc, carried on a sled (Q 67–96).

[1900 OLIVER & BURKE] 12 "Breaking Open the Stores": As they marched up the shore / With their slide loads of hay. . . 1916 MURPHY 21 The old folks used the word *built* when speaking of a big slide load of wood. 1937 DEVINE 50 To swamp a road or path is to build one with a bedding of boughs to be used in hauling slide loads of wood in winter. 1966 FARIS 38 Many slide-loads of 'lungers'. . .are needed for 'bridges' and wharves. . . Most homes need up to 20 'slide-loads' of logs each year, each slide-load averaging 50 'turns'. . .of wood.

slide path: track leading to good stands of timber, made in winter by the traffic of sleds; WOODS PATH.

[1780] P 148–81 [*Colonial Records*] . . .a slide path of 12 feet. 1906 LUMSDEN 121 This was a 'slide-path' used for hauling firewood, and had doubtless been so used in the early part of this very day. M 69–28 After the garden vegetables had been taken up and stored away, the men often took to the woods day after day, cutting piles of wood, which they would haul out later in the winter when the slide-path was good. 1971 NOSEWORTHY 244 Men would go in the woods to cut wood for the winter. The slide-paths would then be frozen and covered with snow. 1975 GUY 147 In the winter, in the woods, coming down the slide paths you would hear the bells jingling on the horses to give anyone coming along the path against them a chance to find a good place to haul off to one side.

slider n   also **slider board**. Cp *EDD* ~ sb 1 So, *DAE* 1 (1887 quot) for sense 2.

1 Movable board or cover placed over ship's companion-way, 'trunk-hole' of a fishing boat, or on the side of a fish-box, etc.

1966 SCAMMELL 39 'Old woman said she thought she heard a motorboat sometime before daylight,' ventured Lige, kicking the slider off the trunkhole. T 453–67 The water'd just keep pourin' [down] the sides of the companion, 'cause it should be that the slider boards, as they call it, were down forrard. We got them down an' stopped most of it. 1971 NOSEWORTHY 244 Slider-board. A board which was placed in the open side of a fish-box as the fish was salted and packed up.

2 Child's home-made sled; SLIDE n.

M 69–6 The best riding was on slider-boards. A kind of toboggan made from barrel staves.

sliding n *DC* ~ 1 (1770). Steep path on the bank of a pond or river made by an otter; OTTER RUB.

[1770] 1792 CARTWRIGHT i, 59 Arriving at the head of Long Pool, I met with the sliding of an otter;. . .and I soon discovered him fishing in the disemboguing of the brook, where it was yet open.

slieveen See SLEEVEEN.

slim n Cp *OED* ~ a 4 b ~ cake 'a kind of plain cake' Ir (1847–). A thin, one-layer cake or bread-stuff; pancake.

1964 *Can Journ Ling* x, 41 Pancakes are often called [slims]. P 148–72 ~ an old-fashioned word meaning a one-layer cake. C 75–146 A slim could be plain or made of fruit, nuts, raisins, etc. P 148–76 ·- A thin molasses pancake, made with grated salt pork.

slime n
1 Exudation of moisture on the surface of a salted cod-fish caused by imperfect drying; cp DUN n, SLIMY.

1953 *Nfld Fish Develop Report* 59 The producers have little control over the quality of their product. In most cases their operations are adversely affected by the weather, which causes 'sun-burn' (skin heating), dampness or 'slime' and, indirectly, over-salting.

2 Comb **slime food**: marine plant and animal organisms fed on by fish.

1900 HARVEY 43 The 'slime-food,' as it is called, sustains the minute crustaceans, and these, in turn, furnish food for the herring.

slimy a Of salted cod-fish, with an exudation of moisture on the surface caused by imperfect drying.

[1909] 1930 COAKER 7 No 4 [grade] to consist of slimy fish. 1979 TIZZARD 294 Another factor was that after a 'spell' of dirty weather the fish would become slimy.

slindge See SLINGE.

slindger See SLINGER.

sling n For phr in sense 1, cp *OED* ~ sb² 1, 2 a and naut senses in SMYTH 632; for comb ~ rock, cp *DC* ~ –ding (1955), *Fisheries of U S* 127.

1 Phr *in slings*: unfinished or held up; cluttered, untidy; in a state of confusion; SLATTER: *slatter and sling*.

[1909 BROWNE 173 A stout line is attached to the harpoon, which is 'payed out' to give the whale 'searoom' until it becomes exhausted. It is then bound up to the side of the steamer by huge chain 'slings' and conveyed to the Factory.] 1925 *Dial Notes* v, 342 ~ Retarded; held up. 1937 DEVINE 29 ~ Delayed; deferred; unfinished or in suspense—like a barrel suspended in the slings while being hoisted from one place to another. C 69–8 To say something was ree-raw would mean it was in an awful mess or again in the slings.

P 108–70 Since the painters came in, the whole place is in slings. P 107–78 The kitchen was all in slings.

go sling, ~ *slingo*, etc: crash! bang!

1925 *Dial Notes* v, 342 To go slingo. Denotes violent action or noise. [1929] 1933 GREENLEAF (ed) 241 "A Crowd of Bold Sharemen": Our skipper carried on to his mainsail too long, / When rounding Cape Charles, sling goes our main boom. P 102–60 He swabbed out the gun, put the bag of powder in and was driving it down tight when sling she goes and he was thrown about 30 feet down off the bank. T 31/5–64 I made a dart now to go along under the other one. And as I did, sling she goes the other one an' took me, an' away I goes out in the water—souse! T 55–64 I stood for a while an' by an' by sling she goes again. An' I jumped. I didn't run though. T 143/4–65¹ We left an' went aboard, got underway—she didn't go far 'fore sling she goes on a rock—bango!

2 Comb **sling line**: light rope with weight attached, thrown from vessel to wharf and used to haul mooring cable ashore (P 127–77).

sling rock: one of a number of stones used to sink a fish-net in the water; LEAD¹ (P 135–74).

slinge v also **slindge** [slɪndʒ] *OED* ~ v dial (1747–); *EDD* v¹ 1 'to slink off or about; lounge about idly' Sc Ir D; *Kilkenny Lexicon*. To avoid one's share of work; to idle, loaf; to play truant from school.

1924 ENGLAND 136 You go alang an' find 'em out, an' ask who's kickin' an' slindgin' [loafing]. I'll do the rest! 1927 *Christmas Messenger* 47 ~ To skulk away from work, or to loaf. 1937 DEVINE 46 ~ To shirk duty; to mooch from school. [1958] 1965 PEACOCK (ed) i, 133 "The Herring Gibbers": For every man is willing but most of them are slack, / They'll work before his face and they'll slinge behind his back. P 127–73 All he did was slinge! P 148–79 They were never working—always slingin' about.

slinger n also **slindger** ['slɪndʒəɪ] *EDD* slinge v¹ 1 (1) sleenger sb 'lounger.' An idler, truant from work.

1924 ENGLAND 179 An' now about this slindgin'. Go alang an' take down the names o' the sick men an' the slindgers. Q 71–15 Slinger [is] one who slinges, or dodges chores.

slingey a ['slɪndʒɪ]. Cowering, drooping; slinking along.

T 368–67¹ He must have had some kind of an illness, maybe palsy. He just scuffed around all the time. He walked in a slingey position, his arms just dangling by his side. His feet were turned in and he just [scuffed].

slink n *EDD* ~ sb² 4, *DC* esp Nfld (1955) for sense 2.

1 A salmon still in fresh water after spawning; a thin salmon in poor condition.

[1771] 1792 CARTWRIGHT i, 132 We had three slinks in the net. 1792 ibid *Gloss* i, xv ~ A salmon which has spawned, and has not yet recovered itself by returning into the sea; till which time, it never will. 1930 *Am*

Speech vi, 57 ~ Thin salmon with pale flesh, not used
as food. 1947 TANNER 738 The pink salmon is reserved
for human consumption, the white salmon [slinks] is
kept as winter food for the dogs. M 68–23 We usually
fished near home around the mouth of the river. There
were always plenty of mud trout, salmon parr and
sometimes even a 'slink' (a thin dark salmon which was
on his way to the sea). These slinks weren't much good
to eat. C 75–61 The rock at the end of the pool was
called 'Slink Rock' because this is where in the spring
of the year a number of slinks used to be caught. 1977
Inuit Land Use 264 Salmon which migrate up-river
remain for the winter in ponds or in steadies. . . When
they return to salt water in spring. . .they are called
slinks. 'They are slimmer and paler than regular
salmon and they have little blood.'

2 A thin cod-fish, esp one caught early in the
spring before summer feeding in coastal waters
(P 243–56).

1955 *Nfld Fisheries Board* No 23 Exceedingly thin
fish ('slinks') shall not be classed as No 1 Labrador.

slinky a *EDD* slink sb 5: slinky 'lean.' Very
thin.

1888 HOWLEY *MS Reminiscences* 57 There was no
mistaking the long slinky foxey, grayish [wolf], which
seemed to walk along with that peculiar hang dog gait
characteristic of his kind. 1924 ENGLAND 258 'Gi' lang
wid ye!' the old man retorted. 'Ye lang, slinky cod hauler, wid legs crooked as a rainbow an' I dare say webbed feet on ye.' P 148–64 [Of a tall boy] long and
slinky. Q 67–20 [riddle] Long, slick, and slender
(slinky) like a trout, / When he bawls, his guts comes
out [Answer: a gun].

slip v Cp *OED* ~ v[1] 26 'to let go' for sense 1.

1 At the seal hunt, to cast off rope from the
shoulder and let go a quantity of seal pelts being
hauled to vessel or shore.

1865 CAMPBELL 64 Our host went out himself, and
slew a lot of seals, with which he was proceeding on his
homeward march, when a cry was raised of, 'Slip your
seals and run.' The ice was opening. 1905 MURPHY 13
There was slipping of 'tows,' there was running for life.
[c1945] TOBIN 40 "Off Southern Head, King's Cove":
. . .and shots rang out, / In code arranged before, no
doubt, / To slip their seals and turn about / To Southern Head. [1923] 1946 PRATT 197 "The Ice-Floes": We
gathered in knots, each man within call / Of his mate,
and slipping our ropes, we sped. 1944 LAWTON &
DEVINE 93 However, the firing on this particular day
was to this effect: Slip your seals and run for the shore.

2 To snare an animal or bird.

T 398–67 He's five times as good shot as what he is to
slip. 1975 LEYTON 21 They used to slip the partridges
then. You used to go in the country, a big copse on the
ridges, and you'd put down your stakes and you'd put
your slip down between them.

slip[1] n Cp *OED* ~ sb[2] 10 b 'newspaper (or part
of one) printed in form of a long slip of paper'
obs (1687–1727), 10 d 'a proof.' A broadside ballad.

P 170–78 [Johnny Burke used to say to Sir Charles

Hutton] 'Charlie, can you loan me some money to get
me slips printed?'

slip[2] n *DC* ~ n 1 Nfld obs (1772), cp *OED* sb[3] 3
b 'noose' obs (1687, 1691) for sense 1; *EDD* 31
'hank of silk or yarn' for sense 2.

1 A snare, arranged like a noose, to catch wild
animals and birds.

[1770] 1792 CARTWRIGHT i, 50 Early in the morning
I sent the furriers out with slips; and they tailed two. . .
I then landed Ned and Charles, and sent them to the
snares on Hare Hill; all of which they found down:
they set them again; and also six more. [1785] ibid iii,
77 She accompanied me in the yawl to the nearest slip,
in which we found a white-bear had been caught, and
from the appearance of the place, I believe it would
have held him, had it been a little stronger. 1792 ibid
Gloss i, xv ~ a snare for catching deer, bears, or other
large animals. They are made of various materials,
accordingly as a man is provided. T 187/9–65 He went
and got some good hay wire, and tailed a slip. The next
morning he had the ol' doe in the slip; she went
through the slip till she got back to her shoulders.
T 202/5–65 The secret was slips, wire slips. You'd find
the fox at lee in the marshes. You'd tail the slip in that.
T 391/3–67 In the fall of the year the youngsters, last
goin' off, put out a lot of slips [to catch rabbits].
P 222–67 ~s. Wire snares tied to a small strong stick in
a rabbit run for the purpose of catching the rabbit. The
rabbit runs into the snare and becomes caught by the
neck. M 68–23 When the rabbit snare was set in an
open area the rabbits could see it on a moonlight night.
To avoid this we sometimes placed a large branch near
the slip in such a way as to cast a shadow on the area
around the slip. 1975 LEYTON 21 You used to go in the
country, a big copse on the ridges, and you'd put down
your stakes and you'd put your slip down between
them. [The partridge would] go in and it'd go round
their neck and you had them.

2 A hank of twine or spun wool.

1940 SCAMMELL 37 "Squarin' Up": Skipper John
Wilkins strolled in to divine / If his credit was good for
a few slips of twine. T 26–64[3] I sent away five pound [of
raw wool] the other day [to be spun]. And yesterday I
had it come: twenty slips—right there on the fence.

3 One of the men operating a 'tow line.'

T 172/5–65 'Go forrard an' tell the slips she'll do it
now.' So I went forrard an' sung out to 'em. I said,
'Alright, boys, skipper said she'll do it.'

4 Comb **slip-place**: location of an animal snare.

[1775] 1792 CARTWRIGHT ii, 125 We also tailed the
two large [traps] in the slip-places, brought the slips
home, and saw the track of a white-bear. [1785] ibid iii,
78 In the mean time I sent the men to look at the other
slips, and then made a slip place on the east side of Slip
Hill.

slip-shod(s): old shoe or boot for casual wear.

[1930 *Am Speech* v, 393 ~s. (Heavy rough shoes
with wooden soles, used when fishermen are working
on deck in fine weather.)] P 222–67 ~s. Rubber boots
which are practically worn out, with the top part cut
off, making them wearable as a conventional shoe;
worn in the summer when one loafed around; used as a

save on shoes. C 71–93 ~s. Old broken-down but comfortable shoes.

slither v   also **slether**. Cp *EDD* ~ v 6 'cause to slide.' To skim a flat stone across surface of water in game of ducks and drakes; SKATE, SKIRR.
1937 DEVINE 19 And a penny to pay the old baker, / A hop and a scotch in another notch, / Sletherum, sletherum [slether 'em] take her. Q 67–89 ~ To skim rocks over water.

slob n   also **slop, slub** *O Sup*[1] ~ sb[1] 1 d Nfld (1920–), *DC* Nfld (1878–) for sense 1, and cp *EDD* sb[1] 2 'sea-mud' Ir, DINNEEN slab 'mud'; *O Sup*[1] sb[1] 4 ~ trout (1930) for sense 2; for combs. in sense 3: *O Sup*[1] 4 ~ ice (1910–), *DC* Nfld ([1836]–); ~ water Nfld (1952).
1 Heavy, slushy, densely packed mass of ice fragments, snow and freezing water, esp on the surface of the sea; sludge; clipped form of **slobice** below; cp SISH.
1846 TOCQUE 194 Sometimes slob, or ice ground up by the action of the waves and covered with snow, is mistaken for hard ice. 1858 [LOWELL] i, 86 We couldn't get into Broad Cove, for the slob an' cakes of ice. 1866 WILSON 282 Sometimes slob, or small loose ice covered with snow, intervenes between the larger ice, on which, if the hunter should chance to step, he must be extricated by the gaff of his friend, or he is ingulfed and perishes in the water. 1884 STEARNS 152 The ice that seriously impedes passage at this season of the year [December] is called here *slob*. It is a thick, consistent mass of frozen salt-water that lies in huge patches all over the surface of the water from land to land. 1895 *Christmas Review* 12 [proverb] Before you leave the sealer's side, the ice or slub must first be tried. [1915] 1972 GORDON 38–9 Salt water ice forms in quite a different way from the fresh water variety. The water seems to thicken with a sugary-looking scum. This is gradually pressed in along the edge of the land and cemented into a tight wedge. Each day the edge of this compressed 'slob,' as it is called, extends further and further until the area of water is completely engulfed. . .the process is more rapid in more snowy and milder weather than when there is a hard frost. 1924 ENGLAND 164 Under the thrust of the stout prow, fissures and crevasses kept constantly opening, through which the sea boiled up, with tangles of slob. 1946 MACKAY (ed) 490 The Newfoundlander has developed a wide vocabulary to describe ice conditions. To him, slush, ice-rind, pancake, sludge, slob, brash, young ice, each has its own characteristic. T 169/70–65[1] An' there've been times years ago in the winter when [the harbour] wasn't frozen over—all this slob around [so] that we wouldn't get a mail for over a month. T 393–67 'Twas late part o' January. An' 'twas all young slob, th' ocean slob.
2 A variety of trout which frequents river estuaries.
1964 SCOTT & CROSSMAN 75 There is probably a third or estuarine form of brook trout which live mainly in the estuaries and river mouths and which go in and out of the lower reaches of the rivers with the tides. Their growth rate is intermediate between that of mud trout and sea trout. These trout are called 'slob' in Labrador.
3 Comb **slob gull**: eastern glaucous gull (*Larus hyperboreus hyperboreus*).
1951 PETERS & BURLEIGH 222–3 Eastern Glaucous Gull. . . Local Names: Slob Gull, Burgomaster. . . It is well named the 'Slob Gull' for it prefers the drift (or slob) ice. When this ice is near shore the Glaucous Gulls become fairly common, and some even come into harbors for garbage and offal. 1967 *Bk of Nfld* iii, 283 Glaucous Gull: Slob Gull (because of its association with slob ice.)

slob hauler, slop ~ : long-handled wooden implement, shaped like a mattock, used to assist a boat through a sea-covering of heavy, slushy ice and snow.
T 172/4–65 We had slop haulers, that was pieces of pork barrel stave sawed off an' a hole put through it; an' a handle into it. P 148–65 A slob hauler is used to drag a boat through thin sea ice or heavy slob which makes normal rowing impossible. Two men (one on either side), each handling a slob-hauler, drag a rodney through the slob by reaching forward with synchronized strokes, digging the blade into the slob, and pulling aft. P 9–73 A pair of slob haulers is necessary for each boat, one for each of two men. They were made from a piece of flour-barrel head, the straight edge of which was between fifteen to eighteen inches long. It had a wood handle.

slob ice: see sense 1 above.
1836 [WIX][2] 25 There is not so much 'slob-ice' during the winter in Placentia and St Mary's bays, as in the northern bays. 1873 CARROLL 19 No matter how thin the ice is during whelping time, seals are sure to whelp on it as long as it will bear their weight, as every moment it will be getting stronger as the 'slob' or 'sish' ice drifts off the land, or drifts in from sea against the shore, pressing such ice together. 1907 TOWNSEND 281 The ice along the seacoast forms a solid highway upon which the inhabitants travel on dog-sledges. . .the breadth of this strip of solid ice along the eastern coast every winter is from twenty to twenty-five miles, while outside of this is the loose 'slob' ice, which drifts back and forth with the winds and tides, varies greatly in thickness and density, and may extend fifty or more miles out to sea. 1965 RUSSELL 84 The island was locked in ice which, at its periphery, had degenerated into slob ice, a tacky mixture of half-ice, half-sludge which was impassable for man or boat. 1975 BUTLER 94 We could not see the edge of the heavy slob ice and could not be sure if we would be able to get through to the land. 1975 *Them Days* i (1), p. 8 When you got to these rapids, and it's freezing-up-time, it keeps ice makin', more ice, more slob ice makin', and it finally accumulates in these rapids and chokes them. 1981 *Evening Telegram* 27 Mar, p. 3 All three captains said the slob ice experienced during mild temperatures after the first four days at the Front off the coast of Labrador was one of the main reasons why they returned.

slob water: slushy mixture of water, ice and half-frozen snow.

1952 BANFILL 75 We were thrown from the komatic and stood waist deep in icy slob water.

slob v

1 To fill or jam a stretch of water with a slushy, dense mass of ice fragments, snow and freezing water. See SLOB n. Cp QUAR(R) v.

1975 *Them Days* i (1), p. 8 More ice, more slob ice makin', and it finally accumulates in these rapids and chokes them. . . To stop the flow of Hamilton River water is a big accomplishment for anybody. So Nature would try it by slobbin' it with ice.

2 Phr *slob haul, slop* ~ : to pull a boat through a sea covering of heavy, slushy ice and snow with a wooden implement shaped like a mattock; cp SLOB HAULER.

1949 FITZGERALD 93 ~ The slow process of hauling a boat through slob with rakelike instruments instead of oars. T 172/4–65 Aboard o' the boat sometimes we'd have to launch, more times we'd have to slop-haul. You get back in the stern o' the boat, one on each side, and those pork barrel staves would go through the ice, an' you would pull the boat.

slobby a Cp *EDD* slob sb[1] 1: slobby 'muddy' and SLOB. Of the sea, covered with a dense, slushy mass of ice fragments, snow and freezing water (Q 67–55).

1973 MOWAT 145 It was all broke up and slobby, but it was ice, and that was some better than black rock!

sloe n Comb **sloe tree**: chokecherry (*Prunus virginiana*) (1956 ROULEAU 37).

slommocky a ['slʌməkɪ] *EDD* slammock sb 1 ~ ; DINNEEN slaimice 'a rag, a tatter.' Of a slovenly, untidy appearance; cp SLAWMEEN*.

P 113–56 Tuck in your shirttail and don't be so slommocky. 1968 DILLON 154 Pad was always slawmeky. P 108–70 She's slawmecky about herself.

sloo See SLEW.

slop[1] n Cod-fish which is split, washed, heavily salted and undried; cp SALT-BULK. Also attrib.

[1912] 1930 COAKER 47 The reason the price was high was because the slop was scarce at St John's. [1914] ibid 84 On the Labrador the usual time for fishing was passed when the coast cleared, the result being that many floaters returned before the fish struck in and those who secured catches, considering time would not permit curing into dry fish, salted their catches heavily. This caused a large over-supply of slop fish. 1966 HORWOOD 350 . . .eying the hundred-odd barrels of slop cod that they had now put down into salt bulk.

slop[2] See SLOB.

sloppy a *OED* ~ a 2 a (1830–). Of snow, wet, half-melting (Q 67–59).

T 178–65 Oh, it was blowin' a howler, and sloppy snow.

slottery a Cp *EDD* slotter v[1] 1 (3) ~ 'wet, dirty' Co D. Of snowflakes, large, heavy, full of moisture.

1897 *J A Folklore* x, 209 Snow falling in large flakes is called *slottery* snow. Such has much moisture in it, easily melts, and makes the ground soft and muddy.

slouch n *EDD* ~ sb[1] 5. A cotton sun-bonnet worn by women for outdoors work; SKULLY.

P 37 ~ A kind of bonnet worn by women for outdoor purposes. In summer it is a large white, thin sun-bonnet; in winter it is of a heavy dark material. T 172/3–65 Way back years ago, the old women used to wear a slouch, an' cover over their faces—tied with a string an' go [back] over their shoulders. 1972 MURRAY 155 Some [women and girls], more careful to their complexions than others, wore a 'slouch' (i.e., sunbonnet) to protect them from sunburn as they worked on the flake or in the garden. P 254–78 Some of the old women used to wear slouches when they was spreading fish.

slough n [slʌf]. In coopering, a strip of material placed over a knot-hole (P 127–76).

T 90–64 And if you had a nasty knot in your stave, you would flatten [this material] out an' then fold it back an' forth, like a dressmaker would fold a piece o' material. An' we call that a slough. Push that down where that nasty knot was an' you'd have a tight barrel.

slouse v [slæuz] *EDD* ~ v. To splash, swill or swish in or under water; cp SOUSE v.

P 148–64 A car was 'slousing' through water which was on the street. T 200/2–65 It's a flat calm night. By an' by, slouse on one side o' the boat, slouse on th' other, an' th' old boat rolled back and forth. T 398/9–67 So I sloused an' sloused an' sloused, an' [struck out for the shore]. P 108–70 Slouse down the bridge while you're at it. C 71–101 If someone had water thrown over him he was said to have been 'sloused.'

sloven n ['slʌvn] *DC* ~ n (1895–); DINNEEN sleamhnán 'slide-car.' A long, low four-wheeled cart, drawn by horses and used to move heavy loads.

1896 *Dial Notes* i, 381 ~ a low truck wagon. 1929 BURKE [11] [advertisement] Charles F Lester. . . Has always for hire Horses, Slovans, Trucks and all tackles required for removing any goods—light or heavy. 1937 DEVINE 46 ~ A long, low horse cart. T 25–64 And then they had another [type of cart] that you'd only see on Water Street at St John's, called a sloven. That's a long thing with four wheels. That would be for taking particularly heavy loads. That would be a pair of horses [required]. C 66–8 These [slovens] were used for transporting heavy freight. There was a single shaft between the two horses. . . The name of these carts was 'slovens'. . . They disappeared, some time after 1940. The wheels were iron rimmed and there was no seat in front for the driver and his helper. 1973 *Daily News* 1 May, p. 4 At the turn of the century. . . Horse-drawn long carts, box carts and slovens, transported goods between the wooden finger wharves and the warehouses.

slowcome n also **slocum** ['slo·ʉkɵm]. Cp *EDD*
~ 'a lagging, stupid, lazy fellow' D Co.

1 A small cod-fish, not large enough to split;
LEGGY, ROUNDER (1968 *Avalon Penin of Nfld*
112).

P 243–73 [At Bay Roberts they call] a small cod-fish
a slocum.

2 Nickname for resident of a section of Herring Neck.

T 172/3–65 When I was a boy they had a name on all
those people. There was always a contention between
the Herring Neck people and the slowcomes—they
were the slowcomes down there.

slub¹ n Cp *EDD* ~ sb¹ 1 'a gelatinous mass; a
slimy wash.'

1 Slimy substance on body of fish; blood,
slime, liquid refuse from process of splitting cod;
cp GURRY.

1897 *J A Folklore* x, 210 With your bag on your back
and your barbel outside, / To keep out the slub from
your poor yeller hide, / In this Newfoundland. [1915]
1930 COAKER 103 The way this fish should be cleaned.
First the slub be removed before splitting. 1937
DEVINE 46 ~ The gelatinous substance on the outside
of fish before washing, after being taken from the boat.
P 211 69 If the fish were plentiful, the slub and gurry
had to be bailed out of the dill. C 71–30 As it was a
rainy day, the fisherman was wet, hair over his eyes,
dirty from the slub of the boat.

2 Deposit of brownish-green mucus or slime
on fish-nets and gear from minute marine animal
(*Larvacean*) (P 245–79).

1956 *Evening Telegram* 12 Dec, p. 11 There has been
a tendency towards use of larger mesh because this
makes the trap lighter and easier to haul, it provides
less area for 'slub' to collect. T 399–67 'I see they got a
lot o' nets in the pond. What's that? To clean the slub?'
'Oh yeah, clean the slub out of 'em. They're salmon
nets.' 'The fresh water cuts the slub off?' 1974 *Evening
Telegram* 14 Oct, p. 4 Some cod were being netted but
no codfish was jigged until August 13, and even then
only in shallow water where 'slub' (a jelly-like form of
sea life that adheres to nets) was not plentiful. 1979
ibid 8 June, p. 1 A number of other explanations have
been put forward to explain the lack of salmon this
year: dirty water, slub on salmon nets, the fact that
caplin haven't begun rolling on the beaches. 1979
NEMEC 249 Some maintain, in addition, that [Dog
Days coincide] with the appearance of 'slub,' a variety
of scum or flotsam formed from miniscule marine
plants, organisms and other debris which collects on
gillnets and clogs the 'meshes.'

slub² See SLOB.

slubby a Cp *EDD* slub sb¹ 1: slubby 'slimy.'
See also SLUB¹.

1 Covered with fish slime (P 148–63).

2 Of the sea, marked by concentrations of the
minute marine animal *Larvacean Oikapleura*
(P 245–79); see CLEAN.

T 194/5–65 An' you was able to see bottom just so
plain as I can see that cookin'; an' the water slubby.

slue See SLEW.

slut n

1 A tin kettle, often one with a large flat bottom and tapering to the top, used to boil water
on an open fire; cp PIPER, SMUT.

1924 ENGLAND 11 Some were drawing water at an
icicled faucet near the cropping shed, bringing 'sluts'
(kettles) aboard, and brewing tea. 1937 DEVINE 46 ~
A large tin teakettle. P 102–60 Everybody would line
up 3 times a day for salt meat, potatoes and figgy duff
or saltfish and brewis and a slut full of boiled tea, no
milk but good old Barbados molasses, no sugar.
P 54–67 A hotwater kettle, of the familiar type locally
made by tinsmiths and much used on outdoor picnics,
hunting trips etc, is called a slut—especially the very
large sort, holding about 4 gallons and made of sheet
copper, used on board the old sealing steamers, being
always kept full of boiling water on the galley stove,
whence sealers would take small kettlesful to take to
their bunks and brew tea with. 1973 MOWAT 69 Twice a
week. . .we got duff, made out of condemned flour put
into bags and boiled in a slut—a big kettle—with a bit
of salt pork.

2 Attrib **slut kettle**: see sense 1 above.

T 181–65 An' we had a large kettle [that was shaped]
up like that. They used to call 'em the slut kettle.

slut tea: strong tea brewed in the kettle in
which the water is boiled.

P 145–74 There was nothing on the table but bread,
molasses and slut tea.

smack¹ n Cp *EDD* ~ sb² 2 'an instant' obs
(1809). A short while (P 133–58).

1925 *Dial Notes* v, 342 We'm 'll be out a *smack* yet.

smack² n Cp *OED* ~ sb³ naut 1 'single-masted
sailing vessel, chiefly employed as a coaster';
DAE 'fishing vessel having a well in which fish
may be kept alive' (1891). A small decked vessel
sailing between settlements to collect fish from
fishermen for export; COLLECTOR, FISHING
SMACK.

1895 *Christmas Review* 18 It was meant as the highest tribute to the boat-building capabilities of Jim
Leary, whose handiwork, whether displayed in the
construction of baitskiff, smack, skiff, punt or rodney,
was always superior to what any other man in the settlement could turn out. 1901 *Christmas Review* 2 The
Hopewell, more like a transport ship than a fishing
smack, cast her moorings for home. M 68–20 The
smack *Alice Jean* was a popular means of transportation for the people of Richards Harbour. 1971
CHIARAMONTE 7 Two alternative modes of travel are
the Canadian National Railways coastal boats and the
'smack,' a fish-collecting boat stationed at the fish plant
in Community 2. 1975 BUTLER 71–2 The small skiffs
which we used to buy and collect lobsters from other
parts of the bay were called lobster smacks.

small a Cp LARGE.

1 In various grades or culls of dried and salted cod: fish of a certain specified size, freq with designation of quality or 'cure': ~ MADEIRA, ~ MERCHANTABLE, ~ THIRDS¹, WEST a: ~ INDIA.

[1909] 1930 COAKER 7 No 1 small same qualifications as in No 1 large, from under [14] inches. . .to 18 inches. 1955 *Nfld Fisheries Board* No 39 Small fish 12″ to 18″. T 36–64 Extra large from twenty one, small from fourteen to eighteen. . . An' when you sell this fish for market there used to be choice, large an' small; and 'extra large'; 'large'; 'small'; 'small Madeira'; 'small West Indee'; 'small thirds'; 'small merchantable.' T 410–67 There was small Madeira, large Madeira; small thirds an' large thirds; small West Indee; tomcods. . .Italian—too many grades for me!

2 Designating a stage of an animal's growth: ~ BEDLAMER, ~ MIDDLER/MEDLER.

T 84–64 This year they're a bellamer—small bellamer, an' the next year they're a big bellamer. [1783] 1792 CARTWRIGHT iii, 22 The second [year beavers are called] small medlers.

3 With nouns forming a comb used attrib: ~ BOAT, ~ **seed**.

1927 DOYLE (ed) 71 "The Newfoundland Fishermen": The small boat men though easy, / Their toil to those mentioned before, / What man dare say they are lazy / Or sleep away time on the shore. 1963 *Nfld Record* ii, 15 No sensible man would wish today to incur these [perils] in the same degree as men did for so long in the small-boat fishery on the fishing banks of the Northwest Atlantic. 1967 FIRESTONE 107 *Small seed* beds are made by first turning over all the ground to be used with mattocks and shovels.

smallagen n A mature male seal (1925 *Dial Notes* v, 342).

1924 ENGLAND 303 Big gangs were out on very loose ice, hunting innumerable thousands of 'de rale ole smallagins, now'—that is to say, very large seals.

smallwood n Attrib **smallwood boot**: leather boot, worn esp by fishermen; TONGUE BOOT.

[c1885] 1973 SMALLWOOD 22–3 They were made mostly by hand and in three styles; one came well above the ankles, the other came up to the knees, and the third pretty well to the thighs. . . Verses were printed on cards and distributed in large quantities, and they came to be very well known. I remember one: Smallwood's Boots are the best of leather, / Smallwood's Boots they suit all weather, / Smallwood's Boots they are so grand, / They are the best in Newfoundland! T 84–64 There was all Smallwood boots then, for fishin' boots, all Smallwood boots, no rubbers. T 191–65 An' they'd wear what they call the half leg boots, you know. They're hard leather boots—that was before, just before the Smallwood boots came out; and the moleskin clothes, an' the swanskin cuffs, you know. So they were well fitted, and. . .they could stand up to a pretty good storm. M 70–15 Another type of boot worn a great deal by fishermen was known as the 'three-quarters' or the 'smallwood' boot (named after the St John's manufacturer). It was made of very heavy leather, and when well greased with cod-oil it was waterproof. 1975 BUTLER 89 I was wearing knee high Smallwood boots, and I unstrapped my oilskins from my suitcase and put them on.

smart a *OED* ~ a 9 for sense 1; *EDD* 12, *DAE* 1 NE (1788–) for sense 2. Cp CLEVER.

1 Lively, alert, active, vigorous.

1792 PULLING *MS* Aug But, added Peckford, there are some smart fellows gone around to Matthew Ward's in New Bay now for the Indians. [1833] 1927 DOYLE (ed) 15 "Come All Ye Jolly Ice-Hunters": We had twenty-eight as smart a lads as ever crossed the main. [1856] 1977 WHITELEY 32 He was a smart little boy. 1873 CARROLL 25 An old seal when on level ice will outstrip a smart fellow in a distance of 60 yards, provided the seal is ten or twelve feet ahead of him. [1896] SWANSBOROUGH 14 "December": December comes when days are short, / To do much work we must be smart. 1964 BLONDAHL (ed) 77 "Sealing Cruise of the *Lone Flier*": Peter Trooke, a smart young man, was working in the hold, / When a cask of oil fell through the hatch and gave him a severe blow. / Edmond Hines was a smart young man, and everything went well, / Until we donkeyed him five times and he got mad as hell. T 187–65 The only thing about Eskimos—they couldn't stand no sickness. They was alright, robust, smart as anything while they was well, but the least bit o' sickness take 'old to un, he was gone.

2 In good health.

1937 DEVINE 46 ~ In good health; much the same as *clever* in this sense. P 245–56 'How's your mother, Joe?' 'She's smart, thank you.' T 172–65 [He's] not as smart as me, 'cause he got an 'eart condition, an' I haven't.

smatchy a *EDD* smatch sb 1: ~ . Of food, esp salt or pickled pork, beef, etc, tainted, spoiled, improperly cured. Cp FOUSTY.

1897 *J A Folklore* x, 210 A fisherman will complain of the pork supplied him being *smatchy*. 1924 ENGLAND 53 And I have heard some of the men growl that more than once they had 'got home wid not'in' but a bundle o' dirty clo'es an' a gad of smatchy [tainted] flippers!' 1937 DEVINE 46 ~ Mouldy; unpalatable. Said of meats insufficiently salted, in particular. Bad taste or flavour in pork etc. C 71–105 ~ Used to describe certain foods such as meat, and especially fat-back pork (salt) when it became stale and unfit to eat. C 71–129 ~ used in connection with salt meat which somehow had the pickle taken from it. When the meat was boiled it had a taste my father always called 'smatchy.'

smatter v also **smather*** *OED* ~ v 1 obs (13. .–1600) for sense 1; *EDD* 1 for sense 2; DINNEEN smeadar 'a mess,' smeádár 'heavy blow'; *Kilkenny Lexicon* smather: lick for smather.

1 To dirty, smear.

1968 DILLON 154 Look, girl, you have paint smaddered all over that.

2 To break, smash.

P 148–69 I smaddered up the glasses [on the table when he pushed me on top of them].

3 Phr *smather my eyes*: exclamation.

1968 DILLON 154 Smadder me eyes, boy! Do you think I'm a liar?

lick for smatter: blow for blow; hammer and tongs (P 8–55).

1968 DILLON 154 Well a couple o' the boys had lick for smadder there last night. C 71–8 They went at it lick for smatter.

smeachy a Cp *EDD* smeech sb 7: smeechy (2) 'tainted' So D Co. Unpleasant in smell or taste; SMATCHY.

1964 *Evening Telegram* 26 May, p. 2 Yes b'y, cold ribs, cold pease puddin', smeachy tea and a bit of cake!

smear n [smiəɹ]. A number (of birds); cp SIGN.

T 389–67[1] Yes, sir, there was a smear o' birds on the water, a smear o' birds on the water! I didn't think there was so many as there was.

smell n Cp *EDD* ~ sb 2 (2) ~ smock 'wood anemone.' Comb **smell bottle, smelling ~, smell-smock**. Leafy white orchid (*Platanthera dilatata*); BOG LILY (1898 *J A Folklore* xi, 280; 1956 ROULEAU 37).

1979 *Evening Telegram* 14 July, p. 13 If it's damp that should be a good place [in the woods] for smell bottles. 1981 ibid 16 May, p. 20 All they had to do was get under the longer fence, and make their way to the first marshy place and there they were, lovely smell bottles with a scent fit for a queen.

smeller n Cp *OED* ~ 3 'esp one of the whiskers of a cat' for sense 1.

1 Whisker of a seal (1925 *Dial Notes* v, 342).

1924 ENGLAND 231 As a souvenir I plucked out one of the [dog seal's] whiskers—'smellers,' the men call them. A peculiar, horn-like structure it was, somewhat corrugated, and of a peculiar gray-brown tint with darker brown spots.

2 Mobile feeler of a lobster (P 77–74).

smert* n *EDD* smirt W So. A sharp stinging sensation; painful spot; smart.

P 148–62 I have a smert on the finger. C 71–38 Many people use the word smirt instead of the word smart for a stinging pain, such as that felt from a burn or iodine on a cut or scratch.

smert v [sməɹt]. Cp *OED* smart v 1 obs var smert. To pain or sting.

1937 DEVINE 46 Smerte. To pain, smart or suffer from a wound. 1958 *Nfld Dishes* 66 Be careful when frying fat, if it splatter on your hand it smerts. 1966 FARIS 178 The needles makes her smert. C 71–130 When a cut or bruise would pain we would say that it really smirts.

smoke n

1 Esp in pl, gusts of wind and spray.

1977 BUTLER 26 There were white smokes of wind as high as the hills and water blew over the vessel in sheets.

2 Comb **smoke heap**: smudge fire.

1876 MURRAY & HOWLEY 449 The more recent destruction [of the forest] is in many cases clearly traceable to the most culpable neglect, on the part of trappers, lumber explorers or 'rhynders,' in omitting to extinguish their camp fires, or smoke heaps, which they had used to drive off flies.

smoke leader: device placed in front of a fireplace to lead smoke up the flue.

P 127–78 ~ A wooden stick hung down from the mouth of a fire-place flue to lead the smoke upward in the right direction. Such an implement even though used in some homes, was most commonly used in tilts where the flue was usually made of wood.

smoked p ppl [ˌsmoʊkɪd ˈkɒt͡ʔn̩, ˌsmoʊkɪd ˈkɒt͡ʔn̩, ˌsmoʊkɪd ˈdæːb]. In comb **smoked cotton, ~ dab**: cheap remnant or second of cloth, spoiled in dyeing and resembling smoke-damaged goods.

T 199–65 The smoke cotton, 'twas only about twenty cents a pound. 'Twas ends of material, when 'twas going through the looms, there was ends that was spoiled. When they were dyeing it, 'twould be misprints and the pattern would be all blurred. 'Twas damaged cotton, but the women'd call it smoked cotton, and more of 'em 'd call it smoked dab, and there was a tremendous outlet for that.

smoky a Comb **smoky jack**: puff-ball (*Lycoperdon gemmatum*); HORSE(S) FART.

C 75–2 A type of brown, spongy ball, very soft, and found in the marshes. When one squeezed it a smoke would come from it; for this reason it was given the name 'smoky jack.' It was used as a blood stopper and cleanser, for it sealed a wound, keeping out infection.

smoochin' n Cp *DAE* smooch v 'to smear.' Heavy, odorous mixture used by men to dress hair.

1896 *J A Folklore* ix, 29 ~ Hair-oil, or pomade. A young man from abroad, commencing as a clerk in an establishment at one of the [outports], was puzzled by an order for a 'pen'orth of smoochin'. 1937 DEVINE 46 ~ A hair oil used by men, formerly called Bear's grease.

smop See MOP*.

smother n Cp *DAE* ~ 'potpie' (1852–). Pastry covering; SOD.

P 13–74 ~ The pastry that covers the stew as in a meat-pie, rabbit-pie, etc.

smothered p ppl Esp of fish, killed by prolonged entanglement in net.

1883 SHEA 25 Every time the trawl was hauled on board there was a large portion, amounting to 60 or 70 per cent., wasted, being either smothered or of uneatable kinds, or too small for the market. . . 1975 BUTLER 47 I got a axe and he got a big bait chopper and we used to go down underwater and chop and hack as long as we could stop down, and come up and go down again. I don't know how long we were at it—drowned, smothered. 1979 NEMEC 267 Although smothered fish has discolored flesh because of the blood suffused through it, and as such is less attractive to consumers, processing plants have not evinced any serious concern over smothered fish.

smouch v *EDD* smooch v 1. To prowl about in a furtive manner with a view to mischief.

1976 MATTHEWS 113 [He] used to be around smouching here and there as far as I could understand. Trying to persuade people to move according to what I heard.

smut n
  1 A tin kettle, esp one used to boil water on an open fire (P 148–64); SLUT.
  1973 BARBOUR 94 We also had one for the grate which we called the 'smut.'
  2 In pl, charred trees still standing after a forest fire (P 10–56).

smutty n also **smutty-nose harp**. A harp seal in the stage when its fur becomes dark.
  1909 ROBINSON 75 Then we have the smutty-nose harp, with a black head and nose and a spotted body. 1925 *Dial Notes* v, 342 ~ a seal just forming its saddle.

snagle n Cp *EDD* ~ sb 'a snail' obs. A variety of periwinkle, family *Littorinidae*; WRINKLE[1].
  M 68–13 'Snagle, snagle come out of your hole, / If you don't I'll make your father and mother black as any crow.' This rhyme is chanted by the boys and girls as they go to the sea-shore to pick the snagle (snail).

snail n also **snailer** *OED* ~ sb[1] c; cp *EDD* snailer 'a snail.' A variety of sea-snail; esp periwinkle, family *Littorinidae*; WRINKLE[1].
  P 148–64 Snails are salt-water fleshy animals in spiral shells, up to half an inch in diameter. M 68–7 Sometimes boys of my age and I would go picking snails in the harbour. . . Everyone would be singing their favourite snailer song. 'Snailer, snailer come out your hole / If you don't I beat your father and mother black as [any] coal. C 69–5 Sometimes we picked up rinkles (small round shells) containing a tiny creature which we called a snail.

snake n
  1 Common name of two small, elongated varieties of salt-water fish: (a) rock gunnel or tansy (*Pholis gunnellus*); (b) radiated shanny (*Ulvaria subbifurcata*) (1971 *RLS* 3, pp. 3, 4).
  2 Cpd **snakehead**: swamp pink (*Arethusa bulbosa*) (1956 ROULEAU 37).
  snakeroot: canker-root (*Coptis groenlandica*) (1893 *N S Inst Sci* viii, 363).
  C 69–6 For ulcers on the tongue, use snakeroot. C 75–142 Snakeroot was also steeped for a cough medicine.

snap-apple n *DC* ~ night (1912). Attrib **snap-apple night**: Hallow-e'en or eve of All Saints'

Day (31 Oct) when children play bob-apple (P 133–58); cp COLCANNON.
  T 347/50–67 Snap-apple night, or hallow-e'en or colcannon night.

snapper n Cp FARMER & HENLEY (1903) ~ 'a braggart' US, BOWEN *Sea Slang* (1929) ~ -rigged 'ship which is poorly rigged and found, or a man with few clothes' E Can and Amer, BERREY 437 ~ rig 'second-hand suit,' *Am Speech* v, 391 herring- ~ 'New Foundlander or Nova Scotian; sometimes an inhabitant of Maine.'
  1 A skilled, successful fisherman; also attrib.
  [1906] GRENFELL 51–2 Tom was a 'snapper fisherman,' and if any boat in the harbor got a load it was as certain as daylight that Tom's punt did not go home empty. 1910 ibid 36 If there was one ocean-going skipper on the coast known to be more of a 'snapper' than the rest, that man was Elijah Anderson. [1911] ibid 69 Every year the 'snapper' fishermen were pushing further and further north, where the coast is not only unlighted and unmarked but also unsurveyed and uncharted.
  2 Attrib, comb **snapper boat**: a type of boat fishing with long lines.
  M 68–3 In the 1940's another type of boat was added to the skiff, 'snapper boats' (long-liner type which was from forty to forty-five feet in the keel). Those were still in use when the Trepassey fishery failed. The men owning those two types of boats carried on the fishery away from home. The snapper boats at first went to the Glace Bay and Dingwall areas of Nova Scotia from April to November. They fished by means of long lines and sold their catches to the fresh-fish producing plants in that area.
  snapper-rigged: dressed unconventionally.
  P 269–64 ~ dressed up funny, as of a child wearing a short coat over a skirt over a pair of pants. P 189–66 ~ of one's dress, untidy.

snappering ppl Cp *EDD* snapper v[2] 'crackle.' Comb **snapperin' bough**: a dead conifer branch which has turned red; BLASTY BOUGH.
  P 207–67 They could hear the snappern boughs snap and crackle in the fire. P 127–79 Her hair was as red as a snappern bough.

snarbuckle n ['snæːɹbʌkl].
  1 (a) A tightly tied knot (1955 ENGLISH 36); (b) a tangled or twisted rope (Q 73–4).
  2 Burnt or charred remnant (of food).
  1955 ENGLISH 36 ~ burnt to a cinder. P 230–66 The potatoes are roasted to a snarbuckle. P 212–73 I forgot my piece of toast, and when I went to take it off the stove, it was burned to a snarbuckle.

snarly n *EDD* snaily: var snarley So. A snail (C 67–13).

snatch v To slake lime by adding water (P 245–67).

snaz n   also **snas**. A meddlesome, cranky old maid.

1925 *Dial Notes* v, 342 Snas. Old maid. 1937 DEVINE 46 ~ An old maid who likes to poke her nose into everybody's business.

snig n   Cp *EDD* ~ sb¹ 1 'eel, esp young or small' for sense 1.

1 Small freshwater cod-fish; TOM COD.

1964 SCOTT & CROSSMAN 86 Until 1962, a freshwater capture of tomcod had been reported only once from Newfoundland. . . Jeffers also noted that the fish (locally called 'snig') was abundant during the winter in Pistolet Bay.

2 A flick.

P 118–67 He gave him a snig [on the face] with his hand.

3 Children's game in which a stick is flicked into the air and must be struck by opposing side (M 71–97).

4 Comb **snig stick**: stick used in game (see sense 3 above).

M 71–97 Each person had a snig-stick, a narrow stick about three feet long and pointed at one end. A gooster was set up and a 'catball' was made. The catball was laid across the 'gooster,' the 'snig stick' placed under it and it was thrown as far as possible. The persons on the other team would be placed anywhere from thirty to one hundred feet out away from the 'gooster.' They had to try and hit the catball and drive it back in as close to the 'gooster' as possible.

snig v   *EDD* ~ v¹ 1, 5 for senses 1, 2; DINNEEN sniogaim for sense 3.

1 To cut or chop (P 113–56).

1937 DEVINE 46 ~ To cut off a small piece.

2 To haul logs out of woods by hand.

P 13–74 I have to snig those logs to the road before lunch.

3 To drain the milk of a cow or goat to the last drop.

1968 DILLON 155 They used to snig the goat.

4 To flick a button with thumb and forefinger.

C 66–1 You'd put your button where your 'malver' landed and then you'd snig 'em all like that.

snip v   *OED* ~ v 1 obs (1586–1674). To snatch.

T 375–67 They has a handkerchief on the floor in the middle. Somebody got to take it and run to the corner, and if they tags the corner, somebody else got to go out and try to snip it.

snite n   *OED* ~ sb¹ 1 now dial; *EDD* sb¹ Co D So. Wilson's common snipe (*Capella gallinago delicata*) (1967 *Bk of Nfld* iii, 283).

1895 *J A Folklore* viii, 34 The snipe is called a *snite*, which is the Old English form. 1959 MCATEE 29 ~ Common Snipe (. . .Nfld).

sno* interrog [snou, snɔʉ]. Cp J GARTON *The Guest* (1932), p. 42 's'no 'dost thou know' So; N ROGERS *Wessex Dialect* (1979), p. 24 sno 'dost

know' W. A contraction of 'Dost thou know?' (P 152–58).

T 14/7–64 'Snow, boy,' he said. 'I'll follow ye in!' T 141/65–65² Ron had a berth, snow, with Fred Parsons one summer. T 178/80–65 Well now I don't hardly know where we was to, but I can mind about that now you come to speak of it, snow. 1969 *Trans Dev Assoc* ci, 187–8 Snaw. (An abbreviation of 'Dost thou know,' used at the beginning of an utterance) [Nfld]. C 70–15 'He's goin' to sell some, he told me.' 'How much, 'sno?'

snock v   Cp *EDD* snack v: var snock 'to snap, bite.' To make a snapping noise or biting movement, esp with the jaws of a hobby-horse in Christmas mumming.

T 284–66 His mouth'd come open down here an' you'll haul this line an' he'd snock so hard. Perhaps you get hold o' their dresses; you snock 'em up and catches their dress, you'll tear a piece right out of un, see, with those nails. T 265–66² They'd be comin' towards you, an' you hear 'em snock together when the mouth close; those big jaws might be a foot long. They'd come together, snockin! They had nails for teeth. 1969 *Christmas Mumming in Nfld* 66 You could tell that it was a horsey-hops outside by his jaws snocking [knocking] together: snock, snock.

snog v   To hit, strike; esp to club a seal; BAT v.

1929 *Nat Geog* July, p. 125 Young seals are saucy and will come for a man until he snogs them with his bat. P 243–59 Snog un. Bat 'im, i.e. hit seal on the snout with a bat. P 7–79 We'll snog 'im in the head.

snop v   [snɒp] *EDD* ~ v 1 'chip, break.' To break off a projecting part.

T 84–64 He took off my gaff just the same as I'd snopped the end off o' that bottle, just as quick.

snot See BEAT.

snotty a   Comb **snotty var**: the balsam-fir (*Abies balsamea*); VAR, SPRING²: ~ VAR.

1957 *Beaver* Autumn, p. 29 An old fir-tree, with resin clotted on the bark, is often called a 'snotty-var.' P 148–61 In those places they burn snotty var. P 148–65 Snotty var is too greasy to be good for cutting for winter fuel. All the sap comes out. C 70–15 Fir wood was coated with turpentine and was usually called snotty var because it was sticky.

snow n   For combs. in sense 2: *DC* ~ house (Nfld: 1771–), ~ hut (1823–), ~ road (1829–1883).

1 Prov phr *a year of snow a year of plenty* (1937 DEVINE 66).

2 Comb **snow deathfall**: animal trap covered with snow to deceive animal; cp DEATHFALL.

[1770] 1792 CARTWRIGHT i, 46 In our return we found two old furriers' tilts, and snow death-falls; which appeared to be of Canadian construction.

snow drop: northern white violet (*Viola pallens*) (1956 ROULEAU 38).

snow dwy: see DWY.

snow hole: deep snow-pit formed as temporary shelter.

[1919] 1972 GORDON 147 I was thus introduced for the first time to what is locally described as a 'Snow-hole.' First, a big log fire was kindled on a bank of snow, and we stretched out in our sleeping-bags beside it. Then, as the snow began to melt, the fire and ourselves gradually sank down until we touched ground. After this, it was the nearest approach to living in a chimney that I have ever experienced. Ten feet below the upper level, and nearly blinded with the smoke, one was warm enough, but I was thankful when light appeared above, and we were able to climb out to the fresh air.

snow house: dwelling or shelter constructed with blocks of snow.

[1771] 1792 CARTWRIGHT i, 96 I looked at my traps down the river, and then proceeded to Lyon Head, where I visited my Indian friends in their snowhouse. 1782 LA TROBE 2 When pinched with hunger, [the dogs] will swallow almost anything; and on a journey, it is necessary to secure the harness within the snow-house overnight, lest by devouring it they should render it impossible to proceed in the morning. 1916 HAWKES 58 The art of building snow-houses is still practised by the Labrador Eskimo north of Hopedale. In Southern Labrador, the custom has so nearly died out that the missionaries hold snow-building contests to keep alive the ancient art. T 187–65 All Usquimaux was [living] into a snow house or canvas tent or place dug into a bank of turf. That's where they'd live then.

snow hut: see **snow house**.

1861 DE BOILIEU 98 We built a snow hut, by cutting blocks of snow, and placing them one upon another, gradually inclining to the top centre. 1895 GRENFELL 153 At night on travel a snow hut is built. . . The snow is cut in blocks. . .from the inside of the circle chosen for the house. Thus the hut goes down and up at the same time. A hole is left at the top for the air, while a block is cut to fit into the door from the outside, after all are in.

snow path: trail or pathway for winter travel; cp SLIDE PATH, WOODS ~ .

[1896] SWANSBOROUGH 5 "March": If snow paths to the woods hold on / Men find there's something to be done. / A sudden thaw will come some day / And take the snow path all away. 1972 MURRAY 99 They had to go over the meadow land inch by inch, picking up stones or any other debris that might have collected on the field during the winter. For, often, when snow covered the fields and fences, short cuts or 'snow paths' were taken across anyone's land.

snow racket: snowshoe.

1819 PANL CS 1 28 May I. . .found what he had told me to be correct, and near the Tilt I discovered part of an Indians Snow Racket.

snow road: frozen surface or track used as a road in winter.

T 43/7–64 But the wagon sleds, now, there was two o' them because they were only used in the winter, an' you had a ice road or a snow road.

snowchy a Snuffling; congested.

1897 *J A Folklore* x, 210 When a person has his nasal passages stuffed up by a cold, he is said to be all *snowchy*.

snowly a Of the weather, presaging or threatening snow.

1960 FUDGE 9 It was looking snowly with a heavy swell running from the southeast.

snub¹ n also **snubby**. Cp *OED* ~ sb³ 1 'a snub nose.' A cod-fish with a rounded, blunt snout, believed to be a sign of good luck; SEAL-HEAD COD. Cp TALLY¹ n: ~ FISH.

C 66–3 A snubby is a cod-fish with an abnormal snout, longer than normal and slightly upturned. The fishermen consider catching one of these in their trap as a sign of a good season. They treat it as a sort of amulet by cutting off the head and hanging it on the fishing stage door and it is not to be taken down. C 69–23 Whenever you have a snub (a fish with a deformed head, cod-fish) in your trap, you will hear the old fishermen say that you will have luck, and that you can expect a few large catches of cod-fish. C 75–141 Old fishermen will hang the head of a snub up in the stage. It was a sign of a [good] load of fish, and it would turn the direction of the wind.

snub² n Cp *NID* ~¹ v 3 c 'restrain the motion of (an animal).' Horse's halter.

T 96/7–64¹ When you go in the barn night time you take off your [horse's] winkers, what you have in the day with the bit in his mouth; take that off, put on the snub—go on over his head, strap around, hook un in the stall. And in the morning you take that snub off.

snubber v Cp SMYTH 637 snubbing her 'bringing a ship up suddenly with an anchor. . .without jerking.' To slow down horse; to brake (a vehicle) going downhill (Q 71–8).

Q 67–95 When going downhill with a full load of wood it was necessary to pull back on the reins so that the horses would hold the load, and prevent it from careering down the slope. [The order was] 'Snubber her!'

snubby See SNUB¹.

so intens used in comparisons. *EDD* ~ 3 n and s counties. Equally.

1878 HOWLEY *MS Reminiscences* 3 So soon as we had all settled away and dinner over, I started off to see the new find. M 64–3 [He is] so big as the side of a house. T 313/5–66 That was just so hard as somebody took a load of lumber on their back. 1972 *Evening Telegram* 19 May, p. 3 'Just so much lip as ever, I see,' replied the doughty dowager of the gowithy.

soak v *EDD* ~ v¹ 5 'with *along*: of riding, driving: to go at a steady, continuous pace' for senses 1, 2. Cp SOG.

1 To walk slowly along.

1907 MILLAIS 37 [The caribou] seems indifferent to his safety, especially when in the company of others, and the Newfoundland expression of 'soakin' along' seems to exactly express his solemn, lazy mode of progression. 1937 DEVINE 46 ~ To walk along heavily and slowly. P 141–72 ~ To walk slowly or aimlessly down the road. C 75–140 I must soak home and get a bite to eat.

2 Of a vessel, to sail steadily and smoothly; JOG.

1917 *Christmas Bells* 10 After two days cruising, they sighted a fine brig soaking along before a fair wind. 1937 DEVINE 46 There was very little wind but we were soaking along down the coast. T 143–65[1] There was a little wind. Soaked on down the reach an' about, oh, four mile from our place there's a island called Hunch Island.

3 To haul a net, mooring, etc, using the slow roll of the boat as leverage; cp DRAW v (Q 67–87).

soaker n Cp SOAK v senses. A very large trout, cod-fish, etc (C 71–128); LOGY n, SADDLER.

C 71–129 When he caught hold of an obviously large fish he said to me 'I've latched on to an old soaker here now.'

sod n *EDD* ~ sb[1] 2 (1) Ir for sense 3; for combs. in sense 4: cp *OED* sb[1] 5 a ~ house (1832 quot), *DC* (1953), *OED* ~ hut (1896 quot), *DC* (1921–).

1 Cap or flat hat (P 148–69).

M 71–91 Someone took off his cap (or sod as it was locally called).

2 Pastry covering; SMOTHER.

C 71–120 ~ A paste put over a rabbit stew. C 71–128 ~ Pastry made from flour, baking powder, etc, and laid over steaming vegetables in a skillet—a thick, fluffy pastry, unlike the thin, brittle pastry for pies.

3 Phr *on the sod*: exactly.

P 148–63 He is his father on the sod (just like his father).

4 Comb **sod house**: root cellar; smoke-house.

M 69–13 A sod house is used for [storing crops] but is built from sods, and it is usually built at the foot of a hill near the house. P 77–74 'Smokers' are herring which have been smoked in a sod house.

sod hut: dwelling built or covered with sods.

M 69–17 The early settlers at Muddy Brook, according to my informant, lived in sod huts. 1974 SQUIRE 7 There is a record of one sod-hut. This was built by Samuel Napier, just above Rocky Cove on the south side of Eastport. He fashioned his home around a flat slab of rock that protruded through the ground to a height of several feet. This rock served as the back for his open fireplace and can still be seen at the site.

sod tilt, sodden ~ : see **sod hut**; TILT.

P 148–61 Sodden tilt [dwelling] made with sods. M 71–103 [He] became a stationer and lived in a sod tilt at Salmon Cove while fishing from the shore. . . The sod tilts were constructed of a framework of wood covered with sods and lined inside with bark.

sod v *EDD* ~ v[1] 9. To throw sods or chunks of peat at an opponent.

T 80/2–64 If you got caught up there with a maid,

'twas murder! Snowballed and sodded or whatever time o' the year 'twas! Q 71–8 A more common practice was to sod rather than to ballast. Using dry, peaty sods as missiles was less dangerous than ballasting and hence much more frequently done. 1976 CASHIN 7, 8 When Sir Edward rose to address the gathering he was greeted with boos and was eventually sodded. . . 'They have sodded Morris in Bay Bulls tonight.'

soddy a Beneath proper size.

1897 *J A Folklore* x, 210 The trout are *soddy* to-day; that is, they are small and not worth taking.

soft a ['sɒf brɛd, 'sɑːf bred, 'sɒˑəf bred, 'sɒˑəf brɛd] *OED* ~ a 23 b ~ bread (1745 quot); SMYTH 637 ~ tack; *EDD* 1 (35) ~ Tuesday. Cp HARD.

Comb **soft-bread**: perishable bread baked on vessel or ashore, as distinguished from ship's biscuit; LOAF.

1854 [FEILD] 53 Sent some flour to be baked by one of the fishermen's wives, which is our usual mode of obtaining occasional supplies of softbread. We have been more than a week at one time with only biscuit. 1900 DEVINE & O'MARA 115 Mr Vail arrived here in the early fifties, and started a small bakery for soft bread; making a little money, he soon embarked in the hard bread business, which, at that time, was supplied from Hamburg. 1924 ENGLAND 151 I mind the time. . .when the men didn't use to get no soft bread at ahl. T 198–65 We'd have plenty o' soft bread, we'll say, loaf, but all he wanted was hard bread, hard bread an' tea. T 393/4–67 What you had in your bread box, brother, was hard bread. Not too much soft bread was carried out in boat. 1975 BUTLER 90 We bought our supplies at a store in Lewisporte—flour, sugar, tea, hard bread, pork, and some tobacco for the boys. . . We did not have any soft bread or butter, no vegetables, no beef.

soft cure, ~ **cured**: cod-fish prepared for market by salting but with a short drying period; LABRADOR.

1925 *Journ of Assembly* 142 The price of soft cured Labrador [fish] reached $8.00 in the local market, while the shore cured article fetched as high as $11.00 per quintal. 1978 *Evening Telegram* 16 Dec, p. 14 He was lost after the [vessel] he was on then was coming up from the Labrador with a load of soft cure and ran ashore on the Offer Wadhams.

soft tack: see **soft bread**.

T 104–64 No soft tack at all, not in th' early days, the real early days, no soft tack; all hard bread. T 194–65 We couldn't give 'em soft tack, you know; the cook wouldn't have enough, would he? But we give 'em more hard bread [than] they'd a mind to eat.

soft tuesday: Shrove Tuesday.

C 67–5 Pancake Day is called Soft Tuesday. Soft Tuesday is the day before Ash Wednesday. M 69–5 Soft Tuesday and Ash Wednesday were not observed as holidays. On Soft Tuesday many families had pancakes for dinner. 1972 MURRAY 231 On Shrove Tuesday (also called Soft Tuesday), everyone ate pancakes for supper. 1979 TIZZARD 274–5 The pancakes on Shrove (we always called it 'soft') Tuesday contained a ring, a button, and a five cent piece. I sort of dreaded that day because I certainly didn't want to get the button for that meant I would not be married, but be a bachelor all my life.

softs n pl *ADD* ~ 2 Nfld. Bare feet (1925 *Dial Notes* v, 342).

[c1894] 1924 ENGLAND 131 "Betsey Brennan's Blue Hen": May corns and soft bunions as big as small onions / Make him walk on his softs before women and men!

sog v *OED* ~ v 1 a (1538, 1722), *EDD* v² 1 for sense 1; *EDD* v³ 2 'to ride easily or lazily' D Co for sense 2. Cp SOAK.

1 To become soaked or saturated with water.

P 148–63 [She became heavy] from the sogging in the salt water. P 245–73 Pine is better than spruce [for outside planks of a dory], it don't sog and get heavy.

2 Phr *sog along*: to walk slowly and in a leisurely fashion.

P 207–67 The old man was just soggin' along.

sog down: (a) to sail steadily but slowly; (b) to settle or sink.

[1906] GRENFELL 26 The life buoy was fastened to the stern of the boat by a half-inch hemp line, and every time a sea came along the old boat sogged down under water and dragged me with it. T 143–65² By an' by, 'fore we sogged down, it was just only a little wind—the other skiff. P 108–70 Sog her down for the night—stay and have a bed.

soil See SEAL.

soiler See SEALER¹.

soiree n [sə'riː]. Cp *OED* ~ sb 'an evening party' (1820–), swarry (1837–); *EDD* surree sb Sc Ir 'a social gathering; a subscription dance.' (a) A special social gathering at night sponsored by an organization or fraternal society; (b) a party, large gathering, or community social with singing, dancing and feasting. Cp SCOFF, TIME.

1851 *Newfoundlander* 6 Mar, p. 3 The Sons of Temperance gave their first *soiree* on Thursday evening last. [1882] 1900 DEVINE & O'MARA 59 Sons of St Crispin held their first Soiree here, 1882. 1900 *Daily News* 19 Apr, p. 4 The Kelligrews Soiree. The S U F held a very enjoyable dance at their hall at Kelligrews on Easter Monday night. . .15 couples. A regular 'breakdown' time was held at Mr Joe Tilley's the same night. . .35 couples. 'Old Uncle Abe' occupied a conspicuous place in the corner, and made fun for the 'youngsters.' It was amusing to see men of 60 and 70 years of age stepping it out in the old-fashioned reel. Ibid p. 4 The British Society Soiree took place last night [tea, dancing, refreshments at 12, dancing till 4]. [c1904] 1960 BURKE (ed White) 23 "The Kelligrews Soiree": Boiled duff, cold duff, / Apple jam was in a cuff, / I tell you boys, we had enough / At the Kelligrews Soiree. 1934 *Public Bureau Christmas No* 23 The volume of city trade was very large in Christmas week, all were in good humour anticipating the great day and

making their plans for Bonnet Hops, Soirees and the big Ball at Jocelyn's. T 175/6–65 The soirees and socials then at them times [would start] after dark; seemed that you couldn't start anything before after dark.

soldier n A performer of the Christmas mummers' play.

[c1900] 1949 *Newfoundlander* Dec, p. 2 [title] Soldiers Acting at Christmas. T 139–65 No, I never took any part as a soldier. Used to see 'em when they come round, you know. T 141/65–65² There was always mummers, goin' around you know, house to house. But years ago they used to call 'em soldiers. 1969 *Christmas Mumming in Nfld* 221 ~s. Term for the performers of the play.

soldier See OLD SOLDIER.

solid a Cp *OED* ~ a 5 'of rain, etc, steady; continuous.' Of the wind, blowing steadily and strongly from the same direction.

1895 PROWSE 491 Within the memory of man there has never been such an ice blockage; for weeks and weeks it blew a 'solid' north-easter.

solly* See SALLY V.

solomon gosse proper n Cp SEARY *Family Names* (1976), p. 198 for 18–19th cent 'planters' of that name. In phr ~*'s birthday*: designating day(s) of the week when a boiled dinner of salt meat, pudding, etc, is customarily served; DUFF¹: ~ DAY; ~*'s dinner*: the meal so served.

1896 *J A Folklore* ix, 33 Solomon Gosse's birthday. . .is applied to Tuesdays and Fridays as pudding-days, when at the seal or cod fishing. 1937 *Bk of Nfld* i, 232 Pork-and-duff days were Tuesdays, Thursdays and Sundays among the early fishermen in the cookroom. When the cook, influenced by the men, served this meal on any other day it was called 'Solomon Gosse's Birthday,' the excuse originally given to the economical grub-saving planter when the rule was first broken. The name became common all over Newfoundland. C 69–20 Solomon Gosse's birthday is either Tuesday or Thursday. The meal would be pork and cabbage. 1975 *Evening Telegram* 21 June, p. 17 My son, mind Solomon Gosse's dinner, as Thursday was called, pork and cabbage?

some intens *EDD* ~ adv 'very,' *DAE* adv 1 (1804–); cp RIGHT. Very; to a high degree, unexpectedly, extraordinarily; WONDERFUL.

P 69–63 Boy, it's some good! P 148–64 That sounds some funny. T 12–64 I was some pleased to see him. P 224–67 That bread is some fungy—full of air-holes. 1971 NOSEWORTHY 80–1 Some perky. 1972 MOWAT 99 She [the whale] turned so quick she heeled right over on her side, and she was *some* big! 1973 WIDDOWSON 204 You're some bad, my son; if you are not careful the 'Old Boy' will get you. 1977 *Decks Awash* vi (3), p. 55 We had to slide it on skids. It was some heavy.

something n *ADD* ~ . Phr *something another*: one thing or another; something or other.

T 1–63¹ If you hook a square block, or you hook a rolls, or you hook a scroll or something another.
T 26–64² Every mummer carried a stick of some sort, or maybe a gun, a toy gun, or a club or something another. T 187/9–65 An' we'd have a yarn about something another.

some(times) See MORE det: ~ (TIMES).

son n *EDD* ~sb 1, cp DINNEEN a mhic 'my lad.' Phr *my son*:
1 Among males, a familiar, friendly mode of address regardless of relationship or age.
1924 ENGLAND 257 A lot of 'em went home bare. An' dat was crool hard, me son. 1930 *Am Speech* vi, 58 ~ All the small girls and boys address their younger baby brothers in this way. 1969 *Christmas Mumming in Nfld* 68–9 Males call each other 'my dear,' 'boy,' 'my son,' and females are generally addressed as 'maid' or, less frequently, 'my maid.' 1973 PINSENT 86 [to old man:] Ya don't have to tell me 'bout ya, my son.
2 Exclamation expressing wonder or surprise.
T 54/65–64 Oh, there's thousand o' fox now, you know. Oh my son, yes, you could go away now in here, in open season, get dozens. T 141/66–65² Blackberry wine, my son, 'tis kicky—more so than blueberry wine.

sook n also **sooky** [sɵ·k, 'sɵkɩ·, 'sɵ·kɩ] *EDD* suck int 21, sucky sb 6; *ADD* suke, etc, for sense 1.
1 A call to cow, calf or sheep; the animal itself.
T 255/6–66 We always call a sheep 'nanny' [but] over to Parsons Pond they call 'em 'sookies.' 1968 DILLON 155 Sookie. A cow or calf, a call to a cow or calf.
2 A babyish child (1968 DILLON 155).

sooky a Whining, petulant; jealous.
P 269–64 A sooky baby is a cry-baby. P 266–74 She told me that another reason for putting these activities together was that they make the people from the other school. . .'sukey' (jealous).

sooky n See SOOK.

sound n *OED* ~ sb¹ 2 'swimming bladder of certain fish' (14.. quot 'sowndys of stok-fysch,' 1655 'Cod. . .sowne'), *Fisheries of U S* 182 for sense 1; *Cent* ~ (1891) for sense 2.
1 The air bladder, or hydrostatic organ, of a cod-fish, removed during splitting and salted as a delicacy.
[1771] 1792 CARTWRIGHT i, 170 In the morning Condon came up and brought some cod tongues and sounds. [1794] 1968 THOMAS 173 From Ten to Forty pounds is given, with a free Passage out, and some petty gratuitys are sometimes admit'd, such as a Cask of Codd Sounds. 1819 ANSPACH 432 The tongues and sounds are sometimes reserved either for domestic uses or for sale. 1842 BONNYCASTLE ii, 179 Cod, mackerel, herrings, capelin, cod's tongues and sounds, salmon, train-oil, seal-oil, seal-skins, some little peltry, with staves, constitute the chief items of export. 1937 DEVINE 46 *Sounds* are often stripped off the bones,

when fish are split, salted and dried for food. Their texture is tougher than the rest of the fish. 1965 RUSSELL 157 With the cod cleaned, he split the fish, then ran his knife along the backbone, isolating a narrow strip of white gristle. 'This is what we call the sound,' he said. T 347–67 We had fish heads, fish tongues, sounds, flatfish, and then the usual dry salt fish. 1975 *The Rounder* Sep, p. 12 Sounds, in the natural state, comprise the gas-filled bladder running along the inside of the spinal columns [of the cod-fish]. It controls the fish's [buoyancy]. Bearing a striking resemblance to tripe, sounds are normally sold salted and must be soaked over-night in fresh water before use.
2 Comb **sound-bone**: backbone of a cod-fish, to which the air bladder is attached.
[1663] 1963 YONGE 57 [They] throw up their fish, which is split, salted, &c. They throw away the heads and sound bones. 1819 ANSPACH 431 The splitter then taking the fish with his left hand, cuts it with the right, beginning at the nape down by the sound-bone to the navel. [1828] 1979 O'FLAHERTY 58 Instead of the hoops, nailed to the table, out of which they sparingly eat their cod's heads and sound bones with more than Spartan temperance. . . 1937 DEVINE 46 Sound [is] the tegument covering the back bone of a codfish on the inside (*the sound bone*). 1946 MACKAY (ed) 81 As soon as possible after the fish is caught it must be beheaded, eviscerated and split, that is, have the backbone or 'sound bone' removed. 1960 FUDGE 26 It was wonderful fishing and every morning my men, weary with work, slept in their dories on the stern, and as I dropped them each day, I woke them with fishes heads and sound bones, for we fished twelve straight days. 1973 COOK 42 Pete splits, guts and removes the sound bones of the fish.

souse av [sæuz, sauz, sɑuz, sɐuz] *OED* ~ av² 'with a sudden deep plunge,' *EDD* av¹ 9. Directly, suddenly; with a splash or bump; bump! splash!
T 31/5–64 And as I did, sling goes the other one and took me, and—souse! 'Way I goes out in the ocean. T 141/65² [He] goes clean over the head of her, right on. Souse out into the tickle. T 178/80–65 We used to run so far an' we'd go souse into a gert bank o' snow, we boys did. 1976 GUY 31 Then down they goes in the hole, souse-O!

souse v [sauz, sɐuz] *OED* ~ v¹ 6 'to go plunging in water,' *EDD* v¹ 1 for sense 1; *OED* v² 1 dial, *EDD* v² 1 for sense 2.
1 To fall over; cp SLOUSE.
T 141/66–65² He soused over [into the water].
2 To knock, strike or push; thrust.
1931 BYRNES 174 I was soused against the clapboards, I was pummelled in the drain, / When I 'gearied' Billy's 'ally' in Kenawitch's Lane. 1976 GUY 54 Then I saw my chance, grabbed [the rat] by the tail and soused him into a small plastic bag.

southard n *OED* southwards sb (1618–1728); *EDD* ~ 1 Sh I. Southward.
1977 RUSSELL 83 He said there's a big tide in our ocean always runnin' to the southard that takes the

drift ice on past the Sou' West Coast without lettin' it come in to block us off.

souther a also **suther** *OED* ~ a obs (c900–1622). Esp in place-names, the more southerly of two points; to the south.

1895 *Christmas Review* 19 The forward boat now rounded Suther Point and, pulling her sheets more taut, stood well in the harbour. 1953 *Nfld & Lab Pilot* ii, 91 From Hants head the south-eastern shore of Trinity bay trends south-westward. . .to Souther point, the southern entrance point of Heart's Content. M 69–23 On the south side of the entrance to the harbour is Souther (Southern) Head which deflects any wind from the southeast, south and southwest. 1977 *Nfld Qtly* Winter, p. 20 Soon the wind have increased so strong we got to take in the mains'le and face it. And over to under fores'le, and jumbo again, and put her head up the souther.

southern a, av

1 In Labrador and northern Newfoundland, of or relating to the northeast coast and the Avalon Peninsula.

[1912] 1930 COAKER 68 The improved cure of fish is about the most pressing matter now facing the Colony, and I regret that the Southern fishermen and business men failed to grasp the importance of establishing a standard cull for fish. 1942 *Little Bay Islands* 14 He made the cod-trap out of his cod-seine after seeing cod-traps being used on the Labrador by fishermen of the southern bays. 1971 CASEY 153 The 'Southern people,' that is, the summer fishing crews who came to Pillier and North-East Crouse from Conception and Notre Dame Bays. . .

2 Phr *go southern*: to sail southward.

1924 ENGLAND 228 They better go suddren [south] again, pick up a few scattered hoods, an' burn down for the night. T 23–64 There was two more vessels come out of Gibraltar when we did, going to St John's; and they went away southern and we come over western and took a gale of wind.

3 Comb **southern coast**: south coast of Newfoundland from Cape Ray to Cape Race.

1874 *Maritime Mo* iii, 205 A clergyman here assures me that when he resided at Lamaline, on the Southern Coast, in the winter of 1870, the bodies of two cuttles were cast ashore.

southern patch: concentration of harp or hooded seals breeding on the ice-floes off the northeast coast of Newfoundland. Cp NORTHERN PATCH.

1905 CHAFE 7 Because of this unusual condition the most of the captains that sailed from northern ports were baffled in their attempts to locate the 'southern patch' of seals. 1924 ENGLAND 24 Some of the seals are scattered; some lie in immense patches. . . There is supposed to be a 'northern patch' and a 'southern patch,' but discussion about this is endless and sterile.

southern shore: (a) see **southern coast**; (b) coast of the Avalon Peninsula from Cape Spear to Cape Race.

1708 OLDMIXON 6 [The French] were suffer'd in his time first to settle on the Southern Shoar of *Newfoundland*, to fortify themselves at *Placentia*, St Peter's, and other Places. 1874 *Maritime Mo* iii, 210 Lamaline, on the southern shore. 1936 DEVINE 51 The founder of the firm was to all intents a practical fisherman himself, and in practical work laid the foundation of his business at Renews on the Southern Shore. 1969 MOWAT 4 Two days later he informed me that he had found the perfect vessel. She was, he said, a small two-masted schooner of the type known generally as a jack-boat and, more specifically, as a Southern Shore bummer.

southern turr: Atlantic common murre (*Uria aalge aalge*) (1959 MCATEE 39).

southerner n

1 Inhabitant of the south coast of Newfoundland, esp one who fishes on the Grand Banks; BANK FISHERMAN.

1920 WALDO 83 The 'Southerners' go to the Grand Banks for their fishing; the others go to the Labrador.

2 Fisherman of the northeast coast of Newfoundland who migrates north for the summer fishery on the Labrador; FLOATER, STATIONER.

[c1945] TOBIN 9 "The Lighthouse": Near the busy turn of the century. . . / When 'the Southerners,' in spring and fall, / Put store clerks on the hustle. 1909 BROWNE 271 The ledges here were the favorite fishing grounds of Captain Nathan Norman of *Brigus*, a celebrated sealer, who was one of the first southerners to locate north of *Hamilton Inlet*, having settled at *Indian Harbor* about 1835. 1909 GRENFELL[2] (ed) 79 November. The last of the southerners leave.

3 Inhabitant of the southern coast of the Labrador Peninsula.

[1918–19] GORDON 48 The Southerners do not look after their dogs like the Northerners.

south-wester See SOU'WESTER.

sou'wester n also **south-wester**. *DAE* south-wester 1 (1840–), SMYTH 639 for sense 1.

1 A fisherman's waterproof hat with a broad brim, elongated and sloping at the back, with side flaps tied under the chin; CAPE ANN, LINCOLN, OIL HAT.

1836 [WIX][2] 124 The distribution of a south-wester, a fox-trap, or a pair of mokasins, was not a. . .matter for Divine interference. 1855 WHITE *MS Journal* 31 May 1 Souwester 2/9. 1858 [LOWELL] i, 208 Besides a battered 'sou-wester'. . . 1874 *Maritime Mo* iii, 548 He was evidently bent on his ordinary avocations as a fisherman, having on his well-patched canvass jacket and sou'wester, and carrying with him all his fishing gear. 1936 DEVINE 115 He sold. . .oil clothing, which was a specialty and included south-westers, Cape Anns and 'Lincolns.' 1940 SCAMMELL 9 "Squid Jiggin' Ground": God bless my sou'wester, there's skipper John Chaffey. 1978 *Evening Telegram* 9 Sep, p. 14 A linkum is an oil hat with a long back on it to protect your shoulders and the round oil hat that was tied underneath your chin was the sou'wester.

2 Attrib, comb **sou'wester block**: wooden form

or pattern used in making fisherman's water-proof hat.

[1884] 1897 *Nfld Law Reports* 8 Bequeaths him 'one thousand pounds instead of twelve hundred in stock and cash, the stock to be computed at first cost, souwester block and sewing machines to be included at inventory value.'

sou'wester hat: see sense 1.

1955 DOYLE (ed) 43 "My Father's Old Sou'wester": He said to me before he died, / 'There's one request I'll make: / Go take that old sou-wester hat / And wear it for my sake.'

spall n also **spawl*, spaw*** [spɒːl]. Cp *EDD* ~ sb 1 'a chip. . .of wood or stone' esp s w cties and Ir.

1 A gouge, nick or cut.
[1900 OLIVER & BURKE] 63 "The Wedding Cake": When they loaded an old rusty gun, / To blow a spaul off the side. P 205–55 ~ Nick in the edge of an axe. P 148–60 There are numerous spawls in the table.

2 Small, thin sliver of wood used as kindling. Cp SPLIT n (C 71–123).
P 37 ~s Kindling for fire. P 68–54 I have to get my spawls for the morning.

span n
Comb **span board**: board fastened across the centre of a 'fish barrow' to strengthen the surface on which the load is carried (1975 BUTLER 183).

span line: rope running from main buoy to the 'leader' of a cod-trap (1975 BUTLER 178).

1936 SMITH 84 At last they arrived, took up the span-line and overhauled the cod-trap. T 43/7–64 Span line goes from the end of the leader across the trap through the centre keg. When you go to haul the trap you get this span line up across the skiff and then you pull up your doors. T 194/5–65 When I went up and hooked the span line, old man, the dawn was broke, and the moon was shining; 'twas almost daylight. P 9–73 The spanline is fastened to the offshore end of the leader and it in turn is fastened to the centre buoy and mooring; the mooring is then run out and the anchor or grapnel is dropped overboard. The spanline is picked up by the boat with the cod trap on board, in such a way that it is across her middle. From the middle of the spanline four ropes are laid out, one for each corner. P 9–73 The boat comes up to the trap and the second hand (mate) stands by with the boathook, he hooks up the spanline buoy and lifts the line over the boat's head and passes it back to her middle.

span v Cp *EDD* ~ v¹ 11 'to tether or fetter horses or cattle' Co. To hobble a domestic fowl; SPANCEL v.
[1952] 1965 PEACOCK (ed) i, 130 "For the Fish We Must Prepare": Go span your hens, the cock will crow, / More rain, it goes too slow.

spancel n Cp *EDD* ~ sb 1 'a fetter' for sense 1.

1 A device to hinder the movement of a domestic animal or fowl.
1895 *J A Folklore* viii, 31 ~ a rope to tie a cow's hind legs. 1937 DEVINE 47 ~ A cord tying the fore leg and hind leg of an animal; also applied to the yoke of a goat; or, in the case of a fowl, a stick thrust into the breast feathers to prevent it getting through fences. Also a cord used to hobble its legs, to the same laudable end. 1940 *Dal Rev* xx, 65 You meet flocks of goats in the outports with wooden yokes or *spancels* on their necks, to keep them out of gardens. P 113–56 ~ a cord tying the legs of a fowl.

2 A drag on a sled (P 271–67).

spancel v Cp *EDD* ~ v 2 'to fetter with a rope.' To hobble a domestic animal or fowl; SPAN v.
1895 *J A Folklore* viii, 31 ~ To tie [a cow's legs] with a rope. 1937 DEVINE 47 I got to spancel my goat. P 113–56 Now that the seed is sown, we'll have to spancel the hens.

spanish a
1 A grade or 'cull' of dried and salted cod-fish prepared for the markets of Spain and Portugal; clipped form of **spanish fish**. Cp MERCHANTABLE.
T 43–64 Our fish used to go to Spain, an' Portugal and the West Indies. Now Spanish was number one. 1971 NOSEWORTHY 246 ~ Highest grade of fish.

2 Comb **spanish cure**: see sense 1; CURE.
P 243–58 Spanish cure is a variety of dried, salted cod-fish.

spanish fish: lightly salted, dried cod-fish of the highest quality or 'cure.' Cp SHORE¹: ~ FISH.
1928 *FPU (Twillingate) Minutes* 5 Oct [He] spoke about the price of fish and that shore fish was $8 and Spanish fish $9. 1937 *Seafisheries of Nfld* 47–8 Shore fish of the grade suitable for Spain, known as Spanish Fish. . . Spanish fish must be extra thick, of an amber colour, with an even surface, thoroughly clean on both back and face, without showing salt, and only [seven-eighths] dry. T 192/3–65 The ones that didn't show the salt—that's number one—kind of a yellow cast; that's the Spanish fish. 1965 *Evening Telegram* 5 Nov, p. 6 Good Spanish shore fish will never be low in price again.

spanish room: in place-names, a tract of land on the water-front of a cove or harbour from which the fishery was prosecuted by Spaniards; ROOM.
1837 BLUNT 43 On the eastern side, at about three miles from the entrance [to Mortier Bay] is an exceedingly good harbor, called Spanish Room. 1951 *Nfld & Lab Pilot* i, 117 Spanish Room is situated on the eastern side of a peninsula the south-western extremity of which, known as Spanish Room point, lies about one mile northward. . . A small town stands on its shores.

spanner n *OED* ~¹ 1 obs (1639–1688; 1863). A device used to wind the firing mechanism of a wheel-lock musket.
T 210/12–65 One Tom used to use—a great long gun, inch bore; that's the hammer, see, an' the spanner and trigger.

spantickle n also **spannytickle*, spannistickle*,**

spanicle*, spanny*; sparnytickle*, sparnicle*, sparny*; spawnykettle, spawnytickle*, spawn. LEIM & SCOTT *Fishes of Atlantic Coast* (1966), p. 181 ~ 'threespine stickleback.' Any of a variety of sticklebacks (*Gasterosteus* spp); small fish found in fresh or brackish water; PRICKLY: PRICKLEY.

1960 *Evening Telegram* 4 Aug, p. 3 The new species of sticklebacks (sometimes locally known as 'spantick-le' or 'pinfish') were located in different parts of the island. 1966 PADDOCK 93 Spawnykettles, spawns—very small freshwater fish. P 130–67 Spannystickle—small fish about 1½ inches long. They have thorn-like projections on their back. M 69–1 These sparnytickles we would catch and bring home and keep for pets. C 71–110 Sparnytickle or sparny—minnow or a very small trout.

spar n Cp *OED* ~ sb¹ 6 ~ naked for sense 2.
1 Leg, usu pl.
[1894–1929] 1960 BURKE (ed White) 42 "We'll Have to Splice to Get a Flask": I waited there for three long hours / And on my spars I had to stand.
2 Phr *stripped to a spar*: naked to the waist.
1901 *Christmas Bells* 11 The scene for such a fight was either the pond or the field, no matter how biting the frost; stripped to a 'spar' the duel was the test of the best man.

spar v Cp *OED* ~ v³ 2 naut. To fit a vessel with masts.
T 169–65² They was goin' to spar the vessel. So they sparred [her], an' the vessel then cost three hundred an' twenty dollars to put the spars in her an' to repair the mainsail.

sparable n also **sparble** ['sparəbl̩, 'spæːɹbl̩, 'spaːɹbl̩]. Cp *EDD* sparrable 'headless nail; spar-rowbill.'
1 A short nail or cleat, used to stud heel and sole of a boot to prevent slipping on the ice; hob-nail; CHISEL, FROSTER.
1842 JUKES i, 275 I had not got my boots properly fitted [for walking on ice] with 'sparables' and 'chisels.' 1906 LUMSDEN 204 To provide against the slippery ice the soles of our leather boots were covered with spara-bles. 1922 *Sat Ev Post* 195 (2 Sep), p. 126 For the most part, the sparables or calks in the Eskimo skin boots did good service. The men gained safer pans, and away they went, copying—jumping—from cake to cake, out over the slow-heaving ice. 1925 *Dial Notes* v, 343 ~s. Sharp nails; hob nails in boots.
2 Ordinary shoemaker's nail which has worked its way through the heel or sole of a boot or shoe (P 245–61).
T 12–64 Sparables is the [word] we use. It's just a small sprig which gets into the sole of the shoe. 1966 SCAMMELL 26 The Customs officer hobbled down on the ball of one foot and the heel of the other. He had a festered toe caused by a 'sparbel' in his shoe and a day's berry picking. P 224–67 Sparrables are small nails that sometimes work out of your shoes and hurt your feet. [They are not] called sparables when they are in your shoe properly—only when they have worked out of your shoe and are now sticking in your feet.

sparabled p ppl *EDD* sparrable sb (2) ~ Co D. Of a shoe or boot, with the sole or heel studded with hobnails.
1931 BYRNES 53 You pass out of the little door, and into the cove, your 'sparrabeld' heels clicking noisily upon the cobble stones.

sparble See SPARABLE.

sparchy a Cp *EDD* sparch 'brittle.' Comb **sparchy bough**: dry red or brown branch of a spruce or fir; BLASTY BOUGH.
C 70–12 Because the sparchy bough is quite dry it was used for spreading on the flakes; the fish could be placed on something [allowing] the air to get at it. The boughs were also used for lighting fires because they were so easy to [ignite].

spare road excl phr. Get out of the way; gang-way! (1925 *Dial Notes* v, 343).
1924 ENGLAND 276 Cries of 'Spare road!' sounded, as some carried the dangling, dripping carcasses for-ward, to chop them apart on planks laid across barrels.

sparkle v *OED* ~ v² 4 b 'to overlay or daub with cement' (1805); cp *EDD* sparkling vbl n (1787); *NID* spackle v. To cover crack with plas-ter; to smooth a surface before painting (P 148–59).

sparrow n Eastern snow bunting (*Plectrophenax nivalis nivalis*).
1846 TOCQUE 202 On the 26th of this month (March, 1843) I saw a flock of sparrows (*Fringilla Nivalis*), called snow birds in America.

spaug n DINNEEN spág 'leg or foot,' JOYCE 331. A big, clumsy foot (1937 DEVINE 47); SPROG.
1968 DILLON 155 Haul your two big spaugs out o' the way. You'll have to hoof it over the harbour tonight in your two bare spaugs. P 108–70 Take your big spaugs off that chair.

spawn n Comb **spawn herring**: mature herring which migrates to coastal waters to spawn; cp HERRING.
1960 FUDGE 51 The spawn herring in Fortune Bay became contaminated with the rotten herring.

spawn v
Phr *spawn abroad*: of an ice-field, to break up, separate into loose pans; cp ABROAD.
T 187/8–65 An' [the vessel] bid there then till the ice all spawned abroad, an' went down an' she settled down herself.
be spawn(ed) out: to be thin and weak after spawning.
P 148–73 When the caplin are all spawned out.

spawny a Of a female lobster, with spawn.

T 139–65 That's the way the most of 'em could be [caught]. And they hooked spawny ones too, you know. Q 71–3 A berried hen [is what] we call a spawny lobster.

spell v also **spill*** *DC* ~ v 2 Nfld (1920–). To carry a burden on one's shoulders, usu halting from time to time for a rest; to carry by other methods; drag; HAUL v.

1866 WILSON 215 If wood be wanted before the snow fall, it must be 'spelled out,' that is, carried on men's shoulders. 1895 *St Nicholas* [N Y] Apr, p. 451 The Newfoundland seal-hunters always speak of seals as 'swiles,' and for our word carry they say 'spell.' A school-master, who had been listening to a seal-hunter's story, said sneeringly: 'Swiles! How do you spell swiles?' 'We don't spell 'em,' replied the hunter; 'we most generally hauls 'em!' 1896 *J A Folklore* ix, 25 ~ In Newfoundland. . .it is used especially to denote carrying on the back or shoulders. 'He has just *spelled* a load of wood out,' meaning, he has carried it on his back. [1906] GRENFELL 167 Pete had left one bag behind because he was physically unable to 'spell' the two on his back at once. [1915] 1972 GORDON 37 To begin with, one had to spell the wood up from the landwash, where it had been stuck up to dry during the summer. 1924 ENGLAND 249 Dey spilled [brought] deir gaves an' ropes alang. 1952 STANSFORD 137 I spent most of my time spelling and cutting wood. T 55/6–64 Women 'd spell youngsters in a kozak [cassock] on their back. 1964 *Evening Telegram* 17 July, p. 22 She spelled more water from the Hamilton Street tank than any other two women. T 43–64 That would be probably up to forty quintals o' fish, see, that he'd have to spell out on the flake. T 185–65 We used to have to spell all up over this hill in handbar then, an' have to make [the fish] ashore. 1966 HORWOOD 157 Course, a man *can* spell out a moose, even ten or fifteen mile, once 'e's quartered. C 75–48 The men cut their own firewood and spelled it home on their backs.

spell n also **spill***. Cp *ADD* ~ n 3 for sense 1 (a); *DC* 2 (1869–), *Dict Aust Colloq* (1845–), cp *EDD* sb³ 1 So for sense 2.

1 (a) A short distance, esp that between the resting places of a man with a heavy burden on his back; cp SPELL v, SHOULDER ~ ; (b) the burden itself so carried; BACK¹: ~ LOAD, TURN n.

1863 MORETON 30 Short distances are in common speech measured by spells. 1896 *J A Folklore* ix, 25 ~ It is also applied to distance. 1931 *Nfld Magazine* 24 I went towards the river (i.e. Rennie's River) and crossing it went out a spell on the bridle path leading to Portugal Cove. T 172/5–65 That time you could go up and you could cut firewood probably half a spell, some places. Half a spell would be half the distance you could carry [the wood] without havin' a spell. P 54–67 ~ a back-load (of wood, etc). P 245–79 Go bring a spell of water from the well.

2 A period of time when people cease to work, travel, etc, in order to rest; a blow. Freq in phr *take a spell*.

1863 MORETON 30 A 'spell' is. . .a time of rest. 1907 MILLAIS 234 When packing, the usual plan is to walk in

line steadily for half-an-hour, and then to take a short rest. During one of these 'spells,' as they are called, Martin again made an excellent 'spy,' noticing the head of a stag. 1920 GRENFELL & SPALDING 41 I have the greatest admiration for the women of this coast. They work like dogs from morning till nightfall, summer and winter, with 'Ne'er a spell,' as one of them told me quite cheerfully. 1937 DEVINE 47 ~ A rest, taken during work or from carrying a load. 'To take a *spell*.' 1953 JOB 38 Robert Job was instrumental in abolishing the old custom of keeping 'Rum on Tap' at the mercantile wharves in St John's, which had resulted in very frequent 'mug-ups' of that locally popular liquor, while, in the local vernacular, the labourers took 'another spell.' T 49–64 He says, 'We better have a spell now before we hauls out the trap.' I said, 'No, we won't. If I goes now an' lies down anywhere,' I says, 'you won't get me no more.' T 411/13–67 And there might be so much as what we call a dozen spells. A spell would be a time when the corpse would be rested on the ground, an' the coffin of course, and somebody else from the congregation would assist in bringing the corpse another hundred or so feet. 1975 *Evening Telegram* 28 June, p. 16 God be with the old days when fellas our age could lean on a gump and take a spell.

spelling vbl n Cp *DC* ~ place (1872, 1912). Comb **spelling rock**: a large rock on a path where men stop to rest.

P 99–64 ~ A rock not far from the community on which men, returning with a 'turn' of wood, would rest the burden. P 41–68 About half-way there was usually a spelling rock where he took a blow. P 227–72 ~ A rock usually situated on a hill where people would rest.

sperking See SPIRKING.

spile v also **spoil**. Cp *OED* spiling vbl sb² 'dimensions of the curve or sny of a plank's edge' (1846–). To taper a plank at the end.

T 48–64 The way we used to spile off the plank, when you'd get up to the filler, you had a rule staff. That was a thin batten that would go the length o' your boat, and you'd spile off from each side, from the top one and from the bottom one. 1969 *Nfld Qtly* July, p. 20 Spoil—to taper wood. 1972 MURRAY 236 'We was plankin' a boat up there see, and I was spilin' the plank with the drawin' knife and had me hand like that, spilin' and he took holt and give it the pluck, and the knife went along and took me finger.'

spill n also **spiller** *OED* ~ sb² 1 obs (1594–1615); *EDD* sb² 4 So D Co. Small cylinder on which yarn is wound.

1979 POCIUS 20 After the spindle was filled, the thread was slipped onto another rod the approximate size and shape of the spindle. In fact, this rod also was frequently called a spindle. Again, there were local variations: . . .'spiller' (Brigus), 'spill' (Brigus).

spill v Cp *EDD* ~ v¹ 2 (2). To rain heavily.

P 127–75 The rain was spilling down all day. It's spilling rain outside.

spill* See SPELL n, v.

spiller See SPILL n.

spilter See SPLITTER.

spilting See SPLITTING.

spirking n also **sperking**. Cp *OED* spirket² obs (1711), spirketting naut 2 (1846 quot). A strip of wood covering the space between the floor-board of a boat and the inside plank at the water-line (P 127–75).
1966 *Evening Telegram* 14 Nov, p. 11 I have never forgotten the thrill that came to me when I read therein that in one of Anson's ships 'the spirketing' had become decayed, for it was my first encounter of the standard term and spelling spirket or spirketing for that part of a fishing boat that I had heard all my life called by my neighbours 'the spirk'ns.' Q 67–34 Spirkins. A covering board to prevent any dirt from getting underneath the ceiling of a fishing boat. 1969 *Nfld Qtly* July, p. 20 Sperkings. Short pieces of board nailed inside at the water line between the edge of the ceiling and the plank.

spirt See SPURT.

spit n *EDD* ~ sb³ 2, and cp JOYCE 332 for sense 2; cp *EDD* sb¹ 13, JOYCE 142 for sense 3.
1 Frothy secretion enclosing the eggs deposited by a fly or insect on a drying cod-fish or other host object; cuckoo-spit.
T 36–64 You know what a fly-blow is? That's spit, where the flies spits those white lumps and [they] turns to maggots. C 70–28 The foam seen clinging to the base of the bud is called fly spit.
2 A spadeful (of potatoes) (P 48–60).
3 Phr *like the spit out of one's mouth*: identical (P 148–71).
4 Cpd **spit jack**: rove beetle (*Creophilus maxillosus*).
1979 TIZZARD 76 [In the outhouse] the buzzing of a few flies, the smell of the 'spit jack,' or the crawling of the woodlice on the floor, would be minimized by the heat of the sun.

spit v *EDD* ~ v¹ 4 for sense 1; cp *EDD* v³ 6 'to dig; to turn over the ground with a spade' esp s w cties for sense 2.
1 Of a fly or insect, to deposit eggs within a protective coating of froth.
See T 36 quot at SPIT n.
2 To set potatoes (P 162–69).

spity a ['spɛɪtɪ, 'spɛɪtʊ] *ADD* ~ a NE (1891). Bad- or hot-tempered; fiery.
P 148–61 Because of solitude [old people] are spity. T 393/5–67 We had a couple o' girls here, an' brother, you talk about spity! They had some fire in 'em, I tell you. 1974 CAHILL 12 The spitey old bitch.

splayer n A device to draw together staves of a barrel so as to fit on the hoops (P 127–75).

splice v To join with others in the purchase and drinking of liquor.
1929 BURKE [21] "We'll Have to Splice to Get a Drink": And the poor devil / A drink trying to bum / When the boys have no money / To splice for the Rum. C 66–8 Two or three people, or possibly four, will pool their money and buy a bottle between them. In sharing it they don't say 'We shared it' but 'We spliced it.'

splice n Joint purchase of a bottle of liquor by two or three people.
C 66–8 'Do you want to go in on a splice?'. . . The cork will be removed, the first party will take the bottle and put his thumb as a marker, hold the bottle for all to look at, and then drink, with remarkable accuracy, to the top of the thumb and pass it to the next person where it will be repeated.

splinter n *OED* ~ sb 2 obs (1597–1820) for sense 1.
1 A surgical splint.
T 207–65 He chopped off his two fingers. He come in and hold 'em up. His father took the two of 'em and stuck 'em on, and splintered 'em up with splinters, and they growed on.
2 Comb **splinter boat**, ~ **fleet**: type of wooden ship (P 245–64).
1973 HORWOOD 93 His position included supervision of a fleet of boats known locally as the Splinter Fleet, but officially as the Clarenville Fleet. 1976 *Evening Telegram* 31 Jan, p. 2 The 90-foot boat was built in Nova Scotia about 17 years ago and Capt Bennett said she is a 'double-ender,' that is the stern is similar to the bow, and she resembles the well-known 'splinter boats' that were built years ago in Newfoundland, although they were normally bigger. 1979 *Evening Telegram* 15 Oct, p. 6 He was offered the command of the wooden motor vessel *Trepassey* (one of Newfoundland's wartime built 'splinter fleet') in which he took a naval crew and scientific party to the Falkland Islands.

splinter v *OED* ~ v 2 obs (1594–1720). To set or fasten with splints.
T 198–65 There was people around here able to splinter un up. If you break your leg or your ankle, they get those little strips o' wood, and bandage it all around. See T 207 quot at SPLINTER n.

split v Cp *NID* ~ v 1 a for sense 1.
1 To cut around the backbone of a cod-fish, opening the fish for salting and drying; to remove the gills and guts of a herring or mackerel; cp GIB v.
[1663] 1963 YONGE 57 When the header had done his work, he thrusts the fish to the other side of the table, where sits a. . .splitter, who with a strong knife splits it abroad, and with a back stroke cuts off the bone. . . There are some that will split incredibly swift, 24 score in half an hour. [1680] 1976 HEAD 80 They

split and Salt Theyr fish on Shore. [1766] 1971 BANKS 134 [The splitter's] business is to split the fish beginning at the head and opening it Down to the tail. At the next cut he takes out the Larger Part of the Back Bone. 1819 ANSPACH 431 The splitter. . .cuts [the fish] with the right hand, beginning at the nape down by the sound-bone to the navel, and giving the knife a little turn to keep as close to the bone as possible, he continues cutting to the end of the tail; then raising the bone with the knife, he pushes the fish so split into the drudge-barrow. 1837 BLUNT 15 A little south of the Cape is Shoe Cove, a place used in bad weather for splitting and salting fish. 1902 HOWLEY *MS Reminiscences* 8 At Boutitou the boats had just come in from the traps, some with considerable fish and the crews were busy nearly all night splitting it. [1915] 1930 COAKER 103 The way this fish should be cleaned: First the slub be removed before splitting, then split the fish, remove the inside also the blood from the bone, then a slight slit each side of the bone, the bone should not be removed as it causes the fish to break if taken away. 1937 *Seafisheries of Nfld* 45 In the dry salting method, the fish, having been split, are placed with the flesh upwards side by side, usually head to tail alternately, until a space in the curing stage about three feet in width and varying from four to twelve feet in length is covered; dry salt is then spread over the surface of the fish. T 43–64 Well, the gut had to come out o' the fish an' the head had to come off, an' then the splitter would split it down one side o' the backbone [and] up the other, and he was ready then for washing an' saltin'. 1973 COOK 42 Pete splits, guts and removes the sound bones of the fish.

2 Phr *split the fish*: game in which a person is put on a table and undergoes in mime all the things a fish undergoes when it is split (T 245–66).

split p ppl *DC* ~ a 3 (1890).

1 Of cod-fish, with head and guts removed and backbone sliced, open and flat for salting and drying.
1964 BLONDAHL (ed) 14 "Hard, Hard Times": When you've got some [fish] split and hung out for to dry, / It will take all your time for to brush off the fly; / To brush off the flies it is more than you'll do, / Then out comes the sun and she all splits in two. 1975 BUTLER 36 [I suggested we go to] Merasheen and buy fresh split fish and salt it on board.

2 Of herring or mackerel, prepared for curing in a variety of ways involving removal of gill and gut.
1941 SMALLWOOD 272 Herring. . .Pickled, Split. 1975 BUTLER 73, 75 There'd be other packs. There was split herring; they'd be cleaned right out. . . Now in the spring. . .they'd pack 'em for the West India market and they would be split herring. . . It would take one hundred and sixty split mackerel to fill one barrel and two hundred and thirty five when filleted.

3 Hence n: a variety of 'cure' or method of processing (herring, mackerel).
1953 *Nfld Fish Develop Report* 46 In the United States, and generally throughout North America. . .the

market for the traditional splits and 'Scotch'-cure has all but disappeared.

4 Phr *split-tail coat*: swallow-tail coat.
1924 ENGLAND 143 It was Hickson who once, when he had an infected finger, called for a 'tom'awk' and implacably chopped that finger off, 'standin' dere on de ship's brudge, sir, bare-handed an' in a green split-tail coat.'

split n Cp *OED* ~ sb[1] 2 'a piece of wood separated or formed by splitting'; *EDD* sb[1] 10 'long, thin pieces of bogwood used as lights' Ir (1892). A thin piece of wood, about twelve to fourteen inches (30–36 cm) long, used chiefly as kindling; BAVIN. Also attrib.
1858 [LOWELL] i, 74 . . .the fire, where the round bake-pot stood, covered with its blazing 'splits.' 1866 WILSON 353 Making a fire was quite an art, and required back-junks, fore-junks, middle-junks, triggers, splits and brands. 1919 GRENFELL[1] 198 'Get a few more splits, then, boy,' she replied, 'and I'll be cutting t' pork t' while.' 1936 DULEY 194 With difficulty Joe Perry had cleaved some splits, and because they had no paper Uncle Seth had whittled some shavings with his knife. T 12–64 A whiten is the rampike or very dry stick used for making splits. T 140–65 You carried a junk o' wood an' a few splits under your arm every morning. 1965 *Evening Telegram* 30 Nov, p. 10 Mind the Paradise splitmen? [who sold kindling in St John's]. 1966 ibid 19 Apr, p. 17 Since Joey took over everyone is usin' oil. No need of splits nowadays. T 246–66 [The jannies] carry a split to defend themselves, see, an' anybody that'd make battle at them, they'd stop 'em with their split. 1967 READER 16 During the depression he used to get wood and made what were called 'splits' (kindling for starting a fire) and he used to go around from door to door selling these bundles of splits. C 70–12 Splits were pieces chopped only from dry wood because they were used to light the fire in the morning. . . After they had begun to burn, the person lighting the fire would put on regular wood. 1973 PINSENT 5 His half-wool, half-holes sweater [was] hooked on a splinter from the 'splits' in his arms. P 181–80 [proverb] There is favour in hell if you come armed with splits.

splitter n also **spilter** *OED* ~ sb[2] 1 b (Nfld: 1623–); *DC* Nfld (1784–) for sense 1.
1 Member of a fishing crew who cuts around the backbone of cod-fish brought ashore to be dressed, opening the fish for salting and drying; SHOREMAN; one who removes gills and entrails of herring or mackerel.
1612 *Willoughby Papers* 71a/96 [They] were sent hether, with only thirtie fishermen and foure Spilters, there are here already eight that are fishermen, and one spilter, and the rest here will serve for land men. 1623 WHITBOURNE 82 Seven are to be skilful headders, and splitters of fish. [1663] 1963 YONGE 57 When the header has done his work, he thrusts the fish to the other side of the table, where sits a spilter, or splitter, who with a strong knife splits it abroad, and with a back stroke cuts off the bone, which falls through a hole into the sea. 1760 CO 194:15 To 1 Splitter. . . £20.

[1766] 1971 BANKS 134 The Splitter [stands opposite and] his business is to split the fish beginning at the head & opening it Down to the tail at the next cut he takes out the Larger Part of the Back Bone which falls through the Floor into the water. 1842 JUKES i, 227 The splitter, who by a dexterous movement cuts out the backbone from the neck nearly to the tail, and thus lays the fish entirely open and capable of being laid flat on its back. 1851 *Journ of Assembly* Appendix, p. 150 The fishermen and splitters of this establishment are brought from the Bay of Chaleur every year about the middle of June, and are sent back there again about the middle of August, the fishing being then over. T 43–64 Well, the gut had to come out o' the fish an' the head had to come off, an' then the splitter would split it down one side o' the backbone [and] up the other, and he was ready then for washin' an' saltin'. T 175/6–65 I cut throats for two splitters, two fast splitters, [when I was] just fourteen years of age. One feller was a sixty barrel splitter an' th'other man was, well, up round forty. 1969 HORWOOD 82 A good splitter can keep a steady flow of fish moving across his table, spending no more than four or five seconds on each.

2 A type of knife used to lay open a cod-fish and cut around the backbone; SPLITTING KNIFE.

1765 WILLIAMS 19 Six Splitters and four Cutters [among stores for the boats].

3 Comb **splitter's mitt**: type of mitten worn on one hand when 'splitting' fish.

1973 BARBOUR 67 During splitting operations [the splitters] wore on their left hand a splitter's mitt, made of swan skin or canvas, with just a narrow band around the thumb to help keep the mitt on; there were no fingers to these mitts for the man needed freedom of movement to [split] the fish. 1979 POCIUS 23–6 A special type of mitt was knitted that was used by fishermen while taking off the head of a fish, called a 'splitter's mitt.' [It] resembled the normal mitt, with the exception that either the thumb, or the thumb and the index finger remained uncovered.

splitting vbl n also **spilting**. For combs. in sense 2: *DC* ~ cuff Nfld (1965); *DAE* ~ knife (1634–).

1 In processing cod-fish, slicing of the backbone between nape and vent, opening the fish for salting and drying.

1819 ANSPACH 432 This process of splitting is performed with considerable rapidity, though with the utmost care, because the value of the fish depends in a material degree upon its being correctly performed: for if ruffled by frequent or interrupted cuttings, the fish would be disfigured. T 43–64 Well, that was the guttin' an' the splittin', and then 'twould be washed.

2 Designating var garments, esp hand coverings, used when splitting cod-fish: **splitting cuff** [see CUFF[1]], ~ **glove,** ~ **mitt** [see MITT]; ~ **pants.**

1965 LEACH 5 On his left hand the splitter wears a 'splittin' cuff,' a kind of fingerless wool mitten. 1612 *Willoughby Papers* 16a/18 One yeard of cloth for spilting gloves. T 26–64[3] When he was goin' on the Labrador I'd have twelve, fifteen an' sixteen splittin' mitts for un. 1972 MURRAY 107–8 One of the first items a girl would be expected to knit (after learning 'garter stitch,'

i.e. plain knitting, on a head band or garters) was a pair of long stockings for herself, or, she might do a 'splitting mitt' for her father. P 118–67 Well, he put on his splitting pants [rubber trousers].

3 Comb **splitting knife**: knife with a short, curved blade used to cut around the backbone of a cod-fish.

1612 *Willoughby Papers* 16a/18 [Guy's Journal, 13 Oct] And comming togeather the foremoste of them presented unto him a chaine of leather full of small perreincle shelles, a spilting knife [etc]. [1622] 1954 INNIS 58 [inventory] Heading and splitting knives £1/5. 1863 *Journ of Assembly* 444 The cure of Fish. . .may be much improved, by washing it immediately after it passes from the splitting-knife, and salting it while fresh. 1905 DUNCAN 156 'The splittin' knife slipped,' he said, feeling of the scar on her wrist. T 185–65 Somebody told me one time that he builded a boat with the splittin' knife; cut out all the timbers with a splittin' knife. 1969 HORWOOD 82 You split [the fish] open on a wooden table with a splitting knife—a curved, square-ended, exceedingly sharp instrument a little like a cobbling knife—taking out the guts and a large piece of bone with a single sweep, and push them off the table into a barrel or tub to be taken to the salting shed. 1971 NOSEWORTHY 247 ~ A knife with a blade curved like a half-moon, with both left and right handed types, used to take the *sound-bones* out of fish. 1978 *Evening Telegram* 11 Mar, p. 3 On the evening following a new candidate's declaration to stand for election he should be taken down behind a fish store and a splitting knife held to his throat.

splitting stage: section of fishing premises where fish is processed; STAGE (Q 67–43).

splitting table: table in a fishing stage where cod or salmon are processed before salting and drying.

1842 JUKES ii, 127 ~ A table on which the salmon are split, previously to their being salted. 1852 *Morning Post* 12 Feb, p. 2 Mr Rowe, then, studied his law at the 'splitting' table. (Laughter) Yes, that hon. Executive Councillor cut throats in his time. 1866 WILSON 205 Entering the stage from the stage-head, we first see the splitting-table. This is usually on the right hand. [1890] P 102–60 Previous to 1890. . .the S.S. *Nimrod* and S.S. *Diana* [sealing vessels] would be at Blanc Sablon for the summer and if a poor fishery around the first of August would be fitted with cod traps, boats, splitting tables, etc, and a number of fishery servants with sufficient supplies for a month or two. T 43–64 There'd be what they call a cut-throat an' a header an' two splitters, an' possibly you'd have a girl or a woman or somebody keepin' the fish box full, to the end of the splittin' table. C 68–17 Fishermen believe it is unlucky to play cards on a splitting table. 1977 BURSEY 167 I had made large pounds to take heavy salted fish, and a splitting table thirty feet long.

splitting tee: see **splitting stage**; TEE.

1972 MURRAY 242–3 Bringing approximately 200 pounds of fish at a time in a 'tub-bar' from the 'stage-head' (the wharf onto which the fish were thrown from the boat) to the 'splitting tee.'

splitting tub: see TUB.

spoil See SPILE.

spot n Cp *Cent* ~ n 8 'a small fishing ground' for sense 3.

1 A concentration of harp or hooded seals on the ice-floes; PATCH.

1871 WHITE *MS Journal* 6 Apr Saw spot [of] old seals, took 150. Saw very large spot. 1873 CARROLL 24 Spots of all kinds of seals are often considered by ice hunters to extend one hundred miles and from one to four miles wide. 1924 ENGLAND 206 Now, though the ship toil through ice and storm for six days, finding but 'a scatterin' few,' and then on Sunday run into a wondrous spot of fat, perhaps the 'main patch' itself—no man will touch gun, gaff, or blade. 1925 *Dial Notes* v, 343 ~ A herd of seals.

2 A school of fish; SCULL, SHOAL[2].

1975 BUTLER 74 The mackerel needed to be near the land where the seine would reach bottom in order to get them. When we came to a spot of mackerel swimming along by the shore, we would fasten the end of the seine ashore by means of a small grapnel to hold it fast to the land and Joe would row the dory around the mackerel. 1979 NEMEC 277 A crew will ordinarily go. . .wherever they think there may be a 'spot of fish' to jig.

3 A shoal frequented by fish; cp GROUND.

1953 *Nfld & Lab Pilot* ii, 244 These [shoals] include. . .Chitman Spot; Harbour bank; Shoal Ground; Paddy Outside Spot; and Outside Spot. Ibid ii, 276 Those [shoals] eastward include John Hewlett Spot and William Hewlett rock, and those westward include The Field, Eli Burton ground, John Hewlett ground, and Thomas Hewlett ground.

4 A stand of timber.

M 68–17 When men wanted lumber for building a house, or boat or dory plank they would buddy up (several would get together), take their pit saw and go back into the woods. They would find a suitable 'spot' of logs, build a pit in the midst of the logs and saw the required amount of lumber.

5 Comb **spot buoy**: float used to fix the location of stationary fishing-gear; MARK(ER) BUOY.

Q 67–21 ~ a buoy with a long staff attached to it located at a distance from the main buoy; its purpose is to permit fishermen to locate their nets.

spotted p ppl

Comb **spotted loo**: greater common loon (*Gavia immer immer*) (1870 *Can Naturalist* v, 411); LOO.

spotted seal: harbour seal (*Phoca vitulina*); BAY SEAL.

1880 *Standard* [London] 20 May, p. 3 Four or five species are pursued off the shores of Newfoundland and in the Arctic Regions proper, viz:—the 'ground' or 'grown' seal, the saddle-back, or harp seal, so called from the saddle or harp-shaped mark on the back of the males, the blubber-nose, and the floe rat—which is the smallest species found in the North Atlantic, and much more rarely the spotted seal, or 'kassigiak' of the Eskimo.

spotted wolf: catfish (*Anarhichas minor*) (1971 *RLS* 3, p. 3).

spottedy a *ADD* ~ Nfld. Of a harp seal's fur, spotted during the colour change from 'white-coat' to young adult; cp RAGGED-JACKET, RAGGEDY COAT.

1924 ENGLAND 102 'Whitecoats'. . . When 'dey rolls de white off, an' gets spottedy,' they are said to be 'buttoned up the back.'

spotter n An observer on an airplane sent out to locate seal herds on the ice-floe.

[1954] 1979 *Evening Telegram* 14 Mar, p. 8 Captain Ken Barbour, official spotter on the sealing plane, says Newfoundland is going to lose her sealing industry. 1957 *Daily News* 16 Oct To top this off, spotters had flown over the vast expanse of ice to the north, reported sighting large herds of seals, the approximate position of which were given to the skippers of the fleet.

spraddle v Cp *EDD* ~ v 'to straddle' D; *ADD*. Comb **spraddle-swing**: a board suspended in the middle by a rope so that children can sit astride each end and swing about (1964 *Can Journ Ling* x, 43).

spraw-foot n Variety of grebe, an aquatic bird.

1951 PETERS & BURLEIGH 49–51 [*Colymbus grisegena holböllii*. . . *Colymbus auritus*. . . Toes individually webbed. . .*Podilymbus podiceps podiceps*] Local name: Sprawfoot. Ibid 51 It has to splash and run along the water for a long distance before attaining sufficient speed for flight. . . This 'Spraw-foot' feeds upon small fish, aquatic insects, crayfish and other crustaceans. 1959 MCATEE 3 ~ Horned Grebe.

sprayed p ppl *OED* ~ ppl a[2] (1869, 1911); *EDD* spray v, spreathe v, sb s w cties. Chapped; red and tender from exposure to cold and wet.

1895 *J A Folklore* viii, 39 ~ describing chapped hands or arms. 1924 ENGLAND 180 Presently Jonas entered, twisting his cap in both 'sprayed' [chapped] hands. 1937 DEVINE 47 ~ Chapped by exposure to cold, said of the hands, especially. P 121–67 My hands were sprayed with the salt water. M 71–86 Sprayed or chapped hands were treated by dipping one's hands in cod liver oil.

spread v

1 To place split and salted cod-fish on a flat expanse, usu a 'flake,' turning it at intervals to dry by exposure to sun and wind; DRY[1], TURN v.

[1726] 1976 HEAD 73–4 As they catch the fish they Split them & Salt 'em then lay 'em down in the Ships hold, where they lay till they goe into the Harbour, then they take them out & Spread them upon the Fleakes. [1766] 1971 BANKS 135 When the Fish are tolerably dry they Put them in Round Piles of 8 or ten Quintals Each Covering them on the top with bark in these Piles they remain 3 or 4 days or a week to sweat after which they are again Spread & when dry Put up in

Larger heaps Coverd with Canvass. [1774] 1792 CARTWRIGHT ii, 17 The people were employed on the buildings, and in spreading fish. [1856] 1976 WHITELEY 122 Fine day—spread fish to dry. 1895 *Christmas Rev* 12 [proverb] The planter's eye spreads the 'water horse.' [1900 OLIVER & BURKE] 69 He wants a wife can spread the fish. 1924 ENGLAND 267 There they labour all day, making up the fish, carrying it on dredge barrows, spreading and turning it; while along the stages 'headers' and 'splitters' are busily at work. 1958 *Evening Telegram* 11 Feb Maud Muller on that summer's day / Spread the fish instead of the hay, / And she looked up as the sun grew duller, / And she thought about the government culler. T 43–64 Well, then you'd spread that an' you'd come back an' get another barrowful an' take that out an' spread it, so it was a good life. 1979 TIZZARD 294 If it was late in the day when the fish was washed it would remain on the barrow in the stage all night to be spread on the flakes at sun-up the next day.

2 To stretch an animal skin on a wooden frame to dry.

[1771] 1792 CARTWRIGHT i, 125 I killed a pair of shell-birds; skinned and spread an otter.

3 Comb **spread-sail punt**: small undecked boat with sail supported by a pole instead of gaff or boom (1975 BUTLER 55, 160).

spread n A pole used on small sailing craft as a substitute for gaff or boom (P 94–57); SPREADER.

T 50/1–64 So I was stood up—I was ready to let go o' the spread, give her the shoulder o' mutton [sail]. T 192–65 [We were] out in our trap skiff with no spreads in the sail; there was too much wind for us to put spread in the sail. 1969 *Nfld Qtly* July, p. 20 ~ a wooden sprit for extending a sail, usually at the after part of a boat. 1975 BUTLER 55 Since there were no gaffs or booms on those sails, a long stick called a spread from fourteen to fifteen feet long was used to hoist sail. This spread would be put in a loop in the peak of the sail and pushed up until the sail came tight.

spreader n

1 A stick used to keep strip of fatty meat from contracting during cooking.

1872 HOWLEY *MS Reminiscences* 7 Another small stick notched at each end was used as a spreader to keep the sheet of [beaver] meat extended and prevent its shrinking up by the head [in cooking]. This spreader was placed on the outside and extended from the upper to the lower skewer, which were caught by the notched ends. The meat was very fat.

2 A pole used on small sailing craft as a substitute for gaff or boom; SPREAD n (P 243–55).

3 Comb **spreader buoy**, ~ **pole**: wooden stick used to keep the ends of a gill-net apart (Q 67–4; P 135–74).

spreading n A quantity of split and salted codfish sufficient to cover a given drying area.

1936 SMITH 31 Anyway we didn't have any fish to make, only about one spreading for our crew.

spring[1] n also **springe** pl: ['sprʌndʒɨz] *OED* ~ sb[1] 13 b. One of the tides, occurring twice in each lunar month, which rise highest and fall lowest from the mean tide level, esp the highest of these when boats are most easily launched or hauled up; spring-tide. Usu pl.

1837 BLUNT 29 The tides here, and also upon all the eastern coast of Newfoundland, have nearly the same rising, the springs being about 6 feet, neaps 4 feet, but these are much influenced by the winds. 1938 MACDERMOTT 254 Word goes round that she will be launched next 'Springis'—Spring Tide. P 127–79 An' we'd be able to haul up our boats, see, because [of] the springes.

spring[2] n *OED* ~ sb[1] 6 a *spring of the year* obs (1530–1828), b (1547–) for sense 1; cp *OED* 6 f for sense 2; *OED* 25 ~ flask (1812), ~ hook (1688–), ~ stick (1880) for sense 4; cp *EDD* 2 (12) ~ heeled Jack 'a highwayman' for sense 5; for combs. in sense 6: *DC* ~ herring (1861–), ~ salmon (1869–).

1 The first season of the year, freq in phr *spring of the year*; the period extending from March to May or June regarded as the time of preparation for and prosecution of the cod, herring and seal fisheries; FISHING SEASON, SEASON.

[1611] 1895 PROWSE 126 When April came our spring began. 1620 WHITBOURNE 34 . . .or else to hire the like Ship to serve for the passing of people, victuals, and provisions, in the Spring of the yeere. 1708 OLDMIXON 14 The Fishing-season is from *Spring* to *September*. [1766] 1976 HEAD 87 There was a greater number of poor Irish Men brought here this Spring from Waterford, than has been known in one year before, for 14 years past. [1794] 1968 THOMAS 173 Poole and Newton Bushell are the Emporiums for the Two Countys [of Devonshire and Dorsetshire]. Lads from the Plow, Men from the Threshing Floor and persons of all sizes, Trades and ages and from the Manufactorys flock annually, in the Spring, to Newfoundland. [1815] 1976 O'NEILL ii, 920 Should he experience that support which he has been taught to hope for, it is his intention in the ensuing Spring, to enlarge his stock very generally. 1913 *Nfld Qtly* July, p. 30 He spent the Springs of 1884–5 at the ice. 1924 ENGLAND 53 Sometimes a seal hunter, after his travelling expenses are paid, will clear only $15 or $20 for his 'spring.' 1934 *Nfld Qtly* July, p. 30 In speaking on the seal fishery I quoted an old adage: 'A frosty winter for a fat spring.' [1954] 1966 DOYLE (ed) 28 "I'se the B'y": Codfish in the spring o' the year / Fried in maggoty butter. T 39/40–64 First thing you do in the spring o' the year is go cut a load o' wood, a couple of loads o' wood for to burn, you know, in the summer, aboard the boat an' in the house. 1975 LEYTON 77 Because every other year I used to start to get a bit better in the spring of the year. 1979 *Evening Telegram* 15 Oct, p. 6 [He] spent nearly seventy springs at the icefields and died in 1961 in his 94th year. 1981 ibid 19 Oct, p. 6 In the spring of the year when [the fishermen] are putting out their cod traps, salmon nets and lobster pots. . .

2 Used with epithets and numerals to indicate

a definite period or particular year, esp in sealing.
1874 *Maritime Mo* iii, 544–5 Captain Rideout, who
has been 'forty springs to the ice'. . .admits that the
parson is 'a wonderful knowin' man about soils.' [1909]
1916 MURPHY 29 The spring of 1832 was called the
'spring of the cats,' on account of such a large number
of immature seals brought in. . . 1853—the White Bay
spring, 1857—the frosty spring, 1862—the first Green
Bay spring, 1838—the spring of the three suns. . .'the
red jacket spring.' 1924 ENGLAND 248–9 Many of the
sealers reckon time not by dates, as with us, but by reference to certain springs. 'De disaster spring,' for
example, refers to 1914 when the *Newfoundland* suffered such tragedy and the *Southern Cross* went down.
'De spring o' the Wadhams' means a certain year when
seals were very plentiful off the Wadham Islands. 1971
CASEY 308 A minor event is dated as before or after
'the spring of White Bay' [in 1923 there was a major
catch of seals in White Bay]. 1977 *Inuit Land Use* 225
One year, remembered as the 'Hungry Spring,' rock
cod was the only food available. The people would jig
for this fish through the ice into the spring when. . .a
new range of resources becomes available.

3 Phr *lose one's spring*: to experience a failure
at fishing or sealing; cp SUMMER.
[1896] SWANSBOROUGH 34 "The Seal Fishery":
They've been kept outside of the ice, / And been
driven southward twice; / Have lost a topmast or a
yard, / Have lost their spring, and think it hard. 1937
DEVINE 63 A sealer applied for a job in a factory and
gave the boss as his reason for coming from Newfoundland to look for work that he had *lost his Spring*. . .
The applicant 'was out to the seal fishery with Skipper
Sam Blandford in March and April and got no seals.'
1964 *Evening Telegram* 28 Mar, p. 6 The fishermen
found, however, that if the sealing season was late,
they could not get off to the Banks in time and were in
danger of losing their spring.

4 Designating var devices involving a mechanical spring: **spring flask, ~ hook, ~ snare, ~
stick**.
[1776] 1792 CARTWRIGHT ii, 207 As they use no
measure for their powder, but throw it in by hand, they
generally over-charge; a spring-flask, with a ball made
up in a cartridge would be a much better way, but
those flasks come too high for the Indian market;
therefore they are furnished with the cow-horn, such as
are provided for ship's use. [1775] ibid ii, 128 I tailed
four more [fox traps], shifted the spring-hook, and
brought the cod-hook home. [1774] ibid i, 169 We
tailed a spring-snare at the lower end of the path.
[1774] ibid i, 179 A fox had broken the snare, the
spring-stick being too weak.

5 Designating an imaginary prowler with pret-
ernatural ability to leap off the ground: **spring
heel(ed) Jackson, ~ legs, ~ man**.
1973 WIDDOWSON 267 Springheeled Jackson—in St
John's. . . He was supposed to have springs on his
shoes and was often seen to jump over fences quite
easily. C 69–17 When I was a boy there was sure to be
an unknown person roaming around at night. He came
in the spring and was referred to as 'springlegs' for
those who saw him said that he [bounded] around as if

he had springs on his feet. . . But it was really believed
that such a man was on the prowl and most people took
all precautions to keep him away from their homes or
children. 1973 WIDDOWSON 392 Spring Legs had a
pumpkin-shaped body and springs for feet enabling
him to jump ten to fifteen feet at a time. Ibid 392
Around autumn when boys were raiding apple and
plum trees at night there was a rumour spread of a
'Spring-man.' He was supposed to be a man with
springs attached to his feet and he leaped several feet
into the air. It is also believed that he looked into windows at night.

6 Attrib, comb **spring avens**: golden ragwort
(*Senecio aureus*) (1956 ROULEAU 38).

spring baiting: quantity of frozen caplin, herring, etc, taken in spring aboard vessel at one
time for use as bait in trawl-fishing; a fishing voyage to the Banks, duration of which is fixed by
the supply of bait aboard; BAITING.
1960 FUDGE 19 The first week in April the winter
trip was over and we returned home to get ready for
the spring baiting. Herring was very scarce in Fortune
Bay and the only herring was secured by purse seines
for bait. 1964 *Evening Telegram* 25 Mar It is now when
south coast activities and thoughts would be centered
around the preparation and sailing of the banking fleet
on what was the beginning of the voyage and known as
the 'spring baitings.' . . .The spring or frozen baitings
usually were of from three to six weeks duration and
extended from the Western Banks to the Grand Banks.

spring fish: fish, esp salmon, migrating inshore
in the spring; cp SUMMER FISH.
[1771] 1792 CARTWRIGHT i, 135 We caught the first
spring-fish this evening. 1792 ibid *Gloss* i, xv ~ A
salmon which is in perfect season.

spring fishery: cod-fishery on the Banks using
herring or frozen bait; early inshore fishery; cp
SUMMER FISHERY.
1916 LENCH 14 We have what is known as the Spring
fishery, which commences in the later part of March, or
the beginning of April, in which they are away for the
space of seven or eight weeks.

spring herring: herring schools which migrate
to inshore waters in spring. Also attrib. Cp FALL
HERRING.
1842 JUKES i, 225 Towards the middle or end of May
the first shoal of herrings, called by the natives the
spring herrings, appear. 1873 HOWLEY *MS
Reminiscences* 15 The chief business of [Sandy Point]
was the spring herring fishery, all the product being
salted and packed in barrels and shipped to Halifax.
1960 FUDGE 49 Long Harbour, the home of the spring
herring, was frozen to many feet thick, and soon the
long month of March came in.

spring hunt: trapping season in the Labrador
interior.
1947 TANNER 716 In the middle of February, however, the wilderness again calls its faithful children.
Muscles swell, snowshoes are strapped on and the trapper starts out on his so-called spring hunt, which usually lasts till the middle of April.

spring run: large number of seals (and fish)

migrating in coastal waters early in the fishing season; cp RUN n.

1909 BROWNE 56 This [seal] fishery is carried on from May to June 10 (spring 'run'), and from 20th November to 10th December (fall 'run').

spring salmon: see **spring fish** above.

[1772] 1792 CARTWRIGHT i, 228 Had a spring salmon to-day.

spring snowshoe: small, light snowshoe.

1933 MERRICK 329 Edward had two pairs of snow-shoes we used to josh him about, a big pair called his 'winter snowshoes' and a little pair called his 'spring snowshoes.'

spring trip: first of the annual periods of fishing on the offshore banks.

M 70–27 The names of our trips [to the Banks] were as follows: Spring trip, fished mostly on the Grand Banks. . .

spring var: balsam fir (*Abies balsamea*); SNOTTY VAR, VAR.

M 68–16 Once the fall fishery is over, the men go in the woods and [haul] out their spring var, pile it up, cut paths to it in order to make it easier for hauling out when the snow comes. M 69–14 Some of this [wood] was hauled 'green' or undried, while in late winter and early spring they would cut what was known as spring var. This was cut during the spring, left lying all summer with the limbs still attached where it dried. The following winter it was limbed and hauled out to provide dry firewood for the winter. C 71–22 [Two men] went in over the hills on Merasheen Island to cut their spring var. 1976 *Daily News* 24 Feb, p. 3 The one-room where I began teaching in Fortune Bay was heated by a black, pot-bellied stove that glowed when primed with good splits and fed with dry spring var.

spring vessel: English West-Country fishing and trading vessel.

[c1830] 1890 GOSSE 71 The arrival of the spring vessels from Poole [to Carbonear].

spring weakness: malnutrition resulting from the exhaustion of the winter's supply of food (C 75–21).

spring winter: snow-fall in late March (1971 NOSEWORTHY 248); cp PATRICK, SHEILA.

springe See SPRING[1].

sprinkle[1] n, usu pl also **brinkle*, prinkle***. See also PRICKLE. Needle of spruce or fir (P 148–62).

T 175/7–65 Next summer that limb was dried up an' perhaps the sprinkles, what we call the sprinkles—the things on the bough—is fell off an' dried up. 1966 PADDOCK 87 Prinkles, sprinkles. The prickley leaves of the local conifirs such as spruce and fir. T 398–67 Spruce buds, she'd boil 'em. She'd put in the liquor an' the buds what she'd strained off, clear o' the sprinkles an' all that: she'd take that all out. P 148–70 [When they brought in blasty boughs] the room was full of bough brinkles.

sprinkle[2] n also **sprinkler**. Cp PRICKLY: PRICKLEY. Stickleback (*Gasterosteus* spp) (P 245–56); SPANTICKLE.

P 130–67 Sprinkles are the ones with thorns. They have sharp projections on their back.

spritsail n *OED* ~ 2 c: ~ v (1835–1867). Comb **spritsail yard** v: to disable a fish regarded as useless or predatory by thrusting a piece of wood through its gills (1842 BONNYCASTLE i, 272).

1818 CHAPPELL 16 The fishermen of Newfoundland are much exasperated whenever an unfortunate *hallibut* happens to seize upon their baits: they are frequently known, in such cases, to wreak their vengeance on the poor fish, by thrusting a piece of wood through its gills, and in that condition turning it adrift upon the ocean. . .spritsail yarding.

sprog n [sprɑg] *EDD* ~ sb[2] Sc. A big clumsy foot; SPAUG.

T 12–64 Sprogs. P 130–67 Get your big sprogs out of the way.

sprong n *OED* ~ now dial (1492–1756; 1870–), *EDD* sb[1] 2 'a prong' K So, *Kilkenny Lexicon* for sense 1. See also PRONG n.

1 A manure fork (1974 MANNION 177).

2 A long stick with one or two tines used in transferring cod-fish from boat to 'fishing stage,' etc; PEW[1].

P 148–59 The fish is then thrown into the moistured area of the wharf by a sprong, a sharp-pointed instrument with two fork-like spikes and a handle about five feet long.

sprong v See also PRONG v. To pierce fish with a long fork and pitch them from boat into the fishing stage; FORK v, PEW v.

P 148–59 Another fisherman then sprongs the fish into the stage.

spruce n *OED* ~ sb 4 (1670–), *DAE* 1 (1630–) for sense 1; for combs. in sense 3: *OED* ~ beer b (1690–), *DAE* (1706–), *DC* (1741–); *DAE* 6 ~ bird (1900); *DC* ~ game (Nfld: 1770); *OED* 5 ~ partridge (1774–), *DC* (1771–); *DC* ~ tea (1783–).

1 Spruce fir, a coniferous tree of the genus *Picea*, freq with specific epithets *black, scrub, white*.

1613 *Willoughby Papers* 16a/70 The turpentine that commeth from the firr and pine and frankincense of the spruce is likewise sent. 1620 WHITBOURNE 10 There are Firre and Spruce trees, sound, good, and fit to mast Ships withall; and as commodious for boords and buildings as the Spruce and Firre trees of *Norway*; and out of these came abundance of Turpentine. [1663] 1963 YONGE 56 As soon as we resolve to fish here, the ship is all unrigged, and in the snow and cold all the men go into the woods to cut timber, fir, spruce, and birch being here plentiful. 1708 OLDMIXON 11 As for the Product of the Country, Fir and Spruce Trees are the most remarkable, being reckon'd as fit for Masts. [1766] 1971 BANKS 120 The Countrey is Covered with wood fir is the only Tree which can yet be distinguished of which I observed 3 sorts (1) Black Spruce [*Picea*

mariana (Mill.) B S P] of which they Make a liquor
Called Spruce Beer. [1794] 1968 THOMAS 59 The
Spruce Tree is the most prevalent wood of this
Country. . . It answers for a great many purposes; of it,
they have no Domestic article but what the Spruce has
some concern. The following is a list of the principal
uses to which This Tree is applicable in Newfoundland:
Yeast, to raise Bread with / Essence of Spruce, the
common drink here / Building Houses / Bark to cover
their Houses with / Firing / Building Fish Flakes / Preserve the Sails of their Vessels / Oars, for their Boats /
Masts and Yards for Ships / Cattle browse on its tender
Branches / Making Pudings with. 1842 BONNYCASTLE
i, 291–2 The pinus nigra or black spruce, is also not a
very large tree. . .in this country. . . It is used here for
fences, posts, and other small work, as well as in ship
building in parts not exposed. From its boughs or
sprigs, essence of spruce, in Canada, and spruce beer,
the common beverage here, are made. Ibid The pinus
alba or white spruce, is very abundant, and grows to a
good size. . . This species of fir or spruce is largely
employed in Newfoundland in shingles or wooden
slates for covering roofs, for staves for fish and oil barrels, and for many of the builder's uses. 1905 PROWSE
145 Spruce is particularly plentiful, and I am of opinion
that this Island is bound to become a large pulp-produ-
cing area. [1951] 1965 PEACOCK (ed) iii, 749 "Gerry
Ryan": It's hard for a man to make money / When
there's only scrub spruce to be found. 1967 BEARNS
42–3 White Spruce [*Picea glauca*]. . .is found in only
scattered amounts throughout Newfoundland and
Labrador. . . Black Spruce [*Picea mariana*] because of
its high wood density. . .is the most valuable pulpwood
species in the Province. 1976 *Evening Telegram* 10 Jan,
p. 3 When a large segment of the peasantry was gra-
ciously taken on to slash down black spruce at 85 cents
per cord to fuel the newspaper barons of Britain, every
maggot in the mess-camp beans was hailed as a special
bonus.

2 Designating parts of the spruce fir used for
various purposes: **spruce bud** [see BUD[1]], ~
longer [see LONGER], ~ **paddle,** ~ **pole,** ~ **top**.
T 141/67–65[2] [The bark would] be all done with buds,
spruce buds. 1971 BOWN 120 With their spruce-bud
'tea' and bread and fish, they made a welcome meal.
1881 WHITE *MS Journal* 28 Feb 6 Spruce longers 6s.
Q 67–103 The stages were made of spruce longers.
T 181/2–65 There's nothing only a spruce paddle then.
1873 HOWLEY *MS Reminiscences* 26 Cutting some hard
spruce poles and sharpening them at one end, we three
spent a couple of hours up to our waists in water chasing the salmon from one end of the pool to another.
[1771] 1935 *Can Hist Rev* xvi, 57 It was continually eating one thing or another, blubber, raw cod, spruce
tops, &c. 1936 DEVINE 113 The beer was made of
spruce tops and good West Indian molasses.

3 Attrib, comb **spruce bark**: concoction of
spruce buds and boughs, used as a preservative
for nets and sails; BARK n.
T 141/67–65[2] There was no such thing as cutch. [The]
only thing that they knew to preserve linnet an' rope
was the spruce bark.

spruce beer: fermented drink made from an
infusion of the boughs and 'buds' of the black
spruce.

[1712 (1895) PROWSE 273 Beer brewed with
molasses and spruce.] [1766] 1971 BANKS 139 Spruce
Beer [is] the Common Liquor of the Country The
receipt for making it take as follows as Perfectly as I
can get it Take a copper that Contains 12 Gallons fill it
as full of the Boughs of Black spruce as it will hold
Pressing them down pretty tight Fill it up with water
Boil it till the Rind will strip off the Spruce Boughs
which will waste it about one third take them out &
add to the water one Gallon of Melasses Let the whole
Boil till the Melasses are disolvd take a half hogshead
& Put in nineteen Gallons of water & fill it up with the
Essence. work it with Barm & Beergrounds & in Less
than a week it is fit to Drink. [1776] 1792 CARTWRIGHT
ii, 152 Why I should now have the scurvy I cannot
imagine, as I have tasted very little salt flesh, or fish for
these twelve months past; have drank great plenty of
good spruce-beer, but no drams of any kind, nor have I
been the least heated with liquor. [1794] 1968 THOMAS
119 Our people were ashore at this place brewing
Spruce Beer, Cutting Wood. 1832 MCGREGOR i, 221
Spruce beer is a very common and excellent beverage,
particularly for people who live so much on fish and
salt meat. [c1851] 1954 INNIS 402 The establishment of
De Quetteville and Brothers, of Jersey, bring about 50
men every year from Jersey, and engage 5 or 6 more
with their boats, to fish during the season, at payment
of 4s per hundred fish, with firewood and spruce beer,
the parties finding themselves in everything else. 1936
DEVINE 111 Not to say gallons, but barrels and barrels
of spruce beer could be sold out in a day. T 222–66 Frequently during these dances spruce beer would be
served, which is a drink made from spruce buds, and
not too alcoholic. 1970 PARSONS 124 Sometimes [they]
make Spruce Beer and get drunk; in such a case a fight
usually starts, and only the priest is able to handle the
situation.

spruce bird: any of several birds, crossbill,
grosbeak, etc, which frequent spruce forests.
1870 *Can Naturalist* v, 156–7 The spruce birds (*Loxia
leucoptera*) have a very pleasing note, much resembling
the song of the canary. 1959 MCATEE 62 ~ Pine Grosbeak (Nfld., 'Labr.') Ibid 63 ~ Dusky Redpoll (As
feeding on the seeds of spruces. Nfld.). 1964 *Evening
Telegram* 28 Oct, p. 5 The black-polled warbler, one of
our commonest birds, but rather shy and secretive, is
called the 'spruce bird.' This too, is an excellent local
name, for the little bird seems to spend most of its time
in spruce trees of all sizes. 1967 *Bk of Nfld* iii, 283 Red
Crossbill: Spruce Bird (from feeding on the seeds of
spruce.)

spruce bread: bread made with a concoction of
spruce boughs as yeast. See 1794 quot in sense 1
and **spruce yeast** below.
M 69–76 Spruce bread was made the same way as the
Hop bread only preparing the Spruce was a little different than preparing the hops. Small spruce branches
[were] put in the old iron pot and let it steep for about
three to four hours. It was put in a large jar with three
potatoes cut in small pieces. The potatoes made it work
fast. After this was done the jar was put away in a

warm place for about three days until it worked. It was then ready for the flour.

spruce game: see **spruce partridge** below.

[1770] 1792 CARTWRIGHT i, 21 But I got shots at an otter, a black-duck, and a spruce-game, with my Hanoverian rifle, and killed them all. 1792 ibid *Gloss* i, xv ~ A bird of the grouse genus.

spruce mope: Newfoundland red crossbill (*Loxia curvirostra pusilla*) (1964 JACKSON 14); cp MOPE.

1951 PETERS & BURLEIGH 382 ~ The crossbill is so named from its peculiarly crossed bill. It seems to be adapted for prying open the tightly closed spruce or pine cones in order to extract the seeds.

spruce partridge: Canada or spruce grouse (*Canachites canadensis*) (1959 MCATEE 24).

[1771] 1935 *Can Hist Rev* xvi, 57 There are more spruce Partridges in the woods than I have seen any-where in this country. 1818 CHAPPELL 224 There is a bird very common in the woods of this country, which is called, by the settlers, 'a spruce partridge.' 1861 DE BOILIEU 75 Before heavy frost sets in, we are busily engaged in trapping—chiefly for their furs—animals and birds of all kinds, such as. . .white and spruce par-tridges, and the ptarmigan. 1908 HUBBARD 155 On the way back four red-throated loons, two old and two young, and a spruce partridge were taken.

spruce tea: drink made from an infusion of spruce boughs.

1881 *Nineteenth Century* ix, 92–3 Suppose my tea give out, perhaps make some spruce tea. [1883] 1963 GARLAND 26 All the time that I sat there they fed me on bread and hot spruce tea.

spruce yeast: fermenting mixture made from black spruce boughs. See **spruce bread** above.

[1794] 1968 THOMAS 59 The people of this Country use Spruce yeast and nothing else to raise their Bread with.

spry n *OED* spray sb²: spry(e) (1621–1818). Fine drops of water blown from the tops of waves; spray.

1937 DEVINE 65 Contempt for a boasting but indif-ferent fellow fisherman is thus expressed: 'I'd drown 'en with the spry of me nippers.' T 141/68–65² I used to chew when I used to knock around a schooner, spe-cially when I was steerin'. It was blowin' an' spry an' stuff like that; I'd put in a chew then.

spuddle v Cp *EDD* ~ v¹ 3 'to muddle' Ha So W D. To do something in a clumsy, awkward man-ner.

P 148–64 Did you see how he spuddled down there then? [skated clumsily].

spudgel n also **spudget***, **spudgin***, **spudgy*** ['spʌdʒl̩, 'spʌdʒɨl, 'spʌdʒɨl] *EDD* ~ sb 1 'a wooden bowl with a long handle used for bailing' Gl IW Do So; *DC* Nfld (1775, 1937) for sense 1.

1 Small wooden bucket with a long handle, used to bail water from a deep-keeled boat; PIGGIN.

[1775] 1792 CARTWRIGHT ii, 73 The boat proved so

leaky, that the spudgel was scarce ever out of hand. 1792 ibid *Gloss* i, xv ~ A small bucket fixed to the end of a pole, to throw the water out of a boat, which has no pump. 1897 *J A Folklore* x, 210 ~ a small bucket used for dipping the water out of the dill and bailing their boats. [c1900] 1978 *RLS* 8, p. 26 ~ a boat bailer consisting of a bucket with a long handle through it. 1937 DEVINE 47 Spudgell. A bailing bucket. It is differ-ent from a *piggin* in being tub shaped and having a long handle—somewhat like a corn-cob pipe. 1951 *Nfld & Lab Pilot* i, 208 Otter Rub point, with Spudgell cove close north-eastward of it, lies 1¼ miles east-north-eastward of the entrance to Pays cove; Spudgell Cove rocks extend three-quarters of a cable southward. P 102–60 If a man was a bit of a cooper [he would go] to the coopershop and make piggins and spudgils out of pork barrel staves. The difference between a piggin and a spudgil: one was about 10 or 12 inches high with one stave about 5 or 6 inches longer than the others to use as a handle; the spudgil was about the same size but through the handle stave was bored a hole about one inch in size through which was passed a round stick from the top and fastened to the bottom and about 4 or 5 feet long so as the man using it did not have to stoop down to bail out water from the dill in the after part of the boat. T 43/7–64 A piggin got the handle attached, an' the spudgel is the one with [the handle] on an angle. T 90–64 The spudgel [is] the little tub with a long stick in it for the larger boats, to throw the water over the gunnel. 1971 NOSEWORTHY 248 ~, spudgin, spud-gy. A ten-pound tub with a long wooden handle, 5 or 6 ft. long, nailed on. It is used for bailing out deep, keeled boats. P 209–73 Spuggal. A large wooden con-tainer with a long handle used to bail water from a boat. 1975 BUTLER 38–9 I had two big long-handled spudgels aboard. I said 'Jack, here, take one of those and,' I said, 'if you ever worked in your life, work now, if you don't want to drown.'

2 Metal or wooden container with a long han-dle, often larger than a boat bailer, used to dip water from a well, hot bark in the tanning of nets, and for other purposes.

T 14/19–64 You'll take your spudgel and you'll dip out your tan out of the boiler and throw it on your twine and let it remain there all night. T 94/5–64 An' in the summer when [the well would] go a bit low they'd have a spudgel, a big can on a wooden machine they made—a long stick went right through from side to side so it wouldn't come off—and you'd fill up your buckets with that. C 71–103 The kind of spudgel that was used to draw water for a well consisted of a large can and a long wooden handle [that] went through a hole in the side and on down to the bottom. 1973 BARBOUR 51–2 ~ It is made of wood, shaped like a bucket, and has a long handle which goes through the bucket slantwise, or, as a fisherman would say, 'scow ways.' At Blanc Sablon the spudgel was used to dip water from over the side of the wharf in order to wash down the troughs and wharf. In lots of places the spudgel is used mainly to dip fresh water from deep wells. 1979 TIZZARD 55 This water was usually drawn up or taken from the well by a spudgel, a small tub or can made fast to the end of a long pole.

spur-shore n *OED* spur sb[1] 12 b (1846 naut quot). A stout post, often placed diagonally to support wharf, fishing-stage, etc; SHORE[2].

1792 CARTWRIGHT *Gloss* i, xv ~s. Very long shores, to support the wall-plate of the roof of a codstage. T 14/16–64 Piles is drove today so close as they can go, but for the old-time wharf it was strouters a couple of feet apart. And spur-shores, we used to call them, would go at an angle from, say the east side of the wharf and the ends will rest on the west side [so] the wharf can't shift from east to west. P 127–76 ~s. Beams which are attached diagonally across the vertical supporting shores of a wharf. P 245–78 If the pile [of dried fish] shows signs of falling one way, a spur shore (post) may be placed against that part to hold it up.

spurt n also **spirt** *OED* ~ sb[1] 1 b freq in 17th c; now dial (1591–), *EDD* 2 for sense 1; cp *OED* 2 for sense 2; cp *Cent* spurt[1] n, spirt 4 'school of shad' Conn, PIERCE 118, 262 for sense 3; *OED* 2 e (1885) for sense 5.

1 An interval or short period of time.

1858 [LOWELL] i, 149 I couldn' rightly say, Pareson Wellon, how long it was, sir; not to say gezac'ly, sir; but it were a short spurt. 1862 *Atlantic Mo* ix, 370 An' so I set out, walkun this way, for a spurt, an' then t' other way. 1895 *J A Folklore* viii, 37 ~ meaning a short time. 'Excuse me for a spurt.' 'How long did you stay?' 'A short spurt.' 1937 DEVINE 47 Spirt. Brief space of time. T 187–65 An' then there was another man belonged here one time but he shift up in [Burnt] Arm for a spurt.

2 A brief period of a certain kind of habitual activity; one's share with another of an activity, SPELL n.

1887 *Colonist Christmas No* 17 It is a fine day in August; the skiffs are on the fishing-ground, as usual. Many of their occupants are asleep, for the morning 'spurt' is over. 1907 DUNCAN 118 'I 'low I'll stay ashore, the morrow,' says my uncle, 'an' have a spurt o' yarnin' along o' that there ol' bully.' 1937 DEVINE 47 ~ Very active work of short duration. 'A good *spurt* of fishing.' Q 67–106 [of the life of a Newfoundlander]: Spurt of work in summer. Spurt of religion in spring. Spurt of laziness in winter. C 71–90 Let me have a spurt [chopping wood]. C 71–99 [She] had a family of boys and when they had been making the fish on the flake, she would go down and give the men a spurt.

3 The sudden appearance or schooling of fish in inshore waters; a quantity of fish so appearing; a quantity of seals; RUN n.

1842 JUKES i, 226 [He] throws out his line again. When they get what they call a good spurt of fish, each person will sometimes be fully employed hauling in one line after another. 1882 TALBOT 24 [The] fishermen. . .worked two lines, and sometimes three when a good spurt occurred. 1891 PACKARD 133 When I asked him what the people would do if the hunting and fishing continued to fall off, he replied hopefully, and in his fisherman's dialect, 'Oh, we'll have a spurt by and by.' 1906 GRENFELL 51 It was his greatest delight to be first on the fishing grounds, and he was ever the last to leave when a 'spurt o' fish' was running.

1924 ENGLAND 79 'Look like we'm handy to young fat,' said Kelloway. 'Look like de first spurt comin', 'treckly.' 1936 SMITH 20 By the time all this work was done it was the middle of July, and the skipper thought it too late to go back to Bluff Head, as he expected the spurt to be nearly over, so he decided to go down the shore. M 68–24 I had to wait for dark and the sunset spurt, and after jigging some two or three hundred squid, bring them ashore, clean out the punt, and start back the five miles to Elliston.

4 A brief interval of a certain kind of weather.

1870 HOWLEY *MS Reminiscences* 28 It seems to have set in for a spurt of very bad weather. 1902 *Christmas Bells* 2 Luckily a few days before Christmas the hard 'spurt' appeared to be over and the weather turned mild. [1918–19] GORDON 43 There is every indication of a mild spurt of weather. [c1945] TOBIN 26 "November Slips Away": This spurt isn't going to stay, / It's too early in the year / For winter to be settled here! T 175/7–65 If you struck a bad spurt o' weather that fish'd go bad quicker if 'twas in a big heavy lot, [than] 'twould in just a few fish together. 1978 *Evening Telegram* 29 July, p. 16 'Begar, Mr English,' sez I, 'now that we are gettin' a spurt of warm weather do you ever hanker after a dish of that grand ice cream they used to make up to Power's on the Middle Street.'

5 A frolic; TIME.

C 71–106 We had a fine spurt over to Tom's last night.

spurt v Of fish, to appear in inshore waters in large numbers; school.

1868 *Roy Geog Soc* xxxviii, 277 The capelin and cod 'spurted' on the 10th of June, and the vessels did not arrive until July.

spurwink See SKERWINK.

spy n, v *OED* ~ sb 5 ~ Wednesday Ir (1842), JOYCE 333.

Comb **spy bucket**, ~ **glass**: device with glass in bottom for viewing fish underwater; FISH GLASS.

1895 *St Nicholas* [N Y] Apr, p. 449 A curious implement of fishing in these waters is a spy-glass with plain window-glass in place of a lens. A man in the bow of a fishing-boat thrusts the glass in the water [and peers through it]. 1936 SMITH 45 On Sunday, the 26th, I got in the punt and sculled in to the trap and looked down with the spy bucket; the trap was filled with fish, and it was a great temptation to haul it.

spy master: crewman sent aloft to look out for seals; BARREL-MAN.

1924 ENGLAND 51 Her 1922 complement. . .comprised: Captain, second hand, barrel men (or spy masters), scunners. 1925 *Dial Notes* v, 343 ~ Barrel master; a man who spies for seals. 1928 *Nfld Qtly* Oct, p. 31 He was spy master and I was bridge master.

spy wednesday: day before Maundy Thursday.

C 67–21 She supposed Spy Wednesday was called that because on that day the Jews sent out men to spy on Christ and see if there were any way of capturing him.

squabby a ['skwɒbɪ]. Cp *EDD* squab sb³ 1: ~ 'fat, loose in figure' So. Soft, flabby; pliant.

1955 ENGLISH 35 ~ soft as jelly. T 391/2–67 But [the skin of] a old hood [seal] is no good [for making boots]; it's too squabby.

squad n Cp *EDD* ~ sb¹ 'a quantity of anything.' A large number (of seals); PATCH.

1924 ENGLAND 108 The seals was in livin' squads on the ice. . . So I got evvery man's mother's son out, an' we clapped a lickin' to that spot o' seals, I'm tellin' you! Ibid 167 Dat'm de rig-out she drapped de message in. Now I 'spects dis-un'll get squads o' swiles! 1925 *Dial Notes* v, 343 ~ A large lot.

squail* See SQUOIL.

squall See FAIRY SQUALL.

squalling ppl Comb **squalling hawk**, **squealing** ~ : American rough-legged hawk (*Buteo lagopus s. johannis*).

1891 PACKARD 425 American Rough-legged Hawk. Both light and dark phases, with their eggs, young, and adults, collected at Fort Chimo. Apparently more abundant on eastern and northern shores than on the southern portions of Labrador. Downy young were also obtained, of the black phase, July 17, 1882, at Davis Inlet. Termed 'Squalling Hawk' by the planters. 1959 MCATEE 21 ~ squealing hawk.

square a Cp *DAE* bender (1846–); *OED* square a 14 b ~ flipper (1883), *DC* Nfld (1774–).

Comb **square beam**: perfect balance of scales when a quantity of dried cod-fish is weighed.

1966 *Evening Telegram* 20 May, p. 5 The scales were so far even. Would the balance hold? 'Square beam' thought Ned wryly, his mind fastening on a local phrase that the fishermen used when weighing off their salt cod in the merchant's storage shed.

square bender: drinking spree (1925 *Dial Notes* v, 343).

1924 ENGLAND 31 To-day's de proper day fer de whiskey. Dough I don't go on no t'ree-days' square-benders [drunks], I belang to de breed to drink everlastin', sir.

square-body: horse-drawn carriage with front and back seat.

T 25–64 There'd be buggies, just a one-seat affair, and the other ones they called them square-bodies. There had to be two seats in the carriage.

square flipper, ~ **fipper**, ~ **phipper**, ~ **phripper**: large migratory seal of northern waters, 'flippers' blunt at the tip; bearded seal (*Erignathus barbatus*). Also attrib. See FLIPPER.

[1766] 1971 BANKS 145 The Fishermen. . .divide them into five sorts which they Call Square Phipper Hooded Seal [etc]. Square Phipper they say is the Largest sometimes weighing 500 weight as they tell you rough like an English Water Dog. [1774] 1792 CARTWRIGHT ii, 38 A squarephripper was caught in a net to-day, but got away as one of the people was clearing him out. 1846 TOCQUE 194 The square fipper,

which is perhaps the great seal of Greenland. . .is now seldom seen. 1891 PACKARD 444 It is probably the species which is called by the sealers the 'Square Flipper.' It is very rare, and much the largest species known. The young weigh 140–150 pounds, while the adult will weigh 500–600 pounds. [1918–19] GORDON 76 Bobbie Williams of North River has killed a square-fripper seal, which means a chance to get some fat for our dogs and a meal of meat for ourselves. 1924 ENGLAND 103 Perhaps twice in a blue moon a 'square fipper' also heaves in view. T 191–65 The ol' harp skin they'd have most generally for the bottom [of a sealskin boot], but when they get the square fipper bottom. . .that's what they'd always wear them times. 1967 *Bk of Nfld* iii, 328 Other common seals found in Newfoundland and Labrador waters are the Harbour Seal or 'ranger,' the Ringed Seal or 'jar,' the Bearded Seal or 'square-flipper,' and the Grey Seal. 1977 *Inuit Land Use* 173 Square-flipper seals are found primarily along the floe edge from November until May.

square n

1 In street names of St John's, Harbour Grace, etc, a short, wide residential street, sometimes blocked at the end.

[1864] 1965 *Am Speech* xl, p. 166 British Square, Brennan's Square, Dick's Square, Lyons Square. [1871] 1930 BARNES 28–9 My grandfather, 'Old Captain Tom Allen'. . .made money hand over hand and my grandmother put the money in land and houses. . . However, when my grandfather died my grandmother had a great big estate, it was called 'Allen's Square.' This was quite a large place with houses all around it. A big hill went down from that square; they used to call it 'Allen's Hill.' [1900 OLIVER & BURKE] 22 He made tracks down the square double quick. 1936 DEVINE 107 After conducting a temporary office in the British Square grounds and on the King's Beach, the plant later passed to Andrew Wright. 1979 TIZZARD 357 After trying unsuccessfully for a boarding house for some time in the afternoon we did get accommodation at 9 Brazil Square.

2 A lot, field; a kin-group house cluster around an ancestral farmstead.

1974 MANNION 51–2 The only evidence of an orderly arrangement of houses is in Branch and, in one or two cases, in St Brides, where dwellings were disposed linearly or grouped compactly around an open space. It is difficult to say if the word 'square' originally referred to the lay-out pattern of the kin-group clusters in these settlements. . . In the settlements near St John's the word 'square' is used to designate a piece of land, e.g. 'a fine "square" of land' or 'a "square" of potatoes.'

3 Sweet baked delicacy, often made into two-inch square pieces.

[1894 BURKE] 78 Now I'm going to bring in a tart on a plate, I'll give a square to Ethel, a square to Maud. . .and a square to Arthur. 1958 *Nfld Dishes* 42 Raisin Squares, Date Squares [etc].

square v Cp *OED* ~ v 5 d 'to settle (a debt) by means of payment'; *DAE* 1 b 'to settle accounts' for sense 1.

1 In the non-cash, or 'truck,' system of the

Newfoundland fishery, to total the credits and debits of a fisherman's account as kept by the supplying merchant (P 267–58); STRAIGHTEN (UP).

1940 SCAMMELL 38 "Squarin' Up": Now come all you men who have squared up your bills, / With not enough left to buy Injun Root pills; / If you must have enough to keep body and soul / The only chance left is to go on the 'dole.' 1966 PHILBROOK 63 'Squaring off' marks the climax of the fishery season. At this time all accounts between merchant and crew are settled. M 69–13 In the [fall] when they were squaring up with the merchants, it seems that they never had any money to the good. 1969 MENSINKAI 5 This may end up with the 'squaring up' of accounts at the end of the season, after which cash transactions may be resorted to.

2 Comb **squaring-up day**, ~ **time**: end of fishing season when a man's account with merchant is balanced to determine amount owed to one or the other; FALL OF THE YEAR.

1940 SCAMMELL 37 "Squarin' Up": 'Tis squarin' up time inside the big shop, / The clerks are kept busy and right on the hop; / The men are all anxious to see what they've done, / For they all want a bottle of Hudson Bay rum. 1966 HORWOOD 16 He might not be able to supply for the fishery, come April, since he might not be able to get the stocks of food and gear that would be needed to carry the fishermen on credit until square-up time in the fall. 1967 Bk of Nfld iv, 235 In the autumn the fish had to be shipped, gardens taken up, wood brought down from the bay and at 'squarin-up time' groceries procured to last till spring. M 71–40 October 1st—Squaring Up Day—the men came 'out of collar.' On this day the fishermen settled with the merchant and the sharemen of the fishing crews were free to go about their own work. The fishing voyage had ended. 1977 Union Forum June, p. 12 It was a tremendous improvement to fishermen to know what the price would be in the spring, rather than have to wait till the squaring-up time as had been the case in the past.

squarefore n   Cp OED square sb 17, 18 'quarrel' obs. An argument, disagreement (P 54–57); STAND V: STAND-BACK.

P 20–55 They had a regular squarefore.

squashberry n   Gray's Botany 1341 ~, NID. An edible orange-red berry, easily crushed; the shrub bearing these berries (Viburnum edule) (1956 ROULEAU 38); BUTTON BERRY; also attrib.

1842 JUKES i, 142 [They were] a kind the men called 'squash-berries,' a bright red berry, the size of a currant, growing on a straggling bush six or eight feet high. They were pulpy, sharp, and juicy, and not unpleasant. 1868 HOWLEY MS Reminiscences 41 Squash berries were very abundant along this brook and I eat my fill of them. [1886] LLOYD 102–3 The partridge-berry, squashberry, foxberry, and marshberry, although differing from each other in some respects, are nevertheless much alike. They are small, red, and when ripe are very good. They grow on small shrubbery on the barrens and marshes. 1898 N S Inst Sci ix, 367–8 ~ few-flowered viburnum. [1914] 1946 MUNN 16

The Squashberry bush is a shrub with thin stem about four feet high. The berries grow in bunches, and when ripe are of a brilliant red colour; they remain on the bush all winter. They have a delicious tart taste, and the fruit of the berry is almost wholly juice and often made into wine. 1933 GREENE 295 Quantities of 'bake-apple' and 'squash-berry' (a red berry with a white stone which makes delicious jelly), and the 'capillaire' berry (a small white berry rather difficult to find as it grows on a sort of vine amongst the grasses, but has a wonderfully delicate and scented flavour) are scattered all over the interior. P 246–60 Squash-berry wine is made from fruit of the squash-berry bush. T 14/19–64 The squashberry is very, very bitter and sour, and a kernel into un. He's not much good for anything apart from making jelly; makes beautiful jelly, beautiful. But it's in November before they're really ripe.

squashy n   Variety of kelp.

T 727–68 The kelp comes over on un—what the old people used to call squashy. Great big long cabbage come up on un. You often sees it in the winter time, comin' up for a storm o' wind.

squat v   [skwɑt, skwɒt] OED ~ v 1 now dial (1300–1722); EDD v¹ 1 esp s w cties for sense 1.

1 To crush, bruise; squeeze; flatten.

1897 J A Folklore x, 210 ~ as a verb means to crush, as 'I got my finger squat'; that is, crushed. 1920 WALDO 161 Instead of 'squashed,' 'squatted' is a common word, as in the expression 'I squatted my finger.' P 148–60 I had to squat my way into the door. T 80/1–64 An' they left Twillingate, see, and come out here an' cut a patch o' seals, an' drove away in th' ice, an' got squat up; had the bottom tore out of her. T 141/68–65² Well the train'd be goin' through sometime that night, an' we put our coppers on the track, an' the weight o' the train, see, squat 'em out. P 157–73 Don't squat the parcel, there's eggs in it. 1976 GUY 98 And a newspaper. . .is where they cuts down trees and squats them out flat for to make paper and then prints stuff on them.

2 To chop or hew one or more flat surfaces on a log.

1869 HOWLEY MS Reminiscences 24 The main or living room was a space of some 10 or 20 feet square with an open fire-place at one end, on either side of which were rough benches or settles made of squatted sticks. 1897 J A Folklore x, 210 ~ To flatten a stick of timber by hewing the one side of it. [c1900] 1968 RLS 8, p. 26 ~ To flatten a piece of timber with an axe, trim down on the sides a round stick. 1937 DEVINE 47 ~ To chop two flat faces on opposite sides of a rail or piece of timber. 1974 MANNION 147 Each pole was 'squatted' on a timber stand, barked and trimmed, then sawn lengthways with a pit-saw, or split with hammer and wedges.

squatter n   Migratory Newfoundland fisherman who moves to the coast of Labrador and prosecutes the summer fishery from a shore base or 'room'; STATIONER.

1909 BROWNE 62 'Stationers' (sometimes called 'Squatters'). 1924 ENGLAND 261 Thousands of outport men migrate almost as regularly as the seals themselves. With small, home-built schooners. . .they take up the sea trek every summer and go down the Labrador. If they pick some berth and settle down, they're called 'stationers,' 'squatters,' or 'roomers.' If they keep on the move, they're 'floaters.' 1936 SMITH 24 Our crew was the same as the year previous, nine men and two girls, and we took along the same number of crews from Conception Harbour who were bound for Splitting Knife, Labrador. These people were what we called 'squatters.'

squatum n ['skwɑtəm, 'skwɒtəm]. Cp SQUAT 'squeeze.' A drink or home-brewed wine made from the juice of crushed berries.
1964 *Evening Telegram* 24 Dec, p. 29 '[Christmas] really started the end of August when we picked the whorts for squatum,' says he. 'Squatum,' sez I, 'what's that?' 'Oh shucks,' sez the skipper, 'whort wine or what you now call blueberry wine. It was called that because the woman had to squat up the berries with a potato masher,' sez he. T 222–66 Before going to bed they would want some refreshment, and a nice drink of squattum would be in order. That is a drink made of partridge berries. You would need lots of sugar in it because it would be bitter as the varge. Q 67–49 ~ blueberry wine. P 81–70 He was going to see his brother to get a bit of squatum. This meant he was going to get some partridge berry drink. He did not know what else was added but he did not think it was without a bit of liquor.

squeaker n Cp *OED* ~ 3 b (1878 quot). A blade of grass held upright between the thumbs and producing a shrill vibration when blown upon (P 97–67).

squealing hawk See SQUALLING HAWK.

squeezy a Comb **squeezy gull**: ring-billed gull (*Larus delawarensis*).
1870 *Can Naturalist* v, 408 *Ring-billed Gull. . .provincial name 'squeezy gull.'*

squid n also **squede** *OED* ~ sb 1 (Nfld: 1613–), *DAE* (1851–), *DC* (Nfld: 1578–) for sense 1; cp *NID* giant squid for sense 2; for combs. in sense 4: *OED* 4 ~ hound (1812); ~ jig (1883), *DAE* (1861–); *OED* 4 ~ jigger (1875); ~ jigging (1881–), *DC* Nfld (1905–); *DC* ~ jigging ground Nfld (1936–); *OED* 4 ~ line (1867); ~ school (1884). For similar words with the sense 'squirt' see squib, squiddle, squit, squitter in *OED* and *EDD*.
1 A pelagic mollusc or cephalopod, esp the short-finned squid (*Illex illecebrosus*), which appears inshore during July and August and is taken for bait and human consumption; freq in place-names and proverbs. Pl often *squids*.
[1578] 1935 *Richard Hakluyt* 130 [Parkhurst's letter] [There is] also a fish like a Smelt which cometh on shore, and another that hath the like propertie, called a Squid. [1620] 1887 MASON 152 Hering-Hoggs, Squides a rare kinde of fish, at his mouth squirting mattere

forth like Inke. . . [1663] 1963 YONGE 60 After the capling [in June] come the squids, a fish like soaked leather. [1712] 1895 PROWSE 273 [They] catch fish with hook and line, first part of year their bait is muscles and lances; about middle of June bait is capeling, squid, and fresh herring, and end of year they fish with herring only—nets purposely for taking the sort of bait. [1794] 1968 THOMAS 182 Its weight and length is about equal to a small Herring, its composition is a transparent jelly with a small substance in the middle. It is called a Squid. Its formation is very singular. Its Tail is like the Fluke of an anchor; from the head part extends Six fibrous and [glutinous] tubes ending in a point, the inner part looking like a saw has the property of adhering to any pungent substance it toucheth. 1819 ANSPACH 407 The squid is also called ink-fish, from its singular faculty of throwing up, when disturbed, a black liquid which suddenly darkens the water, conceals him most effectually from sight, and thereby secures his retreat. [(1852) 1971 SEARY 286 Squib Point.] 1858 [LOWELL] i, 198 'Do 'ee think, now, would n' the squids do better a little furderer up?' I says. 1884 DEMING 87 A squid-fishing fleet of boats, closely grouped, so as to keep the schools of lively octopi collected, is an animated sight. Each man tends three or four lines, and has all he can do when squid are around. 1895 *Christmas Review* 12 When you haul a squid in, look out for your chin. 1904 *Daily News* 18 July By 'Jabers' the Frenchman that would stand before me, / 'Clane' out of his boots 'goes the squid eatin' toad.' 1911 ROGERS 209 The central object in an allegorical picture which symbolized Newfoundland would be the cod-fish, and around it would be grouped its favourite bait the herring, the caplin. . .and the squid. 1937 DEVINE 62 [proverb] The dirt of a squid can be washed off, but the dirt of a tongue sticks and stays. 1951 *Nfld & Lab Pilot* i, 334 Squid cove is entered between a point about 8½ cables south-eastward of Castor point, and a point about 7 cables south-south-eastward. [1952] 1964 PEACOCK (ed) i, 144 "Skipper Tom": We had a whipping fine mainsail and a sporting fine jib, / A crooked-nosed punt and she sailed like a squid. 1955 ENGLISH 39 You can't tell the mind of a squid. [This proverb] refers to an unreliable person. A squid can move backwards or forward. 1940 SCAMMELL 37 "Squarin' Up": O the fish are all caught, and the squids are all jigged, / And the traps are cut up, and the schooner's unrigged. 1979 *Evening Telegram* 6 July, p. 2 There is a high probability that squid will be abundant in inshore Newfoundland waters [this summer]. Ibid 31 July, p. 20 [advertisement] Wanted to Buy: Dried Squid. 1979 TIZZARD 300 While waiting for the squids to strike some men slept, some yarned, while others just kept working their jiggers to try and tow [toll] the squids around.
2 The giant squid, calamary or devil-fish, up to forty feet in length (*Architeuthis dux*); usu with epithet *big*.
[1785] 1792 CARTWRIGHT iii, 44 It proved to be a large squid, which measured seven feet, exclusive of the head, which broke off in hoisting it in; when gutted, the body filled a pork barrel, and the whole of it would have filled a tierce. [1873] 1883 HATTON & HARVEY 240 It proved to be a gigantic cuttle-fish or

calamary, and is called by the fishermen a 'big squid.' The two long arms or tentacles were found to measure each twenty-four feet, and to be three inches in circumference; the eight shorter arms were each six feet in length, and at the point of junction with the central mass, were ten inches in circumference.

3 In exclam *squid-o*: cry to fishermen that 'squid bait' have arrived in inshore waters and are rising to the jigger.

P 118–66 ~ A signal to let other fishermen know that the squid are taking the hook. M 68–24 When the first man shouts 'squid-o' every fisherman jumps to his feet and begins to jig. This continues until the squid slacks off. On a good night each man might jig four or five hundred squid.

4 Attrib, comb, cpd **squid bait**: see sense 1 above.

1919 *Journ of Assembly* 404 Trawling in August and September was short in its returns, owing to the fact that squid bait was late in putting in its appearance. [1953] 1978 *Evening Telegram* 1 Aug, p. 5 A boat. . .was scheduled to leave Grand Bank last night for Rencontre West to load 20,000 pounds of squid bait for the Grand Bank depot. 1973 HORWOOD 9–10 It was too late in the year to expect fish to be caught in traps so the hook and line with squid bait were employed, and that year proved to be successful.

squid baiting: supply of bait squid secured by a schooner; BAITING n.

1960 FUDGE 19 After a few days rest, we left again to look for a baiting of squid. This secured, we anchored on the eastern part of the Grand Banks on August 10th, where we secured five hundred, and proceeded to Harbour Grace, went on dock and painted. From there we proceeded to Holy Rood, where we secured a squid baiting for the Labrador, and there made a trip worth while. 1976 CASHIN 65 Later in the season these vessels bought squid baiting, paying at that time a price of around twenty cents for every hundred squid.

squid barrel: type of wooden container used to pack dried squid for export.

T 90–64 We used to make 'em for squid—a squid barrel; that's [a] package about the size of the barrels we pack tom-cods in, you see; around twenty seven inches, with a sixteen-inch head. 1979 TIZZARD 81 He also made squid barrels; these were to contain two hundred pounds of dried squid.

squid finger, ~ **hand**: inflammation and swelling of hand caused by handling squid, cutting them for bait, etc; erysipeloid (P 148–66). Cp SEAL FINGER.

1979 *Salt Water, Fresh Water* 31 If you have any kind of an allergy to [squid juice] your hands become very sore and they bleed. The only relief to the excruciating pain of squid hands was your own urine and salt water.

squid ground: area of inshore waters with seasonal abundance of the short-finned squid; GROUND.

[c1945] TOBIN 12 "Home Again": And boys who caught trout, or went out to 'squid ground,' / Will bring back account city chums to amaze. [1960] 1965 PEACOCK (ed) i, 123 "Fish and Brewis": With our fish

put away we'll go on the squid ground, / And in a few minutes our jiggers are down.

squid hand: see **squid finger**.

squid hook: metal shank with a number of hooks used unbaited to jig squid for bait; cp **squid jigger** below.

1612 *Willoughby Papers* 16a/12 For our fishing voiage. . .won dosen of squidhookes. [1622] 1954 INNIS 58 [inventory] Squid hooks and squid line 5s. 1765 WILLIAMS 19 Squede Hooks.

squid hound: name variously given to porpoise, small whale, or tuna which pursues squid in coastal waters.

[1794] 1968 THOMAS 183 Whenever Squids are found is also found a Fish called Jumpers, or Squid Hounds, from the avidity with which they pursue and eat Squids. 1908 DURGIN 35 . . .chasing each other through the water and leaping clear, so their entire bodies could be seen, much as a salmon jumps. These were what our crew called 'squid hounds,' but I knew them for the great horse mackerel. 1937 DEVINE 67 When squid-hounds and porpoises leap out of the water in large schools it is a sign of a gale of wind from the direction the porpoises go. P 243–57 ~ Pothead whale. 1966 FARIS 237 Squid Hound—(porpoise)—*Phocaena phocaena*. P 1–69 ~ bluefin tuna.

squid jig: see **squid jigger**.

1861 *Harper's* xxii, 459 The bait used is either soft-shell clams (salted and barreled) or squid. These last are caught by means of a 'squid-jig'—a piece of pewter run on a paper of hooked pins.

squid jigger: metal shank with twenty to forty tiny hooks used unbaited to catch short-finned squid; JIGGER.

1930 RANDELL 12 We dashed away after our squid jiggers. We dashed back to the beach, got a punt, rowed to the squid ground and went to work. M 68–7 ~ A small jigger weighing approximately one ounce, with many small hooks or prongs. There are about twenty prongs on it.

squid jigging: occupation of catching bait squid with a 'squid jigger'; JIGGING.

1883 *Fish Exhibit Cat*[4] 174 [caption to a drawing:] Squid Jigging. 1905 DUNCAN 105 Jack told me much of the lore of lobster-catching and squid-jigging. T 141/64–65[2] Well now they'd have to lose so much time squid jiggin', an' if the squids was uncertain there'd be lots o' times there'd be no bait to get, see.

squid-jigging ground: see **squid ground** above.

1940 SCAMMELL 9 "Squid Jiggin' Ground": They congregate here on the squid-jiggin' ground. 1964 *Daily News* 15 May, p. 4 Too young to get up at four in the morning but was taken out on the squid-jigging ground, and what an experience. T 54–64 An' he used to shout out to the boys on the squid jigging ground, 'were they any squids yet?' T 141/64–65[2] An' up in [the] bay that was the squid jiggin' ground. 1969 HORWOOD 178 I once took a canoe out the bay from Rushoon to the squid jiggin' ground, and paddled around the surprised trap boat fishermen, who were there in a group, waiting for the squid. 1979 TIZZARD 77 Best of all we would watch the boats on the squid jigging ground.

squid juice: inky secretion of short-finned squid.

1940 SCAMMELL 10 "Squid Jiggin' Ground": There's poor Uncle Billy his whiskers are spattered / With spots of the squid juice that's flyin' around. 1979 *Salt Water, Fresh Water* 31 He'd get squid juice on his hands, [his] hands become very sore and they bleed.

squid line: (a) strong, light line about four to fifteen fathoms long to which jigger is attached in fishing for bait squid; (b) length of line on which squid are hung to dry.

1612 *Willoughby Papers* 16a/24 3 bundels of small squidlynes. [1622] 1954 INNIS 58 [inventory] Squid hooks and squid line 5s. 1765 WILLIAMS 19 Squede Lines. 1940 SCAMMELL 9 "Squid Jiggin' Ground": All sizes of figures, with squid lines and jiggers, / They congregate here on the squid jiggin' ground. 1979 TIZZARD 295 My father and I jigged, cleaned and hung on the squid lines 330 squid.

squid pole: long, thin wooden pole between uprights on which the short-finned squid are hung to dry for export.

[c1945] TOBIN 37 "A Tale of Squid": Then if the morn, or eve, be fine / Squid-poles and fences all will shine. P 218–68 ~ A long slender pole formerly used in drying squid.

squid-sail v: to move backward, esp on all fours, like a squid in motion.

T 54–64 I had to crawl under the bed to get the candle. Now this is what they called squid-sailing. I had to come stern foremost to get out—that's how a squid goes, stern foremost. I squid-sailed from under the bed.

squid scull, ~ **school**: appearance in coastal waters of large concentrations of short-finned squid in early summer; SCULL.

1866 WILSON 209 The caplin scull. . .is followed by the squid scull. The squid comes upon the coast in the beginning of August, and continues until the middle of September. 1902 *Nfld Qtly* Sep, p. 21 It was the time between mowing and squid-skull. 1914 *Cadet* 7 Learned modern writers say 'school' of fish—the caplin school, squid school, etc.

squid season: period of late summer when bait squid appear in coastal waters; SEASON.

[1964] 1979 *Evening Telegram* 3 July, p. 14 The squid season usually begins in Newfoundland the first part of August. M 68–24 [They] had what they called a squid season. Late in August and in the month of September most fishing crews spent the hours from about seven p.m. till eleven p.m. jigging squid.

squid shit: see **squid juice** (1971 NOSEWORTHY 248).

squid squall: see SQUID SQUALL.

squid stick: see **squid pole**.

M 68–24 I recall seeing a very large mummer carry little ones on either end of a squid-stick.

squid trap: device to capture schooling squid.

[1930] 1980 *Evening Telegram* 4 Aug, p. 6 The squid trap which was causing so much trouble at Holyrood, was removed to Bay Roberts last week, caught only 150 squid on the first haul on Saturday. 1981 *Evening Telegram* 2 Sep, p. 2 Officials. . .are meeting with Trin-

ity Bay fishermen tonight to discuss an experiment to be set up to keep pothead whales away from the squid traps.

squid trip: voyage to the 'Banks' using squid as bait in trawl-fishing for cod.

1977 *Nfld Qtly* Dec, p. 17 The banking schooner cod fishing year for most vessels operating from Grand Bank was organized in three phases, each according to the main bait species used, viz. herring in the Spring, caplin in the Summer, and squid in the Fall. The men spoke of the 'herring trip,' 'caplin trip,' and 'squid trip,' though each bait phase might embrace several journeys between ports and fishing grounds before actual completion. These three trips then composed the yearly 'voyage.'

squid v Cp *NID* ~ 1 'to fish with or for squid.' To catch squid for bait with a jigger.

1940 SCAMMELL 10 "Squid Jiggin' Ground": Now if ever you feel inclined to go squiddin' / Leave your white shirts and collars behind in the town. 1940 *Fortnightly* cliii, Apr, p. 408 All the men in the boats were squidding for bait, and the water was red with their teeming plenty. 1966 SCAMMELL 68 An' a crowd of us was gettin' ready to go squiddin' when we heard the *Hummin' Bird* comin'. M 67–10 I also went squiddin' with my father in the skiff and the snapper boat.

squidding vbl n

1 Fishing for bait squid.

1955 DOYLE (ed) 83 "When Our Boys Gave Up Squiddin'": Our boys gave up squiddin', they all joined the Navy / To fight for old England, her King and her Crown.

2 Comb **squidding ground**: area of inshore waters with seasonal abundance of the short-finned squid; SQUID n: ~ GROUND (P 148–66).

P 9–73 It was a real nuisance to fishermen living along the shore of the tickle and many a cuss word must have rent the early morning air when some fisherman at 4 a.m. was heading for the squidding ground and found his boat missing.

squid squall n also **squid squad,** ~ **squaw***, etc. ['skwɪd skwɑːl, 'skwɪd skwɒəl, 'skwɪd skwɑː]. Cp *DAE* sunsquall (1859–84); *OED* sun 13 b ~ squall, ~ squaw U S (1865, 1897), squalder obs rare (1659, 1682). A variety of small jelly-fish or *Medusa*: BUBBLY SQUALL.

1842 JUKES ii, 157 Shoals of Medusae (called in Newfoundland squid-squalls). 1878 TOCQUE 496 The waters of Newfoundland, during the autumn, are thick with jelly fishes, or sea nettle (*Medusae*); these fish are also called sea blubbers, but in Newfoundland they are called by the singular name of 'Squid-squads.' 1895 *J A Folklore* viii, 34 The medusae, or sea-nettles, are called *squidsquads*, sometimes *squidsqualls*. 1905 DUNCAN 6 . . .the ways of lobsters and tom cod, the subtle craft of dories, the topography of the wilderness under broad flakes, the abiding places of star-fish and prickly sea-eggs, the significance of squid-squalls, and the virulence of squid. 1937 DEVINE 49 ~s. The umbrella-like medusae floating on the surface of the sea in squid season. P 1–67 Squid squaw: jelly-fish. 1968 DILLON 139

There'd be squid squalls there in galores. C 71–6 When he was out fishing with the other men and any of them saw big jelly-fish come up to the surface of the water nearby they all believed it was a sign of north-east wind and rain and would go ashore. The big jelly-fish were known to the fishermen as squit-squa's. 1979 COOPER 11 "The Boy and the Piggin": I likes de little brown piggin I do / I dips up squid-squalls wid'n.

squile See SQUOIL.

squirt v Of a squid, to eject a dark ink-like juice.

[1620] 1887 MASON 152 What should I speake of. . .Squids a rare kind of fish, at his mouth squirting mattere forth like Inke. . .[?] 1846 TOCQUE 317 The moment the squid is drawn from the water they 'squirt,' as it is termcd, ejecting the black fluid in the face, and over the clothes of the fishermen. 1924 ENGLAND 179 'Dat Jonas,' volunteered the bosun, 'ain't doin' a thing. He ain't worth his salt, sir. An' if ye speak to un, he mind ye of a squid squirtin'.' 1940 SCAMMELL 9 "Squid Jiggin' Ground": But a squid in the boat squirted right down his throat, / He's swearin' like mad on the squid-jiggin' ground.

squirts n pl EDD ~ sb 2 Ha IW So. Diarrhoea (P 54–67).

squish See ASQUISH.

squoil v also **squail***, **squile** [skwɒɪl, skwɔɪl]. Cp EDD squail: squoil Ha W 4 squailing 'awkward, irregularly shaped.'
1 To wear down a heel so that boot or shoe is mis-shapen; often with *down, over*.
1897 J A Folklore x, 211 'The heel of my boot is *squoiled*,' it is twisted and worn on one side. [c1900] 1978 RLS 8, p. 25 Squail or squoiled, gone one side on a boot heel etc. 1937 DEVINE 49 Squile. To turn over a shoe on the foot. P 118–67 Don't squile over your shoes. P 207–67 The heels on his boots were squoiled down. C 70–21 If they should get worn down on one side of the heel so that you couldn't walk in them properly, they were said to be [squoiled] over.
2 Comb **squail-legs** (fig.): pigeon-toed person.
P 127–73 She was a real old squail-legs.
squail's shoe: shoe worn down on one side.
P 127–73 She always wore squail's shoes.

stabber n
1 Harpoon; a long pole with nail in end used by boy to spear fish in shallow water.
T 393/4–67 An' the next thing I know I see him comin' down the stage with his stabber. We call it a stabber, seal stabber—harpoon. M 69–14 To stab these flat fish we used a stabber made simply by getting a long pole and attaching a large sharpened four-inch nail to one end.
2 Comb **stabber pole**: iron-shod pole used to push loose pans of ice away from a sealing vessel (1925 *Dial Notes* v, 343). Also attrib.
1924 ENGLAND 186 'If dis un get froze in yere, solid,

de divil himself couldn't get us out. We might bide a fartnight in dis jam.' . . .All hands looked alive. Masses of men grabbed 'starber' [stabber] poles and tumbled over the rails from the barricade. Ibid 189 Yelling, the stabber-pole crew come running back and fall to work.

stag¹ n
1 One of the two wooden bars fastened as handles on the sides of a tub or half-barrel (P 148–62).
T 43–64 Now the handbarrow was made with two stags, one on each side and you'd load up the barrow [with] what you thought the two people were able to carry, an' you'd take it up by the stags and carry it out on the flake an' dump it off.
2 Protruding end of the runner of a sled or 'komatik.'
T 43/7–64 [There'd be] two stags on the rear end of it, you know, for guidin' 'em. If the thing is empty you sit on an' guide her with your feet, but if you're loaded you stand behind and just guide your komatik with your two stags behind.
3 Comb **stag barrow**: device with two projecting wooden shafts for moving hay (P 269–64).
stag tub: wooden tub or half-barrel with handle on each side, carried by two men (P 269–64); BARROW¹: ~ TUB.

stag² n OED ~ sb² (1775, 1867). A submerged rock (P 148–62).
1951 Nfld & Lab Pilot i, 113 Stag rock, with a depth of less than 6 feet over it, lies 2½ cables [away].

stage n Cp OED ~ sb 4 f 'platform and other apparatus for drying fish' (1535–), DAE (1633–), DC 1 Nfld (1620–) for sense 1; for comb in sense 2: DAE ~ room (1628, 1713).
1 An elevated platform on the shore with working tables, sheds, etc, where fish are landed and processed for salting and drying, and fishing gear and supplies are stored; FISHING STAGE.
[1589] 1972 PARMENIUS 175 [tr HAKLUYT] Beares also appeare about the fishers stages of the Countrie. 1613 Willoughby Papers 17a/ 1/2 Here is a good beach and the fishing neare, to be assured of a good place to fish and a beach, boats and stage may be worth more than one or tow hundreth pounds yearely for a shipp. 1620 WHITBOURNE 25 And if such Pinnaces and such Stages and Houses may be maintained and kept in such readinesse yeerely, it would be the most pleasant, profitable, and commodious trade of fishing, that is at this time in any part of the world. [1663] 1963 YONGE 56 The stages are begun on the edge of the shore, and built out into the sea, a floor of round timber, supported with posts, and shores of great timber. The boats lie at the head of them, as at a key, and throw up their fish, which is split, salted, &c. [1693] 1793 REEVES ii . . .and liberty to go on shore on any part of Newfoundland. . .for the curing, salting, drying, and husbanding of their fish, and for making of oil, and to cut down wood and trees there for building and making or repairing of stages. [1766] 1971 BANKS 134 When the Fish are Catchd they are Carried to the Stage which

is built with one End Hanging over the water for the Sake of throwing away the offals into the sea & of their boats being able to Come close to them & Discharge their fish with. . .little [trouble]. 1819 ANSPACH 430 The place where the operation of curing the cod-fish is performed, is a *stage* or covered platform erected on the shore. 1865 CAMPBELL 88 The stage, a long low building of fir poles and branches, is perched on the rocks, so as to project over the sea. It is like a long windowless house on a wooden pier. In this long room a number of double-beaked tin lamps hung flaring from the roof. 1868 HOWLEY *MS Reminiscences* 8 One man brought me through his stage to see the fish and I must confess I never saw so much green fish together before. 1924 ENGLAND 255 [proverb] An empty stage, an empty stomach. T 43–64 A stage now was a big building [that] was put up, 'twould be possibly fifty or seventy feet long and about thirty feet wide. Well now, that was built a-purpose for curin' your fish in. When you'd start gettin' fish you'd be in the stage both day an' night. 1977 *Decks Awash* vi (3), p. 28 It's a lot easier to handle our fish on our own stages. I can prong the fish from the boat to the truck when the water is high. 1979 NEMEC 257 A 'stage' is a plain wooden structure located above the high tide line and next to the 'landwash' or tidal zone. A wooden 'tramway' or plank walkway connects it to a wharf located at the water's edge. . . A stage functions primarily as a storage shed for 'saltbulk fish' and salt in the summer and nets and gear in the winter. 1980 *Evening Telegram* 20 Sep, p. 1 [The large catch] has caused a problem because many fishermen in the outer stations [of Labrador] have their stages full of salted cod and have been unable to sell it.

2 Attrib, comb **stage beam**: upright post supporting a fishing stage.

[1786] 1792 CARTWRIGHT iii, 224 Where the soil is pretty good [the trees] run clear and tall, and attain substance sufficient for shallop's-oars, skiff's-oars, stage-beams, rafters, longers, and other purposes, for which length is principally required.

stage door: entrance to a fishing stage on the landward side.

1977 RUSSELL 105 Grampa went to the stage door to make sure no one was listenin'.

stage head: see STAGE HEAD.

stage lamp, ~ **light**: makeshift lamp used in a fishing stage when handling the catch at night; FLARE-UP.

1934 *Nfld Qtly* Apr, p. 12 "Jenkins the Fisherman": Work by the stage-light till the coming of daybreak. 1937 DEVINE 22 Flirrup—A stage lamp of large size. 1972 MURRAY 203 In summertime, if there was much nightwork in the stage, the women had to see that the 'stagelamps' and lanterns were trimmed as well. These 'stagelamps' were simply tin kettles holding perhaps a pint of kerosene. The flames from the wicks were not covered and the light given off was a reddish-yellow glow. There was a handle attached to the rim so that the lamp could be suspended above the working area by means of a wire.

stage loft: area of fishing stage or premises where gear is repaired and stored; LOFT (P 209–73).

stage longer: long, thin wooden pole used as flooring, etc, of a fishing stage; LONGER.

1896 *J A Folklore* ix, 32 Stage-longers [are] from five to seven inches in diameter, forming the floor or platform of the fishing stage.

stage pole: see **stage longer**.

1866 WILSON 205 Upon these posts are nailed the stage-poles horizontally, which are the only floor of the building.

stage room: tract or parcel of land on the waterfront of a cove or harbour on which a fishing stage is erected; ROOM.

[1740–3] 1954 INNIS 96 [No planter is permitted] to keep any more stage room than he hath fishing men in possession for the managing of it. 1760 CO 194:15 Allowed to a Single Boat: Stage room 16 feet wide & 70 feet Long.

stage work: collectively, all the operations of landing and processing fish for salting and drying.

1972 MURRAY 247 'Stage work' was a communal activity and was lightened by a yarn, a song, a joke. Laughter helped the work along. 1977 *Them Days* ii (3), p. 28 I used to do all the work in the house and then do me stage. . .work long with it.

stage head n [steɪdʒ 'ɪd, steʊdʒ 'ed, steɪdʒ 'hed] *DAE* ~ (1677–1752), *DC* (1799–) for sense 1.

1 End of a fishing stage which extends over the water where fish is landed.

[1663] 1963 YONGE 57 [The boat's crew] bring the fish at the stage head, the foreshipman goes to boil their kettle, the other two [master and midshipman] throw up the fish on the stage-head. [1777] 1792 CARTWRIGHT ii, 261 The *Hautboy*, riding at the stage head, parted her road and drove on shore near the salthouse. 1819 ANSPACH 430 The place where the operation of curing the cod-fish is performed, is a *stage* or covered platform erected on the shore, with one end projecting over the water, which is called the *stage-head*. [1833] 1976 O'NEILL ii, 584 As Snow was coming in from the stage-head, Mandeville claimed he stepped aside, and Spring fired the fatal shot. Spring claimed that he was unable to bring himself to do the deed and when he dropped the gun Mandeville picked it up and shot Snow in the breast, from a distance of three or four yards, as the man was advancing from the stage-head. 1863 HIND i, 303 At one end of [the stage] is a wharf, called the stage head, extending far enough into the sea for boats loaded with fish to come alongside of it at low water. 1907 DUNCAN 143 'Twas dark when we moored the punt to the stage-head. 1927 DOYLE (ed) 65 "Three Devils for Fish": O we left the stage-head and we steered her so straight. 1936 SMITH 42 We had our eight crews on board, and everything done but taking in the stage-heads and hauling up the boats. 1957 *Nfld Qtly* Sep, p. 4 He told Mark, his older brother about it when they were taking up the salt over the stagehead in waterbuckets. T 36/8–64 You were supposed to build your flakes, when you had the collar on; build your flakes, build your stage heads, tar your roof, go in the woods an' cut rines for to cover up your fish. T 175/6–65 An' puttin' out their wharves, what we call stage heads. They'd have the wharf way in on the beach, all o' fifty feet sometimes, with a stage head out. That'd all have to come down in the fall. 1976 WINSOR 96 When they reached their 'stage-head' (wharf), one of the women who had gathered there, looking down at the caplin, said 'Aunt Matilda, you got your caplin.' 'Yes, my child,' she replied. 'Where did you get them?' 'Pouch Island,' she answered. 'Who hauled them for you?' Shaking her head slowly, and with her heart full of thankfulness, she replied: 'I don't know, but it must have been the angel Gabriel, and his brother.' 1979 *Evening Telegram* 16 July, p. 4 If the producers lose their independence [from the large fish companies] it'll be in the market place and not on the stagehead.

2 Attrib **stage-head clerk**: sea-lawyer; know-it-all.

1937 DEVINE 49 ~ A dude or prate-box who knows how to do everything except work.

stage-head rail: one of a number of wooden poles fastened one above the other at the end of a fishing stage to form a type of ladder (P 148–76).

stage-head step: see **stage-head rail** (Q 67–33).

stain n Small amount of a liquid; drop; freq after negative.

1924 ENGLAND 321 Stain o' rum—drink or small quantity of rum. [1929] 1933 GREENLEAF (ed) 241 "The Crowd of Bold Sharemen": For we were bound fishing in the Strait of Belle Isle, / Our skipper wouldn't give us one stain of our ile. T 393/4–67 Well, a tierce is around 44 gallons or 45, and when the molasses is out of that tierce, there's hardly a stain in it. P 148–69 Not a stain of oil [in the car]. 1976 GUY 67 I do believe I'll have another little stain out of that bottle if you don't mind.

stake n *EDD* ~ sb¹ (9) ~ maul Gl.

Comb **stake and longer fence**: fence constructed of poles or 'longers' fastened horizontally to heavy posts; LONGER FENCE.

1974 MANNION 85 'Stake and longer' fences dominated the Avalon at the end of the last century. A post or stake was driven into the ground every 8 feet or so and 2 or 3 horizontally placed posts or 'longers,' each around 16 feet in length, were tied to the posts with withes or *gads*. Alternatively the longers were tied to the upright posts by homemade tree-nails or 'trunnels,' or secured with strips of bark.

stake driver: heavy wooden maul used to drive posts into the ground.

Q 71–10 We used the stake driver to drive the posts.

stake fence: type of fence constructed of thin poles fastened upright to horizontal pieces nailed to heavy posts (1971 NOSEWORTHY 249).

stake maul, ~ mall: see **stake driver**.

1977 RUSSELL 30 Uncle Jonas was handlin' his stake mall like 'twas a tack-hammer.

stake v To drive stakes through a beaver-house to trap the animal.

[1786] 1792 CARTWRIGHT iii, 169 They kill beavers by watching for, and shooting them; or, by staking

their houses. . . If the pond, where the beaver house is, be not capable of being drawn dry, they cut a hole through the roof of the house into the lodging, to discover the angles; they then run stakes through at the edge of the water, where the house is always soft, parallel to each other, across each angle, and so near together that no beaver can pass between. The stakes being all fitted in their places they draw them up to permit the beavers to return into the house, (the hole on the top being covered up so close as not to admit any light) and then hunt with their dogs, backwards and forwards, round the edges of the pond to discover where they have hid themselves under the hollow banks; taking especial care, not to go near the house, until they can find them no longer any where else. They then approach it very cautiously, replace the stakes with the utmost expedition, throw the covering off the hole, and kill them with spears made for the purpose.

stalk* n also **stock***.

1 The core of an apple (1966 PADDOCK 117; P 11–79).

2 Phr *stocks on you!*: let me have some of your apple (P 148–79).

stalk n [stælk] DINNEEN stailc 'a sulk'; JOYCE 335 sthallk. Stubbornness in a horse; sulkiness.

1968 DILLON 156 My horse took a stalk and he kicked out of his harness.

stalkish See STALKY.

stalky a also **stalkish, sterriky*** ['stælkɪ] DINNEEN stailceach 'stubborn.' Of a horse or person, stubborn, obstinate; STIRTY.

1968 DILLON 156 I wouldn't buy that foal because the mare was stalky. . . Years ago, Larry had an old sterriky horse. P 191–73 Stalkish—morose, obstinate, sulky.

stall n *EDD* ~ sb¹ 5. A covering for thumb or finger to protect a cut or prevent chafing; FINGER-STALL, NIPPER².

1937 DEVINE 49 ~ A rag covering for a sore finger or thumb. T 43/7–64 Nippers [are] made of wool, they're knitted like a stall. M 68–24 He always laughed at the fishermen who wore thumb-stalls on their fingers. P 209–73 ~ wool-knitted thumb support while splitting fish.

stall fed a *EDD* stall sb¹ 8 (1). Of a person, fed to satiety.

P 108–70 'He hasn't much appetite for his meals, he's stall-fed.' Isn't hungry because he's already been picking at food.

stalligan* See STARRIGAN.

stamp n A printed slip pasted on government form administered by an employer, recording amount of unemployment benefits due to employee, esp a fisherman; FISHING STAMP.

1955 *Handbook on Unemployment Insurance* 5 Your
employer buys unemployment insurance stamps
through the post office, so as to record in your insurance book the combined contributions made by him as
employer and by you as employee. . . If you find that
your employer has not put stamps in your book as
required, or that stamps have been placed in error in
your book, advise the local office. 1966 FARIS 143 The
method of assessing a man's eligibility for Unemployment benefits is based on having a sufficient number of
'stamps,' which are issued him by the buyer each time
he sells or ships codfish, lobsters, salmon or seal. 1975
GUY 129 I'm only a fisherman myself, although I didn't
get enough stamps last year. P 182–79 When cod oil
was [being bought] for around forty dollars a barrel,
you'd get a week's stamps for it when you'd settle up in
the fall of the year.

stanchion n Cp *OED* ~ sb 1 'an upright bar,
stay, prop or support' for all senses.

1 Wooden upright to hold a pile of pulp-wood
in place.

T 43/8–64 Your stanchion, we used to call it, would
keep your wood from fallin' out over. In the spring,
when they'd do the drive, all they had to do was chop
off that stanchion an' there'd be cords an' cords o'
wood go out on the river on its own. 1965 PETERS
Gloss ~ Most commonly called 'upstands,' or, less frequently, 'uprights.' Vertical sticks to support a pile of
wood, usually pulpwood.

2 The rib or frame on the inside of a dory
(1971 NOSEWORTHY 249).

3 Right-angled brace forming the body of a
sled and an upright at the side.

Q 67–45 On a home-made slide which the men carried their loads of wood on, there were braces coming
up from the side or runner and running so far across
the slide so as to brace it and make it stronger. These
braces were in one piece (made of wood) and had a
right-angular shape. When these were fashioned out of
an old tree in this shape they were called knees but
when they became part of the slide they were called
stanchions.

stand v Cp *OED* ~ v 41 'to endure, last' for
sense 1.

1 To remain unimpaired, in good condition; to
continue in good supply.

1873 CARROLL 39 Herrings taken in nets are far
superior, as they are not deprived of their silvery coat,
and by no means injured inside: and not only that, but
Herrings taken in nets will stand good longer without
salt than those taken in seines. T 54/9–64 An' by an' by
he said, 'How's the rum standin'?' I said, 'There's
about a good drink left in the bottle.' 'Well,' he said,
'boy, we'll finish it.' T 141/68–65² But the planters'
schooners always had barked sails down here. The canvas stood longer, see.

2 Phr *stand against the salt*: to go towards
meeting the expense of an undertaking
(P 54–59).

stand on its legs: of a seal net, to remain taut in
a vertical position.

[1802] 1895 PROWSE 419 The seals bolt into the nets
while ranging at the bottom in quest of food, which
makes it necessary to keep the nets to the ground,
where they are made to stand on their legs, as the
phrase is, by means of cork fastened at equal distances
along the head ropes.

3 Cpd **stand-back**: argument, confrontation.

T 141/66–65² 'An' who in the name of fortune wrote
it, then, if you didn't write it?' And they havin' the real
stand-back, see.

stander n Cp *OED* ~ 6 'an upright support' obs
(1552–1711); *EDD* sb 2 'pillar, support.' Upright
stem on the bench of a spinning-wheel to which
the wheel is attached.

T 50/2–64 An' a hub in the middle, see. That'd go in
over the spindle on the stander that's stickin' up from
the bench o' the wheel.

standing ppl, vbl n

Comb **standing edge**: seaward side of ice-cover
extending out from the shore; OUTSIDE EDGE,
STRAIGHT ~ .

1910 GRENFELL 67 Our little mail steamer, paying us
her last visit for the winter, was lying far out in the ice.
Her crew was slinging out, onto the standing edge, for
want of a better landing stage, such poor freight as our
people's slender stock of money could buy for the winter. 1916 GRENFELL 168 The wind had pinned the runnin' ice ag'in the standin' edge.

standing flake: platform built on poles and
spread with boughs for drying cod-fish on the
foreshore; FLAKE.

[1766] 1971 BANKS 134 They are Carried to the Last
operation of Drying them which the English Do upon
Standing flakes. . .in some Places as high as twenty feet
from the ground. 1819 ANSPACH 435 The fish is spread
out on boughs in the open air to dry, head to tail, the
open side being exposed to the sun. This is done either
upon a beach, or upon the ground which is called
laying-room; but more generally upon standing
flakes. . .of two sorts, namely, hand and broad flakes.

standing ice: solid stretch of ice extending outward from the shore; fast-ice; SHORE¹: ~ ICE. Cp
RUNNING ICE.

[1886] LLOYD 48–9 [The northern seal-hunters] walk
out over the 'standing ice' which lies along the coast to
a distance of three, four, or more miles, to what is
known as the 'running ice,' i.e. that which lies in the
current of the Strait, and which is always in motion.
This runnning ice does not, like the standing ice, consist of an extensive unbroken field, but is split up into
small floes, or 'pans.' 1924 ENGLAND 115 'An' I 'ave
yeard tell o' ships makin' fast to islands of ice, an' gettin' towed troo de standin' ice.' 1940 DOYLE (ed) 6
"The Loss of the *Ellen Munn*": Next morning then our
hearts were light. / We ran her up for the standin' ice.
1967 FIRESTONE 100 In going out after them [seals in
the Strait] one must first cross the *standing ice* which is
locked to the land and extends one half to two thirds of
a mile into the Strait. 1978 *Evening Telegram* 10 Mar,
p. 1 The four Newfoundland. . .sealing vessels have

been unable to penetrate the standing ice, a term used to describe the non-moving 'ice frozen on shore.'

standing room: compartment between the thwarts of an undecked fishing boat; ROOM.

1857 MOUNTAIN 6 [The fishing punt] is about six-feet keel, and six feet wide, with 'standing rooms' to row in, and the midships and stern, where the fish is stowed. [c1880] 1927 DOYLE (ed) 29 "The Ryans and the Pittmans": I can handle a jigger, and cuts a big figure / Whenever I gets in a boat's standing room. 1895 *Christmas Review* 9 In a small decked skiff, of about eighty quintals carrying capacity, with two caulked wells or standing rooms, one forward for the cable, and one aft, where stood the two brothers; the decks covered with ice, the sea constantly adding to it, no light, no shelter, and miles from the mainland—they seemed to be doomed to utter destruction. T 393/4–67 An' th' other feller, instead o' goin' back aft to steer, he goes up forrard in the standin' room, an' he steers the boat from there. 1971 CASEY 67 While in the boat, the boys cut the tails off the fish they caught for ease of identification or they placed their catch in a separate part of the boat, for example, in the 'afterroom' or 'standin' room.' 1975 BUTLER 54 They were open boats with the center part of the boat covered with boards called gang boards laid on the thwarts. There was a place in the aft and forward part of the boat called standing rooms for the fishermen to stand in when fishing.

standing well: see **standing room**.

1973 *Decks Awash* May, p. 28 'Standing Wells' are used by the crew while fishing. There are generally three.

staneen n   Cp DINNEEN stanna 'vat, barrel.' A makeshift keg for fresh water.

1937 DEVINE 49 ~ A water keg, made from a piece of a log. A section, with a stout limb near the end, was scooped out by chisel, and the inside surface hardened and dried over a fire and then scraped clean. The limb was then made into a spout by burning a hole through its length with a red hot wire or stocking needle. A cross section of the same log, bounded with a split withe, made the cover. The staneen was carried full of fresh water every day in boat at the fishery in the early days when cooper's kegs were scarce and dear.

staple n   Comb **staple room**: area of merchant's premises where dried and salted cod are graded and stored for export; STORE.

[1929] 1933 GREENLEAF (ed) 304 "The Merchants of Fogo": Let you go down to the staple room, and there you will see fun. / When he stands to the culling board, his neighbours do him shun; / When he stands to the culling board, he'll say it is no use.

stark intens Cp *OED* ~ naked sb 2 'unadulterated spirit.' Comb **stark-naked tea**: tea without milk or sweetening (1896 *J A Folklore* ix, 36).

starky a   *OED* ~ a dial (1697–1787; 1863). Stiff and hard; not pliable.

T 141/67–65² I uses cutch for the rounds and leader of a cod trap, but now for the bottom I uses tar because it

makes the linnet right starky an' hard. When it dries 'tis almost like a wire netting.

starrigan n   also **stalligan***, **starigan**, **statigan***, **sterigan** ['stærɪgən, 'stærɨgən, 'stælɪgən, 'stælɨgən, 'stalɨkɨn] DINNEEN stairricín 'a stump or stick, an obstacle, a junk or piece'; R BREATNACH *Déise Irish* (1961), p. 376: stearagán 'a stumble, a delay, an obstacle'; F DAY *Rockbound* (1928), p. 220 stargon N S; *ADD* (Nfld).

1 A small young evergreen, esp a fir, often cut for firewood and for other uses; a trunk of a fir tree, a stick.

1895 *J A Folklore* viii, 39 ~ a young fir tree, which is neither good for firewood nor large enough to be used for timber, hence applied with contempt to anything constructed of unsuitable materials. 1895 *Dial Notes* i, 381 Starigan—a small green fir or spruce tree, cut for firewood; common in the phase 'a load of starigans.' [c1900] 1978 *RLS* 8, p. 26 Starigan—a green stick, especially a var of small [dimensions]. Also called a green lick. 1903 *Nfld Qtly* Dec, p. 5 He could get nothin' there but a few green var starrigans, or dun boughs. 1907 ibid Dec, p. 2 A 'seine gallows'. . .was a sort of 'horse' or trestle made of rough rails or *starrigans*, and was used for drying nets on. 1920 GRENFELL & SPALDING 94 Light snow has fallen during the night, and every 'starigan,' every patch of 'tuckamore' is 'decked in sparkling raiment white.' 1956 ROULEAU 38 Sterigans—*Picea glauca, P. Mariana.* P 94–57 ~ young fir, very wet, with resin. T 191–65 He'd be pokin' the wood in the stove, what the old fellers 'd call stalligans, those little bough stuff that they cut in on the hills. T 141/65–65² Take a piece o' board then, and get a stalligan or something and paddle [the tub] across tickle. 1966 PADDOCK 89 Some stated that a fir is called a *starrigan* only after being cut down for firewood. C 66–12 A stalligan is a long thin tree often cut to be used as a fish-pole or flake-pole. C 71–8 Stalligans are pieces of firewood which have just been cut, still green and sap running out of them. P 13–74 Statigans are young slender trees such as those cut and trimmed out to make 'longers.' 1977 *Decks Awash* vi (6), p. 64 "Uncle Josh": De bull would get de tacklin / An off 'e'd go for starrigans / Wid frosty snow acracklin.

2 An old gnarled, twisted evergreen tree; a dead evergreen tree or stump; a dead tree left standing after a forest fire; CRUNNICK.

[c1894] PANL P4/14, p. 198 Dry wood is *staragons* or *crunnocks*. 1907 MILLAIS 339 ~s, small decayed sticks of trees; boughs of burnt fir-trees; a word of contempt. A mean building of the Reformed Church of England in one out-harbour was always known as the *Starrigan* Church. 1925 *Dial Notes* v, 343 ~s, stunted trees. P 46–63 'Thin as a starrigin.' A starrigin is a sort of post left standing in the ground after a forest fire and is a thin, stark sight. 1964 *Nfld Herald* 26 Jan ~s. actually dry tree stumps which formed an important source of fuel in the depression days. 1969 *Nfld Essays* 33 ~ : small, stunted dwarf-trees, usually blasted on their seaward sides, to which the dialect terms 'cronnick' and 'starrigan' are given.

3 Attrib **starrigan grease**: resin of a conifer;
TURPENTINE (P 127–80).

start v In comb **start-the-cask-out-of-the-cargo**:
a kind of game.

1944 LAWTON & DEVINE 23 There was a great variety of indoor games to fill in the long nights such as Forfeits, Hide-the-button, Hunt-the-slipper, Ride-the-gray-Mare, Start-the-cask-out-of-the-Cargo, and My-man-John.

start n *EDD* ~ sb[2] 'point; a projection' Do So
W. A projection, point, spike or spur; STUD.

1861 DE BOILIEU 155 We generally wear what on the coast are called 'creepers,' which are made in the shape of a cross with thick 'starts,' and which are much the same as cricketers wear in England. 1924 ENGLAND 115 '[Icebergs] has mud an' dirt on de bottom, mostly, an' lang starts [points] under water, too, so it ain't safe to get nigh ner handy to 'em.' 1925 *Dial Notes* v, 343 ~ the straight point of a gaff. T 84–64 I had a gaff that was made out of a fish prong; he was a nice slender gaff, and the start on it was exactly the same as a fish prong. P 113–79 ~s. The spikes projecting from a sea urchin.

starve v

Comb **starve guts**: very thin person (1971
NOSEWORTHY 249).

starve month: March.

P 11–79 March was usually called 'starve month' because it was in March that the year's crop (vegetables and potatoes) began to run out as well as meat, and the fishing season had not yet begun.

statigan* See STARRIGAN.

station n Cp *OED* ~ sb 13 'place where men are stationed and apparatus set up for some kind of work' (1823–); *DC* Nfld (1892–); *Shetland Truck System*, p. 5 for sense 1.

1 A cove or harbour with space on the foreshore for the erection of facilities for the conduct of the fishery in adjacent coastal waters; FISHING STATION; cp ROOM.

[1786] 1975 *Evening Telegram* 22 Dec, p. 6 Five shallops arriving in 1786 from the station of Noble, Kingsworth and Company on the coast of Labrador. 1864 *Times* [London] 2 Jan, p. 1 [Ballard Bank, near Cape Race] will, no doubt, prove good fishing-ground and be of much advantage to the different stations along the coast, where, mostly, punt-fishing prevails close to the shore. 1870 HOWLEY *MS Reminiscences* 8 On an island in the mouth of Gaultois is a station for cutting up and trying out whales. 1895 GRENFELL 68 In one case, after the best berths had thus been taken, the nets to complete the traps did not turn up till after the prescribed four days. . . Again, some men were landed with 'leaders' on one station late at night. 1907 *Tribune Christmas No* 8 The firm have branches in Trinity, King's Cove, Elliston, Greens[pond], and at [Batteaux], Webber's, Orleans, Hawk's Harbor, and other stations on the Labrador. [1946] 1976 *Evening Telegram* 12 Jan, p.

6 She sailed from Queen's Lakes on July 4 and soon after reaching her station [in Northern Labrador] the crews began fishing. 1954 INNIS 184 The number of stations reported in the fishery increased from 20 in 1764 to 28 in 1768. T 178–65 And he had his canoe now up to the station, and now he come out down to the norrard of it. 1980 *Evening Telegram* 20 Sep, p. 1 [He] said the fishery [on the Labrador], both salmon and cod, was exceptionally good and many of the stations had a record year for catching cod.

2 A coastal settlement and adjacent inhabited coves and harbours forming an ecclesiastical parish or mission.

[1825] 1866 WILSON 319 The following is the list of stations as appears in the minutes for 1825: St John's, Carbonear, Harbor Grace, Black Head and Western Bay, Island Cove and Perlican. . .Indian Mission. . .on the Labrador Coast. 1849 [FEILD] 30 The winters are long. . .on the Moravian stations. 1900 *Tribune Christmas No* 3 Like Archdeacon Forristal, and other priests of his day, it was Father Kyran Walsh's lot to labor on almost every station in the island, from St Mary's Bay to the Far North. 1926 HARVEY [3] It was my pleasure to work on various stations where the Rev Thomas Fox had labored.

stationary a Comb **stationary fisherman**: STATIONER.

1971 CASEY 178 . . .the Bay Roberts people, who along with people from Bonavista and Trinity Bays, were stationary fishermen at North-East Crouse and Pillier during the summer. 1977 *Nfld Qtly* Winter, p. 18 Some of the stationary fishermen from Conception Bay fishing in the vicinity asked him to transport them and their catch to their destinations as he sailed homeward.

stationer n Cp *OED* ~[2] 'one who has been some time on a particular station' naut, rare (1867); *DC* Nfld (1905–). See also STATION. Migratory fisherman from Conception Bay and the north-east coast who conducts summer fishery from a cove or harbour in northern Newfoundland and Labrador; also attrib.

1905 GRENFELL 113 A single crew remains on the schooner, and goes on a fishing trip further north. At the end of the voyage with all the fish, split and salted, stowed away in the hold, this solitary crew returns to the station. The men that have remained are called 'stationers'; the others are green-fish catchers. 1909 BROWNE 62 The fishery on the Labrador coast is prosecuted chiefly by men from the northern and eastern bays of Newfoundland, and they are divided into two classes: 'Floaters'. . .and 'Stationers'. . . The latter are located in some harbor, creek, or 'bight' where they own a 'Room.' 1924 ENGLAND 261 Thousands of outport men migrate almost as regularly as the seals themselves. . . If they pick some berth and settle down, they're called 'stationers,' 'squatters,' or 'roomers.' 1939 LODGE 52 'Stationers' on the Labrador are fishermen who work in groups of two or three in small boats which are left permanently on the coast, the fishermen themselves finding their way from and to Newfoundland on the coastal steamers. Their fishery is prosecuted in much the same fashion as the Newfoundland

shore fishery. 1942 *Little Bay Islands* 14 Many stationers went to the French Shore each summer. 1953 *Nfld
Fish Develop Report* 20 While almost 90 per cent of the
floater crews and about 70 per cent of the stationer
crews fish for cod only 60 per cent of the livyer crews
fish for both salmon and cod. T 80–64 She went down
[to Labrador] as a stationer, see, with the Carbonear
people. T 141/63–65² An' then there's Cape
Harrison—big place, and used to be filled years ago
with stationers. 1967 FIRESTONE 29 The larger settlements on the Labrador side of the Strait, then, had
quite an unstable population in contrast with those on
the Newfoundland side as long as the stationer system
lasted. In the latter the summer could find the arrival
and departure of most of the population. 1970
PARSONS 28 While in Chateau Bay we met the first
'stationers' from Newfoundland. They were all residents of Carbonear, and were spending the summer
fishing on the coast. One man had been making the
annual voyage for over forty years and had never
missed a summer. 1979 *Salt Water, Fresh Water* 319 I
had a crew of five men and I had twenty-five stationers,
that is, fishermen that go on the Labrador. . .and I was
bringing them home on the vessel, and we got caught
in a gale of wind off St Anthony.

stave n Attrib **stave-slide**: a child's sled made
with barrel staves for runners (1971
NOSEWORTHY 249).
1974 *Evening Telegram* 13 Feb, p. 3 You could randy
on anything. Bits of old floor canvas and pieces of cardboard boxes. Stave slides which your father made out
of old barrels.

stawkin* See STOOKAWN.

stay up v phr Cp *OED* stay v² 1 'to support, sustain, hold up,' 1 c with *up* rare for sense 1.
   1 At the seal hunt, to hoist and fix in place a
marker indicating ownership of a catch of seals;
FLAG v.
1924 ENGLAND 293 How many flags did ye stay up,
Tom? Siventeen, eh? I branched off to west'ards, but I
seen ye workin' like a flyin' scaldy, I did.
   2 To sit by body during the night hours; to be
present at a wake.
1972 MURRAY 295–6 Neighbours came to 'stay-up'
voluntarily. . . It was generally the more mature people
in the settlement who 'stayed-up'. . . All who stayed up
were given a cup of tea and something light to eat during the night.

steady a Cp *EDD* ~ v 9 'to keep quiet' D. Phr
be/hold steady: be or keep quiet.
C 70–12 'Be steady' [he always said] when he meant
for me to be quiet. C 71–124 'Hold steady' [she sometimes utters] unconsciously to quiet a class of students.

steady n, a also **stiddy, studdy**. Cp *OED* ~ sb 1
'something which is steady' (Nfld: 1792), *DC*
Nfld (1792–) for sense 1.
   1 A stretch of still water in a brook or river;
pool; STILL.

[1783] 1792 CARTWRIGHT iii, 16 We there landed
and. . .walked up by the side of [a strong, rattling
brook]. We soon found some fresh cut sticks in the
water, three or four small ponds, or steadies. . .and
two old houses. 1792 ibid *Gloss* i, xv Steady in a river.
A part where the bed widens, inclining to a pond, and
there is no perceptible stream. 1843 JUKES 47 A succession of 'steadies,' with occasional rapids, may be met
with for twelve miles. 1868 HOWLEY *MS Reminiscences*
29 There are two long smooth reaches on the river
above, called 'Steadies.' The first of these is about 3
miles from our camp, but between the latter and the
steady the river is very rugged and broken by falls,
chutes and rapids. 1877 *Royal Geog Soc* xlvii, 281 A
succession of rapids and steadies took us up to Rosetta
Island, a pretty fork in the river. 1879 HARVEY 20 At
times we come to what the men called a 'stiddy' or
'study'—a long stretch of deep still water which seemed
almost like a little lake. These 'stiddies' afford the men
a welcome breathing time, but they are 'like angels
visits—short and far between.' 1902 *Christmas Bells* 14
A small stream. . .forming a pretty little cascade, ending in a long narrow pool or steady, bordered on the
one side by an overhanging bank of alder bushes, and
on the other, by a sandy beach, over the point of which
the water was slowly oozing into and forming the first
pool of the creek. 1923 GRENFELL 225 Hauling two
canvas boats, they were able to make use of not a few
still unfrozen 'steadies' in the big river along whose
banks they often kept for miles at a time, and up some
of which they could still tow their packs in the boats,
although the ponds, as our folks still call lakes, were
frozen hard. 1972 MURRAY 113–14 And for the children of Elliston during the period 1900–1950, the road-
side, the 'drungs' (narrow lanes between gardens),
under the flakes, the brooks and 'steadies' (where a
brook widens out and deepens), the cliffs, and the
beach, were the playgrounds.
   2 A small fresh-water pond; cp GULLY¹.
1892 *Christmas Review* 25 The moss-carpeted,
flower-bespangled glen; the lazy, stately, sweeping river; the calm, clear, mirror-like mountain 'studdy'; the
bustling, scurrying, rippling, trout-haunted
brooklet. . . 1937 DEVINE 49 ~ A small lake or pond.
P 229–67 A steady is a very small pond that joins a
larger pond. 1973 BARBOUR 55 If there were any ice
formed on the 'steady' of Gotts Cove Pond, father
would suggest that we take our skates, and walk the
mile and a half to the 'steady.'
   3 Comb **steady water**: see sense 1 above; freq
in names of rivers and streams.
1843 JUKES 47 Above this [rapid] is 'steady water,'
for six miles, navigable for a punt. 1848 *Journ of
Assembly* 263 Steady Water River. 1888 HOWLEY *MS
Reminiscences* 11 Here we found some pretty tough
rapids. . .till we reached a point where a short portage
has to be made [until] we reached the steady water
above. 1944 LAWTON & DEVINE 33 A forest fire broke
out on Plate Cove Road—west of the settlement—and
fanned by a smart breeze, soon swept down towards
'Steady Water' valley about half a mile west of the harbor.

steam n

1 Attrib **steam box,** ~ **pot**: a container with boiling water producing steam to enable one to bend wood into a desired curve or shape.

T 172/5–65 Now that spring we lanched a new schooner, a new schooner in dock building that summer. And when I was goin' to school, I'd have to spend Saturdays in dock tendin' a steam-pot, and drawin' trunnels. P 245–68 We'd put the big oak planks into a steam-box, soften 'em up that way and then give 'em the proper bend to nail on the vessel. 1975 *Can Antiques Collector* x (2), 44 One item of expense at first puzzled me: 'steaming rail.' This was the process by which the hardwood handrails of the stairway were worked into curves by immersion in a steam-box. 1979 *'Twas a way of life* 23 There's a special rig called a steam box. It's got a big boiler to hold water. This is covered with a wooden lid that has a pipe going up into a box seven feet long.

2 On the South Coast of Newfoundland, smuggled or illicitly obtained raw alcohol.

M 69–12 The drinks usually consisted of alcohol, or steam as it is still called, and strong rum. 1971 *Time (Canada)* Sep 20, p. 10 Tonight Sean was going after 'steam'—a pure alcohol that sells for $25 per 2½-gal. can. The can produces 15 bottles, which in turn can be cut three-to-one.

steam v To immerse (a plank, rail or timber) in steam in order to bend it into a desired curve or shape.

1878 WHITE *MS Journal* 16 Oct [To] Davies [for] steaming rail. . .9s. 1979 *'Twas a way of life* 23 The bow pieces [of the snowshoe] have to be steamed so that they get pliable enough to turn.

steamer n A horse-drawn cart.

1936 DEVINE 111 In summer time. . .the men and women came to town from Torbay, Pouch Cove, Outer Cove etc., with loads of dried codfish on carts or 'steamers' as they were called.

stearin n also **stearine, stearing, stearn, steerin(e), steering, stern** ['steˑrɪn, 'steˑərɪn] *OED* stern sb¹ 'the tern' (c800–1896). Northern common tern (*Sterna hirundo*); arctic tern (*S. paradisaea*); PAYTRICK; freq in place-names.

1870 *Can Naturalist* v, 409 [Wilson's tern and arctic tern] Both are called 'steerings' by the settler—a name which their cry suggests. Some few small islands round the coasts of Newfoundland have been named 'Steering' Islands from the number of terns which breed on them. 1878 *Nfld Pilot* 50 Steering rocks. Ibid 122 Stern rocks. Ibid 296 Steering island. 1896 *J A Folklore* ix, 36 Steerins—marine birds. 1907 TOWNSEND 318 'Steerine.' Common summer resident in southern Labrador. 1951 PETERS & BURLEIGH 244 Fishermen, and others, do not distinguish between Arctic and Common Tern, but call all of them 'Stearin.' 1959 MCATEE 38 ~ common Tern. T 410–67 I've seen stearins, I seen a one come in here last year and went down on the bottom. 1975 COOK 87 You [stop] to point out the bank swallows, the terns. Steerings, we used to call them. 1981 GUY 118 Soon the steerins will come along diving and

fluttering after the liver which is drifting into range. Ready your rocks. Heave at steerins.

steel n A metal bar, spike or hand-drill used in early mining operations to make a hole in a rock face.

T 187/9–65 I've seen 'em, sir, start some o' them holes an' dull up so much as six or seven steels, an' you wouldn't have a mark not no bigger than you make wi' your finger.

steel v *EDD* ~ v 9 Bk. To sharpen a knife on a special steel rod (1925 *Dial Notes* v, 343).

1924 ENGLAND 171 One day a good-humoured fellow showed me his steel and explained: 'Dat's for steelin' a knife, sir.'

steerin(g) See STEARIN.

steering vbl n Comb **steering stick**: a long pole jutting out from the front of a sled-load of wood and held by the man hauling the load so as to control the movement of the vehicle over the snow; GUIDER.

T 50/2–64 Get a couple o' turns of [the 'hauling rope'] around arm, an' a steerin' stick stickin' out through the wood, see—a long one. That's what you'd guide her by—come over the hills. T 409–67 'How d'you ever do it, hold on the steerin' stick one hand?' 'One hand, one hand; put me drugs on inside here on the level, and let her come! Hold on the steerin' stick.' C 70–15 The wood would be piled until the snow came and the ponds were frozen and then it was hauled on slides called catamarans or simply 'cats.' The men fastened a rope called a 'hauling rope' to the 'forward' beam of the catamaran and guided the load of wood with one stick of wood jutting out from the other sticks and called a 'steering stick.'

steeve v Cp *EDD* stave v¹ 10 'to move quickly and noisily,' 11 'to go about aimlessly' Sc Co. To walk silently (1925 *Dial Notes* v, 343).

1937 DEVINE 49 ~ to walk softly. P 127–76 Steevin' around—sneaking about.

stem n Cp *OED* ~ sb² naut 'at the bow of a vessel.'

1 The front or bow of a sled.

T 264–66 Oh, you got to bawl at her, an' go to the stem o' the slide, see. An' get 'em all ready an' go to the stem o' the slide, and start singin' out to 'em, 'Come on, come on.' Everything come to their legs then.

2 Comb **stem plate**: iron sheathing fastened to the bow of a sealing vessel for protection in ice.

1852 *Morning Post* 12 Feb, p. 4 Towlines—fit for Sealers. . . Stemplates. . . Sealing Guns.

stent See STINT.

step v Cp *EDD* ~ v 1 (2) ~ away 'die.' Phr *step aside*: to die (1863 MORETON 37).

step clumpers, ~ *copy*, ~ *pans*: in children's

pastime, to jump from one pan of ice to another; COPY.

1971 NOSEWORTHY 250 Stepping clumpers. M 68–21 Stepping copy is always popular. Q 67–44 Stepping pans: jump from one ice pan to another.

step it out: to perform the variety of steps characteristic of a step-dance; STEP-DANCE.

1900 *Daily News* 19 Apr, p. 4 It was amusing to see men of 60 and 70 years of age stepping it out in the old-fashioned reel. T 222–66 During an intermission in the dance somebody who was talented in that art would perform a step dance, or it would be said that he would 'step it out.' C 71–44 The one who was considered the best dancer was the one who could step it out.

step n *OED* ~ sb ~-dance (~-dancing 1886). Cpd **step-dance** v: to perform a dance usu solo, involving the quick and intricate movement of the feet.

1964 *Evening Telegram* 23 July, p. 18 The woman thought I might be ast to step-dance.

stephenses day See ST STEPHEN.

stepmother n *EDD* step- pref (8) Ir; *Trans Phil Soc* (1899), p. 104 'cutting north wind in winter' Ulster; JOYCE 139. Comb **stepmother's breath**: a cold draught (P 91–63).

steppy cock n See STEP, COPY PAN: COCKY*. Children's game of jumping from one ice-pan to another (1973 WIDDOWSON 262).

M 68–24 Don't let me catch you playing steppy-cock on the ice.

stern n Comb **stern bore**: movement or drift astern.

T 192–65 She didn't have enough [of a way] ahead to come around, you see, an' she made a stern bore—she went astern, the wind, a little flaw, upset her.

sterriky* See STALKY.

stick n Cp *OED* ~ sb[1] 3 'stem or thick branch of a tree (1386–1707); *EDD* sb[1] 13 esp s w cties; *DC* ~[1] 1 b (1829–).

1 A timber-tree; the trunk of a tree used for var building purposes, fuel, etc; freq in phr *stick of wood*, and with defining words *plank, wharf*, etc.

1774 *Trans Roy Soc* lxiv, 374–5 Up some of the deep bays, and not far from the water, it is said, however, there are a few sticks of no inconsiderable size. [1794] 1968 THOMAS 118 It was fenced in with Sticks and Poles of the Spruce Tree, which was sufficient entablature to point out the Sacred spot. 1853 *Ecclesiologist* xiv, June, p. 160 I cannot help thinking that we shall be obliged to make more use of stone for churches and houses than is now done, as proper sticks for building are getting very scarce in the neighbourhood of St John's, and round Conception Bay. 1868 HOWLEY *MS Reminiscences* 31 This is where the people of the bay procure their material for house and boat building.

Many of the sticks are large enough for schooners spars. They come up in winter cut all they want, drag it out to the river deposit it on the ice, and await the spring thaws to float it out to the salt water. . . We saw many fine sticks hung up on the rocks at intervals as we came up [the river]. 1897 *J A Folklore* x, 210 Squat [means] to flatten a stick of timber by hewing the one side of it. [1900 OLIVER AND BURKE] 46 [There was] a haul of wood every winter for the R C Bishop. . . The skipper and his crew with a band and the boys would cheerily haul them. . .1000 sticks and more in some loads. [1918–19] GORDON 11–12 By 2.30 we had a nice pile of 300 sticks on the bank below the Parsonage, and some of us had stiff shoulders. [For the sake of the uninitiated, a stick or 'turn' of wood is a fair-sized tree with its limbs lopped off.] 1929 *FPU (Twillingate) Minutes* 30 Jan Then there was quite a discussion about the Crow Head breakwater sticks, about who tendered for the sticks and who got them to cut. T 12–64 A whitin' is the rampike or very dry stick used for making splits. T 141/68–65[2] An' the same way you lay it on a wharf stick, see, if you was goin' to plank out a wharf. You lay birch rine over your stick [to] preserve it from the water seepin' into it. T 437–65 Jack said, 'By God,' Jack said, 'there's a big stick there, a fine stick, a elm stick.' M 68–10 [märchen] Sure enough, when Jack got back the punt was timbered out. 'Now,' said the old witch, 'cut me a plank stick.' Jack went off to cut a plank stick. When he got back she was all planked. 1975 BUTLER 43 Looked up and I put the whole load in the mainmast, a BC stick too, beautiful; black hole with the powder burnin' it around. 1977 BURSEY 25 I had three hundred sticks of wood for my share then my brother and I must saw it into six thousand four hundred junks and split it to dry.

2 A length of whalebone.

[1771] 1792 CARTWRIGHT i, 141 They brought me one stick of whalebone, and the skins of six rangers, two hares, and one deer. [1783] ibid iii, 7 I purchased thirty-eight sticks of good whalebone and a few sealskins.

3 Phr *get a stick on*: of a vessel, to steam faster (1925 *Dial Notes* v, 343).

1924 ENGLAND 69 The *Sagona* now lay astern of us as we ground slowly northward 'wid a little better stick [speed] on us,' under steam and sail; the *Eagle* was racing us, off our starboard bow.

stick and string navigation: navigation by log and line.

1962 SPARKES 9 It must be remembered that it [1834] was still the day of 'stick and string' navigation.

4 Comb **stick fence**: fence made of thin trunks, with branches lopped off, standing in vertical position (1963 WILLIAMS i, 87); PICKET FENCE.

[1786] 1792 CARTWRIGHT iii, 181 We landed the goods, had the top of the stick-fence of the garden cut even.

sticking ppl

Comb **sticking bud**: cockle-bur (*Xanthium* spp); dried pod for seeds that sticks to clothing.

P 148–67 ~s: burrs or balls, about half-inch in diameter, that stick to your pants as you walk through country. P 245–76 ~s. Burrs with spike-like formations, produced by a weed and used as missiles by children.

sticking tommy: funnel-shaped metal candleholder used in an outhouse for illumination at night (P 182–76).

stiel n [ʃtiːl]. Cp DINNEEN stiallaim 'I cut in strips, rend.' A rip, tear, slash.
1968 DILLON 156 Who put that stiel in your coat?

stiffle v ['stʊfl, 'stʊft] *EDD* ~ v¹ Ha So D. To suffocate.
T 100/1–64 An' the track an' everything burned over us. [It's a] wonder we hadn't stiffled with smoke, but we didn't. T 141/64–65² And if it hadn't been for that crowd, all the rest would have had a tight nip whether they got out of the house [covered with snow]—stiffled and buried alive.

still n *OED* ~ sb² 3 'a still pool' obs (1681). A stretch of smooth water in a brook or river; pool; STEADY n.
1938 MACDERMOTT 57 'Still' is the wide and smooth-flowing part of a river. P 245–61 ~ A pond in a river.

sting v Cp *OED* ~ v¹ 2 d 'to rob or cheat' obs (1812, 1823); PARTRIDGE. To purloin; collect or gather surreptitiously; BUCK v.
1931 BYRNES 161 "The Old Picket Fence": Oh, don't you remember the days we went 'stingin' / The turnips, the apples, from Graham McNeil's. 1964 *Evening Telegram* 26 May, p. 2 Seems an awful price we had to pay f'r stingin' one apple. 1970 *Daily News* 13 July, p. 4 Those who still recall their youth are aware that a young turnip, 'stung' from a farmer's field and eaten raw, was a delight. P 245–77 Late in the summer we'd creep under the fence around the farmer's field in the evening stingin' rumpers.

stinker n Sulphur-tipped match.
T 147–65 We used to have the old matches them days, what they call stinkers—comb matches wi' the brimstone on 'em—stink like the devil! 1975 RUSSELL 65 Uncle Dudley sold a few things a bit cheaper. . . things like sewin' cotton, kerosene oil, soap and a few combs of stinkers. 'Combs of stinkers?' said I. 'Matches,' said Grampa, 'before they sold 'em in boxes.'

stint n also **stent** *OED* ~ sb¹ 9 (Nfld: 1792); *DC* Lab (1788). A beaver-dam; stretch of deep water into which or from which a stream flows.
[1770] 1792 CARTWRIGHT i, 60 [I] soon met with a pool, which had a new stint across the foot of it. [1778] ibid ii, 325–6 The stint was the longest and completest I ever saw; it extended across a small vale, through which ran a narrow rill of water, by which means a pond, of about an acre, was formed; that is often the practice of those industrious animals. 1792 ibid *Gloss* i, xv ~ The dam made by beavers across a stream to raise the water to a height convenient for their purpose. P 13–73 The ice is treacherous in the stent.

stirty* a ['stəːɹti']. Cp *EDD* starty 'apt to start'

Sc. Of a horse, easily startled. Cp STALKY: STERRIKY*.
T 100/1–64 A horse was kind o' wild, you know, stirty and quick to jump at anything.

stock n *OED* ~ sb¹ 1 b obs (c1000–1806); *EDD* 1 for sense 1.
1 A heavy log or beam.
[1774] 1792 CARTWRIGHT ii, 23 Four hands went up the river to cut skiff-timber and some stocks. 1792 ibid *Gloss* i, xv Stock of timber. A piece of timber, intended to be sawed. T 25–64 This house is 109 years old. But they put stock in houses then that they don't get to put in them today. . . We were making some repairs here. . .and there's sticks like spars down here. I think it's good for another hundred years if it's like that.
2 See STALK [= core of an apple].
3 Comb **stock chest**: container in which logs are placed for pulping.
1964 BLONDAHL (ed) 38 "The Business of Makin' the Paper": Well, the 'furnish' is made, so we'd best move along / To the 'stock-chests' ahead, and I'll say in my song. . .

stog v *DC* ~ Nfld ([1836], 1937) for sense 1; cp *EDD* v¹ 2 'to surfeit with food' W for sense 3; *OED* v² 1, *EDD* v¹ 1 Bk Ha So D Co for sense 4.
1 To fill the chinks in a log-house with moss; to insulate a house; CHINSE.
1836 [WIX]² 53 The structure of the winter tilt, the chimney of which is of upright studs, stuffed or 'stogged' between with moss. [1886] LLOYD 76 They are merely log huts, but are always rendered warm and comfortable. The chinks between the logs are calked, or 'stogged,' as they say, with moss previously gathered and dried. 1895 HOWLEY *MS Reminiscences* 7 Before the weather became too cold and stormy we constructed a very substantial log tilt composed of old sleepers stood upright and well stogged with moss. 1897 *J A Folklore* x, 211 ~ To stuff moss in the seams between the studs in houses, barns, or cellars. In this sense it seems peculiar to Newfoundland. 1906 GRENFELL 176–7 By the Christmas following Rube had up a tiny studded house, well stogged with dry moss and shingles, clapboarded, and only waiting a mistress. 1937 DEVINE 49 ~ To chinse moss between the logs in a log house to keep out draughts. T 43/7–64 Now this is where the shim comes in—stoggin' these camps. You stog 'em with moss. We'd have possibly a man or two away pickin' moss, and a man or two stoggin' as 'cordin' as the carpenters would put on a log, you stog the seams. 1973 *Evening Telegram* 25 Oct, p. 3 It might be worth anyone's while even in this day and age to have [a] bedchamber that is not stuffed and stogged up with insulation and double window glass.
2 To block or clog an aperture; STOP v.
T 158–65 Next night or two we went over, you know, we stogged his funnel. Got up in the morning—black with smoke. T 360/1–67 And I remember once somebody climbed up on top of the place in the night, an' stogged the pipe, an' in the morning this person got up; he'd smoked her out! P 198–67 The sink is all stogged up. C 71–125 To stog means to plug up an opening. For

example a person suffering from a head cold is likely to say that his nose is stogged or stogged up.

3 To fill completely.

c 66–3 I wouldn't go so far as to stog a cellar with him. P 130–67 Stog the fire; it may stay in till we get back. P 108–70 I'm stogged to the gills [with food].

4 To be stuck in boggy ground or snow.

1897 *J A Folklore* x, 211 Stogged. . .describes one stuck in the snow, mire, or a bog. 1937 DEVINE 49 ~ To be caught in boggy ground—said of cattle, especially. T 12–64 Old Kitty Dobbin from Leatherhill came, / With her hammer and saw, chisel and plane; / The wind from the westward began to blow / And old Kitty Dobbin got stogged in the snow. M 69–6 If hard frosts did not come before the snow to freeze the bogs, lungers had to be laid across them to keep the animals from getting stogged. c 70–21 There is a boggy, dangerous spot about a mile or so from our settlement where. . .a cow became trapped in the mire, i.e. was stogged.

stogger n Cp STOG.

1 A large, heavy steamed pudding; DUFF[1]. Also attrib.

1903 *Daily News* 1 Apr He gave a big 'stogger' to each 'pettifogger,' / While we hardly can jog, or keep the wolf from the door. 1909 BROWNE 268 'Stoggers' and 'Alexanders' are huge balls of dough. . .served with. . .'Codcy.' 1959 *Evening Telegram* 9 Oct, p. 4 When the cutthroats came back with the plant (Alexander) they went looking for they would be regaled with a pork and 'stogger' dinner with boiled 'Alexanders' as a tidbit. The women got this ready while the men were ashore.

2 A hearty filling of food.

[1900 OLIVER & BURKE] 12 "Breaking Open the Stores": But I'm bound to get my stogger / Of molasses, pork and tea.

stoggy a *EDD* stog v[1]: stoggy 'muddy, sticky' W D. Of a moving part, stiff, sluggish (P 148–64).

stomach n *OED* ~ sb 10 b ~ sick (1613–1664) for sense 2.

1 The lungs, esp if congested (1925 *Dial Notes* v, 344).

1924 ENGLAND 210 'I ain't bodily sick, sir, but I got a sore stummick.' Investigation revealed that the men's stummicks were always their lungs. So after I had painted one stummick and brought the man out of bronchitis or something, others began to come. P 245–61 I've got a rattling on the stomach. T 222–66 When people had bad colds on their chest, they used to say they had 'wonderful impression on their stomach.'

2 Comb **stomach-sick**: nauseated; sick to one's stomach.

P 148–64 I'm not stomach-sick—just a head-ache. 1975 *Evening Telegram* 23 Aug, p. 14 I was often on a trip and the poor mortals would make your heart bleed, right stummick sick, and their poor eyes as heavy as lead. 1976 GUY 26 Delights now streaming down upon the heads of outharbour juveniles, awash and brimming over, blinding as the sun before dinner

and as dizzying as a game of 'Turning Around and Around Until We Gets Stomach Sick.'

stomachy a *EDD* stomach 7 (2) ~ So Co. Irritable, belligerent.

T 194/5–65 An' the fish never come there before the twenty-second of August, before the fish struck. Aha, my son, that was a hard let. That made me stomachy. P 184–67 It's a wonder they didn't have a row, [he] is so stomachy. P 13–78 He was too stomachy to come in out of the rain.

stone n *OED* ~ 18 c: ~-berry (1837).

Comb **stone berry**: dwarf cornel; BUNCHY-BERRY; CRACKER ~ ; PIGEON ~ (*Cornus canadensis*).

[1794] 1968 THOMAS 140 Here also are Stone Berrys, Gooseberrys, Raspberrys, Currants and Cranberrys, with a great number of other Berrys which produce excellent food. [c1830] 1890 GOSSE 107 Here the scarlet stoneberry (*Cornus Canadensis*) was abundant. 1840 GOSSE 299 The Scarlet Stoneberry. . .is a low and pretty plant, having a white flower, resembling that of a strawberry, and four large oval green leaves on the ground. At present they were crowned with the little cluster of bright red berries, which were ripe, and we ate many. 1860 TAYLOR 286 There was another fruit, called the 'stoneberry,' a bunch of small, scarlet berries, which are much less insipid to the eye than to the palate.

stone chat: northern slate-coloured junco (*Junco hyemalis hyemalis*).

1891 PACKARD 418–19 Black Snowbird. Not observed in the Ungava district. Common in the eastern and southern portions of Labrador. Breeds at Davis Inlet and Rigolet. Known as the 'Stone Chat' on the east coast.

stone curlew: greater yellow-legs; AUNTSARY[1]; TWILLICK (*Totanus melanoleucus*) ([1766] 1971 BANKS 371).

stone hurt: a variety of blueberry; see HURT.

[1794] 1968 THOMAS 117 Here are also Wild Pear Trees and plenty of Currants, with Partridge Berrys, Stone Hurts and Maidenhair Berrys in vast quantitys.

stookawn n also **stawkin***, **stucaun**, **stukawn** [stuːˈkɒn, stuːˈkɔːn, ˈstɒkən] *EDD* ~ simpleton Ir; DINNEEN stuacán 'foolish fellow.' Dull stupid person; a careless, lazy person.

1966 *Evening Telegram* 8 Feb, p. 15 'Get out you lazy stucauns.' P 245–66 Lazy stawkins—a slow, rather idle and tardy person. 1966 *Evening Telegram* 26 Apr, p. 32 'Don't mind him. If he didn't talk he'd bust. A bigger stukawn never lived.' 1968 DILLON 156 Don't mind him; he's a real stookawn. He can't understand you. Q 73–9 ~ a name often given to a lazy or careless person: 'You're a regular stookawn.'

stool n *EDD* ~ sb[1] 4 for sense 1; cp *OED* 11 Sc and north for sense 2.

1 A bench.

T 43/7–64 The stool would be a long thing, you know, that a dozen could sit on, and they used them at the side of the table for the children to sit on. It was just a piece o' wood with two legs under it.

2 Carpenter's horse or trestle (1971 NOSEWORTHY 250).

stop v *OED* ~ v 36, *EDD* 5 for sense 1; *OED* 14 d for sense 2.

1 To stay, abide; remain at home.

[1794] 1968 THOMAS 158 If you propose to stop all the year round you must pay 10/- under the same regulation as the first. 1860–1 *Journ of Assembly* Appendix, p. 533 No man would like to stop on the ice of a frosty, dirty night, when his ship may not be more than a hundred yards from him. [1891] [c1977] WINSOR (ed) 48 Very soon I wouldn't have any strength to leave [the rock]. I'd perish if I stopped an' I could only perish if I fell through the ice. 1900 *Tribune Christmas No* 7 Some of the women. . .declared they had seen Old Martin walking about his late residence, that lights were seen there at nights, that none of the dogs would go by the place, and that Bill Evoy's dog had stopped all one night within a few yards of Martin's house, and howled most mournfully, refusing to go home with his master. P 245–55 I said if she stop, all right; if she come on home, *that's* all right. C 71–116 I stopped home all last summer. 1975 BUTLER 47 I got a axe and he got a big bait chopper and we used to go down underwater and chop and hack as long as we could stop down, and come up and go down again.

2 To stanch (bleeding).

T 50/2–64 This feller here now can stop blood. You're bleedin' bad with a cut: he can stop it. T 175/6–65 He was seventh son. He was supposed to be able to put away warts and stop blood an' all this.

3 Cpd **stop-short**: snack given to a hungry person before a meal (P 25–67).

stop n Cp *OED* ~ sb² 29 (a) ~ net 'a net thrown across a river or tidal channel to intercept fish' (1634–1881), *EDD* 1 (6) Co.

Comb **stop net**: part of a net used to catch migrating seals; STOPPER NET. See also SEAL NET.

[1886] LLOYD 53 The [seal] nets are variously named. That which runs parallel with the land is known as the 'barrier,' that on the right side the 'stop-net'; that on the left as the 'heave-up net.' This last-mentioned net is the special feature of the frame. The barrier and the stop-net are always kept floating in a perpendicular position by means of the above-mentioned floats.

stop tide: high tide.

[1774] 1792 CARTWRIGHT ii, 23 Weighing at daylight we worked up the bay, and anchored to stop tide opposite to Atkinson Island.

stopper n *DC* ~ Lab (1771) for sense 1; *OED* sb 10: ~ net (Nfld: 1792); *DC* ~ net Lab (1861).

1 A net used to catch seals migrating in coastal waters; STOP n: STOP NET. See also SEAL NET.

[1770] 1792 CARTWRIGHT i, 64 The whole consist[s] of twelve shoal nets, of forty fathoms by two; and three stoppers, of a hundred and thirty fathoms by six. 1972

SANGER 241 ~ A trap used to catch seals on their coastal migration.

2 A bottle cap (P 266–64).

1976 *Evening Telegram* 19 June, p. 3 He used to be a dab hand at algebra [in school] and at nipping the stoppers off beer bottles with his teeth.

3 Comb **stopper net**: see sense 1 above.

1792 CARTWRIGHT *Gloss* i, xv ~ A large net for catching seals, which is made to fit the place in which it is fixed; the foot lies upon the ground, and the head floats on the surface of the water, by means of buoys. The farther end is made fast to an island (where there is one) or to the head-rope of a long net which is moored parallel to the shore, and the near end is raised or lowered at pleasure, by means of capstans. Several of these nets being placed at certain distances from each other, form so many pounds. 1861 DE BOILIEU 87 There is another method of catching the seal by what is called the stopper-net. Under this process one net is permanently fixed across a small channel—say between two islands—and another, called the entrance-stopper, is placed about one hundred yards to the north, one end being fastened to the opposite island and the other end attached to a long piece of rope in such a way as to allow the net to sink entirely out of sight.

store n Cp *OED* ~ sb 11 'a place where stores are kept' (1667–), *DC* 2 (1959) for sense 1; for comb in sense 2 see *OED* store sb 13 b ~ loft (1852 quot).

1 A building forming part of a merchant's, planter's or fisherman's waterfront premises or 'room' where supplies and gear are stored for use or trade; esp place where dried and salted codfish are held for shipment; FISH STORE.

[1696 (1895) PROWSE 232 [tr] From there we went to Old Perlican; there were there nineteen houses, several stores, more than thirty head of horned cattle, and a number of sheep and pigs.] [1791] 1976 HEAD 231 I was, on my arrival this year, forcibly struck with the change which had taken place at St John's, where the trade has increased to such a degree that the north side of the harbour is now taken up with Merchants' Stores Wharfs etc for the purpose of trade. [1794] 1968 THOMAS 77 Here are some good Stores and much Trade is carry'd on in Fish. 1819 ANSPACH 437 [The fish] is left some time in that state, then again spread out, and the same day, towards the evening, lodged in stores or put on board the vessels. 1832 MCGREGOR i, 188 But the appearance of the town altogether, indicates at once what it was intended for—a kind of lodging-place for a convenient time; a collection of stores for depositing fish, with wharfs along the whole shore for the convenience of shipping. 1849 [FEILD] 32 A store, the largest in the place, was put at our disposal for that purpose by Mr Seallur, the Agent. 1857 MOUNTAIN 4 Wealthy merchants. . .built large fishing establishments or 'stores,' as they are styled. 1868 HOWLEY *MS Reminiscences* 25 He has a large shop and store and has a good deal of fish collected. 1937 DEVINE 41 Room [is] a fishing premises: stage, flakes and store. 1977 BURSEY 30 When they came back expecting to land their fish at March's store they found that the premises had been burned out of recognition with every thing on the waterfront from Bowring's to the East end of St John's harbour. 1977 *Them Days* ii (3), p. 23 [At Mary's Harbour] there was stages, flakes, houses, men and youngsters. . . There was a big store, under the bank, over forty feet long.

2 Comb **store keeper**: merchant's agent.

[1764] 1976 HEAD 173 The Families that remain [in Trinity] During Winter being Store-Keepers. [1765] 1954 INNIS 155–6 [Other imports were] engrossed by a few opulent merchants, store keepers, and considerable boat keepers who retail them to the rest of the inhabitants and to those they employ under them in the fishery, at exorbitant prices.

store loft: area or room on fishing premises for the storage and repair of gear; LOFT, STAGE ~ .

1936 SMITH 28 After spending our Christmas holidays and enjoying ourselves until Old Twelfth Day, we went to work on the store loft repairing the cod traps, etc, for another season. 1966 FARIS 239 The upper story of a two-story fisherman's storage structure is the 'store loft.' The 'loft' is where cod traps are stored and where net mending takes place during the winter. The 'loft' usually contains a small stove for warmth. P 150–68 The store loft was a place of joy and curiosity. It means the top floor (second floor) of a store which might contain stored wood, fish, salt beef and other supplies on the first floor, and the top floor would be a carpenter's workshop used for making things, with shavings on the floor and all kinds of carpenter tools around and pieces of wood which one could cut and chip as a boy likes to do. 1972 MURRAY 52–3 In the late spring 'trapmen' would be busy in their 'store lofts' mending the linnet. . . [It was the] area where cod traps, trawls, and other fishing equipment were stored in winter, and where dry fish was stored during the curing process in late summer and early fall.

storm n Cp *OED* ~ sb 6 d ~ light 'lurid light seen in a stormy sky' for comb in sense 2.

1 Phr *storm of wind*: a severe gale; BREEZE, LINER.

[1929] 1933 GREENLEAF (ed) 279 It came on to snow and there was five storms of wind all blowing right on the land. 1972 BROWN 38 It comes a wonderful starm o' wind an' frost, sir, the like ye never see, an' in spite o' the ice shelters an' the fires, a lot o' men died. Some got weak in the mind, and walked off an' never come back. 1977 BURSEY 16 He and his eldest son George. . .were adjusting a trap-buoy in a storm of wind. 1979 NEMEC 254 'Storms of wind,' 'breezes,' or 'August Gales' as they are variously called, can create. . .rough surface seas.

2 Comb **storm-hood**: garment worn over head and shoulders in winter; CASSOCK 3, NORTH-WESTER.

1916 YOUNG 76 My travelling outfit, in addition to my ordinary clothes, consisted of a pair of seal-skin pants, a sweater, an adikey, a pair of seal-skin mittens, a pair of moccasins, and a storm-hood.

storm light: St Elmo's fire.

T 453–67 We had a couple o' fellers aboard, young hands; they didn't even know what a storm light were—never seen one. I don't know what it is, but I've a-seen 'em; seen 'em that time too, right by the port

light in the riggin'; goes right to the mast head if it's goin' to be a high storm. Storm light is the right name.

storm v Phr *storm the kettle*: to boil water hastily in a kettle for a 'mug up' or cup of tea (1937 DEVINE 49).

stout n Cp *EDD* ~ sb s w cties; *OED* sb¹ b Nfld (1903, 1905) for sense 1.

1 Gad-fly; deer fly (*Chrysops excitans*).

1884 HOWLEY *MS Reminiscences* 16 Flies as usual very bad all day and the big ferocious stouts or deer flies are now putting in an appearance. Those brutes are nearly as large as a bee and give such a savage bite as to cause one to jump with pain. 1895 *J A Folklore* viii, 33 A large vicious fly is called *stout*. 1907 WALLACE 74–5 The 'bulldogs' or 'stouts,' as they are sometimes called, which are as big as bumblebees, are very vicious, and follow the poor caribou in swarms. [1924] 1933 GREENLEAF (ed) 251 "Change Islands Song": The weather still got hotter, plenty nippers, flies and stout; / A decision they arrived at and a cod-trap was put out. P 245–64 When the stouts arrive, good salmon fishing.

2 Rove beetle (*Staphylinus villosus*); FISH-FLY.

1937 DEVINE 49 ~ A large black fly that gives trouble to the fish curers in summer by depositing its eggs on the fish.

stouter See STROUTER.

stoutish a Tempestuous (1925 *Dial Notes* v, 343).

stove n *DC* ~ cake (1941). Comb **stove cake**: bread-dough baked on a hot stove; FUNNEL CAKE.

1975 *Them Days* i (1), p. 5 And, you'd get up maybe two hours before daylight and you'd boil your kettle and have breakfast—usually a light breakfast of just tea and stovecake (the trapper's baking powder bread) and pack your grub bag for the day, with just a light amount of food.

strad n Cp *EDD* ~ 'a piece of leather tied around the leg, to serve as a gaiter' w country. A piece of calf-skin leather.

1925 *Dial Notes* v, 343 ~ The upper leather of a shoe. 1927 *Christmas Messenger* 48 [When a fisherman] says 'I bought a fine "Strad" at Bowring's,' he means a well-selected cut of calfskin leather to make a pair of long boots. M 71–120 [Sheep] were marked. Some people put tickets around their sheep's neck. These tickets were made from 'strad' or calf-skin leather. The family name would be on those tickets.

strad v also ~ **up**. Cp *EDD* strat sb¹ 'short rope made of hay or straw' Wxf, and STRAD n; see *DC* n [servicing of a cable]. To wind rope or other protective material tightly around a cable to prevent chafing; to serve (P 113–73); SERVICE.

stradding n See STRAD n, v. Protective wrapping around a cable to prevent chafing; service.

M 68–26 Straddin' is brin, or canvas, wrapped around a ship's hawser for about seven fathoms from the clinch.

straight a also **strait**.

1 Of a stretch of coast, without coves, harbours or anchorage.

1832 MCGREGOR i, 201 And then, along the strait of Belle Isle to Cape Norman, the most north-westerly point of Newfoundland, a straight shore prevails, along which an old Indian path is observable. 1912 *Nfld Qtly* Summer, p. 15 The West Coast of Newfoundland is, on the whole, a very straight one and Bonne Bay is the last opening or harbour of safety going north for roughly a hundred miles. 1933 GREENLEAF 278 Between Port Saunders and Bonne Bay the steamer stops and anchors off three ports of call, but on that whole seventy five mile stretch there is no safe harbor, and the shore is straight. 1975 BUTLER 94–5 The shore was straight with no cove to get in out of the ice and the cliff was too perpendicular to climb.

2 Comb **straight edge**: seaward side of an ice-floe; OUTSIDE EDGE.

1909 BROWNE 298 At the end of [December] a straight edge, known as the 'fast ice' is formed from island or rocks several miles from shore, outside which ice flows continuously from December to June. 1924 ENGLAND 79 The seals may be gone to the straight edge. I'd give a wonderful lot to find where them to!

straight shore: (a) stretch of coast from Cape Freels to Farewell Head; (b) from Port Saunders to Bonne Bay; see sense 1 above.

1792 PULLING MS Aug I saw about a dozen Indians together on the Strait shore four years ago but they ran into the woods. 1875 *Maritime Mo* v, 513 A Red Indian who had been killed on the 'Straight Shore'. . . 1887 BOND 123 We must have drifted in the night along the very worst part of the Straight Shore, and I needn't tell you, friends, what that place is like in a gale of wind and heavy sea. 1896 HOWLEY *MS Reminiscences* 31 We were at [Daniel's] Harbour and Belburns early, before I was up. As they are very insignificant places on the straight shore, there was no inducement to see them. 1912 *Nfld Qtly* Summer, p. 15 We. . .make our way along the straight shore to Port Saunders. No harbours, no boats. M 69–2 Wesleyville was the last good harbour near the 'straight' shore.

straight shaft: dory with keel attached and engine held at stern by a connecting rod (M 68–3).

straighten v Cp *EDD* ~ v 2 'to settle accounts'; *NID* v b. In the mostly non-cash, or 'truck,' system of the Newfoundland fishery, to total the credits and debits of a fisherman's account as kept by the supplying merchant; usu with *up*, *out*; SQUARE UP.

1924 ENGLAND 257 Once the men 'fall back,' they are sometimes never again able to 'put up money' or to 'straighten up,' i.e., pay their bills. 1936 SMITH 27 Before going to St John's all hands got straightened up

and we made $175.00, which was considered fairly good. 1937 DEVINE 49 A fisherman was *'straightened out'*—to use his own words—when he got his account from the supplying merchant and was paid the balance due him. C 70–12 It was the custom for the fishermen to straighten up in the fall of the year. This meant that they sold their summer catch to the merchant who had supplied them during the summer, the merchant gave the fisherman whatever he saw fit for the fish and often charged him the highest prices. At this time of year men would put in for supplies for the winter. One always fixed up his account in October. M 71–95 When the fishing season was over the men had to straighten up, which was to pay the fish merchant or other supplier the amount owed him for the goods he had been buying since May 'on account' and to get the balance of his fish money.

strain n When at sea, the line of latitude of the nearest land.

1888 TALBOT 18 We sailed away in a south-easterly direction until we reached the strain or parallel of Cape Bollard, near Cape Race. [1891] [c1977] WINSOR (ed) 46 We left port about the fifth of March, and near the strain of the Grey Islands, we got about half a load of seals. [1902] 1916 MURPHY 13 The gales drove them south fifty miles or more, to the outer edge of the Banks in the strain of Cape Broyle. 1932 BARBOUR 11 We were now beyond Trinity Bay and in the 'strain' (a Newfoundland term for the same line of latitude) of Cape Bonavista. 1937 DEVINE 50 ~ Vicinity. A maritime word. 'In the *strain* of the Funks.'

straits n pl

1 The narrow passage between the northern tip of Newfoundland and Labrador; clipped form of Strait of Belle Isle.

1839 TUCKER 107 The more common mode of sealing of late years, however, is to fit out vessels, and search for these amphibia in the straits and along the Gulf. 1863 HIND ii, 224 The fish which supply the Straits and the Labrador fisheries consist for the most part of two large shoals, one of which, entering the Gulf off Cape Ray in April or May, passes through the Straits down the Labrador shore. 1886 HOWLEY *MS Reminiscences* 3 All the craft are ready to leave for the Straits and Labrador. 1959 SAMSON 78 ~ A short expression mainly applying to the Strait of Belle Isle. 1971 JUPP 114 The other Grenfell Mission boat *Cluett* ran into trouble, and the *Maraval* had been standing by at Forteau ready to help her to cross the Straits if necessary.

2 Comb **straits fish**: cod-fish taken and cured in the Strait of Belle Isle.

P 34–74 It was [in September] that the new salt fish began to come in, and vessels and boats carrying Shore, Labrador and Straits fish were coming to St John's consigned to the various merchants.

straits fishery: cod-fishery prosecuted in the Strait of Belle Isle; cp NORTHERN FISHERY.

[1888] 1975 WHITELEY 158 W H Whiteley, Esq., will commence to ship his crew for the Straits fishery for the coming summer on Monday next.

strange a *EDD* ~ adj 1 for sense 1; *OED* 13 b
to make strange obs (1456–1727) for sense 2.

1 Reserved, shy.

C 70–13 That baby is very strange (easily upset by
strangers). P 157–73 ~ shy, slow to make friends.

2 Phr *make strange*: to behave in a distant, shy
manner; usu in the negative.

1937 DEVINE 33 ~ To be afraid or timid. 'Don't
make strange,' said to a guest sitting down to eat.

3 Comb **strange shake-hands**: a meeting with
an unfamiliar person.

C 71–126 If your left hand itches this means that you
are going to have a 'strange shake-hands,' in other
words meet some stranger.

stranger n *OED* ~ sb 10 a (Nfld: 1792); *DC*
Nfld (1776). A variety of waterfowl.

[1776] 1792 CARTWRIGHT ii, 178 We brought in a
beaver, a goose, a bottle-nosed diver, five ducks, four
strangers, and three hundred and seventeen eggs. 1792
ibid *Gloss* i, xv ~ A water-fowl of the duck kind.

strap n Cp *OED* strop sb 2 'ring of rope with its
ends spliced together' naut.

1 Band of rope used as a purchase for tackle in
hoisting a load of seal pelts aboard a vessel; a
load of seal pelts so hoisted; also attrib.

1924 ENGLAND 88 The straps passed through a
bunch of sculps, and the 'wire' or rope from the winch
dragged out from its pulley on a spar, by the whip-line,
eager men hook the strap of seals to the wire. Ibid 140
In the lurid gloom, the 'strap o' swiles' hit the rail
mushily, flattened, swung clear. The swinging dangle
of sculps slid down the quivery mass that filled the deck
from rail to hatch coaming. . . Black figures cast waver-
ing, grotesque shadows as they dragged sculps, stooped
to unstrap the pelts, wallowed in fat, and threw out the
strap-lines again. 1925 *Dial Notes* v, 344 ~ 1. An endless rope to haul skins aboard with a winch. 2. A reckoning of ten skins.

2 A catch of trout slung on a flexible branch
through the gills; GAD n.

1972 NEMEC 128 Children reciprocated by giving
[the priest] berries they had picked, a 'strap' of trout
they had caught.

3 Rope handle on a tub (1971 NOSEWORTHY
251).

4 A length of rope attached from one of the
corners of a cod trap to a supporting buoy; BUOY
LINE (P 127–80).

T 43/7–64 You make your rope straps and put [them]
on there, when you get [the cod trap] measured up,
and you gather up the corners [tight] to make a corner.

straw n *DC* straw oil Nfld (1966) for sense 2.

1 Phr *have a straw in one's nose*: to speak with
an acquired New England, esp Boston, accent.

P 108–70 She's back from the States with a straw in
her nose.

2 In designations of a variety of pale or straw-
coloured seal oil; PALE (OIL).

1873 CARROLL 31 When seal oil is drawn off out of

tank all the oil rendered out of the young seals fat is
sure to come first, which is called pale seal, and under
the young seal oil the old seal's fat oil is called straw
colour. 1888 STEARNS 186 In one corner of the platform was a big iron kettle where the men were hastening the process of oil making by boiling, and forming a
different kind of oil—the two kinds being known as the
'brown oil' and the 'straw or pale oil.'

3 Comb **straw broom**: commercially marketed
household broom as opposed to a home-made
'birch besom.'

T 43/7–64 I'm sure there was no straw brooms then,
'twas all birch brooms. Ye'd go in the woods an' pick
the small birch, an' make your broom. Of course when
the straw brooms came in it replaced those.

straw flower: (a) everlasting (*Anaphalis
margaritacea*); (b) thrift (*Armeria maritima*)
(1956 ROULEAU 38).

straw-legs: one with spindly legs (C 67–6).

stray-line n Cp *OED* ~ 4 'submerged or
floating line fastened at one end only' (1888
quot); *EDD* stray a 1 (1) ~ line 'line attached to
anything which is let down into the sea' Do. A
length of line attached to various types of fish-
nets, traps, etc.

C 66–5 [A] pryor is a pole about thirty feet long
which is fastened to the buoy-rope (strayline) in winter
time. Q 67–7 Stray lines [are] ropes that you haul net
up with. P 241–68 There is also a stray line which keeps
the headin' in the [lobster] pot by tying it onto the
inside of the pot. M 69–27 Where gill nets were used,
they were fastened to the land by a rope called a stray-
line; at the other end of the net, an anchor was dropped to prevent the net from drifting around. P 127–77
~ On a trawl, the rope attached to the trawl anchor
and the running-line.

streel n *EDD* ~ sb 'untidy, dirty person' Ir;
JOYCE 336–7; DINNEEN sraoille: straoille. See
STREEL v. A dirty, slovenly person, esp a wom-
an; RAG-MOLL (1925 *Dial Notes* v, 344).

1937 DEVINE 50 ~ A term of contempt for a lazy or
slovenly woman. P 148–68 Spoken by a man: I didn't
want to look like a streel. 1968 DILLON 156 She's an
awful streel around the house. C 71–92 Like all dirty St
John's streels / He dressed his head before his heels.

streel v also **streal** *OED* ~ Anglo-Irish; *EDD* v
2 'to drag along the ground; to trail or hang untidily' Ir; DINNEEN sraoillim: straoillim 'I trail,
dangle.' To drag behind one; to soil by dragging.

1902 *Christmas Bells* 14 Jack, who was just round a
bend of the river below us, had a nice landing place,
and streeled his fish on shore without any trouble.
P 130–67 Stop streelin' your coat on the ground. 1968
DILLON 156 A spell ago, the dresses used to streel on
the ground an' they walkin'. He was streelin' along
behind us all the way home. 1975 BUTLER 47 Her cable
was coiled up on the bow, that broke off, that was
strealin' astern.

streelish a   also **streely**. Of a woman, untidy or
slatternly in appearance.
  P 244–56 Streely—untidy. 1968 DILLON 157 That's a
woman wasn't streelish.

street n   See BEAT 2: *beat the paths/roads/streets*
and BEATER 2. Comb **street-beater** (also
path-beater, ~-**walloper**): a girl who wanders the
streets seeking attention or social activity, esp at
night.
  C 71–89 He would call me a path-beater—always
out. P 108–70 Path-walloper—a girl or woman who is
seen frequently walking along the roads or streets with
various 'followers,' or on the look-out for them.
C 69–19 Street-beater—a girl who is always tearing
around with a lot of fellows.

stretcher n   Cp *OED* ~ 9 'a folding bed.' An
upholstered couch; SETTLE n.
  1971 NOSEWORTHY 251 ~ Old name for couch. 1974
MANNION 153 The settle or 'stretcher,' often with
carved back and arm rests or 'pumbles,' was used only
as daytime seats in the Avalon kitchen.

stribbins* See STRIPPINGS.

strife n   Cp *OED* ~ 1 c transf now rare for
sense 1.
  1 Force or blast of wind.
  P 148–64 [He] built the fence to stop the strife of the
wind. P 148–64 The strife of the wind blows down the
bay.
  2 Comb **strife breeder**: (a) a gossip; (b) a false
tale; BAM (1971 NOSEWORTHY 251).

strike v   Cp *OED* ~ v 68 'to come upon, reach'
U S & Colonial (1798–) for sense 1; *OED* 46 e
'bewitched' dial, *EDD* struck 2 Ir for sense 2;
OED 80 h: strike in (Nfld: 1888) for sense 3;
OED v 57 (1780 quot); *EDD* 18; *DC* struck Nfld
(1944), salt struck Nfld (1957) for sense 4.
  1 Of a sealing vessel, to reach the seal herds on
the ice-floes.
  1882 TALBOT 16 We left port in the forenoon of one
day and struck the ice on the following
morning. . .probably twenty miles from the mouth of
Bonavista Bay. 1905 CHAFE 7 It was known that, as a
consequence of the steamers striking the seals early in
the spring, large numbers of immature seals were
brought in. 1924 ENGLAND 80 The *Thetis* and *Diana*
dogged our every 'jife' and 'cut.' They spied on us. Not
if they could help it should Cap'n Kean steal a march
on them. He, 'admiral of the fleet,' should not be
allowed to strike the fat and leave them out of it. [1929]
1933 GREENLEAF (ed) 247 "Sealing Cruise of the *Lone
Flier*": We motored until three o'clock, and then we
struck the fat, / Herbert Legge picked up a seal,
Claude Hawkins got a cat. 1964 BLONDAHL (ed) 75 "A
Noble Fleet of Sealers": Though last to leave the Harbour she was first to strike the patch, / And by the
twenty-ninth of March she'd loaded every hatch. 1979
Salt Water, Fresh Water 53 Usually the ships would get

down twenty-five or thirty miles north of [Funk Island]
and would strike the seals.
  2 Of a fairy, to bewitch (someone), esp to
cause an ailment; cp BLAST, FAIRY STRUCK.
  T 50/5–64 They meet you anywhere, you know. They
strike lots o' people—cripple you.
  3 Of fish (or seals), to appear in coastal waters
in large schools, esp in phr *strike in*.
  1826 *Edin New Phil J* i, 35 As we advance northward
from the Gulf of Saint Lawrence, the migrations of the
cod assume a more decided character, and it strikes in
in greater abundance. 1839 TUCKER 84 This bait is furnished by a small species of fish called capling, which
strike in shore at that season of the year, and are usually followed by immense shoals of cod fish, which feed
upon them. 1866 WILSON 208–9 The fishery commences about the middle of May. The first bait used is
herring. These are taken in herring-nets; but the cod
has not yet struck in for the shore, and is therefore only
taken in small quantities. About the first of June, the
caplin strikes in, and then is the Newfoundland harvest. 1884 DEMING 100 Some years ago, during an
otherwise bad season, the seals 'struck in' on the ice
near the Newfoundland coast while the steamers were
away. Women and children, leaving the shore,
engaged in the slaughter, and during a few days sixty-
four thousand head were killed within a few miles of St
John's. [1914] 1930 COAKER 84 On the Labrador the
usual time for fishing was passed when the coast
cleared, the result being that many floaters returned
before the fish struck in. 1937 DEVINE 45 Skool
[means] to cry warning on the coast when the herring
strike in. [1964] 1979 *Evening Telegram* 3 July, p. 14
Squid will strike inshore in Newfoundland waters in
large quantities this season. T 194/5–65 An' the fish
never come there before the twenty-second of August,
before the fish struck. . . Aha, my son, that was a hard
let. That made me stomachy. 1977 BURSEY 79 Then
the cod-traps must be repaired and barked to be ready
to be put into the water before the fish would 'strike
in.'
  4 Of fish, to impregnate with salt in the curing
process.
  1839 TUCKER 85–6 The boats return to the vessel
about nine o'clock in the morning to breakfast, put
their fish on board, salt and split them, and after having fished for several days, in which time the salt has
struck sufficiently into the fish first caught, they carry
them on shore and spread and dry them on the rocks or
temporary flakes. 1873 CARROLL 41 As soon as the
Vats are erected, caulked and covered, let them be
filled with strong pickle, so that when the herring is
brought alongside, in place of putting them on deck,
exposed to the weather, let them be deposited at once
in the Pickle, and there left until properly struck, which
can be easily ascertained by the stiffness of the herring.
1957 *Can Geog J* lv (Oct), 129 The fish were left in the
stage until they became 'salt struck,' then the family
removed the fish from salt. 1975 WHITELEY 345 The
fish, if heavy salted, is kept in the stage until struck,
that is, until salt and water are uniformly mixed
throughout the fish. This process generally takes not
less than twenty-one days.

5 Phr *strike up*: of a trap, to snap up so as to kill an animal; to release the catch on a trap.

[1770] 1792 CARTWRIGHT i, 74 They found the deathfalls all struck down and choked with snow; the trap in the beaverhouse struck up; and the pond flooded. [1774] ibid ii, 25 Mr Parker. . .went with me to visit the traps: we found both the small ones struck up, and the others so clogged with dirt, that they could not strike up, although deer had been over three of them. 1933 MERRICK 193 As we go along the shores we come to a trap every five or ten minutes. This he unsets and hangs up on its chain stake, for he is 'striking up' his path, preparatory to going home. 1977 *Inuit Land Use* 151 At the end of the season, the hunter struck up his traps and left them tied together, ready for use the next year.

striker n Part of flail used in hand-threshing; swingle.

1974 MANNION 98 The flail comprised two slender sticks fastened together by a flexible joint or link. . . It was often made out of a soft wood such as spruce. The 'thresher' or 'striker' was usually heavier and shorter and was fashioned out of birch, ironwood, or some other hardwood.

string n *OED* ~ sb 1 a 'in early use sometimes a rope of any thickness' for sense 1; *OED* 2 a for sense 2; cp SKEIN for phr in sense 3.

1 A cable (1925 *Dial Notes* v, 344).

1924 ENGLAND 190 'Rise up dat spring, you—hayve un off dat clumper—so! . . .Fire dat string to 'ell's flames out o' dere!' The *Terra Nova* shudders as an acre or two of ice begins to creak and shift. Perilously the hawser tautens; vibrates like a fiddlestring and seems about to snap, but holds.

2 Animal ligament or tendon.

T 29–64 There was nothing better than ever you put inside o' your mouth any better than that seal was. In between the strings, you know, the meat, it's fat, and we wouldn't eat it.

3 Phr *string of ice*: long, narrow strip of floating ice.

1855 WHITE *MS Journal* 1 Mar Passing through strings of Ice at day light on second morning. [1891] [c1977] WINSOR (ed) 46 We was forced to put into the ice for shelter—that is, sir, into a string of loose runnin' ice, about three or four miles off the shore. 1924 ENGLAND 275–6 'See arr sign? Is there arr good string of ice out to east-nordeast?' was the first question I heard from the bridge very early next morning. The ship was drifting in loose ice under a gray sky. 1934 *Nfld Qtly* July, p. 30 In the mild winter they can find open water everywhere, with strings of ice where they can rest; but with very severe frost the ocean is frozen over and the seals are driven to the Southern edge of the ice. 1956 *Nfld & Lab Pilot, Supplement* No 3, p. 10 Stream/Strip/String [ice] long narrow area of pack-ice/-drift ice, about half a mile or less in width, usually composed of small fragments. 1977 BURSEY 23 The Bay was full of strings of ice and there was fog about. But the wind was fair. But strings of ice, fog and night coming on was not about to stop Skipper Tom Strong. 1981 *Evening Telegram* 24 Mar, p. 1 The ice field, smallest

in many years and consisting of loose strings close to the Labrador coast, was broken and drifting.

string of seals: long line of migrating seals; PATCH.

1922 *Sat Ev Post* 195, 2 Sep, p. 11 Why, no one knows; but the strings of hoods always swim to seaward of the harps, either in the gulf or at sea. These two species always migrate in company, but never mix. 1924 ENGLAND 295 Morning brought a report from the barrel that the spymaster could 'rise de smoke o' de *Nipshun* on de 'orizon,' storming after us to catch our own private string o' swiles. 1972 BROWN 31 A string of seals sixty miles long had passed south-east the day before, just a few miles off the land. They could plot their position accurately within three of four miles.

string v
1 Of ice, to arrange in an elongated pattern under the force of tide and wind.

1873 CARROLL 21 West wind will blow it off the land, N. and N.E. wind will string it along, S. tide will separate it.

2 Phr *string into*: of a group of seamen, to form a line in order to carry out a task.

1932 BARBOUR 60 'Come on and let us get the sail up, it is now getting daylight.' So in a few minutes we all strung into the sail and carried it along to the foremast, and in a short time we had it bent.

strip v In Christmas mumming, to take off facial disguise after one's identity has been guessed; to remove a mummer's disguise; THROW UP.

1966 SZWED 113 When identification is positively made, mummers are expected to 'strip'—to remove their masks—not to do so is considered an affront to the hosts. 1976 HOLLETT 16 We started talking myself and three other young fellows. . . She says we is going to strip you now.

striped-head n White-throated sparrow (*Zonotrichia albicollis*) (1959 MCATEE 66).

strippings n pl also **stribbins***. Cp *OED* stripping vbl sb[1] 2 'something stripped off.' Slivers (of wood); boughs from a tree, dried and used as fire-wood and kindling; cp BLASTY BOUGH.

T 141/69–65[2] But we'd had the bottom tore out of un an' the sides; bottom was tore to strippins, and a good bit o' the sides was tore up. M 71–117 [They used] to haul a load of dry boughs to be cut up into stribbins for a quick fire to bake bread or boil the kettle of a hot summer's day. Q 73–9 In Avondale, stribbins refers to the boughs when [the branches] have been cut off. However, in Harbour Main, stribbins mean all of a bough. 'I'll put some stribbins in the barn for the cow to lie on.' P 154–78 Stribbins: limb of a tree stripped out.

strong a Cp *OED* ~ 26 (b) strong-back naut. Comb **strongback**: ridge-pole of a dwelling.

1974 MANNION 147 In the settlements north of St

John's the settlers sometimes used a ridgepole, or 'strongback,' which ran the length of the house.

stroud* n See JOYCE 335–6 for Irish words in *sr-* becoming *str-* in English. Shroud, winding sheet; cp HABIT.

M 68–10 The 'stroud' is large enough to cover the shoulders and face of the body. This is made of white cloth about a yard square. The part which is used to cover the face is cut full of small diamond-shaped holes. 1971 CASEY 300 The older women would always make a 'stroud' [shroud] or winding sheet which was placed in the coffin and wrapped over the face before closing the lid. This shroud was made of white material which had been cut or scalloped in a certain way. There were a number of crosses cut into the material at the corners.

strouter n also **stouter** *OED* stouter (Nfld: 1792), *DC* stouter Nfld (1779–); cp LONGER, based on *long*; cp *EDD* strout v 2: strouter 'support in the side of a wagon' W Do So; strut v 2: strouter sb 'a strut' W Do So for sense 1.

1 One of several heavy posts placed vertically to support and strengthen the head of a fishing stage or wharf; cp SHORE².

[1777] 1792 CARTWRIGHT ii, 234 Part of the people were at work on the stage, and the rest went up the bay, cut some stouters, posts, shores, etc. 1792 ibid *Gloss* i, xv Stouters, strong shores, which are placed round the head of a stage or wharf, to prevent them from being damaged by ships or boats. 1819 ANSPACH 430 The place where the operation of curing the codfish is performed, is a *stage* or covered platform erected on the shore, with one end projecting over the water, which is called the *stage-head*, and which is fortified with stouters. 1895 *J A Folklore* viii, 31 ~s. The outside piles of a wharf, which are larger and stronger than the inner ones, which are called *shores*. 1937 DEVINE 50 ~s. The perpendicular posts at the front end of a fishing stage, jammed firmly into the sea bottom, and having rails nailed across to make the ladder for getting into and out of boats. 1973 *Evening Telegram* 25 Oct, p. 3 You could hear a tin can bonking against the strouters on the rocks down there in the landwash. 1975 BUTLER 61 For the shores [of a wharf] there'd be strouters. They'd be called strouters and they'd be a little larger, probably seven or eight inches in diameter.

2 Fence post (1925 *Dial Notes* v, 344).

3 Comb **strouter post**: see sense 2 above (1914 *Cadet* 7).

stud n Cp *OED* ~ sb¹ 1 'one of the upright timbers in the wall of a building' for sense 1; sb¹ 5 'a boss or nailhead' for sense 2.

1 A log, round, roughly hewn or 'squatted,' placed upright next to other such logs to form the wall of a building.

1776 COUGHLAN 17 The houses there. . .are all wood; the Walls, so called, are Studs put into the Ground close together, and between each, they stop Moss, as they call it, to keep out the Snow. 1819

ANSPACH 467–8 Others are built of logs left rough and uneven on the inside and outside, the interstices being filled with moss. This filling with moss the vacancies between the studs to keep out the weather, is there called *chinsing*. . . Tilt-backs, or *linneys*, are sheds made of studs, and covered with boards or with boughs. 1853 *Ecclesiologist* xiv, 157 A number of studs (i.e. sticks from four to six inches thick) are set upright on a sill as close together as possible, and the interstices filled up with moss. 1866 WILSON 216 The Newfoundland tilt can lay no claim to any ancient order of architecture, but is in its style perfectly original. The walls are formed of rough spruce sticks, called studs, of about six inches in diameter, the height of the sides six feet, and of the gables about ten or twelve feet. The studs are placed perpendicularly, wedged close together, and the chinks or interstices filled with moss. . . The floor is made with round studs like the walls, which are sometimes hewed a little with an adze. [1929] 1949 ENGLISH 48 An ordinary fisherman's home in the mid eighteenth century. . .was built of 'studs' or logs of fir, square hewn and placed upright side by side. Two or three small windows were set in the sides. T 172–65 Cut off your stud eight feet or whatever 'twas, and then right where he'd sit to in your sill you would cut a groove an' he'd sit down in this mortise. M 69–14 All three types of these houses were built mostly with the use of studs or logs sawn or chopped into approximately two-inch thickness and placed side by side thus forming all of the walls. Clapboard was then nailed on the outside while it was boarded up inside and covered with either sheathing paper or patterned wall-paper. 1972 MURRAY 181 All early homes were built of studs (i.e., 2″ x 4″ timbers, roughed out with an axe.

2 Projecting metal point of a sealer's 'gaff.'

T 156/7–65 The after guards galley was locked, see. I stood off an' I put the stud o' my gaff in between the lock an' the face an' I give the prise.

3 Comb **stud camp**: shelter or bunk-house constructed of vertically placed logs; TILT (C 71–32).

stud-house: house constructed with walls of vertical logs instead of planks.

1853 *Ecclesiologist* xiv, 157 [In addition to 'frame-houses'] there are also 'stud-houses' and 'plank-houses.'

stud¹ v *OED* ~ v 1 'to build with studs' (1505, 1511, 1849). To construct the walls of a building with roughly-hewn logs or planks, set vertically side by side; often with epithets *full, round*.

[1775] 1792 CARTWRIGHT ii, 85 In the course of the day we studded the salt-room, made four killicks, started most of the salt, altered the nets. 1886 HOWLEY *MS Reminiscences* 8 The old house built by him is large and roomy and must have been very comfortable as timber was plentiful it is all studded inside and then clapboarded outside. [1906] GRENFELL 176 He was gradually building a pile of good stout sticks. . .he would spend the spare time chopping and squaring some of 'they sticks.' It was a sure sign enough. For 'them sticks could only be for studding a house wi'.' 1927 RULE 32 This fall I have had a School-chapel built at John's Beach. The men have worked at it well. It is what they call *studded*. 1960 FUDGE 36 It was an old fashioned studded house, a very nice place. P 65–64 A person can stud a camp out of any kind of wood. T 36/8–64 They used to have round-studded houses. T 181–65 The stores is over there what my grandfather builded, an' you'll see 'em all full studded right around, with pine.

stud² v   also **study** *EDD* ~ v² 2 Ha W So D; study v 1. To think or meditate; ponder.

1863 MORETON 36 I can't tell, and I can't think, and I can't stud whatever I've done with it. T 54/9–64 An' I thought I seed th' arms movin' under the sheet. An' I said, that's imagination. So I studied, you know, an' by an' by sure enough—he was movin'. By an' by he turned his head, an' he looked out.

studden a   *EDD* -en 'added. . .to denote the material of which anything is made.' See STUD n. Built with upright timbers set next to each other.

C 69–18 The minister went to visit a man who lived in a studden tilt.

studdle n   also **stuttle**. Cp *OED* ~ sb 'a post,' 3 in mining 'a prop' Co. One of the vertical timbers in the frame of a boat (P 127–75).

1969 *Nfld Qtly* July, p. 20 Stuttle—the upper curved part of the timbers between the fore hook and the after hook.

studdy See STEADY n.

stump n
1 Apple core; STALK (P 155–64).
2 Cpd **stump pile** v: to fell, cut and pile timber at one place (1965 PETERS *Gloss*).

stump v   Phr *stump the baby*: to dress in shorter clothes; SHORTEN.

C 71–18 Young babies were always dressed in long clothes which they wore until the age of six weeks. Then a ceremony called 'stumping the baby' took place. . .the two long petticoats and the extra-long nightgown or dress that was wound around the baby were replaced by two short petticoats and a short dress and knitted woollen socks.

stun a   also **stunned** [stɔn, stʌn, stɔnd, stʌnd, 'stɔnpoɵl, 'stʌnpoul, 'stʌndpoɵl]. Collocations fashioned on *OED* stunpoll 'blockhead' (1794–) D, *EDD* 1 'stupid fellow' Ha Do So D; cp *EDD* stunt 6 'unyielding. . .sulky; impassive; stupid'; PARTRIDGE stunned for sense 2.
1 Foolish, stupid, naïve.
1863 MORETON 33 Stunned—dull of apprehension, stupid. 1924 ENGLAND 146 'Now see here, Cap'n, ye stunned fool, sir,' says de engineer, 'you ain't got de sense of a suckin' pig.' 1925 *Dial Notes* v, 344 Stunned—extremely foolish; silly. 1927 *Christmas Messenger* 47 A person will say to the teacher, 'Master, that's a cruel "stun boy."' [1954] 1972 RUSSELL 39 Ah, I was stun, sir. . . But Lizzie was smarter. 1955 ENGLISH 41 Stunned as an owl. T 69–64 You come home an' if you were anyway smart you'd learn [your

lessons] quick, and if you weren't, if you were kind of stunned, they'd take ya all night. 1971 *Evening Telegram* 21 May, p. 3 'My what a head that man got,' said the skipper to his missus. 'Yes, sir, I will admit it,' I replied modestly, 'but I'm only a stunned-poll alongside of some.' 1976 *Daily News* 22 Jan, p. 3 Anyone who knows anything might be inclined to the conclusion that [he] is just another stunned Newf. 1980 *Evening Telegram* 8 Nov, p. 6 That walk over the hills to the berry grounds was real pretty [but] we were too stunned to appreciate it.
2 Intoxicated (1924 ENGLAND 321).
T 187/8–65 'Let's carry home Uncle Jack. He's gettin' pretty stunned.'
3 In comb **stunned whooper**: Newfoundland pine grosbeak; MOPE (*Pinicola enucleator eschatosus*).
1964 *Evening Telegram* 28 Oct, p. 5 In this part of the country, though, it is called a 'stunned hooper' or perhaps it is supposed to be 'stunned whooper.' The 'stunned' part of the name is, of course, a reference to its lack of caution, to the fact that it can easily be killed with an air rifle, a sling shot, or a thrown stone.

stun v   *EDD* ~ v 2 'render incapable of growth,' 4 adj 'incapable of growth' Ha W So. Gnarled, twisted, stunted.
1892 *Christmas Review* 25 I tripped in a snag of an old stunned var [fir]. P 37 Stun var. P 61–66 Stunned wood—a tree which had gone dry and was partly covered with moss, thus making excellent burning material.

stun breeze n   A sea wind blowing about 20–25 knots (P 187–73).
T 393/5–67 When we got there the wind was nor'west—just stun breeze, you know. We didn't want too much.

stunned See STUN a.

suad See SUD LINE.

suant a, av   also **suent** [suːənt] *OED* ~ a 3 now dial; *EDD* 1 'smooth, even, regular' s w cties.
1 Of a tree or structure, straight, true; TANT.
1863 MORETON 32 ~ Well continued, without irregularities. Spoken of any work or building in which the lines are true and unbroken. 1897 *J A Folklore* x, 211 ~ evenly and uniformly made. [c1900] 1978 *RLS* 8, p. 22 ~ a term used to denote regular proportions, shape &c as instance a suant Stick, i.e. nice straight clean grown tree, a suant Curve, regular well defined curve or bend &c. 1937 DEVINE 50 Suent. Regular, smooth or straight, as applied to an object like timber. . . 'A suent plank or tree.' C 71–44 It was often said that the tree was tant and suant.
2 Of a curve, esp in the hull of a vessel, smooth, graceful, with a correct sheer (P 94–57).
T 43/8–64 Sheerin' her meant now that there was so much rise to give her forrards, to bring her in proportion, and so much rise to give her aft down the counter, an' you'd bring that along suent on the timbers an'

make sure that you had it equally alike on both sides. P 99–69 She's a suent and dilly boat.

3 Smooth, even.

1937 DEVINE 50 Suent. Applied to motion. 'Cod liver oil runs suent.' 1958 *Nfld Dishes* 31 Suent. Smooth. 'A nice suent batter.' P 4–59 [We had] a suent time [sailing] around the cape this morning. C 71–94 A suant grade in the road is one that goes up constant without any large dips.

4 Pliant (1897 *J A Folklore* x, 211).

1925 *Dial Notes* v, 344 Suent. Bending; pliant. 1937 DEVINE 43 Newfoundland usage, suent, pliable.

sud line n also **sed, sid*, sud** [sʌd, sɤd, 'sɑːəd]. Cp Dorset County Record Office, 1799 Gundry inventory (D203/A6) Long Seds. . .Short [Seds]; WILCOCKS 135 'snood, or sid' s w cties; *EDD* zid 'bit of silk attached to a hook' D; *Cent* sed² (Maine).

1 A grade of line used for attaching hooks to a trawl-line, and for various other purposes.

1760 CO 194:15 To 3 dozen Fishing Lines @ 6ᶜᵉ each. . . To 10 [dozen] Suad [Lines] @ 10ᶜᵉ. 1937 DEVINE 43 Sed. . .a fine line used with smaller fish hooks, especially for catching squid. P 158–63 As thin as a sud line. T 203/6–65 You'll take up the linnet [of the cast-net] below the horn, and take hold to your suds, or threads, your lines, and you'll haul it right in over the gunwale. P 126–67 The sid of a lobster pot. M 68–26 A sud line is roughly ⅛ in. in diameter. There were two kinds of sud lines sold and used at Hr Buffett—the four-pound sud and the five-pound sud. The line came in coils called 'hanks,' and one hank was thirty fathoms long. A four-pound sud could hold a weight of about twenty pounds; a five-pound sud could hold about twenty-five to thirty pounds. It was generally used as jigger line or for trawls. 1972 *Evening Telegram* 18 May, p. 3 [The door latch] was made of wood. . . If you were inside. . .you pulled on a piece of sud line coming in through two small holes in the door and tied to the latch outside.

2 In trawl-fishing, one of the short lines from which single hooks are suspended at intervals from the trawl-line; snood; cp GANGEING.

1937 *Seafisheries of Nfld* 32 These hooks are fastened to the heavy [trawl] line by short lines about three feet long, called 'seds,' and are spaced about three or four feet apart. P 148–59 A few new seds hung over the coil. T 50/2–64 The suds are so far apart, but when they comes together, this one comes this way, and this one goes this way—they haven't got to meet. They had to be far enough apart so that they wouldn't meet. T 203–65 Now this here, the lower end, they'd put what they calls a sud, a piece of line about so long. P 121–67 Each line of gear contains fifty suds. 1973 *Evening Telegram* 10 Oct, p. 3 What did they expect them to do? Stretch a sed line across from Bread and Cheese?

3 Comb **sud knot**: type of knot used to secure hook to the length of line suspended from a trawl (P 113–79).

sugar n *OED* sugar-loaf 2 b (1691–).

Attrib, comb **sugar-berry**: nodding trillium,

with sweet-scented flower (*Trillium cernuum*) (1956 ROULEAU 38).

sugar hurt, ~ **whort**: dwarf bilberry (*Vaccinium cespitosum*); HURT (1898 *J A Folklore* xi, 273).

sugar-loaf: in designation of a prominent hill resembling in its shape a cone of refined sugar; TOLT. Also attrib.

[c1625] *Willoughby Papers* 1/60 [He] may Fish ther att [New Perlican], or sugarloafe [cove] near [adjoined] wher is vsually as good Fishing as is any in the land. [1669] 1963 YONGE 117 The wind south and fair weather, we stand in for the Sugar Loaf (a high headland between St John's and Torbay, resembling a sugar loaf). [1786] 1792 CARTWRIGHT iii, 207 The extremity of Cape Ray is a low, flat point; close to which is the most remarkable sugar-loaf hill I ever saw: it rises so very steep to a sharp point, that the sides are streaked with small stones by the rain washing away the earth. 1842 JUKES ii, 299 Three remarkable sugar-loaf hills rise from the low land which forms the projecting point of [Cape Ray]. 1951 *Nfld & Lab Pilot* i, 366 Several detached summits, known as the Sugar Loaves, are situated within 1½ miles north-eastward of the head of Goose arm.

sugar tea: tea sweetened with sugar, rather than molasses, for special occasions.

T 49–64 Well, you might have a pound or two, just for anyone that come in, a stranger or anything come in, give him a cup o' sugar tea. T 187/8–65 I never drinked a cup o' sugar tea, not for forty years, I suppose. An' I never drinked [a] cup o' molasses tea for forty years or over.

sulick* n ['suːlɪk] DINNEEN súghlach 'juice. . .gravy'; *Kilkenny Lexicon* sulach 'fluid from dunghill or cow-byre.' The liquid obtained from cooking various meats, fish; a liquid from decayed organic materials used as fertilizer.

C 71–106 Sulick is the juices which remain in a frying pan after beef or poultry has been fried, to which water, onions, and other seasonings have been added. It forms the basis for gravy. It is served as a kind of sauce over pastry or home-made bread. Q 71–12 ~ juices formed by mixing caplin, fish, etc, in water to make fertilizer and letting the whole mess rot, and then pour the juices on the plants or vegetables.

sulky n Cp *OED* ~ 'light two-wheeled carriage seated for one person' (1756–). Comb **sulky sleigh**: horse-drawn sleigh.

1836 [WIX]² 10 Being driven in a sulky sleigh as far as the new road to Topsail Beech. . .I then proceeded with my knapsack. . . A 'sulky sleigh' takes two persons, in seats, one behind the other, and is drawn by a horse.

summer n also **sommer**. Cp *OED* ~ sb¹ 1 'the second and warmest season of the year' for sense 1; *OED* 2 now only poet. for sense 2; cp *EDD* sb¹ 1 (34) ~ lodge 'a fisherman's hut' Sh I for sense 4; for combs. in sense 5: *DAE* 1 (1789 quot for ~ fish); *DC* ~ road (1820–); *NID* ~ time 'chiefly Brit'; cp FALL n, SPRING[2], WINTER.

1 The principal season, beginning in May or June, for the prosecution of the cod and other fisheries and the processing of the catch on shore; FISHING SEASON, SEASON.

1612 *Willoughby Papers* 1/15, 11 All this sommer I have assisted Master roberts in the fishing vaige what possible I could. 1620 WHITBOURNE 42 Hee is to have a single share allowed unto every man alike of such fish as is taken, whilest they labour together in the Summer time with the ships company with whom they are. [1663] 1963 YONGE 56 The masters pay in fish at the end of the summer. [1669] ibid 120 Nothing happened memorable in the season but that I got by private practice above 4 score pounds, that we made a reasonable voyage, so that I think for my summer's work I might have above £100. [1706] 1895 PROWSE 266 The English have at all times used this Fishery on the Eastern coast and in Harbours and Fishing places on that side, wherein they are protected against the French in the Summer Season by yearly convoys and men of war sent thither. 1895 *Christmas Review* 12 [proverb] Slave in the summer—sleep in the winter. 1924 ENGLAND 321 ~ The cod-fishing season, or work. 1936 SMITH 71 It generally takes a crew a week to get ready properly for the summer's work. All the men had then to go up the bay in boats to secure enough wood for cooking purposes. 1960 FUDGE 7 This was the first two hundred dollars made at the cod fishery business in Fortune Bay and it was considered a big summer. P 9–73 With a load of codfish from their Summer's work [they] were on their way south.

2 In pl, with numeral, used for *year*.

1936 SMITH 27 Little did I think then that I was going to buy a fishing room there and spend thirty-two summers of my life fishing. 1977 *Decks Awash* vi (3), p. 50 Before my father died I used to go across the Bay fishing with him in a 'bully,' and after he died my uncle took over the bully and we went across the Bay for three summers. 1977 RUSSELL 16 He went fishin' when he was seven or eight years old and hasn't had a summer ashore since—that's seventy-five summers fishin'.

3 Phr *lose one's summer, lose one's time in summer*: to experience a failure at fishing; cp SPRING.

1612 *Willoughby Papers* 1/15, 11 I have loussed my tyme this summer. [1919] P 124–71 To proceed at once would cause these humble folk to lose their summer at the fishery. 1937 DEVINE 33 To lose one's summer. To be out of employment during the season named, or to come off with a loss or poorly from the season's work. 1967 *Bk of Nfld* iv, 237 People who through illness 'lost their summer' would be looked after by the more fortunate.

4 Designating a structure or location from which the seasonal cod-fishery is conducted: **summer house, ~ place, ~ shack, ~ station** [see STATION], **~ tilt** [see TILT].

[1822] 1928 CORMACK 107 I was here fortunate in finding a very respectable industrious inhabitant. . .still occupying his summer house at the shore, with his fishing-boat or shallop not yet dismantled for the win-

ter. 1836 [WIX][2] 53 A very decent young man, B.L. and his wife, having only left their winter tilts that morning, had cleaned up their neat summer house, and lighted a good fire. 1977 *Inuit Land Use* 209 The three generations of Perraults maintained. . .a summer house at Newfoundland Cove. 1901 *Christmas Bells* 8 Summer hut, Holton, Labrador. [1918–19] GORDON 40 Bob and two Woody Point men also went off to Plant's Bight for the night, but Jim and I decided to see it out in an old summer shack on the point. 1814 KOHLMEISTER & KMOCH 10 We found several of our Esquimaux, who had here their summer-station. 1842 BONNYCASTLE ii, 125 But even this hut is good, compared with some of the summer tilts, which are constructed to carry on the fishery in the little harbours and coves, where, very often, a huge boulder or projecting rock forms the gable, or actual rere-dosse, as our ancestors called the only chimney, or substitute for a chimney, and from this chimney-rock, a few slight poles built up erect in an oblong form, with a pole-roof sloping against a bank, or rock, the whole covered with bark, when it can be had, which is seldom, or with turf; and with turf piled up against the side walls, without a window, and with only an apology for a door; and the whole interior scarcely affording standing room.

5 Attrib, comb **summer agent**: man in charge of a merchant's fishing premises.

1936 SMITH 42 A few minutes later we were safely anchored off the salt store at Indian Harbour, all well. . . When we did get ashore there were six feet of snow from the wharf up to the winter man's residence. Messrs Job Bros & Co owned Indian Harbour in those days, and Mr Joseph Simms was their summer agent.

summer cod-fish, ~ fish: cod taken in coastal waters in the summer fishery.

[1676] 1895 PROWSE 206 From England Ireland France & Spain & Portugal & New Eng'd have vessels come to Newfoundland in November & Dec'r & have loaden oyle summer fish & winter fish out of the houses & gone out some of them three days before Christmas. 1957 *South Coast Commission* 81 East of [Hermitage and Fortune Bay] the summer codfish population seems to be largely those which winter at St Pierre Bank and in channels between St Pierre Bank and Grand Bank [and] which migrate inshore in the spring.

summer fishery: principal cod-fishery; cp SPRING[2]: ~ FISHERY.

[1653] 1895 PROWSE 167 You are upon the close of this summers fishery to returne back into England. [1676] ibid 207 [They] have by leave of the former Governors and Proprietors erected severall stages and Roomes for their winter and summer fisheries and support. [1802] ibid 419 About fifty pounds weight of strong twine will be required to make a [seal] net, the half worn small hawsers, which the boats have used in the summer fishery, serve for foot ropes. 1910 GRENFELL 201 We had just been doctoring among the numbers of fishermen that make this their headquarters for the summer fishery. 1936 SMITH 13 Finally the paddle-boat *Cabot* came alongside and gave us a big hawser and towed us up to Rogerson's wharf, where we took salt and supplies for the summer fishery. We left St John's 25th May for Brigus and arrived in good time. 1975 POCIUS 8 In communities along Conception

Bay, sheep were set loose at the beginning of the summer before the family moved to Labrador for the summer fishery.

summer herring: herring schools which migrate to inshore waters in summer; cp SPRING[2]: ~ HERRING.

1873 CARROLL 38 Up to the present date many and various were the opinions given, both written and verbal, as to the best possible mode of preserving the Spring, Summer, and Fall Herrings that resort to this Island.

summer inhabitant: migratory fisherman or servant from the British Isles engaged for a specified period in the Newfoundland fishery; cp SERVANT.

[1794] 1968 THOMAS 174 Summer Inhabitants who came from England and Ireland 28,018.

summer mole: freckle (1937 DEVINE 50).

summer people: migratory fishermen from Newfoundland conducting seasonal operation in Labrador waters; FLOATER, STATIONER.

1975 *Them Days* i (1), 37 The English teachers were always such wonderful teachers. They taught us how to speak properly. When the summer people came, the Newfoundland fishermen, we would slip into their way of talking.

summer road: road opened into a wood-cutting area and suitable for use throughout the year.

T 43/8–64 When you're cut back to the back of his block, you're shifted to a new road. There was no summer roads then. All the work was done in the winter.

summer time: daylight-saving time.

[1929] 1979 *Evening Telegram* 3 May, p. 13 Summer time will come into effect May 5 when the gun on Signal Hill will be fired at 10 p.m. to notify the public to advance the time to 11 p.m.

sun n Cp *OED* weather-gall; *EDD* ~ sb 1 (24) ~ hound.

Comb, cpd **sun burn**: discoloration and breaking of salted cod through excessive exposure to the sun in drying.

1953 *Nfld Fish Develop Report* 59 The producers have little control over the quality of their product. In most cases their operations are adversely affected by the weather, which causes 'sun-burn' (skin heating), dampness or 'slime' and, indirectly, over-salting. T 36–64 There'd be a spot on un here or a broken fin on un there, or a bit o' sunburn on the back or something like that.

Hence **sunburn** v: of salt cod, to become discoloured and broken in texture through excessive exposure to the sun in curing; BURN. Freq as **sunburned, sunburnt** p ppl: of cod-fish and seal-skins.

[1749] 1755 DOUGLASS i, 302 No sun-burnt, salt-burnt, or that have been a considerable time pickled before dried, are to be deemed merchantable fish. 1819 ANSPACH 440 [Fish] is also liable to become *sun-burnt*, when spread out on a hot calm day, whether on flakes or on beaches. 1873 CARROLL 33 The first evil is, that

if the weather. . .is fine and the sun shines out strongly [the sealskins] are sure to be sun burnt. 1924 ENGLAND 232 [The seal] also revealed traces of being 'sunburned' as a result of riding the ice. Its skin was exceedingly soft. 1957 *Nfld Qtly* Sep, p. 4 'Look here, see this? Every one sunburnt on the backs.' He showed where [the cod] had been split with too much sun. T 43–64 Every year you'd have to renew the boughs [on the flake]—you couldn't have your fish resting on the wood because it would sunburn and spoil. T 170–65 Broken an' sunburnt [fish] was sold down in the West Indies. That's why 'twas called cullage.

sun-gall: sun-dog; bright gleams in vicinity of the sun.

C 66–5 Sun-galls means it is going to blow hard.

sun hound: see **sun-gall**; WIND HOUND.

1924 ENGLAND 245–6 The sun. . .glowed through a shining mist that blued the pinnacles with evanescent marvels of colour, and as the sun died, it gave up its ghost in a miracle of beauty that took a form known to us of warmer seas. 'Sun hounds,' the sealers call such spectacles. Sinking through mists, the sun projected itself gradually in duplicated spheres. Down from its flattened disk, and up and sideways, it flung rosy hands so that a flaming cross glowed against the west. 1937 DEVINE 70 When the yellow streamers called 'sun hounds' surround the sun after its rising and extend right down to the surface of the ocean the fishermen say: 'The sun is drawing water and that a storm is pending.' C 65–4 The old man commented on the sun hounds in the sky—red balls of cloud that may appear before or after the setting sun.

sunday n Attrib **sunday man**: man on a sealing vessel who refrains from hunting seals on the Sabbath.

1924 ENGLAND 205–6 The Sabbath law [of 1892] may add vastly to the length and hardships of the voyage. Before it went into effect, most of the men killed. Even then, however, certain men refused; and these were then called 'Sunday men.' Nowadays I believe the 'Sunday men' are those who refuse any kind of duty.

sunken p ppl *OED* ~ ppl a 1 (1743 quot for sunken rock).

Comb **sunken pound**: framework of heavy logs or beams, filled with rocks, forming the crib of a wharf or 'stage'; POUND (P 121–67).

sunken rock: submerged rock over which the sea breaks; BREAKER, HARRY, SUNKER.

[c1756] 1927 DOYLE (ed) 35 "Wadham's Song": But N.N.W. 7 or 8 miles / Lies a sunken rock near the Barracks Isles. 1774 [LA TROBE] 7 They were obliged, on account of storms, to run into bays between numberless islands and sunken rocks, with which this coast abounds. [1786] 1792 CARTWRIGHT iii, 209 There was a great sea along shore; the sunken rocks in the bay broke very high. 1837 BLUNT 14 Take care to keep the point of Ferryland Head open to the eastward of Bois, by which means you will avoid a sunken rock having only 2 fathoms water over it. 1866 WILSON 20 St Shotts [is] the most dangerous place on the whole coast; dangerous not because of either sunken rocks or shoal water, but because of the irregular current and under-

tow. 1915 *Nfld Qtly* Oct, p. 32 We went in over a sunken rock and the jib-boom landed on the cliff at Mistaken Point. 1951 *Nfld & Lab Pilot* i, 193 Puddy rock; Uncle Joe rock, awash, Outside rock, above-water, and Sunken rock, with a depth of less than 6 feet over it. T 141/69–65² An' them sunken rocks was breakin', every cast. 1975 BUTLER 115 About three quarters of a mile up the shore there is a sunken rock that comes above water about half a cable length from the shore.

sunken wharf: see **sunken pound**; BALLAST n: ~ WHARF.

1837 *Journ of Assembly* 452 That bridge is necessarily 320 feet long upon eleven sunken wharves. 1976 GUY 107 If fish are scarce, you can pick some wrinkles (snails) off the rocks or the sunken wharves and crack them.

sunker n also **sunker rock** *DC* ~ Nfld (1955–) for sense 1.

1 A submerged rock over which the sea breaks; familiar form of SUNKEN ROCK; BREAKER; GROUNDER.

[c1880] 1927 DOYLE (ed) 29 "The Ryans and the Pittmans": We'll rant and we'll roar like true Newfoundlanders, / We'll rant and we'll roar on deck and below, / Until we see bottom inside the two sunkers / When straight thru the Channel to Toslow we'll go. 1896 *J A Folklore* ix, 33 ~ a breaker. 1937 DEVINE 50 ~ A dangerous rock or shoal having only a few feet of water on it at high tide. 1951 *Nfld & Lab Pilot* i, 134 These latter include Duck Rock shoal, about 4 cables north-eastward of Eastern head and Anchor Cove Sunkers, about one mile farther north-north-eastward; both these dangers have depths of less than 6 feet over them. [1952] 1965 PEACOCK (ed) i, 143 "Skipper Tom": Down to the sunker I anchored so fair, / Hand over me lines and never one tear. T 141/69–65² But she struck fair, broadside, on the loo-ward sunker. 1966 SCAMMELL 62 I'm not much of a hand at public meetings. The words don't seem to have a clear channel from me brain to me lips. Too many sunkers for 'em to ground on, I spose. T 727–68 There's a sunker over there—a sunken rock. You know, when the water's high, it bees under water, but when the water falls down low, real low tide, the kelp comes on un. 1974 PITTMAN 15 The sunkers of Merasheen are the world's worst curse to mothers and mariners alike. When the sea is still, they lie like sleeping monsters below the surface at the harbour's mouth and only a master mariner can tell that they are there at all. But when they are breaking, when the sea erupts over them in a boiling mass of white foam smashing itself to smithereens high in the harbour air, their deadly presence is plain for all to see. High on the cliffs along the northern rim of the harbour, all the white crosses, glistening now in the uncertain morning sun, mark with grim fidelity the unmarkable graves of seamen killed by the sunkers. 1977 BUTLER 76 We were among the Follock rocks and sunkers were breaking mountains high all around us.

2 A dumpling in a bowl of soup (C 66–4).

sunning vbl n Cpd **sunning-tank**: a tank, open at

the top, in which seal oil is refined in natural sunlight (1924 ENGLAND 293).

supercargo n Cp *OED* ~ 'officer aboard merchant ship. . .to superintend the cargo.' One employed by a merchant aboard a vessel collecting fish to sort the dried and salted cod into grades by quality and size; CULLER.

1936 SMITH 17 After the next time spread it would be shipped on board the dry fish vessel and the supercargo would inspect it and pass his verdict; there was no talk then of bad cargoes. 1977 BUTLER 38 I want you to be skipper, supercargo (or clerk) and obtain a fish culler's licence. 1981 HUSSEY 101 My father went as supercargo on a dry fish collector [i.e.] a man aboard the ship to keep account and tally every quintal of fish that went into the hold.

superior n A school organized for teaching beyond the elementary levels; also attrib.

1942 *Little Bay Islands* 9, 10 In 1922 a branch of the N.G.I.T. was organized by Miss Georgine Roberts, superior teacher at that time. . . The school became a Superior in 1919.

surrogate n Cp *OED* ~ sb 1 c 'one appointed to act as judge in the vice-admiralty court in place of a regular judge' (1816, 1867 quots); *DC* Nfld (1793, 1818), ~ court Nfld (1818). Naval officer appointed to act as a judge by the governor; also attrib.

[1788] 1895 PROWSE 347 . . .a much greater man than his master and governs this Island as he thinks fit, of which all the surrogates complain loudly. 1793 REEVES 154 The governor conferred on them the title of *surrogates*, an idea taken from the admiralty-law; to which, and which alone the naval governors were in the habit of looking. . . A *surrogate* is well known in Newfoundland, as legally deputed by the governor, to act as his deputy. [1810] 1971 ANSPACH 16 No house to be built, or enclosure erected by virtue of any grant, unless previously registered in the surrogate records. 1810 STEELE 89–90 About the same time [1789], surrogates were deputed by the Governor to assist him in his arduous duties; and they are now always sent into the out-harbours, to hear causes and adjust differences. 1826 [GLASCOCK] i, 147 It was the bowman of the boat's duty, on reaching the beach, to hoist a spare ship's ensign, as a signal for holding a court. Shortly after followed the captain's or lieutenant's coxwain, laden with a cloak-bag filled with books; the surrogate officer. . .attended by two of the resident magistrates, a couple of midshipmen, the captain's clerk as registrar of the court, and a few fishermen of the place as criers and tipstaves. [1831] 1916 *Nfld Law Reports* 110 The Governor may appoint Courts of Civil Jurisdiction called Surrogate Courts, to be Courts of Record, and 'shall determine according to the law of England, as far as the same can be applied to suits and complaints, arising in the Islands and places aforesaid.' 1861 DE BOILIEU 71 In September we generally had a visit from a Surrogate magistrate, in a schooner, but this is done away with; in fact it was a mere farce of a court. The judge was a retired post-captain in the navy, and the court was held on board a schooner hired for the purpose. 1906 *Nfld Qtly* Dec, p. 14 At one time I was district Judge, police-magistrate, by statute also police-inspector, Chairman of the Board of Health, surrogate of the [Admiralty] Court, president of the Royal Marine Court of Inquiry, and, to crown all, they appointed me Naval Commander of the Bait Squadron! 1937 DEVINE 50 ~ In the late 18th century, a deputy of the Governor, having authority to administer the fishery and shipping regulations and the law generally. Naval officers on the Newfoundland station were frequently thus appointed and used to hold court in the various harbors on the coast. T 75/7–64 The English fleet'd come over and would be in charge of a surrogate—fellow in charge of so many ships. T 342/6–67² It's from the old surrogates' records that their families were here fifty-five years before they got their grant from the surrogates.

surrogating vbl n Cp *OED* surrogate v 3: ~ (1679). The conduct of legal hearings in coastal settlements by naval officers appointed by the governor.
  1793 REEVES 154 The time of surrogating was looked forward to as a season when all wrongs were to be redressed against all oppressors; and this naval judicature was flown to by the poor inhabitants and planters, as the only refuge they had from the west country merchants.

suther See SOUTHER.

swab n [swɑ·b] *OED* ~ sb¹ 1 b for sense 1.
  1 A mop, usu with burlap tied to the end, used for 'washing out' salt fish, moistening staves when making a barrel, etc.
  [c1900] 1978 *RLS* 8, p. 24 ~ long handled mop used with Ramshorn to wash the fish. T 141/67–65² Now you rigs out and makes your swabs and makes your fish boxes an' splittin' tables. C 70–12 ~ This was an object used to wash out fish with. The swab was about two feet long and had a piece of brin on one end. P 127–75 ~ A brush used in coopering to wet the staves when the barrel is being steamed. It is normally made from a birch handle with a piece of brin (gunny sacking) on one end.
  2 A stick, similar to the mop used on fishing boats, with various objects attached to one end, carried as a mock-sceptre by mummers during Christmas revels; cp BLADDER.
  [1885] 1962 *Evening Telegram* 21 Dec, p. 22 Many a time have I seen a 'Fool,' whom the mob tried to 'run,' pull off his cap, take the handle of his 'swab' and clean out some two or three hundred persons. 1895 PROWSE 402 The 'swabs' [carried by the fools or mummers] were made of a bladder, covered with canvas or a switch, made sometimes of a cow's tail fastened to a stick. 1957 *Atlantic Advocate* xlviii, 23 A 'swab' was a bladder—taken from a codfish more often than not—which was blown up like a balloon. It contained a number of pebbles and was fastened to a short stick. The mummers used their 'swabs' to belabour the spectators as they passed by.

swab v [swɒ·b]. Cp *EDD* ~ v¹ 5 'to go about in idle fashion.' Phr *swab around*: to lounge idly.
  T 141/59–65² We swabbed around. Anyhow directly we'm getting pretty hungry.

swaddler n *OED* ~ Ir (1747–); *EDD* (1) Ir. Term of opprobrium for a Methodist.
  1866 WILSON 156 The society which Mr Hoskins formed [c1780] in Old Perlican was called *Hoskinites* by their enemies; and sometimes the cognomen Swaddlers, imported from Ireland, was shouted, as the members went or returned from their religious meetings.

swaddling ppl *OED* ~ Ir (1747–); *EDD* (2) Ir. Hypocritical; canting.
  [c1820] 1912 MURPHY 2 "Quigley on Picco": When he found out both my name and nation, / He boldly seized me and turned me out; / Had I been a heathen or a 'swaddling' preacher, / He'd entertain me without a doubt.

swale See SEAL.

swaling See SEALING.

swallow n Cpd **swallow-tail**: a cod-fish with an angular cut made in the tail to mark ownership; cp CUT v: ~-TAIL.
  1937 DEVINE 75 If it was necessary to make a further distinction and keep another lot separate a cut was made on each side and then we had 'swallow tail.' This might be codnet fish or bultow fish.

swamp n Attrib **swamp bottom**, also **swamp**: a small, flat-bottomed row-boat; FLAT n (P 127–73).
  1957 *Daily News* 24 Sep The motor boat, swamp bottom and the dory will soon be dragged up behind the stage on the roadside or in the meadow. 1969 MOWAT 109 We were anchored on the edge of a fleet of trap skiffs, swamps (small rowboats), seagoing dories, and two small coastal schooners.

swamper n A good boat-load of fish; SAGGER; cp BATTY (P 148–61).

swank v To lug; to carry with a great deal of exertion (P 13–75).
  P 148–63 We have to swank [the heavy object] down the stairs.

swanskin n *OED* ~ 2 'fine thick kind of flannel' (1694–1706 quots for clothing), *DAE* (1744–1904); W BARNES *Dorset Dialect* (1886), p. 107 'cloth or flannel. . .mainly for the wear of fishermen out in Newfoundland.'
  1 Fine, thick, flannel used for articles of clothing.
  [1795] 1974 SQUIRE 84 4 yds. swanskin 10s. 1836 [WIX]² 51 I was glad to procure a pair of 'cuffs,' or mittens, made in this bay, of a kind of thick woollen or swan-skin. 1855 WHITE *MS Journal* 1 Aug 1 yd swans-

kin 2/6. 1866 WILSON 214 The cuff is for the hand, made like a mitten, but the substance is a stout, white cloth, called 'swanskin'. . . The buskin is for the leg, to keep out the snow. . .also made of swanskin. 1914 *Cadet* Apr, p. 7 Hamburg boots and bluchers were all the go and the swanskin or buskin when worn over the latter made a tidy, warm and comfortable footwear, except in wet weather. 1937 DEVINE 65 . . .nippers, swanskin or knitted bands around the palms of the hand to avoid being made sore by the chafing of the fishing lines. T 141/68–65[2] That was a familiar thing to see, Jack, a great roll o' swanskin, double breadth, rolled up high as that table. T 210–65 This swanskin [was] a material made an eighth of an inch thick, nearly pure white. Do you know the nature of flannel? Very much that nature; a kind of woolly nature, and very wonderful stuff for the north.

2 In designations of the articles of clothing made from swanskin: **swanskin coat,** ~ **cuff** [see CUFF[1]], ~ **drawers,** ~ **mitt** [see MITT].

T 31–64 In walks a fine-lookin' maid, you know, Uskimaux maid, in through the door, an' she had on a swanskin coat—heavy swanskin, see. 1914 *Cadet* Apr, p. 7 Swanskin cuffs, with a separate place for the thumb only, were worn on the hands and the headgear in winter was a warm, if awkward-looking cap made of fur. T 185–65 In my father's day, an' even in my day, we used to have what they call swanskin cuffs. You hear talk o' that? Made out 'o swanskin; they'd come up here to your elbow, an' a thumb in 'em. 1914 *Cadet* Apr, p. 7 Rough clothing was worn in those days including swanskin trousers, moleskin trousers. T 141/68–65[2] It'd be swanskin drawers, then, an' red flannel shirts. All your clothes was made out o' swanskin. 1959 *Daily News* 13 Feb, p. 20 One longs for a pair of those 'swanskin' gauntlet mitts that travellers wore in winter on the coast. T 172/3–65 I don't know whether you've ever seen that or not, swanskin? Material, very heavy. I've had swanskin mitts made, goin' to the ice, when I was first goin' [as a] boy.

swarve* v Cp *OED* swerve v 5: swarve 'rove' (1543–1698 quots). To stroll aimlessley (P 37).

P 40–78 ~ Can apply to animals as well as humans. 'I always got to be swarvin' around.'

swatch n [swɒtʃ, swɒtʃ]. Cp *OED* ~ sb[3] local 'a passage or channel of water lying between sand-banks or between a sandbank and the shore' (1626–); *EDD* sb[1] 'a narrow channel through a shoal.'

1 An expanse of open water in an ice-field; SLATCH. Merges in some contexts with sense 2.

1909 BERNIER 7 ~ a small pool of open water in the ice. 1916 GRENFELL 165 After a long and unsuccessful day on the ice, the wind being too much on shore, and the 'swatches,' or open water, being mostly closed. . . 1920 GRENFELL & SPALDING 150–1 Sea-birds have also come in the 'swatches' of open water between the pans. 1924 ENGLAND 148 Why, those fellers [sealers] could jump over swatches [open water]. They could jump over a ship without touchin' narr rail. [1929] 1933 GREENLEAF (ed) 247 "Sealing Cruise of the *Lone Flier*": Some of us took oilclothes and one of us took a

watch, / He had it for to see the time, while he was at the swatch. T 141/59–65[2] Blind Tickle never freezes up. There's a little eddy tide there, an' [it] leaves a swatch, see, even at the coldest winters. C 71–104 Be careful going across that harbour tonight. There's a swatch just off Murray's wharf. 1972 BROWN 178 The ice had loosened, showing dark swatches of water, swatches that would have presented no problem to fresh, able sealers, but that looked as wide as the ocean to these dying men.

2 An area of open water frequented by seals; BOBBING-HOLE; also attrib.

1887 BOND 65 I was out swatchin', as we calls it, that's shooting siles as they comes up through the swatches—them's the holes in th' ice. 1895 *Dial Notes* i, 381 ~ hole in the ice through which seals come up. [c1900] 1978 *RLS* 8, p. 23 Swatch hole: water in ice [floe] where seals come up to blow. T 27–64 So he [took] chase after un with the skeets on the slippery ice, and when he made the kick at un he went into a swatch of water. He never seed un afterwards. T 84–64 Spring o' the year when they're shootin' at a seal in swatch, always at un throat-on. T 187/9–65 They bid there then around a swatch lookin' all day, walked in Sleepy Cove again, wi' their punt, launched she, an' got aboard the car. 1978 *Decks Awash* vii (1), p. 52 A swatch is a large or small hole of open water among the ice [floes]. This time there was one large lake, several miles long. Men were scattered here and there along the edge on both sides, waiting for a seal to show.

swatch v To lie in wait for, and shoot, seals in the 'swatches' or areas of open water in an ice-field.

1883 *Fish Exhibit Cat*[4] 175 Swatching and Trolling Old Hoods. [See 1887 quot at SWATCH n.] 1895 *Dial Notes* i, 381 ~ To watch for seals at the holes in order to shoot them. 1924 ENGLAND 174 In a pause, loading sculps, Joe Stirge went overside to swatch. 1955 ENGLISH 36 ~ To shoot seals in pools amid icefloes.

swatcher n One who hunts seals with a gun on the ice-floes near patches of open water or 'swatches'; WATCHER (1925 *Dial Notes* v, 344); cp LANDSMAN.

swatching vbl n ['swɒtʃən] *OED* ~ vbl sb 'a method of taking seals' (Nfld: 1883, 1901). Shooting seals as they appear in the 'swatches' or areas of open water in an ice-field (1895 *J A Folklore* viii, 39).

1895 GRENFELL 161–2 Once alongside the floe, the men jump off on to the ice, and at once the work begins. Sometimes they work in pairs, one man shooting the seals, and his chum, who is called 'the dog,' following up, cutting off the tail from the dead seal to 'mark it,' and then gathering them in heaps, and putting up a pole with a flag or a piece of liver as a claim. These are then said to be 'panned.' This is technically called 'swatching.' [c1900] 1978 *RLS* 8, p. 23 ~ Shooting seals in swatch holes. 1916 GRENFELL 164 'There be plenty of good herrin' for the dogs, and you and me can have a day's swatchin''—which means trying to shoot old seals in the holes of water among the pack ice. 1933 GREENE 166 And everything of all sorts must be made ready for any one of the emergencies that may arise at the Ice—not only for 'swilin'' in the Patch, or 'swatching' in the lanes of the Floe—but for the off-chance of the ship being nipped, or of some other bad accident or jamming. T 141/67–65² An' then in the spring, winter time, when the seals would come along again, there'd be another period of swatchin', we called it. Ice was on the land, you go out if there was a'r hole o' water made where th' ice would pan around an' leave a hole o' water, you'd put in hours an' days upon days waitin' for a seal to come up. 1978 *Decks Awash* vii (1), p. 52 On another day my friend and his uncles were out swatching. . . This time there was one large lake, several miles long. Men were scattered here and there along the edge on both sides, waiting for a seal to show.

sweat n
1 The moisture and salt particles exuded by salted cod-fish in the drying process (P 148–62).
2 Comb **sweat hole**: among the Labrador indians, a cavity used for medicinal sweating; sweat-house.
1907 WALLACE 124–5 On the lake shore were some other camping places that had been used within a few months, and at one of them a newly made 'sweat hole,' where the medicine man had treated the sick. These sweat holes are much in favor with the Labrador Indians, both Mountaineers and Nascaupees. They are about two feet in depth and large enough in circumference for a man to sit in the center, surrounded by a circle of good-sized bowlders. Small saplings are bent to form a dome-shaped frame for the top. The invalid is placed in the center of this circle of bowlders, which have previously been made very hot, water is poured on them to produce steam, and a blanket thrown over the sapling frame to confine the steam.
sweat-pad: stuffed material worn as part of horse's harness.
T 100/1–64 An' they also used another pad they [called] a sweat-pad, so as the horse wouldn't gall his shoulders here, front shoulders.

sweat v Cp *OED* ~ v 10 b 'of products set aside to exude their moisture.' In the curing of fish, esp cod, to exude salt; to spread thoroughly through the fish by pressure of the pile; WORK.
[1663] 1963 YONGE 58 When well dried, it's made up into prest pile, where it sweats; that is, the salt sweats out, and corning, makes the fish look white. [1766] 1971 BANKS 135 When the Fish are tolerably dry they Put them in Round Piles of 8 or ten Quintals Each Covering them on the top with bark in these Piles they remain 3 or 4 days or a week to sweat after which they are again Spread & when dry Put up in Larger heaps Covered with Canvass & Left till they are put on board & ready for the Mediterranean trade. 1819 ANSPACH 437 After the fish has been first spread on the flake, four good days out of seven, (which is considered as better than four successive good days, because it then works or, as the fishermen express it, *sweats* the better), will be sufficient to save it from any material damage. 1861 *Harper's* xxii, 595 After this they are piled in

'kenches' again for a day to 'sweat' them—that is to remove remaining moisture—and are again thrown upon 'flakes' for a day. They are then ready to be stowed in bulk in the vessel.

sweep v *EDD* ~ v¹ 3. Phr *sweep in*: to haul stacks of hay to the barn with a rope.
1974 MANNION 101 In the Avalon hay cocks were also 'swept in' on the ground to the yard by means of a long rope tied around the base of the stack.

sweet a Cp *OED* ~ adj 3 'free from taint or noxious matter' for comb in sense 3.
1 In the names of sweet-flavoured baked foods, often prepared with molasses, raisins or 'figs,' esp those prepared for Christmas or other special occasions: **sweet bread, ~ cake, ~ loaf** [see also LOAF].
1875 *Maritime Mo* i, 443 Oh, what a sad Christmas Eve and Christmas Day it is for me! I think I can see you making the sweet-bread and preparing everything comfortable for to-morrow. 1893 *Christmas Review* 5 Now the table is set with jugs, glasses, and decanters, and plates of 'sweet bread,' apples and oranges. 1931 BYRNES 104 . . .heaping plates of home made 'sweet bread' were passed around. T 74/5–64 I can picture [her], he says, makin' the sweet-breads for Christmas. 1971 NOSEWORTHY 252 Sweet bread: A type of bread made of flour, salt, yeast, butter, molasses and raisins, which is mixed with water. 1866 WILSON 355 [Funerals] were always attended by large bodies of people. . . Spirits and sweet-cake were given at the house. [1886] LLOYD 88 Plum puddings, which are known as 'figgy pudden,' are in great demand, as is also what is called 'sweetcake,' a concoction of flour, yeast, and molasses. [1904] 1927 DOYLE (ed) 5 "Wedding in Renews": They'll have sweet cake and turnip tops. T 50/3–64 Oh well, come in an' dance. Dance an' sing an' ask for sweet cake an' sweet bread an' bigar after beer! 1972 MURRAY 227 Usually too there was raisin bread and many people tried to have 'sweet cake' (layer cake, jam tart, etc.) to provide a finish to the meal. 1893 *Christmas Greeting* 17 . . .while rosy cheeked maidens with deft and nimble fingers busied themselves in decorating the interiors of their homes, and providing the 'sweet loaf' and other Christmas necessaries.
2 In the names of sweet-scented or sweet-flavoured plants: **sweet flower, ~ leaf** [see also SWEETIE], **~ pea, ~ more** [see also MORE n], **~ root, ~ sally** [see also SALLY²], **~ william**.
1956 ROULEAU 38 Sweet-flower: *Moneses uniflora*. 1956 ibid 38 Sweet-leaf: *Rumex Acetosella*. 1975 SCOTT 15 Most children in Newfoundland have enjoyed the refreshing taste of the Sheep Sorrel and it is too bad that this habit is lost with childhood. The Sheep Sorrel is known as Sweet Leaf or Laddie Suckers or Sally Suckers. 1956 ROULEAU 35 Sweet Pea: *Lathyrus japonicus*. C 75–132 To cure a lost appetite a tonic was made from helder berries, juniper bush, beaver roots, bog beans, sweet mores, sassparella roots and Indian tea, all steeped together. The person would take two spoonfuls before each meal. 1956 ROULEAU 38 Sweet-root: *Sanguisorba canadensis*. P 148–63 Sweet Sally:

Rumex Acetosella. 1956 ROULEAU 38 Sweet William: *Sisyrinchium angustifolium*.

3 In comb **sweet seal oil**: processed seal oil free from odour; cp PALE SEAL OIL (1883 *Fish Exhibit Cat*[4] 173).

sweetie n Sheep-sorrel (*Rumex Acetosella*); LEAF, SALLY[2], SWEET LEAF (1956 ROULEAU 38).

P 61–67 Sweeties: a low, weed-like plant growing from the ground as a single leaf with a sweet taste, often eaten by children.

swile See SEAL.

swiler See SEALER[1].

swiling See SEALING.

swing v *EDD* ~ 1 (5) e ~ swong Ir; J E WALSH *Ireland Sixty Years Ago* (1847), p. 82: swing-swong ['hangman's rope'].

Comb, cpd **swing-bunk**: section of a two-piece sled; SWINGING BUNK.

T 96/7–64[1] Wagon sleds some called 'em, an' bunks on 'em, see, swing-bunk. Put on your wood in your forrard bunk, then you [swing] how you like.

swing-line: STRAY-LINE (M 69–23).

P 127–76 The swing-line is one of the ropes attaching the four corner-mooring buoys to the surface corners of a cod-trap.

swing net: fishing net fastened to the shore at one end only.

[1777] 1792 CARTWRIGHT ii, 240 They still caught some poolers there, under the leap, in a swing net.

swing-swong: board suspended from a tree by a rope, used as a swing (P 148–61).

P 108–74 He rigged up a swing-swong out in the yard. 1977 *Lore and Language* ii (6), p. 23 We used to get, sometimes now, after we quit school, or even in the summer time, as 'twas a wet day. You'd get in one of the barns, you know, and perhaps you'd have hide'n'seek, or you'd have swing-swong, or. . .something like that.

swing n

1 Cross-bar behind horse to which traces and plough are attached; BOGGAN* (Q 71–13).

P 148–61 ~ single cross-piece behind horse to which traces attach. Centre of swing fastens to plow.

2 Length of line attached to various types of fish-net, trap, etc; STRAY-LINE.

C 75–63 The lobster pot 'swings' were prepared in the kitchen. Lobster pot swings are the line connected to a pot so that it can be hauled out of the water. The swing contained a buoy at the end and a bobber in the middle. A bobber was a small buoy [that] was always under water and the purpose was to keep the swing from hooking into the bottom.

3 Phr *at swing*: of a fishing net, with only one end made fast.

[1776] 1792 CARTWRIGHT ii, 200 We left the net at swing, in the lower pool. 1792 ibid *Gloss* i, xv A net is

said to be at *swing*, when one end only of it is made fast.

swinge v *EDD* ~ v[2]; *ADD*. To singe, scorch; to burn the down off sea-birds after plucking the feathers.

1896 *J A Folklore* ix, 25 ~ the same as *singe*. . .is the only form heard here. 1924 ENGLAND 221 Dat feller was so nigh an' handy to hell's flames ye could smell un swindgin'. 1937 DEVINE 50 ~ To singe, to char. 1975 RUSSELL 94 'These cooks. . .did they use a hot poker or did they use scaldin' water? . . .they must have used one or the other. . .' 'No' said I, 'they didn't.' 'Well then,' said Grandma, 'how did they swinge 'em?' 'Swinge who?' said I. 'The turrs' said she. 1976 *Daily News* 24 Feb, p. 3 After all day on the bay, and coming back with seventy or eighty turrs, we'd have a feed of hearts and livers in the stage head that night, cleaning the birds by dumping them in scalding hot water, pluckin' off the feathers and then swinge the down. Swinge, which rhymes with hinge, meant running a hot iron over the down, the best way to remove it.

swingeing vbl n Comb **swingeing stick**: slender stick used as a kind of spit to hold a plucked sea-bird while singeing its down preparatory to cooking.

P 127–75 When you swinge a bird, you take a swingein' stick, push it through the mouth down into the stomach and hold it over a wood fire. [1976 GUY 60 We ate turrs (impaled on a sharpened broomstick and held over the damper hole to singe off the fuzz).]

swinging ppl

Comb **swinging bunk**: section of a two-piece sled; SWING-BUNK (Q 67–59).

T 100/1–64 On the front sleigh of the two bob-sleds was what they used to call a swingin' bunk. That bunk was bolted down with a bolt and whichever way the slide moved it slew one way or the other but this bunk'd stay straight.

swinging chair: infant's chair suspended by a rope from above.

P 269–64 ~ a hand-made wooden chair, with a bar of wood across front to keep baby in. Made of small pieces of wood held together by a line passing through four corners of the chair and knotted under the seat. Chair is suspended from ceiling by the lines through the corners, and baby placed in chair.

swinging gear: horse's harness used to pull a sled without shafts.

T 43/8–64 They usen't to use any shafts on the bob-sleds them times. 'Twas what was known as swingin' gear, and you get your load on the bob-sled and of course the rear end would be draggin' on the ground.

swinging rope: length of line attached to various types of fish-net, etc; STRAY-LINE, SWING-LINE.

M 68–7 ~ rope tied from the buoy to the bank line (rode). This piece of rope was in length of approximately three or four fathoms.

swish[1] n Cp [1929] BOWEN 20 bulling a cask

(similar sense). Liquor produced by pouring water into a recently emptied rum barrel.

1973 *Daily News* 2 May, p. 4 "Swish": Into the barrels from the Store / So much hot water you would pour / A three buck deal, but now it's more / Swish will cost ten dollars. / Liquor soaked into the wood / Drawn out by water as it should / A swishy product makes that good / Swish will cost ten dollars. C 75–130 Water [is] put in a rum barrel and left to stand. The alcohol comes out of the wood and forms swish.

swish² See SISH.

switch n   A rough sea; cp LOP².

T 178–65 And some o' the boys went up on the mast head. There was a good bit o' switch on but not much wind.

switch v   *EDD* ~ v¹ 8. To jerk (something) suddenly.

T 43–64 Sometimes he'd let the foresail jive, or possibly the mainsail; that would be an awful crash. You're likely to get switched overboard that way because the whole sheet had to come right over your head back to the wheel.

switchel n   also **switchel tea**. Cp *DAE* ~ 'a drink of molasses and water often seasoned with vinegar and ginger' (1790–); *OED* swizzle 'various compounded intoxicating drinks' (1813–). Tea, esp that once drunk by fishermen and sealers at sea.

1897 *J A Folklore* x, 211 ~ a mug of weak tea given to the sailors between meals when at the seal fishing. 1924 ENGLAND 50 Some were devouring beans and salt meat; others, gulping tea that steamed. 'Switchel,' this tea was; that is, boiled-over tea whereto now and again fresh leaves are added. 1927 *Christmas Messenger* 47 ~ cold tea, not strong, sweetened with molasses. The word is used in contempt, as 'I had a miserable drop of "switchel" for breakfast this morning.' P 20–55 ~ tea which is not just steeped, but which has been boiled. [1959] 1965 PEACOCK (ed) iii, 898 "Young Chambers": [of men in jail] For butter and molasses we did not get a mite,. . . / Then at four o'clock in the morning we're looking out for day, / We're heaving out of our hammocks for a cup of switchel tea. P 48–60 ~ weak, cold, left-over tea. P 118–66 This tea is not bad but the stuff next door is switchel. 1973 HORWOOD 40 ~ is a fisherman's name for tea without milk and sweetened with molasses.

swivel n   *EDD* ~ sb 1 (2) ~ tree obs.

1 Spike driven into the butt-end of a log to which a rope is fastened for a horse to haul (Q 67–68).

2 Comb **swivel tree**: cross-bar attached to collars of a pair of horses, for hauling a 'catamaran' or sled.

T 43/8–64 They had a pole between the two horses, and they were shackled to the outside end o' this pole from a swivel tree comin' across from each collar, and this was where they used to take their load. The swivel tree [would] swing in any direction she wanted to go in.

swoil(e) See SEAL.

swoiler See SEALER¹.

swoiling See SEALING.

swordfish n   Killer whale (*Orcinus orca*).

1976 PINHORN 50 The characteristic high, spiked, dorsal fin distinguishes the species and accounts for its local vernacular name of 'swordfish.' 1977 *Inuit Land Use* 258 The local term for males is swordfish, and the term for females is thrasher. Swordfish travel in pairs but thrashers are usually seen in schools of five to eight animals.

synagogue n   A sealer's bunk or berth; bed; PEW².

1924 ENGLAND 177–8 I loves swilin', me son; an' after I'm on ice, I loves to lay back in my synagogue an' dror de vog [draw the fog, i.e., smoke]. C 71–107 [Go to] synagogue: a favourite expression of my father's when he wanted me to go to bed. His parents used it on him also.

syrup n   A sweet, fruit-flavoured commercial cordial; a drink prepared from such a cordial diluted with water; CLINGY.

1860–1 *Journ of Assembly* Appendix, p. 535 I paid one shilling and eight pence for four glasses of rum punch and two glasses of syrup. 1892 *Evening Herald* 5 Nov They demanded another [drink], but were given syrup. [1900 OLIVER & BURKE] 57 "The Topsail Geisha": Lemon syrup / For the gentlemen. 1951 *N Y Folklore Qtly* vii, 272 [During Christmas everybody served] whiskey and wine for the men, and, for the ladies, big bottles of syrup to which hot water was added. T 365–67 An' somebody'd come along an' offer you some sweets an' a glass of syrup maybe. 1976 GUY 61 Glasses of lemon crystals or strawberry syrup or lime-juice. 1979 TIZZARD 222 After the [Christmas] presents were given out and the concert was over there would be syrup and cake—always red syrup, so it was either raspberry or strawberry flavor. The syrup was made by Purity Factories Ltd, St John's.

T

t- See note at TH-.

T See TEE.

tabanask n   LEMOINE *Dictionnaire Français-Montagnais* 248: utāpānāshk ['native sled']; *DC* ~ (Labr: 1933–). Sledge with flat bottom rather than runners.

1933 MERRICK 135 John claims old Mathieu will make him a better *tabanask* than that [simple slide], but I don't believe it. 1947 TANNER ii, 714–15 The trapper packs his skins and his tackle on to a tabanask, and this he himself must drag in all weathers; in a thaw, which is not rare if a cyclone comes and softens the snow, the tabanask can be unbearably heavy on account of its large friction surface.

tabbety* See TAFFETY.

tabby n   A small floating ice-pan in boys' sport of jumping across the ice or 'copying'; TIPPY n (Q 67–74).

tabby v   To jump from one floating ice-pan to another; COPY, TIPPY v (C 65–4).
P 207–67 The boys thought they could tabby across the harbour.

table n   Cp OED ~ sb 17 f and tabling vbl sb 8 for sense 1.
1 A piece of canvas sewn on the selvage or edge of a sail to strengthen the points where the grummets are placed (P 113–76).
T 141/66–65² An' Uncle Ben, see, was to the wheel, I had he to the wheel. I said, 'Keep her tight.' An' directly I seed the table bust, the table bust on the hanks, you know, where the hanks was banded on.
2 Comb **table butter**: dairy butter in contrast with margarine (P 234–59).
1958 *Nfld Dishes* 22 In Newfoundland fortified Margarine with colour added is generally used in all recipes which call for butter or shortening. In fact Margarine is often referred to as 'butter' and fresh or dairy butter is called 'good butter' or 'table butter.'
table-land: stretch of salt-water marsh along the sea-shore (1971 NOSEWORTHY 253).

tack¹ n   EDD ~ sb² 3 esp Ir; cp OED sb¹ 4 'a stitch.' Clothes, esp the barest covering of garments; SCREED.
P 168–64 [proverb] Sew on your back and you'll never have a tack. 1968 DILLON 157 I haven't got a tack to put on me. P 148–74 [It was so wet out hunting] I had to shift my tack.

tack² n   Phr *a tack with the sun*: a course away from the shore in a clockwise direction; cp quots at BELAY, SLEW v.
1958 HARRINGTON 91 He noted how the vessel made a short reach across the harbour, 'a tack with the sun,' which he learned was a time-honoured custom which, if not fulfilled, would be a bad omen.

tacker n   also **tacking*** EDD tack v² 2 (2) ~ Do So D; (4) tacking. Cobbler's waxed thread.
1937 DEVINE 51 ~ A waxed thread with a bristle at the end, used by shoemakers. 1955 ENGLISH 36 ~ waxed hemp for sewing boots. T 94–64 An' then they had to get the awl an' the tacker an' run a thread around there to tighten it, to bring it in to a nice shape. T 194–65 Well all right, tomorrow morning I'll get up, an' seven o'clock I sit down with my awl an' tacker to make these boots. P 167–67 Tackin: waxed hemp used by cobblers. C 71–119 He had hair on his chest like tacker.

tackle v   EDD ~ v 3. To fish with a net.
1964 BLONDAHL (ed) 93 "The Change Islands Song": They're tackling for the salmon and / The herring and the cod.

tackling n   Cp OED ~ vbl sb 2 b 'horse's harness' obs (1645–1787); DAE 1 'harness of a draft animal' obs (1641–1775) for sense 1.
1 The harness of a sled-dog, horse, etc.
1937 DEVINE 51 Tacklin'. A dog's harness. 1972 MURRAY 275 In the early days, when many families had dogs for hauling firewood, the dog's 'tackling' or harness was often made by the women of the household. Rope, string and cloth were used in making such a harness. 1977 *Decks Awash* vi (6), p. 64 "Uncle Josh": A saucy harse had Uncle Josh / Dat sometimes proved crossacklin / But Uncle Josh would wast no time / De bull would get de tacklin / An off 'e'd go for starrigans / Wid frosty snow acracklin.
2 Clothing; RIG n.
1964 BLONDAHL (ed) 91 "The Spotted Islands Song": The boys jumped in their 'tackle'n', / And their shoes began to shine / For a dance in Spotted Islands / In the good old Fishin' Time!

taffety a   also **tabbety*** OED taffeta, taffety 2 fig.; EDD ~ 1 esp s w cties. Fastidious or particular, esp about one's food (P 152–58).
T 222–66 For your midday meal then you might perhaps have a nice piece of swile, or seal, or if you are taffety and can't come that, or in other words are fussy about your food and have no appetite, you might like instead a tickleace or turr, with perhaps toutons for dessert. C 75–136 ~ Used in referring to a delicate child [who] is very fussy and does not eat very much. P 40–78 No matter what you puts on the table you won't please her; she's some tabbety.

tail n   OED ~ sb¹ 4 e 'stern of a ship or boat' obs (1553–1709) for sense 2.
1 The broad appendage at the rear of a seal; small tip of this cut off for subsequent reckoning of the number of seals taken.
1861 DE BOILIEU 94 The knife was soon found, and the tail of the animal cut close off to the body. 1924 ENGLAND 290 Tails of shot seals have to be counted, you must understand, as the Cap'n himself explained, 'We don't want to lose time lookin' for seals the gunners claimed they shot but didn't. If we knows the number o' tails, we can tell how many we got to pick up an' not leave any on ice.' Ibid 291 The tails were small and triangular. Only a bit of the tip was brought in.
2 The stern of a boat or canoe.
1878 HOWLEY *MS Reminiscences* 4 A shark made a rush at him and barely missed striking the tail of the canoe.
3 The narrow end of a pit-saw.
T 393/403–67 [He] was a good top-man. Went out, you know, an' caught hold the tail of his saw.
4 Phr *tail on*: of a squid, moving back-foremost.
T 54/9–64 A squid can swim head on or tail on. He can go faster tail on than he can head on.

5 Comb tail counting

1972 SANGER 241 ~ Tabulation of the number of seals taken at the end of each day during the second and [third] stages [of] the sealing operation.

tail-drag v: to haul logs on a small sled, the ends dragging on the ground.

P 65–64 In the spring when the snow is soft, or in early autumn when there is only a little snow, pulpwood is 'tail dragged' over the main road. The sled used for tail dragging is made from a single bunk sled in front; two sticks have their butts [larger ends] on the bunks—the tops are allowed to drag. T 43/7–64 The bob sleds used to tail drag the stuff. In the woods there'd be one end draggin' on the ground, see, an' the other chained onto the bunk of the sled, the bob sled.

tail pound: stern compartment of an open boat; POUND, ROOM.

P 122–73 There was a buoy, some hooks and a long piece of line in the tail pound of the dory.

tail rope: (a) length of rope used to haul seals across the ice; cp HAULING-ROPE, TOW v: ~ ROPE; (b) trace on a dog cart.

T 31/5–64 I caught [the] tail rope, a rope on the tail of the seal we used to have [for] hauling up, and I caught un and got up on the seal. 1979 TIZZARD 64 When ready for the road a tail rope or trace would be fastened to one end of this harness and the other end to the bridle rope on the cart and the pup forced to go and. . .pull the cart along.

tail-saw v: to remove the sawn planks from the conveyor-belt in a sawmill.

P 65–64 The person who stands behind the [main] saw and takes away the lumber and sends it on its way to another part of the mill is 'tail sawing.'

tail stick: cross-bar behind horse to which traces are secured (P 148–63); BOGGAN*.

T 100/1–64 There was two shafts'd go up on the horse, and a chain trace to hook on the collar, and coming back to a kind of a tail stick on the end.

tail strap: leather strip joining the traces of a horse's harness at the rear (Q 71–8).

tail[1] v Cp OED ~ v[1] 13 for *tailing to the collar*; OED 20 b for *tail on*.

Phr *tailing to the collar*: of a small boat, taut to its mooring; see COLLAR 1.

C 66–2 If a fisherman looks out through his window and sees the boat *tailing* to its *collar* with the stern out, he has to go to the other shore to fish.

tail off: to assign (to a task).

1924 ENGLAND 182 You'll come into collar, from now on, an' when you're tailed off to do a job, you'll do it?

tail on: to take hold (of a line) and haul.

1924 ENGLAND 152 An' we had tillers an' wheel ropes, an' sometimes the men used to get knocked out. There'd be three or four men on each side, tailed on to the ropes. Ibid 185 Rains came, and the hunters disguised themselves in black or yellow oilskins that gleamed as they *tramp-tramp-tramped* the decks, or tailed on rope hauling up ballast.

tail[2] v also **teel** OED ~ v[3] local var of till

(1862–1901); *EDD* teel v[1] 4: var tail, teil s w cties; *DC* esp Nfld (1770–1941). To bait or set a trap or snare; to place a weapon so that game is shot when the device is triggered.

[1770] 1792 CARTWRIGHT i, 28 We observed many signs of porcupines and several rubbing places: I tailed a couple of old traps on two of them, near the entrance of the creek. [1776] ibid ii, 153 I shot a grouse and tailed two guns for the wolf, which had not been in my walk last night. 1819 ANSPACH 378 The common expression for fixing properly this engine of destruction is, *to tail a trap*. [1886] 1915 HOWLEY 270 He ran back towards his salmon house where he had a gun tailed, but he fell dead before reaching it. 1916 GRENFELL 12 This particular trap had been tailed, as he knew, on the top of an old stump which they had fixed in a very narrow part of the pathway. The stump had been selected to prevent the trap from being snowed deep under. 1937 DEVINE 51 Tail a trap. To set a trap. Also *tale, teel*. T 143/4–65[1] He tailed a gun for the wolf an' killed un. T 203/5–65 Well the secret of gettin' the fox was tailin' the slips out on the sticks across the river. We tailed five slips on one river there an' we was gone from 'em a week. An' when we went back we had two foxes. 1967 FIRESTONE 106 A man may go out alone to *teel slips* [set snares]. . . The single man will teel his slips out over a certain section and is careful to remember the location of each one. M 70–28 They found some fresh rabbit's 'buttons' and this was the lead they needed. Then they 'tailed' a slip. They did this by hanging the slip from the limb near the ground or from a stick, driven at an angle into the ground. The slip was camouflaged with boughs. Running along the lead a rabbit would stick its neck in the slip. 1973 GOUDIE 50 I travelled with my father when I was growing up, fishing and tailing rabbit snares.

tailing n A short length of rope attaching the ring of a small anchor, or 'graple,' to the mooring rope.

P 127–77 The purpose of the tailing is to ensure the retrieval of the grapelin if its claws become hooked in the sea-bed. The rode is tied to the claws of the grapelin and attached to the opposite, the ring end, by the tailing. If the grapelin snags, the strain to retrieve it will break the tailing (which is usually made from a much smaller rope than the rode) and the grapelin can then be pulled away from the direction of the grapelin hooks, thus freeing it.

taint v also **tant***, **tint*** [tɛint, 'tɛntɹd, 'tæntɹd]. To remove hair from animal skins by storing in a warm, moist place for a few days (P 13–79).

P 236–59 ~ to cure sealskins for making 'skin boots' by a process of drying and bleaching. T 94–64 First they had to taint it. They had to get the hair off. . . It's confined there, no air at it. 'Tis tainted. The skin is tainted and we got to bark it. T 199–65 I've heard the old fellers say, you know, they'd soak [it in] water because [the skins] were tanted and the hair was pulled out of the skin. If you pull the hair out, the hair makes a hole in the outside part of the skin, and the water soaks in through the pores in the flesh, because 'tis a 'tented' skin. P 54–67 Tinted [describes] a skin whose fur hairs have come out. P 13–79 Take off that cap, or your head will tint!

taiscown See TAYSCAUN.

take v Cp *OED* ~ v 5 'to strike, hit, impinge upon' for sense 1; cp *OED* 7 e for sense 2; for phr in sense 5 cp *DAE* 7 a to take hold 'to apply oneself'; *Cent* v: to take up (m) for sense (b).

1 To receive the force of a storm or the pressure of ice.

[1862] 1916 MURPHY 30 I then took the ice with a heavy breeze of wind from the N.N.E to E.N.E and a tremendous sea running. T 23–64 And there was two more vessels come out of Gibraltar when we did, out through the Straits of Gibraltar, going to St John's; and they went away southern and we come over western and took a gale of wind.

2 To suffer (an illness).

1960 FUDGE 44 I took an attack of paralysis, and now in 1956, at the age of 76, I am practically an invalid. T 50/1–64 But she sove his life by goin'. The day he got ready to go he took a wonderful pain across his stomach, an' when he got in Lewisporte he was nearly delirious with pain. T 54/63–64 He buried 'em all as 'cordin' as they died. But after they were all dead an' buried, he took the flu.

3 To reach or achieve a certain age.

T 187–65 I took my eighty-second year the thirteenth day o' July gone.

4 To become angry or irritable.

1924 ENGLAND 144 He used to take [get angry] at de laysses' little t'ing. He'd swear at ye one minute, an' give ye a piece of his heart, de nex'. 1937 DEVINE 51 Call that fellow 'Foxey' and he'll *take* right away. P 245–55 To take [means] to become angry at teasing.

5 Phr *take hold* imp [tɛɪk 'oʊɫd, teɪk 'oʊɫ]: to set to.

1887 *Evening Telegram Christmas No* 9 Draw over now, and take hold. You must want your supper, I'm sure. P 237–77 'Take hold' is often said by a member of the household to a stranger or visitor while eating a meal. In this context the phrase implies 'don't be shy! Help yourself to whatever you see on the table.' 'Take hold' is often used in a work situation involving father and son. They might be sawing wood, the father having hold [of] one end of the bucksaw while the son just looks on. It is then common for the father to say to the son, 'take hold, boy.'

take to go: to run away.

P 148–66 We saw the man coming, and we took to go.

take trouble: to sorrow, grieve (for another); cp TROUBLE.

1937 DEVINE 51 ~ To sorrow, especially over bereavement.

take up: (a) to remove split and salted cod from the drying flake in order to place it in a 'pile': see 1972 quot; (b) to obtain supplies up to the value of the fish delivered to the merchant or on credit against the next season's catch.

1887 *Colonist Christmas No* 5 I settled down in a good place in Trinity Bay, cleared land every year,

bought a horse, cattle and sheep. I never took up any supplies; sold all my fish for cash, and bought everything for ready money. 1895 PROWSE 439 A graphic account is given of the outfitting, tallying, seals, and settling the shareman's accounts, the wrangle over what was 'took up'; all the phases of out-harbour life in the thirties are admirably told. 1917 *Christmas Echo* 18 Having 'taken up' a third of his summer's wages in an outfit for the fishery, the youngster was quartered among the sharemen in the cookroom. 1972 MURRAY 248 There was a certain pattern to be followed in spreading and 'taking up' fish at different stages of cure. It was first taken up with a small fish placed over a large one, both back up. Care had to be taken with big 'pickle' fish when taking them up for the first time, especially if it were a Saturday. Sunday might be hot and the big ones might sunburn if left unshielded. Next evening we put four fish together, heads and tails. 1975 BUTLER 61 Two cents, that was the price at that time. No cash. Had to take it up [i.e. take payment in kind], for example, if you wanted tobacco or something. 1976 HOLLETT 9 Well they would give you a note, a slip, blue note we call it. According as you want any you go over. . .to pass him in. [Well] you take him up, take up all the note. 1979 TIZZARD 306 No cash was given [for our lobsters] so we had to 'take it up'; it was a barter business. That day I brought home a pound of tea, five pounds of sugar [etc].

take n See TAKE v 4. A touchy, easily-offended person.

1925 *Dial Notes* v, 344 ~ One who easily takes offense. P 245–55 Oh, don't be such a take!

taker n In the game of marbles, a marble or ally pitched so close to that of an opponent that ownership can be claimed.

C 70–20 If the second ally alighted in a spot so near that of the former that the second player was able to 'completely cover' both allies with the fingers of one hand, it was declared a *taker*. . .and the second player promptly claimed the ally of this opponent.

talk v *EDD* ~ v 1 (8) ~ to a woman Ir; *ADD* v 2 talk to for sense 1.

1 Esp in phr *talk to*: of a young man, to court (a girl).

1924 ENGLAND 251–2 *I* didn't know he was talkin' to [courting] de girl I danced wid. P 108–70 He is talking to Mary since the month of May. C 70–16 'They're talking' means that a particular couple is 'going steady.' C 75–140 If a fellow was going with a girl for a year or so my grandmother would say that he was 'talking to her' for a year or so now.

2 In various collocations, *don't talk, you talk (about)*: an expression of wonder, disbelief.

T 283–66 'Oh,' he said, 'don't be talkin',' he said, 'miss.' 'I've got a handsome fish,' he said, 'prettier than they two I got.' C 71–128 'I got tired and went home and who should I find waiting for me? John Smith!' [listener:] 'You talk about that!' 1975 BUTLER 47 We got forty two fathoms. Now talk about. Not many navigators could do that. I couldn't believe it hardly. He was right, that's where we were to.

tally¹ n   *OED* ~ sb¹ 5 d (1886–), *EDD* 6 for sense 1; for combs. in sense 2: *EDD* sb 1 (1) ~ board; cp *OED* tallyman 2 (1888–); *OED* sb¹ 9 ~ stick (1895).

1 In keeping account of the number of seal pelts, dried cod, etc, being handled, the last of a sequence of numbers, esp *five*, forming a single group.

[c1830] 1890 GOSSE 58 One of the crew that has climbed up begins to lay [the seal pelts] one by one, fur downward, on the barrow; singing out, as he lays down each, 'One-two-three-four-tally,' I at each one making a mark on my paper. . .instead of the word 'five,' the word 'tally' is used, for then I am to make a diagonal line across the four marks, and this formula is called 'a tally.' 1924 ENGLAND 275 What's the other pound take? Two or three tallies, eh? Good enough! 1933 GREENE 192 An extra pelt being added to each twenty sculps to complete a sealing 'tally.' T 393–67 An' they wouldn't weigh their fish puttin' it 'board. They always counted their fish—so many fish, whatever 'twas, an' then they'd say, 'Tally.' You know what tally means—the five strokes. M 67–16 For each tub [of fish] salted a stroke would be marked on the stage wall. When five tubs had been dipped out, this would warrant a tally. You would then hear two or three men sing out at the same time, 'Tally.' C 71–130 When it came time to 'take up' the potatoes, [he] always prepared to keep tally. As each bucket of potatoes was brought to the cellar door he would make a stroke with a pencil on a piece of paper or on a board. Four parallel strokes would be crossed with a fifth stroke.

2 Cpd, comb: **tally board**: (a) plank or wooden table on which dried cod-fish are placed for counting and grading; CULLING BOARD (P 40–78); (b) flat board on which the count of fish caught by a Bank fisherman is marked (P 2–82); cp **tally stick**.

tally fish: cod with colour markings on its back resembling the slant strokes made in keeping count, and thought to presage a good catch; SNUB¹.

C 69–5 [He] believed that if he caught a tally fish there was a skiff-load of codfish forthcoming. A tally fish is one that has a lot of bright black marks on its sides.

tally-man: man employed by fish merchant or sealing firm to keep record of salted cod, seal pelts, etc, handled.

1857 *Courier* 6 May [p. 2] [He was appointed] tally man as the authorized agent of the owner. 1860 TAYLOR 283 He even consented to keep tally of the quintals of dried codfish which his men were carrying on board of a schooner lying below his storehouse, in order that his tally-man, John Butt by name, might act as our pilot over the marshy hills. 1894 CHAFE 7 John Rowe, Tallyman. [c1921] 1960 BURKE (ed White) 15 "Cotton's Patch": The merchants assembled, the great Board of Trade, / And ten cents a seal was the price that they paid, / For every seal that the tally man gave, / And so far we haven't the price of a shave. 1966 *Daily News* 16 Feb, p. 4 He replied that 'my grandfather was engaged in the fishing industry.' This left me

open to wonder if the old gent was a fish merchant, a culler, a tallyman. . . 1976 CASHIN 50–1 Each evening the tallyman came to the office and gave in his returns to Jim Foley, who had charge of the large fish book. This book gave the names, the quantities in quintals of the various qualities of fish received from each dealer or fisherman, as the case may be. When the receipts were made out and each quality priced by one of the Messrs Bowring, the total values were extended and checked.

tally stick: stick notched in keeping count of seal pelts, salted cod, etc; cp **tally board** (b).

1924 ENGLAND 141–2 . . .a vague figure at the hatchway, tallying the sculps. He held in his hands a 'tally stick' and a clasp knife, and cut a notch for every five pelts, a groove for every twenty-one, that in the final reckoning would count only as twenty.

tally² n   also **tally man**. Cp BERREY 52 ~ 'Italy.' Person with swarthy complexion and foreign features.

P 245–55 Tallies are St John's citizens of Syrian descent. P 148–61 [He's] a tally man, right dark. P 245–79 Do you remember him? He was the tally lived on Middle Street.

tally³ n   See TILLY.

tally¹ v   *OED* ~ v¹ 1 'to notch (a stick) so as to make a tally' obs (c1440–1706); *EDD* 13 'to reckon by fives.' To keep count of the number of cod-fish, seal pelts, logs, etc, being handled usu by making notches on a stick, particularly in sequences of five; often with *down, in*.

1905 GRENFELL 124 The fish when dried and 'tallied in' to the merchant on our return are sent to the Mediterranean and Brazilian markets, and to the West Indies. 1913 *FPU (Twillingate) Minutes* 19 Sep It [was] then proposed and second[ed] that the man who bought a ton of coal should pay 5 cents per ton to pay for the man who tallys them. There was an amendment made that 5 cents be deducted from the bill to pay for tallying. 1924 ENGLAND 52 As for the common hands, they have nothing much to do except steer, shift ballast and coal, hunt seals, kill them, skin them and drag the sculps aboard, load sculps and tally them down, and do a lot of other painful, dangerous and laborious tasks. 1925 *Dial Notes* v, 344 To tally down. To note (one's number of seals) on a tally stick. T 393/4–67 There's five strokes, if you are tallyin' fish. C 68–26 This man also 'tallied' (i.e. kept count of the number of hogsheads brought out). 1976 CASHIN 62 I was ordered by father to tally the number of pieces of ice hauled by each horse and slide, whilst in addition I was compelled to work in the ice house stowing the ice. P 231–76 The men had to discharge [seals] when they come in, they had to throw them in a jig, an old fashioned jig, and they were weighed on a swinging beam, and the tally man would tally it down. P 245–78 I saw him tally the logs by putting one chip of wood in his pocket for each log, and then transferring the chips to another pocket each time he had accumulated five.

tally² v

1 To jump from one floating ice-pan to another; COPY; cp TABBY v, TIPPY v (Q 67–14).

C 75–132 Tallying is the art of jumping from ice pan to ice pan. Children usually tally in a protected cove in shallow water.

2 Comb **tally pan**: small pan of floating ice on which boys leap in the sport of 'copying' (M 71–104).

C 75–132 Tally pans [are] small ice pans used to float on in shallow water.

tallying vbl n The keeping count or record of the number of cod-fish, seals, etc, received by a merchant.

1895 PROWSE 439 A graphic account is given of the outfitting, tallying, seals, and settling the shareman's accounts, the wrangle over what was 'took up'; all the phases of out-harbour life in the thirties.

tallywack n Rascal; scalawag.

1970 JANES 144 'How case-hardened are they a-tall!' he squealed. 'How pig-headed! Even this young tallywack. . . I might just as well be talkin' to the stove.'

tallywacking vbl n Cp *EDD* talliwap sb obs 'a blow.' A thrashing given to a misbehaving child.

P 89–66 ~ Whacking with a slipper; spanking.
P 108–70 Come in this minute, or I'll give you a good tallywackin'!

tal qual av phr also **all quall, tal squal, tol squoll**. Cp *NID* ~ [L *talis qualis* 'such as'] 'just as they come.' Designating a quoted price for a whole catch of dried and salted cod sold without differentiation of quality or size; sometimes used as a noun and attrib; cp CULL v.

[c1894] PANL P4/14, p. 196 Tal qual, sometimes called *all qualls*, fish bought without culling is clearly the Latin *talis qualis*, 'such as it is.' 1896 *J A Folklore* ix, 31 In the prices current in the newspapers one may see fish distinguished as *tol squolls* or *tal squals* and quoted at certain figures. [1911] 1930 COAKER 30 Fish would not have advanced beyond $5.50 talqual this season if the FPU did not exist. [1913] 1954 INNIS 462 It may truthfully be said that there is no cull of fish to be standardized, all fish being bought tal qual. 1928 *FPU (Twillingate) Minutes* 5 Oct [He] said that tal qual fish was $8.20 and Spanish $9 and cullage $5 in Port Union today. 1933 *Nfld Royal Commission Report* 105 During the War years, quantity rather than quality became the ruling consideration; the 'cull' was therefore dispensed with and fish were bought on what is known as the 'tal-qual' system, viz., an average price was fixed for the whole of a fisherman's catch without any exact regard to the varying qualities of the fish comprising the catch. 1937 DEVINE 51 ~ As to qualities of fish, it means taking the good and middling at the same price. P 127–73 He bought thirty quintals of tal qual. P 209–73 ~ Good and bad fish together.

tan n Cp *OED* ~ sb¹ 2 'the astringent principle contained in oak-bark; tannin.' Comb **tan boiler**, ~ **pot**: iron cauldron in which an infusion of the bark and 'buds' of conifers is prepared for the preservation of nets, sails, etc; BARK n: ~ POT.

P 140–70 Tan Pot. Large pot for boiling tan. Nets are then dipped into it to strengthen the twine. 1975 BUTLER 76 The house owners would get one hundred gallon size tan boilers, clean them out spotless clean and set them up outdoors.

tangler n Cp *OED* ~ (c1520); *EDD* 7 'thriftless, slatternly person.' A clumsy, disorganized person (P 148–62).

P 108–74 He's a proper tangler. Why, he'd tangle up the Lord himself! C 75–15 ~ A person who, no matter what he went at, he fooled it up. He couldn't do anything right.

tank n A water receptacle with tap for public use in a neighbourhood.

[1851] 1976 O'NEILL ii, 476 In 1851 four public tanks and reservoirs were erected in the town. . . A second reservoir on Cuddihy Street, which became known as Tank Lane, held thirty thousand gallons of water. 1891 *Holly Branch* 19 "Tank Talk": To wait their 'turn' and scold, and talk, / Around the public tank. 1927 [BURKE] "Stoppage of Water" [broadside]: It is hard on [the] poor who must go to the tanks, / And their water works stopped just to please a few cranks. 1973 *Evening Telegram* 26 May, p. 8 It's a wonder that the people of substance don't have a Gosling's jam pot or a tank outside the door.

tannel* n also **tanner***. Cp *talon*. Cat's claw; by extension, child's finger-nail (P 235–70).

tanner*¹ See TANNEL*.

tanner*² See TURNER.

tansy¹ n *EDD* ~ sb¹ 4 'leaf of the tansy'; 1 (4) ~ tea. The leaves of the common yarrow (*Achillea millefolium*), an infusion of which is used in home-remedies and cooking; also attrib.

[1766 (1971)] BANKS 303 *Achillea millefolium* 1 grassy Places Croque.] 1916 HAWKES 37 ~ Makes an effective tea for colds. 1919 GRENFELL² 145 [He was] amazed to see many of his erstwhile patients wending their way seawards, each with one eye treated on his prescription [for snow-blindness] but the other (for safety's sake) doctored after the long-accepted methods of the talent of the village—tansy poultices and sugar being the acknowledged favourites. T 50/2–64 [When] you get swellin', they call information, on your limbs, they dry tansy an' steep that out, bathe it in that hot liquor, tansy water. Good for swellin'. T 187/8–65 My mother had my throat all done right up wi' tansy poultice for to pitch the swellin'. C 68–23 She remembered drinking tansy tea when she was young. One of the boys would go out and pick what we used to call tansy leaves. [She] used to steep the leaves just like you steep tea. We used to drink it for colds. 1972 MURRAY 257 They grew herbs like tansy, mints, and chives, used in medicines and cooking. 1979 TIZZARD 141 The remedy [for snow-blindness] was tansy boiled and a poultice made from this and put on the eyes.

tansy² n *EDD* ~ sb² D. Rock gunnel, a small eel-like salt-water fish (*Pholis gunnellus*); also attrib.

1937 DEVINE 51 ~ A tiny, eel-like fish living in small salt water pools on the beaches, called 'tansy ponds.' T 36–64 Well, he looks like a small eel, but not so round. Thin and flat—tansy, we call un. An' they live under the rocks. When you rise up a rock below water now probably you see three or four of them. 1967 *Nfld Qtly* June, p. 10 And when one foraged along the edge of the sea, peering in pools, gently lifting kelp fronds to surprise what might lurk beneath, collecting tansies (which I presume are blennies) in cans of sea water, marvelling at the flowering anemones (which we called suckers), which at the merest touch became blobs of red brown jelly. . . 1973 WIDDOWSON 540 We were really scared of getting in the water, which was salt bay water, and feeling a tansy around our feet. They are long thin fish that coil around you like a snake and I think they live only in salt water. 1975 GUY 15 A tansie is a small thing like an eel brown on the back and yellowish sort of on the gut and they are under rocks, too.

tant a also **taunt**. Cp *OED* taunt a 2 'of masts, excessively tall or lofty' naut (1622–) for sense 1.

1 Of a mast, tall; straight, slender, well-proportioned; cp SUANT.

[c1900] 1978 *RLS* 8, p. 23 ~ Tall & straight, such as. . .a tant mast. 1937 DEVINE 51 ~ Tall, graceful; said of the mast of a vessel. C 71–44 ~ said when talking about the mast of a ship. P 245–76 Mr Berkshire have a new boat and she's some tant.

2 Of a tree, tall, slender, straight; collectively of timber-land forested with such trees.

1861 *Harper's* xxii, 747 'Did these masts grow up the Bay?' 'I suppose. Big tant wood up the bay.' [c1900] 1978 *RLS* 8, p. 23 ~ Tall & straight, such as a tant tree. 1919 GRENFELL² 231 The problem was all the more interesting as we struck only 'taunt' timberwoods with no undergrowth to halt the wind. 1923 GRENFELL 277 He's been away in the country cutting saw logs in the 'tant' (tall) woods, I reckon. T 26–64³ 'Twas trees growing here as big as mastes for schooners; all woods, my son; all big, tant place—big, tant trees. 1965 *Evening Telegram* 5 Feb, p. 6 Older readers may know that a 'tant' tree is a firm, straight tree, from which a mast of a vessel could be made. T 210–65 That was birch anywhere from eight to nine feet in length, an' would be about four inches in the top, or perhaps not that; an' a very tant stick. P 109–70 We moved from tuck bushes into tant woods. T 283/968–71 'Well now,' he said, 'as I was goin' along,' he said, 'there was a big tant tree.' He said, 'An' I climbed right into the top o' the tree.' P 148–72 When a logger talks about getting into tant spruce or fir, he means good wood for pulpwood.

tant* See TAINT.

tap n Cp *EDD* ~ sb¹ 6 'sole of a boot' Do D Co. Phr *come to one's taps*: to get to one's feet.

T 54/60–64 Anyhow, I come to my taps an' I started

to run. I runned about hundred yards. Q 73–2 ~ Suddenly getting on one's feet.

tar n Cp *OED* ~ sb 4 ~ pot (a) 'a pot containing tar' (1573, 1641 quots).

Comb **tar barrel**: container for tar, set ablaze as a signal or to celebrate 5 November; cp BONFIRE NIGHT.

[1891] [c1977] WINSOR (ed) 49 So they determined to get him off [the rock], if possible. They set fire to a tar barrel so that the man on the rock might see it. 1977 *Decks Awash* vi (3), p. 54 On bonfire night he used to have a tar barrel put outside for the boys who'd be going around getting stuff for the bonfire. . . They would set the tar barrel afire then, and you could see the fire for miles around.

tar mop: swab used to apply tar to roof, boat, etc.

[1952] 1965 PEACOCK (ed) i, 130 "For the Fish We Must Prepare": Oh tar-mops and bark-pots, / And fishin' caplin to the rocks. T 39–64 Now that was a good item, a pink London smoke, at that time. You wouldn't use [it] for a tar-mop now! P 6–79 I cut off two tar mops one mornin'. I was hardy den goin' to school all de time. I went down one mornin' I wadn't able to get de fire goin'.

tar pot: (a) heavy iron vessel with heated preservative for fishing gear; BARK n: ~ POT (1971 NOSEWORTHY 254); (b) large box anchored in water and filled with live lobsters; LOBSTER BOX (1971 NOSEWORTHY 254).

tare n Cp *OED* ~ sb² 'the weight of the wrapping. . .containing goods, which is deducted from the gross in order to ascertain the net weight.' In valuing seal 'pelts,' the number of pounds deducted from the total weight for the worthless flesh adhering to the skin and blubber; BACK av: ~ WEIGHT.

[1843] 1923 CHAFE 40 Bought of Captain Azariah Munden. . .Tare 1½ lb. on young seals and tare on old seals as may appear. 1924 ENGLAND 170 They may grouse a bit concerning the low price of fat and extortion of 'tare,' or 'back weight,' for adherent flesh that sticks to the fat; that is always reckoned as sticking to it, no matter how clean they peel the sculps. That tare is counted off at the rate of from a pound and a half on white coats up to seven pounds on old dog hoods. 1929 *Nat Geog* July, p. 130 There's usually a pound to a pound and a half of meat and hair to a whitecoat sculp. This is called tare.

tatie n also **tatey, teddy*, tetty*, tiddy*, titty***, etc. ['tɛ·tɪ·, 'tɛʊ̯t̪i·] *EDD* ~ sb 'potato', 1 (16) ~ cake (Co quot 'fat pork an' tatie-cake').

1 Potato, usu pl; PRATIE.

1920 GRENFELL & SPALDING 41 The women hang forever over the stove or the washtub, go into the stages to split the fish, or into the gardens to grow 'taties.' P 259–67 I'm going to peel some taties now. C 71–40 My teddies didn't turn out good this year. C 71–130 Aside from forming part of every dinner and most suppers, taties kept us busy from spring to fall.

There was the ground preparation, the spreading of manure, drilling, setting of the potato cutting, spreading of fertilizer, covering with clay from the drills, weeding, spreading caplin.

2 Comb **tatie pork-cake**: variety of cake or bun made with flour, mashed potatoes and pork; freq in children's rhyme when playing ducks and drakes.

P 267–58 ~s. Small baked cakes of potato, pork, flour. C 66–7 In Grand Bank they usually have pea soup for dinner on Saturday, [but] sometimes they substitute titty pork cakes made of potato and pork fried in a pan. 1976 *Daily News* 24 Feb, p. 3 It was considered a respectable effort if your stone skimmed the surface long enough for you to recite, not too fast: 'A duck and a drake and a tatey pork cake and a dory's stern'. . . The recipe, if I remember correctly, called for potatoes, fat back pork, flour and baking powder.

tatie shovel: long-handled spade with triangular blade.

C 71–123 The tatie shovel was used most often for shovelling up drills for potato plants.

tatter n Phr *every tatter*: every stitch of canvas or sail.

1936 SMITH 12 The next command was to loosen the two top gallant sails, and it wasn't long before Skipper Job. . .had every tatter on her.

tattle-tongue n Cp *NID* tattletale. Child who tells tales on another.

1971 NOSEWORTHY 254 ~ A children's nickname for one who tattles. P 11–79 ~ a person who cannot keep things to himself.

tatty v To jump from one floating ice-pan to another (P 148–67); cp TABBY v.

taunt See TANT.

taut a Of an ice-floe, tight against (the land); solidly frozen; cp SLACK v.

1887 BOND 59 The ice will be taut on the land.

taut* n See TAWT.

tavern n Long-stemmed tobacco pipe with large bowl (Q 67–8).

T 70/2–64¹ They'd get [pipes] that length—taverns, they used to call 'em. You'd have to reach your arms out to the bowl. That was the thing to smoke out o'!

tawt n also **taut, thawt, thort** [ðɑːt, tɒːt, tɔːt] *OED* thought², thaught now dial (1622–1886), thoft north dial (1000–); ELMER 106–8 [thoughts] s and e coasts of England, [tawts] two ports in Wales. See *OED* thwart sb² (1736–) for the unclear relations between that standard term and thought².

1 A board across an undecked boat on which rower sits, often with specifying word *after, forward, midship*; thwart.

1937 DEVINE 51 Thorts. Seats of rowers on a boat;

thwarts. P 133–58 Taut: thwart. T 14/6–64 And the aft-tawt will be about two inches shorter than the midship-tawt because the after-tawt goes on the bed of timber between the after-hook and the midship timber. T 43/8–64 From the bow tawt to the after tawt is her carrying capacity, plus a small after room. 1966 HORWOOD 147 If I had to make you into either a book-keeper or a fisherman I'd see you stay in the trap boat until your arse grew fast to the taut!

2 Proverb *your tawts are too far aft*: you are very wrong in your opinion [with a play on *t'oughts*] (1955 ENGLISH 40).

tayscaun n also **taiscown** JOYCE 340 thiescaun; DINNEEN taoscán 'small quantity.' A small amount of anything.

1925 *Dial Notes* v, 344 Taiscown—a small bit of pork. 1937 DEVINE 51 A poor woman would say: 'Would you give me a tayscaun of tea[?]' 1968 DILLON 157 ~ a small amount of wood, hay, liquor, etc., half a load. 'Twas a poor path today; I only had a tayscawn. That drop he gave me, sure that was only a tayscawn.

T D n also **T D pipe** *DA* T II 2 ~ (1889, 1947). Brand-name of a type of clay tobacco-pipe; SCOOTER.

1898 *Christmas Bells* 14 Men of Tom's position were quite autocratic. . .smoked a wooden pipe with a bone mouthpiece, connected by a brass ferule, while the ordinary hands used only a 'T.D.' [1901] 1927 DOYLE (ed) 9 "The Outharbour Planter": And he hooked a coal from the bar-room stove, and set his T.D. pipe aglow. 1937 DEVINE 51 T.D. pipe. A common clay pipe. T 208–65 An' there was an' ol' jostler there   call him an' ol' feller—he had a whisker, you know, an' a home-knit guernsey on, little T.D. pipe stuck in his face, not sayin' nothing. M 68–11 At a wake, T.D. pipes were placed with a dish of tobacco on a table. As the men came, they took a pipe, filled it with tobacco and smoked. These clay pipes cost two cents each. 1973 JELKS 74 The pipes [excavated at the fort on Signal Hill] are of fine-textured, white earthenware paste. None are glazed. . . These pipe bowls have initials or other markings that evidently were intended to identify the maker or distributor. . .seven bear only the initials TD on the proximal side of the bowl roughly a third of the way down the length of the bowl.

tea n Cp *OED* ~ sb 4 'a meal or social entertainment at which tea is served' for senses 1, 2; *OED* 5 for sense 3; for combs. in sense 4: *EDD* sb 1 (21) ~ meeting Bk Co; (36) ~ towel. See also CUP OF TEA, MUG UP.

1 The principal domestic evening meal.

1893 *Christmas Bells* 14 Well, when we got home with a full load of about thirty qtls round fish, it was nearly evening and I said we'd commence to split after tea. 1910 *Nfld Qtly* Oct, p. 23 A hurried tea, and out with our boats! 1924 ENGLAND 65 That night, after tea (they never have 'supper' aboard a sealer), the Doctor entertained us with some natural history. 1932 POLUNIN 30 Over an early and very good 'tea'—the main meal of the day, after midday dinner—the whole business was discussed. 1945 *Atlantic Guardian* Jan, p.

16 Then he found out that the 'Newfies,' as the islanders are sometimes called by one another and by the Americans, refer to supper as 'tea.' 1970 JANES 37 Our tea, as we always called our evening meal. . . 1973 WIDDOWSON 240 She wanted do go down town one day and I said, 'We'll go next week after tea when the stores are lit up and all the lights on.'

2 An afternoon or early evening communal gathering at which a light meal is offered for sale; the food so offered; commonly with defining word *meat, turkey*, etc; cp TIME.

1964 *Evening Telegram* 2 Oct, p. 2 The president informed the members of the 'take out turkey teas' to be held Oct 15. M 66–10 There [were] also plain and meat teas. The meat teas included ham, salad and tea. The plain tea was just tea and cake and cookies and bread. P 148–66 The most important social function for the year [was] the temperance tea. 1975 GUY 90 Generally they had Meat Teas or Soup Suppers [at the Sale of Work]. This was bully beef and potato salad of different sorts. Then jelly and blanc mange and partridge berry tarts and cakes and figgy buns and tea. 1979 TIZZARD 223 Sometime in January the Orangemen would set a date for their parade, church service and tea.

3 An infusion of the leaves, roots, etc, of a variety of plants, other than the tea-plant, used medicinally or as a drink. See INDIAN TEA, LABRADOR ~ , SAFFRON, SPRUCE TEA, TANSY[1].

1778 DE CASSINI 140 The most common plant I met with at St Pierre, is a kind of tea; (at least the inhabitants call it so) its leaf is woolly underneath, and it greatly resembles our rosemary, both in leaf and stalk. [1883] 1963 GARLAND 25 Instead. . .she brewed a tea by steeping young spruce boughs in hot water. C 68–23 She used to boil the roots of dogwood trees [and] always had plenty of this tea on hand for anyone who had the worms.

4 Attrib, comb **teaberry**: crowberry; CURLEW BERRY (*Empetrum* spp) (1956 ROULEAU 38).

tea bun: small cake or soft biscuit served with tea (P 148–61).

1974 PINSENT 77 They had their refreshments, which included tea-buns and bakeapple jam.

tea fish: caplin for domestic consumption; cp BREAKFAST FISH.

P 108–70 Caplin were called 'tea fish' because they were supposed to make you sleepy after eating them, so they were eaten at the evening meal, 'tea,' instead of the middle of the day.

tea-flower: purple-stemmed aster (*Aster puniceus*) (1956 ROULEAU 38); PITNAGEN.

tea-meeting: prayer-meeting with tea and cake served.

1936 DULEY 55 If you'd go to the tea-meetin's with your friends you wouldn't be so silent.

tea towel: cup-towel.

1958 *Nfld Dishes* 29 Turn into a clean tea towel sprinkled with icing sugar.

teak n Cp *OED* teague [teg] 'nickname for an Irishman'; *EDD* teague 'contemptuous name for an Irishman. . .a plague of a person'; DINNEEN tadhg 'Teague or Thady. . .the typical Irishman.'

1 One of the elaborately dressed pranksters who go about during Christmas holidays; FOOL, JANNY n, MUMMER n, OWNSHOOK.

1896 *J A Folklore* ix, 36 . . .*old teaks* and *jannies*, boys and men who turn out in various disguises and carry on various pranks during the Christmas holidays.

2 Attrib **teak day**: January 6th; Old Christmas day, on which certain mummers customarily appeared.

C 70–25 The last day of Christmas was called teak day. It was usually celebrated by children [who] dressed up in old clothes and with a stick; they went about cracking everyone they saw. C 71–21 Teak day was the sixth of January when everyone had to wear a piece of green ribbon anywhere on their person as long as it was visible to the young people outdoors. Children would be ready with sticks to crack you if you dared to go outdoors without a piece of green ribbon.

tee n A T-shaped, roofed section of fishing premises where fish is processed; SPLITTING STAGE, ~ TEE.

M 69–17 In the drawing the splitting table is in the stage itself, but it was more customary at Elliston to have a place called a 'Tee' right on the stage head, as in the picture of Bonavista; and it was here that the splitting took place.

teel See TAIL[2].

teeveen n also **theeveen*** [tiːˈviːn, ˈtiːviːn, θiːˈviːn] JOYCE 340 theeveen; DINNEEN taobh 'side,' taoibhín 'side-patch, a side-wedge.' A patch put on the upper part of a shoe or boot; a wedge put in the sole of a shoe.

1925 *Dial Notes* v, 344 ~ A patch on a boot. 1937 DEVINE 51 ~ a small patch on a boot. P 148–65 When he wanted a shim or wedge inserted between the inner and outer sole of his shoe in order to throw the shoe inward and outward to correct a foot ailment he would request the cobbler to put in a teeveen. 1968 DILLON 157 ~ leather patch on the upper part of a boot or shoe, sewn on with needle and thread. C 71–99 Instead of casting the boots aside, a theeveen was sewed over the hole and the boots were worn again as if new.

tell the roast See BLOW THE ROAST.

terrible a, intens *EDD* ~ adv 3, *ADD* 2 for sense 1; *ADD* adj Nfld for sense 2.

1 Very, extremely.

1863 MORETON 33 A terrible kind man. 1895 *J A Folklore* viii, 40 One may be described as 'terrible good.' Q 67–97 Terrible nice fellow.

2 Remarkable (1925 *Dial Notes* v, 344).

th- *Note*: Words with *th*, as in *thin* and *then*, are often pronounced and written locally with some variant of *t* or *d*. They are entered here according to the standard spelling.

thank v Cp *OED* ~ v 3 f thank one for nothing
(1703–1754). Phr *I thank you*: (a) indeed; you
know; (b) an ironical expression.
1968 DILLON 158 She got another new dress on 'er
today, I thank you. Ibid 'Here,' he says, 'I got a present for you.' A present, I thank you, and he payin' me
me own money.

that sg subs *EDD* ~ 5 (1) and that 'and so forth';
JOYCE 10–11: that's what he is.
   Phr *and that*: 'you know what I mean'; and so
on.
T 158–65 Plenty of grass, a nice place to live. A tickle
to go down through with the boats and that. T 375–67
A bunker is a great big ally, an' there's all colours and
that. 1977 *Inuit Land Use* 212 They're going to want
seal to eat, and that, you know, and all that thing.
   that it is, etc: affirmative following a sentence;
indeed.
1906 *Nfld Qtly* Dec, p. 5 'I'm sure in your experience
you've seen and heard some queer things.' 'That I
have,' said the [Captain]. 1939 DULEY 14 'Woman,
[the baby is] powerful light from stem to stern.' 'That
she is, Benedict!' C 70–12 'Dat it is' was used at the
beginning of a conversation when the person didn't
want any interruption or any contradiction. It was a
sign that he knew without question what he was talking
about.

thatch n Clothing; gear or equipment; RIG n;
TACKLING.
[1900 OLIVER & BURKE] 46 . . .coming in from the
outports with their thatch (box, bag and gun). 1937
DEVINE 51 ~ Clothing. P 207–67 When she went out
she wore her best bit of tatch.

thaw See SILVER THAW.

thawt See TAWT.

the: the once; the year See TO.

theeveen* See TEEVEEN.

them pl det Those, used when specifying past
times; THESE; contrasts systematically with the
local use of THOSE.
1924 ENGLAND 148 Not much socialism an' ah-ner-
chism, in them days. T 41–64 So we used the curb
hooks at that day, them days. Now the hook you get
those days [= now] has a little eye into it, a little hole
in it. T 54/65–64 There was no radio, no telephone, no
nothing them times. T 246/7–66 Them days, if you knit
a pair o' mitts or a pair of socks, they were right fluffy.
1978 *Sat Night* Dec, p. 28 *Them Days* is a quarterly
magazine of oral history, circulation 4,000, published
out of Happy Valley.

thert* See ATHWART.

these pl det *EDD* ~ dem adj 3 'those.' Those,
used when specifying past times; THEM.
1909 BROWNE 178 Enormous 'bills' were made by
sealers in these days, and I have often heard old fisher-

men tell of the years they 'made a hundred pound'
($400.00). [c1928] BURKE "Don't You Remember the
Dump, Maggie" [broadside]: Oh, these were fine
happy days, Maggie, / The fine happy days that I spent.
1935 KEAN 127 As late as 1795 the total catch of seals
for Newfoundland only amounted to 4,900. In these
days the mode of prosecuting was by ice-boats.
T 43/8–64 In these days the wood was too heavy, but
now they can go out there an' pick off, pick off [wood].
P 143–74 Salt fish was real nice roasted on the open
wood fire when you boil up for lunch in the woods on
winter days—these happy days are gone forever.

thick a *OED* ~ a 7, *EDD* 4, *Atlantic Mo*
lxxxviii (1901) 53 thick o' fog (Maine) for sense
1; cp *OED* 4 'dense, crowded' for sense 2.
   1 Of the weather, with restricted visibility;
dense with fog, mist, rain or snow; esp phr *thick
o' fog*, etc.
[1668] 1963 YONGE 114 At 4 in the morning the wind
sprung up at E.S.E. and S.E. and by noon blew fresh
with rainy thick weather. [1771] 1792 CARTWRIGHT i,
168 Small rain in general, with thick weather. 1792
Liverpool MS July 30 They generally choose foggy
weather when they come near any place where our
people live; and it is wonderful how they find their way
about in the thickest fogs as they do. They will go to
the Funk Island, which is 15 leagues from the Main
Land, and return from it in the thickest weather. [1794]
1968 THOMAS 98–9 Had they been known the weather
was so thick that they could not a been made out.
[1857] 1916 MURPHY 28 We made Brigus, it was very
thick and heavy with snow, and sea, and in wearing her
around, they unhooked the throat halyards of the
mainsail. 1863 MORETON 36 In foggy weather it is said
to be 'tick o' vog.' [1886] LLOYD 119 Hardly ten minutes had elapsed, before we were overwhelmed in the
most furious snow-storm I had yet experienced in Newfoundland. So thick was it, that it was an impossibility
to see the dogs just a few feet before us. 1907 DUNCAN
100 ''Tis grown thick,' said he. ''Twill blow from the
east with fog an' rain.' T 70/1–64¹ They said she passed
there. Well, if she did she was lost. . .shoal ground,
inside the shoal ground. Made in there—thick, see.
T 194/5–65 An' I sot my course outside—thick, see, ol'
man. 1973 MOWAT 23 Come thick o' fog or starm o'
wind and snow, 'twere hard enough to make the land.
1977 *Nfld Qtly* Winter, p. 19 You couldn't see twice the
length of the vessel for wind and fog. It was right thick.
Ibid p. 20 It fell down thick a snow the last couple of
hours. You couldn't see a hand before you.
   2 Of fish, seals, mosquitoes, etc, in large numbers; NUMEROUS; THOUSAND.
1924 ENGLAND 77 Early next morning whitejackets
still were bawling not far off; not enough, perhaps, for
a 'rally,' but harbingers of 'de t'ick patch.' Q 67–12 The
fish is some thick today. C 68–24 [tall tale] I took off me
Cape Ann and me oil-jacket and put them on the
dought ['tawt']; the skitties (mosquitoes) was so thick
that when I slooed around they was lugging away me
clothes; one bunch had the Cape Ann, and another had
me oil-jacket. P 245–79 The squid were in and out [of
Trinity Bay] all summer, but now they're thick and
everybody is at [the fishing].

3 Designating a condition of the sea with a concentration of plankton in the upper layer of water obscuring a view of the bottom and favourable for fishing (P 245–79).

[1946] 1976 *Evening Telegram* 12 Jan, p. 6 Before anybody could lift a finger she had grounded by the stern on a large boulder which they had been unable to see because of 'thick water.'

thief n   Newfoundland grey jay (*Perisoreus canadensis sanfordi*).

1959 MCATEE 51 ~ Grey Jay (As a camp robber. Nfld., 'Labr.').

thigh n   Comb **thigh rubber**: rubber boot reaching to the thigh; LONG RUBBER, RUBBER (P 157–67).

1977 BUTLER 12–13 Billy lay on the bunk, his cap pulled over his ears, [woollen] mittens on his hands and thigh rubbers on his feet. He was unconscious. I thought at first he was dead. P 148–80 He is going to have to get his t'igh rubbers on to tow the car [from that boggy ditch].

thimble n   *EDD* ~ sb 1 (2) ~ pie. Comb **thimble pie**: a tap given, or threatened, with a thimble.

1973 WIDDOWSON 68 If you torment me when I'm sewing, I'll give you a thimble pie!

thirds n pl

1 A grade of dried and salted cod-fish, ranking in quality below 'merchantable' and 'madeira.'

1953 *Nfld Fish Develop Report* 42 Newfoundland's most important market in the Caribbean is Puerto Rico. It was developed originally as an outlet for semi-dried Labrador fish. . .but much the larger quantity exported there now consists of shore-cure fish of 'thirds' grade and 'tomcods.' 1955 *Nfld Fisheries Board No 23* ~ Hard-dried fish which cannot be classified as Madeira because of any or all of the following defects: excessively thin, very rough surface, badly split, over-salted, slightly cracked on face, slightly sunburnt or skin-heated, sound fish touched with dun or sound fish from which dun has been removed. T 36–64 The broken [fish] was West India, an' the thirds would be a little worse than Madeira an' a little better than West Indee. There'd be a spot on un here or a broken fin on un there, or a bit o' sunburn on the back or bit o' skin off. T 410–67 But the thirds now, that was not the low grade because the West Indee is the lowest grade, but thirds was the next to it.

2 Phr *catch thirds*: see CATCH v 3.

on the thirds, over the ~ : of the fastening of a fish-net, in a certain traditional fashion; cp HALF n: ON THE HALVES.

P 9–73 The number of feet or fathoms covered by ninety-eight meshes would depend on whether the linnet was brought to (fastened to) on the halves, the thirds, a bit under or over the halves or thirds. Ibid About four or five fathoms back from the doorway, the leader linnet along the head is stretched to over the thirds to take up any slack. Slack linnet here can close the doorway and keep the fish out.

this det *EDD* ~ dem adj 'used with *sing.* or *pl.* nouns denoting time.' Phr *this years*, ~ *weeks*: for the period of (time).

T 45–64 No one ever mentioned mummers' rhymes to me this years. But if they did, and I kept on singin' 'em, I might know 'em. P 259–67 He's been dead this twenty year. P 141–74 I haven't seen them this two weeks or more.

thole-pin See TOLE PIN.

thornback n   also **thorny back***, etc *OED* ~ 1, *DAE* (1674–1806) for sense 1; *EDD* thorn sb 2 (1) ~ back (a), thorny adj 1 (1) ~ back (a) for sense 2.

1 Atlantic prickly skate; thorny skate (*Raja radiata*).

[1578] 1935 *Richard Hakluyt* 129 [Parkhurst's letter:] As touching the kindes of fish beside Cod, there are. . .Thornebacke. . . 1687 [BLOME] 240 Herrings, Salmone, Thorn-back, Oysters. . . 1846 TOCQUE 317 ~ *Raia clavata*. 1971 *RLS* 3, p. 1 Thorny skate. . .tarn back.

2 Any of a variety of sticklebacks (*Gasterosteus* spp); small fish found in fresh or brackish water; SPANTICKLE; PRICKLY: PRICKLEY (P 148–63).

[1766 (1971) BANKS 120 . . .saw a small Fish in the Brooks Very like English Stiklebacks.] 1966 PADDOCK 93 ~s. Very small freshwater fish. P 97–67 Torny backs. Small fish with thorns. C 71–32 Tarney-batts is the name given to tiny fish found in the shallow water of ponds. They were about the size of a goldfish, were brown in colour, and very fast-moving. Q 72–16 Our local word for minnows is thornbat. It is pronounced tarn-bat. It is a small fish with a thorn on its fin on its back which sticks in your hand when you try to grab it. 1979 TIZZARD 327 We always called them 'darn banks,' but really they were thornbacks, so called because of the little thorn on their backs.

thort See TAWT.

those pl det COL. O'CRITICAL *Don't Pat* (1885) 'those for these' Ir. These, used when specifying present times; contrasts systematically with the local use of THEM, THESE.

[1900 OLIVER & BURKE] 46 Congregations [in 1850's] were as devout as they are in those days. 1924 ENGLAND 112 'E ain't no smart rooster. Dey putts some quare hands navigatin', doze days [now]! T 54/65–64 I mean, 'twas—if it happened those days they'd be crucified. T 88–64 [Then] when you [used] sawdust on your floor, and your mother put on a barbel and scrubbed the floor, that's not coming to pass those days, is it? T 141/64–65² An' course years ago, not so much those days, but years ago, you'd always have a gun line. P 212–65 You will [need the insurance], one of those days.

thousand n Cp *OED* ~ sb 2 'used vaguely. . .for a large number'; *EDD* 2 'plenty'; *ADD* 2 'large size or amount.' Used hyperbolically in pl for a large quantity or amount.

1924 ENGLAND 177 I load up me ole birdin' gun wid a span o' two fingers powder an' more 'an a t'ousand shot, an' wad 'em wid tarry oakum, an' go down to me gaze, an' de birds pitch by t'ousands just after de sun risin'. . . Jeeze, what a big burst o' birds down on de landwash! I strick 'em down an' snick 'em down by de t'ousands! T 43/4–64 There's also places that was never cleared—it's just as green as it is out in our yard. Thousands o' land. Q 67–98 'There's thousands of water in the river' [this year]. 'I like thousands o' grease [when] frying bacon and eggs.' 1977 *Inuit Land Use* 137 But out around here, there was thousands of fish, eh? Right into the rocks.

thrashberry n also **thrasher-wood** ~ , **trash** ~ . Northern wild raisin; GADBERRY, WITHE-ROD (*Viburnum cassinoides*); highbush cranberry; *V. trilobum* (1956 ROULEAU 38–9).

1898 *N S Inst Sci* ix, 368 Trash berry: local term for High-bush Cranberry; thrash-berry.

thrasher n A length of chain or other metal device which, when shaken, drives fish into a net; TROUNCER (P 113–56).

thrasher-wood berry See THRASHBERRY.

thread v Cp *EDD* ~ v 9: ~ the needle 'a game.' Comb **threading the needle**: one of the figures of a cotillion; cp GOAT.

C 75–141 The cotillion consisted of eight people, four girls and four boys. It includes (i) through the bushes (ii) figure eight (iii) down the Labrador & (iv) threading the needle.

threaten v *EDD* ~ v; *NID* 5. To promise; announce as intended.

1925 *Dial Notes* v, 344 ~ Promise; as, he *threatened* to give me money. 1937 DEVINE 51 ~ To intend. 'I've been *threatening* to go there a long spell.' 'I threatened to see the doctor.' It is never used in the present tense. P 68–54 I've been *threatenin'* to go there for years. C 71–89 I was threatening to go over to visit you but I didn't get time.

three num *OED* three parts 'almost.'

Comb **three-ball shot**: a certain distance; three gun-shots.

1909 *Christmas Annual* 15 'How far were you then from Captain B's seals?' Turning to the Judge, as directed by Counsel to do, 'Well, me Lard, about a three-ball shot.' Had he said 'three gun-shots,' no doubt the Court would understand right away. 1937 DEVINE 53 ~ An expression of distance; three times as far as a rifle shot.

three handed: of a boat, manned by a crew of three; cp CROSS HANDED, HAND.

1964 BLONDAHL (ed) 68 "The Six-Horsepower Coaker": We turned to go in—in the teeth of the wind— / With a three-handed dory in tow. C 74–114 [It] happened one night that he was bringing the priest back to Admiral's Beach in the jack, a three-handed boat.

three leg: uncompleted mesh of a fish-net, having three corner knots and one loose strand of twine (Q 67–87).

T 187/90–65 So I started to bring to the leader, three leg linnet. An' by an' by the skipper come wi' this man. I had the leader hung up, an' bringin' un to. P 127–78 A three leg is used for scunning leaves of twine together. The loose strand is joined to new twine to form the fourth side of a right mesh, thus joining two separate pieces of netting.

three parts: almost, nearly, esp in phr indicating degree of tipsiness.

T 12–64 [He was] three parts full. T 141/66–65² [He] was three parts on an' he didn't know whether he had a cape ann or a straw hat. 1965 LEACH (ed) 298 "Kelly and the Ghost": Maurice Kelly one night was three parts loaded. P 121–67 He was three parts when I saw him.

three-quarter boot: leather boot reaching to the knee; cp SMALLWOOD BOOT.

P 102–60 When the Newfoundland Boot and Shoe [factory] started manufacturing the three-quarter, those who could afford it bought a pair for Sundays as they had a nice bright red band around the top. They called them the Sunday-go-meeting boot. T 50/2–64 Three-quarter boot, they used to call 'em. Straps in 'em for haulin' 'em on. They wear them mostly Sundays. M 70–15 Another type of boot worn a great deal by fishermen was known as the 'three-quarters' or the 'Smallwood' boot. . . It was made of very heavy leather, and when well greased with cod-oil it was waterproof. 1976 CASHIN 66 I was fitted out with a suit of oil clothes, a pair of what was called in those days three-quarter leather boots which were locally manufactured, and other working clothes appropriate for the job.

three-quarter gun: long-barrelled muzzle-loading fire-arm.

T 172–65 They have their old three-quarter guns and their powder horns, and they'd fire four or five rounds of powder.

throat v Cp *OED* ~ v 2 'to cut the throat of' obs (1382). Cp CUT v: ~ *throats*. To cut the throat of a cod-fish and slit the belly open from gills to vent.

M 69–17 The man on the right is 'throating,' heading and gutting; usually this is done by two men. P 143–74 The men were responsible for throating, heading, and splitting.

throater n *Cent* ~ n N B; *DC* (1923). Member of shore crew who cuts the throat of a cod-fish and slits the belly open from gills to vent; CUT v: ~-THROAT.

1895 GRENFELL 59 The green fish are hove up on to the stage with pitchforks, seized by a woman who cuts off the head—'the header,' and passed on to one who opens the throat—'the throater.' P 143–74 On the cut-

ting table, the throater slit the throat of each fish and
passed it to the header, who removed the head.

thronger n   Cp *OED* ~ 'one who throngs'
(1648, 1908). An unexpected visitor who
intrudes on a gathering (P 245–55).
   P 197–76 ~ a gate-crasher at a party.

throttles n pl Cp *OED* throttle sb 3 'act of throt-
tling, choking' obs rare (1622); *EDD* throttle sb
1 'throat, windpipe.' Ailment affecting the throat
or windpipe, esp diphtheria.
   [1774] 1969 MOWAT 54–5 Inked in a flowery and
faded script at the end of Deuteronomy was a recipe
for the cure of 'throttles' (diphtheria). It called for the
patient to smoke a clay pipe loaded with oakum
(teased-out strands of tarred hemp rope) which had
first been soaked in brimstone. After smoking this mixture he or she was to swallow a pint of black rum drawn
straight from the keg.

through prep Phr *through the bushes*: one of the
figures in a cotillion; cp GOAT.
   C 75–141 [There is] a dance which in some areas of
the province is known as the cotillion. It consisted of
eight people, four girls and four boys. It includes (i)
through the bushes (ii) figure eight (iii) down the
Labrador & (iv) threading the needle.

throw v
   Phr *throw out*: to place split and salted cod-fish
on a flat expanse, usu a 'flake,' turning it at intervals to dry by exposure to sun and wind; MAKE,
SPREAD v.
   [1775] 1792 CARTWRIGHT ii, 178, 180 The women
and I threw the dry fish out to the sun, and then stowed
it in the store-room. . . Some dry fish were thrown out
to the sun.
   throw up: to remove one's mask or head cover
when one's identity has been discovered in
Christmas mumming; STRIP (1969 *Christmas
Mumming in Nfld* 213).
   P 269–63 When a janny 'throws up' he exposes his
masked or veiled face. 'Name us first,' a janny may
say, 'and we'll throw up.'

thrum n   *OED* ~ sb² 7 b ~ cap; *EDD* sb¹ 1 (2)
thrumming cap (a) 'cap or bonnet made
of. . .weaver's ends.'
   Comb **thrum cap**: in place-names.
   1951 *Nfld & Lab Pilot* i, 202 Thrum Cap or No Name
island. . .is situated. . .north-westward of Farmers
Cove head.
   thrum mitt: woollen mitten, the back padded
with strands of unspun wool; cp MITT.
   1979 POCIUS 26 Several women explained that they
knitted a special type of mitt containing a small compartment on the back of the hand. In this compartment, strands of unspun wool were woven, padding the
spot, and providing a great deal of additional warmth.
These mitts were called 'thrum mitts.'

thumb n

Comb **thumb bird**: yellow palm warbler
(*Dendroica palmarum hypochrysea*) (1959
MCATEE 58).
   thumb stall: see STALL.

thumby n   Heavy fingerless mitten.
   1979 POCIUS 23 A mitt is commonly called a
'cuff'. . .although [one] woman called them thumbies.

thunder n   Cp *EDD* ~ n 1 (14) ~ gowl 'the
grumbling of distant thunder.' Comb
thunder-growl: a noise like distant thunder.
   1846 TOCQUE 119 This sound [unexplained rumble
about 1830] is termed by the inhabitants of Bonavista
and Bird-Island Cove, 'the thunder-growl.'

thwart v   Cp *OED* ~ v 2 'to lay (a thing) athwart or across' obs (1522–1632). Phr *thwart up*:
to haul a boat ashore and lay her broadside to
the water for the winter.
   [1771] 1792 CARTWRIGHT i, 177 A punt with two
men from St Lewis's Bay, came up for Baskem's wife,
and to borrow a couple of men to thwart their shallop
up. [1774] ibid ii, 32 We thwarted up the batteau for
the winter. 1792 ibid *Gloss* i, xv Thwart up a boat. To
move a boat out of the reach of the tide, by the assistance of leavers or bodily strength, when she is laid
broadside to the shore.

tibbage n   also **tibeesh, tibbish**. B FABVRE
([c1695] 1970) *Montagnais* Attibis 'petite tissure
des 2 [bouts de raquette].' Fine strips of animal
hide plaited in ends of a snowshoe. See also
BABBISH*.
   [1886] LLOYD 78 The spaces outside the bars are severally the toe and heel of the snow-shoe. These are
filled with more finely cut skin than the middle space,
the Indian term for which is *tibeesh*, while the coarser
filling of the middle space is called *babeesh*. 1897 *J A
Folklore* x, 203 ~ the small filling in at the toe [of the
snowshoe]. 1979 *'Twas a way of life* 28 Skin tibbish and
babbish is put in wet, so before you fill your racquet
you soak the skin overnight.

tibbish See TIBBAGE.

tibeesh See TIBBAGE.

tib's eve n   also **tips*** ~ and, by folk etym, **tipsy
eve** *OED* tib sb 5 ~ dial (1785–1902), *EDD* tib-
(b)'s eve, JOYCE 342 for sense 1; cp *EDD* Co
quot for sense 2. For details of St Tibba, see
Archer Taylor, 'On Tib's Eve, neither before
nor after Christmas' in *Studia Germanica tilläg-
nade Ernst Albin Kock* (1934), pp. 385–6.
   1 A day that will never come; never.
   1896 *J A Folklore* ix, 25 Till Tibs Eve—never. 1924
ENGLAND 79 'Can't dem foolies to de wheel kipp us
cl'ar when us goes 'starn? If it's 'pend on *dey* to putt us
in de fat, us'll get dere on Tib's eve [never], I'm t'in-
kin'!' 1931 BYRNES 121 Aye indeed, sure you'll get it
on Tibb's Eve. C 67–21 'It will be Tibb's Eve before
you get that done.' If the person asked, 'when is Tibb's

Eve?' you would reply, 'Tibb's Eve is neither before Christmas nor after.' M 68–24 I don't care if he's there till Tibb's Eve, he won't get out of that room till he knows every word of his lesson.

2 A day or two before Christmas.

P 245–55 ~ Dec 24, a period when 'anything goes.' P 174–68 ~ It means, or meant once, a specified date, the day before Christmas Eve. M 71–115 Tipsy Eve, December 23rd. What a day! School is out. Christmas has begun. . . Though I'm only guessing, I've always assumed that the name *Tipsy Eve* originated from this custom of the men going from house to house on the afternoon of December 23rd to test or taste each other's brew. M 71–122 Christmas really starts in my home on Tipps Eve which is the day before Christmas Eve. I have heard that it is called Tipps Eve because when men used to put up their own homebrew etc. they wouldn't drink it before Christmas. 1974 GREEN 83 Nevertheless, the first of the twelve days at Christmas, December 23, was known locally by the picturesque name of 'Tipsey Eve' and there would always be a dance to go with the 'near beer' in somebody's kitchen.

tick v In phr *ticking and tacking*: keeping busy.

1979 TIZZARD 42 Apart from being the upstairs maid and the cook, she would have the. . .mat frame in the kitchen and every spare moment would be spent ticking and tacking at that. It kept her busy all the time.

tickalass See TICKLACE.

tickelace See TICKLACE.

ticket n

1 Authorization for a place or 'berth' on a sealing vessel.

1920 WALDO 150–1 The little boys practice jumping across rain-barrels and mud-puddles, because some day they hope to get a 'ticket' (a berth on a sealer) and go to the ice. 1924 ENGLAND 7 The captains 'give out tickets' and so do the officers; and these tickets, entitling men to berths, are as eagerly sought as if some great prize were being conferred instead of merely the chance for week after week of unbelievable hardship and peril, with only a few dollars' reward at the end. 1936 SMITH 49 The next morning we signed articles and got our ticket and crop note. Ibid 100 He then gave us our sealing tickets, 'wetting' the same for good luck, and before we left he made us 'wet the other eye.' 1972 BROWN 2 The boy had got his 'ticket' only because of his father's reputation.

2 Phr **hard ticket**: see HARD.

3 Comb **ticket man**: seaman with an official certificate of competence.

1924 ENGLAND 113 'We'm ahl ticket men,' said he. 'Us master watches ahl has to have stifkits [certificates] from the Gov'ment. It takes ahl of a man to be master watch. If anyt'ing happen your men, t'ink of ahl de widders y're 'sponsible fer, an' de little ones.'

ticklace n also **tickalass, tickelace, tickelelse, tick-i-lace, ticklas, tickleace, tickle-ass, ticklelace, titlas**, etc ['tɪkļeis, 'tɪklæs] DC tickle-ace

Nfld (1956–). Perhaps, like *kittiwake*, imitative of the bird's cry. Atlantic black-legged kittiwake, a small pearl-grey gull, common resident nesting upon cliffs; PINYOLE (*Rissa tridactyla*).

[1819] 1977 *Lgs in Nfld* 16 Titlass—Gotheyet. [1885] 1915 HOWLEY 305 Gotheyet *ticklas*, a bird. . . 1889 HOWLEY *MS Reminiscences* 3 They were chiefly Murres, Turres, Pigeons and Ticklaces. 1896 *J A Folklore* ix, 36 . . .marine birds known as *ticklaces* and *steerins*. [1907 TOWNSEND 312 At Hamilton Inlet thousands of ticklers covered the water, and, as we steamed on, they rose in bodies of five hundred or more and whirled about like gusts of snow driven by the wind.] 1909 BROWNE 207 The Kittiwake. . .is known to fishermen as 'Tickelelse' ('Ticklers'). 1932 BARBOUR 53 The only thing alive, to be seen, was a tickalass, and we tried with poles to kill it, to eat. 1940 SCAMMELL 26 "The Shooting of the Bawks": But if they keep this law that's passed, they will not get a taste / Of bawk or noddy, tinker, tur, and not a tickleace. 1937 DEVINE 53 Tickelace—a kittiwake. 1945 *Can Field-Naturalist* lix, 141 The local name [is] 'tickle-ace' or 'tick-i-lace,' a name which is probably the local interpretation of the call of the bird which is elsewhere interpreted as kittiwake. 1951 PETERS & BURLEIGH 235 Atlantic Black-legged Kittiwake. . . Local names: Tickle-lace, Tickle-ace, Tickle-ass. T 31–64 Soon as we see the first tickle-ace, first little bird come yer [i.e. here] in the Spring —like, you would see 'em round the rocks—that'd be our mark, that'd be his mark, see, tickleace and a sarun—a sarun is a fish-bird. 'Time to get away now! Time to go on now.' P 113–66 Late like the tickleass. T 391/3–67 Tickleace [is] the best. I suppose you been eat the tickleace, have you? P 127–74 The tickleace is slightly smaller than a gull, all pale blue on the wing, with a white breast. 1975 RUSSELL 23 There'd been a few ticklaces around that morning while I was hauling my nets, and being as how I like ticklace soup as well as the next man, I wished I'd had my breech-loader and a few cartridges.

tickle a *OED* ~ a 5 'uncertain, unreliable'; *EDD* a 3 'variable, uncertain, esp of the weather'; cp TICKLE n. Uncertain, hazardous, treacherous, esp in place-names; RAGGED.

[c1630–40] 1971 SEARY 60 [This] is a shift name from Tickle Harbour. . .'in the South corner of Tickle Bay, at the entrance of a salt water lake. . .protected by a small islet and a reef of rocks.' [1786] 1792 CARTWRIGHT iii, 140–1 I was this morning seized with another violent sciatic fit. . . I was so well to-day, as to be able to sit up, but am in a very tickle state. 1842 JUKES i, 81 We met some fishing-boats that told us Tickle Harbour was a bad place to lie in, and one boat piloted us into a small cove called Chance Cove. 1953 *Nfld & Lab Pilot* ii, 127 From Western head the south-eastern shore of Bonavista bay, which is steep and bold, trends about 2¾ miles south-south-westward to the entrance to Tickle cove, a fishing village where it is low, rugged, and bordered by rocks extending 2 cables offshore.

tickle n *OED* ~ sb¹ Nfld 'narrow difficult strait' (1770–); *DC* 1 a, b esp Nfld (1770–); see SEARY

141–2; cp TICKLE a. A narrow salt-water strait, as in an entrance to a harbour or between islands or other land masses, often difficult or treacherous to navigate because of narrowness, tides, etc; a 'settlement' adjoining such a passage; also attrib. Cp REACH, RUN n.

[1770] 1792 CARTWRIGHT i, 64 There is a narrow tickle of twenty yards in width, between this island and the continent; across which a net is fixed, to stop the seals from passing through. [1770] 1971 SEARY 141 Tickle, in the form Tickles, is first cited in *OED* in Cook and Lane 1770 [1775] B, repeated in Lane 1773, for a locality at the head of St Mary's Bay. 1792 PULLING *MS* Aug, p. 29 He had been out in his boat a few weeks before, and rowing through a tickle not far from the cove, he saw a canoe of Indians coming through another tickle and nearly meeting him. 1812 BUCHAN *MS* 17 July I proceeded thro' the Ladle tickle for New bay and return'd again by dark, from Wards island to the head of New bay must be twenty miles. On the 14th I set out for Halls bay by way of Pretty tickle passage, this is form'd by the Tritons and the projecting heads of Bajer and Seal bay, and the Mainland from the latter to Halls bay. 1837 BLUNT 29 This harbor is very secure, with good anchorage in any part, above the Harbor Rock; it has two Tickles, so called, in Newfoundland, and intended to describe narrow passages between islands and rocks. 1842 JUKES ii, 31 What the origin of this word Tickle may be I am at a loss to conjecture; but it is applied all over Newfoundland to a narrow passage or strait between two islands, or other points of land. [1870] 1973 KELLY 27 The Captain, seeing that we were in a little difficulty in getting under weigh in the narrow Tickle, kindly sent his men for this purpose. 1876 HOWLEY 19 The word Tickle appears to refer to a narrow channel between two or more islands, or between islands and the mainland, through which the tide runs with considerable force. 1907 DUNCAN 142 'Twas wild enough, wind and sea, beyond the tickle rocks. 1920 GRENFELL & SPALDING 13 We have turned into a 'tickle,' and around the bend ahead of us are a handful of tiny whitewashed cottages clinging to the sides of the rocky shore. 1940 SCAMMELL 9 "The Squid Jiggin' Ground": There's men from the harbour; there's men from the tickle. 1947 TANNER 285 As has been said the tides are of no great size at the Atlantic coast, but they are sufficient to produce strong tidal currents in the archipelagos and channels of different orders: runs, tickles and rattles. 1951 *Nfld & Lab Pilot* i, 143 [The two islands] are separated from the eastern side of Long island by narrow channels, passable only by boats, and on the shores of which stands a township known as the Tickles. T 50/1–64 There's only a notch comin' in through, you know, when you comes to the tickle, an' if a stranger didn't know nothing about it he'd be liable to run the lighthouse close, see. Ibid An' she got in a tide rip when she got in the shoal tickle in Lewisporte, an' they had like to make a big mess of it. Down she had like to go. 1968 SCHULL 85–6 Nearly four thousand men of the city and the outports, the Tickles and the Guts and the Reaches and the Coves of Newfoundland, were bound to the age-old rendezvous of the ships and the moving ice.

tickleace See TICKLACE.

tickle-ass See TICKLACE.

ticklesome a *OED* ~ a 1 now dial (1585–1604; 1898); *EDD* tickle 2: ~ . Difficult; requiring care; ticklish; TICKLE 1.

1888 HOWLEY *MS Reminiscences* 71 Fortunately there was plenty of water now and the numerous rocks with the water boiling over them were all plainly visible so we were thus enabled to avoid them. But it was ticklesome work and several times we shipped a lot of water.

tiddle v To strike, hook or tip into the air the short stick used in the game of 'tiddly.'

T 246/9–66 They put [the stick] down over their hole and then they'll tiddle it—hit the end of the stick. T 458–67[1] You had your stick across that and you had a rock here for tiddling on. You stood behind and you flicked these out.

tiddly n Perhaps transferred from *OED* tiddlywink 2 b (1870–).

1 A children's game in which a stick, balanced on a rock or over a hole, is hooked or flicked into the air and struck with another; PIDDLY (P 148–65).

T 272–66[1] We used to call it tiddly. You'd have a stick about that long and another stick about so long for hooking it. T 417/9–67 In tiddly you had to hit the stick, pop it in the air and [then] hit it. The distance [driven] was your score—you had it marked off with rocks. M 71–97 The game of tiddly is enjoyed by both boys and girls. It's played by using two sticks; one about a foot long, the tiddly stick, and another about three feet long. Two stones are arranged so that the ends of the tiddly stick rest on them. The other stick is used to hook the tiddly stick as far as possible. If a member of the opposing team catches it, you're out. P 40–78 ~ a child's game involving two or several players using a long stick of about three or four feet to project a smaller stick of about six or eight inches as far as possible by various means such as hooking, striking and so on. It also involves two rocks or junks of wood placed about six inches apart and various other rules for scoring.

2 Attrib **tiddly stick**: either of the two sticks, but esp the short one, used in the game of tiddly.

M 68–12 First we would go hand over hand up the long tiddly-stick to see who [would have first try]. M 69–26 Since he is allowed three trials at batting the short tidley stick, he rarely misses. C 71–115 You put your 'puss stick' across the hole and if the person who picked up your tiddley-stick could throw it and hit your puss stick, you were out.

tide n Comb **tide-watcher**: spotted sandpiper; BEACHY BIRD (*Actitis macularia*) (1976 *Avifaunal Survey* 125).

tidy a Of a stretch of water, esp fishing

grounds, subject to the turbulence of ocean currents and the ebb and flow of the tide.

1931 *Am Speech* vi, 290 ~ Swift; 'a right tidy place with a won'erful lop,' meaning a swift current or tide rip with very high waves. P 148–68 Some places is tidy [and difficult to set cod-traps in].

tie v Comb **tie-out stake**: peg to which the guy-rope of a tent is fastened.

P 9–73 The shanks of [fine-textured boughs] made six tie-out stakes, one for each corner and one for the middle of each side of the tent.

tier n Cp *NID* ~¹ n 1 'a row, rank, or layer of articles.' Layer.

P 269–63 [He had] three or four tiers of clothing [on]. T 50/2–64 Take a block an' an axe an' chop it all up, heave in so much water, an' fold your skin back an' forth, and put a tier o' that [bark] over it. Bark good! T 55–64 The old house got damp an' where there were so much tiers of house paper then on had let go from the boards. 1965 PETERS *Gloss* Brow. A pile of sawlogs near water. The logs are piled parallel to the water, with each tier of logs resting on two or more slender poles laid across the preceding tier. 1979 TIZZARD 54 In these tubs, mother would put a tier of salt and a tier of eggs.

tiffin* n also **sintiffin*** ['tʊfɪn, 'tʊfən, sɪn'tʊfɪn, sɪn'tθʊfən, sɪn'tʊfn̩]. Cp *EDD* tough (1) ~-cake '[cakc] baked on a girdle'; 'cakes. . .made of dough which has been prepared for bread'; perhaps influenced by *OED* tiffin 'light midday meal.' Small cake made of bread-dough, usu fried on stove lid; TOUTIN; see DAMPER combs.

T 94/5–64 He used to make these big piece o' dough, just some bakin' powder in there and salt and flour and water, and mix it up and lay it right on the cover of the stove. He'd be cookin', he said, 'I got a sintiffin on there now.' C 71–28 We would always have tiffins when Mom made bread. C 71–97 ~s. Small pieces of bread dough which were fried in a greased frying pan until cooked.

tight a *OED* ~ B 3 ~ work (1892) for sense 2.
1 Of the air, close, stuffy (P 148–65).
2 Comb **tight work**: in coopering, a type of waterproof construction used in barrels for shipping pickled fish.

T 90–64 An' there's another tool you'd use in tight work. P 127–71 ~ The making of watertight barrels which will be used to hold salted or pickled herring or mackerel.

tighten v Cp *OED* tight v³ 1 a obs (1611). To make (a vessel) watertight.

T 156/7–65 An' they went up to haul her in, an' there's no way [to] tighten her 'cause the [bulkheads] come out [of her].

tiller n Cp *OED* ~ sb² 2 'horizontal bar or beam attached to the rudder-head.' Comb **tiller-stick**: stick attached to the head of the rud-

der permitting one man to steer boat while also tending engine amidships.

Q 67–48 The tiller stick fits into a hole in the rudder and [is] used to steer with. [It is] especially used by those who fish cross-handed [who] use one which reaches to the engine house. C 71–94 The practice in Cape La Hune was to make all tiller sticks from a dogwood tree [in] the belief that the cross on which Jesus died was made [of dogwood].

tilly n also **tally** *EDD* ~ sb Ir; JOYCE 342; DINNEEN tuilleadh 'increase, addition.' A small amount over and above quantity purchased, presented as a gift; cp BAIT 2, DRAININGS.

[1894–1929] 1960 BURKE (ed White) 35 "Playing for the Boneen": Jerry from Harry a one and two carry, / At least wrote O'Mally, when counting his game, / Seven from Billy, thrown in as a tilly / Take Nathan from Denis, nothing remains. P 54–57 Tally. An extra allowance or measure over and above what one has paid for. P 148–65 Ten gallons [of molasses] and one for tally [because it was cold]. 1968 DILLON 158 Now give me a little tilly. I'll give you a tilly over. P 191–73 ~ A little bit added to a required weight. Generally given as a token of good will and in the case of shopkeepers as an incentive to customers to come again.

tilt n Cp *OED* ~ sb¹ 1 'tent' (c1440–1771), 2 'awning over a boat' (1611–), 4 'fisherman's or wood-cutter's hut' (Nfld: 1895, 1906); *DC* n 1 a esp Lab (1753–), 2 a, b (1770–; 1842–) for sense 1; *DC* tilt-back Nfld (1819) for comb in sense 4. See also SEARY 289–90; *Habitat* (1968) xi (5), pp. 14–17.

1 (a) A temporary shelter, covered with canvas, skins, bark or boughs; LEAN-TO; (b) a small single-roomed hut constructed of vertically-placed logs, used seasonally by fishermen, furriers and woodsmen; freq with defining word indicating material of construction, location and season of use (BAY TILT, BOG ~ , BOUGH ~ , SOD ~ , STUDDEN ~ , SUMMER ~ , WINTER ~); common in place-names.

1612 *Willoughby Papers* 1/62/9 They had made a tilte with a sayle, that they got from some Christian. [1676] 1895 PROWSE 206 [They] go in their boats after the fish from three to eighteen leagues each side their harbours mouth there salt their fish in tilts on shore, after carry and dry it where their shipps ride in guard of forts. [1771] 1792 CARTWRIGHT i, 121 After making a tilt with some seal skins which I borrowed at Chateau, I took a walk across the point. 1792 PULLING *MS* Aug, p. 20 James Lilly furred last winter. . .higher up the Main Brook. They had their tilts pitched about ten miles from each other and the last was near forty miles up the Rattling Brook. 1819 ANSPACH 468 They call *tilts* temporary log houses, which they erect in the woods to pursue there their winter occupations. 1842 JUKES i, 69 [It led] in about fifty yards to a very good 'tilt.' This was formed of trunks of trees placed upright on the ground close together, and larger ones for the corner-pieces, and a good strong gable-end roof formed of a frame of roughly squared beams. The corner pieces and beams were nailed together, and the rest driven in tight with wooden wedges wherever necessary. The interstices of those trunks which formed the walls were filled up with moss tightly rammed between them; and the roof was covered by long strips or sheets of birch bark, laid tile-like over one another, and kept down by poles or sticks laid across them. . . In this way a tolerable room, twelve or fourteen feet by eight or ten, is formed. 1863 HIND ii, 162 The planters on the Atlantic coast call their houses 'tilts.' They are generally formed of stakes driven into the ground, chinked with moss, and covered with bark. They are warmed with stoves. 1866 WILSON 216 The winter houses are called tilts. . . The tilt has seldom any window. 1891 PACKARD 141 On every square rod of flat rock on the steep sides of the harbor was a Newfoundlander's 'tilt' or summer house. The sides made of logs or plank, the roof of turf, a square chimney of wood and mud, the four corner-posts projecting above. 1908 TOWNSEND 139 The houses or tilts of the fishermen ashore, the 'freighters' or 'stationers,' vary in character as do the houses of the liveyers. Like the houses of the latter, they are generally rough structures, square in shape, built of poles or planks, covered with green or flowering sods. The freighters often bring birch bark from Newfoundland, with which the frame is spread before the sods are applied. 1933 MERRICK 22 When a man has blazed his trails and built his little cabins (tilts), each a day's walk apart, and set out his two or three hundred traps, that land is his to hunt, and no one else's. 1947 TANNER 731 Early in the spring [the settlers] would move down to their summer homes—'tilts'—at the coast, for from 25th of March to the 4th of June they devoted themselves to seal-hunting. 1951 Nfld & Lab Pilot i, 194 Tilt hill rises to an elevation of 287 feet one mile north-eastward of Bluff point. . . Tilt cove lies close southward of Harbour-my-God point. T 436–65 We used to get in dory an' go to north end, an' stop in tilts over here on the shore, perhaps a week a time, and cut some wood in 'cross the mish. T 398/9–67 So we got ashore all right, [went] up in the tilt an' dried ourselves. 1977 Inuit Land Use 221 When away from home, the trappers spent their nights in a series of tilts: small cabins built a half-day's or a day's walk apart along the trap line.

2 The distance between the shelters built by a trapper on his 'fur path' or 'trap line.'
1973 GOUDIE 99 We had to go four tilts distance—roughly fifty miles one way. 1977 Them Days ii (3), p. 17 We'd go six tilts distance in the country.

3 Prov phr *sit in one end of a tilt and burn the other*: to live improvidently (1937 DEVINE 62).
1863 MORETON 40 He sits in one end of the tilt and burns the other. This. . .admirably expresses to their apprehension the folly of shiftless expedients. I once saw the literal fulfilment of this proverb. A poor shiftless family, too lazy to work, actually, while living in the forest, burned parts of one end of their house to warm themselves sitting at the other.

smoke like a tilt: (a) of a chimney or stove, to emit thick smoke; (b) to consume tobacco copiously (P 54–68).
P 108–70 'Smokes like a bay tilt.' A bay tilt is a rough cabin used for cutting logs in winter. Its stove was usu-

ally full of holes and the room was often full of smoke. It is applied to one who smokes a lot. C 71–120 A tilt is a house in the woods often filled with smoke, hence 'to smoke like a winter's tilt' is used to refer to heavy smoker.

4 Comb **tilt-back**: shed with sloping roof attached to a house; BACK TILT; LINNY.
1819 ANSPACH 468 Tilt-backs, or *linneys*, are sheds made of studs, and covered either with boards or with boughs, resembling the section of a roof, fixed to the back of their dwellings towards the wind.

tilt line: series of shelters built by a trapper on his 'fur path' or 'trap line.'
1972 HORWOOD 11 By freeze-up he had established a tilt line along the southern branch of the river all the way to its source. His tilts were built on high ground about seven miles apart—a day's journey under the worst conditions. . . Each had a food cache set high above the ground. . .he would rarely be more than three or four miles from food and shelter.

tilt v To construct, or use, a shelter or hut for any of the purposes of a TILT.
[1689] 1971 SEARY 75 Southwood describes Shoe-Cove (NTS Pouch Cove), as a place 'where Boats use to come a Tilting. . .that is to split and salt the Fish they catch, and blowing hard and bad weather, cannot get to the places they belong to in time.' More precisely 'a Tilting' would mean to erect a tilt.

timber v Cp OED ~ v 1 'to build a house, shop, etc' obs (1565–73). Phr *timber in/out*: in building a boat or vessel, to fasten in place the timbers which form the ribs of the craft (1969 Nfld Qtly July, p. 20).
T 43/8–64 You'd divide up your body frame an' that. An' you'd make these pitchers—after pitchers an' forward pitchers—an' finish timberin' her out from your after-hook to the counter, an' from your fore-hook to the stem. M 68–10 [märchen] Sure enough, when Jack got back the punt was timbered out. 'Now,' said the old witch, 'cut me a plank stick.' Jack went off to cut a plank stick. When he got back she was all planked.

time n DC ~ n (1950, 1963); cp DAE 10: on a time 'spree' (1855 quot), NID 12 c 'carousal.' A party or celebration, esp a communal gathering with dancing, entertainment, etc; cp SCOFF n.
1878 HOWLEY MS Reminiscences 2 But. . .while on a visit to Bett's Cove [he] got on a time and 'let the cat out of the bag.' 1933 GREENLEAF xxii To raise money for the schoolhouse and the church, the Sally's Cove people held a 'toime' on Orangemen's Day, which took the form of an all-day fair and was held in the schoolhouse. [1956] 1981 Evening Telegram 28 Aug, p. 6 The people of Lance Cove are going to hold a 'time' for a Lance Cove man [who] will be going away to camp shortly. T 200–66 An' the most years now there'd be a time in the hall that night. An' now then all the boys go to the hall, take the wren with us an' tie it on the Christmas tree. An' then you'd dance till the sunrise. T 222–66 In the smaller places during the fall and winter months almost every night there is some kind of a 'time' on, as any social function is called. It might be a

dance or a concert, a church supper an' so on; whatever it is, it's called a time. And everybody goes to
these times. 1967 *Bk of Nfld* iv, 236 The women too
had their meetings, the highlights for us being their two
semi-annual 'Times' in the Lodge. Here would be the
big cooked scoff of salt-water birds or pork and cabbage with a grand assortment of vegetables. . . Crowds
of children would congregate around the 'fish-pond'
and try their luck. 1969 *Christmas Mumming in Nfld*
133 Essentially, a 'time' is an occasion of sanctioned
deviation—thus, mummers mean a 'time,' and drinking
(frowned upon except at sanctioned occasions, such as
weddings and Christmas) means a 'time.' If a wedding,
for example, did not have much 'brew,' people will say,
'We didn't really have a time, did we?' 1976 *Decks
Awash* v (5), p. 9 People on the island would occasionally visit friends to have games of cards or checkers.
And there were the usual 'times.'

timmy noggy* See TOMMY NOGGIN.

tinker n   also **tinker duck** and (in place-names)
tinkershare *OED* ~ sb 3 e 'razor-billed auk'
(Nfld: 1861), f 'guillemot'; tinkershere 'local
name for common guillemot' (1799–); *DC* 1
(1771–), ~ duck (1916). The razor-billed auk
(*Alca torda*); occas other similar birds, as guillemot, PIGEON or MURRE[1]. Freq in place-names.
[1771] 1792 CARTWRIGHT i, 128 Milmouth and Bettres went to Eyre Island with traps; where they killed a
duck and a tinker, and gathered thirty-three eggs.
[1773] 1971 SEARY 290 Tinker's Point (Lane 1773).
[1784–7] 1971 BANKS 449 These birds breed on rocky
islands which lay near the coasts of Newfoundland,
where they are called Tinkers. They creep under hollow rocks where they lay one egg on the bare rock,
which is bluish white, spotted black and weighs near
four ounces. 1854 [FEILD] 16 . . .a tub full of the large
eggs of the turrs and tinkers, (sea-fowl which breed
upon the neighbouring islands). 1870 *Can Naturalist* v,
414 Common. . .until driven south by the drift
ice. . .[the] 'tinker.' 1883 HOWLEY *MS Reminiscences* 4
The chief distinction between the Turr (Tinker) and
the Murr is that the latter has a white band all around
the neck and a spot behind the eye while the former
has all the head, neck and back coal black. 1909
BROWNE 207 'Tinker' is the name by which the
Razor-bill auk is known to fishermen. . . It sits bolt
upright on the rocks, and in the water has a habit of
cocking its tail. 1916 HAWKES 33 Small birds, particularly the little sea-pigeon. . .and 'Tinker' duck are
secured in summer with the bird dart or net and added
to the winter store. 1940 SCAMMELL 26 "The Shooting
of the Bawks": But if they keep this law that's passed,
they will not get a taste / Of bawk or noddy, tinker,
tur, and not a tickleace. 1951 *Nfld & Lab Pilot* i, 124
Tinkershare island, which is small and wooded, is situated close westward of Yardie island. 1951 PETERS &
BURLEIGH 251 The [tinker] is rather curious and often
may be enticed near a boat by shouting or waving a
handkerchief. A number are shot for food around the
coast. 1977 *Inuit Land Use* 177 The outer coastal
islands are the preferred nesting and feeding area for
eider ducks, gulls, murres (tinkers), puffins, terns,
black guillemot (pigeons), and razorbill auks (turres).

tinnen a   *OED* ~ a obs (c1000–1653). Made or
consisting of tin.
1971 NOSEWORTHY Tinnen suitcase. P 108–79 She
was talking about all the clothes her mother used to
wash in her big wash-tub. I said, 'I suppose it was a big
wooden one with handles.' And she said, 'No, it was
tinnen.'

tint* See TAINT.

tintacks* n   Cp pron of *ten*. Child's game
(T 375–67).
P 148–68 ~ said in a game played by youngsters. One
person faces away from the others and counts as fast as
possible from 1 to 10, and turns around on the last
word *tintacks*. The others try to run forward while he is
counting but freeze before he finishes and turns
around. Anyone seen still moving is made to go back
to the starting line.

tip v
    1 To reach the top (of a hill) and begin a
descent.
T 43/8–64 Well, when she'd tip the hill to go down
with her load she'd sit back an' take the weight in the
breechin' an' ease herself down over the hill.
    2 Phr *go tip over tally*: to turn head over heels
(Q 67–60).
    3 Cpd **tip-over**: somersault.
1964 *Can Journ Ling* x, 43 Turning [tip-overs] somersaults.

tippy n   also **tibby, tippy pan**. A small flat pan
of floating ice in boys' sport of 'copying.'
P 213–55 Tippy pans [are] small pans of ice, so-called
by boys who copy. C 67–2 A tibby is a small piece of ice
[in] the game of jumping from ice-pan to ice-pan.
P 245–79 Tippy pan: piece of drift ice, large enough to
support a person. They were used as sort of a raft.
Sometimes they would tip over, hence *tippy pans*.

tippy v   also **tibby, tipsy**. To jump from one
floating ice-pan to another; COPY.
C 67–2 The game was called tippying because the
pans tilted so easily. C 69–2 One of our favourite pastimes when we were boys was tippying. When the ice
used to come in during the late winter or spring we
would jump from one ice-pan to the other. C 71–97
Tipsying is simply jumping from ice-pan to ice-pan
when the ice breaks into pans.

tipsy See TIPPY v.

tipsy eve See TIB'S EVE.

tished p ppl Of a body of water, barely frozen
with a thin layer of ice; cp CATCH (OVER), SISH
(Q 67–22).
C 68–19 I once heard him look at a slightly iced-over
pond and say it was just tissed (pronounced tished).

tiss v imit *EDD* ~ v So D for sense 1. Cp SISS.

1 To hiss; to fizz.

1937 DEVINE 53 ~ To make a hissing noise when being cooked on a pan. 1941 DULEY 104 Salty as her grandfather was, he 'tissed' for the first time over weather—wondering if he was getting old. P 148–61 [When firing a muzzle-loading gun] you have to watch the tissing there. T 398–67 By an' by you'd hear [the moonshine] tissin', tissin'; put it in a jug then. 1975 GUY 74 [Female cats] snarling and tissing at one another back there.

2 To test the hotness of a laundry iron.

P 207–67 She showed Susan how to tiss the iron [by putting a wet finger on it to see if it's getting hot].

tissy a

1 Angry, irritable; cp TISS.

P 121–67 She got tissy with me.

2 Stingingly cold, chilly; cp TISHED.

P 148–65 [At five or six o'clock in the morning when the fire had died down] that's when it gets tissy.

tissy n Rock gunnel, a small, elongated salt-water fish (*Pholis gunnellus*); TANSY[2].

1966 LEIM & SCOTT 304 Rock gunnel. . . Other common names: gunnel, butterfish, tansy, tissy, rock eel.

titter* n *EDD* tetter sb 2. A small wart (Q 67–60).

to prep, prefix also **de*, the** *EDD* the 12, with *day, morn, night*, &c 'this, to-' general, POOLE *Glossary. . .of Forth and Bargy* (1867), p. 118 t' year 'this year' Wxf, *ADD* the 5 'this; to-' for sense 1; *EDD* once 1 (13) to once w cty, Do, *ADD* to 4 to once for sense 2.

1 The present (time period); the coming (time period).

1888 HOWLEY *MS Reminiscences* 15 It is really too bad, we may not get such good chances [to shoot game] again the season. [c1894] PANL P4/14, p. 200 *To* year is this year, used like today, tonight, tomorrow. 'I ain't had a cruise to-year.' 1898 *Christmas Bells* 16 All he tells we is the Queen ain't sent out enough money for the poor widdies *to year*, because she've had a poor *voyage* too. 1907 DUNCAN 117 There wasn't ar another man landed by the mail-boat the day, was they? P 229–67 We'll go in berry pickin' the mar. M 68–20 I don't spose there's e'er store open the day, is there? P 245–76 We didn't have much snow the year an' I'm afraid we may have no rain the summer.

2 Phr *the once, to* ~ [də 'wɔns]: as soon as possible, right away; DIRECTLY; in a short while.

1861 *Harper's* xxii, 753 She let go her two anchors to onst. 1896 *J A Folklore* ix, 25 The use of *to*, as meaning this, as in *to-day*. . .is continued in. . .*to once* for at once. [1906] GRENFELL 123 So I took it that the splint fitted, and was able to insist on Pat getting a nap 'to oncst.' 1937 DEVINE 51 The once—at once. T 80/2–64 And the once, see, I get sick. Smoking, I suppose, and glutching the smoke. T 222–66 If we are going to do something almost immediately we would say we are going to do it de once. T 309–66 He started off next

morn. Got to this pond. Stowed away and looked away to the mountain top. The once he seen this little cloud, you know, risin'. P 17–69 *The rackly* means 'the once.'

tobacco n also **baccy*, backy**. In names of various plants and berries: **tobacco berry, ~ hurt** [see also HURT], **~ leaf**.

1898 *J A Folklore* xi, 281 Tobacco berries. *Maianthemum canadense* [false lily-of-the-valley]. Ibid 282 *Smilacina trifolia* [false solomon's-seal]. 1898 *N S Inst Sci* ix, 383 Ground hurt. On the Labrador, tobacco hurt (*Vaccinium angustifolium*). 1931 *Am Speech* vi, 291 Backy hurts—another variety of blue berries on a higher shrub [than ground hurts]. 1956 ROULEAU 39 Tobacco leaf: *Sanguisorba canadensis* [Canadian burnet].

tod n *EDD* ~ sb[5] 4 Gl Do So for sense 1.

1 A small bundle of hay; cp POOK n (P 148–65).

2 A small number of dried and salted cod piled on a 'fish-flake'; cp FAGGOT n, PILE n.

T 175/7–65 The first time you make it up you [put] it in tods, perhaps three or four fish on top of one another. If you struck a bad spurt of weather that fish'd go bad quicker if 'twas in a big lot. P 229–67 We'll put the fish up in tods—a tod is a small pile of salt cod that has been spread out on the flake for a day.

todger n A piece of wood with hooks in it for retrieving a shot bird from the water; DOG[2] 3, GLY.

1972 NEMEC 223 The community's hunters shot scores of ducks 'to wing,' of which 72 were retrieved with 'gaffs' and 'todgers.'

toggle[1] n Cp *OED* ~ sb 1 'short pin passed through a loop, etc, to keep it in place' naut for sense 1.

1 A home-made latch for a door or gate (Q 73–7).

P 229–67 Put the toggle across the door and bar it. P 40–78 Don't forget to turn the toggle on the gate when you goes out to-night.

2 Coat with ornamental fastenings or frogs; also attrib.

1901 *Christmas Review* 19 When, at the last moment, they arrived, in their best toggles, with crape streamers two yards long flying from their beavers or satin hats. T 194/7–65 Here comes a feller wi' a toggle coat on. Well, he was a Church of England minister.

toggle[2] n Atlantic common cormorant (*Phalacrocorax carbo carbo*); SHAG.

1967 *Nfld Qtly* June, p. 11 I have not told you about toggles and wobbies.

token n *EDD* ~ sb 6 esp s w cties. Death-omen; apparition; FETCH.

1900 *J A Folklore* xiii, 297 Seeing an absent friend is a 'vision' or 'token' that one will die within a year. 1928 *Nfld Qtly* Dec, p. 16 'Jake' had stumbled on the ice, and the contents of his gun had swept through his body like a tornado. That night he died. Did the seeing of his

'Token' have any connection with his death? T 272–66[1] Oh, I've seen tokens. Yes, sir! An' once or twice I thought I knew what it meant. . . I thought then there was something up home, an' about an hour or so after that this feller come in an' told me that [X] was just about gone. So that was the token [I saw]. T 313/5–66 I think that was the token o' two sisters. I knowed them. They was dressed in white, sir, just so white as the holland. Their clothes was never starched no brighter, no whiter than what it was. The snow never fell from the heavens so white as that was. C 70–15 Very early in my childhood I heard about 'tokens,' or strange occurrences being heard or seen shortly before the death of some person usually a member of the family, or some relative. The 'tokens' usually took the form of strange noises, moving lights, vanishing figures (human or animal), voices calling from a distance, and a variety of others.

tole pin n also **thole-pin, towpin*** ['toɒlpɪn, 'toulpɪn, 'doʉlpin, 'toɒpin, 'toupɪn, 'ţoʉpiɪn, 'doɒpiən, 'doʉpiɪn] OED thole-pin 2 (1598, 1725, 1859). Thole or wooden peg, often used in pairs, set vertically in the gunwale of a boat and serving as fulcrum for an oar which is usu secured to it by a 'withe' or thong formed by a flexible branch, rope or leather strap; freq in prov and phr.

[1856] 1977 WHITELEY 37 'The modus operandi' is simply for the boats to anchor on either side of the bag. . .draw it up, fastening the ends to the thole pins of both boats and then pitch out the cod. 1896 *Outing* Jan, p. 330 As the boat 'righted' one oar slipped out from between the clumsy thole-pins and drifted away on the current. 1901 *Christmas Bells* 14 Oars would be made, tholepins, killocks, tillers and even small boats constructed, and launched slide-fashion before the snow would disappear from the ground. 1909 BROWNE 220 A fisherman once told me that the island was so barren that one 'couldn't cut a thole pin for a rodney.' This is a fisherman's expression for things diminutive. 1937 DEVINE 51 Thole-pin. A wooden peg holding an oar in the rowlock with a withe. T 70–64[1] An' he said if he had let him come on, he'd make [it as far as] th' after tole pin, as far as he knew. C 64–5 [It is believed] that having broom handles on board for tolepins or any purpose is unlucky. T 194/6–65 An' my sling hooked in the tow pin, old man, an' I hauled hard an' broke the string o' my cape ann, lost my cape ann. P 113–66 Dumb as a thole pin. Q 67–80 Starved like a toepin. 1971 NOSEWORTHY 256 Tow-pins. Small, round pegs in the sides of a dory to keep the oars from slipping back and forth. 1981 *Livyere* i (1), p. 41 I'm rowin' away from it all, with the water lappin' constantly against the plankin' and the worn paddles squeakin' in the tole-pins.

toll v also **tole, tow** [toɒl, toɒ] OED ~ , tole v[1] now dial, U S, EDD v[2] 1, 2 esp s w cties for sense 1; DAE 1 (1835–1893) for sense 2; NID v[3] 3 for sense 3.

1 To entice, draw, allure; esp with *away*, to lead astray; cp FAIRY-LED.

1924 *Cadet* Feb, p. 17 The captain. . .was one of the best-natured men that ever lived. . .but when the lone widows of the coast began to 'tole' the dog away, purposely, to kill sheep which they never had, in order to get money from the owner, [he] thought it was time to draw the line. C 63–1 When picnicking or berry-picking or fishing in the woods, as children we often turned a coat or a sweater inside out so that the fairies would not tow us away. P 244–64 You should never feed another man's dog; you are tolling him away. The light will toll him in (i.e. attract an undesirable visitor to the door). C 70–15 Every now and again when I was a boy somebody would get lost on the barrens or in the woods while berry-picking. As soon as the word got around the older people would be sure to say that the lost people were tolled away by fairies.

2 To lure game within gun-shot.

1842 JUKES i, 129 Sulleon saw one of these ducks on the wing a long way off, and, pulling me down with him into some bushes, he pinched his nose with his finger and thumb, and then quacked so naturally that the bird flew right over us, and I shot him as he passed. Any device which induces wild animals to come within shot is called 'tolling them.' 1885 KENNEDY 162 It is often necessary to *tole* a big stag, to induce him to leave the hinds, and present a shot. . . *Toleing* the caribou is the reverse process to 'calling' the moose. In the latter the cry of the female is imitated; in the former, the male. . . *Toleing* is not difficult; all the Indians can do it with more or less success: the cry is a shuffling kind of grunt. 1897 J A *Folklore* x, 212 *Tole* or *toll*. . .meaning to allure by some bait. It is quite generally used in Newfoundland in the same sense. 'Throw out some liver to *tole* the gulls.' 1937 DEVINE 53 Tole. To lead or decoy. . .birds. . .by imitating their cries.

3 To entice fish with bait.

[1833] 1918 TOWNSEND 331 [Shattuck's letter:] They throw out pieces of mackerel to toll the fish, put on bait to their hook which lasts all day, and throw the fish on the deck without touching hands to them. 1842 JUKES i, 192 Harvey said he did it to 'toll' or entice the fish. 1937 DEVINE 53 Tole. To. . .decoy fish. . .with bait. P 121–67 He tried to tow the fish nearer the shore. 1979 TIZZARD 300 While waiting for the squids to strike some men slept, some yarned, while others just kept working their jiggers to try and tow the squids around.

toll n See TOLL v. Imitation of an animal- or bird-call used to lure game.

[1822] 1928 CORMACK 71 The Indians. . .have a call or toll for every kind of beast and bird, to bring them within shot.

toller n also **toler**. Cp OED ~[2] 2 'a decoy,' DAE tol(l)er for sense 2.

1 Small sac in the upper throat of a caribou.

1907 MILLAIS 312 I killed a very large stag [caribou] near Shoe Hill, and whilst removing the neck skin my knife slipped and disclosed a very curious sac about five inches long and two broad; this contained growing hair on the inner skin, and the cavity was full of a mass of compressed hair soaking in a watery mucus. This skin bag was situated in a thin vellum of the inner skin in the region of the upper throat. The Indians call this little bag 'Piduateh,' and the few white men who know of its existence the 'Toler' (i.e. crier or bell).

2 A lure (to attract wild animals and birds); an enticement.

P 245–71 Toler. A lure, especially of wild animals or birds, e.g. a dead tickleass would be thrown into the sea to attract other birds within range. Ibid Molasses or jam would be called a 'toler' in a steady diet of pork and duff.

tol squoll See TAL QUAL.

tolt n *EDD* toll sb²: tolt Nfld [1895]; *DC* Nfld (1905–); cp *EDD* towte 'low, rounded hill' Do So, toot sb⁵ 6 'hilly promontory' Do; from *EDD* toot v² 'to peep. . .to spy': toot-hill; SEARY 104. A prominent rounded hill rising above the surrounding terrain; freq in place-names; also attrib; cp BUTTER POT, SUGAR-LOAF.

1836 [WIX]² 19 Before one p.m. I was again upon my way, on foot, through the woods, leaving the remarkable hill, called the Chapel Tolt, behind, and the Long Hill Deer country, on my left. 1842 JUKES ii, 221 The principal of these [elevations] are called. . . Little Gut Outlook, the Tolt, and the Monument. 1868 HOWLEY *MS Reminiscences* 34 In the far distance some high hills or tolts are visible rising like gigantic hay pooks above the tree tops. 1895 *J A Folklore* viii, 39 ~ a solitary hill, usually somewhat conical, rising by itself above the surrounding country. [c1900] 1978 *RLS* 8, p. 23 ~ A rounded conical isolated hill standing above the general level. Like a hay pook. Seems to correspond nearly with the S.A. 'kopj' but smaller. 1953 *Nfld & Lab Pilot* ii, 2–3 On the eastern coast hummocks of granite protrude and are known locally as Tolts. 1965 *Evening Telegram* 31 Dec He reveals only that he climbs to the top of a 1,822-foot tolt on the Gaff Topsails. 1971 NOSEWORTHY 256 ~ A hill standing alone in flat country. ('*Hill*—highest, *tolt*—next highest, then *knap*.') P 245–79 She lives in on the Tolt Road [near St John's].

tom n

Comb **tom cod**: see TOM COD.

tom conner, tommy ~ : blue perch (*Tautogolabrus adspersus*), a bottom-feeding fish of inshore waters, esp common around wharves and fishing stages; CONNER.

M 70–27 The tommy conner is the local name for a conner. C 71–93 Tom conners [are] small fishes of a greyish colour usually found around wharves where cod are landed.

tom fox: eastern fox sparrow (*Passerella iliaca iliaca*); FOXY TOM.

1959 MCATEE 66 ~ Fox sparrow (From its colour; the most widespread subspecies has a good deal of chestnut-rufous spotting, striping, and washing. Nfld. 'Labr.', N.S.)

tom-tee: tom-tit; black-capped chickadee; PIG-A-WEE (*Parus atricapillus bartletti*) (1959 MCATEE 52).

tom cod n ['tɑm kɑd, 'tɒm kɒd, 'tɒm kɔd] *OED*

~ d 'a young codfish' (Nfld: 1883); *DC* 1 (1779–); cp *EDD* tom sb 10 (5) ~ cod 'a large kind of cod' Do for sense 1.

1 A small immature cod-fish (*Gadus morhua*); COD², FISH.

[1766] 1971 BANKS 134 200 Quintals a boat is Calld a saving Voyage, but not under Their Bait are small Fish of all Kinds when they Can gett them Herring Capelin Lance Tom Cod or young Cod. [1779] 1792 CARTWRIGHT ii, 476 At sun-set we hauled the seine by the stage, but took only a few lance and small tomcods. 1792 ibid *Gloss* i, xvi ~ Young codfish. 1826 *Edin New Phil J* i, 33 The young cod, tom-cod, or podley, swarms in summer in all the harbours and shallowwaters. 1858 [LOWELL] i, 203 The King (ef 'twas the king 'isself that doned it) might as well take a squid or a tom-cod for a magistrate, as some 'e'd amade. 1888 HOWLEY *MS Reminiscences* 6 On our way we picked up a dead fish I never saw before. Leslie says it is a Ling. It is much like a Tomcod, but has a somewhat flattened head, and a very narrow tapering tail. 1895 PROWSE 62 The Scot, however, is a long way behind the genuine native, who has been practising it from a small boy; copying, jigging tomcods, and going in the woods trouting, being the popular amusements of the native boy. 1951 *Nfld & Lab Pilot* i, 249 Clam bank. . .and Tom Cod rock [lie] south-south-westward. . .of West Flat island. [1952] 1965 PEACOCK (ed) i, 126 "The Fisherman's Alphabet": 'T' stands for tom-cod, the tide they do stem. T 90–64 And there was other sizes that we had for a few years, barrels for tom cods and other things. P 148–66 He has a gut like a harbour tomcod. P 130–67 ~ A small cod; this includes cod up to twenty inches. There is no set distinction. What one person may call a small fish another may call a big tom-cod. C 70–12 ~ A fish which is too small to be called a cod fish or sold as one, but too big to be called a rounder. [It] is from 12–15 inches in length. It can be split, which means the sound bone can be taken out, this is not possible in the rounder. 1971 *RLS* 3, p. 2 A young, immature cod is called a tomcod and as such must be distinguished from the true Atlantic tomcod Microgadus tomcod. 1979 NEMEC 238 ~ [a cod] under 12 inches.

2 A grade or 'cull' of dried and salted cod-fish; dried cod of small size; cp LEGGY, ROUNDER.

1953 *Nfld Fish Develop Report* 42 Newfoundand's most important market in the Caribbean is Puerto Rico. It was developed originally as an outlet for semi-dried Labrador fish. . .but much the larger quantity exported there now consists of shore-cure fish of 'thirds' grade and 'tomcods.' 1955 *Nfld Fisheries Board* No 23 ~s. Fish 8 to 12 inches in length both inclusive and may be either Merchantable or Madeira quality, or a mixture of both. T 36–64 'Extra large' [was] from 21 to 24 [inches long], 'large' from 18 to 21, 'small' from 14 to 18, 'tom-cod' from 12 to 14. T 410–67 There was small madeira, large madeira; small thirds an' large thirds; small West Indee; tomcods. . .Italian—too many grades for me! 1979 TIZZARD 295 There it would be thrown upon the wharf to be culled into different grades: large merchantable, small merchantable, large Madeira, small Madeira, tom cod and cullage.

tommy n Cp *EDD* ~ sb 3 'loaf of bread'; cp *OED* timenoguy naut 'rope [on board ship, with specialised functions]' (1794–1867), *O Sup*[1] (1880–1925); cp *NID* sticking tommy.

Comb **tommy bun**: small round loaf or ball of bread.

c 75–138 [Dough left over when making bread] is usually taken and rolled in a ball and baked in the oven to form a tommy bun.

tommy conner: see TOM CONNER.

tommy dancer: topmost staysail of a schooner.

1906 DUNCAN 117 The *Rescue* had rounded the cape at dawn, with all sails set, even to her topmast-staysail, which the Newfoundlanders call the 'Tommy Dancer.'

tommy noggin, ~ **nogger, timmy noggy***: frame of a weighing device on which dried cod, seal pelts, etc, are placed; JIG n, MACHINE.

1897 *J A Folklore* x, 212 *Tommy noggin* or *tommy nogger*; a frame usually of wood, but sometimes of iron, on which to rest the fish-barrow when the fish is being weighed. P 8–55 Timmy-noggy—Platform on which draught of codfish is placed for weighing.

tommy-sticker: makeshift candle-holder.

T 14/20–64 When we'd want to stick the candle up for to burn, where he wouldn't burn the wood, we had a tommy-sticker. There's a cone-shape in the top-end large enough for the candle to go into, and a point, a spear on the end, and another spear on the side where we could stick him up perpendicular or stick him up on the side of the ship, or anywhere.

ton n Cp *OED* ~[1] 3 a 'a measure of capacity for timber, equivalent for hewn timber [to] 50 cubic feet.' Comb **ton timber**: a tree of large size, shipped in hewn or 'squatted' form.

1876 MURRAY & HOWLEY 432 I was informed while at Gambo that a certain Captain Wright, of Liverpool, had cut ton timber on that river, and brought to market in 1875, 583 tons of the same; and it is rumoured that similar operations are now going on at the Gander Lake. 1877 SEARS 9 It is computed that there will be at least 20,000 barrels of herring shipped at the opening of navigation, besides large quantities of tow [ed emend: ton] timber and sawed lumber. 1952 SMITH 30 Something less than a century ago expert woodsmen from the mainland were shipping 'tun timbers,' three and four feet thick and so-called from their weight, to England and the United States, almost forgotten evidence that forests of great trees once covered the land. M 68–17 Older residents of Gillams recall having heard their fathers and grandfathers talk of Jerseymen who once came to Gillams for loads of square-timber—what the Jerseymen called 'ton-timber.' The banks of the large brook which flows into the bay at Gillams are forested with very large [trees] and according to these residents, Jerseymen came, cut down this timber, 'squared it down' and took whole ship-loads away.

tongue n Cp *EDD* ~ sb 2 (1) a dish of tongue for sense 3; for comb in sense 4 *OED* 15 c ~-bang (1824–).

1 A device which releases the mechanism of an animal trap.

[1770] 1792 CARTWRIGHT i, 52 In the afternoon I made twenty-four bridges and tongues for deathfalls, and caught two jays on the porch, with birdlime. 1792 ibid *Gloss* i, ix A piece of board placed within a deathfall; one end of which is hung to a small stake by a piece of twine, and the other end is supported in an horizontal position by a peg (called a tongue.) When an animal treads on it, the peg is drawn out, which sets the cat-killer at liberty, and that falls upon the back of the creature and kills it.

2 COD TONGUE.

[1840] 1842 BONNYCASTLE ii, 205 [exports] Tongues and sounds. . . £256. 1861 MRS BEETON 120 The tongues [of cod taken in the Newfoundland fishery] are also cured and packed up in barrels. 1882 TALBOT 30 There are exported. . .lobsters, sounds, and tongues. 1975 *The Rounder* Sep, p. 12 Best known is the tongue, much prized in certain circles for its [glutinous], jelly-like consistency. Young children in many fishing communities make extra pocket money by cutting out the tongues and selling them by the dozen, door to door.

3 Phr *feed of tongue(s), meal of* ~ : a scolding.

[1900 OLIVER & BURKE] 61 She called on Mrs Young and gave a meal of tongue. P 148–61 I'll give him a 'feed of tongue' when he comes home. T 54/8–64 Every time he'd come home drunk, his wife'd always meet him with a big sour look an' give him a feed o' tongues.

4 Comb **tongue-banging**: severe scolding; tongue-lashing.

1924 ENGLAND 48 As usual in such cases, [stowaways] got a 'tongue-banging,' and were then turned over to be serfs for the firemen; to clean the firemen's quarters in the to'gal'n house and bring them food. P 148–62 Father gave some tongue-banging. T 54/8–64 He said, 'I'll get a tongue-bangin' anyhow when I goes home.' 1970 JANES 144 He limited himself to one crack over the head and another good 'tongue bangin'.

tongue boot: fisherman's leather boot reaching above the knee; SMALLWOOD BOOT (P 83–77).

T 29/30–64 One time, instead o' rubber boots they used to wear leather boots, the big tongue boots. I had one pair the first year I was on the Labrador.

toothache n Comb **toothache string**: charm worn around the neck to prevent toothache.

1910 GRENFELL 21 I perceived that he had a string, as of a scapular, around his neck. . . I asked him the meaning of it. 'Sure, 't is a toothache-string, sir,' he replied. 'Sure, I never had the toothache sunce I worn un.'

tooting ppl Comb **tooting owl**: American hawk owl (*Surnia ulula caparoch*) (1977 *Inuit Land Use* 377).

1967 *Bk of Nfld* iii, 283 ~ Hawk Owl (from its cries).

top n Cp *OED* ~ sb[1] 6 (1485–1858) for sense 1.

1 Esp in pl, the branches and upper part of a spruce or fir.

T 14/9–64 We would take the bark off a vir tree or black spruce tops, the small wood, say, and you boil out the boughs. T 84/5–64 I darted in the woods an' I clawed hold to a top an' I comes out o' the woods wi'

this old top, boughs an' everything. 1974 SQUIRE 73
One of our last tasks before leaving home would be to
secure several tops of spruce trees laden with buds
which we carried with us to the fishery. At intervals the
buds would be taken and put into a wooden barrel with
a quantity of water and molasses. When this brewed
the desired length of time, it produced a refreshing
drink, quenching thirst better than anything I know of.

2 The lid of a wood or coal stove.

C 70–21 During my childhood our kitchen stove was
a black shiny iron one, in which we burnt coal and
wood. Naturally lots of soot gathered on the 'tops' or
stove lids.

3 Attrib, comb, cpd **topbearer**: man who helps
carry the pall in funeral procession;
OVERBEARER.

1967 FIRESTONE 78 The overbearers, or topbearers,
are an equal number who hold the pall, a large white
sheet upon which a black cross has been sewn, over the
coffin.

top 'em all: gunwale (P 127–77).

top house: clipped form of topgallant-house;
fo'c's'le.

1924 ENGLAND 10–11 I penetrated the fo'c's'le, or
'top house' and found a V-shaped, whitewashed space;
a tiny cracked bogey, or stove; low beams; narrow,
dark, and dirty bunks in tiers; dim lamps gleaming.

top linnet: upper part of a cod-trap; see
LINNET.

T 43/7–64 You stick a pin in under the risin' somewhere in the boat, an' you make sure that you're not
goin' to lose the top linnet because if there's any fish in
it you'd lose that.

top load: a heavy cargo (of seal pelts).

1978 *Evening Telegram* 15 Apr, p. 6 The old sealers
and fishermen said that [the *Southern Cross*] possibly
went around the cape that evening getting into the big
heavy rollers with a top load of 'live' fat (i.e. that which
is not frozen or settled down.) The seals' live fat slid
forward, broke the bulkheads.

top loft [tɑp 'lɑf, tɒp 'lɒf]: upper room in
house or building; see LOFT.

1899 ENGLISH 9 On this beach was a large store, and
into it Norrie crept, climbed up a ladder to the top loft
where there was one small window. 1910 GRENFELL 33
He and his family were so thoroughly frightened that
they always slept in the top loft of their house, with
loaded revolvers and rifles beside them. T 141/59–65²
There's a ladder there, an' we sticks up the ladder an'
shoved up the trap hatch an' gets up in the top loft.
1972 MURRAY 182 Carpenters who built peaked roof
houses at this time made both sides of the gable roof
the same length. Now ceilings upstairs could be of uniform height, and, in addition, there was an attic, or
'top loft,' directly under the roof which could be used
for storage.

top-man ['tɒpmən]: man at the upper end of a
pit-saw in sawing operation.

T 393/403–67 [He] was a good top-man. Went out,
you know, an' caught hold the tail of his saw.

top tank: water tank aboard sealing vessel in
which fresh-water ice is melted; PINNACLE n: ~
TANK.

1924 ENGLAND 77 Rig and deck gleamed frozen
white. At the 'top tanks,' otherwise called 'pinnacle
tanks,' grimy sealers were drawing rusty red and very
dirty water into their slut kettles for matutinal tea. In
those tanks ice blocks were melted by steam coils; and
once one grew accustomed to rust, dirt, and brackish
taste, one didn't mind the water—much.

top v

1 To rig a vessel with sails.

1924 ENGLAND 150 In four days they had new masts
in her an' topped her down again. 'Twas ahl a loyal
fitout an' they left again fer the ice on the fourth day.
1964 *Can Journ Ling* x, 39 When the upper sails are in
position the vessel is said to be topped.

2 Phr *top off/up*: to fill (a container) to the
brim.

1976 GUY 131 By and by out comes this miserable little dribble which takes five minutes to top off a small
dipper. 1975 BUTLER 43 Come home then, put out our
nets out home, topped up what herrin' Mr Bert had not
topped up. So that ended up that winter. P 127–77 I'm
going to top off that bucket of berries.

topsail n SEARY 291. Attrib **topsail rose**: variety
of cultivated rose associated with Topsail and
adjacent settlements in Conception Bay.

1938 AYRE 3 Hayman's white roses of York and red
roses of Lancaster, which we call 'Topsail roses,' are
found in all the gardens around Conception Bay.

torbay n [= a fishing community north of St
John's] SEARY 291.

Attrib **torbay deal**: a particular sequence followed by dealer in distribution of cards to players.

C 69–18 [She] dealt the cards two to each player, two
more to each player, then one to each player, saying
'I'm going to give you a Torbay deal now.'

torbay hawk: American peregrine falcon
(*Falco peregrinus anatum*).

1612 *Willoughby Papers* 1/13 Touching the cost of
Torbay hawkes which the Falkener and the boy hath
one falcon. . .

torbay mitt: type of mitten hand-knitted from
home-spun wool; MITT.

P 108–70 Torbay mitts were hand-knit from wool of
[local] sheep, carded and spun by hand. [They were]
usually black and white standard pattern, some with
thumb and one finger, some with just the thumb.

torbay nag: small, rough-haired Newfoundland horse (1925 *Dial Notes* v, 345).

1904 *Daily News* 15 Apr "Franky's Little Pony":
Frank Morris gets the boodle 'swag' / While you must
climb the ridges, / He loves a foxy Torbay nag / And
not your roads and bridges. P 108–70 Torbay nags were
the small horses people from Torbay, and people from
Logy Bay, Outer Cove and places nearby drove to
town with fish, splits, etc. 1975 GUY 3 I knocked
together a rough likeness of that beast of burden. It
looked something like a cross between a Torbay nag
and a Newfoundland dog.

torch n Comb **torch night**: November 4th, the eve of Guy Fawkes Day; cp BONFIRE NIGHT.

C 68–15 The night before Bonfire Night when it started to get dark you would see boys 10–15 years of age roaming the roads and lanes with torches lit. . . Torch Night had no particular significance to us except that it signified Bonfire Night was to be the following night. C 71–110 We celebrated the night of the fourth of November as Torch Night. There was a general belief that on that night we were to light torches. These torches were made by us and consisted of a stick (2 or 3 feet long) around which a piece of rubber, cloth, or birch bark was wrapped and then ignited.

tossel* n, v Cp *OED* tassel: tossel dial 19th c, *ADD* ~ 'tassel (as of corn).'

1 To hang strips of cloth, paper or hair on something as an ornament.

T 55/7–64 They'd make big birch rind masks and tossel them and trim them—whiskers and everything on them.

2 Attrib **tossel-cap**: knitted circular cap, topped with a knob formed with strands of wool (P 158¹–81).

[T 172–65 He had a round cap on with a little tossel on, on the top.]

totty n See also WOP TOTTY. Dandelion flower.

P 229–66 The garden is covered with totties. 1972 MURRAY 116 They were rarely called dandelions. To many they were 'piss-a-beds' and to others less 'vulgar' they were 'totties.'

tough a Comb **tough ladder***: rind on salt beef; anything hard to chew (P 148–63).

toutin n also **toutan, touten, touton, towtent** ['tæutʃn̩, 'taʊtʃn̩, 'tæutənz, 'tæutʃn̩z, 'tɛutʃn̩z]. Cp *DAE* dough cake 'flapjack or a kind of cake made with bread dough' (1839–) and doughnut (1805–).

1 A piece of bread dough fried in fat; DAMPER DOG.

1891 *Holly Branch* 12 Skipper Tom and crew. . .remained longer at home whenever they came with a little 'gob,' stopped on the 'jigging ground' and fry 'toutins' till the smoke of the fat. . .had almost set him mad. 1915 *Nfld Qtly* Oct, pp. 32–4 The old captain could not eat hard bread, so we would have toutons for breakfast, sweet pudding for dinner and toutons again for supper. 1937 DEVINE 53 Toutan—a fried cake with bits of fat pork in it. 1966 HORWOOD 166 . . .*toutins*, which are pieces of bread dough fried golden-brown in fat. T 94/5–64 Toutins is rose dough. You knead it down, and cut off little pieces an' you poke your finger through 'em and you have something, bacon or fatback, and lay 'em on. P 130–67 It's been a long time since we had toutins for breakfast. It was usually served for breakfast because with slow rising yeast, bread was mixed in the evening, allowed to rise during the night. P 127–77 ~ A dough pancake, made by

wrapping a piece of dough around a piece of baloney and frying. 1981 *Evening Telegram* 15 Aug, p. 21 I was [in the kitchen] waiting for the toutons to brown.

2 A bun made with flour, molasses and bits of pork (P 267–58); cp BANGBELLY, combs. with MOLASSES, PORK.

1896 *J A Folklore* ix, 36 Towtents—pork cakes made of pork chopped fine and mixed with flour. T 30/3–64¹ Toutins. . .dough mixed up with pork cut up in little small pieces and baked. T 96–64² Take the flour an' put the pork in and the bakin' powders an' then roll them an' bake. That's the toutins. M 69–17 The toutin was the traditional food of woodsmen, for if they contained enough pork, they did not freeze as other food did. 1978 *Decks Awash* vii (1), p. 51 Their food for the day would have consisted of molasses toudons (buns) or plain toudons with diced fat back pork mixed and baked in.

tow v

1 To haul seal pelts over the ice with a length of rope.

1906 DUNCAN 282–3 The skins, with the blubber adhering, were piled in heaps of six or more, according to the strength of the men who were to 'tow' them to the edge of the field, where the ship was to return in the evening. 1916 MURPHY 40 The men killed and sculped, the women and children 'towed' the fatty piles ashore. 1976 CASHIN 86 Then we towed them [seal sculps] with a special tow-rope to special spots or ice-pans, placing the ship's flag on such a pan. They then could be picked up by the ship or, if not, towed again to the vessel.

2 Cpd, comb **tow chain**: stout chain used to fasten sections of a sled together when hauling wood.

T 43/7–64 With the wagon sleds there's two, and you can lengthen out your tow chains, and if you're pulling long stuff you can have [the sleds] as far apart as you like.

tow line: a length of rope, carried coiled over the shoulder, and used by sealers to drag seal pelts over the ice; HAULING-ROPE.

1852 *Morning Post* 12 Feb, p. 4 Towlines—fit for Sealers. . .Sealing Guns. 1905 MURPHY 13 There was a gathering of 'tow-lines' in haste. 1922 *Sat Ev Post* 195, Sep, p. 10 Such a shouting, such a running, such a buckling on of sheath knives, grabbing of towlines and murderous-looking gaffs you never could imagine.

tow rope: see **tow line**; HAULING-ROPE.

1924 ENGLAND 49 On those stanchions, and on steampipes that overhead extended to the winches, oilskins, tow ropes, sou'westers, jackets, gaffs, jumpers, boots and caps were swaying with the slow roll of the ship. 1933 GREENE xv Are the sculps dragged on 'tow-ropes' to the ship or 'Pan-flags' on the Floe. 1972 BROWN 33 The men went over the sides by watches, each in charge of a master watch. They carried gaffs and sculping knives, honed to a razor-edge during the long hours of inactivity of the past few days. They carried tow ropes and lunch bags, with hard tack, oatmeal and raisins, for they might be long on the ice.

tow¹ n Cp *EDD* ~ sb¹ 3 'flax or hemp prepared for spinning.' Absorbent cotton; cotton-wool.

M 67–16 Above the sink stood a medicine cabinet which usually contained remedies for all complaints [and] cotton wool (called woo and tow). 1972 MURRAY 238 For earache some women put warm olive oil on 'tow' (cotton wool) and placed it in the ear.

tow² n See TOW v.

1 A number of sealskins with blubber attached, laced together and hauled over the ice by a rope; freq in phr *tow of fat, ~ of seals*.

1860–1 *Journ of Assembly* Appendix, p. 527 A great many old Seals were killed in Green Bay and not got; my crew killed about 1300 and only got one tow out of the lot. [1862] 1916 MURPHY 31 A man named George King and his two sons took their tows a short distance further than myself. [1870] 1899 *Nfld Law Reports* 328 The crew of the *Brothers* went to the seals on that day and brought one small tow on board. 1889 *Nineteenth Century* xxv, 520 But even if no floating pans are within reach, they are at no loss what to do; the 'tows' (each containing five or six sealskins with the blubber attached) are flung into the water, the blubber causes them to float, and the men use them as stepping-stones. 1895 GRENFELL 164 Six pelts is a full 'tow' for one man. [1900 OLIVER & BURKE] 12 He didn't know the first thing. . . / Not even to lace up a tow. 1924 ENGLAND 86 Open came the loops of the lines; swiftly the nimrods laced their 'tows.' They cut holes in the edges of the sculps, passed the ropes back and forth through these, and made a peculiar complicated knot. A turn of rope served as a grip for the left hand. The long end was passed over the right shoulder, wrapped round the arm, and firmly held by the right hand. Lacing a tow is something of a trick in itself. 1936 SMITH 54 'My God, men, it is like picking up two-dollar bills off the ice; every half-hour you can get a tow of seals worth eight dollars, every seal weighing fifty pounds. This cannot be done in any other part of the world.' 1964 BLONDAHL (ed) 75 "A Noble Fleet of Sealers": Though times are getting hard again our men have not gone soft / They'll haul their tows o'er ice-block floes, or briskly go aloft. 1972 BROWN 59 The man obediently slipped his tow of seals, planted the flag, and stood waiting for the others.

2 A device serving as a brake on a sled; DRUG.

C 70–12 ~ This was the name given to a big stick of wood which would be used to slow down the kometik when coming over a large hill. The tow was tied on to the end of the kometik by means of a piece of rope.

tow* a Bitterly cold; hardly bearable.

P 115–56 'It's cold out today.' 'Yes, it's pretty tow.' P 178–72 It's tow out tonight.

tow* See TOLL v.

town n Transferred from A-I usage: cp DINNEEN *baile* 'a town. . .a place'; see SEARY 146. In place-names, a street or neighbourhood in St John's and other communities on the Avalon Peninsula; cp SQUARE n.

[1846] 1976 O'NEILL 631 About seven o'clock on the evening of Tuesday, October 19, a fire broke out in the residence of a cooper named Summers, in an area of the city called Tarahan's Town. This was roughly that section between Gower Street and Queen's Road, bounded by Prescott and Cathedral Streets. The name came from a local merchant who owned the property. [1875] 1924 MURPHY 14 Hugh Gemmell opened machine and boiler works at Holyestown. 1891 *Holly Branch* 6 Who did not feel a pang of regret when parting forever with. . . 'Dogs' Town'. . .and a number of other euphonious and never-to-be-forgotten names? 1895 TOCQUE 89 He is a native of Irish Town, Carbonear, Newfoundland. 1937 *Bk of Nfld* ii, 27 'Tubrid's Town' was in the vicinity of Barnes Lane. 1977 *Evening Telegram* 26 Jan, p. 4 [Funds] could be available to the Georgetown area of St John's.

towny n also **townie** *OED* ~ B (1828), *NID* ~¹ 'townsman'; *DC* townie Nfld (1958–); *OED* 3 'fellow-townsman' (1865–) for sense 2.

1 A native of St John's, esp a male; usu derisive, and contrasting with BAY MAN. See also CORNER BOY, CRIBBY.

1924 ENGLAND 250 De baymen an' de townies'd fight, an' you couldn't stop it no ways. P 185–64 The townies will be here tonight [to compete in a sport]. C 68–20 There were no St John's people present, [and] someone brought up something about townies thinking St John's is just 'it.' Someone said, 'I'll have to remember that to tell some of the townies.' 1976 SHEA 36 [The election] had shown that the Tories, at least on the surface, had become a Provincial voice, instead of the squeak from the Townie side of the Overpass, or the City Boundary. 1981 *Evening Telegram* 31 Jan, p. 10 What struck me as a 'townie,' as we drove to and from the camp. . .was the appreciation the people of central Newfoundland have for their beautiful countryside.

2 Phr *put the towny on*: to claim to come from the same town (as a person).

1937 DEVINE 38 When an Irish emigrant was rebuked for wasting his time on a stranger and treating him with unusual hospitality, he would, in certain circumstances, be able to plead, 'Sure, he *put the townie on me*,' meaning the stranger had claimed to have come from the same county in the Old Country. This feeling was strong with the early immigrants.

tow pin* See TOLE PIN.

towtent See TOUTIN.

towy a ['tɔuwɪ]. Cp *OED* ~ a. Soft and fluffy, like cotton wool. See TOW¹.

T 246/7–66 Them days, if you knit a pair o' mitts or a pair of socks they were right fluffy, right towy.

track n *EDD* ~ sb² 4 'order; health' Gl Do So. Physical condition, state.

P 54–67 You'm in an awful track (said to a child with muddy clothes).

tracking n Footprints (of an animal); track; FOOTING.

[1771] 1792 CARTWRIGHT i, 188 In my walk I saw much old trackings of foxes, but none new. [1777] ibid ii, 278 He saw some slot of deer not very old, a prodigious deal of fox trackings, one fox, and several otters.

trade n *DC* ~ n 2 Nfld (1828, 1964). Merchant firm engaged in supplying men for the fishery and in the purchase and export of the catch; the aggregate of such firms; FISH TRADE, NEWFOUND-LAND ~ .

1810 STEELE 141 All was bustle and activity in the trade. [1817] 1953 JOB 23 I have no doubt myself but that the trade will continue to send out supplies if they get the two shillings bounty per quintal, but not else. T 43/4–64 They'd ship [the fish] to the trade. P 54–67 Trade means business firm: Ryan's trade. 1972 NEMEC 161 Their local. . .was not legally certified to bargain with 'the trade.'

trader n
1 Entrepreneur and vessel owner who purchases fish from fishermen in exchange for cash or supplies, operating outside the established merchant structure and truck system; merges in some contexts with sense 3 below; PEDLAR.

1765 WILLIAMS 8–9 Unfortunately [the troops were taken away and] by this Means the Traders and Inhabitants were left to shift for themselves. 1850 [FEILD] 48 [He was] intending to ask us if we would take their dried fish, having concluded that we were traders. 1888 STEARNS 165 'Where do you get your syrup from?' asked Mr Jacobs. 'It comes in cakes from Quebec,' said the good woman; 'the traders bring it to us. It is real maple sugar melted down, and they gets the best of maple sugar in Canada,' added she. [c1894] PANL P4/14, p. 198 *Trader*, it must be known is not a *livier* in a harbor, but a stranger come to do a little bartering. 1896 *J A Folklore* ix, 30 ~ Limited to a person visiting a place to trade, in contrast with the resident merchant. 1908 DURGIN 23 A Newfoundland trader goes up and down the coast in a schooner, entering all the bays, their arms, coves and harbors, wherever a few fisherfolk live or there are towns. His schooner is laden with flour, pork, molasses, and other provisions. 1937 *Seafisheries of Nfld* 54 It is also the practice of some persons to visit fishing settlements in schooners and purchase fish and other produce from the fishermen, paying cash or goods in exchange for the produce. This class of collector is usually known as a 'Trader.' T 55/6–64 You call 'em traders—goin' round sellin' stuff all the whole summer. Traders—in an' out o' every port.

2 Vessel engaged in collecting fish from fishermen and in carrying supplies.

[1856] 1975 WHITELEY 237 Go aboard the trader which ran in here yesterday and anchored astern of us. 1907 DUNCAN 225 When, in the spring of that year, the sea being open, the *Quick as Wink* made our harbor, the first of all the traders, Tumm, the clerk, was shorthanded for a cook, having lost young Billy Rudd overboard, in a great sea. 1912 *Nfld Qtly* Summer, p. 14 The isolation is complete. No steamer calls; not even a trader includes it in its list. 1942 *Little Bay Islands* 11 He sent a trader around the Bay each summer supply-

ing the people who were not in contact with merchants of other places. 1975 BUTLER 30 In later years, as skipper of a trader, I visited all the harbours and coves where inhabitants lived from St Lawrence on the west to Placentia on the east. 1981 *Evening Telegram* 19 Sep, p. 6 Christmas at Gaultois in its prime is something to recall: a four day trip in Garland's Trader at 'Settlin' Time.'

3 Smuggler.
1898 PROWSE 140 If, however, the Preventive Officers are active and vigilant smuggling will become a very risky business,—so dangerous that none but very small traders and very small craft will run their chances of being caught. 1909 BROWNE 78 The name 'trader' was in early years synonymous with 'smuggler,' and it retained this meaning up to within recent years.

trading vbl n Sailing to fishing settlements and collecting fish in exchange for cash and supplies outside the established merchant structure and truck system. Cp TRADER.

T 139/40–65 He used to do some business there. And in the fall o' the year he used to generally go round in a schooner—what they call tradin'. . .sellin' goods. 1977 BUTLER 38 'I want you to go trading for me this summer as I want to keep my good dealers around the Bay supplied with goods and I have a lot of dried fish to collect in and I wish to buy all the dried fish I can get.' To fit our schooner for trading, the cabin was to be fitted with shelves and a small counter to weigh and measure goods. The shelves were to be stocked with an assortment of all goods in stock in the merchant's store.

train[1] n Cp *DC* ~[1] n 'a low runnerless sled' obs (1783–1841), [traineau 'F *traîneau* sled'], ~[2] n obs (esp 1918 quot). Sled used for hauling objects or for sledding (M 68–7).

M 69–6 A big boy piled a load [of fire wood] on a train. He then dragged it to the church and packed it in the required place at the back. The 'train' is a long sleigh locally built and was used mostly for country travel hitched to two dogs. . . It is a wooden sleigh strongly built and with 'iron shoes' (steel bands) along the bottom of the runners. An average size train was seven feet long, six or seven inches high and about two feet wide.

train[2] n also **traine, trayne, train-oil** *OED* ~ sb[3] obs (1497–1802), ~-oil (c1553–1895), *EDD* 'fish-oil' Co, *DAE* ~ oil (1637–1866) for sense 1; *OED* ~ fat (Nfld: 1698–), ~-oil lamp (1865) for combs. in sense 2.

1 Oil rendered from the blubber of whales; oil from other marine creatures, esp fish; COD OIL, OIL. Attrib **train-oil**.

[1580] 1895 PROWSE 84 It is agreed this day betwixt Wm Massie and Thomas Tetlow, merchants of city of Chester, of the one part, and Wm Dale, master of ye good ship called *ye William of London*, of the other part, and doth bargain and sell 34,000 Newland fish, merchantable at 10s. the 100, current money in England, also four tonnes traine at £12 per tonne. [1583] 1940 *Gilbert's Voyages and Enterprises* ii, 406 [Hayes'

narrative] Abundance of Whales, for which also is a
very great trade in the bayes of Placentia & the Grand
bay, where is made Traine oiles of the Whale. 1610
Willoughby Papers 13a/99 Yf you would by store of
trayne oyle at [£]8 or under 9 the tonne yt would yeeld
good Proffitt. 1611 ibid 1/3, 83 [inventory] 6 pipes of
traine in ou[r] stage. 1620 WHITBOURNE 2 They are
ready to assist them with great labour and patience, in
the killing, cutting, and boyling of Whales; and making
the Traine-oyle. 1626 [VAUGHAN] *The Golden Fleece*,
pt 3, p. 24 But for the Fish, specially the Cod
[Newfoundland] is most wonderful, and almost incredible, unlesse a man were there present to behold it. Of
these, three men at Sea in a Boat, with some on shoare
to dresse and dry them, in thirty days will kill commonly betwixt five and twenty and thirty thousand,
worth with the Traine oyle arising from them, one hundred or sixe score pounds. 1720 FISHER 61 At a Penny
a Fish, with the Train Oil at five Pounds, comes to a
hundred and thirty Pounds. [1766] 1971 BANKS 135
Lastly Let us remember their Train Oyl for by that
name they distinguish it from Whale or Seal oyl which
they Call Fat Oyle Which is sold at a Lower Price being
only usd for the Lighting of Lamps than the train oyl
which is usd by the Curriers. 1802 *Trans Soc Arts* xx,
212 The cod-oil, or common train, brought from
Newfoundland.[*OED*] 1842 BONNYCASTLE i, 189
Train-oil, per ton, export. . .£22/8.10. 1937 DEVINE 53
~ Cod-oil—generally heard in the phrase '*train* oil.'
   2 Attrib **train bucket**: wooden container for
rendered oil of whale blubber.
   1612 *Willoughby Papers* 16a [receipt] 3 boate buck-
etts 4 boles 1 trayne buckett 8 fisher kniues.
   train-fat: see **train vat** below.
   [1634] 1745 OSBORNE 785 Fifthly, That no person
cut out, deface, or any way alter, or change the marks
of any boats or train-fats, whereby to defraud the right
owneres. [1663] 1963 YONGE 57 A train fatt is a great
square chest the corners of which are frythed athwart,
the liver is thrown into the middle, which melting, the
train leaks through this fryth and is by tappe drawn out
and put into cask. [1693] 1793 REEVES ii . . .and liberty
to go on shore on any part of *Newfoundland*, or any of
the said islands. . .for making of oil, and to cut down
wood and trees there for building and making or
repairing of stages, ship-rooms, train-fats. . .and other
necessaries for themselves and their servants, seamen,
and fishermen.
   train house: structure on fishing premises in
which cod livers, seal and whale blubber are rendered; OIL HOUSE.
   [1676] 1895 PROWSE 205 [He] forced several Masters
of Shipps, even their admiral for one to build up again
their trayne houses, themselves had cut down contrary
to their order.
   train-oil lamp: lamp fuelled with whale, seal or
cod oil.
   [c1875] 1977 *Evening Telegram* 14 Feb, p. 6 All at
once, the traine-oil lamp began to flicker and wane
until, according to the minister, they had only a 'dim
religious light' that the poet Milton described.
   train vat: large box-like trough in which whale
blubber, cod livers, etc, are placed to render oil.
   1895 PROWSE 59 [Men were] left behind every winter

to cut timber for building cook-rooms, stages, train
vats, wharves, and for the construction of boats.

tramps v   *EDD* ~ v 'walk about' So. To walk
clumsily; trample.
   P 74–67 Don't tramps on me flowers.

trap¹ n   Cp *DAE* ~¹ n 3 'trap-net' (1888, 1911),
Fisheries of U S 599, 601–2 for a variety of
pound-net used in coastal fishing in New England, for sense 1; for combs. in sense 2: *DC* Nfld:
~ berth (1905), ~ boat (1922–), ~ fisherman
(1904), ~ skiff (1958–). See also COD TRAP. For
fur-trade terms, see TRAP².
   1 A type of fixed fishing-gear used in inshore
waters, box-shaped, with a length of net stretching from shore to entrance through which
migrating cod (and salmon) enter and are trapped.
   1863 HIND [i], 297 On the day of our visit he took
9,000 cod fish out of his traps. . . A shoal of fish coming
in either direction in thirty to forty feet of water, the
depth of the net, find their course intercepted; some of
the fish pass round the seaward side of the net and
escape; the others or some of them, coming landwards,
enter the first compartment, swim round its side, and a
portion pass into the second compartment, swim round
its side, and, always pursuing a straight course, ultimately enter the third compartment, and finally the
pound or fourth compartment. The fish, when swimming round the sides of the net, are observed to pass
by the narrow doors, keeping always 'straight ahead';
so that, if the doors are always *flush* with the sides of
the net, the fish swim straight on and do not turn out of
their course to pass through them, and consequently
remain in the pound when once there. It is needless to
say that the net is *floored* with net, and really forms a
gigantic bag with square sides and narrow perpendicular inlets. [c1875] 1975 WHITELEY 153 [He] used the
first trap in Newfoundland made by American Net &
Twine Co Boston for Job Bros & Co from plan furnished by Capt James Joy—dimensions taken from my
trap at Bonne Esperance—the following year the same
firm had traps made for Indian Harbor; these were the
first traps used on the Labrador. 1884 DEMING 90 The
local title of 'trap' is applied to a contrivance much like
our fish-pounds, but made entirely of nets. 1889
HOWLEY *MS Reminiscences* 3 Reports of wreckage,
especially the destruction of traps and other fishing
gear, were heard of all along. [1905] 1912 *Nfld Law
Reports* 158 An agreement for dissolution of partnership in 1905, which shows the property to be of considerable value, consisting of land at Brigus and Labrador, goods, wares, merchandize, houses, stores, flakes,
boats, fishing gear, fourteen traps, salt, several schooners, and other fishing property. 1908 TOWNSEND 130 A
wall of net called the 'leader,' anchored at the bottom
and held up by cork floats, extends from some rocky
point to a square or diamond shaped trap of nets which
is held in place in the same way. The fish coming in
contact with the 'leader' at once turn to swim into deep
water, but instead of that find themselves in the trap,
from which they are too stupid or frightened to escape.
[1929] 1979 *Evening Telegram* 9 July, p. 11 There is a

good sign of fish with trawls between Fortune and Carmel and traps are averaging five quintals a haul. 1953
Nfld Fish Develop Report 49 On the whole, the most
productive instrument in the inshore cod fishery is the
trap. T 250–66 He had salmon nets, and an old man to
Norris Point, he was in the salmon business and he recommended the salmon trap. Where you'd get one in
the net, you'd get three or four or five in the trap. 1979
Evening Telegram 2 June, p. 6 One of my first customers, he was a real pioneer and an eager man; a great
producer and was not the last to go haul his traps. 1981
ibid 15 July, p. 2 Fishermen in the lower part of Trinity
Bay. . .have had to keep their traps out of the water
[because of the scarcity of cod-fish].

2 Attrib, comb **trap berth**: a particular area
inshore suitable for setting a cod-trap and
assigned by custom or lot to a vessel, boat, crew
or family; BERTH.

1905 GRENFELL 121–2 We cannot take our nets to
the fish, and therefore have to place them where the
fish are sure to pass [and] the Government has had to
pass a law forbidding any mark to be put out claiming a
'trap berth,' as it is called, before a certain day and
hour. 1936 SMITH 148 They came to me and asked if I
were satisfied to draw for trap-berths. 1953 *Nfld Fish
Develop Report* 49 Trap berths are located in water
from about 10 fathoms to about 20 fathoms in depth, at
points with a deep approach shoreward. In general,
these locations are found off headlands and islands and
at distances of a few yards to five miles or more from
the nearest fishing port or base of operations—usually
inside the inshore line-fishing areas. T 172/4–65 At that
time, to take a berth [you'd] take a rope, tie a bobber
on un, hang un in your trap berth. That was your trap
berth. Every Newfoundlander'd respect that. 1966
SCAMMELL 35 A good trap berth generally meant the
difference between a steady supply of fish when it
struck, or small disheartening hauls. 1975 *Evening
Telegram* 1 Feb, p. 11 This year there has been such little interest in the trap fishery that the normal Jan 15
draw for trap berths was postponed until the middle of
May.

trap boat: see **trap skiff** below.

1905 GRENFELL 124 The fishermen keep a watch on
the shore, and are soon off in the large trap-boat. 1910
PRICHARD 58 I at length prevailed upon the head of
the settlement, Capt Tom Spracklin, to lend me a trap-
boat with a crew to row her. 1936 SMITH 19 We put the
bottoms in our traps there, and painted up our trap
boat and cod seine boat. 1953 *Nfld Fish Develop
Report* 50 The trap boats or skiffs are usually from 25
to 30 feet in length. The largest represents an investment of perhaps $1,000. T 49–64 There was three
brothers with my father—four of us—we used to go in
the one boat. We had big trap boat. T 175/6–65 Everyone builded their own trap boats. An' still do.

trap buoy: any of a variety of buoyant objects
used both to mark the position of a cod trap and
to suspend it in the water; BUOY.

1913 *Christmas Chimes* 25 Every business place had
lost its wharf, every stage was down, the broken timber
of all these washing about the beaches, mixed with
pieces of broken up skiffs and boats, masts, oars, trap
buoys, corks, linnet and one does not know what else.

1971 NOSEWORTHY 256 ~ A small barrel used to float
a cod trap. 1977 BURSEY 16 He and his eldest son
George. . .were adjusting a trap-buoy in a storm of
wind.

trap cod (fish): see **trap fish** below.

1977 *Union Forum* June, p. 3 For grade A gillnet
and trap cod, 24 inches and over, the price has gone
from 12½ cents last year to 15 cents. . . For 16 to 24
inch gillnet and trap codfish, the price has increased
from 9½ cents last year to 12½.

trap crew: a number of men engaged on the
share system to fish under a 'skipper' with cod
traps; CREW.

1937 *Seafisheries of Nfld* 35 The units of production
in the Shore Fishery [include] the trap crew of from
three to six men. 1966 PHILBROOK 60 Nippers Harbour
crews engaged in catching and curing fish are of two
types: the trap crew made up of a skipper and three to
five crew men; and the fishing crew, usually two men
and formed by pairing of trap crew members. 1976
CASHIN 64 A trap crew came into service around the
middle of May. They were hired, or as we called it in
those days, 'shipped,' for a period of two months or
until August the 5th or 10th. 1977 BUTLER 53 In the
Spring of '35 [he] outfitted ten trap-crews at Flat
Islands for the trap-fishery.

trap fish: cod-fish, esp of a smaller size, taken
in a cod trap; FISH.

1907 MILLAIS 153 A quintal is 112 lbs, and it takes
about. . .a hundred trap fish, to realise this weight.
1957 *Nfld Qtly* Sep, p. 4 But there's a job for you Parsons if you want it, in about a week's time when the
trap fish starts to come in. T 175/7–65 But the feller gettin' a fair amount o' trap fish he couldn't afford to light
salt it, because it had to stay in salt a long time, he had
to put a lot o' salt on it, an' you couldn't get number
one fish out o' that. 1975 *Evening Telegram* 7 June, p. 6
We were informed this spring that they did not want
small trap fish this year at all but would buy it for offal
at 1 cent per pound. 1977 *Inuit Land Use* 261 These
young cod, or trap fish as they are called locally, were
caught until August when they migrate north. 1978
Decks Awash vii (1), p. 3 Trap fish, especially, stand to
benefit from this increased efficiency of handling.
Taken close to shore in shallow water, the fish are
warmer than their deeper water relatives, and deterioration starts very quickly in hot summer weather.

trap fisherman: fisherman who fishes for cod
with a stationary cod trap during the summer
season.

1975 *Evening Telegram* 21 June, p. 2 Inshore catches
on the Burin Peninsula have overloaded some of the
fish plants in that area and some trap fishermen are
unable to sell their catches.

trap fishery: seasonal fishery for cod during
their migration to coastal waters, using fixed
gear.

1957 *Evening Telegram* 1 Aug, p. 13 The trap fishery
in the [Bishop's Cove] area has been a complete failure
this year. T 175/7–65 That was something was used for
trap fishery mostly—the mitts, you know, heavy mittens used for the trap fishery. 1978 *Evening Telegram* 4
Mar, p. 19 Our trap fishery is the envy of every nation
in the world [for its low-cost productivity].

trap fishing: see **trap fishery**.

[1929] 1979 *Evening Telegram* 27 June, p. 40 Trap fishing on the local grounds was not good today. Only a small run of fish was had for the morning haul. 1953 *Nfld Fish Develop Report* 19 On the fishing grounds, the schooner is used as a depot or base for trap-fishing. Several berths may be utilized during the season at different points along the coast.

trap gear: floats, marker, buoys, leader, etc, used in placing a cod trap in the water; GEAR.

1936 SMITH 55 We put the bottoms in our cod-traps, painted our boats and set our trap gear in the water to hold the berths.

trap glut: seasonal surplus of cod-fish taken in cod traps during migration to inshore waters; GLUT.

1978 *Decks Awash* vii (1), p. 4 The net bag idea [is] adaptable to inshore trapboats and longliners, would help the trap glut that now plagues the fishery and is relatively easy and cheap for the fisherman.

trap keg, ~ **cag**: see **trap buoy** above (Q 67–46).

trap lead: lead weight used to fix a cod trap in place; LEAD[1] (Q 67–34).

trap leader: a length of net stretching from the shore to a cod trap to guide fish into the entrance; LEADER.

1895 GRENFELL 68 While the ice was still on the shores of Labrador, a steamer was sent ahead with numbers of men, each armed with 'a trap leader,' to get ahead of the sailing schooners which were working their perilous way along inside the ice floe.

trap linnet: 'twine' knitted into meshes to form a cod trap; LINNET.

T 43/8–64 If you were knittin' trap linnet you'd put up your linnet one hundred meshes deep. 1966 SCAMMELL 32 We used to knit trap linnet during the winter to pay our school fees.

trap loft: room or area of fishing premises where cod traps and other nets are kept for winter storage and repair; NET n: ~ LOFT, TWINE LOFT.

T 91/2–64 We had one rigged up down in our trap loft.

trap man: see **trap fisherman** above.

T 168/70–65 We had three hundred accounts o' fishermen—for the schooners an' their sharemen, and then the trapmen home here, an' the hook-and-line men. 1966 SCAMMELL 36 I know some places up on the South Coast where the trapmen draws lots for berths. That's the fairest way. T 393/4–67 The trap men went right to Cape Cove where they goes now, wi' their oars; six men in a skiff then—one man with a scullin' oar an' the other fellers with the five oars across her. 1972 MURRAY 52–3 In the late spring 'trapmen' would be busy in their 'store lofts' mending the 'linnet' (that is, replacing older, weak sections in the cod trap). 1977 BURSEY 35 The *Lady Irene* would be hauled in and each trapman would bring along from twenty five quintals, a small shipment to seventy five quintals of hard dried pickled fish. This would command a good price.

trap master: member of a Labrador fishing crew in charge of setting and hauling a cod trap.

1895 GRENFELL 67 A long telescope, with a plain glass bottom—the fish glass—is pushed down into the room, through which the trap-master is peering to see how many finny prisoners there are. Now the door is pulled up, and now the floor is rising—rising—rising, being passed right over the boat, until all the frightened captives are huddled together in one seething mass near the surface. P 102–60 [There were] fourteen trap boats with five men and a trapmaster for each.

trap mooring: anchoring device, line and buoy to secure a cod trap in place in the water.

T 172/5–65 I passed the tow line around the rigging; when I got back to the quarter I took a turn around a grump head to heave down a end o' towline to a trap moorin'.

trap-net: see sense 1.

1883 *Fisheries Exhibit* xiii, 51–2 But the seine-nets are being gradually superseded by trap-nets. The trap-net consists of a rectangular trap of netting, into which the fish are conducted by a leader of netting running from some rock on the foreshore.

trap season: late June to early August; see **trap fishery** above.

1975 *Evening Telegram* 2 July, p. 3 [He] explained that the plants were at capacity level which happens every year 'from a few days to a couple of weeks' during the six-week trap season.

trap skiff: a large undecked fishing boat, propelled by oar, small sail or engine and used in the coastal fishery to set and haul nets, esp cod traps; SKIFF.

1907 DUNCAN 138 My uncle had manned a trap-skiff at dawn (said they) to put a stranger across to Topmast Point. 1937 *Seafisheries of Nfld* 29 The gear most favoured by the Shore fishermen are cod-traps, cod-nets, hand lines, trawls and jiggers, and the boats used are schooners, trap skiffs, jack-boats, dories and punts; many of those are now propelled by motor engines. 1956 *Evening Telegram* 12 Dec, p. 11 Exactly the right boat for the job, the trapskiff has no peer when it comes to hauling a trap. Ranging in size from 25 to 30 feet, give or take a foot or two, it handles easily, manoeuvres readily, does not impose too great a strain on ropes and mesh, offers excellent convenience for this fishing method and provides good carrying capacity in relation to its size. 1963 TEMPLEMAN & FLEMING 55 In many areas. . .the inshore grounds are so productive of cod by longline in the late summer and autumn that a combined trap-skiff-longliner, a smaller boat than that required for long-distance offshore work, could provide a very satisfactory operation using traps in the early summer and longline later in the year. T 43/7–64 Now a trap skiff, you couldn't have any deck on her, see. 1979 *Signal* 12 Oct, p. 3 E F Barnes Ltd in St John's has almost completed construction of a steel trapskiff—the first ever in Newfoundland. The boat, which is 25 feet long with an eight-foot-11-inch beam, will be powered by a diesel engine and is expected to carry 12,000 pounds of fish.

trap skipper: see **trap master**.

M 68–26 The frame of the trap was set first. Some trap skippers put out the leader anchor first.

trap system: see **trap fishery** above.
1939 LODGE 52 The trap system may give large catches; it may give none. The return depends on the vagaries of the cod and not on the skill or assiduity of the fishermen.

trap time: see **trap season** (P 148–62).
1975 BUTLER 68 *Iris and Verna*—thirty four tons, four dories and nine crewmen, powered with gas engine, fished with cod trap at Golden Bay and fished the Grand Banks after trap time.

trap vee: see VEE.

trap voyage: the enterprise or period of the summer fishery in coastal waters in which cod traps are used; the catch so taken; VOYAGE.
1964 *Daily News* 1 July, p. 2 Although it is getting late for a good trap voyage yet there have been seasons when big trap voyages have been secured in the month of July. T 191–65 He an' his brother was goin' fishing and it was after the trap voyage—it was hook an' line fishing in September month. 1977 BUTLER 72 At Cape Cove, Island Head and Northern Head, dogfish were so numerous the trap voyage was almost a failure.

trap² n   DC ~ house (1931); trapline (1913–). In designations of areas and devices for the taking of wild animals: **trap headland, ~ house, ~ line** [FUR PATH, TILT LINE], **~ station**.
1921 CABOT vii . . .the fine trap headland at the west end of Mistastin Lake. 1933 MERRICK 141 From here on we stopped about every fifteen minutes to dig out a trap, bait it, set it and fix the trap house if necessary. 1977 *Inuit Land Use* 284 You build your cabins, you had your traps—there was quite a bit of work to setting each trap, like a trap house to get the animal to go in for your bait. 1947 TANNER 710 This [fur-path] is not a path in the ordinary meaning, but a zig-zagging, uncleared line, with a row of traps, and for that reason it is called a trap-line. This line must be blazed with an axe at such distances that it is possible to see from one mark to the next; a triangular mark is made in the tree beside each trap in order to find it again after the snow falls. 1975 BUTLER 90 Now, the most important thing was to plan our trap lines. 1977 *Inuit Land Use* 240 Trap lines belonged to individual trappers by virtue of their continued use of an area. 'We all had different places. We weren't allowed to go where somebody else had their traps.' Ibid 303 Trap lines. . .run inland or follow the shores of the saltwater areas. The trap lines that run inland generally follow the courses of rivers and streams, and they trapped mixed populations of aquatic fur-bearing animals. The coastal trap lines generally took coloured fox, and traps set in spring on the ice in Groswater Bay or around the islands east of Holton generally took white fox. [1786] 1792 CARTWRIGHT iii, 115–16 I visited my nearest trap-station, and sat watching about half an hour, but saw nothing.

trap v   In the coastal fishery, to take cod or salmon with a type of fixed gear or 'trap.'
M 68–26 No one, for example, in Hr Buffett (except, perhaps, some of the younger people) would say the *MacDonald* had gone to Golden Bay fishing that summer. They would say 'trapping.' 1972 MURRAY 244 A

woman's workday in summer was governed largely by whether her husband was 'handlining' or 'trapping.' 1975 BUTLER 68 [The vessel] thirty eight tons, six dories and fourteen men, powered with fifty [h.p.] Bolinder diesel engine, trapped Golden Bay and fished the Grand Banks. 1975 LEYTON 35 I went trapping after that, fishing with the Farrells. 1977 *Inuit Land Use* 338 The Winters and the Edmunds trapped there [in the bay]. That's theirs.

trapping vbl n See TRAP¹ n, v.
Attrib, comb **trapping berth**: a particular area of the fishing grounds assigned by custom or lot to a vessel, boat, crew or family; BERTH, TRAP¹: ~ BERTH.
[1940] 1954 INNIS 430 [This was] in contrast with the free fishery of Newfoundland and its numerous disputes as to trapping berths. 1977 *Inuit Land Use* 169 Because cod always returned to the good feeding areas, trapping berths in these areas were the object of competition between local skippers and the Newfoundland schoonermen.

trapping crew: a group (of persons) engaged or 'shipped' by a merchant, planter or skipper to conduct afloat and on shore the various branches and operations of taking and processing cod with fixed gear or 'traps'; CREW, TRAP¹: ~ CREW.
1972 MURRAY 245 The routine followed by a 'trapman's' wife was very different from that of the 'handliner's' wife, when fish were plentiful. As a member of a large 'trapping crew,' she would have a specialized job to attend to, but she would have to handle thousands of fish in a single boatload and there might be five boatloads to 'put away' in a single day.

trapping season: period of the summer, June to early August, when cod (and salmon) are taken in coastal waters by means of stationary nets; see SEASON.
1964 *Daily News* 22 July, p. 4 The fall voyage can compensate for a poor trapping season. 1977 BURSEY 132 All the fishermen. . .took up their traps and gave it up for a bad trapping season.

trapping voyage: the enterprise or period of the summer fishery in coastal waters during which cod traps are used; TRAP¹: ~ VOYAGE, VOYAGE.
M 69–27 One, of course, cannot mention fishing without referring to the trapping voyage. This was a period during June when the fish were usually very near the surface of the water after caplin.

travel v   At the seal hunt, to search the ice-floes for seals.
[1907] 1979 *Nfld Qtly* Fall, p. 26 We can see the men a long way off still travelling, which indicates they have not come across any seals yet.

travel n   Cp OED ~ sb 2 b 'a journey' now only pl exc dial; EDD 6. A foray on the ice (after seals); RALLY (1925 *Dial Notes* v, 345).

traveller n

1 A seal moving purposively over the ice toward a distant point.

1916 YOUNG 153 This [large bedlamer] seal was called by the natives a 'traveller,' and it had travelled for sixty miles or more over the ice. P 245–74 ~ A seal searching for a 'swatch' or patch of open water. They travelled in a straight line, often for long distances, in search of open water and safety.

2 A louse; spider; a crawling creature.

T 96/9–64¹ 'You see that spider,' he said, 'a big spider,' he said, 'traveller.' T 417–67 Just lice—travellers.

3 Wooden device or stick for hauling a trawl-line; RUNNING-STICK (1971 NOSEWORTHY 257).

trawl n *Cent* ~ n 1 'a buoyed line, of great length, to which short lines with baited hooks are attached at intervals'; *DAE* 1 (1860–); see BULTOW. In designation of various parts and operations of a trawl, esp in the Bank fishery: **trawl bobber** [see BOBBER], ~ **gear** [see GEAR], ~ **hook, ~-hook set** [see HOOK-SET], ~ **knot,** ~ **tub** [see TUB].

1957 *Evening Telegram* 16 Aug Perhaps 'tis a trawl-bobber. No, there's no place to fasten the moorin'. 1977 RUSSELL 113 He rowed up closer and figgered that, unless it happened to be a German bomb-shell, it'd come in handy for a trawl bobber. . . 'Twas laced up just like a boot, although he'd never seen anyone with a foot *that* shape. He shook it, but it seemed all hollow inside, so he figgered 'twas a trawl bobber sure enough, and he brought it in. 1960 FUDGE 11 With the coming of winter, men were busy taking food and trawl gear on board. T 50/2–64 Ye'd be watchin' that feller—'fraid he'd drive one o' them hooks in his hand—go right through, see them trawl hooks. 1966 SCAMMELL 23 'Did you eat all those raw onions I put in your bread-box?' The old man avoided her glance. He was thinking of how he had hooked those same onions on the last five trawl-hooks when his caplin ran out. P 113–76 A trawl-hook set [is] a wooden device used by dory-fishermen on the Banks to straighten bent trawl-hooks. T 50/2–64 Trawl line is a big line. They'd be all put together—go to what they call a trawl knot. It'll never slip. M 67–10 The seine, dip-net, trawl-tub, scoop, and oars are the main things in the flat. 1971 NOSEWORTHY 257 Trawl tub. One half or three quarters of a flour barrel with two rope handles, used for holding *trawl lines*. ('Sawed off at top hoop.')

tread n Comb **tread-pole**: one of a number of sticks placed across a stream as a temporary bridge.

T 50–64 All hands had to put tread poles across the little brooks, they were so high with water, to get across 'em.

treaty n Comb **treaty shore,** ~ **coast**: northern coast-line of Newfoundland, and the West coast, where French held fishing and curing rights until 1904; FRENCH SHORE.

1895 PROWSE 257 The French fisherman builds his temporary hut and erects his stage on the treaty shore of Newfoundland. 1899 *Tribune Christmas No* 4 If arrangements can be satisfactorily carried out Sir Henry contemplates residing at Bay of Islands during some of the summer months, and from that point would visit the several settlements on the Treaty Coast. 1903 DES VOEUX ii, 139 By the treaty signed in the latter year [1783] the Treaty of Utrecht was confirmed, except that the 'Treaty shore' was differently defined as the coast between Cape St John round the north of the island down to Cape Ray at its south-western extremity. 1912 *Nfld Qtly* Dec, p. 28 At Griquet is my treaty-shore home. 1920 GRENFELL & SPALDING 15 We are out of the ice field and steaming past Cape St John. This was the dividing line between the English and French in the settlement of their troubles in 1635. North of it is called the French or Treaty Shore, or as the French themselves so much more quaintly named it, 'Le Petit Nord.' It is at the north end of Le Petit Nord that St Antoine is located. 1955 DOYLE (ed) 34 "John Yetman": There is none so brave who fished the waves as the man from Treaty Shore. 1964 *Evening Telegram* 1 Apr, p. 6 Newfoundlanders are always hearing or reading about the French or Treaty Shore. Originally it was established as stretching from Cape Bonavista and Point Riche on the Northwest Coast; but the Treaty of Versailles Declaration of 1783 changed the limits to Cape St John and Cape Ray.

treckly See DIRECTLY.

trench v Cp *OED* ~ v 3 b 'to lay (land) in trenches and ridges alternately' agricul. To spade or hoe soil between rows of potatoes up on the plants, esp after applications of caplin, manure, etc.

T 36–64 What we call top manure is before we trench the potatoes. We earth 'em up the second time. Then we put the caplin on 'em. M 69–5 The crops had to be manured. Kelp, caplin, or codfish guts had to be [be] lugged into the gardens. The potatoes had to be trenched. 1970 JANES 11 Here the child Saul grew up and here, from the time when he could turn a fish or trench a potato, he knew one thing only: work. P 143–74 In August, the men spread caplin in the larger gardens and trenched the plots (threw more soil over the re-fertilized vegetables).

trenching vbl n Spading or hoeing soil on rows of potato plants.

1937 DEVINE 53 ~ A second hoeing of potatoes or other vegetables after they have sprouted above the surface. At this stage the caplin or fish offal, widely used as fertiliser, is applied, being earthed over as laid on the rows. M 69–7 The manure was also used for the potatoes, but there was extra work here because the potatoes and manure had to be covered up again. This was called trenching.

trend n *EDD* ~ sb 2 D. The turning and winding of a stream or estuary.

P 148–61 A tug going up the trend was described.

triangle v Cp *OED* ~ sb 2 l 'tripod. . .to which soldiers were. . .bound to be flogged.' To flog (a person) tied to a tripod or triangle.

1895 PROWSE 226 Mr Pearce, of Twillingate, who died not long ago, remembered as a boy seeing a man triangled—tied by the outstretched arms—and whipped by order of a fishing admiral.

trigger n

1 Piece of kindling used to support wood of various sizes in preparing a fire on an open hearth; cp BAVIN, CHOVY*, SPLIT n.

1866 WILSON 353 Making a fire was quite an art, and required back-junks, fore-junks, middle-junks, triggers, splits and brands. T 156–65 And then one corner [was] fulled [with] triggers an' the other fulled wi' wood.

2 Comb **trigger mitt**: woollen mitten with sheaths for both thumb and index finger; cp MITT (P 148–76).

trim v Cp *OED* ~ v 2 'to put into proper condition; prepare' obs (1517–1725) for sense 1; 11 b (1895, 1901) for sense 2.

1 To pack (something) neatly in a cask.

[1772] 1792 CARTWRIGHT i, 241, 251 [I] ordered the cooper and another man to that place to trim the oil, and stow both it and the skins in the house. . . I sent Baskem and another man to the Lodge, for the cooper to trim the salmon, and to collect the traps.

2 To move along close by (something); to hug, skirt.

1812 BUCHAN *MS* 27 Jun . . .on the following day having trimmed along the ice for twenty miles towards the Funk Islands, in expectation of gaining an outside passage, but found this impracticable. [1916] 1972 GORDON 52 Coming down from the neck-path, we had once again to trim the land-wash and met much the same lumpy going as before. T 43–64 When the fish swim round the trap they'd strike up against the linnet every time, but the fish trimmin' the leader an' goin' for the trap had an open doorway. 1977 *Nfld Qtly* Summer, p. 9 They put the flag up in the cliff but we didn't see the flag; and they sent the men out but we didn't see the men. But we trimmed on down by the shore and when they seen us trimming on down by the shore they went back again. P 254–78 We would wait for the ducks to trim in around the shore. 1979 NEMEC 276 Boats returning from fishing frequently will 'trim the shore' in order to see ('spy') whether any worthwhile quantities of driftwood have accumulated since their last visit.

trip n Cp *Cent* ~[1] n 7 'the catch. . .of fish caught during a voyage' (1891); *Fisheries of U S* 3 'a big trip' [of halibut] N E. The total catch of fish, seals, etc, taken during a single voyage; cargo; the proceeds of the catch; freq with specifying word CAPLIN, HERRING, SALT, SAVING; cp VOYAGE.

1866 WILSON 211 The quantity of fish in the water-horse is indefinite; it simply means one put or trip of fish, that had been washed from the salt the day before, and left to drain; sometimes it is not more than two or three quintals, sometimes it is ten or twelve. 1873 CARROLL 36 It is strange to say, but not the less

true, that the longer a man takes charge of an ice hunting vessel the less he knows where to obtain a trip of old and young seals. [1896] SWANSBOROUGH 5 "March": They labour hard through cold and wet, / But in a week their trip may get. / When they come in and seals have sold / Some men get forty pounds in gold. [1898] 1905 *Nfld Law Reports* 295 What prospect the *Kite* had of securing a trip or part of a trip of seals. . . 1924 ENGLAND 71 Us goin' to bore up wid a full trip o' fat, a logger load. 1934 *Nfld Qtly* July, p. 30–1 On February last they launched out in the deep again, and added the S.S. *Beothic* to their fleet, and as a reward to their energy and push she brought in the largest trip she ever had. 1937 DEVINE 54 Trip of bait (spruce, seals, fish, etc). The word trip here has a quantity meaning: a cargo or load. 1960 FUDGE 7 Our vessel, after discharging her trip of cod fish, fitted to go to Newfoundland for a trip of frozen herring.

trip v To capsize (a boat).

1977 *Nfld Qtly* Summer, p. 7 When it came daylight and no sign of us he thought we were after tripping our boat and we thought he was after tripping his. We had a sail on her then and just let her dodge on before the wind to see if we could see anything coming behind us.

trouble n Euphemism for bereavement; cp TAKE v: ~ *trouble*.

P 54–67 They've had a lot o' trouble. M 68–11 You greet the [bereaved] family by saying 'Sorry for your trouble.' P 108–70 The undertaker, when called in his line of business, would doff his stove-pipe hat and deliver his famous salutation: 'Sorry-for-your-trouble-what's-the-length-of-the-corpse?'

trounce v To drive fish in a desired direction by thrashing the water with a noise-making device.

T 80/3–64 He motions with his hand to heave away a rock. Then [the cod would] roll this way, roll that way and that's what we done: we trounced it right in the trap.

trouncer n A device used to drive fish in a desired direction by thrashing the water; DOUSER, THRASHER.

1937 DEVINE 54 ~ A bar of iron, stick of wood, grapnel, etc, used to thrash the water in order to drive fish into a net or narrow gulch. 1956 *Evening Telegram* 12 Dec, p. 5 Sometimes a 'trouncer' (a length of chain attached to a rope) was used as a flail underwater to keep the fish in the bunt of the net. 1967 FIRESTONE 96 A *trouncer*, an iron ring about the size of a racket bow with 15 or 20 iron rings attached to it, was thrown in to frighten the fish back toward the perimeter of the [seine] so as to keep them from escaping through the hole formed by the taking up of the foots. T 80/3–64 An' of course we never had nar regular trouncer, you know. I means them fellers had trouncers; a gert ring made wi' iron rings on un. An' you let un go down the bottom an' you'd hear un for a mile, all those rings rattlin' over the rocks. That was a proper trouncer. P 9–73 The trouncer was a gadget used when hauling the seine to keep the fish away from the opening near the boat where the foots of the seine came on board over the gunwale. It was made from half-inch iron rod and had several rings attached. About three or four fathom of small six-thread rope was fastened to it, to haul it back when it was thrown overboard.

trout n Cp *OED* ~ sb[1] 1 'freshwater fish of the genus *Salmo*,' *DAE* 1 (1588–) for senses 1, 2.

1 Eastern brook trout (*Salvelinus fontinalis*), both the freshwater fish (MUD TROUT) and the saltwater type or sea-trout; also attrib.

[1583] 1940 *Gilbert's Voyages & Enterprises* ii, 406 [Hayes' narrative] With incredible quantities, and no lesse varietie of kindes of fish in the. . .fresh waters, as Trouts, Salmons and other fish to us unknowen. 1620 WHITBOURNE 10 The Rivers also and Harbours are generally stored with delicate Fish, as. . .Troutes the fairest, fattest and sweetest, that I have seene in any part of the world. [1766] 1971 BANKS 120 Took great Plenty of small Trouts. [1770] 1792 CARTWRIGHT i, 59 I soon discovered [the otter] fishing in the disembogu-ing of the brook, where it was yet open. I sat watching for an hour; in which time he caught plenty of small trouts. [1771] ibid i, 134 I went in the punt [from the estuary] up the stream, and killed one slink and a brace of trout. 1819 ANSPACH 400 Its numerous lakes and ponds abound in divers kinds of excellent trout, partic-ularly the salmon species. 1877 ROCHFORT 78 Exports: Trout. . .1950 brls. [1892] 1896 *Consolidated Statutes of Nfld* 920 No person shall catch, kill, or take any kind of trout, char. . .landlocked salmon, or any fresh-water or migratory fish in any lake, river or stream of this col-ony between [15 Sep and 1 Dec]. [1894–1929] 1960 BURKE (ed White) 37 "The Trouting Liar": And they'd leap for anything at all, / Such trout you never saw, / He caught three dozen on a rag, / Oh lads do you hear the chaw. 1909 GRENFELL[2] (ed) 146 Dr Grenfell reports that the trout [of Hamilton River] bite freely all summer. The fish appear to be sea-run, although their sojourn in salt water is probably short, for they do not lose their markings as do the trout of the St Lawrence. 1921 CABOT 222 A cloud of lance, eel-like fish five or six inches long, were held in the little trout trap. 1966 LEIM & SCOTT 114 Brook trout. *Salvelinus fontinalis*. Common Names: speckled trout, sea trout. . . Colour strikingly different in sea trout and those in fresh water. 1975 RUSSELL 8 You'll see him and his biggest boy out in their punt on fine days hand lining in shoal water. Other times you'll see him goin' in over the hills with his trout pole.

2 Arctic char of Labrador (*Salvelinus alpinus*); also attrib.

1916 HAWKES 88 For trout. . .the Eskimo fish with an iron hook set into a piece of wood and bound fast with sinew. [1935–6] 1977 *Inuit Land Use* 107 Trout may be caught quite easily in almost any harbour, but to catch them one needs nets. 1966 LEIM & SCOTT 112–13 Arctic char. *Salvelinus alpinus*. Common Names: sea trout, Hudson Bay salmon. . . The arctic char may be distinguished from the brook trout by its distinctly forked tail and by the lack of marbling on the back. 1977 *Inuit Land Use* 123 Some people would fill a few barrels with salted trout [char]. Because cod drew more money than trout, the people would leave trout fishing as soon as there were cod around to get.

3 Familiar form of address.

P 259–67 'Me old trout,' a term to denote friendli-ness. Q 67–105 Come here, my little trout. 1975 *Evening Telegram* 6 June, p. 4 The defence witness brought down the house when, in replying affirma-tively to questions by Magistrate Hugh O'Neill, he said: 'That's right, me old trout.'

trouter n Comb **trouters' train,** ~ **special**: des-ignating passenger train which stops at any point requested by anglers on holiday excursion, esp on 24 May.

1911 PROWSE 70 One of the unique features of the holiday season in St John's is that 'Trouters' trains' are run from the capital to points within easy reach along the railway line, and it is not uncommon for several hundred men and boys to engage in this pastime, and to return in twenty-four hours with thousands of doz-ens of fish. P 108–70 The Trouters' Special was a train of several cars which left St John's on the eve of the 24th of May with trouters for the various ponds of their choice, dropping them off wherever they wished along the railway line, and picking them up the following night to bring them back, with their catches, hang-overs, fly-bites, chills, etc.

trouting vbl n *OED* ~ (1768, 1827). The wide-spread pastime of angling for freshwater trout, esp brook trout, as distinguished from FISHING for cod, etc; also attrib.

1865 *Atlantic Mo* xv, 47 Next day there was trouting, with a little. . .better than the usual minnow result. [1877] 1898 *Christmas Bells* 17 The working system of the place in which I was employed was such as afforded a plentiful supply of holidays, and on all such occasions trouting was the 'order of the day.' 1883 *Fish Exhibit Cat*[4] 176 Trouting Lines. [1886] LLOYD 72 Trout teem in every river and brook. . .on stormy days when the cod fishery cannot be prosecuted. . .the fishermen go 'trouting,' as they say. . . The Newfoundlander's 'trout-ing pole' is a gigantic affair, and very much resembles a telegraph post. 1895 PROWSE 62 The Scot [as a sealer] is a long way behind the genuine native, who has been practising it from a small boy; copying, jigging tom-cods, and going in the woods trouting, being the popu-lar amusements of the native boy. 1910 *Nfld Qtly* Oct, p. 17 [He] had gone for a wee bit of troutin'. 1969 HORWOOD 223–4 Of all the varieties of sports fishing available at St John's, trouting remains by far the most popular. On May 24th, the fisherman's holiday, the city is practically empty of men. 'Going trouting' on that day is not just a sport, it is a ritual, a religion. M 70–9 'Have you got era troutin' bag, Aubrey?' 'Na, I'm going to string mine on a skiver.' 1973 SMALLWOOD 63 We children had some glorious adven-tures pursuing the great Newfoundland pastime, trout-ing. (We never did call it trout fishing, except when we wanted foreigners to know what we meant, for how could you expect aliens and strangers to know that trouting meant trout fishing?) 1978 *Evening Telegram* July 29, p. 16 . . .boilin' up a boiler of corned beef and cabbage. Not only in troutin' season but in berry pic-kin' time especially.

truck[1] n Cp *OED* ~ sb[1] 2 'payment. . .other than in money' (1743–), 5 ~ system (1830–); *DC* ~ system (1849–); *Shetland Truck System* (1872). Arrangement by which a fisherman and his family are supplied by a merchant with provisions, gear, etc, against the season's catch; goods and supplies so received; also attrib: **truck agent, ~ system**; CREDIT SYSTEM.

[1851] 1954 INNIS 404 Payment is made in truck, 3 quintals of green fish at 3s 3d per quintal, livers included, counting for one quintal of cured fish; some of the fishermen complained of being compelled to deal in this manner, as the truck agents of Nicolle of Jersey were not allowed salt to sell them. 1872 DASHWOOD 247 The truck system is universal in this country, and the fisherman, after paying all expenses of outfit and provisions for the season, has but little left in cash. 1892 *Christmas Bells* 18 'Now, Mary Jane, where's that pretty little hat you had last fall?' 'Didn't take up no head truck at all, sir, last fall.' [1911] 1930 COAKER 33 The stores will sell for cash, and it won't be many years before the credit and truck system will disappear, and every dollar spent will secure a full dollar's worth in value. 1913 *Morning Post* 12 My great business at first was to carry out the law that compelled balances to be paid in cash. In Harbour Grace truck lasted much longer. 1937 DEVINE 54 The system of receiving payment from the merchant for fish or labour given him, by taking goods in exchange—'taking it up in truck.'

truck[2] n
   Comb **truck cart**: horse-drawn wheeled vehicle used to transport heavy goods; CAR.
   1936 DEVINE 163 John Brien had a stable and worked truck carts in the next building to Renolds.
   truckman: owner and operator of a 'truck cart.'
   T 731–70 A truckman meant a man that had a horse and long cart and stood in the coves until he was hired. 1976 CASHIN 84 His avocation in life was that of what is termed nowadays a truckman. He had left his horse and cart in front of the old mechanics' hall on Water Street, imbibed a little too freely, then he came aboard to see a friend of his off to the sealing voyage. . .

truckle v *EDD* ~ v 1 s w cties. To trundle or roll (a wheeled toy); CHUCKLE, RUCKLE.
   C 70–25 When the car or truck was pushed along. . .it was called *truckling* the car. In fact the name of the game was 'truckling cars.'

truckle n *OED* ~ sb 4 'low-wheeled car' Ir (1689–); *EDD* sb[1] Ir obs. A small cart with four wheels; TRUCKLY-MUCK.
   1937 DEVINE 54 ~ A home made hand cart with small solid wheels. M 68–24 He was on a home-made cart (truckels) with four wheels drawn by a very obedient dog.

truckly-muck n also **chuckle-de-muck***, **trucklemuck, truckly**. Cp *EDD* truckly-mux D; truck-amuck sb 1 'trolly,' 2 'farm-cart' D for sense 1.
   1 A small cart with four wheels; TRUCKLE.

1895 *J A Folklore* viii, 39 ~ a small two-handed car for dogs, with a handle for a man to keep it straight. [c1900] 1978 *RLS* 8, p. 26 Trucklemuck. A small two wheeled hand car with a guiding stick in front, usually used with dogs to haul while the owner also hauls with a rope over one shoulder & his other hand holding the handle or tiller. 1937 DEVINE 54 Truckley-muck. A home made hand cart with small solid wheels. P 267–58 ~ Four-wheeled cart used on the [fishing] stage.
   2 Various toys pushed or trundled by children.
   P 148–65 Truckly. A small barrow, with flat cross-pieces, two small wheels at end, pushed by boy. M 70–25 [He] made a truckley muck for me. It was a long piece of wire, about the size of a clothes hanger on the round. Around this wire there was strung a number of milk cans by pushing the wire through the top of the milk can and out through the bottom. The bottom two cans were on bent wire and as they rolled, all the others turned. C 71–127 Truckly-mucks were carts [with] wheels and were used by the children of the area for pulling each other around, for racing, etc.

trumpet n Comb **trumpet flower**: twin-flower (*Linnaea borealis*) (1898 *J A Folklore* xi, 228).

trunk n Cp *OED* ~ sb 10 'box-like passage for light, air, water, or solid objects' (1610–); *DC* Nfld (1819). Comb **trunk hole**: opening in the floor of a fishing stage through which offal and waste are thrown and salt water drawn up.
   [1766 (1971)] BANKS 134 [His] business it is to gut the Fish & cut of its head which he does by Pressing the Back of the head with Both hands against the side of the table made sharp for the Purpose when both head and Guts fall through a hole in the Floor into the water.] [1810] 1971 ANSPACH 21 [The header] throws [the guts] into the *trunk-hole* under him through the stage floor. 1866 WILSON 206 [The splitting-table] has a trunk-hole for dropping the heads and offal of the fish into the sea. 1937 DEVINE 54 ~ A trap in the floor of a stage through which fish offal is thrown away and water drawn up in a bucket. 1966 SCAMMELL 140 Trunkhole. Trapdoor in fish stage for drawing water, etc. 1972 MURRAY 202 Male members of the family rarely made use of inside [toilet] facilities. . . The 'trunk-hole' (a hole about one and a half feet square in the floor through which a bucket was lowered to bring up sea water) in the stage was their toilet seat. P 66–75 A trunk hole is a hole in the floor of the stage where you salted fish. It was always near the splitting table and you used it for drawing up water and for throwing away offal.

tub n Cp *DAE* ~ n 2 trawl tub (1884 quot); *Fisheries of U S* 163, 175 'tubs of fish,' 'tub o' trawl' for sense 1.
   1 A wooden container, usu a barrel sawn off at the first hoop above the middle, in which trawl-lines are coiled in dory fishing; a quantity of trawl-lines or of fish caught with the lines; similar container used for other fisheries purposes, usu with defining word: BAIT, FISH, PUNCHEON, etc.

[1952] 1965 PEACOCK (ed) i, 143 "Skipper Tom": And down o'er the bank I steered 'er so straight, / With a whipping fine breeze and a tub of fresh bait. 1960 FUDGE 9 My brother Edward was hauling and I was coiling our handlines and we just had one tub of gear. 1971 CHIARAMONTE 36 He and his dory-mate had set four 'tubs' of trawl line and had lost two four-line tubs of gear. 1975 BUTLER 56 All those boats would use four six line tubs of trawls. They would fish up the Southern Shore of Placentia Bay. 1976 CASHIN 9 He gathered his followers together, collected a few tubs of rotten squid (commonly called soldiers) and waited at the foot of Tors Cove Hill. 1979 TIZZARD 330 This made a total of seventy tubs or 35 barrels of codfish we caught from October 6th to November 6th.

2 Attrib, comb **tub barrel**: see **tub barrow**.

P 254–78 ~ Tub made of half-barrel; with two side shafts for two men to carry.

tub barrow: wooden container, or half barrel, with handles attached, carried by two persons; BARROW TUB.

1972 MURRAY 106 She had to take part in several other operations connected with handling the fish, including bringing them in 'tub-bars' (200 pounds or more at a time) from the stagehead to the splitting area.

tub knot: special knot tied at end of the series of linked lines forming a trawl, and serving to mark its end.

1960 FUDGE 9 While untying the tubknot I looked over my shoulder and our vessel, running before the wind and swell, was nearly upon us, coming right for the middle of our dory.

tuck v   Cp *OED* ~ v[1] 5 'to take the fish from (the seine) by means of a tuck-net'; *EDD* v[2] 7 Co. To enclose fish in a net by drawing the openings together; CAST.

1955 DOYLE (ed) 85 "When the Caplin Come In": The caplin to slaughter they rush for the water / And toss their nets as they tuck every throw. C 71–21 When you're casting caplin, you tuck the net and nips the net so that the caplin won't slip out. 1975 BUTLER 58 They would then haul up the foot of the seine and tuck the fish up in the bunt of the seine until it could be dipped on board the skiff in dip nets. 1979 COOPER 15 "Caplin Time": Some are caught in dip nets / Or tucked in castnets.

tuck[1] n   Cp *OED* ~ v[1] 5, and TUCK v.

1 One of the lines drawn tight in a 'cast-net' when catching caplin.

T 198–65 'Tis all tucks, you know; ten or fifteen tucks in the cast-net. P 127–76 Tucks. A number of lines, usually 10–15, attached to the bottom of a cast net and the tucking line. The tucks serve the function of closing the net when the tucking line is tightened.

2 Quantity of fish taken in one haul (of a net); PUT(T).

1955 DOYLE (ed) 86 "When the Caplin Come In": A tuck full o' caplin got hitched in a grapnel, / And now me old net is gone right from the horn. P 148–61 [We got an] extra big tuck of fish. M 67–16 His trap may not

have been made especially for that berth, but he was able to set it in such a way to get a tuck of fish when there was any around. M 69–17 When the caplin are sighted, the net is thrown forward by the right hand, and over the caplin; then a tug on the rope traps the caplin in a sort of bag. If the fisherman was lucky, he would say, 'B'y that was a good tuck of caplin.' P 75–19 We had a big tuck of fish this morning.

tuck[2] n   Prob shortened from TUCKAMORE, sense (b). A dense clump of small, stunted evergreen trees or scrub; also attrib.

[c1900] 1978 *RLS* 8, p. 23 ~ A patch of Tucking Bushes. 1963 MERCER 10 McGrath thinks that the greater interspersion of 'tucks' on Brunette Island as compared to St Shott's may have been a factor [in the partridge population]. T 12/348–64 People here get all their wood in this area. And this area is just a patchwork of bush an' bog an' trees—naps, naps or tucks of trees, as we call 'em. P 131–70 We moved from tuck bushes into tant woods. P 182–79 In addition to burnt over areas of formerly forested land, the barren ground also contains variegated zones marked by small tucks or copses of conifers. 1980 *Evening Telegram* 8 Nov, p. 6 What happens of course is that the moose are driven from the tucks and drokes far back into the country into the thick woods.

tuckamore n   also **tuckamil, tucken-more, tuckermel, tuckermill, tuckermore** *DC* ~ Nfld (1895–). For **tucken-more**, see TUCKING BUSH and MORE n. See also TUCK[2]. (a) Small stunted evergreen tree with gnarled spreading roots, forming closely matted ground-cover on the barrens; also attrib; (b) collectively, low stunted vegetation; scrub.

1863 MORETON 31 Tucken-mores. Small low-grown shrubs and creeping plants. 1866 WILSON 37 In the hollows are the tuckermore bushes, which is a dwarf juniper, with strong branches at right angles to the stem, and closely interlacing each other: the tops of these bushes are level, as if they had been clipped. To walk upon these tuckermores, or penetrate their branches, is equally impracticable. 1868 HOWLEY *MS Reminiscences* 9 The country is nearly level with scarcely any woods except occasional patches of tucking bushes (Tuckamores). 1891 PACKARD 84 Half-way down, as [the vale] widens out, [it becomes] choked with a stunted spruce and fir growth, or what the people call 'tucking,' or 'tuckermel-bush.' 1895 *J A Folklore* viii, 39 ~ , in some places *tuckamil*, a clump of spruce, growing almost flat on the ground and matted together, found on the barrens and bleak, exposed places. Ibid viii, 288 I drawed down to the tuckamores aside the pond and got twict thirty and varty yards from un. I lets drive and the loo' dove. 1919 GRENFELL[2] 229 He had gone through his snow racquets and actually lost the bows later, smashing them all up as he repeatedly fell through between logs and tree-trunks and 'tuckamore.' 1927 RULE 70 Travelling alongshore between Bonne Bay and Cow Head, I sometimes used the sloping surface of tuckermill as a couch to rest upon. 1970 *Evening Telegram* 21 May, p. 3 We proceeded as usual to the Witless Bay

Line. . .and from thence some 13 miles on foot in over the tuckamores. C 70–12 Tuckamore is a sort of low bush which grows in the marshes and in the small valleys. It is in the tuckamore that the path of a rabbit is most likely to be found. 1971 NOSEWORTHY 258 Tuckamoors or tuckamoor trees [are] low bushes on the barrens, about knee-high. 1981 *Evening Telegram* 17 Oct, p. 8 A good (and bad) cross-section of ptarmigan habitat (i.e. prostrate balsam, tuckamores, high plant or shrub cover, open tundra, rock exposures, marshes, etc).

tucken-more See TUCKAMORE.

tuckermel, tuckermill See TUCKAMORE.

tucking¹ vbl n Comb **tucking line**: one of the lines of a fish-net drawn tight to enclose the catch; cp TUCK¹ n, v.
   1971 CASEY 63 When four or five 'doucers' were lowered overboard and pulled up and down by a line or were allowed to strike the ocean floor, they produced a loud noise which drove the cod into the 'bunt' or the loose bag of netting of the seine. The 'bunt' could be closed and the seine with the catch taken on board by the aid of ropes known as 'tuckin' lines.' 1974 SQUIRES 21 Tucking lines affixed to the bottom and top [of the cast-net] would close the net. P 127–76 ~ The main line of a cast-net—used for closing and retrieving the net after it has been cast. The tuckin line is attached to the tucks.

tucking² ppl Cp *OED* tuck v¹ 4 'to tug at; to snatch, pluck, pull' obs; *EDD* tuck v³ 1 'to pull, jerk'; *DAE* tucking 1 (Nfld: 1890 quot); *DC* tucking bush Nfld (1842). Comb **tucking bush**, ~ **spruce**: low-growing, stunted evergreen, forming closely matted ground-cover; TUCKAMORE. Cp TUCK².
   [1822 (1915)] HOWLEY 155 [W E CORMACK:] The larch. . .creeps along the ground to leeward, where neither the birch nor spruce can exist. It is thus sometimes only a few inches in height, and many feet in length. The spruce fir-thickets are often only a few inches in height, the trees hooked and entangled together in such a manner as to render it practicable to walk upon, but impossible to walk through them.] 1843 JUKES 22–3 A bed of dwarf juniper is met with, which goes in Newfoundland by the name of 'tucking bushes.' These grow about breast high with strong branches at right angles to the stem and stiffly interlacing, their tops being flat and level as if they had been mown off. They are so stiff, that in some places one can almost walk upon them. 1868 HOWLEY *MS Reminiscences* 9 The country is nearly level with scarcely any woods except occasional patches of tucking bushes (Tuckamores). 1889 ibid 15 Saw some splendid soil, but the highest part of the ridge between the two rivers was apparently poor as it was covered only with small tucking spruce. [c1900] 1978 *RLS* 8, p. 23 Tucking bushes, low timber, usually stunted spruce, so tangled as to be difficult to walk through, as they catch or tuck one in at every step. Usually found on high barren ground in the hollows. 1905 *Geog J* xxvi, 192 . . .tucking bushes, a thick

growth of stunted spruce and juniper. P 182–79 Tuckenbushes [are] small, low spruce [with] green boughs that one could walk on or through (but with difficulty). Tuckenbush Pond [west of Trepassey] was called that by the old fellas because it was surrounded by tuckenbushes.

tuir See TURR.

tumble n Esp in phr *a big tumble*: condition of the sea marked by a quick succession of large waves; cp LOP², LUMP.
   M 70–29 ~ Long rolling waves which just seem to tumble along unlike waves driven by wind. P 148–74 [There's a] big tumble on. 1979 NEMEC 263 And even if the tide is not running, 'snags' can still be cleared if there is a 'tumble' (large waves with deep troughs but still not a rough sea).

tumbly a See TUMBLE. Of the sea, with large waves or swells; KNOBBLY.
   1979 *Salt Water, Fresh Water* 215 A long-liner will definitely roll in the wind, you know, and if the water is tumbly, she'll roll. P 250–80 You only gets a little wind lop, more or less, up here, but down there you gets the ocean swell and the water is really tumbly, noddy water, we'll say.

tun n *EDD* ~ sb² Gl Ha W Do So. Chimney (P 171–65).
   1975 MILLS 63 The most common chimney or 'tun' was of crude brick construction.

turbot n also **newfoundland** ~ . A flat fish with eyes on one side, esp Greenland halibut (*Reinhardtius hippoglossoides*) (1966 LEIM & SCOTT 401).
   [1583] 1940 *Gilbert's Voyages & Enterprises* ii, 406 [Hayes' narrative] There are sundry other fish very delicate, namely the Bonito, Lobsters, Turbut, with others infinite.

turn v *EDD* ~ v 1 (2) D Co for sense 3 to turn after; cp *OED* turncoat A 'one who changes his principles or party' for cpd in sense 4.
   1 In curing salted cod on a flat expanse, esp a 'flake,' to turn it over to dry in sun and wind; cp MAKE, SPREAD v.
   [1578] 1935 *Richard Hakluyt* 132 [Parkhurst's letter] [The wild animals] take away our flesh before our faces, within lesse then halfe a paire of buts length, where foure and twentie persons were turning of drie fish, and two dogges in sight. 1613 *Willoughby Papers* 1/10 I tooke something Sharp unto him and have mak him carry the barry with me and Torne fishe as I have done. 1849 [FEILD] 36 They do not commonly fish on that day; but there is an express proviso in the articles they sign, that they shall work on Sundays if required. They turn the fish on the flakes, if necessary, and go in quest of bait. 1861 DE BOILIEU 37 The fish having been 'turned' each evening, about the third day they are put in faggots, about a dozen fish being laid one upon the other, their backs upwards, as a defence from wet or the dampness of the night. 1924 ENGLAND 267 They

labour all day, making up the fish, carrying it on dredge barrows, spreading and turning it. 1970 JANES 11 Here the child Saul grew up and here, from the time he could turn a fish or trench a potato, he knew one thing only: work.

2 Of a harp seal, to undergo a change to the darker markings of the adult stage; see **turncoat** (b) below, and TURNING.

1873 CARROLL 16 Harp seals when whelped are called white coats, on account of the fur or hair being of a cream colour. When 16 days old they begin to shed their hair; they then become dark about the eyes and hinder flippers. Once they begin to turn they are called 'ragged jackets,' the skins are then not of as much value. T 84–64 He's turnin' into be a harp. He's turnin' from a bellamer to a harp.

3 Phr *turn after*: to closely resemble, look like (another).

P 148–65 They turns right after their father.

turn in: to hand over the produce of a fishing voyage to the merchant who has advanced credit and supplies for the operation; hence *turning-in*.

[1833] 1966 PITT 61 The second method [of raising income for the Methodist Church] is by what is called in the commercial phrase of this Country 'turnings in,' that is those of our Congregations who have not cash at command give in to the Merchants stores of fish or oil and this is transferred to the credit of the Missionaries and as it is produce taken from the Planter in the account current for the year and not at cash prices we cannot *demand cash* from the *Merchant*. [1881] 1898 *Nfld Law Reports* 257 Plaintiff supplied this vessel for the season, but on defendant's credit, and her voyage was to be 'turned in' to plaintiff, to defendant's credit. . . The plaintiff says as to this, the defendant did not carry out his arrangement of 'turning in the voyage' to the plaintiff. 1975 BUTLER 66 But, if you were a good dealer and the merchant was carryin' ya, 'tis not so bad as it sounds because. . .say I was dealin' with you, well I turned in all my dealings with you and I took out all I needed for the summer and turned in all I had in the fall of the year and the books were balanced.

4 Cpd **turn around**, in phr *take a turn around*: to be changeable; to be sometimes plentiful, sometimes scarce.

1977 *Inuit Land Use* 261 Some summers the fish were plentiful, and others there was hardly anything. . .some summers it's plenty. It's like everything else, it takes a turn around.

turncoat: (a) one who changes his religious affiliation from one denomination to another; (b) TURNER, a type of seal (C 70–12 quot).

P 148–61 [Our family are] all turncoats from the Church of England to the Salvation Army. 1966 PADDOCK 120 ~ derogatory term applied to a person who changes his religious affiliations. C 70–12 ~ Name given to a seal which has shed its white coat and taken on the appearance of a young harp. 1971 NOSEWORTHY 258 ~ A person who changes from one church to another.

turn-out, attrib **turn-out hat**: bride's going-away hat.

T 92/3–64 A white hat trimmed with a big band o'

ribbon, and a big bow, and then flowers—that was your turn-out hat. It wasn't very small either.

turn n *EDD* ~ sb 1 W So D Co for sense 1; cp *OED* sb 19 for sense 2; *OED* 37, *EDD* 7 Ha IW Co [Nfld], *DAE* 2 (1800–) for sense 3.

1 The large spinning wheel in the device for spinning wool.

1979 POCIUS 14 [She] can remember the older people referring to the spinning wheel as a 'turn.'

2 A religious conversion.

1919 GRENFELL[1] 53 [He] took a sudden 'turn.' This expression on our coast usually means a religious 'turn.'

3 A load, esp as much (wood, water, etc) as can be carried by a person at one time; BACK[1]: ~ LOAD, ~ TURN, BURN.

[1783] 1792 CARTWRIGHT iii, 24 So thou mayest take up thy turn of firewood and go home about thy business. 1792 ibid *Gloss* i, xvi Turn of timber. So much as a man can carry on his shoulders. [c1830] 1890 GOSSE 41 . . .coming up from the 'landwash' with a 'turn' of sand for her mother's kitchen floor. 1861 DE BOILIEU 110 He was condemned to supply the room with six turns of wood; implying he should go to the stack of wood six times, which was at the foot of the hill, about three hundred yards off. 1896 *J A Folklore* ix, 25 The word *turn* is used to denote what a man can carry. 'He went into the country for a turn of wood,' that is, as much as he can carry on his back. [1918–19] GORDON 11–12 By 2.30 we had a nice pile of 300 sticks on the bank below the Parsonage, and some of us had stiff shoulders. (For the sake of the uninitiated, a stick or 'turn' of wood is a fair-sized tree with its limbs lopped off.) 1937 DEVINE 54 ~ A load especially of wood; two buckets of water carried with a hoop are a *turn*. T 36/8–64 You're supposed to bring two dozen of these [rines]—that was your turn. T 43/7–64 In carryin' the turn o' water with the hoop all the weight was on your arms. C 69–30 She was lying awake late at night—when she heard the sound of someone letting fall a 'turn' of lumber very close to the house. 1975 RUSSELL 8 I was busy trying to finish a herring net and I had a few turn of birch wood in my back yard that I wanted to have sawed and clove.

4 A quantity of 'sculps' or sealskins, with blubber attached, hauled over the ice; TOW[2]; a boat-load (of fish).

1861 DE BOILIEU 199–200 After a man has killed as many [seals] as he can conveniently walk off with, he drags them alongside the schooner, and walks off after another 'turn,' as it is termed. 1866 WILSON 282 When the seals are found, they are not always close to the vessel, but have to be brought a distance of some miles, when hauling a *turn* of soils over the big hummocks, or ice-hillocks, makes the labor exceedingly toilsome. [1872] 1899 *Nfld Law Reports* 455 The defendant claimed the right to take those seals because Capt White had told some of his crew when they were going for their last turn, and when he appears to have abandoned the taking of them himself, to tell the defendant that he might have them. 1882 TALBOT 16–17 They did not return until two or three o'clock in the afternoon, when they came alongside with their *turns*, as they call the skulps which they haul with their ropes. These *turns* happened to be small, only one or two skulps in each. 1958 *Evening Telegram* 19 June, p. 4 He had killed a turn of seals. [1959] 1965 PEACOCK (ed) iii, 971 "The Sally's Cove Tragedy": We leaved our homes on Tuesday, the day was bright and clear, / And for to get a turn of bait away all hands did steer.

5 A quantity of bread baked at one time.

P 143–74 And that'd make two turns of bread. (A 'turn' of bread was the number of loaves that would fit in an oven at one time; in this case a 'turn' was four loaves of bread.)

turned p ppl Of the eyes, crossed (P 148–64).

turner n   also **tanner*** *Cent* ~[1] n 3 (Nfld: 1891). A young harp seal, undergoing a change to the darker markings of the adult stage; cp RAGGED-JACKET; also attrib. See TURN v 2.

T 84–64 I had five shots an' I killed the five of 'em. I floated the five of 'em—never lost one: old harps an' turners. T 210/11–65 The next year, the third year, they're a turner. An' the next year when they'll be four year old in the spring, that winter they're a harp; there's a plain harp on their back. T 391/2–67 A turner seal—that's a three yeared seal—[is good] for legs [of a skin boot]. 1967 FIRESTONE 102 ~ three to four [-year old harp seal]; can barely see the saddle of the adult on back. P 245–76 [This year] we only got tanners, no beaters. P 40–78 ~ A harp seal whose fur is changing in the process of it becoming an old harp. P 148–79 They took [our raggedy jackets] as tanners.

turning ppl *DC* ~ harp Nfld (1880). Comb **turn-ing harp**, ~ **seal**: a young harp seal undergoing a change to the darker markings of the adult stage; see TURN v. Cp RAGGED JACKET.

1873 CARROLL 16 When 2 years old [harp seals] are called turning harps. 1952 STANSFORD 54 We killed and secured for our day's work two turning seals (called 'Rusties').

turnip See POISON.

turpentine n   also **turkumtine***, etc. *OED* ~ sb (esp 1576 quot); *DAE* 1 a (1634–). Resin of a conifer, esp fir, used as an ingredient in pitch and for home-remedies; cp FRANKINTINE*, FRAN-KUM, MYRRH, STARRIGAN GREASE.

[1583] 1940 *Gilbert's Voyages & Enterprises* ii, 406 [Hayes' narrative] The trees for the most in those South parts, are Firre-trees, pine and Cypresse, all yeelding Gumme and Turpentine. 1613 *Willoughby Papers* 1/2, 69 The turpentine that commeth from the firr and pine and frankincense of the spruce is likewise sent. 1620 WHITBOURNE 10 There are Firre and Spruce trees. . .and out of these came abundance of Turpen-tine. 1682 COLLINS 98 And out of these Woods may be had, Pitch, Tar, Rosin, Turpentine, Frankincense. [1794] 1968 THOMAS 105 I then, with nothing on but my wet Shirt and Drawers (which stuck as close to my skin as Turpentine doth to the Bark of the Fur Tree) clasped my hands. [c1904] 1960 BURKE (ed White) 22 "The Kelligrews Soiree": There was birch rine, tar

wine, / Sherry wine and turpentine. P 65–64 Turpentine on trees is called 'mur.' Mur is put on cuts to cause a cure. T 255–66 Bread poultice, you know, an' juniper water, an' gum plasters—turkumtine [from] the bladders—fir gum. T 271–66[1] I've seen cuts heal up with a plaster o' turkumtine put on 'em. C 69–11 A home-remedy for a cold is a mixture of turpentine (straight from the tree), Minard's Liniment, Friar's Balsam and molasses. C 75–139 [He] took two hand-kerchiefs, climbed a tree and took some raw turpentine straight from the tree and applied it to my serious cut.

turr n   also **tuir**, etc [təːɹ] *DC* ~ n 1, 2 Nfld ([1856–]). Prob imitative of both the earlier name MURRE[1] and the bird's note. One of sev-eral sea-birds hunted as food; Atlantic common murre; BACCALIEU BIRD (*Uria aalge aalge*); Brünnich's thick-billed murre (*U. lomvia lomvia*).

[1794] 1968 THOMAS 144 Penguins, Hegdowns, Muirs and Tuirs, Ice Birds. . .and a number of other Sea Fowl. [1819] 1977 *Lgs in Nfld* 16 Turr. Goenet. 1846 TOCQUE 11 The Baccalieu birds, Turs, or Merrs. . .have now occupied their isolated breeding places. 1854 [FEILD] 16 . . .a tub full of the large eggs of the turs and tinkers, (sea-fowl which breed upon the neighbouring islands). 1866 WILSON 63 Of sea birds, there are the gull, lazy cormorant, twe [ed emend: tur] or baccalao bird, pin-tailed duck or sea-pheasant, eid-er. 1884 STEARNS 233 They commenced to appear, flying around the boat or resting on the water; all were 'parakeets,' and 'tinkers,' except now and then a soli-tary 'turre.' 1920 GRENFELL & SPALDING 122 One day a load of wood will find its way to his door. The next a few fresh 'turr,' a very 'fishy' sea auk, are left ever so quietly inside his woodshed. 1940 SCAMMELL 26 "The Shooting of the Bawks": But if they keep this law that's passed, they will not get a taste / Of bawk or noddy, tinker, tur, and not a tickleace. 1951 BURLEIGH & PETERS 251, 254 Atlantic Common Murre. . . Local names: Turr, Murre, Baccalieu Bird. Voice: Soft, pur-ring notes, suggesting its local name. [1959] 1965 PEACOCK (ed) i, 102 "Tom Bird's Dog": I don't know how many birds you got, your neighbours never said, / I wish the devil had the turs and Tom Bird's dog was dead. 1960 TUCK 34 A common vernacular name for the murre in Newfoundland is 'turr.' It is used for either species and especially for a bird in winter plu-mage. T 141/2–65[2] We had a chicken or a duck or a turr in the oven. 1982 *Evening Telegram* 10 June, p. 3 The world's largest colony of common murres, or turrs as they are called in Newfoundland, occupies the Funk Island, just off the northeast coast.

turr v   To hunt 'turrs,' common sea birds.

T 194/6–65 We's out turrin', about a mile and a half off Back Harbour Gull Island, out on a bight; a lot o' boats around us.

turring vbl n Hunting 'turrs' from small boats; BIRDING.

C 71–35 Turring is a once a year event in Pt Leam-ington. In the spring, everyone has their bird licence and they go hunting turrs. . . Turring also goes on in the fall.

tuttle line* n A length of line forming part of a 'cast-net' and used to draw the 'tucks' together, closing the net; PULL-ROPE.

T 66/7–64 [Take a] cow's horn, an' you put that down the neck of your net. Now your tuttle line would work up an' down through that. It'll never tangle.

twack v To look at goods, inquire about prices, but buy nothing.

1955 ENGLISH 37 ~ to examine goods and buy nothing. T 222–66 To go twacking [means] just pricing goods. C 71–117 Of people who examine goods or asked prices, obviously without intending to buy, the clerk would say, 'They're twacking.' C 75–134 Whenever we went to the store for the sole purpose of looking at the goods without intention of buying we would say we are going to 'twack.'

twack n A shopper who looks over all the commodities but buys nothing.

1937 DEVINE 54 ~ An importunate shop searcher who buys nothing, but wastes the clerk's time. Q 67–70 They're twacks—old women shoppers who can't make up their minds. P 76–76 ~ A woman who is unable to make up her mind on simple choices especially in a store.

twet See OOISHT.

twig n OED ~ sb[2] 'a draught' (1825 quot); cp EDD v[4] 'to swig' Ha. A small drink.

P 148–61 'Have a drop of something?' 'I'll have a twig.'

twillick n also **twilleck, twillet, twillic, twillig, twillik, twillock**. Cp OED twillock (Nfld: 1620) obs var of willock 'guillemot' (1631–); DC Nfld (1842–) for sense 1.

1 Greater yellow-legs (*Totanus melanoleucus*); occas lesser yellow-legs (*T. flavipes*), and other long-legged birds frequenting sea-shore and streams: plover, snipe; AUNTSARY[1].

[1620] 1887 MASON 151 The Fowles are. . .Teales, Twillockes, excellent wilde Ducks of diuers sorts and aboundance, rare and not to be found in Europe. 1842 JUKES i, 141 We shot a couple of 'twillecks,' a grey long-legged bird, about the size and shape of a plover, that frequents the shores of the lakes and arms of the sea. 1868 HOWLEY MS Reminiscences 25 I spent my day looking around the place, caught some small trout and shot one twillick. 1870 Can Naturalist v, 295 Then they are a perfect nuisance to the sportsman, as they not only keep out of range themselves, but alarm every other bird by their incessant cry of 'twillick,' 'twillick'. . . Provincial names of this bird are 'twillick' [and] 'twillet.' 1907 MILLAIS 86 The greater yellowshank. . .locally known as 'Twillik,' is very common in all the Newfoundland rivers during the summer and autumn. 1910 PRICHARD 59 Several flocks of yellow-shanks, locally known as 'twilligs,' haunted these flat shores in some numbers. 1951 PETERS & BURLEIGH

192 Greater Yellow-legs. . . Local Name: Twillick. Voice: A fast repeated *whee-oodle, whee-oodle*, or *twil-ick, twil-ick*. . . It is a very noisy bird. 1959 MCATEE 27 Twillig. Semipalmated Plover. Ibid 28 Twillic. Common Snipe. 1964 JACKSON 14 'Twillicks' eat small fish and water insects. They used to be a game bird but are now protected.

2 Epithet for a fool; an inexperienced boy.

P 69–63 Don't be such a twillick! P 198–67 He's just a twillick (boy of eight years of age about to go trouting for the first time). C 69–9 Go away, you twillick (fool). P 79–73 The oldest child is real big, but the youngest is a real twillick.

twine n Cp NID ~[1] n 1 for sense 1. See also LINNET.

1 Hemp, cotton or nylon thread, varying in the number of its twisted strands, used in making fish-nets; freq with defining word SALMON, SEAL, etc.

1612 Willoughby Papers 16a, 17 [inventory] v [pounds] weighte of twine. [1622] 1954 INNIS 58 [inventory] Twine to make keipnets etc. [1731] 1976 HEAD 104 Exports of West Country Towns to Newfoundland: Dartmouth: Twine ¼ cwt. Poole: 151 cwt. 1792 PULLING MS 12 Aug Here I saw. . .some of their rope which they make by plaiting four parts of salmon net twine together. [1840] 1842 BONNYCASTLE ii, 201 Imports: Lines, twines, and nets. . .value £20,874. 1873 CARROLL 35 The twine [the nets] are made of is about three times the size of salmon net twine. 1895 PROWSE 510 Until quite recently all these articles were imported, principally from the West of England, latterly from New England. [Now] instead of importing all our cordage from abroad, the bulk of the lines, twines, nets, and cables used [are made in St John's at the Rope Walk]. 1904 Nfld Qtly Dec, p. 17 The paraphernalia of a fisherman's craft, hooks and lines, sails and twines, bultows and barrows, and nets. . . 1975 BUTLER 58 'Tis all called linnet. But, see, 'tis made from fibers. Twine was made from cotton or hemp fibers and spun. In a cod trap the twine would be not smaller than fifteen thread—fifteen, eighteen or twenty one thread.

2 A fish-net, seine or trap; all of these collectively; LINNET.

1909 BROWNE 259 Every gale means serious losses to those who have 'twine' (this is the term used by fishermen for traps, nets and seines), as it is usually badly damaged by these dreadful northeasters. 1912 CABOT 93–4 Then Spracklin's trap had to come out, for some reason, and Jim's likewise, for a two-pointed berg blew in and cut it up badly. . . Now there was 'no twine in the water'; the fisherman's dark day had come. 1936 SMITH 27 After the gale abated we went out to Five Islands in the trap boat to see about our cod-trap that we had left in the water, and I regret to say that the trap was in a very bad condition, all torn up. We saved about half the twine and felt thankful for that. P 245–75 The whales is so many we can't keep our twine in the water. 1976 Evening Telegram 22 May, p. 6 [He was caught] using small mesh gear on a. . .stern trawler. . . A stern dragger fishes the Grand Banks winter and summer. On most trips some twine is lost or worn out. 1979 NEMEC 267 By 1968, St Shotts' fishermen were setting approximately fifteen miles of 'twine' (monofil-ament nets) in the water at one time.

3 Attrib, comb **twine captain**: in the deep-sea trawler fishery, man in charge of nets and fishing-gear.

1976 *Evening Telegram* 22 May, p. 6 It's left to the honesty of the twine captain to put aboard the correct size and amount ordered.

twine gurdy: rotating device from which thread is uncoiled when knitting a fish-net (P 13–75); see **twine throw**.

twine house: see **twine loft**.

M 68–16 The time I was shipped down in Bauline I used to sleep in an old twine house.

twine loft: room or area of fishing premises in which nets are stored and repaired; NET n: ~ LOFT.

1917 *Christmas Bells* 15 Go down to the twine loft and give those fellows working there a dram, but mind you make them mix it with water. 1936 SMITH 181 And of course there were the traps to repair in the twine loft again. T 175/7–65 Some fellers just never considered the skipper man—what he was up against; how much time he put in the twine loft when the shareman was free to go on and make another dollar.

twine mender: NET n: ~- MENDER.

P 102–60 Among the paid fishery servants were. . .boat builders, a blacksmith, twine menders, tin-smith and several wharf builders. Most any of these men were capable of making. . .any kind of tool required for the fish business.

twine needle: device, usu of wood or bone, for 'knitting' fish-nets (P 148–63).

twine store: see **twine loft** above.

1981 *Evening Telegram* 2 Sep, p. 3 Battery fishermen [in St John's] have twine stores in the areas they oper-ate from now.

twine throw: see **twine gurdy**.

P 135–64 ~ The wooden object twine is put on when mending cod traps. The twine throw moves around when you pull on the line.

twist n   also **twister**. Cigarette rolled by the smoker.

P 148–66 Give us a twist. P 135–74 Twister is what the fishermen call a cigarette they roll themselves.

twister n   Cp *OED* ~ sb 1 c 'device by which torsional force is applied.'

1 Stick for tightening rope around load of wood on a sled; BITTING STICK; also attrib (Q 71–8).

P 8–55 Twister stick. Lever used to tighten rope holding load of wood to a sled. M 69–6 A twister was made from a 'rined' fir tree and was about a foot long and about two inches in diameter. A twister was put between two parallel parts (of a binder) that were close and then these parts were twisted around and around each other until the binder bit into the rind of the logs.

2 In coopering, a rope and handle used for forcing the staves into the shape of a barrel (P 127–78).

twite v   [twɛitə, twɛɪt, twɒɪtə] *OED* twit: twite (16–17c); *EDD* v¹ 'to reproach, taunt' Do So. To tease, taunt.

T 156/7–65 Joe would be always twitin' me about the Union, cause Joe and Coaker wouldn't be no man's good friend. T 245/51–66 He's only just married. He was twiting his wife about the men she was going to have while he was gone.

two num   Cp *OED* ~ IV 2 two-blocks 'block and block' for sense 1.

1 Phr *come to two blocks*: to be exhausted (1937 DEVINE 54).

C 65–11 By the way you look today you will come to two blocks tomorrow. P 54–68 Of an animal or person, nearly exhausted or worn out.

2 Comb **two-bar slide**: sled with two transverse timbers built across the runners (C 75–25).

two-bow trap: lobster pot with two curved struts onto which the laths are secured (T 250–66).

two-line tub: see TUB.

two-stemmed boat: small fishing boat with stern shaped like the stem (M 68–17).

two-yeared bedlamer: harp seal in its third year.

T 210/11–65 First 'tis called the young seal, young harp, the next year it's called hopper, and the next year, two-yeared seal, two-yeared bedlamer—'tis bed-lamer all along.

tyer* n   Length of cord tied around cod trap to keep it from getting tangled when moved to or from boat or vessel.

P 9–73 After the bottom [of the cod trap] has been scunned in, it is taken by the middle of the back and stretched lengthwise, a tyer being tied on every four or five or six feet to keep the netting snug for moving from loft to skiff to schooner.

U

un pro   also **en** [n̩, ən] *OED* ~ , 'un¹ (OE *hine* 'him') (1633–); *EDD* en s w cties. See HE. Unstressed equivalent to the stressed *he* in objective positions, referring to a male or to cer-tain inanimate nouns.

1891 *Holly Branch* 15 The other dawg runned away, but we cotched 'en, rips 'en up and *gets the needle*. 1925 *Dial Notes* v, 345 ~ It; him. 1937 DEVINE 65 Contempt for a boasting but indifferent fellow fisherman is thus expressed: 'I'd drown'en with the spry [spray] of me nippers.' T 1–63¹ The wool came right on out as far as you want un to come. He'd make the spindle almost full. T 26–64¹ 'Twasn't mornin', 'twas daylight; see the sun all the time; see the sun steady right for three months, never lose un. . . He had his wife, too, along with un. P 155–64 I started to laugh at en.

uncle n   *OED* ~ sb 2 b (1793–); *EDD* 3. See also AUNT. Title of an older man, used with first or full name; general term of respect used of an older man in the community; SKIPPER 2.

1887 *Evening Telegram Christmas No* 37 It was Christmas Eve, and outside Uncle Joe Burton's cottage, wild and stormy enough. 1895 *J A Folklore* viii, 37 ~ In a community every respectable man of say sixty years of age will be so called by all the other people in it. [1915] 1972 GORDON 14 Such titles as Mr & Mrs are not favoured in Labrador, being replaced by the much more homely ones of Uncle and Aunt. T 54/9–64 By and by he said to me, 'You're a stranger.' 'Look here,' I said, 'uncle, I don't know who you are.' 1979 POTTLE 74 A veteran fisherman, 'Uncle' John Vey, who had just come in from his trawl, was mowing grass in his garden.

unemployment n
1 Sum of money paid to an unemployed worker under the provisions of a social security programme.

1977 *Inuit Land Use* 322 There was no wages [in the old days]. I didn't hear of unemployment until about five years ago, I s'pose. We never used to get unemployment. We used to only get paid for our fish, or whatever we got through working with the fish or salmon.

2 Attrib **unemployment boot**: tight-fitting rubber boot.

P 65–64 Unemployment boots are rubber logans [with several] lace holes in the top. P 21–67 ~s. Almost all hardware stores and general stores sell these light green rubber boots. The legs are about 14 inches long.

unknown a *EDD* ~ adj 2 'strange, unaccountable.' Of a person, odd, strange, slightly deranged.

C 68–7 There was a woman down to Gaultois who was a little unknown; she would steep tea but instead of drinking [it] she would throw away the tea and eat the tea leaves.

unmade a See MAKE. Of cod-fish, split and salted but not dried.

1937 DEVINE 25 The Bank and Labrador cargoes of 'unmade' fish are examples [of green fish].

unstrand v To unwind or separate the twisted fibres of a rope.

T 141/68–65[2] You have some condemned rope every year; well, you'll unstrand that an' use that to keep the rine.

unstrip v *OED* ~ v now dial and rare; *EDD*. To undress, strip.

T 258–66 He said, 'I'll give you a big handful o' money if you was to show me where that woman will unstrip to go to bed.'

up av, prep Cp *OED* ~ adv[1] d [up to London] for sense 1; *OED* upsitting 1 for comb in sense 4. Cp DOWN.

1 Towards or located at the principal 'settlement' of Newfoundland, St John's.

P 245–67 (speaker on South Coast) I'm going up to St John's to see the powers that be. 1973 BARBOUR 9 Newfoundlanders have always said. . .'up to St John's' or 'up to New York,' when they were really going in a southerly direction. 1979 *Salt Water, Fresh Water* 58–9 He'd come up to St John's and discharged [his Labrador fish], and on his way home he was lost on [Cape Bonavista].

2 In a southerly direction; at a southern location.

1957 *Evening Telegram* 13 Mar, p. 4 The Arctic ice was up early. 1977 RUSSELL 23 Up on the South coast where I was born. . .we didn't have the drift ice. 1979 *Salt Water, Fresh Water* 44 If the wind is up from the north-east. . .you won't get very much fish.

3 In a southerly direction (towards or by a place).

1924 ENGLAND 21 The harps keep on down the Labrador coast. 'Up' the Labrador, Newfoundlanders call it, 'up' meaning south.

4 Comb **upalong**: see UPALONG.

uphaul: rope used to draw cod trap to the surface; HAUL v: HAUL-UP.

1936 SMITH 31 At seven o'clock we went out to haul our trap and go through the rules; we weren't long hauling on the 'uphauls' when, behold, up came a score of mashed fish in the doorways. P 9–74 ~ one of the ropes used to haul a cod trap.

up-sitting: occasion on which mother first sits up after birth of child and receives visitors.

1972 MURRAY 75 The tenth day after the birth was the Mother's 'Up-sitting Day.'

upstand: one of the sticks placed vertically to support a pile of pulp-wood (1965 PETERS *Gloss*).

up-sticks: in cribbage, equal in score (P 142–66).

up-the-bay: located in settlement at the innermost part or 'bottom' of a bay or harbour.

1901 *Christmas Review* 5 Now, as most goods go to the outports by rail, the 'up-the-bay man' is getting his innings. 1936 SMITH 19 It didn't take these 'up-the-bay' men long before they had their houses cleaned.

upalong av Cp *EDD* up 2 (3) upalong (a) 'a little way up the street or road' Ha IW Do So D Co, *ADD* ~ Mass for sense 1; *EDD* 2 (3) (b) [to the east of a county] Ha for sense 3.

1 Away from a person or locality; to or on the mainland of Canada or the United States.

1919 GRENFELL[1] 226 So Trader Bourne. . .put to sea one fine afternoon in late November, his vessel loaded with good things for his necessitous friends 'up along.' 1931 BYRNES 45 [On Regatta Day] all roads led to the 'pond' and the crowds from 'up along,' 'down along,' and 'in along' on 'shanks mare' or lolling luxuriously in a closed carriage from the 'stand' left dull care behind. T 70–64[1] And they pulled ashore right up, and enquired from all the boats up along. T 169/212–65[1] Don't suppose we'll ever meet again and you be going upalong now, and we down here. 1970 *Evening Telegram* 11 May, p. 3 They say there are from 8,000 to 10,000 taking off upalong each year. C 71–106 If we visited neighbours who lived some distance from us, we said we were cruising upalong. 1976 *Daily News* 2 Nov, p. 2 Local management is not in charge, he says, and 'someone upalong is directing the scene.' 1976 MURPHY 114 I like to think that in his early days going to this school, Mike, a 'Down-Along,' as east enders were called, often met and conversed with (or perhaps fought with) that boy from 'Upalong,' Johnny Dwyer from the Cross Roads (also born in St John's in 1845) who later became professional heavyweight boxing champion of [America]. 1980 *Evening Telegram* 4 Oct, p. 6 I don't see why our Brian [Peckford] is getting so upset with the boys upalong just because he doesn't think it's a good idea to give our oil away.

2 Hence, **upalong** n: resident farther inland, or one to the south in a settlement.

1931 BYRNES 120 Who can forget the traditional 'scraps' between the 'upalongs' and 'down-alongs'? Heaven help the unfortunate youth found alone in the other fellow's territory. 1976 MURPHY 32 But the clashes between the 'Down-Alongs,' the boys of the East End, and the 'Up-Alongs,' the boys of the West End, that were in being in the sixties, seventies and eighties were reminders of the old faction fight days.

upper n also **hupper** PEACOCK 346 'seal. . .appâ.' Grey seal (*Halichoerus grypus*).

1977 *Inuit Land Use* 275 Grey or Atlantic seals, referred to locally as hupper seals, are hunted occasionally in Groswater Bay in September or October near the islands in the centre and at the head of the bay. Their great size (up to 14 feet) makes them difficult to load into boats, so they are rarely sought.

urge v *EDD* ~ v[2] 1 s w cties. To retch; to vomit.

P 44–66 When the boat tipped, Uncle Rex urged. C 69–7 After being forced to swallow two or three of these balls [of dough, molasses and pepper] the sheep would almost get sick. In any event the coughing or urging brought back the cud.

urrah See RA.

ursena n *Grand Larousse* oursin ['sea-urchin'] (1552–). See OSE EGG. Sea-urchin (*Strongylocentrolus drobachiensis*).

[1620] 1887 MASON 152 Now of shell fish there is Scalupes, Musseles, Vrsenas, Hens, Periwinkles &c.

V

v See VEE.

valentine n in forms **good morning, falten, fauten; mar fallaten, falten, farten, fauten, voleten; mol fol**; etc [maːɹ 'valətʃ ɔ̃n, mæːɹ 'fɑːtʃ ɔ̃n, maːɹ 'fɒːtʃɔ̃n] *EDD* ~ v: to go valentining Nb—'Good morrow, Valentine!'

1 Phr *good morning, valentine*: greeting spoken on the morning of St Valentine's Day in hope of receiving a gift.

M 69–1 If a person was successful in saying 'Mar voleten' before the other person, they expected a gift of some sort from the individual. M 71–4 You had to grab the person and kiss him before he could kiss you. You also had to shout 'Marnen falten.' M 71–105 As soon as they entered the house, they said 'Good morning falton,' to which the lady of the house responded by giving some small gift.

2 April fool!

P 74–67 'Mar fauten! Mar fauten!' was repeated when someone falls for a prank. C 68–24 On April 1 until noon, people get up early in order to 'own' as many people as they can. They creep up on somebody and say: 'Mar follitin.' The person so addressed (owned) must give a small gift to the one who 'owned' him. C 71–125 On the morning of April Fool's Day the children of the community would go from house to house knocking on doors and saying 'Marfoton' as each opened. The houseowner could be expected to respond to this with candy or some other small treat. M 71–37 When a trick is played, mar faulton is sometimes said instead of April Fool.

vamp n Cp *OED* ~ sb[1] 1 'part of hose or stockings which covers foot and ankle' now dial (1225–); *EDD* sb[1] 1 Co for sense 1.

1 A short, thick woollen oversock, worn in boots to prevent chafing or around the house as a slipper.

[1811] 1818 BUCHAN 4 Snow shoes, buskins, vamps, cuffs. 1884 STEARNS 166 [Vamps] are simply cloth-like slippers, and much resemble a stocking cut off just above the instep with the edges bound or sewed over and over with worsted, and a central flap an inch or two long from the middle of the front edge, in which is made a loop and by which the pair are looped and fastened, the one to the other, when they are hung up to dry. [1886] LLOYD 55 [Sealskin boots and moccasins] are worn with two pair of thick swanskin vamps. 1937 DEVINE 55 ~s. Outer stockings. T 210–65 You'd make [the boots] a couple of sizes too large for your foot, and then you'd get on some vamps. Sometimes they'd have skin vamp, and then a woollen one inside, beside the sock. 1975 GUY 60 Vamps came next. Hand-knit from the self-same material these socks came to just above the knobs of the ankles and were worn over the first two sets of hose. 1977 RUSSELL 68 I was sittin' by myself in the kitchen this night about nine o'clock, with my boots off, a pair of woolen vamps hauled on over my socks, and with my feet up on the pan of the stove smokin' my pipe.

2 The bottom of a sock.

1872 HOWLEY *MS Reminiscences* 1 He stood 6 feet 4 inches in his stocking vamps. 1955 ENGLISH 37 ~ The sole of a stocking.

vamp v *OED* ~ v[1] 1 (1599–1755), *EDD* v[1] 5 D Co for sense 1; *OED* 4 now dial (1654–1747), *EDD* v[2] 1 for sense 2; *EDD* 7 D Co for sense 3.

1 To mend, esp to knit new soles in socks.

T 96–64[2] And I even palmed them out, knit palms in [the mitts], and vamped out socks. C 70–21 To vamp it down means to knit a new bottom on a sock. 1979 POCIUS 26 She commented that 'when the heel wear out, when the heel wear off, you'd cut 'em off from here [at the heel] and re-vamp 'em.'

2 To walk, tramp. Hence **vamp** n: a walk or tramp.

1925 *Dial Notes* v, 345 To vamp it. Walk. P 148–60 You've got a good vamp before you. P 51–67 I'm going to vamp on home soon.

3 To add water to (a kettle, tea-pot).

P 207–67 Vamp the kettle: add a little water while the water in the kettle is still boiling. C 71–37 That [tea is] too strong, vamp it down.

vang n also **bang**. Cp *EDD* fang sb 7 'slice, a large piece cut from something'; *SND* fang n² 2 (1750–). Melted fat pork served on cod-fish (1937 DEVINE 35).

[1828] 1979 O'FLAHERTY 58 [What would be the horror] to see [the fishermen] regaling themselves on fish and bang, off the plate of Staffordshire. 1842 JUKES ii, 68 We dined on 'fish and vang,' which being interpreted means cod-fish and salt pork cut into 'junks' and boiled together, and with a mealy potato it is really a most excellent dish. 1914 *Cadet* 23 The rude fare of 'fish and vang' used by the fishermen was [Bishop Fleming's] diet. . . The Bishop had the sleeve of his coat well saturated with fish and vang (pork), for when the meal was cooked it was thrown out of the kettle on to the gangboards. 1955 ENGLISH 37 ~ fried salt pork.

var n [vɔːɹ, væːɹ, vaːɹ, vɑːɹ]; the customary form *fir*, like many words with initial *f-*, is pronounced *vir* in numerous localities. *DC* ~ Atlantic Prov (1793–). The balsam-fir (*Abies balsamea*); the wood of the balsam-fir; freq with defining word SNOTTY, SPRING². Also attrib.

[1829] 1915 HOWLEY 190 For some distance around, the trunks of many of the birch and of that species of spruce pine called here the Var (*Pinus balsamifera*) had been rinded. 1858 [LOWELL] ii, 64 Inland, again, lie mysterious-looking many-coloured mountains of broken rock, shaded with. . .the dark green 'Vars' and other never-changing forest trees. 1904 MURPHY (ed) 52 "The Low-Back-Car": Dear Terra Nova, beloved are thy hill-sides, / Home of the alder, the birch and the 'var.' 1909 BROWNE 68 The fish is spread on 'flakes'—scaffolds made of poles covered with 'spruce' or 'var' boughs. T 12–64 He found only two suitable trees; a birch and a var, and on this var was the cross. T 55/6–64 I slep' on var boughs all my lifetime, an' I was about forty years at that, lumberin'. C 67–6 Var rind is the bark of the var tree which is neatly cut off, dried and used to cover fish drying on the flake. 1979 *Evening Telegram* 14 July, p. 13 Then as your woman left the door open I can get the smell of caplin roastin', and that wafted out on the summer breeze to mix with. . .the smell of var. 1982 ibid 8 Feb, p. 24 Many an axe is biting into a piece of crooked var that will end up as the stem on a punt.

varl See FOREL.

vat n also **fat, vate** [væt, veit]. Cp *OED* ~ sb 1: 1400–1600 *vaat*, 1600–1900 *vate*, with explana-

tion of long vowel; cp 1 b 'vessel. . .containing the liquid used in. . .process' (1548–).

1 A large box-like trough in which whale blubber, cod livers, etc, are placed to render oil; TRAIN²: ~ FAT, ~ VAT.

1623 WHITBOURNE 57 There are also some, who arriving first in Harbor, take away other mens Salt that they had left there the yeere before, and also rippe and spoile the Fats wherein they make their Traine oyle. [1768] 1976 HEAD 187 The 1768 return [CO 194/18, f. 40] notes 'Mostly casks in lieu of Fatts.' [1771] 1792 CARTWRIGHT i, 99–100 These [larch planks], and the other planks, which I have sent down at different times before, are intended to build vatts for the seals' oil, when it is melted out in the spring. 1819 ANSPACH 434 The operation of salting is performed in vats or deep oblong square troughs, with a spigot and fauset near the bottom to draw off the foul pickle. The fish is carefully spread in layers to the top until the vat is filled. 1832 MCGREGOR i, 224 The fat, or seal blubber, is separated from the skins, cut into pieces, and put into frame-work vats, through which, and small boughs inside, the oil oozes on being exposed to the heat of the sun. 1873 CARROLL 41 Persons intending to prosecute the Spring, Summer, or Winter Herring Fishery, in vessels, ought, in the first place, to provide themselves with Vats, the boards used for building the same to be of sufficient thickness to caulk, and so made that such Vats should be in compartments, so as to contain from five to twenty barrels each. The object is, that one day's catch would not be mixed with another. T 36–64 Then the women would get [the fish] in these tubs and vates and wash it out.

2 Shed for storing food for sled dogs.

1967 FIRESTONE 72 The structures which went with keeping dogs still stand near many houses. These are the pound, the scaffold, and the vate. . . The vate is a small shed with a tiny door in which salt fish is put away for the dogs' later use.

vee n Either of two V-shaped corners of a cod trap next to the 'door' or entrance; also attrib.

T 43/7–64 [In making the net] then you come along the side and you get out to where you're goin' to make your vee corner. T 141/63–65² An' when we got out to the vee we picked out four barrels o' [mesh] fish out o' the two vees. He was full; must ha' been a-full. T 194/5–65 I went out an' pulled my trap, and he was right full of herring; there couldn't be no more herring get into un than what was into un. An' they was meshed in the vees, meshed in the skirts. I never witnessed the like. 1967 FIRESTONE 89 The two left hand rodes [of a cod trap] are called the *vees*, and the two right hand ones the *corners*. P 9–73 This part is brought to on the thirds or slightly over, especially after the vee corner (front corner) is turned towards the doorway. The vee-rope [is] one of the ropes used to haul a cod trap. Also called uphauls, haul-ups, it is fastened to one of the corners of the trap and is hauled diagonally. 1979 *'Twas a way of life* 83 You start your knitting on the mouth of the V's and knit across the front, seven and a half fathoms, using eight inch mesh.

veil n

1 Face-covering worn by Christmas mummers; FALSE FACE.

1886 *Colonist Christmas No* 12 'Now mummers, up with your veils, and let us see your faces!' It is the mistress of the house, that speaks; and in obedience to her request, the faces of all the maskers are uncovered. 1969 *Christmas Mumming in Nfld* 150 Mostly they wore just veils or sometimes painted ones. . .a piece of curtain or anything that you could see through.

2 The mask-like coloration and arrangement of the feathers around the eye and throat of the blue jay.

T 31/4–64 He was a good shot. He took off [the jay's] head right o'er the veil.

vein n [vɛin]. Cp *OED* ~ 8 c 'a current of wind; the track in which this moves' (1792–) for sense 1; *OED* 2 c (b) (1587, 1589) for phr in sense 2. See also MAIDEN VEIN, MILK ~ .

1 White area among clouds at night.

T 272–66 'There's a vein comes in the sky here, opens to the westard—milk vein, people calls it. Nine times out of ten the wind'll blow in that next day. If it opens to the westard, the wind'll blow in that vein the next day. Vein in the sky, just like the northern lights last night.' 'I don't know what 'tis, but it's a shape. 'Tis a opening, but not a cloud.' 'Some people calls it milk vein—it's white you see.'

2 Phr *with all the veins of one's heart*: profession of cordial willingness (1863 MORETON 39).

vellum n ['vɛləm] *EDD* ~ sb So D Co. Membrane.

1907 MILLAIS 312 This skin bag was situated in a thin vellum of the inner skin in the region of the upper throat [of the caribou]. T 50/2–64 [In making a football from a sheep's bladder] get a pipe stem or something and put in the neck of it up. Take all the vellum off of it when it [be] dry. 1979 *'Twas a way of life* 62 The *killiotak* is a metal scraper with a wooden handle. It is used for scraping the vellum off the [seal]skin and helps to soften it.

ven n *Note*: *I* and *e* before *n* are often neutralized in varieties of local speech. Fin (of a fish) (1924 ENGLAND 322).

P 102–60 The vens of the fish passed under an apron on both sides [of machine] to keep it flat. T 33–64¹ 'Tis just the same as a mark on the fish, where you caught un just back of the vens, like you'll [leave] your thumb and finger like that on un, so that the mark is on the haddock.

venomous a also **venemous**. Cp *OED* ~ a 4 fig.

1 Vehement, fierce, angry.

1863 MORETON 34 ~ Vehement. To go eagerly and determinedly to work is to be venomous. 1924 ENGLAND 144 De more pain in a tooth, ye know, de more venimis you is to take un out. 1937 DEVINE 55 Venemous. Virile, strong, vehement. 'A *venemous* fellow to work.' Also angry. 'He got *venemous*.'

2 Of the wind, blowing with great force.

1863 MORETON 34 When wind blows strongly, and

seems likely to last and increase, it is said to 'blow venomous.' 1937 DEVINE 55 It blowed *venemous* from the north east. T 31/2–64 And 'twas a storm; 'twas just venomous.

venomy a *OED* ~ a rare; *ADD* 1, 2. Angry, spiteful; strongly impelled, desirous (1925 *Dial Notes* v, 345).

venture See ADVENTURE.

vice-admiral n *DC* ~ n Nfld (1714–). See also ADMIRAL. The master of the second English fishing vessel to reach a harbour in Newfoundland, exercising certain privileges for the season under the 'admiral'; LADY¹.

[1663] 1963 YONGE 55 At Renoose. . .one [man] stuck there. . .who kept 18 boats, in the *Dorcas*, so our master resolved to be his vice-admiral. 1699 *Act of Wm III* 10 & 11 . . .that the Master of every such Second Fishing Ship as shall enter any such Harbour or Creek, shall be Vice-Admiral of such Harbour or Creek during that Fishing Season. [1714] 1793 REEVES 89 I had several complaints from the inhabitants and others, of injustice done them by the admirals, vice-admirals, &c. 1883 HATTON & HARVEY 44 The masters of the second and third following vessels were to be vice-admiral and rear admiral.

vinegar n Cp *OED* ~ 6 (b) 'a mould' (1857) for first comb.

Comb **vinegar plant**, ~ **squall**: bacterial culture growing in a home-fermented vinegar made from toasted bread, molasses, yeast and water; cp SQUID SQUALL.

P 192–67 Put molasses, water and vinegar in a crock and after a while a [vinegar squall] will grow. (The word squall is from squid squall, the name we used for jelly-fish.) M 69–5 If no molasses water is added [from time to time] the growing vinegar [plant] will eventually absorb all the vinegar. 1972 MURRAY 233–4 One item present in many homes was the 'vinegar plant'. . . In olden days they'd get a little piece of bread, you know, about that big [two inches square] and a part of a cake of yeast, not the yeast we uses now, but the dry yeast, the square, and put that in the bottle and leave it alone and after a time the plant'd grow there.

vinegar strip: dessert sauce made by boiling molasses, home-made vinegar, flour and water.

M 69–5 A steamed pudding coated with vinegar strip was the dessert.

vinnied a *OED* ~ a dial (1519–1787); *EDD* vinny a 1 (1) (a) vinnied 'mouldy' s w cties. Stale, mouldy; mildewed (P 37).

virgin a Cp *OED* ~ adj 17 b '[substance] obtained as a first product' (1719–). Comb **virgin oil**: first oil yielded by seal blubber in the process of repeated rendering.

1819 ANSPACH 425 [Seal oil which is rendered from the fat] is called virgin, or white oil, [and] is considered as the best. 1832 MCGREGOR i, 225 The first that runs off the seal blubber is the virgin, or pale oil, and the last, the brown oil.

virtue n   Cp *OED* ~ sb 9 d 'excellence in respect. . .of nature.' Nutritive properties (of a plant).

M 71–39 The hay which was cut and cured in late August was little more than roughage. All the 'virtue' had been dried and bleached from it.

vitrid a   *EDD* vitrit, vitrid 'angry' Ch. Of a person, nasty, vengeful (P 141–75).

voyage n   [vɒidʒ, vɔidʒ, vʌidʒ]. Cp *NID* ~[1] n 5 a for sense 1; *OED* sb 6 c, d (1859, 1897), *DC* n[1] (Nfld: 1771, 1964) for sense 2; *DC* ~ seal Nfld (1861) for comb in sense 5.

1 Enterprise or period of fishing, sealing or whaling; FISHERY; freq with defining word BANKING, CAPLIN, FALL n, SAVING, SEALING, TRAP[1], etc.

[1578] 1935 *Richard Hakluyt* 124 [Parkhurst's letter] They wex welthy, for that thier shares ys worthe thre tymes the waiges they have for france, spayne or denmarke. . . Thus can their wyves, chyldren, servantes and credytors wytnes wth me the sweetnes and proffyt of this viage. 1620 WHITBOURNE 24 And for the want of such fit houses, some mens voyages (to my knowledge) haue been greatly ouerthrowne; and then a meane place to make fish on, will be made more commodious then the best place is now, that men so dangerously and desperately runne for euery yeere. 1682 COLLINS 96 . . .those that come first destroy the Stages (if remaining,) of those that arrive afterwards, to the end they may get a Voyage before them. [1771] 1792 CARTWRIGHT i, 186 The boats made three trips each, and brought on shore a hundred and twenty-five seals, and both the stoppers; and here the voyage concludes. [1786] 1793 REEVES lvi The vessels so arriving next in order of time as aforesaid, shall be so navigated wholly by men going out upon shares, that is to say, receiving a certain share of the profits arising from the voyage in lieu of wages. [1810] 1971 ANSPACH 2 [They] shall within ten days after the conclusion of the respective voyages or fisheries every year pay the same for that purpose under the penalty of twenty pounds. 1861 DE BOILIEU 32 The man who prosecutes, or speculates in, the fishery, is called the Planter; and his mode is generally to hire his men by the voyage, giving them food and lodging, with the use of a boat, for half their labour, retaining, however, the cod-livers for himself. 1881 TALBOT 29 . . .the voyage, as the season's fishery is called. 1933 GREENE 39 The "Voyage to the Ice" has always been to the sealers almost a picnic; the dangers and hardships, to them, are non-existent. 1937 DEVINE 62 Now they must go at large and forage for themselves while the Summer crews of fishermen are shipped on for the voyage and their meals supplied at the cook-room. T 43/7–64 You were allowed to take out anything you needed for your comfort, and at the end of the voyage all this would be deducted from your wages.

2 The catch of fish, seals, etc, taken, or the proceeds of the catch; TRIP.

[1771] 1792 CARTWRIGHT i, 137 I went to Seal Island; where Hezekiah Guy and company delivered to me two thousand seven hundred and five gallons of seals' oil; thirty-two fox, and four otter skins; one wolf and one deer skin, with two bags of feathers; being part of their winter's voyage. [1831] 1916 *Nfld Law Reports* 33 . . .the merchant and fisherman—the former being the supplier and the other (the one actually engaged in and prosecuting the fishery) the supplied, and whose voyage, or catch of fish, for the season, on the credit of which the supplies are advanced, is liable by the law and custom of the fishery, into whatever hands it may come, to the current supplier's demand. 1854 [FEILD] 86 . . .a large quantity of fish on the flakes of the two principal planters, whose crews had just returned from the Labrador with good 'voyages.' 1869 MCCREA 186 The fleet is evidently coming in, and 'Have they made a voyage?' is the awful question on every tongue [during the seal hunt]. [1882] 1898 *Nfld Law Reports* 403 The goods furnished to Falle & Co by the plaintiff were either given out by them on credit to dealers, who were planters or fishermen, upon the faith of their receiving the produce of the voyage of fish and oil when caught and cured in payment. 1901 *Christmas Review* 10 After the voyage had been landed, weighed and stored, he went up with the rest of the crew to be paid off at Job's office. 1937 *Seafisheries of Nfld* 75 The voyages are shared in almost every conceivable way, but the system for shore fishermen is usually two-thirds of the voyage between the sharemen and one-third for the owner. 1953 *Nfld Fisheries Develop Report* 18 In general. . .the owner takes about half the 'voyage' and the other half is divided equally among the members of the crew if they are full sharemen (including the skipper and active partners in the enterprise). T 141/67–65[2] If you was independent enough you take your own voyage and carry it into St John's and get clear of it that way. . . T 148–65 And in the fall o' the year they come back with their voyage, and land their voyage—[their] fish, sometime in September. 1980 *Evening Telegram* 6 Sep, p. 6 My wife and I were denied the right to sell three hundred pounds of fresh fish (our summer's voyage).

3 Figurative extension.

1813 CARSON 19 One half of this sum [£30] he is obliged to pay for his board during the winter, and the remainder is spent in drinking, and nocturnal dissipation. If the strength of his constitution, enables him to weather his winter's voyage, each succeeding season, the same scene is acted over, till at last he falls a premature victim.

4 Phr *lose one's voyage, cure one's ~ , make one's ~ .*

1866 WILSON 219 But you will lose your voyage; for this hot day will certainly spoil every fish that is left in fagot. 1887 *Colonist Christmas No* 14 Only in summer time did the fishing vessels with their crews visit the country, and then only to catch and cure their 'voyage' of fish, as it was then, and is still termed. 1936 SMITH 47 He thought that. . .we would scrape up another hundred or more quintals, and then begin to wash out and make our voyage.

5 Comb **voyage seal**: migrating 'harp seal.'

1861 DE BOILIEU 92–3 The principal seal of the coast

is termed the Voyage seal, while the males are distinctively called Harps, or Blackbacks.

vrore See FRORE.

W

wabble* n also **wobble***. Cp LOO, WHABBY. Red-throated loon (*Gavia stellata*) (P 113–74).
P 176–62 'Wary as a wobble' (a wobble is a very cautious bird). P 245–74 That bird's a wobble.

wabby See WHABBY.

wad n Cp *NID* ~² n 2 a 'a considerable amount.' A concentration of fish or seals; SPOT.
1924 ENGLAND 293 De first little wad [of seals] went off, but de rest bid up. A big spot of 'em. C 75–136 We saw a nice wad of fish out on the point today. P 245–78 There'd be fish in little wads on the grounds, an' you'd take them easy.

wadden n Leather boot, esp one reaching to or above the knee and worn by fishermen; cp SMALLWOOD BOOT, TONGUE ~ .
1936 DEVINE 132 The name of Mr Nicholas Wadden. . .became a household word amongst the fishermen of Newfoundland who used the word 'Waddens' as synonym for a pair of long boots.

waddock n A football.
1898 *The Record* 14 The name Rugby Football is known here as 'Kicking the Cod' and 'Rushing the Waddock.' 1904 MURPHY (ed) 39 But give to me the 'waddock' / As we kicked it on the Mall.

wag n Cp *EDD* ~ sb 12 (4) wag of air 'breath of air' Ha. Slight motion or undulation of the water; usu in phr *not a wag*. Cp FLOBBER.
1873 CARROLL 22 There the brig remained for ten days, and not a wag in the water or amongst the ice. 1924 ENGLAND 322 Wag o' say. A bit of wave or sea. 1937 DEVINE 22 Not a *wag* of sea.

wage n Cp *OED* ~ sb 4: wages-man Austr (1888, 1890); *Cent* rare. Comb **wages man**: one indentured or engaged on wages for a period in the fishery; SERVANT[1] as distinguished from SHAREMAN.
1857 MOUNTAIN 4 These men were in all respects the servants or 'wages men' of the merchant.

wagel n *OED* ~ 'black-backed Gull. . .in its immature state' (1672–). Great black-backed gull (*Larus marinus*).
1959 MCATEE 36 ~ A British folk-name for the young [gull]. Nfld.

wagon n See BRYANT 493 logging sled. Comb **wagon sled**, **double wagon** ~ : heavy double sled used with horses to haul logs; cp BUNK SLED, DOUBLE ~ .
T 96/7–64[1] That was a bunk sled. Wagon sleds, some called 'em. T 43/7–64 One man couldn't twist around one o' these double wagon-sleds. . . The difference between the slide and the wagon-sleds is that with the wagon-sleds there's two, and you can lengthen out your tow chains, and if you're pullin' long stuff you can have 'em as far apart as you like. Q 67–3 When hauling was done by horses [wagon sleds] were used: two sleds, the rear one being attached to the front with chains. If a single one was used to haul long timber, it was called a 'bobsled.'

wagtail n Spotted sandpiper (*Actitis macularia*); BEACH BIRD.
1870 *Can Naturalist* v, 295 A common summer migrant, arriving early in May: breeds on the coast. . .[the] 'wagtail.'

wait-a-minute n Cp *DC* wait-awhile-match (1965). (a) Sulphur-tipped match; COMB; (b) kindling for a fire; BLASTY BOUGH.
T 80/2–64 'Twas hardwood matches at that time, we used to call 'em hardwood wait-a-minutes, 'cause you'd have to scrape 'em on an ass o' your pants, an' he fizz, and fizz, an' by an' by [after] he burn up that brimstone he come to a flame. C 75–146 ~ red or blassy [blasty] boughs. He used to hear men from the North Shore of Conception Bay call the boughs this because you have to wait a minute when you put one into the fire before it catches and burns.

wake n *OED* ~ sb[1] 7 (b) ~ house Ir (1814). Comb **wake-house**, **~ room**: house or room in which corpse is laid out for a wake or vigil.
1910 *Nfld Qtly* Oct, p. 23 I primed myself, pretty well, so well, in fact, that I felt quite equal to the task when I arrived at the wake-house at midnight. I saw the white bed up in the corner and without more ado I went over, knelt down close to the head of the bed; the people fell on their knees and I began the prayers. T 55–64 You go into a wake house and say your prayers for the dead, an' stay an hour or two. C 65–2 She had to pass through the wake-room. M 71–44 It is not often that liquor would be kept in the wake-house, but you could be sure that there would be some around at a neighbour's house.

waking vbl n Following in the wake of another vessel through the 'leads' and channels in an ice-floe (1909 BERNIER 7).

walk v
1 To be without work; to be idle in between periods of activity; cp CRUISE v. Freq in phr *walk about*, *~ around*.
[1766] 1976 HEAD 147 Great part [of the Irish immigrants] could not get Employ in the Fishery, being oblig'd to wander and walk from place to place, unemploy'd the whole Summer. 1905 MURPHY 9 "The Sealers Strike of 1902": . . .the sealers strike the other day in town; / When full three thousand northern men did walk the streets all day. 1924 ENGLAND 236 What'd ye

be doin' at home, fer money, but walkin' de bank? 1930 BARNES 232 Things were very dull down in our country at that time. There were several other captains walking about as well as myself and there was not much fun in that. 1937 DEVINE 55 Walking about. To be unemployed. 'I've been *walking about* all the summer.' P 148–77 'Are you out fishing?' 'No, we're walking around till the weather gets better.' 1977 *Inuit Land Use* 243 I've always been fishing. . .but when you have a lot of young people walking around with nothing to do, you have to find something for them to do.

2 Phr *walk back*: to reverse (a machine).
1925 *Dial Notes* v, 345 *Walk back* de winch.
walk in: to weigh (an anchor).
1895 GRENFELL 88–9 It was quite a sight on leaving harbours to see often fifty men. . .'walking in' the anchor by means of a system of pulleys, each as he came to the stern of the ship trotting back to catch hold of the rope again near the bow, a continuous chain of men being thus maintained, and all singing, as they pulled, one of the old shanty songs to assist them to pull together.

3 Cpd **walk-before**: in a funeral procession, one who walks in front of the casket.
C 73–115 You were invited either as a 'walk-before' (this being the minister and five other people who walked in front of the casket), a bearer (to carry the casket), or a mourner.

walk n   *OED* ~ sb[1] 8 obs (1380–1702). The habitual path or haunt of an animal.
[1770] 1792 CARTWRIGHT i, 53 I visited all the traps, snares, and deathfalls, in Hare Hill walk. [1776] ibid ii, 133 Another [wolf] had gotten into a trap in the east walk.

wall n   Cp *OED* ~ sb[1] 9 (1615, 1879 quots) for sense 1.
1 Either of the two long vertical sections of netting in the box-shaped 'cod trap'; also attrib; SIDE.
Q 67–91 ~ one of the two side parts of a cod trap.
P 9–73 The foot rope of the wall netting is right-hand twist and. . .the edge of the bottom is fastened to the foot of the wall.
2 Comb **walls of troy**: decorative pattern marked on sand spread over kitchen floor (P 162–69).

wallop v   Cp *EDD* wallop v[1] 'to move fast. . .to dance.' Phr **wallop'er down***: to dance vigorously, with much physical activity and stamping; cp BREAK'ER DOWN.
T 45–64 This feller'd start up music an' they'd all wallop her down! Take [her] right off o' the shores!
C 71–129 Come on, boy, wallop'er down!

wamby See WHABBY.

wangle n   A horizontal wooden beam or stick fastened to the bow of a sealing vessel; RAMS (1925 *Dial Notes* v, 345).
1924 ENGLAND 152 'Ye mind, sir,' asked John

Domeney, a master watch, 'how they had wangles for the men to jump an' ride on under the bowsprit, an' push away the ice jams wid their feet an' wid poles?'

wap See WOP[2].

waps See WOP[1].

warm a, n *OED* ~ sb[2] 1 rare; *NID* dial for sense 1; cp *OED* flaw sb[2] 1 b 'fall of rain or snow' for sense 2.
1 Phr *get a warm*: to warm oneself by a fire or with hot food (1925 *Dial Notes* v, 346).
1924 ENGLAND 45 'Twas a spectacle worth seeing, those Viking sons of the North slopping Worcestershire and divers ardent sauces into the 'scouse or over their other tucker. . .then gulping pints of tea. Anything to 'get a wahrm'! 1932 BARBOUR 48 'Take the wheel,' I said, 'and let Edward go down for a warm; he has had the wheel for a long time now.' M 69–5 Often we had to keep a big fire in all day and leave the pit every now and then to get a warm by the fire.
2 Comb **warm flaw**: a worthless fellow (1924 ENGLAND 322).
1937 DEVINE 55 ~ A sarcastic name for a weak or undependable type of man, unable to take his part in work.

warp v   *OED* ~ v 1 'to cast, throw' obs (888–1513). To throw (a person or thing); to put down.
T 139–65 If they didn't stop fighting then they warp 'em over the wharf, four or five of 'em over the one time. P 184–67 [in a card game] Warp it right out there!

warping vbl n Comb **warping chantey**, ~ **song**, ~ **tally**: rhythmic song chanted by men hauling on a line or warp; HAULING CHANTEY.
T 88–64 'An' away, away, my jollies, and we're all bound to go'—that's a part o' one! What we used to call a warpin' chantey, [or] a warpin' tally. T 31/4–64 Sometimes they sing the warping songs—'Heave away, Santyanna!' an' all this kind o' stuff.

wash v   *Fisheries of U S* 132.
1 Esp in phr *wash out*: to immerse split and salted cod in brine at various stages of 'making' dried fish; cp WATER v.
[1663] 1963 YONGE 57 The fish being salted, lies 3 or 4 days, sometimes (if bad weather) 8 or 10 days, and is then washed by the boys in salt or fresh water. [1766] 1971 BANKS 135 They are salted & Lie in salt & the Salt is washd out of them in the Same manner as the others. 1895 PROWSE 21 The splitting table, the trough, known as the water horse (for washing out the fish after salting). . . 1936 SMITH 47 He thought. . .we would scrape up another hundred or more quintals, and then begin to wash out and make our voyage. 1960 FUDGE 16 Our last trip totalled 420 quintals, and we came home on September 21st and washed out our fish. M 67–16 Waterhorse fish also provided an unpleasant smell around the house. This is the fish which has been salted for 2 or 3 weeks and is now washed

out—soaked and washed in salt water and then spread on the flake to dry. 1979 TIZZARD 294 Coupled with this was the added danger of dirty weather coming after [the cod] was washed out and ready to go on the flake.

2 Cpd **washball(s),** ~ **rock:** in names of submerged or barely submerged rocks; cp SUNKER.

1951 *Nfld & Lab Pilot* i, 74 Washballs, a rock with a least depth of 4½ feet over it, lies on the outer edge of the coastal bank. Ibid 274 Wash rocks, which dry 4 feet, lie at the outer extremity of a spit.

wash n   *OED* ~ sb 16 (1769) for sense 1.

1 The blade of an oar (1969 *Nfld Qtly* July, p. 20).

2 Attrib **wash house:** room or area of fishing premises where salted fish are processed for drying.

1868 *Royal Geog Soc* xxxviii, 266 On entering Indian Harbour every rock was covered with fish drying and curing, men carrying wet fish in barrows from their boats to the 'washhouse.'

washer n   In the preparation of salted cod-fish, member of crew who processes fish in salt water.

1818 CHAPPELL 128 In this state the *fish* continue for a few days; when they are again taken, in barrows, to a sort of wooden box, full of holes, which is suspended from the stage in the sea. The *washer* stands up to his knees in this box, and scrubs the salt off the cod with a soft mop. 1895 GRENFELL 60 [The splitter] with great dexterity cuts out the back-bone and flings the flesh into a tub of water for the 'washer.'

washing vbl n

1 A length of netting connecting the landward end of a cod trap 'leader' to the shore (Q 67–56).

P 127–77 ~ a short leader. When a trap-leader is anchored to the shore, sometimes a piece of old netting is used between the landwash end of the leader and the shore. While this seems to save the main leader from being torn by the rough seas and the rocks, it also guides the fish to the main leader and thus into the trap.

2 Comb **washing tub,** ~ **vat:** wooden container in which salted cod are placed at various stages in preparation for drying; RAM's HORN.

[1810] 1971 ANSPACH 22 The fish is then put into *washing vats,* (wooden vessels generally 7 or 8 feet long, 3½ broad, and 3 deep) first two or three quintals over which they pour a quantity of salt water, and so on successively until the vat is full of fish and water. 1861 DE BOILIEU 31 The cod is now placed in what is called salt-bulk, where it may remain any period of time; for, so long as fish is being caught in the bay, so long will the 'drying' and 'washing'—which constitute the final process—be delayed. 1979 TIZZARD 81 He made almost every kind of a barrel and tub. There were trap kegs, molasses kegs, washing tubs, salt tubs and punts' piggins.

wasp See WOP[1].

watch n   Cp *OED* ~ sb 18 naut for sense 1.

1 One of the groups of men on a sealing vessel organized to hunt seals on the ice-floes; GANG; also attrib.

1862 *Atlantic Mo* ix, 367 But 't was blowun a gale o' wind, an' we under bare poles, an' snow comun agen, so fast as ever it could come; but out the men 'ould go, all mad like, an' my watch goed, an' so I mus' go. [1900 OLIVER & BURKE] 10 After having placed the different watches (about 30 men under a master watch). . . 1924 ENGLAND 123 Presently we strike another patch, and all hands gather in the waist, with gaffs, bristling flags, gear like crusaders. . . 'Take y'r watches an' go,' commands the Old Man. 'Starburd over. Go on, me sons!' [1923] 1946 PRATT 196 "The Ice-Floes": With our shoulders galled we drew them, and cast / Them in thousands around the watch's flag. 1929 *Nat Geog* July, 106 I put one watch crew on the starboard side. 1952 *Atlantic Guardian* Mar, p. 34 Three watches of the ship's company (almost 150 men) were on the ice from the morning of March 31 to April 2, and many of the survivors were maimed for life. 1972 SANGER 241 ~ Major sub-division of sealing crew to facilitate the operation of the vessel and effectively deploy the sealers on ice after the whelping patches have been located.

2 Comb **watch-buoy:** float marking the location and ownership of a fish-net or trap (M 69–23).

1861 DE BOILIEU 28 They are filled from the large net, and moored in the neighbourhood of the hauling-place, a watch-buoy, with the owner's name upon it, being set floating on the water.

watch-dog: hunting dog used in the pursuit of wild ducks and geese.

1861 DE BOILIEU 239–40 The watch-dog lands with you, and, with much caution, examines the shore, and directly he observes ducks, he will instantly lie down and crawl out of their sight, then immediately rise and run towards you, when by his actions you may be sure he has sighted a company.

watch-house: shelter in which hunter conceals himself in taking seals with nets; cp GAZE.

1967 FIRESTONE 103 There is usually a small tilt called a *watch house* by a capstan, in which a man sits and waits for a seal to enter the [seal] frame. When this occurs he raises the enter net and fires at the seal with a rifle.

watcher n   One who hunts seals (or other game), esp with a gun on the ice-floes near patches of open water; SWATCHER.

1861 DE BOILIEU 131, 133–4 In extreme severe winters the Esquimaux from whom the partridges led me—are often hard driven for food; then the toil to procure it sometimes results in the death of the hunter, or 'watcher'. . . Away went the watchers to examine the blow-holes in the bay, in the hopes of returning in the evening with a prize. On these excursions the watchers are provided with a small stool to sit on.

water n   Cp *OED* ~ sb 6 and 7 b *on (the) water* (esp 1758 quot) for sense 1; *OED* 6 b 'pl is often used. . .with reference to flowing water' for sense 2; for combs. in sense 3: *OED* ~ bear obs (1706); ~ dog 1 a; *DAE* ~ haul (1871–), WILCOCKS (1868) 56; *OED* ~ man 5 (1833–); cp *OED* nipper sb¹ 3 'boy who assists. . .workman' (1851–), *EDD* sb 1; *DC* ~ pup (1912); *OED* ~-side 'bank or margin of the sea, or of a river, stream, or lake' (c1400, 1885 quots); ~ whelp: *ADD* whelk 'a welt.'

1 The sea, esp that adjacent to the land, where the fishery is prosecuted; fishing grounds; freq in phr *on the water*; SALT WATER.

[1583] 1940 *Gilbert's Voyages & Enterprises* ii, 407 [Hayes' narrative] Foule both of water and land in great plentie and diversitie. 1620 WHITBOURNE 34 Thus by such meanes divers men have runne so farre at Sea, in some such unfit voyages, that they have brought land to water, and knew not how to shape a course to recover unto land againe. [1794] 1968 THOMAS 52 In Newfoundland the Dogs commonly are their own caterers. They chiefly live on Fish and many of these sturdy race fish for themselves. . . The instant a Fish appears they plunge into the water and seldom come up without their prey. 1858 [LOWELL] i, 44 [He] did not trouble himself about his pupil's slipping off, in a blue jacket, to go out upon the water. 1863 MORETON 42 An old graveyard in Greenspond. . .had certainly sufficient depth of swamp for the purpose, but it was upon the water's edge, and the ice, which in winter formed upon its banks, foundered in large masses in the spring of the year. 1921 CABOT 258 [proverb] When the water burns look out for wind. 1936 SMITH 27 After the gale abated we went out to Five Islands in the trap boat to see about our cod-trap that we had left in the water, and I regret to say that the trap was in a very bad condition, all torn up. T 194/5–65 Now, I've [always] fished home—always fishin'. I get nothin' clear o' fishin', thank God. What I've got I've got out o' the water, man-fashion. 1966 FARIS 23 Men in Cat Harbour are fishermen, not 'seamen' or sailors. Fishing requires 'nerve for the water,' and few men simply 'love to be at it!' . . .Old and retired fishermen who no longer 'go on the water,' express it as 'losing nerve for the water.' 1976 *Decks Awash* v (2), p. 14 Down along the shore, one time, you could see everyone had a garden and every man and his sons were out on the water. 1977 *Inuit Land Use* 240 I was always a fisherman. What I earned, I earned from the water. 1980 *Evening Telegram* 6 Sep, p. 6 In Newfoundland today, due to federal regulations, we see young men who would like to get into the fishery being refused licences and effectively barred from the water.

2 In pl, a series of fresh-water ponds linked by a stream.

1971 SEARY 143 The use of the generic Waters for a succession of ponds linked by a stream, not recorded in *OED*, is confined to NTS Holyrood: Cocoanut Waters, Eastern Waters, Leonards Waters. C 71–115 Brian's Waters included three Brian's Ponds and a Brian's Feeder (River) which flows from the Long Range Mountains inside Hawkes Bay to Portland Creek Pond. It was a trapping area for a man known only as Brian, before Daniels Harbour was settled.

3 Attrib, comb, cpd **water bear**: polar bear; WHITE BEAR (*Thalarctos maritimus*).

[1768] 1828 CARTWRIGHT ii, 323–4 The white or water bear is not to be reckoned amongst the creatures that contribute to the sustenance of the Red Indians. Although this animal is found in Newfoundland in the winter and early in the spring, he is only a stranger from the northern continent. Stimulated at this season by hunger, he will quit the shores and venture many leagues amongst the floating ice, in quest of seals. 1846 TOCQUE 118 When he first heard the sound he took his loaded gun and proceeded in the direction whence the sound came (supposing it had been a water-bear). 1919 LENCH 22 About eighty years ago an unearthly sound was heard in Bonavista and its immediate neighbourhood. . . All night long the inhabitants were going around with their loaded guns on the track of what they called a 'water bear.' 1965 RUSSELL 84 'Water bear! Water bear!' During much of the Newfoundland winter, ice pans flood into the Atlantic from the arctic. These pans bring down arctic foxes and occasionally polar bears. T 143/4–65¹ We chased the water bears round that sheet of ice three or four times and never caught un.

water doctor: water strider of the family *Gerridae*; DOCTOR¹.

P 148–65 Water doctors dart around on top of the water in road-side pools and drains. P 126–67 Water doctors [are] insects found on pools of calm water in a small stream. They swim in quick, jerky motions on top of the water.

water dog: large, usu black, smooth-haired dog with webbed feet, bred to the salt water; NEWFOUNDLAND DOG 2.

[1839] 1975 MOYLES (ed) 115 We remember to have seen in the first year of the Newfoundland Magna Charta a lively portrait of its constitutional assembly, at the moment when its speaker, an interesting water-dog of the largest size, coifed with a pair of flap ears that fell down either shoulder. . .was putting the question. 1861 DE BOILIEU 239 Some are trained as retrievers, watch, house, and water dogs. Still they are all of the same breed. 1928 BRUTON 136 While I was travelling along the 'Cape Shore,' east of Placentia Bay, in 1927, some of these smooth-haired dogs were pointed out to me as 'water-dogs'; they were said to be expert at retrieving birds that were shot, and had fallen into water. [1930] 1946 PRATT 136 "The *Roosevelt* and the *Antinoe*": The baffled liner like a water-dog / Would dip her nose to the sea and then up-rear / Her head with black hawse nostrils keen to flair. T 398/9–67 But a feller had a good water dog, boy, that's all you want. 1973 *MUN Gazette* 14 Dec [for sale] Newfoundland Water Dog Pups.

water fur: fur-bearing animal frequenting lakes and rivers; FUR n.

P 9–73 Mink, otter, muskrat and beaver were called water furs, chiefly because they spent a great deal of time in the water.

water gully: wooden container to hold water; GULLY².

P 207–67 He dipped the water out with a water gully. C 71–37 ~ Water barrel (used beef barrel, washed and painted). 1971 NOSEWORTHY 260 ~ A tub made of a

half-barrel and carried by a rope and a long stick.
P 127–80 We'd have to cut six inches of ice out of the
water gully before we could boil the kettle.

water haul: the pulling of a fish-net or trap to
the surface with no fish enclosed in the device;
HAUL n; any fruitless trip or enterprise.

[1929] BOWEN 148 ~ Among the Grand Banks net-
fishers, when the net brings up absolutely nothing.
1937 DEVINE 55 When a net or seine is hauled and
found to contain no fish, it's a *water haul*. Applied to
failures generally. 1966 SCAMMELL 40 True they got a
few quintals once in a while, but nothing like the boatloads, yes sometimes two or three boatloads that the
Martins used to get there nearly every time they
hauled. Sometimes Blanchard even had a water-haul.
1968 MESHER 88 "Seal Flipper Stew": While nets and
the hand-line are fishermen's tools / There's those who
with cod trap are many times fooled; / Water hauls,
often a summer day long, / Discourage the clergy and
tire the strong. 1975 *Daily News* 3 Jan, p. 11 ABC Taxi
[plans] to keep track of 'no show' calls. . . Nothing
upsot a cabbie more than going on a 'water haul.' 1975
RUSSELL 48 'Uncle Mose,' he said, 'when I went to
school, I didn't learn much. But one thing I did learn
was that John Cabot discovered Newfoundland in
1497. Now if I've got to lose *that* 'twill mean I made a
complete waterhaul.'

water hopper: see **water doctor** above.

P 126–67 ~ Insect found on surface of calm pools of
water usually in a small stream. They resemble a large
spider and swim in quick, jerky motions.

water-horse: see WATER-HORSE.

water-jug: PITCHER PLANT (*Sarracenia
purpurea*) (1956 ROULEAU 40).

water lily: see **water jug** (1956 ROULEAU 40).

water man: supernatural figure inhabiting the
sea or 'salt water.'

M 71–103 The stage as I have already indicated was
situated at the shoreline, and it was along this general
area, around and under the stage that the 'water man'
lived. As children we were told that if we went near the
water alone, that is when the men weren't around, the
water man would get us. Some children claimed to
have actually seen him.

water nipper, nipper: boy, or sometimes an
elderly man, employed to bring drinking water
to men at work.

P 65–64 The water nipper is a person who brings
water to the men. As a professional the water nipper
has practically died out. Once it used to be a man's job
to bring water around to the men as they
worked—especially in summer. The water nipper
would be an old man—often over 70. His job was a sort
of reward for years of service as a lumberjack. T 29–64
My job was what they call water-nipper—water-boy
today, but water-nipper then. That's taking round
water to the men, your own gang.

water pigeon: southern black guillemot
(*Cepphus grylle atlantis*), or common dovekie
(*Plautus alle alle*); PIGEON, ~ DIVER, SALT-
WATER PIGEON.

1792 *Liverpool MS* Just as we got into the cove we
saw a young water pigeon that had its throat partly

stopped, to prevent its diving, as we supposed afterwards that the Indians had placed it there to know if we
had any guns, for if we had they supposed we should
fire at it.

water pup: blister, sore or inflammation common among fishermen, whose skin is often in
contact with salt water. Possibly a playful synonym of **water whelp**. Also attrib.

1909 BROWNE 118 Others, with bandaged hands or
arms 'in a sling' are suffering from sores, deep ugly
ulcers ('water-pups') that need skilled attention. 1920
WALDO 56 So many fishermen get what are called
'water-whelps' or 'water-pups,'—pustules on the fore-
arm due to the abrasion of the skin by more or less
infected clothing. C 65–4 Water pups are a form of boil
[breaking] out on arms that have been rubbed by wet
clothing and salt water. C 69–2 When he was fishing he
never failed to use water pup chains around the wrist.
These were brass chains worn to prevent the wrist and
arm from being chafed by the oil or rubber coat and
causing water pups which he says could be pretty bad.

water set: the placing of an animal trap in a
pond or stream; cp SET n.

P 9–73 Water sets were used to catch mink, otter,
muskrat and beaver.

waterside: sea-shore or coastal strip bordering
the bays, coves, harbours and inlets comprising
the area of European settlement and fishery
enterprise; SHORE[1]. Also attrib.

[1583] 1940 Gilbert's *Voyages & Enterprises* ii, 403
[Hayes' narrative] The Generall granted in fee farme
divers parcells of land lying by the water side, both in
this harbor of S John, and elsewhere, which was to
owners a great commoditie, being thereby assured (by
their proper inheritance) of grounds convenient to
dresse and to drie their fish. [1667] 1895 PROWSE 157
Sir David Kirke. . .compelled them to take estates in
land in severall harbours for erecting of houses and
ffishing places by ye water side. [1790] 1895 ibid 395 I
have considered your request respecting the alteration
which you wish to make in your Storehouse, near the
waterside. [1794] 1968 THOMAS 52 As [hunger] presses
upon [the dogs] they go to the waterside and set on a
Rock, keeping as good a lookout as ever Cat did for a
Mouse. The instant a Fish appears they plunge into the
water and seldom come up without their prey. 1944
LAWTON & DEVINE 4 Handcock had taken in the
waterside at the north end of the Beach. . . Two of Jim
Sullivan's sons settled on the waterside east of their
father. 1960 FUDGE 36 I purchased this spot, which
included a small waterside. . .cleared away all the old
debts and got ready to build a modern retail store, also
a waterside premises, which included a salt store and a
fish store and wharf, about seventy feet long.

water whelp: see **water pup** above. Possibly a
variant of an unattested *water-welt*.

[See 1920 quot at **water pup**.] 1924 ENGLAND 211
'Water welps,' or sores on the hands and arms caused
by salt water, yield to brass chains worn round the
wrists. T 145–65 They say they used it as a cure for the
sea pups or another term for water whelps. It was a
sort of a pimple that would get infected by the much
use of the clothing an' the hands in salt water. 1981
HUSSEY 56 One of the most common ailments among

the crew was called 'water whelps' or 'pups.' These were boils on the wrists [and] the usual remedy was a poultice made of molasses and flour or a mixture of laundry soap and sugar.

water wolf: an organism which gets into well-water, similar to a polychaete worm (P 154–78).

C 70–28 If you swallow one, hold your head over a pan of warm milk and the water wolf will come out of your stomach seeking the milk.

water v *OED* ~ v 6 'to soak in or with water' obs (1398–1675), b *to water out* 'to free from salt by soaking in water' obs (1683). (a) To immerse split and salted cod in water in preparation for drying; WASH v; (b) to soak dried and salted cod (or meat) in water to remove salt preparatory to cooking.

1873 CARROLL 44 Notwithstanding which, the top fish are often light salted, and the bottom fish in the puncheon, are salt-burned and often must be watered before being exposed to the sun for making. 1905 *Daily News* 4 Jan Why don't E P Morris, for Mackinson buy it? / He'd find it best suited for watering *cod*. 1905 DUNCAN 116 We had disposed of Aunt Ruth's watered fish and soaked hard-bread with hunger for a relish. T 55/6–64 There's nothing better than good salted fish, an' well cured fish, watered an' cooked. T 43/8–64 The way they used to water a fish [at] a logging camp [was] they'd take the fish and throw it in the brook on Thursday evening and you'd have that fish for dinner Friday. 1974 *Evening Telegram* 23 Mar, p. 3 We were kindly asked up to one man's home, a well-to-do person in the insurance business, and sure enough he had a bit of watered fish on the stove for his supper. 1980 ibid 5 Jan, p. 11 [There's nothing better than] some home-made buttered bread and a bit of watered fish.

water-horse n *OED* ~ 3 (Nfld: 1792); *DC* n 1, 2 Nfld (1777–; 1818–); *Fisheries of U S* 132. For derivation, see HORSE n 1, and *OED* horse 7 'frame or structure on which something is supported'; or possibly, from its shape, *OED* sea-horse 4 'hippopotamus' obs (1600–1759), water-horse 1 obs (1398–1642). A bulky oblong stack of split and salted cod-fish piled in layers to drain after immersion in brine; cp BULK n, PILE n; occas the 'washing vat' itself or RAM'S HORN; the fish so washed as they are placed on the drying 'flake.' Also attrib.

[(1663) 1963 YONGE 57 The fish being salted, lies 3 or 4 days, sometimes (if bad weather) 8 or 10 days, and is then washed by the boys in salt or fresh water and laid in a pile skin upward on a platt of beach stones, which they call a horse.] [1777] 1792 CARTWRIGHT ii, 242 Fourteen quintals of fish were washed, the water-horse was carried out, and the green fish were spread. 1792 ibid *Gloss* i, xvi ~ Newly washed codfish, which are laid upon each other to drain before they are spread to dry. [1810] 1971 ANSPACH 23 When *green* fish is put to dry on a beach, great care is requisite that the *water horse* (a singular name for the bulk of fish after washing) be spread before the sun has heated the stones. 1819 ANSPACH 446 The bulk of fish left to drain

after being washed and previous to its being spread for drying, is called the *water-horse*, a name which sets at defiance all the penetration and learning of the deepest etymologist. [1856] 1975 WHITELEY 121 Fine day—carried out first waterhorse of fifty quintals of fish. 1866 WILSON 211 Waterhorse. The quantity of fish in the waterhorse is indefinite; it simply means one put or trip of fish, that had been washed from the salt the day before, and left to drain; sometimes it is not more than two or three quintals, sometimes it is ten or twelve. 1882 TALBOT 23 Here the fish is spread out to dry, after having been taken from the stage and washed in a large square wooden vessel or tub called the water-rhorse. 1895 *J A Folklore* viii, 39 Waterhorse: a pile of fish after being washed, usually three or four feet wide, about the same height, and as long as may be. 1895 PROWSE 21 The splitting table, the trough, known as the water horse (for washing out the fish after salting), the flakes (stages raised on piles and covered with boughs), were all in general use from the very commencement of this great industry. [c1900] 1968 *RLS* 8, p. 24 ~ Fish washed out of the salt & ready to go on the flake to dry. 1924 ENGLAND 255 [proverb] The planter's eye spreads the water horse. (The boss of a fish room gets the fish quickly spread.) 1935 KEAN 100 In my early days I was never taught to spread water-horse fish on lungers or rocks until it had first been spread on flakes for two or three days. 1936 SMITH 17 In horsing the fish up, any fish not perfectly clean would be washed over again, then put in the water-horse, back-up, with a slight sprinkling of salt; it would then lie in the waterhorse for twenty-four hours. 1954 INNIS 426 After catching, splitting, and washing, the fish were put into three-quintal tubs along with two gallons of salt per draft. (A 'draft' and a half of fresh fish, or 238 pounds, made about one quintal of fish, or 108 pounds of dried.) On the first day fish were added to the pickle formed by the salt. After four or five days they were washed in the pickle, put into the 'water horse,' allowed to drain, were spread on the floor for six hours, and then put on the flakes or drying racks, with the flesh side up. T 36/8–64 Wash [the fish], throw it in another tub and wash the dirty water off it again, an' then they would put it in waterhorse—put it in the big bulk in the stage. T 43–64 You'd often hear a feller say, 'I got a big water horse to put out tomorrow!' That would be probably up to forty quintals o' fish that he'd have to spell out on the flake. 1973 BARBOUR 68 The fish lay in bulk for a few days, then were taken out, thoroughly washed, and were placed in what was called 'water hoss' which means laid face down on the floor of a store built over the salt water. The floor had space between lungers so that the pickle left in the fish could drain away. 1977 BURSEY 125 He had the reputation of making the best fish that was cured in St John's. Perhaps the credit for this should be given to his wife. . .who kept an open eye on the fish from water-horse to shipping.

water-horse v To place split and salted cod-fish, just removed from a 'washing vat,' in a stack to drain; HORSE v.

T 36–64 An' then the women would get [the fish] in these tubs an' vats, an' wash it out and rinse it in the water, an' water-horse it. 1966 HORWOOD 350 But who's goin' to wash out all that stuff, an' waterhorse it, an' spread it an' yaffle it?

watering vbl n Cp *OED* ~ vbl sb 8. In designations of places where fresh water is available for ships; cp FRESH a: ~ WATER.

[(1766) 1971 BANKS 450 There is exceedingly good Anchors Ground. . .in Pitts Harbour, which must be recommended for Kings Ships, as having the most room & being the most convenient for Wooding and Watering.] 1891 *Holly Branch* 8 Water Street was known as the Lower Path, and terminated rather abruptly at Prescott St, the hill there running out from Duckworth Street to the water's edge, round which, by the landwash, pedestrians travelled, and what is now known as Job's Cove, was the watering cove, where H.M.S. of war and other vessels, obtained their supply of drinking water from a brook that flowed into it. 1953 *Nfld & Lab Pilot* ii, 437 Watering cove, where there is a disused whaling station, is situated in the south-western side of the island.

waubbe See WHABBY.

way n JOYCE 36 *the way, what* ~ for phr in sense 2.

1 Short poles placed to form a path over which heavy objects are hauled.

1836 [WIX]² 36 On this path the 'ways,' or crossbeams, over which the French when they held Placentia, were in the habit of drawing their boats from one bay to the other, are still to be seen. [1916] 1972 GORDON 84 The house was then dragged on board by means of well-blubbered ways and unloaded by the same means near to the proposed site. M 69–6 A trail wide enough for the ox to walk along, was cut and ways (sticks for logs to run over) were put in places where they were needed.

2 In idiomatic phr *by the way of no harm*: casually.

P 108–70 Drop in to Mary's, by the way of no harm, and see how she is.

no way: not well.

1968 DILLON 159 Girl, I'm no way since I had that cold.

the way: in order that.

1968 DILLON 159 They used to put frosters in the heels o' the boots. They'd leave 'em down so far, the way you wouldn't slip of a frosty day.

what way: in what condition?

1968 DILLON 160 I heard your father was shockin' sick. What way is he now?

3 Comb **way ice**: loose or open ice easy for navigation (1924 ENGLAND 346).

weak n A grade or cull of lobsters; a lobster barely meeting minimum requirements of size and weight.

1953 *Nfld Fish Develop Report* 88 About five per cent of the total number of lobsters shipped are condemned. Rather less than 15 per cent are 'weaks' and somewhat over five per cent are 'culls.'

weather n *OED* ~ sb 1 h now dial and naut; *EDD* 1 for sense 1.

1 Storm with high winds and heavy precipitation.

1858 [LOWELL] i, 125 People in this country take no heed of weather, (when they have good reason to be out), except to dress accordingly. 1896 *J A Folklore* ix, 30 ~ beside the usual nautical uses to signify to sail to windward of, and to bear up under and come through, as a storm, is used to signify foul weather, or storm and tempest. 1924 ENGLAND 54 Yes, sir, when it come t'ick, when it come wedder, you'm able to be wonnerful fine on de ice, if you'm knowin'. . .what to do. 1955 DOYLE (ed) 70 "The Hole in the Wall": Now one little girl was late on arriving, / She must have met weather and had to go in. 1955 ENGLISH 39 [proverb] Praise the weather, when you're ashore. T 380–67 'Gainst weather, you know, you'll see it. C 69–17 [If the cat washed its face above its ears] they would remark, 'We are going to have weather (meaning bad) for the cat washed above its ears.'

2 Comb **weather bird**: bird whose call is thought to presage a storm; a person said to bring bad weather.

C 68–16 [He was called] a weather bird because he brings rain whenever he visits [the settlement]. 1975 GUY 148 You would hear the weather birds in the spring in the evenings when you were up playing rounders, and what birds they seemed to be who could fly so high no one could see them but make so loud a noise that everyone could hear them.

weather edge: (a) windward side of an icefield; (b) the side of a house exposed to prevailing wind.

1861 DE BOILIEU 100 It is a sad sight to see a ship on the weather edge of ice not enabled to work off; for when the ice begins to rafter she is thrown up, falls over, and becomes like corn between two millstones, and is literally ground up. 1887 BOND 74 [They tried to] get to the weather edge of the ice. 1924 ENGLAND 233 We're on the weather edge o' the ice, an' there'll be no give-away till it moderates an' goes abroad. T 141/64–65² Here's the funnel, with smoke comin' out of un, an' down over the weather edge o' the house.

weather house: covering on entrance to the fo'c's'le of a decked boat or vessel; cp HOUSE.

1977 BUTLER 78 I raised the height of the cabin house, and put a new roof on it. I built a new weather house on the forecastle.

weather light: gleam or flicker of light at sea thought to presage a storm.

C 65–4 When you can see [weather] lights on the salt water at night, it is a sign of a storm ahead. C 69–6 Weather lights in the riggings of a schooner is the sign of a storm coming. The lights start at the bottom of the riggings and move gradually up to the top where they disappear.

weatherish a *ADD* ~ Nfld. Of the weather, threatening (1925 *Dial Notes* v, 346).

[1918–19] GORDON 61 Sky clouding over, and looking weatherish. 1924 ENGLAND 65 In consonance with the 'wedderish' barometer, and with the men's opinion that 'de kind of a moil [mild spell] is over now,' a roaring blizzard that night screamed furiously out of the northern dark.

web* See WHIP SCULPIN.

wee-gee n, v A sudden movement in a different direction; to make such a movement.
1937 DEVINE 61 The gun is raised, suddenly [the gull] takes a 'wee-gee' and is off in another direction. P 184–67 Did you see him wee-gee around?

ween n Cp *EDD* ~ v¹ 'to whine, whimper' D. Wailing sound, whimper.
M 69–6 The bearers lowered the coffin slowly into the grave. There were pitiful, heart-rending wails, weens and various choked-up sounds. . .especially by the women relatives.

weep v *EDD* ~ v¹ 1 esp Gl So Co. To leak.
1924 ENGLAND 68 'She's too much by the starn, sir,' declared Skipper Nat. 'Ain't ballasted rate. An' weepin' [leaking] a bit, too.'

weft* See WITHE.

weigh-de-buckedy n also **buckety-board***, **wady buckedy (board)**, and, by folk etymology, **wady-buckety**, etc ['wɛɪtɪ, ˌbɒkətɪ] *EDD* wadybuckety, -buckedy (1867–), weigh-de-buckedy (1848–) Ir; DINNEEN bacaideach 'undulating,' bogadach 'moving, stirring,' cranndaidh bogadaigh ['moving wood, board'] 'see-saw.' Child's balancing board; game of see-saw.
1899 ENGLISH 16 So there she stood on [the large stone] playing wady-buckity, 'till she saw Lucy running towards her. [P 148–63 We're weighing de buckety.] 1964 *Can Journ Ling* x, 43 Play see-saw on the weigh-de-buckety. 1968 DILLON 159 Put that on a rock then, one on each end of it, and you'd go wady buckedy. We used to have a wady buckedy board fitted up. C 71–124 I've seen children use one longer of a fence as a wad-ey-buckety by using one of the intact longers as the fulcrum.

weight n Attrib **weight note**: receipt from fish merchant to fisherman recording amount of cod delivered; FISH TICKET.
1861 DE BOILIEU 44–5 The mode of barter is as follows. A man comes to the office of the house, and delivers a 'weight note' or a 'quantity note'—the former for fish, the latter for oil. The price of this is filled in to his credit, and away he takes it to the warehouseman (who on the coast is a very independent sort of individual), and exchanges it for food.

welt n *ADD* Nfld. A copious draught of spiritous liquor (1925 *Dial Notes* v, 346).
1936 SMITH 133 He then sent two men on shore to buy two bottles of 'Old Tom,' as he called it. . . He gave one bottle to the men in the hold. . . They instantly drew the cork and helped themselves. . .and they very soon had another 'welt,' taking a similar dose

of half a tumbler full. T 54/9–64 'Bring me that bottle,' he said, '[so] I gets a welt out of it too.'

wesleyan a Cp METHODIST. Comb **wesleyan bread**, ~ **kettle**, ~ **leg**.
P 92–68 Wesleyan bread [is] raisin bread, so-called because the raisins, like the Wesleyans, are few and far between. C 71–86 [They] called raisin bread 'Wesleyan bread.' It was always eaten at the Christmas season. C 69–20 A Wesleyan kettle is a little tin kettle which holds about five cups of water and like the old Wesleyan churchmen heats up quickly and cools off rather quickly. P 20–55 He can't dance, he has a Wesleyan leg (said of one who drags one foot in square-dancing instead of quickly touching the floor with it).

west a Cp *OED* west country b; *DC* west india Nfld (1818–).
Comb **west country**: attrib in historical designations of various connections between Newfoundland and the south-west counties of England.
[1679] 1895 PROWSE 197 That a Government may be settled to defend them and the Country especially against the French, who are very powerful there, and against some West Country Merchants whom they have long groaned under. [(1794) 1968 THOMAS 173 The Countys of Devonshire and Dorsetshire supply the greatest number of hands for the Newfoundland Fisherys yearly then all the rest put together. Poole and Newton Bushell are the Emporiums for the Two Countys. Lads from the Plow, Men from the Threshing Floor and persons of all sizes, Trades and ages. . .flock annually, in the Spring, to Newfoundland.] 1887 *Colonist Christmas No* 5 'That be hanged for a yarn,' says I; 'you West Country scoundrel.' 1895 PROWSE 297 We still hear a good deal in these records about the bye-boat men—the planters who brought out West Country servants. The late Hon Stephen Rendell has often told me that even when he came to the Colony in 1834, hundreds of sturdy Devonshire lads came out every spring to Rowell's, Boden's, Bulley's, Mudge's, Job's, and many others on the South Side and in Hoyle's Town. . .and to Torbay, Bay Bulls, Petty Harbour, &c. All these 'youngsters' were shipped for two summers and a winter. 1974 MANNION 18 From at least the beginning of the eighteenth century Westcountrymen, who fished for cod each summer on the Grand Banks of Newfoundland, called at Waterford on their outbound journey to purchase provisions and enlist labourers for the season.
west india, ~ **indian**: a grade or 'cull' of dried and salted cod-fish shipped to the West Indies; also attrib.
1818 CHAPPELL 130 *West-India fish*: the refuse of the whole. These last are invariably sent for sale, to feed the *Negroes* of the *Caribbee* Islands. 1819 ANSPACH 442 The common distinction, in Newfoundland, of the fish when completely dried, is not according to its size, but according to its degree of perfection, both in appearance and quality, into *merchantable, Madeira,* and *West Indian*. 1955 DOYLE (ed) 28 "Hard, Hard Times": Seven dollars for large and six-fifty for small; / Pick out your West Indie, you got nothing at all. 1955

Nfld Fisheries Board No 23 ~ Fish which are cracked, but not broken in pieces, may be excessively salted, may show slight slime, sourness, more than slightly skin-heated or sun-burnt, not excessively dun. 1957 *Nfld Qtly* Sep, p. 4 I'll cull the men from the boys just the same as I'll cull the No 1 from the West Indee cullage. T 203/5–65 There's another kind—West Indee, you'd call it. That fish was sunburnt an' different things wrong with it. 1974 *Evening Telegram* 23 May, p. 3 Of course, the very worst cull of fish, 'West Indie' was sent down to them from here.

west n also **wis*** *OED* ~ sb² obs (1569–1705); *EDD* esp W Do So. Inflammation of the eyelid; sty (P 37).
   C 68–10 If I got a wis on my eye, mother would say 'rub it with my gold ring; that will cure it.' C 69–17 A west on one's eye could be cured by making nine crosses on the eye with a gold wedding ring. C 70–15 Sties or wests on the eyes can be cured by rubbing with May snow. C 75–19 Wist. An infection of the eye, commonly called a sty.

wester a *OED* ~ a Sc; *EDD* 1 Sh I Ork D. Western, westward.
   1612 *Willoughby Papers* 1/62, 17 [Guy's Journal] . . .the Cape [on] the wester side of the bay of Placentia. 1920 WALDO 159 'South'ard,' 'north'ard,' 'east'-ard,' 'west'ard' are current maritime usage, and the adjective 'wester' is heard. T 54/62–64 That summer I fished ashore on th' easter side o' Hilliard's Harbour, where th' only fishin' room was on th' easter side o' the harbour. All the rest was on the wester side. T 141–65² If the wind is up you can go on the wester side. T 391/2–67 They used to live over the wester island summer time, fishin'. 1979 NEMEC 269 'Wester Head Shoals' [near St Shotts]. 1979 *Salt Water, Fresh Water* 44 If you get the wind off the shore, like nor'west wind, wester wind, and north-east wind, it seems to turn the cod away from the cod-trap, turn 'em away from the shoreline.

western a Cp *OED* ~ a 2 b for sense 1; *OED* 3 'having a position relatively west,' *DC* western ocean (Nfld: 1958) for sense 2; for comb in sense 4: *DC* ~ boat (Nfld: 1951–).
   1 Of or pertaining to the south-west counties of England, esp in reference to the West Country-Newfoundland migratory fishing enterprise: **western adventurer** [see ADVENTURER]; ~ **charter**: one of several royal documents confirming customary rights and privileges in Newfoundland; ~ **man¹**; ~ **merchant**.
   [1718] 1895 PROWSE 191 The Western adventurers proposed that the inhabitants of Newfoundland should transport themselves to Jamaica. [1677] ibid 208 Masters and Seamen may be directed to forbear any violence to Planters, upon pretence of said Western Charter and suffer them to inhabit and fish according to usage. 1934 LOUNSBURY 71 The charter of 1634 is known as 'the first Western Charter' to distinguish it from a similar patent issued by Charles II in 1661 and the amended patent of 1676. [1578] 1935 *Richard*

Hakluyt [Parkhurst's letter] 128 [The increase in vessels] commeth to passe chiefly by the imagination of the Westerne men, who thinke their neighbours have had greater gaines then in very deed they have. [1618] 1895 PROWSE 100 But their coming is to be believed of their friends being some of the western men who are still willing to help them. . .with provisions. [1674–77] 1976 HEAD 40 The planters have a right to the house they have built and the western men have no authority to disturb them. [1694] 1895 PROWSE 188 To the several wars within these twenty years which have much impoverished the Western Merchants, and reduced them to carry on a great part of that trade at Bottomry. [1793] 1954 INNIS 290 Hence the murmur of the western merchants against hucksters and adventurers, and hence the notion that the [fish] trade is ruined.
   2 Lying to the westward of England and Ireland, esp in the designation ~ **ocean**: the northwest Atlantic.
   1924 ENGLAND 129 Uncle Bill Teller died las' fall, / Young maiden, where ye bound to? / We jigged t'ree days an' niver got one, / Acrost de Western Ocean. 1958 HARRINGTON 3 The *Maranee* spent the next three weeks. . .beating about the Western Ocean (a sailor's term for the northwest Atlantic). 1973 *Evening Telegram* 19 Mar, p. 6 Most stories of long voyages by Newfoundland vessels involved the so-called Western Ocean, i.e., the North Atlantic between the British Isles and the Banks of Newfoundland. That was the main highway travelled by Newfoundland vessels and crews in the 19th century.
   3 To or from the west; used absolutely.
   1975 BUTLER 42 We moored her the best we could, put out sixty fathom of chain out on the big anchor right out to the western, and we put another ashore with the chain on it. 1977 *Nfld Qtly* Winter, pp. 18–19 The barometer was dropping and I figured before the day would be gone the wind would be around from the Western and we would have a fair wind.
   4 In combs. relating to the south coast of Newfoundland, esp the western stretch, and adjacent fishing grounds.
   western banks: extensive area of shoal water to the south and south-west of Newfoundland forming offshore fishing grounds; BANK(S).
   [1920] 1933 GREENLEAF (ed) 227 "The Spirit Song of George's Bank": I've been out in different vessels from Western Banks to Grand. 1960 FUDGE 2 . . .the first trip of fish to be brought from the Western Banks.
   western boat: schooner-rigged fishing vessel, 15–30 tons (13.6–27.2 m t); cp CAPE BOAT.
   1836 [WIX]² 43 He kindly took me, at nine, A.M., of the next day, in a large western boat, by the island of Merasheen, to the Isle of Valen. 1895 PROWSE 404 The first decked vessels for the seal fishery were about the size of ordinary Western boats, 40 to 50 feet keel, and 14 to 15 feet beam. 1923 CHAFE 16 The Small 'Western Boats' with their apple-cheek bows soon developed into the sharp stem with glancing bows that rose on the ice pans of its own accord, and helped to crush the floes with the weight of the heavier vessel. 1946 MACKAY (ed) 80 The larger vessels operate on the Grand Bank and are often away for days, or even weeks, at a stretch. The smaller vessels, known as *Western boats*,

do not go so far to sea and are rarely away from port more than a few days at a time. T 43/7–64 The western boat—they're not used on this coast—but up on the western shore they're used. It's a big boat, about thirty tons, with rudder out o' doors, you know, rudder hung to the stern. 1976 CASHIN 47 The small harbour of St John's was literally crowded with vessels, schooners, western boats and jacks.

western coast: south coast of Newfoundland, west of the Burin Peninsula, esp the western stretch.

[1927] 1960 BURKE (ed White) 43 "Terrible Disaster on the South West Coast": Attention now good people all, / And hark to what I say, / About this sad disaster / That happened on the Western Coast, / Around that rugged shore, / Where families were swept away / To see their friends no more. 1954 INNIS 403 On the 'western coast,' that is, west of St John's, or actually on the south coast, from Channel to Hermitage Bay, Garnish and Placentia, where the fishery could be carried on all the year round, a western boat. . .

western craft: see **western boat**.

1939 DULEY 14 'Woman, she's [baby] powerful light from stem to stern.' 'That she is, Benedict! And a fair treat to wash after them with a stern like a western craft.'

western (cod) fishery: offshore fishery, esp for cod, on the south coast from Cape Race westward.

[1793] 1976 HEAD 229 In the enquiry of [1793], a mention is made of the enlarging of a shallop into a boat for 'the Western Fishery.' 1797 PANL GN2/1/a The few large Boats in [Ferryland] are all on the Western fishery in Placentia and Saint Mary's Bays. [1810] 1971 ANSPACH 24 [The Bank fishery] is carried on exactly in the same manner as the Western Fishery. 1836 [WIX]² 127 There were so many boats and vessels belonging to Fortune Bay, which were bound to the western fishery at anchor here [Port-aux-Basques]. [1857] 1863 HIND ii, 223 We have but two cod fisheries that are of any importance to us—that carried on on our South coast from Cape Race westward, and known as the Western Fishery, and that carried on at the Labrador, between Blanc Sablon and Cape Harrison.

western man²: fisherman of the south and south-west coasts of Newfoundland; cp SOUTHERNER.

1927 DOYLE (ed) 71 "Newfoundland Fishermen": The next it delights me to mention / Are the Western men skilful and sure. C 67–4 Western men [are] the fishermen who came from Placentia Bay, Fortune Bay, etc, to fish in St Mary's Bay during late spring and summer.

western schooner: see **western boat** above.

1884 *Fisheries Exhibit* xiii, 51 The western fishing schooners fish along the coasts, and range from 20 to 30 tons burden.

western shore, wester ~ , westward ~ : see **western coast** above; also attrib.

1866 WILSON 400 But in the year 1841, our mission began to extend by the appointment of William Marshall as a visiting missionary to that extensive tract of country between Fortune Bay and Cape Ray, called the Western Shore. 1902 MURPHY 64 "A Dialogue": At a place people call Isle of Vallen, way down there on the Westward shore, / I suppose you have heard of that outrage, I mean the attack on the store. 1911 *Tribune Christmas No* [n.p.] One of the good old Irish customs of salutation was even in my day religiously observed on the Western Shore—I mean the salutation of 'God save all here,' and the answer, 'God save you, kindly.' 1919 *Journ of Assembly* 416 The Western Shore fishery commenced in January and was fairly successful. . .several of the local bankers from Burin and Fortune Bay district participated. 1933 GREENLEAF (ed) 282 "The *Southern Cross*": St Mary's Bay she never reached, as news came out next morn. / She must have been all night at sea, out in that dreadful storm. / No word came from the *Southern Cross* now twenty days or more; / To say she reached a harbor around the western shore. T 436–65 An' we used to take our fish in boat, sir, small boat. I had one o' them small western shore boats that we used—western shore skiffs we used to call 'em; no power, only sails. 1972 NEMEC 220 'Wester' shore men' i.e., vessels, from Fortune Bay and the South Coast, continued to fish the area adjacent to Trepassey each summer.

western av In a westerly direction.

T 23–64 There was two more vessels come out of Gibraltar when we did, out through the Straits of Gibraltar going to St John's; and they went away southern and we come over western and took a gale of wind. T 141/63–65² But anyhow the wind breezed up. Wind veered off western. P 245–81 If the wind come around western, the ice will slack off.

wet a *OED* ~ a 10 a, b (Nfld: c1580; 1851). Of cod-fish, split and salted but not dried; GREEN.

[1578] 1935 *Richard Hakluyt* [Parkhurst's Letter] 128 There are above 100 saile of Spaniards that come to take Cod (who make all wet, and do drie it when they come home). [1583] 1940 *Gilbert's Voyages & Enterprises* ii, 398 [Hayes' narrative] The Portugals, and French chiefly. . .who commonly beginne the fishing in Apriell, and have ended by July. That fish is large, alwayes wet, having no land neere to drie, and is called Corre fish. 1611 *Willoughby Papers* 1/3 79 [2 thousand] of Wett fish. [1755] DOUGLASS i, 293 3 quintals wet fish make 1 dry. [1770] 1792 CARTWRIGHT i, 26 . . .whither [the *Nimrod*] was bound with wet fish. [1806] 1951 DELDERFIELD 82 Most interesting is an account of the sale of 1,147 Portuguese quintals of Newfoundland fish in 1806. It was listed:-'661 Qtls large, 208 Qtls small, 278 Qtls dumb, wet and broken.' 1895 GRENFELL 52 Meanwhile, the schooner has gone farther north in search of a 'fare' of fish. If successful the fish will be salted, and brought home 'wet,' so that these vessels are called 'green-fish catchers.' 1966 PHILBROOK 59 The type of cure sold by fishermen for mechanical drying, [is] called salt-bulk or wet cure.

wet v *EDD* ~ v 16 for sense 1; for phr in sense 2: *OED* 9 b *wet one's line* (1653, 1898); *Fisheries of U S* 141 *wet one's salt*.

1 To rain (P 48–60).

1979 NEMEC 261 After stowing his personal gear

alongside the engine house (if it is not 'wettin'' and the sea is fairly calm) the man. . .proceeds.

2 Phr *wet one's line*: to fish for fresh-water trout.

1893 *Trade Review Christmas No* 13 Before settling down to the summer fishery in good earnest, the men generally took a day to go out to 'wet their lines.' P 41–68 The older boys made a *mawn*, i.e., a trout bag, from the leg of a discarded pair of pants and was off *to wet the lines* (trouting).

wet (all) one's salt: of a fishing vessel, to deplete the supply of salt aboard on a full catch of fish.

1868 *Royal Geog Soc* xxxviii, 263 The salt was all expended, or, as they term it, 'wet,' and vessels were now 'turning up' hourly; that is, coming from the north, loaded. [1929] BOWEN 150 To wet all her salt. A Grand Banks fishing schooner when she has filled up with fish, used all the salt that she brought out, and turns for home.

wet* See WITHE.

wexford n attrib *NID* ~ a. Pertaining to settlers originally from Co Wexford, Ireland.

1895 PROWSE 430 Mr Keough was a Wexford man, and after that he got every Wexford vote. 1936 DEVINE 82 The late Mr John McCarthy, an influential man of that day [1880], rallied the Wexford boys to his support, and with the help of Withycombe's committee on the South Side, and the sympathy and support of Father Scott (later Monsignor Scott) won the hard political battle. The Wexford vote was very strong in the West End at this time.

whabby n also **wabby, wamby, waubbe, whobby** *DC* ~ Nfld (1770–). See also WABBLE. Red-throated loon (*Gavia stellata*).

[1766] 1971 BANKS 138 [A bird] known here by the name of Whobby. . .is of the Loon Kind & an Excellent Diver but Very often amuses himself especially in the night by flying high in the air and makeing a very Loud & alarming noise at least to those who do not Know the Cause of it. [1771] 1792 CARTWRIGHT i, 143 On discovering a whabby swimming in a small pond, I sent for my rifle, and broke both its thighs at the first shot; Shuglawina then fired and killed it. 1819 ANSPACH 391 The most remarkable of the sea-birds which frequent these coasts are. . .the loon and whabby, both of the diving genus. 1876 HOWLEY 67 There is another Loon, or as it is called here 'Waubbe,' which Mr Reeks thinks is the same bird in its immature plumage. 1886 *Colonist Christmas No* 9 The merry shouts of the children playing on the green, have ceased, and naught disturbs the silence, save, perhaps the mournful cry of the wamby (snipe) from the woods close by. 1918 TOWNSEND 123–4 In one of the lakelets in a flat barren was a pair of red-throated loons. . . The old birds were dressed alike, and wore a handsome livery, pure white below, relieved only by a broad strip of terra-cotta red on the throat. The upper parts are slate blue; the back of the neck is slashed with wavy lines of white. *Whabby* is their name among the English-speaking people of the coast. 1951 PETERS & BURLEIGH 48–9

Red-throated Loon. . . Local names: Wabby, Whabby. . . Voice. A harsh, guttural note, sometimes resembling a goose-like honking. Also a variety of loud, weird cries. . . [It] can be observed most often in coastal water during migrations. 1959 MCATEE 2 ~ Red-throated Loon (spelled also wabby, waby, and wobby. Possibly derived from 'wobble,' a name for the extinct Great Auk, which alluded to the bird's awkwardness on land. . . Nfld., 'Labr.', Que.).

whale n *Cent* ~ bird n 3 Labrador.

Comb **whale bird**: the red or grey phalarope (*Phalaropus fulicarius; Lobipes lobatus*).

1967 *Bk of Nfld* iii, 283 Red Phalarope: Whale Bird (because it was often found in the same places as whales, with some of which it has a common food supply.)

whale factory: see FACTORY.

whaler n Cap with ear flaps, worn at the ice-fields.

1929 *Nat Geog* July, p. 91–5 Some wear sealskin caps and some elsinors or whalers, which are leather, wool-lined caps with ear flaps.

wheel n Comb **wheelsmaster**: helmsman on a sealing vessel; see MASTER.

T 401/2–67 I was wheelsmaster that spring—I had the wheel.

whelp¹ n Newly-born harp seal; WHITE-COAT. Also attrib.

1862 *Atlantic Mo* ix, 370 An' first I good to where my gaff was, by the mother-swile an' her whelp. . . I took the big swile, that was dead by its dead whelp, and hauled it away. 1925 *Dial Notes* v, 346 Whelp bag. A seal's afterbirth.

whelp² n See WATER WHELP. Attrib **whelp chain**: brass or copper chain worn around wrist to prevent inflamed condition caused by chafing and exposure to salt water (1971 NOSEWORTHY 261).

whelp v Cp *OED* ~ v 1 (1775 quot). Of a harp or hooded seal, to give birth.

1842 JUKES i, 302 Among [the seals] was the pelt of a female hood-seal and two young hoods, one of which had not long been whelped. 1852 ARCHIBALD 4 The seals frequenting the coast of Newfoundland are supposed to whelp their young in the months of January and February. 1873 CARROLL 11 The native young seal sheds its fur in the whelping bag, for after it is whelped a lump of white fur, about the size of a large goose egg. . .is seen floating about in the water. 1924 ENGLAND 27 Some old sealing captains say there are big 'patches' that whelp away up along the Labrador and Greenland coasts without ever coming south.

whelping vbl n *DC* ~ ice Nfld (1918–) for comb in sense 2.

1 The annual parturition in late February or early March of the migratory harp and hooded

seal herds on the ice-floes northeast of Newfoundland and in the Gulf of St Lawrence.

[c1900] 1978 *RLS* 8, p. 23 ~ The act of bringing forth
the young in seals. 1978 *Decks Awash* vii (1) [p. ii] ~
the act of birth in a seal.

2 Comb **whelping bag**: female seal's afterbirth
or placenta.

1873 CARROLL 11 However strange it may appear, it
is not the less true, that the native young seal sheds its
fur in the whelping bag. 1924 ENGLAND 97 Gulls and
other sea fowl relish these 'whelping bags' and spots of
seal are sometimes located by flocks of birds.

whelping ground: see **whelping ice**; GROUND.

1842 JUKES i, 299 . . .large patches of ice dirty and
discoloured, in spots where the seals had brought forth
their young, which are called by the men 'whelping-
grounds.' 1873 *Maritime Mo* i, 257 [The seal hunters']
general practice is to push northward till they fall in
with the 'whelping grounds' of the sea, doubling and
beating about in search of them, according to circumstances.

whelping ice: ice-fields on which seals give
birth.

1852 ARCHIBALD 4 This ice, or the whelping ice as it
is termed, from the currents, and prevailing northerly
and north-east winds, trends towards the east and
north-east coast of Newfoundland, and is always to be
found on some part of the coast after the middle of
March, before which time the young seals are too
young to be profitable. 1883 HATTON & HARVEY 296
At that time of year the 'whelping ice' had passed
many weeks, and the young seals having taken to the
water, only a few stragglers came within range. 1944
LAWTON & DEVINE 14–15 Some springs the winds
brought the whelping ice well into Bonavista Bay and
close to the land. Whenever this happened, women
and boys as well as men went on the ice to haul seals.
1972 BROWN 31 But there it was! True whelping ice!
Thousands, tens of thousands of mother harps, moving
among their whitecoats.

whelping pan: see **whelping ice**; PAN n.

1916 GRENFELL 168 There was nothin' but the open
water left—not a whelpin'-pan to hold e'er an old harp
to have her young on. 1977 BURSEY 21 But many of
them would also go out to the whelping pans and bring
home as many seals as they could find or carry.

whelping patch: concentration of harp or hood
seals on the ice-floes for purposes of giving birth;
PATCH (1972 SANGER 241).

whey n Comb **whey belly**: epithet for person
originally from Waterford; member of Newfoundland-Irish faction. Cp YELLOW-BELLY.

1863 PEDLEY 294 Two great Irish factions had established themselves [c1815] in St John's. . . The
watchword. . .of the men of Waterford, 'Whey Belly.'
1895 PROWSE 402 The Waterford 'Whey bellies.'

whiffen, whiffet See BOUGH WHIFFEN.

whig n [= an adherent to the British political
party opposed to the Tory]. Phr *there are whigs*

in that: there is something suspicious going on
(P 54–67).

1937 DEVINE 57 'There's *wigs* in that story.' Something suspected though not yet apparent.

whinker v, n Cp *OED* whicker, whinny. To
neigh.

T 14/7–64 She went on, she never faltered until she
got to the wood, and she stopped and just turned
around and started to whinker. 1966 PADDOCK 103
Winker—The noise a horse makes.

whip n

Cpd, comb **whipline**: in hoisting seal 'pelts'
aboard a vessel, rope stay to hold the cable of
the whip, or hoisting contrivance, clear of the
hull.

1924 ENGLAND 87 Now, 'aul out y'r whipline! Stand
by with that whipline, you—over with it. 1925 *Dial
Notes* v, 346 ~ Rope used in loading sculps, to draw
out the wire and hold sculps from dragging on the
ship's side.

whip sculpin; also **web*** ~ , **whippy*** ~ , **wip***,
etc ['wɪp ˌskʌlpɪn, 'wɛb 'skʌlpɪn]; see SCULPIN
for var pronunciations. Atlantic sea raven, a fish
with large teeth, ragged dorsal spines and skin
covered with prickles (*Hemitripterus americanus*).

P 56–63 Of a person with an enormous paunch: 'He's
got a gut like a whipped sculpin.' (A sculpin tends to
become larger when beaten with a stick.) P 148–64
Wips: type of fish; one foot long; you blow them up,
put rocks in their mouths; they have whips on their
tails. 1966 LEIM & SCOTT 350–1 Atlantic sea raven. . .
Common names: whip sculpin, gurnet, puff-belly,
scratch-belly. . . When taken from the water the belly
usually becomes inflated. M 69–1 We would spend
hours there catching conners, flatfish, whippy sculp-
tons, and other fish.

whirlygig n *OED* whirligig sb 2 (a) 'instrument
of torture' (1477–1623). Revolving cage in which
offenders are placed for punishment.

1757 PANL GN/3B 1 Oct . . .cause the Constable to
apprehend the said Eleanor Moody, & to put her in
Prison 'till 4 o'clock in the afternoon, at which time to
cause her to be put in the Whirlygig, where she is to
remain One Hour, & to be properly punished, & to be
sent out of this Island the first Opportunity, being a
Nuisance to the Publick.

whirra n ['wɪrə]. Cp *EDD* ~ sb So; worra So D
Co 'part of the centre of a spinning wheel.' Small
wheel on spindle of a spinning-wheel.

1979 POCIUS 15 One end of the spindle tapers down
into a point and a grooved wheel is mounted on the
other end of the rod. . . A cord fits into this groove,
and extends around the circumference of the larger
wheel. This small wheel on the end of the spindle is
known in Port de Grave as a 'whirrer.' 1979 *'Twas a
way of life* 56 To twist the two threads together, you
have to cross the string that runs from the wheel to the
whirrer making an X near the whirrer.

whirry-hole* n   Cp *OED* whirly: ~ pool
(1727–); *EDD* whirly 6: ~ pool. Circle in the
water like a small whirlpool (P 148–66).

whisker[1] n   A full beard. Also attrib.
   1895 PROWSE 423 . . .by the advice of his friends he
wore a pair of false whiskers when he went to receive
his commission. 1924 ENGLAND 221 A gray-whisker
man, he was; a rale whisker man wid narr bit o' ha'r on
his 'eed. [1904] 1927 DOYLE (ed) 5 "Wedding in
Renews": The men dressed grand, to beat the band, /
With whiskers to their shoes. 1969 *Christmas Mumming in Nfld* 130 I wore a beard during the period of
field research, which effectively frightened many small
youngsters. Parents would explain 'They think you're a
mummer.' I was also used by many of the same parents
to threaten children: 'We'll let the old whisker man get
you.'

whisker[2] See OLD MAN'S BEARD.

whist excl also **wish(t)** *OED* ~ int[1] now dial;
EDD 1. Keep silence; hush (1937 DEVINE 55).
   1968 DILLON 160 Oh girl whisht! I had it some
bad. . . For the Lord's sake, whisht about it. C 71–99 If
what someone is saying is not agreeable to the listener,
the listener may 'whisht' the speaker and speak himself. C 71–107 Wish, child, hold your tongue!

whistle n   *OED* ~ sb 4 ~ pipe 'whistle for
decoying birds' obs (1570, 1578) for comb in
sense 2.
   1 Fog-horn.
   1979 NEMEC 235 St Shotts' fishermen do not rely on
any mechanical navigation aids except the compass and
fog horns ('whistles').
   2 Comb **whistle diver**: American common
goldeneye (*Bucephala clangula americana*) (1959
MCATEE 14).
   1907 TOWNSEND 329 ~ Common summer resident in
central and southern parts.
   whistle-pipe: short length of alder or 'dogwood' made to produce a whistling sound; also
attrib.
   [c1945] TOBIN 48–9 "Whistle-pipes": Alders are
coming in all day, / . . .It's whistle-pipes from morn to
night. . . / And fathers, too, are commandeered /
Sometimes unto the service / Of peeling bark and carv-
ing wood. M 68–23 Another way which we used to
entertain ourselves was making whistle pipes. . . The
best trees for making whistle pipes were dogwood and
witherod. The piece for the whistle was cut from a
branch and was about 3 in. long and ¾ in. in diameter.
By wetting it and knocking it gently the rind would
come off in a ring. The center of the piece of branch
was cut away for air circulation and the rind replaced.
C 69–28 Whistle-pipe stuff is brush or shrubs. 1973
SMALLWOOD 66 I was taken about the settlement by
the local boys, and in a small boat about the [Renews]
harbour, jigging sculpins and tom-cods, and I was
shown how to make a whistle-pipe from a piece of
alder.

whistling ppl
   Comb **whistling curlew**: Hudsonian whimbrel
(*Numenius phaeopus hudsonicus*).
   [1786] 1792 CARTWRIGHT iii, 228 The birds of that
country, I presume, are common to most of those
which border upon the arctic circle, they are the white-
tail eagle, falcons, hawks, and owls of various kinds;
raven, white-grouse, ptarmigan, sprucegame, whis-
tling-curlew, grey-plover, various kinds of sandpipers,
and other waders; geese.
   whistling diver: American black scoter
(*Oidemia nigra americana*) (1959 MCATEE 18).

white a   For sense 3: *DC* ~ bird (1760–); *OED*
a: ~ game (1678); *OED* 11 ~ partridge obs
(1674–1747), *DC* (1684–); *NID* ~ tailed eagle 1;
for sense 4: *NID* ~ moss for 1765 quot; for
combs. in sense 5: *OED* ~ bear (Nfld: 1613),
DC 1 (1600–); cp *OED* ~ boy 3 b 'member of
secret agrarian assoc. formed in [Ireland]'
(1762–); *OED* ~-coat 2 (Nfld: 1792–), *DC*
(1778–); *EDD* 1 (61) ~ mouth Gl W So D.
   1 Of a caribou, lighter than the customary
brown and darker shades.
   [(1794)] 1968 THOMAS 129 [The deer] are very
numerous, go in Herds, are of a cream colour.] 1905
PROWSE 38 In Newfoundland 'white' deer are said to
come from the northern parts of the Island, but this is,
I am sure, an error, for they are equally numerous
amongst the southern herds. 1911 ibid 43 There is
another type of adult male known as the 'white' stag,
which is more or less a dirty white all over.
   2 Of the sea, covered with white breakers;
shoal water.
   T 70/1–64[1] An' 'twas heave her around. She spun
around just like the top, an' bet off o' the land. She was
right in the white sea. T 185–65 An' when they are
goin' in 'gain the wharf she blew away over on what
they call white ground, an' got aground.
   3 In names of birds with white colouring: **white
bawk, ~ bird, ~ cap, ~ game, ~ hawk, ~ jay, ~
minister** [see MINISTER GULL], **~ partridge,
~-tail eagle, ~-throated loo, ~-winged diver, ~
winter gull**.
   1959 MCATEE 4 White bauk [*Puffinus gravis*].
Greater Shearwater (Nfld). Ibid 67 White bird
[*Plectrophenax nivalis*]. [Eastern] snow bunting (Labr).
Ibid 64 White-cap [*Zonotrichia leucophrys*]. White-
crowned Sparrow (Nfld, 'Labr,' Que). [1778] 1792
CARTWRIGHT ii, 284 All the sealers came here, and
brought with them seventeen white game (grouse and
ptarmigans). 1876 HOWLEY 54 *Greenland Falcon*. . .a
winter migrant; called in Newfoundland the 'White
Hawk.' 1959 MCATEE 22 White hawk. Gyrfalcon
[*Falco rusticolus obsoletus*]. Ibid 57 White jay [*Lanius
excubitor borealis*]. Northern Shrike. (It is largely
bluish-grey, paler below; but it is no jay. Nfld., 'Labr.')
1832 MCGREGOR i, 204 Ptarmigan, or white partridges,
abound on them; and the most plentiful cod-fishing
surrounds their shores. 1861 DE BOILIEU 75 Before
heavy frost sets in, we are busily engaged in
trapping—chiefly for their furs—animals and birds of

all kinds, such as. . .white and spruce partridges, and the ptarmigan. [1786] 1792 CARTWRIGHT iii, 228 The birds of that country. . .are the white-tail eagle, falcons, hawks, and owls. 1959 MCATEE 2 White-throated loo (*Gavia immer immer*). Common Loon (Nfld). 1893 HOWLEY *MS Reminiscences* 53 They were ducks I never remember seeing before but the lads call them white-winged divers. They have a white feather in each wing, a rusty brown back and a white ring around the base of the bill, the latter is very small and flat towards the tip. Altogether a pretty little duck. 1977 RUSSELL 87 He eat two turrs and a white winged diver. 1959 MCATEE 36 White winter gull (*Larus hyperboreus hyperboreus*). Glaucous Gull ('Labr').

4 In names of plants, shrubs and trees with white or whitish flowers, wood of light colour, etc: **white daisy,** ~ **flower,** ~ **lily,** ~ **maple,** ~ **moss,** ~ **musk,** ~ **snow-drops,** ~ **spruce** [see SPRUCE], ~ **top,** ~ **wood.**

1956 ROULEAU 29 White Daisy: *Anaphalis margaritacea*. Ibid 40 White-flower: *Loiseleuria procumbens*. Ibid 40 White Lily: [*Platanthera*] *dilatata*. Ibid 34 White Maple: *Acer spicatum*. 1765 ROGERS 6 The soil of this island, as hath been hinted, is very barren (excepting some glades upon the banks of rivers) in the inland parts of it, rising into hills, or sinking into bogs and swamps, and where not covered with water, affords nothing but shrubs, spruce, and white moss [*Leucobryum glaucum*]. [1779] 1792 CARTWRIGHT ii, 473 It is a mistaken notion that [caribou] will not eat grass, or scarcely any thing but white moss [*Usnea barbata*]. 1971 NOSEWORTHY 262 White moss: DEAD MOSS. 1978 ROULEAU 91 White musk: *Anaphalis margaritacea*. 1956 ibid 40 White Snow-drops: *Viola pallens*. 1956 ibid 40 White Top: *Anaphalis margaritacea*. 1865 CAMPBELL 137 The food [of the beaver] is 'white wood' [mountain maple: *Acer spicatum*] and birch, about a couple of inches thick. 1956 ROULEAU 40 White-wood: *Viburnum trilobum*. White-wood berry: *V. edule*.

5 Comb **white bear:** polar bear, an infrequent visitor to Newfoundland (*Thalarctos maritimus*); WATER BEAR.

[1587] 1958 HAKLUYT 333 In the morning we saw three or foure white beares, but durst not go on shore to them for lacke of a good boat. [1779] 1792 CARTWRIGHT ii, 410 Not a single track of a white-bear has been seen for a long time past, which makes me think that those creatures keep out upon the outer edge of the ice during the winter; for, there they may meet with seals. When they come on shore, I presume it is chiefly on the outer islands; yet I have sometimes known them go far into the country. 1846 TOCQUE 197–8 The white or polar bear (*Ursus Maritimus*, or *Arcticus*) at this season [March] is sometimes seen on the coast, regardless of the ocean storm and the intense cold. This animal roams among the rifted ice in search of food. In 1841 one of these animals was killed near St John's. 1909 BROWNE 280 The islands are said to have been favorite haunts of the White Bear in former years. 1977 *Them Days* ii (3), pp. 5–6 Then all to once I seen a white bear crossing the harbour down below. They was scravellin' to get their guns. I runned up for the old man's gun and took off after them.

white boy: boisterous, aggressive Irish fishery 'servant.'

[1767] 1976 HEAD 169 [He] reported 490 Protestants and 425 Roman Catholics in 1764, but the number of Irish appears to have swelled in the late 1760s as this missionary reported in 1767 and 1768 that the area was 'so incorporated with Numbers of White Boys that have lately come from Ireland that the Honest & Industrious can hardly live.'

white-coat: young 'harp seal,' with white fur soon shed, hunted for its blubber; also attrib.

[1776] 1792 CARTWRIGHT ii, 159 Jack and I went round our traps; his dog caught a white-coat, but he let it go again. 1792 ibid *Gloss* i, xvi ~ A young seal, before it has cast its first coat, which is white and furry. 1846 TOCQUE 189 I have seen these beautiful 'white coats,' laying six and eight on a pan of ice. 1897 HARVEY 118 On the floating fields of Arctic ice the seals bring forth their young about the end of February. In four or five weeks these 'white coats,' as the young are called, are in the best condition for being taken and their fat then yields the finest oil. 1955 DOYLE (ed) 52 "Sealers' Song": Our boys for fat, would gaff and bat, / And make the whitecoats rattle. T 43/4–64 The young one is the white coat; when 'tis pupped 'tis called a pup. Then after she gets nursed a little bit she begins to perk up an' she gets a beautiful coat on it. ['Tis a] beautiful lookin' thing to look at. 1937 DEVINE 69 Expect a heavy fall of snow when seals whelp (about March). This snow is said to be a bed and nourishment for the whitecoats, and the more snow the more seals. P 148–75 White-coat patch. A light snowfall just after the birth of the white-coats. The old fishermen say the baby seals feed on this. If no snow fell, they would perish. 1978 *Evening Telegram* 10 Mar, p. 1 By the time the vessels reach the whitecoats the seals may have matured to beaters, seals 18 days of age and older and capable of taking to the water. 1981 ibid 10 Mar, p. 2 Whitecoats are at their prime about 10 days old when they weigh up to 32 kilograms.

white-end: see WHITING.

white fish: see WHITE FISH.

white jacket: see **white-coat** above.

1924 ENGLAND 37 Ye don't need to hit de whitejackets very hard. Deir skulls is ondly a kind of cristle.

white mouth: disease in which the mouth and lips have white flecks; thrush.

M 69–12 If a person didn't contract the white mouth when a child, he would get it nine days before he died. 1972 MURRAY 86 Sometimes children were born with what was called 'white mouth.' The midwife's cure for this was to put molasses on the child's tongue.

white-nose: term applied to one indentured in the West Country migratory fishery after his first winter in Newfoundland.

1866 WILSON 207 When [the youngsters] have spent one summer and one winter, they receive the title of *white nose*. 1937 DEVINE 57 A youngster who has graduated in the school of winter experience thus: Himself not knowing how severely frost could freeze and whiten his nose, his companions kept him in ignorance till he suffered the ordeal 'unknowest.' They enjoyed the joke at his expense, and surprised him by applying snow to the part. Then, with a clap on the back, they told him he was a *youngster* no longer but a whitenose.

white oil: first oil yielded by seal blubber in the process of repeated rendering.

1819 ANSPACH 425 [Seal oil which is rendered by the fat] is called virgin, or white oil, [and] is considered as the best.

white owl: snowy owl (*Nyctea scandiaca*).

1870 *Can Naturalist* v, 45 The 'white owl'. . .is a bold, rapacious bird, and not easily driven from its slaughtered prey.

white water: rain-water collected from hollows in rocks and used for washing and drinking in areas in which the alternative is bog-water (P 233–79).

1863 MORETON 17 Water [which drains from swamps] at times becomes scarce, or even altogether fails. People then gather carefully all the water which can be found in the hollows of rocks after rain, which is named 'white water.'

white-wing(ed) diver: eastern white-winged scoter (*Melanitta deglandi deglandi*).

1870 *Can Naturalist* v, 302 Common, and. . .individuals may be seen throughout the summer. . . [the] 'Whitewinged diver.'

white-fish n

1 Variety of dolphin found in Labrador waters (*Lagenorhynchus* spp).

1792 CARTWRIGHT *Gloss* i, xvi ~ A fish of the Porpoise kind. 1814 KOHLMEISTER & KMOCH 17 Our people had caught a large white-fish, and pressed us much to be their guests.

2 Smelt (*Osmerus mordax*).

1873 CARROLL 18 White fish is considered the principal food of the seal. It is the first fish that swarms along the northern coast of Newfoundland in the spring of the year, and the last that leaves the northern coast in the fall. 1924 ENGLAND 275 'Them swiles is feedin' heavy, too,' reported Arthur Roberts. 'Full o' swile bait. One I cut open had buckets o' whitefish in 'er.' 1969 *Christmas Mumming in Nfld* 65 People avidly wait for 'a feed of mushels' (mussels) or 'whitefish' (smelt) in the spring. 1979 TIZZARD 326 Whitefish averaged between six to eight inches long. They came to the brooks in Dildo Run the first or second high tide in May.

3 Caplin after spawning.

1971 *RLS* 3, p. 2 The spent (post spawning) capelin and also the immature capelin which stay in the Bay during the winter are sometimes washed on shore after being killed by cold water temperatures. These caplin may also be found quite frequently in the stomachs of turrs, puffins or seals. In any case these capelin are referred to as whitefish.

whiting n   also **whitin'**, and a re-interpretation, **white-end** ['wɔitʔn, 'wɛitn̩, 'wɛitend, 'wʌitend] *OED* ~ sb 4 (Nfld: 1792), *DC* (Nfld: 1792–). A standing tree with the bark removed, for use on the 'fish flake,' leaving the peeled tree white; a tree killed as a result of the removal of the bark;

any dead tree suitable for fire-wood; rampike. Cp CRUNNICK.

[1774] 1792 CARTWRIGHT ii, 29 Having filled up the boat with whitings, pryor-poles and killick-rods, at high water we sailed home. 1792 ibid *Gloss* i, xvi ~s. Trees which have been barked, and left standing. 1836 [WIX]² 50 Even the sight of a 'whiting' in the woods, that is, of a tree stripped of its bark for the uses of the fishery. . .which tells of the place's having been visited, though in the preceding summer, or a year or two before, by the foot of man. . . [c1900] 1968 *RLS* 8, p. 26 Witing, white end: a tree from which the rind has been stripped such as fir or spruce. 1903 *Nfld Qtly* Dec, p. 56 He went to the wood-pile and selected a nice handy looking whiting and cut it up into junks about two feet long, just sufficient to lay nicely across the dog-irons. 1937 DEVINE 57 ~s. Standing fir or spruce trees stripped of the lower part of their rind for use in covering dry fish. When later cut down for firewood or lumber, they have become quite dry throughout. Also *white ends*. P 245–61 White-end. A spruce tree, with limbs and bark removed, then dried and cut for fuel. T 12–64 'Dry as a whiten.' A whiten is the rampike or very dry stick used for making splits. T 141/67–65² An' then there was rindin'—you had to go up an' rind your white-ends, rind your rind, sir. That was only thing then to cover fish with. C 68–4 They would find some whitings (trees that were cut and placed in piles). M 69–17 The rinds were taken from standing trees, and as a result that part of the tree from which the bark was removed became dry and was then called white ends, and was cut and used as kindling.

whittle n   *EDD* ~ sb² Do D So Co. Heavy flannel or quilted material wrapped around a baby.

T 911–71 We had our children bound up till dey git two or t'ree months old, in whittles dey used to call it you see. 1972 MURRAY 89 Then, winter and summer, children were bound up in 'whittles,' night and day, for two or three months at least, though after this period they were given more freedom of movement during the day. Putting a child in 'whittles' or 'whetals' was also termed 'dressing them up for the night.'

whittled p ppl *OED* whittle v² 3: whittled (Nfld: 1792). Of wood, barked or chipped.

1792 CARTWRIGHT *Gloss* i, xvi Whittled-sticks. Sticks from which beavers have eaten the bark.

whizgigging vbl n also **wisgiggin***, **willigiggin** ['wɪzgɪgn̩]. Cp *OED* whizgig [sb] 'object that whizzes around' (1848–), fizgig (1529–); *EDD* whiz-a-gig sb, v 'to lark about.' Boisterous, silly laughing; engaging in foolish actions; cp GALE v.

1896 *J A Folklore* ix, 36 Willigiggin: half between a whisper and a giggle. 1937 DEVINE 55 Whisgigging—whispering and giggling in such a way as to annoy, especially old people. P 15–64 Stop that whizzgigging, you'll be crying the once. P 219–72 If children are laughing and giggling, parents would say they were 'whizgeeing for a storm.'

who int pro Cp SMYTH 732 Who says amen?;

Kilkenny Lexicon who shall 'the last hand in a rubber.' In phr, comb *who says*: uttered signal to a crew to haul together.

C 65–11 When men get together for various tasks such as pulling up a boat, someone usually sings or shouts so that everyone will pull in harmony. This is awaited for before the work starts and in many cases the men tend to act shy, hesitating and waiting for the other fellow. It is at this moment someone poses the question 'Now then men, who says?' Thus this becomes the 'starter' for the task.

who-shall, ~ shallyroo*: (a) boisterous good fun (P 195–65); (b) an argument; (c) in playing cards, the deciding game.

T 12–64 He raised a who-shall. P 108–71 We're two games apiece, so we'll have to play the who-shall. P 196–74 The who shallyroo—in auction, the deciding game.

whobby See WHABBY.

whooper See STUN a: ~ WHOOPER.

whore's egg See OSE EGG.

whort See HURT.

wib* See WHIP SCULPIN.

wicker n *EDD* ~ sb⁴ Gl. Ear; ear-flap on a boy's cap; WIG.

C 71–100 Very small children (aged 2–6) refer to their ears as 'wickers.' Q 73–4 ~ ear-covering on caps.

widdy See WITHY.

widow n *EDD* ~ sb 1 (3) ~ gentleman; JOYCE 350; *EDD* 1 (10) ~ woman, JOYCE 350.

Comb **widow man**: widower ([c1894] PANL P4/14, p. 2; P 148–64).

widow woman: widow (P 148–60).

1846 TOCQUE 113 He crouched in a little thicket of bushes, opposite the door of a tilt inhabited by a poor widow woman. 1900 *Tribune Christmas No* 10 The house belonged to Mrs Anne Fitzpatrick, a widow woman, who kept a very respectable place of entertainment.

wif(t)* See WITHE.

wig n *EDD* ~ sb². Ear; WICKER (P 154–78).

wild a *OED* ~ a 6 (esp 1813 quot) for sense 2.

1 Of the coast and waters adjacent to a coastal 'settlement,' without good anchorage; with an exposed harbour.

[1813] 1972 MURRAY 32 I wish it were not such a 'wild' place for craft to ride in. [1845] ibid 40 The road from this place to Catalina has been opened but that to Bonavista has not yet been begun, and both would be most useful to the people; for this cove being, as it is called 'wild' those two harbours of Bonavista and Catalina are the emporia whence they principally derive

their supplies. 1972 ibid 28 It is a 'wild' place in the sense that it has no proper harbour, being quite as open to the Atlantic as Cape Bonavista itself.

2 Of game-birds and animals, watchful, wary; YARY.

1868 HOWLEY *MS Reminiscences* 50 Here we saw a great number of wild geese in the lagoon inside the beach but it was impossible to get within shooting distance of them, these birds are so wild and extremely yarry. 1870 *Can Naturalist* v, 295 Sometimes [twillicks] are very tame and take little notice of men or dogs; at other times they are so wild that I know no bird more difficult to approach. 1874 WHITE *MS Journal* 1 May Seals on ice, all Boats out Seals very wild took 212 young. P 245–77 The birds [partridge] were wild today.

3 In names of plants, shrubs, etc: **wild calceolaria, ~ carrot, ~ cranberry, ~ cucumber, ~ daisy, ~ hyacinth, ~ ivy, ~ parsnip, ~ pear, ~ poppy, ~ thimble, ~ tobacco.**

1898 *J A Folklore* xi, 280 Wild Calceolaria: *Cypripedium acaule*. 1956 ROULEAU 40 Wild Carrot: *Heracleum maximum*. Ibid 40 Wild Cranberry: *Ribes glandulosum*. Ibid 40 Wild cucumber: *Streptopus amplexifolius; S. roseus*. Ibid 40 Wild Daisy: *Erigeron hyssopifolius*. Ibid 32 Wild Hyacinth: *Platanthera dilatata*. 1898 *J A Folklore* xi, 275 Wild Ivy: *Convolvulus sepium*. 1839 TUCKER 104 A species of long coarse grass, the wild parsnip, and a variety of other vegetables are found in the deep valleys, where they are sheltered from the northern blasts, and nourished by the sun's rays. 1956 ROULEAU 40 Wild Parsnip: *Angelica atropurpurea, Heracleum maximum*. [1794] 1968 THOMAS 142 Here are Wild Pears, Cherrys and Plumbs. 1956 ROULEAU 40 Wild Pear: *Amelanchier* spp. 1898 *J A Folklore* xi, 227 Wild Poppy: *Sedum roseum*. Ibid 273 Wild Thimbles: *Campanula rotundifolia*. 1843 *Journ of Assembly* 463 I met with rich alluvial flats along the side of brooks, covered with a weed which is commonly called Wild Tobacco, from three to six feet high. 1956 ROULEAU 39 Wild Tobacco: *Epilobium angustifolium; Verbascum thapsus*.

4 Comb **wild cat**: pine marten (*Martes americana*); CAT².

[1794] 1968 THOMAS 73 'Put yourself in a posture of defence! It is a wild Catt'. . . The heads of these Catts are exactly like the tame ones, their bodys are larger. They were of a dark brown colour, the tips of the ears red. The body and tail the shape and motion of a Greyhound.

wild indian: member of a tribe of indians formerly inhabiting Newfoundland ?–1829 A.D.; BEOTHUK, RED INDIAN.

[1785] 1792 CARTWRIGHT iii, 55 It is a very extraordinary thing (yet a certain fact) that the Red, or Wild Indians, of Newfoundland should every year visit [Funk Island]. [1827] 1913 *Christmas Chimes* 16 This was the retreat of the Boeothuks, or red, or wild Indians, until the last [four] or five years.

wild pigeon: southern black guillemot (*Cepphus grylle atlantis*); PIGEON (1959 MCATEE 40).

willem* n   also **wellem*** ['wɪləm]. Cp *OED*
walm sb¹ obs: welm 1 'surging of waves,' *EDD*
walm sb 1 obs. Turbulent water at stern of a vessel (P 154–78).

P 155–64 I saw the wilm of her propeller.

willow n
  Comb **willow bird**: Newfoundland pine gros-
beak (*Pinicola enucleator eschatosus*) (1959
MCATEE 62).
  willow perfume: bog candle, a type of orchid
(*Platanthera dilatata*) (1956 ROULEAU 40).

wincy* n   ['wɪnsɪ, 'wɪnsɪɫ, 'wɪntʃɪ]. In phr *go
one's wincy*: (a) to proceed as fast as possible;
(b) to behave in a loose manner; (c) in card
game, to play one's best card to win (C 71–106).

T 222–66 Sometimes a girl steps aside from conventional habits and it's said of her that 'she's going her
wincy.' Sometimes as a result there is a child born out
of wedlock. P 141–73 Go your wincy—hurry!

wind n   *DC* ~ -charger (1946–) for comb in
sense 2.
  1 In fishermen's weather proverbs.
1895 *Christmas Review* 12 When the wind is inshore,
don't go out any more. ([Excuse used by] A lazy fellow.) 1937 DEVINE 66 If the wind's in the east on Candlemas Day / There it will stick till the first of May.
Ibid 67 When rain comes before the wind, / Halliards,
sheets and reef-points mind. Ibid 67 When the wind
veers against the sun, / Trust it not, for back 'twill run.
  2 Comb **wind-bag**: small sail rigged between
the masts of a two-masted schooner.
1932 BARBOUR 10 It was now only too plain that we
ought to brail our gaff topsail, and we proceeded to do
so without delay, and also to lower down our 'wind-
bag.' P 209–73 ~ Small sail hoisted between two poles
of a two poler.
  wind-charger: generator driven by wind power.
1941 SMALLWOOD 52 [advertisement] Windchar-
gers. 1975 RUSSELL 12 I was up to their house, listening to Grampa's new radio, the old one used dry batteries. Now he's got one with a wet battery and his own
wind-charger. 1976 GUY 136 Then along came the
windcharger. These five-foot wooden propellers
attached to small twelve-volt generators were mounted
where they would catch the most wind. Some people
placed them on the house top, others on the roof of a
nearby shed and others on a twenty-five foot wooden
tower in the yard. The windcharger spun around in the
breeze and pumped two twelve-volt car batteries in the
kitchen full of juice.
  wind gall: same as **wind hound**.
P 154–78 He went out fishing, saw the wind galls to
the east'ard and come on home again.
  wind hound: bright gleam in vicinity of the sun
thought to presage a storm (C 70–26); SUN
HOUND.
  wind-jack: length of wood with movable blade
at one end which rotates when carried as a child's

toy and indicates velocity of wind when fastened
to a post.
P 140–70 A wind-jack is the name of a small piece of
wood, cut in the shape of a fan. These are usually three
to six inches in length and one-half to one and a half
inches in width. When held up into the wind they
rotate like a propeller. A nail is usually driven through
the center to act as an axle. Very common among small
boys and sometimes adults place larger ones in conspicuous places such as, on the top of the clothesline pole,
on the gate post, on the eave of the stable. 1976 GUY
43 The furnace was spouting steam and water like a
beached whale and the pump had gone berserk cutting
in and out at five-second intervals with the pressure
gauge spinning around like a windjack.
  wind light: gleam of light moving over surface
of ocean; WEATHER LIGHT (C 67–10).
  wind lop: rough surface of the sea caused by a
stiff wind and marked by a quick succession of
short breaking waves; LOP², TUMBLE.
[1870] 1973 KELLY 18 Even in harbour, what the sailors call 'the wind lop' was so great, and the squalls at
times so heavy, that the *Star* dragged the single anchor
by which she was riding, and we were obliged to let go
the large anchor in addition. [1954] 1972 RUSSELL 37 It
wasn't too bad goin' home. Just a dirty wind lop and a
drop of spr'y back in the stern. T 50/3–64 [It's] a good
harbour, but believe me it can blow—wind lop, that's
all, no sea. 1966 FARIS 49 Wind lop (rough surface due
to wind action) is simply considered annoying, but if
the sea becomes 'heavy' (rolling and breaking. . .) it
may be quite difficult to get in from the grounds.
T 396–67 You'll get northerly wind right in the harbour. It makes a big lop, what we call a wind lop.

windly a   also **wingly*** *EDD* ~ a Gl Do. Of a
plant, tall, stalky, spindly.
P 207–67 The stem of the flower was windly.
P 127–76 When a plant has a long stalk, long leaf stems,
and sparsely leafed it is referred to as being wingly.

window n   Cp *OED* ~ sb 5 ~ leaves
(1466–1758); *EDD* sb¹ 1 (15) ~ tacking.
  Comb **window-leaf**: one of the two wide sections of a door opening off the seaward side of a
fishing stage.
[1778] 1792 CARTWRIGHT ii, 369–70 Fearing a priva-
teer's crew might be in her, I armed all my people with
guns, sticks or stones, and placed them in ambush
behind one of the window-leaves of the stage. [1779]
ibid ii, 467 The shoremen covered in the stage head,
fresh hung the window-leaves, and did other work.
T 141/65–65² [He] is in the stage now and looking out
through the window leaf. P 113–76 ~ , pl window leafs.
  window tapping: boy's prank.
M 68–24 We played many types of pranks on a family
which believed in ghosts. Our favourite was what we
called 'window-tapping.' We used to get a very long
piece of black sewing cotton, a large pin and a button
to make the rapping and tapping noise.

wing n

Comb **wing fence**: long fence arranged to lead deer into a central area or trap; HAWK.

[1770] 1792 CARTWRIGHT i, 8–9 The other kind of fence is always built on the North side of the river, and is so constructed, that a herd of deer having once entered, it is almost impossible for one of them to escape. . . They erect two high, and very strong fences, parallel to each other, forming a narrow lane of some length, and stretching into the country. From the farther end of each, they extend two very long wing-fences, the extremities of which are from one mile or two, or more, asunder. The deer travel in small companies, few of them exceeding a dozen head, and when they meet with these hawk, or wing-fences, they walk along them, until they are insensibly drawn into the pound, as partridges are into a funnel net.

wing pound: storage area for seal 'pelts' below deck; POUND.

1924 ENGLAND 161–2 A gang was heaving out ballast rocks, making place for a 'wing pound' of sculps.

wing v Cp *OED* ~ v 2; *NID* ² v 10. To sail a vessel, esp directly before the wind; in phr *wing a cove abroad*: to sail directly towards the entrance to a harbour with the wind right aft.

T 194/5–65 An' when she come, she come about east-north-east. An' I winged her out, sir, an' here she goes now. C 67–7 The sailors talk about winging a cove abroad. This means sailing so that the entrance of the harbour becomes directly visible, and right through into the cove.

winging vbl n Comb **winging point**, ~ **island**: a landmark towards which a vessel sails directly (to shelter) with the wind right aft. Cp WING v.

1902 *Christmas Bells* 14 We located the 'winging point,' as the old man called it, and finding a nice sheltered bight, we safely moored our good ship. 1951 *Nfld & Lab Pilot* i, 272 Kitty island. . .lies 2¼ cables west-south-westward of Winging island.

wink n *EDD* ~ sb¹ s w cties. Handle of a grindstone.

T 43/7–64 There's a wink got to go on the outside end of it for turning [the grindstone]. T 75–64 There was a fellow got one o' those small cheese[s] out of her, an' thought 'twas a grindstone. Put a wink in it!

winker See WHINKER.

winnish See OUANANICHE.

winter n *OED* ~ sb¹ 5 b ~ duck (1804), ~ moth (1869) for sense 2; for combs. in sense 4: cp *EDD* sb¹ (9) ~ fish 'salt ling' Sh I, *DC* 1 Nfld (1822); cp *OED* ~-house (1000–); *DC* ~ road 1 (1801–). See also FALL n, SPRING², SUMMER.

1 The season, on most stretches of the coast, following the conclusion of the summer and fall fishery when activities are taken up on land, including preparation for the next fishing season.

1620 WHITBOURNE 43 It will be a great good ease to the Common-wealth, to leave so many there all the Winter; & after this rate proportionably from divers ships, great companyes may commodiously and beneficially be raysed to remaine there in little time, from such as will voluntarily and willingly entertaine their certaine places to make their fish on, and plant. [1663] 1963 YONGE 60 In the winter, the planters employ themselves in getting fish, sawing deal boards, making oars, catching beaver, and fowling. [1775] 1955 *Journeys* (ed Harvey) 63 The few that remains in the land the Winter goes and builds a house in the Woods and when the Weather will permit they Work at Boat Building. [1794] 1968 THOMAS 122 Thus from the affinity of Newfoundland to the Continent of Labrador the cold, in some particulars, receives additional strength so that here Winter reigns in great and mighty force for Seven months of the year. . . The seasons here are divided into two parts—Summer and Winter. 1866 WILSON 206–7 The merchants were accustomed, early in the spring, to bring a number of young men from England or Ireland, who are engaged, or shipped in their native land for the fishery; and the time for which they are shipped is two summers and one winter. 1936 SMITH 14 After discharging the winter's supplies and mooring the vessel for the winter, all hands settled down for the winter and I returned to school again. This was the last week in October.

2 In names of birds, plants, etc: **winter duck, ~ gull, ~ moth, ~ pear**.

[1775] 1792 CARTWRIGHT ii, 61 The water being open, I saw many winter-ducks [*Clangula hyemalis*]; also one flock of king-ducks, which are the first I have heard of this year. 1959 MCATEE 37 Winter gull. Ivory Gull (*Pagophila eburnea*). Common Kittiwake (*Rissa tridactyla tridactyla*). 1840 GOSSE 333 The Winter Moth (*Cheimatobia Vulgaris*), and little Autumnal Case-fly, (*Phryganea —?*) both Newfoundland insects, have also appeared, but these are rather indicative of cold weather than of mild. 1956 ROULEAU 40 Winter Pear (*Aronia prunifolia*).

3 In designations of a structure or location in which the activities characteristic of the winter season are conducted: **winter cabin, ~ house, ~ place, ~ quarters, ~ room** [see ROOM 1], **~ shack, ~ station** [see STATION], **~ tilt** [see TILT], **~ wigwam**.

1974 SQUIRE 6 Although permanent settlement commenced in 1868, [Eastport] was well known to the inhabitants of Salvage long before. Many families had winter cabins, mainly because of the ease with which fuel could be secured, as the area at that time was a veritable forest. [1771] 1792 CARTWRIGHT i, 162 [On this isthmus my tent was pitched] in a pleasant grove of young larch trees, we found two old winter-houses of the Esquimaux. [1822] 1928 CORMACK 96 The inhabitants at the Barachois River were now in their winter houses under the shelter of the woods, having recently left their summer residences at the shore. 1857 MOUNTAIN 5 About twenty or thirty men being retained [over winter] for the necessary labour of the 'Rooms,' or to go into the 'Winter House,' to cut a sufficient supply of firewood. 1909 GRENFELL¹ 36 The people had all, as usual, migrated to the winter houses up the bay, where they get together for schooling and social purposes. T 257–66 People in them days used to go to winter houses. They live out [on the coast] summer time; in the winter time they live in the woods. 1975 *Them Days* i (1), p. 35 We had a winter place and a summer place. We liked shifting from one to the other. We found that real good. It was always good to get back to the summer place in June. [1918–19] GORDON 12 The bay people are just gathering in before going further up to their winter quarters in the shelter of the woods. 1967 FIRESTONE 28 De Quetteville 'supplies most of the winter rooms and resident fishermen with goods, clothes, and stores much to his profit.' 1939 EWBANK 28 I will not attempt to describe the conditions under which they live in these winter shacks, but the necessity of moving to a place where they can keep warm gives them no choice. 1814 KOHLMEISTER & KMOCH 15 We now steered for *Kangertluksoak*, a winter-station of the Esquimaux, where several of our people had pitched their tents. 1910 GRENFELL 137 I pointed to the mere semblance of a boat that was all they had to convey their family over a hundred miles in up to their winter station. 1836 [WIX]² 53 There were houses, and a very decent young man, B.L. and his wife, having only left their winter tilts that morning, had cleaned up their neat summer house, and lighted a good fire, as though for my reception. 1863 MORETON 82 Their houses in the woods, named winter tilts, and required only to serve for one winter's use, are of very simple construction. 1919 GRENFELL¹ 194 . . .hauling food into the country for the winter tilts along his fur-path on the Grand River. C 75–130 [She] smokes like a winter's tilt. [1829] 1915 HOWLEY 190 Every winter wigwam has close by it a small square mouthed or oblong pit, dug in the earth about four feet deep, to preserve their stores, &c in.

4 Attrib, comb **winter credit**: in the 'truck system,' arrangement by which a fisherman is supplied for the winter with provisions against the season's catch; CREDIT.
1869 MCCREA 184 All had a stake [in the seal hunt]. The merchant in his ships, stores, and winter credits to the fishermen; the fishermen to pay these debts, in order (and in order solely) to obtain more credit for the summer cod-fishery.

winter crew: group (of persons) engaged or 'shipped' by merchant or planter to conduct on shore the preparatory activities for the next year's fishery and other seasonal operations; CREW.
[1773] 1792 CARTWRIGHT i, 279 Early this morning a boat of Slade's arrived from Twillingate with supplies for his winter crews. [1788] 1974 MANNION 18 Our winter crews are all gone into the woods where I hope they will be able to make good returns for the vast quantity of provisions they consume. [1811] 1818 BUCHAN 4 The winter crew have their house on the south shore. 1895 PROWSE xvii The first settlements were made by small detached parties of Englishmen known in the island parlance as 'winter crews,' who remained on the coast to cut wood for building houses, flakes, stages, cook-rooms, and boats for the spring.

winter diet: provisions for the winter months; DIET.
1892 *Christmas Review* 16 Only his son-in-law and his nephew appeared to have got their winter's diet out

of [the vessel]. 1895 PROWSE 18 Except for very rich people, who had game, there was no fresh meat to be had all through the winter. Fish, fresh and salted, formed the chief article of winter diet. [1906] GRENFELL 52 No man can't be sure o' getting a winter's diet with only a cross-hand skiff to work in. 1966 FARIS 42 [Formerly] families put in a 'winter's diet,' which consisted of vegetables, local berries, salt fish, flour, molasses, salt beef and salt pork. 1977 *Nfld Qtly* Fall, p. 36 A family of four or five, picking berries at ten cents a gallon. . .could put in a winter's diet of flour.

winter dieter: see DIETER.

winter(s) fat: catch of seals taken in winter months; FAT.
[1867] 1899 *Nfld Law Reports* 206 The letter informed McLea that Thomas and William Kough 'send their winter's fat to him by James McGrath.'

winter fish: (a) cod-fish caught in late fall or winter months; (b) cod-fish kept for winter consumption; FISH.
[c1675] 1976 HEAD 18 At least one source indicates that 'the winter fish is the best.' [1822] 1928 CORMACK 106 The cod caught in October, November, and December [on the south coast] are called winter fish. 1910 GRENFELL 160 'What else did you lose beside the gun, Allan?' 'Only our winter fish and some flour,' he said. P 245–66 We uses the big ones for winter fish. 1979 NEMEC 285 They will occasionally go jigging on Sundays as a favor to one or two relatives who need 'winter fish.'

winter fishery: (a) cod-fishery in coastal waters during fall and early winter; (b) 'bank fishery' off south and south-west coasts.
[1676] 1895 PROWSE 207 Such. . .as come to trade there and have by leave of the former Governors and Proprietors erected several stages and Roomes for their winter and summer fisheries and support. [1764] 1976 HEAD 161 In the winter many of the inhabitants of Fortune and Grand Bank repaired across the Bay to the Harbour of St Jacques to their 'several temporary Stages and Hutts' which they used 'for the benefit of the Winter Fishery.' 1883 HATTON & HARVEY 324 In Fortune Bay also this is the case, and there an extensive winter fishery is carried on. 1919 *Journ of Assembly* 404 The winter fishery on the West Coast began as usual in January, with good catch, plentiful supply of bait and successful returns. 1933 *Nfld Royal Commission Report* 101–2 The Winter Fishery. . .is strictly a 'Bank Fishery' since it is prosecuted on the small banks off the western portion of the South Coast, which is free from ice all the year around. The fishery is not, however, included in the Bank Fishery, since the vessels engaged in it are not true 'Bankers'; they are more nearly akin to the Labrador schooners. 1937 *Seafisheries of Nfld* 35 The units of production in the Shore Fishery [include] the small skiffs that operate the winter fishery with crews of three men.

winter ice: sea-ice formed in a single season.
1956 *Nfld & Lab Pilot* Supplement No 3, p. 11 Winter-ice.

winter issue: see **winter credit** above.
1937 *Seafisheries of Nfld* 73 When the fisherman is not fortunate enough to secure a sufficiently large catch

to pay his summer's account with his merchant, or to provide a surplus for the purchase of his requirements until the following fishing season, it is the custom for him to look to his merchant for a further supply of goods on credit. This is usually known as a 'winter's issue.'

winter justice: justice of the peace appointed to administer the law during the seasonal absence of naval officers and migratory West Country 'admirals.'

1793 REEVES 106 The admirals told the justices, *they were only winter justices*, and seemed to doubt of the governor's authority for appointing. 1895 PROWSE 287 The admirals declared the justices were only *Winter Justices*, and accordingly they had licensed public-houses, seized, fined, and whipped at their pleasure, and entirely set aside his new-fledged magistrates.

winter man: see **winter crew** above; DIETER.

[1775] 1792 CARTWRIGHT ii, 84 Some of the people were cutting wood for a salmon-house, and others rinding; the winter men had done nothing. 1866 WILSON 216 One year, the writer failed in getting wood in the fall, he had therefore himself to 'haul the slide,' accompanied by his 'winter man.' 1895 PROWSE 59 Whitbourne gives us quite a homily on the necessity of winter crews; and it is obvious to anyone acquainted with our shore fishery that it could not be carried on to any extent successfully without winter men. 1936 SMITH 42 When we did get ashore there were six feet of snow from the wharf up to the winter man's residence. Messrs Job Bros & Co owned Indian Harbour in those days, and Mr Joseph Simms was their summer agent. 1972 NEMEC 34–5 Winter 'dieters' or 'winter men,' as they were referred to. A 'dieter' was a man who fished in the summer, and in the absence of employment in the winter, joined a household on an informal basis. In many cases, if a dieter had been a shareman, he might remain with his crew skipper for the duration of the winter.

winter path: track leading to good stands of wood made by the traffic in winter of men, draft animals and sleds; foot-path between coastal 'settlements'; WOODS PATH.

1835 *Journ of Assembly* 147 Both the summer and winter path to Petty Harbor commence at the base of the South Side Hill. P 118–67 ~ A path in woods cut for the purpose of reaching a stand of timber.

winter road: place of habitual passage in winter when the sea and water-ways are frozen.

1910 GRENFELL 158 He was so close to the winter road they fair ate him out o' house and home last winter. 1979 TIZZARD 129–30 People were always ready to go for the doctor, for the bay would be frozen over and there was always a good winter road across Twillingate Island.

winter seal: variety of non-migratory seal; BAY SEAL, HARBOUR ~ .

[1776] 1792 CARTWRIGHT ii, 155 . . .he saw many marks of otters, and abundance of winter seals in the tickle.

winter servant: see **winter crew**, ~ **man**.

1793 *Report on Nfld Trade* Appendix. Dieters—Men who remain in the Island during the winter. . .without engaging as Winter Servants. 1819 ANSPACH 180 And what he says farther, that no master ever kept more winter-servants than the occasion of his situation compelled him to do.

winter side: area of bay or harbour occupied during fall and winter months.

T 246/7–66 You'd always move over here for the winter. They used to call this winter side one time.

winter snowshoe: large snowshoe used in heavy drifts.

1933 MERRICK 329 Edward had two pairs of snowshoes we used to josh him about, a big pair called his 'winter snowshoes' and a little pair called his 'spring snowshoes.'

winter(s) voyage: term used to express the whole of what any group of men make, catch, or procure in the course of a winter ([1771] 1792 CARTWRIGHT i, 137); TRIP, VOYAGE.

winter(s) work: habitual activities necessary for subsistence during winter months, including preparation for the fishing season ahead; the whole of what is built or procured in the course of a winter; cp WOODS WORK.

1792 CARTWRIGHT iii, [15] "Labrador: A Poetical Epistle": The Woodmen now with Sledges, on the Snow, / Their Winter's Work draw out and homeward go. / What's yet to do, must instantly be done, / For other Work must shortly be begun. Shallops now launched, the Crews no longer stay, / But in their Boats, bring all their Work away. 1812 BUCHAN *MS* 25 July The very extraordinary season we have experienced prevented our settlers from quitting their winter houses until a late period, and it is only within this ten days that they have ceased to bring out their winters work. [1829] P 54–67 Winter's work. June 13, 1829. [This term] is the quantitative one for the total of sticks, lumber, rinds and so on that a man would produce while living with his family away from his settlement 'in the woods for the winter.' 1866 WILSON 214 In many harbors to the west, it is a custom for a number of families to go to the woods during the winter, to do a winter's work, as building boats, cutting hoop-poles, or making staves for barrels. Sometimes they migrate for the sole object of catching fresh meat. 1901 *Christmas Bells* 4 It is a common thing for those who go in the bottoms of the Bays 'on winter works' to stay up all night to watch the caribou kneeling on the snow. 1936 SMITH 120 It was a winter's work for one man to repair four cod-traps. T 43/7–64 Apart from the wagon sleds now for winter work there was the slide. Well, it could be a horse slide or a hand slide.

winterer n *DC* ~ n 1 Nfld (1766). A permanent resident of Newfoundland as distinguished from a seasonal migratory fisherman; LIVYER, SETTLER.

[1766] 1971 BANKS 151 In the year 1762 when the french took this Place [St John's] 700 irish immediately entered into their service the number of winterers in the whole island are recond at 10000. 1976 HEAD 11 Towards the end of the seventeenth century and into the beginning of the eighteenth century, frequent counts of the inhabitants—the winterers—were taken.

wit* See WITHE.

witch n   *EDD* ~ sb[1] 4 for sense 1.
1 One believed to possess supernatural power or insight.
1966 FARIS 176 (see quot below). C 70–28 Before we were married a male witch in Lady Cove told my wife's fortune with a deck of card.
2 A fish overlooked when boat is unloaded.
1937 DEVINE 69 If a fish remains forgotten in a boat when the others are taken out, it is a sign of bad luck for the catcher; such a fish is called a 'witch,' and some fishermen making the discovery would not fish on that day.
3 Phr *shoot the witch's heart*: to remove a spell cast by a witch.
1966 FARIS 176 'Shooting the witch's heart' (a local cure for witchcraft) is no good for a jink.

witch-hazel n   also **wych-hazel**. Yellow or grey birch (*Betula lutea*); also attrib.
[1765] 1973 *Can Hist Rev* liv, 265 At the head of Bay Despair, Cook found 'many thousands of acres of land well clothed with all sorts of wood peculiar to this country, such as pine, fir, birch, witchhazle, and kinds of spruce, etc.' [1822] 1928 CORMACK 91 The young black birch, as far as observation went, is called [in St George's Bay] the 'witch-hazel.' 1837 *Journ of Assembly* 451 The road passes through much heavy timber, consisting of birch and witch-hazel. 1874 HOWLEY *MS Reminiscences* 46 These flats possess excellent soil and are over-grown with. . .yellow Birch (witch hazel). 1896 SWANSBOROUGH 28 With good water we are supplied, / From lake and rivers, on whose side / Grow birch, wych-hazel and large pine. 1951 *Nfld & Lab Pilot* i, 210 Witch Hazel point is situated about half a mile northward of Doughball cove. 1967 HORWOOD 108–9 Once a magnificent stand of witch hazel birch, giving its name to Witch Hazel Ridge and the Witch Hazel Line, this land belongs to the Portugal Cove Parish, and was logged out for firewood a generation ago when churches were still heated by wood stoves. C 69–6 He went into the woods and cut a witch hazel which he hoped to make a big schooner's keel out of. 1974 PITTMAN 19 None of the men will put to sea unless they have a branch of witchhazel somewhere on board.

withe n   also **weft***, **wet***, **wif(t)***, **wit***, **with** [wit, wιt]. Cp *OED* withe, with: wifte, wef, etc. 1 'a band, tie, or shackle consisting of a tough flexible twig or branch, or of several twisted together.' See also GAD, WITHE-ROD, WITHY. A flexible branch or root, or a rope, usu formed into a circle and used for var purposes: to hold an oar to the 'tole pin,' to form the entrance to a lobster pot, etc; one of a number of twigs used for making brooms or starting fires.
[c1900] 1978 *RLS* 8, p. 24 ~ A [peculiar] twisted ring of sapling or root of tree used with one toll pin for rowing a boat. 1937 DEVINE 51 [A tole pin is] a wooden peg holding an oar in the rowlock with a withe. P 94–57 Wit—a rope-ring to hold oar of punt to single tole pin.

P 23–63 A long [thin] root of a tree was used by the old people to make 'wits' which are used in rowing a boat. T 14/20–64 When you knit your head, your lobster head, you knit un the shape you want un, and you'll skiver your wit through, on the mashes, in the centre. The hole is in the centre of the head. T 39/40–64 There's a little round—what they call a wit in there—hole for [the lobsters] to shoot in. M 68–7 Wift—a dogwood twisted to make a circle to put over the rods of the killeck to keep them together at the smallest end. C 70–15 The withes were made from long slender witherod or willow saplings. The saplings were peeled and three or four were twisted into a circular form. They were then placed in pickle to toughen the fibres and later in cod-liver oil or blubber for seasoning. 1971 NOSEWORTHY 263 Withs—small twigs used for making brooms. C 71–21 Men went in the woods to get a turn of whits [to burn].

withe-rod n   also **with-rod**, **wit-rod***, etc ['wιtrαd, 'wιt?rαd]. Cp *DAE* ~ [*Viburnum nudum*] (1847–). See WITHE, WITHY. A shrub with thin, pliant branches; northern wild raisin; GADBERRY, THRASHBERRY (*Viburnum cassinoides*) (1956 ROULEAU 40); the branch from this shrub; also attrib.
[1776] 1792 CARTWRIGHT ii, 215 The people came down from the lodge, and brought five hundred killick-rods, fifty pryer-poles and a bundle of white-rods [ed emend: whit-rods]. [1894–1929] 1960 BURKE (ed White) 37 "The Trouting Liar": He was forced to put five dozen [trout] / On the limb of a wit rod stick. 1937 DEVINE 30 Killock—a home made anchor, consisting of a frame of witherods enclosing one or two oblong stones. . . Layers [are] pieces of whitrod or young firs to make a fence. P 148–65 Baskets were used to heave coal out of the pounds in the sealing vessels, from one man to the next. They were made of straw, wit-rods; and held ten to twelve pounds. P 148–65 Wit-rods [used to make] a garden-rod fence. P 126–67 Cut some witrods and make a witrod broom. 1975 BUTLER 61 A witrod. . .is a small flexible tree. . . You can even tie knots in 'em. . . Used to use 'em for brooms, twist them together for to put down. . .flake longers.

withy n   also **widdy** ['wιtι, 'wιdι] *OED* ~ 'willow,' cp widdy Sc and n; *EDD* gen.
1 Variety of willow, or a similar sort of shrub; SALLY[1] (1898 *J A Folklore* xi, 279); also attrib.
[c1894] PANL P4/14, p. 195 The word 'stick,' too, is applicable to all kinds and dimensions of trees, from those that are to be 'masts of some tall admiral' down to a withy. 1956 ROULEAU 40 Widdy: *Cornus stolonifera*. T 70/2–64[1] They used to gather brushwood for a fire, I suppose widdy, as we get for widdy brooms. C 75–132 Widdies are small willow bushes growing on the side of a stream or lake.
2 Shrubby cinquefoil (*Potentilla fructicosa*). Cp GOLD-WITHY.
1970 FERNALD 806 Shrubby C. Widdy (in Nfld.). P 4–59 Widdy—a bush with yellow flower which grows in sand in river banks and will make a fire at any time.

wit-rod* See WITHE-ROD.

wizard n Cp *OED* ~ sb 2 'medicine man.' A man with the power to cure ailments; DOCTOR[1].

1966 FARIS 178 'Wizards' or 'doctors' (both terms are used in Cat Harbour) are always men. This is an *all good* category, and those possessing this quality are able to 'charm' (stop) blood, cure warts, toothache, stomach upset, and find lost objects.

wobble* See WABBLE*.

woman n

1 Phr *woman's knot, cowardly* ~ *mooring*: knot which comes untied; mooring which slips off (1966 FARIS 96).

2 Comb **woman box**: wooden compartment fitted on sled, esp for transporting a sick person; COACH BOX.

1933 GRENFELL 326 The journey by land. . .seemed almost impracticable. However, a 'woman box' was speedily ready, a willing band of men volunteered to draw a sledge, as it was too much of an undertaking for a dog-team, and the party set off [with the sick man].

wonderful a, intens *EDD* ~ adj 'great,' adv 'very, extremely'; *ADD* adv 2 'very,' 3 'terribly.' Cp CRUEL, SOME.

1 Great; extreme.

1902 *Christmas Bells* 3 'Tis a skipper beatin' a 'prentice. They does it a wonderful lot. 1905 DUNCAN 203 'I'm troubled a wonderful sight with the rheumatiz in me knees,' said Jabez. 1920 WALDO 176 The winter of 1918–19 was especially terrible—or 'wonderful' as would be said here—because of the visitation of the 'flu.' P 152–58 ~ used for dreadful. A stormy day is referred to as a wonderful day. T 54/63–64 'My dear man, you have a wonderful temperature, wonderful temperature,' he said. 'You have a hundred an' four degrees.' 1979 *Evening Telegram* 24 Nov, p. 15 'My land,' sez Mag, 'did you 'see the convention for the PCs? I got a big lump in me throat when Mr Moores came on. He's a wonderful loss to Newfoundland.'

2 Very, extremely.

1874 *Maritime Mo* iii, 544–5 Even Captain Rideout, who has been 'forty springs to the ice,' and caused the death of more seals than any other seal-hunter within a hundred miles, admits that the parson is 'a wonderful knowin' man about soils.' 1904 DUNCAN 282 I'm sorry for the cook. . .wonderful sorry. 1905 WALLACE 301 'Tis wonderful sad, 'tis wonderful sad t'have he die so. 1920 GRENFELL & SPALDING 177 The Prophet has encouraged me with the observation that 'nearly all the female ladies what comes aboard her do be wonderful sick.' 1933 MERRICK 9 A trapper admitted to me, rather sheepishly in a moment of rare confidence, that although 'the people from away' seemed to accomplish some marvelous feats such as making guns and radios, he could not see that the few who had come to this bay, the Methodists, the sportsmen, the Catholic priests who visit the Indians once a year and even the mission workers, were all so 'wunnerful fine.' P 148–61 They don't have a wonderful long service at funeral. 1970 JANES 257 Sometimes he gets wonderful crooked and I can't get no sense out of him. 1981 *Evening Telegram* 20 Jan, p. 2 'It's wonderful hard,' he remarked, 'when you've got to throw away ,that beautiful mackerel and herring.'

wooden a Cp *OED* ~ a 8 ~ walls 'ships or shipping as a defensive force.' Comb **wooden walls**, ~ **fleet**: wooden vessels, up to 700 tons (635 m t), powered by sail and steam, used in the prosecution of the seal fishery and with heavy sheathing to withstand the pressure of the ice-fields.

1924 ENGLAND 234 De warriors o' de wooden fleet, / Dey soon will sail away, / In charge of 'ardy swilin' crews, / Wid colours flyin' gay! 1933 GREENE xv The Wooden Walls. The name given to the oak and greenheart steam sealing Fleets of Newfoundland. 1968 *Avalon Penin of Nfld* 29 One cause was the introduction of large steamships in the 1860's, the famous Wooden Walls, requiring an investment difficult to recoup in the off-season, for few of the great ships were designed for anything other than the seal fishery and arctic and antarctic voyages. 1972 BROWN 14 The other Newfoundland merchants, impressed by the new steel ship, began adding their own steel ships to the fleet of 'woodenwalls.' By 1914, Newfoundland was the only country in the world with a fleet of ice-breakers. 1982 *Evening Telegram* 19 Apr, p. 6 His father went in the S.S. *Neptune*, one of the old wooden walls, for several years with Blandford.

wood(s) n, n pl *DC* wood cat (1768–) for (a); cp *EDD* gallows sb 5 'frame. . .against which planks or boards are set. . .to dry' Ha. See also LUMBER-WOODS.

Attrib, comb, cpd **wood-cat**: (a) pine marten (*Martes americana*); WILD CAT; (b) heavy sled; CATAMARAN (see 1896 quot).

1846 TOCQUE 108 I saw a very fine marten or wood-cat. . .which was caught in a trap a few days ago. 1889 HOWLEY *MS Reminiscences* 21 Presently I saw it was a woodcat or martin, the first live one I had ever seen. [1896] SWANSBOROUGH 3 ''January'': Now wood cats and nice painted sleighs / Travel the main roads and bye-ways. 1932 BARBOUR 14 He was a brave as well as a nimble seaman and raced up the rigging like a wood cat.

wood chick: Newfoundland winter wren (*Troglodytes troglodytes*) (1959 MCATEE 53).

wood gallows ['wɒd ˌgælǝs]: framework to support vertically placed sticks to be used for firewood; the sticks so placed to dry (P 205–55); GALLOWS.

C 71–118 The sticks were piled vertically one against the other in a wood gallase or wood pile, waiting to be sawed. A wood gallase is built by putting two large sticks in the ground in a vertical position. Another stick is nailed across the two sticks. The wood then is laid up one by one against this stick.

wood path, woods ~ : track leading to good stands of timber for fuel; PATH, SLIDE ~ , WINTER ~ .

1836 [WIX][1] 14–15 As we could ascertain the points of the compass by observing the inclination of the topmost branches of the juniper or larch-trees, we regained our path some time after dark; and by a slippery wood-path, on which we had many falls, we reached the south shore of Conception Bay. 1896 SWANSBOROUGH 3 "January": We look to have good woodpaths now, / And frozen lakes, and roads o'er snow. [1916] 1972 GORDON 42 Our route took us over the frozen bight across the run to Earl Island, where we struck a wood-path which led up the steep face of Earl Island Mount and ran as steeply down to the ice on Diver Tickle. C 70–15 There was an abundance of wood on the Mizzin Hill which lay just back of the community, and the most of the men of the community would go there to cut firewood. Thus it was that dozens of woodpaths traversed the Mizzen Hill and every path had a special name. Most of the men used the same paths year after year and it became a kind of tradition. Not only that, but it was looked upon as trespassing for anybody to move in on another's territory even though the woods were free for all. 1972 MURRAY 312 Even now many old wood's paths have become impassable.

woodpecker: eastern brown creeper (*Certhia familiaris americana*) (1959 MCATEE 53).

wood pile: stack of long, vertically placed sticks to be dried and cut for fuel.
[1886] LLOYD 77 At a short distance from the house stands the 'wood pile,' where 'one hand is kept cuttin'' all the day.' Q 67–50 After hauling the wood home, it is carefully piled into stacks or what is known as wood piles. 1973 HORWOOD 10 He made a wood pile near the Lambert's back door.

wood slide: (a) declivity over which logs are rolled into a body of water; SCRAPE[1]; (b) sled used esp for carting wood in winter; CATAMARAN, SLIDE n.
1877 *Royal Geog Soc* xlvii, 280 . . .crossing three ravines running to the north, debouched on the sea-coast at the head of a steep wood-slide, with the little settlement lying below on the shingle beach at our feet, and H.M.S. *Eclipse* anchored in Gold Cove. T 175/7–65 Just a knee slide, sir, proper wood slide—the same thing as they use for pulling wood.

woods path: see **wood path** above.

woods racket: see RACKET[2].

woods road: one of a series of intersecting roads used in cutting pulp-wood (1963 HEAD 96).
1966 PHILBROOK 166 In cutting operations, a main or access road, suitable for winter use is cut through the forest. The pulpwood is then cut from lines laid out perpendicular to this road. These 'woods roads' vary in respect to the terrain and timber growth.

woods rope: stout line used to secure load of wood to a sled, to haul the sled, etc. Cp HAULING-ROPE (P 41–68).

woods town: settlement from which logging operations are conducted.
1966 PHILBROOK 123 While the mine buildings constitute distinctive features, the physical character and ecology of the former 'woods town' still dominate [Baie Verte]. The physical attributes of a logging industry appear in the line of log piers in the bay for securing the holding boom.

woods work: (a) the cutting of timber for household use; (b) pulp-wood operations. Cp WINTER WORK.

1953 *Nfld Fish Develop Report* 21 This conclusion would not apply, of course, or would apply only with substantial modification, to areas where fishing is unusually successful or where supplementary sources of cash income (such as woods work) are unusually accessible. T 43–64 So every spring, 'twould be handy about the last woods work would be done [and we'd] get the flake boughs. T 49–64 There was no woods work there done, an' people get their own firewood an' their stuff for fencin'. 1966 FARIS 39 'Woods work' usually starts soon after the first snows in October or early November and lasts intermittently until April. To haul wood out by slide it is necessary that the bogs and ponds be frozen deep enough to support the weight of a horse and fully-loaded slide, and that there be enough snow to enable the slide to function.

woods worker: lumber-jack (1951 PETERS & BURLEIGH 303).
1963 WILLIAMS 92 Table 8 indicates that woods workers and lumbermen are not interested in garden cultivation.

wooge* See WOOLAGE*.

woolage* n also **wooge*** ['wɒlɪdʒ]. Cp *ADD* wudge 'little bunch'; woodgy 'tousled.' Head of hair that is too long or tousled; person with untidy hair.
P 148–63 I look like a woolage. P 130–67 What time are you going to get that woolage cut? C 75–146 If our hair was messy, we would say, 'What a wooge I got!'

wop[1] n also **wap, wapse, wops** *EDD* wasp: var wap D, wopse Gl So D Co, wops Do Gl So. See also BAY WOP.
1 Wasp, or similar stinging insect.
1895 *J A Folklore* viii, 33 Wasps they call *waps*. 1929 MILLER 24 We foun' a wopses' nest. 1933 GREENLEAF xxv So, too, 'wapse' is used for 'wasp.' 1937 DEVINE 57 ~ A bee, a wasp. 1956 *Daily News* 21 June We have often heard the expression 'a girt wop.' P 167–66 The big wop stung me. 1967 *Bk of Nfld* iv, 244 Everybody cast aside the gruelling summer jobs associated with fishing and enjoyed the picnic atmosphere of outdoor cooking and berry-gathering, despite the nippers and 'wops.'
2 Comb **wap totty**: dandelion flower; TOTTY (P 94–57).

wop[2] n Volunteer worker from other countries doing odd jobs at the International Grenfell Mission, Labrador.
[1917] 1972 GORDON 99 Due to arrive any minute. . .were a species known as WOPS. They represented the unskilled Volunteer force that Grenfell gathered in from the universities and other sources of supply. They willingly undertook all the odd jobs that were so necessary to the running of the Hospitals, such as stoking, digging, unloading freight, or anything else. 1920 WALDO 145 'Bill' Norwood—one of the volunteer 'wops' building the Battle Harbour reservoir. 1941 WITHINGTON 170 The work of these 'wops,' the word for the aides who came in the summer *WithOut Pay*, was very desultory—unloading cargoes of supplies,

sorting clothes and arranging them for sale, and doing odd chores. P 130–67 ~s: summer workers, usually students, who work at the Grenfell Hospital without pay.

wops See WOP[1].

word v   *OED* ~ v 2 obs (13..–1663); *ADD* ~ out Nfld. Esp in phr *word off/out*: to recite, rather than sing, a ballad or song (1925 *Dial Notes* v, 346); RHYME v.
1924 ENGLAND 126 'But I can word out a piece for ye. I can just mind "Willy March", an' I'll rhyme it off.' 'No, ye got to sing!' insisted George. T 45–64 My father would word off every rhyme, and the men would write 'em down in the book. T 70/2–64[1] He used to word it for me, an' by an' by I got ahold to [the song]. 1971 CASEY 206 The informant learned this song by someone 'just wordin' it out.'

work v
1 Of cod-fish (a) to be plentiful enough and so located as to be easily taken; (b) when split, salted and placed in a 'pile,' to undergo the curing process; SWEAT v.
[1886] LLOYD 64 If the fish 'work well,' as the people say, a voyage is easily and rapidly secured. T 36–64 When [the fish] gets dry enough to work, you put it in a pile, a round pile, say about five or ten quintals. Then with the weight of so much fish, if there's a'r drop o' pickle in [it] would press out. Now they say this fish is workin'—the water's workin' out of it. T 80/3–64 I asked this feller how the fish was workin', was it comin' down—where he was gettin' it, in his inside door or outside door. Didn't know!
2 Phr *work seals*: to pursue, kill and 'sculp' seals on the ice-floe.
1924 ENGLAND 191 A few of her hunters were still 'working scattered seals on the sheet' in which, with broken tailshaft, she lay imprisoned. 1933 GREENE 42 He had to be able to handle his men as well on the crowded ship as when they were 'working the seals' in the Patch. 1936 SMITH 50 On the 23rd the barrelman spied two steamers to the north-west, about twenty miles away, supposed to be working seals. P 245–71 We needs the gaff to work the seals. 1979 *Salt Water, Fresh Water* 103 Captain Westbury Kean had told his men that they were to stay aboard his father's ship for that night and he would pick them up the following day; they would stay up there and work the seal.
work twine: to 'knit' a fish-net or trap.
T 347–67 They didn't say knit [fish nets], they said work twine, work the twine.

wormul n   Cp *EDD* wornil sb: ~ Co. Swelling on the back of cattle caused by larvae of the gad-fly.
1846 TOCQUE 203 Mr Clouter has been today feeling the backs of his cattle for what he calls 'wormuls,' which is the larvae of the ox gad-fly (*Oestrus Bovis*).

wrangle-gangle a   Cp *DAS* 645 rangle-dangle 'to wrangle.' Rowdy; boisterous.
T 194/6–65 Seems I was a little bit above the other

feller—the wrangle-gangle crowd. Never tangled up with that crowd.

wrapper n   *OED* ~ sb 6 a (Nfld: 1792) for sense 1.
1 Woollen covering, worn around arm and wrist in winter.
1792 CARTWRIGHT *Gloss* i, xvi ~s. Loose sleeve-pieces to button round the wrists, to defend them from the frost. [1811] 1818 BUCHAN 3–4 . . .blankets, thirty; woollen wrappers, nine.
2 Comb **wrapper bag**: burlap sack; BRIN BAG (1971 NOSEWORTHY 264).
C 66–13 Fortune gallies and the Grand Bank shags, / All tied up in wrapper bags.

wreck n   *OED* ~ sb[1] 11 b ~ commissioner (1876); cp *DAE* wrecking: ~ gang.
Attrib, comb **wreck commissioner**: one appointed to take charge of a wrecked vessel or its cargo.
1901 *Christmas Bells* 13 The *Mercade* was driven on shore at the back of the Downs and the balance of her cargo, excepting some of the coals, was removed by the wreck commissioner, and she was subsequently towed off and brought here to St John's. 1941 SMALLWOOD 218 [list of] Wreck Commissioners. 1972 NEMEC 57 Many dories were acquired from the 'wreck commissioner' or direct from shipwrecks themselves.
wreck-crew shack: small cabin for accommodation of railway maintenance workers.
T 43/4–64 I was lookin' after him there in a wreck-crew shack, they call it, but 'twas a nice comfortable place just the same.

wren n   [ræn] *OED* ~ 3 ~ boys (1800–), *EDD* sb[1] (1) ~ boys Ir D for comb in sense 2. For customs related to sense 1, see C SWAINSON *The Folk Lore and Provincial Names of British Birds* (1886) 36–43.
1 Figure of a bird carried in procession on St Stephen's Day; the celebration of hunting the wren so carried out (1893 *Christmas Bells* 15).
1842 BONNYCASTLE ii, 139 So rise up, kind madame, and give us a treat. / Up with the kettle, and down with the pan; / A penny, or twopence, to bury the [wran]. T 45–64 The wran used to be out an' the feller'd carry that. He'd have a stick an' have a big rooster marked out on the top. T 200–65 Most years there'd be a time in the hall that night, an' all the boys go to the hall, take the wren with us an' tie it on the Christmas tree. An' then you'd dance till the sunrise an' that was the end o' the wren.
2 Comb **wren beer**: home-brewed beer made for the celebration of St Stephen's Day.
1969 *Trans Dev Assoc* ci, 195 The brewing of home-made beer, both 'home-brew' and 'spruce beer' is still very popular. In at least one predominantly Irish community a special brew called 'Wren beer' is made for the St Stephen's Day custom of Hunting the Wren, when a bush with a bird tied to the top is carried from door to door.

wren boys: those who walk in procession with the figure of wren (P 160–64).

wriggle See RIDDLE n.

wring v Phr *wring one's mitt*: of a male, to urinate. Cp MITT (P 13–74).
M 68–24 Most men went outside to 'have a leak,' 'wring the mitt,' urinate, or what have you, before going to bed.

wrinkle[1] n *OED* ~ sb[2] s w dial (1589–); *EDD* sb[2] D Co for sense 1.
1 A variety of periwinkle, family *Littorinidae*; SNAGLE, SNAIL.
1846 TOCQUE 72 The sea-shore exhibits to our view the sea urchin. . .and the wrinkle. 1924 ENGLAND 266 Then, too, you can scent tubs of bait, including 'mushels,' 'wrinkles' (periwinkles), and 'cock an' 'ens,' another kind of shellfish. 1969 HORWOOD 187 In a cove just outside Clay Hole we found a bed of small white clams. Beyond low-water mark huge sea snails, periwinkles, or 'wrinkles' as some Newfoundlanders call them, crawled over the rocks. Some of them were monsters of their kind, fully three inches in diameter. M 71–118 We used to say, 'Wrinkle, Wrinkle, blow out your horns. If you don't I'll kill your mother and father.' 1976 GUY 107 If fish are scarce, you can pick up some wrinkles (snails) off the rocks or the sunken wharves and crack them.
2 Comb **wrinkle net**: device to trap periwinkles.
1979 TIZZARD 322 My father used to get [wrinkles] out of his herring net when it dragged on the bottom at times. Then he made a 'wrinkle' net. This was made from an iron hoop from a beef or pork barrel and into this hoop he would sew a piece of burlap bag. Some kind of bait, herring usually, was fastened to this burlap and then the whole thing was lowered to the bottom about a hundred yards or so offshore. Each day it was pulled I remember there would be several 'wrinkles' in it.

wrinkle[2] n Cp *OED* ~ sb[1] 9 'untruth, fib, lie.' Esp in phr *old wrinkle, old woman's* ~ : tale, explanation, superstitious saying; folk wisdom.
T 175/6–65 There's lots o' th' old wrinkles an' stuff a fellow could [remember], especially when he's prodded a bit. C 68–10 I've often heard her say 'That's old women's wrinkles, that's all that is.' 1982 *Evening Telegram* 5 June, p. 8 If the skippers on Galilee years ago. . .could only come back, they'd give Premier Peckford many a useful wrinkle that would help him solve all his problems.

with n Cp *OED* frith sb[2] 4 'frith, with. . .freath, or vreath' Co; *EDD* frith sb 3 'brushwood, underwood'; *OED* ~ Do (1844). Beaver's store of winter food.
[1770] 1792 CARTWRIGHT i, 60 I found the beavers in a large new house, with plenty of writh before it. [1783] ibid iii, 19–20 At a little distance from the angle, is [the beavers'] magazine of provisions, which consists

of the roots of water-lilly, and the branches of trees; the butt-ends of the latter they stick into the mud, where there is any. The whole is termed *writh*, and I have seen as much as a cart would hold

Y

yaffle n *EDD* yafful sb 1 'a handful; an armful' D Co (1842, 1880); *ADD* Nfld; *Cent* n[2] 2 Mass; *SED* iv (1), p. 251 yafful 'armful of hay' two points in Co and D; *EDD* jaffle sb[1] 'handful' Co (1880). Possibly a development from the base in *OED* jag sb[2] 1 [i e *jagful] 'a load (usually a small cart-load) of hay, wood, etc' (1597–): see well-supported senses in *EDD* jag(g) sb[1], jagger, *DAE* jag (1633–).
1 An armful (of dried and salted cod-fish, kindling, etc); a load.
1862 *Daily News* 28 Apr [p. 2] [He] was charged with having purloined a quantity, known in this land as a yaffle of dry fish. [c.1894] PANL P4/14, p. 198 'To *spell* a *yafful* of *crunnocks*' is to gather an armful of dry wood for kindling purposes. 1896 *J A Folklore* ix, 25 ~ an armful, applied especially to gathering up the fish which have been spread out to dry. 1903 *Daily News* 6 May "The False Prophet": Last fall I trow, we had to go / And sell fish by the 'yaffle.' 1937 DEVINE 57 ~ An armful, especially of dried fish. P 65–64 Wood is brought into the cook-house by the 'yaffle.' T 185–65 They'd go out alongside and throw the fish up in yaffles and put it on a bar and dump it right down in the hold o' the vessel. 1966 SCAMMELL 83 Ned plumped another yaffel (armful) of fish on the culling board. 'You're heavin' out too many cullage. I'm not standin' by and watchin' a greenhorn crucify my fish like this.' 1979 TIZZARD 88 The evening the fish was ready to carry in the under store, someone, usually the father, would take it up in little yaffles and we would carry it in an armful at a time.
2 Fig. a small bundle or bunch; a handful (of people).
1964 *Evening Telegram* 4 May, p. 7 Get over to Lester's field and get another yaffle of dandelions.
3 Phr *yaffle at hand*, ~ *up*: call used by men loading dried cod when an armful is gathered together.
T 192/3–65 The men down in the hold'd be yaffling up the fish, and they'd yaffle so much to get enough for the weight to make the draft on the bar, and then there'd be 'yaffle at hand. Yaffle at hand.'. . . Down Fogo you call 'yaffle up.' 1977 BURSEY 35–6 Several boys like myself would yaffle the fish and one would cry out 'Yaffle in hand' and someone aboard would receive it and stow it in the hold of the schooner, each man's separately.

yaffle v *EDD* yafful v 3 Co; *Cent* v[2] Mass for sense 1.
1 To gather an armful (of dried and salted cod, kindling, etc); also phr *yaffle and throw*, ~ *up*.
1891 *Holly Branch* 19 Titivates herself to meet her

beau who daily 'yaffles' fish. 1892 *Christmas Review* 16 After this imposing ceremonial the Magistrate proposed three cheers for the new member, which was responded to by the three parties and three or four small boys that were yaffling fish. 1937 DEVINE 57 We're going to *yaffle* them boughs now. T 139–65 When I was a boy I used to go down to yaffle fish—get three cents an hour, Saturdays. T 192/3–65 The men down in the hold'd be yaffling up the fish. 1979 TIZZARD 295 My father would be down in the punt while I yaffled the fish and threw it down to him. I became expert in yaffling and throwing the fish and my father became a good, expert catcher.

2 To gather, 'spread,' and 'pile' salted cod in the drying and curing process.

1925 *Dial Notes* v, 346 ~ To gather or [pile] (a yaffle). T 175/7–65 And then the next thing, when it got perhaps two or three days' sun on it, good days, you put it in what they call a pile. You go around, all yaffle around, around. All tails inside, all the napes o' the fish out around. 1966 HORWOOD 350 But who's goin' to. . .yaffle it an' pile it? 1966 SCAMMELL 30 As we got old 'nough to work on the 'room' at ten or twelve cents an hour, 'yaffling fish' we got a huge kick out of taking up the value of our earnings in those little personal necessities which meant to us gracious living. 1981 HUSSEY 40 The younger or weaker ones spread the fish in the morning and yaffled it in the evening for the men to take to the bulk.

yaffling vbl n The action of gathering and stowing armloads of dried and salted cod-fish (P 37).

1937 DEVINE 57 Yaffling used to be a large part of the work of loading a vessel's cargo of fish in bulk.

yankee a Cp *NID* slack[5] n (screening of coal).

Comb yankee barge: see BARGE.

yankee slack: American soft coal (1925 *Dial Notes* v, 346).

1976 CASHIN 84 We carried, in addition to full bunkers of coal, an additional supply of what we called 'Yankee slack' in the hold.

yardel n, v (a) Tangled twine or yarn (1897 *J A Folklore* x, 212); (b) to tangle (ibid).

yarkin(g) n also **yorkin(g)*** ['jaːɹkɪn, 'jɔːɹkən]. Cp *OED* yerk, yark v 'to draw stitches tight. . .as a shoemaker in sewing' (1430–1822); *EDD* yark v[1] 14 'to bind tightly' Sc; yarkin(g) sb 'side seam of a shoe' Sc Nb.

1 A line passed through the meshes of a fish-net and fastened to the rope attached to floats which suspend the net in the water.

1955 ENGLISH 37 Yarkin—lines to fasten a net to the head rope. P 243–56 Yorking—a fastening of mesh of a net to a head-rope. T 43/8–64 You take your mesh [of cod trap] here and one yorkin. . .now yorkins they call those, would go that way.

2 Comb **full yarkin(g)**: the fastening of every mesh of a fish-net to the 'head-rope' (Q 67–87).

Q 71–8 A yarkin is the line used to tie the meshes of a herring net to the head-rope. Hence 'full

yarkin'—tying every mesh as opposed to every tenth one.

yarkin(g) mesh: that part of fish-net which is fastened to the 'head-rope' (P 127–76).

yary a also **yarry** ['jæɹɪ, 'jæɹɪ, 'jæːri] *EDD* ~ 'ready; smart, quick; sharp, cunning; wary' Nf K D; *Kilkenny Lexicon*.

1 Of animals and game-birds, watchful, WILD; of persons, wary (1863 MORETON 35).

1868 HOWLEY *MS Reminiscences* 50 Here we saw a great number of wild geese in the lagoon inside the beach but it was impossible to get within shooting distance of them, these birds are so wild and extremely yary. 1881 *Evening Telegram* 20 Sep, p. 1 We don't find the cruising war-ships of our yarry neighbours the French and the Americans, lying in port for weeks at a time. 1937 DEVINE 57 ~ wary, watchful, alert. T 84/5–64 I'll tell ya a trick was played on me one time, and he was a good one. And I was pretty damn yary over those damn tricks. P 113–66 Yary as a night-owl. P 218–68 Ducks difficult to hunt are yary ducks. C 71–39 If a sheep or young cow was wild or elusive or hard to hold we would say it is yary. P 245–75 I guess [the calf] was a little bit too yary for [the rustlers] because they let he go.

2 Alert, energetic; rising early to get to one's tasks.

1896 *Dial Notes* i, 381 Yarry: smart, quick. 'He'll have to be pretty *yarry* to catch up with him.' 1906 DUNCAN 256 'Hi, b'y! Get yarry (wide awake)!' cried the captain in the morning. 1907 MILLAIS 339 ~ pronounced *yarry*; means a careful, early-rising man. 1924 ENGLAND 52 Never was there so 'yary' a man as our bosun. 1966 SCAMMELL 90 That would be Skipper John Elliott, yary as ever, hi-tailing it for Jacob's ground before the Eastern Tickle crowd got the choice berths for the day.

yawny a Pale.

P 167–67 He looked yawny.

ye pro [jiː]. From A-I: JOYCE 88 'They always use *ye* in the plural. . . In like manner. . .*yeer*'; *Kilkenny Lexicon* yeer. Cp DINNEEN tú 'thou,' pl: sibh. The persons addressed; second person plural pronoun, used in contrast with the singular forms *you, ya*.

1869 MCCREA 112 Well, boys, glad to see ye all back again; and what luck? 1897 WILLSON 83 'An' I've taken risks with ye all. . . An' what ha' ye done for me, faith?' [1961] 1965 PEACOCK (ed) iii, 916 "George's Banks": Ye roving boys of Newfoundland draw near and lend an ear. P 148–59 I'm going to tell ye boys something. P 148–61 Why not ye? T 1–63[1] I'm not going to chase ye. 1964 BLONDAHL (ed) 14 "Hard, Hard Times": Then next comes the doctor the worst of them all, / Saying, 'What be the matter with all of ye this fall?' P 148–64 That's what ye loves, isn't it? Q 67–54 Yeer—possessive plural. P 148–78 The next game is yeers.

yellow a P KENNEDY *Legendary Fictions of the*

Irish Celts, 2nd ed (1891), p. 312 ~ belly [nickname for Wexfordian].

Comb **yellow-belly**: epithet for person originally from Wexford; member of Newfoundland-Irish faction; cp WHEY BELLY. Also attrib.

1863 PEDLEY 295 The great Irish factions had established themselves [c1815] in St John's [one of which was called] 'Yellow-bellies,' significant of the Wexford men. 1895 PROWSE 402 The Tipperary 'clear airs,' the Waterford 'whey bellies,' and Cork 'dadyeens' were arrayed against the 'yallow belly' faction—the 'Doones' or Kilkenny boys, and the Wexford 'yallow bellies.' 1915 *Cadet* [28] Water Street from 'Yellow Belly' Corner, to high water mark, down in Kent's Cove, was thronged with people, the residents of each county, Waterford, Wexford, Tipperary, Killkenny, etc, that were already settled here.

yellow hammer: Newfoundland yellow warbler; also the black-polled warbler (*Dendroica petechia amnicola; D. striata*).

1870 *Can Naturalist* v, 154 A common summer migrant. . .'Yellow-hammer'. . .makes a pretty little nest in low bushes. 1951 PETERS & BURLEIGH 342 This all-yellow bird is locally known as 'Yellow-hammer,' but this name seems to be applied to all small birds showing yellow in their plumage. 1959 MCATEE 58 ~ Black-capped Warbler. . . Yellow Warbler (British name of the yellow bunting transferred by colonists to a variety of birds having yellow in their plumage. Nfld.) 1964 *Evening Telegram* 28 Oct, p. 5 The name 'yellow hammer,' brought to Newfoundland by some traveller, was applied without reason to the Newfoundland yellow warbler, one of several yellow birds which not only does not hammer on anything, but would be quite incapable of doing anything other than tap very gently with its tiny warbler's beak. Other yellowish warblers are also indiscriminately called 'yellow hammers.'

yellow jacket: variety of horse-fly; deerfly (*Chrysops excitans*).

1957 *Daily News* 15 July, p. 2 Besides the mosquitoes, there were myriads of what I knew as Yellow Jackets. Some people call them moose flies.

yellow mores, ~ **snakeroot**: bog plant with a yellow threadlike underground stem used in home remedies (*Coptis groenlandica*) (1956 ROULEAU 40). See also MORE n, SNAKEROOT.

yes-ma'am n   Cp *DAE* thank-you-ma'am (1849–). Dip, bump or rut in a road; rut in snow, esp on a 'woods path.'

P 8–55 There was about twenty yes-ma'ams [in the snow] in the road. P 61–67 Yes-ma'ams [are] very quick dips in the snow. C 75–146 ~ Gulch or hole in the snow. P 40–78 ~ A place where the snow has been worn out in a woods road in winter, causing problems for horse-sleds travelling over it because the road dips too quickly in such places.

yess n   also **iss** *EDD* easse: yes(se) 'large earthworm' So Ha Gl Do; *NID* eaceworm. Earthworm.

1895 *J A Folklore* viii, 34 Earthworms are termed yesses. [c1900] 1978 *RLS* 8, p. 26 Yāsis—a term used in

Bonavista Bay for. . .earth worm. 1937 DEVINE 29, 57 Isses. . .yesses.

yoke n   *OED* ~ sb 2; *EDD* sb¹ 4 for sense 2.

1 Harness fitted on each of the animals in a dog-team.

1849 [FEILD] 49 He drives from six to twelve dogs, with a leader, and remains out with them days and nights together. . . Each dog [pulling the sled] has a yoke.

2 Wooden frame placed around the neck of sheep or goat to prevent it from entering fenced gardens; wooden device placed on a hen for similar purpose; SPANCEL n.

1924 ENGLAND 263 The fences are maintained to keep vagrant goats and sheep. . .from ravaging the meagre gardens. These animals often wear yokes; so too, the hens. A yoke on a hen is something of a novelty. At first I could not understand why so many of the domestic fowl had sticks lashed horizontally under their wings. T 43/8–64 There was a law passed for everybody to yoke their goats. They'd make this yoke oblong, and they bore two holes in it, and put a nail through from the outside. 1971 NOSEWORTHY 265 ~ Same as goats' collar. ('Looks like a triangle.') 1975 RUSSELL 9 The Ranger. . .measured the height of Grampa Walcott's fence and even brought the goat into court and measured his yoke.

yop n, v   (a) A quick bite and swallow; (b) to snap, bite.

P 148–65 A horse will yop your hand right off with his teeth if he is wild. P 108–77 She nearly yopped my head off when I told her I wouldn't do it. 1977 *Nfld Qtly* Summer, p. 9 That's all they give us. Well in one yop that was gone. We wanted more [to eat and drink], but the doctor said, 'no.'

yorkin(g)* See YARKIN(G).

young a   *OED* ~ a 5 c (1774, 1853), *DC* ~ ice (Nfld: 1835–) for sense 2.

1 Of various species of seal, designating an animal before breeding age: **young fat** [see FAT¹], ~ **harp** [see HARP], ~ **hood** [see HOOD], ~ **seal** [see SEAL].

1915 *FPU (Twillingate) Minutes* 5 Mar The Chairman then read a circular letter from the President urging among other things that men do not sign any agreement which would give them only 3.75 for young fat as he claims fat is worth today 4.75. 1924 ENGLAND 16 The 'young fat' brings higher prices than the old. . .all [sealing steamers] aim to hit the young fat as early as possible. [1766] 1971 BANKS 145 The Bedlamer [is] Quite dusky without any mark [the fishermen] themselves tell you that the Bedlamer is the young harp. 1852 ARCHIBALD 4–5 The best and most productive seal taken is the young harp. There are generally four different qualities in a cargo of seals,—namely, the young harp, young hood, old harp and bedlamer (the latter is the year old hood), and the old hood. 1955 DOYLE (ed) 74 "The Spring of '97": We struck the seals off Cabot Isle / . . .Eleven thousand prime young harps, / We put on board that day. T 141/2–65² 'Take thy gun,' he said, 'take thy gun and come on; there's a swile out there on the pan, a young harp.' [See 1852 quot above: Young hood.] 1868 WHITE *MS Journal* 30 Mar All hands on ice at daybreak took 1800 young Hoods and old [Hoods]. 1924 ENGLAND 24 Whitecoats and young hoods—which shed their white jacket in the whelping bag and are not white at birth—are swarming by the hundreds of thousands some two weeks before the legal date for the open season on seals—March 15th. T 68–64 By and by I seen one, a young hood, there ahead o' me. [1802] 1895 PROWSE 420 The five succeeding years may be averaged at six thousand each, and three-fourths of these may be reckoned young seals. T 172/3–65 They'd have their seal bottles, made out of sealskin, dried; and they'd have their old seal oil in certain bags, and they'd have their young seal oil, what they had for mixing their bread and their flour in, in [another bag].

2 Of salt-water ice, from 2–6 inches (5–15.2 cm) thick, newly-formed in the bays and harbours.

1836 [WIX]² 101 [They] were up at four a.m., and rowed me through 'the young ice,' which, from the frost at night, was, in some places, very thick, to Fachieu Harbour. 1916 GRENFELL 57 Day by day slipped by, and no westerly gale came to clear the coast of the young 'slob.' 1924 ENGLAND 20 The 'making' of the young ice is [the seals'] dispossess notice, evicting them from their summer home. 1944 LAWTON & DEVINE 95 We met some young ice just below Goose Head and rushed up into the South East Arm, where we met ice of two nights freezing. 1956 *Nfld & Lab Pilot* Supplement No 3, p. 11 Young ice. Newly-formed level ice generally in the transition stage of development from ice-rind, or pancake ice to winter-ice; thickness from 2 inches to 6 inches, as a rule impassable and unsafe for travel either by man or dogs, or in the case of aircraft for ski or wheel landings. Ibid Young shore ice. Primary stage of formation of shore ice: it is of local formation (at shore) and usually consists of ice-rind or thin young ice. T 393–67 'Twas early part o' January. And 'twas all young slob.

3 Phr *get in young*: see GET.

4 Comb **young fellow**: see YOUNG FELLOW.

young fellow n

1 Unmarried male under middle age; bachelor.

1900 *Tribune Christmas No* 10 The young fellows of St John's would make up little pleasure parties for 'Kitty's' and have 'a good time.' 1909 ibid 14 Many old time fishermen of the 19th century used to relate with gusto how on such and such an occasion, when he was a fine strapping young fellow, he opened the ball, by leading the 'Governor's Lady.' [1929] 1933 GREENLEAF (ed) 303 "The Cooks of Torbay": Come all ye young fellows wherever ye be, / I'll sing ye a verse on the cooks of Torbay. C 69–21 It is customary in Cow Head to call a man a 'young fellow' before he is married [regardless of age]. 1979 *Salt Water, Fresh Water* 83 I was supposed to be in Grade Six that September but now I was a full-fledged shareman, getting a full share, and had to be up in the morning at two

o'clock and go out and [jig] squid and the like and go fishing, and that's where I started as a young fellow.

2 Son; FELLOW.

1913 *Christmas Chimes* 15 Do 'ee min' how Abe slobbered th' stage 'ead wid blubber th' night Marchant Tom's young feller comed over yer fr'm Blow-me-down t' coort Libby? 1966 SZWED 130 I'm tired of supporting everybody's young fellow while he looks for jobs. 1973 PINSENT 3 I never told you what Wilf Anstey's young fellow said to me when I went to St John's. P 148–74 Phil's young fella; their young fellow. 1976 MATTHEWS 104 The young fellow cry when he got to go aboard the [school] bus in the morning for Lourdes.

3 Term of address to a male whose name is unknown; BUDDY.

P 148–60 Hey young f'la. C'm'ere, I wantcha.

youngster n *DC* ~ n Nfld (1792, 1964). (a) In the British migratory fishery in Newfoundland, inexperienced man brought out or 'shipped' for two summers and a winter; cp BOY, FRESH a: *fresh man*, GREEN MAN, WHITE-NOSE; (b) a novice at the seal hunt (1924 ENGLAND 323).

[1774] 1792 CARTWRIGHT ii, 25 From thence she is to proceed to Sandwich Bay with Joseph Friend, a youngster, and an apprentice, where they are to remain during the winter, to kill furs; and in the spring, to prepare for a salmon-fishery. [1776] 1976 HEAD 89 [advertisement in *Hibernian Chronicle* 1 Apr] For Harbour-Grace in Newfoundland. The *Hannah and Lydia* of Cork. . .will be ready to sail the 10th of April. For passage apply to said Master at Cove. Fishermen, Shoremen, and Youngsters are wanted. 1792 CARTWRIGHT *Gloss* i, xvi ~ A novitiate; a person in the first year, or early part of his servitude; one who has his business to learn. [1823] 1944 LAWTON & DEVINE 10 I have to suggest the propriety of sending to Mr Richard Fogarty to order him to ship three or four youngsters for us in Waterford next Spring and send them out by some vessel bound to St John's. He could choose stout country fellows that would be inured to hard labour. 1870 HOWLEY *MS Reminiscences* 8 Newman and Company an old English firm have extensive establishments both here and at Harbour Britain. The fishery is carried on by them on a real old time plan. Every year they bring out in their vessels a number of English boys or youngsters who are apprenticed for 3 or 4 years on small wages. 1893 *Trade Review Christmas No* 13 The term 'youngster,' as used among the planters and understood by the early settlers, did not necessarily imply youthfulness; on the contrary, many youngsters were stalwart, full-bearded sons of Erin and Britannia, whose inexperience in the fisheries of the country caused them to be classed as youngsters. 1937 DEVINE 57 ~ The term applied to the young English and Irish apprentices to the fishery. They were generally engaged for two summers and the intervening winter for about £18, their keep and a pair of long boots. C 68–7 Many of the older people in Grole talk about the youngsters who came out from England. There was one fellow. . .who had a few of these youngsters. [The people] had heard that many of these youngsters had been treated very bad by their master.

Z

zad* n *EDD* ~ sb s w cties. The letter Z (see
INTRODUCTION: The Dictionary and English
Language Variation in Newfoundland).

Corrections to the First Edition

Some three score corrections of the 1982 text of the Dictionary are set forth as follows: first in arabic or roman numerals the page reference, with the letter *a* or *b* indicating respectively the left- or right-hand column, then the erroneous reading closed by a square bracket, and finally the corrected reading of the text.

xxxvi a 1708 Nickolson] Nicholson
xxxix b 1864 1811–1885] 1810–1884
xl a [after TUCKER] 1878 *Nfld Pilot = The New-foundland Pilot, Comprising also the Strait of Belle Isle, and North-east Coast of Labrador* (London: Hydrographic Office, Admiralty, 1878)
xliv b [after BURKE] 1927 DOYLE = Gerald S. Doyle, 1892-1956, *The Old Time Songs and Poetry of Newfoundland* (St John's: [Manning & Rabbitts,] 1927)
xlv b [after LODGE] 1940 DOYLE = Gerald S. Doyle, *Old-time Songs and Poetry of Newfound-land*, 2d ed (St John's: Gerald S. Doyle, 1940)
xlvi b [after RUSSELL] 1955 DOYLE = Gerald S. Doyle, *Old-time Songs of Newfoundland*, 3d ed (St John's: Gerald S. Doyle, 1955)
xlix b 1917,] 1908-1984
lii a 1978 *Songs and Poetry of the*] *Songs and Poetry in the History of the*
liv a [after Douglass] Doyle, Gerald S. (1927); (1940); (1955)
lxi b P 2 Minnesota] Chicago
lxiii b P 190 Hungary/] Poland/
lxvi b [after T 393] T 395-67 R. Morey; La Scie
lxix b Kipness] Kipnis
lxx a [after Morey, R. T 393-67] , T 395-67
10 a arsed p ppl] arsed a
17 a bake-pot I forgot] I've forgot
17 b ball power and ball] powder and ball
26 b barrel tub *Nfld Magazine*] *Nfld Magazine & Advertiser*
27 b BARRICADE n.] BARRICADE v.
39 b 1976 TUCK 76] 75
42 a biff (Delete everything after n. Insert:)

Lapland longspur (*Calcarius lapponicus*) (P 88-161)
43 a bim Barbadoes] Barbados
53 b boat master] boat(s) master
80 b canadian [1776]] [1766], 1828] 1826
89 b 1879 TUCKER] [1847] 1877 TUCKER
126 b See CRUISE v for sense 2 and 3] See CRUISE n for sense 3
134 a daps* n pl] n
148 b down (folk) for sense 4.] (folk) for sense 3.
149 a Comb] 3 Comb
149 b draft] draft¹
150 a insert draft² See IN: IN-DRAFT
152 b drew* T 43/8] T 48
154 b 1881 KENNEDY of woods] of wood
163 a ellan] Delete entry
166 a 2 Comb, phr] 4 Phr etc
 [new division] 5 Comb *face-and-eye berry*, etc, *face clock*, etc
168 a fairy pipe Soctia] Scotia
187 a flacoon n [fl...] flacoon n pl: [fl...
188 a flake beam vertically] horizontally
193 b flouse n T 194/6-65] 194-65
216 b glavaun n] glauvaun n
222 b graple 'ta-k-'] 'tak'
233 a gunning Delete 1909 quot
238 b hand-gaff (7.6 cm)] (91.44 cm)
265 a see ice-glim above; LOOM.] see ice-glim above.
302 b lesser newfoundland] Delete entry
308 a livyer MILLIER] MILLYER; 1868...7] 1868...15 July
309 a loaf I forgot] I've forgot
327 b merchantable: ['məɹtʃn̩təbl̩]
343 a newfie 1976 WHALLEY] 1978 WHALLEY
381 a pitty n] pitty a
382 a planter 1610 adventures] adventure[r]s
431 a salt-bulk: see SALT-BULK] salt bulk: see SALT BULK.
434 b salt water 1977 COOK] 1975 COOK
455 b sealing Delete [1798] quotation
462 a settlement their old Harbours] their old [?out] Harbours

482 b **sinks** n pl] **sink** n; ~s The lead
495 a **slob** form of **slobice**] form of **slob ice**
520 a **squalling** ~/:] ~:/
542 a **strouter** 1973: on the rocks] or the rocks
557 a **talqual** $5.50] $5.30
572 a **tolt** kopj] kopje

Supplement

Preface to the Second Edition

The Dictionary which appeared in November 1982 and was subsequently thrice reissued was based on materials which had been assembled during the several decades preceding its publication and the volume represented a selection from a file of evidence considerably larger than that which we presented in print. The principles the selection was based on are set forth in the opening section of the original Introduction (Scope of the Dictionary) in which, discussing the place of the regional lexicon within the world community of English, we indicated our particular search for words and idioms which appear to have been recorded first, or solely, in Newfoundland; words characteristically Newfoundland by having continued in use here after they died out or declined elsewhere, or by having acquired a different form or developed a different meaning, or by displaying a distinctly higher or more general degree of use. We might, for the benefit of the unexpectedly broad readership which appears to have found the Dictionary of interest, have phrased these principles in another way as well, by indicating briefly the kinds of lexical usage current in Newfoundland but deliberately excluded from our published record.

The Dictionary omits, under our guiding principles, that part of the vocabulary common to. the general English-language speech-community, hence no main entry for *Felis catus*, but half a dozen **cat** entries or cross-references in other senses; no entry for *Canis familiaris*, but a dozen **dog** entries in assorted senses, collocations and combinations common to the region, and many other articles (**labrador dog**, **newfoundland dog**, **water dog**) for particular breeds principally associated with Newfoundland and Labrador. Such exclusions need no more than a bare mention here, but there are others which, because they involve words which frequently appear only in the largest and most comprehensive dictionaries, or in the great national dictionaries of English-speaking countries, or in specialized technical dictionaries, may not always be immediately recognized as of such widespread international or North American currency as to place them beyond the proper bounds of a rigorous regional dictionary. A large part of the task of editing our collections has been the winnowing process described in the Introduction and illustrated in Figure 1 (p. xiii) displaying how we handled such a large and diverse corpus of evidence. What needs to be remembered is that many of the activities around which a people's vocabulary develops and grows are introduced to particular regions from outside and therefore frequently come equipped with a specialized terminology which may, of course, be modified and adapted in local use but is rarely replaced. This is particularly true of introduced modern industrial operations: mining, logging and paper-making, for example, the industrial deep-sea fishery, oil exploration and exploitation and the like; and while all but the latter (too recent in Newfoundland to have given rise to any discernible local linguistic creations) have left their mark in special verbal invention or adaptations which of course the Dictionary records, just as often we have excluded other words because they are as common in similar industries elsewhere as they are in Newfoundland and therefore belong to the domain of general lexicography.

The second edition is a reissue of the 1982 work with a Supplement which has been compiled generally upon the same principles as the Dictionary of which it is an expansion and consolidation.

The sources upon which it rests are also, in general, of the kinds drawn upon in the earlier work: printed books and journals, manuscript material, and oral evidence in the form of tape-recordings and transcriptions, and field records, though the proportions of these differ somewhat from those indicated in the Dictionary (see Figure 3, p. xxvi). Central to the Supplement have been the full original Dictionary files. These have been thoroughly reviewed, particularly the material only partly used for the 1982 work: the substantial file of questionable items withheld earlier because many seemed insufficiently attested to warrant being published in authoritative form but which subsequent reports now authenticate; and occasionally the file of withdrawn words which, re-examined for one reason or another, we have been led to change our minds about including. (In a small number of instances we have also now suggested withdrawing a few entries from the Dictionary.)

More important, however, is the fresh material that has been gathered since the original work went to press: field notes from another decade of collecting; transcription of tape-recordings (often from unexcerpted tapes of interviews with informants already named in the 1982 publication, but with others as well); and, in proportions somewhat greater than in the Dictionary, printed evidence, augmented by fresh historical manuscripts. These are incorporated in the chronological list of printed sources, stretching from the late fifteenth century onward. The printed quotations draw from time to time on some works used in the earlier Dictionary but also come from

many others available to us for the first time, particularly works which have been published since the Dictionary left our hands towards the end of 1980. The steady increase of printed material relating to Newfoundland and Labrador which began in the 1940s continued unabated during the 1980s so that when, between January 1988 and April 1990, the Supplement was being written we were able to draw upon a large corpus of poems, fiction, personal reminiscence, biography, history, technical reports and specialist studies, as well as contemporary newspapers, as we monitored the language and selected the evidence for presentation. This is not the place to draw in a formal way the conclusions this recently available material suggests, except to remark that we find little evidence of the retreat of the traditional vocabulary which is so often predicted and that many regional writers are actively extending the metaphoric uses of the Newfoundland vocabulary.

The presentation of the dictionary articles in this Supplement follows, with some necessary and mostly self-evident exceptions, that of the Dictionary. New entries appear in precisely the manner of the parent work: the Main Word in **bold type**, variant spellings where they exist, part of speech, comparative evidence on occasion, definitions, and illustrative quotations from printed and oral sources. There are scores of these new entries in the Supplement throughout the whole alphabetical range from **a-** to **zosweet**, and many hundreds if one also reckons the numerous additional phrases and new combinations, each with its definition and illustration. Readers should also note the considerable number of articles which present substantial revisions of entries in the Dictionary made possible by fresh evidence; examples include **bakeapple**, **catamaran**, **jackatar**, **killick**.

A large proportion of the Supplement articles, however, fall into another category and it is one which may be included for any one of a number of reasons. Most frequent is that the additional data enables us to antedate, post-date, or fill out intervening evidence with fresh quotations now added to the record.

Some of these are historically of considerable importance, enabling us to push back the date of earliest occurrence by a century or more (**desperate, mosquito, scattered**), or to find in recent literature an item not previously recorded in modern times (e.g. **chinsing, filling, papoose, post**). All of them enable us to present a more complete word history, and in the simplest examples the form of presentation is restricted to that purpose, the definition is not repeated from the Dictionary nor is other material from the headnote of the entry given again. Sometimes, however, the discovery of further quotations has also enabled us to revise or refine the earlier definition, and this may be signalled by a definition beginning 'Also:', or else by a newly numbered sense. Frequently we have been able to record additional material helpful in relating the Newfoundland term to usage elsewhere, as when we now add to the evidence of the *English Dialect Dictionary* (1905) data from the southwest counties presented in the *Survey of English Dialects* of Orton and Wakelin (1967). The 1980s have been remarkable for either the completion or the launching of a number of major English dictionaries: hence the Supplement systematically records in the headnotes relevant material from such recent works as the *Dictionary of Bahamian English* (1982), volume I of the *Dictionary of American Regional English* (1985), *The Australian National Dictionary* (1988), the *Dictionary of Prince Edward Island English* (1988), as well as the final two volumes of *A Supplement to the Oxford English Dictionary* (1982, 1986) and the *Oxford English Dictionary*, Second Edition (1989). Readers of the Supplement should understand that the form of entries is necessarily varied, and although many of the articles are complete and self-explanatory, others call upon an interested reader to consider them in light of the main Dictionary entry which is being supplemented in the present work; comparison of one with the other is, therefore, a recommended systematic procedure.

Since the appearance of the Dictionary colleagues and readers have offered comments and quotations and answered questions on matters in specialized fields. Without this freely given assistance, many fine points in the Supplement would not be so confidently treated. The editors express their gratitude to the following at Memorial University of Newfoundland: Frederick A. Aldrich, Raoul Andersen, Donald R. Bartlett, Tom Dawe, Herbert Halpert, W. Gordon Handcock, Leslie Harris, Robert C. Hollett, Alan Macpherson, Elizabeth Miller, William A. Montevecchi, Patrick O'Flaherty, Peter Pope, Hans Rollman, the late E.R. Seary, Peter Scott, and Michael Wilkshire. And to other scholars and correspondents elsewhere: Frederic G. Cassidy (Wisconsin), Niels W. Jannasch (Nova Scotia), Harry Orsman (Wellington, New Zealand), W.S. Ramson (Canberra), Philip E.L. Smith (Montreal), Janet Story (St John's), Russell Tabbert (Fairbanks).

In the final phase of our work the editors were greatly helped in processing the Supplement with a computer-assisted technology by Laura Taylor.

Attention is drawn to the list of Corrections of the 1982 Dictionary which precedes this Supplement in the book. We once again invite readers to draw our attention to any errors or omissions.

G.M. STORY
W.J. KIRWIN
St John's, Newfoundland

J.D.A. WIDDOWSON
Sheffield, England

April 1990

Bibliography

PRINTED SOURCES

Chronological List

[c1497–1522] 1962 *Cabot Voyages* (ed Williamson) = *The Cabot Voyages and Bristol Discovery under Henry VII*, ed James Alexander Williamson, b 1886 (Cambridge: Published for the Hakluyt Society, 1962)

[1578] 1935 *Richard Hakluyt* [Parkhurst's letter] = *The Original Writings & Correspondence of the Two Richard Hakluyts*, vol. i, ed E.G.R. Taylor (London: The Hakluyt Society, 1935)

[1610–30] 1982 CELL (ed) = Gillian T. Cell (ed), *Newfoundland Discovered: English Attempts at Colonisation, 1610-1630* (London: The Hakluyt Society, 1982)

[c1610–1634] *Willoughby Papers* = a collection of inventories and letters relating to the colony at Cupids, preserved in the Middleton MSS (Mi X) at Nottingham University.

1626 [VAUGHAN] *The Golden Fleece* = Sir William Vaughan, 1575–1641, *The Golden Fleece ...Transported from...the Newfoundland, by Orpheus Iunior* (London: Printed for Francis Williams, 1626)

[1663–70] 1963 YONGE = James Yonge, 1647–1721, *The Journal of James Yonge, Plymouth Surgeon*, ed F.N.L. Poynter (London: Longmans, 1963)

1689 *English Pilot* = *The English Pilot, The Fourth Book* (London: Printed for William Fisher and John Thornton, 1689)

1703 LAHONTAN (ed Thwaites) = *Lahontan's New Voyages to North-America, 1666–1715?*, ed Reuben Gold Thwaites, 2 vols. (New York: Burt Franklin, 1905; rpt 1970)

1708 OLDMIXON = John Oldmixon, 1673–1742, *The British Empire in America*, 2 vols. (London: J. Nicholson, B. Tooke, 1708)

1724 TREBY = Henry Treby, *A Narrative of the Shipwreck and Distress Suffered by Mr Thomas Manson, of Lympson in Devon, and His Ship's Crew, near the Coast of Newfoundland, in the Year 1704* (Exon: Andrew Brice, 1724)

[1766] 1971 BANKS (ed Lysaght) = Sir Joseph Banks, 1743–1820, *Joseph Banks in Newfoundland and Labrador 1766: His Diary, Manuscripts and Collections*, ed A.M. Lysaght (Berkeley: University of California Press, 1971)

[1768] 1828 CARTWRIGHT = F.D. Cartwright (ed), *The Life and Correspondence of Major [John] Cartwright, [1740–1824]*, 2 vols. (London: Colburn, 1826)

[1783] 1955 GARDNER = James Anthony Gardner, 1770-1846, *Above and under Hatches: being Naval Recollections in shreds and patches with strange reflections*, ed Christopher Lloyd (London: The Batchworth Press, 1955)

[1792] 1989 PULLING (ed Marshall) = Ingeborg C.L. Marshall, *Reports and Letters by George Christopher Pulling Relating to the Beothuk Indians of Newfoundland, [1766–1819]* (St John's: Breakwater Books, 1989)

[1794] 1968 THOMAS = Aaron Thomas, Able Seaman in H.M.S. *Boston*, b 1762, *The Newfoundland Journal of Aaron Thomas*, ed Jean M. Murray (London: Longmans, 1968)

[1799] 1801 [THORESBY] = *A Narrative of God's Love to William Thoresby*, b 1763?, 2nd ed (Redruth: Printed by J. Bennett, 1801)

[1807] 1971 HERIOT = George Heriot, 1766–1844, *Travels through the Canadas* (London: Richard Phillips, 1807; rpt. Toronto: Coles Publishing, 1971)

1818 CHAPPELL = Edward Chappell, 1792–1861, *Voyage of His Majesty's Ship* Rosamond *to Newfoundland and the Southern Coast of Labrador* (London: Printed for J. Mawman, 1818)

1819 ANSPACH = Lewis Amadeus Anspach, *A History of the Island of Newfoundland* (London: Printed for the Author, 1819)

1821–24 LATHAM = John L. Latham, 1740–1837, *A General History of Birds* (Winchester: Jacob and Johnson, 1821–24)

1832 MOSS *MS Diary* = Moss Diary, 1832: 'Remarks at Battle Harbor [Labrador] from 9th. Feb. 1832 until 7th. Sept. 1832.' (P3/B/3, PANL)

[1833–47] 1984–86 BAYFIELD = Henry Wolsey Bayfield, 1795–1885, *The St Lawrence Survey Journals of Captain Henry Wolsey Bayfield*, 2 vols, ed Ruth McKenzie (Toronto: The Champlain Society, 1984, 1986)

1837 BLUNT = Edmund M. Blunt, 1770–1862, *The American Coast Pilot*, 13th ed (New York: Edmund and George W. Blunt, 1837)

1837–42 ENGLAND *MS Journal* = Rev. James England, ?1815–1878, manuscript journal of Wesleyan missionary activities largely in Conception Bay, in possession of Edward Chafe

1839 TUCKER = Ephraim W. Tucker, b 1821, *Five Months in Labrador and Newfoundland* (Concord: I.S. Boyd and W. White, 1839)

1842 BONNYCASTLE = Sir Richard Henry Bonnycastle, 1791–1848, *Newfoundland in 1842*, 2 vols. (London: H. Colburn, 1842)

1842 JUKES = Joseph Beete Jukes, 1811–1869, *Excursions in and about Newfoundland, during the Years 1839 and 1840*, 2 vols. (London: John Murray, 1842)

[1846–50] 1983 [ROUSE] (ed Street) = *The Journal of Oliver Rouse Anglican Missionary in Newfoundland: September 1846 to May 1850*, [1820–1869], ed John C. Street (Madison, Wis.: John C. Street, 1983)

1849 TOCQUE = Rev. Philip Tocque, 1814–1899, comp *Newfoundland Almanack, for...1849* (St John's: Philip Tocque, 1849)

1854 MOSS *MS Journal* = William P. Moss, b 1838, manuscript journal deposited in Centre for Newfoundland Studies Archives

1857–1864 LIND *MS Diary* = Rev. Henry Lind, 1805-1870, manuscript diary of residence at Sandy Point, St George's Bay, deposited in Centre for Newfoundland Studies

[?1858 GREY] = William Grey, 1819–1872, *Sketches of Newfoundland and Labrador* (Ipswich: S.H. Cowell, [1858])

1858 [LOWELL] = Robert Lowell, 1816–1891, *The New Priest in Conception Bay*, 2 vols. (Boston: Phillips, Sampson and Company, 1858)

1861 DE BOILIEU = Lambert De Boilieu, *Recollections of Labrador Life* (London: Saunders, Otley & Co., 1861; Toronto: Ryerson Press, 1969)

1863 HIND = Henry Yule Hind, 1823–1908, *Explorations in the Interior of the Labrador Peninsula*, 2 vols. (London: Longman, Green, Longman, Roberts & Green, 1863)

1863 MORETON = Rev. Julian Moreton, b 1825, *Life and Work in Newfoundland: Reminiscences of Thirteen Years Spent There* (London: Rivingtons, 1863)

1865 [CAMPBELL] = J.F. Campbell, 1822–1885, *A Short American Tramp in the Fall of 1864* (Edinburgh: Edmonston and Douglas, 1865)

1866 WILSON = Rev. William Wilson, 1800?–1870, *Newfoundland and Its Missionaries* (Cambridge, Mass.: Dakin & Metcalf, 1866)

[1867] 1989 CHIMMO (ed Kirwin) = *William Chimmo's Journal of a Voyage to the N.E. Coast of Labrador during the Year 1867* ed William J. Kirwin (St John's: The editor, 1989)

1871 [JUKES] = *Letters and Extracts from the Addresses and Occasional Writings of J. Beete Jukes* [ed C.A. Browne] (London: Chapman and Hall, 1871)

1871 LOVELL = *Lovell's Province of Newfoundland Directory for 1871* (Montreal: John Lovell, [1871?])

1878 *Nfld Pilot* = *The Newfoundland Pilot, Comprising also the Strait of Belle Isle, and Northeast Coast of Labrador* (London: Hydrographic Office, Admiralty, 1878)

1883 HATTON & HARVEY = Joseph Hatton, 1841–1907, and Rev. M. Harvey, 1820–1901, *Newfoundland: The Oldest British Colony, Its History, Its Present Condition, and Its Prospects in the Future* (London: Chapman and Hall, Limited, 1883)

1884 DEMING = Clarence Deming, 1848–1913, *By-Ways of Nature and Life* (New York: G.P. Putnam's Sons, 1884)

1885 TUTTLE = Charles R. Tuttle, b 1848, *Our North Land* (Toronto: C. Blackett Robinson, 1885)

1895 PROWSE = D.W. Prowse, 1834–1914, *A History of Newfoundland from the English, Colonial, and Foreign Records* (London: Macmillan and Co., 1895)

1896 SARSON = Sarson [Sarson C.J. Ingham] *Adelaide's Treasure* (London: Wesleyan Conference Office, 1880)

[1896] SWANSBOROUGH = W. Swansborough, *Newfoundland Months* (St John's: G.S. Milligan, Jr., [1896])

1902 [MURPHY] = [James Murphy, 1867–1931] *Songs and Ballads of Newfoundland, Ancient and Modern* (St John's: [James Murphy], 1902)

1904 MCALPINE = *McAlpine's Newfoundland Directory for 1904* (Halifax: McAlpine Publishing Company, Limited, 1904)

1904 PEDDEL = N[icholas] Peddel, '*Home Sweet Home'; Newfoundland Poems* (n.p.: Standard Press, 1904)

1906 MURPHY = James Murphy, comp *The Musty Past* (St John's: Barnes' Print, 1906)

1907 MILLAIS = J.G. Millais, 1865-1931, *Newfoundland and Its Untrodden Ways* (London: Longmans, Green and Co., 1907)

1907 TOWNSEND & ALLEN = Charles W. Townsend, M.D., b 1859, and Glover M. Allen, *Birds of Labrador* (Boston: Printed for the Society [of Natural History], 1907) = *Proceedings of the Boston Society of Natural History*, vol. xxxiii, no. 7, 277–428

1909 BROWNE = Rev. P.W. Browne, 1864–1937, *Where the Fishers Go: The Story of Labrador* (New York: Cochrane Publishing Company, 1909)

1910 MOUBRAY = J.M. Moubray, *Notes on Some of the Common Minerals to be Found in Labrador and Newfoundland. For the Use of Fishermen and Liviers More Particularly in Labrador* (St John's: J.M. Moubray, 1910)

1912 DUNCAN = Norman Duncan, 1871–1916, *The Best of a Bad Job: A Hearty Tale of the Sea* (New York: Fleming H. Revell Company, 1912)

1913 THOMAS = William S. Thomas, b 1858, *Trails and Tramps in Alaska and Newfoundland* (New York: G.P. Putnam's Sons, 1913)

1915 HOWLEY = James P. Howley, 1847–1918, *The Beothucks or Red Indians; The Aboriginal Inhabitants of Newfoundland* (Cambridge: Cambridge University Press, 1915)

1919 GRENFELL[2] = Wilfred Thomason Grenfell, 1865–1940, *A Labrador Doctor: The Autobiography of Wilfred Thomason Grenfell* (Boston: Houghton Mifflin Company, 1919)

1923 MOSDELL = H.M. Mosdell, 1883–1944, *When Was That? A Chronological Dictionary of Important Events in Newfoundland* (St John's: Trade Printers and Publishers, Limited, 1923)

1924 ENGLAND = George Allan England, 1877–1936, *Vikings of the Ice* (Garden City: Doubleday, Page & Company, 1924)

1924 MARS = P.C. Mars, *The Call of Terra Nova* (London: Whitehead Morris, 1924)

1925 TURNER = George E. Turner, *Map of Newfoundland* ([St John's:] Government of Newfoundland, 1925)

1929 TRICOCHE = George Nestler Tricoche, b 1859?, *Terre-Neuve et alentours; îles de la Madeleine, Labrador, St Pierre-et-Miquelon* (Paris: P. Roger, [1929])

1930 COAKER = *Twenty Years of the Fishermen's Protective Union of Newfoundland from 1909–1929*, compiled by Hon. Sir W.F. Coaker, 1871–1938 (St John's: Advocate Publishing Co. Ltd, 1930 [facsimile rpt 1984])

1930 KENT = Rockwell Kent, 1882–1971, *N by E* (Cornwall, N.Y.: The Cornwall Press, 1930)

1932 AUSTIN = Oliver Luther Austin, Jr., *The Birds of Newfoundland Labrador* (Cambridge: Nuttall Ornithological Club, Memoir No. 7, 1932)

1933 *Nfld Royal Commission Report* = [Lord Amulree], *Newfoundland Royal Commission 1933 Report* (London: H.M. Stationery Office, 1933)

1936 SMITH = Nicholas Smith, b 1866, *Fifty-two Years at the Labrador Fishery* (London: Arthur H. Stockwell, 1936)

1937–75 *Bk of Nfld* = *The Book of Newfoundland*, ed J.R. Smallwood, b 1900, vols. i, ii (St John's: Newfoundland Book Publishers, Ltd., 1937); iii, iv (St John's: Newfoundland Book Publishers (1967) Ltd., 1967); v, vi (St John's: Newfoundland Book Publishers (1967) Ltd., 1975)

1937 DEVINE = P.K. Devine, 1859–1950, *Devine's Folk Lore of Newfoundland in Old Words, Phrases and Expressions, Their Origin and Meaning* (St John's: Robinson & Co., Ltd., 1937)

[1937] 1983 FROUDE = John W. Froude, *On the High Seas: The Diary of Capt. John W. Froude, Twillingate—1863–1939* (St John's: Jesperson Press, 1983)

1937 JUNEK = Oscar Waldemar Junek, *Isolated Communities; A Study of a Labrador Fishing Village* (New York: American Book Company, 1937)

1937 *Seafisheries of Nfld* = [Hon. Mr Justice Kent et al], *Report of the Commission of Enquiry Investigating the Seafisheries of Newfoundland and Labrador Other than the Sealfishery 1937* (St John's: Dicks & Co., Ltd., 1937)

1938 [MACDERMOTT] = [Hugh MacDermott], *MacDermott of Fortune Bay, Told by Himself* (London: Hodder and Stoughton, Limited, 1938)

1939 ALDRICH & NUTT = John W. Aldrich and David C. Nutt, 'Birds of Eastern Newfoundland.' *Cleveland Museum of Natural History Scientific Publications*, vol. iv, no. 2 (1939), 13–42

1941 SMALLWOOD = J.R. Smallwood (ed), *Hand Book, Gazetteer and Almanac* (St John's: Long Bros., [1941])

1945 MARTIN = Ronald Martin, ed and comp *Poems of Action, Sentiment and Reflection* (St John's: [Manning & Rabbitts], 1945)

1945 SCAMMELL = A.R. Scammell, b 1913, *Mirrored Moments* (Montreal: [privately printed], 1945)

1949 FITZGERALD = L.G. Fitzgerald, 1898–1965, *Lone Eagles of God* (New York: The Exposition Press, 1949)

1961 ROULEAU = Ernest Rouleau, b 1915, comp *A Gazetteer of the Island of Newfoundland* ([Montreal,] 1961)

1965 PEACOCK (ed) = Kenneth Peacock (ed), b 1922, *Songs of the Newfoundland Outports*, 3 vols. (Ottawa: The National Museum of Canada, 1965)

1966 FARIS = James C. Faris, *Cat Harbour: A Newfoundland Fishing Settlement* (St John's: Memorial University ISER, 1966)

1966 GUNN = Gertrude E. Gunn, b 1923, *The Political History of Newfoundland 1832–1864* (Toronto: University of Toronto Press, 1966)

1966 SCAMMELL = A.R. Scammell, *My Newfoundland: Stories, Poems, Songs* (Montreal: Harvest House, 1966)

1968 KEATING = Bern Keating, *The Grand Banks* (Chicago: Rand McNally & Company, 1968)

1968 SMITH = Marjorie Smith, 'Newfoundland, 1815–1840: A Study of Merchantocracy' (St John's: Memorial University M.A. Thesis, 1968)

1968 MOWAT & DE VISSER = Farley Mowat, b 1921, and John De Visser, *This Rock within the Sea: A Heritage Lost* (Boston: Little Brown, 1968)

1970 JANNASCH = Hans-Windekilde Jannasch, *Erziehung zur Freiheit; Ein Lebensbericht* (Göttingen: Vandenhoeck & Ruprecht, 1970)

1971 SEARY = E.R. Seary, 1908–1984, *Place Names of the Avalon Peninsula of the Island of Newfoundland* (Toronto: University of Toronto Press, 1971)

1971 TULK = Bob Tulk, *Newfoundland Jokes* (Mount Pearl: Nfld., 1971)

1972 ANDERSEN & WADEL (eds) = Raoul Andersen and Cato Wadel (eds), *North Atlantic Fishermen: Anthropological Essays on Modern Fishing* (St John's: Institute of Social and Economic Research, Memorial University of Newfoundland, 1972)

1972 DE VOLPI = Charles P. De Volpi, b 1910, *Newfoundland; A Pictorial Record...1497–1887* ([Don Mills:] Longman Canada Limited, 1972)

1973 BARBOUR = Florence Grant Barbour, *Memories of Life on the Labrador and in Newfoundland* (New York: Carlton Press, 1973)

1973 PINSENT = Gordon Pinsent, b 1930 *The Rowdyman* (Toronto: McGraw-Hill Ryerson Limited, 1973)

1974 MOAKLER = Michael J. Moakler, *Roll On, Grand Banks! The Saga of the Grand Banks of Newfoundland* (n.p.: Michael J. Moakler, 1974)

1975 BUTLER = Victor Butler, 1896–1981, *The Little Nord Easter: Reminiscences of a Placentia Bayman*, ed W. Wareham (St John's: Memorial University, 1975)

1975 'Labrador Childhood' = From *Erziehung zur Freiheit*, Autobiography of Hans-Windekilde Jannasch, trans. L.H. Neatby (TS, 1975)

1976 HEAD = C. Grant Head, *Eighteenth Century Newfoundland: A Geographer's Perspective* (Toronto: McClelland and Stewart Limited, 1976)

1976 HOLLETT = Robert Hollett, 'Allegro Speech' (St John's: Memorial University M.Phil. essay, 1976)

1976 MERCER = Paul Mercer, comp *Newfoundland Songs and Ballads in Print 1842–1974: A Title and First-line Index* (St John's: Memorial University of Newfoundland, 1979)

1977 LAMB = James B. Lamb, *The Corvette Navy* (Toronto: Macmillan of Canada, [1977])

1977 WHITELEY = Albert S. Whiteley, *A Century on Bonne Espérance; The Saga of the Whiteley Family* (Ottawa: the author, 1977)

1977 *Nfld Hist Soc*, Winton File MS = Name File, Records of the Newfoundland Historical Society, Colonial Building, St John's

1977 *Peopling of Nfld* = The Peopling of Newfoundland: Essays in Historical Geography, ed John J. Mannion, b 1941 (St John's: Memorial University ISER, 1977)

1979 COOPER = Georgiana Cooper, 1885–1980, *The Deserted Island; Newfoundland Verse and Paintings*, ed Harry A. Cuff and Everard H. King (St John's: [Harry Cuff,] 1979)

1979 GRAHAM = Frank W. Graham, *'We Love Thee, Newfoundland': Biography of Sir Cavendish Boyle* (St John's: Valhalla Press, 1979)

1979 PORTER = Helen Porter, *Below The Bridge: Memories of the South Side of St John's* (St John's: Breakwater, 1979)

1980 COX = Gordon S.A. Cox, *Folk Music in a Newfoundland Outport* (Ottawa: National Museums of Canada, 1980)

1980 *Halpert Festschrift* = Folklore Studies in Honour of Herbert Halpert: A Festschrift, ed Kenneth S. Goldstein and Neil V. Rosenberg (St John's: Memorial University of Newfoundland, 1980)

1980 HOLMES = Albert N. Holmes, *A Boat of My Own* (St John's: Harry Cuff Publications, 1980)

1980 JANES = Percy Janes, b 1922, *Light and Dark: Poems* (St John's: Harry Cuff Publications, 1980)

1981 DAWE = Tom Dawe, *Island Spell: Poems by Tom Dawe* (St John's: Harry Cuff Publications Limited, 1981)

1981-84 *Encyclopedia of Nfld and Labrador* = Encyclopedia of Newfoundland and Labrador, first 2 vols., Joseph R. Smallwood, ed in chief (St John's: Newfoundland Book Publishers (1967) Limited, 1981, 1984)

1981 MAJOR = Kevin Major, *Hold Fast* (New York: Dell Publishing Company, 1981)

1981 PADDOCK = Harold Paddock, *Tung Tyde* (St John's: Harry Cuff Publications, 1981)

1981 SPARKES = R.F. Sparkes, b 1906, *The Winds Softly Sigh* (St John's: Breakwater Books, 1981)

1982 BURKE (ed Kirwin) = *John White's Collection of the Songs of Johnny Burke*, ed William J. Kirwin (St John's: Harry Cuff Publications Limited, 1982)

1982 BURSEY = Wallace Bursey, *No Right of Spring* (St John's: Harry Cuff Publications Limited, 1982)

1982 DAWE = Tom Dawe, *A Gommil from Bumble Bee Bight and Other Nonsense Verse* (St John's: Harry Cuff Publications Limited, 1982)

1982 JACKSON = Lawrence Jackson, *Bounty of a Barren Coast; Resource Harvest and Settlement in Southern Labrador* (Happy Valley: Labrador Institute of Northern Studies, 1982)

1982 *Lgs in Nfld* = *Languages in Newfoundland and Labrador*, 2nd version, ed Harold J. Paddock (St John's: Memorial University, Department of Linguistics, 1982)

1982 MCDOOLING = Jim William McDooling, 'The Fishermen: Transition in a Northeast Coastal Community in Newfoundland' (Fredericton: University of New Brunswick M.A. Thesis, 1982)

1982 MADISON (ed) = R.D. Madison (ed), *Newfoundland Summers: The Ballad Collecting of Elisabeth Bristol Greenleaf* (Westerly, R.I.: Utter Company, 1982)

1983 DAWE & FICKEN = Tom Dawe and Sylvia Ficken, *Angishore, Boo-man and Clumper: A Newfoundland Folk Alphabet* (St John's: Harry Cuff Publications Limited, 1983)

1983 *Gazetteer of Canada: Nfld* = *Gazetteer of Canada: Newfoundland*, 2nd ed (Ottawa: Energy, Mines and Resources Canada, 1983)

1983 *Gazetteer of Undersea Feature Names* = *Gazetteer of Undersea Feature Names* (Ottawa: Department of Fisheries and Oceans, 1983)

1983 MARTIN = Wendy Martin, *Once Upon a Mine: Story of Pre-Confederation Mines on the Island of Newfoundland* (Montreal: The Canadian Institute of Mining and Metallurgy, 1983)

1983 NEARY & O'FLAHERTY = Peter Neary and Patrick O'Flaherty, *Part of the Main: An Illustrated History of Newfoundland and Labrador* (St John's: Breakwater Books, 1983)

1983 PEDDLE = Walter W. Peddle, *The Traditional Furniture of Outport Newfoundland* (St John's: Harry Cuff Publications Limited, 1983)

1983 ROWE = C. Francis Rowe et al, *The Currency and Medals of Newfoundland* (Willowdale, Ont.: The Numismatic Education Society of Canada, 1983)

1983 SOUTH (ed) = G. Robin South (ed), *Biogeography and Ecology of the Island of Newfoundland* (The Hague-Boston-London: Monographiae Biologicae, vol. 48, Dr W. Junk Publishers, 1983)

1983 WARNER = William W. Warner, *Distant Water: The Fate of the North Atlantic Fisherman* (Boston: Little, Brown and Company, 1983)

1984 BYRNE (ed) = Cyril J. Byrne (ed), *Gentlemen-Bishops and Faction Fighters: The Letters of Bishops O Donel, Lambert, Scallan and Other Irish Missionaries* (St John's: Jesperson Press, 1984)

1984 GOUGH = William Gough, *Maud's House* (St John's: Breakwater, 1984)

1984 KALLEO = Josephina Kalleo, *Taipsumane: A Collection of Labrador Stories* (Nain, Labrador: Torngâsok Cultural Centre, 1984)

1984 KELLAND = Otto P. Kelland, b 1904, *Dories and Dorymen* (St John's: Robinson-Blackmore, 1984)

1984-87 PITT = David G. Pitt, b 1921, *E.J. Pratt: The Truant Years 1882–1927; E.J. Pratt: The Master Years 1927–1964* (Toronto: University of Toronto Press, 1984, 1987)

1984 PITTMAN = Al Pittman, *The Boughwolfen and Other Stories* [St John's: Breakwater, 1984]

1984 POWELL = Ben Powell, *Labrador by Choice* (St John's: Jesperson Press, 1984)

1984 ROBERTSON = Margaret R. Robertson, *The Newfoundland Mummers' Christmas House-Visit* (Ottawa: National Museum of Canada, 1984)

1984 WRIGHT = Guy David Wright, *Sons and Seals: A Voyage to the Ice* (St John's: Institute of Social and Economic Research, Memorial University of Newfoundland, 1984)

1985 ASHTON = John Ashton, 'A Study of the Lumbercamp Song Tradition in Newfoundland' (St John's: Memorial University Ph.D. Thesis, 1985)

1985 BUSCH = Briton Cooper Busch, *The War against the Seals: A History of the North American Seal Fishery* (Kingston and Montreal: McGill-Queen's University Press, 1985)

1985 *Canadian Sealers Assoc* = *The Canadian Sealers Association Presentation to The Royal Commission, Feb. 4*

1985 DOMSTAD = Maureen Domstad and Udayakanthie Wijewanthe, *Folk Medicine in the Bonne Bay Area* ([Canada: The authors], 1985)

1985 GOSSE = John S.R. Gosse, *Whitbourne, Newfoundland's First Inland Town: Journey Back in Time 1884–1984* [Whitbourne: Intercollegiate Press, 1985]

1985 GUY = Ray Guy, *This Dear and Fine Country*, ed Eric Norman (St John's: Breakwater Books Ltd, 1985)

1985 JOHNSTON = Wayne Johnston, *The Story of Bobby O'Malley* (Toronto: Oberon Press, 1985)

1985 LEHR & BEST (eds) = Genevieve Lehr and Anita Best (eds), *Come and I Will Sing You: A Newfoundland Songbook* (Toronto: University of Toronto Press, 1985)

[1985] MAHER = Alfred V. Maher, *My Memoirs; Memories of Sixty Years 1922–1982* (St John's: The author, 1985)

1985 NEWHOOK = Cle Newhook, *Mostly in Rodneys* (St John's: Harry Cuff Publications Limited, 1985)

1985 QUIGLEY = Colin Quigley, *Close to the Floor: Folk Dance in Newfoundland* (St John's:

Memorial University of Newfoundland Folklore and Language Publications, 1985)

1985 RUSTED = Nigel Rusted, *It's Devil Deep Down There: 50 years ago on the M.V.* Lady Anderson, *a mobile clinic on the S.W. coast of Newfoundland* (St John's: Occasional Papers in the History of Medicine No. 5, Memorial University of Newfoundland, 1985)

1985 TAYLOR = V.R. Taylor, *The Early Atlantic Salmon Fishery in Newfoundland and Labrador* (Ottawa: Department of Fisheries and Oceans, 1985)

1985 *Terminology of Loggers* = *The Terminology of Early Newfoundland Loggers.* Co-ordinator, George F. Draskoy ([St John's:] Government of Newfoundland and Labrador, Dept. of Culture, Recreation and Youth, 1985)

1985 *A Yaffle of Yarns* = *A Yaffle of Yarns: Five Newfoundland Writers* (St John's: Harry Cuff Publications Limited, 1985)

1986 *Biblio of Nfld* = *Bibliography of Newfoundland*, comp Agnes C. O'Dea, ed Anne Alexander, 2 vols. (Toronto: University of Toronto Press, in association with Memorial University of Newfoundland, 1986)

1986 FELTHAM = John Feltham, *The Islands of Bonavista Bay* (St John's: Harry Cuff Publications Limited, 1986)

1986 GOUDIE = Ed Goudie, 1869–1944, with Robert E. Johns, *Log of a Sealer* (Seattle: Robert E. Johns, 1986)

1986 HISCOCK = Philip Douglas Hiscock, 'Folklore and Popular Culture in Early Newfoundland Radio Broadcasting: An Analysis of Occupational Narrative, Oral History and Song Repertoire' (St John's: Memorial University M.A. Thesis, 1986)

1986 NARVÁEZ = Peter Narváez, 'The Protest Songs of a Labor Union on Strike against an American Corporation in a Newfoundland Company Town; A Folkloristic Analysis' [Ph.D. Dissertation, Indiana University] (University Microfilms International, Ann Arbor, Mich., 1986)

1986 *Nfld's Deepsea Fishery* = *The Social Impact of Technological Change in Newfoundland's Deepsea Fishery* ([St John's:] Institute of Social and Economic Research, Memorial University of Newfoundland, 1986)

1986 RYAN = Shannon Ryan, *Fish out of Water: The Newfoundland Saltfish Trade 1814–1914* (St John's: Breakwater Books, 1986)

1986 SAUNDERS = Gary L. Saunders, *Rattles and Steadies: Memoirs of a Gander River Man* (St John's: Breakwater Books, 1986)

1986 SIDER = Gerald M. Sider, *Culture and Class in Anthropology and History: A Newfoundland Illustration* (Cambridge: Cambridge University Press, 1986)

1987 DAWE = Tom Dawe, *Alley-Coosh, Bibby and Cark: A Second Newfoundland Folk Alphabet* (St John's: Harry Cuff Publications Limited, 1987)

1987 FELT = Lawrence F. Felt, *'Take the "Bloods of Bitches" to the Gallows': Cultural and Structural Constraints upon Interpersonal Violence in Rural Newfoundland* (St John's: Memorial University of Newfoundland, Institute of Social and Economic Research, Research and Policy Papers, No. 6, 1987)

1987 FIZZARD = Garfield Fizzard, *Unto the Sea: A History of Grand Bank* (Grand Bank: Grand Bank Heritage Society, 1987)

1987 HORWOOD = Harold Horwood, *Dancing on the Shore: A Celebration of Life at Annapolis Basin* (Toronto: McClelland and Stewart, 1987)

1987 JOHNSTON = Wayne Johnston, *The Time of Their Lives* (Toronto: Oberon Press, 1987)

1987 KIMIECIK = Kathryn Mary Kimiecik, 'Aspects of Contemporary Courtship in a Rural Newfoundland Community' (St John's: Memorial University M.A. Thesis, 1987)

1987 KING (ed) = *Modern Newfoundland Verse: Poems from* The Newfoundland Quarterly *1971–1987*, Selected and Edited by Everard H. King (St John's: Harry Cuff Publications Limited, 1987)

1987 MCDONALD = Ian D.H. McDonald, *'To Each His Own': William Coaker and the Fishermen's Protective Union in Newfoundland Politics, 1908–1925*, ed J.K. Hiller (St John's: Institute of Social and Economic Research, Memorial University of Newfoundland, 1987)

1987 MONTEVECCHI & TUCK = William A. Montevecchi and Leslie M. Tuck, *Newfoundland Birds: Exploitation, Study, Conservation* (Cambridge, Mass.: The Nuttall Ornithological Club, No. 21, 1987)

1987 O'FLAHERTY = Patrick O'Flaherty, *Summer of the Greater Yellowlegs* (St John's: Breakwater, 1987)

1987 PEYTON = Amy Louise Peyton, *River Lords: Father and Son* (St John's: Jesperson Press, 1987)

1987 POOLE = George Poole, *A Lifetime Listening to the Waves: Memoirs of a Labrador Fisherman* (St John's: Harry Cuff Publications Limited, 1987)

1987 POWELL = Benjamin W. Powell, Sr., *The Letter That Was Never Read: A History of the Labrador Fishery* (St John's: Good Tidings Press, 1987)

[1987] QUINLAN = 'Uncle' Allan Quinlan, *Reflections of Birchy Bay* [Birchy Bay: The author, 1987]

1987 RAPPORT = Nigel Rapport, *Talking Violence: An Anthropological Interpretation of Conversation in the City* (St John's: Institute of Social and Economic Research, Memorial University of Newfoundland, 1987)

1987 REEVES = William George Reeves, '''Our Yankee Cousins'': Modernization and the New-foundland-American Relationship, 1898–1910' (Ph.D. Thesis, University of Maine at Orono, 1987)

1987 STEELE (ed) = *Early Science in Newfound-land and Labrador*, ed D.H. Steele (St John's: Avalon Chapter of Sigma Xi, 1987)

1987 STRONG = Cyril W. Strong, *My Life as a Newfoundland Union Organizer: The Memoirs of Cyril W. Strong 1912–1987* (St John's: Committee on Canadian Labour History, Department of History, Memorial University of Newfoundland, 1987)

1987 WILLIAMS = Alan F. Williams, *Father Baudoin's War: D'Iberville's Campaigns in Acadia and Newfoundland 1696, 1697* (St John's: Department of Geography, Memorial University, 1987)

1988 DOHANEY = M.T. Dohaney, *The Corrigan Women* (Charlottetown: Ragweed Press, 1988)

1988 ELLIOTT = David Elliott, *The Edge of Beulah* (St John's: Breakwater Books, 1988)

1988 GALE = Donald Gale, *Sooshewan; Child of the Beothuk* (St John's: Breakwater Books Limited, 1988)

1988 GOSSE = Eric Martin Gosse, *The Settling of Spaniard's Bay* (St John's: Harry Cuff Publications Limited, 1988)

1988 HANRAHAN = Maura Hanrahan, *Living on the Dead: Fishermen's Licensing and Unemployment Insurance Programs in Newfoundland* (St John's: Institute of Social and Economic Research, 1988)

1988 MOMATIUK & EASTCOTT (eds) = Yva Momatiuk and John Eastcott (eds), *This Marvellous Terrible Place: Images of Newfoundland and Labrador* (Camden East, Ont.: Camden House, 1988)

1988 NADEL-KLEIN & DAVIS (eds) = Jane Nadel-Klein and Dona Lee Davis (eds), *To Work and to Weep: Women in Fishing Economies* (St John's: Institute of Social and Economic Research, Memorial University of Newfoundland, 1988)

1988 NEARY = Peter Neary, b 1938, *Newfound-land in the North Atlantic World, 1929–1949* (Kingston and Montreal: McGill-Queen's University Press, 1988)

1988 PORTER = Helen [Fogwill] Porter, *january, february, june or july: a novel* (St John's: Breakwater Books Limited, 1988)

1988 RUSSELL (ed Miller) = *A Fresh Breeze from Pigeon Inlet: The Best of Ted Russell, No. 3*, ed Elizabeth Russell Miller (St John's: Harry Cuff Publications, 1988)

1988 SINCLAIR (ed) = Peter R. Sinclair (ed), *A Question of Survival: The Fisheries and New-foundland Society* (St John's: Institute of Social and Economic Research, Memorial University of Newfoundland, 1988)

1988 TIERNEY = Pat Tierney, *Ten Sheets to the Wind* (St John's: Tinker Press, 1988)

1988 *Women, Work and Family* = *Women, Work and Family in the British, Canadian and Norwegian Offshore Oilfields*, ed Jane Lewis, Marilyn Porter, and Mark Shrimpton (New York: St Martin's Press, 1988)

1989 BENNETT = Margaret Bennett, *The Last Stronghold: Scottish Gaelic Traditions in Newfoundland* (St John's: Breakwater Books, 1989)

1989 CANDOW = James E. Candow, *Of Men and Seals: A History of the Newfoundland Seal Hunt*, Studies in Archaeology, Architecture and History (Hull: Environment Canada, National Historic Parks and Sites, Canadian Parks Service, 1989)

1989 *East Coast Marine Weather Manual* (Ottawa: Minister of Environment, 1989)

1989 ROWE = William Rowe, *The Temptation of Victor Galanti* [a novel] (Toronto: McClelland & Stewart, 1989)

Alphabetical Index of Authors, Newspapers and Periodicals, and Selected Titles

Acadiensis
Adelphian
Aldrich, John W., and Nutt, David C. (1939)
Am[erican] Speech
Amer[ican] Morris Newsletter
Andersen, R., and Wadel, C. (1972)
Anspach, Lewis Amadeus (1819)
Arctic
Ashton, John (1985)
Assoc[iation of] Am[erican] Geog[raphers]. Annals.
Atlantic Co-operator
Atlantic Insight
Atlantic Mo[nthly]
Austin, O.L., Jr. (1932)
Banks, Joseph (1766)
Barbour, Florence Grant (1973)
Bayfield, Henry Wolsey (1833–47)
Beaver
Bennett, Margaret (1989)
Biblio of Nfld (1986)
Bk of Nfld (1937–75)
Blunt, Edmund M. (1837)
Bonnycastle, Richard Henry (1842)
Books in Canada
Browne, P.W. (1909)
Burke, Johnny (1982)
Bursey, Wallace (1982)

Busch, Briton Cooper (1985)
Butler, Victor (1975)
Byrne, Cyril J. (1984)
Cabot Voyages (ed Williamson) (c1497–1522)
Canadian Folklore canadien
Can[adian] Geog[raphical] J[ournal
Canadian Illustrated News
Can[adian] Med[ical] Ass[ociation] J[ournal]
Canadian Sealers Association (1985)
Candow, James E. (1989)
Canoma
Cartwright, John (1768)
Cell, Gillian T. (1610-30)
Centenary Mag[azine]
Chappell, Edward (1818)
Chimmo, William (1867)
Christmas Bells
Christmas Review
Coaker, W.F. (1930)
Colonist = The Daily Colonist
Colonist Christmas Number
Commercial Annual
Cooper, Georgiana (1979)
Cox, Gordon S.A. (1980)
Daily Mail (London)
Daily News
Dawe, Tom (1981); (1982); (1987)
Dawe, Tom, and Ficken, Sylvia (1983)
De Boilieu, Lambert (1861)
Decks Awash
Deep Sea Fishers = Among the Deep Sea Fishers
Deming, Clarence (1884)
Devine, P.K. (1937)
De Volpi, Charles P. (1972)
Dohaney, M.T. (1988)
Domstad, Maureen, and Wijewantha,
   Udayakanthie (1985)
Duncan, Norman (1912)
East Coast Marine Weather Manual (1989)
Elliott, David (1988)
Encyclopedia of Nfld and Labrador (1981–84)
England, George Allan (1924)
England, James (1837–42)
English Pilot (1689)
Eve[ning] Herald
Evening Telegram
Faris, James C. (1966)
Felt, Lawrence F. (1987)
Feltham, John (1986)
Fitzgerald, L.G. (1949)
Fizzard, Garfield (1987)
Folk Life
Froude, John W. (1937)
Gale, Donald (1988)
Gardner, James Anthony (1783)
Gazette (Memorial University)
Gazetteer of Canada: Nfld (1983)
Gazetteer of Undersea Feature Names (1983)

Geog[raphical] J[ournal]
Gosse, Eric Martin (1988)
Gosse, John S.R. (1985)
Gough, William (1984)
Graham, Frank W. (1979)
Grenfell, Wilfred Thomason (1919)
Grey, William (1858)
Gunn, Gertrude E. (1966)
Guy, Ray (1985)
Halpert Festschrift (1980)
Hanrahan, Maura (1988)
Harper's
Hatton, Joseph, and Harvey, M. (1883)
Head, C. Grant (1976)
Heriot, George (1807)
Hind, Henry Youle (1863)
Hiscock, Philip Douglas (1986)
Holly Branch
Holmes, Albert N. (1980)
Holy Cross Annual (St Alban's)
Horwood, Harold (1987)
Howley, James P. (1915)
Howley, M.F. (1888)
Jackson, Lawrence (1982)
Janes, Percy (1980)
Jannasch, Hans-Windekilde (1970)
Johnston, Wayne (1985); (1987)
J[ournal of] A[merican] Folklore
Journ[al] of Assembly = Journal of the [New-
   foundland] House of Assembly
Jukes, Joseph Beete (1842); (1871)
Junek, Oscar Waldemar (1937)
Kalleo, Josephina (1984)
Keating, Bern (1968)
Kelland, Otto P. (1984)
Kent, Rockwell (1930)
Kimiecik, Kathryn Mary (1987)
King, Everard H. (1987)
'Labrador Childhood' (1975)
Lahontan (1703)
Lamb, James B. (1977)
L[an]g[uage]s in Nfld (1982)
Latham, John L. (1821–24)
Lehr, Genevieve, and Best, Anita (1985)
Lind, Henry (1857–64)
Lore and Language
Lovell (1871)
Lowell, Robert (1858)
Luminus (Memorial University Alumni Assoc)
McAlpine, Charles D. (1904)
MacDermott, Hugh 1938
McDonald, Ian D.H. (1987)
McDooling, Jim William (1982)
Madison, R.D. (1982)
Maher, Alfred V. (1985)
Major, Kevin (1981)
Maritime Anthro[pological] Studies
Mars, P.C. (1924)

Martin, Ronald (1945)
Martin, Wendy (1983)
Medical Post
Mercer, Paul (1976)
Metro, The
Millais, J.G. (1907)
Moakler, Michael J. (1974)
Momatiuk, Yva, and Eastcott, John (1988)
Montevecchi, William A., and Tuck, Leslie M. (1987)
Moreton, Julian (1863)
Mosdell, H.M. (1923)
Moss, William P. (1854)
Moss *MS Diary* (1832)
Moubray, J.M. (1910)
Murphy, James (1902); (1906)
Muse, The (Memorial University)
Nadel-Klein, Jane, and Davis, Dona Lee (1988)
Narváez, Peter (1986)
Nat[ional] Geog[raphic]
Neary, Peter (1988)
Neary, Peter, and Patrick O'Flaherty (1983)
Networker
Newhook, Cle (1985)
Newfoundlander
Nfld Herald
Nfld Hist[orical] Soc[iety] (1977)
Nfld LifeStyle
Nfld Pilot (1878)
Nfld Qtly
Nfld Royal Commission Report (1933)
Nfld Studies
Nfld's Deepsea Fishery (1986)
N[ova] S[cotian] Inst[itute of] Sci[ence]
O'Flaherty, Patrick (1987)
Oldmixon, John (1708)
Outing
Paddock, Harold (1981)
Papers in Ling[uistics]
Peacock, Kenneth (1965)
Peddel, Nicholas (1904)
Peddle, Walter W. (1983)
Peopling of Nfld (1977)
Peyton, Amy Louise (1987)
Pitt, David G. (1984–87)
Pittman, Al (1984)
Poole, George (1987)
Porter, Helen (1979); (1988)
Powell, Ben (1984); (1987)
Prowse, D.W. (1895)
Pulling, George Christopher (1792)
Quigley, Colin (1985)
Quinlan, Allan (1987)
Rapport, Nigel (1987)
Recreation Program Dep[artmen]t
Reeves, William George (1987)
Richard Hakluyt (1578)
Robertson, Margaret R. (1984)

Rouleau, Ernest (1961)
Rouse, Oliver (1846–50)
Rowe, C. Francis (1983)
Rowe, William (1989)
Royal Gazette
Russell, Ted (1988)
Rusted, Nigel (1985)
Ryan, Shannon (1986)
Sarson (1896)
Saunders, Gary L. (1986)
Scammell, A.R. (1945); (1966)
Seafisheries of Nfld (1937)
Seary, E.R. (1971)
Seniors' News
Sider, Gerald M. (1986)
Sinclair, Peter R. (1988)
Smallwood, J.R. (1941)
Smith, Marjorie (1968)
Smith, Nicholas (1936)
South, G. Robin (1983)
Sparkes, R.F. (1981)
SPG Series Letters & Reports
Steele, D.H. (1987)
Strong, Cyril W. (1987)
Sunday Express
Sunday Telegram = *Evening Telegram*, Sunday edition
Swansborough, W. (1896)
Taylor, V.R. (1985)
Terminology of Loggers (1985)
Terra Nova Advocate
Them Days
This Land
This Rock within the Sea (1968)
Thomas, Aaron (1794)
Thomas, William S. (1913)
Thoresby, William (1799)
Tierney, Pat (1988)
Tocque, Philip (1849)
Toilers of the Deep
Townsend, Charles Wendell, and Allen, Glover M. (1907)
Trade Review
Trans[actions of the] Roy[al] Soc[iety] of London]
Trans[actions of the] Soc[iété] Guernesiaise
Treby, Henry (1724)
Tribune Ch[ristmas] Ann[ual]
Tricoche, George Nestler (1929)
Tucker, Ephraim W. (1839)
Tulk, Bob (1971)
Turner, George E. (1925)
Tuttle, Charles R. (1885)
Union Forum
Vaughan, William (1626)
Warner, William W. (1983)
Whiteley, Albert S. (1977)
Williams, Alan F. (1987)
Willoughby Papers (1612)

Wilson, William (1866)
Women, Work and Family (1988)
Wright, Guy David (1984)
Yaffle of Yarns, A (1985)
Yonge, James (1663-70)

CONTEMPORARY COLLECTIONS AND
COLLECTORS

Collections

An explanation of resources in the Memorial University of Newfoundland Folklore and Language Archive used in compiling the Dictionary can be found on page lix.

C 63–16   H. Coates; Bay Roberts
C 66–4   D. Curran; Gambo
C 67–13   B. MacDonald; Scarborough
C 67–4   M. Fagan; St Mary's
C 69–19   T. McCarthy; Bar Haven
C 70–15   M. Hopkins; Heart's Content
C 71–18   C. Hewitt; Corner Brook
C 71–93   J. Dobbin; St Joseph's
C 71–95   G. Dwyer; Marystown
C 71–100   E. Hiscock; Flat Island
C 71–110   W. Lodge; Deer Lake
C 71–122   E. Smith; Port-aux-Basques
M 64–3   C. Williams; USA/Long Pond
M 68–3   J. Dollimount; François
M 68–11   Z. Johnson; Renews
M 68–13   O. Langdon; Seal Cove, F.B.
M 68–16   A.F. O'Brien; Cape Broyle
M 68–17   R. Park; Gillams
M 68–23   H. Stroud; Glovertown
M 69–5   W. Canning; Williamsport
M 69–6   E. Cokes; Head Bay d'Espoir
M 70–9   L. Badcock; Shearstown
M 70–27   K. Sullivan; Calvert
M 78–54   J. James; Trepassey
P 1   F.A. Aldrich; New Jersey/St John's
P 10   R. Barrett; Old Perlican
P 13   D. Bartlett; Rattling Brook
P 14   H. Beck; Carbonear
P 30   H. Carew; St John's
P 51   J. Courage; Fortune Bay
P 54   N.C. Crewe; Elliston
P 65   C. Decker; Roddickton
P 68   V. Dillon; Mobile
P 76   J.D. Eaton; St John's
P 106   B. Haines; Kelligrews
P 108   J. Halley; St John's
P 113   L. Harris; St. Joseph's, P.B.
P 124   E. Hiscock; Flat Island
P 127   R. Hollett; Spencer's Cove
P 131   J. Hutchings; Cow Head
P 133   G. Jeffers; Freshwater, C.B.

P 148   W.J. Kirwin; Newport, R.I./St John's
P 161   B. Mactavish: St John's
P 191   A. O'Brien; St John's
P 197   P. O'Flaherty; Long Beach, C.B.
P 222   R. Rideout; Buchans
P 231   S. Ryan; Riverhead, Harbour Grace
P 237   L. Small; Moreton's Harbour
P 245   G.M. Story; St John's
P 266   J.D.A. Widdowson; Sheffield, U.K./St John's
P 277   J. Acreman; St Anthony
P 278   C. Benoit; Stephenville Crossing
P 279   A. Best; Merasheen Island
P 280   Shirley Burt; Bay Roberts
P 281   Stella Burt; Bay de Verde
P 282   D. Butler; Kelligrews
P 283   P. Byrne; Great Paradise
P 284   R. Carpenter; Port Union
P 285   L. Cassell; St John's
P 286   G. Chaulk; Elliston
P 287   A. Cooper; Grate's Cove
P 288   E. Cunningham; Freshwater, P.B.
P 289   T. Dawe; Long Pond, Manuels
P 290   S. Farrell; Little Bay, Marystown
P 291   R. Ford; Happy Valley, Labrador
P 292   N. Fosnaes; Badger
P 293   M. Furey; St Joseph's
P 294   K. Goldstein; Philadelphia
P 295   C. Griffin; Corner Brook
P 296   G. Handcock; Trinity
P 297   E. Hearn; Petty Harbour
P 298   E. Hewitt; Corner Brook
P 299   E. Hicks; Central Nfld
P 300   E. Hollett; Spencer's Cove
P 301   D. Howse; Hare Bay
P 302   G. Kinden; Lewisporte
P 303   A. King; Hickman's Harbour
P 304   M. Lovelace; Dorset/St John's
P 305   R. McCormack; St John's
P 306   M. Macdonald; Woody Point
P 307   A. Macpherson; Scotland/St John's
P 308   R. Manuel; Campbellton
P 309   S. Manuel; Lewisporte
P 310   A. Martin; New Perlican
P 311   S. Morgan; Kelligrews
P 312   B. O'Dwyer; St John's
P 313   D. Oldford; Trinity Bay
P 314   M. Oldford; Elliston
P 315   G. Penney; Keels
P 316   L. Piercey; Winterton
P 317   H. Ralph; Flat Island
P 318   M. Russell; Coley's Point
P 319   M. Scammell; Change Islands
P 320   M. Seward; New Perlican
P 321   S. Sexton; St Mary's
P 322   P. Smith; Fortune
P 323   M. Snook; Grand Bank
P 324   A. Snow; North River

Alphabetical Index of Collectors and Contributors

This is a name index to the classified sources listed above. For the codes following the names, see the explanation on page lix.

Dictionaries and Other Works Cited

The list excludes a number of authors or works cited only once or twice; for these, specific bibliographical information is provided in the relevant headnote.

AND   *The Australian National Dictionary; A Dictionary of Australianisms on Historical Principles*, ed W.S. Ransom (Melbourne: Oxford University Press, 1988)

Anglo-Manx Dialect   *A Vocabulary of the Anglo-Manx Dialect*, comp A.W. Moore et al (Oxford: Oxford University Press, 1924)

Beothuk Vocabularies   John Hewson, *Beothuk Vocabularies: A Comparative Study* (St John's: Newfoundland Museum, 1978)

BERREY   *The American Thesaurus of Slang*, comp Lester V. Berrey and Melvin Van den Bark (New York: Thomas Y. Crowell, 1943)

BRYANT   Ralph Clement Bryant, *Logging: The Principles and General Methods of Operation in the United States*, 2nd ed (New York: John Wiley & Sons, Inc., 1923)

COHEN   Anthony P. Cohen, *Whalsay: Symbol, Segment and Boundary in a Shetland Island Community* (Manchester: Manchester University Press, 1987)

DA   *A Dictionary of Americanisms on Historical Principles*, ed Mitford M. Mathews (Chicago: University of Chicago Press, 1951)

DAE   *A Dictionary of American English on Historical Principles*, eds William A. Craigie and James R. Hulbert, 4 vols. (Chicago: University of Chicago Press, 1938–1944)

DARE   *Dictionary of American Regional English*, Chief Editor, Frederic G. Cassidy, vol. i, A–C (Cambridge: Belknap Press of Harvard University Press, 1985)

DAS   *Dictionary of American Slang*, 2nd supplemented ed, eds Harold Wentworth and Stuart Berg Flexner (New York: Thomas Y. Crowell Company, 1975)

DBE   John A. Holm with Alison Watt Shilling, *Dictionary of Bahamian English* (Cold Spring, N.Y.: Lexik House Publishers, 1982)

DC   *Dictionary of Canadianisms on Historical Principles*, editor-in-chief, Walter S. Avis (Toronto: W.J. Gage Limited, 1967)

DINNEEN   *Foclóir Gaedhilge agus béarla; An Irish-English Dictionary*, ed Patrick S. Dinneen (Dublin: Educational Company of Ireland, 1927; rpt 1965)

DJE   *Dictionary of Jamaican English*, eds F.G. Cassidy and R.B. Le Page (Cambridge: The University Press, 1967; 2nd ed, 1979)

EDD   *The English Dialect Dictionary*, ed Joseph Wright, 6 vols. (Oxford University Press, 1898-1905; rpt 1961)

EDD Sup   'Supplement' in vol. vi of *The English Dialect Dictionary* (Oxford University Press, 1905)

JOYCE   P.W. Joyce, *English as We Speak It in Ireland* (London: Longmans, Green & Co., 1910)

LEMOINE   Geo. Lemoine, *Dictionnaire français-montagnais avec un vocabulaire montagnais-anglais* (Boston: W.B. Cabot and P. Cabot, 1901)

MED   *Middle English Dictionary*, eds Hans Kurath, Sherman M. Kuhn, John Reidy and others, A–Spr (Ann Arbor: University of Michigan Press, 1956–1989)

NID	*Webster's Third New International Dictionary*, editor-in-chief, Philip Babcock Gove (Springfield: G. & C. Merriam Company, 1961)
OED	*The Oxford English Dictionary*, ed James A.H. Murray and others, 12 vols. (Oxford: At the Clarendon Press, 1884–1928; corrected reissue, 1933)
OED 2nd ed	*Oxford English Dictionary* Second Edition, prepared by J.A. Simpson and E.S.C. Weiner, 20 vols. (Oxford: Clarendon Press, 1989)
O Sup[1]	*The Oxford English Dictionary; Supplement and Bibliography* (Oxford: At the Clarendon Press, 1933)
O Sup[2]	*A Supplement to the Oxford English Dictionary*, ed R.W. Burchfield, 4 vols. (Oxford: At the Clarendon Press, 1972–1986)
PEACOCK	*English-Eskimo Dictionary*, ed F.W. Peacock (St John's: Memorial University of Newfoundland, [1974])
PRATT	*Dictionary of Prince Edward Island English*, ed T.K. Pratt (Toronto: University of Toronto Press, 1988)
SED	*Survey of English Dialects; The Basic Material*, 4 vols. in 12 parts, ed Harold Orton and others (Leeds: E.J. Arnold & Son Limited, 1962–71)
SMYTH	*The Sailor's Word-Book: An Alphabetical Digest of Nautical Terms*, ed W.H. Smyth (London: Blackie and Son, 1867)
SND	*The Scottish National Dictionary*, eds William Grant and David Murison, 10 vols. (Edinburgh: The Scottish National Dictionary Association Ltd, [1931]–1976)
SORDEN	L.G. Sorden, *Lumberjack Lingo* (Spring Green: Wisconsin House, Inc., 1969)
Trésor de la langue française	*Trésor de la langue française; Dictionnaire de la langue du XIXe et du XXe siècle (1789–1960)*, [directed by] Paul Imbs (Paris: Editions du centre national de la recherche scientifique, 1971–)
WAKELIN	Martyn F. Wakelin, *The Southwest of England* (Amsterdam: John Benjamins Publishing Company, 1986)

Abbreviations

Below are listed the abbreviations employed in the Supplement, especially in the references found in the headnotes. For a key to the abbreviations used in quoting the sources for the Supplement, see the BIBLIOGRAPHY.

a, adj   adjective, adjectival
A.D.   anno Domini
A-I   Anglo-Irish
arch   archaic
attrib   attributive(ly)
Austr   Australia
aux   auxiliary
av   adverb
b   born
Brk   Berkshire
c.   approximately; century
C   item in MUNFLA Card Collection
cm   centimetre
Co   Cornwall
CO   Colonial Office [Series]
comb(s)   combination(s)
commun   communication
comp   compiler
Conn   Connecticut
cp   compare with the following term or reference
CPCGN   Canadian Permanent Committee on Geographical Names
cpd   compound
cty, cties   county, counties
cwt   hundredweight
D   Devon
def   definition
det   determiner
dial   dialect
Do   Dorset

ed(s)   editor(s), edited by; edition
ed conject   editorial conjecture
ed emend   editorial emendation
esp   especially
exc dial   except dialect
ff   and the following pages
fig.   figurative
Fr   French
freq   frequent(ly)
Gl   Gloucestershire
Ha   Hampshire
He   Hereford
Hist.   historical
ibid   the same source
inc   including
infreq   infrequent
int   interjection, interrogative
intens   intensifier
Ir   Ireland, Irish
ISER   Institute of Social and Economic Research
Labr   Labrador
m   metre
M   item in MUNFLA Manuscript Collection
MS(S)   manuscript(s)
MUNFLA   Memorial University of Newfoundland Folklore and Language Archive
n   noun; note
N Amer   North America
N&Q   Notes & Queries
naut   nautical
N E   New England
neg   negative
Nfld   Newfoundland
no   northern
No.   number
Nr Car   North Carolina

N S   Nova Scotia
num   numeral
N Z   New Zealand
obs   obsolete
orig   original
p(p).   page(s)
P   item submitted by a person
PANL   Provincial Archives of Newfoundland and
   Labrador
phr   phrase(s)
plu   plural
ppl   present particle
ppl a   participial adjective
p ppl   past participle
prep   preposition(al)
pro   personal pronoun
pron(s)   pronunciation(s)
prov   proverb(ial)
Prov   Provence
Q   item obtained from a questionnaire
qtl   quintal
quot   quotation
ref   reference
rpt   reprint
s   southern
sb   substantive
Sc   Scotland
Sh I   Shetland Islands
sing.   singular
So   Somerset
SPG   Society for the Promotion of the Gospel
spp   species
Sr   Surrey
subs   substitute
s w   southwest
Sx   Sussex
T   item in MUNFLA Tape Collection
TCH   Trans-Canada Highway
tr   translator, translation, translated by
transf   transferred sense
TS   typescript
U K   United Kingdom
U S   United States
usu   usually
v   verb
var   various; variant
vbl n   verbal noun
vol(s).   volume(s)
W   Wiltshire

*   a spelling not attested in printed sources; a
   spelling devised to suggest an approximate
   pronunciation: **graunyer***

( )   an optional spelling or inflectional ending
   occurs: **shaving(s)**

=   the preceding term means: **example** [=**gloss**]

~   'the word being defined'; 'the word just mentioned': **drudge**, ~ **barrow**

[ ]   phonetic transcription; editorial correction or
   emendation; a relevant quotation which does
   not contain the word being illustrated; date of
   first appearance, writing, or, if a ballad, performance.

SUPPLEMENT TO THE
DICTIONARY OF NEWFOUNDLAND ENGLISH

A

a- Cp *OED* ~ prep[1] 13 a and b, 'with verb of motion.' A- and verb forms with -*ing* appear in historical texts ('to come a Tilting,' treated at TILT v), ballad and verse idioms, and the oral vernacular.

1689 *English Pilot* 16 It is not a Mile broad there, as I was informed by the Planters...who usually go a Furring there in the Winter. 1797 PANL GN 2/1/a vol 12, 8 June A few small Bankers are on the Banks a fishing. 1862 *Atlantic Mo* ix, 366 'I 'ould n like to go a-swilun for gain.' 1901 *Christmas Review* 5 "The Outport Planter": 'The winter seed him mend his nets, the summer seed him go a-fishin'.' T 1-63 Well, my son, you talk about girls goin' a-screechin'! 1965 PEACOCK i, 94 "The Sealer's Ball": 'Be ye much of a hand ab'ard a vessel/ A-peltin' the puppy swiles, sir.' T 266-66 And we always bees be frightened. You wouldn't catch us to go out a-singin'.

aa See AW.

able a
3 Phr *able for*
1989 ROWE 75 'High or low, Jane,' said Freeman, 'you're able for that river.'

according ppl Cp *DARE* 'as 'cording to' prep (1966).
1987 FIZZARD 130 'You put your legs over the sail and you slide the sail down and you lace it in to the topmast as you were pressing it in according as you come down.'
according to: a dish of leftovers; HASH.
P 318-82 Aunt Clara was often force put to clobber up a feed of "cardin' to' for supper.

ackley n Rock formation in which the metallic element molybdenum occurs.
1983 MARTIN 35 The [Rencontre East] mine's most active period were the years just before World War II. Employees...lived for a time on the shores of Rencontre Lake in a cabin called 'Ackley City' after a company director, John W. Ackley... One permanent legacy of the mine remains: 'Ackley' has become the official geological name of the granite in which the molybdenum occurs.

admiral n Cp *Anglo-Manx Dialect* ~ 'the fisherman who has charge of the herring fleet.'
2 1689 *English Pilot* 14 About half way into the Bay on the North side (where the Planters live, and the Admirals stage is) there is a ledg of Rocks.

adventure n
[1937] 1945 SCAMMELL 19 "Tommy Decker's Venture": I couldn't arg with Tommy, he's smart, that boy, I'll say/And if the fish holds on a bit, he'll make the venture pay.

adventurer n
1 [1583] 1895 PROWSE 76 [title page]: [Wherein is briefly set down] the great and manifold Commodities, that is likely to grow thereby, to the whole Realme in generall, and to the Adventurers in particular.

after prep also **afther**. Cp PRATT ~ *to be after doing*.
1839 TUCKER 82 'Indade ye wasn't after thinking the Irish cod fools enough for that, was ye!' 1858 [LOWELL] ii, 211 'It's meself that's afther getting good rason to wish longer acquainten wid ye,' said [Croonan], in an easy way. 1987 *Evening Telegram* 9 May, p. 15 I went up on the deck and I looked. Here I saw this big red light and it flashing right on the bow of the ship and she loaded. I said, 'We're after cutting down a boat.' ...Someone said, 'We're after running ashore on Peckford Island.'

after a Cp *OED* after-guard 'men stationed on the quarter-deck and poop, to work the after sails.' Comb **afterguard**: senior officers of a sealing vessel, accommodated aft.
1985 BUSCH 73 The 'afterguard' of captain, second hand...the doctor (if any), 'Marconi'...and the chief engineer lived separately.

ag a Comb **agstone**: limestone processed for agricultural use.
1983 MARTIN 45 Some limestone quarried by the company became processed into the agricultural limestone or 'agstone' needed to neutralize Newfoundland's extremely acidic soils.

agent n
1982 MCDOOLING 76 There was no way that the fishermen [in Conche] could try for a better price [for fish] from another agent while he still owed money to the local buyer.

ain't neg Pron forms: *an't*, *en't*; [ant], [ɛnt]. See BE.
T 284-66 'No,' Jack said, 'I don't want no dinner. I ant goina eat no dinner.' ibid 'Jack,' he said, 'there's a barn out there. He ant been cleaned out for two year.' 1983 FROUDE 122 This disaster may have been caused by a single stroke of a match which shows that all things eant done by mite but by pr[u]dence. 1988 DOHANEY 17 'Of course her bread ent sour,' Ned offered easily, his tone intended to make Bertha feel better. 1989 ROWE 27 'Buddy drivin' dis is a queer hand, b'y,' en't 'e?'

air n Cp *OED* ~ 19 'a piece of music...to be sung or played as a "solo".' A tune, known to a group of singers or performers by its title, to which a newly composed ballad may be sung.
[1894] 1982 BURKE (ed Kirwin) 11 "The July Fire": Air: McGinty. 1895 *Eve Herald* 17 Dec These songs are all sung to airs which have a strong family likeness to each other. 1902 *Daily News* 6 Dec, p. 3 [song by James Murphy] "The Short and Long of It": AIR:— 'A Pretty Kettle of Fish.' [1929] 1982 MADISON (ed) 11 [On seeing lady writing down musical notes] 'Look well, b'ys,' said a man once, 'for you never seed anything to equal it. Them scratches is the 'h'air.' 1985 ASHTON 149 'Often the final words of the song are spoken. Emphasis within the [Newfoundland song] tradition is upon the words rather than the tune (or "air").'

alarm v Cp *DBE* ~ (1918). To set an alarm clock to go off at a certain time.

P 148-89 I forgot to alarm the clock last night.

alder n Cp BRYANT 469 alder grab 'stem of an alder...bent over...to hold a boom or logs inshore.' Comb **alder-grabber**: a logger inexperienced in the spring log drive.

C 66-4 Alder-grabbers are loggers who are afraid to go out on the logs when they are being floated downstream. P 292-83 'It's better to be a live alder grabber than a dead bubble walker.' 1985 *Terminology of Loggers* 2 ~ a person who lingers around the shore during a *drive* trying to avoid going out on the river.

alley-coosh v

1987 DAWE [8] A is for alley-coosh,/Going to bed,/When a dusty old sandman/Skirrs close to your head.

american a Comb **american shore**: stretch of coast from Ramea Islands to Cape Ray and thence up the west coast to Quirpon Island, along which U S vessels formerly held right to take bait; cp FRENCH SHORE.

1987 REEVES 155 Technically, American fishing vessels possessed the right to fish for their own bait on only one part of the Newfoundland coast, the so-called 'American Shore.'

angishore n

2 1983 DAWE & FICKEN 10 A is for angishore,/Weak, puny chap;/When the men go out fishing,/He goes for a nap.

angle n

2 Also: a sharp bend in a river.

P 13-83 ~ Sharp corner in a river. The current may run strong there or the water may be quite 'steady' with the fast water passing on further offshore. 1986 SAUNDERS vi [Gander River names] Bridge's Angle, Long Angle Island, Lush's Angle.

anguish n

1985 *A Yaffle of Yarns* 94 She frequently announced... that she had a 'wonderful anguish in her neck,' however a 'shockin' pain in me quarter' seemed to be the complaint that afflicted her most often.

anti-confederate n

1987 JOHNSTON 50 Though everyone, the anti-Confederates especially, laughed at her, she claimed that the thought of returning, after her illness to a Newfoundland that was now a part of Canada had kept her going.

apast prep *DARE* ~ (1894-).

P 148-87 [It's the] first right apast K Mart.

aps n

1986 SAUNDERS 48 I sat up and listened to the wind rustling the leaves of the small aps and birch on the bank behind us.

apse n *SED* ~ iv, 732 So D.

apsy a also **apsey**.

1871 LOVELL 221 Apsey Cove...Fogo.

arch n

[1860] 1988 *Sunday Express* 5 June, p. 13 [The *Courier* reported that] the order of procession [for Edward, Prince of Wales] was quickly and efficiently formed. Outside the Government wharf gate a colorful and magnificent triumphal arch had been erected. 1987 POWELL 64 By dark we had the arch built right across the wharf. First we built a wooden frame, then fitted the green trees together. All that remained to be done was the 'Welcome' banner [for Premier Smallwood].

arg v *DARE* ~ (1914).

[1937] 1945 SCAMMELL 19 "Tommy Decker's Venture": I couldn't arg with Tommy, he's smart, that boy, I'll say/And if the fish holds on a bit, he'll make the venture pay. P 245-85 'Don't you arg with me!'

arn substitute. *SED* iv, 821, 839 So W Do Ha.

arse n See REDDEN: ~ one's arse.

1 1987 JOHNSTON 66 'Give Tom a hand with his coat,' she'd say, 'get off yer arse.'

arsed a See RAGGEDY. Comb **raggedy-assed.**

1988 *Evening Telegram* 27 Aug, p. A4 'We're a raggedy-assed crowd, you know.'

article n *SED* iv, 1041 Ha.

aspy a also **aspey**. See APSY. Thick with aspen trees; in place-names.

1961 ROULEAU 4 Aspey Brook; Aspy Cove.

athwart prep also **turt**.

1895 *Evening Herald* 17 Dec [p. 4] Uncle Garge is turt de bay,/To get a kag of sugar.

aunt n

1 1984 POWELL 35 When Christmas Day finally came, we were invited to Uncle Alex's and Aunt Maggie Campbell's.

aw int also **aa**.

1984 KALLEO 2 This man steers the sled... To stop the team, he shouts, 'Aa, Aa.'

awful a

1985 ASHTON 128 We'd have a [game of] law suit nearly every week. And I never seen, 't'was awful fun except one time there was...a fight over it.

B

babbish* n also **babiche**, **vabish**.

1981 SPARKES xiii [Snowshoes] were made of a frame of tough birch saplings and 'filled' with deerskin cut into fine strips called babiche. 1985 *Decks Awash* Jan-Feb, p. 25 The tail and head webbing was called *tibish* and the middle rawhide was called *vabish*.

baccalieu n also **barcaliau**.

1 1895 *Evening Herald* 17 Dec, [p. 4] He set his compass and he set it true/For Cape St Francis and for Baccalieu,/And the Almighty being at hand,/'Twas short after we made the shore,/And what should it be but the Labrador.

2 1861 DE BOILIEU 15 [see sense **1** above] From Certain movements...of the bird, known on the coast as the Barcaliau bird,—that is to say, from its flying the whole day in the same direction,—we knew it was migrating to the Funk or Bird Island for the purpose of breeding. 1987 MONTEVECCHI & TUCK 161 The local name 'Baccalieu Birds' has been applied to the multitudes of puffins that raft in huge offshore flocks near the island.

back² n *DBE* ~ 3 (1977) for sense **2**.

back v *EDD* ~ v 2; *DARE* 2 (1840-). To carry on one's shoulders or back; SPELL v.

1987 POOLE 26 You would take all your things up to the head of the pond in this small boat before backing it in to the tilt.

back a

2 Comb **back cove**.

1837 BLUNT 48 To the northward of this head is Lally Back Cove, where ships may anchor in 14 or 16 fathoms water. 1987 *Nfld Qtly* lxxxii (3), 3 Where in 1938 a handful of smugglers landed their boats after sundown in such back coves as Spencer's Dock and Payne's Cove, thousands of Newfoundlanders would be crossing into the country by causeway.

back-end: see VEE.

back run: a smaller branch of a river, as around an island (P 13-83). See RUN n 2.

back side.

1987 KIMIECIK 84 [A favourite meeting place is the] shop before the road continues on to what is called 'the backside' of the community.

back av Comb **back flaw**: a sudden gust of wind from a contrary direction.

1983 FROUDE 170 I did not mind it much as I knew it was only a nother back flaw that I was well acquainted With while sailing down the river of time.

bag n

2 Also: a specific quantity of fish taken in a cod-net.

1987 FIZZARD 211 'During the course of hauling the [otter] trawl or "taking back," as it was commonly called, the knot would be tied and untied according to the number of bags of fish in the net. Every 2,500 or 3,000 pounds of fish constituted a bag.'

3 Canvas sack containing numbers from which inshore fishermen draw by lot a fishing location or 'berth.' See DRAW v, n.

1987 POOLE 84 He was the first to put his hand into the bag to draw.

bait n Attrib **bait jack**.

1984 KELLAND 82 When the meal was over, the two young men loaded their bait jack with caplin and went out to underrun their gear.

bait v

1 1987 FIZZARD 127 Having 'baited up,' the schooners left for the Grand Banks.

2 [1977] 1985 LEHR & BEST (eds) 51 ''The Dole Song'': We'll take on board our caplin boys, and we'll then bait up our gear;/We'll stick her to the Western Grounds if the weather it do keep clear. 1987 *Nfld Life-Style* June, p. 54 You had to see who could bait the hooks and trawls the fastest.

baiting n

1 1984 KELLAND 115 Apparently the squid had struck off for other areas. He was therefore, obliged to pick up a baiting of lancelet. 1987 FIZZARD 127 The summer trips were usually made up of several 'baitings' [of caplin].

bakeapple n also **baygapple**. The first element was borrowed and modified in Labrador from an Eskimo word, now *appik*, in the 1770s and combined with English *apple*. Cp *Labrador Inuit* 21 appik 'bakeapple'; *DARE* baked-apple berry [1889]-1981 [Alaska]; PRATT ~ (1916-).

2 [1867] 1989 CHIMMO (ed Kirwin) 24 [In the schooner cabin were] a small square table in the centre, a dish containing bake-apples (which grow in abundance on shore) which [the women] were picking for a stew! [(c1889) 1970 JANNASCH 47 Vor den Hundebeeren wurde gewarnt, denn sie sollten Leibweh und Erbrechen verursachen, weshalb auch Lea unsre Sammelergebnisse sorgsam prüfte. Die köstlichste aller Beeren aber war die Apik-Beere (norweg. Multebeer). Sie war in grösserer Zahl im sumpfigen Uferstreifen am Fusse der Sophie zu finden.] [1975 ''Labrador Childhood,'' trans. L.H. Neatby, 63 There were several kinds of fruit to be picked of which the blueberry and the whortleberry were the most desired. We were cautioned against the 'Hundebeere' as apt to cause colic and vomiting, so Leah took careful note of what we were picking. The tastiest of all these fruits was the Apik-Beere (in Norwegian the Multebeere). It was plentiful along the swampy banks at the foot of Mount Sophie.] 1909 BROWNE 200 The berry which is so characteristic of Labrador is the succulent Cloudberry, here called 'Bakeapple'... It is supposed to be a sovereign remedy for scorbutic diseases; and is in great use amongst the Esquimaux, who call it *Akbik*. ... We find several places named *Akbik*, *Akbiktok*, i.e., places where the Bakeapple grows. 1924 *Deep-Sea Fishers* xxi (4), 139 Bake apples—baygapple—Warted red berries, ripening late in the summer on low growing plants. The principal berry on the Labrador coast and widely used. 1983 *Gazetteer of Canada: Nfld* 1 Akpiksai Bay; Akpiktok Island. 1985 *Evening Telegram* 6 July, p. 5 Travellers on the [Bonavista Bay] barrens report that good crops of blueberries, bakeapples, etc, can be expected this year.

baker n Cp *DARE* ~ bread (1802-). Comb **baker's loaf**; see LOAF.

1837 BLUNT 26 The largest of these [islands] is named the Baker's Loaf.

ballicatter n also **ballycator**.
3 1986 SAUNDERS 36 Copying was considered boy's
work. Girls mostly played among the ballycators around
the shore.

ballroom n
1985 BUSCH 73 The 'ballroom' or fo'c'sle could only
house a small percentage of such big [sealing] crews.

banana n The root of the cinnamon fern (*Osmunda cinnamomea*), pulled up and eaten by young
people (P 148-84); BUTTER PLANT.

bangbelly n
1985 *Terminology of Loggers* 2 ~ a pork and molasses
cake made with soda that could be baked, fried, or boiled
in a stew like dumplings.

bank n
1 1984 KELLAND x They had to put up with dense
fogs, high seas, sudden storms and racing tides: the same
conditions that their counterparts faced on the Banks.
2 1987 FIZZARD 14 It is thought that this name [Grand
Bank] was given to the location because of the high bank
which extends from Admiral's Cove to the harbour at the
water's edge.
3 Attrib, comb **bank line**.
[1925] 1986 *Them Days* xi (4), 6 There were jiggers,
cod lines, bank lines, rope, tar, pitch.

banker n Cp *DARE* ~ n 2 (1704-) for sense 1.
1 1984 KELLAND 75 The snow thinned out for a few
minutes, which enabled them to sight a banker in the
distance.

banking vbl n
1 1987 FIZZARD 135 'Banking was the big thing in
Grand Bank. There'd be times there was so many schooners in the harbour, we could hardly get in the gut with
our dories. 'Twould be packed with schooners.'
2 Attrib, comb **banking skipper**, SKIPPER n 1,
~ **voyage**, VOYAGE.
[1936] 1986 *Evening Telegram* 13 Feb, p. 6 Capt.
Kennedy for a number of years operated as master on the
South West Coast and is one of the most outstanding
banking skippers of the country. 1984 KELLAND 30 Before a banking voyage commenced both dories and dorymen were assigned to port or starboard sides.

banner n Small square candy in cellophane wrapper, sold two for one cent (P 30-89).
1979 PORTER 32 Most of the time I figured my money
would go for a Graham Sandwich bar and a cent's worth
of banner caramels.

bantam n Bantam occurs four times in Nova
Scotia place-names. An offshore shoal or rock.
1983 *Gazetteer of Canada: Nfld* 6, 26, 145 The Bantam,
Bantam Banks, ~ Rock, Bullhead Bantam, Renews ~.

bar[1] n See BAR v 2.
4 Comb **bar seine**: a net which is hauled in to
entrap herring.

1987 POWELL 14 Herring and codfish were our main
sources of fishing. We used big bar seines that took
hundreds of barrels of herring.

barachois n also **barachoix**. Cp PRATT ~ (1901-).
1904 MCALPINE 487 Fortune Bay District...Barachoix
Cove. 1986 *Evening Telegram* 6 Feb, p. 4 Phase two
would start next spring with the building of the dock and
loadout facilities, breaching of the barrachois and dredging of the channel and Freshwater Bay Pond.

barasway n also **barsway**. For a similar eighteenth-century pronunciation of Fr -*ois* as -*way*, see
shalloway (from *charroy*).
1984 KELLAND 15 The barrisway...was an excellent
area on whose waters young people both male and female
could learn to row as well as sail boats. It is a miniature
inland sea, completely landlocked with the exception of a
narrow gut that connects it with the waters of the harbour
and through which its tides rise and fall. 1985 *Nfld Qtly*
lxxxi (1), 19 There was skating on the 'barsway,' a corruption of the French word barachois, meaning shallow
inlet.

barber n *DARE* ~ (1832-) for sense 2.

barge n
[1895] 1977 WHITELEY 52 In 1895 Bossy Whiteley
applied for bounties on 30 fishing boats, each of which
was 20 ft. long, and also on his barges which he said
were about 3 tons each and equipped with sails.

bark n See PATENT BARK.
1 1986 *Them Days* xi (4), 21 After two days and
nights of soaking in bark, as it was called, the nets were
taken out, drained and hung on poles to dry.
2 Comb **bark pot**.
1985 *Evening Telegram* 7 Sep, p. 13 Other improvements will be carried out...to accom[m]odate several
historic items on the grounds, including a...bark pot.

bark v
1989 *Evening Telegram* 16 May, p. 7A The rest of the
[trouting] equipment consisted of around 30 or 40 feet of
cod trap line which had been 'barked' or tanned.

barked p ppl
2 Comb **bark[ed] sail duff**; DUFF[1] n.
1985 *Terminology of Loggers* 2 ~ steamed molasses
pudding with spices.

barking vbl n
2 Comb **barking house**, ~ **kettle**, ~ **pot**.
1837 *Royal Gazette* 5 Dec [advertisement:] a stone
built barking house (with kettle, etc) about 35' by 16.
1975 BUTLER 76 Originally [the tan boiler] was referred
to as a barking kettle. That was the appropriate name, a
barking kettle to bark twine and sails in. 1988 *Evening
Telegram* 27 Aug, p. A4 'Are you suggesting...that your
true-blue Barking Kettle fellow is a chap with the arse
out of his trousers?' 1987 POOLE 78 I had a man to help
me bring the traps to the barking pot and help me to
bring them back when they were finished.

barley over int also **barrel over**. Cp *DARE* barley 'in children's games: time out!'
1985 *A Yaffle of Yarns* 132 The reference to woods
had to do with a game of hide and seek called barrel-over
and not to any serious sins of the flesh.

barm n *DARE* ~ n[1] (1859, 1975).

barnystickle n also **barnstickle, barnytickle*,
branchy*, branstickle***. Cp *OED* banstickle; *DBE*
banny-sinkle. See SPANTICKLE. Small fish found in
fresh or brackish water; PRICKLY.
1966 PADDOCK 93 Barn-stickles—very small freshwater
fish. 1967 *Bk of Nfld* iv, 243 We learnt to swim in a little
salt-water pond, called Barney Pond because it had
barneystickles in it. P 41-68 In late spring the children
took to the brooks with a tin can to trap branchies, about
one inch long. 1986 SAUNDERS 21 Beyond that [was] the
beach where we could capture barneystickles with our
hands in the rock pools.

barrack n *DARE* ~ (1697-).

barrel n
1 [1841] 1985 TAYLOR 37 Each barrel [of pickled fish
shall contain] two hundred pounds...weight. [1937] 1987
Evening Telegram 5 Jan, p. 6 S.S. *Portia* which left
English Harbour on Sunday for Halifax took 926 casks of
codfish, 642 one-quintal boxes of fish, and 1,529 two-
quintal barrels of fish, besides 9 casks of cod oil and 11
barrels of pickled salmon. P 245-90 'We got two barrels
[of cod-fish] today, not much, we've got up to six a day
last week.'
2 1987 *Evening Telegram* 27 Apr, p. 7 [The barrel]
stood six feet high and was about 30 inches in diameter.
It had a hatch in the bottom and it was strong because a
man's life depended on it, 70 or 80 feet in the air. The
man would go up to the bottom, push up the hatch and
when he was inside the hatch would fall down and he
would stand on it. That was the last barrel I made.
3 Comb **barrel chair**, ~ **man**, ~ **stove**.
1988 DOHANEY 15 Bertha recalled the old woman she
had left downstairs sitting in the barrel chair by the stove,
all hunched over in a black shawl. 1897 *Christmas Review* 2 ''Half an Hour with the Barrel-Man on Board
Steamship 'Grand Lake'.'' 1985 BUSCH 74 The other
subordinate officers had to be capable—they included the
second hand, 'barrelman,' who had the responsibility of
spotting seals from the crow's nest [etc]. 1988 SINCLAIR
(ed) 142 Protesters and their supporters brought a baseball
dugout, which they walled in and equipped with a barrel
stove.

barrener n
1987 MONTEVECCHI & TUCK 237 ~ Rock ptarmigan.

barricade n
1987 POOLE 7 By this time the waves were breaking
over our barrack head and the deck of the *Polly* was
covered with water.

barricado n also **batty catter**.
2 1986 FELTHAM 98 From December to March,

freezing spray and raftering slob ice piled up a rampart
of 'batty catters' along the shore line. When the water
warmed in the April sun, the lower part of this icy ring
that girded the islands melted, leaving overhanging ice.

barrow[1] n
1 1987 POWELL 104 They told me of the time when
they carried all their fish to the flakes in one barrow load.
1990 *Evening Telegram* 9 Jan, p. 4 [I am] one who
carried many a barrow of fish from the flake and saw it
shipped away on vessels from Placentia Bay.

barvel n *DARE* ~ n 1 N E (1629-).
1987 *Evening Telegram* 27 Apr, p. 7 [tape transcript]
[The seal skinners] wore a barbel (barvel) made out of
calfskin with the fur inside. There was no heat in the
building where we were skinning the pelts so when your
hands got cold you just put them inside the barbel so
they'd get warm.

bat n
2 Comb **bat(s)man**:
1985 BUSCH 55 The two middle men—'batsmen,' for
they did little but row and carry a gaff or 'bat' when on
the ice—came cheaply.

batch n
P 317-75 The finer the snow, the bigger the batch.
1984 POWELL 81 The nearest firewood was five miles
inland. This was so small that they almost had to dig it
out of the snow after a big batch. 1986 SAUNDERS 24
One of his favourite stories was about 'The Seventh of
April Batch,' a snowfall so heavy that one of the Horwood Lumber Company's horses perished.

bateau n also **batto**.
[(1765) 1971 BANKS 205 They also brought one of
their Women's Boats or Skin Battoes with near 20
Women with their Children in it.] 1837 BLUNT 36 At the
eastern side of [Belle Isle] is another cove called Batteaux
Creek, frequented occasionally by shallops.

batty catter See BARRICADO.

bavin n *SED* iv, 543 Brk Ha.

bawbeen* n Cp *OED* bawbee 'Scotch coin of
base silver'; *DARE* 'a trifle'; perhaps influenced by
similar forms **crubeen, gombeen, sleeveen**. Very
small object or amount.
P 297-83 Times were so bad, we never had a bawbeen
left in the pantry.

bawk n
1986 FELTHAM 71 Towards the end of May, some
fishermen periodically made trips to the outer banks to try
for cod, and at the same time, kill a meal or two of
'bawks.'

bawl v *SED* iv, 344-5 So W D.
1986 SAUNDERS 187 We stayed there until we heard
the first robin bawl in the morning, then we left for
home. 1988 DOHANEY 13 She lay awake in the back

bedroom of the Corrigans' house, listening to the fog horn on the beach bawl like a caged bull.

bawn n

2 1988 *Evening Telegram* 18 May, p. 19 A bawn was a level, dry area of beach, sometimes used instead of flakes.

3 1987 *Evening Telegram* 4 July, p. 56 [tape transcript] We couldn't get a fish and we never saw a seal. We did nothing only make a bit of bawn and waited.

bay n

1 1987 FIZZARD 54 As the largest settlement in the bay, [Grand Bank] must have been a tempting target [for the French].

3 Phr

[1937] 1983 FROUDE 124 I baught a stock of dry goods and went Around the bay to sell them. 1987 PEYTON 116 He travelled around the bay for the government, placing floating incubators of lobster roe from the hatchery at Dildo, Trinity Bay, in various locations.

[proverb]

1986 *Evening Telegram* 2 Jan, p. 13 Although no longer in Newfoundland, the islanders [at Fort McMurray, Alberta] never forget where they came from. 'They say you can take the boy from the bay...but you can't take the bay out of the boy.'

[child's rhyme]

1979 PORTER 8 Married in grey, you'll live in the bay.

4 Attrib, comb **bay boy, ~ caplin, ~ ice, bayman, ~ noddy, ~ run**: rock band tour to various communities, **~ seal, ~ stock**: concentration of year-round cod population in coastal waters, **~ wop.**

[1985] MAHER 6 [My mother closed up the house and went to Heart's Desire.] That's how I became a bay boy for the first six years of my life! 1987 POWELL 122-3 I found that [the cod] were living mainly on bay caplin, which is a small fish that stayed in the bay. 1986 *Evening Telegram* 7 Apr, p. 2 People living in the community of Hampden [White Bay] don't want the ice broken up [by the ice-breaker] as people there are involved in logging during the winter and spring and use the bay ice for a roadway. 1988 PORTER 161 'Take the baymen out of St John's and you wouldn't have much left,' said the male voice. 1987 O'FLAHERTY 31 Someone else in the [St John's family] termed him 'a bay-noddy.' So he was. 1986 *Nfld Herald* 27 Dec, p. 30 There's a workable circuit on what bands affectionately call the 'bay run,' but there's an embarrassing shortage of live venues —especially for rock bands—in the capital city. 1986 SAUNDERS 63 We always carried our shotguns in case we spotted some sea ducks or a bay seal. P 245-87 'The inshore fishery report recommends that fisheries scientists investigate the existence and status of the various bay stocks.' 1987 *Nfld Herald* 14 Nov, p. 5 Up until a few years ago, people of the outports were looked down upon and referred to as 'baywops' by certain segments of the St John's population.

baygapple See BAKEAPPLE.

be v Cp *EDD* be VIII 5 do be (Ir); *DBE* be[1] bes, doesn't be; be[2] does be (white), ~ (boiling); *DARE*

be: B 1 g 'habitual action or usual condition' (1917-81); C 1 b isn't; C 2 a wasn't; C 2 d weren't. See AIN'T.

be's, bee's:

1927 *Christmas Messenger* 13 ''Big Davey's 'Come-All-Ye's' '': Sometimes we be's gathered about the stage-door. T 266-66 And we always bees be frightened. T 1052-72 So she was goin to the high school an' he bes [bɪz] in the lower school. P 306-73 I be's right tired.

don't be:

T 236-66 And now I don't be tellin this story, ya see. T 245-66 Don't be talkin! 1982 MCDOOLING 115 [Irish settlement] Some of them [berths] don't be very good.

isn't pronunciations: [cp AIN'T: ent]

T 70-64 That's a great cuffer, int it? That's a great story, isn't it? T 171-65 'Art, boy, I got a bottle o' syrup!' 'Nah!' he said, ''Tidn't a bottle o' syrup!' And I said, ''Tis!' C 71-100 'Id'n'em, squid'n'em?' asked an elderly fisherman speaking to another who had just come in from his lobster pots and who replied, 'Narn, all et up.' [Cp MAJOR below.] 1973 BARBOUR 85 from the back of the little school chapel boomed a thundering voice, 'Naw, naw, dat idden de number I put on de paper.' 1981 MAJOR 36 'Grandfather,' I said after a while, 'squiddin is a lot o' fun, idn't it?' 'Yes, b'y, it is so.' 1985 *A Yaffle of Yarns* 94 'I idn't half nor quarter well dis marnin' 'cos I didn't close a ''heye'' last night.' 1987 FIZZARD 189 I said 'That's a good one, e'den it? We won't be long going down if they do change their mind on us.'

wasn't pronunciations:

T 409-67 There was plenty o' fish, but you couldn't fish...at them times down there. You wadden allowed to fish. T 449-67 (Were the children ever afraid of the mummers?) Yes, some was, and some...some more waddent. T 751-70 Clear o' that there wadden nobody knowed un clear of I. 1985 *Nfld LifeStyle* iii (1), 24 If 'twoodin fer Wilson Earle and Twillingate eye school, I [wouldn't have] ben able to read yer recipe on page 29.

weren't pronunciations:

T 47-64 If you werdn't up to the standard, we'll say if you couldn't do either [any] job reasonably, they'd send ya down. T 541-67 When you go on dole, I call it, you werd'n allowed to catch n'ar fish. No, that you werd'n.

being pronunciations:

1929 [1982] MADISON (ed) 13 ''The Wreck of the S.S. *Ethie*'': [One brave man] says he can guide her safely on the shore./Walter Young been our purser, as you may understand/Volunteered for to guide her safely into the land. P 148-63 [sign in store] Everything been sold at rock bottom prices.

be prep See BY.

beach n Cp *Seafisheries of Nfld* (1937), pp. 50-1 for the operation of curing fish on beaches.

1 Also: in phr *build beaches* (cp BAWN: *make bawn*), *point of beach* (place-names).

1987 FIZZARD 116 The harbour was shallow except for an area opposite the 'Point of Beach,' where the present fish plant is located. ibid 139 Winter was also the season for building beaches. Merchants who were starting up operations or needing to expand their beaches, hired men to bring gravel from the natural beach to the flat grassy area nearby... The process was repeated until the new beach was at a depth of about two feet. The rate of pay for this work was about ten cents a barrel. P 245-90 'You'd just try to get a place on the beach' [curing cod].

2 Attrib, comb **beach racket,** ~ **rock,** ~ **room,** ~ **woman.**

1987 FIZZARD 132 'On the beaches the women take charge. Soon after Christmas the "beach racket," starts. The women wonder with whom they will be working this year. One woman is the boss and she has a crew of nine.' 1988 DOHANEY 46 'And that's as sure as God made beachrocks.' 1837 *Royal Gazette* Dec 5 [ad] Together with spacious wharves with beach room for curing fish and mfg. oil. 1987 FIZZARD 159 Throughout the community...there was less and less demand for beach women, longshoremen, sail makers and all others whose livelihoods were tied to the bank fishery. P 245-90 'On the shore the job became the responsibility of the beach women.'

beat v

1 1985 *Canadian Sealers Association* 6 'After the young seals become 6 to 8 weeks old, they start their journey north, which is known as beating their way north.'

2 Phr

1977 MOAKLER 138 We pulled our dory, sleeping as we rowed/...The sunset found us chilled and be't to snots. 1987 KIMIECIK 99 '"On the roads," "beating the paths," "on the prowl," all describe the custom of just going out and walking around, at night, either with a girl or looking for one.'

beater

1 1985 BUSCH 44 Now the mother deserts the pup, which soon takes to the water itself, at this point having shed all traces of its whitecoat, as a 'beater' with a black-spotted light grey coat. 1986 *Evening Telegram* 22 Apr, p. 3 This year [Carino Co] will buy only adult beater pelts, and they will pay up to $15 per pelt.

beaver[1] n Attrib, comb **beaver hat,** ~ **house,** also freq in names of ponds, ~ **tail.**

1985 BUSCH 50 Many schooner-rigged vessels of 60-80 tons used for various fishing chores were turned into 'beaver hats' for the seal fishery, with one large temporary foremast topsail rigged to help through the ice and to back the vessel when jammed. 1904 *McAlpine* 570 Beaver House Road, (St John's West). 1961 ROULEAU 13 Beaver House Pond, Englee. 1985 *Decks Awash* Jan-Feb, p. 25 There are several different designs [of snowshoes]: roundtails, which they call bear-paws now, beavertails and porcupine tails with the curved tails and rattails with the one long point.

bedlamer n

1 1988 *Sunday Express* 20 Nov, p. 12 And right up to the end [of November] there has always been thousands of fish... But this year around the 28th of October, we found 17 or 18 bedlamer seals in our nets and the fish had disappeared. **2** 1986 FELTHAM 102 During the late fall, winter and early spring, dawn invariably found the 'bedlamer' boy

hidden snugly on an island point waiting for the eider ducks to fly.

been v 'being.' See BE.

bee's See BE.

beetle n *SED* iv, 129 So D Do Ha.

belay v

2 1949 FITZGERALD 33 'Keep her off a point;/B'lay on the bow and pull the cuddy oar.'

belk v *SED* iv, 753-4 So W Co D Do Ha.

1985 *A Yaffle of Yarns* 107 Well, I ya'ns and I ga'ps and I ga'ps and I ya'ns and bime-by I 'belks' up wind, 'saving your presence.'

bell n

1986 *Them Days* xi (4), 10 In addition to the various stores and warehouses [in Rigolet], there was the Manager's dwelling; a handsome, bell-roofed building which housed my father and his large family, plus one to three clerks or apprentices.

belong v

2 1988 *Evening Telegram* 31 May, p. 11 I kept in touch with Charlie till he died about five years ago. He swore to the last that my rescuers did not belong to Labrador.

bench n A ledge or shelf of some size jutting out from a vertical rock formation.

1983 *Gazetteer of Canada; Newfoundland* 11 [The] Bench (Hill). 1987 MONTEVECCHI & TUCK 163 [feature name] Anthony's Bench, Shooting Bench.

beothuk n Current commercial names have var spellings: **beothic, beothick, beothuck, beothuk** [bɪ'ɒtɪk]

1 1981 MAJOR 74 All the teacher asked him was how he thought the Beothucks would be treated if there was some still alive today. 1983 NEARY & O'FLAHERTY 18 Recent archaeological excavation at Cape Freels shows that the Beothucks were living in coastal Newfoundland from A.D. 200 to 750. Thus, somewhat surprisingly, they co-existed for about four centuries with the Dorset Eskimo culture.

berry[1] n Attrib, comb **berry acki**: see also ~ **ocky,** ~ **barrens** [see BARRENS n pl 2], ~ **bucket,** ~ **ground.**

1924 *Deep Sea Fishers* xxi (4), 139 Berryacki—A drink made from partridge berries. 1988 *Evening Telegram* 25 June, p. 13 [He] said the new dump site will not be detrimental to the berry barrens, wild life or nearby fishing ponds. 1981 DAWE 9 "A Fairy Tale": She carries a berry bucket/and cries/because she has no money/to drive the fairies away. 1986 FELTHAM 88 Expeditions to the berry grounds of other islands were common.

berth n

1 1987 *Evening Telegram* 18 Apr, p. 23 [tape

transcript] He had so many berths sent him from Bowring Brothers. I went out and got a berth on the *Viking* from him.

3 1984 POWELL 23 The [salmon] nets were sixty fathoms long, so we joined them together and put two in a berth, then ran the nets about seventy-five fathoms straight. 1987 POOLE 75 I had no berths; everybody at Fox Harbour considered that the berths were theirs, as their fathers and grandfathers fished them and that the berths belonged to them.

5 Attrib, comb ~ **money**.

1985 BUSCH 55 Owners, with limited supply to meet considerable demand, found they could charge the men a fee, 'berth money,' merely for the privilege of stepping aboard [a sealing vessel].

berth v To moor or place a fish-net or 'trap' on an inshore fishing station.

1977 MOAKLER 65 We berthed our codtrap in the Kettle Pike,/The cod and caplin swarming round the set.

be's See BE.

bib n

3 Attrib, comb **two-bibbed lamp**: oil lamp with spouts for placing wicks.

1885 *Terra Nova Advocate* 21 Oct Our mind wanders back to the time when the 'two-bibbed' cod oil lamp swung in the stage, and a brown penny candle graced our dining room.

bibby n

1987 DAWE [10] B is for bibby,/A small outdoor kettle,/As black as the soot,/It has tin for its metal.

biff n Revised entry: Lapland longspur (*Calcarius lapponicus*).

P 161-88 It is a common spring and fall migrant and often fed in old potato gardens and I often heard people in L'Anse aux Meadows call them 'Biffs.'

biggest kind n phr Colloquial formula indicating general approval; in the best state, quantity or condition; FINEST KIND.

1987 FIZZARD 188 'We had the biggest kind of day's work of fish.'

billy n also **belly**. Comb **billygale, ~ knocker**.

[1905] 1987 REEVES 517 'Billygale' was a 'sobriquet to designate the laborers or peasantry of Newfoundland who came to Cape Breton to work' ([Corner Brook] *Western Star* 1 Feb 1905). A term used in this period, 'Billygale' was derived from a Newfoundlander named William Gale, a 'rough' and 'uncouth' character supposedly driven ashore in Cape Breton during a storm. 1986 *Evening Telegram* 14 Jan, p. 4 He felt [he] had the right to 'resist that unlawful arrest' by two [policemen] with 'belly knockers,' referring to the police batons.

birch n Attrib, comb **birch broom, ~ junk, ~ rind**.

[1900] 1989 *Nfld Qtly* lxxxv (2), 25 The homemade

birchbroom that was used by the hired girl to scrub the flagstone walks that crisscrossed in an intricate pattern to reach every building on our farm stood at the back door. 1986 FELTHAM 175 Many Labrador schoonermen augmented their income by cutting birch junks...during the winter and taking them to St John's, to be sold in the spring. 1986 SAUNDERS 146 Birch rind—I mean big sheets of birch rind...the kind you get off a white birch you can just get your arms around—was all we ever used.

birchy a

1 1987 POWELL 173 I didn't even notice that the sun had already gone behind the big birchy hill. I would have to get moving towards home.

bird[1] n

1 1986 *Evening Telegram* 31 Jan, p. 2 Bird hunters in three different areas [off Port aux Basques, in Trinity Bay, and off Grand Bank] of the province were on the missing list Thursday but they were all safe and sound this morning.

2 Attrib **bird rock**.

1895 *Xmas Review* 4 [poem] "The Bird Rock."

birding vbl n

1 1986 SAUNDERS 63 We decided to do a little birding at Farewell Head, which was only five miles or so [away].

birth v To act as midwife toward; to deliver; BORN.

1985 *Nfld Qtly* lxxx (4), 28 She improved the gardens and the nutrition and she comforted the mothers and birthed the babies.

bitch n See PORK: *pork bitch*.

2 [1900] 1989 *Nfld Qtly* lxxxv (2), 27 As a dessert [on sealing vessel], hard tack, broken with a hammer or marling pick, was soaked for a few minutes in water, then briefly heated in a pan with molasses and a bit of butter. This mess was rudely labelled 'bitch.'

bivver v *SED* biver(ing) iv, 758 So.

1914 *Deep Sea Fishers* xii, July, p. 59 The people were all 'bivering' with the cold.

black a Cp *DARE* black ice n 1 (1944-), PRATT ~ 1 for sense 1; *Anglo-Manx Dialect* for phr *black stranger* in sense 2; *DARE* ~ fly (1776-) for cpd in sense 4.

2 1989 *Evening Telegram* 14 June, p. 2 She also criticized Newfoundlanders for the way they raise their children. 'The child was nothing. The blackest kind of stranger could come off the street and he would be treated better.' 1990 *Sunday Telegram* 11 Feb, p. 5 I remember the [Catholic] religious pageantry, the uniforms, the dedicated nuns and the special feeling of being different from the 'black' Protestants.

3 T 437-65 'Well' he said 'old man I was just aimin' at a black shot o' ducks' he says 'in th' other world.' P 278-87 The men just home from the lumber camps are black ardent, the women say.

4 In names: **black bawk, ~ bird, ~ fly, ~ marling spike**: pomarine jaeger.

1986 FELTHAM 94 The sooty shearwater, or 'black bawk'...could dive down to the trawls if they were set in shallow water. 1987 MONTEVECCHI & TUCK 243 Blackbird. European starling. [1847] 1986 BAYFIELD ii, 320 Lieut. Hancock returned with face swelled, and eyes nearly closed from the bites of Black Flies & 'Gally nippers.' 1988 *Evening Telegram* 2 June, p. 13 'Take lots of insect repellent,' she said, 'the black flies will attack you by the millions.' [1879] 1987 MONTEVECCHI & TUCK 239 Black marling spike. Pomarine jaeger.

6 Comb **black ball**.

1984 KELLAND 180 The [dory] buoys carried flags, usually circular in shape, which were commonly called black balls, as in most cases they were painted black with a white oversized dot in the center, on those white centers were painted numbers which corresponded with the numbers on the bows of the dories that carried them.

black n

1985 JOHNSTON 101 Whenever it started raining, Dola would say, 'Here comes a bath for de blacks.' Her way of saying that it had been raining for some time was, 'De Prodestins must be down to last year's dirt by now.' 1985 *Nfld LifeStyle* 3 (1), 26 'You're marrying one of them Mainlanders and he's a black, too?'

blackberry n

1 Also attrib.

1898 *J A Folklore* xi, 279 *Empetrum nigrum*, L., ...red berry, black berry, rock berry...Newfoundland... Labrador. 1987 FIZZARD 179 The first [berries] to ripen were the blackberries, which grew profusely, especially on the Cape, and were used mainly for blackberry grunts.

2 1982 MCDOOLING 81-2 In the summer of 1981... much of the 'blackberry fish' had to be salted... These fish are no good for freezing but they can be saved if they are split and salted. 1990 *Evening Telegram* 14 Jan, p. 19 What happens when the U.S. market takes a dip and the collectors don't want to go there; or when there is black berry in the fish?

bladder n

2 1985 DOMSTAD 18 To clean cuts take turkumtine blathers from a green balsom tree.

blare v *SED* iv, 342 So W Do Ha, 344 So D Do Ha for sense 1.

2 1930 *Am Speech* v, 389 ~ v. or n. The crying of birds or a baby, or may be used to indicate the sound of a steam or compressed-air whistle.

blasty a Comb **blasty bough**, cp SPRAY.

1980 *Gazette* 18 Sep, p. 8 'Some [of the trees] may have gone a bit blasty, but they appear to be doing quite well.' 1982 BURSEY 22 "No Sadness of Farewell": Fall days cutting winter wood,/Sweet-smelling wood of birch and alder,/Fir, spruce and juniper;/Blasty boughs cremated/To warm feet and fingers. 1988 *Evening Telegram* 30 Sep, p. 6 Well, fellow Newfoundlanders of like mind, are we too green to burn or has the time come to bring on the blasty boughs?

blocked p ppl

1988 *Women, Work and Family* 97 '[The messroom of

the oil rig] is blocked—with men. They watch you from the minute you walk in, they watch what you eat, where you sit.' 1989 *Networker* July p. 7 Tuesday, Wednesday, and Thursday evenings [at the music conservatory] are blocked.

blood n

1 1981 MAJOR 78 'You blood-of-a-bitch!' I fired down my books and grabbed into the last fellow who spoke. 1987 FELT 1 'Take the bloods of bitches to the gallows' [fisherman instructing his son to take some 'slubbed'— and hence unfishable—nets to the drying rack].

2 Comb ~ **end**: that part of the 'sound bone' of a cod which is removed when the fish is split, a portion of the flesh adhering to the bone and cooked as a delicacy (P 113-87); RISE END.

P 300-89 ~ the end of the sound bone closest to the tail.

bloody a

1986 *Evening Telegram* 22 Mar, p. 4 The departure was [watched by] thousands of people lining the [St John's waterfront] to wish the sealers 'bloody decks and a safe return.'

blow n *AND* ~ n[4] (1855-), *SED* iv, 864 So D Do Ha.

1986 FELTHAM 166 A hundred yards, a short 'blow,' two hundred yards, a longer 'spell' and hour after hour the men got nearer and nearer to their home tickle [over the ice]. P 245-89 'I was just standin' there for a while havin' a blow.'

blow-me-down n

1971 *Can Geog J* lxxxii, 165 Names along the north Labrador coast are a delight: Cutthroat Tickle; Slambang Bay; Blow-Me Down Mountain.

blubber n

1 Add: the residue left after the extraction of the oil; SCRUNCHIONS.

1986 *Them Days* xi (4), 45-6 [After straining out the oil] they'd take that, the scrunchions or blubber, whatever was left, and put that in bags [for pressing]. They'd throw away those old scrunchions then, or blubber as we called it. 1988 *Atlantic Co-operator* Feb, p. 14 The plant...is equipped with machinery which removes blubber and cleans the [seal] skins.

3 1981 PADDOCK 26 "Stink": Both bellies filled, her man and I proceed/Some lobster bait to boil—/The dregs scraped from his blubber barrel/And three half-putrid fish. 1984 POWELL 128 So we decided to go down to the stage and beat up the blubber puncheons.

4 Comb **blubber yard**: area on the shore for landing and processing of seal 'pelts' and 'fat.'

[1919] 1989 *Nfld Qtly* lxxxv (1), 13 'I managed to get out again and opened the blubber yard so as to give the dogs something to eat to save them attacking the people.' 1984 KALLEO 38 Paul's Island was a haven for schooners. It even had a blubber yard because it was a good sealing place in the fall.

blue a

1 blueback.

1984 WRIGHT 75 In 1979, a first-class blueback pelt
was worth $56, whereas a first-class whitecoat pelt was
worth only $26.

2 Also blue wavy.

[1888] 1907 TOWNSEND & ALLEN 340-1 Blue Goose...
According to Indian report, a great breeding-ground for
the blue wavy is the country lying in the interior.

4 Comb ~ bunch, ~ card: see **~ note.**

1985 *Terminology of Loggers* 3 Blue-bunch. A prime
stand of timber. 1987 POWELL 88 Each fisherman received a little book. Then the [fish] buyer obtained the
stamps from the post office and they were recorded in the
fisherman's book. Little blue cards were also available.
In some cases, when the fisherman did not have his book
available, the fish buyers would put the stamps on the
blue card and then give it to the fisherman to enclose in
his little book.

boat n
2 See FLAG[1]: flag boat.
3 Comb ~ keeper, ~ share: see SHARE n 1.

[1670] 1963 YONGE 135-6 Amidst my study here I
revised the rough draft of some occasional meditations I
had made before, and also observed what was true of the
complaints against boat-keepers, and collected arguments
pro and con, intending to publish them in behalf of the
latter, I mean the byboats. 1982 MCDOOLING 109 The old
system is one where the proceeds [from the catch] are
divided equally among the crew members and each man
is equally responsible for contributing to the 'boat share.'

bobber n
1 1987 POWELL 123 It looked strange to go up the bay
and see the red bobbers of a big cod trap in the shallow
water at the bottom of the bay.

bobbing vbl n
2 Comb ~ hole: also fig.

1988 *Nfld Qtly* lxxxiii (4), 14 I'll expose your belief
fer what it really is: a 'bobbin' hole' of superstition you
can conveniently slip down through whenever reality
threatens.

body n Cp *DARE body (boots) and britches*;
FACE: *face and eyes*. Phr *body and bones*: the
whole body.

P 311-83 There was a tradition of carrying a man,
body and bones if necessary, to the public house if he
was caught doing anything, such as chopping wood, on
St Stephen's Day (Boxing Day).

bog n Attrib ~ **tree** 'spruce tree growing in
boggy land, hence scraggy, yellowish' (P 148-86),
~ **water.**

1985 *Metro* 1 Sep, p. 16 [These imported beers have]
the taste of bog water.

bogger n
1984 *Nfld Herald* 25 Aug, p. 4 After school I could be
found playing in the courtyard or doing 'boggers' with
my less agile friends on the hillside—my mother called
them cliffs—that bordered the school.

bogie n
[c1891] 1988 *Canoma* xiv (2), 11 Bogy Ledge, ~
Reef [area of Eastern Shoals]. 1986 FELTHAM 50-1
[Later] a shelter was built on the front of the [seine skiff]
called a 'cuddy,' a small wood-burning stove called a
'bogey' was installed and the fishermen had shelter,
warmth and a means of cooking simple meals. 1988
Evening Telegram 25 June, p. 13 The vestry was heated
by a small iron stove called a 'bogey.'

boil v *AND* ~ v[2] (1923-).

1984 KALLEO 2 We'd stop to boil up and eat frozen
seal-meat. After lunch, we're off again! 1986 SAUNDERS
86 Just above The Works there's this stretch of calm
water where he and a companion stopped one summer
day to boil the kettle.

boiler n *DARE* ~ n[1] (1903-) for sense 1.
1 [1987] QUINLAN 7 Cooking gear consisted of boilers,
bake pots, tea pots, frying pans and sauce pans. 1987
POOLE 61 We were working late that evening and didn't
have time to get any wood for our little camp stove, so
we got a boiler from one of our neighbours and put on
our scoff of pork and cabbage.
3 Person who tends a pot.

1983 MARTIN 55 [At the Bell Island mine] young boys
worked the year around as ore cobbers or as 'boilers,'
boilers being responsible for keeping tea pots full for
thirsty miners.

boil-up n *AND* ~ (1934-).
1984 POWELL 58 As I got to the far end [of the lake],
as usual it was boil-up time.

bonfire n
1987 *Evening Telegram* 6 Nov, p. 2 Guy Fawkes
Night, or bonfire night as it is more commonly called,
kept the St John's Fire Department busy as they
responded to 64 calls [last night], most of them bonfire-
related.

boo n
4 Comb ~ bagger, ~ man.
1983 DAWE & FICKEN 12 He's a boo-bagger
devil,/Some people might say;/He waits to snatch
children/And swoosh them away. ibid B is for boo-
man/Who lurks in the dark;/He's blacker than soot/And
he's quick as a spark.

book n
1987 *Nfld Qtly* lxxxiii (2), 43 The *first class* of the
school was the class of the older pupils—approximately
age 10—and their Reading curriculum used Old Testament and the Fourth Book of the Irish National series.
The *Second class* (age 8) handled New Testament and the
Third Book of the Irish National Series. The Third Class
(age 7) used Union Book and Second Book of Irish
National Series.

born v *DARE* ~ 2, 3. Cp BIRTH.
1979 PORTER 95 My grandmother and her mother
before her had been 'borning' babies as far back as
anyone could remember.

bottle n Comb **bottle-nosed drake**.
1987 MONTEVECCHI & TUCK 235 ~ King eider.

bottom[1] n
1 1987 POWELL 49-50 In late April or early May they would leave the bottom of the bay where their winter homes were—where there was shelter from the winter storms and plenty of firewood—and go to their summer homes. 1989 *Evening Telegram* 14 Dec, p. 1 'The average earnings for a lobster fisherman at the bottom of Fortune Bay could be around $5,200 and that in itself accounts for maybe 80 or 85 per cent of his fishing income.'
2 Also: the lower portion of a trawl net; hence comb **bottom roller**: one of the steel balls or rubber disks, 40.6 to 61 cm in diameter, that are mounted on the bottom of the net (1986 *Nfld's Deepsea Fishery* 650).
[1899] 1977 WHITELEY 40 'Finding this worked well the bottom net or "trap" was first tried in 1871 with great success.' 1986 *Nfld's Deepsea Fishery* 650 A horseshoe [is] a raised semi-circular portion of the trawl deck on some stern trawlers... Bottom rollers fit snugly around it when the net is yanked back on deck.

bough n Cp *AND* ~ 'used attrib. in combs to denote a type of structure' for sense 2.
1 1987 FIZZARD 172 'You'd get out [of the motor car] when you saw a mud hole. You'd cut some boughs and put in the holes. And if she got stuck, we'd put tackle on the tree and haul her out and go on again.'
2 Comb **bough bed, ~ whiffen, ~ whiffet**.
1986 *Nfld Herald* 12 Apr, p. 22 [We] would go off into the wilderness along the Southern Shore and set up camps from scratch. I used to make the bough bed. 1981 MAJOR 195 We might a gone off in the woods somewhere, away from the campsites altogether and fixed up a shelter out of boughs—a boughwiffen we calls it. 1986 SAUNDERS 81 Since a two-man wigwam only took two hours or so to put up and a bough whiffet much less, we were never stuck for shelter.

bough v
1832 MOSS *MS Diary* 12 June Hands finishing boughing the flake.

bow[1] n [bou]
2 1987 *Evening Telegram* 24 Oct, p. 14 The bows are made of laminated material together with the rings [which] are brought in from the mainland.

boxy a PRATT, p. 23.
1984 POWELL 145 Even a slab from a boxy stick could hurt anyone who came too close [to the saw].

boy n Cp *Anglo-Manx Dialect* for sense 1.
2 [1983] 1985 LEHR & BEST (eds) 53 "The Drunken Captain": Our mate came up with the devil's fright/ Sayin': 'B'ys she's filling through the big skylight.' 1986 SAUNDERS 186 'Leave me here, b'ys,' he kept saying. 'I'm all right.' But he...was full of water and his face and hands were cold as ice. 1987 JOHNSTON 26 And while Dad, with half a dozen men holding him, swore

and shouted, Murchie was hustled out of the kitchen. 'Have ya got no better sense b'y,' the men said.

brail v Also: to transfer fish from a seine or cod-trap to a boat using a 'dip-net.'
1984 *Evening Telegram* 22 Mar, p. 5A The netting is then fastened to the trap boat and to one of the smaller boats in position at the back of the trap. The fish are then brailed into the trap boat with long-handled dipnets.

brailer n A net used to transfer fish from a 'trap' or 'seine' to a boat.
P 245-89 'A few hauls with the brailer and you've got a load [of caplin] from the seine.'

bran See BRAND.

brand n also **bran**. Cp *OED* ~ sb 2 'a piece of wood that has been burning on the hearth'; *EDD* sb[1] 1 'a log of wood for burning.' In making a fire on an open hearth, the smallest of the pieces of wood laid for lighting with 'bavins' or 'chovies'; ignited, or 'live,' such a log used in a Christmas Eve ceremony (second 1937 quot), and, in query to a hurried visitor, *come for a brand*? phrasal use.
1866 WILSON 353 The fire was made upon the hearth, and the wood supported by dog-irons. If the fire required a second tier of wood, it was supported upon the lower tier, by small sticks called triggers, which were placed crossways. A large stick was placed against the back, a smaller one in front, and a lesser one still in the middle. The wood was sometimes quite green, and hence making a fire was quite an art, and required back-junks, fore-junks, middle-junks, triggers, splits, and brands; and the fishermen would sometimes say whoever can build a good fire with green fir can build a boat. 1901 *Christmas Bells* 4 On the 'French Shore,' at midnight on Christmas Eve, a live brand from the Yule-log is solemnly taken out doors and thrown over the house, to preserve it from being burnt down the coming year. 1937 DEVINE 10 Bran. [Probably] Brand; a log of wood afire. c 67-4 'What's yer hurry? What did ye come for, a bran?' Often heard when a visitor leaves long before he or she is expected to leave. This probably goes back to the days before matches, when people might come to a neighbouring house for fire. P 288-82 When [she] called to invite someone over to the house for a short visit, she'd say, 'Come for a bran.'

brazil n
1983 FROUDE 24 We squared the yards and set our course for the brazils away down in the southern seas. 1989 *Evening Telegram* 18 Dec, p. 5 [The *Earlshall*] was lost while 'coming home from the Brazils' in 1915.

breach n Cp *OED* sb 6 'the leaping of a whale clear out of the water'; BREACH v.
1924 *Deep Sea Fishers* xxi (4), 138 ~ A swirl in the water by a fish.

bread n Comb ~ **box**.
[1622] 1982 CELL (ed) 174 Whitbourne's *Discourse*:

[inventory] Flaskets, and bread boxes. 1961 ROULEAU 26
Bread Box Island. 1981 SPARKES 185 Food [for the crew]
was carried in a breadbox, which was not a box at all,
but a twenty-two pound butter tub reversed, big end
down, and fitted with a waterproof cover.

breaker n
[1983] 1985 LEHR & BEST (eds) 151 "The *Old
Smite*": Scarce had those words been spoken as we were
passing by—/Our man up on the lookout cried: 'Breakers,
ahoy!' 1987 FIZZARD 154 'Well, we kept her off the
land until 1 a.m., when we grounded in the breakers.'

breaking ppl
1984 POWELL 95 This was a small cove on the outside
of the island with a rock in the tickle that stuck out of
water at low tide. Now with this sea on, it would be a
breaking rock, and there would only be one chance out of
a hundred that we might make it.

bream n Cp *AND*, *DARE* 4 (1887-).

bream v See BRIM v.

breast n Comb ~ **work**: also, a wharflike raised
area around a railway station.
[1895] 1985 GOSSE 14 The old platform that surrounded the [railway station] has been taken away and a breastwork, filled with clay substituted. 1984 KELLAND 12
I was playing around near our back door [in sight of] a
breastwork of stout logs placed tightly together and
driven ends down deep into the beach.

breeches n pl *Anglo-Manx Dialect* britches 'the
roe of a [cod] fish.'
1989 *Evening Telegram* 4 July, p. 13 I mean good
fresh northern cod: steak, scrod, cheek and tongues,
britches, tomcods, sounds, any part of the fish, provided
it was to be fried, stewed with scrunchions, or stuffed
and baked.

breeder n
1988 *Evening Telegram* 12 May, p. 12A I felt what
appeared to be another six ouncer [trout, but] I had
hooked the Breeder.

breeks n pl
1986 SAUNDERS 132 [He was] dressed in his homespun
gray wool sweater and mitts, with khaki breeks and skin
boots.

breeze n *DARE* ~ N E (1945); *DBE*; PRATT 24.
Freq in phr *breeze of wind*.
1986 SAUNDERS 61 And by the look of those mares'
tails...we're in for a breeze of wind.

breeze[1] v Cp *DARE* breezen 1 (1942-); *South
Shore Phr Bk*.
1986 SAUNDERS 179 When we left Twillingate Harbour
the wind was breezing up from the northeast. 1987 *Evening Telegram* 11 Apr, p. 14 Captain Bartlett came up
and looked. It was snowing pretty thick now and the
wind was...breezing up.

breeze[2] v
1924 *Deep-Sea Fishers* xxi (4), 139 Breeze hard—To
press upon a part of the body.

brew v *OED* ~1 v 4 c '[to bring about] natural
phenomena, as rain, wind, a storm' (1530-1765)
for sense 1; cp GALE v.
1 Of imminent weather disturbance and signs
thought to presage it.
1863 HIND ii, 203 [The seals] often stop to sport when
they find a favourable place for the purpose. It is then
they are seen to dive repeatedly, coming up again almost
immediately, and to roll themselves about, and beat the
water with their hands. The fishermen call this brewing.
1904 *Harper's* cviii, 856 The schooners ride at anchor
with harbor near at hand; while the gales are brewing,
they fly to shelter. [1937 DEVINE 67 Old seals jumping
and making for the water is a sign of wind and snow.] C
69-19 Whenever some of the youngsters would get exceptionally playful and make a lot of noise my mother would
always say 'You're galing for wind tonight. You can look
out for the storm tomorrow.' By this she meant that the
youngsters were brewing for a storm. 1971 CASEY 135
'The sky was red in the East this morning, so I knew the
wind was brewin'.'
2 To come down with a cold.
C 70-15 I often heard [her] say whenever somebody
was getting a cold, 'I know you're brewing a cold
because you are all mops and brooms.'

brewis n Cp *DARE* ~ N E (1857-1939) 'a pud-
ding-like dish of bread crumbs soaked in liquid';
for earlier U K evidence, see DEFOE, *Robinson
Crusoe* (1719), 'He caused some Bisket Cakes to
be dipp'd in the Pot, and soften'd with the Liquor
of the Meat, which they calls Brewes, and gave
[the starving seamen] every one, one, to stay their
Stomachs' (ed J.W. Clark, London: Macmillan,
1896, p. 339).

brickle a *Anglo-Manx Dialect*; *DARE* 1.

bride n Comb **bride(s)boy,** ~ **girl,** ~ **knot.**
1981 SPARKES 149 Written invitations were unheard
of, but the bride's-boys would run round to the houses of
the older people and tell them that they were invited to
the wedding. 1916 *Deep Sea Fishers* xiii, 161 Here the
'brideb'ys' and 'bridegirls' were busy pinning favors on
the guests. 1985 *A Yaffle of Yarns* 99 The bride, on her
way to the church for the ceremony called at the house
where I was boarding and, preserving a total silence,
pinned a 'bride's knot' on me—a small white ribbon
bow—which indicated that I was invited to the wedding
reception.

bridge n
1 1980 HOLMES 43 When the harbour was frozen,
the distance was shortened by almost half a mile because
we could cross directly on the bridge of ice to the
school.

brim n See BREAM n.

brim v also **bream**. *EDD* brime v Co (1854); cp
OED bream v[1] 'to clear (a ship's bottom) of shells
[&c] by singeing' (1626-1875). To make the hull
of a boat or small vessel watertight by melting and
spreading pitch on the exterior surface.
[1626 Capt. SMITH 3 'For calking, breaming, stopping
leakes.' *OED*.] 1832 MOSS *MS Diary* 23 May Let the 2
large Boats down on their sides in order to brim them
tomorrow, and got the Pots in order to begin boiling
bark. 25 May Brimmed the boats and got them in order
for tanning. 1863 MORETON 36 Bream. pronounced brim.
A nautical term of correct use. To bream a boat is to
broom or brush its bottom. 1937 DEVINE 11 Bream. To
heat, with a birch-rind lighted mop, the bottom of a boat
hauled up and turned over on the shore or beach, melt the
tar already on it and spread it all over anew with a tar
mop. P 316-79 Years ago they used to use everything [to
paint their boats], what they used to call brimmin' her.
Used to make a mop, take a mop and get [it] full of tar
and set it afire and go all over the bottom of her. That's
what they used to call brimmin' her. 1983 *Evening Telegram* 14 Feb, p. 6 He made one observation...about
some of the boats being brimmed up to the gunnels,
which produced a tar-covered and consequently a black
boat, a 'black punt' was [his] term.

brimming vbl n Cp *OED* breaming (1628-1769).
See the inventory of Nfld fishing equipment in
Whitbourne's *Discourse* (1622) in 1982 CELL (ed),
p. 174: 'Fiue hundred waight of Pitch, A barrell of
Tarre, Two hundred waight of blacke Ocome,
Thrummes for Pitch mabs.' The action of spreading pitch on the bottom of a small vessel.
1983 *Evening Telegram* 9 May, p. 6 We then had a
'brimming' tool, which was a stick, six feet long, with a
rubber boot projecting at one end at right angles. The end
of the rubber boot was lighted and gently stroked over the
tarred bottom. As the tar melted and lighted, the tool
soon became a flaming torch and it was stroked from
aft to bow until the whole thing looked 'glazed'... I
[realized] I had witnessed a 'brimming.'

brin n Comb ~ **bag**.
1981 DAWE 38 "The Bridge": Sometimes people
threw cats and dogs/into brin bags/and dropped them
from the bridge/when the tide was going out. 1985 NEW-
HOOK 89 Some [mummers] would be hooded or have
false faces with flowing beards; others would be dressed
in smelly brin bags.

briner n In a fish-plant, one who immerses cod in
brine during processing. Cp SALTER.
1987 FIZZARD 212 'From the skinners the cod went to
the briners, where it was put into a salt solution.'

bring v
2 Phr *bring to*.
[1925] 1986 *Them Days* xi (4), 18 The netting would
come back in during the winter and [he] would 'bring
them to' with new head and foot ropes and corks and
leads. A net improperly 'brought to' will not fish properly and is a waste of time and material. 1986 FELTHAM
67-80 Gill nets knitted during the winter were fitted with

head-ropes, floats, foot-ropes and weights... The process
was called 'bringing to' a net.

brook n
1 [1610] 1982 CELL (ed) 62 *Willoughby Papers*: He
tolde me likewise of a brooke towards the south of
Reanose, with in tow leagues, that hath a kind of shelfish, in it which he calleth Clammes.
2 Comb ~ **hopper**: water strider of the family
Gerridae; WATER DOCTOR.
1985 NEWHOOK 29 By far and away the most notice-
able [form of insect life on the brook] was the brook
hopper. These were caught and put in a can.

browsy a also **browsey**. Pertaining to the bushes
and shoots eaten by wild animals; see BROWSE n.
P 108-76 The rabbits have a nice browsy flavour. 1987
MONTEVECCHI & TUCK 180 In 1952 Tuck located the first
large colony [of ring-billed gulls] on Browsey Island,
where more than 500 pairs were nesting.

brush n
1989 *Evening Telegram* 20 Mar, p. 1 Legend has it St
Patrick had a wife—or sister, mother or acquaint[a]nce
—named Sheilagh, and that still somehow she gets angry
enough at the good man to whack him about the ears...
perhaps with a 'brush.' Hence, 'tis said, the name long
given the late-winter storm.

bubble n Comb ~ **treader**, ~ **walker**: logger
adept at the work of the log 'drive.'
1985 *Terminology of Loggers* 3 Bubble treader—a man
who can run quickly over logs on rough water. P 292-83
Bubble walker: experienced logger who worked the
middle of the river during a log jam. 'One dead bubble
walker can do the job of two live alder grabbers.'

buckly a
1985 NEWHOOK 27 Like all rivers and brooks in Newfoundland, it freezes over in the winter and offers a range
of pastimes like skidding, skating and running over the
'buckly' places.

bud[1] n
1914 *Deep Sea Fishers* xi, 24 We have [used] native
spruce buds for dyeing and the people tell me the rock
and tree 'liver' (lichen) make a lovely brown. 1985 DOM-
STAD 27 Pick the buds from a withey tree... When the
buds on the White Spruce trees are green, pick them.

bud[2] n Cp *EDD* Supplement ~ sb[4], *DBE* bud[1].

buddy n
1981 MAJOR 73 We didn't get much of a chance to
speak to each other because as soon as we went in the
classroom the teacher came in and started talking. Not
even a chance to find out buddy's name. 1988 *Sunday
Express* 12 June, p. 1 The Prince did not buy a burger,
but reportedly made quite an impact. 'One girl was so
excited she kept saying "buddy went by the window"','
[the] owner said. 1989 ROWE 27 'Buddy drivin' dis is a
queer hand, b'y, en't 'e?'

bulk n
4 Also: a quantity of logs, stored for winter fuel.

1936 SMITH 15 I had to abandon school that winter and go in the woods to secure fuel for the home for the winter and coming summer. We didn't have far to go in those days, so I had a large bulk of wood in the backyard when the snow went in March.

6 Phr *in bulk*; *bulk pen*: on a trawler, a large pen or 'pound' for placing cod-fish in layers of ice.

1987 FIZZARD 160 Unlike the old markets where fish was sent in bulk, the new markets [of the 1930s] wanted their fish packed in wooden [casks]. 1986 *Nfld's Deepsea Fishery* 649 Bulk pen icing.

bulk v
2 (a)
1984 KELLAND 158 [The fish] then were lugged up over the crop of the beach and bulked in waterhorses.

bulking vbl n The placing of 'seal pelts' in a pile on the ice for later collection by a vessel; PANNING.

1986 *Evening Telegram* 31 Mar, p. 6 Devine declared that when the panning and bulking of seals became general, many seal pelts never got aboard any of the ships.

bull n
2 Comb ~ **bird**, ~ **cook**: cook's assistant in a logging camp.

1983 DAWE & FICKEN 36 Some call it a dovekie,/And that's a good guess,/But to us it's a bull-bird,/No more and no less. 1988 MOMATIUK & EASTCOTT (eds) 139 The little bull-bird, that's a fantastic little bird. It comes in the early winter. There are little ears on it, and they stick up like the horns on a bull. 1985 *Terminology of Loggers* 3 Bull cook—the cook's helper, who usually carried the [boat's] kettle to the lunchground.

bullet See NEWFIE.

bully[1] n
1 1986 FELTHAM 51 These ['offer' fishing banks] ranged from four to fifteen miles from the land [and] led to the evolution of the 'bully'... The Bonavista Bay bully was a small decked schooner of from twelve to sixteen tons. Initially, they had four lower sails; mainsail, foresail, jib and stay-sail as well as the main topsail and fore topsail. Early in the twentieth century small marine engines were installed and the topsails and topmasts were discarded. 1988 GOSSE 48-9 Another...development was the Newfoundland 'bulley.' Evolved from ketches and yawls, this beautiful fishing craft was usually about 30 to 32 feet in overall length and little more than 9 feet in the beam. Her slender lines were similar to Yankee schooners... Deep in the keel, she drew a lot of water for her size; high masted, she was tender and required sufficient permanent ballast to keep her stiff enough to withstand sudden squalls and gale force winds.
2 Comb **bully boat**; HIGH-RAT.
1986 SAUNDERS 31 And of course there was Father's little schooner or bulley boat that he used for carrying lumber... She was forty feet long and about eighteen tons. 1987 *Evening Telegram* 4 July, p. 56 [tape transcript] In the fall, after the trap season [on Labrador], the

men used to go out in the high-rats jigging. These high-rats or bully boats had a big sail and a jib and carried two men. There was also a rowing oar and a sculling oar.

bultow n
1982 DAWE 17 A sculpin who swam in Sop's Arm,/ Stirred up quite a bit of alarm,/When he dragged a bultow/All the way to Forteau,/And never recovered his calm. 1987 FIZZARD 95 The change in the vessels was accompanied by an addition to the fishing gear, when in about 1862 the trawl, or the 'bultow' was introduced. 1988 GOSSE 20 Also in common use were long lines of 50 fathoms or more to which were attached hooked lines three feet in length and spaced at approximately one-fathom intervals. Each hook was baited and the whole paid out from the boat with buoyed graplins at either end. This fishing gear was known as bultows or hand trawls.

bumper n
4 Attrib ~ **crop**.
1985 BUSCH 58 Sealing was a way of mastering the environment, exemplified in common words deliberately managerial and exploitive as the sealer sailed in search of a good 'harvest' or a 'bumper crop.'

bunchy-berry n also **bunch berry**. *DARE* bunchberry n 1.
1985 DOMSTAD 23 Take the leaves from a bunch berry bush [to relieve pain].

burn v
1 1987 *Evening Telegram* 27 Apr, p. 7 [tape transcript] Then there were deductions for holes [in the seal pelts]: 10 cents for a single hole, 20 cents for a double hole, maybe 80 cents or a $1 if the fur was burnt.
2 1986 FELTHAM 54 Heavy salted cod burnt more easily than that which was light salted.
5 [1898] 1985 *Evening Telegram* 31 Mar, p. 6 'Around 8:30 p.m. there were still about eight pans out and the ship was "burnt down" until morning, as she was now too deep in the water to risk steaming after nightfall.' 1937 *Bk of Nfld* ii, 255 "The Old Ship's Medicine Chest": We'll dress your wounds when all burnt-down, the ship at midnight rides. 1985 BUSCH 58 The real work came when the patch was found and the ship was 'burned down in the fat.'

burn[2] n
2 A measure of four 'rings' of barrel or cask hoops; twenty-four.
1981 SPARKES xiv Like the rinds, hoops had their own special table of measure. They were counted by rings, burns and bundles. Six hoops made a ring, four rings made a burn.

busy a Comb ~ **bee**.
1987 POWELL 113 The town was invaded by what was called the fish fly, a fly a little smaller than the busy bee.

butter n Comb **butter-ball**: bufflehead (*Bucephela albeola*); SPRITE.
1951 PETERS & BURLEIGH 106 The 'Butter-ball,' so-

called because of its fat, tasty flesh, is one of the best divers among the ducks, disappearing with the quickness of a grebe.

by prep [bɪ] in unstressed positions; also **be**.
P 222-67 Pass me that two be four. 1987 FIZZARD 193 'When the war was over, I was brought to San Francisco with the Englishmen. And then I come be train to Halifax.'

by-boat n
1 1675 CO 1/65 (27), 103 'By reason of Inhabitants and by Boats which carry away all our choise men Wee have not One third of the number of Ships on this Employment as formerly.'
2 Comb **by(e)-boat keeper**.
1680 CO 1/46 (8ii), 22 'An accot. of the By boat keepers in St John's Harbour each of them keeping stages, the Number of Men and Boats they Keepe & Employ what quantity of Fish they Catch what Train they make & how many Fats they have to do it.' 1986 RYAN 32 These men, called *bye boat keepers*, left their boats in Newfoundland during the winter and found transportation for themselves and their crews to and from Newfoundland on the fishing ships.

C

callibogus n *DARE* calibogus (1758-).
1988 GOSSE 24 The favourite refreshment was a 'callibogus' consisting of a tot of rum in a mug of spruce beer.

camp n
1984 POWELL 61 When I got back to the camp, there was a spruce partridge sitting on the tent pole right over the camp door.

canada n
1 1984 GOUGH 6 'Yes, but I've travelled. I've seen all the New England states and I've been over to Canada.' 1988 *Evening Telegram* 18 June, p. 12 [tape transcript] [In Boston] you'd go into the office with your overalls on and your cap on and they would talk to you just the same, not like up around Canada.

cape ann n
1984 GOUGH 97 She sees Ern's sou'wester and Cape Ann hanging on a hook and, underneath, his fishing boots.

cape race n *DARE* ~ n (1835-).

caplin n Cp *Trésor de la langue française* capelan, from Prov (1558-): capelan, or poor cod *Trisopterus minutus* [*OED* power-cod, *O Sup²* poorcod (1828-)]; *DARE* capelin (1824-).
1 1990 *Evening Telegram* 23 Jan, p. 5 Now Bishop's Beach is deserted, not one caplin rolls ashore to spawn.
2 Attrib, comb **caplin baiting**, ~ **fishery**, ~ **glut**: a great abundance of fish appearing in

inshore waters; GLUT, ~ **season**, ~ **skiff**: large undecked boat employed to catch caplin; BAIT-SKIFF, ~ **trip**: a period at sea using caplin for bait.
1895 *Evening Telegram* 25 July The banking schooners along the coast have returned from the grounds with from 400 to 500 quintals of fish for the caplin baiting. 1988 *Evening Telegram* 15 June, p. 3 Fishing boats are gathering near Holyrood and Harbour Grace today for the opening of the caplin fishery. 1986 FELTHAM 73 By the first week of August the cod has begun its trek back to the ocean banks. No longer sluggish from the caplin glut, they can again be caught by jigger. [1837] 1987 FIZZARD 83 Of course, during the caplin season, very large prices are held out to our fishermen to bring them over. 1986 *Evening Telegram* 2 Aug, p. 12 During the caplin season the plant [at Trouty, T.B.] produced about 100,000 pounds of caplin for the Japanese market. 1981 DAWE 49 "Poor Peter": The sirens of the south wind/called a sleek, grey shark/long as a caplin skiff/to tangle, roll up, and die/in the waiting mesh. 1984 KELLAND 82 The vessel which was owned by a Grand Bank firm had gone out on a caplin trip, that is to say, she had onboard caplin for bait.

caplin scull n
1 1981 DAWE 38 "The Bridge": Once we had a wooden bridge/that took us across a salt pond/to the caplin scull/and a crescent of beach stones. 1988 *Evening Telegram* 15 June, p. 3 The fishermen had converged from across the province on St Mary's Bay for the caplin scull during the weekend.
2 1987 *Evening Telegram* 24 Oct, p. 14 The inshore fishery was poor during the caplin scull and through the summer but picked up during the fall.
4 Attrib **caplin-scull weather**:
[1963] 1988 *Evening Telegram* 16 June, p. 6 Weatherwise Newfoundlanders could sense it. The fog and drizzle this past three or four days added up to one singular thing. It was 'caplin scull' weather.

capsize v *SED* ~ iv, 172 Do Ha; *DBE*.
1918 *Deep Sea Fishers* xvi, 95 [The peg for the one-legged man] worked well, but the useless joint stuck out behind like a rudder, and seriously added to the weight he had to carry and the risk of capsizing.

car n
3 Phr *on the cars*: by a special means of rail transport.
1983 *Nfld Qtly* lxxix (2), 15 A door the railway did open for Bonavista was a unique adaptation of Newfoundland's traditional winter migration to the woods, 'going in on the cars.' ... Once the snows and frost came 100-150 families loaded the furnishings for the winter camp on railway flatcars and migrated *en masse* to their winter homes 'on the cars.'
4 Comb ~**boy**: great cormorant (*Phalacrocorax carbo*), ~ **man**.
1987 MONTEVECCHI & TUCK 234 ~boy: Great cormorant. 1893 *Evening Telegram* 22 Mar This morning a carman with a load of lumber, in trying to take a short cut from Water Street through a small lane, experienced a complete breakdown. The slide went to pieces under the

load. [1940] 1990 *Evening Telegram* 5 Feb, p. 4 A car-man pleaded guilty to having no bells on his horse or slide. Sentence was suspended.

carey's chicken n
1 1986 SAUNDERS 36 Almost every November, usually on a storm of easterly wind and rain, the carey chicks (petrels) would come skimming in along the landwash and we would sling rocks at them, and always miss.

caribou n   also **carabou**.
1 1818 CHAPPELL 70 'Me get [musket] of Scotchee ship: me givee de Captain one carabou (deer) for um.' 1986 *Evening Telegram* 1 Mar, p. 14 Starting later this month, 14 hunters will harvest 1,000 caribou in the Nain area [in the first commercial harvest of the Labrador George River herd].
2 Attrib ~ **fly**.
1895 *Evening Herald* 17 Dec ''Newfoundland's Rocky Shore'': And list to the boom of the caribou fly/You can't keep him off whatever you try.

cark n, v   See CORK.

carry v   Cp *DARE* ~ v 1 N E (1861-) for sense 2.

casing n
P 303-82 ~ The gunwale of a boat.

cask n   Cp *OED* ~ sb 1 'general term for a wooden vessel of cylindrical form'; see BARREL, DRUM, PUNCHEON. A type of wooden container made specifically for the shipment of dried and salted cod to the Mediterranean and West Indies markets, containing four cwt of fish. Also attrib **cask fish**.
[1936] 1986 *Evening Telegram* 10 July, p. 6 The SS *Prospero*...left Marystown yesterday en route to Halifax, loaded 182 casks of dry shore fish and two barrels of Labrador from Williams and Co. Bay Bulls, for trans-shipment to the West Indies. [1940] 1990 ibid 7 Mar, p. 4 A string of ponies and slides from Pouch Cove came to town this morning hauling cask fish for export. The load for each pony was one four-quintal cask. 1987 ibid 27 Apr, p. 7 [tape transcript] Fish was packed in half-drums, drums, casks, donkeys, and various kinds of barrels... [A] cask held four quintals of dry or five quintals of Labrador. 1987 FIZZARD 170 'One time we went to Lunenburg and took a load of cask fish.' 1990 *Evening Telegram* 14 Jan, p. 14 I have packaged fish where I had a total 452 casks (four quintals per cask).

cast v
1897 *Evening Telegram* 28 Aug She reports caplin plentiful in Trinity on Wednesday last, the men casting large quantities of them—late as the season is. [1937] 1945 SCAMMELL 37 ''Payne's Cove Bait Skiff'': Yester-day mornin', up there to the head/You could cast all you like, so said Skipper Fred. 1990 *Evening Telegram* 23 Jan, p. 5 The beaches around the coast of this island of ours were a hive of activity when men, women and children were seen casting caplin, dipping caplin, as multitudes of the small fish rolled on the beaches to spawn.

cast-net n
1 1988 GOSSE 21 The cast net, conical in shape and leaded on the foot rope, was thrown by a single fisher-man in a circular motion over a school of caplin in shal-low water. A good haul would yield 100 pounds of fish.

cat[1] n
1 Comb **cat's claws**: cockle-bur (*Xanthium* spp); STICKING BUD (P 148-87).

cat[2] n
2 Comb ~ **house**.
1986 SAUNDERS 141 [He showed me] how to entice a lynx or a weasel into your trap by building a little V-shaped cat-house of logs with a birch rind roof to keep out the rain and snow and some rotten meat or fish in back of the trap.

cat[3] n
1984 WRIGHT 66 He pulled me aside to a spot where chunks of ice hid a small, stillborn seal pup or 'cat' that he wanted to take on board for a souvenir.

catamaran n   also **cat**. The catamaran, 'fire-ship or instrument of naval warfare' (*OED* ~ 2 1804-), was reported in England six years before the term appeared in print in Nfld, connected with the farms in St John's owned by military and naval officers. *Catamaran* 'sledge' is reported in New Zealand from 1902 and *cat* from 1951 (Harry Orsman, personal commun).
1 1811 *Royal Gazette* 14 Nov For sale...3 catamarans Best's Farm. 1903 *Nfld Qtly* iii (3), 5 Three or four 'cat' loads [of birch] could easily be secured in one winter's day by starting for the 'woods' before daylight. [1928] 1982 BURKE (ed Kirwin) 69 ''Don't You Remember the Dump'': And the sport that we had on them nights, Maggie,/On Jim Tracey's old catamaran.

catch v   Cp *DARE* ~ v 6.
1 Phr *catch (over)*.
1984 POWELL 90 Very often the ocean will catch over as far as your eye can see, if winds are calm for several nights and it is frosty. 1986 FELTHAM 105 The tickles separating Bragg's Island, Deer Island and Greens Island 'caught' only when it was extremely cold and when there was an absence of ocean swell.

chain v
Phr *chain off*: see quot.
1986 *Nfld's Deepsea Fishery* 649 Chaining off the warp: a fishing operation connected with fishing in the ice on boats without hydraulic ice davits. This operation involves moving the warps from their normal position above the stern down into the stern ramp for shooting away and then back up again as the net is hauled back.

channel n   See *South Shore Phr Bk* makin' chan-nel, tending channel. In the log drive, the unim-peded flow of water carrying the logs downstream. In combs **channel tender, ~ tending**.
1985 *Terminology of Loggers* 5 Channel tender—the

man stationed on the riverbank to keep the logs moving during a drive. P 13-83 Channel tending, a preventive measure: several drivers are stationed at known trouble spots along the shore—a narrow channel, a particular rock, etc—to keep the logs moving and thus prevent a 'plug.' 1987 QUINLIN 32 The fellow channel tending had it easy as long as the timber kept coming.

charm v
1 1981 DAWE 12 "The Potato Ground": the old woman who charmed toothache/and banished big, seedy warts/from everybody's hands:/in white shopping-line/one knot/for every wart/and bury that line/in the damp potato ground.

charm n
2 1986 SAUNDERS 74 And in the morning a charm of birds to wake you up.

charmer n
1988 *Evening Telegram* 28 May, p. A1 [I mean] people who are charmers. The kind who put away warts...and cure toothache.

charming vbl n
1985 DOMSTAD 11 [It is] necessary for the person who requires the healing to believe the folk medicine and charming works.

cheek n
1 1989 *Evening Telegram* 4 July, p. 13 I mean good fresh northern cod: steak, scrod, cheek and tongues, britches, tomcods, sounds, any part of the fish, provided it was to be fried, stewed with scrunchions, or stuffed and baked.

chin n Attrib ~ music.
1986 HISCOCK 176 Since the song is sung here, it seems likely it is one of the 'textual' rather than 'tunc' songs. As "The Nanny Goat" it is a widespread chin music tune in Newfoundland. 1989 *Sunday Telegram* 11 June, p. 4 Surely there must be somebody on the back benches who can play the mouth organ? No? Even a bit of chin music would help.

chinker n
1987 PEYTON 15 Their houses were individual tilts, makeshift shelters built entirely of logs, the seams or chinks ('chinkers') stuffed or 'stodged' with sphag[n]um moss to block the drafts and keep out the weather.

chinse v
2 1986 FELTHAM 63 The cabins were built in thick woods not far from the shore. The spaces between the logs were chinched with moss.

chinsing vbl n also chinching.
1986 SAUNDERS 145 For chinching we used a blunt wooden chisel and a wooden mallet, both homemade.

chip n Cp *DARE* chip pile n 1. Comb ~ bank: in a logging camp the place where firewood and lumber were cut.

1985 *Terminology of Loggers* 5 Most arguments that came to blows were settled [near the chip bank].

chisel[1] n
1 1988 GOSSE 32 All hands drove thin pieces of steel into the heels of their boots. These steel slivers, usually three in number, protruded approximately one-quarter of an inch and measured the same amount in width. These were known as 'chisels' and, like the nails or 'sparbles' extending from the soles, prevented slipping on the ice.

chitlings n pl *SED* iv, 361 So W Do Ha.

choice a
1 1988 *Evening Telegram* 26 July, p. 3 Salt fish is given one of three possible grades: choice, standard and cullage.
2 [1915] 1930 COAKER 98 Such a movement [to equip Labrador schooners with motors] would drive hundreds [of vessels] out of the race for fish, as only a few would secure engines thereby monopolizing to a large extent the choice trap berths along the coast. 1960 *Assoc Am Geog* l, 274 The codtrap berths were graded choice, prime, seconds, and fly, in that order, according to the run of fish taken from them. The choice berths provided large catches and were fairly dependable from year to year. 1987 POWELL 82 At that time of summer all the choice trap berths were taken by the local fishermen [on the Labrador].

choke v Cp *DARE* ~ v[1] 'to put a line tightly around a log'; BRYANT choker 'noose of wire rope.' Phr *choke your bag*: to tie the mouth of clothes bag before leaving logging camp (1985 *Terminology of Loggers* 5).

chooky n Cp *EDD* choogey sb 1 'child's name for a pig' So D Co, 2 'a call to pigs' Co; *SED* iv, 339 Sr Co.
1 1987 QUINLAN 29 [caption to a drawing of a pig] Chukey, chukey.
2 Comb chooky-pig: an untidy person.
P 295-83 'Don't be such a chooky-pig!'

chop v
2 Phr *chop the beam*.
1981 SPARKES 167 I have often heard the man of the house say to a friend who had not visited for some time, 'You are quite a stranger. I must chop the beam.'

chop n
1985 ASHTON 192 "A Trip up to Sixth Pond": Come back after Christmas for a couple months more,/Then by that time our chop will be o'er.

chovy* n Cp 1961 ROULEAU 42 Chiffy Cove, Point, Chuffy's Head.

christmas n Cp *DARE* ~ n 1 a for sense 2.
1 1987 JOHNSTON 32-3 My mother remembers that he would go out mummering all twelve nights of Christmas.
2 1988 PORTER 199 'I'll be over tonight, before I goes

to the party. I got a little gift for you. I s'pose you'll give me my Christmas, will you?' 'Syrup and cake?'

4 Attrib, comb ~ **fish**: also, a small freshwater fish, so-called locally on the Burin Peninsula.

1989 *Evening Telegram* 14 Jan, p. 10 It struck me that it was 60 years, almost to the day, since I had taken my first 'Christmas fish.' The many 'Christmas fish' I caught were on average about nine inches long and almost an exact replica of a small tomcod, without any of the light brown shade.

christmas-box n *DARE* (1810-96) arch or obs.

2 1984 POWELL 94 The following Christmas I came out of the country to spend Christmas at home. Somehow Uncle Alex learned that there was a Christmas box down at Mr Turnbull's at New York Bay, so he asked me if I would go along with him to get the box, as there was very little for the children for Christmas.

chuck v To act as driller's helper in mining.

1988 *Nfld Qtly* lxxxiii (4), 12 [I would catch] a 7:30 tram to the bottom of Number 3 mine. There I'd begun 'chuckin' ' for 'Big Jim' Shaw.

chuckle² See TRICKLE*.

chuckley a Comb ~ **pear**.

1987 *Sunday Express* 13 Sep, p. 30 Chuckley pears are the slightly shiny, large, purple berries which are found growing...on bushes by roadsides, clearings, creeks and trails all over Newfoundland.

chute n also **shoot**. Cp *DARE* ~ n 'small channel usu between an island and the main landmass' (1859-).

1 [1768] 1988 *Canoma* xiv (1), 7 Shoot Brook, Shoot Brook Hills. 1986 SAUNDERS vi Little & Big Chutes [Gander River].

2 1987 POOLE 25-6 We had real fun carrying our things up the Long Shute as the path was called. You would take all your things up to the head of the pond in this small boat before backing it in to the tilt. Now Long Shute would be your fancy place for carrying the stove.

civil a *DARE* ~ a 2 for sense 1, 1 for sense 3.

1 1986 *Them Days* xi (4), 59 We left St Anthony the following Monday morning. It was quite civil, though a grey morning.

2 1988 ELLIOTT [19] "Going Up Shore": The sea was one blue and the sky another,/As civil a day as I ever saw in my life.

clave v Participial usage is variable.

1 1984 POWELL 23 The next chore was to get the firewood, cut it, and clave it up for the summer. ibid 175 On the other side [of the stove] would be the splits all claved up small. ibid 177 Each of those pickets that [the Indians] drove into the mud had to be clove in two so it would make two pieces.

clean a

1 1989 *Evening Telegram* 3 June, p. A4 The water is

too clean; the water is too dirty. The fish aren't migrating [or] are migrating in the wrong direction.

clear a *DARE* ~ a 1 3 *clear thing* (1951) N E. Phr *clear of*, *clear thing*.

1982 MCDOOLING 130 'It's not too far to go [to get salmon]. Clear of the fellers out around the Gray Islands.' P 245-89 'There's not much here clear of the fishery.' 1986 FELTHAM 109 'What am I offered for this beautiful apron? The clear thing for you, Garge, to wear when you are cooking a scoff of rabbits and duff.'

clergy n

[1937] 1983 FROUDE 124 I was married at tomwalls Harbour Exploits [and] I paid the old clergy four dollars to splice Us. [1977] 1985 LEHR & BEST (eds) 141 "Mr Costler": Jacky Dominy was one, the engineer made two/And the clergy for Burgeo this made up his crew. 1987 POOLE 19 My mother would have about five pounds of sugar in the fall and about a half dozen tins of sweet milk, which was used for the doctor or the Clergy or the nurse if they happened to come along during the winter.

clew v Phr *clew up*.

1988 *Muse* 7 Oct, p. 15 Well choreographed and note for note, this totally in control band clued up the set with powerful selections from [Nazareth, etc].

clit n

1985 *A Yaffle of Yarns* 107 If a person's hair was tangled there were 'clits' in it.

clitty a *SED* iv, 647 W D So Ha.

coach n Comb ~ **box**.

1917 *Deep Sea Fishers* xv, 107 It was my first long komatik ride and I felt like some polar queen embarking on a journey when I got into the 'coach box' dressed in my kossik and sealskin mitts.

co-adventurer n Cp *OED* co-adventure: 'a co-adventurer in that expedition' (1645). In the industrial deep-sea fishery, crew member whose earnings depend on the value of the catch rather than on a fixed wage; cp ADVENTURER, SHARE-MAN.

1972 ANDERSEN & WADEL (eds) 133-4 At the time of writing, Newfoundland trawler fishermen were legally classified as 'co-adventurers,' and not employees. They have been denied the right to union organization...by the Newfoundland Board of Labour, which bases its position on a federal judicial opinion. 1986 SIDER 143 Factories hire the labor for their boats as 'co-adventurers'—which means that they are paid with a share of the catch, rather than a wage. 1987 FIZZARD 218 Previously [to 1974] the amount paid to the [trawler] fishermen was dependent on the amount of fish brought in by their vessel: more fish meant more wages; less fish meant lower wages. Called the 'co-adventurer' system, it required the individual fisherman to share the risk of the voyage with the owner.

coaker n

1985 ASHTON 204-5 "The Gambo Way": We called

into Fair Islands, took a pilot for Hare Bay. /The old Coaker gave no trouble, she hurled us up that day.

coast n
1 1977 WHITELEY 29 [When he] came to the coast in 1856 James Buckle had his establishment on 'John's Island.' 1984 POWELL 72 Very often when the Newfoundlanders came on the coast in the spring they would say, 'What were you doing all winter, sleeping?' 1988 *Evening Telegram* 31 May, p. 11 Things weren't much different along the coast in 1940 than they were in the first war. That ended in November, 1918 but we didn't know it was over till January of 1919 and then only because two veterans from up around Mud Lake on Hamilton Inlet were walking home.

coastal a Phr *coastal boat*.
1984 POWELL 119 These were two things we just had to have, but this was the last trip of the coastal boat for the season. 1987 KING (ed) 112 "The Southern Shore": Like wild sea birds/these people come/across my imagination/went up the south coast/by coastal boat one summer.

coasting vbl n
1 1987 FIZZARD 189 'So we came in and cleared out and carried our men home and we went coasting then. We took fluorspar from St Lawrence and carried it in to Sydney and brought back a load of coal for Harbour Grace.' 1988 *Evening Telegram* 18 June, p. 12 [tape transcript] My father...fished on the Labrador when he was only a young man but he didn't follow it up his whole lifetime. Perhaps he'd go coasting or up around Halifax and then he went to the States.
2 Attrib ~ **schooner**, ~ **vessel**.
1984 KELLAND 22 They often brought [their dories] into St John's on the decks of the coasting schooners skippered by friends who were voyaging to the capital. [1811] 1987 FIZZARD 72 [Trouble arose] from import of liquors, spirits and wine in particular from St John's by Bye Boatkeepers and coasting vessels going to and forth with fish.

cob v *DARE* ~ v[1] 1 (1872, 1968). In mining, to separate rock from the ore.
1983 MARTIN 13 After the blasted rock had been hauled to the surface [of the copper mine], long lines of boys and young men 'cobbed' it by striking away barren rock from the ore-rich portions with a small hammer.

cock n Cp *OED* ~ sb[1] 20 'penis' (1730-) for new sense **1**: Genitals of the male 'hooded seal' (*Cystophora cristata*).
1984 WRIGHT 82 Two Japanese men turned up in a pick-up truck, and Isaac carried out the buckets of 'cocks'—the genitals of the male hooded seals. They would be sold in the Orient as aphrodisiacs, apparently at a huge profit.

cod[2] n For combs in sense 3: *O Sup*[2] ~ line (1634-).
1 1990 *Evening Telegram* 17 Jan, p. 3 He said cod normally feed on caplin and if caplin supplies dwindle it

will have an effect on cod stock already in a depletion stage.
2 Prov *no cod, no cash* ([1916] 1924 ENGLAND 255).
3 Comb **cod block**: fresh filleted cod, packaged frozen, ~ **cheek**: fleshy part of cod's head; CHEEK, ~ **farmer**: aquaculturalist or one who operates a facility where cod are raised to maturity, ~ **fish farm**: net enclosure, in sheltered inshore waters, where cod are raised for market, ~ **glut**: catch of cod in excess of the capacity to handle or process; GLUT, ~ **jigger**, ~ **line**, ~ **net**, ~ **oil**, ~ **run**: movement of cod to inshore waters; RUN n, ~ **tongue**, ~**-whanger**: see WHANGER, ~ **worm**: parasitic aquatic annelid transferred to cod-fish by seals; SEAL WORM.
    1988 *Evening Telegram* 24 Mar, p. A8 There were 24^1/$_2$ million pounds of cod blocks lying around [in unsold inventories]. 1988 ibid 10 Sep, p. 13 There are strong markets for cod tongues and cod cheeks as well as other products. 1987 *Evening Telegram* 9 Oct, p. 2 Because cod cannot be trapped alive in any quantity outside the province...the process also gives Newfoundland cod farmers a unique advantage over competitors elsewhere. 1988 ibid 11 June, p. 3 The operators of the province's first codfish farm in Bay Bulls have received [money] to build four more farms in Newfoundland. 1989 ibid 17 June, p. 1 The [vessel] was brought in to alleviate what is known as the cod glut—a three or four-week period when inshore fishermen are unable to sell their cod because inshore processors concentrate on the lucrative caplin fishery. 1987 POWELL 19 The cod trap season was over and now the fishing boats were using trawls and cod jiggers. 1900 *Tribune Chr Annual* 11 "A Briny Bumper to the Sea": Who has heard the cod-line singing o'er the bow? 1987 JOHNSTON 85 My father and his father would work, pulling traps, hauling mile-long cod-lines hand over hand. 1988 GOSSE 20-1 Most fishermen also used nets with meshes of five to six inches. These were leaded at intervals along the foot ropes, while cork floats... supported and kept the net fully extended when anchored to the bottom of the fishing grounds. The type of cod net used so extensively today looks very similar. 1987 MCDONALD 32 On several occasions, the Trading Company forced increases in the price of seal fat, cod oil and herring. 1960 *Assoc Amer Geog* l, 273 North of Groswater Bay the cod-run began from July 15 to 30 and continued to August 15 or 30. 1989 *Sunday Express* 19 Mar, p. 7 Our winter's pocket money [was] earned door to door: first rank, those who sold cod tongues by the bucket—the quick and skillful. 1989 *Evening Telegram* 26 June, p. 1 The co-called seal worms, also known as cod worms, have a life cycle that is thought to include the stomachs of harbour seals and the flesh of some fish.

cod end n *OED* cod sb[1] 1 'a bag' (c1000-), 8 cod-end (1871-).
1 The part of a trawl net where the fish are collected when hauling; fig.
    1974 *Daily News* 15 July, p. 16 The [Fishermen's Union] will show everyone where the 'political totempole' begins...at the 'cod end.'
2 Comb **cod-end knot**, ~ **line**.

1930 *Am Speech* v, 389 ~ An ingenious knot for keeping the cod-end closed until it is filled with fish and then releasing it after the bag has been hoisted aboard. 1987 FIZZARD 211 'As the [otter] trawl was pulled across the deck, the fish were forced back into the cod-end. As the cod-end filled, a small warp was tightened making the cod-end into a bag-like shape. This bag was then hoisted on board. The cod-end knot was then slipped and that part of the catch fell onto the deck.' ibid 210 'The bottom part of the otter trawl was known as the cod-end. This pointed part was tied together tightly by a short rope called the cod-end line.'

cod-seine n
1 1986 FELTHAM 50 The most common way of catching cod during the early days of [Bonavista Bay] island settlement was by 'cod-seine.' These were long nets that were shot around schools of cod in shallow water.
2 Attrib **cod-seine skiff**.
1988 GOSSE 26 This in turn required a cod-seine skiff, which was towed astern, since they were usually too large and cumbersome to be carried on deck.

cod trap n
1 1990 *Evening Telegram* 14 Jan, p. 14 I've bought the twine, knit it, made cod-traps, caught cod fish, dried it, and exported it.
2 Attrib, comb ~ **berth**, ~ **crew**, ~ **fish**: cod taken in inshore waters by the stationary 'trap', ~ **fishery**, ~ **line**: see ~ TWINE, ~ **season**.
1987 POOLE 20 That morning my dad set out his leader for his cod trap berth. 1986 *Evening Telegram* 15 Feb, p. 9 There are 15 cod trap crews [in Bonavista] with a total of 46 fishermen. 1988 ibid 11 June, p. 3 The farms will enable undersized codtrap fish to be utilized, thus reducing the dumping of fish during glut period. 1988 ibid 24 May, p. 3 With prices for the...codtrap fishery hovering around 31 cents a pound...the job of negotiating [this year] won't be an easy one. 1989 ibid 16 May, p. 7A The rest of the equipment consisted of around 30 or 40 feet of cod trap line which had been 'barked' or tanned. 1987 POWELL 19 The cod trap season was over and now the fishing boats were using trawls and cod jiggers.

colcannon n
1979 PORTER 41 I heard Nanny say [this] to Mom one Hallowe'en when they were preparing the turnip and cabbage for colcannon. 1989 *Sunday Express* 29 Oct, p. 35 The Newfoundland and Irish versions of colcannon taste quite different, but each is excellent in its way.

collar n Cp *DARE* ~ v phr *get in the collar* 'to start working' (1967-) for sense 3.
1 1986 FELTHAM 69 The schooners and bullies that were moored in safe harbours for the winter and allowed to freeze in can now be taken to their summer moorings. The 'collars' removed from the water during the late fall now have to be set out again. 1987 KING (ed) 32 ''Grandmother Figure 1'': She cried without quakes,/without sobs, looking out past orange-lichened rocks/and trap-skiffs restless as boys in chafing hemp collars/on a blue sea.
2 1986 SAUNDERS 277 A bulley boat...drew too much water to tie up at the wharf [so] they would take the

lumber out in a scow to where she was moored off on her collar in midstream.
3 Phr *get off the collar*: to conclude a period of shore work preparatory to actual fishing.
1981 SPARKES 183 The coming of spring was the time to 'go in collar again'. Fishing crews were now to be shipped (signed on) for the work of setting up the great bark-pots, painting boats, setting in order the trawls, nets and cod-traps and repairing flakes. 1987 *Evening Telegram* 4 July, p. 56 [tape transcript] In the fall the men would have to go out no matter how bad the weather was; they had to get off the collar, get clear of the stagehead and go somewhere [on the water to fish].
4 Attrib ~ **time**.
1986 FELTHAM 69 May was 'collar' time for the crews of the many schooners engaged in the Labrador fishery.

collector n Also: a boat used to transport live cod from a 'cod trap' to a 'cod farm'; attrib **collector boat**: see COLLECTING BOAT.
1987 POOLE 93 The big boss had taken over Snug Harbour and I was the second hand and did not go on the collector but stayed on the room all summer. 1988 *Evening Telegram* 24 Oct, p. 6 Another addition to the [cod-farming] company this year was an aluminum collector boat that was used to take the fish from the cod-trap. There is a trap door in the boat's holding tank which allows the fish to be transferred directly to the pens without injury. 1990 ibid 14 Jan, p. 19 What happens when the U.S. market takes a dip and the collectors don't want to go [to Labrador]; or when there is black berry in the fish?

colony n
1 1679 CO 1/43 (121), 216 The Colony & bye boats are supplyed with wine, Brandy, salt, linnen cloath &c from France, Spaine, Portugall and the Ilands.
2 [1964] 1989 *Evening Telegram* 13 Mar, p. 4 Said Premier Smallwood...'as Britain's most ancient colony...we take great pride in our intense loyalty to our sovereign.'

colours n pl *DARE* ~ (1883-).
1979 PORTER 19 Soft evenings [in summer we spent] playing Colours down by Whitten's Shop.

commission n
1987 FIZZARD 173 In 1935 [the Fishermen's Hospital at Grand Bank] became part of the new Cottage Hospital System, established by the new Commission of Government.

company n
1 1987 POWELL 50 Sometimes when big companies of birds start towards land, almost within shooting distance, the Saddleback gulls make noises. ibid 143-4 They saw something on the ice that looked like a company of caribou lying down.

concert n
1917 *Deep Sea Fishers* xv, p. 108 A detachment of Harrington school children [took] part in the Christmas concert in the Mission Hall [and] begged to be allowed to present...our celebrated three-act play, for the people of

the Barrachois. 1987 FIZZARD 152 'At the concert there was singing and skits and recitals.'

conch n *DBE* conch-shell 'used as a signal' (1978).

1 [(1847) 1982 [ROUSE] (ed Street) 128 The men of this place (Romanists and Protestants) to the number of from 60 to 70, assembled at the sound of the horn (a shell) and the firing of guns.] [1859] 1987 *Nfld Qtly* lxxxiii (2), 44-5 Children were usually called to school by the raising of a flag or by a bell, though Inspector Haddon records one instance where 'on the morning of my arrival the children were summoned to school by the sound of a conch...a cheap substitute for a flag or a bell.' 1984 KELLAND 181 In addition, the dories carried a conche shell (shell of a mollusk which produced a loud booming sound when a fisherman blew into it).

confederation n
1987 JOHNSTON 45 The talk at gatherings in the early fifties was almost always about the Confederation debates—not the public debates, but the private ones, the family disagreements. 1988 DOHANEY 158 'What were ye fightin' about?' Bertha asked crossly. 'Not Confederation again.'

conkerbill n *SED* iv, 877 conkerbells So.

conner n *DARE* cunner n[1] 1 N E (1672-). Also attrib ~ **pot**.
1984 GOUGH 57 'You got anything better to do with your time? Like counting connors?' 1985 *Newfoundland LifeStyle* iii (1), 46 I've caught quintals of conners in my time but that's as far as it goes. P 231-87 Conner pot. A round hoop 3^1/$_2$ feet diameter covered with netting, lowered, with bait tied in centre, for catching lobsters. 1990 *Evening Telegram* 14 Jan, p. 5 He said sculpins and connors can be found [in St John's harbor], but very rarely.

cook room n Cp *DARE* ~ n 'kitchen, orig one separate from a house' (1649-).
1983 FROUDE 167 We layed the keels of five Vessels on the blocks builded a cook room and bunk house.

copper n Comb **copper-fasten** v.
1986 *Evening Telegram* 9 June, p. 6 The railway (copper fastened under the Terms of Union with Canada) was to become a permanent part of the Canadian National Railway system. 1987 POOLE 40 It was then that I knew for sure that our love for each other was iron-bound and copper-fastened and we had made no mistake.

copy v also **copsy***.
1 1986 SAUNDERS 36 After school we would make for the pans and copy from one to the other behind a leader, back and forth, showing off for the girls and occasionally falling in.

copying vbl n
1 1988 *Evening Telegram* 23 Apr, p. 8 Like their grandfathers and fathers before them, these four lads [in the photograph] couldn't resist the hazardous activity

of 'copying' across ice pans in Spaniard's Bay [last week].
2 1987 *Evening Telegram* 2 Mar, p. 6 Meantime, the ice drifted close to the shore and the Deckers scrambled to safety over small pieces of ice, 'copying' I suppose you could call that method of travel.

cork[1] n also **cark**.
1 Oakum used to fill the seams of a boat or other wooden structure to be made watertight.
M 68-13 He would pitch the seams so that they wouldn't leak. He would put cark in the seams also. He would do the same job with the coffin as with a dory so that it wouldn't leak. 1987 DAWE [12] C is for cark/In the seams of a boat;/Some folks call it oakum,/And that's no misquote.
2 Comb **cark iron**.
T 166-65 I never seed a'r cark iron. And I went back up and I said, 'He isn't there.'

cork[2] n also **cark***, **kork** [kæːɹk]. Cp *OED* calk sb[1] 1, 2. Protruding metal point to hold (something) in place.
P 65-64 Carks are driven into the bunks to keep the bottom logs from rolling around [on the sled]. Carks are spikes with the sharp part up. [1987] QUINLAN 31 [The loggers] had iron korks in the boots to stick into the wood.

cork v also **cark*** [kaːɹk, kɑːɹk]. Cp *OED* caulk v 1; *DARE* ~ v[2] 4 'to make tight against leakage; to caulk' (1823-). To wedge (material) in seams to prevent leakage; hence vbl n **carking iron** [ˈkaːɹkʔn ˌaiəɹn]: metal chisel used to wedge oakum in seams of a boat or other object, **corking mallet**.
1945 MARTIN [5] Yes, please God! the month of May will hear my corkin' mallet ring. T 58-64 The coffin was leaky. And I hauled it ashore and I corked it and I tarred it. T 203-65 They roll it till they gets a little thread about a half inch big. They'll lay it along the seam and cark it in with the carkin' iron. 1984 POWELL 24 We built a new house for the winter. This was a studded one, caulked [for carked*] with moss. 1988 GOSSE 21 Crews would first cork and pitch their boats, and if necessary repair or replace standing and running gear.

corker n American bittern (*Botaurus lentiginosus*).
1870 *Can Naturalist* v, 292 The American bittern makes a curious thumping noise, very much resembling the noise made by fishermen when driving oakum into the seams of their boats: hence...'corker' (?caulker) in Newfoundland.

corner n *DARE* corners (1970) for sense 2.
3 Comb ~ **boy**.
1897 *Evening Telegram* 20 Feb A young an[d] inoffensive man from the higher levels was tripped up last night at 9:30 near the corner of Springdale Street by a crowd of corner boys. When [he] regained his feet the scoundrels had flown. 1986 *Sunday Express* 23 Nov, p. 2 In times not long past, the city's corner boys took a similar attitude to their profession. They spent their days

leaning against the old General Post Office. Without their support it would surely fall down.

cor(r)e fish n Cp *DARE* corfish n 'whole cod pickled in brine' (1975).

[1807] 1971 HERIOT 19-20 The fish which is salted without being dried, is termed Core-fish, or green cod.

cottage n *OED* ~ 6: ~ hospital (1860, 1890). Comb ~ **hospital**: small hospital with non-specialist medical and nursing service for 'outport' community, ~ **roof**.

1933 *Nfld Royal Commission Report* 212 The twelve hospitals in the Island, of which six are in St John's, are generally well-equipped and managed, but in view of the distances which patients have to travel there is room in many parts of the coast for the establishment of small hospitals of the 'Cottage Hospital' type. 1941 SMALL-WOOD 157 Cottage Hospitals [listed at] Old Perlican, Markland, Argentia, Come by Chance, Burin, Grand Bank, Harbor Breton, Stephenville Crossing, Burgeo, Bonne Bay, Port Saunders. 1988 NEARY 52 By the end of 1936, cottage hospitals were...in operation at Old Perlican, Argentia, Come-by-Chance, Grand Bank, Harbour Breton, and Burgeo. 1989 *Nfld Herald* 15 July, p. 12 The St Lawrence hospital [is] the only cottage hospital...built without government assistance. It was built by the American government...in appreciation [of the rescue of] American sailors who went down with their ships the U.S.S. *Truxton* and the U.S.S. *Pollux* during a naval disaster in 1942. 1987 FIZZARD 143 Around the early 1920s we find the first examples of smaller houses [in Grand Bank] with four sided roofs. In some instances the four sides met in a point to form a pyramid; in others, the four sides met in a ridge to create what is known as a 'cottage' roof.

cotterall n *SED* iv, 535 Ha.

country n Cp *DARE* ~ n 2 d ~ man (1931-) for comb in sense 3.

1 1987 *Nfld Studies* iii (2), 252 [In the Second World War] the country was headed for the greatest boom it had ever known.

2 1984 POWELL 38 I had my dickie hauled over my sweater, which was all I wore back in the country. Back there you spent most of your time in heavy forest, which was warmer. 1986 SAUNDERS 21 Other men harnessed teams of dogs to loaded slides and went 'in the country' to trap lynx and otter and fox.

course n Also: in phr *set the course*: to lay a course to assigned fishing area drawn by lot.

1987 FIZZARD 128 'Everybody got their course by the course they drawed. Every course was put on a ticket and all the tickets were put in one box. The course would be two points or two points and a half apart. Each dory skipper would then draw a ticket and that's the course he'd set. The course was made out of pieces of wood that would last all year.'

court n Attrib ~ **work**.

1987 POOLE 102 But maybe you will think justice was done when in the summer we had court work and that man was fined $19.00.

cove n

1 [1857 GREY 1] Portugal Cove, 'The Cove,' as it is often called, is distant 10 miles West from St John's. 1920 *Deep Sea Fishers* xviii (4), 123 'Well, Doctor, you're welcome to this cove.' 1984 GOUGH 52 That was until Pastor Roberts arrived in the cove. Came first with what looked like a circus tent...and all the children on their way home from school stopped by to watch the flapping and the billowing. 1987 STRONG 75 To solve the problem [of accurate lists of union membership we devised a system] based on the cove or village where the member resided so that all the members who came from a particular area got the letter assigned to that area.

2 [1985] MAHER 22 We also got a part of the Tidal Wave [of 1929]...the harbour water had risen about two feet over the tops of the wharves. All the coves on Water Street were almost covered in water.

crack[2] v Phr *cry crack*.

1985 GUY 127 'I minds the time...when the snow was chock to your hips by the middle part of October. It sot in early that year...and it never cried crack until...' [listener interrupts]

cracker n *DARE* crackerberry n 1 (1900-). Comb ~ **berry**.

1988 *Evening Telegram* 11 June, p. A1 And in the late summer and fall the fruits of chuckley-pear, blueberry, crackerberry [etc] are abundant [for the ruffed grouse].

cracky n

1895 *Outing* xxvii, p. 23 'Sartenly knowed as 'ow a rat ud feel wens [once] a crackey nipped aholt!' T 966-71 Bill went out, an' the cracky went out with un. Well the cracky start goin' around, well he was runnin' around, he'd run over five or six acres o' land in a day. 1986 FELTHAM 168 The dog was small as 'crackies' go [and] was coal black except for his four paws. 1987 JOHNSTON 61 Nick would smile, puff on his pipe and ask my father if he knew that he had a 'saucy crackie' for a wife.

cramp a For sense 2, see GEO. BORROW, *Wild Wales* ([1862], London: Collins, 1978), 508: 'Ochone! that's the meaning of [those words], sure enough. They are cramped words.'

cramp n *DARE* ~ knot N E (1978); *South Shore Phr Bk*; cp *OED* cramp sb[1] d cramp-stone 'a stone used as a charm against cramp' (1629). Attrib **cramp knot**.

1985 *Terminology of Loggers* 5 ~ a gnarled lump of wood which loggers used to ease foot cramps by rolling it on the ground underneath the cramped foot.

credit n Comb **credit system**.

1985 BUSCH 53 The 'credit' system differed from the earlier 'truck' system in that the merchant was providing credit, not the actual goods.

crew n

1 1987 FIZZARD 149 'The crews of women were going

back on the beaches after dinner to turn each fish so that not one would be sunburned.'

2 1985 QUIGLEY 42 Well, we started 'er up again an' Jack got his crew on d' floor an started t' tread d' needle set.

cribby a, n Cp *OED* crib 13 'frame of logs... secured under water to form a pier, dam.' Designating rocks offshore which form a barrier. Comb **cribby rocks** (1983 *Gazetteer of Canada: Nfld* 40, near Tors Cove), also **cribbies**.

P 68-64 Cribbies—a natural breakwater.

crip n Cp *EDD* ~ v, sb s w cties for discards in sheep-shearing. Edging cut from timber to square it for further processing (P 325-83).

[1872] 1985 TAYLOR 15 I regret to be again under the necessity of bringing before your notice the large quantity of crip and loose drift timber drifting about the Exploits during the salmon season. 1986 SAUNDERS 22 Climbing aboard, and using a piece of mill edging—what we called crip—for a pole, I pushed out into the current.

crit[2] n A person dressed in best clothes (Q 67-110).

P 318-84 ~ a person all dressed up. 'You're a real crit!'

croochy* v also **crouchy**.

1985 GUY 66 What he was at, see, he was crouchied down with his ear to the window trying to hear what we were talking about.

crooked a *AND* ~ a 'esp. in phr *crooked on*' (1942-).

1986 SAUNDERS 45 I knew he was crooked because the light in his hand commenced to quiver. 1987 *Evening Telegram* 22 Dec, p. 3 'I don't know what it is. People are either too lazy, too crooked or too tired to park in the designated parking zones,' he said.

crop[1] n

1 Also: the chit or authorization for such fishing or sealing equipment; **crop note**.

1900 *Evening Telegram* 10 Mar Having secured his berth from the captain..he left Harbor Grace without his 'crop,' thinking that it could be secured here in St John's. 1987 ibid 14 Mar, p. 10 [tape transcript] The father helped the boy choose a whole 'fitout' of warm clothes, and used part of his own crop to pay for them.

crop[2] n Cp *OED* ~ sb 6 'the top of anything material' Sc. The topmost part of a beach.

1984 KELLAND 126 By this time [they] had disappeared over the crop of the beach to the west and it dawned on us then that the three men had bravely gone up to face the terror which we had run away from. ibid 158 [The fish] then were lugged up over the crop of the beach and bulked in waterhorses.

crop[2] v

1987 *Evening Telegram* 14 Mar, p. 10 [tape transcript] Each man was 'cropped'...by Job's to the tune of 9 dollars, for which $12 were deducted from his share at

the end of a successful voyage but for which nothing was owed if the voyage was a failure... Articles in demand from our counter were long rubbers, goggles... Nansen caps, warm underwear, overalls, and home-knit mitts.

cross n *DARE* ~ fox n (1917); cp *DARE* cross-haul n 3. Comb ~ **fox**, ~ **hauls**: 'chains connecting two sleds which are crossed in the middle to facilitate the turning of the sleds' (1985 *Terminology of Loggers* 5).

1984 POWELL 66-7 I looked at the hairs on the stick where the wire was attached and saw that a cross fox had been in it but had gotten away. 1986 SAUNDERS 25 [He] built four cages, and got three cross foxes for breeder stock.

cross v Phr *cross the line*: seaman's metaphor for 'to die.'

1983 FROUDE 140 The few remarks which I am about to note down here May be of some value to my boys when I have crossed The line and gone.

cross-handed av

4 Comb **cross-handed dory**.

1984 KELLAND 29 The Portuguese Banks fishermen showed a preference for the cross-handed or single man dory.

croucher n Red knot (1987 MONTEVECCHI & TUCK 238).

crouchy See CROOCHY.

crousty a

1982 DAWE 44 A crousty old fellow from Crouse,/ Prowled outside a rich widow's house;/But she swung a salt fish,/That reclined on a dish,/And gave him a wonderful douse.

crowd n

1 Also: phr *crowd of hands*; cp HAND.

1983 WARNER 25 To set [the cod trap] in place takes two boats 'with a good crowd of hands' working for four or five hours in reasonably calm weather. 1987 POOLE 22 When the fish was all shipped, George settled up for the crowd, with Baine Johnston of Battle Harbour, their merchant.

2 Also: such a group from one's own community.

1987 FIZZARD 156 'When the Americans joined the war in 1917, I came home [to Grand Bank] and signed up. I wanted to join up with our own crowd rather than with the Americans [and] I enlisted in the Newfoundland Regiment in May 1917.'

3 1987 JOHNSTON 84 My mother and father and their crowd, as their children came of an age when they could either be left at home to look after themselves or could easily be managed at a gathering, began going out to bars and clubs again. 1988 ELLIOTT [15-6] "Grandma's Lullaby": And someone roars, 'Dass Jim Parsons' crowd,/ Dass been so long away.'

crown n *OED* ~ sb IV 'top or highest part.' On a fishing 'ground' a shoal area.

1986 FELTHAM 54 The shallowest part of a fishing 'spot' was called the 'crown' and any point that got gradually deeper and narrower was called the 'tail.'

cruel a, intens. *DARE* ~ adv 'very' (1803-) for sense 2.

1 1985 GUY 77 I was always subject to a cruel sight of bunions right here on me left foot. If there's weather coming up they smarts something fierce.

cruise v Cp *Anglo-Manx Dialect* ~ 'stroll' in sense 1.

3 1986 FELTHAM 51 In the spring, before the fishing season began, the bullies were used to 'cruise' home the firewood cut during the previous winter.

crunnick n PRATT ~ 'rare.'

1983 DAWE & FICKEN 48 High up in the cliffs/Where they keep to themselves,/The clusters of crannicks/Are dragons and elves. 1986 FELTHAM 106 Most of the islands were partly covered with saplings from eight to ten feet in height. At times these were cut for firewood and were known as 'crunnicks.'

cuddy n

1 1981 SPARKES 184 In the stern portion of the boat (the after cuddy) was the bottom of an old stove, or discarded oven door, anything that was fire-safe. 1985 NEWHOOK 107 'Billy, get out the oil clothes from the cuddy.' 1987 POOLE 58 He took his bail bucket and dipped up some gas and water and brought it forward onto the cuddy of the boat.

cue n *AND* ~ n (1902-) for sense 1.

2 1981 SPARKES 190 To prevent the heels from wearing unevenly, steel protectors, "U" shaped, were nailed to them. They were called 'Qs.'

cue v *AND* ~ v (1902-).

cuff¹ n

1 1986 SAUNDERS 142 On our hands we wore doubleknit cuffs, or mitts, with a finger on them so you could tail slips or shoot a gun without taking them off.

4 Phr *foolish as a cuff* (P 280-84).

cuffer n *Anglo-Manx Dialect* ~ 'a lie'; *AND* 'a tall story' (1887-1916) for sense 1.

1 1984 WRIGHT 34 These stories, or 'cuffers,' might stretch the truth somewhat. Isaac often seemed to take some artistic licence with his tales. But I never caught him in a bold-faced lie, and sometimes the far-fetched stories have proved truthful.

2 1981 MAJOR 31 By the end of a few weeks he looked and acted a whole lot better. Some nights we'd have a real cuffer... There we was, carrying on what you could call a sensible conversation.

cuffer v

1 1981 MAJOR 32 That's what we was talking about mostly—squids. When Grandfather came in on the two of

us cuffering away there in the bedroom, it must a been ten o'clock or later.

cugger* v *EDD* Ir, DINNEEN cograim 'I whisper.' To converse; to whisper.

P 191-73 ~ to whisper in a sly or suspicious manner. P 288-82 Me and my girlfriends were cougaring all the time when we were in high school.

cull v

1987 POOLE 102 That's what I got for taking the Oath—that I cull fish without fear, favour, partiality or affection.

cullage n

1988 *Evening Telegram* 26 July, p. 3 'When we shipped the [salt bulk fish] to Argentia they downgraded our fish from standard to cullage' [he] said.

culler n

[1807] 1971 HERIOT 19 A person, denominated *culler* or inspector, attends the loading of each vessel [for Europe] in order to see that no fish which is not perfectly cured, be introduced into the cargo. 1987 FIZZARD 133 'The culler separates the small, medium, large; good and cullage.'

culling vbl n Cp *SED* iv, 353 ~ 'selecting animals from a flock'; *DARE* ~ board 'table used for grading oysters for market' (1968-70).

curby See KIRBY*.

curlew n *DARE* ~ berry n (1900-) in sense 2.

1 1987 HORWOOD 84 Meanwhile, that other curlew of the east, the Hudsonian, also a companion of the golden plover, seems to have survived fairly well. Unlike the similar Eskimo curlew, it is a wild bird, difficult to approach.

cut v Cp *DARE* ~ v 5 'to separate or remove (one or more animals from a herd' (1869-) for sense 1.

1 1914 *Deep Sea Fishers* xii, 64 This year [steamers] went in [the Gulf] and 'cut them up,' as they call it.

2 Phr *cut tails*; *cut throats*.

1984 *Evening Telegram* 22 Dec, p. 6 My brother and I 'cut tails,' and cleaned our small catch. 1988 ELLIOTT [29] ''To Gerry Squires'': And in my youth I was a fisherman,/first, cutting tails, then shareman. 1987 *Evening Telegram* 7 Mar, p. 10 During my last summer at the Battery, when I was eleven years old, I had graduated to 'cutting throats' which...included slitting the fish from gills to vent. 1988 MOMATIUK & EASTCOTT (eds) 153 'How do you think Doris would work out cutting throats?' Mum said, 'Well, why don't you ask her?'

3 Comb **cut-throat(er)**.

1988 *Evening Telegram* 18 May, p. 19 The colorful terms cut-throater, header and splitter were the names applied to people who carried out the first three steps in the processing of fish. 1989 *Nfld Qtly* lxxxiv (1), 42 ''The Mug-Up'': There were wild beards of oakum, and cork floats/That made perfect hand-guards for cut-throats.

cut n
2 1985 BUSCH 74 Meanwhile the vessel moved on to leave other watches, which might be fanning out as far as three or four miles from the vessel's track or 'cut.'

cutter¹ n One who fillets cod, etc; filleter.
[1963] 1988 *Evening Telegram* 22 June, p.6 About 50 fish fillet cutters, employees of Job Brothers, St John's, walked off their jobs Friday in a demand for higher wages. 1987 FIZZARD 212 'The cod was then sent into the cuttin' tables. At first we had two cuttin' tables and twelve cutters to fillet the fish.'

cutter² n Cp *DC* ~ n 1 'a low, light one-horse sleigh'; *DARE* n¹ 1 for sense 1.
1 Commercially marketed child's sled or 'slide.'
M 69-6 The very rare 'bought' slides became called 'cutters,' due to the ability of the narrow steel runners to cut through snow. 1985 *Nfld Qtly* lxxxi (1), 19 'Cutter ridin'' which was sledding on the hills [in winter] was very popular.
2 A pointed steel bar projecting down from a sledge onto ice to prevent it from sliding sideways (C 63-16).

D

da n *Anglo-Manx Dialect* daa 'father, elderly man.'
1949 FITZGERALD 44 Somehow, I'd kinda sooner when he used to call me Da. 1988 PORTER 132 'She did think I should tell Mom, but I don't believe she said anything about Da...my Father.'

damp a
1903 *Trade Review* "Newfoundland's Maud Muller": For the fish was damp, and the weather dull. [1909] 1930 COAKER 7 Qualities...No. 2, large and small. No. 3, No. 4 and damp... The damp fish of all sizes and qualities to go together at 40 c. per qtl. below the price of No. 1 small.

damper n For sense 1 see BAILEY & GÖRLACH, *English as a World Language* (1982), p. 201: *damper*: 'the metal circle on a wood-burning stove that lifts out so that wood may be put in' Nr Car. Cp *AND* ~ 1 'a simple kind of bread' (1825), and combs ~ **bread,** ~ **cake**; cp *OED* 1 b 'something that takes off the edge of appetite.'
1 1987 *Nfld Qtly* lxxxiii (1), 15 She took the kettle... back to the stove, took up a damper and placed the kettle over the hole to bring it to a quick boil. 1989 ROWE 240 The mother was just putting the damper back on the stove after putting in a piece of wood, when the ball of fire headed for her.
2 Comb ~ **dog.**
1984 POWELL 35 We were living well on beaver meat, and we dipped our damper dogs in the beaver [fat like] butter.

damsel n *Anglo-Manx Dialect* ~ 'damson.'

dandy n *SED* iv, 474-5 daddy-long-legs.

daps* n *SED* iv, 932 W Co D.

darby n
1984 ROBERTSON xvii In a few communities, other words are known as well as or instead of mummers or janneys [for example] *darbies* in Avondale, C.B., Colinet, S.M.B., Mount Carmel, S.M.B.

dark a Comb ~ **one.**
1983 DAWE & FICKEN 16 D is for dark-one,/A mummer or janny,/Rigged up in old clothes,/He looks somewhat uncanny.

dart n
1 1774 *Trans Roy Soc* lxiv, p. 378 Observing that the seal-darts of every [Esquimaux] Indian were headed with the teeth of the SEA-COW, I was led to inquire, how they came by them.
3 Phr *make a dart*.
1987 *Nfld Qtly* lxxxii (3), 15 'But every once in a while [the mouse would] work up 'nuff courige tuh make a dart fer it.'

darting vbl n The activity of spearing (fish).
[1768] 1989 *Nfld Qtly* lxxxv (1), 21 Darting Rattle.

dead a Comb ~ **box**: seaman's wooden chest; ~ **head wind**: at sea, a breeze straight ahead.
1983 PEDDLE 99 Occasionally a large pine travelling box...is found in the outports. It is generally believed that these were used by the skippers of schooners... On the Port de Grave peninsula they are often referred to as 'dead boxes,' by those who surmise they served a dual purpose. 1987 POOLE 13 As we got out, the wind seemed to draw in through the bight so we had to beat a dead head wind. When the Captain decided to tack and bring her on a starboard tack the vessel was doing fine, but when she got close enough to the land on the southern side of Spear Harbour Bight she [mis-stayed] and went ashore again.

dealer n
1 1984 PITT 16 Most of the outports had a merchant or 'dealer,' the larger ones several. He was usually a general provisioner who was often also the chief fish entrepreneur for the community, supplying the fisherman and his family on credit, the debt to be paid in the currency of the product when it was harvested.
2 1986 SIDER 58 For the most part, except for his own employees, the merchant referred to all these people as his 'dealers,' that is, the people with whom he dealt.

deepwater n Cp *OED* deep IV a phr deep-water [land waterways]. An area of water with great depressions in the sea bottom.
[c1891] 1988 *Canoma* xiv (2), 10 Deepwater Bank [area of Virgin Rocks]. 1977 WHITELEY 46 [Other cod trap berths] have derived their names from experiences such as Lunatic and Deepwater. 1983 *Gazetteer of*

Canada: Nfld 44-5 Deep Water Bank, Deepwater Island, Deepwater Point, etc.

delco n
1987 FIZZARD 188 'We had our lights up. I was at the table splitting fish. I heard something like a delco going.'

desperate a
[1669] 1963 YONGE 114 At noon [wind] veered to the westward, and continued shifting to and fro with many desperate gusts of hail and spouts, often compelling us to lower all amain. 1988 *Muse* 16 Sep, p. 15 The original recording of this song suffered from desperate production.

devil n
2 Comb **devilskin**.
P 266-89 That [politician] is a devilskin.

dialogue n
1979 PORTER 48 Aunt Viley...often took part in those concerts. She and her friend...did sketches or dialogues, which leaned heavily on the American rural tradition.

dickie See DICKY².

dicky¹ n
[1976] 1985 LEHR & BEST (eds) 36 ''Chrissy's Dick'': He started off for Hay Cove, the dicky for to find,/But when he got about half ways over he heard 'en cry behind.

dicky² n also **dickie**.
1 1984 KALLEO 3 These three people are living in 1919. The dress—white dickies and white boots—were worn on holidays. 1984 POWELL 38 I had my dickie hauled over my sweater, which was all I wore back in the country.

diet n
[1849] 1983 [ROUSE] (ed Street) 181 Having talked over the matter I agreed to give [him] £10 Currency for the Summer; he being to fish for us, and to remain up to the next Caplin Skull for his diet alone. 1903 *Deep Sea Fishers* Oct, p. 12 [Families] not only had already a 'summer diet' assured, but had also [ready money for next winter].

diet v Cp *OED* ~ v 1 'to feed, esp in a particular way' (1362-). To provide food, and sometimes accommodation, for members of a fishing crew, esp in non-fishing season.
1879 *Journ of Assembly* Appendix p. 129 [Money] paid Margaret Carew for dieting one of the crew three weeks, at 1s. per meal.

dieter n
2 Phr *dieter's knees*: threadbare trouser knees.
[1960] 1982 BURKE (ed Kirwin) 133 He left me an old pair of trousers,/In the knees like the dieters are seen.

dill¹ n
2 Attrib, comb ~ **thwart**: in an undecked boat

that one of the boards on which rower sits which is placed over the well of the craft; 'midship tawt.'
1986 FELTHAM 175 When I had finished I sat on the 'dill' thwart and 'shoved' towards the motor-boat.

dill² n *SED* iv, 341-2 s w cties.

dilly-dalls n pl also **dilly dolly**. Cp *OED* dilly-dally v. Periods of a dead calm at sea.
1904 *Nfld Qtly* iii (4), 9 [in comment on Dildo Run, near Exploits River] Our people, speaking of a ship in the doldrums, say 'she is in the *Dilly dollies*.' 1924 *Deep Sea Fishers* xxi (4), 138 Dilly-dalls. [A] calm.

dip v PRATT dip net for cpd in sense 5.
1 [1889-93] 1987 PEYTON 7 This congregation of salmon in the dammed shallow pool allowed easy access for someone to dip them from the weir. It was not unusual to dip approximately 250 to 300 pounds of salmon in one hour. 1986 SAUNDERS 21 [He] and a crew of fishermen had been dipping salmon out of their 'rake-works' or rock weir. 1987 *Evening Telegram* 7 Mar, p. 10 Plenty of you have hauled a cod-trap...and you will know the thrill of dipping in as many quintals as will fit between the thwarts [of the boat]. 1990 ibid 23 Jan, p. 5 The beaches around the coast of this island of ours were a hive of activity when men, women and children were seen casting caplin [and] dipping caplin.
4 1986 FELTHAM 80 The young harp seals after they 'dipped' and were no longer on the ice where they whelped were called 'beaters.'

dipper n PRATT ~ for sense 1.
1 Also: such a saucepan for collecting berries; EMPTER, PICKER.
1987 *Lore and Language* vi (1), 27, 33 [She] went across the brook to pick a dipper of berries to make a pudding for supper... All they could find was one of her red socks up in a tree and a dipper of blueberries on the ground.

dirty a Cp *AND* ~ a 'resentful' (1965-) for sense 4.
1 1985 *Evening Telegram* 6 July, p. 5 Fishermen report the water slubby and dirty. 1986 ibid 7 June, p. 50 Longliner skippers operating out of [Catalina] have been experiencing a much better start to the fishing season... but the water on the offshore is becoming dirty and this is expected to affect catches. 1989 ibid 3 June, p. A4 The water is too clean; the water is too dirty. The fish aren't migrating [or] are migrating in the wrong direction.
2 1987 *Evening Telegram* 11 Apr, p. 14 Captain Forward went down to Captain Bartlett and he said, 'I believe we are going to have a dirty night. I don't like the look of it.' 1989 ibid 13 July, p. 3 'We'll be here for another couple of days, but if the weather gets too dirty, we'll have to head home.'
4 1981 MAJOR 34 And how the old man got so dirty with me for being careless. Although he let me steer the boat back into the wharf just the same.
5 Fouled with excrement.
1987 MONTEVECCHI & TUCK 163 Dirty Cliff.

do v [duːz] *SED*, throughout vol iv, has many quotations with weakly stressed auxiliary *do* in s w cties, for example in animal cries, 345-52: [bulls da moo], etc.

1 To carry out (an action).

T 133-64 'Whatever you dooz,' he said, 'don't sell the bridle.' T 547-68 'No odds what he dooz,' [she] said. 'All he dooz [is] plank the money out, pay it, and go on.' 1976 HOLLETT 1 'Say the salmon weigh ten pound, you only get paid for nine. And if he weigh twenty pound you get paid for nineteen, always doed that.' [1970s] 1988 *Maritime Anthro Studies* i, p. 98 'You're goin' to take the small fish, 'cause that's what countin' dooz.'

2 Aux (level of stress not recoverable from printed sources); **do be, don't be**: see BE.

1903 *Daily News* 7 Oct ''Where your Money Goes'': Oh, where do our money go.../For the *voters* like to know. [1977] 1985 LEHR & BEST (eds) 51 ''The Dole Song'': We'll take on board our caplin boys, and we'll then bait up our gear;/We'll stick her to the Western Grounds if the weather it do keep clear. 1987 FIZZARD 189 'I said ''That's a good one, e'den it? We won't be long going down if they do change their mind on us''.'

3 Pro-verb.

1924 ENGLAND 179 'An' if ye speak to un, he mind ye of a squid squirtin'.' 'Oh, he do, do he?' The Old Man bridled with virtuous indignation. [1932] 1987 *Nfld Qtly* lxxxiii (1), 2 ''The Morning Lesson'': I hope/They know their lessons. Mary do I know/By the easy way she rattles off the words. P 148-83 What they don't know don't hurt 'em, do it?

doctor n

2 1988 *Evening Telegram* 28 May, p. 7 If the fish 'doctor' cannot swim how does it get to the wounded fish? And is this phenomenon only found in the codfish species?

5 Comb **doctor's box**.

P 302-88 There'd be one big [kit], it was called the doctor's box then...and he'd be filled with bandages and curichrome, washing soap.

dodding See DOTING.

dodge v Cp SMYTH 255 'to watch or follow a ship from place to place' for sense 2.

1 1924 *Deep Sea Fishers* xxi (4), 139 Dodge up. To drop around; go on an errand. 1984 POWELL 44 We kept dodging along [through the forest]. The travelling was getting better. 1986 SAUNDERS 21 When we got big enough we dodged along the landwash looking for interesting shells and rocks and especially fool's gold. 1987 *Lore and Language* vi (1), 28 Sometimes, he'd be in view sometimes he wouldn't be in view. When we'd be in a hollow, he'd be on a hill. And we started singing out 'Skipper! ... hey!hey!hey!' like you would. But he kept dodging on, dodging on.

2 [1792] 1989 PULLING (ed Marshall) 129 When they presented either of their pieces at the Indians they dodg'd behind the Clifts & made sport of them.

dog[1] n

1 1989 CANDOW 15 The adult male hood ('dog') weighs in the neighbourhood of 900 pounds.

3 1988 GOSSE 33 Later in the spring when attention was turned to the old harps, the gunners, accompanied by two helpers or 'dogs,' led the hunt.

dog[2] n Cp BRYANT 480 ~ n 'short, heavy piece of steel...used for many purposes in logging' for new sense 5.

5 In logging operations, an iron peg used to attach chain connecting boom logs (P 325-83). Also comb ~ **beater,** ~ **ears** (see quots).

1985 *Terminology of Loggers* 6 Dog beater: an old-fashioned stick for measuring lumber. Dog ears: pointed projections left on a stump by someone who was unable to change hands while cutting down a tree, and so changed sides instead, leaving opposite notches on the stumps.

dogberry n

1982 BURSEY 59 ''A Bunch of Dogberries'': A stranger/Brought a bunch of dogberries. /I can see the orange glow,/Not the shape;/In my mind is the shape—/Berry [b]eads on nature's necklace. 1989 *Nfld Qtly* lxxxiv (1), 22 Aunt Liz and her mother are sitting on the back steps on a summer's day. The dogberry tree was a lot smaller then.

dole n Cp *O Sup*[2] ~ sb[1] 6 a 'popular name for the various kinds of weekly payments...to the unemployed' (1919-). Attrib ~ **bread,** ~ **flour**: unrefined, enriched flour, ~ **order**: chit authorizing the provision of supplies to the needy.

1979 PORTER 33 The Government allotted only brown flour to the people on relief, and the never-to-be-forgotten resentment toward 'dole bread' was widespread at that time. [1936] 1986 *Evening Telegram* 21 Nov, p. 6 SS *Nova Scotia* arrived from Liverpool [bringing] 33 passengers and a large general cargo including 10,000 sacks of dole flour. 1987 POWELL 52 The food that was stored at [Frenchman's Island] was of no help to them. The men had to go to Battle Harbour and get what was called 'dole order' from the Ranger.

dominion n

1982 *Evening Telegram* 2 Nov, p. 1 But Newfoundland Premier Brian Peckford, claiming the province joined Confederation in 1949 as a separate dominion with control over resources, rejected the federal offer as a power grab. 1986 SAUNDERS 43 Bishop Feild College had a reputation as one of the best schools in the Dominion of Newfoundland, sending graduates to universities in England and the United States.

donkey n

1 1987 *Evening Telegram* 27 Apr, p. 7 [tape transcript] Fish was packed in half-drums, drums, casks, donkeys, and various kinds of barrels.

4 Phr *donkey's breakfast*: sealer's mattress.

1989 CANDOW 88 The sealer's mattress, known as a 'donkey's breakfast,' consisted of a cloth sack stuffed with straw or wood chips, and each man had to supply the stuffing himself.

donkey v Cp *AND* donkey-lick v 'to defeat (an opponent, etc).' To manhandle another in rough play.

[1929] 1982 MADISON (ed) 31 Everything went well/ Until we donkeyed him five times/And he got mad as hell... When a man is donkeyed, he has to be trimmed up with feathers etc. When he got mad, they tied his arms and legs and dumped him in his bunk.

door n
1 1989 *Sunday Express* 19 Mar, p. 7 From the land-wash to the doors of a cod trap is usually not more than 100 fathoms.

dory n
1 [1887] 1984 KELLAND 47 *Colonist*: 'To fill the orders which have poured in this spring [the staff of The Excelsior Wood Factory] had to work day and night, from February the second, when the first order was received until nearly the end of May, one hundred and sixty-four dories had been produced.' 1891 *Evening Telegram* 1 Aug Captain Yetman reports that, on the 26th of July, he picked up a dory containing a single fisherman.
2 Attrib, comb **dory factory, ~ fisherman, ~ jig, ~ mallet, ~ man, ~ plug, ~ scoop**.
1987 FIZZARD 143 When he gave up the operation, [he] established his own dory factory and developed his own style of dory, which had a reputation for being an exceptionally fine craft. Over the years he and his sons built over 3,000 dories. 1988 *Sunday Express* 5 June, p. 3 The son of a dory fisherman from the southwest coast, [he] help[ed] found Breakwater Books Ltd. 1984 KELLAND 185-6 [The dories] were not dropped into the water immediately, however, but would remain suspended, held up by their burtons or hoisting tackle on the ends of which were four foot long iron hooks, called dory jigs (or as the dorymen used to say, they would be kept in slings). 1987 FIZZARD 160 'We'd make a lot of little things like tow-pins, dory plugs, dory mallets [etc].' ibid 126 [He] says that when he was a doryman, he shipped three years in a row with Captain John. 1984 KELLAND 10 From the work benches of those stores there were manufactured...hand tubs, trawls tubs...dory scoops [etc].

dotard n also **dotter**. Also: high frequency in coastal place-names.
1983 *Gazetteer of Canada: Nfld* 43, 46, 48 Daughter Cove, Doater Cove, Doater Point, Doter Cove, Dotter Cove. 1984 POWELL 19 There was one seal in [the net], a small doter. 1987 ibid 24 There were always lots of seals in that bay. This is the bay seal, not the harp seal. It is the seal which we call the doter, and the young one is called the ranger.

doting ppl also **dodding**. The probable pron is dotin', doat'n. An adjective or attributive of untraced meaning, occurring frequently in place-names.
1871 LOVELL 246 Doting Cove (Fogo). 1878 *Nfld Pilot* 68 Dodding Head, ~ Rock. 1961 ROULEAU 59-60 Doting Cove, ~ Head, ~ Hole.

double a Comb **~ blader**: see **double bitter**, **~ (ball) mitt, ~ sled, ~ spruce**: SPRUCE BEER.
1985 ASHTON 190 "The Indian Bay Song": Grind up your double blader men, your landings clear away. 1949 FITZGERALD 55 And get yourself homespuns and good heavy socks,/With warm double mitts. 1985 *Nfld LifeStyle* 3 (1), 22 A Sunday afternoon will find me beside the swimming pool...knitting a pair of double ball mitts. 1984 POWELL 133 First we hauled in the wheels, then the motor was placed on the big double sleds with two tiers of planks. [1785] 1955 GARDNER 33 The poor fellow was at last made sensible it was a joke, and had some double spruce given to him to make amends which had the desired effect.

douse v
2 1984 KELLAND 134 The two dorymen doused their first anchor and buoy a hundred fathoms from the little schooner, running out the trawl, they dropped the second anchor.

down av *DBE* **~** adv 1 'towards the north' for sense 1; and cp *AND* 1 a to go (come) down, 4 a phr down south, *O Sup*[2] 27 down along 'in or to the West Country' for comb in sense 3.
1 1984 POWELL 13-4 Sometimes they would give us potatoes for it that they had brought down from Newfoundland [to Labrador]. 1987 *Evening Telegram* 9 May, p. 15 [tape transcript] 'Where are you bound Captain Winsor?' 'I'm bound down,' he says, 'to the northern fleet on the Labrador.' 1988 ibid 2 July, p. 14 At a debate some years ago at St Bonaventure's College the expressions 'Down North' and 'Down on the Labrador' were successfully defended. The victor in the debate... argued that: 'Motion to the centre of gravity is downwards...the Earth is flattened at the Poles and expanded at the Equator. So you go down North from the Equator as you go down South from the same location. You go up to the Equator from both Poles.'
2 [1939] 1989 *Evening Telegram* 13 Mar, p. 4 Conception Bay is filled with heavy slob ice and yesterday people walked from Bell Island to the mainland. The ice extends down the shore and there is a considerable body off this port. 1979 PORTER 5 From the church all the way down the road, not much of the harbour could be seen. 1985 JOHNSTON 60 On Sundays, once the roads were free of snow, my father took us driving, up the Shore, sometimes, on rainy days, on fine ones down to Sounder's Bay, around the ponds a mile east inland. 1987 O'FLAHERTY 5 Having decided that labour would dull pain, he set about putting a new fence around his property, with the help of a muscular and blessedly taciturn fellow from down the shore.
3 Comb **down the banks, ~ the line**: homeward from a logging camp (1985 *Terminology of Loggers* 6).
1905 *Adelphian* ii, p. 127 Mrs Moriarty skinned the poor girl alive... Oh, poor Sara got down the banks and no mistake.

dows'y poll n
1987 DAWE [14] D is for dows'y poll,/Moth of the night;/He sloos at my window in search of

the light;/Some call him a miller,/But where is his mill?

drain n

[1841] 1987 FIZZARD 88 Width of 16 ft, but like other outport roads, the stumps of the trees have been left standing. About 400 perches of drains are made and in progress in the wettest parts. [1934] 1984 *Evening Telegram* 26 Feb, p. 6 A large number of laborers are employed by the Council today clearing the [gullies] and drains from the inclines leading to the main streets.

drashel* n *SED* iv, 515 So D Do.

draw v

1 1984 GOUGH 99 [Ern's berth] was a sweet one and had been in the family for as long as anyone could remember. Other coves might draw for their berths—but here they were passed down as secure and as placed as a pew. 1987 POOLE 69 That spring when the fishermen came they wanted me to draw for berths, but I was too stubborn to draw... They drew for the berths that were left, the ones that I didn't have.

3 Phr *draw/dry up*.

[1856] 1977 WHITELEY 37 'The modus operandi is...to anchor on either side of the bag...draw it up, fastening the ends to the thole pins.' [1937] 1945 SCAMMELL 38 "Payne's Cove Bait Skiff": A good winter's diet for Skipper Phil's sow,/But we've dried up enough in the seine, anyway. 1981 SPARKES 187 To haul the trap the doors are hauled up, thus enclosing permanently all the fish within the trap. Then the sides are hauled up and the fish are said to be 'dried up' and so they are dipped into the skiffs by men using large dipnets. 1984 *Evening Telegram* 22 Mar, p. 5A The haul is complete when the fish have been dried up in a corner at the back of the trap. 1989 *Sunday Express* 26 Mar, p. 7 I could now better understand what trapmen had meant when they could say, even when we dried up 2,000 pounds—a full ton of protein in a single haul—'Well, you can't call this fish.' P 245-89 'The men were hard at it, drying up the twine at the caplin fishery.'

4 Comb **draw-bucket**.

1986 FELTHAM 105 The container used [to secure sea water to wash cod in the stage] was called a 'draw-bucket.'

draw n

1984 GOUGH 99 Most people thought if he wasn't going to use [the berth] he should put it up for grabs. Maybe then they could have a draw for it.

drawing vbl n

1 1987 POOLE 79 I soon found out that the younger fishermen considered they had nothing to lose by drawing.

2 Attrib **drawing/drying up** (area).

1988 GOSSE 48 Here the mesh size of the netting was only three to four inches to prevent the fish from escaping and was described as the drying or dry up area [of the cod-trap].

dress v PRATT ~ v for sense 2.

1 1987 FIZZARD 129 'So when you got your fish on board, you'd have to dress it [and] probably you'd get about three hours of rest through the night.'

4 Phr *dress in the fools*: see FOOL; *to dress up*; hence vbl n.

1858 LIND *MS Diary* 6 Jan I am sorry to find that the majority of the young people (& some of the married ones) are busy in dressing up to act as 'mummers.' 1987 FIZZARD 152 'He would come into the house on all fours and sit under the kitchen table making noises like an animal. The house would be filled with mummers, all dressed up.'

5 Cpd **dress-up** (a).

1984 ROBERTSON xvii In a few communities, other words are known as well as or instead of mummers or jannies [for example] *dress-ups* in Port Rexton, T.B., Swift Current, P.B., Twillingate, N.D.B., and Dark Cove, B.B.

drew n See DROO*.

dribble n

1983 *Gazetteer of Canada: Nfld* 48, 56 Dribble Brook...First Dribble Pond, Fischells Dribble.

drift n PRATT drift ice (1853-).

7 Comb **drift-ice**.

1984 POWELL 7 'I want to get to Fishing Ship's Harbour before the drift ice moves back on the coast.'

drite* n See *SED* iv, 883 for s w English parallels.

drive v

1 Also, of ice, *drive out*.

[1777] P 307-83 [Moravian records] The ice in our Bay Broke loose and Drove out but the wind Brought it Back. 1984 POWELL 30 There was a little too much wind for me to make the land with the sculling oar and I was driving off the land. 1987 POOLE 4 The rest of the schooners being close to the north side [of Carbonear Harbour], drove out and were smashed to splinters on Flamber Head and Harbour Rock. The *Polly*, the one we used to go to Labrador on drove out and I don't think she was ever seen again.

2 Phr *drive works*.

1987 POOLE 11 There was one young man among them that was always driving works. He picked up a sod and threw it at this older man [and then] another.

driving vbl n Comb ~ **season**: spring of the year when high water levels are necessary for the logging drive.

1986 SAUNDERS 203 Depending on the year, a full driving season could last from early April, with snow squalls and ice still lingering along the shore, right into the end of May, when the nippers and blackflies would make life hellish.

droke n

1 1983 *Gazetteer of Canada: Nfld* 48 Drook, Drook Cove, Drook Hill, etc. 1989 *Evening Telegram* 23 July, p. A12 There is [in the photograph of Cape Broyle] a good example of the 'saltbox' house and what appears to be a droke leading down from the residence.

2 Phr *droke of woods/spruce*, etc.

P 245-86 '[He] approached the droke o' woods towards the bear's [winter] den.' 1986 SAUNDERS 29 She...left the road and plowed into a thick droke of spruce until the cart brought up against a stump. 1989 *Evening Telegram* 20 Dec, p. 5 As it got late in the evening we'd go into a droke of thick forest and with this piece of duck [for shelter] we could weather the worst storms.

droo* n also **drew**. Possibly developed from a form of *through*, with initial *dr-*. See *EDD droo* forms in s w cties.

1 In 'knitting' a fish-net, a certain number of meshes formed in a row.

T 48-64 Then you'd slip that off o' your card—'twas a bit tedious first until you get three or four drews, they called it, knit up; that was three or four back an' forth—the hundred meshes. Q 73-1 [There are] ninety-eight meshes in a drew. 1986 FELTHAM 94 One of my sisters knit a 'drew' as fast as any male around.

2 A quantity of dried and salted cod-fish equal to the length of a storage pound.

T 395-67 [We'd] turn over the fish what was there, turn over one drew, right the length o' that pound; instead of face up, they'd be back up.

drop v Cp *OED* ~ v 13 b to drop anchor. To lower a small anchor or 'graple' with buoy attached as signal that a particular fishing area is occupied for the season.

1981 SPARKES 188 When a man went to fish on a certain ground, he 'threw away' his grapnel, that is, he anchored. He is then said to be 'dropped' there, and when a man had dropped, it was extremely bad manners for somebody else to come and drop near him.

drudge v

3 Comb ~ **barrow**.

1984 *Evening Telegram* 22 Dec, p. 6 My brother and I...cleaned our small catch—headed, gutted and split the fish, washed them in a 'dredge-barrow,' salted them away.

drug n *SED* iv, 170 Co D Do Ha.

1984 POWELL 85 So I called the dogs to one side of the trail and put the drag over the nose of the kamutik to stop her. 1985 *Terminology of Loggers* 7 Drug or drag: a chain with a pin which was put around the *runner* of a sled for use as a braking device on hills.

drum n

1987 *Evening Telegram* 27 Apr, p. 7 [tape transcript] Fish was packed in half-drums, drums, casks, donkeys, and various kinds of barrels... [A] drum [held] 128 pounds to the Brazil market. 1986 RYAN xxii [Salt] fish for...Brazil was packaged in drums and half-drums. (Officially, a drum contained four Portuguese arrobas for a total of 129.517 lbs, avoirdupois, but 128 lbs was often the weight used by the Newfoundland shippers.)

drung n *SED* iv, 96, 426 drangway D So.

1983 *Daily News* 14 June, p. 14 The once quiet drung [Maunder's Lane], located off Torbay Road at the top of Coaker's Hill [is to undergo major upgrading]. 1988

GOSSE 4 This wharf was located in a small cove at the end of a fairly wide drung, known as Dock Lane.

duckish n

1986 SAUNDERS 48 Around duckish we pulled in to the shore of a large island [and] he said 'We camp here.'

duckish a

T 965-71 And they walked on. And begin to get duckish, gettin' on awards [towards] dark. 1987 *Lore and Language* vi (1), 26 Nan noticed it was getting 'duckish' [twilight] and she was getting scared and began to cry.

duff¹ n

1 1984 WRIGHT 15 These meals usually consisted of salt fish or meat, with 'duffs' of steamed flour. Sweet duff—with a bit of molasses—was served [the sealers] Sundays.

duff² n

P 301-83 'I'll give you a hard duff.'

dumb a Comb ~ **cake**.

1981 SPARKES 168 A less frequently used form of divination was the baking of a 'dumb cake' on Midsummer Eve. Three girls were necessary to participate and, as the name implies, it was made and eaten in silence... If all had been done properly and in strict silence, they would see in their dreams their future husbands.

dump n In logging, a wooden peg used to jam chains in hole at the end of a boom log (P 325-83).

dun a

1 1986 FELTHAM 87 A considerable amount of dried cod was stored by late July, which periodically had to be taken out to be aired, for if it were kept in storage while damp it would eventually become 'dun.'

dunch¹ a

1 1985 GUY 128 When he gets the bit between his china clippers he's good for an hour on any subject from cutting cats to the Boer War. I was good and dunch by the time he came up for air.

E

eat v Phr *eat the rocks*.

1981 SPARKES 187 'The fish are eating the rocks,' indicating plenty, as does, 'I could have loaded with a one claw jigger.'

eddy n Comb ~ **flaw**.

1987 DAWE [16] E is for eddy flaw,/Turn in the breeze,/A contrary puff/That's quick as a sneeze.

edge n Cp *OED* sb ~ 11 'brink or verge of a bank or prccipicc.' That part of an undersea 'bank' or 'ground' forming the sharp boundary between shoal and deep water and frequented by ground-fish.

1983 *Gazetteer of Canada: Nfld* 52 Edge of Ground. 1986 FELTHAM 54 There were 'edges' running for miles that was the dividing line of deep and shallow water. The fisherman had to be able to set his gear precisely along such edges simply by knowing the cross-bearings of every point along their length.

edger n *OED* ~ 3 'circular saw by which the bark [is] ripped from slab-boards' (1874). Comb **edgerman**: in a sawmill, one who operates saw which trims the rough edges of boards.
1981 SPARKES 175 Another [man] placed [the logs] on a bench of rollers which fed them to another saw called the Edger. The man who operated this saw was called the edgerman. He did exactly that. He trimmed off the rough edge of the board or plank and passed it on to the cut-off man.

e'er det
1 1985 *A Yaffle of Yarns* 8 Sir, will we be called anything? Is there ar title for this?
2 T 309-66 Old witch couldn't get ar bit handy into un at all.

egg See CALLIBOGUS: *egg calli*.

egger n
1983 DAWE & FICKEN 18 E is for egger/Who climbs way up high,/Where seabirds are nesting/And cliffs nudge the sky. 1987 MONTEVECCHI & TUCK 161 Baccalieu Island has long been a favored spot of eggers and bird hunters.

either det
1981 MAJOR 54 'Got either copy of *Playboy*?' I said to him for a laugh. 1988 PORTER 198 'Have you got either present for me?' His blue eyes had a hopeful glint in them.

elevener n
1983 *Evening Telegram* 15 Jan, p. 32 Brian Boru often dropped in for his elevener.

embayed ppl a Cp *OED* ~ 1. Of the spring ice floes, close to shore; 'jammed.'
1878 *Royal Gazette* 20 Aug [Chamber of Commerce Report, headed 'Seal fishery poor'] This arose mainly from the prevalence of East winds, and the ice on which the seals were [located] becoming embayed.

empt v *SED* iv, 606 So Co [ɛnt].

empter* n Also: PICKER.

eskimo n Attrib ~ **curlew**.
1987 MONTEVECCHI & TUCK 203 Of these [recent extinctions] only the Eskimo Curlew, which apparently still exists in extremely low numbers elsewhere, is known to have definitely occurred in Newfoundland.

evening n *DBE* ~ (1966-), PRATT 52 for sense 1.
1 [1976] 1985 LEHR & BEST (eds) 55 "The *Ella M. Rudolph*": At five o'clock in the evening through the Tickles she did pass.

excursion n Comb ~ **bread**.
1904 *Nfld Qtly* iv (1), 11 He also handles our hard bread and excursion bread, and gets it from the Rennie Baking Co.

F

face n *DBE* ~ n for sense 3.
4 Phr *face and eyes*.
1985 GUY 103 And just at that I slipped. Me good foot struck a sketch of ice...there on the concrete and down I goes on me face and eyes.

factory n
1983 FROUDE 126 [On] July the 14 we arived in Snooks arm where the men On shore were engaged arecting a Whale factory. 1986 *Them Days* xi (4), 45 There was a liver factory here one time... The old feller that was operatin'...used to get about $50 or $60 for a 45 gallon drum [of cod liver oil].

faggot n also **flacket**. *DC* flacket n (1818, 1840).
1818 CHAPPELL 128 From thenceforward [the cod] are kept constantly turned during the day, and piled up in small heaps, called *flackets*, at night. 1987 FIZZARD 133 'In the evening they put it in faggots—about half a dozen fish in a pile—for the night.'

faggot v
1987 FIZZARD 133 '[The fish] is fagotted for a few nights. Then it is graded.'

fair a Of the lines of a boat, with the correct curve or sheer; SUANT.
P 290-89 [The builder made] certain the outer surface of the boats he constructed were 'suent,' that is, possessed a fair, smooth curve.

fair v Cp *OED* ~ v 3 'to make fair or level' [in ship-building]. Phr *to fair off*: of hair, to trim evenly (P 314-83).

fairety n Equitable treatment, justice (1924 ENGLAND 315).
1916 *Deep Sea Fishers* xiii, 156 'It's not fair to the children, and I believe in fairety to ivery wan.'

fairy n For the fairy belief system, see P. NARVÁEZ "Newfoundland Berry Pickers 'In the Fairies': The Maintenance of Spatial and Temporal Boundaries through Legendry," *Lore and Language* vi (1), 15-49.
1 Phr *(to be) in the fairies*: to be in the domain of, or under the various influences or powers attributed to, fairies.
1987 *Lore and Language* vi (1), 23 Once 'in the fairies,' the victim might sometimes successfully take protective measures during the ordeal...but on other occasions mortals might be captured, experience fairy scenes, suffer mental and physical injury ('fairy-struck'), obtain artistic gifts.

2 Attrib, comb ~ **cap,** ~ **led,** ~ **path,** ~
taking: FAIRY LED, ~ STRUCK.

1988 *Nfld Qtly* lxxxiii (4), 15 [There was] a shadowy
world of dank mosses, pungent 'fairy caps,' bleak barrens
and gnarled spruces. 1989 *Sunday Express* 23 July, p. 7
A fellow might think he was fairy-led, coming on that
vast strange landscape rather suddenly. 1981 DAWE 34
''Ishmael Remembers'': a boy in sweaty wool,/listening
to old Aunt Grace/sooty-handed by her oil lamp,/telling
the youngsters/of the fairy-paths/and the man-in-the-
moon. 1987 *Lore and Language* vi (1), 23 'There were
many instances of ''fairy-taking'' in my town and when I
was a youngster my parents were always worried this
could happen to me.'

fall v Phr *fall back*: to revert to previous religious
state or belief (P 322-88).

fall n Cp *OED* ~ sb¹ 5 'a sinking down, subsidence' for phr *fall of ground*; *SED* iv, 828 fall of
the year.

1 Phr *fall of ground*: collapse of a mine shaft.

1983 MARTIN 79 The union did not mention the
problem of the rockfalls that plagued the mines' underground reaches. Several men had been killed already by
what miners called a 'fall of ground.' The ghosts of the
victims, it was said, sometimes appeared to men working
alone.

fall of the year.

1984 POWELL 176 From being under the snow since
the fall of the year, the carcass would be turned right
green. 1987 POOLE 74 He fished off Murray's Harbour
for many years trawling in the fall of the year.

2 Attrib, comb ~ **fish,** ~ **fishery,** ~ **herring**.

1983 DAWE & FICKEN 20 F is for fall fish,/The finest
fat cod;/They arrive in the autumn,/One big hungry wad.
1988 *Evening Telegram* 20 Aug, p. 23 Cod is still scarce
on the inshore grounds [at Melrose], and unless the fall
fishery picks up it will not be a good season for most
fishermen. ibid 5 Aug, p. 2 The fall herring fishery in
the...Newfoundland region will open Aug 15.

false a *Anglo-Manx Dialect* false-face 'a mask.'
Comb ~ **face**.

1981 SPARKES 120 And in they would come, all
masked, some with false faces made of paper bags or
muslin painted with all sorts of weird expressions. 1985
NEWHOOK 89 Some would be hooded or have false faces
with flowing beards. 1988 MOMATIUK & EASTCOTT (eds)
137 We had on the real store-bought false faces. When
you put on one of them, it's not very often anybody
knows you.

farewell v Cp *EDD* ~ sb for var late-summer
plant names; PRATT (1908-). Comb ~ **summer**:
variety of fireweed (*Epilobium angustifolium*).

[1867] 1989 CHIMMO (ed Kirwin) 58 [1 Sept] An old
Lady [brought me] some wild flowers, very like a
Hyacinth, but what they called 'farewell summer' being
the last of the wild flowers which bloom. 1924 *Deep-Sea
Fishers* xxi (4), 139 Farewell summer—Reddish purple
fireweeds blossoming in August.

farm v To raise cod-fish, taken 'wild' in 'traps,'
to marketable size in sheltered inshore enclosures;
FISH n: ~ **farm**.

1987 *Evening Telegram* 9 Oct, p. 2 [The company]
has been granted an exclusive Canadian right to farm cod
using methods it developed at its Bay Bulls farming
operation...the process [involving] capturing live cod,
transporting them to the pens and growing them for
market.

fashion n *Anglo-Manx Dialect* ~ 'habit.'

fat a

2 Comb **fatback (pork)**.

1949 FITZGERALD 55 Get fat-back and dumplings
under your belt. 1987 FIZZARD 174 In the meantime [to
treat diphtheria] she said, 'Get some fatback pork and
take two slices of it and put one piece in flannel and heat
it on a plate on the stove and put it around his throat.
One off and one on.'

fat¹ n

2 1987 *Evening Telegram* 11 Apr, p. 14 [tape tran-
script] The wind came right from the eastard and we had
a heavy load of fat [aboard the vessel]. 1990 *Sunday
Telegram* 4 Mar, p. 16 When the hunt was in its heyday,
the men lived in the hold of their ship and slept on the
fat, where the blood and gurry soon permeated their
clothes.

fegary n Cp PRATT faigarie, flagarie, frigarie.

fellow n

1 1986 HISCOCK 115 'I got down to the marsh and my
coat was all filled with snow. The young fella was there,
only that height, waiting for us to knock the snow... A
little fella about twelve years old.' 1988 *Muse* 29 July, p.
10 [I read the] *ABC Book* to my little fellow who turned
one year old on Saturday.

2 In pl comb **we fellows**: the people (in a family
or community).

P 245-89 [woman interviewed on television] 'If she
had to go to Corner Brook hospital she wouldn't last long
without we fellers to be there to see her.'

felt n Cp *O Sup²* roofing felt (1894-). Also: comb
~ **tin(t)**: convex metal disc of galvanised metal,
with central indentation through which nail is
driven to secure roofing material.

T 498-68 So three or four days after he was buried, the
will was read, and she went to the bag an' here was
nothing in it only felt tints. P 13-85 Oh the little round
things you use with the small nails—felt tins we call
them. If you hit the nail too hard they bend up. P 197-85
Yes, they're felt tints. I've nailed a good many of them
in my time. [1987] QUINLAN 6 The roof [of the tilt]
consisted of felt placed on round rafters.

fever n Attrib ~ **ship**: vessel used for the
isolation and treatment of those with typhoid, etc;
floating fever hospital.

[1891] 1977 WHITELEY 67 'These men contracted

this disease [typhoid] on board the *Volunteer* which boat is at present and had been for a long time—a fever ship.'

fiddler n
1 1981 SPARKES 96 At two o'clock the fiddler folds his accordion and the few remaining young men and women close up the place and go home.

fig n
2 Comb **fig pudding**.
1915 *Deep Sea Fishers* xiii, 64 There is fig pudding made of poor broken rice, currants and raisins (the figs), boiled with water.

figgy a
For ~ duff cp SMYTH figgie-dowdie 'West Country pudding made with raisins and much in vogue at sea among Cornish and Devon men.' Attrib, comb ~ **bread,** ~ **duff**.
1981 SPARKES 127 Raisin bread, commonly called 'figged bread,' was eaten several times throughout the year, but chiefly as a special treat on Sunday. ibid 131 The pot was put on for the dinner of 'pork and cabbage' complete with viggy duff and peas pudding.

figure n
Cp *OED* eight a, sb 3 figure (of) eight 'anything in the form of an eight.' Comb **figure eight**: in logging, a chain crossed to form two loops, one of which passes around the 'bunk' of a sled, the other around the load of timber on the cross-beams (1985 *Terminology of Loggers* 7).

fill v
2 1981 SPARKES xiii [Snow-shoes] were made of a frame of tough birch sapling and 'filled' with deerskin cut into fine strips called babiche.
3 1987 POOLE 17 That fall Dad had gotten one hundred pounds of cotton twine to knit for his cod trap the next summer. My mother and younger brothers would fill all the needles for me.

filling n
1984 POWELL 35 We had our snowshoes and some spare filling for them. 1986 SAUNDERS 150 You could mend the [snowshoe] frame with wire or rivets, and we always carried a roll of pre-cut hide for filling.

finest kind n phr
South Shore Phr Bk.

finger n
3 Comb **fingernail bird**: red-necked grebe (1987 MONTEVECCHI & TUCK 233).

fire n
2 Cpd **fire-pot**.
1987 FIZZARD 135 'First goin' off, we used to go in punts. They...were practically open boats, just a place covered to put your fish in and a little place in the back of her to put your fire pot. That was a big iron pot, and you had your fire in that and that's how you'd cook your meal when you were out.'

firk v
1 1981 MAJOR 54 I was in there firking around through his books to see all what he had, when in he came that first time and seen me. 1985 *A Yaffle of Yarns* 107 It is unlikely that any woman when talking of her household duties [today] would say 'I be's busy brushin' and firkin'.'

first num
1985 GUY 63 [He] saw her down in the middle of the road, but he didn't take much notice first going off. He thought she might have dropped a five cent piece. 1987 FIZZARD 135 'I fished on Green Island for 34 summers. First goin' off, we used to go in punts.' 1989 *Evening Telegram* 4 July, p. 2 First off what the actual work means to our members and if it's worth our while to give consideration to a freeze on wages and fringe benefits for the next 14 months in order to get that work [for the shipyard].

fish n
1 1987 POOLE 77 I did not get very much salmon but did very well with the fish despite the fact that I did not have any good berths.
2 In var collocations and phr *first fish*: first in the competition, *fish and brewis, fish in summer fun in winter, fish in the punt, pork in the pot* ([1916] 1924 ENGLAND 255), *fish or no fish, no fish, no dollar, when the fish eat, we all eat* ([1916] 1924 ENGLAND 256).
[1925] 1986 *Them Days* xi (4), 21-2 He prided himself on being 'first fish' each season and there were not very many when he wasn't... 'Spect I got the first a'gin, Missus.' 1989 *Evening Telegram* 15 July, p. A9 There's a fish and brewis supper after which the [Trinity Bay] festival will end with a lip sync contest at the Parish Hall. 1990 ibid 9 Feb, p. 5 While the demerit driving system may not be as desirable as fish and brewis to many Newfoundlanders, it should not pose any problems for good drivers. 1968 KEATING 74 'Used to be fish in the summer and fun in the winter,' the skipper said, 'but it's fish the year around now, so the lads have to grab their fun when they can.' P 331-83 She decided to buy the canvas, fish or no fish. 1988 MOMATIUK & EASTCOTT (eds) 124 'The more fish you saw, the more you liked it. That was your dollar. No fish, no dollar.'
3 Attrib, comb **fish cask,** ~ **company**: cp FISH MERCHANT, ~ **crate**: wooden container in which cod are processed in the Bank fishery, ~ **drum,** ~ **farm**: sheltered area in a bay or harbour where cod are raised to maturity in netted enclosures for market, ~ **fly,** ~ **frame**: residue of a filleted cod, ~ **gull**: ring-billed gull, ~ **hold**: storage area on a deep-sea fishing vessel for the catch, ~ **jigger**: JIGGER 1, ~ **killer, fish('s) pea(s),** ~ **plant**: FISHING ROOM, ~ **pound**: also: area of inshore waters with extensive nets for the temporary holding of live cod, ~ **room,** ~ **stage,** ~ **store,** ~ **top,** ~ **trimmer**: one engaged in filleting fresh cod, ~ **truck**: vehicle engaged in transportation of fresh cod, etc, ~ **tub**.
1987 FIZZARD 193 'When we got to the bridge they

had this big archway all made up with fish casks. And they had "Welcome Home" on it.' 1988 *Evening Telegram* 6 May, p. 1 Mr. Cashin said he is anxious to begin contract negotiations with fish companies for the caplin fishery and spring fishery. 1984 KELLAND 152 [There] were four large fish crates in which fish were cut, throated and headed on the Banks. 1893 *Evening Telegram* 22 Mar The schooner *Edith* arrived from Carbonear last evening...with a load of fish drums. 1988 ibid 11 June, p. 3 Department of Fisheries experiments at the Bay Bulls fish farm last year indicate the starting stock will grow at a rate of 23 per cent every month from June to November. 1987 POWELL 113 Then to add to the smell the town was invaded by what was called the fish fly, a fly a little smaller than the busy bee. 1988 *Networker* Dec, p. 1 Little use has been found for fish frames—the skeleton left after the fillets are removed—even though they contain significant amounts of fish flesh. 1987 MONTEVECCHI & TUCK 239 Fish gull. 1972 ANDERSEN & WADEL (eds) 125 Assuming the shipboard, fish-hold log is the most accurate, the daily hail is seen to differ from 'actual' catch by as much as fifty to seventy thousand pounds. 1986 *Nfld's Deepsea Fishery* 649 fishhold: an insulated portion of the vessel where the fish is stored in ice. 1981 SPARKES xii The lead from a broken fish jigger and that which lined the chests in which tea came was saved and melted down into gun-balls for the great long, Birmingham muzzle-loading guns. 1983 WARNER 28 Unlike many Newfoundland localisms, fish killer is easily translated. It means what the rest of the English-speaking fishing world calls a high liner, a top-earning fisherman. 1987 O'FLAHERTY 41 [title] "Fish Killer." ibid 42 Now seventy-five, Abe had once been the fish killer on the shore. 1989 *Sunday Express* 19 Mar, p. 7 Our winter's pocket money [was] earned door to door: first rank, those who sold cod tongues by the bucket—the quick and skillful; second rank, those who sold 'fish's peas' (cod roe)—the industrious but fumble-fingered. 1987 POWELL 96 He wanted me to take the balance of the salt that was left on board. It was hard for me to say no to the skipper, so they landed several thousand bags of it in my fish plant. 1981 PADDOCK 35 "Pronging Fish on the Stage Head": In the ground they are at her by now,/And in the fish-pound, too, the maggots writhe. 1989 *Evening Telegram* 12 July, p. 4 Fishermen at Petty Harbour... have devised a fish pound made of twine wherein the surplus cod from the traps may be held alive until the plants are ready to process it. 1984 POWELL 7 Mr Dawe, who lived in Bay Roberts and operated a fish room at Fishing Ship's Harbour in Labrador, had already contacted my father and my brother Max and offered them salmon nets and some supplies. [1763] 1987 FIZZARD 37 [inventory of property] a fish stage w[ith] conveniences. 1986 *Metro* 29 June, p. 17 A tour around New World Island...will uncover a living history that still survives in the unusual construction of root cellars and the old time 'fish top' still used to cover curing saltfish from the elements. 1987 RAPPORT 63 Leo needs a job, the fish-plant has advertised for fish-trimmers and packers. 1988 SINCLAIR (ed) 134 Others bring us loads of wood to keep us/Warmed up in our little shack/Two fish trucks have left empty but/We're ready for them when they do come back. 1984 KELLAND 152 Two large tubs were placed onboard, those were made by sawing an extra large puncheon in two. They were usually called fish tubs

because they were used to wash dressed fish in before it was sent down to the holds to be salted.

fish v

1 Also: of a fish-net, trap, etc, placed or operated in a manner appropriate for the catching of fish.

[1833] 1984 BAYFIELD i, 261 Before the french came [Wm. Birge] fished the river (as it is termed) for a Mr. Gange also a Brittish subject. [1894] 1977 WHITELEY 52 [We saw] fishermen fishing their traps near them. 1982 MCDOOLING 102 Those fishermen who do still have licenses may only fish the number of nets stated on the license. 1984 *Evening Telegram* 22 Mar, p. 5A The cod trap, once set, can be left to fish on its own while the fishermen pursue other tasks. 1987 POOLE 12 The company had a crew of men fishing salmon nets for them. 1988 *Nfld Qtly* lxxxiii (4), 19 They decided to drive to Western Bay in the pick-up to see if the nets were afloat and fishing.

2 Phr *to fish on the fly*: in the Bank schooner fishery, to fish by dropping dories in rapid succession and setting and hauling trawl-lines; see FLYING SET, SET.

1987 FIZZARD 129 'When you were fishing on the fly, you'd have one set a day. You wouldn't have as much gear when you're setting from the schooner as you would when you were fishing on the fly.'

to fish for stamps.

[1963] 1988 *Evening Telegram* 4 June, p. 6 'The day will come when Newfoundland fishermen may have to stop fishing for stamps and work at their trade all year round,' [he said]. 1986 ibid 23 Oct, p. 6 One of the largest fishing settlements turned to 'fishing for stamps,' which became something like a major industry.

fisherman n

1 Phr *fisherman follows the fish*: indicating the fisherman's right to receive payment (or credit) for the catch before other disbursement of money by the merchant.

1966 GUNN 6 The hired fishermen claimed the right to 'follow' the planter's fish and oil into the hands of his supplier, the produce of the voyage being by law... subject in the first place to payment of wages. 1984 *Encyclopedia of Nfld* i, p. 271-2 The expression 'follow the fish' refers to the custom of a person engaged in the fisheries, having the right to ensure payment for his services, by a claim on the fish and oil. 1986 SIDER 52 Servants' wages were thus given first lien on the catch even when the merchant possessed the fish. In the oft-repeated words of Newfoundland courts, servants had the right to 'follow the fish' to the merchant, and their wages must be paid in full before any other creditor could be satisfied.

2 Attrib, comb **fisherman's brewis, fisherman logger**: one who divides his seasonal work between 'summer fishery' and 'woods work' in winter, **~'s ticket**: reduced fare offered on coastal boat to those engaged in the Labrador fishery.

1949 FITZGERALD 79 (Let epicures scoff if they choose);/ Cod's tongues, pickled sounds or fresh salmon, or a plate full of fisherman's brewis. 1987 *Evening Tele-*

gram 21 Mar, p. 5 There was no time to go home for supper, so Mother brought it down to the stage—a great huge pot of fishermen's brewis. 1981 SPARKES 183 To the fishermen-loggers [spring] was like a resurrection. 1988 *Evening Telegram* 18 May, p. 19 The fishermen's ticket was a specially reduced rate that fishermen paid on the Labrador boat.

fishery n
1 1989 *Evening Telegram* 6 Jan, p. 6 If the additional 13,000 tonnes that has been taken from the offshore is the price for getting the inshore over-capacity under control, then perhaps our loss will have long-term bene-fits for everyone in the fishery.
2 Attrib **fishery salt**: see SALT.

fishing vbl n
2 Attrib, comb ~ **berth**, ~ **establishment**, ~ **ground**, ~ **post**, ~ **premises**, ~ **room**, ~ **salt**, ~ **schooner**, ~ **season**, ~ **settlement**: SETTLEMENT, ~ **ship**, ~ **stage**, ~ **station**, ~ **vessel**.
1986 *Evening Telegram* 2 Aug, p. 12 Some fishermen have removed traps from famous fishing berths and taken them to the other side of Bonavista Bay in the Newman's Cove-Blackhead area west of Bonavista where Fishing is a little better. [1833] 1984 BAYFIELD i, 257 Observed fishing establishments all the way from Black Bay to Forteau and many schooners at anchor. 1985 *Evening Telegram* 7 Sep, p. 13 Bad weather is a major problem with inshore fishermen only being able to get to the fishing grounds two or three times a week. 1990 ibid 4 Jan, p. 4 I would like to comment on a statement...about the trawlers destroying the fishing grounds. 1987 POWELL 76 He knew the ones who had the most fish and the ones who stayed the longest on the fishing grounds. By doing this he knew the hard workers and was ready to help them in any way. 1977 WHITELEY 34 It is not known how Bossy Whiteley acquired the fishing post at Bonne Espérance. 1987 POOLE 14 Driven by the Great Depres-sion and the need to fix up his fishing premises, he had set out to spend one last winter on the Labrador. 1987 *Evening Telegram* 4 July, p. 56 They took it all in the vessel the next spring and put it together on their fishing rooms on the two [Labrador] islands. 1987 POWELL 34 From this high hill I could see my little house beneath me, my store, stage and wharf and one little boat moored just off the stage. I was proud of my fishing room; it was all I owned. ibid 96 My store was almost full of fishing salt, leaving little room to handle anything else. [1847] 1986 BAYFIELD ii, 325 This morning [in Trepassey] we counted 65 Sail of small fishing schooners, from 25 to 30 Tons each. 1987 POOLE 58 A fishing schooner in the harbour just down from where we were belonged to a first cousin of mine. 1988 GOSSE 47 These fishing rooms formed a temporary settlement in most sheltered harbours and coves along the Labrador coast. Supplied by mer-chants in Conception and Trinity Bays, they were only occupied during the fishing season. 1880 *Canadian Illus-trated News* 29 May [caption] Cape Ray...A fishing settlement and signal station. 1986 RYAN 32 These men, called bye boat keepers, left their boats in Newfoundland during the winter and found transportation for themselves and their crews to and from Newfoundland on the fishing ships. 1987 KING (ed) 111 "Resettlement": Empty

houses/and broken windows,/Fields unattended and overgrown/because of forced/evacuation. A fishing stage/stands bitter/against the elements. [1925] 1986 *Them Days* xi (4), 8 The nets were stored in separate bunks on each side of the loft and each bunk had the name of the fishing station in elegant script carved and painted on a board over the door. 1982 JACKSON 45 The winter site offered lumber and fuel, and every man's chief occupation in the spring was to cut and haul wood to his summer fishing station. 1986 *Evening Telegram* 1 Feb, p. 4 Five residents of Burnt Islands were on the fishing vessel *June Bernice* when it ran aground and sank 2.5 miles from the community in May of 1984.

fishocracy n
1986 *Evening Telegram* 27 Jan, p. 7 Just as our grand-fathers and great-grandfathers were indentured to the 'fishocracy' of Water Street, so it seems that [Mayor] Murphy and Mr Crosbie would wish to continue and strengthen the stranglehold of their city over the rest of the province.

fist v *OED* ~ v[1] 3 (1607-1870) now esp naut. To grasp firmly with clenched fingers or fist.
1898 *Trade Review* "The Old Oaken Shutters": No later life's pleasures can suit me as well,/As the joy of those mornings we fisted those shutters. [1904] 1982 BURKE (ed Kirwin) 32 "The Night We Played Cards for the Little Boneen": Then Galwan fisted his pig by the tail. [1928] ibid 39 "The Sealers Gained the Strike": With happy hearts they fisted bags,/as lightly they did trip. 1977 MOAKLER 30 The skipper turned us out to shorten sail./We fisted canvas in the sodden pall.

fit-out n
1 [1914] 1930 COAKER 83 [The refusal of firms to purchase fish from independent fishermen] was poor encouragement to those who purchased their fit-out for cash in the Spring and are trying to keep their heads above water. 1987 *Evening Telegram* 14 Mar, p. 10 The father helped the boy choose a whole 'fitout' of warm clothes [for the sealing voyage].
3 P 266-88 We always had to get new clothes for Easter. We did Water Street for a new fit-out.

fixed ppl Comb ~ **gear**: fishing net, 'trap,' etc, anchored or buoyed in a stationary position.
1976 *Daily News* 22 Dec, p. 2 Inshore herring fisher-men using fixed gear will take an estimated 900 metric tons. 1977 *Union Forum* June, p. 18 Longliner captains fishing fixed gear outside the three mile limit in the areas being covered by the program are asked to provide the local fisheries officer with positions of gear as soon as possible, and on a weekly basis from then on. 1982 MCDOOLING 102 Quotas on fixed gear (traps, nets and longlines) have been instituted by regulation in other areas of the Newfoundland fishery. 1988 *Evening Tele-gram* 13 Feb, p. 2 Fixed gear fishermen involved in the west coast's winter fishery have rejected the latest price offer from processors... Both fixed gear and otter trawl fishermen have decided to tie up their boats.

flacket See FAGGOT.

flag[1] n *OED* ~ sb[1] 1 'member of the genus *Iris*.'

Comb ~ **boat**: the 3-angled ovary of the blue flag, a toy boat in children's pastime; also BOAT.

1985 NEWHOOK 29 Another aquatic pursuit was the making and sailing of flag boats... They were made from the Iris flower flags which grew in abundance on the marsh by the boat.

flag² n
1984 WRIGHT 56-7 The master watch thought there would be more seals a little further on, so he departed... leaving Norman, Victor and myself at the first flag.

flag v
1 1986 *Evening Telegram* 31 Mar, p. 6 I was very interested in the diary entries concerning the claiming of the pelts panned and flagged by the *Iceland*'s crew by some members of the crew of the S.S. *Aurora*.

flake n PRATT ~ n (1895-).
1 1984 POWELL 29 He shouted to some men that were on the flake piling fish together. 1988 *Evening Telegram* 18 May, p. 19 Flakes were platforms of rough wooden posts and rails, sometimes covered with boughs, on which fish were spread to dry in the sun.
2 Phr *on (the) flake*.
1981 SPARKES 188 If a woman said, 'I spent the whole summer on flake' it meant that she spent her whole time drying fish.

flan v Cp *OED* ~ v dial a. 'of a vessel, etc.: to expand towards the top'; *EDD* ~ 3 'to widen upwards.' Of a boat or vessel, to curve at the bow in a fine flare.
1985 NEWHOOK 9 [The trap skiffs] had good, strong, straight keels, raking out of the water up to the stemhead. The bows 'flanned' up and out from the water in a graceful curve.

flanker n
1985 GOSSE 122 A man equipped with merely a water pail and shovel walked the railway line on guard for burning 'flankers' from the old steam engine. 1986 SAUNDERS 23 There we huddled all one night...watching the flames and flankers going up along the whole western sky. 1987 *Evening Telegram* 2 May, p. 8 The room was full of flankers for awhile, but it was great fun stamping them out and seeing your footprints in the soot.

flashet n
P 313-83 'We had to criss-cross the bog because of the many flashes.'

flat n
1984 KELLAND 102 They were clinker or lap strake built, having the raking ends and flaring sides of an ordinary dory, although their sheer is considerably more crooked. The feature which disqualifies these fine craft from being classed as dories, lies in their sterns... They are now and always have been called flats by our south coast fishermen. 1987 PEYTON 80 [He] had many such small boats that he referred to as 'flats'; lightweight, flat bottoms, square ends, which he himself had always used

and found to be invaluable for cruising the shallow brooks and for easy portage.

fleet n Cp COHEN, p. 85 for sense 2.
1 1982 MCDOOLING 103 If you had two fleets of [salmon] nets, or one hundred and sixty fathoms, on your license, well that's all you'd ever get. 1987 POWELL 63 This [storm] had set one of my fleets of salmon nets adrift, and if we couldn't get the nets that evening they would be lost or tangled by an iceberg going south.
2 1984 KELLAND 183 In setting a trawl preparatory to underrunning it, an anchor with the main trawl line, keg buoy, buoyline (called a haul-up line), moorings and slablines were dropped. The entire fleet of gear was then run out.

flipper n
1 1988 *Muse* 6 June, p. 4 I have no vested interest in the seal hunt except perhaps one or two flippers a year which I get anyway.
2 Comb ~ **pie**.
1987 *Evening Telegram* 27 Oct, p. 19 Following a meal of Newfoundland caribou, cod, and flipper pie [the delegates] were congratulated by Mr [John] Crosbie.

flipsy v Also: in logging, to run lightly from one log to another during the river drive.
1983 *Books in Canada* Aug/Sep, p. 8 'Can Uncle John still flipsy?' [is] a question asked to gather opinions that tell whether or not an aging riverman can *copy* from *junk* to *junk* across a *sack boom* of *fours*. 1986 FELTHAM 97 The skill demonstrated by Newfoundland seal hunters in travelling over loose ice was undoubtedly developed while 'copying' or 'flipsying' over the harbour pans in their teen-age play.

floater n
1 1984 KELLAND 112 The men who fished [on the Labrador] from schooners were known as floaters. 1988 *Evening Telegram* 18 May, p. 19 Floaters were the other type of fishermen who spent summers on the Labrador coast, following the fish in schooners, which served as a work place, home, and storage area.
2 1987 POWELL 74 The Labrador Coast was a vanishing frontier [in the 1940s]. The same went for the sailing fleet, known as the floaters.
5 Attrib ~ **fleet**: see sense 2 above.
1987 POWELL 71 Then there was what they called the floater fleet which sailed up to Labrador from Conception Bay, Trinity Bay, Bonavista Bay and Notre Dame Bay.

floating ppl Comb ~ **crew**: see FLOATER CREW.
1901 *Evening Telegram* 20 July Floating crews, too, have met with poor success [and] one hundred schooners passed through Domino run on Wednesday.

flobber n Also in coastal names.
1925 TURNER *Map of Newfoundland* Flobber Co[ve]. 1983 *Gazetteer of Canada: Nfld* 58 Flobber Cove, Flobber Cove Island.

flouse v also **flowse**.
1987 *Nfld Qtly* lxxxii (4), 10 Laughing uproariously, and half-soaked anyway, the kid flowsed down into the pool with a joyous bellyflop.

flouser n Paddle-wheel on a water-turned mill
(1985 *Terminology of Loggers* 7).

flowers n pl
1988 *Nfld Studies* iv (2), 138 A floral passage (like the
one in Milton's *Lycidas*) [follows] built with grim economy on a pun: *flowers*, along that stretch of coast, rever-
berates with echoes of *fleur* in the place names of the old
French Shore, meaning 'a rock that is awash'—the grim
sunker of other parts of Newfoundland.

flummy n
1987 DAWE [18] F is for flummy,/A kind of flat
bread/For men in the woods,/Like old Trapper Fred.

fly³ n Phr *to fish on the fly*: see FISH v 2.

fly a Of a specific area in inshore waters,
habitually poor in concentration of fish. Cp CHOICE
2, PRIME 2.
1960 *Assoc Am Geog* 1, p. 274 The codtrap berths
were graded choice, prime, seconds, and fly, in that
order, according to the run of fish taken from them...
The fly berths provided poor catches even when the
[Labrador] coast experienced a good run of fish. Although the fly berths represented the lowest grade of
berths, they indicated places where the cod approached
close to the shore and where a trap could be set.

flying ppl Attrib ~ **set**.
1984 KELLAND 132 The vessel carried twelve dories.
One morning Captain Follett made a flying set, putting
over eleven dories. 1987 FIZZARD 127 In the spring and
fall, when weather conditions were especially harsh, they
used a method [of fishing] called 'the flying set,' in
which the schooner dropped off its dories as it continued
along under sail. The men set out their gear in straight
lines, and at the end of the day they took in their gear
before being picked up by the schooner, still under
sail.

fog n In prov phr *no fog, no fish, out of the fog
and into the fat, the more fog, the more fish*
([1916] 1924 ENGLAND 255-6; P 245-89).

follow v
1 1858 [LOWELL] i, 129 Then I got up...and follyed
right out to see ef I could find what had becomed of her.
2 Phr *follow on*: to continue without interruption
(cp *go on*), *follow the fish*: see FISHERMAN.
1987 *Evening Telegram* 11 Apr, p. 14 [tape trans-
cript] 'So all right,' he says, 'if you think we will make
St Lawrence we'll go back. It's a poor night to follow
on.'

fool n
2 Phr *to dress (in) the fools*.
1985 NEWHOOK 89 As was the case in many other
outports, the twelve days after Christmas were taken up
by a tradition known variously as 'jennying up,' 'mummering,' or 'dressing the fool.'

for prep
2 Phr *for to*.
[1976] 1985 LEHR & BEST (eds) 89 "The Hoban
Boys": The bait being very plentiful, and the weather
acting fine/And for to have another set we all felt well
inclined. 1982 MCDOOLING 87 Its only three or four
years ago they had fourteen million back from the government for to upgrade their plants.

fore- prefix Comb ~**-cuddy**, ~**-lock** v (see first
1985 quot), ~**-peak**.
1988 GOSSE 18 Being fitted out with a larger fore-
cuddy and gang-boards, [the longer skiffs] were more
seaworthy and not restricted to fishing grounds close to
the foreshore. 1985 *Terminology of Loggers* 7: [Fore-
lock—of a horse, to hook his hind shoe into the shoe of a
front hoof.] [1930] 1985 ASHTON 99 [One bunkhouse]
they call 'forepeak.' Now, in the forepeak, the skipper
would stay and what they called the 'second-hand.'

foreign av
2 Comb **foreign-going**.
1987 POOLE 4 A lot of small vessels [were] all moored
up for the winter including W.J. Moore's foreign-going
vessel which [was] loaded with fish.

fork v
1984 KELLAND 155 They did, however, enjoy a full
breakfast after they had returned from the first trip and
had forked the fish up on deck. 1987 *Evening Telegram* 7
Mar, p. 10 My job was forking the fish up to my
grandfather and his two men [on the stage] as they
cleaned and split.

fouly a
[1937] 1945 SCAMMELL 37 "Payne's Cove Bait
Skiff": 'Tis foully bottom out here on this reef,/What
say if we tucks 'em aboard o' the skeef.'

founder v
1986 FELTHAM 98 Jumping on the overhanging edge
[of the batty catter] or throwing large rocks on it, caused
it to break away from the shore and fall with a considerable crash. This [boys'] activity was called 'foundering
batty catters.'

four num Comb **four-quintal cask**. Cp CASK.
[1940] 1990 *Evening Telegram* 7 Mar, p. 4 A string of
ponies and slides from Pouch Cove came to town this
morning hauling cask fish for export. The load for each
pony was one four-quintal cask. 1987 FIZZARD 160 'We
had several makes of barrels. There'd be half-quintal
drums, quintal drums, two-quintal barrels, and four-quintal casks.'

fousty a *South Shore Phr Bk*.
1924 *Deep Sea Fishers* xxi (4), 139 Fowsty—Mouldy.
1984 POWELL 124 When [the hay] was put into the hold
of the ship in the warm, it heated and went mouldy and
fousty. 1988 PORTER 10 Shirley crouched down to look
in the cupboard under the sink. 'Haven't we got any pot
cleaners? Cripes, this place is fousty. There's even
beetles crawlin' around down here.'

fox n

2 Comb ~ **set**: baited snare to capture fox, ~
slip: see SLIP[2] n 1, ~ **snare**: FOX SLIP, ~ **trap**.

1986 SAUNDERS 149 So a piece of meat or fish in a
lynx house or a fox set smelled pretty good to a dog.
ibid 144 I can hear him now—'Tail a fox slip in that lead
there.' 1984 POWELL 62 I took a fox snare and wired it
up in a tree. 1832 MOSS *MS Diary* 7 Mar Mr Simon set 2
fox traps off on the Gull Island. 1984 POWELL 38 The
next day I was supposed to go out the bay ten miles and
pick up some fox traps that we had out there. 1987
POOLE 25 In the meantime my brother Fred and I set out
our fox traps, thinking that if by chance he would get a
fox that would help to buy food.

foxed ppl a Cp *OED* ~ 5 Ir cite (1880). Phr *foxed
down*: of a sealskin boot, with sole and heel
strengthened with leather. See FOX BOOT.

1981 SPARKES xiii Some schooner men preferred
'foxed down' boots to the more usual leather sea or deck
boot. Foxed down boots were skin-boots to which soles
and heels of leather had been fixed.

foxy a

1 1878 *Nfld Pilot* 433-4 Foxy islands are two conical
mounds covered with grass over rocks of a reddish hue,
lying just south of Cut-throat island. 1982 *Gazette* 15
Apr, p. 5 The many white spruce trees planted in the
library's vicinity will be sprayed for weed control this
year. How have they survived the winter? Too early to
tell, says Mr Dunne, 'some are a bit blasty and foxy but
all in all they look pretty good.' 1988 DOHANEY 24 And
when Vince was young he had sort of foxy-coloured hair.

frame n

1 1985 BUSCH 47 The seal 'frame' was also common
[working] on the same principle [as] a net...firmly
anchored...to the shore.

frankum n

1840 ENGLAND *MS Journal* 9 Feb Before I entered
upon the morning sermon I desired the 'frankum'
chewers, with whom I have often been disgusted, to lay
it aside. 1981 SPARKES 36 From any little scar in the bark
[of the red spruce], a gum exudes which hardens on
exposure to the air. Those hardened blobs melt to proper
chewing consistency when held in one's mouth and make
the finest, certainly the purest, chewing-gum in the
world. First, when you get it started, it is a creamy yellow, but when chewed for a while it turns pink. 1985
NEWHOOK 102 Then early one morning, unannounced,
[father] would return [from the lumber woods] bearing
presents of tins of 'frankum,' which is the sap of the
spruce tree coagulated into hard pink knobs on the bark.
We chewed it for gum and loved it.

frape n Also: attrib ~ **line**.

1988 *Evening Telegram* 21 Mar, p. 6 They rigged up a
'frape' line to lead the boat in bow first to keep it from
swinging broadside and overturning in the rollers.

frape v

2 P 266-89 She had her all fraped up [dressed in a
fancy, old fashioned way].

freely n

1984 ROBERTSON 101 *Winker* or *freely* was a mixture
of bakeapples, sugar, and water. It was delicious.

french a Attrib ~ **shore**.

1983 MARTIN 30 The majority of [nineteenth-century
mines] lay upon Newfoundland's northwest and west
coasts, referred to at the time as the 'French Shore.'
1989 *Sunday Express* 26 Mar, p. 7 Elsewhere all along
the French Shore the fishery was a disaster.

fresh n

1983 FROUDE 28 Our fresh we baught hear for 3 cents
per pound. P 308-88 They'd have peas, duff and the
potatoes and salt meat, plenty of it, but they didn't have
no fresh.

fresh a

2 Comb ~ **fishery**, ~ **frozen (fish)**, ~ **water
shellbird**.

1987 FIZZARD 219 The change from the salt fishery to
the fresh fishery just about coincided with the union of
Newfoundland and Canada. [1950] 1987 *Nfld Studies* iii,
258 Perhaps the most important [development] on a
long-term view is the striking progress which has been
made with the fresh-frozen fish industry over the last few
years. 1987 MONTEVECCHI & TUCK 236 Fresh-water
shellbird. Common merganser.

front n

1 [(1620) 1982 CELL (ed) 90 Mason's *A Briefe Discourse*: The Countrie commonly knowne and called by
the name of Newfoundland...is an Iland or Ilands...
situate on the front of *America*.]
2 1986 *Evening Telegram* 22 Mar, p. 4 March sig-
nalled the beginning of the annual voyage to the harp seal
herds on The Front, off Labrador.

frost n Cpd **frostburn**.

1987 PEYTON 40 The severity of the cold winds
coupled with low temperatures often caused 'frost burn,'
extreme cases when the flesh, benumbed with cold, was
rendered without feeling.

froster n

1985 BUSCH 71 The decks were protected with a layer
of boarding, without which the 'chisels' or 'frosters'
attached to sealers' boots for traction on the ice would
knife the deck to splinters.

full n

1908 *Daily News* 7 Feb, p. 4 [In the Legislature] the
question fiend has drifted towards the east, and Capt.
Bonia had 'the full of the order paper,' as one of the
outside officials put it. They dealt with the Premier's
political aspirations respecting Confederation, and afforded an opportunity to Sir Robert [Bond] of a display
of political pyrotecnics.

full v *SED* iv, 873 D Ha.

funk n

1 1977 MOAKLER 100, 167 Funks. Bad odours or

vapours... Bolting our grub and retching in our bunks,/The cabin reeking with the vomit funks.

funnel n
1 1987 *Evening Telegram* 2 May, p. 8 [Putting gun-powder in the stove] wasn't all that dangerous, not unless you happened to be leaning over the stove when she went off. Then you might get a damper in the teeth or a hot funnel on your head.

fur n Cp *DC* ~ post (1820, 1957) for comb in sense 2.
1 1774 *Trans Roy Soc* lxiv, p. 380 [The Moun-taineers'] chief employment is to catch fur. 1984 POWELL 20 We did well with the furs, the most of which were very good mink... We had otters, foxes, beavers, and only two lynx.
2 Comb **fur (and fish) post**: a settlement or 'station' from which both the fur trade and sea fisheries are conducted, ~ **mark**: stamped impres-sion on the pelt of a fur animal designating the area in which it was trapped.
[1925] 1986 *Them Days* xi (4), 5 Rigolet, at that time, was a 'Fur and Fish' Post. ibid The fur mark 'E.B.' was known throughout the Fur Trade as being the finest. E.B. represents Eskimo Bay.

fur v
1 1986 SAUNDERS 144 Although Uncle Stan took me furring, it was Billy who sold me on the trapper's life.

furrier n
[1987] QUINLAN 16 [Bona fide] furriers were given a monopoly on a certain area of land on which other fur-riers were not permitted to hunt or trap.

furring vbl n
1 1689 *English Pilot* 16 It is not a Mile broad there, as I was informed by the Planters...who usually go a Furring there in the Winter. [1734] 1987 *Nfld Studies* iii, p. 190 [Dealers at St Malo] Supply them with almost every thing Needfull, to carry on the Cod-Fishery, Seal-Fishery, and Furring.

G

gad n PRATT (1981) for sense 1.
1 1988 *Evening Telegram* 17 May (*Supplement*), p. 6. I can remember setting out to catch a gad of trout.
4 Phr *as tough as a gad*.
1987 DAWE [42] He loves a big fight;/He's tough as the gad. 1987 *Evening Telegram* 25 July, p. 20 At 78 years...George Furey of St Joseph's is as tough as a gad and still travels the land and sea.

gaff n
1 1984 GOUGH 33 The fishermen walk toward the hole where the casket is lying and each breaks a wooden gaff across his knee. When the wood parts they throw the broken pieces in on top of the coffin and then the dirt starts showering, rattling and then sticking to the wooden

lid. 1987 FIZZARD 160 'We'd make a lot of little things like tow-pins, dory plugs, dory mallets, tide-sticks, rollers, gaffs and trawl-kegs.'
2 1986 *Evening Telegram* 24 Mar, p. 6 They passed hauling ropes and gaffs on the ice that obviously belonged to the dead men. 1987 ibid 2 Mar, p. 6 After a lapse of several months the gaff was handed to Mr Arthur Hodge of Twillingate.

gaff v PRATT ~ (1980) for sense 3 'to steal.'
1 1984 KELLAND 156 While he was fishing on the Grand Bank, one day when he and his dorymate underran their trawl every fish they gaffed aboard was of an excep-tionally large size. 1986 FELTHAM 65 During the winter and early spring when the water was cold and the seal was insulated with a thick layer of fat, it floated when killed and could be 'gaffed' by the hunter and hauled aboard his boat.

gaffer n
1980 JANES 16 "Salvage": He took me once as gaffer, but it seemed that I became a jinker to his trade. 1987 *Evening Telegram* 3 Jan, p. 4 When I was a young gaffer growing up on the North East coast, mummering was...a major reason for having Christmas at all.

gaffle v
1986 SAUNDERS 166-7 When I went back in Jack and the officer were gaffling into their supper. 1988 *Nfld Qtly* lxxxii (4), 40 [review] And we would have liked a gloss-ary: sufficient 'gafflings,' [quiffs], 'tant spruces,' and 'bough whiffets' pop up to puzzle non-Newfoundland readers.

gale n Comb ~ **bird**, **gill** ~.
1983 SOUTH (ed) 479 The two species of phalaropes, often referred to as 'Gale or Gill birds' or 'swimming snipes,' are shorebirds which are circumpolar breeders and which spend the majority of the non-breeding season in the southern hemisphere well out to sea. 1983 *Gazet-teer of Canada: Nfld* 65 Gill Bird Rock.

gale v
1982 DAWE 23 There once were a couple of cats,/Who fought on the flakes of Joe Batts,/And scratching together,/They galed up the weather,/Those tattered old sky-larkin' cats. 1988 PORTER 15 The next thing the two of them were laughing helplessly, holding on to each other for support. 'Galin',' Nan called it.

galley n Also: area in the cook-house of a lumber camp where the men sit and eat (1985 *Terminology of Loggers* 8).
1895 PROWSE 404 There was no fire below deck; the cooking apparatus, or galley [on the 18th-century English shallop], was built of stone, and was generally on the forecastle. 1987 JOHNSTON 85 They would gut and fillet a codfish, peel some potatoes, then light a fire in the old, cast-iron tub they called the galley. 1988 GOSSE 45 The usual galley made of stones in a puncheon tub was fixed to the foredeck to provide hot food and boiled water for the female passengers [on the voyage to Labrador from Conception Bay].

gallon n   Also: a dry measure for salt.
1987 POOLE 22 He found that the company had
charged him with ten gallons of salt, which they
had used to salt Paul's body in for shipment to Carbonear... Ten gallons of salt would cost about 70 or 80
cents.

galloper n   also **galouper**.
[1799] 1801 [THORESBY] 69 The people are busy in
making galoupers, boats, skiffs, and punts of various
sizes; and likewise making nets, and sails, masts, oars,
and mending their craft of all sorts. 1878 *Nfld Pilot* 68
Galloper rock.

gallows n   also **gallis** ['gælɨs], ['gɑləs]. Cp *OED* ~
5 b 'frame for stowing away the booms or spars'
(1769, 1867) for sense 3.
1 1987 FELT 1 'Take the bloods of bitches to the
gallows' [fisherman instructing his son to take some
'slubbed'—hence unfishable—nets to the drying rack].
2 1984 POWELL 22 After cutting down the trees with
the bucksaw and flattening the top and bottom with the
axe, you'd roll them up on a high gallows, then you'd
mark with a powder line where you were going to make
each saw cut.
3 Device on a fishing craft for setting an otter
trawl.
1986 *Nfld's Deepsea Fishery* 649 ~ a reinforced section
of the trawler where the trawl doors are hung and through
which the main warps normally run. On a side trawler,
these are located on two steel frames, one forward and
one to the rear of the vessel. On a stern trawler, there is a
rear gantry with a gallows on each vessel. 1987 FIZZARD
211 'Several steps were followed in setting the [otter]
trawl [the fourth being when] the engine was stopped and
the two doors were unhooked from the gallows and
lowered ten to fifteen fathoms into the water.'

gally n   Cp *SED* iv, 200 gallybagger.

galore n
1937 *Bk of Nfld* ii, 259 [They achieved] sufficient
coppers at once to bury the wren and buy galores of
'bulls-eyes' at Mother Brian's. 1985 ASHTON 196 "Beans
by Galore": But the beans they were thousands, they
were there by galore.

gam[1] n   1821-8 LATHAM assertion about gam
drake dates from Joseph Banks's Newfoundland
investigations; see [1766] 1971 BANKS 98-100.
[1766] 1821-8 LATHAM 265 In Newfoundland [the
eider duck is called] Gam Drake.

gam[2] n   In mining, a steel bar used to drill holes
in rock face.
1983 MARTIN 13 Mining techniques used in Tilt Cove
closely resembled those of the Cornish mines and were
practised in subsequent Notre Dame Bay copper mines.
Three men drilled explosive holes: one held a steel bar or
'gam' while two others alternately hammered the gam.
Explosives were then inserted and ignited to loosen the
rock.

gander n   Comb ~ **bay boat**, ~ **river** ~. A large
canoe designed for use on the Gander River.
1986 SAUNDERS 152 But I couldn't budge her. A
Gander Bay boat has several hundredweight of plank and
ribs and keel and nails in her. 1988 *Sunday Express* 10
July, p. 30 We had two Gander River boats, special craft
which look like big canoes. They are built especially for
running the Lower Gander River, to carry 'sports' and
their guides to the salmon pools below Glenwood. Fitted
with a motor, these boats can carry a big load easily and
safely.

gandy n
1983 DAWE & FICKEN 22 G is for gandy,/A piece of
bread dough/All done in a frypan/And garnished just so.

gang-board n
1988 GOSSE 19 The cargo space or hold [of the
shallops], located in the waist between the cuddies, was
not decked but covered with removable planks known as
gang-boards.

gange v
1832 MOSS *MS Diary* 16 Feb People...are ginging
Leads, Hooks etc.

ganny n   also **gannie**. Cp *EDD* ganny sb[1] 'a
turkey' W Do So D. Gannet (*Morus bassanus*).
P 245-78 Gannie: gannet. 1983 *Gazetteer of Canada:
Nfld* 63 Ganny Cove. 1987 MONTEVECCHI & TUCK 163
Gannie Cliff.

gansey n   *Anglo-Manx Dialect* gansy; COHEN, p.
85 'Women [in Shetland] spun wool from the
fleeces of the croft's own sheep, from which they
knitted 'garnseys,' socks, undergarments and
shirts'; PRATT ~ (1956).

gap n   Cp *EDD* ~ sb 2 'a cleft in a cliff.'
2 Narrow, precipitous entrance to a harbour; the
Narrows of St John's.
[1928] 1982 BURKE (ed Kirwin) 82 "Who Put the Herring on the Booze?": We're leaning o'er the rail...as she
cut out through the gap.

garden n
1 1981 SPARKES 27 The potato grounds were always
referred to as 'the gardens.' Because of this, most children always associated the word 'garden' with potatoes...
One of the questions [the visiting clergyman] asked them
afterwards was, 'What were Adam and Eve doing in the
garden?' A small girl instantly piped up, 'Diggin' praties,
Sir!' 1987 FIZZARD 139 'And one section [of the chute]
we would take up if anybody with a horse wanted to go
across the beach, say, if they had gardens on the Cape.'
4 Attrib, comb ~ **ground**: see GROUND 3, ~
party.
1837 *Royal Gazette* 5 Dec [advertisement] Together
with spacious wharves...with extensive meadows &
garden grounds immediately contiguous. 1897 *Evening
Telegram* 28 Aug Mrs Nangle and her lady assistants at
the Littledale garden party, acknowledge, with many
thanks, contributions in money and fruit. 1987

O'FLAHERTY 31 If she hadn't cajoled him into taking her to the garden party and then, having gone, insisted on actually playing one of the damned games of chance while being pelted by rain in the school yard, the incident wouldn't have happened.

garnipper n also **galleynipper, gally** ~. QUINN and QUINN (eds), *The English New England Voyages 1602–1608* (1983), 310 [1625] 'A Garnepo fly, Chussuah.'
[1835] 1888 HOWLEY 316 [Bishop Fleming] I had stuffed my clothes along in the spaces [in the house] to keep out the musquitoes and galleynippers. [1847] 1986 BAYFIELD ii, 320 Lieut. Hancock returned with face swelled, and eyes nearly closed from the bites of Black Flies & 'Gally nippers.' 1987 PEYTON 1 The purpose of [the Beothuk use of red ochre] has not been fully understood, whether to ward off mosquitoes (gallinippers), evil spirits or used just as a tribal ritual.

gatch n
1988 *Nfld Qtly* lxxxiii (4), 12 'Ah, it's only one o' your goddam "gatches"!'

gatch v
1988 PORTER 17 Eileen always got mad when she thought she heard Heather, or anyone else, putting on airs. 'I hates anyone gatchin',' was the way she explained it.

gatcher n
1979 GRAHAM 133 Patrons of the [theatre] gallery have little time for such 'gatchers' [who occupy expensive circle seats].

gawmoge n
1983 *Evening Telegram* 15 Jan, p. 32 When he got the job of driving for a prominent gentleman, he got pure beside himself with gamogues and notions.

gaze n
1 1986 FELTHAM 64 Daylight each morning would find each young man and many of the older boys with their long muzzleloaders, shot bags and powder horns in a 'gaze' on one of the many protruding points, hoping to get a shot at a flock of passing eider ducks.
2 1983 *Gazetteer of Canada: Nfld* 64 Gaze Point, The Gaze.

gear n
1 1983 FROUDE 15 [We] went to the banks again for another trip [and] we set our gare. 1987 *Evening Telegram* 5 Mar, p. 10 The otter trawl and fixed gear fishermen have reached an agreement which should avoid gear conflicts. P 245-90 'We'll be headed north [from Twillingate] as soon as we get our gear out of the water.'

geary v Cp *Anglo-Manx Dialect* garry 'to gather way.'

geezer n Cp *EDD* guiser, guizard sb 1. Disguised and costumed Christmas mummer.
1984 ROBERTSON xvii Other words are known as well

as or instead of mummers or janneys [including] geezers in Little Bay East, F.B.

ghost n Comb ~ **net**.
1987 DAWE [20] G is for ghost-net/Adrift on the ocean,/All day and all night,/It's forever in motion.

gib v *SND* gip v 'to gut…herring' [gilping 1788-]; PRATT gib v 'to clean fish' (1901-).

gib n *SND* gip n[2] 2 'herring guts' (1914-).

gig n
2 1986 *Them Days* xi (4), 45 'Come back and get your man. Your man is drowned.' … There was not a gig in buddy. They brought…'en to.

gilson n ['dʒɛlsn̩] A fibre or wire rope that runs through an overhead block, used for lifting objects on the deck of a trawler (1986 *Nfld's Deepsea Fishery* 649).

girl n *DBE* ~ n 2 'informal term of address.'
[1901] 1982 BURKE (ed Kirwin) 28 "How Kelly Fought the Ghost": He then told his wife how he fought with a stranger,/'As strong as a bull, Ellen, girl, almost.' 1985 JOHNSTON 43 'You were busy today, were ye Dola?' 'Yes girl.' 'You were too busy to wash my dress, were ye?' 'I was girl, yes.'

glitter n
1 1984 POWELL 59 The trees were loaded with glitter and snow, and I was only a half mile from the tilt. 1988 *Evening Telegram* 17 Feb, p. 1 Rain and freezing rain [last night] created coats of glitter close to a foot thick that hauled down power lines, knocked out communications, and caused damage to buildings.
2 Attrib ~ **storm**.
P 245-82 'We're used to the [power] lines down because of a glidder storm, but this [unexplained failure in electrical service] is ridiculous.'

glut n
1988 *Evening Telegram* 25 June, p. 3 He said the only option is to get Canadian vessels to buy the glut fish.

glutted p ppl Also: of the fishery, overcrowded with participants.
1987 JOHNSTON 6 In the years following the first world war, when the local fishery was glutted, Dad and Mom and about a hundred other young men and women left Harbour Deep to take up a new life of farming on the Meadows.

gly n
1985 NEWHOOK 12 Sometimes there would be definite jobs to get on with, like baiting a few glys for gulls.

go v
3 Phr *go on*; *how's she going*: polite phr of interrogative greeting; how are you? (P 51-66).
1987 *Evening Telegram* 11 Apr, p. 17 [tape transcript]

'Captain,' I said, 'if you don't make the light don't blame me.' That's all he said. He went on. 1987 FIZZARD 129 'What you'd do then was haul your dory in under [the gear], take the fish off the hooks, bait it and go on again.' 1985 *Nfld Qtly* lxxxi (1), 17 As I was alighting from the elevator who should be getting on but one of my co-workers from the year before. 'Didham! How's she going, man?'

goat n
2 1985 QUIGLEY 113 The Goat has just about disappeared and is replaced with a few belly rubs, a swing or two, a bit of arm swinging and finger cracking and the dance is over.
4 Attrib, comb ~ **house**: small wooden structure to house the animal in winter or in transportation by sea, ~ **rubber**.
1987 POWELL 71 They also had goats which were kept in little goat houses. The goats would be let out on deck long enough to be milked, then put back in the house again. 1988 *Evening Telegram* 27 May, p. 17 As for me, when my time rolls around I shall wear my goat rubbers and even deliver the convocation address if requested to do so. 1989 *Nfld Qtly* lxxxiv (4), 39 I had on my goat rubbers and just ploughed on through [the mud puddles].

gob² n *Anglo-Manx Dialect* ~ 'mouth' for sense 1; *Macquarie Dictionary* for comb ~-stick in sense 2.
2 Comb ~ **music**: humming to provide lively, rhythmic accompaniment for others to dance; MOUTH MUSIC, ~-**stick**.
1985 QUIGLEY 83 The young people might dance on the bridge until late afternoon using instruments or gob music. 1981 SPARKES 184 As the trawl came in, one man removed the fish, using hand-gaff and gobstick, while the other rebaited the hooks and sent them over the other side.

gob-stick v To club or stun a fish with a 'gob-stick.'
1977 MOAKLER 53 We gobsticked flapping cod against the strakes/And baited hooks as fast as they were clear.

gold-withy n also **goodwithy, goudie, go-worthy, guidy**.
1906 *Geog J* xxvii, 385 The 'open ground' or 'country' is covered with 'Indian tea' bush, goudie (*Kalmia glauca*), a lovely flowering shrub [etc]. 1983 *Gazetteer of Canada: Nfld* 66 Goodwithy Harbour. 1985 *Terminology of Loggers* 8 Go-worthy. Small evergreen shrubs with leathery green leaves bearing pink flowers; lambkill. 1986 SAUNDERS 184 Suddenly, up ahead they saw this old birch sticking out of the water where it was growing on one of the submerged guidy islands.

gommel n
1983 DAWE & FICKEN 38 O is for omaudaun,/ Chucklehead cove;/He acts like a gommel,/All squabby and stun. 1987 *Nfld Qtly* lxxxii (3), 17 They drag the poor creature ashore, winch him noisily up a wharf, and unto a tripod o' spruce 'longers'; there they weigh him,

and finally this 'gommil'—he's usually some urbanite… has his picture taken.

googy* n also **goggy***. *EDD* goggy 'child's name for an egg' for sense (a); *AND* goog (1941-), googie (1903-). Comb **googie-egg**: (a) hen's egg (1968 DILLON 143); (b) small white berry of the creeping snowberry; CAPILLAIRE (1968 DILLON 143).
P 295-83 Goggy egg. Child's name for a hen's egg. C 71-93 Googie egg. This is a small white berry found on miniature leaves on mossy hills under fir trees anywhere in St Mary's Bay. It has a sweet taste.

goudie See GOLD-WITHY.

government n Attrib ~ **bull**, ~ **man**: one holding a government appointment, ~ **meal**: corn-meal distributed to the poor, ~ **wharf**.
1903 *Nfld Qtly* iii (3), 13 I can send them a 'Government Bull' that will terrorize the neighbourhood. 1987 FIZZARD 149 'Farmer Sam Bradley had land and cattle there and was the keeper of this government bull, which was provided for the area.' 1987 JOHNSTON 48 Raymond liked to carry on about my father being a 'government' man. This was in reference to the fact that my father now worked with the federal department of fisheries. [1847] 1983 [ROUSE] (ed Street) 133 I agreed to give Phillips 2 Barrels of Government meal and 5 Gallons Molasses. [1860] 1988 *Sunday Express* 5 June, p. 13 [The *Courier* reported that] the order of procession [for Edward, Prince of Wales] was quickly and efficiently formed. Outside the Government wharf gate a colorful and magnificent triumphal arch had been erected. 1986 *Evening Telegram* 4 Apr, p. 4 The illegal strike by public servants is threatening to leave 800 Newfoundland fishing boats high and dry on government wharves.

gowdy a Cp *EDD* gowdie sb in phr (1) *heels o'er gowdy*: topsy-turvy. Of an ill-co-ordinated, clumsy person.
1983 DAWE & FICKEN 38 An oonshick so gowdy/ Wherever he goes,/ He falls on his gob/When he trips in his toes.

gozzard n
1987 MONTEVECCHI & TUCK 236 Gosser. Common merganser.

grand a Comb ~ **bank(s)**.
1988 DOHANEY 12 She had been [widowed] when her skipper husband drowned off the Grand Banks.

granny n Cp *EDD* ~ sb 1 (6) ~ hoods for comb in sense 4.
4 Comb **granny's bonnet**: columbine.
1986 *Atlantic Insight* Feb, p. 44 [The name] Granny's bonnets (*aquilegia [vulgaris]*) [evokes the memory of those old [Nfld] cottage gardens].

graple n *DBE* grapple obs (1807); cp *EDD* grape sb 'a grapnel' D Co.

1 Also: freq in coastal place-names.

[1620] 1982 CELL (ed) 161 They did further present...Two small Boats, Anchors, and a small Grapple, that were found in the Sea vpon that Coast. [1766] 1971 BANKS (ed Lysaght) 145-6 Those who Lie in open harbours are obligd to Content themselves with setting a number of netts up & down in the harbour both the Upper & under Lines of which are moord with Graplins. 1983 *Gazetteer of Canada: Nfld* 68, 79 Grapnel Island, Grappling Island, Grappling Point...Hell Grapple Head. 1984 POWELL 23 We made the trip to Fishing Ship's Harbour for summer supplies, ropes, graplins, and six more salmon nets. 1988 MOMATIUK & EASTCOTT (eds) 153 All the shore-fasts were out and the lead ropes, so I just had to row the net out there, tie it on and put out one grapelin.

2 Phr *throw away (one's) grapnel*: in the inshore fishery, to lower an anchor with float attached as indicator of occupancy of a particular 'berth' or 'ground'; cp *douse the killick*.

1981 SPARKES 188 When a man went to fish on a certain ground, he 'threw away' his grapnel, that is, he anchored. He is then said to be 'dropped' there.

grass n
1 1875 [MOSS] *MS Journal* 24 Aug Margann Boyde here cuting grass, brought the first grass down from the Uper Garden. 1987 POWELL 20 When they left Labrador to go home in the fall, they emptied the straw [hay in their mattresses] and it blew around their premises. In the spring the seed would take root and the long grass would grow.

2 Comb ~ **work**: objects woven or sewed using hay or wild grasses.

1985 *Decks Awash* Jan-Feb, pp. 26-7 'We used to send our grasswork to Cartwright but we'd get paid in clothes rather than money.'

grass v *South Shore Phr Bk* grassin'. Hence vbl n.

1986 FELTHAM 114 The young men and women met and associated with their counterparts of the other island...and perhaps sometime during the visit managed to enliven their stay with a short period of 'grassing.'

graunuail n also **granua uile, graunyer whale**. For a summary discussion of the allusion to Grace O'Malley (1530?-1600?), queen of the O'Malleys of Connaught whose proper name in Irish was Grainne Ni Mhaille, Grania Uaile in the popular form, and the shift to the later personification, see G.M. STORY, ''A Tune beyond Us as We Are,'' *Nfld Studies* iv, p. 134-5; and for further oral variant **granny whale**, cp GEORGE BORROW, *Wild Wales* (1862), Ch. 25. In ballad usage: Ireland, Hibernia, freq *old graunuail*.

[1835] 1988 *Nfld Studies* iv, p. 134 ''Croppy Winton'': chorus With a fol-de-mi-iddle a fol-de-mi-ail/The fox in the trap he was caught by the tail/So fill up your bumpers my lads without fail/And drink to the health of Old Graunuail. 1902 *Songs and Ballads of Nfld* (ed James Murphy) 10 ''The Fate of Rev. Dr. O'Regan'': And in

answer to the ocean, a once glad western vale/Sends up this cry to Heaven, and forth to ''Granua Uile.'' 1977 *Nfld Hist Soc*, Winton File MS, ''Winton's Ears'': So drink up your glasses, boys, and don't fail/For here's a success to ol' Graunyer whale/For the fox in the trap was caught by the tail.

gravel n
1987 FIZZARD 3 The beaches themselves were formed over thousands or millions of years as the pounding of the waves against the rocky shore broke the softer rocks into smaller pieces, slowly smoothing their edges to create the gravel of the modern beaches.

grease v Phr *grease the river*: to try out the first log-drive down a river.
1986 SAUNDERS 204 The first run of logs would 'grease the river' for the rest.

greasy a
2 Comb ~ **jacket**.
1989 CANDOW 37 Vessel and crew became covered in blood and grease, giving rise to the name 'greasy-jacket' to describe a sealer.

great a Comb ~ **auk**.
1987 HORWOOD 51 The people who exterminated the great auks for fish bait and lamp oil were the products of a vision which saw man as top predator in a natural order.

green a
3 Phr *be too green to burn*.
[1901] 1982 BURKE (ed Kirwin) 26 ''Sammy, Ain't You Glad You Joined the Navy'': You come from Newfoundland,/You are too green to burn. 1988 *Evening Telegram* 30 Sep, p. 6 Well, fellow Newfoundlanders of like mind, are we too green to burn or has the time come to bring on the blasty boughs?

4 Comb ~ **fish**, ~ **hand**: greenhorn; inexperienced sealer.
1986 SAUNDERS 60 At other wharves green fish was being forked from skiffs and punts onto stageheads where men were busy at the splitting table. 1984 WRIGHT 33 The younger and less experienced the newcomer, the more important the relationship became. The most intense and obvious play between 'old hand' and 'green hand' grew between Billy and Isaac.

greenland n Attrib ~ **halibut**.
1986 *Evening Telegram* 29 Mar, p. 5A Turbot (Greenland Halibut) are believed to be spawning in deep warm waters south of the Davis Strait Ridge.

grepe n also **grip**.
1983 *Gazetteer of Canada: Nfld* 71, 72 Cape Greep, Greep Head; Gripe Cove, Gripes Nest, Grip [Cove, Head, Island, Nest, etc]. 1990 *Sunday Express* 21 Jan, p. 9 [He] offers a piece of caplin to a grebe...which was found along the Cape Shore with its plumage full of oil.

grin n *OED* ~ sb[1] 2 b 'a halter' obs (1000–1591). A rope or halter to restrain a horse.

1985 *Terminology of Loggers* 8 ~ a rope twisted around the muzzle of a horse in such a way that any movement of the horse's head will be painful; this is to discourage the animal from kicking while he is being shoed.

grip[1] n See ICE-GRIP.

grip[2] n See GREPE.

gripe[1] n See GREPE.

gripe[2] n *OED* ~ sb[1] 8 naut (1762-1867). Rope to secure a dory or other small craft in its place aboard a vessel. Usu pl.
1984 KELLAND 144 The cradles were equipped with ringbolts at each end and on both port and starboard sides. One end of stout ropes, called gripes, was spliced into the ringbolts on one side while the free end which contained a heart shaped grommet or a ring was thrown over the nested dories to the opposite side, where they were hauled tight and lashed securely... The gripes were placed there...to prevent the dories from becoming denested and smashed or washed overboard during rough weather.

groaner n Cp H. GARDNER, *The Composition of Four Quartets* (1978), p. 120 [T.S. Eliot, 1941, on 'the heaving groaner' in line 34 of "The Dry Salvages"]: 'It is the New England word for a "whistling buoy," which by some arrangement of valves, makes a groaning noise as it rises and falls on the swell.'
[1950] 1988 *Seniors' News* Oct, p. 13 The sound of the groaner at Sagona added little to the lonesome scene, but for me the worst was yet to come.

grog n Comb ~ **bit**.
P 245-88 [for sale] Grog bits 75¢ each.

gronyer* n also **graunyer***. An old man, esp one with a marked presence or carriage; *old gronyer*.
P 99-69 Graunyer. A doddering old man. P 277-89 Old gronyer. Elderly man with a distinctive look; crusty, formal [in dress or manner].

ground n *DAE* ~ n[2] 1 (1792-), *DBE* ~ n 'a field; a piece of farmland,' WAKELIN 131 'fields' for sense 3.
1 1986 *Evening Telegram* 19 Feb, p. 3 If they lose access to these grounds [the Placentia Bay spokesman said] they will continue to fish...but they won't have as much gear fishing. 1986 FELTHAM 125 The term 'ground' was used in two different senses. In the broader connotation it was a large fishing area that included many 'spots' such as the Fair Island Ground. In the limited sense, it was used to describe a shallow underwater plain of considerable area, such as Pittsound Ground, which was one of the many fishing spots found on the Offer Gooseberry Ground [in Bonavista Bay].
2 1984 POWELL 38 We needed more traps for the new grounds.
3 [1622] 1982 CELL (ed) 200 Whitbourne's *Discourse*:

I haue, since my comming, beene a little abroad, and finde much good ground for Medow, Pasture, and arable, about *Aquafort*. 1837 *Royal Gazette* 5 Dec [Spacious wharves, commodious flakes and beach room,] with extensive meadows and garden grounds immediately contiguous. 1981 SPARKES 27 The potato grounds were always referred to as 'the gardens.'
6 Attrib ~ **hurt**, ~ **juniper**, ~ **plover**.
1981 SPARKES 28 In our garden there were several little patches of a small, low-growing blueberry called 'ground hirts.' 1985 DOMSTAD 24 Steep ground juniper in water and drink. 1987 MONTEVECCHI & TUCK 238 Ground plover. Lesser golden-plover.

grout n also **groat**.
2 1924 *Deep-Sea Fishers* xxi (4), 139 Groat. Term applied to scrubby trees.

growl n
P 312-88 ~ a game of cards, sometimes known as 120.

growler n
1988 *Evening Telegram* 30 July, p. 7 I don't believe it's possible to prevent a gigantic 'growler' from ripping apart any seabed [oil] installation.

grub n Attrib ~ **bag**, ~ **box**.
1986 SAUNDERS 52, 76 We took our rifles, ammunition, grub bag and axe and walked two miles uphill along the south side of the brook... A few feet away was my grub box.

grum a
[1979] 1985 LEHR & BEST (eds) 85 "Gull Cove": When we arrived at Gull Cove, everything it did look grum—/Our traps lay in good order, also our skiff and all.

guardian n
1 [1833] 1984 BAYFIELD i, 263 The French all leave this coast before the commencement of winter leaving their Fishing Establishments, buildings, fish flakes, &c. in charge of a guardian who is usually an inhabitant of Newfoundland (Brittish) who is half hunter or fur trader and half fisherman.
2 1986 *Evening Telegram* 12 Feb, p. 4 Before the two guardians took the stand...a fisheries officer testified no one had been stationed at Twelve Mile Pool prior to or after the week of July 20-27, although patrols were carried out on the river.

guess n Comb ~ **cake**.
[1920] 1982 MADISON (ed) 8 The best part [of a time] is the 'guess-cakes,' big thick cakes, into which the maker has put something...and you get 5¢ a guess and the cake to the lucky guesser.

guider n A long pole fastened to the front of a sled by which a man hauling the load steers the sled (1985 *Terminology of Loggers* 8); STEERING STICK.

guidy n See GOLD-WITHY.

gulch n
1 1832 MOSS *MS Diary* 10 May Killed a duck down in the Gulch. 1982 BURSEY 15 "The Boy's Tale": They found the body/In the gulch,/The cap on a ledge/Halfway down the cliff. 1986 FELTHAM 48 The shoreline is just as it was when he followed it as a boy searching for driftwood, the cliffs and gulches show little signs of change.
2 1987 POOLE 24 There was a salt water pond not very far away from me, about one hundred yards or so, and to get to this pond I had to go through a gulch of alders.
3 1983 *Gazetteer of Undersea Feature Names* 85 Gulch Shoal. 1984 POWELL 13 One net was set...at Crab Gulch at the other end of the tickle. Those were supposed to be master places for salmon.
4 [1937] 1987 *Evening Telegram* 25 Mar, p. 6 Traffic conditions on Torbay Road are very bad, the road being studded with many treacherous gulches.

gulf n Attrib ~ **ice**, ~ **shore**.
1988 *Evening Telegram* 2 Apr, p. 10 The [rabid] fox, believed to have crossed to the Island on gulf ice, was shot and killed by a wildlife officer...in Roddickton a week ago. 1920 *Deep Sea Fishers* xviii (1), 54 They were making about ten per cent of what their fellow trappers were getting on the Gulf shore.

gull n
3 Comb ~ **gaze**: fowler's blind or place of concealment; GAZE n 1.
[1987] QUINLAN 29 [The birds] were shot by men hid in a gull gazze [gaze].

gully¹ n
1 1986 *Evening Telegram* 8 May, p. 16A About 15 miles off the TCH was a chain of ponds that could get us and our supplies by boat to within an hour's hike of several seldom-fished gullies located in a tree-lined bottomland. 1988 ibid 12 Feb, p. 5 Leary's Brook and the small gully near the Health Sciences Centre on Prince Philip Drive have become a haven for a large flock of 70 or more wild black ducks. 1990 ibid 13 Jan, p. 28 Today will find me in my favorite little cove on the first gully behind Triangular Pond.
2 Phr *leave/leff/let her go for the gullies*.
1984 *Nfld Herald* 7 July, p. 23 Batten down the hatches and lef her go fer the gullies! 1987 *Evening Telegram* 3 Jan, p. 15 [He] announced Friday that we can let 'er go for the gullies Jan. 17—the opening date for trouting.

gully² n
2 1981 SPARKES 114 The woodbox is full, a whole 'gully' (cask) of water stands in the porch, all the work is done.

gum n
1 1985 DOMSTAD 18 Squirt the gum from the blathers on the sore.
2 Comb ~ **bucket**: garbage pail (1985 *Terminology of Loggers* 8).

gun n Attrib, comb ~ **ball**, ~ **cap**, ~ **hunter**: one who hunts game with a firearm rather than a snare, ~ **shot**.

1981 SPARKES xii The lead from a broken fish jigger and that which lined the chests in which tea came was saved and melted down into gun-balls for the great, long Birmingham muzzle-loading guns. 1987 POOLE 19 Plenty of gun powder, shot, and gun caps. And plenty of shells. 1986 *Evening Telegram* 5 Mar, p. 5 Gun hunters, after a few hours in the bush with their beagles, often say, 'we only got six [rabbits].' 1987 ibid 4 July, p. 56 [tape transcript] The next spring [they] put [their fishing gear, etc] on their fishing rooms on the two islands which were only about two gunshots apart.

gun v To engage in shooting sea-birds.
1832 MOSS *MS Diary* 21 May 4 hands out gunning, brought 47 birds. 1858 [LOWELL] i, 82 Our poor boys were out agunnun. 1982 BURSEY 15 "The Boy's Tale": Next day/Both went gunning/(Never together). 1984 KELLAND 105 'By cripes, Joe,' ventured a third, 'she'll be a sweet little bastard to go gunnin' in next winter.'

gunner n
1 1988 GOSSE 33 Later in the spring when attention was turned to the old harps, the gunners, accompanied by two helpers or 'dogs,' led the hunt.
2 1832 MOSS *MS Diary* 23 May 2 Gunners brought home 15 birds. 1983 *Gazetteer of Canada: Nfld* 74 Gunner Rock, Gunners Hole. 1986 SAUNDERS 63 From November until April, especially in the spring, gunners travelled there from as far away as Boyd's Cove to the west and Carmanville to the east to hunt the eider ducks and turrs and bullbirds that passed the headland in swarms on their migrations.

gunning vbl n
2 Comb ~ **point**: coastal location from which migrating sea-fowl can be shot, ~ **punt**, ~ **rock**, ~ **rodney**: RODNEY.
1983 *Gazetteer of Canada: Nfld* 75 Gunning Point. 1987 POWELL 50 When one is on an island he watches for this bright sky in the east, goes to a gunning point and waits for the first birds to fly by. 1945 MARTIN [5] Yes, I'm comin', ole white cottage—tell me gunning punt and kittle. 1981 SPARKES 184 If the ice was 'swatchy,' they took a very light small boat with them called a rodney or gunning punt. 1983 *Gazetteer of Canada: Nfld* 75 Gunning Rock. [1987] QUINLAN 31 A gunning rodney used for hunting birds and bay-seals. They were light, easy to row and also easy to capsize.

gurdy n PRATT ~ n (1975-).
1982 MCDOOLING 93 Put a gurdy on your boat so you haven't got no trouble haulin' your trap up.

gurry n *South Shore Phr Bk* (1983) for sense 2; cp PRATT gurry-butt for comb in sense 3; for kid see *OED* ~ sb⁴ ['a tub or container'].
1 Also: kitchen refuse.
1821 PANL GN 2/1 vol. 32, p. 119 A great quantity of American vessels resort to Isle au Bois and Green Island, about Six leagues west of this (where there are also some British Establishments) and that by their (the Americans) throwing *Gurry* overboard the place is much injured as regards getting Caplin for bait. 1981 PADDOCK

23 "Camp Seven": Da food was served on battered plates/Along wi' hearty flies,/While from da gurry een da sink/Da sweetes' odours rise. 1984 KELLAND 153 [They] were used primarily to stow fish offal (gurry).

2 1990 *Sunday Telegram* 4 Mar, p. 16 When the hunt was in its heyday, the men lived in the hold of their ship and slept on the fat, where the blood and gurry soon permeated their clothes.

3 Comb ~ **kid**: wooden container to cart fish offal away, ~ **pot**: on a 'banker,' container in which fish offal, cod-livers, etc, are placed.

1984 KELLAND 153 Gurry kids, which were large wooden boxes or pounds, had to be built on deck. 1977 MOAKLER 18 The early morning air as black as pitch/While rain came down afresh in gurry pots!

H

habit n
1949 FITZGERALD 42 The habit, too, and buryin' clothes, is always stored away. 1982 *Evening Telegram* 31 Dec, p. 14 Mrs Breen of Bambrick Street [used to make] habits for the dead.

hag[1] n *DBE* ~ 2 for sense 1.
1 [1886] 1910 HOWLEY *MS Reminiscences* 23 'Oh' said he, 'Cole has got the Old Hag Sir, thats all.' ... He tried to call out but could not, but just as they were giving him the third and last swing [over the cliff] he made one desperate effort to screech. 1985 *A Yaffle of Yarns* 94 She frequently announced...that she had had the 'old hag' the night before and described the symptoms in great detail. 1985 JOHNSTON 66 The air itself was black and thick and wrapped like arms around me. The hag, to those who have not known her, cannot be described.

3 Comb, cpd ~ **rode**, ~ **wind**: a gale at sea.
1981 SPARKES 166 A person having a nightmare was said to be hagrode. 1977 MOAKLER 22 So blew the hag winds till a mauzy dawn/That left the Banks as peaceful as a bawn. P 308-88 'That's no way to call a man when he is egg rod.'

hag v also **(h)egg***.
P 302-88 You hear a fellow say in the morning he was egged last night.

hail n Cp *OED* hail sb[3] 2 b naut *within hail*. Periodic report by the captain of a fishing vessel on his catch.
1930 *Am Speech* v, 390 Hail n. The total number of pounds of fish which a vessel may have in her hold at the time a declaration is made; daily *hails* are sent in by most company-owned boats each day by radio. 1972 ANDERSEN & WADEL (eds) 125 'I never can be sure just how much a man has on his boat on a given day. You're only fairly certain of his total catch when he gives his last hail for the trip.' The manager's expectation that something is wrong with his information is substantiated by discrepancies apparent in a comparison of recorded daily hails, the manager's estimates of the actual catch by his 'decoding' of the hail, and the hold log kept by the skipper at approximately the same time. 1989 *Networker* 7, p. 10

[The company's first product] was refined and marketed as the DataHail because fishermen radioing their catch for the day call it a 'hail.'

hail v Phr *hail for*. Also: of a 'cod-trap,' to total a certain catch of fish.
1901 *Evening Telegram* 20 July Hook and line men at these harbors have secured no fish yet, but traps hail for ten to seventy quintals.

half n *AND* ~ n 1 a (1829-1896) for phr *on the halves* (a).
1983 *Nfld Qtly* lxxix (2), 16 A number of Bonavista inhabitants were attracted [to sawmilling], having their timber squared, going 'halves' with the sawmill operator. 1987 POOLE 51 She said she had two salmon nets at Battle Harbour and one in Fox Harbour which used to be fished on the halves for her.

half a Comb ~ **barrel**, ~ **door**, ~ **drum**, ~ **gallon**, ~ **quintal**.
[1841] 1985 TAYLOR 37 Each half-barrel [of pickled fish shall contain] one hundred pounds...weight. 1888 *Colonist Christmas Number* 16 [poem] "The Green Half-Door." 1896 *Evening Telegram* 30 Apr The Angwald...has been cleared for market, taking 2,642 drums, and 2,388 half-drums, containing 4,388 4/7 quintals of prime dry codfish. 1987 ibid 27 Apr, p. 7 [tape transcript] Fish was packed in half-drums, drums, casks, donkeys, and various kinds of barrels... [A] half-drum [held] 64 pounds. 1981 SPARKES 190 All fishermen and seamen in those days wore long leather boots called Smallwood boots or, more often, deck boots. Some came halfway up the leg and were called half-gallon boots. 1987 FIZZARD 160 'We had several makes of barrels. There'd be half-quintal drums, quintal drums [etc].'

hamburg n also **hambutt**. Attrib ~ **bread**, ~ **butter**, **hamburg/hambutt pork**, ~ **tack**: HARD TACK.
1956 *Daily News* 5 Mar, p. 9 Hamburg bread and butter and Hamburg pork formed part of the fare of the hardy, strong and robust men who went to the ice in the old sailing vessels. [1902] 1976 *Evening Telegram* 9 Apr, p. 6 He agreed to give them four pounds of hard bread per man, four pounds of butter and two pieces of hambutt pork between the lot of them, twenty-two all told. T 75-64 They used to get a lot o' pork out of her. Fellows used to get this hambutt pork and put it in bags. 1956 *Daily News* 9 Mar, p. 16 The day is not far distant when the tough yarns of seal killers will be condemned as exaggerated tradition [and] the yarns, rhymes, strange whims of these men shall elude the [grasp] of memory: 'When the planter Burke/With his broad back/Fed his men on good pork/And Hambu[rgh] tack.' 1973 BARBOUR 50 Here we kept the barrels of salt beef, hambutt-pork, fat-back pork, and what we were most interested in—the puncheons of molasses.

hand n *DC* ~ logging (1952, 1956); *Anglo-Manx Dialect* han-barra for comb in sense 3.
1 [1898] 1986 *Evening Telegram* 24 Mar, p. 6 All hands were out, including the cook, and they panned about 200 seals close to the ship. 1984 WRIGHT 33 The

experienced 'hands' goaded the newcomers and made them the butt of jokes, asking and giving favours for things big and small. 1987 *Lore and Language* vi (1), 27-8 He went in picking raspberries and didn't come home. So, all hands went looking for him that night yelling out in the woods, so on and so forth—no sign of him.

2 Phr *to (one's) hand.*

[1898] 1986 *Evening Telegram* 24 Mar, p. 6 All hands were out, including the cook, and they panned about 200 seals close to the ship. He got 'seven for his hand.'

3 Attrib, comb, cpd ~ **barrow**, ~ **cobbing**: see COB v, ~ **gaff**, ~ **logging**: logging with hand tools such as axes, ~ **music**: performance by means of cupped hands; cp MOUTH MUSIC, ~ **pat**: with great ease, quickly, without effort, **handsignment**, ~ **slide**, ~ **trawl**: see TRAWL, ~ **tub**, ~ **stick**: one of the wooden sticks used in the game of 'piddly' or 'tiddly' to flick the other.

1987 POWELL 12 They...ended up with only about three quintals of fish. In fact, they said that they put it all on the hand barrow and carried it to the flakes in one trip. 1988 *Evening Telegram* 21 Mar, p. 6 After the poor fellows were landed they were taken to different homes; most of them had to be carried in hand-barrows. 1983 MARTIN 6 [caption] Young men and boys hand-cobbing ore in Tilt Cove with what likely is the East Mine 'rabbit warren' in the background, c1900. 1981 SPARKES 184 As the trawl came in, one man removed the fish, using hand-gaff and gobstick, while the other rebaited the hooks and sent them over the other side. [1909] 1930 COAKER 9 Hand-logging should be immediately prohibited as this evil is rapidly growing. P 113-89 [He recalled] amateur performances in St John's, one performer noted for rendition of "The Road to the Isles" by means of cupped hands—'hand music.' 1987 FIZZARD 130 'The pressure of your legs and your body coming down used to press the duck in alongside the mast head and then you had your hands to hook your line around. So, it came hand pat after you did it a few times.' P 133-58 Hand-signment 'signature.' 1985 NEWHOOK 58 We had to be careful about meeting oncoming horses and slides or hand slides, although the horses always wore bells. 1988 GOSSE 20 Also in common use were long lines of 50 fathoms or more [with hooked lines] spaced at [intervals]. This fishing gear was known as bultows or hand trawls. 1984 KELLAND 10 From the work benches of those stores were manufactured...hand tubs [etc]. [1985] MAHER 24 [In piddly stick] one stick was balanced on the bricks and one end of it was hit by the hand stick and driven thru the air.

handy a, av PRATT (1908-) for sense 1; *O Sup*[2] (1934) for phr in sense 3.

1 1984 POWELL 14 If all those people had lived in one of those places, it never would have brought the outside world any handier to us. The handiest nursing station was over forty miles away. 1986 SAUNDERS xi These moves were made partly for the sake of better schooling for my brother and me, partly so my mother, never robust... could have a doctor handy.

3 Phr *handy by.*

[1867] 1989 CHIMMO (ed Kirwin) 32-3 [Our pilot]

never knew anything, but 'I suppose so' and a term he often used was 'handy-bye' meaning, close to his native place 'Windy tickle.'

4 Comb ~ **ground**: fishing grounds closely adjacent to a settlement.

[1937] 1945 SCAMMELL 18 "Tommy Decker's Venture": And we old codgers wish 'em luck and all the folks around/Will feel right glad if lots o' fish strikes on the handy ground.

hapse[1] n *SED* iv, 512 So W Co D Do Ha.

harbour n

1 Also: the central part, or core, of a settlement; cp COVE.

[1847] 1983 [ROUSE] (ed Street) 112 I find that the only Communicants in the Harbour are T. Hutchings, Mrs Brine [etc]. [c1894] PANL P4/14 'I have been served most ridiculous by the Poor Commissioner in our harbor.' 1985 GUY 82 A few weeks ago there was a big bank [on the northern side of the house] and with the mild weather we had there's not much left of it. But it must be the only patch of snow left in the harbour. 1987 KIMIECIK 98 The central area was called 'the harbour' although it is not near the harbour. You went 'down the harbour' after church on Sunday nights and after weeknight worship service on Friday nights.

3 Attrib, comb ~ **day**: a holiday, ~ **ice**, ~ **punt**: PUNT, ~ **rule**: a local and customary method of selecting fishing areas each season, ~ **seal**.

1924 *Deep Sea Fishers* xxi (4), 139 Harbor day—When rough weather makes it impossible to go out to the nets. 1897 *Evening Telegram* 4 Mar He was copying on the harbor ice when he slipped on a pan and down he went into the cold icy waters of [St John's] harbor. 1984 KALLEO 16 The young men and the married men are playing soccer on the harbour ice. 1977 MOAKLER 59 We shipped our oars and drifted on a swell/That turned our dory to a harbour punt. 1987 POOLE 79 They told me that we could make a harbour rule but it could not be made law; it was up to us to agree amongst ourselves to draw for berths. But if the fishermen wanted to, they could break off any time they wished and take a berth even if it was drawn for. 1989 *Evening Telegram* 26 June, p. 1 The so-called seal worms, also known as cod worms, have a life cycle that is thought to include the stomachs of harbour seals and the flesh of some fish.

hard a For comb ~ **boot** in sense 4, cp *DBE* ~ shoes 'shoes made of leather.'

4 Comb, cpd ~ **boot**, ~ **bread**, ~-**dried**, ~ **tack**, ~ **ticket**.

1981 SPARKES xiii Shop boots other than deck boots were called 'hard boots.' Nobody wore shoes. 1983 LEHR & BEST (eds) 158 "The Prison of Newfoundland": O when my sentence it was passed then I was marched away,/Down to the penitentiary my winter there to stay;/Where I found comrades plentifully as you may understand,/To live on hard bread and cold water in the prison of Newfoundland. [1987] QUINLAN 6 [Rags were] hooked into the fibre of bags in which hard bread had been bought. 1982 MCDOOLING 43 The production of 'hard-dried' salmon and codfish allowed the fishermen at least partial control...over exchange. 1987 *Evening Telegram* 10 Oct, p. 11 I bought some hard tack from Newfoundland in July... Some people like to dunk theirs in their tea, but not me, I like mine straight. 1986 SAUNDERS 157 He must have been a hard ticket, for he kept running afoul of the law. 1988 NADEL-KLEIN & DAVIS (eds) 219 'Ted's got a brother with a good wife. He's a good skipper, best kind. But this Flossie's some hard ticket, I tell you.'

hardy a
1949 FITZGERALD 36 And all the men and hardy boys was haulin' firewood. 1982 MCDOOLING 106 I was doing a man's work when I was twelve years old... When we were growing up...we were hardier than the crowd that's going today.

harrish* v *Anglo-Manx Dialect* ~ 'harass.'

hart n See HURT.

hash n Vegetables, esp potatoes, turnip, cabbage, left over from an earlier meal, chopped up and heated or browned.
1972 MURRAY 223 Since most housewives cooked more than enough vegetables for dinner, there were always left-overs. These were usually all mashed together and heated up in a frying pan, perhaps with onion added, for the main supper dish, 'hash.' 1987 FIZZARD 181 [On Mondays] soup and hash, usually leftovers from Sunday [would be served for dinner, the mid-day and main meal of the day].

haul v
1 Also: to inspect one's rabbit snares or 'slips' (see 1986 quot).
1981 MAJOR 214 He wasn't the one I had seen hundreds of times heave a castnet and haul it to shore loaded with caplin. 1986 *Evening Telegram* 25 Jan, p. 16 'What's the difference in Premier Peckford hauling his rabbit snares on Sunday and me taking my dog up in the woods for a day's shooting?' 1987 POOLE 73 For hauling the trap three times a day, we got nothing only our grub.
2 1987 *Evening Telegram* 11 Apr, p. 14 [tape transcript] Now three seals were as many as you could haul any distance on dry ice, but if the ice was watery you could haul more because they would float along.
3 1839 ENGLAND 11 Feb The Romans were shouting and running with sleighs...they were hauling wood for the priest. 1987 POOLE 66 Before Uncle Will got big enough to handle the horse, [Grandmother] used to take him herself to haul out firewood.
5 See HOUSE: **house-haul(ing)**.
1980 HOLMES 19 When a house was to be hauled or a boat to be pulled up for the winter...it was only necessary to set a day and call for volunteers.
6 1988 MOMATIUK & EASTCOTT (eds) 44 I was trying to educate people to have fillings done. She said she wanted her tooth ''auled,' as in hauling a net.
7 Phr *haul down*: to take a boat or vessel from its 'haul up' winter position ashore and prepare the craft for launching; *haul in* (a), *haul up*.

1986 FELTHAM 69 The schooner was 'hauled down,' its bottom cleared of barnacles and sea-weed and given a coat of copper paint. 1987 *Evening Telegram* 9 May, p. 15 [tape transcript] There was two ships hauled in [at the wharf at Bay Roberts]. I went to one, got down in the hold and I combed and combed [looking for my fishing gear]. 1987 POOLE 26 The next morning it was take the boats out and haul them up for the winter.
8 Cpd **haul off** (b), **haul-up box**, ~ **line**.
P 308-88 The snow would come and they would have to go away to the haul off. That was pull the wood that they had cut in the spring and summer. 1984 KELLAND 101 The box was called a haul up box [fitted to a motorized dory to cover the propeller shaft]. ibid 183 In setting a trawl preparatory to underrunning it, an anchor with the main trawl line, keg buoy, buoyline (called a haul-up line), moorings and slablines were dropped. The entire fleet of gear was then run out.

haul n
1 P 245-89 'A few hauls with the brailer and you've got a load [of caplin] from the seine.'
3 [1849] 1983 ROUSE (ed Street) 179 In consequence of the drift last night the people could not give us a 'Haul' to day.

hauling vbl n Attrib, comb ~ **path**: WOODS PATH, ~ **rope** (a): see first 1986 quot, (b) 1986 quot, (c): fibre rope used to haul the bottom rollers of a trawl net on board (1986 *Nfld's Deepsea Fishery* 650).
1985 NEWHOOK 58 The haulin' path was narrow and sometimes rough. Usually we had to travel a mile or so before we got to good cutting wood. We had to be careful about meeting oncoming horses and slides or hand slides, although the horses always wore bells. 1986 FELTHAM 175 The hauling rope was strung through the flipper holes in such a way that the pelts rested in each other, leaving the smallest possible area of friction with the ice. 1986 SAUNDERS 285 [diagram] hauling rope tied to centre of cross-piece [of sled].

hay n Attrib, comb ~ **bag**: a slattern, ~ **garden**, ~ **stick**.
[1929] 1982 BURKE (ed Kirwin) 99 ''When Your Old Woman Takes a Cramp in Her Craw'': I wed this old hay bag/I called her my wife. 1987 FIZZARD 220 Some of the new houses have been built in spaces among the older houses [of Grand Bank], in what used to be vegetable and hay gardens. 1985 NEWHOOK 42 Then the grass would be spread around the field in order to expose as much of it as possible to the wind and sun. This was done by using either the hands, or a hay stick.

he pro *SED* iv, 125 'with he'; WAKELIN p. 103, l. 19, p. 105, l. 15, p. 170, l. 49.
1 Revision: referring to human and other male creatures and to count nouns, in stressed positions, after BE or as object of a verb or a preposition.
1858 [LOWELL] i, 40 'The road's wide enough to walk on, athout atumblin over, is n' 'e?' T 133-64 Well she said that wasn't he [Jack]. T 438-65 'The next to myself,' he said, 'lives 'bout thirty mile from this.' And he said, 'You'll find he all right.' ibid 'Yes,' Jack said, 'there he

is, this [ring] is he.' 'Yes,' he said, 'right enough. 'Tis he.'

head n
1 [1622] 1982 CELL (ed) 200 Whitbourne's *Discourse*: I...finde much good ground for Medow, Pasture, and arable, about *Aquafort*, as well neere vnto the head of the Harbour, as all the way betweene that and *Ferryland*. 1984 POWELL 113 I felt like going right back to the head of the bay that night and telling the folks what I had heard on the radio. 1987 *Evening Telegram* 2 Mar, p. 6 They...decided to walk back [across the ice] to the Head of the Bay.
3 [1937] 1945 SCAMMELL 37 "Payne's Cove Bait Skiff": Hurry up, close the foots, keep the heads from goin' down,/'Turn 'em out in the bunt, boys.'
4 1986 FELTHAM 69 During the forties, lobsters were shipped live to the United States [and] this development brought other activities to the [Bonavista Bay] islands, for lobster pots had to be made and the 'heads' knitted. 1987 *Evening Telegram* 24 Oct, p. 14 Two men are employed [at Bonavista] making the [lobster] pots while three are knitting heads.
6 Phr *(that's) the head, heads and tails, head boat* (see 1985 quot).
P 281-84 'Young [so-and-so] had a heart attack yesterday?' 'Well, that's the head!' 1987 FIZZARD 133 'The women spread the fish heads and tails on the beach and turn it once a day.' 1985 *Terminology of Loggers* 8 Head boat. This term refers to the boat containing the head works and was called out as a signal for everyone to pull together when hauling heavy objects.

head v
1984 *Evening Telegram* 22 Dec, p. 6 My brother and I...cleaned our small catch—headed, gutted and split the fish, washed them in a 'dredge-barrow,' salted them away.

heart² n See HURT.

heave v
1 1981 MAJOR 214 He wasn't the one I had seen hundreds of times heave a castnet and haul it to shore loaded with caplin. He wasn't the same fisherman at all. 1988 *Evening Telegram* 6 Dec, p. 8 The vessel was drifting helplessly and taking on water [before the longliner] could secure [her] with a towline and take her to safety in Galtois. 'Snow and winds 35 to 40 mph made it difficult but she handled well and we hove her to starboard [and reached port],' said Capt. Saunders.
3 Phr *heave in, heave out* (a) see 1977 quot; (b) call to get out of bed (1985 *Terminology of Loggers* 8).
[1977] 1985 LEHR & BEST (eds) 17 "The Blue Wave": 'Fore ten on Monday morning we received a distress shout,/Coming from the *Blue Wave* saying that she was hove out.
4 Comb **heave-up (shanty)**.
1985 LEHR & BEST (eds) 86 Many of these 'heave-up shanties' were old ballads or contemporary ones, and very often topical verses were made up on the spur of the moment.

heavy a Comb ~ **damp**: see HEAVY FISH, HEAVY SALTED.

1982 MCDOOLING 63 [If fish could not be sun dried,] the fish would be left for a longer period between the salt layers so that as much of the body moisture as possible could be leached out of it. This produced a 'heavy-damp' product that was worth much less on the market than was the hard-dried variety.

hen n Cp *OED* ~ sb 4 'female fish or crustacean' (1855), *EDD* sb¹ 6 'a shell fish' (1888).
1 Bivalve shellfish; see COCK 1.
[1623] 1982 CELL (ed) 122 *Whitbourne's Discourse*: The Harbours are generally stored with...Lobsters, Crafish, Muskels, Hens, and other varietie of Shelfish great store.

herring n *SED* iv, 484 errin s w cties for sense 1.
1 [1960] 1982 BURKE (ed Kirwin) 114 "The Trouting Liar": And others went to Bay Bulls Big,/And herrins! such a load./He filled his basket and a bag/And left them on the road.
2 Attrib, comb ~ **bait**, ~ **baiting**, ~ **trip**.
1987 POWELL 19 The cod trap season was over and now the fishing boats were using trawls and cod jiggers; some had hand lines using herring bait. 1984 KELLAND 233 [Capt] Ansty was heading for either Placentia Bay or St Mary's Bay to pick up another herring baiting. 1987 FIZZARD 127 After one or two herring trips, the schooners changed both their type of bait and their fishing location.

hidey n *AND* ~ 'game of hide-and-seek' (1957-) for sense 1.

high a Comb **high-rat**: Also: in undersea feature names.
1878 *Nfld Pilot* 413 High-rat bank, with 8 fathoms water, lies N 1/4 W one mile nearly from the east point of Stunk island. 1987 *Evening Telegram* 4 July, p. 56 [tape transcript] After the trap season, the men used to go out in the high-rats jigging [on the Labrador]. These high-rats or bully boats had a big sail and a jib and carried two men. There was also a rowing oar and a sculling oar, each one about 20 feet long.

hobby horse n Also: animal disguise, with many local variations, of Christmas mummers.
1987 ROBERTSON 107 The hobby horse, in one shape or another, was the standard animal figure or animal disguise... Hobby horses, hobby cows, hobby goats, hobby sheep, hobby bulls...are recorded as appearing in Newfoundland at Christmas as mummers' costumes or as figures which mummers carried.

hoggelly bog n also **hoggedy bog, oglibog***. Cp *EDD* hogger 'stocking with the foot cut off, used as a gaiter' Sc, N of England. Large boot; cloth footwear with a skin sole.
P 110-68 'Saboos,' 'oglibogs,' 'clunks,' God walkers' are terms used to describe a pair of boots (shoes, rubbers, sneakers, etc) which look rather odd on the person's feet, usually by being too big for him. 1981 SPARKES ix The [swanskin] socks were soled with deerskin or sealskin and worn in winter, not inside but outside the moccasins. They were called 'hoggelly bogs' or 'hoggeddy bogs.'

hoist v Comb hoist-your-sails-and-run.

1979 PORTER 80 Hoist your Sails and Run was, I suppose, a glorified game of After, or a mixture of After and Hiding. 1989 *Evening Telegram* 30 Jan, p. 4 A million dollars per year [to athletes] for swatting or pitching or catching a ball! Anyone out there for hop-scotch? Hoist your sails and run?

hoist n

1 1986 SAUNDERS 160 The other problem with twine was that the rabbit might bite it off and get away... The way the oldtimers got around this was to rig up a hoister.

2 1983 *Nfld Qtly* lxxix (2), 3 I resolved to give that anecdote the hoist for another fifty years.

holly n

1988 MOMATIUK & EASTCOTT (eds) 92 If somebody heard the 'old hollies'—mournful cries made by dead fishermen floating in a dory and wailing an old chantey—he knew that a big breeze of wind was coming. I remember my grandfather walking into a house and saying, 'You can pull your boats in; I just heard the old hollies.' And the men went down and pulled up the boats.

home n

1 Attrib ~ **boat.**

1985 *Evening Telegram* 29 July, p. 6 Many readers... have fond memories of a voyage [from Liverpool to St John's] in the last of the 'Home Boats.'

hood n

1 1985 BUSCH 45 Hood or bladdernose seals, so-called because adult males have a bladder which when inflated in excitement forms a sort of hood.

hook n Comb hook-and-line.

1987 *Evening Telegram* 3 Feb, p. 3 The hook and line fishermen are meeting tonight to vote on a price agreement. 1990 ibid 21 Jan, p. 13 We would [then] see the inshore trap and hook and line fishery in the straits and all along the Northeast Coast booming.

hoop n Cp *DA* ~ n 1 'wooden shoulder-yoke' (1851, 1857) obs for sense 1; *OED* hoop-stick 1 'thin pliable stick or sapling such as is used for making cask-hoops' (1703, 1704) for comb in sense 2.

1 Wooden frame for carrying two pails of water.

[1900] 1989 *Nfld Qtly* lxxxv (2), 23 No one ever thought of carrying water without a hoop and never less than two buckets at a time. The hoop or circle was made from a birch limb, its ends fastened together.

2 Comb ~ **mare,** ~ **stick** (see quot).

1981 SPARKES xiv The hoopstick was smoothed and shaped on a special bench with a tightening device. This bench was a rather intricate contraption and, I suppose because the hoopmaker sat astride it, was called a hoop-mare.

hopper n

2 Also attrib ~ **bedlamer.**

1985 *Canadian Sealers Association* 6 When seals return the next year, they are called a hopper Bedlamer which is a one year old seal.

horn n

1 Also: the tentacle of a lobster; antenna.

[1937] 1987 *Evening Telegram* 11 Mar, p. 6 A lobster caught by...Chester and Alton Green of Wood Island, measured exactly the length of a match, or slightly over two inches from the end of the 'horn' to the top of the tail.

3 1985 *Terminology of Loggers* 9 ~ [one of the] stout upright sticks driven into the four corners of a swinging bunk to keep the load of wood in place.

7 Comb ~ **cat:** HORN SLIDE (P 310-83).

horse n Comb ~ **head,** ~ **shoe** (see 1986 quot), ~ **sled:** see SLED.

1987 HORWOOD 200 I first watched the seals from our beach when we camped here...the year before we built the house, and discovered to my delight that they were grays, 'horseheads.' 1986 *Nfld's Deepsea Fishery* 650 Horseshoe: a raised semi-circular portion of the trawl deck found on some stern trawlers sometimes called 'the arena.' Bottom rollers fit snugly around it when the net is yanked back on deck. 1939 FROUDE 5-6 I sat and listoned to the men each talking of...lumber woods and camps and bogs horses slids [sleds] and old pine logs.

horsy-hops n Also: animal disguise, with many local variations in names, of Christmas mummers; see also HORSE CHOP(S) (a).

1984 ROBERTSON 107 The [hobby horse] was called other names such as Horsechopper, Horsey Hops, Horse Chops, Horsey Chops...hobble horse, or the hoppy horse.

house n

1 1987 MCDONALD 138 The larger houses, cushioned by the multiplicity of their other business interests, were content to accept dwindling profits on their fish until the fishing industry faced an unmistakable general collapse in the 1930s.

4 Comb ~ **hauling.**

1989 *Evening Telegram* 19 Aug, p. A8 During the winter months there would be several houses getting pulled to different places. We certainly enjoyed going to 'house hauling.'

howden n

1885 TUTTLE 188-9 There are black ducks, divers, howdens, eider ducks, and ducks of all kinds.

hud n Cp *EDD* ~ sb² 3 'a lump or clod' W. A piece of cheese (P 289-87).

huit See OO-ISHT.

hungry a

2 Phr *long and hungry month of March* see LONG.

3 Comb ~ **dance** (see quot).

1985 QUIGLEY 58 What other activities might or might not be expected to take place [is indicated by the terms] 'garden party' run by the local parish, or a 'hungry dance' at which no food was to be served.

hurt n also **hart, heart**. Cp *EDD* black 2 (11) ~ heart Ha; T HARDY *The Return of the Native* V ii, 382 (black-heart); *SED* iv, 495 numerous variants, 1002 Ha.

1 1961 ROULEAU 96-8 Hart Island, Heart Cove, Heart Point. 1917 *Deep Sea Fishers* xv (3), 115 [We had] tin cans, in which to gather the precious blue-hearts, baked apples and wild currants. 1985 DOMSTAD 15 Take the leaves from the black berry hearth [for *heart*], steep them in water and drink the liquid.

I

I pro See note at WE.

1 1858 [LOWELL] ii, 201 'I'se agoun up here a bit, sir: did 'ee want any thing wi' I?' said the man.

ice n *SED* iv, 877 ice candle for comb in sense 2.

1 Phr *at, for, to the ice*, etc.

[1939] 1983 FROUDE 6 We leaved twillingate and steered of NE and the next day we got in the ice. 1984 WRIGHT 27 'I haven't been able to sleep at night for thinking about going to the ice' [he admitted]. 1987 MONTEVECCHI & TUCK 36 Newfoundlanders who used to 'go to the ice' to kill Harp Seals in spring often took along...tubes [made from bird bones] to drink from fresh water pools on the ice.

2 Attrib, comb, cpd ~ **candle**, ~ **captain**: ICE MASTER (a), ~ **claw**, ~ **facsimile (machine)** (see 1986 quote), ~ **glim**, ~ **grip**, ~ **hawk**: gyrfalcon (1987 MONTEVECCHI & TUCK 237), ~ **hunting**, ~ **island**: ISLAND 1, ~ **master** (a), ~ **party**, ~ **picking** (see 1988 quote), ~ **ram**: RAMS, SHEARSTICK, ~ **sail**, ~ **voyage**.

1985 NEWHOOK 27 Underneath the ice it is possible to find clear ice candles reaching down to the water which can be sucked on the way to and from school. 1845 *Journ of Assembly*, Appendix 237 The *Lauret*, Captain Harlow, of Boston, was fitted out for the ice; her ice-captain (Morey) and the mate, his son, and many of the crew, belonged to this country. 1989 CANDOW 64 At night, steamers were routinely anchored in the ice field by means of large grapnels called 'ice claws,' or cables wrapped around ice pinnacles. 1986 *Nfld's Deepsea Fishery* 650 Ice facsimile machine: an electronic machine that prints out maps of the pack ice and weather maps. 1987 DAWE [24] I is for ice-glim,/A ghostly white glow/Far out at sea/Where the sky meets the floe. 1987 FIZZARD 138 'Then there'd be a man there to pull [the block of pond ice] out of the water. He'd [have] ice grips.' 1986 *Nfld Qtly* lxxxi (4), 46 Around these small pans he and companions hooted and dared each other as they skipped and leaped from one solid ice-island to another. 1984 WRIGHT 99 [He] looked out the window at the grey water in the harbour. 'Nah! I don't want to go ice huntin' anymore. You can live without going ice huntin'.' ibid 49 Less skillful captains tried to follow respected 'ice masters,' hoping they would be led to the main patch. 1985 BUSCH 74 Leading his men in the designated direction for seals [the masterwatch] pointed subsections, 'ice parties,' this or that way. 1988 *Recre-*

ation Program Dept [St John's] 29 St John's Sledge Hockey and Ice Picking Association...S.H.I.P. is an integrated winter activity that allows disabled and non-disabled individuals to compete on an equal basis. Players sit in specialized sledges and propel themselves across the ice using ice picks. 1920 *Deep Sea Fishers* xviii (4), 122 The crew on the ice-rams (beams slung under her bowsprit) staved her bow off the pans. [1961] 1986 *Evening Telegram* 17 Dec, p. 6 An ancient ice saw [is] among the newest additions to the Newfoundland Museum. This ice saw was used at the Newfoundland sealfishery and is now on display. 1845 *Journ of Assembly*, Appendix 233. Ice voyage.

ignorant a PRATT ~ a.

1987 *Nfld Qtly* lxxxiii (1), 16 But the American tourists are too ignorant to talk about. 1990 *Evening Telegram* 17 Jan, p. 3 'They're not even polite to you anymore when you go up [to that office]. They're ignorant to you now; it's like they think they're doing you a favor.'

in av

2 1987 PEYTON 13 Not only was [the Exploits river] the aborigines' natural 'way out' to the sea coast, but the early pioneer's natural 'way in' to the heart of Beothuck land.

4 Comb **in-draft, in-wind**.

[1870] 1973 KELLY 7 This is a very pretty harbour, or indraught of the sea, the name of which is said to be derived from a little cascade. 1903 *Nfld Qtly* iii (1), 2 Coming yet southward, about one mile and a half from Harbour Rouge, we meet with a long estuary or 'Indraft,' extending about twelve miles inland named [Canada Bay]. 1901 *Evening Telegram* 20 July The trap voyage is now practically over, though with in winds, saving voyages may yet be trapped. 1983 DAWE & FICKEN 26 I is for in-wind/That blows to the shore,/So cold from the sea,/It creeps under your door.

indian n

1 1983 *Gazetteer of Canada: Nfld* 84-5 Indian Arm, Indian Cove, Indian Head, Indian Island, Indian Point [etc].

3 Attrib ~ **string**.

1986 SAUNDERS 147 After deboning the [caribou] meat, he took half of it and tied it up in a woven wool strap about three inches wide and twelve feet long which he called the 'Indian String.' This string, after he had the meat securely tied into a neat bundle, was long enough to make a pair of shoulder straps that worked just like a knapsack.

inner a Inshore, nearer the land; the more landward of two (or more) objects or features. Cp OUTER. Freq in place-names.

1971 *Can Geog J* lxxxii, 164-5 [In Labrador] big ships take the 'outer run'; skippers of local boats prefer the 'inner run' through the maze of coastal islands. 1983 *Gazetteer of Canada: Nfld* 85 Inner Bob Rock, Inner Brandy Rock, Inner Collins Ledge, Inner Narrows [etc].

inshore a Comb ~ **fisherman**, ~ **ground**: see GROUND 1, ~ **season**: see SEASON, ~ **man**: see **inshore fisherman**.

1983 SOUTH (ed) 445 When the cod are concentrated

in shallow water near shore they are available in huge amounts for the Newfoundland inshore fishermen for a short period during the summer. 1985 *Evening Telegram* 6 July, p. 5 Caplin hasn't put in their appearance yet, and fish on the inshore grounds is scarce. ibid 5 Apr, p. 1 Fishermen preparing for the inshore season have been frustrated because they have been unable to get their boats into the 17 [marine service centres] as the result of the illegal strike. 1982 JACKSON 67 'The next day it's just as well for the landsman to stay home, because the long-liners will come down and throw all their nets around, and what's the inshoreman gonna do then?'

inside av

2 Also: adjacent to the landward or sheltered side of an island or headland.

1966 *Assoc Am Geog* 1, 274 Berths were classified as 'inside' or 'outside,' outside being those located on islands or headlands and exposed to rough seas. Inside berths were those that were sheltered from heavy seas and were trapped when the seas were too rough to trap on the outside berths.

4 Attrib ~ **cut,** ~ **room.**

1989 CANDOW 15 When the wind blows from the land, the ice is loose and easier to navigate; there is usually open water between the coast and the landward edge of the ice. This stretch of water, known as the 'inside cut' or the 'cow path,' is the best route to the whelping ice. 1986 FELTHAM 41 The parlor, or 'inside room,' as it was frequently called, was rarely used... It was a place where the bodies of the dead were kept, pending burial.

inside of prep phr

1987 FIZZARD 189 'And while they were hauling in their gear there was a convoy of ships come down inside of us and I'll bet you I watched them sink 25 or 30 ships in sight of us.'

into prep

1985 GUY 83 There's a lot more strength into [moon-shine] than that old slops you gets from the Controllers. P 302-88 [You] did what you could and tried to get what-ever dollars was into it, that you could get for to bring home to your family.

island n also **iland, island of Newfoundland.**

1 The large land-mass east of the Gulf of St Lawrence and south of the Labrador Peninsula; Newfoundland as a political entity; cp BAC-CALAO(S), COUNTRY, (THE) ROCK, TERRA NOVA.

[1622] 1982 CELL (ed) 109 Whitbourne's *Discourse*: Among my vndertakings & imployments in Seafaring, the most part haue been to an Iland, called *New-found-land*. [1769] 1989 CHIMMO (ed Kirwin) 95 The Governor and Commander in Chief of His Majesty's Island of Newfoundland and the Territories depending thereon for the Time being, and all others whom it may Concern, are to take notice [of this]. 1819 ANSPACH 266 During the last war, the island had exported in one year one million two hundred thousand quintals of fish. 1933 *Roy Com Report* 72 Before we pass to a detailed examination of the prospects in the immediate future, we propose to record here our impressions of the present state of the

Island. [1950] 1987 *Nfld Studies* iii, 257 Mr Quinton told me privately that he would resign rather than see the Island revert once again to a policy of borrowing. 1984 POWELL 14 Brother Max decided to give us a hand to build our winter tilt [in Labrador] before he returned to the Island. 1987 FIZZARD 9 First appearing in southern Labrador, they eventually travelled across the Strait of Belle Isle to the Island of Newfoundland.

2 Phr **island of ice.**

[1527] 1895 PROWSE 40 *Rut's Letter*: We ranne in our course to the Northward [where] we found many great Islands of ice and deepe water. 1987 *Evening Telegram* 4 July, p. 56 [tape transcript] This island of ice was out there and my father said, 'We'll go out where that island of ice is, it might be up against a shoal.'

J

jack[1]

1 [1977] 1985 LEHR & BEST (eds) 24 "The Brule Boys": When Harvey saw them coming, he called: 'All hands on deck—/O come and look to wind'ard and see that little jack.'

3 Comb ~ **boat.**

1988 *Nfld Studies* iv (2), 180 Newfoundlanders flocked to the work site [at Argentia], many finding their own floating accommodation in local jack-boats which would normally have been tied up once the fishing season was over.

jackabaun n For the conservative policies of the Roman Catholic hierarchy in Nfld during the Revo-lutionary period see C.J. BYRNE, *Gentlemen-Bishops and Faction Fighters* (1984), p. 162 [letter of 1799] 'Thus have those hot headed Republicans lately returned from France imbibed Jacobin principles & brought indelible infamy upon our holy religion that breaths nothing more than loyalty & obedience to the Laws of God & the constituted authorities of every country.'

1985 GUY 7 You...mortalizing son of an ever-lasting terrified jumping cross-eyed slimy slot-faced jack-a-bon. Go now, will you.

jackass n

1985 BUSCH 50 Many schooner-rigged vessels of 60-80 tons used for various fishing chores were turned into 'beaver hats' for the seal fishery, with one large tempo-rary foremast topsail rigged to help through the ice and to back the vessel when jammed—larger 'jackass brigs' had topsails on all masts, though the variety of local rigs could blur the distinction.

jackatar n Reports in the mid-nineteenth century declare that the people given this name were part of the complex migrations of the Acadians or were French runaways.

Revised def: in the nineteenth century a person on the West Coast believed to be of mixed French and Micmac indian descent; in recent decades an epithet referring to certain individuals of dark complexion, with a French accent and intonation in their speech.

[1846 P 329-90 [Ces familles à St Georges] sont qualifiées du nom de Jacotards et mes recherches sur l'origine de ce mot ont été infructueuses.] [1847 Archives nationales, Colonies Série C11C. vol. 7b. (Mf. F-505 Pub. Arch. Canada) L'autre moitié [de 700] est composé de jacotars et de sauvages, les uns et les autres catholiques.] [1851] 1852 *Journ of Assembly* Appendix 110 [In 1841 about 250 protestants.] The Roman Catholics in [St George's] Bay [are] about half that number, they are a breed of French Canadians and Cape Breton people and called Jack-o-tars... There is a great quantity of eels and lobsters caught here, and in the winter the Jack-o-tars chiefly subsist on the eels; they are a lazy, indolent people, and I am told, addicted to thieving; in the winter and spring they are frequently in very destitute circumstances; they are looked upon by the English and French as a degraded race, thence styled Jack-o-tars or runaways. 1909 BROWNE 344 Ingernachoix, Point Riche and Garganelle are reminiscent of the Frenchman; and occasionally one sees along the coast 'jack-o-tars' (the name by which deserters from the French Navy are known in Newfoundland), who still wear the *sabot* and sport the Breton *casque*. 1961 ROULEAU 107 Jacotar Point [on outskirts of Sandy Point]. 1988 TIERNEY [10] [satiric extension] "The Mainlander's Ballad": You'll never make us be like you/You English Jackitars. [Mainland is a French settlement on the west coast of the Port au Port Peninsula.] 1988 *Sunday Express* 24 Apr, p. 2 He noted that in the forties francophones [in Nfld] suffered discrimination and were labelled 'Jackatars.' 1990 *Evening Telegram* 1 Mar, p. 28 In Newfoundland the French, for centuries living on the West Coast of the province, are still being referred to as Jackatars. (I'm not sure what the term means, but everybody agrees that it is not a term of endearment.)

jacket n Cp [1720] 1854 *Harper's New Monthly Mag* ix, 291 [N E] 'a coat warmer' for phr in sense 2: *a jacket colder*.

jam v
2 1986 *Evening Telegram* 22 Mar, p. 4 That occurred March 16 when the *Ungava* got jammed in ice during a raging storm. 1988 ibid 26 Mar, p. 31 [He] remembers using explosive powder cans...to help free ships when they were stuck or jammed in heavy ice.

jam n
1 Phr *jam of ice*.
1984 POWELL 159 And then I thought of Harry Morris back in his boat in a jam of ice off Ship Harbour Head.

janny n also **jannie**.
1982 BURSEY 37 "Christmas Fear": Another time/The black jannie appeared/In seven houses/ With no tree—/ Blacker than death he was. 1984 ROBERTSON xvii Other words are known as well as or instead of mummers or janneys.

janny v also **jenny**.
1 1982 BURSEY 36 "Christmas Fear": When we were

young/We went jannying at Christmas/Ransacked old trunks/And understairs closets/For outlandish rig. 1985 NEWHOOK 89 People went 'jennying' when darkness came. They would dress up in fearsome disguises.
2 Phr *janny up*.
1985 NEWHOOK 89 The twelve days...were taken up by a tradition known variously as 'jennying up,' 'mummering,' or 'dressing the fool.'

jannying vbl n
1920 *Deep Sea Fishers* xviii (1), 108 We encouraged 'Jannying,' the Christmas custom of mummery. 1987 *Evening Telegram* 3 Jan, p. 4 The practice of mummering, or jannying as it is also known to many, is particularly popular in communities along the Southern Shore, in Placentia, Fortune and St Mary's Bays.

japanese a also **jap**. Comb ~ **cod trap**. A modified type of box-shaped, stationary fishing net, 'knitted' with artificial fibre; see COD TRAP, TRAP[1] n 1.
1982 MCDOOLING 99 There are still a few [cod traps] being used but most of the fishermen have now gone over to the Japanese trap. The 'Jap' trap is more efficient in that it has a door which keeps the fish from swimming over the top of the walls and the entrance (the door of the Newfoundland trap) is funneled inward so that the fish, once they enter, cannot get out again as easily as...from the older model. 1990 *Evening Telegram* 14 Jan, p. 14 One of the biggest ruinations to the fishery is the Japanese cod trap. This trap is allowed to be made with all three and one half mesh so, you can imagine what small fish is caught...and thrown away.

jar[2] n Attrib ~ **skin**.
1984 KALLEO 8 To clean the dried jar skins, we'd take them up to the hill and slide on them.

jaw n *DBE, SED* iv, 673 jaw teeth, So Co D, for comb in sense 2.
2 Comb ~ **locked** (b), ~ **tooth**.
P 330-87 He went jawlocked. He couldn't talk. 1987 POWELL 42 My turn finally came. I told Dr Paddon that I wanted to have a jaw tooth pulled.

jersey n Attrib ~ **brig**: see **jersey ship**, ~ **people**: see ~ **man**.
[1833] 1984 BAYFIELD i, 252 Two Jersey Brigs with yards and topmasts struck lying here moored with nobody onboard of them... The Jersey people have two establishments on the West side of the bay [Forteau].

jib n *South Shore Phr Bk* for sense 1.
1 Also attrib ~ **spot**.
P 289-86 Jib spot: corner of a 'garden' or piece of ground. P 282-88 I've got a piece of land in behind Kelligrews, but the Highway Department won't let me use it. They say they need part of it for the [proposed] new road, but won't say how much—'only a jib' is what they say.

jig v
1 1981 MAJOR 34 'We'd always jig a nice many [squids], wouldn't we, Grandfather?' 1987 *Evening*

Telegram 4 July, p. 56 [tape transcript] There don't be very much fish in around [Indian Harbour] to jig after the trap season is over. [But at the White Bear Islands] they jigged their load of fish and when they got their load jug the stern of the boat was so close to the land that old Neddy Mulley...stood up on the counter of the boat and he jumped ashore. 1990 *Sunday Express* 14 Jan, p. 7 When the squid came, they came in such great numbers that you could jig them anywhere.

jig n
  3 1987 *Evening Telegram* 27 Apr, p. 7 [tape transcript] When the ship would arrive the men had to discharge the pelts. They had to throw them on a jig, an oldfashioned jig, and they were weighted on a swinging beam.

jigger n
  1 1987 *Evening Telegram* 4 July, p. 56 It was nine miles to what they called the Southard Point...they called it the Southard Point and they stopped and they put the jigger overboard and there were lots of fish there, and the biggest kind, right in on top of the rocks.

jigging vbl n
  1 Also: freq in place-names.
  1981 MAJOR 31 Talk about your fun, old man, when the jiggin's good. 1983 *Gazetteer of Canada: Nfld* 89 Jigging Cove [7 occurrences], Jigging Head, Jigging Point.
  2 Comb ~ **ground**, ~ **machine**: electronically operated device to catch cod on lines baited with artificial lures.
  1987 *Evening Telegram* 4 July, p. 56 There were a lot of good jigging grounds around the Bears [on Labrador]. 1987 *Nfld Herald* 17 Oct, p. 18 Fishing for a shoal of fish like cod requires one man and two jigging machines to land as big a catch as six men using manual methods. Earnings from fish caught by electronically controlled jigging machines are at least 25 per cent more per kilo, as they are of higher quality—the fish are alive when they reach the surface.

jinker n also **jinxer**.
  1 1980 JANES 16 "Salvage": He took me once as gaffer, but it seemed that I became a jinker to his trade:/ before we reached Oporto all his fish got waterlogged and not a cent was made. 1988 NADEL-KLEIN & DAVIS (eds) 217 [It is argued that] village exogamy [produces a] consequent...negative hostile [view] of women as polluters and jinxers.

jinxer See JINKER.

jit v
  1 P 314-83 Don't jit the table when I'm writing.

jog v
  [1889-93] 1987 PEYTON 24 After half passage out, the Masters of some of the smarter sailors [ships] got uneasy at the tedious work of jogging along and wished to get away from convoy. 1930 *Am Speech* v, 391 jog v. To keep a vessel into the wind, and under steerage way if

she is powered, when the weather is too rough to fish. 1988 *Evening Telegram* 21 Oct, p. 3 'You don't run from [storm force winds of 30-40 knots],' said a deepsea trawlerman. 'When it comes to blow, you just jog it out.'

joint n Attrib, comb ~ **wood**: 'white-wood' (*Viburnum trilobum*), ~ **wood berry**: 'white-wood berry' (*V. edule*).
  1985 DOMSTAD 21 Take a piece of joint wood [for cure for diarrhoea]. 1898 *J A Folklore* xi, 228 *Viburnum Opulus*, L. (perhaps other species), trash berry, jointwood berry, whitewood berry, Newfoundland.

jolly a Comb ~ **poker**.
  [1987] QUINLAN 18 The Newfoundlanders broke the dead lock and won the tug of war [with the English soldiers, in England, in WWI] by singing the "Jolly Poker."

jostler n
  1983 DAWE & FICKEN 28 J is for jostler,/A jowly old lad,/So rude in his manners,/He never seems glad.

jowler[2] n This term was often used as a name for a dog in the eighteenth century: *OED*; 'Tommy Trip and His Dog Jowler' (1752 chapbook).
  1985 BUSCH 77 It is no wonder that given a choice sealers went with the lucky ship and the lucky captains, the real 'jowlers' who were more likely to be 'highliner' of the fleet.

jump v
  1 1984 KALLEO 35 Children jump ice-pans at the shore. They're learning skills that they will need as hunters.

jumper n Also: transf in local name for inhabitant of Fogo Island.
  1986 SAUNDERS 60 I recalled that all my life I had heard people jokingly called 'Fogo Jumpers.' Now I knew why. Compared to Fogo, Clarke's Head was Sleepy Hollow.

juniper n
  2 1984 POWELL 35 It was always the rule among the people to have big, dry juniper for Christmas; I used to climb up by the side of the hill and cut down those big dry juniper trees, as big around as barrels.

junk n
  1 1987 KING (ed) 115 "Whispers": gossipy jolly kids/fathers sawing junks/or cracking them for splits/in whistling winds.
  2 [1927] 1982 BURKE (ed Kirwin) 72 "Cadwell the Chaw": He speaks of the meat, they must boil it in junks,/The neig[h]bors they use it for hinges for trunks.
  5 Phr *a cold junk*: of one knocked unconscious.
  T 735-70 Buddy jump up an' grabbed an axe up an' let 'em have it!... Over the wall at bottom o' garden, one o' th' ol' hardwood axes. He made that a cold junk. He was no good to his wife afterwards! 1987 *Nfld Qtly* lxxxii (4), p. 10 The witch hazel [stick] cracked the desperado across the skull and he was out, a cold junk.

K

kedgy n also **kedgie, ketchie.**

1985 *Evening Telegram* 21 Jan, p. 6 [Banking vessel crews] frequently included a youth who was planning to become a Banks fisherman. [One of the] youth's job[s] was to stand by to catch the painter or line attached to a dory's bow and stern, whichever was closest to hand— hence the term 'ketchie.' 1987 FIZZARD 164 'When Pop and they were cook they used to have a little kedgie, a young boy for helping out the cook... He was taken on as kedgie on Father's schooner [and] Johnny used to go up on the deck to throw out the slop bucket or something like that.'

keel-log See KILLICK.

keg n also **cag.**

1 Also comb ~ **buoy.**

1984 KELLAND 180 In addition to the four tubs of trawl, each dory was required to carry two anchors...a bait jack (tub to hold bait), two keg buoys, one of these also was attached to each end of the trawl. 1987 POOLE 69 I have 17 grapnels and mooring buoys and cags and four chain shore fasts out there in that ice jam.

key n Comb ~**-foot**: red-necked grebe (*Podiceps grisegena holböllii*); SPRAW-FOOT (1987 MONTE-VECCHI & TUCK 233).

keylock* See KILLICK.

khaki n Comb ~ **dodger**: small bun or biscuit with molasses as an ingredient.

1986 NARVÁEZ 59 They used to make those little buns or biscuits...and one kind they used molasses in them. They called those the 'khaki dodgers' then you know. And the other kind, they used sugar. They were light... They used to call them 'square sets' and 'khaki dodgers.'

kick v Phr *kick the cod*: see COD[1].

kicking vbl n Comb ~ **stick** (see quot.).

1985 *Terminology of Loggers* 9 Each row of beds in the bunkhouse was a single long frame as wide as a man is tall; individual sleeping space was made by laying long sticks, called kicking sticks, crosswise along the bunk.

kill v Cp the similar neutral hunting usage in "A Dictionary of Alaskan English" (in press) p. 162: 'Many Alaska Natives use the transitive verb *catch* to mean "successfully hunt (such and such an animal)".'

1 To catch or harvest fish, sea-birds, or seals.

[1620] 1895 PROWSE [Mason] 106-7 Cods so thicke...I have killed of them with a pike; of these three men to sea in a boat with some on shoare to dress and dry them in 30 days will kill commonlie betwixt 25 and 30,000, worth. [1623] 1982 CELL (ed) 176 Whitbourne's *Discourse*: 40. persons fit for such a voyage...vsually kill aboue twenty fiue thousand fish for euery boat. 1626

VAUGHAN 3rd part, p. 24 I knew one Fowler in a winter, which killed aboue 700. Partridges himselfe at *Renoos*. [1890] 1986 GOUDIE 26 One crew stays on board ship to handle her and hoist aboard the pelts. Then one crew were killing, one taking off pelts, and one hauling the pelts to the pan. 1986 FELTHAM 71 Towards the end of May, some fishermen periodically made trips to the outer banks to try for cod, and at the same time, kill a meal or two of 'bawks.' 1987 MONTEVECCHI & TUCK 36 Newfoundlanders who used to 'go to the ice' to kill Harp Seals in spring often took along...tubes [made from bird bones] to drink from fresh water pools on the ice.

kill n Activity of hunting seals.

[1890] 1986 GOUDIE 26 The next morning the master watchs and their men were over the side for another kill.

killick n also **keel-log, kellock, keylock*.** G. PULMAN, *Rambles, Roamings, and Recollections* (London, 1870) p. 135 kellick 'local name [in Lyme Regis, Do] for the stone used as an anchor for fishing boats'; *Anglo-Manx Dialect* 98 'In oul' times the boat would be anchored with a wooden kellagh that had a big stone in it to sink it'; *AND* kellick (1867-1962); Burton Bradstock, Do 'large stone picked off the beach used as an anchor (P 304-90).

1 1680 CO 1/45 (68i), 252, v 'They launcht a new shalloway from the Adm[ira]lls place & put the rest of theire provisions into her & moord her with 2 kcylocks.' 1688 CO 1/22, 66 [The English fishermen upon the ledges] for feare of being surprized (not then knoweing what the shipp really was) weighed their killicks and came into harbour. 1832 MOSS *MS Diary* 20 Apr Capt. Frederick and myself walked down to the Killick stand. 1836 WIX 82 We came to ice, at the edge of which persons were engaged in boats, fastened to the ice by keel-logs, catching codfish. 1981 SPARKES xv The 'kellock' or 'killick'... was a simple, home-made anchor for nets and, sometimes, for small punts. 1983 *Gazetteer of Undersea Feature Names* 104, 105 Kellick Shoal, Killick Ledge, Killock Shoal. 1987 O'FLAHERTY 50 At Ferryland he was given a large replica of a killick, made by a local craftsman, to take back to St John's.

killing n Harvest (of seals); hunt (for seals).

[1891] 1986 GOUDIE 28 The Captain forced his ship into the ice pack and put his men out on the ice for a big killing.

kirby* n also **curby.**

[1936] 1984 ASHTON 200 "Lumbering Woods in the 30's": Some had beef and butter and flour by the stone,/Mat[t]ress, pillow, curbies, each man had his own.

kit n *OED* kitten sb 1 b (1899). The young of a beaver.

[c1960] P 148-90 Twelve beaver two of which are tiny kits not much larger than a muskrat although they were caught in the late fall.

kitchen n Attrib ~ **parlour (pot)**: lobster trap with three compartments (P 127-89); see PARLOUR

POT; ~ **string**: thin line of twisted fibre of the kind used to tie parcels.

1986 *Evening Telegram* 4 Apr, p. 4 [At Little Seldom, NDB] the words On Strike are scrawled on a small cardboard sign dangling by kitchen string from the gate outside the [marine service] centre.

knap n
1 1983 *Gazetteer of Canada: Nfld* 64 George Deers Nap. 1987 FIZZARD 141 [They] built a new citadel in the Cow Knap area [of Grand Bank].

knit v Cp PRATT ~ v 'to knot twine for the mesh pieces on a lobster trap' (1957-).
1 1986 FELTHAM 59 In a fishing community, every boy and most girls learned to knit twine during their early teens. 1987 POOLE 17 I'd get my work all done for the day, and after supper get my school books and spend a while studying them, and then start knitting twine. 1990 *Evening Telegram* 14 Jan, p. 14 I've bought the twine, knit it, made cod-traps, caught cod fish, dried it, and exported it.

knitting vbl n
2 Attrib **knitting-needle**: implement designed to hold a quantity of 'twine' and used to knot meshes in a fish-net; see NEEDLE.

knob n
2 Also: freq a good 'spot' for fishing.
1986 FELTHAM 125 A 'nob' was a very tiny fishing spot.
3 Also: a chunk of frozen snow or ice; CLUMPER.
1984 POWELL 78 The trail was very rough because there had been a mild a few days before, and the big knobs of snow were in the trail, frozen like rocks... On the very next step I struck one of those knobs of ice with my snowshoe and knocked my ankle right out of place.
5 1987 FIZZARD 194 My mind was set in motion, trying to determine if I could find a copper or two or manage to plead a 5-cent piece out of my mother. If not, I might be able to get one copper for two peppermint knobs from his shop.

komatik n also **cometic, koamatic, komatic**. The standard Inuit spelling is QAMUTIK.
1 1885 TUTTLE 53 With his dogs and skin-covered koamatic, Mr Ford makes winter trips for two or three hundred miles...gathering furs. 1982 MCDOOLING 68 The men would go after [moose and caribou] in the late fall or early winter when the komatiks could be used to transport the meat and when it was cold enough to keep it frozen. 1984 POWELL 38 We had to haul more flour on this trip and the kamutik, which pulled easier than the toboggan.
2 Attrib ~ **box**, ~ **side**.
1984 POWELL 85 Through the seams in the logs I could still see Uncle Alex sitting out on the kamutik box, so I thought this was no place for a patient that needed care. 1987 POOLE 17 The first week in April my dad was using a pit saw to cut a set of komatic sides.

kork n See CORK n, v.

kursheen* n Cp DINNEEN croisín 'small cross... crutch.' A wooden stilt for a child (P 327-87).

L

labrador n also **larberdore**.
1 Esp in phr *the Labrador*.
[1787] 1984 BYRNE (ed) 63 The Apostate Lonergan is gone of[f] I am told to the coasts of the Labrador. 1903 *Deep Sea Fishers* Oct, p. 4 [Visions come and go] of the hundred and one things that go to make up 'life on the Larberdore.' 1988 *Evening Telegram* 18 June, p. 12 [tape transcript] My father, Patrick Russell, fished on the Labrador when he was only a young man.
2 Attrib ~ **cure**, ~ **merchantable**: see MERCHANTABLE.
[1829] 1845 *Journ of Assembly*, Appendix 227 Labrador merchantable [fish]. 1985 GUY 45 Strung up like a draft of Labrador cure in a derrick, she is. 1987 *Evening Telegram* 27 Apr, p. 7 Fish was packed in half-drums, drums, casks, donkeys, and various kinds of barrels... A cask held four quintals of dry or five quintals of Labrador.
3 In name of animal: ~ **otter**.
1983 SOUTH (ed) 537 The Newfoundland otter and the Labrador otter differ more from one another than either does from the race occurring on the mainland of eastern Canada, suggesting that the Newfoundland race is derived from animals that emigrated to the island from the Maritime Provinces.
5 Attrib, comb ~ **box**: home-made wooden box used by Newfoundland fishermen for personal effects on seasonal voyages to Labrador, ~ **current**, ~ **fishery**, ~ **schooner**, ~ **speech**: see NEWFOUNDLAND DIALECT.
1983 PEDDLE 96 Blanket boxes with attached handles to make them portable were referred to by different names depending upon where they were used. For example, the boxes that the fishermen took with them when they fished for cod in summer off the coast of Labrador were called Labrador boxes. 1983 SOUTH (ed) 37 Although the mild Gulf Stream-North Atlantic Drift ocean current system is encountered some 600-700 km southeast of the island, it is the Labrador Current, forming an encircling ribbon of cold ex-Arctic water, that is responsible for many features of Newfoundland climate and weather. 1987 POWELL 16 He told me that he had always liked the Labrador fishery [and] how they fished in a little cove called Indian Bight in the mouth of Alexis Bay. 1986 FELTHAM 52 The Labrador schooner evolved [as larger vessels were needed for the northern fishery, and] in the main, they were a rag-tag assortment of vessels, varying greatly in size, style and rig. 1987 *Evening Telegram* 31 May, p. 11 Leaning over him was an unshaven but most welcome face which introduced itself in lilting Labrador speech.

labrador dog n also **labrador**. *O Sup*^{2} ~ (1829-) for sense 1.

1 1865 [CAMPBELL] 59 The small smooth black Labrador dog is not so much valued [as the Newfoundland dog]. 1883 HATTON & HARVEY 232 The Labrador, or St John's, or Lesser Newfoundland. 1907 MILLAIS 145 The best dogs are of the 'Labrador' type. In winter they are used for hauling logs—one dog will haul 2 or 3 cwt.

labradorian n   also **labradorean**.
1986 *Nat Geog* clxix, p. 697 For Labradoreans as for the salmon, survival in coastal Labrador is a seasonal struggle.

labradorite n
1 1986 *Evening Telegram* 5 Apr, p. 4 The properties of the stone make Labradorite desirable as building material, being three times harder and denser than marble.

labradorman n
1 1985 *Nfld Qtly* lxxx (4), 31 They were beginning to speak of themselves with pride as Labradormen, something quite different from Newfoundlanders or Liveyeres, and at last Doctor Paddon's hope that they might achieve some feeling of political and economic entity was beginning to bear fruit.

labrador tea n
1 A low-growing evergreen of the genus *Ledum* (*L. groenlandicum*), the bruised leaves of which can be steeped for a beverage.
1981 SPARKES x If the supply of molasses ran out they had to do without, but when tea was scarce, that was stretched out with Labrador tea... It grew plentifully everywhere and some leaves were always dried for the winter.

lace v
1986 FELTHAM 165 They 'laced' their seals with their hauling ropes and after a quick snack from their knapsacks set out on their return journey.

lad n   Comb **lad-in-a-bag** (P 293-83).

lady stick See **lazy stick**.

lake n   Phr *lake of water*.
1984 POWELL 130 We could see one lake of water that ran from Soddy Island out in the bay.

lamb n   *EDD* ~ sb 2 (3) (a). Comb **lamb's ears**: the woolly woundwort (*Stachys lanata*).
1986 *Atlantic Insight* Feb, p. 44 For all that, 'Jesus flannel' or 'lambs ears' as we used to call it does more than *Stachys lanata* to evoke those old cottage gardens.

lammy n   Also attrib ~ **coat**: fleece-lined coat.
1977 MOAKLER 102 As nor'west winds came rustling on the seas/...Piercing our lammy-coats like winter gales!

lance n
1 1984 KELLAND 115 He [picked] up a baiting of lancelet, comm[on]ly called lance by Newfoundland fishermen. This diminutive fish...somewhat resembles a female caplin, only it is tinier. 1988 *Evening Telegram*

29 Apr, p. 6 I have watched hundreds, maybe thousands of those [sea]birds fly by on the way to their nest. There would not be a caplin within a hundred miles; their bill of fare would be lance or, as some call them, whitefish.

lanch v
1 1986 SAUNDERS 262 One time we were launching a house from Victoria Cove to Clarke's Head, a distance of five miles. It was...a big two-story house [and] there was nearly two hundred of us gathered there, and several horses. 1989 *Evening Telegram* 19 Aug, p. A8 There might be three or four houses open for men to launch.

lanching vbl n
1 The activity of hauling or pushing (a boat or vessel) over the ice; moving a house over the ground or across a body of water. Cp LANCH v.
[1937] 1983 FROUDE 8 We leaved in the morning and after a long days lanching and pulling [the boat] over the ice we got in harbour round and found the people there very kind.

landing n   Cp BROW.
1987 *Nfld LifeStyle* June, p. 18 In early logging operations, the cut wood was hauled from the cutting area to a landing on the river bank by horse, after the first major snowfall of the season.

landsman n
2 A migratory fisherman from Newfoundland or a permanent resident who fishes from a shore station on the Labrador coast.
1982 JACKSON 67 Longliners come down from Newfoundland... You'd go out there one day and get a couple of quintals of fish and then the next day it's just as well for the landsman to stay home, because the longliners will come down and throw all their nets around, and what's the inshoreman gonna do then?
3 Also attrib ~ **hunt**: SEAL HUNT, ~ **sealer**: SEALER[1] n.
1988 *Atlantic Co-operator* Feb, p. 14 They won't interfere with the landsmen hunt. 1988 ibid p. 13 The [federal ban on large vessels] will have a positive effect for our co-operative, which is made up of landsmen sealers, who hunt from shore-based small boats and longliners.

landwash n
1981 MAJOR 10 To where I could still see the salt water slapping up on the landwash. 1985 *Nfld Qtly* lxxx (4), 40 [The houses] were all flat-topped and clapboarded and their backs rubbed up against the cliff to make room for the road that snaked along on the lee side of the beach, copying the route of the landwash. 1987 POWELL 26 I cut everything for my stage and hauled it to the landwash to have it ready for my boat when the bay ice melted.

lap n   Comb ~ **rock**.
1987 DAWE [30] L is for lap rock/To warm up your bed/On raw winter nights/When Jack Frost weaves his thread.

large a

1 Also: commercially marketable salt-water fish (cod, salmon) of a specified size in fresh condition.

[1978] 1985 LEHR & BEST (eds) 74 "The *Gigantic*": 'Twas five miles up the river our load we did discharge;/One half our fish was small, my boys, the other half was large. 1986 *Evening Telegram* 26 Apr, p. A10 Salmon spending two or three years at sea are called 'large salmon.' 1987 ibid 17 Mar, p. 4 Fishermen will receive...9 cents [per pound for] large and medium [codfish] (over 17 inches to 26 inches). 1990 ibid 14 Jan, p. 14 Fifty-two casks were medium and large fish. Where would you get this today?

larrigan n

1985 ASHTON 181 "Hurling Down the Pine": We all arrived at the shanty, cold hands and wet feet,/We then pull off our larrigans, our suppers for to eat.

last a Phr *last going off, on the last of it, (on) the last shove-off*. Cp FIRST: *first going off*.

P 245-89 At the last going off 'twas the road that made the difference. T 309-66 On the last of it he decided he would. He'd stay and marry her. P 148-86 The last shove off—'in the end.'

lay n Cp *OED* ~ sb⁷ 8 'a share in a venture, esp in whaling' (1850-98). In the seafishery the agreement between owner and crew on the allotment of the profit of a trip; cp SHARE: *on shares*.

1930 *Am Speech* v, 391 ~ the relationship or agreement between vessel-owners and fishermen with regard to the proportionate share of each in the catch. The *lays* of every type of vessel are different.

lazy a

1 Phr *lazy man's load*.

1988 DOHANEY 17 She looked at the armload of food Vince was carrying and sniped, 'Lazy man's load as always.'

2 Comb: also **lady stick**.

1949 FITZGERALD 85 Two helves of picks, for lazy sticks, we broke, with no solution. 1985 ASHTON 122 [We used] what we called a 'lazy stick,' or a 'lady stick.' Two fellows get down, sit on the floor and test of strength it was.

lead² n Cp *AND* ~² 2 'route followed by travelling stock' (1962-) for sense 2.

1 1984 WRIGHT 41 The mate now stood in the 'barrel'...atop the main mast, searching for leads in the ice, weak places or open water where the ship could push through.

2 1984 POWELL 63 After going a few hundred yards I struck good open leads that took me to the big caribou marsh. 1986 *Sunday Express* 14 Dec, p. 36 The rabbits travel on trails—runways or 'leads' as we commonly call them, which are pathways through the forest and underbrush.

leader n

1 1984 POWELL 85 He said that we had a good leader

and we could depend on her as she would remember the trail from coming north the first time.

2 [1894] 1977 WHITELEY 52 [Fishing Regulations] Each cod leader to extend from shore. 1989 *Evening Telegram* 4 Mar, p. 4 One day in particular we tried to raise the leader of our cod trap but we were forced to give up; it was on the bottom of the ocean full of dogfish.

leaf n

1986 FELTHAM 64 The inshore fishermen had to replace some of their nets every year and the Labrador schoonermen had to knit many 'leaves' of 'linnet' to replace rotten or badly torn parts of their traps.

lean-to n Cp BOUGH WHIFFEN, ~ WHIFFET.

1986 SAUNDERS 151 We had to make in a fire for light, and put up a bough lean-to with stuff we cut handy. We used to have several lean-tos or whiffets like that every ten miles or so.

ledge n

1896 *Evening Herald* 19 July About Grate's Cove there is no fish, and none to be seen on the various ledges. 1902 *Daily News* 25 July, [p. 4] A petition was hawked around Petty Harbor for the purpose of having some rule to prevent a codnet being placed on the ledges [of the harbour]. 1983 WARNER 25 In many places, just outside the churn of the surf, were rocky half-tide ledges—'sunkers,' they call them in Newfoundland's lugubrious maritime vocabulary—on which the seas broke heavily. Those who set their pots as close as they dared to the sunkers, it seemed to me, got the most lobsters. 1986 FELTHAM 125 A 'ledge' was a large fishing area with a long straight edge.

leggy n

1986 SAUNDERS 132 I would jig a few meals of fresh cod and bring back a bag of smoked caplin and salted rounders or leggies to enjoy in the winter.

lesser newfoundland n A strong, short-haired dog; LABRADOR DOG, WATER DOG.

1883 HATTON & HARVEY 232 [The other type of Newfoundland dog is] named the Labrador, or St John's, or Lesser Newfoundland.

limb v Phr *limb out*; also transf: to remove everything; to empty.

1981 SPARKES 173 Loggers would go every morning to the woods and fell trees with great, double-bladed axes called 'double bitters.' One blade was tempered for chopping and the other for 'limbing out' the fallen tree. P 298-83 When we got to the store the place was limbed out.

line² n Cp *AND* ~ 1 line of road (1828-), 2 ~ (1837-); *Names* xxxvi (1988) 46, for a different sense of *line* in U S roads.

2 1985 JOHNSTON 40 There was an ongoing feud when I was eight between the Pond and the Line—The Line was the road along which the houses of the old town were situated, and which had to be crossed to get to the Pond. 1986 *Evening Telegram* 3 Apr, p. 6 We...are writing this letter regarding the Line Road connecting Heart's Delight to Carbonear.

line v Phr *line off*.
1985 *Nfld Qtly* lxxxi (2), 36 His cart was always 'lined off' with people hitching a ride to and from Bonavista and numerous packages were transferred as well.

link n
1 1986 SAUNDERS 283 A lynx ('link') house was built to shelter the trap & entice the lynx.

linnet n
1 1986 FELTHAM 64 The Labrador schoonermen had to knit many 'leaves' of 'linnet' to replace rotten or badly torn parts of their traps.

linny n Cp *SED* iv, 173 So Co D for sense 1.
1 Revised def: storage shed or structure attached to the back of a dwelling; PORCH.
2 Comb ~ **yard**: back-yard.
[1835] 1985 *Evening Telegram* 11 Nov, p. 6 [*Royal Gazette*: For Sale at Brigus, a property including] Cooper's shop, linhay yard and quay.

little a
1 Phr *little small*. Also: slender, narrow.
T 283-66 He cut a long pole about forty feet long; little small stick like you would see in the woods.

liver[1] n
3 Comb ~ **butt**: BUTT[1] n.
1984 KELLAND 152 Then other heavy equipment had to be lugged aboard, such as chocks for the liver butts to rest in; those liver butts were large puncheons.

livyer n *MED* liver(e n. (2): (c1378) [*Piers Plowman*] var lyuyers, (?a1425) [*Secreta Secretorum*] lyuyeres; *Trans Dev Assoc* xi (1879) 136, and references in lxiv (1932), 179.
1 [1976] 1985 LEHR & BEST (eds) 57 "The *Elsie M. Hart*": At daybreak there that morning, to their surprise and joy./They saw by their surroundings, some livyers they were nigh. 1987 *Evening Telegram* 10 Oct, p. 11 In the case of our...inshore fishermen, we must develop a modern version of the old 'livyer.' Why shouldn't Newfoundland[ers] be allowed to own, for instance, hundred acre woodlots?
2 1910 MOUBRAY [title] *Notes...for the Use of Fishermen and Liviers More Particularly in Labrador*. 1915 *Deep Sea Fishers* xii (4), 137 The liveyers, or half breed natives. 1924 ibid xxi (4), 138 Liviers—All year round inhabitants of the Labrador coast—akin to stationers.

loader n
1 1985 ASHTON 181 "Hurling Down the Pine": The next comes in is the loaders, all at the break of day,/Load up your sled five-hundred feet, to the river right away.

local a
1989 CANDOW 15-6 Since harp seals prefer 'local' ice (ice formed off Labrador) to the heavier arctic ice farther out to sea favoured by the hoods, access to the inside cut was crucial to the success of the hunt.

loft n
2 1837 *Royal Gazette* 5 Dec [advertisement] A store, 100′ by 30, and 18′ to wall plate...the loft being commodiously divided and fitted in suitable compartments for sails, nets, etc.

log n Comb ~ **tilt**.
1984 POWELL 64 Some day someone would find me in my little log tilt and would never know the cause of my death.

log v *DC* ~ v 2 obs (1897) for sense 2.
2 1984 POWELL 69 I took my big axe and the bucksaw and in one half day I had enough logs cut up to log up the walls [of the tilt].

logan n
1 1984 GOUGH 74 His logans were loose on his feet and he could feel the new young wood press against the side of his feet. 1986 SAUNDERS 142 For footgear we had either sealskin boots greased with cod oil or the newer rubber boots with leather tops, which we called logans.

logy a
1 1987 POWELL 122 When a fisherman cast his fly on the water, he just didn't know what to expect—a fighting salmon or a big logy codfish.
2 1989 *Evening Telegram* 23 May, p. 5 Three days out of [Gibraltar the vessel] was overtaken by a strong north-easter and her reaction was logy and she yawed heavily. Worse she began to leak.
3 1986 SAUNDERS 147 On logy days with no wind [smoke from the fire] hung at shoulder level when you stood up, enough to sting your eyes.

long a *South Shore Phr Bk* hungry March.
2 Phr *long and hungry month of March*.
1924 ENGLAND 66 Morning again, the eleventh of 'de lang, hungry March month.' T 247-66 That's what the sayin' was: 'the hungry month o' March.' T 526-68 'When he came home in the fall the year, he gave his wife a barrel of flour to put away. She said, "What's this for? Why put it away?" "Well" he said, "for the long and hungry month of March".' 1988 *Nfld Qtly* lxxxiv (2), 16 Jenny and Walter were married in late March, the long and hungry month when winter has not made up its mind to leave, nor spring to appear.
3 Comb ~ **cart**, ~**-liner**.
1985 *A Yaffle of Yarns* 124 For [paths which] could only be used on foot in summer could have traffic jams in winter with dog teams and pony and slide, or long carts and sledges pulled by man or beast. 1985 *Evening Telegram* 18 Dec, p. 1 Longliners are vessels that set nets that fish swim into rather than drag[g]ing nets as trawlers do.

longer n PRATT longer fence for comb in sense 2.
1 1839 ENGLAND *MS Journal* 2 Feb He was on the sleigh...coming furiously down the hill. One of the lungers in the garden fence pierced his belly. 1984 GOUGH 59 The last of the longers that made up the fence

have fallen down and they are grey, even the rot is grey and no longer the surprise of brown or gold rot. 1986 FELTHAM 44 [The flake] consisted of large beams, shored up in horizontal positions, eight or ten feet apart and topped with 'longers' arranged as near together as possible.

loodle-laddle* n also **doodle-daddle***.

1990 *Sunday Express* 11 Feb, p. 7 'We're not sayin' we can rattle [French] off like a Dago with his doodle-addle cotch up in a capstan.' P 266-90 If my children ask me something and I want to tell them to mind their own business, I say I'm making a doodle-daddle.

loose a

1 1984 POWELL 158 Then we made slow progress through loose ice until we got almost to Ship Harbour Head. 1986 FELTHAM 97 The skill demonstrated by Newfoundland seal hunters in travelling over loose ice was undoubtedly developed while 'copying'...over the harbour pans in their teen-age play.

lop² n

1 1989 *Nfld Qtly* lxxxiv (4), 12 Bone-chilling cold; cold northwest winds, not too much lop.

loppy a *South Shore Phr Bk*.

1986 SAUNDERS 21 The Bay never seemed to get very loppy.

lord² n *South Shore Phr Bk* lords and ladies.

1988 *Evening Telegram* 26 Mar, p. 28 The birds are Harlequin Ducks, widely known as 'lords and ladies,' and there are likely fewer than a thousand left in eastern North America.

lose v Cp SAVE: *save one's year*.

1 In form *loss*.

1858 [LOWELL] i, 186 On'y two tarrible heavy blows on the same place,—that's lossing 'er before, an' now, agen, lossin' that false, foolish hope. 1949 FITZGERALD 47 'Young fella boy! Don't loss it.' T 1063-72 'Well now,' she said, 'I'll fit ya out once more.' She said, 'And if you losses it this time,' she said, 'that's all I can do for ya.'

2 Phr *lose one's spring/summer/year*: to have an unsuccessful sealing or fishing season.

[1896] SWANSBOROUGH 34 "The Seal Fishery": They've been kept outside the ice,/And been driven southward twice;/Have lost a topmast or a yard,/Have lost their spring, and think it hard. 1937 DEVINE 33 Lose one's spring (summer, fall or winter). To be out of employment during the season named, or to come off with a loss or poorly from the season's work. ibid 63 A sealer applied for a job in a factory and gave the boss as his reason for coming from Newfoundland to look for work that he had *lost his Spring*... The applicant 'was out to the seal fishery with Skipper Sam Blandford in March and April and got no seals.' 1964 *Evening Telegram* 28 Mar, p. 6 The fishermen found, however, that if the sealing season was late, they could not get off to the Banks in time and were in danger of losing their spring. 1612 *Willoughby Papers* 1/15, 11 I have loussed my tyme this summer. [1919] P 124-71 To proceed at once

would cause these humble folk to lose their summer at the fishery. 1967 *Bk of Nfld* iv, 237 People who through illness 'lost their summer' would be looked after by the more fortunate. [1979] 1985 LEHR & BEST (eds) 84 "Gull Cove": But if the codfish fades away as it often done before,/We could lose our year in Gull Cove, where the stormy winds do blow.

lovyer n

1982 BURSEY 25 "Lovyer's Lep": Now visitors are taken to the spot/And gaze and gape and shudder at the tale,/Then turn away and hurry to their cars—/From what is known no more as Pitcher's Hole/But, in the local parlance, Lovyer's Lep.

low a Comb **low-lifed**.

1988 NADEL-KLEIN & DAVIS (eds) 224 Women who let someone 'walk all over you,' a wife who lets her husband do 'just as he wants' and is afraid 'to put her foot down' is called 'low-lifed.'

lum n

1986 FELTHAM 49 [The] 'scull-oar' [was] about twelve feet long with a gentle bend in the wash and a thole-pin about two feet from the 'lum.'

lumber n Comb **~ agent**: one who arranged contracts for the cutting of forest areas, **~-woods**, **lumbering ~**.

[1898] 1985 GOSSE 15 [list of occupations] McDonald, Richard lumber agent. [1939] 1983 FROUDE 5 french shore and labradore/tilt cove and copper ore. lumber woods and camps and bogs. 1986 SAUNDERS 74 Most Gander Bay men were away to work, either on the Exploits main drive if it was in the spring, or a shareman on a codtrap crew down Change Islands way, or in the lumberwoods cutting pulp for the A.N.D. Company. 1985 ASHTON 195 I'll bid adieu to the lumbering woods, the pulpwood and the pine.

lump n

1 Also attrib **~ roe** (P 147-88).

T 1827-75 But when they fired un overboard he... pitched fair on a lump's back. Well this lump, we'll say, come on with un and land un on the land.

3 Also comb **~ boot**.

1985 *Terminology of Loggers* 12 Lump boots. Short rubber boots worn in winter, sometimes in summer.

lumper n

1 1984 KELLAND 157 There was...one way in which a doryman who desired a visit with his family could be granted time off. That was if he hired a lumper to take his place. Lumpers were young boys or youths who, glad of the opportunity to make a few cents, would hire themselves out to any doryman who took shore leave.

lun n also **lunn**.

1924 *Deep Sea Fishers* xxi (4), 139 Lunn—The sheltering side of an island. 1984 POWELL 86 [The snow] was blowing around the house and then lodging in the lund [of] the house. 1988 *Evening Telegram* 21 Mar, p. 6

There were no inlets, not even a point of land to form a 'lun' that would allow a smooth landing to be made.

lun a
1984 POWELL 31 We were far enough ahead that it would be easier to try and get through Ship's Tickle and then make it up under the White Fish Island. We would have it lund until we got to Narrows Islands. 1985 *A Yaffle of Yarns* 134 We would go to some uninhabited cove, keeping on the lun side of the island and spend the afternoon swimming or berry picking.

lunch n *SED* iv, 867 So W D Do Ha for sense 1.
1 1924 *Deep Sea Fishers* xxi (4), 139 [A mug-up is a] mid-morning lunch consisting usually of bread and molasses-sweetened tea. 1983 FROUDE 7 Now when we landed on the island we were tired and hungry wet and cold so we got a warm lunch and a spill. 1987 POOLE 30 As they were just leaving to go down to dinner, the storekeeper asked us over to his house to get a lunch.
2 [1889] 1983 FROUDE 33 You could come in any time of the night and git a lunch. T 978-71 But anyhow there was this ol' feller took un in for the night an' give un a lunch, an' he told un his story.
3 Attrib ~ **ground**: in a logging camp, an area outdoors where tea and a light repast were served (1985 *Terminology of Loggers* 3).

lunch v To partake of a light repast, or 'lunch,' between any of the main meals.
1984 POWELL 43 From so many trappers lunching up at Clifty Lake the wood close to the lake was all cut down.

M

machine n Also: any unusual or unfamiliar object (1924 *Deep-Sea Fishers* xxi (4), 139).
1861 DE BOILIEU 3-4 With a heavy load [on the woodmen's] backs, I have seen them slide down [on homemade skis] erect, and at almost railway speed. I must confess I was foolish enough to try my skill with a pair of these machines on my feet, and was rewarded with a bound of about ten feet down the hill, with sundry bruises for my pains. 1903 *Deep Sea Fishers* Apr, p. 12 [of a thermometer] 'That's a cute little machine, ma'am; what's it fer?' 'To tell me how hot your body is,' replied the Sister. 1987 POWELL 22 'You better put that machine to work. We are among the grass that does not belong on this island.' Mr Brazil set up [his outfit, a machine that could determine minerals].

mad a
3 Intens: very.
1975 BUTLER 113 By the time we had everything secured it was night and blowing a gale and mad rough.

madeira n
1986 RYAN xxi-xxii Brazil bought the medium-quality fish, *Madeira*, which was light-salted, well-dried, and hard, and eighteen inches and under in length... The [designation] *Madeira*...referred to the quality, not the market.

maggoty a
[(1693) 1987 WILLIAMS 45 Capt Christian Lilly's sketchmap of St John's Harbour. Sept. 1693 [showing] Magotts Cove.]

maid n *SED* iv, 925 'girl' So W Co D Do.
1 1983 FROUDE 212 Supreme they rule oer welling hearts/the maids and wives of newfoundland. 1984 GOUGH 49 'Maud, my maid, what would he want with a place like this? Less he floats it up to Toronto on barrels.'

main a Comb ~ **patch**, ~ **warp**: on a deep-sea trawler, the wire rope that connects net to the vessel (1986 *Nfld's Deepsea Fishery* 650).
1985 BUSCH 43 The 'main patch' [of harp seals] may be over 300 miles from St John's or, more rarely, may be so close as to be worked from land.

make v
1 1981 SPARKES 187 After a period in 'salt bulk,' the fish had to be washed by hand with mops and brushes; then it had to be 'made.' 1986 FELTHAM 88 If the inshore fishery was poor or if the greater part of the catch was already cured, the wives of the inshore fishermen [in Bonavista Bay] agreed to 'make' varying amounts of Labrador cod for a fixed rate.
2 1986 SAUNDERS 81 So in late November month, when the ice was making hard on the ponds and coves, we loaded our gear and grub for a month on a slide and took off.
4 Phr *make away with*, ~ *in (a fire)*: to prepare and kindle a fire.
1981 MAJOR 14 And the gun rack me and Dad done up last year. Every other bloody thing was made away with. T 1827-75 Jack made in a fire, you know, and they'd boiled their kettle and they're started eatin'. 1986 SAUNDERS 151 We had to make in a fire for light, and put up a bough lean-to with stuff we cut handy.

mamateek n
1988 GALE [2] Sooshewan...could hear her father... moving around the mamateek, taking his bow and arrows and harpoon down from their hanging places.

man n Often preceded by terms like AMERICAN, NAKED, ROCKY. A certain pinnacle lined up with another land feature in order to locate a fishing ground or 'berth'; MARK 1.
1842 JUKES ii, 98 We anchored under the headland between Freshwater Bay and Cat Bay, and climbed up Man Point Ridge. 1987 O'FLAHERTY 41 Little Bank had been one of Abe Foley's berths in his great days of cod fishing. John recalled his father's precise naming of the marks for the shoal: to the north, Peg's Tolt between the spires of Northern Bay church; to the west, the top of the spire of Broad Cove church in line with the 'man' on Western Bay Point.

manus v

1914 *Daily Mail* [London] 20 Apr, p. 4 Last year when the *Diana* was coaling from the *Nascapie* in the ice floe the *Diana*'s crew gave trouble...while the *Erik*'s crew manussed and compelled the captain to land them at Bonavista; while in 1911 and 1912 the *Diana*'s crew did the same and the voyage had to be abandoned. P 13-89 ~ to attack or gang up on (another).

manussing vbl n On a sealing vessel, the action of refusing to work and forcing the abandonment of the 'voyage.'

1923 MOSDELL 79 Capt Lewis, of the schooner *Mary*, returned from the ice-fields, April 19, 1862, and summoned eleven of his crew for 'manussing,' i.e., refusing to work and forcing him to abandon the voyage; Magistrate Peters, of Harbour Grace, sentenced three of the accused to twenty-eight days' imprisonment and the other eight to fourteen days' imprisonment.

marconi n The inventor's name was incorporated in his company's name in 1900.

1986 HISCOCK 68 The Labrador 'Marconi Stations,' as they were often called, not only carried the daily news as issued by the Government but they also carried messages to and from the people on the Coast. 1987 *Evening Telegram* 14 Mar, p. 10 I think I would have followed in his footsteps as the Wireless Operator or 'Marconi man' on a sealer if war had not come.

mare n Cp H.L. EDLIN, *Woodland Crafts in Britain* (London: Batsford, 1949), p. 73 'The hoop is therefore fixed to a three-legged upright frame, or else to a horizontal wooden structure called a *mare*.' Comb ~ **head**: a cooper's device to hold barrel staves for trimming; cp BENDING HORSE, HORSE n 2.

1986 *Them Days* xi (4), 26 Then you'd go to your mare-head, a thing like a press. You'd take your thousand staves and sit on the bench and [trim them out with the draw-knife].

mark n *Anglo-Manx Dialect* ~ 'a fishing-ground distinguished by land-marks'; COHEN, p. 121 'Navigation at the *eela* is by the use of *meyds* or *marks*, a basic method of triangulation.'

1 [(1867) 1989 CHIMMO (ed Kirwin) 54-5 [We] went to search for the rocks on which so many vessels had struck, when running north; They were both found in the passage... Marks were obtained for clearing them.] T 1064-72 And he come back to the hill again and he... took good marks, and he said to hisself, 'Well now, I'll find un this time.' 1986 FELTHAM 45 At the time when there were no fathometers in fishing boats and fishermen had to rely on cross-bearings to determine their positions, the various churches on the surrounding islands, provided easily remembered, precise 'marks' for various fishing 'spots', 'grounds' and 'rocks.' 1987 *Evening Telegram* 4 July, p. 56 [tape transcript] My father was skipper and fish was scarce. This island of ice was out there and my father said, 'We'll go out where that island of ice is, it might be up against a shoal.' They went out and they got a load of fish and he never let anyone know the

marks of that bank. 1987 O'FLAHERTY 41 Little Bank had been one of Abe Foley's berths in his great days of cod fishing. John recalled his father's precise naming of the marks for the shoal: to the north, Peg's Tolt between the spires of Northern Bay church; to the west, the top of the spire of Broad Cove church in line with the 'man' on Western Bay Point.

market n Comb ~ **passage**, ~ **run**: voyage from fishing grounds to point of export, esp a rapid passage under full sail.

1977 MOAKLER 163 We left the Burgeo scupper-deep with cod/And set a market passage for St. John's. ibid 133 We set our bowsprit for a market run/With lower tops'ils and the fores'il on.

marl v

1983 DAWE & FICKEN 10 While others are busy/ Mending their twine,/He marls by the store-loft/Like one of a kind.

marsh n Cp *SED* iv, 399 'mesh' D for sense 1.

1 1983 SOUTH (ed) 211 A marsh is a mineral or peat-filled wetland which is periodically inundated by standing or slowly moving waters. 1987 DAWE [32] M is for mash,/Or marish or mish,/A wet grassy spot/Where your rubbers go squish.

2 Comb ~ **berry**, ~ **curlew**: see ESKIMO CURLEW, ~ **plover**.

1983 SOUTH (ed) 259 The marshberry or small cranberry (*Vaccinium macrocarpon*, *V. oxycoccus*), although usually not abundant, is often picked for jam. 1986 SAUNDERS 55 What he lived on during that four- or five-day journey I don't know, just marshberries and a scattered trout, I suppose. 1987 MONTEVECCHI & TUCK 238 Marsh curlew. Eskimo curlew. ibid 238 Marsh plover. Lesser golden-plover.

marten n Comb ~ **cat**: pine marten (*Martes americana*); CAT² n 1.

[1819] 1987 PEYTON 41 Came upon a storehouse used by the Indians to store caribou meat. Five 'marten cat' traps, stolen from the furriers, were found inside. [1889-93] ibid 7 He would come to the waterside of Gander Bay to spend Christmas and return to his trap lines until spring. The smallest number of pelts taken by Mr Elliot was documented as being 'thirty dozen Marten cats, besides Beaver and Otter.'

master n *EDD* ~ adj 16; *ADD* 2. Attrib, with sense of large, superior, unrivalled.

1912 CABOT 192 Whitefish...are not quite up to the southern-slope ones, but sometimes they get large ones, the 'master fish,' which are better. [1929] 1982 BURKE (ed Kirwin) 98 "If Your Wife Is Run Down": She's a great master hand/For to make the grub fly. T 88-64 They had lobster cages out, and one morning they got a master lobster. Oh he was that large. T 90-64 You'd ply it out, and slide down your nice piece o' rush on each side and you had a master job done. 1984 POWELL 13 Those were supposed to be master places for salmon. ibid 20 The next trip Roland took the canoe and I carried the three guns. This was supposed to be the master water for fur-bearing animals... We did well with the furs, the most of which were very good mink.

mauze v Of winter condensation, to cover the ground (or other object) with a light coat.
1977 MOAKLER 163 While geese were plashing in the outport ponds,/And winter frosts were mauzing on the sod,/I stood my freezing trick behind the wheel.

mauzy a
1977 MOAKLER 29 We lost the gale sou'east of St Pierre/And lowered dories in the mauzy air. 1988 *Evening Telegram* 17 May, p. 8 The weather was mausy and...I had it on my mind about a rabbit slip that I never had struck up yet the spring and I wanted to get in and see to that.

medium a
1990 *Evening Telegram* 14 Jan, p. 14 Fifty-two casks were medium and large fish. Where would you get this today?

merchant n
  1 1983 FROUDE 14 We...came out just about square on the merchants books. 1988 *Sunday Express* 18 Dec, p. 2 [Labrador] crews who could haul 10,000 pounds a day, waited in line-ups for as much as eight hours only to learn that merchants could buy 1,000 pounds from every fishing vessel. 1990 *Sunday Telegram* 4 Mar, p. 16 The fish merchants didn't take kindly to [the American Bank fishery].
  2 Comb ~ **room**.
1987 POWELL 53 In those days it was no easy task being a manager in any of those merchant rooms.

merchantocracy n The mercantile class, esp the merchants of St John's engaged in the export of cod-fish and the provisioning of fishermen; FISHOCRACY.
1842 BONNYCASTLE ii, 80 The people who had sighed for the honours of a provincial parliament soon found they were as far from it as before, and that the merchantocracy was not quite so foolish or so blinded by the novelty of the thing as to give up one iota of its time-honoured claims and rule. 1968 SMITH 197 Not until the twentieth century would outside forces eventually be strong enough to challenge Newfoundland's 'merchantocracy.'

merry a Comb ~ **dancers**.
1924 *Deep Sea Fishers* xxi (4), 139 Merry dancers— Northern lights.

methodist n Comb ~ **feet**.
1987 FIZZARD 193 They had a big time in the Masonic for me. And there were different things, dances and stuff. But I had Methodist feet—I couldn't dance.

micmac n
1986 SAUNDERS 46 It was Jim John, a full-blooded Micmac, who had taken me on my first real trip in the country...when I was fifteen. We came back two weeks

later with three caribou. I went up a boy and came back a man, that's all there is to it.

middle n Cpd **middle-distance**: relating to the fishery, or vessels engaged in the fishery, intermediate between the local INSHORE and distant OFFSHORE sectors.
1986 *Evening Telegram* 18 Feb, p. 3. The provincial government has unveiled plans to launch two middle distance fishing vessels this year... The reason for introducing the new fleet is to catch fish not presently caught by the inshore small boat and longliner fleet or the off-shore trawler fleet... The middle-distance vessels, which use long lines and hooks to catch fish, have a distinct advantage over longliners which use gillnets. 1987 ibid 19 Nov, p. 3 [He said] the three middle-distance vessels presently fishing in Newfoundland waters have landed more than five million pounds of fish so far this year.

middler n
1984 POWELL 77 We have names for the whole family of beavers. The small one is the papoose, then the small middler, the middler, the large, and then the blanket.

midshore n attrib. Relating to the sea-fishery in vessels of a size and range capable of operating with seasonal flexibility in waters intermediate between local INSHORE 'grounds' and the distant OFFSHORE sector; cp **middle distance**.
1987 POWELL 117 After 1975 the codfish started to pick up in the gill nets and people began to outfit for the midshore fishery. 1988 *Evening Telegram* 24 Mar, p. A5 The Midshore Fleet consists of auto line and longline systems that provide continuity of supply to the smaller inshore processing companies. 1988 SINCLAIR (ed) 3 In between [the inshore and the offshore sectors of the fishery] is the...midshore fleet from 65 to 100 feet [in length].

midsummer n *OED* ~ men (1755, 1877). Comb ~ **man**.
1895 *N S Inst Sci* ix, 95 *Sedum Rhodiola*...Rose root (Midsummer men, on the Labrador, also Houseleek and Scurvy Grass.).

midwater n attrib. Relating to fishing gear operated at intermediate depths of water.
1986 *Nfld's Deepsea Fishery* 650 Midwater drum: a net drum sometimes present on a stern trawler. This often has a gilson wire mounted on it. 1987 FIZZARD 216 From the early 1970s the midwater trawl became an optional feature of the stern trawler.

mild n
1984 POWELL 78 The trail was very rough because there had been a mild a few days before, and the big knobs of snow were in the trail, frozen like rocks.

milk n Comb ~ **maid's path**.
1983 FROUDE 26 earlier The north star the great bear and all the stars in the/northern sky is disapaired to our view and the milk maids path/the majellan clouds and the southern cross is now comming in/sight.

mind v

1988 ELLIOTT [19] "Going Up Shore": I mind in the summer of seventeen eighty three,/Tom and I were going up shore with our muskets.

minister n

1 Also: fig. usage.

'He's a real pickled minister.' A person very fastidious in dress, stuck-up, aloof (P 289-88).

misk n SED iv, 875 So W Do.

1983 FROUDE 175 The rains decend with the misk and fog to hide the land from/Our view.

mitt n

[1936] 1987 FIZZARD 166 Dory marked *Partanna* badly damaged with five oars bulkheads pair mitts marked J.C. 1977 MOAKLER 149 With frozen mitts we thatched our blinded eyes/Against the snow that came in icy pins. P 308-88 We had wool mitts and skin mitts too, put the wool mitts on and put the skin mitts over them.

molasses 'n also **lassy**.

1 1988 *Evening Telegram* 1 June, p. 9 At her invitation I tried molasses as a spread on my bread. 'It's the fancy grade,' she said, 'though even the black-strap tasted good to me as a child.'

3 In designations of food, drink, etc: ~ **ball**, ~ **bread**, ~ **bun**, ~ **jimmy**: cookie, ~ **kiss**: a sweet, ~ **mog**.

[1904] 1982 BURKE (ed Kirwin) 34 "The Kelligrews Soiree": Boiled chicken, cold chicken, lassey balls we kept a lickin. 1914 *Deep Sea Fishers* xii (3), 106 When the cook put raisins and molasses into the [whole wheat] bread, it was hard to equal the demand for 'lassy bread.' 1984 POWELL 96 I beat the ice off the game bag and soon got his bag of molasses buns out. They were full of pork which made them strengthening to eat. 1985 *Nfld Qtly* lxxxi (1), 18 Molasses cookies were [called] 'lassy jimmies.' 1984 GOUGH 55 Inside [the store] there is a smell of apples and of Dustbane and scent of peppermint knobs and lassie kisses. 1988 MOMATIUK & EASTCOTT (eds) 61 My poor old mother, she'd make up this water and molasses and flour and put it in the oven. That's what the people called 'lassy mogs.'

moldow n

1 1987 *Sunday Express* 6 Sep, p. 27 But the most distinctive growth...is the moldow or 'Old Man's Beard,' the pale green mossy growth which hangs almost like rough, colored cotton wool strands from every coniferous tree. 1988 *Evening Telegram* 17 May, p. 20 I stuck some alder branches,/Through that salmon's gills,/And maldow around his body,/As the warden came over the hills.

montagnais n

1987 MONTEVECCHI & TUCK 45 Montagnais began to visit the island from the Labrador region around the end of the 17th century. They hunted in Newfoundland in historical times.

month n

1983 WARNER 26 Down to the Labrador we went. Just this time of year it was, and you don't see us home until October month! 1987 POWELL 29 All June month some fishermen tried to get their traps set around the mouth of the harbour because there were lots of codfish under the ice.

more n SED iv, 500 'root' So Co D Do.

more v Phr *more out*.

1983 FROUDE 201 I have worked in the forest and moared out the timber/and cut down the trees for my own special use.

more a, substitute.

1 1987 *Them Days* xii (4), 191 We fellas, some of us anyway...worked every hour there was work... But there was more fellas who only worked the one shift.

2 In sequence **sometimes...more times**.

1981 MAJOR 58 School is a funny thing. Sometimes I got the best kinda interest in it. More times I wish I could chuck it all up. 1984 POWELL 13 Sometimes the icebergs would put our nets adrift, and more times the nets would drag ashore with the tide.

mosquito n also **muskeito**.

[1623] 1982 CELL (ed) 192 Whitbourne's *Discourse*: Neither are there any Snakes [etc] knowne to hurt any man in that Countrey, but onely a very little nimble Fly, (the least of all other Flies) which is called a Muskeito; those Flies seeme to haue a great power and authority vpon all loytering and idle people.

mother n Comb ~ **fish**.

[1863] 1987 FIZZARD 96 [He] told me that he had seen large numbers of the mother fish, full of spawn, brought in [and] our own men...plead necessity.

mountaineer n

1 1984 POWELL 184 He and the Mountaineer Indians were always good friends.

mouth n Comb ~ **music**: GOB MUSIC, ~ **speech**: also: words not heartfelt.

1988 *Gazette* 21 Apr, p. 9 You [may] spring the noseharp on them. (The noseharp being akin to a comb in making mouth music.) T 258-66 'Well now,' she said, 'you...ask father for me again the night. Ask un three nights follying' she said. 'See what he'll say.' She said, ''Tis only a mouth speech anyhow.'

mud n Comb ~ **lark**: shore lark; horned lark (1907 TOWNSEND & ALLEN 380), ~ **trout**.

1988 *Sunday Express* 10 July, p. 30 There were two breeds in this deep recess, ouananiche, or 'slinks' as the Gambo men called them, and mud trout. 1990 *Evening Telegram* 14 Jan, p. 13 [He displayed] the three mud trout he hooked Saturday during the opening day of the 1990 ice fishing season at Kelly's Pond.

mug up n

1910 *Deep Sea Fishers* July, p. 37 'Mary, Mary, mug-up!' 1981 MAJOR 180 The two of us having a mugup by the open fire, the air a bit cold and frosty. 1984 KELLAND

84 Rowing back to the [vessel] they discharged their catch then went below for a 'mug-up.' 1989 *Evening Telegram* 17 June, p. A10 He was in what he calls the 'mug-up locker' (often called the 'shack locker') and was having a cup of tea when [the vessel] heeled over.

mummer n
1858 LIND *MS Diary* 6 Jan I am sorry to find that the majority of the young people (& some of the married ones) are busy in dressing up to act as 'mummers' commonly & properly called 'Fools.' 1989 BENNETT 112 She also added to the description by saying that whenever they spoke they would use 'mummer's talk,' which was done in a high-pitched tone, while inhaling.

mummer v
1981 DAWE 40 "The Mummer": And through the Christmas spell/I mummered all by myself/across the drifted fields.

mummering vbl n
[1840] 1871 [JUKES] 89 The lower orders keep up the old custom of mumming from Christmas-day to Twelfth-day. 1987 *Evening Telegram* 3 Jan, p. 4 The practice of mummering, or jannying as it is also known to many, is particularly popular in communities along the Southern Shore, in Placentia, Fortune and St Mary's Bays.

murre¹ n
1983 SOUTH (ed) 467 Common and Thick-billed Murres...or turres, and various types of sea ducks...are still a much hunted resource that adds variety to, and supplements, the tablefare in winter. 1989 *Evening Telegram* 12 Jan, p. 1 The birds [killed by the oil spill] were mainly murres (turres) with some eiderducks included. 1990 ibid 5 Feb, p. 4 [They] estimate that between 500,000 and 750,000 murres (turres) are shot annually in the province.

mutinize v
[1937] 1983 FROUDE 29 Seeing that it may be fatal if the boat go over the bar I mutinized and ran the boat ashore on a wild sandy beach.

myrrh n
1981 SPARKES 183 Then came the day when all the brooks were open and the winter cut was in. That was the signal to strip off the myrrh-stiffened logging clothes. 1986 SAUNDERS 176 A fresh-cut fir would have been very uncomfortable indeed [to handle] with all that sticky myrrh, and it liable to break besides.

N

naked a Comb ~ man.
1981 DAWE 20 "The Naked Man": I found his marker to the pond:/"the naked man"/of weathered, wind-honed stones/and snakes of juniper stumps,/a clumsy rock man/leaning back from the sea wind. 1983 *Gazetteer of Canada: Nfld* 120 Naked Man [five occurrences], Naked Man Point.

nan¹ n
1988 PORTER 49 A series of pictures of Nan flashed through Heather's mind, like the Viewmaster slides she'd gotten for Christmas when she was a child. 1989 *Muse* 24 Nov, p. [19] Did you hide your nanny's teeth again?

nape n
1989 *Sunday Express* 19 Mar, p. 7 Our winter's pocket money [was] earned door to door [by] the sale of napes by those who arrived at Battiste's Wharf too late for tongues or peas.

narn neg substitute. *SED* iv, 806-7 So W Do Ha.

naskapi n also **naskaupi, nascopie.**
1 Also: Innu.
1989 *Evening Telegram* 13 May, p. 10 The chief of the Naskaupi Innu band is pressing the provincial government to install water and sewer services [at Davis Inlet]. 1989 *Nfld Qtly* lxxxiv (4), 44 Sometimes it is spelled 'Nascaupee' or 'Nascaupi' (when it signifies a northern Labrador riding of the House of Assembly), sometimes 'Nascopie' (used for the name of a legendary Hudson Bay Company Arctic supply ship).
4 Comb ~ **head**: type of snow-shoe.
1985 *Decks Awash* Jan-Feb, p. 25 And then we used to have one called the Naskapi head. [This snow-shoe] had a round tail and an almost straight front.

native n
1 Cp NEWFOUNDLANDER n 1.
[1784] 1984 BYRNE (ed) 43 I persuade myself that his Mission will be serviceable not alone to the Catholicks from these parts trading to & residing there, but also to many others, particularly to the Natives, those born there, who tho' descended from European Parents, live, & die alas in the most deplorable ignorance of, & insensibility to what regards their salvation.
2 Cp LABRADORIAN n
1988 *Evening Telegram* 30 May, p. 7 Now I knew that my visit to Labrador was not merely to write my own social history of the natives and liveyers.

nature n Cp *DBE* ~ 1 'sexual drive' for sense 2.

nearshore n Pertaining to the fishery in waters and with vessels intermediate between those of the local 'inshore' and the distant 'offshore' sectors
1988 SINCLAIR (ed) 3 In between [the inshore and the offshore sectors of the fishery] is the nearshore or long-liner fleet from 35 to 65 feet.

neck n
1 Also: phr *neck of water*: a passage through an ice-field; LEAD² n 1.
1987 *Evening Telegram* 11 Apr, p. 14 [tape transcript] We passed up around Channel and we sighted the Burnt Islands and there was a neck of water. The Captain put her in the neck of water and we went on and followed that neck of water right in through the Gulf, and we never stopped until we stopped in the patch of seals.
2 Revision: short cut permitting easy passage; also comb ~ **path**.

[1820] 1915 HOWLEY 122 The frost had been very severe for three days which fastened the river above, where we reached by passing over two necks of burnt woods for three miles. 1924 *Deep Sea Fishers* xxi (4), 139 Neckpath—A short cut overland.

needle n Implement designed to hold a quantity of 'twine' and used to knot meshes in a fish-net; KNITTING-NEEDLE.

1987 *Evening Telegram* 7 Mar, p. 10 The needle flew as he tied his swift bowlines, and his chair gradually slid back as the net grew in length from its anchor point on the mantle-piece to his busy hands.

ne'er neg determiner.

1985 *Nfld LifeStyle* 3 (1), 26 He got nar sense of humor at all...jokes just goes right over his 'ead. 1987 *Lore and Language* vi (1), 34 My grandmother said to me, 'berries were plentiful back then and now you can't get ne'er one to sell.'

neither neg determiner.

M 78-54 I brought you neither purse he says/I brought you neither ring/I brought to you de cold winding sheet/Which covers many de weary limb. 1985 ASHTON 172 I wrote off a hundred and six now from memory. I never took neither one of 'em out of a book. 1987 POW-ELL 52 [Securing able-bodied welfare] could only be done through a justice of the peace. With neither one at Frenchman's Island, the food that was stored there was of no help to them.

nest n Cp *OED* ~ sb 6 for sense 2.

1 A breeding shelter for animals used for food.

[1613] 1982 CELL 88 [Crout's letter] Ther is allso in that quarter good store of beaver o[tt]er and Beavers nesses and many Foxes *which* partly nowe we knowe howe to take them. 1837 BLUNT 29 Seals Nests. 1983 *Gazetteer of Canada: Nfld* 77 Hares Nest Barrens. ibid 157 Seals Nest Islets.

2 A stack of the small flat-bottomed 'dories' used on 'banking' schooners in the days of sail and easily so stowed.

1977 MOAKLER 96 The dories smashed to pieces in their nest.

nest v Cp *OED* ~ v 4 b. To stow a number of flat-bottomed 'dories' in a stack on deck or ashore.

1924 ENGLAND 10 Inverted and nested dories... bespoke possibilities of a quick getaway in case of trouble at the icefields. 1977 MOAKLER 103 We pewed our codfish under threat of gales/And nested dories in the nooning light. 1984 KELLAND 22 It had been discovered that dories which had been manufactured by one builder, rarely, if ever nested or fitted into those produced by another builder. This was caused by differences in side flare and in bow and stern rake.

net n Comb ~ **hauler**: mechanical device to haul fish-nets; gurdy, ~ **loft** = ~ **store**, ~ **sounder** (see last quot).

1987 POWELL 117 After 1975...they were building bigger boats and were equipping them with gurdies or net haulers. 1981 SPARKES 183 The net-lofts, building-docks, sail-lofts and carpenter shops of the trap and schooner fishermen had been busy all winter. 1982 MCDOOLING 133 Boats, net stores and the other major building and repairing is still carried out in the early fall. 1987 FIZZARD 216 From the wheel house the captain, with the aid of an echo-sounder (an instrument to detect the depth of the water or the depth of a school of fish) and a net sounder (an instrument to detect the location of the net in relation to a school of fish), is able to adjust the trawl to the exact location of the fish.

never neg

1 1987 FIZZARD 128 You'd get up about one o'clock in the morning, that's if you never had your gear in the water, if you had to bait your gear aboard the schooner in the tubs to get ready to set it. P 308-88 He never got anything out of it.

newfie n GERALD THOMAS, 'Newfie Jokes,' E. FOWKE, *Folklore in Canada* (Toronto, 1976) p. 142-53. Also: the Island of Newfoundland, and further attrib uses ~ **bullet**, ~ **joke** (see quots).

[1938] 1983 *Canadian Folklore canadien* v (1-2), 72 'Nothing like that in your country, eh, Newfy?' [c1959] P 266-90 Even the most rabid Newfoundland patriot seems long ago to have mentally given him the status of a true-blue *Newf*. 1987 *Nfld Qtly* lxxxiii (2), 2 After I arranged my transportation to Whitbourne via what has come to be known as 'The Newfie Bullet,' now unfortunately defused, I stepped out of the CNR Station. 1988 *Evening Telegram* 2 July, p. 52 Her ancient back is broken/and her boilers bend with age/For our great old Newfie Bullet/Has found her final stage. 1971 TULK [title page] *Newfie Jokes*. 1989 ibid 18 Mar, p. 18 One of them asked if we thought Newfie jokes had peaked and would now begin to fade away.

newfoundland n

1 [1965] 1990 *Evening Telegram* 2 Mar, p. 4 The legal name of the province is Newfoundland and not Newfoundland and Labrador, Attorney General L.R. Curtis told the House of Assembly... While Newfoundland and Labrador may be used in all government reference it can't be used on a legal document. 1987 MONTE-VECCHI & TUCK 13 Modern plate tectonics has established that the Appalachians and the Caledonian Mountains of Europe were part of the same system. Newfoundland was closest to where the separation took place when the continents drifted apart about 150 million years ago. By the time the Atlantic Ocean had formed, parts of the Afro-European continent remained welded to Newfoundland's North American western sector.

3 In names of animals: ~ **beaver**, ~ **black bear**, ~ **marten**, ~ **meadow vole**, ~ **muskrat**, ~ **otter**, ~ **pony**, ~ **red fox**, ~ **wolf**.

1983 SOUTH (ed) 514 [He] thought the Newfoundland beaver to be slightly darker than mainland beaver and noted that the 'straight' zygoma was the essential cranial character separating it from other beavers. ibid 520-1 *Newfoundland Black Bear. Ursus americanus hamiltoni Cameron.* Bangs (1913) thought the bear would 'probably prove to be an insular form' and Cameron (1956) designated the subspecies *hamiltoni* as a new race distinguished by 'the greater height of the cranium in the frontal region and the relatively shorter rostrum.' ibid 522-3 *Newfoundland Marten*. Martes americana atrata *Bangs…* The food habits of Newfoundland marten are not known but presumably *Microtus*, which occurs in forested areas and occasionally in high numbers, was and is important. ibid 516 The Newfoundland Meadow Vole was probably referred to by Banks (1766) when he noted on June 14: 'Killed today a kind of mouse which differs scarce at all from English sort, but is rather larger and its ears extremely broad'… Cameron (1958) states that, 'The Newfoundland meadow mouse is the palest of the eastern Canadian forms, and often it has a definite buffy nose patch.' ibid 518 *Newfoundland Muskrat*. Ondatra zibethicus obscurus. Relatively few early writers mention [this] muskrat, probably because it was not of great importance as either fur or food to the Beothuck or MicMac and did not occur in high densities. ibid 524 *Newfoundland Otter*. Lontra canadensis degener *Bangs*. Bangs (1913) considered the [Newfoundland] otter a full species [but others consider it] a subspecies of *canadensis*. 1986 SAUNDERS 25 [He] was what you'd call a Newfoundland pony. He was five to six hundred pounds, about halfway in size between a Shetland and a regular horse. 1983 SOUTH (ed) 519 *Newfoundland Red Fox*. Vulpes deletrix *Bangs*. [This] fox was mentioned by all authors who took note of natural history, from Mason…and Whitbourne… through to the 20th century. 1987 *Evening Telegram* 17 Jan, p. 14 Although it's impossible to say when the last Newfoundland wolf died, Rev. John H. Moss wrote that the last known wolf in the Daniel's Harbour area was killed about 1920.

4 Attrib, comb ~ **cod trap**: COD TRAP, JAPANESE COD TRAP, ~ **fish**, ~ **fishery**, ~ **language**: see ~ **dialect**, ~ **ranger**, ~ **spade** (see last quot).

1982 MCDOOLING 48 Years ago, one cod trap. And that was a Newfoundland cod trap. [1586] 1895 PROWSE 76 [He] takes up for Her Majesty's service in Ireland 20,000 Newfoundland fish. [1799] 1984 BYRNE (ed) 170 Be pleased to accept of a quintal of our best Newfoundland fish for the use of your kitchen. 1989 *Sunday Express* 19 Mar, p. 7 Growing up in Port aux Basques, I was indeed completely ignorant of the 'Newfoundland fishery' or the great bulk of it on the east coast. 1986 *Them Days* xi (4), 55 He did all his talking in Newfoundland out-port language. 1987 POWELL 47 There was lots of stormy weather and many days of traveling were lost, but we finally reached Red Bay where the Newfoundland ranger gave us a paper that read, 'Clear in Ballast.' 1988 *Evening Telegram* 9 June, p. 3 The foundation wanted [Prince Edward] to use a unique tool for the ground breaking ceremony—a Newfoundland spade. The spade is a version of the traditional southern Irish spade, which was brought to Newfoundland with Irish immigrants in the 19th century and the Avalon Peninsula version was still in use until recent years, particularly on the southern shore and north of St John's… The metal sides are straight edged.

newfoundlander n

1 Also: a person from the Island of Newfoundland as distinct from Labrador; *native Newfoundlander*.

1984 KALLEO 38 When the schooners were returning home in the fall, there were a lot of dances between the Inuit and the Newfoundlanders. 1984 POWELL 72 The thought struck my mind very often when the Newfoundlanders came on the coast in the spring they would say, 'What were you doing all winter, sleeping?' 1987 POOLE 19 [These supplies were] used for the doctor or the Clergy or the nurse if they happened to come along during the winter, and so much had to be kept to give the Newfoundlanders a cup of tea when they arrived [in Labrador]. 1988 *Evening Telegram* 22 Apr, p. 3 [He said] the availability of a large number of native Newfoundlanders skilled in the refining trades 'has been one of the greatest things that has happened to us' [in re-opening the oil refinery]. 1989 ibid 22 July, p. A7 [He] is a native Newfoundlander, born at Cape Onion; he was ordained in 1960, and has spent all his ministry in this province.

newfoundlandiana n

1986 *Nfld Herald* 22 Feb, p. 5 While *Notebook* is a break from [Jack Fitzgerald's] crime series, it is valuable to anyone collecting Newfoundlandia because it preserves so many of the romantic, adventurous and fascinating events from our long history. 1989 *Nfld Qtly* lxxxv (3), 41 [*Close to the Floor*] is entirely too academically oriented a volume for the mere lover of nostalgic Newfoundlandiana.

nice a *SED* iv, 903, 904 'a nice lot' Co D Ha.

1981 MAJOR 34 'We'd always jig a nice many [squids], wouldn't we, Grandfather?' 1987 FIZZARD 210 It took a nice bit to get used to working on the trawler. It was all different [from the schooner fishery].

nip n Cp PINCH.

nipper[1] n Cp *DBE* ~ 'sandfly' for sense 1.

1 1984 PITT 80 [The essay's] unlikely subject is 'the ubiquitous mosquito,' the large, northern, insatiable variety known in Newfoundland as the 'nipper.' 1986 SAUNDERS 51 The nippers or mosquitoes there nearly ate me alive. It had rained a little and there was no wind— whatever the reason, the woods were humming with them.

nipper[2] n

1893 P.K. DEVINE "The Keels' Man": He'd drown you with his nippers' spray. 1987 FIZZARD 151 We would knit many things—long johns, sweaters, socks, pants, mittens, and nippers.

nish a *SED* iv, 1045 nesh So, for sense 1.

noddy n

1 1977 MOAKLER 51 A flock of noddies fished a porpoise shoal/And captured hapless caplin on the fly.

2 1986 SAUNDERS 60 No wonder Fogo people [known as 'Fogo Jumpers'] called us 'The Gander Bay Noddies.'

nog-head n Burton Bradstock, Do 'thin, lanky, hungry' for sense 3 (P 304-90).

3 1988 MOMATIUK & EASTCOTT (eds) 23 An orphaned seal grows up to be a dwarf, what we call a 'nog-head.' Its head grows, but its body gets thin and long.

nonia n

1987 *Evening Telegram* 21 Mar, p. 22 This week, Capt. Andop returned to the province to accept a plaque on behalf of NONIA, which will be displayed in NONIA's store on Water Street.

north n Comb ~ **shore**.

1986 *Evening Telegram* 25 Mar, p. 4 [The accused], of Gull Island, on the north shore of Conception Bay, was released on his own recognizance.

norther a also **norder**.

1988 GOSSE 50 [Another prolific fishing spot] was Norder Rock [near Hamilton Banks].

northern a Comb ~ **cod**, ~ **fleet**: sealing vessels prosecuting the seal hunt northeast of Newfoundland, ~ **front**: FRONT n 2, ~ **glut**: see GLUT, ~ **man**, ~ **slob**.

1989 *Evening Telegram* 6 Jan, p. 6 He is expected to announce the 1989 management plan for the northern cod stocks off the coast of Labrador and northeastern Newfoundland by the middle of February. 1987 *Evening Telegram* 9 May, p. 15 [tape transcript] 'Where are you bound Captain Winsor?' 'I'm bound down,' he says, 'to the northern fleet on the Labrador.' [1936] 1986 ibid 25 Mar, p. 6 The sealing steamers *Beothic* and *Imogene* augmented their catch [of seals] on the northern front yesterday. 1988 *Sunday Express* 18 Dec, p. 2 At the height of the northern glut, fishermen landed more cod than plants and collector boats could handle [in Labrador]. 1981 SPARKES 191 Finally, the small boats would be taken onboard—Northern men never used dories—and the vessel was ready to sail. 1903 *Deep Sea Fishers* July, p. 13 We dare not wait, fearing the northern slob may come up at any time.

north-wester n also **nor'wester**.

1863 *Journ of Assembly* Appendix p. 663 [In my seaman's bag were] a coat and jacket, sou'wester, not sure whether it wasn't a norwester.

nose n

1 1985 *Terminology of Loggers* 18 Toecaps [are] pieces of iron placed over the 'noses' of sled runners.

2 The northeast projection of the Grand Bank lying outside the Canadian 200-mile fishing zone; see TAIL n 4.

1988 *Canoma* xiv (2), 12 'Nose of the Bank' is often referred to in scientific literature. It is the northeast portion of The Grand Banks of Newfoundland, just as Tail of the Bank is the southeast part of it. Before approving the name, members [of CPCGN] suggested that old French and Portuguese charts should be consulted for historical support of the name. 1988 *Evening Telegram* 27 Jan, p. 3 EEC fisheries ministers unilaterally decided in late December to allocate member nations a total of 84,000 tonnes of cod during 1988 from an area known as the nose of the Grand Banks, just outside Canada's 200-mile economic zone. 1989 ibid 18 Feb, p. 1 As for charges of foreign over-fishing on the Nose and Tail of the Grand Banks, he said he did not know the precise figures.

3 Comb ~ **strap**: **nose-rope** (b).

1984 KELLAND 25-7 The idea of fitting a dory to take a nose strap in this manner is excellent, as all stress and strain is placed directly on the sturdy hardwood stempost instead of it being placed, partly on the much frailer pine side boards.

nug n

1989 *Nfld Qtly* lxxxiv (4), 39 [They] carried lumber away from [the jack ladder] and hauled slabs, nugs and sawdust away with horses and carts.

number n

1 [1909] 1930 COAKER 7 The Fishermen's Protective Union have given [the matter of a standard cull of codfish] much consideration and we [propose that of] qualities there should be four and damp. No. 1 large and small. No. 2, large and small. No. 3, No. 4 and damp. 1981 SPARKES 187 I asked a skipper once how he knew when a fish was dry enough to be classed as No. 1. He said, 'When you can hold it by the tail and chop off a man's head with it.' 1987 POOLE 101 The man considered his fish to be number one quality, and felt that I had to take it as that.

numerous a

[1942] 1987 *Them Days* xii (4), 55 All we had were outhouses. I mean they were numerous, hundreds of them built all around in the tent area. 1986 *Evening Telegram* 22 Mar, p. 4 The turrs were so numerous they flew towards the search lights we were using and they broke the flange of the search light.

nunchie n

1983 DAWE & FICKEN 36 N is for nunchie,/Small bird of the bay;/It likes to go bobbing/In cold briny spray.

nunny-bag n also **dunnybag**, **nanny bag**.

1981 SPARKES 178 One summer, two of us got permission from our parents to go in [to the saw-mill] for two or three nights, so taking a 'nunny bag' of food and a couple of blankets, we set off. 1984 POWELL 108 So the mail in between this distance was put in the nunny bag and then for the next fifty miles it was sorted.

O

ocky n See BURN v: *burned ocky*.

odds n pl

1 1989 *Sunday Express* 26 Mar, p. 7 We might as well get our favorite catch-phrase, 'What Odds, What Odds,' translated into Latin and stuck up for the Newfoundland motto.

off av

1 Comb **off-wind**: wind blowing from shore to sea; cp IN: **in-wind**.

1924 *Deep-Sea Fishers* xxi (4), 139 Off-wind, in-wind—West wind, East wind [on coast of Labrador].

2 Phr *write off*: to note down, transcribe (words of a song); cp *sketch off*.

M 68-11 There was another man who knew quite a few songs and Mom said she would ask him if he would write off some for me. I received quite a lengthy song from him (dictated by him, written down by his wife). 1971 CASEY 157 They'd sing it, and somebody would like the song, liked to learn it. They'd get that person to write off the song for them, and they'd read it over and over until they'd know it.

offal(s) n, n pl *South Shore Phr Bk* for sense 1.
1 Also: the residue of rendered seal fat, cod-livers, etc.
1964 BLONDAHL (ed) 92 "The Spotted Islands Song": The fore-castle of the *Anderson*—/It was very full to see;/And the 'aw-faw' from the boilers—/It was nearly to your knees. 1983 DAWE & FICKEN 40 He dines with the flounder/Down under the wharf,/Where a pile of old offal/Makes up a fine scoff. 1987 FIZZARD 10 Soon fishermen from fishing ports of France, Spain, Portugal and England were swarming westward like gulls to offal, to converge on the rich fishing grounds off Newfoundland. 1987 *Evening Telegram* 14 May, p. 8 The plants on the Southern Shore have a real problem disposing of their offal.

offer a
1977 MOAKLER 151 We lowered dories on the offer Banks/While arrowed sleet came hissing in the swell. 1986 FELTHAM 68 This is the season [April] too, when numerous eider ducks frequent the 'Offer' islands and provide excellent shooting.

offshore n attrib Also: relating to undersea oil exploration and activities off the coast of Newfoundland.
1988 *Evening Telegram* 24 Mar, p. A21 The recent confirmation of the purchase of six offshore supply vessels...has created a new major player on the local scene in the offshore supply business. Although the fiscal arrangement is the final key to the eventual development in all of the offshore fields, there does appear to be a renewed and guarded optimism. 1988 ibid 27 May, p. 4 He said...the codfish have left the offshore grounds... noting he didn't catch enough to pay for his fuel.

oil n
3 oil store.
[1925] 1986 *Them Days* xi (4), 8 Number Seven was the oil store and seal fat rendering shed. Seal oil had never been exported to any great degree at Rigolet. 1986 ibid xi (4), 8 [That building] was the oil store and seal fat rendering shed.
4 ~ clothes.
1987 FIZZARD 164 I made a pair of oil clothes for [him].

oil v PRATT ~ v. Phr *oil up*: to don 'oil clothes' (1924 *Deep-Sea Fishers* xxi (4), 138).

old a Cp AND old hand 3, *DBE* old man's (beard) for combs in sense 2.
2 Comb ~ **hand**: one experienced in an activity or occupation; HAND 1, ~ **man**: high frequency as

familiar form of address among males, ~ **man's beard**.
1984 WRIGHT 33 The younger and less experienced the newcomer, the more important the relationship became. The most intense and obvious play between 'old hand' and 'green hand' grew between Billy and Isaac. T 149-65 Jack said. 'Look in th' oven old man, see if there isn't somethin' in there.' T 543-68 That's a long story, ol' man. I don't know whether [I can] tell it to ya, ya know. 1988 *Nfld Studies* iv, 67 People would come up to the stage...and say, 'Well, old man, 'tis no harm to say that you had that [song] right 'cause I remember...' 1987 *Sunday Express* 6 Sep, p. 27 But the most distinctive growth...is the moldow or 'Old Man's Beard,' the pale green mossy growth which hangs almost like rough, colored cotton wool strands from every coniferous tree.

omadhaun n *Anglo-Manx Dialect* ~ n, PRATT omadan (1915).
1983 DAWE & FICKEN 38 O is for omaudaun,/Chucklehead one;/He acts like a gommel,/All squabby and stun.

on prep
1 Phr *on the dead*: (c) lacking any means of support or subsistence.
(a) 1860 *SPG Series Letters & Reports* E.8 A-227 The poor men are but too well accustomed to 'dragging their wood on the dead' as they call the snowless path or gravel road. 1985 *Terminology of Loggers* 12 On-the-dead: to pull logs on bare or level ground. (c) P 148-62 I've got four [young fellas] on the dead. P 108-70 The dogs haul the wood in the winter, but we have to keep them on the dead in the summer. They don't earn their keep in the summer and are then a dead loss. 1988 HANRAHAN 13 Fishing is often impossible, due to inshore ice, until June or even July. Said one fisherman: 'We calls it "living on the dead".'

one num PRATT ~ n (1976-).
5 Comb ~ **lunger**.
1984 GOUGH 101 She spins it again and the one-lunger catches. It coughs and spits out a cloud of oil-filled smoke, and the exhaust pipe trembles as the catch holds.

oo-isht int also **huit**.
1984 KALLEO 2 This man steers the sled... To start the team, he shouts, 'Huit!'

open a Comb ~ **spring**.
1854 *Newfoundlander* 2 Mar The excessive frosts experienced so frequently up to this time forbid me to expect what is termed an open spring.

opening vbl n Comb ~ **medicine**, ~ **pills**.
1924 *Deep-Sea Fishers* xxi (4), 139 Opening pills—Laxatives. 1985 DOMSTAD 15 People were given open medicine to clean out their bowels.

order n
[1979] 1985 LEHR & BEST (eds) 85 "Gull Cove": When we arrived at Gull Cove, everything it did look grum—/Our traps lay in good order, also our skiff and all.

ordinary a Comb ~ **cure**.

1987 *Evening Telegram* 17 Mar, p. 4 In the ordinary cure (45 per cent to 50 per cent moisture content) category (choice), fishermen will be paid 10 cents a pound for extra large [cod-fish].

ose egg n also **hose egg**, **oze-egg**.

1904 PEDDEL 16 ''Comic'': Tommy cods and other fry/Passed around with real good will/Oze-egg jam in oyster shell. 1985 GUY 28 What else she might be doing with them pile of hose eggs out in the door yard I wouldn't know. 1985 *A Yaffle of Yarns* 136 We would... catch flat-fish and tansies and jelly-fish and whore's eggs and anything else that swam or crawled.

otter n Comb ~ **rub**, ~ **set**: otter trap, cp SET n 1.

1984 POWELL 105 We [trappers] talk about otter rubs that are worn as smooth as the floor. 1986 SAUNDERS 283 [diagram of an] otter set.

ouananiche n

1988 *Sunday Express* 10 July, p. 30 There were two breeds in this deep recess, ouananiche, or 'slinks' as the Gambo men called them, and mud trout.

ouk int also **auch**.

1924 *Deep-Sea Fishers* xxi (4), 139 Auch, etta— Right, Left—Gee and Haw for dog-team use. 1984 KALLEO 2 This man steers the sled. When he wants the dogs to turn, he shouts, 'Arara! Auk! Auk!'

out av, prep

2 P 245-87 There, at Norman Bay [Labrador], they live in winter until it's time to go out to the coast for the summer fishery. 1987 PEYTON 13 The [Exploits] river became the Indian's chief natural highway. Not only was it the aborigines' natural 'way out' to the sea coast, but the early pioneer's natural 'way in' to the heart of Beothuck land.

3 Phr *out (of) doors*.

1988 GOSSE 19 Rudders [on the shallops] were hung 'out of doors' on the stern post, with a tiller in easy reach of the rear cockpit or 'after standing room.'

outer a

1971 *Can Geog J* lxxxii, 164-5 [In Labrador] big ships take the 'outer run'; skippers of local boats prefer the 'inner run' through the maze of coastal islands. 1977 MOAKLER 50 And as the vessel gained the outer Banks,/ We felt her straining onward to her task.

outfit n

1 1983 FROUDE 14 We got the vessel ready and went to St Johns and took our out fit for the summer.

outfit v

1984 KELLAND 10 [The store] was usually equipped with a long work bench, which in turn was outfitted with all varieties of carpenter's tools necessary for men who were engaged in the fisheries.

out-harbour n

1708 OLDMIXON 12 But they make use still of their old [out *ed conjec*] Harbours also, as their small Settlements here were termed, and not *Towns*, a Name indeed which they did not deserve. [1787] 1984 BYRNE (ed) 63 [He] slipped thro my hands to some out Harbour where he means to lurk in open defyance of all legal authority. 1888 HOWLEY 228 It was, at the time of its erection, considered one of the neatest buildings in the city, and was much admired by the typical 'Out-harbor-man,' on his annual visit to the capital. 1989 *Evening Telegram* 19 Apr, p. 4 In the outharbours [he] may be seen by some as a slick St John's lawyer.

outport n

[1796] 1984 BYRNE (ed) 139 We are not strangers to the many difficulties with which you have from time to time been obliged to encounter even at the risque of your life: in regularly visiting the different out ports within your reach. [1983] 1985 LEHR & BEST (eds) 15 ''The Blow below the Belt'': I'm moving you away from here, employment sure you'll find,/And you won't regret the day you left those outports far behind. 1984 PITT 15 All the outports grew quite unplanned, though usually facing the sea. Simple wooden houses, ranging from primitive one-roomed shacks to substantial but still plain two-storied dwellings, were perched higgledy-piggledy as the terrain allowed, wherever there was space and solid ground for a foundation. Between the houses were foot-worn lanes which passed for streets, giving access to the waterfront.

outporter n

1988 *Amer Morris Newsletter* Spr [issue], n.p. These old ways [folk revivalists] revere for their sense of communal closeness may have very different connotations for an outporter to whom they 'smell of poverty' and a narrow way of life.

outside n, av Cp PRATT ~ av (1910-) for sense 2, AND ~ 2 (1896-) for sense 2, DC (1896-) for sense 3.

2 [1925] 1986 *Them Days* xi (4), 10 The men who trapped on the 'outside' would move their traps to the islands to trap the white foxes that, every year, came down from the north on the floating ice. 1960 *Assoc Amer Geog* l, 274 Berths were classified as 'inside' or 'outside,' outside being those located on islands and headlands and exposed to rough seas. [1977] 1985 LEHR & BEST (eds) 59 ''The *Excel*'': On the rocky shore on the Labrador, where the dreadful deed was done/In a place called the Black Island, outside of Grady's Run.

3 Also: generally, the world beyond Labrador.

1984 KALLEO 1 These barrels are for storing fish. They are called puncheons. When they came in from outside, they were filled with molasses. 1988 *Evening Telegram* 1 June, p. 9 [His] wife was 'outside,' meaning 'not in Labrador,' having gone for a visit to her native Winnipeg.

ownshook n PRATT oshick for sense 1.

1 1983 DAWE & FICKEN 38 An oonshick so gowdy/ Wherever he goes,/He falls on his gob/When he trips in his toes.

P

package n Add: cured herring, etc.
[1918] 1930 COAKER 136 Packers of split herring
should be registered, and every man be compelled to
place his registered signature or name on every package
he packs.

paddy keefe a, av
1984 *Decks Awash* Nov-Dec, p. 57 We didn't die but
we come paddy keefe to it. 1989 *Evening Telegram* 12
Apr, p. A4 That was in 1972 when the Frank Moores/
Joey Smallwood confrontation ended in a draw and a
'draw' is Paddy Keefe close to what this [election] is
going to be on April 20.

pale a Comb **pale (seal) oil**.
1897 *Evening Telegram* 4 Mar An enterprising member
of a certain firm thinks a large quantity of our pale seal
oil might be disposed of as refined codliver oil.

pan n
1 (a)
1985 BUSCH 62 A big vat or 'crib' [for rendering seal
fat] could be 20-30 feet square, and 20-25 feet high, built
over a larger 'pan' of water.
2 1984 POWELL 130 There were now strings of slob
ice reaching across the bay and pans of ice everywhere.
3 1984 WRIGHT 61 We...moved on to another patch of
seals. The ship was nearby, picking up the first pan of
pelts we had collected that morning.
4 Comb ~ **flag**.
[1898] 1986 *Evening Telegram* 24 Mar, p. 6 The SS
Aurora struck a lot of our pan flags and put up theirs in
place of ours.

pank v *SED* iv, 708 So W D Ha.

papoose n
1984 POWELL 77 We have names for the whole family
of beavers. The small one is the papoose.

parting n *SED* iv, 92 partin So W Co D Do Ha.

partridge n *SED* iv, 465 patridge So W Co Do.
1 1985 *Nfld Qtly* lxxx (4), 30 Finally, one of the
hunters up Grand Lake sent two partridges, one for me
and one for the children. It was the first fresh meat we
had seen all winter.

partridge berry n
1986 FELTHAM 76 He used his fishing boat...to reach
some island where the tangy partridge berry grew in
profusion. 1987 KING (ed) 19 "Wild Geese": Today I
watch the two great birds again/rise up as if a bell were
sounding/somewhere across the partridge-berry hills.

passage n
1 1626 VAUGHAN Pt 3, p. 25 And if the party be a
Labourer, it will cost him nothing for his passage, but
rather hee shall receiue foure or fiue pound for his hire to
helpe the Fishermen on the Land for the drying of their

Fish. 1818 CHAPPELL 218-9 In order to procure for themselves a passage across the *Atlantic*, [the Irishmen] enter
into a bond with the master of a trading vessel; whereby they stipulate to pay him a certain sum as passage-
money, immediately subsequent to their having obtained
employment.
2 1689 *English Pilot* 13 You may sail through between *Goose-Island*, which is the middlemost, and *Stone-
Island*, which is the northermost in both these passages, it
is large enough for Ships to sail or turn in or out. 1983
Gazetteer of Canada: Nfld 132 Passage Island, Passage
Islet, Passage Point, Passage Reef, Passage Shoal.

passenger n Cp *OED* ~ 2 'one who travels or is
carried on board ship.' In the Newfoundland fishery, one who is carried seasonally by water to
participate in the fishing enterprise. Cp SERVANT[1]
n, STATIONER.
[1794] 1968 THOMAS 33 [*Mary Ann* of Dartmouth
sank.] There were many Passengers on board, men who
engaged themselves in the Fishing season at Newfoundland for a certain price... They are carry'd free of expense. [1833] 1984 BAYFIELD i, 255 Irishmen from various parts of Newfoundland come over [near Henley I.] as
passengers in the schooners to fish here and on various
other parts of this coast having boats with them and
building huts which they reside in during the summer
months.

patch n
1 1984 WRIGHT 61 By 11:30 a.m., we had moved on
to another patch of seals [and] the ship was nearby, picking up the first pan of pelts we had collected.

patent n Comb ~ **bark**.
1914 *Deep-Sea Fishers* xi, p. 23 [For mats] we have
used the 'paten bark,' a dye used by the fishermen for
coloring the sails of their boats to prevent mildew.

patrick n
1 1818 CHAPPELL 65 [The stranger's] country could no
longer be a secret to us; and presently the genuine *Paddy*
stood confessed, although disguised by an olive complexion, a dark red beard and red mustachios.
2 Comb ~**'s brush**.
1989 CANDOW 37 Sealers called these storms
'brushes,' the two main ones being Paddy's Brush (17
March) and Sheila's Brush (18 March).

paytrick n
1939 ALDRICH & NUTT 23 Common tern. Pietrie. 1983
Gazetteer of Canada: Nfld 133 Paytrick Rock.

pea n
1 See FISH'S PEA(S).
1989 *Sunday Express* 19 Mar, p. 7 Our winter's
pocket money [was] earned door to door [by] the sale of
napes by those who arrived at Battiste's Wharf too late
for tongues or peas.

pedlar n
1 1986 *Evening Telegram* 28 Apr, p. 6 William
Brown's name appears in the Bonavista Registry in 1806.

He came to Bonavista as a poor fisherman [and then] moved to King's Cove to fish and net seals. Because he was buying his supplies from pedlars, he was blacklisted from McBraire's store.

peg n Comb ~-**tooth**: a straight-toothed saw used to clear sawdust from a cut already made in a log (1985 *Terminology of Loggers* 13).

pelt n Cp *SED* iv, 358 So Co D Ha 'of sheep' for sense 1.
  1 1984 WRIGHT 55 By the time I got myself on deck most of the crew were already busy stowing the pelts that had been left on deck to chill overnight. 1987 *Evening Telegram* 6 Mar, p. 17 The [Carino Co] bought a number of pelts in 1984, none in 1985 and about 3,000 last year.

pelt v *O Sup*^{2} ~ v^2 a (1919-).
  1984 WRIGHT 58 After I had been shown how to kill and pelt and was told to try one for myself, I found I just wanted to get the business over with as soon as possible.

penguin n
  1983 *Gazetteer of Canada: Nfld* 133 Penguin Arm (Cove, Harbour, Head, Hills, Island). 1987 MONTE-VECCHI & TUCK 148 The name 'penguin' was first used to refer to the Great Auks of the North Atlantic and was later applied to present-day penguins when European explorers ventured into southern oceans.

pet n *Anglo-Manx Dialect*, PRATT.

pew^1 n *Fish Exhibit Cat* 293 U S.

philandy v, n Cp *Anglo-Manx Dialect* flander 'philander,' to lounge about without any fixed purpose; nonsense.

pick v Cp *OED* ~ v^1 7 'to separate, select carefully' for sense 1; BRYANT 496, 501 for phr in sense 2; *DA* ~ v 8 pickpole (1837-1905) for comb in sense 3.
  1 To separate male from female 'caplin' in a fish-processing plant; select; cp CULL v.
  P 245-89 'We picks the caplin—you know separate out the males and the females. Get a better price then from the plant when we picks them ourselves.'
  2 Phr *pick up the rear*: to follow a log drive and collect logs which have grounded.
  1986 SAUNDERS 205 'Picking up the rear'...was the last job on a drive. It meant going back after the main drive had gone through and picking up stray logs.
  3 Cpd **pick-pole**: a 2.7-3.7 m pole with a spike, used to handle individual logs in a river drive; pike-pole (P 299-56).
  M 68-17 The chief use of the pick-pole is for handling logs while on the drive down stream. 1973 PINSENT 25 Tomorrow, the kids would be down here with their brin bags and pickpoles to gather up wood for the wood-stoves. 1986 SAUNDERS 85 They said Uncle Stan could jump on a log, stick in his pickpole, run to the other end and stand still just looking at it.

picker n Small container used during berry-picking to fill a larger receptacle; EMPTER.
  C 71-122 When we went berry-picking we would always take a picker with us. This wasn't a thing to pick berries with. It was a small container you use to put the berries in and then you empty the berries into a larger container. P 322-88 ~ small berry-picking can.

picket n
  1840 ENGLAND *MS Journal* 2 Dec [The villains] waylaid them with staves and pickets [to prevent voting]. 1903 *Nfld Qtly* iii (3), 13 A spruce picket was lying on the ground, but the bull was on me like a flash. 1984 KELLAND 106 The...property on which the dwelling and the dory were situated was completely surrounded by a picket fence. 1985 LEHR & BEST (eds) 26 ''The Buck Goat Song'': Then I lost all my patience,/And a picket I tore from the fence.

pick-pocket n *EDD* ~ sb 1 inc s w cties. Shepherd's purse (*Capsella bursa-pastoris*) (1893 *N S Inst Sci* viii, p. 366).

pickle n
  1989 *Evening Telegram* 26 Oct, p. 1 'That's the state of the fishing industry at the moment—your arse is in the pickle,' [Hon. John Crosbie] told the Fisheries Council of Canada.

pickle v Also **pickling** vbl n.
  [1825] 1986 SIDER 61 'Supplied him this year on his promise to give up pickling'. 1917 *Commercial Annual* 60 ''Mr W.A. Munn on Pickled Fish.'' 1983 WARNER 27 Fresh-cooked capelin are a highly prized dish and the little fish also 'pickle' well when salted in barrels.

pig n Comb ~ **flower**: groundsel (*Senecio vulgaris*) (1898 *J A Folklore* xi, 230).

pig-a-wee n also **pig-a-pee**. Newfoundland black-capped chickadee (*Parus atricapillus bartletti*) (1959 MCATEE 52); TOM: **tom-tee**.
  1939 ALDRICH & NUTT 29 Pig-a-pee. 1967 *Bk of Nfld* iii, 283 Black-capped Chickadee: Pig-a-wee (from its calls). 1987 MONTEVECCHI & TUCK 242 Pig-a-wee.

pigeon n
  1 1983 *Gazetteer of Canada: Nfld* 135 Pigeon Cove, Pigeon Gulch [etc, with scores of occurrences in coastal names]. 1988 *Evening Telegram* 29 Apr, p. 6 On Round Hill Island, off the Labrador coast, there is a colony of [sea] birds—the pigeons occupy the northeast end (which is rock) and the puffins the southwest end (which is turf).

piggin n
  [1987] QUINLAN 31 [caption] punts piggin used for bailing water.

pile n
  1985 RUSTED 16 We saw on the beach what appeared to be a large flock of sheep, but with our binoculars we found it was numerous large piles of fish covered with white canvas. 1987 FIZZARD 133 'The [fish] is

graded...a dozen or so fish are placed in a circle, the centre is filled in and layers of fish are added until the pile is made.'

pile v
1984 POWELL 29 He shouted to some men that were on the flake piling fish together. 1987 POOLE 45 It was always the custom to try and pile your fish before the sun went down.

pinch n   AND ~ (1846-).

pinky n   AND ~ n² 1 (1904-).
1979 PORTER 62 I'm almost sure I saw him, a battered, hard-faced version of him, drinking pinky with a bunch of friends on the waterfront one cold winter day.

pinnacle n
1 1986 Nfld Qtly lxxxi (1), 46 He had climbed to the top of a bluish pinnacle [of ice]. Wind and driving snow whipped at his face.
2 Comb ~ tea.
1985 BUSCH 74 The ice made drinkable water when melted, but it was brackish and seldom slaked one's thirst even when turned into the strong brew known as 'pinnacle tea.'

pip¹ n
1986 SAUNDERS 25 And many's the load of stinking flatfish, sculpins and salmon peps I hauled on hot summer days.

piper n
1987 Evening Telegram 17 Oct, p. 18 My old copper piper bubbled to a rumbling boil on the back burner.

piss v   SED iv, 190 pissabed So. Comb piss-a-bed.
1984 GOUGH 50 The floor is peeling linoleum, and where one hole has worn through there's another left over bit slid underneath, showing like tired piss-a-beds, the dandelion flowers all a-shine.

pitch v
1 1984 POWELL 61 This time I took the breechloader, 12 gauge, so that if I came upon anything flying or pitched I was going to have it!

pitcher plant n   Cp AND ~ (1818-).
1982 BURSEY 38 "Poetic Symbols I": What is a pitcher plant/Compared to a yard/Covered with chips?

pitty a   Cp OED pit-hole sb b 'a grave' (1621-1768); EDD pit sb¹ 1 (19) (b): pittee-'awl D. Comb pitty hole: grave, esp as used in threats to naughty children.
M 70-9 As my mother used to say when I was very young, 'You'll go down into the pitty hole.' 1973 WIDDOWSON 231 If you don't be good, the hob-goblin will get you and throw you down the pity-hole.

planching n
1949 FITZGERALD 78 His ancient five-foot muzzle

loader is half cocked for immediate use,/With a charge that could rip off her planching, and jar all her trunnelling loose [on the skipper's craft]. T 149-65 Underneath that table, you take up the planchin', you dig down there, an' you'll find three jars of money. 1985 Terminology of Loggers 14 Planching: flooring in a [lumber] camp made of small logs, planed flat with an adze.

play v   See SPOON: play the spoons.

plim v
1 [1900] 1989 Nfld Qtly lxxxv (2), 27 Previously, between the two layers of boards, some bags of hard bread were dumped. When water touched the bread it 'plimmed'—swelled up. Soon a most satisfactory watertight job was achieved. 1984 POWELL 124-5 There was no way that any animal could eat [the mouldy and fousty hay]. It was still plimming and bursting the wire that tied it.
2 1988 Evening Telegram 2 June, p. 13 We pour the Stockholm tar over frayed or shredded hemp to make what all seagoing people refer to as oakum, which is used with a special chisel to caulk the seams between a boat's planks. Then, when the boat is launched into the water, the planks swell or 'plim' against the oakum and the boat can become as watertight as a bottle.

plough n   A device resembling an agricultural plough, with teeth, used to cut out blocks of ice on heavily frozen freshwater ponds or lakes; cp ICE SAW.
1987 FIZZARD 138 Now, to cut the ice [on the pond] we would use a plough. It was like a farmer's plough, only ours had teeth on it. So, it was really a saw. The first cut we would try to make as straight as we could. Now that cut would be down about three or four inches. And there was a guide on the plough, about 18 to 20 inches wide. And on the second cut we would put the guide in that first cut and make another cut with the saw. So we'd repeat that so many times... Three or four men would...make their cuts right through the ice.

plug¹ n
1 1858 [LOWELL] ii, 213 'What water's this?'... 'I think it's the plug is started; whativer made me have one in [the punt] at all?' 1984 KELLAND 48 Finally, a hole through the bottom...as plugs were inserted into them before the dories were dropped down to the water from a fishing schooner or launched from a beach or slipway by shore fishermen.
2 Attrib, comb plug hole, ~ stick: wooden stopper for a molasses keg; MOLASSES SPILE.
1984 KELLAND 48-9 While it was not essential to have plugholes in shore fishing dories, they were a must in nested Banks dories as with their plugs removed they permitted rain and boarding spray to drain off. 1989 Nfld Qtly lxxxiv (4), 16 'This boat is gonna sink just like the one I got out of. The plugs are out. She's fillin' up from the bottom.' 1987 POWELL 38 Then we went into another big store where I brought in my molasses keg and got some molasses. While the gallon measure was filling, Uncle Bobby was licking the plug stick that he had taken out of the hole to allow the molasses to run.

plug[2] n SORDEN 88 ~ n. A log jam on a river. Also **plug punching** vbl n: the activity of clearing an obstruction during a river drive (P 13-83).

1983 *Books in Canada* Aug/Sep, p. 8 'Tomorrow, boat four, you'll spend the day plug punchin'.' 1985 *Terminology of Loggers* 14 Plug: a pile of timber jammed in the river during a *drive*.

pod auger n Cp PRATT poganger days. Phr *pod auger days*.

1981 SPARKES 2 Holes for the trunnels were bored with a T handled pod auger, a tool like a gigantic gimlet in that it had a long, sharpened gouge ending in a screw or 'worm' to carry it into the wood. That tool was the ancestor of the modern and more familiar spiral auger. The expression, 'back in pod auger days,' meaning very old fashioned, refers to the time when pod augers were in use.

point n *OED* B 2 b 'tapering promontory.' Phrasal use in place-names: a projecting land feature associated with another land or sea feature.

1689 *English Pilot* 13 You may go into the *pool* which is a place on the Larboard-side (going in) within a Point of *Beach*. ibid 15 You may turn from side to side by your Lead, till you draw towards a Mile off the Point of the Beach (within which the Ships ride). 1837 *Royal Gazette* Dec 5 [advertisement] That commodiously situated plantation known by the name of Point of Beach Room on the South Side. 1837 BLUNT 19, 44 Point of Tickle, Point of Laun [a settlement]. 1983 *Gazetteer of Canada: Nfld* 85 Inside Point of Cape Boone Cove. 1987 FIZZARD 116 The harbour [of Grand Bank] was shallow except for an area opposite the 'Point of Beach.'

poison n Comb ~ **berry**.

[1839] 1871 JUKES 69 Saw three kinds of poison berries: one a beautiful cerulean blue, growing on leaf and stalk like lily of valley.

poison v

1985 GUY 90 We got to remember to let bygones be bygones and all that. So to put the strict letter on it, some of you poison me a lot less than others. 1989 ROWE 74 And she turns on me, my son, poisoned with me, the mouth on her going like a fifty cent fish.

poker[2] n

1986 SAUNDERS 262 Even so, we had a tough time getting the house started, and had to sing the "Jolly Poker" to do it.

pollard n A tree which has died as a result of having its bark removed (1985 *Terminology of Loggers* 14).

pond n

1 1983 SOUTH (ed) 3 Thousands of shallow lakes (known locally as 'ponds') are scattered across the landscape. 1986 *Evening Telegram* 8 May, p. 16A About 15 miles off the TCH was a chain of ponds that could get us and our supplies by boat to within an hour's hike of several seldom-fished gullies. 1990 ibid 13 Jan, p. 28

The biggest complaint you'll hear from winter fishers, especially those who frequent lakes, ponds and gullies close to the highways and roads, is the scarcity of trout.

2 [1689 *English Pilot* 13 [In Aqua-Fort you] ride on the North-side, and lie Land-lock'd as it were in a Pond, like to *Ferryland-Pool*, but larger.]

3 1986 SAUNDERS 206 With some brooks you have ponds to cross. In the ponds the current is weak, and if there is any wind against you the logs won't move where you want. 1987 KING (ed) 131 "River": The river flows,/Twisting itself around bends and islets,/Rushing swiftly/Down rattles,/Squeezing narrowly/Between steep banks,/Pausing at dark pools,/Widening into ponds and steadies.

4 Comb ~ **boat**: see DORY, **duck**: see POND DIVER.

P 286-82 The word dory is the name of a small flat-bottomed boat, a 'pond-boat' in northern Labrador. 1985 *Evening Telegram* 11 Dec, p. 16 The inland hunting season for pond ducks, geese and snipe concludes Saturday throughout the island portion of the province.

pondy n Great black-backed gull (*Larus marinus*); SADDLEBACK 2, SADDLER 2 (1987 MONTEVECCHI & TUCK 240).

pook n *SED* iv, 248 s w cties for sense 1.

1 1985 NEWHOOK 42 Towards evening [the hay] would be raked together in pooks to protect it from the evening and morning dew.

pop n

1979 PORTER 105 The undertaker came, mumbled a hurried, 'Sorry for your trouble' in Pop's direction, and went upstairs to measure Nanny for her coffin, or casket as Mom and Aunt Viley liked to call it. 1987 FIZZARD 164 'When Pop and they were cook they used to have a little kedgie...for helping out the cook.' 1988 *Evening Telegram* 11 June, p. 1 'Don't tell Poppy (her grandfather) because he'd be ashamed of me.'

porcupine n Comb ~ **tail**: a variety of snowshoe; see ~ RACKET.

1985 *Decks Awash* Jan-Feb, p. 25 There are several different designs [of snow-shoes]: roundtails, which they call bear-paws now, beavertails and porcupine tails with the curved tails and rattails with the one long point.

pork n

1 Comb ~ **cake**, ~ **toutin**.

1987 FIZZARD 181 Then there was the food item most closely associated with Grand Bank—the pork cake, or potato pork cake, or, as it is more commonly known in Grand Bank, the 'por' cake.' 1981 SPARKES 92 The great wood-box is filled with split wood ready for the baking of buns, tarts, gingerbread and pork toutens.

post n

[1858 GREY] 3 About two miles from [the mouth of Eagle River] is the fishery belonging to Messrs. Hunt, where the salmon caught by different fishermen, at their different 'salmon posts,' is cleaned and packed in tins ready for shipment. 1977 WHITELEY 75 The elimination of sun-dried fish made less necessary the migration of the fishermen's family to fishing posts away from the village.

pot n

3 Comb ~ **lid.**

P 308-88 Some people had [pot leds]. [Pot] covers. Like snow-shoes? Something like that. They were made round. They were made from wood. No tails. They'd go around like that and then there were things across and a rope came up through to tie it on.

pound n *SED* iv, 107 Ha 'enclosure.'

1 Also: an area in inshore waters enclosed with netting in which live fish are held for later processing (see 1989 quot).

[1876] 1977 WHITELEY 38 I have been...in the habit of fishing for codfish at this place with an enclosed pound set at the end of my Salmon weir. 1989 *Evening Telegram* 16 July, p. 3 Fishermen [at Petty Harbour] constructed holding pounds which are connected to their codtraps. Those pounds, which can each hold up to 100,000 pounds of fish and are located up to seven miles offshore, are used to hold fish until they can be processed or sold.

2 1984 KELLAND 158 They washed their catch in large crates called pounds. These measured twelve feet by twelve feet by two and one half feet deep... The pounds were let down deeply enough [over the sides of the banking vessel] so as they filled with water, which poured into them through the spaces between laths. 1987 POOLE 99 When evening came I had thirty barrels of herring taken in and in the pounds and roused.

4 1987 *Evening Telegram* 11 Apr, p. 14 [tape transcript] We had a heavy load of fat [aboard] the vessel, and] we had two big pounds on deck and the *Viking* was an old slow ship and she was not making too much headway.

5 1985 BUSCH 62 But such 'cold drawn' oil...rendered only 50-70 per cent of the oil...even after the fat had been turned periodically and shifted among the sections [or] 'pounds' of the crib.

pound v Also: to store such a compartment with produce, etc.

1832 MOSS *MS Diary* 8 Mar Set 2 hands pounding seals' fat.

powder n Comb ~ **can:** explosive device to open a passage through a field of ice, ~ **devil,** ~ **gun,** ~ **line:** REDDENING LINE.

1988 *Evening Telegram* 26 Mar, p. 31 [He] remembers using explosive powder cans...to help free ships when they were stuck or jammed in heavy ice. The can was filled with powder nailed to a long stick and a long fuse was fitted in a small screwed cover on top. It was sealed water tight, and spread over the ice. The stick with the powder can and attached fuse were pushed below the ice... The fuse was lit and when the can exploded it helped break up the ice around the ship. 1980 HOLMES 43 We discovered [the powder horn] contained a quantity of powder which we laid along the floor in thin, winding trails to make 'powder devils.' [1792] PULLING (ed Marshall) 126 Then we fir'd *three Powder* Guns & gave

three Cheers. 1981 SPARKES 149 As soon as the bride emerged from the church porch, she would be greeted by devastating salvoes of powder-guns. 1984 POWELL 22 Then...you'd roll [the logs] up on a high gallows, then you'd mark with a powder line where you were going to make each saw cut. Both the bottom and the top of the log had to be marked with a black line. In order to make the line black, we would put some gunpowder in a can with some snow, then with birch bark the fire would melt the snow.

premises n pl

1986 RYAN 32 Of more importance [winter caretakers] ensured that the owner retained control of his premises because, under the traditional practice of the first arrival every spring having first choice of the *fishing rooms* [, the owner might lose them].

prime a

3 1960 *Assoc Am Geog* 1, 274 The codtrap berths were graded choice, prime, seconds, and fly, in that order, according to the run of fish taken from them. 1982 MCDOOLING 115 The prime trap berths are picked out first... Now everybody gets a shot at the prime berths.

prog n *Anglo-Manx Dialect* prawg, proag 'store [of supplies].' Attrib ~**bag,** ~ **box.**

1985 GUY 7 He slung his prog bag and kettle and a few muskrats down on the floor and got in. 1986 FELTHAM 174 In some parts of Newfoundland [the lunch box] was called a 'prog box,' but to my knowledge this term was never used in Bonavista North.

prong v

1986 *Evening Telegram* 11 Feb, p. 2 As well, fish is still being pronged with pitchforks and this is another factor contributing to low-quality fish.

prosecute v

[1979] 1985 LEHR & BEST (eds) 84 "Gull Cove": Our schooner we got ready, to prosecute did go/The codfish down in Gull Cove, where the stormy winds do blow.

proud a

1 1987 KING (ed) 129 "Gramma's Lullaby": One day Bill Samson said to she,/'Oi'm livin all alone,/'Oi'd be some proud to offer you,/'A dwelling of your own.'

puffin[1] n Also: adopted as the official provincial bird of Newfoundland.

1987 *Evening Telegram* 19 Sep, p. A4 More nearly than the other choices [in the selection of official bird status], the puffin is a bird of Newfoundland. According to Canadian Wildlife Service estimates, as many as 300,000 pairs—more than two thirds of the Atlantic Puffin population of North America—nest on Great Island, Green Island and Gull Island in the Witless Bay Seabird Sanctuary. 1988 ibid 10 May, p. 6 Although caplin are available for a short period in inshore waters, they are available in nearshore and offshore waters through most of the puffin breeding season. Because of their flying and diving ability, Atlantic puffins can search and find food at great distances from their breeding colonies.

pull v

2 To 'haul' (logs).

1985 ASHTON 201 "Lumbering Woods in the 30's":
Soon we settled in our camps and started pulling by the
cord. /A few days of pulling wood and the next day to
the store,/To keep our camp stocked up with food and
our horses stocked with hay.

3 Phr *pull guts*: in the operation of the 'header'
when dressing cod, to remove the head and entrails
of the fish.

1987 FIZZARD 129 'If I was splitting, I'd be splitting to
a certain table every day. The first thing you'd do starting
out was pulling guts.'

pull n In the lumber woods, the 'haul' of logs by
horse and sled or truck.

1985 ASHTON 201 "Lumbering Woods in the 30's":
For when the pull was over we started for home next
day.

pump n, v

2 Comb ~ **car**: **pump-trolley**.

1949 FITZGERALD 82 I'd sometimes flag a pump car if
I needed any aid. 1985 GOSSE 17 At that time our transportation was by hand car, pump car or trolley. They had
to be operated by manpower.

puncheon n

1 [1927] 1982 BURKE (ed Kirwin) 66 "Hold Your
Water": Every spinister in town she would get a
supply,/If her stock got exhausted, a puncheon on
deck/To last all her life till she passed in her check. 1987
Evening Telegram 27 Apr, p. 7 [tape transcript] Years
ago the coopers had to make the 100 gallon puncheons to
ship the seal oil away in. The wood came out from
England in blocks, squared. They had to cleave them and
make the staves...join them and then make the barrel and
hoop it right up... That was tight work.

3 Comb ~ **tub**.

1988 GOSSE 33 A galley was fixed to the deck just aft
of the forecastle scuttle and near the scuttlebutt. It consisted of a forty-gallon puncheon tub filled with rock
which was used to lay wood fires for cooking the grub of
each watch.

punt n

1 1984 KELLAND 103 There were and still are in use in
many parts of Newfoundland, a boat similar to the trap-
skiff, only very much smaller. Newfoundlanders called
this type a punt... In the Kelligrews area of Conception
Bay, these craft are used in two sizes; with the larger
being known as a punt, the smaller a rodney. 1987
FIZZARD 135 'I fished on Green Island for 34 summers.
First goin' off, we used to go in punts. They had four
sails on 'em, 'bout twenty feet long, 'bout six feet, some
seven in width, and they were practically open boats, just
a place covered to put your fish in.'

3 Comb ~ **man**.

1883 *The Newfoundlander* 12 Oct In some places
throughout Placentia Bay the punt men were still catching
some fish [this month].

pup n

1988 MOMATIUK & EASTCOTT (eds) 26 My dad and
me would jig fish in shoal water... By and by, the skin
comes off [your hands], and then the salt water eats away
your flesh... In the morning, they were right stiff. And
pups—boils from your elbows down, from your jacket
rubbing the wet skin.

purdle* n Cp *EDD* pirl v 1 'to whirl, turn
around,' pirler sb 'a fall, a tumble.' A fall or
tumble (P 113-56).

P 131-70 If a child falls: 'Oh, what a purdle.' P 14-72
'I got some purdle when I tripped on the stump.' P 322-
88 ~ a fall.

pure a, av

1 [1898] 1986 *Evening Telegram* 24 Mar, p. 6 It was
'dark as death,' he wrote, 'a pure hurricane.' 1987 FIZ-
ZARD 154 'Before we got there the storm burst on us like
a thunderstorm, pure hurricane with blinding snow.'

2 1985 GUY 96 'Hop the hell out of that, you.' I said,
wringing up my fist at him, 'because you pure poisons
me.' 1988 DOHANEY 18 'That's all I hears around here.
Grand Falls. Grand Falls. Grand Falls. Me ears are
piesoned with the place. Pure piesoned.'

put v

3 In comb with av ~ **away** (a) (b), ~ **back**: to
save for later use, ~ **down**: to construct a sawmill,
~ **up**: also, to process frozen cod fillets.

[1937] 1945 SCAMMELL 19 "Tommy Decker's Venture": For ever since three years ago when she put his
warts away,/Young Tom, he promised her he'd be a
friend to her some day. 1988 *Evening Telegram* 28 May,
p. A1 [I mean] people...who are charmers. The kind who
put away warts...and cure toothache. 1987 *Nfld Qtly*
lxxxiii (1), 15 Before the boat was tied up she was into
her knee rubbers and oil clothes ready to help put the fish
away. Q 68-38 'You stupid fool, I had that put back for
the Spring.' 1981 SPARKES 177 Incidentally, a [saw] mill
is not 'built,' it is 'put down.' 1984 GOUGH 27 Salted
fish are drying on the flakes... The older men can tell
you who put up the fish as surely as if the men had
signed each open fish. 1987 FIZZARD 212 'We could put
up from 25,000 to 35,000 pounds [of frozen cod fillets]
altogether in a day.'

Q

quar(r) v Cp *SED* iv, 433 ~ n W.

quat v *SED* iv, 1012 So Co.

queer a Cp *O Sup*[2] ~ a[1] 1 a *queer fellow* esp in
Ire and in naut contexts; *EDD* 2 (2) *queer stick*.
Comb ~ **hand,** ~ **stick**: one who is of or
cultivates an unusual, humorous character, an odd
manner or behaviour; cp CRAMP a, HAND 1.

P 245-55 Queer stick: an unusual, eccentric person; a
wag—not at all derogatory. P 10-57 Queer hand: peculiar,
humorous person. M 68-16 He was a queer hand with a
bit of the devil in him. T 969-71 And Jack said, 'Good-

night,' he said, 'Father Drumcap.' He used to call him Father Drumcap. Not a word. Never spoke. He said, 'Have some supper Father Drumcap?' Never spoke... 'Huh! You're a damn queer hand!' Jack said. 'Come in,' he said, 'and won't talk to a feller.' [Father Drumcap] got up and he went out through the door again. 1987 JOHNSTON 61 She would play the 'character' to him, the 'queer hand,' encourage a kind of condescending amusement on his part.

quick n Also comb ~ **kettle**.
1985 *Decks Awash* Jan-Feb, p. 17 [These tin kettles have] been called Quick Kettles and Piper Kettles. At one time they were used in fishing boats and in the woods, as well as in people's homes. 1986 SAUNDERS 12 [She would] send me some things I couldn't buy there, like my awl and tacker for sewing leather and my little Newfoundland tea kettle—what we call a 'quick' because it boils water so fast.

quiff n
1985 *A Yaffle of Yarns* 23 Despite the rainstorm that morning, I dressed in my three-piece suit, my raglan and my quiff hat.

quintal n also **kantle**.
1 1931 *Can Geog J* ii, 399 In one year these hardy men took about 500,000 'kantles' of cod (a quintal is 112 pounds). 1983 WARNER 26 A thousand cantles...we fished, and we were all in the family for crew.
2 1987 POWELL 34 In late September my crew and I got the last of our codfish sun-dried. After it was all weighed we had a little less than two hundred quintals, 112 pounds per quintal.
3 1987 *Evening Telegram* 27 Apr, p. 7 The pelts were all weighed by the quintal. Then there were deductions of the weight of the fat for scraps of meat that was left on the [seal] pelts.
4 Comb ~ **drum**.
1987 FIZZARD 160 'We had several makes of barrels. There'd be half-quintal drums, quintal drums [etc].'

quinter v
1988 GOSSE 40 In actual fact Charlie Dawe was coming south in the *Terra Nova* and quintering (picking up scattered seals) off Cape Bonavista that morning.

quism n
1987 DAWE [40] Q is for quism,/Some quaint odd remark/About stuff like omens,/May snow and pitch dark.

R

ra int also **etta**.
1924 *Deep-Sea Fishers* xxi (4), 139 Auch, etta—Right, Left—Gee and Haw for dog-team use.

rabbit n Comb ~ **slip**, ~ **wire**.
1988 *Evening Telegram* 17 May, p. 8 The weather was mausy and...I had it on my mind about a rabbit slip that I

never had struck up yet the spring and I wanted to get in and see to that. 1986 SAUNDERS 240 He gathered the top on a three-inch nail and tied two parts of rabbit wire about six feet long to the nail [and] hung the bag from a nail directly in front of the stove.

race² n
1858 [LOWELL] i, 90 [With his sons] and theirs he would one day have manned his schooner for 'the Larbadore.' He would have been another man at the head of such a race. P 245-87 'Tis almost too bad to talk about [the Great War] to the young race.

rack² n *DA* ~ n¹ 1 obs (1735), *OED* sb² 5 b (1735) for sense 1; cp *OED* 5 a obs (1687) for sense 2.
1 A wooden framework set in a river to impede the passage of salmon. Attrib ~ **work**.
[1856] 1985 TAYLOR 16 Weirs are...formed by placing a beam across the river; racks, resembling those in use in stables for horses, are formed about eight to ten feet long, which extend from the bottom of the river to the top of the beam, these run out from each side to within about three feet of each other...where a passage is left for the ingress of the fish into the pound formed by extending the racks parallel with the banks of the river. 1987 PEYTON 7 The plentiful supply of salmon in the rivers in those early times was caught by using 'rack work' across narrow, shallow channels of the rivers and large brooks.
2 Comb ~ **sticks**: two long sticks, or 'longers,' bolted to the body or bunk of a sled (1985 *Terminology of Loggers* 14).

racket² n
2 1984 WRIGHT 99 Even Isaac remarked after the 1982 hunt, 'I'm tired of the racket. Twenty springs is enough.'

racy a Cp *OED* ~ a 6 *racy of the soil* 'chiefly used with ref to Ire' (1870, 1889). Phr *racy of the soil*: characteristic of Newfoundland and its people.
1891 *Holly Branch* 38 There was not a song, racy of the soil, but [John Halley] knew. [1927] 1978 DOYLE 2 In selecting our Newfoundland songs we have made a special effort to give precedence to those only that are racy of the soil and illustrate the homely joys and sorrows of our people. 1976 MURPHY 150-1 'The excuse that the effusions of James Murphy and his fellow versifiers are racy of the soil will not hold water. Readers of our dailies must stare when they peruse the horrible compositions which adorn their pages.'

raft¹ v *O Sup²* ~ v¹ 5 (1883-1939) for sense 1.
1 1987 *Evening Telegram* 4 July, p. 56 [tape transcript] The next morning the vessel was jammed and we couldn't get her out and the ice kept coming up, coming up, coming up. That day I saw the ice go over one island and rafted about 20 feet when it struck the main islands.
2 Derivative form **rafter** n.
1987 FIZZARD 6 A combination of high water levels in the brook, ice rafters in the spring, high tides, and waves whipped up by northeast gales broadened the mouth of the brook.
3 Vbl n **rafting**.

1985 BUSCH 44 At times bad storms, especially those which produce 'rafting' of one floe upon another, may bring high mortality among newborn pups and even whelping females.

ragged a
1 1837 BLUNT 41 Ragged Harbor is so named from the rough and craggy appearance of the surrounding rocks, which render it unsafe for either boats or ships to enter. 1983 *Gazetteer of Canada: Nfld* 141-2 Ragged [Clift, Cove, Harbour, Head, Island Point, Rock, etc; several score coastal names].
2 Comb ~-**jacket**.
1985 *Canadian Sealers Association* 6 [The pup] then starts to get in the water and becomes a ragged jacket, which means it is starting to [lose] its white fur.

raggedy a
2 Comb ~ **jacket**.
1986 *Evening Telegram* 1 Mar, p. A5 After less than two weeks [following birth] the 'whitecoat' pups are abandoned by their mothers and begin to shed their hair, or to 'molt.' Partially molted pups are called 'raggedy jackets.'

ral n
1982 DAWE 13 A ral who once lived in St Pauls,/Made rackets in all the dance-halls;/He never grew mellow,/ This troublesome fellow,/From kicking out windows and walls.

ram n
1989 CANDOW 33 Many sealing vessels were equipped with rams, two long poles attached to opposite sides of the bow and lashed together just below the bowsprit.

ram-cat n *SED* iv, 371 D. For the development of this [= tom cat] into a threatening figure, cp 1973 quot and 1985.
1985 *Atlantic Insight* Aug, p. 44 [In Placentia Bay] there's an appalling creature in animal form called a 'ram-cat.' It's 10 times the size of an ordinary moggie and so ferocious in appearance that it puts grown men off their feed for a week.

randy n *SED* iv, 853 Do.
1902 *Nfld Qtly* Sep, p. 21-2 Yes, she was out all night, and we all went in looking for her [with] guns and powder, and horns and lanterns: such a randy! 1984 POWELL 89 The greatest randy I ever had with him and his dogs was the first winter that our first baby was born... The trip was only about forty miles, this didn't seem too far when the weather and travelling were good [for the dog team and sled].

ranger n
1 [1768] 1826 CARTWRIGHT i, p. 36 Ranger's river being crost, the deer fence was seldom visible, and all other vestiges discontinued very much. 1987 POWELL 24 There were always lots of seals in [Hawkes Bay]. This is the bay seal, not the harp seal. It is the seal which we call the doter, and the young one is called the ranger.

2 1988 *Evening Telegram* 31 May, p. 11 Since the man said that the matter had been reported to the nearest Ranger, we felt that things were taken care of.

rat n Comb ~**tail**: a type of snow-shoe.
1985 *Decks Awash* Jan-Feb, p. 25 There are several different designs [of snow-shoes]: roundtails...beavertails and porcupine tails with the curved tails and rattails with one long point.

rattle^1 n *O Sup*^{2} sb^1 II 4 e (Nfld: 1776-1975) for sense 1.
1 1986 SAUNDERS 47 We paddled the steadies and poled or portaged the rattles, and even before we crossed The Gut and struck the tide at Dawson's Point my shoulders were aching.
2 (a)
1987 *Evening Telegram* 19 Sep, p. A4 Narrow, shallow runs or tickles between islands, or the constrictions of bays, where the flowing and ebbing tides resemble rapids in a river are called 'rattles' in Labrador.

rattler n
1983 *Gazetteer of Canada: Nfld* 142 Rattler Brook [Rock, Bight—four occurrences].

rattling ppl
[1768] 1989 *Nfld Qtly* lxxxv (1), 21 Great Rattling Brook. 1983 *Gazetteer of Canada: Nfld* 142-3 Rattling Brook [etc, high frequency in river names]. 1984 POWELL 101 Soon I was heading up the Big Lake, about four miles long, and then I had to go down a very rattling brook about one mile where the water emptied into the river.

reach n
1 1987 POOLE 20 He had his fishing room just across the reach called Little Harbour.

red a PRATT redberry for sense 2.
1 In name of bird: ~ **leg(s)**.
1937 *Bk of Nfld* ii, p. 47 Red legs. Ruddy turnstone. 1987 MONTEVECCHI & TUCK 241 Redleg. Black guillemot.
2 In name of berry: ~ **berry**: PARTRIDGE BERRY; also cranberry.
1985 *Nfld Qtly* lxxx (4), 30 For Christmas dinner all they had was a few stewed redberries and some molasses. 1986 *Them Days* xi (4), 7 [At the Hudson's Bay Co.] there were also barrels of red berries (low bush cranberries) and bakeapples or salmon berries that were purchased in the summer.
3 Comb ~ **indian**, ~ **feed (count)**: a condition of caplin when feeding on plankton in or near the harvesting season, leaving them with a reddish coloration, ~ **jack**.
1987 PEYTON 1 The Beothucks...were also called the Red Indians, from the manner in which these natives smeared their faces and bodies and sometimes even their clothing with red ochre. P 245-90 'When the red feed count is up the caplin are no good [for the Japanese market].' 1930 *Am Speech* v, p. 392 Redjacks. Light but

waterproof leather boots; before the advent of rubber boots they were worn universally by the fishermen.

redden v Phr *redden (one's) arse*: to spank (a child); hence *arse-reddening*.

P 320-63 I'm going to give you an ass reddnin'. P 148-89 You're going to get a redden' arse. 1989 *Muse* 24 Nov, p. [19] Don't you dare throw that worm at Mommy or I'll redden your ass.

reddening n Attrib ~ **line**.

1981 SPARKES 1 Next, with the reddening line, one of those sides was struck off into spaces equal to the desired thickness of the plank, plus a little to allow for the saw kerf and the planing.

ree-raw n Cp *Anglo-Manx Dialect* ~ 'irregular or contrary motion' for sense 1.

1 1987 *Nfld LifeStyle* June, p. 54 We all swapped news of each other and everybody talked at the same time. What a ree-raw!

reeve² v Also ppl **reeving**: in imprecations.

1978 *Papers in Ling* xii, p. 328 Cursed Lord reevin. 1985 GUY 7 Now then, you lord lifting hopped-up reeving dying merciful blood of a flaming sawed-off...jack-a-bon.

reeve n Phr *by the reeves*.

1985 *A Yaffle of Yarns* 21 One cold summer's morning and 'raining be the reeves' I walked from my boarding house [to] The Southside.

reeving vbl n Comb ~ **string**.

[1900] 1989 *Nfld Qtly* lxxxv (2), 23 I might cast a net over hundreds of caplin and draw the reeving string before lifting them to a punt of my very own.

riddle n *SED* iv, 93 'riddle sticks' D. Attrib **riddle (rod) fence** ([1987] QUINLAN 30).

1981 SPARKES xv To make a riddle fence, a top and a bottom rail are first nailed to posts or are tied in position with green withes. A middle rail is then set in place. The riddles are forest thinnings of young spruce, about as tall as a man and not much bigger than a man's thumb. They are laced vertically on the three rails in a basket-weave manner. 1988 *Nfld Herald* 4 June, p. 24 Wright had just made a film about a wriggling fence and was asked...to come in and describe what he was up to.

rig v

1 1987 FIZZARD 129 'There'd be four tables rigged up, one table on the starboard side of the forward hold and one on the port side and the same thing on the after hold [of the banking schooner].'

rig n Cp *O Sup²* ~ sb⁶ 3 c 'any apparatus or device' for sense 3.

1 1985 *A Yaffle of Yarns* 26 B'y if you wants to keep up a job wid we fellers, you'll have to get da proper rig-out.

2 1982 BURSEY 36 "Christmas Fear": We went

jannying at Christmas/Ransacked old trunks/And understairs closets/For outlandish rig;/Blanket, sheet or tablecloth/Or long underwear/For overall disguise. 1989 BENNETT 109 If they so wished, they could wear a different 'rig' every night [during Christmas].

3 1987 FIZZARD 170 'There we took on a load of rum in kegs—five and ten gallon kegs. We brought that up just off the coast. We wouldn't go anywhere in that rig. We wouldn't go in too close anyway. A boat used to come out, perhaps fifteen-twenty miles.'

right intens.

[1935] 1985 RUSTED 33 I met a man from one of the nearby settlements, who described several members with 'flu as 'one was very bad, the other right bad and the third proper bad.' 1984 POWELL 27 Then I went back to the boat and found she was dry on the beach and the wind was gone right calm. 1987 *Nfld Qtly* lxxxiii (1), 16 I got right dizzy going up the steps in Cabot Tower.

rightify v PRATT infreq or rare.

T 543-68 'The teacher,' she said, 'give me a sum this evening,' she said, 'and if I can have the sum rightified,' she said, 'the morrow morning,' she said, 'when I goes to school,' she said, 'me education is over.'

rind n

1 1981 SPARKES xiv Those peeled skins of bark [from the fir tree] were called 'rinds' and were not only used to cover fish but also as roofing for pigsties and other shacks and 'tilts.' 1988 GOSSE 21 Other preparatory chores included repairs to fishing stages, such as replacing 'rinds' or tree barks used for roofing.

rind v also **rhind**. Cp *O Sup²* ~ v¹ b (1893, 1962) for sense 3.

1 [1706] 1987 MONTEVECCHI & TUCK 190 'N. of St John's as far as Carbonier and S. as far as Ferryland, the trees have been rinded and woods destroyed.' 1985 DOMSTAD 20 Take the bark from the top of the tree and rind down towards the bottom.

3 [1907] 1982 BURKE (ed Kirwin) 37 "The Twenty Mile Walking Match": While some began to lag behind,/They found their heels begin to rhind. 1988 *Nfld Qtly* lxxxiii (4), 47 [I kicked] and completely rinded my ankle on the edge of the TV stand.

rinded p ppl

[1987] QUINLAN 6 Beds were cotton duck sacks filled with feathers then placed on boards or layers of small rinded sticks.

rinding vbl n

[1621] 1982 CELL (ed) 255 *Letters to Calvert*: Thirdly that the rinding of Trees may be prohibited, but only such as shall bee felled for necessary vses and needefull behoofes.

ring¹ n Cp *OED* ~ sb¹ 3 f 'a measure of boards or staves' (1674, 1867). A bundle of six hoops, enough for one cask.

1981 SPARKES xiv Like the rinds, hoops had their own special table of measure. They were counted by rings, burns and bundles. Six hoops made a ring.

ripper n A short knife used to 'dress' fish; CUT-THROAT (1930 *Am Speech* v, p. 392).

1971 NOSEWORTHY 237 ~ a short, straight, sharp knife, right-handed only, for cutting the throat and stomach of a fish and removing the head.

rise n

3 1918 *Daily News* 28 Oct, p. 4 The planter conscientiously turned over to the supplier the proceeds of the voyage at the current price and the rise.

5 Comb **rise end**: the end of the sound bone closest to the tail (P 300-89); BLOOD: **blood end**.

riser n Comb ~ **hoop**: the first hoop placed around the staves of a cask or barrel.

1986 *Them Days* xi (4), 28 [The hoops] are made to bang the staves together, see. Then you get your riser hoop, first hoop, and you place your staves in...one wide, one narrow and so on.

river n Comb ~ **head**, ~ **warden**: one appointed to supervise and control use of salmon and trout streams, etc, under regulatory control; GUARDIAN 2.

1689 *English Pilot* 14 [The course] goes in the *Bay-Bulls* lying in W.N.W. for at least two Miles, and after that N.W. for about a Mile to the River Head. 1987 POOLE 86 When the *Codroy* arrived here there were ten or twelve people from the river head of Lewis Bay waiting to get some food. [1892] 1985 TAYLOR 13 Two river wardens were appointed in 1890, one each for Gander Bay and the Bay of Exploits. 1903 *Nfld Qtly* iii (2), 16 'I was quite delighted to read your lists of River Wardens and the records of the various catches.'

road[1] n See **line**[2] n 1: *line of road*.

1 1981 PADDOCK 24 "Camp seven": So h'up da road een single line/We goes een merry mood,/Behin' da man who'll take us to/Da roads wid all da wood.

2 In warning cry of children when sliding in winter; also in form **roader**.

C 71-18 Roader. A word shouted out loudly when sliding to warn people to get out of the way. Shouted row-der, each syllable equally accented but the last one more drawn out than the first. P 108-75 When sliding down a hill in winter we would yell 'The *road*!' to warn people out of our path. P 295-83 Roader! Calling to clear the way when sliding on sleds or coasters.

roader See ROAD[1] 2.

roary-eyed See RORY-EYED.

rock n

1 Familiar term or nickname for Newfoundland, freq in form *the (old) rock*.

[1901 DUNCAN *Ainslee's* Dec, p. 428 "In Remote Newfoundland": The shore line is rock, in some places swept, by flood and fire, bare of all soil—grim, naked rock.] 1939 FROUDE 3 I am leaved alone on the old rock on a christmas day the first time in my life. 1968 *This Rock Within the Sea* [book title]. 1985 JOHNSTON 125

'Here, on this rock-bound Elba of the North Atlantic, here, under the ceaseless howl of storm and gale, give me a boy who will make his mark on the rock.' 1987 *Nfld Herald* 12 Dec, p. 18 Born in Halifax [he] moved to Newfoundland with his family at the age of three months, and spent the next 33 years on the Rock. 1989 *Evening Telegram* 22 Feb, p. 4 In his first words upon arriving in Newfoundland, [Mr Turner] referred to our beautiful Island by that insulting sobriquet, 'the rock.' 1990 ibid 21 Mar, p. 4 Now we are hearing from... Newfoundland broadcasting stations such sayings as the Rock, the weather south of The Rock, the road conditions across The Rock, etc. It goes on and on.

2 An isolated underwater rock protuberance, freq a prolific fishing 'spot' or 'ground' for coastal fishermen.

1986 FELTHAM 54 There were 'rocks' or isolated underwater peaks that measured only a few yards in any direction and lay miles from the nearest land. To find these 'rocks,' very precise 'marks' were necessary.

3 Phr *off the rock*: indigenous to or characteristic of Newfoundland.

1989 *Sunday Express* 5 Mar, p. 23 Phrases like CFA and 'Off the Rock' are identified [in the exhibition catalogue] as Newfoundland expressions. The latter a 'term people use to describe their physical and psychical landscape.'

4 Attrib, comb ~ **berry**: black crowberry (*Empetrum nigrum*) (1898 *J A Folklore* xi, 279), ~ **cod**.

1984 KALLEO 8 During the winter, we'd jig for rock-cod, which we'd cook or eat raw and frozen. They're very tasty frozen, dipped in seal oil or eaten with fresh seal blubber.

rode n

1 [1980] 1985 LEHR & BEST (eds) 198 "The *Water Witch*": Punts, rhodes and lanterns they were brought by kind and willing hands,/The shrieks of females in distress those fishermen could not stand. 1986 FELTHAM 55 On the fishing grounds, the motor boats, like the bullies, were moored with 'rodes' and grapnels.

rodney n *O Sup*[2] 3 (Nfld: 1895-1966).

1981 SPARKES 184 If the ice was 'swatchy,' they took a very light small boat with them called a rodney or gunning punt. 1986 FELTHAM 49 The smallest and most commonly used boat [in Bonavista Bay] was the 'punt' or 'rodney.' It was versatile and seaworthy. It varied in length from fourteen to eighteen feet, was narrow in proportion to its length, had a high counter that created very little drag and was generally streamlined at the water-line. Consequently it could sail very well before or across the wind and could be rowed with a minimum of effort. 1987 *Evening Telegram* 7 Mar, p. 10 I well remember Ira, because he could not only scull a rodney forwards but also backwards, a feat I never accomplished.

roll v

1 1899 *Evening Telegram* 4 Aug For the past three days caplin and squid have been rolling along the full length of the beach [at Carbonear]. 1949 FITZGERALD 46

I can see the schools of caplin now that roll along the beaches. [1963] 1988 ibid 16 June, p. 6 Beaches in many parts of the Avalon Peninsula are the scene of that great annual phenomena...millions of caplin rolling in. 1989 *Sunday Express* 19 Mar, p. 7 The vast bulk of our caplin stocks 'roll on the beaches' as part of their spawning ritual. 1990 *Evening Telegram* 23 Jan, p. 5 Now Bishop's Beach is deserted, not one caplin rolls ashore to spawn.

roller[1] n
3 1987 FIZZARD 160 'We'd make a lot of little things like tow-pins, dory plugs, dory mallets, tide-sticks, rollers [etc].'

roller[2] n Also: rope or yarn used for caulking a wooden craft.
1987 DAWE [12] It's spiky old hemp,/So your fingers might itch/When you tuck in the rawlers/And pour on the pitch.

rolling ppl, vbl n Comb ~ **song**: song accompanying the fulling of cloth.
1980 *Halpert Festschrift* 107 [After milling, the cloth] was smoothed out on the table, then rolled onto a board about six inches wide to the accompaniment of 'rolling songs.'

rompse v Also: to romp and tumble.
1924 *Deep-Sea Fishers* xxi (4), 139 Rampsen—Rough play. T 2414-74 As I went out in the field one day/I saw our parson bright and gay/Rampsin Molly on the hay/And he turned her upside down, sir!

roof n Section of netting covering the top of the traditionally open 'cod trap,' devised to prevent fish from escaping.
1982 MCDOOLING 99 There are still a few [cod traps] being used but most of the fishermen have now gone over to the Japanese traps. The 'Jap' trap is more efficient in that it has a roof which keeps the fish from swimming over the top of the walls and the entrance (the door of the Newfoundland trap) is funneled inward so that the fish, once they enter, cannot get out again as easily as...from the older model.

room n
1 1985 ASHTON 203 "Indian Bay": And when we arrived onto the pier, it was there we had no doubt,/For all the men on the room was anxious looking out. 1987 POOLE 93 The big boss had taken over Snug Harbour and I was second hand and did not go on the collector but stayed on the room all summer.
3 1989 BENNETT 84 'The room' was the name always given to the best, and seldom-used, room in the house—a sitting room where the family kept all their finest dishes, ornaments, framed pictures of their forebears, and their most elaborate holy pictures, crucifixes, and usually a very ornate Sacred Heart.

rory-eyed a also **roary-eyed***. From a U S cpd (h)orry-eyed 'drunk': *DAS* oryide (1894), orry-eyed

(1943): BERREY p. 106 hoary-eyed, orie-eyed, *Am Speech* iv (1928-9), p. 102 orie-eyed, 422, v (1930), p. 231; cp *SND* roarie 'drunk' 1865, 1904.
1 Drunk.
P 279-89 We used to say 'He's roary-eyed' when someone was very, very angry, really enraged, and also when someone was roaring drunk.
2 Very angry, furious.
M 64-3 When anyone dared to call him that [nickname] he'd get roary-eyed. T 147-65 He went right crazy, right roary-eyed. C 71-110 She would get rory-eyed meaning that she would get very mad or angry. 1985 *A Yaffle of Yarns* 11 I also realized that...Dad would be 'rory-eyed' and hit the roof if he knew his only son was takin' his life in his own hands.

rote n *South Shore Phr Bk* rout.
1986 FELTHAM 48 They raised their voices to "Jesus, Savior pilot me" but barely competed with the sea wind whistling through the alders; and the scrub fir and the 'rote' of the breakers on the shore nearby.

rotten a *O Sup*[2] ~ a 1 4 c.
1984 POWELL 107 There would be several weeks in the spring when the bay ice would be too thin to travel on to hunt and the snow would be too rotten to get into the woods. 1988 MOMATIUK & EASTCOTT (eds) 122 The sun was beating down and up to us, reflecting off the snow, and I felt as if I had a sunstroke. We were in rotten snow with about 1,800 pounds on each sled, and we really had to work.

rough a Cp *OED* ~ a 20 'of a homely or plain fare, coarse but plentiful' Sc (1721-1818), *EDD* ~ a 1 (19) ~ meat 'cabbage and other green food' D.
3 Comb ~ **grub**: habitual fare of fishermen and loggers.
P 324-89 The food [in the lumber camps] was a simple affair—'rough grub.' The usual meal was salt meat, potatoes, carrot, turnip, cabbage. Tea and bread were present at every meal. P 285-89 Most of the food that was prepared and eaten on the Labrador was rough grub. People would have flour, sugar, molasses, beans, peas and the most important one was fish.

round a
1 Also: of a sealskin, removed in a single unsplit fashion (see 1895 quot).
1895 *Evening Herald* 6 Feb, p. 3 Mostly the bladder [used in harpooning seals] is a young seal skin, skinned round made [tight], to float a seal. 1989 CANDOW 35 Dead whitecoats were brought back 'round' to the vessel and skinned on the deck at night.
2 [1938] 1988 *Evening Telegram* 8 Mar, p. 6 The SS *Magnhild* loaded...113 barrels of dressed and 109 barrels of round herring for New York. 1988 ibid 18 Jan, p. 3 Round fish has to be processed into the salt product, and it takes 2.34 pounds of fresh fish to produce a pound of saltbulk, or salt fish not yet dried.
3 Comb ~ **tail**: also a type of snow-shoe.
1985 *Decks Awash* Jan-Feb, p. 25 There are several different designs [of snow-shoes]: roundtails...beavertails and porcupine tails with the curved tails.

round n

2 Phr *in the round, on the round.*

1988 SINCLAIR (ed) 119 Prior to 1979 the co-operative sold longliner fish 'in the round' to processing plants elsewhere. 1960 *Assoc Amer Geog* 1, 274 The traps varied in size from 40 to 75 fathoms 'on the round,' or the distance around the top of the four rectangular walls of the trap. 1966 FARIS 217 Cat Harbour traps can vary from 40-60 or more 'fathoms on the round,' meaning 40 to 60 fathoms (80 to 100 yards) around the outside perimeter.

rounder n

1 1903 *Daily News* 19 Sep "Cooking Cod": I saw an account in John Bull's *Daily Mail*,/Relating to Tommy [English soldier] who cooked in a pot/Our Tommy Cod rounders at famed Aldershot. 1988 *Evening Telegram* 18 May, p. 19 Leggies, more commonly known as 'rounders,' were small cod which were salted whole.

roundy a *Anglo-Manx Dialect, O Sup² ~ a 1 (1882).*

royal a Comb ~ george.

1987 PITT 391 Requests for copies [of his address, "Poetry and Science"] did, indeed, 'pour in,'...but realizing that he now had a 'Royal George' in his fleet (Methodist preachers' metaphor for a prize sermon used only on very special occasions) he refused to surrender it for general publication.

rubber n

1 1984 KELLAND 24 [The dory] carried a very strong rake at the ends, and her rubbers (protective strips nailed along the outer edge of the gunnels) were rounded.

2 1985 NEWHOOK 24 The last item to be inspected was the 't'igh' rubbers... They were most often tied at the top with a buckle and strap. 1986 SAUNDERS 52 I had on knee rubbers but Jim wore skin boots. 1987 *Evening Telegram* 10 Oct, p. 34 [tape transcript] The trenches used to be wet and soggy...but Mom had long rubbers and that and she used to dig up the potatoes.

run v

2 1985 BUSCH 71 Movement generated heat and thus hastened decomposition [of the seal fat]; a full ship locked in the ice could see its entire cargo start to 'run' as the fat melted.

run n

1 [1938] 1988 *Evening Telegram* 7 June, p. 6 The run of salmon has slacked off at Bay Bulls during the past few days. 1987 FIZZARD 179-80 The winter supply of salt cod was caught and cured in the fall, the season that normally supplied the best run of fish.

2 Also: a common generic in place-names.

[1977] 1985 LEHR & BEST (eds) 59 "The *Excel*": On the rocky shore on the Labrador, where the dreadful deed was done/In a place called the Black Island, outside of Grady's Run. 1987 *Evening Telegram* 9 May, p. 15 [tape transcript] 'Are you calling in to Battle Harbour?' 'No,' he said, 'there's two ice-bergs in the run going in and we can't get in.'

runner n

1 1984 KELLAND 183 The trawl runner or running stick...is made up of a section of plank, five feet long, four inches wide and two and one half inches thick. A foot and a half back from each end of this piece of wood the center is sawn out to the depth of one and a quarter inches which forms a square edged niche two feet long.

running ppl

2 Comb ~ ice, ~ stick: RUNNER 2.

1986 FELTHAM 65 Sometimes the sealers...found it difficult to get to a railway station because the reach separating these islands from the mainland was made impassable by 'running' ice or slob. 1984 KELLAND 184 It was while a trawl was being underrun that the running stick played an important role. It was jammed down in the dory's riser a little aft of midships; when the lines were hauled in over the bow roller they also ran along on the roller in the running stick. The stick not only had the effect of keeping the dory broadside to the trawl, it assisted the man hauling to keep his grip on the lines when the winds and tides were working against him.

S

sac See SACK².

sack² n also sac. Phr *in sack*: laden with supplies or cargo. Attrib, comb ~ boat, ~ boat system.

1689 *English Pilot* 14 [St John's is] the chiefest in the *New-found-land* for the Number of Ships used and employed in Fishing, and for Sacks, as also for the number of Inhabitants here dwelling and remaining all the Year. [(1703) 1963-4 *Nfld Qtly* lxiii (4), 10 [Lahontan memoir] If...there should not come so great a number to Placentia in Saque (Sack), that is to say with Goods, they would find as much Profit in it as in Trading with Commodities which are prejudicial to the Health of the Inhabitants.] 1732 *Calendar State Papers Amer. & W. Indies* 225 Which fish they sell to the British sack ships, for bills of exchange. [*O Sup²*] 1986 *A People of the Sea* (ed Jamieson) 94 By the 1680s and 1690s the [Channel] Islands were also engaged in sending a small number of 'sac' ships to Newfoundland whose purpose was to purchase fish that had already been caught. The 'sac-boat system,' as has been pointed out, 'involved a more highly complex capitalist system than the operations of the fishing captains who caught their own fish yearly and bartered it cheaply for continental goods.'

saddleback n

2 1987 HORWOOD 164 The crows set up a great clatter [along our beach] but carefully kept their distance. Not the saddleback (as the fishermen call him). He hurled his goose-sized body courageously into the air and made straight for the eagle in a power dive.

sail n

2 Comb ~ loft.

1987 FIZZARD 137 New sails were made and damaged

ones repaired in 'saillofts,' such as the one on the top floor of Harris's fish store on the waterfront.

st john's n

2 Comb **st john's (dog)**, ~ **man**: native of the city.

1883 HATTON & HARVEY 232 It is now generally admitted that there are two distinct types of the Newfoundland dog, one considerably larger than the other, and reckoned as the true breed; the other being named the Labrador, or St John's, or Lesser Newfoundland. The latter is chiefly found in Labrador, and specimens are also to be met with in Newfoundland. [1956] 1988 RUSSELL (ed Miller) 16 'Uncle Bobby figgered he was listenin' to a crowd of St John's men repairin' a cod trap.' 1988 *Nfld Qtly* lxxxiii (4), 41 The display of the gas mask (invented by a St John's man) says so much more about the First World War than do other pictures of plaques and memorials.

st peter's n Comb ~ hooch: see ~ gin, ~ rum.

1985 *Nfld Qtly* lxxix (2), 3 He would...note where his sinful neighbors were hiding their Saint Peter's hooch against the merry Yuletide.

salmon n For comb salmon berry in sense 2, see O Sup[2] ~ sb[1] 4 c.

1 1983 *Gazetteer of Canada: Nfld* 152-3 Salmon Bay [Bight, Brook, Cove, Gulch, Hole, Net Head, Point, Pond, River, Rock, Shoal, etc]. 1989 *Evening Telegram* 27 Nov, p. 3 When asked what may be done [to conserve the salmon stock] he replied: 'Fewer large salmon have to go into nets and on the end of rods and hooks and be put on the spawning grounds, that's what has to be done.'

2 Attrib, comb, cpd ~ **berry**: BAKEAPPLE (*Rubus chamaemorus*), ~ **berth**, ~ **box**, ~ **collector**, ~ **depôt**: see ~ **station**, ~ **net**, ~ **station**.

1986 *Them Days* xi (4), p. 7 There were also barrels of red berries (low bush cranberries) and bakeapples or salmon berries that were purchased in the summer. [1889] 1985 TAYLOR 12 In Gander River I was informed that there were eight salmon berths claimed by seven persons in all. These people fish in the river with stake-nets which they put out...about the 12th June, and...[take] in about the 8th August, each year. 1987 POOLE 17 There was a man living in Seal Bight [who] had good salmon berths handed down from his father. 1980 COX 22 [They] get out three or four chunks of ice...chip it with an axe, put the salmon into what we call a salmon box...and coat it with ice and ship it off. 1987 POOLE 63 When the salmon collector came the first time I had quite a few salmon iced down in my stage. [1858 GREY] 3 [Cartwright] is a salmon depôt of Messrs. Hunt, of London, whence their agents ship preserved salmon for England. 1986 SAUNDERS 58 We don't want to run over Uncle John's salmon nets now, do we? 1986 *Them Days* xi (4), 15 [They would] carefully pass up the huge fish (salmon), which had been split down the back and laid out flat for the preliminary salting which took place at the salmon stations [like Rigolet].

salmonier n

1983 *Gazetteer of Canada: Nfld* 152 Salmonier Arm [Bight, Cove, Hill, Island, Lookout, Point, River, etc].

1985 *Nfld Qtly* lxxx (3), 25 He also owned supply stores at Fogo and Tilting Harbour to trade with the planters, salmoniers, furriers and woodsmen of Notre Dame Bay.

salt n

1 [1985] MAHER 39 [The boat] brought a cargo of salt from Cadiz, Spain and landed it here to be used as fishery salt...sold to every part of the island.

2 1989 CANDOW 76 The pelts were stowed in wooden pounds in the holds, laid fat to fat and hair to hair, with crushed sea ice called 'sish' or 'salt' between each layer.

3 Phr *sparing salt, spoiling fish*: see *spare the salt and spoil the scrod*; under *salt*.

1937 DEVINE 73 [proverb] Sparing salt, spoiling fish. 1891 *Evening Telegram* 1 Aug At one harbor, we are told, 'large codfish could be seen swimming about the stage head, almost asking to be taken up and put under salt.' 1986 FELTHAM 43 It was [in the stage] that the cod were cleaned, washed and salted. After a number of days 'under salt' the cod were again washed and spread on the flakes to dry.

4 Attrib, comb ~ **fish/saltfish**, ~ **fishing** vbl n, ~ **rock**: see **salt water rock**, ~ **ship**, **salt (fish) store**, ~ **vessel**.

[1985] MAHER 45 A ship hulk...was used to store salt for the fisheries because...in those times Newfoundland put up and sold salt fish. 1987 FIZZARD 210 'On the draggers you had to make port at a certain time. It was not like when we were salt fishing, you'd wait and get your trip before you'd think about coming to land.' 1985 DOMSTAD 26 A salt rock was heated at night. [1985] MAHER 45 Salt ships arrived from Cadiz, Spain and Italy and tied up along side [the hulk]. 1977 WHITELEY 44 [part of one building in a diagram] salt fish store. 1987 *Evening Telegram* 4 July, p. 56 [tape transcript] The Haydens came back to Conception Bay and that winter they build their shacks, salt stores and bunkhouses. 1987 POWELL 86 There weren't enough vessels to carry all the salt that was needed to look after the fish. As each salt vessel arrived I would share the salt with the many crews in the harbours.

salt v

2 1987 POOLE 11-2 A casket was made for him and his body was salted in and made ready for shipment [from Labrador] to Newfoundland to his home for burial.

salt bulk n also saltbulk.

3 1981 SPARKES 187 After a period in 'salt bulk,' the fish had to be washed by hand with mops and brushes; then it had to be 'made.' 1988 *Evening Telegram* 18 Jan, p. 3 It takes 1.53 pounds of saltbulk to make one pound of dried salt fish because during the drying process, there is a moisture loss resulting in a weight reduction of 60 to 70 percent.

4 Phr *sell salt-bulk*.

1987 *Evening Telegram* 17 Mar, p. 4 About $500,000 is being paid out to fishermen who sold their catches either as fresh split or as saltbulk.

5 Attrib ~ **fish**.

1988 *Evening Telegram* 26 July, p. 3 A large shipment of salt bulk fish...left Argentia by vessel Saturday morning, consigned to a buyer in Portugal.

salter n

[1874] 1977 WHITELEY 42 'Send to St John's for...2 boys for stage, 1 splitter, 1 salter, 1 girl for cook.' 1977 MOAKLER 69 We watched the sunset ember in the west/And split our codfish in the afterglow,/The salters grating in the failing light.

salting vbl n Attrib ~ **bin**: wooden crib in which fisheries salt is stored or partially cured cod are stacked in salted layers.

1987 *Evening Telegram* 7 Mar, p. 10 From the road down to the men's bunkhouse and the flake where I turned acres of drying cod, and finally to the stage and the enclosed salting-bins, there were crude but effective steps.

salt water n

1 1987 POWELL 16 The second trap was left on the wharf and never taken off. The third was never removed from the saltwater.

2 Attrib ~ **duck**, ~ **ice**, ~ **pond**, ~ **shellbird**: red-breasted merganser (*Mergus serrator serrator*); SHELL BIRD (1987 MONTEVECCHI & TUCK 236), ~ **sore**: WATER PUP.

1986 *Evening Telegram* 15 Mar, p. 1 [The hunters] had been camping on the islands [in Notre Dame Bay] for the past couple of weeks and were getting in the last crack at the salt water ducks before the season closed last Monday. 1987 POOLE 16 I would have to go down over a much longer and steeper hill, and then onto salt water ice, and with an iron shoe on your sled it hauls pretty hard on salt water ice. ibid 24 There was a salt water pond not very far away from me, about one hundred yards or so. 1904 *Harper's* cviii, p. 865 One's wrists are then covered with salt-water sores and one's palms are cracked, even though one take the precaution of wearing a brass chain.

salvationer n *Anglo-Manx Dialect.*

sand n Comb ~ **berry**: black crowberry (*Empetrum nigrum*) (1898 *J A Folklore* xi, 279), ~ **lance**: LANCE 1, ~ **plover**.

1988 *Evening Telegram* 24 Mar, p. A2 More typically, [the cod] feed on caplin, herring, sand lance [etc]. 1932 AUSTIN 85 Black-bellied plover...sand plover.

save v See SAVING; cp LOSE: *lose one's spring*, etc.

3 Phr: also *save one's year*: to show a moderate profit at the end of a fishing season.

1988 *Evening Telegram* 27 May, p. 4 Unless he is permitted to fish in the bay, this year's fishery will be a disaster, said Mr Bolt. 'We won't save the year, but we can manage to make a week's pay if we're allowed inside that line to get a bit of redfish.'

saving ppl Comb ~ **voyage**.

1901 *Evening Telegram* 20 July The trap voyage is now practically over, though, with in winds, saving voyages may yet be trapped. [1979] 1985 LEHR & BEST (eds) 85 "Gull Cove": The schooner the *Madonna Hayden* and Tommy in command—/He always got a saving

voyage since he came to Gull Cove strand. 1988 GOSSE 34 With Porter as master, a crew of 60 men took 1400 seal pelts, a number that could barely be classed as a 'saving voyage.'

scad n

2 P 321-83 Even though we only had a scad of snow it looked like Christmas.

scaffold n

1986 SAUNDERS 54 'Hang [the caribou meat] up on a scaffold of spruce poles,' he said. 1986 *Them Days* xi (4), 53 The men would help the driver unharness the dogs, unload the komatik and put things high up on scaffolds where the dogs could not get at it.

scaffold v *DA* ~ v 2 (1799-1808) obs.

1986 SAUNDERS 161 By Christmas, when we went home to wait for freezeup, we had cleaned and scaffolded three hundred [rabbits].

scat v *EDD* ~ v[1] 3 s w cties. To strike, beat, smash. (1924 *Deep Sea Fishers* xxi (4), 139).

scatter v Of a field of ice, to break up, disperse.

1667 YONGE 128 See no ice, till standing Westward till 8, see many shelfs and scattering ice before us. [1937] 1983 FROUDE 10 The ice was heavy and scatern and to rought to lie up when about 12 oclock on the 19. we struck a block of ice and knocked the stem out of our vessel.

scattered p ppl *EDD* ~ 1 ~ few; *SED* iv, 921 Co, ~ few.

1 1986 *Nfld Herald* 15 Mar, p. 33 *Merasheen Farewell* [recording] is available in scattered stores around the province and can be purchased by mail order.

2 1981 PADDOCK 25 "Camp Seven": A scattered spruce is fit ta pile;/But only try ta git it!/You'll 'ave ta cut a t'ousand firs—/Each one will make a picket. 1987 POOLE 1 [We left Carbonear] and the meadows where we used to kick football and win a scattered game of rounders.

schooner n Comb ~ **box**: home-made wooden chest used by fishermen for personal effects at the 'Bank' fishery; cp LABRADOR BOX.

1983 PEDDLE 96 Blanket boxes with attached handles to make them portable were referred to by different names...depending upon where they were used. For example...those used on banking schooners by Newfoundlanders fishing for cod on the Grand Banks were called schooner boxes.

scoff n *O Sup*[2] ~ sb[2]; *Anglo-Manx Dialect.*

1986 FELTHAM 116 It was not uncommon for a number of...the younger set, to gather in a home, usually after the older members of the family had retired for the night, and cook a 'scoff' of turrs or ducks.

scoop n Cp *OED* ~-net (1792-1883), *DA* ~ 3 (1758-1896) for comb in sense 3.

1 1984 KELLAND 128 He boarded the first dory he found that was equipped with oars, tholepins and scoop.

3 Comb ~ **net**: a circular net, resembling a 'dip net' but larger and employed by two men (1975 BUTLER 180).

scotch a Comb ~ **pack**.
[1918] 1930 COAKER 136 Every man [should] be compelled to place his registered signature or name on every package he packs, as is done in connection with Norwegian and Scotch pack. 1975 BUTLER 73 Between 1900 and 1910 when the Scotch pack of herring came to be in great demand in the U.S.A., the merchants really went into packing herring in a big way.

scote v
3 [1976] 1985 LEHR & BEST (eds) 65 "Fishing on the Labrador": Now to conclude those few lines I have wrote,/To make a fair voyage we all had to scote. 1989 *Nfld Qtly* lxxxiv (4), 36 A narrow-gauge line, locomotives struggling to scote in excess of 100 cars up and down long steep grades, and a twisting rail line did not make for [the best] service.

scote n
1 1987 KING (ed) 74 "Away Through Your Wouldland": to turn back as you swung her/head towards home finally the scote/up the hard scrape that added sweat/to your wet shirt.
3 Comb **scote-shore**.
1985 *Terminology of Loggers* 15 ~ a stick used as a brace, sloping against a pile of wood to keep it upright.

scoting vbl n The activity of toiling at a task; 'hauling,' 'heaving.'
1986 SAUNDERS 28 After we got the sleigh unhitched and hauled back to safety we managed, with much scoting and swearing, to get him up on solid ice. ibid 68 After another spell of scoting at the painters they got clear of the sandbar and rocks and found enough water to float the dories.

scrammed p ppl *SED* ~ iv, 758-60 So D Do; 758-60 shrammed So W D Ha.
1 1863 MORETON 34 Schram'd. Cramped, and clammy cold. 1986 SAUNDERS 27 The wire handles [were] cutting into my fingers that were scrammed with the cold.

scrape[1] n
1985 NEWHOOK 44 [He] might let me drive the horse, except along the 'scrape.' This was a place where the track ran close to the edge of the cliff which fell away to the beach. The boys would often go to the scrape to roll rocks down the steep incline. 1988 GOSSE 11 The demarcation line between Northern Cove and Bishop's Cove was Otterbury...known today as 'the scrape.'

scravel v
1 1988 *Evening Telegram* 12 May, p. 12A Tim Raines can scravel from first to second base [as fast as the line on a fishing reel].
2 1981 MAJOR 9 Thousands of [caplin] piling over each other, flicking like mad on the sand when the water went out, flicking to get washed back out with the next wave. Scravelling to stay alive.

screech n Cp *O Sup*[2] ~ sb[2] (1902-79).
1982 DAWE 5 An old man who lived at Bauline,/Was considered quite cranky and mean,/Till he saw a gaunt ghost,/Drinking 'Screech' by a post,/One night in the moon's misty sheen.

screecher n
2 1988 MOMATIUK & EASTCOTT (eds) 23 An orphaned seal grows up to be a dwarf... It starves to death, bawling for its mother. A 'screecher,' some calls it.

scribbler n *O Sup*[2] ~ 2 (1906-) N. Amer. Also attrib ~ **paper**.
1915 *Deep Sea Fishers* xiii, 123 The children preferred sitting on the floor, and using [the benches] as desks, when they had work to do in their scribblers. T 284-66 She said, 'He got more education than teacher got.' [She] said, 'And he put one down,' she says, 'on the scribbler,' [she] said, 'for the teacher.' 1984 GOUGH 37 In pencil [he] begins to write the bill on to the scribbler paper bill of sale...one pound of salt beef, and licks the pencil tip. 1987 *Evening Telegram* 12 May, p. 3A After a nod from the boy as he was finished, [he] took out a dog-eared scribbler, and with the stump of a pencil...began to figure it up.

script n PRATT (1973-).

scrod n
1 1989 *Evening Telegram* 4 July, p. 13 I mean good fresh northern cod: steak, scrod, cheek and tongues.

scroop v also **scrope**.
1985 GUY 24 Me nerves is...raw. I'm all the time like someone was scropeing a rusty nail across a pane of window glass.

scrope See SCROOP.

scrunchins n pl
1 1986 *Them Days* xi (4), 45-6 [After straining out the oil] they'd take that, the scrunchions or blubber, whatever was left, and put that in bags [for pressing]. They'd throw away those old scrunchions then, or blubber as we called it.
2 1989 *Evening Telegram* 4 July, p. 13 I mean good fresh northern cod: steak, scrod, cheek and tongues, britches, tomcods, sounds, any part of the fish, provided it was to be fried, stewed with scrunchions, or stuffed and baked.

scuff n Also: a public dance.
1987 *Evening Telegram* 14 Mar, p. 6 Non-union employees don't have the gads of membership money to lather the palms of the political parties under the guise of donations for gala pre-election scuffs.

scuff v (a) To steer clear of, away from; (b) to dance.
[1929] 1982 BURKE (ed Kirwin) 100 When taking a wife,/Scuff clear of the hay bags/To worry your life. 1985 QUIGLEY 86 Our crowd would go to your house,

you'd go to theirs... And have a dance then this place and scuff that place.

scull n

1 [1576-78] 1987 STEELE (ed) 87 [Frobisher]: They never saw a better scull of fish.

2 1983 WARNER 27 The 'scull,' or arrival, of the inshore [caplin] spawners is an eagerly awaited event.

sculling vbl n

2 Comb ~ **oar.**

1984 POWELL 30 There was a little too much wind for me to make the land with the sculling oar.

scully See SKULLY.

sculp n

1 1985 BUSCH 54 The master [of the vessel] received a set royalty of four to six pence a seal, or...a hundred-weight or quintal...of 'sculps,' the sealskins with attached layer of fat.

sculp v

1 1987 *Evening Telegram* 11 Apr, p. 14 [tape transcript] The Captain [said to one of the hands] 'Take the four of them with you and show them how to sculp.'

sculpin n also **skulpin.**

[1765] 1971 BANKS (ed Lysaght) 209 The Women he sayd fish for Skulpins (as they also do in Greenland) Early in the year when the Ice breaks. 1984 KALLEO 34 At low tide, the children fish for young sculpins amongst the beach rocks. A pebble, wrapped in a piece of seal intestine and tied on with thread, provide them with their fishing tackle. It will be a very tasty treat for mother. 1987 O'FLAHERTY 43 The net at Great Head...showed nothing but three sculpins and plenty of kelp. The sculpins were duly hauled on board, viciously 'softened' by his father on the gunwale with a special stick, and then extricated from the meshes. 1990 *Evening Telegram* 14 Jan, p. 5 He said sculpin and connors can be found [in St John's harbor], but very rarely.

sculping vbl n

3 Comb ~ **knife.**

1987 *Evening Telegram* 14 Mar, p. 10 Articles in demand from our counter [by sealers] were...sculping knives and steels to sharpen them, Nansen caps [etc].

scun¹ v

2 1924 *Deep Sea Fishers* xxi (4), 138 Scun—To be on watch for ice which would endanger boat.

scun² v

3 Also: to dress carelessly; to arrange one's (long) hair rapidly.

P 295-83 'I don't like your hair scunned up in a bun.' 'Her dress was all scunned up around her.'

scunner n

1985 BUSCH 74 The other subordinate officers [on a sealing vessel] included the...'scunner,' who from the foretop watched for leads in the ice.

scunner v To sew or stitch clothing rapidly; SCUN² v 3.

P 319-87 [Describing a young girl's efforts at sewing] she had this cuff scunnered on.

scurr See SKIRR.

scutter n

1984 WRIGHT 65 The flipper holes were large, and the tails of the pelts were cut short where he had been too lazy to trim neatly around the 'scutters' or hind flippers.

sea n DA ~ n 10 b (2) ~ duck (1835-), *South Shore Phr Bk* ~ duck, ~ parrot for combs in sense 2.

1 Phr *follow (or tease) the sea*: to engage in the youthful sport of following and evading the retreat and advance of large waves on the shore.

1984 KELLAND 124 When we were youngsters we used to play a sport we called 'folleyin' the seas'... Our game was to follow each receding wave out until it melted back into the ocean, then race madly to safety ahead of the next comber that rolled in. 1985 NEWHOOK 34 If there was a 'sea on,' some [boys] would rush up and down the beach 'teasing the sea,' chanting various rhymes.

2 Attrib, comb ~ **boot,** ~ **duck,** ~ **fog**: fog formed when warm air moves over colder sea water, ~ **hen** (b), ~ **parrot, sea-run (trout)**: sea trout.

1863 *Journ of Assembly* Appendix 659 They were long seaboots, came over the knee...paid 30 s. for them. 1986 *Them Days* xi (4), 7 The dry goods shelves [at Hudson's Bay shop] carried yellow oilskins...leather and rubber sea boots, shirts. 1985 *Evening Telegram* 11 Mar, p. 16 The sea duck season for eiders, scoters and oldsquaw continues until March 10, 1986. 1989 *East Coast Marine Weather Manual* 50 Unlike radiation fog, which requires calm or light wind conditions, sea fog may form when winds are moderate, and may even persist as winds become strong. And whereas land fog usually burns off during the day, sea fog is affected much less by sunshine. 1939 ALDRICH & NUTT 239 Sea hen. Pomarine jaeger. [1703] 1905 LAHONTAN (ed Thwaites) p. 355 The *Sea-Parrots* bear the name of *Parrots*, upon the account that their Beak is of the same form with that of the Land *Parrot*. They never quit the Sea or the Shoar; and are always flying upon the surface of the Water, in quest of little Fish. Their colour is black, and their size is much the same with that of a Pullet. There are great numbers of 'em upon the bank of *Newfound-Land*, and near the Coast of the Island, which the Seamen catch with Hooks cover'd with a Cod's Roe, and hung over the Prow of the Ship. 1988 *Evening Telegram* 3 Dec, p. 32 [caption] Nick [Taylor] latched onto a six-and-a-quarter-pound sea run beauty while trolling with a Rapala minnow off Manuels.

seal n

1 Phr *get out in the seals*: cp ICE 1: *at, for, to the ice.*

[1939] 1983 FROUDE 9 That ended our sealing trip we tried to git out in the seals but our labour proved in vain.

4 Attrib, comb ~ **bird**: ivory gull (*Pagophila eburnea*) (1987 MONTEVECCHI & TUCK 240), common eider (ibid 235), ~ **fat**, ~ **finger**, ~ **fishery**, ~ **fishing**, ~ **gun**, ~ **net**, ~ **oil**, ~ **oil lamp**, ~ **pelt**, ~ **penis**: see COCK, ~ **worm**: see COD WORM.

1832 MOSS *MS Diary* 2 Apr 2 hands began cutting seal's fat. 1987 MCDONALD 32 On several occasions, the Trading Company forced increases in the price of seal fat, cod oil and herring. 1985 BUSCH 61 A scratch or other open wound...made the sealer liable to an occupational hazard known as 'seal-finger' or 'spekk-finger' (Norwegian for 'blubber finger'). [1734] 1987 *Nfld Studies* iii, p. 190 [Dealers of St Malo] Supply them with almost every thing Needfull, to carry on the Cod-Fishery, Seal-Fishery, and Furring, nay even with green Men. 1985 BUSCH 41 So remarkable was the seal 'fishery' (a natural and useful term, not least because, quite logically, if seals be fish they are not—for Catholic purposes—meat) that over time it has played and still plays a considerable role in the folklore and indeed the psychological make-up of Newfoundlanders. 1937 JUNEK 27 'It's getting the wood that is the hardest job; getting fish is play; and seal-fishing is real fun.' 1981 SPARKES 149 Usually six men would be waiting [outside the church], armed with their great long muzzle-loading seal guns charged with about a handful of powder. 1987 POOLE 15 We did not have any seal nets of our own as that was the first year staying down [on the Labrador]. [1764] 1971 BANKS (ed Lysaght) 191 I believe the Fishery will be the main thing and perhaps some Whale and Swael oil. 1983 MARTIN 59 Mushroom farms and underground oil storage [at the Bell Island mines] seem far removed from the old days of pickaxes and seal oil lamps. 1989 CANDOW 38 When the seal pelts were unloaded, the skinners were the first to take over. Their job was to separate the skin from the fat. 1988 *Evening Telegram* 22 Apr, p. 3 He [noted] that powder made from the seal penis is used as an aphrodisiac. 1989 ibid 26 June, p. 1 The so-called seal worms, also known as cod worms, have a life cycle that is thought to include the stomachs of harbour seals and the flesh of some fish.

sealing vbl n
1 1858 [LOWELL] i, 79 "Is, sir, it may be, in a manner; but not for s'ilun on those waters.' 1986 *Evening Telegram* 2 Apr, p. 3 Some of [the Bonavista fishermen] need their boats for sealing and some more will be putting their crab pots out in a couple of weeks.
2 Attrib, comb ~ **boat**: see BOAT n 1, ~ **gun**, ~ **plant**: facility for the processing of seal 'pelts' and 'blubber' or oil, ~ **season**.
1987 POOLE 18 When I was fourteen I went in the sealing boat with him in the fall of the year. 1981 SPARKES 163 I remember clearly, when I was nine years old, stepping over a man's sealing gun while he was cleaning it. I was promptly and sternly ordered to step backwards over it again. 1988 GOSSE 32 Their muskets, termed 'swilin' guns,' were originally of two types: the smooth-bore flintlock...and the much heavier shotgun. 1987 *Evening Telegram* 27 Apr, p. 7 In 1948 I was appointed manager of the sealing plant that used to manufacture the seals that the ships brought in [to St John's] from the ice-fields. [1962] 1987 *Evening Telegram* 23

June, p. 6 The sealing season officially closed for sealing vessels May 5 [except for] landsmen.

sealskin n
1 1987 *Evening Telegram* 5 Jan, p. 3 The European Economic Community [imposed] a ban on the importation of seal skin products in 1983.
2 Attrib ~ **cap**, ~ **boot**, ~ **house**: structure for the storage and processing of the skin of hair seals.
[1839] 1871 JUKES 58 What would you think of me in a check shirt, sealskin cap, and Indian boots coming up to my knee...pacing the deck, a sea-geologist! 1977 LAMB 89 Where else [but Water Street] could you select a pair of Eskimo-made sealskin boots out of an odoriferous barrel?

season n
1988 *Evening Telegram* 20 Aug, p. 23 Cod is still scarce on the inshore grounds, and unless the fall fishery picks up it will not be a good season for most fishermen [at Melrose].

second num Comb ~ **hand**.
1 1897 *Evening Telegram* 4 Mar The S.S. *Mastiff*, Capt Frank Jackman, was off Renews at about 5.30 last evening, taking her second hand from that place. [1976] 1985 LEHR & BEST (eds) 57 "The *Elsie M. Hart*": Her name it was the *Elsie M. Hart*, Captain March was in command./Steven Pelley from Random Island on her was second hand. 1986 *Evening Telegram* 22 Mar, p. 4 One [turr] flew into the second hand (Jarvis Winsor) and cut his face.
2 1983 *Terminology of Loggers* 16 ~ The assistant to the foreman. 1985 ASHTON 193 'Now in comes Lazarus, he's our second hand,/He's goin' to boil the kettle with the axe in his hand.' 1987 POOLE 93 The big boss had taken over Snug Harbour and I was the second hand and did not go on the collector but stayed on the room all summer.

see v Phr *see one's own time*: to act only in accordance with one's own judgement and imperative.
1863 MORETON 25-6 [of poor people's general character] Having complete command of their time, these people are of strange imperturbable habit. Unaccustomed to move at other men's bidding, they are hardly to be excited to action unless impelled by their own perception of need. 'When I see my own time,' is a phrase continually in their mouths. 1937 DEVINE 62 'When I see my own time.' Asked to do a certain work a person was able to display an enviable spirit of independence when this was said.

seine n
2 Comb ~ **crew**: the number of men required to procure fish with a seine; CREW n 1, ~ **gallows**, ~ **skiff**.
[1937] 1945 SCAMMELL 37 "Payne's Cove Bait Skiff": Hurry up, Uncle John, you don't want a coat,/The rest of the seine-crew are down in the boat. 1987 KING (ed) 119 "The Black Rock": Out of fog/the seamen form,/eyes already in the sheets/and driving hard/by the Seine-Gallows,/rounding Tuck's Point/for the

Channel. 1986 FELTHAM 50 The seine skiff was later used as a trap boat with little if any modification, and eventually became the motor boat.

send v (a).
1902 *Evening Telegram* 4 June A 22 year-old seaman...was sent down for three months with hard labor.

send n Also: an undulating motion of an ice-field caused by waves.
P 293-83 They walked across to the other side of the harbour even though there was a send in the ice.

servant[1] n
[1622] 1982 CELL (ed) 214 Whitbourne's *Invitation*: And that any Aduenturer shall not onely haue his equall part...which may be yeerly gotten there, by the fishing; but also such part of the benefit as may be gotten by the labours and industry of those which shall yeerely bee sent to remaine there, as seruants to you and the Aduenturers, who are to prouide for them.

set v COHEN, p. 121 'Until about twenty years ago *eela* fishermen might also frequently "set" a line, a shorter version of the traditional long line, consisting of several hundred yards of baited hooks anchored by weights and floats.' In cod-fishing, to place a trawl-line in the water with baited hooks.
1930 *Am Speech* v, 391 Make a set, v. phr. To set, tow, and haul-back the trawl. 1977 MOAKLER 54 And as we shipped the oars to set our trawls/The kittiwakes came by in swooping ranks,/Snatching our bait and fouling on the hooks. 1981 SPARKES 184 A trawl was set, or shot, from a trawl tub. 1987 FIZZARD 128 'If you had the tide going with you, you'd set from the schooner, but if the tide was going against you, you'd have to pull out the distance you thought the gear would be and then you'd set back towards the schooner.'

settle n
1983 PEDDLE 80 This settle was found in Branch on the Cape Shore. It was probably made circa 1830. The legs are oak; other wood is pine. 1985 GUY 131 Many's the time I do be laid down on the settle for an hour or so and I says shag this. Enough of this lying around the house for me.

settle v Cp *OED* ~ v 35 'to close an account by money payment'; COHEN, p. 74 'Until recently sprees were held on several fixed festive occasions [and] also...when crews settled on one of the three customary accounting days in the fishing year.' Phr *settle up*: in the older traditional Newfoundland fishery, to total the credits and debits of a fisherman's account as kept by the supplying merchant in the fall of the year; STRAIGHTEN (UP, OUT).
[1857] 1976 WINSOR 11 'The enlargement and decoration of the church has cost one thousand, five hundred dollars, and we feel quite sure of raising this as soon as the people get settled up in the Fall.' 1918 *Deep Sea Fishers* xv, p. 139 If he were not going to volunteer [for the front] he would have settled up the last of his account

with me for the gear. M 68-3 At the beginning the catches were sold to Newman and Company at Gaultois. Under this system the collectors came to Francois each fall in October, brought the supplies required for the next season and collected the fish. Along with this each year in September the fishermen went to Gaultois to 'settle up.' 1984 POWELL 15 [We'd] go to Fishing Ship's Harbour to the merchant, Mr Lewis Dawe, and get what the people called 'settled up' for the summer's catch for salmon and cod. This included getting winter supplies. 1987 FIZZARD 130 '[The bank fishermen would] be charged for that sack of sugar. That was taken off when they settled up in the fall.' 1987 POOLE 22 It was all credit until you settled up in the fall. When the fish was all shipped, George settled up for the crowd, with Baine Johnston of Battle Harbour, their merchant.

settlement n
1984 KELLAND 119 For a while the men at that settlement [St Shotts] could not venture near the wreckage because of the big seas. 1989 *Nfld Qtly* lxxxv (1), 7 The current Government of Newfoundland has announced a policy of amalgamation of municipalities, incorporated settlements and unincorporated places adjacent to each other.

settling vbl n Comb ~ **(up) time**.
1988 GOSSE 75 At 'settling up' time in late fall [the planter] was allowed half the voyage and the remainder he divided with his [sharemen].

shack v Cp *O Sup[2]* ~ v[4] 'to live in a shack' for sense 1.
1 1985 QUIGLEY 84 'But now there was me and another fella, we were shackin' ourselves, cooking for ourselves in a shack.'
2 Comb ~ **locker**.
1989 *Evening Telegram* 17 June, p. A10 He was in what he calls the 'mug-up locker' (often called the 'shack locker') and was having a cup of tea when [the vessel] heeled over.

shag n
1 1983 *Gazetteer of Canada: Nfld* 158-9 Shag Cliff [Island, Ledge, Point, Pond, Rock, Roost, etc].

shallop n
1 Also: in place-names.
1983 *Gazetteer of Canada: Nfld* 159 Shallop Cove, Shallop Point. 1988 GOSSE 19 A few...fishing boats [larger than the punt], classed as shallops and measuring from 35 to 50 feet in overall length, with a beam of 10 to 15 feet, were also constructed at Northern Cove.

shalloway n For a similar eighteenth-century pronunciation of Fr *-oy* or *-ois* as *-way*, see BARASWAY (from *barachois*). The form *shalloway* may have been influenced by another boat name, *shallop*. Freq in place-names.
1680 CO 1/45 (68i), 252, v Their shalloway w[ch] they had of the said Xpher Pollard splitt in two peices & damaged the small remain[dr] of provisions which they had

left soe they launcht a new shalloway from the Adm^{lls} place & put the rest of theire provisions into her & moord her with 2 keylocks. [1767] 1977 *Peopling of Nfld* 108 Our shalloway from Barrow Harbour arrived with a load salt, discharged 30 hogsheads. 1983 *Gazetteer of Canada: Nfld* 159 Shalloway [Brook, Cove, Head, Island, Point, Pond, etc]. 1988 GOSSE 19 While not as durable as their English counterparts, these 'shalloways' were shipshape for more than fifteen years.

shareman n
    1 1981 SPARKES 187 If the skipper owned more than one trap, he would sign on a crew of sharemen. 1986 SAUNDERS 74 Most Gander Bay men were away to work, either on the Exploits main drive if it was in the spring, or a shareman on a codtrap crew down Change Islands way, or in the lumberwoods cutting pulp for the A.N.D. Company. 1987 POWELL 29 I had two sharemen as crew members during my first summer fishing on my own. *Shareman* was the name used when I first started and the name has not changed today. If the fish that was caught and sold was worth $100.00, the amount was cut in half, one for expenses, the other shared equally between the skipper and the sharemen. So in the case of a skipper and two sharemen, they each received $16.75 out of each hundred dollars.

shaves n pl
    1975 BUTLER 46 They had a lot of old shaves there and I got...a good shaft alright, belonged to Acadia engine.

shaving(s) n Comb ~ **broom**: a broom made by whittling slivers at one end of a birch stick in such a manner as to keep them fastened to the stem.
    1975 BUTLER 61 For shavin' brooms they'd get a straight birch stick...and they'd shave the shavings down and let them all hang down together...[then] tie all the shavings together.

she pro *DBE* 1 [a stressed object]; *AND* 2 'in names of plants'; see note at WE.
    1 P 319-88 She [a clock] was goin' on. I let her go on anyway.
    2 1858 [LOWELL] i, 118 'Missis Frank says I'm want-un up at Riverhead, she thinks, and 'ee'll [you will] plase take this pitcher up to *she*.' T 251-66 Now Jack was there; she knowed Jack. Jack didn't know she. T 1827-75 Well she grabbed the coat from un and hove un around she and he again and wished they was back in town. ibid So he grabbed the marble stick out of her hand, made a wheel or two...and struck her and knocked she into a marble. 1987 KING (ed) 129 "Grandma's Lullaby": One day Bill Samson said to she,/'Oi'm livin all alone,/'Oi'd be some proud to offer you,/'A dwelling of your own.'

sheath n also **shathe**.
    1 Also: a wooden knife casing, made by the sealer and often elaborately decorated.
    1852 *Morning Post* 12 Feb, p. 4 [advertisement] Oiled clothing, covered hats and south-westers...also palms, sheaths, and belts. 1984 WRIGHT 42-3 With the acquisition of knives we started a ritual that must be as old as the seal hunt itself. 'Got to make a "shathe" for

that knife now b'y,' Jacob told me... An ordinary leather sheath is not suitable for a sealing knife because it quickly soaks up blood, which freezes. A properly made wooden sheath is less porous and allows the blood to drain away through a small hole cut into the bottom.
    2 Comb ~ **knife**.
    1852 *Morning Post* 12 Feb, p. 4 [advertisement] Also palms, sheaths, and belts, sheath knives, etc. 1986 SAUNDERS 53 After bleeding and paunching the carcass with his sheath knife, he took his axe and chopped [the caribou] in half for carrying.

sheave v
    P 13-83 'Backwater' [is the] command to stop or turn by reverse movement of one's oar. 'Sheave' is the synonym used by fishermen.

shebeen n *O Sup*² S. Africa (1900-) for sense 1.
    2 Comb ~ **keeper**.
    1902 *Daily News* 24 Oct, [p. 4] The case against the shebeen keeper at magistrate's court yesterday resulted in a conviction.

shebeening vbl n Operating an illicit establishment for the sale or consumption of liquor.
    1901 *Daily News* 2 Sep The police raided several houses yesterday which were suspected of shebeening, but nothing of an incriminating nature was discovered in any of the places visited.

sheila n also **sheelah, sheilagh**.
    1 1982 BURSEY 11 "No Right of Spring 1": In Newfoundland/No Pan's pipes/When spring comes;/Sheila's shrieks/Drown all music. 1989 *Evening Telegram* 20 Mar, p. 1 Legend has it St Patrick had a wife—or sister or [acquaintance]—named Sheilagh, and that still somehow she gets angry enough at the good man to whack him about the ears.
    2 Comb **sheila's brush**, ~ **day**.
    1989 *Evening Telegram* 20 Mar, p. 1 Sheilagh's Brush was alive and well this weekend, and if you were looking forward to a balmy first day of Spring, look again. More than 24 cms of snow fell in the [St] John's area...by late Sunday with about another 15 cms expected by later today. 1872 *Times* 20 Mar, p. 3 We imagine we may safely assert that 'St Patrick's brush,' or 'Sheelah's day' if you will, was never more fully developed by the elements than on the day and night of Monday last [the 18th].

shell-bird n Freq in place-names.
    1983 *Gazetteer of Canada: Nfld* 160 Shellbird Cove [Island, Pond, Rapids]. 1987 KING (ed) 132 "River": Then louder, wings in darkness, beating unseen,/The shellbirds going south.

shift v
    2 1918 *Deep Sea Fishers* xvi, p. 67 [We are stopping at New Harbour.] The first of the winter wasent cold anuff to sheft inside so we stop ther. 1987 POWELL 50 Many of their summer houses were built on the rugged coast... The people would shift to those places along the coast mainly to hunt sea birds and seals.

shim n
1 1981 SPARKES xiv By means of a curved oak shim, made for the purpose from a bit of pork barrel stave, the bark of a carefully selected fir tree would be peeled whole, to a height of from five to six feet from the ground. 1986 FELTHAM 70 To remove the 'rind' intact without breaking it, a chisel-like hardwood 'shem' was used.

shimmick n also **shimic**. Also: a native Newfoundlander, a 'bush-born' person.
1871 SPG Series "E" MSS Reports 1870-71, A-238 You must remember that only 'shimics' (real Newfoundlanders) can cross salt water ice with safety, so be careful how you venture.

shinny v
P 106-81 We could go down to shinny on the pans.

ship n
2 Comb ~ **halfpenny**: early nineteenth-century copper coin.
1983 ROWE 12 In 1851 the government prohibited the further import of [Prince Edward Island currency] in vain... Enough remained that when in [1862] certain parties, for their own purposes, refused to receive them and the 'ship' halfpennies, out of the heterogeneous mass of copper in circulation, considerable distress was caused among the poor.

ship v
1 1981 SPARKES 183 Fishing crews were now to be shipped (signed on) for the work. 1987 POWELL 71 Most of the fishermen had crew members who took a share of the voyage. Others had men who had 'shipped' for the summer, often for only $30.00.
2 T 251-66 And he shipped to a feller. Jack was to ship to a feller, and he had two daughters. T 498-68 She was married for quite a while...when she started to feign sick. So he shipped a boy. And the boy was quite young.
3 Also: to transfer, assign for credit, the season's catch.
1984 KELLAND 148 After they shipped their season's catch, they knew exactly what the merchant was going to tell them...'you still owe me quite a bit of money, but I suppose I will have to supply you with a winter's grub.' 1987 POWELL 34 Nobody was paid for fish or salmon until everything was shipped to the merchant.

shipping vbl n Comb ~ **paper**.
1987 POWELL 71 Even at that low price, the men weren't sure of getting their wages unless the local merchant signed the shipping paper.

shoal n
3 Comb ~ **net**.
1985 BUSCH 47 Seal nets really did not have to be fixed to shore or bottom, and 'shoal' nets could be used in the open water where bigger seals might be taken.

shoot[1] v
1 [1937] 1945 SCAMMELL 37 "Payne's Cove Bait Skiff": Alf Gatehouse's baitskiff is here on the spot,/They've shot the seine twice, but they've got no great lot. 1981 SPARKES 184 A trawl was set, or shot, from a trawl tub. 1986 *Nfld's Deepsea Fishery* 650 Shooting away: getting the trawl net into the water at the beginning of the fishing operation.

shore[1] n
1 1985 QUIGLEY 72 Most every night there would be a dance in one community, one place, one community another night. Like all around the shore.
3 Attrib, comb ~ **crew**, ~ **crowd**: those who unload and process the catch of fish ashore, ~ **fast(ener)**, ~ **fish**, ~ **fisherman**, ~ **fishery**, ~ **liner**: a railway branch-line serving the coastal settlements of Conception Bay: **shore train**, ~ **skipper**: also, a wife who keeps a fisherman's accounts, ~ **train**: see ~ **liner**.
1987 FIZZARD 216 [When the trawler returns to port] the men are then relieved of their duties for a forty-eight hour period. The shore crew begin unloading the fish aided by huge vacuum hoses. 1986 SIDER 21 Male kinsmen crewed the boats; women, kin to these men, were the core of the 'shore crowd' that 'made' the fish cure. 1987 POWELL 30 One day...we went to the Cape Shore to look at the salmon nets, John Campbell had his man, Edward Cadwell, landed on the edge of a cliff to tie on the shore fastener. This was the rope to which the salmon net was tied. 1988 MOMATIUK & EASTCOTT (eds) 153 All the shore-fasts were out and the lead ropes, so I just had to row the net out there, tie it on and put out one grapelin. 1986 RYAN xxi The fishermen who fished near their homes around the island were expected to produce a light-salted, hard-dried product referred to as *shore* fish. 1987 *Evening Telegram* 10 Oct, p. 7 If the French are permitted to catch northern cod it will not make much difference to (east coast) shore fishermen because, even without the French catching any northern cod, the shore fishermen who are left are facing ruin. 1984 KELLAND ix-x The terms as they were used by Canadians and Newfoundlanders in days gone by presented two different meanings. When Newfoundlanders referred to the shore fishery they meant that the men who were engaged at the industry were fishing from shore-based premises, not from a schooner; whereas when Canadians used the term inshore fishery it meant that the undertaking was being carried out by men who fished on grounds near the shore, not on the farflung Banks. 1984 *Evening Telegram* 21 Sep, p. 4 The morning train, or the shoreliner, as those who worked the Carbonear branch line called her, left the St John's station at Water Street West Thursday, 9:30 a.m., carrying passengers for the last time. 1988 NADEL-KLEIN & DAVIS (eds) 211 The shore skipper's fishery-related role is also active and instrumental. She keeps the books and accounts for her seabound husband's vessel and acts as his onshore agent. [1935] 1985 *Evening Telegram* 27 Dec, p. 6 The shore train which went out on Christmas Eve to Carbonear in charge of Conductor Lee was crowded with passengers. The run from St John's to Carbonear occupies three hours and fifteen minutes. [1939] 1989 ibid 25 Feb, p. 4 Forty sealers from Bay Roberts and Brigus arrived by the shore train at 11:30 this morning to join the SS *Ranger* which will sail for the Gulf on Tuesday next.

shore² n

1 1987 POWELL 27 Nobody would build [stages] there because there was a long, slanting rock that went to the water and most people thought it would be difficult to keep shores on this rock because of the pounding ice and seas that would throw in from the Atlantic.

shot n B.J. WHITING, *Early American Proverbs and Proverbial Phrases* (Cambridge, Mass., 1977) S184 To have a shot in the locker (1789-1827), and cp SMYTH shot-locker 'a compartment built up in the hold to contain the shot,' for second phrase.

Phr *a shot of ducks*: group of many ducks which can be brought down with a single shot.

1966 SCAMMELL 60 'Shot of ducks coming,' he whispered, his eyes popping. 'About 50 I think, and it looks like they're going to be in shot. Get a cap on the nipple!' 1987 POOLE 42 I passed the coves where I had many a shot of ducks during the winter time. *ibid* 73 I made one good shot of ducks that fall: on Christmas Day I killed 42 ducks one shot.

have a shot in the locker: to have one last chance.

1983 FROUDE 169 As the old saying goes never despair while there is A Shot in the locker.

shuck n

2 [1976] 1985 LEHR & BEST (eds) 168 "Skipper Dan": For in my old clothes-bag some rags I have got;/A pair of old shucks I've tied up to my bunk,/And if rags can buy liquor this night I'll be drunk.

5 The mantle or cone-shaped portion of a squid including the caudal or tail fins; that part of the squid which remains when the viscera, head, arms and tentacles are removed.

P 1-89 [The shuck is] 'what's left of a squid after you take the pip out.' P 326-89 The shuck was eight feet long. P 296-89 'What's a feed of shucks?' 'Squid. The body part. It is gutted, pipped.'

shuck² v Cp EDD ~ v² 5 'to take off husks; to shell peas, beans, etc.' (a) To remove the shell or body casing of shrimps; (b) to remove a boiled pudding from its cloth bag.

[1900] 1989 *Nfld Qtly* lxxxv (2), 27 One cook with a handgaff pulled 'duffs' from the pot and dropped them in a barrel of cold water to cool them enough to 'shuck' or turn them out of the pudding cloths. 1982 MCDOOLING 125 They shipped in shrimps [to Conche] and the women acquired the stamps they needed by shucking shrimps.

shuff v

P 308-88 When you get a load on your 'brow' see you get her shuffed ahead, shoot [a]head, [if] we had a load we could put three or four cords on it see.

side n

2 Comb ~ **stick**.

1984 WRIGHT 56 As the ship sidled up to a sizeable piece of ice, the men clambered onto the 'sidesticks'—the timbers they had prepared and lashed to the side of the ship to form steps.

sideling a Cp AND siding 'alteration of "sideling," a slope or declivity' (1852-).

sign n

1 1986 SAUNDERS xii They sought information about such things as the thickness of the ice, the depth of snow and the abundance or scarcity of 'sign' in this or that trapping area.

2 1987 *Evening Telegram* 1 Aug, p. 4 There is a sign of squid in Petty Harbour and fishermen are hoping a lucrative squid fishery may save what appears to be another disastrous cod fishery. P 245-90 'We're ten miles off shore and there's still not a sign [of cod-fish].'

silk n Comb ~ **jay** (1987 MONTEVECCHI & TUCK 242).

silver n

2 Comb ~ **fox**, ~ **patch fox**: see **silver fox**, PATCH FOX.

1986 SAUNDERS 25 He paid out $150 for a silver fox, male. 1987 POOLE 27 But there was no way out... Still I had this silver patch fox. I was expecting to get $60.00 for it.

silver thaw n

2 1986 *Evening Telegram* 29 Mar, p. 5A A severe ice storm covered all of southeastern Newfoundland with 25 mm of silver thaw during a 2-day storm.

simon saw* n

P 302-88 Axe and bucksaw [that's] what I used. Before that was simon saw, that was before my time.

sin n

1985 QUIGLEY 83 According to one source, it was 'really a sin to say, [but] everybody was delighted there was no fish,' which gave them the opportunity to dance.

sina n also **sinna**.

1971 *Can Geog J* lxxxii, p. 161 In winter, the Eskimos hunted seal at the 'sinna,' the floe edge, shot caribou inland, and trapped. 1982 JACKSON 24 [The Inuit hunted] at the edge of the landfast ice, the sina, often many trackless miles from shore.

sing v DBE sing out v 'to call out.' Phr *sing out*.

1987 *Lore and Language* vi (1), 28 Now this is very hilly country; sometimes, he'd be in view sometimes he wouldn't be in view. When we'd be in a hollow, he'd be on a hill. And we started singing out 'Skipper! ... hey!hey!hey!' like you would.

single a Comb ~**-handed**.

1858 [LOWELL] ii, p. 213 How long was poor, single-handed Ladford...to hold his own against the other two?

sinker n

1983 *Gazetteer of Canada: Nfld* 163 Sinker Rock, The Sinker.

sinna See SINA.

sish n

1983 WARNER 80 How does an ocean freeze, right before your eyes? Well, first it's patches of gray slush... Ship makes pleasant hissing noise passing through. Germans call it *Eisbrei*, 'ice porridge'; Newfoundlanders rather onomatopoetically refer to it as 'sish.' More technically, good old British Admiralty *Arctic Pilot* defines as 'ice spicules and thin plates about one-third of an inch across, known as frazil crystals.' 1989 CANDOW 76 The pelts were stowed in wooden pounds in the holds, laid fat to fat and hair to hair, with crushed sea ice called 'sish' or 'salt' between each layer.

skerry* n Cp *SED* iv, 151 kerry 'a sledge.'

skerwink n also **skirwink**.

1987 MONTEVECCHI & TUCK (eds) 178-9 Manx Shearwaters probably have been much more common than our records suggest. Familiarity with the species is indicated by the use of a local name 'Skirwink' by fishermen in Bonavista Bay.

sketch n

1 1985 GUY 103 And just at that I slipped. Me good foot struck a sketch of ice—just the bare sketch—there on the concrete and down I goes on me face and eyes.

sketch v Phr *sketch off*.

1914 *Deep Sea Fishers* xii, 72 'Skitch me likeness off, mister.'

skid n

2 P 245-90 'They move the [salt] fish down the skid to the wharf [at Lisbon].'

skiddy See SKITTY² .n.

skiff n

1 1987 *Nfld Qtly* lxxxiii (1), 16 They moved off outside and the boys carried us out in the skiff.
2 1988 *Decks Awash* xvii (4), 14 Several families included experienced boatbuilders who designed a 15-ton, two-masted, three-sailed fishing vessel that became known as a Rocky Harbour skiff.
3 Attrib ~**-load**.
1989 *Evening Telegram* 19 Aug, p. A8 Quite often we would have a skiff load of fish.

skin n

1 Phr *skin of fur*: the pelt of a fur-bearing animal; cp FUR n 1.
1918 *Deep Sea Fishers* xv, 137 [He] existed...on a very pauperizing form of 'charity,' with a semi-occasional 'skin of fur.' 1984 POWELL 76 So every time you got a skin of fur, you'd count the nails [driven into a nearby tree to mark the location of the trap]. Sometimes there would be a tie between the waters [frequented by the animals]; other times, between traps. But mostly each year one trap would always keep a little ahead by one skin of fur.
2 Attrib ~ **boot**.
T 1062-72 I had on a pair o' those skin boots, you know, tie up round here. 1984 KALLEO 9 Some women would be cleaning the [seal] skins to make skin-boots because there were no rubbers or shoes when I was a child. 1986 SAUNDERS 52 I had on knee rubbers but Jim wore skin boots—sealskin leggings handsewn to rawhide moccasins.

skin v

1 1987 *Evening Telegram* 27 Apr, p. 7 [tape transcript] In the 1920s the pelts were skinned by hand... One skinner would skin on an average 300-350 young harps a day.

skinner n

1 1987 *Evening Telegram* 27 Apr, p. 7 [tape transcript] The skinners were paid by the pelt: six cents for a young harp; seven cents for a young hood; 10 cents for a bedlamer; 10 cents for an old harp; and 30 cents for an old hood.
2 1987 FIZZARD 212 'From the cutters the fish went to the skinners, who removed the skin from the fillet.'

skinning vbl n

1 Also: in processing cod fillets, the operation of removing the skin.
1987 FIZZARD 212 'Most of the skinnin' was done by hand, but some of it was done mechanically.'
2 Attrib ~ **knife**, ~ **machine**: a mechanical device to separate the blubber from the skin of a seal.
1987 *Evening Telegram* 27 Apr, p. 7 [tape transcript] They each had a skinning knife and a leather stall for your thumb—where you pressed on the back of the knife—and a steel. The knife, [a] 10-inch blade and curved, was sharpened with the steel and we'd always finish the sharpening stroke with the wire edge turning up and not down. 1987 ibid Then the companies got skinning machines to skin the pelts in place of the men [in 1925]. The machines were quicker. We had two and they were capable of doing 6,000 to 7,000 pelts a day. First the pelt would go through a band knife on a conveyor and that would take the fat off down to one-quarter inch of the skin. Then it would go through a flesh[er] which was a cylinder with a rubber roller so it couldn't damage the pelt.

skipper n

1 [1797] 1989 PULLING (ed Marshall) 139-40 The *skipper* who brot me this Letter...is a Brother in law to one of the younkers. 1987 POWELL 29 If the fish that was caught and sold was worth $100.00, the amount was cut in half, one for expenses, the other shared equally between the skipper and the sharemen.
2 1986 *Evening Telegram* 5 Mar, p. 24 'Those trout are too small to keep, I would let them go,' I said. 'I bring them home to the cats, skipper,' said one man.
4 1984 GOUGH 4 Bessie Sheppard paused and sized her up. 'Come on in and meet the Skipper. He's the one who decides if you'll get the job [as maid].'
5 1981 PADDOCK 24 "Camp Seven": Da skipper come—Oh, no, my frien',/Your pardon I must as'—/A second-'and is all we got/To do da skipper tas'! 1985 *Terminology of Loggers* 16 ~ the foreman or boss of a job.

skipper v
1984 PITT 9 Left thus without a command he was easily prevailed upon to skipper an expedition...a voyage along the northeast coasts of Newfoundland and Labrador. 1988 GOSSE 41 [Conception Bay schooners] were often skippered by reliable planters and local fishermen [who] became the sole owners...by the hire-purchase method.

skirr v also **scurr**.
2 1987 DAWE [8] A is for alley-coosh,/Going to bed,/When a dusty old sandman/Skirrs close to your head.
3 Also: vbl n **skirring**.
1985 NEWHOOK 44 There were always good flat round stones for 'scurring,' or long thin ones which buzzed in the air like big angry hornets.

skirwink See SKERWINK.

skitty² n also **skiddy**.
1985 GUY 53 Them tourists and relatives from the mainland are like the skiddies and the nippers. The first bit of warm weather tolls them along.

slab¹ n OED ~ sb¹ 2 a 'rough outside plank cut from a log preparatory to squaring.' Attrib ~ **man**: one employed in a sawmill to handle slabs.
1981 SPARKES 175 A slabman took care of the slabs and another took the boards as they came from the Rotary and placed them on a bench of rollers which fed them to another saw called the Edger.

slab² n Cp OED ~ sb³ naut 'any slack part of a sail hanging down,' slabline 'cord used to truss up a sail.' Attrib **slabline**: long line used to manage 'trawls' in the cod-fishery.
1984 KELLAND 183 The slablines which were eighteen pound lines, reached a length of approximately fifty fathoms. One end of those lines was fastened to the ends of the mooring ropes, the other to the ends of the trawl. Where mooring ropes and slablines joined, the buoylines were attached. 1987 FIZZARD 129 'On the gear we'd have a slab line on each end, a line with no hooks on it, that's the line from the buoy to the bottom; you'd haul the slab line before you come to the gear.'

slack a EDD ~ sb³ 4 for sense 3.
1 Cp SLACK v: phr slack off (1938 quot).
2 Also: of a field of ice: breaking up.
1902 Evening Telegram 19 Mar There is a large field of slack ice in sight [off Fogo]. [1937] 1983 FROUDE 11 [We steered away north] throu slack ice all the time until...we ran her into another block of ice which split the vessel in two. [1976] 1985 LEHR & BEST (eds) 65 "Fishing on the Labrador": But when we got there the ice hove us back,/Went up to Jigger Tickles the ice it was slack.
3 Also: of a still stretch of water in a stream, deep and slow-moving.
1986 SAUNDERS 80 Gull Steadies has these long stretches of low mud banks with slack water, the perfect place for muskrats.

slack v Also: phr slack off: of a 'run' of fish, to diminish in number; slack out: to let go (a line).
[1938] 1988 Evening Telegram 7 June, p. 6 The run of salmon has slacked off at Bay Bulls during the past few days. 1987 FIZZARD 211 'Several steps were followed in setting the [otter] trawl [the third being when] the fifteen fathoms of warp between the trawl and the doors were "slacked out".'

sleepy a Cp Anglo-Manx Dialect sleep 'gummy secretion in the corners of the eye, grume.'

sleeveen n O Sup² ~ (1834-1975) Ir and Nfld.
1986 SAUNDERS 35 As the sleveens raced from his doorstep and up the road he would let fly at them in the dark [with his musket, loaded with split peas]. 1988 Nfld Herald 22 Oct, p. 22 Sleveens are great equalizers. They redistribute property. In addition, where there's open piracy, there's a chance that the booty will get shared more equitably than otherwise.

sleeveen v Also: sleeveening vbl n: behaving in the manner characteristic of a 'sleeveen'; being crafty, adroit.
1988 Nfld Herald 22 Oct, p. 22 Sleveening helps explain the unusual politics of the province. It also helps explain the odd behaviour of many people in the arts.

slew v
1 1930 Am Speech vi, 57 Sluc round—To turn sharply around. 1974 MOAKLER 86 Our vessel sluing in a canyon's pall,/We fought for heading as the tumult roared!

slice n
1 1981 SPARKES xiii Women made their own soap for household and everyday use. In its simplest form, soap is merely a mixture of lye and fat... The mixture was stirred with a 'soap-slice' of wood until it thickened, then it was poured into large moulds and set to harden.
2 1981 SPARKES 176 To get a drink [of rolled oats, water and molasses], you first gave it a stir with a big wooden 'slice.'

slide v Also **sliding** vbl n.
1983 FROUDE 5 Playing ball riding sliding shout and ball pulling[?] sailing in the boat.

slide n SED iv, 151 So for sense 1.
1 1986 HISCOCK 115 'And the young fellas there—I gave them a quarter...to get them to take me down over the hill on a slide.' 1987 FIZZARD 139 And [then the men] would load the horse and slides [with the heavy block of ice].
3 Attrib, comb ~ **load**, ~ **path**.
1858 [LOWELL] i, 81 I was acomun down Backside from the Cosh, hau'ling a slide-load o' timber. 1981 SPARKES 150 When told that there was no charge at all, he said: 'Would it be all right if I gid ee a slide-load o' wood?' 1896 Trade Review Christmas No. 20 Spell... means to carry on the shoulder from the woods to the slide path. 1988 GOSSE 5 Another byroad known as the 'slide path' also connected with the New Harbour Road

and bisected the Neils' extended holdings from south to north.

sling n
  1 Phr *in slings*.
1983 *Nfld Qtly* lxxix (2), 3 Verbal history of this sort is now all in slings.

slink n
  1 Also: 'ouananiche' or landlocked Atlantic salmon.
1988 *Sunday Express* 10 July, p. 30 There were two breeds in this deep recess, ouananiche, or 'slinks' as the Gambo men called them, and mud trout.

slinky a
1987 POWELL 105 A few sculpin, with their mouths and two eyes on top of their head, were on the bottom looking up. Their bellies looked small and slinky. There were no codfish guts on the bottom for them to eat.

slip v
  2 1949 FITZGERALD 85 He chopped the wood, and he melted snow, and slipped rabbits for the pot.

slip² n
  1 1981 MAJOR 181 The first slip I set out, I asked him to go cut me a standard—a stick to tie the slip onto—and he comes back with an old dead stick, old man, that wouldn't hold a shrew, let alone a rabbit. 1985 *Metro* 21 July, p. 15 [They] had tried several times before to catch the bear with slips but each time the animal had managed to escape. 1986 *Sunday Express* 14 Dec, p. 36 Snare-setting is a very common practice and hunters may 'tail out' as many as several hundred slips over several miles of rabbit country.

slob n *O Sup²* ~ sb¹ 1 d (1878-) for sense 1, 4 ~ ice (1835-) for comb in sense 3.
  1 [1832] 1981 *Them Days* vi (4), 37 The slob made so fast in the tickle that abt 10 o'clock a skiff could scarce row through it. 1984 WRIGHT 33 We ran into 'slob' (loosely packed ice) shortly after leaving St John's and starting northward. 1987 POOLE 26 That fall it got frosty early in December and filled the ocean with slob, and the seals did not appear at all.
  3 Comb ~ **gull**, ~ **hauler**, ~ **ice**.
[1987] QUINLAN 30 [caption] There is slob gulls in the water at Birchy Bay Narrows. 1986 FELTHAM 54 Light [seal] hunting punts were hauled through thin ice by means of 'slob-haulers.' 1990 *Evening Telegram* 6 Feb, p. 2 When they started back their boat encountered heavy slob ice but they managed to free themselves and make it safely to shore.

slobby a
1986 *Evening Telegram* 3 Mar, p. 3 A check up [of Rushoon] river this morning revealed slobby ice that has built up and could cause more serious problems if it breaks free.

slouse v Also: phr *slouse on*: to pour or apply liberally; to slosh.

[1976] 1985 LEHR & BEST (eds) 64 "Fishing on the Labrador": Coming up to our vessel the tiller slipped out,/And out in the water he sloused all about. 1987 *Sunday Express* 3 May, p. 2 Lumbermen bound to and from 'the woods' used to stop off at Uncle Sam's where a feature of the dining table was a large basin of jam. 'Now don't make strange men,' Uncle Sam would say. 'Slouse on lots of it.'

slub¹ n
  1 1981 PADDOCK 35 "Pronging Fish on the Stage Head": Stab, heave, and toss/In an ecstasy of motion,/In a surfeit of slub. 1987 *Evening Telegram* 21 Mar, p. 5 And standing up to my backside in slub and blood and guts, I absolutely loved [that first meal of fishermen's brewis, served on the fishing stage].
  2 1924 *Deep Sea Fishers* xxi (4), 138 Slub—Coarse seaweed, or wrack, which gums up the fishing nets. 1985 *Gazette* 26 July, p. 3 Very often 'slub' conditions between April and June in Newfoundland inshore waters aggravate herring, salmon and cod gillnet fishermen... The slime which coats nets, traps, trawls and other fishing gear is produced by a small tadpole-shaped animal of the genus Oikopleura. 1987 FELT 1 'Slub' is a thick algae-like growth which sometimes clings to the nets and impairs their catching ability.

slubby a
  1 1981 MAJOR 195 Fishing was outa the question that time of year. The fish would be too slubby to eat even if we did catch any.
  2 1985 *Gazette* 26 July, p. 3 [The] research scientist with the university's Marine Science and Research Laboratory...not only identified the organism as being the source of the slub problem but also successfully developed and tested a rapid and thorough method for cleaning slubby gear. 1989 *Evening Telegram* 20 May, p. 26 Fishermen in Bonavista and Catalina...who have [started fishing] are blaming cold and slubby waters for the scarcity of fish.

slut n
  1 P 308-88 [They had] big kettles called sluts.

small a
  1 Also: having a certain regulated size.
[1978] 1985 LEHR & BEST (eds) 74 "The *Gigantic*": 'Twas five miles up the river our load we did discharge;/One half our fish was small, my boys, the other half was large. 1987 *Evening Telegram* 17 Mar, p. 4 Fishermen will receive...6.5 cents [per pound] for small codfish (over 14 inches to 17 inches).

smallwood n Attrib ~ **boot**.
1981 SPARKES 190 All fishermen and seamen in those days wore long leather boots called Smallwood boots or, more often, deck boots. Some came halfway up the leg and were called half-gallon boots.

smart a
  1 [1960] 1982 BURKE (ed Kirwin) 116 "Are you Coming Mrs Doolin": For the school boys will assemble,/And at running they are smart. [1987] QUINLAN 32 Some of the Birchy Bay loggers were 'smart on a log.' They could

jump from the bank and land on a log sluiced through the dam and balance themselves.

smeech n also **smitch** *EDD* ~ sb 5 'smoke' So D Co, 7 'smell, stench' So D Co. Smoke of an overpowering nature; stench; also attrib ~ **roof**. Cp SMEACHY.

1984 POWELL 64 But the gravy that had gone over the red-hot stove made smitch enough to knock me out at the first blast. [When I recovered] the fire had gone out and the hol[e] around the stovepipe was carrying away the smitch slowly. 1985 GUY 32 I fair feels the niceness and the mildness coming off me in waves like the heat off a stove damper or the smeech off a pair of lumberwoods stockings. 1986 *Them Days* xi (4), 28 The old cooperage the [Hudson's Bay Co.] had was built out of logs and he had a chimney into 'en with a big smeetch roof for heatin' the tierces.

snare n Comb ~ **line**: TRAP² n: TRAP LINE, ~ **wire**: RABBIT n: RABBIT WIRE.

1988 *This Land* No. 3 (3), 35 [He lost ten pounds] hiking the twelve mile snare-line every day. When checking his snares he can be gone all day. 1985 *Gazette* 14 Feb, p. 6 [For our survival course] we had a snare wire [for catching rabbits].

snig v

2 1985 *Terminology of Loggers* 17 Sniggin'—pulling logs without a sled.

snow n

2 Comb ~ **hole**.

1895 *Toilers of the Deep* 245 It will be sheer madness to leave this island...as at the worst we can make a snow hole for shelter from the wind and drift. 1984 POWELL 97 So we got in the snow hole for a while, but the drifting snow was still bad as it baffled around and came in the hole. It was severely frosty, so we [put] the tent up in the snow hole with the paddles and some old stumps to hold it up.

so intens used in comparisons.

1981 MAJOR 192 [The shrew] was so small that I carried it home dead in my coat pocket. I didn't like it atall having caught something so small as that.

sod n

4 Comb ~ **house**.

1984 KALLEO 41 The [seal] intestines are blown up and dried. They can also be used for sod-house windows and for storing seal blubber.

sod v *Anglo-Manx Dialect* ~ 'to throw sods... "We'll stan' on the hedge and sod him".'

[(1928) 1982 BURKE (ed Kirwin) 134 "The Girl on the Bike": It's a picnic for the youngsters,/As they follow her and shout,/And they'll play the jews harp at her,/As the sods she'll try and dodge.]

soft a Comb ~ **labrador**: see **soft cure**.

[1918] 1930 COAKER 131 I cannot say the same of soft Labrador, for in many cases fish was sold that was never spread.

soiree n

1983 WARNER 27 It was a happy time, no doubt about it. There were many more scoffs and soirees, as the oldest men called the attendant parties and celebrations.

soldier n

2 Purple sandpiper (*Erolia maritima*) (1987 MONTEVECCHI & TUCK 239).

solomon gosse n

1986 *Nfld Herald* 15 Mar, p. 98 Thursday Dinner...was sometimes called a 'Solomon Gosse Day' or 'Solomon Gosse's Birthday' dinner.

some intens *SED* iv, 963 Co.

[1896] 1985 GOSSE 145 'Still,' the delighted little maiden tells her bosom friend in relating all about it, 'I'm some glad I went.' 1986 SAUNDERS 23 'I tell you, I was some frightened by the time they found me.' 1987 JOHNSTON 132 'Yer lookin' some good Hilda,' Nick would say.

something n

1986 *Them Days* xi (4), 45 You didn't get much for [raw livers], about 5¢ or 6¢ a gallon, something another like that.

son n Cp *O Sup²* ~ sb¹ 3 b 'term of familiar address' (1914-) for sense 1.

1 Phr *my son*.

[1785] 1955 GARDNER 35 When in good temper [the father of our mess] would say 'My son,'...when he addressed any of us. 1905 *Adelphian* ii, p. 126 'Be good to yourself me son.' 1924 *Deep Sea Fishers* xxi (4), 139 My son—Common appellation for a man of any age. A lad under ten will address a man of sixty as, 'my son.' 1987 FIZZARD 193 'She said, "Yes, my son," she said, "He was born in Grand Bank. I knows he and I knows his family".'

2 1985 *A Yaffle of Yarns* 4 [We admired] the way he could 'handle' the concertina... My buddy Wallace Verge used to say, '*My* son, he can make 'er talk.'

sook n also **sookie, soukey**. PRATT ~; *AND* ~ n 1 (1941-).

1 1985 JOHNSTON 10 'Sookie calves,' my father said. At breakfast he would moo at me. 'Mooooo-ooooo.'

2 1981 MAJOR 20 He wouldn't stop. 'Cry baby. Cry baby. You big sook!' 1988 PORTER 38 'God, Jason, you're a ton weight. Don't be such a sook, now. Go out in the backyard and look for the nice doggie.' 1989 *Sunday Express* 17 Dec, p. 7 [He] had a battery of 10 or 12 lawyers...and they threatened to nail my pin pricks on the grounds of 'cumulative effect.' Soukey-baby Telegram!

sooky a *AND* ~ a (1901-).

P 148-89 [discussing plans to have a make-up hockey game on Easter Saturday—person says no] That's nothing but a sooky attitude. 1990 *Evening Telegram* 15 Jan, p. 2 [He said] 'for Mayor Murphy to be sooky and raise up big scare tactics [is] a disservice to himself and...to the city of St John's.'

sound n

1 [1697] 1987 WILLIAMS 105 There would be many like Trevorgy of the Board of Trade who believed that the planters 'should not exceed 1,000' because they were 'too well acquainted with roast beef but not with the virtues of codsheads and sounds.'

2 Comb ~**-bone**.

1984 KELLAND 152 Then there were four splitting tables on which the upper portion of the fishes' back bones (commonly called sound bones) were dexterously removed with square topped knives.

southard n

1981 SPARKES 9 My father was 'a man from the South'ard' (that is what the people called any man who came from south of Cape Bonavista).

southern a, av

3 Comb ~ **man**: inhabitant of Newfoundland coast south of Cape Bonavista, esp the 'southern coast'; cp NORTHERN MAN, ~ **shore**.

1984 KELLAND 111 The grudge against the dory persisted [on the northern coast] until about twenty-five years ago, when the men of northern Newfoundland commenced to buy schooners from the southern men. 1989 Evening Telegram 5 Jan, p. 1 In the Southern Shore community of Ferryland, two families left their flooded homes this morning after a breakwater broke.

sou'wester n

1 [1983] 1985 LEHR & BEST (eds) 77 "The Glen Alone": Until we saw one human form was crouched upon her deck,/With an old sou'wester and guernsey on, shipmate, one of the wreck. 1984 GOUGH 97 She sees Ern's sou'wester and Cape Ann hanging on a hook and, underneath, his fishing boots.

span v Also: to secure the moorings of a fish-net in the water, the net itself temporarily removed.

1987 POOLE 69 There was no salmon along yet, so we would take up the nets and span the moorings.

spanker n Woman's shawl, a fig. term from a vessel's fore-and-aft sail.

[1976] 1985 LEHR & BEST (eds) 68 "The Gallant Brigantine": The dress she wore it was snowy white, her spanker it was green,/A silken shawl round her neck her shoulders for to screen.

spantickle n See also BARNYSTICKLE.

sparable n

1 Also: such cleats worn by loggers on the wood-drive.

1986 SAUNDERS 205 On their feet professional drivers wore leather boots with sharp caulks or 'sparbles' that wouldn't slip on the wet logs and slubby rocks. 1988 GOSSE 32 These [steel slivers in the heel of a boot] were known as 'chisels' and, like the nails or 'sparbles' extending from the soles, prevented slipping on the ice.

spear n Root of a molar or 'jaw-tooth.'

1984 POWELL 88 He had some kind of a unit that was

used for pulling teeth, but no doubt it was the old type. But I always managed to get the teeth out with no deadening at all. And he had some big teeth with three spears on them!

spell n SED iv, 865 Co D Do Ha, AND ~ n 1 (1831-) for sense 2.

2 1984 POWELL 19 Roland said I had had spell enough and it was time to move toward the Southwest Feeder of the Hawkes River. 1986 FELTHAM 166 A hundred yards, a short 'blow,' two hundred yards, a longer 'spell' and hour after hour the men got nearer and nearer to their home tickle [over the ice].

spell v

1983 Evening Telegram 26 Feb, p. 12 How wealthy would you be if you have five cents for every fish you spelled west of the Railway Station.

spirit duck See SPRITE.

spity a also **spitey**.

1981 MAJOR 99 But there wasn't one grain of sense in anything that he said. He only done it to make me spitey.

splice v

P 148-81 'I've been down there, splicing for wine.'

splinter n

2 Comb ~ **fleet**.

1988 Evening Telegram 24 Feb, p. 10 The last of 10 Newfoundland cargo vessels which comprised the famed 'Splinter Fleet' is still afloat and is a major tourist attraction in the Owen Sound area of Ontario.

split v

1 [1622] 1982 CELL (ed) Whitbourne's Discourse: [They] spent aboue twenty dayes...in building of their Stages, and other large necessary roomes there, to split, salt and dry their fish in. 1984 Evening Telegram 22 Dec, p. 6 My brother and I...cleaned our small catch—headed, gutted and split the fish, washed them in a 'dredge-barrow,' salted them away. 1987 FIZZARD 129 'I split with Reub...for eight years.'

split p ppl

1 [1623] 1982 CELL (ed) 188 Whitbourne's Discourse: Such fish...will amount to bee worth sixe pound starling, being splitted, salted, and dried. 1986 RYAN 29 To process the cod into saltfish, it was split along the underside, and the head, offal, and part of the backbone were removed so that the fish lay flat. 1987 Evening Telegram 17 Mar, p. 4 The prices for split fish will be 5 cents a pound for extra large (over 27 inches) [cod-fish].

2 [1918] 1930 COAKER 136 Packers of split herring should be registered, and every man be compelled to place his registered signature or name on every package he packs. [1938] 1988 Evening Telegram 8 Mar, p. 6 At Spencer's Cove on Friday the SS Magnhild loaded 191 casks of codfish and 240 barrels of split herring for Puerto Rico.

split n PRATT ~ 1 for sense 1.

1 1984 POWELL 75 In one minute I had the fire going

with dry brush and splits. 1986 SAUNDERS 80 Then we cut some fresh fir boughs for our bunks, collected some wood and splits [and] laid out our gear.

2 Comb ~ **man**, ~ **merchant**: one who supplies kindling.

1983 *Evening Telegram* 15 Jan, p. 32 I minds how your mother used to get someone to pay the splitman as she didn't want to be seen mingling with common people. 1892 ibid 7 Oct [She] had formerly been a resident of a new outlying settlement, and defendant had frequently appropriated to her the naughty title of 'Split-merchant.'

splitter n
1 1984 KELLAND 152 The curved blade enabled the splitter, when he severed the back bone, to raise it easily and lessened the danger of slicing off portions of the fleshy part which could spoil fish for marketing purposes. 1988 *Evening Telegram* 18 May, p. 19 The colorful terms cut-throater, header and splitter were the names applied to people who carried out the first three steps in the processing of fish.

2 Also: in hoop-making, the froe used to split saplings.

1981 SPARKES xiv The hoopmaker's trade was one of great skill... The froe, sometimes called splitter or cleaver, used to split the sapling lengthwise, was often a bit of hard wood with a bevelled edge covered with tin from an old tin can.

splitting vbl n
3 Comb ~ **knife**, ~ **table**.

1984 POWELL 193 "The Loss of the *Blanche Marie II*": She carried a crew of four young men just in the prime of life,/Who knew the game called fishing, and handled the splitting knife. 1987 POWELL 90 That summer a younger son, Lester, had stood to the splitting table and cut the throats of one thousand quintals of fish. He earned enough money to purchase all his school books for the winter.

spoon n usu pl. Phr *play the spoons*: to create a rhythmic sound using two spoons held back to back in one hand, their clicking effect sometimes providing accompaniment to a song and, with virtuoso performers, involving intricate physical adroitness.

M 69-5 Then he fetched two table spoons from the pantry, came back into the porch, sat up on a chair, crossed his legs, and began 'playing the spoons' and singing a song. 1980 COX 159 [Harry Mercer] plays other instruments as well as the guitar; the mouth organ, the saw and the spoons. He plays the spoons expertly and uses his shoulders, his back and his knees in playing them, much to the amusement of the children. 1985 *Evening Telegram* 24 Dec, p. 3 Today as in the past, [mummers] bring along an accordian, guitar, spoons or a harmonica. P 305-89 We drank the beer until seven o'clock (laugh), playin' the spoons—next thing, jigs and reels.

spot n COHEN, p. 119 for sense 2: 'The rower (*andoer*) required great skill, for when the men

were "into fish" it was his responsibility to keep the boat on the 'spot' by controlling its drift.'

2 1903 *Deep Sea Fishers* Oct, p. 9 [Grenfell speaks of a sort of communication or telepathy between the cod.] Herein lies the whole secret of the so called 'spots' of fish. [1937] 1945 SCAMMELL 37 "Payne's Cove Bait Skiff": Alf Gatehouse's baitskiff is here on the spot,/They've shot the seine twice, but they've got no great lot. P 245-89 'But there's only little spots of fish comes in this year.'

3 1858 *Harper's Weekly* 22 May [caption]...near as may be to the many spots of water, or rather bottom, which experience has shown to be the favorite [locations of fish]. 1982 MCDOOLING 115 As with most fishing ventures there are good spots to fish in the harbours but there are also those areas which are not so good. 1986 FELTHAM 54 The several miles of ocean fished by the fishermen of any one settlement had hundreds of fishing 'spots.'

4 1924 *Deep-Sea Fishers* xxi (4), 139 Tuckamore—Little spot of woods—Underbrush.

spraw-foot n Cp *SED* iv, 723 'splay-footed': spraw-footed, ~-vooted So W Brk Sı Do Ha.

spray n Cp *OED* ~ sb[1] a 'small twigs of trees'; *EDD* sb 1 'branch, bough' Sc Ir s w cties. Small, dry branches of spruce or fir, the needles fallen, used as kindling for a quick fire; cp BLASTY BOUGH.

P 231-89 Fuel would consist of small dried branches (called 'spray' in some rural areas today) which would have already been chopped from the spruce and fir trees brought from the woods by the men the previous winter. This type of fuel would give quick heat, ideal for cooking; and the fire would die down just as quickly once the food was cooked. This was important during hot summer days.

spread v
1 1987 POOLE 2 On Saturdays and after school I would work spreading fish at Maddock's for five cents an hour.

2 1984 POWELL 75 As I always had lots of small nails in the camp to use in spreading my furs, I would put a handful in my pocket.

spring[1] n
1987 FIZZARD 186 For days work continued on removing the sand around [the schooner] and putting timber under her keel. On the spring tide 34 men, using chains and steel cables, attempted to release her from her captivity.

spring[2] n *SED* iv, 828 So Co 'spring of the year' for sense 1.

1 1984 KELLAND 111 Like most young men of his time, he did a trick at fishing and spent a few springs at the icefields. 1987 POWELL 50 So the spring of the year is the most difficult time to hunt sea birds for a living.

6 Attrib, comb ~ **baiting**, ~ **bloom**: seasonal occurrence of plankton in the cold coastal waters of the middle latitudes, ~ **business**: merchant-fisherman supply trade in preparation for the seasonal fishery, ~ **fish**, ~ **fishery**, ~ **trip**, ~ **var**.

1987 FIZZARD 149 'Salt fish, landed from the three spring baitings of the many bankers that sailed out of Grand Bank...was spread on the beaches to dry.' 1989 *Gazette* 3 Mar, p. 5 Much of the phytoplankton produced during the spring bloom sinks to the bottom—providing a nutrient-rich benthic layer. This phytoplankton detritus may be eaten by creatures living at the bottom, or may be a reservoir of food that is recirculated into the water column over time, extending the period of abundant production beyond the limited period of the spring bloom. 1896 *Centenary Magazine* [supplement] p. ii Monday, June 15th... Shops closed at six o'clock, p.m., the spring business being over. [1937] 1987 *Evening Telegram* 17 June, p. 6 Negotiations are now being carried on between the Portugal exporters group and the Gremio regarding the sale of spring fish to Portugal. 1988 ibid 6 May, p. 1 Mr Cashin said he is anxious to begin contract negotiations with fish companies for the caplin fishery and spring fishery. 1987 FIZZARD 126-7 Having taken on their bait, which was herring for the spring trips, the schooners were now ready for their first voyage of the season. 1989 *Nfld Qtly* lxxxv (1), 13 "Winter": Spruce and spring var Crackled in the Findlay Oval.

springy a Of animals trapped for their fur, past their winter prime, their pelts in poor condition.

1986 *Them Days* xi (4), 20 By the middle of March the 'coloured fur' was becoming faded and rubbed and the season ended. Mink, otter and lynx were 'springy' and almost valueless, the beaver season was closed.

sprite n also **spirit duck**. Bufflehead (*Bucephala albeola*), from its uncanny diving ability (1967 *Bk of Nfld* iii, p. 282); BUTTER-BALL.

spritsail n For the naval practice relating to **sprit- sail yard** v see also [1833] 1984 BAYFIELD i, 257 'This man yesterday had amused himself in *sprit- sail yarding* Dog Fish, a cruelty which I disap- proved of.'

sprog n PRATT.

spruce n

1 Also: *red spruce*.

1984 POWELL 102 This was a blind valley—all red spruce about the same size. 1987 *Evening Telegram* 10 Oct, p. A1 Many forest sites...seemed to be too dry to support good growth of black spruce, and pine species ...should grow much faster on these sites.

3 Attrib, comb ~ **bird**, ~ **longer**: see LONGER n 1, ~ **partridge**, ~ **root (basket)**, ~ **tuck**: see TUCK² n.

1987 MONTEVECCHI & TUCK 245 Spruce bird. Red crossbill. 1987 *Nfld Qtly* lxxxii (3), 17 'They drag the poor creature ashore, winch him noisily up a wharf, and unto a tripod o' spruce "longers".' 1984 POWELL 61 When I got back to the camp, there was a spruce par- tridge sitting on the tent pole right over the camp door.

1989 *Nfld Qtly* lxxxv (2), 32 Spruce root baskets hung airily from the rafters and rice paper streamers dangled dashingly from the ceiling. 1983 SOUTH (ed) 194 These [barrens] represent important caribou grazing grounds during severe winters with heavy snow accumulation. Ericaceous dwarf shrub heath, black spruce tuck and scrubby forests become more important eastward.

spry n 1858 [LOWELL] *The New Priest in Con- ception Bay* regularly employs a *'y* spelling for most *-ai/ay* words. For other [ai] prons of common words spelled *-ay*, see *SED* iv, 237-8 hay, W Do Ha, and in the questionnaire index daisy, faint, tail, whey, weigh.

1979 COOPER 11 "The Boy and the Piggin": My Da a'ways jigs wid two lines hove out,/De spry flies high when he's jiggin.

spur-shore n

1949 FITZGERALD 57 He figured from steel square, the angle and cut/Of spur shore and rafter, of wall plate and butt.

spurt n

1 1988 *Evening Telegram* 24 May, p. 3 [The] chief of cardiac surgery at the General Hospital said there was 'a spurt where [the Intensive Care Unit] beds were available' but again this week there was yet another heart surgery cancelled.

2 1983 FROUDE 129 Went on shore and had a spirt prospecting. 1985 *A Yaffle of Yarns* 15 On one of my last 'spurts' on that roof I was haunted by the comments that had been made.

4 1990 *Evening Telegram* 6 Feb, p. 2 The recent four- day cold weather spurt...is finally tapering off to more seasonal temperatures.

spy n, v Comb ~ **top**: elevated structure from which to observe approaching fishing vessels; cp LOOK-OUT.

1977 WHITELEY 44 [diagram] Lay-out of Whiteley Fishery Buildings...Spy Top.

square a Comb ~ **flipper**.

1984 KALLEO 22 They'd come home, having caught a seal amongst the ice. If it was a square-flipper, they would have to tow it behind.

square v

1 1981 SPARKES 188 After that came 'squaring up' when the fishermen and merchants settled their accounts.

squashberry n

1988 *This Land* No. 3, vol. iii (1), p. 36 The woods are full of Chuckley pears, wild raisins, squashberries, bakeapples, blueberries and partridgeberries.

squat v

1 T 309-66 Instead o' Jack [sittin' down in un], Hard Ass sat down in 't, and squat everything down on the floor. 1983 WARNER 46 And then we found ways to stop the fish from squatting... We made a double-wing cod end.

squid n Cp Burton Bradstock, Do quiddle, squiddle 'young cuttlefish or squid caught in the seine' (P 304-90); cp *squid-o* in sense 3.

1 1981 MAJOR 31 What we was talking about this one night was squids. It wasn't quite the right time of the year for them then, but we was on to talking about them anyway. 1990 *Sunday Express* 14 Jan, p. 7 When the squid came, they came in great numbers that you could jig them anyway.

4 Attrib, comb ~ **bait**, ~ **jig**, ~ **jigger**, ~ **jigging**, ~ **shit**: see ~ **juice**.

1984 KELLAND 97 Both squid bait and codfish were very plentiful so all hands were reasonably sure of rounding off a good season's work. 1983 WARNER 26 You used little lead weights—squid jigs, you called them—painted red and crowned at their bottoms with twenty or more tines, bent upward and needle-sharp. 1984 KELLAND 10 From the work benches of those stores were manufactured...hand tubs, trawls tubs [and] squid jiggers and handline reels. 1981 MAJOR 31 A good evening of squid jigging in September or October is one of the best bits of fun you can have out on the salt water. ibid 31 Arms like an octopus, only smaller. If anything grabs hold of them, they shoots out this black inky stuff—squid shit.

squid v

1 1981 MAJOR 34 'Grandfather,' I said to him, 'I was just tellin Brent about the times me and you and Dad was out squiddin.'

squid squall n

1987 *Evening Telegram* 28 Mar, p. 12 Other memories of the St John's harbor [are of] 'squid squalls,' a half-dollar sized jelly-fish, in millions just below the surface as we rowed our dory along the Southside.

squirt v

1981 MAJOR 32 Squid shit going everywhere then, cause as soon as they comes up outa the water, they lets fly. That's half the fun of it—getting squirt, or better still seeing someone else getting their faces full.

stack n Cp *OED* ~ sb 1 'pile, heap or group of things...with its constituents arranged in an orderly fashion.' Dry spruce or fir 'sticks,' their branches lopped off, placed vertically, their butts to the ground, in teepee shape for winter storage as fuel.

1977 WHITELEY 23-4 One of the distinguishing features outside was the stack of poles for firewood. These were brought in rafts down the river and were piled in a wigwam shape in the yard.

stage n

1 1983 WARNER 24-5 Their rickety stages, or mooring platform, each year mauled by winter ice, needed much repair.

stage head n

1 1987 *Evening Telegram* 4 July, p. 56 [tape transcript] In the fall the men would have to go out no matter how bad the weather was; they had to get off the collar, get clear of the stagehead and go somewhere [on the water to fish].

stamp n

1985 *Nfld Herald* 14 Sep, p. 21 We've got six stamps so far, and I'm hoping we'll get the ten stamps that is necessary [for fishermen to qualify for unemployment insurance]. 1987 POWELL 88 Each fisherman received a little book. Then the [fish] buyer obtained the stamps from the post office and they were recorded in the fisherman's book. 1990 *Evening Telegram* 17 Jan, p. 3 We feel we have an adverse image problem of being a bunch of stamp collectors scrounging as many dollars as possible from the government.

stand v Cp *OED* ~ v 76 c *stand to* 'to toil without flagging' obs.

2 Phr *stand off*: to stand to one side; *stand to*: to work steadily.

M 68-23 They notice Uncle Sam standing off, rubbing his hands. P 245-82 When the fish was running we'd sometimes stand to the table for sixteen hours until we'd drop. 1987 POWELL 90 That summer a younger son, Lester, had stood to the splitting table and cut the throats of one thousand quintals of fish.

standard a In designations of a quality cure or 'cull' of dried and salted cod-fish; a grade intermediate between 'choice' and 'cullage.'

1988 *Evening Telegram* 26 July, p. 3 Salt fish is given one of three possible grades: choice, standard and cullage.

standard n Cp *OED* ~ sb 20 a 'tree or shoot left standing,' *EDD* 5 'a sapling' He So. Small sapling forming part of the device to snare rabbits.

1981 MAJOR 181 The first slip I set out, I asked him to go cut me a standard—a stick to tie the slip onto.

standing vbl n Comb ~ **room**.

1988 GOSSE 18 In calm weather [the skiffs] were propelled by a long sculling oar protruding from the stern, which often doubled as a rudder, and was operated by the skipper from the after standing room.

starrigan n also **staragan**. *O Sup*[2] ~ Nfld.

1 1896 *Trade Review*, Christmas No. p. 20 'I'm goin' over Sullivan's hill/To cut and spell a load o' staragans! 1985 *Terminology of Loggers* 17 Starrigan: a small green stick [i.e. a standing tree in the woods].

2 1986 SAUNDERS 53 The greyness of the [caribou] hair surprised me. It looked just the same as the bleached old juniper starrigans and weathered rock around us.

start intens Cp *OED* stark a 5 'sheer, absolute' (1400-), start naked a 'entirely naked' obs exc dial (1225-1325; 1892-96). Comb **start (hammer) calm**: of the sea, absolutely calm.

1920 WALDO 161 'Start calm' means perfectly calm, and then they may say expressively 'The wind's up and down the mast.' T 195-65 Start calm; not a draft o' wind... I jumped out o' the rodney and went aboard and called father. P 237-76 Boy, 'tis start hammer calm.

station n *O Sup*[2] ~ sb (1834-) for sense 2.

1 1988 *Evening Telegram* 18 May, p. 19 The station

consisted of a dwelling for the family, a stage, wharf, 'flakes' and 'bawn,' and sometimes included a separate 'shack' for the crew.

2 1971 *Can Geog J* lxxxii, 163 [Difficulties] forced the Moravians to close many of their missions: Zoar, south of Nain...in 1894; and all the stations north of Nain.

3 Post established by the International Grenfell Association offering medical, educational and industrial facilities and services to northern Newfoundland and Labrador settlements.

1914 *Deep Sea Fishers* xii, p. 118 [Then] came a sweet-faced boy from a neighboring 'station.' 1984 POWELL 14 The handiest nursing station was over forty miles away. 1985 *Nfld Qtly* lxxx (4), 28 In a thousand emergencies [Mrs Paddon] filled the gap and ran the hospital—not only the hospital but the clothing store, the industrial, the school, and the station as a whole.

stationer n
1988 *Evening Telegram* 18 May, p. 19 A stationer was a fisherman without a schooner of his own, who operated from a 'station' or 'fishing room' on the shore.

stave n Attrib **stave-slide**: a sled made with barrel staves for runners; such a sled used by children for sliding in winter.
1987 FIZZARD 139 To carry the gravel, they built 'stave slides,' which used three or four staves from a molasses puncheon as runners.

steady n
1 1986 SAUNDERS 47 We paddled the steadies and poled or portaged the rattles, and even before we crossed The Gut and struck the tide at Dawson's Point my shoulders were aching.
2 1984 POWELL 72 The pond was four miles long, then I had to go one mile over a marsh to the steady where the beavers used to build their houses.
3 Comb ~ **brook**.
1988 *Decks Awash* xvii (4), 23 Bowaters later supplied Brookfield's dairy operation from their herd at Steady Brook and that's where we picked up our cattle.

steam n Attrib ~ **box**, ~ **jenny**: device to heat water for the immersion of plank or timber to be bent to a desired shape.
P 284-85 'A steam jenny is a machine that uses oil and is, has a nozzle, something the same as on your oil burner, which is making the flame and, of course, this is boiling the water, and you got to keep the water going into it. And this creates the steam so you can put that steam, hook that right into your steam box.'

steam v Also: **steaming** vbl n.
1986 FELTHAM 61 He cut balsam fir for plank that had a gradual 'suant' curve that would fit without steaming or applying pressure.

stearin n also **stairn**, **starin**.
1977 *Christmas Bells* Dec, p. 13 Sure a gull, or a starin or a tickless can't carry much more den a herrin. 1966 SCAMMELL 91 Hundreds of white birds, starins and

tickleaces (kittiwakes) could be seen. 1985 NEWHOOK 12 There were many things to see [in the sky]—wheeling birds, blue gulls, saddlebacks and screaming terns which we referred to as stairns.

steering vbl n Comb ~ **stick** (1986 SAUNDERS 285).

stick n
1 1832 MOSS *MS Diary* 29 Mar Left this day for the Bay to haul down some sticks for the store. 1984 POWELL 122 The 10 HP [engine] wasn't much power for those big sticks; many we were squaring down into 12'' by 12'' and it was slow work. 1986 *Evening Telegram* 7 Feb, p. 3 [He] said the woman was not physically able to swing a 30-pound mall and manipulate wharf sticks with 10-inch butts.
4 Comb ~ **fence**.
1930 KENT 86 On the rock-terraced hillside facing north straggled the houses, weather-beaten wood, stark, flimsy; stick fences; tottering wharves and fish houses strewn at the water's edge.

stiffle v *SED* iv, 748 So Do.
1894 *Evening Herald* 24 Dec In the winter I was left alone with the lame woman, Sarah by name, and the wether was so cold that father and John Whittle could not get home for the cold and drifting for about a week and I was so afraid I would be stiffelet in the drift geting water, from a distant brook.

still n
1977 MOAKLER 62 We thought of mud trout plashing in the stills.

sting v
1890 *Evening Telegram* 9 Sep He once sent an urchin to the penitentiary for thirty days for taking a turnip out of the field of a well-to-do personage. 'Stinging crabs' is a high misdemeanor in the estimation of this upright magistrate... There would be little wonder if one day he would...sentence the juvenile offenders to be hanged on a sour apple-tree.

stitch v In making a 'bough bed,' to interweave small conifer tips between the larger boughs.
P 308-88 They used to get those little small boughs, little tiny ones...for to stitch in and make [the bunk] a little bit better across... Fill up the spaces between the boughs and they call that stitching.

stock n PRATT stock skate for comb in sense 3.
3 Comb ~ **skate**: homemade skate, the blade embedded in a narrow block of wood.
1986 SAUNDERS 36 [We] had home-made skates made from a file or other piece of hard metal reworked and set in a wooden stock, called stock skates. Stock skates were tied on with leather thongs threaded through holes in the wood.

stodge v *OED* ~ v 1 'to stuff *in* as a filling material' obs. To fill the chinks in a log-house with moss; STOG.

1987 PEYTON 15 Their houses were individual tilts, makeshift shelters built entirely of logs, the seams or chinks...stuffed or 'stodged' with sphag[n]um moss to block the drafts.

stog v PRATT ~ 1 for sense 3.
1 1984 POWELL 70 By the time I got one end of the tilt caulked, the moss was all used. So I thought I could stog the other seams with ground—anything to keep out the frost. **2** 1984 *Nfld Qtly* lxxix (4), 3 Stogging up Drains, a seasonal and universal delight. Stogging them up with sods and mud and rocks until the water creeps up and back into a pond. **3** 1981 MAJOR 28 I had my pockets stogged full with oranges or bananas or something. 1985 GUY 52 And even he got to turn [the gramophone on] with his toes because he got to keep his two fists stogged in his ears. **4** 1986 SAUNDERS 29 Then you have to go with a halter and search for [the horses], hoping all the time they are not stogged in a marsh somewhere.

stogger n
3 A wedge used to pack moss tightly in between the logs of a log-house; SHIM (1985 *Terminology of Loggers* 17).

stogging vbl n The process of filling the chinks of a log-house with moss; STOG v 1.
[1863] 1977 WHITELEY 84 'The seams were caulked with moss, a process called, "Stogging," which, with newspapers pasted on the smooth surface on the inside, rendered the wall considerably tight.'

stomach n
1 1924 *Deep-Sea Fishers* xxi (4), 139 Stomach—Any part of anatomy from knees up and chin down, particularly front of chest.
2 Comb ~-**sick.**
1981 MAJOR 21 It came back to me, back and back and back to me all night. I got stomach sick. But if I had throwed up my guts it wouldn't a made me any better.

stookawn n also **stoopawn***. Cp PRATT stouk.
P 328-87 [He was] walking around like a stupawn.

stoopawn* See STOOKAWN.

stop v *SED* iv, 985 So D for sense 1.
1 1984 POWELL 70 The brown [moss] was what I mostly used [to caulk the seams of the log tilt] as it will stop in the seams for years. **3** Cpd **stop-a-while**: type of early friction match.
1981 SPARKES 8 [After sulphur matches] came friction matches, called 'stop-a-whiles,' 'eight day matches' and, less politely, 'stinkers.'

stopper n
1 1832 MOSS *MS Diary* 11 May Put the 2 stoppers out. [1832] 1981 *Them Days* vi (4), 43 Sounded the tickle for a new stopper. **3** Comb ~ **net.**
1985 BUSCH 47 A series of 'stopper' nets ran perpen-

dicular from this net to the shore, to be raised at the proper moment.

store n
1 1984 KELLAND 10 'Store' in this instance did not mean a shop, but a building set apart from the dwelling house. It was usually equipped with a long work bench, which in turn was outfitted with all varieties of carpenter's tools necessary for men who were engaged in the fisheries. 1987 POOLE 71 In the meantime I bought two stores from a fisherman in Petty Harbour, who had retired from the fishery. These two stores were large and had been a business place when my father was a boy.
2 Comb ~ **keeper,** ~ **loft.**
1985 *Nfld Qtly* lxxx (3), 22 One report suggests that the main winter occupants of Trinity consisted of 'store keepers' and servants of the merchant firms without a woman or child among them. 1987 POWELL 38 So I went back and there in the store loft, in a little room, were lots of motors from 3-horsepower to 8-horsepower.

storm n
1 Phr *storm of wind.*
1984 POWELL 26 There was a storm of wind from the northwest and our little boat wasn't too seaworthy for the Atlantic Ocean in that kind of weather. 1987 FIZZARD 131 'It came up a storm of wind when we were taking in our gear.'

story n Cp *OED* ~ sb[1] I. 1 'narrative, true or assumed to be true...a historical relation or anecdote' obs (1225-1642). Recollected incident of lived experience; a yarn of times past.
1975 *Them Days* i (2) [cover] *Stories of Early Labrador*; p. 1 Many thanks to the people who shared of their time and memories: Their names appear with their stories. 1984 KALLEO [title-page] *Taipsumane: A Collection of Labrador Stories.*

stout n
1 1986 SAUNDERS 73 It was nice for a change to get clear of the stouts or mooseflies. 1988 MOMATIUK & EASTCOTT (eds) 66 Next, we get the stout... He bites hard enough.

straight a
2 Comb ~ **shore** (a).
1988 GOSSE 41 Those who went north soon discovered that the waters just north of Bonavista Bay, known as the 'straight shore,' offered the most promising fishing grounds.

straighten v
1987 FIZZARD 136 'Time you had the expenses paid there wasn't much for two men. You'd fish all summer, take your supplies and straighten up. Sometimes you'd have nothin' left.'

straits n pl *OED* strait B 3 'the word is usually *pl*. with sing. sense.'
1 1988 *Sunday Express* 18 Dec, p. 2 'I'd like to see some (regulation that says) fishermen from the island can't come past the straits,' said Jessie Bird, president of the Combined Councils of Labrador.

2 Attrib ~ **dog**: variety of sled-dog bred on the lower Labrador Coast.

1919 GRENFELL[2] 197 For short...dashes of twenty to thirty miles the lighter built and more vivacious Straits dog is the speedier and certainly the less wolfish.

strange a

2 Phr *make strange*, usu in the negative.

1987 *Sunday Express* 3 May, p. 2 Lumbermen bound to and from 'the woods' used to stop off at Uncle Sam's where a feature of the dining table was a large basin of jam. 'Now don't make strange men,' Uncle Sam would say. 'Slouse on lots of it.'

strap n

1 [1898] 1986 *Evening Telegram* 24 Mar, p. 6 In the battle they cut three of our straps and cut the skins of several seals which were on the last strap hoisted aboard of us. 1984 WRIGHT 83 [He took] the straps off the pelts, while [we] worked in the hold loading pelts onto the straps to be hauled out with the winch.

5 Length of stout rope fastened to the stern of a 'dory' and used to launch and recover the craft; DORY STRAP.

1984 KELLAND 14 The stern straps were fashioned from stout manila rope, the two ends being pushed through holes in the top section of the dory's stern and secured on the outside by the forming of knots, leaving a loop or becket approximately sixteen inches long hanging down on the inside. On Banks fishing vessels they were used to hoist dories outboard and inboard.

strap v To hoist an object on a vessel using a band of rope as a purchase for tackle; cp STRAP n 1.

1984 WRIGHT 65 I was working on the whipline, strapping the panned pelts together in bunches of fifteen, to be hauled aboard by the whipline. 1987 *Evening Telegram* 9 May, p. 15 [tape transcript] 'There's a barrel here,' I said, 'and everything belong to my motor is in this barrel and,' I said 'it got to go up' [on deck]. 'All right boy,' he said, 'put it up.' 'Hold on,' I said, 'send down the hook and I'll strap it and let it go up.' He sent down the hook, I got my barrel and hoisted it up on deck.

streel v

1986 *Metro* 1 June, p. B7 Struggling upright again, the boy fished for his sunken rod, grabbed it and started for shore, strealing the eel behind.

streelish a *O Sup*[2] streel sb[2] chiefly Anglo-Irish; hence streelish a (1936-). Also: of a damaged fish-net.

1987 DAWE [20] It still captures fish,/Though far from a tending;/It's tangled and streely/And badly needs mending.

strike v

1 1983 FROUDE 10 We leaved twillingate and steered away N.E. until we struck the ice...so we leaved the vessel in our small boats we got a few seals in the fore noon.

3 1986 SAUNDERS 127 That day, seals were all the talk

for they had just struck in around Comfort Cove and Newstead. 1989 *Evening Telegram* 16 June, p. 3 Caplin...usually strike in first in St Mary's Bay.

5 Phr *strike off*: in preparing timber for sawing to mark the log with a 'reddening line'; *strike up*.

1981 SPARKES 2 To 'strike off' a log, the string was stretched taut between points at opposite ends of the log and then snapped by a pinch with finger and thumb. The result was a perfectly straight red line from one end of the log to the other. 1984 POWELL 77 Now it was about time to strike up my traps. 1988 *Evening Telegram* 17 May, p. 8 I had it on my mind about a rabbit slip that I never had struck up yet the spring and I wanted to get in [the country] and see to that.

striker n *OED* ~ 3 c (1824). In mining, the man who lands the ore at the shaft-top.

[1886] 1983 MARTIN 22 Miners' wages...were cited as being as follows: strikers...5 shillings and 6 pence.

string n

3 Phr *string of ice*.

1984 POWELL 130 There were now strings of slob ice reaching across the bay and pans of ice everywhere.

stud n

1 [1768] 1826 CARTWRIGHT ii, 309 We found [the square habitation] to be a rectangle framed nearly in the fashion of the English fishing houses, only that the studs were something apart, from which it was evident that they alone could not, in that state, form the shell, as in the English buildings, where they are closely joined together. [1811] 1915 HOWLEY 85 Considerable pains were employed on these I found them in, and which were of the octagonal structure, the diameter of the base being nearly 22 feet, and enclosed with studs of four feet above the surface. 1832 MOSS *MS Diary* 14 Mar Began putting up the studs of the new store.

stud[1] v

1981 SPARKES 173 Some logging families moved in winter to places nearer their work. There they lived in 'winter houses' or 'studded tilts'... The studded tilt was simply a log cabin built by standing the logs on end. It was, therefore, 'studded.' 1984 POWELL 141 This house was all built from 2' plank, studded right around, then sheeted up on the inside and clapboarded on the outside. [1987] QUINLAN 6 The early settlers [in Birchy Bay] lived in 'studded tilts' so called because the logs or studs were placed vertically.

studden a

1980 COX 17 The early days of [Green's Harbour] are referred to today by local residents as 'stud and [i.e. studden] tilt days.'

stumper n Device to remove roots of a tree when clearing land.

1989 BENNETT 42 A team of men then had to dig out the deep roots, using the powerful and ingenious lever device they called a 'stumper.'

stun a *OED* stunpoll [?f. STONE *sb.* + POLL *sb.*[1]] (1794-). Local evidence shows only attributive and predicative examples. Writers in recent decades have apparently felt that *stun* has merged with the verb *stunned*; speech is variable—[stʌn] and [stʌnd]. Cp *O Sup²* stunned ppl a 2 'drunk' Aust, N Z (1919, 1933) for sense 2.

1 1981 MAJOR 29 What use to bug me more than anything was when he'd come home to Mom with these stun stories about me. 1989 *Evening Telegram* 2 Sep. p. 5 [letter] Those so-called educators are so 'stunned' they just can't learn, even after 40 years [of Nfld being in Canada]. 1990 ibid 28 Mar, p. 4 I'm not usually that 'stunned' but it took me a few moments to figure out that I was the person referred to in [a letter to the Editor, March 20].

stun v Cp STUN a.

suant a, av Cp *South Shore Phr Bk* soonth for sense 2.

1 1986 FELTHAM 61 He cut balsam fir for plank that had a gradual 'suant' curve that would fit without steaming or applying pressure.

2 1981 PADDOCK 42 "The Boat Builder": Of perfection in a flawed universe/which drove you to build two hundred boats/In search of the ultimate curve/Of suant wood beneath your searching fingers.

sud line n

1 1985 GUY 198 I got this bit of sed line tied around me finger here...to put me in mind of not saying three little words. 1989 *Evening Telegram* 16 May, p. 7A The rest of the [trouting] equipment consisted of...about four or five feet of braided black sewing thread for a 'sud' or leader.

2 1981 SPARKES 184 A bulltow was simply a long, strong line with hooks attached at regular intervals by short pieces of line called suds. 1986 FELTHAM 67 During the caplin season, the inshore fisherman used miles of trawls and these had to be overhauled and 'seds' replaced where necessary.

summer n

2 1988 MOMATIUK & EASTCOTT (eds) 124 Mike was 3 when he first went down to Labrador. He spent 67 summers there, never missed one.

4 Designating a structure: ~ **house**.

1987 POWELL 50 Many of their summer houses were built on the rugged coast which was little more than one huge ice cap for seven months of the year. The people would shift to those places along the coast mainly to hunt sea birds and seals.

5 Attrib, comb ~ **fish**, ~ **fishery**, ~ **mole**, ~ **servant**: see SERVANT¹ n, ~ **voyage**: see VOYAGE n 1.

[1714] 1987 FIZZARD 24 All the planters and servants [are] bringing their furs and summer fish to sell for purchasing their winter provisions and necessaries. P 245-87 'There, at Norman Bay [Labrador], they live in winter until it's time to go out to the coast for the summer fishery.' 1985 *A Yaffle of Yarns* 7 Even his freckles (which I, like all my Winterton people, used to call 'summermoles') seemed to light up and glisten. 1987 FIZZARD 54 It was during [the French and English war of 1778] that

for the first time there were more Newfoundland servants than English summer servants engaged in the fishery. 1983 WARNER 28 Even the few dory fishermen who still row out to jig the cod will all have a good summer voyage.

sun n

1 In var phrases and proverbs: *turn with (or towards) the sun*, ~ *is splitting the rocks*, etc.

1916 *Deep Sea Fishers* xiii, [p. 162] [passing plates:] Everything must be passed 'with the sun.' 1937 DEVINE 59 A boat or schooner should be turned towards the sun. ibid 70 'When the sun is drawing water,/Better bide home with your wife and daughter.' P 330-89 'It was rainin', and when we got to La Manche Park, the sun was splittin' the rocks.'

2 Comb ~ **burn**.

1987 FIZZARD 149 'The crews of women were going back on the beaches after dinner to turn each fish so that not one would be sunburned.'

sunken p ppl Comb ~ **rock**.

1689 *English Pilot* 13 Renowes is but a bad Harbour, by reason of sunken Rocks going in, lying in the fair way, besides other Rocks on each side.

sunker n *O Sup²* ~ (1880-) Nfld.

1 [1977] 1985 LEHR & BEST (eds) 160 "The *Ravenal*": She may have struck a sunker, but such things we'll never know;/We only know her eighteen men died in the waters cold. 1983 WARNER 25 In many places, just outside the churn of the surf, were rocky half-tide ledges— 'sunkers,' they call them in Newfoundland's lugubrious maritime vocabulary—on which the seas broke heavily. 1987 FIZZARD 56 Finally, ahead of them lay a small island, not much more than a rock, with a string of sunkers near the shore.

surrogacy n Cp *OED* (1811, 1829) rare. The office of a naval SURROGATE.

[1767] 1828 CARTWRIGHT ii, 305 Herewith...the copies of my proceedings in the surrogacy at Trinity.

swally v, n *EDD* ~ sb 1. To swallow (P 54-60); a swallow (of drink).

1966 PADDOCK ~ to cause food to pass down one's throat. P 229-66 The throat is so sore I can hardly swalley. 1989 *Nfld Qtly* lxxxiv (4), 38 Tossing back a drink to toast the many good times proved a little more than some of the old-timers could stand. Silent promises to sell the ['Bullet'] were made and another swally forced back an already beading tear.

swanskin n

1 1981 SPARKES ix The queen of all material was 'swanskin.' That was a thick, woolly, creamy-white cloth used for making drawers, mitts and a special kind of sock.

2 In var designations: ~ **cuff**.

[1937] 1983 FROUDE 6 I got myself ready for the first time to travel on the frozen jam dressing myself with a pair of mole skin pants, home spun jacket, dog skin cap, seal skin boots, swan skin cuffs [etc].

swash See SWATCH.

swatch n also **swash**.
1 Also: a stretch of weak ice.
1949 FITZGERALD 41 'Just slob haul to that open swash, out there to the north-northeast.' 1985 *Terminology of Loggers* 17 Swatch: a weak or open place on ice. 1986 FELTHAM 161 The sealers did not always follow a straight line, for it was often necessary to take advantage of stronger ice near the sides of the various islands or to detour around 'swatches.' [1987] QUINLAN 27 The slide ran over a swatch of bad ice [and the man was drowned].

swatch v
1985 BUSCH 75 When the vessel was 'swatching,' or hunting mature seals in the leads, only the punts...were overboard, with four-man crews selected by each foregunner.

swatchy a Of an ice-field, broken by stretches of open water or weak ice.
1981 SPARKES 184 If the drift ice brought seals to the land, the men went hunting, of course, but on foot or, if the ice was 'swatchy,' they took a very light small boat with them called a rodney or gunning punt.

sweet a
1 In designations of sweet-flavoured foods: ~ **cake**, also (b) adolescent male teasing name for girl.
1985 *Nfld LifeStyle* 3 (1), 22 After the sweet cake and syrup rituals of New Year's Day, [they flock to Florida.] 1987 KIMIECIK 95 It is the adolescent males who become the pests and annoy their opposite sex peers with their blatantly obscene talk and teasing. Comments like, 'Hey, sweetcakes!' are made by the adolescent males anytime, but especially at night.

sweetness n *O Sup²* ~ 1 b (1912, 1920) [Nfld]. A sweetening material, esp used in tea.
1896 *J A Folklore* ix, 36 ~ sweetening for tea; long ~ molasses; short ~ sugar. 1912 DUNCAN 143 T' beg a barrel o' flour an' a gallon o' sweetness. 1919 GRENFELL² 164 The fact that we were without butter, and that 'sweetness' (molasses) was low, was scarcely even noticed. C 71-95 Put a bit of sweetness in your tea.

swinging ppl Comb ~ **gear**.
1985 *Terminology of Loggers* 17 To harness a horse to a sled without shafts was to put it in *swinging gear*.

swish¹ n
1986 *Evening Telegram* 2 Dec, p. 7 It kicks like a testy mule and it's the dregs swished from discarded whiskey or rum barrels. Nova Scotians love it and they call it swish.

switchel n
1987 *Evening Telegram* 8 May, p. 4A After a dandy cup of 'switchel' (that's fishermen talk) and a slice of lassy bread...we agreed on giving the lily pond a try.

syrup n Also attrib ~ **table**.

[1920] 1985 GOSSE 77 The Sisters of the C.E.W.A. took advantage of the [concert party] to sell off some articles left over in their *strong box*, and also provided a 'syrup table' to benefit their society. 1981 DAWE 40 "The Mummer": they shone/with cake crumbs and syrup/on their happy faces.

T

tabanask n
1924 *Deep Sea Fishers* xxi (4), 139 Tabanask—Small sled or toboggan hauled by men.

table n Comb ~ **flake**: platform, about four feet above ground, used to spread and dry cod-fish; HAND n 3: HAND-FLAKE.
[1888] 1956 *Daily News* 19 Nov, p. 13 Table flakes or vigneaux are spread in all directions.

tack n Phr *in tack with*: in touch with (another) as an associate.
1986 SAUNDERS 77 That summer I had the misfortune of coming in tack with a biologist who was sent out from St John's to study the habits of the Atlantic salmon.

tack v Cp *OED* ~ v¹ 7 'to make a run or course' naut. To make a short visit, run an errand; cp DART n 3: phr *take/make a dart*.
P 76-81 'Tack over the store and get a pack of cigarettes.' 'I'll tack over [to] the house.'

tackling n
1 1896 *Trade Review Christmas Number* p. 20 Where're you goin' my silly old man?/Where're you goin' with dogs and tacklins?

tail n Cp *OED* ~ sb¹ 4 g 'the spit or extremity of a reef or sandbank where it slopes under the water' (1761-) for sense 2 (b).
2 (b) A narrow, elongated and descending part of an undersea fishing ground. Cp NOSE n 2.
[1882] 1972 DE VOLPI 169 [*Harper's Weekly*] Great masses of ice move down from the arctic, and crowd about what the sailors call the 'tail of the banks of Newfoundland.' 1983 WARNER 283 Even under normal circumstances the western edge of the Tail of the Bank will be warmer than the eastern, which is more subject to the Labrador current. 1986 FELTHAM 125 A 'point' or 'tail' was a long, narrow protrusion from a fishing ground where the water deepened gradually and a 'nob' was a very tiny fishing spot.
5 Comb ~**-drag** v, ~ **feathers**: the wooden poles used to fasten logging sled to tractor, ~ **rack**: see final 1985 quot.
1985 *Terminology of Loggers* 17 Tail drag: pulling logs on a go-devil with one end of each log dragging behind. ibid 18 Tail feathers [are] those reaches which pass from the 'tail' of the tractor to the first sled. ibid 18 Tail rack. Two sticks fastened to a single sled so that the ends of the sticks trail on the ground.

tail¹ v Phr *to top and tail*: see TOP v.

tail² v
1984 POWELL 56 I was tailing my traps and snares now, all along one side of the lake. 1986 *Sunday Express* 14 Dec, p. 36 Snare-setting is a very common practice and hunters may 'tail out' as many as several hundred slips over several miles of rabbit country.

take v
2 1984 POWELL 138 Then Aunt Louie took a stroke and died.
5 Phr *take astray* (or *away*): to enchant (a solitary child or adult when away from the community); cp FAIRY v: *fairy away*; *take back*: (a) a setback, (b) to haul an otter trawl; *take up* (b).
1973 WIDDOWSON 224 But the little people were supposed to have the power to 'take you away' *i.e.* to drive them out of their minds or make you foolish so that you would go away or lose the path. 1987 *Lore and Language* vi (1), 25 She said she was taken astray by the fairies. She was surrounded by the forest and couldn't find her way out. 1983 FROUDE 174 Now thats another disappointment and another great take back. 1987 FIZZARD 211 During the course of hauling the [otter] trawl or 'taking back,' as it was commonly called, the knot would be tied and untied according to the number of bags of fish in the net. ibid 136 If it had been a good year, the balance sheet was in the worker's favour. That did not always mean they had cash in their pocket; often they were required to 'take it up,' that is to buy goods in the owner's shop equal to the balance in the account.

talk v
2 Phr *you talk (about)*.
1924 *Deep Sea Fishers* xxi (4), 139 Well, you talks about—Exclamation.

tally¹ n Cp *Anglo-Manx Dialect* 183 ~ 'the tally is a single herrin...over the count' for sense 1, and also for tally fish in sense 2.
2 Cpd ~-man.
1986 SAUNDERS 38 [My uncle] had been tallyman [for the lumber firm]. 1987 *Evening Telegram* 27 Apr, p. 7 [tape transcript] There were two tallymen; one for the ship and one for the firm. 1989 CANDOW 76 The tallyman cut a notch in the stick—hung from a nail in the mast—for every five pelts, and a groove when the number reached 21.

tally¹ v
1986 *Them Days* xi (4), 47 Q is for quintal always tallied down. 1987 *Evening Telegram* 27 Apr, p. 7 [tape transcript] The tallymen would tally it down and the pelts would be wheeled away from the ship.

tal qual av phr *O Sup²* ~ Nfld (1732-).
[1732 in *Calendar State Papers, Amer. & W. Indies* (1939) 282 And by carrying a mixt cargoe which is all sold at markett for marchantable fish, when it's only (what in the stile of the fishermen is called Tal Qual) to the shoarmen. *O Sup².*] P 245-87 'The Chairman of the Canadian Saltfish Corporation said that he didn't like it

but that they had to buy tal qual [this year] because of the competition [for cod] from the large fish plants.' 1987 MCDONALD 8 An additional factor that prejudiced good quality was the growing practice of 'tal qual' purchasing, whereby merchants bought all qualities of fish at a flat rate.

tan n *O Sup²* ~ sb¹ c ~ pot (1978) Nfld. Comb ~ **pot**.
1985 GUY 28 She hove together a whole tan boiler full of purging medicine.

tanning vbl n Cp *OED* tan v b 'to treat (fishing-nets, sails, etc.) with...some preserving substance' (1601 quot), tanning vbl sb (1794 quot). Operation of making certain all joints of a boat's hull are pitched; cp BRIM v, BRIMMING.
1832 MOSS *MS Diary* 25 May Brimmed the boats and got them in order for tanning.

tansy¹ n
1981 SPARKES 31 Tansy has all but disappeared from the gardens of Newfoundland...but when I bought an old country place some years ago, I was delighted to find a tansy patch behind the old barn. I have not yet made any poultices or pillows, nor have I flavoured any buns with it, but I do use it at times as a repellant to unwelcome insects.

tansy² n
1986 FELTHAM 98 Under the [rocks in shallow tidal pools] the eel-like 'tansy' hid. Catching these little fish was a common spring-time activity.

tant a
2 1988 *Nfld Qtly* lxxxii (4), 40 [review] And we would have liked a glossary: sufficient 'gafflings'...'tant spruces,' and 'bough whiffets' pop up to puzzle non-Newfoundland readers.

tar n Comb ~ **mop**.
1983 *Evening Telegram* 14 Feb, p. 6 [He] said that the tar 'mops' they used in his day [for brimming a boat] were made out of the remains of wool socks and various scraps of cloth.

tat n Cp *EDD* tata sb 1 'excrement; filth' D obs. Excrement, esp infant term (P 322-88).

tatie n also **taiddie**. *SED* iv, 201 'teddies' etc, s w cties.
1 1985 NEWHOOK 46 The last load of *taiddies* would be piled into the brimming cellar and the horse would be untackled and stabled. Winter would come soon enough, but at least there were sufficient potatoes to see us through.
2 Comb ~ **pork-cake**.
1985 *Nfld Qtly* lxxxi (1), 18 On Saturdays it was customary to have potato cakes, fried in pork fat, for tea (dinner), and these were called 'tiddy pork cakes.'

tavern n
[1977] 1985 LEHR & BEST (eds) 186 "The Tobacco

Song'': If the wind veers northeast then the ice it will go,/We'll all get some 'baccy St Peter's I know;/Every man with his tavern stuck out of his gob,/And to hell we'll shove shavings, spruce rind and withrod!

tawt n
1 1977 MOAKLER 24 We lashed the compass to the after tawt/And watched the needle flutter as we fought. 1987 FIZZARD 131 'We had a doryload of fish with our two tawts turned up and there was no way could we put a sail on her.'

T D n
1885 *Terra Nova Advocate* 21 Oct Thanks to the energy of scientific men our city is today illuminated by Electric Light, which bears about the same relative comparison to gas, as to the obscure light of a T.D. pipe.

tea n
1 1983 FROUDE 13 When finished we expected our tea as usual but was told that there was no tea for us so we all went below supperless.
2 1985 QUIGLEY 69 Typically the fare consisted of a 'soup table' and 'meat tea,' pork and cabbage and preserves.
4 Comb ~**berry**.
1915 *Deep Sea Fishers* xiii, p. 66 There were little white violets blooming close to the snow, tea-berries and bunch-berries, harebells, [and] pyrolas.

tend v See CHANNEL: ~ **tending**.

terra nova n *DC* ~ 'Newfoundland' (1576-1933) Hist. Northeast coast of North America and its adjacent islands, esp the large island situated at the entrance to the Gulf of St Lawrence; NEWFOUNDLAND, NEWLAND. Hence **terranovan**: inhabitant of Newfoundland.
[1508] 1971 SEARY 32 Terra Nova is found as a Latin name [for Newfoundland] in Ruysch 1508. [1578] 1935 *Richard Hakluyt* 128 [Parkhurst's letter] To answer some part of your letter touching the sundry navies that come to New found land, or Terra nova, for fish... [1617] 1895 PROWSE 105 [Mason's letter:] [We hope] that with all *Terra Nova* will produce *dona nova*, to manifest our gratification. 1842 BONNYCASTLE i, 163 And even in a city like St John's, without a regular police, you may walk the streets at all hours of the night, not only without danger amongst these excitable Terranovans, but even without often meeting with any of them after ten or eleven o'clock. 1887 *Evening Telegram*: Christmas Num p. 6 ''A Few Words on Terra Nova'': Terra Nova is grieving for the hearts that are leaving. 1924 MARS 14 ''The Call of Terra Nova'': Dear Terra Nova's calling,/Her mountains, lakes and streams,/Her virgin forests, untrod paths,/Are ever in my dreams. 1962 *Cabot Voyages* (ed Williamson) 142 One would expect to see an English influence in Ruysch's map [and] one name, Baia de Rockas, looks English, and the name given to the New-foundland coast, Terra Nova, is distinctively English. 1976 MERCER 184-5 [ballad titles] Terra Nova (1902), Terra Nova Regatta (1960), Terra Nova's Farewell (1904), Terra Nova's Naval Reservists (1904), Terra

Nova's Patriot (1902), Terra Nova's Welcome (1902), Terra Novean Exile's Song (1905).

that sg subs
1 Phr *and that*.
1987 *Evening Telegram* 10 Oct, p. 34 But Mom had long rubbers and that and she used to dig up potatoes.

these pl det
1987 *Nfld Qtly* lxxxiii (2), 43 It was more than usual, in the absence of church buildings in a community, for the school to be used as a church than for the church to be used as a school in these days. P 302-88 'Well at these years logs that were cut, they saw them and build the camp right there.'

they pro See note at WE.
1858 [LOWELL] i, 86-7 'She looked black, seemunly; an' no colors nor flag. — 'Twas they! Sure enough, 'twas they!'

thick a
1 1987 FIZZARD 210 'We'd have to leave the fishing ground a little bit early sometimes when it was a thick of fog to allow for that.'
2 [1937] 1945 SCAMMELL 20 ''Tommy Decker's Venture'': And there's tom cods round the stages, thick as any boy could wish,/But Tommy Decker and his crew, they're after bigger fish! 1983 WARNER 26 So thick [the squid] were that the whole town went out to fish them.

thigh n also **tie(d)***. Comb ~ **rubber**.
C 67-13 tied rubbers — another expression for hip-waders or long rubber boots. 1984 POWELL 6 He had just had a shipment of thigh rubbers come in and was hanging a pair over the door for display. [1987] QUINLAN 32 When the [A.N.D.] Company reverted to short timber the short leather boots were replaced by thigh and hip length rubbers.

this sg det *SED* iv, 808 'this last few years' Sx.
[1985] MAHER 19 The both of them have passed away this thirty years. 1987 FIZZARD 162 Most people at this time had fewer debts than is common today.

thorn n Cp *OED* ~ sb 3 a 'a spine or spiny process in an animal (1300, 1711, 1860); *EDD* 4 'sharp prickly spine found on [skate]' Sh I. Sharp projections on 'sculpin' (*Myoxocephalus octodecemspinosus*; *M. scorpius*).
1895 *Christmas Review* 12 [proverb] If you squeeze the sculpion, you'll find his thorns. 1987 O'FLAHERTY 43 Sculpins had to be softened; otherwise time would be wasted getting them out of the net and there was the risk of being stabbed by the thorns.

those pl det
[c1894] PANL I have taken this opportunity of writing those few lines to your Worship to inform that I have been served most ridiculous by the Poor Commissioner. [1960] 1982 BURKE (ed Kirwin) 48 ''Lines Written on Michael Power, the Blind Minstrel'': Attention, all kind hearted friends/To those few lines I write. 1982

MCDOOLING 128 'The people have got more money, you know, and now those late years especially, people have more gear.' 1983 FROUDE 207 To do such wonderful things as are accomplished in those days we should all be educated to the truth.

thousand n
1985 ASHTON 196 "Beans by Galore": But the beans they were thousands, they were there by galore. 1988 *Sunday Express* 20 Nov, p. 12 And right up to the end [of November] there has always been thousands of fish... But this year around the 28th of October, we found 17 or 18 bedlamer seals in our nets and the fish had disappeared.

thread v Comb ~ the needle.
1985 QUIGLEY 42 "Thread the Needle" is performed as a final figure in Pouch Cove and Conception Harbour; in the former community it is known as 'spin the needle.'

tibbage n also tibish.
1985 *Decks Awash* Jan-Feb, p. 25 The tail and head webbing was called *tibish* and the middle rawhide was called *vabish*.

ticket n
1 Also (b): piece of wood marked to indicate a specific course direction assigned, by lot, to a dory crew on the Grand Banks.
1984 KELLAND 144 A couple of skippers told me that they always used their hats to hold the wooden course tickets. But Captain George Follett said that he was against using his hat for the ticket drawing because... keen-eyed dory skippers after a quick glance into the hat would be able to select the course which suited them best.

ticklace n also tickle-ace, tickless. *O Sup*[2] tickle-ace (1819-) Nfld & Labr. See TICKLER.
1917 *Christmas Bells* 13 'How kin dey [shoot guns from airplanes]; sure a gull, or a starin or a tickless can't carry much more den a herrin at won toime, an a grepe is de biggest bird ever I seed, and he culdn't carry a small shot gun.' 1981 DAWE 38 "The Bridge": Once this bridge took children/to the swing of the tickle-ace/and the skin of the sculpin's lip. 1985 NEWHOOK 12 If you were lucky you might even spot a tickle ace or squeaker.

tickle n
[1976] 1985 LEHR & BEST (eds) 55 "The *Ella M. Rudolph*": At five o'clock in the evening through the Tickles she did pass/The threatening of a violent storm was showing by the glass. 1987 FIZZARD 210 'We come in to make Green Island and even if it was very thick we'd have to steer across to Pass Island and there were times I went through that tickle and you'd have a job to see both sides at the same time.'

tickler n A devised spelling of ornithologists who heard sg or pl *ticklas* and recorded it as plural *ticklers*. Atlantic black-legged kittiwake; TICKLACE (*Rissa tridactyla*); a type of gull.
1869 *Zoologist* No. 49, p. 1851 I saw gulls (on wing) which I could refer to no other species, and the settlers, to whom I showed specimens of [the kittiwake gull], said they were larger than the 'tickler,'—a small gull with which they evidently seemed familiar, and one which I think will prove to be this species... There is room to doubt the testimony of fishermen, as well as my own, as to the identity of *C. Philadelphia* with the provincial name 'tickler.' 1908 TOWNSEND 111 Kittiwakes, or any small gull or tern, are called here 'ticklers,' possibly because they fly about 'tickles.' 1912 CABOT 83 According to the fishermen it is small, oily bubbles rising from the fish that the ticklers are after.

tide n Comb ~ stick: wooden device placed in side of dory and used to guide the hauling of trawl-line; RUNNER n 1, RUNNING STICK.
P 127-73 ~ stick used to guide the hauling of trawls. 1987 FIZZARD 160 'We'd make a lot of little things like tow pins, dory plugs, dory mallets, tide sticks [etc].'

tie* v See THIGH.

tierce n Cp *OED* ~ sb 4 'an old measure of capacity...also a cask.' In the fish-trade, a wooden container of designated size for the export of fish; cp BARREL, CASK, PUNCHEON.
[1841] 1985 TAYLOR 37 Each tierce of pickled fish shall contain three hundred pounds of fish. 1986 *Them Days* xi (4), 27 A tierce, now, is bigger than a barrel. He's roughly thirty-one inches high, thirty-six or thirty-seven staves and the head is twenty-one inches in diameter.

tilly n *O Sup*[2] sb[2] (1922-).
1987 POWELL 38 While the gallon measure was filling, Uncle Bobby was licking the plug stick that he had taken out of the hole to allow the molasses to run. After I had three gallons, Uncle Bobby said, 'I will give you a little tally rather than wait for all the heavy molasses to drain off the measure.'

tilt n *O Sup*[2] ~ sb[1] 4.
1 1986 SAUNDERS 145 With a whiffet or tilt you just had a sloping frame of small poles covered with overlapping boughs against the weather. 1988 *Evening Telegram* 18 May, p. 19 A tilt was a crude temporary dwelling, sometimes made from sods, and sometimes partially underground, in which the stationer might spend the summer. 1988 GOSSE 26 Tilts or log cabins were built to house the wood cutters [from Spaniard's Bay] and the temporary hamlet was nicknamed 'Tilt Town.'
2 1924 *Deep Sea Fishers* xxi (4), 139 Tilt's distance—About ten miles—a fair day's journey while making the rounds of the fur traps. [1984 POWELL 54 From the very first year I took over the trapline, it was my desire to get better organized. By this I meant to build more tilts, to have one every day's walk apart, so I wouldn't have to be carrying that canvas camp and stove any more than I had to.]
3 Phr *to smoke like a tilt* (b).
1988 *Sunday Express* 14 Aug, p. 3 'They used to sit around and smoke like tilts and drink coffee all day.'

tilt v See further discussion at **a-**: come a Tilting.

timber n Comb ~ **dog**; cp DOG² n 4.
1985 *Terminology of Loggers* 18 ~ a short iron rod with both ends sharpened into spikes and turned down, driven over a log into the supporting wood to help keep the log steady while being chopped or sawn.

time n
1920 *Deep Sea Fishers* xvii (4), 125 The older people told me they were planning some 'times.' ...an old fashioned dance was what I was in for. 1987 FIZZARD 193 'They had a big time in the Masonic for me. And there were different things, dances and stuff [to celebrate my return from the war].'

todge n Cp *EDD* ~ sb 'anything of a thick stodgy consistency' s w cties. Phr *thick as todge*: of a liquid, very thick, dense (P 318-84).

toe n Cp *OED* ~ sb 6 toe-cap 'cap of leather covering the toe of a boot or shoe.' Comb **toe-cap**: strip of iron placed over the 'nose' or front of the runner of a sled (1985 *Terminology of Loggers* 18).

toggle¹ n
1 1924 *Deep Sea Fishers* xxi (4), 139 Toggle—Door latch.

toggle² n
1985 *A Yaffle of Yarns* 134 We would get shell birds, pigeons, toggles and occasionally a wild goose or two and some ducks if lucky.

tole pin n Burton Bradstock, Do 'metal pin attached to the side of boat over which the loom of an oar fitted' (P 304-90).
1858 [LOWELL] ii, 214 'Clap a tole-pin in, then, can't ye? See, that's wan that ye're rowing against,' cried the fisherman. 1987 FIZZARD 160 'Later on we'd make a lot of little things like tow-pins, dory plugs...tide-sticks, rollers, gaffs and trawl-kegs.'

toll v
1 1985 GUY 53 Them tourists and relatives from the mainland are like the skiddies and the nippers. The first bit of warm weather tolls them along.

tolt n
[1768] 1989 *Nfld Qtly* lxxxv (1), 21 Peters Tolt; Tolt Pond. 1987 O'FLAHERTY 6 The alder bushes were so thick that he lost his way twice and had to climb tolts to get his bearings.

tom cod n
1 1989 *Evening Telegram* 4 July, p. 13 I mean good fresh northern cod: steak, scrod, cheek and tongues, britches, tomcods, sounds, any part of the fish, provided it was to be fried, stewed with scrunchions, or stuffed and baked. 1990 *Sunday Express* 14 Jan, p. 7 Guess what [the squid] ate? Tomcods, of course. I used to check to see what was in their stomachs.

tommy n Comb ~ **cod**: see TOM COD 1.
1903 *Daily News* 17 Feb "The Great Inventor Ned": When the three men dined at a table/On which 'tommie cods' were spread. 1904 PEDDEL 16 Tommy cods and other fry.

tongue n
2 1989 *Sunday Express* 19 Mar, p. 7 Our winter's pocket money [was] earned door to door [by] the sale of napes by those who arrived at Battiste's Wharf too late for tongues or peas.
4 Comb **tongue-banging**.
1987 FIZZARD 103 Chances are, more than one dissident suffered a 'tongue banging' from one of the pillars of the church who, while claiming to hate the sin and not the sinner, seemed to be having trouble distinguishing the two.

top v *OED* ~ v¹ 3 ([1794]-1824 berries), *EDD* ~ 19 v (2) turnips, gooseberries, *SED* iv, 204 s cties, swedes for phr in sense 2.
2 Phr *to top (off, up), top and tail*: to hull or shuck (berries).
[1950] 1988 *Seniors' News* Oct, p. 14 Those were busy days and nights, with the cleaning of fires...topping boiler water, transfer of fresh water to daily service tanks. 1989 BENNETT 59 My pleasures included holding hands of wool for winding; mending the odd sock; 'topping and tailing' berries for jam [etc].

torbay n Attrib ~ **nag**.
1881 *Evening Telegram* 14 Dec The locomotive... caused quite a commotion along the line by breaking a man's leg and scaring two 'Torbay nags' almost to death.

touse n *EDD* ~ sb 8 D Co. A fuss, noise.
P 295-83 'What a touse you're making over this.'

tout n *OED* toute obs 'buttocks, posterior' (1305-1460), *EDD* tout sb³. Comb ~ **piece**: backside; ARSE.
T 1175-72 [When] he got up to her he slewed his backside [to it], he give her a flick with his backside and beat un under the tout-piece.

toutin n
1 1987 JOHNSTON 65 She loved toutons, balls of fried dough. I remember her making toutons for herself, grabbing out handful after handful of dough from a big bread pan. 'Dere'll be no bread if ya keeps makin' toutons May,' Raymond would say.
2 [1987] QUINLAN 22 Molasses buns would be made with small chunks of salted fat pork used instead of raisins. They were called pork toutons and were not unpleasant to the taste.

tow v
1 Also (b) in the deep-sea fishery: to steam ahead with net dragging the water for fish (1987 quot).
1985 BUSCH 59 [Each man would have] a line for towing sealskins; and, above all, the sealers' gaff. 1987

FIZZARD 210 'On the draggers we were up all the time. The only break you'd get was when she was towin' and if there was a lot of fish you wouldn't get no sleep.'

tow² n

1 Also (b) in the deep-sea fishery: the period during which a vessel, using an otter trawl or other type of net, drags the water for fish (1987 quot).

1984 WRIGHT 66 He changed the topic immediately. 'He took a tow of five pelts just then.' And he went back to work. 1987 FIZZARD 211 'The speed of the trawler was then reduced to approximately three nautical miles per hour. The speed was maintained during the period of the tow which was generally ninety minutes [when fishing with an otter trawl].'

towny n

1 1988 *This Land* No. 3, vol. 3 (1), 77 [The restaurant is] but a stone's throw from the Newfoundland Hotel, and anybody, townie and out-of-towner, who gets the munchies at two or three o'clock in the morning might show up here.

trade v

[1937] 1983 FROUDE 124 I took a stock of goods and started trading [and] made seven trips during the summer. 1977 BUTLER 38 'I want you to go trading for me this summer as I want to keep my good dealers around the Bay supplied with goods and I have a lot of dried fish to collect in and I wish to buy all the dried fish I can get.'

trader n

1 1981 SPARKES 41-2 The 'traders' came in large schooners of eighty to a hundred tons which carried in their holds provisions and groceries, clothing and fishing gear and a large stock of 'iron ware and cheap tin trays.' ... When a trader came, men and women would go on board and 'price the goods,' then the trader would go ashore with them and assess the fish or fur and the bartering would begin.

train² n

2 Attrib ~**-fat**.

[1621] 1982 CELL (ed) 255 *Letters to Calvert*: Lastly, that no man may bee wronged in their Boats and traine-fats, or in any thing else whatsoever.

trap¹ n

1 See also JAPANESE COD TRAP.

2 Attrib ~ **berth**, ~ **boat**, ~ **cod**, ~ **crew**, ~ **fish**, ~ **fisherman**, ~ **fishery**, ~ **haul**: the pulling of a catch of netted fish to the surface; HAUL n 1, ~**-line**: TRAP MOORING, ~ **man**, ~ **net**, ~ **season**, ~ **skiff**, ~ **voyage**.

1987 POOLE 18 I asked him to try and talk my father into taking a good trap berth the following summer. 1988 *Evening Telegram* 18 June, p. 12 [tape transcript] It was an open boat just like a good sized trap boat with two sails, a mainsail and a jib. ibid 11 June, p. 3 Through the 'revolutionary new method' of codfish farming, small trap cod are purchased by the company, transported alive to controlled conditions, and fed to increase their weight.

1984 KELLAND 13 His father was a member of our trap crew and he had gone out with my father and the other crew members to haul the codtrap. 1987 *Evening Telegram* 1 Aug, p. 4 These landings provide good pay days with 40 cents a pound being paid for trap fish longer than 16 inches. 1989 *Sunday Express* 26 Mar, p. 7 Thousands of trap [fishermen] have observed life in the seas, each, more or less, always at their same traditional spot. 1901 *Evening Telegram* 20 July The result of the trap fishery in St Mary's Bay, so far, shows a poor season. 1989 *Sunday Express* 19 Mar, p. 7 Doesn't the destruction of the trap fishery, the incomes of trap fishermen and their communities, hide some fundamental truths about our attitude towards our past and the rural way of life? P 245-88 'They're just in from their first trap haul for the day.' 1987 KING (ed) 114 "Of Goats and Hills": boats bobbing on the bay/by trap-lines/I could dream a thousand dreams like this. [1937] 1945 SCAMMELL 18 "Tommy Decker's Venture": And the trapmen, they've been takin' berths, the trawlers got to wait/Until the caplin strikes the land to get a bit o' bait. 1989 *Sunday Express* 26 Mar, p. 7 I could now better understand... what trapmen had meant when they kept saying, 'There's no fish left.' [1895] 1977 WHITELEY 53 '[Blandford has at Long Point] 3 trap nets.' 1987 *Evening Telegram* 4 July, p. 56 They got a nice lot of fish there but when the trap season was over there wasn't too much fish to jig. 1903 *Nfld Qtly* iii (3), 19 Our boat is known in Newfoundland as a 'trap-skiff.' Her length is about thirty feet—a comfortable boat and sea-worthy. She had three masts, with as many large sails. 1988 SINCLAIR (ed) 106 Vessel technologies include...inshore 'trap skiffs' (inboard-powered, wooden boats up to 40 feet long). 1901 *Evening Telegram* 20 July The trap voyage is now practically over [in St Mary's Bay]. [1936] 1986 ibid 19 Sep, p. 6 A well-known fisherman of Petty Harbour and his two partners had $12.25 each coming to them. They secured 132 quintals for their trap voyage. 1989 *Sunday Express* 26 Mar, p. 7 A young man with his biology degree from Memorial does not know more than his father with 30 or 40 trap voyages behind him.

trap² n Comb ~ **house**, ~ **line**.

1984 POWELL 62 But I went back—and under the very same tree with the can in it, I made a new trap house and took many hundreds of dollars' worth of those big silvery lynx from it. 1986 SAUNDERS 142 Add to that a gun, a portable tin stove, an axe [etc] and I was ready for the trapline.

trap v Men, fish, and locations all can 'trap.' Also: of cod-fish, to enter a cod trap.

1901 *Evening Telegram* 20 July The trap voyage is now practically over, though, with in winds, saving voyages may yet be trapped. [1936] 1986 *Evening Telegram* 8 July, p. 6 Fishermen with traps report that codfish, though fairly plentiful on the grounds for some time, did not begin to trap in appreciable quantity until a day or two ago. 1960 *Assoc Am Geog* 1, 274 Inside berths...were trapped when the seas were too rough to trap on the outside berths. P 245-87 'This is our first year trapping in three years.' 1987 *Evening Telegram* 1 Aug, p. 4 Last year we started trapping fish around July 20 and we were getting very good landings.

trapper n Comb **trapper's bread** (see quot).

1988 *Evening Telegram* 31 May, p. 11 [He] was glad to accept, and glad also of the thick slice of bread, made delicious by his hunger and by the molasses and raisins which flavoured it. 'Trapper's bread,' said Charlie.

trapping vbl n

1 The operation of catching migrating fish, esp cod and salmon, in a box-like net or 'trap' moored in a stationary position in inshore waters.

[1919] 1930 COAKER 145 Our first port of call was Doting Cove where we landed some freight. The fishery here is an average one. Trapping was about over.

2 Attrib ~ **season**.

1985 *Nfld Herald* 14 Sep, p. 21 We were a bit later getting started this year. Ourselves, the trapping season usually starts around the twentieth of June, or the last week in June.

trawl n Attrib ~ **fish** v cpd: to fish for cod using a trawl or 'bultow,' ~ **tub**.

[1939] 1989 *Evening Telegram* 21 July, p. 4 The banker *Robert Esdale* has returned to Burin from St Pierre and will proceed to Greenland waters to trawl fish. 1981 SPARKES 184 A trawl was set, or shot, from a trawl tub in which it was always stored when not in use. The tub was usually a portion of a barrel but some men made their own trawl tubs.

tread n Comb ~**-pole**.

1985 *Terminology of Loggers* 18 ~ a log placed across a river and used as a foot-bridge.

treason n Cp PADRAIC COLUM, *My Irish Year* (London: Mills & Boon, 1912), pp. 72-75, SEAMUS CLANDILLON and MARGARET HANNAGEN (eds), '*Londubh an Chairn*' being Songs of the Irish Gaels (London: Oxford University Press, 1927), pp. 8, 11, 27, and G.M. STORY, 'A Tune beyond Us as We Are,' *Nfld Studies* iv, p. 137. Comb ~ **song**: a song or ballad of a sectarian nature; a satiric composition attacking or ridiculing an individual or group.

1985 LEHR & BEST (eds) xi-xii There were songs we weren't allowed to tape because the singers thought they were 'treason songs.' These were usually ones showing racial or religious prejudices, or ones ridiculing, even slandering, people still alive or with close relatives still living. Although they were sung privately, for whatever reason the singers would never sing them at a public gathering. P 294-86 [Many of] the most thoughtful and intelligent [informants interviewed] insist that *any* song that attacks or has the potential for disturbing any individual or group is a 'treason song.'

trickle* v also **chuckle**. *EDD* ~ v 'to roll,' truckle 1 v s w cties. To roll (an object).

T 282-66 Jack had a lot o' rocks up in the room. And when they go down after water, Jack'd rise the puncheon. He shove a rock in under un, see, and by and by he got un trickled right up. 1976 *Daily News* 2 Mar, p. 3

I know we played piddly and hooper and hopscotch, and we would chuckle hoops for hours along the boardwalk that extended for several hundred feet along one side of the road in Garnish.

trigger n

2 Comb ~ **mitt**.

P 245-89 ~ Woollen mitten with the thumb and forefinger separate.

trim v Cp *OED* ~ v 3 'to caulk, clean, and dress a ship's bottom' obs (1513-1850), esp 1711 quot for sense 1; cp *OED* 11 for sense 3.

1 Also: phr *trim out*: to prepare a boat for the summer fishery; cp PLIM v.

1819 ANSPACH 426 The oil thus extracted [from the seal blubber] is poured into hogsheads which have been duly trimmed, that is, which have been kept a long time filled up with water. 1987 POOLE 83 I told him that I wanted forty dollars a month and no extra work. I would trim out the boats in the spring and paint them and that was all except run the store.

2 1987 POWELL 98 The trout that try to get back to the spawning grounds usually don't enter the bay the way a ship would come through the channel. The trout trim the shorelines and coves where there are no tides to slow them down.

3 In a fish-plant, to cut irregularities off a fish fillet.

1987 RAPPORT 71 I should get a job [at the fish-plant] 'cause I trimmed fish for years.

trimmer n Cp *OED* ~ 2 'one who trims...makes neat.' In a fish-plant, one who cuts irregularities from a fish fillet.

1987 RAPPORT 71 'And buddy on the phone said they need trimmers.'

trimming vbl n Comb ~ **table**: in a fish-plant, station at which a 'trimmer' removes irregularities and defects from cod-fillets.

1987 FIZZARD 212 'From the cutters the fish went to the skinners [and] from the skinners the cod went to the briners, where it was put into a salt solution. Then the cod went to the trimmin' table. There we had a light table, where the worms and bones were cut out.'

trip n See also COHEN, p. 49 'It is assumed that it will take [the *Langdale*] most of the week to *get their trip*—to catch sufficient [fish] (approximately 350 boxes) to make the journey south worth while.'

1983 FROUDE 15 Leaved with a good trip of fish. 1987 FIZZARD 210 'It was not like when we were salt fishing, you'd wait and get your trip before you'd think about coming to land.'

trouble n

1979 PORTER 105 The undertaker came, mumbled a hurried 'Sorry for your trouble' in Pop's direction, and went upstairs to measure Nanny for her coffin, or casket as Mom and Aunt Viley liked to call it.

trout n
1 1990 *Evening Telegram* 13 Jan, p. 28 No one would suggest ice fishing is a sport because it isn't—the trout usually hook themseles—but it is a lot of fun and trout taste just fine to me, even if they weren't taken on a Silver Doctor or Parmachene Belle.
2 1987 POWELL 98 [He] and another young fellow took ten trout nets and fished from Alexis Bay to Black Bear Bay. They learned that the trout could not survive with only ten trout nets. Just one week in a place and 90% of the trout would be taken. Then they would move to another bay.
3 1985 GUY 40 'Go right in me old trout,' she said, 'and sit right down on me chester feel.'

trout v
1987 FIZZARD 179 Now and then fresh trout were on the table when young boys, and sometimes the men of the family, went 'troutin'.'

trouter n Comb ~s **train**, ~s **special**: (b) a variety of rum, named after the train.
[(1895) 1985 GOSSE 13 Excursion train to Whitbourne. A train leaves Fort William Station this evening at 7 o'clock... This is the best train for trouters to take, tomorrow promises to be a good day.] 1988 *Nfld Qtly* lxxxiii (4), 15 The favorite brew, at that time, was 'Trouters' Special' at $2.00 a bottle.

trouting vbl n
1987 *Evening Telegram* 3 Jan, p. 15 January 15 [is] the opening date for trouting on non-scheduled rivers, lakes and ponds throughout the province.

truck[1] n
1985 BUSCH 53 The 'credit' system differed from the earlier 'truck' system in that the merchant was providing credit, not the actual goods.

truck[2] n Cpd **truckman**.
1911 *Daily News* 5 Dec The truckman, one of a number who stand in Browning's Cove, mixed in trouble with two stokers...and in the mean time Officer Squibb arrived and attempted to arrest the driver. [1937] 1987 *Evening Telegram* 26 Feb, p. 6 With cars parked as they are [on Water Street] the truckmen have to take to the middle of the Street where all the snow has disappeared and where the horses are put to a severe strain to drag their loads.

truckeying vbl n Cp *OED* trucking vbl sb[1] 'exchanging, bartering, trafficking.' The action or process of engaging in trading.
[1937] 1983 FROUDE 130 We had a large Stock of dry goods grocries and provisions on board[.] we Did a lot of truckeying with the Esqumas they made our Vessel their home.

truss n *OED* ~ sb 8 truss-hoop (b) (1877). Comb ~ **hoop**: in coopering, stout wooden hoop to secure staves of a large cask in place.
1986 *Them Days* xi (4), 28 [To put the tierce together] you got to have a truss-hoop. A truss-hoop is a big heavy hoop made out of birch. The birch is stripped down and tied around with spun yarn and it measures about three inches in diameter. You got to have four truss hoops.

tub n
1 1897 *Evening Telegram* 28 Aug On Wednesday he procured a large quantity of squids, and on that day he also caught ten tubs of fish on the bait. [1936] 1986 ibid 11 Mar, p. 6 A meeting of businessmen was held today in the Board of Trade Rooms for the purpose of considering the sale of salt cod fish in tubs. 1985 LEHR & BEST (eds) 52 "The Dole Song": We only got two tubs that day, the rest we could not get;/A man he must be crazy boys, to come up here and sit. 1987 FIZZARD 128 'You'd have four tubs of gear; well, that means every man had to bait two tubs of gear before it come daylight. There were ten lines of gear in a tub. Each line was 60 fathoms.'

tuck[1] n
2 1903 *Deep Sea Fishers* Oct, p. 9 [This makes] all the difference between large 'tucks' in the traps, and not a single fish to eat. [1938] 1945 SCAMMELL 11 "To an Old Newfoundland Fisherman": Lashed to the wheel; of long, disheartening waits/For cod seine tucks and 50 quintal hauls. 1984 KELLAND 17 While we are gone to the trap, you take the new dory, go over to Harris' and bring back a load of salt. Because if we get a big tuck of fish we'll need more salt to stow it away.

tuck[2] n
P 106-87 '[We'd find rabbits] in a little tuck of woods—a little island of woods in the barrens.'

tuckamore n
1983 SOUTH (ed) 190 The tuckamoor vegetation consists almost entirely of *Abies balsamea*. This contrasts strongly with the tuckamoor of the Long Range Mountains which are dominated by *Picea mariana*. 1987 MONTEVECCHI & TUCK 25 On exposed or very wet sites Black Spruce may be dwarfed to a shrub that grows thick and tight to the ground. Such retarded growths of either Black Spruce or Balsam Fir are locally referred to as 'tuckamoor.'

tunnel n Comb ~ **boat**: in logging, a boat which is fitted for use among floating wood by having its propellers operate within a protective iron cage (1985 *Terminology of Loggers* 18).

turn v
1 1987 FIZZARD 149 'The crews of women were going back on the beaches after dinner to turn each fish so that not one would be sunburned.'
4 Cpd **turncoat**.
1979 PORTER 40 But this system [of identifying religious denomination by surnames] was not always entirely reliable. As Aunt Jen said, there were so many turncoats.

turn n
3 T 438-65 An' she said, 'You go off an' get a turn o' birds of any kind; it makes no difference what kind of a bird [you] fire at.' 1987 POWELL 172 I started to feel as if I had not kept my promise. A turn of wood is what could

be carried all at one time [and] I felt a little guilty going home with only one little stick on my back.

turner n
1985 *Canadian Sealers Association* 6 'Next we have a three year old seal which is called a turner, this is the year most female seals become pregnant.'

turpentine n
1987 DAWE [50] Its turpentine sticky/Is cure for a cut.

turr n
1989 *Evening Telegram* 12 Jan, p. 1 The birds [killed by the oil spill] were mainly murres (turres) with some eiderducks included.

turt See ATHWART.

twack n
1898 *Trade Review* "The Old Oaken Shutters": The basket brigade, all beshawled, from the country,/The twack, and the room paper matcher, as well.

twelfth-cake n also **twelfth bun**. *OED* ~ (1774-1838). Cake prepared for celebration of Twelfth Night, January 6th; cp CHRISTMAS n 1.
T 11-63 Those twelve nights [of Christmas] we'd be at it, and the last night we['d] make a pan of sweet buns, twelfth buns, and give 'em to the people. Every house we'd go to we'd give 'em a bun for Twelfth Night. 1981 SPARKES 123 I have heard my grandmother (born 1835) talk about the 'Twelfth Cake,' and an old gentleman of about the same age, but living in a different part of the island, told me that he had heard his father say that it was the custom to make twelve small bonfires in the village on Twelfth Night. His ancestors came from Gloucestershire.

twice av *O Sup*^{2} [food cooked a second time] (1777-); SMYTH 'salt-fish...potatoes' (1867). Cpd **twice-laid**: a dish of cod mashed with potatoes.
1896 SARSON 4-5 ...that agreement betwixt boiled cod and potatoes, which has made 'Twicelaid' a favourite breakfast and supper dish among rich and poor. 1903 *Nfld Qtly* iii (3), 10 From the old people we learn that...'Twice Laid' (salt fish mashed with potatoes, butter, salt, etc.), 'Vang' (fat pork cut up into small squares and fried in batter)...were among the dishes in vogue.

twillick n
1987 O'FLAHERTY 8 The bird was a greater yellowlegs! He never before seen one. Inquiry established that the species, once known locally as twillicks, had been common along the coast three or four decades ago.

twine n
1 1987 FIZZARD 210 [The otter trawl was] made of manila twines and ropes. 1990 *Evening Telegram* 14 Jan, p. 14 I've bought the twine, knit it, made cod-traps, caught cod fish, dried it, and exported it.
2 1987 *Nfld Herald* 12 Dec, p. 6 Each year we as fishermen are using more and more twine and going further and further to sea to catch less and less fish.

P 245-89 'The men were hard at it, drying [=drawing] up the twine at the caplin fishery [with a caplin seine].'
3 Attrib, comb ~ **loft**, ~ **needle**, ~ **shed**: see **twine loft**, ~ **store**.
1987 POWELL 16 So the first cod trap was taken up and dried, then put away in the twine loft. 1987 O'FLAHERTY 42 [He] took his bucket of twine needles, knives, and other equipment to the bow and stored it away carefully. 1987 *Evening Telegram* 7 Mar, p. 10 I somehow paddled my way to the shallow launchway and crawled ashore to present myself to my grandfather in his twine shed at flake level. 1987 POWELL 132 Most of the fishermen had gathered together in a big twine store.

twitchen n Cp *EDD* twitch sb^3 'a narrow way or passage,' twitchell sb 'a narrow footpath,' 1943 *N&Q* 9 Oct, p. 234 twichen 'narrow lane or alley in a town.' A narrow road or path; cp DRUNG, LEAD^2 n 2.
1913 THOMAS 184 A guide employed, we made a trip up a long valley by the old 'Twitchen' road, used years ago and grown up with alder, fir, and balsam so as to be almost closed; up the old caribou path, worn at some places three feet deep in the moss and soft black mire by countless herds of caribou that had passed beyond.

two num
2 Comb **two-quintal barrel**: wooden container with capacity to hold two quintals of salted and dried cod; see BARREL, QUINTAL, **two-yeared bedlamer**.
1987 FIZZARD 160 'We had several makes of barrels. There'd be half-quintal drums, quintal drums, two-quintal barrels [etc].' 1985 *Canadian Sealers Association* 6 'Next we have a two year old seal which is called a two yeared Bedlamer.'

U

un pro
1858 [LOWELL] i, 20 'An' so, when 'e'd agot back to the w'y, agen, an' thowt 'twas all easy, then God let un go down, and brought un up again, athout e'er a thing belonging to un but 'e's life and 'e's son's.' 1981 MAJOR 82 'He use to stick names on me. That was most of it.' 'Did you have a crack at en or what?' 'I thought about it a lot.'

uncle n
1984 POWELL 35 When Christmas Day finally came, we were invited to Uncle Alex's and Aunt Maggie Campbell's.

underrun v *OED* ~ v 2 c (1883, 1897), *DAE* (1880, 1896), developed from *OED* v 2 a naut 'to overhaul or examine (a cable) on the underside' (1547-1867). To raise a trawl-line or 'bultow' over the dory in order to remove the catch, re-bait hooks and 'set' the line in the water again.
1884 DEMING 90 Two men in a boat, often several

times a day, 'underrun' the trawl—the man in front draw-ing up and taking off the fish, while his companion baits. [1886] 1972 DE VOLPI 180 The 'Bankers' fish with trawl lines, each having about 1000 hooks, and the lines are underrun and rebaited if the fishing is good. 1938 [MACDERMOTT] 170 When fish is plentiful the men 'under-run' the trawls; that is, they just pass the trawl across the dory, rebaiting the hooks as they pass it over, and without actually taking the gear into the dory. 1977 MOAKLER 53 We shipped our oars and underran our trawls. /The fishhooks pricked our hands like darting awls. 1984 KELLAND 184 The underrunning of the trawl gear and hauling of it were two distinct operations. For while the gear being underrun remained moored, in the hauling process it did not, but was taken back onboard the dory and coiled into the tubs as the fishermen proceeded. P 283-89 You dry up your trawl near your buoy and you work along. So your boat is running under your trawl—that's underrunning.

underrun n The raising of a trawl-line to clear the catch, re-bait and 'set', see UNDERRUN v.
1960 FUDGE 11 We [set] our trawls for the underrun, and to our surprise all brought loads of very large fish.

up av
5 Phr *up in glee*: excited, very satisfied.
1924 ENGLAND 63 [When we go sealing] I'll get ye some good offers [chances] as'll putt ye up in glee. [1983 FROUDE 18 She pitched in full glee in a fandango way and danced on the white foaming seas.]
up in cheer: in good spirits (1937 DEVINE 55).
up in gee: associated with the influential and high social classes (P 148-60).
P 108-70 I can't afford that, it's away up in gee—too expensive.

upalong av
1 1987 *Nfld Qtly* lxxxiii (2), 2 I thank God for my faith else I would have thought they were going to wipe out this man from up-along.

V

vabish See BABBISH*.

vamp n
1 1986 FELTHAM 84 The wool was carded and spun into a strong, heavy yarn and knitted into socks, vamps, mittens [etc].
2 P 133-58 ~ sole of a stocking.

vamp v
3 Phr *vamp down*.
P 133-58 ~ 'to dilute.'

vang n Also: comb **vang-board**.
[1835] 1888 HOWLEY 316-7 [Bishop Fleming] [I was] leaning forward on that part of the false deck where the people laid the board for our meals; and even while par-taking of their rude fare, as it was flung out of the pot

upon the board,—for it usually consisted of pork and fish boiled together, which they call 'fish and vang'... [My sleeve] having been considerably impregnated with the juice of the fishermen's food, imbibed from the 'vang-board,' the entire sleeve, from the elbow, was eaten away by the dogs or the rats.

var n also **vir**. See *SED* iv, 103 vir, So W. Other examples of a lowered vowel before -r in the Eng-lish West Country are fern(s) (*SED* iv, 492-3 D Ha Sx) and hurt 'bilberry' (*SED* iv, 495 Do Ha); see HURT.
C 69-25 If you are ever in the woods and cut yourself with an axe or something take a quick look around for a vir tree. Break the mur [myrrh] blatter and stick the cut together. 1986 SAUNDERS 54 'Make...a smokey fire from green var boughs and moldow off the trees.'

vat n
1 1985 BUSCH 62 A big vat or 'crib' [for rendering seal fat] could be 20-30 feet square, and 20-25 feet high, built over a larger 'pan' of water.

vee n Also: **back-end vee**: an arrangement of a salmon net with a V-angled section at the seaward end to entrap fish (P 127-89).
1984 POWELL 23-4 The [salmon nets] were sixty fathoms long, so we joined them together and put two in a berth, then ran the nets about seventy-five fathoms straight and the balance of the twine was used to make what we called 'back [end] vee,' a harpoon-like shape. The salmon would swim along the straight part of the net only to find themselves surrounded by twine.

veerable a *OED* ~ (1670-1742). Of the wind, changeable.
1854 [MOSS] *MS Journal* 4 May Fine day wind vearable 4 more people from Greenspond.

vir See VAR.

voyage n
1 1986 *Evening Telegram* 22 Mar, p. 4 March sig-nalled the beginning of the annual voyage to the harp seal herds on The Front, off Labrador.
2 1987 POOLE 9 My uncle Jim was very well off—he used to get big voyages of fish each summer and never did anything else for a living.

W

wabble n also **whobble**, **whobbler**.
1987 MONTEVECCHI & TUCK 233 Whobble, whobbler: common loon.

wad n
1982 MCDOOLING 122 'Look over the bow of the boat there'd be nothing only just a blue wad of caplin all the way under the boat.' 1990 *Evening Telegram* 13 Feb, p. 5 A news reporter recently had John Cabot lowering a bucket overboard on the Grand Banks and landing a wad

of cod. This is a special kind of fish story. For a bucket can only hold a very few small codfish or just the livers of a very few big ones.

wage n *AND* ~ (1871-1962). Comb **wage(s) man**.

1918 *Deep Sea Fishers* xv, 139 [The merchant was] employing ten Labrador men as sharemen or wagemen.

wagon n Comb ~ **sled**.

1985 *Terminology of Loggers* 19 ~ a combination of two sleds fastened together by cross-hauls.

walk v

1 Phr *walk around*.

1983 *Evening Telegram* 3 May, p. 6 That was the queerest spring of all—unemployed Newfoundlanders walking around with their hands in their pockets; mines closed down; paper mills closed down; fish plants closed down; economic disaster on every hand, no jobs to be had.

wall n

1 1975 BUTLER 58 The walls of the trap are made of twine with a twine bottom sewn in. 1982 MCDOOLING 99 The 'Jap' trap is more efficient in that it has a door which keeps the fish from swimming over the top of the walls.

warm n

1 Phr *get a warm*.

1895 *Toilers of the Deep* 245 We halted [the komatik] just to get a warm and some tea. 1907 *Deep Sea Fishers* July, p. 18 'We'll rest there, and you can go in and get a warm.' 1986 *Them Days* xi (4), 19 We would slide... until dark then run to the dogs' feed house to get a warm.

wash v

1 [1622] 1982 CELL (ed) 179 Whitbourne's *Discourse*: Three men may fetch a-land salt, and tend to wash fish, and dry the same. 1981 SPARKES 187 After a period in 'salt bulk,' a fish had to be washed by hand with mops and brushes; then it had to be 'made.' 1987 POWELL 33 The first of September all the fishermen started to wash their codfish, then carry it to the flakes or rocks to be dried.

wash n SMYTH (1867) for sense 1.

1 P 315-82 ~ the portion of an oar which comes in contact with the water; the blade.

2 Attrib ~ **porch**: room or 'linny' attached to the rear of a dwelling, opening off the kitchen and used for various purposes; cp PORCH.

1985 *Nfld Qtly* lxxx (4), 40 She prodded and poked until she was satisfied she had bullied it enough to catch fire and then she hollered out in the direction of the wash porch.

water n Cp *EDD* watery a 1 (1) ~ haul Co, and PRATT (lobster fishing) for comb in sense 3.

1 1987 JOHNSTON 51 May told my mother that Raymond had been quick enough to get his sea-legs, did not mind being out on the water, but, as for the work itself...he seemed to have no 'inclination' for it. 1990 *Evening Telegram* 16 Jan, p. 5 [Fishermen] are out of

their beds at 3 a.m. and out on the water while we...are in our beds.

2 Also: the drainage system of a river (see 1984 quot).

[1820] 1915 HOWLEY 124-5 [Peyton] made one of my party on our new route which we began on the 21st, entered upon the Badger Bay waters at 10 A.M. and soon discovered the track of a racket and sledge. 1984 POWELL 35 We left our canoe at the feeder, as the water was starting to freeze, and moved to the southern waters of the Hawkes River.

3 Attrib, comb, cpd ~ **bear**, ~ **bird**: SALT-WATER BIRD, ~ **dog**, ~ **gully**, ~ **haul**, ~ **pup**, ~ **welt**, **waterside**, **water white (seal oil)**: variety of light-coloured oil made from seal blubber; see also WHITE OIL.

1987 *Evening Telegram* 4 July, p. 56 By and by they saw him coming and he was shouting. He had walked right up on a water bear and it was chasing him. 1987 FIZZARD 180 Through the winter, when the weather permitted, the men of the family tried to supplement their supply of fresh meat, especially with rabbits and water birds. 1984 KELLAND 109 [These dogs] would plunge into the icy water without the slightest hesitation as a shotgun boomed to bring down a duck, then swimming swiftly out, they would seize the dead bird in their powerful jaws returning it to the dory or the beach. They were commonly called water dogs. 1981 SPARKES 183 There, welcoming neighbours gladly lend a hand at the unpacking, filling the water-gullies. 1989 *Evening Telegram* 4 Mar, p. 4 Cod was very, very scarce, even back then. In fact there were days when you had one water haul after another. 1986 FELTHAM 91 The men were exposed to more danger, endured more hardship, suffered the unending misery of the never-healing 'water pups.' 1987 FIZZARD 132 'Sometimes they would have their hands full right up to their elbow with what they called water-welts, boils. I've had 'em sometimes so big two would go into one.' 1987 PEYTON 7 He would come to the waterside of Gander Bay to spend Christmas and return to his trap lines until spring. 1987 *Evening Telegram* 27 Apr, p. 7 [tape transcription] They'd put [the seal oil] in shallow tanks with a glass roof on it and they'd bleach the oil by sun and ship it away in wooden barrels. It was called 'water white' seal oil. A good lot of it at them times was shipped around the world to the various churches and they'd have a floating light. It was also used for the manufacture of soap.

water v (b).

1986 FELTHAM 88 The fat, Atlantic salmon, pickled when quite fresh and watered for a day or two before being cooked in January or February, with dry, home grown potatoes, made a welcome change in the winter's diet.

water-horse n *O Sup*^{2} ~ 3 Nfld.

1984 KELLAND 158 When the dories had been fully loaded they were rowed across to the beaches or flakes and placed on barrows, then were lugged up over the crop of the beach and bulked in waterhorses. 1988 *Evening Telegram* 18 May, p. 19 Water-horse was a bulky, obl[o]ng stack of split and salted codfish piled in layers to drain after washing. The word also was used to denote the box or tub in which the fish was washed.

watering vbl n
1987 FIZZARD 167 'She struck, without warning, a point of land forming the west end of Watering Cove, a cove three miles west of St Shotts.'

watery a Of a field of ice, melting on the surface, covered with a film of water.
1984 POWELL 178 The young ice started to get watery so I made a short cut for the camp. 1987 *Evening Telegram* 11 Apr, p. 14 Now three seals were as many as you could haul any distance on dry ice, but if the ice was watery you could haul more because they would float along.

wave n Comb ~ **gate**: piece of steel at the top of the stern ramp on a trawler, used to stop water from coming aboard (1986 *Nfld's Deep Sea Fishery* 651).

wavy n See BLUE.

way n Cp *OED* ~ sb¹ 3 pl b 'parallel wooden rails...for heavy loads to slide down upon' (1868) for sense 1.
1 Usu pl.
1985 NEWHOOK 13 [The boats] were heavy to haul up. There were no winches available, only manpower and 'weighs' [i.e. ways] which were sappy, slimy, small logs.

we pro Nominative forms of pronouns (*I, he, she, they*) customarily appear, in stressed positions, after BE or as object of a verb or a preposition.
[c1894] PANL P4/14 All [the Poor Commissioner] tells we is the Queen ain't sent out enough money for the poor widdies [this] year. T 269-66 'Don't tell no more,' she said. 'I knowed,' she said 'you was goin' to get we in trouble.' P 287-77 He blew the whistle three times. He knew it was we. And we sailed with the gun. 1985 *A Yaffle of Yarns* 26 B'y if you wants to keep up a job wid we fellers, you'll have to get de proper rig-out. 1987 *Nfld Qtly* lxxxiii (2), 2 [They] welcomed into their midst, housed and fed one who, being a mainlander, was not one of their own, but because he was a Priest of God was accepted 'as one of we.' 1988 *Muse* 29 July, p. 5 In one of the [softball] semi-finals, the BoSox beat Da's We in two straight games.

weather n
1 1982 MCDOOLING 116 There might be 'weather' in the harbour (fog and rain).
2 Comb ~ **light**.
[1987] QUINLAN 17 There was also a phenomenon that the old folks called a 'weather light,' it appeared in advance of a storm.

web n A length, or quantity, of 'twine' for knitting a fish-net.
1982 MCDOOLING 69-70 'We'd knit [the twine]. We'd have a hundred webs of twine or two hundred webs of twine. Two hundred webs was a lot of knitting. Salmon nets the same way.'

west a Comb ~ **country**, ~ **england**, ~ **india**.
[1623] 1982 CELL (ed) 203: Whitbourne's *Discourse:* Wee stand in need of...a conuenient number of West-country labourers to fit the ground for the Plough. [1892] 1977 WHITELEY 42 'Blandford has lots [of salt] if short borrow prepare load West England fish.' 1986 RYAN xxii The inferior produce, *West India*, was sent to the Caribbean. The [designation] *West India* referred to the quality, not the market.

wester n Also: a westerly wind.
1977 MOAKLER 116 A chilling wester crept along the swells,/Our nostrils smarting with the smell of snow.

western a
2 Comb ~ **boat**, ~ **fishery**, ~ **shore**.
1984 KELLAND 28-9 The Monk dory was a great favourite with fishing skippers and dorymen who conducted operations from small, usually tan-sailed schooners known as western boats, that followed their avocations on the stormy seas off Cape St Mary's, the Virgin Rocks and even out on the far flung Grand Banks. 1845 *Journ of Assembly* Appendix, p. 233 The fishery now carried on by the British is almost entirely confined to the in-shore, Labrador and Western Fisheries...[the last] in large half deck'd boats with six hands, and others that are termed jacks. [1977] 1985 LEHR & BEST (eds) 44 ''The Wreck of the *Danny Goodwin*'': Saying good-bye to friends at home, and all whom they adore,/Never dreaming that they'd meet their doom upon the western shore. 1987 FIZZARD 110 [He] owned at least one schooner and was probably engaged in trading and some long distance fishing on the western shore.

wet v
2 Phr *wet one's line*: also, to fish for cod.
1918 *Deep Sea Fishers* xvi, p. 94 I couldn't wet a line all summer.

whabby n also **wobby**.
1987 *Arctic* xl, p. 62, n 4 Other birds include...turr (murre tinker [sic]...and wobby (red-throated loon). 1987 MONTEVECCHI & TUCK 233 ~ common loon.

whanger n also **cod-~**. *OED* cites 1867 quot below; see the curious cod-banger 'fishing vessel' (1864) in *OED*. A resident of Newfoundland involved in processing cod on shore; cp LANDSMAN 1; SHOREMAN 1.
[1819] 1826 [GLASCOCK] i, p. 160 'Where half-starv'd pigs and puppies run/In quest of fish; and when it's on the fork,/Ye *whangers*!* judge how savory is the pork!' ... [A newly married man] Bows to a yoke his better sense despises/Sinks into *nothing*, and a whanger rises. *Slang of the colony for fish-curers. ibid i, 163-4 'Have mercy, LITERATI!/On this *our* community,/Else ''*Whangers*'' will have at ye.' 1867 SMYTH 728 Whangers, or cod-whangers. Fish-curers of Newfoundland.

wheel n Comb ~ **keg**: wooden cask fastened in wheelbarrow frame and used to transport water from a well to house; see KEG (P 322-87).

whelp v *SED* iv, 369-70, of a bitch.

1984 WRIGHT 8 The Gulf [seal] stock 'whelps,' or bears its young, on newly formed pack-ice. 1989 CANDOW 9 Except when they moult, breed, and give birth (whelp), harp seals spend all their time in the water.

whelping vbl n

2 Comb ~ **ground**, ~ **ice**, ~ **patch**.

1989 CANDOW 14 In recent years the whelping grounds at the Front have tended to be located farther north. 1986 *Nfld Qtly* lxxxi (4), 44 The [boy] had quit before May had melted into June and 'whelpin' ice' from Labrador had drifted down past the cove. 1984 WRIGHT 10 Men from southeastern Newfoundland began sealing from small boats, searching for the southward drifting whelping patches.

whip n Cpd **whipline**.

1984 WRIGHT 65 We had finished picking up the seals near the ship, and I was working on the whipline, strapping the panned pelts together in bunches of fifteen, to be hauled aboard by the whipline.

whisker[1] n

1984 POWELL 10 Several boys were there, and one older fellow with a big foxy whisker.

white a

3 In names of birds: ~ **bawk**, ~ **beachy bird**: see BEACH BIRD (c), ~ **jacket**: common eider (1987 MONTEVECCHI & TUCK 235).

1945 *Can Field-Naturalist* lix, p. 138 White bawk: greater shearwater. 1987 MONTEVECCHI & TUCK 238 White beachy bird. Sanderling.

4 In names of plants, etc: ~ **wood**.

1898 *J A Folklore* xi, p. 228 *Viburnum Opulus*, L. (perhaps other species), trash berry, jointwood berry, whitewood berry, Newfoundland.

5 Comb ~ **bear**, ~ **boy**: also, local name for Christmas mummer or 'janny,' ~-**coat**, ~ **oil**, ~ **seal**: see **white-coat**.

1987 *Evening Telegram* 25 Apr, p. 35 Another big white bear took up residence for a couple of weeks in the Grey River area, on the south coast, back in 1978 and was spotted on the shoreline by dozens of fishermen as they passed by in their boats. 1984 ROBERTSON xvii Other words are known as well as...mummers or janneys...white boys in Clarke's Beach. 1985 *Canadian Sealers Association* 5 'Only one year did I take part in the white coat hunt.' 1985 BUSCH 62 The first, best 'virgin' or 'white' oil, known in the oil trade as 'pale seal oil' (and sold by the pound, not the gallon...) took some two months to self-cure. 1989 *Nfld Qtly* lxxxiv (3), 45 [The groups had] a focus on alleged cruelty to white seal pups.

white-fish n

2 1988 *Evening Telegram* 29 Apr, p. 6 I have watched hundreds, maybe thousands of those [sea]birds fly by on the way to their nest. There would not be a caplin within a hundred miles; their bill of fare would be lance or, as some call them, whitefish.

whiting n

1985 *Terminology of Loggers* 19 White end: the butt of a rinded tree. 1986 FELTHAM 70 The trees from which the bark was removed were called 'whitings,' and within a year or two would become quite dry and make excellent firewood.

who int pro Phr *who-shall* (c).

P 277-89 'This hand [of cards] is the who shall!'

widow n PRATT (1972). Comb ~ **woman**.

[1870] 1973 KELLY 15 Mr Mather baptized a grandchild, of the widow-woman before mentioned. 1986 *Evening Telegram* 3 Apr, p. 6 The high handed and callous treatment by city council of a widow woman on Flowers Hill...reflects a long entrenched attitude at city hall which, in this case, is being carried to the extreme.

wild a

1 1984 KELLAND 100 Men who fished from a wild shore (no harbour) were forced to keep up this practice [of hauling their dories up each night on a beach or slipway] owing to storms which often suddenly blew up.

2 Also: of cod-fish, in their natural state.

[1794] 1968 THOMAS 129 In Newfoundland the wild Deer has a set of foes more implacable then the Buckhound or the Huntsman, and these are the Wolves. 1989 *Sunday Express* 9 July, p. 8 Being a cod farmer, using wild trap cod for starting stock, I've become used to the reaction of fish to everything from light [etc].

3 In names of shrubs: ~ **gooseberry**: *Ribes hirtellum* ([1822] 1929 BRUTON).

4 Comb ~ **cat**.

1895 PROWSE 16 This animal was the Canadian lynx, called in Newfoundland 'wild cat.'

willem* n Cp Burton Bradstock, Do wellum 'rings on the surface of water made by a fish breaking surface or an underwater spring' (P 304-90).

wind n *OED* ~ sb[1] 31 wind-dog (1860), *South Shore Phr Bk* windlop for combs in sense 2.

2 Comb ~-**bag**, ~-**charger**, ~-**dog**: see **wind hound**, ~-**jack**.

1984 KELLAND 151 The remaining sails [on a banking schooner included the] topmast staysail (called fisherman's staysail by Lunenburgers and windbags by northern Newfoundlanders). 1983 *Canadian Folklore canadien* v, 69 'Without electricity they had to use battery sets and you'd see wind chargers all around the island, people revving up their batteries.' 1949 FITZGERALD 37 With wind-dogs slantin' in the sky—the sure sign of a blow. 1986 FELTHAM 98-9 Late spring...was the time when every boy carried a home-made 'windjack' and the buzzing sound of the whirling blades of those nailed to the fence posts could be heard near every home.

windshook ppl a *OED* wind-shook ppl a rare (1784). Of standing timber, cracked and shaken by the wind; wind-shaken.

1986 SAUNDERS 72 These pines were usually twice as tall as anything else, but not much good because they were windshook—cracked in the heartwood from having been exposed to the storms after G.L. Phillips logged those stands thirty years before.

wine n Comb ~ **berry**: crowberry (*Empetrum nigrum*) (1898 *J A Folklore* xi, 279).

wing n See SORDEN, p. 141 '*wing*: small log jam intentionally caught on a rock or other obstruction for the effect of a sluiceway.' Comb ~ **log**, ~ **man** (see quot.).
1986 SAUNDERS 204-5 A fourth group were the wing men, fellows who went ahead of the drive to set up 'wings' or guide logs where they figured the logs would run aground or get snagged in bushes... 'Picking up the rear'...was the last job on a drive. It meant going back after the main drive had gone through and picking up stray logs, including boom logs and wing logs.

wing v Phr *winged out* p ppl: see quot.
1984 KELLAND 209 Then Walters swung his mainsail and foresail wing and wing, which meant that one sail was dragged over to port, the other to starboard. Wung out, as the Lunenburgers called it, and winged out as the Newfoundlanders called it.

winker² n
1 One of two panels or 'leaves' of netting attached to the 'door' of a cod-trap to keep the entrapped fish in the central box.
1981 *Encyc of Nfld & Labr* (ed Smallwood) i, 475 In recent years...attempts have been made to improve the cod trap by the addition of winkers. These are additional leaves which are parallel to the leader but attached to the sides of the doorway and directed inward toward the centre of the trap. They are to confuse the fish in an effort to keep them from leaving. 1984 *Evening Telegram* 22 Mar, p. 5A [A new doorway was made] by adding to the old doorway a set of net panels, called winkers, which intruded into the trap on a decreasing angle, looking much like a partly-opened double house door.
2 Red-necked grebe (*Podiceps holböllii*); SPRAW-FOOT (1987 MONTEVECCHI & TUCK 233).

winter n
1 Also: (b) in pl, with numeral, used for *year*; (c) in prov *winter's thunder means summer's hunger* (1937 DEVINE 66).
1988 *Evening Telegram* 31 May, p. 11 About four winters ago six of the men went inland to look for caribou because their families were hungry at home.
3 In designations of a structure or location for the season: ~ **house**, ~ **home**, ~ **place**, ~ **tilt**.
[1765] 1971 BANKS (ed Lysaght) 207 They...desired when we came to live among them we might come to the Winter Houses & tell them more good words of their Creator. 1987 POWELL 37 I now had two houses—one winter house and a summer house at Square Islands where I fished. [1950] 1963 DIACK 39 All the people on that part of the coast moved 'into the bays' in winter;

there, in the shelter inland, they had another house, their 'winter home.' 1895 *Evening Herald* 6 Feb, p. 3 People that dont try to get anything in the summer will not have much to carry off to their winter places, our winter house and gardens is about 70 or eighty miles from here. 1984 POWELL 14 [He] decided to give us a hand to build our winter tilt before he returned to the Island.
4 Attrib, comb ~ **diet**: see DIET n, ~ **fish** (a), ~ **fishery** (b), ~ **stock**: food laid in for the winter, ~ **work**.
[1825] 1986 SIDER 62 Do not see that they can make it out [pay their bill] if they have credit for winter diet. 1895 *Evening Herald* 6 Feb, p. 3 We are now going to get our winter fish while we can, men, women, and children does all they can to get something for the winter. 1981 DAWE 12 "The Potato Ground": where more cold fingers hurried/knotting stiff cod-lines/for the long trawls/of the winter fish. 1989 *Evening Telegram* 5 Jan, p. 3 The fishermen's union is confident a price agreement will be secured before the start of the winter fishery on the province's southwest coast. 1987 FIZZARD 180 Other foods were added to the larder, and by the time the winter stock was in, one could find a gourmet's delight in the houses and stores of most Grand Bankers. P 302-88 None of that now, no good work winter time now, not in the woods, no winter work.

witch-hazel n
1983 *Gazetteer of Canada: Nfld* 194 Witch Hazel Brook (Hill, Point, Pond, Ridge, Rock). 1987 *Nfld Qtly* lxxxii (4), 10 The witch hazel [stick] cracked the desperado across the skull and he was out, a cold junk.

withe n
1842 PEACH *MS Diary* 6 Sep, p. 22 Punt very leaky... By this time we were half full of water, one of the pins broke and let the man backwards in the bow of the punt. The withes gave out so that we had to cut off the painter to make new ones, a pretty predicament this. 1986 FELTHAM 49 The paddles [used in a punt or rodney] were about eight feet long, shaped from fir or spruce and attached to the thole-pins by 'withes' made from rope.

withe-rod n *O Sup²* withe-rod (1819-).
[1977] 1985 LEHR & BEST (eds) 186 "The Tobacco Song": I can't smoke the stuff I sees some people smoke/Such as withrod and shavings and strands of old rope.

withy n *SED* iv, 489 s w cties.
1 1985 DOMSTAD 25 A withey tree (a small tree found in the woods).

wobby See WHABBY.

wood(s) n, n pl Comb ~ **path**.
1987 POOLE 87 One day I went into the woods to cut a load of wood. I had my dogs drive up the wood path.

wop¹ n *SED* waps iv, 471 s w cties.
1 1924 *Deep-Sea Fishers* xxi (4), 139 'Crispy' becomes 'cripsy'; 'wasp' becomes 'waps'; 'clasp' becomes 'claps,' and 'asp' is converted to 'aps.'

word v
1985 ASHTON 170 '[If he couldn't write out the song,] he just word it out and I'd write it down myself.'

wrinkle[1] n
2 Comb ~ **basket**: see **wrinkle net**.
1987 FIZZARD 113-4 [The French] could still get at least some bait illegally from Newfoundland; for another, by using 'wrinkle baskets' on the banks, they were able to get shell fish to use as bait.

Y

yaffle n   *SED* iv, 251 Co D, 908 D.
1 1986 *Evening Telegram* 27 Jan, p. 6 Upon going to the house with a yaffle of firewood I mentioned to my mother that 'something funny just happened.' 1986 FELTHAM 96 They drew the water used to wash the fish and arranged the drying cod in 'yaffles' when it was time to pile it for the night.

yaffle v
1 1986 FELTHAM 96 Boys could be of considerable help too, when the dried cod was shipped. They 'yaffled' in the storeroom to load on the 'fish barrows.' 1987 *Evening Telegram* 17 Oct, p. 18 I'll never forget sticking my face into [grandfather's well] and quenching my thirst after a hot summer's day, yaffling salt fish at Crosbie's yard.

yarkin(g) n   Burton Bradstock, Do 'bindings of twine joining the two lines at the top and bottom of a seine net to fix the corks and weights' (P 304-90).

yary a   *O Sup*[2] ~ a dial (chiefly Nfld).
2 1987 DAWE [48] But he's some yarry man/With his rubber boots on. 1988 NADEL-KLEIN & DAVIS (eds) 224 Women pride themselves in being 'yary.' Men and women alike enjoy feisty women.

ye pro   See YOUSE*.
T 735-70 If a man tried to tell you were dead and I come in now, ye was frightened o' me, see. 1985 ASHTON 181 "Hurling Down the Pine": 'Arise oh ye teamsters, it's time that ye are out.' 1988 DOHANEY 158 'What were ye fightin' about?' Bertha asked crossly. 'Not Confederation again.'

yellow a   Comb ~ **belly** (a), (b) brown jug with a yellow stripe (see 1888 quot), ~ **hammer**.
1888 HOWLEY 227 [The custom of rum three times a day] is to the present day continued on some of the old English and Jersey houses. Every 'hand,' boy or man, had his brown jug, with a yellow stripe around the middle, called a 'yallow-belly,' and when the time for the 'mornin',' 'the eleven o'clocker,' and the 'evenin',' arrived he approached the rum-puncheon, and, drawing the spile, filled his 'yallow-belly.' 1988 *Evening Telegram* 27 July, p. 3 From Yellow Belly Corner in downtown St John's to the city's historic sites and buildings...

walking tours leave nothing out when presenting the downtown's colorful history to visiting tourists. 1903 *Nfld Qtly* iii (1), 2 Whether they may have seen some of our little 'yellow-hammers'...it would be difficult to decide.

yess n   *SED* iv, 477 yess So.

young a
1 Comb ~ **swile** [seal].
[1797] 1982 PULLING (ed Marshall) 124 [She was] sprawling into the snow...*just like a young swile*.
2 1984 POWELL 178 The young ice started to get watery so I made a short cut for the camp.

young fellow n
1 1986 *Them Days* xi (4), 15 [The salted salmon] were washed in a large trough [with Blake] in charge of several young fellows to do the washing.

youse* pro, usu pl. Taped and transcribed examples of this form (ending in [s] or [z]) are scanty. See also YE.
P 148-63 'Youse all right' [pl]. ibid 'Youse leavin'?' [pl]. T 38-64 And then say yous [jɒs] fish four five days on the squid before the squid would be used, because you generally take eight thousand. T 438-65 Give him a kiss, you know, like yous [jʉuz], you see, yes. T 246-66 My goodness! Yous all go outdoors every ways now! T 258-66 And when I leaved I come on to Sally's Cove, and now I'm up here tellin' yous the yarn. P 309-88 You'd sing a song...getting together bring youse together.

yo-yo n   Comb ~ **winch**: type of winch used on deep-sea trawlers.
1986 *Nfld's Deepsea Fishery* 651 ~ auxiliary winches mounted near the stern ramp (one on each side). These are used for shooting the net away and for emptying the cod end. They are found only on stern trawlers, not on sides.

yuck v   also derived noun **yuckings**. To vomit (1955 ENGLISH 37).
1966 PADDOCK 133 Yuk [to vomit, one response]. 1977 MOAKLER 168 We fought for sea legs as the storm winds roared/And spewed our yuckings on the cleansing wind.

Z

zosweet n   1978 *Beothuk Vocabularies* 160 Partridge susut; zosweet; zosoot. Beothuk term for Allen's willow ptarmigan, Welch's rock ptarmigan; PARTRIDGE.
1903 *Nfld Qtly* iii (1), 3 "The Last of the Boeothics' Lament": [They] must away ere the stars on the dark blue shall pale/Must speed ere the zosweet first utters its cry.